PEARSON

COMMON CORE

Literature

THE AMERICAN EXPERIENCE

PEARSON

HOBOKEN, NEW JERSEY • BOSTON, MASSACHUSETTS
CHANDLER, ARIZONA • GLENVIEW, ILLINOIS

Acknowledgments

Grateful acknowledgment is made to the following for copyrighted material:

Advancement Project "10 Things Every Florida Poll Worker Should Know" from *http://www.advancementproject.org*. Used by permission.

Archaeology Magazine "A Community's Roots" by Samir S. Patel from *http://www.archaeology.org*. Copyright © 2006 by The Archaeological Institute of America. Used by permission.

Arte Publico Press "The Latin Deli: An Ars Poetica" by Judith Ortiz Cofer from *The Latin Deli*. Used with permission from the publisher of "The Americas Review" (Copyright © 1992 Arte Publico Press-University of Houston).

The James Baldwin Estate "The Rockpile" is collected in *Going to Meet the Man*, © 1965 by James Baldwin. Copyright renewed. Published by Vintage Books. Used by arrangement with the James Baldwin Estate.

Susan Bergholz Literary Services "Antojos" by Julia Alvarez from *Antojos*. Copyright © 1991 by Julia Alvarez. Later published in slightly different form in *How the Garcia Girls Lost Their Accents*, Copyright © 1991 by Julia Alvarez. Published by Plume, an imprint of Dutton Signet, a division of Penguin USA, Inc., and originally in hardcover by Algonquin Books of Chapel Hill. "Straw into Gold: The Metamorphosis of the Everyday" by Sandra Cisneros from *The Texas Observer*. Copyright © 1987 by Sandra Cisneros. First published in *The Texas Observer*, September 1987. Used by permission of Susan Bergholz Literary Services, New York, NY and Lamy, NM. All rights reserved.

BOA Editions Limited "The Gift" by Li-Young Lee from Rose. Copyright © 1986 by Li-Young Lee. All rights reserved. "Study the Masters" by Lucille Clifton from *Blessing the Boats: New and Selected Poems 1988–2000*. Copyright © 2000 by Lucille Clifton. Used with the permission of BOA Editions, Ltd. www.boaeditions.org.

Brooks Permissions "The Explorer" by Gwendolyn Brooks from *Blacks*. Used by permission of Brooks Permissions. Copyright © 1991 by Gwendolyn Brooks, published by Third World Press, Chicago.

The California Council for the Humanities "California Council for the Humanities/Our Mission/Our History" from *http://www.calhum.org*. Courtesy of the California Council for the Humanities and its California Stories Initiative. Copyright © 2007 by The California Council for the Humanities. Used by permission.

California Department of Water Resources "California Water Plan Highlights" from *Department of Water Resources Bulletin 160-05*. Copyright © 2005 California Department of Water Resources.

California Secretary of State "Poll Worker Advertisement" from *www.sos.ca.gov/elections/outreach/posters/pollworker.pdf*. Used by permission.

Sandra Dijkstra Literary Agency "Mother Tongue" by Amy Tan from The Joy Luck Club. Copyright © 1989 by Amy Tan. Used by permission of the author and the Sandra Dijkstra Literary Agency. Copyright © 1989 by Amy -Tan. First appeared in *Threepenny Review*.

Doubleday "Cuttings (later)" by Theodore Roethke from Collected Poems of Theodore Roethke. "Cuttings" by Theodore Roethke from *The Collected Poems of Theodore Roethke. The Collected Poems of Theodore Roethke by Theodore Roethke*, copyright © 1946 by Editorial Publications, Inc. Used by permission of Doubleday, a division of Bantam Doubleday Dell Publishing Group.

Richard Erdoes "When Grizzlies Walked Upright" by Modoc Indians from *American History Customized Reader*. Used by permission.

Faber and Faber Limited "Mirror" by Sylvia Plath from *Crossing the Water*. Copyright © 1963 by Ted Hughes. Used by permission.

Farrar, Straus & Giroux, LLC "Losses" by Randall Jarrell from *The Complete Poems by Randall Jarrell*. Copyright © 1969, renewed 1997 by Mary von S. Jarrell. "The Death of the Ball Turret Gunner" by Randall Jarrell from *The Complete Poems of Randall Jarrell*. Copyright © 1969, renewed 1997 by Mary von S. Jarrell. "The First Seven Years" by Bernard Malamud from *The Magic Barrel*. Copyright © 1950, 1958 and copyright renewed 1977, 1986 by Bernard Malamud. "Coyote v. Acme" by Ian Frazier from *Coyote v. Acme*. Copyright © 1996 by Ian Frazier. "One Art" by Elizabeth Bishop from *Geography III*. Copyright © 1979, 1983 by Alice Helen Methfessel. "Filling Station" by Elizabeth Bishop from *The Complete Poems 1927–1979* by Elizabeth Bishop. Copyright © 1979, 1983 by Alice Helen Methfessel. Used by permission of Farrar, Straus and Giroux, LLC.

Florida Master Site File from *http://www.flheritage.com*. Used by permission.

Fulcrum Publishing "The Earth on Turtle's Back" by Joseph Bruchac and Michael J. Caduto from *Keepers of the Earth: Native American Stories and Environmental Activities for Children*, © 1998. Used by permission of Fulcrum Publishing, Inc.

Georgia State University "Georgia State University's Web Accessibility Policy," copyright © 2006 is used with permission from the University System of Georgia by and on behalf of Georgia State University.

Graywolf Press "Traveling Through the Dark" by William Stafford from *Stories That Could be True: New and Collected Poems*. Copyright 1962, 1998 by the Estate of William Stafford. Used from *The Way It Is: New and Selected Poems* with the permission of Graywolf Press, Saint Paul, Minnesota.

Harcourt, Inc. "Chicago" by Carl Sandburg from *Chicago Poems*, copyright © 1916 by Holt, Rinehart and Winston and renewed 1944 by Carl Sandburg. "Grass" by Carl Sandburg from *Chicago Poems*. Copyright © 1916 BY Holt, Rinehart and Winston and renewed 1944 by Carl Sandburg. "Everyday Use" by Alice Walker from *In Love & Trouble: Stories of Black Women*, copyright © 1973 by Alice Walker. "The Jilting of Granny Weatherall" by Katherine Anne Porter from *Flowering Judas and Other Stories*, copyright © 1930 and renewed 1958 by Katherine Anne Porter. "The Life You Save May Be Your Own" by Flannery O'Connor from *A Good Man is Hard to Find and Other Stories*, copyright © 1953 by Flannery O'Connor and renewed 1981 by Regina O'Connor. "A Worn Path" by Eudora Welty from *A Curtain of Green and Other Stories*, copyright 1941 and renewed in 1969 by Eudora Welty. Used by permission of Harcourt, Inc. This material may not be reproduced in any form or by any means without the prior written permission of the publisher.

HarperCollins Publishers, Inc. From "Dust Tracks on a Road" by Zora N. Hurston. Copyright © 1942 by Zora Neale Hurston; renewed © 1970 by John C. Hurston. "Mirror" by Sylvia Plath from *Crossing the Water*. Copyright © 1963 by Ted Hughes. Originally appeared in The New Yorker. "Where Is Here?" by Joyce Carol Oates. Copyright © 1992 by The Ontario Review, Inc. Used by permission of HarperCollins Publishers. Excerpt from *Black Boy* by Richard Wright. Copyright © 1944, 1945 by Richard Wright.

Harvard University Press "Because I could not stop for Death (#712)", "I heard a Fly buzz—when I died (#465)", "My life closed twice before its close— (#1732)", "The Soul selects her own Society (#303)", "There's a certain Slant of light (#258)", "There is a solitude of space (#1695)", by Emily Dickinson from *The Poems of Emily Dickinson*. Used by permission of the publishers and the Trustees of Amherst College from *The Poems of Emily Dickinson*, Thomas H. Johnson, ed., Cambridge, Mass.: The Belknap Press of Harvard University Press, Copyright (c) 1951, 1955, 1979 by the Presidents and Fellows of Harvard College.

Acknowledgments continue on page R74, which constitutes an extension of this copyright page.

COVER: Alan Copson/JAI/Corbis

PEARSON

ISBN-13: 978-0-13-326859-1
ISBN-10: 0-13-326859-4
7 8 9 10 11 12 13 V057 18 17 16 15 14

PEARSON COMMON CORE Literature

THE AMERICAN EXPERIENCE

PEARSON

HOBOKEN, NEW JERSEY • BOSTON, MASSACHUSETTS
CHANDLER, ARIZONA • GLENVIEW, ILLINOIS

PEARSON COMMON CORE Literature

THE AMERICAN EXPERIENCE

PEARSON

HOBOKEN, NEW JERSEY • BOSTON, MASSACHUSETTS
CHANDLER, ARIZONA • GLENVIEW, ILLINOIS

Contributing Authors

The contributing authors guided the direction and philosophy of Pearson Common Core Literature. *They helped to build the pedagogical integrity of the program by contributing content expertise, knowledge of the Common Core State Standards, and support for the shifts in instruction the Common Core will bring. Their knowledge, combined with classroom and professional experience, ensures* Pearson Common Core Literature *is relevant for both teachers and students.*

William G. Brozo, Ph.D., is a Professor of Literacy in the Graduate School of Education at George Mason University in Fairfax, Virginia. He earned his bachelor's degree from the University of North Carolina and his master's and doctorate from the University of South Carolina. He has taught reading and language arts in the Carolinas and is the author of numerous articles on literacy development for children and young adults. His books include *To Be a Boy, To Be a Reader: Engaging Teen and Preteen Boys in Active Literacy; Readers, Teachers, Learners: Expanding Literacy Across the Content Areas*; *Content Literacy for Today's Adolescents: Honoring Diversity and Building Competence; Supporting Content Area Literacy with Technology* (Pearson); and *Setting the Pace: A Speed, Comprehension, and Study Skills Program*. His newest book is *RTI and the Adolescent Reader: Responsive Literacy Instruction in Secondary Schools*. As an international consultant, Dr. Brozo has provided technical support to teachers from the Balkans to the Middle East, and he is currently a member of a European Union research grant team developing curriculum and providing adolescent literacy professional development for teachers across Europe.

Diane Fettrow spent the majority of her teaching career in Broward County, Florida, teaching high school English courses and serving as department chair. She also worked as an adjunct instructor at Broward College, Nova Southeastern University, and Florida Atlantic University. After she left the classroom, she served as Secondary Language Arts Curriculum Supervisor for several years, working with more than 50 of the district's high schools, centers, and charter schools. During her time as curriculum supervisor, she served on numerous local and state committees; she also served as Florida's K–12 ELA content representative to the PARCC Model Content Frameworks Rapid Response Feedback Group and the PARCC K–12 and Upper Education Engagement Group. Currently she presents workshops on the Common Core State Standards and is working with Pearson on aligning materials to the CCSS.

Kelly Gallagher is a full-time English teacher at Magnolia High School in Anaheim, California, where he has taught for twenty-seven years. He is the former co-director of the South Basin Writing Project at California State University, Long Beach, and the author of *Reading Reasons: Motivational Mini-Lessons for Middle and High School; Deeper Reading: Comprehending Challenging Texts, 4–12; Teaching Adolescent Writers;* and *Readicide: How Schools Are Killing Reading and What You Can Do About It.* He is also a principal author of *Prentice Hall Writing Coach* (Pearson, 2012). Kelly's latest book is *Write Like This* (Stenhouse). Follow Kelly on Twitter @KellyGToGo, and visit him at www.kellygallagher.org.

Elfrieda "Freddy' Hiebert, Ph.D., is President and CEO of TextProject, a nonprofit that provides resources to support higher reading levels. She is also a research associate at the University of California, Santa Cruz. Dr. Hiebert received her Ph.D. in Educational Psychology from the University of Wisconsin-Madison. She has worked in the field of early reading acquisition for 45 years, first as a teacher's aide and teacher of primary-level students in California and, subsequently, as a teacher educator and researcher at the universities of Kentucky, Colorado-Boulder, Michigan, and California-Berkeley. Her research addresses how fluency, vocabulary, and knowledge can be fostered through appropriate texts. Professor Hiebert's research has been published in numerous scholarly journals, and she has authored or edited nine books. Professor Hiebert's model of accessible texts for beginning and struggling readers—TExT—has been used to develop numerous reading programs that are widely used in schools. Dr. Hiebert is the 2008 recipient of the William S. Gray Citation of Merit, awarded by the International Reading Association; is a member of the Reading Hall of Fame; and has chaired a group of experts on early childhood literacy who served in an advisory capacity to the CCSS writers.

Donald J. Leu, Ph.D., is the John and Maria Neag Endowed Chair in Literacy and Technology and holds a joint appointment in Curriculum and Instruction and Educational Psychology in the Neag School of Education at the University of Connecticut. Don is an international authority on literacy education, especially the new skills and strategies required to read, write, and learn with Internet technologies and the best instructional practices that prepare students for these new literacies. He is a member of the Reading Hall of Fame, a Past President of the National Reading Conference, and a former member of the Board of Directors of the International Reading Association. Don is a Principal Investigator on a number of federal research grants, and his work has been funded by the U.S. Department of Education, the National Science Foundation, and the Bill and Melinda Gates Foundation, among others. He recently edited the *Handbook of Research on New Literacies* (Erlbaum, 2008).

Ernest Morrell, Ph.D., is a professor of English Education at Teachers College, Columbia University, and the president-elect of the National Council of Teachers of English (NCTE). He is also the Director of Teachers College's Harlem-based Institute for Urban and Minority Education (IUME). Dr. Morrell was an award-winning high school English teacher in California, and he now works with teachers and schools across the country to infuse multicultural literature, youth popular culture, and media production into standards-based literacy curricula and after-school programs. He is the author of nearly 100 articles and book chapters and five books, including *Critical Media Pedagogy: Achievement, Production, and Justice in City Schools* and *Linking Literacy and Popular Culture*. In his spare time he coaches youth sports and writes poems and plays.

Karen Wixson, Ph.D., is Dean of the School of Education at the University of North Carolina, Greensboro. She has published widely in the areas of literacy curriculum, instruction, and assessment. Dr. Wixson has been an advisor to the National Research Council and helped develop the National Assessment of Educational Progress (NAEP) reading tests. She is a former member of the IRA Board of Directors and co-chair of the IRA Commission on RTI. Recently, Dr. Wixson served on the English Language Arts Work Team that was part of the Common Core State Standards Initiative.

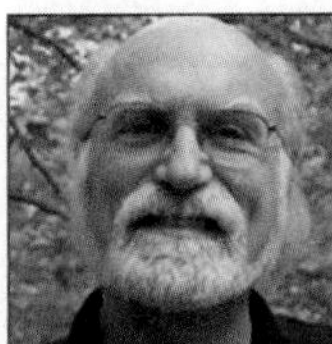

Grant Wiggins, Ed.D., is the President of Authentic Education in Hopewell, New Jersey. He earned his Ed.D. from Harvard University and his B.A. from St. John's College in Annapolis. Grant consults with schools, districts, and state education departments on a variety of reform matters; organizes conferences and workshops; and develops print materials and Web resources on curricular change. He is perhaps best known for being the co-author, with Jay McTighe, of *Understanding by Design* and *The Understanding by Design Handbook*, the award-winning and highly successful materials on curriculum published by ASCD.

Contents in Brief

The selections in this book are presented through the lens of three Essential Questions:

What makes American literature American?

What is the relationship between literature and place?

How does literature shape or reflect society?

A Gathering of Voices

Literature of Early America (Beginnings to 1800)

★ INFORMATIONAL TEXT HIGHLIGHTED

PART THREE TEXT SET: A NATION IS BORN

DIGITAL ASSETS KEY

These digital resources, as well as audio and the Online Writer's Notebook, can be found at **pearsonrealize.com.**

- Interactive Whiteboard Activities
- Virtual Tour
- Close Reading Notebook
- Video
- Close Reading Tool for Annotating Texts
- Grammar Tutorials

A Growing Nation

Literature of the American Renaissance (1800 to 1870)

PART FOUR TEXT SET: **AMERICAN MASTERS**

Extended Study: Poetry

DIGITAL ASSETS KEY

These digital resources, as well as audio and the Online Writer's Notebook, can be found at **pearsonrealize.com.**

- Interactive Whiteboard Activities
- Virtual Tour
- Close Reading Notebook
- Video
- Close Reading Tool for Annotating Texts
- Grammar Tutorials

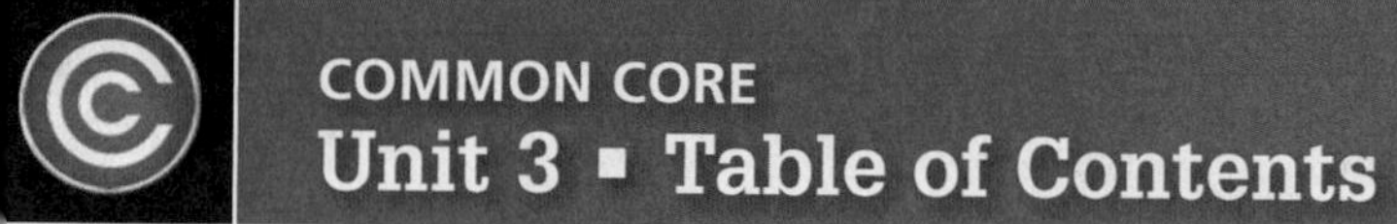

Division, Reconciliation, and Expansion

Literature of the Civil War and the Frontier (1850 to 1914)

DIGITAL ASSETS KEY

These digital resources, as well as audio and the Online Writer's Notebook, can be found at **pearsonrealize.com**.

- **Interactive Whiteboard Activities**
- **Virtual Tour**
- **Close Reading Notebook**
- **Video**
- **Close Reading Tool for Annotating Texts**
- **Grammar Tutorials**

Disillusion, Defiance, and Discontent

Literature of the Modern Age (1914 to 1945)

COMMON CORE
Unit 4 ▪ Table of Contents

PART TWO TEXT SET: **FROM EVERY CORNER OF THE LAND**

PART THREE TEXT SET: **THE HARLEM RENAISSANCE**

DIGITAL ASSETS KEY

These digital resources, as well as audio and the Online Writer's Notebook, can be found at **pearsonrealize.com.**

- **Interactive Whiteboard Activities**
- **Virtual Tour**
- **Close Reading Notebook**
- **Video**
- **Close Reading Tool for Annotating Texts**
- **Grammar Tutorials**

Prosperity and Protest

Literature of the Post-War Era (1945 to 1970)

DIGITAL ASSETS KEY

These digital resources, as well as audio and the Online Writer's Notebook, can be found at **pearsonrealize.com**.

- Interactive Whiteboard Activities
- Virtual Tour
- Close Reading Notebook
- Video
- Close Reading Tool for Annotating Texts
- Grammar Tutorials

New Voices, New Frontiers

Literature of the Contemporary Period (1970 to Present)

Multiple Perspectives on the Era

PART THREE TEXT SET: CONTEMPORARY NONFICTION

DIGITAL ASSETS KEY

These digital resources, as well as audio and the Online Writer's Notebook, can be found at **pearsonrealize.com.**

- Interactive Whiteboard Activities
- Virtual Tour
- Close Reading Notebook
- Video
- Close Reading Tool for Annotating Texts
- Grammar Tutorials

Range of Reading: Complete Contents by Genre

Literature

Stories

Adventure Stories

Allegories

Graphic Novels

Humor/Satire

Myths

Realistic Fiction

Science Fiction/Fantasy/Gothic

Drama

Multi-Act Plays

Screenplays

Poetry

Ballads

Dramatic Monologue

Epics

Formal Verse

Free Verse

Lyrical Poems

Informational Text—Literary Nonfiction

▶ Argument

Opinion Pieces

Speeches/Sermons

▶ Exposition

Essays About Art, Literature, and Language

Essays About Ideas

Historical Accounts

Range of Reading: Complete Contents by Genre

Informational Text—Literary Nonfiction

Historical and Literary Background

The American Experience—Reading in the Humanities

Literature in Context—Reading in the Content Areas

Range of Reading: Complete Contents by Genre

▶ World Literature Connections

▶ Literary History

Skills Workshops

Writing Workshops

Speaking and Listening

Language Study

Text Set Workshops

Test-Taking Practice

Common Core State Standards Overview

The Common Core State Standards will prepare you to succeed in college and your future career. They are separated into four sections—Reading (Literature and Informational Text), Writing, Speaking and Listening, and Language. Beginning each section, the College and Career Readiness Anchor Standards define what you need to achieve by the end of high school. The grade-specific standards that follow define what you need to know by the end of your current grade level.

Common Core Reading Standards

College and Career Readiness Anchor Standards

Key Ideas and Details

1. Read closely to determine what the text says explicitly and to make logical inferences from it; cite specific textual evidence when writing or speaking to support conclusions drawn from the text.
2. Determine central ideas or themes of a text and analyze their development; summarize the key supporting details and ideas.
3. Analyze how and why individuals, events, and ideas develop and interact over the course of a text.

Craft and Structure

4. Interpret words and phrases as they are used in a text, including determining technical, connotative, and figurative meanings, and analyze how specific word choices shape meaning or tone.
5. Analyze the structure of texts, including how specific sentences, paragraphs, and larger portions of the text (e.g., a section, chapter, scene, or stanza) relate to each other and the whole.
6. Assess how point of view or purpose shapes the content and style of a text.

Integration of Knowledge and Ideas

7. Integrate and evaluate content presented in diverse formats and media, including visually and quantitatively, as well as in words.
8. Delineate and evaluate the argument and specific claims in a text, including the validity of the reasoning as well as the relevance and sufficiency of the evidence.
9. Analyze how two or more texts address similar themes or topics in order to build knowledge or to compare the approaches the authors take.

Range of Reading and Level of Text Complexity

10. Read and comprehend complex literary and informational texts independently and proficiently.

Grade 11 Reading Standards for Literature

Key Ideas and Details

1. Cite strong and thorough textual evidence to support analysis of what the text says explicitly as well as inferences drawn from the text, including determining where the text leaves matters uncertain.

2. Determine two or more themes or central ideas of a text and analyze their development over the course of the text, including how they interact and build on one another to produce a complex account; provide an objective summary of the text.

3. Analyze the impact of the author's choices regarding how to develop and relate elements of a story or drama (e.g., where a story is set, how the action is ordered, how the characters are introduced and developed).

Craft and Structure

4. Determine the meaning of words and phrases as they are used in the text, including figurative and connotative meanings; analyze the impact of specific word choices on meaning and tone, including words with multiple meanings or language that is particularly fresh, engaging, or beautiful. (Include Shakespeare as well as other authors.)

5. Analyze how an author's choices concerning how to structure specific parts of a text (e.g., the choice of where to begin or end a story, the choice to provide a comedic or tragic resolution) contribute to its overall structure and meaning as well as its aesthetic impact.

6. Analyze a case in which grasping point of view requires distinguishing what is directly stated in a text from what is really meant (e.g., satire, sarcasm, irony, or understatement).

Integration of Knowledge and Ideas

7. Analyze multiple interpretations of a story, drama, or poem (e.g., recorded or live production of a play or recorded novel or poetry), evaluating how each version interprets the source text. (Include at least one play by Shakespeare and one play by an American dramatist.)

8. (Not applicable to literature)

9. Demonstrate knowledge of eighteenth-, nineteenth-, and early-twentieth-century foundational works of American literature, including how two or more texts from the same period treat similar themes or topics.

Range of Reading and Level of Text Complexity

10. By the end of grade 11, read and comprehend literature, including stories, dramas, and poems, in the grades 11–CCR text complexity band proficiently, with scaffolding as needed at the high end of the range.

Grade 11 Reading Standards for Informational Text

Key Ideas and Details

1. Cite strong and thorough textual evidence to support analysis of what the text says explicitly as well as inferences drawn from the text, including determining where the text leaves matters uncertain.

2. Determine two or more central ideas of a text and analyze their development over the course of the text, including how they interact and build on one another to provide a complex analysis; provide an objective summary of the text.

3. Analyze a complex set of ideas or sequence of events and explain how specific individuals, ideas, or events interact and develop over the course of the text.

Craft and Structure

4. Determine the meaning of words and phrases as they are used in a text, including figurative, connotative, and technical meanings; analyze how an author uses and refines the meaning of a key term or terms over the course of a text (e.g., how Madison defines *faction* in *Federalist* No. 10).

5. Analyze and evaluate the effectiveness of the structure an author uses in his or her exposition or argument, including whether the structure makes points clear, convincing, and engaging.

6. Determine an author's point of view or purpose in a text in which the rhetoric is particularly effective, analyzing how style and content contribute to the power, persuasiveness, or beauty of the text.

Integration of Knowledge and Ideas

7. Integrate and evaluate multiple sources of information presented in different media or formats (e.g., visually, quantitatively) as well as in words in order to address a question or solve a problem.

8. Delineate and evaluate the reasoning in seminal U.S. texts, including the application of constitutional principles and use of legal reasoning (e.g., in U.S. Supreme Court majority opinions and dissents) and the premises, purposes, and arguments in works of public advocacy (e.g., *The Federalist,* presidential addresses).

9. Analyze seventeenth-, eighteenth-, and nineteenth-century foundational U.S. documents of historical and literary significance (including The Declaration of Independence, the Preamble to the Constitution, the Bill of Rights, and Lincoln's Second Inaugural Address) for their themes, purposes, and rhetorical features.

Range of Reading and Level of Text Complexity

10. By the end of grade 11, read and comprehend literary nonfiction in the grades 11–CCR text complexity band proficiently, with scaffolding as needed at the high end of the range.

Common Core Writing Standards

College and Career Readiness Anchor Standards

Text Types and Purposes

1. Write arguments to support claims in an analysis of substantive topics or texts, using valid reasoning and relevant and sufficient evidence.

2. Write informative/explanatory texts to examine and convey complex ideas and information clearly and accurately through the effective selection, organization, and analysis of content.

3. Write narratives to develop real or imagined experiences or events using effective technique, well-chosen details, and well-structured event sequences.

Production and Distribution of Writing

4. Produce clear and coherent writing in which the development, organization, and style are appropriate to task, purpose, and audience.

5. Develop and strengthen writing as needed by planning, revising, editing, rewriting, or trying a new approach.

6. Use technology, including the Internet, to produce and publish writing and to interact and collaborate with others.

Research to Build and Present Knowledge

7. Conduct short as well as more sustained research projects based on focused questions, demonstrating understanding of the subject under investigation.

8. Gather relevant information from multiple print and digital sources, assess the credibility and accuracy of each source, and integrate the information while avoiding plagiarism.

9. Draw evidence from literary or informational texts to support analysis, reflection, and research.

Range of Writing

10. Write routinely over extended time frames (time for research, reflection, and revision) and shorter time frames (a single sitting or a day or two) for a range of tasks, purposes, and audiences.

Grade 11 Writing Standards

Text Types and Purposes

1. Write arguments to support claims in an analysis of substantive topics or texts, using valid reasoning and relevant and sufficient evidence.

a. Introduce precise, knowledgeable claim(s), establish the significance of the claim(s), distinguish the claim(s) from alternate or opposing claims, and create an organization that logically sequences claim(s), counterclaims, reasons, and evidence.

b. Develop claim(s) and counterclaims fairly and thoroughly, supplying the most relevant evidence for each while pointing out the strengths and limitations of both in a manner that anticipates the audience's knowledge level, concerns, values, and possible biases.

c. Use words, phrases, and clauses as well as varied syntax to link the major sections of the text, create cohesion, and clarify the relationships between claim(s) and reasons, between reasons and evidence, and between claim(s) and counterclaims.

d. Establish and maintain a formal style and objective tone while attending to the norms and conventions of the discipline in which they are writing.

e. Provide a concluding statement or section that follows from and supports the argument presented.

2. Write informative/explanatory texts to examine and convey complex ideas, concepts, and information clearly and accurately through the effective selection, organization, and analysis of content.

a. Introduce a topic; organize complex ideas, concepts, and information so that each new element builds on that which precedes it to create a unified whole; include formatting (e.g., headings), graphics (e.g., figures, tables), and multimedia when useful to aiding comprehension.

b. Develop the topic thoroughly by selecting the most significant and relevant facts, extended definitions, concrete details, quotations, or other information and examples appropriate to the audience's knowledge of the topic.

c. Use appropriate and varied transitions and syntax to link the major sections of the text, create cohesion, and clarify the relationships among complex ideas and concepts.

d. Use precise language, domain-specific vocabulary, and techniques such as metaphor, simile, and analogy to manage the complexity of the topic.

e. Establish and maintain a formal style and objective tone while attending to the norms and conventions of the discipline in which they are writing.

f. Provide a concluding statement or section that follows from and supports the information or explanation presented (e.g., articulating implications or the significance of the topic).

3. Write narratives to develop real or imagined experiences or events using effective technique, well-chosen details, and well-structured event sequences.

a. Engage and orient the reader by setting out a problem, situation, or observation and its significance, establishing one or multiple point(s) of view, and introducing a narrator and/or characters; create a smooth progression of experiences or events.

b. Use narrative techniques, such as dialogue, pacing, description, reflection, and multiple plot lines, to develop experiences, events, and/or characters.
c. Use a variety of techniques to sequence events so that they build on one another to create a coherent whole and build toward a particular tone and outcome (e.g., a sense of mystery, suspense, growth, or resolution).
d. Use precise words and phrases, telling details, and sensory language to convey a vivid picture of the experiences, events, setting, and/or characters.
e. Provide a conclusion that follows from and reflects on what is experienced, observed, or resolved over the course of the narrative.

Production and Distribution of Writing

4. Produce clear and coherent writing in which the development, organization, and style are appropriate to task, purpose, and audience.

5. Develop and strengthen writing as needed by planning, revising, editing, rewriting, or trying a new approach, focusing on addressing what is most significant for a specific purpose and audience.

6. Use technology, including the Internet, to produce, publish, and update individual or shared writing products in response to ongoing feedback, including new arguments or information.

Research to Build and Present Knowledge

7. Conduct short as well as more sustained research projects to answer a question (including a self-generated question) or solve a problem; narrow or broaden the inquiry when appropriate; synthesize multiple sources on the subject, demonstrating understanding of the subject under investigation.

8. Gather relevant information from multiple authoritative print and digital sources, using advanced searches effectively; assess the strengths and limitations of each source in terms of the task, purpose, and audience; integrate information into the text selectively to maintain the flow of ideas, avoiding plagiarism and overreliance on any one source and following a standard format for citation.

9. Draw evidence from literary or informational texts to support analysis, reflection, and research.
a. Apply *grades 11–12 Reading standards* to literature (e.g., "Demonstrate knowledge of eighteenth-, nineteenth-, and early-twentieth-century foundational works of American literature, including how two or more texts from the same period treat similar themes or topics").
b. Apply *grades 11–12 Reading standards* to literary nonfiction (e.g., "Delineate and evaluate the reasoning in seminal U.S. texts, including the application of constitutional principles and use of legal reasoning [e.g., in U.S. Supreme Court Case majority opinions and dissents] and the premises, purposes, and arguments in works of public advocacy [e.g., *The Federalist*, presidential addresses]").

Range of Writing

10. Write routinely over extended time frames (time for research, reflection, and revision) and shorter time frames (a single sitting or a day or two) for a range of tasks, purposes, and audiences.

Common Core Speaking and Listening Standards

College and Career Readiness Anchor Standards

Comprehension and Collaboration

1. Prepare for and participate effectively in a range of conversations and collaborations with diverse partners, building on others' ideas and expressing their own clearly and persuasively.
2. Integrate and evaluate information presented in diverse media and formats, including visually, quantitatively, and orally.
3. Evaluate a speaker's point of view, reasoning, and use of evidence and rhetoric.

Presentation of Knowledge and Ideas

4. Present information, findings, and supporting evidence such that listeners can follow the line of reasoning and the organization, development, and style are appropriate to task, purpose, and audience.
5. Make strategic use of digital media and visual displays of data to express information and enhance understanding of presentations.
6. Adapt speech to a variety of contexts and communicative tasks, demonstrating command of formal English when indicated or appropriate.

Grade 11 Speaking and Listening Standards

Comprehension and Collaboration

1. Initiate and participate effectively in a range of collaborative discussions (one-on-one, in groups, and teacher-led) with diverse partners on *grades 11–12 topics, texts, and issues,* building on others' ideas and expressing their own clearly and persuasively.

a. Come to discussions prepared, having read and researched material under study; explicitly draw on that preparation by referring to evidence from texts and other research on the topic or issue to stimulate a thoughtful, well-reasoned exchange of ideas.

b. Work with peers to promote civil, democratic discussions and decision-making, set clear goals and deadlines, and establish individual roles as needed.

c. Propel conversations by posing and responding to questions that probe reasoning and evidence; ensure a hearing for a full range of positions on a topic or issue; clarify, verify, or challenge ideas and conclusions; and promote divergent and creative perspectives.

d. Respond thoughtfully to diverse perspectives; synthesize comments, claims, and evidence made on all sides of an issue; resolve contradictions when possible; and determine what additional information or research is required to deepen the investigation or complete the task.

2. Integrate multiple sources of information presented in diverse formats and media (e.g., visually, quantitatively, orally) in order to make informed decisions and solve problems, evaluating the credibility and accuracy of each source and noting any discrepancies among the data.

3. Evaluate a speaker's point of view, reasoning, and use of evidence and rhetoric, assessing the stance, premises, links among ideas, word choice, points of emphasis, and tone used.

Presentation of Knowledge and Ideas

4. Present information, findings, and supporting evidence, conveying a clear and distinct perspective, such that listeners can follow the line of reasoning, alternative or opposing perspectives are addressed, and the organization, development, substance, and style are appropriate to purpose, audience, and a range of formal and informal tasks.

5. Make strategic use of digital media (e.g., textual, graphical, audio, visual, and interactive elements) in presentations to enhance understanding of findings, reasoning, and evidence, and to add interest.

6. Adapt speech to a variety of contexts and tasks, demonstrating a command of formal English when indicated or appropriate. (See grades 11–12 Language standards 1 and 3 for specific expectations.)

Common Core Language Standards

College and Career Readiness Anchor Standards

Conventions of Standard English

1. Demonstrate command of the conventions of standard English grammar and usage when writing or speaking.
2. Demonstrate command of the conventions of standard English capitalization, punctuation, and spelling when writing.

Knowledge of Language

3. Apply knowledge of language to understand how language functions in different contexts, to make effective choices for meaning or style, and to comprehend more fully when reading or listening.

Vocabulary Acquisition and Use

4. Determine or clarify the meaning of unknown and multiple-meaning words and phrases by using context clues, analyzing meaningful word parts, and consulting general and specialized reference materials, as appropriate.
5. Demonstrate understanding of figurative language, word relationships, and nuances in word meanings.
6. Acquire and use accurately a range of general academic and domain-specific words and phrases sufficient for reading, writing, speaking, and listening at the college and career readiness level; demonstrate independence in gathering vocabulary knowledge when considering a word or phrase important to comprehension or expression.

Grade 11 Language Standards

Conventions of Standard English

1. Demonstrate command of the conventions of standard English grammar and usage when writing or speaking.
   a. Apply the understanding that usage is a matter of convention, can change over time, and is sometimes contested.
   b. Resolve issues of complex or contested usage, consulting references (e.g., *Merriam-Webster's Dictionary of English Usage, Garner's Modern American Usage*) as needed.
2. Demonstrate command of the conventions of standard English capitalization, punctuation, and spelling when writing.
   a. Observe hyphenation conventions.
   b. Spell correctly.

Knowledge of Language

3. Apply knowledge of language to understand how language functions in different contexts, to make effective choices for meaning or style, and to comprehend more fully when reading or listening.

a. Vary syntax for effect, consulting references (e.g., Tufte's *Artful Sentences*) for guidance as needed; apply an understanding of syntax to the study of complex texts when reading.

Vocabulary Acquisition and Use

4. Determine or clarify the meaning of unknown and multiple-meaning words and phrases based on *grades 11–12 reading and content*, choosing flexibly from a range of strategies.

a. Use context (e.g., the overall meaning of a sentence, paragraph, or text; a word's position or function in a sentence) as a clue to the meaning of a word or phrase.

b. Identify and correctly use patterns of word changes that indicate different meanings or parts of speech (e.g., *conceive, conception, conceivable*).

c. Consult general and specialized reference materials (e.g., dictionaries, glossaries, thesauruses), both print and digital, to find the pronunciation of a word or determine or clarify its precise meaning, its part of speech, its etymology, or its standard usage.

d. Verify the preliminary determination of the meaning of a word or phrase (e.g., by checking the inferred meaning in context or in a dictionary).

5. Demonstrate understanding of figurative language, word relationships, and nuances in word meanings.

a. Interpret figures of speech (e.g., hyperbole, paradox) in context and analyze their role in the text.

b. Analyze nuances in the meaning of words with similar denotations.

6. Acquire and use accurately general academic and domain-specific words and phrases, sufficient for reading, writing, speaking, and listening at the college and career readiness level; demonstrate independence in gathering vocabulary knowledge when considering a word or phrase important to comprehension or expression.

COMMON CORE WORKSHOPS

- BUILDING ACADEMIC VOCABULARY
- WRITING AN OBJECTIVE SUMMARY
- COMPREHENDING COMPLEX TEXTS
- ANALYZING ARGUMENTS
- CONDUCTING RESEARCH

Common Core State Standards

Reading Literature 2, 10
Reading Informational Text 2, 4, 5, 6, 8
Writing 1.a, 1.b, 1.e, 7, 8, 9, 9.b
Language 6

Building Academic Vocabulary

Academic vocabulary is the language used in school, on standardized tests, and—often—in the business world. Academic terms are more formal and specific than the informal vocabulary most people use among friends and family members. Success in school and later in work requires a clear understanding of different types of academic language. The Common Core State Standards require that you acquire and use grade-appropriate academic words and phrases.

Technical Domain-Specific Academic Vocabulary The literary concepts you will learn throughout this book are one type of academic language. These words are specific to the content area—the subject or discipline—of literature. Other disciplines, such as social studies, the sciences, mathematics, and the arts, have their own academic vocabularies. Some content-area words cross disciplines, or have different meanings when applied to different areas of study.

Technical words are an even more specialized type of domain-specific academic vocabulary. These are words and phrases, such as the following, that identify a precise element in the content area and usually do not appear in other disciplines:

Science: pipette; genome
Music: clef; libretto

Critical Reading and Thinking Terms Many academic terms define modes of thinking, discussing, or writing about ideas. In this book, these words appear in the Critical Reading questions at the ends of the selections. Such academic terms also appear in instructions and writing prompts.

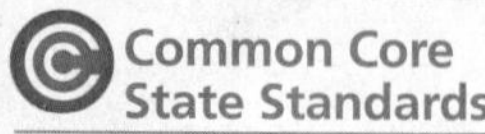

Language

6. Acquire and use accurately general academic and domain-specific words and phrases, sufficient for reading, writing, speaking, and listening at the college and career readiness level; demostrate independence in gathering vocabulary knowledge when considering a word or phrase important to comprehension or expression.

A Note on Etymology

Etymology is the branch of linguistics that deals with word origins and the development of languages. Etymologists trace the history of a word in its own language, and then to even earlier sources in other, more ancient languages. Knowledge of a word's etymology will contribute to your understanding of its meaning and help you determine the meaning of other words that share its history. Etymological information for content-area words appears in the charts on the following pages.

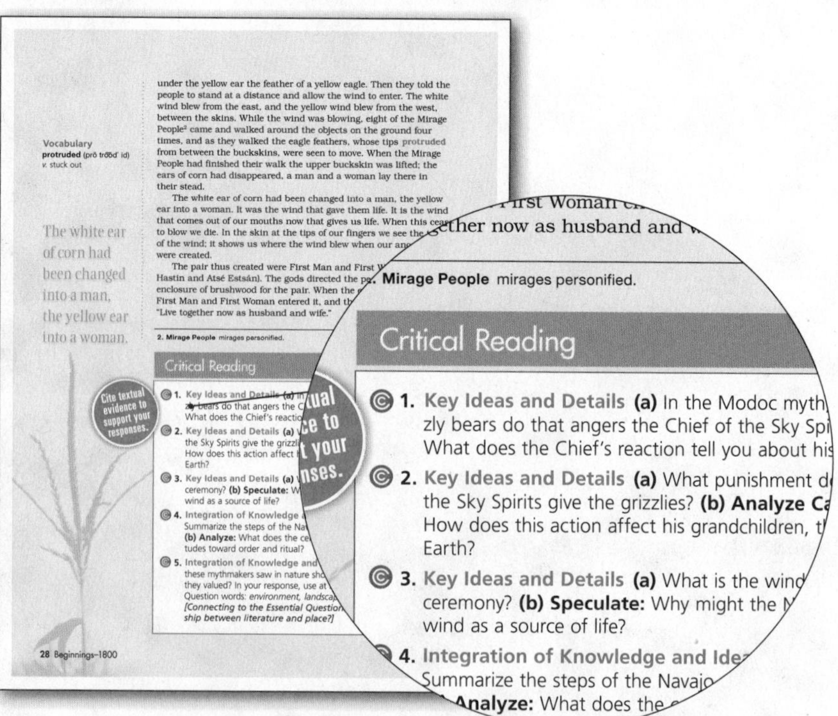

Technical Domain-Specific Academic Vocabulary

Knowledge of technical content-area academic words, and the roots and affixes that compose them, will help you in all of your school courses. As you review the charts below, recognize words that apply to content areas other than those specified here.

Technical Domain-Specific Academic Vocabulary: Science

Term	Meaning	Root/Affix
Accelerate	*v.* increase speed	Latin root *-celer-* = swift Words with the same root: accelerator *n.*; celerity *n.*
Catalyst	*n.* something that acts to bring about a result	Latin root *-cata-* = down; away Words with the same root: cataclysm *n.*; catapult *n.*
Chlorophyll	*n.* green pigment found in plant cells	Greek root *-chloro-* = green Words with the same root: chlorine *n.*; chlorosis *n.*
Chromosome	*n.* strand of proteins that carries the genes of a living creature	Greek prefix *chromo-* = color; pigment Words with the same prefix: chromatic *adj.*; chromate *n.*
Cytoplasm	*n.* colorless substance of a cell; outside the nucleus	Greek suffix *-plasm* = molded; formed Words with the same suffix: bioplasm *n.*; protoplasm *n.*
Entropy	*n.* lack of order that increases over time in a system	Greek root *-tropos-* = turning; deviation Words with the same root: tropical *adj.*; trophy *n.*; heliotrope *n.*
Enzyme	*n.* chemical substance produced by living cells that causes changes in other chemicals	Greek suffix *-zyme* = leavening (an agent that causes fermentation) Words with the same suffix: vitazyme *n.*; microzyme *n.*
Mitosis	*n.* method of cell division	Greek suffix *-osis* = action; process Words with the same suffix: prognosis *n.*; psychosis *n.*
Thermometer	*n.* instrument for measuring temperature	Greek root *-therme-* = hot Words with the same root: thermonuclear *adj.*; thermostat *n.*
Viscous	*adj.* having a thick and sticky fluid consistency	Latin prefix *visco-* = sticky Words with the same prefix: viscometer *n.*; viscosity *n.*

Ordinary Language: Ice cubes placed in water will begin to **break down.**

Academic Language: Ice cubes placed in water will begin the process of **entropy.**

Exploring Academic Vocabulary: Science

The word *thermometer* combines the Greek roots *-therme-*, which means "heat," and *-metr-*, which means "measure." Using this knowledge, determine the meaning of the following words derived from the same roots:

dynameter **odometer** **hypothermia** **thermography**

Then, use a dictionary to confirm the definitions you proposed. If a general dictionary is not sufficient, consult a specialized science dictionary to find the information you need. Explain how the meaning of each word relates to those of its Greek origins.

Technical Domain-Specific Academic Vocabulary: Mathematics

Term	Meaning	Root/Affix
Correlate	*v.* show mutual relationship between items	Latin prefix *cor-* = together; with Words with the same prefix: correspond *v.*; corrosion *n.*
Exponent	*n.* symbol placed above and to the right of a number or letter to show how many times that quantity is to be multiplied by itself	Latin suffix *-ponent* = to put; place; set Words with the same suffix: component *n.*; proponent *n.*
Inflection	*n.* change of a curve or arc from convex to concave or the reverse	Latin root *-flectere-* = to bend Words with the same root: reflection *n.*; deflect *v.*
Logarithm	*n.* power to which a base must be raised to produce a given number	Greek prefix *logos-* = word; speech; reason Words with the same prefix: logic *n.*; logotype *n.*
Statistics	*n.* numerical facts or data	Latin root *-stat-* = condition; position; state Words with the same root: statistical *adj.*; static *adj.*
Permutation	*n.* one of the ways in which a set of things can be arranged or ordered	Latin root *-mutare-* = change Words with the same root: mutable *adj.*; mutation *n.*
Estimate	*v.* calculate approximately	Middle French root *-estimer-* = value; appraise Words with the same root: estimation *n.*; esteem *v.*
Graphic	*adj.* relating to the use of diagrams, graphs, curves	Greek root *-graph-* = writing; drawing Words with the same root: telegraph *n.*; biography *n.*; autograph *n.*
Configure	*v.* construct; arrange	Latin root *-figura-* = shape; form; figure Words with the same root: disfigure *v.*; effigy *n.*

Ordinary Language:
We arranged the **numerical information** in different charts.

Academic Language:
We incorporated **statistical data** into charts.

Exploring Academic Vocabulary: Mathematics

The word *correlate* is built on the Latin prefix *cor-* (also *com-* or *con-*), which means "with" or "together." Using this knowledge, determine the meaning of the following words derived from the same prefix:

correspond **concert** **compress** **congruent**

Then, use an online or print dictionary to confirm the definitions you proposed. Explain how the meaning of each word relates to that of its Latin ancestor.

Technical Domain-Specific Academic Vocabulary: Social Studies

Term	Meaning	Root/Affix
Corporation	*n.* organization of many people authorized to act as a single person	Latin root *-corpus-* = body Words with the same root: corporeal *adj.*; incorporate *v.*
Demography	*n.* study of human populations	Greek prefix *demos-* = people Words with the same prefix: demographic *n.*; democracy *n.*
Economy	*n.* system by which a country's money and goods are used and produced	Greek suffix *-nomy* = law; received knowledge Words with the same suffix: economy *n.*; taxonomy *n.*
Invest	*v.* give money to a company in order to receive a profit	Latin root *-vestire-* = dress; clothe Words with the same root: vestment *n.*; investigation *n.*
Admiral	*n.* high-ranking Naval officer	Arabic root *-amir-* = leader Words with the same root: emirate *n.*; admiralship *n.*
Curfew	*n.* law requiring a population to stay indoors at a stated hour	Old French root *-covrir-* = to cover Words with the same root: covert *adj.*; coverlet *n.*
Lieutenant	*n.* someone who substitutes for another person of greater authority	Old French root *-lieu-* = place Word with the same root: milieu *n.*
Absolutism	*n.* system of government in which a ruler has unlimited power	Latin prefix *ab-* = away; from Words with the same prefix: absolve *v.*
Civic	*adj.* of a city, citizens, or citizenship	Latin root *-civ-* = citizen Words with the same root: civilian *n.*; civilization *n.*

Ordinary Language: The government urges citizens to **put money into** local businesses.

Academic Language: The government urges citizens to **invest in** local businesses.

Exploring Academic Vocabulary: Social Studies

The word *economy* is built on the Greek suffix *–nomy*, which means "law; body of received knowledge." Using this knowledge, determine the meaning of the following words derived from the same suffix:

taxonomy **autonomy** **astronomy** **gastronomy**

Then, use an online or print dictionary to confirm the definitions you proposed. Explain how the meaning of each word relates to that of its Greek ancestor.

Technical Domain-Specific Academic Vocabulary: Technology

Term	Meaning	Root/Affix
Gigabyte	*n.* unit of storage capacity in a computer system, equal to 1,073,741,824 bytes	Greek prefix *giga-* = giant Words with the same prefix: gigahertz *n.*; gigantic *adj.*
Macro	*n.* single computer instruction that represents a sequence of operations	Greek prefix *macro-* = long, tall, deep, large Words with the same prefix: macrobiotic *adj.*; macrocosm *n.*
Pixel	*n.* smallest unit of an image on a television or computer screen	Old French suffix *-el* = small one Words with the same suffix: satchel *n.*; model *n.*
Processor	*n.* central part of a computer that does the calculations needed to deal with the information it is given	from Latin root *-cedere-* = to go Words with the same root: proceed *v.*; recede *v.*
Simulation	*n.* situation that produces conditions that are not real but appear real	Latin root *-sim-* = like derived through Indo-European base *sem-/som-* = same; as one Words with the same root: ensemble *v.*; simultaneous *adj.*
Streaming	*n.* method of transmitting data so that it can be delivered and received in a steady stream	German root *-strom-* = current; river Words with the same root: mainstream *n.*; streamline *v.*
Transmitter	*n.* equipment that sends out radio or television signals	Latin prefix *trans-* = across Words with the same prefix: transportation *n.*; transcontinental *adj.*
Debug	*v.* find and correct defects	Latin prefix *de-* = down; from Words with the same prefix: defuse *v.*; defrost *v.*
Export	*v.* in computers, to save data in a format usable by another program	Latin root *-portare-* = to carry Words with the same root: import *v.*; airport *n.*
Binary	*adj.* made up of two parts or things; twofold	Latin root *-bin-* = together; double Words with the same root: binocular *n.*; binomial *n.*

Ordinary Language:
I asked the technician to **remove the defects from** my computer.

Academic Language:
I asked the technician to **debug** my operating system.

Exploring Academic Vocabulary: Technology

The word *simulation* comes from the Latin root *-sim-,* which means "like." This Latin root derives from the Indo-European base *sem-/som-,* which means "same; as one." Using your knowledge of these origins, determine the meaning of the following words derived from the same roots:

resemble **facsimile** **verisimilitude** **semblance**

Then, use a dictionary to confirm the definitions you proposed. Explain how the meaning of each word relates to that of its Indo-European base.

Technical Domain-Specific Academic Vocabulary: The Arts

Term	Meaning	Root/Affix
Allegro	*adv.* faster than allegretto but not so fast as presto	Latin root *-alacer-/-alacris-* = lively; brisk Words with the same root: allegretto *adj.*; *adv.*; alacrity *n.*
Alignment	*n.* arrangement in a straight line	Old French root *-lignier-* = to line Words with the same root: align *v.*; realign *v.*
Craftmanship	*n.* skill used in making handmade objects	Middle English suffix *-schipe*; derived through Anglian suffix *-scip* = state; condition; quality Words with the same suffix: friendship *n.*; dictatorship *n.*
Decrescendo	*n.* gradual decrease in volume	Old French *creissant*; derived through Latin root *-crescere-* = come forth; spring up; grow; thrive Words with the same root: crescent *n.*; increase *v.*
Baritone	*n.* male singing voice lower than a tenor and higher than a bass	Latin root *-tonus-* = sound; tone Words with the same root: monotone *n.*; intonation *n.*
Medium	*n.* material or technique used in art	Latin root *-medius-* = middle Words with the same root: media *n.*; mediate *v.*; median *adj.*
Musicality	*n.* sensitivity to, knowledge of, or talent for music	Latin suffix *-ity* = quality; state; degree Words with the same suffix: normality *n.*; publicity *n.*
Technique	*n.* method or procedure in rendering an artistic work	Indo-European prefix *tek-* = shape; make Words with the same prefix: technical *adj.*; technician *n.*
Tempo	*n.* speed at which a composition is performed	Latin root *-tempus-* = time Words with the same root: temporal *adj.*; temporary *adj.*

Ordinary Language: The dancers moved in a perfectly **straight line.**

Academic Language: The dancers moved in perfect **alignment** on stage.

Exploring Academic Vocabulary: The Arts

The word *craftsmanship* is built on the Anglian suffix *-scip*, which means "state, condition, quality." Using this knowledge, determine the meaning of the following words derived from the same suffix:

musicianship **readership** **friendship** **partnership**

Then, use an online or print dictionary to confirm the definitions you proposed. Explain how the meaning of each word relates to that of its Anglian ancestor.

Vocabulary Across Content Areas

You might recognize words that apply to content areas other than those specified in the charts on the previous pages. For example, notice how the word *accelerator* relates to two different content areas:

Science: accelerator *n.* nerve or muscle that speeds up a body function

Automotive Technology: accelerator *n.* device, such as the foot throttle of an automobile, for increasing the speed of a machine.

While the objects referred to in each definition are different, both of their functions relate to the Latin root *-celer-*, meaning "swift." As you read texts for school, recognize similarities in roots or affixes among words in different content areas. This will help you better understand specific terms and make meaningful connections among topics.

Academic Vocabulary: Critical Thinking Terms

Throughout this book, you will encounter academic vocabulary related to the process of critical thinking. Unlike content-area vocabulary, these words apply equally in all school studies. Being familiar with these academic vocabulary words will be useful as you approach high-stakes standardized tests such as the SAT and ACT. Academic vocabulary will also aid you as you encounter business materials in the workplace.

Term (verb form)	Meaning	Root/Affix
Advocate	Speak or write in support of	Latin root *-voc-* = speak; call Related words: advocate *n.*; advocacy *n.*
Anticipate	Prepare for or signal something	Latin prefix *ante-* = before Related words: anticipatory *adj.*; anticipation *n.*
Arrange	Put into order or sequence	Old French root *-rang-* = rank Related words: arrangement *n.*
Assess	Determine importance, size, or value	Latin root *-sed-/-sess-* = sit Related words: assessment *n.*
Categorize	Place in related groups	Greek prefix *kata-/cata-* = down; against Related words: category *n.*; categorical *adj.*
Compare	Examine in order to discover similarities	Latin root *-par-* = equal Related words: comparison *n.*; comparable *adj.*
Conclude	Determine through logical reasoning	Latin root *-clud-* = shut Related words: conclusion *n.*; conclusive *adj.*
Contrast	Examine in order to discover differences	Latin prefix *con-/com-* = with; together Related words: contrastable *adj.*
Debate	Discuss opposing reasons; argue	French root *-batre-* = to beat Related words: debatable *adj.*
Deduce	Infer from a general principle	Latin root *-duc-* = to lead Related words: deduction *n.*; deductive *adj.*
Defend	Maintain or support in the face of argument	Latin root *-fend-* = to strike; push Related words: defense *n.*; defendant *n.*

Term (verb form)	Meaning	Root/Affix
Describe	Represent in words	Latin root *-scrib-* = to write Related words: description *n.*; descriptive *adj.*
Design	Create; fashion or construct according to plan	Latin root *-sign-* = to mark Related words: design *n.*; designer *n.*
Devise	Form in the mind by new combinations of ideas; invent	Latin root *-vid-* = to separate Related words: devisable *adj.*
Differentiate	Recognize a difference	Latin suffix *-ate* = act Related words: different *adj.*; differentiation *n.*
Evaluate	Determine significance, worth, or condition through careful study	Old French root *-val-* = worth; value Related words: evaluation *n.*; evaluative *adj.*
Format	Arrange according to a design or plan	Latin root *-form-* = form, shape Related words: format *n.*; formation *n.*
Generalize	Draw a larger principle from details	Latin root *-genus-* = stock; kind Related words: generalization *n.*
Hypothesize	Develop a theory about	Greek prefix *hypo-* = under, beneath Related words: hypothesis *n.*; hypothetically *adv.*
Illustrate	Give examples that support an idea	Latin root *-lus-* = brighten; illuminate Related words: illustration *n.*; illustrative *adj.*
Interpret	Explain the meaning of	Latin root *-inter-* = between Related words: interpretation *n.*; interpreter *n.*
Investigate	Make a systematic examination	French root *-vestige-* = mark; trace; sign Related words: investigation *n.*; investigative *adj.*
Paraphrase	Express in one's own words what another person has said or written	Greek prefix *para-* = beside Related words: paraphraser *n.*
Predict	Foretell on the basis of observation, experience, or reason	Latin root *-dic-* = speak, tell, say Related words: prediction *n.*; predictable *adj.*
Refute	Prove an argument or statement false or wrong	Latin root *-fut-* = beat Related words: refutable *adj.*; refutably *adv.*
Sort	Put in place according to kind, class, or nature	Old French root *-sortir-* = allot; assort Related words: sorter *n.*
Speculate	Use evidence to guess what might happen	Latin root *-spec-* = look at; view Related words: speculation *n.*; speculative *adj.*
Structure	Create a general plot or outline	Latin root *-struct-* = to build; assemble Related words: structure *n.*; structural *adj.*
Validate	Prove to be factual or effective	Latin root *-val-* = be strong Related words: valid *adj.*; validity *n.*

Ordinary Language: She **explained the meaning of** the story's symbols.

Academic Language: She **interpreted** the meaning of the story's symbols.

Writing an Objective Summary

The ability to write objective summaries is important in college course work and in many careers, such as journalism, business, law, and research work. Writing an effective objective summary involves recording the key ideas of a text as well as demonstrating your understanding.

Common Core State Standards

Reading Informational Text

2. Determine two or more central ideas of a text and analyze their development over the course of the text, including how they interact and build on one another to provide a complex analysis; provide an objective summary of the text.

Reading Literature

2. Determine two or more themes or central ideas of a text and analyze their development over the course of the text, including how they interact and build on one another to produce a complex account; provide an objective summary of the text.

Characteristics of an Objective Summary

An effective objective summary is a concise overview of a text. Following are important elements of an objective summary:

- It is **focused,** relaying the main theme or central idea of a text. It includes specific, relevant details that support that theme or central idea, and it leaves out unnecessary supporting details.
- It is **brief,** although the writer must be careful to balance brevity and thoroughness and not misrepresent the text by eliminating important parts.
- It is **accurate** and captures the essence of the longer text it is describing.
- It is **objective.** The writer should refrain from inserting his or her own opinions, reactions, or personal reflections into the summary.

Remember that an objective summary is *not* a collection of sentences or paragraphs copied from the original source. It is *not* a long retelling of every event, detail, or point in the original text. Finally, a good summary does *not* include evaluative comments, such as the reader's overall opinion of or reaction to the selection.

Checklist for Writing an Objective Summary

Before writing an objective summary, be sure you are well acquainted with the text.

- **Understand the entire passage.** You must clearly understand the text's meaning, including any advanced or technical terminology. In your summary, refer to details from the beginning, middle, and end of the text.
- **Prioritize ideas and details.** Determine the main or central ideas of a text and identify the key supporting details. Make sure you recognize which details are less important so that you do not include them in your objective summary.
- **Identify the author's audience and purpose.** Knowing what the author intended to accomplish in the text as well as what audience it was designed to reach will help you summarize accurately.

INFORMATIONAL TEXT

Model Objective Summary

Note the key elements of an effective objective summary, called out in the sidenotes. Then, write an objective summary of a text you have recently read. Review your summary, and delete any unnecessary details, opinions, or evaluations.

Summary of "The Open Window"

"The Open Window," by Saki, ~~the pen name of H.H. Munro~~, is a short story about a nervous man by the name of Framton Nuttel. Set in rural England during the Victorian-Edwardian period, the story tells of a visit that Mr. Nuttel makes to a neighboring estate.

Mr. Framton Nuttel, who has been ordered by his physicians to rest and avoid excitement, has gone to the country for a "nerve cure." His sister has given him letters of introduction to various acquaintances of hers. Framton reluctantly takes his sister's suggestion and calls on the Sappletons.

When Framton arrives at the Sappleton estate, he is met by Mrs. Sappleton's fifteen-year-old niece, Vera. ~~She is quite a character.~~ Vera points to an open window and relates a tragic tale. She tells Framton that exactly three years ago, Mr. Sappleton, Mrs. Sappleton's two younger brothers, and their spaniel went out to hunt, leaving through that very window, and met their death in the bog. Their bodies have never been recovered. The niece explains that her aunt keeps the window open because she expects her husband and brothers to return some day.

Soon thereafter, Mrs. Sappleton enters the room and begins to speak of the hunters. Alarmed, Framton tries to change the topic. He rambles on about his health, noticing that Mrs. Sappleton keeps glancing out of the open window. Suddenly, Mrs. Sappleton exclaims, "Here they are at last!" Framton sees a look of horror in Vera's eyes. Then he turns and sees the figures of three men and a dog approaching. He frantically gathers his belongings and runs away.

As Mr. Sappleton enters through the window, he greets his wife and inquires about the man he spotted running away. Mrs. Sappleton responds that Framton Nuttel was a strange man who dashed off as if he had seen a ghost.

Then Vera mentions that Mr. Nuttel was most likely frightened by the dog. She says that he confided in her that he was once terrified by a pack of wild dogs.

The story ends with this sentence: "Romance at short notice was her specialty."

Eliminate unnecessary details.

A one-sentence synopsis highlighting the theme or central idea of the story can be an effective start to a summary.

This sentence states the writer's opinion and should not be included in an objective summary.

Relating the development of the text in chronological order makes a summary easy to follow.

The writer quotes the final sentence of the story because it is the key to understanding the plot.

Comprehending Complex Texts

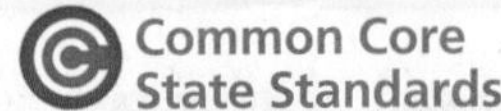

Reading Literature 10. By the end of grade 11, read and comprehend literature, including stories, dramas, and poems, in the grades 11-CCR text complexity band proficiently, with scaffolding as needed at the high end of the range.

During the final years of high school, you will be required to read increasingly complex texts in preparation for college and the workplace. A complex text features one or more of the following qualities:

- challenging vocabulary
- long, complex sentences
- figurative language
- multiple levels of meaning
- unfamiliar settings and situations

The selections in this textbook provide you with a range of readings in many genres. Some of these texts will fall within your comfort zone, but others will be, and should be, more challenging. In order to comprehend and interpret complex texts, practice the reading strategies described here.

Strategy 1: Multidraft Reading

Good readers develop the habit of rereading texts in order to comprehend them completely. To fully understand a text, try this multidraft reading strategy:

1st Reading

The first time you read a text, read to gain its basic meaning. If you are reading a narrative text, look for the basics of the plot: what is happening, and to whom. If the text is nonfiction, look for central ideas and key supporting details. If you are reading poetry, first read to get a sense of who the speaker is. Also take note of the setting and situation.

2nd Reading

During your second reading of a text, focus on the artistry or effectiveness of the writing. Also take note of text structures and organizational patterns. Think about why the author made those choices and what effects they created. Then, examine the author's creative uses of language and the effects of that language. For example, has the author used rhyme, figurative language, or words with negative connotations? If so, to what effect?

3rd Reading

After your third reading, compare and contrast the text with others of its kind you have read. For example, you might compare poems from a certain time period or compare poems written by a single author. Evaluate the text's overall effectiveness and its central idea or theme.

Independent Practice

As you read this sonnet by William Shakespeare, practice the multidraft reading strategy by completing a chart like the one below.

Sonnet 27

Weary with toil, I haste me to my bed,
The dear repose for limbs with travel tired;
But then begins a journey in my head
To work my mind, when body's work's expired:
For then my thoughts—from far where I abide—
Intend a zealous pilgrimage to thee,
And keep my drooping eyelids open wide,
Looking on darkness which the blind do see:
Save that my soul's imaginary sight
Presents thy shadow to my sightless view,
Which, like a jewel hung in ghastly night,
Makes black night beauteous, and her old face new.
Lo! thus, by day my limbs, by night my mind,
For thee, and for myself, no quiet find.

Multidraft Reading Chart

	My Understanding
1st Reading Look for key ideas and details that unlock basic meaning.	
2nd Reading Read for deeper meanings. Look for ways in which the author used text structures and language to create effects.	
3rd Reading Read to integrate your knowledge and ideas. Connect the text to others of its kind and to your own experience.	

Strategy 2: Close Read the Text

Complex texts require close reading—a careful analysis of word choices, phrases, and sentences. An awareness of literary techniques and elements, such as allusion, symbolism, analogy, and text structure, contributes to a deep understanding of a complex text. However, a starting point for close reading is comprehension, which is the foundation for interpretation and analysis. Use the following tips to comprehend the text:

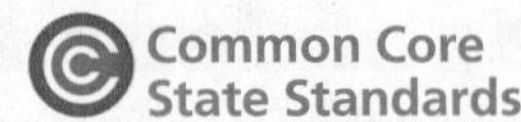
Common Core State Standards

Reading Informational Text
4. Determine the meaning of words and phrases as they are used in a text, including figurative, connotative, and technical meanings; analyze how an author uses and refines the meaning of a key term or terms over the course of a text (e.g., how Madison defines *faction* in *Federalist* No. 10).

Tips for Close Reading

1. **Break down long sentences** into parts. Look for the subject of the sentence and its verb. Then identify which parts of the sentence modify, or give more information about, its subject.

2. **Reread passages.** When reading complex texts, be sure to reread passages to confirm that you understand their meaning.

3. **Look for context clues.** There are several types of context clues, such as the following:
   - **a.** Restatement of an idea. For example, in the sentence below, "to help . . . understand" restates the verb *clarify.*
     The sportscaster tried to **clarify** the offsides violation to help the spectators understand the referee's call.
   - **b.** Definition of sophisticated words. In this sentence, the words *goes beyond* define the verb *transcends.*
     The watercolor painting **transcends,** or goes beyond, the expectations of the viewers.
   - **c.** Examples of concepts and topics.
     The menu listed green beans, corn, and okra as side dishes.
   - **d.** Contrasts of ideas and topics. In the following sentence, the example helps you understand the meaning of *claustrophobia.*
     Adam is **claustrophobic;** he cannot tolerate being cooped up in small spaces.

4. **Identify pronoun antecedents.** If long sentences contain pronouns, reread the text to make sure the pronoun references are clear. The pronoun *its* in the following sentence refers to Yosemite National Park, not to the U.S. government.
   Yosemite National Park was set aside by the U.S. government so people could enjoy **its** natural beauty.

5. **Look for conjunctions,** such as *and, or, yet,* and *however,* to understand relationships between ideas.

6. **Paraphrase,** or restate in your own words, passages of difficult text in order to check your understanding. Remember that a paraphrase is essentially a word-for-word restatement of an original text; it is not a summary.

INFORMATIONAL TEXT

Close-Read Model

As you read this document, take note of the sidenotes that model ways to unlock meaning in the text.

from "The Perils of Indifference" by Elie Weisel

What is indifference? Etymologically, the word means "no difference." A strange and unnatural state in which the lines blur between light and darkness, dusk and dawn, crime and punishment, cruelty and compassion, good and evil.

What are its courses and inescapable consequences? Is it a philosophy? Is there a philosophy of indifference conceivable? Can one possibly view indifference as a virtue? Is it necessary at times to practice it simply to keep one's sanity, live normally, enjoy a fine meal and a glass of wine, as the world around us experiences harrowing upheavals?

Of course, indifference can be tempting—more than that, seductive. It is so much easier to look away from victims. It is so much easier to avoid such rude interruptions to our work, our dreams, our hopes. It is, after all, awkward, troublesome, to be involved in another person's pain and despair. Yet, for the person who is indifferent, his or her neighbors are of no consequence. And, therefore, their lives are meaningless. Their hidden or even visible anguish is of no interest. Indifference reduces the other to an abstraction. . . .

In a way, to be indifferent to that suffering is what makes the human being inhuman. Indifference, after all, is more dangerous than anger and hatred. Anger can at times be creative. One writes a great poem, a great symphony, one does something special for the sake of humanity because one is angry at the injustice that one witnesses. But indifference is never creative. Even hatred at times may elicit a response. You fight it. You denounce it. You disarm it. Indifference elicits no response. Indifference is not a response.

Indifference is not a beginning, it is an end. And, therefore, indifference is always the friend of the enemy, for it benefits the aggressor—never his victim, whose pain is magnified when he or she feels forgotten. The political prisoner in his cell, the hungry children, the homeless refugees—not to respond to their plight, not to relieve their solitude by offering them a spark of hope is to exile them from human memory. And in denying their humanity we betray our own.

Indifference, then, is not only a sin, it is a punishment. And this is one of the most important lessons of this outgoing century's wide-ranging experiments in good and evil. . . .

This list of contrasts helps you to know that "compassion" is the opposite of "cruelty."

Look for antecedents. The abstract noun *indifference* is referred to by the pronouns *its* and *it*.

Search for context clues. The words in blue are context clues that help you infer the meaning of the word that appears in yellow.

Break down this long sentence into parts. The text highlighted in yellow conveys the basic meaning of the sentence. The text highlighted in blue provides additional information.

The examples highlighted in pink help you understand that the word *plight* means "bad situation."

Strategy 3: Ask Questions

Be an attentive reader by asking questions as you read. Throughout this text, we have provided questions for you following each selection. Those questions are sorted into three basic categories that build in sophistication and lead you to a deeper understanding of the texts you read. Here is an example from this text:

Some questions are about **Key Ideas and Details** in the text. To answer these questions, you will need to locate and cite explicit information in the text or draw inferences from what you have read.

Some questions are about **Craft and Structure** in the text. To answer these questions, you will need to analyze how the author developed and structured the text. You will also look for ways in which the author artfully used language and how those word choices impacted the meaning and tone of the work.

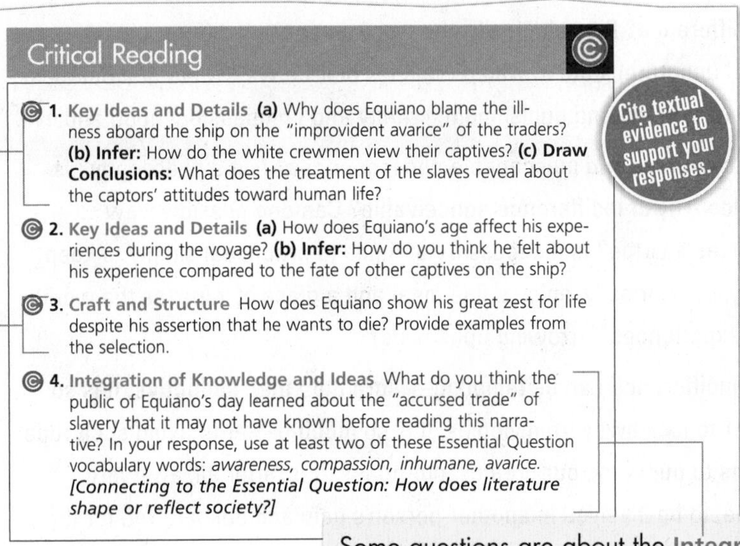

Critical Reading

1. Key Ideas and Details (a) Why does Equiano blame the illness aboard the ship on the "improvident avarice" of the traders? **(b) Infer:** How do the white crewmen view their captives? **(c) Draw Conclusions:** What does the treatment of the slaves reveal about the captors' attitudes toward human life?

2. Key Ideas and Details (a) How does Equiano's age affect his experiences during the voyage? **(b) Infer:** How do you think he felt about his experience compared to the fate of other captives on the ship?

3. Craft and Structure How does Equiano show his great zest for life despite his assertion that he wants to die? Provide examples from the selection.

4. Integration of Knowledge and Ideas What do you think the public of Equiano's day learned about the "accursed trade" of slavery that it may not have known before reading this narrative? In your response, use at least two of these Essential Question vocabulary words: *awareness, compassion, inhumane, avarice.* ***[Connecting to the Essential Question: How does literature shape or reflect society?]***

Cite textual evidence to support your responses.

Some questions are about the **Integration of Knowledge and Ideas** in the text. These questions ask you to evaluate a text in many different ways, such as comparing texts, analyzing arguments in the text, and using many other methods of thinking critically about a text's ideas.

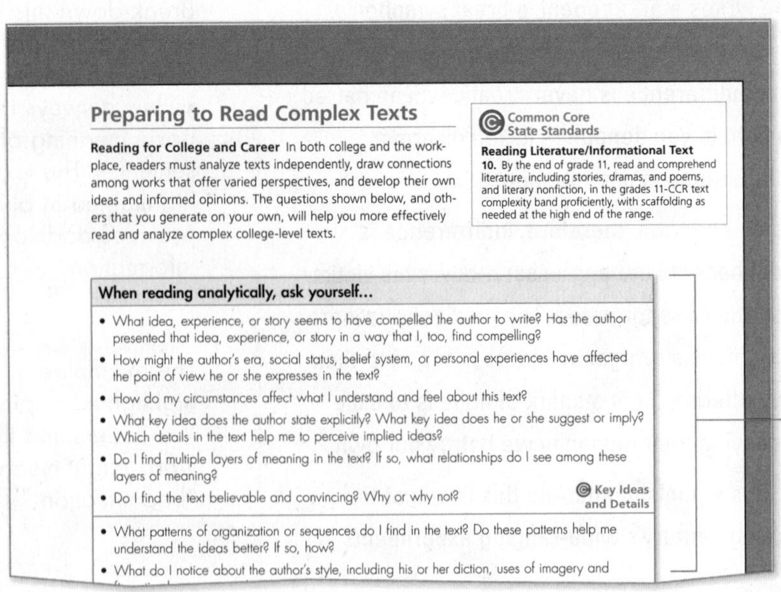

Preparing to Read Complex Texts

Reading for College and Career In both college and the workplace, readers must analyze texts independently, draw connections among works that offer varied perspectives, and develop their own ideas and informed opinions. The questions shown below, and others that you generate on your own, will help you more effectively read and analyze complex college-level texts.

Common Core State Standards

Reading Literature/Informational Text
10. By the end of grade 11, read and comprehend literature, including stories, dramas, and poems, and literary nonfiction, in the grades 11-CCR text complexity band proficiently, with scaffolding as needed at the high end of the range.

When reading analytically, ask yourself...

- What idea, experience, or story seems to have compelled the author to write? Has the author presented that idea, experience, or story in a way that I, too, find compelling?
- How might the author's era, social status, belief system, or personal experiences have affected the point of view he or she expresses in the text?
- How do my circumstances affect what I understand and feel about this text?
- What key idea does the author state explicitly? What key idea does he or she suggest or imply? Which details in the text help me to perceive implied ideas?
- Do I find multiple layers of meaning in the text? If so, what relationships do I see among these layers of meaning?
- Do I find the text believable and convincing? Why or why not?

Key Ideas and Details

- What patterns of organization or sequences do I find in the text? Do these patterns help me understand the ideas better? If so, how?
- What do I notice about the author's style, including his or her diction, uses of imagery and

As you read independently, ask similar types of questions to ensure that you fully enjoy and comprehend texts you read for school and for pleasure. Look for and use the sets of questions provided for Independent Reading at the end of each unit.

Model

Following is an example of a complex text. The call-out boxes show sample questions that an attentive reader might ask while reading.

from *1776* by David McCullough

On January 14, two weeks into the new year, George Washington wrote one of the most forlorn, despairing letters of his life. He had been suffering sleepless nights in the big house by the Charles. "The reflection upon my situation and that of this army produces many an uneasy hour when all around me are wrapped in sleep," he told the absent Joseph Reed. "Few people know the predicament we are in."

Filling page after page, he enumerated the same troubles and woes he had been reporting persistently to Congress for so long, and that he would report still again to John Hancock that same day. There was too little powder, still no money. . . . So many of the troops who had given up and gone home had, against orders, carried off muskets that were not their own that the supply of arms was depleted to the point where there were not enough for the new recruits.

Sample questions:

Key Ideas and Details What central idea is revealed in this passage?

Craft and Structure Why does David McCullough use a direct quotation? What image does Washington create with the words "wrapped in sleep"?

Integration of Knowledge and Ideas What insight does this passage give you about Washington as a general? What insight do you gain about the Revolutionary War?

INFORMATIONAL TEXT

Independent Practice

Write three to five questions you might ask yourself as you read this passage from a speech delivered by James Bryant Conant, president of Harvard University, in 1940.

from "What Are We Arming to Defend?" by James Bryant Conant

. . . The history of this republic has been unique. And the uniqueness of our way of life rests not so much on constitutional democracy as on our social system—a system which is the embodiment of the golden mean of which I speak. I believe that fundamentally it is this unique form of society that we are really arming to defend. I believe that the ambition of every thoughtful citizen of this republic is to assist in keeping inviolate the free way of life which has developed on this continent in the last two hundred years.

. . . Let me examine for a moment the phrase "social mobility," for this is the heart of my argument. If large numbers of young people can develop their own capacities irrespective of the economic status of their parents, then social mobility is high. . . . Such is the American ideal.

Analyzing Arguments

The ability to evaluate an argument, as well as the ability to make one, are critical skills for success in college and in the workplace.

What Is an Argument?

An *argument* is a presentation of a controversial or debatable issue. In a formal, written argument, the writer logically supports a particular belief, conclusion, or point of view. A good argument is supported with sufficient and valid reasoning and evidence.

Purposes of Argument

There are three main purposes for writing a formal argument:

- to change the reader's mind about an issue
- to convince the reader to accept what is written
- to motivate the reader to take action, based on what is written

Common Core State Standards

Language

6. Acquire and use accurately general academic and domain-specific words and phrases, sufficient for reading, writing, speaking, and listening at the college and career readiness level; demonstrate independence in gathering vocabulary knowledge when considering a word or phrase important to comprehension or expression.

Reading Informational Text

5. Analyze and evaluate the effectiveness of the structure an author uses in his or her exposition or argument, including whether the structure makes points clear, convincing, and engaging.

6. Determine an author's point of view or purpose in a text in which the rhetoric is particularly effective, analyzing how style and content contribute to the power, persuasiveness, or beauty of the text.

Elements of Argument
Claim (assertion)—what the writer is trying to prove *Example: Students should wear uniforms to public high schools.*
Grounds (evidence)—the support used to convince the reader *Example: Students will focus less on what they and others are wearing and more on learning.*
Justification—the link between the grounds and the claim; why the grounds are credible *Example: The purpose of school is to learn.*

Evaluating Claims

When reading or listening to an argument, critically assess the claims that are made. Analyze the argument to identify claims that are based on fact or that can be proved true. Also evaluate evidence that supports the claims. If there is little or no reasoning or evidence provided to support the claims, the argument may not be sound or valid.

Analyzing and Evaluating Structures

As you read an argument, look for ways in which the writer uses structures. For example, the organizational structure, or order in which the writer presents claims and evidence, focuses and shapes the argument. Stylistic structural choices such as repetition and parallel structure can lend emotional power to an argument. Evaluate whether those structures strengthen or detract from the argument's effectiveness.

Model Argument

from *The American Forests* by John Muir

The forests of America, however slighted by man, must have been a great delight to God; for they were the best he ever planted. The whole continent was a garden, and from the beginning it seemed to be favored above all the other wild parks and gardens of the globe . . .

. . . In the settlement and civilization of the country, bread more than timber or beauty was wanted; and in the blindness of hunger, the early settlers . . . regarded God's trees as only a larger kind of pernicious weeds, extremely hard to get rid of. Accordingly, with no eye to the future, these pious destroyers waged interminable forest wars; chips flew thick and fast; trees in their beauty fell crashing by millions, smashed to confusion, and the smoke of their burning has been rising to heaven more than two hundred years. . . . Thence still westward the invading horde of destroyers called settlers made its fiery way over the broad Rocky Mountains, felling and burning more fiercely than ever, until at last it has reached the wild side of the continent, and entered the last of the great aboriginal forests on the shores of the Pacific . . . Clearing has surely now gone far enough; soon timber will be scarce, and not a grove will be left to rest in or pray in. . . .

Every other civilized nation in the world has been compelled to care for its forests, and so must we if waste and destruction are not to go on to the bitter end . . . [T]he forest plays an important part in human progress, and . . . the advance in civilization only makes it more indispensable. . . . But the state woodlands are not allowed to lie idle. On the contrary, they are made to produce as much timber as is possible without spoiling them. In the administration of its forests, the state righteously considers itself bound to treat them as a trust for the nation as a whole, and to keep in view the common good of the people for all time. . . .

Notwithstanding all the waste and use which have been going on unchecked like a storm for more than two centuries, it is not yet too late, though it is high time, for the government to begin a rational administration of its forests. . . .

In their natural condition, or under wise management, keeping out destructive sheep, preventing fires, selecting the trees that should be cut for lumber, and preserving the young ones and the shrubs and sod of herbaceous vegetation, these forests would be a never failing fountain of wealth and beauty. . . .

The outcries we hear against forest reservations come mostly from thieves who are wealthy and steal timber by wholesale. They have so long been allowed to steal and destroy in peace that any impediment to forest robbery is denounced as a cruel and irreligious interference with "vested rights" . . .

The introduction shows Muir's fondness for the forests of America.

As evidence, Muir describes the millions of trees that have been destroyed over the past 200 years.

Muir draws the logical conclusion for the audience that the trees will be gone if they continue to be cut down at the current rate.

Muir cites other civilized nations' actions as evidence that we must do the same.

Justification: Sustainable and productive forests are a national resource kept for the common good of the people.

Claim: It is time for the government to begin a rational administration of the forests.

The opposition is addressed and refuted.

The Art of Argument: Rhetorical Devices and Persuasive Techniques

Rhetorical Devices

Rhetoric is the art of using language in order to make a point or to persuade listeners. Rhetorical devices such as the ones listed below are accepted elements of argument. Their use does not invalidate or weaken an argument. Rather, the use of rhetorical devices is regarded as a key part of an effective argument.

Examples of Rhetorical Devices	
Repetition The repeated use of certain words, phrases, or sentences	We are compelled to fight the **injustice** of low wages, the **injustice** of long hours, and the **injustice** of child labor.
Parallelism The repeated use of similar grammatical structures	Children should spend their time **playing active games, reading good books,** and **writing imaginative stories.**
Rhetorical Question Calling attention to the issue by implying an obvious answer	Aren't all people created equal?
Sound Devices The use of alliteration, assonance, rhyme, or rhythm	The savage settlers sowed only the seeds of greed to replace the trees they destroyed.
Simile and Metaphor Comparing two seemingly unlike things or asserting that one thing *is* another	Is **America** a **melting pot** or a **tossed salad**?

Persuasive Techniques

Persuasive techniques are often found in advertisements and in other forms of informal persuasion. Although techniques like the ones below are sometimes found in formal arguments, they should not be regarded as valid evidence.

Persuasive Techniques	
Bandwagon Approach/Anti-Bandwagon Approach Appeals to a person's desire to belong; Encourages or celebrates individuality	Our clothes are as unique as you are.
Emotional Appeal Evokes people's fear, anger, or desire	Soon, all you will see will be strip malls and parking lots.
Endorsement/Testimony Employs a well-known person to promote a product or idea	"I support this just cause. You should too!"
Loaded Language The use of words that are charged with emotion	The child laborers are slaves; their childhoods are owned by the factories.
"Plain Folks" Appeal Shows a connection to everyday, ordinary people	"My parents immigrated to this great land and started a new life."
Hyperbole Exaggerates to make a point	All the money in the world wouldn't solve the problem.

INFORMATIONAL TEXT

Model Speech

The excerpted speech below includes examples of rhetorical devices and persuasive techniques.

from *Strike Against War* by Helen Keller

. . . I think the workers are the most unselfish of the children of men; they toil and live and die for other people's country, other people's sentiments, other people's liberties and other people's happiness! The workers have no liberties of their own; they are not free when they are compelled to work twelve or ten or eight hours a day. They are not free when they are ill paid for their exhausting toil. They are not free when their children must labor in mines, mills and factories or starve, and when their women may be driven by poverty to lives of shame. They are not free when they are clubbed and imprisoned because they go on strike for a raise of wages and for the elemental justice that is their right as human beings. . . .

As civilization has grown more complex the workers have become more and more enslaved, until today they are little more than parts of the machines they operate. Daily they face the dangers of railroad, bridge, skyscraper, freight train, stokehold, stockyard, lumber raft and mine. Panting and training at the docks, on the railroads and underground and on the seas, they move the traffic and pass from land to land the precious commodities that make it possible for us to live. And what is their reward? A scanty wage, often poverty, rents, taxes, tributes and war indemnities. . . .

It is your duty to insist upon still more radical measures. It is your business to see that no child is employed in an industrial establishment or mine or store, and that no worker is needlessly exposed to accident or disease. It is your business to make them give you clean cities, free from smoke, dirt and congestion. It is your business to make them pay you a living wage. It is your business to see that this kind of preparedness is carried into every department on the nation, until everyone has a chance to be well born, well nourished, rightly educated, intelligent and serviceable to the country at all times.

Strike against all ordinances and laws and institutions that continue the slaughter of peace and the butcheries of war. Strike against war, for without you no battles can be fought. Strike against manufacturing shrapnel and gas bombs and all other tools of murder. Strike against preparedness that means death and misery to millions of human beings. Be not dumb, obedient slaves in an army of destruction. Be heroes in an army of construction.

Helen Keller uses parallelism to emphasize her point.

The continued use of repetition gives the speech rhythm and emphasizes her points.

The metaphor compares the workers to the machine parts.

The alliteration gives variety to the speech.

Helen Keller answers the rhetorical question to drive home the irony of the word *reward.*

The continued parallelism and repetition show the increasing passion of her argument.

The repetition in the conclusion calls the audience to action; Keller is now using commands.

The emotional appeal and loaded words add intensity to the argument.

Analyzing Legal Meanings and Reasoning

Reading historical and legal texts requires careful analysis of both the vocabulary and the logical flow of ideas that support a conclusion.

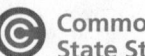

Common Core State Standards

Reading Informational Text

4. Determine the meaning of words and phrases as they are used in a text, including figurative, connotative, and technical meanings; analyze how an author uses and refines the meaning of a key term or terms over the course of a text.

8. Delineate and evaluate the reasoning in seminal U.S. texts, including the application of constitutional principles and use of legal reasoning and the premises, purposes, and arguments in works of public advocacy.

Writing

9. Draw evidence from literary or informational texts to support analysis, reflection, and research.

9.b. Apply grades 11–12 Reading standards to literary nonfiction.

Understanding Legal Meanings

The language of historical and legal documents is formal, precise, and technical. Many words in these texts have specific meanings that you need to understand in order to follow the flow of ideas. For example, the first amendment to the U.S. Constitution states that "Congress shall make no law respecting an establishment of religion, or prohibiting the free exercise thereof; or abridging the freedom of speech, or of the press..." To understand this amendment, it is important to know that in this context *exercise* means "practice," *abridging* means "limiting," and *press* means "media." To understand legal meanings:

- Use your knowledge of word roots to help you understand unfamiliar words. Many legal terms have familiar Greek or Latin roots, prefixes, or suffixes.
- Don't assume that you know a word's legal meaning: use a dictionary to check the meanings of key words to ensure that you are applying the correct meaning.
- Replace difficult words with synonyms to help you follow the logic of the argument.

Delineating Legal Reasoning

Works of public advocacy, such as court decisions, political proclamations, proposed laws, and constitutional amendments, use careful reasoning to support conclusions. These strategies can help outline the basic meanings of these texts:

- State the **purpose** of the document in your own words to help you focus on the writer's primary goal.
- Look for the line of reasoning that supports the **arguments** presented. To be valid and persuasive, key arguments should be backed up by clearly stated logical analysis. Be aware of persuasive techniques, such as citing facts and statistics, referring to expert testimonials, and using emotional language with strong connotations.
- Identify the **premises,** or evidence, upon which a decision rests. In legal texts, premises often include **precedents,** which are earlier examples that must be followed or else specifically overturned. Legal reasoning is usually based on the decisions of earlier trials. Be sure you understand precedents in order to identify how the court arrived at the current decision.

Writing About Legal Meanings

After reading the selection on the next page, write a detailed analysis of the meanings of the words *waive* and *waiver* in the *Miranda* v. *Arizona* decision. Explain the definitions of the terms as they are used in this context and provide an example that illustrates a situation in which a suspect "waives effectuation" of the rights outlined by this Supreme Court decision.

INFORMATIONAL TEXT

Model Court Decision

Note the strategies used to evaluate legal meanings and reasoning in this Supreme Court decision from 1966 regarding the rights of criminal suspects. The court addressed the admissibility of information obtained by police.

from *Miranda* v. *Arizona,* Opinion of the Supreme Court

We dealt with certain phases of this problem recently in *Escobedo* v. *Illinois.* There . . . law enforcement officials took the defendant into custody and interrogated him in a police station for the purpose of obtaining a confession. The police did not effectively advise him of his right to remain silent or of his right to consult with his attorney. Rather, they confronted him with an alleged accomplice who accused him of having perpetrated a murder. When the defendant denied the accusation . . . they handcuffed him and took him to an interrogation room. There, while handcuffed and standing, he was questioned for four hours until he confessed. During this interrogation, the police denied his request to speak to his attorney, and they prevented his retained attorney, who had come to the police station, from consulting with him. At his trial, the State, over his objection, introduced the confession against him. We held that the statements thus made were constitutionally inadmissible. . . .

. . . Our holding will be spelled out with some specificity in the pages which follow, but, briefly stated, it is this: the prosecution may not use statements, whether exculpatory or inculpatory, stemming from custodial interrogation of the defendant unless it demonstrates the use of procedural safeguards effective to secure the privilege against self-incrimination. By custodial interrogation, we mean questioning initiated by law enforcement officers after a person has been taken into custody or otherwise deprived of his freedom of action in any significant way. As for the procedural safeguards to be employed, unless other fully effective means are devised to inform accused persons of their right of silence and to assure a continuous opportunity to exercise it, the following measures are required. Prior to any questioning, the person must be warned that he has a right to remain silent, that any statement he does make may be used as evidence against him, and that he has a right to the presence of an attorney, either retained or appointed. The defendant may waive effectuation of these rights, provided the waiver is made voluntarily, knowingly and intelligently. If, however, he indicates in any manner and at any stage of the process that he wishes to consult with an attorney before speaking, there can be no questioning. Likewise, if the individual is alone and indicates in any manner that he does not wish to be interrogated, the police may not question him. The mere fact that he may have answered some questions or volunteered some statements on his own does not deprive him of the right to refrain from answering any further inquiries until he has consulted with an attorney and thereafter consents to be questioned.

The court cites and describes a **precedent**—an earlier court decision in which a suspect's confession was found inadmissible.

The word root *culp-* means "guilt," as in *culpable.* Context and prefixes combine to show that *exculpatory* means "proving innocence" and *inculpatory* means "proving guilt."

The **purpose** of the decision is stated: to guarantee that a suspect's statements are made in accordance with the rights granted by the U.S. Constitution. This **argument** is detailed and supported in the court decision. The context of the argument is the case summarized in the first paragraph.

Composing an Argument

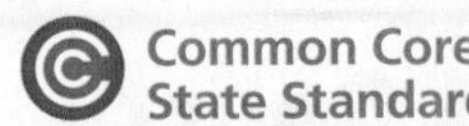

Common Core State Standards

Writing

1.a. Introduce precise, knowledgeable claim(s), establish the significance of the claim(s), distinguish the claim(s) from alternate or opposing claims, and create an organization that logically sequences claim(s), counterclaims, reasons, and evidence.

1.b. Develop claim(s) and counterclaims fairly and thoroughly, supplying the most relevant evidence for each while pointing out the strengths and limitations of both in a manner that anticipates the audience's knowledge level, concerns, values, and possible biases.

1.e. Provide a concluding statement or section that follows from and supports the argument presented.

Choosing a Topic

As you prepare to write an argument, choose a topic that interests you. The topic should be debatable or controversial to some degree.

Then, check to be sure you can make an arguable claim. Ask yourself:

1. What am I trying to prove? What ideas do I need to get across?
2. Are there people who would disagree with my claim? What counterclaims would they make?
3. Do I have evidence to support my claim? Is my evidence sufficient and relevant?

If you are able to put into words what you want to prove and answered "yes" to questions 2 and 3, you have an arguable claim.

Introducing the Claim and Establishing Its Significance

Before you begin writing, determine how much your audience already knows about your chosen topic. Then, provide only as much background information as necessary. If there are issues surrounding your topic, you will need to clarify them for your audience and narrow the focus to your specific claim. Remember that you are not writing a summary of the issue—you are crafting an argument. Once you have provided context for your argument, you should clearly state your claim, or thesis.

Developing Your Claim with Reasoning and Evidence

Now that you have made your claim, support it with evidence, or grounds, and reasons for your claim. A valid argument should have multiple pieces of evidence to support the claim. Evidence can range from personal experience to researched data or expert opinion. Knowing your audience's knowledge level, concerns, values, and possible biases can help you decide what kind of evidence will have the strongest impact. Make sure your evidence is up to date and comes from a credible source. Be sure to credit your sources.

You should also address the opposing counterclaim within the body of your argument. Consider points you have made or evidence you have provided that a person might challenge. Decide how best to refute these counterclaims. One technique for defusing an opponent's claims is to agree with selected parts of them.

Writing a Concluding Statement or Section

Restate your claim in the conclusion of your argument, and summarize your main points. The goal of a concluding section is to provide a sense of closure and completeness to an argument. Make your concluding statement strong enough to be memorable and to leave the reader thinking.

Practice

Exploring both sides of an issue can be a good way to start planning an argument. Complete a chart like the one below to help you plan your own argument.

Topic: **Issue:** ______________________________ ______________________________	
Claim:	**Counterclaim:**
Grounds (Evidence): **1.** ____________ **2.** ____________ **3.** ____________	**Grounds (Evidence):** **1.** ____________ **2.** ____________ **3.** ____________
Justification: **1.** ____________ **2.** ____________ **3.** ____________	**Justification:** **1.** ____________ **2.** ____________ **3.** ____________

When you have completed the chart and developed your own precise claim, consider the following questions:

1. Who is your audience? What type of evidence can you use to best convince those who do not agree with your claim?
2. Is your evidence strong and difficult to dispute? If not, how can you strengthen it or find better evidence?
3. How will you refute the counterclaim? Are there any parts of the counterclaim you agree with?

Conducting Research

Today, information is plentiful. However, not all information is equally useful, or even accurate. Developing strong research skills will help you locate and utilize the valid, relevant, and interesting information you need.

Short-Term Inquiries and Long-Term Investigations

You will conduct many different kinds of research throughout this program, from brief Internet searches to extended, in-depth projects.

- **Short-term research** can help you answer specific questions about a text or extend your understanding of an idea. You will conduct targeted short-term inquiries on a regular basis.
- **Long-term research** allows you to dive into a topic and conduct a detailed, comprehensive investigation. An organized research plan will help you gather and synthesize information from multiple sources.

Research Topics and Questions

Any research project, whether large or small, needs a clear and concise focus in order to avoid wasting your time and energy.

Narrowing Your Focus Before You Begin Research You can avoid many problems by focusing your research before you begin. For example, you might want to learn more about the American wilderness, but that topic is too broad and vague. If you started researching this subject, you could easily end up overwhelmed by the vast amount of information available. Head off trouble before you begin by thinking of a narrower, more manageable topic that interests you.

Narrowing As You Go Preliminary research can help you refine your topic. Your initial findings can help you choose a specific topic to pursue, such as a person, event, or theme.

Formulating a Question A research question can guide your research toward a specific goal and help you gauge when you have gathered sufficient information. Decide on your question, and refer to it regularly to check that your research is on track. Here are three examples of specific questions that could focus an investigation:

- What features of the American wilderness attracted early explorers and settlers?
- Did early settlers view the wilderness as an obstacle to be overcome or as a resource to be appreciated?
- How do first-person accounts of the early-settlement period reflect attitudes toward Native Americans?

Common Core State Standards

Writing

7. Conduct short as well as more sustained research projects to answer a question (including a self-generated question) or solve a problem; narrow or broaden the inquiry when appropriate; synthesize multiple sources on the subject, demonstrating understanding of the subject under investigation.

8. Gather relevant information from multiple authoritative print and digital sources, using advanced searches effectively; assess the strengths and limitations of each source in terms of the task, purpose, and audience; integrate information into the text selectively to maintain the flow of ideas, avoiding plagiarism and overreliance on any one source and following a standard format for citation.

General Subject

The American Wilderness

Focused Topics

- A writer, journalist, or artist who created works about the American wilderness
- A specific region or geographic feature, such as the Missouri River
- One event, expedition, or law related to the American wilderness
- Depictions of American landscapes in pioneer diaries

Planning Your Research

You will have more success in your longer-term research work if you create and follow a **research plan.** A good plan will include the elements shown in the following chart.

Elements of a Research Plan	
Research Question	Begin with an initial question, but be open to modifying your question as you learn more about your subject.
Source List	Create a list of sources you intend to consult. Plan to use a variety of sources. Add sources to your plan as you discover them. Place a check mark next to sources you have located, and then underline sources you have consulted thoroughly.
Search Terms	Write down terms you plan to investigate using online search engines. Making these decisions before you go online can help you avoid digressions that take you away from your topic.
Deadlines	Break a long-term project into short-term goals in order to avoid stress and achieve success.

Multiple Sources It is important not to rely too heavily on a single source. The creativity and originality of your research depends on how you combine ideas from many places. Plan to include a variety of these resources:

- **Primary and Secondary Resources** Primary resources—including journals, news accounts, autobiographies, pamphlets, documentary footage, and interviews—are texts or media created during the time period you are studying. These first-hand impressions offer authentic perspectives of the time. Secondary resources, such as encyclopedia entries and nonfiction books, interpret and analyze known facts.
- **Print and Digital Resources** The Internet allows fast access to data, but print resources are often edited more carefully. Include both print and digital resources in your research to guarantee that your work is accurate.
- **Media Resources** Documentaries, television programs, podcasts, and museum exhibitions are rich sources of information. Public lectures by people knowledgeable on a topic offer opportunities to hear an expert's thoughts.
- **Original Research** You may wish to conduct original research to include among your sources. For example, you might interview experts or eyewitnesses or conduct a survey.

Online Search Tip Type a word or phrase into a general search engine and you may get thousands of results. Using quotation marks can help you focus a search. Place a phrase in quotation marks to find pages that include exactly that phrase. To limit your search to .edu, .org, or .gov sites, use the search command "site:" followed by the extension. For example, enter "site:.edu" and "Lewis and Clark" and you will get a list of .edu (education) sites that include that phrase.

Finding Authoritative Sources

You need to evaluate your sources to make sure that they will give you information that is both relevant and reliable.

Determining Relevance Not every source you uncover will have information that is related to your investigation. Preview each source to determine its relevance. Scanning a table of contents, a preface, illustration captions, or an index can help you decide whether or not a source will help you answer your research question. When searching for information from magazine or Internet articles, you may come across *abstracts*, which are precise summaries of an article's contents. An abstract is short enough to read carefully and completely. Once you have read it, you can decide whether or not the abstracted article is likely to contain information you can use.

Remember that you do not need to include ideas from every source you consult. Be sure to allow yourself enough time to read and reject information that is not relevant.

Evaluating Reliability You also need to consider whether or not each source provides *accurate* information. Use the following ABC criteria to evaluate any print or digital sources:

- **Authority** Examine the credentials of both the author and the publisher or sponsoring institution. Checking an author's citations in other sources is one way to establish authority. Awards, professional memberships, and other recognitions can also support an author's or a work's credibility. When evaluating Internet sources, prefer those sponsored by educational, nonprofit, or government organizations (which have URLs ending in .edu, .org, or .gov.). Be wary of .com sites, which are commercial or personal.

- **Bias** Most sources strive to be objective, but few are completely without bias. Strong partiality in a source is not always a reason to reject it, though you may want to acknowledge that bias in your analysis. To check for bias, notice sources of funding, including advertising on .com sites. Follow hyperlinks to learn about professional affiliations of writers. These can help you identify possible reasons for biased or selective information.

- **Currency** Use recent sources whenever possible. Outdated content is likely to have been replaced by more recent research. Check the publication date of both print and digital sources. Electronic publications may show that a site has been updated—include both the original date and the most current date in your consideration.

Reliability Checklist

Ask yourself these questions about sources you find.

Authority

- Is the author well-known?
- What are the writer's credentials?
- Does the tone of the writing inspire confidence? Why or why not?

Bias

- Does the author have any obvious biases?
- What is the author's purpose for writing?
- Who is the target audience?

Currency

- When was the work created? Has it been revised?
- Is there more current information available?

Taking Notes

Learning to take complete and thoughtful notes as you research is a key to success. Good notes keep a clear record of your sources and capture ideas and facts. They can also help you summarize.

Notes do not need to be written in complete sentences, but be sure to state your ideas clearly enough so you will understand them when you review and draft.

Index Cards Many researchers find that index cards help them organize information. You will create different types of cards:

Source cards list complete bibliographical information for a source (author, title, place of publication, publisher, date). Create one source card for each source.

Sample Source Card

Rhodes, Richard. John James Audubon: The Making of an American.
New York, NY: Alfred A. Knopf, 2004.

Summary cards provide an overview of main ideas in a section. Write a short form of the source's title and author at the top of the card. Adding a topic can help you organize ideas when you write. Summarize the main idea and significant details of the passage. At the bottom of the card, include the location of the information.

Sample Summary Card

Rhodes, Audubon

topic: recording nature

Chapter 7
Rhodes explains Audubon's big change: He stopped following the tradition of painting birds in stiff poses, started painting them flying.

It took him several years to get better at this (not very much formal art training).
pp. 90–106

Quotation cards record an author's exact words. Include the same information as on a summary card, but write down the quotation as it appears. You may note how you might use the quotation in your writing.

Sample Quotation Card

Rhodes, Audubon

topic: science vs. art

Chapter 7
"With his breakthrough to drawing birds in flight, Audubon at twenty-seven abandoned strict illustration and committed himself to expressive art."

Use this quote to support the idea that Audubon's bird paintings are not mainly scientific illustrations.

p. 102

Providing Appropriate Citations

To avoid plagiarism, you must give credit for the information and ideas you collect during research. Plagiarism is presenting someone else's words or ideas as your own. Whether plagiarism is intentional or not, it is dishonest and illegal. Avoid it by being careful to cite your sources thoroughly. Follow the format your teacher recommends, such as Modern Language Association (MLA) style.

Deciding What to Cite Common knowledge does not require citation. If a fact appears in three or more sources, it is probably common knowledge. Facts that reflect one person's research or opinion should be cited, as shown in the chart to the right.

Works-Cited List (MLA Style) A works-cited list, or bibliography, must include the following information about each source: the name of the author, editor, and/or translator; title; place and date of publication; publisher.

Model: Works-Cited List

Rhodes, Richard. *John James Audubon: The Making of an American*, New York, NY: Knopf, 2004.

Gebhardt, Kristin, "John James Audubon (1785–1851)," *Museum of Nebraska Art*, 2004. Accessed December 15, 2012.

http://monet.unk.edu/mona/artexplr/audubon/audubon.html

John James Audubon: Drawn from Nature, Dir. Lawrence R. Hott. Florentine Films/Hott Productions, 2007

Parenthetical Citations (MLA Style) Use parenthetical citations to integrate your research smoothly into your writing. A parenthetical citation appears in the body of your text and briefly identifies the source. The source is fully identified on your works-cited list. You may need to add paraphrases within brackets to place quotations or edited words in context.

Model: Parenthetical Citations

John James Audubon knew that careful observation alone would not be enough to achieve his goal of capturing nature. He needed to find a way "to copy her in her own way, alive and moving!" (Audubon, p. 760) Audubon's early paintings did not satisfy him because he was following the tradition of painting stuffed birds with their wings clamped against their bodies. In May of 1812, he drew a flying whippoorwill. Although it took him many years to perfect his pictures of birds in flight, it was with this "breakthrough [that Audubon]... abandoned strict illustration and committed himself to expressive art." (Rhodes, pp. 101–102)

Common Knowledge

- John James Audubon painted hundreds of birds in their natural habitats.
- Audubon was born in France and moved to the United States when he was 18.
- The first edition of *The Birds of America* was published in 1827.

Facts to be Cited

- Audubon often observed birds in the wild for days before beginning a painting. (Source: Richard Rhodes, *John James Audubon*)
- Audubon used many strategies to sell his work, helping it to reach a wide audience. [Source: Kristin Gebhardt, "John James Audubon (1785–1851)]"

For more information on research and citing sources, see the Writing Workshop on research papers (pp. 664–675) and resource pages on citations (R21–R23).

Practice

Creating a research plan can help you organize a long-term research project. Complete a chart like the one below to plan research and collect details. Begin by choosing a topic that interests you, or use the chart to prepare a research assignment from your classwork. Then, draft a research question that you will answer through investigation.

Topic:

Research Question:

Sources

- Identify sources you will consult for information. Describe the type of source (i.e., encyclopedia, biography, museum Web site, or documentary).
- Tell how you will locate the source. For Internet sites, write the words or phrases you will enter in a search engine.
- Write one or two questions you will ask about each source to determine whether or not it is relevant and reliable.

Print	Digital/Media
Type of source: How you will locate it: Relevance/Reliability:	Type of source: How you will locate it: Relevance/Reliability:
Type of source: How you will locate it: Relevance/Reliability:	Type of source: How you will locate it: Relevance/Reliability:
Type of source: How you will locate it: Relevance/Reliability:	Type of source: How you will locate it: Relevance/Reliability:

Answer these questions before you begin your research:

- How can I be sure that I will not plagiarize any of my sources?
- What deadlines must I meet in order to achieve my goal?
- How will I compile notes so that I can remember and organize the information I find?
- What steps will I take to make sure that my final work reflects my own thoughts and is not overly dependent on one source?

Essential Questions in American Literature

Sometimes, as you read individual stories, poems, or essays, you might feel as if you are acquiring small pieces of a puzzle. Each piece is brightly colored and interesting, but you cannot see how they all fit together. You may wonder, Why does this piece of literature matter? How does it relate to what I already know? You try to fit the new pieces into a bigger picture and give them meaning.

This textbook will help you create that bigger picture. On the following pages, you will find these three Essential Questions, tools for creating meaning from the literature you read:

- **What makes American literature American?**
- **What is the relationship between literature and place?**
- **How does literature shape or reflect society?**

On the next three pages, the Essential Questions are accompanied by descriptions to guide your thinking. These questions re-appear throughout the introductions to units, at the end of every unit, and at the beginning and end of literary selections. You will have opportunities to reconsider them in the light of new information about a literary period or a new experience reading a literary work.

The questions do not have "yes" or "no" answers. They are meant to encourage you to take positions. Different people can answer them in different ways at different times. These large, open-ended questions will

- keep you thinking and making judgments about what you read,
- help you relate literary selections to one another and to larger ideas,
- provide a framework for discussing the selections with your classmates, and
- prompt you to create your own meaningful picture of American literature.

This symbol will guide you to the Essential Questions in this book.

What makes American literature *American?*

In one sense, anything written in America is American. But in a deeper way, literature is "American" because it says something fundamental about our identity as Americans. In fact, literature may be the most powerful creative expression of our national and cultural identity.

The selections in this book will spread before you styles, images, expressions, characters, themes, and stories that are uniquely American. By addressing this Essential Question in different ways throughout the book, you will find yourself getting to the heart of American literature.

As you read, keep in mind what it means to be "American." After all, it is American literature that enables us to tell ourselves who we are.

Thematic Vocabulary

To help as you explore this Essential Question, use words like these:

beliefs	**heritage**	**liberty**
diversity	**immigration**	**self-reliance**
freedom	**individualism**	

"What then is the American, this new man?"

—Michel-Guillaume Jean de Crèvecoeur

What is the **relationship** between literature and *place?*

Europeans imagined America before they knew it. Columbus envisioned a fabled land of gold and spices. Ponce de León dreamt that Florida was the home of a Fountain of Youth. Puritans escaping persecution planned to build a City on a Hill where freedom would reign. Meanwhile, Native Americans told stories inspired by the natural world in which they dwelled.

To dwell in a place is to live in it fully, to merge its real life with the imaginative life you live there. As Emily Dickinson wrote, "I dwell in Possibility." How do Americans shape and reflect all the possibilities of their dwelling place on the earth? How does geography help make literature? Do Americans respond to nature in a unique way?

As you read the selections in this book, consider what it means to live—and to create literature—in a particular place at a particular time.

Thematic Vocabulary

To help as you explore this Essential Question, use words like these:

environment	**natural**	**resources**	**urban**
frontier	**range**	**rural**	**wilderness**
landscape	**region**		

"...offer thanks to the earth where men dwell..."

—The Iroquois Constitution

How does **literature** shape or reflect *society?*

Literature is a product of the society from which it springs, reflecting the values, concerns, and spirit of a people. However, literature can be more than a passive mirror. It can act as a force that changes or shapes a society. Novels, stories, plays, poems, and literary nonfiction made by writers can entertain, inform, persuade, challenge, and move readers, both singly and in great numbers. Writers are the entertainers who amuse, the critics who confront, the teachers who share wisdom, and—sometimes—the visionaries who lead the way to the future. Every day, writers celebrate America, define it, defy it, and tell its story. As you read this textbook and keep asking this Essential Question, you will become aware of the defining interactions between American society and its literature.

Thematic Vocabulary

To help as you explore this Essential Question, use words like these:

humorist	**regionalism**	**storytelling**
myth	**satire**	**vernacular**
persona	**social critic**	**visionary**

"In bombers named for girls, we burned The cities we had learned about in school—"

—Randall Jarrell

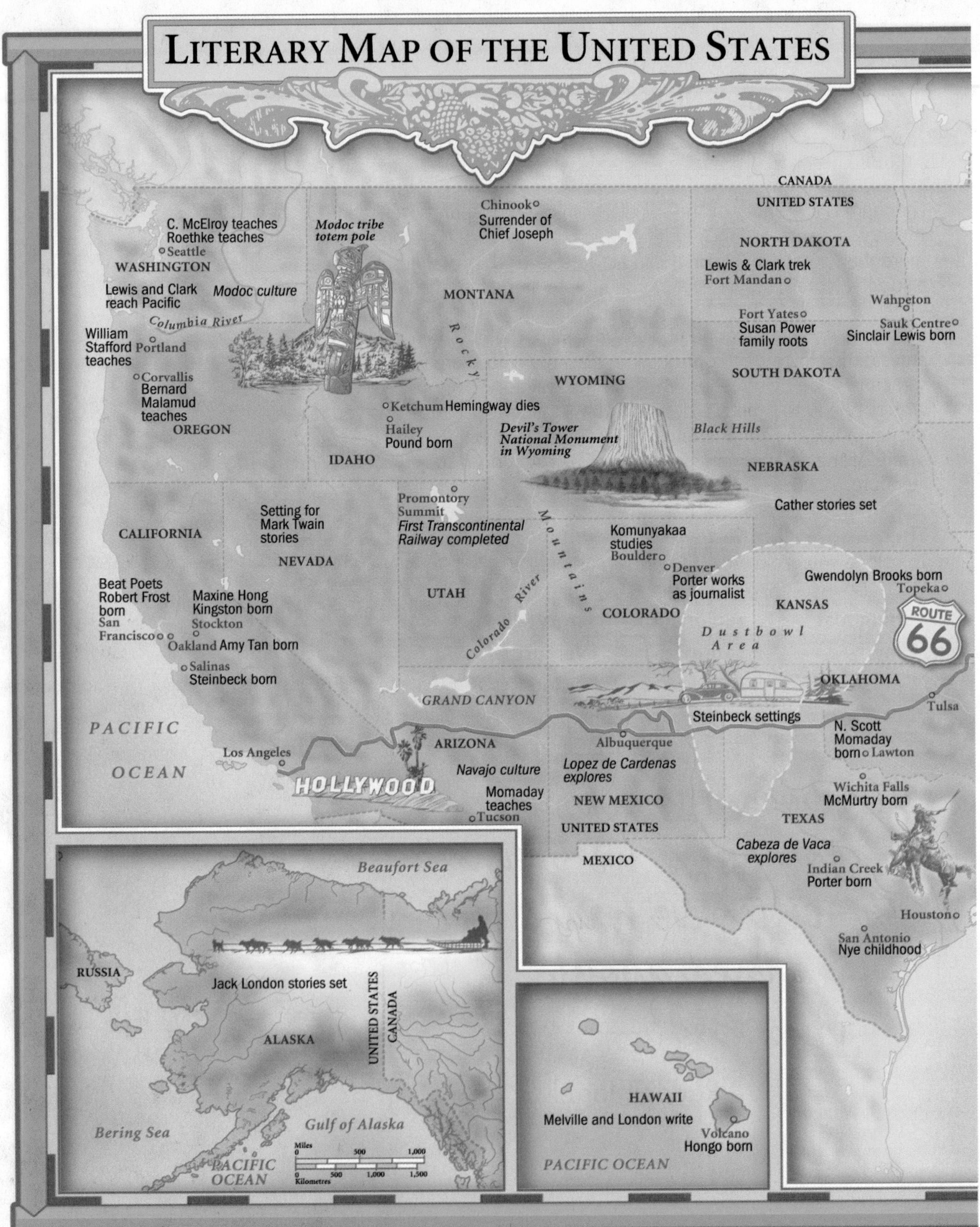
LITERARY MAP OF THE UNITED STATES
CANADA
UNITED STATES
Chinook
Surrender of Chief Joseph
C. McElroy teaches
Roethke teaches
Seattle
WASHINGTON
Modoc tribe totem pole
Modoc culture
Lewis and Clark reach Pacific
Columbia River
William Stafford teaches
Portland
Corvallis
Bernard Malamud teaches
OREGON
MONTANA
Rocky
NORTH DAKOTA
Lewis & Clark trek
Fort Mandan
Wahpeton
Fort Yates
Susan Power family roots
Sauk Centre
Sinclair Lewis born
SOUTH DAKOTA
WYOMING
Ketchum Hemingway dies
Hailey
Pound born
IDAHO
Devil's Tower National Monument in Wyoming
Black Hills
NEBRASKA
Cather stories set
Promontory Summit
First Transcontinental Railway completed
Mountains
Setting for Mark Twain stories
CALIFORNIA
NEVADA
UTAH
Komunyakaa studies
Boulder
Denver
Porter works as journalist
Gwendolyn Brooks born
Topeka
KANSAS
Beat Poets
Robert Frost born
San Francisco
Maxine Hong Kingston born
Stockton
Oakland Amy Tan born
Salinas
Steinbeck born
Colorado River
COLORADO
ROUTE 66
Dustbowl Area
OKLAHOMA
GRAND CANYON
Steinbeck settings
Tulsa
PACIFIC OCEAN
Los Angeles
HOLLYWOOD
ARIZONA
Navajo culture
Momaday teaches
Tucson
Albuquerque
Lopez de Cardenas explores
NEW MEXICO
UNITED STATES
MEXICO
N. Scott Momaday born
Lawton
Wichita Falls
McMurtry born
TEXAS
Cabeza de Vaca explores
Indian Creek
Porter born
Houston
San Antonio
Nye childhood
Beaufort Sea
RUSSIA
Jack London stories set
UNITED STATES
CANADA
ALASKA
Bering Sea
Gulf of Alaska
PACIFIC OCEAN
Miles
0 500 1,000
0 500 1,000 1,500
Kilometres
HAWAII
Melville and London write
Volcano
Hongo born
PACIFIC OCEAN

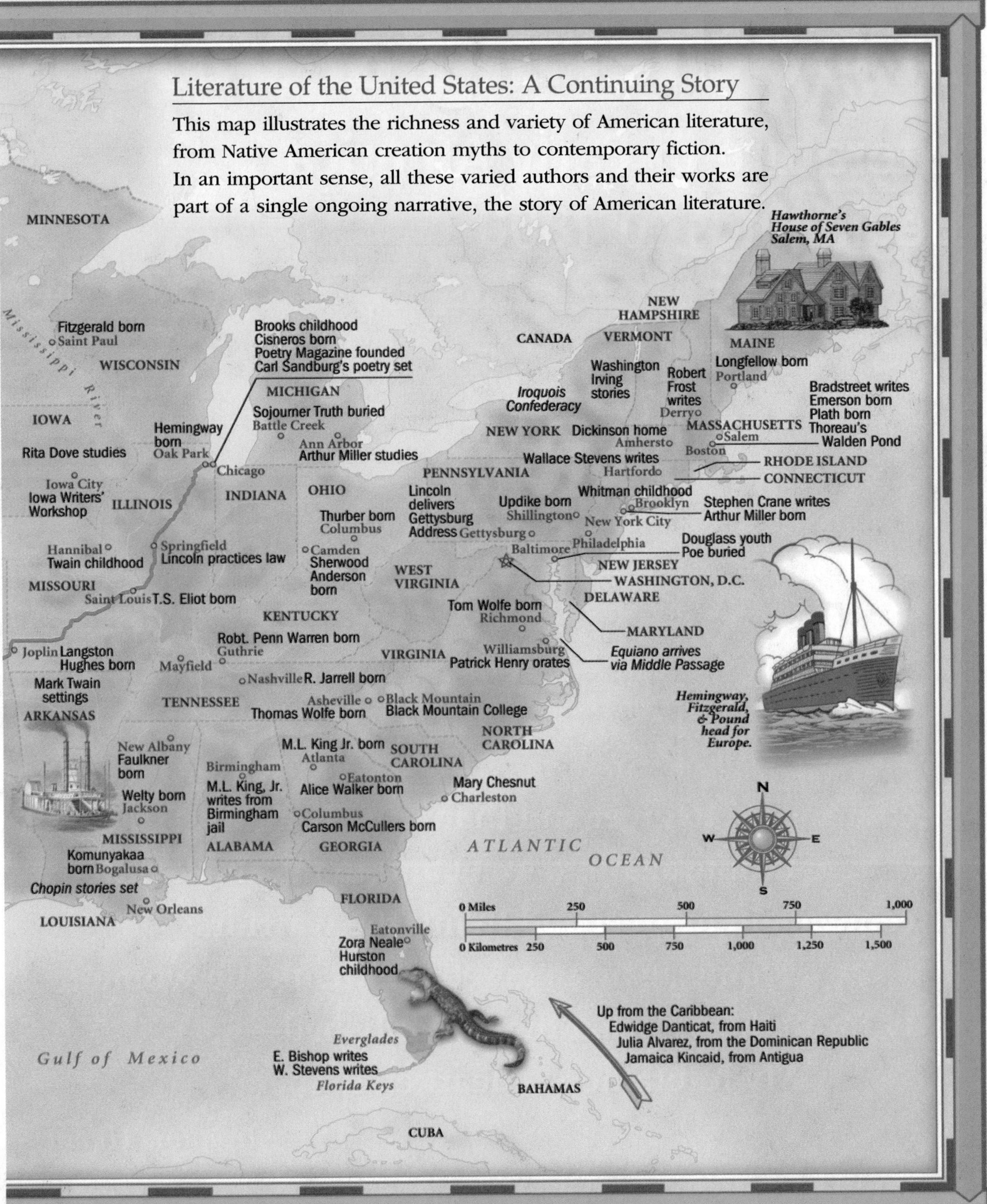
Literature of the United States: A Continuing Story
This map illustrates the richness and variety of American literature, from Native American creation myths to contemporary fiction. In an important sense, all these varied authors and their works are part of a single ongoing narrative, the story of American literature.
MINNESOTA
Mississippi River
Fitzgerald born
Saint Paul
WISCONSIN
Brooks childhood
Cisneros born
Poetry Magazine founded
Carl Sandburg's poetry set
MICHIGAN
Sojourner Truth buried
Battle Creek
Ann Arbor
Arthur Miller studies
IOWA
Hemingway born
Oak Park
Chicago
Rita Dove studies
Iowa City
Iowa Writers' Workshop
ILLINOIS
INDIANA
OHIO
Thurber born
Columbus
Camden
Sherwood Anderson born
Hannibal
Twain childhood
Springfield
Lincoln practices law
MISSOURI
Saint Louis
T.S. Eliot born
KENTUCKY
Robt. Penn Warren born
Guthrie
Joplin
Langston Hughes born
Mayfield
Nashville
R. Jarrell born
Mark Twain settings
ARKANSAS
TENNESSEE
Asheville
Thomas Wolfe born
Black Mountain
Black Mountain College
New Albany
Faulkner born
Birmingham
M.L. King, Jr. writes from Birmingham jail
M.L. King Jr. born
Atlanta
Eatonton
Alice Walker born
Columbus
Carson McCullers born
Welty born
Jackson
MISSISSIPPI
ALABAMA
GEORGIA
Komunyakaa born
Bogalusa
Chopin stories set
New Orleans
LOUISIANA
FLORIDA
Eatonville
Zora Neale Hurston childhood
Everglades
E. Bishop writes
W. Stevens writes
Florida Keys
Gulf of Mexico
BAHAMAS
CUBA
CANADA
Iroquois Confederacy
NEW YORK
PENNSYLVANIA
Lincoln delivers Gettysburg Address
Gettysburg
Updike born
Shillington
WEST VIRGINIA
VIRGINIA
Tom Wolfe born
Richmond
Williamsburg
Patrick Henry orates
NORTH CAROLINA
SOUTH CAROLINA
Mary Chesnut
Charleston
NEW HAMPSHIRE
VERMONT
Washington Irving stories
Robert Frost writes
Derry
MAINE
Longfellow born
Portland
Hawthorne's House of Seven Gables Salem, MA
MASSACHUSETTS
Dickinson home
Amherst
Salem
Boston
Bradstreet writes
Emerson born
Plath born
Thoreau's Walden Pond
RHODE ISLAND
CONNECTICUT
Wallace Stevens writes
Hartford
Whitman childhood
Brooklyn
New York City
Stephen Crane writes
Arthur Miller born
Philadelphia
Baltimore
Douglass youth
Poe buried
NEW JERSEY
WASHINGTON, D.C.
DELAWARE
MARYLAND
Equiano arrives via Middle Passage
Hemingway, Fitzgerald, & Pound head for Europe.
ATLANTIC OCEAN
N
S
E
W
0 Miles 250 500 750 1,000
0 Kilometres 250 500 750 1,000 1,250 1,500
Up from the Caribbean:
Edwidge Danticat, from Haiti
Julia Alvarez, from the Dominican Republic
Jamaica Kincaid, from Antigua

A Gathering of Voices

Literature of Early America Beginnings to 1800

I come again to greet and thank the League;
    I come again to greet and thank the kindred;
I come again to greet and thank the warriors;
    I come again to greet and thank the women.
My forefathers—what they established—
    My forefathers—hearken to them!

- Iroquois Hymn

Unit 1

PART 1 TEXT SET

MEETING OF CULTURES

PART 2 TEXT SET

THE PURITAN INFLUENCE

PART 3 TEXT SET

A NATION IS BORN

CLOSE READING TOOL

Use this tool to practice the close reading strategies you learn.

ONLINE WRITER'S NOTEBOOK

Easily capture notes and complete assignments online.

STUDENT eTEXT

Bring learning to life with audio, video, and interactive tools.

■ Find all Digital Resources at **pearsonrealize.com**.

Snapshot of the Period

In 1492, North America was already populated by several hundred Native American tribes. More than 12,000 years before Christopher Columbus reached North America, nomadic peoples had migrated across the Bering Land Bridge from Asia and settled across the continent. These people spoke different languages and had very different cultures, but the Europeans called them all by one name: "Indians." In the centuries after Columbus, more and more Europeans ventured to the New World. Among them were explorers, fortune-seekers, missionaries, and those fleeing religious persecution. There were also enslaved Africans who made the journey against their will. Individuals from these groups wrote accounts of their experiences, creating the first written literature of North America. By 1699, European colonies dotted the entire Eastern seaboard and extended as far west as New Mexico. In 1776, thirteen of those colonies declared their independence from England.

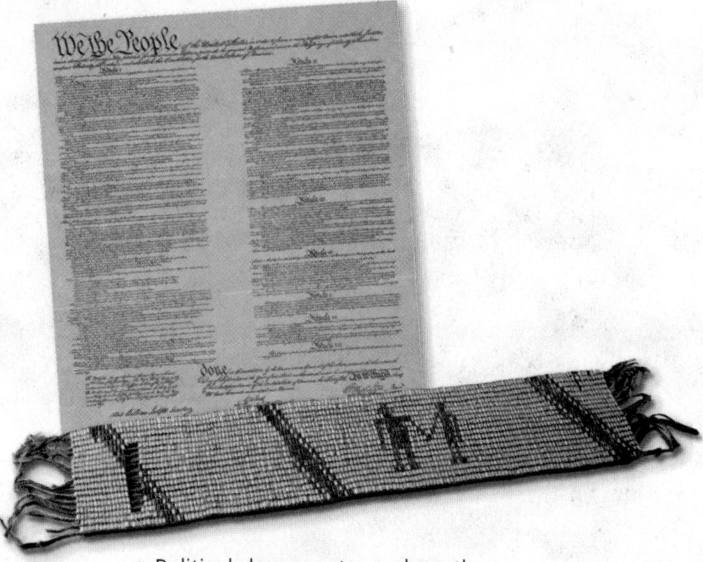

▲ Political documents, such as the Constitution, recorded the new nation's founding principles. Wampum belts recorded important treaties of Eastern tribes.

The Iroquois

Bradstreet

Wheatley

Jefferson

Equiano

Franklin

As you read the selections in this unit, you will be asked to think about them in view of three key questions:

What is the **relationship** between literature and *place?*

How does **literature** shape or reflect *society?*

What makes **American** literature *American?*

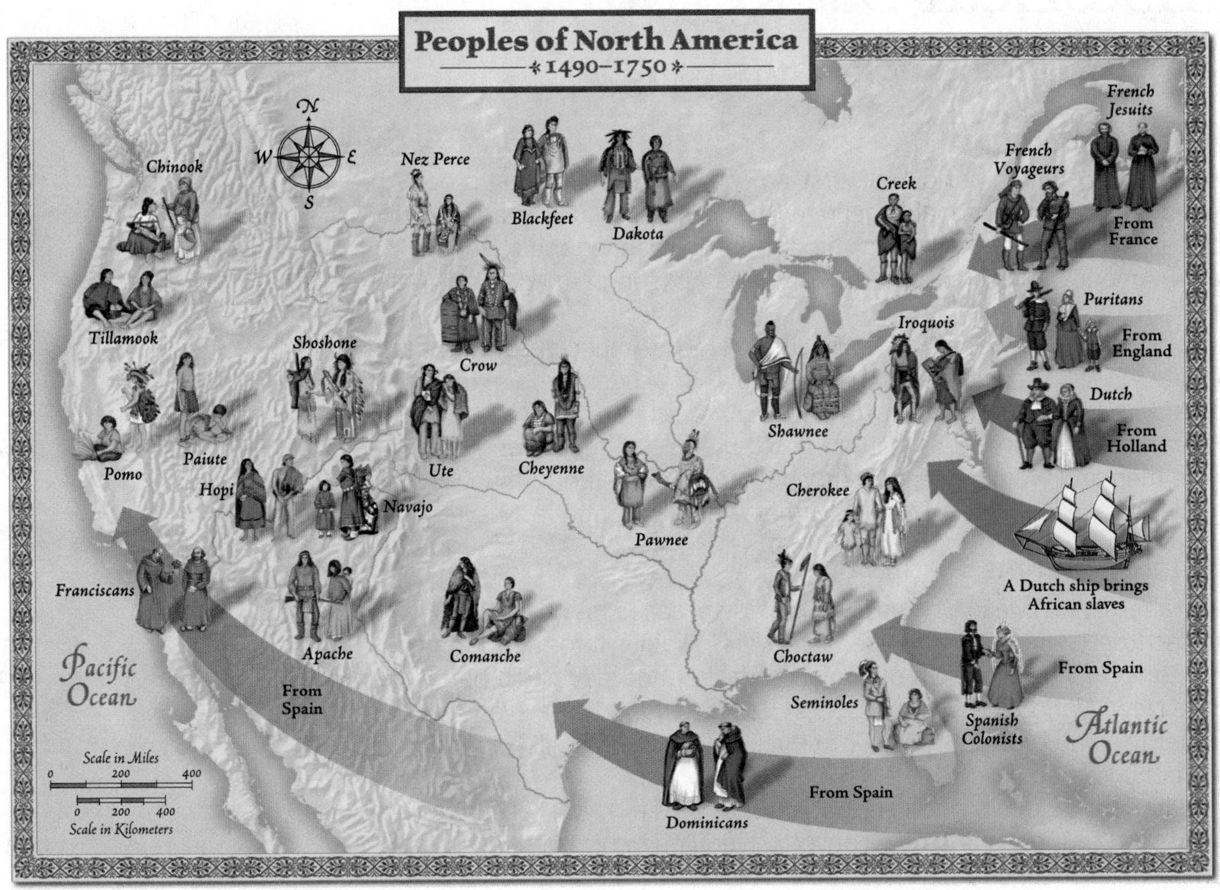

European exploration of North America quickly led to settlement and colonization. The Spaniards settled in Florida, then sent Jesuit and Franciscan missionaries to California and Texas. The French settled in Maine and along the Gulf of Mexico, while the Dutch established New Amsterdam (New York) and communities reaching south to Delaware. English Puritans settled Virginia, New England, and Pennsylvania and later took over the Dutch and French colonies and Florida. This influx of Europeans had a lasting impact on Native Americans, whose lifestyles and territories were increasingly restricted.

Integration of Knowledge and Ideas Based on the information in this map, what can you predict about the interactions among these various groups? Think about the ways in which different groups might form alliances, react to newcomers, or protect their territories. Explain your predictions.

 COMMON CORE ▪ MULTIPLE PERSPECTIVES ON THE ERA

Historical Background

Early America (Beginnings to 1800)

The First Americans

No one knows when or how the first Americans arrived in what is now the United States. It was probably between 12,000 and 70,000 years ago. The rich cultural presence of Native American tribes spanned the continent, and Native American oral literature—myths, legends, songs—begins our American literary heritage.

Colonists from Europe did not reach the North American continent until the late 1500s. The Europeans who settled at St. Augustine, Florida, in 1565 and at Jamestown, Virginia, in 1607 learned agriculture and woodcraft from the Native Americans. They learned about maize and squash and bark canoes. These men and women were tough and hardy, but without the help of those who knew the wilderness intimately, they would probably not have survived.

Puritans, Pilgrims, Planters

After a terrifying ocean voyage, the *Mayflower* sailed into harbor at Plymouth, Massachusetts, in 1620. Its passengers were religious reformers who had tried to "purify" the Church of England but thought they had a better chance in the New World. These Puritans, now called Pilgrims, gave every ounce of energy—and often their lives—to build a "city upon a hill," a model community based on the Bible.

Puritanism gradually declined, but around 1720 a revival called the Great Awakening brought some new converts. Genuine old-fashioned Puritanism never reawakened, although the "Puritan ethic" of hard work and self-discipline remained a basic American value.

The Southern Colonies differed from New England in climate, crops, social organization, and religion. Large plantations, not small farms, were the core of the economy, and slaves, who had been first brought to Virginia in 1619, were the core of the plantations. Planters thought of themselves as hardworking but aristocratic, and their way of life was more sociable and elegant than that of the Puritans.

TIMELINE

1490

1492: Christopher Columbus lands in the Bahamas. ▶

▲ 1499: **England** 20,000 die in London Plague.

The Age of Reason

The Enlightenment shocked Puritan beliefs. Inspired by brilliant scientists such as Galileo and Newton, and philosophers such as Voltaire and Rousseau, the thinkers of this time valued science, logic, and reason over faith. They believed that people are good by nature and capable of building a better society. They spoke of a "social contract" that forms the basis of government, an idea that laid the groundwork for the American Revolution.

The Birth of the Nation

Taxes, taxes, and more taxes imposed by Britain kept beating down American colonists. The Stamp Act, the Townshend Acts, the Tea Act, the Coercive Acts—by 1774 the colonists had had enough. They met in Philadelphia for the First Continental Congress, and in 1775, minutemen at Lexington and Concord fired "the shot heard 'round the world."

Six long years of bloodshed followed. At Bunker Hill, Saratoga, and many other sites, colonists fought alongside French and African American soldiers, until the British finally surrendered at Yorktown in 1781. Even then, the "united" states disagreed fiercely among themselves until the Constitution and Bill of Rights were ratified.

Heroes of the Revolution—Washington and Adams—became the first two presidents. Thomas Jefferson, a hero of the Enlightenment, became the third. By 1800, the United States of America had firmly established its political identity. It would soon establish its cultural identity as well.

Key Historical Theme: Creating a Nation

- Europeans came to America to create a "city upon a hill," an ideal community founded on moral and religious values.
- Colonists, with the help of Native Americans, learned to make the wilderness productive, on both small farms and large plantations.
- The United States arose from Enlightenment ideas—that people are basically good and can use reason to create a better society.

1508: Italy Michelangelo begins painting ceiling of Sistine Chapel. ▼

1513: Juan Ponce de León lands on the Florida peninsula.

1513: Vasco Nuñez de Balboa reaches the Pacific Ocean.

▲ **1519:** Magellan begins voyage around the world.

1519: Spain Chocolate introduced to Europe.

1521: Mexico Cortés conquers the Aztecs.

1555

Essential Questions Across Time

Early America (Beginnings to 1800)

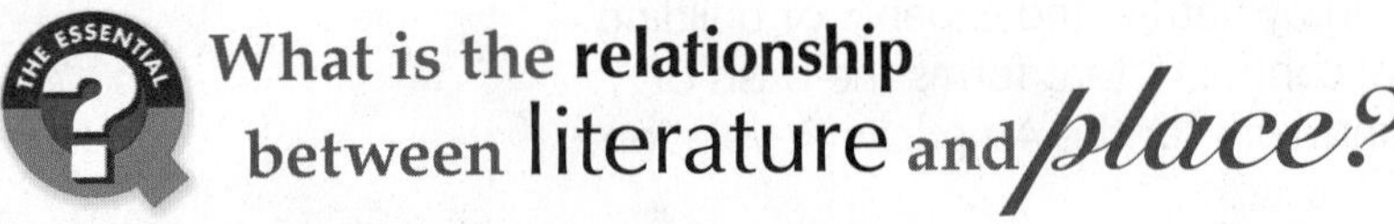
THE ESSENTIAL
What is the relationship between literature and place?

What was the New World's natural environment?

About one century before the colonists arrived in North America, many people thought that crossing the Atlantic Ocean meant sailing off the edge of the earth. Instead, the first European colonists found a continent more magnificent, strange, and dangerous than any of them had ever imagined.

Place of Wonder The colonists discovered long shores and sandy beaches backed by vast forests. They found ranges of mountains and fertile valleys and an astounding variety of plants, fish, birds, and animals. Nature in America was built on an immense scale. The wilderness looked endless. Nevertheless, for all its intimidating size and wild variety, this new place had one overwhelmingly satisfying quality: It was not Europe.

At One with the Place From the beginning, then, America was a place apart—but it was not so in the eyes of the Native Americans. In fact, for most Native American cultures, the people belonged to the land. The deep forests and wide plains were simply to be used and cared for by the human beings who lived in them temporarily. The lands and waters were life-giving environments, and the animals were part of the community. The facts of nature could be harsh, but they were also to be celebrated in myths, rituals, and songs. Nature was not to be feared as an enemy or overcome as an obstacle, but honored as the source of life.

TIMELINE

1555

1558: **England** Elizabeth I inherits throne.

1565: **St. Augustine, Florida** First permanent settlement in U.S., founded by Pedro Menendez. ◀

1570: Iroquois Confederacy established to stop warfare among the Five Nations.

▲ 1587: English colony at Roanoke Island disappears; known as the Lost Colony.

What were the colonists' attitudes toward the New World environment?

For the colonists, the people did not belong to the land. Quite the opposite: Land belonged to people, and this land was to be claimed by Britain, France, and Spain. It was measured, divided, bought, sold, and governed as the property of European kings and trading companies. The Puritans, filled with religious zeal, may have wanted to build a "city upon a hill," but the hill would still belong to the King of England.

Dream vs. Reality During the seventeenth century, the colonists' attitude toward the American environment was a blend of dream and reality. The dream was to create a theocracy, an earthly community governed by religious principles. The reality was to avoid starving to death or falling prey to cold, disease, or animals. The colonists saw the continent's raw beauty, rich resources, and awe-inspiring possibilities. They also felt every day the hard facts of staying alive.

Independent Place and People By the eighteenth century, Europeans had gained a more secure foothold in America. Tree by tree, they had tamed a portion of the wilderness and built towns, roads, schools, and churches. They began to worry less about survival and more about self-government. They began to ask, "We live in an independent place, so why aren't we an independent people?" The effects of the Enlightenment began to set in, and people realized that they could belong to themselves rather than to a monarch. The spirit of self-reliance that had faced down the wilderness was the same spirit that would face down European kings. The place itself had taught Americans how to be Americans.

The American EXPERIENCE

A LIVING TRADITION

Anne Bradstreet and John Berryman

In the 1950s, American poet John Berryman responded powerfully to the life and work of Puritan poet Anne Bradstreet, who had lived 300 years earlier. In his long poem of praise called "Homage to Mistress Bradstreet," he reveals his understanding of her struggle to survive and to be a writer in seventeenth-century America. He imagines her winter ordeals and asserts that he is more sympathetic to her poetry than was her busy husband, Simon.

from "Homage to Mistress Bradstreet"

Outside the New World winters in grand dark
white air lashing high thro' the virgin stands

foxes down foxholes sigh,
surely the English heart quails, stunned.
I doubt if Simon than this blast, that sea,
spares from his rigor for your poetry
more. We are on each other's hands
who care. Both of our worlds unhanded us.
Lie stark,

thy eyes look to me mild. Out of maize & air
your body's made, and moves. I summon, see,
from the centuries it. . .

1588: **Spain** The Spanish Armada is defeated by English fleet. ▼

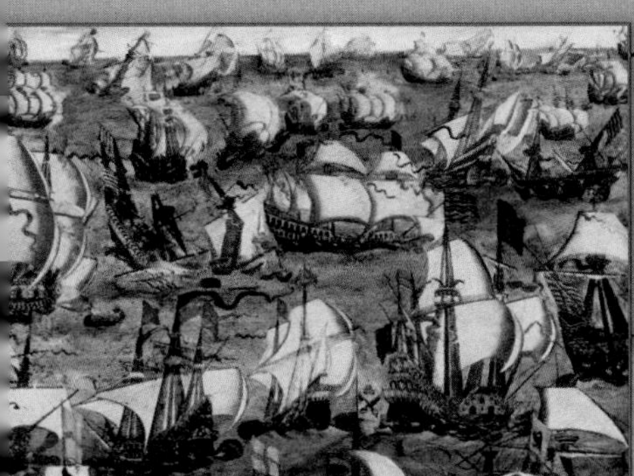

1595: **England** Shakespeare completes *A Midsummer Night's Dream.*

1605: **Spain** Cervantes publishes Part I of *Don Quixote.*

1607: First permanent English settlement at Jamestown, Virginia.

◀ 1609: **Italy** Galileo builds first telescope.

1620

How did attitudes toward nature show up in literature?

The close relationship between Native Americans and nature showed up in myths and legends. In these stories, people communicate with mountains and rivers. People and animals talk with each other and sometimes even change into each other. Human beings and nature live in harmony.

When the earliest explorers searched the continent, their responses to the land appeared in their journals and in the reports and letters they sent back home. Cabeza de Vaca recorded the natural wonders of the New World. William Bradford's *Of Plymouth Plantation*, the finest written work of the first European Americans, is filled with detailed descriptions of creating a colony in a place so delightful and so dangerous.

"Errand into the Wilderness" America's first literary family—Richard, Increase, and Cotton Mather—saw the environment from a religious point of view. Their writings describe a mission to combat evil in an "uncivilized" place. In time, this idea of the wilderness as a dark place of evil profoundly affected other writers. Forests and wild places play a large role, physically and symbolically, in the writings of American writers who would come later, including Washington Irving, James Fenimore Cooper, Nathaniel Hawthorne, and Mark Twain.

Place and Nation As the colonies developed, the power of reason began to make the continent a more hospitable place. Technology improved and agriculture flourished. In *Letters from an American Farmer*, Jean de Crèvecoeur even used the imagery of growing plants to emphasize the important idea that living in this particular place turned Europeans into Americans: "In Europe they were as so many useless plants … they withered and were mowed down by want, hunger, and war; but now by the power of transplantation, like all other plants they have taken root and flourished!" The very name of the new nation reveals the influence of place: The "United States of America" is made of separate distinct places (states) united into one—a federal republic.

ESSENTIAL QUESTION VOCABULARY

These Essential Question words will help you think and write about literature and place:

magnificent (mag nif′ə sənt) *adj.* grandly beautiful; impressive

obstacle (äb′stə kəl) *n.* something that impedes progress

resources (rē′ sôrs əs) *n.* natural sources of wealth, such as land or minerals

TIMELINE

1620

1620: Pilgrims land at Plymouth, Massachusetts. ▼

1632: **India** Mughal Emperor Shah Jahan begins building the Taj Mahal as tomb for his wife Mumtaz. ▶

"For we must consider that we shall be a city upon a hill. The eyes of all people are upon us."
—John Winthrop, Governor of the Massachusetts Bay Colony from 1629–1649

1639: First printing press in English-speaking North America arrives in Massachusetts.

1640: *Bay Psalm Book* published; first book printed in the colonies.

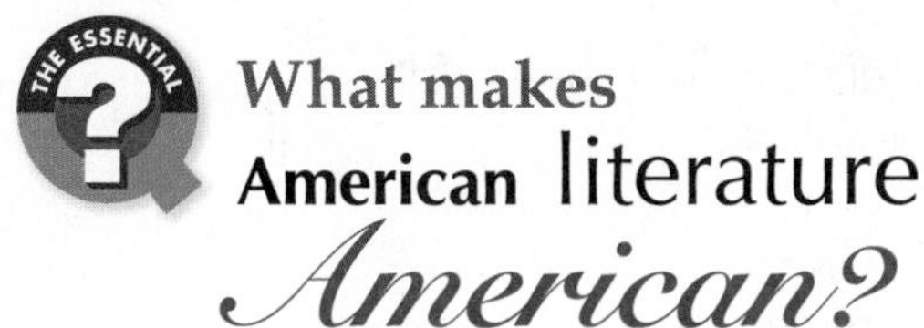

What makes American literature *American?*

American literature, naturally, shares the basic characteristics of all literature—characters, plots, settings, images, and themes. However, American literature is much more than literary works written by Americans. It also embodies certain ideas, evokes certain places, and tells stories of certain kinds of characters. There are qualities that distinguish American literature and make it a unique cultural expression.

What is a theme, and how does it find expression in literature?

A theme is the central idea, message, or insight that a literary work reveals. A theme is not the subject of a work, but rather the insight that the work reveals about the subject. A work reveals its themes through characters' words and actions, through details of setting and plot, through imagery, and even through language and style.

What were early American themes?

Three themes dominate early American writing:

Wilderness Writers revealed insights into the nature and meaning of the wilderness by the details they used to describe it and by the stories they told of their physical, political, and spiritual struggles with it.

The American EXPERIENCE

DEVELOPING AMERICAN ENGLISH

Our Native American Heritage by Richard Lederer

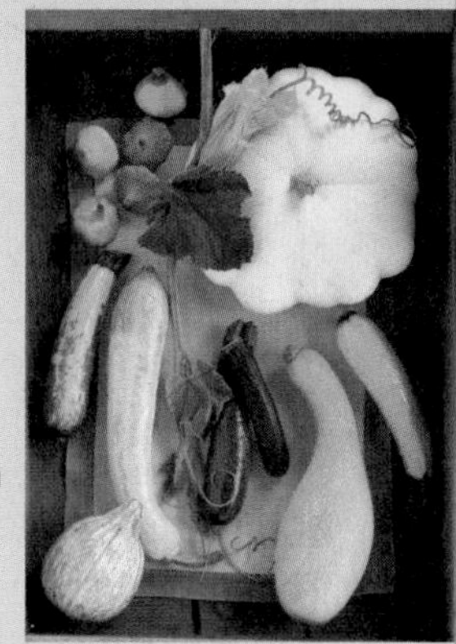

If you had been a settler in North America, you would have found many things in your new environment unknown to you. The handiest way of filling voids in your vocabulary would have been to ask local Native Americans what words they used. Colonists began borrowing words from Native Americans almost from the moment of their first contact, and many of those shared words have remained in our everyday language. They are part of what makes American literature American.

Anglicizing Pronouncing many of the Native American words was difficult for the colonists, so they often shortened or simplified the words. For example, *askútasquash* became "squash," *otchock* became "woodchuck," *rahaugcum* turned into "raccoon," and the smelly *segankw* transformed into "skunk." The North American menagerie brought more new words into the English language, including *caribou* (Micmac), *chipmunk* (Ojibwa), *moose* (Algonquian), and *muskrat* (Abenaki).

The Poetry of Place Names Some of our loveliest place names—*Susquehanna, Shenandoah, Rappahannock*—began life as Native American words. Such names are the stuff of poetry. Colonists freely used words of Indian origin to name states (half of all of them), cities, towns, mountains, lakes, rivers, and ponds.

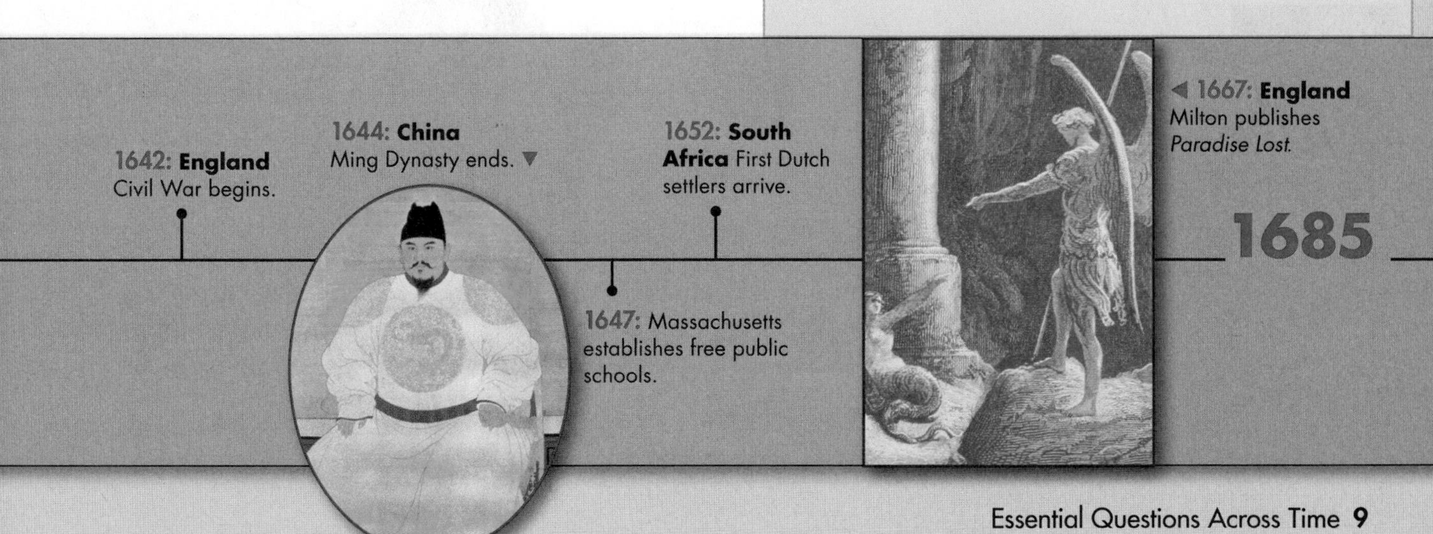
1642: **England** Civil War begins.
1644: **China** Ming Dynasty ends. ▼
1647: Massachusetts establishes free public schools.
1652: **South Africa** First Dutch settlers arrive.
◀ 1667: **England** Milton publishes *Paradise Lost.*
1685

Community In public writing such as pamphlets and newspapers, colonists and patriots conveyed the central message that America was a unique combination of community and independence.

Individualism In history and memoir, and in everything from laws to lyric poems, writers made clear that self-reliance and individualism are fundamental American values.

What is uniquely American about those themes?

The Place Americans recognized that they were in a unique place, a New World, only a small part of which they had even seen. Nothing in their European experience had prepared them for the splendors and the terrors of the American wilderness. Sometimes, America seemed to be the Garden of Eden, a newly created place of natural wealth. Sometimes, it seemed to be an enemy, a punishment, or a source of fear and death. These themes entered into the American literary imagination.

The Past When Americans wrote, they were aware of the many traditional European subjects and themes that were now of no importance to them. After all, there had been no Middle Ages or Renaissance in America. Europeans had medieval romances that told tales of knights and chivalry; Americans did not. Europeans had Shakespeare's tragedies of kings and princes; Americans did not. Europeans had a heritage of elegant and witty writing; Americans had a plain, straightforward way of writing. Americans did have histories and journals, prayers and sermons, speeches and essays. They even had some poems, but all of these imitated European styles. With the turn of the nineteenth century, American writers would begin to forge unique ways of expressing their unique experience.

The Vision The themes of independence and self-reliance are at the heart of Americans' vision of themselves as a new and unique people. They knew they were creating not only a new nation but a new kind of nation. That sense of newness marked Americans as a people of youth, innocence, optimism, risk-taking, and boundless originality.

ESSENTIAL QUESTION VOCABULARY

These Essential Question words will help you think and write about American literature:

independence (in′dē pen′ dəns) *n.* freedom from the control of others

straightforward (strāt for′ wərd) *adj.* direct; clear-cut

optimism (äp′ tə miz′ əm) *n.* hopefulness; a tendency to anticipate the best

TIMELINE

1685

1690: **India** Calcutta founded by the British.

1692: Salem witchcraft trials result in the execution of twenty people. ▼

▲ 1721: **Germany** Bach composes *The Brandenburg Concertos.*

1726: **England** Jonathan Swift publishes *Gulliver's Travels.* ▼

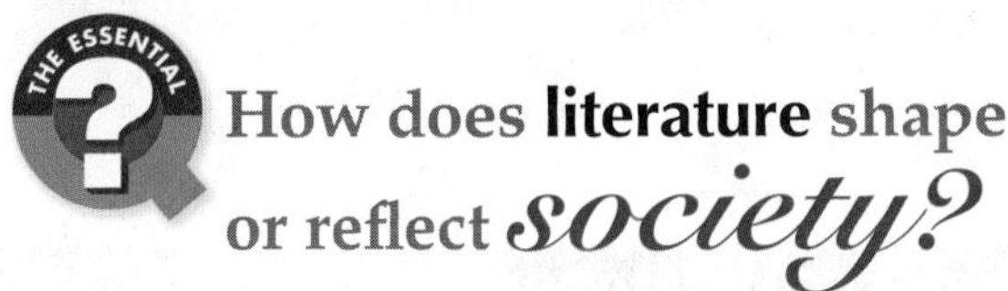

How does literature shape or reflect *society?*

What social and political forces affected early American literature?

Puritanism From the first, Puritanism influenced just about every aspect of colonial life. The impulse to escape to a New World and build a reformed and uncorrupted society shaped Puritan lawmaking, social relations, and daily life. Belief in predestination—John Calvin's doctrine that God has already decided who will be saved—made Puritans search every thought, action, and word for signs of grace. In hymns, sermons, histories, journals, and autobiographies, they aimed only for self-examination and spiritual insight.

The Enlightenment By the eighteenth century, the power of reason asserted itself in America. In speeches, pamphlets, essays, and newspaper articles, the spirit of the times called for debate, clear thinking, and reorganization of the political situation. The Declaration of Independence, for example, is not an outcry or an anarchic demand. It is a reasoned document, a controlled statement of the rational argument for independence.

Native Americans and African Americans Relations with Native Americans and the continued enslavement of African Americans left deep marks in American literature. In histories and captivity narratives, we have some record of relationships between colonists and Native

The American EXPERIENCE

CLOSE-UP ON HISTORY

African Americans and Women in the Revolution

In 1776, more than half a million African Americans lived in the colonies. At first, the Continental Congress did not permit enslaved or free African Americans to join the American army. However, when the British offered to free any male slave who fought for the king, George Washington changed American policy and allowed free African Americans to enlist. About 5,000 African Americans fought against the British. As this eyewitness account demonstrates, they fought with great courage:

Three times in succession, [African American soldiers] were attacked . . . by well-disciplined and veteran British troops, and three times did they successfully repel the assault, and thus preserve our army from capture.

Women also helped in the struggle for independence from Great Britain. When men went off to war, the women took on added work. They planted and harvested crops, and they made shoes and blankets and uniforms. Many followed their husbands and brothers to the front, where they washed, cooked, and cared for the wounded. Some even took part in battle, including a brave woman named Mary Hays, who carried water on the battle lines and became known as Molly Pitcher.

1727: Brazil First coffee plants cultivated. ▼

1735: John Peter Zenger acquitted of libel, furthering freedom of the press.

1741: Great Awakening, a series of religious revivals, begins to sweep the colonies.

▲ **1741:** Jonathan Edwards first delivers his sermon "Sinners in the Hands of an Angry God."

1748: France Montesquieu publishes *The Spirit of the Laws*, which later influences the U.S. Constitution.

1750

The American EXPERIENCE

CONTEMPORARY CONNECTION

Thomas Paine: Essayist, Hero of the Revolution...Father of the Internet?

Thomas Paine believed that knowledge is power and that it belongs to all people, not just the wealthy or privileged. He believed that through knowledge, ordinary people could guarantee their own freedoms. Even at a time when the printed word was slow to publish and distribute, Paine's fiery words brought change, fueling both the American and the French revolutions.

While this pamphleteer and passionate advocate of communication is often seen as a pioneer of investigative journalism, perhaps his true legacy is the Internet. Writing in *Wired News* (issue 3.05–May 1995), journalist Jon Katz observed that regarding the Internet, Paine's "ideas about communications, media ethics, the universal connections between people, and the free flow of honest opinion are all relevant again, visible every time one modem shakes hands with another."

Paine once said, "Such is the irresistible nature of truth that all it asks, and all it wants, is the liberty of appearing." When the Internet is used in its best and highest forms, truth becomes available to anyone with a computer. Thomas Paine, advocate of "all mankind," might recognize the Internet as the true product of his own ideals.

TIMELINE

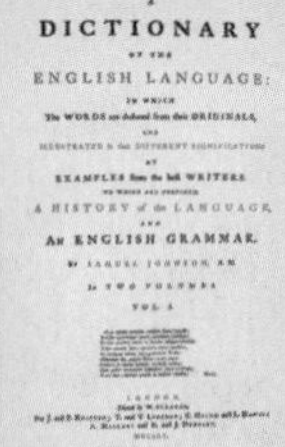
DICTIONARY
OF THE
ENGLISH LANGUAGE:
A HISTORY of the LANGUAGE,
AND
AN ENGLISH GRAMMAR.

◀ **1755: England** Samuel Johnson publishes *Dictionary of the English Language.*

1750

1754: French and Indian War begins.

1773: Parliament's Tea Act prompts Boston Tea Party. ▼

▲ **1775:** American Revolution begins.

Americans, relationships that ranged from trust to distrust, from friendship to hatred. In narratives left by both slaves and slaveholders, we find heartrending stories of individuals, families, and communities scarred by slavery.

What were the major roles of early American writers?

Writers not only reflect the social and political forces of their societies, they also influence those forces. They are not just the mirrors of their cultures and their communities; they can also be the fires that make those communities burn with hope, anger, love, idealism, and creativity.

Writer as Oral Poet and Historian Native American oral poets held places of vital importance for their tribes. They told each community's story, related its history, and honored its heroes. Those European Americans who wrote journals and histories fulfilled a similar role—recording the social and political events that gave meaning to their community's experience. The narratives of de Cárdenas and Cabeza de Vaca, as well as William Bradford's *Of Plymouth Plantation,* give us perspective on our own heritage.

Writer as Preacher and Lawmaker The writers of hymns and sermons believed that their role was to articulate the will of God. Cotton Mather and Jonathan Edwards explained for their communities the working of divine Providence in the wilderness, and they did their utmost to instill the fear of God into every member of their trembling audiences. The writers of America's laws and political documents had a different role—to articulate the will of the people. Thomas Paine's pamphlets, Patrick Henry's speeches, and Thomas Jefferson's multifaceted writing survive today not only as a part of history but also as literature.

Writer as Autobiographer The autobiographer's role goes beyond answering the basic question, "What did I do and why did I do it?" The autobiographer also asks, "Why should you be interested in my life? What did I learn from it? What can you learn from it?" The slave narrative of Olaudah Equiano helped Americans face their own history and ultimately do something about it. Benjamin Franklin's *Autobiography* combined a fascinating life story with explorations of essential American values.

ESSENTIAL QUESTION VOCABULARY

These Essential Question words will help you think and write about literature and society:

rational (rash′ən əl) *adj.* based on reason, not emotion

articulate (är tik′ yo͞o lāt) *v.* express in words

idealism (ī dē′ əl iz′ əm) *n.* belief that one should live according to one's ideals, or high principles

1776: Second Continental Congress adopts Declaration of Independence.

"Any people that would give up liberty for a little temporary safety deserves neither liberty nor safety." —*Benjamin Franklin*

1786: **Austria** Wolfgang Amadeus Mozart creates the comic opera *The Marriage of Figaro.* ▶

1787: Constitutional Convention meets in Philadelphia to draft the Constitution.

1800

▲ 1789: George Washington elected first President of the United States.

Recent Scholarship

America Begins with a Promise and a Paradox

William L. Andrews

It's not just a coincidence that America's earliest literature is highly autobiographical. Nor is it by accident that autobiography emerged as a literary form about the same time that the United States became a new nation. Autobiography and America were made for each other.

The Promise: A New Person and a New Country

The revolution in the United States created a new person, as well as a new country. At least that's what the great spokesmen and propagandists of the Revolution, especially Thomas Jefferson, Patrick Henry, and Benjamin Franklin, claimed. Franklin, who wore a coonskin cap to the royal courts of Europe, became famous for inventing everything from streetlights to eyeglasses. But we read him today because his greatest invention was himself. Franklin gave the new nation (which he also helped to invent) its first literary classic. *The Autobiography of Benjamin Franklin* is the first great American success story: a tale of a poor boy who made good.

About the Author

William L. Andrews is an award-winning scholar and teacher whose work focuses on the historical links between white and black writers in the formation of American literature. In addition to his many scholarly publications, he has co-edited three major literature anthologies: *The Norton Anthology of African American Literature, The Oxford Companion to African American Literature,* and *The Literature of the American South: A Norton Anthology.* Andrews is currently the E. Maynard Adams Professor of English at the University of North Carolina, Chapel Hill.

The Paradox: Freedom and Slavery

In 1789 Franklin, head of Pennsylvania's largest antislavery society, signed a petition to Congress advocating an end to slavery. In the same year, a pioneering African American autobiography, *The Interesting Narrative of the Life of Olaudah Equiano,* adapted the success story to antislavery purposes. Before the American Revolution got under way, Phillis Wheatley, an African-born slave in Boston, published a book of poetry, written in the learned and ornate style of the day to show that the enslaved were just as intelligent and capable as their so-called masters. Yet when the revolutionary orator Patrick Henry demanded in 1775, "Give me liberty or give me death!" no one asked whether the slaves he held on his Virginia plantation deserved the same freedom he so passionately proclaimed.

When I was in the sixth grade in a public school not far from Patrick Henry's plantation, I studied Virginia history, a mandatory subject at the time. I remember learning then that my home state was "the mother of presidents." My teacher didn't mention that all of Virginia's great heroes, including Washington and Jefferson, were slaveholders as well. No one, not even the framers of the U.S. Constitution in 1787, had found a way to justify the presence of slavery in a land supposedly dedicated to freedom. Eventually the only solution to America's political paradox was civil war.

▲ Critical Viewing What image of the founding fathers—Franklin, Adams, and Jefferson—does this painting create? Which details support your response? **ANALYZE**

America's Destiny and a Persistent Question

Ever since the founding of the United States, Americans have trumpeted the new country's special destiny: to create a new form of government, democracy, that would reform humankind itself. The transplanted Frenchman Jean de Crèvecoeur believed that democracy would inspire in all who had immigrated to America an "original genius" that would bind them together in a shared national identity. America's dedication to human rights, particularly "life, liberty, and the pursuit of happiness," would give the new people of America a grand ideal and mission. The most important writers of the early Republic extolled the nation's founding ideals but often questioned the national commitment to them. Then as now we ask of ourselves: Has America become what Jefferson and Crèvecoeur imagined?

Speaking and Listening: Collaboration

William L. Andrews raises an important question at the end of his essay: Has the United States become the country early citizens imagined? Conduct a **full-class discussion** about this issue. Work together to achieve the following goals:

- Determine the ideals held by Jefferson and his contemporaries.
- Come to a consensus about whether modern America has fulfilled these ideals.

As you conduct your discussion, work to engage everyone equally. Respond thoughtfully to different opinions and perspectives and resolve any contradictions. Cite specific examples from multiple relevant sources to support your opinions.

Integrate and Evaluate Information

1. Use a chart like the one shown to determine the key ideas expressed in the Essential Question essays on pages 6–13. Fill in two ideas related to each Essential Question, and note the groups most closely associated with each concept. One example has been done for you.

Essential Question	Key Concept	Group
Literature and Place		
American Literature	Self-determination	Revolutionaries like Thomas Jefferson
Literature and Society		

2. How do the visual sources in this section—illustrations, photographs, and maps—add to your understanding of the ideas expressed in words? Cite specific examples.

3. The Enlightenment belief in human goodness fueled the politics and literature of the American Revolution. How do other Revolutionary themes reflect a similar view of human nature? What conflicts with this optimism do you find in Puritan attitudes or other aspects of early colonial life? In your answer, cite evidence from the multiple sources presented on pages 4–15.

4. **Address a Question** William L. Andrews states that the American Revolution created "a new person, as well as a new country." What do you think "a new person" means? Does this idea still inform American identity? Integrate information from this textbook and other sources to support your ideas.

Common Core State Standards

Reading Informational Text
7. Integrate and evaluate multiple sources of information presented in different media or formats as well as in words in order to address a question or solve a problem.

Speaking and Listening
1.b. Work with peers to promote civil, democratic discussions and decision-making, set clear goals and deadlines, and establish individual roles as needed. *(p. 15)*

Speaking and Listening: Oral Presentation

The spoken word had great power in early America. With a small group, research one of the early American spoken forms listed below. Then, develop an **oral presentation** in which you perform an example of the form.

- Native American oral histories
- Early American speeches
- Puritan sermons or hymns
- Revolutionary War songs

Solve a Research Problem: This assignment requires you to locate texts from the oral tradition, many of which predate recording devices. Formulate a plan to meet this research challenge. Identify print and media sources that provide reliable information about the content and style of forms in the oral tradition. Consider primary sources, such as journals, newspapers, and illustrations from the colonial era. Also consider secondary sources, such as writings by historians, interviews with scholars, and modern recordings, plays, or other dramatic interpretations. As part of your presentation, explain the process you used to identify information and solve the research problem.

ESSENTIAL QUESTION VOCABULARY

Use these words in your responses:

Place and Literature
wilderness
splendor
terrors

American Literature
independence
optimism
community

Literature and Society
govern
doctrine
heritage

For definitions and pronunciations, see the Glossary, pp. R1–R7.

TEXT SET

Meeting of Cultures

Part 1

Building Knowledge and Insight

The Earth on Turtle's Back* • *When Grizzlies Walked Upright* • from *The Navajo Origin Legend

Connecting to the Essential Question These myths reveal the deep connections Native Americans saw between human society and the natural world. As you read, notice the qualities attributed to natural elements. Doing so will help as you consider the Essential Question: **What is the relationship between literature and place?**

Common Core State Standards

Reading Literature

2. Determine two or more themes or central ideas of a text and analyze their development over the course of the text, including how they interact and build on one another to produce a complex account.

Close Reading Focus

Origin Myths and Archetypes

An **origin myth** is a traditional story that explains how life began. Often, origin myths also explain how a feature of the world was formed or how a specific social custom began. As part of the *oral tradition,* myths were shared by generations of storytellers before being written down.

Like other stories, myths express **themes,** insights about life or the human condition. Because they have many layers of meaning, myths may even convey multiple themes. Often, myths from different places and times express similar themes. Such universal messages may be conveyed in **archetypes**—symbols, patterns, or character types that repeat across cultures. For example, these myths place archetypal significance on the cardinal directions:

> *Then they told the people to stand at a distance and allow the wind to enter. The white wind blew from the east, and the yellow wind blew from the west.*

Comparing Literary Works As you read these myths, look for patterns of events, images, or character types that might be *archetypes.* Compare and contrast the themes these archetypes carry in each myth.

Preparing to Read Complex Texts When you **establish a purpose for reading,** you determine the main reason for which you are reading a particular work—to learn, to be entertained, and so on. One purpose for reading these myths would be to learn about the *cultural characteristics* of Native American peoples. As you read, look for details that show how the people of each culture live, think, or worship. Use a chart like the one shown to record your observations.

Details	Cultural Characteristics
Chief says wife's dream has power.	Onondaga believe dreams convey messages.

Vocabulary

The words below appear in the texts that follow. Copy the words into your notebook, sorting them into words you know and words you do not know.

unconscious	**ancestors**
depths	**protruded**

ONONDAGA Tellers of **"The Earth on Turtle's Back"**

The Onondaga were key members of the Five Nations, or Iroquois Confederacy, in what is now upstate New York. Like other Iroquois, they lived in villages of wood-and-bark long houses occupied by related families. After siding with the British during the American Revolution, some Onondaga left for Canada after the British defeat. However, the majority returned to their ancestral valley in central New York state, near the lake that bears their name.

MODOC Tellers of **"When Grizzlies Walked Upright"**

The Modoc traditionally lived in what is now southern Oregon and northern California. There they farmed, fished, hunted, and became famous for their weaving. In the mid-nineteenth century, when the government tried to force the Modoc onto a reservation, they fought the resettlement under a leader known as Captain Jack. After several years of hostilities with United States troops, Captain Jack and his followers were forced to relocate to Oklahoma, although some were later able to return to Oregon.

NAVAJO Tellers of **"The Navajo Origin Legend"**

The largest Native American nation in the United States, the Navajo settled in the Southwest about a thousand years ago. Fierce warriors and hunters, they learned weaving and farming from the nearby Pueblo peoples, with whom they intermarried. Today, many Navajo live on a reservation that covers 24,000 square miles in Arizona, Utah, and New Mexico. Many Navajo still carry on their ancient customs, living in cone-shaped structures called hogans and practicing their tribal religion.

THE EARTH ON TURTLE'S BACK

ONONDAGA-NORTHEAST WOODLANDS
RETOLD BY MICHAEL CADUTO
& JOSEPH BRUCHAC

BACKGROUND Native Americans have great respect for the natural world. They believe that each living thing possesses a unique power that sustains it and affects others. This power is part of a greater power, which many Native American cultures recognize as a Great Spirit—the source of all life. These beliefs are reflected in Native American myths, such as the stories that follow.

Before this Earth existed, there was only water. It stretched as far as one could see, and in that water there were birds and animals swimming around. Far above, in the clouds, there was a Skyland. In that Skyland there was a great and beautiful tree.

▶ **Critical Viewing**
What story could you tell to explain the markings on the turtle shell in this picture? **APPLY**

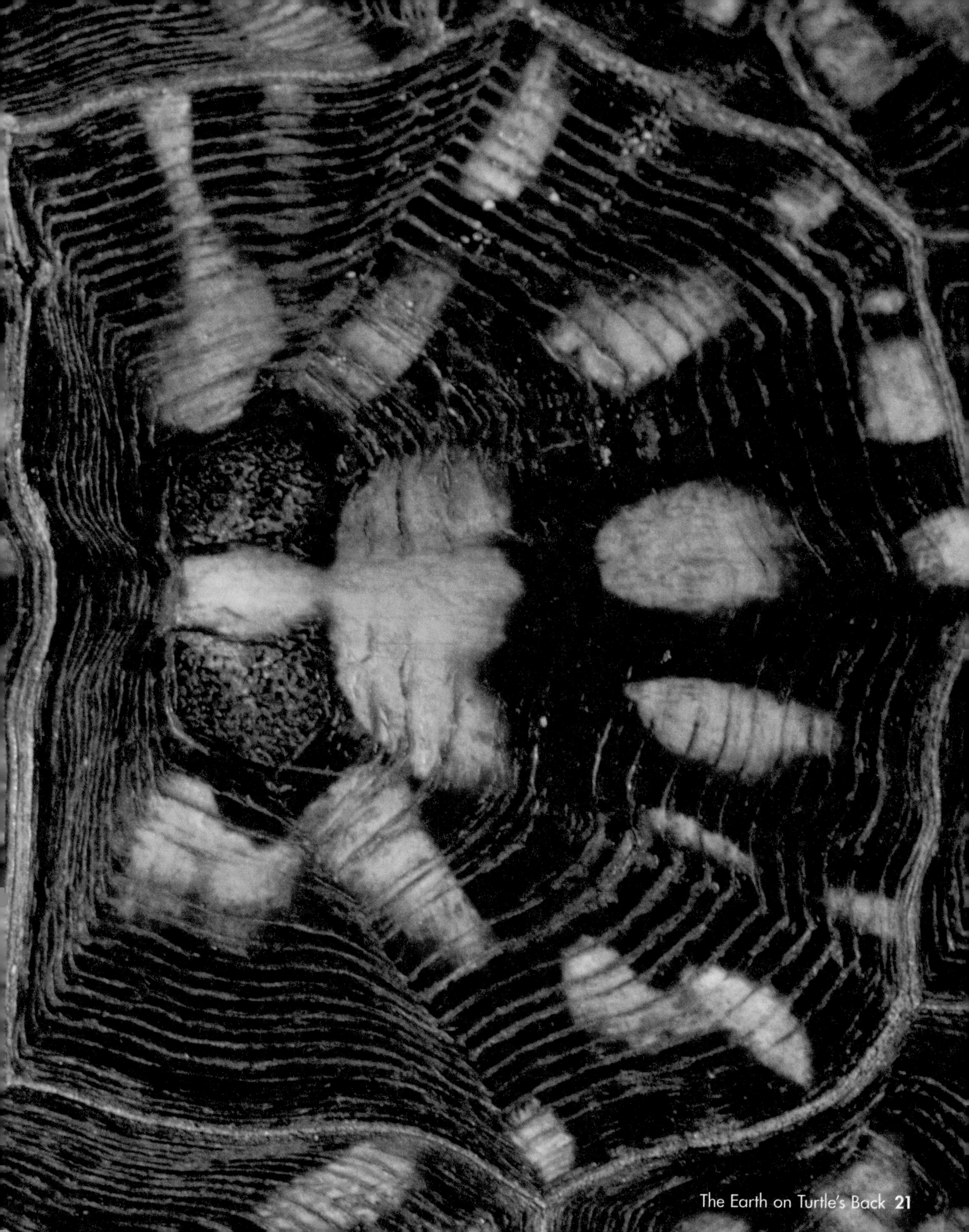

"Skyland" = heaven

It had four white roots which stretched to each of the sacred directions,[1] and from its branches all kinds of fruits and flowers grew.

There was an ancient chief in the Skyland. His young wife was expecting a child, and one night she dreamed that she saw the Great Tree uprooted. The next day she told her husband the story.

He nodded as she finished telling her dream. "My wife," he said, "I am sad that you had this dream. It is clearly a dream of great power and, as is our way, when one has such a powerful dream we must do all we can to make it true. The Great Tree must be uprooted."

Origin Myths
How do the opening words of this story identify it as an origin myth?

Then the Ancient Chief called the young men together and told them that they must pull up the tree. But the roots of the tree were so deep, so strong, that they could not budge it. At last the Ancient Chief himself came to the tree. He wrapped his arms around it, bent his knees and strained. At last, with one great effort, he uprooted the tree and placed it on its side. Where the tree's roots had gone deep into the Skyland there was now a big hole. The wife of the chief came close and leaned over to look down, grasping the tip of one of the Great Tree's branches to steady her. It seemed as if she saw something down there, far below, glittering like water. She leaned out further to look and, as she leaned, she lost her balance and fell into the hole. Her grasp slipped off the tip of the branch, leaving her with only a handful of seeds as she fell, down, down, down, down.

Purpose for Reading: Cultural Characteristics
What does the chief's reaction to his wife's dream tell you about Onondaga beliefs?

Far below, in the waters, some of the birds and animals looked up.

"Someone is falling toward us from the sky," said one of the birds.

"We must do something to help her," said another. Then two Swans flew up. They caught the Woman From The Sky between their wide wings. Slowly, they began to bring her down toward the water, where the birds and animals were watching.

"She is not like us," said one of the animals. "Look, she doesn't have webbed feet. I don't think she can live in the water."

"What shall we do, then?" said another of the water animals.

"I know," said one of the water birds. "I have heard that there is Earth far below the waters. If we dive down and bring up Earth, then she will have a place to stand."

So the birds and animals decided that someone would have to bring up Earth. One by one they tried.

The Duck dove first, some say. He swam down and down, far beneath the surface, but could not reach the bottom and floated back up. Then the Beaver tried. He went even deeper, so deep that it all was dark, but he could not reach the bottom, either. The Loon tried, swimming with his strong wings. He was gone a long long time, but he, too, failed to bring up Earth. Soon it seemed that all had tried and all had failed. Then a small voice spoke.

"I will bring up Earth or die trying."

Origin Myths
Why might characters in creation myths have generic names like "the Duck" or "the Beaver"?

1. **the sacred directions** North, South, East, and West.

They looked to see who it was. It was the tiny Muskrat. She dove down and swam and swam. She was not as strong or as swift as the others, but she was determined. She went so deep that it was all dark, and still she swam deeper. She swam so deep that her lungs felt ready to burst, but she swam deeper still. At last, just as she was becoming **unconscious**, she reached out one small paw and grasped at the bottom, barely touching it before she floated up, almost dead.

When the other animals saw her break the surface they thought she had failed. Then they saw her right paw was held tightly shut.

"She has the Earth," they said. "Now where can we put it?"

"Place it on my back," said a deep voice. It was the Great Turtle, who had come up from the **depths**.

They brought the Muskrat over to the Great Turtle and placed her paw against his back. To this day there are marks at the back of the Turtle's shell which were made by the Muskrat's paw. The tiny bit of Earth fell on the back of the Turtle. Almost immediately, it began to grow larger and larger and larger until it became the whole world.

Then the two Swans brought the Sky Woman down. She stepped onto the new Earth and opened her hand, letting the seeds fall onto the bare soil. From those seeds the trees and the grass sprang up. Life on Earth had begun.

Vocabulary

unconscious (un kän′ shəs) *adj.* temporarily lost awareness; in a faint

depths (depths) *n.* the deepest areas

...THE TREES AND THE GRASS SPRANG UP. LIFE ON EARTH HAD BEGUN.

Critical Reading

Cite textual evidence to support your responses.

1. **Key Ideas and Details (a)** What happens to the young wife after the chief uproots the Great Tree? **(b) Interpret:** Why does this event generate concern among the animals?
2. **Key Ideas and Details (a)** What actions do the animals take when they realize the wife of the chief cannot live in water? **(b) Generalize:** How do these actions exhibit the best aspects of human nature?
3. **Craft and Structure (a)** What does the description of the Muskrat stress about her physical qualities? **(b) Interpret:** What message about human achievement is conveyed by the success of the Muskrat after the other creatures could not accomplish the same task?
4. **Integration of Knowledge and Ideas (a)** How would you characterize the Muskrat's swim and her decision to make it? **(b) Apply:** How does society benefit from actions like those of the Muskrat?

When Grizzlies Walked Upright

Modoc

Retold by
Richard Erdoes
and Alfonso Ortiz

Before there were people on earth, the Chief of the Sky Spirits grew tired of his home in the Above World, because the air was always brittle with an icy cold. So he carved a hole in the sky with a stone and pushed all the snow and ice down below until he made a great mound that reached from the earth almost to the sky. Today it is known as Mount Shasta.

Then the Sky Spirit took his walking stick, stepped from a cloud to the peak, and walked down the mountain. When he was about halfway to the valley below, he began to put his finger to the ground here and there, here and there. Wherever his finger touched, a tree grew. The snow melted in his footsteps, and the water ran down in rivers.

The Sky Spirit broke off the small end of his giant stick and threw the pieces into the rivers. The longer pieces turned into beaver and otter; the smaller pieces became fish. When the leaves dropped from the trees, he picked them up, blew upon them, and so made the birds. Then he took the big end of his giant stick and made all the animals that walked on the earth, the biggest of which were the grizzly bears.

Now when they were first made, the bears were covered with hair and had sharp claws, just as they do today, but they walked on two feet and could talk like people. They looked so fierce that the Sky Spirit sent them away from him to live in the forest at the base of the mountain.

Pleased with what he'd done, the Chief of the Sky Spirits decided to bring his family down and live on earth himself. The mountains of snow and ice became their lodge. He made a big fire in the center of the mountain and a hole in the top so that the smoke and sparks could fly out. When he put a big log on the fire, sparks would fly up and the earth would tremble.

Late one spring while the Sky Spirit and his family were sitting round the fire, the Wind Spirit sent a great storm that shook the top of the mountain. It blew and blew and roared and roared. Smoke blown back into the lodge hurt their eyes, and finally the Sky Spirit said to his youngest daughter, "Climb up to the smoke hole and ask the Wind Spirit to blow more gently. Tell him I'm afraid he will blow the mountain over."

As his daughter started up, her father said, "But be careful not to stick your head out at the top. If you do, the wind may catch you by the hair and blow you away."

The girl hurried to the top of the mountain and stayed well inside the smoke hole as she spoke to the Wind Spirit. As she was about to climb back down, she remembered that her father had once said you could see the ocean from the top of their lodge. His daughter wondered what the ocean looked like, and her curiosity got the better of her. She poked her head out of the hole and turned toward the west, but before she could see anything, the Wind Spirit caught her long hair, pulled her out of the mountain, and blew her down over the snow and ice. She landed among the scrubby fir trees at the edge of the timber and snow line, her long red hair trailing over the snow.

There a grizzly bear found the little girl when he was out hunting food for his family. He carried her home with him, and his wife brought her up with their family of cubs. The little red-haired girl and the cubs ate together, played together, and grew up together.

When she became a young woman, she and the eldest son of the grizzly bears were married. In the years that followed they had many children, who were not as hairy as the grizzlies, yet did not look exactly like their spirit mother, either.

All the grizzly bears throughout the forests were so proud of these new creatures that they made a lodge for the red-haired mother and her children. They placed the lodge near Mount Shasta—it is called Little Mount Shasta today.

After many years had passed, the mother grizzly bear knew that she would soon die. Fearing that she should ask of the Chief of the Sky Spirits to forgive her for keeping his daughter, she gathered all the grizzlies at the lodge they had built. Then she sent her eldest grandson in a cloud to the top of Mount Shasta, to tell the Spirit Chief where he could find his long-lost daughter.

Origin Myths
What natural feature of the world does the Sky Spirit create in this passage?

"But be careful not to stick your head out at the top. If you do, the wind may catch you by the hair and blow you away."

Comprehension
Who finds the red-haired daughter of the Sky Spirit?

Purpose for Reading: Cultural Characteristics
What does the Sky Spirit's reaction to his daughter and grandchildren suggest about Modoc attitudes toward obedience?

Vocabulary
ancestors (an´ ses´ tərz) *n.* people from whom other people descend

When the father got this news he was so glad that he came down the mountainside in giant strides, melting the snow and tearing up the land under his feet. Even today his tracks can be seen in the rocky path on the south side of Mount Shasta.

As he neared the lodge, he called out, "Is this where my little daughter lives?"

He expected his child to look exactly as she had when he saw her last. When he found a grown woman instead, and learned that the strange creatures she was taking care of were his grandchildren, he became very angry. A new race had been created that was not of his making! He frowned on the old grandmother so sternly that she promptly fell dead. Then he cursed all the grizzlies:

"Get down on your hands and knees. You have wronged me, and from this moment all of you will walk on four feet and never talk again."

He drove his grandchildren out of the lodge, put his daughter over his shoulder, and climbed back up the mountain. Never again did he come to the forest. Some say that he put out the fire in the center of his lodge and took his daughter back up to the sky to live.

Those strange creatures, his grandchildren, scattered and wandered over the earth. They were the first Indians, the **ancestors** of all the Indian tribes.

That's why the Indians living around Mount Shasta would never kill a grizzly bear. Whenever a grizzly killed an Indian, his body was burned on the spot. And for many years all who passed that way cast a stone there until a great pile of stones marked the place of his death.

"Get down on your hands and knees. You have wronged me, and from this moment all of you will walk on four feet and never talk again."

from The Navajo ORIGIN LEGEND

Retold by Washington Matthews

On the morning of the twelfth day the people washed themselves well. The women dried themselves with yellow cornmeal; the men with white cornmeal. Soon after the ablutions were completed they heard the distant call of the approaching gods.[1] It was shouted, as before, four times—nearer and louder at each repetition—and, after the fourth call, the gods appeared. Blue Body and Black Body each carried a sacred buckskin. White Body carried two ears of corn, one yellow, one white, each covered at the end completely with grains.

The gods laid one buckskin on the ground with the head to the west: on this they placed the two ears of corn, with their tips to the east, and over the corn they spread the other buckskin with its head to the east; under the white ear they put the feather of a white eagle,

1. **the approaching gods** the four Navajo gods: White Body, Blue Body, Yellow Body, and Black Body

under the yellow ear the feather of a yellow eagle. Then they told the people to stand at a distance and allow the wind to enter. The white wind blew from the east, and the yellow wind blew from the west, between the skins. While the wind was blowing, eight of the Mirage People[2] came and walked around the objects on the ground four times, and as they walked the eagle feathers, whose tips protruded from between the buckskins, were seen to move. When the Mirage People had finished their walk the upper buckskin was lifted; the ears of corn had disappeared, a man and a woman lay there in their stead.

Vocabulary
protruded (prō trood′ id)
v. stuck out

The white ear of corn had been changed into a man, the yellow ear into a woman. It was the wind that gave them life. It is the wind that comes out of our mouths now that gives us life. When this ceases to blow we die. In the skin at the tips of our fingers we see the trail of the wind; it shows us where the wind blew when our ancestors were created.

The white ear of corn had been changed into a man, the yellow ear into a woman.

The pair thus created were First Man and First Woman (Atsé Hastin and Atsé Estsán). The gods directed the people to build an enclosure of brushwood for the pair. When the enclosure was finished, First Man and First Woman entered it, and the gods said to them: "Live together now as husband and wife."

2. **Mirage People** mirages personified.

Critical Reading

Cite textual evidence to support your responses.

1. **Key Ideas and Details (a)** In the Modoc myth, what do the grizzly bears do that angers the Chief of the Sky Spirits? **(b) Analyze:** What does the Chief's reaction tell you about his character?
2. **Key Ideas and Details (a)** What punishment does the Chief of the Sky Spirits give the grizzlies? **(b) Analyze Cause and Effect:** How does this action affect his grandchildren, the people of the Earth?
3. **Key Ideas and Details (a)** What is the wind's role in the Navajo ceremony? **(b) Speculate:** Why might the Navajo have viewed the wind as a source of life?
4. **Integration of Knowledge and Ideas (a) Summarize:** Summarize the steps of the Navajo creation ceremony. **(b) Analyze:** What does the ceremony show about Navajo attitudes toward order and ritual?
5. **Integration of Knowledge and Ideas** What do the qualities these mythmakers saw in nature show about the human traits they valued? In your response, use at least two of these Essential Question words: *environment, landscape, profound, cultivate.* ***[Connecting to the Essential Question: What is the relationship between literature and place?]***

Close Reading Activities

The Earth on Turtle's Back* • *When Grizzlies Walked Upright* • from *The Navajo Origin Legend

Literary Analysis

Common Core State Standards

Writing

3. Write narratives to develop real or imagined experiences or events using effective technique, well-chosen details, and well-structured event sequences. *(p. 30)*

Language

3.a. Vary syntax for effect. *(p. 31)*

4.a. Use context as a clue to the meaning of a word or phrase. *(p. 30)*

1. **Key Ideas and Details** Assume that your **purpose for reading** these myths was to learn about the Native American cultures that produced them. **(a)** Identify at least two *cultural characteristics* that you learned from each myth. **(b)** What does each characteristic reveal about the general attitudes of the culture that produced it?
2. **Integration of Knowledge and Ideas** What similarities and differences do you see in the cultural attitudes expressed in these three myths? Explain your answers, citing details from the selections.
3. **Key Ideas and Details** What are two other purposes you might have for reading these myths? Explain your answers.
4. **Key Ideas and Details** **(a)** In which **origin myth** is the creation of the Earth unintentional, or almost an accident? **(b)** In which myth is the world's creation the result of a deliberate series of actions? Explain your answers.
5. **Key Ideas and Details** **(a)** Which of the myths portrays the spirits or gods as generous and kind? **(b)** Which myth sees them as vengeful? Support your answers with details from the text.
6. **Integration of Knowledge and Ideas** **(a)** In addition to the origins of life on Earth, what features of the land does the Modoc myth explain? **(b)** What social customs does the myth explain? **(c)** What does the myth suggest about the ways members of the Modoc tribe may have felt about the place in which they lived?
7. **Integration of Knowledge and Ideas** **(a)** In which myth is the world's creation the result of cooperation? **(b)** In which myth is it the result of aggression? **(c)** Do you think these differences suggest different views of life? Explain.
8. **Comparing Literary Works** **(a)** Using a chart like the one shown, note patterns, symbols, or character types that are similar in all three myths. **(b)** What common **themes** do these **archetypes** help express? Explain your thinking.

Details	Turtle's Back	Grizzlies	Navajo
Patterns			
Symbols			
Characters			

Close Reading Activities Continued

Vocabulary Acquisition and Use

Word Analysis: Latin Root *-trud-* / *-trus-*

The Latin root *-trud-,* also spelled *-trus-,* means "push" or "thrust." Something that *protruded* was pushed out from where it was supposed to be. Use the context clues and your knowledge of the root *-trud-* / *-trus-* to explain the meaning of each italicized word below. Then, explain how the word's meaning reflects the meaning of the root.

1. Last night an *intruder* broke into the warehouse and robbed it.
2. The pastry bag *extruded* icing when the baker squeezed it.
3. In the quiet library, a noisy child is *obtrusive.*
4. Some uninvited guests are welcome, but others are simply *intrusive.*

Vocabulary: Context Clues

Answer each question. Then, explain how the context clues, or surrounding words and phrases, helped you determine your answer.

1. If Lola were *unconscious,* would you give her smelling salts or ask her to smile?
2. Which lives in the *depths* of the sea, an insect on the surface or a fish far below it?
3. Do people's *ancestors* usually inherit their money?
4. If a person's toes *protruded* from a sandal, could you see them, or would they be hidden?

Writing to Sources

Narrative Text Choose one of the three myths and turn it into a **play** that a group of classmates can perform for an audience.

Prewriting Reread the myth, listing each character and noting details about his or her appearance and personality. Also, list the various settings and jot down the actions that take place in each one. Then, decide if you will include a narrator who provides the audience with background information and transitions between scenes, or if you will rely solely on dialogue to tell the story.

Drafting List the characters. Then, organize the action into separate scenes that take place in each setting. Turn character's remarks or thoughts into dialogue. Use capital letters for the character names. Set stage directions that describe characters' behavior, tone, or actions in parentheses or brackets. Use italics to distinguish stage directions from dialogue.

Model: Setting Dialogue and Stage Directions

SPIRIT CHIEF [*angrily, stamping his feet*]: You have wronged me! You will now walk on all fours for eternity! [*The "bears" sink to their hands and knees and walk around the stage growling.*]

The use of italics and brackets clearly separates stage directions from dialogue.

Revising Read your draft aloud. If you find that some of the dialogue is hard to say, rewrite those sections so they sound more natural.

Conventions and Style: Coordinating Conjunctions

Include compound sentences in your writing by using **coordinating conjunctions** to combine short, choppy sentences. Coordinating conjunctions are words like *and, but, for, so,* and *yet* that connect words, phrases, or clauses of equal rank. Each coordinating conjunction shows a different relationship. For example, *and* shows addition or similarity, *but* and *yet* indicate contrast, and *or* and *nor* indicate a choice. *For* and *so* show a result.

Combining Sentences with Coordinating Conjunctions

Choppy: There was a great tree in Skyland. There was an ancient chief there, too.
Combined: There was a great tree *and* an ancient chief in Skyland.

Choppy: Several animals tried to swim the water's depths. The Muskrat succeeded.
Combined: Several animals tried to swim the water's depths, *but* the Muskrat succeeded.

Choppy: The Chief of the Sky Spirits must be strong. This being is in a position of power.
Combined: The Chief of the Sky Spirits must be strong, *for* he is in a position of power.

Punctuation Tip: If you use a coordinating conjunction to join two independent clauses, *place a comma before the coordinating conjunction.*

Practice In items 1–5, identify each coordinating conjunction and the words it connects. In items 6–10, combine the two sentences using a coordinating conjunction.

1. The Iroquois were five different tribes, yet they united to form one Indian nation.
2. The Sky Woman carries the seeds and allows them to fall.
3. The grizzlies were not supposed to act independently or challenge the chief.
4. Settlers conquered the Indians, but some tribes have survived.
5. Did the Modoc live in New York state or in Oregon?
6. The Chief of the Sky Spirits pledges to make the dream true. The Chief of the Sky Spirits is saddened by this pledge.
7. The chief has great power. He also has great responsibilities.
8. In one myth, an uprooted tree forms a hole in the sky. In another, a stone forms a hole.
9. They wanted potential allies to see the fire. They kept it burning constantly.
10. The woman gives her thanks to the swans. The woman gives her thanks to the turtle.

Writing and Speaking Conventions

A. Writing For each word pair listed below, write a sentence in which you link the two words or word groups using a coordinating conjunction. Then, tell what relationship is indicated by the conjunction.

1. swans—muskrat
2. under the sky—below the waters
3. the roots spread in all directions—they support the world

Example: swans—muskrat
Sentence: The swans and the muskrat display strength in different ways.
Relationship: similarity

B. Speaking Write and present a list of rules for your class. Use three different coordinating conjunctions. If you combine two independent clauses, remember to use a comma before the coordinating conjunction.

Themes Across Centuries: Author's Insights

Susan Power Introduces

MUSEUM INDIANS

Bringing the Spark of Your Own Imagination The origin myths of the Onondaga, Modoc, and Navajo tribes, recounted on pages 20–28 of this textbook, are examples of the oral tradition, stories repeated within a community, passed down from one generation to the next, keeping them alive. These spoken stories are meant to be performed, acted out with great drama before a circle of avid listeners of all ages. Each retelling of the story changes it a little, the performer emphasizing one episode over another, choosing slightly different words each time. These stories are meant to be flexible, interactive—modified according to the present audience's mood and tastes.

So as you read these tales, try to imagine them being acted out. Try to hear the storyteller's voice changing as different characters speak, rising with excitement, falling to a whisper. Your imaginative spark is needed to bring these stories fully to life.

Exposed to Two Cultures I am a grateful listener, eager to hear a gripping yarn, but I myself am not a traditional storyteller. I was very shy as a child and found it difficult to stand before people and speak aloud either a story or an idea. I was silent in my classes, unless called upon, and preferred committing my words to quiet paper rather than the storm of conversation. I was raised to be both Native (Yanktonnai Dakota) and American, and so I was exposed not only to traditional Native American stories, songs, ceremonies, and dances, but also to the culture of mainstream America and the wider world.

Meet the Author

Susan Power is a member of the Standing Rock Sioux Tribe of Fort Yates, North Dakota. Her novel, *The Grass Dancer,* won the PEN/Hemingway Award for First Fiction. She has also written a book of stories and autobiographical essays entitled *Roofwalker.*

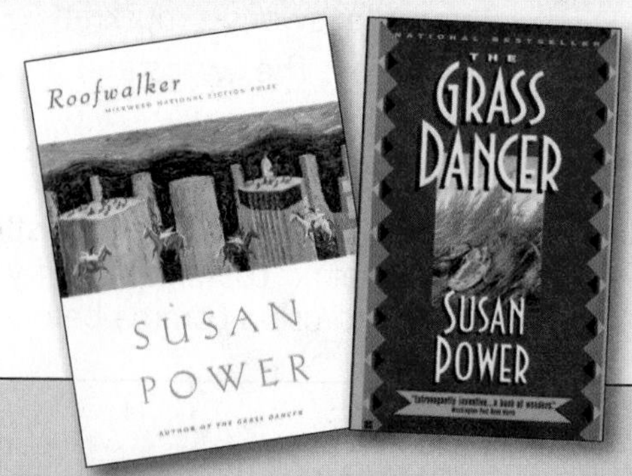

I loved reading and graduated from pop-up books and comics to the Nancy Drew mystery series and the *Chronicles of Narnia*. When I was about twelve, I began listening to recordings made of the plays of William Shakespeare and would memorize long passages that I delighted in performing privately, with no one but my mother and our cats to overhear. I didn't understand much of what was being spoken in the famous plays, but I was fascinated with the rhythmic poetry of the words, the dramatic plot lines, and thought to myself that Shakespeare would have felt at home in the Native world, dramatic as our oral literature can be.

Looking for My Own Experience I began writing my own poems, stories, essays, and political songs when I was very young—five or six years old. Perhaps I needed to write because, although I heard traditional stories of the people who came before me and inhabited this continent prior to European contact, and although I read dozens of books that taught me what it was like to live everywhere else in the world, I never found myself, my own experience, in either of these literatures: the oral tradition or the novels of the world. Where were the stories of little girls who attended church as well as a Native ceremony in the deep Wisconsin woods? Where were the books that told of a child who could perform a variety of traditional dances at an intertribal powwow and also excel in her ballet classes? I could not find myself on the literary map, and so I had to develop my own literature, plot my own place in this world.

But is my writing more Native than American? In my fiction and essays, Native American themes are emphasized—my characters believe, as I do, that everything is potentially alive, a creature of spirit, whether it be a person, an animal, a family car, a stone. But the language I use is English, the paintbrush of words I wield to draw you a picture of what I see with my eyes.

Oral Literature and Print The essay that follows, "Museum Indians," is a brief examination of my childhood in cultural terms—specifically, what it was like to be Native American in the city of Chicago. Notice that even though I have *written* several scenes describing adventures I shared with my mother, employing narrative strategies familiar to any reader of books, my mother is constantly *telling* me stories within the piece—instances of our own family oral tradition still in practice today. So I have captured the oral literature with my printed words.

Critical Reading

1. **Key Ideas and Details (a)** What reason does Power give to explain why she is not a traditional storyteller? **(b) Connect:** What life experiences do you think contributed to Power's decision to become a writer?
2. **Key Ideas and Details (a)** How does Power solve the problem of not finding her own experience in the literature she read as a child? **(b) Interpret:** According to Power, how do the dual influences of her childhood show up in her writing?

As You Read "Museum Indians" . . .

3. **Integration of Knowledge and Ideas** Look for details in the essay that show the contrast between the "Native" and the "American" that Power describes here.
4. **Integration of Knowledge and Ideas** Consider the ways in which Power is like her mother and the ways in which she is different.

MUSEUM INDIANS

Susan Power

She is so tall, a true DAKOTA WOMAN; she rises against the sun like a **SKYSCRAPER,** and when I draw her picture in my notebook, she takes up the **ENTIRE PAGE.**

◀ **Critical Viewing**
How is the portrayal of the woman in this painting similar to and different from the author's description of her mother? **COMPARE AND CONTRAST**

A snake coils in my mother's dresser drawer; it is thick and black, glossy as sequins. My mother cut her hair several years ago, before I was born, but she kept one heavy braid. It is the three-foot snake I lift from its nest and handle as if it were alive.

"Mom, why did you cut your hair?" I ask. I am a little girl lifting a sleek black river into the light that streams through the kitchen window. Mom turns to me.

"It gave me headaches. Now put that away and wash your hands for lunch."

"You won't cut my hair, will you?" I'm sure this is a whine.

"No, just a little trim now and then to even the ends."

I return the dark snake to its nest among my mother's slips, arranging it so that its thin tail hides beneath the wide mouth sheared by scissors. My mother keeps her promise and lets my hair grow long, but I am only half of her; my thin brown braids will reach the middle of my back, and in maturity will look like tiny garden snakes.

My mother tells me stories every day: while she cleans, while she cooks, on our way to the library, standing in the checkout line at the supermarket. I like to share her stories with other people, and chatter like a monkey when I am able to command adult attention.

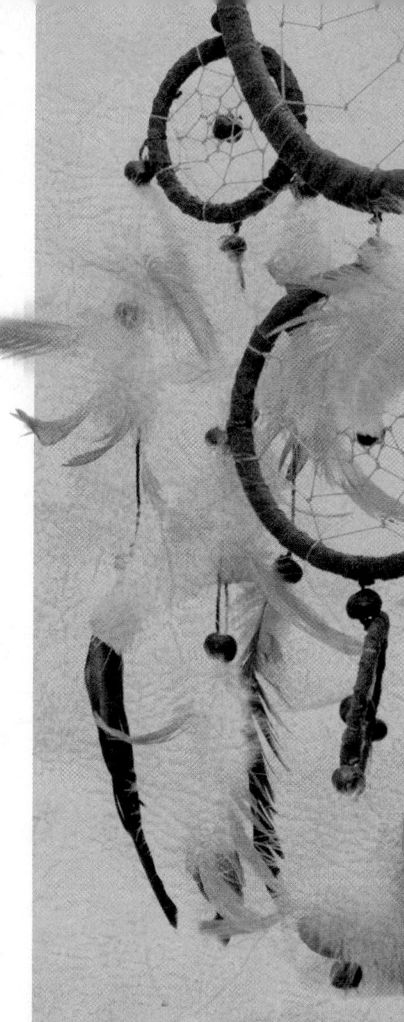

Susan Power
Author's Insight
I compare my mother's braid to my own—hers is a "sleek black river," mine are "tiny garden snakes"—to underscore my childhood impression that I was so much smaller and weaker, a diluted version.

Comprehension
What does the author's mother do every day?

Susan Power
Author's Insight
I describe my mother as a "skyscraper" so the reader will have a visual image of my child's-eye view of her as a towering force.

Vocabulary

integral (in′ tə grəl) *adj.* essential

petrified (pe′ trə fīd′) *adj.* paralyzed as with fear

shrouded (shroud′ əd) *v.* wrapped

intrigues (in′ trēgz′) *n.* secrets

"She left the reservation when she was sixteen years old," I tell my audience. Sixteen sounds very old to me, but I always state the number because it seems integral to my recitation. "She had never been on a train before, or used a telephone. She left Standing Rock to take a job in Chicago so she could help out the family during the war. She was petrified of all the strange people and new surroundings; she stayed in her seat all the way from McLaughlin, South Dakota, to Chicago, Illinois, and didn't move once."

I usually laugh after saying this, because I cannot imagine my mother being afraid of anything. She is so tall, a true Dakota woman; she rises against the sun like a skyscraper, and when I draw her picture in my notebook, she takes up the entire page. She talks politics and attends sit-ins, wrestles with the Chicago police and says what's on her mind.

I am her small shadow and witness. I am the timid daughter who can rage only on paper.

We don't have much money, but Mom takes me from one end of the city to the other on foot, on buses. I will grow up believing that Chicago belongs to me, because it was given to me by my mother. Nearly every week we tour the Historical Society, and Mom makes a point of complaining about the statue that depicts an Indian man about to kill a white woman and her children: "This is the only monument to the history of Indians in this area that you have on exhibit. It's a shame because it is completely one-sided. Children who see this will think this is what Indians are all about."

My mother lectures the guides and their bosses, until eventually that statue disappears.

Some days we haunt the Art Institute, and my mother pauses before a Picasso.

"He did this during his blue period," she tells me.

I squint at the blue man holding a blue guitar. "Was he very sad?" I ask.

"Yes, I think he was." My mother takes my hand and looks away from the painting. I can see a story developing behind her eyes, and I tug on her arm to release the words. She will tell me why Picasso was blue, what his thoughts were as he painted this canvas. She relates anecdotes I will never find in books, never see footnoted in a biography of the master artist. I don't even bother to check these references because I like my mother's version best.

When Mom is down, we go to see the mummies at the Field Museum of Natural History. The Egyptian dead sleep in the basement, most of them still shrouded in their wrappings.

"These were people like us," my mother whispers. She pulls me into her waist. "They had dreams and intrigues and problems with their teeth. They thought their one particular life was of the utmost significance. And now, just look at them." My mother never fails to brighten. "So what's the use of worrying too hard or too long? Might as well be cheerful."

The Old Guitarist, Pablo Picasso, 1903 (reproduction), The Art Institute of Chicago, ©2004 Estate of Pablo Picasso/Artists Rights Society (ARS), New York

◀ Critical Viewing
Compare and contrast the effect of the color blue in this painting and in the dress on page 38. **COMPARE AND CONTRAST**

Before we leave this place, we always visit my great-grandmother's buckskin dress. We mount the stairs and walk through the museum's main hall—past the dinosaur bones all strung together, and the stuffed elephants lifting their trunks in a mute trumpet.

The clothed figures are disconcerting because they have no heads. I think of them as dead Indians. We reach the traditional outfits of the Sioux in the Plains Indian section, and there is the dress, as magnificent as I remembered. The yoke is completely beaded—I know the garment must be heavy to wear. My great-grandmother used blue

Vocabulary
disconcerting (dis′ kən sʉrt′ iŋ) *adj.* upsetting

Comprehension
What do the author and her mother always do before leaving the museum?

beads as a background for the geometrical design, and I point to the azure[1] expanse.

"Was this her blue period?" I ask my mother. She hushes me unexpectedly, she will not play the game. I come to understand that this is a solemn call, and we stand before the glass case as we would before a grave.

"I don't know how this got out of the family," Mom murmurs. I feel helpless beside her, wishing I could reach through the glass to disrobe the headless mannequin. My mother belongs in a grand buckskin dress such as this, even though her hair is now too short to braid and has been trained to curl at the edges in a saucy flip.

We leave our fingerprints on the glass, two sets of hands at different heights pressing against the barrier. Mom is sad to leave.

"I hope she knows we visit her dress," my mother says.

There is a little buffalo across the hall, stuffed and staring. Mom

Susan Power
Author's Insight
"Was this her blue period?" my character asks, to draw a connection between Picasso's art (one phase of Picasso's painting is called his "blue period") and the exquisite beadwork of Native American women.

---

1. **azure** (azh′ ər) *adj.* sky blue.

doesn't always have the heart to greet him. Some days we slip out of the museum without finding his stall.

"You don't belong here," Mom tells him on those rare occasions when she feels she must pay her respects. "We honor you," she continues, "because you are a creature of great endurance and great generosity. You provided us with so many things that helped us to survive. It makes me angry to see you like this."

Few things can make my mother cry; the buffalo is one of them.

"I am just like you," she whispers. "I don't belong here either. We should be in the Dakotas, somewhere a little bit east of the Missouri River. This crazy city is not a fit home for buffalo or Dakotas."

I take my mother's hand to hold her in place. I am a city child, nervous around livestock and lonely on the plains.

I am afraid of a sky without light pollution—I never knew there could be so many stars. I lead my mother from the museum so she will forget the sense of loss. From the marble steps we can see Lake Shore Drive spill ahead of us, and I sweep my arm to the side as if I were responsible for this view. I introduce my mother to the city she gave me. I call her home.

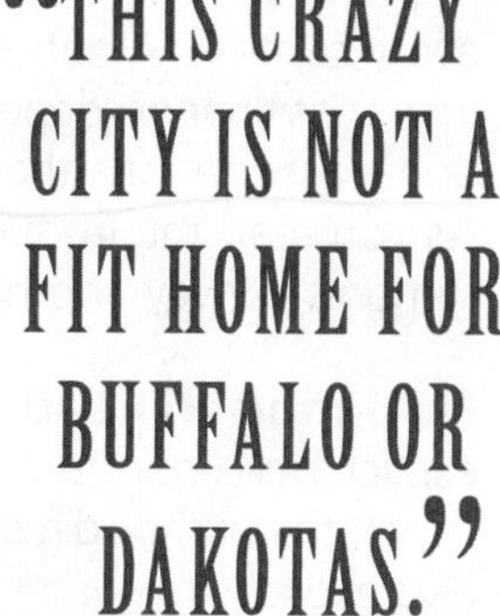
"THIS CRAZY CITY IS NOT A FIT HOME FOR BUFFALO OR DAKOTAS."

Critical Reading

1. **Key Ideas and Details (a)** What is the snake in Power's mother's dresser drawer? **(b) Interpret:** Why does she keep it there?
2. **Key Ideas and Details (a)** What complaint does Power's mother make about the statue at the Historical Society? **(b) Analyze:** What is the effect of her complaints? **(c) Contrast:** How does the statue contrast with the exhibit at the Art Institute?
3. **Key Ideas and Details (a)** What is unique about Power's relationship to the buckskin dress at the Art Institute? **(b) Interpret:** What is her mother's attitude toward seeing the dress there?
4. **Integration of Knowledge and Ideas (a)** In what ways does her mother identify with the buffalo? **(b) Contrast:** How is Power different from her mother? **(c) Generalize:** What does the final paragraph tell you about the relationship between the writer and her mother and their relationship with the city? Explain.
5. **Integration of Knowledge and Ideas** How do you think Power's mother influenced her as a writer? Base your answer on this essay.

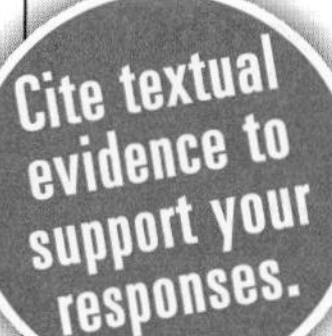
Cite textual evidence to support your responses.

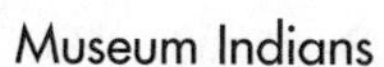

Building Knowledge and Insight

ANCHOR TEXT
from the *Iroquois Constitution*

Connecting to the Essential Question The makers of this document use natural imagery to describe society and government. As you read, find details related to the forces of nature and consider whether nature provides a sound model for human society. This will help as you consider the Essential Question: **What is the relationship between literature and place?**

Close Reading Focus

Political Documents; Symbols

The Iroquois Constitution is a **political document** that defines the structure and practices of a political organization—the Iroquois Confederacy. One of the document's prominent features is its use of symbols. A **symbol** is a person, place, animal, or object that represents something else, often an abstraction. For example, in the Iroquois Constitution, a tree symbolizes the peace established among the uniting tribes:

> *I am Dekanawidah and with the Five Nations' confederate lords I plant the Tree of the Great Peace.*

Some symbols have a fixed meaning, representing the same thing in every context. A national flag is such a symbol. Other symbols have meanings that change depending on their context. Often, symbols have emotional associations that affect people more than the abstract ideas alone. As you read the Iroquois Constitution, think about the abstract ideas the symbols convey and how they intensify the emotional impact of the text.

Preparing to Read Complex Texts Political documents may express *explicit philosophical assumptions and beliefs*. These are statements in which the author directly states his or her point of view. A document may also express the writer's *implicit philosophical assumptions and beliefs,* or points of view that are suggested but not stated. To **analyze philosophical assumptions and beliefs,** follow the steps in the chart shown here.

Vocabulary

The words listed here are critical to understanding the text that follows. Copy the words into your notebook and note which words are nouns. What clue indicates this part of speech?

disposition
constitute
tempered
deliberation
oblivion

Common Core State Standards

Reading Informational Text

1. Cite strong and thorough textual evidence to support analysis of what the text says explicitly as well as inferences drawn from the text.

6. Determine an author's point of view or purpose in a text in which the rhetoric is particularly effective, analyzing how style and content contribute to the power, persuasiveness or beauty of the text.

Step One
Look for words that are negative or positive, such as *just*, *goodness*, or *evil*.
Step Two
Find statements that show specific ideas of right and wrong.
Step Three
Look for ideas that someone could argue against.

The Iroquois

Authors of the **Iroquois Constitution**

The Iroquois are a group of Native American tribes with closely related languages and cultural traditions. They often call themselves the People of the Long House, a reference to the long communal homes in which they traditionally lived. The Iroquois united in the sixteenth century or perhaps earlier, when—according to legend—a mystic and prophet named Dekanawidah traveled from village to village in what is now upstate New York, urging the tribes to stop fighting and band together. The result was a confederacy, or united group, often called the Five Nations. The confederacy initially included the Seneca, Cayuga, Onondaga, Oneida, and Mohawk tribes. In 1722 a sixth tribe, the Tuscarora, joined the group, which became known as the Six Nations.

A Colonial Power Even though their numbers were relatively small, unification made the Iroquois a powerful force in the colonial era. They gained control over many other Native American tribes and kept the Dutch and British from spreading much beyond New York's Hudson River. They often fought the French, who had allied with their enemies, the Algonquins and Hurons. The Iroquois, in turn, allied with the British, helping them win the French and Indian War (1754–1763). The American Revolution divided the Iroquois. While most tribes remained loyal to the British, the Oneida and some Tuscarora supported the colonists. After the war, some Iroquois resettled in Canada, and many Oneida moved to Wisconsin.

The Great Binding Law The agreement that united the Iroquois established a framework of laws and practices that helped make them the most highly organized Native American political body in colonial North America. Known as the Great Binding Law or Great Law of Peace, it was passed down orally for generations and recorded in shell beads called wampum that served as a memory device for oral recitation. The current version, now often called the Iroquois Constitution, was written down in the nineteenth century.

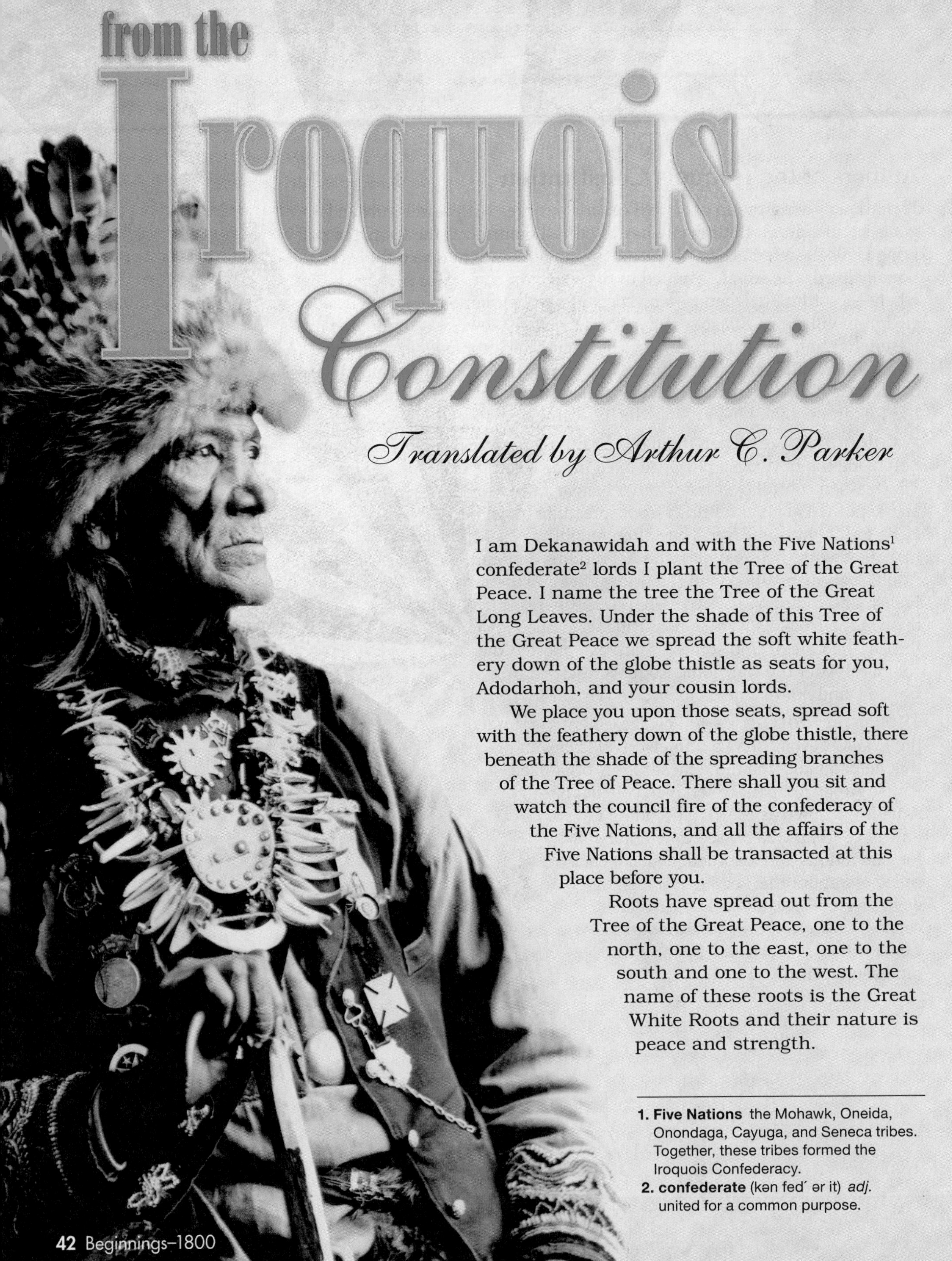

from the Iroquois Constitution

Translated by Arthur C. Parker

I am Dekanawidah and with the Five Nations[1] confederate[2] lords I plant the Tree of the Great Peace. I name the tree the Tree of the Great Long Leaves. Under the shade of this Tree of the Great Peace we spread the soft white feathery down of the globe thistle as seats for you, Adodarhoh, and your cousin lords.

We place you upon those seats, spread soft with the feathery down of the globe thistle, there beneath the shade of the spreading branches of the Tree of Peace. There shall you sit and watch the council fire of the confederacy of the Five Nations, and all the affairs of the Five Nations shall be transacted at this place before you.

Roots have spread out from the Tree of the Great Peace, one to the north, one to the east, one to the south and one to the west. The name of these roots is the Great White Roots and their nature is peace and strength.

---

1. **Five Nations** the Mohawk, Oneida, Onondaga, Cayuga, and Seneca tribes. Together, these tribes formed the Iroquois Confederacy.
2. **confederate** (kən fedʹ ər it) *adj.* united for a common purpose.

If any man or any nation outside the Five Nations shall obey the laws of the Great Peace and make known their **disposition** to the lords of the confederacy, they may trace the roots to the tree and if their minds are clean and they are obedient and promise to obey the wishes of the confederate council, they shall be welcomed to take shelter beneath the Tree of the Long Leaves.

We place at the top of the Tree of the Long Leaves an eagle who is able to see afar. If he sees in the distance any evil approaching or any danger threatening he will at once warn the people of the confederacy.

The smoke of the confederate council fire shall ever ascend and pierce the sky so that other nations who may be allies may see the council fire of the Great Peace . . .

Whenever the confederate lords shall assemble for the purpose of holding a council, the Onondaga lords shall open it by expressing their gratitude to their cousin lords and greeting them, and they shall make an address and offer thanks to the earth where men dwell, to the streams of water, the pools, the springs and the lakes, to the maize and the fruits, to the medicinal herbs and trees, to the forest trees for their usefulness, to the animals that serve as food and give their pelts for clothing, to the great winds and the lesser winds, to the thunderers, to the sun, the mighty warrior, to the moon, to the messengers of the Creator who reveal his wishes and to the Great Creator who dwells in the heavens above, who gives all the things useful to men, and who is the source and the ruler of health and life.

Then shall the Onondaga lords declare the council open . . .

All lords of the Five Nations' Confederacy must be honest in all things . . . It shall be a serious wrong for anyone to lead a lord into trivial affairs, for the people must ever hold their lords high in estimation out of respect to their honorable positions.

When a candidate lord is to be installed he shall furnish four strings of shells (or wampum)[3] one span in length bound together at one end. Such will **constitute** the evidence of his pledge to the confederate lords that he will live according to the constitution of the Great Peace and exercise justice in all affairs.

When the pledge is furnished the speaker of the council must hold the shell strings in his hand and address the opposite side of the council fire and he shall commence his address saying: "Now behold him. He has now become a confederate lord. See how splendid he looks." An address may then follow.

Vocabulary

disposition (dis′ pə zish′ ən) *n.* an inclination or tendency

constitute (kän′ stə to͞ot) *v.* serve as the parts or basis of; form; comprise

Analyzing Philosophical Assumptions and Beliefs

What implicit beliefs are expressed in this paragraph?

Comprehension

What does the speaker say is the nature of the Great White Roots?

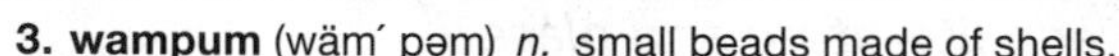

3. wampum (wäm′ pəm) *n.* small beads made of shells.

Political Document and Symbol
What agreement do the strings of shells, or wampum, symbolize?

Vocabulary

tempered (tem´ pərd) *v.* treated to achieve just the right strength or balance

deliberation (di lib´ ər ā´ shən) *n.* careful consideration

oblivion (ə bliv´ ē ən) *n.* the condition of being completely forgotten

At the end of it he shall send the bunch of shell strings to the opposite side and they shall be received as evidence of the pledge. Then shall the opposite side say:

"We now do crown you with the sacred emblem of the deer's antlers, the emblem of your lordship. You shall now become a mentor of the people of the Five Nations. The thickness of your skin shall be seven spans—which is to say that you shall be proof against anger, offensive actions and criticism. Your heart shall be filled with peace and good will and your mind filled with a yearning for the welfare of the people of the confederacy. With endless patience you shall carry out your duty and your firmness shall be **tempered** with tenderness for your people. Neither anger nor fury shall find lodgement in your mind and all your words and actions shall be marked with calm **deliberation**. In all of your deliberations in the confederate council, in your efforts at law making, in all your official acts, self-interest shall be cast into **oblivion**. Cast not over your shoulder behind you the warnings of the nephews and nieces should they chide you for any error or wrong you may do, but return to the way of the Great Law which is just and right. Look and listen for the welfare of the whole people and have always in view not only the present but also the coming generations, even those whose faces are yet beneath the surface of the ground—the unborn of the future nation."

Critical Reading

Cite textual evidence to support your responses.

1. **Key Ideas and Details (a)** What do the lords plant to commemorate their meeting? **(b) Analyze:** What do the roots of this plant symbolize?
2. **Integration of Knowledge and Ideas (a)** According to the Iroquois Constitution, what must confederate lords do to open a council meeting? **(b) Infer:** What does this decree suggest about the Iroquois?
3. **Integration of Knowledge and Ideas (a) Summarize:** Summarize the qualities and conduct required of council lords by the Iroquois Constitution. **(b) Synthesize:** How well do these qualities apply to leaders in the modern world?
4. **Integration of Knowledge and Ideas** Do you agree with and support the ideas presented in the Iroquois Constitution? Why or why not?
5. **Integration of Knowledge and Ideas** In what ways, both practical and spiritual, do the Iroquois rely on the natural world? Use these Essential Question words in your response: *cultivate, civilization, sacred. **[Connecting to the Essential Question: What is the relationship between literature and place?]***

Close Reading Activities

from the *Iroquois Constitution*

Literary Analysis

Common Core State Standards

Language

4.a. Use context as a clue to the meaning of a word or phrase.

1. **Key Ideas and Details (a)** Note one way in which this **political document** creates a structure for Iroquois society. **(b)** Note one way in which this document determines how the Iroquois will react to external threats.
2. **Craft and Structure (a)** Use a chart like the one shown to list three **symbols** in the document and explain the abstract idea each one represents. **(b)** Which of these symbols has fixed meanings sometimes found outside of Iroquois culture? Cite examples to support your answer.

Symbol	Abstract Idea

3. **Integration of Knowledge and Ideas (a) Analyze explicit philosophical assumptions and beliefs** in this document by explaining how the Iroquois see the ideal relationship between a lord and his people. **(b) Analyze implicit philosophical assumptions and beliefs** by explaining the views of nature that underlie many of the statements.
4. **Integration of Knowledge and Ideas** Based on the details in the last paragraph, what philosophical beliefs did the Iroquois hold about the qualities that make one a good leader?

Vocabulary Acquisition and Use

Sentence Completions Use the context clues, or surrounding words and phrases, to choose a word from the vocabulary list on page 40 that best completes each sentence. Explain your choices. Use each word only once.

1. Oil and vinegar ______ the main ingredients of that salad dressing.
2. To make a good decision, emotion must be ______ with reason.
3. I came to my conclusion after careful ______.
4. Someone with amnesia may live in a continuous state of ______.
5. Clio has a lazy ______, while her brother is inclined to work hard.

Writing to Sources

Found Poem A found poem is a poem created from writing or speech not intended to be poetry. Choose a passage from the Iroquois Constitution that you think is especially strong or beautiful. Turn it into a poem by rewriting it with line breaks like those of poetry. Organize the stanzas and place the line breaks where you feel they create the most impact. Read your poem aloud to verify your choices; revise them if necessary.

Building Knowledge and Insight

from *A Journey Through Texas* • *Boulders Taller Than the Great Tower of Seville*

Connecting to the Essential Question These accounts describe early meetings between Europeans and Native Americans. As you read, find details that show how the explorers and the native peoples react to each other. Doing so will help as you think about the Essential Question: **What is the relationship between literature and place?**

Reading Informational Text
5. Analyze and evaluate the effectiveness of the structure an author uses in his or her exposition or argument, including whether the structure makes points clear, convincing, and engaging.

Close Reading Focus

Exploration Narratives

The Europeans who first came to the Americas related their experiences in **exploration narratives**—firsthand accounts of their travels. These accounts generally provide information in **chronological order,** describing events in the order in which they occurred. By creating a clear sequence of events, the explorers allowed readers back home in Europe to follow their journeys, step by step.

Comparing Literary Works Every journey presents conflicts and problems. As you read, use a chart like the one shown to *compare and contrast the problems* each explorer faced and the solutions he found.

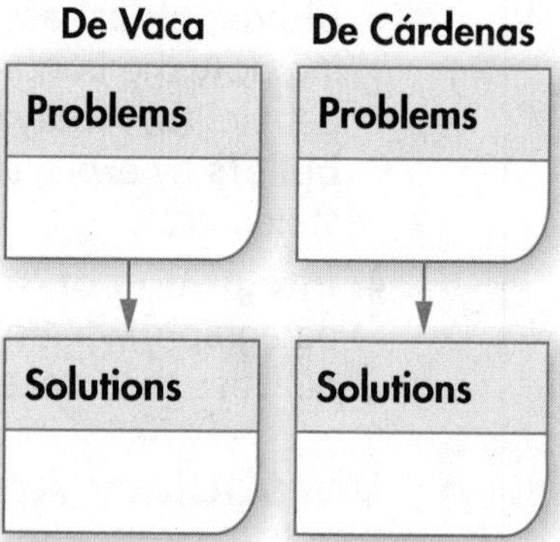

Preparing to Read Complex Texts When reading narrative accounts, analyze and evaluate the structure by making sure you are clear about the sequence in which events occur and the ways in which each event changes a situation. Pause and try to state events in order. To help, **recognize signal words** that clarify relationships of time and sequence, reason, or contrast.

Time: *After five days,* they had not *yet* returned.

Sequence: . . . and so we endured these seventeen days, *at the end of which* we crossed the river. . . .

Contrast: . . . *although* this was the warm season, no one could live in the canyon because of the cold.

Vocabulary

The words below are key to understanding the texts that follow. Copy the words into your notebook and note which ones are adjectives. How can you tell?

entreated
feigned
subsisted
successive
advantageous
traversed

Alvar Núñez Cabeza de Vaca

(1490?–1557?)

Author of *A Journey Through Texas*

In 1528, Pánfilo de Narváez and 400 Spanish soldiers landed near Tampa Bay and set out to explore Florida's west coast. Alvar Núñez Cabeza de Vaca (äl′ bär no͞on′ yes kä bā′ sä dā bä′ kä) was second in command. Beset by hostile natives, illness, and the prospect of starvation, Narváez and his men then set sail for Mexico in five flimsy boats, but he and most of the men drowned. Cabeza de Vaca and a party of about sixty survived and reached the Texas shore near present-day Galveston.

Shipwrecked without supplies, only fifteen of the group lived through the winter. In the end, Cabeza de Vaca and three others survived. They were captured by natives and spent the next several years in captivity. During that time, Cabeza de Vaca gained a reputation as a medicine man and trader. The four Spaniards finally escaped and wandered for eighteen months across the Texas plains. In 1536, the survivors finally reached Mexico City.

Invitation to Others Cabeza de Vaca's adventures and his reports on the richness of Texas sparked exploration of the region. In "A Journey Through Texas," he speaks of Estevanico, the first African to set foot in Texas.

In 1541, Cabeza de Vaca also led a 1,000-mile expedition through the south of present day Brazil to Asunción, the capital of Río de la Plata. He was appointed governor of the Río de la Plata region (now Paraguay), but he was ousted two years later as a result of revolt.

Through his journals, Cabeza de Vaca encouraged others, including Francisco Vásquez de Coronado, to explore America.

García López de Cárdenas

(c. 1540)

Author of *Boulders Taller Than the Great Tower of Seville*

García López de Cárdenas (gär sē′ ä lō′ pes dā kär′ dā näs) is best remembered as the first European to visit the Grand Canyon. As a leader of Francisco Vásquez de Coronado's expedition to New Mexico (1540–1542), Cárdenas was dispatched from Cibola (Zuni) in western New Mexico to see a river that the Moqui Native Americans of northeastern Arizona had described to one of Coronado's captains. The river was the Colorado. López de Cárdenas departed on August 25, 1540, reaching the Grand Canyon after a westward journey of about twenty days. He became the first European to view the canyon and its river, which from the vantage of the canyon's rim appeared to be a stream merely six feet wide! Unable to descend to the river, they took back to Europe descriptions that attempted to record the magnitude of the sight. López de Cárdenas reported that boulders in the Grand Canyon were taller than the 300-foot high Great Tower of Seville, one of the world's tallest cathedrals.

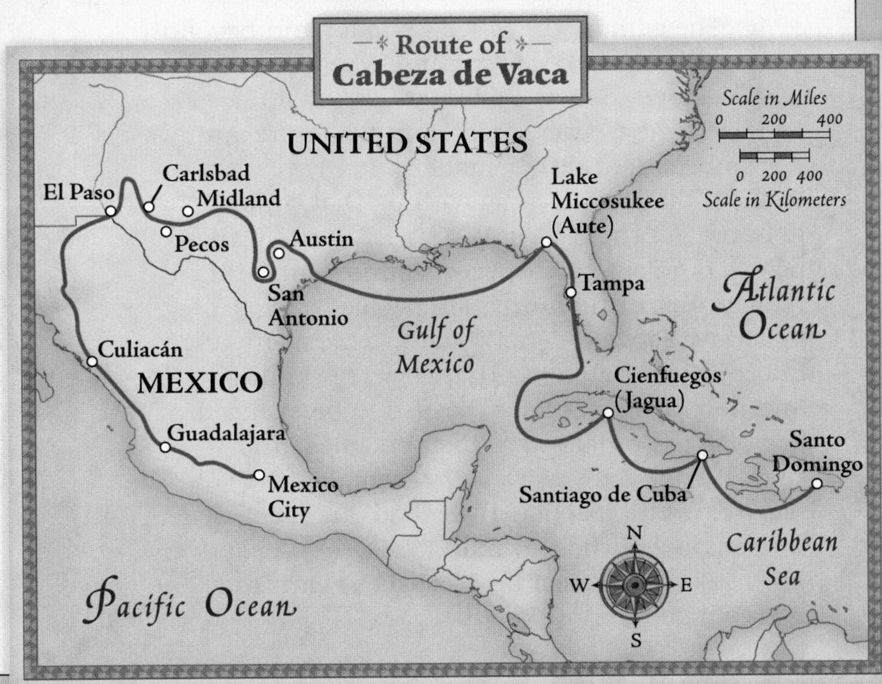

from

A JOURNEY THROUGH TEXAS

Alvar Núñez Cabeza de Vaca

BACKGROUND Alvar Núñez Cabeza de Vaca and three countrymen wandered for months through Texas as they journeyed toward the Spanish settlement in Mexico City. In the course of their travels, Cabeza de Vaca healed a Native American by performing the first recorded surgery in Texas. His resulting fame attracted so many followers that Cabeza de Vaca noted in his journal: "The number of our companions became so large that we could no longer control them." As the party continued traveling westward, they were well received by the native people they encountered.

The same Indians led us to a plain beyond the chain of mountains, where people came to meet us from a long distance. By those we were treated in the same manner as before, and they made so many presents to the Indians who came with us that, unable to carry all, they left half of it. . . . We told these people our route was towards sunset, and they replied that in that direction people lived very far away. So we ordered them to send there and inform the inhabitants that we were coming and how. From this they begged to be excused, because the others were their enemies, and they did not want us to go to them. Yet they did not venture to disobey in the end, and sent two women, one of their own and the other a captive. They selected women because these can trade everywhere, even if there be war.

We followed the women to a place where it had been agreed we should wait for them. After five days they had not yet returned, and the Indians explained that it might be because they had not found anybody. So we told them to take us north, and they repeated that there were no people, except very far away, and neither food nor water. Nevertheless we insisted, saying that we wanted to go there, and they still excused themselves as best they could, until at last we became angry.

One night I went away to sleep out in the field apart from them; but they soon came to where I was, and remained awake all night in great alarm, talking to me, saying how frightened they were. They entreated us not to be angry any longer, because, even if it was their death, they would take us where we chose. We feigned to be angry still, so as to keep them in suspense, and then a singular[1] thing happened.

On that same day many fell sick, and on the next day eight of them died! All over the country, where it was known, they became so afraid that it seemed as if the mere sight of us would kill them. They besought[2] us not to be angry nor to procure the death of any more of their number, for they were convinced that we killed them by merely thinking of it. In truth, we were very much concerned about it, for, seeing the great mortality, we dreaded that all of them might die or forsake us in their terror, while those further on, upon learning of it, would get out of our way hereafter. We prayed to God our Lord to assist us, and the sick began to get well. Then we saw something that astonished us very much, and it was that, while the parents, brothers and wives of the dead had shown deep grief at their illness, from the moment they died the survivors made no demonstration whatsoever, and showed not the slightest feeling; nor did they dare to go near the bodies until we ordered their burial. . . .

The sick being on the way of recovery, when we had been there already three days, the women whom we had sent out returned, saying that they had met very few people, nearly all having gone after the cows, as it was the season. So we ordered those who had been sick to remain, and those who were well to accompany us, and that, two days' travel from there, the same women should go with us and get people to come to meet us on the trail for our reception.

The next morning all those who were strong enough came along, and at the end of three journeys we halted. Alonso del Castillo and Estevanico,[3] the negro, left with the women as guides, and the woman who was a captive took them to a river that flows between mountains, where there was a village, in which her father lived, and these were the first abodes we saw that were like unto real houses.

1. **singular** *adj.* strange.
2. **besought** (bē sôt´) *v.* pleaded with.
3. **Estevanico** (es´ tā vä nē´ kō) Of Moorish extraction, Estevanico was the first African man to set foot in Texas.

◀ Critical Viewing

In what ways might a landscape like the one in the photograph on the facing page pose difficulties for an expedition? **INTERPRET**

Vocabulary

entreated (en trēt´ əd) *v.* begged; pleaded

feigned (fānd) *v.* pretended

Recognizing Signal Words

Which words in this paragraph signal time and sequence relationships?

Comprehension

Why do the Indians fear going on ahead?

Castillo and Estevanico went to these and, after holding parley[4] with the Indians, at the end of three days Castillo returned to where he had left us, bringing with him five or six of the Indians. He told how he had found permanent houses, inhabited, the people of which ate beans and squashes, and that he had also seen maize.

Of all things upon earth this caused us the greatest pleasure, and we gave endless thanks to our Lord for this news. Castillo also said that the negro was coming to meet us on the way, near by, with all the people of the houses. For that reason we started, and after going a league and a half met the negro and the people that came to receive us, who gave us beans and many squashes to eat, gourds to carry water in, robes of cowhide, and other things. As those people and the Indians of our company were enemies, and did not understand each other, we took leave of the latter, leaving them all that had been given to us, while we went on with the former and, six leagues beyond, when night was already approaching, reached their houses, where they received us with great ceremonies. Here we remained one day, and left on the next, taking them with us to other permanent houses, where they **subsisted** on the same food also, and thence on we found a new custom.

▲ Critical Viewing
What does this drawing suggest about the relationship between Cabeza de Vaca's party and the Native Americans? **INTERPRET**

Vocabulary
subsisted (səb sist′ əd) *v.* remained alive; were sustained
successive (sək ses′ iv) *adj.* one after another, in sequence

The people who heard of our approach did not, as before, come out to meet us on the way, but we found them at their homes, and they had other houses ready for us. . . . There was nothing they would not give us. They are the best formed people we have seen, the liveliest and most capable; who best understood us and answered our questions. We called them "of the cows," because most of the cows die near there, and because for more than fifty leagues up that stream they go to kill many of them. Those people go completely naked, after the manner of the first we met. The women are covered with deer-skins, also some men, especially the old ones, who are of no use any more in war.

Exploration Narratives
What information about the region and its people do you learn from this paragraph?

The country is well settled. We asked them why they did not raise maize, and they replied that they were afraid of losing the crops, since for two **successive** years it had not rained, and the seasons were so dry that the moles had eaten the corn, so that they did not dare to plant any more until it should have rained very hard. And they also begged us to ask Heaven for rain, which we promised to do. We also wanted to know from where they brought their maize, and they said it came from where the sun sets, and that it was found all over that country, and the shortest way to it was in that direction.

4. **holding parley** (pär′ lē) conferring.

We asked them to tell us how to go, as they did not want to go themselves, to tell us about the way.

They said we should travel up the river towards the north, on which trail for seventeen days we would not find a thing to eat, except a fruit called *chacan*, which they grind between stones; but even then it cannot be eaten, being so coarse and dry; and so it was, for they showed it to us and we could not eat it. But they also said that, going upstream, we could always travel among people who were their enemies, although speaking the same language, and who could give us no food, but would receive us very willingly, and give us many cotton blankets, hides and other things; but that it seemed to them that we ought not to take that road.

In doubt as to what should be done, and which was the best and most advantageous road to take, we remained with them for two days. They gave us beans, squashes, and calabashes.[5] Their way of cooking them is so new and strange that I felt like describing it here, in order to show how different and queer are the devices and industries of human beings. They have no pots. In order to cook their food they fill a middle-sized gourd with water, and place into a fire such stones as easily become heated, and when they are hot to scorch they take them out with wooden tongs, thrusting them into the water of the gourd, until it boils. As soon as it boils they put into it what they want to cook, always taking out the stones as they cool off and throwing in hot ones to keep the water steadily boiling. This is their way of cooking.

After two days were past we determined to go in search of maize, and not to follow the road to the cows, since the latter carried us to the north, which meant a very great circuit, as we held it always certain that by going towards sunset we should reach the goal of our wishes.

So we went on our way and traversed the whole country to the South Sea,[6] and our resolution was not shaken by the fear of great starvation, which the Indians said we should suffer (and indeed suffered) during the first seventeen days of travel. All along the river, and in the course of these seventeen days we received plenty of cowhides, and did not eat of their famous fruit (*chacan*), but our food consisted (for each day) of a handful of deer-tallow, which for that purpose we always sought to keep, and so endured these seventeen days, at the end of which we crossed the river and marched for seventeen days more. At sunset, on a plain between very high mountains, we met people who, for one-third of the year, eat but powdered straw, and as we went by just at that time, had to eat it also, until, at the end of that journey we found some permanent houses, with plenty of harvested maize, of which and of its meal they gave us great quantities, also squashes and beans, and blankets of cotton. . . .

Vocabulary

advantageous (ad′ van tā′ jəs) *adj.* favorable, profitable

traversed (trə vʉrst′) *v.* moved over, across, or through

Exploration Narratives

What might readers back in Europe have thought about the group's determination to find maize?

Comprehension

With what information does Castilo return?

---

5. **calabashes** (kal′ ə bash′ əz) *n.* dried, hollow shells of gourds used to hold food or beverages.
6. **the South Sea** the Gulf of Mexico.

BOULDERS TALLER THAN THE GREAT TOWER OF SEVILLE

FROM AN ACCOUNT BY GARCÍA LÓPEZ DE CÁRDENAS RETOLD BY PEDRO DE CASTAÑEDA

Information was obtained of a large river and that several days down the river there were people with very large bodies. As Don Pedro de Tovar had no other commission, he returned from Tusayán and gave his report to the general.

The latter at once dispatched Don García López de Cárdenas there with about twelve men to explore this river. When he reached Tusayán he was well received and lodged by the natives. They provided him with guides to proceed on his journey. They set out from there laden with provisions, because they had to travel over some uninhabited land before coming to settlements, which the Indians said were more than twenty days away. Accordingly when they had marched for twenty days they came to gorges of the river, from the edge of which it looked as if the opposite side must have been more than three or four leagues[1] away by air. This region was high and covered with low and twisted pine trees; it was extremely cold, being open to the north, so that, although this was the warm season, no one could live in this canyon because of the cold.

The men spent three days looking for a way down to the river; from the top it looked as if the water were a fathom[2] across. But, according to the information supplied by the Indians, it must have been half a league wide. The descent was almost impossible, but, after these three days, at a place which seemed less difficult, Captain Melgosa, a certain Juan Galeras, and another companion, being the most agile, began to go down. They continued descending within view of those on top until they lost sight of them, as they could not be seen from the top. They returned about four o'clock in the afternoon, as they could not reach the bottom because of the many obstacles they met, for what from the top seemed easy, was not so, on the contrary, it was rough and difficult. They said that they had gone down one-third of the distance and that, from the point they had reached, the river seemed very large, and that, from what they saw, the width given by the Indians was correct. From the top they could make out, apart from the canyon, some small boulders which seemed to be as high as a man. Those who went

FROM THE TOP THEY COULD MAKE OUT, APART FROM THE CANYON, SOME SMALL BOULDERS WHICH SEEMED TO BE AS HIGH AS A MAN.

Comprehension
Who is dispatched to explore the river?

1. **leagues** (lēgz) *n.* units of measurement of approximately three miles.
2. **fathom** (fa*th*′ əm) *n.* a unit of measurement equal to six feet.

▲ **Critical Viewing** Do the photographs on these two pages help you understand the explorers' confusion about the scale of the Grand Canyon? Explain. **CONNECT**

Recognizing Signal Words

What change do the words "up to that time" signal?

THOSE WHO WENT DOWN AND WHO REACHED THEM SWORE THAT THEY WERE TALLER THAN THE GREAT TOWER OF SEVILLE.

down and who reached them swore that they were taller than the great tower of Seville.[3]

The party did not continue farther up the canyon of the river because of the lack of water. Up to that time they had gone one or two leagues inland in search of water every afternoon. When they had traveled four additional days the guides said that it was impossible to go on because no water would be found for three or four days, that when they themselves traveled through that land they took along women who brought water in gourds, that in those trips they buried the gourds of water for the return trip, and that they traveled in one day a distance that took us two days.

This was the Tizón river, much closer to its source than where Melchior Díaz and his men had crossed it. These Indians were of the same type, as it appeared later. From there Cárdenas and his men turned back, as that trip brought no other results.

---

3. **great tower of Seville** The Giralda, the tower on the Cathedral of Seville in Spain, rises above the cathedral more than twice its height.

Critical Reading

Cite textual evidence to support your responses.

1. **Key Ideas and Details (a)** In the Cabeza de Vaca narrative, what conflict in the party occurs immediately before the Native Americans begin to fall ill? **(b) Draw Conclusions:** What do the Native Americans believe is the cause of their sickness? Explain.
2. **Key Ideas and Details (a)** Why do the native people in the settled areas no longer plant corn? **(b)** What do they ask the Spaniards to do to fix this problem? **(c) Interpret:** What does this request suggest about the Native Americans' view of the Spaniards?
3. **Key Ideas and Details (a)** In the Cárdenas narrative, what natural feature are Cárdenas and his men sent to explore? **(b) Infer:** Why do you think Coronado sends the group on this mission? Explain.
4. **Key Ideas and Details (a) Compare and Contrast:** How does the appearance of the river and the boulders from the top of the gorge differ from the reality close up? **(b) Identify Cause and Effect:** In what ways do these differences in perspective affect the explorers?
5. **Integration of Knowledge and Ideas** Judging from these accounts, what are some of the challenges Europeans faced in exploring—and understanding—the Americas? In your response, use at least two of these Essential Question words: *perspective, values, respect, alter.* ***[Connecting to the Essential Question: What is the relationship between literature and place?]***

Close Reading Activities

from *A Journey Through Texas* • *Boulders Taller Than the Great Tower of Seville*

Literary Analysis

1. **Key Ideas and Details** Which details in these **exploration narratives** suggest how the Native Americans viewed the Europeans? Explain your choices.
2. **Craft and Structure** What type of relationship (time, sequence, reason, or contrast) is indicated by each of the italicized **signal words** in this passage? "*Nevertheless* we insisted, saying that we wanted to go there, and they *still* excused themselves as best they could, *until* at last we became angry."
3. **Craft and Structure (a)** Use a chart like this one to list four events from each account in **chronological order. (b)** Why might each explorer have felt a responsibility to create a clear sequence of events for his readers?

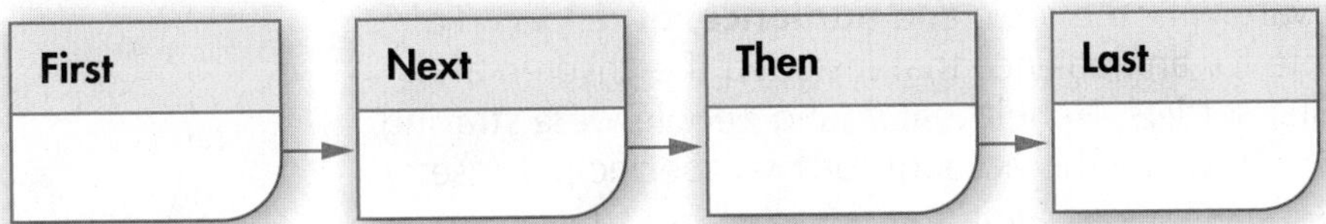

4. **Comparing Literary Works (a)** Note two problems each explorer faced and the solutions each found. **(b)** How were they similar and different?
5. **Integration of Knowledge and Ideas (a)** Why do you think the explorers in the Cárdenas party compare the boulders to the great tower of Seville? **(b)** What does this comparison suggest about the ways in which people understand new experiences?

Common Core State Standards

Writing
2.d. Use precise language.

Language
5. Demonstrate understanding of figurative language, word relationships, and nuances in word meanings.

Vocabulary Acquisition and Use

Use New Words Use the following word pairs correctly in sentences:

1. entreated/danger
2. feigned/surprise
3. advantageous/win
4. traversed/journey
5. successive/days
6. subsisted/food

Writing to Sources

Explanatory Text Imagine that you are exploring a new territory. Write an **explorer's journal entry** that provides precise details about your discoveries. Choose a specific location and gather details through research so that your description is authentic. Share your draft with a partner. If your reader cannot "see" your description, replace weak words with vivid choices.

Weak word choice: The river *was* ten miles from end to end.
Strong word choice: The river *cut through* the mountains for ten miles.

Building Knowledge and Insight

from *Of Plymouth Plantation*

Connecting to the Essential Question William Bradford's account reveals courage and perseverance in the face of harsh circumstances. As you read, find details that show how the Pilgrims face and overcome challenges. Doing so will help as you consider the Essential Question: **What makes American literature American?**

Common Core State Standards

Reading Informational Text
6. Determine an author's point of view or purpose in a text in which the rhetoric is particularly effective, analyzing how style and content contribute to the power, persuasiveness, or beauty of the text.

Close Reading Focus

Author's Purpose; Audience

An **author's purpose** is his or her reason for writing. General purposes for writing are *to inform, to entertain,* and *to persuade*. Authors also have specific purposes that vary with the topic and **audience,** or readers. For example, Bradford wrote for an audience that included the children and grandchildren of the first settlers. He felt that young people were straying from the Pilgrims' faith. He wrote this account for two specific purposes:

- **To inform:** Bradford sought to tell the new generation about the Pilgrims' history.
- **To persuade:** Bradford sought to inspire the new generation to uphold Puritan values.

As you read, consider how the language, style, and content of the text help to advance Bradford's purposes for writing.

Preparing to Read Complex Texts Bradford wrote in *Puritan Plain Style*, which is relatively straightforward, but his writing can be challenging to modern readers. As you read, *monitor your understanding*. If you find you are not completely sure of the sequence of events or Bradford's insights, clarify the meaning by **breaking down long sentences.** To do so, separate a complex sentence into its essential parts—the subject (who or what) and the verb (action). This will help you isolate the main idea. As you read, use a chart like the one shown to analyze and interpret the meaning of complex sentences.

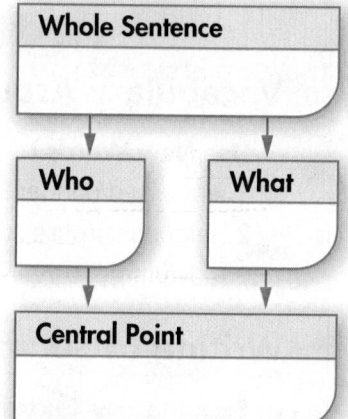

Whole Sentence

Who | What

Central Point

Vocabulary

The words below are important to understanding the text that follows. Copy the words into your notebook. List other words you know related to the word *habitation*.

peril
habitation
subject to
adversity
calamity
relent

William Bradford (1590–1657)

Author, *Of Plymouth Plantation*

Survival in North America was a matter of endurance, intelligence, and courage. William Bradford had all three qualities. Thirteen years after the first permanent English settlement was established in Jamestown, Virginia, Bradford helped lead the Pilgrims to what is now Massachusetts.

Seeking Freedom Bradford, who was born in Yorkshire, England, joined a group of Puritans who believed that the Church of England was corrupt. This group wished to separate from the church. In the face of stiff persecution, they eventually fled to Holland and from there sailed to North America. In *Of Plymouth Plantation,* Bradford provides an account of the experiences of these early settlers. Historians consider this account to be accurate.

A Long Leadership After the death of the colony's first leader, the Pilgrims elected Bradford governor. He was reelected thirty times. During his tenure, he organized the repayment of debts to financial backers, encouraged new immigration, and established good relations with the Native Americans, without whose help the colony never would have survived. He also instituted the town meeting within the colonies, a democratic process that continues to take place in state government today. Bradford was largely responsible for leading the infant colony through many hardships to success.

In 1630, Bradford began writing *Of Plymouth Plantation,* a firsthand account of the Pilgrims' struggle to endure, sustained only by courage and unbending faith. The work, written in the simple language known as Puritan Plain Style, was not published until 1856.

Our fathers were Englishmen which came over this great ocean, and were ready to perish in this wilderness.

from Of Plymouth Plantation

William Bradford

BACKGROUND In September of 1620, the tiny ship *Mayflower* set sail from Plymouth, England, bound for the Jamestown settlement in Virginia. The ship carried 102 Pilgrims, many of them members of a separatist religious congregation. During the stormy Atlantic crossing, the ship was blown off course, which forced it to miss its intended destination. The boat finally set anchor near Cape Cod, Massachusetts, in mid-November.

from Chapter 9

Of Their Voyage and How They Passed the Sea; and of Their Safe Arrival at Cape Cod

[1620] SEPTEMBER 6 . . . After they[1] had enjoyed fair winds and weather for a season, they were encountered many times with cross-winds, and met with many fierce storms, with which the ship was shrewdly[2] shaken, and her upper works made very leaky; and one of the main beams in the mid ships was bowed and cracked, which put them in some fear that the ship could not be able to perform the voyage. So some of the chief of the company, perceiving the mariners to fear the sufficiency of the ship, as appeared by their mutterings, they entered into serious consultation with the master and other officers of the ship, to consider in time of the danger; and rather to return than to cast themselves into a desperate and inevitable peril. And truly there was great distraction and difference of opinion amongst the mariners themselves; fain[3] would they do what could be done for their wages' sake (being now half the seas over), and on the other hand they were loath to hazard their lives too desperately. But in examining of all opinions, the master and others affirmed they knew the ship to be strong and firm under water; and for the buckling of the main beam, there was a great iron screw the passengers brought out of Holland, which would raise the beam into his place; the which being done, the carpenter and master affirmed that with a post under it, set firm in the lower deck, and other ways bound, he would make it sufficient. And as for the decks and upper works, they would caulk them as well as they could, and though with the working of the ship they would not long keep staunch,[4] yet there would otherwise be no great danger, if they did not over-press her with sails. So they committed themselves to the will of God, and resolved to proceed.

In sundry of these storms the winds were so fierce, and the seas so high, as they could not bear a knot of sail, but were forced to hull,[5] for diverse day together. And in one of them, as they thus lay at hull, in a mighty storm, a lusty[6] young man (called John Howland) coming upon some occasion above the gratings, was, with a seele[7] of the ship thrown into [the sea]; but it pleased God that he caught hold of the topsail halyards,[8] which hung overboard, and ran out at length; yet he held his hold (though he was sundry

◀ Critical Viewing
How does this photograph of a *Mayflower* replica help you better understand the Pilgrims' experience? **CONNECT**

Ship took damage

Vocabulary
peril (per′ əl) *n.* danger

Comprehension
How is the ship damaged in the storm?

1. **they** Even though Bradford is one of the Pilgrims, he refers to them in the third person.
2. **shrewdly** (shro͞od′ lē) *adv.* severely.
3. **fain** (fān) *adv.* gladly.
4. **staunch** (stônch) *adj.* watertight.
5. **hull** *v.* drift with the wind.
6. **lusty** *adj.* strong; hearty.
7. **seele** *n.* rolling; pitching to one side.
8. **halyards** (hal′ yərdz) *n.* ropes for raising or lowering sails.

The American EXPERIENCE

HISTORY CONNECTION

The *Mayflower* was the British ship on which 102 Pilgrims sailed from Southampton, England, to North America during September, October, and November of 1620. In November, the Pilgrims disembarked at the tip of Cape Cod. Shortly before Christmas, they moved to the more protected site of Plymouth, Massachusetts. According to historians' estimates, the square-rigged *Mayflower* probably measured about 90 feet long and weighed 180 tons.

Connect to the Literature

What details in *Of Plymouth Plantation* suggest the kinds of challenges the travelers faced on the journey? What other challenges do you think travelers might face on a ship this size?

fathoms under water) till he was held up by the same rope to the brim of the water, and then with a boat hook and other means got into the ship again, and his life saved; and though he was something ill with it, yet he lived many years after, and became a profitable member both in church and commonwealth. In all this voyage there died but one of the passengers, which was William Butten, a youth, servant to Samuel Fuller, when they drew near the coast.

But to omit other things (that I may be brief), after long beating at sea they fell with that land which is called Cape Cod; the which being made and certainly known to be it, they were not a little joyful. After some deliberation had amongst themselves and with the master of the ship, they tacked about[9] and resolved to stand for the southward (the wind and weather being fair) to find some place about Hudson's River for their **habitation**. But after they had sailed that course about half the day, they fell amongst dangerous shoals[10] and roaring breakers, and they were so far entangled therewith as they conceived themselves in great danger; and the wind shrinking upon them withal,[11] they resolved to bear up again for the Cape, and thought themselves happy to get out of those dangers before night overtook them, as by God's providence they did. And the next day they got into the Cape harbor,[12] where they rid in safety. . . .

Being thus arrived in a good harbor and brought safe to land, they fell upon their knees and blessed the God of heaven, who had brought them over the vast and furious ocean, and delivered them from all the perils and miseries thereof, again to set their feet on the firm and stable earth, their proper element. . . .

But here I cannot but stay and make a pause, and stand half amazed at this poor people's present condition; and so I think will the reader too, when he well considers the same. Being thus passed the vast ocean, and a sea of troubles before in their preparation (as may be remembered by that which went before), they had now no friends to welcome them, nor inns to entertain or refresh their weather-beaten bodies, no houses or much less towns to repair to, to seek for succor.[13] It is recorded in Scripture[14] as a mercy to the apostle and his shipwrecked company, that the barbarians

Vocabulary

habitation (hab′ i tā′ shen) *n.* place to live; group of homes or dwellings

9. **tacked about** sailed back and forth so the wind would hit the sails at the best angles.
10. **shoals** (shōlz) *n.* sandbars or shallow areas that are dangerous to navigate.
11. **withal** (with ôl′) *adv.* also.
12. **Cape harbor** now called Provincetown Harbor.
13. **succor** (suk′ ər) *n.* help; relief.
14. **Scripture** In Acts 27–28, when the Apostle Paul and a group of other Christians are shipwrecked on the island of Malta, they are treated kindly by the "barbarians" who live there.

showed them no small kindness in refreshing them, but these savage barbarians, when they met with them (as after will appear) were readier to fill their sides full of arrows then otherwise. And for the season it was winter, and they that know the winters of that country know them to be sharp and violent, and subject to cruel and fierce storms, dangerous to travel to known places, much more to search an unknown coast. Besides, what could they see but a hideous and desolate wilderness, full of wild beasts and wild men? And what multitudes there might be of them they knew not. . . . What could now sustain them but the spirit of God and his grace? May not and ought not the children of these fathers rightly say: *Our fathers were Englishmen which came over this great ocean, and were ready to perish in this wilderness;*[15] *but they cried unto the Lord, and He heard their voice, and looked on their adversity, etc.*[16] *Let them therefore praise the Lord, because He is good, and His mercies endure forever. . . .*

from Book 2[17]

[1620] In these hard and difficult beginnings, they found some discontents and murmurings arise amongst some, and mutinous speeches and carriages in others; but they were soon quelled and overcome by the wisdom, patience, and just and equal carriage of things by the Governor[18] and better part, which cleaved faithfully together in the main. But that which was most sad and lamentable was that in two or three months' time, half of their company died, especially in January and February, being the depth of winter, and wanting houses and other comforts; being infected with the scurvy[19] and other diseases, which this long voyage and their inaccommodate[20] condition had brought upon them; so as there died sometimes two or three of a day, in the foresaid time; that of one hundred and odd persons, scarce fifty remained.

And of these in the time of most distress, there was but six or seven sound persons, who, to their great commendations be it spoken, spared no pains, night nor day, but with abundance of toil and hazard of their own health, fetched them wood, made them fires, dressed them meat, made their beds, washed their loathsome clothes, clothed and unclothed them; in a word, did all the homely[21] and necessary offices for them which dainty and queasy stomachs

Vocabulary

subject to (sub´ jikt to͞o) *adj.* likely to be affected by something

adversity (ad vʉr´ si tē) *n.* hardship; difficulty

Comprehension

What season was it when the Pilgrims arrived in Cape Cod?

---

15. **wilderness** Bradford is comparing the Pilgrims to the ancient Hebrews, who wandered in the desert after fleeing Egypt and before reaching the Promised Land.
16. **they cried . . . etc.** Bradford is paraphrasing a passage from the Hebrew Bible (Deuteronomy 26:7).
17. **Book 2** Here Bradford switches from chapter divisions to book divisions.
18. **Governor** John Carver (c. 1576–1621) was the first governor of Plymouth Colony but died during his first year of office. Bradford succeeded him as governor.
19. **scurvy** (skʉr´ vē) *n.* disease cause by a vitamin C deficiency.
20. **inaccommodate** (in´ ə käm´ ə dāt´) *adj.* unfit.
21. **homely** *adj.* domestic.

Vocabulary

calamity (kə lam′ ə tē) *n.* disaster; catastrophe

Author's Purpose

Why do you think Bradford describes in such detail the different reactions of the crew and the Pilgrims to the illness?

Vocabulary

relent (ri lent′) *v.* become less harsh; be more merciful

cannot endure to hear named; and all this willingly and cheerfully, without any grudging in the least, showing herein their true love unto their friends and brethren. A rare example and worthy to be remembered. Two of these seven were Mr. William Brewster,[22] their reverend Elder, and Myles Standish,[23] their Captain and military commander, unto whom myself, and many others were much beholden in our low and sick condition. And yet the Lord so upheld these persons, as in this general **calamity** they were not at all infected either with sickness, or lameness. And what I have said of these, I may say of many others who died in this general visitation,[24] and others yet living, that whilst they had health, yea, or any strength continuing, they were not wanting to any that had need of them. And I doubt not but their recompense is with the Lord.

But I may not here pass by another remarkable passage not to be forgotten. As this calamity fell among the passengers that were to be left here to plant, and were hasted ashore and made to drink water, that the seamen might have the more beer, and one[25] in his sickness desiring but a small can of beer, it was answered that if he were their own father he should have none; the disease began to fall amongst them also, so as almost half of their company died before they went away, and many of their officers and lustiest men, as the boatswain, gunner, three quartermasters, the cook, and others. At which the master was something stricken and sent to the sick ashore and told the Governor he should send for beer for them that had need of it, though he drunk water homeward bound.

But now amongst his company there was far another kind of carriage[26] in this misery then amongst the passengers; for they that had been boon[27] companions in drinking and jollity in the time of their health and welfare began now to desert one another in this calamity, saying they would not hazard their lives for them, they should be infected by coming to help them in their cabins, and so, after they came to die by it, would do little or nothing for them, but if they died let them die. But such of the passengers as were yet aboard showed them what mercy they could, which made some of their hearts **relent**, as the boatswain (and some others), who was a proud young man, and would often curse and scoff at the passengers; but when he grew weak, they had compassion on

22. **William Brewster** (1567–1644) one of the Pilgrim leaders.
23. **Myles Standish** (c. 1584–1656) professional soldier hired by the Pilgrims to be their military advisor. He was not originally a Puritan but later became a member of the congregation.
24. **visitation** *n.* affliction.
25. **one** Bradford is referring to himself.
26. **carriage** *n.* behavior.
27. **boon** *adj.* close.

him and helped him; then he confessed he did not deserve it at their hands, he had abused them in word and deed. O! saith he, you, I now see, show your love like Christians indeed one to another, but we let one another lie and die like dogs. . . .

All this while the Indians came skulking about them, and would sometimes show themselves aloof of, but when any approached near them, they would run away. And once they stole away their tools where they had been at work, and were gone to dinner. But about the 16th of March a certain Indian came boldly amongst them, and spoke to them in broken English, which they could well understand, but marveled at it. At length they understood by discourse with him that he was not of these parts, but belonged to the eastern parts, where some English ships came to fish, with whom he was acquainted, and could name sundry of them by their names, amongst whom he had got his language. He became profitable to them in acquainting them with many things concerning the state of the country in the east parts where he lived, which was afterwards profitable unto them; as also of the people here, of their names, number, and strength; of their situation and distance from this place, and who was chief amongst them. His name was Samoset;[28] he told them also of another Indian whose name was Squanto,[29] a native of this place, who had been

▲ Critical Viewing
Do you think this picture is an accurate representation of the first Thanksgiving? Why or why not? **JUDGE; SUPPORT**

Comprehension
Who is Samoset, and how do the Pilgrims meet him?

28. **Samoset** (sam´ ə set´) (d. 1655) a Pemaquid tribal chief from Maine.
29. **Squanto** (skwän´ tō) (d. 1622) a member of the Pawtuxet tribe who in 1614 had been kidnapped by an English sea captain and taken to Spain to be sold as a slave. He escaped and eventually returned to Massachusetts in 1619, only to find that his home village had been destroyed by plague.

Breaking Down Long Sentences
What is the essential action described in the sentence beginning "Being, after some time..."?

Author's Purpose
Why do you think Bradford refers to Squanto as a "special instrument"?

could speak English very well

in England and could speak better English then himself. Being, after some time of entertainment and gifts, dismissed, a while after he came again, and 5 more with him, and they brought again all the tools that were stolen away before, and made way for the coming of their great sachem,[30] called Massasoit,[31] who, about four or five days after, came with the chief of his friends, and other attendance, with the aforesaid Squanto. With whom, after friendly entertainment, and some gifts given him, they made a peace with him (which hath now continued this 24 years)[32] in these terms:

1. That neither he nor any of his should injure or do hurt to any of their people.
2. That if any of his did any hurt to any of theirs, he should send the offender, that they might punish him.
3. That if anything were taken away from any of theirs, he should cause it to be restored; and they should do the like to his.
4. If any did unjustly war against him, they would aid him; if any did war against them, he should aid them.
5. He should send to his neighbors confederates, to certify them of this, that they might not wrong them, but might be likewise comprised in the conditions of peace.
6. That when their men came to them, they should leave their bows and arrows behind them.

After these things he returned to his place called Sowams,[33] some 40 mile from this place, but Squanto continued with them and was their interpreter, and was a special instrument sent of God for their good beyond their expectation. He directed them how to set their corn, where to take fish and to procure other commodities, and was also their pilot to bring them to unknown places for their profit, and never left them till he died. He was a native of this place, and scarce any left alive besides himself. He was carried away with diverse others by one Hunt,[34] a master of a ship, who thought to sell them for slaves in Spain; but he got away for England and was entertained by a merchant in London and employed to Newfoundland and other parts, and lastly brought hither into these parts. . . .

---

30. sachem (sā′ chəm) chief.
31. Massasoit (mas′ ə soit′) (c. 1580–1661) the supreme sachem (chief) of the Wampanoag peoples.
32. now . . . 24 years The treaty actually lasted until King Philip's War began in 1675.
33. Sowams (sō′ ämz) present site of Warren, Rhode Island.
34. Hunt Thomas Hunt was captain of one of the ships in John Smith's expedition to Virginia.

[1621] . . . They began now to gather in the small harvest they had,[35] and to fit up their houses and dwellings against winter, being all well recovered in health and strength, and had all things in good plenty; for as some were thus employed in affairs abroad, others were exercised in fishing, about cod and bass and other fish, of which they took good store, of which every family had their portion. All the summer there was no want. And now began to come in store of fowl, as winter approached, of which this place did abound when they came first (but afterward decreased by degrees). And besides water fowl, there was great store of wild turkeys, of which they took many, besides venison, etc. Besides they had about a peck of meal a week to a person, or now since harvest, Indian corn to that proportion. Which made many afterwards write so largely of their plenty here to their friends in England, which were not feigned, but true reports.

---

35. They . . . had This section of Bradford's narrative is often titled "The First Thanksgiving."

Critical Reading

Cite textual evidence to support your responses.

1. **Key Ideas and Details** **(a)** What were some of the hardships the Pilgrims faced during their trip across the Atlantic and their first winter at Plymouth? **(b) Interpret:** What do their troubles tell you about the climate and landscape of Plymouth?
2. **Key Ideas and Details** **(a) Draw Conclusions:** What message do you think Bradford is trying to convey in this narrative? **(b) Apply:** How might the message have meaning for people today?
3. **Integration of Knowledge and Ideas** **Hypothesize:** In what ways might this account have been different if the Pilgrims had settled farther south?
4. **Integration of Knowledge and Ideas** **Evaluate:** Has this account changed your impression of the Pilgrims? Explain your answer.
5. **Integration of Knowledge and Ideas** How are the Pilgrims' values and beliefs evident in the ways they respond to problems? In your response, use at least two of these Essential Question words: *just, commitment, gratitude, conviction.* ***[Connecting to the Essential Question: What makes American literature American?]***

Close Reading Activities

from *Of Plymouth Plantation*

Literary Analysis

1. **Key Ideas and Details (a)** Choose three sentences from the narrative that you find particularly challenging to understand. **(b) Break down the long sentences** into their essential parts—the subject and the verb. **(c)** Write the meaning of each sentence as you understand it.
2. **Craft and Structure** Complete these sentences to describe Bradford's **purpose** for writing and the **audience** he wanted to reach:
   - Bradford wrote *Of Plymouth Plantation* in order to ______.
   - He wrote this historical account for an audience that included ______.
3. **Craft and Structure** Use a chart like the one shown to explore how specific details in Bradford's account help him achieve his purpose for writing. **(a)** Choose four details, descriptions, or incidents that you think are especially important to Bradford's narrative. **(b)** For each one, explain why you think Bradford chose to include it and how it helped him achieve his overall purpose for writing.

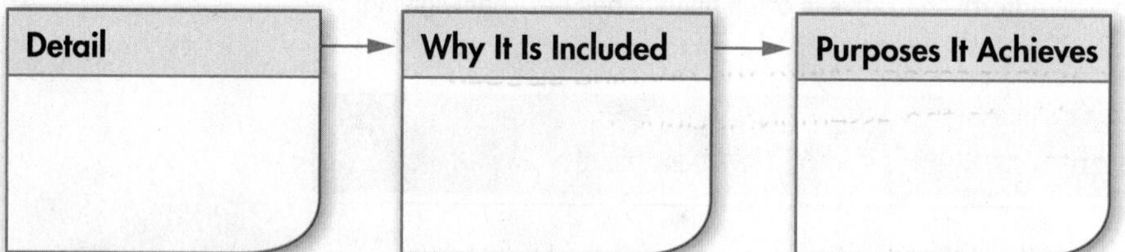

4. **Integration of Knowledge and Ideas (a)** At what points does Bradford see religious or spiritual meaning in incidents that happen to the Pilgrims as a whole or to individuals? **(b)** In what ways do these details both reflect his beliefs and support one of his purposes for writing?
5. **Integration of Knowledge and Ideas** Do you think Bradford succeeded in writing a document that fulfilled his original purpose? Explain why or why not.
6. **Integration of Knowledge and Ideas** Using details from the text, state Bradford's moral and religious goals in writing. Do you think a modern audience would respond to Bradford's work in the way he originally intended? Explain.
7. **Integration of Knowledge and Ideas (a)** List details from the text that Bradford uses to describe Native Americans. **(b)** How might Bradford's first audience have responded to his depiction of Native Americans? **(c)** In what ways do today's readers bring a different perspective to this element of his narrative?

Writing

7. Conduct short as well as more sustained research projects to answer a question or solve a problem; narrow or broaden the inquiry when appropriate; synthesize multiple sources on the subject, demonstrating understanding of the subject under investigation. *(p. 67)*

Speaking and Listening

6. Adapt speech to a variety of contexts and tasks, demonstrating a command of formal English when indicated or appropriate. *(p. 67)*

Language

4.b. Identify and correctly use patterns of word changes that indicate different meanings or parts of speech. *(p. 67)*

Vocabulary Acquisition and Use

Word Analysis: Related Forms of *peril*

The word *peril* comes from the Latin word *periculum*, which means "danger." Using your knowledge of the base word, fill in each blank with the word that best completes the sentence.

a. perilous **b.** perilously **c.** imperiled

1. Undertaking the risky voyage ______ the Pilgrims' lives.
2. The ship tossed ______ in the waves.
3. Building a new home in the wilderness was a ______ undertaking.

Vocabulary: Antonyms or Synonyms

Antonyms are words that have opposite meanings. Synonyms are words that have similar meanings. Decide whether the words in each of the following pairs are antonyms or synonyms. Then, explain your reasoning.

1. calamity, misfortune
2. relent, intensify
3. subject to, prone
4. adversity, ease
5. peril, safety
6. habitation, dwelling

Writing to Sources

Explanatory Text Imagine that time travel is possible and William Bradford is coming to speak at your school. Write the opening **speech** that will be used to introduce him to the assembly. Include information about his life and achievements, and explain why his perspective will be valuable to the audience.

Prewriting Reread the biography of Bradford on page 57 and the excerpt from his narrative. In a chart like the one shown, record questions you still have about Bradford. Then, use both print and electronic sources to find answers to these questions. Document answers and sources in your chart.

Using Clear Research Questions

Research Question	Answer	Source
1.		
2.		
3.		

Drafting As you draft, strike a tone that is informative and respectful, but friendly. Avoid using words that are either too complicated or too casual. Use appropriate formal English, but try to sound natural and fresh, rather than stiff or overly proper. To check your tone, pause to read your work aloud to yourself.

Revising Reread your introduction and make sure that all of the facts you have included are accurate. Double-check specific details and correct them as needed. Finally, read your work aloud as though you are delivering it for an audience. Replace words or sections that sound artificial or forced.

CONTEMPORARY CONNECTION

Exploration Past and Present

When producer Gene Roddenberry pitched a classic adventure drama to the NBC television network, his mission was to get the money he needed to explore new worlds on television. His series *Star Trek* debuted in 1966, and its opening phrase, "to boldly go where no man has gone before," became instantly memorable.

If space was a final frontier in twentieth-century science fiction, then Mars is "where no man has gone before" in twenty-first-century science fact. Just as the North American continent lured European explorers in the sixteenth century, the planet Mars lures scientists like Steve Squyres, the chief investigator for NASA's Mars Exploration Rover (MER) Project.

The rovers *Spirit* and *Opportunity* are twin robots that were launched toward Mars in 2003 to search for answers about the history of water on the Red Planet. From the moment they landed in early 2004, they began to send back amazing pictures, allowing people on Earth to see such Martian wonders as the floor of Victoria Crater: "We're still feeling a little awestruck," Squyres reports in his September 28, 2006, blog entry. López de Cárdenas probably felt the same when he first gazed upon the Grand Canyon.

Steve Squyres Scientist / Blogger

Steve Squyres became a geologist because he liked science and loved to climb mountains. However, he discovered his true passion when he was a graduate student at Cornell University. Looking for a subject for a term paper, he found a "room where they kept all the pictures from the *Viking* missions." Intending to look at these images of Mars explorations for a few minutes, Squyres says, "I was in that room for four hours." For the man who is now a professor at Cornell and also oversees the science operations of both Mars rovers and a team of 170 researchers at NASA's Jet Propulsion Laboratory, the Mars mission to seek "evidence concerning whether or not it once had liquid water and a habitable environment" was a success. However, Squyres is still not satisfied, saying he wants to "bring back samples." And that will require another mission, at least.

MISSION UPDATE

MARS BLOG BY STEVE SQUYRES

SEPTEMBER 28, 2006

Wow.

The last couple of days have been among the most exciting of the entire mission. The only other events I can compare this to are the two landings and the arrival of *Opportunity* at Endurance Crater. And in terms of sheer visual impact, this beats those.

Opportunity has arrived at Victoria Crater. As we expected, we came upon the view quite abruptly . . . it went from just the very tops of distant cliffs to a full-blown vista of the crater floor in just a handful of sols. And now we are perched just back from the lip of the crater at Duck Bay, with the whole thing laid out below us.

BLOG CONTINUES >>>

Our first order of business here, obviously, is going to be to take a very big Pancam panorama. We'll be starting on that very shortly, though of course it will take quite a while to get it all back to Earth. After that has been shot, we're heading for our next location . . . Cape Verde. We were considering both Cape Verde and Cabo Frio, and when we looked at all the factors together, Cape Verde won out. Wherever we stop next is where the rover will spend "superior conjunction"—the upcoming period when Mars will be out of sight behind the Sun, making communications impossible for a short while. Conjunction is coming soon, so we want to get to our conjunction spot quickly, and Cape Verde looked like an easier drive than Cabo Frio. Another factor is that we want to be parked on rock over conjunction, so that we can do some work on rock with the IDD. There seems to be good exposure of rock

BLOG CONTINUES >>>

- The distance between Earth and Mars varies from 33,900,000 to 249,000,000 miles because the two planets are orbiting the Sun at different speeds.
- Mars, named for the Roman war god, has two little moons: Phobos (fear) and Deimos (panic).
- Winds on Mars can blow up to 80 miles per hour, and dust storms sometimes blanket the planet for months.
- The gravity on Mars is only 38% as strong as the gravity on Earth.
- The temperature on Mars can be as warm as 80° Fahrenheit or as cold as -199° Fahrenheit.
- A Martian day is called a sol and lasts 24 hours, 39 minutes, and 35 seconds. A Martian year lasts 686.98 earth days.

MARS ROVER

Spirit took seven months to reach Mars from Earth.

Scientists communicate with the rovers twice per day, sending commands via the morning "uplink" and gathering data via the afternoon "downlink."

The rovers work on solar power that is absorbed during the day and stored in rechargeable batteries.

Data sent back by the rovers provides evidence that water once flowed across the surface of Mars.

There are two rovers—*Spirit* and *Opportunity*. Together, they have sent back more than 100,000 images of Mars.

Each rover carries specialized cameras, microscopic imagers, spectrometers, and rock abrasion tools.

at Cape Verde, but little or none of it at Cabo Frio. So Cape Verde it is. And how about that view?!? We're still feeling a little awestruck. The analytical part of my brain looks at that and is already doing science analysis and planning. The rest of me, though, just wants to sit back for a little while and take in the scenery.

This doesn't mean that we're going to traverse clockwise around the crater . . . we won't make that decision for quite a while yet. And it also doesn't mean we'll never go to Cabo Frio. And, to be honest, we can't even say for sure that we'll make it all the way to Cape Verde before conjunction . . . you have to be very careful when driving near cliffs this big! So we'll be driving slowly and cautiously. But Cape Verde is the next thing we're going to head off toward after we finish shooting the pan.

Critical Reading

1. **(a)** Note the names of two Martian locations or geographical features Squyres mentions. **(b) Describe:** What similarities do these names have to place names on Earth? **(c) Draw Conclusions:** Why might the scientists have chosen these names for each place?
2. Which details in the blog make it seem like Squyres is actually there on the planet instead of viewing it remotely? Explain your answer.
3. **(a) Analyze:** Which details in the text convey Squyres's excitement? Explain. **(b) Interpret:** What image of science and scientists does this blog convey? Explain.

Use these questions to hold a group discussion of "Mission Update":

4. **(a)** What are the risks of modern exploration—whether into space or into the deep sea? **(b)** Are the results worth the risks? Explain.
5. After reading this excerpt from Squyres's blog, how do you think our concepts of exploration and explorers have changed since Europeans first traveled in the Americas? In what way have those concepts remained the same as they once were?

TEXT SET

The Puritan Influence

Part 2

To My Dear and Loving Husband

Connecting to the Essential Question The Puritans valued religious devotion, work, and duty over private emotions. Yet, Bradstreet's poems are filled with her feelings. As you read, notice details in this poem that refer to private feelings and those that refer to community or shared belief. Doing so will help as you consider the Essential Question: **What makes American literature American?**

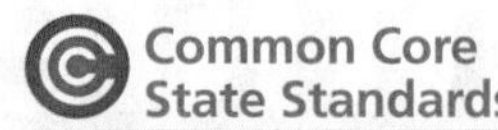

Reading Literature

5. Analyze how an author's choices concerning how to structure specific parts of a text contribute to its overall structure and meaning as well as its aesthetic impact.

Language

3.a. Apply an understanding of syntax to the study of complex texts when reading.

Close Reading Focus

Puritan Plain Style

The Puritans' beliefs in modesty, hard work, and religious devotion were reflected in all aspects of their lives, from the simple, dark clothes they wore, to the spare furnishings they used, to the literature they wrote. The **Puritan Plain Style** is characterized by short words, direct statements, and references to everyday objects and experiences. Consider the simple, direct statements in these lines from Bradstreet's poem:

If ever two were one, then surely we,
If ever man were lov'd by wife, then thee.

Bradstreet's style may seem less plain to modern readers because of the outdated language, like the use of *thee* for *you*, and the **syntax,** or structure, of her sentences. She sometimes omits words, such as the verb *are* after *we* in the first line above, that we would include today. Her syntax also uses **inversion,** or the placing of sentence elements out of normal position. For example, instead of "let's so persevere in love," she says, "in love let's so persevere."

Preparing to Read Complex Texts To better understand a poem's *essential meaning*, **paraphrase** it, or restate it in your own words. Rewrite each sentence or clause in language and word order you understand. If necessary, consult the footnotes or a dictionary to clarify unfamiliar terms. Use a graphic organizer like the one shown to help clarify the lines of your paraphrase.

Poet's Version

My love is such that rivers cannot quench, Nor ought but love from thee, give recompense.

Paraphrase

My love is so strong that rivers cannot relieve its thirst; only your love will satisfy me.

Vocabulary

The words below are important to understanding the text that follows. Copy the words into your notebook, and note which of them have three syllables.

quench
recompense
manifold
persevere

Anne Bradstreet *(1612–1672)*

Author of **"To My Dear and Loving Husband"**

Anne Bradstreet and her husband, Simon, arrived in the Massachusetts Bay Colony in 1630, when she was only eighteen. Armed with the convictions of her Puritan upbringing, she left behind her hometown of Northampton, England, to start afresh in America. It was not an easy life for Bradstreet, who raised eight children, suffered through multiple illnesses, and faced many hardships.

A Private Writer Made Public Despite the difficulties she endured, Bradstreet was able to devote her spare moments to the very "unladylike" occupation of writing. She wrote for herself, not for publication. Nevertheless, in 1650, John Woodbridge, her brother-in-law, arranged for the publication in England of a collection of her scholarly poems, *The Tenth Muse Lately Sprung Up in America, By a Gentlewoman of Those Parts.* Generally considered to be the first collection of original poetry written in colonial America, the book examined the rights of women to learn and express themselves. Bradstreet's later poems, such as "To My Dear and Loving Husband," are more personal, expressing her feelings about the joys and difficulties of everyday Puritan life. In one, she wrote about her thoughts before giving birth. In another, she wrote about the death of a grandchild.

Bradstreet's poetry reflects the Puritans' knowledge of the stories and language of the Bible, as well as their concern for the relationship between earthly and heavenly life. Her work also exhibits some of the characteristics of the French and English poetry of her day.

In 1956, the poet John Berryman wrote "Homage to Mistress Bradstreet," a long poem that pays tribute to this first American poet.

There is no object that we see; no action that we do; no good that we enjoy; no evil that we feel, or fear, but we may make some spiritual advantage of all: and he that makes such improvement is wise, as well as pious.

To My Dear and Loving Husband

Anne Bradstreet

Paraphrasing

How would you paraphrase these first two lines?

Vocabulary

quench (kwench) *v.* satisfy a thirst

recompense (rek′ əm pens′) *n.* repayment; something given or done in return for something else

manifold (man′ ə fōld′) *adv.* in many ways

persevere (pʉr′ sə vir′) *v.* persist; be steadfast in purpose

If ever two were one, then surely we.
If ever man were lov'd by wife, then thee;
If ever wife was happy in a man,
Compare with me ye women if you can.

I prize thy love more than whole mines of gold,
Or all the riches that the East doth hold.
My love is such that rivers cannot **quench**,
Nor ought[1] but love from thee, give **recompense**.
Thy love is such I can no way repay,

The heavens reward thee **manifold**, I pray.
Then while we live, in love let's so **persevere**,[2]
That when we live no more, we may live ever.

1. **ought** (ôt) *n.* anything whatever.
2. **persevere** pronounced (pʉr′ sə vir′) in the seventeenth century, and thus rhymed with the word *ever*.

Critical Reading 

1. **Key Ideas and Details** **(a)** What does the speaker value more than "whole mines of gold"? **(b) Distinguish:** What other images suggest the richness and abundance of the love the speaker and her husband share?
2. **Key Ideas and Details** **(a) Analyze:** What is the apparent contradiction in the last two lines? **(b) Draw Conclusions:** What does the last stanza reveal about Puritan beliefs in the afterlife?
3. **Craft and Structure** **(a)** Note where Bradstreet uses repetition in the first stanza. **(b) Analyze:** How does her use of repetition suggest a growing emotional intensity?
4. **Integration of Knowledge and Ideas** Which aspect of the speaker is more important in this poem—the private or the public self? Use at least two of these Essential Question words in your response: *community, personal, unique, social.* ***[Connecting to the Essential Question: What makes American literature American?]***

▲ Critical Viewing
How does this painting present Bradstreet as both poet and Puritan housewife?
ANALYZE

Cite textual evidence to support your responses.

WORLD LITERATURE IN CONTEXT

The Tenth Muse

THE TENTH MUSE Lately fpring up in AMERICA. OR Severall Poems, compiled with great variety of VVit and Learning, full of delight. Wherein efpecially is contained a compleat difcourfe and defcription of The Four Elements, Conftitutions, Ages of Man, Seafons of the Year. Together with an Exact Epitomie of the Four Monarchies, viz. The Affyrian, Perfian, Grecian, Roman. Alfo a Dialogue between Old England and New, concerning the late troubles. With divers other pleafant and ferious Poems. By a Gentlewoman in thofe parts.

Title page of *The Tenth Muse* by Anne Bradstreet, London, 1650 ▶

Anne Bradstreet's first book of poetry was published in England under the title *The Tenth Muse Lately Sprung Up in America.* In Greek Mythology, the original nine Muses were goddesses, daughters of Zeus, the ruler of the gods. The Muses were thought to be the source of inspiration for all artists, poets, musicians, dancers — and even philosophers. The Muses each had a specialty, as shown in the chart.

In Greek antiquity, the philosopher Plato referred to Sappho, the noted lyric poet, as The Tenth Muse because her poetry was so beautiful. The label lived through the centuries. Gifted, forward-thinking women writers are sometimes called "Tenth Muse." Anne Bradstreet was hailed as a Tenth Muse, as was her Mexican contemporary, Sor Juana Inés de La Cruz. Sor Juana was a noted poet and playwright, a fierce intellectual, and a woman of faith. She spent most of her adult life as a nun in the Convent of the Order of Saint Jerome. In 1689, an anthology of her poetry was published in Spain titled *The Overflowing of the Castalian Spring, by the Tenth Muse of Mexico.*

MUSE	SHE INSPIRED
CALLIOPE *"... beautiful of voice"*	*Eloquence and Epic Poetry*
ERATO *"... amorous"*	*Love Poetry, Lyrics, and Wedding Songs*
CLIO *"... glorious"*	*History*
EUTERPE *"... charming"*	*Music and Lyric Poetry*
MELPOMENE *"... the chanting one"*	*Tragedy*
POLYHYMNIA *"... the singer of many hymns"*	*Sacred Music*
TERPSICHORE *"... delighted with dance"*	*Choral Song and Dance*
THALIA *"... the blossoming one"*	*Comedy and Pastoral Poetry*
URANIA *"... the celestial one"*	*Astronomy*

CONNECT TO THE LITERATURE

Do you think that Tenth Muse is a fitting title for Anne Bradstreet? Why or why not?

◀ Sappho (c. 630 – c. 570 B.C.) Fresco painting Pompeii, Italy, 1st century A.D.

Sor Juana Inés de la Cruz, 18th century painting by Miguel Cabrera ▶

▼ Dance of Apollo with the Nine Muses (tempera on panel)

Close Reading Activities

To My Dear and Loving Husband

Literary Analysis

1. **Key Ideas and Details** **Paraphrase** the last stanza as though you were explaining it to a friend.
2. **Craft and Structure** Use a chart like the one shown to explore aspects of the poem that are typical of the **Puritan Plain Style.**

Style Element	Example
Short Words	
Direct Statements	
Familiar Objects/Experiences	

3. **Craft and Structure** **(a)** Which lines of the poem have customary **syntax? (b)** Which lines present examples of **inversion?** Explain your answers.
4. **Integration of Knowledge and Ideas** Which aspects of the poem do not reflect the plainness of the Puritan ethic? Explain.

Common Core State Standards

Writing

2. Write informative/explanatory texts to examine and convey complex ideas, concepts, and information clearly and accurately through the effective selection, organization, and analysis of content.

Language

5. Demonstrate understanding of figurative language, word relationships, and nuances in word meanings.

Vocabulary Acquisition and Use

Word/Phrase Relationships Choose the letter of the situation that best reflects the meaning of the italicized word or phrase. Then, explain your answers.

1. *quench:* **(a)** filling up on snacks before dinner, **(b)** enjoying a glass of cool water after a long walk, **(c)** calming an unruly group of kids
2. *hard-earned recompense*: **(a)** getting a flat tire on the way to the dentist, **(b)** getting a day off after working late, **(c)** cleaning a messy room after a hard day
3. *increase manifold:* **(a)** receiving a small raise, **(b)** adding a drop to a full bucket, **(c)** getting a 300-percent return on an investment
4. *persevere:* **(a)** quitting when you get tired, **(b)** practicing until you improve, **(c)** arguing with a referee

Writing to Sources

Explanatory Text Write a brief **essay** in which you interpret the speaker's view of love and reward in this poem. First, review the poem for details relating to luxury and abundance. Then, explain how these images of wealth help the speaker express the depth of her love for her husband. Cite details from the text to support your ideas.

Building Knowledge and Insight

Huswifery

Connecting to the Essential Question For most Americans, the values of working hard and being useful are important. Both can be traced back to the Puritans, who believed that all activity should have a practical purpose. As you read this poem, notice details that stress the usefulness of activity. This will help as you consider the Essential Question: **What makes American literature American?**

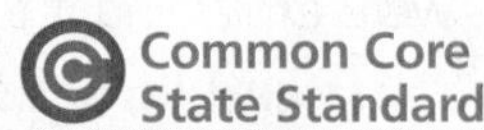

Reading Literature
5. Analyze how an author's choices concerning how to structure specific parts of a text contribute to its overall structure and meaning as well as its aesthetic impact.

Close Reading Focus

Metaphor; Conceit

A **metaphor** is a figure of speech in which two very different subjects are shown to have a point of similarity. A metaphor may liken an abstract idea, such as love or friendship, to a concrete image:

> *Langston Hughes: "Life is a broken-winged bird."*
> *Emily Dickinson: "Hope is the thing with feathers."*

A **conceit,** also called an **extended metaphor,** is a metaphor taken to its logical limit. With a conceit, the metaphor does not end in a single line or image, but builds throughout the work. In this poem, Taylor uses the *poetic structure* itself to extend the metaphor of the spinning wheel into a conceit. Most poems are structured in individual **lines** organized into stanzas. A **stanza** is a group of consecutive lines that form a unit. Like a paragraph in prose, a stanza usually introduces and develops a new idea. Use a chart like the one shown to analyze how Taylor builds his conceit line by line and stanza by stanza.

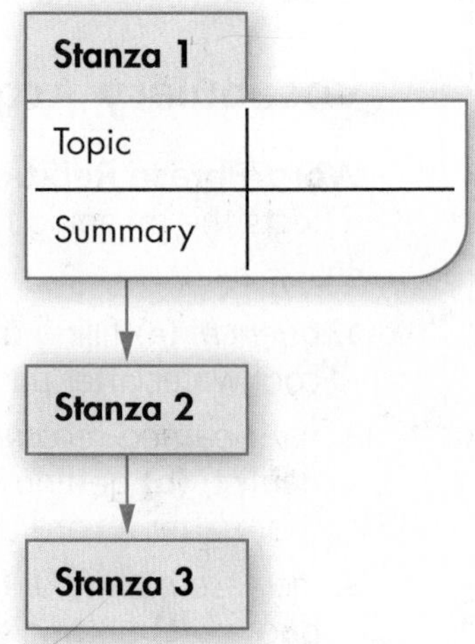

Preparing to Read Complex Texts The language of poetry is rich and dense, so you may find poetry more challenging than prose. As you read, monitor your comprehension to make sure you understand how Taylor builds his meaning. If you find the poem difficult, **adjust your reading rate** by slowing down. When you get to a complex image, you may slow down even more and take the time to form a clear, specific picture before you continue reading.

Vocabulary

The words below are important to understanding the text that follows. Copy the words into your notebook and consider the word *judgment*. What other forms of this word do you know?

affections **judgment**
ordinances **apparel**

Edward Taylor (1642–1729)

Author of "Huswifery"

Puritanism was a religious reform movement that began in England in the sixteenth century. The Puritans sought to reform the Church of England and to reshape English society according to their beliefs. These efforts led to both civil strife and government persecution of the Puritans. In response, many Puritans, including Edward Taylor, fled to the American colonies.

Before his emigration to America, Edward Taylor worked as a teacher in England. Upon arriving in Boston in 1668, Taylor entered Harvard College as a sophomore, graduating in 1671. After graduation, he accepted the position of minister and physician in the small frontier farming community of Westfield, Massachusetts, and then walked more than one hundred miles, much of it through snow, to his new home.

Harsh Life in a New World Life in the village of Westfield was filled with hardships. Fierce battles between the Native Americans and the colonists left the community in constant fear. In addition, Taylor experienced many personal tragedies. Five of his eight children died in infancy; then, his wife died while she was still a young woman. He remarried and had five or six more children. (Biographers differ on the exact number.)

Edward Taylor is now generally regarded as the best of the North American colonial poets. Yet, because Taylor thought of his poetry as a form of personal worship, he allowed only two stanzas to be published during his lifetime. Some believe that he chose not to publish his poems because their joyousness and delight in sensory experience ran counter to Puritan attitudes that poetry be for moral instruction only. One of his nineteenth-century descendants donated Taylor's writings to Yale University. The stash of poems was discovered in the 1930s and, in 1939, *The Poetical Works of Edward Taylor* was published. Most of Taylor's poetry, including "Huswifery," uses extravagant comparisons, intellectual wit, and subtle argument to explore religious faith and affection.

*Oh! that I ever felt what I profess.
'Twould make me then the
happi'st man alive.*

Huswifery

Edward Taylor

Make me, O Lord, Thy spinning wheel complete.
Thy holy word my distaff[1] make for me.
Make mine **affections** Thy swift flyers[2] neat
And make my soul Thy holy spoole to be.
My conversation make to be Thy reel
And reel the yarn thereon spun of Thy wheel.

Make me Thy loom then, knit therein this twine:
And make Thy holy spirit, Lord, wind quills:[3]
Then weave the web Thyself. The yarn is fine.
Thine **ordinances** make my fulling mills.[4]
Then dye the same in heavenly colors choice.
All pinked[5] with varnished flowers of paradise.

Then clothe therewith mine understanding, will,
Affections, **judgment**, conscience, memory
My words, and actions, that their shine may fill
My ways with glory and Thee glorify.
Then mine **apparel** shall display before Ye
That I am clothed in holy robes for glory.

Vocabulary

affections (ə fek′ shənz) *n.* emotions

ordinances (ôrd′'n əns əz) *n.* sacraments or religious rites

judgment (juj′ mənt) *n.* power to form an opinion well; good sense

apparel (əp per′ əl) *n.* clothing

1. **distaff** *n.* staff on which flax or wool is wound for use in spinning.
2. **flyers** *n.* part of a spinning wheel that twists fibers into yarn.
3. **quills** *n.* weaver's spindles or bobbins.
4. **fulling mills** *n.* machines that shrink and thicken cloth to the texture of felt.
5. **pinked** *v.* decorated with a perforated pattern.

Critical Reading

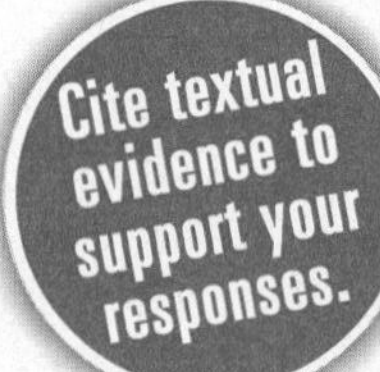
Cite textual evidence to support your responses.

1. **Key Ideas and Details (a)** What household activities are described in the first two stanzas? **(b) Analyze:** How do these images contribute to the idea of being "clothed in holy robes for glory," stated in the third stanza?
2. **Key Ideas and Details (a) Interpret:** What images in this poem may have contradicted the Puritan requirement that clothing be dark and plain? **(b) Deduce:** What do these images suggest about the speaker's feelings about God?
3. **Integration of Knowledge and Ideas** Do you think the Puritans would have considered this poem useful? In your answer, use at least two of these Essential Question words: *expression, practical, spiritual, labor.* ***[Connecting to the Essential Question: What makes American literature American?]***

Close Reading Activities | *Huswifery*

Literary Analysis

1. **Key Ideas and Details** Look back at how you **adjusted your reading rate** as you read the poem. Use a chart like the one shown to classify which lines you read at your usual speed and which you read more slowly. Use your chart to guide a second reading of the poem.

Average speed	More slowly

2. **Key Ideas and Details** Explain how you integrated footnotes into your readings of the poem.
3. **Craft and Structure** **(a)** In the first line, what request does the speaker make? **(b)** Explain how this is a **metaphor**—what two dissimilar things are being compared? **(c)** What is the point of similarity between the two dissimilar things?
4. **Integration of Knowledge and Ideas** Explain how the metaphors developed in each **stanza** build to a **conceit** for the poem as a whole.

Vocabulary Acquisition and Use

True or False Decide whether each statement below is true or false. Explain each answer.

1. It is always possible to control your **affections,** regardless of the situation.
2. **Ordinances** should be fulfilled with respect and care.
3. Sleep deprivation can impair your **judgment.**
4. Wool, cotton, and polyester are examples of fine **apparel.**

Writing to Sources

Explanatory Text Taylor's poem describes the processes of turning raw materials into clothing. It works on two levels—as a description of an ordinary activity and as a metaphor for religious devotion. In a **reflective essay,** describe the procedure of a common household chore and explore how that task suggests a larger, or metaphoric, meaning. Include these elements:

- a complete, step-by-step description of the task from beginning to end
- vivid sensory details that appeal to the five senses
- a thoughtful insight about the meaning the task holds for you

Common Core State Standards

Writing

2. Write informative/explanatory texts to examine and convey complex ideas, concepts, and information clearly and accurately through the effective selection, organization, and analysis of content.

2.d. Use precise language, domain-specific vocabulary, and techniques such as metaphor, simile, and analogy to manage the complexity of the topic.

Building Knowledge and Insight

ANCHOR TEXT

from *Sinners in the Hands of an Angry God*

Connecting to the Essential Question This sermon had a powerful effect on its original audiences. As you read, note passages that you think most affected listeners. This will help as you consider the Essential Question: **How does literature shape or reflect society?**

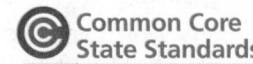

Common Core State Standards

Reading Informational Text

6. Determine an author's point of view or purpose in a text in which the rhetoric is particularly effective, analyzing how style and content contribute to the power, persuasiveness, or beauty of the text.

Language

4. Determine or clarify the meaning of unknown and multiple-meaning words and phrases based on *grades 11–12 reading content.*

4.a. Use context as a clue to the meaning of a word or phrase

Close Reading Focus

Sermon; Archetypes

A **sermon** is broadly defined as a speech given from a pulpit in a house of worship. Like its written counterpart, the essay, a sermon conveys the speaker's message or point of view. As a form of **oratory,** or formal public speaking, sermons almost always display the following elements:

- They are *persuasive*, inspiring listeners to take action.
- They address the needs and concerns of the *audience,* or listeners.
- They *appeal to the emotions.*
- They include *expressive and rhythmic language.*

Often, orators also include images, patterns, characters, or stories from the Bible, myth, or classical literature. These **archetypes** add a deeper dimension for listeners who apply the ancient meanings to the new message. As you read, look for these elements of oratory in the sermon.

Preparing to Read Complex Texts As you read, monitor your comprehension of unfamiliar words and look for **context clues**—other words, phrases, and sentences—that can help you understand. For example, take the word *abominable* in this passage: "You are ten thousand times more abominable in his [God's] eyes, than the most hateful venomous serpent is in ours...." Edwards likens the way God views the sinner with the way we view a snake. From this clue, you can figure out that *abominable* must be close in meaning to *disgusting* or *horrible.* As you read, use a chart like the one shown to define other unfamiliar words by using context clues.

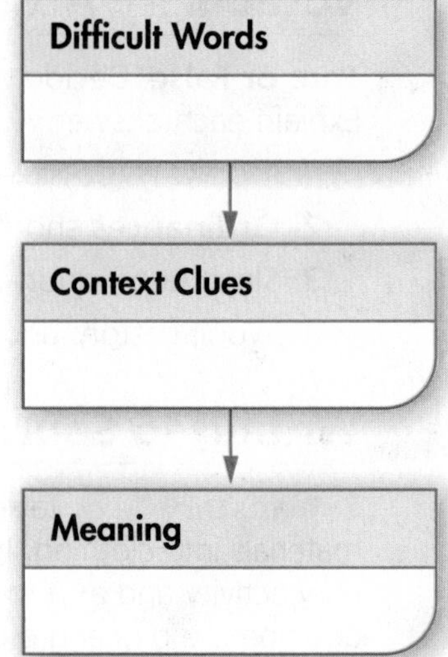

Vocabulary

The words below are important to understanding the text that follows. Copy the words into your notebook. Which one means *all-powerful*?

constitution
prudence
omnipotent
mediator
induce

Jonathan Edwards *(1703–1758)*

Author of "Sinners in the Hands of an Angry God"

The sermons of Jonathan Edwards were so filled with "fire and brimstone"—a phrase symbolizing the torments of hell endured by sinners—that his name alone was enough to make many eighteenth-century Puritans shake in their shoes. Yet, Edwards was not just a stone-faced religious zealot. He was also a man who believed in science and reason and who saw in the physical world the proof of God's presence and will.

A Born Preacher This great American theologian was born in East Windsor, Connecticut, where he grew up in an atmosphere of devout discipline. As a young boy, he is said to have demonstrated his religious devotion by preaching sermons to his playmates. He also displayed academic brilliance, learning to speak Latin, Greek, and Hebrew before he was twelve. Edwards entered the Collegiate School of Connecticut (now Yale University) at the age of thirteen and graduated four years later as valedictorian. He went on to earn his master's degree in theology.

The Great Awakening Edwards began his preaching career in 1727 as assistant to his grandfather, Solomon Stoddard. Stoddard was pastor of the church at Northampton, Massachusetts, one of the largest and wealthiest Puritan congregations. Edwards became the church pastor two years later when his grandfather died. Committed to a return to the orthodoxy and fervent faith of the Puritan past, Edwards became one of the leaders of the Great Awakening, a religious revival that swept the colonies in the 1730s and 1740s.

Fall from Favor As pastor of the church at Northampton, Edwards had instituted disciplinary proceedings against members of his congregation for reading what he considered improper books. In his sermons he denounced by name those he considered sinners. Such actions drew criticism and, in 1750, a council representing ten congregations dismissed Edwards as pastor.

After his dismissal, Edwards moved to Stockbridge, Massachusetts, where he preached to the Native Americans and wrote his most important theological works. He continued to preach and write until his death in 1758, shortly after becoming president of the College of New Jersey (now Princeton University). Although in most of his writings Edwards appeals to reason, his emotional sermon "Sinners in the Hands of an Angry God" is by far his most famous work. It demonstrates Edwards's tremendous powers of persuasion and captures the religious fervor of the Great Awakening.

▶ Critical Viewing

Edwards preached in churches similar to this. What values do you think are reflected in the style of this building? **ANALYZE**

from Sinners in the Hands of an Angry God

Jonathan Edwards

BACKGROUND Jonathan Edwards delivered this famous sermon to a congregation in Enfield, Connecticut, in 1741. Surprisingly, he spoke quietly and without emotion. According to one account, he read the six-hour work in a level voice, staring over the heads of his audience at the bell rope that hung against the back wall "as if he would stare it in two." Despite his calm manner, his listeners are said to have screamed in terror, and Edwards had to stop several times to ask for silence.

This is the case of every one of you that are out of Christ:[1] That world of misery, that lake of burning brimstone, is extended abroad under you. There is the dreadful pit of the glowing flames of the wrath of God; there is Hell's wide gaping mouth open; and you have nothing to stand upon, nor anything to take hold of; there is nothing between you and Hell but the air; it is only the power and mere pleasure of God that holds you up.

You probably are not sensible of this; you find you are kept out of Hell, but do not see the hand of God in it; but look at other things, as the good state of your bodily **constitution**, your care of your own life, and the means you use for your own preservation. But indeed these things are nothing; if God should withdraw his hand, they would avail no more to keep you from falling than the thin air to hold up a person that is suspended in it.

Vocabulary
constitution (kän′ stə to͞o′ shən) *n.* physical makeup of a person

Comprehension
Of what does Edwards believe his congregation is not "sensible"?

1. **out of Christ** not in God's grace.

The American EXPERIENCE

Biblical Imagery
Jonathan Edwards's frightening imagery of God's potential for wrath and destruction recalls stories of fires, floods, and divine retribution in the Old Testament of the King James Bible. While this imagery terrified Edwards's audience, they would have found it quite familiar. In fact, in 1741, when Edwards delivered this sermon, the King James Bible had been in wide circulation for 130 years. The first English version of the Bible to include both the Old and New Testaments, the King James Bible had been produced at the express request of the Puritans in England in 1611. This Bible, with its haunting language and powerful imagery, would have been common daily reading for most of Edwards's listeners.

Connect to the Literature

How do you think a contemporary audience of worshippers would react to this type of "fire and brimstone" biblical imagery?

Your wickedness makes you as it were heavy as lead, and to tend downwards with great weight and pressure towards Hell; and if God should let you go, you would immediately sink and swiftly descend and plunge into the bottomless gulf, and your healthy constitution, and your own care and prudence, and best contrivance, and all your righteousness, would have no more influence to uphold you and keep you out of Hell, than a spider's web would have to stop a fallen rock. Were it not for the sovereign pleasure of God, the earth would not bear you one moment . . . The world would spew you out, were it not for the sovereign hand of Him who hath subjected it in hope. There are black clouds of God's wrath now hanging directly over your heads, full of the dreadful storm, and big with thunder; and were it not for the restraining hand of God, it would immediately burst forth upon you. The sovereign pleasure of God, for the present, stays[2] his rough wind; otherwise it would come with fury, and your destruction would come like a whirlwind, and you would be like the chaff of the summer threshing floor.

The wrath of God is like great waters that are dammed for the present; they increase more and more, and rise higher and higher, till an outlet is given; and the longer the stream is stopped, the more rapid and mighty is its course, when once it is let loose. It is true, that judgment against your evil works has not been executed hitherto; the Hoods of God's vengeance have been withheld; but your guilt in the meantime is constantly increasing, and you are every day treasuring up more wrath; the waters are constantly rising, and waxing more and more mighty; and there is nothing but the mere pleasure of God, that holds the waters back, that are unwilling to be stopped, and press hard to go forward. If God should only withdraw his hand from the floodgate, it would immediately fly open, and the fiery floods of the fierceness and wrath of God, would rush forth with inconceivable fury, and would come upon you with omnipotent power; and if your strength were ten thousand times greater than it is, yea, ten thousand times greater than the strength of the stoutest, sturdiest devil in Hell, it would be nothing to withstand or endure it.

The bow of God's wrath is bent, and the arrow made ready on the string, and justice bends the arrow at your heart, and strains the bow, and it is nothing but the mere pleasure of God, and that of an angry God, without any promise or obligation at all, that keeps the arrow one moment from being made drunk with your blood. Thus all you that never passed under a great change of heart, by the mighty power of the spirit of God upon your souls; all you that were never born again, and made new creatures, and raised from being dead in sin, to

Vocabulary

prudence (pro͞o´ dəns) *n.* carefulness; caution

omnipotent (äm nip´ ə tənt) *adj.* all-powerful

2. **stays** (stāz) *v.* restrains.

a state of new, and before altogether unexperienced light and life, are in the hands of an angry God. However you may have reformed your life in many things, and may have had religious affections, and may keep up a form of religion in your families and closets,[3] and in the house of God, it is nothing but His mere pleasure that keeps you from being this moment swallowed up in everlasting destruction. However unconvinced you may now be of the truth of what you hear, by and by you will be fully convinced of it.

Those that are gone from being in the like circumstances with you, see that it was so with them; for destruction came suddenly upon most of them; when they expected nothing of it, and while they were saying, peace and safety: now they see, that those things on which they depended for peace and safety, were nothing but thin air and empty shadows.

The God that holds you over the pit of Hell, much as one holds a spider, or some loathsome insect over the fire, abhors you, and is dreadfully provoked: his wrath towards you burns like fire; he looks upon you as worthy of nothing else, but to be cast into the fire; he is of purer eyes than to bear to have you in his sight; you are ten thousand times more abominable in his eyes, than the most hateful venomous serpent is in ours. . . .

O sinner! Consider the fearful danger you are in: it is a great furnace of wrath, a wide and bottomless pit, full of the fire of wrath, that you are held over in the hand of that God, whose wrath is provoked and incensed as much against you, as against many of the damned in Hell. You hang by a slender thread, with the flames of divine wrath flashing about it, and ready every moment to singe it, and burn it asunder; and you have no interest in any **mediator**, and nothing to lay hold of to save yourself, nothing to keep off the flames of wrath, nothing of your own, nothing that you ever have done, nothing that you can do, to **induce** God to spare you one moment. . . .

When God beholds the ineffable[4] extremity of your case, and sees your torment to be so vastly disproportioned to your strength, and sees how your poor soul is crushed, and sinks down, as it were, into an infinite gloom; he will have no compassion upon you, he will not forbear the executions of his wrath, or in the least lighten his hand; there shall be no moderation or mercy, nor will God then at all stay his rough wind; he will have no regard to your welfare, nor be at all careful lest you should suffer too much in any other sense, than only that you shall *not suffer beyond what strict justice requires*. . . .

God stands ready to pity you; this is a day of mercy; you may cry now with some encouragement of obtaining mercy. But once the day of mercy is past, your most lamentable and dolorous[5] cries and shrieks

3. closets *n.* small, private rooms for meditation.
4. ineffable (in ef′ ə bəl) *n.* inexpressible.
5. dolorous (dō′ lər əs) *adj.* sad; mournful.

Vocabulary

mediator (mē′ dē ā tər) *n.* one who reconciles opposing groups

induce (in do͞os′) *v.* cause; bring about

Comprehension

According to Edwards, what is "but thin air and empty shadows"?

will be in vain; you will be wholly lost and thrown away of God, as to any regard to your welfare. God will have no other use to put you to, but to suffer misery; you shall be continued in being to no other end; for you will be a vessel of wrath fitted to destruction; and there will be no other use of this vessel, but to be filled full of wrath. . . .

Thus it will be with you that are in an unconverted state, if you continue in it; the infinite might, and majesty, and terribleness of the omnipotent God shall be magnified upon you, in the ineffable strength of your torments. You shall be tormented in the presence of the holy angels, and in the presence of the Lamb,[6] and when you shall be in this state of suffering, the glorious inhabitants of Heaven shall go forth and look on the awful spectacle, that they may see what the wrath and fierceness of the Almighty is; and when they have seen it, they will fall down and adore that great power and majesty. . . .

Using Context Clues

What clue does the reference to "forever" provide to the meaning of *boundless*?

It would be dreadful to suffer this fierceness and wrath of Almighty God one moment; but you must suffer it to all eternity. There will be no end to this exquisite horrible misery. When you look forward, you shall see a long forever, a boundless duration before you, which will swallow up your thoughts and amaze your soul; and you will absolutely despair of ever having any deliverance, any end, any mitigation, any rest at all. . . .

How dreadful is the state of those that are daily and hourly in the danger of this great wrath and infinite misery! But this is the dismal case of every soul in this congregation that has not been born again, however moral and strict, sober and religious, they may otherwise be. Oh that you would consider it, whether you be young or old! . . . Those of you that finally continue in a natural condition, that shall keep you out of Hell longest will be there in a little time! Your damnation does not slumber; it will come swiftly, and, in all probability, very suddenly upon many of you. You have reason to wonder that you are not already in Hell. It is doubtless the case of some whom you have seen and known, that never deserved Hell more than you, and that heretofore appeared as likely to have been now alive as you. Their case is past all hope; they are crying in extreme misery and perfect despair; but here you are in the land of the living and in the house of God, and have an opportunity to obtain salvation. What would not those poor damned hopeless souls give for one day's opportunity such as you now enjoy!

And now you have an extraordinary opportunity, a day wherein Christ has thrown the door of mercy wide open, and stands in calling and crying with a loud voice to poor sinners; a day wherein many are flocking to him, and pressing into the kingdom of God. Many are daily coming from the east, west, north and south; many that were very lately in the same miserable condition that you are in,

6. the Lamb Jesus.

are now in a happy state, with their hearts filled with love to him who has loved them, and washed them from their sins in his own blood, and rejoicing in hope of the glory of God. How awful is it to be left behind at such a day! To see so many others feasting, while you are pining and perishing! To see so many rejoicing and singing for joy of heart, while you have cause to mourn for sorrow of heart, and howl for vexation of spirit! . . .

Therefore, let everyone that is out of Christ now awake and fly from the wrath to come. The wrath of Almighty God is now undoubtedly hanging over a great part of this congregation: let everyone fly out of Sodom.[7] "Haste and escape for your lives, look not behind you, escape to the mountain, lest you be consumed."[8]

---

7. **Sodom** (säd′ əm) In the Bible, a city destroyed by fire because of the sinfulness of its people.
8. **"Haste . . . consumed"** from Genesis 19:17, the angels' warning to Lot, the only virtuous man in Sodom, to flee the city before they destroy it.

Critical Reading

Cite textual evidence to support your responses.

1. **Key Ideas and Details** **(a)** According to the opening paragraph, what keeps sinners from falling into hell? **(b) Interpret:** According to Edwards, what do his listeners mistakenly feel keeps them from falling into hell?
2. **Key Ideas and Details** **(a)** What words in the sermon's title suggest the emotional focus of Edwards's message? **(b) Analyze:** What additional traits does Edwards attribute to God as the sermon progresses?
3. **Key Ideas and Details** **(a)** Toward the end of the sermon, what does Edwards say sinners can obtain? **(b) Analyze Cause and Effect:** What must sinners do to obtain these things?
4. **Integration of Knowledge and Ideas** Given his purpose and the audience of worshipers to whom he spoke, do you think Edwards's sermon was effective? Why or why not?
5. **Integration of Knowledge and Ideas** This sermon played a significant role in reinvigorating Puritan faith during the 1740s. Why? State your opinion, using at least two of these Essential Question words: *powerful, beliefs, doctrine, faithful.* ***[Connecting to the Essential Question: How does literature shape or reflect society?]***

Close Reading Activities

ANCHOR TEXT
from ***Sinners in the Hands of an Angry God***

Literary Analysis

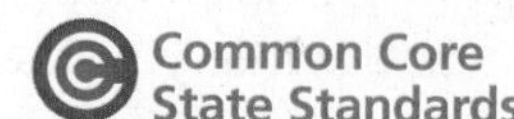

Common Core State Standards

Writing

1. Write arguments to support claims in an analysis of substantive topics or texts, using valid reasoning and relevant and sufficient evidence. *(p. 93)*

Language

3.a. Vary syntax for effect. *(p. 94)*

5. Demonstrate understanding of figurative language, word relationships, and nuances in word meanings. *(p. 93)*

1. **Key Ideas and Details** For each item below, **use context clues** to define the italicized words. Then, explain in your own words what each passage means.
   - **a.** "you are every day treasuring up more wrath; the waters are constantly rising, and *waxing* more and more mighty"
   - **b.** "The God that holds you over the pit of Hell, much as one holds a spider, or some *loathsome* insect over the fire, *abhors* you, and is dreadfully provoked."
   - **c.** "and you will absolutely despair of ever having any deliverance, any end, any *mitigation*, any rest at all"
2. **Key Ideas and Details (a)** What message is Edwards conveying in this **sermon? (b)** Note two places where he directly states his purpose and message.
3. **Craft and Structure** Explain how the purpose and message of Edwards's **oratory** are *persuasive*. What does he want his listeners to do or think?
4. **Craft and Structure (a)** What is the main *emotional appeal* Edwards uses in his effort to move his congregation? **(b)** Considering Edwards's purpose, why is this an appropriate choice? Explain your answer.
5. **Craft and Structure (a)** What does Edwards seem to feel about those who maintain a "form of religion" or who seem "moral and strict"? **(b)** How does this part of his message show that Edwards understands his *audience* well?
6. **Craft and Structure (a)** Choose two passages that you find very powerful. **(b)** Analyze the reasons for your choice: are you responding to the message itself, to the *rhythmic and expressive language* in which it is framed, or to both?
7. **Craft and Structure** Why are images of the destructive power of nature appropriate to Edwards's message?
8. **Integration of Knowledge and Ideas** **(a)** Use a chart like the one shown to identify Biblical **archetypes**—images, patterns, characters, or stories—Edwards uses to describe God's wrath. **(b)** How does each archetype add to the power of Edwards's message?

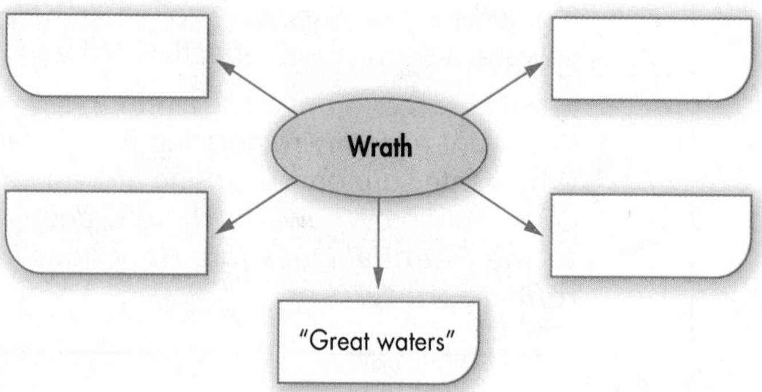

Vocabulary Acquisition and Use

Word Analysis: Latin Prefix *omni-*

The Latin prefix *omni-* means "all" or "every." *Omnipotent,* then, means "all-powerful." Each of the adjectives below contains the prefix *omni-*. Use the information in parentheses to match each adjective with the situation to which it best applies.

1. omniscient (*sciens* = knowing)
2. omnivorous (*vor* = to eat)
3. omnipresent (*praesens* = present)

a. how a zoologist might describe an animal that eats both meat and plants

b. how a student might describe a brilliant teacher

c. how someone lost in the desert might describe the sun

Vocabulary: Analogies

Analogies show the relationship between pairs of words. Complete each analogy using a word from the vocabulary list on page 84. In each, your choice should create a word pair that matches the relationship between the first two words given. Then, explain your answers.

1. *Brilliant* is to *smart* as ______ is to *powerful.*
2. *Soul* is to *spiritual* as ______ is to *physical.*
3. *Translator* is to *languages* as ______ is to *enemies.*
4. *Argue* is to *reconcile* as ______ is to *prevent.*
5. *Loyalty* is to *faithless* as ______ is to *reckless.*

Writing to Sources

Argument A speaker's choice of persuasive techniques should depend on the audience and the occasion. Write an **evaluation** of the persuasive techniques that Edwards uses. Discuss the response he evokes in an audience and the ways he achieves it.

Prewriting To focus your writing, jot down examples of Edwards's uses of imagery, logical reasoning, and emotional appeals. Make sure all of your choices are relevant and provide sufficient support for your claims. Then, write one statement in which you evaluate their effectiveness in reaching an audience.

Drafting Use the statement you wrote as the basis for a strong, focused opening paragraph. Support your main point in the paragraphs that follow.

Model: Building Unity

Jonathan Edwards appealed to his audience's vulnerability by using powerful, elemental images of nature run amok. His images of air, water, and fire terrified his audience by summoning up mental pictures of unlimited natural destruction.

The paragraph contains a general statement followed by details of specific images used by Edwards.

Revising Read your evaluation as though you are seeing it for the first time. Eliminate any information that is unrelated to the main idea.

Close Reading Activities Continued

Conventions and Style: Correlative Conjunctions

The use of *varied sentence structures* makes your writing more sophisticated and gives it a better flow. If you tend to use many short sentences, combine the ones that express related ideas into longer units. Correlative conjunctions can help you do this. A **correlative conjunction** is a word pair that is used to connect similar words or groups of words. Different correlative conjunctions show different relationships between ideas.

Using Correlative Conjunctions

Choppy Sentences: The sermon was frightening. The sermon was inspiring.
Combined: The sermon was *not only* frightening *but also* inspiring.

Choppy Sentences: The waters will be held back. If not, the flood gates will open.
Combined: *Either* the waters will be held back *or* the floodgates will open.

Common Correlative Conjunctions	
Both/and	Not only/but also
Either/or	Whether/or
Neither/nor	As/as

Tip: Use parallel grammatical structures after both parts of the correlative conjunction.

Practice In items 1–5, fill in the blanks with appropriate correlative conjunctions. In items 6–10, combine the two sentences using a correlative conjunction.

1. ______ the arrow will be released ______ it will not.
2. The sermon appeals ______ to people's fears ______ to their hopes.
3. Who decides ______ a person will go to heaven ______ burn in hell?
4. According to Edwards, ______ moral strictness ______ church attendance will reduce God's wrath.
5. The storm, ______ furious ______ dreadful, can be released at any time.
6. The sinner will not be spared. The serpent will not be spared.
7. He preached to Puritans. He also preached to Native Americans.
8. The storm imagery is eloquent. The storm imagery is powerful.
9. People could choose to be saved. They could choose to endure eternal suffering.
10. He can hold you out of the fire. He can withdraw His hand and let you fall.

Writing and Speaking Conventions

A. Writing For each word pair, write a sentence in which you link the two words or word groups using a correlative conjunction. Make sure to use the same grammatical structures after both parts of the correlative conjunction.

1. anger—mercy
2. miserable—eternal
3. to endure suffering—to rejoice in hope

Example: anger—mercy
Sentence: He can show either anger or mercy.

B. Speaking As a member of Edwards's congregation, write and present to the class a response to the sermon. Include two correlative conjunctions.

TEXT SET

A Nation is Born

Part 3

SPEECH IS POWER: SPEECH IS TO PERSUADE, TO CONVERT, TO COMPEL.

— RALPH WALDO EMERSON

In This Section

For more practice analyzing speeches see pages 86, 538, 622, and 1104.

Defining Speeches

A **speech** is a nonfiction work that is delivered orally to an audience. Some speeches are fully composed before the speaker reads them aloud. Others are planned in notes or an outline to which the speaker refers as he or she talks.

Types of Speeches There are countless appropriate settings and purposes for speeches. Common types of speeches include the following:

- **Political Speech:** a speech focusing on an issue relating to government
- **Address:** a formal speech prepared for a special occasion, such as the dedication of a memorial or the inauguration of a new leader
- **Sermon:** a speech intended to provide religious instruction

Rhetorical Devices Regardless of the occasion, speeches typically include rhetorical devices—patterns of words and ideas that create emphasis, clarify meaning, and stir listeners' emotions. There are numerous rhetorical figures, including the following types.

- **Restatement:** expressing the same ideas using different words
  Abraham Lincoln: "…we can not dedicate—we can not consecrate—we can not hallow—this ground."
- **Anaphora:** repetition of the same word or group of words at the beginning of successive sentences, clauses, or phrases
  Winston Churchill: "We shall go on to the end, we shall fight in France, we shall fight on the seas and oceans…"
- **Rhetorical Questions:** questions asked for effect rather than answers
  Benjamin Franklin: "From such an assembly can a perfect production be expected?"

Close Read: Rhetorical Devices

These rhetorical devices appear in the Model text at right.

Repetition: restating an idea using the same words *Example: "The war is inevitable—and let it come! I repeat it, sir, let it come!" (Patrick Henry)*	**Antithesis:** juxtaposition of strongly contrasting words, images, or ideas *Example: "…ask not what your country can do for you—ask what you can do for your country." (John F. Kennedy)*
Parallelism: repeating a grammatical structure *Example: "With malice toward none; with charity for all…" (Abraham Lincoln)*	**Exclamation:** an emotional statement, often indicated in texts by an exclamation mark *Example: "…as for me, give me liberty or give me death!" (Patrick Henry)*

Model

About the Text Frederick Douglass (ca. 1818–1895) escaped from slavery and became a writer, orator, and abolitionist. On July 5, 1852, he delivered a speech at a celebration of the signing of the Declaration of Independence. In the speech he states, "This Fourth of July is *yours*, not *mine*. You may rejoice, I must mourn."

from **"What to the Slave Is the Fourth of July?"**
Frederick Douglass

Fellow Citizens, I am not wanting in respect for the fathers of this republic. The signers of the Declaration of Independence were brave men. They were great men too—great enough to give fame to a great age. It does not often happen to a nation to raise, at one time, such a number of truly great men. The point from which I am compelled to view them is not, certainly, the most favorable; and yet I cannot contemplate their great deeds with less than admiration. They were statesmen, patriots and heroes, and for the good they did, and the principles they contended for, I will unite with you to honor their memory.

They loved their country better than their own private interests; and, though this is not the highest form of human excellence, all will concede that it is a rare virtue, and that when it is exhibited, it ought to command respect. He who will, intelligently, lay down his life for his country, is a man whom it is not in human nature to despise. Your fathers staked their lives, their fortunes, and their sacred honor, on the cause of their country. In their admiration of liberty, they lost sight of all other interests.

They were peace men; but they preferred revolution to peaceful submission to bondage. They were quiet men; but they did not shrink from agitating against oppression. They showed forbearance; but that they knew its limits. They believed in order; but not in the order of tyranny. With them, nothing was "settled" that was not right. With them, justice, liberty and humanity were "final;" not slavery and oppression. You may well cherish the memory of such men. They were great in their day and generation. Their solid manhood stands out the more as we contrast it with these degenerate times.

How circumspect, exact and proportionate were all their movements! How unlike the politicians of an hour! Their statesmanship looked beyond the passing moment, and stretched away in strength into the distant future. They seized upon eternal principles, and set a glorious example in their defense. Mark them!

Fully appreciating the hardship to be encountered, firmly believing in the right of their cause, honorably inviting the scrutiny of an on-looking world, reverently appealing to heaven to attest their sincerity, soundly comprehending the solemn responsibility they were about to assume, wisely measuring the terrible odds against them, your fathers, the fathers of this republic, did, most deliberately, under the inspiration of a glorious patriotism, and with a sublime faith in the great principles of justice and freedom, lay deep the corner-stone of the national superstructure, which has risen and still rises in grandeur around you.

Repetition Repeated use of the word "great" supports the idea that Douglass honors the nation's founders. This allows listeners to more readily accept the argument he will later present that the founders' greatness does not excuse their support of slavery.

Antithesis Douglass's use of opposing ideas emphasizes the complexity of the founding fathers' beliefs and actions.

Exclamation Douglass uses exclamation to show the urgency of his feelings and to stir emotion in his audience.

Parallelism Douglass uses parallelism to add urgency to his accounting of the founding fathers' wisdom and courage.

Building Knowledge and Insight

Speech in the Virginia Convention • Speech in the Convention

Connecting to the Essential Question These speeches prompted great change. Henry's words spurred the American Revolution, and Franklin's helped to shaped our government. As you read, notice how each speaker stresses the need to deal in realities rather than illusions. Doing so will help as you think about the Essential Question: **How does literature shape or reflect society?**

Common Core State Standards

Reading Informational Text

6. Determine an author's point of view or purpose in a text in which the rhetoric is particularly effective, analyzing how style and content contribute to the power, persuasiveness, or beauty of the text.

9. Analyze seventeenth-, eighteenth-, and nineteenth-century foundational U.S. documents of historical and literary significance for their themes, purposes, and rhetorical features.

Close Reading Focus

Rhetorical Devices

In these *persuasive* speeches, Henry and Franklin employ many of the **rhetorical devices** defined on page 96, including **restatement, repetition, parallelism,** and **rhetorical questions.** These devices serve to emphasize key points, make speeches memorable, and move listeners' emotions.

Persuasive orators like Henry and Franklin also use **allusions,** references to well-known people or events from history, literature, the Bible, and other sources. For example, in this passage, Patrick Henry alludes to the biblical figure of Judas, who betrayed Jesus "with a kiss":

> *Trust it not, sir; it will prove a snare to your feet. Suffer not yourselves to be betrayed with a kiss.*

As you read, notice examples of rhetorical devices and allusions and analyze how they contribute to the power and persuasiveness of each speech.

Comparing Literary Works To better appreciate these speeches about America's struggle for independence, **analyze the speakers' political assumptions**—the political ideas they take for granted. As you read, note the authors' beliefs about human nature and the role of government.

Preparing to Read Complex Texts While some listeners agree with a speaker, others may strongly disagree. A persuasive speech is effective when it both holds a friendly audience and convinces a hostile one. As you read these speeches, use a chart like the one shown to **critique their appeal to friendly and hostile audiences.**

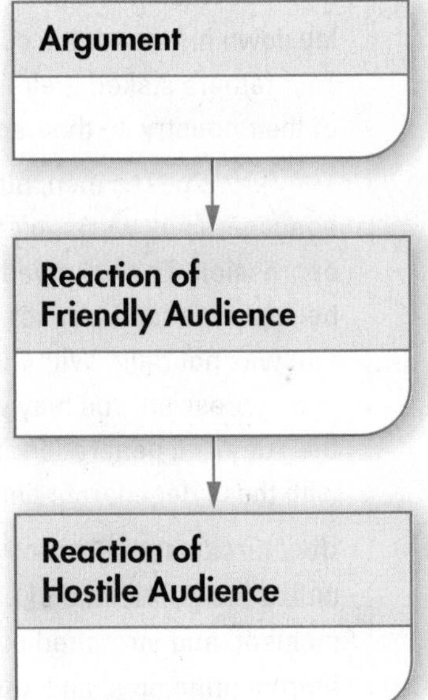

Vocabulary

The words below are key to understanding the texts that follow. Copy the words into your notebook. Then, find the word that is a synonym for *watchful.*

insidious
privileges
vigilant
despotism
salutary
unanimity

Patrick Henry *(1736–1799)*

Author of "**Speech in the Virginia Convention**"

It was said that Patrick Henry could move his listeners to anger, fear, or laughter more easily than the most talented actor. Remembered most for his fiery battle cry—"Give me liberty or give me death"—Henry is considered to be the most powerful orator of the American Revolution. He helped to inspire colonists to unite in an effort to win their independence from Great Britain.

Voice of Protest In 1765, Henry was elected to the Virginia House of Burgesses. Shortly after his election, he delivered one of his most powerful speeches, declaring his opposition to the Stamp Act. The Stamp Act, which was passed by the British Parliament, required American colonists to pay a tax on every piece of printed paper they used. Legal documents, newspapers, and even playing cards were all subject to the tax. Over the protests of some of its most influential members, the Virginia House adopted Henry's resolutions.

A Call to Arms In 1775, Henry delivered his most famous speech at the Virginia Provincial Convention. While most of the speakers that day argued that the colony should seek a compromise with the British, Henry boldly urged armed resistance to England. His speech had a powerful impact on the audience, feeding the revolutionary spirit that led to the signing of the Declaration of Independence.

In the years that followed, Henry continued to be an important political leader, serving as governor of Virginia and member of the Virginia General Assembly.

Give me liberty or give me Death!

Speech in the Virginia Convention

Patrick Henry

Patrick Henry Before the Virginia House of Burgesses, Peter F. Rothermel. Red Hill, The Patrick Henry National Memorial.

BACKGROUND In this famous speech, Patrick Henry denounces the British king and urges the colonists to fight for independence. Making such a declaration took tremendous bravery. England was the world's most powerful country at the time, and the odds against the colonists were overwhelming. If the colonies had failed to win independence, Henry could have been executed for treason.

◀ Critical Viewing
Which details in this painting suggest the power of Patrick Henry's oratory? **ANALYZE**

Mr. President: No man thinks more highly than I do of the patriotism, as well as abilities, of the very worthy gentlemen who have just addressed the house. But different men often see the same subject in different lights; and, therefore, I hope it will not be thought disrespectful to those gentlemen, if, entertaining, as I do, opinions of a character very opposite to theirs, I shall speak forth my sentiments freely and without reserve. This is no time for ceremony. The question before the house is one of awful moment[1] to this country. For my own part, I consider it as nothing less than a question of freedom or slavery. And in proportion to the magnitude of the subject ought to be the freedom of the debate. It is only in this way that we can hope to arrive at truth, and fulfill the great responsibility which we hold to God and our country. Should I keep back my opinions at such a time, through fear of giving offense, I should consider myself as guilty of treason toward my country, and of an act of disloyalty toward the Majesty of Heaven, which I revere above all earthly kings.

Mr. President, it is natural to man to indulge in the illusions of hope. We are apt to shut our eyes against a painful truth, and listen to the song of that siren till she transforms us into beasts.[2] Is this the part of wise men, engaged in a great and arduous struggle for liberty? Are we disposed to be of the number of those who having eyes see not, and having ears hear not,[3] the things which so nearly concern their temporal salvation? For my part, whatever anguish of spirit it may cost, I am willing to know the whole truth; to know the worst and to provide for it.

I have but one lamp by which my feet are guided, and that is the lamp of experience. I know of no way of judging of the future but by the past. And judging by the past, I wish to know what there has been in the conduct of the British ministry for the last ten years to justify those hopes with which gentlemen have been pleased to solace themselves and the house? Is it that **insidious** smile with which our petition has been lately received? Trust it not, sir; it will prove a snare to your feet. Suffer not yourselves to be betrayed with a kiss.[4]

Speeches and Allusions
Why do you think Henry makes allusions to Homer's *Odyssey* and the Bible?

Vocabulary
insidious (in sid′ ē əs) *adj.* deceitful; treacherous

Comprehension
Does Henry agree or disagree with those who spoke before him?

1. **moment** importance.
2. **listen . . . beasts** In Homer's *Odyssey*, the enchantress Circe transforms men into swine after charming them with her singing.
3. **having eyes . . . hear not** In Ezekiel 12:2, those "who have eyes to see, but see not, who have ears to hear, but hear not" are addressed.
4. **betrayed with a kiss** In Luke 22:47–48, Jesus is betrayed with a kiss.

Spiral Review

Metaphor Cite details from throughout the speech that liken the growing tensions to an oncoming storm. How does this metaphor add to Henry's message?

Speeches and Rhetorical Questions

What is the effect of the five rhetorical questions in this paragraph?

Vocabulary

privileges (priv′ lij əz) *n.* special rights; advantages

The battle, sir, is not to the STRONG alone; it is to the vigilant, the active, the brave.

Ask yourselves how this gracious reception of our petition comports with those warlike preparations which cover our waters and darken our land. Are fleets and armies necessary to a work of love and reconciliation? Have we shown ourselves so unwilling to be reconciled that force must be called in to win back our love? Let us not deceive ourselves, sir. These are the implements of war and subjugation—the last arguments to which kings resort.

I ask gentlemen, sir, what means this martial array, if its purpose be not to force us to submission? Can gentlemen assign any other possible motive for it? Has Great Britain any enemy in this quarter of the world, to call for all this accumulation of navies and armies? No, sir, she has none. They are meant for us: they can be meant for no other. They are sent over to bind and rivet upon us those chains which the British ministry have been so long forging.

And what have we to oppose to them? Shall we try argument? Sir, we have been trying that for the last ten years. Have we anything new to offer upon the subject? Nothing. We have held the subject up in every light of which it is capable; but it has been all in vain. Shall we resort to entreaty and humble supplication? What terms shall we find which have not been already exhausted? Let us not, I beseech you, sir, deceive ourselves longer. Sir, we have done everything that could be done to avert the storm which is now coming on. We have petitioned; we have remonstrated; we have supplicated; we have prostrated ourselves before the throne, and have implored its interposition[5] to arrest the tyrannical hands of the ministry and Parliament. Our petitions have been slighted; our remonstrances have produced additional violence and insult; our supplications have been disregarded; and we have been spurned with contempt from the foot of the throne! In vain, after these things, may we indulge the fond[6] hope of peace and reconciliation. There is no longer any room for hope. If we wish to be free, if we mean to preserve inviolate those inestimable **privileges** for which we have been so long contending, if we mean not basely to abandon the noble struggle in which we have been so long engaged, and which we have pledged ourselves never to abandon until the glorious object of our contest shall be obtained—we must fight! I repeat it, sir, we must fight! An appeal to arms and to the God of Hosts is all that is left us!

They tell us, sir, that we are weak—unable to cope with so formidable an adversary. But when shall we be stronger? Will it be the next week, or the next year? Will it be when we are totally disarmed, and when a British guard shall be stationed in every house? Shall we gather strength by irresolution and inaction? Shall we acquire the means of effectual resistance by lying supinely on our backs and hugging the delusive phantom of hope until our enemies shall have

5. **interposition** intervention.
6. **fond** foolish.

bound us hand and foot? Sir, we are not weak, if we make a proper use of those means which the God of nature hath placed in our power. Three millions of people, armed in the holy cause of liberty, and in such a country as that which we possess, are invincible by any force which our enemy can send against us. Besides, sir, we shall not fight our battles alone. There is a just God who presides over the destinies of nations and who will raise up friends to fight our battles for us. The battle, sir, is not to the strong alone;[7] it is to the vigilant, the active, the brave. Besides, sir, we have no election;[8] if we were base enough to desire it, it is now too late to retire from the contest. There is no retreat but in submission and slavery! Our chains are forged! Their clanging may be heard on the plains of Boston! The war is inevitable—and let it come! I repeat it, sir, let it come!

It is in vain, sir, to extenuate the matter. Gentlemen may cry, "Peace, peace"—but there is no peace. The war is actually begun! The next gale that sweeps from the north[9] will bring to our ears the clash of resounding arms! Our brethren are already in the field! Why stand we here idle? What is it that gentlemen wish? What would they have? Is life so dear, or peace so sweet, as to be purchased at the price of chains and slavery? Forbid it, Almighty God! I know not what course others may take; but as for me, give me liberty or give me death!

Vocabulary

vigilant (vij′ ə lənt) *adj.* alert to danger

7. **The battle . . . alone** "The race is not to the swift, nor the battle to the strong." (Ecclesiastes 9:11)
8. **election** choice.
9. **The next gale . . . north** In Massachusetts, some colonists had already shown open resistance to the British.

Critical Reading

1. **Key Ideas and Details** **(a)** What measures does Henry say the colonists have already tried in their dealings with England? **(b) Analyze:** What examples does he provide to support his position that compromise with the British is not a workable solution?
2. **Key Ideas and Details** **(a)** What course of action does Henry want the colonists to take? **(b) Draw Conclusions:** What is Henry's answer to the objection that the colonists are not ready to fight the British?
3. **Integration of Knowledge and Ideas** **(a)** Do you think Henry was prepared to stand behind his words when he exclaimed, "Give me liberty or give me death"? Why, or why not? **(b) Deduce:** What does his willingness to make such an assertion reveal about his character? **(c) Extend:** If you had been in his place, would you have made such a statement? Why, or why not?
4. **Integration of Knowledge and Ideas** **Speculate:** What types of people living in the colonies at the time of Henry's speech might have reacted negatively to his words? Why?

Cite textual evidence to support your responses.

BENJAMIN FRANKLIN

(1706–1790)

Author of **"Speech in the Convention"**

No other colonial American better embodied the promise of America than Benjamin Franklin. Through hard work, dedication, and ingenuity, Franklin was able to rise out of poverty to become a wealthy, famous, and influential person. Although he never received a formal education, Franklin made important contributions in the fields of literature, journalism, science, diplomacy, education, and philosophy.

A Persuasive Diplomat Franklin was a leader in the colonial movement for independence. In 1776, Congress sent him to France to enlist aid for the American Revolution. Franklin's persuasive powers proved effective, as he was able to achieve his goal. This turned out to be a pivotal breakthrough that may have been the deciding factor in the war.

Helping Forge a Nation In 1783, Franklin signed the peace treaty that ended the war and established the new nation. He returned home to serve as a delegate to the Constitutional Convention in Philadelphia. There, as politicians clashed over plans for the new government, Franklin worked to resolve conflicts and ensure ratification of the Constitution.

In spite of his contributions in so many other fields, Franklin is best remembered as a statesman and diplomat. He was the only American to sign all four documents that established the new nation: the Declaration of Independence, the treaty of alliance with France, the peace treaty with England, and the Constitution. (For more on Franklin, see pp. 136–137.)

"I confess, that I do not entirely approve of this Constitution at present…"

SPEECH *in the* CONVENTION

BENJAMIN FRANKLIN

BACKGROUND Following the American Revolution, each of the newly independent states created its own constitution. While Congress was able to pass limited laws, it had no power to tax the states or regulate issues, such as trade, that were affected by state boundaries. These problems led to the Constitutional Convention in 1787. Representatives from twelve states met to approve a national constitution. At the age of eighty-one, Benjamin Franklin represented Pennsylvania.

MR. PRESIDENT,

I confess, that I do not entirely approve of this Constitution at present; but, Sir, I am not sure I shall never approve it; for, having lived long, I have experienced many instances of being obliged, by better information or fuller consideration, to change my opinions even on important subjects, which I once thought right, but found to be otherwise. It is therefore that, the older I grow, the more apt I am to doubt my own judgment of others. Most men, indeed, as well as most sects in religion, think themselves in possession of all truth, and that wherever others differ from them, it is so far error. . . . Though many private Persons think almost as highly of their own infallibility as of that of their Sect, few express it so naturally as a certain French Lady, who, in a little dispute with her sister, said, "But I meet with nobody but myself that is *always* in the right." *"Je ne trouve que moi qui aie toujours raison."*

In these sentiments, Sir, I agree to this Constitution, with all its faults,—if they are such; because I think a general Government necessary for us, and there is no form of government but what may be a blessing to the people, if well administered; and I believe, farther, that this is likely to be well administered for a course of years, and can only end in despotism, as other forms have done before it, when the people shall become so corrupted as to need despotic government, being incapable of any other. I doubt, too, whether any other Convention we can obtain, may be able to make a better constitution; for, when you assemble a number of men, to have the advantage of their joint wisdom, you inevitably assemble with those men all their prejudices, their passions, their errors of opinion, their local interests, and their selfish views. From such an assembly can a *perfect* production be expected? It therefore astonishes me, Sir, to find this

Critiquing Appeal to Audiences In his reference to "faults," is Franklin appealing to those who are happy with the Constitution or those who are not? Explain.

Vocabulary
despotism (des′ pət iz′ əm) *n.* absolute rule; tyranny

Comprehension
What does Franklin confess as he begins his speech?

WE THE PEOPLE

system approaching so near to perfection as it does; and I think it will astonish our enemies, who are waiting with confidence to hear, that our councils are confounded like those of the builders of Babel, and that our States are on the point of separation, only to meet hereafter for the purpose of cutting one another's throats. Thus I consent, Sir, to this Constitution, because I expect no better, and because I am not sure that it is not the best. The opinions I have had of its *errors* I sacrifice to the public good. I have never whispered a syllable of them abroad. Within these walls they were born, and here they shall die. If every one of us, in returning to our Constituents, were to report the objections he has had to it, and endeavour to gain Partisans in support of them, we might prevent its being generally received, and thereby lose all the **salutary** effects and great advantages resulting naturally in our favour among foreign nations, as well as among ourselves, from our real or apparent **unanimity**. Much of the strength and efficiency of any government, in procuring and securing happiness to the people, depends on *opinion*, on the general opinion of the goodness of that government, as well as of the wisdom and integrity of its governors. I hope, therefore, for our own sakes, as a part of the people, and for the sake of our posterity, that we shall act heartily and unanimously in recommending this Constitution, wherever our Influence may extend, and turn our future thoughts and endeavors to the means of having it *well administered.*

On the whole, Sir, I cannot help expressing a wish, that every member of the Convention who may still have objections to it, would with me on this occasion doubt a little of his own infallibility, and, to make manifest our *unanimity*, put his name to this Instrument.

◀ Critical Viewing

How is this painting of the ratifying of the Constitution similar to a literary allusion to classical mythology? **ANALYZE**

Vocabulary

salutary (salʹ yoo terʹ ē) *adj.* beneficial; promoting a good purpose

unanimity (yooʹ nə nimʹ ə tē) *n.* complete agreement

Critical Reading

Cite textual evidence to support your responses.

1. **Key Ideas and Details (a)** Why does Franklin feel that unanimity among the delegates is essential to the success of the United States? **(b) Analyze:** What is his purpose in suppressing his "opinions" for the "public good"?
2. **Key Ideas and Details (a)** According to Franklin, why would any document created by committee be faulty? **(b) Generalize:** What is Franklin saying about human nature?
3. **Craft and Structure (a)** What three reasons does Franklin give for finally agreeing to accept the Constitution? **(b) Evaluate:** How effectively does he convey the thought process that brought him from doubt about the Constitution to a decision to accept it? Explain.
4. **Integration of Knowledge and Ideas** What connections do both Henry and Franklin make between the ability to face hard realities and ideas of loyalty to one's nation? In your response, use at least two of these Essential Question vocabulary words: *patriotism, responsibility, dispute, wisdom.* ***[Connecting to the Essential Question: How does literature shape or reflect society?]***

Close Reading Activities

Speech in the Virginia Convention • Speech in the Convention

Literary Analysis

Common Core State Standards

Writing

2. Write informative/explanatory texts to examine and convey complex ideas, concepts, and information clearly and accurately through the effective selection, organization, and analysis of content. *(p. 109)*

2.a. Introduce a topic; organize complex ideas, concepts, and information so that each new element builds on that which precedes it to create a unified whole. *(p. 109)*

Language

5. Demonstrate understanding of figurative language, word relationships, and nuances in word meanings. *(p. 109)*

1. **Key Ideas and Details** Explain the persuasive message in each **speech:** What do Henry and Franklin want audiences to think and do?
2. **Craft and Structure** For each speech, note one argument that the speaker designed to appeal to a friendly audience and one intended to reach a hostile audience. Explain your choices.
3. **Craft and Structure** In what ways does each speaker use "concession," or the acknowledgment of opposition arguments?
4. **Craft and Structure** Use a chart like the one shown to note examples and describe the effects of each speaker's use of these **rhetorical devices: restatement, repetition, parallelism.**

	Example	Effect
Restatement		
Repetition		
Parallelism		

5. **Craft and Structure** **(a)** Identify at least two **rhetorical questions** from these speeches. **(b)** Explain how each question intensifies the emotion of the speech, clarifies an idea, or emphasizes a point.
6. **Craft and Structure** Explain the meanings each of the following classical and biblical **allusions** add to the speech:
   - Henry's allusion to sirens from Greek mythology
   - Henry's allusion to Judas's betrayal of Jesus in the Bible
   - Franklin's allusion to the builders of the Tower of Babel
7. **Integration of Knowledge and Ideas** **(a)** How is Franklin's experience as a diplomat reflected in his argument and the types of language he uses? **(b)** How is Henry's experience as a lawyer reflected in his?
8. **Comparing Literary Works** **(a)** What **political assumptions** does Henry make about the nature of government? **(b)** Does Franklin make similar assumptions? Defend and clarify your interpretation with elements from the texts.
9. **Integration of Knowledge and Ideas** Critique each speaker's appeal to friendly and hostile audiences. Which speech do you conclude was more effective in holding a friendly audience and in reaching a hostile one? Explain your choice, citing details from the texts to support your claim.
10. **Analyzing Visual Information** Explain the humor in the cartoon shown on this page.

▼ *"Give me moderation or give me death!"*

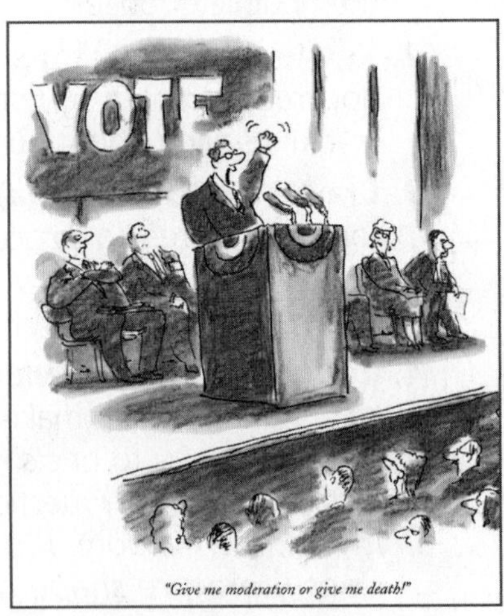

"Give me moderation or give me death!"

Vocabulary Acquisition and Use

Relate New Vocabulary to Familiar Words

The word *unanimity* comes from the Latin word *unanimus*, meaning "of one mind." Franklin did not feel the delegates to the Convention would ever be fully "of one mind." The word combines the prefix *uni-*, meaning "one," with the root *-anima-*, which means "being; soul; mind." Both word parts contribute to other words with which you are probably familiar. Write a definition for each word below. Then, explain how the meaning of the prefix or the root contributes to the meaning of each word.

1. animate
2. animation
3. universe
4. unify
5. unique

Vocabulary: Antonyms

For each vocabulary word, choose the letter of the antonym, or word that most closely expresses an opposite meaning. Then, explain your reasoning.

1. despotism **a.** tyranny; **b.** democracy; **c.** cruelty
2. privileges **a.** freedoms; **b.** fees; **c.** penalties
3. salutary **a.** damaging; **b.** beneficial; **c.** insensitive
4. insidious **a.** innocent; **b.** weary; **c.** sinister
5. unanimity **a.** harmony; **b.** discussion; **c.** discord
6. vigilant **a.** careless; **b.** watchful; **c.** forgetful

Writing to Sources

Explanatory Text Patrick Henry and Benjamin Franklin were master politicians who knew that success sometimes requires persistence and sometimes requires compromise. Write an **essay** in which you compare and contrast their views about when to compromise and when to stand firm.

Prewriting Review each speech, looking for details related to compromise and persistence. Use a chart like the one shown, or make one of your own design to organize your notes. Then, review your notes for patterns of similarity and difference. Write one sentence that states your *thesis*.

Model: Organizing Notes

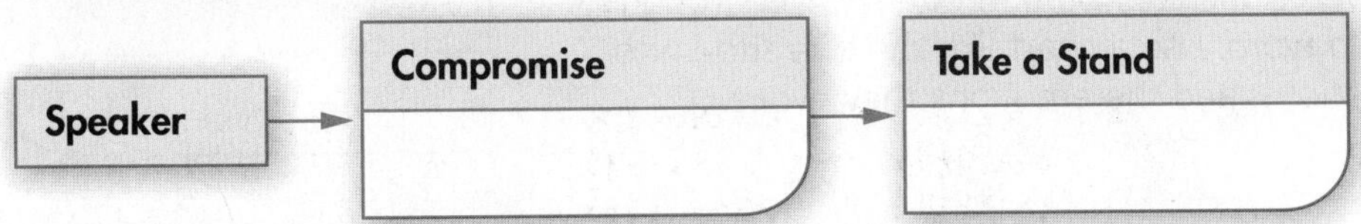

Drafting In your introduction, state the topic and summarize your main points. Then, draft one paragraph about Henry's political approach followed by one paragraph about Franklin's. Support your ideas with quotations.

Revising Reread your essay, making sure you have used sufficient evidence and that your ideas build to a logical conclusion. Check that you have separated longer direct quotations from paragraphs and set off shorter direct quotations with quotation marks.

Building Knowledge and Insight

ANCHOR TEXT
The Declaration of Independence* • from *The American Crisis, Number 1

Connecting to the Essential Question Jefferson and Paine describe ideals that they were willing to fight to protect. As you read, notice the values that both Jefferson and Paine defend. Your observations will help as you reflect on the Essential Question: **What makes American literature American?**

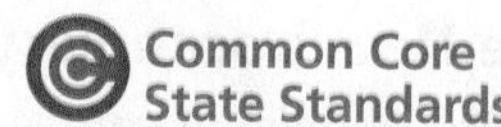

Reading Informational Text

4. Determine the meaning of words and phrases as they are used in a text, including figurative, connotative, and technical meanings; analyze how an author uses and refines the meaning of a key term or terms over the course of a text.

8. Delineate and evaluate the reasoning in seminal U.S. texts and the premises, purposes, and arguments in works of public advocacy.

9. Analyze seventeenth-, eighteenth-, and nineteenth-century foundational U.S. documents of historical and literary significance for their themes, purposes, and rhetorical features.

Close Reading Focus

Persuasion; Argument

Persuasion is writing that presents an *argument*, or message meant to get readers to think or act in a certain way. Effective persuasion uses the following techniques to build arguments:

- *Appeals to emotion* to influence readers' feelings
- *Appeals to logic* to show that an argument is well reasoned
- *Appeals to ethics* to show that an argument is just or fair
- *Appeals to authority* to show that a higher power supports the ideas

As you read, evaluate the reasoning and appeals each writer uses to construct his or her argument.

Comparing Literary Works Jefferson and Paine wrote for different **audiences,** or readers. Some of their readers were friendly and agreed with their ideas, whereas others were hostile and did not. Strong persuasive writers such as Jefferson and Paine attempt to address both types of audience. They anticipate reader concerns and build in counterclaims to address them. As you read, notice how these writers shape their messages to reach different audiences.

Preparing to Read Complex Texts When you **analyze word choice,** you study an author's words and observe how he or she uses and refines key terms over the course of a work. Persuasive writers may use words with strong *connotations* or associations to produce an intense emotional response. For example, the *denotation*, or basic meaning, of "evils" and "wrongs" is similar. However, the connotation of "evils" is stronger, making it a *charged or loaded word.* Use a chart like the one shown to note charged words, connotations, and the emotions they evoke.

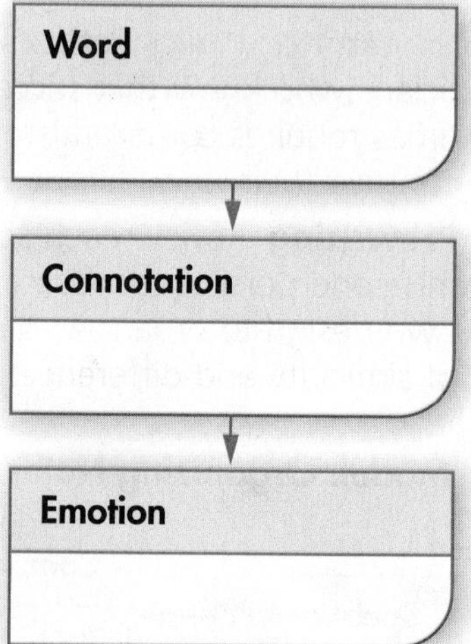

Vocabulary

The words below appear in the texts that follow. Copy the words in your notebook. Which words do you think have negative connotations?

candid
assent
harass
tyranny
redress
acquiesce
rectitude
prudent

Thomas Jefferson *(1743–1826)*

Author of **The Declaration of Independence**

When you look at all of Thomas Jefferson's achievements, it seems almost nothing was beyond his reach. Not only did he help our nation win its independence and serve as its third president, but he also founded the University of Virginia, helped establish the public school system, designed his own home, invented a type of elevator for sending food from floor to floor, and created the decimal system for American money. He was a skilled violinist, an art enthusiast, and a brilliant writer.

Revolutionary Leader Born into a wealthy Virginia family, Jefferson attended the College of William and Mary and went on to earn a law degree. While serving in the Virginia House of Burgesses, he became an outspoken defender of American rights. When conflict between the colonists and the British erupted into revolution, Jefferson emerged as a leader in the effort to win independence.

Valued Statesman When the war ended, Jefferson served as the American minister to France for several years. He then served as the nation's first secretary of state and second vice president before becoming president in 1801. While in office, Jefferson nearly doubled the size of the nation by authorizing the purchase of the Louisiana Territory from France.

On the morning of July 4, 1826, the fiftieth anniversary of the Declaration of Independence, Jefferson died at the age of 83. John Adams, Jefferson's fellow contributor to the Declaration of Independence, died only several hours after his longtime friend. Adams's last words were "Thomas Jefferson still survives."

EXEMPLAR TEXT

The Declaration of Independence, John Trumbull, Yale University Art Gallery

The Declaration of Independence

Thomas Jefferson

BACKGROUND In 1776, Thomas Jefferson was chosen (with Franklin, Adams, and others) to write a declaration of the colonies' independence from England. The draft presented to the Second Continental Congress was largely Jefferson's work. To his disappointment, however, Congress made changes before approving the document. They dropped Jefferson's condemnation of the British for tolerating a corrupt Parliament, and they struck out a strong statement against slavery.

When in the course of human events, it becomes necessary for one people to dissolve the political bands which have connected them with another, and to assume among the powers of the earth, the separate and equal station to which the laws of nature and of nature's God entitle them, a decent respect to the opinions of mankind requires that they should declare the causes which impel them to the separation.

We hold these truths to be self-evident: that all men are created equal; that they are endowed by their Creator with certain unalienable rights; that among these are life, liberty and the pursuit of happiness; that to secure these rights, governments are instituted among men, deriving their just powers from the consent of the governed; that whenever any form of government becomes destructive of these ends, it is the right of the people to alter or to abolish it, and to institute new government, laying its foundation on such principles and organizing its powers in such form, as to them shall seem most likely to effect their safety and happiness. Prudence, indeed, will dictate that governments long established should not be changed for light and transient causes; and accordingly all experience hath shown, that mankind are more disposed to suffer while evils are sufferable than to right themselves by abolishing the forms to which they are accustomed. But when a long train of abuses and usurpations, pursuing invariably the same object, evinces a design to reduce them under absolute despotism,[1] it is their right, it is their duty, to throw off such government, and to provide new guards for their future security. Such has been the patient sufferance of these colonies; and such is now the necessity which constrains them to alter their former systems of government. The history of the present king of Great Britain is a history of repeated injuries and usurpations, all having in direct object the establishment of an absolute tyranny over these states. To prove this, let facts be submitted to a candid world.

He has refused his assent to laws the most wholesome and necessary for the public good.

He has forbidden his governors to pass laws of immediate and pressing importance, unless suspended in their operation till his assent should be obtained; and when so suspended, he has utterly neglected to attend to them.

He has refused to pass other laws for the accommodation of large districts of people, unless those people would relinquish the right of representation in the legislature, a right inestimable to them and formidable to tyrants only.

He has called together legislative bodies at places unusual, uncomfortable, and distant from the depository of their public records, for the sole purpose of fatiguing them into compliance with his measures.

He has dissolved representative houses repeatedly, for opposing with manly firmness his invasions on the rights of the people.

He has refused for a long time after such dissolutions to cause others to be elected, whereby the legislative powers, incapable of annihilation, have returned to the people at large for their exercise, the state remaining in the mean time exposed to all the dangers of invasion from without, and convulsions within.

He has endeavored to prevent the population of these states; for that purpose obstructing the laws for naturalization of foreigners, refusing to pass others to encourage their migration hither, and raising the conditions of new appropriations of lands.

He has obstructed the administration of justice, by refusing his assent to laws for establishing judiciary powers.

1. **despotism** (des′ pət iz′ əm) *n.* tyranny.

Persuasion

Why does Jefferson introduce the idea that one does not change a government for "light" causes?

Vocabulary

candid (kan′ did) *adj.* honest

assent (ə sent′) *n.* agreement

Comprehension

Why did Jefferson write this long list of facts?

The American EXPERIENCE

Philosophical Influence: John Locke and the Social Contract

In writing the Declaration of Independence, Jefferson drew on a theory of government devised by earlier European political thinkers, especially the Englishman John Locke (1632–1704). Locke argued that all people are born with certain *natural rights* that are not the property of governments. Locke's concept of the *social contract* also contributed to Jefferson's notion that governments derive their power from "the consent of the governed." According to Locke, when a ruler breaks the social contract by acting abusively, the people have the right to revolt against his rule. In 1776, that is what the American colonists did.

Connect to the Literature

Where in the Declaration does Jefferson echo Locke's idea that the people have the right to overthrow a government that breaks the social contract?

He has made judges dependent on his will alone, for the tenure of their offices, and the amount and payment of their salaries.

He has erected a multitude of new offices, and sent hither swarms of officers to harass our people and eat out their substance.

He has kept among us in times of peace standing armies without the consent of our legislatures.

He has affected to render the military independent of, and superior to, the civil power.

He has combined with others to subject us to a jurisdiction foreign to our constitution and unacknowledged by our laws, giving his assent to their acts of pretended legislation: for quartering large bodies of armed troops among us; for protecting them by a mock trial from punishment for any murders which they should commit on the inhabitants of these states; for cutting off our trade with all parts of the world; for imposing taxes on us without our consent; for depriving us, in many cases, of the benefits of trial by jury; for transporting us beyond seas to be tried for pretended offenses; for abolishing the free system of English laws in a neighboring province,[2] establishing therein an arbitrary government, and enlarging its boundaries, so as to render it at once an example and fit instrument for introducing the same absolute rule into these colonies; for taking away our charters, abolishing our most valuable laws, and altering fundamentally the forms of our governments; for suspending our own legislatures, and declaring themselves invested with power to legislate for us in all cases whatsoever.

He has abdicated government here, by declaring us out of his protection and waging war against us.

He has plundered our seas, ravaged our coasts, burned our towns, and destroyed the lives of our people.

He is at this time transporting large armies of foreign mercenaries to complete the works of death, desolation, and tyranny, already begun with circumstances of cruelty and perfidy scarcely paralleled in the most barbarous ages, and totally unworthy the head of a civilized nation.

He has constrained our fellow citizens taken captive on the high seas to bear arms against their country, to become the executioners of their friends and brethren, or to fall themselves by their hands.

He has excited domestic insurrections amongst us, and has endeavored to bring on the inhabitants of our frontiers, the merciless Indian savages, whose known rule of warfare is an undistinguished destruction of all ages, sexes, and conditions.

In every stage of these oppressions we have petitioned for redress in the most humble terms. Our repeated petitions have been answered only by repeated injury.

Vocabulary

harass (hər´ əs) *v.* attack; bother

tyranny (tir´ə nē) *n.* oppressive power

redress (ri dres´) *n.* compensation for a wrong done

Analyzing Word Choice Why do you think Jefferson uses the words "ravaged" and "executioners"?

2. **neighboring province** Quebec.

A prince whose character is thus marked by every act which may define a tyrant is unfit to be the ruler of a free people.

Nor have we been wanting in attentions to our British brethren. We have warned them from time to time of attempts by their legislature to extend an unwarrantable jurisdiction over us. We have reminded them of the circumstances of our emigration and settlement here. We have appealed to their native justice and magnanimity and we have conjured[3] them by the ties of our common kindred to disavow these usurpations which would inevitably interrupt our connections and correspondence. They too have been deaf to the voice of justice and of consanguinity. We must therefore **acquiesce** in the necessity which denounces our separation and hold them, as we hold the rest of mankind, enemies in war, in peace friends.

We, therefore, the representatives of the United States of America in general congress assembled, appealing to the Supreme Judge of the world for the **rectitude** of our intentions, do in the name and by authority of the good people of these colonies, solemnly publish and declare that these united colonies are and of right ought to be free and independent states; that they are absolved from all allegiance to the British Crown, and that all political connection between them and the state of Great Britain is and ought to be totally dissolved; and that as free and independent states, they have full power to levy war, conclude peace, contract alliances, establish commerce, and to do all other acts and things which independent states may of right do.

And for the support of this declaration, with a firm reliance on the protection of divine providence, we mutually pledge to each other our lives, our fortunes and our sacred honor.

Vocabulary

acquiesce (ak′ wē es′) *v.* agree without protest

rectitude (rek ti tōōd) *n.* correctness; righteousness

3. **conjured** *v.* solemnly appealed to.

Critical Reading

Cite textual evidence to support your responses.

1. **Key Ideas and Details** **(a)** What points about human rights does Jefferson make at the beginning of the Declaration? **(b) Analyze:** Why does he begin with these observations before addressing the colonists' situation?
2. **Craft and Structure** **(a) Evaluate:** What is the most convincing evidence that Jefferson cites to support his points? Explain. **(b) Evaluate:** How would you rate the overall effectiveness of his argument? Why?
3. **Integration of Knowledge and Ideas** **Synthesize:** The period in which this document was written is often referred to as the Age of Reason because of the emphasis on logic and discipline at the time. What elements of Jefferson's Declaration reflect a faith in reason?

"I love the man that can **smile in trouble,** that can **gather strength** from distress, and **grow brave** by reflection."

Thomas Paine *(1737–1809)*

Author of **The American Crisis, Number 1**

Thomas Paine met Benjamin Franklin in London, and the introduction changed both his life and American history. Paine emigrated to the colonies from England in 1774. With a letter of introduction from Franklin, Paine began a career as a journalist. In January 1776, he published *Common Sense,* in which he argued that Americans must fight for independence. The pamphlet created a national mood for revolution.

Inspiring Essayist Paine enlisted in the American army toward the end of 1776. At that time, the army had just suffered a crushing defeat by the British in New Jersey and had retreated into Pennsylvania. The soldiers were suffering from freezing weather, a shortage of provisions, and low morale. Paine was writing the first of a series of essays entitled *The American Crisis.* Washington ordered Paine's essay read to his troops before they crossed the Delaware River to defeat the Hessians at the Battle of Trenton.

In 1787, several years after the end of the American Revolution, Paine traveled to Europe and became involved with the French Revolution. Though he wrote in support of the revolutionary cause in *The Rights of Man* (1791–1792), he was imprisoned for pleading against the execution of the overthrown French king. While in prison, he began writing *The Age of Reason* (1794), an attack on organized religion. The book turned American public opinion against him, and when he died in 1809, he was a broken man. Years later, however, Paine was once again recognized as a hero of the Revolution.

from THE AMERICAN CRISIS
NUMBER 1
Thomas Paine

These are the times that try men's souls. The summer soldier and the sunshine patriot will, in this crisis, shrink from the service of his country; but he that stands it now, deserves the love and thanks of man and woman. Tyranny, like hell, is not easily conquered; yet we have this consolation with us, that the harder the conflict, the more glorious the triumph. What we obtain too cheap, we esteem too lightly:—'Tis dearness only that gives every thing its value. Heaven knows how to set a proper price upon its goods; and it would be strange indeed, if so celestial an article as Freedom should not be highly rated. Britain, with an army to enforce her tyranny, has declared, that she has a right (*not only to* TAX) but "*to* BIND *us in* ALL CASES WHATSOEVER," and if being *bound in that manner* is not slavery, then is there not such a thing as slavery

▲ Critical Viewing
In what ways does this cartoon mock Great Britain while celebrating the revolutionaries? **ANALYZE**

Comprehension
What does Paine say is not easily conquered?

Vocabulary

prudent (pro͞o′ dənt) *adj.* sensible; careful

upon earth. Even the expression is impious, for so unlimited a power can belong only to God.

Whether the Independence of the Continent was declared too soon, or delayed too long, I will not now enter into as an argument; my own simple opinion is, that had it been eight months earlier, it would have been much better. . . .

I once felt all that kind of anger, which a man ought to feel, against the mean[1] principles that are held by the Tories:[2] A noted one, who kept a tavern at Amboy, was standing at his door, with as pretty a child in his hand, about eight or nine years old, as most I ever saw, and after speaking his mind as freely as he thought was **prudent**, finished with this unfatherly expression, "*Well! give me peace in my day.*" Not a man lives on the Continent but fully believes that a separation must some time or other finally take place, and a generous parent would have said, "*If there must be trouble, let it be in my day, that my child may have peace;*" and this single reflection, well applied, is sufficient to awaken every man to duty. Not a place upon earth might be so happy as America. Her situation is remote from all the wrangling world, and she has nothing to do but to trade with them. A man may easily distinguish in himself between temper and principle, and I am as confident, as I am that God governs the world, that America will never be happy till she gets clear of foreign dominion. Wars, without ceasing, will break out till that period arrives, and the Continent must in the end be conqueror; for, though the flame of liberty may sometimes cease to shine, the coal never can expire.

America did not, nor does not, want force; but she wanted a proper application of that force. Wisdom is not the purchase of a day, and it is no wonder that we should err at first sitting off. From an excess of tenderness, we were unwilling to raise an army, and trusted our cause to the temporary defence of a well meaning militia. A summer's experience has now taught us better; yet with those troops, while they were collected, we were able to set bounds to the progress of the enemy, and, thank God! they are again assembling. . . .

. . . I turn with the warm ardour of a friend to those who have nobly stood, and are yet determined to stand the matter out: I call not upon a few, but upon all; not on THIS State or THAT State, but on every State; up and help us; lay your shoulders to the wheel; better have too much force than too little, when so great an object is at stake. Let it be told to the future world, that in the depth of winter, when nothing but hope and virtue could survive, that the city and the country, alarmed at one common danger, came forth to meet and to repulse it. Say not, that thousands are gone, turn out your tens of thousands; throw not the burden of the day upon Providence, but "*show your faith by your works,*" that God may bless you. It matters not where you live, or what rank of life you hold, the evil or the blessing will reach you all. The far and the near, the home counties and the back, the rich and the poor,

1. **mean** *adj.* small-minded.
2. **Tories** colonists who remained loyal to Great Britain.

shall suffer or rejoice alike. The heart that feels not now, is dead: The blood of his children shall curse his cowardice, who shrinks back at a time when a little might have saved the whole, and made *them* happy. I love the man that can smile in trouble, that can gather strength from distress, and grow brave by reflection. 'Tis the business of little minds to shrink; but he whose heart is firm, and whose conscience approves his conduct, will pursue his principles unto death. My own line of reasoning is to myself as straight and clear as a ray of light. Not all the treasures of the world, so far as I believe, could have induced me to support an offensive war, for I think it murder; but if a thief break into my house, burn and destroy my property, and kill or threaten to kill me, or those that are in it, and to "*bind me in all cases whatsoever,*" to his absolute will, am I to suffer it? What signifies it to me, whether he who does it, is a king or a common man; my countryman or not my countryman? whether it is done by an individual villain, or an army of them? If we reason to the root of things we shall find no difference; neither can any just cause be assigned why we should punish in the one case, and pardon in the other. . . .

There are cases which cannot be overdone by language, and this is one. There are persons too who see not the full extent of the evil that threatens them; they solace themselves with hopes that the enemy, if they succeed, will be merciful. It is the madness of folly to expect mercy from those who have refused to do justice; and even mercy, where conquest is the object, is only a trick of war: The cunning of the fox is as murderous as the violence of the wolf; and we ought to guard equally against both.

These are the times that try men's souls.

Critical Reading

Cite textual evidence to support your responses.

1. **Key Ideas and Details** **(a)** In the first paragraph, how does Paine say the "summer soldier" and the "sunshine patriot" will react to the American crisis? Why? **(b) Interpret:** In that same paragraph, with what ideas does Paine justify the struggle of revolution?
2. **Key Ideas and Details** **(a)** In the third paragraph, what anecdote, or story, does Paine tell? **(b) Draw Conclusions:** What point is Paine making by relating this anecdote?
3. **Integration of Knowledge and Ideas** Are the ideals Jefferson and Paine defend in these writings still important to Americans? Explain. In your response, use at least two of these Essential Question words: *patriotism, service, authority, equality. [Connecting to the Essential Question: What makes American literature American?]*

Close Reading Activities

The Declaration of Independence • from The American Crisis, Number 1

Literary Analysis

1. **Key Ideas and Details** Use a chart like the one shown to identify elements of **persuasion** in these selections. Classify the types of appeals Jefferson and Paine use to advance their arguments.

	Emotion	Logic	Ethics	Authority
Jefferson				
Paine				

2. **Key Ideas and Details** **(a)** What specific beliefs does each writer want his readers to hold? **(b)** What actions does each writer want his readers to take? Note details that support your answers.
3. **Craft and Structure** **Analyze word choice** by examining *denotation* and *connotation:* **(a)** Write the denotative meaning of each numbered word below. **(b)** Write a suggested, or connotative, meaning for each word. **(c)** Explain the emotions each word evokes in you. **(d)** Which of these words is charged or loaded? Explain.
   1. liberty **2.** justice **3.** honor **4.** barbarous
4. **Craft and Structure** In describing the colonists' British rulers, how does Paine's use of the word "thief" evoke a different response than would the word "supporters"?
5. **Craft and Structure** **(a)** Name two emotions to which Paine appeals in this excerpt. **(b)** Does he appeal more to emotion or to reason? Support your answer with examples from the text.
6. **Craft and Structure** What persuasive purpose does Paine's anecdote about the Tory serve?
7. **Integration of Knowledge and Ideas** Jefferson presents a long list of grievances against King George. What counterclaim do you think the list attempts to answer? Explain, citing details from the text to support your reasoning.
8. **Comparing Literary Works** Both Jefferson and Paine use the charged words "tyrant" and "tyranny" frequently. Do these words carry the same meanings for both writers? Explain.
9. **Comparing Literary Works** **(a)** Who are the intended **audiences** for each of these works? **(b)** What kinds of supporting evidence would you expect to see in writing meant for each audience? **(c)** Are your expectations borne out in these selections? Explain your reasoning.

Common Core State Standards

Writing

1. Write arguments to support claims in an analysis of substantive topics or texts, using valid reasoning and relevant and sufficient evidence. *(p. 121)*

Language

4.b. Identify and correctly use patterns of word changes that indicate different meanings or parts of speech. *(p. 121)*

Vocabulary Acquisition and Use

Word Analysis: Latin Word Parts *-rect-* and *-tude*

The word "rectitude" combines the Latin root *-rect-*, meaning "straight," with the suffix *-tude*, meaning "having or possessing." Thus, a person who displays rectitude possesses ethical or moral straightness. For each item below, notice the meanings of the word parts in parentheses. Combine these meanings with those of the root *-rect-* or the suffix *-tude* to write definitions for each numbered word.

1. rectify (suffix *-ify* = make, cause)
2. correct (prefix *co-* = with)
3. indirect (prefix *in-* = without)
4. aptitude (root *-apt-* = fit, suited)
5. fortitude (root *-fort-* = strength)
6. solitude (root *-sol-* = alone)

Vocabulary: True or False

Indicate which of the statements below are true and which are false. Explain your answers.

1. If a child *acquiesces* about being put to bed, she accepts her bedtime.
2. Public support for a radical cause is one form of *tyranny.*
3. There is no need for *redress* if no wrong has been committed.
4. A *candid* opinion is the same as a fact.
5. To judge the *rectitude* of an action, you must consider whether or not it is justified.
6. It is likely that any nation will automatically *assent* to a colony's request for independence.
7. Governments should *harass* citizens who do not agree with specific laws.
8. A *prudent* leader will consider the needs of the public before making a decision.

Writing

Argumentative Text Like Jefferson and Paine, you can change your world with the persuasive use of words. Consider a problem facing your school or community. Write an **editorial** to appear in a local newspaper in which you explain why the situation needs attention and how it should be corrected.

Prewriting List the elements of the problem. Write facts, examples, and explanations that present a solution. Categorize your ideas to identify those that provide strong emotional, logical, and ethical appeals. Consider sources, such as local leaders, whom you might cite in an appeal to authority.

Drafting As you write, structure your ideas so that they flow logically and support them with precise and relevant examples. Demonstrate respect by avoiding name-calling and inappropriate language.

Revising Review your editorial and check that your language is forceful and direct. Replace imprecise or weak language with more persuasive choices.

Model: Revising Language

Separate lounges for upper- and lowerclassmen reflect ~~good~~ *superior* planning. ~~Everyone~~ *Wise thinkers* recognizes that each group needs a place to pursue ~~their own~~ *age-appropriate* activities.

Terms such as *superior* and *wise thinkers* add force to the argument. *Age-appropriate* adds more information.

Building Knowledge and Insight

To His Excellency, General Washington

Connecting to the Essential Question In her poems, Phillis Wheatley often paid tribute to America, its leaders, and the ideals the new country represented to her. As you read, find details that show the qualities Wheatley most admires in George Washington. This will help as you consider the Essential Question: **What makes American literature American?**

Common Core State Standards

Reading Literature
5. Analyze how an author's choices concerning how to structure specific parts of a text contribute to its overall structure and meaning as well as its aesthetic impact.
9. Demonstrate knowledge of eighteenth-century foundational works of American literature.

Close Reading Focus

Heroic Couplets; Classical Mythology

Phillis Wheatley wrote in **heroic couplets,** a traditional *poetic form,* or structure. Heroic couplets were introduced into English literature by the poet Chaucer in the fourteenth century, but they earned their name from their use by sixteenth-century poets in dramatic works about heroes. Heroic couplets have the following elements:

- They are written in a sequence of rhyming *couplets,* or pairs of lines.
- Each couplet expresses a complete thought.
- They have *end rhyme,* or full rhyme at the end of each line.
- They are written in *iambic pentameter,* a meter in which five unstressed syllables are each followed by a stressed syllable.

The influence of traditional literature is also evident in Wheatley's many references to *archetypal figures* from **classical mythology.** In this poem, she even creates a new goddess, Columbia, to symbolize America. As you read, think about how these references add to Wheatley's presentation of Washington as a hero of mythic grandeur.

Preparing to Read Complex Texts As you read, monitor your comprehension. If you find you are unsure of the meaning of lines or sections, **reread** to clarify your understanding. You may need to reorder words or determine the nouns that confusing pronouns replace. As you reread, use a chart like the one shown to clarify the poem's meaning.

Original Sentence
How pour her armies through a thousand gates

Her refers to Columbia. Her armies is the subject of pour.

Clarified Meaning
How Columbia's armies pour through a thousand gates

Vocabulary

The words below are key to understanding the text that follows. Copy the words into your notebook, sorting them into words you know and words you do not know.

propitious
tempest
martial
implore
pensive
lament

Phillis Wheatley (1753?–1784)

Author of **"To His Excellency, General Washington"**

In an era when few women and even fewer slaves could read and write, Phillis Wheatley, a female slave, became one of the finest American poets of her day. A West African native, Wheatley was brought to America on a slave ship when she was about eight. She was lucky enough to be purchased by a Boston family who valued her intelligence and taught her to read and write. The Wheatleys converted their young slave to Christianity and gave her the Bible, Latin and Greek classics, and contemporary English poetry to read. Soon Wheatley was writing her own verse, publishing her first poem when she was just thirteen.

Fame Abroad at an Early Age In 1770, Wheatley won fame through a poem about the death of a celebrated English clergyman, George Whitehead. Three years later, two British aristocrats helped her publish a volume of poetry in London. Called *Poems on Various Subjects: Religious and Moral,* the book was probably the first published work by an African in the colonies. However, it was not published in America until 1786, two years after Wheatley's death.

A Falling and Rising Star Freed from slavery in 1773, Wheatley's final years were filled with hardship and sorrow. Three of her children died in infancy, and her husband was imprisoned for debt. Though she assembled a second collection of poetry, the manuscript was lost before publication, and Wheatley fell into obscurity as a poet. In the centuries since her death, however, her star has again risen. She is now seen as a noteworthy poet of early America and the first writer of African origin to gain a voice in American literature.

The world is a severe schoolmaster, for its frowns are less dangerous than its smiles and flatteries, and it is a difficult task to keep in the path of wisdom.

FIRST in WAR,
FIRST in PEACE,
&
FIRST in the HEARTS
OF HIS
COUNTRYMEN.

Liberty and Washington, New York State Historical Association, Cooperstown

To His Excellency, General Washington

Phillis Wheatley

BACKGROUND In the early days of the American Revolution, Phillis Wheatley wrote a poem addressed to the commander of the American forces, George Washington. She sent him the poem in October of 1775, and he responded with sincere thanks and expressions of admiration. He also explained the reason he did not try to publish the poem was because it praised him so highly he was concerned he would appear vain.

Celestial choir! enthron'd in realms of light,
    Columbia's scenes of glorious toils I write.
While freedom's cause her anxious breast alarms,
She flashes dreadful in refulgent arms.
See mother earth her offspring's fate bemoan,
And nations gaze at scenes before unknown!
See the bright beams of heaven's revolving light
Involved in sorrows and the veil of night!
    The goddess comes, she moves divinely fair,
Olive and laurel binds her golden hair:
Wherever shines this native of the skies,
Unnumber'd charms and recent graces rise.
    Muse![1] bow **propitious** while my pen relates
How pour her armies through a thousand gates,
As when Eolus[2] heaven's fair face deforms,
Enwrapp'd in **tempest** and a night of storms;
Astonish'd ocean feels the wild uproar,
The refluent surges beat the sounding shore;
Or thick as leaves in Autumn's golden reign,
Such, and so many, moves the warrior's train.
In bright array they seek the work of war,
Where high unfurl'd the ensign[3] waves in air.

1. **Muse** A Greek goddess, in this case Erato, who is thought to inspire poets. She is one of nine muses presiding over literature, the arts, and the sciences.
2. **Eolus** (ē´ ə ləs) the Greek god of the winds.
3. **ensign** (en´ sin) flag.

◄ Critical Viewing

Noting the symbols of the Revolutionary conflict, explain the action of the painting. **INTERPRET**

Vocabulary

propitious (prō pish´ əs) *adj.* favorably inclined or disposed

tempest (tem´ pist) *n.* A violent storm with high winds

Comprehension

What army is the poet celebrating?

Shall I to Washington their praise recite?
Enough thou know'st them in the fields of fight.
Thee, first in peace and honors,—we demand
The grace and glory of thy **martial** band.
Fam'd for thy valor, for thy virtues more,
Hear every tongue thy guardian aid **implore**!
    One century scarce perform'd its destined round,
When Gallic[4] powers Columbia's fury found;
And so may you, whoever dares disgrace
The land of freedom's heaven-defended race!
Fix'd are the eyes of nations on the scales,
For in their hopes Columbia's arm prevails.
Anon Britannia[5] droops the **pensive** head,
While round increase the rising hills of dead.
Ah! cruel blindness to Columbia's state!
Lament thy thirst of boundless power too late.
    Proceed, great Chief, with virtue on thy side,
Thy ev'ry action let the goddess guide.
A crown, a mansion, and a throne that shine,
With gold unfading, WASHINGTON! be thine.

Vocabulary
martial (mär′ shəl) *adj.* relating to war
implore (im plôr′) *v.* ask or beg earnestly; plead
pensive (pen′ siv) *adj.* thinking deeply or seriously
lament (lə ment′) *v.* feel sorrow for; mourn

---

4. **Gallic** (gal′ ik) French. The colonists, led by Washington, defeated the French in the French and Indian War (1754–1763).
5. **Britannia** England.

Critical Reading

Cite textual evidence to support your responses.

1. **Key Ideas and Details (a)** In lines 9–12, how is Columbia described? **(b) Deduce:** What does this image of Columbia suggest about the speaker's view of America?
2. **Key Ideas and Details (a)** In lines 13–20, to what natural phenomenon is the American army compared? **(b) Interpret:** What does this comparison suggest about the power of American military forces in battle?
3. **Key Ideas and Details (a)** Which details in the last two lines reflect the influence of the British political system? **(b) Deduce:** What position in a new government does the speaker assume Washington will occupy? **(c) Synthesize:** How do these details hint at the debate about the kind of government to be established after the war?
4. **Integration of Knowledge and Ideas** Do the qualities Wheatley attributes to Washington represent typically American values? In your response, use at least two of these Essential Question vocabulary words: *valor, boldness, principles, character. [Connecting to the Essential Question: What makes American literature American?]*

Close Reading Activities

To His Excellency, General Washington

Literary Analysis

1. **Key Ideas and Details** **Reread** lines 35–38 to clarify their meaning. **(a)** To whom or what does the pronoun *thy* in line 38 refer? **(b)** Whose cruel blindness is the speaker talking about?
2. **Key Ideas and Details** Reread the last four lines. **(a)** To whom does the pronoun *thy* refer? **(b)** Rewrite line 40 in a word order that is easier to understand.
3. **Craft and Structure** To illustrate Wheatley's use of **heroic couplets,** select two lines from the poem. **(a)** Explain what the couplet means. **(b)** Identify the *rhyme*. **(c)** Indicate the patterns of stressed and unstressed syllables.
4. **Integration of Knowledge and Ideas** Use a chart like the one shown to list three **mythological references** in the poem. **(a)** Define each reference. **(b)** Explain what each reference adds to Wheatley's portrayal.

Mythological Reference	What It Contributes

Common Core State Standards

Writing

1. Write arguments to support claims in an analysis of substantive topics or texts, using valid reasoning and relevant and sufficient evidence.

Vocabulary Acquisition and Use

Sentence Completions Complete each sentence with a word from the vocabulary list. Then, explain your choice.

1. We ______ the loss of these brave soldiers.
2. The good weather made it ______ to start the voyage.
3. The soldier knew a lot about ______ matters but little about daily life.
4. Her thoughtful expression reflected her ______ mood.
5. If captured, we must ______ our enemies to treat us with mercy.
6. The ship was tossed back and forth during the ______.

Writing to Sources

Argument A **memo** is a piece of *business writing* that usually begins with these headings: TO: recipients' names; FROM: your name; DATE: date of writing; SUBJECT: your topic. These headings are followed by text organized in paragraphs. Imagine that you are part of the team working on Washington's presidential campaign. Someone has proposed using Wheatley's poem in the campaign. Write a memo supporting or rejecting the idea. Defend your position using details from the poem.

Analyzing Functional and Expository Texts

Manual • Public Service Advertisement

About the Texts

A **manual** is an informational document that organizations publish to instruct readers in how to use a product or perform a task. Most manuals contain a statement of purpose; step-by-step instructions; and a list of requirements, tools, regulations, or suggestions.

A **public service advertisement** (PSA) presents information to the general public about issues that affect the common good. Unlike commercial advertisements, PSAs are broadcast or distributed for free. They may appear on posters, in newspapers, or on signs; be broadcast on TV, radio, or podcast; or appear on Web sites.

Common Core State Standards

Reading Informational Text

5. Analyze and evaluate the effectiveness of the structure an author uses in his or her exposition or argument, including whether the structure makes points clear, convincing, and engaging.

Preparing to Read Complex Texts

To be effective, functional and expository texts present information clearly so readers can understand and apply the information. To ensure a logical flow of ideas, writers may use specific patterns of organization, including the following structures:

- *Cause and effect* describes the results of an action.
- *Chronological order* identifies the sequence in which steps in a task should be performed.
- *Problem and solution* outlines a problem the text will help readers solve.

Text features—such as headings and subheads, boldface and italic type, bulleted lists, and images—help readers navigate the text. As you read these documents, **evaluate text features,** noting how they emphasize specific sections and help readers grasp the organizational structures. Use a chart like the one shown to identify text features and evaluate their purposes.

Content-Area Vocabulary

These words appear in the selections that follow. They may also appear in other content-area texts.

candidate (kan´ də dāt) *n.* person who seeks election to a political position

legislature (leg´ is lā´ chər) *n.* group of lawmakers who represent a state or nation

candid (kan´ did) *adj.* outspoken; open and sincere

officials (ə fish´ əlz) *n.* people who hold government offices or positions

Basic Elements		Purpose
Headings and subheads	Yes ❑ No ❑	
Boldfaced or italicized text	Yes ❑ No ❑	
Numbered or bulleted lists	Yes ❑ No ❑	
Photos or illustrations	Yes ❑ No ❑	

LEAGUE OF WOMEN VOTERS
Making Democracy Work

HOW TO WATCH A DEBATE

The title indicates the task being addressed.

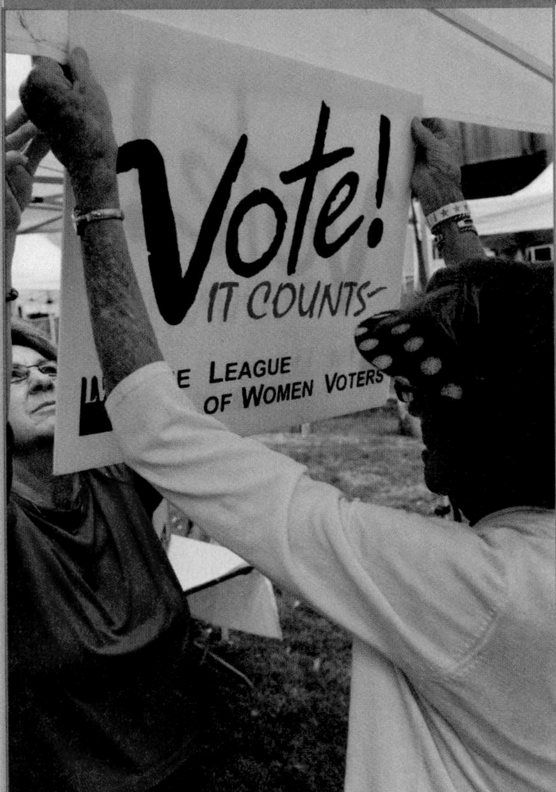

Stay Informed

Sign up for the League's e-newsletter and get all the latest information delivered to your inbox.

How to Watch a Debate

Headings guide readers through a step-by-step process.

Candidate debates have a long history in American politics. At every level of government—from city council to state **legislature**, from Congress to president of the United States—candidates participate in debates to help voters understand who they are and what they stand for.

Watching debates is an important way for voters to learn more about the candidates and the issues before the election, so that they can cast an informed vote. At the same time, voters need to view debates with a careful eye to get the most information. Candidates rehearse thoroughly for debates, making it hard to get **candid**, spontaneous answers. Debates can emphasize form over substance, such as the candidates' appearance instead of their stands on the issues. You may watch a debate and still not get answers to the questions you have about the candidates and issues.

Before the Debate

It will help if you take some time before the debate to

- follow the campaign to learn about the candidates and their backgrounds;
- find out what the important campaign issues are;
- decide what issues are most important to you;
- think about the questions you may have and the information you want to get from the debate to help you in your decision making;
- open your mind to new opinions/impressions of the candidate regardless of party affiliation.

You may want to make plans to get together with friends or family to watch the debate. Watching the debate in a group and discussing it afterward helps to clarify your thoughts about what was said in the debate and how the candidates performed.

A debate might not include all of the candidates for the office. Before the debate, note which candidates are included and which are not. If all candidates are not participating, try to find out why. Some debates include only candidates who have significant support, on the theory that the voters should be able to compare the candidates with a realistic chance of winning. Others invite all candidates who have qualified for the ballot. Sometimes candidates who are invited choose not to participate. Candidates with a strong lead might refuse to participate because they think there is no advantage to be gained by debating a lesser-known opponent.

During the Debate

When watching the debate, ask yourself questions like these to help you judge the fairness of the debate and the performance of the candidates:

The debate format and questions:

Italicized text emphasizes the importance of subheads.

- Does the format give each candidate an equal opportunity to speak and respond to questions?
- Are the questions clear, fair, and equally tough on all candidates?
- Do the questions cover the issues that are important to you?
- Is the moderator in control of the debate? Does the moderator need to say less and let the candidates say more?

The candidates:

- Do they answer questions directly, or do they evade them or fail to answer the specific question?
- Do they give specifics about their stands on the issues, or do they speak in generalities? Do they support their positions and arguments with facts and figures?
- Do they talk about their own policies and positions, or do they mostly attack their opponents?
- Are their proposals realistic? Can they actually carry out the promises they are making?
- Do they appear sincere, confident, and relaxed?
- Do they show how their backgrounds and experience qualify them to hold the office?
- Are their answers consistent with their previous positions, and if not, do they explain why?
- What image are they trying to create?
- Do their responses appear overly rehearsed or "canned"?

Bulleted lists provide a breakdown of important questions and steps.

Media coverage:

- If you are watching the debate on television, are reaction shots or other techniques used to create a sense of drama or conflict?
- Are you being influenced by comments made by reporters and commentators immediately before and after the debate?

Photographs add visual interest.

After the Debate

It will help clarify your thoughts about the candidates and the issues if you take some time after the debate to reflect on what you have just seen and heard. You can do this by

- comparing your impressions with those of others who watched the debate;
- asking yourself, based on the information you got from watching the debate, which candidate appears most qualified for the office;
- identifying the issues on which you agree with a candidate and those on which you disagree, and deciding whether that makes you more or less likely to vote for a particular candidate;
- asking yourself if you learned something new about the issues or the candidate;
- thinking about whether you have more questions about the issues or the candidates that you want to follow up;
- getting more information about the candidates' positions from news reports, candidate Web sites and nonpartisan voter information Web sites; and
- watching later debates for more information or to confirm your current impressions of the candidates.

Conclusion

A conclusion summarizes the information covered in the manual.

Candidate debates give voters a chance to hear the candidates speak and respond to their opponents. They give candidates a chance to present their message directly to a wide audience. As a voter, asking yourself the right questions before, during, and after the debate can help you make the most of this opportunity to learn about the candidates and the issues.

Public Service Announcement

HELP NORTH TEXAS VOTE COLLEGE PROGRAM

Headings help readers follow the problem-and-solution organizational structure.

The problem-and-solution organizational structure is established immediately.

Did You Know?

Not having enough poll workers can force a polling site to close or lead to delays at the voting booth. According to election **officials**, the result could prevent people from exercising their right to vote.

Election Day Is Coming Soon

Sign up to become part of the *Help North Texas Vote College Program* and take on a larger role in the United States election process. The right to vote is the foundation of our democracy, and assuring access in all our communities is critical. Because of this, it is imperative that the election process run smoothly for everyone. A large part of this includes the people that actually work the polls on Election Day. By signing up on the HNTV Web site, you will provide your name to the county in which you are registered to vote, and if there is a need for poll workers in that county, it is very possible that you will be called upon to serve on Election Day.

The Need for Poll Workers

The number of poll workers serving on Election Day is consistently not adequate, according to the election officials in Dallas, Denton, and Tarrant counties. While an inadequate number of poll workers is a significant problem of its own, an added burden results from the lack of bilingual poll workers, including both Spanish and Vietnamese-speaking workers.

How to Become a Poll Worker

It's easy! Sign up on the *Help North Texas Vote* Web site and your information will be transferred to the county in which you are registered. Once the county officials receive your information, they will determine that county's need. Those needed will be called upon to attend poll-worker training. Training is typically held for a few hours over the course of one day. After you are trained, you are qualified to serve as a poll worker on Election Day.

Poll-Worker Requirements

Requirements for election poll workers are similar for Dallas, Denton, and Tarrant counties:

- Workers must be registered to vote in the county where they wish to work.
- Workers must not be an elected official or be an employee of an elected official.
- Workers must be able to arrive at their assigned polling site before the polls open and must remain until the polls are closed and results are either called in or transported.
- Workers should enjoy interaction with the public, be detail-oriented, be able to take direction well, and not be easily distracted.

What's in It for You?

Beyond the opportunity to fulfill a civic duty that aids fellow Texans, there are other advantages to working the polls on Election Day. If you are called and asked to become a poll worker, you will be compensated for your training and the days that you work. Additionally, we encourage students to work with faculty members to arrange criteria for extra credit where applicable.

The average age of a U.S. poll worker is 72, according to the U.S. Election Assistance Commission, and the numbers of active poll workers are dwindling. It has been reported that the current number of poll workers is well short of the 2 million needed for a national election.

Critical Reading

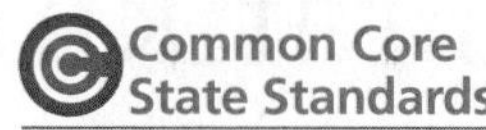

Common Core State Standards

Writing

1. Write arguments to support claims in an analysis of substantive topics or texts, using valid reasoning and relevant and sufficient evidence.

10. Write routinely over extended time frames and shorter time frames for a range of tasks, purposes, and audiences.

1. **Key Ideas and Details** **(a)** Which organizational structure is used in the manual—chronological order, cause-and-effect, or problem-and-solution? Explain. **(b)** Why is this structure appropriate—and common—in a "how-to" text such as this manual?
2. **Craft and Structure** Evaluate the text features used in the manual by considering whether they clarify or obscure the information. Explain your observations.
3. **Craft and Structure** **(a)** What organizational structure is used in the PSA? **(b)** In what ways do specific text features clarify that structure and emphasize distinct pieces of information?
4. **Content-Area Vocabulary (a)** Explain how the meaning of the Middle Dutch word *pol* ("head, top") contributes to the meaning of our English word *pollster.* **(b)** Determine the meaning of the following words derived from the same linguistic root: *outpoll, pollee.*

Timed Writing

Argument [40 minutes]

Format

An **argumentative essay** is not a piece of writing in which you start a fight. An argument is a well-reasoned position or opinion. In an essay, you must explain and support your argument.

These texts provide information intended to get readers more involved in the election process—a key requirement of good **citizenship**. Write an **argumentative essay** in which you take a position about the importance of **civic** involvement. Use evidence from these texts, as well as your own experience and knowledge, to defend your position.

Academic Vocabulary

The prompt asks you to address **citizenship** and **civic** involvement. Focus your response on ideas of community responsibility, rather than on personal benefits.

5-Minute Planner

Complete these steps before you begin to write.

1. Read the prompt carefully. List key words.
2. Draft a thesis that clearly responds to the prompt.
3. Skim the text for details you can use as evidence. **TIP** Organizational structures and text features can be used as evidence if they help support your thesis.
4. Reread the prompt, and draft your essay.

Literary History: Franklin's World

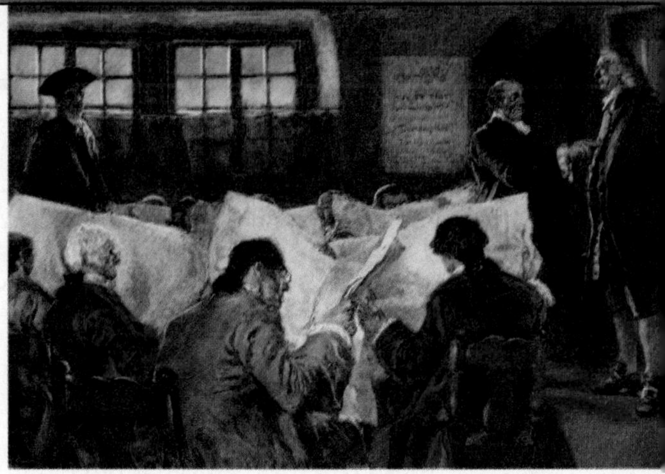

The American Revolution would not have happened when it did without the efforts of colonial newspapers, including those published by the Franklin brothers.

All the News That's Fit to Print

"EXTRA! EXTRA! Read all about it! Newspapers banned! Journalists Jailed! Americans Fight for a Free Press!" Those might have been the headlines blaring from your local newspaper if you had lived in eighteenth-century America. Might have been, that is, if colonial newspapers had used headlines. America's earliest newspapers bore little resemblance to those we know today. They were crudely printed on wooden presses and contained only a clumsy illustration or two. Most were one or two pages, and their stories were often just a list of ship arrivals. Despite their primitive character, these early newspapers laid the groundwork for a uniquely American phenomenon: a free press that could criticize the government.

Trailblazers The first American newspaper, printed in Boston on September 25, 1690, was titled *Publick Occurrences, Both Foreign and Domestick*. The remarkable thing about *Publick Occurrences* was that it existed at all. England had no history of a free and independent press. If a newspaper criticized the crown, it could be shut down. Yet *Publick Occurrences* was published without British approval, and printed stories that the Massachusetts royal governor found offensive. As a result, it lasted exactly one issue.

Americans waited 14 years for another newspaper. In 1704, the Boston *News-Letter* appeared. Approved by the governor of Massachusetts, the *News-Letter* was little more than a British mouthpiece, careful not to offend colonial authorities.

The Franklin Brothers In contrast, other papers sought controversy. For example, the New England *Courant*, founded in 1721 by James Franklin, appeared without British approval. The paper jabbed mercilessly at the royal governor, and eventually landed Franklin in jail. He handed control of the paper to his 16-year-old brother, Benjamin—someone who would play his own significant role in our nation's history.

In 1729, Benjamin Franklin, now living in Philadelphia, founded the Pennsylvania *Gazette*. It was the first newspaper to carry weather reports, interviews, and cartoons, and it became the most successful paper in the colonies.

▲ **Critical Viewing**
What does this scene of a coffee house and the facing samples of early newspapers indicate about the role of newspapers in colonial life? **ANALYZE**

Freedom of the Press Is Born A landmark legal case helped establish freedom of the press in America. In 1733, John Peter Zenger, a German immigrant, began publishing the *New York Weekly Journal.* The paper immediately ran afoul of the royal governor by publishing articles critical of his policies. One year later, Zenger was thrown in jail for libel.

In his 1735 trial, Zenger's lawyer, Andrew Hamilton, argued that while Zenger had indeed printed material offensive to the governor, the material was true and, therefore, not libelous. Under British law, even true statements against the government could be legally silenced. Hamilton made an impassioned plea to the jury to defend the "cause of liberty . . . both of exposing and opposing arbitrary power . . . by speaking and writing truth."

The jury found Zenger innocent. As a result of the case, the British stopped prosecuting American journalists, even when their criticisms of the government grew intense in the years leading up to the American Revolution.

Revolutionary Journalists Most historians agree that the American Revolution would not have happened when it did without the efforts of colonial newspapers. Newspapers stoked the flames of revolution, coining phrases like "taxation without representation" and influencing public perception of England as an enemy. When the British Stamp Act of 1765 imposed a heavy tax on all printed materials, the press denounced the legislation and refused to pay the tax. Even though the Stamp Act was repealed in 1766, it united editors and publishers in support of independence. Indeed, in 1776, most newspapers printed the Declaration of Independence on their front page.

During the Revolution, newspapers brought accounts of military developments to an eager readership. By the end of the war, newspapers had gained enormous strength. American newspapers represented something the world had never before seen: a press committed to telling the truth, not pleasing the government.

In This Section

THE New-York Weekly JOURNAL

The Boston News-Letter.

Published by Authority.

Speaking and Listening: Media Review

Comprehension and Collaboration Today, electronic media, including TV, the Internet, and even cell phones, provide constant access to news. With a small group, read, watch, and listen to news presented in electronic formats. Divide the labor so that each person is responsible for a different media form. Prepare a set of guiding questions, such as those listed here, to focus your review:

- What is the quality of information provided by each media form?
- Are the same stories presented very differently in different formats?
- Is the coverage across media platforms equally objective and fair?

Organize your observations into a **report** to share with the class.

Benjamin Franklin (1706–1790)

From his teen years until his retirement at age forty-two, Benjamin Franklin worked as a printer. He got his start as an apprentice to his brother James Franklin, a Boston printer. By the time he was sixteen, Ben was not only printing, but writing parts of his brother's newspaper. Using the name "Silence Dogood," he wrote letters satirizing daily life and politics in Boston. When he was seventeen, Franklin moved to Philadelphia to open his own print shop. This move gave birth to one of his most enduring contributions to American culture, *Poor Richard's Almanack.* This annual publication, which was published from 1732 to 1757, contained information, observations, and advice and was a colonial bestseller.

The "Write Reputation" Just as he had signed "Silence Dogood" to the letters he wrote for his brother's paper, Franklin created a fictitious author/editor for the *Almanack.* The chatty Richard Saunders, or Poor Richard, first appeared as a dull and foolish astronomer. However, over the years his character developed, becoming more thoughtful, pious, and funny.

Secret to Success Like most almanacs, *Poor Richard's Almanack* contained practical information about the calendar, the sun and moon, and the weather. It also featured a wealth of homespun sayings and observations, or aphorisms, many of which are still quoted today. It was these aphorisms that made the *Almanack* a bestseller. Franklin included an aphorism at the top or bottom of most of the *Almanack*'s pages. The wit and brevity of these sayings allowed him to weave in many moral messages, while also entertaining his readers.

Man of Science When Franklin was forty-two, he retired from the printing business to devote himself to science. He proved to be as successful a scientist as he had been a printer. Over the course of his life, Franklin was responsible for inventing the lightning rod, bifocals, and a new type of stove. He confirmed the laws of electricity, charted the Gulf Stream, and contributed to the scientific understanding of earthquakes and ocean currents. In spite of all these achievements, Franklin is best remembered for his career in politics.

Statesman and Diplomat Franklin played an important role in drafting the Declaration of Independence, enlisting French support during the Revolutionary War, negotiating a peace treaty with Britain, and drafting the United States Constitution. In his later years, he was the United States ambassador to England and then to France. Even before George Washington earned the title, Franklin was considered to be "the father of his country."

The Autobiography Franklin wrote the first section of *The Autobiography* in 1771 when he was sixty-five years old. At the urging of friends, he wrote three more sections—the last shortly before his death—but succeeded in bringing the account of his life only to the year 1759. Though never completed, his *Autobiography*, filled with his opinions and advice, provides not only a record of his achievements but also an understanding of his extraordinary character.

"If you would ***NOT BE* Forgotten,** As soon as you are dead and rotten, Either *write things* **worthy of reading,** Or ***DO things* worth the writing."**

FRANKLIN'S FIRSTS

Benjamin Franklin was an inventions superstar. Practical yet inspired, Franklin never patented his inventions, writing that he was "glad of an opportunity to serve others by any invention of ours; and this we should do freely and generously."

Swim fin/fan: (Ben's childhood) Young Franklin thought he needed a bit more oomph during his swims. To increase his speed in the water, he concocted a fin, shaped like a lily pad, that he wore over his hands.

Fire Department: 1736 Franklin created the first fire department in Philadelphia. Sixteen years later, he set up the first fire insurance company.

Lightning Rod: 1752 Franklin's insight that lightning is a form of electricity led to his design of a pointed metal rod that attached to the top of a building with a wire running into the ground. Elegant and simple, this device reduced property damage and the numbers of lives lost to the fires caused by lightning strikes.

Glass Armonica: 1761 A more sophisticated version of filling up glasses with water and "playing" them by running your fingers around the edge of each, the armonica could produce chords and melodies. These instruments are still in use.

Glass Armonica ▼

Odometer: 1775 As postmaster of Philadelphia, Franklin wanted to boost efficiency by learning which routes were fastest. To measure distances, he attached an instrument to his carriage that counted the rotations of the axles, giving him the information he needed.

Bifocals: 1784 After getting frustrated with the need to keep switching between eyeglasses (one for seeing close up and one for seeing distances), Franklin had each pair cut in half horizontally and put one half of each lens into one frame. Many people use bifocals to this day.

Daylight Savings Time: 1784 Whether in jest or thrift, Franklin invented Daylight Savings Time, an idea that helps us spring forward and fall back each year as we make the most of natural light.

Building Knowledge and Insight

from *The Autobiography* • from *Poor Richard's Almanack*

Connecting to the Essential Question Scholar William L. Andrews has called Franklin's *Autobiography* "the first great American success story." As you read, notice the goals that Franklin set for himself, and think about how they reflect his values. This will help as you reflect on the Essential Question: **What makes American literature American?**

Common Core State Standards

Reading Informational Text

3. Analyze a complex set of ideas or sequence of events and explain how specific individuals, ideas, or events interact and develop over the course of the text.

9. Analyze eighteenth-century foundational U.S. documents of historical and literary significance for their themes, purposes, and rhetorical features.

Close Reading Focus

Autobiography; Aphorisms

The word **autobiography** is composed of three Greek roots: *-auto-*, which means "self," *-bio-*, which means "life," and *-graph-*, which means "write." Hence, an autobiography is a life history written by its subject. To later readers, an autobiography may provide a more intimate view of history than one might find in an official report or political document.

As an elder statesman, Franklin wrote his life story to serve as an example for young people and to offer advice. A similar motivation is at work in his writing of the **aphorisms**—short sayings with a message—for *Poor Richard's Almanack*. Like his life story, the aphorisms help to paint a portrait of Franklin's attitudes and the world he inhabited. As you read, use a chart like the one shown to record details that help you understand Franklin's values and the times in which he lived.

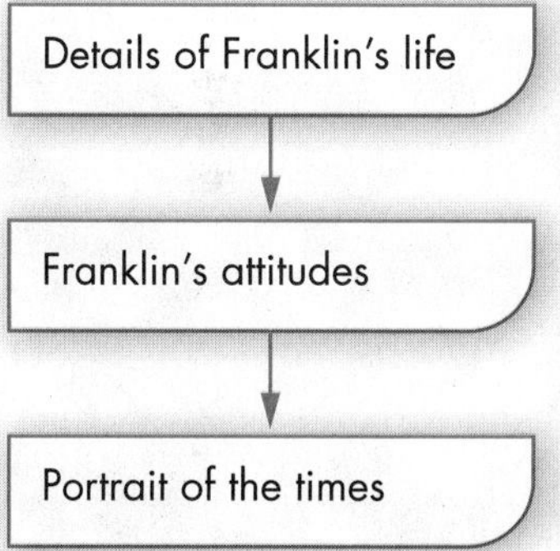

Preparing to Read Complex Texts In *The Autobiography*, you will read about Franklin's plan for self-improvement and the changes it made in his life. His plan can be seen as a *cause*, or the reason something happens, while each change may be seen as an *effect*, or the result. Some cause-and-effect relationships are simple.

Cause: Franklin wanted to organize his time

Effect: He prepared a notebook with a 24-hour schedule.

However, other cause-and-effect relationships are more complex. Many events have more than one cause or more than one effect. As you read, **analyze cause and effect** by pausing at important events and deciding, Why did this happen? What occurred as a result?

Vocabulary

The words below are critical to understanding the texts that follow. Copy the words into your notebook, and find the word that is an antonym of *easy*.

arduous
avarice
vigilance
incorrigible
posterity
squander

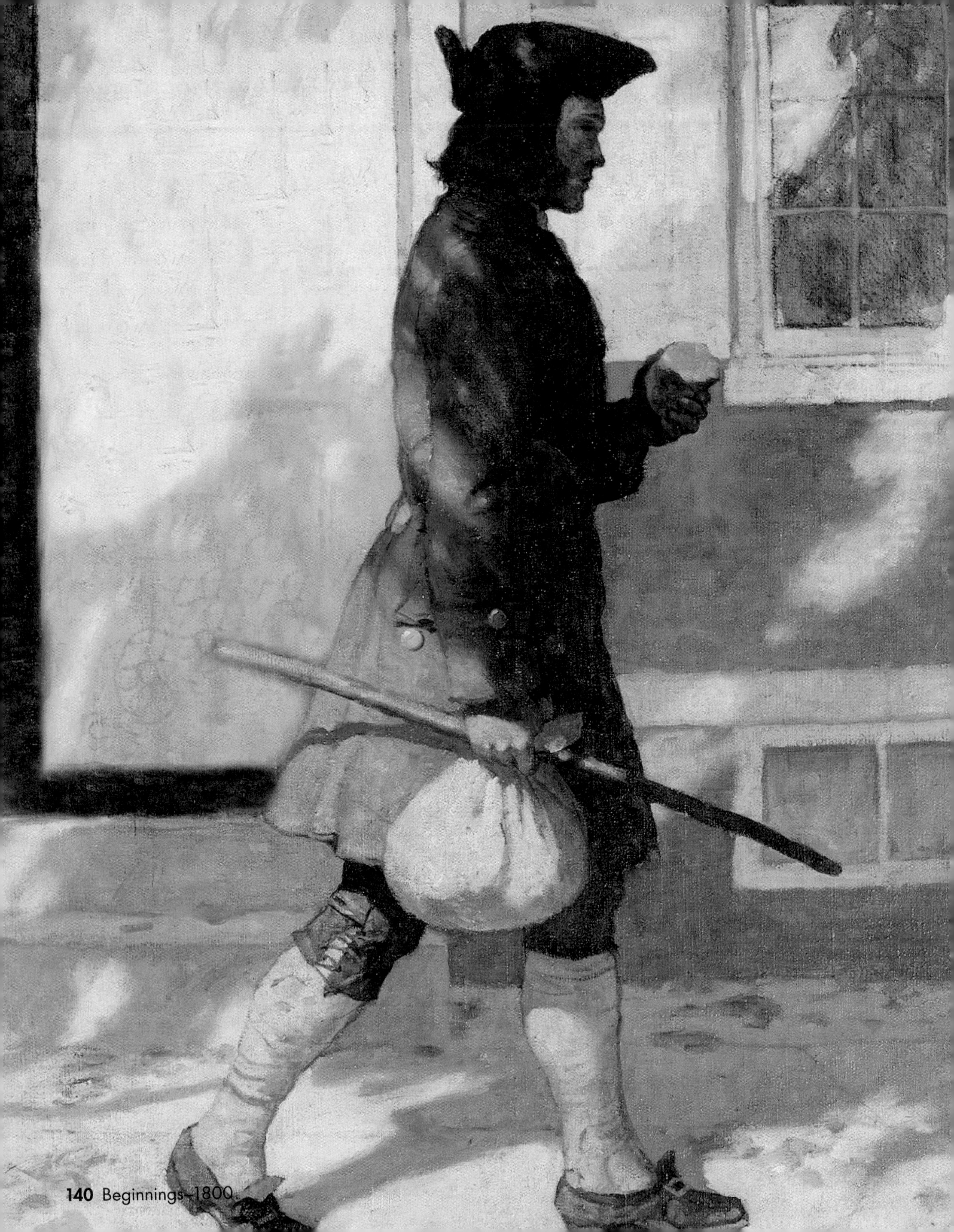

from The Autobiography

Benjamin Franklin

Background Benjamin Franklin arrived in the city of Philadelphia in 1723 at the age of seventeen. He knew no one, and he had little money and fewer possessions. However, his accomplishments shaped the city in ways that are still visible today. He helped establish Philadelphia's public library and fire department, as well as its first college. In addition, through his efforts, Philadelphia became the first city in the colonies to have street lights. While Franklin was a brilliant man, some of his success can be attributed to sheer self-discipline, which is evident in this excerpt.

◄ Critical Viewing
This painting shows young Franklin arriving in Philadelphia, carrying all he owns. What point about Franklin might the artist be making? **DRAW CONCLUSIONS**

It was about this time I conceived the bold and arduous project of arriving at moral perfection. I wished to live without committing any fault at any time; I would conquer all that either natural inclination, custom, or company might lead me into. As I knew, or thought I knew, what was right and wrong, I did not see why I might not always do the one and avoid the other. But I soon found I had undertaken a task of more difficulty than I had imagined. While my care was employed in guarding against one fault, I was often surprised by another; habit took the advantage of inattention; inclination was sometimes too strong for reason. I concluded, at length, that the mere speculative conviction that it was our interest to be completely virtuous was not sufficient to prevent our slipping; and that the contrary habits must be broken, and good ones acquired and established, before we can have any dependence on a steady, uniform rectitude of conduct. For this purpose I therefore contrived the following method.

In the various enumerations of the moral virtues I had met with in my reading, I found the catalog more or less numerous, as different writers included more or fewer ideas under the same name.

Vocabulary
arduous (är′ jo͞o əs) *adj.* difficult

Autobiography
What does Franklin's goal of moral "perfection" suggest about the values of the time period?

Comprehension
What project does Franklin undertake?

LITERATURE IN CONTEXT

World Literature

Socrates

A Greek philosopher and teacher who lived in the fifth century B.C., Socrates pioneered the kind of self-reflection that Benjamin Franklin undertakes with his moral improvement plan. Socrates believed that only through self-knowledge can people achieve virtue. Though he led many Athenians in searching for truth and defining rules for moral conduct, Socrates' criticism of the government resulted in his execution.

Connect to the Literature

Do you see any humor or irony in Franklin's plan for achieving humility—namely, by imitating Jesus and Socrates? Explain.

Vocabulary

avarice (av´ ə ris) *n.* greed

Temperance, for example, was by some confined to eating and drinking, while by others it was extended to mean the moderating every other pleasure, appetite, inclination, or passion, bodily or mental, even to our avarice and ambition. I proposed to myself, for the sake of clearness, to use rather more names, with fewer ideas annexed to each, than a few names with more ideas; and I included under thirteen names of virtues all that at that time occurred to me as necessary or desirable, and annexed to each a short precept, which fully expressed the extent I gave to its meaning.

These names of virtues, with their precepts, were:

1. TEMPERANCE Eat not to dullness; drink not to elevation.
2. SILENCE Speak not but what may benefit others or yourself; avoid trifling conversation.
3. ORDER Let all your things have their places; let each part of your business have its time.
4. RESOLUTION Resolve to perform what you ought; perform without fail what you resolve.
5. FRUGALITY Make no expense but to do good to others or yourself; i.e., waste nothing.
6. INDUSTRY Lose no time; be always employed in something useful; cut off all unnecessary actions.
7. SINCERITY Use no hurtful deceit; think innocently and justly, and, if you speak, speak accordingly.
8. JUSTICE Wrong none by doing injuries, or omitting the benefits that are your duty.
9. MODERATION Avoid extremes; forebear resenting injuries so much as you think they deserve.
10. CLEANLINESS Tolerate no uncleanliness in body, clothes, or habitation.
11. TRANQUILLITY Be not disturbed at trifles, or at accidents common or unavoidable.
12. CHASTITY Rarely use venery but for health or offspring, never to dullness, weakness, or the injury of your own or another's peace or reputation.
13. HUMILITY Imitate Jesus and Socrates.

My intention being to acquire the *habitude* of all these virtues, I judged it would be well not to distract my attention by attempting the whole at once but to fix it on one of them at a time; and, when I should be master of that, then to proceed to another, and so on, till I should have gone through the thirteen; and, as the previous acquisition of some might facilitate the acquisition of certain others, I arranged them with that view, as they stand above. *Temperance* first, as it tends to procure that coolness and clearness of head, which is so necessary where constant **vigilance** was to be kept up, and guard maintained against the unremitting attraction of ancient habits and the force of perpetual temptations. This being acquired and established, *Silence* would be more easy; and my desire being to gain knowledge at the same time that I improved in virtue, and considering that in conversation it was obtained rather by the use of the ears than of the tongue, and therefore wishing to break a habit I was getting into of prattling, punning, and joking, which only made me acceptable to trifling company, I gave *Silence* the second place. This and the next, *Order,* I expected would allow me more time for attending to my project and my studies. *Resolution,* once become habitual, would keep me firm in my endeavors to obtain all the subsequent virtues; *Frugality* and *Industry* freeing me from my remaining debt and producing affluence and independence, would make more easy the practice of *Sincerity* and *Justice,* etc., etc. Conceiving then, that, agreeably to the advice of Pythagoras[1] in his *Golden Verses,* daily examination would be necessary, I contrived the following method for conducting that examination.

I made a little book, in which I allotted a page for each of the virtues. I ruled each page with red ink, so as to have seven columns, one for each day of the week, marking each column with a letter for the day. I crossed these columns with thirteen red lines, marking the beginning of each line with the first letter of one of the virtues, on which line and in its proper column I might mark, by a little black spot, every fault I found upon examination to have been committed respecting that virtue upon that day.

I determined to give a week's strict attention to each of the virtues successively. Thus, in the first week, my great guard was to avoid every[2] the least offense against *Temperance,* leaving the other virtues to their ordinary chance, only marking every evening the faults of the day. Thus, if in the first week I could keep my first line, marked *T.* clear of spots, I supposed the habit of that virtue so much strengthened, and its opposite weakened, that I might venture extending my attention to include the next, and for the following week keep both lines clear of spots. Proceeding thus to the last, I could go through a course complete in thirteen weeks, and four courses in a year. And like him who, having a garden to weed, does not attempt to eradicate all the bad herbs at once, which would exceed his reach and his strength, but works on one of the beds at a time, and, having accomplished the first, proceeds to a second, so I should have, I hoped, the encouraging pleasure of seeing on my pages the progress I made in virtue, by clearing successively my lines of their spots, till in the end, by a number of courses, I should be happy in viewing a clean book, after a thirteen weeks' daily examination. . . .

Vocabulary
vigilance (vij´ ə ləns) *n.* watchfulness

Autobiography
What does the care with which Franklin makes his book tell you about his character?

Comprehension
What does Franklin hope to achieve in 13 weeks?

---

1. **Pythagoras** (pi thag´ ə rəs) Greek philosopher and mathematician who lived in the sixth century B.C.
2. **every** even.

The precept of *Order* requiring that *every part of my business should have its allotted time,* one page in my little book contained the following scheme of employment for the twenty-four hours of a natural day.

The Morning	5	Rise, wash and address Powerful Goodness! Contrive day's business and take the resolution of the day; prosecute the present study, and breakfast.
Question. What good shall I do this day?	6	
	7	
	8	
	9	
	10	Work.
	11	
Noon	12	Read, or overlook my accounts, and dine.
	1	
	2	Work.
	3	
	4	
	5	Put things in their places. Supper. Music or diversion, or conversation. Conversation. Examination of the day.
	6	
Evening	7	
Question. What good have I done today?	8	
	9	
	10	Sleep.
	11	
	12	
Night	1	

I entered upon the execution of this plan for self-examination, and continued it with occasional intermissions for some time. I was surprised to find myself so much fuller of faults than I had imagined; but I had the satisfaction of seeing them diminish. To avoid the trouble of renewing now and then my little book, which, by scraping out the marks on the paper of old faults to make room for new ones in a new course, became full of holes, I transferred my tables and precepts to the ivory leaves of a memorandum book, on which the lines were drawn with red ink that made a durable stain, and on those lines I marked my faults with a black-lead pencil, which marks I could easily wipe out with a wet sponge. After a while I went through one course only in a year, and afterward only one in several years, till at length I omitted them entirely, being employed in voyages and business abroad, with a multiplicity of affairs that interfered; but I always carried my little book with me.

My scheme of *Order* gave me the most trouble; and I found that, though it might be practicable where a man's business was such as to leave him the disposition of his time, that of a journeyman printer, for instance, it was not possible to be exactly observed by a master, who must mix with the world and often receive people of business at their own hours. *Order*, too, with regard to places for things, papers, etc., I found extremely difficult to acquire. I had not been early accustomed to it, and, having an exceeding good memory, I was not so sensible of the inconvenience attending want of method. This article, therefore, cost me so much painful attention, and my faults in it vexed me so much, and I made so little progress in amendment, and had such frequent relapses, that I was almost ready to give up the attempt, and content myself with a faulty character in that respect, like the man who, in buying an ax of a smith, my neighbor, desired to have the whole of its surface as bright as the edge. The smith consented to grind it bright for him if he would turn the wheel; he turned, while the smith pressed the broad face of the ax hard and heavily on the stone, which made the turning of it very fatiguing. The man came every now and then from the wheel to see how the work went on, and at length would take his ax as it was, without farther grinding. "No," said the smith, "turn on, turn on; we shall have it bright by and by; as yet, it is only speckled." "Yes," says the man, "*but I think I like a speckled ax best.*" And I believe this may have been the case with many, who, having, for want of some such means as I employed, found the difficulty of obtaining good and breaking bad habits in other points of vice and virtue, have given up the struggle, and concluded that "*a speckled ax was best*"; for something, that pretended to be reason, was every now and then suggesting to me that such extreme nicety as I exacted of myself might be a kind of foppery in morals, which, if it were known, would make me ridiculous; that a perfect character might be attended with the inconvenience of being envied and hated; and that a benevolent man should allow a few faults in himself, to keep his friends in countenance.

Autobiography
What does this anecdote about the man with the ax reveal about Franklin's sense of humor?

In truth, I found myself incorrigible with respect to *Order*; and now I am grown old, and my memory bad, I feel very sensibly the want of it. But, on the whole, though I never arrived at the perfection I had been so ambitious of obtaining, but fell far short of it, yet I was, by the endeavor, a better and a happier man than I otherwise should have been if I had not attempted it; as those who aim at perfect writing by imitating the engraved copies, though they never reached the wished-for excellence of those copies, their hand is mended by the endeavor, and is tolerable while it continues fair and legible.

Vocabulary
incorrigible (in kôr′ ə jə bəl) *adj.* impossible to correct

Comprehension
Which virtue did Franklin hope to achieve by planning each day's activity?

It may be well my **posterity** should be informed that to this little artifice, with the blessing of God, their ancestor owed the constant felicity of his life, down to his seventy-ninth year in which this is written. What reverses may attend the remainder is in the hand of Providence; but, if they arrive, the reflection on past happiness enjoyed ought to help his bearing them with more resignation. To *Temperance* he ascribes his long-continued health, and what is still left to him of a good constitution; to *Industry* and *Frugality*, the early easiness of his circumstances and acquisition of his fortune, with all that knowledge that enabled him to be a useful citizen, and obtained for him some degree of reputation among the learned; to *Sincerity* and *Justice*, the confidence of his country, and the honorable employs it conferred upon him; and to the joint influence of the whole mass of the virtues, even in the imperfect state he was able to acquire them, all that evenness of temper, and that cheerfulness in conversation, which makes his company still sought for, and agreeable even to his younger acquaintance. I hope, therefore, that some of my descendants may follow the example and reap the benefit.

Spiral Review

Audience For whom is Franklin writing? How do you think his sense of audience helped to shape this account of his life?

Vocabulary

posterity (päs ter ə tē) *n.* all future generations

THE AMERICAN EXPERIENCE

BENJAMIN FRANKLIN *in Our World*

In *The Autobiography*, Benjamin Franklin describes his attempts to become a completely virtuous person. Though he thought he failed, Americans *do* view Franklin as a man of many virtues. He was civic-minded, intelligent, inquisitive, practical, and industrious. He embodies much that Americans value, which may be why his image is so visible in our world today. He is, in fact, an American icon.

Benjamin Franklin National Memorial, The Franklin Institute, Philadelphia, PA ▶

Cartoon illustration of Ben Franklin from *Liberty's Kids* ▶

Ben Franklin Action Figure ▶

U.S. currency: $100 bill ▲

CONNECT TO THE LITERATURE

What would you choose as Benjamin Franklin's most inspiring quality? Explain.

Critical Commentary

Ben Franklin, America's Everyman

William L. Andrews

William L. Andrews, an award-winning scholar and teacher, is the E. Maynard Adams Professor of English at the University of North Carolina, Chapel Hill.

...his greatest INVENTION was himself.

It's not just a coincidence that America's earliest literature is highly autobiographical. Nor is it by accident that autobiography emerged as a literary form about the same time that the United States became a new nation. Autobiography and America were made for each other.

The revolution in the United States created a new person, as well as a new country. At least that's what the great spokesmen and propagandists of the Revolution, especially Thomas Jefferson, Patrick Henry, and Benjamin Franklin, claimed. Franklin, who wore a coonskin cap to the royal courts of Europe, became famous for inventing everything from street lights to eyeglasses. But we read him today because his greatest invention was himself. *The Autobiography* of Benjamin Franklin is the first great American success story: a tale of a poor boy who made good.

A New American Franklin's *Autobiography* has served for many generations as a blueprint for a new American man. This man was energetic, adaptable, shrewd, and, as the *Autobiography* makes very clear, success oriented. Industrious, frugal, temperate, orderly, and resolute, Franklin modeled for Americans a hero fulfilled by the work of this world, not longing for deliverance to the next. Yet in Franklin's autobiographical mirror his readers could see that success was not to be measured simply by acquiring the goods of this world but by "doing good" for the practical benefit of one's fellow Americans too.

An Achievable Good Franklin's "project of arriving at moral perfection," which he undertook when he was in his mid-twenties, epitomizes his audaciously American can-do spirit in at least two ways. First, it appears that the young Franklin really thought he could divest himself of all his faults simply by putting his mind and will to the task. Second, he seems to have been confident of success by approaching the task as a "project," not unlike some he'd already wrapped up, including the founding of the first lending library and the publication of *Poor Richard's Almanack*. Franklin doesn't hesitate to admit that he failed, but he insists that the effort he exerted was just as valuable to his character development as his unattained goal. Thus, as if following Poor Richard's counsel to "write injuries in dust, benefits in marble," Franklin's autobiographical account of his perfection project points finally to an achievable good, not an unreachable ideal.

Key Ideas and Details According to Andrews, why have generations of Franklin's readers treasured this episode of failure in a life of so many successes?

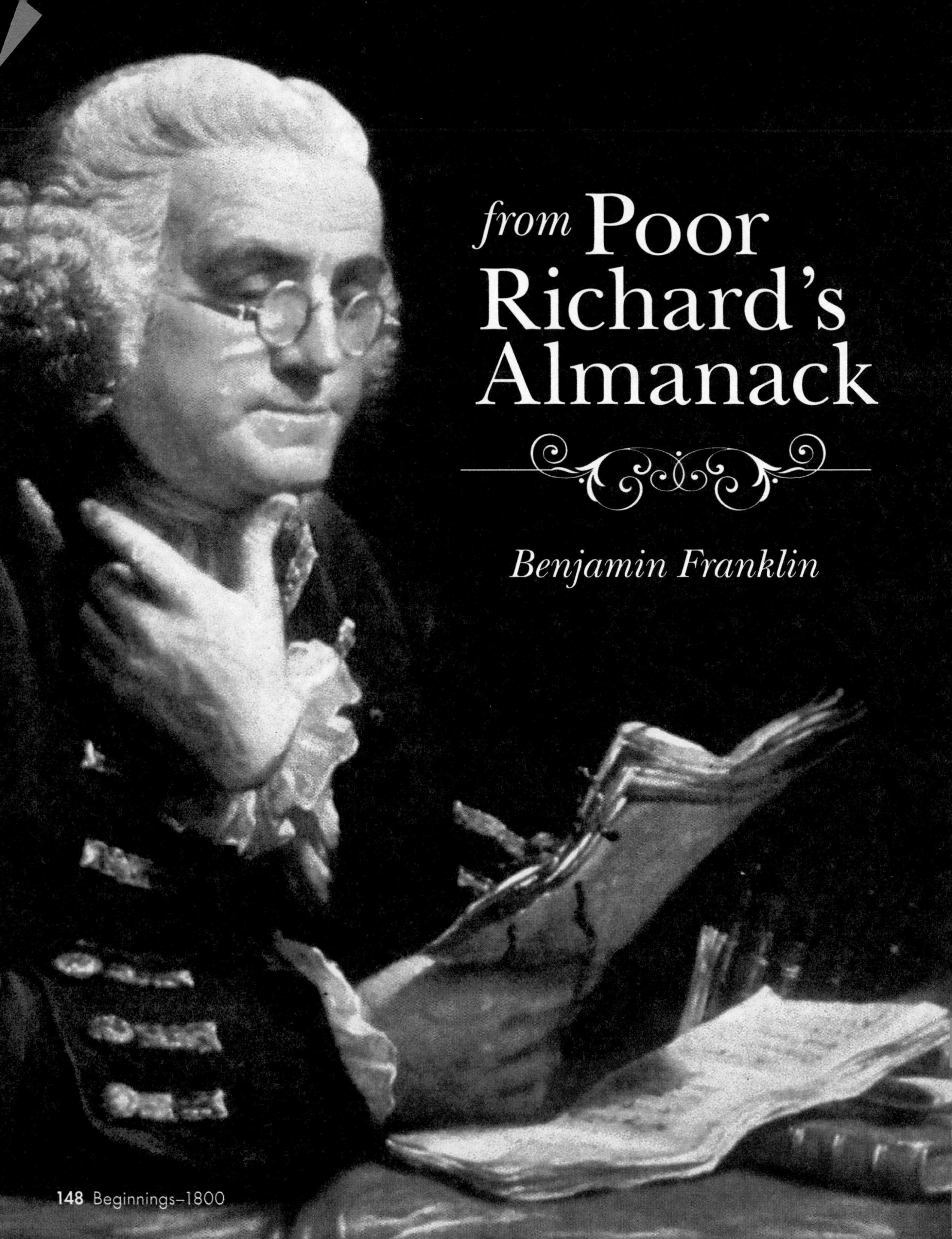

from Poor Richard's Almanack

Benjamin Franklin

- Fools make feasts, and wise men eat them.
- Be slow in choosing a friend, slower in changing.
- Keep thy shop, and thy shop will keep thee.
- Early to bed, early to rise, makes a man healthy, wealthy, and wise.
- Three may keep a secret if two of them are dead.
- God helps them that help themselves.
- The rotten apple spoils his companions.
- An open foe may prove a curse; but a pretended friend is worse.
- Have you somewhat to do tomorrow, do it today.
- A true friend is the best possession.
- A small leak will sink a great ship.
- No gains without pains.
- Tis easier to prevent bad habits than to break them.
- Well done is better than well said.
- Dost thou love life? Then do not squander time; for that's the stuff life is made of.
- Write injuries in dust, benefits in marble.
- A slip of the foot you may soon recover, but a slip of the tongue you may never get over.
- If your head is wax, don't walk in the sun.
- A good example is the best sermon.

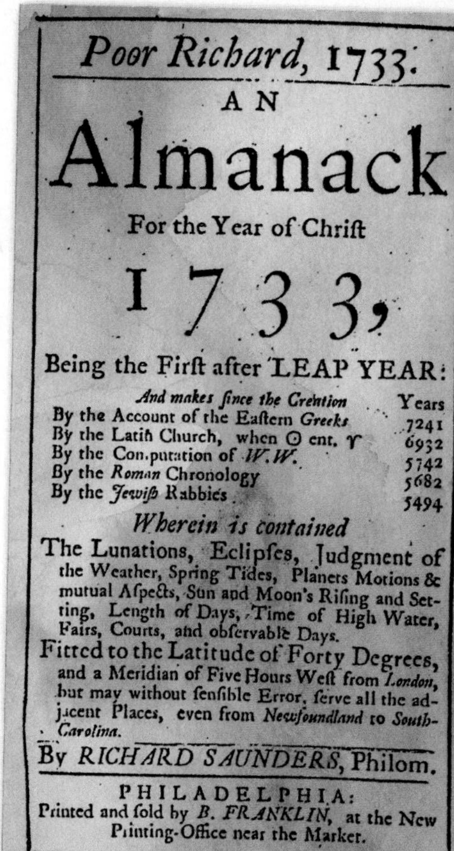

Poor Richard, 1733.

AN

Almanack

For the Year of Chriſt

1733,

Being the Firſt after LEAP YEAR:

And makes ſince the Creation	Years
By the Account of the Eaſtern *Greeks*	7241
By the Latin Church, when ☉ ent. ♈	6932
By the Computation of *W.W.*	5742
By the *Roman* Chronology	5682
By the *Jewiſh* Rabbies	5494

Wherein is contained

The Lunations, Eclipſes, Judgment of the Weather, Spring Tides, Planets Motions & mutual Aſpects, Sun and Moon's Riſing and Setting, Length of Days, Time of High Water, Fairs, Courts, and obſervable Days.

Fitted to the Latitude of Forty Degrees, and a Meridian of Five Hours Weſt from *London*, but may without ſenſible Error, ſerve all the adjacent Places, even from *Newfoundland* to *South-Carolina*.

By *RICHARD SAUNDERS*, Philom.

PHILADELPHIA:
Printed and ſold by *B. FRANKLIN*, at the New Printing-Office near the Market.

▲ Critical Viewing

The abbreviation "Philom." is short for *philomath*. The root *-philo-* means "love" and the suffix *-math-* means "learn." Can you infer what the word means? **INFER MEANING**

Vocabulary

squander (skwän′ dər) *v.* spend or use wastefully

Comprehension

Which aphorisms offer advice about using time wisely?

❧ A good EXAMPLE is the best SERMON.

- ❧ Hunger is the best pickle.
- ❧ Genius without education is like silver in the mine.
- ❧ For want of a nail the shoe is lost; for want of a shoe the horse is lost; for want of a horse the rider is lost.
- ❧ Haste makes waste.
- ❧ The doors of wisdom are never shut.
- ❧ Love your neighbor; yet don't pull down your hedge.
- ❧ He that lives upon hope will die fasting.

Critical Reading

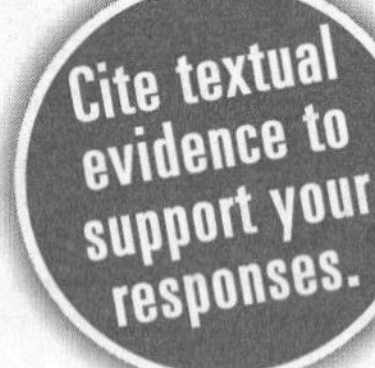
Cite textual evidence to support your responses.

1. **Key Ideas and Details (a)** What efforts does Franklin make to become more orderly? **(b) Infer:** Is he successful? Explain. **(c) Analyze:** What aspect of his attempt to become more orderly is illustrated by the anecdote of the man with the speckled ax?
2. **Key Ideas and Details (a)** When Franklin began his project, he was a young man. How do you think he felt at the time about his chances of attaining moral "perfection"? **(b) Compare and Contrast:** What insights does Franklin gain about the goal of achieving perfection as he gets older?
3. **Key Ideas and Details (a)** Note three aphorisms that deal directly with friendship. **(b) Analyze:** Is Franklin's message about friendship consistent? Explain.
4. **Key Ideas and Details (a)** According to the aphorism, what happens to a person who "lives upon hope"? **(b) Speculate:** What more reliable value would Franklin say a person can successfully "live upon"?
5. **Integration of Knowledge and Ideas** In what ways can analyzing one's own behavior contribute to personal growth?
6. **Integration of Knowledge and Ideas** With which of Franklin's aphorisms do you most strongly agree and disagree? Why?
7. **Integration of Knowledge and Ideas** In what ways do the goals Franklin sets for himself and the aphorisms he wrote express values that are still widely held in America? Explain. Use at least two of these Essential Question words: *individualism, thrifty, practical, humorous.* ***[Connecting to the Essential Question: What makes American literature American?]***

WORLD LITERATURE CONNECTION

PROVERBS
THE WISDOM OF MANY

◀ Wooden helmet mask with beard (Congo)

The memorable aphorisms that Benjamin Franklin presents in *Poor Richard's Almanack* are grounded in the rich oral tradition of proverbs. A proverb is a traditional saying that offers a practical truth about life, work, love, death, and other universal experiences. Each proverb is a bit of cultural wisdom. A society's proverbs reflect the attitudes and worldviews of its people. Proverbs are handed down through generations and can be used to teach children, offer advice, settle arguments, or even help resolve legal disputes. The proverbs presented here are from various cultures on the African continent.

CONNECT TO THE LITERATURE

What similarities and differences do you notice between the African proverbs and Franklin's aphorisms?

AFRICAN PROVERBS

UGANDA: THE BAGANDA PEOPLE
Where there are no dogs, the wild cats move about freely.

LIBERIA: THE JABO PEOPLE
The butterfly that flies among the thorns will tear its wings.
~
Children are the wisdom of the nation.

SOUTH AFRICA: THE ZULU PEOPLE
There is no foot, which does not stumble.

GHANA: THE ASHANTI PEOPLE
Rain beats on a leopard's skin,
but it does not beat out the spots.
~
One falsehood spoils a thousand truths.

NIGERIA: THE YORUBA PEOPLE
He who is being carried does not
realize how far the town is.

TANZANIA AND KENYA: THE MASAI PEOPLE
The zebra cannot do away with his stripes.
~
Do not repair another man's fence
until you have seen to your own.

Mask with horns (Nigeria) ▶

Close Reading Activities

from ***The Autobiography*** •
from ***Poor Richard's Almanack***

Literary Analysis

1. **Key Ideas and Details** **(a)** Why do you think Franklin devoted such a large chunk of his **autobiography** to a discussion of his failures to achieve perfect virtue? **(b)** What message do both his efforts and his failures convey?
2. **Key Ideas and Details** **(a)** Do you think Franklin achieved the virtue of humility? Why or why not? **(b)** Do you find any evidence of pride—humility's opposite—in this account of his life?
3. **Craft and Structure** How do you think *The Autobiography* would be different if it were written about Franklin rather than by him?
4. **Integration of Knowledge and Ideas** **(a)** Note two details from this section of *The Autobiography* that reveal an aspect of ordinary daily life in colonial America. **(b)** In what ways does this excerpt shed light on Franklin's era?
5. **Integration of Knowledge and Ideas** Use a chart like this one to match three aphorisms with virtues from *The Autobiography*. Explain each choice.

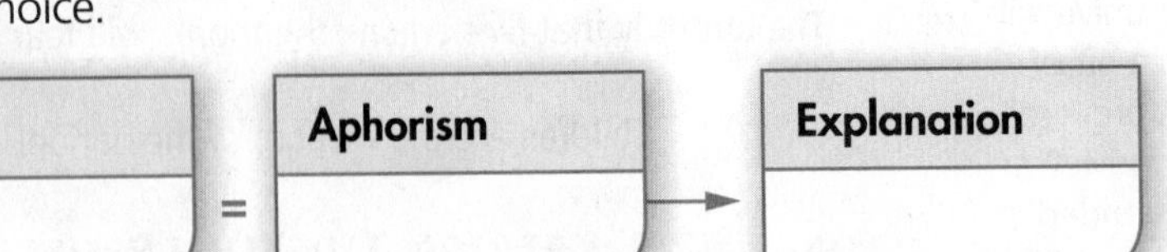
Virtue
=
Aphorism
Explanation

6. **Comparing Literary Works** **(a)** Are Franklin's struggles to improve himself related to the advice he offers in the **aphorisms**? **(b)** Do these aphorisms seem to be written by the same person who wrote *The Autobiography*? Why or why not?
7. **Integration of Knowledge and Ideas** Analyze cause and effect in the anecdote about the man with the ax. **(a)** What goal propels the man to take an action? **(b)** What is the result of that action? **(c)** How does that result become the cause of another action or decision?
8. **Integration of Knowledge and Ideas** Choose one of Franklin's aphorisms and explain how it suggests a cause-and-effect relationship. For example, "No gains without pains" suggests that only through hard work (cause) can you achieve your goals (effect).
9. **Analyzing Visual Information** Based on what you know of the genre of autobiography, explain the humor in the cartoon shown on this page.

Common Core State Standards

Language

4.b. Identify and correctly use patterns of word changes that indicate different meanings or parts of speech. *(p. 153)*

5. Demonstrate understanding of word relationships and nuances in word meanings. *(p. 153)*

▼ *"I called for you creative people because I feel it's time to begin my autobiography."*

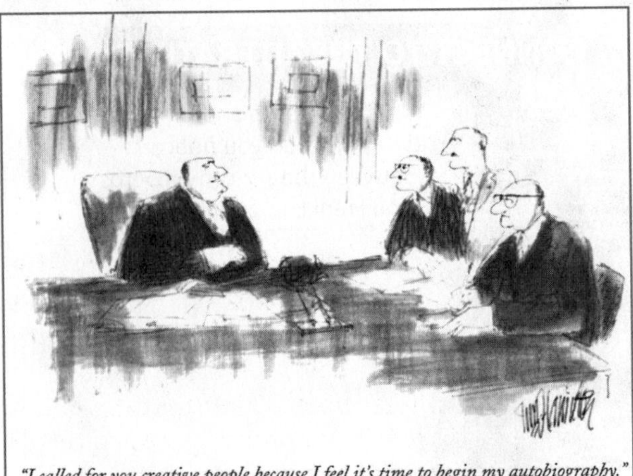
"I called for you creative people because I feel it's time to begin my autobiography."

Vocabulary Acquisition and Use

Word Analysis: Patterns of Word Changes

The noun *vigilance*, meaning "watchfulness," contains the suffix *-ance*. Whenever you see a word with the *-ance* or *-ence* ending, you can be sure it is a noun. That suffix is a *pattern that indicates the word's function*. Words exhibit other patterns that indicate different meanings or functions. Write a definition for each italicized word below. Then, explain the word's function—noun, adjective, or adverb. Based on your answer, identify the letter pattern that indicates the word's function.

1. He was *vigilant* in his efforts to reform.
2. Through the night, the soldier stood watch *vigilantly*.
3. He showed great *avarice* in his drive for wealth.
4. Many great stories exist about *avaricious* characters.

Vocabulary: Analogies

Analogies show the relationships between pairs of words. Complete each analogy using a word from the vocabulary list on page 139. In each, your choice should create a word pair that matches the relationship between the first two words given. Then, explain your answers.

1. *Permission* is to *authorization* as ______ is to *greed*.
2. *Tragedy* is to *comedy* as ______ is to *negligence*.
3. *Contemporary* is to *now* as ______ is to *future*.
4. *Rare* is to *common* as ______ is to *easy*.
5. *Criticize* is to *praise* as ______ is to *save*.
6. *Fresh* is to *trite* as ______ is to *curable*.

Using Resources to Build Vocabulary

The Language of Failed Attempts

Although Franklin strives for moral perfection, he openly acknowledges his failure to meet his goals. Consider how these words help Franklin describe his failed attempt to be perfect:

debt	reverses
prattle	slipping
punning	temptations
relapses	vexed

Use a print or electronic dictionary to find a meaning for each word as it is used by Franklin. Then, write a short advice column in which you give readers suggestions that will help them avoid failure. Include each word at least once. You might use a question-and-answer format. Vocabulary words may appear in both the questions and answers.

Close Reading Activities Continued

Writing to Sources

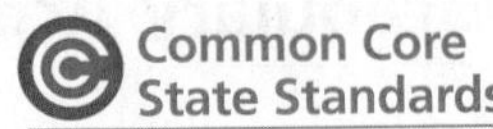
Common Core State Standards

Writing

2.a. Introduce a topic; organize complex ideas, concepts, and information so that each new element builds on that which precedes it to create a unified whole.

2.c. Use appropriate and varied transitions and syntax to link the major sections of the text, create cohesion, and clarify the relationships among complex ideas and concepts.

2.f. Provide a concluding statement or section that follows from and supports the information or explanation presented.

Language

3.a. Vary syntax for effect.

Informative Text In both life and literature, cause-and-effect relationships are far more complex than "A caused B." Often, one cause has multiple effects. Likewise, an effect can prompt other results, or new effects. In addition, while some effects can be anticipated, many are unforeseen and even surprising. Write an **analytical essay** in which you identify and explain the multiple effects of Benjamin Franklin's plan for self-improvement.

Prewriting Review *The Autobiography,* looking for events, changes, and insights that happened as a result of Franklin's plan. Use a chart like the one shown to identify multiple effects. After completing the chart, rank the effects from most important to least important.

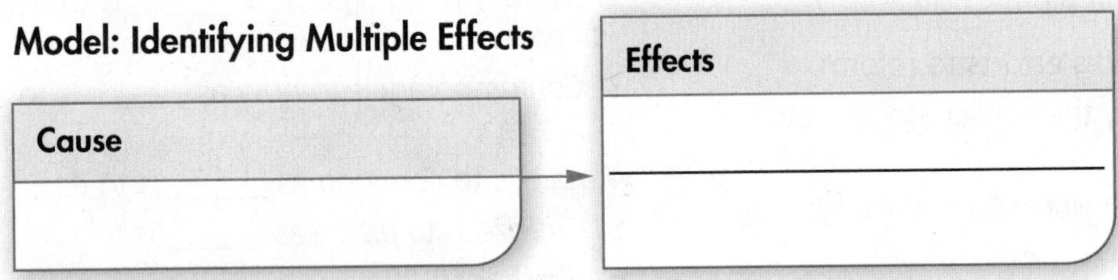

Drafting Start with a strong first sentence. You might use one of Franklin's aphorisms as a launching point. In the opening paragraph, state the topic of your essay and your *thesis*, or main idea. Then, follow these steps to structure the body of your essay:

- Describe the effects of Franklin's plan, devoting one paragraph to each effect. Make sure that each paragraph has a clear main idea.
- Follow *order-of-importance organization*, beginning with the least important effect and building toward the most important effect.
- In your conclusion, *summarize* the cause-and-effect relationships you have discussed.

Revising Reread your essay, making sure you have carefully explained the connections among your ideas. Consider reading your essay aloud so that you can hear sections that sound awkward or do not flow logically. Locate points in the text where the addition of *transitional words and phrases* will help clarify the flow of your ideas.

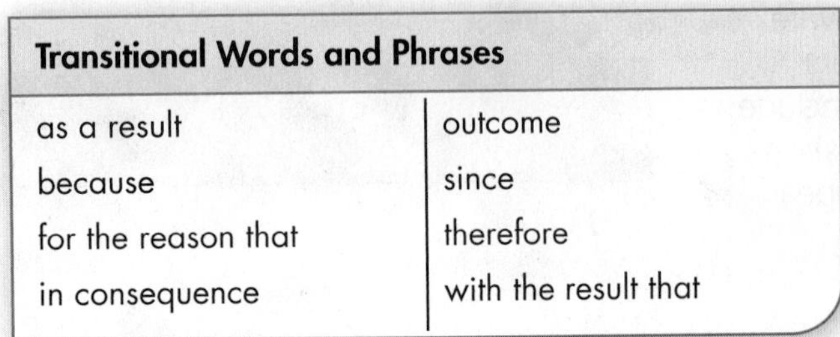

Transitional Words and Phrases	
as a result	outcome
because	since
for the reason that	therefore
in consequence	with the result that

Conventions and Style: Subordinating Conjunctions

To increase the sentence variety in your writing, use subordinating conjunctions to combine short sentences. **Subordinating conjunctions** are words or phrases that join two complete ideas by making one idea subordinate to, or dependent on, the other. When you use **subordination,** you show which idea is more important.

Common Subordinating Conjunctions			
after	as though	if	unless
although	because	since	until
as if	before	so that	when
as long as	even though	than	where

Using Subordinating Conjunctions

Short Sentences: Ben Franklin moved to Philadelphia. He had very little money.
Combined: Benjamin Franklin had very little money *when* he moved to Philadelphia.

Short Sentences: Franklin used a pseudonym. Franklin became known as a good writer.
Combined: *Even though* he used a pseudonym, Franklin became known as a good writer.

Short Sentences: He would have to be more careful. He wanted to attain moral perfection.
Combined: He would have to be more careful *if* he wanted to attain moral perfection.

Punctuation Tip: When the dependent clause comes first in a sentence, use a comma between the clauses. When the independent clause comes first, do not separate the clauses with a comma.

Practice In items 1–5, add a subordinating conjunction to complete each sentence. In items 6–10, combine the two sentences using a subordinating conjunction.

1. Do not speak ______ you have something beneficial to say.
2. Practice temperance ______ you eat and drink.
3. Franklin worked on improving himself ______ it were his life's project.
4. ______ you speak, make sure your words are sincere.
5. ______ a line has no marks, he is improving in that particular category.
6. All things should have a place and time. Order is important.
7. Franklin listed the virtues in a certain order. This way, he could work through them methodically.
8. He tried. He did not achieve moral perfection.
9. People enjoyed the *Almanack.* The proverbs were entertaining.
10. You should use your time wisely. There is never enough of it.

Writing and Speaking Conventions

A. Writing For each item, write a sentence that joins the two ideas using an appropriate subordinating conjunction.

1. he wrote the book—his friends encouraged him
2. Franklin made a chart—he could track his progress
3. you follow these rules—you will be a better person

Example: He wrote the book *after* his friends encouraged him.

B. Speaking Make up two aphorisms that could each be a refrain for a song. Correctly use subordinating conjunctions in your refrains.

A GALLERY OF *Autobiography*

Self-Portraits in American Literature

Benjamin Franklin
(1706–1790)
The Autobiography

Henry David Thoreau
(1817–1862)
Walden

Frederick Douglass
(1817–1895)
My Bondage and My Freedom

Zora Neale Hurston
(1891–1960)
Dust Tracks on a Road

Richard Wright
(1908–1960)
Black Boy

Maya Angelou
(1928–)
I Know Why the Caged Bird Sings

Frank McCourt
(1930–2009)
Angela's Ashes

N. Scott Momaday
(1934–)
The Names: A Memoir

Maxine Hong Kingston
(1940–)
The Woman Warrior

Sandra Cisneros
(1954–)
Straw Into Gold: The Metamorphosis of the Everyday

Comparing Literary Works

from ***The Autobiography*** by Benjamin Franklin • ***"Straw Into Gold: The Metamorphosis of the Everyday"*** by Sandra Cisneros

Comparing Autobiographies Past and Present

Autobiographical Writing The first autobiography was the *Confessions* of St. Augustine, which was written in Latin sometime around A.D. 400. The form did not appear in English, though, until the late 1700s. It was during this "Golden Age" of nonfiction that Benjamin Franklin wrote his *Autobiography.* In doing so, he created a model for the American success story.

Over the next two centuries, major American autobiographies such as the *Narrative of the Life of Frederick Douglass* (1845) and Zora Neale Hurston's *Dust Tracks on a Road* (1942) paved the way for other related forms of nonfiction. These include *memoirs,* which are smaller in scope and less formal in tone, and *autobiographical essays,* which focus on a small slice of the writer's life in order to explore larger ideas. "Straw Into Gold," by Sandra Cisneros, is an example of an autobiographical essay.

These selections highlight some of the ways that American autobiography has evolved. They reflect vastly different historical periods and cultures as well as changing attitudes toward social status and gender. Despite these differences, both address a powerful American *theme*—success. As you read "Straw Into Gold," use a chart like the one shown to compare and contrast Franklin's and Cisneros's ideas about success.

	Franklin	Cisneros
What is success?		
What are its costs?		
What are its rewards?		

Common Core State Standards

Reading Informational Text
3. Analyze a complex set of ideas or sequence of events and explain how specific individuals, ideas, or events interact and develop over the course of the text.

Language
6. Demonstrate independence in gathering vocabulary knowledge when considering a word or phrase important to comprehension or expression.

Gather Vocabulary Knowledge

Sandra Cisneros uses related forms of the words *venture, nomad,* and *vagabond.* Use a **dictionary** to find each word's part of speech and definition. Then, employ other references to further explore these words:

- **History of Language:** Use a history of English to research each word's origins. Write a paragraph about the word's emergence in English.
- **Book of Quotations:** Use an online or print collection of quotations to find a statement or passage containing one of the words. In a paragraph, explain nuances in meaning that are evident from the context of the quotation.

Comparing References Compare and contrast what you learn about the words from each specialized reference.

Sandra Cisneros (b. 1954)

Author of **"Straw Into Gold: The Metamorphosis of the Everyday"**

Sandra Cisneros was born in Chicago into a large Mexican American family. Because her family was poor, Cisneros moved frequently and lived for the most part in small, cramped apartments. To cope with these conditions, she retreated into herself and spent much of her time reading fairy tales and classic literature.

Embracing Her Heritage Cisneros attended Loyola University in Chicago and, later, the prestigious Writer's Workshop at the University of Iowa. During her college years, Cisneros met writers from many other backgrounds. At first uncomfortable about her family's struggles, she soon realized that her heritage provided her with something unique. She began writing about her childhood in a book of connected short stories. *The House on Mango Street,* published in 1984, ushered Cisneros into the literary limelight.

Charting Her Success Cisneros's second book, *Woman Hollering Creek* (1991), confirmed her status as an important American writer. Since then, Cisneros has penned dozens of books, essays, poems, articles, and collections. Her most recent novel, *Caramelo* (2002), was selected for the Today Show Book Club and as notable book of the year by *The New York Times Book Review,* among others. Of her desire to write about her family and community, Cisneros has said, "I feel like a cartographer; I'm determined to fill a literary void."

All Autobiography? Translated into more than a dozen languages and taught in schools and universities around the world, Cisneros's works have not only filled a literary void, but charted new territory for writers who work in a semi-autobiographical vein. Frequently asked whether her fictional stories are "true" and whether she is their "main character," Cisneros responds: *"Yes, but no. . . . . I write what I see . . . or what happened to me that I can't forget, but also what happened to others I love, or what strangers have told me happened to them. . . . I take all of this and cut and paste it together to make a story, because in real life a story doesn't have shape, and it's the writer that gives it a beginning, a middle, and an end."*

Straw into Gold:

The Metamorphosis Of The Everyday

SANDRA CISNEROS

BACKGROUND The term "essay" from the French *essai*, meaning "try," historically described an exploratory piece of writing that lacked finish. Eventually, the essay lost its original "unfinished" sense and became a polished form of writing. Here, Sandra Cisneros recounts part of her own growth from "unfinished" to accomplished writer.

When I was living in an artists' colony in the south of France, some fellow Latin-Americans who taught at the university in Aix-en-Provence[1] invited me to share a home-cooked meal with them. I had been living abroad almost a year then on an NEA[2] grant, subsisting mainly on French bread and lentils while in France so that my money could last longer. So when the invitation to dinner arrived, I accepted without hesitation. Especially since they had promised Mexican food.

1. **Aix-en-Provence** (eks än prō väns´) city in southeastern France.
2. **NEA** National Endowment for the Arts.

Comparing Autobiographies

Are the challenges Cisneros describes similar in any way to those Franklin set for himself? Explain.

Vocabulary

intuitively (in to͞o´ i tiv lē) *adv.* without having to be taught; instinctively

capable (kā´ pə bəl) *adj.* having the skills needed to do something

What I didn't realize when they made this invitation was that I was supposed to be involved in preparing this meal. I guess they assumed I knew how to cook Mexican food because I was Mexican. They wanted specifically tortillas, though I'd never made a tortilla in my life.

It's true I had witnessed my mother rolling the little armies of dough into perfect circles, but my mother's family is from Guanajuato,[3] *provinciales*,[4] country folk. They only know how to make flour tortillas. My father's family, on the other hand, is chilango,[5] from Mexico City. We ate corn tortillas but we didn't make them. Someone was sent to the corner tortilleria to buy some. I'd never seen anybody make corn tortillas. Ever.

Well, somehow my Latino hosts had gotten a hold of a packet of corn flour, and this is what they tossed my way with orders to produce tortillas. *Asi como sea.* Any ol' way, they said and went back to their cooking.

Why did I feel like the woman in the fairy tale who was locked in a room and ordered to spin straw into gold? I had the same sick feeling when I was required to write my critical essay for my MFA[6] exam—the only piece of noncreative writing necessary in order to get my graduate degree. How was I to start? There were rules involved here, unlike writing a poem or story, which I did intuitively. There was a step-by-step process needed and I had better know it. I felt as if making tortillas, or writing a critical paper for that matter, were tasks so impossible I wanted to break down into tears.

Somehow though, I managed to make those tortillas—crooked and burnt, but edible nonetheless. My hosts were absolutely ignorant when it came to Mexican food; they thought my tortillas were delicious. (I'm glad my mama wasn't there.) Thinking back and looking at that photograph documenting the three of us consuming those lopsided circles I am amazed. Just as I am amazed I could finish my MFA exam (lopsided and crooked, but finished all the same). Didn't think I could do it. But I did.

I've managed to do a lot of things in my life I didn't think I was capable of and which many others didn't think me capable of either.

Especially because I am a woman, a Latina, an only daughter in a family of six men. My father would've liked to

---

3. **Guanajuato** (gwä´ nä hwä´ tō) state in central Mexico.
4. **provinciales** (prō bēn sē ä´ lās) "country folk" (Spanish).
5. **chilango** (chē län´ gō) "city folk" (Spanish).
6. **MFA** Master of Fine Arts.

La molendera (The grinder), Diego Rivera (1886–1957), 1926, oil on canvas, Museo Nacional de Arte Moderno, Instituto Nacional de Bellas Artes, Mexico City, D.F., Mexico, ©Banco de Mexico Diego Rivera & Frida Kahlo Museums Trust, Av. Cinco de Mayo No. 2, Col. Centro, Del. Cuauhtemoc 06059, Mexico, D.F., reproduction authorized by the Instituto Nacional de Bellas Artes y Literatura.

◀ Critical Viewing

Judging from this painting by Mexican artist Diego Rivera, explain the challenge tortilla making would present to someone who had never done it before. **CONNECT**

have seen me married long ago. In our culture, men and women don't leave their father's house except by way of marriage. I crossed my father's threshold with nothing carrying me but my own two feet. A woman whom no one came for and no one chased away.

To make matters worse, I had left before any of my six brothers had ventured away from home. I had broken a terrible taboo. Somehow, looking back at photos of myself as a child, I wonder if I was aware of having begun already my own quiet war.

I like to think that somehow my family, my Mexicanness, my poverty all had something to do with shaping me into a writer. I like to think my parents were preparing me all along for my life as an artist even though they didn't know it. From my father I inherited a love of wandering. He was born in Mexico City but as a young man he traveled into the U.S. vagabonding. He eventually was drafted and thus became a citizen. Some of the stories he has told about his first months in the U.S. with little or no English surface in my stories in *The House on Mango Street* as well as others I have in mind to write in the future. From him I inherited a sappy heart. (He still cries when he watches the Mexican soaps—especially if they deal with children who have forsaken their parents.)

Vocabulary

taboo (ta bōō´) *n.* something forbidden within a particular society or culture

Comprehension

What Mexican dish was Cisneros asked to prepare?

My mother was born like me—in Chicago but of Mexican descent. It would be her tough, streetwise voice that would haunt all my stories and poems. An amazing woman who loves to draw and read books and can sing an opera. A smart cookie.

When I was a little girl we traveled to Mexico City so much I thought my grandparents' house on La Fortuna, Number 12, was home. It was the only constant in our nomadic ramblings from one Chicago flat to another. The house on Destiny Street, Number 12, in the colonia Tepeyac,[7] would be perhaps the only home I knew, and that **nostalgia** for a home would be a theme that would obsess me.

Vocabulary
nostalgia (nä stal´jə) *n.* a longing for something

My brothers also figured greatly in my art. Especially the oldest two; I grew up in their shadows. Henry, the second oldest and my favorite, appears often in poems I have written and in stories which at times only borrow his nickname, Kiki. He played a major role in my childhood. We were bunkbed mates. We were co-conspirators. We were pals. Until my oldest brother came back from studying in Mexico and left me odd-woman-out for always.

What would my teachers say if they knew I was a writer? Who would've guessed it? I wasn't a very bright student. I didn't much like school because we moved so much and I was always new and funny-looking. In my fifth-grade report card, I have nothing but an avalanche of C's and D's, but I don't remember being that stupid. I was good at art and I read plenty of library books and Kiki laughed at all my jokes. At home I was fine, but at school I never opened my mouth except when the teacher called on me, the first time I'd speak all day.

When I think how I see myself, it would have to be at age eleven. I know I'm thirty-two on the outside, but inside I'm eleven. I'm the girl in the picture with skinny arms and a crumpled shirt and crooked hair. I didn't like school because all they saw was the outside me. School was lots of rules and sitting with your hands folded and being very afraid all the time. I liked looking out the window and thinking. I liked staring at the girl across the way writing her name over and over again in red ink. I wondered why the boy with the dirty collar in front of me didn't have a mama who took better care of him.

I think my mama and papa did the best they could to keep us warm and clean and never hungry. We had birthday and graduation parties and things like that, but there was another hunger that had to be fed. There was a hunger I didn't even have a name for. Was this when I began writing?

Comparing Autobiographies
Why do you think Cisneros does not go into greater detail about the nature of her "hunger"?

7. **colonia Tepeyac** (cô lō´ nēä tā pā´ yäc) district of Mexico City.

In 1966 we moved into a house, a real one, our first real home. This meant we didn't have to change schools and be the new kids on the block every couple of years. We could make friends and not be afraid we'd have to say goodbye to them and start all over. My brothers and the flock of boys they brought home would become important characters eventually for my stories—Louie and his cousins, Meme Ortiz and his dog with two names, one in English and one in Spanish.

My mother **flourished** in her own home. She took books out of the library and taught herself to garden, producing flowers so envied we had to put a lock on the gate to keep out the midnight flower thieves. My mother is still gardening to this day.

This was the period in my life, that slippery age when you are both child and woman and neither, I was to record in *The House on Mango Street*. I was still shy. I was a girl who couldn't come out of her shell.

How was I to know I would be recording and documenting the women who sat their sadness on an elbow and stared out a window? It would be the city streets of Chicago I would later record, but from a child's eyes.

I've done all kinds of things I didn't think I could do since then. I've gone to a prestigious university, studied with famous writers, and taken away an MFA degree. I've taught poetry in the schools in Illinois and Texas. I've gotten an NEA grant and run away with it as far as my courage would take me. I've seen the bleached and bitter mountains of the Peloponnesus.[8] I've lived on a Greek island. I've been to Venice[9] twice. In Rapallo, I met Ilona once and forever and took her sad heart with me across the south of France and into Spain.

I've lived in Yugoslavia. I've been to the famous Nice[10] flower market behind the opera house. I've lived in a village in the pre-Alps[11] and witnessed the daily parade of promenaders.

I've moved since Europe to the strange and wonderful country of Texas, land of polaroid-blue skies and big bugs. I met a mayor with my last name. I met famous Chicana/o artists and writers and *politicos*.[12]

Texas is another chapter in my life. It brought with it the Dobie-Paisano Fellowship, a six-month residency on a 265-acre ranch. But most important Texas brought Mexico back to me.

Vocabulary
flourished (flur′ isht)
v. grew strong, healthy, and happy; prospered

Comprehension
What happened to change Cisneros's life in 1966?

---

8. **Peloponnesus** (pel′ ə pə nē′ səs) peninsula forming the southeastern part of the Greek mainland.
9. **Venice** (ven′ is) seaport in northern Italy.
10. **Nice** (nēs) seaport and resort in southeastern France.
11. **pre-Alps** foothills of the Alps, a mountain range in south-central Europe.
12. **politicos** (pō lē′ tē cōs) "politicians" (Spanish).

Sitting at my favorite people-watching spot, the snaky Woolworth's counter across the street from the Alamo,[13] I can't think of anything else I'd rather be than a writer. I've traveled and lectured from Cape Cod to San Francisco, to Spain, Yugoslavia, Greece, Mexico, France, Italy, and finally today to Seguin, Texas. Along the way there is straw for the taking. With a little imagination, it can be spun into gold.

13. **the Alamo** (al´ ə mō´) mission in San Antonio, Texas, that was the scene of a famous battle between Texans and Mexican troops in 1836.

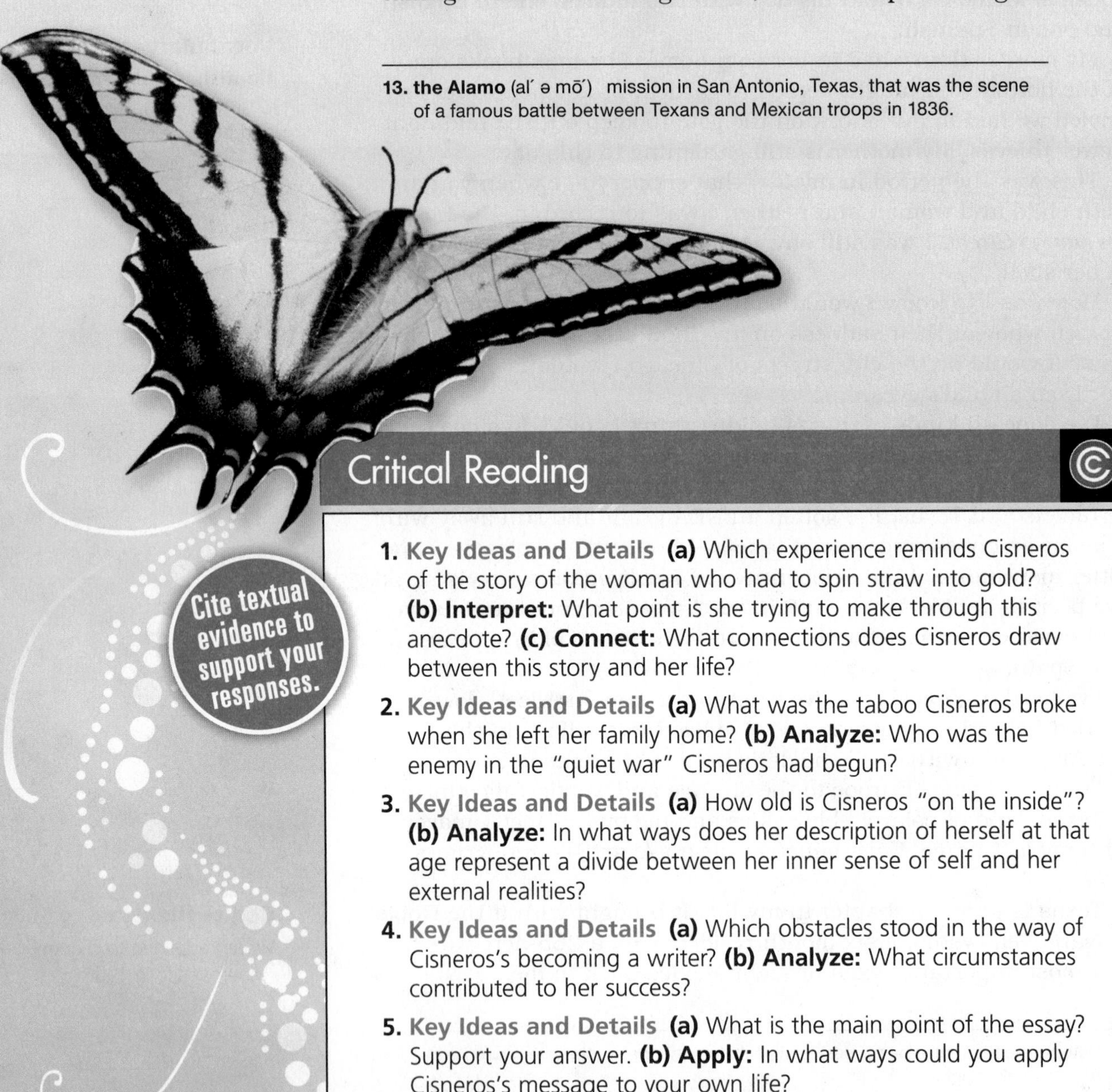

Critical Reading

Cite textual evidence to support your responses.

1. **Key Ideas and Details (a)** Which experience reminds Cisneros of the story of the woman who had to spin straw into gold? **(b) Interpret:** What point is she trying to make through this anecdote? **(c) Connect:** What connections does Cisneros draw between this story and her life?
2. **Key Ideas and Details (a)** What was the taboo Cisneros broke when she left her family home? **(b) Analyze:** Who was the enemy in the "quiet war" Cisneros had begun?
3. **Key Ideas and Details (a)** How old is Cisneros "on the inside"? **(b) Analyze:** In what ways does her description of herself at that age represent a divide between her inner sense of self and her external realities?
4. **Key Ideas and Details (a)** Which obstacles stood in the way of Cisneros's becoming a writer? **(b) Analyze:** What circumstances contributed to her success?
5. **Key Ideas and Details (a)** What is the main point of the essay? Support your answer. **(b) Apply:** In what ways could you apply Cisneros's message to your own life?

Close Reading Activities

from ***The Autobiography*** **•** ***Straw Into Gold***

Comparing Autobiography Past and Present

1. **Key Ideas and Details** **(a)** What facts about Franklin do you learn from reading his **autobiography** on pages 141–146? **(b)** What facts about Cisneros do you learn from reading her **autobiographical essay**?
2. **Key Ideas and Details** What information other than basic facts do you learn about each writer from these works? Cite details to support your answers.
3. **Key Ideas and Details** **(a)** What details does Cisneros include that you would find surprising in Franklin's writing? **(b)** Is this due to the time period, the writer's gender, the writer's cultural background, or another element? Explain.
4. **Integration of Knowledge and Ideas** **(a)** Judging from these two texts, how has American autobiography changed from the eighteenth to the twenty-first centuries? **(b)** In what ways is the genre the same? Support your answers with details from the texts.

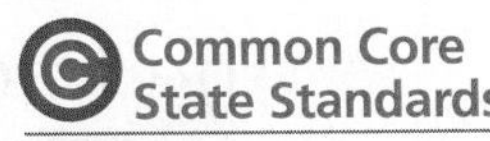

Common Core State Standards

Writing

9. Draw evidence from literary or informational texts to support analysis, reflection, and research.

10. Write routinely over exended time frames and shorter time frames for a range of tasks, purposes, and audiences.

Timed Writing

Explanatory Text: Essay

Even though Franklin and Cisneros faced different obstacles, the *theme* of success—how to achieve it, what it is, and what it means—is a key element in both of their autobiographical works.

Assignment: Write an **essay** in which you *compare and contrast* each writer's ideas about success. Cite evidence from the texts to support your ideas. Use these questions to focus your analysis. **[40 minutes]**

- What challenges does each writer face? Are the challenges self-imposed, or do they come from without?
- What conclusions about success does each writer draw?
- Do these autobiographical works reveal connections between American identity and ideas of achievement or success?

Organize your ideas logically. You might focus on the features of one selection and then the features of the other. Alternatively, you might focus on points of similarity and difference, moving back and forth between the two selections.

USE ACADEMIC VOCABULARY

As you write, use academic language, including the following words or their related forms:

categorize
examine
insight
perception

For more on academic language, see the vocabulary charts in the introductory unit in this book.

5-Minute Planner

Complete these steps before you begin to write:

1. Read the assignment carefully. List key words and phrases.
2. Scan the autobiographies for evidence that relates to the ideas in your list. **TIP** As you scan the texts, jot down quotations or details that you might use in your essay.
3. Create a rough outline for your essay.
4. Reread the prompt, and draft your essay.

William L. Andrews Introduces

The Interesting Narrative of THE LIFE OF OLAUDAH EQUIANO

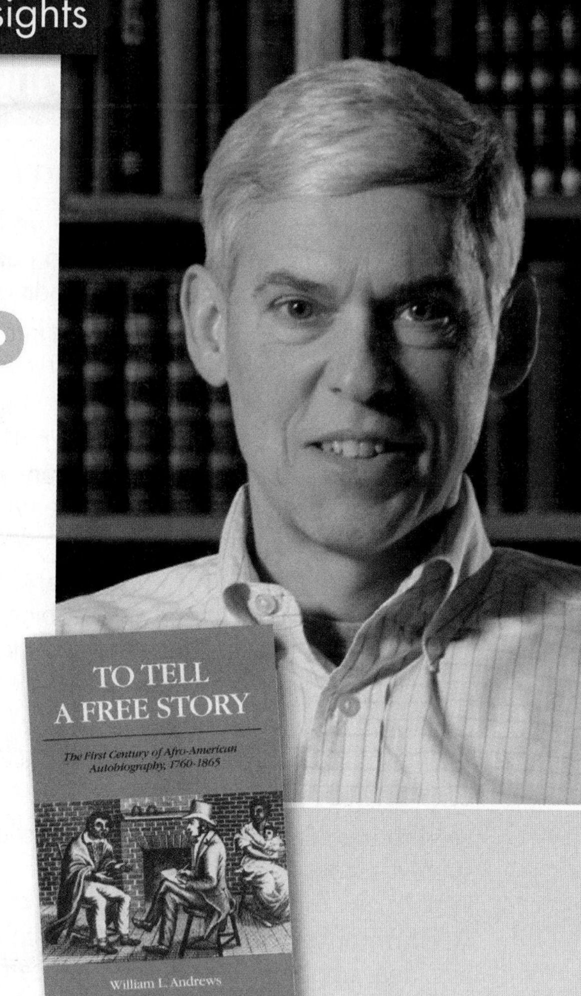

A Rare Firsthand Account of the Middle Passage One of the most astonishing facts about the Middle Passage—the Atlantic crossing of enslaved Africans to the Americas—is that, although millions of Africans endured it, and as many as one in eight died from it, history has preserved almost no firsthand accounts of it. *The Interesting Narrative of the Life of Olaudah Equiano* contains one of the rare detailed reports of the catastrophic journey that survives in English. Imagine how hard it would be for someone who had been through such a horrifying experience to write about it. Writing about past trauma almost certainly requires a person to relive it.

A Virtual Tour of the Slave Ship Equiano's account of the Middle Passage directly thrusts his reader, who Equiano expected would be either English or American, into a terrifying situation. Whatever Equiano's white readers thought about slavery, we can be pretty sure that they didn't want to think about how the Africans got to the Americas. By taking his reader on a virtual tour of the slave ship above and below decks, Equiano seems determined to confront his reader with the hideous—and generally hidden—truth about life aboard a slave ship.

The first stop is the ship's suffocating hold, where its human cargo was stored for most of the transatlantic voyage. Here we can see, hear, feel, and, especially, smell how "loathsome" a place it really was. Hell on earth would not be too strong a term to describe the hold of a slave ship.

Equiano doesn't confine us long in the miserable hold before taking us up into the fresh air, where we might hope for some relief from the horrors we've experienced. However, we soon find ourselves accompanied by dying Africans who've been brought up to the deck to perish of the illnesses they've contracted in the hold. Meanwhile, the European ship hands merely watch and wait, supremely indifferent to the suffering they witness.

About the Author

William L. Andrews is the series editor of North American Slave Narratives, Beginnings to 1920. His book *To Tell a Free Story* is a history of African American autobiography up to 1865.

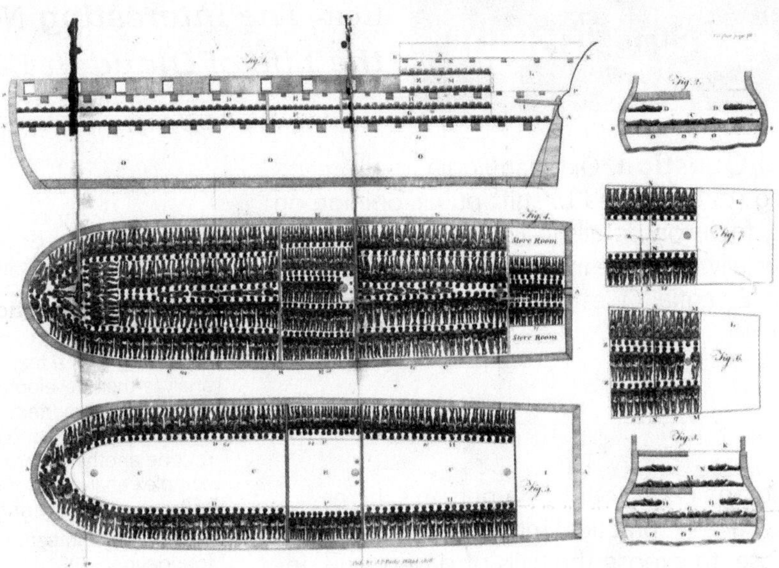

◀ **Critical Viewing** What do these design drawings of a slave ship tell you about slave traders' attitudes toward their captives? **ANALYZE**

Identifying With the Abused Africans The cruelty of the whites aboard the slave ship must have shocked Equiano's readers, particularly since, as whites themselves, they would likely have felt more in common with the Europeans on the ship than the Africans. But Equiano's storytelling gradually alienates his reader from the brutal whites while helping the reader to identify with the abused Africans.

Through the point of view of the ten-year-old African narrator, we inevitably feel the same shock and dread that the innocent African boy felt. Our sympathy with the narrator goes beyond pitying him as a victim, however. We follow as the curious African boy steps forward to take a peek through the ship's quadrant. As an unimagined world opens up to him, we realize that no matter how unjustly that new world may treat him in the future, Equiano the inquisitive, resilient traveler, will survive.

Thinking About the Commentary 

1. **Key Ideas and Details (a)** What was the Middle Passage? **(b) Speculate:** Why do you think firsthand accounts of it are so rare?

2. **Key Ideas and Details (a)** What does Equiano show readers? **(b) Infer:** What do you think was his purpose in conducting this "virtual tour"?

As You Read *The Interesting Narrative of the Life of Olaudah Equiano . . .*

3. **Key Ideas and Details** Identify details that justify Andrews's description of Equiano as "inquisitive" and "resilient."

Building Knowledge and Insight

from ***The Interesting Narrative of the Life of Olaudah Equiano***

Connecting to the Essential Question Olaudah Equiano wrote about a personal ordeal. In doing so, he helped to shift public opinion on the issue of slavery. As you read, focus on details in Equiano's writing that you think would have been especially effective in changing public opinion. This will help as you consider the Essential Question: **How does literature shape or reflect society?**

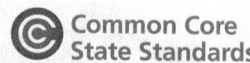

Common Core State Standards

Reading Informational Text
2. Determine two or more central ideas of a text and analyze their development over the course of the text, including how they interact and build on one another to provide a complex analysis; provide an objective summary of the text.
9. Analyze eighteenth-century foundational U.S. documents of historical and literary significance for their themes, purposes, and rhetorical features.

Close Reading Focus

Slave Narratives

A **slave narrative** is an autobiographical account of a person's life as a slave. Written when slavery was a legal practice, most slave narratives have an *implicit* persuasive purpose: to expose the evils of slavery and, in so doing, turn the public against it. Equiano's account speaks powerfully against the slave trade. His style includes descriptive language that appeals to readers' emotions. Notice, for example, how descriptive words such as "shrieks" and "groans" evoke readers' sympathy and outrage in this description of the slave ship that brought Equiano from Africa:

> *The shrieks of the women, and the groans of the dying, rendered the whole a scene of horror almost inconceivable.*

As you read, recognize details that both convey Equiano's perceptions and experiences and register as strong emotional appeals against the institution of slavery. Consider how each detail contributes to the implicit case Equiano is building against the entire institution of slavery.

Preparing to Read Complex Texts Some literature written long ago may be challenging to read. You can improve your comprehension by **summarizing to identify the main, or central, idea.** To do so, identify only the most important ideas and details in a passage. Include key information from the beginning, middle, and end. Then, gather that information into a brief statement. As you read, use a chart like the one shown to summarize.

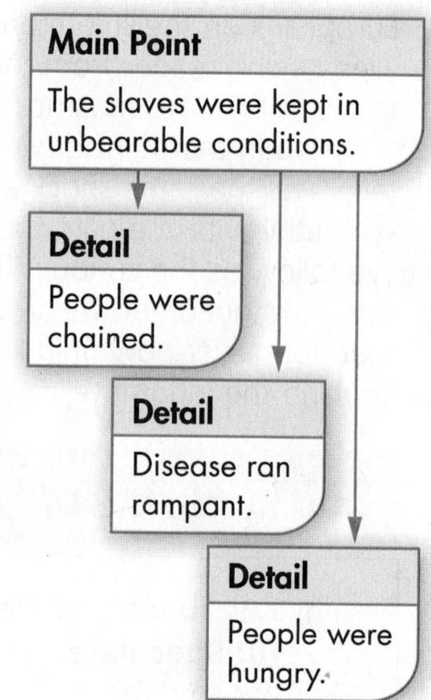

Main Point
The slaves were kept in unbearable conditions.

People were hungry.

Vocabulary

You will encounter the words listed here in text that follows. Copy the words in your notebook. Can you determine which two words have similar meanings?

People were chained.

Disease ran rampant.

copious	**inseparable**
wretched	**heightened**
dejected	**pacify**

Olaudah Equiano

(1745–1797)

Author of *The Interesting Narrative of the Life of Olaudah Equiano*

"I believe there are few events in my life, which have not happened to many: it is true the incidents of it are numerous; and, did I consider myself an European, I might say my sufferings were great: but when I compare my lot with that of most of my countrymen, I regard myself as a particular favorite of Heaven, and acknowledge the mercies of Providence in every occurrence of my life."

When it was first published in 1789, the autobiography of Olaudah Equiano (ō lä o͞o′dā ek′wē ä′ nō) created a sensation. A best seller on both sides of the Atlantic, it made society face the cruelties of slavery and contributed to the banning of the slave trade in both the United States and England.

Childhood Interrupted The son of a West African tribal elder, Olaudah Equiano might have followed in his father's footsteps had he not been sold into slavery. Instead, when he was eleven years old, he and his sister were kidnapped from their home and sold to British slave traders. Separated from his sister, Equiano—like millions of other Africans—was shipped across the Atlantic Ocean under horrendous conditions. He was taken first to the West Indies and later brought to Virginia, where he was purchased by a British captain and employed at sea.

The Struggle for Liberty Renamed Gustavus Vassa, Equiano was enslaved for nearly ten years. After managing his master's finances and making his own money in the process, he amassed enough to buy his own freedom. In later years, he settled in England and devoted himself to the abolition of slavery. In addition to writing his two-volume autobiography to publicize the plight of slaves, he lectured and rallied public sympathies against the cruelties of slavery. He was also involved in the founding of Sierra Leone, the famous British colony established on the west coast of Africa for freed British slaves.

from The Interesting Narrative of THE LIFE OF OLAUDAH EQUIANO

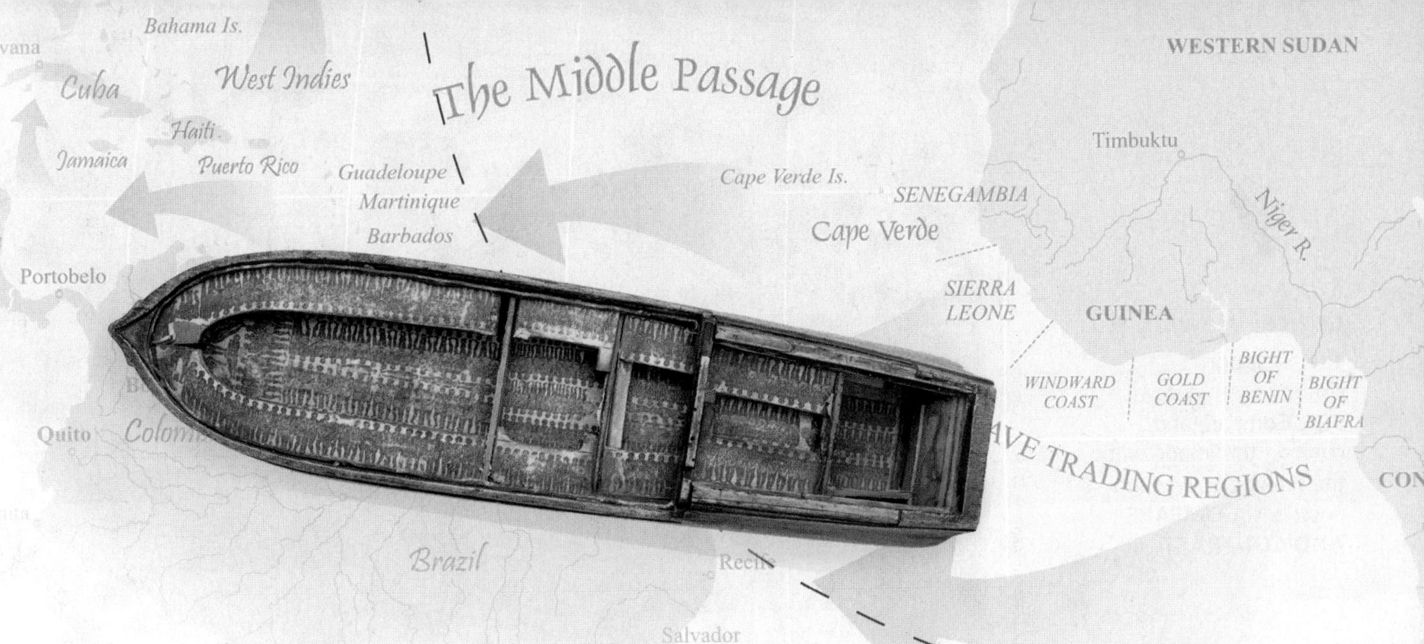

BACKGROUND In the first several chapters of his narrative, Olaudah Equiano describes how slave traders kidnapped him and his sister from their home in West Africa and transported them to the African coast. During this six- or seven-month journey, Equiano was separated from his sister and held at a series of way stations. After reaching the coast, Equiano was shipped with other slaves to North America. The following account describes this horrifying journey.

◄ ▲ Critical Viewing
In what ways do these images of slave ships help prove Equiano's point that the slavers were motivated by extreme greed? **VERIFY**

At last when the ship we were in, had got in all her cargo, they made ready with many fearful noises, and we were all put under deck, so that we could not see how they managed the vessel. But this disappointment was the least of my sorrow. The stench of the hold while we were on the coast was so intolerably loathsome, that it was dangerous to remain there for any time, and some of us had been permitted to stay on the deck for the fresh air; but now that the whole ship's cargo were confined together, it became absolutely pestilential. The closeness of the place, and the heat of the climate, added to the number in the ship, which was so crowded that each had scarcely room to turn himself, almost suffocated us.

Comprehension
According to Equiano, why does the hold become "pestilential"?

Critical Viewing ▶

The artist portrays conditions on a slave ship. Compare and contrast this image with the scene that Equiano describes. **COMPARE AND CONTRAST**

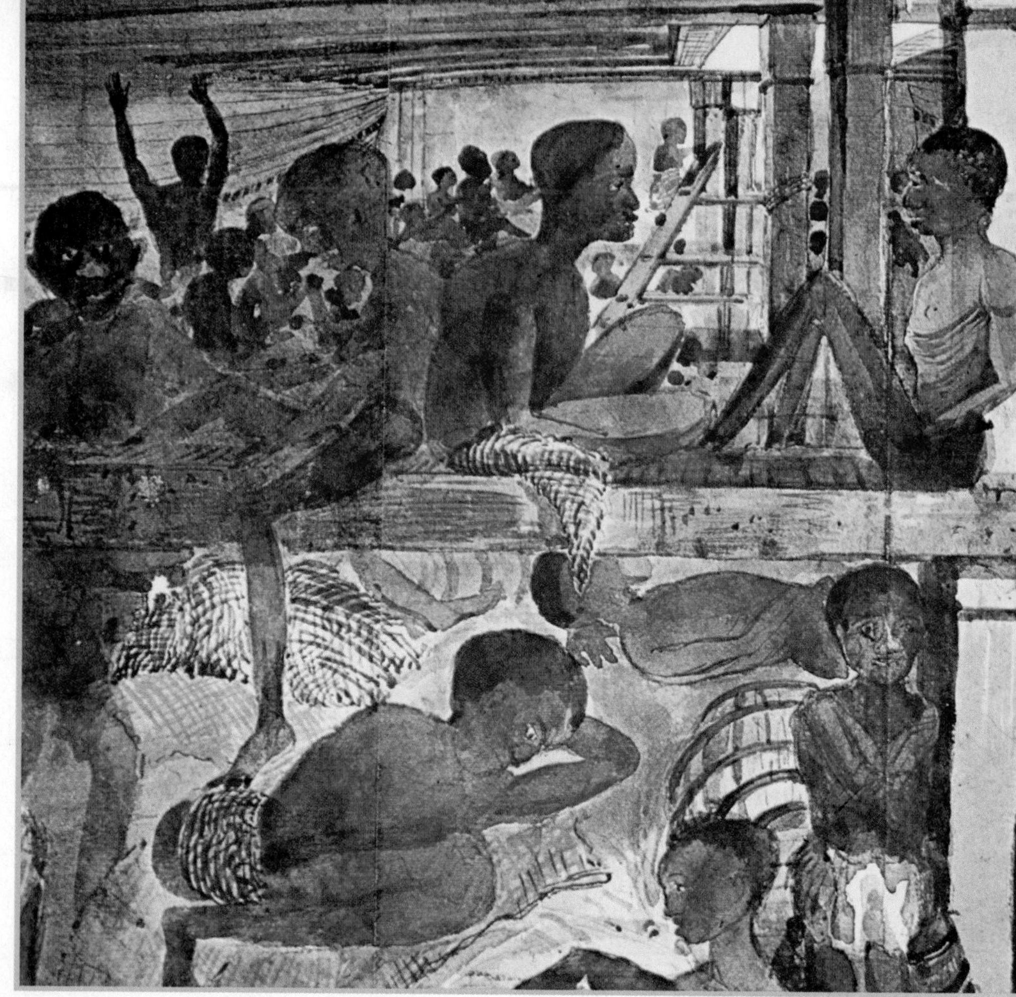

Slaves Below Deck (detail), Lt. Francis Meynell, National Maritime Museum, Greenwich

Vocabulary

copious (kō′ pē əs) *adj.* plentiful; abundant

wretched (rech′ id) *adj.* deeply distressed; miserable

William L. Andrews

Scholar's Insight

The wasteful greed of European slave traders makes them so callous that they don't even care about the profits they lose when slaves die in transit aboard their ships. The words *improvident avarice* help Equiano portray slavery as both inhuman and unprofitable.

This produced copious perspirations, so that the air soon became unfit for respiration, from a variety of loathsome smells, and brought on a sickness among the slaves, of which many died—thus falling victims to the improvident avarice, as I may call it, of their purchasers. This wretched situation was again aggravated by the galling of the chains, now become insupportable, and the filth of the necessary tubs, into which the children often fell, and were almost suffocated. The shrieks of the women, and the groans of the dying, rendered the whole a scene of horror almost inconceivable. Happily perhaps, for myself, I was soon reduced so low here that it was thought necessary to keep me almost always on deck; and from my extreme youth I was not put in fetters.[1] In this situation I expected every hour to share the fate of my companions, some of whom were almost daily brought upon deck at the point of death, which I began to hope would soon put an end to my miseries. Often did I think many of the inhabitants of the deep much more happy than myself.

1. **fetters** (fet′ ərz) *n.* chains.

I envied them the freedom they enjoyed, and as often wished I could change my condition for theirs. Every circumstance I met with, served only to render my state more painful, and heightened my apprehensions, and my opinion of the cruelty of the whites.

One day they had taken a number of fishes; and when they had killed and satisfied themselves with as many as they thought fit, to our astonishment who were on deck, rather than give any of them to us to eat, as we expected, they tossed the remaining fish into the sea again, although we begged and prayed for some as well as we could, but in vain; and some of my countrymen, being pressed by hunger, took an opportunity, when they thought no one saw them, of trying to get a little privately; but they were discovered, and the attempt procured them some very severe floggings. One day, when we had a smooth sea and moderate wind, two of my wearied countrymen who were chained together (I was near them at the time), preferring death to such a life of misery, somehow made through the nettings and jumped into the sea; immediately, another quite dejected fellow, who, on account of his illness, was suffered to be out of irons, also followed their example; and I believe many more would very soon have done the same, if they had not been prevented by the ship's crew, who were instantly alarmed. Those of us that were the most active, were in a moment put down under the deck; and there was such a noise and confusion amongst the people of the ship as I never heard before, to stop her, and get the boat out to go after the slaves. However, two of the wretches were drowned, but they got the other, and afterwards flogged him unmercifully, for thus attempting to prefer death to slavery. In this manner we continued to undergo more hardships than I can now relate, hardships which are inseparable from this accursed trade. Many a time we were near suffocation from the want of fresh air, which we were often without for whole days together. This, and the stench of the necessary tubs, carried off many.

William L. Andrews

Scholar's Insight

The inexplicable cruelty of the Europeans, contrasted with the pleading and praying of the Africans, is designed to challenge the prejudices of Equiano's readers. These readers would have expected the supposedly heathen Africans, not the Christian Europeans, to be indifferent to human need.

Vocabulary

dejected (dē jek′ tid) *adj.* in low spirits; downcast; depressed

inseparable (in sep′ ə rə bəl) *adj.* not able to be divided; linked

Comprehension

What do some slaves do to escape the misery of the Middle Passage?

The American EXPERIENCE

ECONOMICS

The Slave Trade

While some people came to the Western Hemisphere in search of a better life, others were brought against their will to be sold as slaves. The map shown here indicates the major slave trade routes.

The Atlantic crossing, known as the Middle Passage, was brutal. Africans were chained below decks in cramped, filthy spaces. Overcrowding, disease, and despair claimed many lives. Some Africans mutinied; others tried to starve themselves or jump overboard.

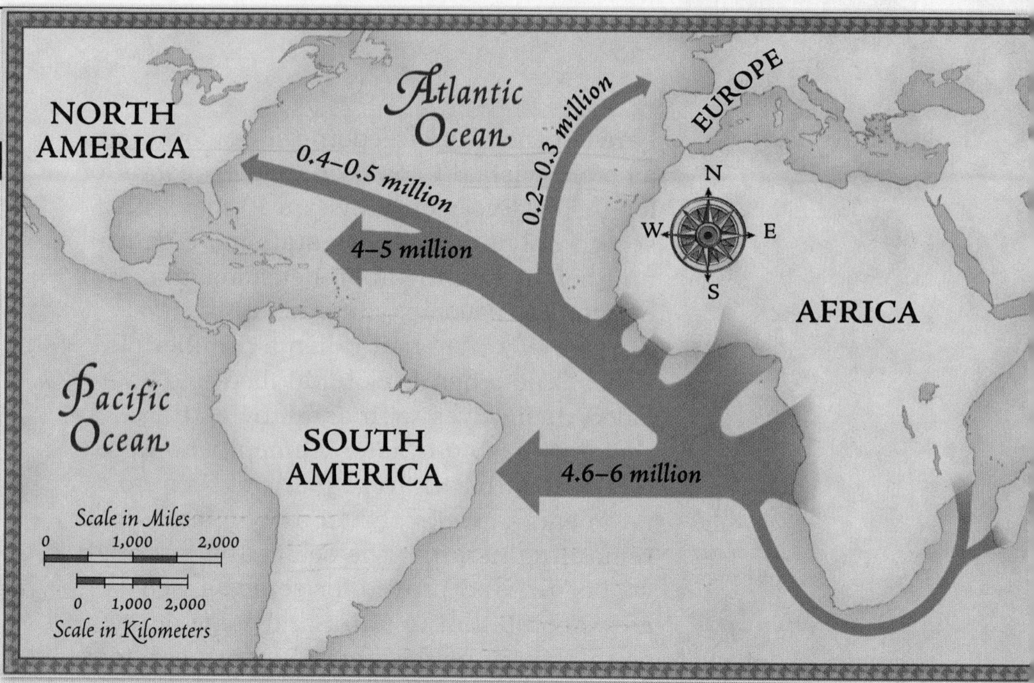

Atlantic Slave Trade Routes
1502–1870

Connect to the Literature

What seems to be Equiano's attitude toward the captives who preferred death to slavery?

During our passage, I first saw flying fishes, which surprised me very much; they used frequently to fly across the ship, and many of them fell on the deck. I also now first saw the use of the quadrant;[2] I had often with astonishment seen the mariners make observations with it, and I could not think what it meant. They at last took notice of my surprise; and one of them, willing to increase it, as well as to gratify my curiosity, made me one day look through it. The clouds appeared to me to be land, which disappeared as they passed along. This **heightened** my wonder; and I was now more persuaded than ever, that I was in another world, and that every thing about me was magic. At last, we came in sight of the island of Barbados, at which the whites on board gave a great shout, and made many signs of joy to us. We did not know what to think of this; but as the vessel drew nearer, we plainly saw the harbor, and other ships of different kinds and sizes, and we soon anchored amongst them, off Bridgetown.[3] Many merchants and planters now came on board, though it was in the evening. They put us in separate parcels,[4] and examined us attentively. They also made us jump, and pointed to the land, signifying we were to go there.

Vocabulary
heightened (hīt′ ənd) *v.* raised the level of

2. **quadrant** (kwä′ drənt) *n.* an instrument used by navigators to determine the position of a ship.
3. **Bridgetown** *n.* the capital of Barbados.
4. **parcels** (pär′ səlz) *n.* groups.

We thought by this, we should be eaten by these ugly men, as they appeared to us; and, when soon after we were all put down under the deck again, there was much dread and trembling among us, and nothing but bitter cries to be heard all the night from these apprehensions, insomuch, that at last the white people got some old slaves from the land to pacify us. They told us we were not to be eaten, but to work, and were soon to go on land, where we should see many of our country people. This report eased us much. And sure enough, soon after we were landed, there came to us Africans of all languages.

We were conducted immediately to the merchant's yard, where we were all pent up together, like so many sheep in a fold, without regard to sex or age. . . . We were not many days in the merchant's custody, before we were sold after their usual manner, which is this: On a signal given (as the beat of a drum), the buyers rush at once into the yard where the slaves are confined, and make choice of that parcel they like best. . . .

Vocabulary
pacify (pas′ ə fī′) *v.* to calm or soothe

William L. Andrews
Scholar's Insight
This reversal of the well-established European stereotype of the African as cannibal is one of Equiano's most effective ironies.

Critical Reading

Cite textual evidence to support your responses.

1. **Key Ideas and Details** **(a)** Why does Equiano blame the illness aboard the ship on the "improvident avarice" of the traders? **(b) Infer:** How do the white crewmen view their captives? **(c) Draw Conclusions:** What does the treatment of the slaves reveal about the captors' attitudes toward human life?
2. **Key Ideas and Details** **(a)** How does Equiano's age affect his experiences during the voyage? **(b) Infer:** How do you think he felt about his experience compared to the fate of other captives on the ship?
3. **Craft and Structure** How does Equiano show his great zest for life despite his assertion that he wants to die? Provide examples from the selection.
4. **Integration of Knowledge and Ideas** What do you think the public of Equiano's day learned about the "accursed trade" of slavery that it may not have known before reading this narrative? In your response, use at least two of these Essential Question vocabulary words: *awareness, compassion, inhumane, avarice.* ***[Connecting to the Essential Question: How does literature shape or reflect society?]***

Literary Analysis

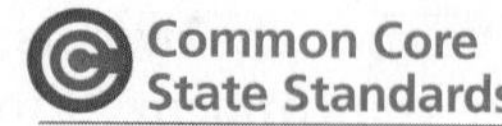

Common Core State Standards

Writing

7. Conduct short as well as more sustained research projects to answer a question or solve a problem; narrow or broaden the inquiry when appropriate; synthesize multiple sources on the subject, demonstrating understanding of the subject under investigation. *(p. 177)*

Language

4.d. Verify the preliminary definition of the meaning of a word or phrase. *(p. 177)*

1. **Key Ideas and Details** A summary of the first paragraph of the excerpt appears below. Revise this summary by deleting one piece of information that is not important enough to include, and adding one detail that is too important to omit.

   On the ship that took Equiano from Africa to the Americas, the slaves were kept in miserable conditions. It was hot and crowded. People were chained. Equiano wished he were a fish or another inhabitant of the deep.

2. **Key Ideas and Details** **(a)** In his **slave narrative,** which physical hardships does Equiano say the captives suffered during the Middle Passage? **(b)** What emotional torments does he describe? **(c)** In what ways do these descriptions serve as appeals to readers' emotions? Explain.
3. **Key Ideas and Details** **(a)** Cite two examples of the slave traders' cruelty to the slaves. **(b)** What effect do you think this information would have had on readers in Equiano's day?
4. **Key Ideas and Details** **(a)** Cite two examples that show the slave traders' concern for the slaves. **(b)** What seems to motivate this concern? **(c)** Would you say this is genuine concern or something else? Explain.
5. **Key Ideas and Details** **(a)** In **summarizing** the excerpt as a whole, what three central ideas would you include? **(b)** What is the single most essential message of Equiano's autobiographical account?
6. **Key Ideas and Details** **(a)** Summarize the events that occur after the ship reaches Bridgetown. **(b)** What is the central idea or essential message in that section of the narrative?
7. **Craft and Structure** **(a)** Using a chart like the one shown, identify three examples of *descriptive language* in the narrative. **(b)** Explain how each example serves as a strong emotional appeal to the reader.

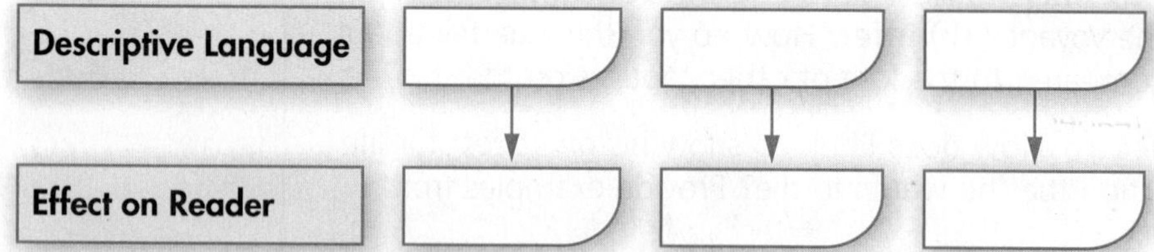

8. **Integration of Knowledge and Ideas** Based on your reading of this selection, do you think it is better for people who are victims of injustice to record and even publicize their experiences or to maintain their privacy? Make a claim and support it, using references to the text as you present your argument.

Vocabulary Acquisition and Use

Word Analysis: Latin Root *-ject-*

The word *dejected* contains the Latin root *-ject-*, which means "throw." Someone who is *dejected* is thrown down, or downcast, by disappointment or sorrow. Use context clues and knowledge of the root *-ject-* to explain the meaning of each italicized word below. Also make clear how the word's meaning reflects the meaning of the root.

1. I was disappointed when the publisher *rejected* my manuscript.
2. The nurse gave me an *injection* in my arm.
3. Tanya *projected* her voice across the room.
4. We did not know the answer, but we offered our *conjectures* in a brainstorming session.
5. Pablo and Luisa were conversing when Celia *interjected* some remarks.
6. The guard *ejected* the misbehaving children.

Vocabulary: Categorize Key Vocabulary

Review the list of vocabulary words on page 168. Then, analyze the relationship between the italicized word and the words that follow it in each item below. For each grouping, determine a logical category, such as *synonyms, antonyms and synonyms,* or another category that you can defend. Explain your reasoning. Consult a dictionary if necessary.

1. *copious,* sparse, meager
2. *wretched,* desolate, pitiful
3. *dejected,* cheerful, lively
4. *inseparable,* divisible, isolated
5. *heightened,* sensitive, keen
6. *pacify,* agitate, incite

Writing to Sources

Informative Text Write the information for a large **museum placard** that visitors might read at the beginning of a museum exhibit about Olaudah Equiano and the slave trade during the eighteenth century. Use details from Equiano's narrative, as well as facts and data about the North American slave trade that you gather through research in other sources.

Prewriting Conduct research at the library or online to find public documents that *verify and clarify facts* and observations Equiano presents in his narrative. Organize your findings, perhaps drawing a map to trace the slave trade routes or marking dates and other key details on a timeline. Identify any *specialized vocabulary* you may need to define in order to make the material clear to a general reader.

Drafting As you draft, *consider your audience and purpose.* Begin with strong information, such as a startling anecdote or fact, that will draw the public into the exhibit. Remember that your audience probably has little prior knowledge about your topic. Use a chart like the one shown to anticipate readers' questions.

Revising Review your work, making sure you have clarified all unfamiliar facts or data. Add explanations as needed.

Model: Assessing Audience Knowledge

Detail	Prior Knowledge?	Action
Location of West Africa	Probably not	Explain
Average duration of Middle Passage	No	Provide data

Primary Sources

Letter
Letter from the President's House

Letter
Letter from the New White House

Floor Plan
President's House

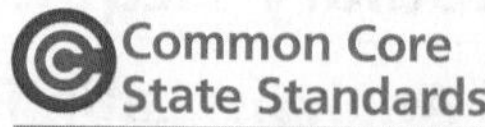

Reading Informational Text
9. Analyze seventeenth-, eighteenth-, and nineteenth-century foundational U.S. documents of historical and literary significance for their themes, purposes, and rhetorical features.

About the Text Forms

Today, you might send an IM or an e-mail to a distant friend, or simply make a phone call. In the past, though, people relied on **letters** to keep in touch. Private letters tend to be informal, spontaneous, and intended only for the reader to whom they are addressed. Most letters are not meant for publication. However, some letters, such as these by John and Abigail Adams, contain firsthand accounts of historical events and so are regarded as important primary source documents.

A **floor plan** is a diagram of one level of a building shown from an aerial point of view. It is usually drawn to scale and shows the relationships between rooms and other features. While this floor plan is an interesting primary source document in its own right, you may also use it to *verify and clarify* information the Adamses include in their letters.

Preparing to Read Complex Texts

A writer's circumstances and point of view are often referred to as his or her "perspective." **Analyzing a writer's perspective** in a primary source document can help you step more fully into the time period in which he or she lived. For example, these letters describe the White House as it is being built. As you read, picture the structure exactly as the writers describe it. Analyze the perspectives using questions such as these:

- Does the writer have positive or negative feelings about the subject?
- Are broader *philosophical, religious, ethical, social, or historical events* influencing his or her perspective?
- Does the perspective seem appropriate, given the circumstances?

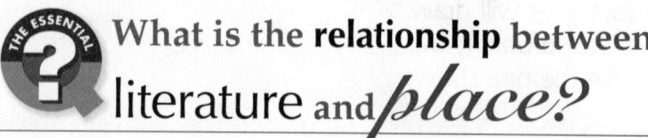

What is the **relationship** between literature and *place?*

Today, the White House is recognized as a symbol of power and democracy, but in 1800 it was just an unfinished structure. As you inspect these texts, notice details that express how the President and First Lady felt in such an environment as well as their hopes for the future.

Note-Taking Guide

Primary source documents are a rich source of information for researchers. As you read these documents, use a note-taking guide like the one shown to organize relevant and accurate information.

1 Type of Document (check one)

☐ Newspaper ☐ Advertisement ☐ Telegram ☐ Letter
☐ Floor Plan ☐ Diary or Journal ☐ E-mail ☐ Report

2 Date(s) of Document ______________________

3 Author of Document ______________________

4 Who is the intended audience for the work? ______________________

____

5 What is the main subject of this work? ______________________

____

6 List three observations or details in this document that you think are important:

a ______________________

b ______________________

c ______________________

7 Based on your answers to items 4–6, how would you describe the writer's perspective on the subject?

____

____

Analyzing a Writer's Perspective
A writer's perspective is often affected by his or her audience. As you study each document, ask yourself whether the relationship between writer and audience is intimate or formal, and how this relationship influences the work's content.

This guide was adapted from the **U.S. National Archives** document analysis worksheet.

Vocabulary

account (ə count´) *n.* a report or description (p. 181)

commissioners (kə mish´ ə nərz) *n.* government officials (p. 181)

inspection (in spek´ shən) *n.* examination (p. 181)

unabated (un ə bāt´ əd) *adj.* not lessened or reduced (p. 181)

interspersed (in´ tər spurst´) *v.* placed here and there (p. 182)

scale (skāl) *n.* the extent or size of something (p. 182)

establishment (ə stab´ lish mənt) *n.* a household or business (p. 182)

contract (kän´ trakt´) *n.* a written agreement (p. 183)

procure (prō kyoor´) *v.* bring about through some effort (p. 183)

recourse (rē´ kôrs´) *n.* access to a form of help or aid (p. 183)

THE STORY BEHIND THE DOCUMENTS

President John Adams

Abigail Adams

Benjamin Henry Latrobe

In 1790—two years after the ratification of the Constitution and one year after George Washington was elected the nation's first president—the U.S. Congress passed the Residence Act. This act established a permanent national capital in a 10-square-mile tract of land along the Potomac River. Washington himself selected the site for the President's House, later known as the White House, in a wooded area on the banks of the river. In 1792, a competition was held to choose an architect for the presidential residence. It was hoped that the design would reflect the nation's noble ideals. Irishman James Hoban (1762–1831) won the competition.

Hoban's design for the President's House was a basic rectangular structure. The classic simplicity of this design would allow later presidents to make alterations according to the needs of the day. Thomas Jefferson, for one, would ask architect **Benjamin Henry Latrobe (1764–1820)** to complete and extend Hoban's design. Latrobe transformed Hoban's boxy original into the grand house with columns and covered entrances that today is widely recognized as the home of the President of the United States.

Construction of the original President's House began on October 13, 1792. The house would not near completion until some eight years later, when the second President of the United States, **President John Adams (1735–1826)** and his wife **Abigail Smith Adams (1744–1818)** took up residence there in November, 1800. Although their stay in the house would be brief, the Adamses graciously made do with less-than-perfect living conditions. Many of the walls were still unplastered. A giant hole marked the place where the grand staircase would someday be, and the six out of thirty-six rooms that were habitable were poorly lit and drafty. To keep the house even mildly warm, President Adams paid for firewood out of his own pocket. Unwilling to have the president's laundry hung about the yard, Abigail had lines strung in the large, unfinished East Room.

These were trying times for the Adamses. John was on the brink of losing his reelection to Thomas Jefferson, and Abigail had been ill. The couple was no doubt bolstered by their close companionship, a relationship documented in their letters. Throughout their courtship and marriage, John and Abigail wrote more than one thousand letters to one another. Although their letters are often affectionate and even playful, they also reflect the couple's underlying awareness that they were key players in the unfolding of history.

Letter from the PRESIDENT'S HOUSE

John Adams

BACKGROUND As John Adams wrote this letter, the outcome of the election of 1801, in which Thomas Jefferson was his opponent, was still uncertain. Anxious for the company and consolation of his wife, Adams seems to sense that defeat is likely.

President's house,
Washington City,
Nov. 2. 1800

My Dearest Friend,

We arrived here last night, or rather yesterday, at one o Clock and here we dined and Slept. The Building is in a State to be habitable. And now we wish for your Company. The **Account** you give of the melancholly State of our dear Brother Mr. Cranch [1] and his family is really distressing and must severely afflict you. I most cordially Sympathize with you and them. I have seen only Mr. Marshall and Mr. Stoddert, General Wilkinson and the two **Commissioners** Mr. Scott and Mr. Thornton.[2] I shall say nothing of public affairs. I am very glad you consented to come on, for you would have been more anxious at Quincy[3] than here, and I, to all my other Solicitudines Mordaces as Horace[4] calls them i.e. "biting Cares" should have added a great deal on your Account. Besides it is fit and proper that you and I should retire together and not one before the other. Before I end my Letter I pray Heaven to bestow the best of Blessings on this House and all that shall hereafter inhabit it. May none but honest and wise Men ever rule under this roof. I shall not attempt a description of it. You will form the best Idea of it from **Inspection**. Mr. Brisler[5] is very anxious for the arrival of the Man and Women and I am much more so for that of the Ladies. I am with **unabated** Confidence and affection your

John Adams

Vocabulary

account (ə cσunt′) *n.* a report or description

commissioners (kə mish′ ə nərz) *n.* government officials

inspection (in spek′ shən) *n.* examination

unabated (un ə bā′ təd) *adj.* not lessened or reduced

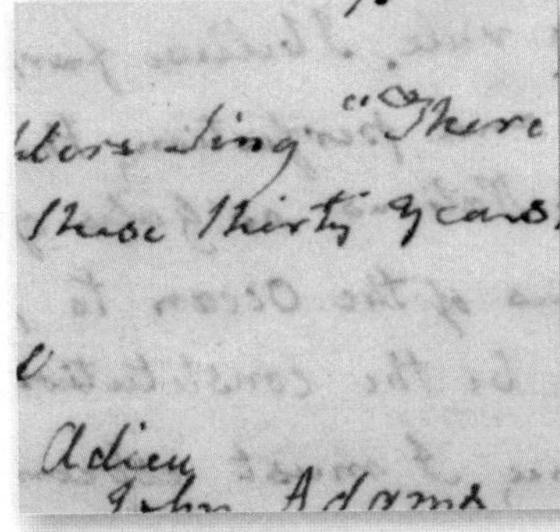

▲ sample of John Adams's handwriting

1. **Richard Cranch** President Adams's brother-in-law.
2. **Mr. Marshall. . . Mr. Thornton** Various officials and cabinet members.
3. **Quincy** the Adamses' hometown in Massachusetts.
4. **Horace** classical Roman poet.
5. **John Brisler** President Adams's servant.

Letter to Her Daughter from the NEW WHITE HOUSE

Abigail Adams

Washington,
21 November, 1800

My Dear Child:

I arrived here on Sunday last, and without meeting with any accident worth noticing, except losing ourselves when we left Baltimore and going eight or nine miles on the Frederick road, by which means we were obliged to go the other eight through woods, where we wandered two hours without finding a guide or the path. Fortunately, a straggling black came up with us, and we engaged him as a guide to extricate us out of our difficulty; but woods are all you see from Baltimore until you reach the *city*, which is only so in name. Here and there is a small cot, without a glass window, **interspersed** amongst the forests, through which you travel miles without seeing any human being. In the city there are buildings enough, if they were compact and finished, to accommodate Congress and those attached to it; but as they are, and scattered as they are, I see no great comfort for them. The river, which runs up to Alexandria,[1] is in full view of my window, and I see the vessels as they pass and repass. The house is upon a grand and superb **scale**, requiring about thirty servants to attend and keep the apartments in proper order, and perform the ordinary business of the house and stables; an **establishment** very well proportioned to the President's salary. The lighting of the apartments, from the kitchen to parlors and chambers, is a tax indeed; and the fires we are obliged to keep to secure us from daily agues is another very cheering comfort. To assist us in this great castle, and render less attendance necessary, bells are wholly wanting, not one single one being hung through the whole house, and promises are all you can obtain. This is so great an inconvenience, that I know not what to do, or how to do. The ladies from Georgetown[2] and in the city have many of them visited me. Yesterday I returned fifteen visits—but such a place as Georgetown appears—why, our Milton[3] is beautiful. But no comparisons—if they will put me up some bells and let me have wood enough to keep fires, I design to be pleased. I could content myself almost anywhere three

Vocabulary

interspersed (in′ tər spurst′) *v.* placed here and there

scale (skāl) *n.* the extent or size of something

establishment (ə stab′ lish mənt) *n.* a household or business

1. **Alexandria** city in northeastern Virginia.
2. **Georgetown** section of Washington, D.C.
3. **Milton** town in Massachusetts.

months; but, surrounded with forests, can you believe that wood is not to be had because people cannot be found to cut and cart it? Briesler entered into a **contract** with a man to supply him with wood. A small part, a few cords only, has he been able to get. Most of that was expended to dry the walls of the house before we came in, and yesterday the man told him it was impossible for him to **procure** it to be cut and carted. He has had **recourse** to coals; but we cannot get grates made and set. We have, indeed, come into a new country. You must keep all this to yourself, and, when asked how I like it, say that I write you the situation is beautiful, which is true. The house is made habitable, but there is not a single apartment finished, and all withinside, except the plastering, has been done since Briesler came. We have not the least fence, yard, or other convenience without and the great unfinished audience room I make a drying-room of, to hang up the clothes in. The principal stairs are not up, and will not be this winter. Six chambers are made comfortable; two are occupied by the President and Mr. Shaw; two lower rooms, one for a common parlor, and one for a levee room. Upstairs there is the oval room, which is designed for the drawing room, and has the crimson furniture in it. It is a very handsome room now; but, when completed, it will be beautiful. If the twelve years, in which this place has been considered as the future seat of government had been improved, as they would have been if in New England, very many of the present inconveniences would have been removed. It is a beautiful spot, capable of every improvement, and, the more I view it, the more I am delighted with it. Since I sat down to write, I have been called down to a servant from Mount Vernon,[4] with a billet[5] from Major Custis, and a haunch of venison, and a kind, congratulatory letter from Mrs. Lewis, upon my arrival in the city, with Mrs. Washington's love, inviting me to Mount Vernon, where, health permitting, I will go before I leave this place. Affectionally, your mother,

Abigail Adams

4. **Mount Vernon** home of George Washington, located in northern Virginia.
5. **billet** (bil′ it) *n.* brief letter.

Vocabulary

contract (kän′ trakt′) *n.* a written agreement

procure (prō kyoor′) *v.* to bring about through some effort

recourse (rē′ kôrs′) *n.* access to a form of help or aid

Primary Sources

Letters

In what ways does Mrs. Adams's statement about coming into a "new country" suggest a moment in time that is both historically and personally significant?

American stagecoach, mid-nineteenth century ▼

Floor Plan of the PRESIDENT'S HOUSE

Benjamin Henry Latrobe

Shown here is a floor plan of the President's House as it existed in 1803. Latrobe created this floor plan as a proposal for work that remained to be done on the house. Below is a detail showing all the rooms on the first floor; at right is the entire original drawing, including Latrobe's comments. Latrobe's original notations are blurred with age.

▼ Detail of Latrobe drawing

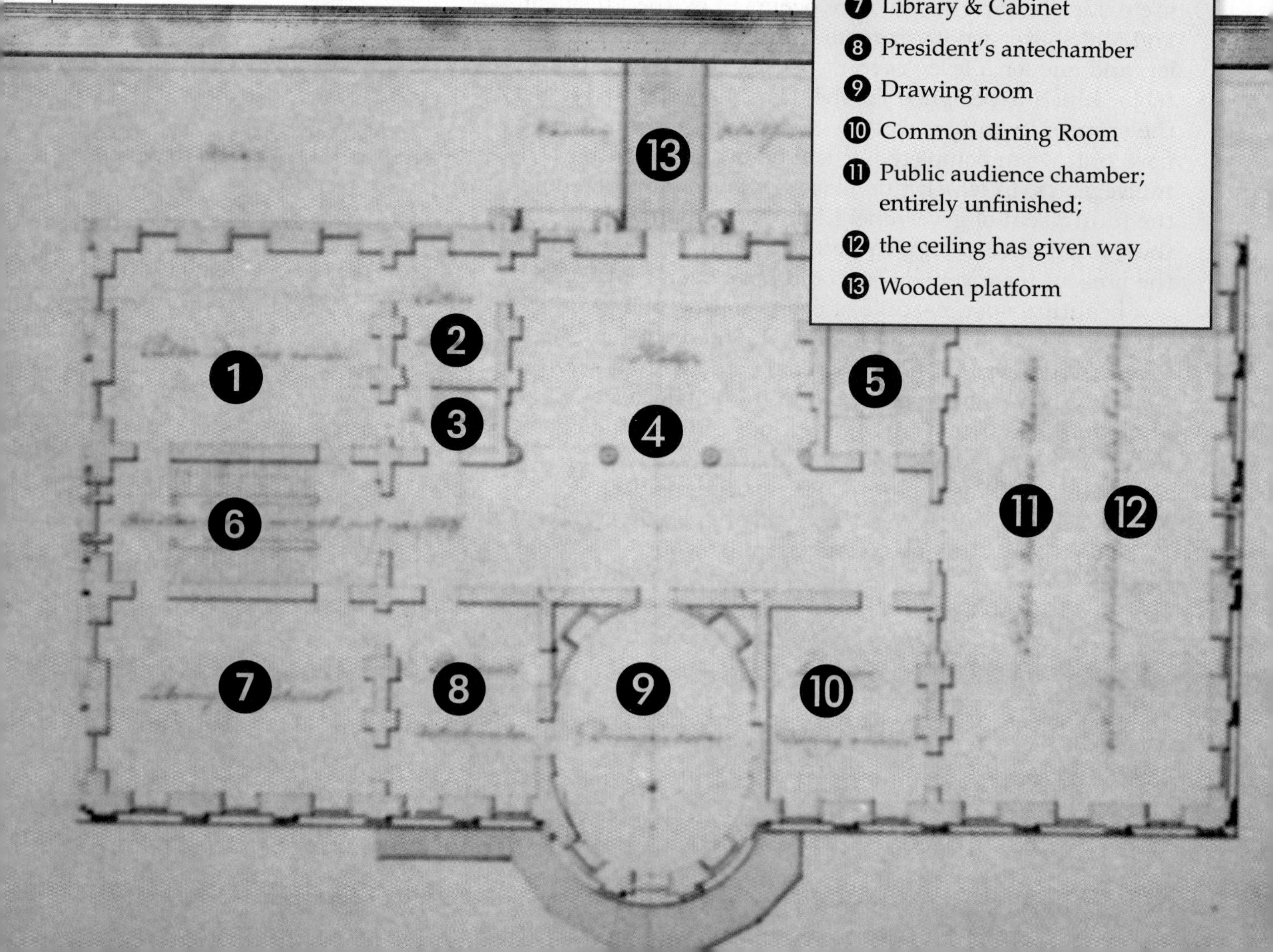

Latrobe's Notations

1. Public dining room
2. Porters Lodge
3. Private stairs
4. Hall
5. Staircase
6. This staircase is not yet put up
7. Library & Cabinet
8. President's antechamber
9. Drawing room
10. Common dining Room
11. Public audience chamber; entirely unfinished;
12. the ceiling has given way
13. Wooden platform

Latrobe's notes above and below the drawing contain observations about the President's House and its grounds. The drawing is signed and dated.

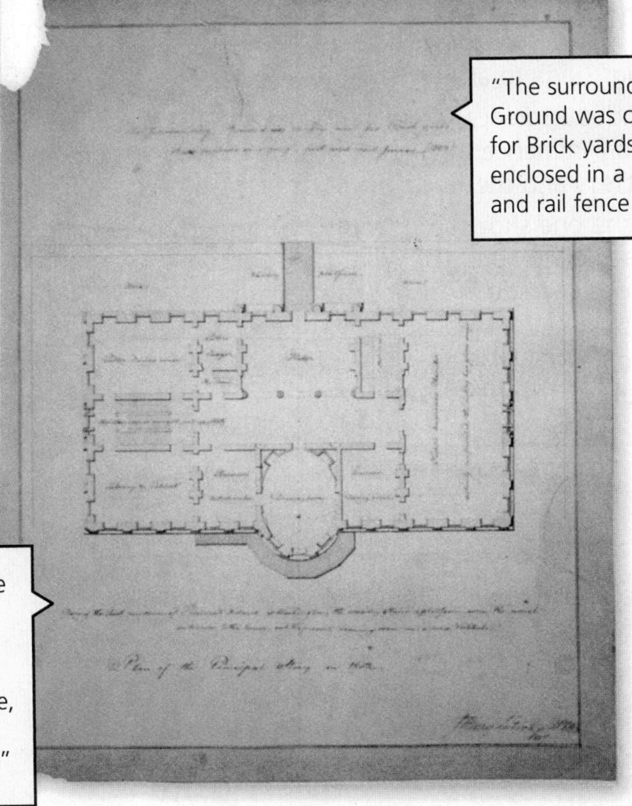

"The surrounding Ground was chiefly used for Brick yards, it was enclosed in a rough post and rail fence (1803)"

◀ Full image of Latrobe's original drawing of the White House floor plan

"During the short residence of President Adams at Washington, the wooden stairs & platform were the usual entrance to the house, and the present drawing room was a mere vestibule"

Critical Reading 

1. **Key Ideas and Details (a)** What is John Adams's stated wish for the house? **(b) Infer:** What does this wish tell you about the President's values and expectations?
2. **Key Ideas and Details (a)** What does Abigail Adams instruct her daughter to tell those who ask about the White House? **(b) Speculate:** Why might Mrs. Adams be greatly concerned about the opinions of others?
3. **Craft and Structure Analyze:** Which elements of the Latrobe floor plan show that the White House was designed to function as both a private residence and a public meeting place?
4. **Integration of Knowledge and Ideas (a)** Today, how are the White House and the city of Washington, D.C., different from the way they were when the Adamses lived there? **(b) Synthesize:** What do these differences tell you about changes in the United States since the eighteenth century?

Cite textual evidence to support your responses.

Letters • Floor Plan

Comparing Primary Sources

Refer to your Note-Taking Guide to answer these questions.

1. **(a)** Who is the intended audience for each document? **(b)** How did the audience probably influence the type and style of information presented in the **letters** and the **floor plan**?
2. **(a)** Use a chart like the one shown to identify one important detail or observation from each document. **(b)** What **perspective** toward the President's House does each detail or observation reflect?

Source	Detail or Observation	Attitude It Reveals
John Adams		
Abigail Adams		
Benjamin Latrobe		

3. Which details do the Adamses present in their letters that you can verify or clarify by reviewing the floor plan and its notes? Explain.

Vocabulary Acquisition and Use

Synonyms For each item, replace the italicized word with a synonym, or word of similar meaning, from the vocabulary list on page 179. Use each word once.

1. In a letter to her mother, Holly gave a(n) *description* of her train ride.
2. The scenery consisted of farmhouses with cows *scattered* in between.
3. The train station was a primitive *structure* with no indoor plumbing.
4. Holly felt *strong* pleasure at the idea of a week in the country.

Content-Area Vocabulary Answer each question. Explain your answers.

5. Do *commissioners* most likely work at a school or a state capitol?
6. How might restaurant owners prepare for an *inspection*?
7. Which group is more concerned with *scale*, city planners or dancers?
8. Would you use a *contract* to get a ride from a friend?
9. Should a successful campaign *procure* votes or voters?
10. Would you have *recourse* to the law if you had broken it?

Etymology Study The word *contract* comes from the Latin words *com*, which means "together," and *trahare*, which means "to draw." Explain how these meanings relate to both the noun and the verb form of *contract*. Then, use a dictionary to locate other words with the same Latin word parts.

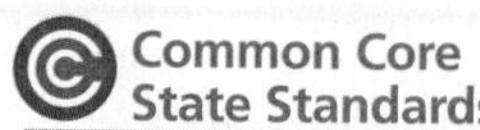

Writing

7. Conduct short as well as more sustained research projects to answer a question or solve a problem; narrow or broaden the inquiry when appropriate; synthesize multiple sources on the subject, demonstrating understanding of the subject under investigation.

8. Gather relevant information from multiple authoritative print and digital sources, using advanced searches effectively; assess the strengths and limitations of each source in terms of the task, purpose, and audience; integrate information into the text selectively to maintain the flow of ideas, avoiding plagiarism and overreliance on any one source and following a standard format for citation.

Language

6. Acquire and use accurately general academic and domain-specific words and phrases, sufficient for reading, writing, speaking, and listening at the college and career readiness level; demonstrate independence in gathering vocabulary knowledge when considering a word or phrase important to comprehension or expression.

Research Task

Topic: The Changing White House

Like America itself, the White House has come a long way since Abigail Adams hung her family's clothes to dry in "the great unfinished audience room." Starting with what you have learned from the Adams letters and the Latrobe floor plan, research the history of the building.

Assignment: Construct an annotated and illustrated timeline of the White House. Include each of these types of items:

- Architectural changes and additions
- Technological changes and additions
- Historical events that altered the building
- Influential presidents and first ladies
- Visual images—photos, drawings, diagrams

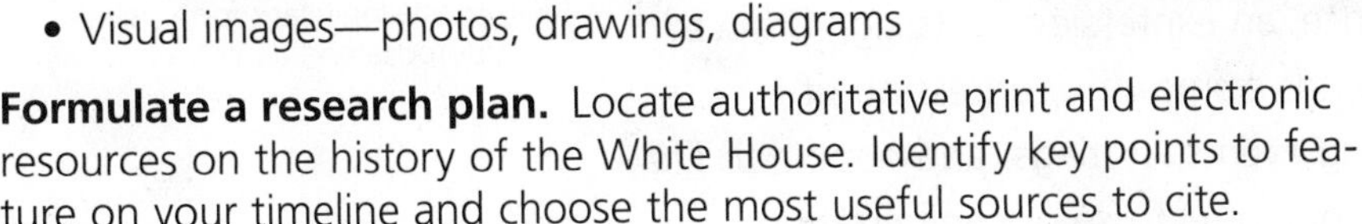

Formulate a research plan. Locate authoritative print and electronic resources on the history of the White House. Identify key points to feature on your timeline and choose the most useful sources to cite.

Narrow the inquiry. Focus your research by listing questions, such as the following: When was electrical wiring installed? Who changed the house the most? What do specific changes to the White House say about our changing culture? Work to answer your specific questions.

Gather sources. Assemble the information in a systematic way, taking accurate notes, and separating factual data from opinions. Make sure to follow appropriate principles of citation (see pp. R21–R23 for details on how to cite varied sources.)

Synthesize multiple sources. When you synthesize information, you assemble data from varied sources and organize it into a unified presentation. As you work, critique your process. You may need to discard some details or continue researching to find additional information.

Model: Synthesizing Information with a Flexible Timeline

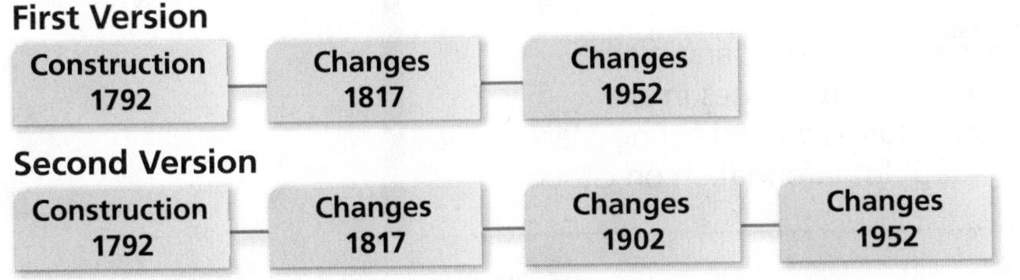

Present your ideas. Make sure your timeline contains all of the essential information. Then, add annotations, quotations, and visuals.

RESEARCH TIP

As you research, you may find it helpful to distinguish between interior and exterior changes to the White House.

Use a checklist like the one shown to evaluate your work.

Research Checklist

- ☐ Have I addressed all of my research questions?
- ☐ Have I clearly shown changes over time?
- ☐ Do my annotations support the basic facts?
- ☐ Do my visuals clearly illustrate historical changes?

Write a Narrative

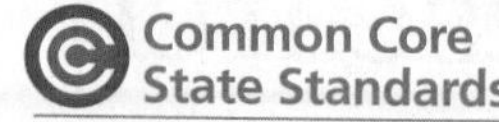

Writing

3. Write narratives to develop real or imagined experiences or events using effective techniques, well-chosen details, and well-structured event sequences.

3.a. Engage and orient the reader by setting out a problem, situation, or observation and its significance, establishing one or multiple point(s) of view, and introducing a narrator and/or characters; create a smooth progression of experiences or events.

5. Develop and strengthen writing as needed by planning, revising, editing, and rewriting, or trying a new approach, focusing on addressing what is most significant for a specific purpose and audience.

Autobiographical Narrative Writers are often told to write about what they know. This advice has produced some of the best stories in literature. While some are pure works of imagination, others are true tales about the writer's own life. Such nonfiction stories are called autobiographical narratives. Autobiographical narratives often use the same types of narrative techniques you are used to seeing in works of fiction. Follow the steps outlined in this workshop to write your own autobiographical narrative.

Assignment Write an autobiographical narrative about a special or memorable experience.

What to Include Your autobiographical narrative should include the following elements:

- You, the writer, as the main character and other developed characters
- A clear depiction of a problem or situation
- An insight about the experience, an expression of its significance
- A logical organization that builds a smooth progression of events
- Narrative techniques that bring events, settings, and people to life
- Error-free conventions, including correct use of capitalization

To preview the criteria on which your autobiographical narrative may be assessed, see the rubric on page 195.

Focus on Research

Research can enrich narrative texts in the following ways:

- by bringing more precise information to descriptions
- by adding accurate historical details about setting and time
- by broadening the scope of the narrative to go beyond the personal

Be sure to note all sources you use in your research, and credit appropriately. Refer to the Conducting Research pages in the Introductory Unit as well as the Citing Sources and Preparing Manuscript pages in the Resource section (R21–R23) for information on citation.

Prewriting and Planning

Choosing Your Topic

Choose an event from your life that is meaningful to you, interesting to readers, and not awkward or painful to share. It may be an experience that showed you a different aspect of yourself, solved a problem, or gave you a new perspective. To find a topic, use one of these strategies:

- **Interview yourself.** List ten questions you might ask a stranger about his or her life. Add follow-up questions that would help you get deeper answers. Then, use your list to interview yourself.

Model: Interviewing Yourself

Main Question: What was the most surprising thing that ever happened to you?
Follow-Ups: How did you react? Would you react the same way today? Why or why not?

- **Make memory notes.** Go through a photo album or scrapbook and jot down notes about the events recorded there. Add details about what you did and how you felt at those times. Talk to a relative who might remember those moments from a different perspective.

Narrowing Your Topic

Find the turning point. Once you have chosen a basic topic, sharpen your focus. Narrow in on a moment—something that became a turning point in your life. Use an event chart like the one shown to locate such a key event. In the chart shown, the writer has highlighted the turning point in yellow.

We moved to CA when Dad got a promotion.
Lost my friends; felt afraid of new situations
Mom gave us surfboards and lessons.
I began to love the ocean.
I decided to study oceanography in college.

Gathering Details

Engage and orient the reader. Your purpose in writing is to explore your thoughts and feelings about an experience and to share your insights with readers. Once you have chosen a topic, gather details that will help your readers understand your meaning. To do so, answer questions like the following:

- What *background information* do my readers need to have in order to understand my experience?
- What *descriptive details* will bring my experience to life for my readers?
- What do readers need to know about what this experience means to me?

Drafting

Shaping Your Writing

Order events. Most autobiographical narratives relate events in *chronological order*, or the sequence in which they happened. They also center on a *conflict*, or problem, that is somehow resolved. As the conflict develops, the tension should increase until it reaches the *climax,* or point of greatest intensity. After that, the tension should decrease as you move toward the ending, or *resolution*. Within this overall structure, consider using narrative techniques. For example, you may jump back in time with a *flashback* or forward in time with a *flash-forward*. Use a plot diagram like the one shown here to order your events.

Begin with a strong lead. Write a simple but intriguing sentence that catches the reader's curiosity. Notice how these lead sentences *foreshadow*, or drop hints about the story to follow:

- ***My grandfather walked in and suddenly the room was silent.***
- ***My dog probably wouldn't want me to tell you this story.***

Common Core State Standards

Writing

3.b. Use narrative techniques such as dialogue, pacing, description, reflection, and multiple plot lines, to develop experiences, events, and/or characters.

3.c. Use a variety of techniques to sequence events so that they build on one another to create a coherent whole and build toward a particular tone and outcome.

3.e. Provide a conclusion that follows from and reflects on what is experienced, observed, or resolved over the course of the narrative.

Climax

Show the conflict at its height.

Build the intensity of the conflict.

Rising Action

Falling Action

Start to end the conflict.

Exposition

Introduce the situation and conflict.

Resolution

Settle the conflict.

Provide a meaningful conclusion. End your narrative with a reflection, observation, or insight that confirms the importance of the experience.

Providing Elaboration

Use thought shots. As you write, follow these steps to expand your ideas:

- Scan your draft for uses of the word *I*. For each one, ask yourself how you reacted to what you described.
- For each reaction, draw a circle, or *thought shot*, in the margin. Inside the circle, jot details about what you saw, heard, felt, or thought.

Model: Using "Thought Shots"

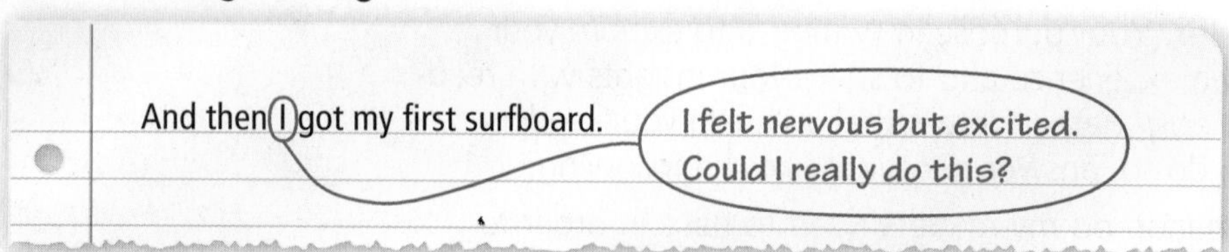

And then I got my first surfboard.
I felt nervous but excited.
Could I really do this?

Include dialogue. One of the best ways to make your writing more vivid is to include dialogue. People's words bring them alive as characters and help advance the story's conflict and climax.

Writers on Writing

Susan Power On Choosing the Right Words

Susan Power is the author of "Museum Indians" (p. 34).

"Finding the precise word can be tricky."
—Susan Power

Beginnings are always difficult for me. I'll have an idea for a story, or, as in this excerpt from a nonfiction essay, a memory from childhood, but I won't know where to start. Here I wanted to write about the body of water where I'd spent many happy hours—Lake Michigan. Should I begin with hard facts, its depth and circumference? No. After many drafts, I began with my mother's stories.

from "Chicago Waters," from *Roofwalker*

My mother used to say that by the time I was an old woman, Lake Michigan would be the size of a silver dollar. She pinched her index finger with her thumb to show me the pitiful dimensions.

"People will gather around the tiny lake, what's left of it, and cluck over a spoonful of water," she told me.

I learned to squint at the 1967 shoreline until I had carved away the structures and roads built on landfill and could imagine the lake and its city as my mother found them in 1942 when she arrived in Chicago. I say *the lake and its city* rather than *the city and its lake*, because my mother taught me another secret: the city of Chicago belongs to Lake Michigan.

> I mention that I'm looking at "the 1967 shoreline" so the reader will know the time frame, when I was a child.

But which of my mother's pronouncements to believe? That Chicago would swallow the Midwestern sea, smother it in concrete, or that the lake wielded enough strength to outpolitick even Mayor Richard Daley?

> I rely on the dictionary and thesaurus to help me find the precise, specific word. First I tried *sayings*, but that didn't exhibit my mother's strength as much as *pronouncements*.

> Wrestling with word choice again, I used *beat* initially but later selected *outpolitick*—more appropriate when describing a politician.

Mayor Daley, Sr. is gone now, but the lake remains, alternately tranquil and riled, changing colors like a mood ring. I guess we know who won.

When my mother watches the water from her lakeside apartment building, she still sucks in her breath. "You have to respect the power of that lake," she tells me. And I do now. I do.

Revising

Revising Your Overall Structure

Connect the past to the present. Your autobiographical narrative should show how the experience you are describing helped you become the person you are today. Make sure you have included details that help the reader understand what you learned or how you changed as a direct result of the experience you narrate. To strengthen those connections even more, follow these steps:

- Highlight passages in your draft that state or hint at how the experience affected you in a long-term way.
- ✔ Put a check mark beside those passages that could be clearer or explained better.
- Strengthen the checked passages by adding transitions to clarify connections, sensory details to make them more vivid, or a better explanation.

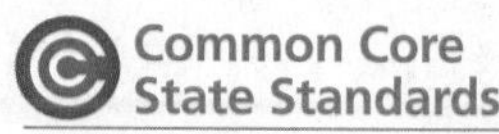

Writing
3.d. Use precise words and phrases, telling details, and sensory language to convey a vivid picture of the experiences, events, setting, and/or characters.

Language
3.a. Vary syntax for effect.

Model: Revising to Connect the Past to the Present

I had never had a lot of friends, and now I had none.
✓Moving away from the place I had always lived was hard. ^
I was lonely and bored. My mom told me it would get better,
but I thought I would never be happy again. ^
Eventually, my mom, a surfboard, and an open mind
would change all that, but—for now—I was miserable.

These additions clarify the writer's conflict and hint at the importance of the experience.

Revising Your Sentences

Use subordination to give characters depth. Carefully reread the sentences that introduce the people in your story. If they seem bland and uninformative, use subordinate clauses to expand simple sentences and provide more information about who your characters are, what they are like, and how they affect the events of your narrative.

Simple Sentence: Alison taught me how to surf.

Complex Sentence: Alison, my mother's best friend, saw me fumbling in the waves, so she took pity on me and taught me how to surf.

Simple Sentence: She helped me a lot.

Complex Sentence: By showing that someone cared, she helped me a lot.

Peer Review: Have a partner review your draft, identifying sentences that introduce or describe characters. Answer questions your partner poses about the characters' personalities, their behavior or statements, and their roles in your narrative. Use your answers to expand the sentences your partner identified.

Developing Your Style

Improving Word Choice

If your writing is not as clear, sharp, or fresh as it should be, a careful look at your **word choice** might help. The use of strong verbs, precise nouns, and specific adjectives will make your writing come alive. It will also help you avoid clichés and say exactly what you mean.

Dull, Vague Words	Lively, Precise Words
The dog ran through the woods.	The terrier bounded through the underbrush.
I fell into the rough water.	I tumbled into the churning foam.
People yelled at the mayor.	Irate citizens harangued the mayor.

Find It in Your Reading

Read the excerpt from *The Interesting Narrative of the Life of Olaudah Equiano* on page 171.

1. Identify at least one specific noun, active verb, vivid adjective, and effective adverb.
2. Make a list of the words and identify their parts of speech.
3. Choose one word you think is a particularly good choice. Write a sentence or two in which you explain your reasons.

Apply It to Your Writing

Review the draft of your autobiographical narrative. Follow these steps for each paragraph:

1. Underline any nouns or verbs that seem vague or weak. Note each use of the verb *to be* (*am, is, are, was,* and *were*). In the margin, jot down a few interesting alternates for each bland word, and then choose the best replacement.
2. Highlight phrases that are wordy, and think about what you are really trying to say. Then, find one or two punchy words that mean the same thing but express your idea more forcefully.
3. Check to see if there are any sentences with no underlining or highlighting. Take a look at these sentences again. Challenge yourself to find places where you could add vivid words to create a clearer picture or convey a stronger attitude.

Student Model: Branden Boyer-White, Palm Springs, CA

Discovering Poetry

My mother was a night owl. She worked nights as a nurse at the hospital. She liked it; the schedule suited her. The nights she was off, she maintained her nocturnal routine—active at night and asleep in the early part of the day.

One early morning, I went into the living room to find my mother reading a thick book called *Best Loved Poems to Read Again and Again.* My interest was piqued solely by the fact that the word *Poems* appeared in big, hot pink letters.

Branden uses concrete details to set the scene.

"Is it good?" I asked her.

"Yeah, " she answered. "There's one you'll really like." She began to thumb through the grainy white pages. She finally stopped and asked, "Ready?" I certainly was! I leaned forward.

"'Patty Poem,'" she read the title. *Who is Patty?* my mind buzzed. The poem began:

She never puts her toys away,
Just leaves them scattered where they lay, . . .

The poem was just three short stanzas. The final one came quickly:

When she grows and gathers poise,
I'll miss her harum-scarum noise,
And look in vain for scattered toys,
And I'll be sad.

Excerpts from the poem help readers understand the writer's emotional reaction to what she heard.

A terrible sorrow washed over me. Whoever Patty was, she was a dreadful, mean girl. Then, the bombshell.

"It's you, honey," my mother sentimentalized.

To my mother, the poem captured a parent's nostalgic love when her child grows up and leaves. To me, the "she" in the poem was a horror. It was my mama who would be sad. It was so terrible I burst into tears.

"What's wrong?" my mother asked.

"Oh Mama," I babbled. "I don't want to grow up ever!"

Dialogue makes the narrative more realistic and poignant.

She smiled. "Honey, it's okay. You're not growing up anytime soon. And when you do, I'll still love you, okay?"

"Okay," I hiccuped. My panic had subsided. But I could not stop thinking about that silly poem. After what seemed like a safe amount of time, I read the poem again and was mystified. It all fit so well together, like a puzzle. The language was simple, so simple I could plainly understand its meaning, yet it was still beautiful. I was now transfixed by the idea of poetry, words that had the power to make or break a person's world. . . .

I have since fallen in love with other poems, but "Patty Poem" remains my poem. It was my first, and it will be mine to the end, because it brought me my love for poetry. This is a great testimony to the poignancy of the art. After all, "Patty Poem" gave me my love for poetry not because it was the verse that lifted my spirits, but because it was the one that hurt me the most.

Branden clearly demonstrates the significance of this experience.

Editing and Proofreading

Language
2.b. Spell correctly.
Speaking and Listening
6. Adapt speech to a variety of contexts and tasks.

Check your narrative for errors in grammar, usage, punctuation, and spelling.

Focus on capitalization. Double-check the capitalization of names and places. Common nouns name general categories and are lowercase. Proper nouns name specific people, places, or things and are capitalized.

Focus on spelling. The one-syllable word *full* has two *l's*. However, the suffix *-ful* has only one *l*. The orthographic, or spelling, rule is as follows: Words with two or more syllables, like *cheerful* and *successful*, end with the one-*l* suffix. Check your spelling of any words that end with this suffix.

Spiral Review: Conventions Earlier in this unit, you learned about coordinating conjunctions (p. 31), correlative conjunctions (p. 94), and subordinating conjunctions (p. 155). Check your narrative to be sure you have used those conventions correctly.

Publishing, Presenting, and Reflecting

Consider one of the following ways to share your writing.

Deliver an oral presentation. Turn your narrative into an oral presentation and deliver it to the class. To do so, mark up a copy of your finished work, underlining words and phrases to emphasize. Also, identify places where you can add drama by changing your tone of voice or pausing. If you wish, choose photographs to display as a backdrop.

Create an illustrated class anthology. With classmates, combine several narratives in a binder. Include photographs or artwork that capture the mood or setting of each narrative.

Reflect on your writing. In a writer's journal, jot down your thoughts about the experience of writing an autobiographical narrative. Begin by answering these questions: *Which part of the process did you enjoy most and least? Did the work make you look at your life differently? If so, how?*

Rubric for Self-Assessment

Evaluate your reflective essay using the following criteria and rating scale.

Criteria	Rating Scale *not very* — *very*
Purpose/Focus: How clearly do you depict the conflict, its resolution, and your insight?	1 2 3 4
Organization: How clear and logical is the progression of events?	1 2 3 4
Development of Ideas/Elaboration: How well do you build on your ideas with details and reactions?	1 2 3 4
Language: How effectively do you vary sentences and add details to bring characters alive?	1 2 3 4
Conventions: How correct are your grammar and mechanics, especially your use of capitalization?	1 2 3 4

Speaking and Listening

Evaluate Persuasive Speech

Persuasive speech, also called *argument*, is the language people use when they want to convince us to think or act in a certain way. Advertisers use it to spread interest in their products; lawyers use it to establish the innocence of clients; and politicians use it to attract our support.

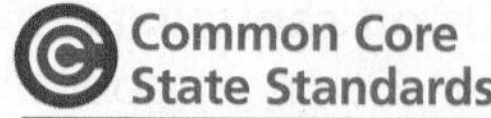

Speaking and Listening
3. Evaluate a speaker's point of view, reasoning, and use of evidence and rhetoric, assessing the stance, premises, links among ideas, word choice, points of emphasis, and tone used.

Types of Content and Positions

There are four main types of argumentation, or persuasive speech: propositions of fact, value, problem, and policy. All use language, reasoning, and proof differently in order to achieve specific ends.

Propositions	What They Establish	Examples
Fact	That something is so, or has happened	In fact, the defendant fled the scene.
Value	That something is good or bad, better or worse	Jazz is America's best music.
Problem	That something is a problem	The parking situation is a problem because...
Policy	That something should be done	Latin should be a required subject.

Types of Appeals and Evidence

Persuasive Appeals More than 2,000 years ago, Aristotle identified three types of appeals, or techniques, that can occur in any argument:

- **Ethos, or appeal to authority,** cites the speaker's credibility, or authority; for example, a noted scientist discussing issues in medical ethics.
- **Pathos, or appeal to sympathy,** engages the audience's emotions.
- **Logos, or appeal to logic,** applies reasoning and facts to build convincing arguments.

Some strategies may be more useful than others in certain situations. For example, a speaker asking for donations may use pathos more than logos.

Evidence Effective arguments employ strong evidence.

- **Facts:** data, statistical information, scientific observations
- **Anecdotes:** stories that illustrate a point
- **Expert Testimony:** statements by people who are widely viewed as authorities on a subject

When listening to persuasive speech, identify the speaker's position and evaluate the quality of the evidence he or she uses to support ideas.

Negative Persuasive Techniques

Logical fallacies are types of reasoning that may seem convincing but contain inherent flaws. Be alert to arguments built on such faulty reasoning.

- **Ad Hominem:** an attack on a person's character, not his or her ideas
- **False Causality:** an assumption that because A happened before B, A caused B
- **Red Herring:** something a speaker tosses into an argument to distract listeners from a more important issue or question
- **Overgeneralization:** a conclusion based on too little evidence
- **Bandwagon:** the assumption that something is right because it is popular

Propaganda, another negative technique, presents one-sided information and does not fairly represent an opposing view. It aims to win, but not to educate or invite discussion.

Activities: Evaluate Persuasive Speech

Comprehension and Collaboration For both activities, use an evaluation form like the one shown below.

A. Watch or listen to a persuasive speech. You may listen to a speech given by a classmate, find one in a movie, or locate one on the Internet.

B. With a partner, select two speeches that argue similar propositions but to different audiences. Critique their uses of appeals and evidence. Notice whether they use any negative persuasive techniques, and to what effect.

Evaluation Form for Persuasive Speech

Name of Speech ______________________________

Media Type ______________________________

Intended Audience ______________________________

Purpose ______________________________

Type of Proposition ______________________________

Types of Appeals:

Ethos: ☐ Example: ______________________________

Pathos: ☐ Example: ______________________________

Logos: ☐ Example: ______________________________

Specific Forms of Evidence: ______________________________

Special Uses of Language: ______________________________

Negative Persuasive Techniques: no ☐ yes ☐

Which Ones? ______________________________

Language Study

Using a Dictionary and Thesaurus

A **dictionary** is a reference work containing words and information about them. Dictionaries can help you find the exact meaning of a word or understand the different ways in which a word might be used. A print dictionary is arranged alphabetically. To use an **electronic dictionary,** you enter the word for which you are searching. **Specialized dictionaries** are those that define terms used in a particular field, such as law or business.

Common Core State Standards

Language

1.b. Resolve issues of complex or contested usage, consulting references as needed.

4.a. Use context as a clue to the meaning of a word or phrase.

4.c. Consult general and specialized reference materials, both print and digital, to find the pronunciation of a word or determine or clarify its precise meaning, its part of speech, its etymology, or its standard usage.

5.b. Analyze nuances in the meaning of words with similar denotations.

Sample Dictionary Entry

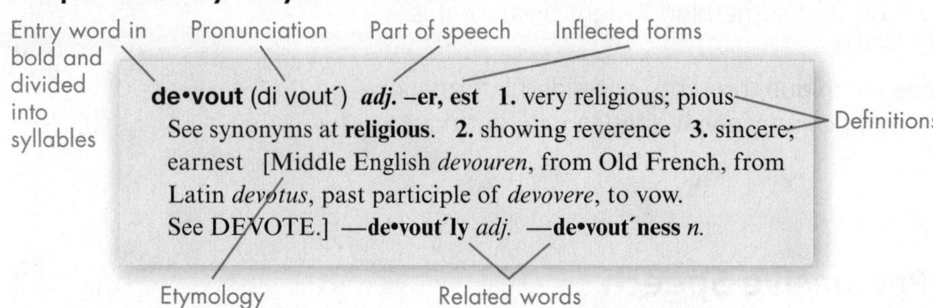

A **thesaurus** is a book of synonyms, or words with similar meanings. All of the synonyms listed for a word share denotation, or surface meaning, but their connotations, or shades of meaning, will probably vary. When writing, use a thesaurus to help vary your word choice. However, check your choices in a dictionary to make sure both their denotative and connotative meanings accurately represent your ideas.

Sample Thesaurus Entry

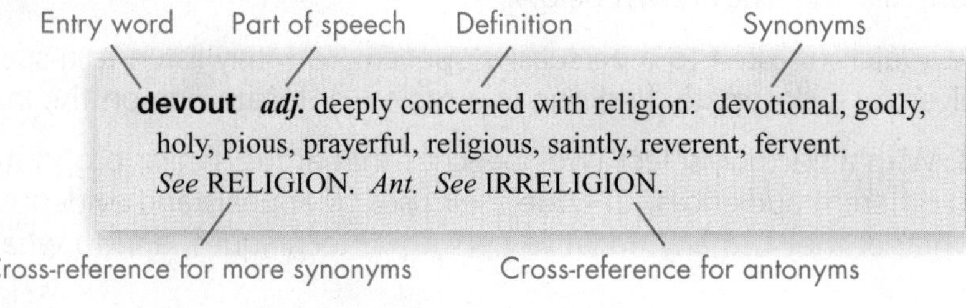

Practice

Directions: Refer to the sample entries to answer questions 1 and 2. Use a print or electronic dictionary and thesaurus to answer question 3.

1. Trace the path by which the word *devout* entered the English language. Explain whether its meaning has changed or stayed the same.
2. **(a)** Analyze the context to determine which synonym for *devout* best completes this sentence: *Their hushed voices showed the pilgrims'* ___ *attitude.* **(b)** Explain the nuances in word meanings that allowed you to make your choice.
3. Find two synonyms for *earnest* that have positive connotations and two that have negative connotations. For each synonym, write a sentence that reflects its connotative meaning.

Vocabulary Acquisition and Use: Context Clues

Context clues are words or phrases that help readers clarify the meanings of unfamiliar words in a text. Even fluent readers may not always know the dictionary definition of every word they read. By using context clues, readers make educated guesses, or inferences, about unfamiliar word meanings. This skill is often assessed on standardized tests.

Practice

This exercise is modeled after the Sentence Completion questions that appear in the Reading Comprehension section of the SAT.

Directions: Each of the following sentences is missing one or two words. Choose the word or set of words that best completes each sentence.

> **Test-Taking Tip**
> Immediately rule out any answer choices you *know* are wrong.

1. Many colonists felt that more ___?___ was necessary before war against Britain was declared.

A. disposition
B. provision
C. oblivion
D. deliberation
E. recompense

2. Revolutionaries such as Thomas Paine attempted to rouse the colonists' ___?___ desires for freedom and self-determination.

A. brittle
B. unconscious
C. tempered
D. omnipotent
E. vigilant

3. Paine and others argued that only a full split with Britain would create a peaceful world for ___?___.

A. posterity
B. tyranny
C. unanimity
D. diversity
E. urgency

4. With no sign of ___?___ for their complaints, colonial leaders declared independence from the crown.

A. privilege
B. vigilance
C. redress
D. peril
E. allegiance

5. Though the ___?___ of war would last for years, few would ___?___ the freedom it secured.

A. tempest . . . lament
B. assent . . . implore
C. tempest . . . relent
D. apparel . . . implore
E. privileges . . . redress

6. Nevertheless, the work of crafting a ___?___ for the new nation proved ___?___.

A. judgment . . . incorrigible
B. mediator . . . prudent
C. provision . . . copious
D. constitution . . . arduous
E. judgment. . . pensive

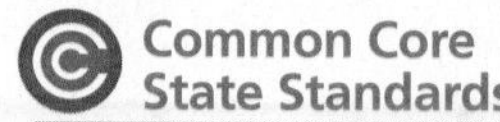

Writing

1. Write arguments to support claims in an analysis of substantive topics or texts, using valid reasoning and relevant and sufficient evidence.

4. Produce clear and coherent writing in which the development, organization, and style are appropriate to task, purpose, and audience.

5. Develop and strengthen writing as needed by planning, revising, editing, and rewriting, or trying a new approach, focusing on addressing what is most significant for a specific purpose and audience.

From Text to Understanding

You have studied each part of Unit 1 as a set of connected texts. In this workshop, you will have the chance to further explore the fundamental connections among these texts and to deepen your essential understanding of the literature and its social and historical context.

PART 1: Meeting of Cultures

Writing: Argumentative Essay When the European explorers first arrived in North America, they encountered indigenous, or native, peoples whose social organizations and cultures were highly diverse. The first encounters affected both individuals and entire cultures in many different ways and continue to resonate in our society.

Assignment: Review Part One selections, focusing especially on the Anchor Text, the excerpt from *The Iroquois Constitution*. Consider the idea of the early contact between cultures and the impact that one culture might have upon another. Develop and defend a claim on a topic related to this Unit Part, such as one of the following:

The early contact between Native Americans and Europeans set the tone for a long-standing cultural relationship of inequality.

or

The early contact between Native Americans and Europeans showed that Native American culture had much to offer the young American culture that was growing on the North American continent.

Structure ideas. As you reread selections, focus on two or three that best support your claim. Use these as your sources in writing your argument. Record details that you can use as you build your argument.

Consider the evidence. Make sure to include information on all relevant perspectives. Present counterarguments and make sure that you have good evidence to support your claim against them.

Structure your writing. Once you have established your claim and gathered supporting evidence, decide on the most effective structure for your essay. For example, you may decide that a cause-and-effect structure best presents your argument, or that focusing on one selection at a time is stronger. Whatever structure you choose, begin by clearly stating your claim.

Use academic words. As you write, use specific academic vocabulary. Thematic words such as *influence*, *values*, *perspective*, and *indigenous* can help develop your ideas.

Writing Checklist

☐ Sustained and logical structure

Explain why: ___________

☐ Multiple relevant perspectives

Example: ___________

☐ Clear claim

Identify: ___________

☐ Valid, reliable, and relevant sources

Examples: ___________

PART 2: The Puritan Influence

Research: The American Dream The Puritans came to North America in search of religious freedom and the opportunity to lead their lives according to their own principles. Though the term had not yet been coined, they were pursuing the original American Dream.

Review the selections and background materials in Part 2, focusing especially on the Anchor Text, the excerpt from *Sinners in the Hands of an Angry God*. Consider what an achievement it was for Edwards to have the freedom to think and preach as he did.

Assignment: With a small group, design and conduct a survey that will help you assess the ways in which the idea of the American Dream has changed over time. First, describe the "original" American Dream. Use this text set and research beyond it to formulate a statement of what the original European settlers wished to achieve. Then, ask questions about how that definition compares to today's idea of the American Dream. Follow the Survey Research Plan to prepare and conduct your survey. After you have gathered your data, present and discuss it. Include an analysis of your results and draw conclusions based on your analysis.

Survey Research Plan

- ☐ **Identify the objective.** What do you want to learn?
- ☐ **Choose a target group.** Select a population that is large enough to provide a meaningful set of information.
- ☐ **Choose a method.** Will you conduct your survey in-person or by phone? Will you use paper, e-mail, or a web page? If you want to use an electronic format, make sure your target group has access to the Internet.
- ☐ **Write questions.** Include both open- and close-ended questions. Open-ended questions cannot be answered "yes" or "no." Close-ended questions give a limited list of possible answers. Formats include multiple-choice, categorical, ordinal, numerical, and scale ranking.
- ☐ **Pretest.** Try your questionnaire out on a small group first. Fix any errors or problems.
- ☐ **Conduct the survey and analyze the data.** Extract the important information from the data you have collected and write a report that summarizes your findings.

PART 3: A Nation Is Born

Listening and Speaking Project: Press Conference
Review the selections in Part 3, paying special attention to the Anchor Texts, *The Declaration of Independence*, and the excerpt from Thomas Paine's first volume of *The American Crisis*. These foundational documents, carefully considered, reveal truths about the early American nation and the people that founded it. Based on your readings, what would you argue are the values that the founders held most dear?

Assignment: As a class, conduct a press conference in which the past speaks to the present about the importance of American ideals. Half of the students will play early American figures who have time-traveled to the present. The other half will be 21st century journalists. One person should serve as the organizer. Follow these steps to conduct the press conference:

Historical Figures: Choose the historical figure you will be playing. Review the text to find details about that person's attitude toward ideals such as freedom, the role of government, and citizenship. Take notes on the text to provide talking points at the press conference. Explain your ideas about freedom in a statement to be read at the conference.

Journalists: Write a list of 5–10 questions to ask each historical figure. Your questions should reflect an understanding of the content of each speaker's statement and the evidence used in support of their positions.

Organizer: Introduce each historical figure. After they read their statements, open the floor to questions from the journalists.

Test-Taking Practice

Reading Test: Social Science Passages

Social science reading passages are one type of reading selection found on standardized tests. The social sciences include disciplines such as anthropology, economics, geography, history, political science, and psychology. These passages tend to be tightly written and logically organized. They are informational, but they also express the author's point of view either directly or indirectly. Questions following these passages usually address elements such as structure, main idea, or author's purpose.

Common Core State Standards

RI.11-12.1, RI.11-12.4, RI.11-12.6; L.11-12.1, L.11-12.2, L.11-12.3, L.11-12.4.a
[For the full wording of the standards, see the standards chart in the front of your textbook.]

Practice

This exercise is modeled after the ACT Reading Test, Social Science section.

Directions: Read the following passage, taken from *The American Crisis* by Thomas Paine. Then, choose the best answer to each question.

I once felt all that kind of anger, which a man ought to feel, against the mean principles that are held by the Tories: a noted one, who kept a tavern at Amboy, was standing at this door, with as pretty a child in his hand, about eight or nine years old, as I ever saw, and after speaking his mind as freely as he thought was prudent, finished with this unfatherly expression, *"Well! give me peace in my day."* Not a man lives on the continent but fully believes that a separation must some time or other finally take place, and a generous parent should have said, *"If there must be trouble let it be in my day, that my child may have peace"*; and this single reflection, well applied, is sufficient to awaken every man to duty. . . .

I turn with the warm ardor of a friend to those who have nobly stood, and are yet determined to stand the matter out: I call not upon a few, but upon all; not on *this* state or *that* state, but on *every* state; up and help us; lay your shoulders to the wheel; better have too much force than too little, when so great an object is at stake. Let it be told to the future world, that in the depth of winter, when nothing but hope and virtue could survive, that the city and the country, alarmed at one common danger, came forth to meet and to repulse it. Say not that thousands are gone, turn out your tens of thousands; throw not the burden of the day upon Providence, but *"show your faith by your works,"* that God may bless you. It matters not where you live, or what rank of life you hold, the evil or the blessing will reach you all.

Strategy

Scan, then read.

- **First, scan the passage.** Take 20 seconds to skim the text. Look for a main topic and a few key terms.
- **Second, read the passage in full.** Ask yourself: *What is the author's purpose? What information is most important?*

1. The author includes the story about the father and child in order to:
   A. entertain his readers.
   B. shame his readers into action.
   C. stir up noble feelings in his readers.
   D. persuade his readers to do nothing.

2. The author uses the word *unfatherly* in reference to the tavern owner because he feels the man is:
   F. putting his child in danger.
   G. being selfish.
   H. behaving immaturely.
   J. ignoring his child.

3. What is the best summary of this passage?
   A. Let us band together to defend ourselves.
   B. We must labor to improve the lives of our children.
   C. The separation of one continent from another is inevitable.
   D. If we do good deeds, we will be blessed.

4. In the phrase "lay your shoulders to the wheel," what does the wheel symbolize?
   F. the Tories
   G. one's fellow soldiers
   H. Thomas Paine himself
   J. the task of war

5. When the author writes "I call not upon a few, but upon all; not on *this* state or *that* state, but on *every* state," which rhetorical device is he using?
   A. repetition
   B. restatement
   C. a rhetorical question
   D. an allusion

6. This passage LEAST resembles:
   F. a speech.
   G. an origin myth.
   H. a political document.
   J. a sermon.

7. According to the passage, what kind of anger does Paine believe is justified?
   A. anger at Tories
   B. anger at low-minded principles
   C. anger at bad parents
   D. anger at those who show little faith

8. Based on the passage, Paine's approach to his topic can best be characterized as:
   F. flexible and unbiased.
   G. contemplative and expansive.
   H. skeptical and tentative.
   J. passionate and uncompromising.

9. When the author urges his readers to "'*show your faith by your works,*' that God may bless you," he is using:
   A. a logical appeal.
   B. an emotional appeal.
   C. an ethical appeal.
   D. a political appeal.

10. Paine's overall purpose in this passage is to:
    F. urge Tories to defend themselves against abuse and ignorance.
    G. entertain soldiers who have recently returned from war.
    H. persuade colonists to fight in the cause of freedom.
    J. provide religious instruction to those who are troubled by anger.

Grammar and Writing: Editing in Context

In some tests you will encounter a passage with numbered sentences or parts of sentences, some of which contain errors in grammar, style, and usage. Your task is to choose the best version of the sentence from the choices offered. Some questions may also refer to the passage as a whole.

Practice

This exercise is modeled after the ACT English Test.

Strategy

Try out each answer. Mentally test each answer before you choose one of them. The one that sounds the best is probably correct.

Directions: For each underlined sentence or portion of a sentence, choose the best alternative. If an item asks a question about the underlined portion, or about the passage as a whole, choose the best answer to the question.

[1]

Most people know that the mature Franklin <u>was an important statesman but also</u> (1) an innovative scientist. What they may *not* know is that even the young Franklin lived a noteworthy life.

[2]

As one of seventeen children and the son of a poor soap maker, the odds were against young Ben. [2] As a small boy, he taught himself to read; and though he had only two years of formal education, he stored the knowledge away for future use. <u>When</u> (3) he was apprenticed at age twelve to his brother, a printer, Franklin took his education into his own hands. He spent his spare moments copying essays out of a discarded literary magazine, translating them into poetry, translating them back into prose, and then memorizing them. He knew that good writing <u>was rare, and could</u> (4) lead him to both fame and fortune.

[3]

Finally, at age sixteen, Franklin saw himself in print. Adopting the persona of a widow named Silence Dogood, he penned a series of essays that poked fun at various aspects of colonial <u>life that included</u> (5) education, etiquette, and fashion. All fourteen essays were printed in his brother's newspaper, the *New-England Courant*. In fact, readers were so charmed by Silence Dogood that the nonexistent widow received several written proposals of marriage. [6]

SAT® PREP ACT

1. **A.** NO CHANGE
   B. either an important statesman or
   C. both an important statesman and
   D. whether an important statesman nor

2. At this point, the writer is considering inserting the following: Nevertheless, he proved self-reliant from early on. Should the writer make this insertion?
   F. No, because the sentence directly expresses the essay's main idea.
   G. No, because the sentence distracts from the paragraph's main focus.
   H. Yes, because the sentence refers to Franklin's later writings.
   J. Yes, because the sentence provides a transition between two ideas.

3. What is the function of this word?
   A. It has no function and should be deleted.
   B. It is used as a subordinating conjunction.
   C. It is used as a correlative conjunction.
   D. It is used as a coordinating conjunction.

4. **F.** NO CHANGE
   G. is rare, but could
   H. was rare, as if it could
   J. though rare, could

5. **A.** NO CHANGE
   B. life and which included
   C. life, yet including
   D. life, including

6. Upon reviewing paragraph 3, the writer considers deleting the preceding sentence. If the writer were to delete the sentence, the paragraph would primarily lose:
   F. a humorous commentary that helps underscore Franklin's success.
   G. a colorful detail that shows how naive eighteenth-century readers were.
   H. a good-natured hint that Franklin's writing may have lacked clarity.
   J. nothing; it should be deleted.

7. This question asks about the passage as a whole.
   Review paragraphs 1 through 3. The text structure of this passage is:
   A. cause and effect.
   B. chronological order.
   C. problem and solution.
   D. comparison and contrast.

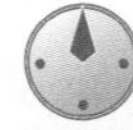

Timed Writing: Position Statement [25 minutes]

Consider these two commentaries on success:

I wished to live without committing any fault at any time; I would conquer all that either natural inclination, custom, or company might lead me into.

—Benjamin Franklin, *Autobiography*

I've managed to do a lot of things in my life I didn't think I was capable of and which many others didn't think me capable of either.

—Sandra Cisneros, "Straw Into Gold"

In your view, is success doing something perfectly, or doing something new and unexpected? Write an essay in which you develop your point of view on this issue. Support your position with reasoning and examples taken from your reading, studies, or experience.

Academic Vocabulary

An **issue** is a debatable idea. There is no right or wrong opinion. Choose the position for which you can offer the strongest support.

Constructed Response

Follow the instructions to complete the tasks below as required by your teacher. As you work on each task, incorporate both general academic vocabulary and literary terms you learned in this unit.

Common Core State Standards

RL.11-12.2, RL.11-12.9; RI.11-12.2, RI.11-12.4, RI.11-12.8, RI.11-12.9; W.11-12.9.a, W.11-12.9.b, W.11-12.10; SL.11-12.1.a, SL.11-12.1.b, SL.11-12.4, SL.11-12.5; L.11-12.2.b, L.11-12.3.a

[For the full wording of the standards, see the standards chart in the front of your textbook.]

Writing

Task 1: Literature [RL.11-12.2; W.11-12.9.a; L.11-12.3.a]

Analyze the Development of Theme

*Write an **essay** in which you determine two or more themes in a literary work from this unit.*

- Identify at least two themes in the work. Analyze how each theme is introduced and developed.
- Discuss similarities and differences among the insights each theme expresses.
- Note ways in which the themes interact and build on one another, and discuss how this interaction creates a complex account or deeper meaning.
- To ensure that readers understand your analysis, include an objective summary of each literary work.
- Vary your syntax by using coordinating or correlative conjunctions to combine short, choppy sentences.

Task 2: Informational Text [RI.11-12.2; W.11-12.9.b; L.11-12.3.a]

Analyze the Development of Central Ideas

*Write an **essay** in which you analyze the development of two or more central ideas in a work of literary nonfiction from this unit.*

- Clearly identify and explain at least two central ideas expressed in the work.
- Discuss how the author introduces and develops each idea.
- Identify specific details that shape and refine each central idea.
- Consider how the central ideas interact and build on one another to create a complex analysis of a topic.
- To ensure that readers understand your analysis, include an objective summary of the work.
- Vary your syntax by using subordinating conjunctions to combine sentences.

Task 3: Informational Text [RI.11-12.9; W.11-12.9.b; L.11-12.2.b]

Analyze Foundational U.S. Documents for Themes, Purposes, and Rhetorical Features

*Write an **essay** in which you analyze one of the foundational U.S. documents that appears in this unit, identifying its theme, purpose, and key rhetorical features.*

- Explain which document you chose and why you chose it.
- Identify the theme, or central idea, expressed in the document. If there are multiple themes or ideas, explain what they are and how they interact.
- Discuss the author's main purpose for writing as well as any secondary purposes.
- Analyze notable rhetorical features, considering how they help communicate the themes and advance the author's purpose for writing.
- Add to the strength of your writing and the clarity of your ideas by using strong verbs, precise nouns, and specific adjectives. Spell correctly.

Speaking and Listening

Task 4: Literature [RL.11-12.9; W.11-12.9.a; SL.11-12.5]

Demonstrate Knowledge of Foundational Works of American Literature

*With a partner, deliver an **oral presentation** in which you analyze how two or more literary works from this unit treat similar themes or topics.*

- Explain which works you will discuss and why you chose them.
- Identify the topics each work addresses and describe how each work presents characters, settings, and ideas.
- Explain the theme each work expresses and analyze the reasons for any similarities or differences.
- Incorporate digital media that enhances your presentation. For example, consider images, audio, graphics, or textual elements that help illustrate and clarify your ideas or those expressed in the works under discussion.

Task 5: Informational Texts [RI.11-12.8; SL.11-12.1.a, SL.11-12.1.b]

Evaluate the Reasoning in Seminal U.S. Texts

*Conduct a **panel discussion** in which you delineate and evaluate the reasoning in a seminal U.S. text from this unit.*

- Assign each member of the panel a specific role in the discussion.
- Each presenter should address at least one of the following elements: the text to be discussed and the reasons for the choice; the author's purpose for writing; the author's premises, reasoning, and arguments; the ways in which the author builds transitions and establishes meaningful connections among ideas; the types of evidence the author uses to support ideas and the quality of that evidence.
- As a group, ensure that the discussion is civil and democratic, or equally shared.
- As a group, ensure that each panel member has read the materials and completed any research needed to participate fully.

Task 6: Informational Text [RI.11-12.4; SL.11-12.4]

Determine the Meaning of Words and Phrases as They Are Used in a Text

*With a partner, conduct a **colloquy,** or formal discussion, about the meaning of a key term as it is used and refined in a text from this unit.*

- Explain which text you chose and why you chose it. Identify the key term you will discuss and explain why it is essential to the author's ideas.
- Discuss how the author introduces and defines the key term. Explain how the author then develops and refines that definition.
- Consider how the author incorporates connotations, or nuances, in the term's meaning as well as any figurative or technical meanings.
- As you speak, present information, findings, and evidence clearly so that listeners can follow your line of reasoning.
- Make sure your use of language, speaking style, and content are appropriate for a formal discussion.

What is the relationship between literature and place?

First Encounters When Europeans first arrived in North America, the native peoples had been living here for thousands of years. The first encounters between various groups not only affected the early settlements but continue to resonate in our society.

Assignment Choose at least two writers from this unit who describe an early encounter between two different groups. Write a **comparison-and-contrast essay** about the perspectives reflected in each text.

Titles for Extended Reading

In this unit, you have read a variety of precolonial and early American literature. Continue to read works related to this era on your own. Select books that you enjoy, but challenge yourself to explore new topics, new authors, and works offering varied perspectives or approaches. The titles suggested below will help you get started.

LITERATURE

Native American Literature
Pearson Prentice Hall

Anthology The literature of Native Americans is a rich collection of myths, legends, poems, histories, personal experiences, dreams, and songs. More than fifty such selections are collected in this anthology.

The Complete Writings
Phillis Wheatley

EXEMPLAR TEXT 

Poetry Wheatley was the first enslaved African and the third woman in the United States to publish a book of poems. Wheatley's verse, including the poem "On Being Brought From Africa to America," explores religion, death, and the struggles of enslaved Africans.

[Wheatley's poem, "To His Excellency, General Washington," appears on p. 124 of this book. Build knowledge by reading Wheatley's complete works.]

INFORMATIONAL TEXTS

Historical Texts

Chronicle of the Narváez Expedition
Alvar Núñez Cabeza de Vaca;
translated by Fanny Bandelier

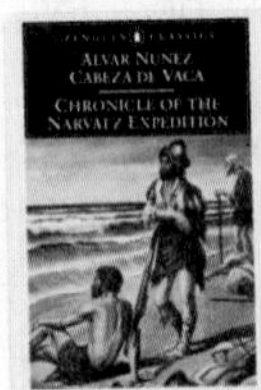

Narrative Account In the early sixteenth century, Spain sent the Narváez expedition to what is now the southern United States to claim vast territories for the Spanish empire. Cabeza de Vaca, who went on this journey, describes the fate of the nine-year expedition.

[An excerpt from de Vaca's account appears on p. 48 of this book. Build knowledge by reading the full text.]

Letters From an American Farmer
J. Hector St. John de Crevecoeur;
translated by Gerald Bevan

Epistolary Letters Early America's physical and cultural landscape is captured in these impassioned and engaging epistles, or essays fashioned as letters.

The Interesting Narrative of The Life of Olaudah Equiano
Olaudah Equiano

Autobiography Written in 1789, Equiano's autobiography is one of the most widely read "slave narratives." The author describes his childhood in eighteenth-century Guinea, Africa, where he was first enslaved. He also recounts his later experiences as a freedman and abolitionist in the United States.

[An excerpt from Equiano's autobiography appears on p. 170 of this book. Build knowledge by reading the full text.]

Democracy in America
Alexis de Tocqueville;
translated by Gerald Bevan

EXEMPLAR TEXT 

Political Science In 1831, Alexis de Tocqueville, a twenty-five year old Frenchman, traveled throughout the United States for nine months. He had been sent by his government to observe American prisons, but he wound up taking notes about all aspects of American society. The resulting two-volume work, published in 1835 and 1840, is now a classic of political science.

Contemporary Scholarship

American Colonies: The Settling of North America
Alan Taylor

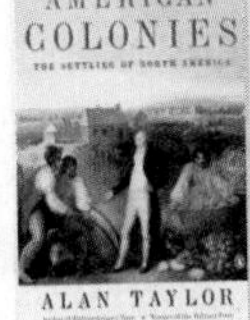

History The settling of the American colonies was not a simple story but an interweaving of many narratives. Pulitzer Prize–winning author Alan Taylor does justice to this multifaceted history by explaining the roles that different peoples played in this process.

1776
David McCullough

EXEMPLAR TEXT 

History Esteemed historian McCullough describes the turbulence and promise of this most important year in American history.

Preparing to Read Complex Texts

Reading for College and Career In both college and the workplace, readers must analyze texts independently, draw connections among works that offer varied perspectives, and develop their own ideas and informed opinions. The questions shown below, and others that you generate on your own, will help you more effectively read and analyze complex college-level texts.

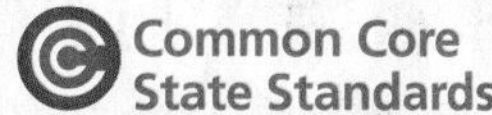

Reading Literature/Informational Text
10. By the end of grade 11, read and comprehend literature, including stories, dramas, and poems, and literary nonfiction, in the grades 11-CCR text complexity band proficiently, with scaffolding as needed at the high end of the range.

When reading analytically, ask yourself...

- What idea, experience, or story seems to have compelled the author to write? Has the author presented that idea, experience, or story in a way that I, too, find compelling?
- How might the author's era, social status, belief system, or personal experiences have affected the point of view he or she expresses in the text?
- How do my circumstances affect what I understand and feel about this text?
- What key idea does the author state explicitly? What key idea does he or she suggest or imply? Which details in the text help me to perceive implied ideas?
- Do I find multiple layers of meaning in the text? If so, what relationships do I see among these layers of meaning?
- Do I find the text believable and convincing? Why or why not?

Key Ideas and Details

- What patterns of organization or sequences do I find in the text? Do these patterns help me understand the ideas better? If so, how?
- What do I notice about the author's style, including his or her diction, uses of imagery and figurative language, and syntax?
- Do I like the author's style? Is the author's style memorable? Why or why not?
- What emotional attitude does the author express toward the topic, the story, or the characters? Does this attitude seem appropriate? Why or why not?
- What emotional attitude does the author express toward me, the reader? Does this attitude seem appropriate? Why, or why not?
- What do I notice about the author's voice—his or her personality on the page? Do I like this voice? Does it make me want to read on?

Craft and Structure

- Is the work fresh and original? How do I know?
- Do I agree with the author's ideas entirely or are there elements I find unconvincing?
- Do I disagree with the author's ideas entirely, or are there elements I can accept as true?
- How does this text relate to others I have read on the same or a similar topic?
- Based on my knowledge of American literature, history, and culture, does this work seem distinctly American? Why, or why not?

Integration of Ideas

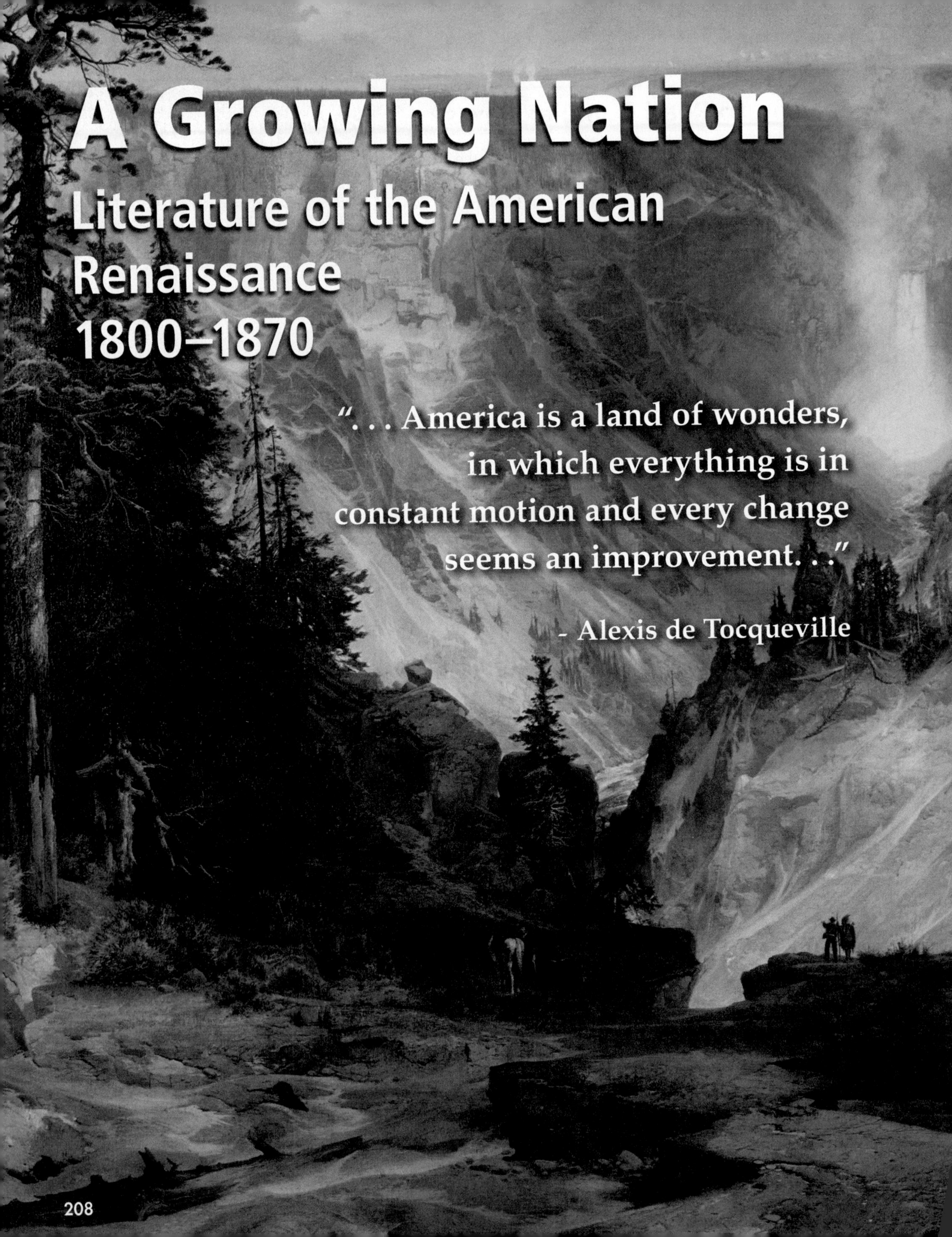

A Growing Nation

Literature of the American Renaissance 1800–1870

"... America is a land of wonders, in which everything is in constant motion and every change seems an improvement..."

- Alexis de Tocqueville

Unit 2

PART 1 TEXT SET

FIRESIDE AND CAMPFIRE

PART 2 TEXT SET

SHADOWS OF THE IMAGINATION

PART 3 TEXT SET

THE HUMAN SPIRIT AND THE NATURAL WORLD

PART 4 TEXT SET

AMERICAN MASTERS

CLOSE READING TOOL

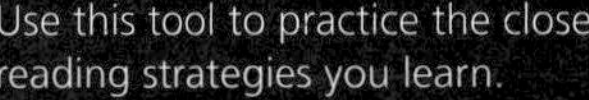

Use this tool to practice the close reading strategies you learn.

ONLINE WRITER'S NOTEBOOK

Easily capture notes and complete assignments online.

STUDENT eTEXT

Bring learning to life with audio, video, and interactive tools.

- Find all Digital Resources at **pearsonrealize.com**.

Snapshot of the Period

1804 Filter Coffee Pot

In 1831, the French writer Alexis de Tocqueville (shown at right) traveled to America to write about its prisons. He was so enchanted by the bustling spirit of the young nation that he chose to write instead about American culture. While he celebrated the country's energy, Tocqueville also noted that America "has produced very few writers of distinction … [The literature of England] still darts its rays into the forests of the New World." By 1870, industrialism, population growth, economic changes, and the Civil War had all aged the nation's spirit. Along with that maturity came a new generation of writers who were the equal of any Europe had produced. Irving, Poe, Emerson, Thoreau, Dickinson, Whitman, and others shone their distinctly American light into and far beyond the "forests of the New World."

Hawthorne

Whitman

Poe

Emerson

Dickinson

Thoreau

As you read the selections in this unit, you will be asked to think about them in view of three key questions:

What is the **relationship** between literature and *place?*

How does **literature** shape or reflect *society?*

What makes **American** literature *American?*

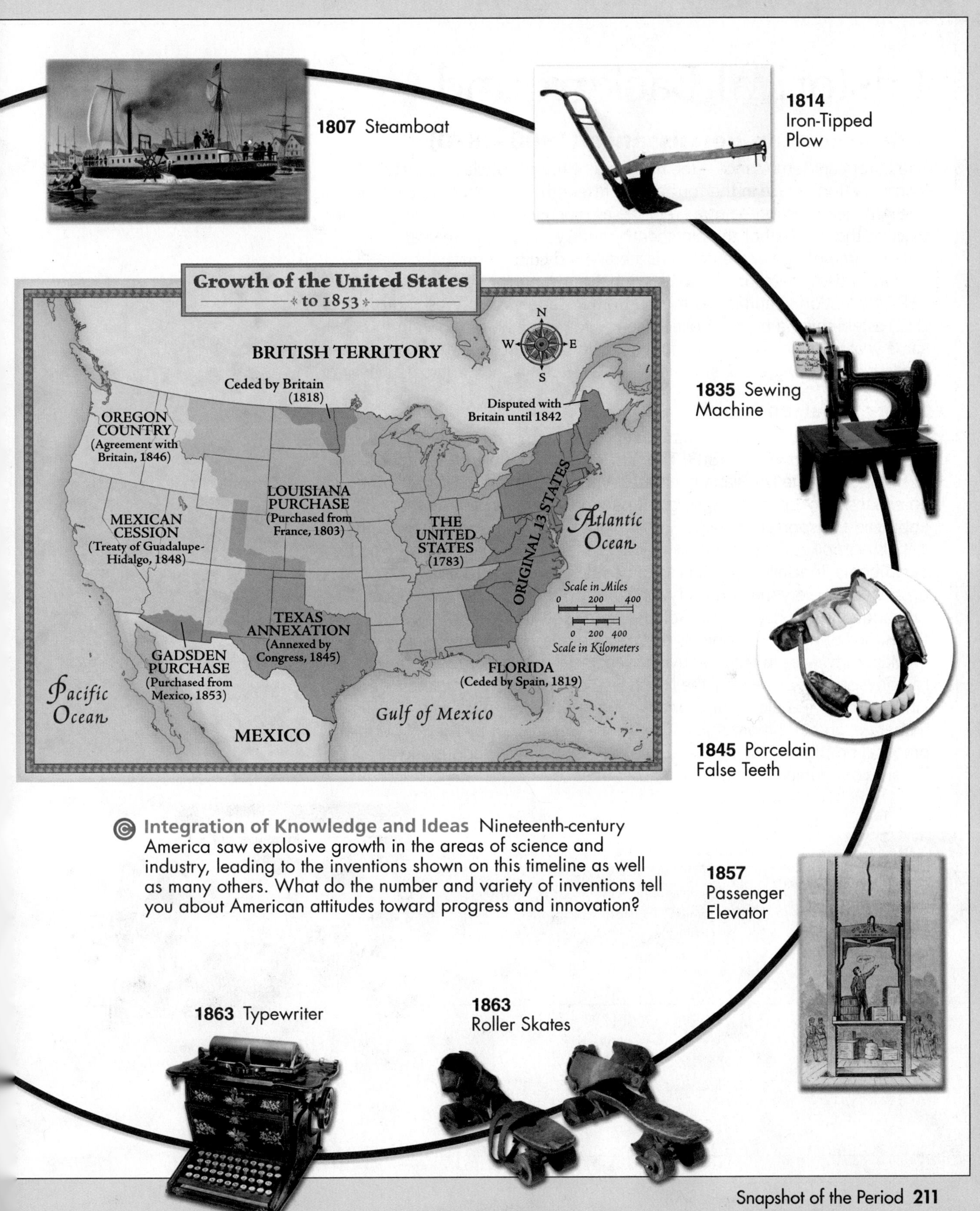

Integration of Knowledge and Ideas Nineteenth-century America saw explosive growth in the areas of science and industry, leading to the inventions shown on this timeline as well as many others. What do the number and variety of inventions tell you about American attitudes toward progress and innovation?

Historical Background

The American Renaissance (1800–1870)

The European Renaissance—the magnificent rebirth of classical art and learning—took place in the fourteenth, fifteenth, and sixteenth centuries. The American version—not a "rebirth" as much as a first flowering—took place in the first half of the nineteenth century. During these years, the nation came of age and entered its literary and cultural maturity.

Two turn-of-the-century events symbolized America's growing up. In 1800 the nation's capital was moved from Philadelphia to Washington, D.C., establishing a unique political center for a unique republic. In the same year, Americans founded the first cultural institution in the capital, the Library of Congress, a storehouse of law, scholarship, and creativity.

Steam, Steel, and Spirit

Underpinning the American cultural renaissance was sheer physical and technological growth. In 1803, Thomas Jefferson doubled the nation's size by signing the Louisiana Purchase. With the expansion of size came an expansion of spirit, an upsurge of national pride and self-awareness. Improved transportation helped bind the old and the new states together. Canals, turnpikes, and especially railroads—"the iron horse"—multiplied. Steamboats and sailing packets sped people and goods to their destinations. Everyone and everything was on the move. After California was added to the nation, the Gold Rush of 1849 drew hundreds of thousands of hopeful people to the western edge of the continent.

Major advances in technology spurred social and cultural change. Factories sprang up all over the Northeast, creating new industries, new kinds of jobs, and plenty of economic profit. The steel plow and the reaper encouraged more aggressive frontier settlement by making farming practical on the vast, sod-covered grasslands. The telegraph made almost instant communication possible across America's great distances.

TIMELINE

1800

1803: Louisiana Purchase extends the nation's territory to the Rocky Mountains.

"The object of our mission is to explore the Missouri River ."
—Thomas Jefferson

▲ **1804:** Lewis and Clark begin expedition exploring and mapping vast regions of the West.

The Slow March of Democracy

The 1828 election of Andrew Jackson, "the People's President," ushered in the era of the common man, as property requirements for voting began to be eliminated. Only white males, however, benefited from these democratic advances. Little political attention was paid to women, and most African Americans remained enslaved. The tragic policy of "Indian removal" forced the westward migration of Native Americans as their tribal lands were confiscated. On the 1838 "Trail of Tears," for example, thousands of Cherokee perished on the trek from Georgia to Oklahoma.

On the World Stage

The first decades of the 1800s were hopeful ones. The War of 1812 convinced Europeans that the United States was on the world stage to stay. The Monroe Doctrine of 1823 warned Europe not to intervene in the new Latin American nations. In the 1830s, the U.S. became embroiled in a conflict over the secession of Texas from Mexico. When Texas was admitted to the Union in 1845, the resulting war with Mexico ended in a United States victory, adding more territory to the nation, including California.

Winds of Change

At mid-century the United States faced trouble as well as promise. The new prosperity unleashed fierce competition, leading to factories scarred by child labor and unsafe working conditions. Women's rights gained some ground, but the deepest social divide remained slavery. Advocates of states' rights argued that the federal government could not bend states to its will. Abolitionists, on the other hand, insisted that slavery was morally wrong. In 1861, the gathering storm finally burst into civil war.

Key Historical Theme: Coming of Age

- Physical expansion and technological progress lay the foundation for an American cultural flowering.
- Democracy advanced, although women, Native Americans, and African Americans did not fully share in it.
- The conflict over slavery eventually led to civil war.

1807: Robert Fulton's steamboat makes first trip from New York City to Albany. ▶

1810

◀ **1804: France** Napoleon Bonaparte declares himself emperor.

Essential Questions Across Time

The American Renaissance (1800–1870)

What did Americans discover as they explored the continent?

Starting as thirteen eastern seaboard colonies, hemmed in by mountain barriers blocking easy access to the interior, the United States gradually extended itself west. The Louisiana Purchase in 1803, the Mexican Cession of 1848, and the additions of Texas and the Oregon Territory filled out the nation and needed to be explored, surveyed, documented, and celebrated.

Size and Diversity Americans were inspired by the sheer size of the land. Vast open prairies in the Midwest, demanding deserts in the Southwest, unbroken forests in the Northwest, grand mountains and canyons in the West—the land ended only at an ocean. Explorers and settlers found countless natural resources. It seemed enough to last forever.

What attitudes developed toward the American land?

Commerce Americans covered the continent in a spirit of acquisition and pride of ownership. The land seemed to demand optimism and practical invention, calling continuously for one more step west. With exploration came exploitation. Commercial possibilities were as wide as the landscape.

Grandeur At the same time, many Americans developed an attitude that went beyond practical matters. The land struck them with awe. To them its spiritual possibilities, not its commercial ones, were as wide as the landscape. Its physical grandeur inspired them to reach for the sublime.

ESSENTIAL QUESTION VOCABULARY

These Essential Question words will help you think and write about literature and place:

barrier (bar′ē ər) *n.* something that prevents movement or separates

acquisition (ak′wə zish′ən) *n.* the act of obtaining something

exploration (eks′ plə rā′ shən) *n.* investigation of new lands

TIMELINE

1810

1812: U.S. declares war on Great Britain; early battles in War of 1812 are at sea.

1813: **England** Jane Austen publishes *Pride and Prejudice.* ▶

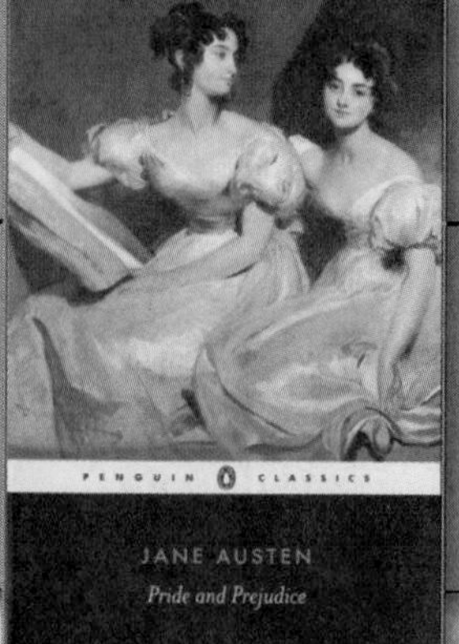

▲ 1814: Bombardment of Fort McHenry inspires Francis Scott Key to write "The Star-Spangled Banner."

How did these attitudes show up in literature?

An American Mythology Explorers such as Meriwether Lewis and Captain William Clark recorded the facts of their expeditions in colorful words and drawings that made the farthest reaches of the continent accessible to every American, at least in imagination. Fiction writers Washington Irving and James Fenimore Cooper helped to create an American mythology by setting tales in the forests, towns, and outposts of the American landscape. In his exciting narrative poems, Henry Wadsworth Longfellow populated the wilderness with colonial Americans, Native Americans, and Revolutionary War heroes.

The American Masters The greatest of American writers—those whose work created the American Renaissance—were all profoundly involved in the American landscape. Edgar Allan Poe, Nathaniel Hawthorne, and Herman Melville saw the dark side of the wilderness, while Ralph Waldo Emerson and Henry David Thoreau emphasized its sublimity. Emily Dickinson explored the universal qualities of her local landscape, while Walt Whitman merged his all-encompassing self with the entire nation.

Nature and Culture The American place affected a wide variety of cultural figures. Thomas Cole and the other Hudson River painters based their work on the romantic and sublime features of the landscape. John James Audubon applied both science and art to American wildlife. Frederick Law Olmsted even found a way to bring nature into the city with his landscape design of New York City's Central Park.

The **American EXPERIENCE**

CLOSE-UP ON HISTORY

Sacajawea, Guide for Lewis and Clark

In 1804, a Shoshone woman named Sacajawea was staying with the Mandan Indians near present-day Bismarck, North Dakota. Meriwether Lewis and William Clark, who had been asked by President Thomas Jefferson to explore the new lands of the Louisiana Purchase, were spending the winter with the Mandans. Sacajawea offered to guide them in the spring across the Rocky Mountains, where the Shoshones lived. She knew the region well and she could translate for them in their encounters with different Indian tribes.

Sacajawea contributed greatly to the success of the expedition, gathering wild vegetables and advising the men where to fish and hunt. She also knew about the healing qualities of different herbs. When the party reached the mountains, Sacajawea recognized the lands of her people, and she persuaded her relatives to support the expedition with food and horses.

After crossing the Rockies, the explorers reached the west coast and returned to St. Louis in 1806. Thanks largely to Sacajawea, their relations with Indians had been almost entirely peaceful. Sadly, however, the westward movement inspired by the expedition would eventually lead to "Indian removal" and confiscation of Indian lands.

1817: William Cullen Bryant publishes early draft of "Thanatopsis" in a Boston magazine. ▶

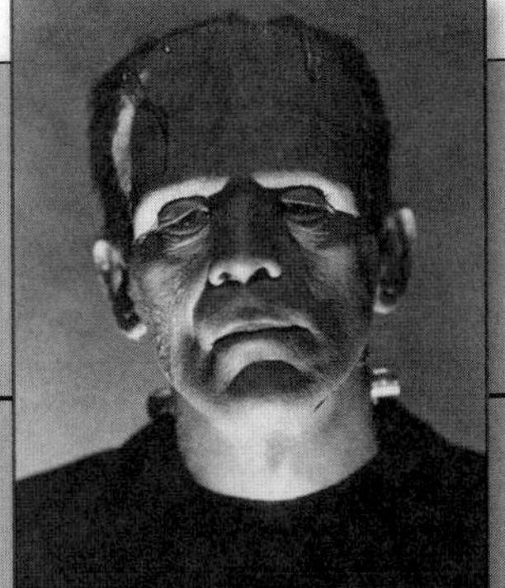

1818: England Mary Wollstonecraft Shelley creates a legend with *Frankenstein.* ▲

1820

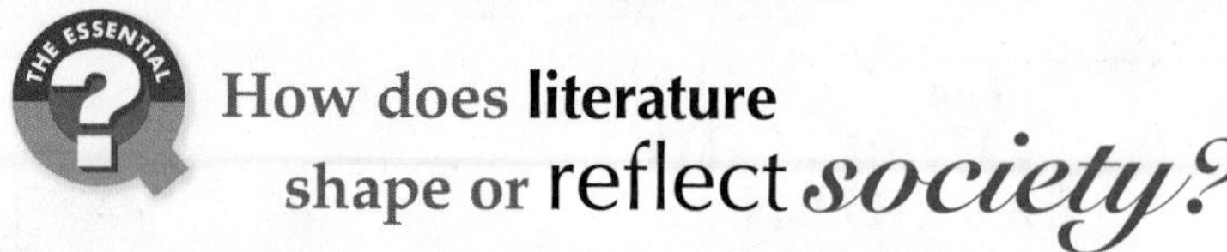

How does literature shape or reflect *society?*

What social forces shaped America during this period?

Technology Bigger, better, stronger, faster—everything in America was rolling on the fast track, especially on the iron network of railroad tracks that crisscrossed the country. Railroads allowed farmers to get their crops to larger markets, and they made almost every corner of America a potential market. Factories made cities grow, and cities then built more factories. Shipbuilding, fishing, and whaling flourished. Inventions of all kinds made life easier: the telegraph and Morse code, the steamboat, the reaper, vulcanized rubber, powerful looms and lathes, the sewing machine, the elevator. Even the word *technology* was coined during this period.

Democracy As the nineteenth century moved forward in America, the right to vote was still largely restricted to white males who owned land. The election of Andrew Jackson as president and the rise of Jacksonian Democracy, however, signaled the rise of the common man to positions of unprecedented power. It was no longer necessary to be wealthy and highly educated to wield political authority in America. At the same time, the women's rights movement gained momentum, spurred on by the Seneca Falls Convention in 1848. Native Americans, on the other hand, felt the continuing hardship of forced removal from their traditional homelands.

Slavery The institution of slavery remained the most profound controversy in America. Eventually, slavery would be the social and political issue that would have the greatest effect on the lives—and deaths—of Americans.

What did nineteenth-century Americans read?

Americans had broken away from Britain politically, but they still devoured British literature, including the adventure tales of Walter Scott and the serial novels of Charles Dickens. However, no British author came close in popularity to two Americans. Harriet Beecher Stowe's anti-slavery novel *Uncle Tom's Cabin* became a national—and international—phenomenon, and Longfellow became the best-selling poet in the English language.

ESSENTIAL QUESTION VOCABULARY

These Essential Question words will help you think and write about literature and society:

market (mär′ kit) *n.* region in which goods can be bought and sold

invention (in ven′ shən) *n.* something originated by experiment; new device

technology (tek näl′ ə jē) *n.* scientific or industrial methods or products

TIMELINE

1820

1820: Missouri Compromise bans slavery in parts of new territories. ▼

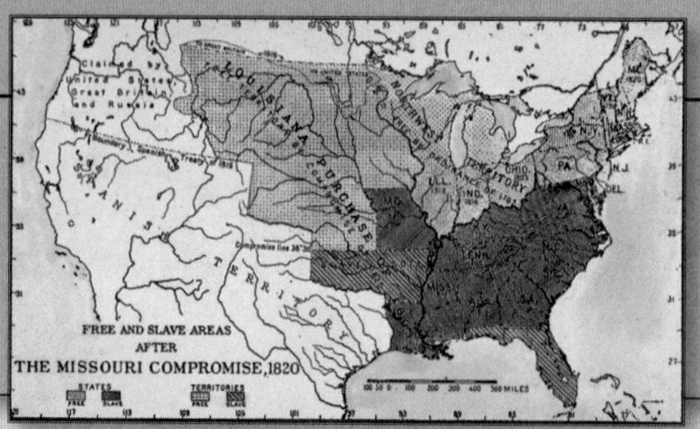

▲ 1825: Completion and success of Erie Canal spurs canal building throughout the nation.

What did American writers want to achieve?

The Social Vision Thomas Jefferson's vision of America was grand, and the Louisiana Purchase helped make that vision a reality. The reports sent by Lewis and Clark and other explorers encouraged the country's physical, political, and commercial growth. At the same time, American journalism fed the idea that the New World could rival the Old World in every way. In lectures, essays, speeches, debates, pamphlets, editorials, and songs, Americans presented what they thought and felt about women's rights, slavery, treatment of Native Americans, land use, immigration, trade, and taxes. Public writing enabled America to define a public self.

The Romantic Vision Romanticism made clear that exploration of the private self was as important as exploration of the land. In prose and poetry, American writers described individual quests for self-definition. Romantic writers elevated imagination over reason, feeling over fact, and nature above all. The fantastical tales of Washington Irving and Edgar Allan Poe, and the agonized heroes of Nathaniel Hawthorne and Herman Melville made the Romantic vision an essential part of the American Renaissance.

The Transcendental Vision Literature, philosophy, and religion merged in New England Transcendentalism, producing a native blend that was Romantic, intuitive, and ethically engaged. For Transcendentalists, real truths lay outside sensory experience. Ralph Waldo Emerson explored those truths in brilliant, wide-ranging essays. Henry David Thoreau put his finger on those truths by merging nature writing and spiritual autobiography. Thoreau's *Walden* remains central to American literature.

The American EXPERIENCE

A LIVING TRADITION

Walden Pond and Tinker Creek

About 120 years after Thoreau embarked on the experiment of living "alone, in the woods ... on the shore of Walden Pond," Annie Dillard undertook a similar experiment with nature and solitude: "I live by a creek, Tinker Creek, in a valley in Virginia's Blue Ridge." Just as Thoreau wrote *Walden* to describe his experiences, she, too, wrote a book about what she saw and thought, the best-selling *Pilgrim at Tinker Creek*. Near the beginning of the book, she describes the home base for her observations:

"An anchorite's hermitage [hermit's secluded retreat] is called an anchor-hold; some anchor-holds were simple sheds clamped to the side of a church like a barnacle to a rock. I think of this house clamped to the side of Tinker Creek as an anchor-hold. It holds me at anchor to the rock bottom of the creek itself and it keeps me steadied in the current, as a sea anchor does, facing the stream of light pouring down. It's a good place to live; there's a lot to think about. The creeks—Tinker and Carvin's—are an active mystery, fresh every minute."

▲ **1827:** Edgar Allan Poe publishes *Tamerlane*, his first collection of poems.

1829: England George Stephenson perfects a steam locomotive for Liverpool-Manchester Railway.

1831: France Victor Hugo publishes *Notre Dame de Paris.* ▶

1830

"OUR FIELD IS THE WORLD."
LIGHT DRAFT. SUPERIOR DESIGN.
CLEAN AND RAPID CUTTER.
McCormick Harvesting Machine Co., Chicago.
ESTABLISHED 1831.

◀ **1831:** Cyrus McCormick invents mechanical reaper.

The American EXPERIENCE

CONTEMPORARY CONNECTION

EMILY DICKINSON: POET, RECLUSE . . . GAMER?

In 2005, three prominent video-game designers set themselves a challenge to create games based on something surprising: the poetry of Emily Dickinson.

Clint Hocking, lead designer of *Splinter Cell*, created a game called *Muse*. Players would collect symbols based on Dickinson's Massachusetts. They would then assemble the symbols to make poems within a certain amount of time.

Peter Molyneux, designer of *Black & White*, created a game using a house modeled on Dickinson's. Players would wander around the house, trying to unlock Dickinson's experiences.

Will Wright, creator of *The Sims*, believes that Dickinson and hi-tech are a natural combination. "If she were alive today," he said, "she'd be an Internet addict, and she'd probably have a really amazing blog." The game Wright designed would be stored on a USB flash drive. The player and Emily would write to each other. Emily would appear randomly with IMs, e-mails, or desktop appearances. Ultimately, she could delete herself from the memory stick.

Wright's game won the challenge.

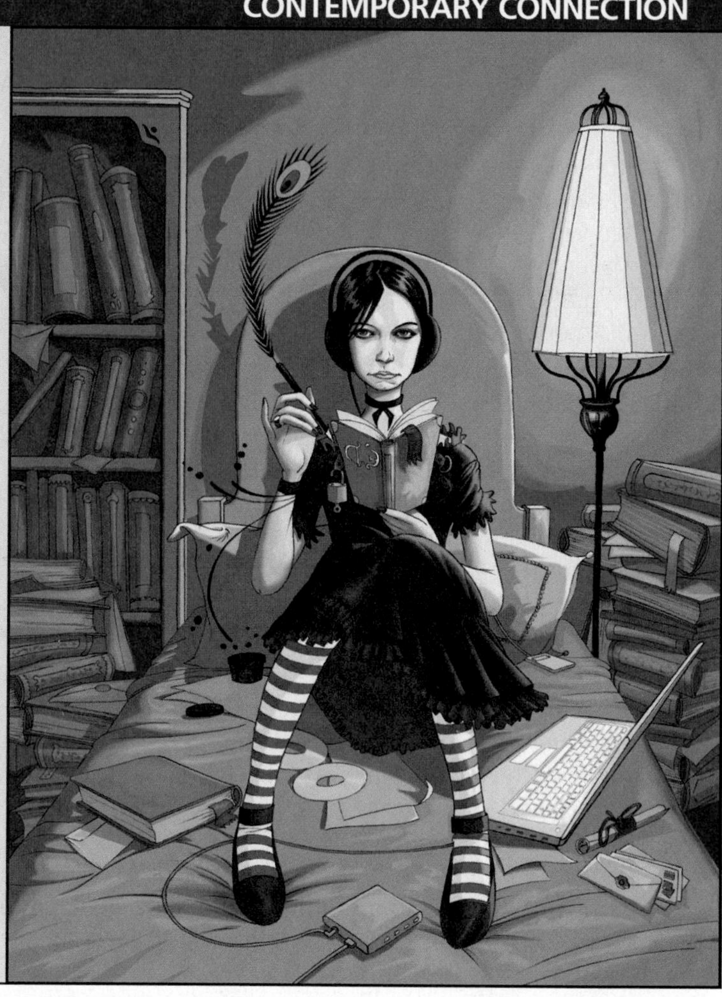

TIMELINE

1835

1837: Samuel F.B. Morse patents electromagnetic telegraph. ▶

1838: U.S. Army marches Cherokees of Georgia on long "Trail of Tears" to Oklahoma. ▶

1841: Antarctica is first explored by Englishman James Ross. ▶

1842: Asia Hong Kong becomes a British colony.

THE ESSENTIAL
What makes
American literature American?

What qualities made American literature sound American?

American English Most Americans, descended from English colonists, spoke English, but gradually the American way of speaking and writing took on many unique features. Dialects, the products of local communities, developed around the country, and local grammar and syntax often drove out standard British English. Spanish, French, Dutch, and Native American languages added to the mix, and Americans coined new words to describe their land, weather, plants, animals, and ways of daily life.

Triumph of the Colloquial American English, both spoken and written, became more colloquial, or informal, than British English. Contractions such as *can't, don't,* and *couldn't* were acceptable. Colorful idioms enlivened everyday speech. Americans might *set a spell, take a fork in a road,* or *bark up the wrong tree.* The British thought that Americans were ruining the language, but, like the nation itself, American English was intensely alive to change, variety, and new additions.

The "Barbaric Yawp" During the American Renaissance, American writers found their own voices. Emerson, Thoreau, Poe, Dickinson—each contributed to a recognizably American style, but no one sounded as utterly American as Walt Whitman. He was unafraid to sound his "barbaric yawp" across the continent. His style incorporated the plain and the elegant, the high and the low, the foreign and the native. It mixed grand opera, political oratory, journalistic punch, everyday conversation, and biblical cadences. Whitman's sound was the American sound.

What literary character types emerged during this period?

The Frontiersman As the frontier continued to open, the men and women who faced it head-on entered into the nation's literary imagination. Real-life backwoodsmen such as Daniel Boone and Davy Crockett were mythologized in almanacs and folktales, and Americans delighted in tall tales about

ESSENTIAL QUESTION VOCABULARY

These Essential Question words will help you think and write about American literature:

individualist (in′də vij′o͞o əl ist) *n.* one who lives life his or her own way, not influenced by others

colloquial (kə lō′kwē əl) *adj.* conversational; informal

self-reliant (self-ri lī′ənt) *adj.* depending upon one's own judgments and abilities

◀ 1845: **Ireland** Famine results from failure of potato crop.

1845: **Florida** becomes the twenty-seventh state in the United States.

◀ 1848: Women's Rights Convention held in Seneca Falls, New York.

1848: Mexican War ends; United States expands borders.

1848: Gold Rush begins in California. ▶

1848: Karl Marx and Friedrich Engels publish *The Communist Manifesto.*

1850

the superhuman lumberjack Paul Bunyan, the rowdy riverboat man Mike Fink, and the African American steel-driver John Henry. In fiction, the essential frontiersman was Natty Bumppo, the hero of James Fenimore Cooper's *Leatherstocking Tales*. At one with the wilderness, these hardy characters helped define the American identity as bold, self-reliant, and "uncorrupted" by civilization.

The Romantic Individualist Romanticism emphasized the individual over the institution and the person over the community. The American Romantic hero took many forms. In *The Scarlet Letter*, Nathaniel Hawthorne's Hester Prynne dared to put love and honor over the repressive rule of her town. In *Moby-Dick*, Herman Melville's Captain Ahab let nothing stand in the way of his obsession with the white whale. In *Leaves of Grass*, Walt Whitman's ecstatic self celebrated its own joyful existence at the center of the universe.

The Transcendental Seeker One type of Romantic individualist was the person who sought to reach the sublime, a feeling of oneness with all that is beautiful and good. This private soul craved unity with the Oversoul, a universal force that might be identified as the mind of God. As Emerson wrote, "the individual is the world," and an individual could reach the sublime through the world of nature. Emerson and Thoreau defined this character type, but other writers and artists contributed to the quest for the sublime. Margaret Fuller edited the Transcendentalist magazine *The Dial*, and the Hudson River school of visual artists painted landscapes that inspired a sense of the sublime in all who saw them.

What literary themes emerged during this era?

Westering The myth of America began as "a city upon a hill," but by the nineteenth century it had become "the garden of the world." The sheer bulk of the continent, with its treasury of natural resources, made continuous Western expansion a fundamental part of the national identity. Many Americans considered this movement west as a continental destiny. It became the right and duty of Americans to explore, expand, and exploit. However, if America was a garden, it was one being invaded by machines. This is a theme that continues to resonate in American literature.

TIMELINE

1850

1850: Nathaniel Hawthorne publishes *The Scarlet Letter.*

1850: England Elizabeth Barrett Browning publishes *Sonnets from the Portuguese.* ▶

◀ **1851:** Herman Melville publishes *Moby-Dick.*

1851: Nathaniel Hawthorne publishes *The House of Seven Gables.*

1851: Australia Gold discovered in New South Wales.

Bright and Dark Romanticism Romanticism had two faces, one bright and optimistic, the other dark and shadowed by evil. Emerson and Thoreau emphasized "the sun is but a morning star" aspect of Romanticism. They saw human beings as fundamentally good. Poe, Hawthorne, and Melville, on the other hand, were deeply disturbed by what they saw in the human heart. They believed that crime, cruelty, guilt, and self-destruction were the true earmarks of human nature. During the American Renaissance, writers explored both sides of the Romantic impulse.

Self-Reliance "Trust thyself," Emerson advised. Think for yourself, and act on what you think. "Live deliberately," Thoreau advised. Make your own choices, and do not let others choose for you. These principles had been built into American democracy, and they became fundamental themes of American culture. What applied to individuals also applied to the nation as a whole. The eighteenth century had seen the Declaration of Independence. The nineteenth century saw declarations of cultural independence. Self-reliance is key to why the American Renaissance happened at all. Literary culture had begun to grow; journalism and education prepared the ground. But it was extraordinary individuals who made it happen—self-reliant men and women who thought for themselves and refused to let social, political, religious, or cultural institutions overwhelm them.

The **American EXPERIENCE**

DEVELOPING AMERICAN ENGLISH

The Truth About O.K. by Richard Lederer

Americans seem to have a passion for stringing initial letters together. We use *A.M.* and *P.M.* to separate light from darkness and *B.C.* and *A.D.* to identify vast stretches of time. We may listen to a deejay or veejay on *ABC* or *MTV*, or a crusading *DA* quoting the *FBI* on *CNN*.

Perhaps the most widely understood American word in the world is *O.K.* The explanations for its origin have been imaginative and various. Some claim that *O.K.* is a version of the Choctaw affirmative *okeh*. Others assert that it is short for the Greek *olla kalla* ("all good") or *Orrin Kendall* crackers or chief *Old Keukuk*.

The truth is that in the 1830s there was a craze for initialisms, like our currently popular *T.G.I.F.* and *F.Y.I.* The fad went so far as to generate letter combinations of intentional misspellings: *K.Y.* for "know use," *O.W.* for "oll wright." *O.K.* for "oll korrect" followed.

Ultimately, *O.K.* survived because of a presidential nickname. President Martin Van Buren was born in Kinderhook, New York, and dubbed "Old Kinderhook." "O.K." became the rallying cry of the Old Kinderhook Club that supported him for re-election in 1840. Van Buren was defeated, but the word honoring his name remains what H. L. Mencken identified as "the most shining and successful Americanism ever invented."

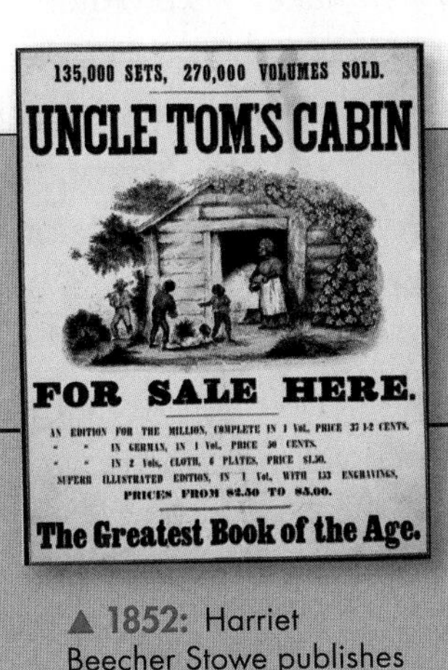
135,000 SETS, 270,000 VOLUMES SOLD.
UNCLE TOM'S CABIN
FOR SALE HERE.
The Greatest Book of the Age.

▲ **1852:** Harriet Beecher Stowe publishes *Uncle Tom's Cabin.*

1854: Henry David Thoreau publishes *Walden.* ▼

1855: England Robert Browning publishes *Men and Women.*

1855: Walt Whitman publishes *Leaves of Grass.* ▶

Leaves of Grass.

1858: Abraham Lincoln and Stephen Douglas run for Illinois Senate seat and conduct a series of famous debates.

1870

Recent Scholarship

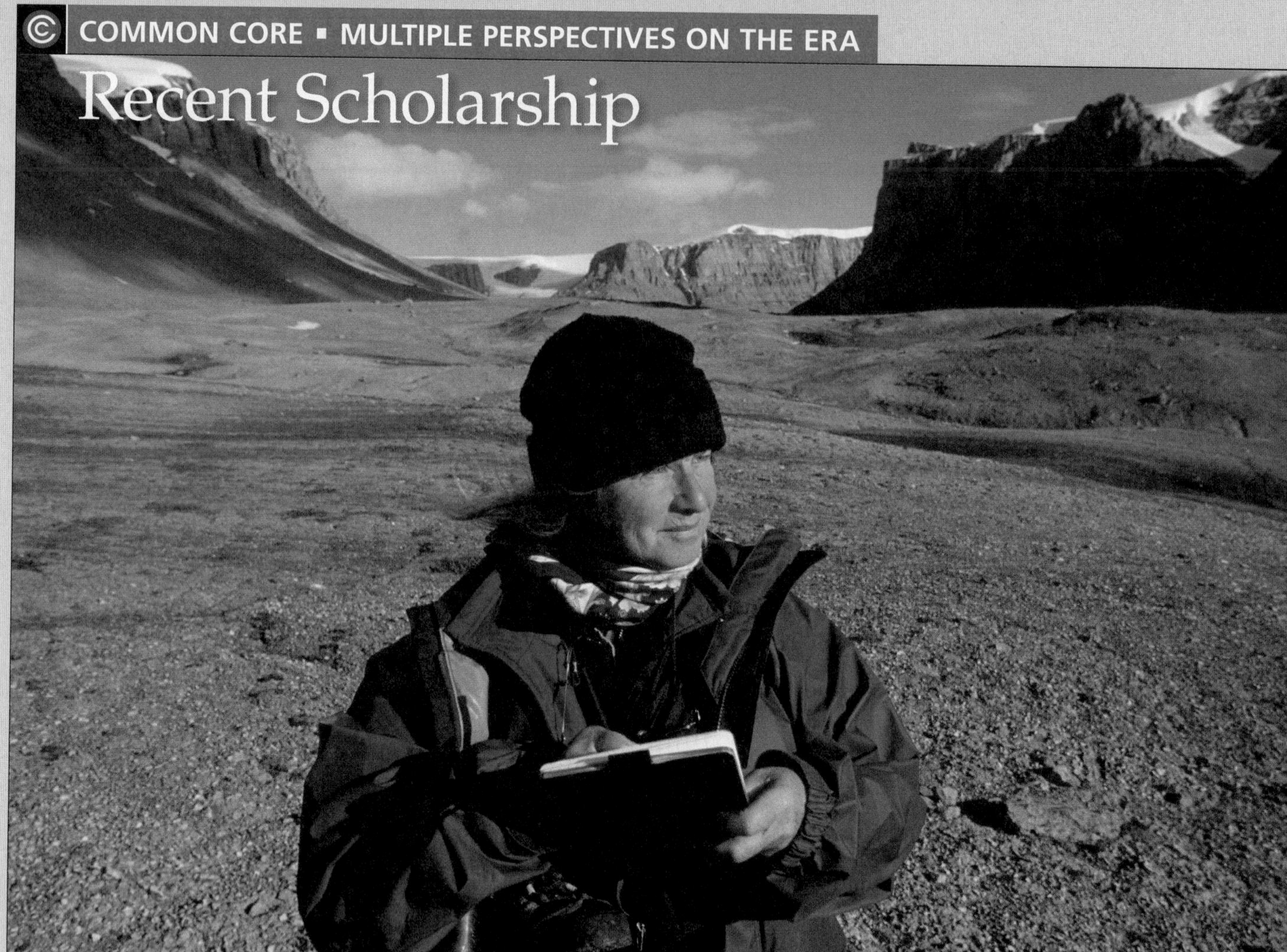

Inspired by Nature

Gretel Ehrlich

We are all born on a particular spot on the planet with its unique seasons, weather, and topography. Mountains, rivers, rocks, storms, glaciers, skies, trees, and grasses, as well as all living things, help shape who we are, how we see, how we move through our days, and how we know who we are. Those of us who have been called "nature writers" are simply people who observe and write about the living planet, who witness the birth and death of its residents, who understand that we all share the earth equally, and who tell the stories that come from the earth.

About the Author

Gretel Ehrlich was born in California. She has worked as a ranch hand, a sheepherder, and a documentary filmmaker. As a writer, she has been profoundly influenced by living in Wyoming, a place of intense extremes and breathtaking beauty. Ehrlich is the author of 13 books, including three collections of essays, a memoir, and three books of poetry. Her many honors include the 2010 PEN Thoreau Award. She is best known for her nature writing, which has focused most recently on the island of Greenland.

From Natural Fact Comes Human Meaning

The Inuit people of northern Greenland have a word, *sila*, that means "the power of nature, weather, and human and animal consciousness as one and the same": no separation between the "emotional weather" inside ourselves and the natural forces on the outside that affect us. Nature writers are always writing about two things at once: the ecosystem and continent that is our mind and body, and the greater one of the world surrounding us. They show us how human meaning can come from natural fact.

A One-Room Cabin on Walden Pond

Henry David Thoreau was one of the great natural history writers of all time. Broken-hearted over a lost love, he went to live on Walden Pond in Concord, Massachusetts, for two years and two months. His friend and mentor, Ralph Waldo Emerson, a brilliant essayist, bought an eleven-acre field on the north shore of the pond, and in March of 1845, Thoreau, with Emerson's encouragement, built a ten-by-fifteen-foot one-room cabin. Then, he borrowed a horse and plow and planted two acres in white beans, corn, and potatoes.

An Inventory of the Natural World

Thoreau was twenty-eight at the time, and he wanted to be free from the constraints of family and society. Reading widely, walking locally, writing obsessively—those were his priorities. He was not a great adventurer—others at the time were searching for the Northwest Passage in the Arctic, sailing the seas of the world, traveling by covered wagon across the country. Thoreau knew that his inventory of the natural world and his insights into human consciousness could be achieved right where he was: on Walden Pond. He wanted to live simply and quietly, to live deeply, to listen and observe, to become intimate with a place. In so doing, he allowed the outer landscape to shape the prose that came from within.

Where We Live Holds the Secrets of the Universe

"I went to the woods because I wished to live deliberately," he wrote, "to front only the essential facts of life, and see if I could not learn what it had to teach, and not, when I came to die, discover that I had not lived." What we learn from Thoreau's life and writings is that anywhere we happen to live is good enough. We don't have to go to some exotic place to find ourselves or understand the world. It's all right here, for each of us. Each place holds all the secrets of the universe, the history of the world in a raindrop.

Collaboration: Speaking and Listening

One lesson of Thoreau's writing, according to Gretel Ehrlich, is that natural wonders exist in every corner of the natural world:

"What we learn from Thoreau's life and writings is that anywhere we happen to live is good enough... Each place holds all the secrets of the universe, the history of the world in a raindrop."

Hold a **small group discussion** about Ehrlich's ideas in the quoted passage. Decide whether you agree or disagree with her statement. Select a point person to share your ideas with the class.

Integrate and Evaluate Information

1. Use a chart like the one shown to determine the key ideas expressed in the Essential Question essays on pages 214–221. Fill in two ideas related to each Essential Question and note the authors most closely associated with each concept. One example has been done for you.

Essential Question	Key Concept	Key Author
Literature and Place	A kinship with nature	Thoreau
American Literature		
Literature and Society		

2. How do the visual sources in this section—artifacts, paintings, photographs, and illustrations—add to your understanding of the ideas expressed in words? Cite specific examples.
3. The vast, unexplored American West sparked the American imagination. Describe some of the different attitudes that developed toward the American land and its settlement, citing evidence from the multiple sources on pages 210–223. In your view, have these attitudes helped shape contemporary American culture? If so, how? If not, why not?
4. **Address a Question** In her discussion of Thoreau, Gretel Ehrlich writes: "We don't have to go to some exotic place to find ourselves or understand our world.... Each place holds all the secrets of the universe." How might this idea challenge certain values, such as the importance of progress, innovation, and expansion, that are often seen as essentially American? Integrate information from this textbook and other sources to support your ideas.

Common Core State Standards

Reading Informational Text
7. Integrate and evaluate multiple sources of information presented in different media or formats as well as in words in order to address a question or solve a problem.

Speaking and Listening
6. Adapt speech to a variety of contexts and tasks.

Language
6. Acquire and use accurately general academic and domain-specific words and phrases.

Speaking and Listening: Slide Presentation

During the nineteenth century, technology leaped forward. Using a variety of print and electronic resources, research one of the following nineteenth-century inventions. Then, write and deliver a **slide presentation** that explores the impact of the invention on American life:

- the mechanical reaper
- the cotton gin
- the steam locomotive
- the telegraph
- the bicycle

Your slide presentation should answer the following questions: What aspects of American life did the invention affect or change? What ripple effects did the invention cause? Whom did the invention most benefit? Whom, if anyone, did the invention harm?

Solve a Research Problem This assignment requires you to understand and integrate technical terms into your writing. To do so, find reliable print and online sources for definitions and explanations. Also, consult writings by scientists, inventors, and historians. As you present, make sure to explain technical terms that may be unfamiliar to your audience.

ESSENTIAL QUESTION VOCABULARY

Use these words in your responses:

Literature and Place
barrier
acquisition
exploration

American Literature
individualist
colloquial
self-reliant

Literature and Society
market
invention
technology

TEXT SET

Fireside and Campfire

Part 1

Building Knowledge and Insight

ANCHOR TEXT

The Devil and Tom Walker

Connecting to the Essential Question This dark yet comic story centers on greedy Tom Walker, who cares only for himself in his pursuit of riches. As you read, look for details that criticize selfishness and greed. This will help as you consider the Essential Question: **How does literature shape or reflect society?**

Common Core State Standards

Reading Literature

3. Analyze the impact of the author's choices regarding how to develop and relate elements of a story or drama (e.g., where a story is set, how the characters are introduced and developed).

9. Demonstrate knowledge of nineteenth-century foundational works of American literature.

Close Reading Focus

Characterization

Characterization is the creation and development of a character. In **direct characterization,** a writer tells you what a character is like. In **indirect characterization,** the writer reveals a character's personality through the character's speech, thoughts, actions, appearance, and other characters' reactions. For example, Irving uses direct characterization when he tells the reader that Tom Walker was "not a man to be troubled with any fears." He uses indirect characterization in Tom's reply to the Devil, who has threateningly suggested that Tom is trespassing:

> *"Your grounds!" said Tom with a sneer, "no more your grounds than mine; they belong to Deacon Peabody."*

Indirect characterization provides valuable information and adds to a story's action, drama, or humor. As you read, notice Irving's use of characterization.

Preparing to Read Complex Texts Works of fiction are often shaped by the concerns of the historical period in which they are set. These may involve philosophical trends, religious beliefs, ethical issues, or social problems. As you read, **evaluate the influences of the historical period** on characters, plot, and settings. For example, the characters in this story hold attitudes common to New Englanders in the 1720s, when the story is set. Through his narrator, Irving criticizes some of those attitudes while accepting others. Use a chart like the one shown to track the effects of specific cultural attitudes on the characters, plot, and settings of this story.

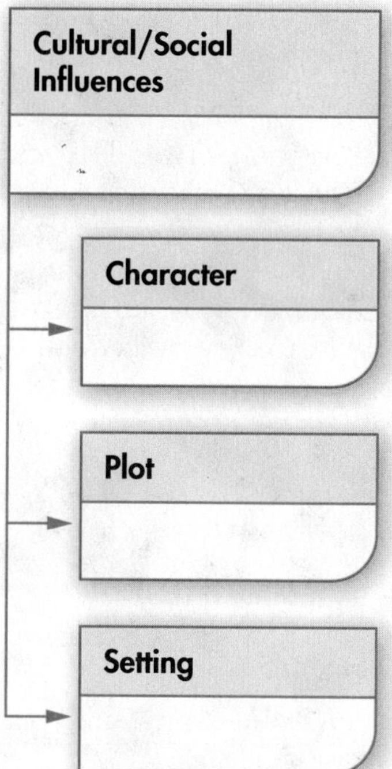

Vocabulary

The words below are important to understanding the text that follows. Copy the words into your notebook. Which word is a synonym for *dangerous*?

prevalent
discord
treacherous
extort
ostentation
parsimony

Washington Irving *(1783–1859)*

Author of "The Devil and Tom Walker"

Named after President George Washington, Washington Irving became the first American fiction writer to achieve an international reputation. Irving was born into a wealthy New York family right at the close of the American Revolution. Although he planned to be a lawyer, he grew more interested in travel and writing and devoted his life to both pursuits.

A Career Blooms From 1807 to 1808, Irving wrote satirical essays under the pen name Jonathan Oldstyle. With his brother William, he anonymously published the magazine *Salmagundi*, named after a spicy appetizer. In 1809, he produced his first major work, *A History of New York From the Beginning of the World to the End of the Dutch Dynasty*. This humorous examination of New York in colonial times made Irving so famous that to this day native New Yorkers are known as "Knickerbockers" after Diedrich Knickerbocker, the character Irving created to narrate the work.

Americanizing Europe's Folklore Traveling in Europe from 1815 to 1832, Irving encountered European folklore that helped inspire his own writing. Two of his best-known works, "The Legend of Sleepy Hollow" and "Rip Van Winkle," turn German folk tales into distinctly American narratives set in New York's Hudson Valley. Their main characters—Ichabod Crane, the nervous Sleepy Hollow schoolteacher harassed by a headless horseman, and Rip Van Winkle, the lazy colonist who slept for decades—have become classic figures of American literature.

I am endeavoring to serve my country. Whatever I have written has been written with the feelings and published as the writing of an American. . . . If I can do any good in this world it is with my pen.

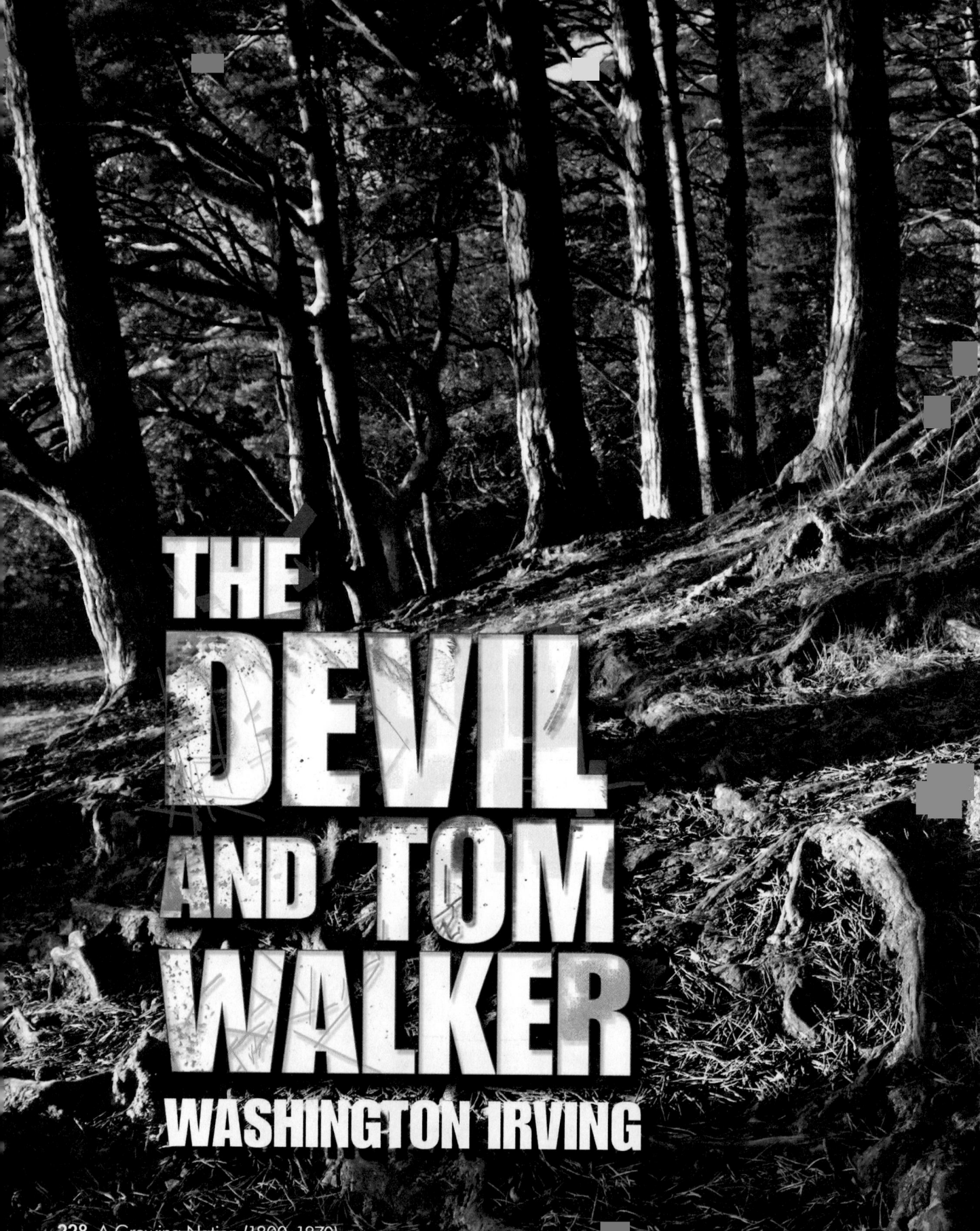

THE DEVIL AND TOM WALKER

WASHINGTON IRVING

BACKGROUND This story appeared in 1824, when the American economy was booming. Advances in technology and transportation and the rapid growth of cities created large markets for goods. For the first time, manufactured items were widely available and people had money to buy them. Irving's story retells the European tale of Faust, a scholar who sold his soul for wisdom. Tom Walker, Washington Irving's American Faust, has no interest in wisdom; he is simply after riches. Irving may have set this story in an earlier America, but he revealed the materialism of his own era.

A few miles from Boston in Massachusetts, there is a deep inlet, winding several miles into the interior of the country from Charles Bay, and terminating in a thickly wooded swamp or morass. On one side of this inlet is a beautiful dark grove; on the opposite side the land rises abruptly from the water's edge into a high ridge, on which grow a few scattered oaks of great age and immense size. Under one of these gigantic trees, according to old stories, there was a great amount of treasure buried by Kidd the pirate.[1] The inlet allowed a facility to bring the money in a boat secretly and at night to the very foot of the hill; the elevation of the place permitted a good look-out to be kept that no one was at hand; while the remarkable trees formed good landmarks by which the place might easily be found again. The old stories add, moreover, that the Devil presided at the hiding of the money, and took it under his guardianship; but this it is well known he always does with buried treasure, particularly when it has been ill-gotten.

Be that as it may, Kidd never returned to recover his wealth; being shortly after seized at Boston, sent out to England, and there hanged for a pirate.

About the year 1727, just at the time that earthquakes were prevalent in New England, and shook many tall sinners down upon their knees, there lived near this place a meager, miserly fellow, of the name of Tom Walker. He had a wife as miserly as himself: they were so miserly that they even conspired to cheat each other. Whatever the woman could lay hands on, she hid away; a hen could not cackle but she was on the alert to secure the new-laid egg. Her husband was continually prying about to detect her secret hoards, and many and fierce were the conflicts that took place about what ought to have been common property.

Evaluate Influences of the Historical Period
What does this reference to the Devil and treasure suggest about period attitudes toward wealth?

Vocabulary
prevalent (prev´ ə lənt) *adj.* widely existing or occuring

Comprehension
What is buried under one of the gigantic trees?

1. **Kidd the pirate** Captain William Kidd (1645–1701).

They lived in a forlorn-looking house that stood alone, and had an air of starvation. A few straggling savin trees, emblems of sterility, grew near it; no smoke ever curled from its chimney; no traveler stopped at its door. A miserable horse, whose ribs were as articulate as the bars of a gridiron, stalked about a field, where a thin carpet of moss, scarcely covering the ragged beds of puddingstone, tantalized and balked his hunger; and sometimes he would lean his head over the fence, look piteously at the passerby, and seem to petition deliverance from this land of famine.

▲ Critical Viewing

How does this picture compare to Irving's description of the Walkers' home? **COMPARE AND CONTRAST**

The house and its inmates had altogether a bad name. Tom's wife was a tall termagant,[2] fierce of temper, loud of tongue, and strong of arm. Her voice was often heard in wordy warfare with her husband; and his face sometimes showed signs that their conflicts were not confined to words. No one ventured, however, to interfere between them. The lonely wayfarer shrunk within himself at the horrid clamor and clapperclawing;[3] eyed the den of **discord** askance; and hurried on his way, rejoicing, if a bachelor, in his celibacy.

Vocabulary

discord (dis´ kôrd´) *n.* lack of harmony; conflict

treacherous (trech´ ər əs) *adj.* dangerous

One day that Tom Walker had been to a distant part of the neighborhood, he took what he considered a shortcut homeward, through the swamp. Like most shortcuts, it was an ill-chosen route. The swamp was thickly grown with great gloomy pines and hemlocks, some of them ninety feet high, which made it dark at noonday, and a retreat for all the owls of the neighborhood. It was full of pits and quagmires, partly covered with weeds and mosses, where the green surface often betrayed the traveler into a gulf of black, smothering mud; there were also dark and stagnant pools, the abodes of the tadpole, the bullfrog, and the watersnake; where the trunks of pines and hemlocks lay half-drowned, half-rotting, looking like alligators sleeping in the mire.

Tom had long been picking his way cautiously through this **treacherous** forest; stepping from tuft to tuft of rushes and roots, which afforded precarious footholds among deep sloughs; or pacing carefully, like a cat, along the prostrate trunks of trees; startled now and then by the sudden screaming of the bittern, or the quacking of a wild duck, rising on the wing from some solitary pool. At length he arrived at a piece of firm ground, which ran out like a peninsula into the deep bosom of the swamp. It had been one of the strongholds of the Indians during their wars with the first colonists. Here they had thrown up a kind of fort, which they had looked upon as almost impregnable, and had used as a place of refuge for their squaws and children. Nothing remained of the old Indian fort but a few embankments, gradually sinking to the level of the surrounding earth, and already overgrown in part by oaks and other forest trees, the foliage of which formed a contrast to the dark pines and hemlocks of the swamp.

2. **termagant** (tʉr´ mə gənt) *n.* quarrelsome woman.
3. **clapperclawing** (klap´ ər klô´ iŋ) *n.* clawing or scratching.

It was late in the dusk of evening when Tom Walker reached the old fort, and he paused there awhile to rest himself. Anyone but he would have felt unwilling to linger in this lonely, melancholy place, for the common people had a bad opinion of it, from the stories handed down from the time of the Indian wars; when it was asserted that the savages held incantations here, and made sacrifices to the evil spirit.

Tom Walker, however, was not a man to be troubled with any fears of the kind. He reposed himself for some time on the trunk of a fallen hemlock, listening to the boding cry of the tree toad, and delving with his walking staff into a mound of black mold at his feet. As he turned up the soil unconsciously, his staff struck against something hard. He raked it out of the vegetable mold, and lo! a cloven skull, with an Indian tomahawk buried deep in it, lay before him. The rust on the weapon showed the time that had elapsed since this deathblow had been given. It was a dreary memento of the fierce struggle that had taken place in this last foothold of the Indian warriors.

"Humph!" said Tom Walker, as he gave it a kick to shake the dirt from it.

"Let that skull alone!" said a gruff voice. Tom lifted up his eyes, and beheld a great black man seated directly opposite him, on the stump of a tree. He was exceedingly surprised, having neither heard nor seen anyone approach; and he was still more perplexed on observing, as well as the gathering gloom would permit, that the stranger was neither Negro nor Indian. It is true he was dressed in a rude half-Indian garb, and had a red belt or sash swathed round his body; but his face was neither black nor copper color, but swarthy and dingy, and begrimed with soot, as if he had been accustomed to toil among fires and forges. He had a shock of coarse black hair, that stood out from his head in all directions, and bore an ax on his shoulder.

He scowled for a moment at Tom with a pair of great red eyes.

"What are you doing on my grounds?" said the black man, with a hoarse growling voice.

"Your grounds!" said Tom with a sneer, "no more your grounds than mine; they belong to Deacon Peabody."

"Deacon Peabody be d—d," said the stranger, "as I flatter myself he will be, if he does not look more to his own sins and less to those of his neighbors. Look yonder, and see how Deacon Peabody is faring."

Tom looked in the direction that the stranger pointed, and beheld one of the great trees, fair and flourishing without, but rotten at the core, and saw that it had been nearly hewn through, so that the first high wind was likely to blow it down. On the bark of the tree was scored the name of Deacon Peabody, an eminent man, who had waxed wealthy by driving shrewd bargains with the Indians. He now looked round, and found most of the tall trees marked with the name of some great man of the colony, and all more or less scored by the ax. The one on which he had been seated, and which had evidently just been hewn down, bore the name of Crowninshield: and he recollected a mighty

Evaluate Influences of the Historical Period

What do details in the first two paragraphs on this page reveal about colonial attitudes toward Native Americans?

Mistreatment of Indians

Comprehension

Where does Tom pause to rest?

rich man of that name, who made a vulgar display of wealth, which it was whispered he had acquired by buccaneering.

"He's just ready for burning!" said the black man, with a growl of triumph. "You see I am likely to have a good stock of firewood for winter."

"But what right have you," said Tom, "to cut down Deacon Peabody's timber?"

"The right of a prior claim," said the other. "This woodland belonged to me long before one of your white-faced race put foot upon the soil."

"And pray, who are you, if I may be so bold?" said Tom.

"Oh, I go by various names. I am the wild huntsman in some countries; the black miner in others. In this neighborhood I am known by the name of the black woodsman. I am he to whom the red men consecrated this spot, and in honor of whom they now and then roasted a white man, by way of sweet-smelling sacrifice. Since the red men have been exterminated by you white savages, I amuse myself by presiding at the persecutions of Quakers and Anabaptists;[4] I am the great patron and prompter of slave dealers, and the grandmaster of the Salem witches."

"The upshot of all which is, that, if I mistake not," said Tom, sturdily, "you are he commonly called Old Scratch."

"The same, at your service!" replied the black man, with a half-civil nod.

Such was the opening of this interview, according to the old story; though it has almost too familiar an air to be credited. One would think that to meet with such a singular personage, in this wild, lonely place, would have shaken any man's nerves; but Tom was a hard-minded fellow, not easily daunted, and he had lived so long with a termagant wife, that he did not even fear the Devil.

It is said that after this commencement they had a long and earnest conversation together, as Tom returned homeward. The black man told him of great sums of money buried by Kidd the pirate, under the oak trees on the high ridge, not far from the morass. All these were under his command, and protected by his power, so that none could find them but such as propitiated his favor. These he offered to place within Tom Walker's reach, having conceived an especial kindness for him; but they were to be had only on certain conditions. What these conditions were may easily be surmised, though Tom never disclosed them publicly. They must have been very hard, for he required time to think of them, and he was not a man to stick at trifles where money was in view. When they had reached the edge of the swamp, the stranger paused—"What proof have I that all you have been telling me is true?" said Tom. "There is my signature," said the black man, pressing his finger on Tom's forehead. So saying, he turned off among the thickets of the swamp, and seemed, as Tom

"And pray, who are you, if I may be so bold?" said Tom.

Characterization

Identify the direct characterization in the paragraph beginning "Such was the opening of this interview . . ."

4. Quakers and Anabaptists two religious groups that were persecuted for their beliefs.

said, to go down, down, down, into the earth, until nothing but his head and shoulders could be seen, and so on, until he totally disappeared.

When Tom reached home, he found the black print of a finger, burnt, as it were, into his forehead, which nothing could obliterate.

The first news his wife had to tell him was the sudden death of Absalom Crowninshield, the rich buccaneer. It was announced in the papers with the usual flourish, that "A great man had fallen in Israel."[5]

Tom recollected the tree which his black friend had just hewn down, and which was ready for burning, "Let the freebooter roast," said Tom, "who cares!" He now felt convinced that all he had heard and seen was no illusion.

He was not prone to let his wife into his confidence; but as this was an uneasy secret, he willingly shared it with her. All her avarice was awakened at the mention of hidden gold, and she urged her husband to comply with the black man's terms and secure what would make them wealthy for life. However Tom might have felt disposed to sell himself to the Devil, he was determined not to do so to oblige his wife; so he flatly refused, out of the mere spirit of contradiction. Many and bitter were the quarrels they had on the subject, but the more she talked, the more resolute was Tom not to be damned to please her.

Characterization
What does Mrs. Walker's reaction to Tom's news reveal about her character?

At length she determined to drive the bargain on her own account, and if she succeeded, to keep all the gain to herself. Being of the same fearless temper as her husband, she set off for the old Indian fort towards the close of a summer's day. She was many hours absent. When she came back, she was reserved and sullen in her replies. She spoke something of a black man, whom she had met about twilight, hewing at the root of a tall tree. He was sulky, however, and would not come to terms: she was to go again with a propitiatory offering, but what it was she forbore to say.

The next evening she set off again for the swamp, with her apron heavily laden. Tom waited and waited for her, but in vain; midnight came, but she did not make her appearance: morning, noon, night returned, but still she did not come. Tom now grew uneasy for her safety, especially as he found she had carried off in her apron the silver teapot and spoons, and every portable article of value. Another night elapsed, another morning came; but no wife. In a word, she was never heard of more.

Comprehension
What does Tom's wife determine to do?

What was her real fate nobody knows, in consequence of so many pretending to know. It is one of those facts which have become confounded by a variety of historians. Some asserted that she lost her way among the tangled mazes of the swamp, and sank into some pit or slough; others, more uncharitable, hinted that she had eloped with the household booty, and made off to some other province;

5. **A . . . Israel** a reference to II Samuel 3:38 in the Bible. The Puritans often called New England "Israel."

while others surmised that the tempter had decoyed her into a dismal quagmire, on the top of which her hat was found lying. In confirmation of this, it was said a great black man, with an ax on his shoulder, was seen late that very evening coming out of the swamp, carrying a bundle tied in a checked apron, with an air of surly triumph.

The most current and probable story, however, observes that Tom Walker grew so anxious about the fate of his wife and his property, that he set out at length to seek them both at the Indian fort. During a long summer's afternoon he searched about the gloomy place, but no wife was to be seen. He called her name repeatedly, but she was nowhere to be heard. The bittern alone responded to his voice, as he flew screaming by; or the bullfrog croaked dolefully from a neighboring pool. At length, it is said, just in the brown hour of twilight, when the owls began to hoot, and the bats to flit about, his attention was attracted by the clamor of carrion crows hovering about a cypress tree. He looked up, and beheld a bundle tied in a checked apron, and hanging in the branches of the tree, with a great vulture perched hard by, as if keeping watch upon it. He leaped with joy; for he recognized his wife's apron, and supposed it to contain the household valuables.

"Let us get hold of the property," said he, consolingly to himself, "and we will endeavor to do without the woman."

As he scrambled up the tree, the vulture spread its wide wings, and sailed off screaming into the deep shadows of the forest. Tom seized the checked apron, but woeful sight! found nothing but a heart and liver tied up in it!

Such, according to the most authentic old story, was all that was to be found of Tom's wife. She had probably attempted to deal with the black man as she had been accustomed to deal with her husband; but though a female scold is generally considered a match for the Devil, yet in this instance she appears to have had the worst of it. She must have died game, however; for it is said Tom noticed many prints of cloven feet deeply stamped about the tree, and found handfuls of hair, that looked as if they had been plucked from the coarse black shock of the woodsman.

▼ Critical Viewing

The narrator describes "a great vulture" and a checked apron hanging in a tree. What do you think happened to Tom Walker's wife? **INFER**

Tom knew his wife's prowess by experience. He shrugged his shoulders, as he looked at the signs of a fierce clapper-clawing. "Egad," said he to himself, "Old Scratch must have had a tough time of it!"

Tom consoled himself for the loss of his property, with the loss of his wife, for he was a man of fortitude. He even felt something like gratitude towards the black woodsman, who, he considered, had done him a kind-ness. He sought, therefore, to cultivate a further acquaintance with him, but for some time without success; the old blacklegs played shy, for whatever people may think, he is not always to be had for calling for: he knows how to play his cards when pretty sure of his game.

At length, it is said, when delay had whetted Tom's eagerness to the quick, and prepared him to agree to anything rather than not gain the promised treasure, he met the black man one evening in his usual woodsman's dress, with his ax on his shoulder, sauntering along the swamp, and humming a tune. He affected to receive Tom's advances with great indifference, made brief replies, and went on humming his tune.

By degrees, however, Tom brought him to business, and they began to haggle about the terms on which the former was to have the pirate's treasure. There was one condition which need not be mentioned, being generally understood in all cases where the Devil grants favors; but there were others about which, though of less importance, he was inflexibly obstinate. He insisted that the money found through his means should be employed in his service. He proposed, therefore, that Tom should employ it in the black traffic; that is to say, that he should fit out a slave ship. This, however, Tom resolutely refused: he was bad enough in all conscience, but the Devil himself could not tempt him to turn slave-trader.

Finding Tom so squeamish on this point, he did not insist upon it, but proposed, instead, that he should turn usurer; the Devil being extremely anxious for the increase of usurers, looking upon them as his peculiar[6] people.

To this no objections were made, for it was just to Tom's taste.

"You shall open a broker's shop in Boston next month," said the black man.

"I'll do it tomorrow, if you wish," said Tom Walker.

---

6. peculiar particular; special.

World LITERATURE IN CONTEXT

The Faust Legend

"The Devil and Tom Walker" is a variation of the Faust legend—a tale about a man who sells his soul to the Devil for earthly benefits. The legend was inspired by a real person, a wandering scholar and conjurer named Faust who lived in early sixteenth-century Germany. *Faustbach*, the first printed version of a Faust legend, was published in 1587. That story proposed that Faust had made a pact with the Devil for knowledge and power on Earth. Over the years, many variations of the Faust legend have appeared. Each retelling involves a person who trades his soul for experience, knowledge, or treasure. Adaptations do not share the same ending—in some, the protagonist is doomed; in others, he is redeemed.

Connect to the Literature

How do Irving's changes to the Faust story reveal the themes and issues of his era, in contrast to those of 16th century Europe?

Comprehension

What service does Tom refuse to provide for the Devil?

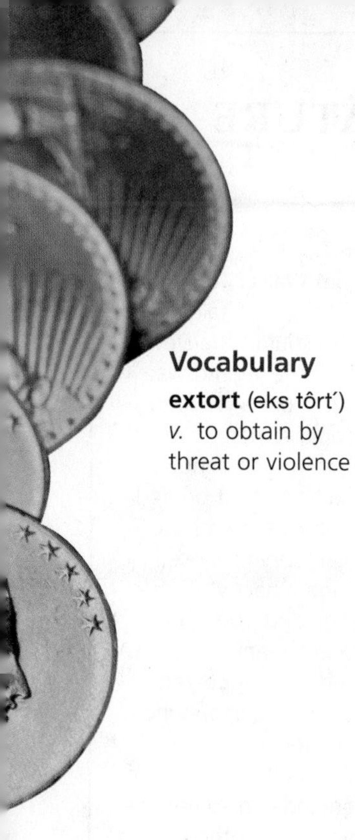

Vocabulary
extort (eks tôrt′)
v. to obtain by threat or violence

"You shall lend money at two per cent a month."

"Egad, I'll charge four!" replied Tom Walker.

"You shall extort bonds, foreclose mortgages, drive the merchant to bankruptcy—"

"I'll drive him to the D——l," cried Tom Walker.

"You are the usurer for my money!" said the blacklegs with delight. "When will you want the rhino?"[7]

"This very night."

"Done!" said the Devil.

"Done!" said Tom Walker. So they shook hands and struck a bargain.

A few days' time saw Tom Walker seated behind his desk in a countinghouse in Boston.

His reputation for a ready-moneyed man, who would lend money out for a good consideration, soon spread abroad. Everybody remembers the time of Governor Belcher,[8] when money was particularly scarce. It was a time of paper credit. The country had been deluged with government bills; the famous Land Bank[9] had been established; there had been a rage for speculating; the people had run mad with schemes for new settlements, for building cities in the wilderness; land jobbers[10] went about with maps of grants, and townships, and El Dorados,[11] lying nobody knew where, but which everybody was ready to purchase. In a word, the great speculating fever which breaks out every now and then in the country, had raged to an alarming degree, and everybody was dreaming of making sudden fortunes from nothing. As usual the fever had subsided; the dream had gone off, and the imaginary fortunes with it; the patients were left in doleful plight, and the whole country resounded with the consequent cry of "hard times."

At this propitious time of public distress did Tom Walker set up as usurer in Boston. His door was soon thronged by customers. The needy and adventurous, the gambling speculator, the dreaming land jobber, the thriftless tradesman, the merchant with cracked credit, in short, everyone driven to raise money by desperate means and desperate sacrifices, hurried to Tom Walker.

Thus Tom was the universal friend of the needy, and acted like a "friend in need"; that is to say, he always exacted good pay and good security. In proportion to the distress of the applicant was the hardness of his terms. He accumulated bonds and mortgages; gradually squeezed his customers closer and closer, and sent them

---

7. **rhino** (rī′ nō) slang term for money.
8. **Governor Belcher** Jonathan Belcher, the governor of Massachusetts Bay Colony from 1730 through 1741.
9. **Land Bank** a bank that financed transactions in real estate.
10. **land jobbers** people who bought and sold undeveloped land.
11. **El Dorados** (el′ də rä′ dōz) *n.* places that are rich in gold or opportunity. El Dorado was a legendary country in South America sought by early Spanish explorers for its gold and precious stones.

at length, dry as a sponge, from his door.

In this way he made money hand over hand, became a rich and mighty man, and exalted his cocked hat upon 'Change.[12] He built himself, as usual, a vast house, out of ostentation; but left the greater part of it unfinished and unfurnished, out of parsimony. He even set up a carriage in the fullness of his vainglory, though he nearly starved the horses which drew it; and as the ungreased wheels groaned and screeched on the axletrees, you would have thought you heard the souls of the poor debtors he was squeezing.

Vocabulary

ostentation (äs′ tən tā′ shən) *n.* boastful display

parsimony (pär′ sə mō′ nē) *n.* stinginess

As Tom waxed old, however, he grew thoughtful. Having secured the good things of this world, he began to feel anxious about those of the next. He thought with regret on the bargain he had made with his black friend, and set his wits to work to cheat him out of the conditions. He became, therefore, all of a sudden, a violent churchgoer. He prayed loudly and strenuously, as if heaven were to be taken by force of lungs. Indeed, one might always tell when he had sinned most during the week, by the clamor of his Sunday devotion. The quiet Christians who had been modestly and steadfastly traveling Zionward,[13] were struck with self-reproach at seeing themselves so suddenly outstripped in their career by this new-made convert. Tom was as rigid in religious as in money matters; he was a stern supervisor and censurer of his neighbors, and seemed to think every sin entered up to their account became a credit on his own side of the page. He even talked of the expediency of reviving the persecution of Quakers and Anabaptists. In a word, Tom's zeal became as notorious as his riches.

Evaluate Influences of the Historical Period

How do religious attitudes of the day inform Tom's feelings as he gets older?

Characterization

What do you learn about Tom's character from the narrator's description of his religious zeal?

Still, in spite of all this strenuous attention to forms, Tom had a lurking dread that the Devil, after all, would have his due. That he might not be taken unawares, therefore, it is said he always carried a small Bible in his coat pocket. He had also a great folio Bible on his countinghouse desk, and would frequently be found reading it when people called on business; on such occasions he would lay his green spectacles in the book, to mark the place, while he turned round to drive some usurious bargain.

Some say that Tom grew a little crackbrained in his old days, and that fancying his end approaching, he had his horse newly shod, saddled and bridled, and buried with his feet uppermost; because he supposed that at the last day the world would be turned upside down, in which case he should find his horse standing ready for mounting, and he was determined at the worst to give his old friend a run for it. This, however, is probably a mere old wives' fable. If he really did take such a precaution, it was totally superfluous; at least so says the authentic old legend, which closes his story in the following manner.

Comprehension

As he gets older, what does Tom always carry in his pocket?

12. 'Change exchange where bankers and merchants did business.

13. Zionward (zī′ ən wərd) toward heaven.

One hot summer afternoon in the dog days, just as a terrible black thunder-gust was coming up, Tom sat in his countinghouse in his white linen cap and India silk morning gown. He was on the point of foreclosing a mortgage, by which he would complete the ruin of an unlucky land speculator for whom he had professed the greatest friendship. The poor land jobber begged him to grant a few months' indulgence. Tom had grown testy and irritated, and refused another day.

"My family will be ruined and brought upon the parish," said the land jobber.

"Charity begins at home," replied Tom; "I must take care of myself in these hard times."

"You have made so much money out of me," said the speculator.

Tom lost his patience and his piety—"The Devil take me," said he, "if I have made a farthing!"

Just then there were three loud knocks at the street door. He stepped out to see who was there. A black man was holding a black horse, which neighed and stamped with impatience.

"Tom, you're come for," said the black fellow, gruffly. Tom shrunk back, but too late. He had left his little Bible at the bottom of his coat pocket, and his big Bible on the desk buried under the mortgage he was about to foreclose: never was sinner taken more unawares. The black man whisked him like a child into the saddle, gave the horse the lash, and away he galloped, with Tom on his back, in the midst of the thunderstorm. The clerks stuck their pens behind their ears, and stared after him from the windows. Away went Tom Walker, dashing down the streets, his white cap bobbing up and down, his morning gown fluttering in the wind, and his steed striking fire out of the pavement at every bound. When the clerks turned to look for the black man he had disappeared.

Tom Walker never returned to foreclose the mortgage. A countryman who lived on the border of the swamp, reported that in the height of the thunder-gust he had heard a great clattering of hoofs and a howling along the road, and running to the window caught sight of a figure, such as I have described, on a horse that galloped like mad across the fields, over the hills and down into the black hemlock swamp towards the old Indian fort; and that shortly after a thunderbolt falling in that direction seemed to set the whole forest in a blaze.

The good people of Boston shook their heads and shrugged their shoulders, but had been so much accustomed to witches and goblins and tricks of the Devil, in all kind of shapes from the first settlement of the colony, that they were not so much horror struck as might have been expected. Trustees were appointed to take charge of Tom's effects. There was nothing, however, to administer upon.

On searching his coffers all his bonds and mortgages were found reduced to cinders. In place of gold and silver his iron chest was filled with chips and shavings; two skeletons lay in his stable instead of his half-starved horses, and the very next day his great house took fire and was burned to the ground.

Such was the end of Tom Walker and his ill-gotten wealth. Let all griping money brokers lay this story to heart. The truth of it is not to be doubted. The very hole under the oak trees, whence he dug Kidd's money, is to be seen to this day; and the neighboring swamp and old Indian fort are often haunted in stormy nights by a figure on horseback, in morning gown and white cap, which is doubtless the troubled spirit of the usurer. In fact, the story has resolved itself into a proverb, and is the origin of that popular saying, so prevalent throughout New England, of "The Devil and Tom Walker."

Critical Reading

Cite textual evidence to support your responses.

1. **Key Ideas and Details (a)** What does the Devil offer Tom Walker? **(b) Analyze:** Why does Tom at first refuse?
2. **Key Ideas and Details (a)** What happens to Tom's wife? **(b) Interpret:** What do you learn about Tom, based on his reaction to the loss of his wife?
3. **Key Ideas and Details (a)** What agreement does Tom Walker ultimately make with the Devil? **(b) Draw Conclusions:** As the story progresses, why do you think Tom begins to go to church and carry a Bible with him at all times?
4. **Key Ideas and Details (a)** What does Tom do to cause the narrator to call him a "violent churchgoer"? **(b) Interpret:** In what way is Tom's approach to religion similar to his approach to financial dealings?
5. **Integration of Knowledge and Ideas (a) Take a Position:** Do you feel that Tom Walker deserved his fate? Explain. **(b) Defend:** Would you have felt more sympathy for Tom if he, like the original Faust, had sold his soul for knowledge instead of money? Explain.
6. **Integration of Ideas and Knowledge** Judging from the events of this story, what do you think Washington Irving might say about the effects of greed on society? In your response, use at least two of these Essential Question words: *avarice, failure, divide, charitable. **[Connecting to the Essential Question: How does literature shape or reflect society?]***

Close Reading Activities

The Devil and Tom Walker

Literary Analysis

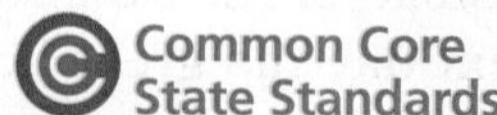

Writing
3. Write narratives to develop real or imagined experiences or events using effective technique, well-chosen details, and well-structured event sequences. *(p. 241)*
3.d. Use precise words and phrases, telling details, and sensory language to convey a vivid picture of the experiences, events, setting, and/or characters. *(p. 241)*

Language
2.a. Observe hyphenation conventions. *(p. 241)*

1. **Key Ideas and Details** Identify three things you learn about Tom Walker through **direct characterization.**
2. **Key Ideas and Details** **(a)** Use a chart like the one shown to record dialogue, thoughts, actions, and other details that help reveal the key traits of Tom's personality. **(b)** What do these examples of **indirect characterization** show to be his chief personality traits?

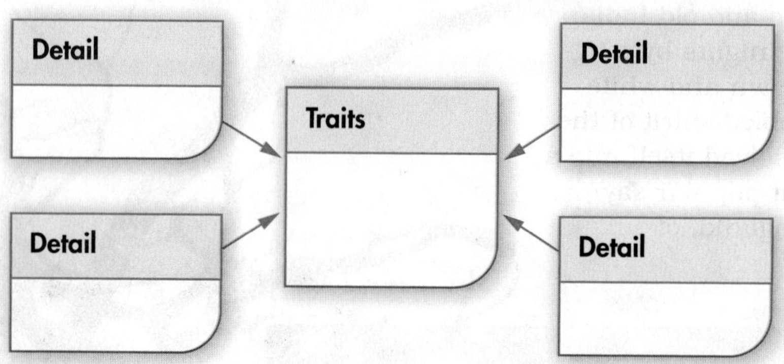

3. **Key Ideas and Details** **(a)** Describe Tom's wife based on the narrator's comments. **(b)** What do you learn about the relationship between Tom and his wife through indirect characterization? Explain.
4. **Key Ideas and Details** **(a)** What does the Walkers' home early in the story show about their personalities and values? **(b)** What does the home Tom builds later show about him?
5. **Craft and Structure** How would you describe the narrator's attitude toward Tom and his wife—for example, does he admire them? Is he amused by them? Cite details to support your answer.
6. **Integration of Knowledge and Ideas** **Evaluate the influences of the historical period** on characters, plot, and settings by identifying elements of the story that reflect an excessive concern for wealth in 1720s New England. **(a)** Note two characters who are driven by a desire for wealth. **(b)** Note at least one setting that demonstrates characters' concerns for the appearance of wealth. **(c)** Explain how the plot as a whole can be seen as an exploration of the dangers of excessive concern for wealth.
7. **Integration of Knowledge and Ideas** Does Irving effectively criticize this attitude? Cite details to support your evaluation.
8. **Integration of Knowledge and Ideas** **(a)** What does the story reveal about social attitudes toward Native Americans among New Englanders of European background in the 1720s? **(b)** Does Irving criticize these views? Cite story details to illustrate your thoughts.

Vocabulary Acquisition and Use

Word Analysis: Latin Prefix *ex-*

When used without a hyphen, the Latin prefix *ex-* means "out; out of; away from." In the word *extort*, for example, it combines with the Latin root *-tort-*, meaning "twist," to form a verb meaning "to twist out of" or "to force." For each item below, form a word that combines the prefix *ex-* with the specified Latin root. You may need to make small changes to the spelling of the root. Explain the meaning of each word you form.

1. *-clam-*, "to cry; to shout"
2. *-hal-*, "to breathe"
3. *-tend-*, "to stretch"

When the prefix *ex-* is used with a hyphen, it means "former," as in ex-Governor. Write three words that correctly use the prefix *ex-* with a hyphen.

Vocabulary: Sentence Completions

Use a word from the vocabulary list on page 226 to complete each sentence, and explain your choice. Use each word only once.

1. Walking on that crumbling bridge is ______.
2. During those years of ______, politicians quarreled all the time.
3. Hurricanes in the Gulf of Mexico are ______ in summer but rare in winter.
4. The building's gold trim and ornate stone carvings were marks of ______.
5. The miser's ______ irritated his neighbors.
6. He would ______ money by threatening to harm those who would not pay.

Writing to Sources

Narrative Text Write a new version of Irving's **story,** updating it in a way that addresses a modern audience. Keep Irving's theme and the conflict of someone selling his or her soul to the devil for worldly gain.

Prewriting Use a two-column chart to plan your story. Reread Irving's tale, listing plot events, characters, and settings in the left column. Put a check next to details you want to update. Then, decide on the best way to update those details and write your ideas in the right-hand column. Finally, write down ideas for sensory details that will bring the new settings and characters to life for the reader.

Drafting Write your story using the updated details. Pay particular attention to the *concrete sensory details* you listed and take care to describe the specific actions, movements, gestures, and feelings of the characters. Consider using *interior monologue,* in which a character shares his or her thoughts with the reader but keeps them hidden from other characters.

Revising Confirm that your new version balances the original story elements with new details. Check to see that the conflict and message are the same, while the language and setting reflect today's world.

Model: Updating a Story

Tom was sitting at his computer, downloading promissory notes. Suddenly, he saw a pair of beady eyes glaring at him from the screen. Then, pixel by pixel, a strange-looking face took shape.

While maintaining the intent of the story, modern elements such as "pixel" and "computer" update the setting.

Primary Sources

Government Document
Commission of Meriwether Lewis

Field Report
Crossing the Great Divide

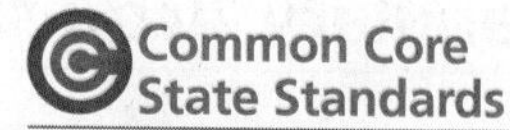

Common Core State Standards

Reading Informational Text

9. Analyze nineteenth-century foundational U.S. documents of historical and literary significance for their themes, purposes, and rhetorical features.

About the Text Forms

The word *commission* has different meanings in different contexts. In a financial context, it refers to a payment based on percentages of a sale; in a legal context, it refers to the perpetration of a crime. When referring to a written work, a **commission** is a type of **government document** in which an official person or institution assigns a special task to someone. In this commission, Thomas Jefferson, then president of the United States, describes Meriwether Lewis's main goal and assigns him specific responsibilities. The language Jefferson uses reflects his position as leader of the young country, as well as an almost scientific curiosity about the vast territories acquired in the Louisiana Purchase.

A **field report** is a first hand record of observations and data written by researchers or explorers at the site of their work, or "in the field." Field reports present objective information and may also contain notes on personal thoughts. Depending on their subjects, writers of field reports may use *specialized scientific or technical language*, as well as graphs, charts, maps, or illustrations. Lewis's detailed report reflects his commitment to meeting Jefferson's expectations.

Preparing to Read Complex Texts

The *general purpose* of any written work may be *to inform, to entertain, to persuade, to describe*, or *to reflect*. The documents you are about to read were written to inform. However, their *specific purposes* and intended *audiences,* or readers, are different. Jefferson was sending Lewis on a mission. His commission describes the details of the task. Lewis was reporting his progress to his boss. As you read, **identify the writer's purpose** and the ways in which it shapes the text.

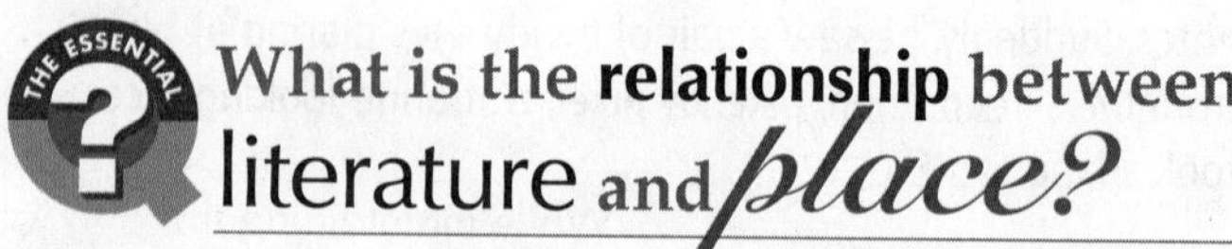
THE ESSENTIAL
What is the relationship between literature and place?

Reading these documents will help you understand how some nineteenth-century Americans felt about the vast continent they were beginning to explore. Notice details that show President Jefferson's interest in the resources provided by the new lands. Also, note details that tell you what Meriwether Lewis felt as he explored the wilderness.

Note-Taking Guide

Primary source documents are a rich source of information for researchers. As you read these documents, use a note-taking guide like the one shown to systematically organize relevant and accurate information.

1 Type of Document (check one)
☐ Newspaper ☐ Letter ☐ Map ☐ Memorandum ☐ Press release
☐ Report ☐ Government document ☐ E-mail ☐ Advertisement ☐ Other

2 Date(s) of Document ______

3 Author of Document ______
Author's Position or Title ______

4 Audience: For whom was the document written? ______

5 Purpose and Importance:

a **Why was this document written?** ______
Write down two details that support your answer: ______

b List two important ideas, statements, or observations from this document: ______

c What does this document show about life in the time and place in which it was written? ______

Purpose
A primary-source document may be written for more than one reason, or purpose. As you read, think about the different purposes each document may have served.

This guide was adapted from **U.S. National Archives** document-analysis worksheets.

Vocabulary

celestial (sə les′ tē əl) *adj.* of or in the sky, as planets or stars (p. 245)

practicable (prak′ ti kə bəl) *adj.* practical; possible (p. 245)

latitude (lat′ ə to͞od′) *n.* distance north or south from the equator (p. 245)

longitude (län′ jə to͞od) *n.* distance east or west on the earth's surface (p. 245)

membranes (mem′ branz′) *n.* thin, soft layers serving as coverings or linings (p. 247)

conciliatory (kən sil′ ē ə tôr′ ē) *adj.* intended to make peace or to reconcile; friendly (p. 249)

discretion (dis kre′ shən) *n.* judgment (p. 249)

dispatched (di spach′d′) *v.* sent off, usually on official business (p. 251)

prospect (pros′ spekt) *n.* something hoped for or expected (p. 251)

conspicuous (kən spik′ yo͞o əs) *adj.* obvious; easy to see or perceive (p. 252)

THE STORY BEHIND THE DOCUMENTS

President Thomas Jefferson

As the 19th century dawned, Ohio was the westward frontier of the United States, but that was not long to be. In 1803, **President Thomas Jefferson (1743–1826),** then the nation's third president, negotiated with France to buy a tract of land extending from the southern coast of Louisiana north into what is now Canada. This vast expanse included all of present-day Arkansas, Missouri, Iowa, Oklahoma, Kansas, and Nebraska. It also included parts of Minnesota, most of North and South Dakota, northeastern New Mexico, northern Texas, and portions of Colorado, Montana, and Wyoming. This enormous real-estate deal became known as **The Louisiana Purchase** and was one of the defining achievements of Thomas Jefferson's presidency. In a single treaty, Jefferson added more than 800,000 uncharted square miles to the holdings of the nation, effectively doubling the size of the country.

Jefferson had long wanted to pursue exploration of the Pacific Northwest. The completion of the Louisiana Purchase strengthened his resolve. He convinced Congress to allocate $2,500 to fund an expedition, writing:

The river Missouri, and Indians inhabiting it, are not as well known as rendered desirable by their connection with the Mississippi, and consequently with us. . . . An intelligent officer, with ten or twelve chosen men. . . might explore the whole line, even to the Western Ocean. . . .

Captain Meriwether Lewis

The "intelligent officer" he had in mind was his secretary, **Captain Meriwether Lewis (1774–1809).** On June 20, 1803, Jefferson wrote Lewis's commission to lead an expedition. He assigned Lewis the job of exploring the new territories with the particular objective of finding a water route from the Missouri River to the Pacific Ocean. Jefferson instructed Lewis to collect scientific data along the way, trace the boundaries of the Louisiana Territory, and claim the Oregon Territory for the United States. He also charged Lewis with the responsibility of recording almost every detail of his experiences.

Lewis had honed his leadership skills in the army. In preparation for the journey, he studied botany, biology, and cartography (map making). **Captain William Clark** became co-leader of the group, which numbered thirty-three people and one Newfoundland dog. Between 1804 and 1806, the team—which was known as **The Corps of Discovery**—completed an 8,000-mile trek from St. Louis to the source of the Missouri River, across the Rocky Mountains to the Pacific coast, and back to Missouri. Lewis started writing his report in May of 1804. Clark also maintained a journal in which he drew pictures of the people, plants, and animals the expedition encountered.

Commission of
MERIWETHER LEWIS

Thomas Jefferson

▲ Compass used by Lewis and Clark

To Meriwether Lewis,

Esquire, captain of the first regiment of infantry of the United States of America: Your situation as secretary of the president of the United States, has made you acquainted with the objects of my confidential message of January 18, 1803, to the legislature; you have seen the act they passed, which, though expressed in general terms, was meant to sanction those objects, and you are appointed to carry them into execution.

Instruments for ascertaining by **celestial** observations the geography of the country, through which you will pass, have been already provided. Light articles for barter, and presents among the Indians, arms for your attendants, say for from ten to twelve men, boats, tents, and other traveling apparatus, with ammunition, medicine, surgical instruments and provisions you will have prepared with such aids as the Secretary at War can yield in his department; and from him also you will receive authority to engage among our troops, by voluntary agreement, the number of attendants abovementioned, over whom you, as their commanding officer, are invested with all the powers the laws give in such a case...

The object of your mission is to explore the Missouri river, and such principal streams of it, as, by its course and communication with the waters of the Pacific ocean, whether the Columbia, Oregan [*sic*], Colorado, or any other river, may offer the most direct and **practicable** water-communication across the continent, for the purposes of commerce.

Beginning at the mouth of the Missouri, you will take observations of **latitude** and **longitude**, at all remarkable points on the river, and especially at the mouths of rivers, at rapids, at islands, and other places and objects distinguished by such natural marks and characters, of a durable kind, as that they may with certainty be recognized hereafter. The courses of the river between these points of observation may

Vocabulary

celestial (sə les′ tē əl) *adj.* of or in the sky, as planets or stars

practicable (prak′ ti kə bəl) *adj.* practical; possible

latitude (lat′ə to͞od′) *n.* distance north or south from the equator

longitude (län′jə to͞od) *n.* distance east or west on the earth's surface

Comprehension

What preparations for the journey does Jefferson instruct Lewis to make?

▲ Primary Source: Map How does this period map clarify your understanding of Jefferson's interest in the newly acquired lands? **[Connect]**

be supplied by the compass, the log-line, and by time, corrected by the observations themselves. The variations of the needle, too, in different places, should be noticed.

The interesting points of the portage between the heads of the Missouri, and of the water offering the best communication with the Pacific Ocean, should also be fixed by observation; and the course of that water to the ocean, in the same manner as that of the Missouri.

Your observations are to be taken with great pains and accuracy; to be entered distinctly and intelligibly for others as well as yourself; to comprehend all the elements necessary, with the aid of the usual tables, to fix the latitude and longitude of the places at which they were taken; and are to be rendered to the war-office, for the purpose of having the calculations made concurrently by proper persons within the United States. Several copies of these, as well as of your other notes, should be made at leisure times, and put into the care of the most trustworthy of your attendants to guard, by multiplying them against the accidental losses to which they will be exposed. A further guard would be, that one of these copies be on the cuticular membranes of the paper-birch, as less liable to injury from damp than common paper.

The commerce which may be carried on with the people inhabiting the line you will pursue, renders a knowledge of those people important. You will therefore endeavor to make your self acquainted, as far as a diligent pursuit of your journey shall admit, with the names of the nations and their numbers;

The extent and limits of their possessions;
Their relations with other tribes or nations;
Their language, traditions, monuments;
Their ordinary occupations in agriculture, fishing, hunting, war, arts, and the implements for these;
Their food, clothing, and domestic accommodations;
The diseases prevalent among them, and the remedies they use;
Moral and physical circumstances which distinguish them from the tribes we know;
Peculiarities in their laws, customs, and dispositions;
And articles of commerce they may need or furnish, and to what extent.

And, considering the interest which every nation has in extending and strengthening the authority of reason and justice among the people around them, it will be useful to acquire what knowledge you can of the state of morality, religion, and information among them; as it may better enable those who may endeavor to civilize and instruct them, to adapt their measures to the existing notions and practices of those on whom they are to operate.

Other objects worthy of notice will be—The soil and face of the country, its growth and vegetable productions, especially those not of the United States;

The animals of the country generally, and especially those not known in the United States;
The remains and accounts of any which may be deemed rare or extinct;

The mineral productions of every kind, but more particularly metals, limestone, pitcoal, and saltpeter; salines and mineral waters, noting the temperature of the last, and such circumstances as may indicate their character;

Vocabulary
membranes (mem′ branz′) *n.* thin, soft layers serving as coverings or linings

Captain Clark's magnet and compass ▼

Comprehension
What does Jefferson tell Lewis to look for between the heads of the Missouri River and the Pacific Ocean?

 COMMON CORE ▪ RESEARCH PROJECT

To Meriwether Lewis esquire, Captain of the 1st regiment of infantry of the United States of America.

Your situation as Secretary of the President of the United States has made you acquainted with the objects of my confidential message of Jan. 18. 1803. to the legislature; you have seen the act they passed, which, tho' expressed in general terms, was meant to sanction those objects, and you are appointed to carry them into execution.

Instruments for ascertaining by celestial observations the geography of the country thro' which you will pass, have been already provided. light articles for barter, & presents among the Indians, arms for your attendants, say for from 10. to 12. men, boats, tents, & other travelling apparatus, with ammunition, medicine, surgical instruments & provisions you will have prepared with such aids as the Secretary at War can yield in his department; & from him also you will recieve authority to engage among our troops, by voluntary agreement, the number of attendants above mentioned, over whom you, as their commanding officer are invested with all the powers the laws give in such a case.

As your movements while within the limits of the U.S. will be better directed by occasional communications, adapted to circumstances as they arise, they will not be noticed here. what follows will respect your proceedings after your departure from the U.S.

Your mission has been communicated to the Ministers here from France, Spain, & Great Britain, and through them to their governments; and such assurances given them as to it's objects, as we trust will satisfy them. the country of Louisiana having been ceded by Spain to France, the passport you have from the Minister of France, the representative of the present sovereign of the country, will be a protection with all it's subjects; and that from the Minister of England will entitle you to the friendly aid of any traders of that allegiance with whom you may happen to meet.

The object of your mission is to explore the Missouri river, & such principal stream of it, as, by it's course & communication with the waters of the Pacific ocean, may offer the most direct & practicable water communication across this continent, for the purposes of commerce.

Beginning at the mouth of the Missouri, you will take observations of latitude & longitude, at all remarkable points on the river, & especially at the mouths of rivers, at rapids, at islands, & other places & objects distinguished by such natural marks & characters of a durable kind, as that they may with certainty be recognised hereafter. the courses of the river between these points of observation may be supplied by the compass, the log-line & by time, corrected by the observations themselves. the variations of the compass too, in different places, should be noticed.

The interesting points of the portage between the heads of the Missouri & the water offering the best communication with the Pacific ocean, should also be fixed by observation, & the course of that water to the ocean, in the same manner as that of the Missouri.

Your observations are to be taken with great pains & accuracy, to be entered distinctly, & intelligibly for others as well as yourself, to comprehend all the elements necessary, with the aid of the usual tables, to fix the

22884

▲ Shown above is the original letter of commission President Jefferson wrote to Captain Lewis. The clarity of Jefferson's handwriting has been blurred by time.

Volcanic appearances;

Climate, as characterized by the thermo-meter, by the proportion of rainy, cloudy, and clear days; by lightning, hail, snow, ice; by the access and recess of frost; by the winds prevailing at different seasons; the dates at which particular plants put forth, or lose their flower or leaf; times of appearance of particular birds, reptiles or insects....

In all your [dealings] with the natives, treat them in the most friendly and conciliatory manner which their own conduct will admit; allay all jealousies as to the object of your journey; satisfy them of its innocence; make them acquainted with the position, extent, character, peaceable and commercial dispositions of the United States; of our wish to be neighborly, friendly, and useful to them, and of our dispositions to a commercial [relationship] with them; confer with them on the points most convenient as mutual emporiums, and the articles of most desirable interchange for them and us. If a few of their influential chiefs, within practicable distance, wish to visit us, arrange such a visit with them, and furnish them with authority to call on our officers on their entering the United States, to have them conveyed to this place at the public expense. If any of them should wish to have some of their young people brought up with us, and taught such arts as may be useful to them, we will receive, instruct, and take care of them. Such a mission, whether of influential chiefs, or of young people, would give some security to your own party. Carry with you some matter of the kine-pox; inform those of them with whom you may be of its efficacy as a preservative from the small-pox, and instruct and encourage them in the use of it. This may be especially done wherever you winter.

As it is impossible for us to foresee in what manner you will be received by those people, whether with hospitality or hostility, so is it impossible to prescribe the exact degree of perseverance with which you are to pursue your journey. We value too much the lives of citizens to offer them to probable destruction. Your numbers will be sufficient to secure you against the unauthorized opposition of individuals, or of small parties; but if a superior force, authorized, or not authorized, by a nation, should be arrayed against your further passage, and inflexibly determined to arrest it, you must decline its further pursuit and return. In the loss of yourselves we should lose also the information you will have acquired. By returning safely with that, you may enable us to renew the essay with better calculated means. To your own discretion, therefore, must be left the degree of danger you may risk, and the point at which you should decline, only saying, we wish you to err on the side of your safety, and to bring back your party safe, even if it be with less information. . . .

Vocabulary

conciliatory (kən sil′ ē ə tôr′ ē) *adj.* intended to make peace or to reconcile; friendly

Primary Sources

Commission In what ways do Jefferson's instructions to Lewis regarding the native peoples show his official interest in matters of public concern?

Vocabulary

discretion (dis kre′ shən) *n.* judgment

Crossing the GREAT DIVIDE

Meriwether Lewis

Lewis and Clark With Sacagawea at the Great Falls of the Missouri, Olaf Seltzer, The Thomas Gilcrease Institute of Art, Tulsa, Oklahoma

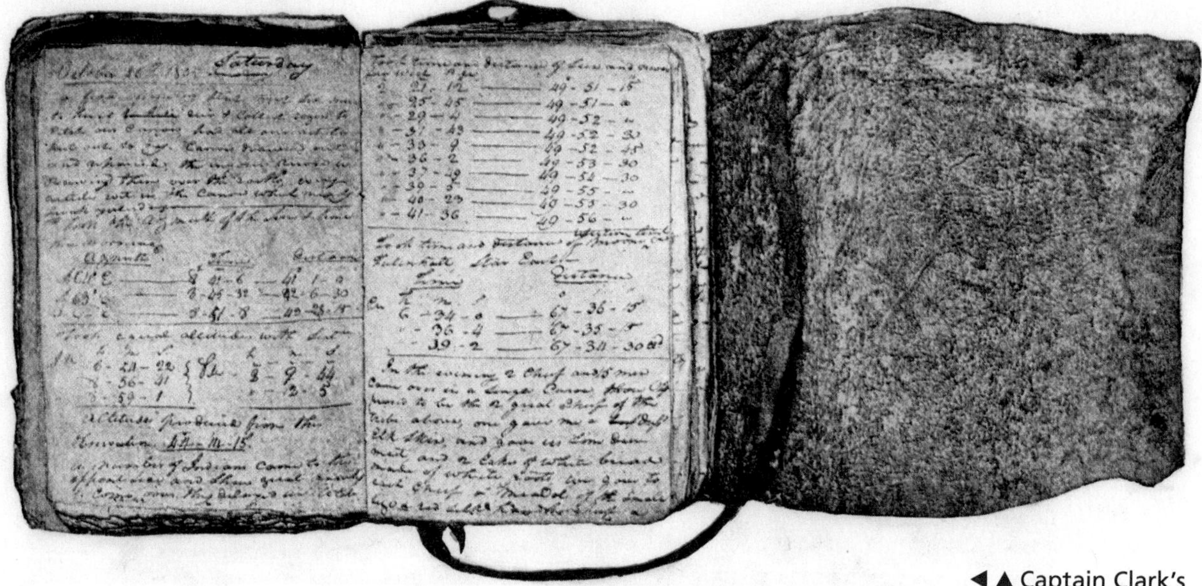

◀▲ Captain Clark's journal is shown here both closed (left) and open (right).

Saturday, August 17th, 1805

This morning I arose very early and dispatched Drewyer and the Indian down the river. Sent Shields to hunt. I made McNeal cook the remainder of our meat which afforded a slight breakfast for ourselves and the Chief. Drewyer had been gone about 2 hours when an Indian who had straggled some little distance down the river returned and reported that the white men were coming, that he had seen them just below. They all appeared transported with joy, and the chief repeated his fraternal hug. I felt quite as much gratified at this information as the Indians appeared to be. Shortly after Capt. Clark arrived with the Interpreter Charbono, and the Indian woman, who proved to be a sister of the Chief Cameahwait. The meeting of those was really affecting, particularly between Sah-ca-ga-we-ah and an Indian woman, who had been taken prisoner at the same time with her, and who had afterwards escaped from the Minnetares and rejoined her nation. At noon the canoes arrived, and we had the satisfaction once more to find ourselves all together, with a flattering prospect of being able to obtain as many horses shortly as would enable us to prosecute our voyage by land should that by water be deemed unadvisable.

Vocabulary

dispatched (di spach'd´)
v. sent off, usually on official business

Vocabulary

prospect (pros´ spekt)
n. something hoped for or expected

Comprehension

What information does the Indian bring to Lewis and his group?

◀ **Primary Source: Art** What does this painting of Lewis and Clark with Sacagawea suggest about the relationships among the people in it? Does Lewis's journal support the suggestion? **INFER; SUPPORT**

▲ **Primary Source: Art** What do the placement and size of these sketches in William Clark's journal reveal about his purpose in making them? **INTERPRET**

Identifying Writer's Purpose

Which of Lewis's specific purposes for writing are evident in this paragraph?

Vocabulary

conspicuous (kən spik′ yo͞o əs) *adj.* obvious; easy to see or perceive

We now formed our camp just below the junction of the forks on the Lard. side[1] in a level smooth bottom covered with a fine turf of greensward. Here we unloaded our canoes and arranged our baggage on shore; formed a canopy of one of our large sails and planted some willow brush in the ground to form a shade for the Indians to sit under while we spoke to them, which we thought it best to do this evening. Accordingly about 4 P.M. we called them together and through the medium of Labuish, Charbono and Sah-ca-ga-we-ah, we communicated to them fully the objects which had brought us into this distant part of the country, in which we took care to make them a **conspicuous** object of our own good wishes and the care of our government.

1. **Lard. side** abbreviation for larboard, the port side of a ship. From their perspective, they camped on the left side of the river.

We made them sensible of their dependence on the will of our government for every species of merchandise as well for their defense and comfort; and apprised them of the strength of our government and its friendly dispositions towards them. We also gave them as a reason why we wished to penetrate the country as far as the ocean to the west of them was to examine and find out a more direct way to bring merchandise to them. That as no trade could be carried on with them before our return to our homes that it was mutually advantageous to them as well as to ourselves that they should render us such aids as they had it in their power to furnish in order to hasten our voyage and of course our return home.

▲ **Primary Source: Art**
Why do you think Clark used less detail in these sketches than in his drawings of plants and animals? **INFER**

Sextant used for celestial navigation by the expedition ▶

Critical Reading

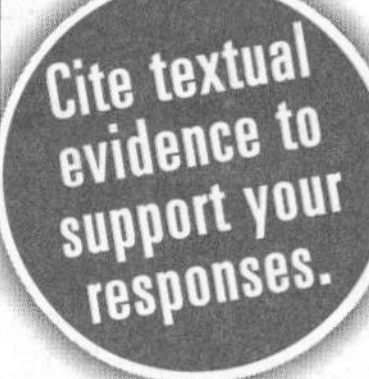
Cite textual evidence to support your responses.

1. **Key Ideas and Details** **(a)** In the Commission, what information did Jefferson tell Lewis to write out in multiple copies? **(b)** To what office of the government was Lewis instructed to render these copies? **(c) Infer:** What do these instructions suggest about the importance of this information to Jefferson and the United States government? Explain.
2. **Key Ideas and Details** **(a)** In his report, how did Lewis feel about being reunited with his party? **(b) Analyze:** What are his reasons for feeling as he did?
3. **Key Ideas and Details** **(a)** Note two tasks that Jefferson instructed Lewis to perform. **(b) Evaluate:** Judging from this excerpt, how well do you think Lewis fulfilled his assignment?
4. **Integration of Knowledge and Ideas** **(a)** What did Lewis tell the Indians to expect from the United States government? **(b) Speculate:** In what ways does his dialogue with the Indians reflect specific instructions from Jefferson?

COMMON CORE • RESEARCH PROJECT

Government Document • Field Report

Comparing Primary Sources

Refer to your Note-Taking Guide to complete these questions.

1. **(a)** Find two details from the commission that show Jefferson is writing as a government official, not a private person. **(b)** In this excerpt, is Lewis writing from an official or a personal perspective? Explain.
2. **(a)** Using a chart like the one shown, identify one statement from each document and explain what it shows about life in the early 1800s. **(b)** From which document do you learn more? Explain.

Author	Statement	Life in early 1800s
Jefferson		
Lewis		

3. **(a)** Note one fact you learn from the commission about Jefferson's reasons for exploring the new lands. **(b)** Locate one statement in Lewis's report that *verifies or clarifies* that fact. Explain your choice.
4. **(a)** Identify two similarities and two differences in how these documents describe the Lewis and Clark expedition. **(b)** Explain the reasons for these similarities and differences.

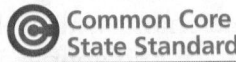

Common Core State Standards

Writing

7. Conduct short as well as more sustained research projects to answer a question or solve a problem; narrow or broaden the inquiry when appropriate; synthesize multiple sources on the subject, demonstrating understanding of the subject under investigation. *(p. 255)*

8. Gather relevant information from multiple authoritative print and digital sources, using advanced searches effectively; assess the strengths and limitations of each source in terms of the task, purpose, and audience; integrate information into the text selectively to maintain the flow of ideas, avoiding plagiarism and overreliance on any one source and following a standard format for citation. *(p. 255)*

Vocabulary Acquisition and Use

Use New Words Correctly For each word pair, write a sentence in which you use both words correctly.

1. conspicuous/discretion
2. prospect/dispatched
3. conciliatory/practicable

Content-Area Vocabulary Answer each question. Then, explain your reasoning.

4. Would an astronomer or a biologist be more interested in ***celestial*** bodies?
5. Can a city change its ***latitude***?
6. Would a sailor be concerned about ***longitude***?
7. Would the outer bark of a tree be considered a ***membrane***?
8. Can a ***mineral*** be a living organism?

Etymology Study The word *celestial* comes from the Latin word *caelestis,* which means "heaven" or "sky." It often appears in opposition to the word *terrestrial.* Research the history of the word *terrestrial,* locate its root, and write a definition. Then, identify two other words that share the same root.

Research Task

Topic: The Life of Sacagawea

Sacagawea, the Shoshone woman who traveled with Lewis and Clark, was an invaluable source of help and information to the explorers. While some parts of Sacagawea's life are well documented, there is scarce and sometimes conflicting information about other periods of her life. She is, therefore, an intriguing topic for research.

Assignment: Write a biographical narrative designed as a **book for young readers** on the life of Sacagawea. As you research, differentiate between the theories about Sacagawea and the evidence that supports them. Determine the quality of the evidence you find for each theory in order to decide whether to include that information in your narrative.

Formulate a research plan. Working alone or in a group, formulate questions, such as the following, to answer through research:

- What are the basic facts of Sacagawea's life?
- What did she do on the Lewis and Clark expedition?
- What happened to her after the expedition?
- How does the popular cultural view of Sacagawea differ from the provable facts?

Gather sources. Use online and library sources to follow your research plan and find answers to your questions. Collect the information in a systematic way, grouping items about Sacagawea in categories such as "Family," "Accomplishments," and "Personal Qualities."

Synthesize information. When you synthesize information, you evaluate, assemble, and combine it in order to create a cogent argument—in this case, a reliable biography. Use a graphic organizer like the one shown to differentiate between theories about Sacagawea and the weak or strong evidence that supports them.

Model: Differentiating Between Theories and Evidence

Theory	Evidence	Evaluation of Evidence
Sacagawea was calm and brave under pressure.	Personal diaries of members of the expedition agree.	Strong, reliable first-hand evidence from multiple sources.

Organize and present ideas. As you write, remember that you are addressing young readers. This means you may use shorter sentences and easier vocabulary and should plan to include useful visuals. However, a narrative for young readers should never be so simplified that it becomes incorrect or misleading. Make sure your facts are accurate according to the best sources. Include a Works Cited list in which you cite your sources, both print and electronic, correctly. (For more information on correct citations, see page R21 in this textbook.)

RESEARCH TIP

Pay careful attention to sources of online information. A Web site administered by a university or a recognized scholar is likely to be more reliable than one sponsored by a blogger, a club, a commercial company, or a popular media outlet.

Use a checklist like the one shown to be sure your research results in a reliable biographical narrative.

Research Checklist

- ☐ Have I answered all my research questions?
- ☐ Have I differentiated between theories and evidence?
- ☐ Have I included strong evidence throughout?
- ☐ Do my visuals adequately illustrate the narrative?

Building Knowledge and Insight

from *The Song of Hiawatha* • *The Tide Rises, The Tide Falls* • *Thanatopsis* • *Old Ironsides*

Connecting to the Essential Question The Fireside Poets' work helped to create a mythology of early American heroes. As you read, notice details that praise or celebrate American settings or characters. This will help as you consider the Essential Question: **What makes American literature American?**

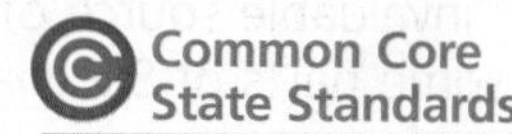

Reading Literature
5. Analyze how an author's choices concerning how to structure specific parts of a text contribute to its overall structure and meaning as well as its aesthetic impact.

Close Reading Focus

Meter

In poetry, the systematic arrangement of stressed (´) and unstressed (˘) syllables is called **meter.** The basic unit of meter is the **foot,** which usually consists of one stressed and one or more unstressed syllables. The most frequently used foot in American verse is the *iamb*—one unstressed syllable followed by a stressed syllable. The type and number of feet in the lines of a poem determine its meter. For example, a pattern of five iambs per line is known as *iambic pentameter*, as in this line from Bryant's "Thanatopsis":

> The youth in life's green spring, and he who goes

In "The Song of Hiawatha," Longfellow uses the *trochee*, a stressed syllable followed by an unstressed syllable. This line has four trochees, a meter called *trochaic tetrameter*:

> Ye who love the haunts of Nature

Comparing Literary Works The meter of a poem can affect the **mood,** or emotional quality, it evokes in a reader. Meter can also contribute to a poem's meaning. For example, the drum-like rhythm of the trochees in "The Song of Hiawatha" reflects the Native American subject and adds to the poem's intensity. To better hear and understand these metered poems, read them aloud, listening for patterns. Identify the meter and compare the moods each helps to evoke. For each poem, consider how the meter contributes to the work's overall meaning.

Preparing to Read Complex Texts To check your understanding of what you have read, **summarize** the work or parts of the work by briefly stating the main ideas and supporting details in your own words. As you read, use a graphic organizer like the one shown to summarize each poem.

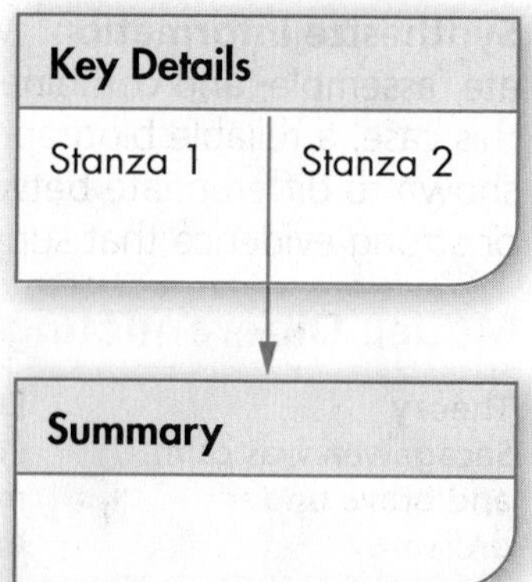

Vocabulary

The words listed here are key to understanding the texts that follow. Copy the words into your notebook, and note which words have three syllables or more.

efface **pensive**
eloquence **venerable**

Henry Wadsworth Longfellow (1807–1882)

Author of "The Song of Hiawatha"; "The Tide Rises, The Tide Falls"

Henry Wadsworth Longfellow enjoyed a long and successful career as a poet, publishing his first collection of poems, *Voices in the Night,* in 1839. By writing poetry that soothed and encouraged readers, Longfellow became the first American poet to reach a wide audience and create a national interest in poetry. His popular anthology *The Poets and Poetry of Europe,* published in 1845, accomplished his goal of bringing non-English poetry to the ordinary American reader.

Born and raised in Portland, Maine, Longfellow graduated from Bowdoin College and went on to teach modern languages at Harvard University for eighteen years, often writing and publishing his own textbooks for his classes. He also translated foreign literature into English, finding in foreign poetry inspirational models for his own work.

Longfellow experimented with adapting traditional European verse forms and themes to uniquely American subjects. Many of his narrative poems, such as "The Song of Hiawatha" (1855), "The Courtship of Miles Standish" (1858), and "Paul Revere's Ride" (1860), gave a romanticized view of America's early history and democratic ideals.

The Poet's Legacy Longfellow's poetry has been criticized for being overly optimistic and sentimental. Yet it was his optimism and sentimentality that made Longfellow the most popular poet of his day. In fact, Longfellow was so popular in his time that his seventy-fifth birthday was celebrated as if it were a national holiday.

"Talk not of wasted affection; affection never was wasted."

from *The Song of* HIAWATHA

Henry Wadsworth Longfellow

BACKGROUND "The Song of Hiawatha" is a long narrative poem based on a legend of the Ojibway, a Native American people of the Great Lakes region. Hiawatha was actually an Iroquois chief who joined with Dekanawidah (page 41) in efforts to unite the Iroquois people. In the Ojibway version, Hiawatha takes on godlike, heroic qualities. Published in 1855, Longfellow's famous poem contains over twenty sections recounting Hiawatha's adventures. The following lines are from the prologue, or introduction, to the poem.

Prologue

Should you ask me, whence these stories?
Whence these legends and traditions,
With the odours of the forest,
With the dew and damp of meadows,
With the curling smoke of wigwams,
With the rushing of great rivers,
With their frequent repetitions,
And their wild reverberations,
As of thunder in the mountains?

I should answer, I should tell you:
'From the forests and the prairies,
From the great lakes of the Northland,
From the land of the Ojibways,
From the land of the Dacotahs,[1]
From the mountains, moors, and fenlands,[2]
Where the heron, the Shuh-shuh-gah,[3]
Feeds among the reeds and rushes.
I repeat them as I heard them
From the lips of Nawadaha,
The musician, the sweet singer.'

Summarizing In two sentences, summarize the question and answer in lines 1–20.

1. **Dacotahs** *n.* a Native American people living near the Ojibway; usually spelled *Dakotas*. Minniehaha, Hiawatha's wife in Longfellow's poem, is Dacotah.
2. **moors . . . fenlands** swampy areas.
3. **Shuh-shuh-gah** Longfellow's attempt to spell the Ojibway word for the great blue heron, a large water bird.

Ye who love the haunts of Nature,
Love the sunshine of the meadow,
Love the shadow of the forest,
Love the wind among the branches,
And the rain-shower and the snowstorm,
And the rushing of great rivers
Through their palisades[4] of pine-trees,
And the thunder in the mountains,
Whose innumerable echoes
Flap like eagles in their eyries;[5]
Listen to these wild traditions,
To this Song of Hiawatha!

Ye who love a nation's legends,
Love the ballads of a people,
That like voices from afar off
Call to us to pause and listen,
Speak in tones so plain and childlike,
Scarcely can the ear distinguish
Whether they are sung or spoken;
Listen to this Indian Legend,
To this Song of Hiawatha!

4. **palisades** (pal´ ə sādz) *n.* stakes of a fence; used figuratively here.
5. **eyries** (ā´ ər ēz *or* ē´ rēz) *n.* high nests; often spelled *aeries*.

LITERATURE IN CONTEXT

Literary Connection

The Fireside Poets

The Fireside Poets—Henry Wadsworth Longfellow (1807–1882), Oliver Wendell Holmes (1809–1894), James Russell Lowell (1819–1891), and John Greenleaf Whittier (1807–1892)—got their nickname because their works were widely read as family entertainment at American firesides. The four poets—all New England born and bred—chose uniquely American settings and subjects but drew heavily on English tradition for their themes, meter, and imagery. Though this reliance on traditional styles prevented them from being truly innovative, the Fireside Poets were literary giants in their day and ranked for decades among America's best-loved poets.

Connect to the Literature

Fireside reading often meant oral recitation. Review the poems by the Fireside Poets (pages 258, 260, and 266) and list three qualities that make them well suited to oral recitation.

Critical Reading

1. **Key Ideas and Details (a)** According to this prologue, what are the sources of the Hiawatha legend? **(b) Analyze:** What details in lines 1–20 stress the authenticity of this retelling?
2. **Key Ideas and Details (a)** What attitude toward nature does the prologue say a reader who appreciates "The Song of Hiawatha" will have? **(b) Analyze:** What attitude toward nature does the prologue convey?
3. **Key Ideas and Details (a)** What attitude toward traditional legends and ballads is expressed in this prologue? **(b) Evaluate:** Based on this prologue, what values do you think the poem will express?

Cite textual evidence to support your responses.

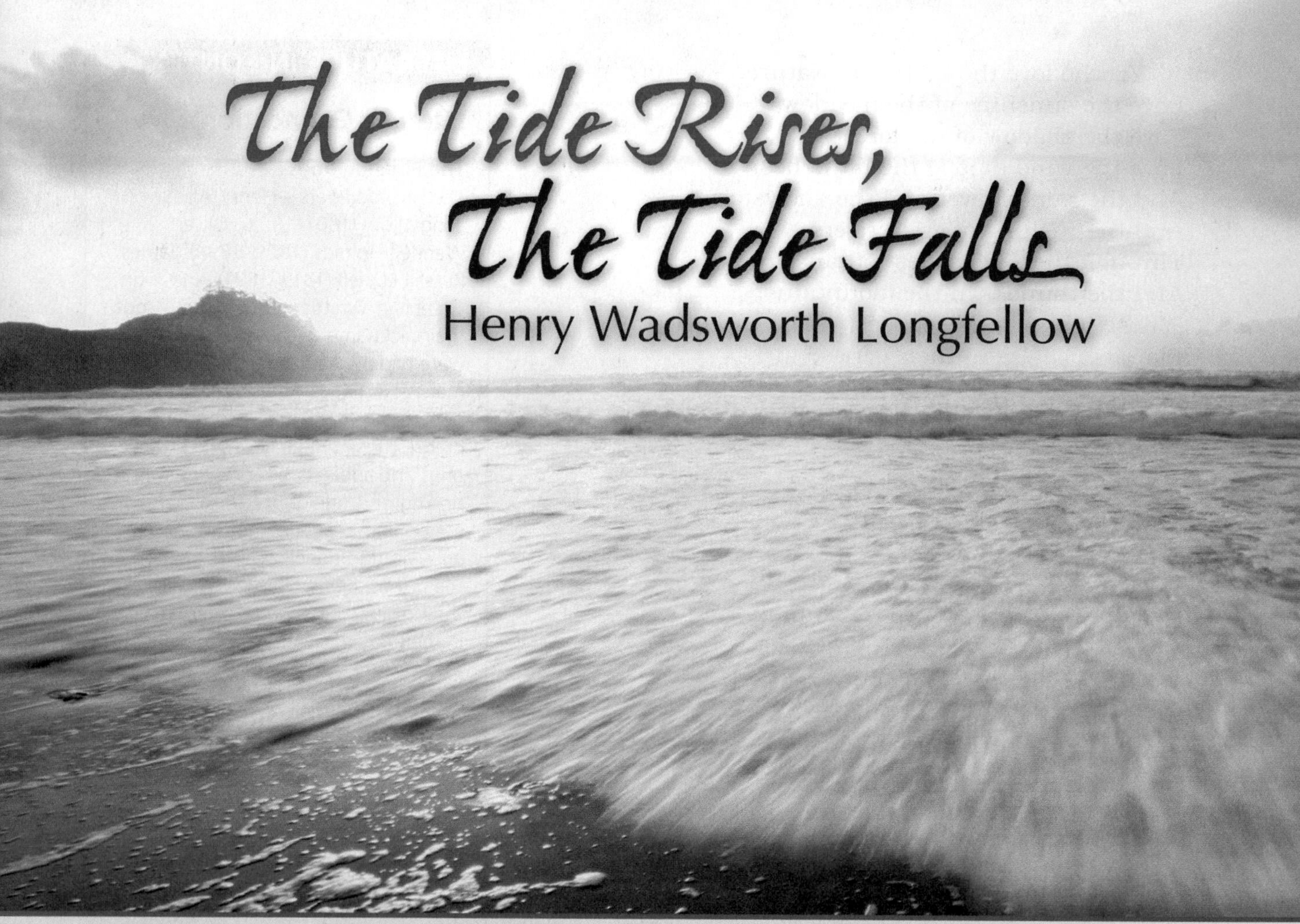

The Tide Rises, The Tide Falls

Henry Wadsworth Longfellow

Meter
How does the broken meter in lines 1, 5, 10, and 15 reflect the content of those lines?

Vocabulary
efface (ə fās′) *v.* erase; wipe out

The tide rises, the tide falls.
The twilight darkens, the curlew[1] calls;
Along the sea sands damp and brown
The traveler hastens toward the town,
    And the tide rises, the tide falls.

Darkness settles on roofs and walls,
But the sea, the sea in the darkness calls:
The little waves, with their soft, white hands,
Efface the footprints in the sands,
    And the tide rises, the tide falls.

The morning breaks; the steeds in their stalls
Stamp and neigh, as the hostler[2] calls:
The day returns, but nevermore
Returns the traveler to the shore,
    And the tide rises, the tide falls.

---

1. **curlew** (kʉr′ lo͞o) *n.* large wading bird associated with evening.
2. **hostler** (häs′ lər) *n.* person tending the horses at an inn or a stable.

William Cullen Bryant (1794–1878)

Author of "Thanatopsis"

As a journalist and political activist, William Cullen Bryant fought to ensure that industrialization did not obscure America's democratic values. Bryant began writing poetry at the age of nine and drafted the first version of "Thanatopsis," his most famous poem, when he was only nineteen. To support himself, Bryant practiced law for ten years while continuing to write poetry in his spare time. In 1825, he moved to New York City and became a journalist; by 1829, he had become editor-in-chief and part owner of the New York newspaper the *Evening Post.*

Voice for Justice Bryant used his position as an influential journalist to defend human rights and personal freedoms. He was an outspoken advocate of women's rights and a passionate foe of slavery. Bryant was the first American poet to win worldwide critical acclaim, and his work helped establish the Romantic Movement in America.

Romantic Influence Romanticism was an artistic and philosophical movement that stressed emotion over reason and celebrated individuality and the human imagination. Critical of science and the new industrial age, Romantic writers turned instead to nature as a source of spiritual comfort and guidance. Bryant was influenced by the work of the British Romantics William Wordsworth and Samuel Taylor Coleridge, whose 1798 publication of *Lyrical Ballads* revolutionized British poetry. After reading Wordsworth and Coleridge, Bryant incorporated aspects of romanticism into his poem "Thanatopsis."

"To me it seems that one of the most important requisites for a great poet is a luminous style."

Thanatopsis

William Cullen Bryant

▲ Critical Viewing

What moods or emotions does this painting capture for you? Explain. **INTERPRET**

Vocabulary

eloquence (el′ ə kwəns)
n. expressiveness

BACKGROUND The poem's title, which comes from Greek, means "a view or meditation on death." Bryant wrote his first draft of "Thanatopsis" while still a teenager, revised it often, and published his final longer version in 1821.

To him who in the love of Nature holds
Communion[1] with her visible forms, she speaks
A various language; for his gayer hours
She has a voice of gladness, and a smile
And eloquence of beauty, and she glides
Into his darker musings, with a mild
And healing sympathy, that steals away
Their sharpness, ere[2] he is aware. When thoughts
Of the last bitter hour come like a blight
Over thy spirit, and sad images
Of the stern agony, and shroud, and pall,
And breathless darkness, and the narrow house,[3]
Make thee to shudder, and grow sick at heart—
Go forth, under the open sky, and list
To Nature's teachings, while from all around—
Earth and her waters, and the depths of air—
Comes a still voice—Yet a few days, and thee

1. **Communion** (kə myo͞on′yən) *n.* the act of sharing one's thoughts; intimate conversation.
2. **ere** (er) *conj.* before.
3. **narrow house** coffin.

The all-beholding sun shall see no more
In all his course; nor yet in the cold ground,
Where thy pale form was laid, with many tears,
Nor in the embrace of ocean, shall exist
Thy image. Earth, that nourished thee, shall claim
Thy growth, to be resolved to earth again,
And, lost each human trace, surrendering up
Thine individual being, shalt thou go
To mix forever with the elements,
To be a brother to the insensible rock
And to the sluggish clod, which the rude swain
Turns with his share,[4] and treads upon. The oak
Shall send his roots abroad, and pierce thy mold.

Yet not to thine eternal resting place
Shalt thou retire alone, nor couldst thou wish
Couch[5] more magnificent. Thou shalt lie down
With patriarchs of the infant world—with kings,
The powerful of the earth—the wise, the good,
Fair forms, and hoary seers of ages past,
All in one mighty sepulcher.[6] The hills
Rock-ribbed and ancient as the sun—the vales
Stretching in **pensive** quietness between;
The **venerable** woods—rivers that move
In majesty, and the complaining brooks
That make the meadows green; and, poured round all,
Old Ocean's gray and melancholy waste—
Are but the solemn decorations all
Of the great tomb of man. The golden sun,
The planets, all the infinite host of heaven,
Are shining on the sad abodes of death,
Through the still lapse of ages. All that tread
The globe are but a handful to the tribes
That slumber in its bosom. Take the wings
Of morning,[7] pierce the Barcan[8] wilderness,
Or lose thyself in the continuous woods
Where rolls the Oregon,[9] and hears no sound,
Save his own dashings—yet the dead are there:
And millions in those solitudes, since first
The flight of years began, have laid them down
In their last sleep—the dead reign there alone.

Meter Identify two places in the first fifteen lines where the poem does not use perfect iambic pentameter.

Mood Describe the shift in mood that occurs in line 31.

Vocabulary

pensive (pen′ siv) *adj.* expressing deep thoughtfulness

venerable (ven′ ər ə bəl) *adj.* worthy of respect

Comprehension
Who has "a voice of gladness" and a "healing sympathy"?

---

4. **clod, which . . . share** lump of earth, which the simple country youth turns with his plowshare.
5. **Couch** bed.
6. **sepulcher** (sep′ əl kər) *n.* tomb.
7. **Take . . . morning** a reference to Psalm 139:9.
8. **Barcan** (bär′ kən) *adj.* referring to Barca, a desert region in North Africa.
9. **Oregon** river flowing between Oregon and Washington State, now called the Columbia River.

So shalt thou rest, and what if thou withdraw
In silence from the living, and no friend
Take note of thy departure? All that breathe
Will share thy destiny. The gay will laugh
When thou art gone, the solemn brood of care
Plod on, and each one as before will chase
His favorite phantom; yet all these shall leave
Their mirth and their employments, and shall come
And make their bed with thee. As the long train
Of ages glide away, the sons of men,
The youth in life's green spring, and he who goes
In the full strength of years, matron and maid,
The speechless babe, and the gray-headed man—
Shall one by one be gathered to thy side,
By those, who in their turn shall follow them.

So live, that when thy summons comes to join
The innumerable caravan, which moves
To that mysterious realm, where each shall take
His chamber in the silent halls of death,
Thou go not, like the quarry-slave at night,
Scourged[10] to his dungeon, but, sustained and soothed
By an unfaltering trust, approach thy grave,
Like one who wraps the drapery of his couch
About him, and lies down to pleasant dreams.

Summarizing

Briefly state the poet's message in the final nine lines of the poem.

10. **Scourged** (skʉrjd) *v.* whipped.

Critical Reading

Cite textual evidence to support your responses.

1. **Key Ideas and Details** **(a) Analyze:** Which details in the second and third stanzas of "The Tide Rises..." suggest that the traveler has died? **(b) Interpret:** What does the contrast between the traveler and the waves suggest about human life?
2. **Craft and Structure** **(a)** What does the "still voice" in line 17 of "Thanatopsis" say will happen to the individual being? **(b) Analyze:** In what ways do the images in lines 27–30 reinforce this idea?
3. **Integrate Ideas and Knowledge** **(a) Connect:** Explain the connection between Bryant's poem and its title, which combines the Greek words *thanatos* ("death") and *opsis* ("view or vision"). **(b) Draw Conclusions:** What is the speaker's overall attitude toward death and the role nature plays in it?

Oliver Wendell Holmes *(1809–1894)*

Author of "Old Ironsides"

Another of the so-called Fireside Poets, Oliver Wendell Holmes penned humorous and celebratory verse with wide audience appeal. Famous for prose as well as poetry, he was also a significant figure in the world of medicine, serving as a professor of anatomy and physiology as well as dean of the Harvard Medical School and producing many important medical tracts.

A Cambridge Man A descendant of the poet Anne Bradstreet (page 75), Holmes grew up near Harvard in Cambridge, Massachusetts, where his father was a Congregationalist minister. After a brief flirtation with the law, he switched to medicine, studying at Harvard and also for two years in Paris. He obtained his medical degree in 1836, the same year he published his first collection of poetry.

A Keen Wit Whether lecturing at Harvard or rubbing elbows with Emerson, Longfellow, and other leading writers of the day, Holmes was known for his brilliant skills as a speaker. He found a way to exhibit those skills in written form in his best-known prose work, *The Autocrat of the Breakfast-Table*, a series of supposed dinner-table conversations at a fictional Boston boarding house that wittily examine a wide range of interesting topics. The popular work was serialized in *The Atlantic Monthly*, the influential magazine of art, literature, and politics that Holmes helped found with his friend and fellow Fireside Poet James Russell Lowell.

"One's mind, once stretched by a new idea, never regains its original dimensions."

Old Ironsides

Oliver Wendell Holmes

BACKGROUND The battleship *Constitution* earned its nickname of "Old Ironsides" for withstanding British attacks during the War of 1812. By 1830, having outworn its usefulness, the ship was slated for demolition. Holmes wrote this poem to protest this decision. The popular verse saved the ship and won Holmes early fame as a poet.

Ay, tear her tattered ensign[1] down!
Long has it waved on high,
And many an eye has danced to see
That banner in the sky;
Beneath it rung the battle shout,
And burst the cannons roar;—
The meteor of the ocean air
Shall sweep the clouds no more.

Her deck, once red with heroes' blood,
Where knelt the vanquished foe,
When winds were hurrying o'er the flood,
And waves were white below,
No more shall feel the victor's tread,
Or know the conquered knee;—
The harpies[2] of the shore shall pluck
The eagle of the sea!

Oh, better that her shattered hulk
Should sink beneath the wave;
Her thunders shook the mighty deep,
And there should be her grave;
Nail to the mast her holy flag.
Set every threadbare sail,
And give her to the god of storms,
The lightning and the gale!

◀ Critical Viewing
To celebrate the 200th anniversary of her 1797 launch, the U.S.S. *Constitution* took a five-hour sail around Massachusetts Bay in 1997. The ship had not sailed in more than 116 years. Which lines from the poem still apply to "Old Ironsides" today? **APPLY**

Meter Identify the three-syllable foot that breaks the iambic meter in line 7.

1. **ensign** (en′ sin′) *n.* the national flag displayed on a ship.
2. **harpies** (här′ pēz) *n.* a term for greedy, grasping people that comes from the name of the sharp-clawed half-bird, half-woman monsters in Greek mythology.

Critical Reading

1. **Key Ideas and Details (a) Infer:** Who or what are "the harpies of the shore" in line 15? **(b) Interpret:** What does the word *harpies* suggest about their motives in demolishing the ship?
2. **Key Ideas and Details (a) Draw Conclusions:** Why does the speaker think it would be better to let the ship sink? **(b) Evaluate:** Do you agree? Explain.
3. **Integration of Knowledge and Ideas** How is the subject matter of the poems in this grouping distinctly American? In your response, use at least two of these Essential Question words: *native, heroic, landscape.* ***[Connecting to the Essential Question: What makes American literature American?]***

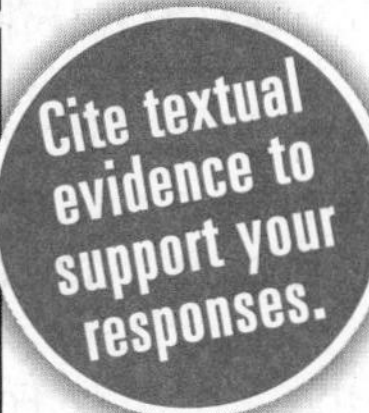
Cite textual evidence to support your responses.

Close Reading Activities

from ***The Song of Hiawatha* • *The Tide Rises, The Tide Falls* • *Thanatopsis* • *Old Ironsides***

Literary Analysis

1. **Key Ideas and Details** **(a)** What is the main idea of the excerpt from "The Song of Hiawatha"? **(b)** What are three supporting details? **(c) Summarize** the excerpt.
2. **Craft and Structure** **(a)** Copy the first two lines of "The Song of Hiawatha" and mark the syllables to show the **meter** (trochaic tetrameter). **(b)** What **mood** does line after line of trochaic tetrameter help establish? Explain.
3. **Craft and Structure** **(a)** In "Old Ironsides," which lines are in iambic tetrameter (four iambs)? **(b)** Which are in iambic trimeter (three iambs)? **(c)** The first two lines do not follow the exact metrical pattern. What effect does breaking the meter create?
4. **Craft and Structure** **(a)** Using a chart like the one shown, analyze the meter of two lines of poetry. **(b)** Which meter sounds the most like natural speech? Explain.

Line #	Stresses	# of feet	Meter
58 (Thanatopsis)			
9 (Old Ironsides)			

Common Core State Standards

Writing
2. Write informative texts to examine and convey complex ideas, concepts, and information clearly and accurately through the effective selection, organization, and analysis of content.

Language
5. Demonstrate understanding of word relationships.

Vocabulary Acquisition and Use

Antonyms For each numbered word, choose the letter of its antonym, or word of opposite meaning. Then, explain your choice.

1. **venerable** **(a)** greedy **(b)** disregarded **(c)** quick **(d)** current
2. **efface** **(a)** clarify **(b)** insert **(c)** retire **(d)** loose
3. **eloquence** **(a)** slurring **(b)** persuasive **(c)** powerful **(d)** fearful
4. **pensive** **(a)** shallow **(b)** deep **(c)** curious **(d)** creative

Writing to Sources

Informative Text Choose two passages from the poems you have just read that evoke distinct moods in the reader. The passages should be between five and ten lines long. Write a **compare-and-contrast essay** in which you describe the mood evoked by each passage and discuss the *stylistic devices* the poet uses to create those moods. For example, in addition to meter, consider each poem's subject, striking images or word choices, and other aspects that you find noteworthy. Support your comparisons and contrasts with details from the passages.

TEXT SET

Shadows of the Imagination

Part 2

Building Knowledge and Insight

ANCHOR TEXT
The Minister's Black Veil

Connecting to the Essential Question Nathaniel Hawthorne wrote about America's Puritan past with puzzlement and shame but also with fascination. As you read this story, notice details that express specific attitudes toward Puritan New England. This will help as you consider the Essential Question: **What is the relationship between literature and place?**

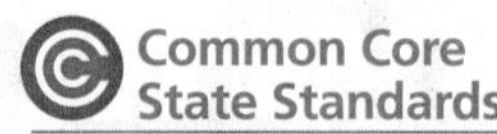

Reading Literature
1. Cite strong and thorough textual evidence to support analysis of what the text says explicitly as well as inferences drawn from the text, including determining where the text leaves matters uncertain.

Close Reading Focus

Parable; Ambiguity; Symbol

Hawthorne called "The Minister's Black Veil" a **parable,** or story that teaches a moral lesson. However, unlike religious parables such as those in the Bible, Hawthorne's parable teaches a lesson full of **ambiguity,** or uncertain meaning. Much of the ambiguity stems from the story's use of a symbol that is subject to different interpretations. A **symbol** is an object, setting, or even a character that has meaning as itself but also stands for something greater—often an abstract idea. The central symbol in this story is an article of clothing that the main character vows never to remove:

> *Swathed about his forehead, and hanging down over his face ... Mr. Hooper had on a black veil.*

The veil's meaning is a mystery for both the characters in the story and the reader. As you read, look for details that will help you decide on your own interpretation of this ambiguous symbol.

Preparing to Read Complex Texts An inference is a logical guess you make about aspects of a text that are not explicitly, or directly, stated. You draw inferences by applying your own life experience to story details. To *interpret the essential meaning* of this story, **draw inferences** by noting descriptions, dialogue, and characters' actions and assessing them in view of your own understanding of human nature. As you read, use a chart like the one shown to draw inferences.

Description/Dialogue
"A sad smile gleamed faintly from beneath the black veil, . . ."

↓

Inference
The minister has suffered a loss.

Vocabulary

The words listed here are important to understanding the text that follows. Copy the words into your notebook, sorting them into words you know and words you do not know.

inanimate	**impertinent**
venerable	**obstinacy**
pathos	**imperceptible**

Nathaniel Hawthorne

(1804–1864)

"Happiness is a butterfly, which when pursued, is always just beyond your grasp, but which, if you will sit down quietly, may alight upon you."

Author of "The Minister's Black Veil"

Sometimes called an "anti-Transcendentalist," Nathaniel Hawthorne admired Transcendentalists like Ralph Waldo Emerson but could not adopt their optimistic world view. Instead, as the descendant of New England Puritans who prosecuted witches and persecuted Quakers, Hawthorne was shaped by a sense of inherited guilt that gave him a darker vision. He believed that evil was a powerful force in the world, a sentiment that infuses most of his fiction.

A Shaky Start Hawthorne was born in Salem, Massachusetts, 112 years after the famous witchcraft trials in which one of his ancestors was a judge. After graduating from Bowdoin (bō´din) College in Maine, he secluded himself in his mother's home, determined to become a writer. In 1828 he published a novel, *Fanshawe,* but was so displeased with the effort that he tried to burn all the copies. Continuing to toil at his craft, he produced a story collection, *Twice-Told Tales* (1837), that won him critical regard but sold poorly.

Struggling to Earn a Living Hawthorne lived briefly at the Transcendentalist commune at Brook Farm and then at the Old Manse in Concord, Massachusetts, where he produced another story collection, *Mosses from an Old Manse* (1846). Still, to support his family, he was forced to accept a political post at the custom house back in Salem. A change of administrations lost him the job, but his stint there helped inspire his masterpiece, *The Scarlet Letter* (1850), a novel of sin and guilt among the early Puritans.

A Final Appointment When his college friend, Franklin Pierce, became president, Hawthorne was named American consul in Liverpool, England. He spent several years abroad, his travels in Italy inspiring his novel *The Marble Faun* (1860). Four years later, on a tour of New Hampshire with Franklin Pierce, Hawthorne died suddenly in his sleep.

The Minister's BLACK VEIL

A PARABLE ∾ NATHANIEL HAWTHORNE

BACKGROUND Set in the 1600s, in a typical village of Puritan New England, this story reflects Nathaniel Hawthorne's deep awareness of his Puritan ancestry. The Puritans lived stern lives, emphasizing hard work and religious devotion. They believed that only certain people were predestined, or chosen, by God to go to heaven. This belief led them to search their souls continually for signs that God had selected them. At the same time, those who behaved unusually were often thought to be controlled by evil forces. This attitude contributed to the Salem witchcraft trials of 1692, during which at least twenty accused witches were executed. In this story, Hawthorne explores how such attitudes probably led to other, more commonplace acts of cruelty.

The sexton[1] stood in the porch of Milford meetinghouse, pulling busily at the bell rope. The old people of the village came stooping along the street. Children, with bright faces, tripped merrily beside their parents, or mimicked a graver gait, in the conscious dignity of their Sunday clothes. Spruce bachelors looked sidelong at the pretty maidens, and fancied that the Sabbath sunshine made them prettier than on weekdays. When the throng had mostly streamed into the porch, the sexton began to toll the bell, keeping his eye on the Reverend Mr. Hooper's door. The first glimpse of the clergyman's figure was the signal for the bell to cease its summons.

"But what has good Parson Hooper got upon his face?" cried the sexton in astonishment.

All within hearing immediately turned about, and beheld the semblance of Mr. Hooper, pacing slowly his meditative way towards the meetinghouse. With one accord they started, expressing more wonder than if some strange minister were coming to dust the cushions of Mr. Hooper's pulpit.

"Are you sure it is our parson?" inquired Goodman[2] Gray of the sexton.

"Of a certainty it is good Mr. Hooper," replied the sexton. "He was to have exchanged pulpits with Parson Shute, of Westbury; but Parson Shute sent to excuse himself yesterday, being to preach a funeral sermon."

◀ Critical Viewing
How might a community react if a respected person were to wear a veil like the one shown in this illustration? **SPECULATE**

Comprehension
As the story begins, what weekly event is about to take place?

1. **sexton** (seks′ tən) *n.* person in charge of the maintenance of a church.
2. **Goodman** title of respect similar to "Mister."

The cause of so much amazement may appear sufficiently slight. Mr. Hooper, a gentlemanly person, of about thirty, though still a bachelor, was dressed with due clerical neatness, as if a careful wife had starched his band, and brushed the weekly dust from his Sunday's garb. There was but one thing remarkable in his appearance. Swathed about his forehead, and hanging down over his face, so low as to be shaken by his breath, Mr. Hooper had on a black veil. On a nearer view it seemed to consist of two folds of crape,[3] which entirely concealed his features, except the mouth and chin, but probably did not intercept his sight, further than to give a darkened aspect to all living and inanimate things. With this gloomy shade before him, good Mr. Hooper walked onward, at a slow and quiet pace, stooping somewhat, and looking on the ground, as is customary with abstracted men, yet nodding kindly to those of his parishioners who still waited on the meetinghouse steps. But so wonderstruck were they that his greeting hardly met with a return.

Vocabulary
inanimate (in an′ ə mit) *adj.* not alive; lifeless

"I can't really feel as if good Mr. Hooper's face was behind that piece of crape," said the sexton.

"I don't like it," muttered an old woman, as she hobbled into the meetinghouse. "He has changed himself into something awful, only by hiding his face."

"He has changed himself into something awful, only by hiding his face."

"Our parson has gone mad!" cried Goodman Gray, following him across the threshold.

A rumor of some unaccountable phenomenon had preceded Mr. Hooper into the meetinghouse, and set all the congregation astir. Few could refrain from twisting their heads towards the door; many stood upright, and turned directly about; while several little boys clambered upon the seats, and came down again with a terrible racket. There was a general bustle, a rustling of the women's gowns and shuffling of the men's feet, greatly at variance with that hushed repose which should attend the entrance of the minister. But Mr. Hooper appeared not to notice the perturbation of his people. He entered with an almost noiseless step, bent his head mildly to the pews on each side, and bowed as he passed his oldest parishioner, a white-haired great-grandsire, who occupied an armchair in the center of the aisle. It was strange to observe how slowly this venerable man became conscious of something singular in the appearance of his pastor. He seemed not fully to partake of the prevailing wonder, till Mr. Hooper had ascended the stairs, and showed himself in the pulpit, face to face with his congregation, except for the black veil. That mysterious emblem was never once withdrawn. It shook with his measured breath, as he gave out the psalm; it threw its obscurity between him and the holy page, as he read the Scriptures; and while he prayed, the veil lay heavily on his uplifted countenance. Did he seek to hide it from the dread Being whom he was addressing?

Vocabulary
venerable (ven′ ər ə bəl) *adj.* commanding respect

Parable and Symbol
The passage beginning "That mysterious emblem" is the first suggestion that the veil is a symbol. What might the veil symbolize?

3. **crape** (krāp) *n.* piece of black cloth worn as a sign of mourning.

Such was the effect of this simple piece of crape, that more than one woman of delicate nerves was forced to leave the meetinghouse. Yet perhaps the palefaced congregation was almost as fearful a sight to the minister, as his black veil to them.

Mr. Hooper had the reputation of a good preacher, but not an energetic one: he strove to win his people heavenward by mild, persuasive influences, rather than to drive them thither by the thunders of the Word. The sermon which he now delivered was marked by the same characteristics of style and manner as the general series of his pulpit oratory. But there was something, either in the sentiment of the discourse itself, or in the imagination of the auditors, which made it greatly the most powerful effort that they had ever heard from their pastor's lips. It was tinged, rather more darkly than usual, with the gentle gloom of Mr. Hooper's temperament. The subject had reference to secret sin, and those sad mysteries which we hide from our nearest and dearest, and would fain conceal from our own consciousness, even forgetting that the Omniscient[4] can detect them. A subtle power was breathed into his words. Each member of the congregation, the most innocent girl, and the man of hardened breast, felt as if the preacher had crept upon them, behind his awful veil, and discovered their hoarded iniquity of deed or thought. Many spread their clasped hands on their bosoms. There was nothing terrible in what Mr. Hooper said, at least, no violence; and yet, with every tremor of his melancholy voice, the hearers quaked. An unsought **pathos** came hand in hand with awe. So sensible were the audience of some unwonted attribute in their minister, that they longed for a breath of wind to blow aside the veil, almost believing that a stranger's visage would be discovered, though the form, gesture, and voice were those of Mr. Hooper.

At the close of the services, the people hurried out with indecorous confusion, eager to communicate their pent-up amazement, and conscious of lighter spirits the moment they lost sight of the black veil. Some gathered in little circles, huddled closely together, with their mouths all whispering in the center; some went homeward alone, wrapt in silent meditation; some talked loudly, and profaned the Sabbath day with ostentatious laughter. A few shook their sagacious heads, intimating that they could penetrate the mystery; while one or two affirmed that there was no mystery at all, but only that Mr. Hooper's eyes were so weakened by the midnight lamp, as to require a shade. After a brief interval, forth came good Mr. Hooper also, in the rear of his flock. Turning his veiled face from one group to another, he paid due reverence to the hoary heads, saluted the middle-aged with kind dignity as their friend and spiritual guide, greeted the young with mingled authority and love, and laid his hands on the little children's heads to bless them. Such was always

Drawing Inferences

Has Mr. Hooper truly changed? What inferences can you draw based on this description of his sermon?

Vocabulary

pathos (pā´ thäs´ or thōs´) *n.* quality that arouses pity, sorrow, or sympathy in others

Comprehension

What change has occurred in Mr. Hooper's appearance?

---

4. Omniscient (äm ni´ shənt) all-knowing God.

The American EXPERIENCE

Jonathan Edwards, Puritans, and Sermons of Fear

The congregation's fear of Mr. Hooper's veil recalls Jonathan Edwards, one of the greatest preachers of the colonial period. Edwards used his sermons to inspire fear of eternal damnation in the minds of his listeners. He insisted that the evidence they saw as proof of God's grace in their lives was false. According to Edwards, personal comfort, success, health, and a sense of being a good person were no proof that one was saved. Rather, these satisfactions in the earthly realm were mere distractions, providing comfort, but no substance, to the ignorant.

Though Hawthorne describes Mr. Hooper as a mild and benevolent preacher—certainly no spouter of fire-and-brimstone like Edwards—his veil inspires a similar fear and trembling among the villagers. You can read an excerpt of Jonathan Edwards's "Sinners in the Hands of an Angry God" on page 86.

Connect to the Literature

People in Hooper's congregation are taught to fear eternal damnation and to look for signs of evil in themselves and others. Why would they be inclined to fear anything that appears to be a mark of sin?

his custom on the Sabbath day. Strange and bewildered looks repaid him for his courtesy. None, as on former occasions, aspired to the honor of walking by their pastor's side. Old Squire Saunders, doubtless by an accidental lapse of memory, neglected to invite Mr. Hooper to his table, where the good clergyman had been wont to bless the food, almost every Sunday since his settlement. He returned, therefore, to the parsonage, and, at the moment of closing the door, was observed to look back upon the people, all of whom had their eyes fixed upon the minister. A sad smile gleamed faintly from beneath the black veil, and flickered about his mouth, glimmering as he disappeared.

"How strange," said a lady, "that a simple black veil, such as any woman might wear on her bonnet, should become such a terrible thing on Mr. Hooper's face!"

"Something must surely be amiss with Mr. Hooper's intellects," observed her husband, the physician of the village. "But the strangest part of the affair is the effect of this vagary, even on a sober-minded man like myself. The black veil, though it covers only our pastor's face, throws its influence over his whole person, and makes him ghostlike from head to foot. Do you not feel it so?"

"Truly do I," replied the lady; "and I would not be alone with him for the world. I wonder he is not afraid to be alone with himself!"

"Men sometimes are so," said her husband.

The afternoon service was attended with similar circumstances. At its conclusion, the bell tolled for the funeral of a young lady. The relatives and friends were assembled in the house, and the more distant acquaintances stood about the door, speaking of the good qualities of the deceased, when their talk was interrupted by the appearance of Mr. Hooper, still covered with his black veil. It was now an appropriate emblem. The clergyman stepped into the room where the corpse was laid, and bent over the coffin, to take a last farewell of his deceased parishioner. As he stooped, the veil hung straight down from his forehead, so that, if her eyelids had not been closed forever, the dead maiden might have seen his face. Could Mr. Hooper be fearful of her glance, that he so hastily caught back the black veil? A person who watched the interview between the dead and living, scrupled not to affirm, that, at the instant when the clergyman's features were disclosed,

the corpse had slightly shuddered, rustling the shroud and muslin cap, though the countenance retained the composure of death. A superstitious old woman was the only witness of this prodigy. From the coffin Mr. Hooper passed into the chamber of the mourners, and thence to the head of the staircase; to make the funeral prayer. It was a tender and heart-dissolving prayer, full of sorrow, yet so imbued with celestial hopes, that the music of a heavenly harp, swept by the fingers of the dead, seemed faintly to be heard among the saddest accents of the minister. The people trembled, though they but darkly understood him when he prayed that they, and himself, and all of mortal race, might be ready, as he trusted this young maiden had been, for the dreadful hour that should snatch the veil from their faces. The bearers went heavily forth, and the mourners followed, saddening all the street, with the dead before them, and Mr. Hooper in his black veil behind.

"Why do you look back?" said one in the procession to his partner.

"I had a fancy," replied she, "that the minister and the maiden's spirit were walking hand in hand."

"And so had I, at the same moment," said the other.

Drawing Inferences
What inferences can you draw from this dialogue about the veil's intensifying impact on the villagers?

That night, the handsomest couple in Milford village were to be joined in wedlock. Though reckoned a melancholy man, Mr. Hooper had a placid cheerfulness for such occasions, which often excited a sympathetic smile where livelier merriment would have been thrown away. There was no quality of his disposition which made him more beloved than this. The company at the wedding awaited his arrival with impatience, trusting that the strange awe, which had gathered over him throughout the day, would now be dispelled. But such was not the result. When Mr. Hooper came, the first thing that their eyes rested on was the same horrible black veil, which had added deeper gloom to the funeral, and could portend nothing but evil to the wedding. Such was its immediate effect on the guests that a cloud seemed to have rolled duskily from beneath the black crape, and dimmed the light of the candles. The bridal pair stood up before the minister. But the bride's cold fingers quivered in the tremulous hand of the bridegroom, and her deathlike paleness caused a whisper that the maiden who had been buried a few hours before was come from her grave to be married. If ever another wedding were so dismal, it was that famous one where they tolled the wedding knell.[5] After performing the ceremony, Mr. Hooper raised a glass of wine to his lips, wishing happiness to the new-married couple in a strain of mild pleasantry that ought to have brightened the features of the guests, like a cheerful gleam from the hearth. At that instant, catching a glimpse of his figure in the looking glass, the black veil involved his own spirit in the horror with which it overwhelmed all others. His frame shuddered, his lips grew white, he spilt the untasted wine upon

Comprehension
How does Mr. Hooper's veil affect the wedding party?

---

5. If . . . knell reference to Hawthorne's short story "The Wedding Knell." A knell is the slow ringing of a bell, as at a funeral.

the carpet, and rushed forth into the darkness. For the Earth, too, had on her Black Veil.

The next day, the whole village of Milford talked of little else than Parson Hooper's black veil. That, and the mystery concealed behind it, supplied a topic for discussion between acquaintances meeting in the street, and good women gossiping at their open windows. It was the first item of news that the tavernkeeper told to his guests. The children babbled of it on their way to school. One imitative little imp covered his face with an old black handkerchief, thereby so affrighting his playmates that the panic seized himself, and he well nigh lost his wits by his own waggery.

Vocabulary
impertinent (im pur′ tə nənt) *adj.* not showing proper respect; saucy

It was remarkable that of all the busybodies and **impertinent** people in the parish, not one ventured to put the plain question to Mr. Hooper, wherefore he did this thing. Hitherto, whenever there appeared the slightest call for such interference, he had never lacked advisers, nor shown himself averse to be guided by their judgment. If he erred at all, it was by so painful a degree of self-distrust that even the mildest censure would lead him to consider an indifferent action as a crime. Yet, though so well acquainted with this amiable weakness, no individual among his parishioners chose to make the black veil a subject of friendly remonstrance. There was a feeling of dread, neither plainly confessed nor carefully concealed, which caused each to shift the responsibility upon another, till at length it was found expedient to send a deputation of the church, in order to deal with Mr. Hooper about the mystery, before it should grow into a scandal. Never did an embassy so ill discharge its duties. The minister received them with friendly courtesy, but became silent, after they were seated, leaving to his visitors the whole burden of introducing their important business. The topic, it might be supposed, was obvious enough. There was the black veil swathed round Mr. Hooper's forehead, and concealing every feature above his placid mouth, on which, at times, they could perceive the glimmering of a melancholy smile. But that piece of crape, to their imagination, seemed to hang down before his heart, the symbol of a fearful secret between him and them. Were the veil but cast aside, they might speak freely of it, but not till then. Thus they sat a considerable time, speechless, confused, and shrinking uneasily from Mr. Hooper's eye, which they felt to be fixed upon them with an invisible glance. Finally, the deputies returned abashed to their constituents, pronouncing the matter too weighty to be handled, except by a council of the churches, if, indeed, it might not require a general synod.[6]

But there was one person in the village unappalled by the awe with which the black veil had impressed all beside herself. When the deputies returned without an explanation, or even venturing to demand one, she, with the calm energy of her character, determined to chase away the strange cloud that appeared to be settling round Mr. Hooper,

---

6. synod (sin′ əd) *n.* high governing body in certain Christian churches.

every moment more darkly than before. As his plighted wife,[7] it should be her privilege to know what the black veil concealed. At the minister's first visit, therefore, she entered upon the subject with a direct simplicity, which made the task easier both for him and her. After he had seated himself, she fixed her eyes steadfastly upon the veil, but could discern nothing of the dreadful gloom that had so overawed the multitude: it was but a double fold of crape, hanging down from his forehead to his mouth, and slightly stirring with his breath.

"No," said she aloud, and smiling, "there is nothing terrible in this piece of crape, except that it hides a face which I am always glad to look upon. Come, good sir, let the sun shine from behind the cloud. First lay aside your black veil; then tell me why you put it on."

Mr. Hooper's smile glimmered faintly.

"There is an hour to come," said he, "when all of us shall cast aside our veils. Take it not amiss, beloved friend, if I wear this piece of crape till then."

"Your words are a mystery, too," returned the young lady. "Take away the veil from them, at least."

"Elizabeth, I will," said he, "so far as my vow may suffer me. Know, then, this veil is a type and a symbol, and I am bound to wear it ever, both in light and darkness, in solitude and before the gaze of multitudes, and as with strangers, so with my familiar friends. No mortal eye will see it withdrawn. This dismal shade must separate me from the world: even you, Elizabeth, can never come behind it!"

"What grievous affliction hath befallen you," she earnestly inquired, "that you should thus darken your eyes forever?"

"If it be a sign of mourning," replied Mr. Hooper, "I, perhaps, like most other mortals, have sorrows dark enough to be typified by a black veil."

"But what if the world will not believe that it is the type of an innocent sorrow?" urged Elizabeth. "Beloved and respected as you are, there may be whispers that you hide your face under the consciousness of secret sin. For the sake of your holy office, do away this scandal!"

The color rose into her cheeks as she intimated the nature of the rumors that were already abroad in the village. But Mr. Hooper's mildness did not forsake him. He even smiled again—that same sad smile, which always appeared like a faint glimmering of light, proceeding from the obscurity beneath the veil.

"If I hide my face for sorrow, there is cause enough," he merely replied; "and if I cover it for secret sin, what mortal might not do the same?"

And with this gentle, but unconquerable **obstinacy** did he resist all her entreaties. At length Elizabeth sat silent. For a few moments she appeared lost in thought, considering, probably, what new methods might be tried to withdraw her lover from so dark a fantasy,

7. **plighted wife** fiancée.

"There is an hour to come," said he, "when all of us shall cast aside our veils."

Drawing Inferences
In his reply to Elizabeth, what does Mr. Hooper suggest about the veil's meaning?

Vocabulary
obstinacy (äb′ stə nə sē) *n.* stubbornness

Comprehension
Are the villagers able to confront Mr. Hooper directly about the veil?

Winter Sunday in Norway, Maine, Unidentified artist, New York Historical Association, Cooperstown

▲ Critical Viewing In what ways does the atmosphere in this painting reflect the mood of the story? **CONNECT**

which, if it had no other meaning, was perhaps a symptom of mental disease. Though of a firmer character than his own, the tears rolled down her cheeks. But in an instant, as it were, a new feeling took the place of sorrow: her eyes were fixed insensibly on the black veil, when, like a sudden twilight in the air, its terrors fell around her. She arose, and stood trembling before him.

"And do you feel it then, at last?" said he mournfully.

She made no reply, but covered her eyes with her hand, and turned to leave the room. He rushed forward and caught her arm.

"Have patience with me, Elizabeth!" cried he, passionately. "Do not desert me, though this veil must be between us here on earth. Be mine, and hereafter there shall be no veil over my face, no darkness between our souls! It is but a mortal veil—it is not for eternity! O! you know not how lonely I am, and how frightened, to be alone behind my black veil. Do not leave me in this miserable obscurity forever!"

"Lift the veil but once, and look me in the face," said she.

"Never! It cannot be!" replied Mr. Hooper.

"Then farewell!" said Elizabeth.

She withdrew her arm from his grasp, and slowly departed, pausing at the door, to give one long shuddering gaze, that seemed almost to penetrate the mystery of the black veil. But, even amid his grief, Mr. Hooper smiled to think that only a material emblem had separated him from happiness, though the horrors, which it shadowed forth, must be drawn darkly between the fondest of lovers. From that time no attempts were made to remove Mr. Hooper's black veil, or, by a direct appeal, to discover the secret which it was supposed to hide. By persons who claimed a superiority to popular prejudice, it was reckoned merely an eccentric whim, such as often mingles with the sober actions of men otherwise rational, and tinges them all with its own semblance of insanity. But with the multitude, good Mr. Hooper was irreparably a bugbear.[8] He could not walk the street with any peace of mind, so conscious was he that the gentle and timid would turn aside to avoid him, and that others would make it a point of hardihood to throw themselves in his way. The impertinence of the latter class compelled him to give up his customary walk at sunset to the burial ground; for when he leaned pensively over the gate, there would always be faces behind the gravestones, peeping at his black veil. A fable went the rounds that the stare of the dead people drove him thence. It grieved him, to the very depth of his kind heart, to observe how the children fled from his approach, breaking up their merriest sports, while his melancholy figure was yet afar off. Their instinctive dread caused him to feel more strongly than aught else, that a preternatural[9] horror was interwoven with the threads of the black crape. In truth, his own antipathy to the veil was known to be so great that he never willingly passed before a mirror, nor stooped to drink at a still fountain, lest, in its peaceful bosom, he should be affrighted by himself. This was what gave plausibility to the whispers, that Mr. Hooper's conscience tortured him for some great crime too horrible to be entirely concealed, or otherwise than so obscurely intimated. Thus, from beneath the black veil, there rolled a cloud into the sunshine, an ambiguity of sin or sorrow, which enveloped the poor minister, so that love or sympathy could never reach him. It was said that ghost and fiend consorted with him there. With self-shudderings and outward terrors, he walked continually in its shadow, groping darkly within his own soul or gazing through a medium that saddened the whole world. Even the lawless wind, it was believed, respected his dreadful secret, and never blew aside the veil. But still good Mr. Hooper sadly smiled at the pale visages of the worldly throng as he passed by.

Among all its bad influences, the black veil had the one desirable effect, of making its wearer a very efficient clergyman. By the aid of his mysterious emblem—for there was no other apparent cause—he became a man of awful power over souls that were in agony for sin. His converts always regarded him with a dread peculiar to them-

Parable

What message is conveyed by the passage beginning "But, even amid his grief,..."?

Drawing Inferences

Based on this description of the townspeople's reactions, what inferences can you draw about Mr. Hooper's happiness in life?

Comprehension

What one desirable effect does the veil have?

---

8. **bugbear** *n.* something causing needless fear.
9. **preternatural** (prēt´ ər nāch´ ər əl) *adj.* supernatural.

selves, affirming, though but figuratively, that, before he brought them to celestial light, they had been with him behind the black veil. Its gloom, indeed, enabled him to sympathize with all dark affections.

The Puritan, Frank E. Schoonover

▲ **Critical Viewing**
Does this image of a Puritan reflect Mr. Hooper's character? Explain.
CONNECT

Dying sinners cried aloud for Mr. Hooper, and would not yield their breath till he appeared; though ever, as he stooped to whisper consolation, they shuddered at the veiled face so near their own. Such were the terrors of the black veil, even when Death had bared his visage! Strangers came long distances to attend service at his church, with the mere idle purpose of gazing at his figure, because it was forbidden them to behold his face. But many were made to quake ere they departed! Once, during Governor Belcher's[10] administration, Mr. Hooper was appointed to preach the election sermon. Covered with his black veil, he stood before the chief magistrate, the council, and the representatives, and wrought so deep an impression that the legislative measures of that year were characterized by all the gloom and piety of our earliest ancestral sway.

In this manner Mr. Hooper spent a long life, irreproachable in outward act, yet shrouded in dismal suspicions; kind and loving, though unloved, and dimly feared; a man apart from men, shunned in their health and joy, but ever summoned to their aid in mortal anguish. As years wore on, shedding their snows above his sable veil, he acquired a name throughout the New England churches, and they called him Father Hooper. Nearly all his parishioners, who were of mature age when he was settled, had been borne away by many a funeral: he had one congregation in the church, and a more crowded one in the churchyard; and having wrought so late into the evening, and done his work so well, it was now good Father Hooper's turn to rest.

Several persons were visible by the shaded candlelight, in the death chamber of the old clergyman. Natural connections[11] he had none. But there was the decorously grave, though unmoved physician, seeking only to mitigate the last pangs of the patient whom he could not save. There were the deacons, and other eminently pious members of his church. There, also, was the Reverend Mr. Clark, of Westbury, a young and zealous divine, who had ridden in haste to pray by the bedside of the expiring minister. There was the nurse, no hired handmaiden of death, but one whose calm affection had endured thus long in secrecy, in solitude, amid the chill of age, and would not perish, even at the dying hour. Who, but Elizabeth! And there lay the hoary head of good Father Hooper upon the death pillow, with the black veil still swathed

10. **Governor Belcher** Jonathan Belcher (1682–1757), the royal governor of the Massachusetts Bay Colony, from 1730 to 1741.
11. **Natural connections** relatives.

about his brow, and reaching down over his face, so that each more difficult gasp of his faint breath caused it to stir. All through life that piece of crape had hung between him and the world: it had separated him from cheerful brotherhood and woman's love, and kept him in that saddest of all prisons, his own heart; and still it lay upon his face, as if to deepen the gloom of his darksome chamber, and shade him from the sunshine of eternity.

For some time previous, his mind had been confused, wavering doubtfully between the past and the present, and hovering forward, as it were, at intervals, into the indistinctness of the world to come. There had been feverish turns, which tossed him from side to side, and wore away what little strength he had. But in his most convulsive struggles, and in the wildest vagaries of his intellect, when no other thought retained its sober influence, he still showed an awful solicitude lest the black veil should slip aside. Even if his bewildered soul could have forgotten, there was a faithful woman at his pillow, who, with averted eyes, would have covered that aged face, which she had last beheld in the comeliness of manhood. At length the death-stricken old man lay quietly in the torpor of mental and bodily exhaustion, with an **imperceptible** pulse, and breath that grew fainter and fainter, except when a long, deep, and irregular inspiration seemed to prelude the flight of his spirit.

The minister of Westbury approached the bedside.

"Venerable Father Hooper," said he, "the moment of your release is at hand. Are you ready for the lifting of the veil that shuts in time from eternity?"

Father Hooper at first replied merely by a feeble motion of his head; then, apprehensive, perhaps, that his meaning might be doubtful, he exerted himself to speak.

"Yea," said he, in faint accents, "my soul hath a patient weariness until that veil be lifted."

"And is it fitting," resumed the Reverend Mr. Clark, "that a man so given to prayer, of such a blameless example, holy in deed and thought, so far as mortal judgment may pronounce; is it fitting that a father in the church should leave a shadow on his memory, that may seem to blacken a life so pure? I pray you, my venerable brother, let not this thing be! Suffer us to be gladdened by your triumphant aspect as you go to your reward. Before the veil of eternity be lifted, let me cast aside this black veil from your face!"

And thus speaking, the Reverend Mr. Clark bent forward to reveal the mystery of so many years. But, exerting a sudden energy, that made all the beholders stand aghast, Father Hooper snatched both his hands from beneath the bedclothes, and pressed them strongly on the black veil, resolute to struggle, if the minister of Westbury would contend with a dying man.

"Never!" cried the veiled clergyman. "On earth, never!"

"Dark old man!" exclaimed the affrighted minister, "with what horrible crime upon your soul are you now passing to the judgment?"

Vocabulary
imperceptible (im′ pər sep′ tə bəl) *adj.* not easy to perceive; unnoticeable

Parable and Symbol
What does the minister of Westbury's question suggest about the veil's symbolic meaning?

Comprehension
On his deathbed, does Mr. Hooper wish the veil to be removed?

Father Hooper's breath heaved; it rattled in his throat; but, with a mighty effort, grasping forward with his hands, he caught hold of life, and held it back till he should speak. He even raised himself in bed; and there he sat, shivering with the arms of death around him, while the black veil hung down, awful, at that last moment, in the gathered terrors of a lifetime. And yet the faint, sad smile, so often there, now seemed to glimmer from its obscurity, and linger on Father Hooper's lips.

Spiral Review
Characterization What aspects of Mr. Hooper's character, especially his motivations, does this final speech reveal?

"Why do you tremble at me alone?" cried he, turning his veiled face round the circle of pale spectators. "Tremble also at each other! Have men avoided me, and women shown no pity, and children screamed and fled, only for my black veil? What, but the mystery which it obscurely typifies, has made this piece of crape so awful? When the friend shows his inmost heart to his friend; the lover to his best beloved; when man does not vainly shrink from the eye of his Creator, loathsomely treasuring up the secret of his sin; then deem me a monster, for the symbol beneath which I have lived, and die! I look around me, and, lo! on every visage a Black Veil!"

While his auditors shrank from one another, in mutual affright, Father Hooper fell back upon his pillow, a veiled corpse, with a faint smile lingering on the lips. Still veiled, they laid him in his coffin, and a veiled corpse they bore him to the grave. The grass of many years has sprung up and withered on that grave, the burial stone is moss-grown, and good Mr. Hooper's face is dust; but awful is still the thought that it moldered beneath the Black Veil!

Critical Reading

1. **Key Ideas and Details** **(a)** How did his congregation regard Mr. Hooper before he began wearing the veil? **(b) Analyze:** In what ways does the veil affect Mr. Hooper's relationship with his congregation?
2. **Key Ideas and Details** **(a)** What is the subject of Mr. Hooper's sermon on the day he first wears the veil? **(b) Compare and Contrast:** What emotions does Mr. Hooper evoke in his congregation that he never did before? **(c) Draw Conclusions:** To what do you attribute Mr. Hooper's newfound ability to affect his listeners?
3. **Craft and Structure** **(a)** According to the narrator, how does the "lawless wind" respond to the veil? **(b) Draw Conclusions:** Why is it significant that nature, as represented by the wind, has this reaction?
4. **Integration of Knowledge and Ideas** Does the portrait this story paints of Puritan New England seem too sympathetic, too harsh, or simply accurate? Explain. In your response, use at least two of these Essential Question words: *severe, powerful, community, struggle.* ***[Connecting to the Essential Question: What is the relationship between literature and place?]***

Close Reading Activities

The Minister's Black Veil

Literary Analysis

Writing

2.b. Develop the topic thoroughly by selecting the most significant and relevant facts, concrete details, quotations, or other information and examples appropriate to the audience's knowledge of the topic. *(p. 286)*

2.c. Use appropriate and varied transitions and syntax to link the major sections of the text, create cohesion, and clarify the relationships among complex ideas and concepts. *(p. 286)*

Language

1. Demonstrate command of the conventions of standard English grammar and usage when writing or speaking. *(p. 287)*

3.a. Vary syntax for effect. *(p. 287)*

5. Demonstrate understanding of word relationships. *(p. 286)*

1. **Key Ideas and Details** **(a)** From the description in the opening paragraph, **draw inferences** about the town of Milford's physical setting and its inhabitants. **(b)** How critical is the setting to the essential meaning of this story?
2. **Key Ideas and Details** **(a)** Based on her actions in the story, what inferences can you draw about Elizabeth's personality and overall character? **(b)** Explain which of her actions lead you to draw your inferences.
3. **Key Ideas and Details** A **parable** is a story that conveys a message. What message does this story convey? Support your answer with details from the text.
4. **Craft and Structure** **(a)** By calling this story a parable, what expectation does Hawthorne set up for the reader? **(b)** Does the story meet that expectation? Explain your response.
5. **Craft and Structure** What does Hawthorne's parable show about the way communities may treat those who are different or who behave oddly? Explain your answer.
6. **Craft and Structure** Explain how the veil might be a **symbol** of each of these abstract ideas: **(a)** sin or guilt, **(b)** sorrow or mourning, **(c)** isolation, **(d)** the mystery of the self. Use a chart like the one shown to gather details from the story that support each interpretation.

Sin/Guilt	Sorrow/Mourning	Isolation	Mystery

7. **Craft and Structure** **(a)** Identify at least one other symbol in the story besides the veil. **(b)** Explain what this additional symbol might represent.
8. **Integration of Knowledge and Ideas** Hawthorne never makes it clear why Mr. Hooper chooses to wear the veil. **(a)** By leaving the causes of Mr. Hooper's choice uncertain, what might Hawthorne be saying about relationships among people? **(b)** Do you agree with this implicit message? Explain.
9. **Integration of Knowledge and Ideas** Do you think Hawthorne's intentional use of **ambiguity,** or uncertain meaning, makes the story more effective or less effective? Explain your reasoning.
10. **Integration of Knowledge and Ideas** On his deathbed, when Mr. Clark asks him to remove the black veil, Mr. Hooper replies, "On earth, never!" **(a)** What inference can you draw about when he *will* remove the veil? **(b)** What does this inference suggest about the essential meaning or significance of the veil?

Close Reading Activities Continued

Vocabulary Acquisition and Use

Word Analysis: Greek Root *-path-*

The word *pathos* contains the Greek root *-path-*, which means "suffering," "feeling," or "disease." Although the root appears in words related to the emotions, it is often found in *scientific and medical terminology*. Match each *-path-* word on the left with its definition on the right. Then, use each word in a sentence.

1. empathy
2. pathetic
3. pathogen
4. pathology
5. sympathetic

(a) caring about the feelings and suffering of others
(b) a microorganism that causes disease
(c) the branch of medicine that studies the nature of disease
(d) ability to experience the emotions of another person
(e) arousing feelings of pity in others; pitiful

Vocabulary: Word/Phrase Relationships

For each item, indicate the letter of the choice that best illustrates the phrase containing the italicized word. Explain your thinking.

1. an ***inanimate*** object: **(a)** a flower **(b)** a puppy **(c)** a rock **(d)** a dancer
2. a ***venerable*** figure: **(a)** a village elder **(b)** a criminal **(c)** an insect **(d)** a spoiled brat
3. a nearly ***imperceptible*** movement: **(a)** a twirl **(b)** a lurch **(c)** a blink **(d)** a stride
4. a play full of ***pathos:*** **(a)** a comedy **(b)** a tragedy **(c)** a fantasy **(d)** a farce
5. an ***impertinent*** act: **(a)** bowing **(b)** smiling **(c)** shaking hands **(d)** teasing
6. a creature of ***obstinacy:*** **(a)** a fickle friend **(b)** a puzzled student **(c)** a timid mouse **(d)** a stubborn mule

Writing to Sources

Explanatory Text Like Mr. Hooper's congregation, critics and general readers alike have puzzled over the uncertainties of the black veil in Hawthorne's story. Write an **interpretive essay** in which you explore the veil's significance. Explain the ambiguity that surrounds the veil, and give your own interpretation of its meaning.

Prewriting Reread the story, listing descriptions, dialogue, and character's actions relating to the veil. Review the details you listed, and look for relationships among them. Then, write a sentence in which you state your interpretation of the veil's meaning. Underline the details on your list that point to your interpretation.

Model: Using Exact Quotations

Hawthorne never tells us why Parson Hooper decides to wear the veil. We know only that the veil [, which Hawthorne describes as a "gloomy shade,"] conceals his entire face except for his chin and mouth.

The most effective way to cite details from a literary work is to use word-for-word quotations.

Drafting Begin with a statement about the veil's ambiguity and the meaning that you give it. Then, defend your interpretation using the details you underlined as supporting evidence. *Use transitions* such as *first*, *next*, *in addition*, and *finally* to make the sequence of your examples clear.

Revising Reread your essay and make sure you have included enough passages or details from the story to support your ideas. Add additional direct quotations as needed to strengthen your work.

Conventions and Style: Adjective and Adverb Clauses

Sentence variety and flow are important elements of all good writing. Add to the fluidity of your writing by combining sentences with adjective or adverb clauses. An **adjective clause** is a subordinate clause that modifies a noun or pronoun by telling *what kind* or *which one*. An **adverb clause** is a subordinate clause that modifies a verb, adjective, adverb, or verbal by telling *where, when, in what way, to what extent, under what condition*, or *why*.

Starter Words for Types of Clauses

Adjective Clause: the relative pronouns *that, which, who, whom,* and *whose;* the relative adverbs *where, when*

Adverb Clause: the subordinating conjunctions *after, although, because, even though, so that, though, when*

Using Clauses to Combine Sentences

Choppy: The Puritans valued self-discipline. The Puritans devoted their lives to hard work.
Combined with adjective clause: The Puritans, *who valued self-discipline*, devoted their lives to hard work.

Choppy: People saw Mr. Hooper in his veil. People felt shocked.
Combined with adverb clause: People felt shocked *when they saw Mr. Hooper in his veil.*

Practice In items 1–5, identify each adjective clause or adverb clause. State what type of clause it is and tell what word or words it modifies. In items 6–10, use an adjective or adverb clause to combine the two sentences.

1. The sexton, who was the first to see Mr. Hooper, cried out in astonishment.
2. The sight that drew everyone's attention was a black veil.
3. The congregation stirred as the minister entered the church.
4. Although the villagers were curious, no one asked him about the veil.
5. As long as Mr. Hooper lived, he kept the veil on his face.
6. He would not remove the veil. His fiancée pleaded with him.
7. He would not answer Elizabeth's questions. Elizabeth left.
8. Through the veil, they could sometimes see a smile. The smile was melancholy.
9. The children were also there. The children seemed more frightened than the adults.
10. The mysterious preacher's sermon was powerful. The preacher's sermon upset his parishioners.

Writing and Speaking Conventions

A. Writing Use each subordinate clause in a sentence. Tell what word the clause modifies and what type of clause it is.

1. who had died young
2. which hid most of his face
3. after he delivered the sermon

Example: who loved him
Sentence: Elizabeth, who loved him, never understood Mr. Hooper's choice.
Word Modified: Elizabeth; **Type of Clause:** adjective

B. Speaking Write and present to the class a eulogy to be read at Reverenc Hooper's funeral. Include at least one adjective clause and one adverb clause.

EDGAR ALLAN POE (1809–1849)

When Edgar Allan Poe died, Rufus Griswold, an editor and fellow writer who had an uneasy relationship with Poe, wrote a slanderous obituary that began, "Edgar Allan Poe is dead . . . . This announcement will startle many, but few will be grieved by it" (*New York Tribune*, October 9, 1849, p. 2). He went on to claim that Poe had been expelled from college, that he had neither good friends nor good qualities, and that he committed flagrant acts of plagiarism. Suspicious of this unconventional obituary, some speculated that Poe orchestrated the death notice himself to keep his name in the public eye. Yet, Poe's real life was almost as dark and dismal as the false obituary described it.

A TROUBLED CHILDHOOD Poe was born in Boston in 1809, the son of impoverished traveling actors. Shortly after Poe's birth, his father deserted the family; a year later, his mother died. Young Edgar was taken in—though never formally adopted—by the family of John Allan, a wealthy Virginia merchant. Poe lived with the Allans in England from 1815 to 1820, when they returned to the United States. It was from John Allan that Poe received his middle name. The Allans also provided for Poe's education; however, when his stepfather refused to pay Poe's large gambling debts at the University of Virginia, the young man was forced to leave the school.

BUILDING A LITERARY CAREER

In 1827, after joining the army under an assumed name, Poe published his first volume of poetry, *Tamerlane and Other Poems*. Two years later, he published a second volume, *Al Aaraaf.* In 1830, John Allan helped Poe win an appointment to the United States Military Academy at West Point. Within a year, however, Poe was expelled for academic violations, and his dismissal resulted in an irreparable break with his stepfather.

In This Section

STRUGGLING, WITH LITTLE REWARD During the second half of his short life, Poe pursued a literary career in New York, Richmond, Philadelphia, and Baltimore, barely supporting himself by writing and working as an editor for several magazines. After his third volume of poetry, *Poems* (1831), failed to bring him either money or acclaim, he turned from poetry to fiction and literary criticism. Five of his short stories were published in newspapers in 1832, and in 1838 he published his only novel, *The Narrative of Arthur Gordon Pym*.

AN UNHAPPY ENDING Although his short stories gained him some recognition, and his poem "The Raven" (1845) was greeted with enthusiasm, Poe could never escape from poverty. He suffered from bouts of depression and madness. His beloved wife, Virginia, seemed to be his one source of happiness. In 1846, he wrote these words to her: "[M]y little darling wife you are my greatest and only stimulus now, to battle with this uncongenial, unsatisfactory and ungrateful life...." Virginia died in 1847, at the age of 24. Some critics believe that Poe's despair over Virginia's lingering illness and death explains his fascination with doomed female characters, such as the lost Lenore of "The Raven" and the tormented Madeline Usher of "The Fall of the House of Usher." Two years after Virginia's death, Poe died in Baltimore, alone and unhappy.

A BOUNTIFUL LEGACY Since his death, Poe's work has been a magnet for attention and has influenced writers and artists of all types. His story "The Murders in the Rue Morgue" is widely accepted as the first detective story, making Poe the founder of an entire literary and theatrical genre. His psychological thrillers have been imitated by scores of modern writers, translated into nearly every language, and adapted for dozens of films. Since 1946, the Mystery Writers of America have honored their best and brightest by conferring upon them the Edgar Award for achievement in mystery writing. Today, Poe is regarded as a brilliant original whose tireless exploration of altered mental states and the dark side of human nature changed the landscape of literature, both in America and around the world.

ALL THAT WE SEE OR SEEM, IS BUT A DREAM WITHIN A DREAM.

Edgar A Poe

POE & POP CULTURE

Ever since his death in 1849, Poe's legend has grown. He has become a pop icon—a status usually reserved for movie stars or musicians. Consider this sampling of Poe's modern-day appearances:

- Poe is pictured on the Beatles' famous Sergeant Pepper album cover, and is referred to in the lyrics of "I Am the Walrus."
- Other musicians who have recorded Poe-related songs include Lou Reed, Joan Baez, Judy Collins, Iron Maiden, Good Charlotte, Public Enemy, Green Day, the Alan Parsons Project, and Japanese pop star Utada Hikaru.
- The 1990 Halloween edition of the TV show The Simpsons featured "The Raven." Poe is credited as a writer on the episode.
- Dozens of movies have been based on Poe's stories, including the famous films directed by Roger Corman.
- The Baltimore Ravens football team takes its name from Poe's famous poem.
- In the 1960s sitcom *The Munsters*, a raven often emerged from a cuckoo clock to squawk, "Nevermore, Nevermore."

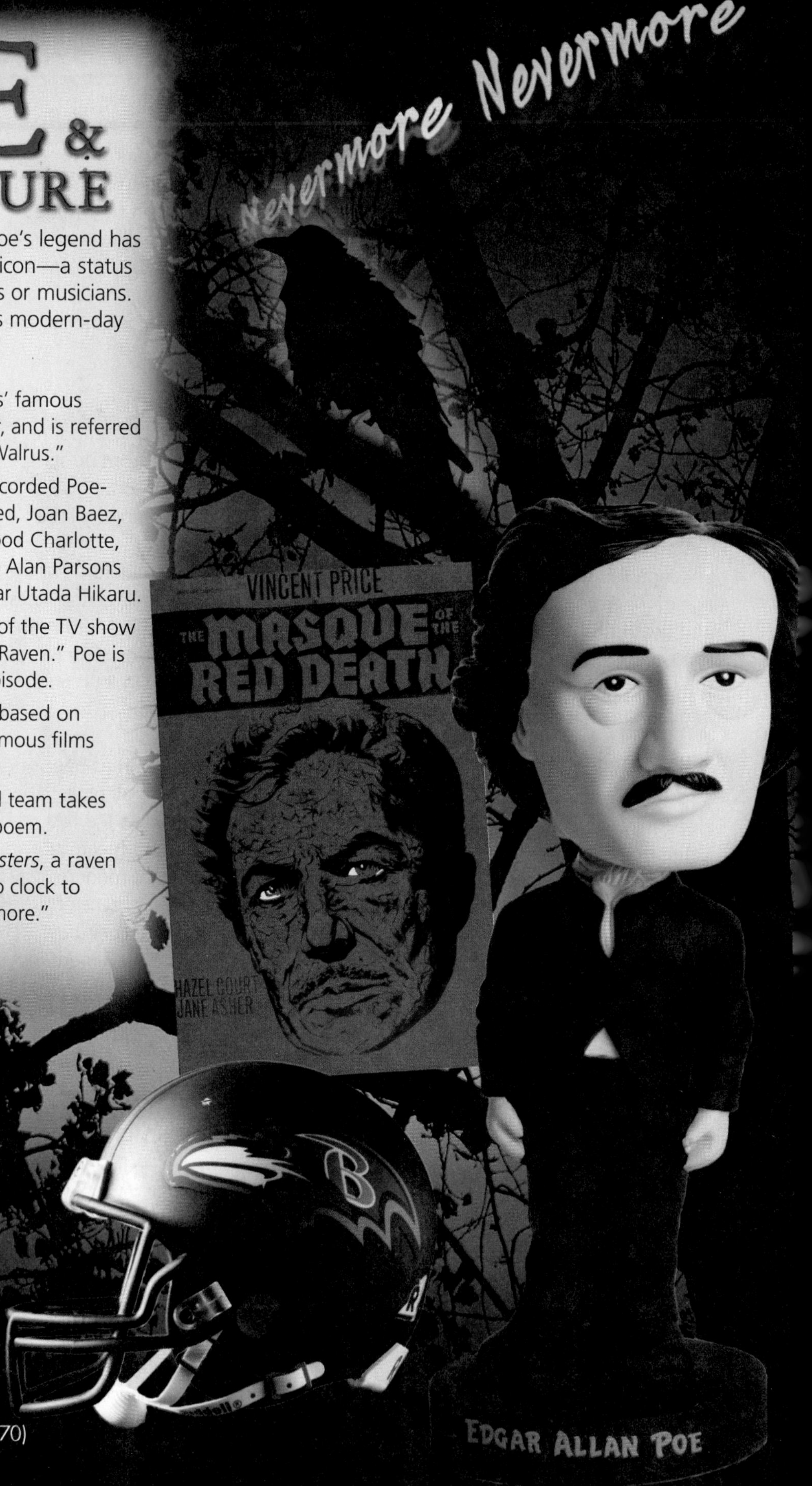

Nevermore Nevermore

VINCENT PRICE
THE MASQUE OF THE RED DEATH
HAZEL COURT
JANE ASHER

EDGAR ALLAN POE

Building Knowledge and Insight

The Fall of the House of Usher • The Raven

Connecting to the Essential Question Poe explored boundaries between reality and dreamlike states. The settings in his stories and poems are fantastic mental landscapes. As you read, find details that portray the setting as unreal or dreamlike. This will help as you think about the Essential Question: **What is the relationship between literature and place?**

Reading Literature

1. Cite strong and thorough textual evidence to support analysis of what the text says explicitly as well as inferences drawn from the text, including determining where the text leaves matters uncertain.

3. Analyze the impact of the author's choices regarding how to develop and relate elements of a story.

9. Demonstrate knowledge of nineteenth-century foundational works of American literature, including how two or more texts from the same period treat similar themes or topics.

Close Reading Focus

Gothic Literature; Single Effect

This story and poem are examples of **Gothic literature,** a literary genre that began in England in the late 1700s. The word *Gothic* comes from architecture, where it describes castles and cathedrals that served as the mysterious settings for early Gothic fiction. The Gothic style, which has the following elements, appealed to Edgar Allan Poe's dark view of the world:

- Bleak or remote settings
- Macabre or violent incidents
- Characters in psychological and/or physical torment
- Supernatural or otherworldly elements
- Strong language full of dangerous meanings

Poe's literary contributions extend beyond his stories. He was an important critic, who argued that a narrative should achieve a "certain unique or **single effect.**" He felt that every detail in a short story, play, or poem should contribute to one impression. In Poe's work, the single effect is usually one of fear and a disturbing ambiguity about what is real. As you read, notice Gothic elements in both works that contribute to a single, unified effect.

Preparing to Read Complex Texts As you read, *monitor your comprehension* of Poe's complex sentences. If you are unsure of the meaning, **break down long sentences** into logical parts. First, look for a sentence's subject and verb. Then, look for clues in punctuation, conjunctions, and modifiers. Use a chart like the one shown to break Poe's intricate sentences into smaller parts.

Sentence

As if . . . there had been found the potency of a spell, the huge antique panels to which the speaker pointed threw slowly back, upon the instant, their ponderous and ebony jaws.

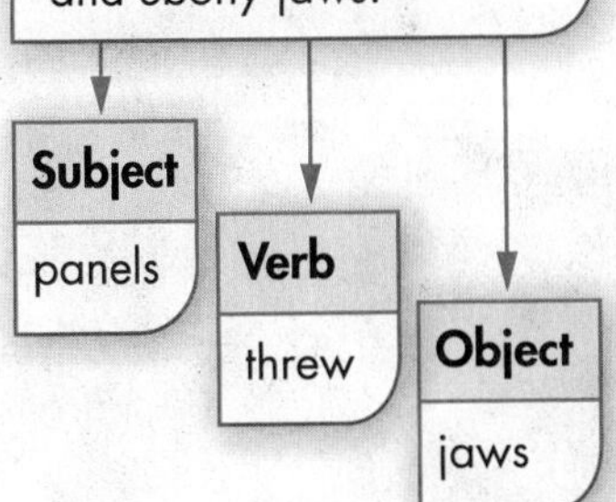

Vocabulary

The words listed here are important to understanding the text that follows. Copy the words into your notebook. Note which words have four syllables.

importunate
munificent
equivocal
specious
anomalous
sentience

▲ Critical Viewing
What does this opening illustration suggest about the events that will take place in this story? **PREDICT**

THE FALL OF THE HOUSE OF USHER

EDGAR ALLAN POE

BACKGROUND In 1839, Edgar Allan Poe lived in Philadelphia and became coeditor of *Burton's Gentleman's Magazine*, a journal that published essays, fiction, reviews, and poems, as well as articles on sailing, hunting, and cricket. Poe's articles ran the gamut of topics. He explained the parallel bars, mused about the mysteries of Stonehenge, and reviewed more than eighty books on varied topics. It was in this magazine that he first published "The Fall of the House of Usher."

Son Coeur est un luth suspendu:
Sitôt qu'on le touche il résonne.[1]

During the whole of a dull, dark, and soundless day in the autumn of the year, when the clouds hung oppressively low in the heavens, I had been passing alone, on horseback, through a singularly dreary tract of country, and at length found myself, as the shades of evening drew on, within view of the melancholy House of Usher. I know not how it was—but, with the first glimpse of the building, a sense of insufferable gloom pervaded my spirit. I say insufferable; for the feeling was unrelieved by any of that half-pleasurable, because poetic, sentiment, with which the mind usually receives even the

Comprehension
What does the narrator feel at his first glimpse of the House of Usher?

1. ***Son . . . résonne*** "His heart is a lute strung tight: As soon as one touches it, it resounds." From "Le Refus" by Pierre Jean de Béranger (1780–1857).

sternest natural images of the desolate or terrible. I looked upon the scene before me—upon the mere house, and the simple landscape features of the domain—upon the bleak walls—upon the vacant eyelike windows—upon a few rank sedges[2]—and upon a few white trunks of decayed trees—with an utter depression of soul, which I can compare to no earthly sensation more properly than to the after-dream of the reveler upon opium—the bitter lapse into everyday life—the hideous dropping off of the veil. There was an iciness, a sinking, a sickening of the heart—an unredeemed dreariness of thought which no goading of the imagination could torture into aught[3] of the sublime. What was it—I paused to think—what was it that so unnerved me in the contemplation of the House of Usher? It was a mystery all insoluble; nor could I grapple with the shadowy fancies that crowded upon me as I pondered. I was forced to fall back upon the unsatisfactory conclusion, that while, beyond doubt, there are combinations of very simple natural objects which have the power of thus affecting us, still the analysis of this power lies among considerations beyond our depth. It was possible, I reflected, that a mere different arrangement of the particulars of the scene, of the details of the picture, would be sufficient to modify, or perhaps to annihilate its capacity for sorrowful impression; and, acting upon this idea, I reined my horse to the precipitous brink of a black and lurid tarn[4] that lay in unruffled luster by the dwelling, and gazed down—but with a shudder even more thrilling than before—upon the remodeled and inverted images of the gray sedge, and the ghastly tree stems, and the vacant and eyelike windows.

THERE WAS AN ICINESS, A SINKING, A SICKENING OF THE HEART.

Nevertheless, in this mansion of gloom I now proposed to myself a sojourn of some weeks. Its proprietor, Roderick Usher, had been one of my boon companions in boyhood; but many years had elapsed since our last meeting. A letter, however, had lately reached me in a distant part of the country—a letter from him—which, in its wildly **importunate** nature, had admitted of no other than a personal reply. The MS[5] gave evidence of nervous agitation. The writer spoke of acute bodily illness—of a mental disorder which oppressed him—and of an earnest desire to see me, as his best and indeed his only personal friend, with a view of attempting, by the cheerfulness of my society, some alleviation of his malady. It was the manner in which all this, and much more, was said—it was the apparent *heart* that went with his request—which allowed me no room for hesitation; and I accordingly obeyed forthwith what I still considered a very singular summons.

Although, as boys, we had been even intimate associates, yet I really knew little of my friend. His reserve had been always excessive and habitual. I was aware, however, that his very ancient family had

Vocabulary
importunate (im pôr′ che nit) *adj.* insistent

▶ Critical Viewing
Which details in this illustration reflect the description of the narrator's first impression of the house? **CONNECT**

2. **sedges** (sej′ iz) *n.* grasslike plants.
3. **aught** (ôt) anything.
4. **tarn** (tärn) *n.* small lake.
5. **MS.** *abbr.* manuscript.

Vocabulary
munificent
(myo͞o nif´ ə sənt)
adj. generous

Vocabulary
equivocal (i kwiv´ ə kəl)
adj. having more than one possible interpretation

Gothic Literature
How do the setting and mood of the story so far reflect Gothic literary style?

been noted, time out of mind, for a peculiar sensibility of temperament, displaying itself, through long ages, in many works of exalted art, and manifested, of late, in repeated deeds of **munificent** yet unobtrusive charity, as well as in a passionate devotion to the intricacies, perhaps even more than to the orthodox and easily recognizable beauties, of musical science. I had learned, too, the very remarkable fact, that the stem of the Usher race, all time-honored as it was, had put forth, at no period, any enduring branch: in other words, that the entire family lay in the direct line of descent, and had always, with very trifling and very temporary variations, so lain. It was this deficiency, I considered, while running over in thought the perfect keeping of the character of the premises with the accredited character of the people, and while speculating upon the possible influence which the one, in the long lapse of centuries, might have exercised upon the other—it was this deficiency, perhaps of collateral issue,[6] and the consequent undeviating transmission, from sire to son, of the patrimony[7] with the name, which had, at length, so identified the two as to merge the original title of the estate in the quaint and **equivocal** appellation of the "House of Usher"—an appellation which seemed to include, in the minds of the peasantry who used it, both the family and the family mansion.

I have said that the sole effect of my somewhat childish experiment—that of looking down within the tarn—had been to deepen the first singular impression. There can be no doubt that the consciousness of the rapid increase of my superstition—for why should I not so term it?—served mainly to accelerate the increase itself. Such, I have long known, is the paradoxical law of all sentiments having terror as a basis. And it might have been for this reason only, that, when I again uplifted my eyes to the house itself, from its image in the pool, there grew in my mind a strange fancy—a fancy so ridiculous, indeed, that I but mention it to show the vivid force of the sensations which oppressed me. I had so worked upon my imagination as really to believe that about the whole mansion and domain there hung an atmosphere peculiar to themselves and their immediate vicinity—an atmosphere which had no affinity with the air of heaven, but which had reeked up from the decayed trees, and the gray wall, and the silent tarn—a pestilent and mystic vapor, dull, sluggish, faintly discernible and leaden-hued.

Shaking off from my spirit what *must* have been a dream, I scanned more narrowly the real aspect of the building. Its principal feature seemed to be that of an excessive antiquity. The discoloration of ages had been great. Minute fungi overspread the whole exterior, hanging in a fine tangled web-work from the eaves. Yet all this was apart from any extraordinary dilapidation. No portion of the masonry had fallen; and there appeared to be a wild inconsistency between

---

6. collateral (kə lat´ ər əl) **issue** descended from the same ancestors but in a different line.
7. patrimony (pat´ rə mō´ nē) *n.* property inherited from one's father.

its still perfect adaptation of parts, and the crumbling condition of the individual stones. In this there was much that reminded me of the **specious** totality of old woodwork which has rotted for long years in some neglected vault, with no disturbance from the breath of the external air. Beyond this indication of extensive decay, however, the fabric gave little token of instability. Perhaps the eye of a scrutinizing observer might have discovered a barely perceptible fissure, which, extending from the roof of the building in front, made its way down the wall in a zigzag direction, until it became lost in the sullen waters of the tarn.

Noticing these things, I rode over a short causeway to the house. A servant in waiting took my horse, and I entered the Gothic[8] archway of the hall. A valet, of stealthy step, then conducted me, in silence, through many dark and intricate passages in my progress to the studio of his master. Much that I encountered on the way contributed, I know not how, to heighten the vague sentiments of which I have already spoken. While the objects around me—while the carvings of the ceilings, the somber tapestries of the walls, the ebon blackness of the floors, and the phantasmagoric[9] armorial trophies which rattled as I strode, were but matters to which, or to such as which, I had been accustomed from my infancy—while I hesitated not to acknowledge how familiar was all this—I still wondered to find how unfamiliar were the fancies which ordinary images were stirring up. On one of the staircases, I met the physician of the family. His countenance, I thought, wore a mingled expression of low cunning and perplexity. He accosted me with trepidation and passed on. The valet now threw open a door and ushered me into the presence of his master.

The room in which I found myself was very large and lofty. The windows were long, narrow, and pointed, and at so vast a distance from the black oaken floor as to be altogether inaccessible from within. Feeble gleams of encrimsoned light made their way through the trellised panes, and served to render sufficiently distinct the more prominent objects around; the eye, however, struggled in vain to reach the remoter angles of the chamber, or the recesses of the vaulted and fretted[10] ceiling. Dark draperies hung upon the walls. The general furniture was profuse, comfortless, antique, and tattered. Many books and musical instruments lay scattered about, but failed to give any vitality to the scene. I felt that I breathed an atmosphere of sorrow. An air of stern, deep, and irredeemable gloom hung over and pervaded all.

Upon my entrance, Usher arose from a sofa on which he had been lying at full length, and greeted me with a vivacious warmth which

Vocabulary

specious (spē′ shəs) *adj.* seeming to be but not actually sound

Comprehension

What flaw in the house might a careful observer find?

---

8. Gothic *adj.* high and ornate.

9. phantasmagoric (fan taz′ mə gôr′ ik) *adj.* fantastic or dreamlike.

10. fretted (fret′ id) *adj.* ornamented with a pattern of small, straight, intersecting bars.

had much in it, I at first thought, of an overdone cordiality—of the constrained effort of the *ennuyé*[11] man of the world. A glance, however, at his countenance convinced me of his perfect sincerity. We sat down; and for some moments, while he spoke not, I gazed upon him with a feeling half of pity, half of awe. Surely, man had never before so terribly altered, in so brief a period, as had Roderick Usher! It was with difficulty that I could bring myself to admit the identity of the wan being before me with the companion of my early boyhood. Yet the character of his face had been at all times remarkable. A cadaverousness of complexion; an eye large, liquid, and luminous beyond comparison; lips somewhat thin and very pallid, but of a surpassingly beautiful curve; a nose of a delicate Hebrew model, but with a breadth of nostril unusual in similar formations; a finely molded chin, speaking, in its want of prominence, of a want of moral energy; hair of a more than weblike softness and tenuity—these features, with an inordinate expansion above the regions of the temple, made up altogether a countenance not easily to be forgotten. And now in the mere exaggeration of the prevailing character of these features, and of the expression they were wont to convey, lay so much of change that I doubted to whom I spoke. The now ghastly pallor of the skin, and the now miraculous luster of the eye, above all things startled and even awed me. The silken hair, too, had been suffered to grow all unheeded, and as, in its wild gossamer texture, it floated rather than fell about the face, I could not, even with effort, connect its Arabesque[12] expression with any idea of simple humanity.

Breaking Down Long Sentences

In your own words, restate the meaning of the sentence beginning "The silken hair. . ."

In the manner of my friend I was at once struck with an incoherence—an inconsistency; and I soon found this to arise from a series of feeble and futile struggles to overcome an habitual trepidancy—an excessive nervous agitation. For something of this nature I had indeed been prepared, no less by his letter than by reminiscences of certain boyish traits, and by conclusions deduced from his peculiar physical conformation and temperament. His action was alternately vivacious and sullen. His voice varied rapidly from a tremulous indecision (when the animal spirits seemed utterly in abeyance) to that species of energetic concision—that abrupt, weighty, unhurried, and hollow-sounding enunciation—that leaden, self-balanced, and perfectly modulated guttural utterance, which may be observed

11. ***ennuyé*** (än′ wē ā′) *adj.* bored (French).
12. **Arabesque** (ar′ ə besk′) *adj.* of complex and elaborate design.

in the lost drunkard, or the irreclaimable eater of opium, during the periods of his most intense excitement.

It was thus that he spoke of the object of my visit, of his earnest desire to see me, and of the solace he expected me to afford him. He entered, at some length, into what he conceived to be the nature of his malady. It was, he said, a constitutional and a family evil and one for which he despaired to find a remedy—a mere nervous affection,[13] he immediately added, which would undoubtedly soon pass off. It displayed itself in a host of unnatural sensations. Some of these, as he detailed them, interested and bewildered me; although, perhaps, the terms and the general manner of their narration had their weight. He suffered much from a morbid acuteness of the senses; the most insipid food was alone endurable; he could wear only garments of certain texture; the odors of all flowers were oppressive; his eyes were tortured by even a faint light; and there were but peculiar sounds, and these from stringed instruments, which did not inspire him with horror.

To an **anomalous** species of terror I found him a bounden slave. "I shall perish," said he, "I *must* perish in this deplorable folly. Thus, thus, and not otherwise, shall I be lost. I dread the events of the future, not in themselves, but in their results. I shudder at the thought of any, even the most trivial, incident, which may operate upon this intolerable agitation of soul. I have, indeed, no abhorrence of danger, except in its absolute effect—in terror. In this unnerved, in this pitiable, condition I feel that the period will sooner or later arrive when I must abandon life and reason together, in some struggle with the grim phantasm, FEAR."

I learned, moreover, at intervals, and through broken and equivocal hints, another singular feature of his mental condition. He was enchained by certain superstitious impressions in regard to the dwelling which he tenanted, and whence, for many years, he had never ventured forth—in regard to an influence whose supposititious[14] force was conveyed in terms too shadowy here to be restated—an influence which some peculiarities in the mere form and substance of his family mansion had, by dint of long sufferance, he said, obtained over his spirit—an effect which the physique of the gray walls and turrets, and of the dim tarn into which they all looked down, had at length, brought about upon the morale of his existence.

He admitted, however, although with hesitation, that much of the peculiar gloom which thus afflicted him could be traced to a more natural and far more palpable origin—to the severe and long-continued illness—indeed to the evidently approaching dissolution—of a tenderly beloved sister, his sole companion for long years, his last and only relative on earth. "Her decease," he said, with a bitterness

13. affection affliction.
14. supposititious (sə päz′ ə tish′ əs) *adj.* supposed.

Gothic Literature

In what ways do Usher's mental state and the house itself typify a work of Gothic literature?

Vocabulary

anomalous (ə näm′ ə ləs) *adj.* odd; out of the ordinary

Comprehension

In what ways has Roderick Usher changed since the narrator last saw him?

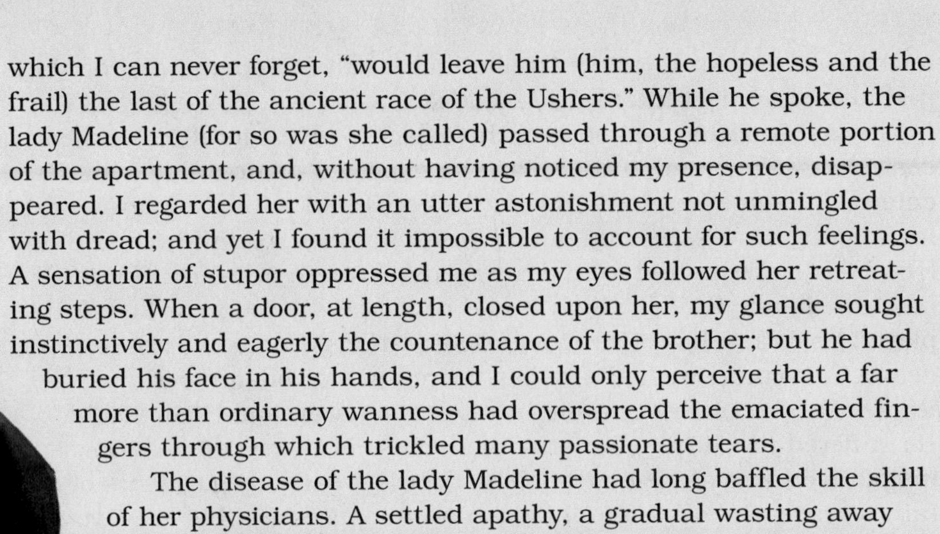

which I can never forget, "would leave him (him, the hopeless and the frail) the last of the ancient race of the Ushers." While he spoke, the lady Madeline (for so was she called) passed through a remote portion of the apartment, and, without having noticed my presence, disappeared. I regarded her with an utter astonishment not unmingled with dread; and yet I found it impossible to account for such feelings. A sensation of stupor oppressed me as my eyes followed her retreating steps. When a door, at length, closed upon her, my glance sought instinctively and eagerly the countenance of the brother; but he had buried his face in his hands, and I could only perceive that a far more than ordinary wanness had overspread the emaciated fingers through which trickled many passionate tears.

The disease of the lady Madeline had long baffled the skill of her physicians. A settled apathy, a gradual wasting away of the person, and frequent although transient affections of a partially cataleptical[15] character were the unusual diagnosis. Hitherto she had steadily borne up against the pressure of her malady, and had not betaken herself finally to bed; but on the closing in of the evening of my arrival at the house, she succumbed (as her brother told me at night with inexpressible agitation) to the prostrating power of the destroyer; and I learned that the glimpse I had obtained of her person would thus probably be the last I should obtain—that the lady, at least while living, would be seen by me no more.

For several days ensuing, her name was unmentioned by either Usher or myself; and during this period I was busied in earnest endeavors to alleviate the melancholy of my friend. We painted and read together, or I listened, as if in a dream, to the wild improvisations of his speaking guitar. And thus, as a closer and still closer intimacy admitted me more unreservedly into the recesses of his spirit, the more bitterly did I perceive the futility of all attempt at cheering a mind from which darkness, as if an inherent positive quality, poured forth upon all objects of the moral and physical universe in one unceasing radiation of gloom.

I shall ever bear about me a memory of the many solemn hours I thus spent alone with the master of the House of Usher. Yet I should fail in any attempt to convey an idea of the exact character of the studies, or of the occupations, in which he involved me, or led me the way. An excited and highly distempered ideality[16] threw a sulfureous[17] luster over all. His long improvised dirges will ring forever in my ears. Among other things, I hold painfully in mind a certain singular perversion and amplification

---

15. **cataleptical** (kat´ əl ep´ tik əl) *adj.* in a state in which consciousness and feeling are suddenly and temporarily lost and the muscles become rigid.
16. **ideality** (ī dē al´ i tē) *n.* something that is ideal and has no reality.
17. **sulfureous** (sul fyo͞or´ ē əs) *adj.* greenish-yellow.

of the wild air of the last waltz of von Weber.[18] From the paintings over which his elaborate fancy brooded, and which grew, touch by touch, into vaguenesses at which I shuddered the more thrillingly, because I shuddered knowing not why—from these paintings (vivid as their images now are before me) I would in vain endeavor to educe more than a small portion which should lie within the compass of merely written words. By the utter simplicity, by the nakedness of his designs, he arrested and overawed attention. If ever mortal painted an idea, that mortal was Roderick Usher. For me at least, in the circumstances then surrounding me, there arose out of the pure abstractions which the hypochondriac contrived to throw upon his canvas, an intensity of intolerable awe, no shadow of which felt I ever yet in the contemplation of the certainly glowing yet too concrete reveries of Fuseli.[19]

One of the phantasmagoric conceptions of my friend, partaking not so rigidly of the spirit of abstraction, may be shadowed forth, although feebly, in words. A small picture presented the interior of an immensely long and rectangular vault or tunnel, with low walls, smooth, white and without interruption or device. Certain accessory points of the design served well to convey the idea that this excavation lay at an exceeding depth below the surface of the earth. No outlet was observed in any portion of its vast extent, and no torch or other artificial source of light was discernible; yet a flood of intense rays rolled throughout, and bathed the whole in a ghastly and inappropriate splendor.

I have just spoken of that morbid condition of the auditory nerve which rendered all music intolerable to the sufferer, with the exception of certain effects of stringed instruments. It was, perhaps, the narrow limits to which he thus confined himself upon the guitar which gave birth, in great measure, to the fantastic character of his performances. But the fervid facility of his impromptus could not be so accounted for. They must have been, and were, in the notes, as well as in the words of his wild fantasias (for he not unfrequently accompanied himself with rhymed verbal improvisations), the result of that intense mental collectedness and concentration to which I have previously alluded as observable only in particular moments of the highest artificial excitement. The words of one of these rhapsodies I have easily remembered. I was, perhaps, the more forcibly impressed with it as he gave it because, in the under or mystic current of its meaning, I fancied that I perceived, and for the first time, a full consciousness on the part of Usher of the tottering of his lofty reason upon her throne. The verses, which were entitled "The Haunted Palace," ran very nearly, if not accurately, thus:

◀ Critical Viewing

Which of the qualities described by the narrator are captured in this illustration of Madeline Usher? **INTERPRET**

Gothic Literature and Single Effect

What effect does this description of Usher's artwork help to create? Explain.

Comprehension

What conclusion does the narrator draw about Usher's mental state?

---

18. von Weber (fôn vä′ bər) Karl Maria von Weber (1786–1826), a German Romantic composer whose music was highly emotional and dramatic.

19. Fuseli (fo͞o ze′ lē) Johann Heinrich Fuseli (1741–1825), also known as Henry Fuseli, Swiss-born painter who lived in England and was noted for his depictions of dreamlike and sometimes nightmarish images.

Gothic Literature and Single Effect

Which details of this poem mirror the narrator's sense of Usher's mental instability?

I

In the greenest of our valleys,
By good angels tenanted,
Once a fair and stately palace—
Radiant palace—reared its head.
In the monarch Thought's dominion—
It stood there!
Never seraph[20] *spread a pinion*
Over fabric half so fair.

II

Banners yellow, glorious, golden,
On its roof did float and flow
(This—all this—was in the olden
Time long ago)
And every gentle air that dallied,
In that sweet day,
Along the ramparts plumed and pallid,
A winged odor went away.

III

Wanderers in that happy valley
Through two luminous windows saw
Spirits moving musically
To a lute's well-tunéd law;
Round about a throne, where sitting
(Porphyrogene!)[21]
In state his glory well befitting,
The ruler of the realm was seen.

IV

And all with pearl and ruby glowing
Was the fair palace door,
Through which came flowing, flowing, flowing
And sparkling evermore,
A troop of Echoes whose sweet duty
Was but to sing,
In voices of surpassing beauty,
The wit and wisdom of their king.

---

20. seraph (ser′ əf) angel.
21. Porphyrogene (pôr fər ō jēn′) born to royalty or "the purple."

V

But evil things, in robes of sorrow,
Assailed the monarch's high estate;
(Ah, let us mourn, for never morrow
Shall dawn upon him, desolate!)
And, round about his home, the glory
That blushed and bloomed
Is but a dim-remembered story
Of the old time entombed.

VI

And travelers now within that valley,
Through the red-litten[22] *windows see*
Vast forms that move fantastically
To a discordant melody;
While, like a rapid ghastly river,
Through the pale door,
A hideous throng rush out forever,
And laugh—but smile no more.

I well remember that suggestions arising from this ballad led us into a train of thought wherein there became manifest an opinion of Usher's which I mention not so much on account of its novelty (for other men have thought thus), as on account of the pertinacity with which he maintained it. This opinion, in its general form, was that of the **sentience** of all vegetable things. But, in his disordered fancy the idea had assumed a more daring character, and trespassed, under certain conditions, upon the kingdom of inorganization.[23] I lack words to express the full extent, or the earnest abandon of his persuasion. The belief, however, was connected (as I have previously hinted) with the gray stones of the home of his forefathers. The conditions of the sentience had been here, he imagined, fulfilled in the method of collocation of these stones—in the order of their arrangement, as well as in that of the many fungi which overspread them, and of the decayed trees which stood around—above all, in the long undisturbed endurance of this arrangement, and in its reduplication in the still waters of the tarn. Its evidence—the evidence of the sentience—was to be seen, he said (and I here started as he spoke), in the gradual yet certain condensation of an atmosphere of their own about the waters and the walls. The result was discoverable, he added, in that silent yet importunate and terrible influence which for centuries had molded the destinies of his family, and which made him what I now saw him—what he was. Such opinions need no comment, and I will make none.

Vocabulary
sentience (sen′ shəns) *n.* capacity of feeling

Comprehension
What is "The Haunted Palace"?

---

22. litten lighted.
23. inorganization (in′ ôr gə ni zā′ shən) *n.* inanimate objects.

Our books—the books which, for years, had formed no small portion of the mental existence of the invalid—were, as might be supposed, in strict keeping with this character of phantasm. We pored together over such works as the *Ververt et Chartreuse*[24] of Gresset; the *Belphegor* of Machiavelli; the *Heaven and Hell* of Swedenborg; the *Subterranean Voyage of Nicholas Klimm* by Holberg; the *Chiromancy* of Robert Flud, of Jean D'Indaginé and of De la Chambre; the *Journey into the Blue Distance* of Tieck; and the *City of the Sun* of Campanella. One favorite volume was a small octavo edition of the *Directorium Inquisitorium*, by the Dominican Eymeric de Gironne; and there were passages in Pomponius Mela, about the old African Satyrs and Œgipans, over which Usher would sit dreaming for hours. His chief delight, however, was found in the perusal of an exceedingly rare and curious book in quarto Gothic—the manual of a forgotten church—the *Vigilae Mortuorum secundum Chorum Ecclesiae Maguntinae*.

HE STATED HIS INTENTION OF PRESERVING HER CORPSE FOR A FORTNIGHT.

I could not help thinking of the wild ritual of this work, and of its probable influence upon the hypochondriac, when, one evening, having informed me abruptly that the lady Madeline was no more, he stated his intention of preserving her corpse for a fortnight (previously to its final interment), in one of the numerous vaults within the main walls of the building. The worldly reason, however, assigned for this singular proceeding, was one which I did not feel at liberty to dispute. The brother had been led to his resolution (so he told me) by consideration of the unusual character of the malady of the deceased, of certain obtrusive and eager inquiries on the part of her medical men, and of the remote and exposed situation of the burial ground of the family. I will not deny that when I called to mind the sinister countenance of the person whom I met upon the staircase, on the day of my arrival at the house, I had no desire to oppose what I regarded as at best but a harmless, and by no means an unnatural precaution.

Breaking Down Long Sentences

Clarify the main idea of the sentence beginning "The vault in which we placed it. . ."

At the request of Usher, I personally aided him in the arrangements for the temporary entombment. The body having been encoffined, we two alone bore it to its rest. The vault in which we placed it (and which had been so long unopened that our torches, half smothered in its oppressive atmosphere, gave us little opportunity for investigation) was small, damp, and entirely without means of admission for light; lying, at great depth, immediately beneath that portion of the building in which was my own sleeping apartment. It had been used, apparently, in remote feudal times, for the worst purposes of a donjon-keep, and, in later days, as a place of deposit for powder, or some other highly combustible substance, as a portion of its floor, and the whole interior of a long archway through which we reached it, were carefully sheathed with copper. The door, of massive

24. *Ververt et Chartreuse*, etc. All the books listed deal with magic or mysticism.

iron, had been, also, similarly protected. Its immense weight caused an unusually sharp, grating sound, as it moved upon its hinges.

Having deposited our mournful burden upon trestles within this region of horror, we partially turned aside the yet unscrewed lid of the coffin, and looked upon the face of the tenant. A striking similitude between the brother and sister now first arrested my attention; and Usher, divining, perhaps, my thoughts, murmured out some few words from which I learned that the deceased and himself had been twins, and that sympathies of a scarcely intelligible nature had always existed between them. Our glances, however, rested not long upon the dead—for we could not regard her unawed. The disease which had thus entombed the lady in the maturity of youth, had left, as usual in all maladies of a strictly cataleptical character, the mockery of a faint blush upon the bosom and the face, and that suspiciously lingering smile upon the lip which is so terrible in death. We replaced and screwed down the lid, and, having secured the door of iron, made our way, with toil, into the scarcely less gloomy apartments of the upper portion of the house.

And now, some days of bitter grief having elapsed, an observable change came over the features of the mental disorder of my friend. His ordinary manner had vanished. His ordinary occupations were neglected or forgotten. He roamed from chamber to chamber with hurried, unequal, and object-less step. The pallor of his countenance had assumed, if possible, a more ghastly hue—but the luminousness of his eye had utterly gone out. The once occasional huskiness of his tone was heard no more; and a tremulous quaver, as if of extreme terror, habitually characterized his utterance. There were times, indeed, when I thought his unceasingly agitated mind was laboring with some oppressive secret, to divulge which he struggled for the necessary courage. At times, again, I was obliged to resolve all into the mere inexplicable vagaries[25] of madness, for I beheld him gazing upon vacancy for long hours, in an attitude of the profoundest attention, as if listening to some imaginary sound. It was no wonder that his condition terrified—that it infected me. I felt creeping upon me, by slow yet uncertain degrees, the wild influences of his own fantastic yet impressive superstitions.

It was, especially, upon retiring to bed late in the night of the seventh or eighth day after the placing of the lady Madeline within the donjon, that I experienced the full power of such feelings. Sleep came not near my couch—while the hours waned and waned away. I struggled to reason off the nervousness which had dominion over me. I endeavored to believe that much, if not all of what I felt, was due to the bewildering influence of the gloomy furniture of the room—of the dark and tattered draperies, which, tortured

Comprehension

What does the narrator notice about Madeline's appearance in her coffin?

25. vagaries (vā′ gər ēz) *n.* odd, unexpected actions or notions.

Gothic Literature

Which elements of Gothic literature are present in this description of the narrator's sleepless night?

into motion by the breath of a rising tempest, swayed fitfully to and fro upon the walls, and rustled uneasily about the decorations of the bed. But my efforts were fruitless. An irrepressible tremor gradually pervaded my frame; and, at length, there sat upon my very heart an incubus[26] of utterly causeless alarm. Shaking this off with a gasp and a struggle, I uplifted myself upon the pillows, and, peering earnestly within the intense darkness of the chamber, hearkened—I know not why, except that an instinctive spirit prompted me—to certain low and indefinite sounds which came, through the pauses of the storm, at long intervals, I knew not whence. Overpowered by an intense sentiment of horror, unaccountable yet unendurable, I threw on my clothes with haste (for I felt that I should sleep no more during the night), and endeavored to arouse myself from the pitiable condition into which I had fallen by pacing rapidly to and fro through the apartment.

I had taken but few turns in this manner, when a light step on an adjoining staircase arrested my attention. I presently recognized it as that of Usher. In an instant afterward he rapped, with a gentle touch, at my door, and entered, bearing a lamp. His countenance was, as usual, cadaverously wan—but, moreover, there was a species of mad hilarity in his eyes—an evidently restrained hysteria in his whole demeanor. His air appalled me—but anything was preferable to the solitude which I had so long endured, and I even welcomed his presence as a relief.

"And you have not seen it?" he said abruptly, after having stared about him for some moments in silence—"you have not then seen it?—but, stay! you shall." Thus speaking, and having carefully shaded his lamp, he hurried to one of the casements, and threw it freely open to the storm.

The impetuous fury of the entering gust nearly lifted us from our feet. It was, indeed, a tempestuous yet sternly beautiful night, and one wildly singular in its terror and its beauty. A whirlwind had apparently collected its force in our vicinity; for there were frequent and violent alterations in the direction of the wind; and the exceeding density of the clouds (which hung so low as to press upon the turrets of the house) did not prevent our perceiving the lifelike velocity with which they flew careering from all points against each other, without passing away into the distance. I say that even their exceeding density did not prevent our perceiving this—yet we had no glimpse of the moon or stars, nor was there any flashing forth of the lightning. But the under surfaces of the huge masses of agitated vapor, as well as all terrestrial objects immediately around us, were glowing in the unnatural light of a faintly luminous and distinctly visible gaseous exhalation which hung about and enshrouded the mansion.

"You must not—you shall not behold this!" said I, shuddering,

---

26. incubus (iŋ′ kyə bəs) *n.* something nightmarishly burdensome.

to Usher, as I led him, with a gentle violence, from the window to a seat. "These appearances, which bewilder you, are merely electrical phenomena not uncommon—or it may be that they have their ghastly origin in the rank miasma[27] of the tarn. Let us close this casement:—the air is chilling and dangerous to your frame. Here is one of your favorite romances. I will read, and you shall listen:—and so we will pass away this terrible night together."

The antique volume which I had taken up was the *Mad Trist* of Sir Launcelot Canning;[28] but I had called it a favorite of Usher's more in sad jest than in earnest; for, in truth, there is little in its uncouth and unimaginative prolixity which could have had interest for the lofty and spiritual ideality of my friend. It was, however, the only book immediately at hand; and I indulged a vague hope that the excitement which now agitated the hypochondriac, might find relief (for the history of mental disorder is full of similar anomalies) even in the extremeness of the folly which I should read. Could I have judged, indeed, by the wild overstrained air of vivacity with which he hearkened, or apparently hearkened, to the words of the tale, I might well have congratulated myself upon the success of my design.

I had arrived at that well-known portion of the story where Ethelred, the hero of the Trist, having sought in vain for peaceable admission into the dwelling of the hermit, proceeds to make good an entrance by force. Here, it will be remembered, the words of the narrative run thus:

"And Ethelred, who was by nature of a doughty heart, and who was now mighty withal, on account of the powerfulness of the wine which he had drunken, waited no longer to hold parley with the hermit, who, in sooth, was of an obstinate and maliceful turn, but feeling the rain upon his shoulders, and fearing the rising of the tempest, uplifted his mace outright, and, with blows, made quickly room in the plankings of the door for his gauntleted hand; and now pulling therewith sturdily, he so cracked, and ripped, and tore all asunder, that the noise of the dry and hollow-sounding wood alarumed and reverberated throughout the forest."

At the termination of this sentence I started and, for a moment, paused; for it appeared to me (although I at once concluded that my excited fancy had deceived me)—it appeared to me that, from some very remote portion of the mansion, there came, indistinctly to my ears, which might have been, in its exact similarity of character, the echo (but a stifled and dull one certainly) of the very cracking and ripping sound which Sir Launcelot had so particularly described. It was, beyond doubt, the coincidence alone which had arrested my attention; for, amid the rattling of the sashes of the casements, and the ordinary commingled noises of the still increasing storm, the sound, itself, had nothing, surely, which should have interested or

"YOU MUST NOT—YOU SHALL NOT BEHOLD THIS!"

Comprehension
What odd or unnatural sight does the narrator see when the curtains are opened?

---

27. miasma (mī az′ mə) *n.* unwholesome atmosphere.
28. *Mad Trist* of Sir Launcelot Canning fictional book and author.

disturbed me. I continued the story:

"But the good champion Ethelred, now entering within the door, was sore enraged and amazed to perceive no signal of the maliceful hermit; but, in the stead thereof, a dragon of a scaly and prodigious demeanor, and of a fiery tongue, which sate in guard before a palace of gold, with a floor of silver; and upon the wall there hung a shield of shining brass with this legend enwritten—

Who entereth herein, a conqueror
hath bin;
Who slayeth the dragon, the shield
he shall win.

And Ethelred uplifted his mace, and struck upon the head of the dragon, which fell before him, and gave up his pasty breath, with a shriek so horrid and harsh, and withal so piercing, that Ethelred had fain to close his ears with his hands against the dreadful noise of it, the like whereof was never before heard."

Here again I paused abruptly, and now with a feeling of wild amazement—for there could be no doubt whatever that, in this instance, I did actually hear (although from what direction it proceeded I found it impossible to say) a low and apparently distant, but harsh, protracted, and most unusual screaming or grating sound—the exact counterpart of what my fancy had already conjured up for the dragon's unnatural shriek as described by the romancer.

Oppressed, as I certainly was, upon the extraordinary coincidence, by a thousand conflicting sensations, in which wonder and extreme terror were predominant, I still retained sufficient presence of mind to avoid exciting, by an observation, the sensitive nervousness of my companion. I was by no means certain that he had noticed the sounds in question; although, assuredly, a strange alteration had, during the last few minutes, taken place in his demeanor. From a position fronting my own, he had gradually brought round his chair; so as to sit with his face to the door of the chamber; and thus I could but partially perceive his features, although I saw that his lips trembled as if he were murmuring inaudibly. His head had dropped upon his breast—yet I knew that he was not asleep, from the wide and rigid opening of the eye as I caught a glance of it in profile. The motion of his body, too, was at variance with this idea—for he rocked from side to side with a gentle yet constant and uniform sway. Having rapidly taken notice of all this, I resumed the narrative of Sir Launcelot, which thus proceeded:

Breaking Down Long Sentences

Summarize the action of the paragraph-long sentence beginning "And now, the champion. . ."

"And now, the champion, having escaped from the terrible fury of the dragon, bethinking himself of the brazen shield, and of the breaking up of the enchantment which was upon it, removed the carcass from out of the way before him, and approached valorously over the silver pavement of the castle to where the shield was upon the wall; which in sooth tarried not for his full coming, but fell down at his feet upon the silver floor, with a mighty great and terrible ringing sound."

No sooner had these syllables passed my lips, than—as if a shield of brass had indeed, at the moment, fallen heavily upon a floor of silver—I became aware of a distinct, hollow, metallic, and clangorous, yet apparently muffled, reverberation. Completely unnerved, I leaped to my feet; but the measured rocking movement of Usher was undisturbed. I rushed to the chair in which he sat. His eyes were bent fixedly before him, and throughout his whole countenance there reigned a stony rigidity. But, as I placed my hand upon his shoulder, there came a strong shudder over his whole person; a sickly smile quivered about his lips; and I saw that he spoke in a low, hurried, and gibbering murmur, as if unconscious of my presence. Bending closely over him I at length drank in the hideous import of his words.

"Not hear it?—yes, I hear it, and have heard it. Long—long—long—many minutes, many hours, many days, have I heard it—yet I dared not—oh, pity me, miserable wretch that I am!—I *dared* not—I dared not speak! *We have put her living in the tomb!* Said I not that my senses were acute? I *now* tell you that I heard her first feeble movement in the hollow coffin. I heard them—many, many days ago—yet I dared not—*I dared not speak!* and now—tonight—Ethelred—ha! ha!—the breaking of the hermit's door, and the death cry of the dragon, and the clangor of the shield—say, rather, the rending of her coffin, and the grating of the iron hinges of her prison, and her struggles within the coppered archway of the vault! Oh! wither shall I fly? Will she not be here anon? Is she not hurrying to upbraid me for my haste? Have I not heard her footstep on the stair? Do I not distinguish that heavy and horrible beating of her heart? Madman!"—here he sprang furiously to his feet, and shrieked out his syllables, as if in the effort he were giving up his soul—*"Madman! I tell you that she now stands without the door!"*

As if in the superhuman energy of his utterance there had been found the potency of a spell, the huge antique panels to which the speaker pointed threw slowly back, upon the instant, their ponderous and ebony jaws. It was the work of the rushing gust—but then without those doors there *did* stand the lofty and enshrouded figure of the lady Madeline of Usher. There was blood upon her white robes, and the evidence of some bitter struggle upon every portion of her emaciated frame. For a moment she remained trembling and reeling to and fro upon the threshold—then, with a low moaning cry, fell heavily inward upon the person of her brother, and in her violent and now final death agonies, bore him to the floor a corpse, and a victim to the terrors he had anticipated.

From that chamber, and from that mansion, I fled aghast. The storm was still abroad in all its wrath as I found myself crossing the old causeway. Suddenly there shot along the path a wild light, and I turned to see whence a gleam so unusual could have issued; for the vast house and its shadows were alone behind me. The radiance

Gothic Literature and Single Effect

What effect does the description of Usher trembling and rocking help to create?

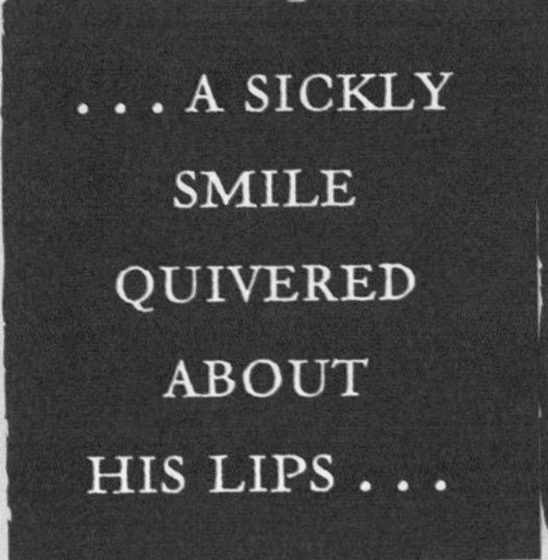
. . . A SICKLY
SMILE
QUIVERED
ABOUT
HIS LIPS . . .

Gothic Literature

Which aspects of Gothic literature are apparent in this description of Madeline Usher?

Comprehension

What unusual sounds does the narrator hear as he reads aloud?

was that of the full, setting, and bloodred moon, which now shone vividly through that once barely discernible fissure, of which I have before spoken as extending from the roof of the building, in a zigzag direction, to the base. While I gazed, this fissure rapidly widened—there came a fierce breath of the whirlwind—the entire orb of the satellite burst at once upon my sight—my brain reeled as I saw the mighty walls rushing asunder—there was a long tumultuous shouting sound like the voice of a thousand waters—and the deep and dank tarn at my feet closed sullenly and silently over the fragments of the *"House of Usher."*

Critical Reading

1. **Key Ideas and Details** **(a)** Why has the narrator gone to visit Usher? **(b) Assess:** Does the narrator succeed in his purpose? Explain.
2. **Key Ideas and Details** **(a) Interpret:** What beliefs about the "sentience" of matter does Usher express to the narrator? **(b) Analyze:** How are Usher's beliefs and fears borne out by the final events of the story?
3. **Craft and Structure** **(a) Analyze:** In the description of the exterior of the house, which words suggest the presence of decay in the structure itself? **(b) Connect:** In what ways does this description foreshadow, or hint at, the ending of the story?
4. **Craft and Structure** **(a) Interpret:** Which descriptive details of the interior of the house suggest that the narrator has entered a realm that is very different from the ordinary world? **(b) Infer:** Which details in Usher's appearance suggest that he has been cut off from the outside world for many years? **(c) Connect:** In what ways is the appearance of the interior of the house related to Usher's appearance and to the condition of his mind?
5. **Integration of Knowledge and Ideas** **(a) Analyze:** What is the significance of the detail that the narrator finds himself becoming affected by Usher's condition? **(b) Evaluate:** Do you think the narrator is a reliable witness of the events he describes? Explain your opinion.

Critical Commentary

On Writing "The Raven"

Edgar Allan Poe

Poe's most famous poem, "The Raven," was an instant popular and critical hit. Just as people today are interested in "behind-the-scenes" information about their favorite movies or songs, Poe's fans wanted to know how their favorite poem was written. Poe obliged with an essay explaining that he wrote "The Raven" with almost mathematical precision. First, Poe explains that he wanted to write a poem that was short enough to be read in one sitting, but long enough to have an impact:

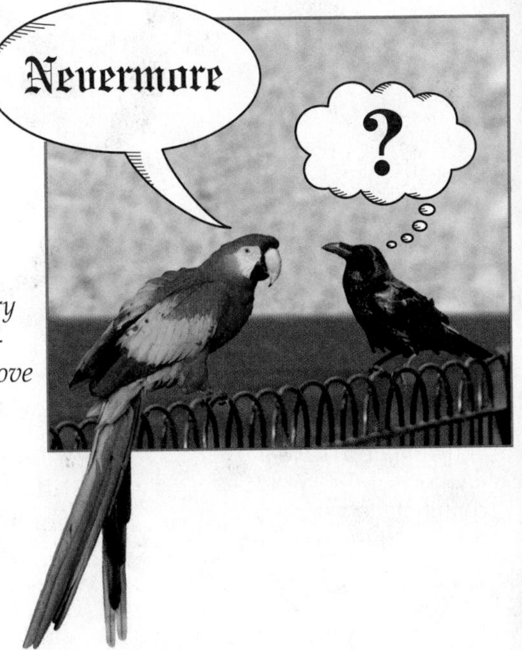

> *... there is a distinct limit, as regards length, to all works of literary art—the limit of a single sitting.... Holding in view these considerations, as well as that degree of excitement which I deemed not above the popular, while not below the critical, taste, I reached at once what I conceived the proper length for my intended poem—a length of about one hundred lines. It is, in fact, a hundred and eight.*

Poe goes on to tell how he chose both his subject matter and the mood of melancholy, or sadness, he wanted to convey:

> *Beauty of whatever kind, in its supreme development, invariably excites the sensitive soul to tears. Melancholy is thus the most legitimate of all the poetical tones.*

Poe then says that he wanted a **refrain,** or repeated set of phrases or lines, containing the *o* and *r* sounds, but he needed to find the right word:

> *... it became necessary to select a word embodying this sound, and at the same time in the fullest possible keeping with that melancholy which I had predetermined as the tone of the poem. In such a search it would have been absolutely impossible to overlook the word "Nevermore." In fact, it was the very first which presented itself.*

Now Poe had a problem: what kind of creature would speak the refrain?

> *Here, then, immediately arose the idea of a non-reasoning creature capable of speech; and, very naturally, a parrot, in the first instance, suggested itself, but was superseded forthwith by a Raven, as equally capable of speech, and infinitely more in keeping with the intended tone.*

Key Ideas and Details

- What tone did Poe want to achieve in "The Raven"?
- What subject did Poe believe is the most suitable for poetry?
- Why did Poe choose a Raven and not a parrot to deliver the refrain "Nevermore"?

The Raven

Edgar Allan Poe

Gothic Literature

In the very first line of the poem, which words contribute to a dark, mysterious Gothic mood?

Once upon a midnight dreary, while I pondered, weak and weary,
Over many a quaint and curious volume of forgotten lore—
While I nodded, nearly napping, suddenly there came a tapping,
As of some one gently rapping, rapping at my chamber door.
"'Tis some visitor," I muttered, "tapping at my chamber door—
Only this, and nothing more."

Ah, distinctly I remember it was in the bleak December;
And each separate dying ember wrought its ghost upon the floor.
Eagerly I wished the morrow;—vainly I had sought to borrow
From my books surcease[1] of sorrow—sorrow for the lost Lenore—
For the rare and radiant maiden whom the angels name Lenore—
Nameless *here* for evermore.

And the silken, sad, uncertain rustling of each purple curtain
Thrilled me—filled me with fantastic terrors never felt before;
So that now, to still the beating of my heart, I stood repeating
"'Tis some visitor entreating entrance at my chamber door—
Some late visitor entreating entrance at my chamber door;—
This it is and nothing more."

Presently my soul grew stronger; hesitating then no longer,
"Sir," said I, "or Madam, truly your forgiveness I implore;
But the fact is I was napping, and so gently you came rapping,
And so faintly you came tapping, tapping at my chamber door,
That I scarce was sure I heard you"—here I opened wide the door;—
Darkness there and nothing more.

Breaking Down Long Sentences
Summarize the action of the stanza-long sentence beginning "Presently my soul grew stronger. . ."

Comprehension
For whom is the speaker grieving?

1. **surcease** (sur sēs′) end.

Deep into that darkness peering, long I stood there wondering, fearing,
Doubting, dreaming dreams no mortal ever dared to dream before;
But the silence was unbroken, and the stillness gave no token,
And the only word there spoken was the whispered word, "Lenore?"
This I whispered, and an echo murmured back the word, "Lenore!"
Merely this and nothing more.

Back then into the chamber turning, all my soul within me burning,
Soon again I heard a tapping somewhat louder than before.
"Surely," said I, "surely that is something at my window lattice;
Let me see, then, what thereat is, and this mystery explore—
Let my heart be still a moment and this mystery explore;—
'Tis the wind and nothing more!"

Open here I flung the shutter, when, with many a flirt and flutter,
In there stepped a stately Raven of the saintly days of yore;
Not the least obeisance made he; not a minute stopped or stayed he;
But, with mien of lord or lady, perched above my chamber door—
Perched upon a bust of Pallas[2] just above my chamber door—
Perched, and sat, and nothing more.

Gothic Literature
What element of Gothic literature does the Raven's speaking introduce into the poem? Explain.

Then this ebony bird beguiling[3] my sad fancy into smiling,
By the grave and stern decorum of the countenance[4] it wore,
"Though thy crest be shorn and shaven, thou," I said, "art sure no craven,
Ghastly grim and ancient Raven wandering from the Nightly shore—
Tell me what thy lordly name is on the Night's Plutonian[5] shore!"
Quoth the Raven, "Nevermore."

Much I marveled this ungainly fowl to hear discourse so plainly,
Though its answer little meaning—little relevancy bore;
For we cannot help agreeing that no living human being
Ever yet was blessed with seeing bird above his chamber door—
Bird or beast upon the sculptured bust above his chamber door,
With such name as "Nevermore."

But the Raven, sitting lonely on the placid bust, spoke only
That one word, as if his soul in that one word he did outpour.
Nothing farther than he uttered—not a feather then he fluttered—

---

2. **Pallas** (pal´ əs) Pallas Athena, the ancient Greek goddess of wisdom.
3. **beguiling** (bi gīl´ iŋ) *part.* charming.
4. **countenance** (koun´ tə nəns) *n.* facial expression.
5. **Plutonian** (plo͞o tō´ nē ən) *adj.* like the underworld or infernal regions; refers to Pluto, Greek and Roman god of the underworld.

Till I scarcely more than muttered, "Other friends have flown before—
On the morrow *he* will leave me, as my Hopes have flown before."
Then the bird said, "Nevermore."

Startled at the stillness broken by reply so aptly spoken,
"Doubtless," said I, "what it utters is its only stock and store
Caught from some unhappy master whom unmerciful Disaster
Followed fast and followed faster till his songs one burden bore—
Till the dirges of his Hope that melancholy burden bore
Of 'Never—nevermore.'"

But the Raven still beguiling my sad fancy into smiling,
Straight I wheeled a cushioned seat in front of bird, and bust and door;
Then, upon the velvet sinking, I betook myself to linking
Fancy unto fancy, thinking what this ominous[6] bird of yore—
What this grim, ungainly, ghastly, gaunt, and ominous bird of yore
Meant in croaking "Nevermore."

This I sat engaged in guessing, but no syllable expressing
To the fowl whose fiery eyes now burned into my bosom's core;
This and more I sat divining, with my head at ease reclining
On the cushion's velvet lining that the lamp-light gloated o'er,
But whose velvet-violet lining with the lamp-light gloating o'er,
She shall press, ah, nevermore!

Then, methought, the air grew denser, perfumed from an unseen censer
Swung by seraphim whose foot-falls tinkled on the tufted floor.
"Wretch," I cried, "thy God hath lent thee—by these angels he hath sent thee
Respite—respite and nepenthe[7] from thy memories of Lenore;
Quaff, oh quaff this kind nepenthe and forget this lost Lenore!"
Quoth the Raven, "Nevermore."

"Prophet!" said I, "thing of evil!—prophet still, if bird or devil!—
Whether Tempter sent, or whether tempest tossed thee here ashore,
Desolate yet all undaunted, on this desert land enchanted—
On this home by Horror haunted—tell me truly, I implore—
Is there—*is* there balm in Gilead?[8]—tell me—tell me, I implore!"

Gothic Literature
How is the speaker's psychological distress increasing?

Comprehension
What does the speaker want from the Raven?

---

6. **ominous** (äm′ ə nəs) *adj.* threatening; sinister.
7. **nepenthe** (ni pen′ thē) *n.* drug that the ancient Greeks believed could relieve sorrow.
8. **balm in Gilead** (gil′ ē əd) in the Bible, a healing ointment made in Gilead, a region of ancient Palestine.

Quoth the Raven, "Nevermore."

"Prophet!" said I, "thing of evil!—prophet still, if bird or devil!
By that Heaven that bends above us—by that God we both adore—
Tell this soul with sorrow laden if, within the distant Aidenn,[9]
It shall clasp a sainted maiden whom the angels name Lenore—
Clasp a rare and radiant maiden whom the angels name Lenore."
Quoth the Raven, "Nevermore."

"Be that word our sign of parting, bird or fiend!" I shrieked, upstarting—
"Get thee back into the tempest and the Night's Plutonian shore!
Leave no black plume as a token of that lie thy soul hath spoken!
Leave my loneliness unbroken!—quit the bust above my door!
Take thy beak from out my heart, and take thy form from off my door!"
Quoth the Raven, "Nevermore."

And the Raven, never flitting, still is sitting, *still* is sitting
On the pallid bust of Pallas just above my chamber door;
And his eyes have all the seeming of a demon's that is dreaming;
And the lamp-light o'er him streaming throws his shadow on the floor;
And my soul from out that shadow that lies floating on the floor
Shall be lifted—nevermore!

◀ Critical Viewing

In this illustration of the poem's opening scene, how do the details in the setting and the angle of the image itself add to a sense of the speaker's fear and distress? **ANALYZE**

9. **Aidenn** (ā′ den) Arabic for *Eden* or *heaven*.

Critical Reading

Cite textual evidence to support your responses.

1. **Key Ideas and Details (a)** With what emotion does the speaker first greet the Raven? **(b) Interpret:** As the poem progresses, how does the speaker's attitude toward the Raven change? **(c) Analyze Cause and Effect:** In what way is the word *nevermore* related to the emotional changes?
2. **Key Ideas and Details (a)** What does the speaker eventually order the Raven to do? **(b) Analyze:** At the end of the poem, what does the speaker mean when he says the Raven "still is sitting" above the door?
3. **Craft and Structure (a) Interpret:** What is the relationship between the Raven's shadow and the speaker's soul at the end of the poem? **(b) Analyze:** In your opinion, what does the Raven finally come to represent?
4. **Craft and Structure** Review your list of details that make Poe's settings seem dreamlike. Then, write a paragraph describing the power of Poe's landscapes. In your response, use at least two of these Essential Question words: *fantastic, personal, terrors, realistic. **[Connecting to the Essential Question: What is the relationship between literature and place?]***

Close Reading Activities

The Fall of the House of Usher • The Raven

Literary Analysis

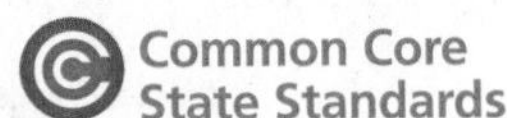

Common Core State Standards

Language

4.c. Consult general and specialized reference materials, both print and digital, to find the pronunciation of a word or determine or clarify its precise meaning or its standard usage. *(p. 319)*

1. **Key Ideas and Details Break down this long sentence** from the story and restate it in your own words:

   At times, again, I was obliged to resolve all into the mere inexplicable vagaries of madness, for I beheld him gazing upon vacancy for long hours, in an attitude of the profoundest attention, as if listening to some imaginary sound.

2. **Key Ideas and Details** Choose another long sentence from the story or poem. Break the sentence down and restate it in your own words.
3. **Craft and Structure** Use a chart like the one shown to identify the **Gothic** elements in "The Fall of the House of Usher" and "The Raven."

Gothic Element	House of Usher	Raven
Setting		
Violence		
Characterization		
The Supernatural		

4. **Craft and Structure** Describe the ways in which the following elements contribute to the **single effect** of a sense of terror in "The Fall of the House of Usher": **(a)** description of the house, **(b)** Madeline's entombment, **(c)** the storm.
5. **Integration of Knowledge and Ideas (a)** In what ways is the ending of the story intentionally *ambiguous*? What does Poe leave uncertain? **(b)** What are some possible interpretations of the ending? **(c)** Which do you support, and why?
6. **Integration of Knowledge and Ideas** In "The Raven," how do both the sound of tapping and the Raven's fiery eyes contribute to the speaker's deteriorating emotional state?
7. **Integration of Knowledge and Ideas (a)** When Madeline appears at the end of the story, is she actually there, or is she a hallucination? Explain. **(b)** At the end of "The Raven," do you think the bird is actually in the room? Why or why not?
8. **Analyzing Visual Text** Explain the humor in the cartoon.

Vocabulary Acquisition and Use

Word Analysis: Latin Root *-voc-*

The word *equivocal* contains the Latin root *-voc-*, which derives from the Latin word *vox*, meaning "voice." Combined with the Latin prefix *equi-*, meaning "equal," *equivocal* can be defined as "having two equal voices" or "having more than one possible interpretation." Consider the meaning of these words containing *-voc-*. Then, answer the questions.

advocate *v.* speak or argue in favor of

equivocate *v.* avoid making a clear statement

vociferous *adj.* noisy or aggressive in making one's feelings known

1. The council *advocates* banning parking near the bridge. Is the council for or against it? Explain.
2. When the reporter asked the mayor about the new law, the mayor *equivocated.* Did the reporter like the mayor's answer? Explain.
3. Several citizens were *vociferous* in their response to the law. Do you think the mayor heard them? Why or why not?

Vocabulary: True or False?

Indicate which of the statements below are true and which are false. Explain your answers.

1. If historians decide that a document is *specious*, they will probably write a paper about its importance.
2. The quality of *sentience* is evident in rocks and other inanimate matter.
3. If a senator's position in a debate is *equivocal*, he probably believes strongly in his argument.
4. Misers are *munificent* and often give to the needy.
5. Someone who is in desperate need might be *importunate* about a request.
6. A professional's *anomalous* behavior will make others feel confident about using his or her services.

Using Resources to Build Vocabulary

Gothic Style: Words For a Character in Torment

In drawing a picture of his tormented friend, the narrator of "The Fall of the House of Usher" uses the following words:

agitation	leaden
feeble	tremulous
futile	trepidancy

Reread the last paragraph on page 298 to see these words in context. Then, *use a dictionary and a print or electronic thesaurus* to find synonyms for each word. On your own paper, rewrite the paragraph by replacing each of the words shown above with a duller, more ordinary word. Now, compare the original paragraph with your version. Write several sentences in which you describe the differences between the two versions.

Close Reading Activities Continued

Writing to Sources

Explanatory Text Since its original publication in 1839, "The Fall of the House of Usher" has prompted varied critical opinions. Some see the story as entirely symbolic, while others take it at face value as a tale of sheer horror. These passages represent two differing critical views:

Edward H. Davidson: The three characters are unique people with distinct characters, but they are tied together by the same type of "mental disorder." All of them suffer from insanity....

H. P. Lovecraft: "The Fall of the House of Usher"... displays an abnormally linked trinity of entities at the end of a long and isolated family history—a brother, his twin sister, and their incredibly ancient house all sharing a single soul ...

While both critics note strong connections among the characters, they see different meanings in these connections. Do you agree with Davidson that all the characters are separate, insane personalities, or do you prefer Lovecraft's analysis, that the brother, sister, and house represent different aspects of a single personality? Write an **essay** in which you evaluate these views and state your own judgment about Poe's story.

Common Core State Standards

Writing

2.c. Use appropriate and varied transitions and syntax to link the major sections of the text, create cohesion, and clarify the relationships among complex ideas and concepts.

9.a. Apply *grades 11-12 Reading standards* to literature.

Language

1. Demonstrate command of the conventions of standard English grammar and usage when writing or speaking. *(p. 321)*

Prewriting Review the story to develop your perspective. As you read, gather details that relate to the two critical views. Jot down details, looking for patterns among them. Then, determine which viewpoint—Davidson's or Lovecraft's—is more persuasive. Remember that *ambiguities, nuances, and complexities* are an integral part of Poe's writing. While you may not be able to fully explain them, assess the effect they have on the story's meaning.

Model: Using Transitions to Clarify Meaning

The idea that all the characters in the story are insane is intriguing. It would explain the story's strangeness. **After all,** if the narrator is mad, he would not be able to relate events clearly.

This idea is intriguing. **; however,** ~~It~~ it is not convincing.

Use transitional words and phrases to make the flow of your ideas clear.

Punctuation Tip: The word "however" joins two complete sentences. When you combine sentences with a transitional word or phrase, use a semicolon.

Drafting Establish a logical organizational pattern for your essay. In your introduction, summarize the two critical viewpoints and state which one you support. Elaborate upon your reasoning in each body paragraph, citing details that are substantial, specific, and relevant to your position.

Revising Reread your essay, making sure you have established a logical flow of ideas. Improve the logic by adding transitional words and phrases at points where relationships among ideas are not perfectly clear.

Conventions and Style: Comparative and Superlative Adjectives and Adverbs

In academic writing, you will often be asked to explain how things are similar and different. To do so, use modifiers showing comparison and contrast correctly. Adjectives and adverbs can take three forms: **positive, comparative,** and **superlative.**

Positive	Comparative	Superlative
dark	darker	darkest
weary	wearier	weariest
nervous	more nervous	most nervous
painfully	more painfully	most painfully
bad	worse	worst
good	better	best

Using Comparative and Superlative Forms

Use the comparative degree to compare *two* persons, places, or things.

Comparative Adjective: Madeline is even *spookier* than her brother.
Comparative Adverb: The narrator describes Roderick *more fully* than he does Madeline.

Use the superlative degree to compare *three or more* persons, places, or things.

Superlative Adjective: The underground chamber is the *worst* place in the house.
Superlative Adverb: Usher's home is the *most elaborately* described mansion in all of literature.

Practice Complete each sentence below by supplying the correct form of the adjective or adverb shown in parentheses.

1. In your opinion, who is the ______ writer, Edgar Allan Poe or Stephen King? (*good*)
2. He got into trouble ______ than his friend did. (*frequently*)
3. Some scholars have criticized Poe's work ______ than others have. (*harshly*)
4. Of all the writers we have studied so far, I think Edgar Allan Poe had the ______ life. (*sad*)
5. Which deteriorated ______, the house or Usher's mental state? (*quick*)
6. He considers the narrator his ______ friend in the world. (*close*)
7. His last night at the mansion was by far the ______ one. (*bad*)
8. The second time he heard the tapping, it was ______ than before. (*loud*)
9. "The Raven" may be the ______ of Poe's poems. (*popular*)
10. Both selections are scary, but I think the poem is the ______ of the two. (*terrifying*)

Writing and Speaking Conventions

A. Writing For each item listed, write two sentences. In one, use the comparative form, and in the other, use the superlative form.

1. damp **2.** desperately **3.** sick **4.** gloomy **5.** hesitantly

Example: cold
Comparative: The bedroom is colder than the kitchen.
Superlative: The attic is the coldest place in the house.

B. Speaking Write and recite an alternate ending to the story in which you use at least one comparative form and one superlative form.

The Gothic Family Tree

British Author
Horace Walpole
(1717–1797)
The Castle of Otranto (1764)

BRITISH

Ann Radcliffe
(1764–1823)
Mysteries of Udolpho (1794)

Mary Shelley
(1797–1851)
Frankenstein, or the Modern Prometheus (1818)

Bram Stoker
(1847–1912)
Dracula (1897)

Daphne du Maurier
(1907–1989)
Rebecca (1938)

AMERICAN

Charles Brockden Brown
(1771–1810)
Wieland, or The Transformation (1798)

Edgar Allan Poe
(1809–1849)
Tales of the Grotesque and Arabesque (1839)

Detective/ mystery stories

H. P. Lovecraft
(1890–1937)
The Colour Out of Space (1927)

MODERN GOTHIC

Joyce Carol Oates
(b. 1938)
Bellefleur (1980)

Anne Rice
(b. 1941)
Interview with the Vampire (1976)

Peter Straub
(b. 1943)
Ghost Story (1979)

Stephen King
(b. 1947)
The Dark Tower
(series: 1982–2004)

Comparing Literary Works

"The Fall of the House of Usher" by Edgar Allan Poe • "Where Is Here?" by Joyce Carol Oates

Comparing Gothic Literature Past and Present

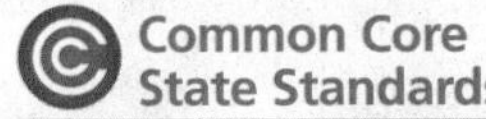

Common Core State Standards

Reading Literature
3. Analyze the impact of the author's choices regarding how to develop and relate elements of a story.

Language
4.c. Consult general and specialized reference materials, both print and digital, to find the precise meaning of a word and its etymology.

Gothic Literature Edgar Allan Poe's work has roots deep in European Gothic literature. Horace Walpole's *The Castle of Otranto: A Gothic Tale* (1764) and Ann Radcliffe's *Mysteries of Udolpho* (1794) are just two of the books that probably influenced Poe (see the Gothic Family Tree on page 322). In a similar way, modern writers such as Joyce Carol Oates, author of "Where Is Here?," look back to Poe as the founding voice of an American Gothic tradition. The legacy of traditional Gothic literature cuts across genre classifications, and its elements can be found in poetry, drama, novels, and short stories. Regardless of the genre, traditional Gothic writing such as Poe's has these elements:

- A bleak or remote setting; often grand, such as a castle or mansion
- A gloomy atmosphere; a sense of impending doom
- Characters in physical or psychological torment
- Horrific or violent incidents
- Supernatural elements

Modern Gothic literature uses the same elements but does so with more subtlety or with details that reflect modern life. As you read "Where Is Here?," use a chart like the one shown to examine how Oates puts a new spin on traditional Gothic features.

	Traditional: Poe	Modern: Oates
Setting	a crumbling mansion	
Characters	Roderick Usher, who is ghostly and tormented	
Violence	Burying sister in vault	
The Supernatural	Link between house and Usher	

Gather Vocabulary Knowledge

Joyce Carol Oates uses related forms of the words *perplex*, *disturb*, and *resent*. Use a **dictionary** to define each word. Then, employ other references to further explore these words:

- **History of Language:** Use a book on the history of English to research each word's origins. Write a paragraph about the word's emergence in English.
- **Glossary of Affixes:** Consult a print or online list of affixes. For each word, explain how the addition of a specific affix modifies its meaning.

Comparing References Compare and contrast what you learn about the words from each reference.

Joyce Carol Oates

(b. 1938)

Author of "**Where Is Here?**"

Joyce Carol Oates was born in 1938 in Lockport, New York, a small, rural town. Though she grew up without many books, she always had a strong attraction to storytelling and began drawing picture stories even before she knew how to write.

Oates's elementary school years were spent in a one-room schoolhouse. At age 14, she received a typewriter as a gift and began writing in earnest. She was soon producing one book after another. In her college days, she would write one novel using one side of the paper, then write another novel on the reverse side. Then, she would throw the papers away.

Early Success Oates won the *Mademoiselle* short story contest, an important national fiction prize, while still in college, and published her first book at the age of twenty-five. Today, she is renowned not just for the quality of her work, but for her immense literary output. She has averaged two books a year during the course of her career. Her many honors include the National Book Award and three separate nominations for the Pulitzer Prize.

A Taste for the Gothic Oates's discovery of the Gothic novels of Ann Radcliff, an English writer, and of Edgar Allan Poe's remarkable short stories sparked her interest in Gothic fiction. Though she has written fiction and nonfiction in a wide variety of styles, she always returns to the Gothic. "Horror," she says, "Is a fact of life. As a writer I'm fascinated by all facets of life." Over her desk she keeps a quote from Henry James, another American master, which reads: "We work in the dark—we do what we can—we give what we have. Our doubt is our passion, and our passion is our task. The rest is the madness of art."

"Horror is a fact of life."

Where Is Here?

Joyce Carol Oates

For years they had lived without incident in their house in a quiet residential neighborhood when, one November evening at dusk, the doorbell rang, and the father went to answer it, and there on his doorstep stood a man he had never seen before. The stranger apologized for disturbing him at what was probably the dinner hour and explained that he'd once lived in the house— "I mean, I was a child in this house"—and since he was in the city on business he thought he would drop by. He had not seen the house since January 1949 when he'd been eleven years old and his widowed mother had sold it and moved away but, he said, he thought of it often, dreamt of it often, and never more powerfully than in recent months. The father said, "Would you like to come inside for a few minutes and look around?" The stranger hesitated, then said firmly, "I think I'll just poke around outside for a while, if you don't mind. That might be sufficient." He was in his late forties, the father's approximate age. He wore a dark suit, conservatively cut; he was hatless, with thin silver-tipped neatly combed hair; a plain, sober, intelligent face and frowning eyes. The father, reserved by nature, but genial and even *gregarious* when taken unaware, said amiably, "Of course we don't mind. But I'm afraid many things have changed since 1949."

So, in the chill, damp, deepening dusk, the stranger wandered around the property while the mother set the dining room table and the father peered covertly out the window. The children were upstairs in their rooms. "Where is he now?" the mother asked. "He just went into the garage," the father said. "The garage! What does he want in there!" the mother said uneasily. "Maybe you'd better go out there with him." "He wouldn't want anyone with him," the father said. He moved **stealthily** to another window, peering through the curtains. A moment passed in silence. The mother, paused in the act of setting down plates, neatly folded paper napkins, and stainless-steel cutlery, said impatiently, "And where is he now? I don't like this." The father said, "Now he's coming out of the garage," and stepped back hastily from the window. "Is he going now?" the mother asked. "I wish I'd answered the door." The father watched for a moment in silence then said, "He's headed into the backyard." "Doing what?" the mother asked. "Not doing anything, just walking," the father said. "He seems

Vocabulary

stealthily (stel′ thə lē) *adv.* slowly so as to avoid notice

Comprehension

Who invites the stranger in to the house?

to have a slight limp." "Is he an older man?" the mother asked. "I didn't notice," the father confessed. "Isn't that just like you!" the mother said.

She went on worriedly, "He could be anyone, after all. Any kind of thief, or mentally disturbed person, or even a murderer. Ringing our doorbell like that with no warning and you don't even know what he looks like!"

The father had moved to another window and stood quietly watching, his cheek pressed against the glass. "He's gone down to the old swings. I hope he won't sit in one of them, for memory's sake, and try to swing—the posts are rotted almost through." The mother drew breath to speak but sighed instead, as if a powerful current of feeling had surged through her. The father was saying, "Is it possible he remembers those swings from his childhood? I can't believe they're actually that old." The mother said vaguely, "They were old when we bought the house." The father said, "But we're talking about forty years or more, and that's a long time." The mother sighed again, involuntarily. "Poor man!" she murmured. She was standing before her table but no longer seeing it. In her hand were objects—forks, knives, spoons—she could not have named. She said, "We can't bar the door against him. That would be cruel." The father said, "What? No one has barred any door against anyone." "Put yourself in his place," the mother said. "He told me he didn't *want* to come inside," the father said. "Oh—isn't that just like you!" the mother said in **exasperation**.

Vocabulary
exasperation (eks äs pə rā′ shun) *n.* annoyance; frustration

Without a further word she went to the back door and called out for the stranger to come inside, if he wanted, when he had finished looking around outside.

They introduced themselves rather shyly, giving names, and forgetting names, in the confusion of the moment. The stranger's handshake was cool and damp and tentative. He was smiling hard, blinking moisture from his eyes; it was clear that entering his childhood home was enormously exciting yet intimidating to him. Repeatedly he said, "It's so nice of you to invite me in—I truly hate to disturb you—I'm really so grateful, and so—" But the perfect word eluded him. As he spoke his eyes darted about the kitchen almost like eyes out of control. He stood in an odd stiff posture, hands gripping the lapels of his suit as if he meant to crush them. The mother, meaning to break the awkward silence, spoke warmly of their satisfaction with the house and with the neighborhood, and the father concurred, but the stranger listened only politely, and continued to stare, and stare hard. Finally he said that the kitchen had been so changed—"so modernized"—he almost didn't recognize it. The floor tile, the size of the windows, something about the position of the cupboards—all

Comparing Gothic Literature
Which details in the description of the stranger create a sense of his agitation or distress?

were different. But the sink was in the same place, of course; and the refrigerator and stove; and the door leading down to the basement— "That is the door leading down to the basement, isn't it?" He spoke strangely, staring at the door. For a moment it appeared he might ask to be shown the basement but the moment passed, fortunately—this was not a part of their house the father and mother would have been comfortable showing to a stranger.

Finally, making an effort to smile, the stranger said, "Your kitchen is so—pleasant." He paused. For a moment it seemed he had nothing further to say. Then, "A—controlled sort of place. My mother— When we lived here—" His words trailed off into a dreamy silence and the mother and father glanced at each other with carefully neutral expressions.

On the windowsill above the sink were several lushly blooming African violet plants in ceramic pots and these the stranger made a show of admiring. Impulsively he leaned over to sniff the flowers— "Lovely!"—though African violets have no smell. As if embarrassed he said, "Mother too had plants on this windowsill but I don't recall them ever blooming."

The mother said tactfully, "Oh they were probably the kind that don't bloom—like ivy."

In the next room, the dining room, the stranger appeared to be even more deeply moved. For some time he stood staring, wordless. With fastidious slowness he turned on his heel, blinking, and frowning, and tugging at his lower lip in a rough gesture that must have hurt. Finally, as if remembering the presence of his hosts, and the necessity for some display of civility, the stranger expressed his admiration for the attractiveness of the room, and its coziness. He'd remembered it as cavernous, with a ceiling twice as high. "And dark most of the time," he said wonderingly. "Dark by day, dark by night." The mother turned the lights of the little brass chandelier to their fullest: shadows were dispersed like ragged ghosts and the cut-glass fruit bowl at the center of the table glowed like an exquisite multifaceted jewel. The stranger exclaimed in surprise. He'd extracted a handkerchief from his pocket and was dabbing carefully at his face, where beads of perspiration shone. He said, as if thinking aloud, still wonderingly, "My father was a unique man. Everyone who knew him admired him. He sat *here*," he said, gingerly touching the chair that was in fact the father's chair, at one end of the table. "And Mother sat *there*," he said, merely pointing. "I don't recall my own place or my sister's but I suppose it doesn't matter. . . . I see you have four place settings, Mrs. . . .? Two children, I suppose?" "A boy eleven, and a girl thirteen," the mother said. The stranger stared not at her but at the table, smiling. "And so too we were—I mean, there were two of us: my sister and me."

Comparing Gothic Literature

How do the stranger's halted, or unfinished, statements affect your reading of his character?

Vocabulary

impulsively (im puhl′ siv lē) *adv.* spontaneously

fastidious (fa stid′ ē əs) *adj.* careful; meticulous

cavernous (cav′ ərn nəs) *adj.* cavelike; vast

Comprehension

What similarity does the stranger notice between his own family and that of the house's current occupants?

The mother said, as if not knowing what else to say, "Are you—close?"

The stranger shrugged, distractedly rather than rudely, and moved on to the living room.

This room, cozily lit as well, was the most carefully furnished room in the house. Deep-piled wall-to-wall carpeting in hunter green, cheerful chintz drapes, a sofa and matching chairs in nubby heather green, framed reproductions of classic works of art, a gleaming gilt-framed mirror over the fireplace: wasn't the living room impressive as a display in a furniture store? But the stranger said nothing at first. Indeed, his eyes narrowed sharply as if he were confronted with a disagreeable spectacle. He whispered, "Here too! Here too!"

. . . Who was this man, and how could they tactfully get rid of him?

He went to the fireplace, walking, now, with a decided limp; he drew his fingers with excruciating slowness along the mantel as if testing its materiality. For some time he merely stood, and stared, and listened. He tapped a section of wall with his knuckles—"There used to be a large water stain here, like a shadow.

"Was there!" murmured the father out of politeness, and "Was there!" murmured the mother. Of course, neither had ever seen a water stain there.

Then, noticing the window seat, the stranger uttered a soft surprised cry, and went to sit in it. He appeared delighted: hugging his knees like a child trying to make himself smaller. "This was one of my happy places! At least when Father wasn't home. I'd hide away here for hours, reading, daydreaming, staring out the window! Sometimes Mother would join me, if she was in the mood, and we'd plot together—oh, all sorts of fantastical things!" The stranger remained sitting in the window seat for so long, tears shining in his eyes, that the father and mother almost feared he'd forgotten them. He was stroking the velvet fabric of the cushioned seat, gropingly touching the leaded windowpanes. Wordlessly, the father and mother exchanged a glance: who was this man, and how could they tactfully get rid of him? The father made a face signaling impatience and the mother shook her head without seeming to move it. For they couldn't be rude to a guest in their house.

Comparing Gothic Literature
In this and the next two paragraphs, what is odd or unsettling in the stranger's responses? Explain.

The stranger was saying in a slow, dazed voice, "It all comes back to me now. How could I have forgotten! Mother used to read to me, and tell me stories, and ask me riddles I couldn't answer. 'What creature walks on four legs in the morning, two legs at midday, three legs in the evening?' 'What is round, and flat, measuring mere inches in one direction, and infinity in the other?' 'Out of what does our life arise? Out of what does our consciousness arise? Why are we here? Where *is* here?' "

The father and mother were perplexed by these strange words and hardly knew how to respond. The mother said uncertainly, "Our daughter used to like to sit here too, when she was younger. It *is* a lovely place." The father said with surprising passion, "I hate riddles—they're moronic some of the time and obscure the rest of the time." He spoke with such uncharacteristic rudeness, the mother looked at him in surprise.

Hurriedly she said, "Is your mother still living, Mr. . . .?" "Oh no. Not at all," the stranger said, rising abruptly from the window seat, and looking at the mother as if she had said something mildly preposterous. "I'm sorry," the mother said. "Please don't be," the stranger said. "We've all been dead—*they've* all been dead—a long time."

The stranger's cheeks were deeply flushed as if with anger and his breath was quickened and audible.

The visit might have ended at this point but so clearly did the stranger expect to continue on upstairs, so purposefully, indeed almost defiantly, did he limp his way to the stairs, neither the father nor the mother knew how to dissuade him. It was as if a force of nature, benign at the outset, now uncontrollable, had swept its way into their house! The mother followed after him saying nervously, "I'm not sure what condition the rooms are in, upstairs. The children's rooms especially—" The stranger muttered that he did not care in the slightest about the condition of the household and continued on up without a backward glance.

The father, his face burning with resentment and his heart accelerating as if in preparation for combat, had no choice but to follow the stranger and the mother up the stairs. He was flexing and unflexing his fingers as if to rid them of stiffness.

On the landing, the stranger halted abruptly to examine a stained-glass fanlight—"My God, I haven't thought of this in years!" He spoke excitedly of how, on tiptoe, he used to stand and peek out through the diamonds of colored glass, red, blue, green, golden yellow: seeing with amazement the world outside so *altered*. "After such a lesson it's hard to take the world on its own terms, isn't it?" he asked. The father asked, annoyed, "On what terms should it be taken, then?" The stranger replied, regarding him levelly, with a just perceptible degree of disdain, "Why, none at all."

It was the son's room—by coincidence, the stranger's old room—the stranger most wanted to see. Other rooms on the second floor, the "master" bedroom in particular, he decidedly did not want to see. As he spoke of it, his mouth twisted as if he had been offered something repulsive to eat.

Comprehension

Which room on the second floor does the stranger want to see and which does he "decidedly" not wish to see?

The mother hurried on ahead to warn the boy and to straighten up his room a bit. No one had expected a visitor this evening! "So you have two children," the stranger murmured, looking at the father with a small quizzical smile. "Why?" The father stared at him as if he hadn't heard correctly. "'Why'?" he asked. "Yes. *Why?*" the stranger repeated. They looked at each other for a long strained moment, then the stranger said quickly, "But you love them—of course." The father controlled his temper and said, biting off his words, "Of course."

No one had expected a visitor this evening!

"Of course, of course," the stranger murmured, tugging at his necktie and loosening his collar, "otherwise it would all come to an end." The two men were of approximately the same height but the father was heavier in the shoulders and torso; his hair had thinned more severely so that the scalp of the crown was exposed, flushed, damp with perspiration, sullenly alight.

With a stiff avuncular formality the stranger shook the son's hand. "So this is your room, now! So you live here, now!" he murmured, as if the fact were an astonishment. Not used to shaking hands, the boy was stricken with shyness and cast his eyes down. The stranger limped past him, staring. "The same!—the same!—walls, ceiling, floor—window—" He drew his fingers slowly along the windowsill; around the frame; rapped the glass, as if, again, testing materiality; stooped to look outside—but it was night, and nothing but his reflection bobbed in the glass, ghostly and insubstantial. He groped against the walls, he opened the closet door before the mother could protest, he sat heavily on the boy's bed, the springs creaking beneath him. He was panting, red-faced, dazed. "And the ceiling overhead," he whispered. He nodded slowly and repeatedly, smiling. "And the floor beneath. That is what *is*."

He took out his handkerchief again and fastidiously wiped his face. He made a visible effort to compose himself.

The father, in the doorway, cleared his throat and said, "I'm afraid it's getting late—it's almost six."

The mother said, "Oh yes I'm afraid— I'm afraid it *is* getting late. There's dinner, and the children have their homework—"

Comparing Gothic Literature
Which details suggest that the stranger's psychological torment has continued to intensify?

The stranger got to his feet. At his full height he stood for a precarious moment swaying, as if the blood had drained from his head and he was in danger of fainting. But he steadied himself with a hand against the slanted dormer ceiling. He said, "Oh yes!—I know!—I've disturbed you terribly! —you've been so kind." It seemed, surely, as if the stranger *must* leave now, but, as chance had it, he happened to spy, on the boy's desk, an opened mathematics textbook and several smudged sheets of paper, and impulsively offered to show the boy a mathematical riddle—"You can take it to school tomorrow and surprise your teacher!"

So, out of dutiful politeness, the son sat down at his desk and the stranger leaned familiarly over him, demonstrating adroitly with a ruler and a pencil how "what we call 'infinity' " can be contained within a small geometrical figure on a sheet of paper. "First you draw a square; then you draw a triangle to fit inside the square; then you draw a second triangle, and a third, and a fourth, each to fit inside the square, but without their points coinciding, and as you continue—here, son, I'll show you—give me your hand, and I'll show you—the border of the triangles' common outline gets more complex and measures larger, and larger, and larger—and soon you'll need a magnifying glass to see the details, and then you'll need a microscope, and so on and so forth, forever, laying triangles neatly down to fit inside the original square *without their points coinciding*—!" The stranger spoke with increasing fervor; spittle gleamed in the corners of his mouth. The son stared at the geometrical shapes rapidly materializing on the sheet of paper before him with no seeming comprehension but with a rapt staring fascination as if he dared not look away.

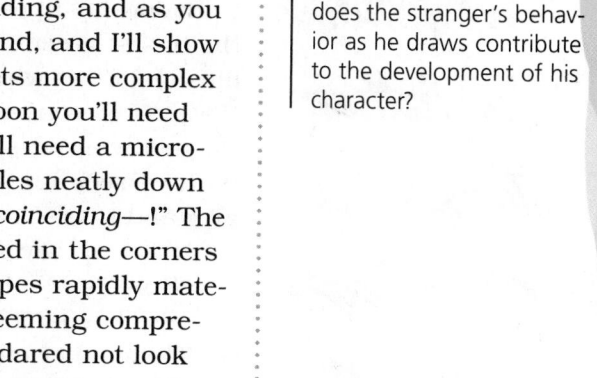

Spiral Review
Characterization How does the stranger's behavior as he draws contribute to the development of his character?

After several minutes of this the father came abruptly forward and dropped his hand on the stranger's shoulder. "The visit is over," he said calmly. It was the first time since they'd shaken hands that the two men had touched, and the touch had a galvanic effect upon the stranger: he dropped ruler and pencil at once, froze in his stooped posture, burst into frightened tears.

Now the visit truly was over; the stranger, at last, *was* leaving, having wiped away his tears and made a stoical effort to compose himself; but on the doorstep, to the father's astonishment, he made a final, preposterous appeal—he wanted to see the basement. "Just to sit on the stairs? In the dark? For a few quiet minutes? And you could close the door and forget me, you and your family could have your dinner and—"

The stranger was begging but the father was resolute. Without raising his voice he said, *"No. The visit is over."*

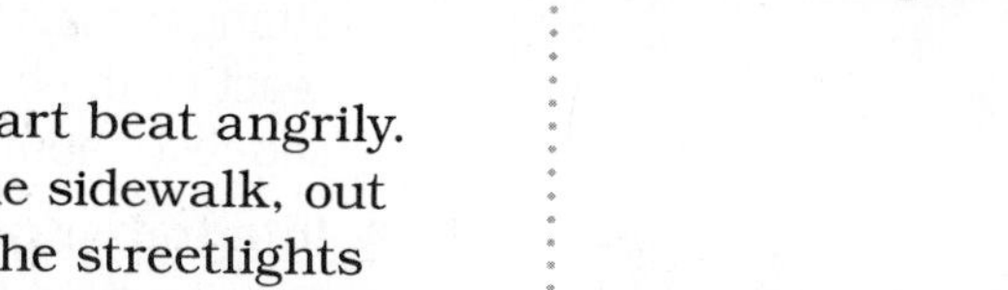

He shut the door, and locked it.

Locked it! His hands were shaking and his heart beat angrily.

He watched the stranger walk away—out to the sidewalk, out to the street, disappearing in the darkness. Had the streetlights gone out?

Behind the father the mother stood apologetic and defensive, wringing her hands in a classic stance. "Wasn't that *sad!* Wasn't that—*sad!* But we had no choice but to let him in, it was the only

Comprehension
Before he leaves, what request does the stranger make?

Everywhere the father looked, a pulse beat mute with rage.

decent thing to do." The father pushed past her without comment. In the living room he saw that the lights were flickering as if on the brink of going out; the patterned wallpaper seemed drained of color; a shadow lay upon it shaped like a bulbous cloud or growth. Even the robust green of the carpeting looked faded. Or was it an optical illusion? Everywhere the father looked, a pulse beat mute with rage. "*I* wasn't the one who opened the door to that man in the first place," the mother said, coming up behind the father and touching his arm. Without seeming to know what he did the father violently jerked his arm and thrust her away.

"Shut up. We'll forget it," he said.

"But—"

"We'll forget it."

The mother entered the kitchen walking slowly as if she'd been struck a blow. In fact, a bruise the size of a pear would materialize on her forearm by morning. When she reached out to steady herself she misjudged the distance of the door frame—or did the door frame recede an inch or two—and nearly lost her balance.

In the kitchen the lights were dim and an odor of sourish smoke, subtle but unmistakable, made her nostrils pinch.

She slammed open the oven door. Grabbed a pair of pot holders with insulated linings. "*I* wasn't the one, . . ." she cried, panting, "and you know it."

Critical Reading

1. **Key Ideas and Details (a)** At what time of day does the stranger arrive at the house? **(b) Analyze:** In what ways does this choice add to the air of mystery surrounding the stranger?
2. **Key Ideas and Details (a) Describe:** How does the father react to the stranger's request to look around? **(b) Analyze Cause and Effect:** What conflict does this decision set up between the father and mother? **(c) Analyze Cause and Effect:** At the end of the story, how does the stranger's visit continue to affect the family?
3. **Integrate Knowledge and Ideas (a) Interpret:** How does the stranger react to the window seat? **(b) Interpret:** How does he react to the boy's bedroom? **(c) Speculate:** What do these details suggest about his relationship to his own father?
4. **Integrate Knowledge and Ideas (a) Deduce:** What apparent mistake does the stranger make when he responds to the mother's question about whether his family is still living? **(b) Make a Judgment:** Is this a ghost story? Explain your answer.

Close Reading Activities

The Fall of the House of Usher • Where Is Here?

Comparing Gothic Literature

1. **Craft and Structure** **(a)** Which character in Poe's story is most tormented? Explain. **(b)** Which character in Oates's story is tormented? **(c)** In what ways does the tormented character affect other characters in each story?
2. **Craft and Structure** **(a)** Where do readers first encounter a hint of the supernatural in Oates's story? **(b)** What are some supernatural elements in "The Fall of the House of Usher?" **(c)** Explain how these elements are both similar and different in the two stories.
3. **Integration of Knowledge and Ideas** **(a)** What violent acts occur in "The Fall of the House of Usher?" **(b)** In what more subtle ways does Oates's story suggest the occurrence of mysterious but equally awful events?

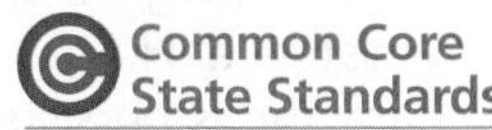

Writing

9.a. Apply *grades 11-12 Reading standards* to literature.

10. Write routinely over shorter time frames for a range of tasks, purposes, and audiences.

Timed Writing

Explanatory Text: Analytical Essay

The castles and mansions that provide the settings for traditional Gothic tales are full of grandeur, darkness, and decay. These settings are one of the most recognizable elements of traditional Gothic fiction. Is setting equally important in a modern Gothic story?

Assignment: Write an **analytical essay** in which you explore the importance of setting in these two stories. Prewrite by answering the questions listed below to generate ideas and focus your analysis. **[40 minutes]**

- How are the settings in each story described? Note specific words each author uses to paint a picture of the setting.
- What *mood*, or atmosphere, does each setting have? Does this mood or atmosphere change as the story progresses? Explain.
- Which details in "Where Is Here?" show the setting as ordinary and which give it a frightening quality?
- Are the settings of "The Fall of the House of Usher" and "Where Is Here?" equally important to the events of each story? Explain.

As you write, support your ideas with detailed references to the stories.

5-Minute Planner

Complete these steps before you begin to write:

1. Read the prompt carefully. Underline key words and phrases.
2. Skim the stories and jot down notes about elements that address the focus questions in the prompt.
3. Write an outline to structure your ideas. **TIP** As part of your outline, note specific textual details you will use in each paragraph.
4. Reread the prompt, and draft your essay.

USE ACADEMIC VOCABULARY

As you write, use academic language, including the following words or their related forms:

quote
distinguish
illustrate
compare

For more on academic language, see the vocabulary charts in the introduction to this book.

from *Moby-Dick*

Connecting to the Essential Question Americans tend to admire persistence. However, Captain Ahab, Herman Melville's most famous character, is persistent to the point of obsession. As you read, notice details that suggest the dark side of Ahab's determination. This will help as you consider the Essential Question: **What makes American literature American?**

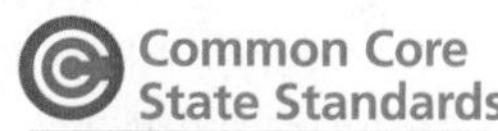

Reading Literature
2. Determine two or more themes or central ideas of a text and analyze their development over the course of the text, including how they interact and build on one another to produce a complex account; provide an objective summary of the text.

Close Reading Focus

Symbol; Theme

A **symbol** is a person, place, or thing that has its own meaning and also represents something larger, usually an abstract idea. The main symbol in Melville's great novel—the whale that gives the book its title—is complex. To understand it as a symbol, reflect on all aspects of the whale's behavior and appearance, including the following qualities:

- Moby-Dick is enormous and powerful.
- Moby-Dick seems unpredictable but is controlled by natural laws.
- Moby-Dick seems immortal and indifferent to human suffering.

Analyzing the symbol of the whale will help you identify the novel's **theme,** its central message or comment on life. A writer develops theme through symbols, descriptions, characters, and imagery. A long and complex novel like *Moby-Dick* may have multiple themes. As you read, look for details related to concepts of good, evil, sacrifice, and revenge.

Preparing to Read Complex Texts Melville builds symbolic meaning and theme through details. As you read, **identify relevant details to determine the essential message.** Look for characters, settings, objects, and dialogue that suggest larger ideas. For example, Ahab's description of Moby-Dick provides a clue to the whale's essential meaning: "I see in him outrageous strength, with an inscrutable malice sinewing it." As you read, use a chart like the one shown to identify relevant details that will lead you to the novel's essential meanings.

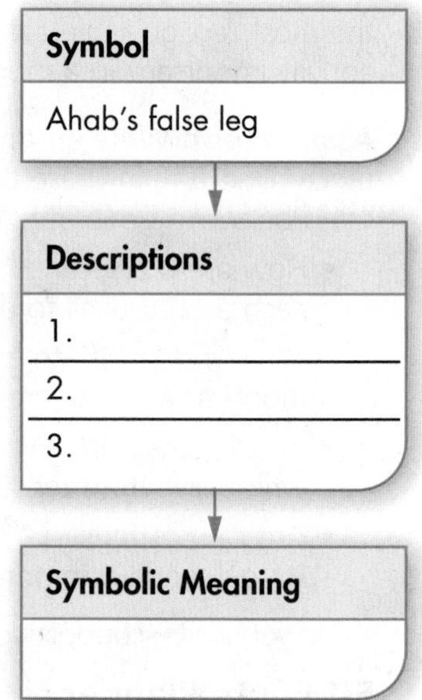

Vocabulary

You will find the following words in the text that follows. Copy the words in your notebook and note which ones are adjectives. What clues indicate that these words are adjectives?

pedestrian
impulsive
inarticulate
inscrutable
maledictions
prescient

HERMAN MELVILLE *(1819–1891)*

Author of *Moby-Dick*

One of America's greatest novelists, Herman Melville was born in New York City, the son of a wealthy merchant. His family's comfortable situation changed drastically in 1830, however, when his father's business failed. Two years later, Melville's father died, leaving the family in debt. Melville spent the rest of his childhood working as a clerk, a farmhand, and a teacher to help support his family.

Whaling in the South Pacific Melville became a sailor at the age of nineteen and spent several years working on whaling ships in the South Pacific. He returned to the United States in 1844, after a brief period of service in the navy. Soon thereafter, Melville began his writing career, using his adventures in the South Seas as material for his fiction. He produced two popular novels, *Typee* (1846) and *Omoo* (1847), both set in the Pacific islands. His third novel, *Mardi* (1849), was more abstract and symbolic. When readers rejected the book, Melville grew melancholy. He continued writing, however, turning out two more novels over the next two years.

Writing in the Berkshires Using the profits from his popular novels, Melville bought Arrowhead, a farm near Pittsfield, Massachusetts. There, he befriended the author Nathaniel Hawthorne, who lived nearby. Encouraged by Hawthorne's interest, Melville redoubled his creative efforts. In 1851, he published his masterpiece, *Moby-Dick,* under the title *The Whale.*

A Moment of Pride *Moby-Dick* is a complex novel with several layers of meaning. On the surface, it is the story of the fateful voyage of a whaling ship. On another level, it is the story of a bitter man's quest for vengeance. On still another level, it is a philosophical examination of humanity's relationship to the natural world. When he finished the book, Melville sensed the magnitude of his achievement. Unfortunately, nineteenth-century readers rejected the book. They also spurned his next two novels and Melville fell into debt. The job he took as an inspector at the New York customs house became another experience that would inform his fiction, especially the story "Bartleby, the Scrivener."

Rediscovered In the latter part of his life, Melville privately published several volumes of poetry, a handful of short stories, and the novella *Billy Budd.* He died in 1891, unappreciated and unnoticed. In the 1920s, however, his work was rediscovered, and he finally received the recognition he deserved. Today, *Moby-Dick* is widely regarded as one of the finest novels in all of American literature.

FROM

MOBY-DICK

HERMAN MELVILLE

BACKGROUND *Moby-Dick* is the story of a man's obsession with the dangerous and mysterious white whale that years before had taken off one of his legs. The man, Captain Ahab, guides the *Pequod,* a whaling ship, and its crew in relentless pursuit of the whale, Moby-Dick. Among the more important members of the crew are Starbuck, the first mate; Stubb, the second mate; Flask, the third mate; Queequeg, Tashtego, and Daggoo, the harpooners; and Ishmael, the young sailor who narrates the story. When the crew signed aboard the *Pequod,* they believed the voyage to be a business venture. However, in the following excerpt, Ahab makes clear that his real purpose is to seek revenge against Moby-Dick.

◀ Critical Viewing
Which elements of this illustration emphasize human weakness in the face of nature? **ANALYZE**

FROM THE QUARTER-DECK

One morning shortly after breakfast, Ahab, as was his wont, ascended the cabin gangway to the deck. There most sea captains usually walk at that hour, as country gentlemen, after the same meal, take a few turns in the garden.

Soon his steady, ivory stride was heard, as to and fro he paced his old rounds, upon planks so familiar to his tread, that they were all over dented, like geological stones, with the peculiar mark of his walk. Did you fixedly gaze, too, upon that ribbed and dented brow; there also, you would see still stranger footprints—the footprints of his one unsleeping, ever-pacing thought.

But on the occasion in question, those dents looked deeper, even as his nervous step that morning left a deeper mark. And, so full of his thought was Ahab, that at every uniform turn that he made, now

Comprehension
Why are the *Pequod's* planks dented?

at the mainmast and now at the binnacle,[1] you could almost see that thought turn in him as he turned, and pace in him as he paced; so completely possessing him, indeed, that it all but seemed the inward mold of every outer movement.

"D'ye mark him, Flask?" whispered Stubb; "the chick that's in him pecks the shell. 'Twill soon be out."

The hours wore on—Ahab now shut up within his cabin; anon, pacing the deck, with the same intense bigotry of purpose[2] in his aspect.

It drew near the close of day. Suddenly he came to a halt by the bulwarks, and inserting his bone leg into the auger hole there, and with one hand grasping a shroud, he ordered Starbuck to send everybody aft.

"Sir!" said the mate, astonished at an order seldom or never given on shipboard except in some extraordinary case.

"Send everybody aft," repeated Ahab. "Mastheads, there! come down!"

When the entire ship's company were assembled, and with curious and not wholly unapprehensive faces, were eyeing him, for he looked not unlike the weather horizon when a storm is coming up, Ahab, after rapidly glancing over the bulwarks, and then darting his eyes among the crew, started from his standpoint; and as though not a soul were nigh him resumed his heavy turns upon the deck. With bent head and half-slouched hat he continued to pace, unmindful of the wondering whispering among the men; till Stubb cautiously whispered to Flask, that Ahab must have summoned them there for the purpose of witnessing a **pedestrian** feat. But this did not last long. Vehemently pausing, he cried:

"What do ye do when ye see a whale, men?"

"Sing out for him!" was the **impulsive** rejoinder from a score of clubbed voices.

"Good!" cried Ahab, with a wild approval in his tones; observing the hearty animation into which his unexpected question had so magnetically thrown them.

"And what do ye next, men?"

"Lower away, and after him!"

"And what tune is it ye pull to, men?"

"A dead whale or a stove[3] boat!"

More and more strangely and fiercely glad and approving, grew the countenance of the old man at every shout; while the mariners began to gaze curiously at each other, as if marveling how it was that they themselves became so excited at such seemingly purposeless questions.

▲ Critical Viewing
How does this portrait of Ahab compare with your mental image of him? **COMPARE AND CONTRAST**

Vocabulary

pedestrian (pi des´ trē ən) *adj.* going on foot; walking

impulsive (im pul´ siv) *adj.* done without thinking

1. **binnacle** (bin´ ə kəl) *n.* case enclosing a ship's compass.
2. **bigotry of purpose** complete single-mindedness.
3. **stove** *v.* broken; smashed.

But, they were all eagerness again, as Ahab, now half-revolving in his pivot hole, with one hand reaching high up a shroud,[4] and tightly, almost convulsively grasping it, addressed them thus:

"All ye mastheaders have before now heard me give orders about a white whale. Look ye! d'ye see this Spanish ounce of gold?"—holding up a broad bright coin to the sun—"it is a sixteen-dollar piece, men. D'ye see it? Mr. Starbuck, hand me yon topmaul."

While the mate was getting the hammer, Ahab, without speaking, was slowly rubbing the gold piece against the skirts of his jacket, as if to heighten its luster, and without using any words was meanwhile lowly humming to himself, producing a sound so strangely muffled and inarticulate that it seemed the mechanical humming of the wheels of his vitality in him.

Vocabulary
inarticulate (in′ är tik′ yo͞o lit′) *adj.* unclearly spoken or expressed

Receiving the topmaul from Starbuck, he advanced towards the mainmast with the hammer uplifted in one hand, exhibiting the gold with the other, and with a high raised voice exclaiming: "Whosoever of ye raises me a white-headed whale with a wrinkled brow and a crooked jaw; whosoever of ye raises me that white-headed whale, with three holes punctured in his starboard fluke[5]—look ye, whosoever of ye raises me that same white whale, he shall have this gold ounce, my boys!"

"Huzza! huzza!" cried the seamen, as with swinging tarpaulins they hailed the act of nailing the gold to the mast.

"It's a white whale, I say," resumed Ahab, as he threw down the topmaul: "a white whale. Skin your eyes for him, men; look sharp for white water; if ye see but a bubble, sing out."

All this while Tashtego, Daggoo, and Queequeg had looked on with even more intense interest and surprise than the rest, and at the mention of the wrinkled brow and crooked jaw they had started as if each was separately touched by some specific recollection.

"Captain Ahab," said Tashtego, "that white whale must be the same that some call Moby-Dick."

"Moby-Dick?" shouted Ahab. "Do ye know the white whale then, Tash?"

"Does he fantail[6] a little curious, sir, before he goes down?" said the Gay-Header deliberately.

"And has he a curious spout, too," said Daggoo, "very bushy, even for a parmacetty,[7] and mighty quick, Captain Ahab?"

"And he have one, two, tree—oh! good many iron in him hide, too, Captain," cried Queequeg disjointedly, "all twiske-tee betwisk, like him—him—" faltering hard for a word, and screwing his hand round and round as though uncorking a bottle—"like him—him—"

"Corkscrew!" cried Ahab, "aye, Queequeg, the harpoons lie all twisted and wrenched in him; aye, Daggoo, his spout is a big one, like

Comprehension
What reward does Ahab offer to the man who spots the white whale?

---

4. **shroud** *n.* set of ropes from a ship's side to the masthead.
5. **starboard fluke** (flo͞ok) *n.* right half of a whale's tail.
6. **fantail** *v.* to spread the tail like a fan.
7. **parmacetty** (pär′ mə set′ ē) *n.* dialect for sperm whale, from which spermaceti was derived. Spermaceti is a high quality oil that was once used to make candles and other products.

▲ Critical Viewing
What does this image suggest about the perils involved in whaling? **INTERPRET**

a whole shock of wheat, and white as a pile of our Nantucket wool after the great annual sheepshearing; aye, Tashtego, and he fantails like a split jib in a squall. Death and devils! men, it is Moby-Dick ye have seen—Moby-Dick—Moby-Dick!"

"Captain Ahab," said Starbuck, who, with Stubb and Flask, had thus far been eyeing his superior with increasing surprise, but at last seemed struck with a thought which somewhat explained all the wonder. "Captain Ahab, I have heard of Moby-Dick—but it was not Moby-Dick that took off thy leg?"

"Who told thee that?" cried Ahab; then pausing, "Aye, Starbuck; aye, my hearties all round; it was Moby-Dick that dismasted me; Moby-Dick that brought me to this dead stump I stand on now. Aye, aye," he shouted with a terrific, loud, animal sob, like that of a heartstricken moose; "Aye, aye! it was that accursed white whale that razeed me; made a poor pegging lubber[8] for me forever and a day!" Then tossing both arms, with measureless imprecations he shouted out: "Aye, aye! and I'll chase him round Good Hope, and round the Horn, and round the Norway Maelstrom, and round perdition's flames before I give him up. And this is what ye have shipped for, men! to chase that white whale on both sides of land, and over all sides of earth, till he spouts black blood and rolls fin out. What say ye, men, will ye splice hands on it, now? I think ye do look brave."

"Aye, aye!" shouted the harpooneers and seamen, running closer to the excited old man: "A sharp eye for the white whale; a sharp lance for Moby-Dick!"

"God bless ye," he seemed to half sob and half shout. "God bless

---

8. lubber (lub´ ər) *n.* slow, clumsy person.

ye, men. Steward! go draw the great measure of grog. But what's this long face about, Mr. Starbuck; wilt thou not chase the white whale? art not game for Moby-Dick?"

"I am game for his crooked jaw, and for the jaws of Death too, Captain Ahab, if it fairly comes in the way of the business we follow; but I came here to hunt whales, not my commander's vengeance. How many barrels will thy vengeance yield thee even if thou gettest it, Captain Ahab? it will not fetch thee much in our Nantucket market."

"Nantucket market! Hoot! But come closer, Starbuck; thou requirest a little lower layer. If money's to be the measurer, man, and the accountants have computed their great countinghouse the globe, by girdling it with guineas, one to every three parts of an inch; then, let me tell thee, that my vengeance will fetch a great premium *here!*"

"He smites his chest," whispered Stubb, "what's that for? methinks it rings most vast, but hollow."

"Vengeance on a dumb brute!" cried Starbuck, "that simply smote thee from blindest instinct! Madness! To be enraged with a dumb thing, Captain Ahab, seems blasphemous."

"Hark ye yet again—the little lower layer. All visible objects, man, are but as pasteboard masks. But in each event—in the living act, the undoubted deed—there, some unknown but still reasoning thing puts forth the moldings of its features from behind the unreasoning mask. If man will strike, strike through the mask! How can the prisoner reach outside except by thrusting through the wall? To me, the white whale is that wall, shoved near to me. Sometimes I think there's naught beyond. But 'tis enough. He tasks me; he heaps me; I see in him outrageous strength, with an **inscrutable** malice sinewing it. That inscrutable thing is chiefly what I hate; and be the white whale agent, or be the white whale principal, I will wreak that hate upon him. Talk not to me of blasphemy, man; I'd strike the sun if it insulted me. For could the sun do that, then could I do the other; since there is ever a sort of fair play herein, jealousy presiding over all creations. But not my master, man, is even that fair play. Who's over me? Truth hath no confines. Take off thine eye! more intolerable than fiends' glarings is a doltish stare! So, so; thou reddenest and palest; my heat has melted thee to anger-glow. But look ye, Starbuck, what is said in heat, that thing unsays itself. There are men from whom warm words are small indignity. I meant not to incense thee. Let it go. Look! see yonder Turkish cheeks of spotted tawn—living, breathing pictures painted by the sun. The pagan leopards—the unrecking and unworshiping things, that live, and seek, and give no reasons for the torrid life they feel! The crew, man, the crew! Are they not one and all with Ahab, in this matter of the whale? See Stubb! he laughs! See yonder Chilean! he snorts to think of it. Stand up amid the general hurricane, thy one tossed sapling cannot, Starbuck! And what is it? Reckon it. 'Tis but to help strike a fin; no wondrous feat for Starbuck. What is it more? From this one poor hunt, then, the

Theme
What do Ahab's comments suggest about the value of money compared with great desire?

Vocabulary
inscrutable (in skro͞ot′ ə bəl) *adj.* difficult to know or understand

Comprehension
What is Starbuck's objection to Ahab's desire for vengeance on a "dumb brute"?

best lance out of all Nantucket, surely he will not hang back, when every foremasthand has clutched a whetstone. Ah! constrainings seize thee; I see! the billow lifts thee! Speak, but speak!—Aye, aye! thy silence, then, that voices thee. *(Aside)* Something shot from my dilated nostrils, he has inhaled it in his lungs. Starbuck now is mine; cannot oppose me now, without rebellion."

"God keep me!—keep us all!" murmured Starbuck, lowly.

Identifying Details to Determine Essential Message

What important details in his environment does Ahab fail to notice?

But in his joy at the enchanted, tacit acquiescence of the mate, Ahab did not hear his foreboding invocation; nor yet the low laugh from the hold; nor yet the presaging vibrations of the winds in the cordage; nor yet the hollow flap of the sails against the masts, as for a moment their hearts sank in. For again Starbuck's downcast eyes lighted up with the stubbornness of life; the subterranean laugh died away; the winds blew on; the sails filled out; the ship heaved and rolled as before. Ah, ye admonitions and warnings! why stay ye not when ye come? But rather are ye predictions than warnings, ye shadows! Yet not so much predictions from without, as verifications of the fore-going things within. For with little external to constrain us, the innermost necessities in our being, these still drive us on.

"The measure! the measure!" cried Ahab.

Receiving the brimming pewter, and turning to the harpooneers, he ordered them to produce their weapons. Then ranging them before him near the capstan,[9] with their harpoons in their hands, while his three mates stood at his side with their lances, and the rest of the ship's company formed a circle round the group; he stood for an instant searchingly eyeing every man of his crew. But those wild eyes met his, as the bloodshot eyes of the prairie wolves meet the eye of their leader, ere he rushes on at their head in the trail of the bison; but, alas! only to fall into the hidden snare of the Indian.

"Drink and pass!" he cried, handing the heavy charged flagon to the nearest seamen. "The crew alone now drink. Round with it, round! Short drafts—long swallows, men; 'tis hot as Satan's hoof. So, so; it goes round excellently. It spiralizes in ye; forks out at the serpent-snapping eye. Well done; almost drained. That way it went, this way it comes. Hand it me—here's a hollow! Men, ye seem the years; so brimming life is gulped and gone. Steward, refill!

"Attend now, my braves. I have mustered ye all round this capstan; and ye mates, flank me with your lances; and ye harpooneers, stand there with your irons; and ye, stout mariners, ring me in, that I may in some sort revive a noble custom of my fishermen fathers before me. O men, you will yet see that—Ha! boy, come back? bad pennies come not sooner. Hand it me. Why, now, this pewter had run brimming again, wer't not thou St. Vitus' imp[10]—away, thou ague![11]

"Advance, ye mates! cross your lances full before me. Well done!

---

9. capstan (kap′ sten) *n.* large cylinder, turned by hand, around which cables are wound.

10. St. Vitus' imp offspring of St. Vitus, the patron saint of people stricken with the nervous disorder *chorea* which is characterized by irregular, jerking movements.

11. ague (ā′ gyo͞o) *n.* a chill or fit of shivering.

Let me touch the axis." So saying, with extended arm, he grasped the three level, radiating lances at their crossed center; while so doing, suddenly and nervously twitched them; meanwhile glancing intently from Starbuck to Stubb; from Stubb to Flask. It seemed as though, by some nameless, interior volition, he would fain have shocked into them the same fiery emotion accumulated within the Leyden jar[12] of his own magnetic life. The three mates quailed before his strong, sustained, and mystic aspect. Stubb and Flask looked sideways from him; the honest eye of Starbuck fell downright.

"In vain!" cried Ahab; "but, maybe, 'tis well. For did ye three but once take the full-forced shock, then mine own electric thing, *that* had perhaps expired from out me. Perchance, too, it would have dropped ye dead. Perchance ye need it not. Down lances! And now, ye mates, I do appoint ye three cupbearers to my three pagan kinsmen there—yon three most honorable gentlemen and noblemen, my valiant harpooneers. Disdain the task? What, when the great Pope washes the feet of beggars, using his tiara for ewer? Oh, my sweet cardinals! your own condescension, that shall bend ye to it. I do not order ye; ye will it. Cut your seizings and draw the poles, ye harpooneers!"

Silently obeying the order, the three harpooneers now stood with the detached iron part of their harpoons, some three feet long, held, barbs up, before him.

"Stab me not with that keen steel! Cant them; cant them over! know ye not the goblet end? Turn up the socket! So, so; now, ye cupbearers, advance. The irons! take them; hold them while I fill!" Forthwith, slowly going from one officer to the other, he brimmed the harpoon sockets with the fiery waters from the pewter.

"Now, three to three, ye stand. Commend the murderous chalices! Bestow them, ye who are now made parties to this indissoluble league. Ha! Starbuck! but the deed is done! Yon ratifying sun now waits to sit upon it. Drink, ye harpooneers! drink and swear, ye men that man the deathful whaleboat's bow—Death to Moby-Dick! God hunt us all, if we do not hunt Moby-Dick to his death!" The long, barbed steel goblets were lifted; and to cries and **maledictions** against the white whale, the spirits were simultaneously quaffed down with a hiss. Starbuck paled, and turned, and shivered. Once more, and finally, the replenished pewter went the rounds among the frantic crew; when, waving his free hand to them, they all dispersed; and Ahab retired within his cabin.

After Moby-Dick has been sighted in the Pacific Ocean, the Pequod's *boats pursue the whale for two days. One of the boats has been sunk, and Ahab's ivory leg has been broken off. However, as the next day dawns, the chase continues.*

12. Leyden (līd′ ən) **jar** *n.* glass jar coated inside and out with tinfoil and having a metal rod connected to the inner lining; used to condense static electricity.

Symbol

What is Ahab's symbolic purpose in having his harpooners drink from their weapons?

Vocabulary

maledictions (mal′ ə dik′ shənz) *n.* curses

Comprehension

How do the three mates react to Ahab's gaze?

THE AMERICAN EXPERIENCE

The Golden Age of Yankee Whaling

During the nineteenth century, New England grew prosperous from whaling. Hundreds of ships set out from the ports of Nantucket, New Bedford, Boston, Sag Harbor, and New London and spread out across the world's seas in pursuit of whales. Whale oil and other by-products could make captains and ship owners rich, but whaling was a hard business. Voyages lasted as long as three years and many sailors died at sea. With the invention of the electric lamp (1879) and the development of spring steel (1906), whaling declined. However, during its heyday, whaling created fortunes.

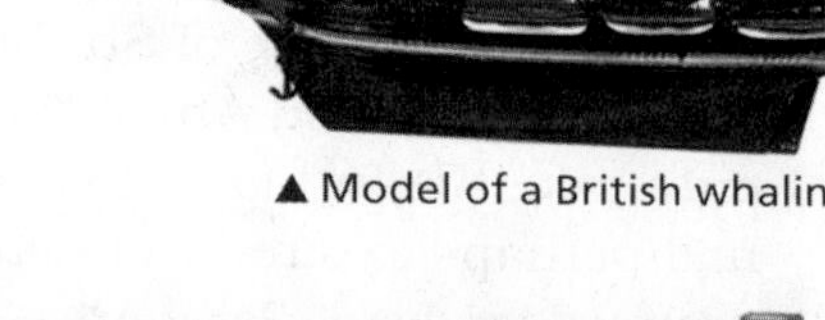

▲ Model of a British whaling shi

CONNECT TO THE LITERATURE

How do these facts about the business of whaling enhance your understanding of *Moby-Dick*?

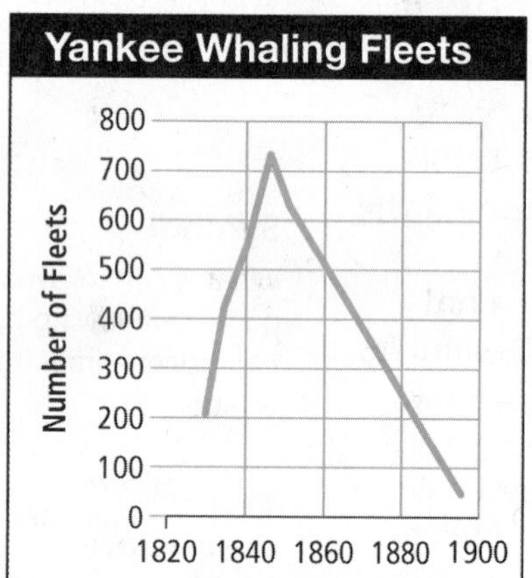

▼ An iron harpoon bent in the hunt

WHALE PRODUCTS

- Corsets (from whale bone)
- Lamp oil
- Candles
- Soaps
- Machine oil
- Vitamin supplement
- Perfume ambergris

▶ Bottle of whale liver oil

- Brushes
- Buggy whips
- Combs
- Hoop skirts
- Fishing rods

Baleen bristles shown with a floorbrush made from them. ▶

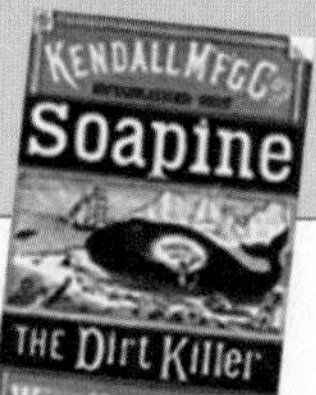

KENDALL MFG CO
Soapine
THE Dirt Killer
WILL NOT INJURE HANDS or FABRIC

◀ Whale oil was used to make soap.

▲ **Whale blubber pot**
After a whale was caught, the crew stripped the blubber and heated it in giant pots like this one.

THE CHASE—THIRD DAY

The morning of the third day dawned fair and fresh, and once more the solitary night man at the foremasthead was relieved by crowds of the daylight lookouts, who dotted every mast and almost every spar.

"D'ye see him?" cried Ahab; but the whale was not yet in sight.

"In his infallible wake, though; but follow that wake, that's all. Helm there; steady, as thou goest, and hast been going. What a lovely day again! were it a new-made world, and made for a summerhouse to the angels, and this morning the first of its throwing open to them, a fairer day could not dawn upon that world. Here's food for thought, had Ahab time to think; but Ahab never thinks; he only feels, feels, feels; that's tingling enough for mortal man! to think's audacity. God only has that right and privilege. Thinking is, or ought to be, a coolness and a calmness; and our poor hearts throb, and our poor brains beat too much for that. And yet, I've sometimes thought my brain was very calm—frozen calm, this old skull cracks so, like a glass in which the contents turned to ice, and shiver it. And still this hair is growing now; this moment growing, and heat must breed it; but no, it's like that sort of common grass that will grow anywhere, between the earthy clefts of Greenland ice or in Vesuvius lava. How the wild winds blow it; they whip it about me as the torn shreds of split sails lash the tossed ship they cling to. A vile wind that has no doubt blown ere this through prison corridors and cells, and wards of hospitals, and ventilated them, and now comes blowing hither as innocent as fleeces.[13] Out upon it!—it's tainted. Were I the wind, I'd blow no more on such a wicked, miserable world. I'd crawl somewhere to a cave, and slink there. And yet, 'tis a noble and heroic thing, the wind! who ever conquered it? In every fight it has the last and bitterest blow. Run tilting at it, and you but run through it. Ha! a coward wind that strikes stark-naked men, but will not stand to receive a single blow. Even Ahab is a braver thing—a nobler thing than *that.* Would now the wind but had a body but all the things that most exasperate and outrage mortal man, all these things are bodiless, but only bodiless as objects, not as agents. There's a most special, a most cunning, oh, a most malicious difference! And yet, I say again, and swear it now, that there's something all glorious and gracious in the wind. These warm trade winds, at least, that in the clear heavens blow straight on, in strong and steadfast, vigorous mildness; and veer not from their mark, however the baser currents of the sea may turn and tack, and mightiest Mississippis of the land swift and swerve about, uncertain where to go at last. And by the eternal poles! these same trades that so directly blow my good ship on; these trades, or something like them—something so unchangeable, and

Symbol
What does the wind symbolize to Ahab?

Comprehension
As the third day dawns, has the whale been sighted?

---

13. fleeces (flēs′ əz) *n.* sheep.

LITERATURE IN CONTEXT

Humanities Connection

The Whale as Archetype

An archetype is an image, a symbol, a character, or a plot that recurs so consistently across cultures and time that it is considered universal. The term comes from Swiss psychologist Carl Jung (1875–1961), who believed that certain human experiences have become a shared genetic memory. According to Jung, this "collective unconscious" explains why archetypes evoke strong feelings in people of all cultures.

The whale had made many appearances in myth, folklore, literature, and art well before Melville used it as a central symbol in *Moby-Dick*. Perhaps the most famous is the biblical tale in which Jonah is swallowed by a whale and then cast ashore. Because the whale is the largest of all animals, its image evokes fear and awe, as well as a sense of the power of nature. In *Moby-Dick*, Melville used these archetypal associations to create fiction of enduring power.

Connect to the Literature

Do you think modern readers react with fear and awe to the image of a whale? Explain.

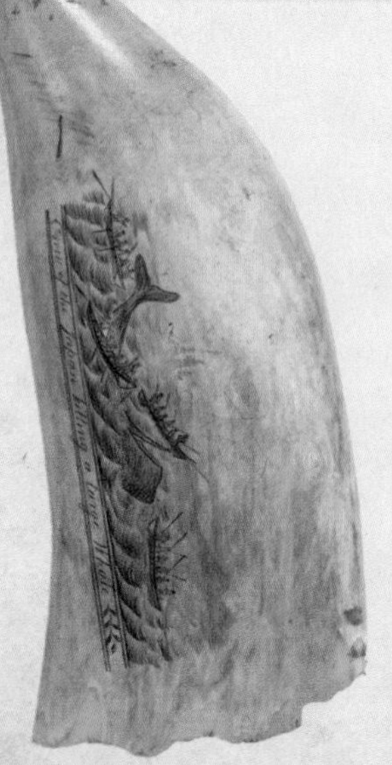

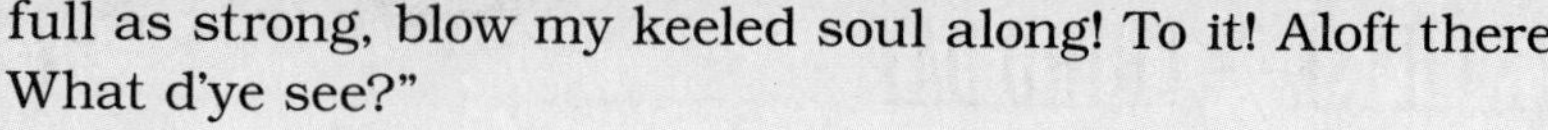
full as strong, blow my keeled soul along! To it! Aloft there! What d'ye see?"

"Nothing, sir."

"Nothing! and noon at hand! The doubloon[14] goes a-begging! See the sun! Aye, aye, it must be so. I've oversailed him. How, got the start? Aye, he's chasing me now; not I, him—that's bad; I might have known it, too. Fool! the lines—the harpoons he's towing.

Aye, aye, I have run him by last night. About! about! Come down, all of ye, but the regular lookouts! Man the braces!"

Steering as she had done, the wind had been somewhat on the Pequod's quarter, so that now being pointed in the reverse direction, the braced ship sailed hard upon the breeze as she rechurned the cream in her own white wake.

"Against the wind he now steers for the open jaw," murmured Starbuck to himself, as he coiled the new-hauled main brace upon the rail. "God keep us, but already my bones feel damp within me, and from the inside wet my flesh. I misdoubt me that I disobey my God in obeying him!"

"Stand by to sway me up!" cried Ahab, advancing to the hempen basket.[15] "We should meet him soon."

"Aye, aye, sir," and straightway Starbuck did Ahab's bidding, and once more Ahab swung on high.

A whole hour now passed; gold-beaten out to ages. Time itself now held long breaths with keen suspense. But at last, some three points off the weather bow, Ahab descried the spout again, and instantly from the three mastheads three shrieks went up as if the tongues of fire had voiced it.

"Forehead to forehead I meet thee, this third time, Moby-Dick! On deck there!—brace sharper up; crowd her into the wind's eye. He's too far off to lower yet, Mr. Starbuck. The sails shake! Stand over that helmsman with a topmaul! So, so; he travels fast, and I must down. But let me have one more good round look aloft here at the sea; there's time for that. An old, old sight, and yet somehow so young; aye, and not changed a wink since I first saw it, a boy, from the sand hills of Nantucket! The same!—the same!—the same to Noah as to me. There's a soft shower to leeward. Such lovely leewardings! They must lead somewhere—to something else than common land, more palmy than the palms. Leeward! the white whale goes that way; look to windward, then; the better if the bitterer quarter. But good-bye, good-bye, old masthead! What's this?—green? aye, tiny mosses in these
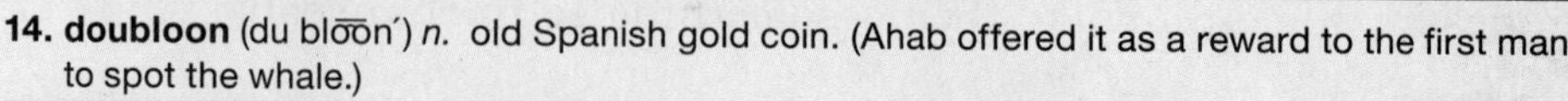
warped cracks. No such green weather stains on Ahab's head! There's

14. doubloon (du blo͞on′) *n.* old Spanish gold coin. (Ahab offered it as a reward to the first man to spot the whale.)

15. hempen basket rope basket. (The basket was constructed earlier by Ahab, so that he could be raised, by means of a pulley device, to the top of the mainmast.)

the difference now between man's old age and matter's. But aye, old mast, we both grow old together; sound in our hulls, though, are we not, my ship? Aye, minus a leg, that's all. By heaven this dead wood has the better of my live flesh every way. I can't compare with it; and I've known some ships made of dead trees outlast the lives of men made of the most vital stuff of vital fathers. What's that he said? he should still go before me, my pilot; and yet to be seen again? But where? Will I have eyes at the bottom of the sea, supposing I descend those endless stairs? and all night I've been sailing from him, wherever he did sink to. Aye, aye, like many more thou told'st direful truth as touching thyself, O Parsee; but, Ahab, there thy shot fell short. Good-bye, masthead—keep a good eye upon the whale, the while I'm gone. We'll talk tomorrow, nay, tonight, when the white whale lies down there, tied by head and tail."

Symbol

What symbolic meaning do you find in the comparison between Ahab and the mast?

He gave the word; and still gazing round him, was steadily lowered through the cloven blue air to the deck.

In due time the boats were lowered; but as standing in his shallop's stern, Ahab just hovered upon the point of the descent, he waved to the mate—who held one of the tackle ropes on deck—and bade him pause.

"Starbuck!"

"Sir?"

"For the third time my soul's ship starts upon this voyage, Starbuck."

"Aye, sir, thou wilt have it so."

"Some ships sail from their ports, and ever afterwards are missing, Starbuck!"

"Truth, sir: saddest truth."

"Some men die at ebb tide; some at low water; some at the full of the flood—and I feel now like a billow that's all one crested comb, Starbuck. I am old—shake hands with me, man."

Their hands met; their eyes fastened; Starbuck's tears the glue.

"Oh, my captain, my captain!—noble heart—go not—go not!—see, it's a brave man that weeps; how great the agony of the persuasion then!"

"Lower away!"—cried Ahab, tossing the mate's arm from him. "Stand by the crew!"

In an instant the boat was pulling round close under the stern.

" The sharks! the sharks!" cried a voice from the low cabin window there; "O master, my master, come back!"

But Ahab heard nothing; for his own voice was high-lifted then; and the boat leaped on.

Yet the voice spake true; for scarce had he pushed from the ship, when numbers of sharks, seemingly rising from out the dark waters beneath the hull, maliciously snapped at the blades of the oars, every time they dipped in the water; and in this way accompanied the boat with their bites. It is a thing not uncommonly happen-

Comprehension

What does Starbuck beg Ahab to do?

Vocabulary

prescient (presh′ ənt) *adj.* having foreknowledge

▼ Critical Viewing

Does this illustration seem like a realistic rendering of an actual situation? Explain. **EVALUATE**

ing to the whaleboats in those swarming seas; the sharks at times apparently following them in the same **prescient** way that vultures hover over the banners of marching regiments in the east. But these were the first sharks that had been observed by the *Pequod* since the White Whale had been first descried; and whether it was that Ahab's crew were all such tiger-yellow barbarians, and therefore their flesh more musky to the senses of the sharks—a matter sometimes well known to affect them—however it was, they seemed to follow that one boat without molesting the others.

"Heart of wrought steel!" murmured Starbuck gazing over the side, and following with his eyes the receding boat—"canst thou yet ring boldly to that sight?—lowering thy keel among ravening sharks, and followed by them, open-mouthed to the chase; and this the critical third day?—For when three days flow together in one continuous intense pursuit; be sure the first is the morning, the second the noon, and the third the evening and the end of that thing—be that end what it may. Oh! my God! what is this that shoots through me, and leaves me so deadly calm, yet expectant—fixed at the top of a shudder! Future things swim before me, as in empty outlines and skeletons; all the past is somehow grown dim. Mary, girl; thou fadest in pale glories behind me; boy! I seem to see but thy eyes grown wondrous blue.[16] Strangest problems of life seem clearing; but clouds sweep between—Is my journey's end coming? My legs feel faint; like his who has footed it all day. Feel thy heart—beats it yet? Stir thyself, Starbuck!—stave it off—move, move! speak aloud!—Masthead there! See ye my boy's hand on the hill?—Crazed—aloft there!—keep thy keenest eye upon the boats—mark well the whale!—Ho! again!—drive off that hawk! see! he pecks—he tears the vane"—pointing to the red flag flying at the maintruck—"Ha, he soars away with it!—Where's the old man now? see'st thou that sight, oh Ahab!—shudder, shudder!"

The boats had not gone very far, when by a signal from the mastheads—a downward pointed arm, Ahab knew that the whale had sounded; but intending to be near him at the next rising, he held on his way a little sideways from the vessel; the becharmed crew maintaining the profoundest silence, as the head-beat waves

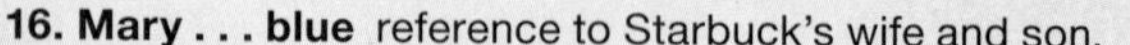

16. Mary . . . blue reference to Starbuck's wife and son.

hammered and hammered against the opposing bow.

"Drive, drive in your nails, oh ye waves! to their uttermost heads drive them in! ye but strike a thing without a lid; and no coffin and no hearse can be mine:—and hemp only can kill me! Ha! ha!"

Suddenly the waters around them slowly swelled in broad circles; then quickly upheaved, as if sideways sliding from a submerged berg of ice, swiftly rising to the surface. A low rumbling sound was heard; a subterraneous hum; and then all held their breaths; as bedraggled with trailing ropes, and harpoons, and lances, a vast form shot lengthwise, but obliquely from the sea. Shrouded in a thin drooping veil of mist, it hovered for a moment in the rainbowed air; and then fell swamping back into the deep. Crushed thirty feet upwards, the waters flashed for an instant like heaps of fountains, then brokenly sank in a shower of flakes, leaving the circling surface creamed like new milk round the marble trunk of the whale.

Symbol
What symbolic meaning is suggested by the description of the whale's behavior as he breaks the water's surface?

"Give way!" cried Ahab to the oarsmen, and the boats darted forward to the attack; but maddened by yesterday's fresh irons that corroded in him, Moby-Dick seemed combinedly possessed by all the angels that fell from heaven. The wide tiers of welded tendons overspreading his broad white forehead, beneath the transparent skin, looked knitted together; as head on, he came churning his tail among the boats; and once more flailed them apart; spilling out the irons and lances from the two mates' boats, and dashing in one side of the upper part of their bows, but leaving Ahab's almost without a scar.

While Daggoo and Queequeg were stopping the strained planks; and as the whale swimming out from them, turned, and showed one entire flank as he shot by them again; at that moment a quick cry went up. Lashed round and round to the fish's back; pinioned in the turns upon turns in which, during the past night, the whale had reeled the involutions of the lines around him, the half-torn body of the Parsee was seen; his sable raiment frayed to shreds; his distended eyes turned full upon old Ahab.

The harpoon dropped from his hand.

"Befooled, befooled!"—drawing in a long lean breath—"Aye, Parsee! I see thee again—Aye, and thou goest before; and this, this then is the hearse that thou didst promise. But I hold thee to the last letter of thy word. Where is the second hearse? Away, mates, to the ship! those boats are useless now; repair them if ye can in time, and return to me; if not, Ahab is enough to die—Down, men! the first thing that but offers to jump from this boat I stand in, that thing I harpoon. Ye are not other men, but my arms and my legs; and so obey me—Where's the whale? gone down again?"

Identifying Details to Determine Essential Message
What does Ahab realize when he sees Parsee's body lashed to Moby-Dick?

But he looked too nigh the boat; for as if bent upon escaping with the corpse he bore, and as if the particular place of the last encounter had been but a stage in his leeward voyage, Moby-Dick was now again steadily swimming forward; and had almost passed the ship—which thus far had been sailing in the contrary direction to him,

Comprehension
What happens to Parsee?

▼ Critical Viewing

Which details from the story did the artist use to create this illustration? **ANALYZE**

though for the present her headway had been stopped. He seemed swimming with his utmost velocity, and now only intent upon pursuing his own straight path in the sea.

"Oh! Ahab," cried Starbuck, "not too late is it, even now, the third day, to desist. See! Moby-Dick seeks thee not. It is thou, thou, that madly seekest him!"

Setting sail to the rising wind, the lonely boat was swiftly impelled to leeward, by both oars and canvas. And at last when Ahab was sliding by the vessel, so near as plainly to distinguish Starbuck's face as he leaned over the rail, he hailed him to turn the vessel about, and follow him, not too swiftly, at a judicious interval. Glancing upwards he saw Tashtego, Queequeg, and Daggoo, eagerly mounting to the three mastheads; while the oarsmen were rocking in the two staved boats which had just been hoisted to the side, and were busily at work in repairing them, one after the other, through the portholes, as he sped, he also caught flying glimpses of Stubb and Flask, busying themselves on deck among bundles of new irons and lances. As he saw all this; as he heard the hammers in the broken boats; far other hammers seemed driving a nail into his heart. But he rallied. And now marking that the vane or flag was gone from the main masthead, he shouted to Tashtego, who had just gained that perch, to descend again for another flag, and a hammer and nails, and so nail it to the mast.

Whether fagged by the three days' running chase, and the resistance to his swimming in the knotted hamper he bore; or whether it was some latent deceitfulness and malice in him: whichever was true, the White Whale's way now began to abate, as it seemed, from the boat so rapidly nearing him once more; though indeed the whale's last start had not been so long a one as before. And still as Ahab glided over the waves the unpitying sharks accompanied him; and so pertinaciously stuck to the boat; and so continually bit at the plying oars, that the blades became jagged and crunched, and left small splinters in the sea, at almost every dip.

"Heed them not! those teeth but give new rowlocks to your oars. Pull on! 'tis the better rest, the sharks' jaw than the yielding water."

"But at every bite, sir, the thin blades grow smaller and smaller!"

" They will last long enough! pull on!—But who can tell"—he muttered—"whether these sharks swim to feast on the whale or on Ahab?—But pull on! Aye, all alive, now—we near him. The helm! take the helm! let me pass"—and so saying, two of the oarsmen helped him forward to the bows of the still flying boat.

At length as the craft was cast to one side, and ran ranging along with the White Whale's flank, he seemed strangely oblivious of its advance—as the whale sometimes will—and Ahab was fairly within the smoky mountain mist, which, thrown off from the whale's spout, curled round his great Monadnock[17] hump; he was even thus close to him; when, with body arched back, and both arms lengthwise high-lifted to the poise, he darted his fierce iron, and his far fiercer curse into the hated whale. As both steel and curse sank to the socket, as if sucked into a morass, Moby-Dick sidewise writhed; spasmodically rolled his nigh flank against the bow, and, without staving a hole in it, so suddenly canted the boat over, that had it not been for the elevated part of the gunwale to which he then clung, Ahab would once more have been tossed into the sea. As it was, three of the oarsmen—who foreknew not the precise instant of the dart, and were therefore unprepared for its effects—these were flung out; but so fell, that, in an instant two of them clutched the gunwale again, and rising to its level on a combing wave, hurled themselves bodily inboard again; the third man helplessly dropping astern, but still afloat and swimming.

Almost simultaneously, with a mighty volition of ungraduated, instantaneous swiftness, the White Whale darted through the weltering sea. But when Ahab cried out to the steersman to take new turns with the line, and hold it so; and commanded the crew to turn round on their seats, and tow the boat up to the mark; the moment the treacherous line felt that double strain and tug, it snapped in the empty air!

"What breaks in me? Some sinew cracks!—'tis whole again; oars! oars! Burst in upon him!"

Hearing the tremendous rush of the sea-crashing boat, the whale wheeled round to present his blank forehead at bay; but in that evolution, catching sight of the nearing black hull of the ship; seemingly seeing in it the source of all his persecutions; bethinking it—it may be—a larger and nobler foe; of a sudden, he bore down upon its advancing prow, smiting his jaws amid fiery showers of foam.

Ahab staggered; his hand smote his forehead. "I grow blind; hands! stretch out before me that I may yet grope my way. Is't night?"

"The whale! The ship!" cried the cringing oarsmen.

"Oars! oars! Slope downwards to thy depths. O sea that ere it be forever too late, Ahab may slide this last, last time upon his mark! I see: the ship! the ship! Dash on, my men! will ye not save my ship?"

But as the oarsmen violently forced their boat through the sledge-hammering seas, the before whale-smitten bow-ends of two planks burst through, and in an instant almost, the temporarily disabled

Symbol
What symbolic connection between his own body and the boat does Ahab seem to feel?

Comprehension
What happens to the boat carrying Ahab when it nears Moby-Dick?

---

17. Monadnock (mə nad′ näk) mountain in New Hampshire.

boat lay nearly level with the waves; its half-wading, splashing crew, trying hard to stop the gap and bale out the pouring water.

Meantime, for that one beholding instant, Tashtego's masthead hammer remained suspended in his hand; and the red flag, half wrapping him as with a plaid, then streamed itself straight out from him, as his own forward-flowing heart; while Starbuck and Stubb, standing upon the bowsprit beneath, caught sight of the down-coming monster just as soon as he.

Symbol
What is symbolized by the red flag streaming out from Tashtego?

"The whale, the whale! Up helm, up helm! Oh, all ye sweet powers of air, now hug me close! Let not Starbuck die, if die he must, in a woman's fainting fit. Up helm I say—ye fools, the jaw! the jaw! Is this the end of all my bursting prayers? all my lifelong fidelities? Oh, Ahab, Ahab, lo, thy work. Steady! helmsman, steady. Nay, nay! Up helm again! He turns to meet us! Oh, his unappeasable brow drives on towards one, whose duty tells him he cannot depart. My God, stand by me now!"

◀ Critical Viewing
How does this illustration emphasize the symbolic aspects of this story? **EVALUATE**

"Stand not by me, but stand under me, whoever you are that will now help Stubb; for Stubb, too, sticks here. I grin at thee, thou grinning whale! Who ever helped Stubb, or kept Stubb awake, but Stubb's own unwinking eye? And now poor Stubb goes to bed upon a mattress that is all too soft; would it were stuffed with brushwood! I grin at thee, thou grinning whale! Look ye, sun, moon, and stars! I call ye assassins of as good a fellow as ever spouted up his ghost. For all that, I would yet ring glasses with thee, would ye but hand the cup! Oh, oh! oh, oh! thou grinning whale, but there'll be plenty of gulping soon! Why fly ye not, O Ahab! For me, off shoes and jacket to it; let Stubb die in his drawers! A most moldy and oversalted death, though—cherries! cherries! cherries! Oh, Flask, for one red cherry ere we die!"

"Cherries? I only wish that we were where they grow. Oh, Stubb, I hope my poor mother's drawn my part-pay ere this; if not, few coppers will now come to her, for the voyage is up."

From the ship's bows, nearly all the seamen now hung inactive; hammers, bits of plank, lances, and harpoons, mechanically retained in their hands, just as they had darted from their various employments; all their enchanted eyes intent upon the whale, which from side to side strangely vibrating his predestinating head, sent a broad band of overspreading semicircular foam before him as he rushed. Retribution, swift vengeance, eternal malice were in his whole aspect, and spite of all that mortal man could do, the solid white buttress of his forehead smote the ship's starboard bow, till men and timbers reeled. Some fell flat upon their faces. Like dislodged trucks, the heads of the harpooneers aloft shook on their bull-like necks. Through the breach, they heard the waters pour, as mountain torrents down a flume.

"The ship! The hearse!—the second hearse!" cried Ahab from the boat; "its wood could only be American!"

Comprehension
What does Moby-Dick finally do to the *Pequod*?

Symbol and Theme

What thematic elements come together in Ahab's climactic speech?

Diving beneath the settling ship, the whale ran quivering along its keel; but turning under water, swiftly shot to the surface again, far off the other bow, but within a few yards of Ahab's boat, where, for a time, he lay quiescent.

"I turn my body from the sun. What ho, Tashtego! let me hear thy hammer. Oh! ye three unsurrendered spires of mine; thou uncracked keel; and only god-bullied hull; thou firm deck, and haughty helm, and Polepointed prow—death-glorious ship! must ye then perish, and without me? Am I cut off from the last fond pride of meanest shipwrecked captains? Oh, lonely death on lonely life! Oh, now I feel my topmost greatness lies in my topmost grief. Ho, ho! from all your furthest bounds, pour ye now in, ye bold billows of my whole foregone life, and top this one piled comber of my death! Towards thee I roll, thou all-destroying but unconquering whale; to the last I grapple with thee; from hell's heart I stab at thee; for hate's sake I spit my last breath at thee. Sink all coffins and all hearses to one common pool! and since neither can be mine, let me then tow to pieces, while still chasing thee, though tied to thee, thou damned whale! *Thus,* I give up the spear!"

The harpoon was darted; the stricken whale flew forward; with igniting velocity the line ran through the groove;—ran foul. Ahab stooped to clear it; he did clear it; but the flying turn caught him round the neck, and voicelessly as Turkish mutes bowstring their victim, he was shot out of the boat, ere the crew knew he was gone. Next instant, the heavy eye splice in the rope's final end flew out of the stark-empty tub, knocked down an oarsman, and smiting the sea, disappeared in its depths.

For an instant, the tranced boat's crew stood still; then turned. "The ship? Great God, where is the ship?" Soon they through dim, bewildering mediums saw her sidelong fading phantom, as in the gaseous fata morgana,[18] only the uppermost masts out of water: while fixed by infatuation, or fidelity, or fate, to their once lofty perches, the pagan harpooneers still maintained their sinking lookouts on the sea. And now, concentric circles seized the lone boat itself, and all its crew, and each floating oar, and every lance pole, and spinning, animate and inanimate, all round and round in one vortex, carried the smallest chip of the *Pequod* out of sight.

But as the last whelmings intermixingly poured themselves over the sunken head of the Indian at the mainmast, leaving a few inches of the erect spar yet visible, together with long streaming yards of the flag, which calmly undulated, with ironical coincidings, over the destroying billows they almost touched—at that instant, a red arm and a hammer hovered backwardly uplifted in the open air, in the act of nailing the flag faster and yet faster to the subsiding spar. A sky hawk that tauntingly had followed the main-truck downwards

18. fata morgana (fät′ə môr gän ə) *n.* mirage seen at sea.

from its natural home among the stars, pecking at the flag, and incommoding Tashtego there: this bird now chanced to intercept its broad fluttering wing between the hammer and the wood: and simultaneously feeling that ethereal thrill, the submerged savage beneath, in his deathgasp, kept his hammer frozen there: and so the bird of heaven, with archangelic shrieks, and his imperial beak thrust upwards, and his whole captive form folded in the flag of Ahab, went down with his ship, which, like Satan, would not sink to hell till she had dragged a living part of heaven along with her, and helmeted herself with it.

Now small fowls flew screaming over the yet yawning gulf; a sullen white surf beat against its steep sides; then all collapsed, and the great shroud of the sea rolled on as it rolled five thousand years ago.

Critical Reading

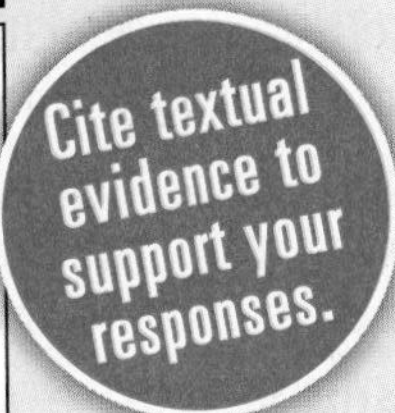
Cite textual evidence to support your responses.

1. **Key Ideas and Details** **(a)** What happened to Ahab in his previous encounter with Moby-Dick? **(b) Interpret:** What does Ahab's obsession with Moby-Dick reveal about his character? **(c) Compare and Contrast:** In what ways is Starbuck different from Ahab?
2. **Key Ideas and Details** **(a)** How does Starbuck interpret Ahab's obsession with Moby-Dick? **(b) Analyze:** Why does Starbuck obey Ahab even though he disagrees with him?
3. **Key Ideas and Details** **(a)** What does Ahab believe exists "behind the unreasoning mask" of all visible things? **(b) Summarize:** Briefly, explain Ahab's beliefs about the nature of creation.
4. **Key Ideas and Details** **(a)** How does Moby-Dick react when the *Pequod* first approaches his flank? **(b) Compare and Contrast:** How does Moby-Dick's reaction illuminate the differences between the whale in reality and in Ahab's imagination?
5. **Integration of Knowledge and Ideas** **Take a Position:** This novel has been called a "voyage of the soul." Would you agree or disagree with that assessment? Explain.
6. **Integration of Knowledge and Ideas** **(a)** What happens to Ahab, Moby-Dick, and the *Pequod* at the story's end? **(b) Analyze:** What does the final paragraph indicate about the relationship between humanity and nature?
7. **Integration of Knowledge and Ideas** Does Ahab's persistence reflect aspects of a distinctly American character, or is it simply human? Explain. In your response, use at least two of these Essential Question words: *individualism, ambition, persistence, extreme.* ***[Connecting to the Essential Question: What makes American literature American?]***

Close Reading Activities from *Moby-Dick*

Literary Analysis

1. **Key Ideas and Details** How does this statement by Ishmael suggest a way to look at the essential meaning of the events he narrates?

   Ah, ye admonitions and warnings! why stay ye not when ye come? But rather are ye predictions than warnings, ye shadows! Yet not so much predictions from without, as verifications of the fore-going things within.

2. **Key Ideas and Details** **Identify relevant details to determine the essential message.** Which events, dialogue, or descriptions in the excerpt lead you to recognize Moby-Dick as a symbol of **(a)** nature's beauty; **(b)** nature's power; and **(c)** nature's immortality? For each meaning, explain your reasoning.
3. **Key Ideas and Details** **(a)** What does Ahab mean when he says "Ahab never thinks; he only feels, feel, feels; that's tingling enough for mortal man! to think's audacity." **(b)** Considering the events that occur as a result of Ahab's feelings, what message do you derive from that statement?
4. **Key Ideas and Details** What omens appear **(a)** as Ahab's whaleboat pulls away from the *Pequod* and **(b)** when Moby-Dick surfaces? **(c)** What is Ahab's reaction to these omens?
5. **Craft and Structure** **(a)** Use a chart like the one shown to compare and contrast the characters of Starbuck and Ahab. **(b)** What message, or **theme,** is Melville expressing through these contrasting characters?

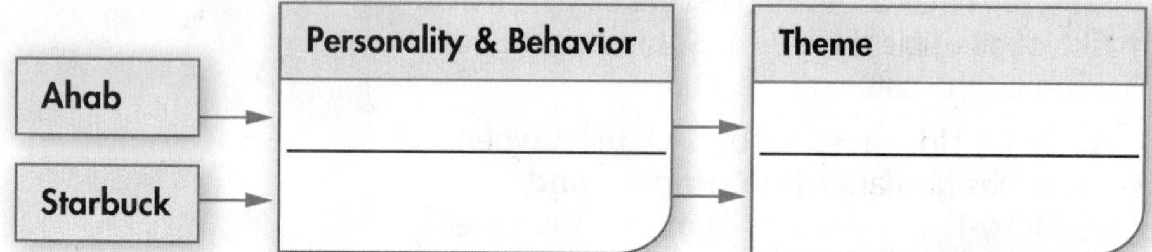

6. **Craft and Structure** The color white is often used as a **symbol** for innocence, as well as for absence and death. What contradictory symbolic meanings does the whale's whiteness convey?
7. **Craft and Structure** If the *Pequod* crew symbolizes humanity and Moby-Dick symbolizes nature, what might the ship's voyage symbolize?
8. **Integration of Knowledge and Ideas** Considering the journey's symbolic meaning and its terrible outcome, speculate about the novel's overall theme, or central idea.
9. **Analyze Visual Information** Explain the humor in this cartoon.

"Have ye seen a whale that matches this swatch?"

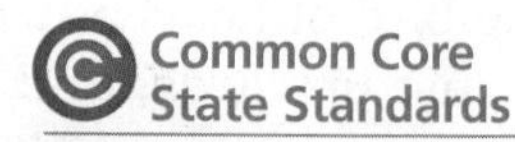

Writing

1. Write arguments to support claims in an analysis of substantive topics or texts, using valid reasoning and relevant and sufficient evidence. *(p. 357)*

1.a. Introduce precise, knowledgeable claim(s), establish the significance of the claim(s), distinguish the claim(s) from alternate or opposing claims, and create an organization that logically sequences claim(s), counterclaims, reasons, and evidence. *(p. 357)*

Vocabulary Acquisition and Use

Word Analysis: Latin Prefix *mal-*

The word "maledictions" combines the Latin prefix *mal-*, which means "bad" or "badly," with the root *-dic-*, which means "to speak." Hence, the word "maledictions" means "bad speech," or curses. Write a definition for each numbered word below. Explain how the meaning of the prefix or root contributes to the meaning of the word.

1. malevolent
2. malice
3. malignant
4. dictate
5. predict
6. diction

Vocabulary: Synonyms

For each vocabulary word, select the best synonym from the column on the right. Then, explain your reasoning.

1. maledictions	**a.** thoughtless
2. prescient	**b.** curses
3. impulsive	**c.** walking
4. inscrutable	**d.** prophetic
5. pedestrian	**e.** inexpressive
6. inarticulate	**f.** mysterious

Writing to Sources

Argument A **character study** is a type of *literary criticism* in which a writer analyzes a character and argues for a certain interpretation of that figure. Often, a character study focuses on a subject, like Ahab, whose behavior can be interpreted in varied ways. For example, some readers feel Ahab's obsession borders on madness, while others feel it borders on greatness. Write an essay in which you analyze Ahab's character and present a convincing argument for your ideas.

Prewriting Review the excerpt and gather details about Ahab's appearance, statements, and behavior. Note what other characters say and feel about him. Use a format like the one shown to assemble the details and look for patterns among them. Write one sentence—your thesis—that expresses your analysis.

Model: Gathering Details and Forming an Opinion

Details:
- Ahab becomes more consumed by his thoughts as the story progresses.
- The crew members notice Ahab's excitement and his wild appearance when he gathers them on the quarter-deck.
- Ahab continues to take greater risks with life and lives of crew members in an effort to kill Moby-Dick.

Thesis: Ahab's obsession with Moby-Dick eventually leads to his madness.

Details taken from the selection as a whole show a character's development.

Drafting In your introduction, state your thesis and provide background information readers may need to understand your ideas. Then, devote one body paragraph to each of your supporting points. Make sure to address alternative explanations of Ahab's character but show why yours is better. Summarize your ideas in your conclusion.

Revising Reread your draft and make sure you have developed your thesis thoroughly. If there are stray details that do not support your thesis, either delete them or strengthen their connections to your main idea.

Close Reading Activities Continued

Conventions and Style: Participles, Gerunds, and Infinitives (Verbals)

Your writing will be more interesting if you use varied sentences. Participles, gerunds, and infinitives, also called *verbals*, are good tools for creating sentence variety. A **participle** is a verb form, usually ending in *-ing* or *-ed*, that can be used as an adjective. A **gerund** is a verb form ending in *-ing* that acts as a noun. An **infinitive** is a verb form that appears with the word "to" and acts as a noun, an adjective, or an adverb. All of these verbals can be used with modifiers and complements to make a **phrase,** a group of words that lacks a subject or verb but adds detail to a sentence.

Varying Sentences with Verbals

Choppy: Ahab is filled with vengeance. Ahab chases Moby-Dick.
Combined Using Participial Phrase: *Filled with vengeance*, Ahab chases Moby-Dick.

Choppy: They are hunting whales. It is dangerous.
Combined Using Gerund Phrase: *Hunting whales* is dangerous.

Choppy: Their first task is clear. They must find the whale.
Combined Using Infinitive Phrase: Their first task is *to find the whale.*

Punctuation Tip: Always place a comma after an introductory participial phrase.

Practice In items 1–5, identify the italicized phrase as a participial, gerund, or infinitive phrase. In items 6–10, use the type of phrase indicated in parentheses to combine the two sentences into a single more detailed sentence.

1. Captain Ahab wants *to kill Moby-Dick.*
2. *Angering a huge whale* is not a good idea.
3. *To hunt whales for profit* was the men's original plan.
4. *Damaged by the sharks' bites,* the oars were useless.
5. Starbuck, *doubting the wisdom of his captain,* quietly mutters a prayer.
6. They use the basket. They lift Ahab to the top of the mainmast. (infinitive)
7. Most of the crew were eager. They wanted to obey the captain's orders. (infinitive)
8. Captain Ahab is obsessed with one thing. He is obsessed with getting revenge. (gerund)
9. The sailors follow Ahab's lead. They are motivated by their desire for the gold piece. (participial)
10. The whale initially swims away from the ship. The whale shows no aggression toward the men. (participial)

Writing and Speaking Conventions

A. Writing Use each phrase in a sentence and explain what type of phrase it is.

1. pacing the deck
2. to use their harpoons
3. obeying orders

Example: spying the whale
Sentence: Spying the whale, the men on watch shout out.
Type of Verbal: participial

B. Speaking Describe the final scene of the excerpt from Moby-Dick's point of view. As you speak, use at least one participial phrase, one gerund phrase, and one infinitive phrase.

TEXT SET

The Human Spirit and the Natural World

Part 3

Literary History: Transcendentalism

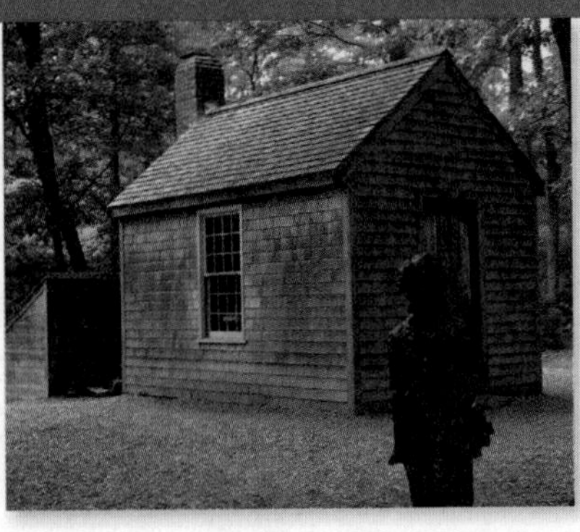

▲ **Critical Viewing**

How might Thoreau feel about this statue and replica of his cabin that stand today at Walden Pond State Reservation? **SPECULATE**

According to Ralph Waldo Emerson, the preeminent Transcendentalist of his day, the human mind is so powerful it can unlock any mystery, from the intricacies of nature to the wonder of God.

Transcendentalism: The Seekers

For the Transcendentalists, the loose-knit group of writers, artists, and reformers who flourished in the 1830s and 1840s, the individual was at the center of the universe, more powerful than any institution, whether political or religious. So it is fitting that the most influential literary and philosophical movement in American history began with the struggles of one man.

A Crisis of Confidence In the early 1830s, a young Boston pastor found himself wrestling with his faith. His beloved wife had died, and he began questioning his beliefs. At the time, many institutions downplayed the importance of the individual. The Industrial Revolution had shown that machines could actually replace people, that individuals did not matter.

The pastor was troubled by this notion. He believed, on the contrary, that the human mind was the most important force in the universe. The pastor was so passionate about his search for a new way of thinking that he resigned his position and traveled to Europe to visit with some of the great philosophers of the day.

That pastor was Ralph Waldo Emerson, and his crisis of confidence became a revolution in American thought. When Emerson returned to the United States in 1833, he helped forge the Transcendentalist movement.

The Individual Is the World The Transcendentalist movement lasted a mere ten years and produced only two major books—Emerson's *Nature* (1836) and Thoreau's *Walden* (1854). Yet its influence on American life and letters continues to this day. According to Emerson, the human mind is so powerful it can unlock any mystery, from the intricacies of nature to the wonder of God. To Emerson, "the individual is the world." This was a radical thought in an age that gave all authority to the organized institutions of government, religion, and education.

Emerson first proposed his ideas in 1833 in a speech at Harvard University. Then, he took his ideas further, proposing that every soul and all of nature was part of an "Over-Soul," a universal spirit to which all beings return after death. In other words, every being is part of God's mind.

Meetings of Great Minds Many people denounced Emerson as a heretic, but his supporters flocked to his home in Concord, Massachusetts. During the height of Transcendentalist activities, Concord attracted so many great minds that it was dubbed the "Athens of America."

Among Emerson's admirers was **Amos Bronson Alcott**, whose beliefs about education revolutionized American schools. Alcott insisted that students should not be taught through routine memorization, but should instead be challenged to think, debate, and discuss. Feminist author and editor **Margaret Fuller** was another eminent Transcendentalist. Along with Emerson, Fuller was the driving force behind the Transcendentalist journal *The Dial.*

Emerson's most famous protégé was **Henry David Thoreau.** As a twenty-year-old student, Thoreau heard Emerson speak at Harvard and was thrilled by his ideas. Not content merely to discuss Transcendentalist philosophy, Thoreau wanted to put it into action. In 1845, he built a rough cottage in the woods at Walden Pond and went there to live alone, in harmony with nature, untied to material things. Thoreau lived at Walden Pond for two years and wrote about his experiences in his collection of essays, *Walden.*

A Lasting Legacy Like other Transcendentalists, Thoreau was a fierce abolitionist. To protest slavery and the Mexican War, he refused to pay taxes and was imprisoned. Although Thoreau spent only one night in jail, the experience gave him insights into the relationship of individuals to government. The theory of nonviolent civil disobedience that he developed has had a profound effect on society throughout the world. During India's struggle for independence in the 1940s, **Mahatma Gandhi** adopted Thoreau's ideas. In America, nonviolent protest served as the guiding principle for **Martin Luther King, Jr.,** during the civil rights movement.

The influence of the Transcendentalists is so woven into the fabric of American culture that we take it for granted. Yet whenever we celebrate the individual, look to the natural world as a mirror of human lives, or state a belief in the power of intuition to grasp fundamental truths, we owe a debt to the great, brief meeting of minds in Concord.

In This Section

Speaking and Listening: Small Group Discussion

Comprehension and Collaboration The Transcendentalists believed that no institution should be as powerful as the individual. With a small group, discuss the role of the individual in our society today. Use these questions to guide your discussion:

- How much power do formal institutions have in our society? Support your position with examples.
- In what ways do individuals make a difference in our society?
- Should individuals have more power than they do? Why or why not?

Choose a point person to share your group's conclusions with the class.

Themes Across Centuries: Scholar's Insights

Charles Johnson on Ralph Waldo Emerson

Emerson Gave Me Permission to Question Everything At age sixteen, when I was an Illinois boy trying to figure out where my place might be in the tempestuous, rapidly changing decade of the 1960s, and long before I became a black American novelist and philosopher, my teachers at Evanston Township High School placed the essays of Ralph Waldo Emerson in front of me. I'm thankful they did.

In grand fashion, "Self-Reliance" gave me permission to be a free thinker and to rigorously question *every*thing around me—from the status quo to social cliques in my school, from neighborhood gangs to eighty-year-old social "conventions" that enshrined racial segregation in the South and in the North. Emerson gave me the courage to resist the pressure to conform to things that were unreasonable, to always trust myself, to dream "impossible dreams," and to value my own individual voice and vision, even if doing so resulted in disapproval and being unpopular with the hip "in crowd."

Challenging Us to Go Beyond the Ordinary Just as he served me well in my teens, Emerson's belief in "the infinitude of the private man," and his identification with all forms of life, proved to be reliable guides during my adult years. First, that's because he defined so beautifully the values that eight generations of Americans regard as the basis for our national character and core beliefs, particularly his devotion to what he called "the republic of Man." He condemned the institution of slavery, championed the right of women to vote, and spoke out against the "wicked Indian policy."

In his journal, Emerson dreamed of an America that would one day be an "asylum of all nations, the energy of Irish, Germans, Swedes, Poles & Cossacks, & all the European tribes—of the Africans, & of the Polynesians [who] will construct a new race, a new religion, a new State, a new literature, which will be as vigorous as the new Europe which came out of the smelting pot of the Dark Ages. . . ." He truly believed, and made *me* see, how "It is our duty to be discontented, with the measure we have of knowledge & virtue, to forget the things behind & press toward those before."

Meet the Author

Charles Johnson has published in a wide variety of genres, including cartoons, philosophical and literary criticism, screenplays, and novels. His novel *Middle Passage* won the National Book Award in 1990.

Secondly, Emerson has long inspired me—as he does anyone with an adventurous spirit—because he challenges us to be flexible and resourceful, like the "sturdy lad from New Hampshire or Vermont, who in turn tries all the professions, who *teams* it, *farms* it, *peddles*, keeps a school, preaches, edits a newspaper, goes to Congress, buys a township, and so forth, in successive years, and always, like a cat, falls on his feet" (from "Self-Reliance").

All those *are* our possibilities. There is nothing, Emerson says, that we cannot achieve if we believe in ourselves. As a Transcendentalist, he was a restless and superbly civilized man who went beyond (or transcended) the ordinary, the outdated, and the unoriginal, for, in his own words, he chose to "unsettle all things. No facts are to me sacred, none are profane; I simply experiment, an endless seeker, with no Past at my back" (from "Circles").

▲ Critical Viewing

This print shows Emerson delivering a lecture. What details reveal what he might have been like as a speaker? **ANALYZE**

Critical Reading

1. **Key Ideas and Details** **(a)** When Johnson was a teenager, what three important lessons did he learn from Emerson? **(b) Connect:** What important life lessons have you learned from a favorite author?
2. **Key Ideas and Details** **(a)** What two qualities does Emerson's "sturdy lad from New Hampshire or Vermont" display? **(b) Speculate:** Are these qualities still part of our "core beliefs" as Americans? Why or why not?

As You Read the Selections by Emerson . . .

3. **Integration of Knowledge and Ideas** Think about whether Emerson's work is still as relevant to today's high school students as it was to the young Charles Johnson.

Building Knowledge and Insight

from ***Nature*** • from ***Self-Reliance***
Concord Hymn

Connecting to the Essential Question Emerson's ideas about individualism were radical to many people during his lifetime and remain challenging to many people today. As you read, look for passages in which Emerson alludes to the difficulty of being true to oneself. This will help as you consider the Essential Question: **How does literature shape or reflect society?**

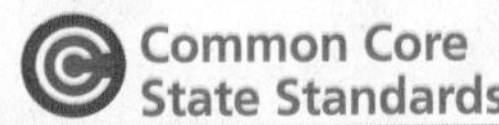

Common Core State Standards

Reading Informational Text
4. Determine the meaning of words and phrases as they are used in the text, including figurative, connotative, and technical meanings.

Language
5.a. Interpret figures of speech in context and analyze their role in the text.

Close Reading Focus

Figurative Language

Figurative language, which is also called **figures of speech,** is language that is used imaginatively instead of literally. Types of figurative language include the following:

- **Metaphor:** a stated similarity between two or more unlike things that does not use the words *like* or *as*
  Example: "Society is a joint-stock company."
- **Synecdoche:** the use of a part of something to stand for the whole
  Example: "the shot heard round the world" [The shot stands in for the whole of the Revolutionary War and the spread of American revolutionary ideals.]

In both his poetry and his prose, Emerson uses metaphor and synecdoche to clarify ideas and stir readers' emotions. He also uses **imagery,** or word pictures, and is sensitive to the *sounds of words*. For example, the long *e* sounds in the phrase "the dark stream which seaward creeps" add to the beauty of the image. As you read, notice how figures of speech, images, and sound affect what you understand and feel about Emerson's ideas.

Preparing to Read Complex Texts As you read, check your understanding of Emerson's ideas by **challenging,** or **questioning,** the text. To do so, do not simply accept his arguments and evidence but evaluate them against your own experiences and other reading. As you read, use a chart like the one shown to record your challenges or questions and responses.

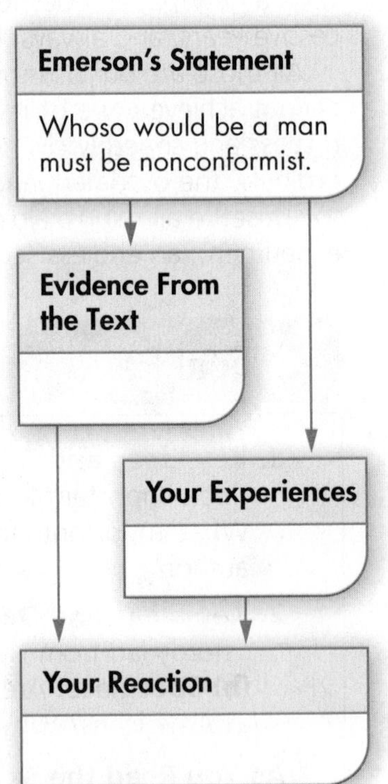

Vocabulary

The words listed here are key to understanding the texts that follow. Copy the words into your notebook. Which word is a synonym for *peaceful*?

perpetual
decorum
tranquil
conviction
chaos
aversion
absolve

RALPH WALDO EMERSON *(1803–1882)*

Author of "Nature" • "Self-Reliance" • "Concord Hymn"

Individuality, independence, and an appreciation for the wonders of nature are just a few of the principles that Ralph Waldo Emerson helped to instill in our nation's identity. Although his ideas were sometimes considered controversial, they continue to inspire people to this day. Throughout his life, Emerson's mind was constantly in motion, generating new ideas and defining and redefining his view of the world. His natural eloquence in expressing these ideas—in essays, lectures, and poetry—makes him one of the most quoted writers in American literature.

A New England Childhood The son of a Unitarian minister, Emerson was born in Boston. When Emerson was seven, his father died. The boy turned to a brilliant aunt, Mary Moody Emerson, who encouraged his independent thinking. At fourteen, Emerson entered Harvard, where he began the journal he was to keep all his life. After postgraduate studies at Harvard Divinity School, he became pastor of the Second Church of Boston.

Finding His Niche Emerson's career as a minister was short-lived. Grief-stricken at the death of his young wife, and dissatisfied with Unitarianism, Emerson resigned after three years. He then went to Europe, where he met the English writers Thomas Carlyle, Samuel Taylor Coleridge, and William Wordsworth. On his return to the United States, Emerson settled in Concord, Massachusetts. He married Lydia Jackson of Plymouth and began to write seriously. Slowly, the Emerson household began to welcome a widening circle of friends and admirers that included many of the country's most important thinkers. In time, Emerson became widely sought as a lecturer.

Emerson first achieved national fame in 1841, when he published *Essays*, a collection based on material from his journals and lectures. He went on to publish several more volumes of nonfiction, including *Essays, Second Volume* (1844), *Representative Men* (1849), and *The Conduct of Life* (1860).

Though Emerson was known mostly for his essays and lectures, he considered himself a poet. "I am born a poet," he once wrote, "of a low class without doubt, yet a poet. That is my nature and my vocation." He published two successful volumes of poetry, *Poems* (1847) and *May-Day and Other Pieces* (1867). Like his essays, Emerson's poems express his beliefs in individuality and in humanity's spiritual connection to nature.

FROM NATURE

RALPH WALDO EMERSON

BACKGROUND *During the 1830s and 1840s, Emerson and a small group of like-minded friends gathered regularly in his study to discuss philosophy, religion, and literature. Among them were Emerson's protégé, Henry David Thoreau, as well as educator Bronson Alcott, feminist writer Margaret Fuller, and ex-clergyman and author George Ripley. The intimate group, known as the Transcendental Club, developed a philosophical system that stressed intuition, individuality, and self-reliance. In 1836, Emerson published Nature, the lengthy essay excerpted here that became the Transcendental Club's unofficial statement of belief.*

Nature is a setting that fits equally well a comic or a mourning piece. In good health, the air is a cordial of incredible virtue. Crossing a bare common,[1] in snow puddles, at twilight, under a clouded sky, without having in my thoughts any occurrence of special good fortune, I have enjoyed a perfect exhilaration. I am glad to the brink of fear. In the woods, too, a man casts off his years, as the snake his slough, and at what period soever of life is always a child. In the woods is **perpetual** youth. Within these plantations of God, a **decorum** and sanctity reign, a perennial festival is dressed, and the guest sees not how he should tire of them in a thousand years. In the woods, we return to reason and faith. There I feel that nothing can befall me in life—no disgrace, no calamity (leaving me my eyes), which nature cannot repair. Standing on the bare ground—my head bathed by the blithe air and uplifted into infinite space—all mean egotism vanishes. I become a transparent eyeball; I am nothing; I see all; the currents of the Universal Being circulate through me; I am part or parcel of God. The name of the nearest friend

Vocabulary

perpetual (pər pech′ o͞o əl) *adj.* lasting forever

decorum (di kôr′ rəm) *n.* rightness; suitability

Comprehension

What effect does Emerson believe nature has on all people regardless of age?

1. **common** *n.* piece of open public land.

◀ **Critical Viewing** What different emotions might the natural setting shown in this photograph evoke in people? Explain. **INTERPRET** sounds then foreign and accidental: to be brothers, to be acquaintances, master or servant, is then a trifle and a disturbance. I am the lover of uncontained and immortal beauty. In the wilderness, I find something more dear and connate than in the streets or villages. In the tranquil landscape, and especially in the distant line of the horizon, man beholds somewhat as beautiful as his own nature.

Vocabulary
tranquil (traŋ′ kwəl) *adj.* calm, quiet, still

The greatest delight which the fields and woods minister is the suggestion of an occult relation between man and the vegetable. I am not alone and unacknowledged. They nod to me, and I to them. The waving of the boughs in the storm is new to me and old. It takes me by surprise, and yet is not unknown. Its effect is like that of a higher thought or a better emotion coming over me, when I deemed I was thinking justly or doing right.

Questioning the Text
What question or challenge might you pose to Emerson's idea that one is not alone in nature?

Yet it is certain that the power to produce this delight does not reside in nature, but in man, or in a harmony of both. It is necessary to use these pleasures with great temperance. For nature is not always tricked[2] in holiday attire, but the same scene which yesterday breathed perfume and glittered as for the frolic of the nymphs is overspread with melancholy today. Nature always wears the colors of the spirit. To a man laboring under calamity, the heat of his own fire hath sadness in it. Then there is a kind of contempt of the landscape felt by him who has just lost by death a dear friend. The sky is less grand as it shuts down over less worth in the population.

2. **tricked** *v.* dressed.

Critical Reading

Cite textual evidence to support your responses.

1. **Key Ideas and Details** Under what circumstances, according to Emerson, does "mean egotism" vanish? **(b) Define:** How would you define Emerson's idea of "mean egotism"? **(c) Analyze Cause and Effect:** In nature, what emotion does Emerson believe replaces "mean egotism"?
2. **Key Ideas and Details** **(a)** When does Emerson become a "transparent eyeball"? **(b) Analyze:** What are the characteristics of this experience? **(c) Connect:** In what ways does this description reflect Transcendentalist belief in an Over-Soul?
3. **Integration of Knowledge and Ideas** **(a)** Where does the power to produce nature's delight come from? **(b) Define:** In describing a harmony between human beings and nature, do you think Emerson means the relationship is always serene? Explain.

FROM

SELF-RELIANCE

RALPH WALDO EMERSON

There is a time in every man's education when he arrives at the conviction that envy is ignorance; that imitation is suicide; that he must take himself for better, for worse, as his portion; that though the wide universe is full of good, no kernel of nourishing corn can come to him but through his toil bestowed on that plot of ground which is given to him to till. The power which resides in him is new in nature, and none but he knows what that is which he can do, nor does he know until he has tried. Not for nothing one face, one character, one fact makes much impression on him, and another none. This sculpture in the memory is not without preestablished harmony. The eye was placed where one ray should fall, that it might testify of that particular ray. We but half express ourselves, and are ashamed of that divine idea which each of us represents. It may be safely trusted as proportionate and of good issues, so it be faithfully imparted, but God will not have his work made manifest by cowards. A man is relieved and gay when he has put his heart into his work and done his best; but what he has said or done otherwise, shall give him no peace. It is a deliverance which does not deliver. In the attempt his genius deserts him; no muse befriends; no invention, no hope.

Trust thyself: every heart vibrates to that iron string. Accept the place the divine providence has found for you; the society of your contemporaries, the connection of events. Great men have always done so and confided themselves childlike to the genius of their age, betraying their perception that the absolutely trustworthy was stirring at their heart, working through their hands, predominating in all their being. And we are now men, and must accept in the highest mind the same transcendent destiny; and not minors and invalids in a protected corner, but guides, redeemers, and benefactors. Obeying the Almighty effort and advancing on chaos and the Dark. . . .

Society everywhere is in conspiracy against the manhood of every one of its members. Society is a joint-stock company in which the members agree for the better securing of his bread to each shareholder, to surrender the liberty and culture of the eater. The virtue in most request is conformity. Self-reliance is its aversion. It loves not realities and creators, but names and customs.

Vocabulary
conviction (kən vik′ shən) *n.* strong belief

Figurative Language
How does the metaphor of tilling soil help clarify Emerson's ideas in this opening paragraph?

Vocabulary
chaos (kā′ äs′) *n.* disorder of matter and space, supposed to have existed before the ordered universe

aversion (ə vʉr′ zhən) *n.* object arousing an intense dislike

Comprehension
According to Emerson, what have great men always done?

Vocabulary
absolve (ab zälv′) *v.* pardon; free from guilt

Whoso would be a man must be a nonconformist. He who would gather immortal palms must not be hindered by the name of goodness, but must explore if it be goodness. Nothing is at last sacred but the integrity of your own mind. Absolve you to yourself, and you shall have the suffrage of the world. . . .

A foolish consistency is the hobgoblin of little minds, adored by little statesmen and philosophers and divines. With consistency a great soul has simply nothing to do. He may as well concern himself with his shadow on the wall. Speak what you think now in hard words and tomorrow speak what tomorrow thinks in hard words again, though it contradict everything you said today. "Ah, so you shall be sure to be misunderstood?"—is it so bad, then, to be misunderstood? Pythagoras was misunderstood, and Socrates, and Jesus, and Luther, and Copernicus, and Galileo, and Newton,[1] and every pure and wise spirit that ever took flesh. To be great is to be misunderstood. . . .

1. **Pythagoras ... Newton** individuals who made major contributions to scientific, philosophical, or religious thinking.

Critical Reading

Cite textual evidence to support your responses.

1. **Key Ideas and Details (a)** What terms does Emerson use to describe society? **(b) Interpret:** According to Emerson, what is society's main purpose? **(c) Draw Conclusions:** In what ways does Emerson believe people should be affected by the way others perceive them?
2. **Key Ideas and Details (a) Interpret:** According to Emerson, what role does the "divine" have in determining each person's circumstances? **(b) Generalize:** What would Emerson say is each person's reason for living? Explain.
3. **Craft and Structure (a) Make a Judgment:** How important is Emerson's use of the adjective "foolish" in his discussion of consistency? **(b) Speculate:** Do you think there are any circumstances in which Emerson would advocate the benefits of consistency? Explain.
4. **Integration of Ideas and Knowledge** Which passage in these essays best expresses belief in the importance of the individual? Explain the reasons for your choice. In your response, use at least two of these Essential Question words: *conformity, integrity, society, agreement.* ***[Connecting to the Essential Question: What makes American literature American?]***

CONCORD HYMN

SUNG AT THE COMPLETION OF THE BATTLE MONUMENT, JULY 4, 1837

Ralph Waldo Emerson

By the rude[1] bridge that arched the flood,
    Their flag to April's breeze unfurled,
Here once the embattled farmers stood,
    And fired the shot heard round the world.

The foe long since in silence slept;
    Alike the conqueror silent sleeps;
And Time the ruined bridge has swept
    Down the dark stream which seaward creeps.

On this green bank, by this soft stream,
    We set today a votive[2] stone;
That memory may their deed redeem,
    When, like our sires, our sons are gone.

Spirit, that made those heroes dare
    To die, and leave their children free,
Bid Time and Nature gently spare
    The shaft we raise to them and thee.

---

1. **rude** (ro͞od) *adj.* crude or rough in form or workmanship.
2. **votive** (vōt′ iv) *adj.* dedicated in fulfillment of a vow or pledge.

▼ Critical Viewing
In 1875, the first verse of "Concord Hymn" was carved into the base of this statue commemorating the Minutemen who fought the British at Lexington and Concord on April 19, 1775. What aspects of the sculpture communicate the emotions of the poem? **CONNECT**

Critical Reading

1. **Key Ideas and Details (a)** What event took place by the "rude bridge"? **(b) Interpret:** What does the poet mean by the image of "the shot heard round the world"?
2. **Craft and Structure (a)** What has happened to the bridge since the battle that took place there? **(b) Analyze:** How does the poem's organization reflect a sense of the passage of time?
3. **Craft and Structure (a)** In the last stanza, whom does the poet address directly? **(b) Infer:** In what way does this direct address reflect the Transcendentalist belief in an Over-Soul?
4. **Integration of Knowledge and Ideas Apply:** Which aspects of "Concord Hymn" would be appropriate for the dedication of other war monuments?

Close Reading Activities

from ***Nature*** • from ***Self-Reliance*** • ***Concord Hymn***

Literary Analysis

1. **Craft and Structure** **(a)** Identify one **metaphor** in each essay. **(b)** Explain the abstract idea each metaphor helps Emerson express in concrete terms. **(c)** What emotion do you think Emerson hopes to evoke with each example? Explain.
2. **Craft and Structure** **(a)** Restate the meaning of this sentence: "In the woods, too, a man casts off his years, as the snake his slough." **(b)** How does the repeated *s* sound in the phrase "snake his slough" add to the meaning?
3. **Craft and Structure** In "Nature," Emerson describes the woods as the "plantations of God." What type of figurative language is he using? Explain your thinking.
4. **Craft and Structure** Does the **image** of the "transparent eyeball" effectively convey the Transcendentalist idea of a universal Over-Soul? Explain.
5. **Craft and Structure** In "Self-Reliance," Emerson describes "that divine idea which each of us represents." How do that phrase and the one noted in question 3 represent similar ideas about the relationship of God to nature and people?
6. **Craft and Structure** **(a)** Explain Emerson's use of **synecdoche** in this passage: "Trust thyself: every heart vibrates to that iron string." **(b)** How does this use of synecdoche help to clarify Emerson's point about belief in oneself?
7. **Integration of Knowledge and Ideas** **Challenge or question the text** by answering the questions below about this statement from "Nature": "Nature always wears the colors of the spirit."
   (a) What evidence does Emerson provide to support this statement?
   (b) Is this evidence convincing? Explain.
   (c) What argument can you make against this statement?
   (d) What argument can you make in support of this statement?
8. **Integration of Knowledge and Ideas** "Concord Hymn" commemorates events that happened more than sixty years before the poem was written. **(a)** Note one example each of imagery, metaphor, and synecdoche in the poem. **(b)** Explain how each example helps bring the events of the past and the passage of time to life in the reader's mind.
9. **Integration of Knowledge and Ideas** **(a)** Use a chart like the one shown to compare and contrast Emerson's descriptions of the bonds between people in society and those between people and nature. **(b)** Which bonds would Emerson say are more important? Explain.

People in Society	People and Nature

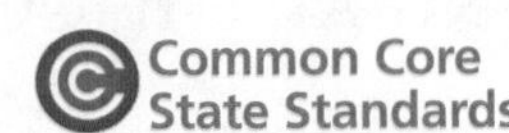

Common Core State Standards

Writing

2. Write explanatory texts to examine and convey complex ideas, concepts, and information clearly and accurately through the effective selection, organization, and analysis of content. *(p. 373)*

2.b. Develop the topic thoroughly by selecting the most significant and relevant facts, extended definitions, concrete details, quotations, or other information and examples appropriate to the audience's knowledge of the topic. *(p. 373)*

Language

5. Demonstrate understanding of word relationships. *(p. 373)*

Vocabulary Acquisition and Use

Word Analysis: Latin Prefix *ab-*

The word *absolve* includes the Latin prefix *ab-* meaning "away" or "from." This prefix contributes to the meaning of *absolve,* which means to take guilt away from someone. When Emerson exhorts his readers to "Absolve you to yourself," he urges them to release themselves from their own guilt or shame.

Explain how the prefix *ab-* relates to the meaning of each of the words below. If any of the words are unfamiliar, refer to a dictionary to clarify their meanings.

1. abnormal
2. absorb
3. abscond
4. abrupt
5. abduct
6. abhor

Vocabulary: Categorize Vocabulary

Review the vocabulary list on page 364. Then, study each item below to categorize each group of words as all synonyms or as a mixture of antonyms and synonyms. If necessary, consult a dictionary. Then, explain your reasoning.

1. chaos, order, clarity
2. conviction, principle, tenet
3. aversion, enticement, attraction
4. absolve, blame, castigate
5. decorum, propriety, politeness
6. perpetual, temporary, impermanent
7. tranquil, turbulent, moderate

Writing to Sources

Explanatory Text Ever since they were first published, Emerson's essays have stirred argument and inspired admiration. Now, it is your turn to add your voice. Write a **critical evaluation** of "Self-Reliance." Include a summary of Emerson's points, an assessment of his uses of *stylistic devices,* such as imagery and figurative language, and a statement of your opinion.

Prewriting Reread the excerpt from "Self-Reliance," noting key ideas, images, and uses of figurative language from the beginning, middle, and end. Then, write one sentence that summarizes Emerson's argument and another sentence that states your opinion about his presentation.

Drafting State the goals of your essay in your introduction. Then, write your summary of Emerson's essay. Follow the summary with a statement of your opinion of his ideas and how he presents them. Support your ideas with accurate and detailed citations from the text.

Model: Using Relevant Citations

Emerson pays tribute to the value of being true to oneself. While most of us would agree with him in theory, how many of us withstand the pressures to conform? Emerson notes, "The virtue in most request is conformity."

Citations specific to the argument keep the writing focused.

Revising As you revise, highlight any citations that do not effectively support your point. Replace weak citations with more relevant support.

Themes Across Centuries: Scholar's Insights

Gretel Ehrlich Introduces *Walden* by Henry David Thoreau

When I was in high school, my parents took me to look at colleges on the East Coast, and on that trip, we visited Walden Pond. I'd bought a collection of Thoreau's essays at a bookstore in Boston, and standing at the edge of the pond, I read *Walden*. My parents had lived nearby before I was born, but I grew up on the central California coast. Thoreau's landscape was not familiar to me, and yet the ideas he expressed in his book-length essay *Walden* spoke to me as no others had.

Living From the Inside Out An essay is essentially a way of asking a question. It is an attempt to understand the nature of things: the human condition and the natural world. Thoreau's questions to me, the reader, asked me to think about where I lived and how I lived in that place. That "owning" land or a house is not as important as becoming friends with that place. That rich and poor are unimportant, but that how you meet your life and how you live from moment to moment, day to day, is most important of all.

Living comes from the inside out, not from an outsider's view of who you are. Life is change. The weather changes, our relationships with one another change, our bodies change. To be static is to be dead. To live in harmony with nature means to roll with those changes daily, yearly, moment by moment.

Contemplating One Ripple in the Pond These days we go about our lives with so much speed and so much extraneous information that it's difficult to contemplate just one thing, one sight, one evening or morning, one ripple in the pond. Thoreau would have us simplify, slow down, become quiet, and burrow into the heart of things with our minds. Not to "dumb down," but the opposite: to stop, listen, and see; to turn off the monologue in our minds; to erase our idea about how things are; to live in others' shoes.

Building a Fire in the Mind Thoreau would have us think like a river, a pond, a tree, another animal or human; to adopt their point of view instead of our own; to build a fire in the mind with real wood and a match that cannot be extinguished. Then, the fresh, dawnlike nature of things—what

Meet the Author

Gretel Ehrlich is the author of more than a dozen works of nonfiction, fiction, and poetry, including *The Solace of Open Spaces* and *A Match to the Heart.* For more information about Ehrlich, see page 222.

Thoreau calls "the auroral character"—will keep radiating, piercing the difficulties in our lives with new songs. A hut in the woods, a still pond, a fresh breeze: these morning winds carry poems, music, love, and loss into our days. Not a dreaminess, but the direct experience of life as it is.

Marching to a Different Drummer Thoreau encourages us to advance confidently in the direction of our dreams. He encourages each of us to be our own person—distinct, unique, thoughtful, precise, and passionate about what we love in the world. It is good to march to "a different drummer," if that's where our feet take us. To live fully, deeply, profoundly, unafraid to be ourselves—this is advice that travels forward for centuries, through all our lives.

▲ Critical Viewing

What details in this early hand-painted photograph of Walden Pond capture what Thoreau calls "the auroral character" of the setting? **CONNECT**

Critical Reading

Cite textual evidence to support your responses.

1. **Key Ideas and Details** **(a)** What do Thoreau's questions ask Ehrlich—and all readers—to think about? **(b) Interpret:** In what way might Thoreau's questions help readers live "from the inside out"?
2. **Key Ideas and Details** **(a)** What would Thoreau have people do in a complex world? **(b) Speculate:** How might following Thoreau's advice change the way you live in the twenty-first century?

As You Read the excerpt from *Walden* . . .

3. **Integration of Knowledge and Ideas** Consider what relevance Thoreau's ideas have in today's world and in your own life.
4. **Integration of Knowledge and Ideas** Think about the ways in which Ehrlich's commentary enriches your understanding of specific passages in Thoreau's essays.

Building Knowledge and Insight

ANCHOR TEXT
from *Walden* •
from *Civil Disobedience*

Connecting to the Essential Question In *Walden*, one of the most famous philosophical works in American literature, Thoreau explains his aim to live a simple life. As you read, look for details that demonstrate Thoreau's goals and values. Doing so will help as you reflect on the Essential Question: **How does literature shape or reflect society?**

Close Reading Focus

Author's Style

An **author's style** is the unique manner in which he or she puts thoughts into words. Elements of style include an author's *diction*, or word choice, and *syntax*, or arrangement of words in sentences. Thoreau's style has a conversational **tone,** or attitude, as though he is talking to a friend. This aspect of his style serves his purpose of enlightening the reader without seeming to lecture or scold. Thoreau also "thinks" in images, often using a series of **figurative expressions** to develop ideas. For example, in *Walden,* Thoreau explains that modern life is too complex. He illustrates the point with a series of concrete examples:

- First, he uses a **metaphor,** a figure of speech that shows a similarity between two or more unlike things without using the words "like" or "as": *In the midst of this chopping sea of civilized life, such are the clouds and storms and quicksands . . .*
- Next, he uses an **analogy,** an extended comparison of relationships: *"Our life is like a German Confederacy, made up of petty states . . ."*

As you read, notice how these elements help to enhance Thoreau's ideas.

Preparing to Read Complex Texts As a reader, you are not obligated to accept everything you see in print. When reading essays of opinion, **analyze the author's implicit and explicit philosophical assumptions**. Implicit ideas are only suggested, while explicit ideas are directly stated. First, ask yourself what fundamental beliefs the author holds about life. Then, identify the support the author provides. Decide if that support is convincing. As you read, use a chart like the one shown to analyze Thoreau's philosophical assumptions.

Vocabulary

The words listed here are important to understanding the texts that follow. Copy the words into your notebook. Which words have four syllables or more?

dilapidated	**magnanimity**
sublime	**expedient**
superfluous	**alacrity**

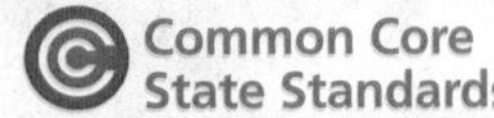

Reading Informational Text

1. Cite strong and thorough textual evidence to support analysis of what the text says explicitly as well as inferences drawn from the text, including determining where the text leaves matters uncertain.

4. Determine the meaning of words and phrases as they are used in the text, including figurative meanings; analyze how an author uses and refines the meaning of a key term or terms over the course of a text.

Language

5.a. Interpret figures of speech in context and analyze their role in the text.

Thoreau's Idea:

People should simplify their lives: "Simplify, simplify."

Supporting Details:

-
-
-

Am I Convinced?

- Yes, because...
- No, because...

Henry David Thoreau

(1817–1862)

Author of *Walden* and "Civil Disobedience"

"Be true to your work, your word, and your friend."

Henry David Thoreau was known by his Concord, Massachusetts, neighbors as an eccentric. As a child he rarely followed rules and was independent and strong-willed. He pursued a formal education at his mother's insistence. Thoreau attended Concord Academy, a college preparatory school, and later enrolled at Harvard University. Although Harvard's dress code required students to wear black coats, Thoreau wore a green one.

Questioning Authority When his objections to corporal punishment forced him to quit his first teaching job, Thoreau and his older brother John opened their own school in Concord. The school was successful, but they had to close it when John became ill.

In 1841, Thoreau moved into the house of another famous Concord resident, Ralph Waldo Emerson. He lived there for two years, performing odd jobs to pay for his room and board. Fascinated by Emerson's Transcendentalist ideas, Thoreau became Emerson's friend and disciple. Rather than return to teaching, he decided to devote his energies to exploring the spiritual relationship between humanity and nature and to living by his political and social beliefs.

On Walden Pond From 1845 to 1847, Thoreau lived alone in a one-room cabin he built at Walden Pond near Concord. This experience provided him with the material for his masterwork, *Walden* (1854). A blend of natural observation, social criticism, and philosophical insight, *Walden* is now generally regarded as the supreme work of Transcendentalist literature and one of the greatest examples of nature writing in American literature.

When he died of tuberculosis at the age of forty-four, Thoreau had received little public recognition. Only *A Week on the Concord and Merrimack Rivers* and some poems had been published—at his own expense—while he was alive. *The Maine Woods, Cape Cod,* and *A Yankee in Canada* were published posthumously. Nevertheless, Emerson knew that future generations would cherish Thoreau. Speaking at his funeral, Emerson said: "The country knows not yet, or in the least part, how great a son it has lost. . . . His soul was made for the noblest society; he had in a short life exhausted the capabilities of this world; wherever there is knowledge, wherever there is virtue, wherever there is beauty, he will find a home."

from Walden

Henry David Thoreau

from Where I Lived, and What I Lived For

At a certain season of our life we are accustomed to consider every spot as the possible site of a house. I have thus surveyed the country on every side within a dozen miles of where I live. In imagination I have bought all the farms in succession, for all were to be bought, and I knew their price. I walked over each farmer's premises, tasted his wild apples, discoursed on husbandry[1] with him, took his farm at his price, at any price, mortgaging it to him in my mind; even put a higher price on it—took everything but a deed of it—took his word for his deed, for I dearly love to talk—cultivated it, and him too to some extent, I trust, and withdrew when I had enjoyed it long enough, leaving him to carry it on. This experience entitled me to be regarded as a sort of real-estate broker by my friends. Wherever I sat, there I might live, and the landscape radiated from me accordingly. What is a house but a sedes, a seat?—better if a country seat. I discovered many a site for a house not

Comprehension
Did Thoreau truly intend to purchase a farm?

1. **husbandry** (huz′ bən drē) *n.* farming.

◀ **Critical Viewing** Based on this picture of Walden Pond, what do you think it would be like to live in such a place? **SPECULATE**

Gretel Ehrlich
Scholar's Insight
Thoreau is saying that every rock is our home, every vista is ours to drink in. And as a result, the landscape comes into us, and pours out again as an image, a poem, a bit of music.

likely to be soon improved, which some might have thought too far from the village, but to my eyes the village was too far from it. Well, there might I live, I said; and there I did live, for an hour, a summer and a winter life; saw how I could let the years run off, buffet the winter through, and see the spring come in. The future inhabitants of this region, wherever they may place their houses, may be sure that they have been anticipated. An afternoon sufficed to lay out the land into orchard woodlot and pasture, and to decide what fine oaks or pines should be left to stand before the door, and whence each blasted tree could be seen to the best advantage; and then I let it lie, fallow[2] perchance, for a man is rich in proportion to the number of things which he can afford to let alone.

My imagination carried me so far that I even had the refusal of several farms—the refusal was all I wanted—but I never got my fingers burned by actual possession. The nearest that I came to actual possession was when I bought the Hollowell Place, and had begun to sort my seeds, and collected materials with which to make a wheelbarrow to carry it on or off with; but before the owner gave me a deed of it, his wife—every man has such a wife—changed her mind and wished to keep it, and he offered me ten dollars to release him. Now, to speak the truth, I had but ten cents in the world, and it surpassed my arithmetic to tell, if I was that man who had ten cents, or who had a farm, or ten dollars, or all together. However, I let him keep the ten dollars and the farm too, for I had carried it far enough; or rather, to be generous, I sold him the farm for just what I gave for it, and, as he was not a rich man, made him a present of ten dollars, and still had my ten cents, and seeds, and materials for a wheelbarrow left. I found thus that I had been a rich man without any damage to my poverty. But I retained the landscape, and I have since annually carried off what it yielded without a wheelbarrow. With respect to landscapes:

> "I am monarch of all I *survey*,
> My right there is none to dispute."[3]

Author's Style and Metaphor
Identify the metaphor Thoreau uses in this paragraph and the idea it helps him develop.

I have frequently seen a poet withdraw, having enjoyed the most valuable part of a farm, while the crusty farmer supposed that he had got a few wild apples only. Why, the owner does not know it for many years when a poet has put his farm in rhyme, the most admirable kind of invisible fence, has fairly impounded it, milked it, skimmed it, and got all the cream, and left the farmer only the skimmed milk.

The real attractions of the Hollowell farm, to me, were: its complete retirement, being about two miles from the village, half a mile from the nearest neighbor, and separated from the highway by a broad field; its bounding on the river, which the owner said protected

---

2. **fallow** (fal´ ō) *adj.* left uncultivated or unplanted.
3. **"I . . . dispute"** from William Cowper's *Verses Supposed to Be Written by Alexander Selkirk*.

it by its fogs from frosts in the spring, though that was nothing to me; the gray color and ruinous state of the house and barn, and the **dilapidated** fences, which put such an interval between me and the last occupant; the hollow and lichen-covered apple trees, gnawed by rabbits, showing what kind of neighbors I should have; but above all, the recollection I had of it from my earliest voyages up the river, when the house was concealed behind a dense grove of red maples, through which I heard the house-dog bark. I was in haste to buy it, before the proprietor finished getting out some rocks, cutting down the hollow apple trees, and grubbing up some young birches which had sprung up in the pasture, or, in short, had made any more of his improvements. To enjoy these advantages I was ready to carry it on; like Atlas,[4] to take the world on my shoulders—I never heard what compensation he received for that—and do all those things which had no other motive or excuse but that I might pay for it and be unmolested in my possession of it; for I knew all the while that it would yield the most abundant crop of the kind I wanted if I could only afford to let it alone. But it turned out as I have said.

All that I could say, then, with respect to farming on a large scale (I have always cultivated a garden) was that I had had my seeds ready. Many think that seeds improve with age. I have no doubt that time discriminates between the good and the bad; and when at last I shall plant, I shall be less likely to be disappointed. But I would say to my fellows, once for all, As long as possible live free and uncommitted. It makes but little difference whether you are committed to a farm or the county jail.

Old Cato,[5] whose "De Re Rustica" is my "Cultivator," says, and the only translation I have seen makes sheer nonsense of the passage, "When you think of getting a farm, turn it thus in your mind, not to buy greedily; nor spare your pains to look at it, and do not think it enough to go round it once. The oftener you go there the more it will please you, if it is good." I think I shall not buy greedily, but go round and round it as long as I live, and be buried in it first, that it may please me the more at last. . . .

I do not propose to write an ode to dejection, but to brag as lustily as chanticleer[6] in the morning, standing on his roost, if only to wake my neighbors up.

When first I took up my abode in the woods, that is, began to spend my nights as well as days there, which, by accident, was on Independence Day, or the fourth of July, 1845, my house was not finished for winter, but was merely a defense against the rain, without plastering or chimney, the walls being of rough weatherstained boards, with wide chinks, which made it cool at night. The upright white hewn studs and freshly planed door and window casings gave

Vocabulary

dilapidated (də lap′ ə dāt′ id) *adj.* in disrepair

Analyzing the Author's Philosophical Assumptions

What do you think the idea of freedom means to Thoreau?

Comprehension

What were the "real attractions" of the Hollowell farm to Thoreau?

---

4. **Atlas** (at′ ləs) from Greek mythology, a Titan who supported the heavens on his shoulders.
5. **Old Cato** Roman statesman (234–149 B.C.). "De Re Rustica" is Latin for "Of Things Rustic."
6. **chanticleer** (chan′ tə klir′) *n.* rooster.

Gretel Ehrlich
Scholar's Insight
Thoreau comes to Walden Pond with a "beginner's mind." He allows the earth to instruct him in its ways, leaving preconceptions behind. That is how writers must approach all things, as a student of the world.

it a clean and airy look, especially in the morning, when its timbers were saturated with dew, so that I fancied that by noon some sweet gum would exude from them. To my imagination it retained throughout the day more or less of this auroral[7] character, reminding me of a certain house on a mountain which I had visited the year before. This was an airy and unplastered cabin, fit to entertain a traveling god, and where a goddess might trail her garments. The winds which passed over my dwelling were such as sweep over the ridges of mountains, bearing the broken strains, or celestial parts only, of terrestrial

7. auroral (ô rōr′ əl) *adj.* resembling the dawn.

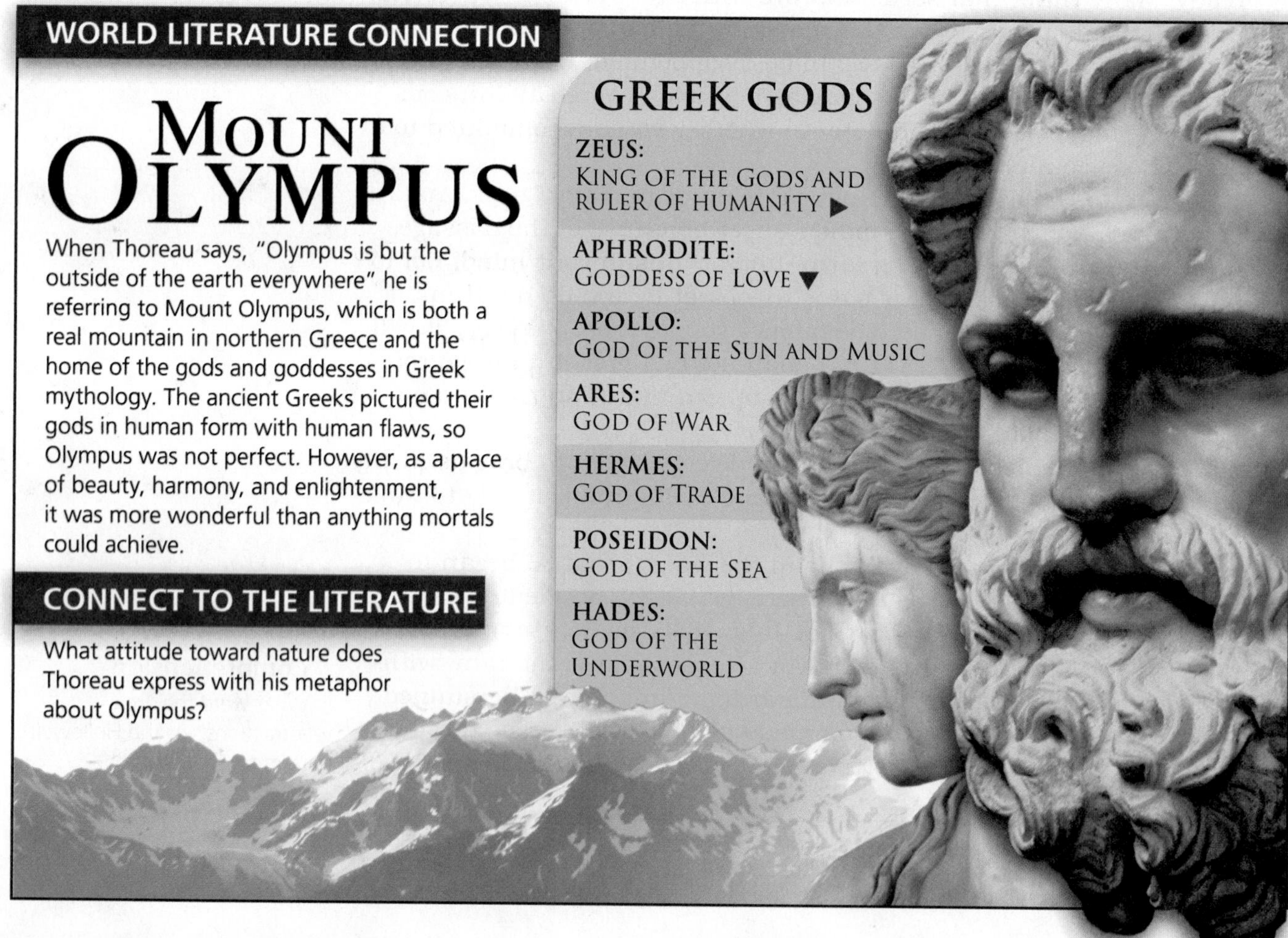

WORLD LITERATURE CONNECTION

Mount Olympus

When Thoreau says, "Olympus is but the outside of the earth everywhere" he is referring to Mount Olympus, which is both a real mountain in northern Greece and the home of the gods and goddesses in Greek mythology. The ancient Greeks pictured their gods in human form with human flaws, so Olympus was not perfect. However, as a place of beauty, harmony, and enlightenment, it was more wonderful than anything mortals could achieve.

CONNECT TO THE LITERATURE

What attitude toward nature does Thoreau express with his metaphor about Olympus?

Greek Gods

Zeus: King of the Gods and Ruler of Humanity ▶

Aphrodite: Goddess of Love ▼

Apollo: God of the Sun and Music

Ares: God of War

Hermes: God of Trade

Poseidon: God of the Sea

Hades: God of the Underworld

music. The morning wind forever blows, the poem of creation is uninterrupted; but few are the ears that hear it. Olympus is but the outside of the earth everywhere. . . .

I went to the woods because I wished to live deliberately, to front only the essential facts of life, and see if I could not learn what it had to teach, and not, when I came to die, discover that I had not lived. I did not wish to live what was not life, living is so dear; nor did I wish to practice resignation, unless it was quite necessary. I wanted to live deep and suck out all the marrow of life, to live so sturdily and Spartanlike[8] as to put to rout all that was not life, to cut a broad swath and shave close, to drive life into a corner, and reduce it to its lowest terms, and, if it proved to be mean, why then to get the whole and genuine meanness of it, and publish its meanness to the world; or if it were **sublime**, to know it by experience, and be able to give a true account of it in my next excursion. For most men, it appears to me, are in a strange uncertainty about it, whether it is of the devil or of God, and have *somewhat hastily* concluded that it is the chief end of man here to "glorify God and enjoy him forever."[9]

Still we live meanly, like ants; though the fable tells us that we were long ago changed into men; like pygmies we fight with cranes:[10] it is error upon error, and clout upon clout, and our best virtue has for its occasion a **superfluous** and evitable wretchedness. Our life is frittered away by detail. An honest man has hardly need to count more than his ten fingers, or in extreme cases he may add his ten toes, and lump the rest. Simplicity, simplicity, simplicity! I say, let your affairs be as two or three, and not a hundred or a thousand; instead of a million count half a dozen, and keep your accounts on your thumbnail. In the midst of this chopping sea of civilized life, such are the clouds and storms and quicksands and thousand-and-one items to be allowed for, that a man has to live, if he would not founder and go to the bottom and not make his port at all, by dead reckoning,[11] and he must be a great calculator indeed who succeeds. Simplify, simplify. Instead of three meals a day, if it be necessary eat but one; instead of a hundred dishes, five; and reduce other things in proportion. Our life is like a German Confederacy,[12] made up of petty

Gretel Ehrlich
Scholar's Insight
Thoreau encourages us to face all that life brings to us, both its painful and beautiful sides. There cannot be one without the other.

Vocabulary

sublime (sə blīm′) *adj.* noble; majestic

superfluous (so͞o pʉr′ flo͞o əs) *adj.* excessive; not necessary

Comprehension

Why did Thoreau go to the woods?

---

8. **Spartanlike** like the people of Sparta, an ancient Greek state whose citizens were known to be hardy, stoical, simple, and highly disciplined.
9. **"glorify . . . forever"** the answer to the question "What is the chief end of man?" in the Westminster catechism.
10. **like . . . cranes** In the *Iliad*, the Trojans are compared to cranes fighting against pygmies.
11. **dead reckoning** navigating without the assistance of stars.
12. **German Confederacy** At the time, Germany was a loose union of thirty-nine independent states, with no common government.

▼ **Critical Viewing**

This picture shows a replica of Thoreau's cabin. How does it help you understand his point that people should work on the quality of their lives rather than the things they own? **INTERPRET**

states, with its boundary forever fluctuating, so that even a German cannot tell you how it is bounded at any moment. The nation itself, with all its so-called internal improvements, which, by the way, are all external and superficial, is just such an unwieldy and overgrown establishment, cluttered with furniture and tripped up by its own traps, ruined by luxury and heedless expense, by want of calculation and a worthy aim, as the million households in the land; and the only cure for it as for them is in a rigid economy, a stern and more than Spartan simplicity of life and elevation of purpose. It lives too fast. Men think that it is essential that the *Nation* have commerce, and export ice, and talk through a telegraph, and ride thirty miles an hour, without a doubt, whether *they* do or not; but whether we should live like baboons or like men, is a little uncertain. If we do not get out sleepers,[13] and forge rails, and devote days and nights to the work, but go to tinkering upon our *lives* to improve *them*, who will build railroads? And if railroads are not built, how shall we get to heaven in season? But if we stay at home and mind our business, who will want railroads? We do not ride on the railroad; it rides upon us. . . .

Time is but the stream I go a-fishing in. I drink at it; but while I drink I see the sandy bottom and detect how shallow it is. Its thin current slides away, but eternity remains. I would drink deeper; fish in the sky, whose bottom is pebbly with stars. I cannot count one. I know not the first letter of the alphabet. I have always been regretting that I was not as wise as the day I was born. The intellect is a cleaver; it discerns and rifts its way into the secret of things. I do not wish to be any more busy with my hands than is necessary. My head is hands and feet. I feel all my best faculties concentrated in it. My instinct tells me that my head is an organ for burrowing, as some creatures use their snout and forepaws, and with it I would mine and burrow my way through these hills. I think that the richest vein is somewhere here- abouts; so by the divining rod[14] and thin rising vapors I judge; and here I will begin to mine. . . .

---

13. **sleepers** (slē´ pərz) *n.* ties supporting railroad tracks.
14. **divining rod** a forked branch or stick alleged to reveal underground water or minerals.

from The Conclusion

I left the woods for as good a reason as I went there. Perhaps it seemed to me that I had several more lives to live, and could not spare any more time for that one. It is remarkable how easily and insensibly we fall into a particular route, and make a beaten track for ourselves. I had not lived there a week before my feet wore a path from my door to the pondside; and though it is five or six years since I trod it, it is still quite distinct. It is true, I fear that others may have fallen into it, and so helped to keep it open. The surface of the earth is soft and impressible by the feet of men; and so with the paths which the mind travels. How worn and dusty, then, must be the highways of the world, how deep the ruts of tradition and conformity! I did not wish to take a cabin passage, but rather to go before the mast and on the deck of the world, for there I could best see the moonlight amid the mountains. I do not wish to go below now.

I learned this, at least, by my experiment; that if one advances confidently in the direction of his dreams, and endeavors to live the life which he has imagined, he will meet with a success unexpected in common hours. He will put some things behind, will pass an invisible boundary; new, universal, and more liberal laws will begin to establish themselves around and within him; or the old laws be expanded, and interpreted in his favor in a more liberal sense, and he will live with the license of a higher order of beings. In proportion as he simplifies his life, the laws of the universe will appear less complex, and solitude will not be solitude, nor poverty poverty, nor weakness weakness. If you have built castles in the air, your work need not be lost; that is where they should be. Now put the foundations under them. . . .

Why should we be in such desperate haste to succeed, and in such desperate enterprises? If a man does not keep pace with his companions, perhaps it is because he hears a different drummer. Let him step to the music which he hears, however measured or far away. It is not important that he should mature as soon as an apple tree or an oak. Shall he turn his spring into summer? If the condition of things which we were made for is not yet, what were any reality which we can substitute? We will not be shipwrecked on a vain reality. Shall we with pains erect a heaven of blue glass over ourselves, though when it is done we shall be sure to gaze still at the true ethereal heaven far above, as if the former were not? . . .

However mean your life is, meet it and live it; do not shun it and call it hard names. It is not so bad as you are. It looks poorest when you are richest. The faultfinder will find faults even in paradise. Love your life, poor as it is. You may perhaps have some pleasant, thrilling, glorious hours, even in a poorhouse. The setting sun is reflected from the windows of the almshouse[15] as brightly as from the rich man's

Author's Style and Metaphor

What metaphor does Thoreau use in the sentence beginning "If a man does not keep pace with his companions . . .?" What idea does it help him develop?

Comprehension

What does Thoreau claim to have learned from his experiment in living?

15. almshouse *n.* home for people too poor to support themselves.

Gretel Ehrlich
Scholar's Insight
To cultivate poverty is a radical thought and one that has been alive throughout history. Poverty in this sense means simplicity, like the "poverty" of an animal that wears only its own fur coat. The mind and the imagination are our true wealth.

Analyzing the Author's Philosophical Assumptions

Thoreau has strong opinions about how people should live, as shown in his advice to "cultivate poverty." Has he convinced you? Explain.

Vocabulary

magnanimity (mag′ nə nim′ ə tē) *n.* generosity

abode; the snow melts before its door as early in the spring. I do not see but a quiet mind may live as contentedly there, and have as cheering thoughts, as in a palace. The town's poor seem to me often to live the most independent lives of any. Maybe they are simply great enough to receive without misgiving. Most think that they are above being supported by the town; but it oftener happens that they are not above supporting themselves by dishonest means, which should be more disreputable. Cultivate poverty like a garden herb, like sage. Do not trouble yourself much to get new things, whether clothes or friends. Turn the old; return to them. Things do not change; we change. Sell your clothes and keep your thoughts. God will see that you do not want society. If I were confined to a corner of a garret[16] all my days, like a spider, the world would be just as large to me while I had my thoughts about me. The philosopher said: "From an army of three divisions one can take away its general, and put it in disorder; from the man the most abject and vulgar one cannot take away his thought." Do not seek so anxiously to be developed, to subject yourself to many influences to be played on; it is all dissipation. Humility like darkness reveals the heavenly lights. The shadows of poverty and meanness gather around us, "and lo! creation widens to our view."[17] We are often reminded that if there were bestowed on us the wealth of Croesus,[18] our aims must still be the same, and our means essentially the same. Moreover, if you are restricted in your range by poverty, if you cannot buy books and newspapers, for instance, you are but confined to the most significant and vital experiences; you are compelled to deal with the material which yields the most sugar and the most starch. It is life near the bone where it is sweetest. You are defended from being a trifler. No man loses ever on a lower level by **magnanimity** on a higher. Superfluous wealth can buy superfluities only. Money is not required to buy one necessary of the soul. . . .

The life in us is like the water in the river. It may rise this year higher than man has ever known it, and flood the parched uplands; even this may be the eventful year, which will drown out all our muskrats. It was not always dry land where we dwell. I see far inland the banks which the stream anciently washed, before science began to record its freshets. Everyone has heard the story which has gone the rounds of New England, of a strong and beautiful bug which came out of the dry leaf of an old table of apple-tree wood, which had stood in a farmer's kitchen for sixty years, first in Connecticut, and afterward in Massachusetts—from an egg deposited in the living tree many years earlier still, as appeared by counting the annual layers

---

16. **garret** (gar′ it) *n.* attic.
17. **"and . . . view"** from the sonnet "To Night" by British poet Joseph Blanco White (1775–1841).
18. **Croesus** (krē′ səs) King of Lydia (d. 546 B.C.), believed to be the wealthiest person of his time.

beyond it; which was heard gnawing out for several weeks, hatched perchance by the heat of an urn. Who does not feel his faith in a resurrection and immortality strengthened by hearing of this? Who knows what beautiful and winged life, whose egg has been buried for ages under many concentric layers of woodenness in the dead dry life of society, deposited at first in the alburnum[19] of the green and living tree, which has been gradually converted into the semblance of its well-seasoned tomb—heard perchance gnawing out now for years by the astonished family of man, as they sat round the festive board—may unexpectedly come forth from amidst society's most trivial and handselled furniture, to enjoy its perfect summer life at last!

I do not say that John or Jonathan[20] will realize all this; but such is the character of that morrow which mere lapse of time can never make to dawn. The light which puts out our eyes is darkness to us. Only that day dawns to which we are awake. There is more day to dawn. The sun is but a morning star.

---

19. alburnum (al bʉr′ nəm) *n.* soft wood between the bark and the heartwood, where water is conducted.

20. John or Jonathan average person.

Critical Reading 

Cite textual evidence to support your responses.

1. **Key Ideas and Details (a)** What advice does Thoreau offer to his "fellows" about ownership of land or property? **(b) Interpret:** What does Thoreau mean by his comment, "It makes but little difference whether you are committed to a farm or the county jail"?
2. **Key Ideas and Details (a)** What advice does Thoreau offer to those who live in poverty? **(b) Analyze:** What does this advice suggest about Thoreau's definition of true wealth?
3. **Key Ideas and Details (a)** According to Thoreau, by what is our life "frittered away"? **(b) Interpret:** What does Thoreau mean by his advice to "simplify, simplify"?
4. **Key Ideas and Details (a) Deduce:** What did Thoreau hope to achieve by living at Walden Pond? **(b) Make a Judgment:** Do you believe Thoreau felt his time at Walden was well spent? Explain.
5. **Integration of Knowledge and Ideas (a) Apply:** How would you define those things that are necessary to the soul? **(b) Take a Position:** Do you agree with Thoreau that "money is not required to buy one necessary of the soul"? Explain.

from

CIVIL DISOBEDIENCE

Henry David Thoreau

BACKGROUND The Mexican War was a conflict between Mexico and the United States that took place from 1846 to 1848. The war was caused by a dispute over the boundary between Texas and Mexico, as well as by Mexico's refusal to discuss selling California and New Mexico to the United States. Believing that President Polk had intentionally provoked the conflict before gaining congressional approval, Thoreau and many other Americans strongly objected to the war. In protest, Thoreau refused to pay his taxes and was forced to spend a night in jail. After that experience, Thoreau wrote "Civil Disobedience," urging people to resist governmental policies with which they disagree.

I heartily accept the motto, "That government is best which governs least";[1] and I should like to see it acted up to more rapidly and systematically. Carried out, it finally amounts to this, which also I believe: "That government is best which governs not at all"; and when men are prepared for it, that will be the kind of government which they will have. Government is at best but an **expedient**; but most governments are usually, and all governments are sometimes, inexpedient. The objections which have been brought against a standing army, and they are many and weighty, and deserve to prevail, may also at last be brought against a standing government. The standing army is only an arm of the standing government. The government itself, which is only the mode which the people have chosen to execute their will, is equally liable to be abused and perverted before the people can act through it. Witness the present Mexican war, the work of comparatively a few individuals using the standing government as their tool; for in the outset, the people would not have consented to this measure.

Vocabulary
expedient (ek spē′ dē ənt) *n.* resource

Spiral Review
Rhetorical Techniques What rhetorical technique does Thoreau use in the sentence beginning "This American government..."? Explain.

This American government—what is it but a tradition, though a recent one, endeavoring to transmit itself unimpaired to posterity, but each instant losing some of its integrity? It has not the vitality and force of a single living man; for a single man can bend it to his will. It is a sort of wooden gun to the people themselves; and, if ever

1. **"That . . . least"** the motto of the *United States Magazine and Democratic Review*, a literary-political journal.

they should use it in earnest as a real one against each other, it will surely split. But it is not the less necessary for this; for the people must have some complicated machinery or other, and hear its din, to satisfy that idea of government which they have. Governments show thus how successfully men can be imposed on, even impose on themselves, for their own advantage. It is excellent, we must all allow; yet this government never of itself furthered any enterprise, but by the alacrity with which it got out of its way. *It* does not keep the country free. *It* does not settle the West. *It* does not educate. The character inherent in the American people has done all that has been accomplished; and it would have done somewhat more, if the government had not sometimes got in its way. For government is an expedient by which men would fain succeed in letting one another alone; and, as has been said, when it is most expedient, the governed are most let alone by it. Trade and commerce, if they were not made of India rubber,[2] would never manage to bounce over the obstacles which legislators are continually putting in their way; and, if one were to judge these men wholly by the effects of their actions, and not partly by their intentions, they would deserve to be classed and punished with those mischievous persons who put obstructions on the railroads.

But, to speak practically and as a citizen, unlike those who call themselves no government men, I ask for, not at once no government, but *at once* a better government. Let every man make known what kind of government would command his respect, and that will be one step toward obtaining it. . . .

Vocabulary
alacrity (ə lak′ rə tē) *n.* speed

2. India rubber a form of crude rubber.

Critical Reading

Cite textual evidence to support your responses.

1. **Key Ideas and Details** **(a)** How does Thoreau define the best possible kind of government? **(b) Draw Conclusions:** According to Thoreau, when will Americans get the best possible kind of government?
2. **Key Ideas and Details** **(a) Summarize:** What is Thoreau asking his readers to do? **(b) Evaluate:** Does Thoreau present a convincing argument for acting on one's principles?
3. **Integration of Knowledge and Ideas** **(a) Criticize:** What arguments might you use to counter Thoreau's objections to the idea of a standing government? **(b) Support:** What examples might support an argument that government benefits individuals?
4. **Integration of Ideas and Knowledge** Do you find it surprising that the goals Thoreau tried to achieve have influenced generations of people around the world? Explain. In your response, use at least two of these Essential Question words: *self-reliance, vision, freedom, principle.* ***[Connecting to the Essential Question: How does literature shape or reflect society?]***

Close Reading Activities

from ***Walden*** •
from ***Civil Disobedience***

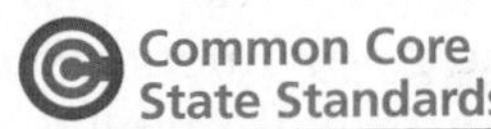

Literary Analysis

1. **Craft and Structure** Explain how the paragraph on simplicity in *Walden* demonstrates the following elements of Thoreau's **style:** **(a)** a conversational **tone**, or attitude; **(b)** a tendency to use a series of **figurative expressions**, including **metaphor** and **analogy**, to develop a key idea.
2. **Key Ideas and Details** **(a)** What is the central idea Thoreau develops in the paragraph on simplicity? Summarize it in one sentence. **(b)** Note another section in *Walden* where Thoreau repeats the idea for emphasis.
3. **Craft and Structure** Thoreau often starts a paragraph with specific examples. He then applies them to a larger truth. **(a)** Identify one such paragraph. **(b)** Do you think this approach is effective? Explain.
4. **Craft and Structure** Choose two metaphors and one analogy from these essays. Use a chart like the one shown to examine the meanings of each one.

Metaphor/Analogy	Things Compared	Meaning
I wanted to live deep and suck out all the marrow of life		

5. **Craft and Structure** In "Civil Disobedience," Thoreau describes government as a "wooden gun." In *Walden,* he describes civilized life as a "chopping sea." **(a)** Explain the meaning of each metaphor. **(b)** Then, explain how the metaphors help Thoreau develop the logic of his ideas.
6. **Craft and Structure** **(a)** In which essay does Thoreau spend more time translating abstract ideas into concrete metaphors and analogies? **(b)** How does this choice reflect the purpose of the essay and the nature of his topic?
7. **Analyze Visual Information** Explain the humor in the cartoon at right.
8. **Integration of Knowledge and Ideas** Thoreau expresses his **explicit philosophical assumption** that people should simplify their lives. **(a)** What support for this belief does he provide? **(b)** How might someone argue against this idea?
9. **Integration of Knowledge and Ideas** **(a)** What evidence does Thoreau use to support his point that "It makes but little difference whether you are committed to a farm or the county jail"? **(b)** What **implicit philosophical assumption** does this statement suggest? **(c)** Do you agree? Explain.

Common Core State Standards

Writing

1. Write arguments to support claims in an analysis of substantive topics or texts, using valid reasoning. *(p. 391)*

Language

4.b. Identify and correctly use patterns of word changes that indicate different meanings. *(p. 391)*

5. Demonstrate understanding of figurative language, word relationships, and nuances in word meanings. *(p. 391)*

▼ *Text in Bubble: "Dear Ralph, Talk about boring!! Nothing to do but take stupid walks in the dreary woods! You'd hate it!! Best regards, Henry" Caption: By Strategic Use of Postcards, Thoreau Manages to Keep Walden Pond Unspoiled.*

Vocabulary Acquisition and Use

Word Analysis: Latin Root *-flu-*

The Latin root *-flu-*, found in words like *fluid,* means "flow." The word *superfluous* means "overflowing" or "exceeding what is sufficient." Consider the meanings of the *-flu-* words listed below. For each word, write an alternate explanation that contains the target word and the word *flow.* Follow the example shown here.

confluence *n.* a merging of two things
alternate definition: A confluence of two rivers occurs when they flow together.

1. affluence *n.* wealth; prosperity
2. fluent *adj.* effortlessly smooth
3. fluctuate *v.* change from high to low levels or change unpredictably
4. influx *n.* a sudden arrival of a large number of people or things
5. flue *n.* a shaft or tube used as an outlet for smoke or gas

Vocabulary: Synonyms

Synonyms are words that have the same or nearly the same meaning. Review the vocabulary list on page 376. Then, select the word below whose meaning is closest to that of the first word. For each answer, explain your reasoning.

1. **dilapidated: (a)** depressed **(b)** rundown **(c)** uneven
2. **sublime: (a)** lovely **(b)** enormous **(c)** awe-inspiring
3. **superfluous: (a)** toxic **(b)** extravagant **(c)** repetitive
4. **magnanimity: (a)** selflessness **(b)** tolerance **(c)** patience
5. **expedient: (a)** expense **(b)** instrument **(c)** barrier
6. **alacrity: (a)** awareness **(b)** preparedness **(c)** quickness

Writing to Sources

Argument In the century and a half since Thoreau wrote *Walden*, life for most Americans has become more complex rather than simpler. Write an **editorial**—a *persuasive article*—in which you argue for or against the relevance of Thoreau's ideas of simplicity in today's world. Refer to *Walden* and "Civil Disobedience" to support your ideas.

Prewriting Decide what you think of Thoreau's ideas, and brainstorm for examples that support your position. Plan to include specific *stylistic elements* to enhance meaning. Like Thoreau, develop *metaphors and analogies* that clarify your ideas.

Drafting Introduce Thoreau and his ideas. Write a statement either advocating or rejecting their relevance today. As you work, *use repetition* for emphasis; vary your wording, but drive home your key points. Conclude with a specific *call to action.*

Revising Reread your editorial, adding examples, anecdotes, or quotations as necessary to sharpen your argument. To complete your work, include photographs or illustrations that capture your ideas visually.

Model: Anticipating Reader's Concerns and Counterclaims

Today, Thoreau's ideas fall on deaf ears because everyone is glued to a cell phone. Instead of hearing his wisdom, people say, "But I can't live without my mobile GPS. It makes my life easier." Yet, people have less time with family, and less time for the simple pleasures of life than ever before.

Anticipating and answering opponents' arguments creates a more persuasive piece of writing.

Analyzing Functional and Expository Texts

Consumer Guide • Report

Reading Informational Text
7. Integrate and evaluate multiple sources of information presented in different media or formats as well as in words in order to address a question or solve a problem.

About the Texts

A **consumer guide** may be prepared by either a government agency or a private organization to educate the public about specific products or services. For a guide to be effective, it must be issued by a reliable source that does not stand to profit from the reporting. Most consumer guides contain basic facts about a product, service, or topic of interest; visual aids such as charts, graphs, or illustrations; and answers to frequently asked questions.

A **report** is a document written to inform officials and the public about issues such as environmental or health concerns. Reports are usually dated because they are often time sensitive. Most reports contain facts, statistics, and other data about an issue; dates and headings that organize the data; and a summary that omits all but the most essential information.

Preparing to Read Complex Texts

Many government and public documents use charts, graphs, and other visual aids to present complex data in an easy-to-read format. As you read, **evaluate the information from charts and graphs** and apply it to the information presented in the text. Notice the features listed in the chart below, and use a checklist like the one shown to identify, interpret, and evaluate the information each feature presents.

Content-Area Vocabulary

These words appear in the selections that follow. They may also appear in other content-area texts.

aquifer (ak´ wə fər) *n.* an underground rock formation in which water collects

contaminant (kən tam´ ə nənt) *n.* material that makes something impure or corrupt by contact or mixture

ecosystem (ē´ kō sis´ təm) *n.* a community of related organisms, together with their physical environment, considered as a unit

hydrologic (hī´ drə laj´ ik) *adj.* relating to the scientific study of water

Basic Elements		Purpose	Effectiveness
Titles and headings	Yes ❑ No ❑		
Charts or graphs	Yes ❑ No ❑		
Photos, maps, or illustrations	Yes ❑ No ❑		
Labels or captions	Yes ❑ No ❑		
Color-coding	Yes ❑ No ❑		
Issue dates	Yes ❑ No ❑		

WATER ON TAP

what you need to know

Where Does My Drinking Water Come From And How Is It Treated?

The headings anticipate questions readers may have.

Your drinking water comes from **surface water** or **ground water**. The water that systems pump and treat from sources open to the atmosphere, such as rivers, lakes, and reservoirs is known as surface water. Water pumped from wells drilled into underground **aquifers**, geologic formations containing water, is called ground water. The quantity of water produced by a well depends on the nature of the rock, sand, or soil in the aquifer from which the water is drawn. Drinking water wells may be shallow (50 feet or less) or deep (more than 1,000 feet). More water systems have ground water than surface water as a source (approx. 147,000 v. 14,500), but more people drink from a surface water system (195 million v. 101,400). Large-scale water supply systems tend to rely on surface water resources, while smaller water systems tend to use ground water. Your water utility or public works department can tell you the source of your public water supply.

How Does Water Get To My Faucet?

An underground network of pipes typically delivers drinking water to the homes and businesses served by the water system. Small systems serving just a handful of households may be relatively simple, while large metropolitan systems can be extremely complex—sometimes consisting of thousands of miles of pipes serving millions of people. Drinking water must meet required health standards when it leaves the treatment plant. After treated water leaves the plant, it is monitored within the distribution system to identify and remedy any problems such as water main breaks, pressure variations, or growth of microorganisms.

How Is My Water Treated To Make It Safe?

Water utilities treat nearly 34 billion gallons of water every day.[1] The amount and type of treatment applied varies with the source and quality of the water. Generally, surface water systems require more treatment than ground water systems because they are directly exposed to the atmosphere and runoff from rain and melting snow.Water suppliers use a variety of treatment processes to remove **contaminants** from drinking water. These individual processes can be arranged in a "treatment train" (a series of processes applied in a sequence). The most commonly used processes include coagulation (flocculation and sedimentation), filtration, and disinfection. Some water systems also use ion exchange and adsorption. Water utilities select the treatment combination most appropriate to treat the contaminants found in the source water of that particular system.

Coagulation (Flocculation & Sedimentation):

Flocculation: This step removes dirt and other particles suspended in the water. Alum and iron salts or synthetic organic polymers are added to the water to form tiny sticky particles called "floc," which attract the dirt particles.

All sources of drinking water contain some naturally occurring contaminants. At low levels, these contaminants generally are not harmful in our drinking water. Removing all contaminants would be extremely expensive, and in most cases, would not provide increased protection of public health. A few naturally occurring minerals may actually improve the taste of drinking water and may even have nutritional value at low levels.

Sedimentation: The flocculated particles then settle naturally out of the water.

Filtration:

Many water treatment facilities use filtration to remove all particles from the water. Those particles include clays and silts, natural organic matter, precipitates from other treatment processes in the facility, iron and manganese, and microorganisms. Filtration clarifies the water and enhances the effectiveness of disinfection.

***Disinfection*:**

Disinfection of drinking water is considered to be one of the major public health advances of the 20th century. Water is often disinfected before it enters the distribution system to ensure that dangerous microbial contaminants are killed. Chlorine, chlorinates, or chlorine dioxides are most often used because they are very effective **disinfectants**, and residual concentrations can be maintained in the water system.

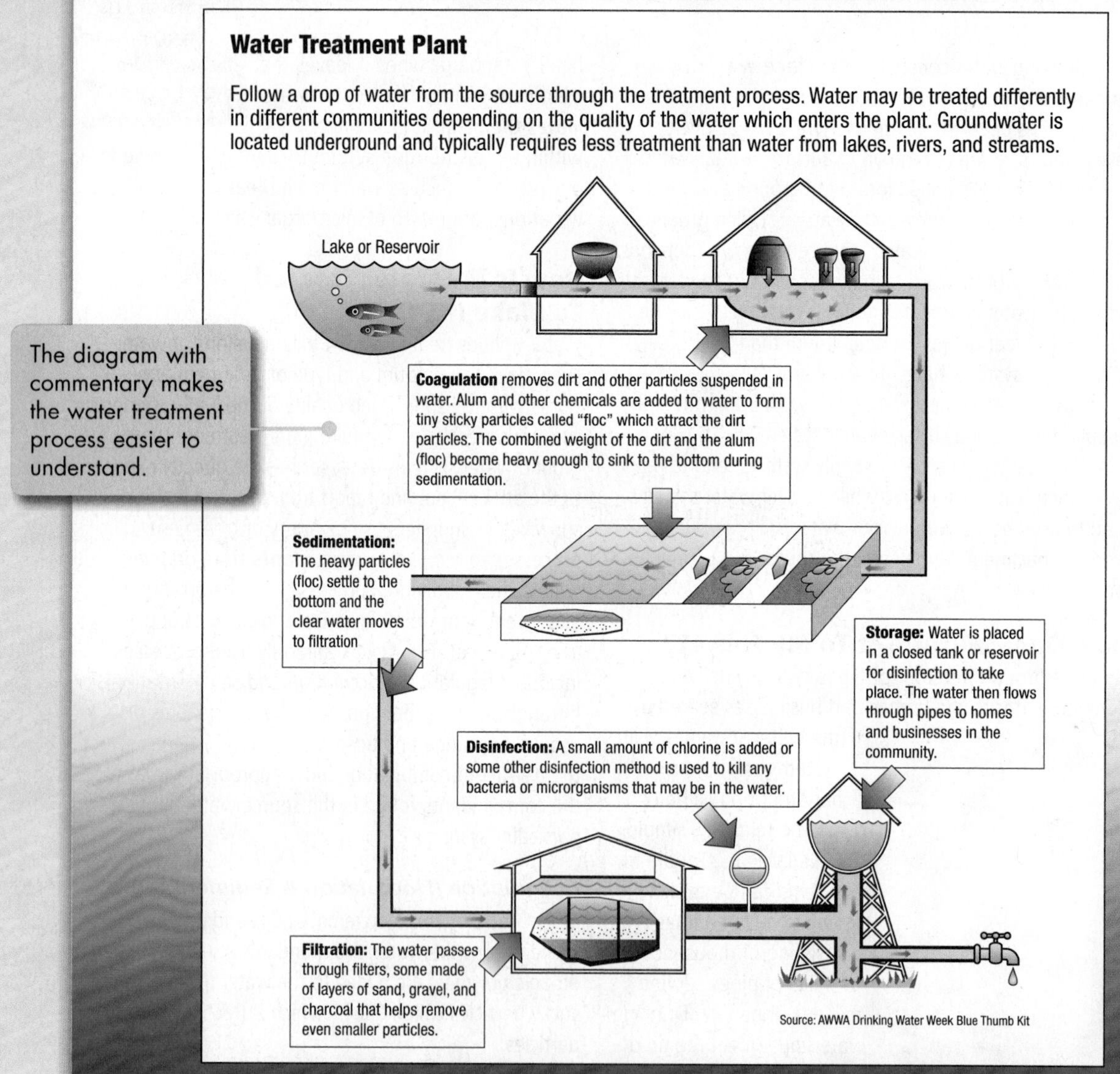

Water Treatment Plant
Follow a drop of water from the source through the treatment process. Water may be treated differently in different communities depending on the quality of the water which enters the plant. Groundwater is located underground and typically requires less treatment than water from lakes, rivers, and streams.
Lake or Reservoir
Coagulation removes dirt and other particles suspended in water. Alum and other chemicals are added to water to form tiny sticky particles called "floc" which attract the dirt particles. The combined weight of the dirt and the alum (floc) become heavy enough to sink to the bottom during sedimentation.
Sedimentation: The heavy particles (floc) settle to the bottom and the clear water moves to filtration
Storage: Water is placed in a closed tank or reservoir for disinfection to take place. The water then flows through pipes to homes and businesses in the community.
Disinfection: A small amount of chlorine is added or some other disinfection method is used to kill any bacteria or microorganisms that may be in the water.
Filtration: The water passes through filters, some made of layers of sand, gravel, and charcoal that helps remove even smaller particles.
Source: AWWA Drinking Water Week Blue Thumb Kit

The diagram with commentary makes the water treatment process easier to understand.

The heading indicates the topic covered in this section of the report.

2007 SOUTH FLORIDA ENVIRONMENTAL REPORT

The report is dated.

KISSIMMEE RIVER RESTORATION AND UPPER BASIN INITIATIVES

Covering approximately 3,000 square miles, the Kissimmee watershed forms the headwaters of the Kissimmee-Okeechobee-Everglades system. This watershed is comprised of a diverse group of wetland aquatic ecosystems within its Upper Basin—and Lower Basin, the Kissimmee River. The meandering Kissimmee River was channelized to prevent catastrophic flooding and much of the original floodplain was drained. However, there were pronounced impacts on the ecosystem—drastic declines in wintering waterfowl, wading bird, and fish populations and loss of ecosystem functions.

Another Year of Above-Average Rainfall In The Kissimmee Basin Poses Regional Water Management Challenges

During WY2006, hydrologic conditions in the Kissimmee watershed were quite variable, particularly due to extreme seasonal rainfall conditions. There were high levels of rainfall in June 2005, followed by a relatively dry spring and another surge of intense rainfall in October 2005 from Hurricane Wilma. The basin also experienced another year of above-average rainfall during WY2006, primarily due to Hurricane Wilma. The total rainfall during WY2006 in the Upper Basin (53 inches) and in the Lower Basin (49 inches) exceeded historical annual averages by about 3 to 4 inches, respectively. During this water year, discharges from the S-65 water control structure into the Kissimmee River peaked near 9,000 cubic feet per second and, were among the highest recorded in nearly 75 years.

The Next Phase of Kissimmee Basin Construction Was Launched In Water Year 2006

The District and the U.S. Army Corps of Engineers are collaborating in the Kissimmee River Restoration and the Kissimmee River Headwaters Revitalization projects.

Together, these large-scale restoration projects will **(1)** reestablish the river-floodplain system's ecological integrity by reconstructing the river's physical form, **(2)** provide the water storage and regulation

schedule modifications needed to approximate the historical flow characteristics of the Kissimmee River system, and **(3)** increase the quantity and quality of shoreline habitat in lakes Kissimmee, Hatchineha, Tiger, and Cypress for the benefit of fish and wildlife.

The first of four major phases of canal backfilling was completed in early 2001, reclaiming almost 6,000 acres of floodplain habitat. Initiated in June 2006, the second phase of construction will backfill 1.9 miles of C-38 canal, remove three weirs, and excavate some portions of river channel. It is projected that all restoration-related construction will be completed by 2012. In total, this project will restore ecological integrity to approximately 20 square miles of river/floodplain habitat and 44 continuous miles of meandering river channel.

Kissimmee River Restoration Produces Promising Results

A key element of the Kissimmee River Restoration is a comprehensive, multi-phased evaluation program for tracking ecological responses to restoration. To address the goal of ecological integrity, the evaluation program has a broad scope encompassing hydrology, water quality, and major biological communities such as plants, invertebrates, fish, and birds. Although restoration efforts only have been under way for a few years and will continue through 2012, many positive responses to the first phase are already being observed. These responses include increases in dissolved oxygen levels, reductions in accumulated sediments, and increased populations of bass and sunfishes in river channels, as well as increased use of the river and floodplain by various birds. Remarkably, the highest densities of both waterfowl and long-legged wading birds, such as white ibis (*Eudocimus albus*), on the restored floodplain were recorded in 2006, almost two times those observed in 2005 (see figure below). Since completion of Phase I construction in 2001, wading bird densities have exceeded the projected restoration expectation in this area.

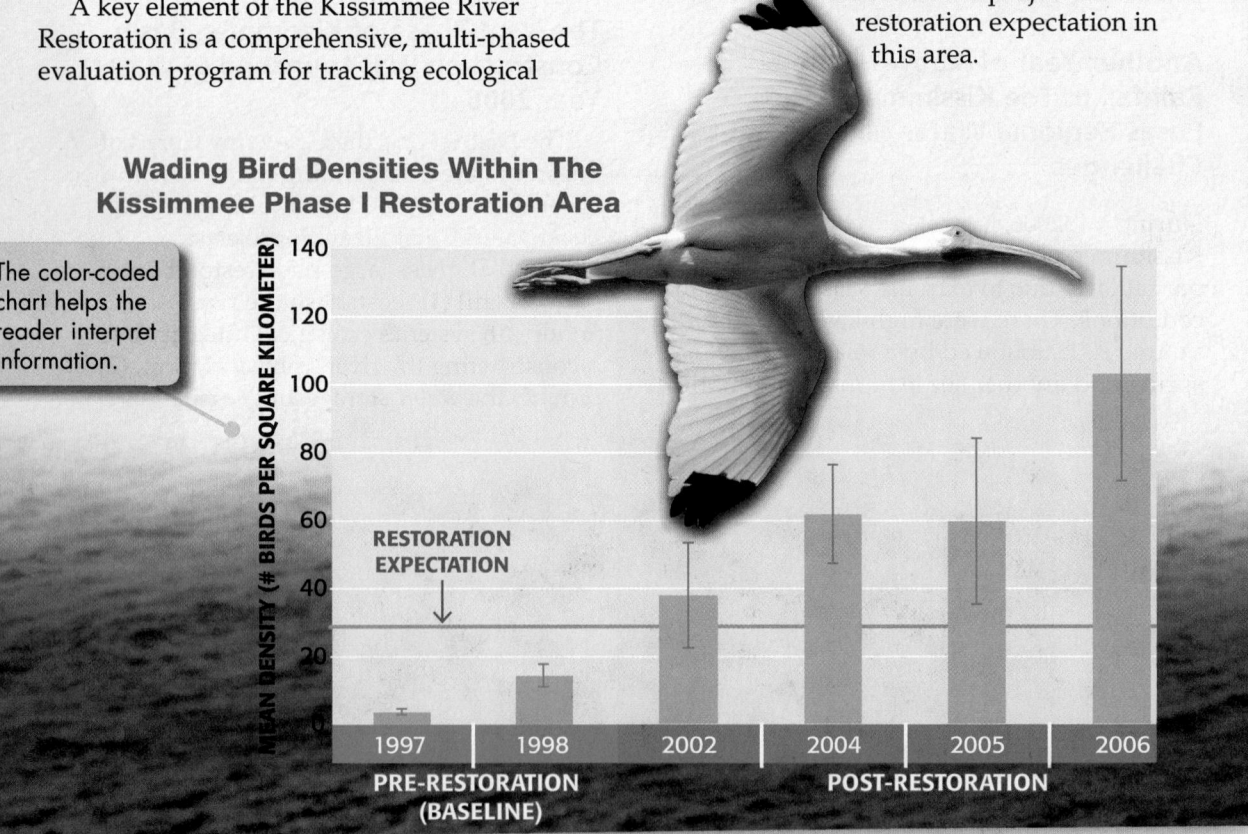

Wading Bird Densities Within The Kissimmee Phase I Restoration Area

The color-coded chart helps the reader interpret information.

Close Reading Activities

Consumer Guide • Government Report

Critical Reading

1. **Key Ideas and Details** **(a)** What public issue or issues does the consumer guide address? **(b)** Cite one fact presented in the guide that a citizen might find reassuring and one that might raise concerns. Explain your choices.
2. **Key Ideas and Details** **(a)** What environmental concern does the project discussed in the report seek to correct? Explain. **(b)** At the time the report was issued, is the project showing clear success? Cite specific details to support your response.
3. **Integration of Knowledge and Ideas** **(a)** Identify two visual elements in each text that clarify or organize information presented verbally. **(b)** For each, explain how the visual element helps you interpret and integrate the information contained in the text.
4. **Content-Area Vocabulary** **(a)** Explain how the Greek prefix *hydro-* ("water") contributes to the meaning of the word *hydrologic.* **(b)** Determine the meaning of the following words that contain this Greek prefix: *hydraulic, hydrate, hydrant,* and *hydroplane.* Use a dictionary to verify the meanings.

Common Core State Standards

Writing

1. Write arguments to support claims in an analysis of substantive topics or texts, using valid reasoning and relevant and sufficient evidence.

1.a. Introduce precise, knowledgeable claim(s) and establish the significance of the claim(s).

10. Write routinely over shorter time frames for a range of tasks and purposes.

Timed Writing

Argument: Persuasive Essay [40 minutes]

Format

In an argument, or **persuasive essay,** you present a well-reasoned position or opinion. In an essay, you must explain and support your argument.

Refer to both the Consumer Guide and the Government Report to write a position statement, a **persuasive essay** in which you state and support an opinion, about the management of **natural resources** both today and in the future. Cite facts, statistics, and quotations from the documents to support your case and persuade readers to agree with your position.

Academic Vocabulary

The prompt asks you to discuss the management of **natural resources.** Focus your response on land, water, and air and ways in which to improve the management of these resources.

5-Minute Planner

Complete these steps before you begin to write:

1. Read the prompt carefully. List key words.
2. Review the texts. Make notes about details pertaining to the management of natural resources. Cite specific details to include in your essay.
3. Draft a rough outline. Note ideas with which to introduce and conclude your essay. **TIP** In your outline, include notes about how to transition smoothly between ideas and evidence to convey meaning clearly and logically.
4. Reread the prompt, and then draft your essay.

Embracing WILDERNESS

Past and Present

In 1846, 1853, and 1857, Henry David Thoreau traveled through vast stretches of Maine wilderness, following ancient canoe routes used by the Wabanaki Indians. In the Maine woods, Thoreau hiked and scaled mountains, writing, "I looked with awe at the ground I trod on...This was the Earth of which we have heard, made out of Chaos and Old Night." These Maine expeditions, far more grueling than Thoreau's walks around Massachusetts, "left such an impression of stern, yet gentle, wildness on [his] memory as will not soon be effaced."

Today, the Thoreau-Wabanaki Trail, as it is now called, is still in use. In the spring of 2005, photographer Bridget Besaw shot a series of photographs featuring people hiking, fishing, canoeing, camping, and climbing on the Thoreau-Wabanaki Trail. The photographs, captioned with quotes from Thoreau's writings, became an exhibit and a book. In her striking images, Besaw shows people rising to the challenges of the wilderness, celebrating its beauty, and standing in awe of its power. Her images suggest that the wilderness remains as important for us today as it was for Thoreau and the Wabanaki before him.

Bridget Besaw / Photographer

Bridget Besaw's award-winning photographs appear in a full spectrum of media: magazines, newspapers, advertisements, documentaries, books, and exhibits. Her current focus is on creating images for use as an advocacy tool for environmental protection.

Give me a WILDNESS whose glance no CIVILIZATION can endure . . .

Henry David Thoreau

Critical Reading

1. **Describe:** Select one of these images and describe the relationship between Besaw's images and Thoreau's words.
2. **(a) Compare and Contrast:** In what ways might a contemporary person's view of the wilderness be both similar to and different from Thoreau's perspective? **(b) Assess:** What circumstances might account for these similarities and differences?

Use this question to focus a class discussion:

3. Bridget Besaw's subject in this series is the north woods of Maine. If your assignment were to celebrate the beauty of nature in photographs, what locale would you select? Explain your choices.

TEXT SET

American Masters

Part 4

IF I FEEL PHYSICALLY AS IF THE TOP OF MY HEAD WERE TAKEN OFF, I KNOW THAT IS POETRY.

— EMILY DICKINSON

In This Section

For more practice analyzing poetry, see numerous pages throughout this textbook, including 82, 125, 256, 312, 428, 636, 643, 708, 722, 874 , 902, 1064, 1072, and 1366.

Defining Poetry

Along with prose and drama, poetry is one of the three major genres, or forms, of literature. Poets usually employ highly charged language and arrange words in lines that form stanzas.

Types of Poetry Most poems fall into one of three categories:

- **Narrative poetry** tells a story and has the same literary elements as works of prose fiction. *Ballads* and *epics* are two types of narrative poem.
- **Dramatic poetry** uses the techniques of drama to present the speech of one or more characters in verse form.
- **Lyric poetry** expresses the thoughts and feelings of a single speaker.

Sound Devices Poets use the innate musical qualities of words to create patterns that emphasize meaning. **Meter,** the regular pattern of beats in a line, is one aspect of poetic sound. Other sound devices are

- **rhyme,** the repetition of sounds at the ends of words (*leaf* and *brief*);
- **consonance,** the repetition of final consonant sounds (*speak* and *break*);
- **assonance,** repetition of similar vowel sounds (*shade* and *ray*).

Alliteration, another sound device, is defined in the chart below.

Images and Figurative Language Images are words and phrases that appeal to the senses. Figurative language is language used imaginatively rather than literally. These, too, are hallmarks of poetry.

Close Read: Poetic Elements

These poetic elements appear in the Model text at right.

Alliteration: repetition of initial identical consonant sounds in accented syllables *Example: "What saint strained so much . . . ?" (Theodore Roethke)*	**Imagery:** language that appeals to the senses, creating word pictures that help to express meaning *Example: "a red wheelbarrow / glazed with rain water" (William Carlos Williams)*
Simile and Metaphor: figures of speech that compare two apparently unlike things. Similes use a connecting word (*like* or *as*); metaphors do not. *Simile: "The child's first step, / as awesome as an earthquake. (Anne Sexton)* *Metaphor: "...the fiery night that's in your eyes..." (Edward Arlington Robinson)*	**Precise Word Choice:** words that carry precise shades of meaning and express tone *Example: "Oh, but it is dirty!—this little filling station . . ." (Elizabeth Bishop)*

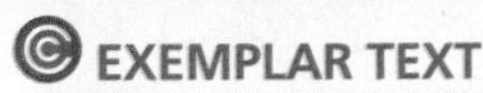

Model

About the Text Billy Collins (born 1941) has written many poems about other art forms. This poem celebrates the musical qualities and artistry of jazz.

"Man Listening to Disc" by Billy Collins

This is not bad—
ambling along 44th Street
with Sonny Rollins for company,
his music flowing through the soft calipers
of these earphones,

as if he were right beside me
on this clear day in March,
the pavement sparkling with sunlight,
pigeons fluttering off the curb,
nodding over a profusion of bread crumbs.

In fact, I would say
my delight at being suffused
with phrases from his saxophone—
some like honey, some like vinegar—
is surpassed only by my gratitude

to Tommy Potter for taking the time
to join us on this breezy afternoon
with his most unwieldy bass
and to the esteemed Arthur Taylor
who is somehow managing to navigate

this crowd with his cumbersome drums.
And I bow deeply to Thelonious Monk
for figuring out a way
to motorize—or whatever—his huge piano
so he could be with us today.

This music is loud yet so confidential
I cannot help feeling even more
like the center of the universe
than usual as I walk along to a rapid
little version of "The Way You Look Tonight,"

and all I can say to my fellow pedestrians,
to the woman in the white sweater,
the man in the tan raincoat and the heavy glasses,
who mistake themselves for the center of the universe—
all I can say is watch your step,

because the five of us, instruments and all,
are about to angle over
to the south side of the street
and then, in our own tightly knit way,
turn the corner at Sixth Avenue.

And if any of you are curious
about where this aggregation,
this whole battery-powered crew,
is headed, let us just say
that the real center of the universe,

the only true point of view,
is full of the hope that he,
the hub of the cosmos
with his hair blown sideways,
will eventually make it all the way downtown.

Alliteration Repetition of initial consonant *p* sounds mimics the popping rhythms of a jazz riff.

Simile The comparisons suggest the changing textures of the sound from sweet and flowing to sharp and jagged.

Imagery Word pictures appeal to the sense of sight. The speaker's head is filled with music, but he sees the world and its people clearly.

Precise Word Choice Precise word choices suggest the speaker's physical movement as he walks, the reality of his listening on a portable CD-player, and the virtuoso precision of the musicians.

Emily Dickinson

(1830–1886)

A unique voice of delicate intensity, Emily Dickinson is invariably named as one of our nation's greatest poets. Yet in her own lifetime, only a small circle of friends and relatives knew of Dickinson's poetic genius.

A Life Apart Born to a prominent family in Amherst, Massachusetts, Dickinson attended Amherst Academy and nearby Mount Holyoke Female Seminary. As a teenager she had an active social life, but over time she became increasingly reclusive, rarely venturing from her home after she was thirty. Devoting most of her time to writing poetry, she saw only the occasional visitor and communicated with friends and family mainly through letters.

Dickinson's Legacy Although she sometimes enclosed poetry in her letters, Dickinson published only a handful of her poems in her lifetime. When she died, her sister Lavinia found over a thousand poems in the drawers of her dresser, neatly tied in bundles known as **fascicles**. Dickinson left instructions that the poems be destroyed, but her family overrode that wish, recognizing that such a valuable legacy should be shared.

◀ This photograph shows the garden view of the Dickinson family homestead in Amherst, Massachusetts. The site is now a museum.

The Johnson Edition Unfortunately, Dickinson's early editors diminished the power of her verse by changing it to be more conventional in language and style. It was not until 1955 that Thomas H. Johnson published an edition of Dickinson's poetry that attempted to present the poems in their original form. With the appearance of the Johnson edition, Dickinson's poetic genius was more fully appreciated, and she is now acknowledged as a visionary who was far ahead of her time.

The Belle of Amherst In the years since the publication of her work, Dickinson has become the subject of plays, novels, and poems that have romanticized her life and celebrated her genius with varying levels of sentimentality and accuracy. In these works, she has been given a public personality that may or may not resemble the truth of who she was. However, in her work itself, the poets who have followed her find no peer.

FIND ECSTASY IN LIFE; THE MERE SENSE OF LIVING IS JOY ENOUGH.

— *Emily Dickinson*

In This Section

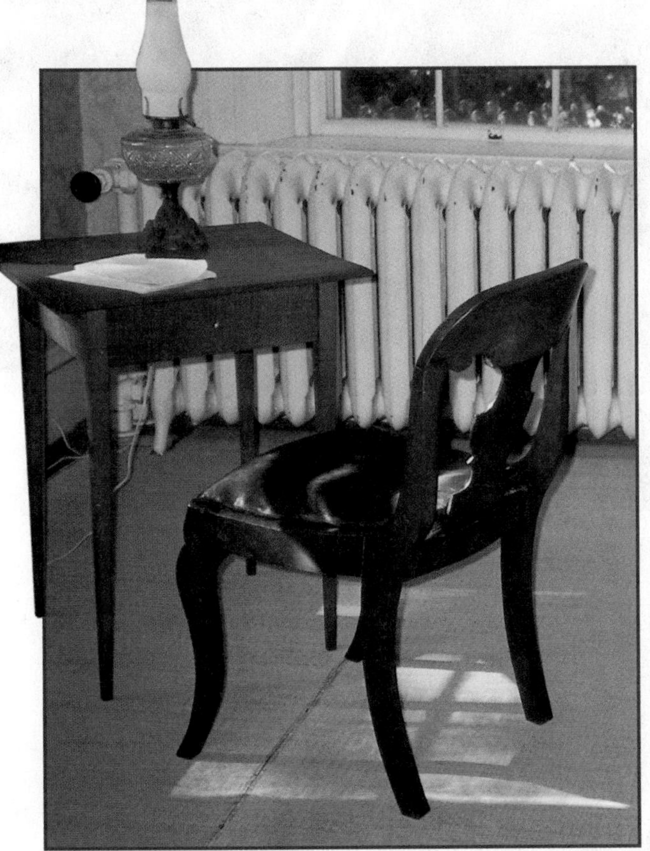

◄ Emily Dickinson's writing desk and chair still stand in her bedroom at the Homestead.

◄ This dress belonged to Emily Dickinson. It is now on display at the Emily Dickinson Homestead Museum.

Dickinson's Style

Uncertain about her abilities, in 1862 Dickinson sent four poems to the influential literary critic Thomas Wentworth Higginson. With the poems she enclosed a card on which she had written her name and the following unsigned letter:

MR. HIGGINSON, *—Are you too deeply occupied to say if my verse is alive? The mind is so near itself it cannot see distinctly, and I have none to ask. Should you think it breathed, and had you the leisure to tell me, I should feel quick gratitude. If I make the mistake, that you dared to tell me would give me sincerer honor toward you. I inclose my name, asking you, if you please, sir, to tell me what is true? That you will not betray me it is needless to ask, since honor is it's own pawn.*

In his response to Dickinson, Higginson recognized Dickinson's talent and encouraged her to keep writing, but he also sought to change her unconventional style. He was especially concerned by her unorthodox use of dashes and capitalization. After Dickinson died, Higginson was one of the early editors of her verse. Along with other early editors, he failed to recognize that Dickinson crafted her poems with great precision and that her eccentric capitalization and punctuation were important elements in her poetry. When Thomas H. Johnson came out with his edition of Dickinson's poetry in 1955, he restored original elements including the dashes and capital letters, so that today we can read the poems as Dickinson meant them to be read.

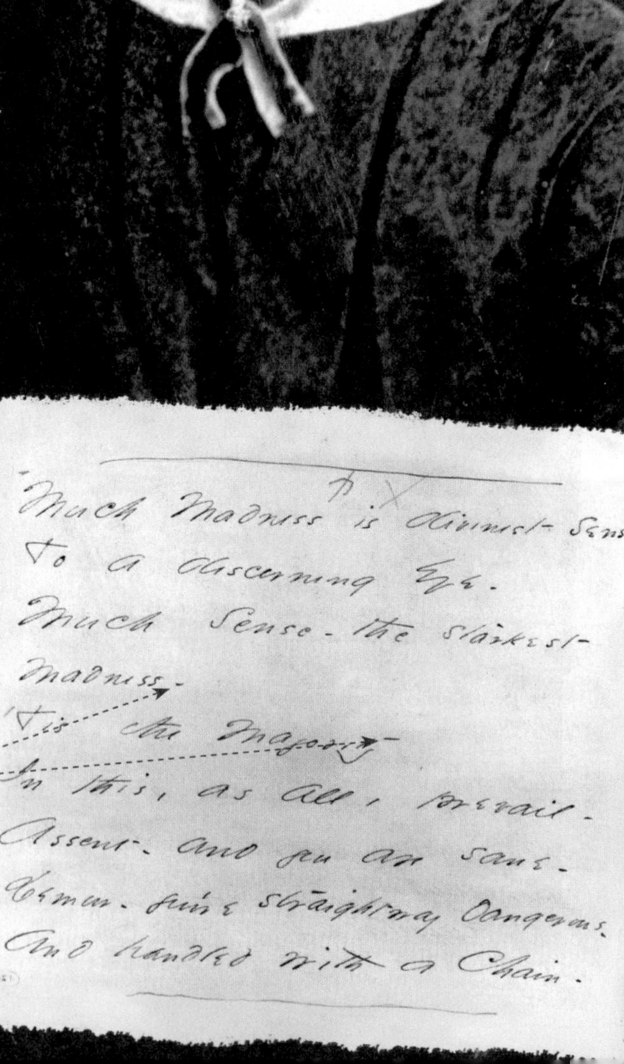

Much Madness is divinest Sense -
To a discerning Eye -
Much Sense - the starkest Madness -
'Tis the Majority
In this, as All, prevail -
Assent - and you are sane -
Demur - you're straightway dangerous -
And handled with a Chain -

This image shows Dickinson's original manuscript of her famous poem "Much Madness is Divinest Sense." Note her unconventional use of dashes throughout the poem.

Building Knowledge and Insight

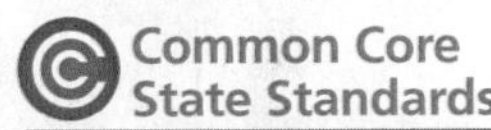

Emily Dickinson's Poetry

Connecting to the Essential Question Emily Dickinson's poems often express a preference for solitude, a value many people would not choose. As you read Dickinson's poems, notice references to the soul and society. This will help as you consider the Essential Question: **What makes American literature American?**

Common Core State Standards

Reading Literature

4. Determine the meaning of words and phrases as they are used in the text, including figurative and connotative meanings; analyze the impact of specific word choices on meaning and tone.

5. Analyze how an author's choices concerning how to structure specific parts of a text contribute to its overall structure and meaning as well as its aesthetic impact.

6. Analyze a case in which grasping a point of view requires distinguishing what is directly stated in a text from what is really meant.

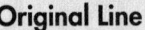

Close Reading Focus

Slant Rhyme; Exact Rhyme; Paradox

Poets use rhyme to stress ideas, make poems musical, convey mood, and unify groups of lines. In **exact rhyme,** two or more words have identical sounds in their final stressed syllables, as in *one/begun*. In **slant rhyme** the final sounds are similar but not identical, as in *one/stone*. Dickinson's frequent use of slant rhyme at points where the reader expects an exact rhyme helps make her poetry surprising:

I've known her—from an ample nation—
Choose One—
Then—close the Valves of her attention—
Like Stone—

Another hallmark of Dickinson's style is her fondness for paradox. A **paradox** is a statement that seems contradictory but actually presents a truth. For example, the statement "The Brain—is wider than the Sky" is a paradox. It seems impossible, but this truth becomes apparent if you consider the brain's capacity to understand. As you read, analyze the effects of rhyme and notice examples of paradox in these poems.

Preparing to Read Complex Texts Dickinson writes with great precision, using carefully chosen words in statements that are dense with meaning. Sometimes she omits words that are expected to be understood. This is called *elliptical phrasing*. To clarify this language, it may be helpful to **reread.** As you reread, mentally fill in words that seem to be missing, and be alert to different possible meanings. Use a chart like the one shown to help as you reread.

Original Line
Water, is taught by thirst.

Possible Meaning
Water is taught **something** by thirst.

Probable Meaning
The concept of water is taught **to us** by thirst.

Vocabulary

The words listed here are key to understanding the texts that follow. Copy the words into your notebook. Which two words are synonyms for *endlessness*?

surmised
eternity
interposed
affliction
ample
finite
infinity

Waiting Outside No. 12, Anonymous, Crane Kalman Gallery

BECAUSE I COULD NOT STOP FOR DEATH

Emily Dickinson

▲ Critical Viewing
In what ways do the details of this painting mirror Dickinson's poem? **ANALYZE**

BACKGROUND *The extent of Emily Dickinson's gift was not generally recognized until 1955, when a new edition of her poems was published under the guidance of Thomas H. Johnson. Previous editors had changed Dickinson's poems to reflect conventional ideas about poetry, but Johnson's edition restored the poet's original versions. For the first time, Dickinson's poetry was printed as she had meant it to be read, and the world experienced the power of her complex mind captured in concrete imagery and simple but forceful language. Dickinson's work is often compared with that of the modern poets, and she is now acknowledged as a visionary who was far ahead of her time.*

Because I could not stop for Death—
He kindly stopped for me—
The Carriage held but just Ourselves—
And Immortality.

We slowly drove—He knew no haste
And I had put away
My labor and my leisure too,
For his Civility—

We passed the School, where Children strove
At Recess—in the Ring—
We passed the Fields of Gazing Grain—
We passed the Setting Sun—

Or rather—He passed Us—
The Dews drew quivering and chill—
For only Gossamer,[1] my Gown—
My Tippet[2]—only Tulle[3]—

We paused before a House that seemed
A Swelling of the Ground—
The Roof was scarcely visible—
The Cornice—in the Ground—

Since then—'tis Centuries—and yet
Feels shorter than the Day
I first **surmised** the Horses' Heads
Were toward **Eternity**—

Reread Clarify the elliptical phrasing in lines 15–16 and restate the poet's meaning.

Vocabulary

surmised (sər mīzd′) *v.* guessed; concluded

eternity (ˈē tʉrn′ə tē) *n.* time without beginning or end

1. **Gossamer** *n.* very thin, soft, filmy cloth.
2. **Tippet** *n.* scarflike garment worn over the shoulders and hanging down in front.
3. **Tulle** (to͞ol) *n.* thin, fine netting used for scarves.

Critical Reading

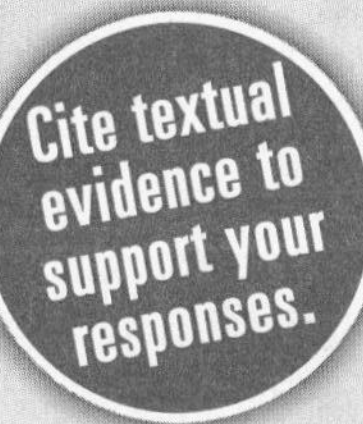
Cite textual evidence to support your responses.

1. **Craft and Structure** **(a)** In the first two lines, what adverb defines Death's actions? **(b) Analyze:** In what sense is this depiction surprising or ironic?
2. **Key Ideas and Details** **(a)** What three scenes does the carriage pass in stanza three? **(b) Interpret:** What meaning do you attribute to these scenes?
3. **Key Ideas and Details** **(a)** How much time passes for the speaker in this poem? **(b) Speculate:** Why do you think the speaker notes that the time "feels shorter than the Day"? **(c) Compare and Contrast:** What does the speaker seem to feel about the experience of death in contrast with life?
4. **Integration of Knowledge and Ideas** **Take a Position:** Do you think this poem has a single meaning or message? Explain your reasoning.

I HEARD A FLY BUZZ— WHEN I DIED

Emily Dickinson

I heard a Fly buzz—when I died—
The Stillness in the Room
Was like the Stillness in the Air—
Between the Heaves of Storm—

The Eyes around—had wrung them dry—
And Breaths were gathering firm
For that last Onset—when the King
Be witnessed—in the Room—

I willed my Keepsakes—Signed away
What portion of me be
Assignable—and then it was
There **interposed** a Fly—

With Blue—uncertain stumbling Buzz—
Between the light—and me—
And then the Windows failed—and then
I could not see to see—

Slant Rhyme What two words form a slant rhyme in the first stanza?

Vocabulary
interposed (in´tər pōzd´) *v.* came between

◄ Critical Viewing
Which details in this painting appropriately illustrate Dickinson's poem? **SUPPORT**

Critical Reading

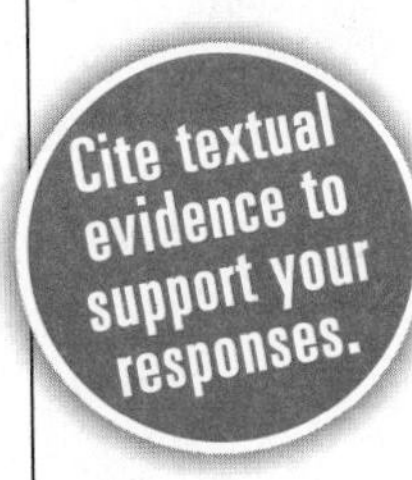
Cite textual evidence to support your responses.

1. **Key Ideas and Details** **(a)** What do the speaker and those in attendance expect to experience when "the last Onset" occurs? **(b)** What happens instead? **(c) Analyze:** In what ways is this turn of events ironic?
2. **Key Ideas and Details** **(a)** What actions has the speaker taken in preparation for death? **(b) Interpret:** Which "portion" of the speaker is "assignable," or able to be willed to others, and which is not?
3. **Craft and Structure** **(a)** In the final stanza, what adjectives does the speaker use to describe the buzzing of the fly? **(b) Draw Conclusions:** What statement about dying is Dickinson making in this poem?
4. **Integration of Knowledge and Ideas** **Speculate:** If you were describing a deathbed scene from the perspective of the dying person, would you mention the buzzing of a fly? Why or why not?

THERE'S A CERTAIN SLANT OF LIGHT

EMILY DICKINSON

There's a certain Slant of light,
Winter Afternoons—
That oppresses, like the Heft
Of Cathedral Tunes—

Heavenly Hurt, it gives us—
We can find no scar,
But internal difference,
Where the Meanings, are—

None may teach it—Any—
'Tis the Seal Despair—
An imperial **affliction**
Sent us of the Air—

When it comes, the Landscape listens—
Shadows—hold their breath—
When it goes, 'tis like the Distance
On the look of Death—

Vocabulary
affliction (ə flik′ shən)
n. anything causing pain or distress

My Life Closed Twice Before Its Close—

Emily Dickinson

My life closed twice before its close—
It yet remains to see
If Immortality unveil
A third event to me.

So huge, so hopeless to conceive
As these that twice befell.
Parting is all we know of heaven.
And all we need of hell.

WORLD LITERATURE CONNECTION

Capturing the Moment

In her poems, Emily Dickinson often seems to capture a moment and hold it still. The tanka is a Japanese form of poetry that also captures the moment. In the original Japanese, tanka is a 31-syllable poem that usually contains at least one distinct pause. This pause is often represented by a dash in English translations. When translated into English, tanka are usually written in five lines, and the syllable count often changes. In Japan, tanka-writing has been popular for more than 1300 years and is still practiced today.

Renowned tanka writers include **Ki Tsurayuki** (died c. 945), an important figure in the Japanese imperial court and a leading poet of his time; **Ono Komachi** (833 – 857), a great beauty whose poems were noted for their passion and energy; and **Priest Jakuren** (1139? – 1202), a Buddhist priest whose poems are filled with beautiful, melancholy imagery.

Tanka

Ki Tsurayuki
translated by Geoffrey Bownas

When I went to visit
The girl I love so much,
That winter night
The river blew so cold
That the plovers
were crying.

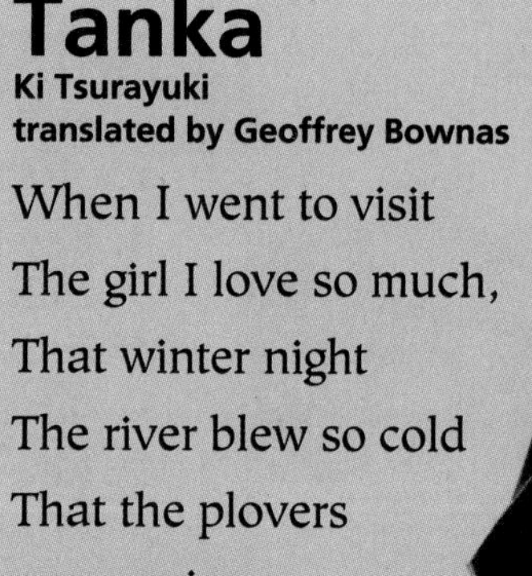

CONNECT TO THE LITERATURE

What similarities do you see in this tanka and the Emily Dickinson poems you have read? In what ways are they different?

The Soul Selects her own Society—

Emily Dickinson

Slant Rhyme What words create slant rhymes in the second stanza?

Vocabulary
ample (am′ pəl) *adj.* large in size; more than enough

The Soul selects her own Society—
Then—shuts the Door—
To her divine Majority—
Present no more—

Unmoved—she notes the Chariots—pausing—
At her low Gate—
Unmoved—an Emperor be kneeling
Upon her Mat—

I've known her—from an **ample** nation—
Choose One—
Then—close the Valves of her attention—
Like Stone—

Critical Reading

Cite textual evidence to support your responses.

1. **Key Ideas and Details (a)** According to the speaker of "There's a certain Slant of light," in what ways does the winter light affect people? **(b) Analyze:** What does this light seem to represent to the speaker?
2. **Key Ideas and Details (a) Interpret:** What is the third event to which the speaker of "My life closed twice before its close—" refers? **(b) Connect:** What is the relationship between the three events?
3. **Key Ideas and Details (a)** In "The Soul selects her own Society," what leaves the soul "unmoved"? **(b) Analyze:** How would you describe the soul's attitude toward the world's attractions?
4. **Key Ideas and Details (a)** What happens after the soul makes her choice? **(b) Assess:** What adjectives would you use to characterize the speaker based on this choice?
5. **Integration of Knowledge and Ideas Relate:** Our culture places a premium on popularity for its own sake. What do Dickinson's poems suggest about other ways to view human relationships?

The Brain— IS WIDER THAN THE SKY—

Emily Dickinson

The Brain—is wider than the Sky—
For—put them side by side—
The one the other will contain
With ease—and You—beside—

The Brain is deeper than the sea—
For—hold them—Blue to Blue—
The one the other will absorb—
As Sponges—Buckets—do—

The Brain is just the weight of God—
For—Heft them—Pound for Pound—
And they will differ—if they do—
As Syllable from Sound—

Paradox What paradoxes do you find in all three stanzas of this poem?

THERE IS A SOLITUDE OF SPACE

EMILY DICKINSON

Vocabulary

finite (fī′ nīt′) *adj.* having measurable or definable limits

infinity (in fin′ i tē) *n.* endless or unlimited space, time, or distance

There is a solitude of space
A solitude of sea
A solitude of death, but these
Society shall be
Compared with that profounder site
That polar privacy
A soul admitted to itself—
Finite Infinity.

Water, is taught by thirst

EMILY DICKINSON

Water, is taught by thirst.
Land—by the Oceans passed.
Transport[1]—by throe[2]—
Peace—by its battles told—
Love, by Memorial Mold[3]—
Birds, by the Snow.

---

1. **Transport** ecstasy; rapture.
2. **throe** spasm or pang of pain.
3. **Memorial Mold** memorial grounds or cemetery.

Critical Reading

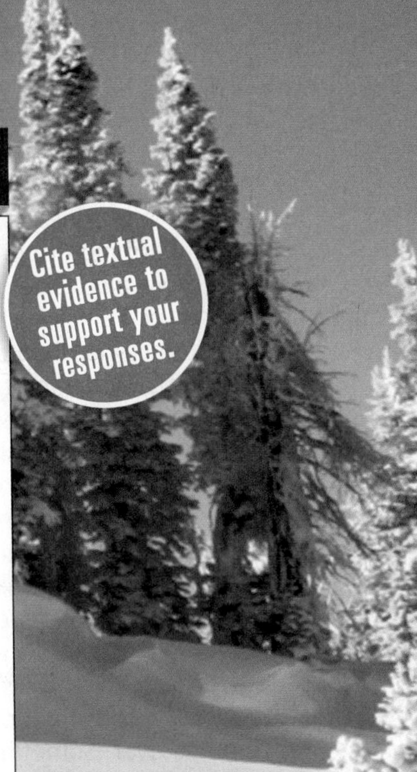
Cite textual evidence to support your responses.

1. **Craft and Structure (a)** What comparisons does the speaker make in "The Brain—is wider than the Sky—"? **(b) Interpret:** What role does a surprising use of scale and size play in these comparisons?
2. **Key Ideas and Details (a)** In "There is a solitude of space," what three things does the speaker compare to "polar privacy"? **(b) Contrast:** How does the solitude of "a soul admitted to itself" differ from other types of solitude?
3. **Craft and Structure (a)** In "Water, is taught by thirst," what is the relationship between each line's first word and the words that follow? **(b) Interpret:** What is the theme or message of this poem?
4. **Integration of Ideas and Knowledge** Is the tension Dickinson sees between individuality and society true for most people, or is it simply the poet's view of her own life? In your response, use at least two of these Essential Question words: *unlimited, limited, social, private, public.* ***[Connecting to the Essential Question: What makes American literature American?]***

Critical Commentary

Reckless Genius

Galway Kinnell

A Pulitzer Prize-winning Poet Pays Tribute to the Belle of Amherst.

Emily Dickinson wrote about the kinds of experience few poets have the daring to explore or the genius to sing. She is one of the most intelligent of poets and also one of the most fearless. If the fearlessness ran out, she had her courage, and after that her heart-stopping recklessness.

More fully than most poets, Dickinson tells how it is to be a human being in a particular moment, in compressed, hard, blazingly vivid poems—which have duende![1] Her greatest seem not sung but forced into being by a craving for a kind of forbidden knowledge of the unknowable.

Being thoroughly conventional, the few literary men of the time who saw Dickinson's poems found nothing very special about them and attributed her experiments in rhyme and rhythm to the naiveté of an untaught lady poet with a tin ear.

Similar figures today think she cannot be considered a major poet because she writes tiny poems. Of course there is nothing inherently minor in smallish poems, and in any case, many of Dickinson's poems are little because she omits the warming-up, preface and situation—and begins where a more discursive poet might be preparing to end. Relative to their small surface, her poems have large inner bulk. And since her themes obsessively reappear, a group of the poems, when read together, sweeps one along inside another's consciousness much as a long poem does.

In my opinion, she could not have accomplished her great work without making two technical innovations.

Dickinson's chosen form requires rhymes, which are scarce in English, at frequent intervals. To avoid using an imprecise word for the sake of rhyme, she made a simple revolutionary innovation: expanding the kinds of echoes that qualify as rhyme. To exact rhyme *(room/broom)* and slant rhyme *(room/brim)* she added assonant rhyme *(room/bruise)*, thus multiplying the supply of rhyme words many times over. Sometimes, perhaps shocked by the rightness of an unrhymable word, she resorted to rhyme by vague resemblance *(freeze/privilege)* or skipped the rhyme entirely.

1. **duende** (dwen´ da) intensity; burning within.

▲ Poet and translator Galway Kinnell is the recipient of the MacArthur Foundation "Genius" Grant and many other honors.

She is one of the most intelligent of poets and also one of the most fearless.

Her other innovation protects the density and dissonance of her poems from the singsong latent in common meter's de dum, de dum, de dum, de dum / de dum, de dum, de dum / de dum, de dum, de dum, de dum / de dum, de dum, de dum. Using wee dashes, she divides lines into clusters of syllables (sometimes a single syllable) that are not unlike William Carlos Williams'[2] "variable feet"—rhythmic units of varying length that are all spoken in approximately the same amount of time.

Saying her poems aloud, we hear two rhythmic systems clashing and twining: the iambic beat, and superimposed upon it, Dickinson's own inner, speech-like, sliding, syncopated rhythm. The latter suggests an urge in her toward some kind of Creeley-like[3] free verse, and it is also what allows her to write in formal verse using all her passion and intelligence.

A poem by Dickinson that I particularly like is the widely admired "I heard a Fly buzz — when I died." Here, through what Keats[4] called "negative capability," Dickinson enters, imaginatively, a dying person and goes with her into death. To write this poem with authority, Dickinson had to "die" a moment in imagination, which may be to say that she had actually to die a little in reality. ... The brilliance of Emily Dickinson's greatest poems may have exacted a high price in emotional stamina and stability, and foreshortened by years that amazingly prolific period (in one year, she wrote 364 poems) when she was writing with her full powers...

To write this poem with authority, Dickinson had to "die" a moment in imagination...

---

2. **William Carlos Williams** (1883-1963) American poet and physician; one of the original Imagist poets, a group whose work stressed simplicity and the use of imagery.
3. **Creeley-like** The work of American poet Robert Creeley (1926-2005) was notable for its very short lines and simple language.
4. **Keats** John Keats (1795-1821), famous British poet whose work centered on the beauty found in ordinary things.

Check Your Comprehension

- According to Kinnell, what does Emily Dickinson do more fully than most other poets?
- What did Dickinson's contemporaries think of her work?
- With what two innovations does Kinnell credit Dickinson?

Close Reading Activities

Emily Dickinson's Poetry

Literary Analysis

1. **Key Ideas and Details Reread** "I heard a Fly buzz—when I died." **(a)** In Dickinson's elliptical style, what words do you understand to be missing from lines 5 and 6? **(b)** Explain your interpretation of the poem's final line.
2. **Key Ideas and Details** Reread "There's a certain Slant of light." What are two possible meanings of the last two lines?
3. **Craft and Structure (a)** Use a chart like the one shown to examine the use of **slant rhyme** and **exact rhyme** in "I heard a Fly buzz—when I died." **(b)** What is the effect of the exact rhyme after so many slant rhymes?

Slant Rhyme	Lines	Exact Rhyme	Lines

4. **Craft and Structure (a)** How do the many slant rhymes in "Because I could not stop for Death" and "The Soul selects her own Society—" reflect the content of those poems? **(b)** How do the many exact rhymes in "The Brain—is wider than the Sky—" suit the content of that poem?
5. **Craft and Structure** Each line of "Water, is taught by thirst" expresses the same basic **paradox.** What is that paradox, and how can it be true?
6. **Craft and Structure (a)** Explain how the first line of "I heard a Fly buzz—when I died" is a paradox. **(b)** Which of the other poems presented here is built around a similar paradox? **(c)** For both poems, what explanation might make the situation possible, even though it seems impossible?
7. **Craft and Structure** A two-word paradox, such as *cruel kindness,* is called an *oxymoron.* Identify an oxymoron in "There is a solitude of space," and explain the apparent contradiction.
8. **Integration of Knowledge and Ideas** What is similar and different about the speaker's attitude toward the self and other people in "My life closed twice before its close—," "The Soul selects her own Society—," and "There is a solitude of space"?
9. **Integration of Knowledge and Ideas (a)** Which poems present human understanding as something boundless or unlimited? **(b)** Which present it as something small and limited? **(c)** How would you define Dickinson's view of the individual self?

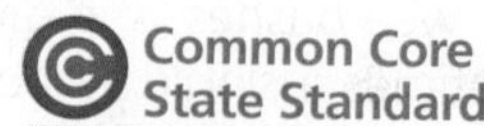

Common Core State Standards

Writing

2. Write explanatory texts to examine and convey complex ideas, concepts, and information clearly and accurately through the effective selection, organization, and analysis of content.

2.b. Develop the topic thoroughly by selecting the most significant quotations or other information and examples appropriate to the audience's knowledge of the topic.

Language

5.a. Interpret figures of speech in context and analyze their role in the text.

Vocabulary Acquisition and Use

Word Analysis: Latin Root *-fin-*

The Latin root *-fin-* means "end." In the word *finite* it combines with the suffix *-ite* to create an adjective meaning "having a definite end." In the word *infinite*, it combines with the suffix *-ite* and the prefix *in-*, meaning "not," to create an adjective meaning "without end." Use your knowledge of the root to explain the meaning of each italicized word below. Make clear how the word's meaning reflects the meaning of the root.

1. Perhaps you can count the stars, but to me they seem *infinite* in number.
2. The musical composition had an introduction, a long middle section, and a grand *finale*.
3. Stop being vague and give me a *definite* answer.
4. The contest began with fifty competitors, but I was one of only three *finalists*.
5. The coarse lad attended a special school, so his manners are now quite *refined*.

Vocabulary: Antonyms

For each numbered item, choose the letter of its antonym, or word that expresses an opposite meaning. Explain your choices.

1. **surmised:** **(a)** concluded **(b)** focused **(c)** asked **(d)** stated
2. **interposed:** **(a)** continuous **(b)** scattered **(c)** between **(d)** above
3. **affliction:** **(a)** poverty **(b)** passion **(c)** warfare **(d)** balm
4. **ample:** **(a)** smooth **(b)** huge **(c)** inhospitable **(d)** insufficient
5. **finite:** **(a)** countless **(b)** meaningless **(c)** worthwhile **(d)** thick
6. **infinity:** **(a)** trivia **(b)** limitation **(c)** confusion **(d)** endlessness

Writing to Sources

Explanatory Text A **blog** is a forum for writing that is part of a web site. Most blogs contain a series of postings on related topics and many have rules for content and posting. Write a blog entry for a poetry site in which you analyze Dickinson's sense of infinity. Plan your work to meet the site's deadlines and other requirements.

Prewriting Reread Dickinson's poems, looking for references to infinity. List details and the poems in which they appear. Study the details, and write a statement in which you interpret patterns. This will serve as your controlling idea.

Drafting Develop your ideas in a logical sequence and support them with details from the poems. Follow correct requirements for citation.

Revising Make sure all the elements of your entry work to develop or support your controlling idea. Delete any stray ideas or unrelated details.

Model: Following Manuscript Requirements

In the "The Brain—is wider than the Sky—," Dickinson suggests that there is no limit to the amount of knowledge the human brain can take in. She compares the brain with the sky, writing, "For—put them side by side— / The one the other will contain."

A short quotation should be set off with quotation marks. If longer than four lines, a quotation should be set off and indented.

Walt Whitman (1819–1892)

In the preface to his first volume of poetry, the 1855 edition of *Leaves of Grass,* Walt Whitman wrote: "The proof of a poet is that his country absorbs him as affectionately as he absorbed it." Whitman's hopes for such proof of his own merit as a poet were deferred: He was harshly denounced for his first volume of poetry, but in the following decades, his poems gained popularity, and he became famous as "the Good Gray Poet" and "the Bard of Democracy." In his later years, Whitman was admired by writers and intellectuals on both sides of the Atlantic. Today, he is widely recognized as one of the greatest and most influential poets the United States has ever produced.

The Poet at Work Whitman was born on Long Island and raised in Brooklyn, New York. His education was not formal, but he read widely, including the works of Sir Walter Scott, Shakespeare, Homer, and Dante. Trained to be a printer, Whitman spent his early years alternating between printing jobs and newspaper writing. When he was twenty-seven, he became the editor of the *Brooklyn Eagle,* a respected newspaper, but the paper fired him in 1848 because of his opposition to slavery. After accepting a position on a paper in New Orleans, Whitman traveled across the country for the first time, observing the diversity of America's landscapes and people.

Whitman soon returned to New York City, however, and in 1850 quit journalism to devote his energy to writing poetry. Impressed by Ralph Waldo Emerson's prophetic description of a new kind of American poet, Whitman had been jotting down ideas and fragments of verse in a notebook for years. His work broke every poetic tradition of rhyme and meter as it celebrated America and the common man. When the first edition of *Leaves of Grass* was published in 1855, critics attacked Whitman's subject matter and abandonment of traditional poetic devices and forms. Noted poet John Greenleaf Whittier hated Whitman's poems so much that he hurled his copy of *Leaves of Grass* into the fireplace. Emerson, on the other hand, responded with great enthusiasm, remarking that the collection was "the most extraordinary piece of wit and wisdom that America has yet contributed."

The Bard of Democracy Though Whitman did publish other works in the course of his career, his life's work proved to be *Leaves of Grass,* which he continually revised, reshaped, and expanded until his death in 1892. The poems in later editions became less confusing, repetitious, and raucous, and more symbolic, expressive, and universal. He viewed the volume as a single long poem that expressed his evolving vision of the world. Using his poetry to convey his passionate belief in democracy, equality, and the spiritual unity of all forms of life, he celebrated the potential of the human spirit. Though Whitman's philosophy grew out of the ideas of the Transcendentalists, his poetry was mainly shaped by his ability to absorb and comprehend everything he observed. From its first appearance as twelve unsigned and untitled poems, *Leaves of Grass* grew to include 383 poems in its final, "death-bed" edition (1892). The collection captures the diversity of the American people and conveys the energy and intensity of all forms of life. In the century since Whitman's death, *Leaves of Grass* has become one of the most highly regarded collections of poetry ever written. There is little doubt that, according to his own definition, Whitman has proven himself as a poet.

"THE UNITED STATES THEMSELVES ARE ESSENTIALLY THE GREATEST POEM."

Building Knowledge and Insight

ANCHOR TEXT

Walt Whitman's Poetry

Connecting to the Essential Question The poetry of Walt Whitman is bold, adventurous, generous, and optimistic. As you read Whitman's poems, note word choices that signal a sense of boldness, adventure, and optimism. This will help as you consider the Essential Question: **What makes American literature American?**

Common Core State Standards

Reading Literature

4. Determine the meaning of words and phrases as they are used in the text, including figurative and connotative meanings; analyze the impact of specific word choices on meaning and tone, including words with multiple meanings or language that is particularly fresh, engaging, or beautiful. *(p. 425)*

5. Analyze how an author's choices concerning how to structure specific parts of a text contribute to its overall structure and meaning as well as its aesthetic impact.

9. Demonstrate knowledge of nineteenth-century foundational works of American literature, including how two or more texts from the same period treat similar themes or topics.

Language

5.a. Interpret figures of speech in context and analyze their role in the text.

Close Reading Focus

Epic Poetry; Style

Traditional **epic poetry** tells a long story about a hero whose adventures embody the values of a nation. Although many of his first readers were shocked by Whitman's *Leaves of Grass*, today the poem is considered a type of *American epic* that expresses national ideals. A true "poet of democracy," Whitman is broadly inclusive in his topics, which range from slavery and the Civil War to romantic love and immortality. Thrumming through these diverse subjects, though, is the constant echo of Whitman's **epic theme**—that all people of all times are connected by their shared experience of life. Whitman's **style** is marked by specific *structural and poetic elements* that contribute to a sense of epic sweep:

- **Free Verse:** Unlike formal verse, which has strict rules, free verse has irregular meter and line length and sounds like natural speech. Although free verse is as old as the Psalms in the Bible, Whitman was the first American poet to use it. It allows him to shape every line and stanza to suit his meaning, rather than fitting his message to a form:

  Do I contradict myself?
  Very well then I contradict myself. . . .

- **Long Lines:** Whitman uses long, sprawling lines for various effects. They may reflect the idea being expressed, capture a broad scene, develop a complex idea, or string together a list of objects:

  I lean and loaf at my ease observing a spear of summer grass.

- **Catalogues,** or **lists:** Whitman's use of catalogues, or lists, of people, objects, or situations, evokes the infinite range of elements that make up human experience. His catalogs create a colorful, inclusive parade of images while simultaneously suggesting that each element is of equal weight and worth. "I am enamor'd," he writes,

  Of men that live among cattle . . .
  Of the builders and steerers of ships and the wielders of axes and mauls, and the drivers of horses...

- **Anaphora,** or the repetition of phrases or sentences with similar structures or meanings: In the preface to *Leaves of Grass*, Whitman writes that America "perceives that the corpse" of old ideas is being moved out of the "house" of the national literature. His use of anaphora in this paragraph creates a tone and rhythm that is almost biblical, even as it delivers a message that is revolutionary:

  ... perceives that it waits a little while in the door ... that it was fittest for its days ... that its action has descended to the stalwart and well-shaped heir who approaches ... and that he shall be fittest for his days.

- **Diction,** or **word choice:** In the example used to illustrate anaphora above, the words *fittest* and *heir* enhance the passage's biblical quality. Whitman chooses other words for their clarity, precision, or sound quality.
- **Onomatopoeia,** or words whose sounds imitate their meanings: Whitman's use of words like *grunting*, *gab*, and *yawp* give his poetry an earthy quality, while also suggesting that his ideas transcend language itself.

Comparing Literary Works As you read, notice Whitman's use of these structural and poetic elements, and compare their effects in different poems. Think about the ideas or emotions individual elements help to emphasize.

Preparing to Read Complex Texts To increase your understanding of Whitman's ideas, **adjust your reading rate.** When a poem's lines are long and dense, read slowly, and when you feel pulled by the rhythm of the verse, read more rapidly. *Read aloud* to hear the flow of Whitman's language and to better appreciate his sprawling lines, evocative sounds, and rhythmic repetitions. As you read, use a chart like the one shown to record passages you read slowly and to note how this strategy enhances your understanding.

Passage
"Song of Myself," lines 10–13

Meaning
Whitman sets aside what he was taught through formal education, but these things cannot be completely forgotten. He will speak openly and freely in the lines to follow.

Vocabulary

The words listed here are key to understanding the texts that follow. Copy the words into your notebook. Which words pertain to the idea of abundant energy?

stirring
abeyance
effuse
bequeath
stealthily
robust

FROM PREFACE TO THE 1855 EDITION OF LEAVES OF GRASS

WALT WHITMAN

BACKGROUND The 1855 edition of was the first edition of Whitman's opus. In the preface to his work, Whitman's prose sings much as his poetry does, full of poetic language, enthusiasm, and energy.

America does not repel the past or what it has produced under its forms or amid other politics or the idea of castes or the old religions. . . . accepts the lesson with calmness . . . is not so impatient as has been supposed that the slough still sticks to opinions and manners and literature while the life which served its requirements has passed into the new life of the new forms . . . perceives that the corpse is slowly borne from the eating and sleeping rooms of the house . . . perceives that it waits a little while in the door . . . that it was fittest for its days . . . that its action has descended to the stalwart and well-shaped heir who approaches . . . and that he shall be fittest for his days.

The Americans of all nations at any time upon the earth have probably the fullest poetical nature. The United States themselves are essentially the greatest poem. In the history of the earth hitherto the largest and most **stirring** appear tame and orderly to their ampler largeness and stir. Here at last is something in the doings of man that corresponds with the broadcast doings of the day and night. Here is not merely a nation but a teeming nation of nations. Here is action untied from strings necessarily blind to particulars and details magnificently moving in vast masses. Here is the hospitality which forever indicates heroes. . . . Here are the roughs and beards and space and ruggedness and nonchalance that the soul loves. Here the performance disdaining the trivial unapproached in the tremendous audacity of its crowds and groupings and the push of its perspective spreads with crampless and flowing breadth and showers its prolific and splendid extravagance. One sees it must indeed own the riches of the summer and winter, and need never be bankrupt while corn grows from the ground or the orchards drop apples or the bays contain fish or men beget children upon women. . . .

Vocabulary
stirring (stur′ iŋ) *adj.* busy; full of energy

Epic Theme What portrait of America does Whitman paint in his references to "roughs and beards and space and ruggedness"?

Critical Reading

1. **Key Ideas and Details (a)** What subject does Whitman address in the first paragraph? **(b) Interpret:** What does Whitman mean when he says "the corpse is slowly borne from the eating and sleeping rooms of the house"?
2. **Key Ideas and Details (a)** According to Whitman, what makes America different from all other nations? **(b) Interpret:** What is the meaning of Whitman's notion that the United States is "a teeming nation of nations"?
3. **Key Ideas and Details (a)** According to Whitman, what is the greatest of all poems? **(b) Analyze:** Based on this statement, how is Whitman redefining the idea of a poem?

Cite textual evidence to support your responses.

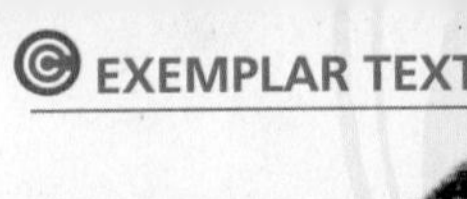

from Song of Myself

WALT WHITMAN

1

I celebrate myself, and sing myself,
And what I assume you shall assume,
For every atom belonging to me as good belongs to you.

I loaf and invite my soul,
I lean and loaf at my ease observing a spear of summer grass.

My tongue, every atom of my blood, formed from this soil, this air,
Born here of parents born here from parents the same, and their parents the same,
I, now thirty-seven years old in perfect health begin,
Hoping to cease not till death.

Creeds and schools in **abeyance**,
Retiring back a while sufficed at what they are, but never forgotten,
I harbor for good or bad, I permit to speak at every hazard,
Nature without check with original energy.

Vocabulary
abeyance (ə bā´ əns) *n.* temporary suspension

6

A child said *What is the grass?* fetching it to me with full hands,
How could I answer the child? I do not know what it is any more than he.

I guess it must be the flag of my disposition, out of hopeful
green stuff woven.

Or I guess it is the handkerchief of the Lord,
A scented gift and remembrancer[1] designedly dropped,
Bearing the owner's name someway in the corners, that we may see
and remark, and say *Whose?*

. . .

What do you think has become of the young and old men?
And what do you think has become of the women and children?

They are alive and well somewhere,
The smallest sprout shows there is really no death,
And if ever there was it led forward life, and does not wait at the
end to arrest it,
And ceas'd the moment life appear'd.
All goes onward and outward, nothing collapses,
And to die is different from what anyone supposed, and luckier.

9

The big doors of the country barn stand open and ready,
The dried grass of the harvest-time loads the slow-drawn wagon.
The clear light plays on the brown gray and green intertinged,
The armfuls are pack'd to the sagging mow.

I am there, I help, I came stretch'd atop of the load,
I felt its soft jolts, one leg reclined on the other,
I jump from the crossbeams and seize the clover and timothy,
And roll head over heels and tangle my hair full of wisps.

14

The wild gander leads his flock through the cool night,
Ya-honk he says, and sounds it down to me like an invitation,
The pert may suppose it meaningless, but I listening close,
Find its purpose and place up there toward the wintry sky.

The sharp-hoof'd moose of the north, the cat on the house-sill,
the chickadee, the prairie dog,
The litter of the grunting sow as they tug at her teats,
The brood of the turkey hen and she with her half-spread wings,
I see in them and myself the same old law.

The press of my foot to the earth springs a hundred affections,
They scorn the best I can do to relate them.

1. remembrancer reminder.

◀ Critical Viewing

This drawing is based on a photograph of Whitman as a young man. What can you conclude about his attitudes and personality from this picture? How are they reflected in this poem? **INFER; SUPPORT**

Epic Theme and Diction

What attitude toward the cycle of life is suggested by Whitman's use of the words "onward," "outward," and "luckier"? Explain.

Comprehension

What aspects of life does the poet celebrate in this poem?

I am enamor'd of growing outdoors,
Of men that live among cattle or taste of the ocean or woods,
Of the builders and steerers of ships and the wielders of axes and mauls, and the drivers of horses,
I can eat and sleep with them week in and week out.

What is commonest, cheapest, nearest, easiest, is Me,
Me going in for my chances, spending for vast returns,
Adorning myself to bestow myself on the first that will take me,
Not asking the sky to come down to my good will,
Scattering it freely forever.

Epic Theme and Anaphora

How does Whitman's use of anaphora in Section 17 emphasize the ideas he is expressing?

17

These are really the thoughts of all men in all ages and lands, they are not original with me,
If they are not yours as much as mine they are nothing, or next to nothing,
If they are not the riddle and the untying of the riddle they are nothing,
If they are not just as close as they are distant they are nothing.
This is the grass that grows wherever the land is and the water is,
This is the common air that bathes the globe.

51

The past and present wilt—I have fill'd them, emptied them,
And proceed to fill my next fold of the future.

Listener up there! what have you to confide to me?
Look in my face while I snuff the sidle of evening,[2]
(Talk honestly, no one else hears you, and I stay only a minute longer.)

Do I contradict myself?
Very well then I contradict myself,
(I am large, I contain multitudes.)
I concentrate toward them that are nigh,[3] I wait on the door-slab.

Who has done his day's work? who will soonest be through with his supper?
Who wishes to walk with me?

Will you speak before I am gone? will you prove already too late?

---

2. **snuff . . . evening** put out the hesitant last light of day, which is moving sideways across the sky.
3. **nigh** near.

52

The spotted hawk swoops by and accuses me, he complains of
my gab and my loitering.

I too am not a bit tamed, I too am untranslatable,
I sound my barbaric yawp over the roofs of the world.
The last scud[4] of day holds back for me,
It flings my likeness after the rest and true as any on the
shadow'd wilds,
It coaxes me to the vapor and the dusk.

I depart as air, I shake my white locks at the runaway sun,
I effuse my flesh in eddies, and drift it in lacy jags.

I bequeath myself to the dirt to grow from the grass I love,

If you want me again look for me under your boot soles.

You will hardly know who I am or what I mean,
But I shall be good health to you nevertheless,
And filter and fiber your blood.

Failing to fetch me at first keep encouraged,
Missing me one place search another,
I stop somewhere waiting for you.

4. **scud** low, dark, wind-driven clouds.

Vocabulary

effuse (e fyo͞oz′) *v.* to pour out

bequeath (bē kwēth′) *v.* to hand down or pass on

Critical Reading

Cite textual evidence to support your responses.

1. **Key Ideas and Details** **(a)** From what does Whitman say his tongue and blood are formed? **(b) Analyze:** How does he view his relationship with nature? **(c) Analyze:** How does he view his relationship with other people?
2. **Key Ideas and Details** **(a)** In Section 17, what natural images does Whitman use to communicate the idea that his thoughts belong to everyone? **(b) Generalize:** Which elements of these images convey a belief in the spiritual unity of all natural forms?
3. **Key Ideas and Details** **(a)** In Section 52, where does the speaker say readers can find him? **(b) Infer:** What does he suggest will happen to his spirit and message after he is gone?
4. **Integration of Knowledge and Ideas** **Evaluate:** In Section 52, Whitman proudly characterizes his poetry as "barbaric yawp." What terms would you use to evaluate his work?

The Lawrence Tree, 1929, Georgia O'Keeffe, Wadsworth Atheneum, Hartford

When I Heard the Learn'd Astronomer

Walt Whitman

▲ Critical Viewing
In what ways does the artist's viewpoint in this painting compare with Whitman's in this poem? **CONNECT**

When I heard the learn'd astronomer,
When the proofs, the figures, were ranged in columns before me,
When I was shown the charts and diagrams, to add, divide and
    measure them,
When I sitting heard the astronomer where he lectured with
    much applause in the lecture room,
How soon unaccountable I became tired and sick,
Till rising and gliding out I wander'd off by myself,
In the mystical moist night air, and from time to time,
Look'd up in perfect silence at the stars.

BY THE BIVOUAC'S Fitful Flame

WALT WHITMAN

By the bivouac's[1] fitful flame,
A procession winding around me, solemn and sweet and slow—but first I note,
The tents of the sleeping army, the fields' and woods' dim outline,
The darkness lit by spots of kindled fire, the silence,
Like a phantom far or near an occasional figure moving,
The shrubs and trees, (as I lift my eyes they seem to be **stealthily** watching me,)
While wind in procession thoughts, O tender and wondrous thoughts,
Of life and death, of home and the past and loved, and of those that are far away;
A solemn and slow procession there as I sit on the ground,
By the bivouac's fitful flame.

Vocabulary
stealthily (stelth′ ə lē) *adv.* slyly or secretively

1. **bivouac** (biv′ wak′) *n.* night guard to prevent surprise attacks.

Critical Reading

Cite textual evidence to support your responses.

1. **Key Ideas and Details (a)** In "When I Heard the Learn'd Astronomer," what does the speaker do in reaction to the lecture? **(b) Connect:** What do his actions reveal about his character?
2. **Key Ideas and Details (a) Compare and Contrast:** In what ways does the "perfect silence" in the last line contrast with the lecture? **(b) Draw Conclusions:** What is the speaker saying about the value of science versus a personal experience with nature?
3. **Key Ideas and Details (a)** In lines 3–4 of "By the Bivouac's Fitful Flame," what sights does the speaker look upon? **(b) Infer:** What is the procession to which he refers in line 2?
4. **Key Ideas and Details (a)** Where does the speaker's mind go as he gazes upon the scene before him? **(b) Analyze:** Is the procession he refers to in line 9 the same one referred to earlier? Explain.
5. **Integration of Knowledge and Ideas Make a Judgment:** Whitman is known as a poet who celebrated life. Are these poems celebratory? If so, of what?

Haystack, 1938, Thomas Hart Benton, Museum of Fine Arts, Houston, Texas, USA, © DACS /Gift of Mr. Frank J. Hevrdejs / The Bridgeman Art Library International/©T.H. Benton and R.P. Benton Testamentary Trusts/Licensed by VAGA, New York, NY

I HEAR AMERICA SINGING

Walt Whitman

I hear America singing, the varied carols I hear,
Those of mechanics, each one singing his as it should be blithe and strong,
The carpenter singing his as he measures his plank or beam,
The mason singing his as he makes ready for work, or leaves off work,
The boatman singing what belongs to him in his boat, the deckhand singing on the steamboat deck,
The shoemaker singing as he sits on his bench, the hatter[1] singing as he stands,
The wood-cutter's song, the ploughboy's on his way in the morning, or at noon intermission or at sundown,
The delicious singing of the mother, or of the young wi
or of the girl sewing or washing,
Each singing what belongs to him or he
The day what belongs to the day—at ni
fellows, robust, friendly,
Singing with open mouths their strong m

Vocabulary
robust (rō bust′) *adj.* strong and healthy; full of life

1. **hatter** person who makes, sells, or cleans hats.

◀ **Critical Viewing** In this painting of farmwork, does the qualities in common with Whitman's style? Explain. **COMPARE**

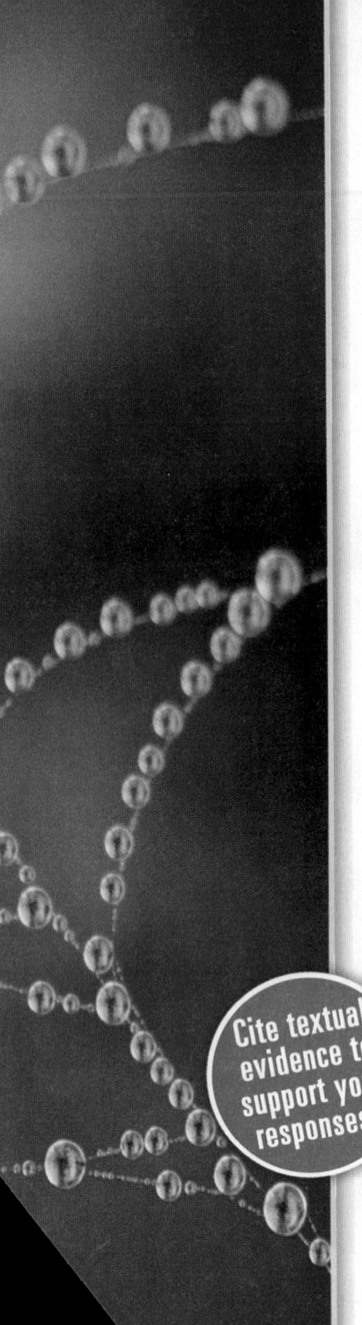
Cite textual evidence to support your responses.

A Noiseless Patient Spider

Walt Whitman

A noiseless patient spider,
I mark'd where on a little promontory it stood isolated,
Mark'd how to explore the vacant vast surrounding,
It launch'd forth filament, filament, filament, out of itself,
Ever unreeling them, ever tirelessly speeding them.

And you O my soul where you stand,
Surrounded, detached, in measureless oceans of space,
Ceaselessly musing, venturing, throwing, seeking the spheres
to connect them,
Till the bridge you will need be form'd, till the ductile anchor hold,
Till the gossamer thread you fling catch somewhere, O my soul.

Critical Reading

1. **Key Ideas and Details** **(a)** In "I Hear America Singing," what occupations does Whitman attribute to Americans? **(b) Draw Conclusions:** What does his catalog of occupations suggest about his vision of America?
2. **Key Ideas and Details** **(a)** What does Whitman describe the laborers doing at night? **(b) Analyze:** Why do you think the poem ends as it does?
3. **Key Ideas and Details** **(a)** In line three of "A Noiseless Patient Spider," what surrounds the spider? **(b) Interpret:** In line 7, what are the "measureless oceans of space" with which the speaker's soul is surrounded?
4. **Craft and Structure** **(a)** What verbs does Whitman use to describe the spider's actions? **(b)** What verbs does he use to describe the activities of his soul? **(c) Compare and Contrast:** How are the two explorations the same, and how are they different?
5. **Integration of Knowledge and ideas** What characteristics of America and the American spirit can you find in all the poems presented here? Use at least two of these Essential Question words in your response: *perseverance, bravery, spirit, unknown.* ***[Connecting to the Essential Question: What makes American literature American?]***

Critical Commentary

America's Epic
James E. Miller, Jr.

James E. Miller, Jr. is the Helen A. Regenstein Professor Emeritus of English at the University of Chicago. He is the author of two important critical studies of Walt Whitman and another focusing on T. S. Eliot.

Did Whitman write the epic for modern America? There have been many who contend that *Leaves of Grass* is merely a collection of lyric poetry, some good, some bad, all of it of a peculiarly personal nature that disqualifies its attitudes and philosophy generally. There have been others who have defended Whitman's book as the embodiment of the American reality and ideal, as superb fulfillment of all the genuine requirements of the national epic.

What did Whitman believe? The answer may be found in a number of prose works, beginning with the 1855 Preface. It is clear in this early work that Whitman desired *Leaves of Grass* to bear a unique relationship with America: "Here [in America] at last is something in the doings of man that corresponds with the broadcast doings of the day and night… It awaits the gigantic and generous treatment worthy of it." It is generally recognized that the entire Preface is a veiled account of Whitman's concept of his own role as a poet. Certainly he includes himself in the category when he asserts: "The poets of the kosmos advance through all interpositions and coverings and turmoils and stratagems to first principles." Although Whitman does not use the term, it is clear throughout the 1855 Preface that he believes his book to have the basic nature and general scope of the traditional national epic.

In *Democratic Vistas*, in the same indirect manner, Whitman again reveals his concept of the nature of his poetry: "Never was anything more wanted than, to-day, and here in the States, the poet of the modern is wanted, or the great literatus of the modern. At all times, perhaps, the central point in any nation, and that whence it is itself really sway'd the most and whence it sways others, is its national literature, especially its archetypal poems" (V, 54–55). Whitman was by this time (1871) acutely aware that America had not accepted his book as he had planned and hoped. There can be little doubt that he conceived *Leaves of Grass* as an "archetypal" poem produced and offered to America at its "central point"—a book "sway'd" by the nation and written to sway others. Such a work as Whitman calls for in *Democratic Vistas* is surely the epic of America. And, basically, it is his own work which he desires to be recognized as such.

Key Ideas and Details What question about Whitman's work does Miller pose? According to Miller, how does Whitman himself answer that question? What evidence does Miller provide to support this answer?

Close Reading Activities

Walt Whitman's Poetry

Literary Analysis

1. **Key Ideas and Details** Explain how you **adjusted your reading rate** as you read "Song of Myself." **(a)** Which stanzas or sections did you read more slowly? Why? **(b)** What new insight did slower reading help you gain?
2. **Key Ideas and Details** **(a)** What reading rate did you use to read "I Hear America Singing"? Why? **(b)** Did your reading rate change over the course of the poem? Explain.
3. **Craft and Structure** How does Whitman's use of **catalog,** or **list,** in the following line from the preface to *Leaves of Grass* help convey his **epic theme?**

   Here are the roughs and beards and space and ruggedness and nonchalance that the soul loves.
4. **Craft and Structure** **(a)** Note two ways in which his use of **free verse** in "Song of Myself" allows Whitman to express his ideas more effectively than a formal structure would. **(b)** Cite a passage that you think is a strong example of the relationship between free verse and meaning. Explain your choice.
5. **Craft and Structure** **(a)** In Section 51 of "Song of Myself," what does the speaker ask of the listener? **(b)** In line 5 of that section, do you think Whitman means exactly what he says? Why or why not? **(c)** In what ways does the **long line** enhance the poet's meaning?
6. **Craft and Structure** How does the use of **anaphora** in lines 1–4 of "When I Heard the Learn'd Astronomer" reinforce the speaker's idea of the astronomer?
7. **Craft and Structure** Note two examples of **word choice,** or **diction,** that add to the dreamlike quality of "By the Bivouac's Fitful Flame." Explain your choices.
8. **Comparing Literary Works** **(a)** Use a chart like the one shown to analyze and compare Whitman's epic theme of shared human experience in "Song of Myself" and at least two other poems in this grouping. **(b)** Based on your analysis, explain your understanding of Whitman's overall message or view of life.

Title	What Is Shared	Shared by Whom
"Song of Myself"	Atom	All, shared by everyone

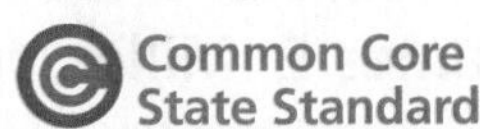

Common Core State Standards

Writing

3.d. Use precise words and phrases, telling details, and sensory language to convey a vivid picture of the experiences, events, setting, and/or characters. *(p. 439)*

4. Produce clear and coherent writing in which the development, organization, and style are appropriate to task, purpose, and audience. *(p. 439)*

Language

4. Determine or clarify the meaning of unknown and multiple-meaning words and phrases based on *grades 11–12 reading and content,* choosing flexibly from a range of strategies. *(p. 439)*

4.d. Verify the preliminary determination of the meaning of a word or phrase. *(p. 439)*

Vocabulary Acquisition and Use

Multiple Meaning Words

Many words in English have more than one meaning. Usually, the meaning of a word changes according to its part of speech. For example, the word *bow* as a noun refers to a tied ribbon, to the implement that is drawn across a violin's strings, or to the front section of a boat. As a verb, it means "to bend one's head or body as a sign of respect." Explain the multiple meanings of each of the numbered words below. Use a dictionary to check your work.

1. stirring **3.** figures

2. note **4.** check

Then, choose two of the words, and use more than one meaning of both words in a brief paragraph describing the daily work of different kinds of Americans.

Vocabulary: Denotations

Denotations are the literal meanings of words, as opposed to their *connotative* meanings, which are the emotional associations the words bring forth. Answer each of the following questions. Then, explain your answers.

1. If a judge hands down a ruling in *abeyance* of a particular law, is she enforcing that law?

2. Does light that *effuses* from a lamp spread softly or shine in a sharply focused beam?

3. If you *bequeath* your bedroom to your little sister, could she use it?

4. If someone gave you a *robust* greeting, would you be likely to hear it?

5. Does a person typically move *stealthily* through a library?

6. If a town is *stirring,* is it peaceful and quiet?

Writing to Sources

Poem Write a poem to be read aloud as part of a group poetry reading honoring Walt Whitman. In addition to the use of free verse, choose several key elements of Whitman's unique style—his use of long lines, catalogs, anaphora, and onomatopoeia—and use them to enhance your own individual voice. Your poem should be your own while also demonstrating your understanding of Whitman's literary achievement.

Prewriting Decide on a "Whitmanesque" topic, and review the traits of free verse. Use a format like the one shown here to list or diagram sensory details and images related to your topic.

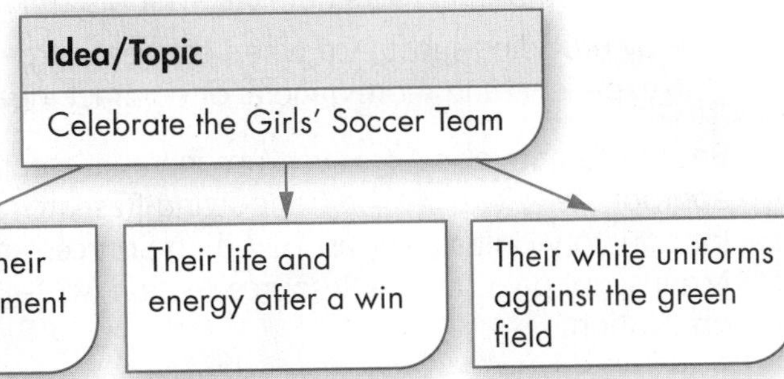

Drafting As you write, let your meaning determine the lengths of lines and stanzas. Be aware of your *tone*, or attitude toward your subject, and make sure your *diction,* or word choice, reflects that tone. Choose vivid words that contribute to the mood you want to evoke.

Revising Read your draft aloud. Listen for natural rhythms of speech rather than formal grammatical structures. Make any changes necessary to maintain natural rhythms and to enhance your meaning. If your word choices could be more precise, use a dictionary or thesaurus to select more effective language.

Write a Reflective Essay

Reflective Essay Ralph Waldo Emerson and Henry David Thoreau wrote essays that do not just report on events but also interpret them and consider their deeper meanings. Their reflective essays make connections between each writer's personal life experiences and the larger world. Follow the steps outlined in this workshop to write your own reflective essay.

Assignment Write a reflective essay in which you explore a personal experience or an event and reflect on its deeper meaning.

What to Include Your reflective essay should have these elements:

- You, the writer, as the main speaker or character
- Your personal feelings and thoughts about a clearly defined topic
- Insights presented in a logical organization
- A balanced approach that presents incidents from your life and connects them to more general or abstract ideas
- Illlustration of your important beliefs
- An appropriate and consistent tone

To preview the criteria on which your reflective essay may be assessed, see the rubric on page 447.

Common Core State Standards

Writing

2. Write informative texts to examine and convey complex ideas, concepts, and information clearly and accurately through the effective selection, organization, and analysis of content.

2.b. Develop the topic thoroughly by selecting the most significant and relevant facts, extended definitions, concrete details, quotations, or other information and examples appropriate to the audience's knowledge of the topic.

Focus on Research

Research can add more depth to reflective essays in the following ways:

- by providing a factual basis for your thinking
- by adding evidence to support your opinions
- by contributing more detail to your discussion
- by providing substance when connecting personal thoughts and experiences to more general or abstract ideas

Be sure to note all sources you use in your research, and credit appropriately. Refer to the Conducting Research pages in the Introductory Unit as well as the Citing Sources and Preparing Manuscript pages in the Resource section (R21–R23) for information on citation.

Prewriting and Planning

Choosing Your Topic

To choose an event for your essay, use one of these strategies:

- **Listing** List the activities that fill your week, paying attention to any incidents that made you pause or that seemed special. Choose one to explore in your essay.
- **Freewriting** Consider the important moments in your life, such as meeting your best friend, or making a tough choice. As you freewrite, ask yourself how this moment changed your life. Choose one moment to explore further.

Narrowing Your Topic

Write a topic sentence. Narrow your focus by identifying a lesson you learned, or the instant you suddenly saw yourself or the world in a new light. Write one sentence about the event and the lesson it taught you.

Model: Expressing an Insight

When I saw how long it took me to walk home, (Event) I marveled at my ancestors who had cleared the land by themselves. (Insight)

Gathering Details

Make connections. Consider how your experience relates to themes in the world at large. Organize your thoughts in a diagram like the one shown below. You might also want to do some research to strengthen your knowledge about your subject. Talk with friends and family, or use the library or the Internet to gather details about past events or issues that relate to your personal experience.

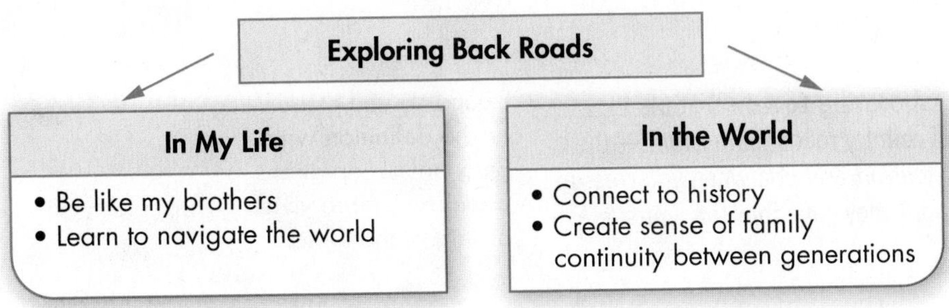

Exploring Back Roads
In My Life
• Be like my brothers
• Learn to navigate the world
In the World
• Connect to history
• Create sense of family continuity between generations

Drafting

Shaping Your Writing

Organize your ideas. Choose an organization that places the incident you are describing in a larger context. The format shown here is one effective way to build a reflective essay.

Model: Organizing Your Essay

Identify an experience from your life.

▼

Describe thoughts or feelings related to the event.

▼

Compare your experiences with other related events.

▼

End with a lesson learned from reflecting on the event.

Common Core State Standards

Writing

2.a. Organize complex ideas, concepts, and information so that each new element builds on that which precedes it to create a unified whole.

2.b. Develop the topic thoroughly by selecting the most significant and relevant facts, extended definitions, concrete details, quotations, or other information and examples appropriate to the audience's knowledge of the topic.

Start with a strong lead. A simple, compelling lead, or opening sentence, provides enough information to activate readers' curiosity and make them want to read your essay. Notice how both of these leads raise questions in your mind:

- *Whenever I hear the song "Memory," I burst into laughter.*
- *My sister refuses to wear the color purple.*

Providing Elaboration

Use the SEE technique. The step-by-step approach of the SEE method can help you add details and develop your ideas. This is what the initials mean:

S **Statement:** Write a sentence to express a main idea.

E **Extension:** Restate or develop the main idea.

E **Elaboration:** Provide further information that amplifies or expands on the main idea.

Be generous as you extend and elaborate. Include sensory details, images, and personal thoughts that will make your writing vivid and interesting.

Model: Extending and Elaborating to Add Details

[*Statement*] They are small country roads [*Extension*] —the ones that change color [*Extension*] and ride when you cross a simple parish line. [*Extension*] They have four-ton limits . . .

Extending and elaborating on the definition with personal observations provides a more vivid picture of the topic.

Writers on Writing

Gretel Ehrlich On Using Layers of Meaning

Gretel Ehrlich is the author of "Inspired by Nature" (p. 222).

These are the closing paragraphs of the title essay of my book *The Solace of Open Spaces*. Here, I stepped back from the details in the essay—those of anecdote and description—to contemplate the larger meaning of "space" and the way it shapes our minds and our experience of the world—the "internal weather" of our lives.

"Writing is an act of seeing through to the other side of our lives, then coming back and putting an expression of that otherness on the page."

—Gretel Ehrlich

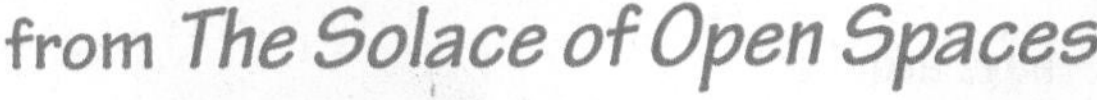

from *The Solace of Open Spaces*

At night, by moonlight, the land is whittled to slivers—a ridge, a river, a strip of grassland stretching to the mountains, then the huge sky. One morning a full moon was setting in the west just as the sun was rising. I felt precariously balanced between the two as I loped across a meadow. For a moment, I could believe that the stars, which were still visible, work like cooper's bands, holding together everything above Wyoming.

Space has a spiritual equivalent and can heal what is divided and burdensome in us. My grandchildren will probably use space shuttles for a honeymoon trip or to recover from heart attacks, but closer to home we might also learn how to carry space inside ourselves in the effortless way we carry our skins. Space represents sanity, not a life purified or dull, or "spaced out," but one that might accommodate intelligently any idea or situation.

In this paragraph, I turn the concept of "space" in four directions: as a spiritual guide, as a healer of physical maladies, as an actual component of our body's makeup, and as a state of mind.

From the clayey soil of northern Wyoming is mined bentonite, which is used as a filler in candy, gum, and lipstick. We Americans are great on fillers, as if what we have, what we are, is not enough. We have a cultural tendency toward denial, but, being affluent, we strangle ourselves with what we can buy. . . . We fill up space as if it were a pie shell, with things whose opacity further obstructs our ability to see what is already there.

Here I take an actual geological substance—bentonite, which is a kind of clay—and use it metaphorically: to indicate the way we pack our heads, hearts, and homes with things we don't need.

Here I am reminding the reader that "space" does not represent an "absence" but something positive.

Revising

Revising Your Overall Structure

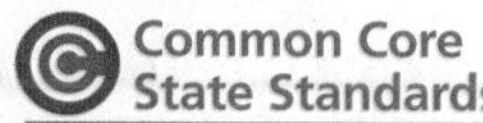

Writing

2.d. Use precise language to manage the complexity of the topic.

2.e Establish and maintain a formal style and objective tone while attending to the norms and conventions of the discipline in which they are writing.

5. Develop and strengthen writing as needed by revising, rewriting, or trying a new approach.

Language

3.a. Vary syntax for effect.

Take a balanced approach. Your reflective essay will have more meaning for readers if you achieve a subtle balance between your personal experiences and broader themes or ideas about life. Use the following strategy to evaluate your draft:

★ Place a blue star next to sentences that describe your personal experiences.

✔ Place a red check next to sentences that refer to outside events or to reflections about the meaning of your experiences.

Check that your draft balances information about your personal experiences with reflections on larger, related themes. If you have too few red checks, revise to include statements that broaden your focus.

Model: Revising for Balance

★ Now I am driving.★ Those old Bienville roads have acquired new meaning. ✓ I know that if I hang a right at the T, I can get to the cemetery that holds my relations from 150 years back, the same people that first helped settle North Louisiana. ★ None of my brothers ever knew about the cemetery, but I do. ★ I even know three ways to get to Minden that my brother Judd did not teach me. ✓ *On the roads that my family has traveled for over a century, I am just starting to find my way of traveling. . . .*

The writer added information that provides insight into the experiences he describes.

Revising Your Sentences

Vary your sentences. Even though your essay is about you, avoid beginning every sentence with *I*. Go through your draft and highlight the first word in every sentence. Make sure you are using a variety of sentence openers. If all or a majority of your sentences begin in the same way, combine or rewrite them to create more interest and variety.

Examples:

Monotonous: ***I remember the door. I remember it was locked. I wanted to get inside. I was nervous about what I might find. I was very curious.***

Varied: ***The door was locked, and I wanted to get in there. While I was nervous about what I might find, I was also curious.***

Peer Review: Exchange drafts with a partner. After you have read each other's essays, meet to discuss them. Focus on the clarity of the events and insights you present throughout your essay. Ask for specific suggestions, such as modifying sentences, omitting or adding transitions, or reordering paragraphs, to improve the logical flow of your ideas.

SIX TRAITS **WRITER'S TOOLBOX** SIX TRAITS

Voice | Organization | Word Choice | Ideas | Conventions | Sentence Fluency

Developing Your Style

Voice: Controlling Your Tone and Diction

Voice is a writer's distinctive "sound" on the page. Voice is partly based on **tone,** the attitude you express toward your subject; and **diction,** your choice and arrangement of words. Your tone may be described as serious, lighthearted, humorous, insincere, soulful, and so on. Your diction may be casual, formal, technical, simple, or complex.

Serious Tone/Formal Diction
To my horror, I realized that I had absentmindedly mailed the urgent letter without a stamp.

Lighthearted Tone/Casual Diction
Oops, I must have goofed and forgotten to put a stamp on that!

Find It in Your Reading

Read the selection from *Walden* by Henry David Thoreau.

1. Describe Thoreau's tone. Note key passages that convey that tone.
2. For each passage you choose, list two words that help express Thoreau's attitude toward his subject or audience.
3. **Discuss:** Choose three of your key words, and replace them with words that have a different tone. With a partner, discuss how these changes in diction affect the overall tone of the writing and create a different sense of voice.

Apply It to Your Writing

For each paragraph in your draft reflective essay, follow these steps:

1. Read your essay aloud, paying attention to specific words that convey your attitude toward your reader or subject. Be sure that the overall tone of your essay is consistent throughout the essay. In addition, make sure your tone is appropriate to both personal reflection and the larger themes you discuss.
2. If your tone seems inappropriate, change it. Informal and friendly tones usually work best with personal observations, whereas formal or distant tones keep your far-reaching comments from sounding flippant or insincere.
3. Identify any words that do not support the tone you would like to have. Replace these words with ones that better express your attitudes. The voice of your essay will shift as a result.

Student Model: Graham Walker, Ruston, Louisiana

Back Roads to Tomorrow

They are small country roads—the ones that change color and ride when you cross a simple parish line. They have four-ton limits assigned to small bridges that hop over waters like Bear Creek and Black Lake Bayou. Their ragged shoulders are missing chunks of pavement and rise three inches above the packed red clay that supports the asphalt. Bright ribbons of tape hang from the lower limbs of pine trees to escort log trucks to jobs. Now and again a color will halt at a worn path entering a clean-bottomed plot of trees, but the others remain loyal to the country road.

> This descriptive language creates a strong sense of place and establishes a personal tone.

These are the roads I grew up on.

It was usually just my oldest brother, Judd, and me. In a blue and gray Ford truck, we would branch out from our home in Taylor, Louisiana, with the windows down. Whether we went and looked at natural gas wells or whether we shot big turtles sunning themselves on logs in a bayou, it never took too much to keep us rolling along on those old Bienville back roads.

> Graham uses sensory details to convey a vivid picture of his experience.

But it was not pure riding experience that I enjoyed so much. It was the infinite knowledge of the roads that I believed I gained from those trips. I was in Back Roads 101: Knowing the Road. I made sure that I asked my brother whether we would take a right here or keep straight at the intersections. I felt that I had to know three different ways to get to Minden, ten miles away, or which way the T below our house would take me in case I wanted to slip off for a spin in my pre–double digit years.

Looking back, I realize it was not my concern for my future driving years that led me to study those roads so intently and to map them in my memory. It was one of the lengths I went to so I could be like my three older brothers. All three of them knew the lay of the pavement throughout the Bienville Parish. They could tell me how to get wherever I wished by a backroad route—even to Shreveport, I am sure. And more than I wanted to get to Shreveport, I wanted to be like them.

> Graham begins to draw connections between the specific experience and a deeper meaning.

So I soon knew most of the roads they knew. I could tell anyone three different ways to get to Minden, or which way the T would take me. But I was mapping more than Bienville Parish.

Now I am driving. Those old Bienville roads have acquired new meaning. I know that if I hang a right at the T, I can get to the cemetery that holds my relations from 150 years back, the same people who first helped settle North Louisiana. None of my brothers ever knew about the cemetery, but I do. I even know three ways to get to Minden that my brother Judd did not teach me. On the roads that my family has traveled for over a century, I am just starting to find my way of traveling. That journey, I now understand, is what all my rides with my brothers were really about.

> Graham extends his personal experience into the abstract realm of family, identity, and history.

Editing and Proofreading

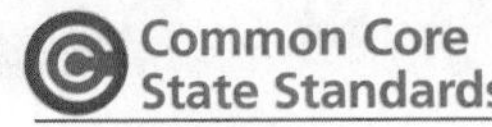

Writing

5. Develop and strengthen writing as needed by editing, focusing on addressing what is most significant for a specific purpose and audience.

Language

1. Demonstrate command of the conventions of standard English grammar and usage when writing.

2.b. Spell correctly.

Check your essay to eliminate errors in grammar, spelling, or punctuation.

Focus on fragments. Look for sentence fragments and correct them.

Fragment: ***Because I wanted to avoid traffic.***
Complete: ***We took the back road because I wanted to avoid traffic.***

Fragment: ***The orchestra uses many types of strings. Cellos, violins, and violas.***
Complete: ***The orchestra uses many types of strings, including cellos, violins, and violas.***

Focus on spelling. In general, use ***–tion*** to spell the sound of ***shun,*** as in ***exploration*** and ***portion***. Use ***–sion*** to spell the sound of ***zhun,*** as in ***vision*** and ***incision***. Check your spelling of any words that end with these suffixes.

Spiral Review: Conventions Earlier in this unit, you learned about adjective and adverb clauses (p. 287) and comparative and superlative adjectives and adverbs (p. 321). Check your reflective essay to be sure you have used those conventions correctly.

Publishing, Presenting, and Reflecting

Consider one of the following ways to share your writing:

Deliver a reflective presentation. Use your reflective essay as the basis for an oral presentation. Select photographs, drawings, or other images to share with your audience, as well as music or sound effects.

Publish a literary magazine. Gather a variety of reflective essays to create a classroom magazine. Assign committees the tasks of designing the format, creating illustrations, proofreading, and distributing copies to other classes.

Reflect on your writing. Jot down your thoughts about the experience of writing a reflective essay. Begin by answering these questions: What new insights into your own life did you have? What did you learn about the effect of diction on your tone?

Rubric for Self-Assessment

Evaluate your reflective essay using the following criteria and rating scale.

Criteria	Rating Scale			
	not very			*very*
Purpose/Focus: How well do you establish yourself as the main character?	1	2	3	4
Organization: How well have you organized your feelings, thoughts, and views?	1	2	3	4
Development of Ideas/Elaboration: How effectively do you use specific incidents to connect to broader themes	1	2	3	4
Language: How well do you describe the insights you gained?	1	2	3	4
Conventions: How correct is your use of grammar, especially your use of complete sentences?	1	2	3	4

Speaking and Listening

Write and Deliver a Persuasive Speech

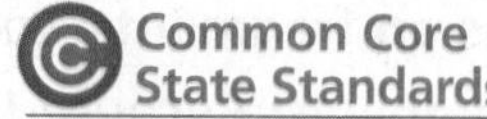

Writing
1. Write arguments to support claims in an analysis of substantive topics or texts, using valid reasoning and relevant and sufficient evidence.

Speaking and Listening
3. Evaluate a speaker's point of view, reasoning, and use of evidence and rhetoric, assessing the stance, premises, links among ideas, word choice, points of emphasis, and tone used.
6. Adapt speech to a variety of contexts and tasks, demonstrating a command of formal English when indicated or appropriate.

Persuasive speech is language designed to influence the way other people think or act. You use persuasive speech often. Perhaps you want to convince a friend to see a certain movie, or a prospective employer to hire you. Both situations require you to speak persuasively. In daily life, persuasive speech is usually spontaneous. However, in formal speaking situations, you must develop persuasion with forethought and organization.

Topic, Focus, and Thesis

To write and deliver a formal persuasive speech, choose a topic that means something to you. Ask yourself, "What do people argue about when they discuss this topic?" The answer will help you narrow your focus. Then, determine your **thesis**—your specific position or claim. This should be a statement with which reasonable people could agree or disagree. *Example thesis:* "The Hillsboro Library is inadequate because it does not have enough computer workstations."

Appeals and Rhetorical Devices

Consider your audience. After defining your topic and thesis, think about your audience and what they may know or feel about your topic. This will help you choose effective *persuasive appeals* to reach them.

- To prove a position, use a **logical argument** that relies on *facts* and sound *reasoning.* Draw facts from credible sources, such as newspapers, journals, encyclopedias, and government Web sites.
- To gain your audience's trust, use an **ethical argument** that establishes your credibility as a speaker. Cite trusted sources and demonstrate knowledge of your topic.
- To move your audience, use an **emotional argument** that evokes sympathy or humor. Relate affecting stories and use vivid language that sets a specific *tone*, or attitude, toward the subject.

Structure your speech. Like an essay, a strong speech has a logical structure. In your **introduction,** engage your audience and show why your topic matters. In the **body** of your speech, develop your ideas point by point. In your **conclusion,** restate your thesis and issue a call to action, or urgent request that your audience do something or think in a new way.

Select language techniques. Make deliberate choices about the *diction*, or word choice, and *syntax*, or grammar and sentence structure, you use. To ensure your ideas are clear, use *formal English*, the version of English taught in school. Use *informal expressions,* such as slang, sparingly to connect to your audience. If your topic is scientific or technical, use *technical language*, such as the specific names of devices or processes.

There is also a rich variety of rhetorical devices and expressive language that can help you convince your audience in a clear and forceful way:

- **Rhetorical Questions:** questions asked for effect, not to get information. "Shouldn't the library be a valuable resource for students?"
- **Parallel Structure:** repeated grammatical patterns that create balance and emphasis. "The books are ancient, the computers are slow, and the lighting is terrible."
- **Concrete Images:** vividly described situations, places, or people
- **Figurative Language:** symbolic or non-literal language, such as similes and metaphors, used to make ideas memorable

Select appropriate persuasive techniques. To support your thesis and keep your audience interested, use a variety of supporting arguments:

- **Characterization:** using evaluative language, such as "essential" or "unfair" to classify a position or a situation
- **Irony:** pointing out incongruities. "The library has more computers for its staff than for the public."
- **Dialogue:** relating conversations or quoting directly from sources

Activities: Deliver and Evaluate Persuasive Speech

Comprehension and Collaboration For both activities, use an evaluation form like the one shown below.

A. Write and deliver a persuasive speech to the class. Have your audience assess your argument.

B. Using your class's responses, develop additional arguments and then present an *impromptu speech* to further defend your thesis.

Peer Evaluation Form for Persuasive Speech

Title of Speech ____________________

Thesis ____________________

Exhibits a Logical Structure: Yes ☐ No ☐

Explain ____________________

Diction and Syntax:

Standard English ☐ Rhetorical Questions ☐ Figurative Language ☐

Informal Language ☐ Parallel Structure ☐

Technical Language ☐ Concrete Images ☐

Examples ____________________

What would the speaker's opponents say in response to this argument?

____

What did the speaker do well? What could be improved? ____________________

____

Language Study

Etymology: Political Science/History Terms

Many events have shaped the development of the English language. The timeline shown here identifies events that brought critical changes:

5th century	6th century	11th century
Angles and Saxons invade the British Isles. Anglo-Saxon becomes the dominant culture and language.	*Christianity spreads into England, adding Latin and Greek words to Anglo-Saxon.*	*Normans invade from France, bringing thousands of French and Latin words.*

The Romans and Greeks introduced numerous political ideas to the world, and English reflects those influences. The Normans became the ruling class of England, and many of their word contributions relate to politics, history, and law. Knowing key affixes and roots will help you define unfamiliar terms you encounter as you study political science and history.

	Word Part	Meaning	Example Words
Prefixes	*con-* (Latin)	with; together	constitution, congress
	auto- (Greek)	self	autocracy, autonomy
	dom- (Latin)	rule	dominion, dominant
Roots	*-belli-* (Latin)	war	bellicose, belligerent
	-dem- (Greek)	people	demographics, democracy
	-polis- (Greek)	city	politician, politics
Suffixes	*-cracy* (Greek)	government; rule	meritocracy, aristocracy
	-hood (Anglo-Saxon)	sharing a condition	statehood, knighthood
	-ism (Greek)	quality or practice of	nationalism, colonialism

Practice

1. Refer to the chart above to define **(a)** autocracy; **(b)** democracy.
2. Write definitions for each italicized word: **(a)** *Bellicose* acts caused greater conflict. **(b)** Members of the convention wrote a *constitution.*
3. Choose a word from the chart above and create a timeline *tracing its etymology,* or development as an English word. Include its language of origin, its movement from one language to another, changes in its meaning, and a discussion of any points at which its usage may have been contested. Consult reference materials, both print and digital, to aid your work.

Common Core State Standards

Language

1.a. Apply the understanding that usage is a matter of convention, can change over time, and is sometimes contested.

4.a. Use context as a clue to the meaning of a word or phrase.

4.c. Consult general and specialized reference materials, both print and digital, to find the pronunciation of a word or determine or clarify its precise meaning, its part of speech, its etymology, or its standard usage.

6. Acquire and use accurately general academic and domain-specific words and phrases.

Vocabulary Acquisition and Use: Context Clues

Sentence Completion questions appear in most standardized tests. One skill that Sentence Completions test is your ability to figure out what a word means by examining its context, or the surrounding words or sentences. In these types of questions, you are given sentences with one or more missing words. Your task is to choose the correct word or words to complete each sentence logically. Try using the following strategy: (1) Read the entire sentence and anticipate a word that would logically complete it. (2) Scan the answer choices for that word. (3) If the word you anticipated is not there, look for a synonym.

Practice

This exercise is modeled after the Sentence Completions exercises that appear in the Critical Reading section of the SAT.

Directions: Each of the following sentences is missing one or two words. Choose the word or set of words that best completes each sentence.

Test-Taking Tip
Before you mark an answer, carefully read the complete sentence to confirm that it makes sense.

1. Both his vengefulness and his __?__ prevent Captain Ahab from surrendering to the white whale.

A. parsimony
B. alacrity
C. obstinacy
D. magnanimity
E. flexibility

2. Those who celebrate the beauty of nature sometimes have an __?__ to industrialization.

A. eloquence
B. aversion
C. expedience
D. attraction
E. affinity

3. In the staid congregations of New England, __?__ was considered not only __?__, but sinful.

A. ostentation . . . indecorous
B. pathos . . . prevalent
C. discord . . . impulsive
D. avarice . . . superfluous
E. obstinacy . . . vengeful

4. Mr. Hooper's reasons for wearing the mysterious veil are __?__ to his parishioners.

A. impertinent
B. ample
C. inscrutable
D. stirring
E. sublime

5. In *Walden*, Thoreau voices his desire to lead a simple life and rid himself of __?__ concerns.

A. ominous
B. venerable
C. imperceptible
D. superfluous
E. essential

6. Though the human mind is limited and __?__, it is able to contemplate __?__.

A. tremulous . . . maledictions
B. finite . . . infinity
C. infinite . . . chaos
D. prescient . . . posterity
E. radiant . . . iniquity

Text Set Workshop

From Text to Understanding

You have studied each part of Unit 2 as a set of connected texts. In this workshop, you will have the chance to further explore the fundamental connections among these texts, and deepen your essential understanding of the literature and its social and historical context.

Common Core State Standards

Writing

1. Write arguments to support claims in an analysis of substantive topics or texts, using valid reasoning and relevant and sufficient evidence.

7. Conduct short as well as more sustained research projects to answer a question (including a self-generated question) or solve a problem; narrow or broaden the inquiry when appropriate; synthesize multiple sources on that subject, demonstrating understanding of the subject under investigation.

9. Draw evidence from literary or informational texts to support analysis, reflection, and research.

Speaking and Listening

1. Initiate and participate effectively in a range of collaborative discussions (one-on-one, in groups, and teacher-led) with diverse partners on *grades 11–12 topics, texts, and issues*, building on others' ideas and expressing their own clearly and persuasively.

PART 1: Fireside and Campfire

Writing: Argumentative Essay The writers in Part 1 contributed to the country's emerging sense of identity. Review the Primary Sources, the writings of the Fireside Poets, and, most closely, the Anchor Text, Washington Irving's "The Devil and Tom Walker." Make a list of elements that are uniquely American. You may note certain types of characters, settings, items, or attitudes.

Assignment: Develop and defend a claim about the character of the young American nation based on the texts in this unit.

Example: The story of Tom Walker introduces a truly American archetype: Tom Walker, in his relationship with the Devil, mirrors America's brashness and boldness.

Interpret the Literature. Develop and support your claim with accurate and relevant references to and quotations from the texts. If you look to secondary sources, such as literary criticism, be sure to cite your sources.

PART 2: Shadows of the Imagination

Writing: Writing to Sources Concealed secrets and fears can become destructive elements in the human psyche and the culture as a whole. Review the selections in Part 2, focusing especially on Nathaniel Hawthorne's "The Minister's Black Veil." Consider what each author might be communicating about individuals and society through his fiction. Look for meaningful points of comparison between the texts.

Assignment: Write an analytical essay in which you compare Hawthorne's Reverend Hooper with a character from one of the other selections in Part 2. Discuss what each character signifies to the larger community and how each character affects society.

Develop your claim. Use details from the texts to develop your comparison. Be sure to present interesting parallels and contrasts.

Organize your writing. Use either point-by-point organization or block organization, in which you discuss first one author, and then the other.

Conclude. State the end result of your analysis in a powerful and thought-provoking paragraph.

Writing Checklist

- ☐ Clear claim
  Identify: ___________
- ☐ References to the text
  Example: ___________
- ☐ Quotations from the text
  Examples: ___________
- ☐ Commentary on quotations from the text
  Examples: ___________

PART 3: The Human Spirit and the Natural World

Research: Poster Series The Transcendentalist writers featured in Part 3 believed in the primacy of the individual. In these texts, each person is charged with cultivating independent thought and developing a personal relationship with nature, for in the natural world one tunes in most fully to one's soul. The consequences of staying true to individual principles, however, are often the rejection of authority and society's expectations.

Review the background materials and selections in Part 3, paying particular attention to the Anchor Texts, excerpts from Henry David Thoreau's *Walden* and "Civil Disobedience." Think about whether or not Thoreau's ideas would have been considered radical at the time.

Assignment: With a small group, research Americans in the arts, politics, and sports who cultivated their individualism and followed their own path. Use ideas found in Thoreau's texts as a framework in which to consider these independent thinkers throughout American history. Create a poster series of American Free Thinkers. First, write a summary of Thoreau's philosophy. Then, create a poster for each free thinker that includes two or three paragraphs about each person and an illustrative image. Explain how that person's ideas and actions reflect Thoreau's principles.

Research Checklist

For Summary of Thoreau:

- ☐ **Explain Thoreau's thesis.** What is his main idea?
- ☐ **Provide examples of Thoreau's ideas in action.** How did his life reflect his principles?
- ☐ **Include quotations.** Use Thoreau's own words to illustrate your discussion of his ideas.

For Each Poster:

- ☐ **Identify subject of report.** Include the person's name in your thesis statement.
- ☐ **Provide background facts.** Where is the person from? What did he or she do? When did the person live?
- ☐ **Explain connection to Thoreau.** How does this person reflect Thoreau's ideas about individualism, his devotion to nature, or both?
- ☐ **Include quotations.** Use quotations that help illustrate how this person can be seen as a descendant of Thoreau's thinking.

PART 4: American Masters

Listening and Speaking: Debate Both Emily Dickinson and Walt Whitman are today acknowledged as poetic geniuses. Review their work, giving special attention to Whitman's "Preface to the 1855 Edition of *Leaves of Grass*." Consider the qualities that make these writers so enduringly great.

Assignment: Establish two debate teams, one focusing on Dickinson and one focusing on Whitman. Prepare to have a debate about which was the greater and more influential of the two poets. Look to secondary sources, including biographies and literary criticism.

- Designate someone to moderate the debate. This person will make sure students from each team speak in order and for equal amounts of time.
- Each debate team should prepare and deliver an opening statement that is lively and to the point, and that presents the team's primary claim.
- Make sure you have evidence to support each of your team's points.
- Anticipate claims opposing team members might make in favor of their poet. Have responses ready to counter these claims.
- Be respectful of others' opinions at all times.

Test-Taking Practice

Reading Test: Paired Passages

Paired reading passages are one type of critical reading passage used on standardized tests. Paired passages may be fiction or nonfiction, prose or poetry, and may vary in length. As you read, keep in mind that the passages will be **compared and contrasted.** Questions following paired passages will refer to each passage individually and to both passages as a unit. Note similarities and differences between the passages, especially the author's attitudes, word choices, and styles.

 **Common Core State Standards**

RI.11-12.1, RI.11-12.2, RI.11-12.3, RI.11-12.4; L.11-12.4, L.11-12.5.a, L.11-12.6

[For the full wording of the standards, see the standards chart in the front of your textbook.]

Practice

The following exercise is modeled after the SAT Paired Passages Critical Reading section. This section usually includes 48 questions.

Directions: Read both passages. Then, answer the questions. Passage 1 is from *Walden* by Henry David Thoreau. Passage 2 is by Gretel Ehrlich.

PASSAGE 1

The life in us is like the water in the river. It may rise this year higher than man has ever known it, and flood the parched uplands. . . . It was not always dry land where we dwell. I see far inland the banks which the stream anciently washed, before science began to record its freshets. Everyone has heard the story which has gone the rounds of New England, of a strong and beautiful bug which came out of the dry leaf of an old table of apple-tree wood, which had stood in the farmer's kitchen for sixty years. . . . From an egg deposited in the living tree many years earlier still, as appeared by counting the annual layers beyond it; which was heard gnawing out for several weeks, hatched perchance by the heat of an urn. . . . Who knows what beautiful and winged life, whose egg has been buried for ages under many concentric layers of woodenness in the dead dry life of society . . . may unexpectedly come forth . . . to enjoy its perfect summer life at last.

PASSAGE 2

These days we go about our lives with so much speed and so much extraneous information that it's difficult to contemplate just one thing, one sight, one ripple in the pond. Thoreau would have us simplify, slow down, become quiet, and burrow into the heart of things without minds. Not to "dumb down," but the opposite: to stop, to listen, and see; to turn off the monologue in our minds; to erase our idea about how things are; to live in others' shoes. Thoreau would have us think like a river, a pond, a tree, another animal or human; to adopt their point of view instead of our own. Then, the fresh, dawnlike nature of things . . . will keep radiating, piercing the difficulties in our lives with new songs.

Strategy

Break the task into parts.

- **Read Passage 1,** and answer the questions that refer only to the first passage.
- **Read Passage 2,** and answer the questions that refer only to the second passage.
- Finally, answer the compare-and-contrast questions.

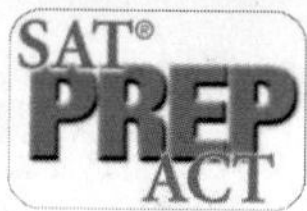

1. What is the best statement of the main idea of Passage 1?
   A. It is unusual that a large bug should hatch from old wood.
   B. One can determine the age of a tree by counting its rings.
   C. Life ebbs and flows, sometimes surprisingly.
   D. Science cannot measure life's force.
   E. Summer is the best season.

2. In Passage 1, the hatched bug is used as a symbol for
   A. life's irrepressibility.
   B. unexpected beauty.
   C. rebelliousness.
   D. the act of writing.
   E. a nightmare.

3. The main idea of Passage 2 is that
   A. people should use less technology.
   B. Americans should be less materialistic.
   C. people are like bodies of water.
   D. the truth can be found only in our minds.
   E. serenity will bring us new understanding.

4. It would be most accurate to say that
   A. Passage 2 is a commentary on Passage 1.
   B. Passage 1 is a commentary on Passage 2.
   C. Passage 1 is an excerpt of Passage 2.
   D. Passage 2 is an unfavorable review of Passage 1.
   E. Passage 1 was written after Passage 2.

5. In Passage 1, Thoreau uses a metaphor to compare
   A. life to water in the river.
   B. New England to a strong, beautiful bug.
   C. the heat of an urn to the heat of the sun.
   D. society to concentric layers of woodenness.
   E. an egg to summer.

6. It can be inferred that the author of Passage 2
   A. struggles to understand aspects of Thoreau's thinking.
   B. embraces some of Thoreau's views, but rejects others.
   C. thinks that Thoreau's philosophy is too simplistic.
   D. has read all of Thoreau's writings.
   E. respects Thoreau's philosophy.

7. In Passage 1, Thoreau's reference to the "parched uplands" (line 2) is
   A. a description of the landscape he is viewing as he writes.
   B. an image that evokes a sense of dryness and thirst.
   C. a metaphor for the story that follows.
   D. an example of synecdoche.
   E. a symbol of summer.

8. Why does Thoreau mention the "dry leaf" (line 7) of the kitchen table?
   A. to remind readers that the table was once a living tree
   B. to create suspense
   C. to create an atmosphere of dry lifelessness
   D. to urge people not to abuse nature
   E. as a metaphor for the page of a book

9. It can be inferred from the phrase "piercing the difficulties in our lives with new songs" that the author of Passage 2
   A. uses straightforward language.
   B. is not in tune with Thoreau's philosophy.
   C. appreciates Thoreau, but does not echo his voice.
   D. is attuned with Thoreau in both thought and writing style.
   E. believes that problem solving is painful.

Grammar and Writing: Editing in Context

Editing in Context segments often appear in the writing sections of standardized tests. The passages or sample sentences used are usually drafts of student essays that may or may not contain errors in grammar, style, and usage. For each question, you must first decide if there is an error and then determine which of four possible answers will best correct a given sentence.

Strategy

"Listen" for errors.

Read the sentence straight through. If you mentally "trip" over one of the underlined portions, it is probably wrong.

Practice

This exercise is modeled after the Identifying Sentence Errors portion of the SAT Writing test.

Directions: Each of the following sentences contains either a single error or no error at all. The error, if there is one, is underlined and lettered. If a sentence contains an error, select the letter of that underlined part. If the sentence is correct, select choice E.

1. Humankind (A) has been fascinated (B) with whales, the greater (C) of all sea mammals, for (D) the entire span of recorded history. No error (E)

A.
B.
C.
D.
E.

2. Byzantine scholar and historian (A) Procopius wrote of a whale who (B) made its way into the inland Sea of Marmara (C), where it happily consumed the fisheries that (D) were maintained there. No error (E)

A.
B.
C.
D.
E.

3. The whale is an (A) archetype that (B) appears repeatedly (C) throughout world religions, cultures, and literature (D). No error (E)

A.
B.
C.
D.
E.

4. The King James Version of (A) the Bible makes (B) several mention (C) of whales (D). No error (E)

A.
B.
C.
D.
E.

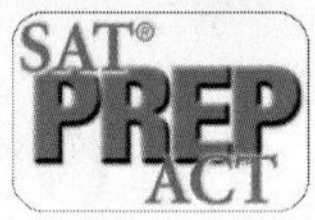

5. The more (A) famous one (B) is the story of Jonah, who is said (C) to have survived three days and nights in the belly of a great (D) whale. No error (E)

A.
B.
C.
D.
E.

6. Because (A) whaling (B) was a lucrative and (C) dangerous industry in nineteenth-century America, it is no surprise so that (D) a whale would become the centerpiece of an American novel. No error (E)

A.
B.
C.
D.
E.

7. Herman Melville's masterwork, *Moby-Dick*, widely regarded (A) as one of the finer (B) novels ever written, uses (C) the whale as a character (D), a symbol, and a force of nature. No error (E)

A.
B.
C.
D.
E.

8. *Moby-Dick* is a rich (A), complex, and (B) entirely American rendition of (C) the archetypal (D) whale. No error (E)

A.
B.
C.
D.
E.

Timed Writing: Position Statement [25 minutes]

Ralph Waldo Emerson wrote, "There is a time in every man's education when he arrives at the conviction that envy is ignorance; that imitation is suicide; that he must take himself for better, for worse, as his portion. . . ."

Write a position statement—an essay in which you express and support an opinion—in response to Emerson's statement. First, explain what the statement means. Then, explain your views: Do you believe the type of individualism he describes is an important value that people should try to develop? This assigment is similar to the essay portion of the SAT Writing Section.

Academic Vocabulary

The prompt asks you to *express,* or state, and *support,* or defend, your opinion.

Constructed Response

Follow the instructions to complete the tasks below as required by your teacher. As you work on each task, incorporate both general academic vocabulary and literary terms you learned in this unit.

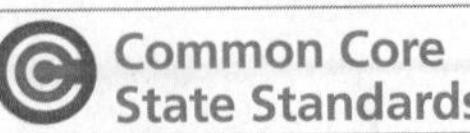
Common Core State Standards

RL.11-12.2, RL.11-12.3, RL.11-12.4, RL.11-12.5, RL.11-12.9; RI.11-12.4; W.11-12.2, W.11-12.9; SL.11-12.6; L.11-12.4, L.11-12.5

[For the full wording of the standards, see the standards chart in the front of your textbook.]

Writing

Task 1: Literature [RL.11-12.3; W.11-12.2]

Analyze the Development of a Story

*Write an **essay** in which you analyze and evaluate the development of a story from this unit.*

- Explain which story you chose and briefly summarize the plot.
- Identify key choices the author made in writing the story. For example, consider where the story is set, how the action is ordered, or how the characters are introduced and developed.
- Analyze the impact of the author's choices, discussing how these decisions affect both the story's meaning and the reader's experience.
- Organize your ideas so that each new idea builds on the one it follows to create a unified whole.
- Provide a concluding section that follows from the explanation presented.

Task 2: Literature [RL.11-12.4; W.11-12.9; L.11-12.4, L.11-12.5]

Analyze Word Choice

*Write an **essay** in which you analyze the word choice in a poem from this unit.*

- Explain which poem you chose and why you chose it.
- Identify specific examples of language in the poem that you find especially effective. Consider the following elements: figures of speech, such as similes or metaphors; specific words that are particularly interesting or beautiful; connotative meanings that are especially rich or striking. Explain your choices and the reasons for them.
- Identify any words in the poem that readers may not understand. Explain the meanings of these words. If any have multiple meanings, explain which ones are most important in this work.
- Consider how the combined word choices in the poem develop the author's tone.
- Cite specific examples from the poems to support your ideas. Quote precisely and accurately.

Task 3: Literature [RL.11-12.5; W.11-12.2]

Analyze Text Structure

*Write an **essay** in which you analyze the structure of a story in this unit.*

- Introduce your essay by discussing the overall structure of your chosen story. For example, does it follow simple chronological order or does it move about in time?
- Identify a specific section or aspect of the story you will analyze in depth. For example, you may discuss how the story begins, how events are ordered, or how it ends (happily, tragically, or inconclusively). Discuss how the specific section or aspect of the story contributes to the overall structure.
- Discuss the aesthetic, or artistic, impact of the author's structural choices. For example, consider how the structure affects the story's overall meaning.
- Choose varied transitional words and phrases to connect your ideas and clearly express the relationships you are analyzing.

Speaking and Listening

Task 4: Literature [RL.11-12.9; SL.11-12.6]

Demonstrate Knowledge of Foundational Works of American Literature

Deliver a ***speech*** *in which you analyze how two or more foundational literary works in this unit treat similar themes or topics.*

- Identify the works you will discuss and explain why you chose them. Discuss why these works are examples of foundational American literature.
- Identify the topic each work addresses and describe how each one presents characters, settings, or ideas.
- Explain the theme, or themes, the two works explore. Discuss similarities and differences—and the reasons for them—in these presentations or portrayals.
- Cite specific details to support your ideas.
- Include graphics or notes to support your analysis and clarify your ideas.
- Adapt your speech as you present. For example, you might slow your pace as you explain complex ideas.

Task 5: Informational Text [RI.11-12.4; SL.11-12.6]

Determine Author's Point of View

Deliver an ***oral presentation*** *in which you analyze the use of language in a nonfiction work from this unit.*

- Introduce the work you chose. Explain the historical context for the work and briefly summarize its central ideas.
- Identify specific word choices that are particularly critical to the writer's overall purpose and expression of ideas. State why you chose these words and phrases, and explain their figurative, technical, or connotative meanings.
- Speak clearly and precisely so that listeners can follow your line of reasoning, including your use of examples to illustrate your ideas.

Task 6: Literature [RL.11-12.2; SL.11-12.6]

Analyze Development of Theme

Deliver an ***oral presentation*** *in which you analyze the development of two or more themes in a work from this unit.*

- Explain which work you chose. Introduce your analysis by summarizing the work and identifying two distinct themes it conveys.
- Explain how the author develops the themes over the course of the work. For example, consider descriptions of the setting, characters' actions and reactions, and specific events. Also, consider symbols, imagery, or other literary elements that add to the development of two or more themes.
- Explain how the two themes interact and build on one another throughout the work.
- As you speak, use both general academic language and literary terms accurately. Employ formal English appropriate to an academic setting.

THE ESSENTIAL

How does literature shape or reflect society?

A Growing Nation Some writers in the 1800s celebrated the growing American nation and contributed to the sense of the country's unlimited potential. Others viewed the growing American culture less positively.

Assignment Choose two or more literary works from this unit that portray distinctly American settings and characters. Write a **comparison-and-contrast essay** in which you analyze these portrayals and characterize their perspective on American culture.

Titles for Extended Reading

In this unit, you have read a variety of literature from the American Renaissance. Continue to read works related to this era on your own. Select books that you enjoy, but challenge yourself to explore new topics, new authors, and works offering varied perspectives or approaches. The titles suggested below will help you get started.

LITERATURE

The Scarlet Letter
Nathaniel Hawthorne

EXEMPLAR TEXT 

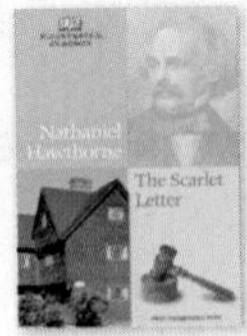

Novel Set in Puritan Boston in the early 1600s, *The Scarlet Letter* tells the story of Hester Prynne, a woman who is branded as an outcast for her sins and must struggle to create her own redemption.

["The Minister's Black Veil" by Hawthorne appears on page 272. Build knowledge by reading a longer work by this author.]

Leaves of Grass
Walt Whitman

EXEMPLAR TEXT 

Poetry A landmark collection of free verse poetry that includes "Song of Myself," *Leaves of Grass* combines heroic and historical themes with deeply personal observations.

[Excerpts from Leaves of Grass *begin on page 426 in this book. Build knowledge by reading the full text.]*

Complete Stories and Poems of Edgar Allan Poe
Edgar Allan Poe
Doubleday, 1984

EXEMPLAR TEXT 

Short Story/Poetry This collection of Poe's short stories and poems reveals his talent for developing mysterious, macabre characters and plots. The collection includes his famous story "The Cask of Amontillado."

[Two of Edgar Allan Poe's works begin on pages 292 and 312 in this book. Build knowledge by reading Poe's complete works.]

The Complete Poems of Emily Dickinson
Emily Dickinson
Back Bay Books, 1976

EXEMPLAR TEXT 

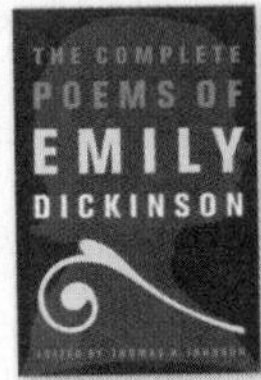

Poetry Emily Dickinson's small, precise poems describe enormous topics, such as mortality and the nature of the imagination. She is one of the great poets of American literature. This volume, which includes "Because I Could Not Stop for Death," presents her collected works.

[Poems by Emily Dickinson appear on pages 408–417 of this book. Build knowledge by reading her complete works.]

INFORMATIONAL TEXTS

Historical Texts

Selected Writings of Ralph Waldo Emerson
Ralph Waldo Emerson
edited by William H. Gilman

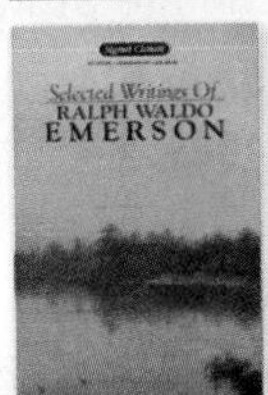

Essay One of the great essayists in American letters, Ralph Waldo Emerson addressed subjects ranging from everyday experiences to the meaning of life.

[Excerpts from Emerson's essays begin on page 366 in this book. Build knowledge by reading the full texts.]

Walden and Civil Disobedience
Henry David Thoreau

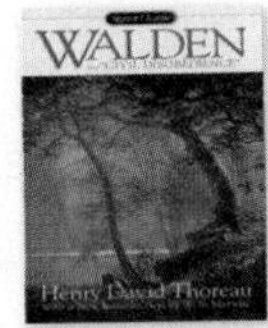

Essay These essays by poet and philosopher Henry David Thoreau are among the most influential works of nonfiction in American literature.

[Excerpts from Thoreau's essays begin on page 378 of this book. Build knowledge by reading the full text.]

Eyewitness to America: 500 Years of American History in the Words of Those Who Saw It Happen
edited by David Colbert

EXEMPLAR TEXT

Primary Source Read first-hand accounts of 500 years of the American experience in this extraordinary book. Subjects range from Horace Porter's description of Robert E. Lee's surrender to Grant to Hunter S. Thompson's discussion of a Super Bowl game.

Contemporary Scholarship

An American Primer
edited by Daniel Boorstin

EXEMPLAR TEXT 

Primary Source and Commentary This collection presents the most important documents in American history, accompanied by commentary from celebrated historians.

Preparing to Read Complex Texts

Reading for College and Career In both college and the workplace, readers must analyze texts independently, draw connections among works that offer varied perspectives, and develop their own ideas and informed opinions. The questions shown below, and others that you generate on your own, will help you more effectively read and analyze complex college-level texts.

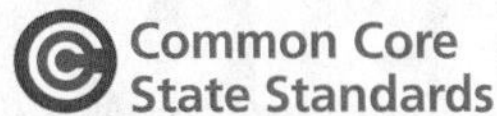

Reading Literature/Informational Text
10. By the end of grade 11, read and comprehend literature, including stories, dramas, and poems, and literary nonfiction, in the grades 11-CCR text complexity band proficiently, with scaffolding as needed at the high end of the range.

When reading complex texts, ask yourself...

- What idea, experience, or story seems to have compelled the author to write? Has the author presented that idea, experience, or story in a way that I, too, find compelling?
- How might the author's era, social status, belief system, or personal experiences have affected the point of view he or she expresses in the text?
- How do my circumstances affect what I understand and feel about this text?
- What key idea does the author state explicitly? What key idea does he or she suggest or imply? Which details in the text help me to perceive implied ideas?
- Do I find multiple layers of meaning in the text? If so, what relationships do I see among these layers of meaning?
- How do details in the text connect or relate to one another? Do I find any details unconvincing, unrelated, or out of place?
- Do I find the text believable and convincing?

Key Ideas and Details

- What patterns of organization or sequences do I find in the text? Do these patterns help me understand the ideas better?
- What do I notice about the author's style, including his or her diction, use of imagery and figurative language, and syntax?
- Do I like the author's style? Is the author's style memorable?
- What emotional attitude does the author express toward the topic, the story, or the characters? Does this attitude seem appropriate?
- What emotional attitude does the author express toward me, the reader? Does this attitude seem appropriate?
- What do I notice about the author's voice—his or her personality on the page? Do I like this voice? Does it make me want to read on?

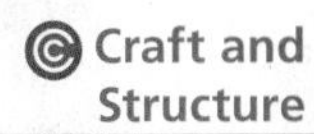

- Is the work fresh and original?
- Do I agree with the author's ideas entirely, or are there elements I find unconvincing?
- Do I disagree with the author's ideas entirely, or are there elements I can accept as true?
- Based on my knowledge of American literature, history, and culture, does this work reflect the American tradition? Why or why not?

Division, Reconciliation, and Expansion

Literature of the Civil War and the Frontier 1850–1914

Unit 3

PART 1 TEXT SET

A NATION DIVIDED

PART 2 TEXT SET

FORGING NEW FRONTIERS

PART 3 TEXT SET

LIVING IN A CHANGING WORLD

Fondly do we hope—fervently do we pray—that this mighty scourge of war may speedily pass away.

– Abraham Lincoln
Second Inaugural Address, 1865

CLOSE READING TOOL

Use this tool to practice the close reading strategies you learn.

ONLINE WRITER'S NOTEBOOK

Easily capture notes and complete assignments online.

STUDENT eTEXT

Bring learning to life with audio, video, and interactive tools.

■ Find all Digital Resources at **pearsonrealize.com**.

Snapshot of the Period

The years between 1850 and 1914 witnessed a transformation of the United States. During those years, America came of age—the country changed from a decentralized, mostly agricultural nation to the modern industrial power that we know today. This transformation began in the period leading up to the Civil War. In that war, Americans took up arms against one another to determine which should prevail: The Union of the North or the Confederacy of the South? The federal Union or states' rights? Freedom or slavery? As the Civil War began, each side possessed significant strengths and notable weaknesses. The North had a tremendous advantage in population and was far more industrialized and thus better prepared to wage war than the agrarian South. However, the Confederacy had the psychological advantage of greater motivation: it was fighting for its very survival. The South also had a strong military tradition and notably fine leaders. When the struggle was over, the North won, the Union held, and slavery was abolished—but all at a devastating cost to the nation.

▲ Abraham Lincoln signed the Emancipation Proclamation in 1863, as the nation approached the third year of Civil War.

Twain

Douglass

Chopin

Crane

Cather

Chief Joseph

As you read the selections in this unit, you will be asked to think about them in view of three key questions:

What is the **relationship** between literature and *place?*

How does **literature** shape or reflect *society?*

What makes **American** literature *American?*

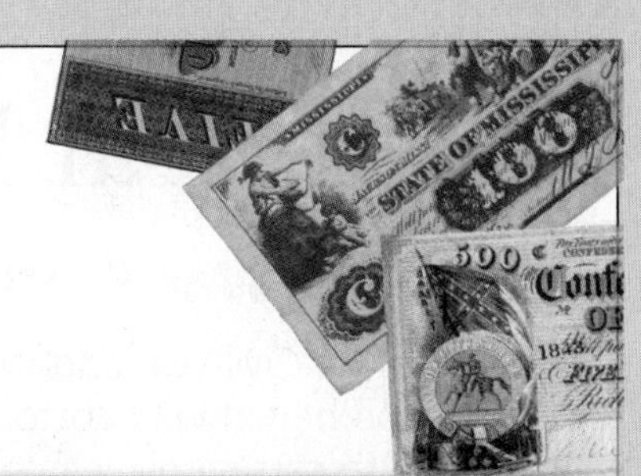

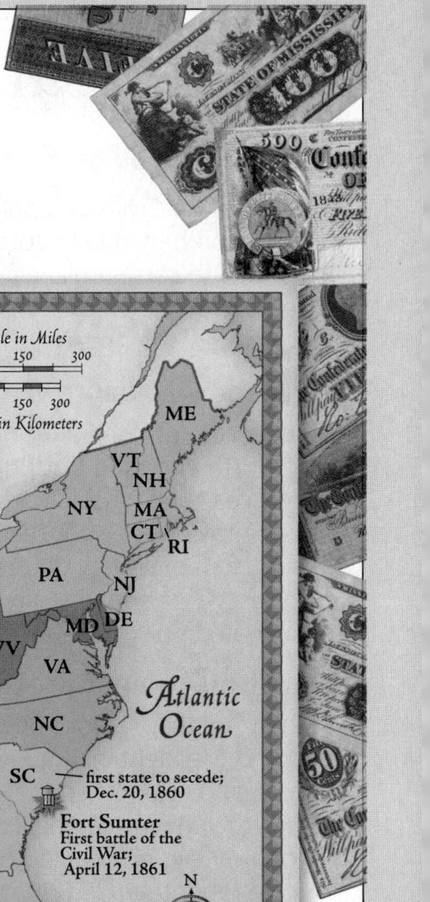

Integration of Knowledge and Ideas What does the information shown in the charts below help you understand about differences between the North and South in their economies, population densities, and overall lifestyles? How do you think these differences affected the outcome of the Civil War?

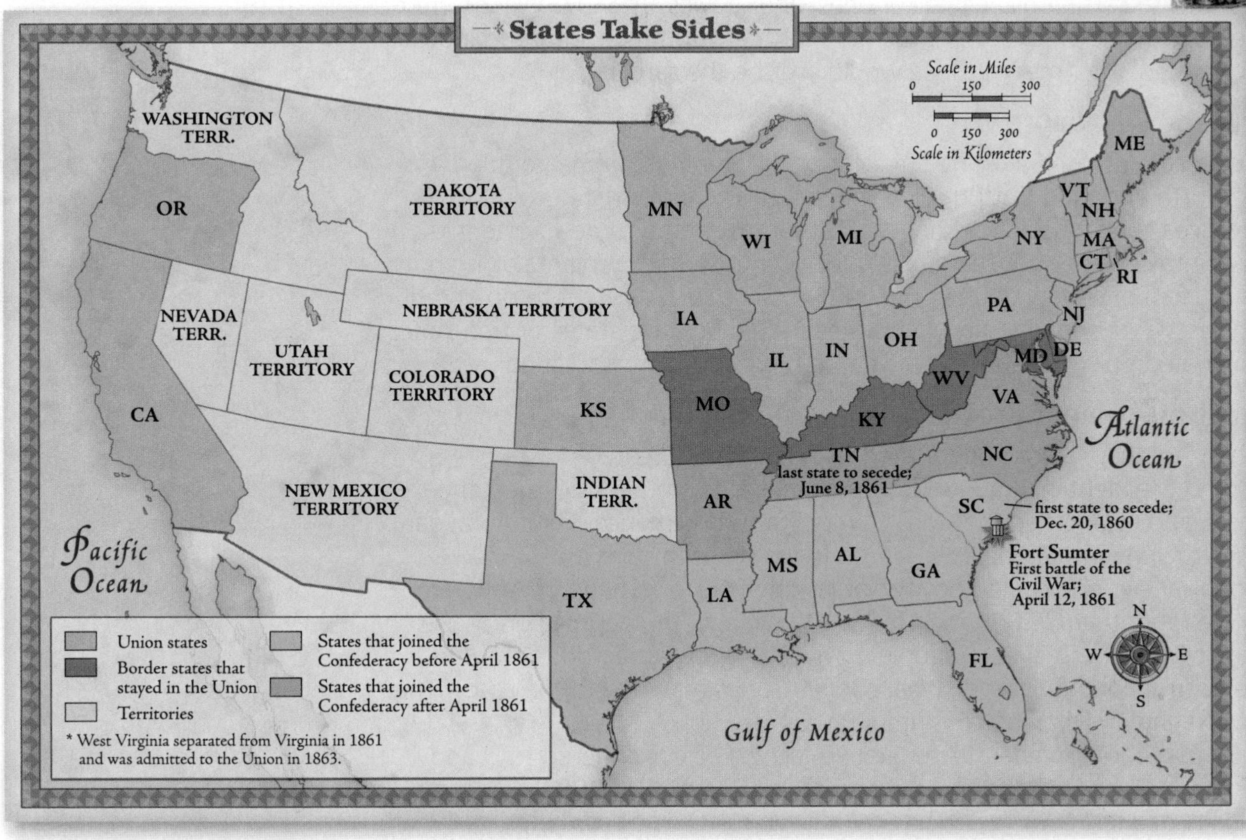

States Take Sides
Scale in Miles
0 150 300
0 150 300
Scale in Kilometers
WASHINGTON TERR.
OR
DAKOTA TERRITORY
MN
WI
MI
ME
VT
NH
NY
MA
CT
RI
PA
NJ
DE
MD
NEVADA TERR.
UTAH TERRITORY
NEBRASKA TERRITORY
COLORADO TERRITORY
IA
IL
IN
OH
WV
VA
CA
KS
MO
KY
TN
last state to secede; June 8, 1861
NC
SC
first state to secede; Dec. 20, 1860
Fort Sumter
First battle of the Civil War; April 12, 1861
Atlantic Ocean
NEW MEXICO TERRITORY
INDIAN TERR.
AR
MS
AL
GA
LA
TX
FL
Pacific Ocean
Gulf of Mexico
N
S
E
W
Union states
Border states that stayed in the Union
Territories
States that joined the Confederacy before April 1861
States that joined the Confederacy after April 1861
* West Virginia separated from Virginia in 1861 and was admitted to the Union in 1863.

U.S. Population, 1860
Number of whites and slaves
25,000,000
20,000,000
15,000,000
10,000,000
5,000,000
0
North
(border states)
South
Whites
Slaves

U.S. Cotton Production, 1860
Bales of cotton produced
6,000,000
5,000,000
4,000,000
3,000,000
2,000,000
1,000,000
0
North
South

U.S. Factories and Employees, 1861
Number of factories and employees
1,000,000
750,000
500,000
250,000
0
North
South
Factories
Employees

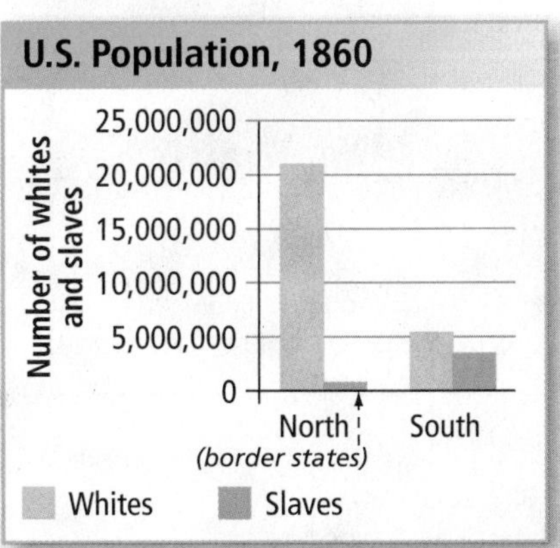

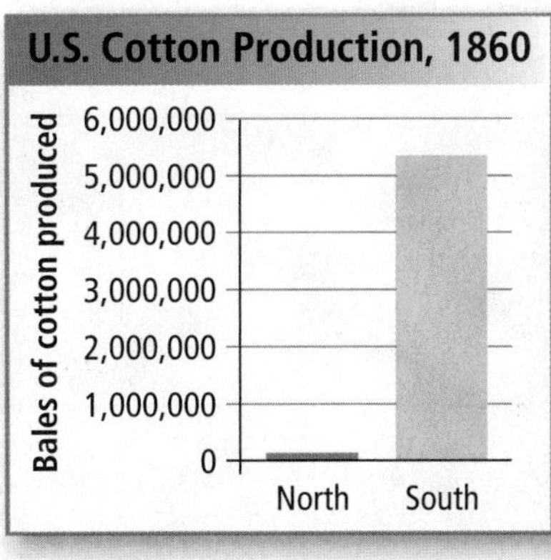

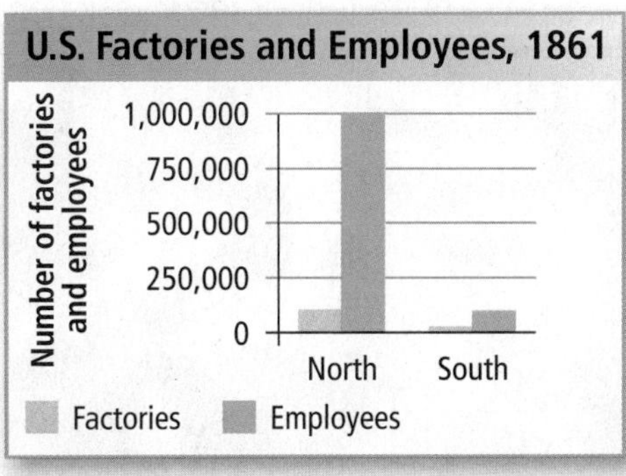

Historical Background

The Civil War Era (1850–1914)

Between the Civil War and World War I, America changed dramatically. The period began with cotton plantations and the Pony Express, and it ended with cars, airplanes, telephones, and movies. The Civil War scarred everyone—soldier, civilian, slave—and the shift from agriculture to industry accelerated. No American's life would ever be the same.

Prelude to War

The North and the South had developed differently. Commerce ruled the North and King Cotton ruled the South. The Industrial Revolution, advances in transportation, and a tide of immigration turned northern cities into centers of bustling activity. By contrast, cotton plantations and the system of slavery defined the South. Issues such as what to do about fugitive slaves and whether new states should be slave states or free states dominated politics. Rage and resentment grew. War was waiting.

Brother Against Brother

When Abraham Lincoln, dedicated to halting the spread of slavery, was elected president in 1860, South Carolina and five other states left the Union and established the Confederate States of America. Fighting began at Fort Sumter, in Charleston Harbor. Many on both sides anticipated a short war. No one could know what lay ahead: the carnage of Antietam, where more than 26,000 men fell in a single day; the deprivation of the siege of Vicksburg, where people survived only by eating dogs and rats; the destruction of Georgia, when Union troops marched to the coast. The devastating civil war lasted four long years.

By the time Confederate general Robert E. Lee surrendered to Union general Ulysses S. Grant in the spring of 1865, over 600,000 American soldiers had lost their lives. The South lay in ruins, its cities, farms, and plantations destroyed. The future looked grim. Just after the surrender, Abraham Lincoln was assassinated, and the exhausted, war-torn nation faced the huge task of reconstruction without him.

TIMELINE

1850

1850: **China** Taiping rebellion begins against the authority of the Qing government.

◀ 1856: **France** Gustave Flaubert publishes *Madame Bovary,* a classic novel of realism.

1857: Dred Scott decision by the U.S. Supreme Court rules that people of African descent cannot become U.S. citizens.

▶ 1859: John Brown, an abolitionist, leads a raid on the federal arsenal at Harpers Ferry, Virginia; he is hanged for treason.

1859: **England** Charles Darwin introduces theory of evolution in *The Origin of the Species.*

Americans Go West

After the Civil War, physical expansion and industrialization transformed the American landscape, economy, and society. The Homestead Act of 1862 promised 160 acres to anyone who would live on the land for a certain period and improve it. This shifted the westward movement into high gear. Half a million farmers, including tens of thousands of emancipated African Americans, staked their claims on the Great Plains. Miners went west, with dreams of gold sparkling in their eyes. In 1869, workers drove the last spike in the transcontinental railroad.

The Frontier Disappears

By 1890, the frontier had ceased to exist. Settlers, railroads, mines, ranches, and the slaughter of the buffalo had transformed the West. In place of open range were ploughed fields, grazing lands, and miles of fences. Gone, too, were the Indian nations; by 1890, almost all Native Americans in the West had been forced from their lands.

The "Electric" Society

When electricity entered the scene in the 1880s, the second Industrial Revolution began. Americans began to enjoy electric lights, telephones, automobiles, motion pictures, and skyscrapers, along with noise, traffic, and air pollution. Urban populations exploded; millions of immigrants provided cheap labor. Low wages, child labor, and disease were the norm for the working class, while a handful of industrial giants lived like kings. Mark Twain perfectly summarized the contradictions of this era when he called it "The Gilded Age."

Key Historical Theme: Painful Growth and Electric Change

- The Civil War left the nation physically, economically, and emotionally devastated as reconstruction began.
- Riding the railroad, Americans moved West and annihilated the frontier.
- The Age of Electricity transformed everyday life. Cities, with all their pleasures and problems, expanded rapidly.

1860: Abraham Lincoln is elected United States president. ▼

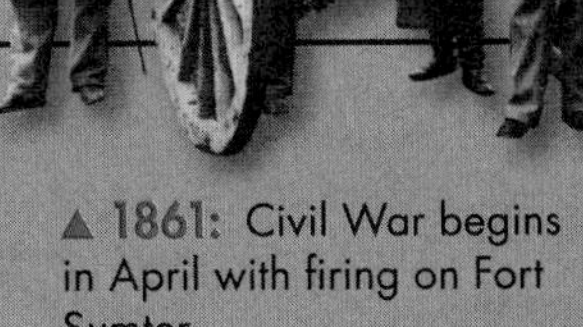

▲ **1861:** Civil War begins in April with firing on Fort Sumter.

1862: Emily Dickinson's poem "Safe in their Alabaster Chambers" is published in the Massachusetts newspaper *The Republican.*

▼ **1862: France** Louis Pasteur proposes modern germ theory of disease.

1865

1863: Lincoln issues the Emancipation Proclamation.

Essential Questions Across Time

The Civil War and the Frontier (1850–1914)

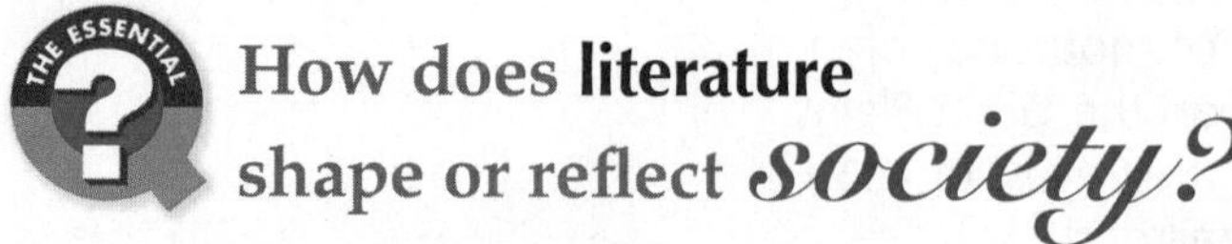
THE ESSENTIAL
How does literature
shape or reflect society?

What literary forms did writers use to discuss social and political issues during this period?

Spirituals Although spirituals were sung, not written down, they were the form of literature that grew directly out of the major social and political issue of the time—slavery. Born in the rhythms of work and based on biblical imagery, spirituals were lyrical expressions of lamentation, comfort, and hope. Songs like "Go Down, Moses" and "Swing Low, Sweet Chariot" made it possible for slaves to at least imagine release into a better life.

Life Stories Nonfiction in which men and women related the dramatic events of their lives also gave literary form to the issues of the era. Sojourner Truth's first-person account of her life and Frederick Douglass's autobiography were true-life narratives of bondage and freedom. Richly detailed diaries, such as the one kept by Confederate wife Mary Chesnut, as well as the journals and letters of countless Civil War soldiers remain valuable and moving literary resources that turn abstract issues into the daily realities of actual human beings.

Fiction and Journalism With Harriet Beecher Stowe's *Uncle Tom's Cabin*, fiction stepped up to play a major role in the politics of the era. Newspapers, too, took stands on a wide variety of issues and provided forums for editorials, essays, and public letters. After the Civil War, investigative journalists called muckrakers wrote blistering exposés of corruption, scandal, and incompetence in American industries.

ESSENTIAL QUESTION VOCABULARY

These Essential Question words will help you think and write about literature and society:

lamentation (lam′ən tā′ shən) *n.* outward expression of grief; wail or cry

forum (fôr′əm) *n.* place for the discussion of public matters

unflinching (un flin′chiŋ) *adj.* steadfast; resolute

TIMELINE

1865

1865: The Thirteenth Amendment, outlawing slavery, is added to the U.S. Constitution.

1865: President Lincoln is assassinated by John Wilkes Booth.

▲ 1865: **England** Lewis Carroll completes *Alice's Adventures in Wonderland.*

▲ 1867: The United States buys the state of Alaska from Russia.

How did popular literature reflect the era's social and political issues?

Rags to Riches As America's cities grew, the struggle against crushing urban poverty became a fact of life for more and more people. Many readers turned to the young adult novels of Horatio Alger to find inspiration on the hard road to success. Alger's rags-to-riches stories of young men finding fame and fortune through right-thinking and moral actions were immensely popular, selling more than twenty million copies.

Twists and Turns William Sydney Porter started out as a journalist, worked in a bank, went to prison for embezzlement, and became a short story writer. Under the name "O. Henry," he published hundreds of tales of ordinary city dwellers and became one of the most popular writers in America. His stories are often humorous episodes that include twists of fate. Beneath the light-hearted surface, however, his ironic surprise endings suggest how much people felt their lives were subject to coincidence and chance.

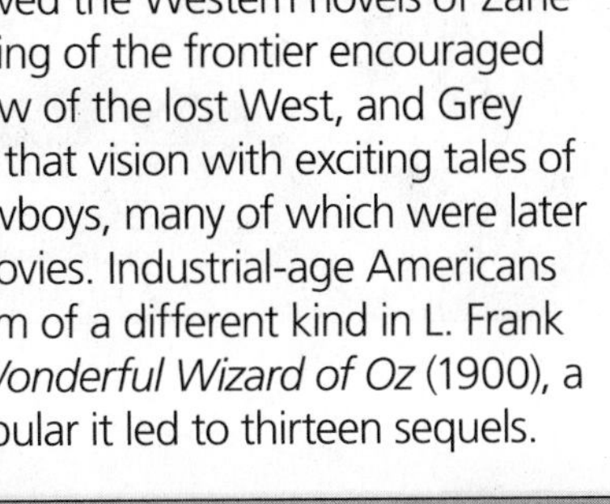

The West and the Wizard Millions of Americans who never set foot on a prairie or an open range loved the Western novels of Zane Grey. The closing of the frontier encouraged a romantic view of the lost West, and Grey capitalized on that vision with exciting tales of self-reliant cowboys, many of which were later turned into movies. Industrial-age Americans found escapism of a different kind in L. Frank Baum's *The Wonderful Wizard of Oz* (1900), a fantasy so popular it led to thirteen sequels.

The **American EXPERIENCE**

ART IN THE HISTORICAL CONTEXT

Realism in Painting: The Ashcan School

At the turn of the twentieth century, a group of artists working in Philadelphia and New York realized that city life was fertile ground for a new kind of imagery. They shared the basic principles and attitudes of Realism, and they developed ways of conveying Realism visually. These painters were aware that America was becoming increasingly urban, and they wanted to depict this new steel-and-concrete reality. They painted the grubby and the drab as well as the hectic and the colorful. These frank and honest painters included Robert Henri, William Glackens, and George Luks. Some critics insultingly called them the Ashcan ("garbage can") School, a label that has endured but is no longer an insult.

One prominent Ashcan painter was John Sloan (1871–1951). Sloan said that he saw the city as a "vast stage set where all sorts of lively business was in progress." His painting *Six O'Clock, Winter* (c. 1912) shows the "lively business" of a New York City rush hour.

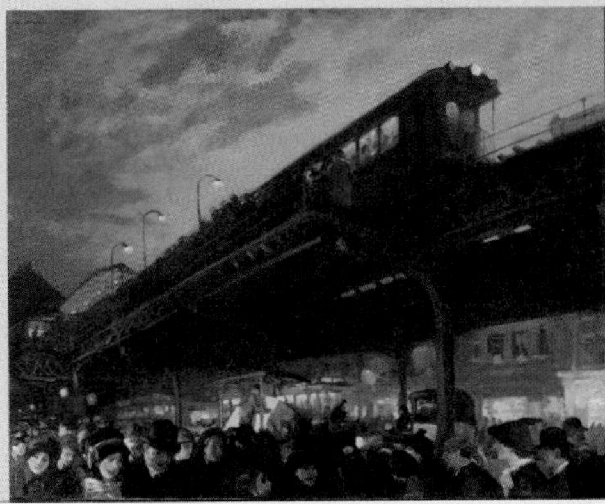

SIX O'CLOCK, WINTER, 1912, JOHN SLOAN, THE PHILLIPS COLLECTION

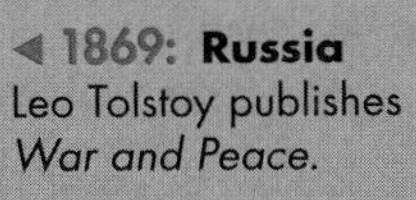

◀ **1869: Russia** Leo Tolstoy publishes *War and Peace.*

1874: France Claude Monet gathers Impressionist painters for first exhibition. ▶

1876: Baseball's National League is founded.

1877: Thomas Edison patents the phonograph.

1877: England First tennis championship held at Wimbledon.

1880

The American EXPERIENCE

CONTEMPORARY CONNECTION

Mark Twain, the Original Time Traveler

In his novel, *A Connecticut Yankee in King Arthur's Court*, Mark Twain places a present-day hero in the distant past. Twain said the idea was inspired by a dream in which he was "a knight errant in armor in the Middle Ages." When the book was published in 1889, *The Boston Herald* raved, "Of all the extraordinary conceits that have germinated in his fruitful imagination, nothing more delicious has ever occurred to Mark Twain than that of running riot among the legendary times of our ancestral race. . . .'"

While he must have enjoyed the book's success, Twain probably never imagined its long-term effect. Indeed, the time travel tale—now a familiar device in science fiction—is widely regarded to have begun with Twain's book. Perhaps because of this, many science fiction writers have a fondness for Twain. He often appears as a character in sci-fi books, films, television shows, and comics, including the following brief list of examples:

- *The Riverworld* series by Philip José Farmer
- *To Sail Beyond the Sunset* by Robert A. Heinlein
- *Star Trek: The Next Generation,* "Time's Arrow" episode
- *The Sandman* graphic novel series by Neil Gaiman
- *The Transformers: Evolutions* "Hearts of Steel" comic book series

TIMELINE

1880

1883: Railroads adopt standard time zones.

◀ 1884: Mark Twain publishes *The Adventures of Huckleberry Finn.*

1888: Great mid-March blizzard in eastern United States piles 30-foot drifts in New York's Herald Square.

1883: The Brooklyn Bridge is opened. ▶

1886: Statue of Liberty dedicated in New York Harbor. ▶

How did social and political issues lead to Realism and Naturalism?

The war was over. The unthinkable had happened: Americans had tried to slaughter each other. Although the outcome of the war had given the nation a hard-won sense of unity, the enormous cost in human life had shattered the nation's idealism. Like the hero of Stephen Crane's *Red Badge of Courage*, Americans had lost their innocence. The youthful sense of enthusiastic optimism that had built the country had faded away. Frustrated, unfulfilled, young writers turned away from the Romanticism that was popular before the war. They threw away their rose-colored glasses and saw the world for what it was. They became Realists.

The Common Life American writers began to focus on creating portrayals of "real life" as ordinary people lived it. They attempted to show characters and events in an honest, objective, almost factual way. In prose, Willa Cather wrote unflinchingly of the loneliness and cultural isolation of life on the prairie. In poetry, Edwin Arlington Robinson created unsparing psychological portraits of a variety of small-town characters. In *Spoon River Anthology*, Edgar Lee Masters presented a disturbingly candid portrait of small-town life in the form of epitaphs spoken by the dead themselves.

Naturalism Like Realists, Naturalists also depicted ordinary people in real-life situations, but they took it a step further. They believed that forces far more powerful than any individual shaped human destinies. Indifferent Nature, blind fate, heredity, pure chance—these determined the lives of men and women. Even fierce self-interest was not enough to guarantee success or survival. Jack London, for example, set much of his fiction in the Alaskan wilderness, where the frigid environment was unforgiving. The Naturalist theme of human endurance in the face of overwhelming natural forces pervades his fiction. The atmosphere of urban life fed Naturalism too, as people recognized that industrialization, mechanization, and anonymity were forces against which individuals were increasingly powerless.

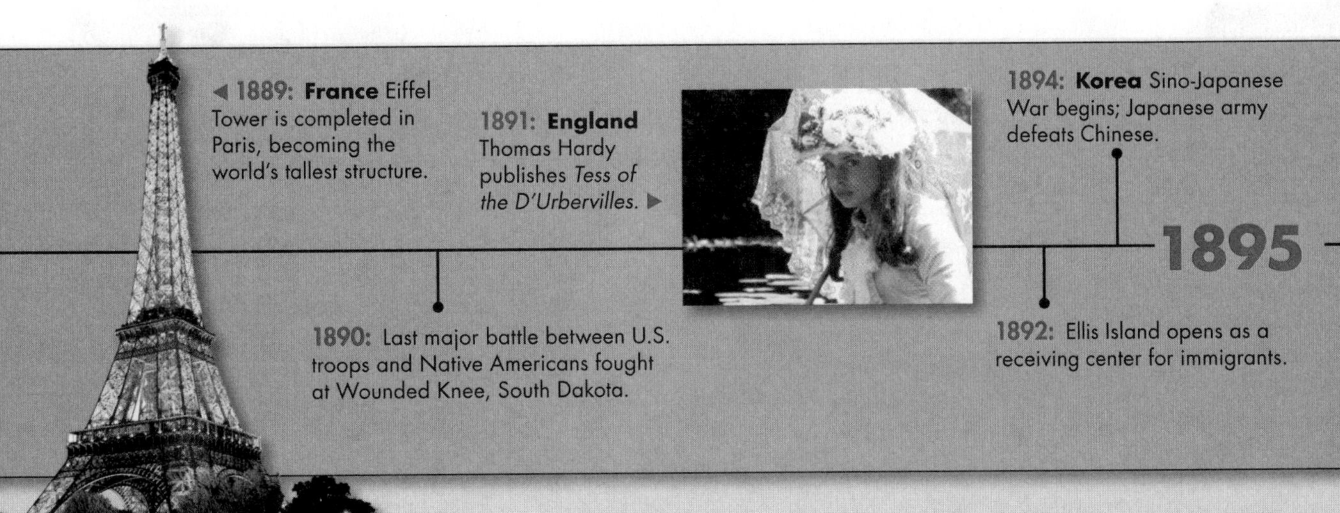

◀ 1889: **France** Eiffel Tower is completed in Paris, becoming the world's tallest structure.
1890: Last major battle between U.S. troops and Native Americans fought at Wounded Knee, South Dakota.
1891: **England** Thomas Hardy publishes *Tess of the D'Urbervilles.* ▶
1892: Ellis Island opens as a receiving center for immigrants.
1894: **Korea** Sino-Japanese War begins; Japanese army defeats Chinese.
1895

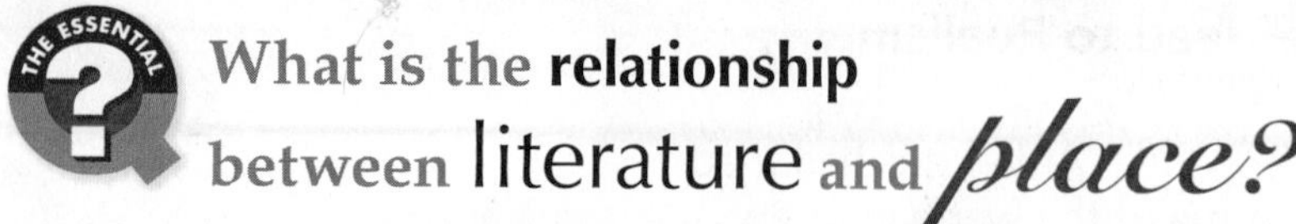
THE ESSENTIAL
What is the relationship
between literature and place?

What elements of the physical environment affected Northern writers' attitudes?

Industry The growth of industry in the North radically changed the landscape, and the landscape profoundly affected the thoughts, attitudes, and values of the people. In fact, change itself became a significant value. Technological advances in manufacturing, transportation, and the conveniences of daily life encouraged Northerners to believe that anything bigger, stronger, faster, and newer was necessarily better.

Urban Life On the other hand, the increased sizes and populations of Northern cities led to a host of urban problems and discontents. Conflicts arose over the treatment of immigrants, the role of organized labor, and the causes and effects of poverty. Writers were particularly sensitive to what was happening to the spirits—the emotions and values—of people crowded into cities and working at mind-numbing jobs in factories.

What elements of the physical environment affected Southern writers' attitudes?

Regionalism The South of course had cities too, but overall it remained a predominantly rural environment. Agriculture had always been at the heart of the economy, but the war had devastated the plantation system and abolished slavery, radically altering the Southern way of life. Nevertheless, Southern writers focused on the distinctive qualities of their geographical setting. Like writers in other parts of the country, Southern regionalists used the features and color of their local landscapes to tell stories that seemed to grow out of the land itself.

How did expressions of place show up in literature?

Local Color Almost as a conscious national reaction to the Civil War, writers all over the country seemed to realize how precious each separate part of the country could be. In the Northeast, South, Midwest, and West,

ESSENTIAL QUESTION VOCABULARY

These Essential Question words will help you think and write about literature and place:

industry (in′dəs trē) *n.* the production of goods; manufacturing enterprises collectively

transportation (trans′pər tā′shən) *n.* system for carrying passengers or goods from one place to another

rural (ro͝or′əl) *adj.* characteristic of the country or farm rather than the city

TIMELINE

1895

1895: **Germany** Wilhelm Roentgen discovers X-rays.

1895: First professional football game played in Latrobe, Pennsylvania. ▶

1896: *The Country of the Pointed Firs,* Sarah Orne Jewett's masterpiece, is published.

1898: **France** Pierre and Marie Curie discover radium and polonium. ▲

1901: **Italy** First transatlantic radio telegraphic message is sent by Marconi.

writers began to feature characters and details that were unique to a particular geographic area. Characters spoke in dialect, linking themselves to a specific locale. Landscapes were so fully integrated into stories that they virtually became characters. Descriptions of customs, clothing, manners, and attitudes all contributed to a literature of local color.

The mining-camp sketches and stories of Bret Harte made the West, especially California, a lively locale in the American literary imagination. Hamlin Garland and Willa Cather found hardship and tragedy, sometimes touched with romance, on the farms of the Midwest. Mark Twain told stories, like *The Adventures of Huckleberry Finn*, that are so deeply entwined with the landscape of the Mississippi River we cannot imagine them happening in any other place. In Maine, Sarah Orne Jewett created delicate and unforgettable New England idylls, and in Louisiana Kate Chopin told wrenchingly realistic stories of life in the bayous.

Urban Sophistication Not all realism, however, was set on farms, in small towns, and on riverboats. Some American writers were also comfortable in elegant drawing rooms. Edith Wharton wrote novels and stories about repressive customs in the Eastern high society into which she had been born. William Dean Howells applied his brand of realism to New England novels of manners and class. Urban subtlety and sophistication found its greatest American analyst in Henry James. Often placing his Americans back in Europe, James probed deeply into characters motivated by complex mixes of desire, honor, ambition, and guilt.

The American EXPERIENCE

DEVELOPING AMERICAN ENGLISH

Mark Twain and the American Language by Richard Lederer

On February 18, 1885, thirty thousand copies of *The Adventures of Huckleberry Finn* were released, and the novel changed the direction of American letters. Twain used everyday speech instead of formal, standard English. He used seven distinct dialects to reflect the speech patterns of his characters, and he showed the vitality of the American idiom in narrative as well as in dialogue. *Huckleberry Finn* is the first novel of world rank written entirely in American.

Readin', Writin', and Twain

Twain held strong opinions about a passel of subjects. Here are a few things he had to say about the American language that he helped to shape.

- *On dialects*: I have traveled more than anyone else, and I have noticed that even the angels speak English with an accent.
- *On choosing words*: The difference between the almost right word and the right word is really a large matter—'tis the difference between the lightning-bug and the lightning.
- *On style* (in a letter to a twelve-year-old): I notice that you use plain, simple language, short words, and brief sentences. That is the way to write English—it is the modern way and the best way. Stick to it; and don't let fluff and flowers and verbosity creep in.

1903: Jack London publishes *The Call of the Wild.*

1903: **Spain** Pablo Picasso paints *The Old Guitarist.* ▶

1903: W.E.B. DuBois publishes *The Souls of Black Folk*, a collection of essays.

1903: Wright Brothers fly 852 feet in their airplane at Kitty Hawk, North Carolina. ▼

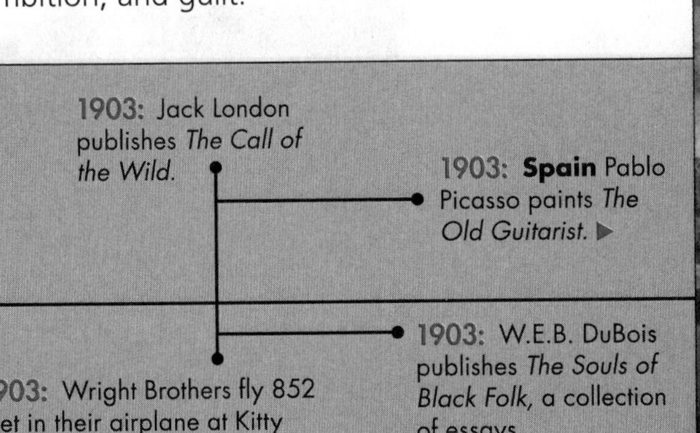

The Old Guitarist, 1903, Pablo Picasso, The Art Institute of Chicago, ©2004 Estate of Pablo Picasso/Artists Rights Society (ARS), New York

1904: Russo-Japanese War begins.

1905

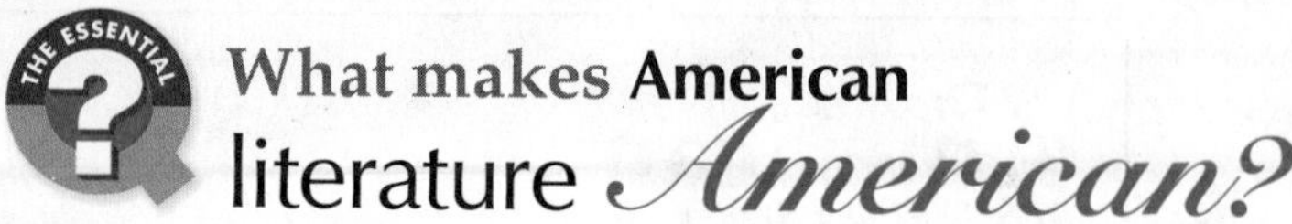

What makes American literature *American*?

What literary elements contributed to an American style?

Settings and Plots Unique local settings were essential in creating the "Americanness" of literature during this period. A Civil War battlefield, a Mississippi riverboat, a Western mining town, a Yukon wilderness—these and other sites grounded American literature in truly American places.

Dialogue and Style Common speech and dialects contributed to an American style. The way characters talked linked them to specific parts of the country and gave them distinct identities. Straightforward, deliberately "unliterary" speech defined a plain and powerful American style.

Humor Mark Twain said, "The humorous story is American." He felt that a good comic story depended on *how* it was told. Twain and other American writers often used humor to expose corruption and dissect human foibles.

What roles did writers play in shaping American identity?

Writer as Realist During the first half of the nineteenth century, Romantic subjectivity dominated American writing. The adventure tales of Irving and Cooper, the romances and fantasies of Hawthorne and Poe, and the otherworldly quests of Emerson and Melville defined American literature. However, after the horrors of the Civil War, the second half of the century saw the rise of a more objective attitude toward the world and human affairs. Hard fact took on more value than the search for the Transcendentalist Oversoul.

Local color writers such as Bret Harte, Sarah Orne Jewett, and Kate Chopin took great pains to depict details of the places they loved. As a result, their readers came to love those places as well. Local colorists were storytellers—Mark Twain the finest of them all—but they were also documentarians, recording life as it was lived.

TIMELINE

1905: **Germany** Albert Einstein proposes his relativity theory. ▼

▲ 1906: The San Francisco earthquake results in the deaths of at least 3,000 people.

1908: Henry Ford builds the first Model T. ▲

1905

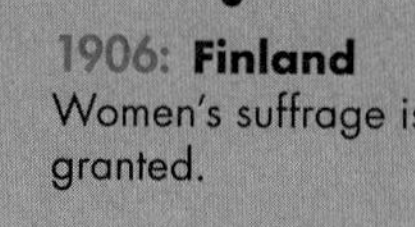

1906: **Finland** Women's suffrage is granted.

1907: Frank Lloyd Wright hosts his first solo exhibition at the Art Institute of Chicago.

1908: The electric washing machine is invented.

These were also the years when a new invention, photography, began to flourish, further feeding the demand for realistic images of life.

Writer as Naturalist The writers associated with Naturalism, including Stephen Crane, Frank Norris, and Jack London, were even more detached. They were deeply influenced by the writings of British naturalist Charles Darwin, German political economist Karl Marx, and French novelist Emile Zola, who believed that heredity, environment, and social conditions determined people's actions. To the American Naturalists, Emerson's self-reliance was an illusion, and the role of the writer was to make that clear.

At the dawn of the twentieth century, what did literature reveal about American attitudes?

Pragmatism The American Romantic impulse had faded. The dream-life expressed by Hawthorne and Poe had given way to a hard-edged pragmatism. Melville's Captain Ahab, an obsessive, tragic figure on a doomed whaling ship, was succeeded by Twain's Huck Finn, a clear-eyed and clear-headed boy on a raft.

Loss of Idealism The Civil War tarnished many of the ideals that had characterized the pre-war nation. In the face of Civil War deaths, postwar poverty, urban crowding, and mass production, Emersonian self-reliance lost its relevance. Henry David Thoreau, living alone at Walden and becoming one with nature, was succeeded by Jack London's doomed Yukon camper in "To Build a Fire."

Democracy Americans continued to put their faith in democracy. Realism emphasized the common person. It praised the everyday and the ordinary, even at the risk of glorifying mediocrity. Hawthorne's Hester Prynne, an exceptional woman reviled by her community, was succeeded by Edgar Lee Masters' Lucinda Matlock, an ordinary woman in small-town America.

Science As the nation entered the twentieth century, science and technology took on ever greater importance. Americans believed in progress and measured it in concrete ways. Over 27 million people visited the 1893 World's Columbian Exposition in Chicago, a massive world's fair that celebrated culture, craft, and commerce. The fair symbolized America's future as a leader in the practical industries that would continue to transform the world and create the Modern Age.

ESSENTIAL QUESTION VOCABULARY

These Essential Question words will help you think and write about American literature:

objective (əb jek´tiv) *adj.* real; actual

realistic (rē ə lis´tik) *adj.* practical or concrete rather than visionary

pragmatism (prag´mə tiz´əm) *n.* quality of being practical, sensible

1909: A multi-racial group of activists founds the National Association for the Advancement of Colored People.

1912: Over 1,500 people die in the sinking of the *Titanic.* ▶

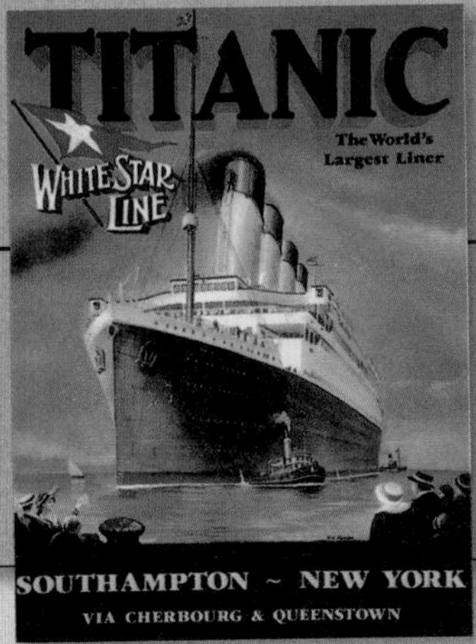

▶ **1913:** Willa Cather publishes *O Pioneers!*

1914

1914: The world's first scheduled airline service begins taking flight from St. Petersburg to Tampa.

Recent Scholarship

Defining an Era

Nell Irvin Painter

One of my most-read books, *Standing at Armageddon: The United States, 1877–1919,* showed me how politics changes as the times change. (The word *Armageddon* in the title refers to the end of the world, and the phrase *Standing at Armageddon* comes from a statement Theodore Roosevelt made in 1912.)

Historians, of course, know that timing is everything. We call one of our specialties "periodization," meaning the breaking up of the past into meaningful chunks of time. Historians decided that certain dates—in this textbook, for example, 1750, 1800, 1850, 1870, 1914, and 1946—carried special meaning, that what came before was different from what came afterward. The periodization in this unit (1850–1914) generally corresponds to the periodization of my book (1877–1919), although this unit includes the Civil War and Reconstruction and my book does not.

I made my own discoveries as I was just starting to work on *Standing at Armageddon.* I had to decide where to start and end a book on the period that covered roughly 1885 to 1915. The years 1885 and 1915 had no particular resonance: Nothing earthshaking occurred in either of those years to change the course of United States history. So I set about finding meaningful years by reading newspapers and news magazines, where I could follow the news of the day as it unfolded, day by day and week by week.

Meet the Author

Introducing Nell Irvin Painter (b. 1942)

Nell Irvin Painter served as the director of Princeton University's Program in African American Studies from 1997 to 2000. She is the author of numerous books, including *Standing at Armageddon: The United States, 1877–1919; Southern History Across the Color Line;* and *Sojourner Truth: A Life, A Symbol.*

A Shift from Land to Labor Issues

At the beginning of the 1870s, the news still bristled with violence related to the politics of the Civil War, as Democrats attacked Republicans and killed off the people associated with Reconstruction. Reconstruction—the reorganization of Southern states from 1867 to 1877—was dying a bloody death in the South, as Democrats took back by force the power they had held before the war. In 1877, however, new conflicts eclipsed the focus on Southern political terrorism. The news also revealed a great deal of labor conflict outside the South. A nationwide strike of railroad workers occurred in 1877 that began a whole new era in which politics revolved around working people and strikes. Before the Civil War, politics had been about land and access to land. After Reconstruction, postwar politics focused on industries and workers; 1877—the year national attention shifted from land to labor—became the starting point for *Standing at Armageddon*.

What about the end? Where should my period and my book end? Still reading the newspapers and news magazines, I found an echo of 1877's strikes and riots in 1919, the year contemporaries called the "Great Upheaval." There was the end of my period, a time in which working people and their issues once again dominated American politics.

Organized Labor Becomes a Force

Before 1877, American politics revolved around questions of land. But after 1877, politics revolved around industry and the people who worked in it. Organized labor became a force in U.S. politics between 1877 and 1919 and, building on this foundation, labor unions would surge to the fore in the 1930s. My periodization of 1877–1919 reflects my belief that working people and their concerns lie at the heart of the politics of the era. I begin and end *Standing at Armageddon* at moments in which workers attract the attention of Americans as a whole.

Speaking and Listening: Collaboration

Nell Irvin Painter discusses "periodization," the breaking up of the past into meaningful time periods. Some periods begin or end with major dramatic events, such as a war or an economic change. The beginning or ending of other periods, such as a "renaissance," are more difficult to pinpoint.

Hold a **small group discussion** about your own time period. What event or events define it? When would you say it started? What name or label would you give it? As a group, arrive at a consensus and then share your ideas with the class.

◀ **Critical Viewing**

Explain how this photograph of a railroad strike reflects Painter's discussion of American workers. **CONNECT**

Integrate and Evaluate Information

1. Use a chart like the one shown to determine the key ideas expressed in the Essential Question essays on pages 466–473. Fill in two ideas related to each Essential Question and note the authors most closely associated with each concept. One example has been done for you.

Essential Question	Key Concept	Key Author
Literature and Place		
American Literature	Influence of heredity and environment	Crane
Literature and Society		

2. How do the visual sources in this section—map, charts, paintings, and photographs—add to your understanding of the ideas expressed in words? Cite specific examples.
3. After the Civil War, Americans were more conscious than ever of their regional identities. How did writers of this era express and preserve the distinct perspectives of Americans across the land? Cite evidence from the various sources presented on pages 462–473 in your answer.
4. **Address a Question:** In her essay "Defining an Era," Nell Irvin Painter states her contention that politics before the Civil War dealt with issues related to land, while politics after the Civil War dealt with issues related to labor. In what ways does her point echo other societal changes occurring during this era? Consider information presented in this textbook about urbanization and industrialization. In addition, integrate information from other sources to support your ideas.

Common Core State Standards

Reading Informational Text
7. Integrate and evaluate multiple sources of information presented in different media or formats as well as in words in order to address a question or solve a problem.

Speaking and Listening
5. Make strategic use of digital media in presentations to enhance understanding of findings, reasoning, and evidence and to add interest.

Speaking and Listening: Oral Presentation

During the Civil War era, speeches and debates played an important role in American life. Research and develop an **oral presentation** about the public-speaking style of one of these famous American orators:

- Abraham Lincoln
- Henry Ward Beecher
- Sojourner Truth
- Mark Twain

Solve a Research Problem: To complete this assignment, you will need to locate examples of and commentaries about the public speaking of a person who lived before the age of sophisticated recording devices. Formulate a plan to meet this research challenge. Consider primary and secondary sources such as:

- Journal and newspaper articles written during the speaker's life
- Writings of later scholars familiar with the speaker's works
- Recordings of other people reenacting the speaker's speeches

As part of your presentation, explain the process you used to identify and evaluate information and solve the research problem. To add interest and evidence to your presentation, use a digital recording of a reenactment of the speaker's words or of an expert discussing the speaker's abilities and ideas.

ESSENTIAL QUESTION VOCABULARY

Use these words in your responses:

Literature and Place
industry
transportation
rural

American Literature
objective
realistic
pragmatism

Literature and Society
lamentation
forum
unflinching

TEXT SET

A Nation Divided

Part 1

Building Knowledge and Insight

An Occurrence at Owl Creek Bridge

Connecting to the Essential Question Everyday locations become charged with strategic importance and danger during times of war. As you read this story, which takes place during the Civil War, notice ominous details about the setting. This will help as you reflect on the Essential Question: **What is the relationship between literature and place?**

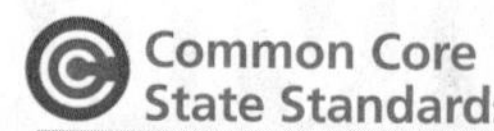

Reading Literature

3. Analyze the impact of the author's choices regarding how to develop and relate elements of a story.

5. Analyze how an author's choices concerning how to structure specific parts of a text contribute to its overall structure and meaning as well as its aesthetic impact.

Close Reading Focus

Point of View; Stream of Consciousness

Point of view is the perspective, or vantage point, from which a story is told. An author's choice of point of view affects every aspect of a story. For example, different points of view convey different types of information to the reader.

- In stories told from an **omniscient point of view,** the narrator is an observer who can relate everything that happens, as well as the private thoughts and feelings of all the characters. The opening scene of this story is related from an omniscient, "bird's eye" perspective: "A man stood on a railroad bridge in northern Alabama . . ."
- In stories told from a **limited third-person point of view,** readers' information is limited to what a single character feels, thinks, and observes: "A piece of dancing driftwood caught his attention . . ."

The point of view in this story shifts from omniscient to limited third-person. As the point of view shifts, so do the emotional tone and sense of time. To emphasize this change, Bierce introduces yet another narrative approach. He uses **stream of consciousness,** a technique in which a character's thoughts are presented as the mind experiences them—in short bursts without obvious logic. As you read, consider which events spark the thoughts and feelings the main character experiences.

Preparing to Read Complex Texts Bierce chooses to structure this story in three sections, each representing a shift in time and in chronological order. Clarify meaning by **analyzing the story's pattern of organization,** or *text structure*. Use a chart like the one shown to identify the time frame and events for each section. Then, analyze how this pattern of organization contributes to the story's meaning and impact.

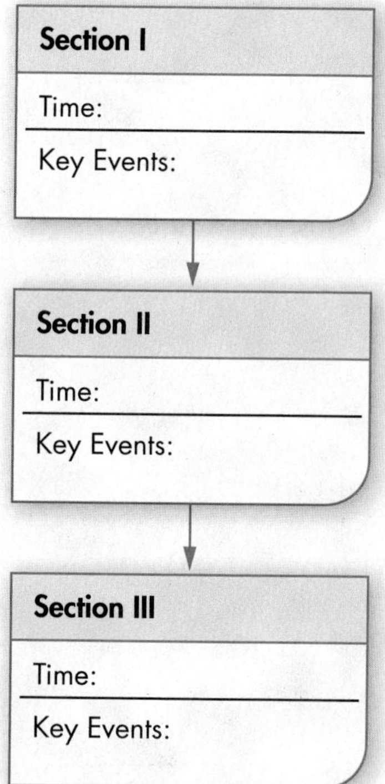

Vocabulary

The words below are important to understanding the text that follows. Copy the words into your notebook, sorting them into words you know and words you do not know.

etiquette **summarily**
deference **apprised**
dictum **ineffable**

AMBROSE BIERCE (1842–1914?)

Author of "An Occurrence at Owl Creek Bridge"

Ambrose Bierce's writing and worldview were shaped by his career as a Union officer in the Civil War. The poverty in which he was raised helped to foster Bierce's unsentimental outlook; the brutality he saw during the war cemented his cynicism. Bierce explored themes of cruelty and death in his writing, earning himself the nickname "Bitter Bierce."

A Civil War Soldier Bierce was born in Ohio and raised on a farm in Indiana. Having educated himself by reading his father's books, he left the farm while in his teens to attend a military academy in Kentucky. When the Civil War broke out, he enlisted in the Union army. Bierce fought in several important battles, rose from private to lieutenant, and won many awards for bravery. Toward the end of the war he was seriously wounded, but he returned to battle a few months later.

Poisoned Pen After the war, Bierce settled in San Francisco as a journalist. His "Prattler" column, which appeared in *The Argonaut* (1877–1879), the *Wasp* (1881–1886), and the *San Francisco Sunday Examiner* (1887–1896), mixed political and social satire, literary reviews, and gossip. The broodingly handsome writer was dubbed "the wickedest man in San Francisco" for his cynical and often malicious commentary. Yet Bierce's dark reputation only added to his personal popularity. He was a magnetic figure who charmed those around him despite the malice of his words.

Establishing His Legacy Although Bierce published many of his finest short stories in his column, he decided in the early 1890s to publish his collected short stories in two volumes entitled *Tales of Soldiers and Civilians* (1891) and *Can Such Things Be?* (1893). The concise, carefully plotted stories in these collections, set for the most part during the Civil War, capture the cruelty and futility of war and the indifference of death.

The Perfect Cynic Writer George Sterling wrote of Bierce, his longtime friend, that he "never troubled to conceal his justifiable contempt of humanity. . . . Bierce was a 'perfectionist,' a quality that in his case led to an intolerance involving merciless cruelty."

While he was successful professionally, Bierce found little happiness in a world where so few people met his expectations. His marriage ended in divorce, and both of his sons died at an early age. In 1913, at age 71, Bierce traveled to Mexico, a country in the midst of a bloody civil war. To this day, his fate is unknown, although a reasonable speculation is that he was killed during the siege of Ojinaga in 1914.

An Occurrence at Owl Creek Bridge

Ambrose Bierce

BACKGROUND *The senseless violence, death, and destruction Ambrose Bierce witnessed during the American Civil War (1861–1865) convinced him that war was terrible and futile. He set much of his best fiction, including this story, against the backdrop of this divisive war in which the agricultural South, whose economy was based on slavery, battled the more industrialized North. Fought mostly in the South, the war caused hundreds of thousands of casualties on both sides.*

I

A man stood upon a railroad bridge in northern Alabama, looking down into the swift water twenty feet below. The man's hands were behind his back, the wrists bound with a cord. A rope closely encircled his neck. It was attached to a stout cross timber above his head and the slack fell to the level of his knees. Some loose boards laid upon the sleepers supporting the metals of the railway supplied a footing for him and his executioners—two private soldiers of the Federal army, directed by a sergeant who in civil life may have been a deputy sheriff. At a short remove upon the same temporary platform was an officer in the uniform of his rank, armed. He was a captain. A sentinel at each end of the bridge stood with his rifle in the position known as "support," that is to say, vertical in front of the left shoulder, the hammer resting on the forearm thrown straight across the chest—a formal and unnatural position, enforcing an erect carriage of the body. It did not appear to be the duty of these two men to know what was occurring at the center of the bridge; they merely blockaded the two ends of the foot planking that traversed it.

Point of View
Which details in the first paragraph show the use of the omniscient point of view? Explain.

Beyond one of the sentinels nobody was in sight; the railroad ran straight away into a forest for a hundred yards, then, curving, was lost to view. Doubtless there was an out-post farther along. The other bank of the stream was open ground—a gentle acclivity[1] topped with a stockade of vertical tree trunks, loopholed for rifles, with a single embrasure through which protruded the muzzle of a brass cannon commanding the bridge. Midway of the slope between bridge and fort were the spectators—a single company of infantry in line, at "parade rest," the butts of the rifles on the ground, the barrels inclining slightly backward against the right shoulder, the hands crossed upon the stock. A lieutenant stood at the right of the line, the point of his sword upon the ground, his left hand resting upon his right. Excepting the group of four at the center of the bridge, not a man moved. The company faced the bridge, staring stonily, motionless. The sentinels, facing the banks of the stream, might have been statues to adorn the

Comprehension
What event is about to take place on the bridge?

1. acclivity (ə kliv′ ə tē) *n.* upward slope.

Vocabulary

etiquette (et′ i kit) *n.* appropriate behavior and ceremonies

deference (def′ ər əns) *n.* respect; courtesy; regard

bridge. The captain stood with folded arms, silent, observing the work of his subordinates, but making no sign. Death is a dignitary who when he comes announced is to be received with formal manifestations of respect, even by those most familiar with him. In the code of military **etiquette** silence and fixity are forms of **deference**.

The man who was engaged in being hanged was apparently about thirty-five years of age. He was a civilian, if one might judge from his habit, which was that of a planter. His features were good—a straight nose, firm mouth, broad forehead, from which his long, dark hair was combed straight back, falling behind his ears to the collar of his well-fitting frock coat. He wore a mustache and pointed beard, but no whiskers; his eyes were large and dark gray, and had a kindly expression which one would hardly have expected in one whose neck was in the hemp. Evidently this was no vulgar assassin. The liberal military code makes provision for hanging many kinds of persons, and gentlemen are not excluded.

The preparations being complete, the two private soldiers stepped aside and each drew away the plank upon which he had been standing. The sergeant turned to the captain, saluted and placed himself immediately behind that officer, who in turn moved apart one pace. These movements left the condemned man and the sergeant standing on the two ends of the same plank, which spanned three of the crossties of the bridge. The end upon which the civilian stood almost, but not quite, reached a fourth. This plank had been held in place by the weight of the captain; it was now held by that of the sergeant. At a signal from the former the latter would step aside, the plank would tilt and the condemned man go down between two ties. The arrangement commended itself to his judgment as simple and effective. His face had not been covered nor his eyes bandaged. He looked a moment at his "unsteadfast footing," then let his gaze wander to the swirling water of the stream racing madly beneath his feet. A piece of dancing driftwood caught his attention and his eyes followed it down the current. How slowly it appeared to move! What a sluggish stream!

He closed his eyes in order to fix his last thoughts upon his wife and children. The water, touched to gold by the early sun, the brooding mists under the banks at some distance down the stream, the fort, the soldiers, the piece of drift—all had distracted him. And now he became conscious of a new disturbance. Striking through the thought of his dear ones was a sound which he could neither ignore nor understand, a sharp, distinct, metallic percussion like the stroke of a blacksmith's hammer upon the anvil; it had the same ringing quality. He wondered what it was, and whether immeasurably distant or near by—it seemed both. Its recurrence was regular, but as slow as the tolling of a death knell. He awaited each stroke with impatience and—he knew not why—apprehension. The intervals of silence grew progressively longer; the delays became maddening. With their greater infrequency the sounds increased in strength and sharpness. They hurt his ear like the thrust of a knife; he feared he would shriek. What he heard was the ticking of his watch.

He unclosed his eyes and saw again the water below him. "If I could free my hands," he thought, "I might throw off the noose and spring into the stream. By diving I could evade the bullets and, swimming vigorously, reach the bank, take to the woods and get away home. My home, thank God, is as yet outside their lines; my wife and little ones are still beyond the invader's farthest advance."

As these thoughts, which have here to be set down in words, were flashed into the doomed man's brain rather than evolved from it the captain nodded to the sergeant. The sergeant stepped aside.

II

Peyton Farquhar was a well-to-do planter, of an old and highly respected Alabama family. Being a slave owner and like other slave owners a politician he was naturally an original secessionist and ardently devoted to the Southern cause. Circumstances of an imperious nature, which it is unnecessary to relate here, had prevented him from taking service with the gallant army that had fought the disastrous campaigns ending with the fall of Corinth,[2] and he chafed under the inglorious restraint, longing for the release of his energies, the larger life of the soldier, the opportunity for distinction. That opportunity, he felt, would come, as it comes to all in war time. Meanwhile he did what he could. No service was too humble for him to perform in aid of the South, no adventure too perilous for him to undertake if consistent with the character of a civilian who was at heart a soldier, and who in good faith and without too much qualification assented to at least a part of the frankly villainous **dictum** that all is fair in love and war.

One evening while Farquhar and his wife were sitting on a rustic bench near the entrance to his grounds, a gray-clad soldier rode up to the gate and asked for a drink of water. Mrs. Farquhar was only too happy to serve him with her own white hands. While she was fetching the water her husband approached the dusty horseman and inquired eagerly for news from the front.

"The Yanks are repairing the railroads," said the man, "and are getting ready for another advance. They have reached the Owl Creek bridge, put it in order and built a stockade on the north

2. Corinth Mississippi town that was the site of an 1862 Civil War battle.

Spiral Review
Characterization
Identify one example of direct and one example of indirect characterization in this paragraph. Explain what you learn about Farquhar from each example.

Vocabulary
dictum (dik´ təm) *n.* formal statement of fact or opinion

Comprehension
In the war that divides his nation, which side does Farquhar support?

Vocabulary
summarily (sə mer′ ə lē) *adv.* without formality; hastily

bank. The commandant has issued an order, which is posted everywhere, declaring that any civilian caught interfering with the railroad, its bridges, tunnels or trains will be **summarily** hanged. I saw the order."

"How far is it to the Owl Creek bridge?" Farquhar asked.

"About thirty miles."

"Is there no force on this side the creek?"

"Only a picket post[3] half a mile out, on the railroad, and a single sentinel at this end of the bridge."

"Suppose a man—a civilian and student of hanging—should elude the picket post and perhaps get the better of the sentinel," said Farquhar, smiling, "what could he accomplish?"

The soldier reflected. "I was there a month ago," he replied. "I observed that the flood of last winter had lodged a great quantity of driftwood against the wooden pier at this end of the bridge. It is now dry and would burn like tow."[4]

The lady had now brought the water, which the soldier drank. He thanked her ceremoniously, bowed to her husband and rode away. An hour later, after nightfall, he repassed the plantation, going northward in the direction from which he had come. He was a Federal scout.

Analyzing Patterns of Organization
Describe the shift in time that occurs between sections II and III.

As Peyton Farquhar fell straight downward through the bridge he lost consciousness and was as one already dead. From this state he was awakened—ages later, it seemed to him—by the pain of a sharp pressure upon his throat, followed by a sense of suffocation. Keen, poignant agonies seemed to shoot from his neck downward through every fiber of his body and limbs. These pains appeared to flash along well-defined lines of ramification[5] and to beat with an inconceivably rapid periodicity. They seemed like streams of pulsating fire heating him to an intolerable temperature. As to his head, he was conscious of nothing but a feeling of fullness—of congestion. These sensations were unaccompanied by thought. The intellectual part of his nature was already effaced: he had power only to feel, and feeling was torment. He was conscious of motion. Encompassed in a luminous cloud, of which he was now merely the fiery heart, without material substance, he swung through unthinkable arcs of oscillation, like a vast pendulum. Then all at once, with terrible suddenness, the light about him shot upward with the noise of a loud plash; a frightful roaring was in his ears, and all was cold and dark. The power of thought was restored; he knew that the rope had broken and he had fallen into the stream. There was no additional strangulation; the

3. **picket post** troops sent ahead with news of a surprise attack.
4. **tow** (tō) *n.* coarse, broken fibers of hemp or flax before spinning.
5. **flash along well-defined lines of ramification** spread out quickly along branches from a central point.

noose about his neck was already suffocating him and kept the water from his lungs. To die of hanging at the bottom of a river!—the idea seemed to him ludicrous. He opened his eyes in the darkness and saw above him a gleam of light, but how distant, how inaccessible! He was still sinking, for the light became fainter and fainter until it was a mere glimmer. Then it began to grow and brighten, and he knew that he was rising toward the surface—knew it with reluctance, for he was now very comfortable. "To be hanged and drowned," he thought, "that is not so bad; but I do not wish to be shot. No; I will not be shot; that is not fair."

He was not conscious of an effort, but a sharp pain in his wrist **apprised** him that he was trying to free his hands. He gave the struggle his attention, as an idler might observe the feat of a juggler, without interest in the outcome. What splendid effort!—what magnificent, what superhuman strength! Ah, that was a fine endeavor! Bravo! The cord fell away; his arms parted and floated upward, the hands dimly seen on each side in the growing light. He watched them with a new interest as first one and then the other pounced upon the noose at his neck. They tore it away and thrust it fiercely aside, its undulations resembling those of a water-snake. "Put it back, put it back!" He thought he shouted these words to his hands, for the undoing of the noose had been succeeded by the direst pang that he had yet experienced. His neck ached horribly; his brain was on fire; his heart, which had been fluttering faintly, gave a great leap, trying to force itself out at his mouth. His whole body was racked and wrenched with an insupportable anguish! But his disobedient hands gave no heed to the command. They beat the water vigorously with quick, downward strokes, forcing him to the surface. He felt his head emerge; his eyes were blinded by the sunlight; his chest expanded convulsively, and with a supreme and crowning agony his lungs engulfed a great draft of air, which instantly he expelled in a shriek!

He was now in full possession of his physical senses. They were, indeed, preternaturally[6] keen and alert. Something in the awful disturbance of his organic system had so exalted and refined them that they made record of things never before perceived. He felt the ripples upon his face and heard their separate sounds as they struck. He looked at the forest on the bank of the stream, saw the individual trees, the leaves and the veining of each leaf—saw the very insects upon them: the locusts, the brilliant-bodied flies, the gray spiders

6. **preternaturally** (prēt′ ər nach′ ər əl ē) *adv.* abnormally; extraordinarily.

LITERATURE IN CONTEXT

History Connection

The Battle of Shiloh

Owl Creek is the stream that runs through Tennessee at the site of one of the bloodiest battles of the Civil War—the Battle of Shiloh—where more than 20,000 soldiers died. Railroad bridges like Owl Creek Bridge were important because they gave the armies access over bodies of water.

Connect to the Literature

Why does Farquhar ask so many questions about the bridge?

Vocabulary

apprised (ə prīzd′) *v.* informed; notified

Comprehension

What surprising event happens after Farquhar first loses consciousness?

▲ Critical Viewing
Explain the connection between the illustrations on this and the facing page and their relationship to the story. **CONNECT**

stretching their webs from twig to twig. He noted the prismatic colors in all the dewdrops upon a million blades of grass. The humming of the gnats that danced above the eddies of the stream, the beating of the dragonflies' wings, the strokes of the water spiders' legs, like oars which had lifted their boat—all these made audible music. A fish slid along beneath his eyes and he heard the rush of its body parting the water.

He had come to the surface facing down the stream; in a moment the visible world seemed to wheel slowly round, himself the pivotal point, and he saw the bridge, the fort, the soldiers upon the bridge, the captain, the sergeant, the two privates, his executioners. They were in silhouette against the blue sky. They shouted and gesticulated, pointing at him. The captain had drawn his pistol, but did not fire; the others were unarmed. Their movements were grotesque and horrible, their forms gigantic.

Suddenly he heard a sharp report and something struck the water smartly within a few inches of his head, spattering his face with spray. He heard a second report, and saw one of the sentinels with his rifle at his shoulder, a light cloud of blue smoke rising from the muzzle. The man in the water saw the eye of the man on the bridge gazing into his own through the sights of the rifle. He observed that it was a gray eye and remembered having read that gray eyes were keenest, and that all famous marksmen had them. Nevertheless, this one had missed.

A counterswirl had caught Farquhar and turned him half round; he was again looking into the forest on the bank opposite the fort. The sound of a clear, high voice in a monotonous singsong now rang out behind him and came across the water with a distinctness that pierced and subdued all other sounds, even the beating of the ripples in his ears. Although no soldier, he had frequented camps enough to know the dread significance of that deliberate, drawling, aspirated chant; the lieutenant on shore was taking a part in the morning's work. How coldly and pitilessly—with what an even, calm intonation, presaging,[7] and enforcing tranquillity in the men—with what accurately measured intervals fell those cruel words:

"Attention, company! . . . Shoulder arms! . . . Ready! . . . Aim! . . . Fire!"

Farquhar dived—dived as deeply as he could. The water roared in his ears like the voice of Niagara, yet he heard the dulled thunder of the volley and, rising again toward the surface, met shining bits of metal, singularly flattened, oscillating slowly downward. Some of them touched him on the face and hands, then fell away, continuing their descent. One lodged between his collar and neck; it was uncomfortably warm and he snatched it out.

As he rose to the surface, gasping for breath, he saw that he had been a long time under water; he was perceptibly farther down stream—nearer to safety. The soldiers had almost finished reloading; the metal ramrods flashed all at once in the sunshine as they were drawn from the barrels, turned in the air, and thrust into their sockets. The two sentinels fired again, independently and ineffectually.

The hunted man saw all this over his shoulder; he was now swimming vigorously with the current. His brain was as energetic as his arms and legs; he thought with the rapidity of lightning.

"The officer," he reasoned, "will not make that martinet's[8] error a second time. It is as easy to dodge a volley as a single shot. He has probably already given the command to fire at will. God help me, I cannot dodge them all!"

Comprehension
How do the soldiers try to stop Farquhar after he dives?

An appalling plash within two yards of him was followed by a loud, rushing sound, *diminuendo,*[9] which seemed to travel back through the air to the fort and died in an explosion which stirred the very river to its deeps! A rising sheet of water curved over him, fell down upon him, blinded him, strangled him! The cannon had taken a hand in the game. As he shook his head free from the commotion of the smitten water he heard the deflected shot humming through the air ahead, and in an instant it was cracking and smashing the branches in the forest beyond.

"They will not do that again," he thought; "the next time they

7. **presaging** (prē sāj′ iŋ) *v.* predicting; warning.
8. **martinet** (märt′ 'n et′) *n.* strict military disciplinarian.
9. **diminuendo** (də min′ yo͞o en′ dō) *adj.* musical term used to describe a gradual reduction in volume.

will use a charge of grape.[10] I must keep my eye upon the gun; the smoke will apprise me—the report arrives too late; it lags behind the missile. That is a good gun."

Point of View and Stream of Consciousness

What clues suggest Farquhar may not be totally reliable as a witness?

Suddenly he felt himself whirled round and round—spinning like a top. The water, the banks, the forests, the now distant bridge, fort and men—all were commingled and blurred. Objects were represented by their colors only; circular horizontal streaks of color—that was all he saw. He had been caught in a vortex and was being whirled on with a velocity of advance and gyration that made him giddy and sick. In a few moments he was flung upon the gravel at the foot of the left bank of the stream—the southern bank—and behind a projecting point which concealed him from his enemies. The sudden arrest of his motion, the abrasion of one of his hands on the gravel, restored him, and he wept with delight. He dug his fingers into the sand, threw it over himself in handfuls and audibly blessed it. It looked like diamonds, rubies, emeralds; he could think of nothing beautiful which it did not resemble. The trees upon the bank were giant garden plants; he noted a definite order in their arrangement, inhaled the fragrance of their blooms. A strange, roseate[11] light shone through the spaces among their trunks and the wind made in their branches the music of aeolian harps.[12] He had no wish to perfect his escape—was content to remain in that enchanting spot until retaken.

Suddenly he felt himself whirled round and round—spinning like a top.

A whiz and rattle of grapeshot among the branches high above his head roused him from his dream. The baffled cannoneer had fired him a random farewell. He sprang to his feet, rushed up the sloping bank, and plunged into the forest.

All that day he traveled, laying his course by the rounding sun. The forest seemed interminable; nowhere did he discover a break in it, not even a woodman's road. He had not known that he lived in so wild a region. There was something uncanny in the revelation.

By night fall he was fatigued, footsore, famishing. The thought of his wife and children urged him on. At last he found a road which led him in what he knew to be the right direction. It was as wide and straight as a city street, yet it seemed untraveled. No fields bordered it, no dwelling anywhere. Not so much as the barking of a dog suggested human habitation. The black bodies of the trees formed a straight wall on both sides, terminating on the horizon in a point, like a diagram in a lesson in perspective. Overhead, as he looked up through this rift in the wood, shone great golden stars looking unfamiliar and grouped in strange constellations. He was sure they were arranged in some order which had a secret and malign significance. The wood on either side was full of singular noises, among which—once, twice, and again, he distinctly heard whispers in an unknown tongue.

---

10. **charge of grape** cluster of small iron balls—"grape shot"—that disperse once fired from a cannon.

11. **roseate** (rō′ zē it) *adj.* rose-colored.

12. **aeolian** (ē ō′ lē ən) **harps** stringed instruments that produce music when played by the wind. In Greek mythology, Aeolus is the god of the winds.

His neck was in pain and lifting his hand to it he found it horribly swollen. He knew that it had a circle of black where the rope had bruised it. His eyes felt congested: he could no longer close them. His tongue was swollen with thirst; he relieved its fever by thrusting it forward from between his teeth into the cold air. How softly the turf had carpeted the untraveled avenue—he could no longer feel the roadway beneath his feet!

Doubtless, despite his suffering, he had fallen asleep while walking, for now he sees another scene—perhaps he has merely recovered from a delirium. He stands at the gate of his own home. All is as he left it, and all bright and beautiful in the morning sunshine. He must have traveled the entire night. As he pushes open the gate and passes up the wide white walk, he sees a flutter of female garments: his wife, looking fresh and cool and sweet, steps down from the veranda to meet him. At the bottom of the steps she stands waiting, with a smile of **ineffable** joy, an attitude of matchless grace and dignity. Ah, how beautiful she is! He springs forward with extended arms. As he is about to clasp her he feels a stunning blow upon the back of the neck; a blinding white light blazes all about him with a sound like the shock of a cannon—then all is darkness and silence!

Peyton Farquhar was dead; his body, with a broken neck, swung gently from side to side beneath the timbers of the Owl Creek bridge.

Vocabulary
ineffable (in ef′ ə bəl) *adj.* too overwhelming to be spoken

Critical Reading

Cite textual evidence to support your responses.

1. **Key Ideas and Details** **(a)** Identify one example of Farquhar's distorted perceptions. **(b) Interpret:** What causes this distortion?
2. **Key Ideas and Details** **(a)** What does Farquhar visualize moments before he is hanged? **(b) Connect:** How is his journey connected with this earlier vision?
3. **Craft and Structure** **(a)** What sensation does Farquhar experience "with terrible suddenness"? **(b) Distinguish:** Which details suggest that Farquhar's escape occurs in his mind?
4. **Key Ideas and Details** **(a)** What does this story suggest about the psychology of a person facing a life or death situation? **(b) Speculate:** Are such insights applicable in daily life, or merely in extreme circumstances, like those of war? Explain.
5. **Integration of Knowledge and Ideas** How does the contrast between the ordinary settings and the awful events of this story add to its power? Explain. In your response, use at least two of these Essential Question words: *heighten, conflict, tension, perspective.* ***[Connecting to the Essential Question: What is the relationship between literature and place?]***

Close Reading Activities

An Occurrence at Owl Creek Bridge

Literary Analysis

1. **Key Ideas and Details** **(a)** What do you learn in Section II about the main character's home life, political loyalties, and motivations? **(b)** How does this detailed information shed light on the scene described in Section I? Explain.
2. **Craft and Structure** Reread the story to find examples of the two different **points of view** Bierce uses. Then, using a chart like the one shown, analyze the effects of these choices.

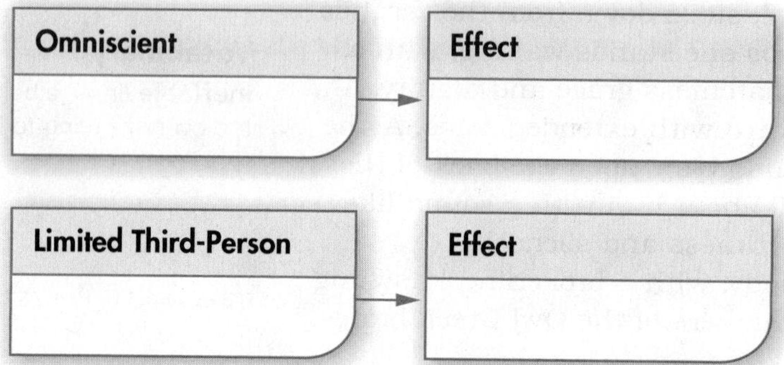

3. **Craft and Structure** **(a)** What point of view does Bierce use in Section III? **(b)** Explain why this choice of point of view is essential to the story's overall impact.
4. **Craft and Structure** What is the effect of the shift in point of view in the last paragraph of the story? Explain.
5. **Craft and Structure** Clarify meaning by **analyzing the story's pattern of organization.** **(a)** Explain how the time frame of the story shifts from Section I to Section II and from Section II to Section III. **(b)** How does the style of writing shift from section to section?
6. **Craft and Structure** **(a)** Which details in the second paragraph of Section III are revealed through the use of **stream of consciousness?** **(b)** What is the "sharp pain" that sparks Farquhar's thoughts? **(c)** In what ways does this passage mimic the natural, jumbled flow of thought?
7. **Integrating Knowledge and Ideas** Why is the stream-of-consciousness technique particularly appropriate for this story?
8. **Key Ideas and Details** At the end of the story, what do you suddenly understand about both the scene described in Section I and the incident described in Section II?
9. **Integrating Knowledge and Ideas** How important do you think the structure of this story is to its overall power and effect on the reader? Explain, citing specific story details in your response.

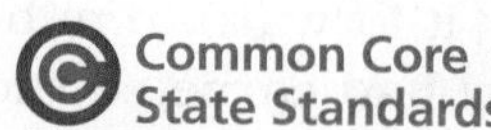

Common Core State Standards

Writing

2. Write explanatory texts to examine and convey complex ideas, concepts, and information clearly and accurately through the effective selection, organization, and analysis of content. *(p. 491)*

2.b. Develop the topic thoroughly by selecting the most significant quotations or other information and examples appropriate to the audience's knowledge of the topic. *(p. 491)*

9.a. Apply *grades 11–12 Reading* standards to literature. *(p. 491)*

Language

3. Apply knowledge of language to make effective choices for meaning. *(p. 491)*

Vocabulary Acquisition and Use

Word Analysis: Latin Root *-dict-*

The noun *dictum* derives from the Latin root *-dict-*, meaning "saying; expression; word." Words that share this root include *verdict* and *dictionary.* Decide whether each of the following statements is true or false and explain each answer. In your explanation, demonstrate your understanding of the meaning of the root *-dict-* in words with different meanings and parts of speech.

1. If two arguments are nearly identical, there is a *contradiction* of terms.
2. An *unpredictable* disaster is one that cannot be avoided.
3. A governmental *edict* is usually written in a formal style.
4. A school board often has *jurisdiction* to establish regulations relating to school safety.
5. Writers who prefer not to type might *dictate* their stories for someone to transcribe.
6. Radio announcers do not need clear *diction* in order to do their jobs well.

Vocabulary: Revising Sentences for Logic

Revise each sentence below so that the underlined vocabulary word is used logically and effectively. Do not change the word.

Example: His preparation for the exam gave him a feeling of apprehension.
Corrected Sentence: His lack of preparation for the exam gave him a feeling of apprehension.

1. He followed proper etiquette and offended nearly everyone in attendance.
2. The judge acted so summarily that we were certain her decision was just.
3. A dictum is likely to use slang or dialect in order to keep an informal tone.
4. In deference to the elders' frailty, we asked them to walk to the reunion.
5. The moment had an ineffable quality that was perfectly described by the soldier.
6. The reporter had not been apprised of the breaking news, so she scooped the story.

Writing to Sources

Explanatory Text Bierce was among the first writers to use stream of consciousness, a *stylistic device* that imitates the natural flow of thoughts and feelings. In an **essay,** explain how Bierce's use of this technique adds to the story's drama.

Prewriting Reread the story and generate a list of selected passages in which the use of stream of consciousness helps you understand Farquhar's thoughts and feelings. Then, select the two or three most significant passages to discuss.

Drafting Focus on one passage at a time. Explain why the use of stream-of-consciousness narration reveals the character's thoughts with heightened realism and drama.

Revising As you review your draft, note points where quotations from the story will help support your opinions and analysis. To assure effective organization, make strong connections between your opinions and each passage you are quoting.

Model: Incorporating Quotations From the Story

Through stream of consciousness, Bierce enables readers to empathize with Farquhar as he desperately imagines a struggle to save his life. The moment of full peace when he reunites with his wife is especially powerful. In his own words, Farquhar thinks he "must have traveled the entire night."

Appropriate quotations from the story create strong connections between the writer's opinions and the text.

Primary Sources

Civil War Diaries and Journals

Mary Chesnut's Civil War

A Confederate Account of the Battle of Gettysburg

Recollections of a Private

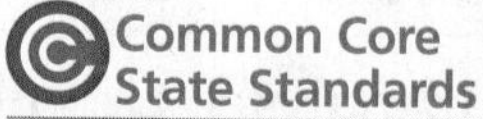

Common Core State Standards

Reading Informational Text

1. Cite strong and thorough textual evidence to support analysis of what the text says explicitly as well as inferences drawn from the text, including determining where the text leaves matters uncertain.

6. Determine an author's point of view or purpose in a text.

9. Analyze nineteenth-century foundational U.S. documents of historical and literary significance for their themes, purposes, and rhetorical features.

About the Text Forms

Diaries and **journals** are personal records of events, thoughts, feelings, and observations. These texts are written informally in a series of dated entries, express the writer's immediate responses to events, and use the first-person pronouns *I* and *we*.

Diaries and journals tell us a great deal about each writer's beliefs, political leanings, values, and experience of life. While most remain unpublished, some that are especially powerful or shed light on historical events, such as these Civil War writings, may be published after the writer's death.

Preparing to Read Complex Texts

Generating questions, or asking questions about a text as you read, can help you focus your reading and better understand the *authors' purposes and perspectives* in historical documents. As you read these diaries and journals, pose questions such as the following:

- *What main purpose prompts the writer to record these experiences?*
- *What does the writer's use of language suggest about his or her position in life?*
- *What does the writer feel or believe about the Civil War? Why? Does the writer express a thematic insight about war in general? If so, how does it relate to those expressed in similar texts?*
- *Does the writer state opinions, feelings, and beliefs directly or implicitly through observation and descriptions?*
- *What clues suggest an opinion or belief is being stated?*

As you read, generate questions to help you better understand each author's position on the Civil War and other aspects of life during that era.

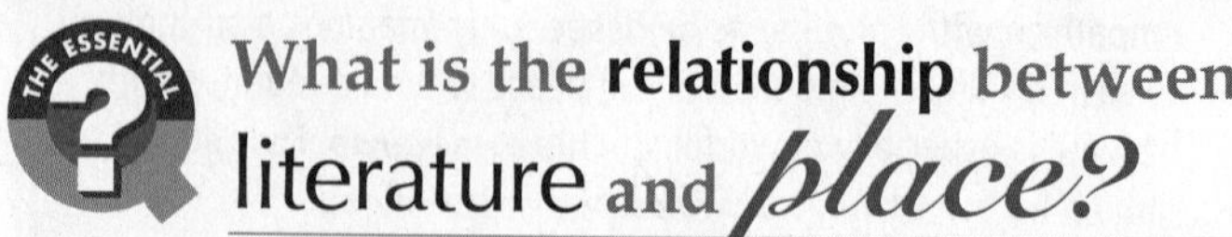
THE ESSENTIAL
What is the relationship between literature and place?

The Civil War was fought on American soil and in American waters. Reading these diary and journal entries will help you see how the war caused people to view their own towns, hillsides, and harbors differently. As you read, note details that describe various locations as being unfamiliar, comforting, strange, or frightening.

Note-Taking Guide

Primary-source documents are a rich source of information for researchers. As you read these documents, use a note-taking guide like the one shown to organize relevant and accurate information.

1 Type of Document (check one)

☐ Newspaper ☐ Advertisement ☐ Telegram ☐ Letter
☐ Press Release ☐ Diary or Journal ☐ E-mail ☐ Report

2 Date(s) of Document ______________________

3 Author of Document ______________________

Author's Position, Title, or Circumstances ______________________

4 Purpose and Audience: Why and for whom was the document written? ______________________

____

5 Document Information

a List two observations or pieces of information given near the beginning of the document that strike you as important. ______________________

____

b Ask a question about each piece of information. ______________________

____

c Identify answers. ______________________

____

d If answers are not clear, explain how you might find them. ______________________

____

____

Generating Questions
A primary source document may raise questions in your mind about a historical event. Pay attention to these questions and use them to focus your reading.

This guide was adapted from the **U.S. National Archives** Document Analysis Worksheets.

Vocabulary

adjourned (ə jurnd´) *v.* closed for a time (p. 495)

convention (kən ven´ shən) *n.* a meeting attended by members or delegates (p. 495)

intercepted (in´ tər sept´ əd) *v.* seized or stopped something on its way from one place to another (p. 496)

obstinate (äb´ stə nət) *adj.* stubborn (p. 497)

recruits (ri kro͞ots) *n.* newly drafted soldiers (p. 500)

fluctuation (fluk´ cho͞o ā´ shən) *n.* a change in level or intensity (p. 500)

spectator (spek´ tāt´ ər) *n.* a person who watches something without taking part in it (p. 501)

offensive (ô´ fen´ siv) *n.* an attitude or position of attack (p. 502)

brigade (bri gād´) *n.* a unit of soldiers (p. 502)

entrenchments (en trench´ mənts) *n.* long, deep holes with steep sides, used as defense against enemy fire (p. 503)

THE STORY BEHIND THE DOCUMENTS

Mary Chesnut

Randolph McKim

In the early days of April 1861, the nation held its collective breath. South Carolina and six other Southern states had recently seceded, or split away; formed their own government; and elected Jefferson Davis as the president of their new Confederacy. Meanwhile, Abraham Lincoln had been inaugurated as president of the United States. When he refused to acknowledge the Confederacy as a separate entity, an armed conflict between the two regions seemed inevitable.

The drama was centered on a massive fort that stood in the harbor of Charleston, South Carolina. Since December 26, 1860, Fort Sumter had housed 85 unwelcome Union soldiers and their commander. In spite of stern warnings from the Confederate army, the Union troops refused to budge. Meanwhile, their food supplies began to dwindle.

It was an uneasy stalemate: neither the North nor the South wanted to fire the first shot. On April 6, President Lincoln ordered supplies sent to Fort Sumter. The gesture was seen as a threat. Southern leaders decided to attack the fort before the shipment arrived.

As the attack began at 4:30 A.M. on April 12, 1861, citizens of Charleston clambered to their rooftops to watch the action. **Mary Boykin Chesnut** (1823–1886) was one of these spectators. Raised in a wealthy aristocratic family, Boykin married James Chesnut, Jr., a senator and a Confederate officer. While her diary provides a detailed account of the events at Fort Sumter, it also conveys the mixture of optimism and dread felt by most Southern aristocrats during the opening days of the war.

Once the war was underway, men hurried to enlist in what most believed would be a swift and glorious conflict. Some saw the military as an opportunity for adventure and advancement, as we learn from the journal of Union soldier **Warren Lee Goss.** Like Goss, most soldiers were young—21 on average—and had no military experience. These naive young men quickly learned that war meant misery, not glory.

Perhaps no other Civil War battle was as painful as the Battle of Gettysburg, in which 51,000 men were either wounded or killed. From July 1 to July 3, 1863, Union and Confederate troops fought near the small town of Gettysburg, Pennsylvania. After Union troops gained control of the nearby hills, the Confederate troops launched a risky attack on the strongest Union position. The attack—described as both "gallant" and "terrible" in the diary of Confederate soldier **Randolph McKim**—was a bitter failure.

Although Chesnut, Goss, and McKim experienced the Civil War in different ways, their diaries and journals reveal profound similarities. They all try to make sense of a fearful unknown, and to contribute, in some way, to the safety and well-being of their loved ones, their companions, and the country and ideals they cherish.

from Mary Chesnut's CIVIL WAR

Mary Chesnut

BACKGROUND As Mary Chesnut notes in the first diary entry below, plans for an attack on Fort Sumter have been made, and the citizens of Charleston wait with both excitement and anxiety for something—or nothing—to happen.

APRIL 7, 1861. Today things seem to have settled down a little.

One can but hope still. Lincoln or Seward[1] have made such silly advances and then far sillier drawings back. There may be a chance for peace, after all.

Things are happening so fast.

My husband has been made an aide-de-camp[2] of General Beauregard.

Three hours ago we were quietly packing to go home. The convention has **adjourned**.

Now he tells me the attack upon Fort Sumter[3] may begin tonight. Depends upon Anderson and the fleet outside. The *Herald* says that this show of war outside of the bar is intended for Texas.

John Manning came in with his sword and red sash. Pleased as a boy to be on Beauregard's staff while the row goes on. He has gone with Wigfall to Captain Hartstene with instructions.

Mr. Chesnut is finishing a report he had to make to the **convention**.

Mrs. Hayne called. She had, she said, "but one feeling, pity for those who are not here."

Jack Preston, Willie Alston—"the take-life-easys," as they are called—with John Green, "the big brave," have gone down to the island—volunteered as privates.

Seven hundred men were sent over. Ammunition wagons rumbling along the streets all night. Anderson burning blue lights—signs and signals for the fleet outside, I suppose.

Primary Sources

Diaries and Journals What details of style and form tell you that you are reading a diary or journal entry?

Vocabulary

adjourned (ə jʉrnd′) *v.* closed for a time

convention (kən ven′ shən) *n.* a meeting attended by members or delegates

Comprehension

What event might happen on the night of April 7, 1861?

1. **Seward** William Henry Seward (1801–1872), U.S. Secretary of State from 1861 through 1869.
2. **aide-de-camp** (ād′ də kamp′) *n.* officer serving as assistant and confidential secretary to a superior.
3. **Fort Sumter** fort in Charleston Harbor, South Carolina. At the time, the fort was occupied by Union troops commanded by Major Robert Anderson.

Bombardment of Sumter, Harper's Weekly, 1861

▶ **Primary Source: Art**
Describe the spectators' differing reactions to the attack on Fort Sumter as shown in this illustration. **DISTINGUISH**

Primary Sources
Diaries and Journals
Judging from her list of dinner guests, what do you understand about Mary Chesnut's social circumstances?

Today at dinner there was no allusion to things as they stand in Charleston Harbor. There was an undercurrent of intense excitement. There could not have been a more brilliant circle. In addition to our usual quartet (Judge Withers, Langdon Cheves, and Trescot) our two governors dined with us, Means and Manning.

These men all talked so delightfully. For once in my life I listened.

That over, business began. In earnest, Governor Means rummaged a sword and red sash from somewhere and brought it for Colonel Chesnut, who has gone to demand the surrender of Fort Sumter.

And now, patience—we must wait.

Why did that green goose Anderson go into Fort Sumter? Then everything began to go wrong.

Now they have **intercepted** a letter from him, urging them to let him surrender. He paints the horrors likely to ensue if they will not.

He ought to have thought of all that before he put his head in the hole.

Vocabulary
intercepted (in′ tər sept′ əd) *v.* seized or stopped something on its way from one place to another

APRIL 12, 1861. Anderson will not capitulate.

Yesterday was the merriest, maddest dinner we have had yet. Men were more audaciously wise and witty. We had an unspoken foreboding it was to be our last pleasant meeting. Mr. Miles dined with us today. Mrs. Henry King rushed in: "The news, I come for the latest news—all of the men of the King family are on the island"—of which fact she seemed proud.

While she was here, our peace negotiator—or envoy—came in. That is, Mr. Chesnut returned—his interview with Colonel Anderson had been deeply interesting—but was not inclined to be communicative, wanted his dinner. Felt for Anderson. Had telegraphed to President Davis[4] for instructions.

What answer to give Anderson, etc., etc. He has gone back to Fort Sumter with additional instructions.

When they were about to leave the wharf, A. H. Boykin sprang into the boat, in great excitement; thought himself ill-used. A likelihood of fighting—and he to be left behind!

I do not pretend to go to sleep. How can I? If Anderson does not accept terms—at four—the orders are—he shall be fired upon.

I count four—St. Michael chimes. I begin to hope. At half-past four, the heavy booming of a cannon.

I sprang out of bed. And on my knees—prostrate—I prayed as I never prayed before.

There was a sound of stir all over the house—pattering of feet in the corridor—all seemed hurrying one way. I put on my double gown and a shawl and went, too. It was to the housetop.

The shells were bursting. In the dark I heard a man say "waste of ammunition."

I knew my husband was rowing about in a boat somewhere in that dark bay. And that the shells were roofing it over—bursting toward the fort. If Anderson was **obstinate**—he was to order the forts on our side to open fire. Certainly fire had begun. The regular roar of the cannon—there it was. And who could tell what each volley accomplished of death and destruction.

The women were wild, there on the housetop. Prayers from the women and imprecations from the men, and then a shell would light up the scene. Tonight, they say, the forces are to attempt to land.

The *Harriet Lane*[5] had her wheelhouse[6] smashed and put back to sea.

Generating Questions
What questions might you ask about Chesnut's daily life?

Vocabulary
obstinate (äb′ stə nət) *adj.* stubborn

Comprehension
What happens at half past four on April 12, 1861?

---

4. **President Davis** Jefferson Davis (1808–1889), president of the Confederacy (1861–1865).
5. **The *Harriet Lane*** federal steamer that had brought provisions to Fort Sumter.
6. **wheelhouse** *n.* enclosed place on the upper deck of a ship, in which the helmsman stands while steering.

We watched up there—everybody wondered. Fort Sumter did not fire a shot.

Today Miles and Manning, colonels now—aides to Beauregard—dined with us. The latter hoped I would keep the peace. I give him only good words, for he was to be under fire all day and night, in the bay carrying orders, etc.

Last night—or this morning truly—up on the housetop I was so weak and weary I sat down on something that looked like a black stool.

"Get up, you foolish woman—your dress is on fire," cried a man. And he put me out.

It was a chimney, and the sparks caught my clothes. Susan Preston and Mr. Venable then came up. But my fire had been extinguished before it broke out into a regular blaze.

Do you know, after all that noise and our tears and prayers, nobody has been hurt. Sound and fury, signifying nothing.[7] A delusion and a snare. . . .

Somebody came in just now and reported Colonel Chesnut asleep on the sofa in General Beauregard's room. After two such nights he must be so tired as to be able to sleep anywhere. . . .

Primary Sources
Diaries and Journals
What do you learn from the entry of April 13, 1861, that you would probably not learn from a textbook?

APRIL 13, 1861. Nobody hurt, after all. How gay we were last night.

Reaction after the dread of all the slaughter we thought those dreadful cannons were making such a noise in doing.

Not even a battery[8] the worse for wear.

Fort Sumter has been on fire. He has not yet silenced any of our guns. So the aides—still with swords and red sashes by way of uniform—tell us.

But the sound of those guns makes regular meals impossible. None of us go to table. But tea trays pervade the corridors, going everywhere.

Some of the anxious hearts lie on their beds and moan in solitary misery. Mrs. Wigfall and I solace ourselves with tea in my room.

These women have all a satisfying faith.

APRIL 15, 1861. I did not know that one could live such days of excitement.

---

7. **Sound . . . nothing** from Shakespeare's *Macbeth*, Act V, Scene v, lines 27–28. Macbeth is contemplating the significance of life and death after learning of his wife's death.
8. **battery** *n.* artillery unit.

They called, "Come out—there is a crowd coming."

A mob indeed, but it was headed by Colonels Chesnut and Manning.

The crowd was shouting and showing these two as messengers of good news. They were escorted to Beauregard's headquarters. Fort Sumter had surrendered.

Those up on the housetop shouted to us, "The fort is on fire." That had been the story once or twice before.

When we had calmed down, Colonel Chesnut, who had taken it all quietly enough—if anything, more unruffled than usual in his serenity—told us how the surrender came about.

Wigfall was with them on Morris Island when he saw the fire in the fort, jumped in a little boat and, with his handkerchief as a white flag, rowed over to Fort Sumter. Wigfall went in through a porthole.

When Colonel Chesnut arrived shortly after and was received by the regular entrance, Colonel Anderson told him he had need to pick his way warily, for it was all mined.

As far as I can make out, the fort surrendered to Wigfall.

But it is all confusion. Our flag is flying there. Fire engines have been sent to put out the fire.

Everybody tells you half of something and then rushes off to tell something else or to hear the last news. . . .

Critical Reading

1. **Key Ideas and Details (a)** What significant events does Chesnut describe in her diary? **(b) Interpret:** What does her diary reveal about daily life during these historical events? **(c) Evaluate:** Do you find anything surprising about Chesnut's depiction of the events themselves or of people's reactions to them? Explain.
2. **Key Ideas and Details (a)** What role does Chesnut's husband play in the events at Fort Sumter? **(b) Infer:** What does his response to the events and the people involved tell you about him? **(c) Hypothesize:** Do you think the Chesnuts' feelings about the events mirror those of most other Southerners? Explain.
3. **Key Ideas and Details (a)** Does Chesnut seem worried about the fate of her hometown, or does she seem to feel safe even in the face of battle? Cite details to support your answer. **(b)** What do you think explains Chesnut's attitude?

▲ **Primary Source: Art**
What attitude toward war does this 1861 painting of a young Civil War soldier convey? Explain. **ANALYZE**

Recollections of A PRIVATE

Warren Lee Goss

In the weeks that followed the attack on Fort Sumter, thousands of men on both sides volunteered to fight. Among the early enlistees was young Warren Lee Goss of Massachusetts.

"Cold chills" ran up and down my back as I got out of bed after the sleepless night, and shaved preparatory to other desperate deeds of valor. I was twenty years of age, and when anything unusual was to be done, like fighting or courting, I shaved.

With a nervous tremor convulsing my system, and my heart thumping like muffled drumbeats, I stood before the door of the recruiting office, and before turning the knob to enter read and reread the advertisement for **recruits** posted thereon, until I knew all its peculiarities. The promised chances for "travel and promotion" seemed good, and I thought I might have made a mistake in considering war so serious after all. "Chances for travel!" I must confess now, after four years of soldiering, that the "chances for travel" were no myth; but "promotion" was a little uncertain and slow.

I was in no hurry to open the door. Though determined to enlist, I was half inclined to put it off awhile; I had a **fluctuation** of desires; I was fainthearted and brave; I wanted to enlist, and yet—Here I turned the knob, and was relieved. . . .

My first uniform was a bad fit: My trousers were too long by three or four inches; the flannel shirt was coarse and unpleasant, too large at the neck and too short elsewhere. The forage cap[1] was an ungainly bag with pasteboard top and leather visor; the blouse was the only part which seemed decent; while the overcoat made me feel like a little nubbin of corn in a large preponderance of husk. Nothing except "Virginia mud" ever took down my ideas of military pomp quite so low.

Vocabulary

recruits (ri kro͞ots) *n.* newly drafted soldiers

fluctuation (fluk′ cho͞o ā′ shən) *n.* a change in level or intensity

1. **forage cap** cap worn by infantry soldiers.

After enlisting I did not seem of so much consequence as I had expected. There was not so much excitement on account of my military appearance as I deemed justly my due. I was taught my facings, and at the time I thought the drillmaster needlessly fussy about shouldering, ordering, and presenting arms. At this time men were often drilled in company and regimental evolutions long before they learned the manual of arms, because of the difficulty of obtaining muskets. These we obtained at an early day, but we would willingly have resigned them after carrying them a few hours. The musket, after an hour's drill, seemed heavier and less ornamental than it had looked to be.

The first day I went out to drill, getting tired of doing the same things over and over, I said to the drill sergeant: "Let's stop this fooling and go over to the grocery." His only reply was addressed to a corporal: "Corporal, take this man out and drill him"; and the corporal did! I found that suggestions were not so well appreciated in the army as in private life, and that no wisdom was equal to a drillmaster's "Right face," "Left wheel," and "Right, oblique, march." It takes a raw recruit some time to learn that he is not to think or suggest, but obey. Some never do learn. I acquired it at last, in humility and mud, but it was tough. Yet I doubt if my patriotism, during my first three weeks' drill, was quite knee high. Drilling looks easy to a spectator, but it isn't. After a time I had cut down my uniform so that I could see out of it, and had conquered the drill sufficiently to see through it. Then the word came: on to Washington! . . .

Generating Questions
What question might you ask about Goss's future as a soldier?

Vocabulary
spectator (spek´ tāt´ ər) *n.* a person who watches something without taking part in it

Critical Reading

1. **Key Ideas and Details (a) Summarize:** Describe Warren Lee Goss's feelings on the day he was to enlist in the army.
   (b) Analyze: How did Private Goss's attitudes and expectations change after he enlisted?
2. **Key Ideas and Details (a)** According to Goss, what takes a long time for a recruit to learn? **(b) Infer:** What do you think happened to cause him to say, "I acquired it at last, in humility and in mud, but it was tough"?
3. **Integration of Knowledge and Ideas (a) Make a Judgment:** In your view, how well suited is Goss for military life? **(b) Generalize:** How similar or different do you think Goss might be to other young men in his situation? Explain.

A Confederate Account of the BATTLE OF GETTYSBURG

Randolph McKim

The Battle of Gettysburg is often referred to as the "turning point" in the Civil War—the point at which the North gained the upper hand. In his diary, Confederate soldier Randolph McKim recounts the bravery of his companions, many of whom were killed or wounded during the advance on Culp's Hill. The advance was led by McKim himself.

Vocabulary

offensive (ô´ fen´ siv) *n.* an attitude or position of attack

brigade (bri gād´) *n.* a unit of soldiers

Then came General Ewell's order to assume the **offensive** and assail the crest of Culp's Hill, on our right. . . . The works to be stormed ran almost at right angles to those we occupied. Moreover, there was a double line of entrenchments, one above the other, and each filled with troops. In moving to the attack we were exposed to enfilading fire[1] from the woods on our left flank, besides the double line of fire which we had to face in front, and a battery of artillery posted on a hill to our left rear opened upon us at short range. . . .

On swept the gallant little **brigade**, the Third North Carolina on the right of the line, next the Second Maryland, then the three Virginia regiments (10th, 23d, and 37th), with the First North Carolina on the extreme left. Its ranks had been sadly thinned, and its energies greatly depleted by those six fearful hours of battle that morning; but its nerve and spirit were undiminished. Soon, however, the left and center were checked and then repulsed, probably by the severe flank fire from the woods; and the small remnant of the Third North Carolina, with the stronger Second Maryland (I do not recall the banners of any other regiment), were far in advance of the rest of the line. On they pressed to within about twenty or thirty paces of the works—a small but gallant band of heroes daring to attempt what could not be done by flesh and blood.

Primary Sources
Diaries and Journals
Which words in this description of the battle show McKim's political leanings?

The end soon came. We were beaten back to the line from which we had advanced with terrible loss, and in much confusion, but the enemy did not make a countercharge. By the strenuous efforts of the officers of the line and of the staff, order was restored, and we re-formed in the breastworks[2] from which we had emerged, there to be again exposed to an artillery fire exceeding in violence that of the

1. **enfilading** (en´ fə lād´ iŋ) **fire** gunfire directed along the length of a column or line of troops.
2. **breastworks** low walls put up quickly as a defense in battle.

◀ **Primary Source: Art** Does this painting of the Battle of Gettysburg help you understand McKim's pride in his brigade? Explain. **CONNECT**

early morning. It remains only to say that, like Pickett's men[3] later in the day, this single brigade was hurled unsupported against the enemy's works. Daniel's brigade remained in the breastworks during and after the charge, and neither from that command nor from any other had we any support. Of course it is to be presumed that General Daniel acted in obedience to orders. We remained in this breastwork after the charge about an hour before we finally abandoned the Federal entrenchments and retired to the foot of the hill.

Vocabulary
entrenchments (en trench′ mənts) *n.* long, deep holes with steep sides, used as defense against enemy fire

3. **Pickett's men** General George Pickett was a Confederate officer who led the unsuccessful attack on the Union position.

Critical Reading

1. **Integration of Knowledge and Ideas (a) Summarize:** Describe in your own words the attack on Culp's Hill. **(b) Speculate:** In your view, who or what was responsible for the Confederates' defeat?
2. **Key Ideas and Details (a)** According to McKim, how was the attack like Pickett's charge later in the day? **(b) Infer:** How do you think McKim felt about his superiors' decisions and orders during the battle? Support your inference with a quotation from the text.
3. **Integration of Knowledge and Ideas Make a Judgment:** Is McKim's account trustworthy? Explain.

Diaries and Journals

Comparing Primary Sources

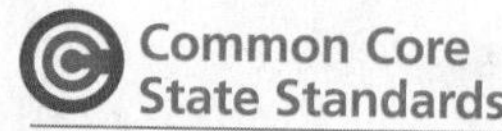

Writing
7. Conduct short as well as more sustained research projects to answer a question or solve a problem; narrow or broaden the inquiry when appropriate; synthesize multiple sources on the subject, demonstrating understanding of the subject under investigation.
8. Gather relevant information from multiple authoritative print and digital sources, using advanced searches effectively; assess the strengths and limitations of each source in terms of the task, purpose, and audience; integrate information into the text selectively to maintain the flow of ideas, avoiding plagiarism and overreliance on any one source.

Language
4.c. Consult general and specialized reference materials to find the etymology of a word.

Refer to your Note-Taking Guide to answer these questions.

1. **(a)** Why do you think each of these writers felt compelled to write a diary or journal? **(b)** What connection do you see between each writer's purpose and the details he or she includes in a diary entry?
2. **(a)** Using a chart like the one shown below, identify one detail or observation from each diary or journal that reveals something important about the writer's beliefs. **(b)** Which writers state their beliefs explicitly? **(c)** Which express their beliefs implicitly? Explain.

Writer	Detail or Observation	What It Reveals
Chesnut		
Goss		
McKim		

3. Write several paragraphs in which you compare and contrast these writers' stations in life and the perspectives they bring to their descriptions of the war. Consider each writer's objectivity, political feelings, and philosophical beliefs.

Vocabulary Acquisition and Use

True or False Indicate whether each sentence below is true or false. Explain your answer.

1. The police would foil a crime if they *intercepted* stolen goods.
2. An *obstinate* person makes a good negotiator.
3. A sudden summer rainstorm can cause a *fluctuation* in temperature.
4. At a sports event, a *spectator* is often responsible for a team's win.

Content-Area Vocabulary Link each word on the left with a set of words on the right. Explain why the word belongs to that set.

5. adjourned
6. recruits
7. brigade
8. offensive
9. convention
10. entrenchments

a. delegates, capitol, elect, legislature
b. combat, campaign, tactic, siege
c. soldiers, enlist, drill, military

Etymology Study The word *adjourned* comes from the Latin word *diurnus*, which means "day" or "daily." Use a dictionary to determine how the words *journal* and *diary* are also related to this Latin root. Then, locate other words that share the same root.

Research Task

Topic: Women and the Civil War

Waiting wives and mourning mothers, fighters and farmers, abolitionists and slaves, nurses and spies—American women during the Civil War played many roles. Before, during, and after the war, women's lives told a vital and often heartrending part of the tragic American story.

▲ Clara Barton traveled behind enemy lines to bring medical care to wounded Union soldiers.

Assignment: Write a **research report** on women and the Civil War. Do not rely strictly on texts written for students; instead, include evidence from texts written by experts for informed, scholarly audiences.

Formulate your research plan. "Women and the Civil War" is a huge topic that cannot be covered adequately in a brief research report. Therefore, narrow the topic to make it manageable and interesting. Alone or in a group, brainstorm for a list of focused topics such as the following:

- women who participated in military action
- the domestic lives of women during the war
- women who worked as spies during the war
- wartime for Northern women vs. Southern women
- one particular woman, such as Mary Chesnut

Choose a focused topic that grabs your interest. Then, formulate a brief list of major questions to answer through research.

RESEARCH TIP

Read author information, often on a jacket flap or back page, to evaluate a writer's authority. On a Web site, read the "About Me" section to evaluate credentials.

Gather sources. Answer your questions using online and library materials. To avoid overreliance on one source, create a chart of the different kinds of information you acquire from a variety of sources.

Model: Researching Using Multiple Sources

Source	Type of Source	Type of Information
"Belle Boyd"	encyclopedia	biographical facts
"Belle Boyd"	history Web site	other women spies
Belle Boyd	2007 biography	details of spy missions

Synthesize information. As you synthesize details from different sources, flexibility is key. You may need to further refine the topic, shift the focus of your research, or add or discard sources. Be prepared to pursue new thoughts and new directions.

Organize and present your ideas. Organize your report into sections identified by subheads. This will clarify the flow of your ideas and information and make the job of writing easier. Add summary statements at the end of each section to make the final report clearer.

Use a checklist like the one shown to ensure the reliability of your research report.

Research Checklist

- ☐ Have I answered all my research questions?
- ☐ Does my evidence come from experts and texts written for informed audiences in the field?
- ☐ Have I avoided relying too much on one source?
- ☐ Is my report clearly organized, with sections, subheads, and summary statements?

Building Knowledge and Insight

An Episode of War

Connecting to the Essential Question Stephen Crane presents the stark realities of war, omitting lofty reflections on honor or courage. As you read, notice details that downplay the drama of war. This will help as you consider the Essential Question: **How does literature shape or reflect society?**

Reading Literature

3. Analyze the impact of the author's choices regarding how to develop and relate elements of a story (e.g., how the characters are introduced and developed).

9. Demonstrate knowledge of nineteenth-century foundational works of American literature, including how two or more texts from the same period treat similar themes or topics.

Close Reading Focus

Naturalism

Naturalism is a literary movement that developed in reaction to *Romanticism*. The horrors of the Civil War caused many American writers to question Romantic ideas about human goodness and nature's beauty. In stark contrast to the Romantic view, Naturalists felt that people's lives are controlled by forces beyond their understanding or control. These forces include heredity, people's surroundings, and sheer chance. In Naturalistic works, characters are often victims of their own instincts or of a violent world, and they endure their suffering with a quiet dignity. For example, the wounded main character in "An Episode of War" wanders aimlessly through a Civil War encampment:

> ***He wore the look of one who knows he is the victim of a terrible disease and understands his helplessness.***

Like other Naturalistic writers, Crane presents a bleak reality without explaining it. Instead, he allows the reader to draw his or her own conclusions. As you read, look for these Naturalistic elements in Crane's story.

Preparing to Read Complex Texts Knowledge of the Civil War era can clarify your understanding of the characters and action in this story. The diaries and journals that appear on pages 494–503, as well as the unit introduction, background note, and other features in this textbook offer valuable insights into the realities of the Civil War experience. As you read, **apply background knowledge** you gain from these texts to clarify details. Doing so will also help you *predict* the story's events. Use a chart like the one shown to record your observations.

Background Knowledge	Story Details

Vocabulary

You will encounter the words below in the text that follows. Copy the words into your notebook. Which words do you think are nouns? What clue indicates this part of speech?

precipitate **disdainfully**
aggregation **sinister**
commotion

STEPHEN CRANE *(1871–1900)*

Author of "An Episode of War"

Stephen Crane had not been born when the last battle of the American Civil War was fought, yet he is best remembered for his compelling depiction of the conflict. During his brief life, Crane established himself as both a leader of the Naturalist movement and one of the greatest writers of his time.

Early in his career, Crane worked as a journalist in New York City. His experiences there inspired his first novel, *Maggie: A Girl of the Streets* (1893). Its grimly realistic portrayal of life in the city's slums was so frank and shocking that Crane was unable to find a publisher, and he printed the book at his own expense.

The Red Badge of Courage Crane's second novel, published in 1895, was *The Red Badge of Courage: An Episode of the American Civil War.* A psychological exploration of a young soldier's mental and emotional reactions under enemy fire, the wildly successful novel earned international acclaim for the twenty-four-year-old writer. Crane had never experienced military combat, but he interviewed Civil War veterans and studied photographs, battle plans, and biographical accounts before writing the realistic battle scenes.

Crane later viewed war firsthand when he served as a newspaper correspondent during the Greco-Turkish War in 1897 and the Spanish-American War in 1898. His war experiences provided material for a collection of poetry, *War Is Kind* (1899), but they took their toll on his health. He died of tuberculosis at the age of twenty-eight.

A Short, Passionate Life Like other Naturalists, Crane depicts characters who are manipulated by forces that are beyond their understanding or control. His most common themes include the harsh reality of war, the degradation of humanity, social rebellion, betrayal, and guilt. Knowing he would not live long, Crane worked intensely in the last years of his life. His novels, short stories, poems, and other writings fill twelve volumes. He is considered a literary prodigy who wrote as quickly and passionately as he lived.

An Episode of War

Stephen Crane

BACKGROUND Until World War II, the American Civil War was the bloodiest conflict in American history. It claimed the lives of 600,000 soldiers. Hundreds of thousands more were left maimed by battle wounds and crude medical care. In fact, the conditions in field hospitals were so primitive that twice as many soldiers died from infections as from combat wounds. As you read this story, keep in mind that amputation was the routine treatment for injured limbs. A wounded soldier knew that he faced the high probability of losing his arm or leg to a surgeon's saw.

The lieutenant's rubber blanket lay on the ground, and upon it he had poured the company's supply of coffee. Corporals and other representatives of the grimy and hot-throated men who lined the breast-work[1] had come for each squad's portion.

The lieutenant was frowning and serious at this task of division. His lips pursed as he drew with his sword various crevices in the heap, until brown squares of coffee, astoundingly equal in size, appeared on the blanket. He was on the verge of a great triumph in mathematics, and the corporals were thronging forward, each to reap a little square, when suddenly the lieutenant cried out and looked quickly at a man near him as if he suspected it was a case of personal assault. The others cried out also when they saw blood upon the lieutenant's sleeve.

He had winced like a man stung, swayed dangerously, and then straightened. The sound of his hoarse breathing was plainly audible. He looked sadly, mystically, over the breast-work at the green face of a wood, where now were many little puffs of white smoke. During this moment the men about him gazed statuelike and silent, astonished and awed by this catastrophe which happened when catastrophes were not expected—when they had leisure to observe it.

As the lieutenant stared at the wood, they too swung their heads, so that for another instant all hands, still silent, contemplated the distant forest as if their minds were fixed upon the mystery of a bullet's journey.

The officer had, of course, been compelled to take his sword into his left hand. He did not hold it by the hilt. He gripped it at the middle of the blade, awkwardly. Turning his eyes from the hostile wood, he looked at the sword as he held it there, and seemed puzzled as to what to do with it, where to put it. In short, this weapon had of a sudden become a strange thing to him. He looked at it in a kind of stupefaction, as if he had been endowed with a trident, a sceptre,[2] or a spade.

Finally he tried to sheathe it. To sheathe a sword held by the left hand, at the middle of the blade, in a scabbard hung at the left hip, is a feat worthy of a sawdust ring.[3] This

The **American EXPERIENCE**

Humanities Connection

Photographer Mathew Brady

Thanks to photography pioneer Mathew Brady (1823?–1896), the Civil War was the first war to be captured on film. As a young man, Brady met Samuel Morse, the inventor of the telegraph. Morse taught Brady how to make daguerreotypes, the forerunners of photographs. By the 1850s, Brady owned a thriving studio in New York City and was known for his portraits of distinguished Americans. When the Civil War broke out, Brady hired twenty photographers and sent them out to document the conflict. Due to the limitations of their technology, the photographers rarely captured battlefield action. Instead, they took pictures of events behind the scenes and of the carnage after battles. **The photographs that illustrate this story were taken by Brady and his team.** Their images, often horrific, forced viewers to face the realities of war more directly than ever before.

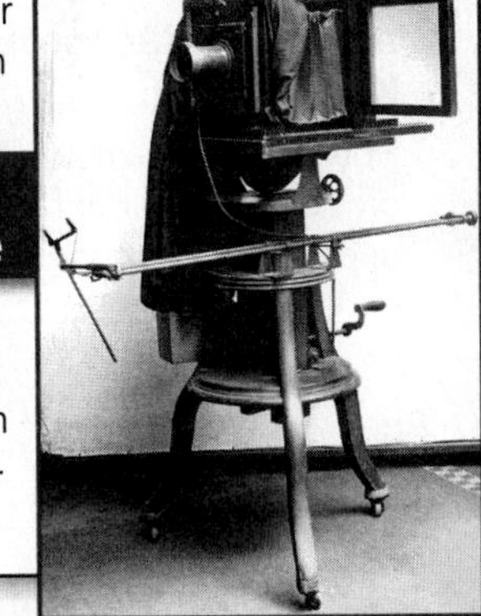

Connect to the Literature

How is documentary photography, like the images on these pages, similar to Naturalism?

1. **breast-work** low wall put up quickly as a defense in battle.
2. **a trident, a sceptre** (trīd′ ənt; sep′ tər) three-pronged spear; decorated ornamental rod or staff symbolizing royal authority.
3. **sawdust ring** ring in which circus acts are performed.

◀ **Critical Viewing** What similarities do you see between this photograph and Crane's description of the wounded lieutenant being helped by his men? **CONNECT** wounded officer engaged in a desperate struggle with the sword and the wobbling scabbard, and during the time of it breathed like a wrestler.

But at this instant the men, the spectators, awoke from their stone-like poses and crowded forward sympathetically. The orderly-sergeant took the sword and tenderly placed it in the scabbard. At the time, he leaned nervously backward, and did not allow even his finger to brush the body of the lieutenant. A wound gives strange dignity to him who bears it. Well men shy from his new and terrible majesty. It is as if the wounded man's hand is upon the curtain which hangs before the revelations of all existence—the meaning of ants, potentates,[4] wars, cities, sunshine, snow, a feather dropped from a bird's wing; and the power of it sheds radiance upon a bloody form, and makes the other men understand sometimes that they are little. His comrades look at him with large eyes thoughtfully. Moreover, they fear vaguely that the weight of a finger upon him might send him headlong, **precipitate** the tragedy, hurl him at once into the dim, grey unknown. And so the orderly-sergeant, while sheathing the sword, leaned nervously backward.

Naturalism
What Naturalist ideas are evident in this passage about the orderly-sergeant's reaction to the lieutenant's wound?

Vocabulary
precipitate (prē sip′ ə tāt′) *v.* cause to happen before expected or desired

There were others who proffered assistance. One timidly presented his shoulder and asked the lieutenant if he cared to lean upon it, but the latter waved him away mournfully. He wore the look of one who knows he is the victim of a terrible disease and understands his helplessness. He again stared over the breast-work at the forest, and then, turning, went slowly rearward. He held his right wrist tenderly in his left hand as if the wounded arm was made of very brittle glass.

And the men in silence stared at the wood, then at the departing lieutenant; then at the wood, then at the lieutenant.

As the wounded officer passed from the line of battle, he was enabled to see many things which as a participant in the fight were unknown to him. He saw a general on a black horse gazing over the lines of blue infantry at the green woods which veiled his problems. An aide galloped furiously, dragged his horse suddenly to a halt, saluted, and presented a paper. It was, for a wonder, precisely like a historical painting.

Applying Background Knowledge
How does your knowledge of the Civil War clarify your understanding of these battlefield details?

To the rear of the general and his staff a group, composed of a bugler, two or three orderlies, and the bearer of the corps standard,[5] all upon maniacal horses, were working like slaves to hold their ground, preserve their respectful interval, while the shells boomed in the air about them, and caused their chargers to make furious quivering leaps.

A battery, a tumultuous and shining mass, was swirling toward the right. The wild thud of hoofs, the cries of the riders shouting

---

4. potentates (pōt′ ən tāts) *n.* rulers; powerful people.
5. corps standard (kôr) flag or banner representing a military unit.

blame and praise, menace and encouragement, and, last, the roar of the wheels, the slant of the glistening guns, brought the lieutenant to an intent pause. The battery swept in curves that stirred the heart; it made halts as dramatic as the crash of a wave on the rocks, and when it fled onward this **aggregation** of wheels, levers, motors had a beautiful unity, as if it were a missile. The sound of it was a war-chorus that reached into the depths of man's emotion.

The lieutenant, still holding his arm as if it were of glass, stood watching this battery until all detail of it was lost, save the figures of the riders, which rose and fell and waved lashes over the black mass.

Later, he turned his eyes toward the battle, where the shooting sometimes crackled like bush-fires, sometimes sputtered with exasperating irregularity, and sometimes reverberated like the thunder. He saw the smoke rolling upward and saw crowds of men who ran and cheered, or stood and blazed away at the inscrutable distance.

He came upon some stragglers, and they told him how to find the field hospital. They described its exact location. In fact, these men, no longer having part in the battle, knew more of it than others. They told the performance of every corps, every division, the opinion of every general. The lieutenant, carrying his wounded arm rearward, looked upon them with wonder.

At the roadside a brigade was making coffee and buzzing with talk like a girls' boarding school. Several officers came out to him

▲ Critical Viewing

What mood do the expressions and body language of these Civil War officers convey? Explain. **ANALYZE**

Vocabulary

aggregation (ag′ rə gā′ shən) *n.* group of distinct objects or individuals

Comprehension

What does the lieutenant stop to watch on his way to the field hospital?

▶ **Critical Viewing**
This is a photograph of a Civil War field hospital. Do you think that soldiers received quality treatment in this setting? Explain. **DEDUCE**

and inquired concerning things of which he knew nothing. One, seeing his arm, began to scold. "Why, man, that's no way to do. You want to fix that thing." He appropriated the lieutenant and the lieutenant's wound. He cut the sleeve and laid bare the arm, every nerve of which softly fluttered under his touch. He bound his handkerchief over the wound, scolding away in the meantime. His tone allowed one to think that he was in the habit of being wounded every day. The lieutenant hung his head, feeling, in this presence, that he did not know how to be correctly wounded.

The low white tents of the hospital were grouped around an old schoolhouse. There was here a singular **commotion**. In the foreground two ambulances interlocked wheels in the deep mud. The drivers were tossing the blame of it back and forth, gesticulating and berating, while from the ambulances, both crammed with wounded, there came an occasional groan. An interminable crowd of bandaged men were coming and going. Great numbers sat under the trees nursing heads or arms or legs. There was a dispute of some kind raging on the steps of the schoolhouse. Sitting with his back against a tree a man with a face as grey as a new army blanket was serenely smoking a corncob pipe. The lieutenant wished to rush forward and inform him that he was dying.

A busy surgeon was passing near the lieutenant. "Good-morning," he said, with a friendly smile. Then he caught sight of the

Vocabulary
commotion (kə mō′ shən) *n.* noisy confusion

▶ **Critical Viewing**
What do the Civil War era surgical instruments shown on the next page suggest about the care the lieutenant will receive? **INFER**

lieutenant's arm, and his face at once changed. "Well, let's have a look at it." He seemed possessed suddenly of a great contempt for the lieutenant. This wound evidently placed the latter on a very low social plane. The doctor cried out impatiently, "What mutton-head had tied it up that way anyhow?" The lieutenant answered, "Oh, a man."

When the wound was disclosed the doctor fingered it **disdainfully**. "Humph," he said. "You come along with me and I'll 'tend to you." His voice contained the same scorn as if he were saying: "You will have to go to jail."

The lieutenant had been very meek, but now his face flushed, and he looked into the doctor's eyes. "I guess I won't have it amputated," he said.

"Nonsense, man! Nonsense! Nonsense!" cried the doctor. "Come along, now. I won't amputate it. Come along. Don't be a baby."

"Let go of me," said the lieutenant, holding back wrathfully, his glance fixed upon the door of the old schoolhouse, as **sinister** to him as the portals of death.

And this is the story of how the lieutenant lost his arm. When he reached home, his sisters, his mother, his wife, sobbed for a long time at the sight of the flat sleeve. "Oh, well," he said, standing shamefaced amid these tears, "I don't suppose it matters so much as all that."

Vocabulary

disdainfully (dis dān′ fəl ē) *adv.* showing scorn or contempt

sinister (si′ nəs tər) *adj.* threatening harm, evil, or misfortune

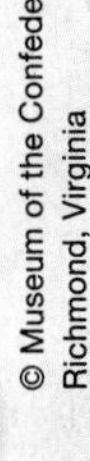

Critical Reading

Cite textual evidence to support your responses.

1. **Key Ideas and Details (a)** What happens to cause the lieutenant's injury? **(b) Analyze:** How do the details of his injury make him a sympathetic character?
2. **Key Ideas and Details (a)** What is the lieutenant's reaction when a soldier offers a helpful shoulder? **(b) Infer:** Why does he react this way?
3. **Integration of Knowledge and Ideas (a)** Note three examples of the lieutenant's distance from the uninjured people around him. **(b) Interpret:** What do these examples suggest about the way others see him and the way he sees himself?
4. **Integration of Knowledge and Ideas** In your view, does society benefit from frank portrayals of suffering? In your response, use at least two of these Essential Question words: *awareness, assumption, reality, despair.* ***[Connecting to the Essential Question: How does literature shape or reflect society?]***

Close Reading Activities **_An Episode of War_**

Literary Analysis

1. **Key Ideas and Details** **(a)** What is the lieutenant doing when he is injured? **(b)** How does this detail reflect the **Naturalist** idea that people are victims of chance?
2. **Craft and Structure** **(a)** Why do you think Crane chooses to have the lieutenant remain nameless? **(b)** Does the lieutenant's namelessness heighten or lessen the emotional impact of the story? Explain.
3. **Craft and Structure** Note two details that show how the lieutenant exhibits a quiet endurance typical of characters in Naturalist works. Explain your choices.
4. **Craft and Structure** **(a)** Identify three descriptions of human actions in the story that could also describe the actions of animals. **(b)** How do these descriptions reflect Naturalist ideas about people's helplessness in the face of nature and circumstance?
5. **Craft and Structure** **(a)** At various points in the story, people make gestures of kindness toward the lieutenant. Use a chart like the one shown to record these details and explain why they fail. **(b)** What Naturalist ideas about the possibility of kindness does this series of details imply?

Event or Detail	Why It Fails	Naturalist Idea

6. **Integration of Knowledge and Ideas** What differences might exist in the mood, events, or outcome of this story if it had been written by a *Romantic* writer who believed in the harmony of humanity and nature? Explain.
7. **Integration of Knowledge and Ideas** **(a) Apply your background knowledge** of Civil War medical practices to explain why the doctor promises the lieutenant he will not amputate. **(b)** How did your background knowledge help you anticipate, or *predict,* the type of medical treatment the lieutenant would receive?
8. **Integration of Knowledge and Ideas** Apply the background knowledge you gain from reading the Civil War documents on pages 494–503. **(a)** List at least three details from the primary sources that relate to the setting, characters, and events in *An Episode of War.* **(b)** For each detail you cite, explain how it adds to your understanding of the story.

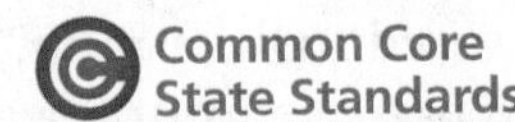

Common Core State Standards

Writing

2. Write informative/explanatory texts to examine and convey complex ideas, concepts, and information clearly and accurately through the effective selection, organization, and analysis of content. *(p. 515)*

2.a. Introduce a topic; organize complex ideas, concepts, and information so that each new element builds on that which precedes it to create a unified whole. *(p. 515)*

Language

4.b. Identify and correctly use patterns of word changes that indicate different meanings or parts of speech. *(p. 515)*

Vocabulary Acquisition and Use

Word Analysis: Latin Root *-greg-*

The word *aggregation* contains the Latin root *-greg-*, meaning "herd" or "flock." An *aggregation* is a group of people or things taken as a whole. A *congregation* is a group, and a *gregarious* person is someone who enjoys being part of a crowd. Copy the paragraph below, filling in each blank with the appropriate *-greg-* word from the list. Be sure to fill in each blank with a word that is appropriate in meaning and part of speech.

aggregate   gregarious   congregated

The wounded soldiers _______ on the steps, waiting to see the doctor. They were silent, except for one _______ private who described his injury in great detail to the rest of the group. In the _______, an orderly reflected, wounded men are a quiet bunch.

Vocabulary: Analogies

Analogies show the relationships between pairs of words. Complete each analogy using a word from the vocabulary list on page 506. In each, your choice should create a word pair that matches the relationship between the first two words given. Then, explain your answer.

1. *Quickly* is to *rapidly* as _______ is to *scornfully*.
2. *Hidden* is to *revealed* as _______ is to *harmless*.
3. *Storm* is to *peace* as _______ is to *serenity*.
4. *Laugh* is to *cry* as _______ is to *delay*.
5. *Sum* is to *parts* as _______ is to *individual*.

Writing to Sources

Explanatory Text Many critics have observed that Crane's fiction asks questions but does not provide answers, challenging readers to evaluate their ideas about people's behavior, feelings, and thoughts. Write an **essay** in which you respond to this assessment of Crane's work. Determine whether "An Episode of War" provides strong support for this critical view.

Prewriting Use a format like the one shown to list assumptions about war that people commonly hold. Then, reread the story. Note details that relate to your list of assumptions. Decide if you think this story poses challenges to those assumptions and whether it provides support for the critical view. Write a statement that summarizes your observations.

Drafting Clearly state the critical assessment of Crane's work. Then, state your position. Using your prewriting notes, devote one paragraph to each assumption and its expression in the story.

Model: Questioning Assumptions

Assumption: Soldiers have what they need to do their job well.
Challenge question: Do soldiers always have what they need?
Related detail: The soldiers are each being rationed a small bit of coffee.

To challenge an assumption, ask, "Is this always true?"

Revising Reread your essay to make sure that your ideas are fully developed, that your ideas flow in a logical order, and that each idea builds on the one that comes before. If necessary, reorder your paragraphs to improve the flow of ideas.

There are events which are so great that if a writer has participated in them his obligation is to write truly rather than assume the presumption of altering them with invention.

~ Ernest Hemingway

In This Section

For more practice analyzing narrative nonfiction, see pages 34, 48, 58, 69, 140, 171, 251, 495, 554, 570, 589, 617, 930, and 1426.

Defining Narrative Nonfiction

Narrative nonfiction is prose writing that tells the stories of real people, places, objects, or events. It features many of the same elements as fiction—including characters, setting, and a sequence of events—but these are based on actual, lived experiences, rather than imagination.

Types of Narrative Nonfiction These are the most common forms of narrative nonfiction:

- **Biography and Autobiography:** works that tell life stories. A biography is a life story written by another person, while an autobiography is an account of the writer's own life.
- **Historical Narrative:** a work that relates historical events that the writer may or may not have experienced firsthand
- **Memoir:** an autobiographical work that focuses on a particular time period or aspect of the writer's life
- **Diary and Journal:** an informal account of the writer's daily experiences
- **Narrative Essay:** a short work that explores ideas while relating a story

Style and Tone Style is a writer's particular way of using language, and tone is his or her attitude toward the audience and subject. Both are key ingredients in narrative nonfiction.

Close Read: Style and Tone

Many literary elements contribute to a writer's style and tone. The following elements appear in the Model Text.

Diction: the types of words a writer favors. Diction may be ornate, plain, familiar, formal, technical, or any combination thereof. *Example: "Why did that green goose Anderson go into Fort Sumter?" (Mary Chesnut)*	**Rhetorical Devices:** meaningful patterns of words and ideas. *Parallelism* is the repetition of the same grammatical structure. *Rhetorical questions* are asked for effect. *Example (parallelism): "She had bread for the hungry, clothes for the naked, and comfort for every mourner. . . ." (Frederick Douglass)*
Syntax: sentence length and complexity. Syntax may involve any combination of long, short, complex, or simple sentences. *Example: "When I was a boy, there was but one permanent ambition among my comrades in our village on the west bank of the Mississippi River. That was, to be a steamboatman." (Mark Twain)*	**Telling Details:** precise details that reveal important information about the characters, setting, or situation. *Example: ". . . she had two shopping bags full of canned peaches, real peaches, beans wrapped in taro leaves, cookies, Thermos bottles, enough food for everybody . . ." (Maxine Hong Kingston)*

Model

About the Text Richard Wright (1908–1960) was one of the first African American writers to achieve international fame. His autobiography, *Black Boy,* was published in 1945, five years after the appearance of his acclaimed first novel, *Native Son.* In this excerpt, he refers to *A Book of Prefaces* by journalist and social critic H. L. Mencken.

from ***Black Boy***
by Richard Wright

That night in my rented room, while letting the hot water run over my can of pork and beans in the sink, I opened *A Book of Prefaces* and began to read. I was jarred and shocked by the style, the clear, clean, sweeping sentences. Why did he write like that? And how did one write like that? I pictured the man as a raging demon, slashing with his pen, consumed with hate, denouncing everything American, extolling everything European or German, laughing at the weakness of people, mocking God, authority. What was this? I stood up, trying to realize what reality lay behind the meaning of the words. Yes, this man was fighting, fighting with words. He was using words as a weapon, using them as one would use a club. Could words be weapons? Well, yes, for here they were. Then maybe, perhaps, I could use them as a weapon? No. It frightened me. I read on and what amazed me was not what he said, but how on earth anybody had the courage to say it.

Occasionally I glanced up to reassure myself that I was alone in the room. Who were these men about whom Mencken was talking so passionately? Who was Anatole France? Joseph Conrad? Sinclair Lewis, Sherwood Anderson, Dostoevski, George Moore, Gustave Flaubert, Maupassant, Tolstoy, Frank Harris, Mark Twain, Thomas Hardy, Arnold Bennett, Stephen Crane, Zola, Norris, Gorky, Bergson, Ibsen, Balzac, Bernard Shaw, Dumas, Poe, Thomas Mann, O. Henry, Dreiser, H. G. Wells, Gogol, T. S. Eliot, Gide, Baudelaire, Edgar Lee Masters, Stendhal, Turgenev, Huneker, Nietzsche,[1] and scores of others? Were these men real? Did they exist or had they existed? And how did one pronounce their names?

Telling Details Specific details, such as "rented room," and "can of pork and beans" clearly establish both the setting and Wright's less than affluent circumstances.

Rhetorical Devices Note the use of parallel structure in Wright's description of Mencken's prose: "slashing," "denouncing," "extolling," and "mocking."

Syntax Wright's syntax—featuring short, staccato sentences—reflects the intensity and speed of his thoughts. It is as though the reader is allowed to experience Wright's internal, highly charged conversation.

Diction Wright uses an idiomatic expression: "how on earth." This strengthens the sense of authenticity in his impassioned, emotional reaction to Mencken's words.

[1]**Anatole France...Nietzche** This list identifies some of the most celebrated European and American philosophers, poets, playwrights, and fiction writers of the 19th and 20th centuries.

Building Knowledge and Insight

ANCHOR TEXT

from *My Bondage and My Freedom*

Connecting to the Essential Question In both his writing and, implicitly, in the example he provided through his own life, Frederick Douglass argued for freedom and equality. As you read, notice details that reveal Douglass's character. Doing so will help as you consider the Essential Question: **How does literature shape or reflect society?**

Close Reading Focus

Autobiography; Author's Purpose

An **autobiography** is a person's account of his or her own life. Most autobiographers feel their lives are noteworthy and can somehow help others. This belief is part of the **author's purpose,** or reason for writing. Douglass's purpose was to show through his own life that African Americans are as intelligent, capable, and feeling as whites:

> *I could talk and sing; I could laugh and weep;*
> *I could reason and remember . . .*

Douglass's formal and dignified writing style, or specific way of using language, contributes to his purpose. It also helps to expresses his *tone*, or attitude, which is both passionate and compassionate. As you read, think about Douglass's purpose for relating the events in this excerpt and analyze how his style contributes to that purpose.

Preparing to Read Complex Texts **Setting a purpose** for reading gives you a concept on which to focus. When reading literature from other eras, one useful purpose is to note how *influences of the historical period shape characters, events, and settings.* Historical influences may include the following broad areas:

- *philosophical ideas* or *religious beliefs* that motivate specific actions
- *political events* or *social problems* that affect individuals or groups
- *ethical issues,* such as the moral conflicts caused by slavery

As you read, identify the historical influences in Douglass's narrative. Record your observations in a chart like the one shown.

Vocabulary

The words listed here are key to understanding the text that follows. Copy the words into your notebook. Which words do you think are adjectives? What is the clue that points to their part of speech?

benevolent	**opposition**
deficient	**consternation**
fervent	**intolerable**

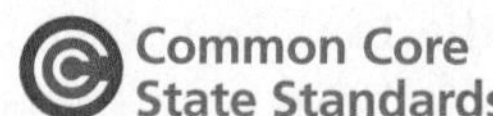

Common Core State Standards

Reading Informational Text

6. Determine an author's point of view or purpose in a text in which the rhetoric is particularly effective, analyzing how style and content contribute to the power, persuasiveness, or beauty of the text.

9. Analyze nineteenth-century foundational U.S. documents for their themes, purposes, and rhetorical features.

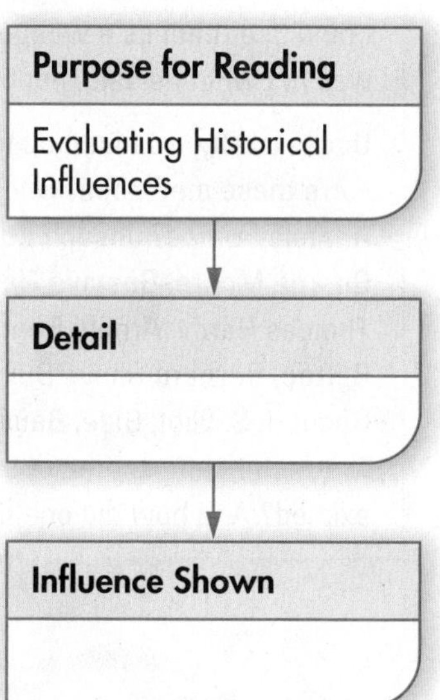

Frederick Douglass (1817–1895)

Author of *My Bondage and My Freedom*

Frederick Douglass rose out of slavery to become one of the most gifted writers and orators of his time. He used his talents to fight for the abolition of slavery and for civil rights. His life served as an inspiration and example for all Americans, both black and white throughout the country.

Early Years Douglass was born on a Maryland plantation. Historians believe that his name at birth was Frederick Augustus Bailey. At the age of eight, he was sent as a slave to the Baltimore home of the Auld family, where he learned to read and write. Learning became an unquenchable thirst for Douglass. As his knowledge grew, so did his desire for freedom. At age twenty, he escaped to Massachusetts, a free state, and took the surname Douglass to avoid arrest as a fugitive.

A Public Life In 1841, despite the fear of being arrested, Douglass began lecturing against slavery and for civil rights for all people. Rumors spread that a man of such eloquence could not possibly have been a slave. In response, Douglass published his first autobiography, *Narrative of the Life of Frederick Douglass, an American Slave, Written By Himself* (1845). Fearing re-enslavement, Douglass then fled to England, where he worked to gain British support for the abolitionist movement in the United States.

Freedom at Last After English friends raised money to buy his freedom, Douglass returned to the United States, founded a newspaper for African Americans, and resumed lecturing. In 1855, he published *My Bondage and My Freedom*, an updated version of his autobiography.

After slavery was abolished, Douglass fought vigorously for civil rights for African Americans. He became a consultant to President Lincoln and held several government positions, including United States minister to Haiti.

A Vision for the Future In 1883, Douglass said "I expect to see the colored people of this country enjoying the same freedom, voting at the same ballot-box, . . . going to the same schools, attending the same churches, . . . proud of the same country, fighting the same foe, and enjoying the same peace and all its advantages. . . ."

from

My Bondage and My Freedom

FREDERICK DOUGLASS

BACKGROUND *Frederick Douglass was perhaps the most prominent African American leader of the nineteenth century, and his influence is still felt. As a crusader for human rights, Douglass served as a role model for African American leaders such as Booker T. Washington and W.E.B. DuBois. In our own era, the civil rights movement has drawn inspiration from Douglass, who opposed segregation decades before other voices were raised. As a young man, Douglass protested segregated seating on trains by sitting in cars reserved for whites until the authorities forcibly removed him. Later, he fought job discrimination against African Americans, protested segregation in school, and fought for civil rights for all Americans.*

The Chimney Corner, 1863, Eastman Johnson, Munson-Williams-Proctor Institute Museum of Art, Utica, New York

I lived in the family of Master Hugh, at Baltimore, seven years, during which time—as the almanac makers say of the weather—my condition was variable. The most interesting feature of my history here, was my learning to read and write, under somewhat marked disadvantages. In attaining this knowledge I was compelled to resort to indirections by no means congenial to my nature, and which were really humiliating to me. My mistress—who had begun to teach me—was suddenly checked in her benevolent design, by the strong advice of her husband. In faithful compliance with this advice, the good lady had not only ceased to instruct me, herself, but had set her face as a flint against my learning to read by any means. It is due, however, to my mistress to say, that she did not adopt this course in all its stringency at the first. She either thought it unnecessary, or she lacked the depravity indispensable to shutting me up in mental darkness.

Vocabulary
benevolent (bə nev′ ə lənt) *adj.* kindly; charitable

Comprehension
Why did Douglass's mistress stop teaching him to read?

◀ **Critical Viewing** What might the light shining on the reader in this painting symbolize? **INTERPRET**

It was, at least, necessary for her to have some training, and some hardening, in the exercise of the slaveholder's prerogative, to make her equal to forgetting my human nature and character, and to treating me as a thing destitute of a moral or an intellectual nature. Mrs. Auld—my mistress—was, as I have said, a most kind and tender-hearted woman; and, in the humanity of her heart, and the simplicity of her mind, she set out, when I first went to live with her, to treat me as she supposed one human being ought to treat another.

It is easy to see, that, in entering upon the duties of a slaveholder, some little experience is needed. Nature has done almost nothing to prepare men and women to be either slaves or slaveholders. Nothing but rigid training, long persisted in, can perfect the character of the one or the other. One cannot easily forget to love freedom; and it is as hard to cease to respect that natural love in our fellow creatures. On entering upon the career of a slaveholding mistress, Mrs. Auld was singularly **deficient**; nature, which fits

Vocabulary
deficient (di fi′ shənt) *adj.* incomplete; defective

▲ Critical Viewing
Is the situation and relationship shown in this image similar to Douglass's? Explain. **DISTINGUISH**

nobody for such an office, had done less for her than any lady I had known. It was no easy matter to induce her to think and to feel that the curly-headed boy, who stood by her side, and even leaned on her lap; who was loved by little Tommy, and who loved little Tommy in turn; sustained to her only the relation of a chattel.[1] I was *more* than that, and she felt me to be more than that. I could talk and sing; I could laugh and weep; I could reason and remember; I could love and hate. I was human, and she, dear lady, knew and felt me to be so. How could she, then, treat me as a brute, without a mighty struggle with all the noble powers of her own soul. That struggle came, and the will and power of the husband was victorious. Her noble soul was overthrown; but, he that overthrew it did not, himself, escape the consequences. He, not less than the other parties, was injured in his domestic peace by the fall.

When I went into their family, it was the abode of happiness and contentment. The mistress of the house was a model of affection and tenderness. Her fervent piety and watchful uprightness made it impossible to see her without thinking and feeling—"that woman is a Christian." There was no sorrow nor suffering for which she had not a tear, and there was no innocent joy for which she did not [have] a smile. She had bread for the hungry, clothes for the naked, and comfort for every mourner that came within her reach. Slavery soon proved its ability to divest her of these excellent qualities, and her home of its early happiness. Conscience cannot stand much violence. Once thoroughly broken down, *who* is he that can repair the damage? It may be broken toward the slave, on Sunday, and toward the master on Monday. It cannot endure such shocks. It must stand entire, or it does not stand at all. If my condition waxed bad, that of the family waxed not better. The first step, in the wrong direction, was the violence done to nature and to conscience, in arresting the benevolence that would have enlightened my young mind. In ceasing to instruct me, she must begin to justify herself *to* herself; and, once consenting to take sides in such a debate, she was riveted to her position. One needs very little knowledge of moral philosophy, to see *where* my mistress now landed. She finally became even more violent in her opposition to my learning to read, than was her husband himself. She was not satisfied with simply doing as *well* as her husband had commanded her, but seemed resolved to better his instruction. Nothing appeared to make my poor mistress—after her turning toward the downward path—more angry, than seeing me, seated in some nook or corner, quietly reading a book or a newspaper. I have had her rush at me, with the utmost fury, and snatch from my hand such newspaper or book, with something of the wrath and consternation which a traitor might be supposed to feel on being discovered in a plot by some dangerous spy.

1. **chattel** (chat´ 'l) *n.* a movable item of personal property, as a piece of furniture or a head of livestock.

Purpose for Reading: Historical Influences

How do the ethical conflicts of slavery affect everyone in the Auld household?

Vocabulary

fervent (fər´ vənt) *adj.* intensely devoted or earnest

Vocabulary

opposition (ä pə zi´ shən) *n.* resistance; hostility

consternation (kän´ stər nā´ shən) *n.* fear or shock that makes one feel helpless or bewildered

Comprehension

What extreme measure does Mrs. Auld take?

Purpose for Reading: Historical Influences

What multiple influences of the period are evident in this paragraph? Explain.

Mrs. Auld was an apt woman, and the advice of her husband, and her own experience, soon demonstrated, to her entire satisfaction, that education and slavery are incompatible with each other. When this conviction was thoroughly established, I was most narrowly watched in all my movements. If I remained in a separate room from the family for any considerable length of time, I was sure to be suspected of having a book, and was at once called upon to give an account of myself. All this, however, was entirely *too late*. The first, and never to be retraced, step had been taken. In teaching me the alphabet, in the days of her simplicity and kindness, my mistress had given me the "inch," and now, no ordinary precaution could prevent me from taking the "ell."[2]

Seized with a determination to learn to read, at any cost, I hit upon many expedients to accomplish the desired end. The plea which I mainly adopted, and the one by which I was most successful, was that of using my young white playmates, with whom I met in the street, as teachers. I used to carry, almost constantly, a copy of Webster's spelling book in my pocket; and, when sent on errands, or when play time was allowed me, I would step, with my young friends, aside, and take a lesson in spelling. I generally paid my *tuition fee* to the boys, with bread, which I also carried in my pocket. For a single biscuit, any of my hungry little comrades would give me a lesson more valuable to me than bread. Not everyone, however, demanded this consideration, for there were those who took pleasure in teaching me, whenever I had a chance to be taught by them. I am strongly tempted to give the names of two or three of those little boys, as a slight testimonial of the gratitude and affection I bear them, but prudence forbids; not that it would injure me, but it might, possibly, embarrass them; for it is almost an unpardonable offense to do anything, directly or indirectly, to promote a slave's freedom, in a slave state. It is enough to say, of my warm-hearted little play fellows, that they lived on Philpot Street, very near Durgin & Bailey's shipyard.

For a single biscuit, any of my hungry little comrades would give me a lesson more valuable to me than bread.

Although slavery was a delicate subject, and very cautiously talked about among grownup people in Maryland, I frequently talked about it—and that very freely—with the white boys. I would, sometimes, say to them, while seated on a curbstone or a cellar door, "I wish I could be free, as you will be when you get to be men." "You will be free, you know, as soon as you are twenty-one, and can go where you like, but I am a slave for life. Have I not as good a right to be free as you have?" Words like these, I observed, always troubled them; and I had no small satisfaction in wringing from the boys, occasionally, that fresh and bitter condemnation of slavery, that springs from nature, unseared and unperverted.[3] Of all consciences let me have those to deal with which have not been bewildered by the cares of

2. ell *n.* former English measure of length, equal to forty-five inches.

3. unperverted (un′ pər vʉrt′ id) *adj.* uncorrupted; pure.

A Home on the Mississippi, Currier & Ives, The Museum of the City of New York

life. I do not remember ever to have met with a *boy*, while I was in slavery, who defended the slave system; but I have often had boys to console me, with the hope that something would yet occur, by which I might be made free. Over and over again, they have told me, that "they believed *I* had as good a right to be free as *they* had"; and that "they did not believe God ever made anyone to be a slave." The reader will easily see, that such little conversations with my play fellows, had no tendency to weaken my love of liberty, nor to render me contented with my condition as a slave.

When I was about thirteen years old, and had succeeded in learning to read, every increase of knowledge, especially respecting the free states, added something to the almost intolerable burden of the thought—"I am a slave for life." To my bondage I saw no end. It was a terrible reality, and I shall never be able to tell how sadly that thought chafed my young spirit. Fortunately, or unfortunately, about this time in my life, I had made enough money to buy what was then a very popular schoolbook, the *Columbian Orator.* I bought this addition to my library, of Mr. Knight, on Thames street, Fell's Point, Baltimore, and paid him fifty cents for it. I was first led to buy this book, by hearing some little boys say they were going to learn some little pieces out of it for the exhibition. This volume was, indeed, a rich treasure, and every opportunity afforded me, for a time, was spent in diligently perusing it. . . . The dialogue and the

▲ Critical Viewing

How does this idealized picture of plantation life contrast with Douglass's experiences as an enslaved African American? **CONTRAST**

Vocabulary

intolerable (in ˈtäl ər ə bəl) *adj.* unbearable; too severe

Comprehension

What beliefs do Douglass's playmates express about slavery?

The
American EXPERIENCE

Slave Narratives

Between 1760 and the end of the Civil War, when slavery was officially abolished, testimonies of hundreds of fugitives and former slaves appeared in the form of slave narratives. These narratives exposed the inhumanities of the slave system as former slaves recorded the harsh conditions they suffered at the hands of their owners. Their writings did more than document their personal experiences for the enlightenment of others. They also served to create permanent reminders that could not be easily ignored by the reunified nation. In the 1920s and 1930s, The Federal Writers Project created an archive of these narratives, preserving the memory of the painful realities of American slavery.

Connect to the Literature

Douglass intended his narrative to be read by both black and white audiences. What do you think his purpose was in describing his white playmates' attitudes toward slavery?

LADIES' DEPARTMENT.

'Am I not a Woman and a Sister?'

White Lady, happy, proud and free,
Lend awhile thine ear to me;
Let the Negro Mother's wail
Turn thy pale cheek still more pale.
Can the Negro Mother joy
Over this her captive boy,
Which in bondage and in tears,
For a life of wo she rears?
Though she bears a Mother's name,
A Mother's rights she may not claim;
For the white man's will can part,
Her darling from her bursting heart.

speeches were all redolent of the principles of liberty, and poured floods of light on the nature and character of slavery. As I read, behold! the very discontent so graphically predicted by Master Hugh, had already come upon me. I was no longer the light-hearted, gleesome boy, full of mirth and play, as when I landed first at Baltimore. Knowledge had come. . . . This knowledge opened my eyes to the horrible pit, and revealed the teeth of the frightful dragon that was ready to pounce upon me, but it opened no way for my escape. I have often wished myself a beast, or a bird—anything, rather than a slave. I was wretched and gloomy, beyond my ability to describe. I was too thoughtful to be happy. It was this everlasting thinking which distressed and tormented me; and yet there was no getting rid of the subject of my thoughts. All nature was redolent of it. Once awakened by the silver trump[4] of knowledge, my spirit was roused to eternal wakefulness. Liberty! the inestimable birthright of every man, had, for me, converted every object into an asserter of this great right. It was heard in every sound, and beheld in every object. It was ever present, to torment me with a sense of my wretched condition. The more beautiful and charming were the smiles of nature, the more horrible and desolate was my condition. I saw nothing without seeing it, and I heard nothing without hearing it. I do not exaggerate, when I say, that it looked from every star, smiled in every calm, breathed in every wind, and moved in every storm.

I have no doubt that my state of mind had something to do with the change in the treatment adopted, by my once kind mistress toward me. I can easily believe, that my leaden, downcast, and discontented look, was very offensive to her. Poor lady! She did not know my trouble, and I dared not tell her. Could I have freely made her acquainted with the real state of my mind, and given her the reasons therefor, it might have been well for both of us. Her abuse of me fell upon me like the blows of the false prophet upon his ass; she did not know that an *angel* stood in the way;[5] and—such is the relation of master and slave—I could not tell her. Nature had made us *friends*; slavery made us *enemies.* My interests were in a direction opposite to hers, and we both had our private thoughts and plans. She aimed to keep me ignorant; and I resolved to know, although knowledge only increased my discontent. My feelings were

4. **trump** trumpet.
5. **blows . . . the way** allusion to a biblical tale (Numbers 22:21–35) about an ass that cannot move, though she is beaten by her master, because her path is blocked by an angel.

not the result of any marked cruelty in the treatment I received; they sprung from the consideration of my being a slave at all. It was *slavery*—not its mere *incidents*—that I hated. I had been cheated. I saw through the attempt to keep me in ignorance. . . . The feeding and clothing me well, could not atone for taking my liberty from me. The smiles of my mistress could not remove the deep sorrow that dwelt in my young bosom. Indeed, these, in time, came only to deepen my sorrow. She had changed; and the reader will see that I had changed, too. We were both victims to the same overshadowing evil—*she*, as mistress, *I*, as slave. I will not censure her harshly; she cannot censure me, for she knows I speak but the truth, and have acted in my opposition to slavery, just as she herself would have acted, in a reverse of circumstances.

I have often wished myself a beast, or a bird—anything, rather than a slave.

Critical Reading

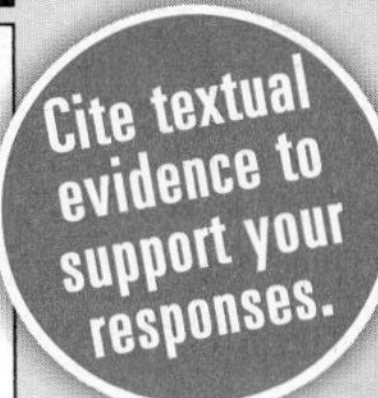
Cite textual evidence to support your responses.

1. **Key Ideas and Details** **(a)** What does Mrs. Auld initially think about Douglass's reading? **(b) Draw Conclusions:** Why do you think she is later "violent in her opposition" to Douglass's reading?
2. **Key Ideas and Details** **(a)** What book does Douglass buy when he is about thirteen years old? **(b) Analyze Causes and Effects:** How does reading this transform Douglass from "light-hearted" to "wretched and gloomy"?
3. **Key Ideas and Details** **(a)** What consumed Douglass once he obtained knowledge? **(b) Support:** How does his experience prove his mistress's belief that education and slavery are incompatible?
4. **Integration of Knowledge and Ideas** What personal qualities do you think helped Douglass become an effective champion of human rights? Use at least two of these Essential Question words in your response: *conviction, determination, goal, justice, humanity.* ***[Connecting to the Essential Question: How does literature shape or reflect society?]***

Close Reading Activities

from *My Bondage and My Freedom*

Literary Analysis

1. **Key Ideas and Details** In approaching this selection, you **set a purpose for reading**—to *evaluate the historical influences that shape the narrative.* Note two specific observations you made as a result of setting this focus. Explain.
2. **Key Ideas and Details** **(a)** Describe the treatment Douglass receives as a slave in the Auld household. **(b)** In what ways does his **autobiography** make a powerful case against slavery?
3. **Craft and Structure** **(a)** Using a chart like the one shown, select three events from this excerpt, and explain the **purpose,** or reason, Douglass includes each one in his narrative. **(b)** How does each event advance his overall purpose for writing?

4. **Craft and Structure** **(a)** Note at least three positive words or phrases Douglass uses to describe Mrs. Auld. **(b)** How does he seem to feel about her? Explain.
5. **Craft and Structure** **(a)** Considering their relationship as owner and slave, what is remarkable about Douglass's *tone* in his discussion of Mrs. Auld? **(b)** What does this suggest about Douglass's purpose in writing his life story?
6. **Integration of Knowledge and Ideas** What *ethical, political, and social* conflicts are evident in Mrs. Auld's changing behavior toward Douglass? Explain.
7. **Integration of Knowledge and Ideas** **(a)** How does his reading of the *Columbian Orator* affect Douglass? **(b)** To what *philosophical* ideas does it awaken him? Provide details to support your response.
8. **Integration of Knowledge and Ideas** As an adult, Douglass was a staunch advocate of human rights. How do you think the philosophical influences he encountered as a child affected his adult decisions? Explain.
9. **Integration of Knowledge and Ideas** Based on this account, how did some people of Douglass's era justify owning slaves?
10. **Integration of Knowledge and Ideas** In what ways would this account be different if it had been written by another member of the Auld household, such as Mrs. Auld? Explain.

Common Core State Standards

Writing

2. Write informative/explanatory texts to examine and convey complex ideas, concepts, and information clearly and accurately through the effective selection, organization, and analysis of content. *(p. 529)*

2.a. Introduce a topic; organize complex ideas, concepts, and information so that each new element builds on that which precedes it to create a unified whole. *(p. 529)*

2.b. Develop the topic thoroughly by selecting the most significant and relevant facts, concrete details, quotations, or other information and examples. *(p. 529)*

2.c. Use appropriate and varied transitions and syntax to link the major sections of the text, create cohesion, and clarify the relationships among complex ideas and concepts. *(p. 529)*

Language

4.b. Identify and correctly use patterns of word changes that indicate different meanings or parts of speech. *(p. 529)*

4.d. Verify the preliminary determination of the meaning of a word or phrase. *(p. 529)*

Vocabulary Acquisition and Use

Word Analysis: Latin Root *-bene-*

The Latin root *-bene-* means "well" or "good." In the word *benevolent*, it combines with a form of the Latin word *velle*, which means "to want," or "to wish." Thus, *benevolent* literally means "a disposition to do good," or "with good wishes." Define each of the numbered words, incorporating the meaning of the root *–bene-* into your definition. If necessary, consult a dictionary to check your work.

1. benefit
2. benefactor
3. benediction
4. beneficence
5. benign

Vocabulary: Sentence Completions

Fill in the blanks in each sentence below with the appropriate vocabulary word from the list on page 518. Then, explain your reasoning.

1. Douglass holds a ______ belief that slavery is morally wrong.
2. His eloquent prose proves that slaves are not ______ in intellect.
3. Douglass argues that slavery is an ______ institution that must be eliminated.
4. His ______ to slavery could not be more firm.
5. Douglass's ______ attitude toward Mrs. Auld suggests his greatness of spirit.
6. The conflicts and ______ of violating her own good nature changes Mrs. Auld's personality.

Writing

Informative Text College applications often require a **reflective essay** about an experience that helped shape you as a person. Just as Douglass described how knowledge freed him, identify a key event in your life, and write an essay communicating its significance. Follow the model Douglass set of combining *narration*, or storytelling, with other rhetorical strategies, such as *description, exposition,* or *explanation,* and—if appropriate—*persuasion.*

Prewriting Outline the details of the event and its effect on you. List details in chronological order to establish organization. Identify points at which your essay will benefit from description, explanation, or persuasion.

Drafting Introduce the experience and explain why it is important. Then, write the body paragraphs to follow your outline. Conclude with a paragraph that insightfully sums up the meaning of the experience in your life.

Revising Review your essay and make sure you have balanced the narrative, or storytelling aspect, with a discussion of its meaning. If necessary, add transitional words, concrete sensory details, or more in-depth explanation to clarify that balance.

Model: Planning a Clear and Logical Organization

A. Experience: I worked in a local campaign office.
B. What happened:
1. met the candidate; was inspired to join her campaign
2. distributed flyers; polled voters
3. phoned residents to encourage voting

C. Outcome: I learned teamwork and the power of democracy.

Chronological order makes it easy for readers to follow events.

Building Knowledge and Insight

Go Down, Moses • *Swing Low, Sweet Chariot*

Connecting to the Essential Question The sense of place in spirituals is often a longed-for promised land that offers delivery from pain. As you read, noticing how settings are described will help as you consider the Essential Question: **What is the relationship between literature and place?**

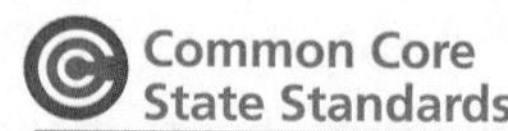

Reading Literature

4. Determine the meaning of words and phrases as they are used in the text, including figurative meanings; analyze the impact of specific word choices on meaning and tone, including language that is particularly fresh, engaging, or beautiful.

5. Analyze how an author's choices concerning how to structure specific parts of a text contribute to its overall structure and meaning as well as its aesthetic impact.

Close Reading Focus

Spirituals; Biblical Allusions; Allegory

Spirituals are folk songs that were often sung by enslaved African Americans. The following structures are shared by virtually all spirituals:

- A **refrain** is a word, phrase, line, or group of lines repeated at regular intervals. A refrain emphasizes key ideas, sets a rhythm, and makes a song easier to remember. Refrains also allowed spirituals to have a call-and-response format in which a leader sang the verses and the rest of the group acted like a chorus and sang the refrain.
- **Biblical allusions** and **allegory:** Spirituals are full of allusions, or references, to people, places, and events from the Bible. These allusions often have allegorical meaning. An allegory is a story in which all the literal elements are also symbols. For example, in the Old Testament story, Moses led the ancient Israelites out of slavery. References to Moses in the spirituals are allegorical; the slaves are referring to both the Biblical story and to their own yearning for a guide who will lead them to freedom. As you read, analyze the meaning of Biblical allusions in specific passages as well as in each spiritual as a whole.

Comparing Literary Works Compare and contrast the messages of freedom expressed in the refrains to these songs. In particular, consider similarities and differences in the emotional quality of those messages.

Preparing to Read Complex Texts Songs are created to be heard; **listening,** therefore, is an especially important skill for appreciating lyrics. Read each spiritual aloud, listening to its *rhythm, rhymes,* and *repeated sounds.* Think about the *moods,* or emotions, these sound devices help to express. Record your observations in a chart like the one shown.

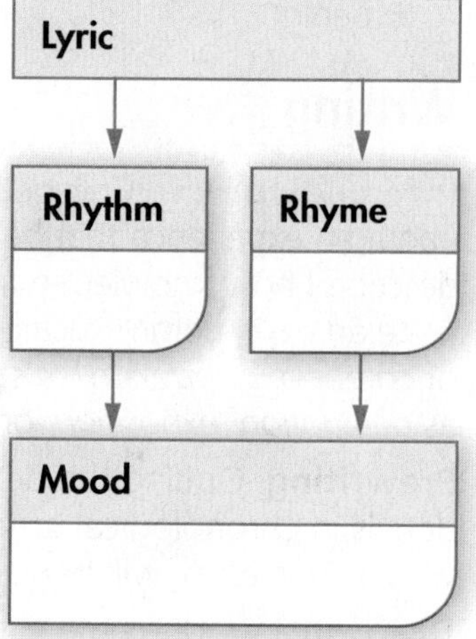

Vocabulary

The words below appear in one of the following texts. Copy the words into your notebook. Which word is a verb in the past tense? How do you know?

oppressed **smite**

SPIRITUALS

Spirituals are folk songs that originated among enslaved and oppressed African Americans. Spirituals took the forms of anthems, ballads, shouts, and jubilees to reflect different moods and circumstances. Containing both social and religious content, spirituals helped to shape the conscious identity of an enslaved people. They also helped slaves persevere under the physical and psychological pressures of their daily lives. These songs conveyed the singers' pain, their yearning for freedom, and their rage against slavery. In doing so, they brought to life the emotional impact of slavery, which divided our nation for decades and played a key role in causing the Civil War. Frederick Douglass, a slave who became one of the most important writers of his time, wrote of the spirituals, "Every tone was a testimony against slavery and a prayer to God for deliverance from chains."

Song of the Fields Plantation owners encouraged field hands to sing, reasoning that people who were busy singing could not plot escape or rebellion. They generally accepted spirituals because of their religious content. The slaves, however, found ways to benefit from singing. These songs provided an outlet for the grief and frustration they often kept bottled up inside. Spirituals also communicated messages of hope and encouragement. Likewise, their traditional African sounds and rhythms helped slaves maintain a connection to their homelands and heritages. In addition, the language in some spirituals provided a means to communicate forbidden thoughts and feelings. For example, songs that referred to the escape of Biblical slaves expressed the slaves' own hope that they would someday escape to a "promised land." Other songs did more than express feelings; they actually provided specific directions for escape. In "Follow the Drinking Gourd," fugitive slaves were advised to follow the Big Dipper north to freedom.

Path to Popularity Spirituals were almost unknown outside the South until after the Civil War. In 1867, a collection of African American music called *Slave Songs of the United States* was published. In 1871, a black choral group, The Jubilee Singers from Fisk University, traveled throughout the United States and to England and Germany singing spirituals to raise money for their school. The Jubilee Singers were extremely gifted and became highly successful, even singing for Queen Victoria in England. Students from other schools followed their example and helped popularize the spiritual. Today, spirituals are performed by singers of all types, and their influence is apparent in contemporary music forms such as blues and jazz.

"Every tone was a testimony against slavery and a prayer to God for deliverance from chains."

—Frederick Douglass

GO DOWN, MOSES

SPIRITUAL

BACKGROUND Africans were first brought to this country as slaves in 1619. Although the slave trade was banned in 1808, slavery itself remained legal. In the years before the Civil War, many enslaved Africans fled captivity. They were hidden and transported by the Underground Railroad, a secret network of activists dedicated to helping fugitives reach freedom in the North and in Canada. One of these activists was Harriet Tubman, who was born a slave around 1820. Tubman's remarkable efforts earned her the name "Moses." In the Bible, Moses led the Israelites out of captivity in Egypt. Tubman escaped slavery via the Underground Railroad and then risked her life to return for her family. She returned to the South repeatedly to rescue other enslaved Africans, eventually leading more than 300 people to freedom.

▲ Portrait of Harriet Tubman, also known as "Moses"

Go down, Moses,
Way down in Egypt land
Tell old Pharaoh
To let my people go.

When Israel was in Egypt land
Let my people go
Oppressed so hard they could not stand
Let my people go.

Go down, Moses,
Way down in Egypt land
Tell old Pharaoh
"Let my people go."

"Thus saith the Lord," bold Moses said,
"Let my people go;
If not I'll smite your first-born dead
Let my people go."

Go down, Moses,
Way down in Egypt land,
Tell old Pharaoh,
"Let my people go!"

Vocabulary

oppressed (ə prest′) *v.* kept down by cruel or unjust power

smite (smīt) *v.* kill by a powerful blow

◀ **Critical Viewing** The Rankin House, shown here, was a stop on the Underground Railroad. How does the mood of this picture reflect the role the home played? **CONNECT**

Swing Low, Sweet Chariot

SPIRITUAL

Swing low, sweet chariot,
Coming for to carry me home,
Swing low, sweet chariot,
Coming for to carry me home.

I looked over Jordan[1] and what did I see
Coming for to carry me home,
A band of angels coming after me,
Coming for to carry me home.

If you get there before I do,
Coming for to carry me home,
Tell all my friends I'm coming too,
Coming for to carry me home.

Swing low, sweet chariot,
Coming for to carry me home,
Swing low, sweet chariot,
Coming for to carry me home.

Listening

Read the song aloud. What is the effect of the repetition of the word *home*?

1. **Jordan** river of the Middle East that flows from the Lebanon Mountains through the Sea of Galilee to the Dead Sea. Many spirituals use the phrase "crossing over Jordan" as a metaphor for crossing the Ohio River to freedom or going to heaven.

Critical Reading

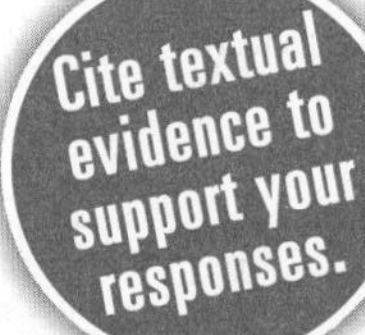
Cite textual evidence to support your responses.

1. **Key Ideas and Details (a)** In "Go Down, Moses," who is oppressed? **(b) Connect:** What connection might these oppressed people have with the slaves?
2. **Key Ideas and Details (a)** Whom does Moses tell to "let my people go"? **(b) Interpret:** If this song is related to the slaves, whom might this figure represent?
3. **Key Ideas and Details (a)** In "Swing Low, Sweet Chariot," who is coming to carry the speaker home? **(b) Interpret:** What might these figures represent?
4. **Key Ideas and Details Interpret:** Knowing that spirituals were often "code" songs for escape, do you see any hidden messages in these songs? Explain.
5. **Integration of Knowledge and Ideas** What qualities do the places described in these songs have? How do they compare to the actual places inhabited by the slaves? In your response, use at least two of these Essential Question words: *escape, desire, respite, expression.* ***[Connecting to the Essential Question: What is the relationship between literature and place?]***

Close Reading Activities

Go Down, Moses • Swing Low, Sweet Chariot

Literary Analysis

1. **Craft and Structure** What **refrains,** both lines and entire stanzas, appear in each **spiritual?**
2. **Craft and Structure** **(a)** Using a chart like the one shown, identify one **Biblical allusion** in each spiritual. **(b)** Explain how each allusion functions as an **allegory.**

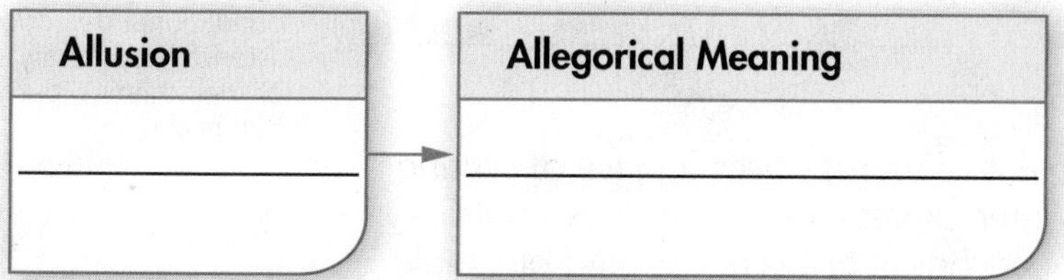

3. **Craft and Structure** Read the spirituals aloud, **listening** to their sound elements. **(a)** Identify the uses of *rhythm, rhyme, and repetition* in both songs. **(b)** Explain how these musical elements help reinforce each song's meaning.
4. **Comparing Literary Works** **(a)** In what ways are the messages about freedom in each song similar and different? **(b)** How are the moods or emotional qualities of each song similar and different? Explain.

Common Core State Standards

Writing
6. Use technology, including the Internet, to produce, publish, and update individual or shared writing products in response to ongoing feedback, including new arguments or information.

Language
5. Demonstrate understanding of word relationships.

Vocabulary Acquisition and Use

Antonyms For each numbered word, select the letter of the answer that is the best antonym, or word of opposite meaning. Explain your choices.

1. oppressed	**(a)** crushed	**(b)** assisted	**(c)** punished
2. smite	**(a)** hit	**(b)** question	**(c)** caress

Writing to Sources

Informative Text Using the Internet and library resources, find recordings of several spirituals and related art or illustrations from the historical period discussed in this unit. Incorporate the recordings and images into a **slide presentation** about spirituals in their historical context. Write a brief introduction for each song and a general introduction to the presentation as a whole. Consider including quotations from the following types of writers or speakers:

- scholars who have written about this genre of music
- important African American figures, such as Harriet Tubman or Frederick Douglass

If possible, post your presentation to an approved Internet site, such as a class or school Web site. Invite constructive comments and incorporate feedback into a revised presentation.

Connecting to the Essential Question These selections were written by two patriotic men on opposite sides of a conflict. As you read, look for ideas that express each writer's patriotism. This will help as you consider the Essential Question: **How does literature shape or reflect society?**

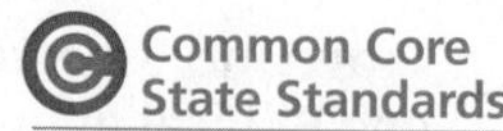

Reading Informational Text
9. Analyze nineteenth-century foundational U.S. documents of historical and literary significance for their themes, purposes, and rhetorical features.

Close Reading Focus

Diction

Diction, the choice and arrangement of words, gives a piece of writing its unique quality and helps the writer express ideas clearly and precisely. Diction may be formal or informal, technical or plain, elevated or simple. Diction is influenced by the *audience, purpose,* and *occasion* for a given text. For example, in this public speech, Lincoln's diction has a formality that suits the occasion and purpose of the event:

> Four score and seven years ago, our fathers brought forth on this continent a new nation . . .

In this private letter to his son, Lee's informal diction suits his audience:

> As far as I can judge by the papers, we are between a state of anarchy and civil war . . .

As you read, note how each writer's diction reflects the audience, purpose, and occasion of his writing.

Comparing Literary Works Each selection communicates a writer's views about the Civil War, but from very different vantage points. Lee, a Southerner, wrote on the eve of conflict, whereas Lincoln, the Union leader, wrote from a battlefield two years into the war. Compare and contrast the insights each writer brings to this painful conflict.

Preparing to Read Complex Texts When reading historical documents, it is helpful to understand the situations that inspired them. **Use your background knowledge** of the Civil War to analyze the ideas these writers express in their historical context. Complete a chart like the one shown to organize your ideas.

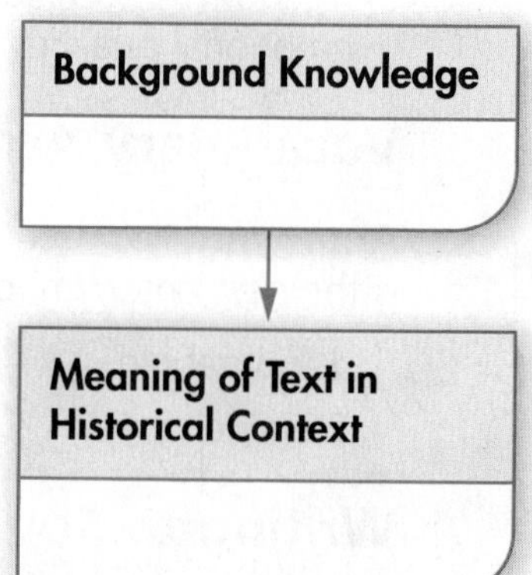

Vocabulary

The words are key to understanding the texts that follow. Copy the words into your notebook. Which word do you think shares the same root as *sacred*?

consecrate **virtuous**
hallow **anarchy**

Abraham Lincoln
(1809–1865)

Author of the Gettysburg Address

Serving as president during one of the most tragic periods in American history, Abraham Lincoln fought to reunite a nation torn apart by war. His courage, strength, and dedication in the face of an overwhelming national crisis have made him one of the most admired and respected American presidents.

Lincoln was born into a family of humble means. As a child, his duties on his parents' farm limited his opportunities to receive a formal education. Still, he was an avid reader and developed an early interest in politics. He served in the Illinois state legislature and the United States Congress, where he earned a reputation as a champion of emancipation. In 1858, he ran for the United States Senate against Stephen Douglas. Lincoln lost the election, but his heated debates with Douglas brought him national recognition and helped him win the presidency in 1860.

Troubled Times Shortly after his election, the Civil War erupted. Throughout the war, Lincoln showed great strength and courage. He also demonstrated his gift for oratory. He was invited to make "a few appropriate remarks" in November 1863 for a dedication of the Gettysburg battlefield as a national cemetery. The world has long remembered what he said there.

Lincoln's great care as a writer shows in the Gettysburg Address, as it does in many of his other speeches. He worked diligently and thoughtfully to prepare messages that would have the effect he desired. Two important aspects of the Gettysburg speech are its brevity—just 272 words—and its reaffirmation of the democratic principles at the heart of American government. Lincoln was killed by an assassin's bullet in 1865 while attending the theater with his wife.

"As I would not be a slave, so I would not be a master. This expresses my idea of democracy. Whatever differs from this, to the extent of the difference, is no democracy."

THE GETTYSBURG ADDRESS

Abraham Lincoln

November 19, 1863

BACKGROUND The battle of Gettysburg, Pennsylvania, fought in July 1863, was an important Union victory and marked a turning point in the war. More than 51,000 soldiers were injured in the battle. On November 19, 1863, while the war still raged, a military cemetery on the battlefield was dedicated. Unsure of President Lincoln's availability, the dedication organizers slated him as a secondary speaker, asking him to make only "a few appropriate remarks." In drafting that brief address, Lincoln wanted to lead the 15,000 American citizens attending the dedication through an emotional, final rite of passage. He also needed to gain continuing support for a bloody conflict that was far from over.

Four score and seven years ago our fathers brought forth on this continent a new nation, conceived in Liberty, and dedicated to the proposition that all men are created equal.

Now we are engaged in a great civil war, testing whether that nation, or any nation so conceived and so dedicated, can long endure. We are met on a great battle-field of that war. We have come to dedicate a portion of that field, as a final resting place for those who here gave their lives that that nation might live. It is altogether fitting and proper that we should do this.

But, in a larger sense, we can not dedicate—we can not consecrate—we can not hallow—this ground. The brave men, living and dead, who struggled here, have consecrated it, far above our poor power to add or detract. The world will little note, nor long remember what we say here, but it can never forget what they did here. It is for us the living, rather, to be dedicated here to the unfinished work which they who fought here have thus far so nobly advanced. It is rather for us to be here dedicated to the great task remaining before us—that from these honored dead we take increased devotion to that cause for which they gave the last full measure of devotion—that we here highly resolve that these dead shall not have died in vain—that this nation, under God, shall have a new birth of freedom—and that government of the people, by the people, for the people, shall not perish from the earth.

Diction

What impression do you get of the speaker from the level of diction in "four score and seven years ago"?

Vocabulary

consecrate (kän′ si krāt′) *v.* cause to be revered or honored

hallow (hal′ ō) *v.* honor as sacred

◀ **Critical Viewing** What do the details in this painting of Lincoln suggest about the esteem in which he was held by people of his time? **INFER**

Robert E. Lee (1807–1870)

Author of "Letter to His Son"

Robert E. Lee was born into a respected Virginia family with a strong military tradition and graduated with high honors from the United States Military Academy at West Point. During the Mexican War, he established a reputation as one of the finest leaders in the United States Army.

Divided Loyalties Despite his military training and talent, the job of commanding the Confederate army during the Civil War was not one that Robert E. Lee wanted. As the dispute over slavery grew, Lee was torn. A descendant of a number of distinguished patriots and statesmen, he believed in the Union and opposed both slavery and secession. Still, when President Lincoln offered him command of the Union forces, Lee refused to lead an army against his native state and resigned from the army, vowing to fight only in defense of Virginia.

A Difficult Task Unlike many Confederate leaders, Lee had no illusions about the South's power. Serving initially as commander of the army of northern Virginia and later of all the Confederate armies, he expected the widespread bloodshed and destruction caused by the war. He was an extraordinary military leader whose accomplishments and personal integrity in the face of overwhelming odds inspired great loyalty in both soldiers and civilians.

An avid letter writer, Lee wrote frequently to family members explaining his actions and expressing his feelings. On the eve of resigning his U.S. Army commission, Lee explored his divided loyalties in "Letter to His Son." After the war, Lee served as president of Washington College (now Washington and Lee) until his death.

"Do your duty in all things. You cannot do more, you should never wish to do less."

Letter to His Son

Robert E. Lee

January 23,1861

I received Everett's[1] *Life of Washington* which you sent me, and enjoyed its perusal. How his spirit would be grieved could he see the wreck of his mighty labors! I will not, however, permit myself to believe, until all ground of hope is gone, that the fruit of his noble deeds will be destroyed, and that his precious advice and **virtuous** example will so soon be forgotten by his countrymen. As far as I can judge by the papers, we are between a state of **anarchy** and civil war. May God avert both of these evils from us! I fear that mankind will not for years be sufficiently Christianized to bear the absence of restraint and force. I see that four states[2] have declared themselves out of the Union; four more will apparently follow their example. Then, if the border states are brought into the gulf of revolution, one half of the country will be arrayed against the other. I must try and be patient and await the end, for I can do nothing to hasten or retard it.

The South, in my opinion, has been aggrieved by the acts of the North, as you say. I feel the aggression and am willing to take every proper step for redress. It is the principle I contend for, not individual or private benefit. As an American citizen, I take great pride in my country, her prosperity and institutions, and would defend any state if her rights were invaded. But I can anticipate

▲ **Critical Viewing**

What sense of Lee as a leader does this painting convey? **INTERPRET**

Vocabulary

virtuous (vʉr´ cho͞o əs) *adj.* characterized by moral virtue

anarchy (an´ ər kē) *n.* absence of government

Comprehension

According to Lee, what is the political state of the country?

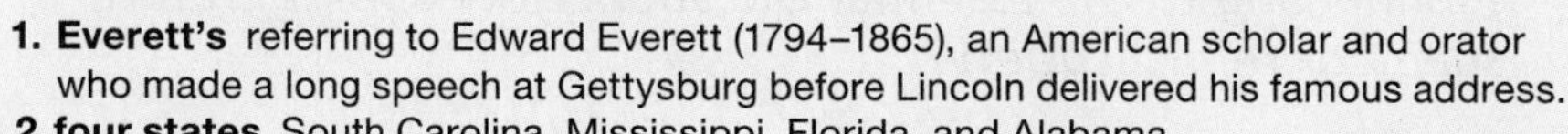

1. **Everett's** referring to Edward Everett (1794–1865), an American scholar and orator who made a long speech at Gettysburg before Lincoln delivered his famous address.
2. **four states** South Carolina, Mississippi, Florida, and Alabama.

Using Background Knowledge
Given what you know about Lee, why was he so committed to both the Union and to Virginia?

> *I* shall mourn for my country and for the welfare and progress of mankind.

no greater calamity for the country than a dissolution of the Union. It would be an accumulation of all the evils we complain of, and I am willing to sacrifice everything but honor for its preservation. I hope, therefore, that all constitutional means will be exhausted before there is a resort to force. Secession is nothing but revolution. The framers of our Constitution never exhausted so much labor, wisdom, and forbearance in its formation, and surrounded it with so many guards and securities, if it was intended to be broken by every member of the Confederacy at will. It was intended for "perpetual union," so expressed in the preamble, and for the establishment of a government, not a compact, which can only be dissolved by revolution or the consent of all the people in convention assembled. It is idle to talk of secession. Anarchy would have been established, and not a government, by Washington, Hamilton, Jefferson, Madison, and the other patriots of the Revolution. . . . Still, a Union that can only be maintained by swords and bayonets, and in which strife and civil war are to take the place of brotherly love and kindness, has no charm for me. I shall mourn for my country and for the welfare and progress of mankind. If the Union is dissolved, and the government disrupted, I shall return to my native state and share the miseries of my people; and, save in defense, will draw my sword on none.

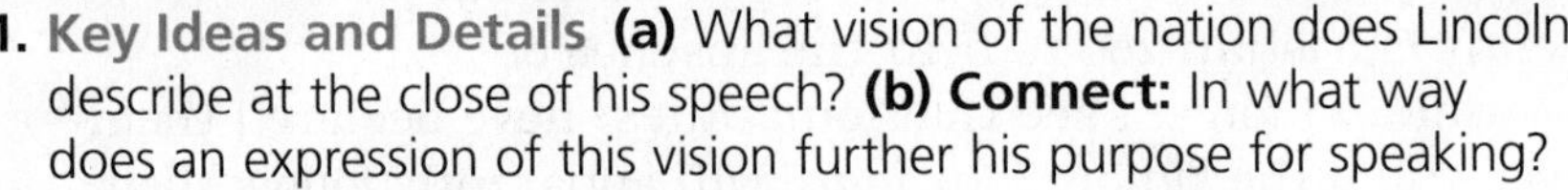

Critical Reading

Cite textual evidence to support your responses.

1. **Key Ideas and Details (a)** What vision of the nation does Lincoln describe at the close of his speech? **(b) Connect:** In what way does an expression of this vision further his purpose for speaking?
2. **Key Ideas and Details (a)** What gift has Lee's son given him? **(b) Connect:** How is Lee's recognition of this gift linked to his feelings about secession? Explain.
3. **Key Ideas and Details (a)** How would you explain Lee's use of the word *Union*? **(b)** In what ways does he clarify or refine the meaning of the word *Union*? **(c) Summarize:** In your own words, explain Lee's argument against secession.
4. **Integration of Knowledge and Ideas** Based on these selections, how do you think both Lincoln and Lee define American patriotism? In your response, use at least two of these Essential Question words: *devotion, unity, conviction, aspiration.* ***[Connecting to the Essential Question: How does literature shape or reflect society?]***

The Gettysburg Address • Letter to His Son

Literary Analysis

1. **Key Ideas and Details** **Using background knowledge,** explain why President Lincoln wrote such a short speech for his address at Gettysburg.
2. **Key Ideas and Details** Why did Lincoln connect the honoring of those who died at Gettysburg with the goal of continuing the war toward a Union victory?
3. **Key Ideas and Details** Why was Lee so opposed to secession?
4. **Craft and Structure** Using a chart like the one shown, analyze how the **diction** used by each writer is appropriate to the audience, occasion, and purpose of the text.

	Examples of Diction	Audience	Occasion	Purpose
Lincoln				
Lee				

5. **Craft and Structure** Which voice do you find more engaging, Lincoln's or Lee's? Explain your reasoning, citing details from the texts.
6. **Integration of Knowledge and Ideas** Choose one passage from each selection in which the diction seems especially effective in expressing and clarifying the writer's meaning. Explain your choices.
7. **Comparing Literary Works** **(a)** What words does Lincoln use to describe the war? **(b)** What words does Lee use to describe it? **(c)** What personal views about the war do you think the two men share?

Common Core State Standards

Writing

2. Write informative/explanatory texts to examine and convey complex ideas, concepts, and information clearly and accurately through the effective selection, organization, and analysis of content.

2.c. Use appropriate and varied transitions and syntax to link the major sections of the text, create cohesion, and clarify the relationships among complex ideas and concepts.

Vocabulary Acquisition and Use

Use New Words in Sentences For each word pair, write one sentence using both words correctly.

1. consecrate/hallow
2. anarchy/virtuous

Writing to Sources

Explanatory Text Abraham Lincoln and Robert E. Lee wrote from different sides of the Civil War conflict, yet both take a historical view about the founding principles of the United States. Write a **compare-and-contrast essay** in which you describe each writer's understanding of the relationship between the Civil War strife of their own generation and the ideas on which the United States was founded. To clarify the flow of your ideas, *use transitional words and phrases* that show contrast or similarity, such as "alternatively," "on the other hand," and "in a similar way."

CONTEMPORARY CONNECTION

Civil War Writings Past and Present

A turbulent and tragic stage in America's story, the Civil War has captured the imaginations of generations of American writers. Ambrose Bierce wrote about the war from firsthand experience as a Union soldier. Stephen Crane steeped himself in knowledge about the war in order to write his vivid stories. Margaret Mitchell set her sweeping 1936 bestseller *Gone With the Wind* during the Civil War. Ken Burns's documentary series, *Civil War*, debuted on public television stations in 1990. With 40 million viewers, it was the most-watched PBS series ever aired.

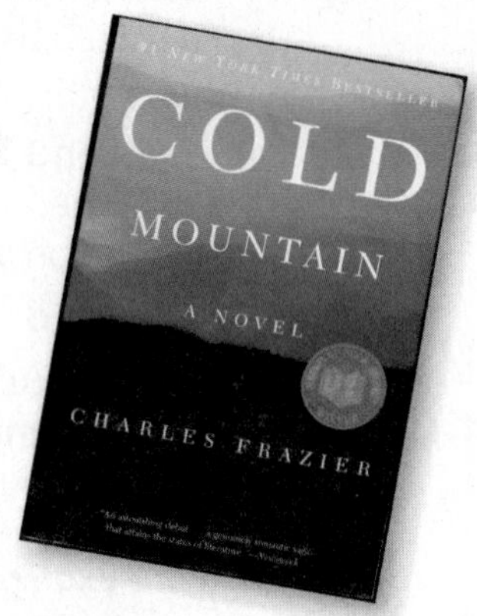

Charles Frazier's novel *Cold Mountain* continues this tradition. The story of a man's quest to return from the battlefield to his home in the Carolina mountains, the book stormed onto bestseller lists when it was published in 1997. In 2003, Nicole Kidman, Jude Law, and Renée Zellwegger starred in the feature film based on the book.

ANTHONY MINGHELLA Screenwriter/Director

British director and screenwriter Anthony Minghella's film career took off in 1990 with the release of *Truly, Madly, Deeply*, a drama he wrote and directed for Britain's BBC. He later wrote the screenplay adaptation of Patricia Highsmith's novel *The Talented Mr. Ripley* and directed the 1999 film starring Matt Damon. In 1996, Minghella won the Academy Award for Best Director for his work on *The English Patient,* a film he adaptated from his friend Michael Ondaatje's novel. Minghella once described a screenplay as "not beautiful in the way a book is beautiful . . . It's much more sort of a plan. So I tried not to even think of the screenplay as a defining document, as a piece of work in itself, but only as a route." Minghella was in Toronto, Canada, when Ondaatje gave him a copy of *Cold Mountain.* Upon his return home to London, he discovered two other people had sent him copies of the novel. He said, "I felt there must be some augury," or prophecy, in the coincidence. The film he wrote and directed was a critical and box office success and received seven Academy Award nominations. Sadly, Minghella's thriving career was cut short by his death in 2008.

JUDE LAW

NICOLE KIDMAN

RENÉE ZELLWEGER

FIND YOUR WAY HOME

from COLD MOUNTAIN

▲ Nicole Kidman plays Ada Monroe, a cultured young woman struggling to survive during the Civil War in the film version of *Cold Mountain*.

from COLD MOUNTAIN

a screenplay by

Anthony Minghella

based on the novel by

Charles Frazier

BACKGROUND The following scenes are set at Black Cove Farm, the home of Ada Monroe. Ada is a privileged young woman who has never had to work the land before. With the Civil War in full force, she has fallen on desperate times. The arrival of capable and tough Ruby Thewes saves both Ada's farm and her life.

79.[1] INT.[2] ADA'S BEDROOM, BLACK COVE FARM. PREDAWN. SUMMER 1864.

Ada wakes up to persistent knocking.

RUBY. (O.S.[3]) Ada? Ada? You up?

---

1. Numbers indicate scene numbers.
2. **INT.** abbreviation for "interior" or a scene shot indoors.
3. **O.S.** off screen, a voice heard without the actor appearing on screen.

▲ Renée Zellweger plays the feisty and practical Ruby Thewes.

ADA. Yes. *(opening her eyes)* It's still dark.

RUBY. (O.S.) Tell the cows that. It's late.

80. INT. KITCHEN, BLACK COVE FARM. PREDAWN. SUMMER 1864.

Ada enters blearily, clutching her novel. Ruby is already busy.

ADA. I have to eat something.

RUBY. Then you have to get up earlier. *(at Ada's book)* What's that?

ADA. A novel.

RUBY. *(heading outside)* You want to carry a book, carry one you can write in—

81. EXT.[4] BLACK COVE FARM. DAWN. SUMMER 1864.

Ruby emerges, followed by Ada, chewing on a carrot.

RUBY. —we got our own story. Called Black Cove Farm : a catastrophe.

She looks back at Ada for a reaction.

RUBY. (CONT.[5]) I can spell it, too. Learned the same place you did, in the schoolhouse. That's one of the first words they taught me. Ruby Thewes, you are a c-a-t-a-s-t-r-o-p-h-e.

They're heading for the stable.

82. INT. STABLE, BLACK COVE FARM. DAY. SUMMER 1864.

Ruby's already pitching hay. Turns to Ada, hands her a rake. Ada, half asleep, accepts obediently, stunned by this energy.

RUBY. Three years I was in school before my daddy—saying God rest his soul is like wishing him what he had in life, 'cause he lived to rest, he was born tired—before my daddy decided there was better use for me than have me sat all day in front of a chalkboard.

83. EXT. A FIELD OF WEEDS, BLACK COVE FARM. DAY.

4. EXT. exterior, a scene shot outdoors.
5. CONT. continued, here dialogue that is interrupted for a moment, but begins again.

SUMMER 1864.

Ruby dictates a list to Ada as they bustle along.

RUBY. Number one—lay out a winter garden for cool-season crops: turnips, onions, cabbage, greens.

Ada scribbles, walks, scribbles.

84. EXT. BARN, BLACK COVE FARM. DAY. SUMMER 1864.

Ruby up a ladder, inspecting the roof.

RUBY. Number two: patch the shingles on the barn roof. Do we have a maul and froe?

ADA. *(writing, holding the ladder)* Maul?

RUBY. Maul. M-a-u-l.

ADA. I have no idea.

85. INT. SPRINGHOUSE, BLACK COVE FARM. DAY. SUMMER 1864.

Ruby cleans out leaves and detritus from the stone channel, allowing the stream to flow free and cool.

RUBY. Number three: clay crocks for preserves. Peppers. Beans. Jams.

86. EXT. BOTTOM FIELD, BLACK COVE FARM. DUSK. SUMMER 1864.

Ruby doing her version of soil analysis, scrunching the earth, tasting it, spitting it out. Ada makes a face.

RUBY. Clear and turn this field. No harm done letting it go fallow, now we'll do well.

87. EXT. OUTBUILDINGS, BLACK COVE FARM. AFTERNOON. SUMMER 1864.

Ruby looks up. Ada catches up with her.

RUBY. Number fifteen—

ADA. Sixteen.

RUBY. Number sixteen: let's hang some gourds for a martin colony. Keep away crows. You got one thing in abundance on this farm, and that's crows. Shut the gate.

88. EXT. APPLE ORCHARD, BLACK COVE FARM. DUSK. SUMMER 1864.

Ruby, delighted, contemplates the bounty of apples.

RUBY. There's survival. On them trees. *(turns to an exhausted Ada)* You got a cider press or would that be wishing on a blessing?

ADA. Actually, yes, I think we do.

Ruby whoops, jogs away. Ada, exhausted, takes a bite of an apple, watching her.

Critical Reading

1. **(a)** When Ruby wakes Ada, what does each woman say about breakfast? **(b) Compare and Contrast:** Explain the similarities and differences in the two women's perceptions of morning. **(c)** What does this suggest about other differences in their characters?
2. **(a)** As Ada and Ruby walk, what does Ruby say about the farm? **(b) Describe:** How does Ada respond? **(c) Infer:** What does each woman know about farming?

Use these questions to focus a class discussion of *Cold Mountain:*

3. Why do you think writers and filmmakers are interested in characters who do not see battle but nevertheless struggle during a war?
4. In what ways are depictions of events in a screenplay different from their presentation in short stories or novels?

 Themes Across Centuries: Scholar's Insights

Nell Irvin Painter Introduces

An Account of an Experience with Discrimination

by Sojourner Truth

A Public Figure Encounters Discrimination Sojourner Truth, an African American abolitionist born in upstate New York in 1797, belonged to a group of antislavery women volunteering with the ex-slave refugees in Washington, D.C., during the Civil War. Poor people from the battlefields of Virginia and from slaveholding Maryland sought protection and jobs in the nation's capital. Volunteers like Truth and her comrades, Josephine Griffing and Laura Haviland, helped them cope with their situation. Although Truth did not read or write, she dictated this account for publication in the antislavery press. In this way, people who cared about human rights would know that one Washington, D.C., streetcar conductor had not stopped for her and another had tried to push her from the platform of the car, even though she was a well-known public figure.

Two American Histories Truth's experience of discrimination in public transportation belongs to two American histories, both beginning in the early nineteenth century and both ending with the passage and enforcement of federal legislation against discrimination in public services in the 1950s and 1960s. The first history is that of Washington, D.C., a Southern city. The second history is that of discrimination against African Americans throughout the United States.

In 1791, President George Washington chose land on the border of Maryland and Virginia near his own home to serve as the nation's capital. In the 1790s, slavery existed in virtually the whole country. But during the early nineteenth century the Northern states abolished slavery, while the institution grew stronger in the South, of which Washington, D.C., was a part. The Washington slave market sat near the capitol building, and slavery flourished in the District until abolition in 1862. The discrimination Sojourner Truth experi-

Meet the Author

Nell Irvin Painter is an award-winning historian and professor. Her book *Sojourner Truth: A Life, A Symbol* was a choice of both the Book of the Month Club and the History Book Club.

enced belonged partly to Washington, D.C.'s Southern traditions. However, even after the abolition of slavery, racial discrimination in transportation remained a national problem. The war between black people and American railroads was national in scope, because racial discrimination was national in scope.

Truth's Experience Was Not Unique Sojourner Truth's painful experience caused her psychic and physical pain—she was in her sixties at the time. However, the insult she suffered was one she shared with many other black people trying to get from one place to another before the middle of the twentieth century.

Before the Civil War, the black abolitionists Frederick Douglass and David Ruggles had traded blows with conductors pushing them out of their seats. During the war, Harriet Tubman, who had guided Union troops during the Civil War, suffered shoulder injuries in New Jersey, when a conductor and three other men dragged her out of her seat and threw her into the baggage car. After the war, Frances Ellen Watkins Harper, the most prominent black woman writer of the era, experienced humiliating and bruising conflicts on railroads and streetcars. George T. Downing, an African American businessman, encountered difficulties in railroad transportation during Reconstruction. The Civil War and Reconstruction ended slavery but not discrimination and exclusion.

Critical Reading

1. **Key Ideas and Details** **(a)** Who was Sojourner Truth? **(b)** What was she doing in Washington, D.C., during and after the Civil War? **(c) Connect:** Was the act of making public her own experience with discrimination related to her purpose for being in Washington? Explain.
2. **Key Ideas and Details** **(a)** According to Nell Irvin Painter, to what two American histories does Truth's experience of discrimination belong? **(b) Speculate:** Why do you think discrimination persisted in both the North and South even after slavery ended?

As You Read "An Account of an Experience With Discrimination" . . .

3. **Integration of Knowledge and Ideas** Identify two ways in which Painter's commentary helps you better understand Sojourner Truth's experiences and reactions.
4. **Integration of Knowledge and Ideas** Decide what an individual who experiences or witnesses discrimination should do.

Building Knowledge and Insight

An Account of an Experience With Discrimination

Connecting to the Essential Question Sojourner Truth showed courage in the face of injustice—one aspect of the American ideal. As you read, notice details that show Truth's reactions to harsh treatment and injustice. Doing so will help as you consider the Essential Question: **What makes American literature American?**

Reading Informational Text
6. Determine an author's point of view or purpose in a text in which the rhetoric is particularly effective, analyzing how style and content contribute to the power, persuasiveness, or beauty of the text.

Close Reading Focus

Author's Purpose; Tone

Every author has both a general and a specific purpose for writing. An **author's general purpose for writing** may be *to inform, to persuade, to entertain,* or *to describe.* Authors also have at least one **specific purpose for writing** any given literary work. For example, in this account Truth seeks to inform readers about a distressing experience. She also has an implicit, or unstated, persuasive purpose: by describing her experiences, she may move readers to put an end to prejudice and injustice.

An author's purpose affects all elements of a literary work, including the **tone,** or attitude, the writer assumes toward the subject and audience. Tone, a key aspect of a writer's style, may be formal or informal, personal or distant, modest or pretentious. For an account of a distressing experience, Truth chooses a surprisingly factual, unemotional tone:

> *A few weeks ago I was in company with my friend Josephine S. Griffing, when the conductor of a streetcar refused to stop his car for me. . . . They dragged me a number of yards before she succeeded in stopping them.*

As you read this account, think about why Truth adopted this even tone and how it helps her achieve her purpose for writing.

Preparing to Read Complex Texts In this account, Truth presents a series of factual events. Taken together, these facts build toward a powerful main idea or **essential message**. As you read, **identify relevant facts and details** to determine the essential message of Truth's account. Use a chart like the one shown to collect important details and identify the essential message of Truth's narrative.

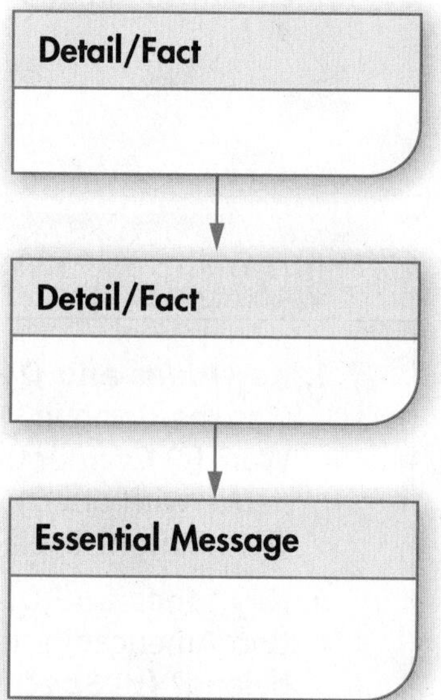

Vocabulary

You will encounter the words listed in the text that follows. Copy the words into your notebook. Which word can be used as both a noun and a verb?

ascended **assault**

Sojourner Truth *(1797–1883)*

Author of "An Account of an Experience With Discrimination"

Sojourner Truth was born into slavery in Ulster County, New York. At the age of nine, she was separated from her family and sold several times, facing abuse at the hands of harsh masters. She was finally bought by John and Sally Dumont. As a slave in the Dumont household, she was forced into marriage with a fellow slave, Thomas, with whom she had at least four children. In 1826, one year before New York state emancipated slaves, Truth escaped from her master's household with her youngest son. She was later able to recover custody of another son, who was illegally sold as a slave in the South. In 1829, Truth and her two youngest children moved to New York City, where she found work as a domestic employee.

A Passion for Preaching Throughout her life, Truth felt a strong commitment to religion. In New York City, she became a missionary, preaching on the streets. Truth was a powerful speaker whose passion and charisma often drew large crowds. In 1843, she assumed the name Sojourner Truth and began preaching along the east coast. She began to travel through the Midwest in 1850, spreading her opinions and beliefs. She dictated her autobiography, *The Narrative of Sojourner Truth,* to Olive Gilbert and sold copies to support her tours.

A Voice for Justice Truth became a noted abolitionist, eloquently arguing against the horrifying injustices of slavery. After the Civil War ended in 1865, she continued to battle the lasting effects of slavery, including discrimination and racism. Working as a counselor, she helped former slaves find employment and build new lives. During her lifetime, Truth also earned fame as an advocate for women's rights and for workplace and prison reform.

> *"That man over there says that women need to be helped into carriages, and lifted over ditches, and to have the best place everywhere. Nobody ever helps me into carriages, or over mud-puddles, or gives me any best place! And ain't I a woman?"*

An Account of an Experience with Discrimination

Sojourner Truth

Background *Although the Civil War brought an end to slavery, the struggle against racial discrimination was far from over. Before the war, Sojourner Truth worked to free slaves. After the war, she fought for a number of causes, including the woman's suffrage movement and the desegregation of public transportation. Once, when a driver of a streetcar refused her passage, she brought a local street to a standstill. With the support of a crowd behind her, the driver was forced to allow her on board. In the following account, dictated by Truth on October 1, 1865, Sojourner Truth describes other encounters with racism.*

A few weeks ago I was in company with my friend Josephine S. Griffing, when the conductor of a streetcar refused to stop his car for me, although [I was] closely following Josephine and holding on to the iron rail. They dragged me a number of yards before she succeeded in stopping them. She reported the conductor to the president of the City Railway, who dismissed him at once, and told me to take the number of the car whenever I was mistreated by a conductor or driver. On the 13th I had occasion to go for

Comprehension
What does Josephine S. Griffing do to help her friend?

◀ **Critical Viewing** In what ways does this image of Sojourner Truth compare with the impression you gain from this account? Explain. **COMPARE AND CONTRAST** necessities for the patients in the Freedmen's Hospital where I have been doing and advising for a number of months. I thought now I would get a ride without trouble as I was in company with another friend, Laura S. Haviland of Michigan. As I ascended the platform of the car, the conductor pushed me, saying "Go back—get off here." I told him I was not going off, then "I'll put you off" said he furiously, clenching my right arm with both hands, using such violence that he seemed about to succeed, when Mrs. Haviland told him he was not going to put me off. "Does she belong to you?" said he in a hurried angry tone. She replied, "She does not belong to me, but she belongs to humanity." The number of the car was noted, and conductor dismissed at once upon the report to the president, who advised his arrest for assault and battery as my shoulder was sprained by his effort to put me off. Accordingly I had him arrested and the case tried before Justice Thompson. My shoulder was very lame and swollen, but is better. It is hard for the old slaveholding spirit to die. But die it must. . . .

Vocabulary

ascended (ə send′ əd) *v.* climbed up

assault (ə sôlt′) *n.* violent attack

Nell Irvin Painter

Scholar's Insight The African American journalist Ida B. Wells went to court in 1884 after being denied first-class passage despite having purchased a first-class ticket. (She won her case, then lost on appeal.)

Critical Reading

Cite textual evidence to support your responses.

1. **Key Ideas and Details** **(a)** What does the streetcar conductor say to Laura Haviland about Sojourner Truth? **(b) Infer:** What does his question reveal about the "old slaveholding spirit"?
2. **Key Ideas and Details** **(a)** What action does Truth take following each incident of discrimination described in her account? **(b) Evaluate:** Do you think this is the best course of action in each situation? Explain.
3. **Key Ideas and Details** **(a)** What happens to the conductor who refuses service to Truth? **(b) Synthesize:** What do details of these events of 1865 have in common with the civil rights movement of the 1950s?
4. **Integration of Knowledge and Ideas** **Take a Position:** Do you think the conductors received appropriate punishments for their acts? Explain.
5. **Integration of Knowledge and Ideas** What does Truth's account suggest about the individual's responsibility to act with courage to promote positive social change? In your response, use at least two of these Essential Question words: *integrity, self-determination, freedom, challenge.* ***[Connecting to the Essential Question: What makes American literature American?]***

Close Reading Activities

An Account of an Experience With Discrimination

Literary Analysis

1. **Key Ideas and Details** **(a)** What is the **essential message** of this account? **(b)** Cite three **relevant details** from Truth's account that support that message.
2. **Craft and Structure** **(a)** Truth's **general purposes** for writing this account were to inform and persuade. How would you describe her **specific purpose for writing?** **(b)** Do you think she achieved that purpose? Explain.
3. **Craft and Structure** **(a)** How would you describe Truth's **tone** in this account? **(b)** Using a chart like the one shown, note three examples that reflect this tone. Then, explain how Truth's tone suits her purpose for writing.

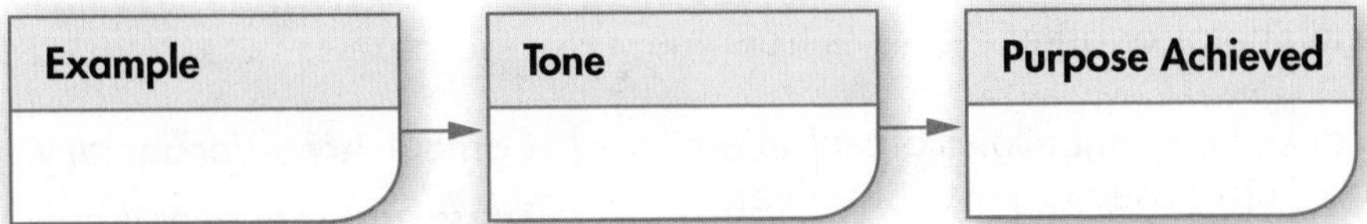

4. **Integration of Knowledge and Ideas** Well-chosen details often shed light on a situation in more than one way. Identify two details Truth includes that do so. Write a paragraph in which you explain and defend your choices.

Vocabulary Acquistion and Use

True or False Determine whether each statement below is true or false. Explain your answers.

1. Someone who experiences an *assault* will have positive feelings.
2. Someone who is trying to get to a rooftop restaurant would take an elevator that *ascended.*

Writing to Sources

Informative Text Rewrite Truth's account as a **newspaper article.** First, determine how the change of form will affect your approach. For example, a newspaper article, written by a reporter rather than a participant, should maintain a formal style and objective, or neutral, tone. As you write your article, incorporate the changes you have outlined. Your article should include

- a *headline* that summarizes the event and engages readers' interest.
- a gripping first sentence, or *lead.*
- relevant facts that identify *who, what, where, when,* and *why.*
- *quotes* from participants and eyewitnesses that shed additional light on the events described.

Common Core State Standards

Writing

2. Write informative/explanatory texts to examine and convey complex ideas, concepts, and information clearly and accurately through the effective selection, organization, and analysis of content.

2.a. Introduce a topic; organize complex ideas, concepts, and information; include formatting when useful to aiding comprehension.

2.b. Develop the topic thoroughly by selecting the most significant and relevant facts, concrete details, quotations, or other information and examples appropriate to the audience's knowledge of the topic.

2.e. Establish and maintain a formal style and objective tone while attending to the norms and conventions of the discipline in which they are writing.

Reading for Information

Analyzing Functional and Expository Texts

Periodical Abstract • Government Form

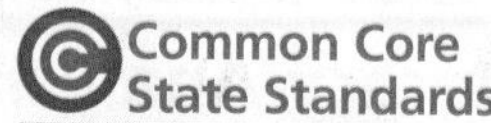

Writing
8. Assess the strengths and limitations of each source in terms of the task, purpose, and audience.

About the Texts

A **periodical abstract** is a summary of a long article from a magazine or scholarly journal. An abstract allows you to quickly evaluate the relevance of a source or gain a general overview of the subject. Abstracts can be found in both print and electronic form. In addition to a summary, most periodical abstracts contain the full article's title, author's name, and publication information; a list of the full article's key points; and photos or other elements from the original article.

A **government form** is a document that allows organizations to compile information efficiently. Forms use quick-response features and a minimal amount of extended text. Basic features include the label or logo of the relevant organization; headings for different categories of information; and checklists, short answer lists, write-on lines, and other text features that capture and organize information.

Preparing to Read Complex Texts

Researchers use abstracts and forms to locate information and evaluate its usefulness. They apply various strategies to assess the quality of information, connect facts and concepts, and outline key points. As you read, **apply systematic strategies to organize and record information.** The chart below highlights strategies you may use at different stages of your own research.

Content-Area Vocabulary

These words appear in the selections that follow. They may also appear in other content-area texts.

archaeology (är´ kē´ äl´ ə jē´) *n.* the study of material evidence from human life in the past

dig (dig) *n.* an archaeological excavation to explore human life from the past

site (sīt) *n.* the place or setting of an event

Note-Taking Strategy	When to Use
Anecdotal Scripting (highlighting texts and making marginal notes)	When first surveying a source (only on a personal copy or photocopy)
Outlining	When you want to extract key points or trace a line of reasoning
Making an Annotated Bibliography	When you want to keep track of information in a wide variety of sources
Concept Mapping (a diagram, using key words and branching lines, that shows relationships among related ideas)	When many concepts are linked

ARCHAEOLOGY

A Publication of the Archaeological Institute of America

abstracts

Volume 59 Number 6, November/December 2006

The title, date, volume, and number of the source magazine for this abstract are clearly identified.

A Community's Roots

by Samir S. Patel

(National Portrait Gallery, Smithsonian Institution/Art Resource)

With Frederick Douglass's help, the past and present come together on a Maryland plantation.

The first section of the abstract includes an element from the article.

In Talbot County, Eastern Shore, State of Maryland, near Easton, the county town, there is a small district of country, thinly populated, and remarkable for nothing that I know of more than for the worn-out, sandy, desert-like appearance of its soil, the general dilapidation of its farms and fences, the indigent and spiritless character of its inhabitants, and the prevalence of ague and fever. It was in this dull, flat, and unthrifty district or neighborhood, bordered by the Choptank river, among the laziest and muddiest of streams surrounded by a white population of the lowest order, indolent and drunken to a proverb, and among slaves who, in point of ignorance and indolence, were fully in accord with their surroundings, that I, without any fault of my own, was born, and spent the first years of my childhood.

—Frederick Douglass,
Life and Times of Frederick Douglass (1881)

The summary of the full article begins here.

Under the boughs of a huge tulip poplar, buried among clumps of roots and piles of oyster shells, is the brick foundation of a building, a remnant of a once-thriving slave community. For 18 months in the early nineteenth century, it was home to a young Frederick Douglass, the future African-American statesman, diplomat, orator, and author. Here, at the age of seven or eight, a shoeless, pantless, precocious Douglass first saw whippings and petty cruelties. Here, he first realized he was a slave. "A lot of the horror that comes through his autobiographies is grounded in those months that he was there," says James Oakes, a historian at the City University of New York who is working on a book about Douglass's relationship with Abraham Lincoln. The modest excavation at Wye House Farm,

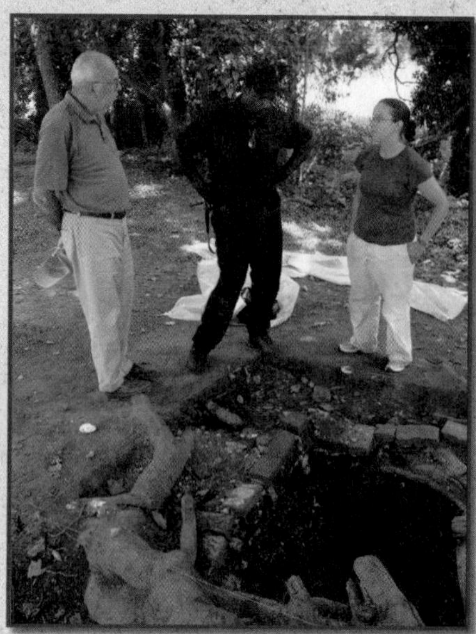

Archaeologist Mark Leone and site supervisor Jenn Babiarz show the site to Derek Lloyd, an engineer at Howard University who may be descended from slaves who lived on the farm. (Samir S. Patel)

a 350-year-old estate on Maryland's Eastern Shore, has yielded sherds, buttons, pipe stems, beads, and precious knowledge about everyday slave life, and is allowing the descendants of that slave community, many of whom live in the nearby rural African-American town of Unionville, to reclaim a lost cultural heritage.

A team of archaeologists and students started digging here in 2005 after archaeologist Lisa Kraus proposed the dig, on the basis of Douglass's descriptions of the site, to Mark Leone, director of the urban archaeology field school at the University of Maryland. Before beginning the excavation, Leone approached St. Stephen's African Methodist Episcopal Church, the social and religious center of Unionville, to ask what the people of the community wanted to learn from the archaeology. "You should ask the people who think it's their heritage what they want to know about it," Leone says. "The answers automatically dissolve the difference between then and now." This, he adds, is the heart of social archaeology, working with descendant communities and understanding that the past and present inform one another. The people of Unionville wanted to know about slave spirituality, what remained of African life, how the owner of the slaves did or did not support freedom, and how slaves found the strength to survive. They are questions a single dig is unlikely to answer, but they have opened an avenue of dialogue between the archaeologists and the people to whom their work matters most.

Photographs and captions from the actual article make this a particularly useful abstract.

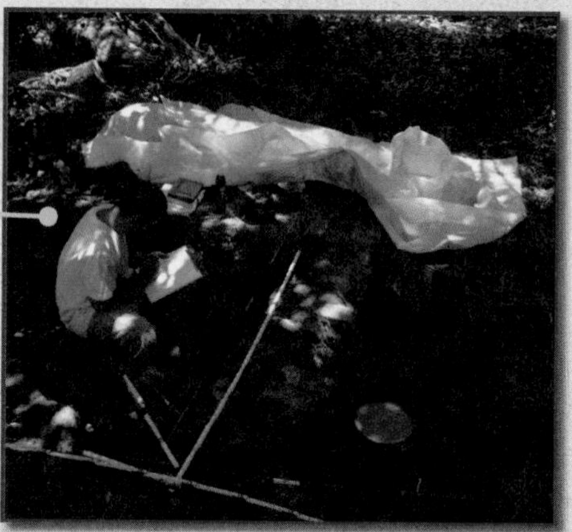

Pete Quantock, a University of Maryland student, profiles the site of a workshop, where slaves probably both slept and worked. (Samir S. Patel)

Samir S. Patel is an associate editor at ARCHAEOLOGY.

Virginia Department of Historic Resources

GENERAL PROPERTY INFORMATION

City/County:

Site Class: _______ Terrestrial, Open Air _______ Terrestrial, Cave/ Rockshelter _______ Submerged

Temporary Designation:

Specialized Contexts:

Resource Name:

Open to public: Y N

Ownership Status: _______ Private
_______ Public/Local
_______ Public/State
_______ Public/Federal

Gov. Modifier:

Checklists provide an efficient way to gather important information.

Cultural Affiliation: _______ African-American
_______ Euro-American
_______ Indeterminate
_______ Native American
_______ Other

LOCATION INFORMATION

Physiographic Province:

Aspect:

Drainage:

Direction:

Landform:

Site Dimensions: _________ × _________ ft

Slope: _________ percent

Survey Description:

Elevation: _______ ft

Site Soils:

Adjacent Soils:

Distance: _______ ft

Nearest Water Source:

Acreage:

SPECIMENS AND FIELD NOTES INFORMATION

Specimens Obtained: ____ Yes ____ No Depository:

Assemblage Description:

Specimens Reported: ____ Yes ____ No

Owner Name: Owner Address:

Assemblage Description:

Field Notes: ____ Yes ____ No Depository:

Headings define the information being collected in each section.

INDIVIDUAL/ORG AGENCY MAILING INFORMATION

Category: Informant Occupant Owner Owner of Specimens Property Mgr. Tenant

Honorific: _________ First Name: _________ Last Name: _________ Suffix: _________

Title: _________ Company: _________ Mailing Address: _________ City: _________

Zip Code: _________ Country: _________ Phone 1/Ext.: _________ Phone 2/Ext.: _________ Surveyor's Notes:

Close Reading Activities

Periodical Abstract • Government Form

Literary Analysis

Writing

1.a. Introduce precise, knowledgeable claim(s), establish the significance of the claim(s), distinguish the claim(s) from alternate or opposing claims, and create an organization that logically sequences claim(s), counterclaims, reasons, and evidence.

1. **Key Ideas and Details** **(a)** If you were to use anecdotal scripting to identify the key points in the abstract, which passages would you highlight? **(b)** Which passages would you note because they contain other important details? Explain.
2. **Key Ideas and Details** **(a)** What information does the government form capture quickly and efficiently? **(b)** What types of workers or professionals would use this form and for what purposes?
3. **Key Ideas and Details** Why do you think the government form attempts to capture specific data about elevation, soils, and water sources?
4. **Craft and Structure** If you were to draw a concept map for both the abstract and the government form, what key concepts would you identify and how would you connect them?
5. **Integration of Knowledge and Ideas** Do you think a government form like the one on page 561 would be useful to the researchers described in the abstract? Cite details to support your response.

Timed Writing

Argument [40 minutes]

Format

In a **persuasive essay**, you build a well-reasoned and compelling argument for a position or claim. Strengthen your argument by introducing counterclaims, or opposing opinions, and demonstrating that your position is more convincing.

Write a **persuasive essay** about the importance of archaeology and whether society has a responsibility to preserve historical sites and objects. Take and **defend** a position about the types of documents, sites, or objects that are most important, and explain your reasons. Support your claims with details from the Periodical Abstract and the Government Form.

Academic Vocabulary

When you **defend** a position, you supply varied, convincing evidence that supports your point of view. Evidence can include facts, quotations from reliable sources, and personal observation.

5-Minute Planner

Complete these steps before you begin to write.

1. Read the prompt carefully. List key words.
2. Scan the texts for details that relate to the prompt.
3. Briefly sketch an outline for your essay. **TIP** In a Timed Writing situation, an outline can be a simple numbered list of key words.
4. Reread the prompt, and draft your essay.

TEXT SET

Forging New Frontiers

Part 2

Literary History: Twain's World

At a time when most American writers were copying European novelists, Twain wrote about American themes.

Mark Twain: The American Bard

In the late 1800s, readers might have known him as Thomas Jefferson Snodgrass, W. Epaminandos Adrastus Blab, or simply Josh. Today, we know Samuel Langhorne Clemens as Mark Twain, his most famous literary pseudonym. Whichever name he used, Twain pulled off a rare literary feat—he created stories, novels, and essays that were both wildly popular in his own day and models of wit and skill more than a century later. Twain was so influential that fifty years after his death, Ernest Hemingway said that "all modern American literature begins" with Twain's novel *The Adventures of Huckleberry Finn.*

Life on the Mississippi Born in 1835, Samuel Clemens grew up in the small river town of Hannibal, Missouri. Steamboat men, religious revivalists, circus performers, minstrel companies, showboat actors, and every other kind of traveler imaginable made appearances in Hannibal. As a boy, Clemens met many of the characters that he would later write about.

After his father's death in 1847, Clemens was forced to leave school and became a printer's apprentice. During the 1850s, he published a few stories and traveled the country. A boat trip down the Mississippi brought back childhood memories, and he decided to become a riverboat pilot. He served as a pilot until 1861, when the Civil War closed the Mississippi to boat traffic.

Mark Twain Is Born In 1862, Clemens took a job as a reporter on a Virginia City newspaper, where he found his calling as a humorist under the byline Mark Twain. The new name, which is actually a signal yelled out by riverboat pilots, freed him to develop a new style. Before becoming "Twain," his work was typical of the low humor of the time, filled with bad puns and intentional misspellings. But in 1865, Twain published a short story entitled "The Notorious Jumping Frog of Calaveras County" (p. 576). The story won

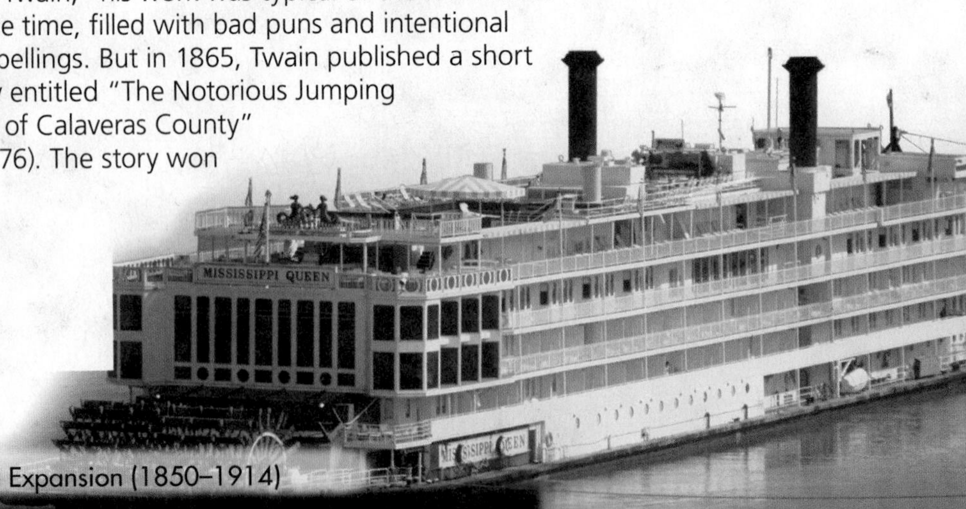

▶ Critical Viewing
What do you think it would have been like to captain a Mississippi riverboat like the one shown in this photograph? **SPECULATE**

the author fame and financial success, and it marked the first appearance of his distinctive comic style.

Ordinary American Speech The targets of Twain's jokes were not new. He distrusted technology and railed against political figures, calling them swindlers and con men. What was new was Twain's feel for ordinary American people and their language. He wrote using the American English that people actually spoke. In that source, he found rich and comic poetry.

Twain's novels, such as *The Adventures of Tom Sawyer* and *The Adventures of Huckleberry Finn*, were unlike any books the world had ever seen. At a time when most American writers were copying European novelists, Twain wrote about American themes. His heroes were dirt-poor and plain-spoken, but in Twain's hands, their moral choices had as much drama as those of any tormented aristocrat in a European novel.

Not everyone appreciated Twain's humor. The author fled Virginia City when a rival journalist, offended by a story, challenged him to a pistol duel. He was chased out of San Francisco by policemen angered by critical articles. Even as his fame grew, some critics dismissed him as little more than a jokester. Yet the American public loved Twain. He made a fortune from his writings, settling with his family into a Hartford, Connecticut, mansion that was decorated to look like the inside of a steamboat.

The Old Man in a White Suit In the late 1800s, the deaths of Twain's wife and daughters left the writer bitter and cynical. Twain became so reclusive that a newspaper reported he was dead. Twain immediately wired the editors: "Reports of my death have been greatly exaggerated." History has not exaggerated Twain's legacy. He was the first, and possibly the greatest, authentically American writer.

In This Section

Speaking and Listening: Oral Presentation

Comprehension and Collaboration Like Twain, contemporary humor writers and comedians find ordinary American life a rich source of material. With a small group, research current humor on television, in movies, in periodicals, and in books. Then, using the research, write and deliver a **formal oral presentation:**

- As a group, prepare a set of focus questions, such as: What roles does comedy play today? What values does current humor transmit? Does contemporary humor challenge or perpetuate stereotypes?
- Use *systematic strategies, such as anecdotal scripting* (underlining, highlighting, and writing notes in the margins of a text) to identify key information.

Select examples to maintain a tone that is appropriate for the classroom. Work together to set goals and deadlines, organize your observations, write the text, and divide up responsibilities for the presentation.

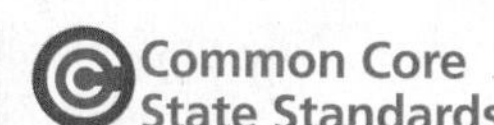

SL.11-12.1.a, SL.11-12.1.b, SL.11-12.1.c, SL.11-12.1.d.

[For the full wording of the standards, see the standards chart in the front of your textbook.]

MARK TWAIN 1835–1910

Although Mark Twain is widely regarded as one of the greatest American writers, the world-renowned author once indicated that he would have preferred to spend his life as a Mississippi riverboat pilot. The comment was probably not entirely serious, but Twain so loved life on the river that, as a young man, he did in fact work as a riverboat pilot for several years. His childhood on the banks of the Mississippi fostered more than a love of riverboats—it also became the basis for many of his most famous works, including *The Adventures of Tom Sawyer* (1876) and *The Adventures of Huckleberry Finn* (1884).

Be good + you will be lonesome.
Clemens
Mark Twain
3-15-

Life on the River

Twain, whose given name was Samuel Langhorne Clemens, felt so closely tied to the Mississippi River that he even took his pen name, Mark Twain, from a river man's call meaning "two fathoms deep," indicating that the river is deep enough for a boat to pass safely. He grew up in the Mississippi River town of Hannibal, Missouri. His father died when he was eleven, and he left school to become a printer's apprentice. He worked as a printer in a number of different cities before deciding at age twenty-one to pursue a career as a riverboat pilot.

IT IS WISER TO FIND OUT THAN SUPPOSE.

A Traveling Man

When the Civil War closed traffic on the Mississippi, Twain went west to Nevada. There, he supported himself as a journalist and lecturer, developing the entertaining writing style that made him famous. In 1865, Twain published "The Notorious Jumping Frog of Calaveras County," his version of a tall tale he had heard in a mining camp in California while he was working as a gold prospector. The story made him an international celebrity.

Following the publication of *The Innocents Abroad* (1869), a successful book of humorous travel letters, Twain moved to Hartford, Connecticut, where he was to make his home for the rest of his life. There, Twain began using his past experiences as raw material for his books. He drew on his travels in the western mining region for *Roughing It* (1872). He turned to his childhood experiences on the Mississippi for *The Adventures of Tom Sawyer, Life on the Mississippi,* and his masterpiece, *The Adventures of Huckleberry Finn.*

A Restless Soul

Twain traveled widely throughout his life, including residential stints in such major American cities as St. Louis, New York, Philadelphia, Cincinnati, and San Francisco. He made extended visits to England, Germany, Switzerland, Italy, and Palestine. His adventures, both at home and abroad, were fuel for a number of books. After living in Europe for several years, he returned home with his family. Following the death of his wife and three of their four children, Twain was unable to reproduce the balance between pessimism and humor that he had captured so brilliantly in *The Adventures of Huckleberry Finn*. In his later works, such as *A Connecticut Yankee in King Arthur's Court* (1889), *Pudd'nhead Wilson* (1894), and *The Man That Corrupted Hadleyburg* (1900), Twain's writing depicted an increasingly pessimistic view of society and human nature. However, he continued to display the same masterful command of language that had already established him as one of America's finest fiction writers.

THE QUOTABLE TWAIN

"CLOTHES MAKE THE MAN," Mark Twain once wrote. In his case, it was words that made the man. From novels to travel correspondence to social commentary, Twain's words were passionately celebrated and hotly criticized. As the great writer and humorist himself declared, "An author values a compliment even when it comes from a source of doubtful competency." What follows are ten more quotable quotes from Twain.

1. "When in doubt, tell the truth."
2. "Let us be thankful for the fools. But for them the rest of us could not succeed."
3. "Don't part with your illusions. When they are gone you may still exist, but you have ceased to live."
4. "It is curious—curious that physical courage should be so common in the world, and moral courage so rare."
5. "It could probably be shown by facts and figures that there is no distinctly native American criminal class except Congress."
6. "We find not much in ourselves to admire, we are always privately wanting to be like somebody else. If everybody was satisfied with himself there would be no heroes."
7. "It is better to keep your mouth shut and appear stupid than to open it and remove all doubt."
8. "All generalizations are false, including this one."
9. "Always do right. That will gratify some of the people, and astonish the rest."
10. "The only way to keep your health is to eat what you don't want, drink what you don't like, and do what you'd rather not."

Building Knowledge and Insight

from *Life on the Mississippi* • *The Notorious Jumping Frog of Calaveras County*

Connecting to the Essential Question Mark Twain portrayed America in a way that continues to define our national character. As you read, look for images, expressions, characters, and ways of thinking that strike you as distinctly American. This will help as you consider the Essential Question: **What makes American literature American?**

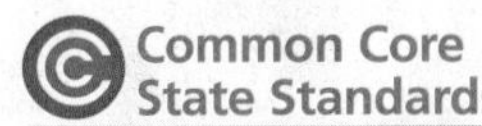

Common Core State Standards

Reading Literature

6. Analyze a case in which grasping a point of view requires distinguishing what is directly stated in a text from what is really meant.

9. Demonstrate knowledge of nineteenth-century foundational works of American literature, including how two or more texts from the same period treat similar themes or topics.

Reading Informational Text

4. Determine the meaning of words and phrases as they are used in a text, including technical meanings.

Language

5.a. Interpret figures of speech in context and analyze their role in the text.

Close Reading Focus

Humor; Dialect

Humor, which may appear in all literary genres, is writing intended to amuse. Humorists use a variety of devices and techniques to achieve that goal:

- **Incongruity,** or differences in logic or degree. For example, a speaker may use a serious tone to describe ridiculous events.
- **Hyperbole,** or the exaggeration of details or embellishment of events beyond what is logical
- **Comic uses of language,** including funny names

Twain's humor is not just funny. Even his most comic works carry an undercurrent of **social commentary,** or critique of society. His social commentary is infused with Twain's keen observations *of human foibles,* or weaknesses, which he usually describes with affection. Twain is also a master of **dialect**—ways of speaking that are specific to a particular area or group of people. This, too, adds to the humor of his writing. As you read, look for these hallmarks of Twain's comic style.

Preparing to Read Complex Texts Twain uses *technical language* to describe steamboats and *dialect* to convey a sense of authentic speech. Both types of language may be unfamiliar to you. To **clarify** technical language, consult footnotes. To **interpret** regional dialect, read unfamiliar words aloud to find that they are simply different pronunciations of words you know. Use a chart like the one shown to translate dialect into modern Standard English.

Regional Dialect

. . . there couldn't be no solit'ry thing mentioned but that feller'd offer to bet on it, and take ary side you please. . . .

Standard English

Not one thing could be mentioned without him offering to bet on it, taking any side.

Vocabulary

You will encounter the words below in the texts that follow. Copy the words into your notebook. Which two words are related to the idea of boredom?

transient
prodigious
eminence
garrulous
conjectured
monotonous
interminable

FROM

LIFE ON THE MISSISSIPPI

MARK TWAIN

BACKGROUND Mark Twain was an eyewitness to the nineteenth-century expansion of the western frontier. He was a young man when wagon trains left his home state of Missouri to cross the prairies, and he later saw the transcontinental railroad built. He traveled throughout the nation, working first on the Mississippi and then in the West, before settling in Connecticut. However, as this excerpt shows, the Mississippi River held a special place in his memory.

The Boys' Ambition

When I was a boy, there was but one permanent ambition among my comrades in our village[1] on the west bank of the Mississippi River. That was, to be a steamboatman. We had transient ambitions of other sorts, but they were only transient.

When a circus came and went, it left us all burning to become clowns; the first Negro minstrel show that came to our section left us all suffering to try that kind of life; now and then we had a hope that if we lived and were good, God would permit us to be pirates. These ambitions faded out, each in its turn; but the ambition to be a steamboatman always remained.

Once a day a cheap, gaudy packet[2] arrived upward from St. Louis, and another downward from Keokuk.[3] Before these events, the day was glorious with expectancy; after them, the day was a dead and empty thing. Not only the boys, but the whole village, felt this. After all these years I can picture that old time to myself now, just as it was then: the white town drowsing in the sunshine of a summer's morning; the streets empty, or pretty nearly so; one or two clerks sitting in front of the Water Street stores, with their splint-bottomed chairs tilted back against the wall, chins on breasts, hats slouched over their faces, asleep—with shingle shavings enough around to show what broke them down; a sow and a litter of pigs loafing along the sidewalk, doing a good business in watermelon rinds and seeds; two or three lonely little freight piles scattered about the levee;[4] a pile of skids[5] on the slope of the stone-paved wharf, and the fragrant town drunkard asleep in the shadow of them; two or three wood flats[6] at the head of the wharf, but nobody to listen to the peaceful lapping of the wavelets against them; the great Mississippi, the majestic, the magnificent Mississippi, rolling its mile-wide tide along, shining in the sun; the dense forest away on the other side; the point above the town, and the point below, bounding the river-glimpse and turning it into a sort of sea, and withal a very still and brilliant and lonely one. Presently a film of dark smoke appears above one of those remote

Vocabulary

transient (tran′ zē ənt) *adj.* not permanent

◀ Critical Viewing

How does this painting convey a sense of the glamour steamboats brought to the Mississippi River? **ANALYZE**

Comprehension

How did the boys' ambitions change with each new visitor to their town?

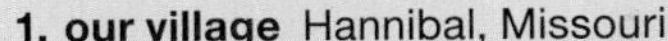

1. **our village** Hannibal, Missouri.
2. **packet** *n.* boat that travels a regular route, carrying passengers, freight, and mail.
3. **Keokuk** (kē′ ə kuk′) town in southeastern Iowa.
4. **levee** (lev′ ē) *n.* landing place along the bank of a river.
5. **skids** *n.* low, movable wooden platforms.
6. **flats** *n.* small, flat-bottomed boats.

▶ Critical Viewing
What does this painting suggest about some of the challenges steamboat captains faced in navigating the river? **INFER**

Vocabulary
prodigious (prə dij′ əs) *adj.* of great power or size

Clarifying and Interpreting Language
How do footnotes clarify your understanding of the technical terms in this paragraph?

points; instantly a Negro drayman,[7] famous for his quick eye and prodigious voice, lifts up the cry, "S-t-e-a-m-boat a-comin'!" and the scene changes! The town drunkard stirs, the clerks wake up, a furious clatter of drays follows, every house and store pours out a human contribution, and all in a twinkling the dead town is alive and moving. Drays, carts, men, boys, all go hurrying from many quarters to a common center, the wharf. Assembled there, the people fasten their eyes upon the coming boat as upon a wonder they are seeing for the first time. And the boat is rather a handsome sight, too. She is long and sharp and trim and pretty; she has two tall, fancy-topped chimneys, with a gilded device of some kind swung between them; a fanciful pilothouse, all glass and gingerbread, perched on top of the texas deck[8] behind them; the paddleboxes are gorgeous with a picture or with gilded rays above the boat's name; the boiler deck, the hurricane deck, and the texas deck are fenced and ornamented with clean white railings; there is a flag gallantly flying from the jackstaff;[9] the furnace doors are open and the fires glaring bravely; the upper decks are black with passengers; the captain stands by the big bell, calm, imposing, the envy of all; great volumes of the blackest smoke are rolling and tumbling out of the chimneys—a husbanded grandeur created with a bit of pitch pine just before arriving at a town; the crew are grouped on the forecastle;[10] the broad stage is run far out over the port bow, and an envied deckhand stands picturesquely on the end of it with a coil of rope in his hand; the pent steam is screaming through the gauge cocks; the captain lifts his hand, a bell rings, the wheels stop; then they turn back, churning the water to foam, and the steamer is at rest. Then such a scramble as there is to get aboard, and to get ashore, and to take in freight and to discharge

7. **drayman** (drā′ mən) *n.* driver of a dray, a low cart with detachable sides.
8. **texas deck** deck adjoining the officers' cabins, the largest cabins on the ship.
9. **jackstaff** (jak′ staf) *n.* small staff at the bow of a ship for flying flags.
10. **forecastle** (fōk′ səl) *n.* front part of the upper deck.

freight, all at one and the same time; and such a yelling and cursing as the mates facilitate it all with! Ten minutes later the steamer is under way again, with no flag on the jackstaff and no black smoke issuing from the chimneys. After ten more minutes the town is dead again, and the town drunkard asleep by the skids once more.

My father was a justice of the peace, and I supposed he possessed the power of life and death over all men and could hang anybody that offended him. This was distinction enough for me as a general thing; but the desire to be a steamboatman kept intruding, nevertheless. I first wanted to be a cabin boy, so that I could come out with a white apron on and shake a tablecloth over the side, where all my old comrades could see me; later I thought I would rather be the deckhand who stood on the end of the stage plank with the coil of rope in his hand, because he was particularly conspicuous. But these were only daydreams—they were too heavenly to be contemplated as real possibilities. By and by one of our boys went away. He was not heard of for a long time. At last he turned up as apprentice engineer or striker on a steamboat. This thing shook the bottom out of all my Sunday school teachings. That boy had been notoriously worldly, and I just the reverse; yet he was exalted to this eminence, and I left in obscurity and misery. There was nothing generous about this fellow in his greatness. He would always manage to have a rusty bolt to scrub while his boat tarried at our town, and he would sit on the inside guard and scrub it, where we could all see him and envy him and loathe him. And whenever his boat was laid up he would come home and swell around the town in his blackest and greasiest clothes, so that nobody could help remembering that he was a steamboatman; and he used all sorts of steamboat technicalities in his talk, as if he were so used to them that he forgot common people could not understand them. He would speak of the labboard[11] side of a horse in an easy, natural way that would make one wish he was dead. And he was always talking about "St. Looey" like an old citizen; he would refer casually to occasions when he "was coming down Fourth Street," or when he was "passing by the Planter's House," or when there was a fire and he took a turn on the brakes of "the old Big Missouri"; and then he would go on and lie about how many towns the size of ours were burned down there that day. Two or three of the boys had long been persons of consideration among us because they had been to St. Louis once and had a vague general knowledge of its wonders, but the day of their glory was over now. They lapsed into a humble silence, and learned to disappear when the ruthless cub engineer approached. This fellow had money, too, and hair oil. Also an ignorant silver watch and a showy brass watch chain. He wore a leather belt and used no suspenders. If ever a youth was cordially

Spiral Review
Tone How would you describe the author's tone in this paragraph? Explain.

Vocabulary
eminence (em′ i nəns) *n.* greatness; celebrity

Clarifying Regional Dialect
What does the apprentice engineer's use of riverboat jargon reveal about him?

Comprehension
What activities and actions of the boy who worked on a steamship inspired envy?

11. **labboard** (lab′ ərd) larboard, the left-hand side of a ship.

admired and hated by his comrades, this one was. No girl could withstand his charms. He cut out every boy in the village. When his boat blew up at last, it diffused a tranquil contentment among us such as we had not known for months. But when he came home the next week, alive, renowned, and appeared in church all battered up and bandaged, a shining hero, stared at and wondered over by everybody, it seemed to us that the partiality of Providence for an undeserving reptile had reached a point where it was open to criticism.

Humor

How does the use of the word *reptile* add to the humor of this passage?

This creature's career could produce but one result, and it speedily followed. Boy after boy managed to get on the river. The minister's son became an engineer. The doctor's and the postmaster's sons became mud clerks; the wholesale liquor dealer's son became a barkeeper on a boat; four sons of the chief merchant, and two sons of the county judge, became pilots. Pilot was the grandest position of all. The pilot, even in those days of trivial wages, had a princely salary—from a hundred and fifty to two hundred and fifty dollars a month, and no board to pay. Two months of his wages would pay a preacher's salary for a year. Now some of us were left disconsolate. We could not get on the river—at least our parents would not let us.

So by and by I ran away. I said I never would come home again till I was a pilot and could come in glory. But somehow I could not manage it. I went meekly aboard a few of the boats that lay packed together like sardines at the long St. Louis wharf, and very humbly inquired for the pilots, but got only a cold shoulder and short words from mates and clerks. I had to make the best of this sort of treatment for the time being, but I had comforting daydreams of a future when I should be a great and honored pilot, with plenty of money, and could kill some of these mates and clerks and pay for them.

Critical Reading

Cite textual evidence to support your responses.

1. **Key Ideas and Details** **(a)** What is the one permanent ambition of the narrator and his boyhood friends? **(b) Connect:** How does this childhood ambition reflect the American spirit that gave rise to the settlement of new frontiers?
2. **Key Ideas and Details** **(a)** How do the people of Hannibal respond to the arrival of the steamboat? **(b) Interpret:** What impression of the town does Twain convey by this response?
3. **Craft and Structure** **(a) Hypothesize:** Do you think Twain could have written so well about riverboat life had he not become a pilot himself? Explain. **(b) Apply:** In what ways do you think Twain's love for the Mississippi River contributed to his success as a writer?
4. **Integration of Knowledge and Ideas** **Evaluate:** The last paragraph suggests that the young Twain was driven by a desire for glory. Is a desire for glory a reasonable motivation in life? Explain.

Critical Commentary

from "How to Tell a Story"

An Essay by Mark Twain

I do not claim that I can tell a story as it ought to be told. I only claim to know how a story ought to be told, for I have been almost daily in the company of the most expert story-tellers for many years.

There are several kinds of stories, but only one difficult kind—the humorous. I will talk mainly about that one. The humorous story is American, the comic story is English, the witty story is French. The humorous story depends for its effect upon the *manner* of the telling; the comic story and the witty story upon the *matter.*

The humorous story may be spun out to great length, and may wander around as much as it pleases, and arrive nowhere in particular; but the comic and witty stories must be brief and end with a point. The humorous story bubbles gently along, the others burst.

The humorous story is strictly a work of art—high and delicate art—and only an artist can tell it; but no art is necessary in telling the comic and the witty story; anybody can do it. The art of telling a humorous story—understand, I mean by word of mouth, not print—was created in America, and has remained at home.

The humorous story is told gravely; the teller does his best to conceal the fact that he even dimly suspects that there is anything funny about it; but the teller of the comic story tells you beforehand that it is one of the funniest things he has ever heard, then tells it with eager delight, and is the first person to laugh when he gets through. And sometimes, if he has had good success, he is so glad and happy that he will repeat the "nub" of it and glance around from face to face, collecting applause, and then repeat it again. It is a pathetic thing to see.

Very often, of course, the rambling and disjointed humorous story finishes with a nub, point, snapper, or whatever you like to call it. Then the listener must be alert, for in many cases the teller will divert attention from that nub by dropping it in a carefully casual and indifferent way, with the pretense that he does not know it is a nub. . . .

But the teller of the comic story does not slur the nub; he shouts it at you—every time. And when he prints it, in England, France, Germany, and Italy, he italicizes it, puts some whooping exclamation-points after it, and sometimes explains it in a parenthesis. All of which is very depressing, and makes one want to renounce joking and lead a better life.

Key Ideas and Details Why does Twain think Americans are skilled at telling humorous stories? What is the difference between a humorous story and a comic story?

THE NOTORIOUS JUMPING FROG OF CALAVERAS COUNTY

MARK TWAIN

Vocabulary

garrulous (gar′ ə ləs) *adj.* talking too much

conjectured (kən jek′ chərd) *v.* guessed

monotonous (mə nät′ ən əs) *adj.* tiresome because unvarying

interminable (in tʉr′ mi nə bəl) *adj.* seeming to last forever

In compliance with the request of a friend of mine, who wrote me from the East, I called on good-natured, **garrulous** old Simon Wheeler, and inquired after my friend's friend, Leonidas W. Smiley, as requested to do, and I hereunto append the result. I have a lurking suspicion that *Leonidas W.* Smiley is a myth; that my friend never knew such a personage: and that he only **conjectured** that if I asked old Wheeler about him, it would remind him of his infamous *Jim* Smiley, and he would go to work and bore me to death with some exasperating reminiscence of him as long and as tedious as it should be useless to me. If that was the design, it succeeded.

I found Simon Wheeler dozing comfortably by the barroom stove of the dilapidated tavern in the decayed mining camp of Angel's, and I noticed that he was fat and baldheaded, and had an expression of winning gentleness and simplicity upon his tranquil countenance. He roused up, and gave me good day. I told him a friend of mine had commissioned me to make some inquiries about a cherished companion of his boyhood named *Leonidas W.* Smiley—*Rev. Leonidas W.* Smiley, a young minister of the Gospel, who he had heard was at one time a resident of Angel's Camp. I added that if Mr. Wheeler could tell me anything about this Rev. Leonidas W. Smiley, I would feel under many obligations to him.

Simon Wheeler backed me into a corner and blockaded me there with his chair, and then sat down and reeled off the **monotonous** narrative which follows this paragraph. He never smiled, he never frowned, he never changed his voice from the gentle-flowing key to which he tuned his initial sentence, he never betrayed the slightest suspicion of enthusiasm; but all through the **interminable** narrative there ran a vein of impressive earnestness and sincerity, which showed me plainly that, so far from his imagining that there was anything ridiculous or funny about his story, he regarded it as a really important matter, and admired its two heroes as men of transcendent genius in *finesse*. I let him go on in his own way, and never interrupted him once.

"Rev. Leonidas W. H'm, Reverend Le—well, there was a feller here once by the name of *Jim* Smiley, in the winter of '49—or maybe it was the spring of '50—I don't recollect exactly, somehow, though what makes me think it was one or the other is because I remember the big flume[1] warn't finished when he first come to the camp; but anyway, he was the curiousest man about always betting on anything that turned up you ever see, if he could get anybody to bet on the other side; and if he couldn't he'd change sides. Any way that suited the other man would suit *him*—any way just so's he got a bet, *he* was satisfied. But still he was lucky, uncommon lucky; he most always come out winner. He was always ready and laying for a chance; there couldn't be no solit'ry thing mentioned but that feller'd offer to bet on it, and take ary side you please, as I was just telling you. If there was a horse race, you'd find him flush or you'd find him busted at the end of it; if there was a dogfight, he'd bet on it; if there was a cat fight, he'd bet on it; if there was a chicken fight, he'd bet on it; why, if there was two birds setting on a fence, he would bet you which one would fly first; or if there was a camp meeting,[2] he would be there reg'lar to bet on Parson Walker, which he judged to be the best exhorter about here and so he was too, and a good man. If he even see a straddle bug[3] start to go anywheres, he would bet you how long it would take him to get to—to wherever he was going to, and if you took him up, he would foller that straddle bug to Mexico but what he would find out where he was bound for and how long he was on the road. Lots of the boys here has seen that Smiley, and can tell you about him. Why, it never made no difference to *him*—he'd bet on *any* thing—the dangdest feller. Parson Walker's wife laid very sick once, for a good while, and it seemed as if they warn't going to save her; but one morning he come in, and Smiley up and asked him how she was, and he said she was considable better—thank the Lord for his inf'nite

▼ Critical Viewing
Would Twain have been amused or offended by this caricature of himself? Explain. **SPECULATE**

Comprehension
What does the narrator suspect about Leonidas W. Smiley?

1. **flume** (flo͞om) *n.* artificial channel for carrying water to provide power and transport objects.
2. **camp meeting** religious gathering at the mining camp.
3. **straddle bug** insect with long legs.

mercy—and coming on so smart that with the blessing of Prov'dence she'd get well yet; and Smiley, before he thought, says, 'Well, I'll resk two-and-a-half she don't anyway.'

Humor
What is funny about this description of the mare?

Thish-yer Smiley had a mare—the boys called her the fifteen-minute nag, but that was only in fun, you know, because of course she was faster than that—and he used to win money on that horse, for all she was so slow and always had the asthma, or the distemper, or the consumption, or something of that kind. They used to give her two or three hundred yards start, and then pass her under way; but always at the fag end[4] of the race she'd get excited and desperate like, and come cavorting and straddling up, and scattering her legs around limber, sometimes in the air, and sometimes out to one side among the fences, and kicking up m-o-r-e dust and raising m-o-r-e racket with her coughing and sneezing and blowing her nose—and *always* fetch up at the stand just about a neck ahead, as near as you could cipher it down.

Humor
Why is the dog's name—Andrew Jackson—funny?

And he had a little small bull-pup, that to look at him you'd think he warn't worth a cent but to set around and look ornery and lay for a chance to steal something. But as soon as money was up on him he was a different dog; his under-jaw'd begin to stick out like the fo' castle[5] of a steamboat, and his teeth would uncover and shine like the furnaces. And a dog might tackle him and bullyrag him, and bite him, and throw him over his shoulder two or three times, and Andrew Jackson—which was the name of the pup—Andrew Jackson would never let on but what *he* was satisfied, and hadn't expected nothing else—and the bets being doubled and doubled on the other side all the time, till the money was all up; and then all of a sudden he would grab that other dog jest by the j'int of his hind leg and freeze to it—not chaw, you understand, but only just grip and hang on till they throwed up the sponge, if it was a year. Smiley always come out winner on that pup, till he harnessed a dog once that didn't have no hind legs, because they'd been sawed off in a circular saw, and when the thing had gone along far enough, and the money was all up, and he come to make a snatch for his pet holt,[6] he see in a minute how he'd been imposed on, and how the other dog had him in the door, so to speak, and he 'peared surprised, and then he looked sorter discouraged-like, and didn't try no more to win the fight, and so he got shucked out bad. He give Smiley a look, as much as to say his heart was broke, and it was his fault, for putting up a dog that hadn't no hind legs for him to take holt of, which was his main dependence in a fight, and then he limped off a piece and laid down and died. It was a good pup, was that Andrew Jackson, and would have made a name for hisself if he'd lived, for the stuff was in him and he had genius—I know it, because he hadn't no opportunities to

4. **fag end** last part.
5. **fo'castle** (fōk′ səl) *n.* the forward part of the upper deck.
6. **holt** hold.

speak of, and it don't stand to reason that a dog could make such a fight as he could under them circumstances if he hadn't no talent. It always makes me feel sorry when I think of that last fight of his'n, and the way it turned out.

Well, thish-yer Smiley had rat terriers,[7] and chicken cocks,[8] and tomcats and all them kind of things, till you couldn't rest, and you couldn't fetch nothing for him to bet on but he'd match you. He ketched a frog one day, and took him home, and said he cal'lated to educate him; and so he never done nothing for three months but set in his back yard and learn that frog to jump. And you bet you he *did* learn him, too. He'd give him a little punch behind, and the next minute you'd see that frog whirling in the air like a doughnut—see him turn one summerset, or maybe a couple, if he got a good start, and come down flatfooted and all right, like a cat. He got him up so in the matter of ketching flies, and kep' him in practice so constant, that he'd nail a fly every time as fur as he could see him. Smiley said all a frog wanted was education, and he could do 'most anything—and I believe him. Why, I've seen him set Dan'l Webster down here on this floor—Dan'l Webster was the name of the frog—and sing out, "Flies, Dan'l, flies!" and quicker'n you could wink he'd spring straight up and snake a fly off 'n the counter there, and flop down on the floor ag'in as solid as a gob of mud, and fall to scratching the side of his head with his hind foot as indifferent as if he hadn't no idea he'd been doin' any more'n any frog might do. You never see a frog so modest and straightfor'ard as he was, for all he was so gifted. And when it come to fair and square jumping on a dead level, he could get over more ground at one straddle than any animal of his breed you ever

▲ Critical Viewing
Which moment of the story is depicted in this illustration?
CONNECT

Humor
What exaggerations in this passage make the description funnier?

Comprehension
What was most unusual about Smiley and his betting habits?

---

7. rat terriers dogs skilled in catching rats.
8. chicken cocks roosters trained to fight.

see. Jumping on a dead level was his strong suit, you understand; and when it come to that, Smiley would ante up money on him as long as he had a red.[9] Smiley was monstrous proud of his frog, and well he might be, for fellers that had traveled and been everywheres all said he laid over any frog that ever *they* see.

'IT MIGHT BE A PARROT, OR IT MIGHT BE A CANARY, MAYBE, BUT IT AIN'T—IT'S ONLY JUST A FROG.'

Well, Smiley kep' the beast in a little lattice box, and he used to fetch him downtown sometimes and lay for a bet. One day a feller—a stranger in the camp, he was—come acrost him with his box, and says:

'What might it be that you've got in the box?'

And Smiley says, sorter indifferent-like, 'It might be a parrot, or it might be a canary, maybe, but it ain't—it's only just a frog.'

And the feller took it, and looked at it careful, and turned it round this way and that, and says, 'H'm—so 'tis. Well, what's *he* good for?'

'Well,' Smiley says, easy and careless, 'he's good enough for *one* thing, I should judge—he can outjump any frog in Calaveras county.'

The feller took the box again, and took another long, particular look, and give it back to Smiley, and says, very deliberate, 'Well,' he says, 'I don't see no p'ints about that frog that's any better'n any other frog.'

'Maybe you don't,' Smiley says. 'Maybe you understand frogs and maybe you don't understand 'em; maybe you've had experience, and maybe you ain't only a amature, as it were. Anyways, I've got *my* opinion, and I'll resk forty dollars that he can outjump any frog in Calaveras county.'

And the feller studied a minute, and then says, kinder sad like, 'Well, I'm only a stranger here, and I ain't got no frog; but if I had a frog, I'd bet you.'

And then Smiley says, 'That's all right—that's all right—if you'll hold my box a minute, I'll go and get you a frog.' And so the feller took the box, and put up his forty dollars along with Smiley's, and set down to wait.

So he set there a good while thinking and thinking to hisself, and then he got the frog out and prized his mouth open and took a teaspoon and filled him full of quailshot[10]—filled him pretty near up to his chin—and set him on the floor. Smiley he went to the swamp and slopped around in the mud for a long time, and finally he ketched a frog, and fetched him in, and give him to this feller, and says:

'Now, if you're ready, set him alongside of Dan'l, with his forepaws just even with Dan'l's, and I'll give the word.' Then he says, 'One—two—three—*git!*' and him and the feller touched up the frogs from behind, and the new frog hopped off lively, but Dan'l give a heave, and hysted up his shoulders—so—like a Frenchman, but it warn't no use—he couldn't budge; he was planted as solid as a church, and he couldn't no more stir than if he was anchored out. Smiley was a good

---

9. a red red cent; colloquial expression for "any money at all."
10. quailshot small lead pellets used for shooting quail.

deal surprised, and he was disgusted too, but he didn't have no idea what the matter was, of course.

The feller took the money and started away; and when he was going out at the door, he sorter jerked his thumb over his shoulder—so—at Dan'l, and says again, very deliberate, 'Well,' he says, 'I don't see no p'ints about that frog that's any better'n any other frog.'

Smiley he stood scratching his head and looking down at Dan'l a long time, and at last he says, 'I do wonder what in the nation that frog throw'd off for—I wonder if there ain't something the matter with him—he 'pears to look mighty baggy, somehow.' And he ketched Dan'l by the nap of the neck, and hefted him, and says, 'Why blame my cats if he don't weigh five pound!' and turned him upside down and he belched out a double handful of shot. And then he see how it was, and he was the maddest man—he set the frog down and took out after that feller, but he never ketched him. And—"

Clarifying and Interpreting Language
How would you rephrase the sentence beginning "And he ketched Dan'l . . ." in Standard English?

Here Simon Wheeler heard his name called from the front yard, and got up to see what was wanted. And turning to me as he moved away, he said: "Just set where you are, stranger, and rest easy—I ain't going to be gone a second."

But, by your leave, I did not think that a continuation of the history of the enterprising vagabond *Jim* Smiley would be likely to afford me much information concerning the Rev. *Leonidas W.* Smiley, and so I started away.

At the door I met the sociable Wheeler returning, and he buttonholed me and recommenced:

"Well, thish-yer Smiley had a yaller one-eyed cow that didn't have no tail, only just a short stump like a bannanner, and—"

However, lacking both time and inclination, I did not wait to hear about the afflicted cow, but took my leave.

Critical Reading

1. **Key Ideas and Details** **(a)** What prompts Simon Wheeler to tell the story of Jim Smiley? **(b) Infer:** Why had the narrator's friend suggested that he ask Wheeler about Leonidas Smiley?
2. **Key Ideas and Details** **(a)** What was Jim Smiley's response to any event? **(b) Infer:** Based on this behavior, what can you infer about his character?
3. **Integration of Knowledge and Ideas** What image of America do both the excerpt from Twain's memoir and this comic story paint? Consider the sense of place, character, and event. In your response, use at least two of these Essential Question words: *adventure, individualism, sincerity, ambition.* ***[Connecting to the Essential Question: What makes American literature American?]***

Cite textual evidence to support your responses.

Close Reading Activities

from *Life on the Mississippi* • *The Notorious Jumping Frog of Calaveras County*

Literary Analysis

1. **Craft and Structure** In the excerpt from *Life on the Mississippi,* how does Twain's use of the word *heavenly* to describe ordinary activities (shaking out a tablecloth or holding a rope) add to the **humor** of his narrative?
2. **Craft and Structure** **(a)** What place and way of life does Twain describe in the excerpt? **(b)** How does humor help Twain avoid sentimentality in dealing with this subject?
3. **Craft and Structure** In the excerpt from *Life on the Mississippi,* the narrator—the older Twain—peppers his account with steamboat terminology. **(a)** Identify two examples of this use of technical language. **(b)** Explain what each example means and how you clarify that information.
4. **Craft and Structure** **(a)** In "The Notorious Jumping Frog of Calaveras County," what basic **incongruity** exists between the narrator and Simon Wheeler? **(b)** How does this contrast add to the story's humor?
5. **Craft and Structure** Use a chart like the one shown to analyze two examples of **hyperbole** in "The Notorious Jumping Frog of Calaveras County."

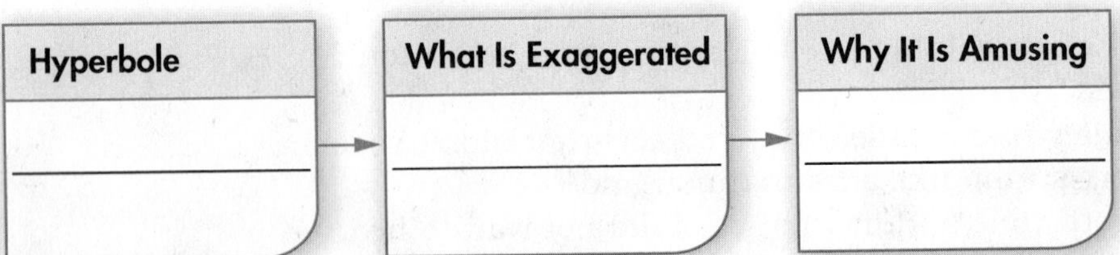

6. **Craft and Structure** **(a)** How does the use of **dialect** in "The Notorious Jumping Frog of Calaveras County" add to the story's humor? **(b)** Why would the story be less effective if Wheeler spoke in Standard English?
7. **Craft and Structure** **Interpret** the regional dialect in this passage by "translating" it into modern Standard English: *...he 'peared surprised, and then he looked sorter discouraged-like, and didn't try no more to win the fight, and so he got shucked out bad.*
8. **Integration of Knowledge and Ideas** **(a)** What is Wheeler's main activity in "The Notorious Jumping Frog..."? **(b)** What **social commentary** about this activity might Twain be making through humor?
9. **Integration of Knowledge and Ideas** In which selection does Twain view the characters' foibles, or weaknesses, with more sympathy? Explain.
10. **Analyze Visual Information** What does this drawing, made after Twain's death, show about his place in American culture?

Common Core State Standards

Language

4. Determine or clarify the meaning of unknown and multiple-meaning words and phrases based on *grades 11–12 reading and content,* choosing flexibly from a range of strategies. *(p. 583)*

4.b. Identify and correctly use patterns of word changes that indicate different meanings or parts of speech. *(p. 583)*

4.c. Consult general and specialized reference materials, both print and digital, to determine or clarify the precise meaning of a word. *(p. 583)*

5. Demonstrate understanding of word relationships and nuances in word meanings. *(p. 583)*

5.b. Analyze nuances in the meanings of words with similar denotations. *(p. 583)*

THERE IS A TIME TO LAUGH AND THERE IS A TIME TO WEEP

Vocabulary Acquisition and Use

Word Analysis: Greek Prefix *mono-*

The Greek prefix *mono-* means "alone," "one," or "single." A *monotonous* storyteller, therefore, uses a single tone, without varying volume or pace. Likewise, a *monosyllabic* word is made up of one syllable, and a *monocle* is a form of eyeglass with only one lens. Add the prefix *mono-* to each word root listed below. Using your understanding of the prefix and the definition of each root, tell the meaning of each newly created word.

1. *theism* = belief in a god or gods
2. *logue* = speech; speaking
3. *lith* = stone
4. *syllable* = unit of sound

Which of the new words best describes Simon Wheeler's tale? Explain.

Vocabulary: Antonyms

Antonyms are words with opposite or nearly opposite meanings. Review the words in the vocabulary list on page 569. Then, select the letter of the word in the right column that is the best antonym for each vocabulary word in the left column. Explain your answers.

1. transient	**a.** varied
2. prodigious	**b.** meager
3. eminence	**c.** quiet
4. garrulous	**d.** permanent
5. conjectured	**e.** verified
6. monotonous	**f.** obscurity
7. interminable	**g.** brief

Using Resources to Build Vocabulary

Funny Business: Words for Overstating the Case

Twain infuses his prose with humor by using overblown words to describe common feelings, experiences, and situations. Here are a few of them:

glorious	heavenly
fragrant	tranquil
grandeur	transcendent

Return to Twain's stories to review these words in context. Then, *use a print or an electronic thesaurus* to find a less inflated synonym for each one. (For example, a milder synonym for *glorious* might be *bright*.) On your own paper, rewrite the sentence in which the word appears by replacing the word with the deflated synonym. Read over your new lines, and, in a sentence or two, explain why they are less amusing than Twain's originals.

Close Reading Activities Continued

Writing to Sources

Expository Text In the essay excerpted on page 575, Twain defines some of the elements that contribute to a humorous story:

> ***The humorous story may be spun out to great length, and may wander around as much as it pleases, and arrive nowhere in particular. . . . [It] is told gravely; the teller does his best to conceal the fact that he even dimly suspects there is anything funny about it.***

Write an **essay** in which you analyze Twain's application of these techniques in his own story "The Notorious Jumping Frog of Calaveras County." Include in your analysis an evaluation of Twain's definition. Determine whether his definition is universal—true in most times and places—or true only in Twain's day and age.

Prewriting Select several humorous passages from the story to analyze according to the main ideas in Twain's definition. Use a chart like the one shown to organize your thoughts.

Model: Organizing to Show Comparison

spins out at length	arrives nowhere	is told gravely	conceals humor

Drafting Organize your essay point by point, connecting Twain's definition to passages from the story. For each passage, do the following:

- Introduce the passage by indicating which aspect of the definition it will illustrate.
- Provide the passage in the form of a quotation. Introduce shorter passages with a colon, and enclose them in quotation marks. Set longer passages off from the text. Include a parenthetical page reference after each quotation.
- Explain the connection between the passage and Twain's definition. Strengthen your analysis by adding your own insights about how and why a certain technique creates humor.

Conclude your draft with an assessment of Twain's definition. To end the essay on a lively note, consider imitating Twain's style or otherwise injecting your own variety of respectful humor.

Revising Review your essay to find ideas that you can support more effectively with additional examples, details, or quotations. Return to your notes or to the story to find additional supporting evidence.

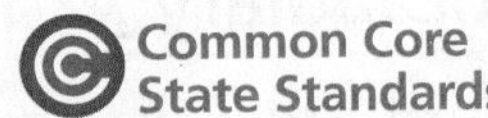

Writing

2. Write explanatory texts to examine and convey complex ideas, concepts, and information clearly and accurately through the effective selection, organization, and analysis of content.

2.a. Introduce a topic; organize complex ideas, concepts, and information so that each new element builds on that which precedes it to create a unified whole.

2.b. Develop the topic thoroughly by selecting the most significant and relevant facts, extended definitions, concrete details, quotations, or other information and examples appropriate to the audience's knowledge of the topic.

2.f. Provide a concluding statement or section that follows from and supports the information or explanation presented.

Language

1. Demonstrate command of the conventions of standard English grammar and usage when writing or speaking. *(p. 585)*

Conventions and Style: Fixing Misplaced and Dangling Modifiers

A **misplaced modifier** seems to modify the wrong word in a sentence because it is too far away from the word it really modifies. A **dangling modifier** seems to modify the wrong word or no word at all because the word it *should* modify is not in the sentence. Misplaced and dangling modifiers can be single words, phrases, or clauses. Your writing will be clearer if you avoid misplaced and dangling modifiers.

Misplaced: *Disappointed*, the riverboat captain ignored the boy.
Fixed: The riverboat captain ignored the disappointed boy.

Misplaced: Twain's adventures inspired a number of books *in foreign countries.*
Fixed: Twain's adventures in foreign countries inspired a number of books.

Dangling: *Full of quailshot*, jumping was impossible.
Fixed: Full of quailshot, the frog could not jump.

Dangling: *While working as a journalist*, an entertaining writing style developed.
Fixed: While working as a journalist, Twain developed an entertaining writing style.

TIP Dangling modifiers most often appear as introductory phrases or clauses.

Practice Rewrite each sentence to fix the misplaced or dangling modifier and make the sentence clear. You may have to change the wording slightly. In items 1–5, the misplaced or dangling modifier is in italics.

1. The frog *only* lost one race.
2. The pup would grab the other dog *to win the fight* by the hind leg.
3. *Determined*, Twain's plan was to work on a steamboat.
4. *Eager to make a bet*, Smiley's frog is left with the stranger.
5. *After his wife's death*, pessimism overcame Mark Twain.
6. The young men were talking about their future jobs on steamboats yesterday.
7. Having found a second frog, the jumping contest was started.
8. Clemens met many characters that he would write about later as a boy.
9. Assembled at the wharf, their eyes were fixed on the handsome steamboat.
10. The boy would become a writer who dreamed of piloting a riverboat.

Writing and Speaking Conventions

A. Writing For each numbered item, write a sentence using the phrase or clause as a modifier. Then, tell what word or words the phrase or clause modifies.

1. near the Mississippi River
2. who envied him
3. gone for a long time
4. placing his bet

Example: near the Mississippi River
Sentence: As a boy, Clemens lived near the Mississippi River.
Word Modified: lived

B. Speaking Describe an occupation you dream of having. Correctly use at least three different types of modifiers.

"School" of American Humor

"Semper Ridere"

Mark Twain, President & Founder
Robert Benchley, Punster & Wordsmith
Dorothy Parker, Resident Wit
James Thurber, Fabulist
S. J. Perelman, Wry *Feuilletonist*
Russell Baker, Memoirist & Humorist
Art Buchwald, Political Satirist

Garrison Keillor, Storyteller
Bill Cosby, Comedian of Stage, Screen, and Print
Erma Bombeck, Humorous Housewife
Dave Barry, Humor Columnist
Bill Bryson, Backpacking Comic

COURSE CATALOGUE

Humor Writing 101

Dry Wit, Dialect, and Local Color
Prof. **Mark Twain**
Meets: M-W-F, 11:00–12:00 *4 credits*

Knowing your audience is the key to effective humor, and Prof. Twain shares his time-tested techniques in this required humor course. Learn to be an observer and develop a keen ear for speech to make your writing richer and funnier.

Humor Writing 102

Bon Mots, Biting Wit, and Blistering Sarcasm
Prof. **Dorothy Parker**
Meets: F 5:00–11:00 *4 credits*

If Oscar Wilde had an American sister, it would have been Prof. Parker. She'll teach you to write satirical fiction, brutal barbs and viciously funny poems. Wield wit as a weapon. Torpedo the double standard. Subvert the status quo. Students will emerge as seasoned professionals. "The most beautiful words in English," says Parker, "are 'check enclosed.'"

Humor Writing 103

Satire, Punch Lines, Cartoons, and Deadpan Delivery
Prof. **James Thurber**
Meets T-TH, 9:00 – 10:00 *4 credits*

Unlock the absurdity in your secret life. Prof. Thurber will show how writing about small, timid protagonists can earn you a whale of a reputation. Humor, as Prof. Thurber will demonstrate, is emotional chaos remembered in tranquility. This is his class and welcome to it.

Humor Writing 104

Humorous Sketches and Absurdist Screenplays
Prof. **S. J. Perelman**
Meets: W 2:00–5:00 *4 credits*

Feuilletons is a French literary term meaning "little leaves." Prof. Perelman shows how he produces his *feuilletons*—brief, amusing sketches for *The New Yorker*. On the syllabus: making wry observations, tossing up non- sequiturs, infusing everyday events with irony, and writing absurdist screenplays a la *Horsefeathers* and *Monkey Business*.

Humor Writing 105

Hyperbole and Screwball Characters
Prof. **Erma Bombeck**
Meets: M-W-F 10:00–11:00 *4 credits*

Learn how to turn mundane household chores into comic opera for a newspaper column. Master screwball characters, down-home hyperbole, and the self-deprecating voice. Prof. Bombeck will show you how to make outrageous claims—such as, "Motherhood is the second oldest profession," —without bursting your own balloon.

Humor Writing 106

Anthropology, Incongruity, and Human Foibles
Prof. **Bill Bryson**
Meets: T-TH 9:00–11:00 *4 credits*

If you look at your own backyard and see an exhibit on alien culture, you may have what it takes to become a best-selling author. After Prof. Bryson leads you on a tour of Main Street USA, it will never seem quite the same again. His tools of the trade include regional detail, hyperbole, embellishment, and comic characters. Wear your walking shoes.

Comparing Literary Works

Mark Twain's Writings* • from *The Life and Times of the Thunderbolt Kid

Comparing American Humor Past and Present

Writing Humor American humor writing falls roughly into two categories: the refined, moral wit of figures such as Benjamin Franklin and Washington Irving; and the folk humor, or "humor of the people," of writers such as Mark Twain and contemporary writer **Bill Bryson.** While the first type of humor is characterized by a subtle, high-minded cleverness, the second makes use of more obvious humorous devices, including the following:

- **hyperbole:** the exaggeration of details or embellishment of events
- **incongruity:** elements that seem not to fit their context
- **regionalism:** language or behaviors specific to a certain part of the country
- **foibles:** a focus on human flaws

When used in conjunction with everyday subject matter, such as making a bet or cooking dinner, these elements produce snapshots of real life that are familiar, funny, and revealing of larger ideas about human nature.

Like Mark Twain, Bill Bryson began his career as a journalist; also like Twain, Bryson used his observational skills in humorous works on a wide range of subjects, including travel. Both authors deal in the humor of the everyday—the amusing aspects of regular folks trying to live in a world that is anything but "regular." Use the following chart to compare and contrast Twain's and Bryson's humor.

Humorous Device	Twain	Bryson
hyperbole	describes an apprentice engineer as an "exalted . . . eminence"	
regional elements	Simon Wheeler's dialect	
comic characters	the "trapped" narrator of "The Notorious Jumping Frog..."	

Common Core State Standards

Reading Informational Text

4. Determine the meaning of words and phrases as they are used in a text, including figurative and connotative meanings.

Language

4.c. Consult general and specialized reference materials, both print and digital, to find the pronunciation of a word or determine or clarify its precise meaning, its part of speech, its etymology, or its standard usage.

5.a. Interpret figures of speech in context and analyze their role in the text.

Gather Vocabulary Knowledge

Bryson uses related forms of the words *explode, perish,* and *recoil* to relate his early experiences with food. Use print or online glossaries and other references to explore these words.

- **Related References**: Using an etymology guide or vocabulary builder, learn more about each word's origin and meaning. Select one word and build a word map for it that includes synonyms, antonyms, and examples of use in sentences.
- **Glossaries:** Refer to the glossary of a cookbook and find three verbs that normally apply to cooking processes. Use the words in a paragraph.

Bill Bryson *(b. 1951)*

Author of ***The Life and Times of the Thunderbolt Kid: A Memoir***

Bill Bryson was born and raised in Des Moines, Iowa, where his father was a sports writer and his mother a home furnishings editor for the daily newspaper the *Des Moines Register*. Bryson's two older siblings had left home by the time he was a teenager, and his busy parents granted Bryson a great deal of freedom: On any given evening he might be given five dollars and told to eat out and catch a movie. This lifestyle suited Bryson, who has led what he describes as a "rootless" life ever since.

Back and Forth In 1972, Bryson abandoned his studies at Drake University in order to spend four months backpacking through Europe. The following year, he returned to England for a longer stay. While working in a psychiatric hospital near London, Bryson met his wife, a nurse. The couple returned to the United States in order for Bryson to complete his college degree. They crossed the Atlantic yet again, settled in northern England, and stayed put for almost twenty years before moving back to the United States in 1995. After eight years in New Hampshire, the couple returned to England, where they remain.

Word Wanderings During his early years in Britain, Bryson worked as a journalist. The work left him restless, though, and he retired from journalism in 1987. Bryson's first book, *The Lost Continent*, appeared two years later. True to its author's ambling spirit, the book describes a visit to the United States—38 of them, to be exact—in search of the perfect American small town. Subsequent books have ranged across the globe and across a wide spectrum of subjects, including travels in Europe, hiking the Appalachian Trail, British culture, the history of the English language, the history of science, and the life of William Shakespeare.

Looking Back Bryson's memoir, *The Life and Times of the Thunderbolt Kid*, is a portrait of his childhood that also provides insight into the stuff of Bryson's humor, which he finds in our chaotic daily lives, in our oddball habits, in those forgotten containers at the backs of our refrigerators. Bryson admits that the memoir is also a kind of lament for the loss of our collective innocence. If you were a kid in the 1950s, he reflects, "You really did expect, any day, that we'd all have jet-packs or be going on vacation to Mars. . . . And now that's completely gone."

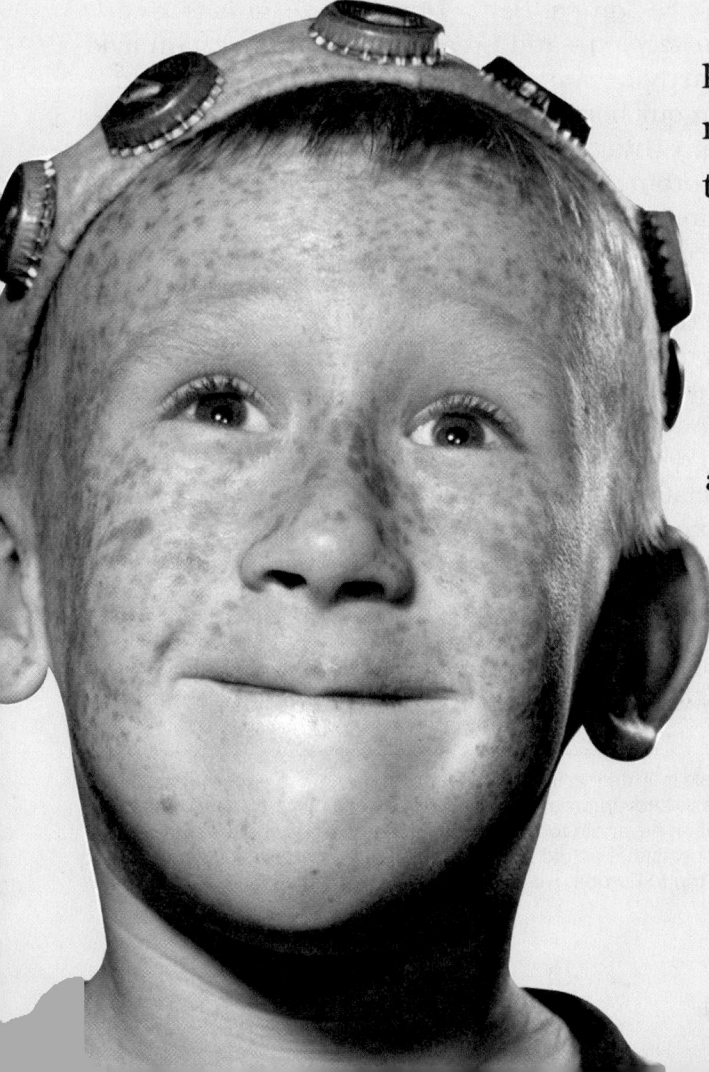

from

The Life and Times of the Thunderbolt Kid

Bill Bryson

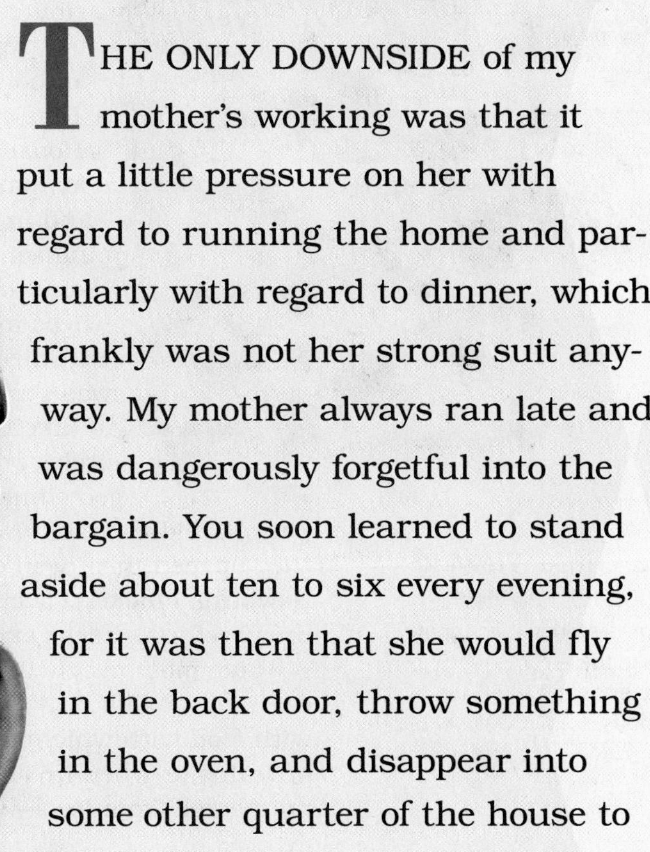

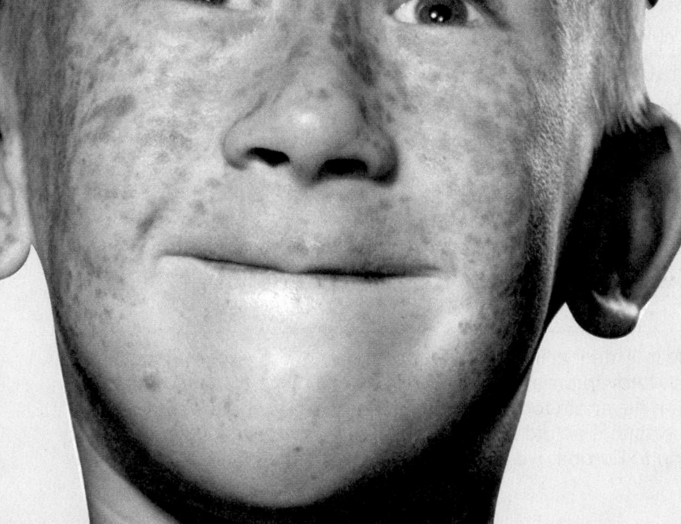

THE ONLY DOWNSIDE of my mother's working was that it put a little pressure on her with regard to running the home and particularly with regard to dinner, which frankly was not her strong suit anyway. My mother always ran late and was dangerously forgetful into the bargain. You soon learned to stand aside about ten to six every evening, for it was then that she would fly in the back door, throw something in the oven, and disappear into some other quarter of the house to

Vocabulary

embark (em bärk′) *v.* to begin a venture, project, or activity

embark on the thousand other household tasks that greeted her each evening. In consequence she nearly always forgot about dinner until a point slightly beyond way too late. As a rule you knew it was time to eat when you could hear potatoes exploding in the oven.

We didn't call it the kitchen in our house. We called it the Burns Unit.

"It's a bit burned," my mother would say apologetically at every meal, presenting you with a piece of meat that looked like something—a much-loved pet perhaps—salvaged from a tragic house fire. "But I think I scraped off most of the burned part," she would add, overlooking that this included every bit of it that had once been flesh.

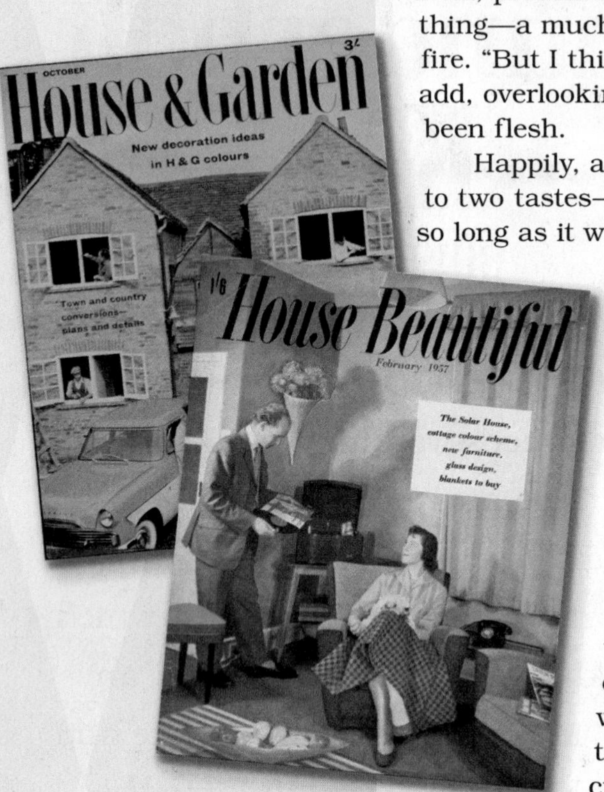

Happily, all this suited my father. His palate only responded to two tastes—burned and ice cream—so everything suited him so long as it was sufficiently dark and not too startlingly flavorful. Theirs truly was a marriage made in heaven, for no one could burn food like my mother or eat it like my dad.

As part of her job, my mother bought stacks of housekeeping magazines—*House Beautiful, House & Garden, Better Homes and Gardens, Good Housekeeping*—and I read these with a certain avidity, partly because they were always lying around and in our house all idle moments were spent reading something, and partly because they depicted lives so absorbingly at variance with our own. The housewives in my mother's magazines were so collected, so organized, so calmly on top of things, and their food was perfect—their *lives* were perfect. They dressed up to take their food out of the oven! There were no black circles on the ceiling above their stoves, no mutating goo climbing over the sides of their forgotten saucepans. Children didn't have to be ordered to stand back every time they opened *their* oven doors. And their foods—baked Alaska, lobster Newburg, chicken cacciatore—why, these were dishes we didn't even dream of, much less encounter, in Iowa.

▲ Critical Viewing

How does the lifestyle presented in magazines like these compare to the realities of Bryson's household? **COMPARE**

Like most people in Iowa in the 1950s, we were more cautious eaters in our house.* On the rare occasions when we were presented with food with which we were not comfortable or familiar—on planes or trains or when invited to a meal cooked by someone who was not herself from Iowa—we tended to tilt it up carefully with a knife

* In fact, like most other people in America. The leading food writer of the age, Duncan Hines, author of the hugely successful *Adventures in Good Eating*, was himself a cautious eater and declared with pride that he never ate food with French names if he could possibly help it. Hines's other proud boast was that he did not venture out of America until he was seventy years old, when he made a trip to Europe. He disliked much of what he found there, especially the food.

and examine it from every angle as if determining whether it might need to be defused. Once on a trip to San Francisco my father was taken by friends to a Chinese restaurant and he described it to us afterward in the somber tones of someone recounting a near-death experience.

"And they eat it with sticks, you know," he added knowledgeably.

"Goodness!" said my mother.

"I would rather have gas gangrene than go through that again," my father added grimly.

All of our meals consisted of leftovers.

In our house we didn't eat

- pasta, rice, cream cheese, sour cream, garlic, mayonnaise, onions, corned beef, pastrami, salami, or foreign food of any type, except French toast
- bread that wasn't white and at least 65 percent air
- spices other than salt, pepper, and maple syrup
- fish that was any shape other than rectangular and not coated in bright orange bread crumbs, and then only on Fridays and only when my mother remembered it was Friday, which in fact was not often
- soups not blessed by Campbell's and only a very few of those
- anything with **dubious** regional names like "pone" or "gumbo," or foods that had at any time been an esteemed staple of slaves or peasants

Vocabulary
dubious (do͞o′ bē əs) *adj.* questionable; suspicious

All other foods of all types—curries, enchiladas, tofu, bagels, sushi, couscous, yogurt, kale, arugula, Parma ham, any cheese that was not a vivid bright yellow and shiny enough to see your reflection in—had either not yet been invented or was yet unknown to us. We really were radiantly unsophisticated. I remember being surprised to learn at quite an advanced age that a shrimp cocktail was not, as I had always imagined, a predinner alcoholic drink with a shrimp in it.

All our meals consisted of leftovers. My mother had a seemingly inexhaustible supply of foods that had already been to the table, sometimes repeatedly. Apart from a few perishable dairy products, everything in the fridge was older than I was, sometimes by many years. (Her oldest food possession of all, it more or less goes without saying, was a fruitcake that was kept in a metal tin and dated from the colonial period.) I can only assume that my mother did all of her cooking in the 1940s so that she could spend the rest of her life surprising herself with what she could find under cover at the back of the fridge. I never knew her to reject a food. The rule of thumb seemed to be that if you opened the lid and the stuff inside didn't make you actually recoil and take at least one staggered step backward, it was deemed okay to eat.

Comprehension
Why was Bryson's parents' marriage "made in heaven"?

My mother routinely washed and dried paper plates...

Both of my parents had grown up during the Great Depression and neither of them ever threw anything away if they could possibly avoid it. My mother routinely washed and dried paper plates, and smoothed out for reuse spare aluminum foil. If you left a pea on your plate, it became part of a future meal. All our sugar came in little packets spirited out of restaurants in deep coat pockets, as did our jams, jellies, crackers (oyster *and* saltine), tartar sauces, some of our ketchup and butter, all of our napkins, and a very occasional ashtray; anything that came with a restaurant table really. One of the happiest moments in my parents' life was when maple syrup started to be served in small disposable packets and they could add those to the household hoard.

Critical Reading

Cite textual evidence to support your responses.

1. **Key Ideas and Details** **(a)** What was the kitchen called in the Bryson house? **(b) Infer:** What does this name suggest about the family?
2. **Key Ideas and Details** **(a)** How does Bryson describe the eaters in his house—and in Iowa in the 1950s? **(b) Infer:** What does this attitude toward food tell you about other aspects of life in Iowa in the 1950s?
3. **Craft and Structure** **Evaluate:** Which word choices or descriptions do you think add most to the humor of this excerpt? Explain.
4. **Craft and Structure** **(a) Distinguish:** What tone, or attitude toward his subject, does Bryson take in this excerpt? **(b) Apply:** Keeping his attitude in mind, write a one-sentence rule for responding to exasperating situations.

Close Reading Activities

***Mark Twain's Writings* •**
from *The Life and Times of the Thunderbolt Kid*

Comparing Humor

1. **Key Ideas and Details (a)** What specific **regional** elements of place and time does Twain bring to light in *Life on the Mississippi*? **(b)** What specific place and time does Bryson bring to life? **(c)** What do the boys in these two different settings have in common?
2. **Key Ideas and Details (a)** Identify a **human foible,** or flaw, that is emphasized in Bryson's memoir. **(b)** Identify a foible Twain spotlights in one of his works. **(c)** For which foible do you have greater sympathy? Why?
3. **Craft and Structure (a)** Note one example each of **hyperbole** and **incongruity** in Bryson's memoir. **(b)** Identify one example of each of these devices in Twain's story "The Notorious Jumping Frog of Calaveras County." **(c)** Which examples do you find funnier? Explain.

Common Core State Standards

Writing

2. Write informative/explanatory texts to examine and convey complex ideas, concepts, and information clearly and accurately through the effective selection, organization, and analysis of content.

2.b. Develop the topic thoroughly by selecting the most significant and relevant facts, extended definitions, concrete details, quotations, or other information and examples appropriate to the audience's knowledge of the topic.

9.a. Apply *grades 11–12 Reading standards* to literature.

Timed Writing

Explanatory Text: Essay

Stock characters, or character "types," are personalities that have become conventional in literature over time. The "overworked career woman" and the conniving trickster are both stock characters. Humor writers use character types to evoke laughter and sympathy and, sometimes, to critique society.

Assignment: Write a **compare-and-contrast** essay in which you examine two character "types" presented by Twain and Bryson. Prewrite by answering the questions listed below to generate ideas and focus your analysis.

- What aspects of each character suggest they are "types"?
- Why is each character funny? What makes each character sympathetic?

As you write, follow the conventions of a strong analytical essay:

- Analyze humorous nuances in the texts.
- Analyze the effects of each author's use of figurative language, such as hyperbole.

5-Minute Planner

Complete these steps before you begin to write.

1. Read the assignment carefully, noting key words and phrases.
2. Scan the selections, looking for details about your chosen characters. **TIP** Jot down details that support your interpretation in two columns, devoting one column to each character.
3. Create a rough outline for your essay.
4. Reread the prompt, and draft your essay.

USE ACADEMIC VOCABULARY

As you write, use academic language, including the following words or their related forms:

compare
contrast
analyze
characterize

For more information about academic language, see the vocabulary charts in the introduction to this book.

Connecting to the Essential Question For "armchair adventurers" at the turn of the twentieth century, this and other stories by Jack London brought to life a distant world of danger and extreme conditions. As you read, note details of extreme peril specific to the setting. This will help as you consider the Essential Question: **What is the relationship between literature and place?**

Reading Literature

3. Analyze the impact of the author's choices regarding how to develop and relate elements of a story or drama.

6. Analyze a case in which grasping a point of view requires distinguishing what is directly stated in a text from what is really meant.

Close Reading Focus

Conflict; Setting; Irony

Conflict, the struggle between opposing forces, can take two forms:

- **Internal,** occurring within the mind of a character
- **External,** occurring between a character and society, nature, another person, God, or fate

A character's efforts to resolve a conflict form the basis for the plot of a narrative. In "To Build a Fire," a man is in the throes of a deadly external conflict, struggling to survive in the bitter cold of the Alaskan wilderness. In this case, the story's **setting**—the time and place of the action—serves as the opposing force against which the protagonist struggles.

Irony involves a discrepancy between what is stated and what is meant, or between what is expected and what actually happens. In the case of **dramatic irony,** there is a contradiction between what a character thinks and what the reader knows to be true. For example, in this story the reader knows that the frigid temperature poses a much greater danger than the man realizes. The result is an ironic quality that permeates the entire story, affecting the reader's understanding of the characters, plot, and setting. As you read, notice passages where it is clear that you understand more than the man does about the conflict he faces.

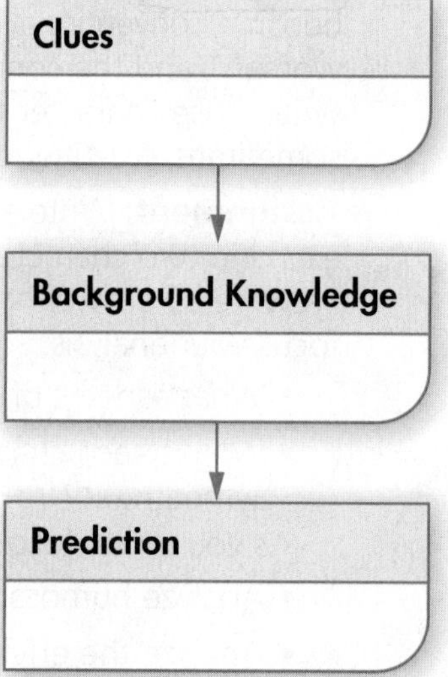

Preparing to Read Complex Texts As you read this story, **predict,** or anticipate, what will happen by noting clues that hint at later events. You can apply your *background knowledge* about the Yukon and survival at extreme temperatures to identify clues. Then, determine what the clues suggest about the main character's plight. Use a chart like the one shown to record your predictions.

Vocabulary

You will encounter the words listed below in the text that follows. Copy the words into your notebook. Which word relates to fire or flames?

conjectural **conflagration**
unwonted **peremptorily**
appendage

JACK LONDON (1876–191

Author of "To Build a Fire"

Jack London had endured more hardships by the age of twenty-one than most people experience in a lifetime. His struggles gave him a sympathy for the working class and a lasting distaste for drudgery. They also provided inspiration for novels and short stories, and became the foundation of his success as a writer.

Difficult Beginnings London grew up in San Francisco in extreme poverty. At the age of eleven, he left school and supported himself through a succession of unskilled jobs. Despite the long hours spent toiling at these jobs, London was able to read constantly, borrowing travel and adventure books from the library.

The books he read inspired London to travel, and he did so as a "tramp," using the name "Frisco Kid." After being arrested for vagrancy near Buffalo, New York, London decided to educate himself and reshape his life. He completed high school in eighteen months and enrolled at the University of California.

After only one semester, however, the lure of adventure proved irresistible. In 1897, London abandoned his studies and traveled to the Alaskan Yukon in an unsuccessful search for gold. His experiences in Alaska taught him about people's desire for wealth and power, and about our inability to control the forces of nature.

A Writing Life Once back in California, London became determined to earn a living as a writer. He rented a typewriter and worked up to fifteen hours a day, spinning his Alaskan adventures into short stories and novels. According to legend, London's stack of rejection slips from publishers grew to five feet in height. Even so, he wrote diligently every morning, setting himself a 1,000-word minimum.

In 1903, London earned national fame when he published *The Call of the Wild*. He soon became the highest-paid and most industrious writer in the country. During his career, London produced more than fifty fiction and nonfiction books, including *The Sea-Wolf* (1904) and *White Fang* (1906), which, along with *The Call of the Wild*, have become American classics.

Recognition by His Peers The well-known writer Upton Sinclair wrote that Jack London "was the true king of our storytellers." London's friend Oliver Madox Hueffer recalled that London "was the ideal yarnster . . . and one reason why I think him likely to be numbered as among the writers of real mark was that he was perfectly unconscious of it. Like Peter Pan, he never grew up, and he lived in his own stories with such intensity that he ended by believing them himself."

…UILD A FIRE

JACK LONDON

BACKGR… nited States purchased Al… m Russia for two cents an acre in 1867. Three decades later, thousands of prospectors, including Jack London, headed north after gold was discovered in the Yukon wilderness. London may have been searching for more than gold. He once commented: "True, the new territory was mostly barren; but its several hundred thousand square miles of frigidity at least gave breathing space to those who else would have suffocated at home."

Day had broken cold and gray, exceedingly cold and gray, when the man turned aside from the main Yukon[1] trail and climbed the high earth-bank, where a dim and little-traveled trail led eastward through the fat spruce timberland. It was a steep bank, and he paused for breath at the top, excusing the act to himself by looking at his watch. It was nine o'clock. There was no sun nor hint of sun, though there was not a cloud in the sky. It was a clear day, and yet there seemed an intangible pall over the face of things, a subtle gloom that made the day dark, and that was due to the absence of sun. This fact did not worry the man. He was used to the lack of sun. It had been days since he had seen the sun, and he knew that a few more days must pass before that cheerful orb, due south, would just peep above the skyline and dip immediately from view.

The man flung a look back along the way he had come. The Yukon lay a mile wide and hidden under three feet of ice. On top of this ice were as many feet of snow. It was all pure white, rolling in gentle undulations where the ice jams of the freeze-up had formed. North and south, as far as his eye could see, it was unbroken white, save for a dark hairline that curved and twisted from around the spruce-covered island to the south, and that curved and twisted away into the north, where it disappeared behind another spruce-covered island. This dark hairline was the trail—the main trail—that led south five hundred miles to the Chilcoot Pass, Dyea,[2] and salt water; and that led north seventy miles to Dawson, and still on to the north a thousand miles to Nulato,[3] and finally to St. Michael on Bering Sea, a thousand miles and half a thousand more.

But all this—the mysterious, far-reaching hairline trail, the absence of sun from the sky, the tremendous cold, and the strangeness and weirdness of it all—made no impression on the man. It was not because he was long used to it. He was a newcomer in the land, a *chechaquo*,[4] and this was his first winter. The trouble with him was that he was without imagination. He was quick and alert in the things of life, but only in the things, and not in the significances. Fifty degrees below zero meant eighty-odd degrees of frost. Such fact impressed him as being cold and uncomfortable, and that was all. It did not lead him to meditate upon his frailty as a creature of temperature, and upon man's frailty in general, able only to live within certain narrow limits of heat and cold; and from there on it did not lead him to the conjectural field of immortality and man's place in the universe. Fifty degrees below zero stood for a bite of frost that hurt and that must be guarded against by the use of mittens, earflaps, warm

Predicting
What do you predict will happen to the "newcomer" who is "without imagination"?

Vocabulary
conjectural (kən jek′ chər əl) *adj.* based on guesswork

Comprehension
Where is the man, and what weather conditions is he experiencing?

1. **Yukon** (yo͞o′ kän) territory in northwestern Canada, east of Alaska; also, a river.
2. **Dyea** (dī′ ā) former town in Alaska at the start of the Yukon trail.
3. **Dawson . . . Nulato** former gold-mining villages in the Yukon.
4. ***chechaquo*** (chē chä′ kwō) slang for newcomer.

moccasins, and thick socks. Fifty degrees below zero was to him just precisely fifty degrees below zero. That there should be anything more to it than that was a thought that never entered his head.

As he turned to go on, he spat speculatively. There was a sharp, explosive crackle that startled him. He spat again. And again, in the air, before it could fall to the snow, the spittle crackled. He knew that at fifty below spittle crackled on the snow, but this spittle had crackled in the air. Undoubtedly it was colder than fifty below—how much colder he did not know. But the temperature did not matter. He was bound for the old claim on the left fork of Henderson Creek, where the boys were already. They had come over across the divide from the Indian Creek country, while he had come the roundabout way to take a look at the possibilities of getting out logs in the spring from the islands in the Yukon. He would be in to camp by six o'clock; a bit after dark, it was true, but the boys would be there, a fire would be going, and a hot supper would be ready. As for lunch, he pressed his hand against the protruding bundle under his jacket. It was also under his shirt, wrapped up in a handkerchief and lying against the naked skin. It was the only way to keep the biscuits from freezing. He smiled agreeably to himself as he thought of those biscuits, each cut open and sopped in bacon grease, and each enclosing a generous slice of fried bacon.

Conflict
With what or whom is the man in conflict?

He plunged in among the big spruce trees. The trail was faint. A foot of snow had fallen since the last sled had passed over, and he was glad he was without a sled, traveling light. In fact, he carried nothing but the lunch wrapped in the handkerchief. He was surprised, however, at the cold. It certainly was cold, he concluded, as he rubbed his numb nose and cheekbones with his mittened hand. He was a warm-whiskered man, but the hair on his face did not protect the high cheekbones and the eager nose that thrust itself aggressively into the frosty air.

Predicting
What prediction can you make based on the description of the dog's instincts?

At the man's heels trotted a dog, a big native husky, the proper wolf dog, gray-coated and without any visible or temperamental difference from its brother, the wild wolf. The animal was depressed by the tremendous cold. It knew that it was no time for traveling. Its instinct told it a truer tale than was told to the man by the man's judgment. In reality, it was not merely colder than fifty below zero; it was colder than sixty below, than seventy below. It was seventy-five below zero. Since the freezing point is thirty-two above zero, it meant that one hundred and seven degrees of frost obtained. The dog did not know anything about thermometers. Possibly in its brain there was no sharp consciousness of a condition of very cold such as was in the man's brain. But the brute had its instinct. It experienced a vague but menacing apprehension that subdued it and made it slink along at the man's heels, and that made it question eagerly every **unwonted** movement of the man as if expecting him to go into camp or to seek shelter somewhere and build a fire. The dog had learned fire, and it wanted fire, or else to burrow under the snow and cuddle its warmth away from the air.

Vocabulary
unwonted (un wän′ tid) *adj.* unusual; unfamiliar

The frozen moisture of its breathing had settled on its fur in a fine powder of frost, and especially were its jowls, muzzle, and eyelashes whitened by its crystalled breath. The man's red beard and mustache were likewise frosted, but more solidly, the deposit taking the form of ice and increasing with every warm, moist breath he exhaled. Also, the man was chewing tobacco, and the muzzle of ice held his lips so rigidly that he was unable to clear his chin when he expelled the juice. The result was that a crystal beard of the color and solidity of amber was increasing its length on his chin. If he fell down it would shatter itself, like glass, into brittle fragments. But he did not mind the appendage. It was the penalty all tobacco-chewers paid in that country, and he had been out before in two cold snaps. They had not been so cold as this, he knew, but by the spirit thermometer[5] at Sixty Mile he knew they had been registered at fifty below and at fifty-five.

Vocabulary
appendage (ə pen′ dij) *n.* an external part of a plant or animal, such as a tail or a limb

He held on through the level stretch of woods for several miles, crossed a wide flat, and dropped down a bank to the frozen bed of a small stream. This was Henderson Creek, and he knew he was ten miles from the forks. He looked at his watch. It was ten o'clock. He was making four miles an hour, and he calculated that he would arrive at the forks at half past twelve. He decided to celebrate that event by eating his lunch there.

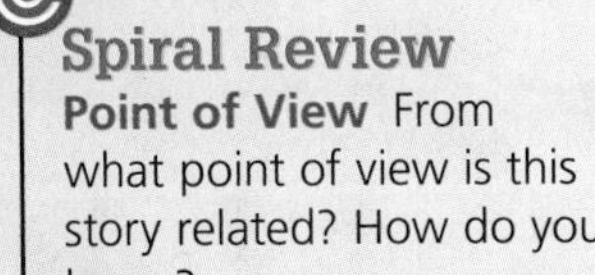

Spiral Review
Point of View From what point of view is this story related? How do you know?

The dog dropped in again at his heels, with a tail drooping discouragement, as the man swung along the creek bed. The furrow of the old sled trail was plainly visible, but a dozen inches of snow covered the marks of the last runners. In a month no man had come up or down that silent creek. The man held steadily on. He was not much given to thinking, and just then particularly he had nothing to think about save that he would eat lunch at the forks and that at six o'clock he would be in camp with the boys. There was nobody to talk to; and, had there been, speech would have been impossible because of the ice-muzzle on his mouth. So he continued monotonously to chew tobacco and to increase the length of his amber beard.

Once in a while the thought reiterated itself that it was very cold and that he had never experienced such cold. As he walked along he rubbed his cheekbones and nose with the back of his mittened hand. He did this automatically, now and again changing hands. But rub as he would, the instant he stopped his cheekbones went numb, and the following instant the end of his nose went numb. He was sure to frost his cheeks; he knew that, and experienced a pang of regret that he had not devised a nose strap of the sort Bud wore in cold snaps. Such a strap passed across the cheeks, as well, and saved them. But it didn't matter much, after all. What were frosted cheeks? A bit painful, that was all: they were never serious.

Comprehension
What physical effects of the cold does the man experience?

Empty as the man's mind was of thoughts, he was keenly observant, and he noticed the changes in the creek, the curves and

5. spirit thermometer thermometer containing alcohol; used in extreme cold.

▲ Critical Viewing

Which words or passages from the story could be used to describe this scene? **ANALYZE**

bends and timber jams, and always he sharply noted where he placed his feet. Once, coming around a bend, he shied abruptly, like a startled horse, curved away from the place where he had been walking, and retreated several paces back along the trail. The creek he knew was frozen clear to the bottom—no creek could contain water in that arctic winter—but he knew also that there were springs that bubbled out from the hillsides and ran along under the snow and on top the ice of the creek. He knew that the coldest snaps never froze these springs, and he knew likewise their danger. They were traps. They hid pools of water under the snow that might be three inches deep, or three feet. Sometimes a skin of ice half an inch thick covered them, and in turn was covered by the snow. Sometimes there were alternate layers of water and ice skin, so that when one broke through he kept on breaking through for a while, sometimes wetting himself to the waist.

Predicting

Based on the description of the creek and hidden pools, what do you predict might happen?

That was why he had shied in such panic. He had felt the give under his feet and heard the crackle of a snow-hidden ice skin. And to get his feet wet in such a temperature meant trouble and danger. At the very least it meant delay, for he would be forced to stop and build a fire, and under its protection to bare his feet while he dried his socks and moccasins. He stood and studied the creek bed and its banks, and decided that the flow of water came from the right. He reflected awhile, rubbing his nose and cheeks, then skirted to the left, stepping gingerly and testing the footing for each step. Once clear of the danger, he took a fresh chew of tobacco and swung along at his four-mile gait.

In the course of the next two hours he came upon several similar traps. Usually the snow above the hidden pools had a sunken, candied appearance that advertised the danger. Once again, however, he had a close call; and once, suspecting danger, he compelled the dog to go on in front. The dog did not want to go. It hung back until the man shoved it forward, and then it went quickly across the white, unbroken surface. Suddenly it broke through, floundered to one side, and got away to firmer footing. It had wet its forefeet and legs, and almost immediately the water that clung to it turned to ice. It made quick efforts to lick the ice off its legs, then dropped down in the snow and began to bite out the ice that had formed between the toes. This was a matter of instinct. To permit the ice to remain would mean sore feet. It did not know this. It merely obeyed the mysterious prompting that arose from the deep crypts of its being. But the man knew, having achieved a judgment on the subject, and he removed the mitten from his right hand and helped tear out the ice particles. He did not expose his fingers more than a minute, and was astonished at the swift numbness that smote them. It certainly was cold. He pulled on the mitten hastily, and beat the hand savagely across his chest.

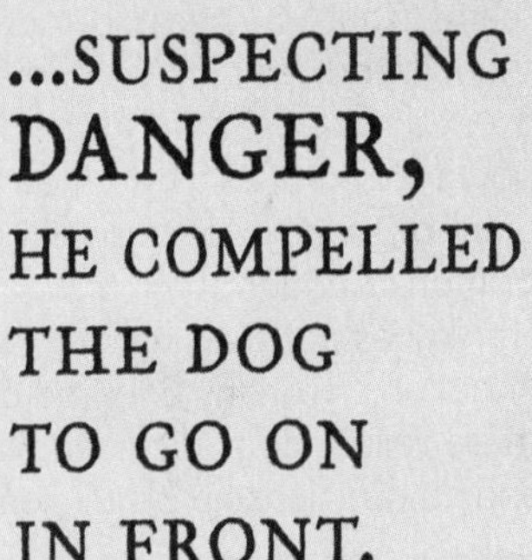
...SUSPECTING
DANGER,
HE COMPELLED
THE DOG
TO GO ON
IN FRONT.

At twelve o'clock the day was at its brightest. Yet the sun was too far south on its winter journey to clear the horizon. The bulge of the earth intervened between it and Henderson Creek, where the man walked under a clear sky at noon and cast no shadow. At half-past twelve, to the minute, he arrived at the forks of the creek. He was pleased at the speed he had made. If he kept it up, he would certainly be with the boys by six. He unbuttoned his jacket and shirt and drew forth his lunch. The action consumed no more than a quarter of a minute, yet in that brief moment the numbness laid hold of the exposed fingers. He did not put the mitten on, but, instead, struck the fingers a dozen sharp smashes against his leg. Then he sat down on a snow-covered log to eat. The sting that followed upon the striking of his fingers against his leg ceased so quickly that he was startled. He had had no chance to take a bite of biscuit. He struck the fingers repeatedly and returned them to the mitten, baring the other hand for the purpose of eating. He tried to take a mouthful, but

Comprehension
Why does the man want to avoid getting his feet wet?

LITERATURE IN CONTEXT

History Connection

Dogs and the Yukon
Dogs like the one in "To Build a Fire" have long played a key role in the Yukon. For centuries, native people in Alaska have bred dogs for a variety of purposes, including transportation. When the Klondike gold rush brought thousands of miners to the Yukon, the problem of transportation became acute. In 1910, the federal government constructed a trail more than 1,000 miles long for use by dog sled teams. That trail became known as the Iditarod.

Sled dogs are among the most powerful draft animals on earth. A team of twenty dogs can pull a ton or more. Though the man in London's story does not treat his dog with affection, for many dog sled drivers these valiant dogs provided warmth and companionship on the long, cold trail.

Connect to the Literature

Why do you think London chooses to portray the dog's thoughts and feelings?

the ice muzzle prevented. He had forgotten to build a fire and thaw out. He chuckled at his foolishness, and as he chuckled he noted the numbness creeping into the exposed fingers. Also, he noted that the stinging which had first come to his toes when he sat down was already passing away. He wondered whether the toes were warm or numb. He moved them inside the moccasins and decided that they were numb.

He pulled the mitten on hurriedly and stood up. He was a bit frightened. He stamped up and down until the stinging returned into the feet. It certainly was cold, was his thought. That man from Sulphur Creek had spoken the truth when telling how cold it sometimes got in the country. And he had laughed at him at the time! That showed one must not be too sure of things. There was no mistake about it, it was cold. He strode up and down, stamping his feet and threshing his arms, until reassured by the returning warmth. Then he got out matches and proceeded to make a fire. From the undergrowth, where high water of the previous spring had lodged a supply of seasoned twigs, he got his firewood. Working carefully from a small beginning, he soon had a roaring fire, over which he thawed the ice from his face and in the protection of which he ate his biscuits. For the moment the cold of space was outwitted. The dog took satisfaction in the fire, stretching out close enough for warmth and far enough away to escape being singed.

When the man had finished, he filled his pipe and took his comfortable time over a smoke. Then he pulled on his mittens, settled the earflaps of his cap firmly about his ears, and took the creek trail up the left fork. The dog was disappointed and yearned back toward the fire. This man did not know cold. Possibly all the generations of his ancestry had been ignorant of cold, of real cold, of cold one hundred and seven degrees below freezing point. But the dog knew; all its ancestry knew, and it had inherited the knowledge. And it knew that it was not good to walk abroad in such fearful cold. It was the time to lie snug in a hole in the snow and wait for a curtain of cloud to be drawn across the face of outer space whence this cold came. On the other hand, there was no keen intimacy between the dog and the man. The one was the toil slave of the other, and the only caresses it had ever received were the caresses of the whiplash and of harsh and menacing throat sounds that threatened the whiplash. So the dog made no effort to communicate its apprehension to the man. It was not concerned in the welfare of the man; it was for its own sake that it yearned back toward the fire. But the man whistled, and spoke to it with the sound of whiplashes, and the dog swung in at the man's heels and followed after.

The man took a chew of tobacco and proceeded to start a new amber beard. Also, his moist breath quickly powdered with white his mustache, eyebrows, and lashes. There did not seem to be so many springs on the left fork of the Henderson, and for half an hour the man saw no signs of any. And then it happened. At a place where there were no signs, where the soft, unbroken snow seemed to advertise solidity beneath, the man broke through. It was not deep. He wet himself halfway to the knees before he floundered out to the firm crust.

He was angry, and cursed his luck aloud. He had hoped to get into camp with the boys at six o'clock, and this would delay him an hour, for he would have to build a fire and dry out his footgear. This was imperative at that low temperature—he knew that much; and he turned aside to the bank, which he climbed. On top, tangled in the underbrush about the trunks of several small spruce trees, was a high-water deposit of dry firewood—sticks and twigs, principally, but also larger portions of seasoned branches and fine, dry, last year's grasses. He threw down several large pieces on top of the snow. This served for a foundation and prevented the young flame from drowning itself in the snow it otherwise would melt. The flame he got by touching a match to a small shred of birch bark that he took from his pocket. This burned even more readily than paper. Placing it on the foundation, he fed the young flame with wisps of dry grass and with the tiniest dry twigs.

He worked slowly and carefully, keenly aware of his danger. Gradually, as the flame grew stronger, he increased the size of the twigs with which he fed it. He squatted in the snow, pulling the twigs out from their entanglement in the brush and feeding directly to the flame. He knew there must be no failure. When it is seventy-five below zero, a man must not fail in his first attempt to build a fire—that is, if his feet are wet. If his feet are dry, and he fails, he can run along the trail for half a mile and restore his circulation. But the circulation of wet and freezing feet cannot be restored by running when it is seventy-five below. No matter how fast he runs, the wet feet will freeze the harder.

All this the man knew. The old-timer on Sulphur Creek had told him about it the previous fall, and now he was appreciating the advice. Already all sensation had gone out of his feet. To build the fire he had been forced to remove his mittens, and the fingers had quickly gone numb. His pace of four miles an hour had kept his heart pumping blood to the surface of his body and to all the extremities. But the instant he stopped, the action of the pump eased down. The cold of space smote the unprotected tip of the planet, and he, being on that unprotected tip, received the full force of the blow. The blood of his body recoiled before it. The blood was alive, like the dog, and like the dog it wanted to hide away and cover itself up from the fearful cold. So long as he walked four

WHEN IT IS SEVENTY-FIVE **BELOW ZERO,** A MAN MUST NOT FAIL IN HIS FIRST ATTEMPT TO BUILD A FIRE—

Comprehension
What does the man do after he falls into the creek?

miles an hour, he pumped that blood, willy-nilly, to the surface; but now it ebbed away and sank down into the recesses of his body. The extremities were the first to feel its absence. His wet feet froze the faster, and his exposed fingers numbed the faster, though they had not yet begun to freeze. Nose and cheeks were already freezing, while the skin of all his body chilled as it lost its blood.

Conflict and Irony

What does the reader understand about the old-timer's advice that the man does not?

But he was safe. Toes and nose and cheeks would be only touched by the frost, for the fire was beginning to burn with strength. He was feeding it with twigs the size of his finger. In another minute he would be able to feed it with branches the size of his wrist, and then he could remove his wet foot-gear, and, while it dried, he could keep his naked feet warm by the fire, rubbing them at first, of course, with snow. The fire was a success. He was safe. He remembered the advice of the old-timer on Sulphur Creek, and smiled. The old-timer had been very serious in laying down the law that no man must travel alone in the Klondike after fifty below. Well, here he was; he had had the accident; he was alone; and he had saved himself. Those old-timers were rather womanish, some of them, he thought. All a man had to do was to keep his head, and he was all right. Any man who was a man could travel alone. But it was surprising, the rapidity with which his cheeks and nose were freezing. And he had not thought his fingers could go lifeless in so short a time. Lifeless they were, for he could scarcely make them move together to grip a twig, and they seemed remote from his body and from him. When he touched a twig, he had to look and see whether or not he had hold of it. The wires were pretty well down between him and his finger ends.

▼ Critical Viewing

What aspects of the Alaskan landscape pictured here clarify the challenge the man faces in building a fire? **CONNECT**

All of which counted for little. There was the fire, snapping and

crackling and promising life with every dancing flame. He started to untie his moccasins. They were coated with ice; the thick German socks were like sheaths of iron halfway to the knees; and the moccasin strings were like rods of steel all twisted and knotted as by some **conflagration**. For a moment he tugged with his numb fingers, then, realizing the folly of it, he drew his sheath-knife.

But before he could cut the strings, it happened. It was his own fault or, rather, his mistake. He should not have built the fire under the spruce tree. He should have built it in the open. But it had been easier to pull the twigs from the brush and drop them directly on the fire. Now the tree under which he had done this carried a weight of snow on its boughs. No wind had blown for weeks, and each bough was fully freighted. Each time he had pulled a twig he had communicated a slight agitation to the tree—an imperceptible agitation, so far as he was concerned, but an agitation sufficient to bring about the disaster. High up in the tree one bough capsized its load of snow. This fell on the boughs beneath, capsizing them. This process continued, spreading out and involving the whole tree. It grew like an avalanche, and it descended without warning upon the man and the fire, and the fire was blotted out! Where it had burned was a mantle of fresh and disordered snow.

The man was shocked. It was as though he had just heard his own sentence of death. For a moment he sat and stared at the spot where the fire had been. Then he grew very calm. Perhaps the old-timer on Sulphur Creek was right. If he had only had a trail mate he would have been in no danger now. The trail mate could have built the fire. Well, it was up to him to build the fire over again, and this second time there must be no failure. Even if he succeeded, he would most likely lose some toes. His feet must be badly frozen by now, and there would be some time before the second fire was ready.

Such were his thoughts, but he did not sit and think them. He was busy all the time they were passing through his mind. He made a new foundation for a fire, this time in the open, where no treacherous tree could blot it out. Next, he gathered dry grasses and tiny twigs from the high-water flotsam. He could not bring his fingers together to pull them out, but he was able to gather them by the handful. In this way he got many rotten twigs and bits of green moss that were undesirable, but it was the best he could do. He worked methodically, even collecting an armful of the larger branches to be used later when the fire gathered strength. And all the while the dog sat and watched him, a certain yearning wistfulness in its eyes, for it looked upon him as the fire provider, and the fire was slow in coming.

When all was ready, the man reached in his pocket for a second piece of birch bark. He knew the bark was there, and, though he could not feel it with his fingers, he could hear its crisp rustling as he fumbled for it. Try as he would, he could not clutch hold of it. And all the time, in his consciousness, was the knowledge that each instant his feet were freezing. This thought tended to put him in a panic, but

Vocabulary

conflagration (kän′ flə grā′ shən) *n.* big, destructive fire

Comprehension

What happens to ruin the man's fire?

he fought against it and kept calm. He pulled on his mittens with his teeth, and threshed his arms back and forth, beating his hands with all his might against his sides. He did this sitting down, and he stood up to do it; and all the while the dog sat in the snow, its wolf brush of a tail curled around warmly over its forefeet, its sharp wolf ears pricked forward intently as it watched the man. And the man, as he beat and threshed with his arms and hands, felt a great surge of envy as he regarded the creature that was warm and secure in its natural covering.

After a time he was aware of the first faraway signals of sensation in his beaten fingers. The faint tingling grew stronger till it evolved into a stinging ache that was excruciating, but which the man hailed with satisfaction. He stripped the mitten from his right hand and fetched forth the birch bark. The exposed fingers were quickly going numb again. Next he brought out his bunch of sulphur matches. But the tremendous cold had already driven the life out of his fingers. In his effort to separate one match from the others, the whole bunch fell in the snow. He tried to pick it out of the snow, but failed. The dead fingers could neither touch nor clutch. He was very careful. He drove the thought of his freezing feet, and nose, and cheeks, out of his mind, devoting his whole soul to the matches. He watched, using the sense of vision in place of that of touch, and when he saw his fingers on each side of the bunch, he closed them—that is, he willed to close them, for the wires were down, and the fingers did not obey. He pulled the mitten on the right hand, and beat it fiercely against his knee. Then, with both mittened hands, he scooped the bunch of matches, along with much snow, into his lap. Yet he was no better off.

Predicting

As the man struggles to light the matches, what do you predict about his success? Why?

After some manipulation he managed to get the bunch between the heels of his mittened hands. In this fashion he carried it to his mouth. The ice crackled and snapped when by a violent effort he opened his mouth. He drew the lower jaw in, curled the upper lip out of the way, and scraped the bunch with his upper teeth in order to separate a match. He succeeded in getting one, which he dropped on his lap. He was no better off. He could not pick it up. Then he devised a way. He picked it up in his teeth and scratched it on his leg. Twenty times he scratched before he succeeded in lighting it. As it flamed he held it with his teeth to the birch bark. But the burning brimstone went up his nostrils and into his lungs, causing him to cough spasmodically. The match fell into the snow and went out.

Conflict

What is the conflict with which the man now struggles desperately?

The old-timer on Sulphur Creek was right, he thought in the moment of controlled despair that ensued: after fifty below, a man should travel with a partner. He beat his hands, but failed in exciting any sensation. Suddenly he bared both hands, removing the mittens with his teeth. He caught the whole bunch between the heels of his hands. His arm muscles not being frozen enabled him to press the hand heels tightly against the matches. Then he scratched the bunch along his leg. It flared into flame, seventy sulphur matches at once!

There was no wind to blow them out. He kept his head to one side to escape the strangling fumes, and held the blazing bunch to the birch bark. As he so held it, he became aware of sensation in his hand. His flesh was burning. He could smell it. Deep down below the surface he could feel it. The sensation developed into pain that grew acute. And still he endured it, holding the flame of the matches clumsily to the bark that would not light readily because his own burning hands were in the way, absorbing most of the flame.

At last, when he could endure no more, he jerked his hands apart. The blazing matches fell sizzling into the snow, but the birch bark was alight. He began laying dry grasses and the tiniest twigs on the flame. He could not pick and choose, for he had to lift the fuel between the heels of his hands. Small pieces of rotten wood and green moss clung to the twigs, and he bit them off as well as he could with his teeth. He cherished the flame carefully and awkwardly. It meant life, and it must not perish. The withdrawal of blood from the surface of his body now made him begin to shiver, and he grew more awkward. A large piece of green moss fell squarely on the little fire. He tried to poke it out with his fingers, but his shivering frame made him poke too far, and he disrupted the nucleus of the little fire, the burning grasses and tiny twigs separating and scattering. He tried to poke them together again, but in spite of the tenseness of the effort, his shivering got away with him, and the twigs were hopelessly scattered. Each twig gushed a puff of smoke and went out. The fire provider had failed. As he looked apathetically about him, his eyes chanced on the dog, sitting across the ruins of the fire from him, in the snow, making restless, hunching movements, slightly lifting one forefoot and then the other, shifting its weight back and forth on them with wistful eagerness.

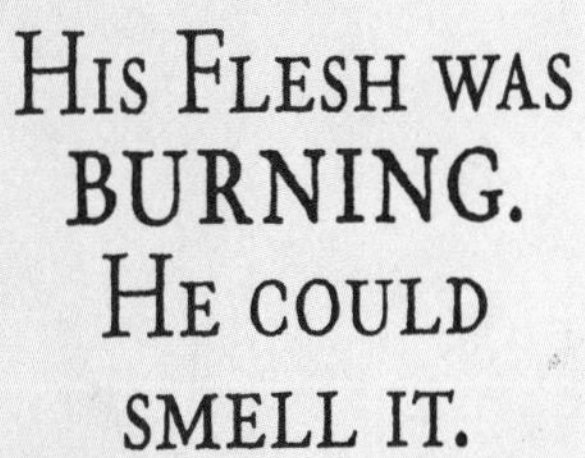
HIS FLESH WAS
BURNING.
HE COULD
SMELL IT.

The sight of the dog put a wild idea into his head. He remembered the tale of the man, caught in a blizzard, who killed a steer and crawled inside the carcass, and so was saved. He would kill the dog and bury his hands in the warm body until the numbness went out of them. Then he could build another fire. He spoke to the dog, calling it to him; but in his voice was a strange note of fear that frightened the animal, who had never known the man to speak in such way before. Something was the matter, and its suspicious nature sensed danger—it knew not what danger, but somewhere, somehow, in its brain arose an apprehension of the man. It flattened its ears down at the sound of the man's voice, and its restless, hunching movements and the liftings and shiftings of its forefeet became more pronounced; but it would not come to the man. He got on his hands and knees and crawled toward the dog. This unusual posture again excited suspicion, and the animal sidled mincingly away.

Conflict
What conflict is intensified in the passage beginning "The sight of the dog . . ."?

The man sat up in the snow for a moment and struggled for calmness. Then he pulled on his mittens, by means of his teeth, and got upon his feet. He glanced down at first in order to assure himself that

Comprehension
What happens to the man's second attempt to build a fire?

Vocabulary
peremptorily (pər emp′ tə rə lē) *adv.* decisively; commandingly

he was really standing up, for the absence of sensation in his feet left him unrelated to the earth. His erect position in itself started to drive the webs of suspicion from the dog's mind; and when he spoke peremptorily, with the sound of whiplashes in his voice, the dog rendered its customary allegiance and came to him. As it came within reaching distance, the man lost his control. His arms flashed out to the dog, and he experienced genuine surprise when he discovered that his hands could not clutch, that there was neither bend nor feeling in the fingers. He had forgotten for the moment that they were frozen and that they were freezing more and more. All this happened quickly, and before the animal could get away, he encircled its body with his arms. He sat down in the snow, and in this fashion held the dog, while it snarled and whined and struggled.

But it was all he could do, hold its body encircled in his arms and sit there. He realized that he could not kill the dog. There was no way to do it. With his helpless hands he could neither draw nor hold his sheath-knife nor throttle the animal. He released it, and it plunged wildly away, with tail between its legs, and still snarling. It halted forty feet away and surveyed him curiously, with ears sharply pricked forward. The man looked down at his hands in order to locate them, and found them hanging on the ends of his arms. It struck him as curious that one should have to use his eyes in order to find out where his hands were. He began threshing his arms back and forth, beating the mittened hands against his sides. He did this for five minutes, violently, and his heart pumped enough blood up to the surface to put a stop to his shivering. But no sensation was aroused in the hands. He had an impression that they hung like weights on the ends of his arms, but when he tried to run the impression down, he could not find it.

A CERTAIN FEAR OF DEATH, DULL AND OPPRESSIVE, CAME TO HIM.

A certain fear of death, dull and oppressive, came to him. This fear quickly became poignant as he realized that it was no longer a mere matter of freezing his fingers and toes, or of losing his hands and feet, but that it was a matter of life and death with the chances against him. This threw him into a panic, and he turned and ran up the creek-bed along the old, dim trail. The dog joined in behind and kept up with him. He ran blindly, without intention, in fear such as he had never known in his life. Slowly, as he plowed and floundered through the snow, he began to see things again—the banks of the creek, the old timber jams, the leafless aspens, and the sky. The running made him feel better. He did not shiver. Maybe, if he ran on, his feet would thaw out; and, anyway, if he ran far enough, he would reach camp and the boys. Without doubt he would lose some fingers and toes and some of his face; but the boys would take care of him, and save the rest of him when he got there. And at the same time there was another thought in his mind that said he would never get to the camp and the boys; that it was too many miles away, that the freezing had too great a start on him, and that he would soon be stiff

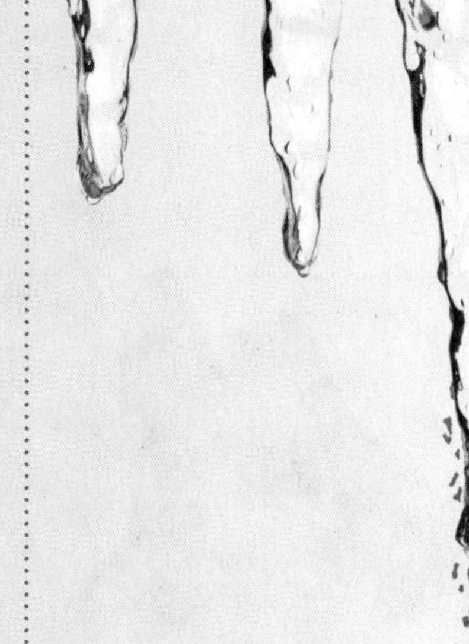

and dead. This thought he kept in the background and refused to consider. Sometimes it pushed itself forward and demanded to be heard, but he thrust it back and strove to think of other things.

It struck him as curious that he could run at all on feet so frozen that he could not feel them when they struck the earth and took the weight of his body. He seemed to himself to skim along above the surface, and to have no connection with the earth. Somewhere he had once seen a winged Mercury,[6] and he wondered if Mercury felt as he felt when skimming over the earth.

His theory of running until he reached camp and the boys had one flaw in it: he lacked the endurance. Several times he stumbled, and finally he tottered, crumpled up, and fell. When he tried to rise, he failed. He must sit and rest, he decided, and next time he would merely walk and keep on going. As he sat and regained his breath, he noted that he was feeling quite warm and comfortable. He was not shivering, and it even seemed that a warm glow had come to his chest and trunk. And yet, when he touched his nose or cheeks, there was no sensation. Running would not thaw them out. Nor would it thaw out his hands and feet. Then the thought came to him that the frozen portions of his body must be extending. He tried to keep this thought down, to forget it, to think of something else; he was aware of the panicky feeling that it caused, and he was afraid of the panic. But the thought asserted itself, and persisted, until it produced a vision of his body totally frozen. This was too much, and he made another wild run along the trail. Once he slowed down to a walk, but the thought of the freezing extending itself made him run again.

Conflict and Irony
As the man begins to feel warm, what does the reader know that the man does not?

And all the time the dog ran with him, at his heels. When he fell down a second time, it curled its tail over its forefeet and sat in front of him, facing him, curiously eager and intent. The warmth and security of the animal angered him, and he cursed it till it flattened down its ears appeasingly. This time the shivering came more quickly upon the man. He was losing in his battle with the frost. It was creeping into his body from all sides. The thought of it drove him on, but he ran no more than a hundred feet, when he staggered and pitched headlong. It was his last panic. When he had recovered his breath and control, he sat up and entertained in his mind the conception of meeting death with dignity. However, the conception did not come to him in such terms. His idea of it was that he had been making a fool of himself, running around like a chicken with its head cut off—such was the simile that occurred to him. Well, he was bound to freeze anyway, and he might as well take it decently. With this new-found peace of mind came the first glimmerings of drowsiness. A good idea, he thought, to sleep off to death. It was like taking an anaesthetic. Freezing was not so bad as people thought. There were lots worse ways to die.

Comprehension
What thought does the man refuse to consider?

6. **Mercury** from Roman mythology, the wing-footed messenger of the gods.

He pictured the boys finding his body next day. Suddenly he found himself with them, coming along the trail and looking for himself. And, still with them, he came around a turn in the trail and found himself lying in the snow. He did not belong with himself any more, for even then he was out of himself; standing with the boys and looking at himself in the snow. It certainly was cold, was his thought. When he got back to the States he could tell the folks what real cold was. He drifted on from this to a vision of the old-timer on Sulphur Creek. He could see him quite clearly, warm and comfortable, and smoking a pipe.

"You were right, old hoss; you were right," the man mumbled to the old-timer of Sulphur Creek.

Then the man drowsed off into what seemed to him the most comfortable and satisfying sleep he had ever known. The dog sat facing him and waiting. The brief day drew to a close in a long, slow twilight. There were no signs of a fire to be made, and, besides, never in the dog's experience had it known a man to sit like that in the snow and make no fire. As the twilight drew on, its eager yearning for the fire mastered it, and with a great lifting and shifting of forefeet, it whined softly, then flattened its ears down in anticipation of being chidden[7] by the man. But the man remained silent. Later, the dog whined loudly. And still later it crept close to the man and caught the scent of death. This made the animal bristle and back away. A little longer it delayed, howling under the stars that leaped and danced and shone brightly in the cold sky. Then it turned and trotted up the trail in the direction of the camp it knew, where were the other food providers and fire providers.

7. **chidden** scolded.

Critical Reading

Cite textual evidence to support your responses.

1. **Key Ideas and Details (a)** What do the dog's instincts tell it about the cold? **(b) Compare and Contrast:** Why does the extreme cold "make no impression" on the man? **(c) Make a Judgment:** Who is better equipped to survive in the cold, the dog or the man? Explain.
2. **Key Ideas and Details (a)** What trap does the man unsuccessfully try to avoid? **(b) Analyze Cause and Effect:** What deadly chain of events does this begin?
3. **Integration of Knowledge and Ideas** What does London suggest about human strength in the face of nature's power? In your response, use at least two of these Essential Question words: *vulnerable, resolve, frailty, wilderness.* ***[Connecting to the Essential Question: What is the relationship between literature and place?]***

Close Reading Activity *To Build a Fire*

Literary Analysis

1. **Key Ideas and Details** Early in the story, the narrator reveals that the man does not really know the temperature outside. What can you **predict** from this clue?
2. **Key Ideas and Details** **(a)** What *background knowledge* about the Yukon did you bring to your reading of the story? **(b)** What predictions were you able to make based on this knowledge? **(c)** Were your predictions correct? Explain.
3. **Key Ideas and Details** **(a)** What information do the man's recollections of his conversation with the old-timer provide? **(b)** What clues about the man can you draw based on his responses to the old-timer? **(c)** How do these clues help you predict what will happen at the end of the story?
4. **Key Ideas and Details** **(a)** At what point did you first predict that the man would not survive his journey? **(b)** On what clues did you base your prediction?
5. **Craft and Structure** Use a chart like the one shown to analyze the **conflict** in "To Build a Fire." **(a)** What **external conflict** drives the plot? **(b)** Identify at least three details in the **setting** that contribute to the central conflict.

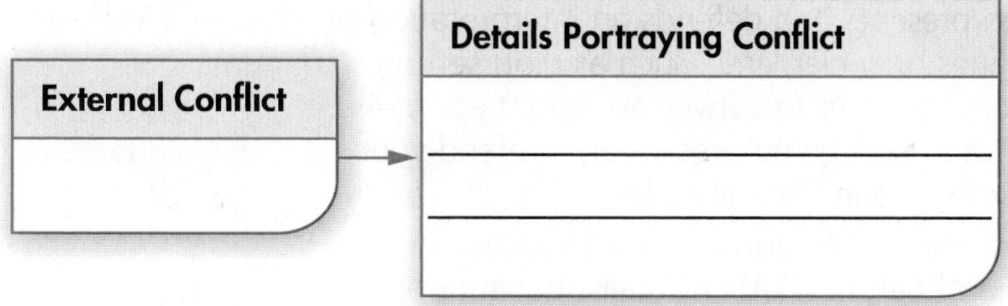

6. **Craft and Structure** In what ways does the main character's awareness of the conflict intensify as the story unfolds? Explain.
7. **Craft and Structure** What **internal conflict** develops as the plot progresses? Explain, using details from the story.
8. **Craft and Structure** What events finally resolve, or settle, the conflict?
9. **Craft and Structure** The man breaks through the snow and steps in the hidden spring. In what ways is this event an example of **irony?**
10. **Craft and Structure** What is ironic about the location in which the man builds his fire?
11. **Craft and Structure** In what way do London's descriptions of the dog's feelings and its instincts about survival increase the story's **dramatic irony?**

Common Core State Standards

Writing

1. Write arguments to support claims in an analysis of substantive topics or texts, using valid reasoning and relevant and sufficient evidence. *(p. 612)*

Language

1. Demonstrate command of the conventions of standard English grammar and usage when writing or speaking. *(p. 613)*

4.b. Identify and correctly use patterns of word changes that indicate different meanings or parts of speech. *(p. 612)*

4.d. Verify the preliminary determination of the meaning of a word or phrase. *(p. 612)*

5. Demonstrate understanding of word relationships. *(p. 612)*

Vocabulary Acquisition and Use

Word Analysis: Latin Root *-pend-*

The Latin root *-pend-* means "to hang." Your *appendages*—your arms and legs, toes and feet—hang or extend from your torso. Likewise, if you *depend* on someone, you may be "hanging on" to him or her for help. Each of the following words contains the root *-pend-*. Write a definition for each word and explain how the idea of hanging or extending relates to the term. If a word is unfamiliar, use a dictionary to clarify its meaning.

1. impending
2. pendulum
3. suspend
4. perpendicular
5. pendant

Vocabulary: Word/Phrase Relationships

Scan the paragraph below. For each blank, write a sentence explaining what type of word—noun, adjective, or adverb—you would expect to find there. Then, fill in the blanks with appropriate words from the vocabulary list on page 594.

A lightning storm in the parched woodland sparked a(n) _______. The tree's dry limbs and branches fell flaming from the trees, and soon the forest floor was covered with charred _______ of the tree. This was a(n) _______ scene for the young and inexperienced fire chief. Yet, he acted _______ ordering all firefighters to work around the clock. His estimates of how long it would take to overcome the fire, however, were _______ at best.

Writing to Sources

Argument Critical writing often presents and defends an interpretation of a literary work. The writer examines how elements, such as plot, setting, character, and point of view, work together to convey an insight about life. Write a work of **literary criticism** in which you present and defend your interpretation of the message expressed in"To Build a Fire."

Prewriting Review the story to identify London's message about the relationship between humanity and nature. Gather details that support your interpretation.

Drafting In your introduction, state your thesis and outline your main points. Focus each body paragraph on one main point. Cite supporting details from the story.

Model: Elaborating to Support an Argument

The dog, equipped by centuries of evolution for life in the bitter cold, serves as a symbolic foil to the man. Unlike the man, who disregards plain evidence,". . . the dog knew; all its ancestry knew, and it had inherited the knowledge. And it knew that it was not good to walk abroad in such fearful cold."

Providing details from the work helps to elaborate on the main point, underlined here.

Revising Review your draft, making sure your thesis is clear and your support is convincing. Look for opportunities to *elaborate ideas through supporting details.*

Conventions and Style: Introductory Phrases and Clauses

To keep your reader's interest, try *varying sentence structures* in your writing. For example, instead of starting every sentence with the subject, begin some sentences with phrases or clauses. A **phrase** is a group of words that acts as a single part of speech and lacks a complete subject and verb. A **clause** is a group of words that has both a subject and verb.

Using Introductory Phrases and Clauses to Vary Sentence Structure

Subject First: He stopped at the top of a steep bank to catch his breath.
Phrase First: *At the top of a steep bank*, he stopped to catch his breath. (prepositional phrase)

Subject First: The dog seemed hesitant as he slinked along behind the man.
Phrase First: *Slinking along behind the man*, the dog seemed hesitant. (participial phrase)

Subject First: He sends the dog ahead to check the thickness of the ice.
Phrase First: *To check the thickness of the ice*, he sends the dog ahead. (infinitive phrase)

Subject First: The spittle crackled and froze when he spit into the air.
Clause First: *When he spit into the air*, the spittle crackled and froze. (adverb clause)

Punctuation Tip: Place a comma after most introductory phrases and clauses.

Practice Revise each sentence by using the italicized part as an introductory phrase or clause. In some sentences, you will have to make slight changes to the original wording.

1. Huskies burrow beneath the snow *to stay warm.*
2. Thousands of prospectors *lured by visions of gold and wealth* headed to the Yukon.
3. His nose and cheekbones turned numb *even though he kept rubbing them.*
4. He could not build a third fire *in spite of all his efforts.*
5. The dog *grew suspicious* and moved away from the man.
6. He heard the crackle of ice *as he came around a bend in the creek.*
7. The dog *curled his tail around his forefeet* and sat there watching the man.
8. The man beat his hands against his sides *to restore feeling to his fingers.*
9. Jack London produced more than fifty books *during his career.*
10. London was *determined to earn a living as a writer*, so he often worked fifteen hours a day.

Writing and Speaking Conventions

A. Writing Use each phrase or clause to begin a sentence.

1. in his pocket
2. to build a fire
3. numbed by the extreme cold
4. after his legs are wet

Example: If he kept the pace
Sentence: If he kept the pace, he would be at the camp by six.

B. Speaking Suppose the dog in the story could speak. Tell the story as he would relate it to the men at the camp. In your story, begin at least four sentences with an introductory phrase or clause.

Primary Sources

Personal History
Heading West

Speech
I Will Fight No More Forever

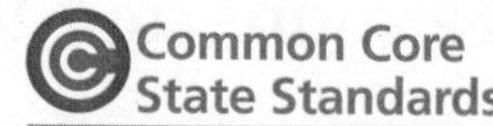
Common Core State Standards

Reading Informational Text

1. Cite strong and thorough textual evidence to support analysis of what a text says explicitly as well as inferences drawn from the text, including determining where the text leaves matters uncertain.

9. Analyze nineteenth-century foundational U.S. documents of historical and literary significance for their themes, purposes, and rhetorical features.

About the Text Forms

A **personal history** is a type of autobiographical nonfiction in which a writer relates his or her experiences during a particular event or era. Personal histories can take many forms, from straightforward narratives to the dated entries of a journal or diary.

A **speech** is a nonfiction work that is delivered orally to an audience. There are many types of speeches, each suited to a different kind of public gathering and setting. Speakers use a variety of strategies to express their ideas and move listeners. They may appeal to listeners' values or emotions, or to their sense of reason and logic.

Preparing to Read Complex Texts

In addition to facts, primary-source documents written by individuals often include subjective statements, such as opinions, beliefs, prejudices, and assumptions. For later readers and researchers, these subjective statements are important for a number of reasons:

- They provide a window into history as it was truly experienced.
- They provide a sense of the principles and values that drove a society.

While authors may state these ideas explicitly, more often they will merely imply, or suggest, them. Teasing out these unstated claims, or **making inferences about an author's implicit and explicit philosophical assumptions and beliefs,** is an important part of reading primary-source documents. As you read these documents, notice references, details, opinions, and other clues to the underlying assumptions that motivate these writers.

THE ESSENTIAL ?

What is the **relationship** between literature and *place?*

Most settlers of the American West were farmers who sought a better life for themselves and their children. This meant settling on fertile land that they could own, cultivate, and pass on to later generations. For Native Americans, however, the land was the source of all life and belonged to no one person. As you read these texts, watch for words and phrases that reflect these competing worldviews.

Note-Taking Guide

Primary-source documents are a rich source of information for researchers. As you read these documents, use a note-taking guide like the one shown to organize relevant and accurate information.

1 Type of Document (check one)

☐ Telegram ☐ Press Release ☐ Personal History ☐ Letter
☐ Speech ☐ Newspaper ☐ Report ☐ E-Mail

2 Date(s) of Document ______

3 Author of Document ______

Author's Position, Title, or Circumstances ______

4 Audience: For whom was the document written? ______

5 Document Information

a What is the main subject of the document? ______

b Find in the document a stated opinion, or belief, about the subject you listed above. Write it here. ______

c List one additional thing the author says that you think is important. ______

d Find in the document an implied—not directly stated—opinion. Write it here. ______

Inferring an Author's Philosophical Assumptions and Beliefs Remember that an opinion is a person's belief or judgment about something. Unlike a fact, an opinion cannot be proved. As you read, look for statements that express feelings, attitudes, or desires.

This guide was adapted from the **U.S. National Archives** document analysis worksheets.

Vocabulary

shares (sherz) *n.* portions of ownership of a company or a piece of property (p. 617)

pervading (per vād´ iŋ) *v.* spreading throughout (p. 618)

levee (lev´ ē) *n.* an embankment built along the side of a river to prevent flooding (p. 618)

emigrants (em´ i grənts) *n.* people who leave one place to settle in another (p. 618)

profusion (prō fyōō´ zhən) *n.* abundance; rich supply (p. 619)

foothold (fo͝ot´ hōld´) *n.* a secure position from which further actions can be taken (p. 619)

prairie (prer´ ē) *n.* a treeless, grass-covered plain (p. 620)

forded (fôrd´ əd) *v.* crossed a river at a low point (p. 620)

ravine (rə vēn´) *n.* a long, deep hollow in the ground; a gully (p. 621)

THE STORY BEHIND THE DOCUMENTS

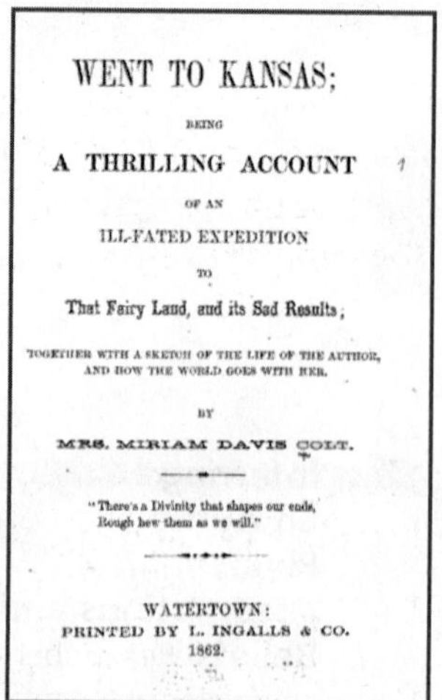

WENT TO KANSAS;

BEING

A THRILLING ACCOUNT

OF AN

ILL-FATED EXPEDITION

TO

That Fairy Land, and its Sad Results;

TOGETHER WITH A SKETCH OF THE LIFE OF THE AUTHOR, AND HOW THE WORLD GOES WITH HER.

BY

MRS. MIRIAM DAVIS COLT.

"There's a Divinity that shapes our ends,
Rough hew them as we will."

WATERTOWN:
PRINTED BY L. INGALLS & CO.
1862.

▲ The title page of Colt's published book

The history of America from its beginnings to 1900 might be summarized in two words: *westward expansion.* For more than 300 years, European explorers, colonial settlers, and American pioneers pushed west from the Atlantic Ocean toward the distant Pacific. Urged onward by curiosity, these travelers—and the ever-strengthening national government behind them—also believed that it was their right and duty to settle the continent. The consequences of this policy came to a dramatic climax during the 1800s, as unprecedented numbers of pioneers flocked westward. **Miriam Davis Colt** (1815–1900) and her family were among them. In 1856, the Colts set out on a month-long journey from upstate New York to Kansas. At the time, Kansas was in turmoil. In 1854, Congress had passed an act giving the people of the territory the freedom to decide for themselves whether to allow slavery. Both anti-slavery Northerners and pro-slavery Southerners streamed there from the East. The resulting conflicts were frequent and bloody.

Aware that their journey was history in the making, many Kansas pioneers kept a written record of their experiences. Some, like Colt, described their journeys in personal histories meant for a public audience, including relatives and future generations. Occasionally, as in Colt's case, the histories were later published as books.

▲ Chief Joseph

Though the settlers often lived harrowing lives, the most endangered people on the western frontier were the American Indians. As the frontier advanced past the Mississippi River, tribe after tribe was driven from its ancient homeland. The cycle was always the same: As white settlers encroached upon new lands, the tribes in that region would resist. United States soldiers would be sent to secure the area, and war would ensue. Eventually, the Indians would be defeated. They would either be forced onto a reservation, or made to sign a treaty in which they were promised food or money in exchange for their lands. More often than not, these promises went unfulfilled.

One such ill-fated tribe was the Nez Percé of the Pacific northwest. When an 1863 treaty reduced the size of the tribe's lands to a small reservation in Idaho, a group of the Nez Percé continued living outside the reservation boundaries in Oregon's Wallowa Valley. They were allowed to do so until 1877, when General Oliver O. Howard issued an ultimatum. Unwilling to concede, Nez Percé leader **Chief Joseph** (1840–1904) and six hundred of his people fled northeast through the mountains of Montana, toward the Canada border. Hotly pursued by legions of soldiers and finally weakened by the onset of winter, the Nez Percé were compelled to admit defeat. The speech in which Chief Joseph surrenders contains some of the most achingly beautiful words ever spoken.

HEADING WEST

Miriam Davis Colt

BACKGROUND Miriam Davis Colt and her family were among a group of families forming a vegetarian commune in the Kansas territory. The personal history from which this excerpt is taken was published in 1862 under the title "Went to Kansas; Being a Thrilling Account of an Ill-Fated Expedition to that Fairy Land, and its Sad Results."

JANUARY 5TH, 1856. We are going to Kansas. The Vegetarian Company that has been forming for many months, has finally organized, formed its constitution, elected its directors, and is making all necessary preparations for the spring settlement. . . . We can have, I think, good faith to believe, that our directors will fulfill on their part; and we, as settlers of a new country, by going in a company will escape the hardships attendant on families going in singly, and at once find ourselves surrounded by improving society in a young and flourishing city. It will be better for ourselves pecuniarily,[1] and better in the future for our children.

▲ Primary Source: Photograph
What does this photograph suggest about the quality of life people led while on the journey west? **ANALYZE**

My husband has long been a practical vegetarian, and we expect much from living in such a genial clime, where fruit is so quickly grown, and with people whose tastes and habits will coincide with our own.

JANUARY 15TH. We are making every necessary preparation for our journey, and our home in Kansas. My husband has sold his farm, purchased shares in the company, sent his money as directed by H. S. Clubb. . . . I am very busy in repairing all of our clothing, looking over bags of pieces, tearing off and reducing down, bringing everything into as small a compass as possible, so that we shall have no unnecessary baggage.

Vocabulary
shares (sherz) *n.* portions into which a company or a piece of property is divided

APRIL 15TH. Have been here in West Stockholm, at my brother's, since Friday last. Have visited Mother very hard, for, in all probability, it is the last visit we shall have until we meet where parting never comes—believe we have said everything we can think of to say.

Comprehension
Why do the Colts decide to travel to Kansas?

---

1. **pecuniarily** (pi kyo͞o′ nē er′ i lē) *adv.* financially.

APRIL 16TH. Antwerp, N.Y. Bade our friends good bye, in Potsdam, this morning, at the early hour of two o'clock.

APRIL 22ND. Have been on the cars[2] again since yesterday morning. Last night was a lovely moonlit night, a night of thought, as we sped almost with lightning speed, along in the moonlight, past the rail fences.

Found ourselves in this miserable hotel before we knew it. Miserable fare—herring boiled with cabbage—miserable, dirty beds, and an odor pervading the house that is not at all agreeable. Mistress gone.

APRIL 23RD. On board steamer "Cataract," bound for Kansas City.

APRIL 24TH. A hot summer day. The men in our company are out in the city, purchasing wagons and farming implements, to take along on the steamer up to Kansas City.

APRIL 28TH. The steamer struck a "snag" last night; gave us a terrible jar; tore off a part of the kitchen; ladies much frightened. Willie is not very well; the water is bad; it affects all strangers.

APRIL 30TH. Here we are, at Kansas City, all safely again on terra firma. Hasten to the hotel—find it very much crowded. Go up, up, up, and upstairs to our lodging rooms.

MAY 1ST. Take a walk out onto the levee—view the city, and see that it takes but a few buildings in this western world to make a city. The houses and shops stand along on the levee, extending back into the hillsides. The narrow street is literally filled with huge merchandise wagons bound for Santa Fe. The power attached to these wagons is seven or eight and sometimes nine pair of long-eared mules, or as many pair of oxen, with a Mexican driver who wields a whip long enough to reach the foremost pair, and who does not hesitate to use it with severity, and a noise, too.

Large droves of cattle are driven into town to be sold to emigrants, who like us, are going into the Territory. Our husbands are all out today buying oxen, provisions and cooking utensils for our ox-wagon journey into the Territory.

This is the anniversary of my wedding-day, and as I review the past pleasant years as they have passed, one after another, until they now number eleven, a shadow comes over me, as I try to look away into the future and ask, "What is my destiny?"

Ah! away with all these shadowings. We shall be very busy this year in making our home comfortable, so that no time can be spared for that dreaded disease, "home-sickness," to take hold of us, and we mean to obey physical laws,[3] thereby securing to ourselves strength of body and vigor of mind.

Vocabulary

pervading (per vād´ iŋ) *v.* spreading throughout

levee (lev´ ē) *n.* an embankment built along the side of a river to prevent flooding

emigrants (em´i grənts) *n.* people who leave one place to settle in another

Primary Sources

Personal History What two contrasting aspects of the pioneers' journey does Colt describe in the May 1st entry?

2. **cars** train cars.
3. **physical laws** community's by-laws that dictated members abstain from alcohol and meat.

MAY 2ND. A lovely day. Our husbands are loading the ox-wagons. . . . Women and children walk along up the hill out of this "Great City," wait under a tree—what a beautiful country is spread out before us! Will our Kansas scenery equal this . . .?

One mile from the city, and Dr. Thorn has broke his wagon tongue;[4] it must be sent back to Kansas City to be mended. Fires kindled—women cooking—supper eaten sitting round on logs, stones and wagon tongues. This I am sure is a "pic-nic." We expect "pic-nic" now all the time. We are shaded by the horse-chestnut, sweet walnut, and spreading oak; flowers blooming at our feet, and grasshoppers in profusion hopping in every direction. This is summer time.

MAY 3RD. The women and children, who slept in their wagons last night, got a good drenching from the heavy shower. It was fortunate for mother, sister, myself and children, that lodgings were found for us in a house. My husband said not a rain drop found him; he had the whole wagon to himself, besides all of our Indian blankets. Father, it seems, fell back a little and found a place to camp in a tavern (not a hotel), where he fell in with the scores of Georgians who loaded a steamer and came up the river the same time that we did. He said he had to be very shrewd indeed not to have them find out that he was a "Free States"[5] man. These Bandits have been sent in here, and will commit all sorts of depredations on the Free State settlers, and no doubt commit many a bloody murder.

Have passed Westport, the foothold for Border-Ruffianism. The town looks new, but the hue is dingy. Our drivers used their goads to hurry up the oxen's heavy tread, for we felt somewhat afraid, for we learned the Georgians had centered here. Here, too, came in the Santa Fe and Indian trade—so here may be seen the huge Mexican wagon, stubborn mule, swarthy driver with his goad-like whip, and the red man of the prairie on his fleet Indian pony, laden with dried meat, furs, and buffalo robes.

"What! fast in the mud, and with our wagon tongue broke?" "Why yes, to be sure." So a long time is spent before my husband and Dr. House can put our vehicle in moving order again. Meanwhile, we women folks and children must sit quietly in the wagon to keep out of the rain—lunch on soda biscuit, look at the deep, black mud in which our wagon is set, and inhale the sweet odor that comes from the blossoms of the crab-apple trees that are blooming in sheets of whiteness along the roadside. . . .

Vocabulary

profusion (prō fyōō′ zhən) *n.* abundance; rich supply

foothold (fo͝ot′ hōld′) *n.* a secure position from which further actions can be taken

Inferring Philosophical Assumptions and Beliefs

What assumptions does Colt hold about the opponents of "Free States" settlers?

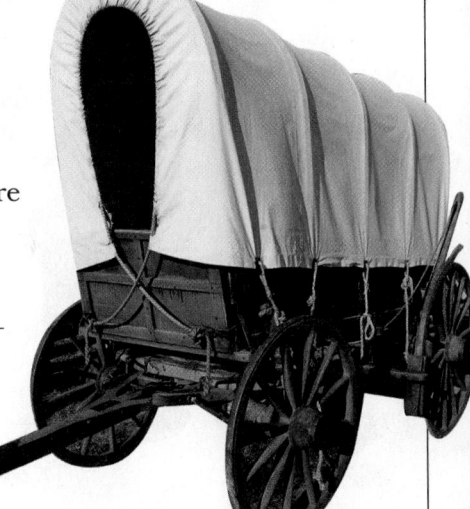

▼ Wagon used by Dr. Marcus and Narcissa Whitman, 19th century pioneers in the Oregon Territory

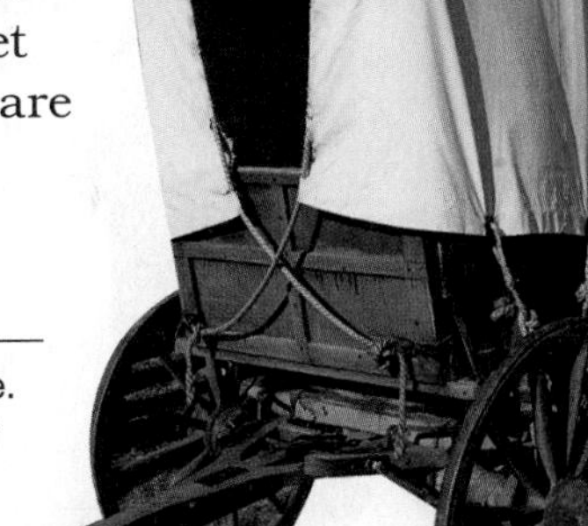

4. **wagon tongue** harnessing pole attached to the front axle of a horse-drawn vehicle.
5. **"Free States"** Free Soil movement; a group whose goal was to keep slavery out of the western territories.

Vocabulary

prairie (prer´ ē) *n.* a treeless, grass-covered plain

forded (fôrd´ əd) *v.* crossed a river at a low point

Inferring Philosophical Assumptions and Beliefs

What beliefs underlie Colt's ironic reference to the owner of the log cabin as the "Lord of the Castle"?

MAY 6TH. Dined on the prairie, and gathered flowers, while our tired beasts filled themselves with the fresh, green grass. . . . Have driven 18 miles to-day . . . so here we are, all huddled into this little house 12 by 16—cook supper over the fire . . . fill the one bed lengthwise and crosswise; the family of the house take to the trundle-bed,[6] while the floor is covered . . . with men, women and children, rolled in Indian blankets like silk worms in cocoons.

MAY 11TH. "Made" but a few miles yesterday. Forded the Little Osage; the last river, they say, we have to ford . . . our "noble lords" complained of the great weight of the wagons. . . . That our wagon is heavily loaded, have only to make a minute of what we have stowed away in it—eight trunks, one valise, three carpet bags, a box of soda crackers, 200 lbs. flour, 100 lbs. corn meal, a few lbs. of sugar, rice, dried apple, one washtub of little trees, utensils for cooking, and two provision boxes—say nothing of mother, a good fat sister, self, and two children, who ride through the rivers. . . .

At nightfall came to a log-cabin at the edge of the wood, and inquired of the "Lord of the Castle" if some of the women and children could take shelter under his roof for the night; the masculine number and whichever of the women that chose, couching in the wagons and under them. He said we could. His lady, who was away, presently came, with bare feet, and a white sack twisted up and thrown over her shoulder, with a few quarts of corn meal in the end that hung down her back. I said to myself—"Is that what I have got to come to?" She seemed pleased to have company—allowed us the first chance of the broad, Dutch-backed fireplace with its earthy hearth, and without pot hooks or trammels,[7] to make ready our simple evening repast. . . .

Are now [May 11th] crossing the 20 mile prairie, no roads—Think Mrs. Voorhees will get walking enough crossing this prairie. She is quite a pedestrian, surely, for she has walked every bit of the way in, so far, from Kansas City, almost 100 miles.

Arrive at Elm Creek—no house to lodge in tonight—campfire kindled—supper cooked, and partaken of with a keen relish, sitting in family groups around the "great big" fire. Some will sleep in wagons, others under the canopy of the blue vault of Heaven. The young men have built some shady little bowers of the green boughs; they are looking very cosily under them, wrapped in their white Indian blankets.

We ladies, or rather, "emigrant women," are having a chat around the camp-fire—the bright stars are looking down upon us—we wonder if we shall be neighbors to each other in the great "Octagon City. . . ."

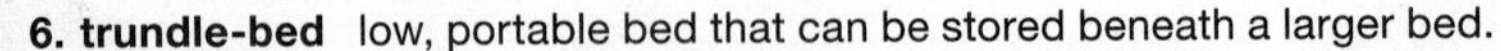

6. **trundle-bed** low, portable bed that can be stored beneath a larger bed.
7. **trammels** (tram´ əlz) *n.* devices for hanging several pothooks in a fireplace.

MAY 12TH. Full of hope, as we leave the smoking embers of our camp-fire this morning. Expect tonight to arrive at our new home.

It begins to rain, rain, rain, like a shower; we move slowly on, from high prairie, around the deep ravine—are in sight of the timber that skirts the Neosho river. Have sent three men in advance to announce our coming; are looking for our Secretary, (Henry S. Clubb) with an escort to welcome us into the embryo city. If the booming of cannon is not heard at our approach, shall expect a salute from the firing of Sharp's rifles, certainly.

No escort is seen! no salute is heard! We move slowly and drippingly into town just at nightfall—feeling not a little nonplused on learning that our worthy, or unworthy Secretary was out walking in the rain with his *dear* wife. We leave our wagons and make our way to the large camp-fire. It is surrounded by men and women cooking their suppers—while others are busy close by, grinding their hominy[8] in hand mills.

Look around, and see the grounds all around the camp-fire are covered with tents, in which the families are staying. Not a house is to be seen. In the large tent here is a cook stove—they have supper prepared for us; it consists of hominy, soft Johnny cake (or corn bread, as it is called here), stewed apple, and tea. We eat what is set before us, "asking no questions for conscience' sake."

The ladies tell us they are sorry to see us come to this place; which shows us that all is not right. Are too weary to question, but with hope depressed go to our lodgings, which we find around in the tents, and in our wagons.

Vocabulary
ravine (rə vēn′) *n.* a long, deep hollow in the ground; a gully

8. **hominy** (häm′ ə nē) *n.* dry corn, usually ground and boiled for food.

Critical Reading

1. **Key Ideas and Details (a)** What financial arrangements did the Colts make as part of their preparations for heading west? **(b) Evaluate:** Do you think they were too naive and trusting? Explain.
2. **Key Ideas and Details (a)** Describe the settler woman Colt mentions in her entry of May 11. **(b) Analyze:** What does this settler woman suggest to Colt about her own future?
3. **Key Ideas and Details Compare and Contrast:** How do Colt's expectations about life at "Octagon City" compare with the reality she finds there?
4. **Integration of Knowledge and Ideas Synthesize:** Based on Colt's experiences, explain which character traits you feel were necessary to being a successful pioneer.

I WILL FIGHT NO MORE FOREVER

Chief Joseph

BACKGROUND *In company with fellow chiefs, Chief Joseph gave this speech on October 4, 1877, to an aide of General Oliver Howard. The aide recorded and delivered the speech to his commander.*

Primary Sources
Speech Chief Joseph appeals to values and beliefs that he hopes his listeners share. What are they?

Tell General Howard I know his heart. What he told me before, I have in my heart. I am tired of fighting. Our chiefs are killed. Looking Glass is dead. Toohoolhoolzote is dead. The old men are all dead. It is the young men who say yes and no. He who led on the young men is dead. It is cold and we have no blankets. The little children are freezing to death. My people, some of them, have run away to the hills and have no blankets, no food; no one knows where they are—perhaps freezing to death. I want to have time to look for my children and see how many I can find. Maybe I shall find them among the dead. Hear me, my chiefs. I am tired; my heart is sick and sad. From where the sun now stands I will fight no more forever.

Critical Reading

1. **Key Ideas and Details** **(a)** What has happened to many of the Nez Percé chiefs? **(b) Infer:** Who has been left to carry on the fight? **(c) Speculate:** Why do you think Chief Joseph directs part of his speech to his chiefs?
2. **Key Ideas and Details** **(a)** What reasons does Chief Joseph give for his surrender? **(b) Evaluate:** Would the speech have been more or less effective had it contained more detailed explanations?
3. **Integration of Knowledge and Ideas** **Synthesize:** Although Chief Joseph delivered this speech to confirm his tribe's surrender, his eloquent words serve another purpose for people today. What is that purpose?

Personal History • Speech

Comparing Primary Sources

Refer to your Note-Taking Guide to answer these questions.

1. **(a)** Note three details you learn about pioneer families from Colt's **personal history. (b)** Note two details you understand about the Native American experience based on Chief Joseph's brief **speech.**
2. **(a)** Use a chart like the one shown to identify one statement from each document about the subject on the left. **(b)** What **philosophical assumption,** or unstated belief, underlies each statement?

	Colt		Joseph	
	Statement	Assumption	Statement	Assumption
leaving home →				
children →				

3. Write three paragraphs in which you compare and contrast each author's understanding of nineteenth-century westward expansion. Explain the reasons for any similarities and differences.

Common Core State Standards

Writing

7. Conduct short as well as more sustained research projects to answer a question or solve a problem; narrow or broaden the inquiry when appropriate, synthesize multiple sources on the subject, demonstrating understanding of the subject under investigation. *(p. 624)*

8. Gather relevant information from multiple authoritative print and digital sources, using advanced searches effectively; assess the strengths and weaknesses of each source in terms of the task, purpose, and audience; integrate information into the text selectively to maintain the flow of ideas, avoiding plagiarism and overreliance on any one source and following a standard format for citation. *(p. 624)*

Language

4.b. Identify and correctly use patterns of word changes that indicate different meanings or parts of speech.

Vocabulary Acquisition and Use

Evaluating Logic Decide whether each sentence below is logical. If not, revise the sentence so that the italicized word is used in a logical way.

1. The smell of wet paint is *pervading* the art room.
2. The *levee* will cause the town to flood when the river rises.
3. A *profusion* of weeds is every gardener's dream.
4. The army established a *foothold* near the border.
5. The hikers *forded* the river by piling large rocks along its bank.

Content-Area Vocabulary Answer each question. Then, explain your answer.

6. Who is more likely to sell *shares*: a stockbroker or a musician?
7. Would *emigrants* be more likely to ask or give directions?
8. Who would have less success on a *prairie*: a lumberjack or a farmer?
9. What might a *ravine* become during heavy rains?

Etymology Study The word *mile* comes from the Latin word *mille*, for "thousand." Use a dictionary to discover how each of the following words are related to "thousand": *millennium, milligram, millimeter, million, millisecond.*

Research Task

Topic: Westward Expansion

Ambition, politics, principles, greed, restlessness, curiosity—all of these motives, and others, drove people West during the nineteenth century. Perhaps even more powerful than practical reasons was the image of the West created by those who wrote about it in government documents, newspaper reports, and personal histories.

Assignment: Make a **display**—a poster, a trifold poster, or a museum-style exhibit—about the Westward Expansion. In your research, investigate the reliability of early media sources that informed people about opportunities in the West. Avoid over-reliance on any one source.

Formulate your research plan. To plan your display, make a list of relevant questions, such as the following:

- How did the government announce opportunities?
- What did people learn from pamphlets and posters?
- What did people learn from newspapers?
- How reliable was word-of-mouth news about the West?
- How reliable were the visual images of the West?

Then, choose a question or questions that will enable you to focus on a limited, manageable topic.

Gather sources. Use online and library searches to find answers to your research questions. Just like a smart American planning to go West, avoid relying too much on one source of information. Consult multiple sources, including texts written by experts in the field for scholarly audiences, as well as primary-source documents. Collect all details needed to prepare accurate citations.

Synthesize information. In deciding which information to use and which to discard, distinguish carefully between reliable and unreliable sources. A text that is awkwardly written may nevertheless be a trustworthy primary source. A source that seems dull may be accurate. A source that is entertaining may be oversimplified.

Organize and present your ideas. When you present information, use parallel structures to communicate parallel, or related, ideas. This will help viewers sift through a variety of data and clearly see your point. For example, you might organize a trifold poster with three parallel headings so that viewers can easily compare and contrast different information.

Model: Using Parallelism to Present Information

What People Learned from the Government — **What People Learned from Newspapers** — **What People Learned from Word of Mouth**

GRAND REAL ESTATE DISTRIBUTION.

AT ATCHISON, KANSAS, MARCH 28, 1876.

2 664 PIECES OF PROPERTY, VALUED AT $770,800 00.

THE CHARTER

"PRICE VILLA."

THE KANSAS LAND AND IMMIGRANT ASSOCIATION

▲ Advertisements such as this one from 1876 captured the imagination of adventurous Americans.

RESEARCH TIP

Set the preferences on your printer so that the full address of each Web site is included on each page you choose to print. In this way, you will have an automatic record of your Web-related sources.

Use a checklist like the one shown to create a display that is reliable, informative, and easy to understand.

Research Checklist

- ☐ Have I answered my research questions?
- ☐ Does my evidence come from experts on the topic and texts written for informed audiences in the field?
- ☐ Have I avoided relying too much on one source?
- ☐ Have I cited all sources according to a standard format?

TEXT SET

Living in a Changing World

Part 3

Building Knowledge and Insight

ANCHOR TEXT

The Story of an Hour

Connecting to the Essential Question Chopin's heroine appears to be mild and dependent, but she secretly hungers for independence. As you read, notice details that emphasize Mrs. Mallard's independence. Doing so will help as you consider the Essential Question: **How does literature shape or reflect society?**

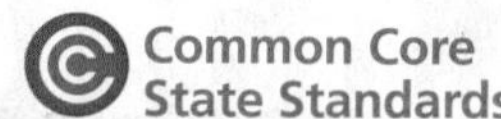

Reading Literature

6. Analyze a case in which grasping point of view requires distinguishing what is directly stated in a text from what is really meant.

Close Reading Focus

Irony; Theme

Irony is a contradiction between appearance and reality, between expectation and outcome, or between meaning and intention. In literature, readers frequently encounter three types of irony:

- **Verbal irony** occurs when someone says something that deliberately contradicts what that person actually means.
- **Situational irony** occurs when something happens that contradicts readers' expectations.
- **Dramatic irony** occurs when the reader or audience is aware of something that a character does not know.

Authors may use irony to create humor or to add an element of surprise to a story. The use of irony may also develop a story's **theme**—its central message. When irony is used in this way, the theme of the work may concern a discrepancy between surface appearances and inner truths. As you read this story, decide which type of irony Chopin primarily uses and whether it functions to create an effect or to develop the theme.

Preparing to Read Complex Texts Kate Chopin was among the first American authors to write with intention about women who suffer from the restrictions imposed on them by society. Her fiction is driven by a philosophy—the belief that men and women are equals but that society denies women their full humanity. As you read this story, **analyze the philosophical argument** that drives the plot. Determine how Chopin's philosophy contributes to the credibility of Mrs. Mallard's character. Note your ideas in a chart like the one shown.

Detail
Louise would "have no one follow her" up to her room.

↓

Related Issue
Women seek independence.

Vocabulary

The words listed are key to understanding the text that follows. Copy the words into your notebook, separating them into words you know and words you do not know.

forestall	**elusive**
repression	**tumultuously**

Kate Chopin (1850–1904)

Author of "The Story of an Hour"

Despite her conservative, aristocratic upbringing, Kate O'Flaherty Chopin (shō´ pan) became one of the most powerful and controversial writers of her time. In her writing, she captured the local color of Louisiana and boldly explored the role of women in society.

Family Life Kate O'Flaherty was born in St. Louis, Missouri, the daughter of a wealthy businessman who died five years later in a railroad accident. When she was twenty, Kate married Oscar Chopin, a Louisiana cotton trader. The couple settled in New Orleans, where they lived for ten years before moving to a plantation in rural Louisiana.

In 1882, Chopin's husband died, leaving her to raise their six children. Chopin carried on the work of the plantation alone until 1884, when she returned with her children to St. Louis. Then, in 1885, Chopin's mother died, leaving her in deep sorrow. Her family doctor, concerned about her emotional health, suggested that she begin to write fiction. Chopin spent the rest of her life in St. Louis, devoting much of her energy to writing.

Chopin the Writer and Rebel Chopin focused on capturing the essence of life in Louisiana in her writing. Her first novel, *At Fault* (1890), was set in a small Louisiana town inhabited by Creoles, descendants of the original French and Spanish settlers, and Cajuns, descendants of French Canadian settlers. Her charming portraits of Louisiana life often obscured the fact that she explored themes considered radical at the time: the nature of marriage, racial prejudice, and women's desire for equality.

The Awakening Chopin's finest novel, *The Awakening* (1899), is a psychological account of a woman's search for independence and fulfillment. Because the novel explored the issue of infidelity, it aroused a storm of protest. The book was eventually banned and Chopin's reputation was badly damaged. Then, in the 1950s, *The Awakening* was resurrected. Today, the book is among the five most-read American novels in colleges and universities. Chopin is now considered an early practitioner of American Realism—a literary style that seeks to avoid sentimental depictions of life. She is widely respected for her portrayal of the psychology of women and her ability to capture local color.

"The bird that would soar above the plain of tradition and prejudice must have strong wings."

THE STORY OF AN *Hour*

Kate Chopin

BACKGROUND "The Story of an Hour" was considered daring in the nineteenth century. The editors of at least two magazines refused the story because they thought it was immoral. They wanted Chopin to soften her female character, to make her less independent and unhappy in her marriage. Undaunted, Chopin continued to deal with issues of women's growth and emancipation in her writing, advancing ideas that are widely accepted today.

Knowing that Mrs. Mallard was afflicted with a heart trouble, great care was taken to break to her as gently as possible the news of her husband's death.

It was her sister Josephine who told her, in broken sentences; veiled hints that revealed in half concealing. Her husband's friend Richards was there, too, near her. It was he who had been in the newspaper office when

▶ **Critical Viewing** This story presents a "subtle and elusive" revelation. What connection do you see between the light shining through the window and such a discovery? **[Connect]**

intelligence of the railroad disaster was received, with Brently Mallard's name leading the list of "killed." He had only taken the time to assure himself of its truth by a second telegram, and had hastened to forestall any less careful, less tender friend in bearing the sad message.

Vocabulary
forestall (fôr stôl′) *v.* prevent by acting ahead of time

She did not hear the story as many women have heard the same, with a paralyzed inability to accept its significance. She wept at once, with sudden, wild abandonment, in her sister's arms. When the storm of grief had spent itself she went away to her room alone. She would have no one follow her.

There stood, facing the open window, a comfortable, roomy armchair. Into this she sank, pressed down by a physical exhaustion that haunted her body and seemed to reach into her soul.

She could see in the open square before her house the tops of trees that were all aquiver with the new spring life. The delicious breath of rain was in the air. In the street below a peddler was crying his wares. The notes of a distant song which someone was singing reached her faintly, and countless sparrows were twittering in the eaves.

There were patches of blue sky showing here and there through the clouds that had met and piled one above the other in the west facing her window.

Irony
Considering the news she has just received, what is ironic about the details Mrs. Mallard notices through her window?

She sat with her head thrown back upon the cushion of the chair, quite motionless, except when a sob came up into her throat and shook her, as a child who has cried itself to sleep continues to sob in its dreams.

She was young, with a fair, calm face, whose lines bespoke repression and even a certain strength. But now there was a dull stare in her eyes, whose gaze was fixed away off yonder on one of those patches of blue sky. It was not a glance of reflection, but rather indicated a suspension of intelligent thought.

There was something coming to her and she was waiting for it, fearfully. What was it? She did not know; it was too subtle and elusive to name. But she felt it, creeping out of the sky, reaching toward her through the sounds, the scents, the color that filled the air.

Vocabulary
repression (ri presh′ ən) *n.* restraint
elusive (ē lo͞o′ siv) *adj.* hard to grasp
tumultuously (to͞o mul′ cho͞o əs lē) *adv.* in an agitated way

Now her bosom rose and fell tumultuously. She was beginning to recognize this thing that was approaching to possess her, and she was striving to beat it back with her will—as powerless as her two white slender hands would have been.

When she abandoned herself, a little whispered word escaped her slightly parted lips. She said it over and over under her breath: "free, free, free!" The vacant stare and the look of terror that had followed it went from her eyes. They stayed keen and bright. Her pulses beat fast, and the coursing blood warmed and relaxed every inch of her body.

She did not stop to ask if it were or were not a monstrous joy that held her. A clear and exalted perception enabled her to dismiss the suggestion as trivial.

She knew that she would weep again when she saw the kind, tender hands folded in death; the face that had never looked save with love upon her, fixed and gray and dead. But she saw beyond that bitter moment a long procession of years to come that would belong to her absolutely. And she opened and spread her arms out to them in welcome.

There would be no one to live for her during those coming years; she would live for herself. There would be no powerful will bending hers in that blind persistence with which men and women believe they have a right to impose a private will upon a fellow creature. A kind intention or a cruel intention made the act seem no less a crime as she looked upon it in that brief moment of illumination.

And yet she had loved him—sometimes. Often she had not. What did it matter! What could love, the unsolved mystery, count for in face of this possession of self-assertion which she suddenly recognized as the strongest impulse of her being!

"Free! Body and soul free!" she kept whispering.

Josephine was kneeling before the closed door with her lips to the keyhole, imploring for admission. "Louise, open the door! I beg; open the door—you will make yourself ill. What are you doing, Louise? For heaven's sake open the door."

"Go away. I am not making myself ill." No; she was drinking in a very elixir of life[1] through that open window.

Her fancy was running riot along those days ahead of her. Spring days, and summer days, and all sorts of days that would be her own. She breathed a quick prayer that life might be long. It was only yesterday she had thought with a shudder that life might be long.

She arose at length and opened the door to her sister's importunities.[2] There was a feverish triumph in her eyes, and she carried herself unwittingly like a goddess of Victory. She clasped her sister's waist, and together they descended the stairs. Richards stood waiting for them at the bottom.

1. **elixir of life** (i liks′ ər) imaginary substance believed in medieval times to prolong life indefinitely.
2. **importunities** (im′ pôr to͞on′ i tēz) *n.* persistent requests or demands.

World
LITERATURE CONNECTION

Challenging Women's Roles

Chopin was one of a growing number of writers in the late nineteenth and early twentieth centuries who challenged women's traditional social roles. A generation earlier in Britain, novelist Mary Ann Evans adopted the pen name **George Eliot** (1819–1880) to explore the theme of women's independence. In France, Amadine Dupin (1804–1876) did the same, publishing as **George Sand.** In 1929, novelist and critic **Virginia Woolf** (1882–1941), pictured below, published the essay "A Room of One's Own" in which she argued that women need community in order to realize their potential as writers. She wrote: "Masterpieces are not solitary births."

Connect to the Literature

Do you think Kate Chopin would have trouble publishing "The Story of An Hour" today? Why or why not?

Comprehension

What does Mrs. Mallard think about while alone in her room?

Someone was opening the front door with a latchkey. It was Brently Mallard who entered, a little travel-stained, composedly carrying his gripsack[3] and umbrella. He had been far from the scene of accident, and did not know there had been one. He stood amazed at Josephine's piercing cry; at Richards's quick motion to screen him from the view of his wife.

But Richards was too late.

When the doctors came they said she had died of heart disease—of joy that kills.

3. **gripsack** (grip′ sak) *n.* small bag for holding clothes.

"Free! Body and soul free!"

Critical Reading 

Cite textual evidence to support your responses.

1. **Key Ideas and Details (a)** At the beginning of the story, what does the narrator call the ailment that afflicts Mrs. Mallard? **(b) Interpret:** In addition to a medical condition, what might the narrator mean by this phrase?
2. **Key Ideas and Details (a)** What does Mrs. Mallard see as she gazes out her window? **(b) Connect:** How does the scene outside the window foreshadow the feelings that sweep over her as she sits in her chair?
3. **Key Ideas and Details (a)** According to the doctors, what causes Mrs. Mallard's death? **(b) Draw Conclusions:** What do you believe is the actual cause of her death? **(c) Speculate:** Why do you think Chopin does not elaborate more about Mrs. Mallard's death?
4. **Integration of Knowledge and Ideas** How does Chopin emphasize differences between Mrs. Mallard's true self and the ways in which she is perceived? In your response, use at least two of these Essential Question words: *perception, subservient, illusion, fragile.* ***[Connecting to the Essential Question: How does literature shape or reflect society?]***

Close Reading Activities | *The Story of an Hour*

Literary Analysis

1. **Craft and Structure** In what ways is Mrs. Mallard's reaction to her husband's death an example of **situational irony?**
2. **Craft and Structure** How might the diagnosis of Mrs. Mallard's cause of death be an example of **dramatic irony?**
3. **Craft and Structure** Use a chart like the one shown to examine elements of irony in the story's descriptive passages.

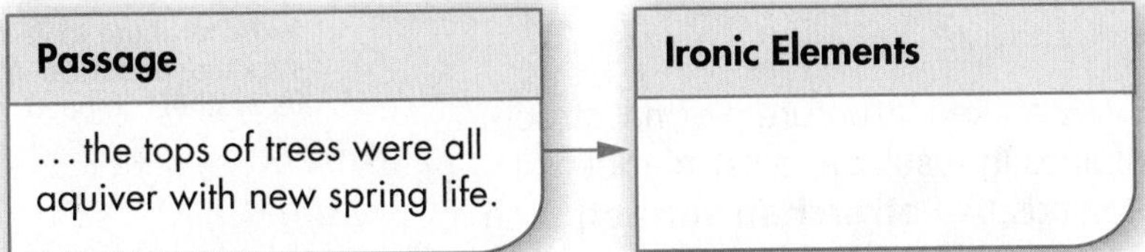

Passage
. . . the tops of trees were all aquiver with new spring life.
Ironic Elements

4. **Integration of Knowledge and Ideas** Reread the paragraph beginning, "There would be no one to live for during those coming years. . . ." **(a) Analyze the philosophical argument** about human interactions Chopin describes in that paragraph. **(b)** How does this argument illuminate Mrs. Mallard's conflict?
5. **Integration of Knowledge and Ideas** Is Mrs. Mallard a *credible* character? Explain, relating story details to Chopin's philosophy regarding women at that time period.
6. **Integration of Knowledge and Ideas** How does the story's central **theme** relate to a discrepancy between perception and reality?

Common Core State Standards

Writing

3. Write narratives to develop real or imagined experiences or events using effective technique, well-chosen details, and well-structured event sequences.

3.c. Use a variety of techniques to sequence events so that they build on one another to create a coherent whole and build toward a particular tone and outcome.

Vocabulary Acquisition and Use

Synonyms For each item, choose the letter of the synonym, or word that most closely expresses the same meaning. Explain your reasoning.

1. forestall	**a.** intercept	**b.** facilitate	**c.** arrange
2. repression	**a.** indulgence	**b.** constraint	**c.** tolerance
3. elusive	**a.** tangible	**b.** vivid	**c.** evanescent
4. tumultuously	**a.** severely	**b.** thoughtlessly	**c.** briskly

Writing

Narrative Text In a **reflective essay,** a writer describes personal experiences and conveys his or her feelings about them. Draw upon your memory and observations to write your own "story of an hour" about a moment when your life dramatically changed. Organize precise details either chronologically or in order of importance. *Create a fresh, authentic tone* by using words and phrases that come naturally to you.

Building Knowledge and Insight

Douglass • We Wear the Mask

Connecting to the Essential Question Paul Laurence Dunbar depicts the struggles of African Americans in "Douglass" and "We Wear the Mask." As you read, take note of the issues that Dunbar raises. Doing so will help as you reflect on the Essential Question: **How does literature shape or reflect society?**

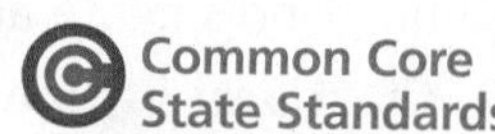

Reading Literature
5. Analyze how an author's choices concerning how to structure specific parts of a text contribute to its overall structure and meaning as well as its aesthetic impact.

Close Reading Focus

Formal Verse

Formal verse is poetry that follows a fixed structure. Formal structures may require a specific number of lines in a stanza, a set number of stanzas, or the use of repeated sounds. A **Petrarchan sonnet,** such as Dunbar's poem "Douglass," has fourteen lines separated into one stanza of eight lines and one of six lines. A sonnet also has a regular **rhyme scheme,** or pattern of rhyming words at the ends of lines. When notating rhyme scheme, the same sounds are indicated with lower case letters:

> Ah, Douglass, we have fall'n on evil days, (a)
> Such days as thou, not even thou didst know, (b)
> When thee, the eyes of that harsh long ago (b)
> Saw, salient, at the cross of devious ways . . . (a)

Poets also use formal structures in poems that do not use a specific fixed form. For example, "We Wear the Mask" is not written in a fixed form, but it has formal elements, including rhyme scheme. Formal elements enhance a poem's meaning and *mood,* or emotion. They also contribute to a poem's *aesthetic qualities*—the sense of art and beauty it conveys. As you read, notice how Dunbar's use of formal elements adds to the meaning, power, and beauty of these poems.

Preparing to Read Complex Texts Dunbar wrote in the decades following the Civil War. To fully appreciate his poems, consider how the period in which he wrote affected his point of view. As you read, **analyze the effect of the historical period** on the ideas, values, and themes that Dunbar expressed. A complete interpretation of the poem will account for both its *universal themes* and the ideas that reflect the poet's historical period. Use a chart like the one shown to record your interpretations.

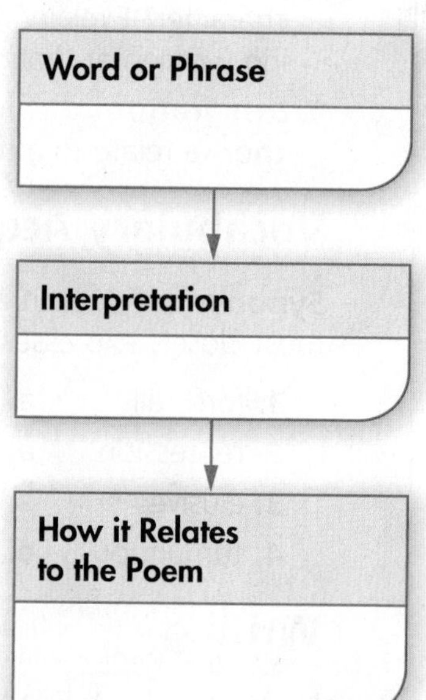

Vocabulary

The words listed here are key to understanding the poems that follow. Copy the words into your notebook. Which word is a synonym for *deception*?

salient
dissension
stark
guile
myriad

Paul Laurence Dunbar *(1872–1906)*

Author of "Douglass" and "We Wear the Mask"

Paul Laurence Dunbar was the first African American author to attain national recognition and support himself entirely with his writing. Throughout his short career, he wrote many books of poetry, as well as four novels and four volumes of short stories.

A Literary Child Dunbar was born in Dayton, Ohio, the son of former slaves. Encouraged by his mother, he began writing poetry at an early age. The only African American student in his high school class, Dunbar served as president of the literary society, class poet, and editor of the school newspaper.

Gaining Recognition After graduation, Dunbar sought work in a newspaper or legal office, but he found it difficult because of his race. He finally took a job as an elevator operator, supporting himself while continuing to write. He first earned recognition among writers and critics in 1892, when he read his poetry during a meeting of the Western Association of Writers. A year later, he took out a loan and published his first collection of poetry, *Oak and Ivy*. In 1895, he published a second collection, *Majors and Minors*. William Dean Howells, the leading critic of the day, was so impressed with the book that he wrote an introduction for Dunbar's next collection, *Lyrics of a Lowly Life* (1896).

Characters, Themes, and Forms Dunbar's fiction often focuses on daily life in the vanished world of the southern plantation. Sometimes, however, his writing revolves around social problems facing African Americans in Midwestern towns and urban ghettoes at the turn of the century. His characters include farmers, politicians, preachers, traders, entertainers, and professionals.

Popularity at a Price Dunbar composed poems in two styles—one formal and elegant, the other informal, using a rural dialect. His gift for re-creating dialect and using it to create believable characters was profound. However, it also drew criticism from those who believed Dunbar was pandering to white readers' desire for stereotypes of prewar African Americans. In poems such as "Douglass" and "We Wear the Mask," however, Dunbar demonstrates a command of the English language that was often overlooked, capturing the struggles of African Americans in a dignified, graceful manner.

An Untimely Death By his late twenties, Dunbar was a nationally recognized poet. Sadly, his life was cut short by tuberculosis in 1906. By the end of his life, his poetry was so popular that he was able to write from Florida, "Down here one finds my poems recited everywhere."

DOUGLASS

Paul Laurence Dunbar

Background *Paul Laurence Dunbar was among the last generation to have an ongoing contact with former African American slaves. As a child, Dunbar heard stories from his father, who had escaped captivity and fought during the Civil War. In his poems, Dunbar expresses the pain of racial injustice and the struggles of African Americans to achieve equality. In "Douglass," he calls upon the memory of Frederick Douglass (1817–1895), the great African-American abolitionist.*

Ah, Douglass, we have fall'n on evil days,
Such days as thou, not even thou didst know,
When thee, the eyes of that harsh long ago
Saw, salient, at the cross of devious ways,
And all the country heard thee with amaze.
Not ended then, the passionate ebb and flow.
The awful tide that battled to and fro;
We ride amid a tempest of dispraise.

Now, when the waves of swift dissension swarm,
And Honor, the strong pilot, lieth[1] stark,
Oh, for thy voice high-sounding o'er the storm,
For thy strong arm to guide the shivering bark,[2]
The blast-defying power of thy form,
To give us comfort through the lonely dark.

1. **lieth** (lī′ eth) *v.* lies.
2. **bark** boat.

Vocabulary

salient (sāl′ yənt) *adj.* standing out from the rest

dissension (di sen′ shən) *n.* disagreement; discord

stark (stärk) *adj.* stiff; rigid

Comprehension

What does the speaker say is the difference between the current time and the time in which Douglass lived?

◀ **Critical Viewing** Do you think this portrait and Dunbar's poem convey similar understandings of Frederick Douglass's character? Explain. **INTERPRET**

We Wear the Mask

Paul Laurence Dunbar

Vocabulary
guile (gīl) *n.* craftiness
myriad (mir′ ē əd) *adj.* countless

We wear the mask that grins and lies,
It hides our cheeks and shades our eyes—
This debt we pay to human **guile**;
With torn and bleeding hearts we smile,
And mouth with **myriad** subtleties.

Why should the world be overwise,
In counting all our tears and sighs?
Nay, let them only see us, while
We wear the mask.

Rhyme Scheme
Where does the poet use exact rhyme? Which lines do not rhyme?

We smile, but, O great Christ, our cries
To thee from tortured souls arise.
We sing, but oh the clay is vile
Beneath our feet, and long the mile;
But let the world dream otherwise,
We wear the mask!

Critical Reading

Cite textual evidence to support your responses.

1. **Key Ideas and Details (a)** In "Douglass," when was Douglass's voice heard by the nation? **(b) Compare:** How does Douglass's message relate to what the speaker of "Douglass" describes?
2. **Key Ideas and Details (a) Infer:** Who is the "we" in "We Wear the Mask"? **(b) Analyze:** What struggles do they face? **(c) Draw Conclusions:** Why do you think they wear the mask?
3. **Integration of Knowledge and Ideas** If Dunbar were alive today, do you think he would still have the views he expresses in these poems? Why or why not?
4. **Integration of Knowledge and Ideas** Based on your reading of these poems, how do you think the expression of personal emotion might lead to social change? In your response, use at least two of these Essential Question words: *bigotry, disclose, endurance, justice.* ***[Connecting to the Essential Question: How does literature shape or reflect society?]***

Close Reading Activities

Douglass • *We Wear the Mask*

Literary Analysis

1. **Craft and Structure** Which words in "We Wear the Mask" rhyme with "lies"? With "guile"?
2. **Craft and Structure** Using a chart, notate the **rhyme scheme** of each poem. Use a lower-case letter to identify each rhyming sound.

Rhyme Scheme →

"Douglass"	"We Wear..."
1	1
2	2
	3

3. **Craft and Structure** **(a)** What elements of **formal verse** does Dunbar use in "We Wear the Mask"? **(b)** How do these elements add to the poem's *mood* and *aesthetic qualities?* Explain.
4. **Craft and Structure** **(a)** What ideas does Dunbar introduce in the first stanza of the **sonnet** "Douglass"? **(b)** How does the second stanza build on these ideas? **(c)** What plea does he make in the final lines?
5. **Integration of Knowledge and Ideas** **Analyze the effect of the historical period** in "Douglass" by noting details that reveal the speaker's understanding of his times.
6. **Integration of Knowledge and Ideas** **(a)** What is the *theme*, or message, of "We Wear the Mask"? **(b)** How does that theme reflect problems African Americans faced during Dunbar's lifetime? Explain.

Common Core State Standards

Writing
1. Write arguments to support claims in an analysis of substantive topics or texts, using valid reasoning and relevant and sufficient evidence.

Language
5. Demonstrate understanding of word relationships and nuances in word meanings.

Vocabulary Acquisition and Use

Antonyms For each word below, select the antonym, or word of opposite meaning, from the vocabulary list on page 634. Explain your answers.

1. inconspicuous
2. agreement
3. few
4. honesty
5. flexible

Writing to Sources

Argument When it was first published, Dunbar's work received mixed reviews. Conduct research to find examples of both positive and negative responses to Dunbar's work. In a report, summarize your findings and take a position about Dunbar's legacy. Examine how ideas held during Dunbar's era—including prejudice—may have influenced critics.

Building Knowledge and Insight

Luke Havergal • Richard Cor
Lucinda Matlock • Richard B

Connecting to the Essential Question The vision of small-town America in these poems is full of contradictions. As you read, notice details that portray the light and dark sides of small-town life. This activity will help as you consider the Essential Question: **What is the relationship between literature and place?**

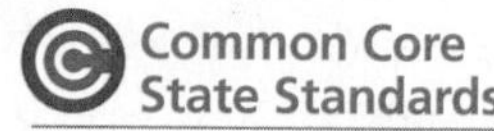

Common Core State Standards

Reading Literature

3. Analyze the impact of the author's choices regarding how to develop and relate elements of a story or drama.

9. Demonstrate knowledge of early-twentieth-century foundational works of American literature, including how two or more texts from the same period treat similar themes or topics.

Close Reading Focus

Narrative Poetry; Speaker

Narrative poetry is poetry that tells a story and includes the same literary elements as narrative prose such as short stories and novels:

- **Plot:** a related sequence of events, driven by a *conflict* or problem
- **Setting:** the time and place in which a story takes place
- **Characters:** people who participate in the action

In some narrative poems, one character acts as the **speaker,** or voice that tells the story. For example, the speakers in the poems from Masters's *Spoon River Anthology* are characters buried in the cemetery of the fictional town of Spoon River: "At ninety-six I had lived enough, that is all. . . ." Instead of using a neutral speaker, Masters lets characters tell their own stories. As you read, notice how the poet's choice of speaker affects the drama and emotional power of each poem.

Preparing to Read Complex Texts **Comparing and contrasting** poems in a group can give you a deeper understanding of each individual poem. It also allows you to see shared elements of works representing a certain region, time period, or literary style. As you read, use a chart like the one shown to compare and contrast the following elements:

- **Poetic Elements:** Which poems use rhyme and meter? To what effect?
- **Point of View:** How are the speakers similar and different?

Poetic Elements	Point of View

Once you have compared and contrasted the poetic elements and points of view in each poem, consider the **theme** conveyed by each. How are the central messages or insights about life in each poem similar and different?

Vocabulary

The words below are key to understanding the texts that follow. Copy the words into your notebook, sorting them into words you know and words you do not know.

repose **epitaph**
degenerate **chronicles**

EDWIN ARLINGTON ROBINSON *(1869–1935)*

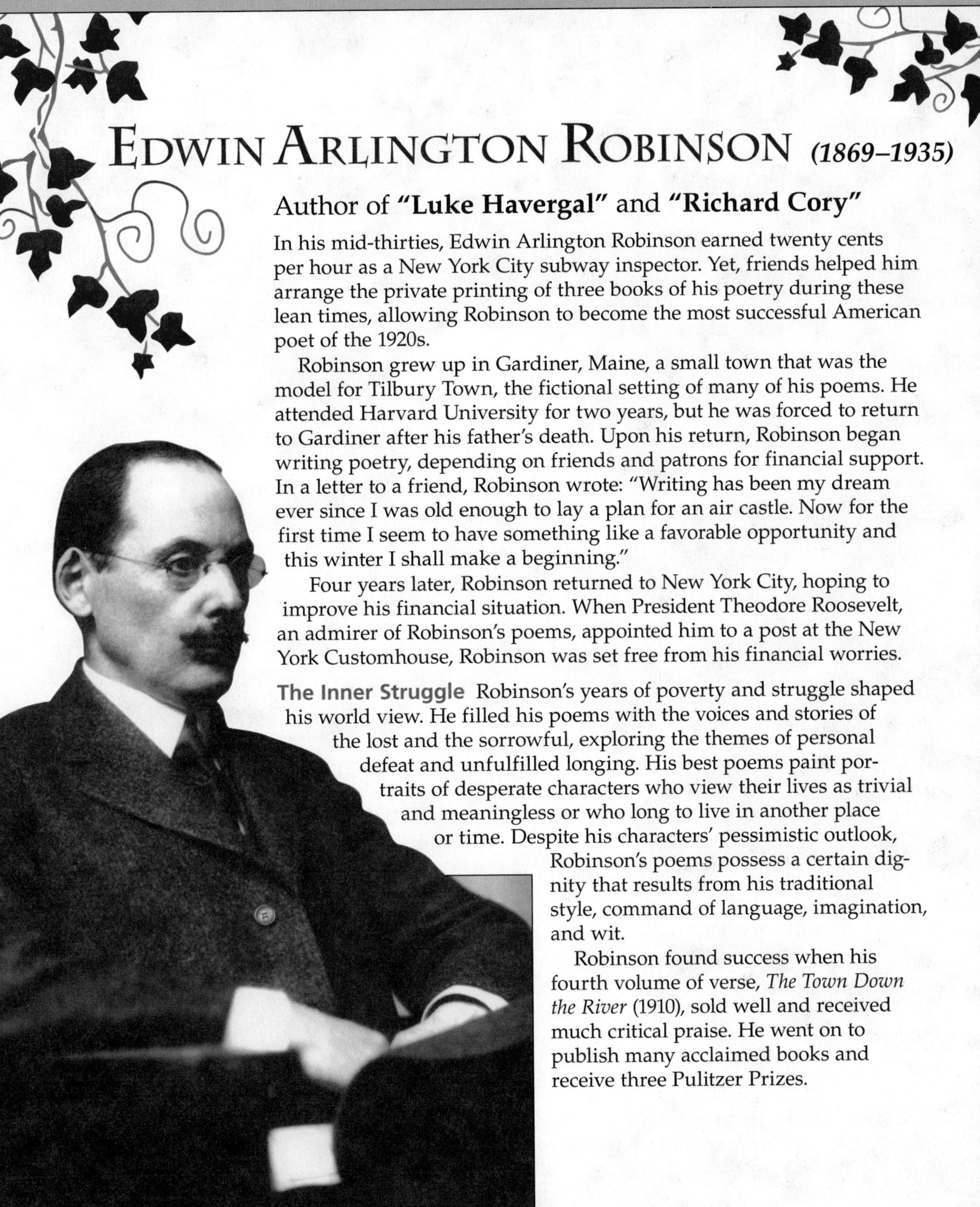

Author of "Luke Havergal" and "Richard Cory"

In his mid-thirties, Edwin Arlington Robinson earned twenty cents per hour as a New York City subway inspector. Yet, friends helped him arrange the private printing of three books of his poetry during these lean times, allowing Robinson to become the most successful American poet of the 1920s.

Robinson grew up in Gardiner, Maine, a small town that was the model for Tilbury Town, the fictional setting of many of his poems. He attended Harvard University for two years, but he was forced to return to Gardiner after his father's death. Upon his return, Robinson began writing poetry, depending on friends and patrons for financial support. In a letter to a friend, Robinson wrote: "Writing has been my dream ever since I was old enough to lay a plan for an air castle. Now for the first time I seem to have something like a favorable opportunity and this winter I shall make a beginning."

Four years later, Robinson returned to New York City, hoping to improve his financial situation. When President Theodore Roosevelt, an admirer of Robinson's poems, appointed him to a post at the New York Customhouse, Robinson was set free from his financial worries.

The Inner Struggle Robinson's years of poverty and struggle shaped his world view. He filled his poems with the voices and stories of the lost and the sorrowful, exploring the themes of personal defeat and unfulfilled longing. His best poems paint portraits of desperate characters who view their lives as trivial and meaningless or who long to live in another place or time. Despite his characters' pessimistic outlook, Robinson's poems possess a certain dignity that results from his traditional style, command of language, imagination, and wit.

Robinson found success when his fourth volume of verse, *The Town Down the River* (1910), sold well and received much critical praise. He went on to publish many acclaimed books and receive three Pulitzer Prizes.

Luke Havergal

Edwin Arlington Robinson

Go to the western gate, Luke Havergal,
There where the vines cling crimson on the wall,
And in the twilight wait for what will come.
The leaves will whisper there of her, and some,
Like flying words, will strike you as they fall;
But go, and if you listen she will call.
Go to the western gate, Luke Havergal—
Luke Havergal.

No, there is not a dawn in eastern skies
To rift the fiery night that's in your eyes;
But there, where western glooms are gathering,
The dark will end the dark, if anything:
God slays Himself with every leaf that flies,
And hell is more than half of paradise.
No, there is not a dawn in eastern skies—
In eastern skies.

Out of a grave I come to tell you this,
Out of a grave I come to quench the kiss
That flames upon your forehead with a glow
That blinds you to the way that you must go.
Yes, there is yet one way to where she is,
Bitter, but one that faith may never miss.
Out of a grave I come to tell you this—
To tell you this.

There is the western gate, Luke Havergal,
There are the crimson leaves upon the wall.
Go, for the winds are tearing them away,—
Nor think to riddle the dead words they say,
Nor any more to feel them as they fall;
But go, and if you trust her she will call.
There is the western gate, Luke Havergal—
Luke Havergal.

Speaker
Who is the "I" who speaks in this poem? Is there more than one possible interpretation?

Comprehension
What will happen at the western gate if Luke Havergal goes there?

The Thinker (Portrait of Louis N. Kenton, 1900), Thomas Eakins, The Metropolitan Museum of Art

▲ **Critical Viewing**
Do you think this painting suggests Richard Cory or the poem's speaker? Explain. **EVALUATE**

RICHARD CORY

EDWIN ARLINGTON ROBINSON

Whenever Richard Cory went down town,
We people on the pavement looked at him:
He was a gentleman from sole to crown,
Clean favored, and imperially slim.

And he was always quietly arrayed,
And he was always human when he talked;
But still he fluttered pulses when he said,
"Good-morning," and he glittered when he walked.

And he was rich—yes, richer than a king—
And admirably schooled in every grace:
In fine, we thought that he was everything
To make us wish that we were in his place.

So on we worked, and waited for the light,
And went without the meat, and cursed the bread;
And Richard Cory, one calm summer night,
Went home and put a bullet through his head.

Critical Reading

Cite textual evidence to support your responses.

1. **Key Ideas and Details** **(a)** Why should Luke Havergal go to the gate? **(b) Speculate:** What might the gate symbolize?
2. **Key Ideas and Details** **(a)** In "Luke Havergal," from where has the speaker come? **(b) Interpret:** What is the speaker's message?
3. **Key Ideas and Details** **(a)** Why was Richard Cory the envy of the town? **(b) Contrast:** In what ways does Richard Cory differ from the other townspeople?
4. **Key Ideas and Details** **(a)** What does Cory do one night? **(b) Infer:** Do you think the town was surprised by his action? Explain.
5. **Integration of Knowledge and Ideas** **(a) Apply:** Why might Richard Cory have been miserable? **(b) Relate:** What does this poem suggest about differences between people's inner realities and their outward appearances? **(c) Extend:** In what ways is the message of this poem applicable to contemporary American culture today? Explain.

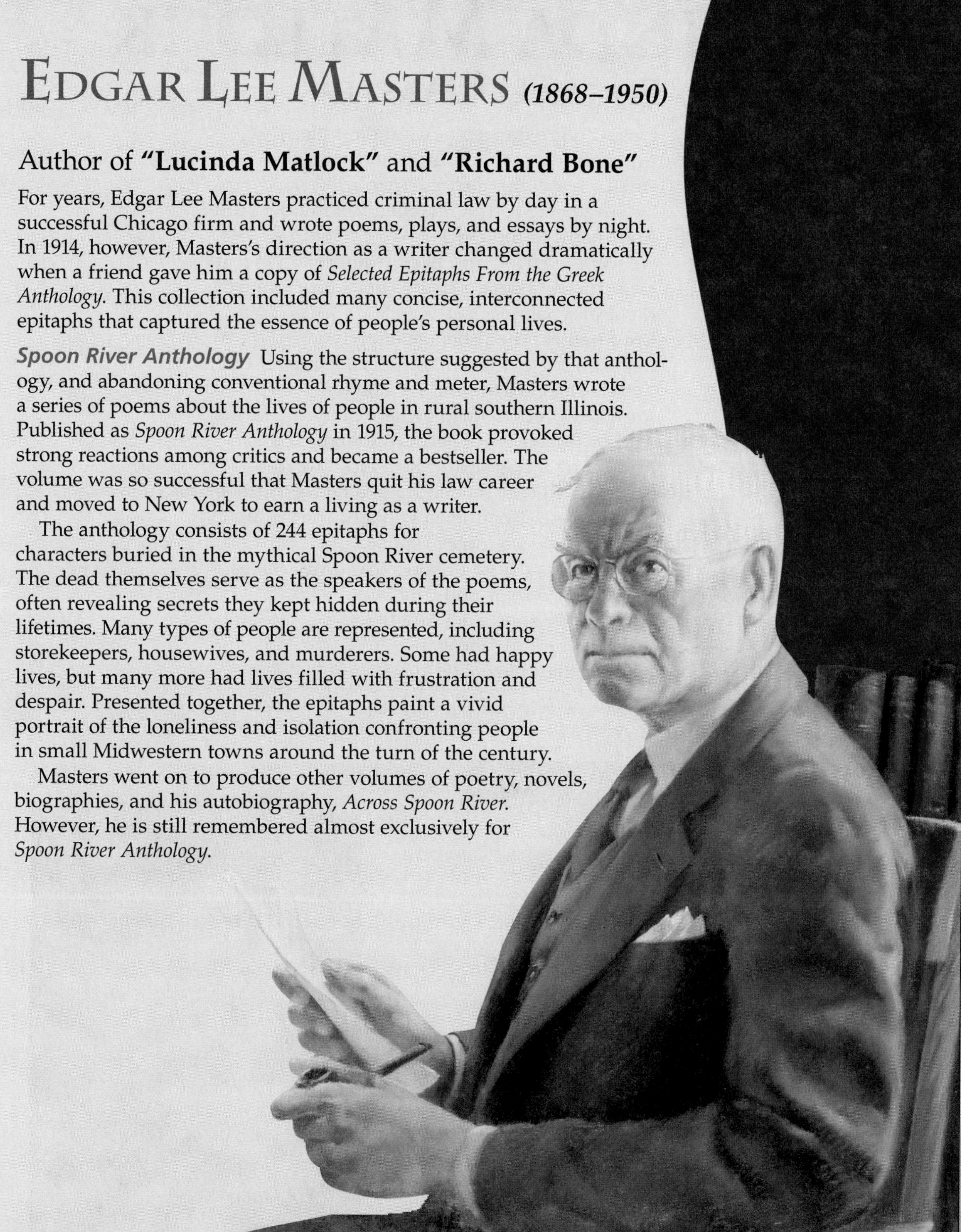

Edgar Lee Masters (1868–1950)

Author of "Lucinda Matlock" and "Richard Bone"

For years, Edgar Lee Masters practiced criminal law by day in a successful Chicago firm and wrote poems, plays, and essays by night. In 1914, however, Masters's direction as a writer changed dramatically when a friend gave him a copy of *Selected Epitaphs From the Greek Anthology.* This collection included many concise, interconnected epitaphs that captured the essence of people's personal lives.

Spoon River Anthology Using the structure suggested by that anthology, and abandoning conventional rhyme and meter, Masters wrote a series of poems about the lives of people in rural southern Illinois. Published as *Spoon River Anthology* in 1915, the book provoked strong reactions among critics and became a bestseller. The volume was so successful that Masters quit his law career and moved to New York to earn a living as a writer.

The anthology consists of 244 epitaphs for characters buried in the mythical Spoon River cemetery. The dead themselves serve as the speakers of the poems, often revealing secrets they kept hidden during their lifetimes. Many types of people are represented, including storekeepers, housewives, and murderers. Some had happy lives, but many more had lives filled with frustration and despair. Presented together, the epitaphs paint a vivid portrait of the loneliness and isolation confronting people in small Midwestern towns around the turn of the century.

Masters went on to produce other volumes of poetry, novels, biographies, and his autobiography, *Across Spoon River.* However, he is still remembered almost exclusively for *Spoon River Anthology.*

LUCINDA MATLOCK

EDGAR LEE MASTERS

I went to the dances at Chandlerville,
And played snap-out[1] at Winchester.
One time we changed partners,
Driving home in the moonlight of middle June,
And then I found Davis.
We were married and lived together for seventy years,
Enjoying, working, raising the twelve children,
Eight of whom we lost
Ere I had reached the age of sixty.
I spun, I wove, I kept the house, I nursed the sick,
I made the garden, and for holiday
Rambled over the fields where sang the larks,
And by Spoon River gathering many a shell,
And many a flower and medicinal weed—
Shouting to the wooded hills, singing to the green valleys.
At ninety-six I had lived enough, that is all,
And passed to a sweet **repose**.
What is this I hear of sorrow and weariness,
Anger, discontent and drooping hopes?
Degenerate sons and daughters,
Life is too strong for you—
It takes life to love Life.

Vocabulary
repose (ri pōz′) *n.* state of being at rest
degenerate (dē jen′ ər it) *adj.* morally corrupt

1. **snap-out** game in which a long line of players who are holding hands spin around in a circle, causing the players on the ends to be flung off by centrifugal force.

WORLD LITERATURE CONNECTION

Dramatic Monologue

The poems from *Spoon River Anthology* are dramatic monologues, a form developed by British poets during the Victorian period. In a dramatic monologue, the speaker of the poem is a character who addresses the reader, just as a character in a play might speak directly to the audience.

The most famous writer of dramatic monologues is Robert Browning, born near London in 1812. Browning first gained celebrity with *The Ring and the Book*, a series of poems spoken by characters that describe a murder case. Today, Browning's best-known poem is "My Last Duchess," a dramatic monologue spoken by a rich Italian duke who unwittingly admits to having killed his wife: "That's my last Duchess painted on the wall, /Looking as if she were alive."

CONNECT TO THE LITERATURE

Do you think the dramatic monologues from *Spoon River Anthology* could provide the basis for an interesting television series? Why or why not?

Proserpine, 1984 Dante Gabriel Rosetti. Tate Gallery

RICHARD BONE

EDGAR LEE MASTERS

When I first came to Spoon River
I did not know whether what they told me
Was true or false.
They would bring me the **epitaph**
And stand around the shop while I worked
And say "He was so kind," "He was wonderful,"
"She was the sweetest woman," "He was a consistent Christian."
And I chiseled for them whatever they wished,
All in ignorance of its truth.
But later, as I lived among the people here,
I knew how near to the life
Were the epitaphs that were ordered for them as they died.

But still I chiseled whatever they paid me to chisel
and made myself party to the false **chronicles**
Of the stones,
Even as the historian does who writes
Without knowing the truth,
Or because he is influenced to hide it.

Vocabulary

epitaph (ep′ ə taf′) *n.* inscription on a tombstone

chronicles (krän′ i kəlz) *n.* stories; histories

Critical Reading

Cite textual evidence to support your responses.

1. **Key Ideas and Details (a)** How old was Lucinda Matlock when she died? **(b) Infer:** Why might she have thought she "lived enough"?
2. **Key Ideas and Details (a)** Whom does she address at the end of the poem? **(b) Interpret:** What is the meaning of Matlock's message to those she addresses?
3. **Key Ideas and Details (a)** What is Richard Bone's occupation? **(b) Infer:** What does he learn after years in Spoon River?
4. **Key Ideas and Details (a) Interpret:** Why does Bone think the epitaphs are "false chronicles"? **(b) Speculate:** Is it likely Bone is correct in his assessment? Explain.
5. **Integration of Knowledge and Ideas** What image of life in small-town America do these poems project? In your response, use at least two of these Essential Question words: *conflict, appearance, secretive, familiar.* ***[Connecting to the Essential Question: What is the relationship between literature and place?]***

Close Reading Activities

Luke Havergal • Richard Cory • Lucinda Matlock • Richard Bone

Literary Analysis

1. **Craft and Structure** **(a)** Use a chart like the one shown to identify the **plot, setting,** and **characters** in the **narrative poem** "Richard Cory." **(b)** Do the same for "Lucinda Matlock."

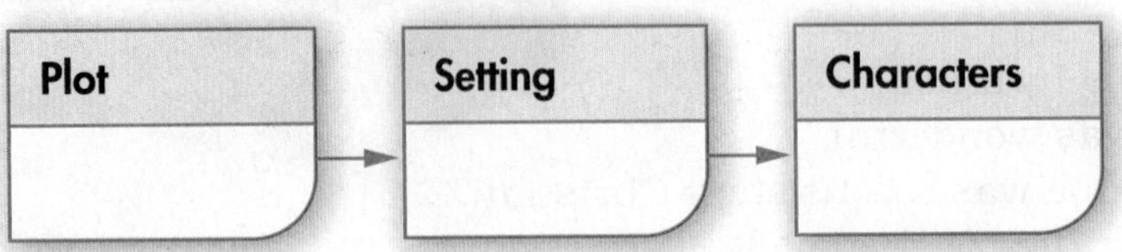

2. **Craft and Structure** **(a)** For each poem in this grouping, identify the *conflict*—the obstacles or problems—the characters face. **(b)** Do all the characters resolve, or solve, their conflicts? Explain.
3. **Craft and Structure** Identify the **speaker** of each poem in this grouping.
4. **Key Ideas and Details** Which details suggest that the speaker of "Richard Cory" is the voice of an entire town? Explain.
5. **Craft and Structure** In what ways does the speaker's admiration for Richard Cory add to the drama and surprise of the poem?
6. **Craft and Structure** **(a)** In what ways might "Lucinda Matlock" be different if Masters had used a different speaker? **(b)** If "Richard Cory" spoke for himself, how might the poem be different?
7. **Integration of Knowledge and Ideas** The speakers in Masters's *Spoon River Anthology* are dead. Why might this allow them to discuss their lives more openly?
8. **Integration of Knowledge and Ideas** **(a)** Write several sentences in which you **compare and contrast** the uses of *rhyme* and *meter* in Robinson's poems and Masters's poems. **(b)** In your opinion, which type of poetic form is better suited to the topic of life in small-town America? Explain.
9. **Integration of Knowledge and Ideas** **(a)** If Richard Bone were to inscribe a true epitaph for each of the four speakers of these poems, including himself, what might each one say? **(b)** Compare and contrast those messages.
10. **Integration of Knowledge and Ideas** Taken together, is there a single *theme* all these poems express? If not, why not? If so, what is that theme?

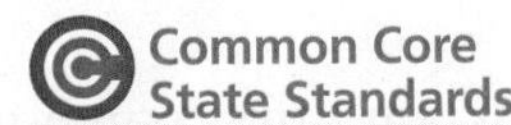
Common Core State Standards

Writing
3. Write narratives to develop real or imagined experiences or events using effective technique, well-chosen details, and well-structured event sequences. *(p. 649)*

Language
4.b. Identify and correctly use patterns of word changes that indicate different meanings or parts of speech. *(p. 649)*

Vocabulary Acquisition and Use

Word Analysis: Latin Root *-genus-*

The word *degenerate* combines the Latin root *-genus-*, meaning "birth, race, species, or kind," with the prefix *de-*, meaning "away from" or "unlike." If a person is *degenerate*, he or she has fallen away from the ancestral qualities of his or her species. Use each of the following *-genus-* words below to complete the sentences. If the meaning of a word is unclear, consult a dictionary.

genetic	genealogy	homogenous
ingenious	generate	general

1. Is the human race truly ____: are we really all alike?
2. We all have a nearly identical ____ makeup.
3. Most of us can ____ good solutions to everyday problems.
4. However, each of us inherits a unique ____.
5. Some of us think in ____ terms, while others dwell on the tiniest of details.
6. And while many of us can be described as "bright," only a few can be considered ____!

Vocabulary: Evaluating Logic

Indicate whether the underlined word in each sentence below is used logically. If it is, explain your answer. If it is not, explain why not and correct the sentence to restore the logic.

1. Just as I drifted off for my afternoon nap, I heard a loud yapping outside the window and was instantly wrenched into a state of annoyed <u>repose</u>.
2. Throwing up the blind, I could see that the source of the yapping was the <u>degenerate</u> beast my neighbor refers to as his pet.
3. I began to fantasize about a small gravestone bearing an <u>epitaph</u> that read *Rover, detested dog of Denton Drive.*
4. Sadly, I thought, the <u>chronicle</u> of my own life will feature a tired grump with an overactive imagination.

Writing to Sources

Narrative Text Choose the poem in this grouping that you think would make the most poignant short story. Then, create an outline that would aid you in translating the verse into a prose narrative.

Prewriting First, use a chart like the one shown to identify the beginning, middle, and end of the story. Refer back to the poem for key story events.

Beginning	Middle	End

Drafting Decide how each part of the story will unfold. Decide what new elements or events would make the beginning more engaging, the middle more suspenseful, and the end more satisfying. As you think of ways to enrich the plot, make notes in the relevant columns of your chart.

Revising Convert the contents of your chart into an outline, using Roman numerals *I, II,* and *III* for the story's beginning, middle, and end. Use the letters *A, B, C,* etc., for details within each section. Organize the story events in chronological order.

Building Knowledge and Insight

A Wagner Matinée

Connecting to the Essential Question In this story, a woman's move to a distant state changes her life and character. As you read, notice how setting affects both Aunt Georgiana and Clark. Doing so will help as you reflect on the Essential Question: **What is the relationship between literature and place?**

Reading Literature
3. Analyze the impact of the author's choices regarding how to develop and relate elements of a story or drama.

Close Reading Focus

Characterization; First-Person Point of View

Characterization is the art of revealing characters' personalities. In **direct characterization,** a writer simply states what a character is like, as in this sentence: "She was a pious woman." In **indirect characterization,** the writer uses the following methods to provide clues about the character:

- descriptions of the character's appearance, manner, and behavior
- the character's own words, inner thoughts, and actions
- comments about the character made by other characters
- the ways in which other characters react to the character

The point of view in which a story is told also affects how readers learn about characters. For example, this story uses **first-person point of view**—the narrator is part of the action and uses the pronouns *I, me,* and *we.* As a result, readers' impressions filter through the narrator's eyes. As you read, notice what characters are like and identify the clues that help you understand them.

Preparing to Read Complex Texts To fully understand a story, **ask questions to clarify meaning.** You might ask the following types of questions: What problems or obstacles do characters face? What motivates characters to think, feel, or act as they do? How do characters respond to cultural or historical influences? Then, to find answers, *reread* or *refer to footnotes and sidebars*. Use a chart like the one shown to ask questions and clarify details as you read this story.

Question
Why did Georgiana go to Nebraska?

Clarifying Strategy
Reread.

Vocabulary

You will encounter the words below in the text that follows. Copy the words into your notebook. Which word contains a prefix that means *before*?

reverential
tremulously
inert
prelude
jocularity

Willa Cather (1873–1947)

Author of "A Wagner Matinée"

Although Willa Cather lived more than half her life in New York City, she turned again and again to the Nebraska prairie of her youth—at the time, a recently settled area of the American frontier—for inspiration and material for her writing. Cather captured with unflinching honesty the difficulties of life on the expanding frontier.

A Prairie Childhood Born in a small town in western Virginia, Cather moved to the Nebraska frontier when she was nine. Many of her new neighbors were immigrants struggling to build new lives while preserving their native cultures. Commenting on the diversity that surrounded her during her childhood, Cather once wrote, "On Sundays we could drive to a Norwegian church and listen to a sermon in that language, or to a Danish or Swedish church. We could go to a French Catholic settlement or into a Bohemian township and hear one in Czech, or we could go to the church with the German Lutherans."

Cather received a rich formal education, studying foreign languages, history, classical music, and opera. In 1891, she left home to study at the University of Nebraska, becoming one of the first women to receive a college education.

"Most of the basic material a writer works with is acquired before the age of fifteen."

The Making of a Literary Giant After her graduation in 1895, Cather worked as an editor at a Pittsburgh newspaper while writing poems and short stories in her spare time. Her first collection of stories, *The Troll Garden,* was published in 1905. In 1906, she moved to New York and joined the editorial staff of *McClure's Magazine.* After her first novel, *Alexander's Bridge,* was published in 1912, Cather devoted herself to writing full-time. She remained in New York for the rest of her life, but her memories of the prairie inspired her greatest work.

Over the next 35 years, Cather produced ten novels, two short-story collections, and two collections of essays. Among her outstanding works are *O Pioneers!* (1913), *My Ántonia* (1918), and *One of Ours* (1922), all of which capture the flavor of life on the Midwestern prairie. *One of Ours* won the Pulitzer Prize in 1923. Cather then shifted her attention from the Midwest to New Mexico in *Death Comes for the Archbishop* (1927) and to seventeenth-century Canada in *Shadows on the Rock* (1931).

A Wagner Matinée

Willa Cather

BACKGROUND When "A Wagner Matinée" first appeared in 1904, Cather's readers would have been as familiar with Richard Wagner (väg nər) as people are today with the Beatles. Wagner, who was German, was one of the nineteenth century's great composers. His operas are characterized by adventurous harmonic language and an innovative intermarriage of music and drama. To many, Wagner represents the idea of high culture. In this story, Cather contrasts the stark realities of frontier life with life in a more cultured world.

I received one morning a letter written in pale ink, on glassy, blue-lined notepaper, and bearing the postmark of a little Nebraska village. This communication, worn and rubbed, looking as though it had been carried for some days in a coat pocket that was none too clean, was from my Uncle Howard. It informed me that his wife had been left a small legacy by a bachelor relative who had recently died, and that it had become necessary for her to come to Boston to attend to the settling of the estate. He requested me to meet her at the station, and render her whatever services might prove necessary. On examining the date indicated as that of her arrival, I found it no later than tomorrow. He had characteristically delayed writing until, had I been away from home for a day, I must have missed the good woman altogether.

The name of my Aunt Georgiana called up not alone her own figure, at once pathetic and grotesque, but opened before my feet a gulf

◀ Critical Viewing
What sort of life do you think the woman depicted in this painting has lived? Explain **INTERPRET**

Comprehension
Why is Aunt Georgiana going to Boston?

◀ ***From Arkansas,*** 1939, George Schreiber, Sheldon Swope Art Museum, Terre Haute, Indiana of recollections so wide and deep that, as the letter dropped from my hand, I felt suddenly a stranger to all the present conditions of my existence, wholly ill at ease and out of place amid the surroundings of my study. I became, in short, the gangling farmer boy my aunt had known, scourged with chilblains and bashfulness, my hands cracked and raw from the corn husking. I felt the knuckles of my thumb tentatively, as though they were raw again. I sat again before her parlor organ, thumbing the scales with my stiff, red hands, while she beside me made canvas mittens for the huskers.

The next morning, after preparing my landlady somewhat, I set out for the station. When the train arrived I had some difficulty in finding my aunt. She was the last of the passengers to alight, and when I got her into the carriage she looked not unlike one of those charred, smoked bodies that firemen lift from the *débris* of a burned building. She had come all the way in a day coach; her linen duster[1] had become black with soot and her black bonnet gray with dust during the journey. When we arrived at my boardinghouse the landlady put her to bed at once, and I did not see her again until the next morning.

Characterization

What do the contrasting details of Aunt Georgiana's life in Boston and Nebraska reveal about her character?

Whatever shock Mrs. Springer experienced at my aunt's appearance she considerately concealed. Myself, I saw my aunt's misshapen figure with that feeling of awe and respect with which we behold explorers who have left their ears and fingers north of Franz Josef Land,[2] or their health somewhere along the upper Congo.[3] My Aunt Georgiana had been a music teacher at the Boston Conservatory, somewhere back in the latter sixties. One summer, which she had spent in the little village in the Green Mountains[4] where her ancestors had dwelt for generations, she had kindled the callow[5] fancy of the most idle and shiftless of all the village lads, and had conceived for this Howard Carpenter one of those absurd and extravagant passions which a handsome country boy of twenty-one sometimes inspires in a plain, angular, spectacled woman of thirty. When she returned to her duties in Boston, Howard followed her; and the upshot of this inexplicable infatuation was that she eloped with him, eluding the reproaches of her family and the criticism of her friends by going with him to the Nebraska frontier. Carpenter, who of course had no money, took a homestead in Red Willow County,[6] fifty miles from the railroad. There they measured off their eighty acres by driving across the prairie in a wagon, to the wheel of which they had tied a red cotton handkerchief, and counting its revolutions. They built a dugout in the red hillside, one of those cave dwellings whose

---

1. **duster** *n.* short, loose smock worn while traveling to protect clothing from dust.
2. **Franz Josef Land** group of islands in the Arctic Ocean.
3. **Congo** river in central Africa.
4. **Green Mountains** mountains in Vermont.
5. **callow** (kal′ ō) *adj.* immature; inexperienced.
6. **Red Willow County** county in southwestern Nebraska that borders on Kansas.

inmates usually reverted to the conditions of primitive savagery. Their water they got from the lagoons where the buffalo drank, and their slender stock of provisions was always at the mercy of bands of roving Indians. For thirty years my aunt had not been farther than fifty miles from the homestead.

But Mrs. Springer knew nothing of all this, and must have been considerably shocked at what was left of my kinswoman. Beneath the soiled linen duster, which on her arrival was the most conspicuous feature of her costume, she wore a black stuff dress whose ornamentation showed that she had surrendered herself unquestioningly into the hands of a country dressmaker. My poor aunt's figure, however, would have presented astonishing difficulties to any dressmaker. Her skin was yellow from constant exposure to a pitiless wind, and to the alkaline water which transforms the most transparent cuticle into a sort of flexible leather. She wore ill-fitting false teeth. The most striking thing about her physiognomy, however, was an incessant twitching of the mouth and eyebrows, a form of nervous disorder resulting from isolation and monotony, and from frequent physical suffering.

Characterization
In this paragraph, which details are examples of indirect characterization?

In my boyhood this affliction had possessed a sort of horrible fascination for me, of which I was secretly very much ashamed, for in those days I owed to this woman most of the good that ever came my way, and had a **reverential** affection for her. During the three winters when I was riding herd for my uncle, my aunt, after cooking three meals for half a dozen farmhands, and putting the six children to bed, would often stand until midnight at her ironing board, hearing me at the kitchen table beside her recite Latin declensions and conjugations, and gently shaking me when my drowsy head sank down over a page of irregular verbs. It was to her, at her ironing or mending, that I read my first Shakespeare; and her old textbook of mythology was the first that ever came into my empty hands. She taught me my scales and exercises, too, on the little parlor organ which her husband had bought her after fifteen years, during which she had not so much as seen any instrument except an accordion, that belonged to one of the Norwegian farmhands. She would sit beside me by the hour, darning and counting, while I struggled with the "Harmonious Blacksmith"; but she seldom talked to me about music, and I understood why. She was a pious woman; she had the consolation of religion; and to her at least her martyrdom was not wholly sordid. Once when I had been doggedly beating out some passages from an old score of "Euryanthe" I had found among her music books, she came up to me and, putting her hands over my eyes, gently drew my head back upon her shoulder, saying **tremulously**, "Don't love it so well, Clark, or it may be taken from you. Oh! dear boy, pray that whatever your sacrifice be it is not that."

Vocabulary
reverential (rev′ ə ren′ shəl) *adj.* showing deep respect and love

Vocabulary
tremulously (trem′ yo͞o ləs lē) *adv.* fearfully; timidly

Comprehension
When Clark was a boy, what subjects did he learn from his aunt?

LITERATURE IN CONTEXT

Music Connection

Wagnerian Opera

Aunt Georgiana has a strong reaction to the music of Richard Wagner, the composer of *The Flying Dutchman* (1843). Wagner rejected some of the traditions of opera. He usually avoided lengthy musical speeches and instead originated the *leitmotif*, a recurring musical theme used to symbolize an emotion or event. Wagner also wrote what he called "music dramas." An entire series of these works, called *The Ring of the Nibelung,* consumed twenty-six years of his life. In "A Wagner Matinée," the audience hears excerpts from *The Ring* and *Siegfried,* an opera based on the adventures of a legendary German hero.

Connect to the Literature

Does the reader need to be familiar with Wagner's operas to understand Aunt Georgiana's response? Explain.

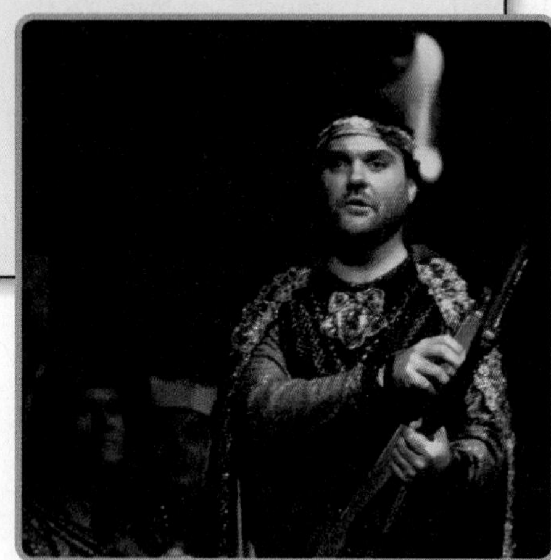

When my aunt appeared on the morning after her arrival, she was still in a semi-somnambulant[7] state. She seemed not to realize that she was in the city where she had spent her youth, the place longed for hungrily for half a lifetime. She had been so wretchedly trainsick throughout the journey that she had no recollection of anything but her discomfort, and, to all intents and purposes, there were but a few hours of nightmare between the farm in Red Willow County and my study on Newbury Street. I had planned a little pleasure for her that afternoon, to repay her for some of the glorious moments she had given me when we used to milk together in the straw-thatched cowshed, and she, because I was more than usually tired, or because her husband had spoken sharply to me, would tell me of the splendid performance of Meyerbeer's *Les Huguenots*[8] she had seen in Paris in her youth. At two o'clock the Boston Symphony Orchestra was to give a Wagner program, and I intended to take my aunt, though as I conversed with her I grew doubtful about her enjoyment of it. Indeed, for her own sake, I could only wish her taste for such things quite dead, and the long struggle mercifully ended at last. I suggested our visiting the Conservatory and the Common[9] before lunch, but she seemed altogether too timid to wish to venture out. She questioned me absently about various changes in the city, but she was chiefly concerned that she had forgotten to leave instructions about feeding half-skimmed milk to a certain weakling calf, "Old Maggie's calf, you know, Clark," she explained, evidently having forgotten how long I had been away. She was further troubled because she had neglected to tell her daughter about the freshly opened kit of mackerel in the cellar, that would spoil if it were not used directly.

I asked her whether she had ever heard any of the Wagnerian operas, and found that she had not, though she was perfectly familiar with their respective situations and had once possessed the piano score of *The Flying Dutchman.* I began to think it would have been best to get her back to Red Willow County without waking her, and regretted having suggested the concert.

From the time we entered the concert hall, however, she was a trifle less passive and **inert**, and seemed to begin to perceive her

Vocabulary
inert (in ʉrt′) *adj.* motionless

7. **semi-somnambulant** (se mī säm′ nam byə lənt) *adj.* resembling a sleepwalker.
8. ***Les Huguenots*** (lāz hyōō′ gə nät′) opera written in 1836 by Giacomo Meyerbeer (1791–1864).
9. **Common** Boston Common, a small park in Boston.

surroundings. I had felt some trepidation[10] lest one might become aware of the absurdities of her attire, or might experience some painful embarrassment at stepping suddenly into the world to which she had been dead for a quarter of a century. But again I found how superficially I had judged her. She sat looking about her with eyes as impersonal, almost as stony, as those with which the granite Ramses[11] in a museum watches the froth and fret that ebbs and flows about his pedestal, separated from it by the lonely stretch of centuries. I have seen this same aloofness in old miners who drift into the Brown Hotel at Denver, their pockets full of bullion, their linen soiled, their haggard faces unshorn, and who stand in the thronged corridors as solitary as though they were still in a frozen camp on the Yukon, or in the yellow blaze of the Arizona desert, conscious that certain experiences have isolated them from their fellows by a gulf no haberdasher could conceal.

The audience was made up chiefly of women. One lost the contour of faces and figures, indeed any effect of line whatever, and there was only the color contrast of bodices past counting, the shimmer and shading of fabrics soft and firm, silky and sheer, resisting and yielding: red, mauve, pink, blue, lilac, purple, ecru, rose, yellow, cream, and white, all the colors that an impressionist finds in a sunlit landscape, with here and there the dead black shadow of a frock coat. My Aunt Georgiana regarded them as though they had been so many daubs of tube paint on a palette.

When the musicians came out and took their places, she gave a little stir of anticipation, and looked with quickening interest down over the rail at that invariable grouping; perhaps the first wholly familiar thing that had greeted her eye since she had left old Maggie and her weakling calf. I could feel how all those details sank into her soul, for I had not forgotten how they had sunk into mine when I came fresh from plowing forever and forever between green aisles of corn, where, as in a treadmill, one might walk from daybreak to dusk without perceiving a shadow of change in one's environment. I reminded myself of the impression made on me by the clean profiles of the musicians, the gloss of their linen; the dull black of their coats, the beloved shapes of the instruments, the patches of yellow light thrown by the green-shaded stand-lamps on the smooth, varnished bellies of the cellos and the bass viols in the rear, the restless, wind-tossed forest of fiddle necks and bows; I recalled how, in the first orchestra I had ever heard, those long bow strokes seemed to draw the soul out of me, as a conjuror's stick reels out paper ribbon from a hat.

The first number was the Tannhäuser overture. When the violins

Characterization
What do Clark's descriptions of his own first reactions to a concert reveal about his character?

Comprehension
What is Clark's initial feeling about being in public with Aunt Georgiana? How does that attitude change?

---

10. trepidation (trep′ ə dā′ shən) *n.* fearful anxiety; apprehension.

11. Ramses (ram′ sēz) one of the eleven Egyptian kings by that name who ruled from c. 1292 to c. 1075 B.C.

drew out the first strain of the Pilgrims' chorus, my Aunt Georgiana clutched my coat sleeve. Then it was that I first realized that for her this singing of basses and stinging frenzy of lighter strings broke a silence of thirty years, the inconceivable silence of the plains. With the battle between the two motifs, with the bitter frenzy of the Venusberg[12] theme and its ripping of strings, came to me an overwhelming sense of the waste and wear we are so powerless to combat. I saw again the tall, naked house on the prairie, black and grim as a wooden fortress; the black pond where I had learned to swim, the rain-gullied clay about the naked house; the four dwarf ash seedlings on which the dishcloths were always hung to dry before the kitchen door. The world there is the flat world of the ancients; to the east, a cornfield that stretched to daybreak; to the west, a corral that stretched to sunset; between, the sordid conquests of peace, more merciless than those of war.

The overture closed. My aunt released my coat sleeve, but she said nothing. She sat staring at the orchestra through a dullness of thirty years, through the films made, little by little, by each of the three hundred and sixty-five days in every one of them. What, I wondered, did she get from it? She had been a good pianist in her day, I knew, and her musical education had been broader than that of most music teachers of a quarter of a century ago. She had often told me of Mozart's operas and Meyerbeer's, and I could remember hearing her sing, years ago, certain melodies of Verdi. When I had fallen ill with a fever she used to sit by my cot in the evening, while the cool night wind blew in through the faded mosquito netting tacked over the window, and I lay watching a bright star that burned red above the cornfield, and sing "Home to our mountains, oh, let us return!" in a way fit to break the heart of a Vermont boy near dead of homesickness already.

I watched her closely through the **prelude** to *Tristan and Isolde*, trying vainly to conjecture what that warfare of motifs, that seething turmoil of strings and winds, might mean to her. Had this music any message for her? Did or did not a new planet swim into her ken? Wagner had been a sealed book to Americans before the sixties. Had she anything left with which to comprehend this glory that had flashed around the world since she had gone from it? I was in a fever of curiosity, but Aunt Georgiana sat silent upon her peak in Darien.[13] She preserved this utter immobility throughout the numbers from the *Flying Dutchman*, though her fingers worked mechanically upon her black dress, as though of themselves they were recalling the piano score they had once played. Poor old hands! They

Asking Questions to Clarify Meaning
What questions might you ask about Clark's description of the plains?

◀ Critical Viewing
In what ways does this painting mirror Clark's description of the audience at the opera house?
CONNECT; COMPARE

Vocabulary
prelude (prel′ yo͞od) *n.* introductory section or movement of a musical work

Comprehension
Describe Aunt Georgiana's musical education.

12. **Venusberg** (vē′ nəs bʉrg′) legendary mountain in Germany where Venus, the Roman goddess of love, held court.
13. **peak in Darien** (der′ ē ən′) mountain on the Isthmus of Panama; from "On First Looking into Chapman's Homer" by English poet John Keats (1795–1821).

were stretched and pulled and twisted into mere tentacles to hold, and lift, and knead with; the palms unduly swollen, the fingers bent and knotted, on one of them a thin worn band that had once been a wedding ring. As I pressed and gently quieted one of those groping hands, I remembered, with quivering eyelids, their services for me in other days.

Soon after the tenor began the "Prize Song," I heard a quick-drawn breath, and turned to my aunt. Her eyes were closed, but the tears were glistening on her cheeks, and I think in a moment more they were in my eyes as well. It never really dies, then, the soul? It withers to the outward eye only, like that strange moss which can lie on a dusty shelf half a century and yet, if placed in water, grows green again. My aunt wept gently throughout the development and elaboration of the melody.

Asking Questions to Clarify Meaning
What questions might you ask about the episode of the farm hand to clarify your understanding of its meaning to Georgiana?

During the intermission before the second half of the concert, I questioned my aunt and found that the "Prize Song" was not new to her. Some years before there had drifted to the farm in Red Willow County a young German, a tramp cow puncher who had sung in the chorus at Bayreuth,[14] when he was a boy, along with the other peasant boys and girls. On a Sunday morning he used to sit on his blue gingham-sheeted bed in the hands' bedroom, which opened off the kitchen, cleaning the leather of his boots and saddle, and singing the "Prize Song," while my aunt went about her work in the kitchen. She had hovered about him until she had prevailed upon him to join the country church, though his sole fitness for this step, so far as I could gather, lay in his boyish face and his possession of this divine melody. Shortly afterward he had gone to town on the Fourth of July, lost his money at a faro[15] table, ridden a saddled Texas steer on a bet, and disappeared with a fractured collarbone.

Vocabulary
jocularity (jäk´ yo͞o lar´ ə tē) *n.* joking good humor

"Well, we have come to better things than the old *Trovatore* at any rate, Aunt Georgie?" I queried, with well-meant **jocularity**.

Her lip quivered and she hastily put her handkerchief up to her mouth. From behind it she murmured, "And you've been hearing this ever since you left me, Clark?" Her question was the gentlest and saddest of reproaches.

"But do you get it, Aunt Georgiana, the astonishing structure of it all?" I persisted.

"Who could?" she said, absently; "why should one?"

The second half of the program consisted of four numbers from the *Ring*. This was followed by the forest music from *Siegfried*[16] and the program closed with Siegfried's funeral march. My aunt wept quietly, but almost continuously. I was perplexed as to what

14. **Bayreuth** (bī roit´) city in Germany known for its annual Wagnerian music festivals.
15. **faro** (fer´ ō) gambling game in which players bet on the cards to be turned up from the top of the dealer's deck.
16. **Siegfried** (sēg´ frēd) opera based on the adventures of Siegfried, a legendary hero in medieval German literature.

measure of musical comprehension was left to her, to her who had heard nothing for so many years but the singing of gospel hymns in Methodist services at the square frame schoolhouse on Section Thirteen. I was unable to gauge how much of it had been dissolved in soapsuds, or worked into bread, or milked into the bottom of a pail.

The deluge of sound poured on and on; I never knew what she found in the shining current of it; I never knew how far it bore her, or past what happy islands, or under what skies. From the trembling of her face I could well believe that the *Siegfried* march, at least, carried her out where the myriad graves are, out into the gray, burying grounds of the sea; or into some world of death vaster yet, where, from the beginning of the world, hope has lain down with hope, and dream with dream and, renouncing, slept.

The concert was over; the people filed out of the hall chattering and laughing, glad to relax and find the living level again, but my kinswoman made no effort to rise. I spoke gently to her. She burst into tears and sobbed pleadingly, "I don't want to go, Clark, I don't want to go!"

"I don't want to go, Clark, I don't want to go!"

I understood. For her, just outside the door of the concert hall, lay the black pond with the cattle-tracked bluffs, the tall, unpainted house, naked as a tower, with weather-curled boards; the crook-backed ash seedlings where the dishcloths hung to dry, the gaunt, moulting turkeys picking up refuse about the kitchen door.

Critical Reading

Cite textual evidence to support your responses.

1. **Key Ideas and Details** **(a)** What part did Boston play in Aunt Georgiana's earlier life? **(b) Compare and Contrast:** In what ways would you compare and contrast life in Boston and life in Red Willow County?
2. **Key Ideas and Details** **(a)** As a boy, what did the narrator practice on the "parlor organ" in the Nebraska farmhouse? **(b) Interpret:** What does Aunt Georgiana mean when she says, "Don't love it so well, Clark, or it may be taken from you"? **(c) Connect:** Do the events of the story reinforce her statement? Explain.
3. **Integration of Knowledge and Ideas** **Take a Position:** Would it have been better for Aunt Georgiana if she had not come to Boston? Explain.
4. **Integration of Knowledge and Ideas** What do you think Cather would say about the importance of artistic and cultural outlets to the health of a community? Do you agree or disagree? Explain. In your response, use at least two of these Essential Question words: *expression, freedom, individualism, self-reliance.* ***[Connecting to the Essential Question: What is the relationship between literature and place?]***

Close Reading Activities A Wagner Matinée

Literary Analysis

1. **Key Ideas and Details (a)** What **questions** might you ask about the difficulties of Aunt Georgiana's life in Nebraska? **(b)** *Reread* to find two details in the story that help you understand Nebraska life at that time in history. In what ways do these details **clarify the meaning** of the story for you?
2. **Key Ideas and Details (a)** What **questions** might you ask about Boston life at the time of the story? **(b)** Which story details provide answers to your questions?
3. **Key Ideas and Details (a)** As you read this story, what questions might you ask about the composer Richard Wagner? **(b)** How do *footnotes or sidebars* help to answer these questions? **(c)** In what ways did learning about Wagner deepen your understanding of the story?
4. **Craft and Structure** Note two examples of **direct characterization** in this story.
5. **Craft and Structure** What do you learn about Aunt Georgiana's personality through **indirect characterization?** Use a chart like the one shown to record your observations.

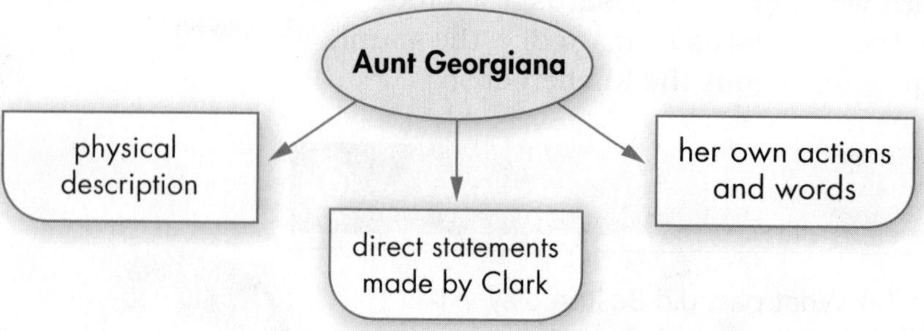

6. **Craft and Structure** What do Clark's thoughts and feelings about his aunt indirectly reveal about his personality? Explain.
7. **Craft and Structure** Aunt Georgiana's husband bought her a "little parlor organ." Explain what this small detail suggests about his character.
8. **Craft and Structure** What effect does Clark's **first-person point of view** have on your perception of Aunt Georgiana?
9. **Key Ideas and Details (a)** Find two examples of events Clark recalls from living with Aunt Georgiana. **(b)** How do these events shape your impressions of her?
10. **Integration of Knowledge and Ideas (a)** How do Clark's feelings toward his aunt change during the story? **(b)** How do his feelings affect your response to her? **(c)** How do Clark's feelings about his aunt affect your attitude toward him as a character?

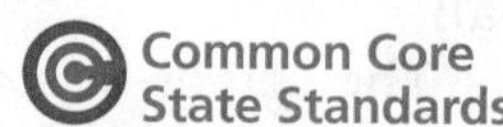

Common Core State Standards

Writing

1. Write arguments to support claims in an analysis of substantive topics or texts, using valid reasoning and relevant and sufficient evidence. *(p. 663)*

5. Develop and strengthen writing as needed by revising, focusing on addressing what is most significant for a specific purpose and audience. *(p. 663)*

Language

4. Determine or clarify the meaning of unknown and multiple-meaning words and phrases based on *grades 11–12 reading and content,* choosing flexibly from a range of strategies. *(p. 663)*

6. Acquire and use accurately general academic and domain-specific words and phrases, sufficient for reading, writing, and speaking at the college and career readiness level. *(p. 663)*

Vocabulary Acquisition and Use

Multiple-Meaning Words from Music

Musical vocabulary often has multiple meanings. For example, a *prelude* can be the introduction to a musical work or preparation for any important matter. For each numbered item below, select the correct definition of the italicized word.

chord: (a) two or more notes played or sung simultaneously, **(b)** an emotional response

concert: (a) a performance of several short compositions, **(b)** working together

harmony: (a) a pleasing combination of musical sounds, **(b)** a peaceful situation

overture: (a) an introductory movement to an extended musical work, **(b)** any first movement

1. We put a *concerted* effort into the game.
2. The chorus sang in glorious *harmony*.
3. He made an *overture* to pay for lunch.
4. The speech struck a *chord* in the audience.

Vocabulary: Word Meanings

Answer the following questions in complete sentences. Be sure to use the underlined words in your responses.

1. If students are reverential toward a teacher, do they ignore or respect her?
2. Who is most likely to speak tremulously—a musician, a truck driver, or a child?
3. What is an example of a substance that is usually—but not always—inert?
4. As a prelude to bad news, would you expect sarcasm or seriousness?
5. Is jocularity more likely to be the trademark of a talk-show host or a funeral director?

Writing to Sources

Argument "A Wagner Matinée" provoked an outcry among Nebraskans who felt Cather had portrayed the state unfairly. Cather responded that the story was a tribute to pioneer strength and endurance. As the editor of a Nebraska newspaper, take a position and write an **editorial** defending your view. Structure your argument in a persuasive way, supported by precise and relevant examples.

Prewriting Review the story. Analyze the details Cather uses to portray Nebraska and Boston. Decide whether you agree with her views. Jot down ideas, observations, and facts that support your opinion.

Drafting Arrange your ideas in order of importance. Include factual evidence and emotional appeals to support your statements.

Revising Reread your work to make sure your language is specific and persuasive and that you present a sustained, unified argument. Replace irrelevant statements, and add support as needed.

Model: Using Specific Language

Cather implies that Boston offers more than Nebraska. While it may be true that Boston is a center for art, Nebraska offers many ~~things~~ cultural resources without the ~~trouble~~ pollution and congestion of a major city.

Specific references such as *cultural resources* and *pollution and congestion* make the editorial clear and persuasive.

Write a Research Report

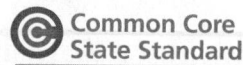

Common Core State Standards

Writing

2. Write informative/explanatory texts to examine and convey complex ideas, concepts, and information clearly and accurately through the effective selection, organization, and analysis of content.

7. Conduct short as well as more sustained research projects to answer a question or solve a problem; narrow or broaden the inquiry when appropriate; synthesize multiple sources on the subject, demonstrating understanding of the subject under investigation.

Historical Investigation Report You can learn a great deal about a literary work by investigating the historical context in which it was written. To focus such an investigation, write a report in which you present information you have gathered, along with your own insights. An effective historical investigation report synthesizes information from multiple sources and connects ideas to form a coherent analysis. Follow the steps outlined in this workshop to write a historical investigation report.

Assignment Write a research report about the historical context in which a literary work or group of related works was written.

What to Include Your research report should have these elements:

- a clear thesis statement or main proposition
- factual support from varied sources, including primary and secondary sources found in both electronic and print texts
- direct quotations and proper citations of sources
- logical organization, including an introduction, body, and conclusion
- a formal bibliography or works-cited list

To preview the criteria on which your research report may be assessed, see the rubric on page 675.

Focus on Research

When you conduct research, you should keep the following strategies in mind:

- Use both print and electronic sources.
- Be sure you use the most current information from reliable sources.
- If you are doing research online, look for sources that have *.gov* or *.edu* in their addresses.
- When possible and appropriate, consider using primary sources.

Be sure to note all sources you use in your research, and credit appropriately. Refer to the Conducting Research pages in the Introductory Unit as well as the Citing Sources and Preparing Manuscript pages in the Resource section (R21–R23) for information on citation.

Prewriting and Planning

Choosing Your Topic

To find a suitable topic, use the following strategies:

- **Notebook and Textbook Review** Flip through your notebooks, literature textbooks, and writing journals, and list selections or authors you find interesting. Write down specific questions you have about the historical context in which your favorite works were written.
- **Research Preview** Once you have several possible topic choices and questions, spend 10–15 minutes researching each one on the Internet or at the library. Seek out both primary and secondary sources. A quick research preview will confirm the availability of information on each topic.

Narrowing Your Topic

Find your focus. Make sure your topic is substantial but not too ambitious for a short research paper. Narrow an overly broad topic by finding a more focused subject that fits within the larger area of interest. Use a flowchart like the one shown to do so.

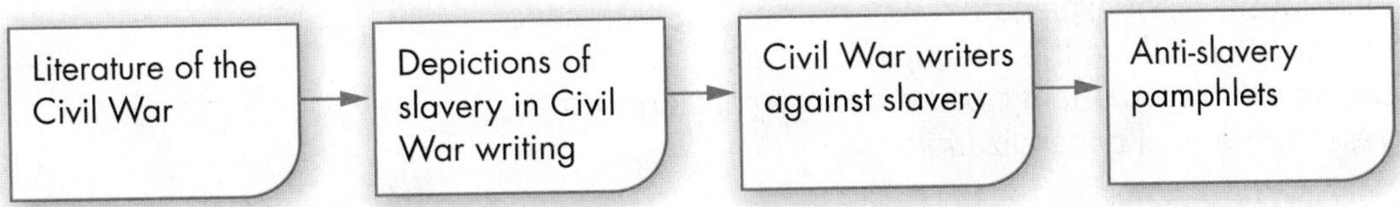

Gathering Details

Organize your notes. As you gather information, use index cards to keep track of important ideas, facts, and scholarly opinions. Write down the general subject, fact or quotation, page numbers, and an identifying letter or number you will assign to the source.

Prepare to credit sources. Use another set of index cards to keep track of your sources. Use one card for each source you consult. Record the author's name, title, publisher, city, and date of publication. Label each source card with a letter or number so you can refer to sources quickly.

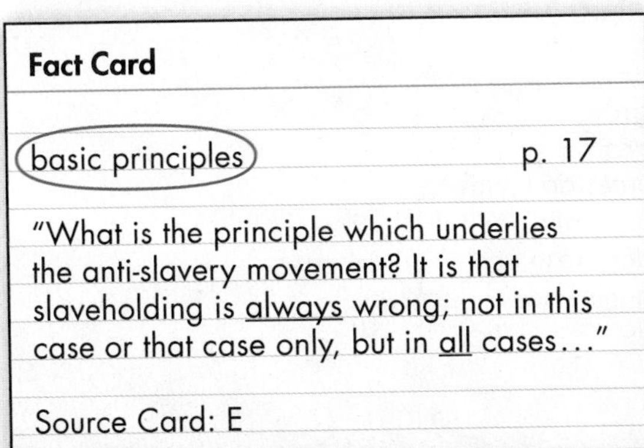

Fact Card

basic principles p. 17

"What is the principle which underlies the anti-slavery movement? It is that slaveholding is always wrong; not in this case or that case only, but in all cases..."

Source Card: E

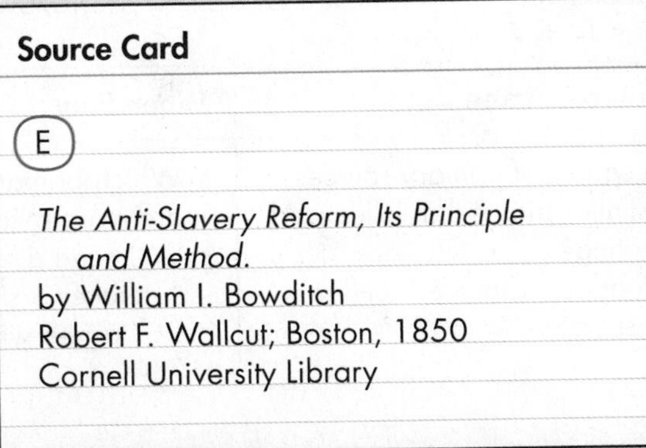

Source Card

E

The Anti-Slavery Reform, Its Principle and Method.
by William I. Bowditch
Robert F. Wallcut; Boston, 1850
Cornell University Library

Drafting

Shaping Your Writing

Propose a thesis statement. Your research report should develop a coherent thesis statement or controlling idea. Review your notes and write a statement that is supported by the evidence you discovered in primary and secondary resources. Your thesis should make a claim that your report will support; it should not state a simple fact.

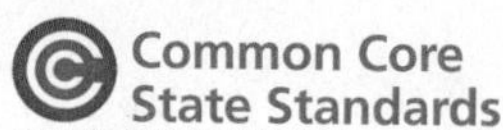

Common Core State Standards

Writing

2.a. Introduce a topic; organize complex ideas, concepts, and information so that each new element builds on that which precedes it to create a unified whole.

2.b. Develop the topic thoroughly by selecting the most significant and relevant facts, extended definitions, concrete details, quotations, or other information and examples appropriate to the audience's knowledge of the topic.

8. Gather relevant information from multiple authoritative print and digital sources, using advanced searches effectively; assess the strengths and limitations of each source in terms of the task, purpose, and audience.

Weak Argument	Strong Argument
• Anti-slavery pamphlets first appeared in 1704. • Pamphlets were very influential in ending slavery.	Beginning in 1704, anti-slavery pamphlets increasingly used the tools of advertising to persuade readers that slavery was immoral.

Write a formal outline. After you have selected a controlling idea, prepare an outline. Consider points at which you might include rhetorical strategies other than exposition, or explanation. For example, use an anecdote, a form of ***narration***, or include the ***description*** of a setting. Note ideas for a conclusion in which you attain closure by summarizing your main points and presenting a final generalization.

Providing Elaboration

Include a variety of sources. As you draft, use direct quotations, paraphrases, and visuals from sources that are reliable, valid, and varied. Do not rely on the ideas or information you find in a single source. Referencing multiple resources gives your writing more validity because it takes into account a variety of perspectives.

Analyze relationships among sources. In your research, you may have encountered differences of opinion in secondary sources or conflicting accounts of the same events in primary sources. Provide analysis and explanation about the reasons for such differences. To present a complete analysis, include answers to the questions listed in the following chart.

When Sources Agree	When Sources Disagree
• Do the writers of primary sources share similar biases that influenced their writing? • Do secondary resources confirm this perspective?	• Which primary sources do I think are more reliable and valid? Why? • Do I have a secondary resource that takes a side on this issue? Do I agree with it?

Developing Your Style

Choosing an Effective Organization

To choose the best pattern of organization for your report, consider your thesis and your findings. Then, structure your report with one of the methods listed in the chart below. You may choose an overall organizational strategy and use other methods to support it. For example, your essay might follow a chronological organization, but an individual paragraph might evaluate the causes and effects of a single important event.

Method	Description
Chronological	Discuss events in the order in which they occurred.
Cause/Effect	Analyze the causes and/or effects of an event.
Problem/Solution	Identify a specific problem and present a solution.
Parts to Whole	Relate elements of a single event or topic to a whole.
Order of Importance	Present your support from most to least important or from least to most important.
Compare and Contrast	Discuss similarities and differences between two topics.

Find It in Your Reading

Review Nell Irvin Painter's introduction to "An Account of an Experience With Discrimination" on page 664.

1. Identify the overall organizational method Painter uses.
2. Note her organization within individual paragraphs. Find examples of chronological and cause-and-effect organizations.

Apply It to Your Writing

To select an appropriate organizational method, follow these steps:

1. Review the strategies listed in the chart and consider their pros and cons. For example, chronological order can present a sequence of events clearly, but it may not establish the importance of a person or event.
2. Choose the overall organizational method that best supports your thesis statement. Draft an outline that reflects that strategy.
3. Think about the organization of information within paragraphs. Consider using cause-and-effect or problem-and-solution organization if relevant to the ideas you are presenting in that paragraph.
4. Use transitions to make your organization clear to readers.

Revising

Revising Your Paragraphs

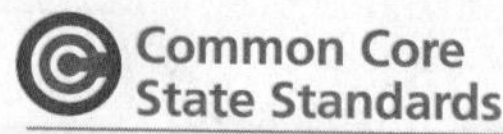

Writing

2.d. Use precise language, domain-specific vocabulary, and techniques such as metaphor, simile, and analogy to manage the complexity of the topic.

4. Produce clear and coherent writing in which the development, organization, and style are appropriate to task, purpose, and audience.

5. Develop and strengthen writing as needed by rewriting, focusing on addressing what is most significant for a specific purpose and audience.

8. Integrate information into the text selectively to maintain the flow of ideas, avoiding plagiarism and overreliance on any one source and following a standard format for citation.

Integrate source material smoothly. A strong research report is not a choppy collection of facts and quotations. It presents a smooth flow of ideas that are supported by valid, researched information. Review your paper, looking for points at which your source material can be integrated better. When you paraphrase another writer's ideas, include a citation that identifies the source of the idea. When you include exact quotations, follow this strategy:

- First, introduce the quotation by naming the writer or by connecting the quotation to the subject being discussed.
- Then, present the quoted material.
- Finally, explain the quotation by showing how it supports the point you are making.

Revising Your Word Choice

Define specialized vocabulary. General readers may not be familiar with specialized terms you have encountered in your research. Some words may be familiar only to experts in the field and will present obstacles to your readers' appreciation of your ideas. To aid readers' understanding, define jargon that is specific to a topic.

- Review your work and identify specialized words, such as *broadsheet* in the example shown. Add necessary definitions.
- Consider whether definitions are sufficient. If necessary, add descriptions or comparisons to more familiar concepts or objects.
- If the terms are still too challenging for your readers, consider replacing the specialized vocabulary with simpler language.

Model: Revising to Define Technical Terms

, large sheets of paper printed on one side and then folded.
Some anti-slavery materials were published as broadsheets^. Others were presented as stapled or folded pamphlets. Some
, or right-hand,
pamphlets included illustrations on recto^ pages and
, or left-hand,
commentary on verso^ pages.

Defining technical terms with more commonly used language clarifies the writer's meaning.

Peer Review: Ask a partner to review your draft and identify specialized terms. Discuss whether each term should be defined, deleted, or simplified.

Writers on Writing

Nell Irvin Painter On Using Research

Nell Irvin Painter is the author of "Defining an Era" (p. 474).

These words come from the introduction to my history of the United States between 1877 and 1919. I wanted to break down gross generalizations about Americans based on race (black/white) and ethnicity (Irish, German, Jewish) by talking about socio-economic class. Men and women experience class in different ways. In order to speak broadly, I had to research the incomes and lifestyles of many kinds of Americans, not just middle-class white people.

The broader your research, the more appealing your writing.

—Nell Irvin Painter

from *Standing at Armageddon, 1877–1919*

In both 1877 and 1919 native-born white Protestant Americans were presumed to belong to the middle (or upper) classes, even though in the South, West, and Midwest large numbers of such people belonged to the agricultural and industrial working classes. The standing of descendants of immigrants changed over time because the arrival of new groups of immigrants altered assumptions about relative class status. The Irish, who had seemed in 1877 to constitute a permanent class of casual laborers and domestic servants, had by 1919 become skilled workers and foremen, while many Irishwomen had become the teachers of eastern and southern European immigrants who early in the twentieth century formed a new industrial working class. Similarly, German Jews, many of whom in the mid-nineteenth century had been itinerant peddlers, were largely middle- and upper-class by the time of heavy Russian Jewish immigration after 1905. And the process continued. By 1920 the children of Europeans who had immigrated in the late nineteenth century had become the teachers and foremen of southern black migrants in the North and Midwest.

I purposefully included the words *white* and *Protestant* to break up an equation that many readers take for granted: that middle-class is the same as white and Protestant. I also did research in sources that discussed the lives of many kinds of people.

I specifically mentioned Irish immigrants, because many readers forget the history of Irish Americans as immigrants. I wanted this section to convey the sense of change over time in the status of Irish Americans in relation to later immigrants.

I used these two particular vocations because one, teachers, is associated with women, and the other, foremen, is associated with men.

Providing Appropriate Citations

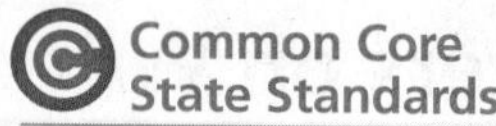

Writing
8. Integrate information into the text selectively to maintain the flow of ideas, avoiding plagiarism and overreliance on any one source and following a standard format for citation.

You must cite the sources for the information and ideas you use in your report. In the body of your paper, include a footnote, an endnote, or a parenthetical citation, identifying the sources of facts, opinions, and quotations. At the end of your paper, provide a bibliography or a works-cited list, a list of all the sources you cite. Follow the format your teacher recommends, such as Modern Language Association (MLA) Style or American Psychological Association (APA) Style. See pages R20–R23 for more information about how to prepare citations for different kinds of sources.

If you do not credit sources accurately, you commit the serious offense of **plagiarism,** presenting someone else's work as your own. Plagiarism is stealing someone else's ideas, so it is both illegal and dishonest. Avoid this problem by fairly and thoroughly citing every source you use.

Deciding What to Cite

You do not need to cite every fact that you report. For example, facts that are considered common knowledge do not require citation. A fact that can be found in three or more sources is probably common knowledge. However, you should cite any facts and statistics that are not common knowledge. The examples in this chart reflect the difference between common knowledge and facts that should be cited.

Common Knowledge
• Slavery was abolished in the United States in 1863. • William Lloyd Garrison was a leader of the abolitionist movement. • *Uncle Tom's Cabin* was published in 1852.
Facts to Be Cited
• From the 17th to 19th centuries, about 12 million Africans were captured and sent as slaves to the Americas. Source: Ronald Segal, *The Black Diaspora: Five Centuries of the Black Experience Outside Africa* (New York: Farrar, Straus and Giroux, 1995, page 4). • Harriet Beecher Stowe's anti-slavery novel *Uncle Tom's Cabin* (1852) increased tensions between the North and the South. Source: Will Kaufman, *The Civil War in American Culture* (Edinburgh: Edinburgh University Press, 2006, page 18).

In your report, give credit for the following:

- ideas, opinions, or theories presented by other writers
- facts or statistics that are not common knowledge
- direct quotations of spoken or written words
- paraphrases of spoken or written words

Notice that you must still provide a citation even if you paraphrase someone else's ideas. It is appropriate to give credit to someone else's thoughts, whether or not you use his or her exact words. In general, it is a good idea to provide more citations rather than risk not providing enough.

Works-Cited List (MLA Style)

A works-cited list must contain the following information:

- name of the author, editor, translator, or group responsible for the work
- title
- place and date of publication
- publisher

For print materials, the information required for a citation generally appears on the copyright and title pages of a work.

Sample Works-Cited List

Blue, Frederic J. *No Taint of Compromise: Crusaders in Antislavery Politics*. Louisiana: Louisiana State University Press, 2006 — Book

Samuel J. May Anti-Slavery Collection, 26 May, 2008 http://dlxs.library.cornell.edu/m/mayantislavery/collection.html — Web site

Roots of Resistance: A Story of the Underground Railroad, Dir. Orlando Bagwell. WGBH Boston, 1989 — Documentary

The Liberty Tree, Chicago: Z. Eastman, 1843 — Anonymous pamphlet

Parenthetical Citations (MLA Style)

A parenthetical citation appears in the body of your text and identifies the source at point of use. It refers the reader to an entry on your works-cited list. A parenthetical citation appears in parentheses. It identifies the source by the last name of the author, editor, or translator. It also gives a page reference, identifying the page of the source on which the information can be found.

Model: Parenthetical Citations

Although most of the anti-slavery pamphlets were expected to exist for only a short time, some rare examples have survived in carefully preserved collections. The founders of one large collection acknowledged the "great importance that the literature of the Anti-Slavery movement... be preserved and handed down..." (Samuel J. May Anti-Slavery Collection, "Collection Description") The variety of opinions reflected in this collection show that there were many divisions among the beliefs of abolitionists. (Blue, p. 1)

Manuscript Preparation

The final copy of your research report should be prepared according to your teacher's recommended style. Here are some common preferences:

- double-spaced lines
- 12-point type (Times New Roman or Courier is often requested.)
- italics to replace underscoring (for example, in titles of novels)
- one-inch margins on each side of the text

Student Model: Lauren Shepherd, Tupelo, MS

The Writing Style of Phillis Wheatley

In an era when African Americans were struggling to carve an identity for themselves, Phillis Wheatley emerged as the first truly significant black poet in American literature. Although many do not consider her to be an important writer, judged by today's values of originality, she persevered through the challenges of her social status to become not only a celebrated poet, but the starting point for the study of African American literature. In this paper, I will discuss her work as a whole and present a detailed analysis of one of her most famous poems, "To His Excellency General Washington."

Lauren clearly states her thesis in the opening paragraph.

Religious Message Wheatley was highly educated for her time and had read the classics as well as the best English poets (Miller, de Dwyer, Wood 48). She was deeply influenced by the work of the great English poet John Milton (1608–1674), who saw himself as a writer in the service of God. Like Milton, Wheatley expressed a constant awareness of "God, His Son, His beneficence and His Power." Almost every one of Wheatley's poems develops around a central theme of religious morality and sometimes has an "air of message from the pulpit" (Mason 15–17). One theme, Christian salvation, underlies nearly everything she wrote (Redding 10).

Lauren provides thorough support for the opinions she expresses in this passage.

Wheatley's religious messages are often conveyed through embellished Bible stories. In fact, a tradition within African American literature of augmenting biblical accounts with creative license and poetic flair can be traced directly to Wheatley. Both her poems "Goliath and Gath" and "Isaiah LXIII" add creative information to a foundation of biblical narrative.

Subheads add to the clarity and order of the essay.

African Influences In addition to the key role of Christian religious messages in Wheatley's work, many of her writings also exhibit a subtle presence of African traditions. For example, Wheatley uses solar imagery throughout her body of poems. Her frequent use of sun imagery in such poems as "A Hymn to the Morning" and "A Hymn to the Evening" suggest that her early religious training in Africa may have consisted of some kind of hierophantic—or sun—worship (Smith, Baechler, Litz 474). Wheatley usually uses such sun imagery as a metaphor for Christian revelation, thus connecting the two essential elements of her religious life.

Lauren provides factual support for an interesting literary analysis.

Also reminiscent of Wheatley's childhood in Africa is her constant interest in panegyric—or praise—poetry. In many of the cultures of Africa, poets were instructed that political praise constituted the very core of their responsibility as writers (Smith Baechler, Litz 476). In keeping with that tradition, the majority of Wheatley's works are directed towards politically and socially prominent individuals, such as George Whitehead, a famous English clergyman, and George Washington (Johnson 29).

Racial Consciousness Although many have ventured to say that Wheatley's "unquestioning embrace of New England and white cultures" prompted her to neglect the issue of slavery (Smith, Baechler, Litz 476), a closer examination of her poetry reveals that she was quite "race conscious" (Davis 192). She refers to herself on several occasions as "Africa's muse," and even uses her skin color and presumed low social status as a reference point for her religious message of salvation (Davis 192–193).

Neoclassical Style The majority of Wheatley's poems adhere to the established patterns of the neoclassical style. Neoclassicism was a widespread movement in the visual and literary arts that began in the 1700s and lasted until the 1840s and 1850s. Classical history and mythology provided much of the subject matter of Neoclassical works. The poetry of Homer, Virgil, and Ovid, and the plays of Aeschylus, Sophocles, and Euripides provided the bulk of classical sources. Neoclassical writers, such as Alexander Pope (1688–1744), stressed order, harmony, and restraint.

Like the Neoclassicists she admired, Wheatley's work was noted for an unfaltering preoccupation with regular rhyme and rhythm (Mason 14). Breaking out of her usual form on only six occasions, Wheatley most frequently wrote using the heroic couplet—two-line stanzas written in iambic pentameter—that Alexander Pope made so effective (Mason 20). Considering that she is labeled as a spontaneous poet who would write during bouts of inspiration, the general regularity of her meter is remarkable. The influence of the Neoclassical writers also shows in Wheatley's use of elevated language (Mason 16) and in her numerous classical and mythological allusions.

"To His Excellency General Washington" The poem "To His Excellency General Washington" serves as a good example of Wheatley's style. Troubled by poor health since her arrival in America in 1761, when she was only eight years old (Perkins et al. 272), Wheatley traveled from Boston to London in 1773 in hope that the sea air would improve her well-being. Upon her return to the rebellious colonies in 1774, she found the fighting in the Boston vicinity had escalated. Wheatley composed her poem to George Washington and crossed the battle lines to deliver it in person. Two years later, Wheatley received a letter from the general himself thanking her for her adulation but insisting that she had placed him on too high a pedestal. In April 1776, Thomas Paine published her poem, its accompanying note, and Washington's reply in Pennsylvania Magazine or American Monthly Museum (Sheeler 8–10).

Although Washington's response to Wheatley's poem was modest, Wheatley gives the reader clear insight as to her opinions of the man. The entire poem is devoted to the veneration of the Continental Army and the leadership of General Washington. Wheatley adheres to her favorite poetic form of heroic couplets. She does not merely revere Washington, she portrays him as a royal figure, referring to him as "Your Excellency," and ascribing to him "a crown, a mansion and a throne that shine."

The essay presents a variety of interpretations of the material.

Necessary background information is essential to the readers' understanding.

Lauren refers to other points of view regarding Wheatley's work.

The essay makes use of a variety of historical documents, including a primary source.

Wheatley resorts to a striking use of personification in the poem. In the opening lines, she mentions the sorrow of "mother earth" at the bloodshed ravaging the land. In line 15, she personifies heaven as a maiden with a "fair face." Her use of alliteration in that image adds to its effect. Wheatley also gives life to the "nations" in line 33 and describes Brittania as a defeated being who "droops the pensive head" (line 35).

Perhaps Wheatley's most notable use of personification lies in her image of the American colonies as the Goddess Columbia (line 9), who is a "native of the skies" (line 11). Wheatley created this new goddess in honor of Christopher Columbus. Later popularized by Revolutionary War poets such as Philip Freneau, the image of Columbia has its first appearance in Wheatley's poem (Jensen).

Wheatley also weaves various allusions into her poem. For example, the European countries in conflict with America are said to be "Gallic powers" (line 30). This allusion refers to the Gallic Wars at the time of Julius Caesar when France was called Gaul. Further evidence of her classical knowledge appears in the reference to "Aeolus," the God of the wind (line 15). Aeolus appeared in Homer's Odyssey (Tripp 24), which Wheatley read in Alexander Pope's famous translation. Wheatley scholars generally agree that Pope's translation of Homer greatly affected her poetry (Mason 16).

Although Phillis Wheatley never achieved a truly original poetic style, she is undoubtedly an important figure in American literature. She transcended racial and language barriers to occupy a significant position in the social and intellectual scene of both Boston and London. If one judges her work based on the impact of her poetry on her contemporaries, she is an important pioneer in the development of American literature.

Lauren concludes by restating her thesis.

Works Cited

Davis, Arthur P. "Personal Elements in the Poetry of Phillis Wheatley." *Phylon: The Atlanta University Review of Race and Culture.* 13 vols. June 1953, pp. 191–198.

Johnson, James Weldon., ed. *The Book of American Negro Poetry.* New York: Harcourt Brace Jovanovich Inc., 1922.

Mason, Julian D., Jr., ed. *The Poems of Phillis Wheatley.* North Carolina: The University of North Carolina Press, 1989.

Miller, James E., Jr., Carlota Cárdenas de Dwyer, and Kerry M. Wood. *The United States in Literature.* Illinois: Scott Foresman and Company, 1985.

Perkins, George, et al., eds. *The American Tradition in Literature.* 1 vol. New York: McGraw-Hill Publishing Company, 1990.

Redding, J. Saunders. *To Make a Poet Black.* New York: Cornell University Press, 1988.

Sheeler, Karissa L. Phillis Wheatley. 11 February 2000. <http://www.kutztown.edu/faculty/reagan/wheat1.html>

Smith, Valerie, Lea Baechler, and A. Walton Litz, eds. *African American Writers.* New York: Charles Scribner's Sons, 1991.

Tripp, Edward. *Cromwell's Handbook of Classical Mythology.* New York: Thomas Y. Cromwell Company, 1970.

A complete works-cited list provides information on the sources Lauren references in the report.

Editing and Proofreading

Writing

5. Develop and strengthen writing as needed by editing, focusing on addressing what is most significant for a specific purpose and audience.

Language

2. Demonstrate command of the conventions of standard English capitalization, punctuation, and spelling when writing.

2.b. Spell correctly.

Review your historical investigation report to eliminate errors in grammar, usage, punctuation, and spelling. Also, check that your report is neatly presented and legible.

Focus on accuracy. Consult your notes to be sure you have quoted material exactly. Check all dates and statistics.

Focus on capitalization and spelling. Make sure you have capitalized proper nouns correctly. Then, check your spelling. Follow this *spelling rule:* If an adjective ends in *-ent*, such as the word *expedient*, its parallel forms end in *-ence (expedience)* or *-ency (expediency)*.

Spiral Review: Conventions Earlier you learned that misplaced and dangling modifiers can be confusing (p. 585). Check your report to make sure you have not used any misplaced or dangling modifiers.

Publishing, Presenting, and Reflecting

Consider the following ways to share and think further about your writing.

Present an oral historical investigation report. Deliver your paper as an oral report. Incorporate visual aids and images to illustrate specific information. Provide classmates with a handout listing your sources.

Submit your paper for publication. Submit your paper to a magazine or Web site that publishes student writing or that covers your research topic.

Reflect on your writing. Jot down your thoughts on the experience of writing a historical investigation report. Begin by answering these questions: What strategies would you use again? How was conducting in-depth research on a topic different from other types of research you have done?

Rubric for Self-Assessment

Evaluate your research report using the following criteria and rating scale.

Criteria	Rating Scale *not very* — *very*
Purpose/Focus: How clearly does your thesis statement guide your report?	1 2 3 4
Organization: How logical and effective is the organization?	1 2 3 4
Development of Ideas/Elaboration: How well do you use a variety of primary and secondary sources to support your thesis?	1 2 3 4
Language: How clear is your writing and how precise is your word choice?	1 2 3 4
Conventions: According to an accepted format, how complete and accurate are your citations?	1 2 3 4

Speaking and Listening

Oral Interpretation of a Literary Work

An *oral interpretation* is a performance of a literary work that highlights its most important qualities as the performer sees, or interprets, them. Generally, oral interpretations do not use scenery or other theatrical effects. Instead, they call upon a performer's ability to analyze a literary work and present it meaningfully, using *tone, vocal inflection, pacing,* and *body language.*

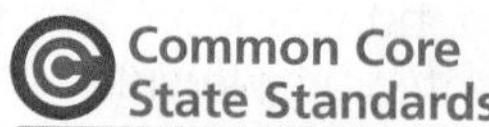

Reading Literature
7. Analyze multiple interpretations of a story, drama, or poem, evaluating how each version interprets the source text.

Writing
2. Write explanatory texts to examine and convey complex ideas, concepts, and information clearly and accurately through the effective selection, organization, and analysis of content.

Speaking and Listening
3. Evaluate a speaker's point of view, reasoning, and use of evidence and rhetoric, assessing the stance, premises, links among ideas, word choice, points of emphasis, and tone used.
4. Present information, findings, and supporting evidence, conveying a clear and distinct perspective, such that listeners can follow the line of reasoning, alternative or opposing perspectives are addressed, and the organization, development, substance, and style are appropriate to purpose, audience, and a range of formal and informal tasks.

Language
2. Demonstrate command of the conventions of standard English capitalization, punctuation, and spelling when writing.
5.a. Interpret figures of speech in context and analyze their role in the text.
5.b. Analyze nuances in the meaning of words with similar denotations.

Prepare an Analysis of a Literary Work

Analyze the literature. To prepare a compelling oral interpretation, start by reading, analyzing, and researching a work of literature. As you read, consider the *stylistic devices* and elements shown in the chart.

Literary Element	Description	How to Identify
Tone	the author's attitude	Determine if the author is serious, playful, or critical.
Language and Style	the manner in which ideas are expressed	Study the lengths and rhythm of sentences, details, repetition, and changes to pronunciation, spelling, or grammar.
Imagery	word pictures that appeal to the senses	Analyze descriptions of places, objects, settings, or experiences.
Theme	a work's central idea, message, or insight about life	Identify the author's purpose and note images or ideas that repeat.
Nuance and Ambiguity	literary elements that can be interpreted in multiple ways	Look for significant words, figurative language, symbols, changes in characters, and the variety of meanings they may have.

Read, analyze, and research. Read your selection closely and analyze how specific literary elements help develop significant ideas and meaning. Consider both denotative, or literal, meanings, and connotative meanings, or the associations or feelings that words suggest. Make sure to address any elements that are open to interpretation. Research the selection by reviewing other texts, such as critical essays, to support your ideas. Then, write a brief analytical essay detailing your findings. Incorporate *rhetorical strategies* into your writing, such as describing your first impressions of the text or recalling conversations you had with others about your selection. You will use this essay to introduce your oral interpretation.

Plan Your Interpretation

Focus on delivery techniques. Your oral interpretation should help listeners understand characters, follow shifts in plot, and hear changes in emotion. Consider how you will use the techniques shown in the graphic to add depth and drama to your interpretation.

Research other ways to enhance your performance by observing the body language and vocalization of an actor, poet, or other polished reader as he or she presents a literary work.

Mark up the selection. Make notes on your copy of the selection indicating how you will use your voice and movement to communicate your understanding of the work. Also, consider using music, images, or sound effects to enhance the artistry of your interpretation.

Practice. Plan *staging and performance details* as you rehearse in front of a mirror or record yourself. For example, consider when to move, use gestures, or include simple props. Then, practice for family or friends and apply their feedback to improve your presentation.

Vocalization

Reflect characters' speech patterns and *dialects*, and enunciate and project your voice.

Appropriate Eye Contact

Look at your listeners and make eye contact with people in the back as well as the front of the room.

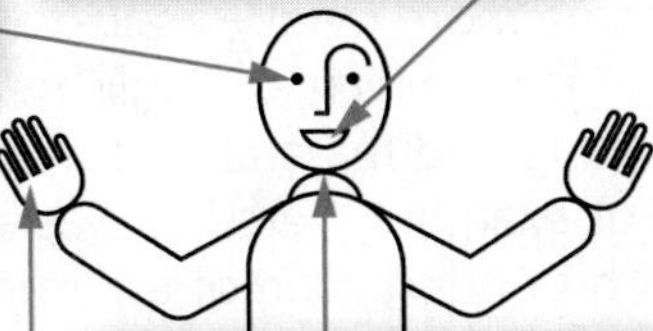

Voice Register

Make characters distinct by using the high, low, and middle tones in your voice.

Gesture/Movement

Use hand gestures and move around your stage to show actions in the work.

Activities: Deliver and Analyze Oral Interpretations

Comprehension and Collaboration For both activities, use an evaluation form like the one shown below.

A. Deliver your oral interpretation to your class. First, read your analytical essay—or a shorter, less formal version—to introduce the literary work. Then, deliver your interpretation. After your performance, apply feedback from listeners to improve your delivery.

B. With a small group, analyze a variety of interpretations of the same literary work. You may use audio or video recordings, your own interpretations, or a combination of the two. Analyze how each version interprets the source text.

Evaluation Form for Oral Interpretation
Title and Author of Literary Work: ______________________
How well does the speaker convey the main idea of the selection? ______________________
How well does the speaker use gestures? Give examples. ______________________
Comment on one effective use of voice. ______________________
How well does the speaker maintain eye contact with the audience? ______________________
What can the speaker improve? ______________________

Language Study

Words from Mythology and Religious Traditions

Language

4.a. Use context as a clue to the meaning of a word or phrase.

5. Demonstrate understanding of word relationships in word meanings.

6. Acquire and use accurately general academic and domain-specific words and phrases, sufficient for reading, writing, speaking, and listening at the college and career readiness level.

Many of the words in the English language have their origins in Greek or Roman mythology or the Bible. They entered the language during the Renaissance, a time when translations of classical and Biblical works became more readily available. Knowing the story behind the figure or event from which an English word developed will help you to infer its meaning and remember it more clearly.

For example, Hercules was an ancient Greek hero noted for his strength and his undertaking of enormous physical tasks. The word *herculean* derives from the qualities of this mythological hero, as seen in the sentence *"I was unable to face the herculean chore of cleaning my room."* Based on the story of Hercules, you can figure out that the job of cleaning the room is huge and challenging. The chart below provides information on the mythological or Biblical origins of some common words.

Word	Origin	Myth
jovial	Roman	**Jove,** the chief Roman god, was believed to be the source of happiness.
mentor	Greek	In Homer's *Odyssey,* the goddess Athena disguises herself as **Mentor,** a human male, and guides Telemachus while his father is away.
nemesis	Greek	**Nemesis** was the goddess who punished mortals for their crimes against the gods.
panic	Greek	**Pan** was the god of untamed nature. His sudden appearance and the sound of his music inspired fear.
scapegoat	Biblical	An **escape goat** was sent into the wilderness to carry away the sins of the people.
tantalize	Greek	**Tantalus,** punished for murdering his son, was surrounded by food and water that moved out of reach whenever he wanted them.

Practice

Directions: Refer to the chart above to complete the **analogies.** Then, write an explanation of the word relationships for each pairing.

1. jovial : happiness :: _______ : panic

a. dark **b.** run **c.** afraid **d.** wild

2. mentor : _______ :: nemesis : enemy

a. lead **b.** teacher **c.** friend **d.** student

Directions: Make a four-column chart tracing the origins of each word below. The column heads should read: "Word," "Meaning Today," "Origin," "Sample Sentence." Use a dictionary as necessary.

1. dire **2.** spartan **3.** nectar

Vocabulary Acquisition and Use: Context Clues

Sentence Completion questions appear in most standardized tests. They are designed to test your ability to understand what a word means from its *context*, or the way it is used in a text. In these types of questions, you are given sentences with one or more missing words. Your task is to choose the correct word or words to complete each sentence logically. Try using the following strategy: (1) Define each word in the answer options. (2) Identify clues to the meanings of words that are unfamiliar. For example, identify root words, prefixes, suffixes, or related words. (3) Test possible meanings by plugging them into the original sentence.

Practice

This exercise is modeled after the Sentence Completion exercises that appear in the Critical Reading section of the SAT.

Test-Taking Tip
Later questions in this section of the test are more difficult than earlier ones.

Directions: Each of the following sentences is missing one or two words. Choose the word or set of words that best completes each sentence.

1. The untrained soldiers, a loose _______ of men, heard a _______ and surged forward.

A. monopoly . . . tempest
B. aggregation . . . commotion
C. congregation . . . spy
D. regiment . . . bark
E. amalgamation . . . whisper

2. The officers in the tent rose in _______ when their commander entered.

A. insubordination
B. alarm
C. deference
D. condemnation
E. disgust

3. Many in the audience yawned as the _______ speaker droned on.

A. intrepid
B. prodigious
C. compelling
D. garrulous
E. fervent

4. The frowning judge _______ banged the gavel to _______ the lawyer's statement.

A. peremptorily . . . forestall
B. aggressively . . . permit
C. repeatedly . . . encourage
D. happily . . . punctuate
E. playfully . . . contradict

5. The philosopher cautioned that fame is a(n) _______ goal.

A. transporting
B. transparent
C. transient
D. transcendental
E. transitional

6. Before dying, the miserly loner made sure to write his own _______ .

A. epigram
B. epitaph
C. epigraph
D. epitome
E. epistle

Text Set Workshop

From Text to Understanding

You have studied each part of Unit 3 as a set of connected texts. In this workshop, you will have the chance to further explore the fundamental connections among these texts and to deepen your essential understanding of the literature and its social and historical context.

Common Core State Standards

Writing
7. Conduct short as well as more sustained research projects to answer a question (including a self-generated question) or solve a problem; narrow or broaden the inquiry when appropriate; synthesize multiple sources on that subject, demonstrating understanding of the subject under investigation.
9. Draw evidence from literary or informational texts to support analysis, reflection, and research.

Speaking and Listening
1. Initiate and participate effectively in a range of collaborative discussions (one-on-one, in groups, and teacher-led) with diverse partners on *grades 11-12 topics, texts, and issues,* building on others' ideas and expressing their own clearly and persuasively.

PART 1: A Nation Divided

Writing: Argumentative Essay Primary sources, such as diaries, journals, and speeches, give readers a first-hand glimpse of life in the past. Works written as literary art also shed light on people's sense of identity and culture, but the effect is generally more intentional than that of a primary source. The Anchor Text of Part 1, the excerpt from Frederick Douglass's *My Bondage and My Freedom* can be seen as a primary source as well as a work of literature.

Review the primary sources and the literature in Part 1, and consider what each selection teaches about the Civil War era. Note differences and similarities between the various primary sources and the unit's literary works.

Assignment: Take a position on whether Frederick Douglass's *My Bondage and My Freedom* is more accurately categorized as a primary source or a work of literature.

Writing Checklist

- ☐ Sustained and logical structure
- ☐ Clear claim
- ☐ Present counterclaim
- ☐ Plentiful support

Gather information in stages. Gathering the information you need to determine your claim will require four steps.

First, list the significant differences between a primary source and a literary work. Conduct research to help develop these lists.

Next, review the various primary source selections and note the various ways in which they reveal information to readers.

Then, review the story "An Occurrence at Owl Creek Bridge." Consider how its style and structure affects readers.

Finally, carefully reread "My Bondage and My Freedom." Determine how it conveys its information to readers. Take notes.

State your claim. Decide whether you will claim that "My Bondage and My Freedom" is essentially a primary source or a work of literature.

Structure your argument. Defend your claim, using examples from texts. Remember to address possible counterclaims. Refer to your lists as well as to your notes. Show your reasoning fully in your writing.

Fine-tune your word choice. As you write, experiment with academic vocabulary. Using precise words, such as *authentic, purpose, stylistic* and *implicit* can help convey your meaning with accuracy.

PART 2: Forging New Frontiers

Argument: Editorial on Westward Expansion The idea of destiny, at a personal and national level, is woven throughout the selections in Part 2. People followed their personal dreams and helped build a nation along the way. Americans often took great risks as they explored the Mississippi, delved into the Yukon, and settled the West. Yet, there is an ethical question regarding Westward Expansion: Did settlers have a right to lay claim to lands?

Review the background materials and selections in Part 2, especially the Anchor Texts, "Heading West" by Miriam Davis Colt and "I Will Fight No More Forever" by Chief Joseph. Consider the two sides of the issue of Westward Expansion.

Assignment: Take a side on the ethics of Westward Expansion and write an editorial presenting your argument. Imagine that you are writing for a newspaper of the mid-1800s. Research to find information to support your claim. Look for primary sources as well as secondary sources. Maintain a formal tone in your writing. Remember to create a Works Cited list to submit with your editorial.

Research and Writing Plan

- ☐ **Choose your position on the issue.** Determine which side you wish to defend.
- ☐ **Research.** Look for valid primary and secondary sources to support your argument, as well as to defend against counterclaims.
- ☐ **Create historical context.** Give your editorial the feel of the time period with accurate references and authentic diction.
- ☐ **Use rhetorical devices.** If appropriate to your argument, use devices such as rhetorical questions or analogies to strengthen your editorial.
- ☐ **Cite sources.** On a separate piece of paper, list and provide information about sources you consulted.

PART 3: Living in a Changing World

Listening and Speaking: Conversation The selections in Part 3 are filled with characters making transitions in their lives or reflecting on what their lives have been. Review these works, especially the Anchor Text, "The Story of an Hour" by Kate Chopin. How do these characters feel about their choices and experiences? How would they define happiness?

Assignment: Work with a partner to prepare a conversation between two characters from these works. For example, what might Mrs. Mallard and Aunt Georgiana have to say to each other? You and your partner should each write the rest of their stories, the inner feelings and opinions that readers do not see. The characters should introduce themselves to each other, so use the background information and other secondary sources, if necessary, to develop the characters' presentation of their circumstances. Then, talk with and listen to your partner as you share information about your characters.

Use the Research Guide shown here to help you as you create your conversation.

Research Guide

Historical and cultural context for character: ______________________

____

Details about character's life: ______________________

____

What character thinks about his or her life: ______________________

____

Test-Taking Practice

Reading Test: Humanities Passage

Humanities passages are one type of reading selection found on standardized tests. These passages may be excerpts from essays, biographies, or memoirs and address diverse topics including the arts, philosophy, and literary criticism. Questions may focus on main ideas and supporting details, the author's tone and style, or on the meanings of particular words or sentences. Some questions may require you to make generalizations or think about causes and effects.

 **Common Core State Standards**

RL.11-12.3, RL.11-12.5, RL.11-12.6; RI.11-12.1, RI.11-12.4, RI.11-12.6; L.11-12.1, L.11-12.2, L.11-12.3, L.11-12.4.a.

[For the full wording of the standards, see the standards chart in the front of your textbook.]

Practice

The following exercise is modeled after the ACT Reading Test, Humanities section. The full test has 40 questions.

Directions: Read the following passage from Frederick Douglass's *My Bondage and My Freedom*. Then, choose the *best* answer to each question.

Strategy

- Look for words and phrases that convey the author's attitude toward the subject. Such words may be clues to nuances in the author's intended meaning or point of view.

Passage 1

It is easy to see, that, in entering upon the duties of a slaveholder, some little experience is needed. Nature has done almost nothing to prepare men and women to be either slaves or slaveholders. Nothing but rigid training, long persisted in, can perfect the character of the one or the other. One cannot easily forget to love freedom; and it is as hard to cease to respect that natural love in our fellow creatures. On entering upon the career of slaveholding mistress, Mrs. Auld was singularly deficient; nature, which fits nobody for such an office, had done less for her than any lady I had known. It was no easy matter to induce her to think and to feel that the curly-headed boy, who stood by her side, and even leaned on her lap; who was loved by little Tommy, and who loved little Tommy in turn; sustained to her only the relation of a chattel. I was *more* than that, and she felt me to be more than that. I could talk and sing; I could laugh and weep; I could reason and remember; I could love and hate. I was human, and she, dear lady, knew and felt me to be so. How could she, then, treat me as a brute, without a mighty struggle with all the noble powers of her own soul. That struggle came, and the will and power of the husband was victorious. Her noble soul was overthrown; but, he that overthrew it did not, himself, escape the consequences. He, not less than the other parties, was injured in his domestic peace by the fall.

1. Which of the following statements best summarizes lines 1–6?
   - **A.** Human history has a long record of slavery.
   - **B.** Slavery is an unnatural condition for both owner and slave.
   - **C.** Slaveholders who treat slaves kindly have been taught to do so.
   - **D.** Slaveholders are uncaring, cruel people.

2. In the context of lines 1–9, it can reasonably be inferred that *singularly* means:
   - **F.** alone.
   - **G.** on one occasion.
   - **H.** notably.
   - **J.** lonely.

3. Which best explains what Douglass means by calling Mrs. Auld "deficient" (line 8)?
   - **A.** She suffered from a disability.
   - **B.** She lacked financial resources.
   - **C.** She wasted few resources when running the home.
   - **D.** She lacked a certain characteristic.

4. In the context of the passage, it can reasonably be inferred that "little Tommy" (lines 11 and 12) is:
   - **F.** Mrs. Auld's favorite pet.
   - **G.** Mrs. Auld's child.
   - **H.** a slave like Douglass.
   - **J.** a neighbor.

5. Which best describes Douglass's overall opinion of Mrs. Auld?
   - **A.** She was a kindly woman with a generous nature.
   - **B.** She was a stiff and uncompromising person.
   - **C.** She stood up to her husband, defying him.
   - **D.** She was difficult to live with due to wild mood swings.

6. In the context of the first part of the passage, it can reasonably be inferred that *chattel* (line 12) means:
   - **F.** a lowly creature.
   - **G.** a kind of house.
   - **H.** constant talking.
   - **J.** a piece of property.

7. The ideas expressed in lines 9 through 15 can best be described as:
   - **A.** Douglass's view of his own situation at the time.
   - **B.** what Douglas came to believe as an adult.
   - **C.** Mrs. Auld's rationale for treating Douglass well.
   - **D.** the general attitude of Southerners toward slaves.

8. In the context of lines 9–21, it can reasonably be inferred that:
   - **F.** Mrs. Auld's treatment of Douglass changed.
   - **G.** Mr. Auld was convinced to be kind to Douglass as well.
   - **H.** Douglass ran away from the home.
   - **J.** Mrs. Auld suffered a nervous breakdown.

9. In the context of lines 18–21, which best describes Mr. Auld's "injury"?
   - **A.** He was struck in the head by a falling object.
   - **B.** The tranquility of his home was shattered.
   - **C.** His wife turned against him.
   - **D.** All his slaves revolted against him.

10. Which of the following statements best describes the structure of the passage?
    - **F.** It begins with an arresting anecdote and then draws general principles from that incident.
    - **G.** It contains several general arguments and supporting details to substantiate each one.
    - **H.** It opens with a generalization that helps explain the events that follow.
    - **J.** It follows a chronological structure and ends with a surprising twist.

Grammar and Writing: Editing in Context

Editing-in-context segments test your understanding of grammar and sentence structure. You may be presented with a reading passage that has numbered sentences, some of which contain errors in grammar, style, or usage. Your task is to choose the best way to correct each sentence.

Practice

The exercise is modeled after the ACT English Test, which usually has 75 questions.

Directions: For each underlined sentence or portion of a sentence, choose the best alternative. If an item asks a question about the underlined portion, choose the best answer to the question.

Strategy

Narrow the answer options.

Make your task simpler by eliminating any answers you know to be incorrect.

[1]

Lincoln begins the Second Inaugural Address formally but he (1) ends with an eloquent plea for reconciliation. In the opening paragraph (2), his use of the passive voice and refusal even to identify himself as an actor in the inaugural drama give the passage a stiff formality. This (3) matches his understated message, which is that he has nothing to say about the previous four years that he hasn't (4) said already.

[2]

When he begins (5) discussing slavery, though, Lincoln injects a moral seriousness into the address that is reinforced by his growing eloquence. Speculated (6) that the war might be divine retribution for decades of suffering endured by enslaved African Americans his speech (7) uses language and rhythms that deepen the impact of his message. Then the opening words of his final paragraph suggest a vision of reconciliation made memorable by his cadences—"With malice toward none; with charity for all" (8)—and the contrasting absolutes of "none" and "all." Lincoln concludes by expressing his sense of mission for the remainder of the war—"to bind up the nation's wounds" and to "achieve a just and lasting peace, among ourselves, and with all nations."

SAT® PREP ACT

1. A. NO CHANGE
   B. formally, but
   C. formally; but,
   D. formally. But

2. What is the function of this phrase?
   F. independent clause
   G. adverbial prepositional phrase
   H. adverbial dependent clause
   J. adjectival phrase

3. A. NO CHANGE
   B. This strategy
   C. This passive construction
   D. This formality

4. F. NO CHANGE
   G. has not
   H. have not
   J. hadn't

5. While reviewing Paragraph 2, the author considers deleting these two words. If the writer were to do so, the sentence would lose:
   A. the idea that the eloquence starts with the discussion of slavery.
   B. the idea that Lincoln views slavery as a moral evil.
   C. the idea that Lincoln delayed discussing slavery for much of the speech.
   D. nothing; they should be deleted.

6. F. NO CHANGE
   G. Speculating
   H. Lincoln speculated
   J. Asserted

7. A. NO CHANGE
   B. his speeches
   C. he speaks
   D. Lincoln

8. In reviewing the draft, the author considers moving this phrase to follow "his final paragraph" in the preceding line. If the writer were to do so, the effect would be:
   F. to misquote Lincoln and distort his meaning.
   G. to gain clarity about which phrases the author has in mind.
   H. to lose the author's emphasis on the rhythm of the phrases.
   J. to underscore Lincoln's moral message.

 Timed Writing: Position Statement [30 minutes]

The Civil War was the first war that people were able to witness through photographs. Some might say that images of war are important because they convey much more than words alone. Others might hold that showing pain and destruction is coldhearted and disrespectful to the victims.

Write an essay in which you express and support an opinion on this question. Whichever side you take, cite specific reasons and examples to support your position. This exercise is similar to the optional ACT Writing Test.

Academic Vocabulary

To "express and support an opinion" you must first decide **what** you think, and then tell **why** you think it.

Constructed Response

Follow the instructions to complete the tasks below as required by your teacher. As you work on each task, incorporate both general academic vocabulary and literary terms you learned in this unit.

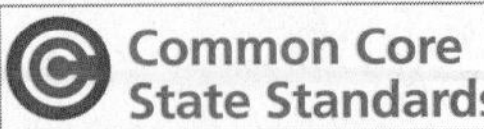

RL.11-12.3, RL.11-12.6, RL.11-12.9; RI.11-12.1, RI.11-12.4, RI.11-12.6, RI.11-12.9; W.11-12.2, W.11-12.9.a, W.11-12.9.b; SL.11-12.1, SL.11-12.4, SL.11-12.6

[For the full wording of the standards, see the standards chart in the front of your textbook.]

Writing

Task 1: Literature [RL.11-12.3; W.11-12.2]

Analyze Characterization in a Story

*Write an **essay** in which you analyze the character development in a story from this unit.*

- Choose a story from this unit with memorable characters.
- Describe one of the main characters. Then, provide at least two examples of indirect and at least two examples of direct characterization from the story to support your description.
- Identify the setting and point of view of the story. Analyze the role each of these choices plays in influencing the development of the main character you chose.
- Describe how the story's plot events influence the main character's development.
- Conclude by briefly restating the impression that the main character creates for the reader and evaluating which story element (setting, point of view, or plot) has the greatest influence in creating that impression.

Task 2: Literature/Informational Text [RL.11-12.4; RI.11-12.4; W.11-12.2]

Analyze Word Choice

*Write an **essay** in which you analyze the meaning and impact of the word choices in a work of fiction or nonfiction from this unit.*

- Choose a work from this unit in which the writer uses a variety of interesting word choices.
- Choose particular passages in the work in order to highlight ones that you find especially effective.
- Analyze word choice by interpreting the meaning of key language in each passage and explaining why it is effective.
- Distinguish between literal meanings and figurative and connotative meanings in each passage you choose. Explain how figurative and connotative meanings add to the power of the passage and the overall work.
- Conclude by explaining how the word choice creates a tone and meaning that is appropriate to the author's audience and purpose.

Task 3: Informational Text [RI.11-12.5; W.11-12.2]

Analyze and Evaluate Text Structure

*Write an **essay** in which you analyze and evaluate the effectiveness of the structure of a work of literary nonfiction from this unit.*

- Choose a work of literary nonfiction from this unit that has a clear organizational structure.
- Identify and analyze the structure of the author's argument. For example, does the author use cause and effect, comparison and contrast, or main idea and details?
- Evaluate the effectiveness of the structure for conveying the author's main argument. Assess whether the structure makes individual points clear and helps make the overall argument convincing.
- Support your analysis with examples from the work.
- Organize your ideas logically, using transitional words, phrases, and clauses to clearly show the link between ideas.

Speaking and Listening

Task 4: Literature/Informational Text [RL.11-12.6; RI.11-12.6; SL.11-12.1]

Analyze Irony

Hold a ***panel discussion*** *in which you analyze various authors' use of irony in works from this unit.*

- Identify all works from this unit in which irony features prominently.
- As a group, discuss why each selection you choose is ironic and identify the type of irony it represents.
- Evaluate what the author's use of irony adds to the theme or meaning of each selection.
- Finally, compare a single author's use of irony in one selection with another author's use of irony in a work from the same unit or in something else you have read or seen.
- Make sure that each person on the panel gets an opportunity to speak. Allow time for follow-up questions and debate, and try to build on each other's ideas to reach a final consensus.

Task 5: Informational Text [RI.11-12.9; SL.11-12.4]

Evaluate a Work of Nonfiction and Two Foundational Documents

Deliver an ***oral presentation*** *in which you assess whether the social injustices described by Frederick Douglass in the excerpt from* My Bondage and My Freedom *were addressed by the Emancipation Proclamation and the Fourteenth Amendment.*

- Review the excerpt from *My Bondage and My Freedom.* Identify the individual injustices that Douglass describes in the excerpt.
- Find the texts of the Emancipation Proclamation and the Fourteenth Amendment online or in print.
- Analyze and compare the purposes, themes, and language of the autobiographical account and the two historical documents.
- Assess the two documents to determine whether they address Douglass's grievances completely, partially, or not at all.
- Organize and present your findings logically, so your audience can easily follow your reasoning.

Task 6: Literature [RL.11-12.3, RL.11-12.6; SL.11-12.4]

Identify and Analyze Point of View

Deliver an ***oral presentation*** *in which you identify and analyze the point of view in a work of fiction from this unit.*

- Choose a story that effectively uses point of view.
- Identify point of view by describing whether a story is written from a first- or third-person and limited or omniscient perspective. Explain to your audience how you made this determination.
- Analyze the impact of the author's choice of point of view on the story. Do this by relating point of view to other elements in the story, such as character development or plot, and to the use of devices such as irony or understatement.
- Present your ideas in a way that makes them easy for listeners to follow.

What makes American literature American?

Primary Sources and Fiction Primary sources, such as journals and speeches, speak to readers with great immediacy, even centuries after they were written. They help us understand how people experienced life in the past. Short stories and poems also shed light on people's sense of identity and aspects of their culture at a particular time in history, but their effect is often different from that of a primary source.

Assignment Choose one primary source and one work of fiction from this unit. Write a **compare-and-contrast essay** about how the two works add to your understanding of American identity during the Civil War era.

Titles for Extended Reading

In this unit, you have read a variety of literature of the Civil War and Frontier eras. Continue to read works related to these eras on your own. Select books that you enjoy, but challenge yourself to explore new topics, new authors, and works offering varied perspectives or approaches. The titles suggested below will help you get started.

LITERATURE

The Adventures of Huckleberry Finn
Mark Twain

Novel Set in pre-Civil War Missouri, this influential novel describes the adventures of two runaways on a raft on the Mississippi River—Huck Finn, who is escaping his abusive father, and Jim, a slave hoping to gain his freedom.

[Works by Twain begin on page 570 of this book. Build knowledge by reading a novel by this author.]

My Ántonia
Willa Cather

Novel The story of Ántonia, a self-reliant, spirited young woman growing up on the Nebraska frontier, is told by her friend and confidant, Jim Burden. *My Ántonia* chronicles their friendship and reveals both the beauty and hardship of frontier life.

[Cather's "A Wagner Matinée" appears on page 652 of this book. Build knowledge by reading a novel by this author.]

Spoon River Anthology
Edgar Lee Masters

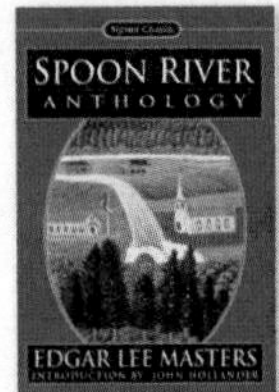

Poetry The former residents of an Illinois town, now long dead, tell the stories of their lives from the graveyard in which they lie.

[On pages 646 and 647, you'll find "Lucinda Matlock" and "Richard Bone," two of the poems from Spoon River Anthology. *Build knowledge by reading the complete anthology.]*

INFORMATIONAL TEXTS

Historical Texts

The Classic Slave Narratives
edited by Henry Louis Gates, Jr.

Autobiographical Narrative This book presents the accounts of two men and two women who had been enslaved and describes their extraordinary experiences, ranging from surviving the dangerous Atlantic Crossing to enduring the brutal, and often short, life of a slave in the Caribbean colonies and in America.

Narrative of the Life of Frederick Douglass
Frederick Douglass

Autobiographical Narrative Born into slavery, Frederick Douglass escaped to become an abolitionist leader as well as a gifted writer and orator. This narrative describes the cruelty of slavery and gives a powerful voice to a disenfranchised people.

[An excerpt from My Bondage and My Freedom *appears on page 520 of this book. Build knowledge by reading Douglass's autobiographical narrative.]*

The American Reader: Words That Moved a Nation
edited by Diane Ravitch
HarperCollins, 1990

EXEMPLAR TEXT

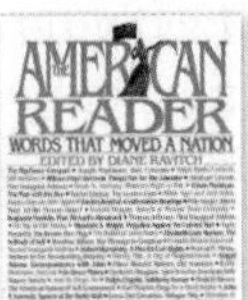

Prose and Poetry This collection of prose and poetry by famous and ordinary Americans from different socioeconomic and racial backgrounds provides the reader with a rich view of American culture and history.

Contemporary Scholarship

Empire Express: Building the First Transcontinental Railroad
David Haward Bain

History On May 10, 1868, the last spike was driven to complete the transcontinental railroad. *Empire Express* describes the race to complete the railroad and presents a fresh view of the history and impact of this engineering triumph.

What They Fought For 1861–1865
James McPherson
Anchor Books, 1995

EXEMPLAR TEXT

History Scholar James McPherson investigates what motivated Civil War soldiers to fight, based on their letters and journals. Through the voices of these long-dead soldiers, McPherson gives readers a strong sense of the intense passions and ideological conflicts of the time.

Preparing to Read Complex Texts

Reading for College and Career In both college and the workplace, readers must analyze texts independently, draw connections among works that offer varied perspectives, and develop their own ideas and informed opinions. The questions shown below, and others that you generate on your own, will help you more effectively read and analyze complex college-level texts.

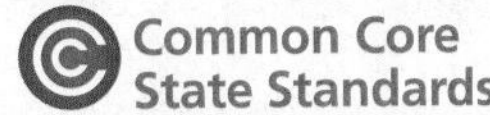

Reading Literature/Informational Text
10. By the end of grade 11, read and comprehend literature, including stories, dramas, and poems, and literary nonfiction, in the grades 11-CCR text complexity band proficiently, with scaffolding as needed at the high end of the range.

When reading analytically, ask yourself...

- What idea, experience, or story seems to have compelled the author to write? Has the author presented that idea, experience, or story in a way that I, too, find compelling?
- How might the author's era, social status, belief system, or personal experiences have affected the point of view he or she expresses in the text?
- How do my circumstances affect what I understand and feel about this text?
- What key idea does the author state explicitly? What key idea does he or she suggest or imply? Which details in the text help me to perceive implied ideas?
- Do I find multiple layers of meaning in the text? If so, what relationships do I see among these layers of meaning?
- How do details in the text connect or relate to one another? Do I find any details unconvincing, unrelated, or out of place?
- Do I find the text believable and convincing?

Key Ideas and Details

- What patterns of organization or sequences do I find in the text? Do these patterns help me understand the ideas better?
- What do I notice about the author's style, including his or her diction, use of imagery and figurative language, and syntax?
- Do I like the author's style? Is the author's style memorable?
- What emotional attitude does the author express toward the topic, the story, or the characters? Does this attitude seem appropriate?
- What emotional attitude does the author express toward me, the reader? Does this attitude seem appropriate?
- What do I notice about the author's voice—his or her personality on the page? Do I like this voice? Does it make me want to read on?

Craft and Structure

- Is the work fresh and original?
- Do I agree with the author's ideas entirely, or are there elements I find unconvincing?
- Do I disagree with the author's ideas entirely, or are there elements I can accept as true?
- Based on my knowledge of American literature, history, and culture, does this work reflect the American tradition? Why or why not?

Disillusion, Defiance, and Discontent

Literature of the Modern Age 1914–1945

"We asked the cyclone to go around our barn but it didn't hear us."

— Carl Sandburg, from *The People, Yes*

Unit 4

PART 1 TEXT SET

FACING TROUBLED TIMES

PART 2 TEXT SET

FROM EVERY CORNER OF THE LAND

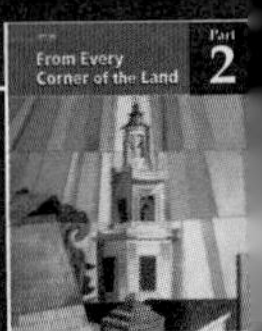

PART 3 TEXT SET

THE HARLEM RENAISSANCE

CLOSE READING TOOL

Use this tool to practice the close reading strategies you learn.

ONLINE WRITER'S NOTEBOOK

Easily capture notes and complete assignments online.

STUDENT eTEXT

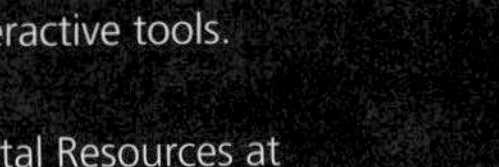

Bring learning to life with audio, video, and interactive tools.

■ Find all Digital Resources at **pearsonrealize.com**.

Snapshot of the Period

The America that entered the twentieth century was a nation achieving world dominance while simultaneously losing some of its youthful innocence. Two world wars, a dizzying decade of prosperity, and a devastating worldwide depression marked this era. With these events came a new age in literature. The upheavals of the early twentieth century ushered in a period of literary boldness and lasting achievement. Many of the monumental figures of American literature, including F. Scott Fitzgerald (shown with his wife, Zelda, at right), William Faulkner, and Ernest Hemingway, rose to prominence during this period. Simultaneously, the movie industry grew from a fledgling experiment into a commercial powerhouse.

In 1919, the 18th Amendment established Prohibition in the United States. The Amendment was repealed in 1933. ▶

Fitzgerald

Hemingway

Faulkner

Porter

Hughes

Hurston

As you read the selections in this unit, you will be asked to think about them in view of three key questions:

What is the **relationship** between literature and *place?*

How does **literature** shape or reflect *society?*

What makes **American** literature *American?*

World Conflicts

Military Deaths

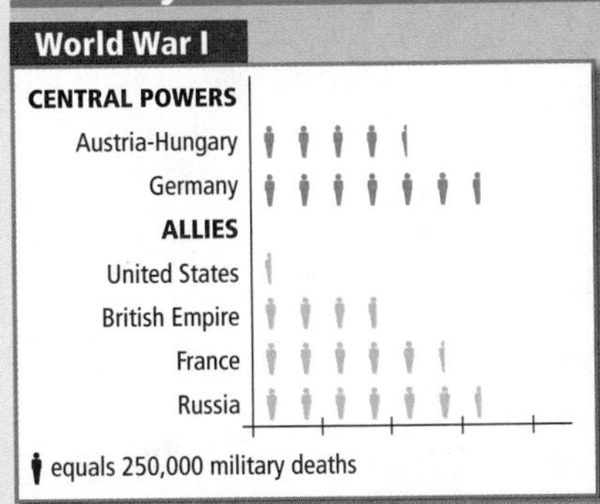

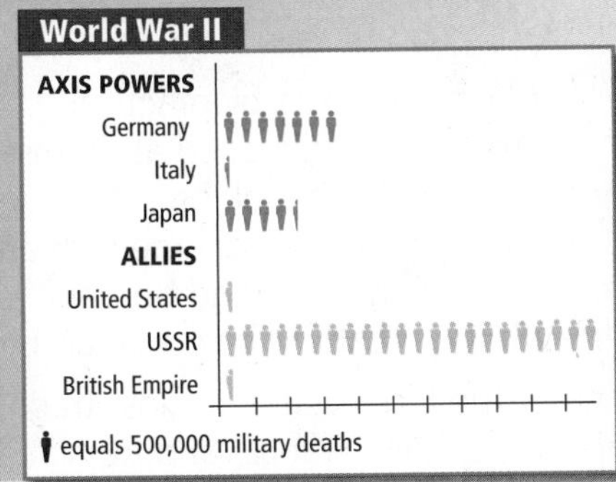

The Great Depression

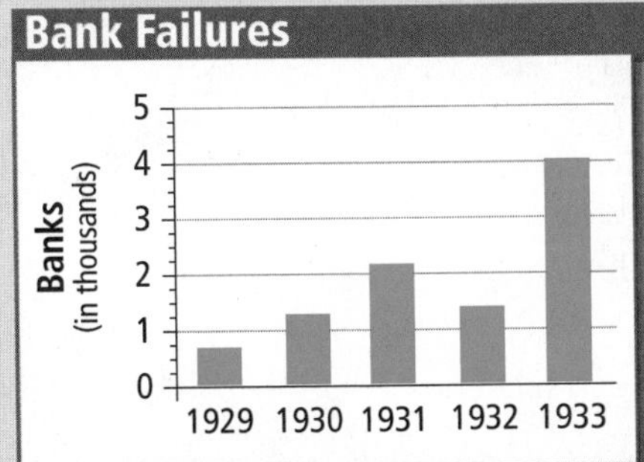

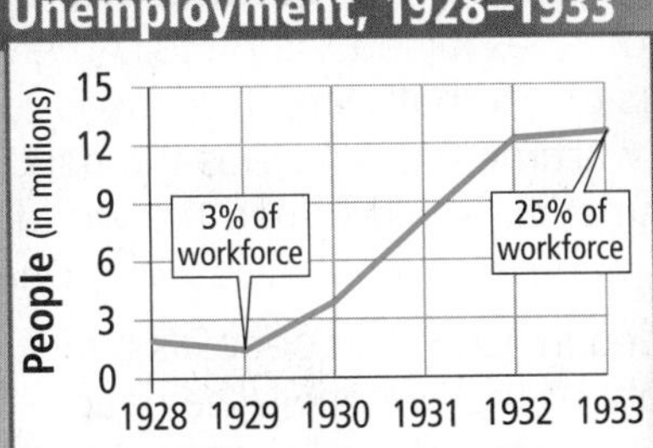

The Movie Industry

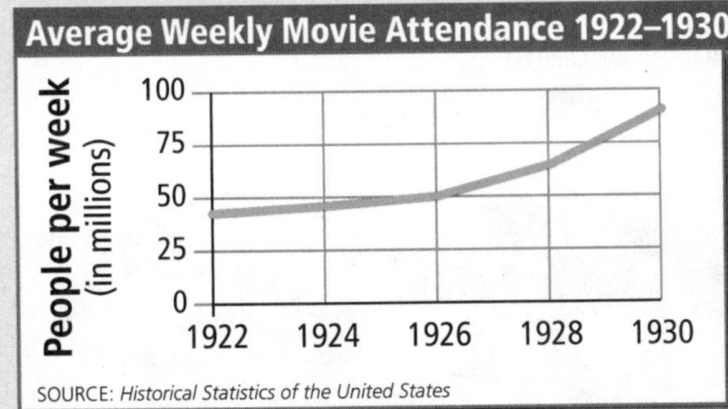

Integration of Knowledge and Ideas Review the data in the top four graphs against the information on movie attendance in the bottom chart. Based on this combination of data, what inferences can you draw about the role movies play in American society, especially during hard times? **[Connect]**

Historical Background

The Modern Age (1914–1945)

The years immediately before World War I were marked by practical optimism. Americans believed they had grown up and looked at themselves realistically. Technological know-how made the future look bright. Social problems could be solved. However, World War I shattered American and European values. The war not only remade governments and borders, it made people all over the world rethink what it meant to be a human being.

The Great War World War I was one of the bloodiest and most tragic conflicts ever to occur. The Allies (primarily Britain, France, and Russia) halted the German advances, but both sides dug trenches and brought the war to a standstill. Machine guns made it impossible to overrun the opponent. Almost an entire generation of European men wasted away.

President Woodrow Wilson tried to remain neutral, but that proved impossible. Eventually, unrelenting German submarine attacks swayed public opinion, and in 1917 the United States joined the Allies. American confidence passed quickly. The horrors of combat were unspeakable, intensified by new technology put to wartime use. This was the dark side of the Modern Age: Europeans and Americans had turned the world into a wasteland. As one soldier/poet put it, "I Have a Rendezvous with Death."

The Roaring Twenties The war ended in 1918, but people's minds and hearts were not at peace. Throughout the Twenties, the nation seemed to go on a binge. The economy boomed, and skyscrapers rose. Prohibition made the sale of liquor illegal, leading to bootlegging and the rise of organized crime. Radio arrived, and so did jazz. Movies became big business, and fads abounded: raccoon coats, flagpole sitting, a dance called the Charleston. People let go as prewar values and attitudes were thrown to the winds. The "roar" of the Roaring Twenties tried to drown out the remembered sound of exploding bombs and the horror of death.

TIMELINE

1914

1914: World War I begins.

1915: Olympic track and field champion Jim Thorpe begins his professional football career. ▶

◀ **1915: England** Because of the war in Europe, travelers are cautioned against transatlantic voyages. The *Lusitania* would be sunk despite these warnings.

"All the News That's Fit to Print."

The New York Times. EXTRA 5:30 A.M.

LUSITANIA SUNK BY A SUBMARINE, PROBABLY 1,260 DEAD; TWICE TORPEDOED OFF IRISH COAST; SINKS IN 15 MINUTES; CAPT. TURNER SAVED, FROHMAN AND VANDERBILT MISSING; WASHINGTON BELIEVES THAT A GRAVE CRISIS IS AT HAND

SHOCKS THE PRESIDENT

Washington Deeply Stirred by the Loss of American Lives.

SOME DEAD TAKEN ASHORE

Several Hundred Survivors at Queenstown and Kinsale.

NOTICE!

TRAVELLERS intending to embark on the Atlantic voyage are reminded that a state of war exists between Germany and her allies and Great Britain and her allies; that the zone of war includes the

1916: *Chicago Poems* by Carl Sandburg appears.

1917: Russia Bolsheviks seize control of Russia in October Revolution.

The Great Depression The boom, of course, could not last. In October 1929, the stock market crashed, spurring the Great Depression. By mid-1932, about 12 million Americans—one quarter of the work force—were out of work. Bread lines formed and soup kitchens opened. Depression became more than an economic fact; it became a national state of mind.

The New Deal In the presidential election of 1932, New York's governor Franklin D. Roosevelt defeated president Herbert Hoover. Roosevelt initiated the New Deal, a package of major economic reforms, to strengthen the economy. People found work on huge public projects, such as building dams and bridges. Roosevelt's leadership and policies helped end the Depression and earned him reelection in 1936, 1940, and 1944.

World War II Only twenty years after the end of World War I, the German invasion of Poland ignited World War II. Even after the fall of France in 1940, the dominant mood in the United States was one of isolationism, with most Americans preferring to stay out of the conflict. However, when the Japanese attacked Pearl Harbor, Hawaii, on December 7, 1941, isolationism and neutrality came to a swift end. The United States declared war on the Axis powers—Germany, Japan, and Italy.

After years of bitter fighting in Europe and in the Pacific, the Allies, which included the United States, Great Britain, France, and the Soviet Union, defeated Nazi Germany. Japan surrendered three months later, after the United States dropped atomic bombs on the cities of Hiroshima and Nagasaki. Peace, and the Atomic Age, had arrived.

Key Historical Theme: War and Its Aftermath

- After the shock of World War I, Americans left behind many of the optimistic attitudes and humane values of the prewar world.
- During the Roaring Twenties, Americans gave way to self-indulgence; during the Thirties, they endured intense economic hardship.
- World War II ushered in the Atomic Age.

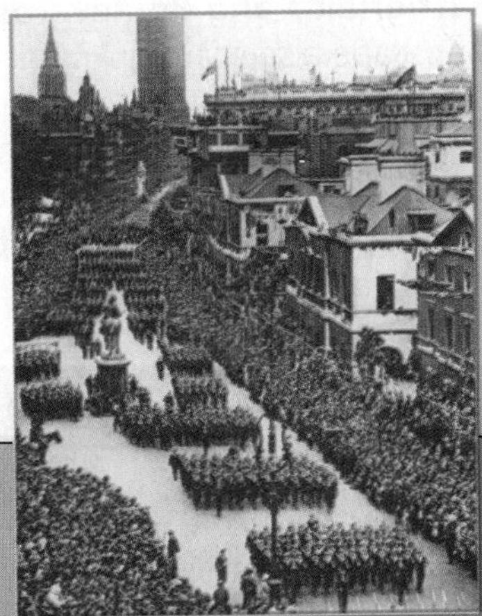

1918: Worldwide influenza epidemic kills as many as 20 million people.

1919: **France** Treaty of Versailles ends World War I. ▶

1921

◀ 1918: President Wilson announces his Fourteen Points in peace plan.

1919: Prohibition becomes law; repealed in 1933.

◀ 1920: Nineteenth Amendment to Constitution gives American women the right to vote.

Essential Questions Across Time

The Modern Age (1914–1945)

What is the **relationship** between literature and *place?*

What American places especially affected American life in the first half of the twentieth century?

Cities Immigration, land development, and technological advances in telephones, building materials, power generators, and cars turned towns into cities and cities into metropolises. Big business thrived and the Twenties "roared" on city streets and in downtown hotspots. However, city life also came to mean crowding, poverty, crime, racism, and anonymity.

Towns and Farms Small-town America changed too, especially after World War I. A popular 1919 song asked, "How you gonna keep 'em down on the farm, after they've seen Paree?" Town populations shrank, and many traditions became the subjects of nostalgia. Farmers suffered terribly in the 1930s when severe drought turned the Great Plains into the Dust Bowl.

What non-American places especially affected American life in the first half of the twentieth century?

Battlefields and Boulevards The trenches that scarred Europe's landscape also scarred Americans' minds, undercutting cherished beliefs, such as the nobility of Western culture. On the other hand, the artistic life that flourished in the studios and cafes of Paris pushed Americans into the Modern Age. The battlefields of World War II, including Hiroshima, would leave their indelible marks on both the American psyche and its politics.

ESSENTIAL QUESTION VOCABULARY

These Essential Question words will help you think and write about literature and place.

development (di vel′ əp mənt) *n.* building up or expansion

metropolis (mə träp′ ə lis) *n.* large city

anonymity (an′ ə nim′ ə tē) *n.* condition of lacking individuality or identity

TIMELINE

1921

◀ 1922: T. S. Eliot publishes *The Waste Land.*

1922: **Ireland** James Joyce publishes *Ulysses.* ▶

1924: The Immigration Act limits the number of immigrants that can enter the United States.

1924: **Germany** Thomas Mann publishes *The Magic Mountain.*

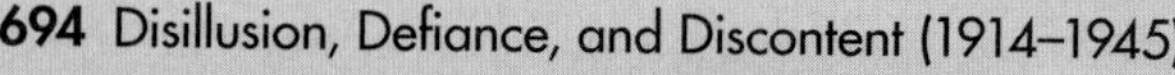

What makes American literature *American*?

What changes in literary elements contributed to American Modernism?

Narrative Conventions Modernist storytellers paid close attention to *how* they told their stories. They often left out transitions between events and omitted the detailed expositions and explanations that readers found in older literature. Sometimes they left plotlines unresolved, refusing to tie up every thread. Readers had to interpret on their own.

Modernists shifted time in their stories, moving among past, present, and future. They also shuttled between inner and outer realities. Influenced by developments in psychology, particularly those of Sigmund Freud and William James, Modernist writers wove characters' dreams and fantasies into their narratives. They tried to create the natural flow of thoughts, memories, and insights—the "stream of consciousness" connected only by associations.

Forms Modernists also broke formal boundaries. Two European giants led the way: Irish writer James Joyce's *Ulysses* (1922) revolutionized the novel with multi-layered chapters based on Homer's *Odyssey*, and French writer Marcel Proust's *In Search of Lost Time* (1913–1927) recaptured his own past in seven free-flowing volumes. Modernists invented new structures, some expansive and encompassing, others compressed. At the small end of the scale, Imagist poets—including Ezra Pound and Hilda Doolittle—created miniatures of hard, clear expression in concrete images.

Themes Most often, works of fiction, poetry, and drama have implied themes. In Modernist works, themes are even more indirect. Readers of modern literature need to pay closer attention, ask more questions, and forge more connections for themselves. In addition, the challenging theme of the nature of art itself often dominated the Modernist imagination.

Tone An overall tone of irony marks many Modernist works. Writers such as Eliot, Hemingway, Fitzgerald, and Faulkner were painfully aware of the gap between the world as it was and the world as it ought to have been.

ESSENTIAL QUESTION VOCABULARY

These Essential Question words will help you think and write about American literature.

consciousness (kän′ shəs nis) *n.* totality of one's thoughts, feelings, and impressions

indirect (in′ də rekt′) *adj.* suggested, not clearly stated or defined

breadth (bredth) *n.* wide range or variety

1936: **Spain** Spanish Civil War begins.

1937: **Japan** invades China, beginning the Second Sino-Japanese War.

1938: The Fair Labor Standards Act establishes a national minimum wage.

1939

1937: Amelia Earhart takes off from Miami for a flight around the world; she disappears over the Pacific Ocean. ▲

1937: Zora Neale Hurston publishes *Their Eyes Were Watching God.* ▶

They were not satirists, mocking the world in order to improve it. They were ironists, dissecting the world simply to make it possible to live in it.

Style In prose, journalism brought a news style into fiction. Most obvious in Hemingway, American style strove for shorter, harder-edged sentences. Snappier dialogue, less flowery descriptions, and everyday American vocabulary gave modern American works a recognizable style. In poetry, free verse enabled such poets as Wallace Stevens, William Carlos Williams, and E. E. Cummings to create new rhythms of variety and surprise.

Imagery High culture and low, domestic and exotic, elegant and vulgar, common and bizarre and everything in between—the twentieth century opened the biggest box of images that writers had ever had. For Ezra Pound, a crowd in a subway could be blossoms on a tree. For F. Scott Fitzgerald, a pair of eyes painted on a billboard could watch a tragedy unfold. For Langston Hughes, a dream could explode. Modernists saw the world with new eyes and helped their readers see it newly too.

Allusion The range of possible allusions grew wider too. T. S.Eliot quoted the Indian Upanishads; Ezra Pound quoted Latin and ancient Greek. Hemingway referred to African tribal customs; Marianne Moore invoked both baseball and basilisks. The reader's familiarity was no longer assumed or even required. The end result was a world-embracing awareness in American literature, a breadth of vision that still amazes us today.

How did the relationship between writers and the public change during the Modernist period?

Modernism began an overall distancing of serious writers from the general reading public. With the rise of mass communication and popular culture, Modernist works were sometimes seen as obscure or elitist. There was no doubt that they made greater demands on readers than Romantic or Realist works. More mental and imaginative effort was required to read Eliot's *The Waste Land* or Stevens's *Harmonium* than to read the Fireside Poets. As a result, some of the literary audience turned away.

TIMELINE

1939: John Steinbeck writes *The Grapes of Wrath* in his California home. ▶

1939: Poland German blitzkrieg invasion of Poland sets off World War II.

1939: *The Wizard of Oz* and *Gone With the Wind* appear in movie theaters. ▶

1940: Civil Aeronautics Board is created to regulate U.S. commercial air traffic.

1940: France French government signs armistice with Germany.

Many writers believe that great literary works teach their readers how to read them. In this sense, Modernist writers also became teachers. In time, people learned how to read Modernist works—how to make the connections, fill in the blanks, listen to new rhythms, and appreciate new images. Modernism gave people new ways to be delighted, and many Modernist devices are now taken for granted in the twenty-first century.

By 1945, what identities had emerged in American literature?

During the Modernist period, the American profile included these varied identities and character types:

- **Denizen of the Waste Land:** wanderer through a war-wearied landscape, spiritually exhausted, in search of new values, defined by T. S. Eliot
- **Member of the Lost Generation:** disillusioned, self-indulgent, escapist, expatriated, embodied by Fitzgerald and Hemingway
- **Triumphant Commoner:** believer in the innate strength of those who remain close to the land, led by Faulkner, Welty, and Steinbeck
- **Poetic Maker:** believer in the saving power of art and imagination, championed by Pound, Stevens, Williams, Cummings, Moore, and Frost
- **African American Artist:** creator of art drawn from the African American experience, represented by Hughes, McKay, Cullen, and Hurston

The American EXPERIENCE

DEVELOPING AMERICAN ENGLISH

Sliding with Slang by Richard Lederer

Slang is hot and slang is cool. Slang is nifty and slang is wicked. Slang is the bee's knees and the cat's meow. Slang is far out, fresh, fly, and phat. Slang is awesome, copacetic, and totally tubular.

Slang is the spice of language. It has added its spice to American literature as American writers, particularly in the Modern Age, have increasingly written in an American voice, using the words and rhythms of everyday American discourse. Listen to the poet Langston Hughes:

Good morning, daddy!
Ain't you heard
The boogie-woogie rumble
Of a dream deferred?

Defining the Lingo The *Dictionary of American Slang* defines slang as "the body of words and expressions frequently used by or intelligible to a rather large portion of the general American public, but not accepted as good, formal usage by the majority." In other words, it is vagabond language that prowls the outskirts of respectable speech, yet few of us can get along without it.

What's in This Name? The word *slang* may have developed from an erroneous past tense (*sling-slang-slung*) or from thieveS' LANGuage or beggarS' LANGuage. Jargon and slang originate with a particular group, but slang gets slung around by the whole population. In fact, slang may now make up a fifth of the American wordscape.

1941: Japanese bomb Pearl Harbor, bringing U.S. into World War II.

1944: Roosevelt is reelected president for an unprecedented fourth term.

◀ **1945:** United Nations Charter signed at end of World War II.

1945

◀ **1945: Germany** Dresden is hit by Allied firebombing raid. Firestorm virtually destroys city.

1945: Atom bombs dropped on Hiroshima and Nagasaki.

Recent Scholarship

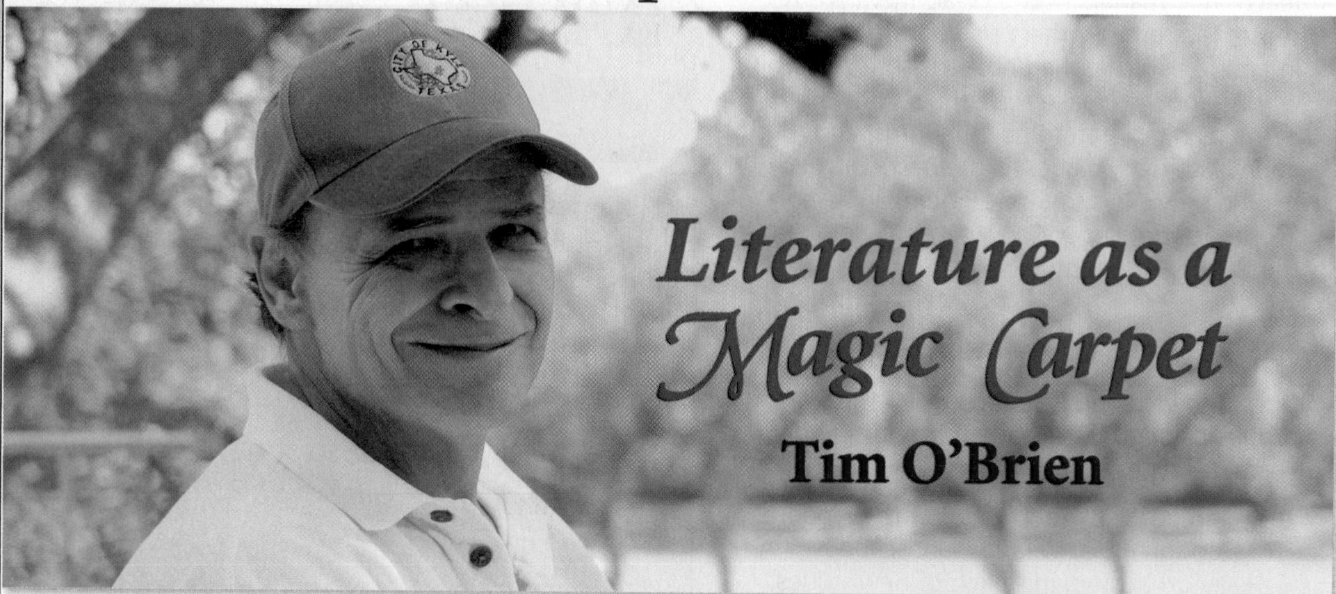

Literature as a Magic Carpet

Tim O'Brien

As a boy of fifteen or sixteen, feeling restless and marooned in a small town on the prairies of southern Minnesota, I began using literature as a kind of magic carpet—a way of flying off to more exciting places on the earth, a way of escaping the brutal Minnesota winters and the dull, drowsy, summertime fields of soybeans and alfalfa and corn. I didn't merely read. I was transported. I *lived* inside stories and novels. Just turn a page—that simple—and I was suddenly a soldier in World War I, or a young man in love during the famous Jazz Age, or a grieving parent, or an aging railroad engineer, or an old African American woman trudging down a path through the frozen woods of Mississippi.

Inventing Stories of My Own

The word "literature," I'll confess, did not mean much to me. It seemed too fancy, too formidable. Even so, by the time I'd graduated from high school, I had read—mostly on my own, mostly for fun—a good many of the stories and poems that appear in this unit. I remember, for instance, my first encounter with Hemingway's "In Another Country" during the summer between my sophomore and junior years. I remember marveling at the water-clear transparency of the prose, the deceptive simplicity of the plot, the quiet, uncomplaining dignity of the characters, those solid nouns, those invigorating verbs, the unspoken and unspeakable emotional pain

About the Author

Tim O'Brien was born in Minnesota. He was drafted after college to fight in the Vietnam War. Although he has written extensively about the war and its aftermath, he resists being labeled a "Vietnam writer." O'Brien's fiction explores the larger themes of betrayal and loss of faith, as well as the tension between truth and fiction. He has been called "the best American writer of his generation."

that hovered like an invisible vapor just above the surface of each page. More than anything, though, I remember thinking: Wow, I want to try this. I want to invent stories of my own. I want to write fiction someday.

Poetry As Explosive As Artillery

Not much later, in the first months of my junior year in high school, these fantasies about becoming a writer were reinforced by the work of two very dissimilar poets, T. S. Eliot and Robert Frost, both of whom are represented in this unit. Until then, I'd stupidly conceived of poetry as something for English teachers and nearsighted librarians. I hadn't realized that a good poem could be as explosive as any artillery round, as powerful as any rocket lifting off for the moon.

Living the Poem

From T. S. Eliot I learned that vivid writing requires vivid imagery, and that vivid imagery requires something unexpected and off the beaten literary path: a patient etherized upon a table; sawdust restaurants; women who come and go, talking of Michelangelo. To this day, Robert Frost's "Stopping by Woods on a Snowy Evening" remains one of my favorite pieces of writing. The words in themselves are ordinary—no need for a dictionary—but the impact of the poem, its pressure on the human spirit, is extraordinary. We feel the cold, snowy dark against our skin. We hear the harness bells, the wind, and the eerie, timeless echo of our own mortality. We don't merely read the poem. We live it. And we come to understand that, one way or another, all of us have promises to keep, and miles to go before we sleep.

Rekindling a Fire

My dream of becoming a writer has come true. And yet rereading these stories and poems has rekindled a fire inside me. I'm a teenager again. I want to write a new novel.

Speaking and Listening: Presentation of Ideas

Tim O'Brien recalls two life-changing effects that literature had on him: It enabled him to escape into other worlds, and it inspired him to write. He remembers the rocket-like effect of reading Hemingway, Eliot, and Frost. While few people go on to become professional writers as O'Brien did, nearly everyone can take off on that literary "magic carpet."

Write a short **testimonial**—a personal statement affirming the value of something—about a literary work you have read. Explain its subject and style and why it is important to you.

▼ **Critical Viewing** In what ways does this young man seem like a reader who uses "literature as a . . . magic carpet," the way Tim O'Brien did? **CONNECT**

Integrate and Evaluate Information

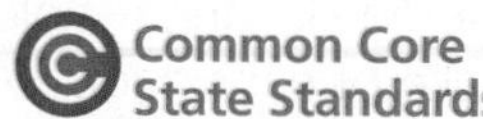
Common Core State Standards

Reading Informational Text
7. Integrate and evaluate multiple sources of information presented in different media or formats as well as in words in order to address a question or solve a problem.

Speaking and Listening
5. Make strategic use of digital media in presentations to enhance understanding of findings, reasoning, and evidence and to add interest.

1. Use a chart like the one shown to determine the key ideas expressed in the Essential Question essays on pages 694–701. Fill in two ideas related to each Essential Question and note the groups most closely associated with each concept. One example has been done for you.

Essential Question	Key Concept	Key Author
Literature and Place		
American Literature		
Literature and Society	Disillusion with the American Dream	Fitzgerald

2. How do the visual sources in this section (pp. 688–703) add to your understanding of the ideas expressed in words? Cite specific examples.
3. During the Modern era, paperbacks and movies helped to create popular culture. At the same time, the challenging nature of Modernism caused some readers to turn away from serious literature. The effect was a divide between popular and "high" culture. Do you think that divide continues today? Consider the effects of television and the Internet in your response.
4. **Address a Question** Tim O'Brien recalls that as a boy he "lived" inside stories. In today's world, is the experience of playing a video-game avatar or character similar to the transport O'Brien describes? As you explain your thinking, integrate information from this textbook and other sources to support your ideas.

ESSENTIAL QUESTION VOCABULARY

Use these vocabulary words in your presentations.

Literature and Place
development
metropolis
anonymity

Literature and Society
disillusion
awareness
cultural

American Literature
consciousness
indirect
breadth

Speaking and Listening: Multimedia Presentation

During the Modern Age, popular culture played a growing role in the lives of Americans. Choose one of these popular culture forms and prepare a brief **multimedia presentation** about its significance during the period of 1914–1945:

- jazz and other popular music
- comic strips
- motion pictures
- science fiction

Solve a Research Problem: The topics listed above are very broad. Conduct preliminary research to narrow your focus and then conduct targeted research on that specialized area. Use your research to answer the following questions: Who were some of the outstanding people in this field and what did they do? What characterized works in this field during the time period? What do these works reveal about Americans during this era? Integrate print, visual, and audio examples into your presentation to communicate your points clearly and to add interest to your presentation.

TEXT SET

Facing Troubled Times

Part 1

Building Knowledge and Insight

The Love Song of J. Alfred Prufrock

Connecting to the Essential Question Prufrock, the speaker of this poem, reveals feelings of insecurity and self-consciousness. As you read, notice details that reflect Prufrock's perceptions of other people's opinions. Doing so will help you think about the Essential Question: **How does literature shape or reflect society?**

Reading Literature

4. Determine the meaning of words and phrases as they are used in the text, including figurative meanings; analyze the impact of specific word choices on meaning and tone, including language that is particularly fresh, engaging, or beautiful.

5. Analyze how an author's choices concerning how to structure specific parts of a text contribute to its overall structure and meaning as well as its aesthetic impact.

Close Reading Focus

Dramatic Monologue; Allusion

A troubled J. Alfred Prufrock invites an unidentified companion, perhaps a part of his own personality, to walk with him as he reflects aloud about his bitter realization that life and love are passing him by. His so-called love song is a **dramatic monologue,** a poem or speech in which a character addresses a silent listener. As Prufrock moves through his evening, images, dialogue, and other details reveal his internal conflicts.

Throughout the poem, Prufrock makes **allusions**, or references, to people and historical or literary events that hold meaning for him. For example, in this passage, he alludes to Shakespeare's *Hamlet*:

No! I am not Prince Hamlet, nor was meant to be;
Am an attendant lord, one that will do
To swell a progress, start a scene or two . . .

These allusions form a literary shorthand that paints a portrait of Prufrock and his society. As you read, use footnotes and guided reading questions to understand these allusions and the meanings they hold for Prufrock.

Preparing to Read Complex Texts This poem contains some of the most haunting passages in literature. One of the reasons the poem affects readers so intensely is its musicality—the sweep and fall of the lines, the repetition and rhyme, and the sounds of the words. To fully appreciate the poem, **adjust your reading rate** to *listen* to the poem's rhythms and language. As you read, use a chart like the one shown to note points where you slow down. Record how the music of those moments contributes to the poem's mood and meaning.

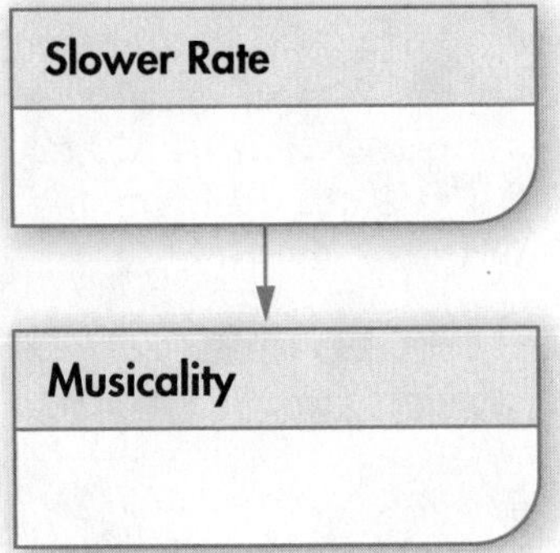

Vocabulary

The words below are important to understanding the text that follows. Copy the words into your notebook. Which words end with the same suffix? Which part of speech are they?

tedious	**malingers**
insidious	**meticulous**
digress	**obtuse**

T.S. ELIOT *(1888–1965)*

Author of "The Love Song of J. Alfred Prufrock"

Always well-spoken and somberly attired, Thomas Stearns Eliot was outwardly the model of convention. His work, in contrast, was revolutionary in both form and content.

Beginnings Born into a wealthy family in St. Louis, Eliot grew up in an environment that promoted his intellectual development. He attended Harvard University, where he published a number of poems in the school's literary magazine. In 1910, the year Eliot received his master's degree in philosophy, he completed "The Love Song of J. Alfred Prufrock."

A Literary Sensation Just before the outbreak of World War I, Eliot moved to England where he became acquainted with Ezra Pound, another young American poet. Pound convinced Harriet Monroe, the editor of *Poetry* magazine, to publish "Prufrock." Shortly thereafter, Eliot published a collection entitled *Prufrock and Other Observations* (1917). Eliot's use of innovative poetic techniques and his focus on the despair of modern urban life caused a sensation in the literary world.

Facing a New World Eliot made his literary mark against the backdrop of a rapidly changing society. Disillusioned with the ideologies that produced the devastation of World War I, many people were searching for new ideas and values. Eliot was among a group of such writers and visual artists who called themselves Modernists. Modernist poets believed that poetry had to reflect the genuine, fractured experience of life in the twentieth century, not a romanticized idea of what life was once like.

In 1922, Eliot published *The Waste Land,* a profound critique of the spiritual barrenness of the modern world. Filled with allusions to classical and world literature and to Eastern culture and religion, it was widely read and greatly affected writers and critics.

A Return to Tradition In his search for something beyond the "waste land" of modern society, Eliot became a member of the Church of England in 1927. He began to explore religious themes in poems such as "Ash Wednesday" (1930) and *Four Quartets* (1943)—works that suggest a belief that religion could heal the wounds inflicted by society. In later years, Eliot wrote several plays and a sizable body of literary criticism. In 1948, he received the Nobel Prize for Literature.

Three White Bluebells, 1920, Paul Klee, Artists Rights Society (ARS), New York

THE LOVE SONG OF J. ALFRED PRUFROCK

T. S. Eliot

▲ Critical Viewing

How does this painting mirror Modernist ideas about experimenting with artistic forms? **INTERPRET**

BACKGROUND In this poem, J. Alfred Prufrock, a stuffy and inhibited man who is pained by his own passivity, invites the reader, or some unnamed visitor, to join him in a journey. Where Prufrock is and where he is going—to a party, a museum, a tea party, or some other gathering—is open to debate. The most important part of this journey, however, takes place within the inner landscape of Prufrock's emotions, memory, and intellect as he meditates on his life.

S'io credessi che mia risposta fosse
a persona che mai tornasse al mondo,
questa fiamma staria senza più scosse.
Ma per ciò che giammai di questo fondo
non tornò vivo alcun, s'i'odo il vero,
senza tema d'infamia ti rispondo.[1]

1. ***S'io credessi . . . ti rispondo*** The epigraph is a passage from Dante's *Inferno,* in which one of the damned, upon being asked to tell his story, says: "If I believed my answer were being given to someone who could ever return to the world, this flame [his voice] would shake no more. But since no one has ever returned alive from this depth, if what I hear is true, I will answer you without fear of disgrace."

Let us go then, you and I,
When the evening is spread out against the sky
Like a patient etherized[2] upon a table;
Let us go, through certain half-deserted streets,
The muttering retreats
Of restless nights in one-night cheap hotels
And sawdust restaurants with oyster-shells:
Streets that follow like a **tedious** argument
Of **insidious** intent
To lead you to an overwhelming question . . .
Oh, do not ask, "What is it?"
Let us go and make our visit.

In the room the women come and go
Talking of Michelangelo.[3]

The yellow fog that rubs its back upon the window-panes,
The yellow smoke that rubs its muzzle on the window-panes,
Licked its tongue into the corners of the evening,
Lingered upon the pools that stand in drains,
Let fall upon its back the soot that falls from chimneys,
Slipped by the terrace, made a sudden leap,
And seeing that it was a soft October night,
Curled once about the house, and fell asleep.

And indeed there will be time[4]
For the yellow smoke that slides along the street
Rubbing its back upon the window-panes;
There will be time, there will be time
To prepare a face to meet the faces that you meet;
There will be time to murder and create,
And time for all the works and days[5] of hands
That lift and drop a question on your plate;
Time for you and time for me,
And time yet for a hundred indecisions,
And for a hundred visions and revisions.
Before the taking of a toast and tea.

In the room the women come and go
Talking of Michelangelo.

And indeed there will be time
To wonder, "Do I dare?" and, "Do I dare?"
Time to turn back and descend the stair,

Vocabulary

tedious (tēd´ ē əs) *adj.* boring and wearisome

insidious (in sid´ ē əs) *adj.* secretly treacherous

Dramatic Monologue and Allusion

What might the allusion to Michelangelo suggest about the women at the party?

Comprehension

At what time of day is the poem set?

---

2. **etherized** (ē´ thə rīzd) *v.* anesthetized with ether.
3. **Michelangelo** (mī´ kəl an´ jə lō) a famous Italian artist and sculptor (1475–1564).
4. **there will be time** These words echo the speaker's plea in English poet Andrew Marvell's "To His Coy Mistress": "Had we but world enough and time . . . "
5. **works and days** Ancient Greek poet Hesiod wrote a poem about farming called "Works and Days."

With a bald spot in the middle of my hair—
(They will say: "How his hair is growing thin!")
My morning coat, my collar mounting firmly to the chin,
My necktie rich and modest, but asserted by a simple pin—
(They will say: "But how his arms and legs are thin!")
Do I dare
Disturb the universe?
In a minute there is time
For decisions and revisions which a minute will reverse.

For I have known them all already, known them all—
Have known the evenings, mornings, afternoons,
I have measured out my life with coffee spoons;
I know the voices dying with a dying fall
Beneath the music from a farther room.
    So how should I presume?

And I have known the eyes already, known them all—
The eyes that fix you in a formulated phrase,
And when I am formulated, sprawling on a pin,
When I am pinned and wriggling on the wall,
Then how should I begin
To spit out all the butt-ends of my days and ways?
    And how should I presume?

And I have known the arms already, known them all—
Arms that are braceleted and white and bare
(But in the lamplight, downed with light brown hair!)
Is it perfume from a dress
That makes me so **digress**?
Arms that lie along a table, or wrap about a shawl.
    And should I then presume?
    And how should I begin?

. . . .

Shall I say, I have gone at dusk through narrow streets
And watched the smoke that rises from the pipes
Of lonely men in shirt-sleeves, leaning out of windows? . . .

I should have been a pair of ragged claws
Scuttling across the floors of silent seas.[6]

. . . .

And the afternoon, the evening, sleeps so peacefully!

Do I dare Disturb the universe?

Vocabulary
digress (dī gres′) *v.* depart temporarily from the main subject

Dramatic Monologue
What do Prufrock's observations of "narrow streets," and "lonely men" suggest he feels about the world?

6. I should . . . seas In Shakespeare's *Hamlet,* the hero, Hamlet, mocks the aging Lord Chamberlain, Polonius, saying, "You yourself, sir, should be old as I am, if like a crab you could go backward" (II.ii. 205–206).

Smoothed by long fingers,
Asleep . . . tired . . . or it **malingers**,
Stretched on the floor, here beside you and me.
Should I, after tea and cakes and ices,
Have the strength to force the moment to its crisis?
But though I have wept and fasted, wept and prayed,
Though I have seen my head (grown slightly bald) brought in
    upon a platter,[7]
I am no prophet—and here's no great matter;
I have seen the moment of my greatness flicker,
And I have seen the eternal Footman[8] hold my coat, and snicker.
And in short, I was afraid.

And would it have been worth it, after all,
After the cups, the marmalade, the tea,
Among the porcelain, among some talk of you and me,
Would it have been worth while,
To have bitten off the matter with a smile,
To have squeezed the universe into a ball
To roll it towards some overwhelming question.
To say: "I am Lazarus,[9] come from the dead,
Come back to tell you all. I shall tell you all"—
If one, settling a pillow by her head,
    Should say: "That is not what I meant at all.
    That is not it, at all."

And would it have been worth it, after all,
Would it have been worth while,
After the sunsets and the dooryards and the sprinkled streets,
After the novels, after the teacups, after the skirts that trail
    along the floor—
And this, and so much more?—
It is impossible to say just what I mean!
But as if a magic lantern[10] threw the nerves in patterns on a
    screen:
Would it have been worth while
If one, settling a pillow or throwing off a shawl,
And turning toward the window, should say:
    "That is not it at all,
That is not what I meant, at all."

. . . . . .

No! I am not Prince Hamlet, nor was meant to be;
Am an attendant lord, one that will do

7. **head . . . platter** a reference to the prophet John the Baptist, whose head was delivered on a platter to Salome as a reward for her dancing (Matthew 14:1–11).
8. **eternal Footman** death.
9. **Lazarus** (laz´ ə rəs) Lazarus is resurrected from the dead by Jesus in John 11:1–44.
10. **magic lantern** an early device used to project images on a screen.

Vocabulary

malingers (mə liŋ´ gərz) *v.* pretends to be ill

Adjusting Reading Rate

When you slow down to read lines 87–98, what do you notice about Eliot's use of rhyme?

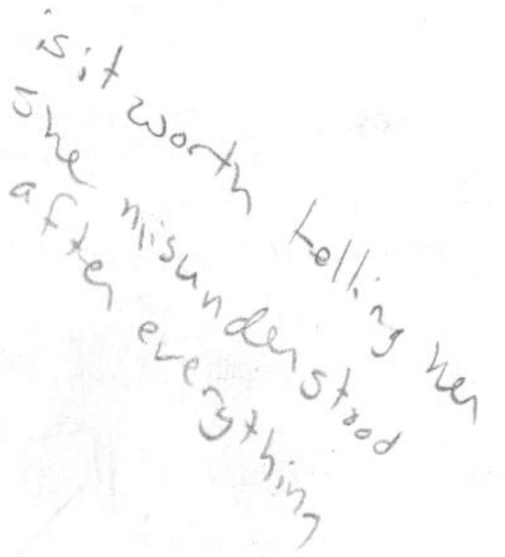

Comprehension

What questions does Prufrock repeatedly ask himself?

Vocabulary

meticulous (mə tik′ yo͞o ləs) *adj.* precise about details

obtuse (äb to͞os′) *adj.* slow to understand or perceive

I have heard the mermaids singing, each to each.

To swell a progress,[11] start a scene or two,
Advise the prince; no doubt, an easy tool,
Deferential, glad to be of use,
Politic, cautious, and **meticulous**;
Full of high sentence,[12] but a bit **obtuse**;
At times, indeed, almost ridiculous—
Almost, at times, the Fool.

I grow old . . . I grow old . . .
I shall wear the bottoms of my trousers rolled.

Shall I part my hair behind? Do I dare to eat a peach?
I shall wear white flannel trousers, and walk upon the beach.
I have heard the mermaids singing, each to each.

I do not think that they will sing to me.

I have seen them riding seaward on the waves
Combing the white hair of the waves blown back
When the wind blows the water white and black.

We have lingered in the chambers of the sea
By sea-girls wreathed with seaweed red and brown
Till human voices wake us, and we drown.

11. To swell a progress to add to the number of people in a parade or scene from a play.
12. Full of high sentence speaking in a very ornate manner, often offering advice.

Critical Reading

Cite textual evidence to support your responses.

1. **Key Ideas and Details (a) Interpret:** In lines 96–97, how does the woman react to Prufrock? **(b) Describe:** In line 125, how does Prufrock describe the mermaids' reactions to him? **(c) Connect:** How does Prufrock seem to feel about women and their interest in him?
2. **Key Ideas and Details (a)** In line 85, who or what does Prufrock see? **(b) Make a Judgment:** Do you think Prufrock is simply afraid of death, or are his fears more complicated? Explain.
3. **Integration of Knowledge and Ideas** Do you think the poem is simply a portrait of one man, or does it represent something deeper in modern society? In your response, use at least two of these Essential Question words: *companionship, reluctance, alienation, self-consciousness.* ***[Connecting to the Essential Question: How does literature shape or reflect society?]***

THE AMERICAN EXPERIENCE

MODERNISM

Modernism, an artistic movement that rejected traditional forms and emphasized bold new ways of expression, revolutionized arts and audiences worldwide. In 1913, the premiere of the ballet *The Rite of Spring* caused a riot in Paris. Members of the audience were horrified by the dissonant music composed by Igor Stravinsky and the angular movements choreographed by Vaslav Nijinsky. Supporters and detractors shouted and threw punches. Soon, the police arrived to break things up, but many remembered that event as the birth of Modernism.

Artistic movements are not really born in a day, though. They develop slowly. The seeds of Modernism sprouted in the decades before World War I, as many artists came to Paris. The young Spanish painter Pablo Picasso arrived in Paris in 1900 and met writers Guillaume Apollinaire, Max Jacob, and Gertrude Stein. French painters Marcel Duchamp and Fernand Léger were already on the scene. American dancer Isadora Duncan spent time in Paris. So did T. S. Eliot, E. E. Cummings, Edward Munch, Piet Mondrian, and Umberto Boccioni. After the war, Ernest Hemingway, Ezra Pound, James Joyce, and Alexander Calder moved to Paris. The ideas of these Modernist pioneers quickly spread across borders. Modernism had become a truly international movement.

▲ Art in Motion
The son and grandson of Philadelphia sculptors, Alexander Calder moved to Paris in 1926, where he designed toys and a miniature circus. When he created a series of sculptures that moved, Marcel Duchamp dubbed them "mobiles."

▲ Cubism Is Born
Picasso was influenced by African art in the development of his Cubist style.

CONNECT TO THE LITERATURE

What evidence of international influences can you find in "The Love Song of J. Alfred Prufrock"?

American Modern
American dancer and choreographer Martha Graham (shown dancing *Letter to the World* in 1940) created the technique and vocabulary for modern dance. In 1944, she choreographed the seminal *Appalachian Spring*, set to music by Aaron Copland. ▶

Close Reading Activities

The Love Song of J. Alfred Prufrock

Literary Analysis

1. **Key Ideas and Details** What do his descriptions of the sky and the city in lines 1–12 suggest about Prufrock's outlook on life?
2. **Key Ideas and Details** **(a)** How can the first line of this **dramatic monologue** be interpreted to suggest that Prufrock sees himself as divided, both seeking and fearing action? **(b)** At what other points does he express a deeply conflicted sense of self?
3. **Craft and Structure** **(a)** At what points in the poem did you **adjust your reading rate** by slowing down to listen for rhyme, repetition, and other sound elements? **(b)** Explain how this strategy helped you better understand the poem.
4. **Craft and Structure** What is the effect of the repetition of "there will be time" in lines 23–34 and again in lines 37–48?
5. **Craft and Structure** Some of Prufrock's **allusions** paint imaginary portraits that reveal his sense of self. Use a chart like the one shown to examine these allusions and what they suggest about Prufrock's self-image.

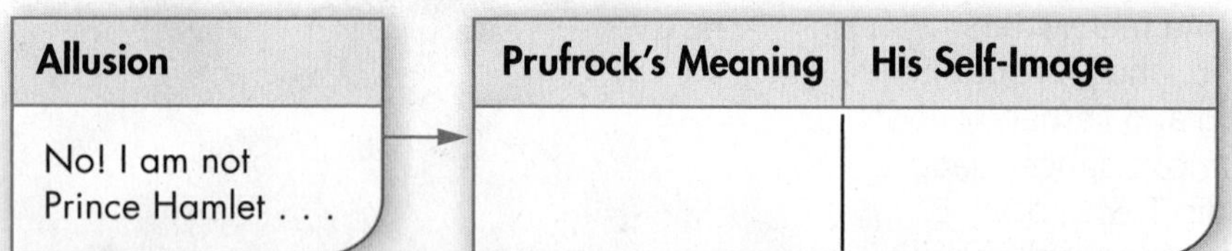

6. **Craft and Structure** **(a)** Review the first footnote and explain the meaning of the opening allusion—the passage from Dante's *Inferno.* **(b)** What does this quotation suggest about the content of the poem that follows?
7. **Craft and Structure** **(a)** What is suggested by the repeated reference to Michelangelo? **(b)** In what ways would the portrayal of Prufrock's world be quite different if that reference were to something less refined?
8. **Integration of Knowledge and Ideas** **(a)** In lines 49–54, what image does Prufrock use to describe how he has "measured out" his life? **(b)** In your own words, explain how Prufrock has lived.
9. **Analyzing Visual Information** Explain the humor in this cartoon.

Common Core State Standards

Writing

1. Write arguments to support claims in an analysis of substantive topics or texts, using valid reasoning and relevant and sufficient evidence. *(p. 715)*

4. Produce clear and coherent writing in which the development, organization, and style are appropriate to task, purpose, and audience. *(p. 715)*

Language

3. Apply knowledge of language to understand how language functions in different contexts, to make effective choices for meaning or style, and to comprehend more fully when reading or listening. *(p. 715)*

5.b. Use the relationship between particular words to better understand each of the words. *(p. 715)*

"I have heard the mermaids singing, each to each. I told them to pipe down."

▲ *"I have heard the mermaids singing, each to each. I told them to pipe down."*

Vocabulary Acquistion and Use

Word Analysis: Greek Prefix *di-*

The Greek prefix *di-* (or *dis-*) means "apart" or "away." The word *digress* means "to move away from a subject." Each of the sentences below includes a word containing the prefix *di-* or *dis-*. Indicate whether each sentence is true or false and write a brief explanation of your choice.

1. A path *diverges* if it branches off.
2. If you are *diverted,* your focus is sharp.
3. If a rumor is *dispelled*, people are likely to believe it.
4. If information is *divulged*, many will have access to it.
5. To *dilate* an object will make it more narrow.
6. A *diverse* menu features many similar foods.
7. A *discerning* person can tell truth from lies.

Vocabulary: Synonyms

Review the words from the vocabulary list on page 706. Then, choose the letter of the word that is the best synonym, or word with a similar meaning, for the first word. Explain your thinking.

1. tedious: **(a)** twisted, **(b)** direct, **(c)** humble, **(d)** engaging
2. insidious: **(a)** innocent, **(b)** wealthy, **(c)** dangerous, **(d)** certified
3. digress: **(a)** wander, **(b)** contain, **(c)** hesitate, **(d)** elaborate
4. malingers: **(a)** fakes, **(b)** studies, **(c)** boasts, **(d)** anticipates
5. meticulous: **(a)** messy, **(b)** absurd, **(c)** careful, **(d)** tart
6. obtuse: **(a)** intense, **(b)** stupid, **(c)** friendly, **(d)** prompt

Writing to Sources

Argumentative Text Ever since Eliot's "Love Song" was published in 1915, J. Alfred Prufrock has fascinated readers. For some, Prufrock is merely a man who fails to achieve his dreams. For others, he embodies larger failings of the modern age—an absence of heroism or a general weariness. Write an **essay** presenting and defending your own analysis of this character.

Prewriting Reread the poem, taking notes about Prufrock's character. Pay attention to details that suggest reasons for Prufrock's passivity and fears, and support your viewpoint through detailed references to the text.

Drafting Begin by noting the title and author of the work. Then, state your opinion about Prufrock's character. Use quotes from the poem and precise language to develop your ideas in each body paragraph.

Revising Review your draft. Highlight any words that seem vague or inaccurate. Use a thesaurus to replace them with more specific words.

Model: Revising Word Choice for Accuracy

Prufrock's lament is ~~big~~ sweeping. He ~~talks about~~ pines for all that he has lost or that he never had—youth and love. He is keenly aware of, ~~and really upset about~~ even tormented by, the passage of time.

Replacing vague words with specific ones makes a piece of writing more accurate and powerful.

The Imagist Poets

Background: Imagism

Imagism was a literary movement established in the early 1900s by Ezra Pound and other poets. As the name suggests, the Imagists concentrated on the direct presentation of images, or word pictures. An Imagist poem expressed the essence of an object, person, or incident, without providing explanations. Through the spare, clean presentation of an image, the Imagists hoped to freeze a single moment in time and to capture the emotions of that moment. To accomplish this purpose, the Imagists used the language of everyday speech.

The Imagists were influenced by traditional Chinese and Japanese poetry. Many Imagist poems bear a close resemblance to the Japanese verse forms of *haiku* and *tanka,* which generally evoke an emotional response through the presentation of a single image or a pair of contrasting images.

The Imagist movement was short-lived, lasting only until about 1918. However, for many years that followed, the poems of Pound, Williams, H.D. and other Imagists continued to influence the work of other poets, including Wallace Stevens, T.S. Eliot, and Hart Crane.

Ezra Pound *(1885–1972)*

Author of **"A Few Don'ts"** and **"In a Station of the Metro"**

As both an editor and a poet, Ezra Pound inspired the dramatic changes in American poetry that characterized the Modern Age. His insistence that writers "make it new" led many poets to discard the forms, techniques, and ideas of the past and to experiment with new approaches to poetry.

After college, Pound traveled to Europe, where he spent most of his life. Settling in London and later moving to Paris, he became a vital voice in the growing Modernist movement. Pound influenced the work of the Irish poet William Butler Yeats, as well as that of T. S. Eliot, William Carlos Williams, H. D., Marianne Moore, and Ernest Hemingway—a "who's who" of the literary voices of the age. He is best remembered, however, for his role in the development of Imagism.

Despite his preoccupation with originality and inventiveness, Pound's work often drew upon the poetry of ancient cultures. Many of his poems are filled with literary and historical allusions, requiring that readers apply background knowledge or use reference sources to fully understand his meaning.

William Carlos Williams (1883–1963)

Author of **"The Red Wheelbarrow," "This Is Just to Say,"** and **"The Great Figure"**

Unlike his fellow Imagists, William Carlos Williams spent most of his life in the United States, where he pursued a double career as a poet and a pediatrician in New Jersey. He felt that his experiences as a doctor provided him with inspiration as a poet, and credited medicine for his ability to "gain entrance to . . . the secret gardens of the self."

The child of immigrants, Williams grew up speaking Spanish, French, and British English. He was enamored of American language and life, and believed that common experience contains the seeds of the extraordinary. In volumes such as *Spring and All* (1923), he focused on capturing the essence of America by depicting ordinary people, objects, and experiences in everyday language.

In his later work, Williams departed from pure Imagism in order to write more expansively. His five-volume poem *Paterson* (1946–1958) explores the idea of a city as a symbol for a man. The poem is based on the real city of Paterson, New Jersey.

Williams continued to write even after his failing health forced him to give up his medical practice. In 1963, he received a Pulitzer Prize for *Pictures from Breughel and Other Poems*, his final volume of poetry.

H.D. (Hilda Doolittle) (1886–1961)

Author of **"Pear Tree"**

In 1913, Ezra Pound reshaped three of Hilda Doolittle's poems and submitted them to *Poetry* magazine under the name "H. D., Imagiste," thus giving birth to the Imagist movement. The publication of the poems also served to launch the successful career of the young poet, who continued to publish under the name H. D. throughout her life.

Like the Greek lyrics that she admired, H. D.'s early poems were brief, precise, and direct. Often emphasizing light, color, and physical textures, she created vivid, emotive images. In 1925, almost all of H. D.'s early poems were gathered in *Collected Poems*, a book that also contained her translations from the *Odyssey* and from the Greek poet Sappho. She also wrote a play, *Hippolytus Temporizes*, which appeared in 1927, and two prose works, *Palimpsest* (1926) and *Hedylus* (1928). During the later stages of her career, she focused on writing longer works, including an epic poem. H. D. is best remembered, however, for her early Imagist work.

Building Knowledge and Insight | *The Imagist Poets*

Connecting to the Essential Question Many Imagist poems focus on a single detail of nature or place. As you read, notice how these poems describe ordinary things in extraordinary ways. Doing so will help as you think about the Essential Question: **What is the relationship between literature and place?**

Reading Literature

4. Determine the meaning of words and phrases as they are used in the text, including figurative and connotative meanings; analyze the impact of specific word choices on meaning and tone, including language that is particularly fresh, engaging, or beautiful.

9. Demonstrate knowledge of early-twentieth-century foundational works of American literature, including how two or more texts from the same period treat similar themes or topics.

Close Reading Focus

Imagism

Imagism was a literary movement begun in the early 1900s by Ezra Pound and other poets. As the name suggests, Imagist poetry evokes emotion and sparks the imagination through the vivid presentation of a limited number of **images,** or words and phrases that appeal to the senses. The poem "In a Station of the Metro," for example, presents just two images in only two lines and fourteen well-chosen words.

Comparing Literary Works In his essay "A Few Don'ts," Ezra Pound describes the image as more than a simple word-picture:

> ***An "Image" is that which presents an intellectual and emotional complex in an instant of time.***

For Pound, the image brings the reader a new way of seeing—on the physical level through the senses, and on higher levels through the emotions and the intellect. As you read these poems, think about which best achieve the effect of "that sense of sudden growth" that Pound believed was the highest achievement of art.

Preparing to Read Complex Texts When reading Imagist poetry, increase your understanding by **engaging your senses.** As you encounter each image, re-create in your mind the sights, sounds, smells, tastes, and physical sensations it evokes. Note that some images may appeal to more than one sense at a time. For example, in "This Is Just to Say," the image of plums as "delicious / so sweet / and so cold" appeals to both taste *and* touch. Use a chart like the one shown to record how you engage your senses as you read these poems.

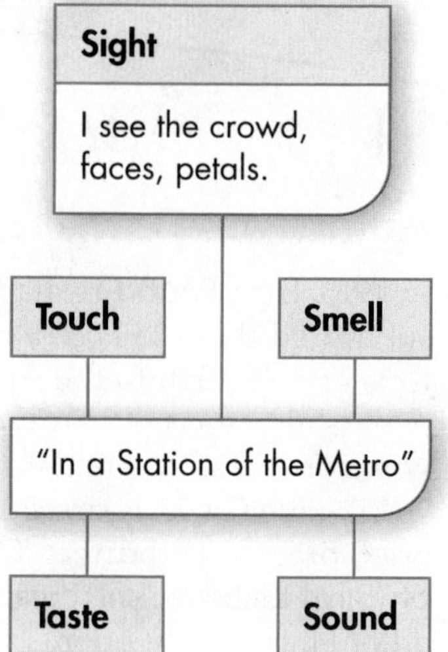

Vocabulary

You will encounter the words listed here in the texts that follow. Copy the words into your notebook. Which word is connected to the idea of visibility? How can you tell?

voluminous **apparition**

dogma

A Few Don'ts

Ezra Pound

BACKGROUND Ezra Pound was one of the leading figures in the Imagist movement. As the name suggests, Imagists concentrated on the focused presentation of images, or word-pictures. For example, Pound's original draft of "In a Station of the Metro" consisted of 30 lines. Pound whittled away at the poem until he arrived at a work of only 14 words of great precision and power. In this essay, Pound discusses his beliefs about what poetry should and should not be.

An "Image" is that which presents an intellectual and emotional complex in an instant of time. I use the term "complex" rather in the technical sense employed by the newer psychologists, such as Hart, though we might not agree absolutely in our application.

It is the presentation of such a "complex" instantaneously which gives that sense of sudden liberation; that sense of freedom from time limits and space limits; that sense of sudden growth, which we experience in the presence of the greatest works of art.

It is better to present one Image in a lifetime than to produce voluminous works.

All this, however, some may consider open to debate. The immediate necessity is to tabulate A LIST OF DON'TS for those beginning to write verses. But I can not put all of them into Mosaic negative.[1]

To begin with, consider the three propositions[2] . . . not as dogma—never consider anything as dogma—but as the result of long contemplation, which, even if it is someone else's contemplation, may be worth consideration. . . .

Vocabulary

voluminous (və lo͞om′ ə nəs) *adj.* of enough material to fill volumes

dogma (dôg′ mə) *n.* authoritative doctrines or beliefs

Comprehension

According to Pound, what is an image?

1. **Mosaic negative** Pound is referring to the Ten Commandments presented by Moses to the Israelites in the Hebrew Bible. Many of the commandments are in the negative and begin with the words "Thou shalt not . . ."
2. **three propositions** Pound is referring to the three rules that English Imagist poet Frank Stuart Flint formulated for the writing of Imagist poetry:
   1. direct treatment of the "thing" either subjective or objective
   2. to use absolutely no word that does not contribute to the presentation
   3. as regarding rhythm: to compose in sequence of the musical phrase, not in sequence of a metronome

LANGUAGE

Use no superfluous word, no adjective, which does not reveal something.

Don't use such an expression as "dim lands *of peace*." It dulls the image. It mixes an abstraction with the concrete. It comes from the writer's not realizing that the natural object is always the *adequate* symbol.

Imagist Poetry
Why is the rule of avoiding abstractions consistent with the goals of Imagist poetry?

Go in fear of abstractions. Do not retell in mediocre verse what has already been done in good prose. Don't think any intelligent person is going to be deceived when you try to shirk all the difficulties of the unspeakably difficult art of good prose by chopping your composition into line lengths. . . .

Don't imagine that the art of poetry is any simpler than the art of music, or that you can please the expert before you have spent at least as much effort on the art of verse as the average piano teacher spends on the art of music. . . .

RHYTHM AND RHYME

. . . Don't imagine that a thing will "go" in verse just because it's too dull to go in prose.

Don't be "viewy"—leave that to the writers of pretty little philo-

▲ **Critical Viewing** What key details might be emphasized in an Imagist poem about this portrait of Ezra Pound? **SYNTHESIZE**

sophic essays. Don't be descriptive; remember that the painter can describe a landscape much better than you can, and that he has to know a deal more about it.

When Shakespeare talks of the "Dawn in russet mantle clad" he presents something which the painter does not present. There is in this line of his nothing that one can call description; he presents. . . .

Don't chop your stuff into separate *iambs.*[3] Don't make each line stop dead at the end, and then begin every next line with a heave. Let the beginning of the next line catch the rise of the rhythm wave, unless you want a definite longish pause.

In short, behave as a musician, a good musician, when dealing with that phase of your art which has exact parallels in music. The same laws govern, and you are bound by no others. . . .

A rhyme must have in it some slight element of surprise if it is to give pleasure; it need not be bizarre or curious, but it must be well used if used at all. . . .

Don't mess up the perception of one sense by trying to define it in terms of another. This is usually only the result of being too lazy to find the exact word. To this clause there are possibly exceptions.

The first three simple proscriptions[4] will throw out nine-tenths of all the bad poetry now accepted as standard and classic; and will prevent you from many a crime of production. . . .

Engaging Your Senses
What physical sensations are suggested by the rhythmic wave Pound advocates?

3. **iambs** (ī´ ambz) *n.* metrical feet, each consisting of an unaccented syllable followed by an accented one.
4. **The first three simple proscriptions** reference to Flint's three rules outlined in footnote #2.

Critical Reading

1. **Key Ideas and Details (a)** What three rules does Pound invite readers to consider? **(b) Define:** What is the difference between dogma and the results of "long contemplation"? **(c) Speculate:** Why might Pound prefer a list of "don'ts" to a list of "do's"?
2. **Key Ideas and Details (a)** What does Pound consider preferable to abstractions? **(b) Analyze:** Why would the use of abstractions be offensive to an Imagist poet?
3. **Key Ideas and Details (a)** Does Pound think Shakespeare's image is an example of description or presentation? **(b) Distinguish:** How does presentation differ from description?
4. **Craft and Structure Make a Decision:** Pound says that defining one sense in terms of another is "usually the result of being too lazy to find the exact word." Do you agree with this statement? Explain your position.
5. **Integration of Knowledge and Ideas Evaluate:** Do you think following Pound's "don'ts" would make it easier or more difficult to write poetry? Explain.

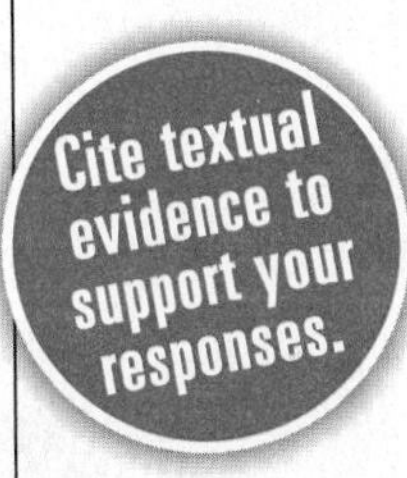
Cite textual evidence to support your responses.

IN A STATION OF THE METRO

Ezra Pound

Vocabulary
apparition (ap′ ə rish′ ən) *n.* act of appearing or becoming visible

The apparition of these faces in the crowd;
Petals on a wet, black bough.

1. **Metro** the Paris subway.

Critical Reading 

Cite textual evidence to support your responses.

1. **Key Ideas and Details (a)** What two things does Pound compare in this poem? **(b) Interpret:** In what ways does this poem capture the essence of a single moment?
2. **Key Ideas and Details Analyze:** Given the poem's setting, why is the image of "petals on a wet, black bough" surprising?
3. **Craft and Structure Infer:** Why do you think Pound chose to use the word *apparition* rather than *appearance*?
4. **Integration of Knowledge and Ideas Evaluate:** How well does "In a Station of the Metro" follow the advice given in "A Few Don'ts"? Explain.

The Red Wheelbarrow

William Carlos Williams

so much depends
upon

a red wheel
barrow

glazed with rain
water

beside the white
chickens.

Image
What two images dominate this poem?

This Is Just to Say

William Carlos Williams

I have eaten
the plums
that were in
the icebox
and which
you were probably
saving
for breakfast

Forgive me
they were delicious
so sweet
and so cold

Engaging Your Senses
To what senses does the central image in this poem appeal?

The Great Figure

William Carlos Williams

Among the rain
and lights
I saw the figure 5
in gold
on a red
fire truck
moving
tense
unheeded
to gong clangs
siren howls
and wheels rumbling
through the dark city.

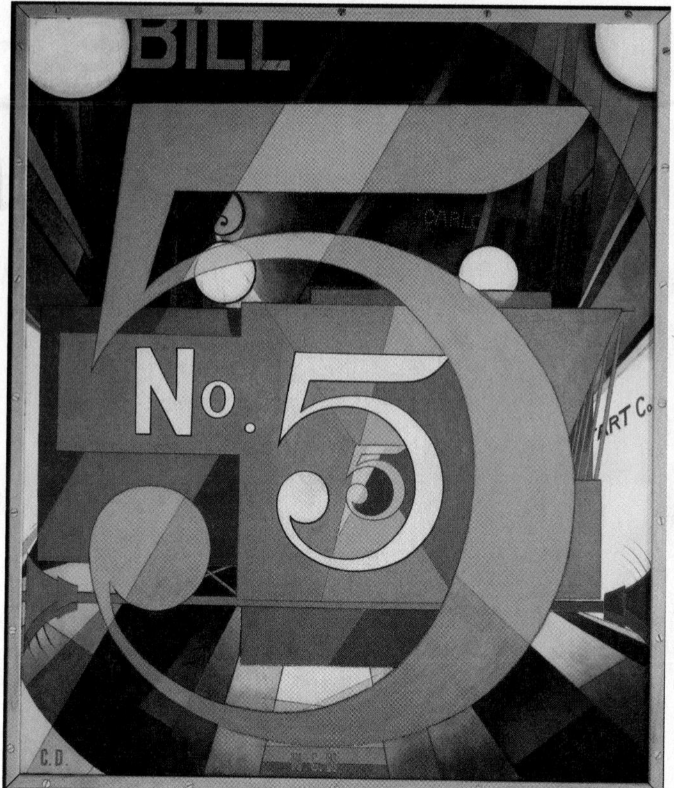

The Figure 5 in Gold, Charles Demuth, Metropolitan Museum of Art

▲ **Critical Viewing** Artist Charles Demuth created this work of art to accompany his friend Williams's poem. What elements of the painting convey the energy and clamor of the poem? **CONNECT**

Critical Reading

1. **Key Ideas and Details (a)** In "The Red Wheelbarrow," what words does Williams split to run on two lines? **(b) Analyze:** What is the effect? Explain.
2. **Key Ideas and Details (a)** What is the intention of the speaker in "This Is Just to Say"? **(b) Connect:** Which details in the second stanza challenge the speaker's sincerity?
3. **Key Ideas and Details (a)** In "The Great Figure," what detail of the fire truck is the focus of the speaker's experience? **(b) Interpret:** In focusing on this detail, what might Williams be saying about beauty and modern life?
4. **Craft and Structure Evaluate:** Which elements of these poems reflect Williams's interest in portraying and celebrating everyday American life?

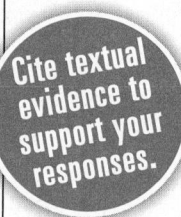

Cite textual evidence to support your responses.

PEAR TREE
H. D.

Silver dust
lifted from the earth,
higher than my arms reach,
you have mounted,
O silver,
higher than my arms reach
you front us with great mass;

no flower ever opened
so staunch a white leaf,
no flower ever parted silver
from such rare silver;

O white pear,
your flower-tufts
thick on the branch
bring summer and ripe fruits
in their purple hearts.

▲ Critical Viewing
Which phrases from the poem best describe this image of a pear tree in full flower? **EVALUATE**

Critical Reading

1. **Key Ideas and Details (a)** What is the "silver dust" referred to in the first stanza? **(b) Interpret:** In what sense is the dust "lifted from the earth"?
2. **Key Ideas and Details (a)** What does the pear tree's blossom anticipate? **(b) Infer:** What time of year is the speaker describing?
3. **Key Ideas and Details Assess:** How would you define the speaker's relationship to nature?
4. **Integration of Knowledge and Ideas** What larger portrait of the American landscape emerges from the common, everyday images in these poems? In your response, use at least two of these Essential Question words: *commonplace, medley, essence, contemplate.* ***[Connecting to the Essential Question: What is the relationship between literature and place?]***

Cite textual evidence to support your responses.

Close Reading Activities *The Imagist Poets*

Literary Analysis

1. **Key Ideas and Details** **Engage your senses** while rereading "In a Station of the Metro." **(a)** To what senses does the image in this poem appeal? **(b)** How does engaging your senses affect your understanding and appreciation of the poem?
2. **Craft and Structure** Of the fourteen words in "In a Station of the Metro," not one of them is a verb. **(a)** How does this absence reflect the criteria Pound lists in his essay? **(b)** How does it affect the reader's experience of the poem?
3. **Key Ideas and Details** In "The Red Wheelbarrow," what do you think is the "so much" that "depends / upon / a red wheel / barrow"? Apply what you know about **Imagist poetry** to answer this question.
4. **Craft and Structure** In what ways would the meaning of the poem be different if Williams had used "the" instead of "a" to identify the wheelbarrow?
5. **Craft and Structure** Using a chart like the one shown, identify **images** of color in the poems by Williams. Explain the differing emotions these uses of color evoke.

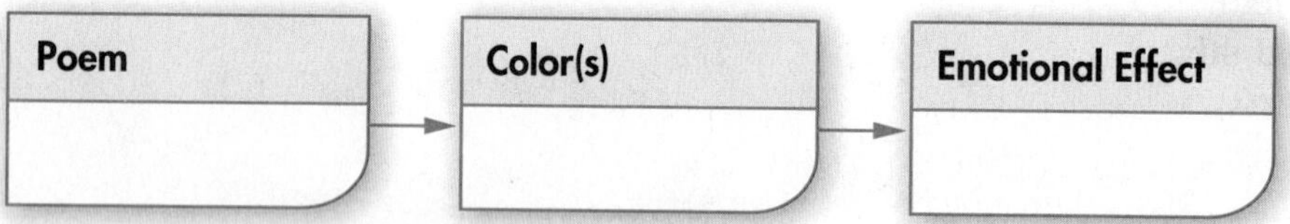

6. **Craft and Structure** **(a)** To what sense does "Pear Tree" mainly appeal? **(b)** To what sense does "The Red Wheelbarrow" mainly appeal? **(c)** Give two examples of passages from each poem that support your answers.
7. **Integration of Knowledge and Ideas** **(a)** Which of the five poems engages the sense of hearing most? Explain. **(b)** How do the sounds in that poem help to sharpen the central image?
8. **Integration of Knowledge and Ideas** Although Pound wrote "the painter can describe a landscape much better than you can," in what ways are these poems like paintings?
9. **Comparing Literary Works** In what ways is Pound's advice to **(a)** avoid abstractions and **(b)** avoid superfluous words evident in all of these poems?
10. **Comparing Literary Works** **(a)** According to Pound, what does a good musician do that a poet should emulate? **(b)** Do H. D. and Williams achieve this skill in their poems? Explain.
11. **Comparing Literary Works** Which of these poems best exemplifies Pound's idea of the image as "that which presents an intellectual and emotional complex in an instant of time"? Explain your choice.

Common Core State Standards

Writing

2. Write explanatory texts to examine and convey complex ideas, concepts, and information clearly and accurately through the effective selection, organization, and analysis of content. *(p. 727)*

2.b. Develop the topic thoroughly by selecting the most significant and relevant facts, extended definitions, concrete details, quotations, or other information and examples appropriate to the audience's knowledge of the topic. *(p. 727)*

2.c Use precise language. *(p. 727)*

Language

4.b. Identify and correctly use patterns of word changes that indicate different meanings or parts of speech. *(p. 727)*

Vocabulary Acquisition and Use

Word Analysis: Forms of *appear*

Several common English words are forms of the verb *appear,* meaning "to come into sight or into being" or "to become understood."

apparent appearance apparition

Complete each of the sentences with the correct word from the list above. Explain your choices.

1. He made a brief ______ at the awards dinner, just long enough to pick up his trophy and say a few words.
2. When midnight found the toddlers still running around the house, it became ______ that the babysitter was not in control.
3. The ______ of a face at the window nearly stopped her heart with fear.

Vocabulary: True or False

Decide whether each statement below is true or false. Explain your answers.

1. You should not accept as dogma everything that a two-year-old says.
2. A person who takes voluminous notes can easily store them in a pocket folder.
3. An apparition will go unnoticed by someone wearing a blindfold.

Writing to Sources

Explanatory Text Imagine that you are a magazine editor who has just received a manuscript from an Imagist poet. Write a **letter** to the poet explaining why you will or will not publish his or her poems. Be simple, honest, and kind, and include constructive criticism.

Prewriting Choose a poet and reread the poem or poems. Take notes on the strengths and weaknesses of each poem, citing relevant passages.

Drafting Write a letter that explains why you will or will not publish the poems. Discuss strengths and identify flaws. Support your viewpoint through detailed references to the poet's work.

Revising Review your draft, highlighting any words that are inaccurate or vague. Use a thesaurus to replace these words with more precise choices.

Model: Revising for Clarity

Your poems are small and ~~not complex~~ ^deceptively simple^, but they are rich in imagery and ideas. I especially enjoyed the ~~incredible~~ ^wry^ tone of "This Is Just to Say."

Replacing vague words with specific words helps to express ideas exactly.

Building Knowledge and Insight

ANCHOR TEXT
Winter Dreams

Connecting to the Essential Question The main character of this story is preoccupied with wealth and all that it brings. As you read, notice Fitzgerald's descriptions of "glittering things." Doing so will help as you think about the Essential Question: **How does literature shape or reflect society?**

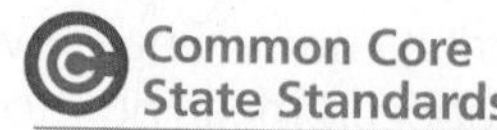

Reading Literature

1. Cite strong and thorough textual evidence to support analysis of what the text says explicitly as well as inferences drawn from the text, including determining where the text leaves matters uncertain.

3. Analyze the impact of the author's choices regarding how to develop and relate elements of a story or drama (e.g., how the characters are introduced and developed).

9. Demonstrate knowledge of early-twentieth-century foundational works of American literature.

Close Reading Focus

Characters; Characterization

All fictional works have **characters,** the personalities represented in a story. Characters fall into two basic categories: **Flat characters** are one-dimensional, with few character traits. Their main role is to advance the action. **Round characters** have many character traits. They are usually the main characters. Authors use these specific strategies to develop characters:

- **Direct characterization:** The narrator simply tells the reader what a character is like. Example: "She is honest."
- **Indirect characterization:** The writer reveals characters through their thoughts, actions, words, and other characters' reactions.

As you read, notice how Fitzgerald brings his characters into sharp focus.

Preparing to Read Complex Texts Fitzgerald often leaves it up to the reader to draw inferences about his characters. To **draw inferences about characters,** combine information from the story with your own knowledge of life. Consider this example:

> *Dexter stood perfectly still . . . if he moved forward a step his stare would be in her line of vision—if he moved backward he would lose his full view of her face.*

If you have ever wanted to hide your interest in someone but could not stop looking, you can draw a strong inference from this scene: Dexter is enthralled by someone. Use a chart like the one shown to draw inferences.

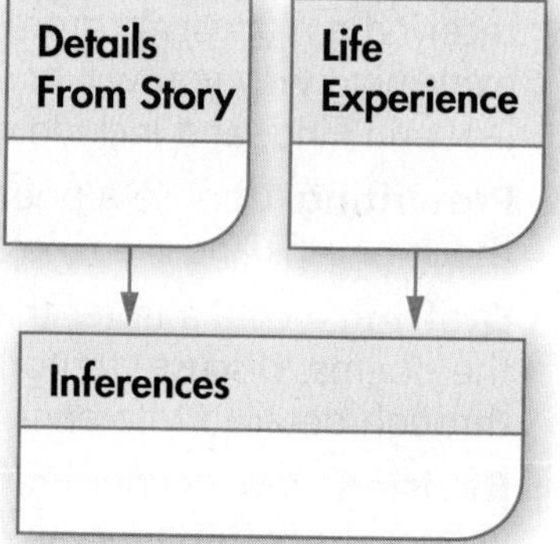

Vocabulary

You will encounter the words listed here in the text that follows. Copy the words into your notebook. Can you infer which two words are nouns? How can you tell?

fallowness	**mundane**
fortuitous	**poignant**
sinuous	**sediment**

F. Scott Fitzgerald *(1896–1940)*

Author of "Winter Dreams"

When you open the pages of one of F. Scott Fitzgerald's books, you are transported back in time to the Roaring Twenties, when many Americans lived with reckless abandon, attending wild parties, wearing glamorous clothing, and striving for fulfillment through material wealth. Yet, this quest for pleasure was often accompanied by a sense of inner despair. Fitzgerald was able to capture the paradoxes of this glittering, materialistic lifestyle because he actually lived it.

A Quick Rise to Fame Francis Scott Key Fitzgerald was born in St. Paul, Minnesota, into a family with high social aspirations but little wealth. As a young man, Fitzgerald was eager to improve his social standing. He entered Princeton University in 1913, where he pursued the type of high-profile social life for which he would later become famous. Fitzgerald failed to graduate and soon enlisted in the army.

His first novel, *This Side of Paradise* (1920), published shortly after his discharge from the service, was an instant success. Buoyed by the fame and wealth the book gave him, Fitzgerald courted Zelda Sayre, a southern belle with whom he had fallen in love while in the army. They married in 1920. Together, they blazed an extravagant trail across New York and Europe, mingling with the rich and famous and spending money recklessly.

An American Masterpiece Despite his pleasure-seeking lifestyle, Fitzgerald remained a productive writer. In 1925, he published *The Great Gatsby*, the story of a self-made man whose dreams of love and social acceptance end in tragedy. The book is widely considered to be Fitzgerald's masterpiece and one of the greatest novels in American literature.

Fortunes Turn After the 1929 stock market crash, Fitzgerald's world began to crumble. His wife suffered a series of nervous breakdowns, and financial problems forced him to seek work as a screenwriter. Despite these setbacks, however, he managed to produce many more short stories and a second novel, *Tender Is the Night* (1934). He was in the midst of writing *The Last Tycoon* when he died of a heart attack in 1940. His editor approached the novelist John O'Hara about finishing the book, but O'Hara declined. In a letter O'Hara wrote to author John Steinbeck, he explained his refusal: "Fitzgerald was a better just plain writer than all of us put together. Just words writing."

WINTER DREAMS

F. Scott Fitzgerald

BACKGROUND Written in 1922, this story unfolds against the background of the Jazz Age. Focusing on Dexter Green's obsession with Judy Jones, a beautiful young woman from a prominent wealthy family, Fitzgerald explores the connections between love, money, and social status. Through Dexter, he shows what life was like in the 1920s for an ambitious young man driven by the desire for "glittering things."

◄ Critical Viewing
Which details in this illustration demonstrate women's newfound freedoms during the Jazz Age? **DEDUCE**

Some of the caddies were poor as sin and lived in one-room houses with a neurasthenic[1] cow in the front yard, but Dexter Green's father owned the second best grocery store in Black Bear—the best one was "The Hub," patronized by the wealthy people from Sherry Island—and Dexter caddied only for pocket money.

In the fall when the days became crisp and gray, and the long Minnesota winter shut down like the white lid of a box, Dexter's skis moved over the snow that hid the fairways of the golf course. At these times the country gave him a feeling of profound melancholy—it offended him that the links should lie in enforced **fallowness**, haunted by ragged sparrows for the long season. It was dreary, too, that on the tees where the gay colors fluttered in summer there were now only the desolate sandboxes knee deep in crusted ice. When he crossed the hills the wind blew cold as misery, and if the sun was out he tramped with his eyes squinted up against the hard dimensionless glare.

Vocabulary
fallowness (fal′ ō nis)
n. inactivity

In April the winter ceased abruptly. The snow ran down into Black Bear Lake scarcely tarrying for the early golfers to brave the season with red and black balls. Without elation, without an interval of moist glory, the cold was gone. Dexter knew that there was something dismal about this Northern spring, just as he knew there was something gorgeous about the fall. Fall made him clinch his hands and tremble and repeat idiotic sentences to himself, and make brisk abrupt gestures of command to imaginary audiences and armies. October filled him with hope which November raised to a sort of ecstatic triumph, and in this mood the fleeting brilliant impressions of the summer at Sherry Island were ready grist to his mill. He became a golf champion and defeated Mr. T. A. Hedrick in a marvelous match played a hundred times over the fairways of his imagination, a match each detail of which he changed about untiringly—sometimes he won with almost laughable ease, sometimes he came

Comprehension
What does Dexter do for pocket money?

1. **neurasthenic** (no͞or′ əs thēn′ ik) *adj.* here, weak; tired.

up magnificently from behind. Again, stepping from a Pierce-Arrow automobile, like Mr. Mortimer Jones, he strolled frigidly into the lounge of the Sherry Island Golf Club—or perhaps, surrounded by an admiring crowd, he gave an exhibition of fancy diving from the springboard of the club raft. . . . Among those who watched him in open-mouthed wonder was Mr. Mortimer Jones.

And one day it came to pass that Mr. Jones—himself and not his ghost—came up to Dexter with tears in his eyes and said that Dexter was the—best caddy in the club, and wouldn't he decide not to quit if Mr. Jones made it worth his while, because every other—caddy in the club lost one ball a hole for him—regularly—

"No, sir," said Dexter decisively, "I don't want to caddy any more." Then, after a pause: "I'm too old."

"You're not more than fourteen. Why the devil did you decide just this morning that you wanted to quit? You promised that next week you'd go over to the state tournament with me."

"I decided I was too old."

Dexter handed in his "A Class" badge, collected what money was due him from the caddy master, and walked home to Black Bear Village.

"The best—caddy I ever saw," shouted Mr. Mortimer Jones over a drink that afternoon. "Never lost a ball! Willing! Intelligent! Quiet! Honest! Grateful!"

Characterization

What methods of characterization does Fitzgerald use in this introduction to Judy Jones?

The little girl who had done this was eleven—beautifully ugly as little girls are apt to be who are destined after a few years to be inexpressibly lovely and bring no end of misery to a great number of men. The spark, however, was perceptible. There was a general ungodliness in the way her lips twisted down at the corners when she smiled, and in the—Heaven help us!—in the almost passionate quality of her eyes. Vitality is born early in such women. It was utterly in evidence now, shining through her thin frame in a sort of glow.

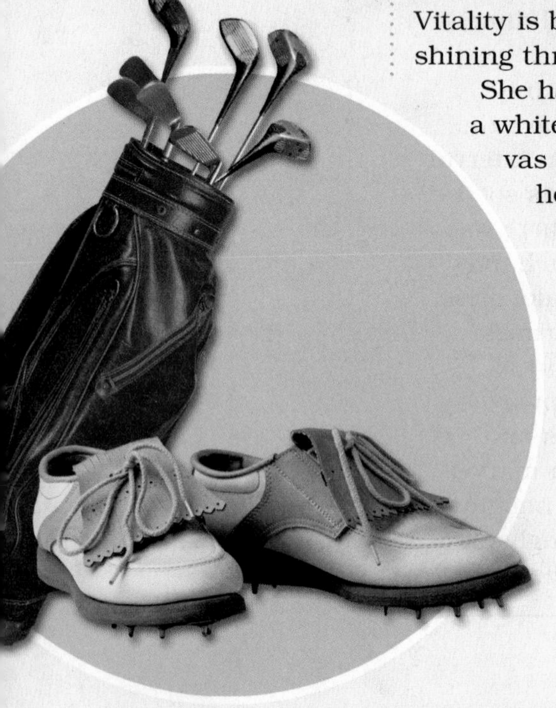

She had come eagerly out on to the course at nine o'clock with a white linen nurse and five small new golf clubs in a white canvas bag which the nurse was carrying. When Dexter first saw her she was standing by the caddy house, rather ill at ease and trying to conceal the fact by engaging her nurse in an obviously unnatural conversation graced by startling and irrelevant grimaces from herself.

"Well, it's certainly a nice day, Hilda," Dexter heard her say. She drew down the corners of her mouth, smiled, and glanced furtively around, her eyes in transit falling for an instant on Dexter.

Then to the nurse:

"Well, I guess there aren't very many people out here this morning, are there?"

The smile again—radiant, blatantly artificial—convincing.

"I don't know what we're supposed to do now," said the nurse looking nowhere in particular.

"Oh, that's all right. I'll fix it up."

Dexter stood perfectly still, his mouth slightly ajar. He knew that if he moved forward a step his stare would be in her line of vision—if he moved backward he would lose his full view of her face. For a moment he had not realized how young she was. Now he remembered having seen her several times the year before—in bloomers.

Suddenly, involuntarily, he laughed, a short abrupt laugh—then, startled by himself, he turned and began to walk quickly away.

"Boy!"

Dexter stopped.

"Boy—"

Beyond question he was addressed. Not only that, but he was treated to that absurd smile, that preposterous smile—the memory of which at least a dozen men were to carry into middle age.

"Boy, do you know where the golf teacher is?"

"He's giving a lesson."

"Well, do you know where the caddy master is?"

"He isn't here yet this morning."

▲ Critical Viewing

How does this painting of two golfers and their caddies compare to your impression of Dexter's experience? **COMPARE AND CONTRAST**

Comprehension

What does Dexter suddenly decide one day?

"Oh." For a moment this baffled her. She stood alternately on her right and left foot.

"We'd like to get a caddy," said the nurse. "Mrs. Mortimer Jones sent us out to play golf, and we don't know how without we get a caddy."

Here she was stopped by an ominous glance from Miss Jones, followed immediately by the smile.

"There aren't any caddies here except me," said Dexter to the nurse, "and I got to stay here in charge until the caddy master gets here."

"Oh."

Characterization
What does the argument between Judy Jones and her nurse reveal about Judy?

Miss Jones and her retinue now withdrew, and at a proper distance from Dexter became involved in a heated conversation, which was concluded by Miss Jones taking one of the clubs and hitting it on the ground with violence. For further emphasis she raised it again and was about to bring it down smartly upon the nurse's bosom, when the nurse seized the club and twisted it from her hands.

"You little mean old *thing*!" cried Miss Jones wildly.

Another argument ensued. Realizing that the elements of the comedy were implied in the scene, Dexter several times began to laugh, but each time restrained the laugh before it reached audibility. He could not resist the monstrous conviction that the little girl was justified in beating the nurse.

Vocabulary
fortuitous (fôr to͞o′ ə təs) *adj.* fortunate

The situation was resolved by the **fortuitous** appearance of the caddy master, who was appealed to immediately by the nurse.

"Miss Jones is to have a little caddy, and this one says he can't go."

"Mr. McKenna said I was to wait here till you came," said Dexter quickly.

"Well, he's here now." Miss Jones smiled cheerfully at the caddy master. Then she dropped her bag and set off at a haughty mince toward the first tee.

"Well?" The caddy master turned to Dexter.

"What you standing there like a dummy for? Go pick up the young lady's clubs."

"I don't think I'll go out today," said Dexter.

"You don't—"

"I think I'll quit."

The enormity of his decision frightened him. He was a favorite caddy, and the thirty dollars a month he earned through the summer were not to be made elsewhere around the lake. But he had received a strong emotional shock, and his perturbation required a violent and immediate outlet.

It is not so simple as that, either. As so frequently would be the case in the future, Dexter was unconsciously dictated to by his winter dreams.

2

Now, of course, the quality and the seasonability of these winter dreams varied, but the stuff of them remained. They persuaded Dexter several years later to pass up a business course at the State university—his father, prospering now, would have paid his way—for the precarious advantage of attending an older and more famous university in the East, where he was bothered by his scanty funds. But do not get the impression, because his winter dreams happened to be concerned at first with musings on the rich, that there was anything merely snobbish in the boy. He wanted not association with glittering things and glittering people—he wanted the glittering things themselves. Often he reached out for the best without knowing why he wanted it—and sometimes he ran up against the mysterious denials and prohibitions in which life indulges. It is with one of those denials and not with his career as a whole that this story deals.

He made money. It was rather amazing. After college he went to the city from which Black Bear Lake draws its wealthy patrons. When he was only twenty-three and had been there not quite two years, there were already people who liked to say: "Now *there's* a boy—" All about him rich men's sons were peddling bonds precariously, or investing patrimonies precariously, or plodding through the two dozen volumes of the "George Washington Commercial Course," but Dexter borrowed a thousand dollars on his college degree and his confident mouth, and bought a partnership in a laundry.

It was a small laundry when he went into it, but Dexter made a specialty of learning how the English washed fine woolen golf stockings without shrinking them, and within a year he was catering to the trade that wore knickerbockers. Men were insisting that their Shetland hose and sweaters go to his laundry, just as they had insisted on a caddy who could find golf balls. A little later he was doing their wives' lingerie as well—and running five branches in different parts of the city. Before he was twenty-seven he owned the largest string of laundries in his section of the country. It was then that he sold out and went to New York. But the part of his story that concerns us goes back to the days when he was making his first big success.

When he was twenty-three Mr. Hart—one of the gray-haired men who like to say "Now there's a boy"—gave him a guest card to the Sherry Island Golf Club for a weekend. So he signed his name one day on the register, and that afternoon played golf in a foursome with Mr. Hart and Mr. Sandwood and Mr. T. A. Hedrick. He did not consider it necessary to remark that he had once carried Mr. Hart's bag over this same links, and that he knew every trap and gully with his eyes shut—but he found himself glancing at the four caddies who trailed them, trying to catch a gleam or gesture that would remind him of himself, that would lessen the gap which lay between his present and his past.

Comprehension
How does Dexter make money after college?

RB

It was a curious day, slashed abruptly with fleeting, familiar impressions. One minute he had the sense of being a trespasser—in the next he was impressed by the tremendous superiority he felt toward Mr. T. A. Hedrick, who was a bore and not even a good golfer any more.

Then, because of a ball Mr. Hart lost near the fifteenth green, an enormous thing happened. While they were searching the stiff grasses of the rough there was a clear call of "Fore!" from behind a hill in their rear. And as they all turned abruptly from their search a bright new ball sliced abruptly over the hill and caught Mr. T. A. Hedrick in the abdomen.

"By Gad!" cried Mr. T. A. Hedrick, "they ought to put some of these crazy women off the course. It's getting to be outrageous."

A head and a voice came up together over the hill:

"Do you mind if we go through?"

"You hit me in the stomach!" declared Mr. Hedrick wildly.

"Did I?" The girl approached the group of men. "I'm sorry. I yelled 'Fore!'"

Her glance fell casually on each of the men—then scanned the fairway for her ball.

"Did I bounce into the rough?"

It was impossible to determine whether this question was ingenuous or malicious. In a moment, however, she left no doubt, for as her partner came up over the hill she called cheerfully:

"Here I am! I'd have gone on the green except that I hit something."

As she took her stance for a short mashie shot, Dexter looked at her closely. She wore a blue gingham dress, rimmed at throat and shoulders with a white edging that accentuated her tan. The quality of exaggeration, of thinness, which had made her passionate eyes and down-turning mouth absurd at eleven, was gone now. She was arrestingly beautiful. The color in her cheeks was centered like the color in a picture—it was not a "high" color, but a sort of fluctuating and feverish warmth, so shaded that it seemed at any moment it would recede and disappear. This color and the mobility of her mouth gave a continual impression of flux, of intense life, of passionate vitality—balanced only partially by the sad luxury of her eyes.

She swung her mashie impatiently and without interest, pitching the ball into a sand pit on the other side of the green. With a quick, insincere smile and a careless "Thank you!" she went on after it.

"That Judy Jones!" remarked Mr. Hedrick on the next tee, as they waited—some moments—for her to play on ahead. "All she needs is to be turned up and spanked for six months and then to be married off to an old-fashioned cavalry captain."

"My God, she's good looking!" said Mr. Sandwood, who was just over thirty.

"Good looking!" cried Mr. Hedrick contemptuously, "she always

◀ Critical Viewing

Golf was once a game reserved for the privileged. How might meeting Judy in a setting like this have affected Dexter's impression of her? **ANALYZE**

Drawing Inferences About Characters

What does Judy's behavior toward the men on the golf course suggest about her character?

Comprehension

What "enormous thing" happens near the fifteenth green?

looks as if she wanted to be kissed! Turning those big coweyes on every calf in town!"

It was doubtful if Mr. Hedrick intended a reference to the maternal instinct.

"She'd play pretty good golf if she'd try," said Mr. Sandwood.

"She has no form," said Mr. Hedrick solemnly.

"She has a nice figure," said Mr. Sandwood.

"Better thank the Lord she doesn't drive a swifter ball," said Mr. Hart, winking at Dexter.

Later in the afternoon the sun went down with a riotous swirl of gold and varying blues and scarlets, and left the dry, rustling night of Western summer. Dexter watched from the veranda of the golf club, watched the even overlap of the waters in the little wind, silver molasses under the harvest moon. Then the moon held a finger to her lips and the lake became a clear pool, pale and quiet. Dexter put on his bathing suit and swam out to the farthest raft, where he stretched dripping on the wet canvas of the springboard.

There was a fish jumping and a star shining and the lights around the lake were gleaming. Over on a dark peninsula a piano was playing the songs of last summer and of summers before that—songs from *Chin-Chin* and *The Count of Luxemburg* and *The Chocolate Soldier*[2]—and because the sound of a piano over a stretch of water had always seemed beautiful to Dexter he lay perfectly quiet and listened.

▼ Critical Viewing
How does the demeanor of the woman in this drawing compare to your impression of Judy Jones? Explain. **COMPARE AND CONTRAST**

The tune the piano was playing at that moment had been gay and new five years before when Dexter was a sophomore at college. They had played it at a prom once when he could not afford the luxury of proms, and he had stood outside the gymnasium and listened. The sound of the tune precipitated in him a sort of ecstasy and it was with that ecstasy he viewed what happened to him now. It was a mood of intense appreciation, a sense that, for once, he was magnificently attuned to life and that everything about him was radiating a brightness and a glamor he might never know again.

A low, pale oblong detached itself suddenly from the darkness of the Island, spitting forth the reverberate sound of a racing motorboat. Two white streamers of cleft water rolled themselves out behind it and almost immediately the boat was beside him, drowning out the hot tinkle of the piano in the drone of its

2. ***Chin-Chin . . . The Chocolate Soldier*** popular operettas of the time.

spray. Dexter raising himself on his arms was aware of a figure standing at the wheel, of two dark eyes regarding him over the lengthening space of water—then the boat had gone by and was sweeping in an immense and purposeless circle of spray round and round in the middle of the lake. With equal eccentricity one of the circles flattened out and headed back toward the raft.

"Who's that?" she called, shutting off her motor. She was so near now that Dexter could see her bathing suit, which consisted apparently of pink rompers.

The nose of the boat bumped the raft, and as the latter tilted rakishly he was precipitated toward her. With different degrees of interest they recognized each other.

"Aren't you one of those men we played through this afternoon?" she demanded.

He was.

"Well, do you know how to drive a motorboat? Because if you do I wish you'd drive this one so I can ride on the surfboard behind. My name is Judy Jones"—she favored him with an absurd smirk—rather, what tried to be a smirk, for, twist her mouth as she might, it was not grotesque, it was merely beautiful—"and I live in a house over there on the Island, and in that house there is a man waiting for me. When he drove up at the door I drove out of the dock because he says I'm his ideal."

Drawing Inferences About Characters

What does Judy's reason for leaving the house suggest about her character?

There was a fish jumping and a star shining and the lights around the lake were gleaming. Dexter sat beside Judy Jones and she explained how her boat was driven. Then she was in the water, swimming to the floating surfboard with a **sinuous** crawl. Watching her was without effort to the eye, watching a branch waving or a sea gull flying. Her arms, burned to butternut, moved sinuously among the dull platinum ripples, elbow appearing first, casting the forearm back with a cadence of falling water, then reaching out and down, stabbing a path ahead.

Vocabulary

sinuous (sin′ yo͞o əs) *adj.* moving in and out; wavy

They moved out into the lake; turning, Dexter saw that she was kneeling on the low rear of the now uptilted surfboard.

"Go faster," she called, "fast as it'll go."

Obediently he jammed the lever forward and the white spray mounted at the bow. When he looked around again the girl was standing up on the rushing board, her arms spread wide, her eyes lifted toward the moon.

"It's awful cold," she shouted. "What's your name?"

He told her.

"Well, why don't you come to dinner tomorrow night?"

His heart turned over like the flywheel of the boat, and, for the second time, her casual whim gave a new direction to his life.

Comprehension

Where is Dexter when he meets Judy for the third time?

3

Next evening while he waited for her to come downstairs, Dexter peopled the soft deep summer room and the sun porch that opened from it with the men who had already loved Judy Jones. He knew the sort of men they were—the men who when he first went to college had entered from the great prep schools with graceful clothes and the deep tan of healthy summers. He had seen that, in one sense, he was better than these men. He was newer and stronger. Yet in acknowledging to himself that he wished his children to be like them he was admitting that he was but the rough, strong stuff from which they eternally sprang.

When the time had come for him to wear good clothes, he had known who were the best tailors in America, and the best tailors in America had made him the suit he wore this evening. He had acquired that particular reserve peculiar to his university, that set it off from other universities. He recognized the value to him of such a mannerism and he had adopted it; he knew that to be careless in dress and manner required more confidence than to be careful. But carelessness was for his children. His mother's name had been Krimelich. She was a Bohemian of the peasant class and she had talked broken English to the end of her days. Her son must keep to the set patterns.

At a little after seven Judy Jones came downstairs. She wore a blue silk afternoon dress, and he was disappointed at first that she had not put on something more elaborate. This feeling was accentuated when, after a brief greeting, she went to the door of a butler's pantry and pushing it open called: "You can serve dinner, Martha." He had rather expected that a butler would announce dinner, that there would be a cocktail. Then he put these thoughts behind him as they sat down side by side on a lounge and looked at each other.

"Father and mother won't be here," she said thoughtfully.

He remembered the last time he had seen her father, and he was glad the parents were not to be here tonight—they might wonder who he was. He had been born in Keeble, a Minnesota village fifty miles farther north, and he always gave Keeble as his home instead of Black Bear Village. Country towns were well enough to come from if they weren't inconveniently in sight and used as footstools by fashionable lakes.

They talked of his university, which she had visited frequently during the past two years, and of the nearby city which supplied Sherry Island with its patrons, and whither Dexter would return next day to his prospering laundries.

During dinner she slipped into a moody depression which gave Dexter a feeling of uneasiness. Whatever petulance she uttered in her throaty voice worried him. Whatever she smiled at—at him, at a chicken liver, at nothing—it disturbed him that her smile could have no root in mirth, or even in amusement. When the scarlet corners of her lips curved down, it was less a smile than an invitation to a kiss.

Then, after dinner, she led him out on the dark sun porch and deliberately changed the atmosphere.

"Do you mind if I weep a little?" she said.

"I'm afraid I'm boring you," he responded quickly.

"You're not. I like you. But I've just had a terrible afternoon. There was a man I cared about, and this afternoon he told me out of a clear sky that he was poor as a church mouse. He'd never even hinted it before. Does this sound horribly **mundane**?"

"Perhaps he was afraid to tell you."

"Suppose he was," she answered. "He didn't start right. You see, if I'd thought of him as poor—well, I've been mad about loads of poor men, and fully intended to marry them all. But in this case, I hadn't thought of him that way, and my interest in him wasn't strong enough to survive the shock. As if a girl calmly informed her fiancè that she was a widow. He might not object to widows, but—

"Let's start right," she interrupted herself suddenly. "Who are you, anyhow?"

For a moment Dexter hesitated. Then:

"I'm nobody," he announced. "My career is largely a matter of futures."

"Are you poor?"

"No," he said frankly, "I'm probably making more money than any man my age in the Northwest. I know that's an obnoxious remark, but you advised me to start right."

There was a pause. Then she smiled and the corners of her mouth drooped and an almost imperceptible sway brought her closer to him, looking up into his eyes. A lump rose in Dexter's throat, and he waited breathless for the experiment, facing the unpredictable compound that would form mysteriously from the elements of their lips. Then he saw—she communicated her excitement to him, lavishly, deeply, with kisses that were not a promise but a fulfillment. They aroused in him not hunger demanding renewal but surfeit that would demand more surfeit . . . kisses that were like charity, creating want by holding back nothing at all.

It did not take him many hours to decide that he had wanted Judy Jones ever since he was a proud, desirous little boy.

Vocabulary
mundane (mun′ dān′) *adj.* commonplace; ordinary

Characterization
What does this conversation reveal about the characters of Dexter and Judy?

Comprehension
Where do Dexter and Judy have dinner?

LITERATURE IN CONTEXT

Cultural Connection

Fitzgerald's Elusive Women
From Daisy in *The Great Gatsby* to Judy Jones in "Winter Dreams," F. Scott Fitzgerald's fictional landscape is populated by elusive women. This theme mirrors Fitzgerald's life, which was deeply bound up in that of his wife, Zelda. When they first met, Zelda Sayre was a young Southern society girl, the darling of Montgomery, Alabama. Although Fitzgerald believed himself to be socially inferior to Zelda, he finally won her. The marriage that ensued was troubled and stormy, made more so by Zelda's mental illness. In Fitzgerald's fiction, the lovely, elusive woman becomes not only an object of desire in her own right but a symbol of all that is desirable in life.

Connect to the Literature

Do you think Dexter would be so obsessed with Judy if she had not both "beckoned him and yawned at him"? Explain.

4

It began like that—and continued, with varying shades of intensity, on such a note right up to the denouement. Dexter surrendered a part of himself to the most direct and unprincipled personality with which he had ever come in contact. Whatever Judy wanted, she went after with the full pressure of her charm. There was no divergence of method, no jockeying for position or premeditation of effects—there was a very little mental side to any of her affairs. She simply made men conscious to the highest degree of her physical loveliness. Dexter had no desire to change her. Her deficiencies were knit up with a passionate energy that transcended and justified them.

When, as Judy's head lay against his shoulder that first night, she whispered, "I don't know what's the matter with me. Last night I thought I was in love with a man and tonight I think I'm in love with you—" it seemed to him a beautiful and romantic thing to say. It was the exquisite excitability that for the moment he controlled and owned. But a week later he was compelled to view this same quality in a different light. She took him in her roadster to a picnic supper, and after supper she disappeared, likewise in her roadster, with another man. Dexter became enormously upset and was scarcely able to be decently civil to the other people present. When she assured him that she had not kissed the other man, he knew she was lying—yet he was glad that she had taken the trouble to lie to him.

He was, as he found before the summer ended, one of a varying dozen who circulated about her. Each of them had at one time been favored above all others—about half of them still basked in the solace of occasional sentimental revivals. Whenever one showed signs of dropping out through long neglect, she granted him a brief honeyed hour, which encouraged him to tag along for a year or so longer. Judy made these forays upon the helpless and defeated without malice, indeed half unconscious that there was anything mischievous in what she did.

When a new man came to town everyone dropped out—dates were automatically canceled.

The helpless part of trying to do anything about it was that she did it all herself. She was not a girl who could be "won" in the kinetic sense—she was proof against cleverness, she was proof against charm; if any of these assailed her too strongly she would immediately resolve the affair to a physical basis, and under the magic of her physical splendor the strong as well as the brilliant played her game and not their own. She was entertained only by the gratification of her desires and by the direct exercise of her own charm. Perhaps from so much youthful love, so many youthful lovers, she had come, in self-defense, to nourish herself wholly from within.

Succeeding Dexter's first exhilaration came restlessness and dissatisfaction. The helpless ecstasy of losing himself in her was opiate rather than tonic. It was fortunate for his work during the winter that those moments of ecstasy came infrequently. Early in their acquaintance it had seemed for a while that there was a deep and spontaneous mutual attraction—that first August, for example—three days of long evenings on her dusky veranda, of strange wan kisses through the late afternoon, in shadowy alcoves or behind the protecting trellises of the garden arbors, of mornings when she was fresh as a dream and almost shy at meeting him in the clarity of the rising day. There was all the ecstasy of an engagement about it, sharpened by his realization that there was no engagement. It was during those three days that, for the first time, he had asked her to marry him. She said "maybe some day," she said "kiss me," she said, "I'd like to marry you," she said "I love you"—she said—nothing.

Characterization
What do Judy Jones's varying responses to Dexter's marriage proposals reveal about her feelings for him?

The three days were interrupted by the arrival of a New York man who visited at her house for half September. To Dexter's agony, rumor engaged them. The man was the son of the president of a great trust company. But at the end of a month it was reported that Judy was yawning. At a dance one night she sat all evening in a motorboat with a local beau, while the New Yorker searched the club for her frantically. She told the local beau that she was bored with her visitor, and two days later he left. She was seen with him at the station, and it was reported that he looked very mournful indeed.

. . . he was glad that she had taken the trouble to lie to him.

On this note the summer ended. Dexter was twenty-four, and he found himself increasingly in a position to do as he wished. He joined two clubs in the city and lived at one of them. Though he was by no means an integral part of the stag lines at these clubs, he managed to be on hand at dances where Judy Jones was likely to appear. He could have gone out socially as much as he liked—he was an eligible young man, now, and popular with downtown fathers. His confessed devotion to Judy Jones had rather solidified his position. But he had no social aspirations and rather despised the dancing men who were always on tap for the Thursday or Saturday parties and who filled in at dinners with the younger married set. Already he was playing with the idea of going East to New York. He wanted to take Judy Jones with him. No disillusion as to the world in which she had grown up could cure his illusion as to her desirability.

Remember that—for only in the light of it can what he did for her be understood.

Comprehension
What does Dexter learn about the number of Judy's suitors?

Character

Is Irene Scheerer a flat character or a round character? Explain.

Spiral Review

Context Clues Which context clues help you define the word "manifested" in the last sentence of this paragraph?

Eighteen months after he first met Judy Jones he became engaged to another girl. Her name was Irene Scheerer, and her father was one of the men who had always believed in Dexter. Irene was light-haired and sweet and honorable, and a little stout, and she had two suitors whom she pleasantly relinquished when Dexter formally asked her to marry him.

Summer, fall, winter, spring, another summer, another fall—so much he had given of his active life to the incorrigible lips of Judy Jones. She had treated him with interest, with encouragement, with malice, with indifference, with contempt. She had inflicted on him the innumerable little slights and indignities possible in such a case—as if in revenge for having ever cared for him at all. She had beckoned him and yawned at him and beckoned him again and he had responded often with bitterness and narrowed eyes. She had brought him ecstatic happiness and intolerable agony of spirit. She had caused him untold inconvenience and not a little trouble. She had insulted him, and she had ridden over him, and she had played his interest in her against his interest in his work—for fun. She had done everything to him except to criticize him—this she had not done—it seemed to him only because it might have sullied the utter indifference she manifested and sincerely felt toward him.

When autumn had come and gone again it occurred to him that he could not have Judy Jones. He had to beat this into his mind but he convinced himself at last. He lay awake at night for a while and argued it over. He told himself the trouble and the pain she had caused him, he enumerated her glaring deficiencies as a wife. Then he said to himself that he loved her, and after a while he fell asleep. For a week, lest he imagined her husky voice over the telephone or her eyes opposite him at lunch, he worked hard and late, and at night he went to his office and plotted out his years.

> She had brought him ecstatic happiness and intolerable agony of spirit.

At the end of a week he went to a dance and cut in on her once. For almost the first time since they had met he did not ask her to sit out with him or tell her that she was lovely. It hurt him that she did not miss these things—that was all. He was not jealous when he saw that there was a new man tonight. He had been hardened against jealousy long before.

He stayed late at the dance. He sat for an hour with Irene Scheerer and talked about books and about music. He knew very little about either. But he was beginning to be master of his own time now, and he had a rather priggish[3] notion that he—the young and already fabulously successful Dexter Green—should know more about such things.

---

3. priggish (prigʹ gish) *adj.* excessively proper and smug.

That was in October, when he was twenty-five. In January, Dexter and Irene became engaged. It was to be announced in June, and they were to be married three months later.

The Minnesota winter prolonged itself interminably, and it was almost May when the winds came soft and the snow ran down into Black Bear Lake at last. For the first time in over a year Dexter was enjoying a certain tranquillity of spirit. Judy Jones had been in Florida, and afterward in Hot Springs, and somewhere she had been engaged, and somewhere she had broken it off. At first, when Dexter had definitely given her up, it had made him sad that people still linked them together and asked for news of her, but when he began to be placed at dinner next to Irene Scheerer people didn't ask him about her any more—they told him about her. He ceased to be an authority on her.

May at last. Dexter walked the streets at night when the darkness was damp as rain, wondering that so soon, with so little done, so much of ecstasy had gone from him. May one year back had been marked by Judy's **poignant**, unforgivable, yet forgiven turbulence—it had been one of those rare times when he fancied she had grown to care for him. That old penny's worth of happiness he had spent for this bushel of content. He knew that Irene would be no more than a curtain spread behind him, a hand moving among gleaming teacups, a voice calling to children . . . fire and loveliness were gone, the magic of nights and the wonder of the varying hours and seasons . . . slender lips, down-turning, dropping to his lips and bearing him up into a heaven of eyes . . . The thing was deep in him. He was too strong and alive for it to die lightly.

Vocabulary
poignant (poin′ yənt) *adj.* sharply painful to the feelings

In the middle of May when the weather balanced for a few days on the thin bridge that led to deep summer he turned in one night at Irene's house. Their engagement was to be announced in a week now—no one would be surprised at it. And tonight they would sit together on the lounge at the University Club and look on for an hour at the dancers. It gave him a sense of solidity to go with her—she was so sturdily popular, so intensely "great."

Drawing Inferences About Characters
What inferences about Dexter's feelings for Irene can you draw from this description of "a sense of solidity"?

He mounted the steps of the brownstone house and stepped inside.

"Irene," he called.

Mrs. Scheerer came out of the living room to meet him.

"Dexter," she said, "Irene's gone upstairs with a splitting headache. She wanted to go with you but I made her go to bed."

"Nothing serious, I—"

"Oh, no. She's going to play golf with you in the morning. You can spare her for just one night, can't you, Dexter?"

Her smile was kind. She and Dexter liked each other. In the living room he talked for a moment before he said good night.

Returning to the University Club, where he had rooms, he stood in the doorway for a moment and watched the dancers. He leaned against the doorpost, nodded at a man or two—yawned.

Comprehension
What does Dexter do eighteen months after he meets Judy Jones?

The American EXPERIENCE

The Jazz Age

When World War I ended in 1918, Americans were desperate for a good time. They roared into the 1920s at breakneck speed, overthrowing rules about clothing, decorum, and personal style. The flapper, with her short dresses, bobbed hair, and complicated social life became a symbol of the times. She rode in sporty automobiles and danced until dawn to the sounds of jazz, a new kind of music critics blamed for a loosening moral code.

F. Scott Fitzgerald's work and life reflected the gaiety of this time, as well as the emptiness many felt when their pleasure seeking did not prove satisfying. Fitzgerald was not only part of the age, he helped to shape it, naming it the Jazz Age. Through both his life and his fiction, he created some of the decade's most enduring images.

Connect to the Literature

How would this story be different if it were *not* set during the Jazz Age?

"Hello, darling."

The familiar voice at his elbow startled him. Judy Jones had left a man and crossed the room to him—Judy Jones, a slender enameled doll in cloth of gold: gold in a band at her head, gold in two slipper points at her dress's hem. The fragile glow of her face seemed to blossom as she smiled at him. A breeze of warmth and light blew through the room. His hands in the pockets of his dinner jacket tightened spasmodically. He was filled with a sudden excitement.

"When did you get back?" he asked casually.

"Come here and I'll tell you about it."

She turned and he followed her. She had been away—he could have wept at the wonder of her return. She had passed through enchanted streets, doing things that were like provocative music. All mysterious happenings, all fresh and quickening hopes, had gone away with her, come back with her now.

She turned in the doorway.

"Have you a car here? If you haven't, I have."

"I have a coupé."

In then, with a rustle of golden cloth. He slammed the door. Into so many cars she had stepped—like this—like that—her back against the leather, so—her elbow resting on the door—waiting. She would have been soiled long since had there been anything to soil her—except herself—but this was her own self outpouring.

With an effort he forced himself to start the car and back into the street. This was nothing, he must remember. She had done this before, and he had put her behind him, as he would have crossed a bad account from his books.

He drove slowly downtown and, affecting abstraction, traversed the deserted streets of the business section, peopled here and there where a movie was giving out its crowd or where consumptive or pugilistic youth lounged in front of pool halls. The clink of glasses and the slap of hands on the bars issued from saloons, cloisters of glazed glass and dirty yellow light.

She was watching him closely and the silence was embarrassing, yet in this crisis he could find no casual word with which to profane the hour. At a convenient turning he began to zigzag back toward the University Club.

"Have you missed me?" she asked suddenly.

"Everybody missed you."

He wondered if she knew of Irene Scheerer. She had been back only a day—her absence had been almost contemporaneous with his engagement.

"What a remark!" Judy laughed sadly—without sadness. She looked at him searchingly. He became absorbed in the dashboard.

"You're handsomer than you used to be," she said thoughtfully. "Dexter, you have the most rememberable eyes."

He could have laughed at this, but he did not laugh. It was the sort of thing that was said to sophomores. Yet it stabbed at him.

"I'm awfully tired of everything, darling." She called everyone darling, endowing the endearment with careless, individual camaraderie.[4] "I wish you'd marry me."

The directness of this confused him. He should have told her now that he was going to marry another girl, but he could not tell her. He could as easily have sworn that he had never loved her.

"I think we'd get along," she continued, on the same note, "unless probably you've forgotten me and fallen in love with another girl."

Her confidence was obviously enormous. She had said, in effect, that she found such a thing impossible to believe, that if it were true he had merely committed a childish indiscretion—and probably to show off. She would forgive him, because it was not a matter of any moment but rather something to be brushed aside lightly.

"Of course you could never love anybody but me," she continued, "I like the way you love me. Oh, Dexter, have you forgotten last year?"

"No, I haven't forgotten."

"Neither have I!"

Was she sincerely moved—or was she carried along by the wave of her own acting?

Drawing Inferences About Characters

Given the information Fitzgerald provides in this conversation, what can you infer about Judy's experiences during her absence?

Comprehension

What does Dexter wonder during his reunion with Judy?

---

4. **camaraderie** (käm´ ə räd´ ə rē) *n.* warm, friendly feelings.

Spiral Review
Setting Identify the analogy Fitzgerald uses in this passage describing the Joneses' house. What does this analogy convey about the setting?

Characterization
What does this wistful remark about her lack of happiness add to Fitzgerald's portrait of Judy's character?

Vocabulary
sediment (sed´ ə mənt) *n.* material that settles to the bottom of a liquid

"I wish we could be like that again," she said, and he forced himself to answer:

"I don't think we can."

"I suppose not. . . . I hear you're giving Irene Scheerer a violent rush."

There was not the faintest emphasis on the name, yet Dexter was suddenly ashamed.

"Oh, take me home," cried Judy suddenly; "I don't want to go back to that idiotic dance—with those children."

Then, as he turned up the street that led to the residence district, Judy began to cry quietly to herself. He had never seen her cry before.

The dark street lightened, the dwellings of the rich loomed up around them, he stopped his coupé in front of the great white bulk of the Mortimer Joneses' house, somnolent, gorgeous, drenched with the splendor of the damp moonlight. Its solidity startled him. The strong walls, the steel of the girders, the breadth and beam and pomp of it were there only to bring out the contrast with the young beauty beside him. It was sturdy to accentuate her slightness—as if to show what a breeze could be generated by a butterfly's wing.

He sat perfectly quiet, his nerves in wild clamor, afraid that if he moved he would find her irresistibly in his arms. Two tears had rolled down her wet face and trembled on her upper lip.

"I'm more beautiful than anybody else," she said brokenly, "why can't I be happy?" Her moist eyes tore at his stability—her mouth turned slowly downward with an exquisite sadness: "I'd like to marry you if you'll have me, Dexter. I suppose you think I'm not worth having, but I'll be so beautiful for you, Dexter."

A million phrases of anger, pride, passion, hatred, tenderness fought on his lips. Then a perfect wave of emotion washed over him, carrying off with it a **sediment** of wisdom, of convention, of doubt, of honor. This was his girl who was speaking, his own, his beautiful, his pride.

Two tears had rolled down her wet face and trembled on her upper lip.

"Won't you come in?" He heard her draw in her breath sharply.

Waiting.

"All right," his voice was trembling, "I'll come in."

5

It was strange that neither when it was over nor a long time afterward did he regret that night. Looking at it from the perspective of ten years, the fact that Judy's flare for him endured just one month seemed of little importance. Nor did it matter that by his yielding he subjected himself to a deeper agony in the end and gave serious hurt to Irene Scheerer and to Irene's parents, who had befriended him. There was nothing sufficiently pictorial about Irene's grief to stamp itself on his mind.

Dexter was at bottom hard-minded. The attitude of the city on his action was of no importance to him, not because he was going to leave the city, but because any outside attitude on the situation seemed superficial. He was completely indifferent to popular opinion. Nor, when he had seen that it was no use, that he did not possess in himself the power to move fundamentally or to hold Judy Jones, did he bear any malice toward her. He loved her, and he would love her until the day he was too old for loving—but he could not have her. So he tasted the deep pain that is reserved only for the strong, just as he had tasted for a little while the deep happiness.

Characterization
What does Fitzgerald reveal about Dexter's state of mind through direct characterization?

Even the ultimate falsity of the grounds upon which Judy terminated the engagement that she did not want to "take him away" from Irene—Judy who had wanted nothing else—did not revolt him. He was beyond any revulsion or any amusement.

He went East in February with the intention of selling out his laundries and settling in New York—but the war came to America in March and changed his plans. He returned to the West, handed over the management of the business to his partner, and went into the first officers' training camp in late April. He was one of those young thousands who greeted the war with a certain amount of relief, welcoming the liberation from webs of tangled emotion.

6

This story is not his biography, remember, although things creep into it which have nothing to do with those dreams he had when he was young. We are almost done with them and with him now. There is only one more incident to be related here, and it happens seven years farther on.

It took place in New York, where he had done well—so well that there were no barriers too high for him. He was thirty-two years old, and, except for one flying trip immediately after the war, he had not been West in seven years. A man named Devlin from Detroit came

Comprehension
How long does Dexter's renewed romance with Judy last?

into his office to see him in a business way, and then and there this incident occurred, and closed out, so to speak, this particular side of his life.

"So you're from the Middle West," said the man Devlin with careless curiosity. "That's funny—I thought men like you were probably born and raised on Wall Street. You know—wife of one of my best friends in Detroit came from your city. I was an usher at the wedding."

Dexter waited with no apprehension of what was coming.

"Judy Simms," said Devlin with no particular interest; "Judy Jones she was once."

"Yes, I knew her." A dull impatience spread over him. He had heard, of course, that she was married—perhaps deliberately he had heard no more.

"Awfully nice girl," brooded Devlin meaninglessly, "I'm sort of sorry for her."

"Why?" Something in Dexter was alert, receptive, at once.

"Oh, Lud Simms has gone to pieces in a way. I don't mean he ill-uses her, but he drinks and runs around—"

"Doesn't she run around?"

"No. Stays at home with her kids."

"Oh."

"She's a little too old for him," said Devlin.

"Too old!" cried Dexter. "Why, man, she's only twenty-seven."

He was possessed with a wild notion of rushing out into the streets and taking a train to Detroit. He rose to his feet spasmodically.

"I guess you're busy," Devlin apologized quickly. "I didn't realize—"

"No, I'm not busy," said Dexter, steadying his voice. "I'm not busy at all. Not busy at all. Did you say she was—twenty-seven? No, I said she was twenty-seven."

"Yes, you did," agreed Devlin dryly.

"Go on, then. Go on."

"What do you mean?"

"About Judy Jones."

Devlin looked at him helplessly.

"Well, that's—I told you all there is to it. He treats her like the devil. Oh, they're not going to get divorced or anything. When he's particularly outrageous she forgives him. In fact, I'm inclined to think she loves him. She was a pretty girl when she first came to Detroit."

A pretty girl! The phrase struck Dexter as ludicrous.

"Isn't she—a pretty girl, anymore?"

"Oh, she's all right."

"Look here," said Dexter, sitting down suddenly. "I don't understand. You say she was a 'pretty girl' and now you say she's 'all right.' I don't understand what you mean—Judy Jones wasn't a pretty girl, at all. She was a great beauty. Why, I knew her. I knew her. She was—"

Devlin laughed pleasantly.

Drawing Inferences About Characters

What inference about Dexter's feelings for Judy can you draw from his response to Devlin?

"I'm not trying to start a row," he said. "I think Judy's a nice girl and I like her. I can't understand how a man like Lud Simms could fall madly in love with her, but he did." Then he added: "Most of the women like her."

Dexter looked closely at Devlin, thinking wildly that there must be a reason for this, some insensitivity in the man or some private malice.

"Lots of women fade just like *that*," Devlin snapped his fingers. "You must have seen it happen. Perhaps I've forgotten how pretty she was at her wedding. I've seen her so much since then, you see. She has nice eyes."

A sort of dullness settled down upon Dexter. For the first time in his life he felt like getting very drunk. He knew that he was laughing loudly at something Devlin had said, but he did not know what it was or why it was funny. When, in a few minutes, Devlin went he lay down on his lounge and looked out the window at the New York skyline into which the sun was sinking in dull lovely shades of pink and gold.

He had thought that having nothing else to lose he was invulnerable at last—but he knew that he had just lost something more, as surely as if he had married Judy Jones and seen her fade away before his eyes.

Comprehension
How does Devlin describe Judy?

The dream was gone. Something had been taken from him. In a sort of panic he pushed the palms of his hands into his eyes and tried to bring up a picture of the waters lapping on Sherry Island and the moonlit veranda, and gingham on the golf links and the dry sun and the gold color of her neck's soft down. And her mouth damp to his kisses and her eyes plaintive with melancholy and her freshness like new fine linen in the morning. Why, these things were no longer in the world! They had existed and they existed no longer.

For the first time in years the tears were streaming down his face. But they were for himself now. He did not care about mouth and eyes and moving hands. He wanted to care, and he could not care. For he had gone away and he could never go back any more. The gates were closed, the sun was gone down, and there was no beauty but the gray beauty of steel that withstands all time. Even the grief he could have borne was left behind in the country of illusion, of youth, of the richness of life, where his winter dreams had flourished.

"Long ago," he said, "long ago, there was something in me, but now that thing is gone. Now that thing is gone, that thing is gone. I cannot cry. I cannot care. That thing will come back no more."

Critical Reading

Cite textual evidence to support your responses.

1. **Key Ideas and Details** **(a)** At the beginning of Section 2, what does the narrator say Dexter wants? **(b) Interpret:** How does Judy embody his ambitions?
2. **Key Ideas and Details** **(a)** What actions does Dexter take as a result of his first two meetings with Judy? **(b) Connect:** Find two examples in the story that demonstrate the effects of Judy's casual behavior on Dexter's life.
3. **Key Ideas and Details** **(a) Interpret:** What is Dexter's response to Judy whenever she reappears in his life? **(b) Analyze:** Why do Dexter's feelings for Judy remain unchanged even after he finally loses her?
4. **Key Ideas and Details** **Evaluate:** Are Dexter's values and ideas influenced by the times in which he lives, or would his feelings for Judy Jones be the same in any era? Explain.
5. **Integration of Knowledge and Ideas** Explain what material success does for Dexter and what it does not do. Based on this story, what observations can you make about a materialistic culture? Explain. In your response, use at least two of these Essential Question words: *commonplace, disillusioned, criticism, realistic, fortune.* ***[Connecting to the Essential Question: How does literature shape or reflect society?]***

Literary Analysis

1. **Craft and Structure** **(a)** Identify two **flat characters** in "Winter Dreams." **(b)** Indicate the most obvious traits of each character. **(c)** Explain how each character helps to advance the story's action.
2. **Craft and Structure** Explain why both Dexter and Judy can be classified as **round characters.**
3. **Craft and Structure** **(a)** What motivates Dexter's drive for success? **(b)** What does Judy want in her life? **(c)** Do their motivations or desires change over the course of the story? Explain.
4. **Integration of Knowledge and Ideas** On the evening of Dexter's first dinner with Judy, she comes downstairs in "a blue silk afternoon dress, and he was disappointed at first that she had not put on something more elaborate." **(a)** **Draw an inference** to explain Dexter's disappointment. **(b)** How does your own knowledge of life help you draw this inference?
5. **Craft and Structure** **(a)** Use a chart like the one shown to note examples of both **direct characterization** and **indirect characterization** in Fitzgerald's portrayals of Dexter and Judy. **(b)** What do you learn about the characters from each example?

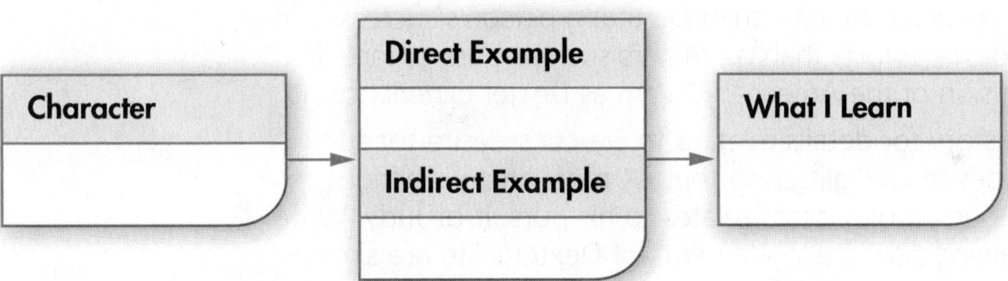

6. **Craft and Structure** **(a)** For both Dexter and Judy, identify an example of direct characterization that Fitzgerald builds on with a specific detail of indirect characterization. **(b)** Based on these examples, summarize the ways in which Fitzgerald uses both types of characterization to create consistent portraits.
7. **Craft and Structure** **(a)** What traits do Dexter and Judy share? **(b)** In what ways are they different? **(c)** Which details of characterization lead you to your answers?
8. **Integration of Knowledge and Ideas** Demonstrate what you have learned about the characters of Dexter and Judy by drawing inferences about their last meeting. What do they say and how do they act as their relationship ends?
9. **Integration of Knowledge and Ideas** Based on this story, what inferences can you draw about Fitzgerald's views of material wealth and social status?

Common Core State Standards

Writing

2. Write informative texts to examine and convey complex ideas, concepts, and information clearly and accurately through the effective selection, organization, and analysis of content. *(p. 754)*

2.b. Develop the topic thoroughly by selecting the most significant and relevant facts, extended definitions, concrete details, quotations, or other information and examples appropriate to the audience's knowledge of the topic. *(p. 754)*

Language

1. Demonstrate command of the conventions of standard English grammar and usage when writing or speaking. *(p. 755)*

Close Reading Activities Continued

Vocabulary Acquisition and Use

Word Analysis: Latin Root *-sed-*

The word *sediment* means "material that settles to the bottom." It is built on the Latin root *-sed-*, which means "to sit." This root frequently appears in *words related to the sciences*.

- In geology, *sedimentary* rocks form when sediments build up and are compressed into layers.
- In biology, *sedentary* organisms do not migrate.
- In medical science, *sedation* induces a state of unconsciousness.

For each word below, write a sentence that might be spoken by a scientist, a doctor, or a patient. The sentence should both include the *-sed-* word and reflect its meaning.

sediment *sedimentary* *sedentary* *sedate*

Vocabulary: Context

Answer each question. Explain your answers.

1. Which is an example of *fallowness:* an empty field or a flourishing vegetable garden?
2. Which is more *fortuitous:* a cancelled test or a difficult test?
3. Which is more *sinuous:* a snake or a ruler?
4. Which is more *mundane:* doing laundry or climbing a mountain?
5. Which is more *poignant:* a wistful memory or a funny joke?
6. Which is more like *sediment:* ocean waves or autumn leaves?

Writing to Sources

Informative Text "Winter Dreams" can be thought of as a commentary on the notion of the American Dream—the idea that a person's success depends more on his or her efforts than on factors such as class or race. In an essay, explore the vision of the American Dream as Dexter experiences it.

Prewriting Scan the story for details relating to Dexter's desire for success. Explain how his desire for "glittering things" motivates his actions, and consider how his pursuit of success relates to his pursuit of Judy. Write a few sentences explaining how these elements of Dexter's life are similar and different.

Drafting In your introduction, name the author and title of the work and clearly state your main idea. In the body of your essay, describe and analyze Dexter's goals. Develop the topic thoroughly by elaborating on your analysis with the most significant and relevant details, quotations, or other information and examples that will help readers understand your ideas.

Model: Elaborating for Information

Dexter is an outsider looking in on an elegant world. He is so close to it he can almost touch it, and that combination of proximity and distance drives him. As Fitzgerald tells us, "He wanted not association with glittering things and glittering people—he wanted the glittering things themselves."

Direct quotations from the text provide support for the analysis.

Revising Make sure every idea expressed in your essay relates to your main idea. If an idea does not relate, take it out.

Conventions and Style Lesson: Subject-Verb Agreement

Subject-verb agreement requires that a subject and a verb agree in number. Follow this rule even when a phrase or clause comes between the subject and the verb.

Singular noun: *A desire* for luxury *motivates* Dexter.
Plural noun: *Desires* for luxury and success *motivate* Dexter.

Compound subjects make subject-verb agreement more challenging to identify. With *either/or* and *neither/nor*, verbs agree with the closest subject.

Compound subject (singular closest): Neither Judy's *outbursts* nor her *indifference changes* Dexter's feelings.

Compound subject (plural closest): Neither Judy's *indifference* nor her *outbursts change* Dexter's feelings.

When the subject is an indefinite pronoun, the rule may vary. Some indefinite pronouns are always singular, but others are plural.

Indefinite pronoun (singular): *Everyone* here *praises* him.

Indefinite pronoun (plural): *Several* of the golfers *notice* Judy.

Practice Choose the verb in parentheses that agrees with the subject of each sentence.

1. There (was, were) something gloomy and dismal about spring.
2. Mr. Jones, along with the other golfers, (is, are) upset when Dexter decides to quit.
3. Neither several business successes nor money (brings, bring) happiness.
4. Everyone at the parties he attends (stops, stop) asking about Judy.
5. There (is, are) about Dexter something hard-hearted and calculating.
6. One of the reasons that Judy draws attention (is, are) her unpredictability.
7. Either his memories of summer or hope for the future (keeps, keep) Dexter going.
8. Golfers who play at the Sherry Island Golf Club (likes, like) to have Dexter as a caddy.
9. Many of Dexter's admirers (gathers, gather) to see him dive from the raft at the Sherry Island Golf Club.
10. The winter that is long and cold (follows, follow) a glorious fall.

Writing and Speaking

A. Writing Revise each sentence to correct the subject-verb agreement.

Example: After the tears come emptiness.
Revision: After the tears comes emptiness.

1. There was elements of comedy in the fight.
2. A wave of emotions wash over Dexter.
3. Dexter seem callous about his broken engagement to Irene.
4. Either crisp days or snow are a sign of winter's arrival.
5. Each of them are happy in spring and summer.

B. Speaking Compose and present a brief character sketch of Judy. Throughout, maintain correct subject-verb agreement.

Building Knowledge and Insight

The Turtle from *The Grapes of Wrath*

Connecting to the Essential Question This selection is part of a novel that changed people's understanding of migrant workers in America. As you read, notice details that portray the turtle's resilience and dignity. Doing so will help as you consider the Essential Question: **How does literature shape or reflect society?**

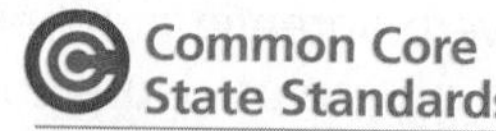

Common Core
State Standards

Reading Literature

1. Cite strong and thorough textual evidence to support analysis of what the text says explicitly as well as inferences drawn from the text, including determining where the text leaves matters uncertain.

4. Determine the meaning of words and phrases as they are used in the text, including figurative meanings.

6. Analyze a case in which grasping a point of view requires distinguishing what is directly stated in a text from what is really meant.

Close Reading Focus

Allegory; Theme

An **allegory** is a narrative in which every literal element has a symbolic meaning. An allegory does not simply contain symbols, but is a symbol in and of itself. For example, this story is the third chapter of Steinbeck's novel *The Grapes of Wrath*. The novel tells the story of the Joads, a family of farm workers struggling to survive the devastating drought in Oklahoma during the Great Depression. Every element in Steinbeck's description of the turtle and the landscape through which it struggles can be related to the Joads and their struggles.

The allegory of the turtle helps Steinbeck express the novel's **theme**—the message, or comment on life. Novelists rarely state their themes directly. Instead, they reveal themes indirectly through these means:

- Characters' statements, beliefs, and actions
- Events in the plot
- The use of literary devices, such as description and symbol

As you read, consider the deeper meanings of the events in this story.

Preparing to Read Complex Texts To interpret this story as an allegory and better understand the theme, **analyze patterns of symbolism.** Identify individual details and then look at their relationships to each other. For example, Steinbeck includes glancing descriptions of two motorists. Their responses to the turtle create a meaningful pattern that sheds light on the deeper meaning of the story. As you read, look for related details and consider them as part of a larger pattern of meaning. Gather clues in a chart like the one shown.

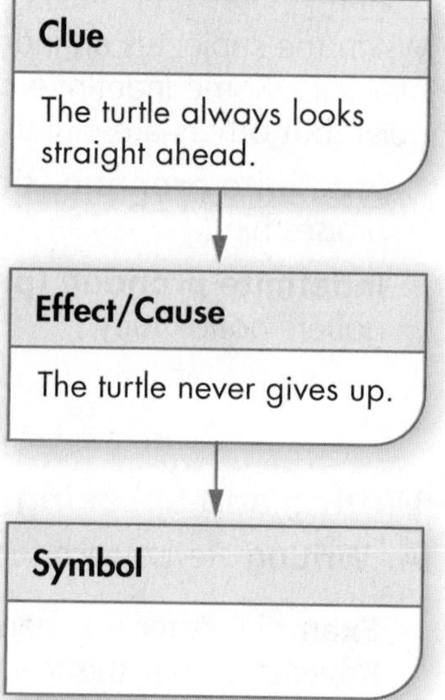

Clue
The turtle always looks straight ahead.
Effect/Cause
The turtle never gives up.
Symbol

Vocabulary

You will encounter the words listed here in the the text that follows. Copy the words into your notebook. Which word is a verb? How can you tell?

dispersal
plodding
embankment
frantic

JOHN STEINBECK (1902–1968)

Author of "The Turtle" *from The Grapes of Wrath*

No writer portrays more vividly than John Steinbeck what it was like to live through the Great Depression of the 1930s. His stories and novels capture the poverty, desperation, and social injustice experienced by many working-class Americans during this bleak period. As in the works of Naturalist writers like Stephen Crane and Jack London, Steinbeck's characters struggle desperately against forces beyond their understanding or control. While many of his characters suffer tragic fates, they almost always exhibit bravery and dignity in their struggles.

Modest Beginnings Steinbeck was born in Salinas, California. By his late teens, he was supporting himself by working as a laborer. After high school, he enrolled at Stanford University. He left before graduating, however, and spent the next five years drifting across the country, working in a variety of odd jobs, including fish hatcher, fruit picker, laboratory assistant, surveyor, apprentice painter, and journalist.

First Success Steinbeck's first three books received little—or negative—attention from critics. This changed in 1935 when he published *Tortilla Flat*. The book received the California Commonwealth Club's Gold Medal for best novel by a California author. Two years later, the author earned even greater recognition and acclaim with *Of Mice and Men* (1937). The novel became a bestseller and was made into a Broadway play and a movie.

The Great Novel Steinbeck went on to write what is generally regarded as his finest novel. *The Grapes of Wrath* (1939) is the story of the Joad family, Oklahoma farmers dispossessed of their land and forced to become migrant workers in California. The novel won the National Book Award and the Pulitzer Prize and aroused public sympathy for the plight of farm workers.

Steinbeck produced several more successful novels during his later years and in 1962 received the Nobel Prize for Literature. In accepting that award, he noted his belief that literature can sustain people through hard times. He added that it is the writer's responsibility to celebrate the human "capacity for greatness of heart and spirit—for gallantry in defeat, for courage, compassion and love."

THE TURTLE

from THE GRAPES OF WRATH

JOHN STEINBECK

BACKGROUND The Great Depression of the 1930s was a time of profound economic distress. In 1932, one quarter of all Americans were out of work. One of many factors contributing to the Depression was a drought in Oklahoma. The drought was so severe that farmland literally blew away in massive dust storms. This is the situation faced by the Joad family, whose story Steinbeck tells in his novel *The Grapes of Wrath*. This tale of the turtle is the third chapter of that epic book.

▼ **Critical Viewing**
What challenges would a landscape like this one present? **DEDUCE**

The concrete highway was edged with a mat of tangled, broken, dry grass, and the grass heads were heavy with oat beards to catch on a dog's coat, and foxtails to tangle in a horse's fetlocks, and clover burrs to fasten in sheep's wool: sleeping life waiting to be spread and dispersed, every seed armed with an appliance of dispersal, twisting darts and parachutes for the wind, little spears and balls of tiny thorns, and all waiting for animals and for the wind, for a man's trouser cuff or the hem of a woman's skirt, all passive but armed with appliances of activity, still, but each possessed of the anlage[1] of movement.

The sun lay on the grass and warmed it, and in the shade under the grass the insects moved, ants and ant lions to set traps for them, grasshoppers to jump into the air and flick their yellow wings for a second, sow bugs like little armadillos, plodding restlessly on many tender feet. And over the grass at the roadside a land turtle crawled, turning aside for nothing, dragging his high-domed shell over the grass. His hard legs and yellow-nailed feet threshed slowly through the grass, not really walking, but boosting and dragging his shell along. The barley beards slid off his shell, and the clover burrs fell on him and rolled to the ground. His horny beak was partly opened, and his fierce, humorous eyes, under brows like fingernails, stared straight ahead. He came over the grass leaving a beaten trail behind him, and the hill, which was the highway embankment, reared up ahead of him. For a moment he stopped, his head held high. He blinked and looked up and down. At last he started to climb the embankment. Front clawed feet reached forward but did not touch. The hind feet kicked his shell along, and it scraped on the grass, and on the gravel. As the embankment grew steeper and steeper, the more frantic were the efforts of the land turtle. Pushing hind legs strained

Vocabulary

dispersal (di spər′ səl) *n.* distribution

plodding (pläd iŋ) *v.* walking or moving heavily; trudging

embankment (em baŋk′ mənt) *n.* mound of earth or stone built to hold back water or support a roadway

frantic (frant′ ik) *adj.* marked by frenzy

Comprehension

What is the turtle trying to do?

1. **anlage** (än′ lä′ gə) *n.* foundation; basis; the initial cell structure from which an embryonic part develops.

Theme
What does the turtle's reaction to the parapet suggest about the story's theme?

and slipped, boosting the shell along, and the horny head protruded as far as the neck could stretch. Little by little the shell slid up the embankment until at last a parapet[2] cut straight across its line of march, the shoulder of the road, a concrete wall four inches high. As though they worked independently the hind legs pushed the shell against the wall. The head upraised and peered over the wall to the broad smooth plain of cement. Now the hands, braced on top of the wall, strained and lifted, and the shell came slowly up and rested its front end on the wall. For a moment the turtle rested. A red ant ran into the shell, into the soft skin inside the shell, and suddenly head and legs snapped in, and the armored tail clamped in sideways. The red ant was crushed between body and legs. And one head of wild oats was clamped into the shell by a front leg. For a long moment the turtle lay still, and then the neck crept out and the old humorous frowning eyes looked about and the legs and tail came out. The back legs went to work, straining like elephant legs, and the shell tipped to an angle so that the front legs could not reach the level cement plain. But higher and higher the hind legs boosted it, until at last the center of balance was reached, the front tipped down, the front legs scratched at the pavement, and it was up. But the head of wild oats was held by its stem around the front legs.

2. **parapet** (par′ ə pet′) *n.* a low wall or edge of a roof, balcony, or similar structure.

Now the going was easy, and all the legs worked, and the shell boosted along, waggling from side to side. A sedan driven by a forty-year-old woman approached. She saw the turtle and swung to the right, off the highway, the wheels screamed and a cloud of dust boiled up. Two wheels lifted for a moment and then settled. The car skidded back onto the road, and went on, but more slowly. The turtle had jerked into its shell, but now it hurried on, for the highway was burning hot.

And now a light truck approached, and as it came near, the driver saw the turtle and swerved to hit it. His front wheel struck the edge of the shell, flipped the turtle like a tiddly-wink, spun it like a coin, and rolled it off the highway. The truck went back to its course along the right side. Lying on its back, the turtle was tight in its shell for a long time. But at last its legs waved in the air, reaching for something to pull it over. Its front foot caught a piece of quartz and little by little the shell pulled over and flopped upright. The wild oat head fell out and three of the spearhead seeds stuck in the ground. And as the turtle crawled on down the embankment, its shell dragged dirt over the seeds. The turtle entered a dust road and jerked itself along, drawing a wavy shallow trench in the dust with its shell. The old humorous eyes looked ahead, and the horny beak opened a little. His yellow toe nails slipped a fraction in the dust.

Analyzing Patterns of Symbolism

What symbolic meaning might you give to the turtle's actions after it is hit by the truck?

Critical Reading

Cite textual evidence to support your responses.

1. **Key Ideas and Details (a)** What obstacles does the turtle encounter? **(b) Make a Judgment:** Which of these is most dangerous?
2. **Key Ideas and Details (a)** What happens to the turtle in his encounter with the two drivers? **(b) Compare and Contrast:** Based on their actions, what kinds of people do the two drivers seem to be?
3. **Key Ideas and Details (a)** What happens to the red ant that slips inside the turtle's shell? **(b) Distinguish:** What does this event suggest about the turtle's capacity to defend itself?
4. **Key Ideas and Details (a)** What happens to the wild oat head at the end of the story? **(b) Analyze:** What is the author suggesting about the relationships between different forms of life?
5. **Integration of Knowledge and Ideas** What does the portrayal of the turtle lead you to expect about Steinbeck's portrayal of the Joads in *The Grapes of Wrath*? Explain. In your response, use at least two of these Essential Question words: *dignity, resilient, migrant, obstacle.* ***[Connecting to the Essential Question: How does literature shape or reflect society?]***

Close Reading Activities

The Turtle from *The Grapes of Wrath*

Literary Analysis

1. **Key Ideas and Details (a)** Use a chart like the one shown to examine the turtle's actions at each stage of its journey. **(b)** What does the turtle's journey symbolize?

	Obstacles	Turtle's Reactions	Symbolic Meaning
climbs embankment			
crosses road			

2. **Craft and Structure** Steinbeck uses the words *dragging, turning aside for nothing,* and *thrashed slowly* to describe the turtle. **(a)** What effect do these words have on your perception of the turtle? **(b)** In what ways do these words create a **pattern of symbolism**?
3. **Integration of Knowledge and Ideas** Why do you think Steinbeck twice describes the turtle's eyes as "humorous"?
4. **Key Ideas and Details** How would you define the story's **theme**? Defend your answer with details from the selection.
5. **Key Ideas and Details** What connection does the image from the first paragraph of "sleeping life waiting to be spread" have to the story's theme?
6. **Craft and Structure** Notice patterns of symbolism that represent the following ideas:
   (a) people's struggle for survival
   (b) challenges to survival that come from nature
   (c) challenges to survival that come from other people or society
7. **Integration of Knowledge and Ideas (a)** Trace the path of the wild oat seeds in this story. **(b)** At the end of *The Grapes of Wrath*, Ma Joad says, "We're the people that live. . . . we're the people—we go on." Explain the ways in which the path of the oat seed expresses similar ideas symbolically.
8. **Craft and Structure** Explain the story of the turtle as an **allegory** for human struggle.
9. **Integration of Knowledge and Ideas** In Chapter 14 of *The Grapes of Wrath*, Steinbeck writes that humanity is defined by the need to struggle toward goals: "Having stepped forward, he may slip back, but only half a step, never the full step back." Explain how the story of the turtle expresses that idea allegorically.

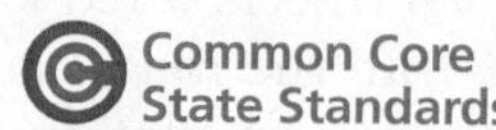

Common Core State Standards

Writing

2. Write informative texts to examine and convey complex ideas, concepts, and information clearly and accurately through the effective selection, organization, and analysis of content. *(p. 763)*

2.b. Develop the topic thoroughly by selecting the most significant and relevant facts, extended definitions, concrete details, quotations, or other information and examples appropriate to the audience's knowledge of the topic. *(p. 763)*

2.c. Use appropriate and varied transitions and syntax to link the major sections of the text, create cohesion, and clarify relationships among complex ideas and concepts.

7. Conduct short as well as more sustained research projects to answer a question; synthesize multiple sources on the subject, demonstrating understanding of the subject under investigation. *(p. 763)*

Language

5. Demonstrate understanding of figurative language, word relationships, and nuances in word meanings. *(p. 763)*

Vocabulary Acquisition and Use

Word Analysis: Latin Prefix *pro-*

In this story, John Steinbeck uses the word *protruded,* which begins with the Latin prefix *pro-*, meaning "forward." Knowing this meaning helps you to define the whole word *protruded,* which means "thrust forward," and other words beginning with the prefix *pro-*.

Add the prefix *pro-* to the word roots below. Then, define each word and use it in a sentence.

1. *-ject*
2. *-ceed*
3. *-gress*
4. *-hibit*
5. *-duce*
6. *-pose*

Vocabulary: Word/Phrase Relationships

Use your knowledge of the words from the vocabulary list on page 756 to determine whether the relationships between the italicized words below and the phrases that follow them are logical. Explain your reasoning.

1. *embankment* the bottom of a lake
2. *plodding* tired during a hike
3. *dispersal* collection of garbage
4. *frantic* nerves before a test

Writing to Sources

Informative Text "The Turtle" is part of Steinbeck's novel *The Grapes of Wrath,* which portrays the struggles of a Depression-era farm family. Steinbeck intended that readers draw parallels between the turtle and the human characters. Write an **essay** connecting the events described in "The Turtle" to the lives of ordinary people during the Great Depression.

Prewriting Use print and online sources to research the Great Depression to learn how people reacted to adverse economic circumstances. Then, review "The Turtle" and draw parallels.

Drafting First, provide information about the Depression. In your body paragraphs, note facts and data and explain parallels you found to "The Turtle." Use transitional words and phrases that clarify the relationships among ideas. For example, *likewise* and *in the same way* indicate similarity, whereas *to the contrary* and *by contrast* indicate difference. Cite the sources of all facts as you draft.

Model: Providing Internal Documentation

The Oklahoma Dust Bowl heightened the effects of the Great Depression for farmers living in that state. The average rainfall in Oklahoma was under 20 inches a year before the early 1930s, when it suffered a severe drought.
(http://www.britannica.com, Dust Bowl)

Citing sources of facts adds credibility.

Revising Review your essay. Make sure that you have provided enough historical context to support your observations. Add information as needed, and provide correct citations about where you found the material.

Primary Sources

Photographs
Migrant Mother

Ballad
Dust Bowl Blues

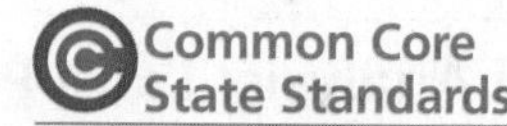
Common Core State Standards

Reading Literature
Reading Informational Text
1. Cite strong and thorough textual evidence to support analysis of what the text says explicitly as well as inferences drawn from the text, including determining where the text leaves matters uncertain.

About the Text Forms

A **photograph** is a visual image created when light falls on a sensitive surface, such as film or an electronic imager. Photographers use the lens of a camera to admit various degrees of light onto this surface and to focus the image as a human eye would. Timing these tasks to capture a small, meaningful slice of reality is known as the art of photography.

A **ballad** is a song or a song-like poem that tells a story—often, a story about adventure or love. Most ballads use simple language, regular meter, rhyme, and a *refrain*, which is a repeated line or group of lines. Sometimes the refrain varies slightly each time it appears. An ancient form, the ballad experienced new popularity in the mid- to late-twentieth century as folk singers used it to reflect and comment on the social upheavals of the time.

Preparing to Read Complex Texts

Drawing inferences can enrich your understanding of a document's meaning. When you draw inferences, you make logical guesses about something that is not directly shown or stated. To draw inferences, notice details. Then, apply your own knowledge about people, the world, or life in general to an interpretation of those details. Consider this example:

- **Document:** A historical photograph shows a long line of adults in tattered clothes waiting outside a city building.
- **Details:** tattered clothes, long line
- **Your Knowledge:** Tattered clothes might indicate poverty; long lines suggest people want or need something badly.

By applying your knowledge to the details in the text, you can infer that the people in the photo are seeking help or employment. You can also infer that at the time the photo was taken, many people were in dire need. As you explore the photographs and the ballad, draw inferences to enrich your understanding.

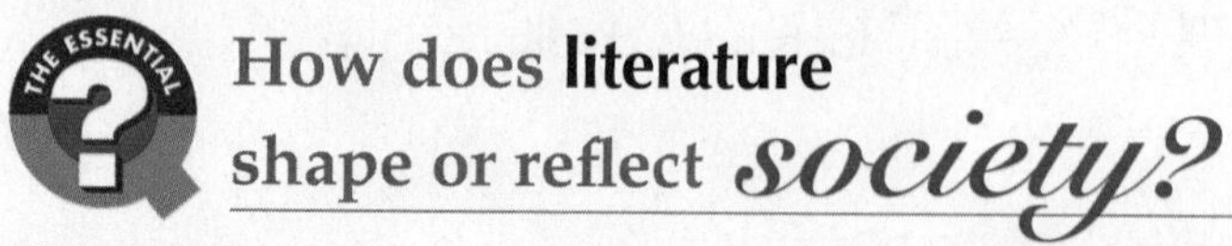

How does **literature** shape or reflect *society?*

These documents present powerful testimony to the challenges people faced at a specific historical moment. At the same time, they express universal ideas about human struggle. As you explore these texts, consider what they reveal about their era and about human experience in general.

Note-Taking Guide

Primary-source documents are a rich source of information for researchers. As you read these documents, use a note-taking guide like the one shown to organize relevant and accurate information.

1 Type of Document (check one)
☐ Newspaper ☐ Advertisement ☐ Photograph ☐ Letter
☐ Press Release ☐ Journal ☐ E-mail ☐ Other ____________

2 Date(s) of Document ____________

3 Maker of Document ____________

Maker's Position, Title, or Circumstances ____________

4 Purpose and Audience: Why and for whom was the document created or written?

____

5 Document Information

a List significant details that you notice about the people and objects included in the document. ____________

b What activities or events are referred to in the document? ____________

c List words or elements that are repeated in the document. ____________

d Based on your notes above, list three inferences you might draw from the photo or ballad. ____________

Drawing Inferences
In photos and in song lyrics, every detail counts. Take the time to consider how each object, shadow, or unusual word adds to the work's meaning and significance.

This guide was adapted from the **U.S. National Archives** Photo and Document Analysis worksheets.

Vocabulary

migrant (mī´ grənt) *adj.* moving from place to place (p. 767)

exposures (ek spō´ zhərz) *n.* sections of film on which light falls when a photograph is taken (p. 767)

huddled (hud´ əld) *v.* gathered closely; nestled (p. 767)

stout (stout) *adj.* strong in body; sturdy (p. 769)

THE STORY BEHIND THE DOCUMENTS

Dorothea Lange

Woody Guthrie

A man caught in a dust storm during the Dust Bowl disaster of the 1930s.

On October 29, 1929, or "Black Tuesday," the United States stock market crashed. The prices of stocks, or shares in companies, plummeted. Hundreds of thousands of people who had purchased stock with borrowed money went bankrupt and the economy ground to a virtual halt.

The domino effects of the crash—collectively known as the Great Depression of the 1930s—were far-reaching. Employers who lost money laid off workers. Workers could not pay their bills and lost their homes. Many moved into crowded quarters with relatives, or built makeshift shanty towns. Teenagers wandered the country, looking for work. Children went hungry.

For Americans living on the Great Plains that extend from the Dakotas south to Oklahoma and Texas, these dire circumstances were made catastrophic by a series of dust storms that began in 1933 and continued through the early 1940s. Decades of over-farming had exposed the prairie soil to the scorching sun. When drought set in, the dry soil turned to dust. Sweeping prairie winds carried massive amounts of dirt eastward, devastating homesteads, destroying crops and livestock, and dumping tons of filth on cities as far east as Boston and New York. The drought-stricken area became known as the Dust Bowl. In desperation, more than a half-million people from the Dust Bowl regions migrated to California.

Living and working among the displaced masses were visual artists, such as photographer **Dorothea Lange** (1895–1965), and musician **Woody Guthrie** (1912–1967). These artists became eyewitnesses to the events of history, producing work that documented the times.

Originally from New Jersey, Lange traveled to San Francisco as a young adult. There, she began capturing stark realities on film. Later, she was hired by the government to photograph the country's rural poor. Lange's *Migrant Mother* series of photos are the most famous of these powerful images. It was said of her work that she "photographed the nation's soul."

Another Great Depression-era artist, singer/songwriter Woody Guthrie, once said, "I ain't a writer . . . I'm just a little one-cylinder guitar picker." His songs tell a different story. Born and raised in Oklahoma, Guthrie experienced the Dust Bowl first-hand, finally migrating to California where he wrote and broadcast his first songs. Among these were his Dust Bowl Ballads—tunes that lamented the difficulties of life on the Plains. The songs resonated with the thousands of displaced "Okies" on the west coast, and soon Guthrie's legend was born.

MIGRANT MOTHER

Dorothea Lange

Dorothea Lange took these photographs in February or March of 1936 in Nipomo, California, while she was on assignment photographing **migrant** farm workers. She later gave this account of the experience:

I saw and approached the hungry and desperate mother, as if drawn by a magnet. I do not remember how I explained my presence or my camera to her, but I do remember she asked me no questions. I made five **exposures**, *working closer and closer from the same direction. I did not ask her name or her history. She told me her age, that she was thirty-two. She said that they had been living on frozen vegetables from the surrounding fields, and birds that the children killed. She had just sold the tires from her car to buy food. There she sat in that lean-to tent with her children* **huddled** *around her, and seemed to know that my pictures might help her, and so she helped me. There was a sort of equality about it.*

Vocabulary

migrant (mī´ grənt) *adj.* moving from place to place

exposures (ek spō´ zhərz) *n.* sections of film on which light falls when a photograph is taken

huddled (hud´ əld) *v.* gathered closely; nestled

DUST BOWL BLUES

Woody Guthrie

Woody Guthrie's first album of original songs, *Dust Bowl Ballads*, was recorded in 1940 in New York City. This album, and those that followed, were celebrated for their "homespun" quality and embraced by Guthrie's fellow artists and musicians. They also opened the door for generations of singer-songwriters who sought to express through their music the social and political ideals of peace, compassion, and equality.

Primary Sources
Ballad What kind of story do you think this ballad will tell?

I just blowed in, and I got them dust bowl blues,
I just blowed in, and I got them dust bowl blues,
I just blowed in, and I'll blow back out again.
I guess you've heard about ev'ry kind of blues,
I guess you've heard about ev'ry kind of blues,
But when the dust gets high, you can't even see the sky.
I've seen the dust so black that I couldn't see a thing,
I've seen the dust so black that I couldn't see a thing,

▼ Oklahomans head to California, June 1935

And the wind so cold, boy, it nearly cut your water off.
I seen the wind so high that it blowed my fences down,
I've seen the wind so high that it blowed my fences down,
Buried my tractor six feet underground.
Well, it turned my farm into a pile of sand,
Yes, it turned my farm into a pile of sand,
I had to hit that road with a bottle in my hand.
I spent ten years down in that old dust bowl,
I spent ten years down in that old dust bowl,
When you get that dust pneumony, boy, it's time to go.
I had a gal, and she was young and sweet,
I had a gal, and she was young and sweet,
But a dust storm buried her sixteen hundred feet.
She was a good gal, long, tall and **stout,**
Yes, she was a good gal, long, tall and stout,
I had to get a steam shovel just to dig my darlin' out.
These dusty blues are the dustiest ones I know,
These dusty blues are the dustiest ones I know,
Buried head over heels in the black old dust,
I had to pack up and go.
An' I just blowed in, an' I'll soon blow out again.

Drawing Inferences

Where did the speaker once live? Explain how you know.

Vocabulary

stout (stout) *adj.* strong in body; sturdy

Critical Reading

1. **Key Ideas and Details Analyze:** Which aspects of all three of Lange's photographs emphasize the family's isolation and powerlessness?
2. **Key Ideas and Details Evaluate:** Do you think Lange's photographs are more or less powerful because they depict a woman and children but no other adults?
3. **Key Ideas and Details (a)** In "Dust Bowl Blues," what happened to the speaker's farm and his "gal"? **(b) Interpret:** Do you think these things happened in just the way the speaker describes them? Explain. **(c) Deduce:** What larger point about the dust storms is Guthrie making?
4. **Craft and Structure (a) Identify:** What line is repeated in the first and last stanzas of the ballad? **(b) Connect:** Which details in Lange's photographs indicate that this line could also apply to the migrant mother and her family?
5. **Integration of Knowledge and ideas Analyze:** Based on Guthrie's lyrics and Lange's photographs, how did the Dust Bowl affect people's lives?

Photographs • Ballads

Comparing Primary Sources

Refer to your note-taking guide to complete these questions.

1. **(a)** What are your main impressions as you scan the "Migrant Mother" photographs? **(b)** What do you learn about the speaker upon first reading the ballad?
2. **(a)** Using a chart like the one shown, identify one detail from each "Migrant Mother" photograph that you noticed after studying it more closely. **(b)** Do the same for the ballad. **(c)** Write one sentence about life during the Great Depression that incorporates these details.

	Detail	Depression-Era Life
Photo 1		
Photo 2		
Photo 3		
Ballad		

3. **(a)** Describe the tent shown in the lower right "Migrant Mother" photograph. **(b)** Do you think the tent is a sound shelter? Explain.
4. **(a)** In the upper right "Migrant Mother" photograph, what detail is visible on the woman's hand? **(b)** How does this detail shed light on the larger story of this family?
5. **(a)** Compare and contrast what you learn about the Depression from the "Migrant Mother" photographs with what you learn from the ballad. **(b)** Explain the reasons for any similarities and differences.

Vocabulary Acquisition and Use

Use New Words Correctly For each item below, write one sentence in which you use the word correctly.

1. huddled **2.** stout

Content-Area Vocabulary Answer each question. Then, explain your answers.

3. Can a *migrant* worker receive regular promotions?
4. Are *exposures* an important part of photography?

Etymology Study The word *migrant* often appears in political science and history texts. The word derives from the Latin word *migrare,* meaning "to move from one place to another." Identify four other words that share this root. Then, use a dictionary to answer these questions: **(a)** Which related word can apply to either people or animals? **(b)** Which two related words can apply *only* to people? Explain.

Common Core State Standards

Writing

7. Conduct short as well as more sustained research projects to answer a question or solve a problem; narrow or broaden the inquiry when appropriate; synthesize multiple sources on the subject, demonstrating understanding of the subject under investigation. *(p. 771)*

8. Gather relevant information from multiple authoritative print and digital sources, using advanced searches effectively. *(p. 771)*

9. Draw evidence from literary or informational texts to support analysis, reflection, and research. *(p. 771)*

Language

6. Acquire and use accurately general academic and domain-specific words and phrases, sufficient for reading, writing, speaking, and listening at the college and career readiness level; demonstrate independence in gathering vocabulary knowledge when considering a word or phrase important to comprehension or expression.

Speaking and Listening

4. Present information, findings, and supporting evidence, conveying a clear and distinct perspective, such that listeners can follow the line of reasoning. *(p. 771)*

Research Task

Topic: The WPA

As the photos of Dorothea Lange and the songs of Woody Guthrie make clear, the Great Depression was a time of crushing poverty. Many Americans survived with the help of the Works Progress Administration (later the Work Projects Administration). Often referred to as the WPA, this federal agency created jobs from writing to road building.

▲ WPA plaque on the Riverwalk in San Antonio, Texas

Assignment: Formulate a research plan related to the WPA. Write a major research question and modify it as necessary to refocus and narrow in on meaningful data. Present an **oral report** in which you discuss the research process itself, as well as your findings on the topic.

Formulate a research plan. Good research begins with a general exploration into a wide area. As you conduct your preliminary research driven by an initial question, you gain perspective on your topic—its outlines, branches, and specific elements that you want to examine in detail. Like an explorer learning a new terrain, you choose one direction rather than another: You revise your research question and refocus your search for useful materials.

Model: Refining a Research Question

Starting Question	Focused Question	Refined Question
What did the WPA do?	What did the WPA do for literature and the arts?	What was the Federal Writers' Project and what did it produce?

Gather sources. Use online and library searches to collect information from a variety of reliable sources. Start with general information, and, as you refine your research question, search more detailed accounts. As you go, critique the research process itself, considering creative steps you might take to acquire more interesting, varied, or reliable information.

Synthesize information. To synthesize is "to bring parts together in order to make a whole." Combine the results of your research to arrive at an idea, a unified whole, that answers your research question.

Organize and present your ideas. For this report, how you proceed is as important as what you find out. Consider presenting your ideas using a cause-and-effect strategy: "Because I found out that . . . , I changed my question to . . . ."

RESEARCH TIP

As part of your preliminary research, read the chapter titles of a book or the section headings on a Web site. These concise expressions may give you good leads on how to refocus and refine your research.

Use a checklist like the one shown to make sure your oral report fulfills the requirements of the assignment.

Research Checklist

- ☐ Have I refined my main research question so that it is specific and manageable?
- ☐ Have I answered my main research question?
- ☐ Does my evidence come from reliable sources?
- ☐ Have I clearly shown the process of my research?

Connecting to the Essential Question In this poem, Auden refers to official statistics that government and other modern institutions use to define people. As you read, think about the view of modern life portrayed in the poem. Doing so will help you as consider the Essential Question: **How does literature shape or reflect society?**

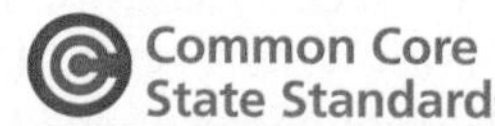

Reading Literature

4. Analyze the impact of specific word choices on meaning and tone.

5. Analyze how an author's choices concerning how to structure specific parts of a text contribute to its overall structure and meaning as well as its aesthetic impact.

6. Analyze a case in which grasping a point of view requires distinguishing what is directly stated in a text from what is really meant.

Close Reading Focus

Satire; Tone

A subgenre found in all forms of literature—poems, essays, novels, plays, and short stories—**satire** is writing that ridicules or exposes the faults of individuals, groups, institutions, or humanity at large. Satirical writings vary in **tone,** or attitude, which may be bitter, harsh, gentle, humorous, sober, or comical. A writer establishes tone through word choice, details, and grammatical structures. For example, in the opening lines of this poem, Auden strings together long, formal phrases full of bureacratic words: *Bureau of Statistics, official complaint, reports, conduct, Greater Community.* These official-sounding words and phrases issue forth from a disembodied speaker to generate a chilling and cynical tone. As you read, identify the object of Auden's satire and note details that add to the speaker's tone.

Preparing to Read Complex Texts Ideas in poetry are not expressed solely in words; often, the structure itself reinforces meaning. Structure includes the following elements:

- *Lines:* Are lines short, long, or varied lengths?
- *Stanzas:* Are stanzas the same length or varied lengths?
- *Grammatical forms:* Does the poet use particular constructions, such as passive voice or collective nouns?

When you **evaluate structure as it relates to meaning,** you understand a poem as a complete whole. As you read, use a chart like the one shown to note structural elements and their relationship to meaning.

Structure	Meaning
Variable rhyme	This creates a sense of imbalance, as though something is wrong with "the system."

Vocabulary

The words below are important to understanding the text that follows. Copy the words into your notebook. What are some other forms of the word *psychology*?

conduct

psychology

sensible

Wystan Hugh Auden *(1907–1973)*

Author of "The Unknown Citizen"

Although he was influenced by the Modernist poets, Wystan Hugh Auden adopted only those aspects of Modernism with which he felt comfortable, choosing to retain many elements of traditional poetry in his work. Throughout his career, he wrote with insight and technical virtuosity about people struggling to preserve their individuality in an increasingly conformist society.

Auden was born in York, England, in 1907, the third of three children. He attended Oxford University, where he made lifelong friendships with two fellow writers, Stephen Spender and Christopher Isherwood. At age twenty-three, Auden published his first volume of poetry, simply titled *Poems*. The book established Auden as the leading voice of a new generation of poets. In the same year, he developed a passionate interest in politics, speaking out against poverty in England and the rise of Nazism in Germany.

A New Country In 1939, just before World War II, Auden moved from England to the United States, where he became a citizen. That move was coincident with his rediscovery of his Christian beliefs. His works *The Double Man* (1941) and *For the Time Being* (1944) depict religion as a way of coping with a disjointed modern society. Despite the comfort he found in religion, Auden became disillusioned with modern life in his later years. He used his poetry to explore the responsibilities of the artist in what he saw as a faithless modern age.

Auden won the Pulitzer Prize in 1948 for his long narrative poem *The Age of Anxiety* (1947), which explores the confusion associated with post–World War II life. He later published several more volumes of poetry and a large body of literary criticism. He also anthologized others' works and coauthored at least one musical composition—a libretto for the opera *The Rake's Progress*. From 1954 to 1973, Auden served as chancellor of the Academy of American Poets. Today, Auden is admired as one of the great poets of the twentieth century.

"A poet is, before anything else, a person who is passionately in love with language."

The Turret Lathe Operator (J. G. Cherry series), Grant Wood, Cedar Rapids Museum of Art, Cedar Rapids, Iowa. © Estate of Grant Wood/Licensed by VAGA, New York, NY

The Unknown Citizen

W.H. Auden

(To JS/07/M/378 This Marble Monument is Erected by the State)

▲ Critical Viewing
Does the man in this painting fit Auden's description of "the unknown citizen"? Explain. **EVALUATE**

Vocabulary
conduct (kän′ dukt)
n. behavior

BACKGROUND Auden wrote this poem five years after the passage of the Social Security Act of 1935, which sought to provide workers with pensions after retirement. The system required that each citizen be assigned a unique number. For skeptics like Auden, the system symbolized a frightening new world controlled by bureaucracy.

He was found by the Bureau of Statistics to be
One against whom there was no official complaint,
And all the reports on his conduct agree
That, in the modern sense of an old-fashioned word, he was a saint,
For in everything he did he served the Greater Community.
Except for the War till the day he retired

He worked in a factory and never got fired,
But satisfied his employers, Fudge Motors Inc.
Yet he wasn't a scab or odd in his views,
For his Union reports that he paid his dues,
(Our report on his Union shows it was sound)
And our Social **Psychology** workers found
That he was popular with his mates and liked a drink.
The Press are convinced that he bought a paper every day
And that his reactions to advertisements were normal in every way.
Policies taken out in his name prove that he was fully insured,
And his Health-card shows he was once in hospital but left it cured.
Both Producers Research and High-Grade Living declare
He was fully **sensible** to the advantages of the Installment Plan
And had everything necessary to the Modern Man,
A phonograph, a radio, a car and a frigidaire.
Our researchers into Public Opinion are content
That he held the proper opinions for the time of year;
When there was peace, he was for peace; when there was war,
he went.
He was married and added five children to the population.
Which our Eugenist[1] says was the right number for a parent of
his generation,
And our teachers report that he never interfered with their
education.
Was he free? Was he happy? The question is absurd:
Had anything been wrong, we should certainly have heard.

Vocabulary

psychology (sī käl′ ə jē) *n.* science dealing with the human mind

sensible (sen′ sə bəl) *adj.* emotionally or intellectually aware

1. **Eugenist** (yo͞o jen′ ist) *n.* a specialist in eugenics, the movement devoted to improving the human species through genetic control.

Critical Reading

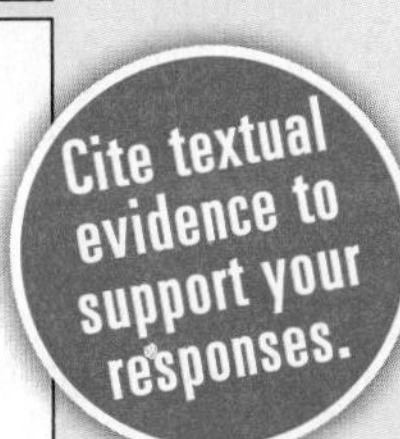
Cite textual evidence to support your responses.

1. **Key Ideas and Details (a)** How does the state identify the unknown citizen in the poem's subtitle? **(b) Interpret:** What do these numbers and letters suggest?
2. **Key Ideas and Details (a)** Identify at least three facts the state knows about the citizen. **(b) Interpret:** In what ways is the citizen "unknown"?
3. **Key Ideas and Details (a)** What questions does the speaker refer to as "absurd"? **(b) Make a Judgment:** Are these questions actually absurd? Explain.
4. **Integration of Knowledge and Ideas** What view of individuals in the modern world does Auden express in this poem? In your response, use at least two of these Essential Question words: *alienation, isolated, community, data.* ***[Connecting to the Essential Question: How does literature shape or reflect society?]***

Close Reading Activities *The Unknown Citizen*

Literary Analysis

1. **Key Ideas and Details** Using a chart like the one shown, name four groups that report on the unknown citizen's life and identify the information they have about him.

2. **Craft and Structure** **(a)** Who is the speaker, or narrator, of this poem? Explain. **(b)** Describe the speaker's **tone.** **(c)** Cite three examples of word choice in the poem that support your description.
3. **Craft and Structure** Begin to **evaluate structure as it relates to meaning** by identifying three examples of each of the following grammatical structures:
   (a) the use of collective nouns, such as "the Press"
   (b) the use of passive voice, such as "He was found"
4. **Craft and Structure** How does Auden's use of the grammatical structures you identified in question 3 help the poet convey his central idea?
5. **Craft and Structure** How does Auden's use of capitalization add to the poem's meaning?
6. **Craft and Structure** **(a)** In what ways do the line lengths make the poem look like prose? **(b)** How does this structural quality add to the poem's meaning?
7. **Craft and Structure** In what ways does the tone of the poem add to or support the satire?
8. **Craft and Structure** **(a)** What societal flaw or folly is the object of Auden's **satire** in this poem? **(b)** Would you characterize this satire as harsh or gentle? Explain.
9. **Integration of Knowledge and Ideas** Do you think this poem implies a call for action or change, or does it simply present a situation? Explain.
10. **Integration of Knowledge and Ideas** **(a)** In what ways is official knowledge of the unknown citizen limited? **(b)** Do you think deeper knowledge of citizens by government or corporate institutions is either possible or desirable in a modern society? Explain your point of view.

Common Core State Standards

Writing

2. Write informative texts to examine and convey complex ideas, concepts, and information clearly and accurately through the effective selection, organization, and analysis of content. *(p. 777)*

2.b. Develop the topic thoroughly by selecting the most significant and relevant facts, extended definitions, concrete details, quotations, or other information and examples appropriate to the audience's knowledge of the topic. *(p. 777)*

2.f. Provide a concluding statement or section that follows from and supports the information or explanation presented.

Language

4.b. Identify and correctly use patterns of word changes that indicate different meanings or parts of speech. *(p. 777)*

Vocabulary Acquisition and Use

Word Analysis: Greek Root *-psych-*

In Greek mythology, Psyche was the daughter of a king and was a person of deep emotion. Her name comes from a Greek word meaning "soul," or "mind." The root *-psych-,* then, means "soul" or "mind" and forms the basis for *psychology* and other English words. Write definitions for the words below. Then, write a sentence in which you use each word correctly.

1. psychiatry
2. psychosomatic
3. psychotic

Vocabulary: Assessing Logic

Decide whether each sentence below is logical. If it is not, rewrite the sentence to fix the logic, but do not replace the italicized word. Explain your answers.

1. Because Mona was interested in sports, she chose to major in *psychology*.
2. Sophia found that her new backpack's *conduct* was bothersome.
3. *Sensible* to the benefits of eating healthfully, Joe ate a candy bar.

Writing to Sources

Informative Text Auden offers a fairly dark vision of modern society. Write an **essay** in which you describe the political nature of the world this poem portrays. Cite specific details from the poem to support your ideas.

Prewriting Reread the poem to address these questions as they apply to the world of the poem: **1.** Do individuals or institutions have power? **2.** How are business and politics connected? **3.** Are individuals able to think for themselves? Record details from the poem that speak to these and other related questions. Then, write a statement summarizing the political nature of the world Auden portrays.

Drafting Include the summary you wrote in your introduction. Then, devote one body paragraph to specific ideas that relate to your summary. Provide quotations from the poem to support your ideas. End with a memorable conclusion in which you restate important ideas from earlier in the essay.

Model: Drafting to Include Quotations

In "The Unknown Citizen," Auden explores the effect of a highly structured society on individuals. In such a society, government policies overwhelm citizens' opinions. The speaker states, "When there was peace, he was for peace; when there was war, he went."

Using direct quotations supports your interpretation of the poem.

Revising Read through your draft to make sure your writing is unified and coherent. Delete stray, unrelated ideas and check that you have supported main points with strong evidence.

Building Knowledge and Insight

old age sticks • anyone lived in a pretty how town

Connecting to the Essential Question E. E. Cummings's poetry was radical in his day. While it is celebrated today, it still presents what many see as a radical vision of poetry. As you read, notice elements that distinguish these poems from traditional verse. Doing so will help as you consider the Essential Question: **How does literature shape or reflect society?**

Reading Literature
4. Determine the meaning of words and phrases as they are used in the text, including figurative and connotative meanings; analyze the impact of specific word choices on meaning and tone, including language that is particularly fresh, engaging, or beautiful.
5. Analyze how an author's choices concerning how to structure specific parts of a text contribute to its overall structure and meaning as well as its aesthetic impact.

Language
3.a. Apply an understanding of syntax to the study of complex texts when reading.

Close Reading Focus

Author's Style

An **author's style** is his or her unique way of writing. Many factors determine style, including word choice, sentence structure, and the arrangement of words on a page. E. E. Cummings's style is among the most distinctive of any American poet. He uses a range of experimental elements and techniques, including the following:

- Unconventional *syntax*, or sentence structure, including the splitting up of words and phrases and the mixing up of parts of speech
- The bending and breaking of grammatical rules
- The unorthodox use of lowercase and uppercase letters
- A minimal or unorthodox use of punctuation
- The elimination of spaces between certain words and characters
- The use of typographical symbols to create visual impact

Cummings's style is not just for show; it is a key part of his meaning and affects how the reader experiences the poems. As you read, think about the effect Cummings's style has on your understanding of each poem.

Preparing to Read Complex Texts The lack of a traditional structure makes the experience of reading an E. E. Cummings poem very different from that of traditional verse. One way to make sure you understand the poet's essential meaning is to **paraphrase,** or restate ideas in your own words. Paraphrasing can help you determine the meaning of passages that may otherwise challenge your comprehension. Use a chart like the one shown to list any unclear phrases or whole passages and paraphrase them.

Passage
"with up so floating many bells down"
Paraphrase
With the airy sound of ringing bells

Vocabulary

The words below are important for understanding the text that follows. Copy the words into your notebook. Are these words nouns or verbs? How can you tell?

sowed **reaped**

E. E. Cummings

(1894–1962)

Author of "old age sticks" and "anyone lived in a pretty how town"

After working in the French ambulance corps and spending three months behind bars as a political prisoner during World War I, Edward Estlin Cummings studied painting in Paris and subsequently began writing poetry in New York City. A graduate of Harvard University, his first published poems appeared in the *Harvard Monthly*. Though some critics attacked the unconventional style of his poetry, Cummings's work was popular with general readers. People admired his playful use of language, his distinctive use of grammar and punctuation, and his interest in a poem's appearance, a sensitivity that might have stemmed from his talent as a painter. Cummings also became known for his concern for the individual and his discerning eye for life's ironies.

Form vs. Content Although Cummings's poems tend to be unconventional in form and style, they generally express traditional ideas. In his finest poems, Cummings explores the customary poetic terrain of love and nature but makes innovative use of grammar and punctuation to reinforce meaning. Many of his poems also contain comic touches as Cummings addresses the confusing aspects of modern life. Cummings was also a skillful satirist who used his poems to challenge accepted notions and fixed beliefs.

Cummings received a number of awards for his work, including the Boston Fine Arts Poetry Festival Award and the Bollingen Prize in Poetry. In 1968, six years after his death, a volume of his poetry, *The Complete Poems, 1913–1968,* was published. At the time of his death, he was the second most widely read poet in the United States, after Robert Frost.

"It takes courage to grow up and become who you really are."

old age sticks

E. E. Cummings

Remember Now the Days of Thy Youth, 1950, Paul Starrett Sample, Hood Museum of Art, Dartmouth College, Hanover, NH

old age sticks
up Keep
Off
signs)&

youth yanks them
down(old
age
cries No

Tres)&(pas)
youth laughs
(sing
old age

scolds Forbid
den Stop
Must
n't Don't

&)youth goes
right on
gr
owing old

▲ **Critical Viewing** Do the elderly men in this painting belong to a group similar to the one Cummings describes, or are they a different sort? On what details do you base your conclusion? **DRAW CONCLUSIONS**

anyone lived in a pretty how town

E. E. Cummings

Background Cummings wrote these poems late in life. After an eventful youth, he settled down to enjoy his family farm in New Hampshire. The poems from this period tend to be gentle and even joyful.

anyone lived in a pretty how town
(with up so floating many bells down)
spring summer autumn winter
he sang his didn't he danced his did.

Women and men(both little and small)
cared for anyone not at all
they **sowed** their isn't they **reaped** their same
sun moon stars rain

children guessed(but only a few
and down they forgot as up they grew
autumn winter spring summer)
that noone loved him more by more

when by now and tree by leaf
she laughed his joy she cried his grief
bird by snow and stir by still
anyone's any was all to her

someones married their everyones
laughed their cryings and did their dance
(sleep wake hope and then)they
said their nevers they slept their dream

Vocabulary

sowed (sōd) *v.* scattered; planted

reaped (rēpt) *v.* gathered; brought in

Paraphrasing

Restate lines 13–14 in your own words.

Comprehension

Which words are repeated in these five stanzas?

Author's Style
How does Cummings's unconventional syntax add to the dream-like quality of the last three stanzas?

stars rain sun moon
(and only the snow can begin to explain
how children are apt to forget to remember
with up so floating many bells down)

one day anyone died i guess
(and noone stooped to kiss his face)
busy folk buried them side by side
little by little and was by was

all by all and deep by deep
and more by more they dream their sleep
noone and anyone earth by april
wish by spirit and if by yes.

Women and men(both dong and ding)
summer autumn winter spring
reaped their sowing and went their came
sun moon stars rain

Critical Reading

Cite textual evidence to support your responses.

1. **Key Ideas and Details** **(a)** In "old age sticks," what actions do old age and youth take? **(b) Compare and Contrast:** Explain the differences Cummings points out between youth and old age.
2. **Key Ideas and Details** **(a)** In the final stanza of "old age sticks," what does the poem say is happening to youth? **(b) Interpret:** Explain the irony in this final stanza.
3. **Craft and Structure** **(a)** In "anyone lived in a pretty how town," what does Cummings name the main male and female characters? **(b) Speculate:** What is the poet suggesting in this choice?
4. **Key Ideas and Details** **(a)** What does Cummings say the people do with their cryings and their dreams? **(b) Interpret:** What does the poet suggest about the townspeople through these statements?
5. **Key Ideas and Details** **Evaluate:** What message does the poet convey about the ideas of individuality and conformity?
6. **Integration of Knowledge and Ideas** Do you think the emergence of new approaches to an art form, such as the experimental verse Cummings wrote, reflects larger changes in a society? Explain. In your response, use at least two of these Essential Question words: *innovation, prevail, expertise, enduring, ambiguity.* ***[Connecting to the Essential Question: How does literature shape or reflect society?]***

Close Reading Activities

old age sticks • anyone lived in a pretty how town

Literary Analysis

1. **Key Ideas and Details** **Paraphrase** the following passages: **(a)** lines 5–8 of "old age sticks"; **(b)** lines 13–16 of "anyone lived in a pretty how town."
2. **Integration of Knowledge and Ideas** Explain how the paraphrasing you did in response to question 1 clarified your understanding of each poem.
3. **Craft and Structure** **(a)** Use a chart like the one shown to identify elements of Cummings's unique **style** as they appear in these two poems. **(b)** Explain how each example adds to the poem's essential meaning.

Element of Style	Example	Meaning
unconventional syntax		
uppercase or lowercase letters		
minimal/unorthodox punctuation		

4. **Craft and Structure** **(a)** In "anyone lived . . . ," identify two points at which the poet mixes up parts of speech. **(b)** For each one, explain how it adds to the meaning and mood, or feeling, of the poem.

Common Core State Standards

Writing

2. Write informative texts to examine and convey complex ideas, concepts, and information clearly and accurately through the effective selection, organization, and analysis of content.

2.b. Develop the topic thoroughly by selecting the most significant and relevant quotations or other information and examples appropriate to the audience's knowledge of the topic.

Language

5. Demonstrate understanding of word relationships.

Vocabulary Acquisition and Use

Analogies Analogies show the relationships between pairs of words. Complete each analogy using a word from the vocabulary list on page 778. In each, your choice should create a word pair that matches the relationship between the first two words given. Then, explain your answers.

1. ____________ is to *gathered* as *destroyed* is to *constructed.*
2. *Calamity* is to *blessing* as ____________ is to *dispersed.*

Writing to Sources

Informative Text Imagine that E. E. Cummings will be giving a poetry reading at a bookstore in your town. As the organizer of the event, write an **introduction** that provides background about the poet and prepares the audience for the poetry they will hear. Select the most relevant and interesting facts about Cummings and include at least one eloquent quotation from the poet. Use a conversational style appropriate to the setting and purpose of the event.

Building Knowledge and Insight

Of Modern Poetry • Ars Poetica • Poetry

Connecting to the Essential Question In these poems, Stevens, MacLeish, and Moore contemplate the art of poetry. As you read, notice details that both suggest and directly state what poetry can and cannot achieve. Your observations will help as you reflect on the Essential Question: **How does literature shape or reflect society?**

Common Core State Standards

Reading Literature

1. Cite strong and thorough textual evidence to support inferences drawn from the text, including determining where the text leaves matters uncertain.

4. Determine the meaning of words and phrases as they are used in the text, including figurative meanings; analyze the impact of specific word choices on meaning and tone, including language that is particularly fresh, engaging, or beautiful.

9. Demonstrate knowledge of early-twentieth-century foundational works of American literature, including how two or more texts from the same period treat similar themes or topics.

Language

5.a. Interpret figures of speech in context and analyze their role in the text.

Close Reading Focus

Imagery; Personification; Simile

Poets combine rich language with poetic devices to develop a poem's *theme,* or central message. The theme of these three poems is poetry itself: what it is, what it does, and what it means to people and societies. These are abstract ideas. To give them weight and shape, the poets use a variety of literary devices, including the following:

- **Imagery:** word pictures that appeal to the senses
- **Personification:** a figure of speech in which a nonhuman idea or thing is given human qualities
- **Simile:** a figure of speech comparing two seemingly different things and using the words *like* or *as*

Comparing Literary Works As you read, compare how each poet draws on these tools to clothe abstract themes in tangible realities that readers can understand and feel.

Preparing to Read Complex Texts These three poems are about poetry itself; each presents a view of life—an artistic philosophy—in which poetry plays a key role. For example, Stevens holds that the making of a poem is also the making of a self and a world. To understand poems about ideas, read with a different critical lens than you use for poems about more everyday concerns. As you read, **analyze philosophical arguments** that support the poet's message. Note a key idea and then make inferences about a broader philosophy that it implies. Use a chart like the one shown to identify and analyze the philosophical ideas these poems express.

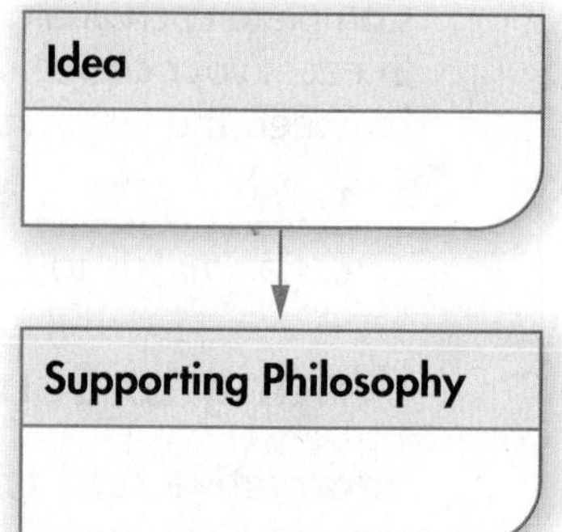

Vocabulary

The words below are important to understanding the texts that follow. Copy the words into your notebook. Write the words you know in one column. What is one similarity that two of the words share?

suffice **palpable**
insatiable **derivative**

Wallace Stevens (1879–1955)

Author of "Of Modern Poetry"

Wallace Stevens believed that the goal of poetry is to capture the interaction between the private, subjective world of the mind and reality. He spent his career writing poems that delve into the imagination and the ways it shapes our perception of the physical world. He uses elaborate imagery and precise language to express his philosophical themes. Stevens depended largely on the natural world for his inspiration because nature, he said, is the only certainty.

Insurance Executive by Day Stevens was born and raised in Reading, Pennsylvania. After completing his education at Harvard University, he took a job at an insurance company in Hartford, Connecticut, and eventually became the company's vice president. He did not publish his first collection of poetry, *Harmonium* (1923), until he was forty-three years old. In *Harmonium* and much of his other work, Stevens uses dazzling imagery to capture the beauty of the physical world while expressing the dependence of that beauty on the perceptions of the observer. Although the book received little public attention, it was praised by critics and launched Stevens's literary career.

Stevens published many volumes of poetry, including *Ideas of Order* (1935), *Parts of a World* (1942), *Transport to Summer* (1947), and *The Auroras of Autumn* (1950). His *Collected Poems* earned him the Pulitzer Prize in 1955. Despite his success as a poet, however, Stevens continued his career in insurance until the end of his life. "It gives a man character as a poet to have this daily contact with a job," he once said. A brilliant and unusual figure, he is now regarded as one of the most important poets of the twentieth century.

Of Modern Poetry

Wallace Stevens

BACKGROUND Wallace Stevens's poetry reflects the influence of the Symbolist literary movement. Originating in the last half of the nineteenth century, Symbolist poets believed that ideas and emotions are difficult to communicate because people perceive the world in such personal ways. These poets tried to convey meaning through symbols—people, places, and objects that represent ideas beyond their concrete meanings. As a result, the work of Symbolist poets like Stevens can often have many interpretations.

Vocabulary

suffice (sə fīs′) *v.* be adequate; meet the needs of

The poem of the mind in the act of finding
What will **suffice**. It has not always had
To find: the scene was set; it repeated what
Was in the script.
Then the theatre was changed
To something else. Its past was a souvenir.

It has to be living, to learn the speech of the place.
It has to face the men of the time and to meet
The women of the time. It has to think about war
And it has to find what will suffice. It has

To construct a new stage. It has to be on that stage
And, like an insatiable actor, slowly and
With meditation, speak words that in the ear,
In the delicatest ear of the mind, repeat,
Exactly, that which it wants to hear, at the sound
Of which, an invisible audience listens,
Not to the play, but to itself, expressed
In an emotion as of two people, as of two
Emotions becoming one. The actor is
A metaphysician[1] in the dark, twanging
An instrument, twanging a wiry string that gives
Sounds passing through sudden rightnesses, wholly
Containing the mind, below which it cannot descend,
Beyond which it has no will to rise.

                                                            It must
Be the finding of a satisfaction, and may
Be of a man skating, a woman dancing, a woman
Combing. The poem of the act of the mind.

Vocabulary

insatiable (in sā′ shə bəl) *adj.* constantly wanting more

1. **metaphysician** (met′ ə fə zish′ ən) *n.* a person versed in philosophy, especially those branches that seek to explain the nature of being or of the universe.

Critical Reading

Cite textual evidence to support your responses.

1. **Key Ideas and Details (a)** In the first stanza, what does the poet say happened to theater? **(b) Interpret:** What does "the theater" represent?
2. **Key Ideas and Details (a) Interpret:** What does the speaker mean when he says that a poem "has to think about war"? **(b) Analyze:** What does the speaker suggest about the connections poetry must have with its time period?
3. **Key Ideas and Details (a) Summarize:** What topics for poetry does the speaker identify in lines 25–26? **(b) Connect:** How do these topics relate to the conception of poetry presented earlier in the poem?
4. **Craft and Structure (a) Speculate:** The opening and closing lines of the poem are sentence fragments. What verbs might meaningfully complete these lines? Explain your choices.
5. **Integration of Knowledge and Ideas Infer:** Do you think the poet believes the work of poetry to be difficult? Explain.

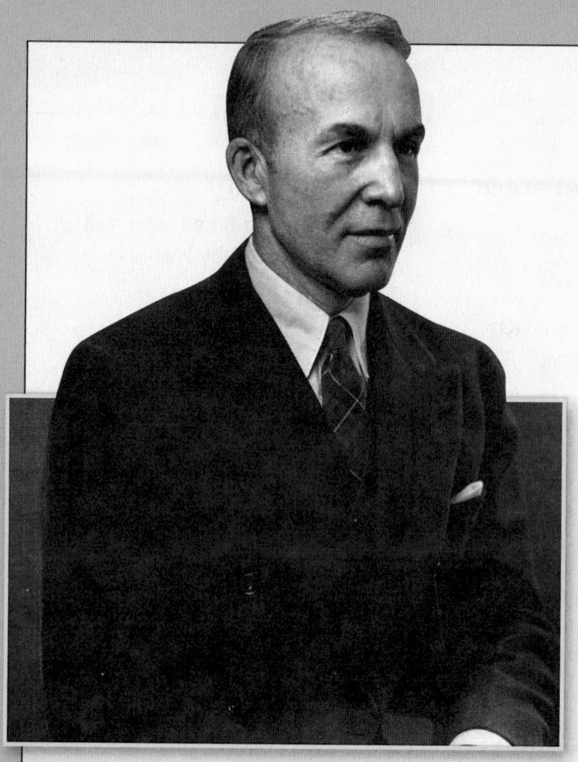

Archibald MacLeish

(1892–1982)

Author of **"Ars Poetica"**

Archibald MacLeish was born in Glencoe, Illinois. He was trained as a lawyer but, unlike Wallace Stevens, turned his back on his first career to devote himself completely to poetry.

MacLeish's early poems, such as "Ars Poetica," are experimental, reflecting the influence of the Modernists. By contrast, his later poems are more traditional and accessible. As unrest spread throughout the world in the 1930s, MacLeish used poetry to explore political and social issues. Over the course of his career, MacLeish produced more than thirty books and won three Pulitzer Prizes.

Marianne Moore

(1887–1972)

Author of **"Poetry"**

Born in Kirkwood, Missouri, Marianne Moore first gained a footing in the literary world as the editor of *The Dial,* a highly regarded literary journal. In that role, she encouraged many new writers by publishing their work. However, she was hesitant to publish her own work, although many noted poets had admired it. In fact, her first book, *Poems* (1921), was published without her knowledge.

As a Modernist, Moore wrote poems that were inventive, precise, and witty. Unlike other Modernists, however, she chose not to write about the state of modern civilization. Instead, she explored subjects such as animals and nature. "Poetry," one of her best-known poems, explores the subject of poetry itself.

Moore published poems and collections regularly, garnering honors and awards along the way. Her *Collected Poems* (1951) won the Pulitzer Prize and the National Book Award in 1952.

Ars Poetica

Archibald MacLeish

BACKGROUND **Ars Poetica** The title is an allusion to the ancient Roman poet Horace's "Ars Poetica," or "The Art of Poetry," which was composed about 20 B.C. For a contemporary *ars poetica,* see Judith Ortiz Cofer's poem on page 1366.

A poem should be palpable and mute
As a globed fruit.

Dumb
As old medallions to the thumb,

Silent as the sleeve-worn stone
Of casement ledges where the moss has grown—

A poem should be wordless
As the flight of birds.

A poem should be motionless in time
As the moon climbs,

Leaving, as the moon releases
Twig by twig the night-entangled trees,

Leaving, as the moon behind the winter leaves.
Memory by memory the mind—

Vocabulary
palpable (pal´ pə bəl)
adj. able to be touched, felt, or handled

Comprehension
According to the speaker, how silent should a poem be?

A poem should be motionless in time
As the moon climbs.

A poem should be equal to:
Not true.

For all the history of grief
An empty doorway and a maple leaf.

For love
The leaning grasses and two lights above the sea—

A poem should not mean
But be.

Critical Reading

Cite textual evidence to support your responses.

1. **Key Ideas and Details (a)** Identify at least three items the speaker compares to poetry. **(b) Analyze:** What do you think the speaker means by saying that a poem should be "palpable and mute," "wordless," and "motionless in time"?
2. **Key Ideas and Details (a)** With what images can a poem show the history of grief, as the speaker states? **(b)** With what images should it show love? **(c) Speculate:** Why do you think MacLeish chooses to focus on these emotions?
3. **Key Ideas and Details (a) Interpret:** What contradiction do you see in lines 7–8? **(b) Analyze:** What do you think this contradiction suggests about the subject, poetry?
4. **Craft and Structure (a) Interpret:** What contrast does the poet make in the final two lines? **(b) Define:** How would you define the difference between *meaning* and *being*?
5. **Integration of Knowledge and Ideas Extend:** In what ways do you think poetry can touch the human spirit? Explain.

Untitled, 1984, Alexander Calder, Solomon R. Guggenheim Museum, New York

Poetry

Marianne Moore

I, too, dislike it: there are things that are important beyond all this
    fiddle.
  Reading it, however, with a perfect contempt for it, one discovers in
  it after all, a place for the genuine.
    Hands that can grasp, eyes
    that can dilate, hair that can rise
      if it must, these things are important not because a

high-sounding interpretation can be put upon them but because
    they are
  useful. When they become so **derivative** as to become
    unintelligible,
  the same thing may be said for all of us, that we
    do not admire what
    we cannot understand: the bat
      holding on upside down or in quest of something to

▲ Critical Viewing
Write a sentence describing this painting "with a perfect contempt for it." Explain what the result shows you about Moore's point in lines 2–3. **CONNECT**

Vocabulary
derivative (də riv′ ə tiv) *adj.* not original; based on something else

Comprehension
Why are the "things" the poet describes in lines 4–5 "important"?

eat, elephants pushing, a wild horse taking a roll, a tireless wolf
under a tree, the immovable critic twitching his skin like a
horse that feels a flea, the base-
ball fan, the statistician—
nor is it valid
to discriminate against "business documents and
school-books"; all these phenomena are important. One must
make a distinction
however: when dragged into prominence by half poets, the result is
not poetry,
nor till the poets among us can be
"literalists[1] of
the imagination"—above
insolence and triviality and can present
for inspection, "imaginary gardens with real toads in them," shall we
have
it. In the meantime, if you demand on the one hand,
the raw material of poetry in
all its rawness and
that which is on the other hand
genuine, you are interested in poetry.

Imagery
What images does the speaker use to describe things that are "genuine"?

1. **literalists** *n.* those who take words at their exact meaning.

Critical Reading

Cite textual evidence to support your responses.

1. **Key Ideas and Details (a)** What does the speaker say happens when poems become derivative? **(b) Synthesize:** What qualities does the speaker believe good poetry should possess?
2. **Craft and Structure (a) Interpret:** What seeming contradiction exists in the phrase "literalists of the imagination"? **(b) Analyze:** How is the meaning of this phrase extended by the image of "imaginary gardens with real toads"?
3. **Integration of Knowledge and Ideas** Based on the ideas these poets express, do you think poets have a significant role to play in today's world? Defend your opinion, using at least three of these Essential Question words: *contemporary, relevant, expression, communicate, depth. **[Connecting to the Essential Question: How does literature shape or reflect society?]***

Literary Analysis

1. **Craft and Structure** **(a)** In "Of Modern Poetry," note two examples of **imagery** that relate poetry to a theater performance. **(b)** In line 18, how does Stevens describe the emotional link between actor and audience? **(c)** What does this suggest about the relationship of a reader to a poem?
2. **Craft and Structure** **(a)** What **simile** does Stevens introduce in line 11? **(b)** How does he develop that simile in the rest of the poem?
3. **Craft and Structure** What example of personification do you find in the first two lines of MacLeish's poem? Explain.
4. **Craft and Structure** **(a)** In "Ars Poetica," note four images that involve the idea of muteness or silence. **(b)** Which images in the poem suggest ideas of stillness? **(c)** How do these images clarify the poet's meaning in the last two lines?
5. **Craft and Structure** **(a)** To what senses do Moore's images of animal behavior appeal? **(b)** How do these images help define poetry for Moore?
6. **Craft and Structure** **(a)** How does Stevens use **personification** to describe the "poem of the act of the mind"? **(b)** How does Moore use it to describe the "genuine"?
7. **Integration of Knowledge and Ideas** **Analyze the philosophical argument** underpinning Stevens's ideas in "Of Modern Poetry." **(a)** In lines 3–4, how did the "poem of the mind" once find "what will suffice"? **(b)** What change has happened, as noted in lines 4–5? **(c)** What ideas about a new relationship between the modern world and the past is Stevens suggesting?
8. **Integration of Knowledge and Ideas** What philosophical idea about the way people understand reality is suggested in the phrase "the poem of the act of the mind"?
9. **Integration of Knowledge and Ideas** **(a)** In Moore's poem, what philosophical outlook about the role of art does her discussion of the "genuine" suggest? **(b)** What concept of the "genuine" does the image she quotes in line 23 support?
10. **Comparing Literary Works** Use a chart like the one shown to interpret each poet's use of imagery and simile to advance his or her theme.

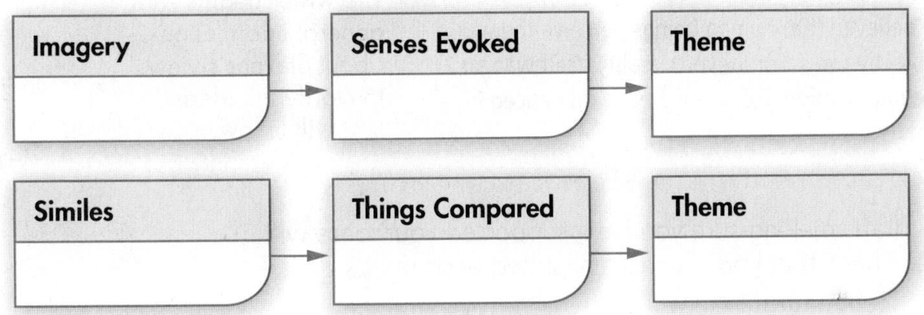

Common Core State Standards

Writing

2. Write informative texts to examine and convey complex ideas, concepts, and information clearly and accurately through the effective selection, organization, and analysis of content. *(p. 794)*

9.a. Apply grades 11–12 Reading standards to literature. *(p. 794)*

Language

4.b. Identify and correctly use patterns of word changes that indicate different meanings or parts of speech. *(p. 794)*

4.d. Verify the preliminary determination of the meaning of a word or phrase. *(p. 794)*

Close Reading Activities Continued

Vocabulary Acquisition and Use

Word Analysis: Latin Root *-satis-*

The word *insatiable* contains the Latin root *-satis-*, which means "enough." Combined with the prefix *in-*, meaning "not," you can determine that *insatiable* suggests "not enough." Use your knowledge of *-satis-* to define each numbered word. Then, use a dictionary to check your definitions.

1. satisfy
2. dissatisfied
3. satisfactory
4. sate
5. satiate
6. unsatisfactory
7. satiety
8. saturate

Vocabulary: Use New Words

Follow the instructions below to write a sentence for each item, using a word from the vocabulary list on page 784. Use each word only once.

1. Describe the quality of a peach in a beautiful painting.
2. Criticize a musician whose work lacks originality.
3. Explain why a minimal amount of nutritious food is not enough to maintain one's health.
4. Criticize someone who always wants more possessions.

Writing to Sources

Informative Text In these three poems, Stevens, Moore, and MacLeish define poetry by example. Write an **essay** in which you compare and contrast the ideas the poets present in two of these poems. Note the distinct ways each poet explains, above all, why poetry is important.

Prewriting Reread each poem and paraphrase the ideas it presents. Briefly state the poets' philosophies by completing these sentences for each poem:

Poetry is ______. It is important because ______.

Choose two poets to compare and contrast. After gathering your points of comparison, select a logical organizing principle and main idea to develop in your essay.

Drafting Introduce each poet by providing a general statement about his or her beliefs about poetry. Then, write a brief statement of your main point. Develop your ideas, using quotations from the poem to support your analysis.

Model: Providing Necessary Background

Wallace Stevens believed that human beings perceive the world in an entirely subjective way. For Stevens, reality itself was an expression of the imagination. This view greatly influenced his philosophy of poetry.

The writer begins with general information about Stevens's views to clarify the ideas that will follow.

Revising Review your draft, making sure you have supported your ideas with appropriate quotations. Check that you have clearly stated each poet's basic philosophy of poetry.

TEXT SET

From Every Corner of the Land

Part 2

In a few pages a good story portrays the complexity of a life . . .

— BERNARD MALAMUD

In This Section

For more practice analyzing short stories, see numerous selections in this book, including those on pages 292, 628, 652, 730, 834, 1011, 1298, 1310, and 1326.

Elements of Short Stories

A **short story** is a brief work of fiction. Short stories have no fixed length, but most can be read in one sitting. A short story includes the key literary elements of fiction.

- **Plot:** the sequence of events that make up the story. A story's plot focuses on a central **conflict,** or struggle that the main character faces. Driven by this conflict, the plot follows a pattern called the "dramatic arc." During the **exposition,** the characters, setting, and conflict are introduced. The conflict intensifies during the **rising action,** reaching its point of highest tension during the **climax.** The intensity of the conflict lessens during the **falling action,** and ends during the **resolution.**
- **Characters:** the personalities who participate in the story. A writer uses techniques of **characterization** to develop and reveal characters.
- **Setting:** the time and place of a story. The setting may serve as the background, or it may play a crucial role in the story.
- **Theme:** the central idea, message, or insight a story explores. The reader may have to piece together different clues to infer the theme.
- **Point of view:** the perspective from which a story is told. With first-person point of view, the narrator is part of the story and refers to himself or herself as *I*. With third-person point of view, the narrator stands outside the story and refers to all the characters as *he* or *she*.

Voice The best short stories do more than simply relate a tale from start to finish. They express an author's distinct voice, or personality on the page. Voice is conveyed through all the elements of the writing, including the author's syntax, tone, characters, plots, and themes. Just as no two singers sound precisely the same, so do author's literary voices differ.

Close Read: Voice in Fiction

These literary elements that contribute to voice appear in the model text at the right.

Description: word portraits of people, places, or things. Descriptive writing uses **images** and may include figurative language. *Example: "She was very old and small and she walked slowly in the dark pine shadows, moving a little from side to side in her steps . . ." (Eudora Welty)*	**Diction/Word Choice:** the writer's use of particular types of words. Diction may be formal, casual, elevated, idiomatic, or any combination thereof. *Example: It was a clear day, and yet there seemed an intangible pall over the face of things . . ." (Jack London)*
Syntax: the length and types of sentences a writer uses *Example: "It was not a matter of live or die. There was no real peril." (Tim O'Brien)*	**Symbolism:** the imbuing of a story element with meaning that is larger than itself. *Example: "Across the street from their house, in an empty lot between two houses, stood the rockpile." (James Baldwin)*

Model

About the Text This classic work by Sarah Orne Jewett (1849–1909) tells the story of Sylvia, a child who lives with her grandmother in rural New England. When a young "sportsman" arrives and offers money for help in finding an elusive white heron, Sylvia's loyalties are tested.

from "A White Heron"

Sarah Orne Jewett

Half a mile from home, at the farther edge of the woods, where the land was highest, a great pine-tree stood, the last of its generation. Whether it was left for a boundary mark, or for what reason, no one could say; the woodchoppers who had felled its mates were dead and gone long ago, and a whole forest of sturdy trees, pines and oaks and maples, had grown again. But the stately head of this old pine towered above them all and made a landmark for sea and shore miles and miles away. Sylvia knew it well. She had always believed that whoever climbed to the top of it could see the ocean; and the little girl had often laid her hand on the great rough trunk and looked up wistfully at those dark boughs that the wind always stirred, no matter how hot and still the air might be below. Now she thought of the tree with a new excitement, for why, if one climbed it at break of day, could not one see all the world, and easily discover from whence the white heron flew, and mark the place, and find the hidden nest? What a spirit of adventure, what wild ambition! What fancied triumph and delight and glory for the later morning when she could make known the secret! It was almost too real and too great for the childish heart to bear.

All night the door of the little house stood open and the whippoorwills came and sang upon the very step. The young sportsman and his old hostess were sound asleep, but Sylvia's great design kept her broad awake and watching.

She forgot to think of sleep. The short summer night seemed as long as the winter darkness, and at last when the whippoorwills ceased, and she was afraid the morning would after all come too soon, she stole out of the house and followed the pasture path through the woods, hastening toward the open ground beyond, listening with a sense of comfort and companionship to the drowsy twitter of a half-awakened bird, whose perch she had jarred in passing. Alas, if the great wave of human interest which flooded for the first time this dull little life should sweep away the satisfactions of an existence heart to heart with nature and the dumb life of the forest!

There was the huge tree asleep yet in the paling moonlight, and small and silly Sylvia began with utmost bravery to mount to the top of it, with tingling, eager blood coursing the channels of her whole frame, with her bare feet and fingers, that pinched and held like bird's claws to the monstrous ladder reaching up, up, almost to the sky itself. First she must mount the white oak tree that grew alongside, where she was almost lost among the dark branches and the green leaves heavy and wet with dew; a bird fluttered off its nest, and a red squirrel ran to and fro and scolded pettishly at the harmless housebreaker.

Description Details paint a word picture of the tree in its setting. They also begin to establish the tree's deeper meaning: it is "the last of its generation," and "a landmark."

Symbol The symbolism of the tree, from where one can "see all the world," intensifies. The tree is also the means by which Sylvia can discover the location of the white heron, yet another of the story's symbols.

Syntax Jewett's long, flowing sentences contribute to her voice. In addition, the piling up of the conjunction *and* in the phrase "triumph and delight and glory" builds a sense of Sylvia's excitement.

Word Choice Jewett's distinctive voice is conveyed in her diction, including the unusual adjective "paling," the reference to Sylvia as "small and silly," and the tree described as a "monstrous ladder."

Building Knowledge and Insight

ANCHOR TEXT
In Another Country

Connecting to the Essential Question The narrator of this story is given a medal he does not believe he deserves. As you read, look for clues that reveal the author's attitude toward war and the glory that is often associated with it. Doing so will help as you reflect on the Essential Question: **What makes American literature American?**

Close Reading Focus

Style; Theme

Ernest Hemingway's style is among the most influential in American literature. It is characterized by economy and "vigorous English," a phrase he encountered in the style guide of a newspaper for which he once wrote. That style has certain specific ingredients:

- **Syntax:** Hemingway's sentences are short, direct, and forceful.
- **Word Choice:** He uses plain language and few, if any, adjectives.
- **Tone:** He suggests emotions but does not explain them or directly state what characters feel. The reader is left to interpret textual clues.

These elements of Hemingway's style are evident in this description of an Italian army officer's reaction to distressing news: "He looked straight past me and out through the window. Then he began to cry."

Hemingway's style marries perfectly with his **themes**—the messages or insights into life that recur throughout his work. Hemingway's themes address ideals of heroism and courage, relationships between young and old, and the loss of innocence in a disappointing and violent world. As you read "In Another Country," look for trademarks of Hemingway's style and the development of two or more of his significant themes. Notice how these themes interact and add to the richness of the story.

Preparing to Read Complex Texts Even if your life differs entirely from those of characters in a story, you can increase your understanding of fiction by **identifying with characters.** To do so, relate their thoughts and feelings to your own and consider how you would feel in similar circumstances. As you read, use a chart like the one shown to help you identify with a story's characters.

Vocabulary

You will encounter the words listed here in the text that follows. Copy the words into your notebook. What is the prefix in each word?

detached **resign**
disgrace

Common Core State Standards

Reading Literature

2. Determine two or more themes or central ideas of a text and analyze their development over the course of the text, including how they interact and build on one another to produce a complex account.

4. Determine the meaning of words and phrases as they are used in the text, including figurative and connotative meanings; analyze the impact of specific word choices on meaning and tone, including language that is particularly fresh, engaging, or beautiful.

9. Demonstrate knowledge of early-twentieth-century foundational works of American literature.

Language

3.a. Apply an understanding of syntax to the study of complex texts when reading.

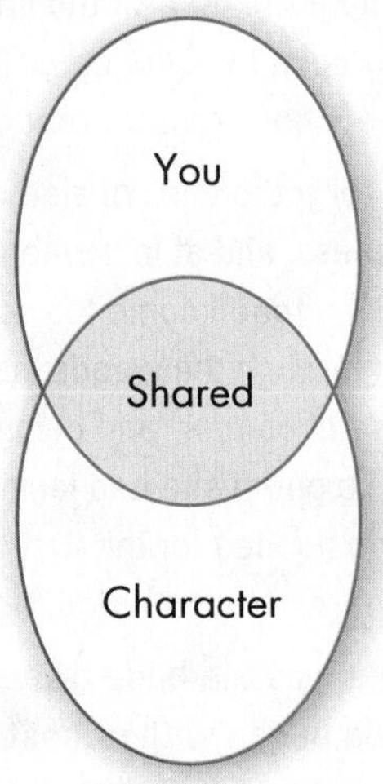

Ernest Hemingway *(1899–1961)*

Author of **"In Another Country"**

Ernest Hemingway's fiction expressed the sentiments of many members of the post-World War I generation. He wrote about people struggling to maintain a sense of dignity while living in a sometimes hostile world.

The Red Cross Hemingway, the son of a physician, was born and raised in Oak Park, Illinois. In high school, he played football and wrote newspaper columns. Eager to serve in World War I, he tried to join the army but was repeatedly turned away due to an eye defect. He joined the Red Cross ambulance corps instead and, in 1918, was sent to the Italian front. Just before his nineteenth birthday, he was severely wounded and spent several months recovering in a hospital in Milan, Italy. These experiences helped shape his view of the world and provided material for his writing, including the story "In Another Country."

Expatriates After the war, Hemingway had a hard time readjusting to life in the United States. To establish himself as a writer, he went to Paris as a foreign correspondent for the *Toronto Star.* In Paris, he befriended Ezra Pound, Gertrude Stein, F. Scott Fitzgerald, and other American writers and artists living overseas. The literary advice of these friends and his work as a journalist helped him develop his concise, concrete, and highly charged writing style.

In 1925, Hemingway published his first major work, *In Our Time,* a series of loosely connected short stories. A year later he published *The Sun Also Rises*, a novel about a group of British and American expatriates trying to overcome the pain and disillusionment of life in the modern world.

A Famous Life Hemingway eventually became as famous for his lifestyle as he was for his writing. Constantly pursuing adventure, he hunted big game in Africa, attended bullfights in Spain, held records for deep-sea fishing in the Caribbean, and participated in amateur boxing.

The full body of Hemingway's work—including *A Farewell to Arms* (1929), *For Whom the Bell Tolls* (1940), and *The Old Man and the Sea* (1952)—earned him the Nobel Prize in Literature in 1954.

In Another Country

Ernest Hemingway

BACKGROUND World War I, the first truly global war, began in Europe in 1914, sparked by nationalist pride and systems of alliances among nations. The Central Powers (Germany, Austria-Hungary, Turkey) fought the Allies (England, France, Russia) with other nations joining one side or the other. The United States entered the war late, on the side of the Allies. Italy, where this story takes place, was not strategically important, but it helped the Allies by drawing Central Power troops away from other battle areas.

The war lasted four brutal years. Throughout most of the conflict, a stalemate existed. Both sides were dug into trenches, and took turns rushing one another. Each rush was greeted by a barrage of machine-gun fire, with thousands falling dead. Other soldiers fell to new weapons—inventions such as airplanes, long-range artillery, and poison gas. Many of the wounded were saved, however, by advances in medical treatment, such as surgical disinfectants and rehabilitative techniques to strengthen injured limbs.

In the fall the war[1] was always there, but we did not go to it any more. It was cold in the fall in Milan[2] and the dark came very early. Then the electric lights came on, and it was pleasant along the streets looking in the windows. There was much game hanging outside the shops, and the snow powdered in the fur of the foxes and the wind blew their tails. The deer hung stiff and heavy and empty, and small birds blew in the wind and the wind turned their feathers. It was a cold fall and the wind came down from the mountains.

We were all at the hospital every afternoon, and there were different ways of walking across the town through the dusk to the hospital. Two of the ways were alongside canals, but they were long. Always, though, you crossed a bridge across a canal to enter the hospital. There was a choice of three bridges. On one of them a woman sold roasted chestnuts. It was warm, standing in front of her charcoal fire, and the chestnuts were warm afterward in your pocket. The hospital was very old and very beautiful, and you entered through a gate and walked across a courtyard and out a gate on the other side. There were usually funerals starting from the courtyard. Beyond the old hospital were the new brick pavilions, and there we met every afternoon and were all very polite and interested in what was the matter, and sat in the machines that were to make so much difference.

Comprehension

Where do the narrator and his companions go each afternoon?

1. **the war** World War I (1914–1918).
2. **Milan** (mi lan′) a city in northern Italy.

◀ Critical Viewing

Does this painting of a World War I ambulance have the same direct, straightforward quality as Hemingway's prose? Explain. **EVALUATE**

The doctor came up to the machine where I was sitting and said: "What did you like best to do before the war? Did you practice a sport?"

I said: "Yes, football."

"Good," he said. "You will be able to play football again better than ever."

My knee did not bend and the leg dropped straight from the knee to the ankle without a calf, and the machine was to bend the knee and make it move as in riding a tricycle. But it did not bend yet, and instead the machine lurched when it came to the bending part. The doctor said: "That will all pass. You are a fortunate young man. You will play football again like a champion."

"You are a fortunate young man. You will play football again like a champion."

In the next machine was a major who had a little hand like a baby's. He winked at me when the doctor examined his hand, which was between two leather straps that bounced up and down and flapped the stiff fingers, and said: "And will I too play football, captain-doctor?" He had been a very great fencer, and before the war the greatest fencer in Italy.

The doctor went to his office in a back room and brought a photograph which showed a hand that had been withered almost as small as the major's, before it had taken a machine course, and after was a little larger. The major held the photograph with his good hand and looked at it very carefully. "A wound?" he asked.

"An industrial accident," the doctor said.

"Very interesting, very interesting," the major said, and handed it back to the doctor.

"You have confidence?"

"No," said the major.

There were three boys who came each day who were about the same age I was. They were all three from Milan, and one of them was to be a lawyer, and one was to be a painter, and one had intended to be a soldier, and after we were finished with the machines, sometimes we walked back together to the Café Cova, which was next door to the Scala.[3] We walked the short way through the communist quarter because we were four together. The people hated us because we were officers, and from a wine-shop someone called out, "A basso gli ufficiali!"[4] as we passed. Another boy who walked with us sometimes and made us five wore a black silk handkerchief across his face because he had no nose then and his face was to be rebuilt. He had gone out to the front from the military academy and been wounded within an hour after he had gone into the front line for the first time. They rebuilt his face, but he came from a very old family and they could never get the nose exactly right. He went to South America and worked in a bank. But this was a long time ago, and then we did not

Identifying With Characters

Have you ever been in a situation like the narrator's in which you did not feel fully accepted or part of a group? How did it make you feel? Explain.

3. **the Scala** (ska´ la) an opera house in Milan.
4. **"A basso gli ufficiali!"** (a ba´ so lye oo fe cha´ le) "Down with officers!" (Italian).

any of us know how it was going to be afterward. We only knew then that there was always the war, but that we were not going to it any more.

We all had the same medals, except the boy with the black silk bandage across his face, and he had not been at the front long enough to get any medals. The tall boy with a very pale face who was to be a lawyer had been a lieutenant of Arditi[5] and had three medals of the sort we each had only one of. He had lived a very long time with death and was a little detached. We were all a little detached, and there was nothing that held us together except that we met every afternoon at the hospital. Although, as we walked to the Cova through the tough part of town, walking in the dark, with light and singing coming out of the wine-shops, and sometimes having to walk into the street when the men and women would crowd together on the sidewalk so that we would have had to jostle them to get by, we felt held together by there being something that had happened that they, the people who disliked us, did not understand.

▲ Wounded Ernest Hemingway (Milan, Italy; 1918)

We ourselves all understood the Cova, where it was rich and warm and not too brightly lighted, and noisy and smoky at certain hours, and there were always girls at the tables and the illustrated papers on a rack on the wall. The girls at the Cova were very patriotic, and I found that the most patriotic people in Italy were the café girls—and I believe they are still patriotic.

The boys at first were very polite about my medals and asked me what I had done to get them. I showed them the papers, which were written in very beautiful language and full of *fratellanza* and *abnegazione*,[6] but which really said, with the adjectives removed, that I had been given the medals because I was an American. After that their manner changed a little toward me, although I was their friend against outsiders. I was a friend, but I was never really one

Vocabulary

detached (di tacht′) *adj.* not emotionally involved

Comprehension

What do the narrator and the "three boys" have in common?

---

5. **Arditi** (är dē′ tē) a select group of soldiers chosen specifically for dangerous campaigns.
6. ***fratellanza*** (frä tāl än′ tsä) **and *abnegazione*** (äb′ nā gä tzyō′ nā) "brotherhood" and "self-denial" (Italian).

▲ Ernest Hemingway is fourth from the right in this photograph of hospital staff and patients (Milan, Italy; 1918).

of them after they had read the citations, because it had been different with them and they had done very different things to get their medals. I had been wounded, it was true; but we all knew that being wounded, after all, was really an accident. I was never ashamed of the ribbons, though, and sometimes, after the cocktail hour, I would imagine myself having done all the things they had done to get their medals; but walking home at night through the empty streets with the cold wind and all the shops closed, trying to keep near the street lights, I knew that I would never have done such things, and I was very much afraid to die, and often lay in bed at night by myself, afraid to die and wondering how I would be when I went back to the front again.

The three with the medals were like hunting-hawks; and I was not a hawk, although I might seem a hawk to those who had never hunted; they, the three, knew better and so we drifted apart. But I stayed good friends with the boy who had been wounded his first day at the front, because he would never know now how he would have turned out; so he could never be accepted either, and I liked him because I thought perhaps he would not have turned out to be a hawk either.

Spiral Review
Characterization
What does the grammar incident reveal about both the narrator's and the major's characters? Explain.

The major, who had been the great fencer, did not believe in bravery, and spent much time while we sat in the machines correcting my grammar. He had complimented me on how I spoke Italian, and we talked together very easily. One day I had said that Italian seemed such an easy language to me that I could not take a great interest in it; everything was so easy to say. "Ah yes," the major said. "Why, then, do you not take up the use of grammar?" So we took up the use of grammar, and soon Italian was such a difficult language that I was afraid to talk to him until I had the grammar straight in my mind.

The major came very regularly to the hospital. I do not think he ever missed a day, although I am sure he did not believe in the machines. There was a time when none of us believed in the machines, and one day the major said it was all nonsense. The machines were new then and it was we who were to prove them. It was an idiotic idea, he said, "a theory, like another." I had not learned my grammar, and he said I was a stupid impossible **disgrace**, and he was a fool to have bothered with me. He was a small man and he sat straight up in his chair with his right hand thrust into the machine and looked straight ahead at the wall while the straps thumped up and down with his fingers in them.

Vocabulary
disgrace (dis grās′) *n.* something that brings shame or dishonor

"What will you do when the war is over if it is over?" he asked me.

"Speak grammatically!"

"I will go to the States."

"Are you married?"

"No, but I hope to be."

"The more of a fool you are," he said. He seemed very angry. "A man must not marry."

"Why, Signor Maggiore?"[7]

"Don't call me 'Signor Maggiore.'"

"Why must not a man marry?"

"He cannot marry. He cannot marry," he said angrily. "If he is to lose everything, he should not place himself in a position to lose that. He should not place himself in a position to lose. He should find things he cannot lose."

He spoke very angrily and bitterly, and looked straight ahead while he talked.

"But why should he necessarily lose it?"

"He'll lose it," the major said.

He was looking at the wall. Then he looked down at the machine and jerked his little hand out from between the straps and slapped it hard against his thigh. "He'll lose it," he almost shouted. "Don't argue with me!" Then he called to the attendant who ran the machines. "Come and turn this damned thing off."

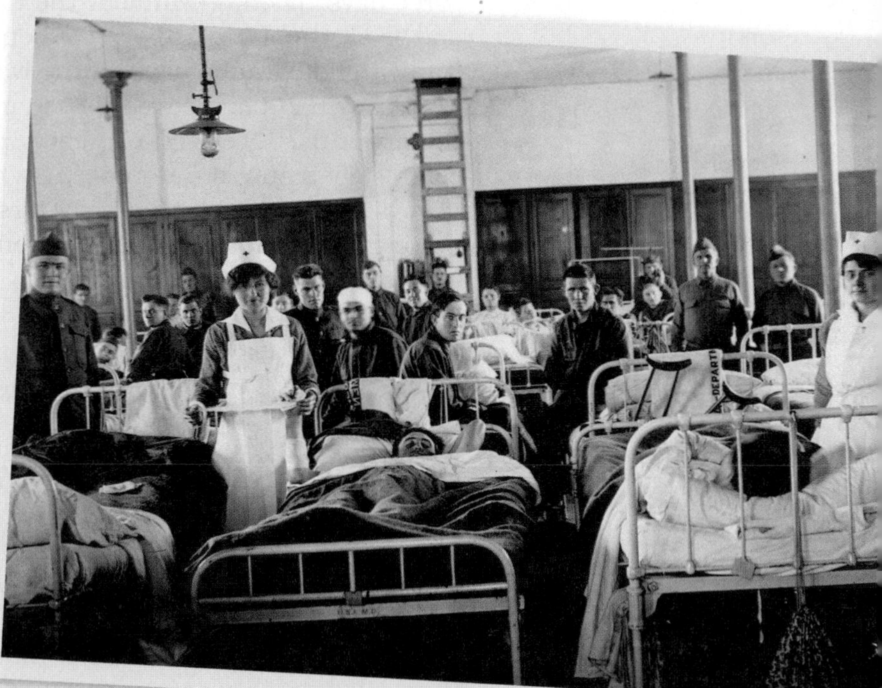

He went back into the other room for the light treatment and the massage. Then I heard him ask the doctor if he might use his telephone and he shut the door. When he came back into the room, I was sitting in another machine. He was wearing his cape and had his cap on, and he came directly toward my machine and put his arm on my shoulder.

"I am so sorry," he said, and patted me on the shoulder with his good hand. "I would not be rude. My wife has just died. You must forgive me."

"Oh—" I said, feeling sick for him. "I am so sorry."

He stood there biting his lower lip. "It is very difficult," he said. "I cannot **resign** myself."

---

7. **Signor Maggiore** (sēn yōr′ mäj jō′ rā) "Mr. Major" (Italian); a respectful way of addressing an officer.

Author's Style

How does Hemingway suggest the major's emotions without explaining them?

▲ Critical Viewing

How does this World War I era hospital compare with the one Hemingway describes? **COMPARE AND CONTRAST**

Vocabulary

resign (ri zīn′) *v.* to accept something as unavoidable; to submit oneself to something negative

Comprehension

Why does the major believe "a man must not marry"?

He looked straight past me and out through the window. Then he began to cry. "I am utterly unable to resign myself," he said and choked. And then crying, his head up looking at nothing, carrying himself straight and soldierly, with tears on both his cheeks and biting his lips, he walked past the machines and out the door.

The doctor told me that the major's wife, who was very young and whom he had not married until he was definitely invalided out of the war, had died of pneumonia. She had been sick only a few days. No one expected her to die. The major did not come to the hospital for three days. Then he came at the usual hour, wearing a black band on the sleeve of his uniform. When he came back, there were large framed photographs around the wall of all sorts of wounds before and after they had been cured by the machines. In front of the machine the major used were three photographs of hands like his that were completely restored. I do not know where the doctor got them. I always understood we were the first to use the machines. The photographs did not make much difference to the major because he only looked out of the window.

Critical Reading

Cite textual evidence to support your responses.

1. **Key Ideas and Details (a)** Why does the narrator go to the hospital every day? **(b) Compare and Contrast:** How do the attitudes of other patients differ from that of the narrator, even though they are facing similar situations? Why?
2. **Key Ideas and Details (a) Infer:** Does the narrator express a pessimistic or optimistic outlook toward the machines at the hospital? **(b) Interpret:** Why do you think he has developed this attitude toward the machines? Explain.
3. **Key Ideas and Details (a)** What happens to the major's wife? **(b)** How does the major react? **(c) Analyze:** What is ironic about the major's situation?
4. **Integration of Knowledge and Ideas Apply:** Do you think this story reflects the sense of disillusionment that arose among writers and artists during World War I? Explain.
5. **Integration of Knowledge and Ideas** Do you think Hemingway presents a typically American view of war in this story? Explain. In your response, use at least three of these Essential Question words: *ideals, exalt, nationality, reflection.* ***[Connecting to the Essential Question: What makes American literature American?]***

Close Reading Activities *In Another Country*

Literary Analysis

1. **Key Ideas and Details** Explain how you might **identify with characters** in this story through these details: **(a)** The narrator is a "boy" far from home. **(b)** He feels the Italian boys were "like hunting-hawks; and [he] was not a hawk."
2. **Craft and Structure** Use a chart like the one shown to identify elements of Hemingway's **style** in this story.

Syntax	Tone	Word Choice

3. **Craft and Structure** The narrator admits that the papers accompanying his medal inflate his bravery through the use of adjectives. How does this realization connect to Hemingway's sparse use of adjectives in the story?
4. **Craft and Structure** **(a)** What are two of the story's **themes**? **(b)** How does Hemingway's style contribute to each theme?
5. **Integration of Knowledge and Ideas** One theme in Hemingway's writing is the loss of innocence and a shift toward disillusionment. How might you interpret the title of this story as a reflection of that theme?

Vocabulary Acquisition and Use

Use New Words Review the words from the vocabulary list on page 798. Then, answer each question below, using the underlined word in your answer.

1. When might you need to <u>resign</u> yourself to doing something you do not want to do?
2. Is it usually a <u>disgrace</u> to make a mistake? Why or why not?
3. How can you tell if someone is <u>detached</u> during a conversation?

Writing to Sources

Informative Text Hemingway once said, "I always try to write on the principle of the iceberg. There is seven-eighths of it underwater for every part that shows." Reread "In Another Country" with Hemingway's statement in mind. Write an **essay** in which you explore how this "iceberg" approach to writing is evident in the story. Clearly demonstrate your understanding of Hemingway's style and the way he achieves it, citing passages from the story as support.

Common Core State Standards

Writing

2. Write informative texts to examine and convey complex ideas, concepts, and information clearly and accurately through the effective selection, organization, and analysis of content.

2.b. Develop the topic thoroughly by selecting the most significant and relevant facts, extended definitions, concrete details, quotations, or other information and examples appropriate to the audience's knowledge of the topic.

Language

4. Determine or clarify the meaning of unknown and multiple-meaning words and phrases based on grades 11–12 reading and content, choosing flexibly from a range of strategies.

4.a. Use context as a clue to the meaning of a word.

Themes Across Time: Author's Insights

Tim O'Brien Introduces "Ambush"

A Short Story That Is Also Part of a Novel

"Ambush" is part of a larger work of fiction, a novel called *The Things They Carried*, but I must quickly add that the story is also meant to stand entirely on its own. It has a beginning, a middle, and an end. It can be understood and appreciated, I hope, with no additional information.

An Invented Character Who Has My Name Although the main character in the story is named Tim, which is my own name, and although many years ago I did in fact serve as an infantryman in Vietnam, "Ambush" is nonetheless a piece of fiction. The events in this story are largely invented. The characters, too, are invented, including the character named Tim. (I don't have a daughter, for example, and until very recently I had no children at all.) As a novelist and short-story writer, I am not limited by what actually happened. In fiction, I am free to write about what did *not* happen. I can write about what almost happened, or what could've happened, or what should've happened.

Fact Versus Fiction While the story is mostly imagined, it is loosely based on a "real life" ambush during the war. The mosquitoes, the trail junction, the dark night, the tension—all that comes from my own experience. In the actual incident, however, I did not throw a hand grenade that killed the young man. As it truly happened, a group of seven or eight of us simultaneously fired our rifles at three shadowy, barely visible enemy soldiers creeping across a rice paddy. One moment the night was silent, the next moment it exploded—gunfire and screams and yellow-white flashes in the dark. Later, when dawn broke, one of my friends discovered a dead Viet Cong soldier. But I did not inspect the body. I did not so much as glance at it. I certainly did not stand gaping like the character in this story.

Meet the Author

Tim O'Brien is an award-winning fiction writer. His novel *Going After Cacciato* won the National Book Award, *The Things They Carried* was a finalist for a Pulitzer Prize, and *In the Lake of the Woods* was named the best novel of 1994 by *Time* magazine.

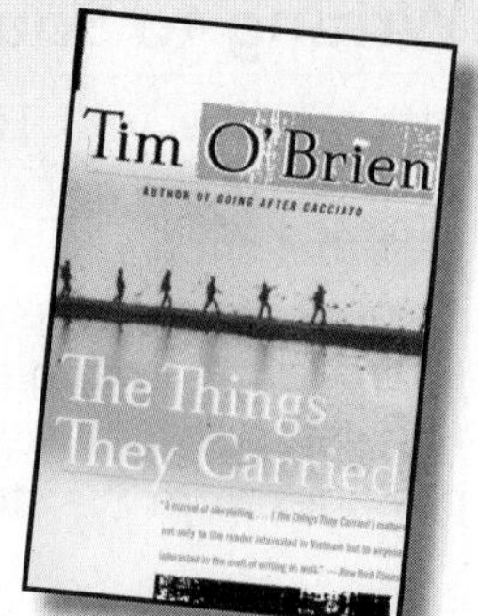

Confession and Lament I will never know whether a bullet from my own weapon killed that young man. Perhaps so, perhaps not. But in the end, it doesn't matter. I was there that night. I pulled the trigger. And I am therefore responsible. In my view, that's what "Ambush" is finally about: responsibility. Even now, like the protagonist in this story, I still have trouble forgiving myself. I still hear the gunfire and the screams. I still have the sour, fruity taste of terror in my mouth. I still feel the guilt. And I suppose that's why I sat down one day to write "Ambush"—as a kind of confession, as a lament, as a way of acknowledging my full personal responsibility for the death of a fellow human being.

◀ **Critical Viewing**
This photograph was taken during the Vietnam War. What thoughts and emotions do you imagine these soldiers are experiencing? **SPECULATE**

Critical Reading

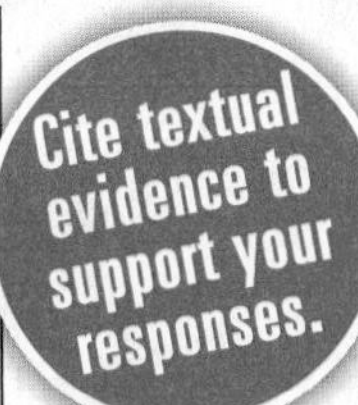
Cite textual evidence to support your responses.

1. **Craft and Structure** **(a)** Why did O'Brien choose to write "Ambush" as fiction? **(b) Take a Position:** Do you think fiction is stronger if it is based on real events? Explain.
2. **Key Ideas and Details** **(a)** What does O'Brien say that "Ambush" is finally about? **(b) Infer:** What effect do you think writing "Ambush" has had on O'Brien's memories of his own experience?

As You Read "Ambush" . . .

3. **Craft and Structure** Compare and contrast the events in the story with the real events that O'Brien describes in this commentary.
4. **Integration of Knowledge and Ideas** Think about the ways in which the main character does and does not resemble O'Brien himself.

AMBUSH

TIM O'BRIEN

When she was nine, my daughter Kathleen asked if I had ever killed anyone. She knew about the war; she knew I'd been a soldier. "You keep writing these war stories," she said, "so I guess you must've killed somebody." It was a difficult moment, but I did what seemed right, which was to say, "Of course not," and then to take her onto my lap and hold her for a while. Someday, I hope, she'll ask again.

But here I want to pretend she's a grown-up. I want to tell her exactly what happened, or what I remember happening, and then I want to say to her that as a little girl she was absolutely right. This is why I keep writing war stories:

◀ **Critical Viewing**
What does this photograph suggest were some of the physical hardships soldiers experienced in Vietnam? **DEDUCE**

Tim O'Brien
Author's Insight
The character of Kathleen, the narrator's daughter, seemed essential to this story. Adults rarely ask a direct, embarrassing question such as: "Did you ever kill anyone?" But a child of nine might easily ask just such a question.

Comprehension
What question does the narrator's daughter ask?

Vocabulary

ambush (am´ bo͝osh´) *n.* lying in wait to attack by surprise

ammunition (am´ yo͞o nish´ ən) *n.* anything hurled by a weapon or exploded as a weapon

muzzle (muz´ əl) *n.* front end of a barrel of a gun

Tim O'Brien
Author's Insight
In these sentences I try to humanize the young enemy soldier—his clothing, his posture, the unhurried and slightly distracted way he walks up the trail.

He was a short, slender young man of about twenty. I was afraid of him—afraid of something—and as he passed me on the trail I threw a grenade that exploded at his feet and killed him.

Or to go back:

Shortly after midnight we moved into the **ambush** site outside My Khe. The whole platoon was there, spread out in the dense brush along the trail, and for five hours nothing at all happened. We were working in two-man teams—one man on guard while the other slept, switching off every two hours—and I remember it was still dark when Kiowa shook me awake for the final watch. The night was foggy and hot. For the first few moments I felt lost, not sure about directions, groping for my helmet and weapon. I reached out and found three grenades and lined them up in front of me; the pins had already been straightened for quick throwing. And then for maybe half an hour I kneeled there and waited. Very gradually, in tiny slivers, dawn began to break through the fog, and from my position in the brush I could see ten or fifteen meters up the trail. The mosquitoes were fierce. I remember slapping at them, wondering if I should wake up Kiowa and ask for some repellent, then thinking it was a bad idea, then looking up and seeing the young man come out of the fog. He wore black clothing and rubber sandals and a gray **ammunition** belt. His shoulders were slightly stooped, his head cocked to the side as if listening for something. He seemed at ease. He carried his weapon in one hand, **muzzle** down, moving without any hurry up the center of the trail. There was no sound at all—none that I can remember. In a way, it seemed, he was part of the morning fog, or my own imagination, but there was also the reality of what was happening in my stomach. I had already pulled the pin on a grenade. I had come up to a crouch. It was entirely automatic. I did not hate the young man; I did not see him as the enemy; I did not ponder issues of morality or politics or military duty. I crouched and kept my head low. I tried to swallow whatever was rising from my stomach, which tasted like lemonade, something fruity and sour. I was terrified. There were no thoughts about killing. The grenade was to make him go away—just evaporate—and I leaned back and felt my mind go empty and then felt it fill up again. I had already thrown the grenade before telling myself to throw it. The brush was thick and I had to lob it high, not aiming, and I remember the grenade seeming to freeze above me for an instant, as if a camera had clicked, and I remember ducking down and holding my breath and seeing little wisps of fog rise from the earth. The grenade bounced once and rolled across the trail. I did not hear it, but there must've been a sound, because the young man dropped his weapon and began to run, just two or three quick steps, then he hesitated, swiveling to

his right, and he glanced down at the grenade and tried to cover his head but never did. It occurred to me then that he was about to die. I wanted to warn him. The grenade made a popping noise—not soft but not loud either—not what I'd expected—and there was a puff of dust and smoke—a small white puff—and the young man seemed to jerk upward as if pulled by invisible wires. He fell on his back. His rubber sandals had been blown off. There was no wind. He lay at the center of the trail, his right leg bent beneath him, his one eye shut, his other eye a huge star-shaped hole.

It was not a matter of live or die. There was no real peril. Almost certainly the young man would have passed by. And it will always be that way.

Later, I remember, Kiowa tried to tell me that the man would've died anyway. He told me that it was a good kill, that I was a soldier and this was a war, that I should shape up and stop staring and ask myself what the dead man would've done if things were reversed.

None of it mattered. The words seemed far too complicated. All I could do was gape at the fact of the young man's body.

Even now I haven't finished sorting it out. Sometimes I forgive myself, other times I don't. In the ordinary hours of life I try not to dwell on it, but now and then, when I'm reading a newspaper or just sitting alone in a room, I'll look up and see the young man coming out of the morning fog. I'll watch him walk toward me, his shoulders slightly stooped, his head cocked to the side, and he'll pass within a few yards of me and suddenly smile at some secret thought and then continue up the trail to where it bends back into the fog.

Tim O'Brien
Author's Insight
This sentence ("And it will always be that way."), for my money, is among the best I have ever written. Only seven very simple words, yet for me the sentence carries the weight of eternity, the permanent and inescapable horror of war.

Tim O'Brien
Author's Insight
As the narrator imagines the young man continuing up the trail to where it bends back into the fog, he is also imagining that the ambush never occurred, that the dead young man has a long and full life ahead of him in a future that will never be.

Critical Reading

1. **Key Ideas and Details** **(a)** What does the narrator say to describe the degree of danger he faced? **(b) Interpret:** What does he mean when he says "And it will always be that way"?
2. **Key Ideas and Details** **(a) Deduce:** How does the narrator react to the killing? **(b) Interpret:** How does Kiowa respond to the narrator's reaction?
3. **Key Ideas and Details** **(a)** At the end of the story, what does the narrator fantasize? **(b) Interpret:** In what ways does this fantasy contribute to the story's power and meaning?
4. **Craft and Structure** **(a) Compare and Contrast:** The narrator tells his story twice. Compare and contrast the short and long versions. **(b) Speculate:** Why do you think the author chose this narrative device?
5. **Integration of Knowledge and Ideas** **Make a Judgment:** Kiowa uses the expression "a good kill." Is there such a thing? Explain.

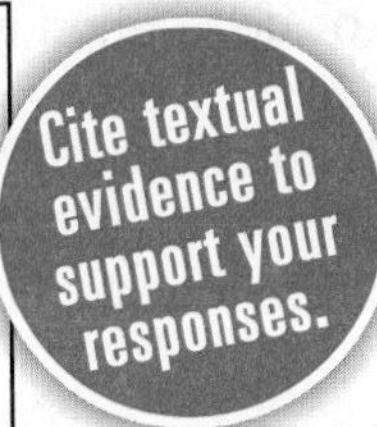
Cite textual evidence to support your responses.

Building Knowledge and Insight

A Rose for Emily • *Nobel Prize Acceptance Speech*

Connecting to the Essential Question In this story, outward appearances conflict in profound ways with the inner world of the main character. As you read, notice details that reveal other people's perceptions of Miss Emily and her family. Doing so will help as you consider the Essential Question: **How does literature shape or reflect society?**

Reading Literature

1. Cite strong and thorough textual evidence to support analysis of what the text says explicitly as well as inferences drawn from the text, including determining where the text leaves matters uncertain.

3. Analyze the impact of the author's choices regarding how to develop and relate elements of a story or drama.

Close Reading Focus

Conflict

A **conflict** is a struggle between opposing forces. It is the engine that drives narrative writing. A conflict achieves **resolution** when the struggle ends and the outcome is revealed. There are two types of literary conflict:

- **Internal conflict** occurs within the mind of a character who is torn by competing values or needs.
- **External conflict** occurs between a character and an outside force, such as another person, society as a whole, nature, or fate.

Internal conflict is at the core of Faulkner's fiction. In his Nobel Prize acceptance speech, he wrote that a writer's responsibility is to address "the problems of the human heart in conflict with itself." As you read "A Rose for Emily," think about its portrayal of a bitterly conflicted human heart. Look beneath the refined surface to find clues about deeper struggles.

Preparing to Read Complex Texts Intentional ambiguity occurs in a literary work when one or more elements can be interpreted in several ways. To **clarify ambiguity,** recognize parts of the action, characterization, or description that the writer may have deliberately left open ended, uncertain, or even inconsistent. Then, look for details or clues in the writing that help you make an interpretation. As you read, use a chart like the one shown to record ambiguous elements. Then, decide which possible interpretation you find most convincing or meaningful.

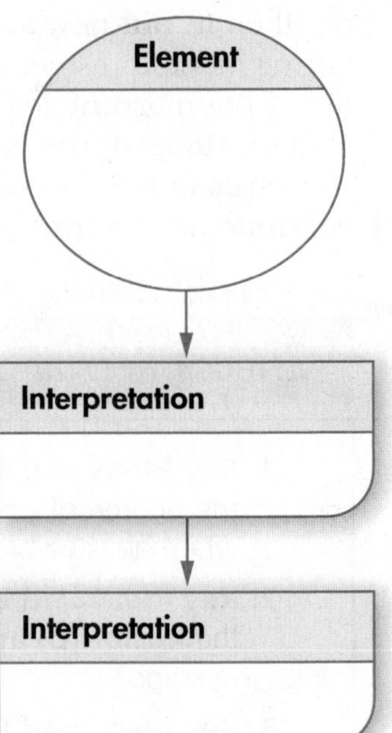

Vocabulary

You will encounter the words listed here in the texts that follow. Copy the words into your notebook. Which words have more than three syllables?

encroached
vanquished
vindicated
circumvent
virulent
inextricable

William Faulkner *(1897–1962)*

Author of "A Rose for Emily" and Nobel Prize Acceptance Speech

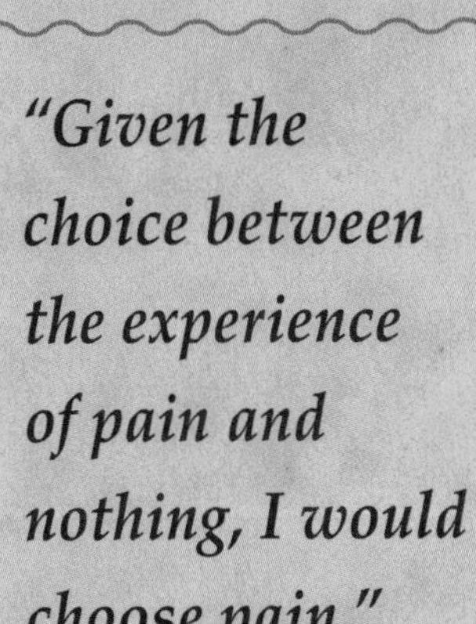

For some writers, the place of their roots is a wellspring of story material. Oxford, Mississippi, was such a place for William Faulkner. It became the basis for the imaginary world of Yoknapatawpha County—the setting of many of his novels and stories.

A Writer's Roots Although Faulkner never finished high school, he read a great deal and developed an interest in writing from an early age. In 1925, after an uninspired stint in the British military, Faulkner moved to New Orleans. There he became friends with author Sherwood Anderson, who helped get Faulkner's first novel, *Soldier's Pay*, published. In 1926, Faulkner returned home to Oxford, Mississippi, to devote himself to his writing.

A Gold Mine of Inspiration In what he called his "own little postage stamp of native soil," Faulkner uncovered a "gold mine" of inspiration. So compelling and complex was this source of inspiration that Faulkner decided to create a "cosmos of my own"—the fictional county of Yoknapatawpha. In Oxford, Faulkner wrote a series of novels about the decay of traditional values as small communities became swept up in the changes of the modern age. He used jumbled time sequences, stream-of-consciousness narration, dialect, page-long sentences, and other challenging techniques in his dense and often dark stories.

Experimenting With Narration The novel that first earned him critical acclaim was *The Sound and the Fury* (1929), a complex book exploring the downfall of an old southern family as seen through the eyes of three brothers, one of whom suffers from severe mental retardation. Other innovative works followed, including *As I Lay Dying* (1930), the story of a poor family's six-day journey to bury their mother. Told from fifteen different points of view and exploring people's varying perspectives of death, the novel was a masterpiece of narrative experimentation.

In some of Faulkner's later works, such as *The Unvanquished* (1938) and *The Hamlet* (1940), he returned to a more traditional style. Yet, in these novels, he continued to develop the history of Yoknapatawpha County and its people.

Faulkner was awarded the Nobel Prize for Literature following the publication of *Intruder in the Dust* (1948), a novel in which he confronted the issue of racism. The narrative techniques he pioneered continue to challenge and inspire writers and readers today.

"Given the choice between the experience of pain and nothing, I would choose pain."

A Rose for Emily

William Faulkner

BACKGROUND Like many of William Faulkner's works, this story is set in the fictional town of Jefferson, which is in the fictional county of Yoknapatawpha (ÿuk′ nə pə tô′ fə) in the actual state of Mississippi. Using his real home of Lafayette County, Faulkner created an amazingly detailed world in his fiction, even down to the map of Yoknapatawpha that he included in one novel. "A Rose for Emily" takes place in Jefferson over the course of more than forty years, from around 1875 to 1920, chronicling the life and death of the reclusive Miss Emily Grierson.

When Miss Emily Grierson died, our whole town went to her funeral: the men through a sort of respectful affection for a fallen monument, the women mostly out of curiosity to see the inside of her house, which no one save an old manservant—a combined gardener and cook—had seen in at least ten years.

It was a big, squarish frame house that had once been white, decorated with cupolas and spires and scrolled balconies in the heavily lightsome style of the seventies,[1] set on what had once been our most select street. But garages and cotton gins had **encroached** and obliterated even the august[2] names of that neighborhood; only Miss Emily's house was left, lifting its stubborn and coquettish decay above the cotton wagons and the gasoline pumps—an eyesore among eyesores. And now Miss Emily had gone to join the representatives of those august names where they lay in the cedar-bemused cemetery among the ranked and anonymous graves of Union and Confederate soldiers who fell at the battle of Jefferson.

Vocabulary

encroached (en krōch′ t) *v.* intruded

Comprehension

As the story begins, what has happened to Miss Emily?

1. **the seventies** the 1870s.
2. **august** (ô gust′) *adj.* dignified; inspiring respect.

Alive, Miss Emily had been a tradition, a duty, and a care; a sort of hereditary obligation upon the town, dating from that day in 1894 when Colonel Sartoris, the mayor—he who fathered the edict[3] that no Negro woman should appear on the streets without an apron—remitted her taxes, the dispensation dating from the death of her father on into perpetuity.[4] Not that Miss Emily would have accepted charity. Colonel Sartoris invented an involved tale to the effect that Miss Emily's father had loaned money to the town, which the town, as a matter of business, preferred this way of repaying. Only a man of Colonel Sartoris' generation and thought could have invented it, and only a woman could have believed it.

When the next generation, with its more modern ideas, became mayors and aldermen, this arrangement created some little dissatisfaction. On the first of the year they mailed her a tax notice. February

▼ Critical Viewing

How is the house in this photograph similar to and different from Miss Emily's house as described on page 817? **COMPARE AND CONTRAST**

3. **edict** (ē′ dikt) *n.* command.
4. **remitted . . . into perpetuity** (pʉr′ pə to͞o′ ə tē) cancelled Emily's taxes forever after her father's death.

San Francisco Museum of Modern Art, Collection of the Sack Photographic Trust (Detail)

came, and there was no reply. They wrote her a formal letter, asking her to call at the sheriff's office at her convenience. A week later the mayor wrote her himself, offering to call or to send his car for her, and received in reply a note on paper of an archaic shape, in a thin, flowing calligraphy in faded ink, to the effect that she no longer went out at all. The tax notice was also enclosed, without comment.

They called a special meeting of the Board of Aldermen. A deputation waited upon her, knocked at the door through which no visitor had passed since she ceased giving china-painting lessons eight or ten years earlier. They were admitted by the old Negro into a dim hall from which a stairway mounted into still more shadow. It smelled of dust and disuse—a close, dank smell. The Negro led them into the parlor. It was furnished in heavy, leather-covered furniture. When the Negro opened the blinds of one window, they could see that the leather was cracked; and when they sat down, a faint dust rose sluggishly about their thighs, spinning with slow motes in the single sun-ray. On a tarnished gilt easel before the fireplace stood a crayon portrait of Miss Emily's father.

They rose when she entered—a small, fat woman in black, with a thin gold chain descending to her waist and vanishing into her belt, leaning on an ebony cane with a tarnished gold head. Her skeleton was small and spare; perhaps that was why what would have been merely plumpness in another was obesity in her. She looked bloated, like a body long submerged in motionless water, and of that pallid[5] hue. Her eyes, lost in the fatty ridges of her face, looked like two small pieces of coal pressed into a lump of dough as they moved from one face to another while the visitors stated their errand.

She did not ask them to sit. She just stood in the door and listened quietly until the spokesman came to a stumbling halt. Then they could hear the invisible watch ticking at the end of the gold chain.

Her voice was dry and cold. "I have no taxes in Jefferson. Colonel Sartoris explained it to me. Perhaps one of you can gain access to the city records and satisfy yourselves."

"But we have. We are the city authorities, Miss Emily. Didn't you get a notice from the sheriff, signed by him?"

"I received a paper, yes," Miss Emily said. "Perhaps he considers himself the sheriff . . . I have no taxes in Jefferson."

"But there is nothing on the books to show that, you see. We must go by the—"

"See Colonel Sartoris. I have no taxes in Jefferson."

"But, Miss Emily—"

"See Colonel Sartoris." (Colonel Sartoris had been dead almost ten years.) "I have no taxes in Jefferson. Tobe!" The Negro appeared. "Show these gentlemen out."

Conflict
Which of Miss Emily's conflicts with the townspeople is introduced in this scene?

Spiral Review
Characterization What do the details describing Miss Emily's appearance indicate about her character?

Comprehension
Why do representatives of the town visit Miss Emily?

---

5. pallid (pal′ id) *adj.* pale.

II

Vocabulary
vanquished (vaŋ′ kwisht) *v.* thoroughly defeated

So she **vanquished** them, horse and foot, just as she had vanquished their fathers thirty years before about the smell. That was two years after her father's death and a short time after her sweetheart—the one we believed would marry her—had deserted her. After her father's death she went out very little; after her sweetheart went away, people hardly saw her at all. A few of the ladies had the temerity[6] to call, but were not received, and the only sign of life about the place was the Negro man—a young man then—going in and out with a market basket.

"Just as if a man—any man—could keep a kitchen properly," the ladies said; so they were not surprised when the smell developed. It was another link between the gross, teeming world and the high and mighty Griersons.

A neighbor, a woman, complained to the mayor, Judge Stevens, eighty years old.

"But what will you have me do about it, madam?" he said.

"Why, send her word to stop it," the woman said. "Isn't there a law?"

"I'm sure that won't be necessary," Judge Stevens said. "It's probably just a snake or a rat that nigger of hers killed in the yard. I'll speak to him about it."

The next day he received two more complaints, one from a man who came in diffident deprecation.[7] "We really must do something about it, Judge. I'd be the last one in the world to bother Miss Emily, but we've got to do something." That night the Board of Aldermen met—three graybeards and one younger man, a member of the rising generation.

"It's simple enough," he said. "Send her word to have her place cleaned up. Give her a certain time to do it in, and if she don't . . ."

"Dammit, sir," Judge Stevens said, "will you accuse a lady to her face of smelling bad?"

So the next night, after midnight, four men crossed Miss Emily's lawn and slunk about the house like burglars, sniffing along the base of the brickwork and at the cellar openings while one of them performed a regular sowing motion with his hand out of a sack slung from his shoulder. They broke open the cellar door and sprinkled lime there, and in all the outbuildings. As they recrossed the lawn, a window that had been dark was lighted and Miss Emily sat in it, the light

The American EXPERIENCE

Two Influential Writers

William Faulkner and Ernest Hemingway were probably the two most influential American writers of the twentieth century, even though they were near-opposites. Although Faulkner longed for adventure as a young man, he settled in a tiny corner of rural Mississippi. His prose was dense and complex and featured long, ornate sentences. Hemingway, on the other hand, lived a life of epic adventure, traveling the world and hunting big game. His prose—precise and unadorned—introduced a new way of writing to American literature.

Both men won the Nobel Prize—Faulkner in 1950 and Hemingway in 1954—and though they shared a grudging respect, they also waged a famous war of words. Hemingway said that Faulkner "wrote like an old grandmother," and Faulkner replied that Hemingway was "afraid to use a word of more than five letters."

Connect to the Literature

In "A Rose for Emily," where does Faulkner use dense, complex language, and where does his prose seem more simple and unadorned?

---

6. **temerity** (tə mer′ ə tē) *n.* foolish or reckless boldness.
7. **diffident deprecation** (dif′ ə dənt dep′ rə kā′ shen) timid disapproval.

behind her, and her upright torso motionless as that of an idol. They crept quietly across the lawn and into the shadow of the locusts[8] that lined the street. After a week or two the smell went away.

That was when people had begun to feel really sorry for her. People in our town, remembering how old lady Wyatt, her great-aunt, had gone completely crazy at last, believed that the Griersons held themselves a little too high for what they really were. None of the young men were quite good enough for Miss Emily and such. We had long thought of them as a tableau, Miss Emily a slender figure in white in the background, her father a spraddled[9] silhouette in the foreground, his back to her and clutching a horsewhip, the two of them framed by the back-flung front door. So when she got to be thirty and was still single, we were not pleased exactly, but **vindicated**; even with insanity in the family she wouldn't have turned down all of her chances if they had really materialized.

Vocabulary
vindicated (vin′ də kāt′ əd) *v.* cleared from blame

When her father died, it got about that the house was all that was left to her; and in a way, people were glad. At last they could pity Miss Emily. Being left alone, and a pauper, she had become humanized. Now she too would know the old thrill and the old despair of a penny more or less.

The day after his death all the ladies prepared to call at the house and offer condolence and aid, as is our custom. Miss Emily met them at the door, dressed as usual and with no trace of grief on her face. She told them that her father was not dead. She did that for three days, with the ministers calling on her, and the doctors, trying to persuade her to let them dispose of the body. Just as they were about to resort to law and force, she broke down, and they buried her father quickly.

We did not say she was crazy then.

We did not say she was crazy then. We believed she had to do that. We remembered all the young men her father had driven away, and we knew that with nothing left, she would have to cling to that which had robbed her, as people will.

III

She was sick for a long time. When we saw her again, her hair was cut short, making her look like a girl, with a vague resemblance to those angels in colored church windows—sort of tragic and serene.

The town had just let the contracts for paving the sidewalks, and in the summer after her father's death they began the work. The construction company came with niggers and mules and machinery, and a foreman named Homer Barron, a Yankee—a big, dark, ready man, with a big voice and eyes lighter than his face. The little boys would follow in groups to hear him cuss the niggers, and the niggers singing

Comprehension
Why do the men break open the cellar door?

8. **locusts** (lō′ kəsts) *n.* locust trees; a hardy tree with hanging flowers in spring.
9. **spraddled** (sprad′ əld) *adj.* seated with spread, sprawling legs.

Conflict and Resolution
What conflict, suggested by references to *noblesse oblige*, do the townspeople have with Emily?

in time to the rise and fall of picks. Pretty soon he knew everybody in town. Whenever you heard a lot of laughing anywhere about the square, Homer Barron would be in the center of the group. Presently we began to see him and Miss Emily on Sunday afternoons driving in the yellow-wheeled buggy and the matched team of bays from the livery stable.

At first we were glad that Miss Emily would have an interest, because the ladies all said, "Of course a Grierson would not think seriously of a Northerner, a day laborer." But there were still others, older people, who said that even grief could not cause a real lady to forget *noblesse oblige*[10]—without calling it *noblesse oblige*. They just said, "Poor Emily. Her kinsfolk should come to her." She had some kin in Alabama; but years ago her father had fallen out with them over the estate of old lady Wyatt, the crazy woman, and there was no communication between the two families. They had not even been represented at the funeral.

"Poor Emily. Her kinsfolk should come to her."

And as soon as the old people said, "Poor Emily," the whispering began. "Do you suppose it's really so?" they said to one another. "Of course it is. What else could . . ." This behind their hands; rustling of craned silk and satin behind jalousies[11] closed upon the sun of Sunday afternoon as the thin, swift clop-clop-clop of the matched team passed: "Poor Emily."

She carried her head high enough—even when we believed that she was fallen. It was as if she demanded more than ever the recognition of her dignity as the last Grierson; as if it had wanted that touch of earthiness to reaffirm her imperviousness. Like when she bought the rat poison, the arsenic. That was over a year after they had begun to say "Poor Emily," and while the two female cousins were visiting her.

"I want some poison," she said to the druggist. She was over thirty then, still a slight woman, though thinner than usual, with cold, haughty black eyes in a face the flesh of which was strained across the temples and about the eyesockets as you imagine a lighthouse-keeper's face ought to look. "I want some poison," she said.

"Yes, Miss Emily. What kind? For rats and such? I'd recom—"

"I want the best you have. I don't care what kind."

The druggist named several. "They'll kill anything up to an elephant. But what you want is—"

"Arsenic," Miss Emily said. "Is that a good one?"

"Is . . . arsenic? Yes, ma'am. But what you want—"

"I want arsenic."

The druggist looked down at her. She looked back at him, erect, her face like a strained flag. "Why, of course," the druggist said. "If

---

10. ***noblesse oblige*** (nō bles´ ō blēzh´) *n.* the presumed duty of the upper classes to behave in a noble and generous way (French).
11. **jalousies** (jal´ ə sēz) *n.* windows or shades with slats that can be adjusted to let in air and light.

▲ **Critical Viewing** Does this portrait match your mental image of Miss Emily? Why or why not? **CONNECT**

that's what you want. But the law requires you to tell what you are going to use it for."

Miss Emily just stared at him, her head tilted back in order to look him eye for eye, until he looked away and went and got the arsenic and wrapped it up. The Negro delivery boy brought her the package; the druggist didn't come back. When she opened the package at home there was written on the box, under the skull and bones: "For rats."

Comprehension
Why do people begin to refer to Miss Emily as "Poor Emily"?

IV

So the next day we all said, "She will kill herself"; and we said it would be the best thing. When she had first begun to be seen with Homer Barron, we had said, "She will marry him." Then we said, "She will persuade him yet," because Homer himself had remarked—he liked men, and it was known that he drank with the younger men in the Elks' Club—that he was not a marrying man. Later we said, "Poor Emily" behind the jalousies as they passed on Sunday afternoon in the glittering buggy, Miss Emily with her head high and Homer Barron with his hat cocked and a cigar in his teeth, reins and whip in a yellow glove.

Then some of the ladies began to say that it was a disgrace to the town and a bad example to the young people. The men did not want to interfere, but at last the ladies forced the Baptist minister—Miss Emily's people were Episcopal—to call upon her. He would never divulge what happened during that interview, but he refused to go back again. The next Sunday they again drove about the streets, and the following day the minister's wife wrote to Miss Emily's relations in Alabama.

So she had blood-kin under her roof again and we sat back to watch developments. At first nothing happened. Then we were sure that they were to be married. We learned that Miss Emily had been to the jeweler's and ordered a man's toilet set in silver, with the letters H. B. on each piece. Two days later we learned that she had bought a complete outfit of men's clothing, including a nightshirt, and we said, "They are married." We were really glad. We were glad because the two female cousins were even more Grierson than Miss Emily had ever been.

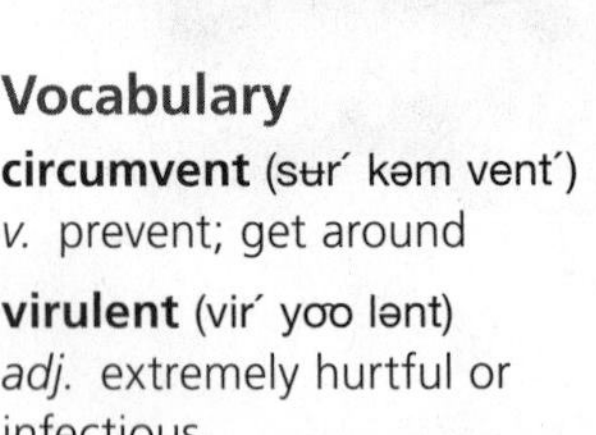

So we were not surprised when Homer Barron—the streets had been finished some time since—was gone. We were a little disappointed that there was not a public blowing-off, but we believed that he had gone on to prepare for Miss Emily's coming, or to give her a chance to get rid of the cousins. (By that time it was a cabal[12], and we were all Miss Emily's allies to help **circumvent** the cousins.) Sure enough, after another week they departed. And, as we had expected all along, within three days Homer Barron was back in town. A neighbor saw the Negro man admit him at the kitchen door at dusk one evening.

And that was the last we saw of Homer Barron. And of Miss Emily for some time. The Negro man went in and out with the market basket, but the front door remained closed. Now and then we would see her at a window for a moment, as the men did that night when they sprinkled the lime, but for almost six months she did not appear on the streets. Then we knew that this was to be expected too; as if that quality of her father which had thwarted her woman's life so many times had been too **virulent** and too furious to die.

Vocabulary

circumvent (sur′ kəm vent′) *v.* prevent; get around

virulent (vir′ yoo lənt) *adj.* extremely hurtful or infectious

---

12. cabal (kə bäl′) *n.* small group of people joined in a secret plot.

When we next saw Miss Emily, she had grown fat and her hair was turning gray. During the next few years it grew grayer and grayer until it attained an even pepper-and-salt iron-gray, when it ceased turning. Up to the day of her death at seventy-four it was still that vigorous iron-gray, like the hair of an active man.

From that time on her front door remained closed, save for a period of six or seven years, when she was about forty, during which she gave lessons in china-painting. She fitted up a studio in one of the downstairs rooms, where the daughters and granddaughters of Colonel Sartoris' contemporaries were sent to her with the same regularity and in the same spirit that they were sent to church on Sundays with a twenty-five-cent piece for the collection plate. Meanwhile her taxes had been remitted.

Then the newer generation became the backbone and the spirit of the town, and the painting pupils grew up and fell away and did not send their children to her with boxes of color and tedious brushes and pictures cut from the ladies' magazines. The front door closed upon the last one and remained closed for good. When the town got free postal delivery, Miss Emily alone refused to let them fasten the metal numbers above her door and attach a mailbox to it. She would not listen to them.

Daily, monthly, yearly we watched the Negro grow grayer and more stooped, going in and out with the market basket. Each December we sent her a tax notice, which would be returned by the post office a week later, unclaimed. Now and then we would see her in one of the downstairs windows—she had evidently shut up the top

Comprehension
What items does Miss Emily order from the jeweler?

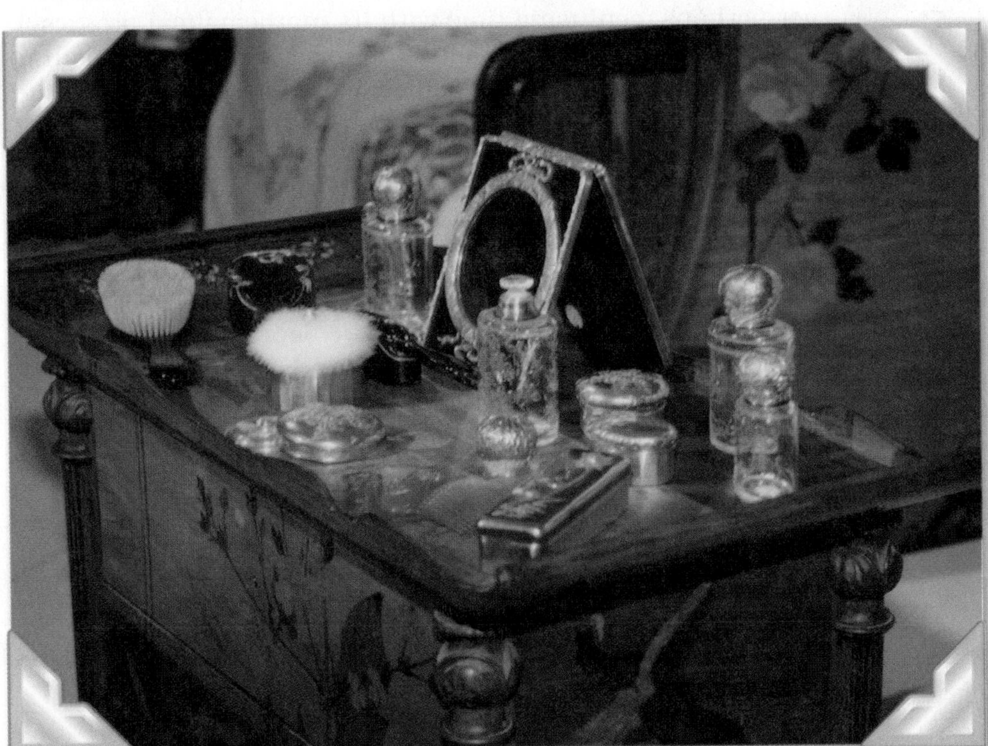

◀ Critical Viewing
What aspects of this image suggest the kind of refinement the townspeople attribute to Miss Emily? **ANALYZE**

floor of the house—like the carven torso of an idol in a niche, looking or not looking at us, we could never tell which. Thus she passed from generation to generation—dear, inescapable, impervious, tranquil, and perverse.[13]

Conflict and Resolution

Is Miss Emily's death the resolution to the conflicts in this story? Explain.

And so she died. Fell ill in the house filled with dust and shadows, with only a doddering Negro man to wait on her. We did not even know she was sick; we had long since given up trying to get any information from the Negro. He talked to no one, probably not even to her, for his voice had grown harsh and rusty, as if from disuse.

She died in one of the downstairs rooms, in a heavy walnut bed with a curtain, her gray head propped on a pillow yellow and moldy with age and lack of sunlight.

V

The Negro met the first of the ladies at the front door and let them in, with their hushed, sibilant[14] voices and their quick, curious glances, and then he disappeared. He walked right through the house and out the back and was not seen again.

The two female cousins came at once. They held the funeral on the second day, with the town coming to look at Miss Emily beneath a mass of bought flowers, with the crayon face of her father musing profoundly above the bier[15] and the ladies sibilant and macabre[16]; and the very old men—some in their brushed Confederate uniforms—on the porch and the lawn, talking of Miss Emily as if she had been a contemporary of theirs, believing that they had danced with her and courted her perhaps, confusing time with its mathematical progression, as the old do, to whom all the past is not a diminishing road but, instead, a huge meadow which no winter ever quite touches, divided from them now by the narrow bottle-neck of the most recent decade of years.

Already we knew that there was one room in that region above stairs which no one had seen in forty years, and which would have to be forced. They waited until Miss Emily was decently in the ground before they opened it.

The violence of breaking down the door seemed to fill this room with pervading dust. A thin, acrid pall[17] as of the tomb seemed to lie everywhere upon this room decked and furnished as for a bridal: upon the valance curtains of faded rose color, upon the rose-shaded lights, upon the dressing

---

13. **perverse** (pər vʉrs′) *adj.* stubbornly contrary or difficult.
14. **sibilant** (sib′ ə lənt) *adj.* making a hissing sound with *s* or *sh* sounds.
15. **bier** (bir) *n.* supporting platform for a coffin.
16. **macabre** (mə käb′ rə) *adj.* gruesome.
17. **acrid pall** (ak′ rid pôl) *n.* bitter and gloomy covering or atmosphere.

table, upon the delicate array of crystal and the man's toilet things backed with tarnished silver, silver so tarnished that the monogram was obscured. Among them lay a collar and tie, as if they had just been removed, which, lifted, left upon the surface a pale crescent in the dust. Upon a chair hung the suit, carefully folded; beneath it the two mute shoes and the discarded socks.

The man himself lay in the bed.

For a long while we just stood there, looking down at the profound and fleshless grin. The body had apparently once lain in the attitude of an embrace, but now the long sleep that outlasts love, that conquers even the grimace of love, had cuckolded[18] him. What was left of him, rotted beneath what was left of the nightshirt, had become **inextricable** from the bed in which he lay; and upon him and upon the pillow beside him lay that even coating of the patient and biding dust.

Then we noticed that in the second pillow was the indentation of a head. One of us lifted something from it, and leaning forward, that faint and invisible dust dry and acrid in the nostrils, we saw a long strand of iron-gray hair.

Vocabulary
inextricable (in eks′ tri kə bəl) *adj.* unable to be separated or freed from

18. cuckolded (kuk′ əld əd) *v.* betrayed by an unfaithful wife or lover.

Critical Reading 

Cite textual evidence to support your responses.

1. **Key Ideas and Details** **(a)** What happened when the judge tried to get Miss Emily to pay her taxes? **(b) Infer:** What does this incident reveal about her relationship to the town?
2. **Key Ideas and Details** **(a)** What had been the position of Miss Emily's family in Jefferson while her father was alive? **(b) Deduce:** How does her position change over time? **(c) Draw Conclusions:** What does she seem to feel about this change?
3. **Key Ideas and Details** **(a) Describe:** What happens when Emily buys arsenic? **(b) Summarize:** What problem do the townspeople notice shortly after that purchase? **(c) Speculate:** What do you think Emily did with the arsenic?
4. **Key Ideas and Details** **(a)** What does the story say about Homer Barron and his relationship with Emily? **(b) Infer:** What probably happened to Homer, and why?
5. **Integration of Knowledge and Ideas** In what ways does this story comment on discrepancies between society's ideas of class, privilege, and respectability and the darker sides of human nature? In your response, use at least two of these Essential Question words: *reputation, conventions, insight, respectability, ambition.* ***[Connecting to the Essential Question: How does literature shape or reflect society?]***

WILLIAM FAULKNER
Nobel Prize Acceptance Speech

BACKGROUND Swedish chemist Alfred Nobel earned fame as the inventor of dynamite. Nobel had intended dynamite to be used safely in mining and construction, but disasters often occurred, and his name became associated with tragedy. Nobel eventually succeeded in making dynamite safer. Later, he established a foundation to encourage achievement and diplomacy. The Nobel Prizes, the world's most prestigious awards, are the result of his efforts. When William Faulkner received the Nobel Prize for literature in 1950, he delivered a speech that is among the most moving examples of oratory in our literature.

Stockholm, Sweden
December 10, 1950

I feel that this award was not made to me as a man, but to my work—a life's work in the agony and sweat of the human spirit, not for glory and least of all for profit, but to create out of the materials of the human spirit something which did not exist before. So this award is only mine in trust. It will not be difficult to find a dedication for the money part of it commensurate with the purpose and significance of its origin. But I would like to do the same with the acclaim too, by using this moment as a pinnacle from which I might be listened to by the young men and women already dedicated to the same anguish and travail, among whom is already that one who will some day stand here where I am standing.

Our tragedy today is a general and universal physical fear so long sustained by now that we can even bear it. There are no longer problems of the spirit. There is only the question: When will I be blown up? Because of this, the young man or woman writing today has forgotten the problems of the human heart in conflict with itself which alone can make good writing because only that is worth writing about, worth the agony and the sweat.

He must learn them again. He must teach himself that the basest of all things is to be afraid; and, teaching himself that, forget it forever, leaving no room in his workshop for anything but the old verities and truths of the heart, the old universal truths lacking which any story is ephemeral and doomed—love and honor and pity and pride and compassion and sacrifice. Until he does so, he labors under a curse. He writes not of love but of lust, of defeats in which nobody loses anything of value, of victories without hope and, worst of all, without pity or compassion. His griefs grieve on no universal bones, leaving no scars. He writes not of the heart but of the glands.

Until he relearns these things, he will write as though he stood among and watched the end of man. I decline to accept the end of man. It is easy enough to say that man is immortal simply because he will endure: that when the last ding-dong of doom has clanged and faded from the last worthless rock hanging tideless in the last red and dying evening, that even then there will still be one more sound: that of his puny inexhaustible voice, still talking. I refuse to accept this. I believe that man will not merely endure: he will prevail. He is immortal, not because he alone among creatures has an inexhaustible voice, but because he has a soul, a spirit capable of compassion and sacrifice and endurance. The poet's, the writer's, duty is to write about these things. It is his privilege to help man endure by lifting his heart, by reminding him of the courage and honor and hope and pride and compassion and pity and sacrifice which have been the glory of his past. The poet's voice need not merely be the record of man, it can be one of the props, the pillars to help him endure and prevail.

I decline to accept the end of man.

Critical Reading

1. **Key Ideas and Details** **(a)** According to Faulkner, why are there no longer problems of the spirit? **(b) Deduce:** What is the physical fear to which he refers?
2. **Key Ideas and Details** **(a)** What alone does Faulkner believe is the subject matter of good writing? **(b) Interpret:** Why does he view most modern literature as ephemeral?
3. **Key Ideas and Details** **(a)** According to Faulkner, will humanity endure or prevail? **(b) Define:** In what way does Faulkner define the difference between enduring and prevailing?
4. **Key Ideas and Details** **(a)** What does Faulkner say is a writer's "duty"? **(b) Interpret:** What distinction does he draw about the role of "the poet's voice"?
5. **Integration of Knowledge and Ideas** **(a) Extend:** What events not long before 1950 gave rise to the fear of which Faulkner speaks? **(b) Hypothesize:** If he were alive today, would he say we have lost or retained that fear? Explain.

Cite textual evidence to support your responses.

Close Reading Activities

A Rose for Emily • *Nobel Prize Acceptance Speech*

Literary Analysis

1. **Key Ideas and Details** Use a chart like the one shown to analyze the **internal** and **external conflicts** that affect Emily's life. **(a)** How is each conflict resolved, if at all? **(b)** What common thread runs through all the conflicts Emily faces?

Conflict	Who vs. Who/What?	Resolution
nonpayment of taxes	Emily vs. town	

2. **Key Ideas and Details** **(a)** What do Emily's external conflicts with the people of Jefferson reveal about her? **(b)** What do they reveal about the town? Explain.
3. **Key Ideas and Details** **(a)** Why are there no suitors available for Emily? **(b)** In what ways is this both an internal and an external conflict for Emily?
4. **Key Ideas and Details** **(a)** What conflict does Emily have with her father? **(b)** Does she ever find **resolution** for this conflict? Explain.
5. **Key Ideas and Details** **(a)** In his Nobel Prize acceptance speech, what conflicts does Faulkner seem to have with the era in which he lives? **(b)** What does he fear will happen to literature—and to humanity?
6. **Craft and Structure** The identity of the narrator in this story is uncertain and unspecified; therefore, it is ambiguous. **(a)** What clues help you **clarify ambiguity** about the narrator's identity? **(b)** Who do you think the narrator is? Explain your interpretation. **(c)** Why do you think Faulkner chose to leave the narrator's identity uncertain and open to interpretation?
7. **Integration of Knowledge and Ideas** **(a)** What event, character, or situation in the story do you find most ambiguous? **(b)** What possible interpretations would clarify that ambiguity? **(c)** Which of these interpretations do you think the text best supports? Explain.
8. **Integration of Knowledge and Ideas** In a 1955 interview, Faulkner explained the story's title: "The meaning was, here was a woman who had had a tragedy, an irrevocable tragedy and nothing could be done about it, and I pitied her and this [the story] was a salute . . . to a woman you would hand a rose." What is Emily's tragedy? Explain.

Common Core State Standards

Writing

1. Write arguments to support claims in an analysis of substantive topics or texts, using valid reasoning and relevant and sufficient evidence.

Language

4.b. Identify and correctly use patterns of word changes that indicate different meanings or parts of speech.

5. Demonstrate understanding of word relationships.

Vocabulary Acquisition and Use

Word Analysis: Latin Prefix *in-*

The Latin prefix *in-* has two basic meanings:

- a location or direction: "in," "into," "within," "on," or "toward," as in *insert, indent,* and *invade*
- a negative: "no," "not," or "without," as in *inextricable, inescapable,* and *inseparable*

When *in-* is used before a word beginning with *p*, the prefix becomes *im-*, as in *impossible*. Write the meaning of the following words, noting whether the prefix in each indicates location or negation.

1. indelible
2. impact
3. insensible
4. inundate
5. impervious
6. intention
7. impress
8. inexhaustible

Vocabulary: Analogies

Complete each analogy with a word from the vocabulary list. In each, your choice should make a word pair that matches the relationship between the first two words given. Explain your answers.

1. encroached : withdrew :: expanded :
   (a) inflated **(b)** collapsed **(c)** magnified
2. vanquished : strength :: comprehended :
   (a) intelligence **(b)** fear **(c)** mystery
3. vindicated : blame :: cured :
   (a) illness **(b)** medicine **(c)** physician
4. circumvent : avoid :: collect :
   (a) scatter **(b)** gather **(c)** repulse
5. virulent : disease :: nauseating :
   (a) weakness **(b)** discomfort **(c)** odor
6. inextricable : separate :: invisible :
   (a) see **(b)** hide **(c)** disappear

Writing to Sources

Argument In his Nobel Prize acceptance speech, Faulkner notes that the writer's duty is "to help man endure by lifting his heart, by reminding him of the courage and honor and hope and pride and compassion and pity and sacrifice which have been the glory of his past." Apply this criteria to a **critical review** of "A Rose for Emily." Consider whether Faulkner fulfills his ideal. Support your opinion with facts, details, quotations, or other information and examples from the story.

Prewriting Review the story, and make notes about whether the author has succeeded or failed, according to Faulkner's own standards.

Model: Elaborating to Explain an Idea Fully
In "A Rose for Emily," Faulkner fulfills his own criteria for writing about "truths of the heart." He accomplishes this by giving dignity to the story of a town recluse. His writing summons feelings of both pity and horror.

Including specific information elaborates on a basic idea.

Drafting Introduce your review with a clear statement of your position. Then, elaborate through detailed and accurate references to the story.

Revising Reread your review to confirm that you have provided solid supporting evidence for your ideas.

Building Knowledge and Insight

The Jilting of Granny Weatherall

Connecting to the Essential Question In this story, Granny Weatherall remembers key moments from her life as it comes to a close. As you read, notice the judgments Granny makes about the life she has lived. Your observations will help you reflect on the Essential Question: **How does literature shape or reflect society?**

Common Core State Standards

Reading Literature

3. Analyze the impact of the author's choices regarding how to develop and relate elements of a story.

5. Analyze how an author's choices concerning how to structure specific parts of a text contribute to its overall structure and meaning as well as its aesthetic impact.

Close Reading Focus

Stream of Consciousness; Flashback

People's thoughts do not flow in neat patterns; they move unpredictably among perceptions, memories, and ideas. During the early 1900s, some writers began using a literary device called **stream of consciousness** to try to capture the natural flow of thought. These narratives usually

- present sequences of thought as if they were coming directly from a character's mind;
- leave out transitional words and phrases found in ordinary prose;
- connect details only through a character's associations.

Stream-of-consciousness narratives often include the use of **flashback,** an interruption in which earlier events are described. A flashback might take the form of a memory, a story told about a character, a dream or daydream, or a switch by the narrator to a time in the past. As you read, trace the path of Granny Weatherall's thoughts and note the details that trigger her memories and observations. Identify points at which a more traditional story would have provided transitions or other connections that smooth the reader's way. Finally, consider how these structural choices contribute both to the story's meaning and to its sense of artistry.

Preparing to Read Complex Texts In the present time of the story, Granny Weatherall is on her deathbed. However, events from her eighty years of life flow throughout the story and do not appear in chronological order. *Monitor your comprehension* of this complex narrative. At points where you are unclear about the relationships between details, **clarify the sequence of events.** Use a graphic organizer like the one shown to place the events of Granny's life in order.

Ordering Events

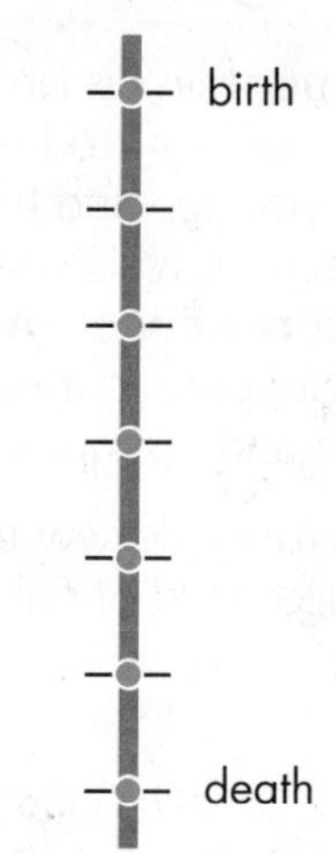

Vocabulary

The words below are important to understanding the text that follows. Copy the words into your notebook, sorting them into words you know and words you do not know.

tactful
piety
dyspepsia

Katherine Anne Porter

(1890–1980)

Author of "The Jilting of Granny Weatherall"

Katherine Anne Porter's life spanned World War I, the Great Depression, World War II, and the rise of the nuclear age, making her deeply aware of what she called "the heavy threat of world catastrophe." For Porter, her fiction was an "effort to grasp the meaning of those threats, to trace them to their sources, and to understand the logic of this majestic and terrible failure of the life of man in the Western world." Her stories were often set in the South and featured characters at pivotal moments in their lives, faced with dramatic change, the constricting bonds of family, and the weight of the past.

A descendant of legendary pioneer Daniel Boone, Porter was born in Indian Creek, Texas. She was raised in poverty and haphazardly educated in convent schools. Porter claimed that her true education came by reading five writers—American authors Henry James, T. S. Eliot, and Ezra Pound, Irish writer James Joyce, and Irish poet W. B. Yeats.

Beginnings as a Writer Porter began writing at an early age, though she did not publish her first book until she was forty years old. As a young adult, she worked as a journalist. Her work took her to many places, including Mexico City, where she lived for eight years. While in Mexico, Porter developed an interest in writing fiction, and in 1922 she published her first story. Eight years later, she published her first book, *Flowering Judas*, a collection of short stories, which earned her critical praise and widespread recognition.

Literary Achievements Porter went on to produce several other major works, including *Noon Wine* (1937); *Pale Horse, Pale Rider* (1939); *The Leaning Tower and Other Stories* (1944); and *Ship of Fools* (1962)—her only novel. Although her body of work was relatively small, it consistently received high praise and earned her a place among the finest writers of the twentieth century. Her *Collected Stories* (1965) was awarded the Pulitzer Prize and the National Book Award.

A First-Rate Artist Critic Edmund Wilson once tried to account for the "elusive" quality that made Porter an "absolutely first-rate artist." He said, "What [these stories] show us are human relationships in their constantly shifting phases and in the moments of which their existence is made. There is no place for general reflections; you are to live through the experiences as the characters do."

"Now and again thousands of memories converge, harmonize, arrange themselves around a central idea in a coherent form, and I write a story."

THE JILTING OF GRANNY WEATHERALL

KATHERINE ANNE PORTER

Garden of Memories, (detail) 1917, Charles Burchfield, The Museum of Modern Art, New York

BACKGROUND Katherine Anne Porter's view of life and the fiction she wrote were shaped by a sense of disillusionment resulting from World War I, the despair of the Great Depression, and the World War II horrors of Nazism and nuclear warfare. Sometimes, as in the novel *Ship of Fools,* Porter focused on political issues such as Nazism. In contrast, works like "The Jilting of Granny Weatherall" pinpointed the dissolving families and communities of the modern age.

She flicked her wrist neatly out of Doctor Harry's pudgy careful fingers and pulled the sheet up to her chin. The brat ought to be in knee breeches. Doctoring around the country with spectacles on his nose! "Get along now, take your schoolbooks and go. There's nothing wrong with me."

Doctor Harry spread a warm paw like a cushion on her forehead where the forked green vein danced and made her eyelids twitch. "Now, now, be a good girl, and we'll have you up in no time."

"That's no way to speak to a woman nearly eighty years old just because she's down. I'd have you respect your elders, young man."

"Well, Missy, excuse me," Doctor Harry patted her cheek. "But I've got to warn you, haven't I? You're a marvel, but you must be careful or you're going to be good and sorry."

"Don't tell me what I'm going to be. I'm on my feet now, morally speaking. It's Cornelia. I had to go to bed to get rid of her."

Her bones felt loose, and floated around in her skin, and Doctor Harry floated like a balloon around the foot of the bed. He floated and pulled down his waistcoat and swung his glasses on a cord. "Well, stay where you are, it certainly can't hurt you."

"Get along and doctor your sick," said Granny Weatherall. "Leave a well woman alone. I'll call for you when I want you. . . Where were you forty years ago when I pulled through milk leg[1] and double pneumonia? You weren't even born. Don't let Cornelia lead you on," she shouted, because Doctor Harry appeared to float up to the ceiling and out. "I pay my own bills, and I don't throw my money away on nonsense!"

She meant to wave good-bye, but it was too much trouble. Her eyes closed of themselves, it was like a dark curtain drawn around the bed. The pillow rose and floated under her, pleasant as a hammock in a light wind. She listened to the leaves rustling outside the window. No, somebody was swishing newspapers: no, Cornelia and Doctor Harry were whispering together. She leaped broad awake, thinking they whispered in her ear.

"She was never like this, never like this!" "Well, what can we expect?" "Yes, eighty years old. . . ."

Well, and what if she was? She still had ears. It was like Cornelia

1. milk leg painful swelling of the leg.

◀ Critical Viewing
Which elements of this surreal illustration of an old woman in her "garden of memories" might represent Granny Weatherall? **CONNECT**

Stream of Consciousness
While Granny is rebuking the doctor, what is really happening in the room?

Comprehension
Where is Granny Weatherall as she speaks to the doctor?

Vocabulary

tactful (takt′ fəl) *adj.* concerned about upsetting or offending others; diplomatic

to whisper around doors. She always kept things secret in such a public way. She was always being **tactful** and kind. Cornelia was dutiful; that was the trouble with her. Dutiful and good: "So good and dutiful," said Granny, "that I'd like to spank her." She saw herself spanking Cornelia and making a fine job of it.

"What'd you say, Mother?"

Granny felt her face tying up in hard knots.

"Can't a body think, I'd like to know?"

"I thought you might want something."

"I do. I want a lot of things. First off, go away and don't whisper."

She lay and drowsed, hoping in her sleep that the children would keep out and let her rest a minute. It had been a long day. Not that she was tired. It was always pleasant to snatch a minute now and then. There was always so much to be done, let me see: tomorrow.

Tomorrow was far away and there was nothing to trouble about. Things were finished somehow when the time came; thank God there was always a little margin over for peace: then a person could spread out the plan of life and tuck in the edges orderly. It was good to have everything clean and folded away, with the hair brushes and tonic bottles sitting straight on the white embroidered linen: the day started without fuss and the pantry shelves laid out with rows of jelly glasses and brown jugs and white stone-china jars with blue whirligigs and words painted on them: coffee, tea, sugar, ginger, cinnamon, allspice: and the bronze clock with the lion on top nicely dusted off. The dust that lion could collect in twenty-four hours! The box in the attic with all those letters tied up, well, she'd have to go through that tomorrow. All those letters—George's letters and John's letters and her letters to them both—lying around for the children to find afterwards made her uneasy. Yes, that would be tomorrow's business. No use to let them know how silly she had been once.

While she was rummaging around she found death in her mind and it felt clammy and unfamiliar. She had spent so much time preparing for death there was no need for bringing it up again. Let it take care of itself now. When she was sixty she had felt very old, finished, and went around making farewell trips to see her children and grandchildren, with a secret in her mind: This is the very last of your mother, children! Then she made her will and came down with a long fever. That was all just a notion like a lot of other things, but it was lucky too, for she had once for all got over the idea of dying for a long time. Now she couldn't be worried. She hoped she had better sense now. Her father had lived to be one hundred and two years old and had drunk a noggin of strong hot toddy on his last birthday. He told the reporters it was his daily habit, and he owed his

LITERATURE IN CONTEXT

History Connection

House Calls

In this story, eighty-year-old Ellen Weatherall dies at home, having been attended by the family doctor. Up until the 1930s, it was a common practice for doctors to deliver most of their services in the home. Medical technology was simple enough that home treatment was as good as—or better than—hospital treatment. However, after World War II, the field of medicine changed dramatically. New techniques for diagnosis and treatment required special technology and facilities. Economic factors also came into play; house calls were considered wasteful of the doctor's time. Today, except in some rural areas, the house call has faded into memory.

Connect to the Literature

How do you think Granny would react if she were moved to a hospital or nursing home? How would Cornelia feel?

long life to that. He had made quite a scandal and was very pleased about it. She believed she'd just plague Cornelia a little.

"Cornelia! Cornelia!" No footsteps, but a sudden hand on her cheek. "Bless you, where have you been?"

"Here, mother."

"Well, Cornelia, I want a noggin of hot toddy."

"Are you cold, darling?"

"I'm chilly, Cornelia. Lying in bed stops the circulation. I must have told you that a thousand times."

Well, she could just hear Cornelia telling her husband that Mother was getting a little childish and they'd have to humor her. The thing that most annoyed her was that Cornelia thought she was deaf, dumb, and blind. Little hasty glances and tiny gestures tossed around her and over her head saying, "Don't cross her, let her have her way, she's eighty years old," and she sitting there as if she lived in a thin glass cage. Sometimes Granny almost made up her mind to pack up and move back to her own house where nobody could remind her every minute that she was old. Wait, wait, Cornelia, till your own children whisper behind your back!

She had fenced in a hundred acres once, digging the post holes herself. . .

In her day she had kept a better house and had got more work done. She wasn't too old yet for Lydia to be driving eighty miles for advice when one of the children jumped the track, and Jimmy still dropped in and talked things over: "Now, Mammy, you've a good business head, I want to know what you think of this? . . ." Old. Cornelia couldn't change the furniture around without asking. Little things, little things! They had been so sweet when they were little. Granny wished the old days were back again with the children young and everything to be done over. It had been a hard pull, but not too much for her. When she thought of all the food she had cooked, and all the clothes she had cut and sewed, and all the gardens she had made—well, the children showed it. There they were, made out of her, and they couldn't get away from that. Sometimes she wanted to see John again and point to them and say, Well, I didn't do so badly, did I? But that would have to wait. That was for tomorrow. She used to think of him as a man, but now all the children were older than their father, and he would be a child beside her if she saw him now. It seemed strange and there was something wrong in the idea. Why, he couldn't possibly recognize her. She had fenced in a hundred acres once, digging the post holes herself and clamping the wires with just a negro boy to help. That changed a woman. John would be looking for a young woman with the peaked Spanish comb in her hair and the painted fan. Digging post holes changed a woman. Riding country roads in the winter when women had their babies was another thing: sitting up nights with sick horses and sick children and hardly ever losing one. John, I hardly ever lost one of them! John would see that in a minute, that would be something he could understand, she wouldn't have to explain anything!

Stream of Consciousness

Notice the path of Granny's thoughts. What are some topics she touches on, and how are they linked in her mind?

Comprehension

What journey did Granny Weatherall take when she was sixty years old? Why?

It made her feel like rolling up her sleeves and putting the whole place to rights again. No matter if Cornelia was determined to be everywhere at once, there were a great many things left undone on this place. She would start tomorrow and do them. It was good to be strong enough for everything, even if all you made melted and changed and slipped under your hands, so that by the time you finished you almost forgot what you were working for. What was it I set out to do? she asked herself intently, but she could not remember. A fog rose over the valley, she saw it marching across the creek swallowing the trees and moving up the hill like an army of ghosts. Soon it would be at the near edge of the orchard, and then it was time to go in and light the lamps. Come in, children, don't stay out in the night air.

Lighting the lamps had been beautiful. The children huddled up to her and breathed like little calves waiting at the bars in the twilight. Their eyes followed the match and watched the flame rise and settle in a blue curve, then they moved away from her. The lamp was lit, they didn't have to be scared and hang on to mother any more. Never, never, never more. God, for all my life I thank Thee. Without Thee, my God, I could never have done it. Hail Mary, full of grace.

Flashback
What do you learn about Granny from this flashback to a time when her children were small?

I want you to pick all the fruit this year and see that nothing is wasted. There's always someone who can use it. Don't let good things rot for want of using. You waste life when you waste good food. Don't let things get lost. It's bitter to lose things. Now, don't let me get to thinking, not when I am tired and taking a little nap before supper. . . .

The pillow rose about her shoulders and pressed against her heart and the memory was being squeezed out of it: oh, push down the pillow, somebody: it would smother her if she tried to hold it. Such a fresh breeze blowing and such a green day with no threats in it. But he had not come, just the same. What does a woman do when she has put on the white veil and set out the white cake for a man and he doesn't come? She tried to remember. No, I swear he never harmed me but in that. He never harmed me but in that . . . and what if he did? There was the day, the day, but a whirl of dark smoke rose and covered it, crept up and over into the bright field where everything was planted so carefully in orderly rows. That was hell, she knew hell when she saw it. For sixty years she had prayed against remembering him and against losing her soul in the deep pit of hell, and now the two things were mingled in one and the thought of him was a smoky cloud from hell that moved and crept in her head when she had just got rid of Doctor Harry and was trying to rest a minute. Wounded vanity, Ellen, said a sharp voice in the top of her mind. Don't let your wounded vanity get the upper hand of you. Plenty of girls get jilted. You were jilted, weren't you? Then stand up to it. Her eyelids wavered and let in streamers of blue-gray light like tissue paper over her eyes. She must get up and pull the shades down or she'd never sleep. She was in bed again and the shades were not down. How could that happen? Better turn over, hide from the light, sleeping in the light

Stream of Consciousness
What memory does Granny try to keep from surfacing? Why?

Don't let your wounded vanity get the upper hand of you. Plenty of girls get jilted.

◀ **Critical Viewing**
In what ways does the mood and subject of this painting reflect Granny's memories of being jilted at the altar? **INTERPRET**

gave you nightmares. "Mother, how do you feel now?" and a stinging wetness on her forehead. But I don't like having my face washed in cold water!

Hapsy? George? Lydia? Jimmy? No, Cornelia, and her features were swollen and full of little puddles. "They're coming, darling, they'll all be here soon." Go wash your face, child, you look funny.

Instead of obeying, Cornelia knelt down and put her head on the pillow. She seemed to be talking but there was no sound. "Well, are you tongue-tied? Whose birthday is it? Are you going to give a party?"

Cornelia's mouth moved urgently in strange shapes. "Don't do that, you bother me, daughter."

"Oh, no, Mother. Oh, no. . . ."

Comprehension
What happened to Granny sixty years ago?

Stream of Consciousness

What actual events are taking place in the room, and in what ways do they affect Granny's thoughts?

Nonsense. It was strange about children. They disputed your every word. "No what, Cornelia?"

"Here's Doctor Harry."

"I won't see that boy again. He just left five minutes ago."

"That was this morning, Mother. It's night now. Here's the nurse."

"This is Doctor Harry, Mrs. Weatherall. I never saw you look so young and happy!"

"Ah, I'll never be young again—but I'd be happy if they'd let me lie in peace and get rested."

She thought she spoke up loudly, but no one answered. A warm weight on her forehead, a warm bracelet on her wrist, and a breeze went on whispering, trying to tell her something. A shuffle of leaves in the everlasting hand of God, He blew on them and they danced and rattled. "Mother, don't mind, we're going to give you a little hypodermic." "Look here, daughter, how do ants get in this bed? I saw sugar ants yesterday." Did you send for Hapsy too?

It was Hapsy she really wanted. She had to go a long way back through a great many rooms to find Hapsy standing with a baby on her arm. She seemed to herself to be Hapsy also, and the baby on Hapsy's arm was Hapsy and himself and herself, all at once, and there was no surprise in the meeting. Then Hapsy melted from within and turned flimsy as gray gauze and the baby was a gauzy shadow, and Hapsy came up close and said, "I thought you'd never come," and looked at her very searchingly and said, "You haven't changed a bit!" They leaned forward to kiss, when Cornelia began whispering from a long way off, "Oh, is there anything you want to tell me? Is there anything I can do for you?"

Yes, she had changed her mind after sixty years and she would like to see George. I want you to find George. Find him and be sure to tell him I forgot him. I want him to know I had my husband just the same and my children and my house like any other woman. A good house too and a good husband that I loved and fine children out of him. Better than I hoped for even. Tell him I was given back everything he took away and more. Oh, no, oh, God, no, there was something else besides the house and the man and the children. Oh, surely they were not all? What was it? Something not given back. . . . Her breath crowded down under her ribs and grew into a monstrous frightening shape with cutting edges; it bored up into her head, and the agony was unbelievable: Yes, John, get the Doctor now, no more talk, my time has come.

When this one was born it should be the last. The last. It should have been born first, for it was the one she had truly wanted. Everything came in good time. Nothing left out, left over. She was strong, in three days she would be as well as ever. Better. A woman needed milk in her to have her full health.

"Mother, do you hear me?"

"I've been telling you—"

"Mother, Father Connolly's here."

"I went to Holy Communion only last week. Tell him I'm not so sinful as all that."

"Father just wants to speak to you."

He could speak as much as he pleased. It was like him to drop in and inquire about her soul as if it were a teething baby, and then stay on for a cup of tea and a round of cards and gossip. He always had a funny story of some sort, usually about an Irishman who made his little mistakes and confessed them, and the point lay in some absurd thing he would blurt out in the confessional showing his struggles between native **piety** and original sin. Granny felt easy about her soul. Cornelia, where are your manners? Give Father Connolly a chair. She had her secret comfortable understanding with a few favorite saints who cleared a straight road to God for her. All as surely signed and sealed as the papers for the new Forty Acres. Forever . . . heirs and assigns[2] forever. Since the day the wedding cake was not cut, but thrown out and wasted. The whole bottom dropped out of the world, and there she was blind and sweating with nothing under her feet and the walls falling away. His hand had caught her under the breast, she had not fallen, there was the freshly polished floor with the green rug on it, just as before. He had cursed like a sailor's parrot and said, "I'll kill him for you." Don't lay a hand on him, for my sake leave something to God. "Now, Ellen, you must believe what I tell you. . . ."

So there was nothing, nothing to worry about any more, except sometimes in the night one of the children screamed in a nightmare, and they both hustled out shaking and hunting for the matches and calling, "There, wait a minute, here we are!" John, get the doctor now, Hapsy's time has come. But there was Hapsy standing by the bed in a white cap. "Cornelia, tell Hapsy to take off her cap. I can't see her plain."

Her eyes opened very wide and the room stood out like a picture she had seen somewhere. Dark colors with the shadows rising towards the ceiling in long angles. The tall black dresser gleamed with nothing on it but John's picture, enlarged from a little one, with John's eyes very black when they should have been blue. You never saw him, so how do you know how he looked? But the man insisted the copy was perfect, it was very rich and handsome. For a picture, yes, but it's not my husband. The table by the bed had a linen cover and a candle and a crucifix. The light was blue from Cornelia's silk lampshades. No sort of light at all, just frippery. You had to live forty years with kerosene lamps to appreciate honest electricity. She felt very strong and she saw Doctor Harry with a rosy nimbus around him.

"You look like a saint, Doctor Harry, and I vow that's as near as

2. assigns persons to whom property is transferred.

. . . get the Doctor now, no more talk, my time has come.

Vocabulary

piety (pī´ ə tē) *n.* devotion to religion

Comprehension

What does Granny want George to know?

you'll ever come to it."

"She's saying something."

"I heard you, Cornelia. What's all this carrying on?"

"Father Connolly's saying—"

Cornelia's voice staggered and bumped like a cart in a bad road. It rounded corners and turned back again and arrived nowhere. Granny stepped up in the cart very lightly and reached for the reins, but a man sat beside her and she knew him by his hands, driving the cart. She did not look in his face, for she knew without seeing, but looked instead down the road where the trees leaned over and bowed to each other and a thousand birds were singing a Mass. She felt like singing too, but she put her hand in the bosom of her dress and pulled out a rosary, and Father Connolly murmured Latin in a very solemn voice and tickled her feet.[3] My God, will you stop that nonsense? I'm a married woman. What if he did run away and leave me to face the priest by myself? I found another a whole world better. I wouldn't have exchanged my husband for anybody except St. Michael[4] himself, and you may tell him that for me with a thank you in the bargain.

Light flashed on her closed eyelids, and a deep roaring shook her. Cornelia, is that lightning? I hear thunder. There's going to be a storm. Close all the windows. Call the children in. . . . "Mother, here we are, all of us." "Is that you, Hapsy?" "Oh, no, I'm Lydia. We drove as fast as we could." Their faces drifted above her, drifted away. The rosary fell out of her hands and Lydia put it back. Jimmy tried to help, their hands fumbled together, and Granny closed two fingers around Jimmy's thumb. Beads wouldn't do, it must be something alive. She was so amazed her thoughts ran round and round. So, my dear Lord, this is my death and I wasn't even thinking about it. My children have come to see me die. But I can't, it's not time. Oh, I always hated surprises. I wanted to give Cornelia the amethyst set—Cornelia, you're to have the amethyst set, but Hapsy's to wear it when she wants, and, Doctor Harry, do shut up. Nobody sent for you. Oh, my dear Lord, do wait a minute. I meant to do something about the Forty Acres, Jimmy doesn't need it and Lydia will later on, with that worthless husband of hers. I meant to finish the altar cloth and send six bottles of wine to Sister Borgia for her **dyspepsia**. I want to send six bottles of wine to Sister Borgia, Father Connolly, now don't let me forget.

Stream of Consciousness

What is the connecting link between Granny's thoughts about her amethyst set, the Forty acres, and the altar cloth?

Vocabulary

dyspepsia (dis pep´ shə) *n.* indigestion

Cornelia's voice made short turns and tilted over and crashed. "Oh, Mother, oh, Mother, oh Mother. . . ."

"I'm not going, Cornelia. I'm taken by surprise. I can't go."

You'll see Hapsy again. What about her? "I thought you'd never come." Granny made a long journey outward, looking for Hapsy. What if I don't find her? What then? Her heart sank down and down, there

3. murmured . . . feet administered the last rites of the Catholic Church.

4. St. Michael one of the archangels.

was no bottom to death, she couldn't come to the end of it. The blue light from Cornelia's lampshade drew into a tiny point in the center of her brain, it flickered and winked like an eye, quietly it fluttered and dwindled. Granny lay curled down within herself, amazed and watchful, staring at the point of light that was herself; her body was now only a deeper mass of shadow in an endless darkness and this darkness would curl around the light and swallow it up. God, give a sign!

For the second time there was no sign. Again no bridegroom and the priest in the house. She could not remember any other sorrow because this grief wiped them all away. Oh, no, there's nothing more cruel than this—I'll never forgive it. She stretched herself with a deep breath and blew out the light.

Critical Reading

Cite textual evidence to support your responses.

1. **Key Ideas and Details** **(a)** Who sits with Granny during her final hours? **(b) Analyze:** What is Granny's attitude toward this person?
2. **Key Ideas and Details** **(a)** What are the names of Granny's children? **(b) Interpret:** Which of her children does Granny long to see? **(c) Deduce:** Why is she unable to see this child?
3. **Key Ideas and Details** **(a)** As she drifts in and out of consciousness, what memory is "squeezed out" of Granny's heart? **(b) Interpret:** How does Granny try to talk herself out of the pain of this memory?
4. **Key Ideas and Details** **(a) Interpret:** What memories and details suggest Granny's physical and emotional strength as a young woman? **(b) Analyze:** Why might the author have chosen "Weatherall" as an appropriate surname for Granny?
5. **Key Ideas and Details** **(a) Infer:** As she nears death, why does Granny say she "can't go"? **(b) Connect:** What is the connection between her experience of having been jilted and her experiences in the final paragraph?
6. **Craft and Structure** **Speculate:** In what ways might this story have been different if Granny had confronted George after he jilted her?
7. **Integration of Knowledge and Ideas** Whose criteria do you think Granny uses to judge her life? Is her assessment of her life accurate or fair? In your response, use at least three of these Essential Question words: *satisfying, fulfillment, judgment, critical, productive.* ***[Connecting to the Essential Question: How does literature shape or reflect society?]***

Close Reading Activities *The Jilting of Granny Weatherall*

Literary Analysis

1. **Craft and Structure** What impact does the use of **stream of consciousness** have on the reader's perceptions of Granny's children and of Doctor Harry?
2. **Key Ideas and Details** **Clarify the sequence of events** presented in this story by completing a timeline of Granny Weatherall's life.
3. **Craft and Structure** Use a chart like the one shown to analyze Granny's thoughts and their associations. **(a)** Identify two points at which Granny's thoughts drift from one subject to another without an obvious transition or connection. **(b)** What possible associations might connect her thoughts in each of these examples?

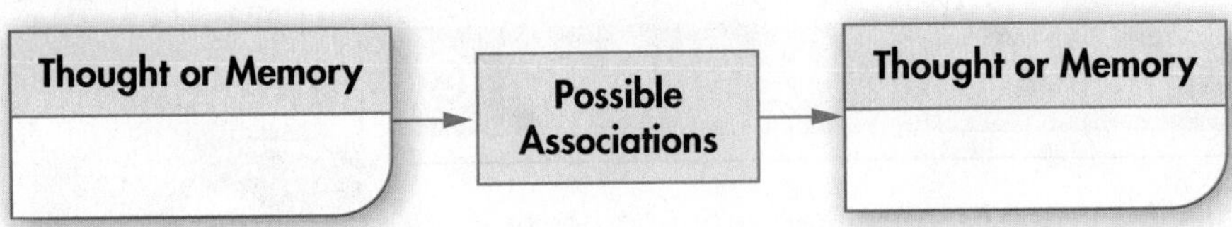

4. **Craft and Structure** Analyze three **flashbacks** in the story. **(a)** Identify the form each flashback takes (dream, memory, and so on). **(b)** Note what you learn from each flashback about Granny's life.
5. **Craft and Structure** **(a)** What details trigger Granny's flashback to lighting the lamps when her children were young? **(b)** What is the connection between this flashback and her experiences in the present?
6. **Craft and Structure** Describe a structure this story might have had if Porter had not used stream of consciousness and flashback. For example, how might Porter have introduced individual characters or narrated specific scenes?
7. **Craft and Structure** **(a)** Based on your response to question 6, what qualities does the use of stream of consciousness and flashback lend to the narrative? **(b)** Overall, do you think these techniques are effective for the telling of this particular tale? Explain.
8. **Integration of Knowledge and Ideas** Do you think Porter's use of stream of consciousness makes Granny's character more or less vivid to the reader? Explain.
9. **Integration of Knowledge and Ideas** Does the jumbled sequence of events as they appear in the story create a complete picture of Granny's life? Explain.

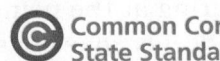

 **Common Core State Standards**

Writing

3. Write narratives to develop real or imagined experiences or events using effective technique, well-chosen details, and well-structured event sequences. *(p.845)*

3.b. Use narrative techniques, such as dialogue, pacing, description, reflection, and multiple plot lines, to develop experiences, events, and/or characters. *(p. 845)*

3.d. Use precise words and phrases, telling details, and sensory language to convey a vivid picture of the experiences, events, setting, and/or characters. *(p. 845)*

Language

4.b. Identify and correctly use patterns of word changes that indicate different meanings or parts of speech. *(p. 845)*

4.d. Verify the preliminary determination of the meaning of a word or phrase. *(p. 845)*

Vocabulary Acquisition and Use

Word Analysis: Greek Prefix *dys-*

The Greek prefix *dys-*, meaning "difficult" or "bad," can help you decipher many unfamiliar words. This prefix is often used in scientific terms involving medical or psychological diagnoses. Write a definition of each word below by combining the meaning of the prefix *dys-* with the clues in parentheses. After you have finished, use a dictionary to check your work and revise as necessary.

1. dysfunctional (*functional* = working properly)
2. dyslexia (*lexis* = word or speech)
3. dysentery (*entery* = intestine)
4. dyspepsia (*pepsis* = digestion)
5. dystopia (*topos* = place)

Vocabulary: Sentence Completions

Select the word from the vocabulary list on page 830 that best completes each sentence below. Then, explain your reasoning.

1. Kelly showed her ______ by attending religious services daily.
2. It is best to be ______ when discussing politics with people you do not know well.
3. I try to avoid eating pizza because it aggravates my ______.

Writing to Sources

Narrative Text A monologue is a dramatic form in which only one person speaks. A stream-of-consciousness monologue is a type of *interior monologue* in that it takes place within the mind of a character. Choose a character from the story or make up a new one. Write a **monologue** in which you use stream of consciousness to portray the character's thoughts.

Prewriting List concrete sensory details—words and phrases related to sight, sound, and smell. Think about gestures, actions, and feelings that come alive through these details. Organize the details into two categories: scenes in the present / scenes in the past.

Drafting Select several memories around which to organize the monologue. Add to the stream-of-consciousness effect by omitting transitions.

Model: Using Details to Create a Vivid Character

Here's the jetway, a chute, really. No going back now. *Fasten your seatbelts.* Night flight without my parents—was I nine, eleven?—daring myself to peek out the scratched plastic oval at the tiny lights below. *Ouch.* My stomach hurts because I buckled my belt so tight.

Using specific images emphasizes the character's feelings.

Revising Read your monologue aloud to make sure it sounds like a genuine, private voice. Add clues to help your audience follow the thought stream and clarify the ideas and memories expressed.

Building Knowledge and Insight *A Worn Path*

Connecting to the Essential Question Phoenix Jackson, the main character in this story, addresses the natural world as if it were an old acquaintance. As you read, look for instances in which Phoenix relates to the landscape like another person. Doing so will help as you consider the Essential Question: **What is the relationship between literature and place?**

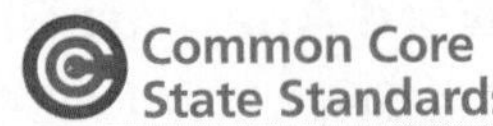

Reading Literature

3. Analyze the impact of the author's choices regarding how to develop and relate elements of a story or drama.

5. Analyze how an author's choices concerning how to structure specific parts of a text contribute to its overall structure and meaning as well as its aesthetic impact.

Close Reading Focus

Archetype; Hero's Quest

An **archetype** is a plot structure, character type, symbol, or idea that recurs in the literature or mythology of many different cultures across the world. The **hero's quest** is one archetypal plot structure. Classic quest tales—from ancient Egyptian myths to the modern-day *Star Wars* stories—typically follow a certain structure and share certain elements.

- The hero is on a journey to obtain something of great value.
- The hero encounters obstacles that test his or her character.
- The hero overcomes these obstacles, often with the aid of others, and often at great sacrifice.
- The hero receives a boon, or benefit, that is used to help others.
- The hero's quest symbolizes the larger journey of life.

As its title suggests, "A Worn Path" features a traveler on a familiar road. Phoenix Jackson, an elderly black woman in Depression-era Mississippi, faces a range of obstacles as she progresses through the landscape. Some of these obstacles are physical and some are societal. As you read, notice elements in the story that mirror the structure of the hero's quest archetype.

Preparing to Read Complex Texts The reason for Phoenix Jackson's journey remains a mystery for much of the story, although various details provide clues about the nature of her quest. As you read, **generate questions** about Phoenix's life and journey. Then, **make predictions** in response to the questions. As the story unfolds, use what you learn to *confirm* whether your predictions were correct. Use a chart like the one shown to generate questions, make predictions, and confirm them.

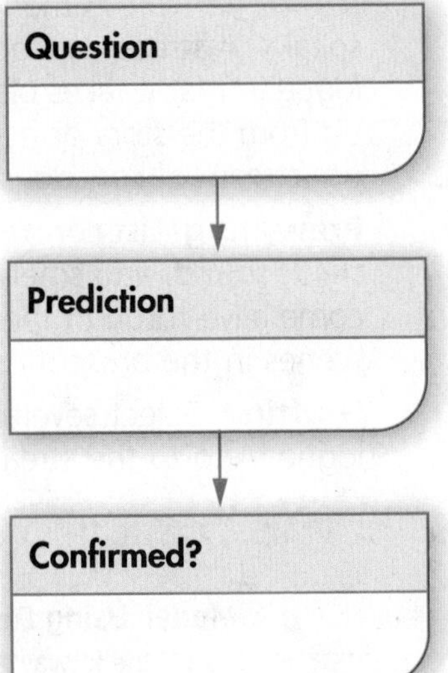

Vocabulary

The words below are important to understanding the text that follows. Copy the words into your notebook. What are some other forms of the word *persistent*?

grave
persistent
limber
obstinate

Eudora Welty (1909–2001)

Author of "A Worn Path"

Eudora Welty's stories and novels capture life in the deep South, creating images of the landscape and conveying the shared attitudes and values of the people. While she often confronts the hardships of life in poor rural areas and depicts people's suffering, her writing remains optimistic.

Welty was born in Jackson, Mississippi, where she spent most of her life. She attended Mississippi State College for Women before transferring to the University of Wisconsin, where she graduated in 1929. Hoping to pursue a career in advertising, she moved to New York City and enrolled at Columbia University's School of Business. However, because of the worsening economic depression, she was unable to find steady employment and returned to Jackson in 1931.

Traveling and Writing After accepting a job as a publicist for a government agency, Welty spent several years traveling throughout Mississippi, taking photographs and interviewing people. Her experiences inspired her to write, and in 1936 her first short story, "Death of a Traveling Salesman," was published.

In her fiction, Welty displays an acute sense of detail and a deep sense of compassion toward her characters. For example, in "A Worn Path," she paints a sympathetic portrait of an old woman whose feelings of love and sense of duty motivate her to make a long, painful journey through the countryside.

One of the leading American writers of the twentieth century, Welty published numerous collections of short stories and novels. In 1973, her novel *The Optimist's Daughter* won the Pulitzer Prize.

A Worn Path

EUDORA WELTY

BACKGROUND This story is set in Mississippi during the Great Depression of the 1930s. Decades after the end of the Civil War and the emancipation of southern slaves, the people of Mississippi still suffered from the social and economic consequences of that war. Many whites continued to reject the idea of a biracial society, and most blacks, though "free," had become trapped in a tenant-farming system that kept them perpetually indebted to the white landowners. It was not a prosperous system for anyone, black or white. By the onset of the Depression in 1929, Mississippi was among the poorest states in the nation, with an average annual income of $287 per capita; by 1933, that average had fallen to $117. Families struggled to make ends meet in a state that could offer neither financial aid nor social services. This is the economic and social landscape through which Phoenix Jackson travels.

It was December—a bright frozen day in the early morning. Far out in the country there was an old Negro woman with her head tied in a red rag, coming along a path through the pinewoods. Her name was Phoenix Jackson. She was very old and small and she walked slowly in the dark pine shadows, moving a little from side to side in her steps, with the balanced heaviness and lightness of a pendulum in a grandfather clock. She carried a thin, small cane made from an umbrella, and with this she kept tapping the frozen earth in front of her. This made a **grave** and **persistent** noise in the still air, that seemed meditative like the chirping of a solitary little bird.

She wore a dark striped dress reaching down to her shoe tops, and an equally long apron of bleached sugar sacks, with a full pocket: all neat and tidy, but every time she took a step she might have fallen over her shoelaces, which dragged from her unlaced shoes. She looked straight ahead. Her eyes were blue with age. Her skin had a pattern all its own of numberless branching wrinkles and as though a whole little tree stood in the middle of her forehead, but a golden color ran underneath, and the two knobs of her cheeks were illumined by a yellow burning under the dark. Under the red rag her hair came down on her neck in the frailest of ringlets, still black, and with an odor like copper.

Now and then there was a quivering in the thicket. Old Phoenix said, "Out of my way, all you foxes, owls, beetles, jack rabbits, coons and wild animals! . . . Keep out from under these feet, little bob-whites[1]. . . . Keep the big wild hogs out of my path. Don't let none of

Vocabulary

grave (grāv) *adj.* serious; solemn

persistent (pər sist′ ənt) *adj.* repeated; continual

Comprehension

What are some of Phoenix Jackson's distinguishing features?

1. **bob-whites** *n.* partridges.

◀ **Critical Viewing** What details in this image suggest Phoenix's strong character? **CONNECT**

Miz Emily, Joseph Holston, Courtesy of Joseph Holston

Vocabulary
limber (limˈ bər) *adj.* flexible

Archetype of the Quest
What first obstacle does Phoenix encounter?

Generating Questions
What question about Phoenix might you ask based on her discussion with the thorns?

those come running my direction. I got a long way." Under her small black-freckled hand her cane, **limber** as a buggy whip, would switch at the brush as if to rouse up any hiding things.

On she went. The woods were deep and still. The sun made the pine needles almost too bright to look at, up where the wind rocked. The cones dropped as light as feathers. Down in the hollow was the mourning dove—it was not too late for him.

The path ran up a hill. "Seem like there is chains about my feet, time I get this far," she said, in the voice of argument old people keep to use with themselves. "Something always take a hold of me on this hill—pleads I should stay."

After she got to the top she turned and gave a full, severe look behind her where she had come. "Up through pines," she said at length. "Now down through oaks."

Her eyes opened their widest, and she started down gently. But before she got to the bottom of the hill a bush caught her dress.

Her fingers were busy and intent, but her skirts were full and long, so that before she could pull them free in one place they were caught in another. It was not possible to allow the dress to tear. "I in the thorny bush," she said. "Thorns, you doing your appointed work. Never want to let folks pass, no sir. Old eyes thought you was a pretty little *green* bush."

Finally, trembling all over, she stood free, and after a moment dared to stoop for her cane.

"Sun so high!" she cried, leaning back and looking, while the thick tears went over her eyes. "The time getting all gone here."

At the foot of this hill was a place where a log was laid across the creek.

"Now comes the trial," said Phoenix.

Putting her right foot out, she mounted the log and shut her eyes. Lifting her skirt, leveling her cane fiercely before her, like a festival figure in some parade, she began to march across. Then she opened her eyes and she was safe on the other side.

"I wasn't as old as I thought," she said.

But she sat down to rest. She spread her skirts on the bank around her and folded her hands over her knees. Up above her was a tree in a pearly cloud of mistletoe. She did not dare to close her eyes, and when a little boy brought her a plate with a slice of marble cake on it she spoke to him. "That would be acceptable," she said. But when she went to take it there was just her own hand in the air.

So she left that tree, and had to go through a barbed-wire fence. There she had to creep and crawl, spreading her knees and stretching her fingers like a baby trying to climb the steps. But she talked loudly to herself: she could not let her dress be torn now, so late in the day, and she could not pay for having her arm or her leg sawed off if she got caught fast where she was.

At last she was safe through the fence and risen up out in the clearing. Big dead trees, like black men with one arm, were standing in the purple stalks of the withered cotton field. There sat a buzzard.

"Who you watching?"

In the furrow she made her way along.

"Glad this not the season for bulls," she said, looking sideways, "and the good Lord made his snakes to curl up and sleep in the winter. A pleasure I don't see no two-headed snake coming around that tree, where it come once. It took a while to get by him, back in the summer."

She passed through the old cotton and went into a field of dead corn. It whispered and shook and was taller than her head. "Through the maze now," she said, for there was no path.

Then there was something tall, black, and skinny there, moving before her.

At first she took it for a man. It could have been a man dancing in the field. But she stood still and listened, and it did not make a sound. It was as silent as a ghost.

"Ghost," she said sharply, "who be you the ghost of? For I have heard of nary death close by."

But there was no answer—only the ragged dancing in the wind.

She shut her eyes, reached out her hand, and touched a sleeve. She found a coat and inside that an emptiness, cold as ice.

"You scarecrow," she said. Her face lighted. "I ought to be shut up for good," she said with laughter. "My senses is gone. I too old. I the oldest people I ever know. Dance, old scarecrow," she said, "while I dancing with you."

She kicked her foot over the furrow, and with mouth drawn down, shook her head once or twice in a little strutting way. Some husks blew down and whirled in streamers about her skirts.

Then she went on, parting her way from side to side with the cane, through the whispering field. At last she came to the end, to a wagon track where the silver grass blew between the red ruts. The quail were walking around like pullets, seeming all dainty and unseen.

"Walk pretty," she said. "This the easy place. This the easy going."

She followed the track, swaying through the quiet bare fields, through the little strings of trees silver in their dead leaves, past cabins silver from weather, with the doors and windows boarded shut, all like old women under a spell sitting there. "I walking in their sleep," she said, nodding her head vigorously.

In a ravine she went where a spring was silently flowing through a hollow log. Old Phoenix bent and drank. "Sweet-gum[2] makes the water sweet," she said, and drank more. "Nobody know who made this well, for it was here when I was born."

The track crossed a swampy part where the moss hung as white as lace from every limb. "Sleep on, alligators, and blow your bubbles." Then the track went into the road.

---

2. sweet-gum *a tree that produces a fragrant juice.*

WORLD LITERATURE CONNECTION

The Hero's Quest

"A Worn Path" tells of Phoenix Jackson's quest to get medicine for her grandson. One of the oldest archetypal forms, the quest plot appears in poetry and folk tales throughout the world. The *Odyssey*, an epic poem that was likely composed by the Greek poet Homer in the 8th century B.C., is one of the most famous examples of the quest plot.

The *Odyssey* tells of the voyage of the Greek warrior Odysseus. After the Trojan War, Odysseus loads his ship and sails for home, where his family awaits him on the island of Ithaca. The voyage turns out to be longer and harder than expected—ten years longer. Powerful winds blow the ship off course, and Odysseus lands on a series of islands, where he encounters frightening giants, monsters, cannibals, beautiful witches and seductive goddesses. These are the obstacles that Odysseus must overcome before reuniting with his family on Ithaca.

Connect to the Literature

Can the world of a rural, impoverished woman like Phoenix Jackson be as challenging as the world of a royal warrior like Odysseus? Why or why not?

Archetype of the Quest

What heroic trait does Phoenix display in her encounter with the "ghost"?

Comprehension

What is Phoenix Jackson's attitude as she walks?

Deep, deep the road went down between the high green-colored banks. Overhead the live-oaks met, and it was as dark as a cave.

A black dog with a lolling tongue came up out of the weeds by the ditch. She was meditating, and not ready, and when he came at her she only hit him a little with her cane. Over she went in the ditch, like a little puff of milkweed.[3]

Down there, her senses drifted away. A dream visited her, and she reached her hand up, but nothing reached down and gave her a pull.

▼ Critical Viewing
Does this image accurately represent the path Phoenix travels? Why or why not? **EVALUATE**

3. milkweed *n.* a plant with pods that, when ripe, release feathery seeds.

So she lay there and presently went to talking. "Old woman," she said to herself, "that black dog come up out of the weeds to stall you off, and now there he sitting on his fine tail, smiling at you."

A white man finally came along and found her—a hunter, a young man, with his dog on a chain.

"Well, Granny!" he laughed. "What are you doing there?"

"Lying on my back like a June bug waiting to be turned over, mister," she said, reaching up her hand.

He lifted her up, gave her a swing in the air, and set her down. "Anything broken, Granny?"

"No sir, them old dead weeds is springy enough," said Phoenix, when she had got her breath. "I thank you for your trouble."

"Where do you live, Granny?" he asked, while the two dogs were growling at each other.

"Away back yonder, sir, behind the ridge. You can't even see it from here."

"On your way home?"

"No sir, I going to town."

"Why, that's too far! That's as far as I walk when I come out myself, and I get something for my trouble." He patted the stuffed bag he carried, and there hung down a little closed claw. It was one of the bob-whites, with its beak hooked bitterly to show it was dead. "Now you go on home, Granny!"

"I bound to go to town, mister," said Phoenix. "The time come around."

He gave another laugh, filling the whole landscape. "I know you old colored people! Wouldn't miss going to town to see Santa Claus!"

But something held old Phoenix very still. The deep lines in her face went into a fierce and different radiation. Without warning, she had seen with her own eyes a flashing nickel fall out of the man's pocket onto the ground.

"How old are you, Granny?" he was saying.

"There is no telling, mister," she said, "no telling."

Then she gave a little cry and clapped her hands and said, "Git on away from here, dog! Look! Look at that dog!" She laughed as if in admiration. "He ain't scared of nobody. He a big black dog." She whispered, "Sic him!"

"Watch me get rid of that cur," said the man. "Sic him, Pete! Sic him!"

Phoenix heard the dogs fighting, and heard the man running and throwing sticks. She even heard a gunshot. But she was slowly bending forward by that time, further and further forward, the lids stretched down over her eyes, as if she were doing this in her sleep. Her chin was lowered almost to her knees. The yellow palm of her hand came out from the fold of her apron. Her fingers slid down and along the ground under the piece of money with the grace and care they would have in lifting an egg from under a setting hen. Then she slowly straightened up, she stood erect, and the nickel was in her apron pocket. A bird flew by. Her lips moved. "God watching me the whole time. I come to stealing."

Archetype of the Quest
What element of the hero's quest might the hunter represent?

Generating Questions
What question might you ask about the nickel's importance in the story?

Comprehension
Who comes along to help Phoenix on her way?

Georgia Red Clay, 1946, Nell Choate Jones, Morris Museum of Art, Augusta, Georgia

The man came back, and his own dog panted about them. "Well, I scared him off that time," he said, and then he laughed and lifted his gun and pointed it at Phoenix.

She stood straight and faced him.

"Doesn't the gun scare you?" he said, still pointing it.

"No, sir, I seen plenty go off closer by, in my day, and for less than what I done," she said, holding utterly still.

He smiled, and shouldered the gun. "Well, Granny," he said, "you must be a hundred years old, and scared of nothing. I'd give you a dime if I had any money with me. But you take my advice and stay home, and nothing will happen to you."

Archetype of the Quest
Does Phoenix pass the "test" of the hunter? Explain.

"I bound to go on my way, mister," said Phoenix. She inclined her head in the red rag. Then they went in different directions, but she could hear the gun shooting again and again over the hill.

She walked on. The shadows hung from the oak trees to the road like curtains. Then she smelled wood-smoke, and smelled the river, and she saw a steeple and the cabins on their steep steps. Dozens of little black children whirled around her. There ahead was Natchez[4] shining. Bells were ringing. She walked on.

In the paved city it was Christmas time. There were red and green electric lights strung and crisscrossed everywhere, and all turned on in the daytime. Old Phoenix would have been lost if she had not distrusted her eyesight and depended on her feet to know where to take her.

She paused quietly on the sidewalk where people were passing by. A lady came along in the crowd, carrying an armful of red-, green- and silver-wrapped presents; she gave off perfume like the red roses in hot summer, and Phoenix stopped her.

"Please, missy, will you lace up my shoe?" She held up her foot.

"What do you want, Grandma?"

"See my shoe," said Phoenix. "Do all right for out in the country, but wouldn't look right to go in a big building."

Generating Questions
What questions might you ask about the big building and the goal of Phoenix's quest?

"Stand still then, Grandma," said the lady. She put her packages down on the sidewalk beside her and laced and tied both shoes tightly.

"Can't lace 'em with a cane," said Phoenix. "Thank you, missy. I doesn't mind asking a nice lady to tie up my shoe, when I gets out on the street."

Moving slowly and from side to side, she went into the big building, and into a tower of steps, where she walked up and around and around until her feet knew to stop.

She entered a door, and there she saw nailed up on the wall the document that had been stamped with the gold seal and framed in the gold frame, which matched the dream that was hung up in her head.

"Here I be," she said. There was a fixed and ceremonial stiffness over her body.

"A charity case, I suppose," said an attendant who sat at the desk before her.

But Phoenix only looked above her head. There was sweat on her

4. **Natchez** (nach´ iz) a town in southern Mississippi.

face, the wrinkles in her skin shone like a bright net.

"Speak up, Grandma," the woman said. "What's your name? We must have your history, you know. Have you been here before? What seems to be the trouble with you?"

Old Phoenix only gave a twitch to her face as if a fly were bothering her.

"Are you deaf?" cried the attendant.

But then the nurse came in.

"Oh, that's just old Aunt Phoenix," she said. "She doesn't come for herself—she has a little grandson. She makes these trips just as regular as clockwork. She lives away back off the Old Natchez Trace." She bent down. "Well, Aunt Phoenix, why don't you just take a seat? We won't keep you standing after your long trip." She pointed.

The old woman sat down, bolt upright in the chair.

"Now, how is the boy?" asked the nurse.

Old Phoenix did not speak.

"I said, how is the boy?"

But Phoenix only waited and stared straight ahead, her face very solemn and withdrawn into rigidity.

"Is his throat any better?" asked the nurse. "Aunt Phoenix, don't you hear me? Is your grandson's throat any better since the last time you came for the medicine?"

With her hands on her knees, the old woman waited, silent, erect and motionless, just as if she were in armor.

"You mustn't take up our time this way, Aunt Phoenix," the nurse said. "Tell us quickly about your grandson, and get it over. He isn't dead, is he?"

At last there came a flicker and then a flame of comprehension across her face, and she spoke.

"My grandson. It was my memory had left me. There I sat and forgot why I made my long trip."

"Forgot?" The nurse frowned. "After you came so far?"

Then Phoenix was like an old woman begging a dignified forgiveness for waking up frightened in the night. "I never did go to school. I was too old at the Surrender,"[5] she said in a soft voice. "I'm an old woman without an education. It was my memory fail me. My little grandson, he is just the same, and I forgot it in the coming."

"Throat never heals, does it?" said the nurse, speaking in a loud, sure voice to old Phoenix. By now she had a card with something written on it, a little list. "Yes. Swallowed lye. When was it?—January—two, three years ago—"

Phoenix spoke unasked now. "No, missy, he not dead, he just the same. Every little while his throat begin to close up again, and he not able to swallow. He not get his breath. He not able to help himself. So the time come around, and I go on another trip for the soothing medicine."

"All right. The doctor said as long as you came to get it, you could have it," said the nurse. "But it's an **obstinate** case."

5. **the Surrender** the surrender of the Confederate army, which ended the Civil War.

"There I sat and forgot why I made my long trip."

Vocabulary
obstinate (äb´ stə nət) *adj.* stubborn

Comprehension
Why is Phoenix at the doctor's office?

"We is the only two left in the world."

"My little grandson, he sit up there in the house all wrapped up, waiting by himself," Phoenix went on. "We is the only two left in the world. He suffer and it don't seem to put him back at all. He got a sweet look. He going to last. He wear a little patch quilt and peep out holding his mouth open like a little bird. I remembers so plain now. I not going to forget him again, no, the whole enduring time. I could tell him from all the others in creation."

"All right." The nurse was trying to hush her now. She brought her a bottle of medicine. "Charity," she said, making a check mark in a book.

Old Phoenix held the bottle close to her eyes, and then carefully put it into her pocket.

"I thank you," she said.

"It's Christmas time, Grandma," said the attendant. "Could I give you a few pennies out of my purse?"

"Five pennies is a nickel," said Phoenix stiffly.

"Here's a nickel," said the attendant.

Phoenix rose carefully and held out her hand. She received the nickel and then fished the other nickel out of her pocket and laid it beside the new one. She stared at her palm closely, with her head on one side.

Then she gave a tap with her cane on the floor.

"This is what come to me to do," she said. "I going to the store and buy my child a little windmill they sells, made out of paper. He going to find it hard to believe there such a thing in the world. I'll march myself back where he is waiting, holding it straight up in this hand."

She lifted her free hand, gave a little nod, turned around, and walked out of the doctor's office. Then her slow step began on the stairs, going down.

Critical Reading 

Cite textual evidence to support your responses.

1. **Key Ideas and Details (a)** How does the young hunter address Phoenix? **(b) Analyze:** What contradictory attitudes toward Phoenix does the hunter express? Explain.
2. **Integration of Knowledge and Ideas Synthesize:** In mythology, the phoenix is a bird that rises from the ashes. Why do you think Welty named the main character of this story Phoenix?
3. **Integration of Knowledge and Ideas (a) Interpret:** At the end of the story, do you think Phoenix's grandson is alive? Explain. **(b) Assess:** Why do you think Welty does not clarify this ambiguity?
4. **Integration of Knowledge and Ideas** Does Phoenix seem more "at home" in the natural landscape or in the social landscape of Depression-era Mississippi? Explain. In your response, use at least two of these Essential Question words: *dignified, charity, perceptions, trials, status.* ***[Connecting to the Essential Question: What is the relationship between literature and place?]***

Close Reading Activities *A Worn Path*

Literary Analysis

1. **Key Ideas and Details** **(a)** What **prediction** did you make about the purpose of Phoenix's journey? **(b)** Was your prediction confirmed partly, fully, or not at all? Explain. **(c)** What unpredictable "gifts" does the end of the story offer?
2. **Craft and Structure** Use a chart like the one shown to analyze the obstacles Phoenix encounters on her **archetypal hero's quest.**

Obstacle	How Phoenix Responds

3. **Craft and Structure** **(a)** Which obstacles listed in your chart are physical? **(b)** Which are social? **(c)** In general, how does Phoenix deal differently with these two types of challenges? Consider her words, tone, and actions.
4. **Craft and Structure** **(a)** What object of great value does Phoenix seek? **(b)** What sacrifices must she make to obtain it?
5. **Craft and Structure** **(a)** What benefit, or boon, does Phoenix receive? **(b)** How is her use of this boon heroic?
6. **Integration of Knowledge and Ideas** In what ways does Phoenix's journey symbolize the journey of life?

Vocabulary Acquisition and Use

Context Clues Review the words from the list on page 846. Then, answer *yes* or *no* to each question below. Explain the context clues that help you.

1. Would someone bringing *grave* news be smiling?
2. If you heard a *persistent* noise, would you go investigate?
3. Would a gymnast need to be *limber* before performing?
4. Would you want to work on a project with an *obstinate* person?

Writing to Sources

Narrative Text Write a **sequel** to this story that describes what happens when Phoenix Jackson gets home. Use specific details and sensory language to create vivid pictures in your story. Use these questions to plan your sequel:

- Is Phoenix's grandson alive?
- What problem or problems does Phoenix face? What is/are its/their significance?
- What does Phoenix feel and do?
- How will your story end?

Common Core State Standards

Writing

3. Write narratives to develop real or imagined experiences or events using effective technique, well-chosen details, and well-structured event sequences.

3.a. Engage and orient the reader by setting out a problem and its significance, establishing one or multiple point(s) of view, and introducing a narrator and/or characters; create a smooth progression of experiences or events.

Language

4.a. Use context as a clue to the meaning of a word.

Building Knowledge and Insight

The Night the Ghost Got In

Connecting to the Essential Question James Thurber is a treasured humorist, known for a comic vision that has a decidedly American quality. As you read, notice elements that you find funny. Doing so will help you think about the Essential Question: **What makes American literature American?**

Reading Informational Text

3. Analyze a complex set of ideas or sequence of events and explain how specific individuals, ideas, or events interact and develop over the course of the text.

4. Determine the meaning of words and phrases as they are used in the text, including figurative, connotative, and technical meanings.

Language

5.a. Interpret figures of speech in context and analyze their role in the text.

Close Reading Focus

Humorous Essay

Humor appears in all forms of literature, from drama to poetry to fiction. A **humorous essay** is a short, funny work of nonfiction. It requires literary skill and the use of specific strategies to translate the comedy of everyday life into an amusing work of writing. Humor writers use the following techniques to make written works funny:

- **hyperbole:** exaggeration or outrageous overstatement
- **understatement:** the opposite of hyperbole; downplaying a dramatic event, or saying less than what is meant
- **idioms:** expressions in which the literal meanings of the words do not add up to the actual meaning ("raining cats and dogs" = downpour)
- **dialect:** ways of speaking that are particular to a region or group

As you read, notice Thurber's use of these techniques and the ways in which they add to the essay's humor.

Preparing to Read Complex Texts A *cause* is the reason something happens; an *effect* is the result. Thurber structures this essay around cause and effect, or the idea that "one thing leads to another." He ratchets up the humor by making each successive moment sillier than the last. By **analyzing cause and effect** as you read, you can trace the flow of events and better appreciate the skill with which Thurber intensifies the humor. As you read, use a chart like the one shown to analyze causes and effects.

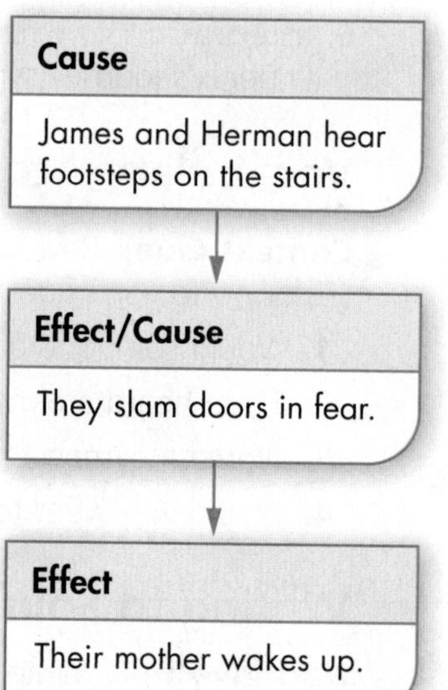

Cause
James and Herman hear footsteps on the stairs.
Effect/Cause
They slam doors in fear.
Effect
Their mother wakes up.

Vocabulary

You will encounter the words listed here in the text that follows. Copy the words into your notebook. Which words are adjectives? How can you tell?

despondent
intervene
reluctant
blaspheming

James Thurber

(1894–1961)

Author of **"The Night the Ghost Got In"**

James Thurber's essays, plays, sketches, cartoons, and short stories generally evolved from his own experiences. In his humorous sketches, Thurber embellishes facts and describes events in an amusing manner. In his short stories, Thurber's characters typically struggle against the unpleasant realities of modern life. In his pen-and-ink illustrations and cartoons, Thurber portrays men, women, and animals—especially dogs—facing the trials of everyday life.

The New Yorker Thurber was born in Columbus, Ohio. After attending Ohio State University, he joined *The New Yorker* magazine staff in 1927 as managing editor. From there, or so he claimed, he quickly worked his way down to writer. Until the end of his life, Thurber regularly contributed stories, essays, drawings, and cartoons to the magazine's pages. He also worked closely with the celebrated writer E. B. White, who wrote numerous essays for the magazine.

Comic Genius Thurber is one of the few humorists whose work is part of the American literary canon. About his comic genius, Thurber was quite modest:

"I write humor the way a surgeon operates, because it is a livelihood, because I have a great urge to do it, because many interesting challenges are set up, and because I have the hope it may do some good."

In much of his work, Thurber's humor reveals an edge of unhappiness, especially in his later years when his failing vision caused him much pain and bitterness. Thurber's many published works include *The Owl in the Attic and Other Perplexities* (1931), *The Seal in the Bedroom and Other Predicaments* (1932), *Fables for Our Time* (1940), and the bestselling *My World and Welcome to It* (1942).

"The wit makes fun of other persons; the satirist makes fun of the world; the humorist makes fun of himself."

The Night the Ghost Got In

James Thurber

He always half suspected that something would get him. by James Thurber

▲ Critical Viewing
The humor in Thurber's drawing echoes the humor in his essay. What makes this sketch funny? **ANALYZE**

Humorous Essay
Which details in the first two paragraphs tell you that this essay is based on actual events from the author's life?

The ghost that got into our house on the night of November 17, 1915, raised such a hullabaloo of misunderstandings that I am sorry I didn't just let it keep on walking, and go to bed. Its advent caused my mother to throw a shoe through a window of the house next door and ended up with my grandfather shooting a patrolman. I am sorry, therefore, as I have said, that I ever paid any attention to the footsteps.

They began about a quarter past one o'clock in the morning, a rhythmic, quick-cadenced walking around the dining-room table. My mother was asleep in one room upstairs, my brother Herman in another; grandfather was in the attic, in the old walnut bed which, as you will remember, once fell on my father. I had just stepped out of the bathtub and was busily rubbing myself with a towel when I heard the steps. They were the steps of a man walking rapidly around the dining-room table downstairs. The light from the bathroom shone down the back steps, which dropped directly into the dining-room; I could see the faint shine of plates on the plate-rail; I couldn't see the table. The steps kept going round and round the table; at regular intervals a board creaked, when it was trod upon. I supposed at first that it was my father or my brother Roy, who had gone to Indianapolis but were expected home at any time. I suspected next that it was a burglar. It did not enter my mind until later that it was a ghost.

After the walking had gone on for perhaps three minutes, I tiptoed to Herman's room. "Psst!" I hissed, in the dark, shaking him. "Awp," he said, in the low, hopeless tone of a despondent beagle—he always half suspected that something would "get him" in the night. I told him who I was. "There's something downstairs!" I said. He got up and followed me to the head of the back staircase. We listened together. There was no sound. The steps had ceased. Herman looked at me in some alarm: I had only the bath towel around my waist. He wanted to go back to bed, but I gripped his arm. "There's something down there!" I said. Instantly the steps began again, circled the dining-room table like a man running, and started up the stairs toward us, heavily, two at a time. The light still shone palely down the stairs; we saw nothing coming; we only heard the steps. Herman rushed to his room and slammed the door. I slammed shut the door at the stairs top and held my knee against it. After a long minute, I slowly opened it again. There was nothing there. There was no sound. None of us ever heard the ghost again.

Vocabulary

despondent (di spän′ dənt) *adj.* without courage or hope

The slamming of the doors had aroused mother: she peered out of her room. "What on earth are you boys doing?" she demanded. Herman ventured out of his room. "Nothing," he said, gruffly, but he was, in color, a light green. "What was all that running around downstairs?" said mother. So she had heard the steps, too! We just looked at her. "Burglars!" she shouted intuitively. I tried to quiet her by starting lightly downstairs.

"Come on, Herman," I said.

"I'll stay with Mother," he said. "She's all excited."

I stepped back onto the landing.

"Don't either of you go a step," said mother. "We'll call the police." Since the phone was downstairs, I didn't see how we were going to call the police—nor did I want the police—but mother made one of her quick, incomparable decisions. She flung up a window of her bedroom which faced the bedroom windows of the house of a neighbor, picked up a shoe, and whammed it through a pane of glass across the narrow space that separated the two houses. Glass tinkled into the bedroom occupied by a retired engraver named Bodwell and his wife. Bodwell had been for some years in rather a bad way and was subject to mild "attacks." Most everybody we knew or lived near had some kind of attacks.

Analyzing Cause and Effect

Describe the chain of cause-and-effect that begins with the slamming doors and ends with a shattered window.

It was now about two o'clock of a moonless night; clouds hung black and low. Bodwell was at the window in a minute, shouting, frothing a little, shaking his fist. "We'll sell the house and go back to Peoria," we could hear Mrs. Bodwell saying. It was some time before mother "got through" to Bodwell. "Burglars!" she shouted. "Burglars in the house!" Herman and I hadn't dared to tell her that it was not burglars but ghosts, for she was even more afraid of ghosts than of burglars. Bodwell at first thought that she meant there were burglars in his house, but finally he quieted down and called the police for us over an extension phone by his bed. After he had disappeared from the window, mother suddenly made as if to throw another shoe, not because there was further need of it, but, as she later explained,

Comprehension

Who does Mother think the intruders are?

Some nights she threw them all. by James Thurber

▲ **Critical Viewing**

Thurber drew this cartoon to illustrate this essay. How does the illustration add to the essay's humor? **ASSESS**

because the thrill of heaving a shoe through a window glass had enormously taken her fancy. I prevented her.

The police were on hand in a commendably short time: a Ford sedan full of them, two on motorcycles, and a patrol wagon with about eight in it and a few reporters. They began banging at our front door. Flashlights shot streaks of gleam up and down the walls, across the yard, down the walk between our house and Bodwell's. "Open up!" cried a hoarse voice. "We're men from Headquarters!" I wanted to go down and let them in, since there they were, but mother wouldn't hear of it. "You haven't a stitch on," she pointed out. "You'd catch your death." I wound the towel around me again. Finally the cops put their shoulders to our big heavy front door with its thick beveled glass and broke it in: I could hear a rending of wood and a splash of glass on the floor of the hall. Their lights played all over the living-room and crisscrossed nervously in the dining-room, stabbed into hallways, shot up the front stairs and finally up the back. They caught me standing in my towel at the top. A heavy policeman bounded up the steps. "Who are you?" he demanded. "I live here," I said. "Well, whattsa matta, ya hot?" he asked. I was, as a matter of fact, cold; I went to my room and pulled on some trousers. On my way out, a cop stuck a gun into my ribs. "Whatta you doin' here?" he demanded. "I live here," I said.

The officer in charge reported to mother. "No sign of nobody, lady," he said. "Musta got away—whatt'd he look like?" "There were two or three of them," mother said, "whooping and carrying on and slamming doors." "Funny," said the cop. "All ya windows and doors was locked on the inside tight as a tick."

Downstairs, we could hear the tromping of the other police. Police were all over the place; doors were yanked open, drawers were yanked open, windows were shot up and pulled down, furniture fell with dull thumps. A half-dozen policemen emerged out of the darkness of the front hallway upstairs. They began to ransack the floor: pulled beds away from walls, tore clothes off hooks in the closets, pulled suitcases and boxes off shelves. One of them found an old zither[1] that Roy had won in a pool tournament. "Looky here, Joe," he said, strumming it with a big paw. The cop named Joe took it and turned it over. "What is it?" he asked me. "It's an old zither our guinea pig used to sleep on," I said. It was true that a pet guinea pig we once had would never sleep anywhere except on the zither, but I should never have said so. Joe and the other cop looked at me a long time. They put the zither back on a shelf.

---

1. **zither** (zith′ ər) *n.* musical instrument with thirty to forty strings stretched across a flat soundboard and played with the fingers.

"No sign o' nuthin'," said the cop who had first spoken to mother. "This guy," he explained to the others, jerking a thumb at me, "was nekked. The lady seems historical." They all nodded, but said nothing; just looked at me. In the small silence we all heard a creaking in the attic. Grandfather was turning over in bed. "What's 'at?" snapped Joe. Five or six cops sprang for the attic door before I could **intervene** or explain. I realized that it would be bad if they burst in on grandfather unannounced, or even announced. He was going through a phase in which he believed that General Meade's men, under steady hammering by Stonewall Jackson, were beginning to retreat and even desert.

Vocabulary
intervene (in′ tər vēn′) *v.* take action in order to prevent something

When I got to the attic, things were pretty confused. Grandfather had evidently jumped to the conclusion that the police were deserters from Meade's army, trying to hide away in his attic. He bounded out of bed wearing a long flannel nightgown over long woolen underwear, a nightcap, and a leather jacket around his chest. The cops must have realized at once that the indignant white-haired old man belonged in the house, but they had no chance to say so. "Back, ye cowardly dogs!" roared grandfather. "Back t' the lines, ye yellow, lily-livered cattle!" With that, he fetched the officer who found the zither a flat-handed smack alongside his head that sent him sprawling. The others beat a retreat, but not fast enough; grandfather grabbed Zither's gun from its holster and let fly. The report seemed to crack the rafters; smoke filled the attic. A cop cursed and shot his hand to his shoulder. Somehow, we all finally got downstairs again and locked the door against the old gentleman. He fired once or twice more in the darkness and then went back to bed. "That was grandfather," I explained to Joe, out of breath. "He thinks you're deserters."

Comprehension
What does grandfather think is happening?

Police were all over the place. by James Thurber

◀ **Critical Viewing**
Compare this illustration with Thurber's description of the police investigation. What makes each funny? **EVALUATE**

Vocabulary

reluctant (re luk′ tənt) *adj.* unwilling; disinclined

blaspheming (blas fēm′ iŋ) *v.* cursing

"I'll say he does," said Joe.

The cops were **reluctant** to leave without getting their hands on somebody besides grandfather; the night had been distinctly a defeat for them. Furthermore, they obviously didn't like the "layout"; something looked—and I can see their viewpoint—phony. They began to poke into things again. A reporter, a thin-faced, wispy man, came up to me. I had put on one of mother's blouses, not being able to find anything else. The reporter looked at me with mingled suspicion and interest. "Just what the heck is the real lowdown here, Bud?" he asked. I decided to be frank with him. "We had ghosts," I said. He gazed at me a long time as if I were a slot machine into which he had, without results, dropped a nickel. Then he walked away. The cops followed him, the one grandfather shot holding his now-bandaged arm, cursing and **blaspheming**. "I'm gonna get my gun back from that old bird," said the zither-cop. "Yeh," said Joe. "You—and who else?" I told them I would bring it to the station house the next day.

"What was the matter with that one policeman?" mother asked, after they had gone. "Grandfather shot him," I said. "What for?" she demanded. I told her he was a deserter. "Of all things!" said mother. "He was such a nice-looking young man."

Grandfather was fresh as a daisy and full of jokes at breakfast next morning. We thought at first he had forgotten all about what had happened, but he hadn't. Over his third cup of coffee, he glared at Herman and me. "What was the idee of all them cops tarry-hootin' round the house last night?" he demanded. He had us there.

Critical Reading

Cite textual evidence to support your responses.

1. **Key Ideas and Details (a)** What event sets off the family's reactions? **(b) Classify:** Describe how each member of the family reacts. **(c) Distinguish:** In what way does Thurber's portrayal of himself in the situation differ from his portrayal of the other characters?
2. **Key Ideas and Details (a)** Why are the police summoned? **(b) Support:** How does this lack of communication contribute to the humor of the essay?
3. **Key Ideas and Details (a)** What does grandfather do when the police burst into his room? **(b) Infer:** Why do you think he does this?
4. **Integration of Knowledge and Ideas Evaluate:** Do you find the essay's conclusion fitting? Why?
5. **Integration of Knowledge and Ideas** This essay describes an event that took place in 1915. Has the American sense of humor changed since that time, or is this still funny? Explain. In your response, use at least two of these Essential Question words: *misunderstanding, slapstick, proportion, unconventional, exaggeration.* ***[Connecting to the Essential Question: What makes American literature American?]***

Close Reading Activities

The Night the Ghost Got In

Literary Analysis

1. **Key Ideas and Details** **Analyze cause and effect** in this essay by tracing the final event back to the event that started the action.
2. **Key Ideas and Details** Are most of the effects reasonable reactions to the causes? Explain.
3. **Craft and Structure** Use a chart like the one shown to identify one example of each literary technique Thurber uses in this **humorous essay.**

Element of Humor	Example
Hyperbole	
Understatement	
Idiom	
Dialect	

4. **Craft and Structure** **(a)** How does the speech of the policemen contrast with the type of language Thurber uses as the narrator? **(b)** In what ways does the policemen's speech add to the essay's humor?
5. **Integration of Knowledge and Ideas** What human behaviors or weaknesses help to explain the escalation of the events to the fever pitch they reach?

Common Core State Standards

Writing

2. Write explanatory texts to examine and convey complex ideas, concepts, and information clearly and accurately through the effective selection, organization, and analysis of content.

2.b. Develop the topic thoroughly by selecting the most significant and relevant facts, extended definitions, concrete details, quotations, or other information and examples appropriate to the audience's knowledge of the topic.

2.f. Provide a concluding statement or section that follows from and supports the information or explanation presented.

Language

4.a. Use context as a clue to the meaning of a word or phrase.

Vocabulary Acquisition and Use

Context Clues Review the vocabulary list on page 858. Then, answer *yes* or *no* to each question. Explain the context clues that help you.

1. If someone were tired, is it likely she would be *reluctant* to sleep?
2. If someone won a contest, would he become *despondent*?
3. If a parent saw a child about to fall, would she *intervene*?

Writing to Sources

Explanatory Text Thurber once wrote that "the humorist makes fun of himself, but in so doing, he identifies himself with people—that is, people everywhere, not for the purpose of taking them apart, but simply revealing their true nature." Write an **essay** in which you apply Thurber's ideas to this selection. To begin, identify points in the essay at which Thurber pokes fun at himself. Then, discuss how these examples relate Thurber to all people. Finally, draw conclusions about human nature and the role of humor in revealing it.

Chicago • Grass

Connecting to the Essential Question In these poems, work represents a source of strength and even redemption. As you read, look for details related to the value of labor and the vitality of workers. Doing so will help as you consider the Essential Question: **What makes American literature American?**

Reading Literature

4. Determine the meaning of words and phrases as they are used in the text, including figurative and connotative meanings; analyze the impact of specific word choices on meaning and tone, including language that is particularly fresh, engaging, or beautiful.

5. Analyze how an author's choices concerning how to structure specific parts of a text contribute to its overall structure and meaning as well as its aesthetic impact.

Language

5.a. Interpret figures of speech in context and analyze their role in the text.

Close Reading Focus

Apostrophe

Apostrophe is a literary device in which a speaker directly addresses a thing, concept, or person who is dead or absent. In the poem "Chicago," the speaker uses apostrophe to address the city:

They tell me you are wicked and I believe them . . .
And they tell me you are crooked and I answer: Yes . . .

Comparing Literary Works Sandburg's portrayal of the city of Chicago relies on a figure of speech called **personification,** in which a nonhuman subject is given human qualities. Chicago is depicted as laughing, sweating, bareheaded, and alive. In "Grass," personification takes a different form. Instead of showing a person speaking to the grass, it shows the grass speaking to the reader. As you read these poems, compare Sandburg's use of personification. Note how the personification affects the meaning of each poem and evokes different emotions in you as you read.

Preparing to Read Complex Texts One way to *clarify meaning in poetry* is to identify ideas that the poet repeats. The structure of repetition may provide a gentle reminder of an idea already expressed or a forceful emphasis of an important point. When you **evaluate the effects of repetition,** you examine the feelings or ideas the repetition emphasizes. As you read, use a chart like the one shown to record repeated words, phrases, ideas, and grammatical forms in each poem and examine their effects on meaning.

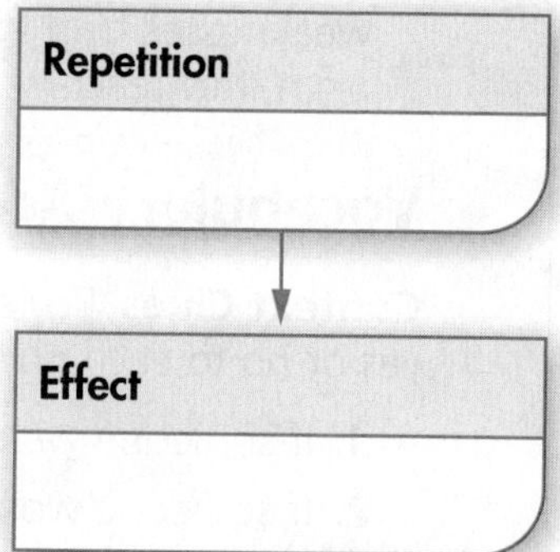

Vocabulary

You will encounter the words listed here in the text that follows. Copy the words into your notebook. Decide whether each word has a positive or a negative connotation.

brutal **cunning**
wanton

Carl Sandburg

(1878–1967)

Author of "Chicago" and "Grass"

Carl Sandburg was an optimist who believed in the power of ordinary people to fulfill their dreams. His poems were concrete and direct, capturing the energy and enthusiasm of industrial America. His vivid portraits of the working class made Sandburg one of the most popular poets of his day.

The son of Swedish immigrants, Sandburg left school after eighth grade to help support his family. He found work as a laborer. When he was nineteen, however, he set out to see the country, hitching rides on freight trains and taking odd jobs wherever he landed. He completed a stint in the Army, then tried college for a few years before hitting the road again.

The Bard of Chicago In 1912, Sandburg settled in the dynamic industrial city of Chicago. He worked as a newspaper reporter and began to publish his poetry in literary magazines. His first book, *Chicago Poems*, gained recognition for both Sandburg and Chicago. Over the next ten years, he published three more successful poetry collections: *Cornhuskers* (1918), *Smoke and Steel* (1920), and *Slabs of the Sunburnt West* (1922).

Collecting Songs While continuing to write poetry, Sandburg started a career as a folk singer. He prepared an anthology of folk songs he collected from cowboys, lumberjacks, factory workers, and hobos as he toured the country. *The American Songbag* appeared in 1927.

Winning Awards During his tours of the country, Sandburg also delivered lectures on Walt Whitman and Abraham Lincoln and collected material for a biography of Lincoln. The resulting multi-volume work earned him a Pulitzer Prize in 1940. In 1951, Sandburg received a second Pulitzer Prize for his *Complete Poems*. He was also awarded the United States Presidential Medal in 1964.

Sandburg offered a variety of definitions of poetry, among them these two: "Poetry is a search for syllables to shoot at the barriers of the unknown and the unknowable" and "Poetry is the opening and closing of a door, leaving those who look through to guess about what is seen during a moment."

"Nothing happens unless first we dream."

Chicago

Carl Sandburg

▼ Critical Viewing
In what ways does this bustling street scene of Chicago reflect Sandburg's poem? **CONNECT**

Hog Butcher for the World,
Tool Maker, Stacker of Wheat,
Player with Railroads and the Nation's Freight Handler;
Stormy, husky, brawling,
City of the Big Shoulders:

They tell me you are wicked and I believe them, for I have seen
your painted women under the gas lamps luring the farm boys.
And they tell me you are crooked and I answer: Yes, it is true I
have seen the gunman kill and go free to kill again.
And they tell me you are **brutal** and my reply is: On the faces of
women and children I have seen the marks of **wanton** hunger.
And having answered so I turn once more to those who sneer at
this my city, and I give them back the sneer and say to them:
Come and show me another city with lifted head singing so proud
to be alive and coarse and strong and **cunning**.
Flinging magnetic curses amid the toil of piling job on job, here is
a tall bold slugger set vivid against the little soft cities;
Fierce as a dog with tongue lapping for action, cunning as a
savage pitted against the wilderness,
Bareheaded,
Shoveling,
Wrecking,
Planning,
Building, breaking, rebuilding,
Under the smoke, dust all over his mouth, laughing with
white teeth,
Under the terrible burden of destiny laughing as a young man
laughs,
Laughing even as an ignorant fighter laughs who has never lost
a battle,
Bragging and laughing that under his wrist is the pulse, and
under his ribs the heart of the people,
Laughing!
Laughing the stormy, husky, brawling laughter of Youth, half-naked, sweating, proud to be a Hog Butcher, Tool Maker,
Stacker of Wheat, Player with Railroads and Freight Handler
to the Nation.

Vocabulary

brutal (brōōt′ əl) *adj.* cruel and without feeling; savage; violent

wanton (wän′ tən) *adj.* senseless; unjustified

cunning (kun′ iŋ) *adj.* skillful in deception; crafty; sly

Personification

In what way is the city like a "young man"?

Critical Reading

1. **Craft and Structure (a)** What names does the speaker use to address the city in the first stanza? **(b) Interpret:** What do the names tell you about the city's economy and atmosphere?
2. **Key Ideas and Details (a)** What are some of the city's faults? **(b) Interpret:** How do these faults affect the speaker's attitude toward the city?
3. **Key Ideas and Details (a) Summarize:** What overall sense of the city does Sandburg portray? **(b) Deduce:** Does Sandburg's portrayal reflect a larger sense of an American national character? Explain.

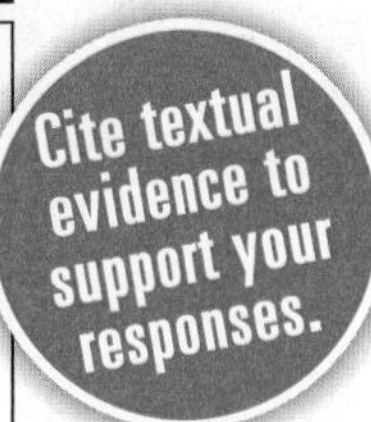
Cite textual evidence to support your responses.

GRASS

CARL SANDBURG

Evaluating Repetition
What idea does the poet emphasize through the repetition of the word "pile"?

Pile the bodies high at Austerlitz and Waterloo.[1]
Shovel them under and let me work—
    I am the grass; I cover all.

And pile them high at Gettysburg
And pile them high at Ypres and Verdun.[2]
Shovel them under and let me work.
Two years, ten years, and passengers ask the conductor:
    What place is this?
    Where are we now?

    I am grass.
    Let me work.

---

1. **Austerlitz** (ôs´ tər lits´) **and Waterloo** sites of battles of the Napoleonic Wars.
2. **Ypres** (ē´ pr) **and Verdun** (vər dun´) sites of battles of World War I.

Critical Reading

Cite textual evidence to support your responses.

1. **Key Ideas and Details** **(a)** In the first stanza, what does the grass claim it is able to do? **(b) Interpret:** What does this claim mean? Support your answer.
2. **Key Ideas and Details** **(a)** What does each place name in the poem represent? **(b) Draw Conclusions:** By focusing on war, rather than death in general, what is Sandburg suggesting?
3. **Integration of Knowledge and Ideas** What do these poems suggest about the value of industry and labor to a society? In your response, use at least two of these Essential Question words: *ambition, magnitude, expansion, regional. **[Connecting to the Essential Question: How does literature shape or reflect society?]***

Close Reading Activities Chicago • Grass

Literary Analysis

1. **Craft and Structure** **(a)** In which lines of "Chicago" does Sandburg address the city directly? **(b)** What is the effect of this use of **apostrophe**?
2. **Craft and Structure** **(a)** Using a chart like the one shown, identify four examples of **personification** in the poem "Chicago." **(b)** For each example, identify the quality it communicates about the city.

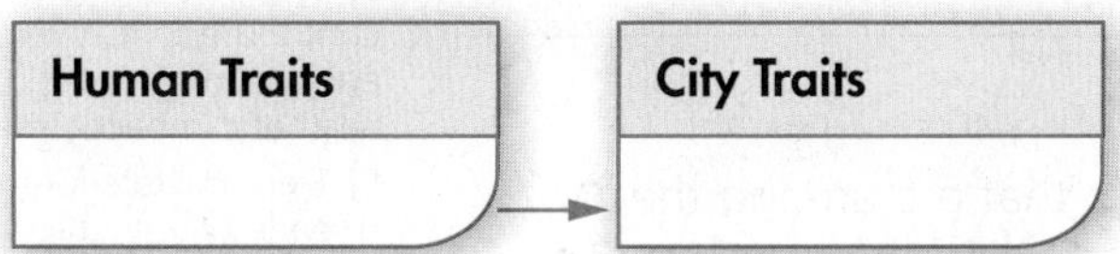

3. **Craft and Structure** **Evaluate the effect of repetition** on meaning in "Chicago." Why do you think "laughing" is repeated near the end of the poem?
4. **Craft and Structure** What entire line is repeated in "Grass" and to what effect?
5. **Comparing Literary Works** **(a)** How do Sandburg's uses of personification in "Chicago" and "Grass" differ? **(b)** In what ways do these different uses of personification serve the distinct goals of each poem?

Common Core State Standards

Writing

2. Write explanatory texts to examine and convey complex ideas, concepts, and information clearly and accurately through the effective selection, organization, and analysis of content.

2.b. Develop the topic thoroughly by selecting the most significant and relevant quotations.

9.a. Apply *grades 11–12 Reading standards* to literature.

Language

4.a. Use context as a clue to the meaning of a word or phrase.

Vocabulary Acquisition and Use

Context Clues Use a word from the vocabulary list on page 866 to complete each sentence below. Use each word only once. Explain the context clues that help you.

1. It was clear that the family had done nothing to deserve the ______ suffering that beset them.
2. That fox was a ______ creature, and the farmer could not figure out how to keep him from stealing eggs.
3. The winter storm was ______, and many members of the herd were lost in the snow.

Writing to Sources

Explanatory Text Review the chart of repeated words and phrases you made while you read these poems. Use those notes as the prewriting stage for an **essay** in which you analyze Sandburg's use of repetition in the poem "Chicago." In your essay, explain how the poet's repetition of words, phrases, sentence structures, and grammatical forms emphasizes particular ideas and heightens specific emotions. Support your ideas with relevant quotations from the poems.

Building Knowledge and Insight

Robert Frost's Poetry

Connecting to the Essential Question Many readers have learned about rural New England from Robert Frost's poetry. As you read, notice details that create a portrait of life in rural New England. This activity will help as you consider the Essential Question: **What is the relationship between literature and place?**

Common Core State Standards

Reading Literature

5. Analyze how an author's choices concerning how to structure specific parts of a text contribute to its overall structure and meaning as well as its aesthetic impact.

9. Demonstrate knowledge of early-twentieth-century foundational works of American literature, including how two or more texts from the same period treat similar themes or topics.

Close Reading Focus

Blank Verse; Pastorals

Robert Frost wove sound and sense into poems that are among the best loved in American literature. He often wrote in **blank verse,** or *unrhymed iambic pentameter,* which mimics the sound of natural speech:

- The basic unit of *meter* is a *foot*, which is usually one stressed syllable (´) and one or more unstressed syllables (˘).
- The most common foot in English is the *iamb*, one unstressed syllable followed by a stressed syllable (˘ ´).
- A line containing five iambs is written in *iambic pentameter.*

The use of iambic pentameter, blank verse, and other meters affects the sound and mood of a poem. Notice these effects as you read.

Many of Frost's poems, including five in this grouping, can be categorized as **pastorals,** or poems that deal with rural settings. Traditional pastorals present idealized views of rural life. In Frost's hands, however, rural life can be fraught with ethical lapses, accident, and conflict. As you read these poems, examine their portrayals of rural life, and notice the ways in which setting contributes to meaning.

Preparing to Read Complex Texts One way to *clarify the essential meaning* of poems is to **read poetry in sentences** rather than in poetic lines. Instead of pausing at the end of each line, follow the punctuation: pause briefly after commas, and pause longer after periods. Use the information in the chart shown here as a guide to your reading. However, as you apply this strategy, remain sensitive to the poem's pattern of organization, noticing how line breaks enrich and extend the meanings of individual sentences.

Sign	Means
(diamond sign with straight arrow)	No punctuation: Continue without pause.
(diamond sign with curved arrow)	Pause for comma, dash, or semicolon and continue.
(stop sign)	Full stop for period

Vocabulary

The words below are important to understanding the text that follows. Copy the words into your notebook. Which word has a root that means "light"?

poise **luminary**
rueful

Robert Frost (1874–1963)

In becoming one of America's most loved and respected poets, Robert Frost displayed the same persistence and determination exhibited by the rural New Englanders he depicted in his poems. Although he eventually received four Pulitzer Prizes and read at a presidential inauguration, Frost's success as a poet did not come overnight or easily. Only after years of rejection by publishers did he achieve the acceptance for which he had worked so hard.

Early Struggles Frost was born in San Francisco, California. His father died when Frost was eleven, and his mother moved the family to the textile city of Lawrence, Massachusetts. After graduating from high school, Frost briefly attended Dartmouth College. Disliking college life, he left school and spent time working as a farmer, mill hand, journalist, and schoolteacher. During his spare time, he wrote poetry and dreamed of someday being able to support himself solely by writing.

"Like a piece of ice on a hot stove the poem must ride on its own melting."

The English Years Frost married and spent ten years farming in New Hampshire. In 1912, unable to get his poems published, he moved his family to England. While living in England, Frost befriended a number of well-known poets, including Ezra Pound, and succeeded in publishing two collections of poetry, *A Boy's Will* (1913) and *North of Boston* (1914). When he returned to the United States in 1915, Frost found that his success in England had spread across the Atlantic, and he was on the road to fame.

Critical Acclaim Frost published several more volumes of poetry, for which he received many awards. He taught and lectured at dozens of schools and continued to farm in Vermont and New Hampshire. In 1960, at John F. Kennedy's invitation, Frost became the first poet to read his work at a presidential inauguration.

Deeper Meanings Frost's poetry was popular with both critics and the general public. He used traditional verse forms and conversational language to paint vivid portraits of New England. Despite their apparent simplicity, however, his poems are filled with profound meanings.

Like his poetry, Frost's personality also had multiple levels. In his public appearances, Frost presented himself as a folksy farmer who just happened to write poetry. In reality, however, Frost was a deep thinker whose darker, complicated personality sometimes mystified those who knew him.

BIRCHES

ROBERT FROST

BACKGROUND Robert Frost spent most of his life in New Hampshire, Vermont, and Massachusetts—a heavily forested region of the United States. One of the most common trees of this region is the birch, a tall, slender tree with white bark and small, dainty leaves. Despite its graceful trunk, though, the birch is by no means delicate. Its wood is dense, hardy, and flexible, and its bark is practically waterproof (which made it a popular canoe covering among Native Americans). In this poem, Frost celebrates the birch's resilience and suggests that the human spirit shares this quality.

When I see birches bend to left and right
Across the lines of straighter darker trees,
I like to think some boy's been swinging them.
But swinging doesn't bend them down to stay
As ice storms do. Often you must have seen them
Loaded with ice a sunny winter morning
After a rain. They click upon themselves
As the breeze rises, and turn many-colored
As the stir cracks and crazes their enamel.
Soon the sun's warmth makes them shed crystal shells
Shattering and avalanching on the snow crust—
Such heaps of broken glass to sweep away
You'd think the inner dome of heaven had fallen.
They are dragged to the withered bracken by the load,
And they seem not to break; though once they are bowed
So low for long, they never right themselves:
You may see their trunks arching in the woods
Years afterwards, trailing their leaves on the ground
Like girls on hands and knees that throw their hair
Before them over their heads to dry in the sun.
But I was going to say when Truth broke in
With all her matter of fact about the ice storm,
I should prefer to have some boy bend them
As he went out and in to fetch the cows—
Some boy too far from town to learn baseball,
Whose only play was what he found himself,
Summer or winter, and could play alone.
One by one he subdued his father's trees
By riding them down over and over again
Until he took the stiffness out of them,
And not one but hung limp, not one was left
For him to conquer. He learned all there was
To learn about not launching out too soon
And so not carrying the tree away
Clear to the ground. He always kept his **poise**

◀ Critical Viewing
Frost's poem expresses the speaker's reaction to birch trees. What response does this photograph of birches evoke in you? **CONNECT**

Blank Verse
Does this poem sound like natural speech? Explain.

Vocabulary
poise (poiz) *n.* balance; stability

Comprehension
What does the speaker think of when he sees "birches bend to left and right"?

To the top branches, climbing carefully
With the same pains you use to fill a cup
Up to the brim, and even above the brim.
Then he flung outward, feet first, with a swish,
Kicking his way down through the air to the ground.
So was I once myself a swinger of birches.
And so I dream of going back to be.
It's when I'm weary of considerations,
And life is too much like a pathless wood
Where your face burns and tickles with the cobwebs
Broken across it, and one eye is weeping
From a twig's having lashed across it open.
I'd like to get away from earth awhile
And then come back to it and begin over.
May no fate willfully misunderstand me
And half grant what I wish and snatch me away
Not to return. Earth's the right place for love:
I don't know where it's likely to go better.
I'd like to go by climbing a birch tree,
And climb black branches up a snow-white trunk
Toward heaven, till the tree could bear no more,
But dipped its top and set me down again.
That would be good both going and coming back.
One could do worse than be a swinger of birches.

Reading Poetry in Sentences

How does reading lines 43–47 as a sentence help clarify its meaning?

Critical Reading

Cite textual evidence to support your responses.

1. **Key Ideas and Details (a)** What is the connection between the ice storm and the bent birches? **(b)** What does the speaker prefer to think when he sees birches "bend to left and right"? **(c) Interpret:** What does the speaker feel about the facts concerning the real causes of the bowed trees?
2. **Key Ideas and Details (a)** What is the connection between the "swinger of birches" and the speaker? **(b) Interpret:** What does the activity of swinging on birches come to symbolize for the speaker in the poem?
3. **Key Ideas and Details (a) Interpret:** What does the speaker say he would like to "begin over"? **(b) Analyze:** What aspects of this poem reflect the speaker's conflicting attitudes about life?
4. **Integration of Knowledge and Ideas Speculate:** What kinds of events, experiences, and feelings in his life might have caused the speaker to make the admission expressed in lines 48–49?

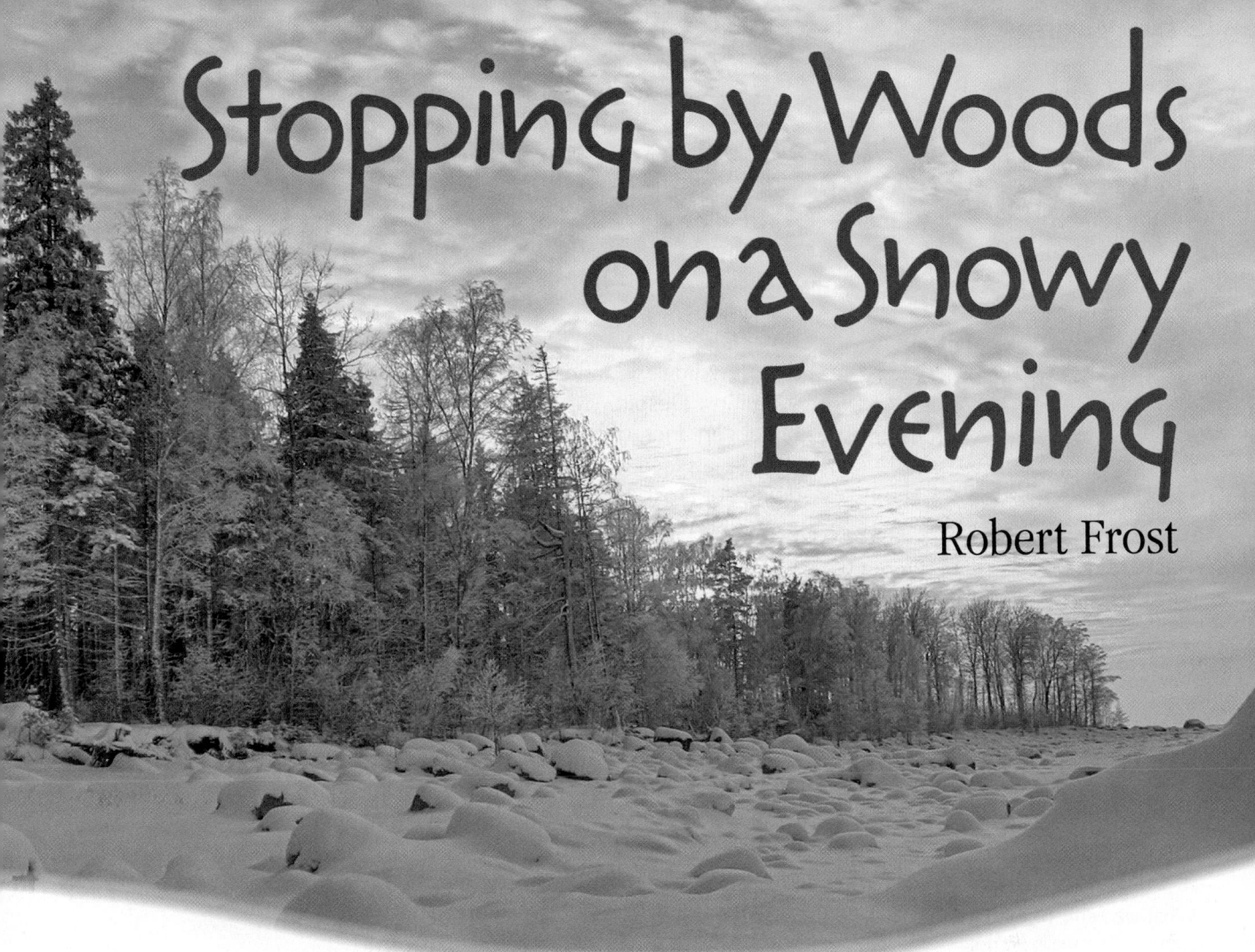

Stopping by Woods on a Snowy Evening

Robert Frost

Whose woods these are I think I know.
His house is in the village though;
He will not see me stopping here
To watch his woods fill up with snow.

My little horse must think it queer
To stop without a farmhouse near
Between the woods and frozen lake
The darkest evening of the year.

He gives his harness bells a shake
To ask if there is some mistake.
The only other sound's the sweep
Of easy wind and downy flake.

The woods are lovely, dark and deep,
But I have promises to keep,
And miles to go before I sleep,
And miles to go before I sleep.

▲ Critical Viewing

What elements of this scene differ from the one the speaker describes? What do the two scenes have in common? **COMPARE AND CONTRAST**

Blank Verse

Is this poem an example of blank verse? Explain.

EXEMPLAR TEXT

Mending Wall

ROBERT FROST

BACKGROUND Much of Frost's poetry reflects not only the New England landscape, but also its distinctive personalities. Despite Frost's city roots, he was able to gain the acceptance of his country neighbors and to enter their world—a place that was usually closed to outsiders. In doing so, Frost gathered a wealth of material for his poetry.

Pastorals

What activities do lines 5–9 suggest are part of rural life?

▼ Critical Viewing

What elements of this picture suggest that walls do not belong in the natural world? **ANALYZE**

Something there is that doesn't love a wall,
That sends the frozen-ground-swell under it
And spills the upper boulders in the sun,
And makes gaps even two can pass abreast.
The work of hunters is another thing:
I have come after them and made repair
Where they have left not one stone on a stone,
But they would have the rabbit out of hiding,
To please the yelping dogs. The gaps I mean,
No one has seen them made or heard them made,
But at spring mending-time we find them there.
I let my neighbor know beyond the hill;
And on a day we meet to walk the line
And set the wall between us once again.
We keep the wall between us as we go.

To each the boulders that have fallen to each.
And some are loaves and some so nearly balls
We have to use a spell to make them balance:
"Stay where you are until our backs are turned!"
We wear our fingers rough with handling them.
Oh, just another kind of outdoor game,
One on a side. It comes to little more:
There where it is we do not need the wall:
He is all pine and I am apple orchard.
My apple trees will never get across
And eat the cones under his pines, I tell him.
He only says, "Good fences make good neighbors."
Spring is the mischief in me, and I wonder
If I could put a notion in his head:
"*Why* do they make good neighbors? Isn't it
Where there are cows? But here there are no cows.
Before I built a wall I'd ask to know
What I was walling in or walling out,
And to whom I was like to give offense.
Something there is that doesn't love a wall,
That wants it down." I could say "Elves" to him,
But it's not elves exactly, and I'd rather
He said it for himself. I see him there,
Bringing a stone grasped firmly by the top
In each hand, like an old-stone savage armed.
He moves in darkness as it seems to me,
Not of woods only and the shade of trees.
He will not go behind his father's saying,
And he likes having thought of it so well
He says again, "Good fences make good neighbors."

Something there is that doesn't love a wall.

Reading Poetry in Sentences
Read lines 28–31 as sentences. In what ways are their meanings clarified?

Critical Reading

1. **Key Ideas and Details** **(a)** In the first stanza of "Stopping by Woods," what does the speaker do? **(b) Infer:** What internal conflict do these actions cause?
2. **Craft and Structure** **(a)** What phrase is repeated in the poem's last two lines? **(b) Analyze:** How does this repetition reinforce the poem's theme?
3. **Key Ideas and Details** **(a)** In "Mending Wall," what two causes of gaps in walls does the speaker identify? **(b) Speculate:** In what ways are these two causes expressions of a general force the speaker struggles to name?

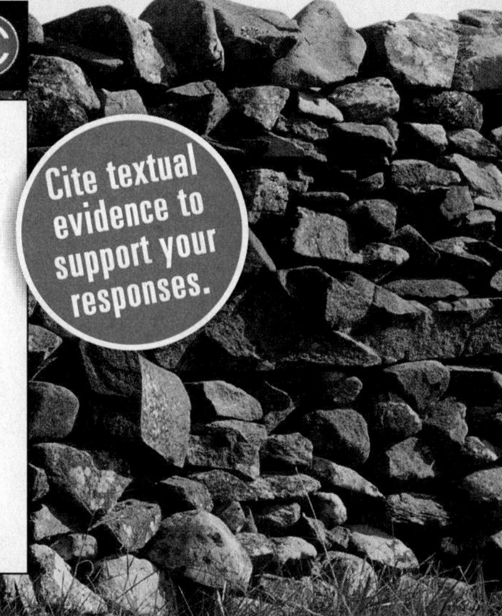
Cite textual evidence to support your responses.

"Out, Out—"

ROBERT FROST

The buzz saw snarled and rattled in the yard
And made dust and dropped stove-length sticks of wood,
Sweet-scented stuff when the breeze drew across it.
And from there those that lifted eyes could count
Five mountain ranges one behind the other
Under the sunset far into Vermont.
And the saw snarled and rattled, snarled and rattled,
As it ran light, or had to bear a load.
And nothing happened: day was all but done.

Blank Verse

Which words or phrases in lines 5–7 capture the rhythms of everyday speech?

Call it a day, I wish they might have said
To please the boy by giving him the half hour
That a boy counts so much when saved from work.
His sister stood beside them in her apron
To tell them "Supper." At the word, the saw,
As if to prove saws knew what supper meant,
Leaped out at the boy's hand, or seemed to leap—
He must have given the hand. However it was,
Neither refused the meeting. But the hand!
The boy's first outcry was a rueful laugh,
As he swung toward them holding up the hand,
Half in appeal, but half as if to keep
The life from spilling. Then the boy saw all—
Since he was old enough to know, big boy
Doing a man's work, though a child at heart—
He saw all spoiled. "Don't let him cut my hand off—
The doctor, when he comes. Don't let him, sister!"
So. But the hand was gone already.
The doctor put him in the dark of ether.[1]
He lay and puffed his lips out with his breath.
And then—the watcher at his pulse took fright.
No one believed. They listened at his heart.
Little—less—nothing!—and that ended it.
No more to build on there. And they, since they
Were not the one dead, turned to their affairs.

Vocabulary

rueful (ro͞o′ fəl) *adj.* feeling or showing someone sorrow or pity

Pastorals

In what ways do lines 19–34 portray a harsh view of rural life?

NO ONE BELIEVED. THEY LISTENED AT HIS HEART.

---

1. **ether** (ē′ thər) *n.* chemical compound used as an anesthetic.

Critical Reading

1. **Key Ideas and Details (a)** At what time of day does the accident occur? **(b) Analyze:** What is ironic about the fact that the boy is cut at precisely that moment?
2. **Key Ideas and Details (a)** What are the boy's first and second responses to the accident? **(b) Interpret:** What does the speaker mean by the expression "the boy saw all" in line 22?
3. **Integration of Knowledge and Ideas Connect:** The title comes from a scene in Shakespeare's *Macbeth* in which Macbeth laments the death of his wife with these words: "Out, out, brief candle! / Life's but a walking shadow, a poor player, / That struts and frets his hour upon the stage, / And then is heard no more." What does this quotation reveal about the poem's theme?

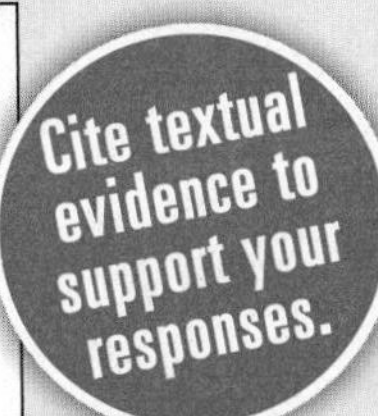
Cite textual evidence to support your responses.

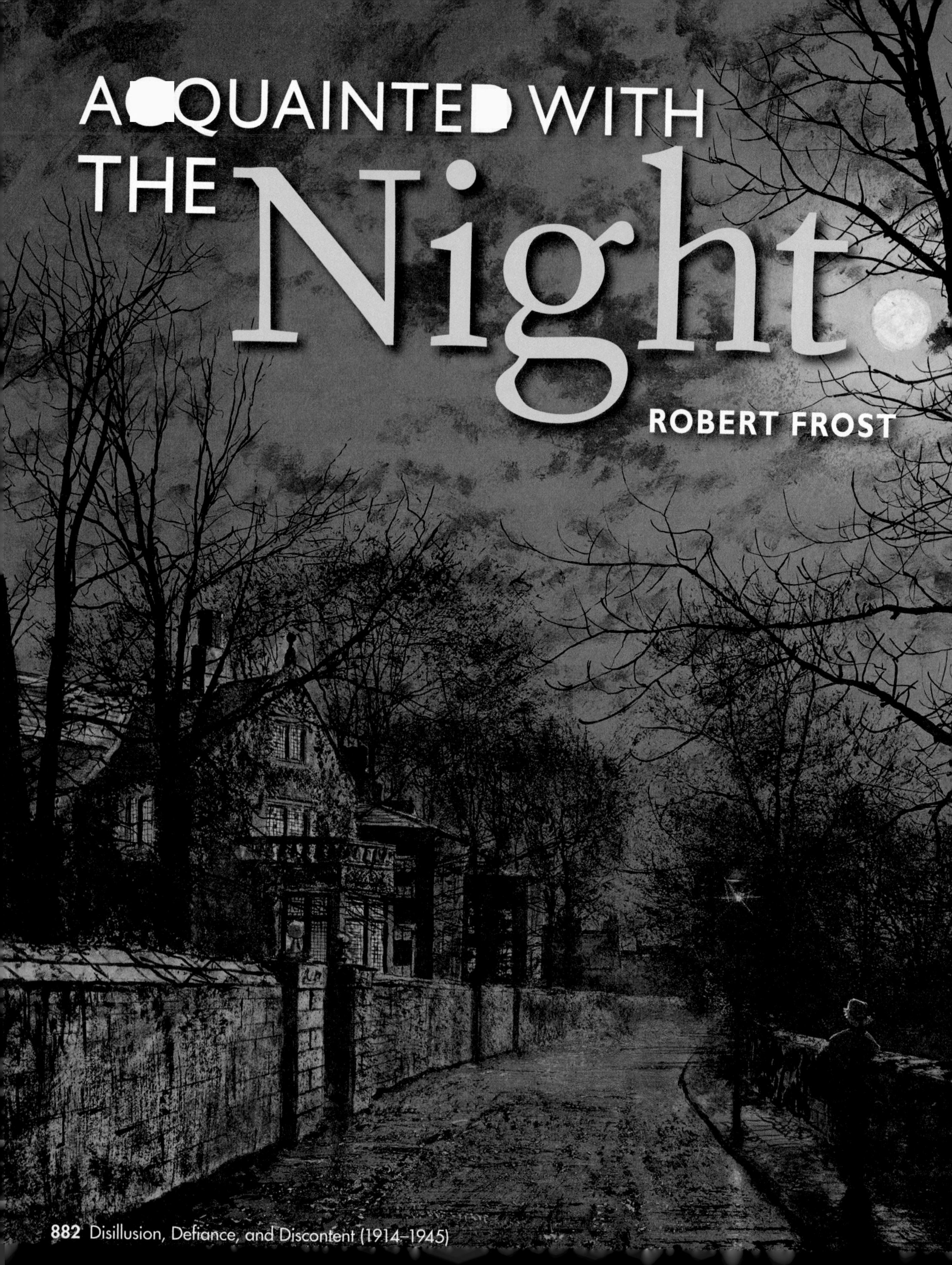

ACQUAINTED WITH THE Night

ROBERT FROST

BACKGROUND: Frost wrote this poem in terza rima, a verse form invented by the Italian poet Dante (see sidebar below). The form is very challenging in English, and Frost's poem is one of only a few examples in American literature.

I have been one acquainted with the night.
I have walked out in rain—and back in rain.
I have outwalked the furthest city light.

I have looked down the saddest city lane.
I have passed by the watchman on his beat
And dropped my eyes, unwilling to explain.

I have stood still and stopped the sound of feet
When far away an interrupted cry
Came over houses from another street,

But not to call me back or say good-by;
And further still at an unearthly height
One luminary clock against the sky

Proclaimed the time was neither wrong nor right.
I have been one acquainted with the night.

Blank Verse

How do you know that this poem is not an example of blank verse?

Vocabulary

luminary (lo͞o′ mə ner′ ē) *adj.* giving off light

WORLD LITERATURE CONNECTION

Terza Rima

Terza rima (Italian for "third rhyme") is a form of poetry consisting of three-line stanzas with the rhyme scheme *aba, bcb, cdc,* and so on. In other words, the first and third lines of each stanza rhyme with each other, and the second line rhymes with the first and third lines of the following stanza. The Italian poet Dante (ca. 1300) was the first to write a long epic poem—his masterpiece, *The Divine Comedy*—in terza rima. This choice was not accidental: in the Christian tradition, the number *3* is symbolic of the divine, and this number informs all levels of the poem's structure. The work is divided into three sections—the "Inferno," "Purgatorio," and "Paradisio"—each of which, in turn, is divided into 33 subsections called cantos. All together, the sections tell the story of the poet's imaginary journey through hell, purgatory, and finally into the light of heaven. In addition to its association with the number *3*, terza rima is a fitting verse structure for Dante's poem: the rhymes, echoing between stanzas and linking one to the next, draw the reader forward, just as the poet himself was compelled forward on his epic journey.

CONNECT TO THE LITERATURE

With its cycling rhyme scheme and reflections of a Christian worldview, terza rima was a meaningful verse form for Dante's epic. Explain how it fits the action and setting of Frost's twentieth-century poem.

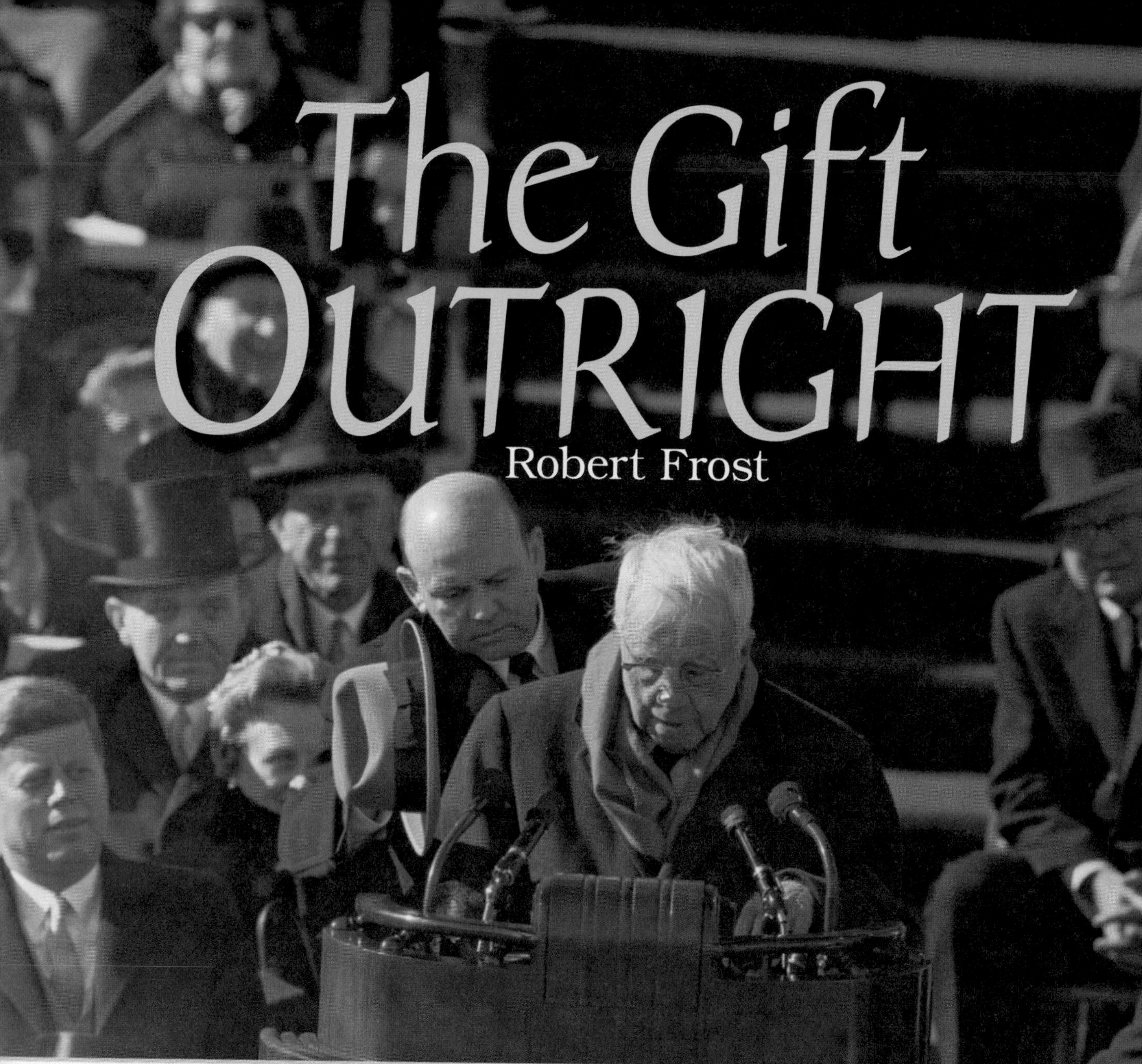

The Gift Outright

Robert Frost

BACKGROUND During the planning stages of John F. Kennedy's presidential inauguration, his staff approached Robert Frost with a request: Would the poet write and recite a poem for the inauguration? Frost declined to write something new but agreed to recite "The Gift Outright." President Kennedy had a second request: Would Frost change the word "would" to "will" in the last line of the poem? The poet agreed. Shortly before the inauguration date, Frost was struck by inspiration and, despite his earlier refusal, drafted a forty-two-line poem, "Dedication," especially for the ceremony. The weather on inauguration day was windy, clear, and sunny. As Frost stood at the podium reading his new poem, the glare of the sun and the whipping wind made it almost impossible for him to see the words on the page. After struggling through the first half of "Dedication," he gave up the effort, and recited "The Gift Outright" from memory.

The land was ours before we were the land's.
She was our land more than a hundred years
Before we were her people. She was ours
In Massachusetts, in Virginia,
But we were England's, still colonials,
Possessing what we still were unpossessed by,
Possessed by what we now no more possessed.
Something we were withholding made us weak
Until we found out that it was ourselves
We were withholding from our land of living,
And forthwith found salvation in surrender.
Such as we were we gave ourselves outright
(The deed of gift was many deeds of war)
To the land vaguely realizing westward,
But still unstoried, artless, unenhanced,
Such as she was, such as she would become.

Reading Poetry in Sentences

In what ways does reading this poem in sentences help clarify its meaning?

Critical Reading

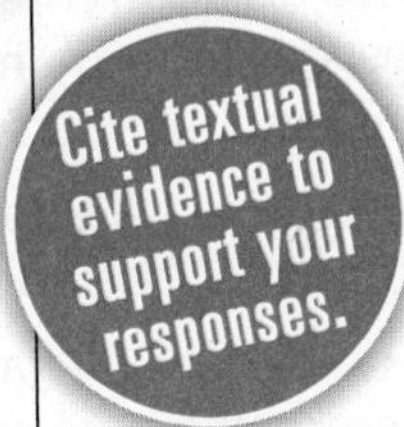
Cite textual evidence to support your responses.

1. **Key Ideas and Details (a)** In "Acquainted with the Night," how does the speaker react to the watchman? **(b) Interpret:** What is the speaker "unwilling to explain"?
2. **Key Ideas and Details (a)** What does the speaker hear in the third stanza? **(b) Infer:** Based on line 10, what does it seem the speaker hoped?
3. **Key Ideas and Details (a)** In "The Gift Outright," what does the speaker say was the relationship between the land and the people in colonial America? **(b) Interpret:** What do you think the speaker means by the phrase "the land was ours"?
4. **Key Ideas and Details (a)** In what action did the early Americans find salvation? **(b) Connect:** What is the meaning of the poem's title?
5. **Integration of Knowledge and Ideas** What understanding of rural New England and America as a whole do these poems convey? Explain. In your response, use at least two of these Essential Question words: *industrious, self-determination, community, courage, severe.* ***[Connecting to the Essential Question: What is the relationship between literature and place?]***

Literary Analysis

Common Core State Standards

Writing

1. Write arguments to support claims in an analysis of substantive topics or texts, using valid reasoning and relevant and sufficient evidence. *(p. 887)*

Language

4.b. Identify and correctly use patterns of word changes that indicate different meanings or parts of speech. *(p. 887)*

5. Demonstrate understanding of word relationships. *(p. 887)*

1. **Key Ideas and Details** Explain how **reading poetry in sentences** clarified your understanding of **(a)** two specific lines; **(b)** the meaning of one poem as a whole.
2. **Craft and Structure** Traditional pastorals present nature and life itself as idyllic. In "Birches," however, nature gives rise to conflicting feelings. Use a chart like the one shown to provide evidence of the speaker's ambivalence.

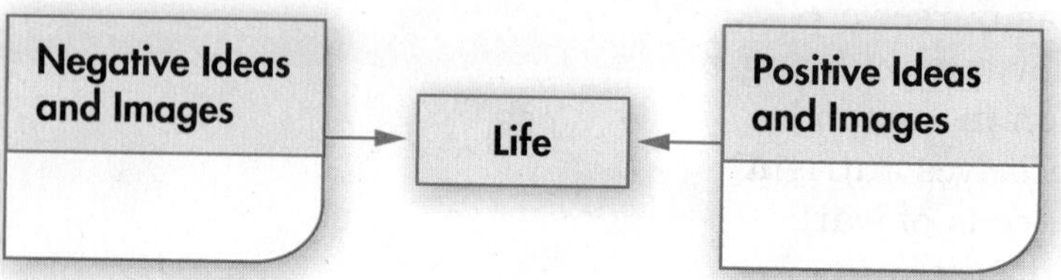

3. **Key Ideas and Details** What ideas about land ownership and boundaries do "Stopping by Woods on a Snowy Evening" and "Mending Wall" express?
4. **Key Ideas and Details** Read "'Out, Out—,'" pausing at the end of each line. Then, read the poem as a series of sentences. How does each reading affect your understanding of the poem?
5. **Craft and Structure** **(a)** Find two instances in "'Out, Out—'" where Frost deviates from **blank verse. (b)** In what ways do these metrical variations emphasize a specific idea or image?
6. **Craft and Structure** **(a)** Rewrite "The Gift Outright" as five prose sentences. **(b)** What is the effect of this approach?
7. **Craft and Structure** **(a)** Which of the poems presented here are not written in blank verse? **(b)** What is one poetic device that distinguishes these poems from the ones written in blank verse? Explain.
8. **Craft and Structure** Which of the poems in this grouping would you classify as **pastorals**? Explain your choices.
9. **Integration of Knowledge and Ideas** Frost's poems often have simple surfaces—plain language and a conversational quality—but complex meanings. Choose one of these poems and explain how it combines apparent simplicity with deeper meanings.
10. **Analyzing Visual Information** Explain the humor in this cartoon.

Vocabulary Acquisition and Use

Word Root: Latin Root *-lum-*

The word *luminary*, which means "giving off light," is based on the Latin root *-lum-*, meaning "light." The same root appears in the words *luminous* and *illuminate*. Complete each sentence with one of the words listed below. Use each word once. Explain each of your decisions.

luminous illuminate illumination

1. Is that small flashlight enough to ______ the entire campsite?
2. Cindy hoped to wear a ______ golden gown, but wound up in her sister's puffy, purple prom dress.
3. The teacher explained that students who are baffled may seek ______ in tutoring sessions.

Vocabulary: Analogies

Analogies show the relationships between pairs of words. Complete each analogy using a word from the vocabulary list on page 872. In each, your choice should create a word pair that matches the relationship between the first two words given. Then, explain your answers.

1. *Scorching* is to *fire* as ______ is to *moon*.
2. *Swiftness* is to *runner* as ______ is to *dancer*.
3. *Joyful* is to *celebrant* as ______ is to *mourner*.

Writing to Sources

Argument Robert Frost wrote during the early- to mid-20th century, an era that saw two world wars, growing industrialization, and increasing urbanization. Write a **critical essay** in which you explore this question: In the 20th and 21st centuries, how can poetry set in natural or rural settings be meaningful? In your essay, consider your own experiences in nature, whether good or bad, and draw conclusions about the relevance of pastoral poetry today.

Prewriting Reread Frost's poems, and make notes about how he describes the countryside. Then, decide whether your own experiences in nature have caused you to have similar or different feelings. Make notes explaining why.

Drafting Begin by stating your opinion on the relevance or importance of the pastoral in today's world. Then, support your opinion with examples from your own experience. In addition, use examples from Frost's poems to bolster your own views or to contrast his worldview with your own.

Revising As you review your work, make sure that you have clearly linked your ideas. Add transitions to introduce examples, where necessary.

Model: Revising to Smooth Transitions

In an age characterized by busyness, speed, and complexity, we sorely need real or imaginative escapes into nature. Robert Frost would agree. ^For example, in "Birches," he admits that he would "like to get away…for awhile" when he is "weary of considerations."

Phrases like *for example* provide transitions that improve clarity.

CONTEMPORARY CONNECTION

Trapped in a Comic Book

Cartoonist/Author

Cartooning as Literature

During the 1920s, James Thurber (p. 860) gave his comic stories an edge by illustrating them with his signature cartoons and drawings. These cartoons, witty, understated, and decidedly highbrow, were appreciated by a broad range of readers. In contrast, comic books, the action-packed, hero-driven tales that became wildly popular in the 1940s and 1950s, were not considered literature. They were frowned upon by many parents and educators. Today, looking at the many combinations of text and art available to readers—graphic novels of many genres, manga, collections of comic strips, and web comics—it becomes clear that the boundary between cartoon and serious literary art has blurred.

Cartoonist Jules Feiffer understands the nuance and power of comics, or "sequential art." He once said, "You can use cartoons to tell the truth about people." Perhaps this is where the connection between cartoons and literature lies. There is nothing more valuable about literature than the truth it contains.

About the Author

Jules Feiffer, born in 1929, is a big believer in pictures. As a lonely child, he filled his days reading the funnies and drawing his own. He worked on other artists' comic books in his early professional years, but he soon developed his distinctive personal style. His output has been exceptional. He drew cartoons for the alternative newspaper *The Village Voice* for decades; he wrote plays and screenplays. He won an Oscar in 1961 for the short animated film "Munro," about a 4-year-old boy drafted into the army. In 1986, Feiffer earned a Pulitzer Prize for editorial cartooning. As politically and socially acute as his creations tend to be, Feiffer also has a playful side and enjoys writing for young people. "Trapped in a Comic Book" shows his approach to a younger audience. Feiffer has thought a lot about what kids do and don't want. "What kids hate most," he insists, "is to be lectured at."

TRAPPED IN A COMIC BOOK

JULES FEIFFER

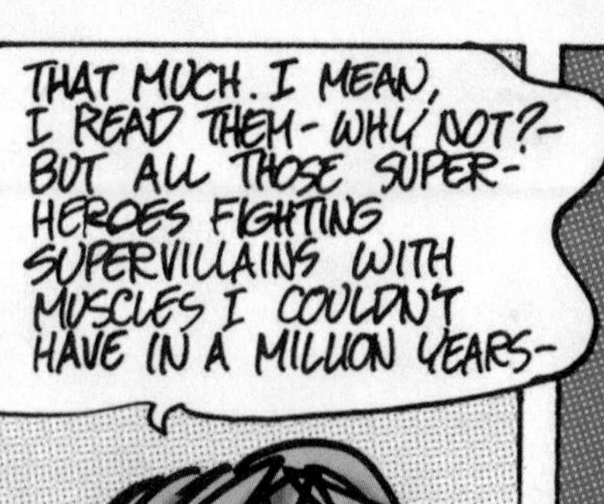

AND THIS IS WHAT I'M EXPLAINING TO THIS CARTOONIST IN HIS STUDIO WHERE I'M ON A SCHOOL VISIT WITH MY CLASS:

SO I THINK IT WOULD BE BETTER IF YOU DREW SOMETHING REAL FOR A CHANGE, LIKE MY LITTLE BROTHER'S ALWAYS GETTING ME IN TROUBLE AND WHEN I PUSH HIM EVEN A LITTLE, WHOSE SIDE DOES MY MOTHER TAKE, EVEN WHEN HE STARTED IT? **HIS!** I MEAN, IF YOU DREW A COMIC ZAPPING A VILLAIN LIKE MY KID BROTHER, THAT'S A STORY KIDS LIKE ME WOULD GO OUT AND BUY.

I'M ONLY TRYING TO HELP HIM, BECAUSE NORMAL KIDS LIKE ME ARE THE ONES WHO READ HIS STUFF, SO **SHOULDN'T** HE WANT TO KNOW WHAT I THINK?

OK, SO I LOOK CLOSER.

BUT THAT'S ALL I SEE, THIS SUPER-HERO FIGHTING THIS SUPERVILLAIN.
AND I'M RIGHT ON TOP OF THEM, AND THEY'RE STILL BEATING EACH OTHER UP.
SO I LOOK EVEN CLOSER AND I SEE A BUNCH OF JUMBLY LINES.
AND I LOOK EVEN CLOSER AND IT'S JUST A BLURRY, FIDGETY, WEIRD AND AWESOME NOTHING.
AND THEN I FALL IN.
AND I'M TOTALLY INSIDE THIS PICTURE—
WHICH IS VERY CLEAR NOW!

BUT WHEN YOU'RE STANDING ONLY A FOOT AWAY FROM FIGHTING SUPERGUYS IT'S NOT WHAT YOU THINK.
THWACK
POW
IT'S LIKE, "THIS IS IT? DON'T YOU DO ANYTHING ELSE?"
THUD
SMASH
WHOMP
AND THE SOUND EFFECTS CAN DRIVE YOU CRAZY!
PLUNGE!
EDOP
SOKK
SO I JUMP PANELS.
BUT THESE TWO NOISY SUPER-JERKS FOLLOW ME EVERYWHERE!
I KNOW IF I WAS READING THIS I'D LOVE IT!
KCHU
WACK
BUT I'M NOT READING IT, I'M TOTALLY IN IT- AND IT'S EVIL, STUPID, BORING PUKE!

Critical Reading

1. **(a) Summarize:** Briefly summarize the superguys' actions. **(b) Interpret:** How does the boy react to these actions? **(c) Interpret:** What is Feiffer saying about comic books and the view of life they represent? Explain.

Use these questions to focus a discussion of the comic strip:

2. Why might Feiffer have chosen to write a comic—rather than a prose story—that makes fun of comics superheroes?

TEXT SET

The Harlem Renaissance

Part 3

Literary History: Langston Hughes and Harlem

Langston Hughes was a leading light of the Harlem Renaissance, an artistic movement in which the voices of African American artists rose to the forefront of American culture.

▲ Critical Viewing

What elements of the lives and works of Langston Hughes and Zora Neale Hurston are expressed in this image of the two writers? **INTERPRET**

The Harlem Renaissance

Harlem in the 1920s: For some, it conjures images of jazz sessions at hot spots like the Cotton Club, of seedy speakeasies like the Clam Bake and the Hot Feet. For others, it brings to mind the artistic genius of writers like Langston Hughes and Zora Neale Hurston and painters like Aaron Douglas. In the 1920s, the New York City neighborhood of Harlem was home to an unprecedented flowering of African American talent that left an astonishing cultural legacy.

A Celebration of African American Life Known as the Harlem Renaissance, this remarkable period marked the first time that African American artists were taken seriously by the culture at large. "Negro life is seizing its first chances for group expression and self determination," wrote sociologist Alain Locke in 1926. Harlem became what Locke termed "the center of a spiritual coming of age," as its artists celebrated their culture and race.

The artists and writers of this renaissance did not share a style. Langston Hughes's realistic poems of downtrodden but determined people bear little resemblance to Countee Cullen's elegant sonnets. Instead, these artists shared the urgent need to document the experiences of their people.

The Center of the World In the early 1900s, hundreds of thousands of African Americans embarked on what has come to be called the Great Migration, moving from the rural South to the industrial cities of the North. As more and more African Americans settled in Harlem, it became a meeting ground for writers, musicians, and artists.

The work they produced was unique. Before the Harlem Renaissance, many African American writers had tried to emulate whites. By contrast, the Harlem writers celebrated their racial identity. The goal was to create, as Hughes put it, "an expression of our individual dark-skinned selves."

An Outpouring of Expression From the 1920s through the mid-1930s, sixteen African American writers published more than fifty volumes of poetry and fiction—an astounding amount of work. Other African Americans made their marks in art, music, and theater. Aaron Douglas incorporated African images into his paintings. Blues singer Bessie Smith performed to packed houses. Musicians Jelly Roll Morton, Louis Armstrong, and Duke Ellington laid the foundations of jazz, a form of music that scholars argue is the only truly American art form.

The movement's most influential advocate may have been Langston Hughes, whose poems combined the rhythms of jazz and blues with stories of Harlem life. Other writers, such as Countee Cullen and Claude McKay, wrote in more classical forms. Novelist Zora Neale Hurston combined African folklore with realistic narratives.

A Powerful Legacy The impact of the Harlem Renaissance has been a subject of debate. Most scholars agree that it opened doors for the acceptance of art and writing by African Americans. However, some say that the Harlem Renaissance artists were too interested in seeking the approval of the white establishment. Even Langston Hughes admitted that few African Americans had read his work.

Still, the Harlem Renaissance gave Americans a language with which to begin a discussion of racism. It also broke ground for mid-century African American writers such as Richard Wright, Ralph Ellison, and James Baldwin. Today, Nobel Prize–winner Toni Morrison, novelist and poet Alice Walker, popular mystery writer Walter Mosley, and hundreds of other writers, painters, and musicians owe a debt to the artists of the Harlem Renaissance. For aspiring writers, artists, and musicians, the Harlem Renaissance was proof that art excludes no one.

In This Section

Speaking and Listening: Group Discussion

Comprehension and Collaboration With a small group, discuss the influence of African Americans on contemporary art and culture.

- Research individual African Americans whose artistic accomplishments are helping to shape contemporary culture.
- Consider how our culture would be different without the contributions of African American artists and writers.
- Consider whether African Americans are fairly represented in all the arts. If not, what could be done to improve their representation?

Work together to establish rules for the discussion and to assign individual roles, such as note-taker and moderator. Respond respectfully to one another's insights and ask meaningful questions. Synthesize your ideas and choose a point person to share them with the class.

Langston Hughes (1902–1967)

Humble Beginnings Langston Hughes emerged from the Harlem Renaissance, a cultural movement of the 1920s, as one of the country's most successful African American writers and one of the major interpreters to the world of the African American experience. His work was anchored in a childhood that was not always easy. Shortly after his birth in Missouri, Hughes's parents separated, and Hughes was raised primarily by his grandmother. After his grandmother's death, he lived with his mother in half a dozen cities, finally settling in Cleveland, Ohio.

Writing and Wandering

After graduating from high school in 1921, Hughes published his poem "The Negro Speaks of Rivers" in an African American magazine called *The Crisis*. He moved to New York, where he attended Columbia University and began to explore Harlem, forming a strong attachment to a place he would later help define. After a year, Hughes quit school to work as a steward on a freighter bound for Africa and then traveled in Europe.

Upon his return to the United States, Hughes took a job working in a hotel restaurant in Washington, D.C. One night in 1925, he put three of his poems beside the plate of poet Vachel Lindsay. The next day, newspapers trumpeted the news that Lindsay had discovered a new writer. Then, in 1926, Hughes's first collection of poetry, *The Weary Blues*, was published, earning him even more recognition. A scholarship followed, permitting Hughes to continue his education.

Renaissance Man In 1926, Hughes also wrote an essay titled "The Negro Artist and the Racial Mountain." This work, which called for African American artists to "express our individual dark-skinned selves without fear or shame," helped define the spirit that motivated the Harlem Renaissance. Hughes became a major player in that movement, writing plays, fiction, musicals, autobiographies, and screenplays.

Over the course of his career, Hughes experimented with a variety of poetic forms and techniques. He often tried to recreate the rhythms of contemporary blues and jazz—two other major artistic expressions of the Harlem experience. However, just as he did not only write poetry, Hughes did not only live in Harlem. He traveled the world, and lived much of his life elsewhere. But Harlem was where he felt most welcome, nourished, and inspired. Today, Hughes is recognized as one of the most popular and enduring African American writers of the twentieth century.

"I have discovered in life that there are ways of getting almost anywhere you want to go, if you really want to go."

Hughes and the Blues

Langston Hughes made *beautiful music* with his words: what he, and others, called *jazz poetry.*

This poet of Harlem riffed with words much like a musician riffs with musical phrases, intentionally echoing the rhythms of American jazz and blues. Those rhythms could be traced back to the work songs and spirituals sung by slaves toiling in the fields of the South, and to older songs from West Africa. Classic blues songs are set to 12 bars of music in 4/4 time, using three simple chords. Hughes used this traditional structure in at least half of his poems.

- Hughes began his career in 1926 with a book of jazz poems, *The Weary Blues*, written to be performed to musical accompaniment.
- In his essay "Songs Called the Blues" (1941), Hughes wrote that the blues were sung by "black, beaten but unbeatable throats."
- A 1958 recording features Hughes reciting his poems to the accompaniment of the great jazz composer and musician Charles Mingus.
- The rhythms of jazz influenced Hughes's 1951 *Montage of a Dream Deferred*, a book-length poem depicting the African-American urban experience.

Building Knowledge and Insight

The Negro Speaks of Rivers • I, Too • Dream Variations • Refugee in America

Connecting to the Essential Question These poems center on issues of racial identity and equality for African Americans. As you read, notice details that reflect pride, sorrow, and anger. This will help as you think about the Essential Question: **What makes American literature American?**

Close Reading Focus

Speaker; Multiple Themes

The **speaker** is the voice of a poem. Often, the speaker is the poet. However, a speaker may also be an imaginary person, a group of people, an animal, or an inanimate object. In some poems, such as many by Langston Hughes, the speaker is a voice that represents an entire people. As you read these poems, use a chart like the one shown to identify clues that suggest the identity of the speaker.

Comparing Literary Works These poems express **multiple themes,** or more than one essential meaning. While Hughes writes consistently about *cultural identity* and the status of African Americans within an oppressive society, his focus shifts from themes of suffering, injustice, and struggle to those of pride and beauty. As you read these poems, compare the images, memories, and attitudes Hughes expresses toward African American cultural identity. Look for clues in each poem that reveal the poem's themes.

Preparing to Read Complex Texts When you **apply a critical perspective** to literature, you read a selection through a particular lens or framing idea, such as the following:

- **Social or historical perspective:** viewing literature as it reflects issues in society at the time it was written
- **Archetypal perspective:** viewing literature as an expression of archetypes—characters, symbols, or patterns that cross cultures
- **Biographical perspective:** viewing literature as an expression of events and issues in a writer's personal life

As you read these poems, use a chart like the one shown to apply different critical perspectives and examine how varied lenses reveal different meanings.

Vocabulary

The words below are important to understanding the text that follows. Copy the words into your notebook. What are some other forms of the word *liberty*?

lulled **liberty**

dusky

Common Core State Standards

Reading Literature

2. Determine two or more themes or central ideas of a text and analyze their development over the course of the text, including how they interact and build on one another to produce a complex account.

9. Demonstrate knowledge of early-twentieth-century foundational works of American literature, including how two or more texts from the same period treat similar themes or topics.

Speaking and Listening

SL.11–12.1.a, SL.11–12.1.b, SL.11–12.1.c, SL.11–12.1.d *(p. 897)*

[For the full wording of the standards, see the standards chart in the front of your textbook.]

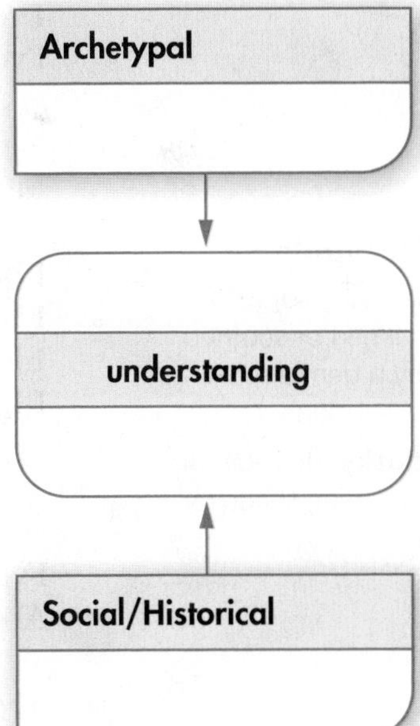

THE NEGRO SPEAKS OF RIVERS

Langston Hughes

BACKGROUND "The Negro Speaks of Rivers" was Langston Hughes's first great poem. He wrote it during the summer after he graduated from high school and it was published a short time later. Hughes considered Carl Sandburg and Walt Whitman to be the greatest American poets. In "The Negro Speaks of Rivers," Hughes follows the model of Whitman's "Song of Myself," using a first-person speaker to express the experience of an entire community.

I've known rivers:
I've known rivers ancient as the world and older than
the flow of human blood in human veins.

My soul has grown deep like the rivers.

I bathed in the Euphrates when dawns were young.
I built my hut near the Congo and it **lulled** me to sleep.
I looked upon the Nile and raised the pyramids above it.
I heard the singing of the Mississippi when Abe Lincoln
went down to New Orleans, and I've seen its muddy
bosom turn all golden in the sunset.

I've known rivers:
Ancient, **dusky** rivers.

My soul has grown deep like the rivers.

Vocabulary

lulled (luld) *v.* calmed or soothed by a gentle sound or motion

dusky (dus′ kē) *adj.* dim; shadowy

Critical Viewing Which details in this painting, *Into Bondage*, by Harlem Renaissance painter Aaron Douglas, connect to Hughes's poem? **CONNECT ▶**

Into Bondage, Aaron Douglas, In the collection of the Corcoran Gallery of Art, Washington, D.C.

I, TOO

LANGSTON HUGHES

Nobody Around Here Calls Me Citizen, 1943, Robert Gwathmey, Collection Frederick R. Weisman Art Museum at the University of Minnesota, Minneapolis, © Estate of Robert Gwathmey/Licensed by VAGA, New York, NY

I, too, sing America.

I am the darker brother.
They send me to eat in the kitchen
When company comes,
But I laugh,
And eat well,
And grow strong.

Tomorrow,
I'll be at the table
When company comes.
Nobody'll dare
Say to me,
"Eat in the kitchen,"
Then.

Besides,
They'll see how beautiful I am
And be ashamed—

I, too, am America.

Applying Critical Perspectives

How does your understanding of this poem change when you read it with different critical perspectives?

◀ **Critical Viewing** Which image in this painting better illustrates the sentiments of this poem—the man or the lion? Explain. **MAKE A DECISION**

Critical Reading

1. **Key Ideas and Details** **(a)** In "The Negro Speaks of Rivers," which four rivers does the speaker mention? **(b) Deduce:** What does the age of these rivers imply about people of African ancestry?
2. **Key Ideas and Details** **(a) Infer:** Why does the speaker in "I, Too" have to eat in the kitchen when company comes? **(b) Interpret:** What does eating in the kitchen represent?
3. **Integration of Knowledge and Ideas** **(a) Interpret:** What does the speaker mean when he says "I, too, am America"? **(b) Synthesize:** Why do you think he refers so directly to Walt Whitman's poem?

Dream Variations

Langston Hughes

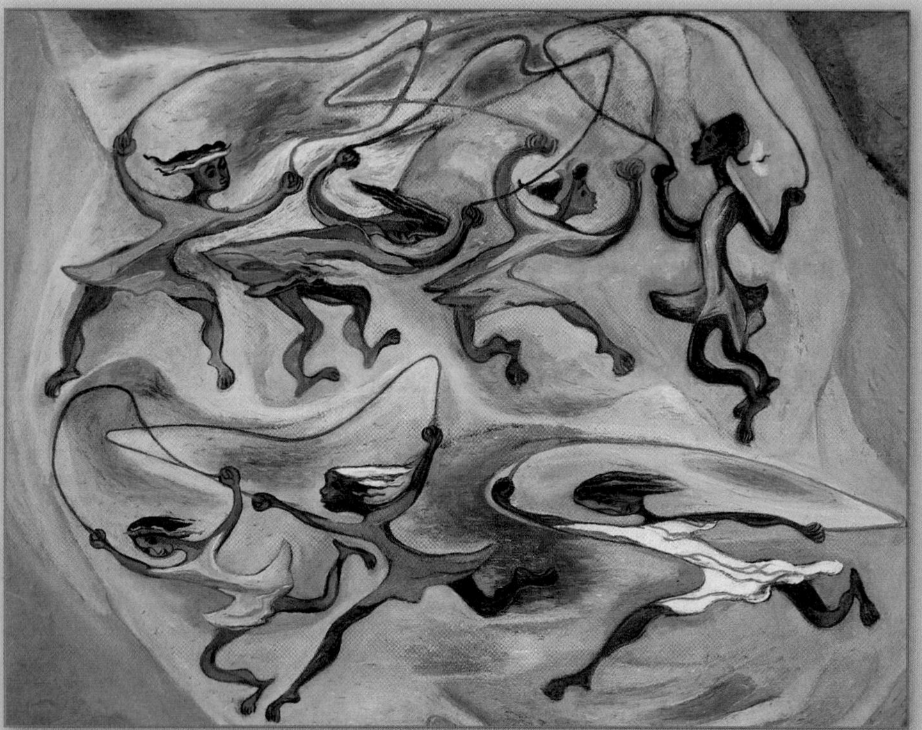

Girls Skipping, 1949, Hale Woodruff, Private Collection. Courtesy of Michael Rosenfeld Gallery, New York

▲ Critical Viewing

How does the motion of the figures in this painting reflect the mood of the poem? **CONNECT**

Speaker

Do you think the speaker in this poem is an individual or a group?

To fling my arms wide
In some place of the sun,
To whirl and to dance
Till the white day is done.
Then rest at cool evening
Beneath a tall tree
While night comes on gently,
    Dark like me—
That is my dream!

To fling my arms wide
In the face of the sun,
Dance! Whirl! Whirl!
Till the quick day is done.
Rest at pale evening . . .
A tall, slim tree . . .
Night coming tenderly
    Black like me.

REFUGEE IN AMERICA

LANGSTON HUGHES

There are words like *Freedom*
Sweet and wonderful to say.
On my heart-strings freedom sings
All day everyday.

There are words like **Liberty**
That almost make me cry.
If you had known what I knew
You would know why.

Vocabulary
liberty (lib′ ər tē) *n.* condition of being free from control by others

Critical Reading

1. **Key Ideas and Details** **(a)** In "Dream Variations," what does the speaker want to do till the "white" day is done? **(b) Analyze:** What double meaning can you identify in the phrase "white day"?
2. **Key Ideas and Details** **(a)** In "Refugee in America," what is the speaker's reaction to words like *freedom* and *liberty*? **(b) Interpret:** In what way does the title of the poem connect these words to the poem itself?
3. **Craft and Structure** **(a)** What words of emotion does the speaker use in "Refugee in America"? **(b) Evaluate:** In what way do these emotions contribute to the mood conveyed by the poem? Explain.
4. **Integration of Knowledge and Ideas** In what ways do these poems capture some of the complexities of the African American experience? In your response, use at least two of these Essential Question words: *perseverance, dignity, homeland, longing.* ***[Connecting to the Essential Question: What makes American literature American?]***

Close Reading Activities

The Negro Speaks of Rivers • I, Too • Dream Variations • Refugee in America

Literary Analysis

1. **Key Ideas and Details (a)** Who is the **speaker** in "The Negro Speaks of Rivers"? **(b)** How does the title help you identify the speaker? Explain.
2. **Key Ideas and Details** What can you infer about the identity and emotions of the speaker in "I, Too"?
3. **Craft and Structure** Walt Whitman, the author of "I Hear America Singing," was a great inspiration to Langston Hughes. How does this information about Hughes's biography affect your understanding of the poem "I, Too"?
4. **Key Ideas and Details (a)** Describe the speaker of "Dream Variations." **(b)** Which details in the poem support your description?
5. **Integration and Knowledge of Ideas (a)** What differences do you find between the speaker in "The Negro Speaks of Rivers" and the speaker in "Refugee in America"? **(b)** To what do you attribute those differences?
6. **Key Ideas and Details** Use a chart like the one shown to identify elements in the poems that reflect the **multiple themes** of racial identity, pride, and perseverance. Record words or phrases for each poem under the themes that they support. (Note: Not all poems have all three themes.)

	Racial Identity	Pride	Perseverance
Rivers			
I, Too			
Dream			
Refugee			

7. **Integration and Knowledge of Ideas** In what ways are the themes of racial identity, pride, and perseverance interconnected?
8. **Integration and Knowledge of Ideas (a)** When you read "Refugee in America" using a **social or historical critical perspective**, how do you understand the poem's last two lines? **(b)** What different interpretation of the poem might a **biographical perspective** provide?
9. **Integration and Knowledge of Ideas (a)** What aspects of "The Negro Speaks of Rivers" does an **archetypal critical perspective** help you interpret? Explain. **(b)** What other critical perspective might help you interpret this poem? Why?

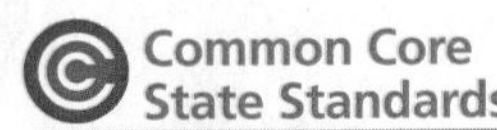

Common Core State Standards

Reading Literature

4. Deterrmine the meaning of words and phrases as they are used in a text, including connotative meanings. *(p. 909)*

Writing

9.a. Apply *grades 11–12 Reading standards* to literature. *(p. 909)*

Language

4.b. Identify and correctly use patterns of word changes that indicate different meanings or parts of speech. *(p. 909)*

5. Demonstrate understanding of word relationships. *(p. 909)*

5.b. Analyze nuances in the meaning of words with similar denotations. *(p. 909)*

Vocabulary Acquisition and Use

Word Analysis: Latin Root *-liber-*

The word *liberty* contains the Latin root *-liber-* or *-liver-*, which means "free." The root is combined with the suffix *-ty,* which means "quality" or "condition." Thus, liberty is the quality or condition of being free. (Note: A different Latin word root that is spelled the same as *-liber-* contributes to the words *library* and *libretto.* Use context clues to confirm meanings when you see words that contain this root.)

Consider the meanings of the words below, that are based on *-liber-* or *-liver-*. Then, answer the questions.

liberate *v.* to release, to free
liberal *adj.* marked by generosity
deliverance *n.* the act of setting free or the state of being set free

1. *Simone was frustrated as she tried to liberate the coat lining from the zipper.* What has happened, and what is Simone trying to do?
2. *If the charity runs low on funds, the board will approach Mrs. Stephens, who has a liberal nature.* How do you think the charity hopes Mrs. Stephens will help? Explain.
3. *The soldiers hear gunfire and hope deliverance is near.* What are the soldiers hoping?

Vocabulary: Analogies

Analogies show the relationships between pairs of words. Complete each analogy using a word from the vocabulary list on page 901. In each, your choice should create a word pair that matches the relationship between the first two words given. Then, explain your answers.

1. *Deliverance* is to *bondage* as *capture* is to ______.
2. *Yellow* is to sunlight as *gray* is to ______.
3. *Dark* is to *light* as *stimulated* is to ______.

Using Resources to Build Vocabulary

Connotation and Denotation: Words for Freedom

Denotation is the direct meaning of a word. *Connotation* is an implied and often subjective meaning. For example, the denotative meaning of *license* is "freedom of action." The connotative meaning suggests a freedom that is used irresponsibly or without regard for rules.

Look up the words *freedom* and *liberty* in a thesaurus to find related words. Then, look up the new words in a dictionary. Make a chart or organize your notes to identify differences in connotation among all the words you find. Finally, rewrite "Refugee in America," with words other than *freedom* and *liberty.* Consider how the connotations of the substituted words alter the meaning of the poem.

Close Reading Activities Continued

Writing to Sources

Explanatory Text In a **multi-genre response** to literature you deliver an interpretation or critical assessment of a literary work in writing and in forms involving video, audio, performance, illustration, or other expressive media.

1. **Analytical Essay** Write an essay about "The Negro Speaks of Rivers" in which you apply historical and archetypal critical perspectives. Analyze Hughes's use of literary elements, such as simile, symbolism, and imagery, to advance meaning and evoke emotions. Follow the writing process instructions below to guide this part of your multi-genre response.
2. **Visual Elements** Add to your analysis of the poem with illustrations, a slide presentation, a series of photographs or drawings, or a poster.
3. **Audio Elements** Select music, spoken-word recordings, or other sound aids to accompany the visual element.
4. **Performance** Consider other ways to present your ideas. For example, you might interpret the poem in dance or set it to music.

To write your analytical essay, follow these steps:

Prewriting Reread the poem *applying a historical perspective.* To aid your work, consult an atlas or encyclopedia to find information about the rivers, objects, and time periods mentioned in the poem. Also, consider other issues in Hughes's era that may have inspired this poem.

Reread the poem again, *applying an archetypal perspective.* Consider what rivers mean to people across cultures. Note what the rivers in the poem symbolize and what their relationship is to the speaker. Identify similes or imagery that express those relationships. Write a clear thesis statement about the poem's meaning when viewed from two different perspectives.

Drafting In your introduction, state your main idea. In the body paragraphs, explain your interpretation. Clearly express the different understandings of the poem you gain from applying two critical perspectives. Use details from the poem and your research to support your ideas.

Revising Review your draft, paying particular attention to word choice. Replace vague or inappropriate words with more precise choices. In addition, make sure you use literary terms accurately.

Model: Revising Word Choice

The Euphrates River was the site of some of the ~~oldest people~~ *most ancient civilizations* in history. Cities were being built on the shores of this river ~~long~~ *thousands of years* ago.

Clear and specific language helps express ideas accurately.

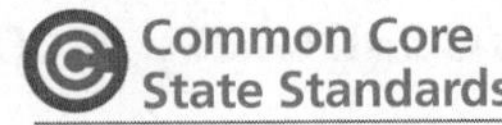

Common Core State Standards

Writing

2. Write informative/explanatory texts to examine and convey complex ideas, concepts, and information clearly and accurately through the effective selection, organization, and analysis of content.

2.d. Use precise language and domain-specific vocabulary to manage the complexity of the topic.

5. Develop and strengthen writing as needed by planning, revising, editing, rewriting, or trying a new approach, focusing on addressing what is most significant for a specific purpose and audience.

Speaking and Listening

5. Make strategic use of digital media in presentations to enhance understanding of findings, reasoning, and evidence and to add interest.

Language

1. Demonstrate command of the conventions of standard English grammar and usage when writing or speaking. *(p. 911)*

Conventions and Style: Pronoun-Antecedent Agreement

Use correct pronoun-antecedent agreement to make your writing logical and clear. Remember that a **pronoun** stands for a noun, and the noun is its **antecedent**. The noun and pronoun should agree in person, number, and gender.

	Singular Pronouns	Plural Pronouns
First Person	I, me, my	we, us, our
Second Person	you, your	you, your
Third Person	he, she, it	they, them, their

The only pronouns that show gender are third-person singular pronouns.

Masculine	Feminine	Neuter
he, him, his	she, her, hers	it, its

Correcting Faulty Agreement

Unintended Shift in Person: Many *students* enjoy poems with images *you* can visualize.
Correct: Many *students* enjoy poems with images *they* can visualize.

Vague Reference: I liked "Dream Variations" because *they* helped me feel the dancing.
Correct: I liked "Dream Variations" because *the poet's words* helped me feel the dancing.

Unclear Reference: Bontemps and Hughes were friends, and after *his* death *he* compiled a book of Hughes's poetry.
Correct: After Hughes died, his friend *Bontemps* compiled a book of Hughes's poetry.

Practice Rewrite each sentence, correcting the problem in antecedent and pronoun agreement.

1. Langston Hughes wrote poetry to express pride in his heritage, which you see honored.
2. Countee Cullen and Claude McKay used images of fruit. That is in their poems.
3. Either Hughes or Cullen published their first poetry in 1925.
4. McKay sees fruit on a window ledge, and you feel like crying.
5. Bontemps and Cullen write poems of planting and reaping. They express despair.
6. Storms are dramatic and vivid. This makes them the subject of many poems and poets.
7. Poetry expresses feelings of sorrow, which not everyone likes.
8. Memories of dewy dawns and blue skies come back. They make the poet write.
9. Bontemps and Hughes corresponded. His letters were donated to a library.
10. The Harlem Renaissance poets celebrated freedom and their ancestors. They were oppressed.

Writing and Speaking Conventions

A. Writing Write a sentence for each noun below. Include one of the following pronouns to refer to the noun: *you, she, he, his, it, its, them, their,* or *they*. Make the pronoun and antecedent agree.

1. rivers **2.** brother **3.** night **4.** children **5.** dream

Example: company
Sentence: If *company* comes, *they* will be welcome.

B. Speaking Present a review of a poem by Langston Hughes. Include at least two sentences that show correct pronoun-antecedent agreement.

POETRY OF IDENTITY

The Harlem Renaissance poets developed an artistic and cultural identity . . .

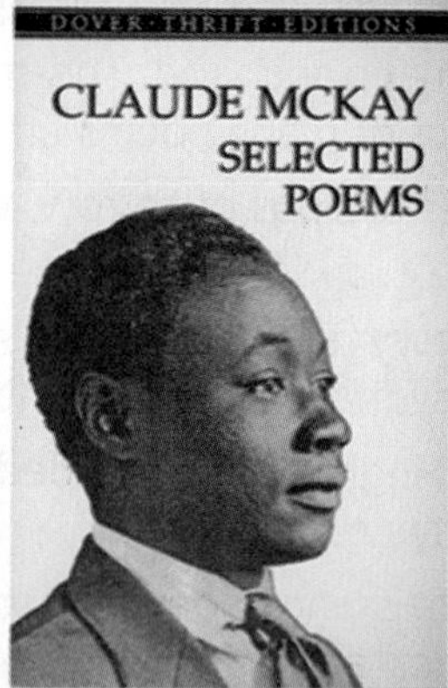

Claude McKay
Poet, journalist, activist

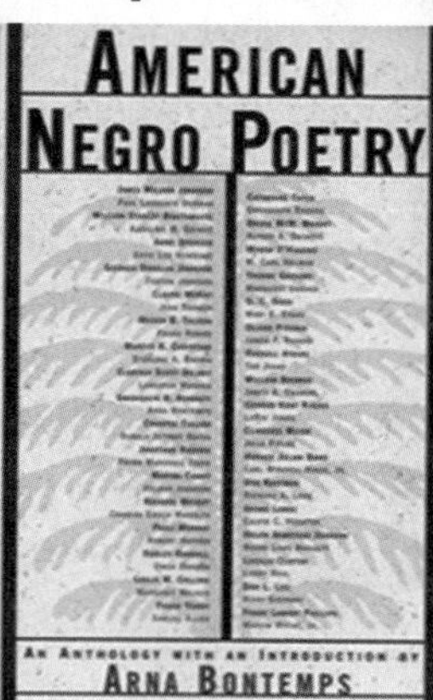

Arna Bontemps
Author of
A Black Man Talks of Reaping.

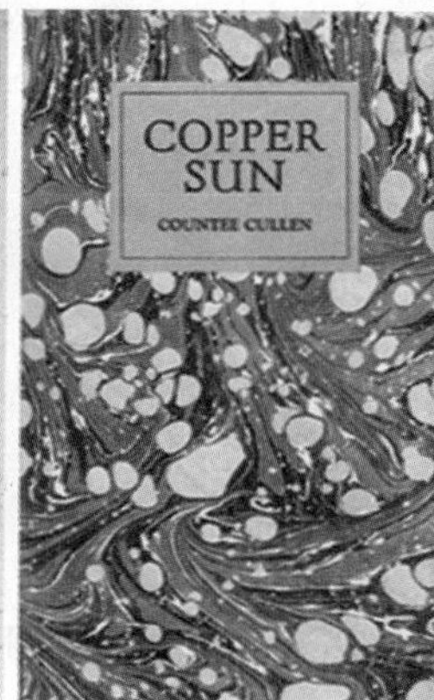

Countee Cullen
Poet and novelist

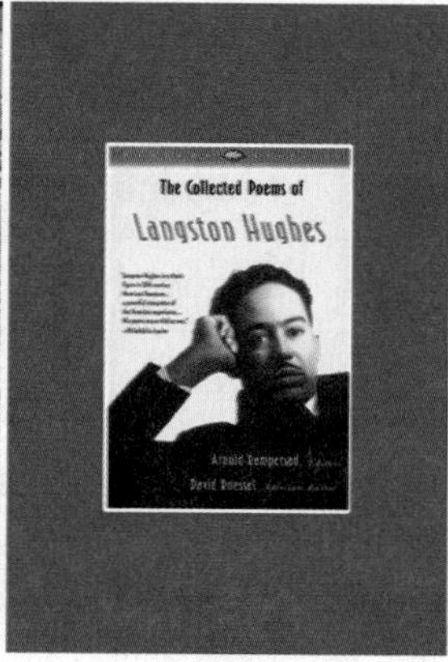

Langston Hughes
A leader of the
Harlem Renaissance

. . . that has grown through generations and will continue.

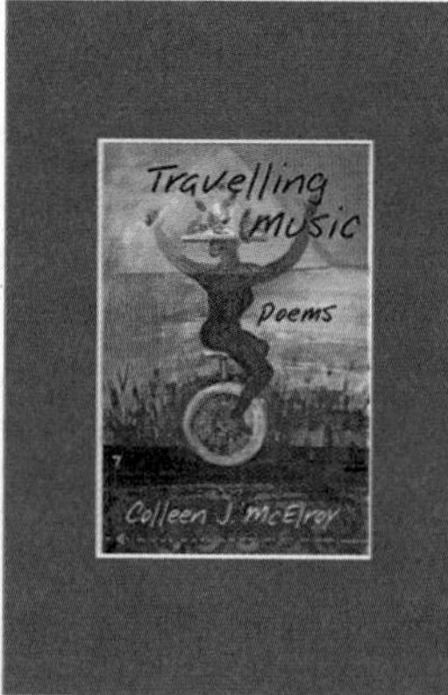

Colleen McElroy
Honors include
two Fulbright Fellowships

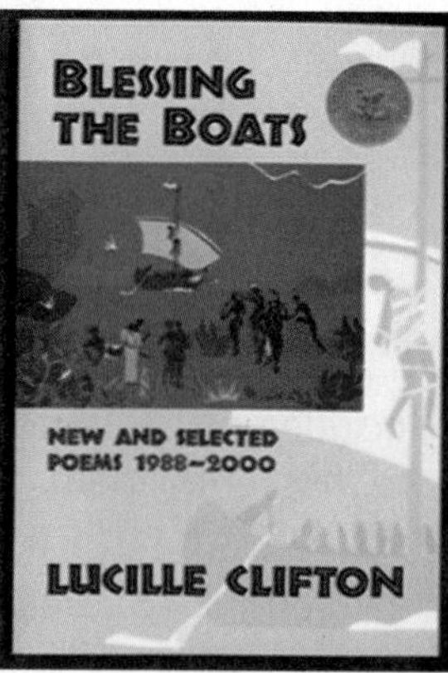

Lucille Clifton
National Book Award in 2000

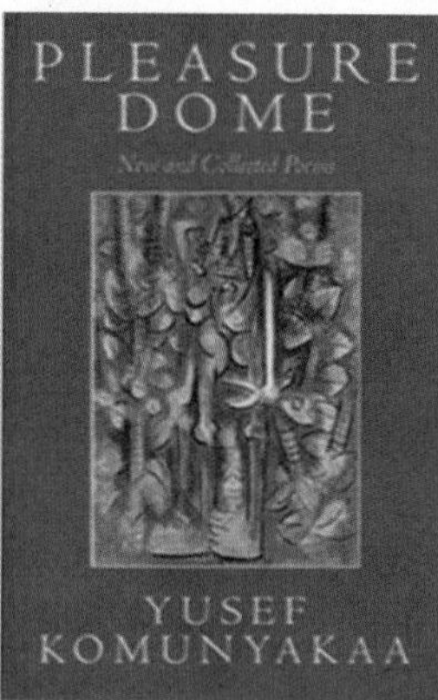

Yusef Komunyakaa
Pulitzer Prize,
Ruth Lilly Poetry Prize

Nikki Giovanni
Honors include
Langston Hughes
Medal for poetry

Comparing Literary Works

The Poetry of Langston Hughes* • *"study the masters" by Lucille Clifton* • *"For My Children" by Colleen McElroy

Comparing Poetry of Cultural Identity

Poetry of Cultural Identity Langston Hughes was famous before poets Colleen McElroy and Lucille Clifton were even born. Yet these three poets share a cultural identity that gives their work a "family resemblance." Cultural identity is a way of defining oneself as part of a culture or ethnic group. Culture, the way of life of a group of people, is expressed through manners, dress, language, rituals, beliefs, art, and food. The following are some of the cultural elements shared by African Americans, as expressed in these poems:

- **Roots and history:** from African origins through the era of slavery to freedom within a primarily white society
- **Values:** the importance of family, history, and cultural pride
- **Language:** the use of specific speech patterns and idioms

Other elements indicating a shared cultural identity include references to specific art forms, goals, beliefs, traditions, or social barriers—anything that establishes a community of common heritage.

In the mid- to late twentieth century, African American women writers sought to distinguish themselves from men because they often faced different problems. For example, women—both black and white—could not vote until long after African American men had won that right. As a result, female poets like McElroy and Clifton often emphasize women's views. Nevertheless, cultural identity is still paramount in their work. As you read these poems, use a chart like the one shown to compare elements in the poems that speak to cultural identity.

	Hughes	Clifton	McElroy
Roots/History	"I built my hut near the Congo…"		
Values	"On my heart-strings freedom sings/All day everyday."		
Goals	"Tomorrow, I'll be at the table"		

Common Core State Standards

Reading Literature

2. Determine two or more themes or central ideas of a text and analyze their development over the course of the text, including how they interact and build on one another to produce a complex account.

4. Determine the meaning of words and phrases as they are used in the text; analyze the impact of specific word choices on meaning and tone, including language that is particularly fresh, engaging, or beautiful.

Gather Vocabulary Knowledge

Clifton and McElroy use related forms of the words *handiwork, heritage,* and *ritual.* Use a **dictionary** to find each word's part of speech and definition. Then, employ other references to further explore these words.

- **History of Language:** Use a history of English to research each word. Write a paragraph about each word's emergence in English.
- **Book of Quotations:** Use an online or print collection of quotations to find a passage containing one of the words. In a paragraph, explain subtleties in meaning that are evident from the context of the quotation.

Compare and contrast what you learn about the words from each reference.

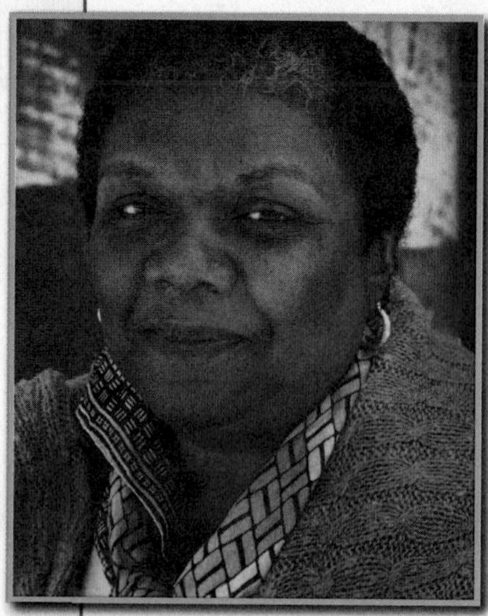

Lucille Clifton (1936–2010)

Author of **"study the masters"**

Lucille Clifton was born in New York. Her father, a steel worker, and her mother, a launderer and homemaker, were not formally educated, but had a love of books and language that they passed along to their daughter.

Lucille was only sixteen when she entered Howard University in Washington, D.C. There she met poets and writers (including Toni Morrison) who both influenced and encouraged her work. She later transferred to Fredonia State Teachers College, worked as an actor, and began to develop the style of poetry for which she would become known. A poet friend entered her work in a competition, which Clifton won. Part of the prize was the publication of her first volume of poems, *Good Times*. *The New York Times* called it one of the best books of 1969.

Clifton's work focuses largely on African American heritage and culture. In addition to her poetry, she has written a memoir and fourteen works of juvenile fiction, one of which received the Coretta Scott King Award in 1984. In 2007, Clifton became the first black woman to win the prestigious Ruth Lilly Poetry Prize.

Colleen McElroy (b. 1935)

Author of **"For My Children"**

An "army brat," McElroy spent much of her youth on the move, living in Missouri, Wyoming, and Germany—and she never seems to have stopped moving. She received her B.A. from Kansas State University, and then headed to Pennsylvania to study speech and language. Next, she headed west, receiving a Ph.D. in ethnolinguistics from the University of Washington. She stayed in Washington to teach English, but was still always on the move, traveling to Europe, South America, Japan, Africa, the South Pacific, and Southeast Asia.

McElroy began writing seriously when she was in her thirties. The many writers she knew encouraged her in her work. Her first collection of poems, *The Mules Done Long Since Gone*, was published in 1973. McElroy continued to both write and teach, and in 1983, she became the first black woman to be made a full professor at the University of Washington. In 1985, her collection *Queen of the Ebony Isles* received the American Book Award.

McElroy has also written short stories and plays, including a drama about Harriet Tubman, but is best known as a poet. She retired from teaching in 2006, but continues to write and travel.

STUDY THE MASTERS

Lucille Clifton

BACKGROUND The expression "study the masters" refers to the practice of looking at the work of great artists in order to learn an art form. In this poem, the master poet may be someone the speaker once studied, but just as she has abandoned the traditions of European poetry, she has also abandoned the idea that these were the only "masters" to be studied. Note that the title is really the first line of the poem. This is a common feature of Clifton's poems.

study the masters
like my aunt timmie.
it was her iron,
or one like hers,
that smoothed the sheets
the master poet slept on.
home or hotel, what matters is
he lay himself down on her **handiwork**
and dreamed. she dreamed too, words:
some cherokee[1], some masai[2] and some
huge and particular as hope.
if you had heard her
chanting as she ironed
you would understand form and line
and discipline and order and
america.

▲ Critical Viewing
In what ways does this painting, like Aunt Timmie's words, say something about "form and line . . . and america"? **ANALYZE**

Vocabulary
handiwork (hand′ dē wʉrk′) *n.* work done by the hands; work done personally

1. **Cherokee** (cher′ ə kē) a Native American people.
2. **Masai** (mä sī′) an African people.

FOR MY CHILDREN

Colleen McElroy

The Madonna and Child (detail), 1990, Momodou Ceesay

▲ **Critical Viewing** In what ways does this painting reflect the heritage that the speaker in the poem seeks to hand on to her children? Explain. **ANALYZE**

BACKGROUND In societies without a written language, oral information that was passed down from one generaton to the next took the place of written historical accounts. The speaker of "For My Children" is a collector of the oral history of African American people. In telling this poem, the speaker sifts through facts, images, and other stories to pass on those with the greatest meaning. In doing so, the speaker connects the present to the past, the living to the dead, and North America to Africa.

I have stored up tales for you, my children
    My favorite children, my only children;
Of shackles and slaves and a bill of rights.
But skin of honey and beauty of ebony begins
    In the land called Bilad as-Sudan,[1]
So I search for a **heritage** beyond St. Louis.

My memory floats down a long narrow hall,
    A calabash[2] of history.
Grandpa stood high in Watusi[3] shadows
    In this land of yearly **rituals** for alabaster beauty;
Where **effigies** of my ancestors are captured
    In Beatle tunes,
And crowns never touch Bantu[4] heads.

My past is a slender dancer reflected briefly
    Like a leopard in fingers of fire.
The future of Dahomey[5] is a house of 16 doors,
The totem of the Burundi[6] counts 17 warriors—
    In reverse generations.
While I cling to one stray Seminole.[7]
My thoughts grow thin in the urge to travel
    Beyond Grandma's tale
Of why cat fur is for kitten britches;[8]
Past the wrought-iron rail of first stairs
    In baby white shoes,
To Ashanti[9] mysteries and rituals.

Comparing Poetry of Cultural Identity
Which details in the first stanza reflect the children's roots in Africa?

Vocabulary

heritage (her′ i tij′) *n.* something handed down from one's ancestors or from the past

rituals (rich′ o͞o əlz′) *n.* established forms of ceremonies; ceremonial acts

effigies (ef′ i jēz) *n.* images or likenesses, especially of people

Comprehension
What has the speaker stored up for her children?

1. **Bilad as-Sudan** (bē läd′ äs so͞o dan′) "land of the blacks," an Arabic expression by which Arab geographers referred to the settled African countries north of the southern edge of the Sahara.
2. **calabash** (kal′ ə bash′) *n.* dried, hollow shell of a gourd, used as a bowl or a cup.
3. **Watusi** (wä to͞o′ sē) a people of east-central Africa.
4. **Bantu** (ban′ to͞o) Bantu-speaking peoples of Africa.
5. **Dahomey** (də hō′ mē) old name for Benin, in west-central Africa.
6. **Burundi** (boo roon′ dē) country in east-central Africa.
7. **Seminole** (sem′ ə nōl′) Native American people from Florida.
8. **Cat fur is for kitten britches** In the South, this was once a common saying used to correct those who pronounced "for" as "fur." If someone asked, "What's that fur?" rather than answering the intended question, the response of "Cat fur is for kitten britches" would remind the questioner to use standard English pronunciation.
9. **Ashanti** (ə shän′ tə) people of western Africa.

Back in the narrow hallway of my childhood.
I cradled my knees
In limbs as smooth and long as the neck of a bud vase,
I began this ancestral search that you children yield now
In profile and bust
By common invention, in being and belonging.

The line of your cheeks recalls Ibo[10] melodies
As surely as oboe and flute.
The sun dances a honey and cocoa duet on your faces.
I see smiles that mirror schoolboy smiles
In the land called Bilad as-Sudan;
I see the link between the Mississippi and the Congo.

Comparing Poetry of Cultural Identity
What physical connections to Africa does the speaker see in the children's faces?

10. Ibo (ē′ bō′) a people of southeastern Nigeria.

Critical Reading

Cite textual evidence to support your responses.

1. **Key Ideas and Details (a)** In "study the masters," what is Aunt Timmie's occupation? **(b) Interpret:** What connection does the speaker make between Aunt Timmie's labor and the master poet?
2. **Key Ideas and Details (a)** What "huge and particular" word does the speaker say Aunt Timmie dreams? **(b) Analyze:** Why is this word so significant?
3. **Key Ideas and Details (a)** In "For My Children," for whom has the speaker "stored up tales"? **(b) Interpret:** Why has the speaker made this effort?
4. **Key Ideas and Details** Are the children solely the speaker's biological children? Explain.
5. **Key Ideas and Details (a)** Identify the cultures in which the speaker searches for evidence of her heritage. **(b) Analyze:** In the second and third stanzas, what impressions of her ancestors does the speaker convey? **(c) Analyze:** What images shape these impressions?
6. **Key Ideas and Details (a)** Which two rivers does the speaker mention in the last stanza? **(b) Interpret:** Why might these two rivers be important to the speaker and to her children?
7. **Integration of Knowledge and Ideas** In what specific ways might educating children about their heritage affect the choices they make in life?

Close Reading Activities

The Poetry of Langston Hughes • study the masters • For My Children

Comparing Poetry of Cultural Identity

1. **Key Ideas and Details (a)** What rivers do both Hughes and McElroy mention? **(b)** What does the inclusion of these two rivers in the poems suggest about the shared cultural identities of the speakers?
2. **Integration and Knowledge of Ideas** What examples of pride in physical appearance do you find in "I, Too," "Dream Variations," and "For My Children"? Explain.
3. **Integration of Knowledge and Ideas** Both "I, Too" and "study the masters" end with the word "America." What does each speaker feel toward America? Explain.

 Timed Writing

Explanatory Text: Essay

Langston Hughes and other artists of the Harlem Renaissance brought African American voices into the mainstream of American society. Today, issues of cultural identity still permeate American letters, as the poems by Clifton and McElroy demonstrate.

Assignment: Write an **analytical essay** in which you compare and contrast the explorations of cultural heritage in the poems by Hughes, Clifton, and McElroy. **[40 minutes]**

Use these questions to focus your analysis:

- What aspects of cultural identity are important in each poem?
- What is the message each speaker expresses?
- Based on these poems, in what ways is cultural identity both a private concern and one with meaning for an entire society?

As you write, incorporate these elements of a strong analytical essay:

- Craft effective introductory and concluding paragraphs, using a variety of sentence structures.
- Use a clear organizational scheme to compare the poems, either poem by poem or point by point.
- Include well-chosen details to support your statements.

5-Minute Planner

Complete these steps before you begin to write:

1. Read the assignment carefully. List key words and phrases.
2. Scan the poems for evidence that supports your ideas. **TIP** As you scan, jot down quotations for inclusion in your essay.
3. Create a rough outline for your essay.
4. Reread the prompt, and draft your essay.

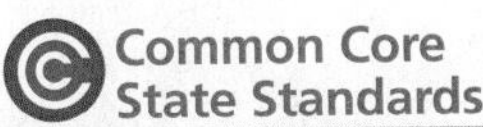

Common Core State Standards

Writing

2. Write explanatory texts to examine and convey complex ideas, concepts, and information clearly and accurately through the effective selection, organization, and analysis of content.

9. Draw evidence from literary or informational texts to support analysis, reflection, and research.

10. Write routinely over extended time frames and shorter time frames for a range of tasks, purposes, and audiences.

USE ACADEMIC VOCABULARY

As you write, use academic language, including the following words or their related forms:

comparison
reveal
categorize
discriminate

For more information about academic language, see the vocabulary charts in the introduction to this book.

Harlem Renaissance Poets

Claude McKay *(1890–1948)*

Author of **"The Tropics in New York"**

In some ways, poet and novelist Claude McKay seemed to be a man without roots. Once, while traveling overseas, he wrote to Langston Hughes, "I write of America as home [although] I am really a poet without a country." Born in Jamaica, he lived in numerous places in the United States and overseas. However, McKay considered Harlem his spiritual home, and it was to Harlem he returned in both his life and his work.

The son of Jamaican farm workers, McKay was able to emigrate to the United States when his first collection of poems, *Songs of Jamaica* (1912) won an award from the Institute of Arts and Letters. McKay moved to Harlem in 1914, after studying at Tuskegee Institute and Kansas State Teachers College. In 1917, McKay published two sonnets, "The Harlem Dancer" and "Invocation." McKay's poetry focused largely on the social injustices experienced by blacks in America. However, poems like "The Tropics in New York" are also marked by nostalgia for his homeland—a feeling echoed in the title of his autobiography, *A Long Way From Home* (1937).

Arna Bontemps *(1902–1973)*

Author of **"A Black Man Talks of Reaping"**

Arna Bontemps was one of the most scholarly figures of the Harlem Renaissance. Throughout his career as an editor, a novelist, a dramatist, and a poet, his commitment to social justice made him "the conscience of an era."

Born in Louisiana and raised in California, Bontemps came to New York during the height of the Harlem Renaissance. After teaching at several religious academies, he wrote *Black Thunder* (1936), a highly acclaimed novel about a Virginia slave revolt. In subsequent years, he published poems, biographies, dramas, and books for young readers. He also ran the library at Fisk University in Nashville, making it a major center for African American studies. In 1967, after the death of his friend Langston Hughes, Bontemps compiled *Hold Fast to Dreams* (1969), a poetry anthology. The bulk of the extensive correspondence between Hughes and Bontemps was donated to Yale University, where scholars can study this vivid chronicle of African American literary life.

Countee Cullen *(1903–1946)*

Author of **"From the Dark Tower"**

Unlike most other poets of his day, Countee Cullen used traditional forms and methods. Yet, no other poet expressed the sentiments of African Americans during the early 1900s more eloquently than did Cullen.

Cullen was born in Louisville, Kentucky, and raised by foster parents in New York. As a high-school student, Cullen's gift for poetry was recognized when he won a city-wide competition for his poem, "I Have a Rendevous With Life." An outstanding student, he also worked on his high-school newspaper and literary magazine. During his undergraduate career at New York University, Cullen's poetry was published in W.E.B. DuBois's magazine, *The Crisis*. Cullen later earned a master's degree in English and French from Harvard University. His first collection of poetry, *Color,* was published in 1925. That volume was followed by *Copper Sun* (1927), *The Ballad of the Brown Girl* (1927), and *The Black Christ* (1929). In 1932, he published *One Way to Heaven,* a satirical novel. In his later years, Cullen published two children's books, *The Lost Zoo* (1940) and *My Lives and How I Lost Them* (1942).

"Nations, like plants and human beings, grow. And if the development is thwarted they are dwarfed and overshadowed."

— Claude McKay

The Tropics in New York • A Black Man Talks of Reaping From the Dark Tower

Connecting to the Essential Question These poems are filled with images of ripeness, but they focus on loss rather than bounty. As you read, look for details that express hope or despair. Doing so will help as you think about the Essential Question: **What is the relationship between literature and place?**

Close Reading Focus

Stanza; Stanza Structure; Imagery

A **stanza** is a group of lines that forms a division of a poem. Often, like paragraphs in prose, each stanza develops a single main idea that adds to a poem's overall meaning. **Stanza structure** refers to the way a poet organizes stanzas, which may vary in length or be evenly ordered. Types of stanzas are identified by the number of lines they contain:

two lines: *couplet* **four lines**: *quatrain*
six lines: *sestet* **eight lines**: *octave*

A **sonnet** is a fourteen-line lyric poem that follows one of two stanza structures. A *Petrarchan sonnet*, such as "From the Dark Tower," is divided into an opening octave followed by a sestet. A *Shakespearean sonnet* is divided into three quatrains and a final couplet. As you read these poems, notice how each poet uses stanza structure to develop his ideas.

Comparing Literary Works These poems contain similar types of **imagery,** or word pictures that appeal to the senses. As you read, compare each poet's use of imagery to express meaning and emotions.

Preparing to Read Complex Texts Literature can be read using a variety of critical approaches. These approaches are like spotlights that illuminate different aspects of a work. **Applying a political approach to literary criticism** allows a reader to interpret a work for its political content and themes. Writers may state political ideas directly or use symbols and other literary devices to suggest political meanings, as these poets do. You will understand these poems better if you read them for the political messages they express. As you read, use a chart like the one shown to note details that suggest political content.

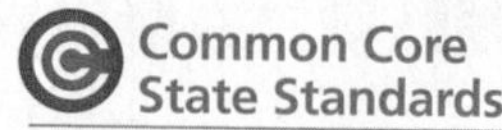

Reading Literature

5. Analyze how an author's choices concerning how to structure specific parts of a text contribute to its overall structure and meaning as well as its aesthetic impact.

9. Demonstrate knowledge of early-twentieth-century foundational works of American literature, including how two or more texts from the same period treat similar themes or topics.

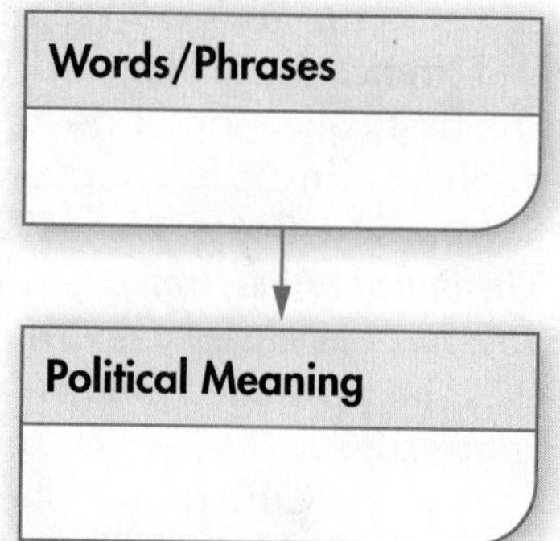

Vocabulary

You will encounter the words listed here in the texts that follow. Copy the words into your notebook, sorting them into words you know and words you do not know.

benediction **countenance**
increment **beguile**

The TROPICS in New York

Claude McKay

BACKGROUND *This poem is marked by nostalgia for Jamaica, where the poet was born and raised.*

Bananas ripe and green, and ginger-root,
    Cocoa in pods and alligator pears,[1]
And tangerines and mangoes and grape fruit,
    Fit for the highest prize at parish fairs,

Set in the window, bringing memories
    Of fruit-trees laden by low-singing rills,[2]
And dewy dawns, and mystical blue skies
    In benediction over nun-like hills.

My eyes grew dim, and I could no more gaze;
    A wave of longing through my body swept,
And, hungry for the old, familiar ways
    I turned aside and bowed my head and wept.

1. **alligator pears** avocados.
2. **rills** (rilz) *n.* little streams or brooks.

Stanza Structure
What type of stanza appears in this poem? Explain.

Vocabulary
benediction (ben e dik′ shen) *n.* prayer asking for God's blessing

A Black Man Talks of Reaping

Arna Bontemps

Hoeing, 1943, Robert Gwathmey, Carnegie Institute Museum of Art, Pittsburgh, Pennsylvania, © Estate of Robert Gwathmey/Licensed by VAGA, New York, NY

▲ **Critical Viewing**

What emotion does this image convey? In what way does it compare with the mood of the poem? **COMPARE AND CONTRAST**

BACKGROUND In addition to poetry, Bontemps wrote numerous works on African American history for younger readers. Planting was a significant part of life for African Americans. In this poem, Bontemps uses this historic reality to explore the political realities of his day.

I have sown beside all waters in my day.
I planted deep, within my heart the fear
that wind or fowl would take the grain away.
I planted safe against this stark, lean year.

I scattered seed enough to plant the land
in rows from Canada to Mexico
but for my reaping[1] only what the hand
can hold at once is all that I can show.

Yet what I sowed and what the orchard yields
my brother's sons are gathering stalk and root;
small wonder then my children glean[2] in fields
they have not sown, and feed on bitter fruit.

Applying a Political Approach
What political realities does the poet speak about symbolically in this stanza?

1. **reaping** (rēp´ iŋ) *v.* cutting or harvesting grain from a field.
2. **glean** (glēn) *v.* collect the remaining grain after reaping. Traditionally, the poor who did not own land gleaned the fields.

Critical Reading

1. **Key Ideas and Details (a)** In "The Tropics in New York," what memories does the fruit stir in the speaker? **(b) Infer:** Why do you think the speaker weeps?
2. **Key Ideas and Details Interpret:** What is ironic about the title as it relates to the message of the poem?
3. **Key Ideas and Details (a)** In "A Black Man Talks of Reaping," why does the speaker plant "deep"? **(b) Draw Conclusions:** What do you think is the meaning of the phrase "stark, lean year"?
4. **Key Ideas and Details (a)** How much of the seed does the speaker scatter? **(b) Infer:** Who reaps what the speaker has sown?
5. **Integration of Knowledge and Ideas Infer:** What does Bontemps suggest about what African Americans have received in exchange for their hard work?

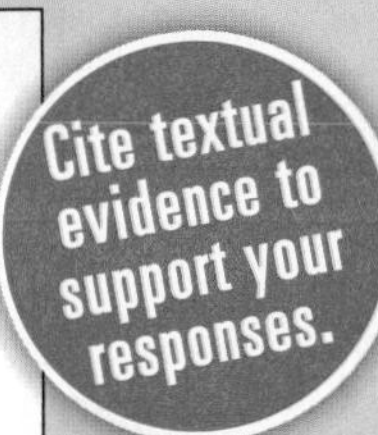
Cite textual evidence to support your responses.

From The Dark Tower

Countee Cullen (to Charles S. Johnson)

Background Countee Cullen dedicated this poem to Charles S. Johnson, an African American sociologist, editor, and author of a landmark study of race relations in the 1920s.

Vocabulary

increment (inˊ crə mənt) *n.* increase, as in a series

countenance (koun´ tə nəns) *v.* approve; tolerate

beguile (bē gīl´) *v.* charm or delight

We shall not always plant while others reap
The golden **increment** of bursting fruit,
Not always **countenance**, abject and mute,
That lesser men should hold their brothers cheap;
Not everlastingly while others sleep
Shall we **beguile** their limbs with mellow flute,
Not always bend to some more subtle brute;
We were not made eternally to weep.

The night whose sable[1] breast relieves the stark,
White stars is no less lovely being dark,
And there are buds that cannot bloom at all
In light, but crumple, piteous, and fall;
So in the dark we hide the heart that bleeds,
And wait, and tend our agonizing seeds.

1. **sable** (sa´ bel) *adj.* black

Critical Reading

Cite textual evidence to support your responses.

1. **Craft and Structure** **(a)** Which word is repeated five times in the first stanza? **(b) Analyze:** What is the effect of this repetition?
2. **Craft and Structure** **(a)** What contrast does the speaker set up in lines 9–10? **(b) Interpret:** What does Cullen mean by "no less lovely being dark?"
3. **Integration of Knowledge and Ideas** Are these poets hopeful or pessimistic about the future for African Americans? Explain. In your response, use at least two of these Essential Question words: *prospect, hurdle, expectation, overcome, surmount.* ***[Connecting to the Essential Question: What is the relationship between literature and place?]***

Close Reading Activities

The Tropics in New York • A Black Man Talks of Reaping • From the Dark Tower

Literary Analysis

1. **Craft and Structure** What type of **stanza** does McKay use in "The Tropics in New York"?
2. **Integration of Knowledge and Ideas** How does a political reading clarify "A Black Man Talks of Reaping"?
3. **Craft and Structure** Using a chart like the one shown, identify the **stanza structure** of "A Black Man Talks of Reaping." Explain how each stanza works to develop the ideas expressed in the poem.

Stanza	Idea It Develops

4. **Integration of Knowledge and Ideas** **(a)** When you **apply a political approach** to "From the Dark Tower" how do you interpret the first stanza? **(b)** The last *couplet?*
5. **Craft and Structure** **(a)** Identify two stanza types in "From the Dark Tower." **(b)** How does the stanza structure of this *sonnet* help develop the poet's meaning?
6. **Comparing Literary Works** **(a)** For each poem, note examples of **imagery** related to planting and reaping. **(b)** Are the messages this imagery helps to express similar or different in each poem? Explain.

Common Core State Standards

Writing

2. Write explanatory texts to examine and convey complex ideas, concepts, and information clearly and accurately through the effective selection, organization, and analysis of content.

2.b. Develop the topic thoroughly by selecting the most significant and relevant facts, extended definitions, concrete details, quotations, or other information and examples appropriate to the audience's knowledge of the topic.

Language

5. Demonstrate understanding of word relationships.

5.a. Interpret figures of speech in context and analyze their role in the text.

Vocabulary Acquisition and Use

Antonyms For each word, choose the letter of the correct antonym, or word of opposite meaning. Explain your choice.

1. benediction: **(a)** curse **(b)** talk **(c)** reap **(d)** bind
2. countenance: **(a)** face **(b)** remember **(c)** hope **(d)** disagree
3. beguile: **(a)** impress **(b)** disgust **(c)** steal **(d)** relate
4. increment: **(a)** tool **(b)** rapidity **(c)** decrease **(d)** multiplication

Writing to Sources

Explanatory Text Although Countee Cullen and Arna Bontemps were associated with the same literary movement, each had a distinct style. In an essay, **compare and contrast** "From the Dark Tower" and "A Black Man Talks of Reaping." Identify specific points of comparison, such as each poet's use of metaphor, and consider each poem's message and sound. Include vivid language and quote sufficiently from the poems to support your ideas.

Building Knowledge and Insight

ANCHOR TEXT

from *Dust Tracks on a Road*

Connecting to the Essential Question Hurston writes of a time when she received encouragement from an unexpected source. As you read, look for details that reveal Hurston's self-confidence to help you think about the Essential Question: **How does literature shape or reflect society?**

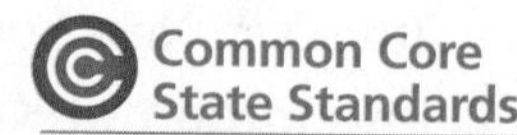

Common Core State Standards

Reading Informational Text

4. Determine the meaning of words and phrases as they are used in a text.

6. Determine an author's point of view or purpose in a text, analyzing how style and content contribute to the power, persuasiveness, or beauty of the text.

Close Reading Focus

Autobiography; Social Context; Dialogue; Dialect

Autobiography is a nonfiction account of a writer's life told in his or her own words. An autobiography documents the writer's feelings about key events and experiences. Because of this personal content, autobiographies often reveal **social context**—the attitudes, customs, and beliefs of the culture in which the writer lived. Hurston's autobiography provides a glimpse into the social context of her African American community in rural Florida during the early years of the twentieth century.

Hurston brings additional life to her characters and their social context by using two literary elements:

- **Dialogue:** the conversations among people
- **Dialect:** the form of a language spoken by people of a particular region or group

Hurston's use of dialogue allows her characters to speak for themselves. Her use of dialect allows them to speak with authenticity. As you read, notice the ways dialogue and dialect add nuance and depth to your understanding of Hurston's experience.

Preparing to Read Complex Texts Hurston's **purpose for writing**—to share her personal experience and show the vitality of the African American community—contributes to the decisions she makes about the events and thoughts to describe in her autobiography. The meaning of the piece is shaped by Hurston's purpose for writing it. As you read, **analyze the effect of the author's purpose** on meaning. Note words, details, characters, actions, and events in a chart like the one shown. Determine how each element helps Hurston meet her overall purpose for writing.

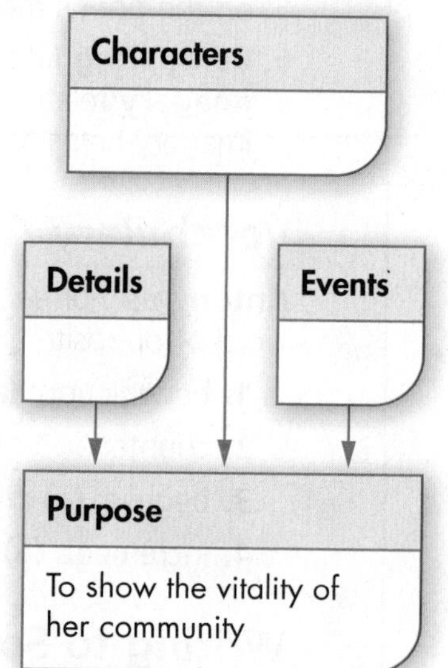

Vocabulary

You will encounter the words listed here in the text that follows. Copy the words into your notebook. What do the suffixes *-ness* and *-tion* tell you about the part of speech of two of the vocabulary words?

brazenness **duration**
caper **exalted**

Zora Neale Hurston *(1891–1960)*

Author of *Dust Tracks on a Road*

Zora Neale Hurston was an influential author and a pioneering force in African American culture. Yet, she died penniless and was buried in an unmarked grave in Fort Pierce, Florida. Hurston was almost entirely forgotten until author Alice Walker set out to locate and mark her grave, recording the experience in a 1975 *Ms.* magazine article. Walker's effort restored Hurston to her rightful place as "the dominant black woman writer" of her time.

Early Influences Hurston grew up in Eatonville, Florida, America's first fully incorporated African American township. One of eight children, she was, by her own account, a spirited, curious child who "always wanted to go." Hurston's childhood abruptly ended when her mother died. She then lived with a series of friends and relatives and, by age fourteen, was supporting herself.

Two Careers Hurston began writing while studying at Howard University. In 1925, she moved to New York City. She soon published a story and a play, firmly establishing herself as one of the bright new talents of the Harlem Renaissance. She attended Barnard College, where her work came to the attention of prominent anthropologist Franz Boas. He convinced Hurston to begin graduate studies in anthropology at Columbia University. With an academic grant, she began a second career as a folklorist.

Preserving a Culture Hurston was one of the first American writers to recognize that a cultural heritage was valuable in its own right. During the Great Migration, when African Americans from the South migrated by the hundreds of thousands to the North, Hurston moved against the tide. She returned to the South for six years to collect African American folk tales. In 1935, she published *Mules and Men*, the first volume of black American folklore compiled by an African American. Her work helped to document the African American connection to the stories, songs, and myths of Africa.

The Road to Obscurity Hurston achieved critical and popular success during the 1930s and 1940s with the novels *Jonah's Gourd Vine* (1934), *Their Eyes Were Watching God* (1937), *Moses, Man of the Mountain* (1939), and her prize-winning autobiography, *Dust Tracks on a Road* (1942).

"There are years that ask questions and years that answer."

from

DUST TRACKS ON A ROAD

Zora Neale Hurston

BACKGROUND In this excerpt from Zora Neale Hurston's autobiography, the young Zora experiences an event that opens her eyes to the world of literature and sets the stage for her career as a writer.

I used to take a seat on top of the gatepost and watch the world go by. One way to Orlando[1] ran past my house, so the carriages and cars would pass before me. The movement made me glad to see it. Often the white travelers would hail me, but more often I hailed them, and asked, "Don't you want me to go a piece of the way with you?"

They always did. I know now that I must have caused a great deal of amusement among them, but my self-assurance must have carried the point, for I was always invited to come along. I'd ride up the road for perhaps a half-mile, then walk back. I did not do this with the permission of my parents, nor with their foreknowledge.[2]

1. **Orlando** (ôr lan′ dō) city in central Florida, about five miles from Eatonville, Hurston's hometown.
2. **foreknowledge** (fôr′ näl′ ij) *n.* awareness of something before it happens or exists.

▲ **Critical Viewing** What elements of this photograph document the economic realities many of these children probably faced? **ANALYZE**

When they found out about it later, I usually got a whipping. My grandmother worried about my forward ways a great deal. She had known slavery and to her my brazenness was unthinkable.

"Git down offa dat gate-post! You li'l sow, you! Git down! Setting up dere looking dem white folks right in de face! They's gowine[3] to lynch you, yet. And don't stand in dat doorway gazing out at 'em neither. Youse too brazen to live long."[4]

Nevertheless, I kept right on gazing at them, and "going a piece of the way" whenever I could make it. The village seemed dull to me most of the time. If the village was singing a chorus, I must have missed the tune.

Perhaps a year before the old man[5] died, I came to know two other white people for myself. They were women.

It came about this way. The whites who came down from the North were often brought by their friends to visit the village school. A Negro school was something strange to them, and while they were always sympathetic and kind, curiosity must have been present, also. They came and went, came and went. Always, the room was hurriedly put in order, and we were threatened with a prompt and bloody death if we cut one caper while the visitors were present. We always sang a spiritual, led by Mr. Calhoun himself. Mrs. Calhoun always stood in the back, with a palmetto switch[6] in her hand as a

Vocabulary

brazenness (brā′ zən nəs) *n.* shamelessness; boldness; impudence

Vocabulary

caper (kā′ pər) *n.* prank

Comprehension

Why does her grandmother worry about Zora's sitting on the gatepost and accepting rides from strangers?

3. **gowine** "going."
4. **"Git down . . . live long"** Hurston's grandmother's fears reflect the belief of many people at the time that it was dangerous for African Americans to be assertive toward whites.
5. **the old man** white farmer who had developed a friendship with Hurston.
6. **palmetto** (pal met′ ō) **switch** whip made from the fan-shaped leaves of the palmetto, a type of palm tree.

squelcher. We were all little angels for the **duration**, because we'd better be. She would cut her eyes and give us a glare that meant trouble, then turn her face towards the visitors and beam as much as to say it was a great privilege and pleasure to teach lovely children like us. They couldn't see that palmetto hickory in her hand behind all those benches, but we knew where our angelic behavior was coming from.

Social Context
What concerns are revealed in this passage about preparation for visitors?

Usually, the visitors gave warning a day ahead and we would be cautioned to put on shoes, comb our heads, and see to ears and fingernails. There was a close inspection of every one of us before we marched in that morning. Knotty heads, dirty ears and fingernails got hauled out of line, strapped and sent home to lick the calf over again.

This particular afternoon, the two young ladies just popped in. Mr. Calhoun was flustered, but he put on the best show he could. He dismissed the class that he was teaching up at the front of the room, then called the fifth grade in reading. That was my class.

Vocabulary

duration (du ra′ shun) *n.* the time during which something continues or exists

exalted (eg zôlt′ id) *adj.* filled with joy or pride; elated

So we took our readers and went up front. We stood up in the usual line, and opened to the lesson. It was the story of Pluto and Persephone. It was new and hard to the class in general, and Mr. Calhoun was very uncomfortable as the readers stumbled along, spelling out words with their lips, and in mumbling undertones before they exposed them experimentally to the teacher's ears.

Then it came to me. I was fifth or sixth down the line. The story was not new to me, because I had read my reader through from lid to lid, the first week that Papa had bought it for me.

Spiral Review
Tone What is Hurston's tone as she describes the visitors? Explain

That is how it was that my eyes were not in the book, working out the paragraph which I knew would be mine by counting the children ahead of me. I was observing our visitors, who held a book between them, following the lesson. They had shiny hair, mostly brownish. One had a looping gold chain around her neck. The other one was dressed all over in black and white with a pretty finger ring on her left hand. But the thing that held my eyes were their fingers. They were long and thin, and very white, except up near the tips. There they were baby pink. I had never seen such hands. It was a fascinating discovery for me. I wondered how they felt. I would have given those hands more attention, but the child before me was almost through. My turn next, so I got on my mark, bringing my eyes back to the book and made sure of my place. Some of the stories I had reread several times, and this Greco-Roman myth was one of my favorites. I was **exalted** by it, and that is the way I read my paragraph.

"Yes, Jupiter had seen her (Persephone). He had seen the maiden picking flowers in the field. He had seen the chariot of the dark monarch pause by the maiden's side. He had seen him when he seized Persephone. He had seen the black horses leap down Mount Aetna's fiery throat. Persephone was now in Pluto's dark realm and he had made her his wife."

The two women looked at each other and then back to me. Mr. Calhoun broke out with a proud smile beneath his bristly moustache, and instead of the next child taking up where I had ended, he nodded to me to go on. So I read the story to the end, where flying Mercury, the messenger of the Gods, brought Persephone back to the sunlit earth and restored her to the arms of Dame Ceres, her mother, that the world might have springtime and summer flowers, autumn and harvest. But because she had bitten the pomegranate[7] while in Pluto's kingdom, she must return to him for three months of each year, and be his queen. Then the world had winter, until she returned to earth.

Mr. Calhoun broke out with a proud smile beneath his bristly moustache . . .

The class was dismissed, and the visitors smiled us away and went into a low-voiced conversation with Mr. Calhoun for a few minutes. They glanced my way once or twice and I began to worry. Not only was I barefooted, but my feet and legs were dusty. My hair was more uncombed than usual, and my nails were not shiny clean. Oh, I'm going to catch it now. Those ladies saw me, too. Mr. Calhoun is promising to 'tend to me. So I thought.

Then Mr. Calhoun called me. I went up thinking how awful it was to get a whipping before company. Furthermore, I heard a snicker run over the room. Hennie Clark and Stell Brazzle did it out loud, so I would be sure to hear them. The smart-aleck was going to get it. I slipped one hand behind me and switched my dress tail at them, indicating scorn.

Analyzing Effect of Author's Purpose

Why do you think Hurston includes this description of her response to taunting classmates?

"Come here, Zora Neale," Mr. Calhoun cooed as I reached the desk. He put his hand on my shoulder and gave me little pats. The ladies smiled and held out those flower-looking fingers towards me. I seized the opportunity for a good look.

"Shake hands with the ladies, Zora Neale," Mr. Calhoun prompted and they took my hand one after the other and smiled. They asked if I loved school, and I lied that I did. There was *some* truth in it, because I liked geography[8] and reading, and I liked to play at recess time. Who ever it was invented writing and arithmetic got no thanks from me. Neither did I like the arrangement where the teacher could sit up there with a palmetto stem and lick me whenever he saw fit. I hated things I couldn't do anything about. But I knew better than to bring that up right there, so I said yes, I *loved* school.

"I can tell you do," Brown Taffeta gleamed. She patted my head, and was lucky enough not to get sandspurs in her hand. Children who roll and tumble in the grass in Florida are apt to get sandspurs in their hair. They shook hands with me again and I went back to my seat.

When school let out at three o'clock, Mr. Calhoun told me to wait. When everybody had gone, he told me I was to go to the Park House,

Comprehension

Why is Zora afraid to approach her teacher after reading so well?

---

7. **pomegranate** (päm′ gran′ it) *n.* round, red-skinned fruit with many seeds.
8. **geography** (je äg′ rə fē) *n.* science that deals with the surface of the earth.

that was the hotel in Maitland,[9] the next afternoon to call upon Mrs. Johnstone and Miss Hurd. I must tell Mama to see that I was clean and brushed from head to feet, and I must wear shoes and stockings. The ladies liked me, he said, and I must be on my best behavior.

Analyzing Effect of Author's Purpose
Why do you think that Hurston includes this incident about her mother preparing her for her meeting with the women?

The next day I was let out of school an hour early, and went home to be stood up in a tub full of suds and be scrubbed and have my ears dug into. My sandy hair sported a red ribbon to match my red and white checked gingham dress, starched until it could stand alone. Mama saw to it that my shoes were on the right feet, since I was careless about left and right. Last thing, I was given a handkerchief to carry, warned again about my behavior, and sent off, with my big brother John to go as far as the hotel gate with me.

First thing, the ladies gave me strange things, like stuffed dates and preserved ginger, and encouraged me to eat all that I wanted. Then they showed me their Japanese dolls and just talked. I was then handed a copy of *Scribner's Magazine*,[10] and asked to read a place that was pointed out to me. After a paragraph or two, I was told with smiles, that that would do.

I was led out on the grounds and they took my picture under a palm tree. They handed me what was to me then a heavy cylinder done up in fancy paper, tied with a ribbon, and they told me goodbye, asking me not to open it until I got home.

My brother was waiting for me down by the lake, and we hurried home, eager to see what was in the thing. It was too heavy to be candy or anything like that. John insisted on toting it for me.

My mother made John give it back to me and let me open it. Perhaps, I shall never experience such joy again. The nearest thing to that moment was the telegram accepting my first book. One hundred goldy-new pennies rolled out of the cylinder. Their gleam lit up the world. It was not avarice[11] that moved me. It was the beauty of the thing. I stood on the mountain. Mama let me play with my pennies for a while, then put them away for me to keep.

That was only the beginning. The next day I received an Episcopal hymn-book bound in white leather with a golden cross stamped into the front cover, a copy of *The Swiss Family Robinson*, and a book of fairy tales.

Social Context
What does Zora's excitement about the books she receives reveal about the social context of her community?

I set about to commit the song words to memory. There was no music written there, just the words. But there was to my consciousness music in between them just the same. "When I Survey the Wondrous Cross" seemed the most beautiful to me, so I committed that to memory first of all. Some of them seemed dull and without life, and I pretended they were not there. If white people liked trashy singing like that, there must be something funny about them that I had not noticed before. I stuck to the pretty ones where the words marched to a throb I could feel.

---

9. **Maitland** (māt′ lənd) city in Florida, close to Eatonville.
10. ***Scribner's Magazine*** literary magazine no longer published.
11. **avarice** (av′ ə ris) *n.* extreme desire for wealth; greed.

A month or so after the young ladies returned to Minnesota, they sent me a huge box packed with clothes and books. The red coat with a wide circular collar and the red tam[12] pleased me more than any of the other things. My chums pretended not to like anything that I had, but even then I knew that they were jealous. Old Smarty had gotten by them again. The clothes were not new, but they were very good. I shone like the morning sun.

But the books gave me more pleasure than the clothes. I had never been too keen on dressing up. It called for hard scrubbings with Octagon soap suds getting in my eyes, and none too gentle fingers scrubbing my neck and gouging in my ears.

In that box were *Gulliver's Travels, Grimm's Fairy Tales, Dick Whittington, Greek and Roman Myths,* and best of all, *Norse Tales.* Why did the Norse tales strike so deeply into my soul? I do not know, but they did. I seemed to remember seeing Thor swing his mighty short-handled hammer as he sped across the sky in rumbling thunder, lightning flashing from the tread of his steeds and the wheels of his chariot. The great and good Odin, who went down to the well of knowledge to drink, and was told that the price of a drink from that fountain was an eye. Odin drank deeply, then plucked out one eye without a murmur and handed it to the grizzly keeper, and walked away. That held majesty for me.

Of the Greeks, Hercules moved me most. I followed him eagerly on his tasks. The story of the choice of Hercules as a boy when he met Pleasure and Duty, and put his hand in that of Duty and followed her steep way to the blue hills of fame and glory, which she pointed out at the end, moved me profoundly. I resolved to be like him. The tricks and turns of the other Gods and Goddesses left me cold. There were other thin books about this and that sweet and gentle little girl who gave up her heart to Christ and good works. Almost always they died from it, preaching as they passed. I was utterly indifferent to their deaths. In the first place I could not conceive of death, and in the next place they never had any funerals that amounted to a hill of beans, so I didn't care how soon they rolled up their big, soulful, blue eyes and kicked the bucket. They had no meat on their bones.

But I also met Hans Andersen and Robert Louis Stevenson. They seemed to know what I wanted to hear and said it in a way that tingled me. Just a little below these friends was Rudyard Kipling in his *Jungle Books.* I loved his talking snakes as much as I did the hero.

I came to start reading the Bible through my mother. She gave me a licking one afternoon for repeating something I had overheard a neighbor telling her. She locked me in her room after the whipping,

12. tam (tam) *n.* cap with a wide, round, flat top and sometimes a center pompom.

The American EXPERIENCE

Zora Neale Hurston Rediscovered
Although she died in a welfare home in 1960 penniless and unknown, the rediscovery of Zora Neale Hurston in the 1970s is among the most dramatic events in American literary history. Hurston became a subject of author Alice Walker's 1983 essay, "In Search of Our Mother's Gardens." Ten years earlier, Walker's article "Looking for Zora" described her 1973 search to find and mark Hurston's unknown grave.

In both of her writings, Walker speaks of the importance of recovering and remembering Hurston as one of the greatest African American folklorists of all time and a major American writer. Walker championed the cause to resurrect Hurston's literary reputation and, once again, give her a prominent place in our literary heritage.

Connect to the Literature

Think about the incident that Hurston describes in this excerpt from her autobiography. Why do you think she became a writer?

Comprehension

Of all the gifts she receives, which gives Zora the most pleasure? Explain.

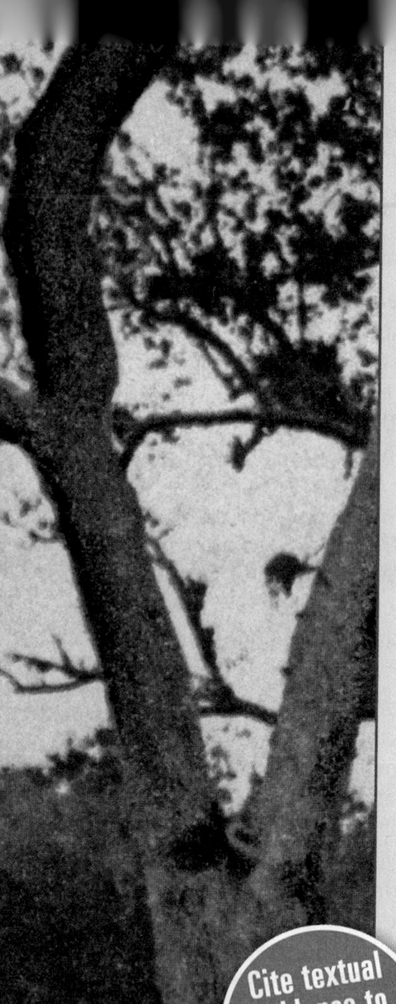

and the Bible was the only thing in there for me to read. I happened to open to the place where David[13] was doing some mighty smiting, and I got interested. David went here and he went there, and no matter where he went, he smote 'em hip and thigh. Then he sung songs to his harp awhile, and went out and smote some more. Not one time did David stop and preach about sins and other things. All David wanted to know from God was who to kill and when. He took care of the other details himself. Never a quiet moment. I liked him a lot. So I read a great deal more in the Bible, hunting for some more active people like David. Except for the beautiful language of Luke and Paul,[14] the New Testament still plays a poor second to the Old Testament for me. The Jews had a God who laid about Him when they needed Him. I could see no use waiting until Judgment Day to see a man who was just crying for a good killing, to be told to go and roast. My idea was to give him a good killing first, and then if he got roasted later on, so much the better.

---

13. David in the Bible, the second king of Israel, the land of the Hebrews.
14. Luke and Paul two Christian Apostles who wrote parts of the New Testament.

Critical Reading

Cite textual evidence to support your responses.

1. **Key Ideas and Details (a)** What does Zora do when white travelers pass by her house? **(b) Infer:** What does this activity tell you about her?
2. **Key Ideas and Details (a)** Who are the two white women Zora meets, and why are they at her school? **(b) Support:** How can you tell that these two women made an impression on Hurston?
3. **Key Ideas and Details (a)** What does Zora find fascinating about the two visitors? **(b) Infer:** What does her fascination suggest about her life experiences so far?
4. **Key Ideas and Details (a)** Describe Zora's response to the gifts she receives. **(b) Infer:** What does her preference reveal about her?
5. **Integration of Knowledge and Ideas** What does this episode from Hurston's childhood suggest about the qualities that helped people of her era succeed despite social barriers, such as those of gender or race? In your response, use at least two of these Essential Question words: *self-reliance, individualism, persistence, dignity, creativity.* ***[Connecting to the Essential Question: How does literature shape or reflect society?]***

Close Reading Activities

from *Dust Tracks on a Road*

Literary Analysis

1. **Key Ideas and Details** In this excerpt from her **autobiography,** Hurston describes her boldness as a child. **(a)** Why was Hurston's grandmother worried about her granddaughter's bold personality? **(b)** What do you understand about the **social context** from the grandmother's statements?
2. **Key Ideas and Details** What do you learn about the social context of Hurston's life from these details? **(a)** the schoolroom's being cleaned for visitors **(b)** students reading mythology **(c)** Hurston's going to school barefoot
3. **Key Ideas and Details** Find three more details that reveal the attitudes of Hurston's culture. Record them in a chart like the one shown.

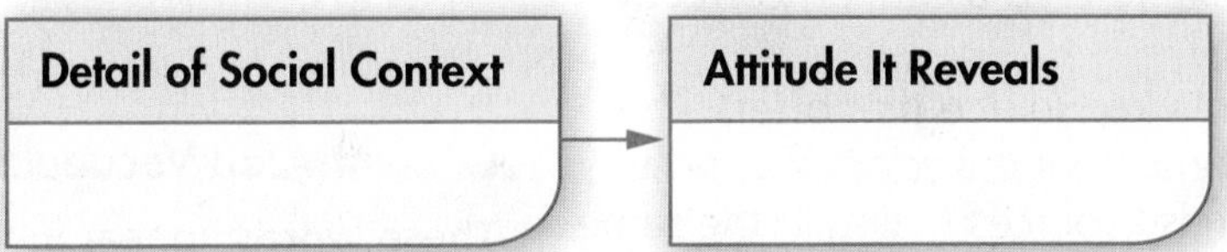

4. **Craft and Structure** **(a)** What information about Hurston is revealed in the opening **dialogue** she has with her grandmother? **(b)** Why do you think Hurston included her grandmother's words in **dialect**?
5. **Key Ideas and Details** **(a)** What details does Hurston use to reveal her independence and passion for learning? **(b)** In what ways does her inclusion of details reflect her **purpose?**
6. **Integration and Knowledge of Ideas** Why do you think Hurston wrote about her experience with the Minnesotans?

Vocabulary Acquisition and Use

Write a sentence for each word pair, using the words correctly.

1. duration/exalted
2. brazenness/caper

Writing to Sources

Narrative Text Write a **reflective essay** that tells a story about a moment in your life that inspired you to pursue something you love. Develop a clear conflict or problem by describing obstacles you faced. Develop a clear resolution by showing the events that inspired you and the changes that occurred as a result. Enhance the plot and develop characters by using a range of literary strategies and devices, including dialogue.

Common Core State Standards

Writing

3. Write narratives to develop real or imagined experiences or events using effective technique, well-chosen details, and well-structured event sequences.

3.a. Engage and orient the reader by setting out a problem, situation, or observation and its signifiance.

3.b. Use narrative techniques, such as dialogue, to develop experiences, events, and/or characters.

3.e. Provide a conclusion that follows from and reflects on what is experienced, observed, or resolved over the course of the narrative.

Reading for Information

Analyzing Functional and Expository Texts

Online Citation Organizer • Online Encyclopedia

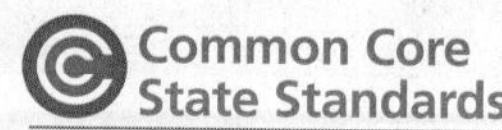

Writing

8. Gather relevant information from multiple authoritative print and digital sources; assess the strengths and limitations of each source in terms of the task, purpose, and audience; integrate information, avoiding plagiarism and following a standard format for citation.

About the Texts

An **online citation organizer** is a Web resource that provides correctly formatted citations to use in bibliographies. This service compiles the citation rules from many style books—MLA, APA, and others—and allows users to choose the style they prefer. Users input research source information and the site returns a citation correctly formatted to a specific style.

An **online encyclopedia** is an electronic source that offers articles on varied topics. Many traditional print encyclopedias now make their content available online; these sources maintain the same authority as their print versions. **Wikipedia** is an online encyclopedia written and edited by users, a practice that has led some to criticize its accuracy. Common features of online encyclopedias include a search engine that allows the user to locate articles, links to other Web pages with related information, and a list of references consulted by the writer or writers.

Preparing to Read Complex Texts

As you use a digital reference tool, it is important to ensure its truthfulness, or validity, and its accuracy, or reliability. To **evaluate validity and reliability,** follow these steps:

- Check references listed within or at the end of an article.
- Consult outside references that you know to be authoritative.
- Assess the authority of the writer or writers, if listed.

As you read, use a chart like the one shown to evaluate the validity and reliability of online reference sources.

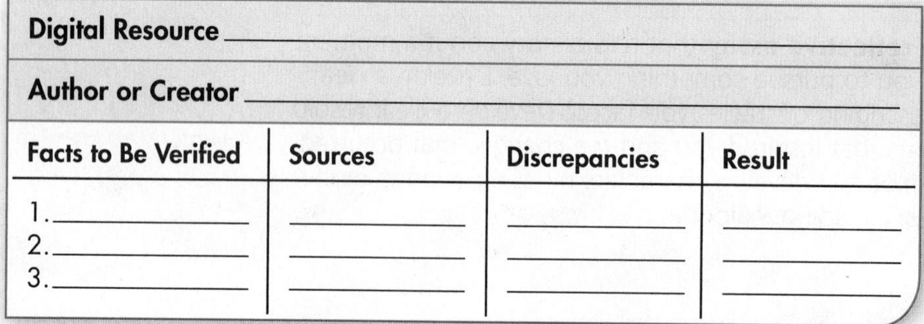

Digital Resource ____________________

Author or Creator ____________________

Facts to Be Verified	Sources	Discrepancies	Result
1. ________	________	________	________
2. ________	________	________	________
3. ________	________	________	________

Content-Area Vocabulary

These words appear in the selections that follow. They may also appear in other content-area texts.

interactive (in′ tər ak′ tiv) *adj.* in computer technology, reacting or responding to the user

software (sôft wer′) *n.* the collection of electronic programming directions that controls a computer's functioning

wiki (wi′ kē) *n.* Web site that can be edited by any user

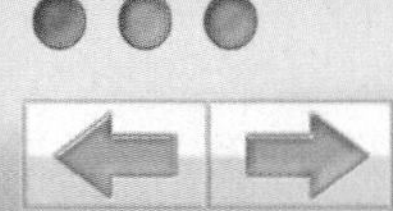

Citation Machine

Landmarks Son of Citation Machine™

▼ **MLA**

Print

- Book: One or More Authors
- Encyclopedia or other reference work
- Journal Article: One or More Authors
- Magazine Article: One or More Authors

Non-Print

- Internet Journal or Magazine Article: One or More Authors
- Web Page
- Online Encyclopedia
- Encyclopedia (CD-ROM)

▼ **APA**

▼ **CHICAGO**

▼ **TURABIAN**

CITATION MACHINE

Serving Students & Teachers

K-12, College, & University

Numbered items show how to use the organizer.

Citation Machine™ is an **interactive** web tool designed to assist high school, college, and university students, their teachers, and independent researchers in their effort to respect other people's intellectual properties. To use Citation Machine™, simply ...

1. Click the citation format you need and then the type of resource you wish to cite.
2. Complete the Web form that appears with information from your source.
3. Click **Make Citations** to generate standard bibliographic and in-text citations.

The primary goal of this tool is to make it so easy for **high school**, **college**, and **university students** and other researchers to credit information sources that there is virtually no reason not to—because **SOMEDAY THE INFORMATION SOMEONE WANTS TO USE WILL BE YOURS.**

Warning: There are many nuances to how citations are formed, and this **software** may not pick up all of the circumstances that influence a citation's proper format. The Citation Machine™ cannot fully guarantee the accuracy of citations generated by this tool.

If you have questions about the proper citation of these or other source types, consult your local copy of:

- MLA Handbook for Writers of Research Papers: 6th Edition or
- Publication Manual of the American Psychological Association: 5th Edition.

Bullets beneath each format or style of citation list additional resources.

There will be copies in your school or public libraries.

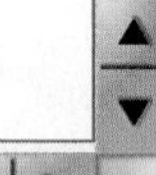

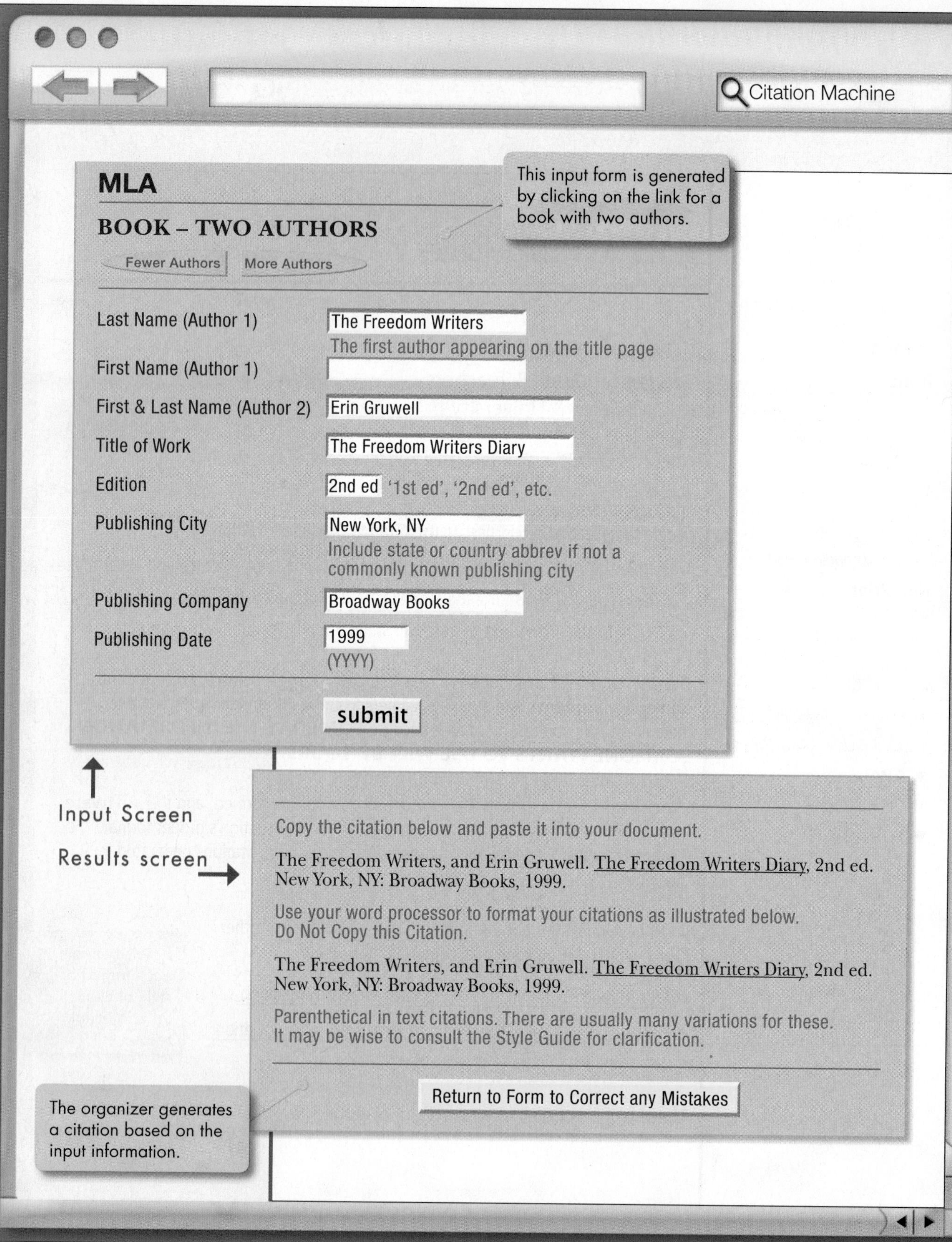
Citation Machine
MLA
BOOK – TWO AUTHORS
Fewer Authors
More Authors
Last Name (Author 1)
The Freedom Writers
The first author appearing on the title page
First Name (Author 1)
First & Last Name (Author 2)
Erin Gruwell
Title of Work
The Freedom Writers Diary
Edition
2nd ed
'1st ed', '2nd ed', etc.
Publishing City
New York, NY
Include state or country abbrev if not a commonly known publishing city
Publishing Company
Broadway Books
Publishing Date
1999
(YYYY)
submit
This input form is generated by clicking on the link for a book with two authors.
Input Screen
Results screen
Copy the citation below and paste it into your document.
The Freedom Writers, and Erin Gruwell. The Freedom Writers Diary, 2nd ed. New York, NY: Broadway Books, 1999.
Use your word processor to format your citations as illustrated below. Do Not Copy this Citation.
The Freedom Writers, and Erin Gruwell. The Freedom Writers Diary, 2nd ed. New York, NY: Broadway Books, 1999.
Parenthetical in text citations. There are usually many variations for these. It may be wise to consult the Style Guide for clarification.
Return to Form to Correct any Mistakes
The organizer generates a citation based on the input information.

Online Encyclopedia

Atlanta Braves

article | discussion | edit this page | history

Atlanta Braves

From **Wiki**pedia, the free encyclopedia

The **Atlanta Braves** are a National League Major League Baseball team based in Atlanta, Georgia since 1966, after having been located first in Boston (1871–1952) and then in Milwaukee (1953–1965). The franchise is one of the only two remaining National League charter members, along with the Chicago Cubs. The Braves compete in the NL East after being in the western division from 1969 to 1993.

The first paragraph defines the topic, provides some history, and suggests other aspects of the topic the reader might explore.

For the last decade and a half, the Braves have been one of the most successful franchises in baseball, winning their division title an unprecedented 14 consecutive times from 1991 to 2005 (omitting the strike-shortened 1994 season in which there were no official division champions), and advancing to the World Series five times in that period, winning it in 1995. In their history, the Braves have won 16 divisional titles, nine National League pennants, and three World Series championships—in 1914 as the Boston Braves, in 1957 as the Milwaukee Braves, and in 1995 while in Atlanta. (The Braves are the only MLB franchise to have won the Series in three different home cities.)

By clicking on a highlighted hyperlink (blue text), the user will be connected to other articles about baseball.

For current news on this topic, see **20--Atlanta Braves season**

Atlanta Braves
Established 1871
Based in Atlanta since 1966

- **National League (1876–present)**
- **East Division (1994–present)**

Current uniform

Retired Numbers

3, 21, 35, 41, 42, 44

Name

- **Atlanta Braves (1966–present)**
- Milwaukee Braves (1953–1965)
- Boston Braves (1941–1952)
- Boston Bees (1936–1940)
- Boston Braves (1912–1935)
- Boston Rustlers (1911)
- Boston Doves (1907–1910)
- Boston Beaneaters (1883–1906)
- Boston Red Stockings (1871–1882)

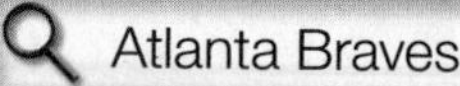

Quick reference information is provided in a list format.

article | discussion | edit this page | history

Ballpark

- **Turner Field (1997–present)**
- Atlanta-Fulton County Stadium (1966–1976)
  - a.k.a. Atlanta Stadium (1966–1976)
- Milwaukee County Stadium (1953–1965)
- Braves Field (1915–1952)
  - a.k.a. National League Park (1936–1941)
- Fenway Park (1914–1915)
- South End Grounds (1894–1914)
- Congress Street Grounds (1894)
- South End Grounds (1871–1894)

NL Pennants (17) 1877 · 1878 · 1883 · 1891 · 1892 · 1893 · 1897 · 1898 · 1914 · 1948 · 1957 · 1958 · 1991 · 1992 · 1995 · 1996 · 1999

East Division titles (11) 1995 · 1996 · 1997 · 1998 · 1999 · 2000 · 2001 · 2002 · 2003 · 2004 · 2005

West Division titles (5) 1969 · 1982 · 1991 · 1992 · 1993

Quick Facts

- **Founded:** 1871 in Boston, Massachusetts as the Boston Red Stockings a charter member of the National Association. The club became a charter member of the National League in 1876 and has remained in the league without a break since then. The Braves are the oldest continuously operating sports franchise in North American sports. Arguably, they can trace their ancestry to the original Cincinnati Red Stockings of 1869–1870, baseball's first openly professional team. When the N.A. formed, Cincinnati's backers declined to field a team in the new league and Red Stockings player-manager Harry Wright along with three of the best players from that team moved collectively to Boston and took the nickname with them.
- **Formerly known as:** Boston Braves (1912–1952), and Milwaukee Braves (1953–1965). Prior to 1912, the Boston team had several unofficial nicknames: "Red Stockings" and "Red Caps" in the 1870s and 1880s; "Beaneaters" in the 1890s and early 1900s; "Doves" (when the Dovey family owned the franchise, 1907–1910) and "Rustlers" (when William Russell owned the franchise, 1911). Following the 1935 season, after enduring bankruptcy and a series of poor seasons, new owner Bob Quinn asked a team of sportswriters to choose a new nickname, to change the team luck. The sportswriters chose "Bees", which was adopted in 1936, though it never really caught on. The team dropped the nickname in 1941, using only the official name "Braves" from 1941 on.
- **Uniform colors:** Navy blue, garnet red, and white
- **Logo design:** The script word "Braves"
- **Team mottos:** "Atlanta's Pastime Since 1966" and "Welcome to the Bigs"

Close Reading Activities

Online Citation Organizer • Online Encyclopedia

Critical Reading

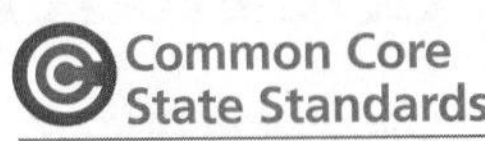

Writing
10. Write routinely over extended time frames and shorter time frames for a range of tasks, purposes, and audiences.

Language
4.d. Verify the preliminary determination of the meaning of a word or phrase.

1. **Key Ideas and Details (a)** Why might an online citation organizer be valuable to someone writing a research paper? **(b)** What advantages and disadvantages does it offer when compared to a traditional print resource?

2. **Key Ideas and Details (a)** What warning does the online citation organizer provide? **(b)** How does this warning help you evaluate the site's reliability and credibility?

3. **Key Ideas and Details (a)** CIte two facts presented in the Wikipedia article about the Atlanta Braves. **(b)** Explain two methods you could use to verify each fact and evaluate the overall reliability and credibility of the article.

4. **Content-Area Vocabulary (a)** Explain how the meaning of the Latin prefix *inter-* ("among or between") contributes to the meaning of *interactive*. **(b)** Determine the meaning of these words derived from the same Latin prefix: *intercom, interdict, intercept.* **(c)** Use a dictionary to verify your preliminary definitions.

Timed Writing

Argument [40 minutes]

Format

An **argumentative essay** advances a thesis, or position supported by logical reasons. State your thesis in the introduction, support it in the body paragraphs, and restate it in your conclusion.

Write an **argumentative essay** in which you persuade readers that it is or is not a good idea to do important research using an online encyclopedia that is written and edited by its users. Consider both the benefits and **issues** such an online tool might present. Cite specific details, including your own observations, to support your argument.

Academic Vocabulary

Issues are the problems, concerns, or consequences created by a situation. Issues are often multifaceted, requiring you to discuss them from more than a single angle.

5-Minute Planner

Complete these steps before you begin to write:

1. Read the prompt carefully. Identify key words.
2. Make a list of varied types of evidence that support your thesis.
3. Sketch an outline of your essay.
4. Reread the prompt, and draft your essay. **TIP** Use transitional words and phrases such as *however* and *on the other hand* to distinguish ideas in your essay and convey your meaning more clearly.

Write a Multimedia Presentation of an Argument

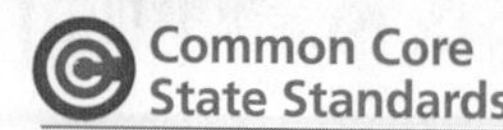

Writing

1. Write arguments to support claims in an analysis of substantive topics or texts, using valid reasoning and relevant and sufficient evidence.

1.b. Develop claim(s) and counterclaims fairly and thoroughly, supplying the most relevant evidence for each while pointing out the strengths and limitations of both in a manner that anticipates the audience's knowledge level, concerns, values, and possible biases.

6. Use technology, including the Internet, to produce, publish, and update individual or shared writing products in response to ongoing feedback, including new arguments or information.

8. Gather relevant information from multiple authoritative print and digital sources, using advanced searches effectively.

Speaking and Listening

5. Make strategic use of digital media in presentations to enhance understanding of findings, reasoning, and evidence and to add interest.

Argumentative Text Today, electronic media dominates the communications landscape. The effect of the wide variety of media on an audience is very different from that of the printed word alone. By combining text, images, and sound in a multimedia presentation, you can bring ideas to life in new ways. For example, you can show video clips of an actual event or an interview with an expert as powerful evidence to support your argument. Follow the steps outlined in this workshop to write and deliver your own multimedia presentation of an argument.

Assignment Write and deliver a multimedia presentation in which you present a claim on a topic and support that claim.

What to Include Your multimedia presentation should feature the following elements:

- Integrated text, audio, and visual components
- The use of a wide range of media, including films, newspapers, magazines, online information, television, and videos
- Innovative use of media to convey concepts
- Reinforcement of key ideas with the use of an appropriate medium
- A scripted and logical organization to present a focused message

To preview the criteria on which your multimedia presentation may be assessed, see the rubric on page 951.

	Sources of Existing Media	Hardware to Generate New Media	Software to Edit Media
Text	books, magazines, newspapers, Web sites, CD-ROMs, e-mails	keyboard; scanner	word processor; multimedia software
Photographs	books, magazines, newspapers, Web sites, CD-ROMs	digital camera; scanner	photo editing software
Illustrations	books, magazines, newspapers, Web sites, CD-ROMs	keyboard; graphics tablet; scanner	graphics programs
Movies	television, DVDs, videos, Web sites, CD-ROMs	digital video camera	digital editor; animation software
Sound	radio, CDs, Web sites, CD-ROMs	microphone; digital instruments	sound/music editor

Prewriting and Planning

Choosing Your Topic

To choose a subject for your multimedia presentation of an argument, use one of the following strategies:

- **List preferences.** Think about topics and local or global issues that you feel passionate about. What argument would you make to convince others to agree with you? What would your claim be? List your potential topics and choose your favorite.
- **Create a media checklist.** Using a chart like the one shown, list the various types of media that are available for several different topics. Note specific media that would best suit your topic in the left-hand column. Review your chart, and choose the topic that offers the richest possibilities.

Media Checklist	Animal Shelters
☑ Music	*Sad or melancholy music*
☑ Videos	*Cats and dogs in cages*
☑ Art	*Sketches of cats and dogs*
☑ Photographs	*People adopting pets*
☐ Web Pages	
☑ Interviews	*Volunteer at the shelter*

Narrowing Your Topic

Find a single example within a broad subject. The general topic you chose is probably too big to be manageable. For example, the topic of animal shelters is too broad to address effectively in an argument. However, volunteering at an animal shelter or adopting a pet is manageable. Be on the lookout for similar slices of a broad subject. Images and sounds can be more difficult to find than text, so continue to research varied material, and make sure you will have enough.

Gathering Materials

Research your topic. As you gather materials, note creative ways to involve viewers. Consult your library for audio or video clips of interviews, documentaries, music, and art resources. Search the Internet for photographs, recordings, cartoons, and archives of periodicals. Keep careful notes about your media sources so you can credit them accurately.

Develop your claim. Review your notes and research materials. Consider the most relevant, authoritative evidence from your research to develop your claim. Which evidence makes your claim the strongest and the most compelling?

Drafting

Shaping Your Presentation

Sketch an outline. Your presentation needs the same solid structure as an argumentative essay or a research paper. Support your claim with a unified approach and a script that details the sequence of ideas. Your final script will orchestrate the presentation of multiple elements—as you draft, though, a breakdown of your presentation's major components will keep you focused and help you avoid oversights.

Writing

1.a. Introduce precise, knowledgeable claim(s), establish the significance of the claim(s), distinguish the claim(s) from alternate or opposing claims, and create an organization that logically sequences claim(s), counterclaims, reasons, and evidence.

Opening Image 1

Audio: "Adagio for Strings" by Samuel Barber
Photo: A sad-looking dog curled up in a blanket

2

Audio: (fade music level)
Photo: Forlorn cat outside
Narration: Animals need a home and someone to play with them.

3

Audio: (increase music level)
Video: Cats and dogs peering out of their cages

Plan your delivery. Remember that your delivery will require a script and format that allow you to use two or more different media at the same time. Consider a two- or three-column chart to diagram what will occur at any given moment. Add stage directions to your diagram as you include text, audio, and video. Also note any props or equipment you will need as you present your work.

2.a. Introduce a topic; organize complex ideas, concepts, and information so that each new element builds on that which precedes it to create a unified whole; include formatting, graphics, and multimedia when useful to aiding comprehension.

4. Produce clear and coherent writing in which the development, organization, and style are appropriate to task, purpose, and audience.

Providing Elaboration

Strike a balance. Too many stimuli will confuse viewers. Aim for a targeted interplay between two or three media at any one time. You want the viewer to be able to absorb primary materials along with any secondary elements, such as music. Consult the sample note cards on this page for guidance.

Keep your narration lively. Your text does more than anchor your presentation: it is an important part of the show. Avoid repeating in words what other media are already communicating to the viewer in sounds or visuals. Your writing should sparkle with lively language that presents your claim and evidence in an interesting way.

Model: Keep Narration Lively

Today, ^there are millions of dogs and cats that ^*yearn for* ~~do not have~~ homes (pause for emphasis; cue video)…and someone needs to show compassion for them as they wait for a new home. (Pause as video plays.)

Livelier words heighten the effect of pauses.

Writers on Writing

Tim O'Brien On Revision

Tim O'Brien is the author of "Ambush" (p. 811).

This is the opening to a novel called ***The Things They Carried,*** and it introduces the book's central motif: the physical and psychological burdens men carry through a war. I revised these sentences twenty or thirty times, sometimes deleting, sometimes adding bits of action to make the opening vivid and concrete.

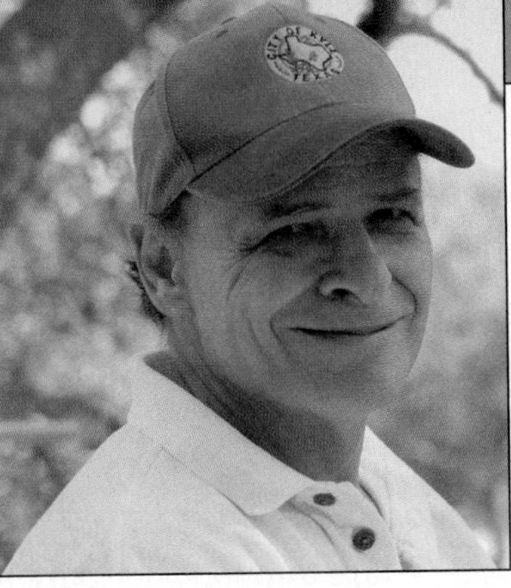

I revised these sentences twenty or thirty times . . .

—Tim O'Brien

from *The Things They Carried*

First Lieutenant Jimmy Cross carried letters from a girl named Martha, a junior at Mount Sebastian College in New Jersey. They were not love letters, but Lieutenant Cross was hoping, so kept them folded in plastic at the bottom of his rucksack. In the late afternoon, after a day's march, he would dig his foxhole, wash his hands under a canteen, unwrap the letters, hold them with the tips of his fingers, and spend the last hour of light pretending. He would imagine romantic camping trips into the White Mountains in New Hampshire. He would sometimes taste the envelope flaps, knowing her tongue had been there. More than anything, he wanted Martha to love him as he loved her, but the letters were mostly chatty, elusive on the matter of love.... She was an English Major at Mount Sebastian, and she wrote beautifully about her professors and roommates and midterm exams, about her respect for Chaucer and her great affection for Virginia Woolf. She often quoted lines of poetry; she never mentioned the war, except to say, Jimmy, take care of yourself. The letters weighed 10 ounces. They were signed Love, Martha, but Lieutenant Cross understood that Love was only a way of signing and did not mean what he sometimes pretended it meant.

Instead of writing abstractly about Jimmy's love for Martha, I inserted this line. These actions, I hope, convey a sense of how precious the letters are to Jimmy Cross.

Although Martha isn't physically present in the scene, I wanted to hint at her character. I also wanted to suggest the vast emotional distance between college life and combat, how Jimmy and Martha are living in two different worlds.

By stating the precise weight of the letters, I hoped the reader might realize that some of the heaviest things we carry through life—letters, memories—can weigh almost nothing.

Revising

Revising Your Overall Structure

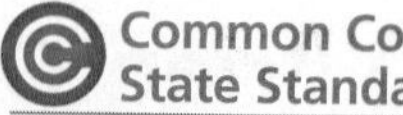

Writing

1.c. Use words, phrases, and clauses as well as varied syntax to link the major sections of the text, create cohesion, and clarify the relationships between claim(s) and reasons, between reasons and evidence, and between claim(s) and counterclaims.

1.d. Establish and maintain a formal style and objective tone while attending to the norms and conventions of the discipline in which they are writing.

Speaking and Listening

2. Integrate multiple sources of information presented in diverse formats and media.

Improve your sequence. A seamless delivery is the goal of any presentation. Because your presentation may involve apparatus that requires time for setup, be organized. Practice in advance. Make sure that the room you will be using is properly lit and equipped for your presentation.

Peer Review: Hold a test run with a partner.

- Run through your presentation, incorporating all audiovisual elements.
- Ask your partner to comment on parts that lack clarity or seem unpolished.

If necessary, revise the sequence to clarify connections between ideas or to smooth awkward transitions. Consider eliminating elements that are distracting or overly complicated.

Model: Revising for Cohesion and Clarifying Relationships

(cue slide) ~~(cue video)~~ ^ Shelter cats and dogs need to be groomed, fed, and loved. Many shelters ^ *often rely on donations and* barely survive on strict budgets. ^ *Still,* they need people to care for and love the animals.	**Video:** cats and dogs in shelter cages or kennels ~~**Photo:** a cat outside looking for food~~

Revising Your Selection of Media

Use a variety of effects. By using a variety of media to enhance your narration, you will spice up your presentation and keep your audience's interest. Review your script for overuse of one form of media. If you decide that your presention lacks variation, replace repetitive elements with different media formats.

Without Variety	With Variety
• Audio interview of quarterback • Audio interview of ballerina • Recording of overture to ballet	• Video footage of quarterback • Audio interview of ballerina • Slides of ballet in performance

Developing Your Style

Integrating Media to Support Ideas

Choose different types of media. Your media must be appropriate for your argument. For example, you would render a serious, thoughtful claim or piece of evidence less effective if you introduced silly cartoons and other lighter fare. Use the following chart as you integrate your media.

Media Element	Claim It Expresses or Supports	Is the Idea Clear? (Include Strategy for Clarifying.)
Audio of interview with volunteer	Volunteering at the shelter is rewarding.	Clear
Video of cats and dogs in cages	Homeless cats and dogs are needy and helpless.	This is not very clear. Add a line of narration to explain the connection.
Sad music	Cats and dogs in a shelter are bored and lonely.	The music I selected may not be quiet enough. I need something that suggests dull days.

Find It in Your Reading

Read or review the Student Model on page 950.

1. Locate elements of the presentation that have been properly integrated. Note the ways in which different media work together.
2. In particular, consider how the audio and video work together toward an appropriate effect.

Apply It to Your Writing

Review the script for your multimedia presentation.

1. Evaluate the effect your media choices will have on the viewer. Consider each aspect separately, as well as its use with other media.
2. Circle each audio and video transition, as well as each stage direction, to make sure that all are working together. Look for ways to emphasize your claim, make your evidence convincing, and clearly show the connections to your argument.
3. Experiment with different combinations of images and music. Varying the content or the order might produce unexpectedly effective results. Add transitions as you try several options to improve the flow of your work. Once you have developed your script, confirm your choices by previewing the presentation.

Student Model: Afton Kapala, Ventura, CA

Wanted: Shelter Volunteers

Text	Video and Audio
(cue video and audio) Millions of homeless cats and dogs enter shelters each year across the nation. They are in need of care as they yearn for new homes.	**Video:** shots of cats and dogs in shelter cages or kennels **Audio:** slow melancholy music, somewhat quiet, even boring
According to the American Society for the Prevention of Cruelty to Animals (ASPCA), **(pause for emphasis; cue video)** . . . about half are euthanized each year. **(pause as video plays)**	**Video:** cats and dogs peering out of cages with zooms of their faces
(cue first slide) Shelter cats and dogs need to be groomed, fed, and loved. **(use pointer to highlight the cat searching for food)** Many shelters often rely on donations and barely survive on strict budgets. Still, they need people to care for and love the animals.	**Slide:** a forlorn cat looking for food outside
(cue audio and second slide) At an animal shelter, volunteers provide an essential service. **(cue third slide)** They clean, feed, and care for the animals. **(cue fourth slide)** They play with the animals, which can make the pets more attractive to potential adopters.	**Slide:** collage of photos showing a volunteer caring for a shelter dog (grooming, feeding, etc.) **Slide:** a volunteer using a toy to play with a puppy while a potential adoption family watches
(cue fifth slide) Volunteering at an animal shelter often may not provide a paycheck, but the rewards it brings are countless and last a lifetime. **(cue video)** Volunteering at an animal shelter is a community service that will not only serve as a highlight on your resume but can also change your life and the lives of others.	**Slide:** a group of teenagers walking together outside of school **Video interview clip with teenage shelter volunteer** **Video morphs to:** the volunteer handing a shelter cat to its new owner

The claim has strong visual and audio elements, which fit a multimedia format.

Afton uses a compelling image to develop his claim and appeal to his audience's values.

The text, audio, and visual elements clarify the relationships between Afton's claims and reasons in a clear, cohesive way.

This vivid image helps to support Afton's concluding statement and his argument that volunteering is needed and rewarding.

Editing and Proofreading

Review your script to eliminate errors in grammar, spelling, and punctuation.

Focus on punctuation and spelling. Make sure the text your audience will actually see—and not just hear—demonstrates correct punctuation and spelling.

Focus on sentence fragments. Look for sentence fragments in your text and fix them by adding the missing subjects or verbs.

Fragment: About half euthanized each year.

Complete Sentence: About half of that number are euthanized each year.

Spiral Review: Conventions Earlier in this unit you learned about subject-verb agreement (p. 755) and pronoun-antecedent agreement. Check your script to make sure you have used these conventions correctly.

Publishing, Presenting, and Reflecting

Share your multimedia presentation in one of the following ways, and reflect on the writing experience:

Stage a showing. Deliver your multimedia presentation to your class, followed by a question and discussion session.

Create a multimedia portfolio. Join with classmates to create a portfolio of multimedia presentations. Include a multimedia table of contents that uses catchy audio and visual components to summarize each presentation. If possible, post your portfolio to a classroom Web site or blog.

Reflect on your writing. Jot down your thoughts on the experience of creating a multimedia presentation. Answer these questions: What did you learn about focusing your presentation? How has creating a multimedia presentation changed the way you look at media? To what extent does media enhance argumentation?

Rubric for Self-Assessment

Evaluate your multimedia presentation using the following criteria and rating scale, or determine your own reasonable evaluation criteria.

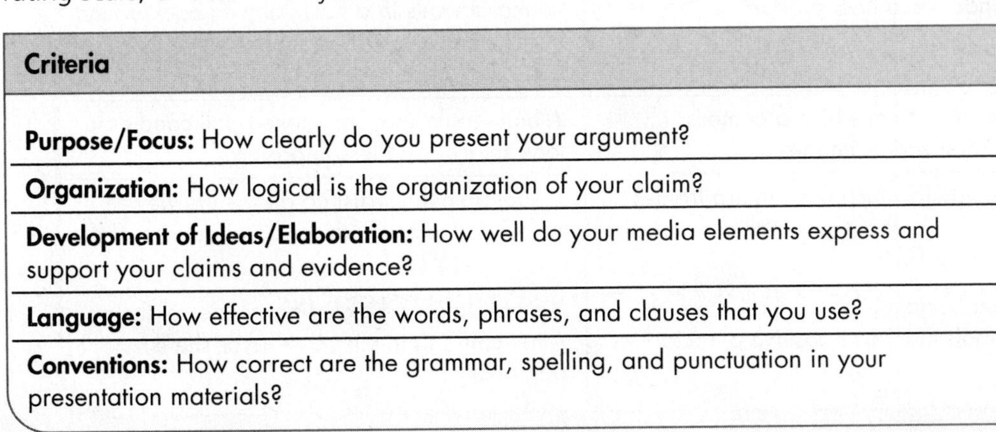

Criteria	Rating Scale *not very* … *very*
Purpose/Focus: How clearly do you present your argument?	1 2 3 4
Organization: How logical is the organization of your claim?	1 2 3 4
Development of Ideas/Elaboration: How well do your media elements express and support your claims and evidence?	1 2 3 4
Language: How effective are the words, phrases, and clauses that you use?	1 2 3 4
Conventions: How correct are the grammar, spelling, and punctuation in your presentation materials?	1 2 3 4

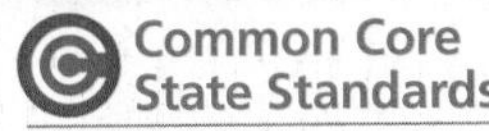

Common Core State Standards

Writing

1.a. Introduce precise, knowledgeable claim(s), establish the significance of the claim(s), distinguish the claim(s) from alternate or opposing claims, and create an organization that logically sequences claim(s), counterclaims, reasons, and evidence.

1.c. Use words, phrases, and clauses as well as varied syntax to link the major sections of the text, create cohesion, and clarify the relationships between claim(s) and reasons, between reasons and evidence, and between claim(s) and counterclaims.

5. Develop and strengthen writing as needed by editing, focusing on addressing what is most significant for a specific purpose and audience.

6. Use technology, including the Internet, to produce, publish, and update individual or shared writing products in response to ongoing feedback, including new arguments or information.

Language

1. Demonstrate command of the conventions of standard English grammar and usage when writing or speaking.

2.b. Spell correctly.

Speaking and Listening

Analyze a Nonprint Political Advertisement

Speaking and Listening
1. Initiate and participate effectively in a range of collaborative discussions with diverse partners on *grades 11–12 topics, texts, and issues,* building on others' ideas and expressing their own clearly and persuasively.

Language
1. Demonstrate command of the conventions of standard English grammar and usage when speaking. *(p. 953)*

If you have turned on a TV or radio during an election cycle, you have surely observed messages explaining why you should vote for a particular candidate. These are **nonprint political advertisements**—a form of broadcast media designed to shape public opinion about candidates and issues. Airing on television and radio and streaming on the Internet, these ads rely on strong images and powerful language. Because they reach vast audiences, they often exert great influence on the outcomes of elections.

Identify Purpose of Political Advertising

At first glance, political ads might seem purely informational. However, like any ad, their purpose is to sell something—not soap or cars, but an issue or candidate. Political ads create name recognition for a candidate and transmit values to potential voters. These ads fall into two basic categories:

- *Issue-based ads* establish a candidate's position on a particular matter of public concern, such as health care, crime, or taxes.
- *Character-based ads* establish an image of the candidate as a person.

Identify Persuasive Techniques

Makers of nonprint political ads seek to convert viewers whose attitudes toward a candidate are neutral or hostile, as well as to reaffirm the opinions of supporters. To meet these goals, they use a number of visual and sound techniques to produce particular images of candidates.

Technique	Description	Effect
Editing	Arranging the sequence of images and sounds into a final product	An ad showing a candidate visiting young patients in a hospital with background music sung by children suggests that the candidate cares about children's health.
Camera Angles	Directions from which a camera operator shoots images	A high-angle shot can make a tall candidate look smaller and less imposing.
Camera Shots	The way in which the camera frames the subject; shot types include close-ups and long shots	A shot from the waist up allows the viewer to feel connected with the candidate.
Symbols	The association of a candidate with symbols that have positive associations	A candidate's ad including images of the American flag implies that he or she is patriotic.

Negative Techniques

Some political ads may use **propaganda,** or biased content, to damage an opponent's credibility or image. Such ads may also rely on **logical fallacies,** which are arguments that sound convincing at first but are based on faulty reasoning. Logical fallacies that may appear in political ads include the following:

- **Mud-slinging or *Ad Hominem* Attacks:** These criticize an opponent's character rather than addressing flaws in positions on issues.
- **Wrong or Incomplete Facts:** Hostile ads sometimes intentionally misrepresent candidates' positions or present only part of a story.
- **Generalizations:** Ads may include unfairly simplified descriptions of an opponent or his or her opinions.

As a citizen, it is your responsibility to understand how political messages are shaped and to determine the reliability of the claims they present.

Activities: Analyze Political Advertisements

Comprehension and Collaboration For both activities, use an evaluation form like the one shown below.

A. Watch a political ad on TV or the Internet and analyze the techniques the ad uses to sway viewers.

B. Research a national election from the past and the effect of advertising on the outcome. Locate an ad used in the campaign. (Organizations such as the American Museum of the Moving Image maintain archives of ads.) Watch the ad and evaluate it using the form shown here. Write a summary of your findings to share in a class discussion. Use the conventions of standard English in your summary.

Evaluation Form for a Political Ad

This ad was produced for ______________________________
(name of candidate)

What type of voter is this ad targeting? ❑ *sympathetic* ❑ *undecided* ❑ *hostile*

Explain. ______________________________

Identify the techniques used to convey the ad's message. Explain how each is used.

Visual and Sound Techniques: ______________________________

Negative Techniques: ______________________________

Are the claims made about the candidate truthful? (Check other sources if necessary.) ______________________________

Would this ad help someone who wants to be informed about this candidate? Explain. ______________________________

Language Study

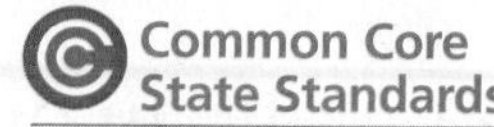

Etymology: Scientific, Medical, and Mathematical Terms

The European Renaissance saw renewed interest in the sciences and mathematics. English scholars turned to the works of the ancient Greeks, Romans, and Arabs to learn more about these subjects. As a result, many Greek and Latin words related to these fields entered the English language. The chart below lists some word parts from Greek, Latin, and Anglo-Saxon often used in scientific, medical, and mathematical matters. Understanding these word parts will help you decode the meanings of unfamiliar terms.

Language

4.c. Consult general and specialized reference materials, both print and digital, to find the etymology of a word.

6. Acquire and use accurately general academic and domain-specific words and phrases, sufficient for reading, writing, speaking, and listening at the college and career readiness level; demonstrate independence in gathering vocabulary knowledge when considering a word important to comprehension or expression.

Prefixes	Roots	Suffixes
bi- (Latin): two *cardio-* (Greek): heart *centi-* (Latin): one-hundredth part; one hundred *micro-* (Greek): small *mono-* (Greek): single, one *pan-* (Greek): all *poly-* (Greek): many *psycho-* (Greek): mind	*-gno-* (Greek): know *-gon-* (Greek): angle *-oculus-* (Latin): eye *-path-* (Greek): feeling; disease; suffering *-ped-* (Latin): foot *-phon-* (Greek): sound; voice; speech	*-ar* (Latin): resembling *-graph* (Greek): something written or drawn *-iatry* (Greek): medical treatment *-ist* (Greek): one who specializes *-logy* (Greek): science, theory, study *-scope* (Greek): instrument for viewing *-teen* (Anglo-Saxon): ten

Practice

Directions: Choose the letter of the word that best fits each numbered definition. Explain your choice with reference to the chart above.

1. identification of a disease a. psychologist b. diagnosis
2. eye specialist a. oculist b. monocle
3. record of heart activity a. seismograph b. cardiograph
4. epidemic affecting a large area a. pandemic b. empathy
5. creature with two feet a. biped b. centipede
6. study of disease a. biology b. pathology
7. figure with many angles a. polygon b. polygraph
8. instrument for viewing small objects a. microphone b. microscope
9. treatment of mental disorders a. prognosis b. psychiatry

Directions: Use a dictionary to locate as many English words as you can that contain the following word parts: **(a)** Latin prefix *centi-*; **(b)** Latin word root *-ped-*; **(c)** Greek suffix *-scope*.

Vocabulary Acquisition and Use: Sentence Completions

Sentence Completion questions appear in most standardized tests. Sentence Completions test your vocabulary skills, as well as your ability to identify word/phrase relationships. In these types of questions you are given sentences with one or more missing words. Your task is to choose the correct word or words to complete each sentence logically.

Use this strategy to improve your results: **1.** Read the whole sentence, looking for signal words that suggest an attitude or emotion. **2.** Determine if the missing word will be positive or negative. **3.** Scan the answer choices for the ones that meet your criteria. Delete the ones that do not fit, and test the others in the sentence.

Practice

This exercise is modeled after the Sentence Completion exercises that appear in the Critical Reading section of the SAT.

Test-Taking Tip
For sentences with two missing words, if one word in an answer choice does not fit, reject that choice.

Directions: Each of the following sentences is missing one or two words. Choose the word or set of words that best completes each sentence.

1. The dire poverty and dislocation the dust storms caused created many ___?___ scenes that moved readers of the photo magazines.

A. poignant
B. passionate
C. mundane
D. fortuitous
E. obtuse

2. The migration of farmers from Oklahoma to California filled refugee camps with ___?___ tents of starving, impoverished, and desperate people.

A. insatiable
B. palpable
C. derivative
D. voluminous
E. detached

3. Many politicians blamed the farmers for poor land management, feeling they ___?___ what they ___?___ when they failed to rest fields between crops.

A. disgraced . . . bequeathed
B. reaped . . . sowed
C. resigned . . . irrigated
D. circumvented . . . extricated
E. beguiled . . . endured

4. Black blizzards, as dust storms were called, brought ___?___ destruction of farmlands, causing ___?___ reactions from those who survived.

A. sensible . . . preposterous
B. virulent . . . inextricable
C. despondent . . . indignant
D. cunning . . . poised
E. wanton . . . rueful

From Text to Understanding

You have studied each part of Unit 4 as a set of connected texts. In this workshop, you will have the chance to further explore the fundamental connections among these texts and to deepen your essential understanding of the literature and its social and historical context.

Common Core State Standards

Writing

1. Write arguments to support claims in an analysis of substantive topics or texts, using valid reasoning and relevant and sufficient evidence.

2. Write informative/explanatory texts to examine and convey complex ideas, concepts, and information clearly and accurately through the effective selection, organization, and analysis of content.

Speaking and Listening

4. Present information, findings, and supporting evidence, conveying a clear and distinct perspective, such that listeners can follow the line of reasoning, alternative or opposing perspectives are addressed, and the organization, development, substance, and style are appropriate to purpose, audience, and a range of formal and informal tasks.

PART 1: Facing Troubled Times

Writing: Argumentative Essay As the Victorian era gave way to the modern world in the early twentieth century, values, art, and even global events began to change. Artists, inspired by changes in society, began to break the boundaries of form and content, which in turn contributed to further shifts in attitudes and behavior. Review the texts, especially F. Scott Fitzgerald's Anchor Text, "Winter Dreams," keeping in mind what each might tell us about social change.

Assignment: Develop a claim that addresses the social status of Dexter Green and Judy Jones in Fitzgerald's "Winter Dreams." Consider the perceived differences between wealth that comes from an individual's success and wealth that is inherited. What sort of impact did awareness of such differences have on the American experience? Consult other texts and background information in Part 1 to support and expand your claim.

Example: America was built on the idea that people are free to make choices that hopefully lead to happiness and fulfillment. In the lives of characters in F. Scott Fitzgerald's "Winter Dreams," however, this concept takes on the taint of superficial striving and leads to disillusionment.

Identify character traits. Use a simple note-taking system like the one shown to identify character traits that can be considered "American."

Character Traits

"Winter Dreams":
Dexter Green: works hard, rises to higher social status; strives for better things but is often superficial

Judy Jones: beautiful; an unattainable ideal rather than a real person

Structure your essay. Explain your view of what defined social class as part of the American experience at the beginning of the twentieth century. Then identify and analyze characters as an expression of or departure from that view.

Demonstrate your familiarity. As you write, demonstrate your familiarity with the Anchor Text and any other works you engage. For example, identify literary elements that might reflect the nation's new Modernist outlook. Explain characters that might be used as metaphors for American ideals.

PART 2: From Every Corner of the Land

Research: Magazine Articles Isolation was an undercurrent of American society and art in the early twentieth century. Review the background materials and selections in Part 2, considering how the forces of society and culture often sever people from a sense of belonging. Consider in particular, the Anchor Text—Ernest Hemingway's "In Another Country and the isolation caused by the pain of war.

Assignment: Working in a small group, design and create a series of magazine articles that examine the idea of isolation in early twentieth-century America. Each person should first choose a selection from Part 2 and think about the lack of social connection apparent in the text. Conduct research on the historical context of the text's setting—e.g. World War I, or the Great Depression—to help explain the factors that kept people from connecting with each other.

Include illustrations or photographs with each article, and model the layout on magazine pieces you have seen. Combine your group's articles into a magazine to share with the class.

Production Checklist:

- ☐ **Thesis.** Include a clear statement of topic.
- ☐ **Title.** Create a concise, engaging title that captures the reader's attention.
- ☐ **Illustrations/Photographs.** Choose images that add meaning to your text.
- ☐ **Typeface.** Choose a typeface that is easy to read and does not distract the reader from your ideas.
- ☐ **Sources.** Include a list of sources at the end of your article.

PART 3: The Harlem Renaissance

Listening and Speaking: Oral Interpretation The writers of the Harlem Renaissance helped forge an artistic community that embraced a variety of styles but a singular purpose, to create art borne of their own experiences and culture.

Review the selections in Part 3, especially the Anchor Text, the excerpt from Zora Neale Hurston's autobiography, "Dust Tracks on a Road." Through their artistic expression, these writers create a cultural identity and define their own history.

Assignment: Listen as these writers speak for themselves. Select and read aloud an excerpt of Hurston's autobiography or one of the poems of a Harlem Renaissance writer. Include an introduction explaining why you chose the work, and conclude with a comment about why the work still matters. To prepare, read the selection aloud to become comfortable with speaking rate, volume, and enunciation. Encourage your audience to ask questions after your presentation.

Notes for Introduction:

Date selection was written/published: ______________________

Why I chose the selection: ______________________

What is powerful about the selection: ______________________

Impact of selection on literature and culture: ______________________

Notes for Conclusion:

Ideas from selection that are important today: ______________________

Feelings expressed in selection that are relevant today: ______________________

Test-Taking Practice

Critical Reading Test: Long Reading Passage

Some critical reading tests present **long passages** that require extended concentration. Passages can be as long as 850 words and can present narrative, persuasive, and expository modes. You should spend more time answering the questions than reading the passage. This requires you to read purposefully to cover the material. If necessary, you can reread later for details.

Common Core State Standards

RL.11-12.1, RL.11-12.2, RL.11-12.3, RL.11-12.4, RL.11-12.5; L.11-12.1, L.11-12.2, L.11-12.4.a, L.11-12.5.b

[For the full wording of the standards, see the standards chart in the front of your textbook.]

Practice

The following exercise is modeled after the SAT Critical Reading section.

Directions: Read the following passage, taken from "Winter Dreams" by F. Scott Fitzgerald. Then, choose the best answer to each question.

He made money. It was rather amazing. After college he went to the city from which Black Bear Lake draws its wealthy patrons. When he was only twenty-three and had been there not quite two years, there were already people who liked to say: "Now *there's* a boy—" All about him rich men's sons were peddling bonds precariously, or investing patrimonies precariously, or plodding through the two dozen volumes of the "George Washington Commercial Course," but Dexter borrowed a thousand dollars on his college degree and his confident mouth, and bought a partnership in a laundry.

It was a small laundry when he went into it, but Dexter made a specialty of learning how the English washed fine woolen golf stockings without shrinking them, and within a year he was catering to the trade that wore knickerbockers. Men were insisting that their Shetland hose and sweaters go to his laundry, just as they had insisted on a caddy who could find golf balls. A little later he was doing their wives' lingerie as well—and running five branches in different parts of the city. Before he was twenty-seven he owned the largest string of laundries in his section of the country. It was then that he sold out and went to New York. But the part of this story that concerns us goes back to the days when he was making his first big success.

Strategy

The content of a paragraph as a whole can be inferred from the first and last sentences.

- **First Sentence:** usually states the main idea of the paragraph
- **Last Sentence:** usually summarizes the major points of the paragraph and restates the main idea
- Scanning first and last sentences will help you identify paragraphs with information you need to answer given questions.

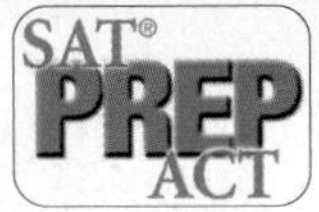

1. Which detail does the author include to show that Dexter was not like other men his age?
   A. investing money their fathers gave them
   B. borrowing money to start a business
   C. selling bonds in a dangerous manner
   D. reading books to learn how to make money
   E. returning to Black Bear Lake

2. One can infer from the mention of golfers wanting a caddy who could find golf balls that
   A. Dexter hired caddies who could find his lost golf balls.
   B. Dexter also could find lost golf balls when he wasn't at work.
   C. they frequently lost golf balls and needed a caddy to find them.
   D. they also wanted a laundry that washed their socks correctly.
   E. they wanted a laundry that could only wash socks and sweaters.

3. In line 5, the word *precariously* means
   A. dangerously
   B. aggressively
   C. illegally
   D. with a careful plan
   E. by instinct

4. What does the author suggest about the way men see Dexter in the mention from line 10, "A little later he was doing their wives' lingerie as well . . ."?
   A. Men thought that Dexter was their social equal.
   B. Men thought that he charged a low price for work.
   C. Men were embarrassed to discuss these matters.
   D. Dexter knew a great deal about women.
   E. Dexter had gained their trust.

5. What does the first sentence of the second paragraph convey to readers?
   A. It shows that Dexter got lucky in business.
   B. It tells the reader how to create a successful business.
   C. It defines the steps Dexter took in business.
   D. It explains how this information relates to his first success.
   E. It explains how he eventually owned five laundries.

6. Which excerpt from the passage best expresses the main idea of the passage?
   A. It was then that he sold out and went to New York.
   B. He made money. It was rather amazing.
   C. But the part of this story that concerns us goes back to the days when he was making his first big success.
   D. After college he went to the city from which Black Bear Lake draws its wealthy patrons.
   E. Men were insisting that their Shetland hose and sweaters go to his laundry.

7. What details about Dexter would the reader know from this passage?
   A. his age
   B. his size
   C. his background
   D. his beliefs
   E. his politics

8. What does the author infer about Dexter by mentioning "his confident mouth" in line 8?
   A. He talked his way through college to get ahead.
   B. He learned how to launder stockings a special way.
   C. He was a great salesman for a variety of products.
   D. He convinced people to lend him money.
   E. He did not doubt what other people said to him.

GO ON

Grammar and Writing: Improving Sentences

Improving sentences exercises often appear in the writing sections of standardized tests. The test items show five different versions of a sentence. Your job is to choose the most effective version. This type of exercise tests your ability to recognize and correct flaws in grammar, usage, and sentence structure.

Practice

This exercise is modeled after the Improving Sentences portion of the SAT Writing section. The full test has 25 such questions.

Directions: Part or all of each of the following sentences is underlined; beneath each sentence are five ways of phrasing the underlined portion. Choice A will always be the same as the original wording; B–E are different options. If you consider the original sentence to be the most effective sentence, select choice A; otherwise, select one of the other choices.

1. Many elderly town residents are entitled to property tax benefits <u>that you might consider</u> enviable.
   A. that you might consider
   B. that she might consider
   C. that he or she might consider
   D. which he or she might consider
   E. which you might consider

2. Faulkner and Hemingway were contemporaries, yet <u>while he won his Nobel Prize in 1950 he would not win</u> this prize for four more years.
   A. while he won his Nobel Prize in 1950 he would not win
   B. while he won his Nobel Prize in 1950 Hemingway would not win
   C. while Faulkner won his Nobel Prize in 1950, Hemingway would not win
   D. while Faulkner won his Nobel Prize in 1950 he would not win
   E. while they won a Nobel Prize in 1950 Hemingway would not win

3. Readers have long wondered about the basis for Faulkner's characters like Miss Grierson <u>because it is so real it had</u> to exist in his hometown.
   A. because it is so real it had
   B. because she is so real it had
   C. because she is so real they had
   D. because they are so real they had
   E. because it is so real they had

Strategy

Pinpoint the Confusion:
The majority of the sentence is correct and the error has to exist in the underlined portion. Usually one word or phrase is wrong while the rest may be misleading.

4. The men spread lime in the basement, because they were doing their civic duty.
   A. because they were doing their civic duty
   B. because it was its civic duty
   C. because he was doing their civic duty
   D. because they were doing our civic duty
   E. because he were doing his civic duty

5. Many elderly people hire an aide to help them or else you would not be able to manage.
   A. them or else you would not be able
   B. them or else they would not be able
   C. them or else she would not be able
   D. her or else she would not be able
   E. him or else it would not be able

6. Miss Emily, like Old Lady Wyatt, lived alone, so when she died two younger cousins buried them.
   A. when she died two younger cousins buried them
   B. when she died their young cousins buried her
   C. when Emily died two younger cousins buried them
   D. when it died two younger cousins buried of them
   E. when she died two younger cousins buried her

7. The druggist sold arsenic to his customers, which you considered dangerous.
   A. his customers, which you considered
   B. her customers, which he considered
   C. his customers, which he considered
   D. their customers, which they considered
   E. its customers, which it considered

8. The servant allowed the cousins into the house yet they were upset by what they found inside.
   A. they were upset by what they found
   B. he was upset by what they found
   C. they was upset by what they found
   D. they were upset by what he found
   E. they were upset by what they finds

9. I love the short story form, although they are often very intense and even eerie.
   A. I love the short story form, although they are
   B. I love the short story form, although it is
   C. You love the short story form, although you are
   D. I love the short story form, although characters are
   E. They love the short story form, although it are

Timed Writing: Position Statement [25 minutes]

In his Nobel Prize acceptance speech of 1950, delivered at a time of world tension and fear, William Faulkner said, "I believe that man will not merely endure: he will prevail . . . because he has a soul, a spirit capable of compassion and sacrifice and endurance."

Would Faulkner express the same confident belief in humanity's future if he were to give his acceptance speech today? Write an essay in which you develop a point of view on this issue. Support your opinion with reasoning and evidence, and examples drawn either from your reading or experience. This assignment is similar to the Essay portion of the SAT Writing section.

Academic Vocabulary

To persuade your reader, you need to provide more than your **opinion,** or personal belief. Provide convincing **evidence** that supports your opinion.

Constructed Response

Follow the instructions to complete the tasks below as required by your teacher. As you work on each task, incorporate both general academic vocabulary and literary terms you learned in this unit.

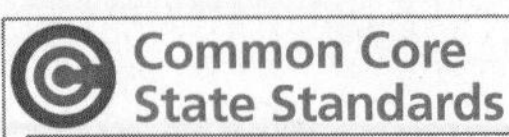
Common Core State Standards

RL.11-12.2, RL.11-12.3, RL.11-12.4, RL.11-12.5, RL.11-12.6; RI.11-12.6; W.11-12.2, W.11-12.5, W.11-12.9.a; SL.11-12.1, SL.11-12.2, SL.11-12.4, SL.11-12.6

[For the full wording of the standards, see the chart in the front of your textbook.]

Writing

Task 1: Literature [RL.11-12.2; W.11-12.2]

Analyze Development of Theme

*Write an **essay** in which you analyze the development of two themes in a work of literature from this unit.*

- Choose a literary work that clearly presents two themes.
- Introduce your essay with an objective summary of the work. Then, identify the two themes you will analyze.
- Identify whether the themes are implied or stated directly. If a theme is stated directly, indicate where this occurs in the text. If it is implied, describe how you inferred the theme based on imagery, events, dialogue, or the actions or interactions of characters in the work.
- Explain how each theme is developed over the course of the story.
- Analyze how the two themes are interconnected. How does this interaction of themes add depth and meaning to the story?

Task 2: Literature [RL.11-12.4; W.11-12.5]

Analyze the Impact of Word Choice

*Write an **essay** in which you analyze the impact of word choice in a poem from this unit.*

- Choose a poem from this unit that contains language that is fresh, engaging, or beautiful. Provide examples that show these qualities.
- Identify words and phrases that have interesting connotations. Interpret the meanings of these words and phrases as they are used in the poem.
- Identify figurative language in the poem. Name the specific type of language used, such as simile, metaphor, or personification. Then, describe the impact of each use of figurative language on the overall meaning and tone of the poem.
- Finally, evaluate whether the poet's use of word choice was successful by giving your overall impression of the language in the work.
- When you are finished drafting your essay, review your work in order to strengthen the points that you think are most significant for your audience.

Task 3: Literature [RL.11-12.5; W.11-12.2, W.11-12.9.a]

Analyze Text Structure

*Write an **essay** in which you analyze how an author's choice of a particular structure adds to the overall meaning and impact of a story in this unit.*

- Choose a story from this unit that has a structure you find interesting. Explain your choice.
- Discuss the overall meaning of the story you have chosen. Explain how the story's structure supports this meaning.
- Analyze the author's choices concerning how to structure specific parts of the story. For example, where did the author choose to begin or end the story? What type of ending did the author choose and what was the impact of that decision?
- Explain how the author's choices concerning structure add to the meaning of the story. Consider how these choices create aesthetic effects, such as humor, horror, or beauty.
- Make sure to state your position clearly at the beginning of your essay in a thesis statement. Support your thesis with examples from the story and provide a concluding statement that follows naturally from the evidence you have provided.

Speaking and Listening

Task 4: Literature [RL.11-12.6; SL.11-12.6]

Analyze Point of View

Deliver an ***oral presentation*** *in which you analyze a work from this unit that uses satire, sarcasm, irony, or understatement to express point of view.*

- Choose a work that includes satire, sarcasm, irony, or understatement.
- Briefly summarize the work to begin your presentation. Explain how the writer uses the literary techniques of satire, sarcasm, irony, or understatement to express a particular perspective on a topic.
- Distinguish what is directly stated in the text from what is really meant. For example, if you are pointing out understatement, you might show how the writer deliberately shows a situation as better or worse than it actually is.
- Explain the underlying meaning or message the writer is attempting to convey through the use of satire, sarcasm, irony, or understatement.
- Rehearse your presentation and adapt word choice as needed to convey your intended tone.

Task 5: Literature [RL.11-12.3; SL.11-12.6]

Analyze Characterization in a Story

Deliver an ***analysis*** *of the impact of author's choices regarding characterization in a story from this unit.*

- Choose a story from this unit with interesting characters, and summarize it.
- Describe the individual characters in the story by identifying their main personality traits.
- Categorize the story's characters as either flat or round, and explain how you made this determination.
- Explain how the author uses direct or indirect characterization, or both, to establish character traits. Draw attention to story elements such as dialogue, plot events, and setting when discussing indirect characterization.
- Finally, describe how certain characters grow or change during the course of the story, and analyze which story elements help produce this change.
- As you present your analysis, be sure to use formal English and an appropriate tone.

Task 6: Literature/Informational Text [RL.11-12.4; RI.11-12.6; SL.11-12.1, SL.11-12.2]

Analyze Authors' Styles

Participate in a discussion group in which you compare and contrast authors' styles in a work of fiction and a work of nonfiction from this unit.

- Choose two works from this unit that provide interesting points to compare and contrast.
- Analyze the various elements that make up the author's style in each of the works. These include word choice, sentence structure, and tone.
- In your discussion, indicate specific examples from each of the texts to support your analysis of the author's style.
- Compare and contrast the two authors' styles by explaining how they create similar or different tones through the use of such devices as figurative language, humorous anecdotes, and lengthy sentences.
- Evaluate which author's style is more effective in achieving its purpose and producing an effect on the reader.
- Allow each person to state his or her view and support that view with evidence. Acknowledge new information by trying to connect it to earlier points or by modifying the group's position.
- Appoint a spokesperson from the group to present your findings to the rest of the class.

How does literature shape or reflect society?

The Modern Reader Modern writers, such as T. S. Eliot and William Faulkner, introduced new levels of innovation and experimentation into American literature. They presented new challenges for readers in their works, expecting more from their readers than did authors of previous eras.

Assignment Choose one Modernist work and one traditional work from this unit. Write a **comparison-and-contrast essay** about the challenges each work presents and the assumptions you feel each author makes about his or her readers.

Titles for Extended Reading

In this unit, you have read a variety of literature of the Modern Age. Continue to read works related to this era on your own. Select books that you enjoy, but challenge yourself to explore new topics, new authors, and works offering varied perspectives or approaches. The titles suggested below will help you get started.

LITERATURE

As I Lay Dying

William Faulkner
Modern Library, 2000

EXEMPLAR TEXT 

Novel This influential novel, told from the perspective of fifteen different narrators, is the story of the death of the matriarch of a poor Southern family and her family's journey to bury her.

[A short story and a speech by Faulkner begin on page 816 of this book. Build knowledge by reading a novel by this author.]

The Great Gatsby

F. Scott Fitzgerald
Scribner, 2004

EXEMPLAR TEXT 

Novel This tragic tale of grand dreams and ruined lives explores self-made millionaire Jay Gatsby's quest to win the love of the wealthy, beautiful—and married—Daisy Buchanan.

[Fitzgerald's short story "Winter Dreams" appears on page 730 of this book. Build knowledge by reading a novel by this author.]

A Farewell to Arms

Ernest Hemingway
Scribner, 1995

EXEMPLAR TEXT 

Novel This story of an American soldier and a British nurse in Italy during World War I is based largely on Hemingway's own experiences as an ambulance driver in the war. The story describes love and loss and the horror of war.

[Hemingway's short story "In Another Country" appears on page 800 of this book. Build knowledge by reading a novel by this author.]

The Complete Poems of Robert Frost

Robert Frost
Henry Holt and Company, 1969

EXEMPLAR TEXT 

Poetry All of poet laureate Robert Frost's books of poetry are collected in this one volume. Among the poems included is "Mending Wall."

[Seven of Frost's poems appear on pages 874–885 of this book. Build knowledge by reading the complete poems of this poet.]

INFORMATIONAL TEXTS

Historical Texts

Dust Tracks on a Road

Zora Neale Hurston
Harper Perennial Modern Classic, 2010

Autobiography Hurston's autobiography tells the story of her childhood in the South and her rise to literary fame as a star of the Harlem Renaissance.

[An excerpt from Dust Tracks on a Road *appears on page 930 of this book. Build knowledge by reading the full text.]*

Contemporary Scholarship

The First World War

John Keegan
Vintage, 2000

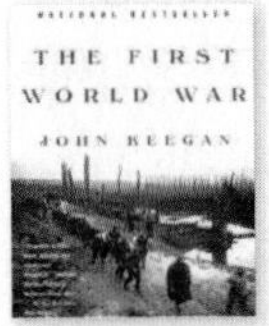

History Using diaries, letters, and action reports, historian John Keegan vividly describes the soldiers, leaders, and battles of what he believes was a tragic, preventable war.

Hard Times: An Oral History of the Great Depression

Studs Terkel
New Press, 2000

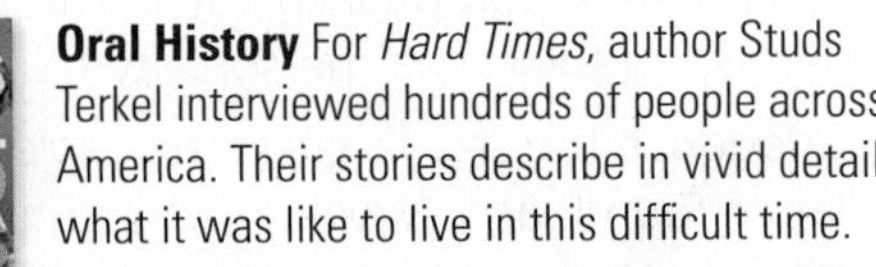

Oral History For *Hard Times,* author Studs Terkel interviewed hundreds of people across America. Their stories describe in vivid detail what it was like to live in this difficult time.

The Reader's Companion to American History

edited by Eric Foner and John A. Garraty
Houghton Mifflin, 1991

Encyclopedia This "readers' encyclopedia" contains almost 1,000 engaging articles about important events, people, and trends in American history. Included in the volume is Ellen Condliffe Lagemann's article "Education."

Preparing to Read Complex Texts

Reading for College and Career In both college and the workplace, readers must analyze texts independently, draw connections among works that offer varied perspectives, and develop their own ideas and informed opinions. The questions shown below, and others that you generate on your own, will help you more effectively read and analyze complex college-level texts.

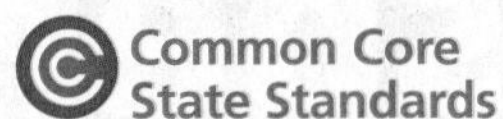

Reading Literature/Informational Text

10. By the end of grade 11, read and comprehend literature, including stories, dramas, and poems, and literary nonfiction, in the grades 11-CCR text complexity band proficiently, with scaffolding as needed at the high end of the range.

When reading complex texts, ask yourself...

- What idea, experience, or story seems to have compelled the author to write? Has the author presented that idea, experience, or story in a way that I, too, find compelling?
- How might the author's era, social status, belief system, or personal experiences have affected the point of view he or she expresses in the text?
- How do my circumstances affect what I understand and feel about this text?
- What key idea does the author state explicitly? What key idea does he or she suggest or imply? Which details in the text help me to perceive implied ideas?
- Do I find multiple layers of meaning in the text? If so, what relationships do I see among these layers of meaning?
- How do details in the text connect or relate to one another? Do I find any details unconvincing, unrelated, or out of place?
- Do I find the text believable and convincing?

Key Ideas and Details

- What patterns of organization or sequences do I find in the text? Do these patterns help me understand the ideas better?
- What do I notice about the author's style, including his or her diction, use of imagery and figurative language, and syntax?
- Do I like the author's style? Is the author's style memorable?
- What emotional attitude does the author express toward the topic, the story, or the characters? Does this attitude seem appropriate?
- What emotional attitude does the author express toward me, the reader? Does this attitude seem appropriate?
- What do I notice about the author's voice—his or her personality on the page? Do I like this voice? Does it make me want to read on?

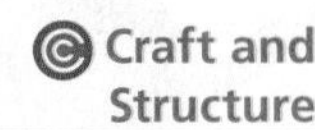

- Is the work fresh and original?
- Do I agree with the author's ideas entirely, or are there elements I find unconvincing?
- Do I disagree with the author's ideas entirely, or are there elements I can accept as true?
- Based on my knowledge of American literature, history, and culture, does this work reflect the American tradition? Why or why not?

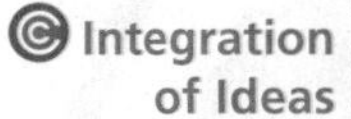

Prosperity and Protest

Literature of the Post-War Era 1945–1970

Unit 5

PART 1 TEXT SET

WAR SHOCK

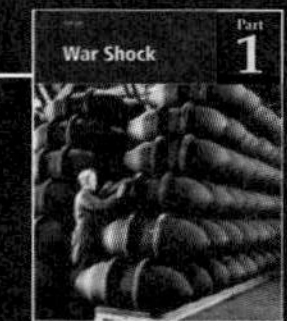

PART 2 TEXT SET

TRADITION AND REBELLION

PART 3 TEXT SET

LITERATURE OF PROTEST

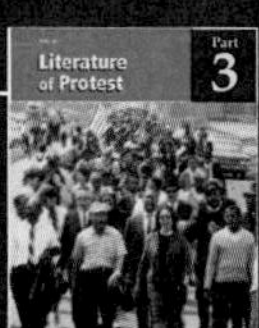

"Sometimes I can see the future stretched out in front of me—just as plain as day. The future hanging over there at the edge of my days. Just waiting for me."

—Lorraine Hansberry

CLOSE READING TOOL

Use this tool to practice the close reading strategies you learn.

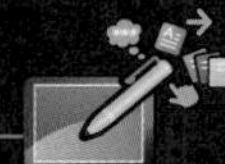

ONLINE WRITER'S NOTEBOOK

Easily capture notes and complete assignments online.

STUDENT eTEXT

Bring learning to life with audio, video, and interactive tools.

Find all Digital Resources at **pearsonrealize.com**.

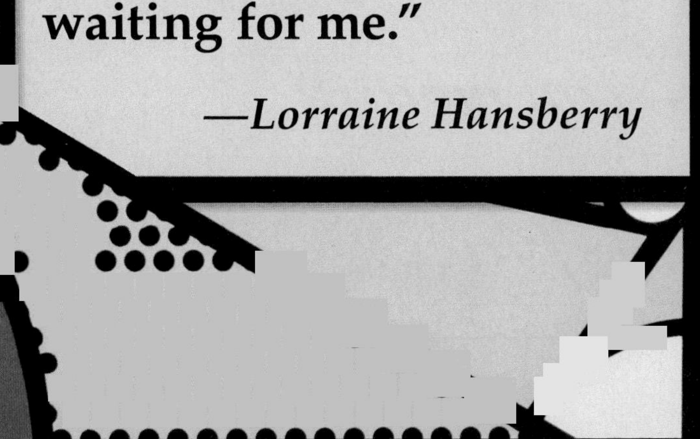

Snapshot of the Period

The 1950s began with a booming consumer economy, the birth of American car culture, and the rise of suburbia as a new lifestyle norm. By the end of the decade, this apparent stability showed signs of strain. In 1957, the Soviet Union, America's cold-war opponent, launched the first earth-orbiting satellite and the United States entered the "Space Race" in dire earnestness. Unrest in the nation over Civil Rights issues led to protests—some organized and peaceful, some violent. The war in Vietnam, begun in 1954, did not end until 1975. It became a focal point of political and generational conflict. A period that began with complacency, ended with a spirit of revolution and the sense of a new age dawning.

A human footprint on the moon and *TIME* magazine's cover featuring Soviet cosmonaut Yuri Gagarin are two indelible images of the space race. ▶

O'Connor

Plath

Baldwin

Bishop

King

Miller

As you read the selections in this unit, you will be asked to think about them in view of three key questions:

How does literature shape or reflect *society*?

What makes American literature *American*?

What is the relationship between literature and *place*?

RIDING FOR FREEDOM

In 1961, a historic moment in the Civil Rights movement took place when a group of Freedom Riders challenged segregation codes in buses and bus terminals. They rode in integrated buses from Washington, D.C., to New Orleans. Along the way, buses were firebombed, riders were beaten, and finally Federal Marshals were called in.

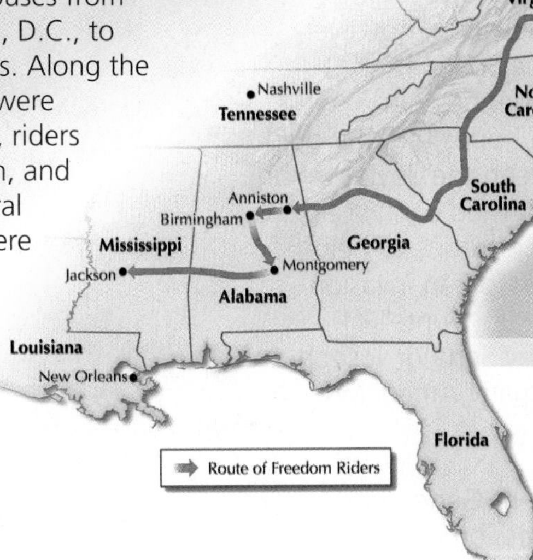

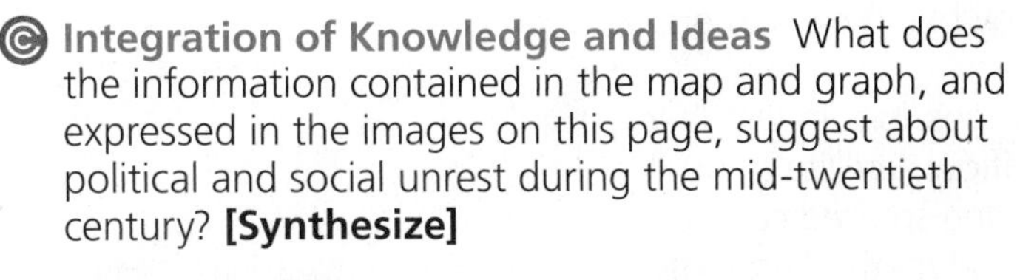

Integration of Knowledge and Ideas What does the information contained in the map and graph, and expressed in the images on this page, suggest about political and social unrest during the mid-twentieth century? **[Synthesize]**

Vietnam War Approval Rates (1965–1971)

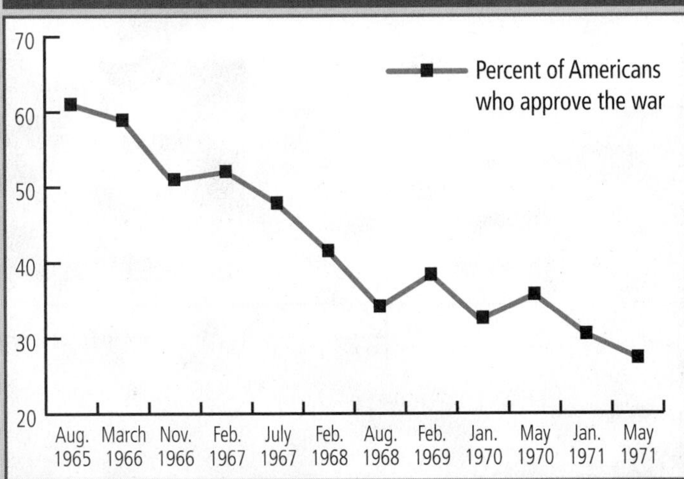

Source: The Gallup Poll

Buttons of the Era

A dove held by white and black hands symbolized racial harmony and world peace.

A march that took place in Jackson, Mississippi, was named for Civil Rights figure James Meredith.

President Kennedy dreamed of an international army of peace workers. This dream led to the creation of the Peace Corps.

The peace movement, lead by Hippies, used flowers as symbols for an alternative to war.

Many Americans believed in the Vietnam War and sought to support the troops overseas.

As the Vietnam War dragged on and more Americans died, support waned.

Historical Background

The Post-War Era (1945–1970)

The United States emerged from World War II as the most powerful nation on Earth. Proud of their role in the Allied victory, Americans now wanted life to return to normal. Soldiers came home, rationing of scarce goods ended, and the nation prospered. Despite post-war jubilation, however, the dawn of the nuclear age and the dominance of the Soviet Union throughout Eastern Europe meant enormous new challenges.

In 1945, the United Nations was created amid high hopes that it would prevent future wars. Nonetheless, the Cold War between the Soviet Union and the West began as soon as World War II ended. Armed conflict arose in 1950 when President Harry S. Truman sent American troops to help anticommunist South Korean forces turn back a North Korean invasion. Within our borders, fear of communism fueled the "witch hunts" of the 1950s, unleashing investigations and accusations by Senator Joseph McCarthy that ruined the careers and reputations of many Americans.

The Complacent Fifties

Americans of the 1950s are sometimes called "the Silent Generation." Many of them had lived through both the Great Depression and World War II, and they were tired to the bone of sacrifice and conflict. When peace finally arrived, they were glad to adopt quiet ways of living. They wanted to stay at home, raise their families, and enjoy being consumers. They wanted to keep life the way it was for a while.

But the march of technology made complacency impossible. In October 1957, the Soviet Union launched Sputnik, the first artificial satellite to orbit Earth. The Space Age had begun, and the Soviet triumph spurred calls for changes in American education, especially in science and math. President John F. Kennedy, elected in 1960, promised to "get the nation moving again," and he set in motion an intense national effort to land an American on the moon.

TIMELINE

1945

1945: The United States drops atomic bombs on Hiroshima and Nagasaki.

1945: The United Nations Charter is signed in San Francisco, California.

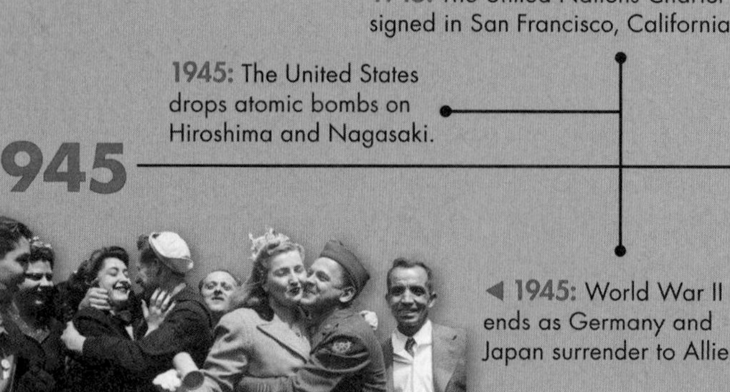

◀ **1945:** World War II ends as Germany and Japan surrender to Allies.

1947: Tennessee Williams's *A Streetcar Named Desire* premiers. ▶

1947: The Cold War between the United States and the Soviet Union begins.

1947: India/Pakistan India and Pakistan granted independence from Great Britain.

The Turbulent Sixties

The assassination of President Kennedy in 1963 was a deeply felt national tragedy. After the assassination came an escalating and increasingly unpopular war in Vietnam. Waves of protest disrupted the country's complacency. Gone were the calm of the 1950s and the high hopes of Kennedy's brief administration. In their place came idealistic but strident demands for an end to the war, progress on civil rights, and greater relevance in education. It was a time of crisis and confrontation, but it also brought genuine progress.

Lasting gains were made in civil rights during these years. In 1954, the Supreme Court had outlawed segregation in public schools, and the Sixties witnessed the continuing battle for racial equality. Tragedy struck again in 1968, however, when civil rights leader Martin Luther King, Jr., was assassinated. Riots broke out in many cities across the nation.

Culture and Counterculture

Through the Fifties and Sixties, television continued to spearhead a revolution in mass communication. By 1960, millions of Americans owned televisions, and masses of people shared common electronic experiences of news, entertainment, and advertising. At the same time, groups of Americans sought lifestyles that opposed the prevailing culture. In music, art, literature, occupations, speech, and dress, these Americans resisted the sameness and anonymity that seemed to be consuming the nation's personality.

Key Historical Theme: Recovery and Rebellion

- During the Fifties, many Americans who had lived through the Great Depression and World War II craved normalcy.
- During the Sixties, many Americans protested against the Vietnam War, racial injustice, and social conformity.

1948: **Israel** United Nations establishes state of Israel.

1949: The North Atlantic Treaty Organization (NATO) is founded to provide security for its member nations. ▶

1950

1948: **Germany** Soviet Union blockades Allied sectors of Berlin.

◀ 1949: *Death of a Salesman* by Arthur Miller is produced.

Essential Questions Across Time

The Post-War Era (1945–1970)

How does literature shape or reflect *society?*

What social and political events affected Americans in the quarter-century after World War II?

The Holocaust and the Atomic Bomb As the war ended, concentration camps were liberated and journalists reported, in shocking words and images, the horrific facts of the Holocaust. In addition, the reality of the atomic bomb gave people all over the world a new fear and a new responsibility for managing international conflict.

Wars, Both Cold and Hot With the rise of the Soviet Union, the Cold War—competition between Eastern bloc countries and the West—became intense. Fear of unchecked Soviet aggression marked the period. Espionage, economic sanctions, treaties, defense measures, and diplomatic conflicts were constantly in the news. In Korea and in Vietnam, many Americans fought and died facing Communist forces.

Civil Rights Struggles and the Women's Movement During the Sixties, protests against racism gave way to riots. Many cities seethed as African Americans demanded change, and television brought the anguish into every living room. During these years, the assassinations of President John F. Kennedy, Malcolm X, Reverend Martin Luther King, Jr., and Senator Robert F. Kennedy underscored the violence of the decade. At the same time, women struggled for greater economic and social power, changing the American work force and the political landscape.

ESSENTIAL QUESTION VOCABULARY

These Essential Question words will help you think and write about literature and society:

international (in´ tər nash´ ə nəl) *adj.* between or among countries

diplomacy (də plō´ mə sē) *n.* the conducting of relations between nations

protest (prō´ test) *n.* demonstration of disapproval; a gathering to voice dissent

TIMELINE

1950

1950: **Korea** North Korean troops invade South Korea, marking the start of the Korean War.

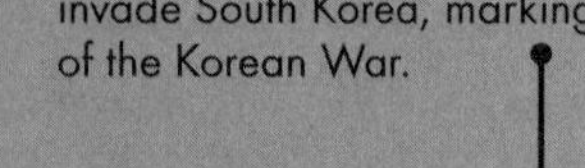

1950: Thousands are falsely accused of treason following McCarthy's claims of Communist spies infiltrating the government. ▶

1951: Julius and Ethel Rosenberg are sentenced to death for conspiracy to commit espionage. ▶

1951: J.D. Salinger publishes *The Catcher in the Rye.*

What values and attitudes grew from these events?

Age of Anxiety vs. Age of Aquarius The fear and violence of the postwar period characterized it as an Age of Anxiety. Americans seemed unable to stop thinking about terrible things that could or might happen. Schools regularly held air-raid drills, and Communists were hunted everywhere. By the late Sixties, however, some Americans put forth an alternative set of idealistic values that called for an "Age of Aquarius"—an era of universal peace and love.

Seeking Conformity During the 1950s, the nation enjoyed widespread prosperity, suburbs expanded, and the consumer society flourished. As a result, many Americans relished, and even demanded, social conformity. Beneath the surface, however, anxiety lurked. For example, in 1954, the United States Information Agency banned Henry David Thoreau's *Walden* from American embassy libraries for being "downright socialistic."

Protesting Conformity As the Sixties wore on, more and more Americans made strong assertions of their individuality. People resisted living with conformity and fear. This new spirit of independence energized the passions for justice and equality that swept the nation.

The American EXPERIENCE

ART IN THE HISTORICAL CONTEXT

The Landscapes of Richard Diebenkorn

After World War II, Abstract Expressionists like Jackson Pollock created paintings that drew attention to the process of how they were made. Their abstract forms emphasized a complex inner reality over a straightforward representation of the outer world. In the 1960s, however, Richard Diebenkorn combined the dynamic energy of abstract forms with shapes that evoked sunny California landscapes.

Diebenkorn captured vibrant West Coast color and light in his pictures. He was able to suggest the land, the sky, the ocean, and the buildings that fragment a scene into blocks of color and yet, at the same time, present a unified, humanized landscape. His 1963 painting *Cityscape I (Landscape No. 1)* fully achieves this blend of abstract thought and warm feeling.

Later in his career Diebenkorn shifted to an even more abstract approach. However, his long series of paintings called *Ocean Park* continued to suggest landscape-like images. Ocean Park is a community near Santa Monica, California, and this particular American place seems to have provided the artist with a firm ground for his stunning abstract visions.

◀ **1952:** Hollywood produces its first feature-length 3D movie to compete with the rising popularity of television.

1952: Ralph Ellison publishes *Invisible Man.*

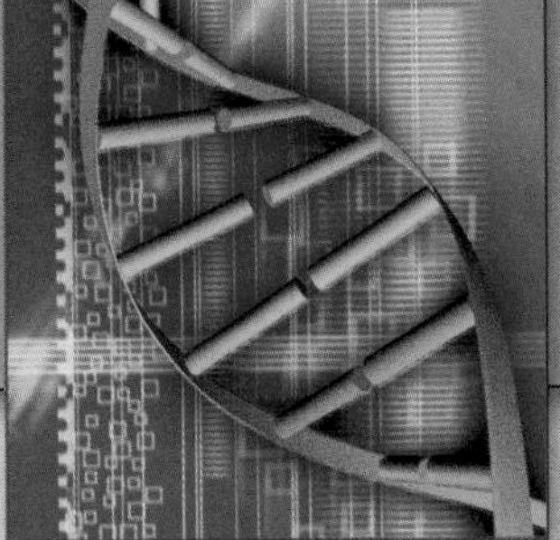

1953: The heart-lung machine is invented, creating treatment options for patients with heart defects.

◀ **1953: England** Francis Crick and James Watson discover DNA.

1954: Supreme Court rules public school segregation to be unconstitutional in *Brown v. Board of Education.*

1954: England *Lord of the Flies* by William Golding is published.

1955

The American EXPERIENCE

CONTEMPORARY CONNECTION

Jack Kerouac: King of the Road Trip

Jack Kerouac was one of the original Beats—a group of cutting edge writers and artists that emerged during the 1950s. Daring, rebellious, intelligent, and mobile, the Beats gave voice to a new generation. Kerouac's best-known work is *On the Road,* a novel inspired by cross-country road-trips. The book was reputedly written in a full-throttle three-week creative frenzy. In fact, the original manuscript of *On the Road* is a continuous scroll made by taping tracing paper end to end. The scroll is typewritten, has no margins, no paragraph indents, and is single-spaced. It still exists; it was purchased by a private collector in 2001, and can be viewed by the public whenever it is on tour. It was displayed at the New York Public Library in 2007 and at the University of Texas at Austin in 2008.

Once Kerouac typed the scroll in 1951, it was not snapped up by publishers. That was not to happen until 1957. After it was published, though, *The New York Times* called *On the Road* "the most beautifully executed, the clearest and most important utterance" of Kerouac's generation.

On the fiftieth anniversary of *On the Road*'s publication, fellow Beat figure Lawrence Ferlinghetti said, "The road doesn't exist anymore in America; there is this huge nostalgia for it. That's one of the reasons *On the Road* is more popular than ever."

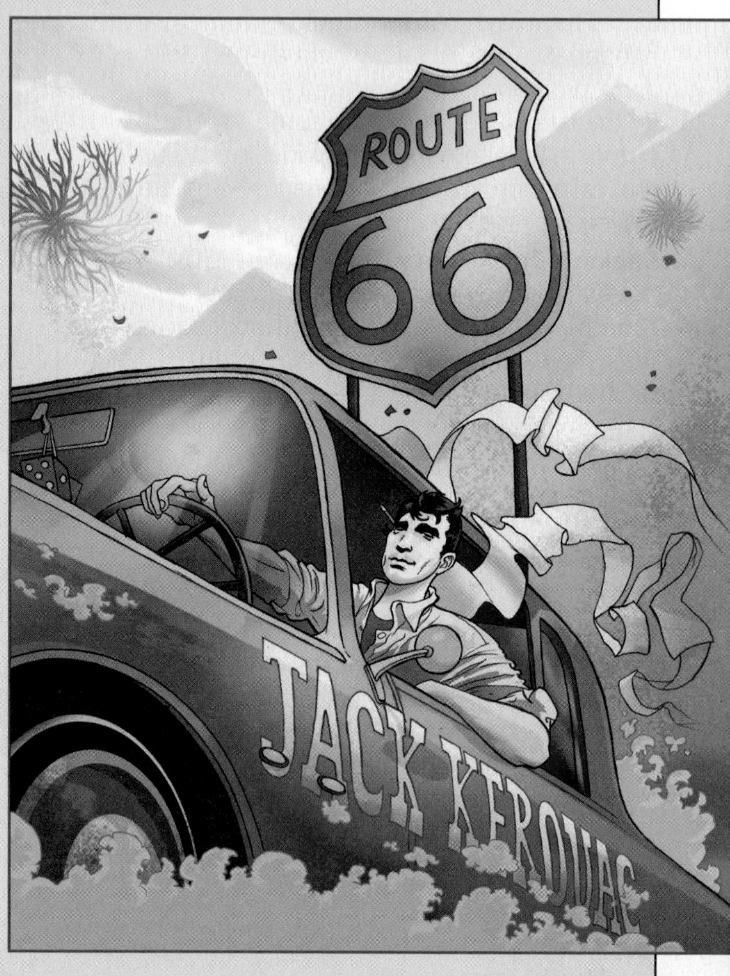

TIMELINE

1955

1955: Flannery O'Connor publishes *A Good Man Is Hard to Find.*

1955: **Argentina** Jorge Luís Borges publishes *Extraordinary Tales.*

1955: Rosa Parks is arrested, triggering the start of the Montgomery Bus Boycott. ▶

"We must learn to live together as brothers or perish together as fools."
— Martin Luther King, Jr.

How did these values and attitudes emerge in literature?

From Anxiety to Irony In the years just after World War II, literature dealt with the grief and shock of the conflict. Journalist John Hersey's *Hiroshima* appeared in 1946, graphically depicting the effects of the atomic bomb on the lives of ordinary Japanese citizens. In 1948, Randall Jarrell published *Losses*, intense poems that captured the feeling of postwar emptiness. By the 1960s, however, some writers were treating the war with tragicomic irony. Joseph Heller's *Catch-22* in 1961 and Kurt Vonnegut, Jr.'s, *Slaughterhouse-Five* in 1969 mixed bitterness with absurdity and fantasy that helped to distance readers from the mid-century violence.

Literature with Purpose The fight for racial equality generated powerful literary statements, including the autobiographical fiction of Ralph Ellison, James Baldwin, and Richard Wright; the poetry of Gwendolyn Brooks and Robert Hayden; the plays of Lorraine Hansberry; and the speeches and essays of Martin Luther King, Jr.

Equality for women was one of the purposes that drove the poems of Sylvia Plath, Adrienne Rich, and Denise Levertov. A general spirit of protest underlay the achievements of Beat poets Allen Ginsberg, Jack Kerouac, and Lawrence Ferlinghetti, while folk musician Bob Dylan produced lyrics that asked piercing social questions. Perhaps the finest socially purposeful literature of the time was Arthur Miller's *The Crucible*—the 1953 play that attacked the anti-Communist Congressional hearings chaired by Wisconsin Senator Joseph McCarthy.

Popular Culture Sails Along On a very different note, the two decades after World War II were high times for the Broadway musical. All over America people were humming tunes from *South Pacific*, *The King and I*, *The Music Man*, *Bye Bye Birdie*, *West Side Story*, *The Sound of Music*, and many other sparkling shows. Fans went crazy with Beatlemania, and families gathered every night around the electronic hearth—the television—to enjoy sitcoms like *I Love Lucy* and *Father Knows Best*, westerns like *Gunsmoke* and *Bonanza*, and the science fiction tales of *The Twilight Zone*.

◀ 1957: **USSR** The first space satellite, *Sputnik 1*, is launched by the Soviet Union.

1957: Dr. Albert Sabin develops an oral vaccine for polio. ▶

1959: Lorraine Hansberry's *A Raisin in the Sun* is produced.

1959: Alaska and Hawaii are admitted to the Union as the 49th and 50th states.

1960

What makes American literature *American?*

What themes did American writers consider important?

Prosperity While the conspicuous consumption of consumer goods seemed to make people's lives easier, it also raised questions about the national character. Writers wondered about the realities of the American Dream. What did "the pursuit of happiness" really mean? The theme of success and its steep price was an important strand in postwar literature.

Rebellion During the 1960s, themes of rebellion ran through American writings. These were not the kinds of rebellious thoughts that Americans had expressed two hundred years earlier. Americans were not rebelling against a colonial government; they were rebelling against a culture they had themselves created. Counterculture movements gave rise to a variety of avant-garde artistic accomplishments with rebellion at their core.

Race After World War II, issues of race took on enormous urgency. When Martin Luther King, Jr., said "I have a dream," many Americans realized that the American Dream itself still needed work. This theme asserted itself in literature just as the civil rights struggle unfolded in American streets.

What roles did American writers play at this time?

The Witness In the literature that looked back at World War II, the writer's role was that of witness to history. Like Randall Jarrell, the writer was the one who had seen the horrors and lived to tell about them. Like John Hersey, the writer was the journalist or historian who could describe what had happened. The writer was also the witness to what was currently happening to the country. When Arthur Miller wrote *The Crucible*, he took on the role of witness to the effects of the rampant fear of Communism.

The Nonconformist Throughout history, writers have often set themselves apart from the mainstream of society. In the 1960s, however,

ESSENTIAL QUESTION VOCABULARY

These Essential Question words will help you think and write about American literature:

prosperity (präs per´ ə tē) *n.* good fortune, wealth

rebellion (ri bel´yən) *n.* defiance of or opposition to authority or control

avant-garde (ə vänt´ gärd´) *adj.* new, unconventional

TIMELINE

1960

1961: **Cuba** The U.S.-supported Bay of Pigs Invasion fails at overthrowing Fidel Castro.

1961: **Germany** East Germany builds Berlin Wall. ▶

1961: Harper Lee wins the Pulitzer Prize for *To Kill a Mockingbird.* ▶

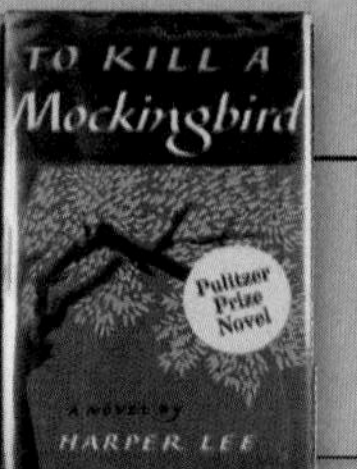

1961: The first American astronaut, Alan Shepard, is launched into space from Cape Canaveral Space Center in Florida. ▶

1962: Environmental protection movement is spurred by Rachel Carson's book *Silent Spring.*

1962: **USSR** *One Day in the Life of Ivan Denisovich* by Alexander Solzhenitsyn is published.

they began to stand apart in greater numbers. These men and women were not "rebels without a cause." They had causes galore. They were anti-war, anti-racism, anti-sexism, anti-materialism, and anti-conformity. Earlier in the century, Modernists had usually confined their rebellions to *artistic* norms. By mid-century, many writers sought to alter *social* norms as well.

The Standard-Bearer Writers took on the vital task of articulating the principles that drove many social movements. They fulfilled this role directly in nonfiction and indirectly in fiction and poetry. Wielding the weapon of words, African American writers such as James Baldwin, Richard Wright, and Ralph Ellison gave definition to the Black experience, inspiring commitment and change. In the works of Sylvia Plath, Gwendolyn Brooks, Adrienne Rich, and many others, the women's movement in America found not only high literary art but also deep pride and energy.

At mid-century, how did writers build on the past?

Enlightening the Present American writers mined American history for parallels to their own era. In *The Crucible*, Arthur Miller shed light on the 1950s by examining a fearful incident of colonial history. In "Frederick Douglass," Robert Hayden looked back to the fight for freedom during the Civil War years to inspire the fight for freedom in the 1960s.

Continuing Forms and Styles Poets such as Robert Lowell, Elizabeth Bishop, and Richard Wilbur composed sonnets and sestinas, framing modern views in traditional forms. Novelists such as John Steinbeck continued to tell realistic stories, and the tradition of the Southern Gothic lived on in the work of William Faulkner, Carson McCullers, Flannery O'Connor, and others.

Keeping Modernism Alive The Modernist impulse that had revolutionized literature earlier in the century marched on into the 1950s. During these years, Modernist artists produced some of their greatest works, including William Carlos Williams's *Paterson*, Wallace Stevens's *The Auroras of Autumn*, and Ernest Hemingway's *The Old Man and the Sea*.

"We need men who can dream of things that never were."
–John F. Kennedy

◀ **1964:** 73 million people tune in to watch the Beatles perform on *The Ed Sullivan Show*.

1965

1963: President John F. Kennedy is assassinated in Dallas. ▶

1964: South Africa Anti-Apartheid leader Nelson Mandela is sentenced to life imprisonment.

1964: IBM produces OS-360, the first mass-produced computer operating system. ▶

What is the relationship between literature and *place?*

How did World War II settings appear in American writing?

The battlefields of Europe, the jungles of the Pacific islands, and the devastated cities of Japan provided settings for great American writing after the war. Randall Jarrell's "The Death of the Ball Turret Gunner," Norman Mailer's novel *The Naked and the Dead*, and John Hersey's *Hiroshima* made readers feel they were standing amid the bloody landscapes. The tone of post–World War II writing, however, did not echo the despair of the literature that had emerged from World War I. War writing in the 1940s and 1950s was filled with pain, but still seemed to hold out the possibility of meaningful courage and even heroism.

How did urban life inspire post-war American literature?

Fiction and Drama In novels, stories, and plays, American writers used the lives of city-dwellers to explore a wide range of twentieth-century issues. The strivings of the middle-class for success, the struggles of immigrants to survive, the uncertainties of adolescents searching for love and independence—these themes and many more grew out of the modern cityscape. In the novels of Saul Bellow, Bernard Malamud, J. D. Salinger, James Agee, and Philip Roth, and in plays such as Arthur Miller's *Death of a Salesman* and Lorraine Hansberry's *A Raisin in the Sun*, urban life had powerful, even fatal, effects on characters.

Poetry The imagery of the city—its steel and glass beauties, its overarching bridges and underground tunnels, its smoke, speed, and noise—appeared often in poems. Brilliant collections by William Carlos Williams, Robert Lowell, Anne Sexton, Gwendolyn Brooks, and Allen Ginsberg define modern America as an increasingly urban place.

How did literature respond to the growth of suburbia?

Selling the American Dream After World War II, a "baby boom" created the need for more new homes. Developers across the nation

ESSENTIAL QUESTION VOCABULARY

These Essential Question words will help you think and write about literature and place.

cityscape (sit′ ē skāp′) *n.* urban scene or landscape

underground (un′ dər ground′) *adj.* beneath the surface

suburbs (sub′ ərbz) *n.* residential areas outside of cities

TIMELINE

1965

1966: **China** Mao Zedong launches Cultural Revolution. ▶

1966: *Ariel*, Sylvia Plath's last collection of poems, is published in the United States.

1967: **Israel** Israel gains territory from Arab states in Six-Day War.

1967: **South Africa** Christiaan Barnard performs the world's first heart transplant; the patient dies 18 days later.

1967: Thurgood Marshall becomes the first black U.S. Supreme Court justice. ▶

built new suburbs and expanded existing ones. Partly urban and partly pastoral, suburbs seemed to make the American Dream accessible for more people, at least for the middle class. Advertising, television, and movies sold the suburbs as the best chance for families to escape urban crowding and the pace and pressure of city life. Literature, however, explored both sides of the coin.

Dissecting the American Dream Many American writers recognized that, for some people, the dream could turn into a nightmare. A popular song of 1962 warned about what happens to people who all live in "little boxes" that "all look just the same." In 1845, Thoreau found peace by building his own house on the shore of a pond. What if, one hundred years later, thousands of people did the same thing, in the same place, at the same time?

Writers such as John Cheever and John Updike saw the dysfunction that could tear apart suburban families. In their novels and stories, they chronicled the symptoms of a new kind of alienation, brought on by too much sameness, too little genuine individuality, too much insistence on "keeping up with the Joneses." Issues that literature had once explored in small-town life in America now became transferred to suburban life.

The American EXPERIENCE

CLOSE-UP ON HISTORY

Rachel Carson and Environmental Writing

Today, most people are aware of the human impact on the environment. While people may disagree about the severity of environmental problems or how to address them, most feel these issues are important. Yet, even that understanding did not always exist. Americans were alerted to the problems facing the environment by a scientist named Rachel Carson.

In 1962, Carson published *Silent Spring*, the book that made millions of people conscious of the dangers of industrial pollution and of the damage it was doing throughout the natural world. In prose that is both scientifically accurate and passionate, Carson explained humanity's place in the world's ecosystem. She described the environmental consequences of technological progress, the chemical "rivers of death" that people allow to flow into the ocean.

Along with the naturalist Aldo Leopold, Rachel Carson sparked the modern environmental movement and also helped found a genre of literature that remains vital today. Writings about the environment—sometimes call eco-literature or green literature—continues to inform contemporary readers.

▲ 1968: Martin Luther King, Jr., civil rights leader, murdered in Memphis.

▲ 1969: Kurt Vonnegut publishes his novel *Slaughterhouse-Five*.

1969: **Northern Ireland** A long period of violence begins between Catholics and Protestants.

1969: Richard Nixon is sworn in as the 37th President of the United States.

1970

1969: Astronaut Neil Armstrong becomes the first person to set foot on the moon. ▶

Recent Scholarship

The Purpose of THEATER

Arthur Miller

After a talk Arthur Miller gave at the University of Michigan, a member of the audience asked him: "What do you think the purpose, the ultimate purpose, of the theater is, really?" Miller responded: "I couldn't even speak in those terms because it's like asking, 'What is the ultimate purpose of the Universe?' To me the theater is not a disconnected entertainment, which it usually is to most people here. It's the sound and ring of the spirit of the people at any one time. It is where a collective mass of people, through the genius of some author, is able to project its terrors and its hopes and to symbolize them. Now how that's done—there are thousands of ways to do it of course. . . . I personally feel that the theater has to confront the basic themes always. And the faces change from generation to generation, but their roots are generally the same, and that is a question of man's increasing awareness of himself and his environment, his quest for justice and for the right to be human. That's a big order, but I don't know where else excepting a playhouse, where there's reasonable freedom, one should hope to see that."

Theater as a Bridge Between Cultures

Arthur Miller once wrote: "In a theater, people are themselves; they come of their own volition; they accept or reject, are moved or left cold not by virtue of reason alone or of emotion alone, but as whole human beings.

About the Author

Arthur Miller (1915–2005) is a legend of the twentieth-century American theater. He chronicled the dilemmas of common people pitted against powerful social forces. His most famous plays are *Death of a Salesman,* for which he won a Pulitzer Prize, and *The Crucible,* one of the most frequently performed plays in the world today.

Literature of the first rank is a kind of international signaling service . . .

▲ **Critical Viewing** What emotions do you think this theater audience is feeling? Explain. **SPECULATE**

"A communion through art is therefore unusually complete; it can be a most reliable indication of a fundamental unity; and an inability to commune through art is, I think, a stern indication that cultures have not yet arrived at a genuine common ground. Had there been no Flaubert, no Zola, no Proust, de Maupassant, Stendhal, Balzac, Dumas;[1] had there been no Mark Twain, or Poe, Hawthorne, Emerson, Hemingway, Steinbeck, Faulkner,[2] or the numerous other American artists of the first rank, our conviction of essential union with France and of France with us would rest upon the assurances of the two Departments of State and the impression of tourists. I think that had there been no Tolstoy, no Gogol, no Turgenev, no Chekov or Dostoyevsky,[3] we should have no assurance at all nor any faint hope that the Russian heart was even ultimately comprehensible to us.

"Literature of the first rank is a kind of international signaling service, telling all who can read that wherever that distant blinker is shining live men of a common civilization."

1. **Flaubert . . . Dumas** influential French writers.
2. **Mark Twain . . . Faulkner** famous American writers.
3. **Tolstoy . . . Dostoyevsky** well-known Russian writers.

Speaking and Listening: Collaboration

Arthur Miller's comments emphasize the unifying power of literature. Just as people are brought together in a theater, they are also brought together when they read. Drama, fiction, and poetry make people aware of each other and lead to "a communion through art."

With a partner, discuss Miller's comments and the implications they have for writers and for audiences. Do you agree or disagree with the comments? Why or why not? What responsibilities does Miller suggest writers have to bear? What responsibilities does he suggest lay with readers and audiences? Gather your ideas into a **written statement** to read for the class.

Integrate and Evaluate Information

1. Use a chart like the one shown to determine the key ideas expressed in the Essential Question essays on pages 970–977. Fill in two ideas related to each Essential Question and note the authors most closely associated with each concept. One example has been done for you.

Essential Question	Key Concept	Key Author
Literature and Place		
American Literature		
Literature and Society	Individuality and nonconformity	Lawrence Ferlinghetti

2. How do the visual sources in this section—map, graphs, timelines, paintings, photographs, and artifacts—add to your understanding of the ideas expressed in words? Cite specific examples.
3. During the 1950s, many Americans craved normalcy; but during the 1960s, many people rebelled against normalcy and conformity. Citing evidence from the multiple sources presented on pages 968–977, explain the underlying reasons for the mood of each decade. How were these moods made manifest in art and popular culture?
4. **Address a Question** Playwright Arthur Miller says that one purpose of theater is to ask and answer questions about "man's increasing awareness of himself and his environment, his quest for justice and for the right to be human." In your view, what other human activity or form of expression shares these purposes? In what other arenas can such goals be effectively pursued? Integrate information from this textbook and other sources to support your ideas.

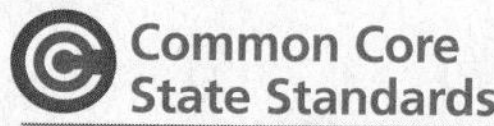
Common Core State Standards

Reading Informational Text
7. Integrate and evaluate multiple sources of information presented in different media or formats as well as in words in order to address a question or solve a problem.

Speaking and Listening
1.a. Come to discussions prepared, having read and researched material under study; explicitly draw on that preparation by referring to evidence from texts and other research on the topic or issue to stimulate a thoughtful, well-reasoned exchange of ideas.
1.c. Propel conversations by posing and responding to questions that probe reasoning and evidence; ensure a hearing for a full range of positions on a topic or issue; clarify, verify, or challenge ideas and conclusions; and promote divergent and creative perspectives.

Speaking and Listening: Interview

The 1960s were turbulent years in America. Conduct an **interview** with someone who lived through that decade. If possible, *use technology,* such as a digital camera or a video recorder, to capture the interview, and a computer to edit it. Present the edited interview to the class. Include a closing statement in which you summarize what you learned.

Solve a Research Problem To conduct an effective interview, you must ask thoughtful, informed questions. Create a research plan to educate yourself about the 1960s before conducting the interview. Use a variety of sources—print, digital, audio, and visual—to learn about this time period. Use the information you gather to write interview questions; for example:

- What were your reactions to the Kennedy and King assassinations?
- How did you feel about the Vietnam War?
- Were you a fan of the Beatles or other musical groups? Why?

ESSENTIAL QUESTION VOCABULARY

Use these words in your responses:

Literature and Place
cityscape
underground
suburbs

American Literature
prosperity
rebellion
avant-garde

Literature and Society
international
diplomacy
protest

TEXT SET

War Shock

Part 1

Building Knowledge and Insight

ANCHOR TEXT

from ***Hiroshima* • *The Death of the Ball Turret Gunner***

Connecting to the Essential Question These selections present unflinching portrayals of war. As you read, note details that emphasize the high costs of armed conflict. Doing so will help as you consider the Essential Question: **How does literature shape or reflect society?**

Close Reading Focus

Theme; Perspective

The **theme** is the central idea or insight in a work of literature. Many nonfiction works present explicitly stated central ideas, while most works of fiction, poetry, and drama express implied themes. The meaning is conveyed through details, characters, events, descriptions, and literary devices. However, some nonfiction works use the same literary techniques as fiction, including an implied or suggested theme. Both of these selections—one a work of journalism and the other a poem—express implied themes about war.

Comparing Literary Works An author's **perspective** is the point of view from which he or she writes. This perspective may be objective and impersonal, subjective and personal, or a mixture of both:

- With an *objective perspective,* the narrator reports events without obvious emotion or bias. *Hersey:* A hundred thousand people were killed by the atomic bomb.
- With a *subjective perspective,* the narrator expresses feelings about the events. *Jarrell:* I woke to black flak and the nightmare fighters.

As you read these selections about World War II, compare how the authors mix objectivity and subjectivity in surprising and effective ways.

Preparing to Read Complex Texts Both Hersey and Jarrell bring strong but unstated political beliefs to their writing. Because of this, **analyzing the writers' political assumptions** can lead you to a deeper understanding of their work. As you read, use a chart like the one shown to consider how key details express both the writers' political assumptions and deeper truths about human beings.

Common Core State Standards

Reading Literature/ Informational Text

1. Cite strong and thorough textual evidence to support analysis of what the text says explicitly as well as inferences drawn from the text, including determining where the text leaves matters uncertain.

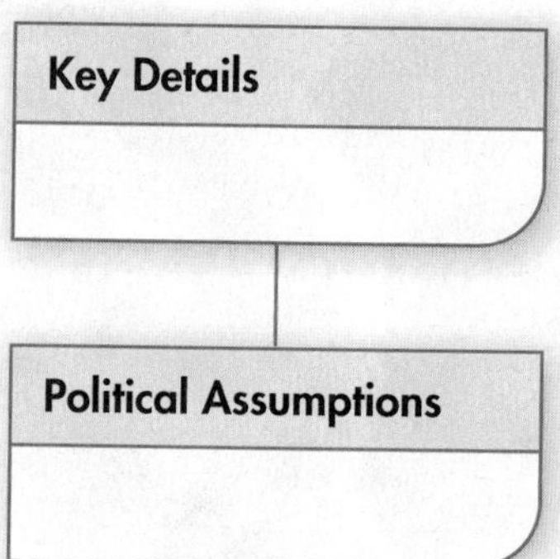

Vocabulary

You will encounter the words listed here in the text that follows. Copy the words into your notebook, sorting them into words you know and words you do not know.

evacuated
volition
rendezvous
incessant
convivial

JOHN HERSEY (1914–1993)

Author of ***Hiroshima***

John Hersey was born in China to American missionary parents. The family lived in China until Hersey was ten years old, when they returned to the United States. In 1936, Hersey graduated from Yale University and became a foreign correspondent in East Asia, Italy, and the Soviet Union. His experiences working as a journalist served as the premise for his twenty-five books and countless essays and articles.

Hersey combined a profound moral sensibility with the highest artistry. His novels and essays not only examine the moral implications of the major political and historical events of his day, they do so with high literary grace. In 1945, Hersey won a Pulitzer Prize for his novel *A Bell for Adano,* in which an American major discovers the human dignity of the Italian villagers who were his enemies in World War II.

The Atomic Bomb During the 1940s, Hersey traveled to China and Japan as a correspondent for *The New Yorker* and *Time* magazines. He also used these visits to gather material for his most famous and acclaimed book, *Hiroshima* (1946), a shocking, graphic depiction of the devastation caused by the atomic bomb that was dropped on the Japanese city of Hiroshima near the end of World War II. This remarkable report, which tells the vivid and detailed stories of victims of the bombing, was first published as a four-part article in *The New Yorker* on August 31, 1946. William Shawn, then editor of *The New Yorker,* made the unprecedented decision to bump all of the magazine's other editorial content in order to publish Hersey's article.

Stories of Inhumanity and Courage In 1950, Hersey published the novel *The Wall,* which tells of the extinction of the Warsaw ghetto by the Germans during World War II. Hersey's later works include *A Single Pebble* (1956), *The War Lover* (1959), *The Child Buyer* (1960), *The Algiers Motel Incident* (1968), *The Writer's Craft* (1974), *Blues* (1987), and *Fling and Other Stories* (1990).

"There is one sacred rule of journalism. The writer must not invent."

from HIROSHIMA

JOHN HERSEY

BACKGROUND In August 1945, American President Harry Truman was faced with a terrible decision. The world had been at war for six years. Germany had surrendered in May, but Japan refused to give up. The United States had just finished developing an atomic bomb. President Truman had to decide whether or not to use this new technology to bring an end to the war. On August 6, Truman ordered that the atomic bomb be dropped on the Japanese city of Hiroshima. Three days later, another bomb was dropped on Nagasaki. These two bombs killed more than 200,000 people and forced the Japanese surrender. Like so many events of World War II, the atomic bomb gave the world a new horror, as John Hersey so carefully documents in this selection.

Exactly fifteen minutes past eight in the morning, on August 6, 1945, Japanese time, at the moment when the atomic bomb flashed above Hiroshima, Miss Toshiko Sasaki, a clerk in the personnel department of the East Asia Tin Works, had just sat down at her place in the plant office and was turning her head to speak to the girl at the next desk. At that same moment, Dr. Masakazu Fujii was settling down cross-legged to read the Osaka *Asahi* on the porch of his private hospital, overhanging one of the seven deltaic rivers which divide Hiroshima; Mrs. Hatsuyo Nakamura, a tailor's widow, stood by the window of her kitchen, watching a neighbor tearing down his house because it lay in the path of an air-raid-defense fire lane . . . and the Reverend Mr. Kiyoshi Tanimoto, pastor of the Hiroshima Methodist Church, paused at the door of a rich man's house in Koi, the city's western suburb, and prepared to unload a handcart full of things he had evacuated from town in fear of the massive B-29 raid which everyone expected Hiroshima to suffer. A hundred thousand people were killed by the atomic bomb, and these [four] were among the survivors. They still wonder why they lived when so many others died. Each of them counts many small items of chance or volition—a step taken in time, a decision to go indoors, catching one streetcar instead of the next—that spared him. And now each knows that in the act of survival he lived a dozen lives and saw more death than he ever thought he would see. At the time, none of them knew anything.

The Reverend Mr. Tanimoto got up at five o'clock that morning. He was alone in the parsonage, because for some time his wife had been commuting with their year-old baby to spend nights with a friend in Ushida, a suburb to the north. Of all the important cities of Japan, only two, Kyoto and Hiroshima, had not been visited

◀ **Critical Viewing** What do you find most disturbing about this photograph of the ruined city of Hiroshima? **TAKE A POSITION**

Vocabulary

evacuated (ē vak′ yo͞o āt′ id) *v.* made empty; withdrawn

volition (vō lish′ ən) *n.* act of using the will

Comprehension

What happened at exactly 8:15 in the morning on August 6, 1945?

in strength by *B-san*, or Mr. B, as the Japanese, with a mixture of respect and unhappy familiarity, called the B-29; and Mr. Tanimoto, like all his neighbors and friends, was almost sick with anxiety. He had heard uncomfortably detailed accounts of mass raids on Kure, Iwakuni, Tokuyama, and other nearby towns; he was sure Hiroshima's turn would come soon. He had slept badly the night before, because there had been several air-raid warnings. Hiroshima had been getting such warnings almost every night for weeks, for at that time the B-29s were using Lake Biwa, northeast of Hiroshima, as a **rendezvous** point, and no matter what city the Americans planned to hit, the Super-fortresses streamed in over the coast near Hiroshima. The frequency of the warning and the continued abstinence of Mr. B with respect to Hiroshima had made its citizens jittery; a rumor was going around that the Americans were saving something special for the city.

Vocabulary
rendezvous (rän′dā vōō′)
n. meeting place

Mr. Tanimoto was a small man, quick to talk, laugh, and cry. He wore his black hair parted in the middle and rather long; the prominence of the frontal bones just above his eyebrows and the smallness of his mustache, mouth, and chin gave him a strange old-young look, boyish and yet wise, weak and yet fiery. He moved nervously and fast, but with a restraint which suggested that he is a cautious, thoughtful man. He showed, indeed, just those qualities in the uneasy days before the bomb fell. Mr. Tanimoto had been carrying all the portable things from his church, in the close-packed residential district called Nagaragawa, to a house that belonged to a rayon manufacturer in Koi, two miles from the center of town. The rayon man, a Mr. Matsui, had opened his then unoccupied estate to a large number of his friends and acquaintances, so that they might evacuate whatever they wished to a safe distance from the probable target area. Mr. Tanimoto had had no difficulty in moving chairs, hymnals, Bibles, altar gear, and church records by pushcart himself, but the organ console and an upright piano required some aid. A friend of his named Matsuo had, the day before, helped him get the piano out to Koi; in return, he had promised this day to assist Mr. Matsuo in hauling out a daughter's belongings. That is why he had risen so early.

Mr. Tanimoto cooked his own breakfast. He felt awfully tired. The effort of moving the piano the day before, a sleepless night, weeks of worry and unbalanced diet, the cares of his parish—all combined to make him feel hardly adequate to the new day's work. There was another thing, too: Mr. Tanimoto had studied theology at Emory College, in Atlanta, Georgia; he had graduated in 1940; he spoke excellent English; he dressed in American clothes; he had corresponded with many American friends right up to the time the war

LITERATURE IN CONTEXT

History Connection

B-29 Bombers

The Second World War saw major advances in the technology of mechanized warfare—warfare that relied heavily on machines. The B-29 Superfortress bomber that Hersey mentions was an aircraft capable of long-range, heavy bombing runs. It was used frequently against Japan during 1944 and 1945. Firebomb B-29 raids against industrial cities in Japan totaled nearly 7,000 flights and dropped 41,600 tons of bombs.

Connect to the Literature

In what way would having more information about the B-29 bomber increase Mr. Tanimoto's anxiety level?

began; and among a people obsessed with a fear of being spied upon—perhaps almost obsessed himself—he found himself growing increasingly uneasy. The police had questioned him several times, and just a few days before, he had heard that an influential acquaintance, a Mr. Tanaka, a retired officer of the Toyo Kisen Kaisha steamship line, an anti-Christian, a man famous in Hiroshima for his showy philanthropies and notorious for his personal tyrannies, had been telling people that Tanimoto should not be trusted. In compensation, to show himself publicly a good Japanese, Mr. Tanimoto had taken on the chairmanship of his local *tonarigumi*, or Neighborhood Association, and to his other duties and concerns this position had added the business of organizing air-raid defense for about twenty families.

Before six o'clock that morning, Mr. Tanimoto started for Mr. Matsuo's house. There he found that their burden was to be a *tansu*, a large Japanese cabinet, full of clothing and household goods. The two men set out. The morning was perfectly clear and so warm that the day promised to be uncomfortable. A few minutes after they started, the air-raid siren went off—a minute-long blast that warned of approaching planes but indicated to the people of Hiroshima only a slight degree of danger, since it sounded every morning at this time, when an American weather plane came over. The two men pulled and pushed the handcart through the city streets. Hiroshima was a fan-shaped city, lying mostly on the six islands formed by the seven estuarial rivers that branch out from the Ota River; its main commercial and residential districts, covering about four square miles in the center of the city, contained three-quarters of its population, which had been reduced by several evacuation programs from a wartime peak of 380,000 to about 245,000. Factories and other residential districts, or suburbs, lay compactly around the edges of the city. To the south were the docks, an airport, and the island-studded Inland Sea. A rim of mountains runs around the other three sides of the delta. Mr. Tanimoto and Mr. Matsuo took their way through the shopping center, already full of people, and across two of the rivers to the sloping streets of Koi, and up them to the outskirts and foothills. As they started up a valley away from the tight-ranked houses, the all-clear sounded. (The Japanese radar operators, detecting only three planes, supposed that they comprised a reconnaissance.) Pushing the handcart up to the rayon man's house was tiring, and the men, after they had maneuvered their load into the driveway and to the front steps, paused to rest awhile. They stood with a wing of the house between them and the city. Like most homes in this part of Japan, the house consisted of a wooden frame and wooden walls supporting a heavy tile roof. Its front hall, packed with rolls of bedding and clothing, looked like a cool cave full of fat cushions. Opposite the house, to the right of the front door, there was a large, finicky rock garden. There was no sound of planes. The morning was still; the place was cool and pleasant.

Implied Theme

In light of the bombing, what is ironic about an air-raid siren indicating only a "slight degree of danger"?

Comprehension

Why does Mr. Tanimoto move all the portable things in his church to a home farther from the town center?

▲ **Critical Viewing**
You may have seen photographs like this one of the aftermath of the Hiroshima bombing. Does Hersey's account change the way you view such pictures? Explain. **RELATE**

Then a tremendous flash of light cut across the sky. Mr. Tanimoto has a distinct recollection that it travelled from east to west, from the city toward the hills. It seemed a sheet of sun. Both he and Mr. Matsuo reacted in terror—and both had time to react (for they were 3,500 yards, or two miles, from the center of the explosion). Mr. Matsuo dashed up the front steps into the house and dived among the bedrolls and buried himself there. Mr. Tanimoto took four or five steps and threw himself between two big rocks in the garden. He bellied up very hard against one of them. As his face was against the stone, he did not see what happened. He felt a sudden pressure, and then splinters and pieces of board and fragments of tile fell on him. He heard no roar. (Almost no one in Hiroshima recalls hearing any noise of the bomb. But a fisherman in his sampan on the Inland Sea near Tsuzu, the man with whom Mr. Tanimoto's mother-in-law and sister-in-law were living, saw the flash and heard a tremendous explosion; he was nearly twenty miles from Hiroshima, but the thunder was greater than when the B-29s hit Iwakuni, only five miles away.)

When he dared, Mr. Tanimoto raised his head and saw that the rayon man's house had collapsed. He thought a bomb had fallen directly on it. Such clouds of dust had risen that there was a sort of twilight around. In panic, not thinking for the moment of Mr. Matsuo under the ruins, he dashed out into the street. He noticed as he ran that the concrete wall of the estate had fallen over—toward the house rather than away from it. In the street, the first thing he saw was a squad of soldiers who had been burrowing into the hillside opposite, making one of the thousands of dugouts in which the Japanese apparently intended to resist invasion, hill by hill, life for life; the soldiers were coming out of the hole, where they should have been safe, and blood was running from their heads, chests, and backs. They were silent and dazed.

Under what seemed to be a local dust cloud, the day grew darker and darker.

Spiral Review
Diction and Tone What do you notice about Hersey's diction and tone as he describes these awful scenes?

Nearly midnight, the night before the bomb was dropped, an announcer on the city's radio station said that about two hundred B-29s were approaching southern Honshu and advised the population of Hiroshima to evacuate to their designated "safe areas." Mrs. Hatsuyo Nakamura, the tailor's widow, who lived in the section called Nobori-cho and who had long had a habit of doing as she was told, got her three children—a ten-year-old boy, Toshio, an eight-year-old girl, Yaeko, and a five-year-old girl, Myeko—out of bed and dressed them and walked with them to the military area known as the East Parade Ground, on the northeast edge of the city. There she unrolled some mats and the children lay down on them. They slept until about two, when they were awakened by the roar of the planes going over Hiroshima.

As soon as the planes had passed, Mrs. Nakamura started back with her children. They reached home a little after two-thirty and she immediately turned on the radio, which, to her distress, was just then broadcasting a fresh warning. When she looked at the children and saw how tired they were, and when she thought of the number of trips they had made in past weeks, all to no purpose, to the East Parade Ground, she decided that in spite of the instructions on the radio, she simply could not face starting out all over again. She put the children in their bedrolls on the floor, lay down herself at three o'clock, and fell asleep at once, so soundly that when planes passed over later, she did not waken to their sound.

Author's Perspective
What do the details about Mrs. Nakamura's tired children suggest about the author's objectivity?

The siren jarred her awake at about seven. She arose, dressed quickly, and hurried to the house of Mr. Nakamoto, the head of her Neighborhood Association, and asked him what she should do. He said that she should remain at home unless an urgent warning—a series of intermittent blasts of the siren—was sounded. She returned home, lit the stove in the kitchen, set some rice to cook, and sat down to read that morning's Hiroshima *Chugoku*. To her relief, the all-clear

Comprehension
Why are Mrs. Nakamura's children so tired?

sounded at eight o'clock. She heard the children stirring, so she went and gave each of them a handful of peanuts and told them to stay in their bedrolls, because they were tired from the night's walk. She had hoped that they would go back to sleep, but the man in the house directly to the south began to make a terrible hullabaloo of hammering, wedging, ripping, and splitting. The prefectural government,[1] convinced, as everyone in Hiroshima was, that the city would be attacked soon, had begun to press with threats and warnings for the completion of wide fire lanes, which, it was hoped, might act in conjunction with the rivers to localize any fires started by an incendiary[2] raid; and the neighbor was reluctantly sacrificing his home to the city's safety. Just the day before, the prefecture had ordered all able-bodied girls from the secondary schools to spend a few days helping to clear these lanes, and they started work soon after the all-clear sounded.

Implied Theme

Why do you think the author included information about the citizens' attempts to defend their city and its population?

---

1. **prefectural government** regional districts of Japan which are administered by a governor.
2. **incendiary** (in sen′ dē er′ ē) *adj.* designed to cause fires.

◀ Critical Viewing

There are no people shown in this photograph—nor in many others—depicting the devastation wrought by the Hiroshima bomb. Does the lack of humanity lessen or intensify the power of the image? Explain. **ASSESS**

Mrs. Nakamura went back to the kitchen, looked at the rice, and began watching the man next door. At first, she was annoyed with him for making so much noise, but then she was moved almost to tears by pity. Her emotion was specifically directed toward her neighbor, tearing down his home, board by board, at a time when there was so much unavoidable destruction, but undoubtedly she also felt a generalized, community pity, to say nothing of self-pity. She had not had an easy time. Her husband, Isawa, had gone into the Army just after Myeko was born, and she had heard nothing from or of him for a long time, until, on March 5, 1942, she received a seven-word telegram: "Isawa died an honorable death at Singapore." She learned later that he had died on February 15th, the day Singapore fell, and that he had been a corporal. Isawa had been a not particularly prosperous tailor, and his only capital was a Sankoku sewing machine. After his death, when his allotments stopped coming,

Comprehension

Why does the prefectural government call for the completion of fire lanes?

Mrs. Nakamura got out the machine and began to take in piecework herself, and since then had supported the children, but poorly, by sewing.

As Mrs. Nakamura stood watching her neighbor, everything flashed whiter than any white she had ever seen. She did not notice what happened to the man next door; the reflex of a mother set her in motion toward her children. She had taken a single step (the house was 1,350 yards, or three-quarters of a mile, from the center of the explosion) when something picked her up and she seemed to fly into the next room over the raised sleeping platform, pursued by parts of her house.

Timbers fell around her as she landed, and a shower of tiles pommelled her; everything became dark, for she was buried. The debris did not cover her deeply. She rose up and freed herself. She heard a child cry, "Mother, help me!" and saw her youngest—Myeko, the five-year-old—buried up to her breast and unable to move. As Mrs. Nakamura started frantically to claw her way toward the baby, she could see or hear nothing of her other children.

In the days right before the bombing, Dr. Masakazu Fujii, being prosperous, hedonistic,[3] and at the time not too busy, had been allowing himself the luxury of sleeping until nine or nine-thirty, but fortunately he had to get up early the morning the bomb was dropped to see a house guest off on a train. He rose at six, and half an hour later walked with his friend to the station, not far away, across two of the rivers. He was back home by seven, just as the siren sounded its sustained warning. He ate breakfast and then, because the morning was already hot, undressed down to his underwear and went out on the porch to read the paper. This porch—in fact, the whole building—was curiously constructed. Dr. Fujii was the proprietor of a peculiarly Japanese institution; a private, single-doctor hospital. This building, perched beside and over the water of the Kyo River, and next to the bridge of the same name, contained thirty rooms for thirty patients and their kinfolk—for, according to Japanese custom, when a person falls sick and goes to a hospital, one or more members of his family go and live there with him, to cook for him, bathe, massage, and read to him, and to offer incessant familial sympathy, without which a Japanese patient would be miserable indeed. Dr. Fujii had no beds—only straw mats—for his patients. He did, however, have all sorts of modern equipment: an X-ray machine, diathermy[4] apparatus, and a

The **American EXPERIENCE**

World War II

World War II began in September 1939, when German forces, following the orders of the dictator Adolf Hitler, invaded Poland. In response to this unprovoked invasion, France and Great Britain declared war on Germany. Just over two years later, the United States entered the war when Japan, a German ally, launched a surprise attack on an American naval base at Pearl Harbor in Hawaii. The war continued to escalate during the early 1940s. More than two dozen nations were eventually drawn into the conflict, and tens of millions of soldiers were killed. By 1945, the tide had turned strongly in favor of the United States and its allies. In early May 1945, the German forces surrendered. Fighting continued in the Pacific, however, as the Japanese refused to give up. The war finally ended in 1945 when the United States dropped two atomic bombs on the Japanese cities of Hiroshima and Nagasaki. The bombs killed more than 200,000 people and forced Japan's surrender.

Connect to the Literature

In what way does getting to know Dr. Fujii and the others affect your feelings about the dropping of the atom bombs on Hiroshima?

Vocabulary

incessant (in ses′ ənt) *adj.* constant; continuing in a way that seems endless

3. **hedonistic** (he de nis′ tik) *adj.* indulgently seeking out pleasure.
4. **diathermy** (dī′ ə thur′ mē) *n.* medical treatment in which heat is produced beneath the skin to warm or destroy tissue.

fine tiled laboratory. The structure rested two-thirds on the land, one-third on piles over the tidal waters of the Kyo. This overhang, the part of the building where Dr. Fujii lived, was queer-looking, but it was cool in summer and from the porch, which faced away from the center of the city, the prospect of the river, with pleasure boats drifting up and down it, was always refreshing. Dr. Fujii had occasionally had anxious moments when the Ota and its mouth branches rose to flood, but the piling was apparently firm enough and the house had always held.

Dr. Fujii had been relatively idle for about a month because in July, as the number of untouched cities in Japan dwindled and as Hiroshima seemed more and more inevitably a target, he began turning patients away, on the ground that in case of a fire raid he would not be able to evacuate them. Now he had only two patients left—a woman from Yano, injured in the shoulder, and a young man of twenty-five recovering from burns he had suffered when the steel factory near Hiroshima in which he worked had been hit. Dr. Fujii had six nurses to tend his patients. His wife and children were safe; his wife and one son were living outside Osaka, and another son and two daughters were in the country on Kyushu. A niece was living with him, and a maid and a manservant. He had little to do and did not mind, for he had saved some money. At fifty, he was healthy, convivial, and calm, and he was pleased to pass the evenings drinking whiskey with friends, always sensibly and for the sake of conversation. Before the war, he had affected brands imported from Scotland and America; now he was perfectly satisfied with the best Japanese brand, Suntory.

Dr. Fujii sat down cross-legged in his underwear on the spotless matting of the porch, put on his glasses, and started reading the Osaka *Asahi.* He liked to read the Osaka news because his wife was there. He saw the flash. To him—faced away from the center and looking at his paper—it seemed a brilliant yellow. Startled, he began to rise to his feet. In that moment (he was 1,550 yards from the center), the hospital leaned behind his rising and, with a terrible ripping noise, toppled into the river. The Doctor, still in the act of getting to his feet, was thrown forward and around and over; he was buffeted and gripped; he lost track of everything, because things were so speeded up; he felt the water.

Dr. Fujii hardly had time to think that he was dying before he realized that he was alive, squeezed tightly by two long timbers in a V across his chest, like a morsel suspended between two huge chopsticks—held upright, so that he could not move, with his head miraculously above water and his torso and legs in it. The remains of his hospital were all around him in a mad assortment of splintered lumber and materials for the relief of pain. His left shoulder hurt terribly. His glasses were gone. . . .

Dr. Fujii hardly had time to think that he was dying before he realized that he was alive...

Vocabulary
convivial (kən viv′ ē əl) *adj.* fond of good company; sociable

Author's Perspective
Is Hersey's description of Dr. Fujii objective or subjective? Explain.

Comprehension
Where is Dr. Fujii when the bomb hits?

▲ Critical Viewing
Based on this image, does survival in this setting seem possible? **ASSESS**

Miss Toshiko Sasaki, the East Asia Tin Works clerk, . . . got up at three o'clock in the morning on the day the bomb fell. There was extra housework to do. Her eleven-month-old brother, Akio, had come down the day before with a serious stomach upset; her mother had taken him to the Tamura Pediatric Hospital and was staying there with him. Miss Sasaki, who was about twenty, had to cook breakfast for her father, a brother, a sister, and herself, and—since the hospital, because of the war, was unable to provide food—to prepare a whole day's meals for her mother and the baby, in time for her father, who worked in a factory making rubber earplugs for artillery crews, to take the food by on his way to the plant. When she had finished and had cleaned and put away the cooking things, it was nearly seven. The family lived in Koi, and she had a forty-five-minute trip to the tin works, in the section of town called Kannonmachi. She was in charge of the personnel records in the factory. She left Koi at seven, and as soon as she reached the plant, she went with some of the other girls from the personnel department to the factory auditorium. A prominent local Navy man, a former employee, had committed suicide the day before by throwing himself under a train—a death considered honorable enough to warrant a memorial service, which was to be held at the tin works at ten o'clock that morning. In the large hall, Miss Sasaki and the others made suitable preparations for the meeting. This work took about twenty minutes.

Miss Sasaki went back to her office and sat down at her desk. She was quite far from the windows, which were off to her left, and behind her were a couple of tall bookcases containing all the books of the factory library, which the personnel department had organized. She settled herself at her desk, put some things in a drawer, and shifted papers. She thought that before she began to make entries in her lists of new employees, discharges, and departures for the Army, she would chat for a moment with the girl at her right. Just as she turned her head away from the windows, the room was filled with a blinding light. She was paralyzed by fear, fixed still in her chair for a long moment (the plant was 1,600 yards from the center).

Everything fell, and Miss Sasaki lost consciousness. The ceiling dropped suddenly and the wooden floor above collapsed in splinters and the people up there came down and the roof above them gave way; but principally and first of all, the bookcases right behind her swooped forward and the contents threw her down, with her left leg horribly twisted and breaking underneath her. There, in the tin factory, in the first moment of the atomic age, a human being was crushed by books.

Critical Reading

1. **Key Ideas and Details (a)** At what time and on what day was the bomb dropped on Hiroshima? **(b) Draw Conclusions:** Why do you think Hersey is so precise in noting the exact date and time?
2. **Key Ideas and Details (a)** In describing each individual's experience, which moment does Hersey refer to again and again? **(b) Interpret:** What is the effect of Hersey's returning to this moment repeatedly?
3. **Key Ideas and Details (a)** Note three details describing the city of Hiroshima in the hours preceding the bomb. **(b) Analyze:** Why does Hersey spend so much time describing the city before the blast?
4. **Key Ideas and Details (a)** By what is Miss Sasaki crushed? **(b) Infer:** What effect do you think Hersey intended when he described Miss Sasaki's experience?
5. **Key Ideas and Details (a) Classify:** Are the people Hersey portrays important decision makers or merely ordinary citizens? **(b) Draw Conclusions:** What is Hersey implying about the fates of individuals in the midst of war?
6. **Integration of Knowledge and Ideas Take a Position:** President Truman's hope that the atomic bomb would end the war proved true but at a great cost. Do you think he made the right decision? Why or why not?

Cite textual evidence to support your responses.

Randall Jarrell (1914–1965)

Author of "The Death of the Ball Turret Gunner"

Randall Jarrell was a gifted poet, literary critic, and teacher whose work was praised by both writers and critics. His literary essays, many of which appear in his book *Poetry and the Age* (1953), have been credited with changing the critical tastes and trends of his time.

Literary Ambitions Born in Nashville, Tennessee, Jarrell graduated from Vanderbilt University, where he studied under writers Robert Penn Warren, Allen Tate, and John Crowe Ransom. All of these men would prove helpful in promoting Jarrell's career. Warren and Tate published Jarrell's early poetry and criticism, and Tate helped land Jarrell his first teaching job at Kenyon College.

During World War II, Jarrell enlisted in the U.S. Air Force. He served only briefly as a pilot and spent the remaining war years as an aviation instructor, training pilots to fly the famed B-29 bombers that helped secure victory. Jarrell's war experiences provided him with the material for the poems in his books *Little Friend, Little Friend* (1945) and *Losses* (1948). These books rank among the finest literature to emerge from the war.

American Language Jarrell was a great admirer of the poetry of Robert Frost, and, like Frost, he wrote poems based on the sounds and rhythms of American speech. Jarrell's collections *The Seven-League Crutches* (1951) and *The Lost World* (1965) focus on childhood and innocence. *The Woman at the Washington Zoo* (1960), for which Jarrell won the National Book Award for poetry, deals with the themes of aging and loneliness. "The Death of the Ball Turret Gunner," a brief poem told in the first person of a soldier experiencing his last moments in a World War II bomber, is one of Jarrell's most famous works. American poet Robert Lowell said of Jarrell, "His gifts . . . were wit, pathos, and brilliance of intelligence. These qualities, in themselves, were often so well employed that he became, I think, the most heartbreaking English poet of his generation."

Photograph by Rollie McKenna

The Death of the Ball Turret Gunner

Randall Jarrell

Background A ball turret was a plexiglass sphere, or circular capsule, in the underside of certain World War II bombers; it held a small man and two machine guns. When the bomber was attacked by a plane below, the gunner, hunched in his little sphere, would revolve with the turret to fire his guns from an upside-down position.

From my mother's sleep I fell into the State,
And I hunched in its belly till my wet fur froze.
Six miles from earth, loosed from its dream of life,
I woke to black flak[1] and the nightmare fighters.
When I died they washed me out of the turret with a hose.

1. **flak** *n.* anti-aircraft fire.

Critical Reading

Cite textual evidence to support your responses.

1. **Key Ideas and Details (a)** Which words does the gunner use to describe his view of life on Earth? **(b) Analyze:** In what way is this view of life related to the "nightmare" in the turret?
2. **Key Ideas and Details (a) Interpret:** To what does the word "State" refer? **(b) Draw Conclusions:** What is the poet suggesting about the relationship between a soldier in a war and the government?
3. **Integration of Knowledge and Ideas Take a Position:** Jarrell based his poem on observations of World War II, a war that has been called "the good war." Is there such a thing as a "good war"? Explain.
4. **Integration of Knowledge and Ideas** How do both the essay by Hersey and the poem by Jarrell create a societal memory of World War II? How important is that societal memory? Explain. In your response, use at least two of these Essential Question words: *encounter, information, repetition, ideals, confront.* *[Connecting to the Essential Question: How does literature shape or reflect society?]*

Close Reading Activities

from *Hiroshima* • *The Death of the Ball Turret Gunner*

Literary Analysis

1. **Key Ideas and Details (a)** Which details in *Hiroshima* provide clues to the **implied theme? (b)** What is that theme?
2. **Key Ideas and Details (a)** How and when is Mrs. Nakamura informed of her husband's death? **(b)** What political assumption about war does Hersey express through this detail?
3. **Key Ideas and Details** Of the survivors whose stories he documents, Hersey writes, "They still wonder why they lived when so many others died." What implied theme about war does Hersey express with this question?
4. **Key Ideas and Details** In "Death of the Ball Turret Gunner," what is the poet saying about the value of an individual human life during war?
5. **Key Ideas and Details** What political assumptions about the value of the individual underlie "The Death of the Ball Turret Gunner"? Explain.
6. **Craft and Structure (a)** Use a chart like the one shown to explore similarities and differences between Hersey's and Jarrell's portrayals of victims in war. **(b)** Do the two selections share a common theme? Explain.

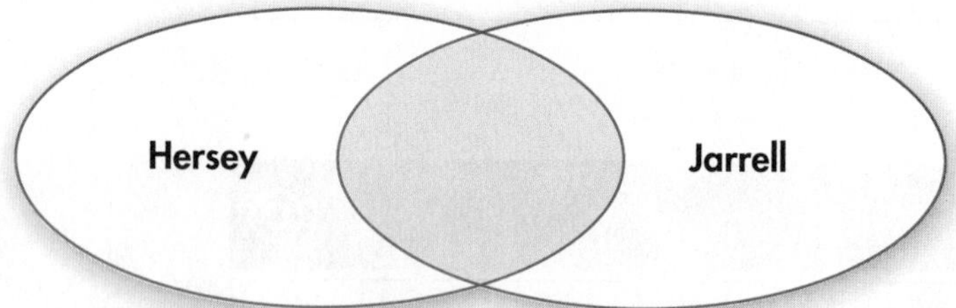

7. **Craft and Structure** In what ways does this quotation by Hersey speak to the implied theme of both selections? "It's a failure of national vision when you regard children as weapons, and talents as materials you can mine, assay, and fabricate for profit and defense."
8. **Integration of Knowledge and Ideas Analyze the political assumptions** Hersey expresses. **(a)** What political assumptions about the Japanese does Hersey challenge in *Hiroshima*? **(b)** How would you describe Hersey's political viewpoint? **(c)** Does Hersey present a consistent viewpoint on war throughout his account?
9. **Comparing Literary Works (a)** In *Hiroshima*, which descriptions evoke the strongest emotions in you? **(b)** Which lines in Jarrell's poem do you find most powerful? Explain. **(c)** For each work, would you characterize the writer's use of **perspective** as primarily objective or primarily subjective? Explain.
10. **Comparing Literary Works** Compare and contrast the effect of each author's use of the objective and subjective perspectives in these works.

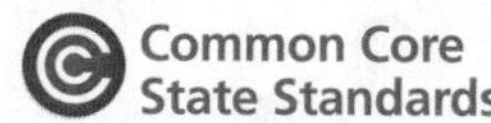

Common Core State Standards

Writing

2. Write explanatory texts to examine and convey complex ideas, concepts, and information clearly and accurately through the effective selection, organization, and analysis of content. *(p. 999)*

2.b. Develop the topic thoroughly by selecting the most significant and relevant facts, extended definitions, concrete details, quotations, or other information and examples appropriate to the audience's knowledge of the topic. *(p. 999)*

2.f. Provide a concluding statement that follows from and supports the information or explanation presented. *(p. 999)*

Language

4.c. Consult general reference materials, both print and digital, to determine or clarify the precise meaning of a word or its standard usage. *(p. 999)*

6. Acquire and use accurately general academic and domain-specific words and phrases, sufficient for reading, writing, speaking, and listening at the college and career readiness level. *(p. 999)*

Vocabulary Acquisition and Use

Military Words From Other Languages

A *rendezvous* was originally a place for the assembling of military troups. The word comes from the French words *rendez vous,* meaning "present yourself." Many English words related to the military and warfare have their origins in other languages. Match each word below with its origin. Then, provide the modern English definition of each word. Use a print or online dictionary to find or confirm the correct definitions.

1. *coup*	**a.** French for "barrel"
2. *barricade*	**b.** Urdu, Persian for "dusty"
3. *blitz*	**c.** French for "act of surveying"
4. *reconnaissance*	**d.** German for "lightning"
5. *khaki*	**e.** French for "blow" or "strike"

Vocabulary: Sentence Completions

Select the word from the vocabulary list on p. 982 that best completes each sentence below. Explain your choices.

1. She took on extra homework out of her own ______.

2. The birds ______ their nest and never returned to it.

3. The child's ______ whining bothered fellow train passengers on the long, slow trip.

4. We will have a ______ tomorrow at noon to compare our research notes.

5. Her ______ personality attracted many friends and admirers.

Writing to Sources

Explanatory Text Both Hersey and Jarrell present powerful themes about war. Write an **essay** to compare and contrast these themes as they are expressed in *Hiroshima* and "The Death of the Ball Turret Gunner."

Prewriting Review each selection and summarize the theme, or essential message about war that it presents. Jot down key similarities and differences between these messages, and note details from the selections that support these interpretations.

Drafting Begin with a vivid opening sentence. Then, summarize the similarities and differences you identified in the authors' themes. In the body of your essay, include detailed references to each selection to support your viewpoint. Restate your main points in a concluding paragraph.

Revising Review your work to make sure you have conveyed a clear sense of both literary works. Determine whether you have appropriately targeted the knowledge level of your expected audience, and revise as needed.

Model: Revising to Incorporate Quotations

Hersey's humane writing makes the city of Hiroshima very real for readers. He makes the day the atomic bomb exploded vivid by describing the lives of four survivors who still "wonder why they lived when so many others died." ~~think about what happened.~~

Adding quotations strengthens the connection between the writer's opinion and the text.

Primary Sources

Poster
Junk Rally Ad

Editorial Cartoon
The Battle of the Easy Chair

Editorial
Backing the Attack

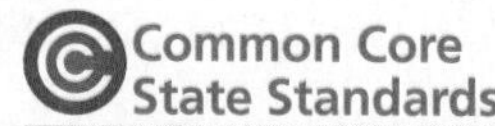

Reading Informational Text

5. Analyze and evaluate the effectiveness of the structure an author uses in his or her exposition or argument, including whether the structure makes points clear, convincing, and engaging.

7. Integrate and evaluate multiple sources of information presented in different media or formats as well as in words in order to address a question or solve a problem.

About the Text Forms

All three of these selections are examples of persuasion—texts meant to convince an audience to take an action or think in a certain way. However, their approaches and structures are very different. An **editorial** is a persuasive essay that appears in a news publication and expresses the opinions of the publication's editor or editorial board. Its purpose is to affect readers' opinions on an issue of public concern. Most editorials are short and tightly structured. All include a clear *thesis*, or main idea, and several pieces of persuasive, high-interest support.

An **editorial cartoon** is a drawing that contains a message or opinion. It emphasizes visual elements such as oversimplified objects and caricatures. These combine with verbal elements, such as *captions* and embedded words, to express opinion, often in a humorous way.

An advertisement is a notice designed to attract customers or participation. Large, free-standing print ads, or **posters,** appear in every sort of public space. Poster ads typically include a heading, contact information or directions, visual elements, and one or more catchy phrases. As you read these texts, consider how their structural elements, both verbal and visual, help to convey the persuasive message.

Preparing to Read Complex Texts

Persuasive texts include many different types of techniques to sway readers or viewers. Among these is the use of visual symbols—pictures that carry strong meanings. For example, to evoke viewers' patriotism, a poster may use an image of the American flag, the bald eagle, or even just the colors red, white, and blue. Visual symbols have a variety of effects:

- They create immediate—and often strong—emotional associations.
- They may appeal to a viewers' sense of country, social group, or family.
- They may appeal to negative emotions, such as biases or fears.

As you review these documents, **evaluate the persuasive use of symbols** by identifying visual elements that are symbolic and assessing their effects on viewers.

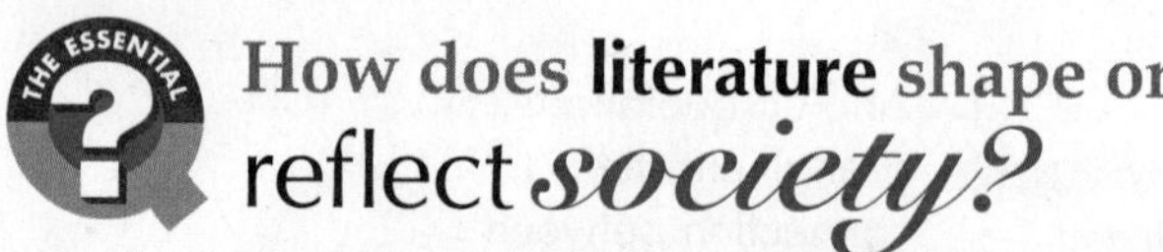
THE ESSENTIAL
How does literature shape or reflect society?

The makers of these documents were deeply concerned about national security during World War II. As you study the documents, identify the different goals each was designed to achieve. Ask what each document reveals about the forces that united and divided the country at war.

Note-Taking Guide

Primary source documents are a rich source of information for researchers. As you read these documents, use a note-taking guide like the one shown to organize relevant and accurate information.

1 Type of Primary Source (check one)

☐ E-mail ☐ Advertisement ☐ Letter ☐ Photograph
☐ Editorial ☐ Diary or Journal ☐ Map ☐ Cartoon

2 Date(s) of Document: ______________________

3 Are the messages in this source mainly visual, verbal, or both?

____

Visual Elements

a Which visual elements are used in the piece?

☐ Objects ☐ People ☐ Colors
☐ Other Design Elements: ______________________

b Which of these elements are symbols, or stand for larger ideas? Explain.

____

____

Evaluating Symbols Images often do more than just decorate a text. They also convey meaning and may have symbolic value.

Verbal Elements

a Which verbal elements are used in the piece?

☐ Title: ____________ ☐ Caption: ____________
☐ Catchy Phrases: ____________ ☐ Main Idea Statement: ____________
☐ Other: ______________________

b Which of these verbal elements seem most important to you? Why?

____

____

4 Summarize the situation depicted in the primary source.

____

____

This guide was adapted from the **U.S. National Archives** poster and document analysis worksheets.

Vocabulary

civilian (sə vil′ yən) *n.* any person who is not a member of the armed forces (p. 1003)

license (lī′ səns) *n.* freedom from rules, appropriate behavior, or appropriate speech (p. 1005)

undertaking (un′ dər tā′ kiŋ) *n.* task or challenge (p. 1005)

canvass (kan′ vəs) *v.* to go through an area asking people for votes, orders, or participation (p. 1005)

collective (kə lek′ tiv) *adj.* gathered into a whole (p. 1005)

expenditures (ek spen′ di chərz) *n.* expenses; uses of money or resources (p. 1006)

estimates (es′ tə mits) *n.* general, careful calculations (p. 1006)

receipts (ri sēts′) *n.* amounts of money received (p. 1006)

THE STORY BEHIND THE DOCUMENTS

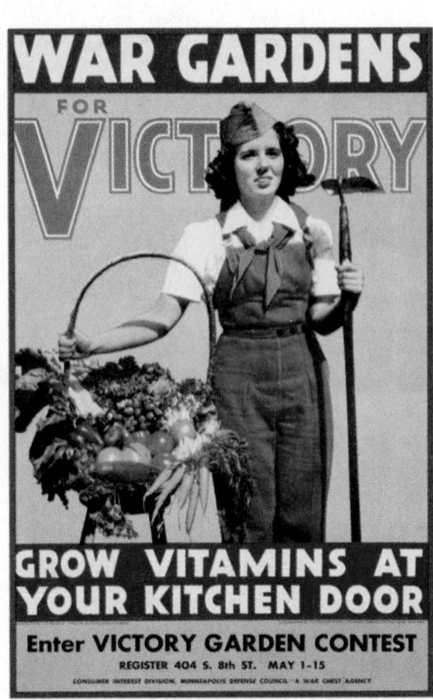

▲ World War II poster campaigns urged citizens to aid the war effort.

▲ Theodor Seuss Geisel, also known as Dr. Seuss

World War II began in Europe in 1939, with the Axis powers of Germany, Italy, and Japan opposing the Allied powers of France, Great Britain, and the Soviet Union. The United States, though sympathetic to the Allies, did not enter the war until December, 1941, after Japanese forces launched a surprise attack on the American naval base at Pearl Harbor, Hawaii.

Prior to the attack on Pearl Harbor, both the American government and the majority of its citizens had embraced a policy of isolationism, or neutrality. Still reeling from World War I and struggling to overcome the economic disaster of the Great Depression, Americans felt that they had few resources and little energy to offer the war effort. However, when 2,300 Americans were killed in the two-hour attack at Pearl Harbor, the mood changed dramatically. America entered the war—and it did so to win.

The United States and its allies fought on two main fronts: in Europe, against the totalitarian governments of Adolf Hitler in Germany and Benito Mussolini in Italy; and in the South Pacific, against fascist Japan. Throughout 1942, the Allies were on the defensive, but by 1943 the tide had turned. At home in the United States public optimism ran high. The war was surely near an end. Or was it?

The truth was that the war was more expensive than any conflict previously fought in American history. The United States government had to convert American optimism into action—and dollars. Appealing to the almost universal patriotism of its citizens, the government launched poster campaigns that urged citizens to support the war effort with their time, money, and even old junk. Efforts to rally the American public were also made by artists, celebrities, and high-profile journalists. The now-famous **Dr. Seuss** (Theodor Seuss Geisel, 1904–1991), for one, served as chief editorial cartoonist for the New York newspaper *PM* from 1941 to 1943. In that role he drew over 400 political cartoons condemning, among other things, isolationism, Hitler, the Japanese, and anti-war Americans. Meanwhile, in tandem with their political cartoonists, newspaper publishers printed editorials urging people not to grow complacent in their expectation of victory.

Americans responded. Families tightened their budgets and used the extra money to purchase war bonds, or government IOUs. Women tied kerchiefs in their hair and went to work in tank and airplane factories. Communities conserved resources by planting "victory gardens," and citizens of all ages hauled unused tires, appliances, and hardware to scrap drives. Participating in the drives made people feel useful, helped them express their patriotism, and boosted their morale.

Junk Rally POSTER

The Winchester Salvage Committee

JUNK RALLY

For WINCHESTER

SATURDAY OCTOBER 3rd. at 2.30 P.M.

MANCHESTER FIELD

CIVILIAN DEFENSE DEMONSTRATION

Auxiliary Firemen
Auxiliary Police
Junior Police
Motor Corps
Medical Units
Canteen
Emergency Public Works Corps

St. Mary's Band Will Play

Junk helps make guns, tanks, ships for our fighting men . . . . Bring in anything made of metal . . .

If you cannot carry it

Call Winchester 0207

Bring your family
Meet your friends

Throw YOUR scrap into the fight!

JUNK MAKES FIGHTING W

One old radiator will provide scrap steel needed for seventeen .30 calibre rifles.

One old lawn mower will help make six 3-inch shells.

One useless old tire will provide as much rubber as is used in 12 gas masks.

One old shovel will help make 4 hand grenades.

Let's Jolt them with Junk from Winchester.

Salvage Committee, Defense Headquarters, 572 Main Street, Winchester 0207

Vocabulary
civilian (sə vil' yən) *n.* any person who is not a member of the armed forces

The Battle of the EASY CHAIR

Dr. Seuss

This cartoon appeared in the newspaper *PM* on December 13, 1941, just five days after Japanese forces attacked the American base at Pearl Harbor, Hawaii. The setting is a members-only club where gentlemen could unwind, talk with friends, eat, and play games. Here, the club member relaxes in the company of his valet, or personal servant.

The Battle of the Easy Chair

"Wake me, Judkins, when the Victory Parade comes by!"

V

WE CAN'T LOSE

HOORAY FOR OUR SIDE

HITLER CAN'T TAKE IT!

Dr. Seuss

BACKING THE ATTACK

The New York Times Editorial

On September 8, 1943, General Dwight D. Eisenhower, commander-in-chief of the Allied forces in the Mediterranean, announced that Italy had surrendered. This news followed closely on the heels of several successful Allied attacks in Japan. Suddenly, it seemed as if the war would come to a rapid end. However, in a radio address from the White House later that evening, President Franklin D. Roosevelt warned Americans that "The time for celebration is not yet . . . This war does not and must not stop for one single instant." Days later, *The New York Times* ran the following editorial. Its main subject is war bonds—certificates that promised a payback of the face value plus interest at a specified future date.

The New York Times

September 12, 1943

The great news you have heard today from General Eisenhower does not give you the ***license*** *to settle back in your rocking chairs and say "Well, that does it. We've got 'em on the run. Now we can start the celebration."*

With these words, President Roosevelt last Wednesday night warned Americans against over-optimism. He spoke on the eve of the Treasury Department's third campaign to sell $15,000,000,000 in war bonds. The next afternoon, to open the two-month drive, the greatest financial **undertaking** in the history of the world, 3,000 men and women of the armed forces, trained Army dogs, jeeps, trucks and war material paraded down New York's Fifth Avenue. There were similar celebrations across the United States. Half a million salesmen in New York City alone, millions more throughout the country, began a **canvass** of American citizens, who already are purchasing $4,600,000,000 in bonds by payroll savings deducted from their **collective** annual income of $140,000,000,000.

Vocabulary

license (lī′ səns) *n.* freedom from rules, appropriate behavior, or appropriate speech

undertaking (un′ dər tā′ kiŋ) *n.* task or challenge

canvass (kan′ vəs) *v.* to go through an area asking people for votes, orders, or participation

collective (kə lek′ tiv) *adj.* gathered into a whole

Comprehension

What enormous effort did the Treasury Department undertake?

Vocabulary

expenditures (ek spen´ di chərz) *n.* expenses; uses of money or resources

estimates (es´ tə mits) *n.* general, careful calculations

receipts (ri sēts´) *n.* amounts of money received

The $15,000,000,000 bond issue will help finance the war. From July 1, 1940, to August 31, 1943, war **expenditures** totaled about $124,000,000,000. (Between 1789 and 1932, the Government spent $108,000,000,000.) The breakdown figure of $71,000,000,000 used for war in 1942 will be increased 80 per cent if **estimates** of $106,000,000,000 needed for military expenses during 1943 are correct.

The new estimate is three times the total cost of the World War, including loans to Allies. Taxes provide but 38 per cent of this. The first two War Bond drives added $31,500,000,000 to Government **receipts**. When the last War Bond is subscribed in this third campaign, the Government should have enough money to pay, at the present average spending rate, for two months of war.

The items of war which varying purchases of war bonds would buy were being listed by speakers at War Bond rallies in every State. The purchase of a hundred dollar bond would just about outfit a sailor. A $40,000,000 bond could build a cruiser; $150 would completely equip a soldier or marine or buy a parachute, $750 would build a bantam jeep, $1,500 would send up a barrage balloon, $3,000 would launch a marine landing barge. For $6,100, a bombsight would be made, for $125,000 a dive bomber. Medium bombers cost $175,000, and heavy bombers $300,000. It cost $436,000,000 to crush Hamburg. It will cost $2,076,000,000 to destroy Berlin.

Critical Reading

1. **Key Ideas and Details (a) Summarize:** Describe the event advertised in the poster. **(b) Connect:** How does the illustration at top right of the poster relate to the event? **(c) Analyze:** To what basic emotions or values does the illustration appeal?
2. **Key Ideas and Details (a) Infer:** What feelings or beliefs about the war does Dr. Seuss address in this editorial cartoon? Explain. **(b) Summarize:** How would you convey that same message in words?
3. **Integration of Knowledge and Ideas Evaluate:** Why do you think the editorial writer presented such a long list of specific items that could be purchased for the war effort?

Poster • Editorial Cartoon • Editorial

Comparing Primary Sources

Refer to your note-taking guide to complete these questions.

1. (a) Use a chart like the one shown to identify one strong visual element in the poster and in the editorial cartoon and one strong verbal element in the editorial. **(b)** Does each element you chose appeal to reason or to a particular emotion? Explain.

Document	Strong Verbal or Visual Element	What It Appeals To
Poster		
Cartoon		
Editorial		

2. (a) What does the junk rally poster reveal about small-town attitudes toward the war effort? **(b)** What does the poster reveal about American attitudes toward the enemy?

3. (a) Summarize the persuasive message of the editorial cartoon. **(b)** Summarize the message of the editorial. **(c)** How are these messages similar and different? Explain, identifying specific structural elements that contribute to the message of each text.

Vocabulary Acquisition and Use

Sentence Completions Use a word from the vocabulary list on page 1001 to fill in each blank, and explain your choice. Use each word only once.

1. This petition will be a big _______. First, let's _______ the neighborhood for signatures.

2. Winning the contest does not give you _______ to gloat.

Content-Area Vocabulary Answer each question. Then, explain your answer.

3. Should an elected official express the *collective* opinion of the voters?

4. To keep a budget balanced, should *expenditures* outweigh *receipts*?

5. How might population *estimates* help a city council?

6. When they are on the job, do *civilians* wear military uniforms?

Etymology Study The word *civilian* comes from the Latin word *civis*, which means "home" or "the place where one dwells." Use an online or print dictionary to locate four other words that come from this root. Explain how the meaning of each word relates to that of its Latin ancestor.

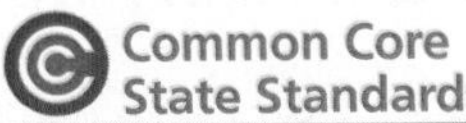

Common Core State Standards

Writing

6. Use technology, including the Internet, to produce individual writing products. *(p. 1008)*

7. Conduct short as well as more sustained research projects to answer a question or solve a problem; narrow or broaden the inquiry when appropriate; synthesize multiple sources on the subject, demonstrating understanding of the subject under investigation. *(p. 1008)*

8. Gather relevant information from multiple authoritative print and digital sources, using advanced searches effectively; integrate information into the text selectively to maintain the flow of ideas. *(p. 1008)*

Language

4.c. Consult general and specialized reference materials, both print and digital, to find the pronunciation of a word or determine or clarify its precise meaning, its part of speech, its etymology, or its standard usage.

6. Acquire and use accurately general academic and domain-specific words and phrases, sufficient for reading, writing, speaking, and listening at the college and career readiness level; demonstrate independence in gathering vocabulary knowledge when considering a word or phrase important to comprehension or expression.

 COMMON CORE ▪ RESEARCH PROJECT

Research Task

Topic: Society and Culture in the Media

Do images affect you more than words do? Politicians, business leaders, advertisers, cartoonists, and film directors all know that visual media may sway people more effectively than words or traditional texts on their own.

Assignment: Create a computer slide show or poster presentation in which you analyze several editorial cartoons. Use historical or contemporary cartoons, and evaluate how messages in the cartoons present social and cultural views differently than do traditional written texts.

▲ This editorial cartoon from 1942 indicates America's military might.

Formulate your research plan. Editorial cartoons address almost every aspect of life, so you need to choose one area to research. Consider politics, sports, education, business, the arts, or an aspect of social life, such as dating. Then, formulate a limited and manageable research question, such as, "What attitudes do editorial cartoons express about schools in my city?"

Gather sources. Use online and library searches to examine editorial cartoons in historical collections or newspaper archives. Maintain accurate records of the source name, date, and page of each cartoon.

Synthesize information. Choose several cartoons to analyze. For each cartoon, use a graphic organizer like the one shown to identify the historical context, the intended audience, the social or cultural message, and the tone.

Model: Analyzing an Editorial Cartoon

Context	Historical: presidential election
Audience	Undecided voters
Message	Candidate does not inspire confidence
Tone	Ironic, humorous

Synthesize your findings about each cartoon into a single statement. Comment on how the use of visuals and humor makes the cartoon more or less effective than a traditional, written editorial. Consider this example:

> This cartoon uses exaggeration to persuade people that we should have a leader who inspires confidence. The cartoon format does this with no words at all, which is very different from a traditional, written text.

Organize and present your ideas. If possible, enlarge the cartoons and be sure all the text, including the captions and text in speech or thought "bubbles," is readable. Use typeface, layout, color, and graphics to make your presentation easy to follow.

RESEARCH TIP

You might find ideas in the huge archive of categorized images available online through the Library of Congress American Memory collection.

Use a checklist like the one shown to evaluate your work.

Research Checklist

- ☐ Have I made my research question manageable?
- ☐ Have I answered my main research question?
- ☐ Have I identified and analyzed the individual elements of each cartoon?
- ☐ Have I synthesized my findings into clear and comprehensive statements?

TEXT SET

Tradition and Rebellion

Part 2

Building Knowledge and Insight

The Life You Save May Be Your Own

Connecting to the Essential Question This story paints a vivid picture of a rural community in the American South. As you read, notice how O'Connor depicts the setting and its influence on the characters. Your observations will help as you reflect on the Essential Question: **What is the relationship between literature and place?**

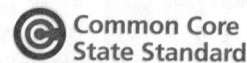

Common Core State Standards

Reading Literature

1. Cite strong and thorough textual evidence to support analysis of what the text says explicitly as well as inferences drawn from the text, including determining where the text leaves matters uncertain.

3. Analyze the impact of the author's choices regarding how to develop and relate elements of a story or drama (e.g., how the characters are introduced and developed).

Close Reading Focus

Grotesque Character; Characterization

The word *grotesque* in literature does not mean "ugly" or "disgusting," as it sometimes does in popular speech. In literature, the **grotesque character** is one who has become bizarre or twisted, usually through some kind of obsession. Grotesque traits may be expressed in a character's physical appearance. Alternatively, they may be hidden, visible only in a character's actions and emotions.

O'Connor creates grotesques in this story through **characterization**—the revelation of personality. In **direct characterization,** the writer simply tells the reader what a character is like. With **indirect characterization,** traits are revealed through these elements:

- the character's words, thoughts, and actions
- descriptions of the character's appearance or background
- what other characters say about him or her
- how other characters react or respond

As you read, examine O'Connor's use of characterization, noting examples of extreme behavior, distortions, and striking oddities that make all three main characters grotesques.

Preparing to Read Complex Texts A *conclusion* is a decision or judgment you make after considering specific information. O'Connor writes with a sharp eye for meaningful details. As you read, **draw conclusions** from these details to deepen your understanding of the meaning of the story as a whole. Use a chart like the one shown to record details and the conclusions you draw from them.

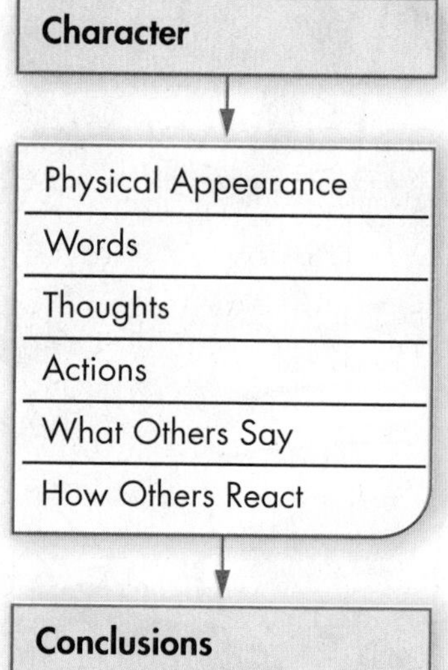

Vocabulary

The words below are important to understanding the text that follows. Copy the words into your notebook. Which two words have the same suffix? What might that suffix indicate?

desolate

listed

ominous

ravenous

morose

Flannery O'Connor

(1925–1964)

Author of **"The Life You Save May Be Your Own"**

Born in Savannah, Georgia, Flannery O'Connor was raised in the small Georgia town of Milledgeville. She earned her undergraduate degree from Georgia State College for Women and then attended the celebrated University of Iowa Writers' Workshop. While still in graduate school, she published her first short story, "Geranium."

Land of the Sick In 1950, O'Connor became ill with lupus, a serious disease that restricted her independence. She moved back to the family farm outside Milledgeville, where she lived with her mother. "I have never been anywhere but sick," she wrote. "In a sense, sickness is a place more instructive than a trip to Europe." Despite her illness, O'Connor committed herself not only to her writing but also to "the habit of art," an enlivened way of thinking and seeing. In 1952, she published her first novel, *Wise Blood*. She would ultimately publish a second novel and two story collections.

A Triumphant Spirit Throughout most of her adult life, O'Connor lived with pain and the awareness that she would probably die young. Despite her condition, she often seemed joyous, entertaining friends at home and painting watercolors of the peacocks that she and her mother raised. Still, her disease set her apart, and O'Connor felt a kinship with eccentrics and outsiders. Many of her characters are social misfits or people who are physically or mentally challenged. Although she paints these characters in an unsentimental way, O'Connor brings to their stories an underlying sense of sympathy, which reflects both her own physical problems and her Catholic faith.

Religious Faith O'Connor was raised as a devout Catholic in a region of the American South that was largely Protestant. She considered herself a religious writer in a world that had abandoned true values. In an effort to point out the spiritual failings of the modern world, she often highlights characters with dubious moral and intellectual capabilities. "The Life You Save May Be Your Own" is a typical O'Connor work. In its grim depiction of a group of outcasts, the story conveys shrewd insights, a powerful moral message, and an urgent sense of the tragic realities of modern life.

"I am a writer because writing is the thing I do best."

Deep Fork Overlook, Joan Marron-LaRue

THE Life YOU Save MAY BE Your Own

Flannery O'Connor

Background Gothic literature, a genre of fiction that developed in Britain in the late 1700s, features horror and violence. Traditional gothic tales are often set against dramatic, gloomy backdrops—remote castles, deserted fortresses, and the like. Such literature acknowledges evil as a real force and ascribes to some characters a dark side that lures them to violent or wicked acts. Flannery O'Connor borrowed some devices from Gothic fiction, such as a foreboding atmosphere and grotesque characters, but she set her stories in an unremarkable American landscape. The story you are about to read is a perfect example of her exploration of the Gothic under the familiar sunlight of the American South.

The old woman and her daughter were sitting on their porch when Mr. Shiftlet came up their road for the first time. The old woman slid to the edge of her chair and leaned forward, shading her eyes from the piercing sunset with her hand. The daughter could not see far in front of her and continued to play with her fingers. Although the old woman lived in this **desolate** spot with only her daughter and she had never seen Mr. Shiftlet before, she could tell, even from a distance, that he was a tramp and no one to be afraid of. His left coat sleeve was folded up to show there was only half an arm in it and his gaunt figure **listed** slightly to the side as if the breeze were pushing him. He had on a black town suit and a brown felt hat that was turned up in the front and down in the back and he carried a tin tool box by a handle. He came on, at an amble, up her road, his face turned toward the sun which appeared to be balancing itself on the peak of a small mountain.

The old woman didn't change her position until he was almost into her yard; then she rose with one hand fisted on her hip. The daughter, a large girl in a short blue organdy dress, saw him all at once and jumped up and began to stamp and point and make excited speechless sounds.

Vocabulary

desolate (des′ ə lit) *adj.* forlorn; wretched

listed (list′ id) *v.* tilted; inclined

Comprehension

Who does the old woman notice coming up the road?

◀ **Critical Viewing** Visually, what is the most important part of this setting—the chickens, the truck, or some other element? Explain. **ANALYZE**

Mr. Shiftlet stopped just inside the yard and set his box on the ground and tipped his hat at her as if she were not in the least afflicted; then he turned toward the old woman and swung the hat all the way off. He had long black slick hair that hung flat from a part in the middle to beyond the tips of his ears on either side. His face descended in forehead for more than half its length and ended suddenly with his features just balanced over a jutting steel-trap jaw. He seemed to be a young man but he had a look of composed dissatisfaction as if he understood life thoroughly.

"Good evening," the old woman said. She was about the size of a cedar fence post and she had a man's gray hat pulled down low over her head.

Grotesque Characters and Characterization
What exaggerated traits do you perceive in this description of the three characters?

The tramp stood looking at her and didn't answer. He turned his back and faced the sunset. He swung both his whole and his short arm up slowly so that they indicated an expanse of sky and his figure formed a crooked cross. The old woman watched him with her arms folded across her chest as if she were the owner of the sun, and the daughter watched, her head thrust forward and her fat helpless hands hanging at the wrists. She had long pink-gold hair and eyes as blue as a peacock's neck.

He held the pose for almost fifty seconds and then he picked up his box and came on to the porch and dropped down on the bottom step. "Lady," he said in a firm nasal voice, "I'd give a fortune to live where I could see me a sun do that every evening."

"Does it every evening," the old woman said and sat back down. The daughter sat down too and watched him with a cautious sly look as if he were a bird that had come up very close. He leaned to one side, rooting in his pants pocket, and in a second he brought out a package of chewing gum and offered her a piece. She took it and unpeeled it and began to chew without taking her eyes off him. He offered the old woman a piece but she only raised her upper lip to indicate she had no teeth.

Grotesque Characters and Characterization
What personality traits are suggested by this description of Mr. Shiftlet's "pale sharp glance"?

Mr. Shiftlet's pale sharp glance had already passed over everything in the yard—the pump near the corner of the house and the big fig tree that three or four chickens were preparing to roost in—and had moved to a shed where he saw the square rusted back of an automobile. "You ladies drive?" he asked.

"That car ain't run in fifteen year," the old woman said. "The day my husband died, it quit running."

"Nothing is like it used to be, lady," he said. "The world is almost rotten."

"That's right," the old woman said. "You from around here?"

"Name Tom T. Shiftlet," he murmured, looking at the tires.

"I'm pleased to meet you," the old woman said. "Name Lucynell Crater and daughter Lucynell Crater. What you doing around here, Mr. Shiftlet?"

He judged the car to be about a 1928 or '29 Ford. "Lady," he said, and turned and gave her his full attention, "lemme tell you something.

There's one of these doctors in Atlanta that's taken a knife and cut the human heart—the human heart," he repeated, leaning forward, "out of a man's chest and held it in his hand," and he held his hand out, palm up, as if it were slightly weighted with the human heart, "and studied it like it was a day-old chicken, and lady," he said, allowing a long significant pause in which his head slid forward and his clay-colored eyes brightened, "he don't know no more about it than you or me."

"That's right," the old woman said.

"Why, if he was to take that knife and cut into every corner of it, he still wouldn't know no more than you or me. What you want to bet?"

"Nothing," the old woman said wisely. "Where you come from, Mr. Shiftlet?"

He didn't answer. He reached into his pocket and brought out a sack of tobacco and a package of cigarette papers and rolled himself a cigarette, expertly with one hand, and attached it in a hanging position to his upper lip. Then he took a box of wooden matches from his pocket and struck one on his shoe. He held the burning match as if he were studying the mystery of flame while it traveled dangerously toward his skin. The daughter began to make loud noises and to point to his hand and shake her finger at him, but when the flame was just before touching him, he leaned down with his hand cupped over it as if he were going to set fire to his nose and lit the cigarette.

He flipped away the dead match and blew a stream of gray into the evening. A sly look came over his face. "Lady," he said, "nowadays, people'll do anything anyways. I can tell you my name is Tom T. Shiftlet and I come from Tarwater, Tennessee, but you never have seen me before: how you know I ain't lying? How you know my name ain't Aaron Sparks, lady, and I come from Singleberry, Georgia, or how you know it's not George Speeds and I come from Lucy, Alabama, or how you know I ain't Thompson Bright from Toolafalls, Mississippi?"

"I don't know nothing about you," the old woman muttered, irked.

"Lady," he said, "people don't care how they lie. Maybe the best I can tell you is, I'm a man; but listen lady," he said and paused and made his tone more **ominous** still, "what is a man?"

The old woman began to gum a seed. "What you carry in that tin box, Mr. Shiftlet?" she asked.

"Tools," he said, put back. "I'm a carpenter."

"Well, if you come out here to work, I'll be able to feed you and give you a place to sleep but I can't pay. I'll tell you that before you begin," she said.

There was no answer at once and no particular expression on his face. He leaned back against the two-by-four that helped support the porch roof. "Lady," he said slowly, "there's some men that some things mean more to them than money." The old woman rocked without comment and the daughter watched the trigger that moved up and down in his neck. He told the old woman then that all most people

"Lady," he said, "people don't care how they lie."

Drawing Conclusions
Why do you think Shiftlet is so concerned about lying?

Vocabulary
ominous (äm′ ə nəs) *adj.* threatening; sinister

Comprehension
Can the young Lucynell speak?

were interested in was money, but he asked what a man was made for. He asked her if a man was made for money, or what. He asked her what she thought she was made for but she didn't answer, she only sat rocking and wondered if a one-armed man could put a new roof on her garden house. He asked a lot of questions that she didn't answer. He told her that he was twenty-eight years old and had lived a varied life. He had been a gospel singer, a foreman on the railroad, an assistant in an undertaking parlor, and he come over the radio for three months with Uncle Roy and his Red Creek Wranglers. He said he had fought and bled in the Arm Service of his country and visited every foreign land and that everywhere he had seen people that didn't care if they did a thing one way or another. He said he hadn't been raised thataway.

Spiral Review
Personification Which words describe the moon as though it were a living creature? Explain.

A fat yellow moon appeared in the branches of the fig tree as if it were going to roost there with the chickens. He said that a man had to escape to the country to see the world whole and that he wished he lived in a desolate place like this where he could see the sun go down every evening like God made it to do.

"Are you married or are you single?" the old woman asked.

There was a long silence. "Lady," he asked finally, "where would you find you an innocent woman today? I wouldn't have any of this trash I could just pick up."

The daughter was leaning very far down, hanging her head almost between her knees watching him through a triangular door she had made in her overturned hair; and she suddenly fell in a heap on the floor and began to whimper. Mr. Shiftlet straightened her out and helped her get back in the chair.

"Is she your baby girl?" he asked.

Grotesque Characters and Characterization
What does this dialogue about her daughter reveal about the old woman?

"My only," the old woman said "and she's the sweetest girl in the world. I would give her up for nothing on earth. She's smart too. She can sweep the floor, cook, wash, feed the chickens, and hoe. I wouldn't give her up for a casket of jewels."

"No," he said kindly, "don't ever let any man take her away from you."

"Any man come after her," the old woman said, "'ll have to stay around the place."

Mr. Shiftlet's eye in the darkness was focused on a part of the automobile bumper that glittered in the distance. "Lady," he said, jerking his short arm up as if he could point with it to her house and yard and pump, "there ain't a broken thing on this plantation that I couldn't fix for you, one-arm jackleg or not. I'm a man," he said with a sullen dignity, "even if I ain't a whole one. I got," he said, tapping his knuckles on the floor to emphasize the immensity of what he was going to say, "a moral intelligence!" and his face pierced out of the darkness into a shaft of doorlight and he stared at her as if he were astonished himself at this impossible truth.

Black Walnuts, 1945, Joseph Pollet, Oil on canvas, 30" × 40", Collection of Whitney Museum of American Art, Purchase, Gift of Gertrude Vanderbilt Whitney, by exchange

The old woman was not impressed with the phrase. "I told you you could hang around and work for food," she said, "if you don't mind sleeping in that car yonder."

"Why listen, lady," he said with a grin of delight, "the monks of old slept in their coffins!"

"They wasn't as advanced as we are," the old woman said.

The next morning he began on the roof of the garden house while Lucynell, the daughter, sat on a rock and watched him work. He had not been around a week before the change he had made in the place was apparent. He had patched the front and back steps, built a new hog pen, restored a fence, and taught Lucynell, who was completely deaf and had never said a word in her life, to say the word "bird." The big rosy-faced girl followed him everywhere, saying "Burrttddt ddb-irrrttdt," and clapping her hands. The old woman watched from a distance, secretly pleased. She was ravenous for a son-in-law.

Mr. Shiftlet slept on the hard narrow back seat of the car with his feet out the side window. He had his razor and a can of water on a crate that served him as a bedside table and he put up a piece of mirror against the back glass and kept his coat neatly on a hanger that he hung over one of the windows.

▲ Critical Viewing

Which aspects of the story are reflected in this painting? **CONNECT**

Vocabulary

ravenous (rav′ ə nəs) *adj.* extremely eager

Comprehension

For what is the old woman "ravenous"?

The girl was nearly thirty but because of her innocence it was impossible to guess.

In the evenings he sat on the steps and talked while the old woman and Lucynell rocked violently in their chairs on either side of him. The old woman's three mountains were black against the dark blue sky and were visited off and on by various planets and by the moon after it had left the chickens. Mr. Shiftlet pointed out that the reason he had improved this plantation was because he had taken a personal interest in it. He said he was even going to make the automobile run.

He had raised the hood and studied the mechanism and he said he could tell that the car had been built in the days when cars were really built. You take now, he said, one man puts in one bolt and another man puts in another bolt and another man puts in another bolt so that it's a man for a bolt. That's why you have to pay so much for a car: you're paying all those men. Now if you didn't have to pay but one man, you could get you a cheaper car and one that had had a personal interest taken in it, and it would be a better car. The old woman agreed with him that this was so.

Mr. Shiftlet said that the trouble with the world was that nobody cared, or stopped and took any trouble. He said he never would have been able to teach Lucynell to say a word if he hadn't cared and stopped long enough.

"Teach her to say something else," the old woman said.

"What you want her to say next?" Mr. Shiftlet asked.

The old woman's smile was broad and toothless and suggestive. "Teach her to say 'sugarpie,'" she said.

Mr. Shiftlet already knew what was on her mind.

The next day he began to tinker with the automobile and that evening he told her that if she would buy a fan belt, he would be able to make the car run.

The old woman said she would give him the money. "You see that girl yonder?" she asked, pointing to Lucynell who was sitting on the floor a foot away, watching him, her eyes blue even in the dark. "If it was ever a man wanted to take her away, I would say, 'No man on earth is going to take that sweet girl of mine away from me!' but if he was to say, 'Lady, I don't want to take her away, I want her right here,' I would say, 'Mister, I don't blame you none. I wouldn't pass up a chance to live in a permanent place and get the sweetest girl in the world myself. You ain't no fool,' I would say."

"How old is she?" Mr. Shiftlet asked casually.

"Fifteen, sixteen," the old woman said. The girl was nearly thirty but because of her innocence it was impossible to guess.

"It would be a good idea to paint it too," Mr. Shiftlet remarked. "You don't want it to rust out."

"We'll see about that later," the old woman said.

The next day he walked into town and returned with the parts he needed and a can of gasoline. Late in the afternoon, terrible noises issued from the shed and the old woman rushed out of the house,

Grotesque Characters and Characterization

What does Mr. Shiftlet's remark about the car reveal about his obsession?

thinking Lucynell was somewhere having a fit. Lucynell was sitting on a chicken crate, stamping her feet and screaming, "Burrddtt! bddurrddttt!" but her fuss was drowned out by the car. With a volley of blasts it emerged from the shed, moving in a fierce and stately way. Mr. Shiftlet was in the driver's seat, sitting very erect. He had an expression of serious modesty on his face as if he had just raised the dead.

That night, rocking on the porch, the old woman began her business, at once. "You want you an innocent woman, don't you?" she asked sympathetically. "You don't want none of this trash."

"No'm, I don't," Mr. Shiftlet said.

"One that can't talk," she continued, "can't sass you back or use foul language. That's the kind for you to have. Right there," and she pointed to Lucynell sitting crosslegged in her chair, holding both feet in her hands.

"That's right," he admitted. "She wouldn't give me any trouble."

"Saturday," the old woman said, "you and her and me can drive into town and get married."

Mr. Shiftlet eased his position on the steps.

"I can't get married right now," he said. "Everything you want to do takes money and I ain't got any."

"What you need with money?" she asked.

"It takes money," he said. "Some people'll do anything anyhow these days, but the way I think, I wouldn't marry no woman that I couldn't take on a trip like she was somebody. I mean take her to a hotel and treat her. I wouldn't marry the Duchesser Windsor," he said firmly, "unless I could take her to a hotel and giver something good to eat.

"I was raised thataway and there ain't a thing I can do about it. My old mother taught me how to do."

"Lucynell don't even know what a hotel is," the old woman muttered. "Listen here, Mr. Shiftlet," she said, sliding forward in her chair, "you'd be getting a permanent house and a deep well and the most innocent girl in the world. You don't need no money. Lemme tell you something: there ain't any place in the world for a poor disabled friendless drifting man."

The ugly words settled in Mr. Shiftlet's head like a group of buzzards in the top of a tree.

He didn't answer at once. He rolled himself a cigarette and lit it and then he said in an even voice, "Lady, a man is divided into two parts, body and spirit."

The old woman clamped her gums together.

"A body and a spirit," he repeated. "The body, lady, is like a house: it don't go anywhere; but the spirit, lady, is like a automobile: always on the move, always . . ."

"Listen, Mr. Shiftlet," she said, "my well never goes dry and my house is always warm in the winter and there's no mortgage on a thing about this place. You can go to the courthouse and see for

Grotesque Characters and Characterization

What is revealed about Mr. Shiftlet and the old woman in this exchange about marriage and money?

Comprehension

What does Mr. Shiftlet do with the old car?

yourself. And yonder under that shed is a fine automobile." She laid the bait carefully. "You can have it painted by Saturday. I'll pay for the paint."

In the darkness, Mr. Shiftlet's smile stretched like a weary snake waking up by a fire. After a second he recalled himself and said, "I'm only saying a man's spirit means more to him than anything else. I would have to take my wife off for the weekend without no regards at all for cost. I got to follow where my spirit says to go."

"I'll give you fifteen dollars for a weekend trip," the old woman said in a crabbed voice. "That's the best I can do."

"That wouldn't hardly pay for more than the gas and the hotel," he said. "It wouldn't feed her."

"Seventeen-fifty," the old woman said. "That's all I got so it isn't any use you trying to milk me. You can take a lunch."

Mr. Shiftlet was deeply hurt by the word "milk." He didn't doubt that she had more money sewed up in her mattress but he had already told her he was not interested in her money. "I'll make that do," he said and rose and walked off without treating with her further.

On Saturday the three of them drove into town in the car that the paint had barely dried on and Mr. Shiftlet and Lucynell were married in the Ordinary's office while the old woman witnessed. As they came out of the courthouse, Mr. Shiftlet began twisting his neck in his collar. He looked **morose** and bitter as if he had been insulted while someone held him. "That didn't satisfy me none," he said. "That was just something a woman in an office did, nothing but paper work and blood tests. What do they know about my blood? If they was to take my heart and cut it out," he said, "they wouldn't know a thing about me. It didn't satisfy me at all."

"It satisfied the law," the old woman said sharply.

"The law," Mr. Shiftlet said and spit. "It's the law that don't satisfy me."

He had painted the car dark green with a yellow band around it just under the windows. The three of them climbed in the front seat and the old woman said, "Don't Lucynell look pretty? Looks like a baby doll." Lucynell was dressed up in a white dress that her mother had uprooted from a trunk and there was a Panama hat on her head with a bunch of red wooden cherries on the brim. Every now and then her placid expression was changed by a sly isolated little thought like a shoot of green in the desert.

"You got a prize!" the old woman said.

Mr. Shiftlet didn't even look at her. They drove back to the house to let the old woman off and pick up the lunch. When they were ready to leave, she stood staring in the window of the car, with her fingers clenched around the glass. Tears began to seep sideways out of her eyes and run along the dirty creases in her face. "I ain't ever been parted with her for two days before," she said.

Mr. Shiftlet started the motor.

...Mr. Shiftlet's smile stretched like a weary snake waking up by a fire.

Vocabulary

morose (mə rōs′) *adj.* gloomy; sullen

Drawing Conclusions

Based on this speech about his dissatisfaction with the law, what conclusions can you draw about Shiftlet?

"And I wouldn't let no man have her but you because I seen you would do right. Goodbye, Sugarbaby," she said, clutching at the sleeve of the white dress. Lucynell looked straight at her and didn't seem to see her there at all. Mr. Shiftlet eased the car forward so that she had to move her hands.

The early afternoon was clear and open and surrounded by pale blue sky. Although the car would go only thirty miles an hour, Mr. Shiftlet imagined a terrific climb and dip and swerve that went entirely to his head so that he forgot his morning bitterness. He had always wanted an automobile but he had never been able to afford one before. He drove very fast because he wanted to make Mobile by nightfall.

Occasionally he stopped his thoughts long enough to look at Lucynell in the seat beside him. She had eaten the lunch as soon as they were out of the yard and now she was pulling the cherries off the hat one by one and throwing them out the window. He became depressed in spite of the car. He had driven about a hundred miles when he decided that she must be hungry again and at the next small town they came to, he stopped in front of an aluminum-painted eating place called The Hot Spot and took her in and ordered her a plate of ham and grits. The ride had made her sleepy and as soon as she got up on the stool, she rested her head on the counter and shut her eyes. There was no one in The Hot Spot but Mr. Shiftlet and the boy behind the counter, a pale youth with a greasy rag hung over his shoulder. Before he could dish up the food, she was snoring gently.

"Give it to her when she wakes up," Mr. Shiftlet said. "I'll pay for it now." The boy bent over her and stared at the long pink-gold hair and the half-shut sleeping eyes. Then he looked up and stared at Mr. Shiftlet. "She looks like an angel of Gawd," he murmured.

"Hitchhiker," Mr. Shiftlet explained. "I can't wait. I got to make Tuscaloosa."

The boy bent over again and very carefully touched his finger to a strand of the golden hair and Mr. Shiftlet left.

He was more depressed than ever as he drove on by himself. The late afternoon had grown hot and sultry and the country had flattened out. Deep in the sky a storm was preparing very slowly and without thunder as if it meant to drain every drop of air from the earth before it broke. There were times when Mr. Shiftlet preferred not to be alone. He felt too that a man with a car had a responsibility to others and he kept his eye out for a hitchhiker. Occasionally he saw a sign that warned: "Drive carefully. The life you save may be your own."

The American EXPERIENCE

Southern Regionalism

While writers have the capacity to invent whole new worlds, they are human beings who are influenced by their environments. Regional writers are those who use specific geographical areas—usually their home turf—as settings. Yet, regionalists do more than simply set their fiction in familiar locales; they incorporate the distinct culture of an area, including characteristic speech patterns, customs, beliefs, history, and folklore into the very fabric of their stories. This marriage of place, sensibility, and style goes beyond mere reporting to present a sophisticated treatment of the culture of a region. With the best regional writers, local detail helps to create stories of universal impact. You need not be from the American South to appreciate the work of such great Southern regional writers as Flannery O'Connor, Truman Capote, Carson McCullers, Tennessee Williams, William Faulkner, Eudora Welty, or Robert Penn Warren.

Connect to the Literature

What details in this story reflect a Southern sensibility? Could this story be set in a different region? Explain.

Comprehension

What does Mr. Shiftlet do when Lucynell falls asleep at The Hot Spot?

▶ Critical Viewing

Does this painting reflect the mood of the story's closing scene? Explain. **EVALUATE**

The narrow road dropped off on either side into dry fields and here and there a shack or a filling station stood in a clearing. The sun began to set directly in front of the automobile. It was a reddening ball that through his windshield was slightly flat on the bottom and top. He saw a boy in overalls and a gray hat standing on the edge of the road and he slowed the car down and stopped in front of him. The boy didn't have his hand raised to thumb the ride, he was only standing there, but he had a small cardboard suitcase and his hat was set on his head in a way to indicate that he had left somewhere for good. "Son," Mr. Shiftlet said, "I see you want a ride."

The boy didn't say he did or he didn't but he opened the door of the car and got in, and Mr. Shiftlet started driving again. The child held the suitcase on his lap and folded his arms on top of it. He turned his head and looked out the window away from Shiftlet. Mr. Shiftlet felt oppressed. "Son," he said after a minute, "I got the best old mother in the world so I reckon you only got the second best."

The boy gave him a quick dark glance and then turned his face back out the window.

"It's nothing so sweet," Mr. Shiftlet continued, "as a boy's mother. She taught him his first prayers at her knee, she give him love when no other would, she told him what was right and what wasn't, and she seen that he done the right thing. Son," he said, "I never rued a day in my life like the one I rued when I left that old mother of mine."

The boy shifted in his seat but he didn't look at Mr. Shiftlet. He unfolded his arms and put one hand on the door handle.

"My mother was a angel of Gawd," Mr. Shiftlet said in a very strained voice. "He took her from heaven and giver to me and I left her." His eyes were instantly clouded over with a mist of tears. The car was barely moving.

The boy turned angrily in the seat. "You go to the devil!" he cried. "My old woman is a flea bag and yours is a stinking pole cat!" and with that he flung the door open and jumped out with his suitcase into the ditch.

Mr. Shiftlet was so shocked that for about a hundred feet he drove along slowly with the door still open. A cloud, the exact color of the boy's hat and shaped like a turnip, had descended over the sun, and another, worse looking, crouched behind the car. Mr. Shiftlet felt that the rottenness of the world was about to engulf him. He raised his arm and let it fall again to his breast. "Oh Lord!" he prayed. "Break forth and wash the slime from this earth!"

The turnip continued slowly to descend. After a few minutes there was a guffawing peal of thunder from behind and fantastic raindrops, like tin-can tops, crashed over the rear of Mr. Shiftlet's car. Very quickly he stepped on the gas and with his stump sticking out the window he raced the galloping shower into Mobile.

Critical Reading

1. **Key Ideas and Details** **(a)** What is Mrs. Crater's first reaction to Shiftlet when she sees him from a distance as the story begins? **(b) Infer:** What object on the Crater farm does Mr. Shiftlet want? **(c) Analyze:** What clues about Mr. Shiftlet's true character does Mrs. Crater not seem to notice?
2. **Key Ideas and Details** **(a)** What arguments does Mrs. Crater use to persuade Shiftlet to marry Lucynell? **(b) Interpret:** What factors cause Shiftlet to agree?
3. **Key Ideas and Details** **(a)** What prayer does Shiftlet offer at the end of the story? **(b) Analyze:** What is ironic about the way in which his prayer is answered? **(c) Generalize:** What does this event suggest about those whose behavior contradicts their professed beliefs?
4. **Integration of Knowledge and Ideas** **Make a Judgment:** When Mrs. Crater decides to marry Lucynell to Shiftlet, the girl seems to have no control over her fate. Do Mrs. Crater's actions have any moral justification? Explain.
5. **Integration of Knowledge and Ideas** Based on this story, a good example of regionalism, do you think there is a single, unified body of American literature? Explain. In your response, use at least two of these Essential Question words: *landscape, vision, commonplace, alienation, identity. [Connecting to the Essential Question: What makes American literature American?]*

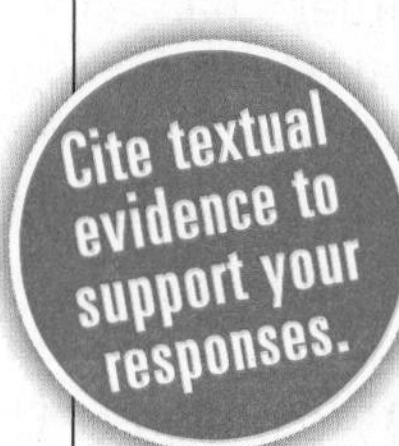
Cite textual evidence to support your responses.

Close Reading Activities

The Life You Save May Be Your Own

Literary Analysis

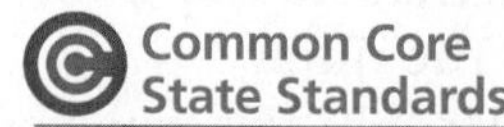

Writing

2. Write informative texts to examine and convey complex ideas, concepts, and information clearly and accurately through the effective selection, organization, and analysis of content. *(p. 1025)*

2.b. Develop the topic thoroughly by selecting the most significant and relevant facts, extended definitions, concrete details, quotations, or other information and examples appropriate to the audience's knowledge of the topic. *(p. 1025)*

2.c. Use appropriate and varied transitions and syntax to link the major sections of the text, create cohesion, and clarify the relationships among complex ideas and concepts. *(p. 1025)*

2.f. Provide a concluding statement that follows from and supports the information or explanation presented. *(p. 1025)*

Language

4.a. Use context as a clue to the meaning of a word or phrase. *(p. 1025)*

4.b. Identify and correctly use patterns of word changes that indicate different meanings or parts of speech. *(p. 1025)*

1. **Key Ideas and Details** Use a chart like the one shown to examine Mrs. Crater and Mr. Shiftlet as **grotesque characters:** **(a)** What primary goal or obsession controls each character? **(b)** What actions does each undertake as a result of the obsession?

Character	→	Goal or Obsession	Actions Undertaken

2. **Craft and Structure** Note two examples of physical description that create an exaggerated, or grotesque, effect for **(a)** Mrs. Crater, **(b)** Mr. Shiftlet, and **(c)** Lucynell.
3. **Craft and Structure** **(a)** Shiftlet twice brings up the image of a human heart—the physical, beating heart of a person. Identify both references. **(b)** What idea does he express both times?
4. **Craft and Structure** **(a)** Note one example of **direct characterization** O'Connor uses to depict Lucynell. **(b)** Note at least two examples of **indirect characterization** that reveal Lucynell's innocence. Explain your choices.
5. **Craft and Structure** How important is the setting in shaping characters and determining their actions?
6. **Key Ideas and Details** **(a) Draw conclusions** about the meaning of Mr. Shiftlet's name by considering his interest in the automobile—a vehicle that allows for fast, ongoing motion. **(b)** In what ways is this meaning very different from that of Crater, the name O'Connor gives to the mother and daughter?
7. **Key Ideas and Details** When Mrs. Crater asks Shiftlet to marry Lucynell, he replies that a "man is divided into two parts, body and spirit." **(a)** According to Shiftlet, what does the spirit want? **(b)** What conclusion can you draw from this detail?
8. **Integration of Knowledge and Ideas** **(a)** What conclusion about his character can you draw from the description of Shiftlet forming "a crooked cross"? **(b)** What conclusions can you draw from the description of Lucynell as an "innocent" and "an angel of Gawd." **(c)** Knowing that O'Connor was a deeply religious writer, what overall conclusions about the story's meaning might you draw from these details?

Vocabulary Acquisition and Use

Word Analysis: Latin Root *-sol-*

The Latin word root *-sol-*, meaning "alone," builds the meaning of these words:

a. *desolate:* uninhabited, deserted

b. *solitary:* alone, without company

c. *soloist:* one who performs by him- or herself

Use your knowledge of the Latin root *-sol-* to answer the following questions.

1. In a *soliloquy*, do two actors have an exchange or does one actor address the audience?
2. Would a pilot have a co-pilot on a *solo* flight?
3. Would a person who usually loves to take long walks alone enjoy the state of *solitude*?
4. How might you *isolate* a sick puppy?
5. If someone is the *sole* survivor, what has happened to the rest of the people?

Vocabulary: Context Clues

For each sentence below, indicate whether the word in italics is used correctly. Explain the context clues that help you decide. If the word is used incorrectly, write a new, correct sentence.

1. There were so many people at the town meeting that the atmosphere was utterly *desolate.*
2. The rickety fence *listed* in the strong winds.
3. In an *ominous* voice, the jury foreperson read the guilty verdict.
4. After the huge dinner, we were *ravenous.*
5. His *morose* reaction showed his delight with the entertainment.

Writing to Sources

Informative Text The title and ending of a story contain essential information that may help you interpret a story's meaning. Write an **essay** in which you explain the fate of each character in O'Connor's "The Life You Save May Be Your Own" and interpret the title.

Prewriting As you reread the story, use a chart like the one shown to analyze the relationships between the characters' fates and the meaning of the title. Jot down notes and look for connections among the ideas.

Drafting Present your interpretation of the story's title in your introduction. Then, write one paragraph about each of the three main characters. Explain how the final image of each character relates to the key idea of the title. Summarize and extend your analysis in your conclusion.

Model: Charting to Organize Ideas

	Mrs. Crater	Lucynell	Mr. Shiftlet
What happens to the character in the end?			
How does the character's fate connect to the title?			

Revising Review your essay, making sure you have presented a balanced, unified discussion. Clarify ideas that seem vague and develop incomplete thoughts more thoroughly. Consider adding transitional phrases, such as "in contrast," and "alternatively," to make comparisons easier to follow.

Connecting to the Essential Question In this story, a parent dreams of a better life for a child—a common theme in American literature. As you read, notice differences in the three main characters' aspirations and goals. Doing so will help you reflect on the Essential Question: **What makes American literature American?**

Common Core State Standards

Reading Literature

2. Determine two or more themes or central ideas of a text and analyze their development over the course of the text; provide an objective summary of the text.

3. Analyze the impact of the author's choices regarding how to develop and relate elements of a story.

5. Analyze how an author's choices concerning how to structure specific parts of a text contribute to its overall structure and meaning as well as its aesthetic impact.

Close Reading Focus

Plot

A story follows a sequence of events called a **plot,** which is organized into distinct phases:

- The **exposition** introduces the setting, characters, and situation.
- An **inciting incident** establishes the central conflict.
- During the **development,** the conflict increases.
- The plot reaches a high point of interest or suspense at the **climax.**
- A **resolution** explains the end of the central conflict. Note that many modern stories, such as this one, have no resolution. Instead, a character may experience an **epiphany,** or moment of insight, that affects the conflict but does not resolve it.

The events that lead up to the climax make up the **rising action.** Those that follow make up the **falling action.** Along the way, writers may also use **foreshadowing,** or clues, to hint at what will happen next. Foreshadowing can increase suspense and help build toward the climax. It also creates a sense of unity in a story as hints planted early in the plot develop into meaningful moments later. As you read, notice how the author builds the conflict through the phases of the plot.

Preparing to Read Complex Texts All of the details in a story, including the events of the plot and the characters' reactions, add up to express deeper meanings, or **themes.** To better understand this process, **summarize** as you read. To summarize, briefly restate the main points in a passage. Pause after significant scenes and review which characters were involved and what happened. Use a chart like the one shown to identify key elements to note as you summarize.

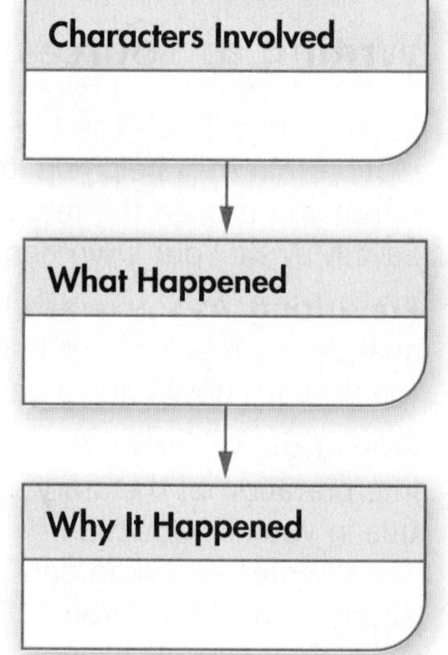

Vocabulary

You will encounter the words listed here in the text that follows. Copy the words into your notebook. Which word is an antonym of *ethical*?

diligence
illiterate
unscrupulous
repugnant
discern

Bernard Malamud (1914–1986)

Author of "The First Seven Years"

Bernard Malamud was born in Brooklyn, New York, the son of Russian immigrants. His father ran a grocery store and worked hard to forge a better life for his family. According to his own account, Malamud's boyhood was "comparatively happy." He grew up hearing the constant mingling of Yiddish and English—an experience that contributed to his fine ear for the rhythms of spoken dialogue. A favored boyhood pastime was listening to his father recount tales of Jewish life in pre-Revolutionary Russia. Young Bernard began to display his father's gift for telling stories when, recovering from pneumonia at age nine, he spent hours in the back room of the family store writing down the stories he had composed to tell his friends.

"LIFE IS A TRAGEDY FULL OF JOY."

A Literary Range Malamud attended City College of New York and Columbia University and began publishing stories in a number of well-known magazines. Despite the strong influence of Yiddish folk tales—many of Malamud's stories are drawn from this tradition—his work depicts a broad range of settings and characters. From the gifted baseball player in *The Natural* (1952), to the handyman living in czarist Russia in the Pulitzer Prize-winning *The Fixer* (1966), all of his characters come across as real and accessible, with universal hopes and concerns. Malamud's other novels include *The Assistant* (1957), *A New Life* (1961), *The Tenants* (1971), and *Dubin's Lives* (1979). He also wrote numerous short stories, many of which were published in *The Magic Barrel* (1958), which won the National Book Award.

A Touch of Magic Malamud tells his stories in spare, compressed prose, sprinkled with flashes of highly charged metaphorical language. He allows magical events to happen in gloomy city neighborhoods, and gives his hard-working characters unexpected flashes of passion. Some Malamud stories move readers to sadness as characters struggle courageously against tragedy. "The First Seven Years" depicts a Polish immigrant's desire to see his daughter achieve a better life. His notion of that life, however, is not the same as hers.

The First Seven Years

BERNARD MALAMUD

BACKGROUND During World War II, millions of Jews were murdered by the Nazis under the direction of German dictator Adolf Hitler. Many Jewish refugees immigrated to the United States, a pattern that continued after the end of the war. This story takes place in the 1950s, when many Holocaust survivors like Sobel, the shoemaker's assistant, struggled to establish new lives in the United States.

Feld, the shoemaker, was annoyed that his helper, Sobel, was so insensitive to his reverie that he wouldn't for a minute cease his fanatic pounding at the other bench. He gave him a look, but Sobel's bald head was bent over the last[1] as he worked he didn't notice. The shoemaker shrugged and continued to peer through the partly frosted window at the near-sighted haze of falling February snow. Neither the shifting white blur outside, nor the sudden deep remembrance of the snowy Polish village where he had wasted his youth could turn his thoughts from Max the college boy, (a constant visitor in the mind since early that morning when Feld saw him trudging through the snowdrifts on his way to school) whom he so much respected because of the sacrifices he had made throughout the years—in winter or direst heat—to further his education. An old wish returned

1. **last** *n.* block shaped like a person's foot, on which shoes are made or repaired.

to haunt the shoemaker: that he had had a son instead of a daughter, but this blew away in the snow for Feld, if anything, was a practical man. Yet he could not help but contrast the **diligence** of the boy, who was a peddler's son, with Miriam's unconcern for an education. True, she was always with a book in her hand, yet when the opportunity arose for a college education, she had said no she would rather find a job. He had begged her to go, pointing out how many fathers could not afford to send their children to college, but she said she wanted to be independent. As for education, what was it, she asked, but books, which Sobel, who diligently read the classics, would as usual advise her on. Her answer greatly grieved her father.

A figure emerged from the snow and the door opened. At the counter the man withdrew from a wet paper bag a pair of battered shoes for repair. Who he was the shoemaker for a moment had no idea, then his heart trembled as he realized, before he had thoroughly discerned the face, that Max himself was standing there, embarrassedly explaining what he wanted done to his old shoes. Though Feld listened eagerly, he couldn't hear a word, for the opportunity that had burst upon him was deafening.

He couldn't exactly recall when the thought had occurred to him, because it was clear he had more than once considered suggesting to the boy that he go out with Miriam. But he had not dared speak, for if Max said no, how would he face him again? Or suppose Miriam, who harped so often on independence, blew up in anger and shouted at him for his meddling? Still, the chance was too good to let by: all it meant was an introduction. They might long ago have become friends had they happened to meet somewhere, therefore was it not his duty—an obligation—to bring them together, nothing more, a harmless connivance to replace an accidental encounter in the subway, let's say, or a mutual friend's introduction in the street? Just let him once see and talk to her and he would for sure be interested. As for Miriam, what possible harm for a working girl in an office, who met only loud-mouthed salesmen and **illiterate** shipping clerks, to make the acquaintance of a fine scholarly boy? Maybe he would awaken in her a desire to go to college; if not—the shoemaker's mind at last came to grips with the truth—let her marry an educated man and live a better life.

When Max finished describing what he wanted done to his shoes, Feld marked them, both with enormous holes in the soles which he pretended not to notice, with large white-chalk x's, and the rubber heels, thinned to the nails, he marked with o's, though it troubled him he might have mixed up the letters. Max inquired the price, and the shoemaker cleared his throat and asked the boy, above Sobel's insistent hammering, would he please step through the side door there into the hall. Though surprised, Max did as the shoemaker requested, and Feld went in after him. For a minute they were both silent, because Sobel had stopped banging, and it seemed they understood neither was to say anything until the noise began again.

◀ **Critical Viewing** How does the young woman portrayed in this painting compare to your impression of Miriam? **COMPARE**

Vocabulary
diligence (dil′ ə jəns) *n* constant, careful effort; perseverance

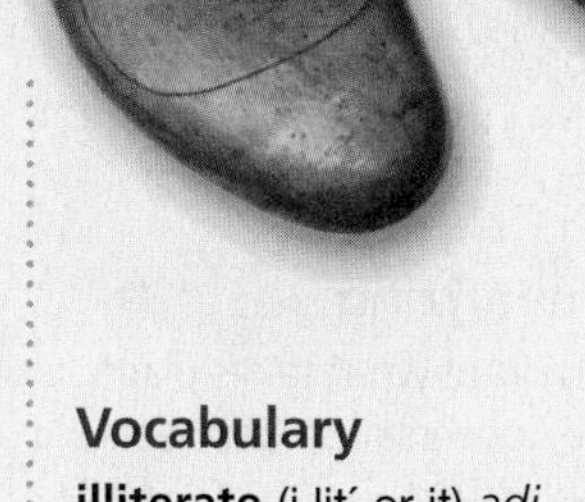

Vocabulary
illiterate (i lit′ ər it) *adj.* unable to read or write

Comprehension
What hope does Feld hold for his daughter Miriam and the college boy Max?

▶ **Critical Viewing**

What does this photograph reveal about the setting of the story? **ANALYZE**

Summarizing

Briefly state what takes place in the conversation between Max and Feld.

When it did, loudly, the shoemaker quickly told Max why he had asked to talk to him.

"Ever since you went to high school," he said, in the dimly-lit hallway, "I watched you in the morning go to the subway to school, and I said always to myself, this is a fine boy that he wants so much an education."

"Thanks," Max said, nervously alert. He was tall and grotesquely thin, with sharply cut features, particularly a beak-like nose. He was wearing a loose, long slushy overcoat that hung down to his ankles, looking like a rug draped over his bony shoulders, and a soggy, old brown hat, as battered as the shoes he had brought in.

"I am a business man," the shoemaker abruptly said to conceal his embarrassment, "so I will explain you right away why I talk to you. I have a girl, my daughter Miriam—she is nineteen—a very nice girl and also so pretty that everybody looks on her when she passes by in the street. She is smart, always with a book, and I thought to myself that a boy like you, an educated boy—I thought maybe you will be interested sometime to meet a girl like this." He laughed a bit when he had finished and was tempted to say more but had the good sense not to.

Max stared down like a hawk. For an uncomfortable second he was silent, then he asked, "Did you say nineteen?"

"Yes."

"Would it be all right to inquire if you have a picture of her?"

"Just a minute." The shoemaker went into the store and hastily returned with a snapshot that Max held up to the light.

"She's all right," he said.

Feld waited.

"And is she sensible—not the flighty kind?"

"She is very sensible."

After another short pause, Max said it was okay with him if he met her.

"Here is my telephone," said the shoemaker, hurriedly handing him a slip of paper. "Call her up. She comes home from work six o'clock."

Max folded the paper and tucked it away into his worn leather wallet.

"About the shoes," he said. "How much did you say they will cost me?"

"Don't worry about the price."

"I just like to have an idea."

"A dollar—dollar fifty. A dollar fifty," the shoemaker said. At once he felt bad, for he usually charged two twenty-five for this kind of job. Either he should have asked the regular price or done the work for nothing.

Later, as he entered the store, he was startled by a violent clanging and looked up to see Sobel pounding with all his might upon the naked last. It broke, the iron striking the floor and jumping with a thump against the wall, but before the enraged shoemaker could cry out, the assistant had torn his hat

and coat from the hook and rushed out into the snow.

So Feld, who had looked forward to anticipating how it would go with his daughter and Max, instead had a great worry on his mind. Without his temperamental helper he was a lost man, especially since it was years now that he had carried the store alone. The shoemaker had for an age suffered from a heart condition that threatened collapse if he dared exert himself. Five years ago, after an attack, it had appeared as though he would have either to sacrifice his business upon the auction block and live on a pittance thereafter, or put

Comprehension
What does Feld ask of Max?

Vocabulary
unscrupulous
(un skrōō′ pyə ləs)
adj. unethical; dishonest

himself at the mercy of some **unscrupulous** employee who would in the end probably ruin him. But just at the moment of his darkest despair, this Polish refugee, Sobel, appeared one night from the street and begged for work. He was a stocky man, poorly dressed, with a bald head that had once been blond, a severely plain face and soft blue eyes prone to tears over the sad books he read, a young man but old—no one would have guessed thirty. Though he confessed he knew nothing of shoemaking, he said he was apt and would work for a very little if Feld taught him the trade. Thinking that with, after all, a landsman,[2] he would have less to fear than from a complete stranger, Feld took him on and within six weeks the refugee rebuilt as good a shoe as he, and not long thereafter expertly ran the business for the thoroughly relieved shoemaker.

BUT JUST AT THE MOMENT OF HIS DARKEST DESPAIR, THIS POLISH REFUGEE, SOBEL, APPEARED ONE NIGHT FROM THE STREET AND BEGGED FOR WORK.

Feld could trust him with anything and did, frequently going home after an hour or two at the store, leaving all the money in the till, knowing Sobel would guard every cent of it. The amazing thing was that he demanded so little. His wants were few; in money he wasn't interested—in nothing but books, it seemed—which he one by one lent to Miriam, together with his profuse, queer written comments, manufactured during his lonely rooming house evenings, thick pads of commentary which the shoemaker peered at and twitched his shoulders over as his daughter, from her fourteenth year, read page by sanctified page, as if the word of God were inscribed on them. To protect Sobel, Feld himself had to see that he received more than he asked for. Yet his conscience bothered him for not insisting that the assistant accept a better wage than he was getting, though Feld had honestly told him he could earn a handsome salary if he worked elsewhere, or maybe opened a place of his own. But the assistant answered, somewhat ungraciously, that he was not interested in going elsewhere, and though Feld frequently asked himself what keeps him here? why does he stay? he finally answered it that the man, no doubt because of his terrible experiences as a refugee, was afraid of the world.

Plot
What inciting incident creates a conflict between Feld and Sobel?

After the incident with the broken last, angered by Sobel's behavior, the shoemaker decided to let him stew for a week in the rooming house, although his own strength was taxed dangerously and the business suffered. However, after several sharp nagging warnings from both his wife and daughter, he went finally in search of Sobel, as he had once before, quite recently, when over some fancied slight—Feld had merely asked him not to give Miriam so many books to read because her eyes were strained and red—the assistant had left the place in a huff, an incident which, as usual, came to nothing for he had returned after the shoemaker had talked to him, and taken

2. landsman *n.* fellow countryman.

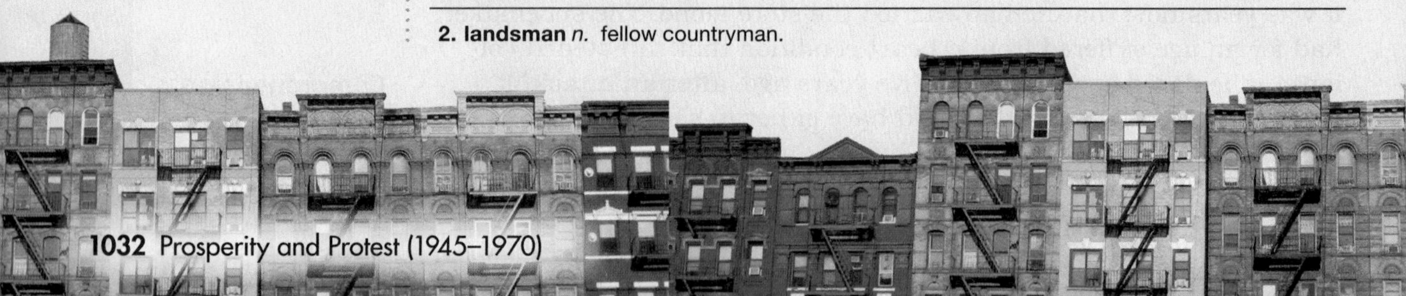

his seat at the bench. But this time, after Feld had plodded through the snow to Sobel's house—he had thought of sending Miriam but the idea became **repugnant** to him—the burly landlady at the door informed him in a nasal voice that Sobel was not at home, and though Feld knew this was a nasty lie, for where had the refugee to go? still for some reason he was not completely sure of—it may have been the cold and his fatigue—he decided not to insist on seeing him. Instead he went home and hired a new helper.

Having settled the matter, though not entirely to his satisfaction, for he had much more to do than before, and so, for example, could no longer lie late in bed mornings because he had to get up to open the store for the new assistant, a speechless, dark man with an irritating rasp as he worked, whom he would not trust with the key as he had Sobel. Furthermore, this one, though able to do a fair repair job, knew nothing of grades of leather or prices, so Feld had to make his own purchases: and every night at closing time it was necessary to count the money in the till and lock up. However, he was not dissatisfied, for he lived much in his thoughts of Max and Miriam. The college boy had called her, and they had arranged a meeting for this coming Friday night. The shoemaker would personally have preferred Saturday, which he felt would make it a date of the first magnitude, but he learned Friday was Miriam's choice, so he said nothing. The day of the week did not matter. What mattered was the aftermath. Would they like each other and want to be friends? He sighed at all the time that would have to go by before he knew for sure. Often he was tempted to talk to Miriam about the boy, to ask whether she thought she would like his type—he had told her only that he considered Max a nice boy and had suggested he call her—but the one time he tried she snapped at him—justly—how should she know?

At last Friday came. Feld was not feeling particularly well so he stayed in bed, and Mrs. Feld thought it better to remain in the bedroom with him when Max called. Miriam received the boy, and her parents could hear their voices, his throaty one, as they talked. Just before leaving, Miriam brought Max to the bedroom door and he stood there a minute, a tall, slightly hunched figure wearing a thick, droopy suit, and apparently at ease as he greeted the shoemaker and his wife, which was surely a good sign. And Miriam, although she had worked all day, looked fresh and pretty. She was a large-framed girl with a well-shaped body, and she had a fine open face and soft hair. They made, Feld thought, a first-class couple.

Miriam returned after 11:30. Her mother was already asleep, but the shoemaker got out of bed and after locating his bathrobe went into the kitchen, where Miriam, to his surprise, sat at the table, reading.

Vocabulary
repugnant (ri pug′ nənt) *adj.* offensive; disagreeable

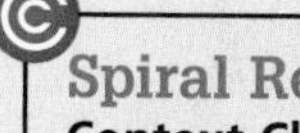

Spiral Review
Context Clues What can you conclude about the meaning of the word *magnitude* as it is used here?

Comprehension
To what extent does Feld trust Sobel?

Plot and Foreshadowing

What might Feld's conversation about Miriam's date with Max foreshadow?

"So where did you go?" Feld asked pleasantly.

"For a walk," she said, not looking up.

"I advised him," Feld said, clearing his throat, "he shouldn't spend so much money."

"I didn't care."

The shoemaker boiled up some water for tea and sat down at the table with a cupful and a thick slice of lemon.

"So how," he sighed after a sip, "did you enjoy?"

"It was all right."

He was silent. She must have sensed his disappointment, for she added, "You can't really tell much the first time."

"You will see him again?"

Turning a page, she said that Max had asked for another date.

"For when?"

"Saturday."

"So what did you say?"

"What did I say?" she asked, delaying for a moment—"I said yes."

Afterwards she inquired about Sobel, and Feld, without exactly knowing why, said the assistant had got another job. Miriam said nothing more and began to read. The shoemaker's conscience did not trouble him; he was satisfied with the Saturday date.

During the week, by placing here and there a deft question, he managed to get from Miriam some information about Max. It surprised him to learn that the boy was not studying to be either a doctor or lawyer but was taking a business course leading to a degree in accountancy. Feld was a little disappointed because he thought of accountants as bookkeepers and would have preferred "a higher profession." However, it was not long before he had investigated the subject and discovered that Certified Public Accountants were highly respected people, so he was thoroughly content as Saturday approached. But because Saturday was a busy day, he was much in the store and therefore did not see Max when he came to call for Miriam. From his wife he learned there had been nothing especially revealing about their meeting. Max had rung the bell and Miriam had got her coat and left with him—nothing more. Feld did not probe, for his wife was not particularly observant. Instead, he waited up for Miriam with a newspaper on his lap, which he scarcely looked at so lost was he in thinking of the future. He awoke to find her in the room with him, tiredly removing her hat. Greeting her, he was suddenly inexplicably afraid to ask anything about the evening. But since she volunteered nothing he was at last forced to inquire how she had enjoyed herself. Miriam began something noncommittal but apparently changed her mind, for she said after a minute, "I was bored."

When Feld had sufficiently recovered from his anguished disappointment to ask why, she answered without hesitation, "Because he's nothing more than a materialist."

"What means this word?"

"He has no soul. He's only interested in things."

He considered her statement for a long time but then asked, "Will you see him again?"

"He didn't ask."

"Suppose he will ask you?"

"I won't see him."

He did not argue: however, as the days went by he hoped increasingly she would change her mind. He wished the boy would telephone, because he was sure there was more to him than Miriam, with her inexperienced eye, could **discern**. But Max didn't call. As a matter of fact he took a different route to school, no longer passing the shoemaker's store, and Feld was deeply hurt.

Then one afternoon Max came in and asked for his shoes. The shoemaker took them down from the shelf where he had placed them, apart from the other pairs. He had done the work himself and the soles and heels were well built and firm. The shoes had been highly polished and somehow looked better than new. Max's Adam's apple went up once when he saw them, and his eyes had little lights in them.

"How much?" he asked, without directly looking at the shoemaker.

"Like I told you before," Feld answered sadly. "One dollar fifty cents."

Max handed him two crumpled bills and received in return a newly-minted silver half dollar.

He left. Miriam had not been mentioned. That night the shoemaker discovered that his new assistant had been all the while stealing from him, and he suffered a heart attack.

Though the attack was very mild, he lay in bed for three weeks. Miriam spoke of going for Sobel, but sick as he was Feld rose in wrath against the idea. Yet in his heart he knew there was no other way, and the first weary day back in the shop thoroughly convinced him, so that night after supper he dragged himself to Sobel's rooming house.

He toiled up the stairs, though he knew it was bad for him, and at the top knocked at the door. Sobel opened it and the shoemaker entered. The room was a small, poor one, with a single window facing the street. It contained a narrow cot, a low table and several stacks of books piled haphazardly around on the floor along the wall, which made him think how queer Sobel was, to be uneducated and read so much. He had once asked him, Sobel, why you read so much? and the assistant could not answer him. Did you ever study in a college someplace? he had asked but Sobel shook his head. He read, he said, to know. But to know what, the shoemaker demanded, and to know, why? Sobel never explained, which proved he read much because he was queer.

Feld sat down to recover his breath. The assistant was resting on his bed with his heavy back to the wall. His shirt and trousers were clean, and his stubby fingers, away from the shoemaker's bench, were strangely pallid. His face was thin and pale, as if he had been shut in this room since the day he had bolted from the store.

"So when you will come back to work?" Feld asked him.

"HE HAS NO SOUL. HE'S ONLY INTERESTED IN THINGS."

Vocabulary

discern (di surn′) *v.* perceive or recognize.

Comprehension

Why is Miriam bored with Max?

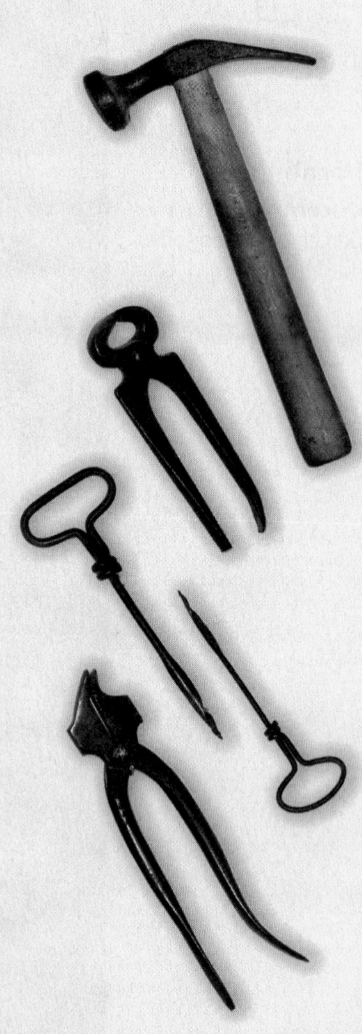

To his surprise, Sobel burst out, "Never."

Jumping up, he strode over to the window that looked out upon the miserable street. "Why should I come back?" he cried.

"I will raise your wages."

"Who cares for your wages!"

The shoemaker, knowing he didn't care, was at a loss what else to say.

"What do you want from me, Sobel?"

"Nothing."

"I always treated you like you was my son."

Sobel vehemently denied it. "So why you look for strange boys in the street they should go out with Miriam? Why you don't think of me?"

The shoemaker's hands and feet turned freezing cold. His voice became so hoarse he couldn't speak. At last he cleared his throat and croaked, "So what has my daughter got to do with a shoemaker thirty-five years old who works for me?"

"Why do you think I worked so long for you?" Sobel cried out. "For the stingy wages I sacrificed five years of my life so you could have to eat and drink and where to sleep?"

"Then for what?" shouted the shoemaker.

"For Miriam," he blurted—"for her."

The shoemaker, after a time, managed to say, "I pay wages in cash, Sobel," and lapsed into silence. Though he was seething with excitement, his mind was coldly clear, and he had to admit to himself he had sensed all along that Sobel felt this way. He had never so much as thought it consciously, but he had felt it and was afraid.

"Miriam knows?" he muttered hoarsely.

"She knows."

"You told her?"

"No."

"Then how does she know?"

"How does she know?" Sobel said, "because she knows. She knows who I am and what is in my heart."

Feld had a sudden insight. In some devious way, with his books and commentary, Sobel had given Miriam to understand that he loved her. The shoemaker felt a terrible anger at him for his deceit.

"Sobel, you are crazy," he said bitterly. "She will never marry a man so old and ugly like you."

Sobel turned black with rage. He cursed the shoemaker, but then, though he trembled to hold it in, his eyes filled with tears and he broke into deep sobs. With his back to Feld, he stood at the window, fists clenched, and his shoulders shook with his choked sobbing.

Watching him, the shoemaker's anger diminished. His teeth were on edge with pity for the man, and his eyes grew moist. How strange and sad that a refugee, a grown man, bald and old with his miseries, who had by the skin of his teeth escaped Hitler's incinerators,[3] should fall in love, when he had got to America, with a girl less than half his

3. **Hitler's incinerators** The furnaces used in concentration camps to burn human bodies during Adolf Hitler's dictatorship.

age. Day after day, for five years he had sat at his bench, cutting and hammering away, waiting for the girl to become a woman, unable to ease his heart with speech, knowing no protest but desperation.

"Ugly I didn't mean," he said half aloud.

Then he realized that what he had called ugly was not Sobel but Miriam's life if she married him. He felt for his daughter a strange and gripping sorrow, as if she were already Sobel's bride, the wife, after all, of a shoemaker, and had in her life no more than her mother had had. And all his dreams for her—why he had slaved and destroyed his heart with anxiety and labor—all these dreams of a better life were dead.

The room was quiet. Sobel was standing by the window reading, and it was curious that when he read he looked young.

"She is only nineteen," Feld said brokenly. "This is too young yet to get married. Don't ask her for two years more, till she is twenty-one, then you can talk to her."

Sobel didn't answer. Feld rose and left. He went slowly down the stairs but once outside, though it was an icy night and the crisp falling snow whitened the street, he walked with a stronger stride.

But the next morning, when the shoemaker arrived, heavy-hearted, to open the store, he saw he needn't have come, for his assistant was already seated at the last, pounding leather for his love.

Plot and Epiphany
What does Feld suddenly understand about Sobel?

Critical Reading

1. **Key Ideas and Details (a)** Under what circumstances does Feld first notice Max? **(b) Interpret:** Why is Max so appealing to Feld?
2. **Key Ideas and Details (a)** To Feld, what values does Max seem to embody? **(b) Interpret:** Does Max really share Feld's values? Explain.
3. **Key Ideas and Details (a)** How does Miriam react to her second date with Max? **(b) Compare and Contrast:** Explain the differences between Miriam's feelings for Max and her feelings for Sobel.
4. **Key Ideas and Details (a)** What is Sobel's background? **(b) Speculate:** In what ways do the events of history that Sobel experienced add to his characterization?
5. **Key Ideas and Details (a) Interpret:** What does education represent to Feld and Max? **(b) Compare and Contrast:** How does Sobel's love of reading compare with both Feld's and Max's feelings about education?
6. **Integration of Knowledge and Ideas** In your view, is Feld's definition of a successful and meaningful life one many Americans share? Explain. In your response, use at least three of these Essential Question words: *prosperity, materialism, idealistic, realistic, independence.* ***[Connecting to the Essential Question: What makes American literature American?]***

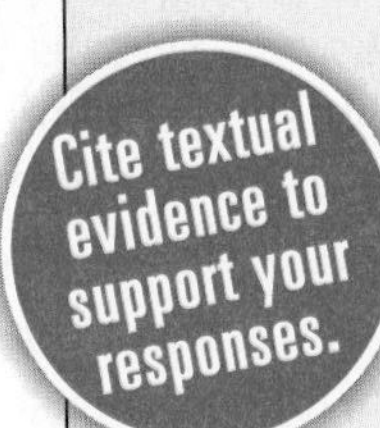
Cite textual evidence to support your responses.

Literary Analysis

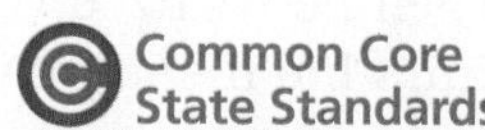

Common Core State Standards

Writing

2.a. Introduce a topic; organize complex ideas, concepts, and information so that each new element builds on that which precedes it to create a unified whole; include graphics when useful to aiding comprehension. *(p. 1039)*

2.b. Develop the topic thoroughly by selecting the most significant and relevant facts, extended definitions, concrete details, quotations, or other information and examples appropriate to the audience's knowledge of the topic. *(p. 1039)*

Language

4. Determine or clarify the meaning of unknown and multiple-meaning words and phrases based on *grades 11–12 reading and content,* choosing flexibly from a range of strategies. (p. 1039)

4.a. Use context as a clue to the meaning of a word or phrase. *(p. 1039)*

4.b. Identify and correctly use patterns of word changes that indicate different meanings or parts of speech. *(p. 1039)*

1. **Craft and Structure** Use a chart like the one shown to outline key events in the **plot** of the story. **(a)** Explain the information contained in the story's **exposition. (b)** Identify the **inciting incident** that introduces the conflict. **(c)** Define the main conflict and explain how it develops to the **climax** and leads to the **resolution.**

Rising Action	Climax	Resolution
Exposition:		
Inciting Incident:		
Conflict:		

2. **Craft and Structure** Explain how the climax of this story is also an **epiphany** for Feld.
3. **Key Ideas and Details** What new ideas does Feld's epiphany introduce that challenge the values and assumptions about life he has always held?
4. **Key Ideas and Details (a)** How might Feld's epiphany affect his attitudes toward Miriam and Sobel in the future? **(b)** To what degree is the central conflict resolved at the end of the story? Explain.
5. **Key Ideas and Details (a) Summarize** what happens in the final scene between Feld and Sobel. **(b)** How does summarizing help you understand and interpret the meaning of the scene?
6. **Key Ideas and Details (a)** Summarize the entire story as briefly as possible. Carefully choose the information you feel is most important to understanding the story's essential meaning. **(b)** Compare your summary with another student's version. Identify elements that only one writer included. Decide whether or not each of these elements should be part of a useful summary.
7. **Craft and Structure** Early in the story, Feld asks to speak to Max privately. As they step into the side room, Sobel stops hammering. How is the detail about Sobel an example of **foreshadowing?**
8. **Craft and Structure (a)** Identify two other examples of foreshadowing in the story. **(b)** Explain how each is a clue for events that later unfold.
9. **Craft and Structure** Based on this story, explain how foreshadowing helps to give a story a sense of unity.
10. **Integration of Knowledge and Ideas (a)** What image of Sobel begins the story? **(b)** What image of Sobel ends it? **(c)** What meaning do you find in the relationship of the beginning of the story to its end?

Vocabulary Acquisition and Use

Word Analysis: Latin Root *-litera-*

The root *-litera-* comes from the Latin word that means "letter." Words that derive from this root often relate to reading and language. Complete each sentence below with a *-litera-* word from the list. Then, explain the meaning of the word you used.

literary	illiteracy
literal	literati

1. He insists on a _____ interpretation of the law.
2. Improved education is one solution to the problem of _____.
3. Her _____ talents are obvious in her poetry.
4. All of the local _____ gathered at the book reading to meet the famous author.

Vocabulary: Context Clues

Review the vocabulary list on p. 1026. Then, select the word you would most likely find in each of these newspaper articles.

1. "Reading Rate Declines Among Adults"
2. "Residents Complain of Dump's Disagreeable Smell"
3. "Hard-Working Teens Turn Vacant Lot into Garden"
4. "Dishonorable Band of Thieves Gets Nabbed"
5. "Girl of Ten Recognizes Error in Mayor's Speech"

Writing to Sources

Informative Text Malamud creates believable and engaging characters in "The First Seven Years." Suppose you are developing a television show based on this story. Write a **personality profile** of one of the characters. The profile could be used by producers or the director to cast an appropriate actor.

Prewriting Your profile should include details about how the character looks, talks, and behaves. Use a cluster diagram like the one shown to jot down physical characteristics and personal qualities you observe in the character you are describing.

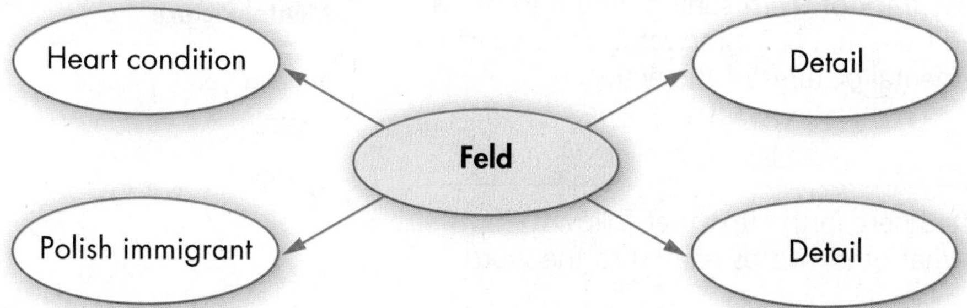

Drafting Begin with an informative detail or image of the character. Expand your profile in layers, referring to your cluster diagram as needed.

Revising Have a classmate create a new cluster diagram based on your profile. Compare it to your prewriting diagram to discover key information you may have omitted.

Building Knowledge and Insight

Constantly Risking Absurdity

Connecting to the Essential Question In this poem, Ferlinghetti says that the poet risks seeming absurd. As you read, consider what types of activities, beliefs, or ideals are worth the risk of appearing absurd. Doing so will help you think about the Essential Question: **How does literature shape or reflect society?**

Reading Literature
4. Determine the meaning of words and phrases as they are used in the text, including figurative and connotative meanings; analyze the impact of specific word choices on meaning and tone, including words with multiple meanings or language that is particularly fresh, engaging, or beautiful.

Language
5. Demonstrate understanding of figurative language, word relationships, and nuances in word meanings.
5.a. Interpret figures of speech in context and analyze their role in the text.

Close Reading Focus

Extended Metaphor; Puns

Ferlinghetti was a member of the "Beat Generation," a group of writers who rebelled against social, political, and literary norms. In an effort to free poetry from the hands of the elite and return it to "the streets," the Beats wrote poems that were playful, earthy, and defiant. Their guiding principle was "first thought, best thought"—the idea that an artist should not censor his or her immediate responses.

Ferlinghetti builds this poem as a single **extended metaphor,** or sustained comparison. In doing so, he demonstrates a poetic balance akin to the physical skills of the acrobat. To mimic the acrobat's agility, Ferlinghetti studs the poem with **puns**—words or phrases with double meanings:

- The acrobat/poet performs "above the heads" of his audience.
- The acrobat/poet climbs on "rime."
- The acrobat/poet balances on "eyebeams."

Puns can be amusing and clever. Under the guidance of a nimble poet, they also deepen the meaning and gravity of this poem.

Preparing to Read Complex Texts In this poem, Ferlinghetti uses phrases and line breaks rather than punctuation to signal units of meaning. As you read, *clarify your comprehension* by **visualizing or picturing the action** being described. If you lose track of the meaning, return to the last line you clearly pictured, and read from that point forward. Use a chart like the one shown to describe your mental pictures of the action.

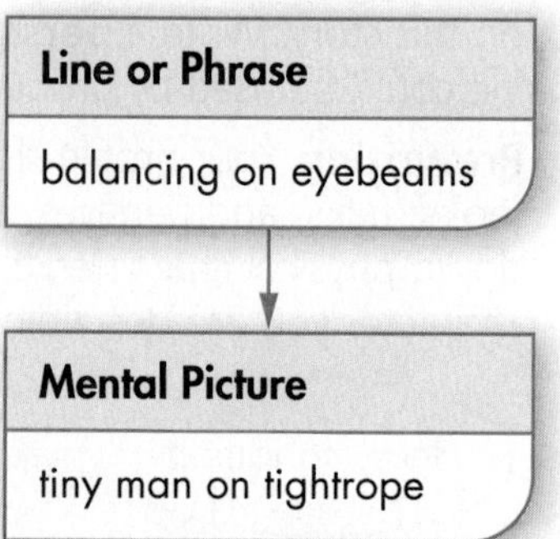

Line or Phrase
balancing on eyebeams
Mental Picture
tiny man on tightrope

Vocabulary

You will encounter the words listed here in the text that follows. Copy the words into your notebook. What other words related to the word *realist* can you list?

absurdity **taut**
realist

LAWRENCE FERLINGHETTI *(b. 1919)*

Author of "Constantly Risking Absurdity"

Lawrence Ferlinghetti was born in Yonkers, New York, six months after the sudden death of his father. The loss left his mother helpless, and Ferlinghetti was raised by a series of relatives and foster parents.

After graduating from the University of North Carolina in 1941, Ferlinghetti joined the Navy and served as a ship's commander for the remainder of World War II. He stocked his ship with a set of small, inexpensive volumes of literature for his men to read. "We had all the classics stacked everywhere," he remembers. The horrors Ferlinghetti saw during the war made him a lifetime pacifist.

After the war, Ferlinghetti completed graduate degrees at Columbia University in New York and the Sorbonne in Paris. As a budding poet in France, Ferlinghetti was heavily influenced by the American expatriates T. S. Eliot and Ezra Pound. Fearful that he was merely imitating the greats, Ferlinghetti struck out in search of new models. He landed in San Francisco, California, the home of an edgy new literary scene that would later become known as the Beat movement.

In the Light Ferlinghetti launched the poetry magazine *City Lights* in 1953. Shortly thereafter, he opened a bookstore by the same name. It was the first store in the country to sell only paperbacks. Small, cheap, and transportable, this medium represented a democratic revolution in literature: Books could be owned, read, and shared by rich and poor alike.

Ferlinghetti also founded a paperback publishing house, City Lights Pocket Poets, in 1955. The fourth volume he produced was *Howl & Other Poems* by Allen Ginsberg, a raw and volatile work that was viewed by many conventional readers as immoral. The publication led to Ferlinghetti's arrest on charges of obscenity, although he was fully cleared in a landmark ruling in favor of free speech. The trial brought national attention to Beat movement writers, and City Lights Books instantly became the epicenter of a new intellectual movement.

"Poetry is more alive when it is about living things."

A Poetry of Living Things In 1958 Ferlinghetti published his first poetry collection, *A Coney Island of the Mind*. Conversational, clear, and good-natured, his poems found a ready audience among those who were weary of the dense, subtle poetry of the Modernists. Ferlinghetti was named the first Poet Laureate of San Francisco in 1998 and received an Author's Guild Lifetime Achievement Award in 2003.

Constantly Risking Absurdity

Lawrence Ferlinghetti

Vocabulary

absurdity (ab sʉr′ də tē) *n.* nonsense; ridiculousness

Constantly risking **absurdity**
and death
whenever he performs
above the heads
of his audience
the poet like an acrobat
climbs on rime[1]
to a high wire of his own making
and balancing on eyebeams

---

1. rime An archaic spelling of the word *rhyme*; also, a thin coating of frost.

above a sea of faces
paces his way
to the other side of day
performing entrechats[2]
and sleight-of-foot tricks
and other high theatrics
and all without mistaking
any thing
for what it may not be
For he's the super **realist**
who must perforce perceive
taut truth
before the taking of each stance or step
in his supposed advance
toward that still higher perch
where Beauty stands and waits
with gravity
to start her death-defying leap
And he
a little charleychaplin man[3]
who may or may not catch
her fair eternal form
spreadeagled in the empty air
of existence

Vocabulary

realist (rē′ ə list) *n.* a person or artist concerned with things as they are, rather than as they could or should be

taut (tôt) *adj.* tightly stretched

2. **entrechats** (än′ trə chä′) In ballet, leaps straight upward in which the dancer crosses and uncrosses the legs a number of times.
3. **charleychaplin man** Charlie Chaplin (1889–1977) was an English comedy actor famous for his character "the Little Tramp," who wore a tight coat, oversized pants and shoes, a derby hat, and a mustache.

Critical Reading

1. **Key Ideas and Details** **(a)** Who is waiting for the poet on the other side of the high wire? **(b) Interpret:** Why is the poet not certain he will catch this figure?
2. **Integration of Knowledge and Ideas** **Interpret:** In what ways is "truth" like a tightrope?
3. **Integration of Knowledge and Ideas** What does this poem suggest about the reasons poetry is important to a society? Explain. In your response, use at least two of these Essential Question words: *expression, unconventional, profound, authenticity, universal.* ***[Connecting to the Essential Question: How does literature shape or reflect society?]***

Cite textual evidence to support your responses.

The BEATS

▲ Jack Kerouac

On an October evening in 1955, a crowd piled into San Francisco's Six Gallery to hear a group of poets read from their work. Poet and publisher Lawrence Ferlinghetti was among those in the audience. Halfway through the evening, a young man with intense brown eyes took the stage to perform a poem. When he ended, the room erupted into wild applause.

That night would go down in history as the debut of Beat literature. The young poet was Allen Ginsberg and his poem was "Howl." The next day, Ferlinghetti sent Ginsberg a telegram: "I greet you at the beginning of a great career." He published "Howl" the following year, and it is now considered one of the seminal works of the twentieth century.

▲ Bob Donlin, Neal Cassady, Allen Ginsberg, Robert LaVigne, and Lawrence Ferlinghetti (left to right) stand outside Ferlinghetti's City Lights Bookstore in San Francisco.

The Beat movement had actually begun in New York City in the 1940s. It was not a formal movement, just a small group of writer friends that included Allen Ginsberg, Jack Kerouac, William Burroughs, and Gregory Corso. In the mid-fifties, Ginsberg and Kerouac traveled to California, where they connected with West Coast poets Kenneth Rexroth, Lawrence Ferlinghetti, and Gary Snyder, and received their first public attention.

For their literary heroes, the Beats looked to figures as diverse as Walt Whitman, English poet William Blake, American novelist Thomas Wolfe, French poet Arthur Rimbaud, Spanish poet García Lorca, and Japanese writer Masaoki Shiki. The jazz riffs of musicians like Dizzy Gillespie and Charlie Parker inspired the rhythms of their poems, which they often performed to music. The Beats wrote about the perils of conformity, urging people to defy convention.

CONNECT TO THE LITERATURE

In what ways does "Constantly Risking Absurdity" express Beat ideas?

Allen Ginsberg ▶

Close Reading Activities

Constantly Risking Absurdity

Literary Analysis

1. **Key Ideas and Details** **(a)** As you **visualize or picture the action** of the poem, does your image of the acrobat change? Explain. **(b)** In what ways does picturing the action help you better understand the poem's meaning?
2. **Craft and Structure** Use a chart like the one shown to interpret the poem's **extended metaphor.** **(a)** List the acrobat's actions. **(b)** For each of the acrobat's actions, explain what corresponding task a poet must perform.

Acrobat's Action	Poet's Task

3. **Craft and Structure** **(a)** Identify and explain two **puns** used in the poem. **(b)** How does wordplay advance or illustrate the poem's underlying meaning?
4. **Craft and Structure** How does the poem's form, or look on the page, reflect the actions it describes?
5. **Integration of Knowledge and Ideas** The Beats believed that the poet should record without censoring his or her perception of the world. Does this poem affirm or challenge the idea of "first thought, best thought"? Explain.

Common Core State Standards

Writing
4. Produce clear and coherent writing in which the development, organization, and style are appropriate to task, purpose, and audience.

Language
4. Determine or clarify the meaning of unknown and multiple-meaning words and phrases based on *grades 11–12 reading and content,* choosing flexibly from a range of strategies.

Vocabulary Acquisition and Use

Use New Words For each word below, write a sentence that illustrates the word's meaning. Then, write one paragraph that uses all three words correctly.

1. realist **2.** taut **3.** absurdity

Writing to Sources

Poem Using Ferlinghetti's poem as a model, write a **poem** using an extended metaphor. In your poem, compare an abstract idea to a concrete object or a physical activity. Before you begin, make a list of ways in which two things are alike. As you write, make sure to meet the following criteria:

- Clearly identify the two things that are being compared.
- Use strong, clear verbs to help your reader picture what is happening.
- Develop a form so that the look of the poem on the page mirrors or illustrates the action of the poem.

Try to avoid revising too much. Instead, retain a sense of freshness and spontaneity, or "first thought" in your poem.

CONTEMPORARY CONNECTION

Artistic Upstarts Past and Present

On his social networking page, Charlie Todd describes himself this way: "In my free time, I'm a prankster." Todd is the founder of Improv Everywhere, a fluid mix of comedians, actors, and interested others. They travel around New York on self-described "missions," which appear to be free-form but are actually scripted and highly organized events.

Improv Everywhere missions are a modern equivalent of 1960s "happenings," artistic gatherings that included performance elements. They also have roots in the Beat Generation's rebelliousness toward set artistic modes. "We do what makes us laugh, but we're also interested in reclaiming public space," says Todd.

One public space perfect for an Improv Everywhere mission was the New York subway system, a setting not known to encourage eye contact or merriment. According to Todd, by staging a mock birthday on the No. 6 Lexington Line train, Improv "agents" hoped to "bring excitement to otherwise unexciting locales and give strangers a story they can tell for the rest of their lives."

CHARLIE TODD

Performance Artist

Charlie Todd graduated in 2001 from the University of North Carolina at Chapel Hill, where he majored in dramatic art. Todd decided that "if giant corporations can slap ads all over town, we should be able to blanket the city with comedy." The key to Improv Everywhere, Todd explained, is to make its stunts "somewhat plausible" and never to break character.

Subway Birthday

Charlie Todd

MISSION

February 2nd, 2002

Surprise!

Featuring: Kinney, Minton, White, Todd, Good, Rainswept, Lovejoy, Richardson, McKinley, Narasimhan, Ries, Boim

With our Subway Series, Improv Everywhere attempts to shatter the mundane and bring excitement and happiness to the underground. To us, the subway is a place where long lost brothers can meet, men can exchange outfits, and pants can be sold for $1.

With the goal of creating total fun, on February 2nd Improv Everywhere agents threw two surprise birthday parties on the 6 train. They came prepared with two 12-foot "Happy Birthday" banners, 24 party hats, and 20 "pin the tail on the donkey" games. IE Agents boarded the 6 train at Brooklyn Bridge. For the first party, agents White, Lovejoy, and Todd were throwing the birthday party for their friend Agent Good. Agent Rainswept, another friend of the birthday boy, was in charge of filming the party. The remaining seven IE Agents played strangers who did not know anyone else. They entered the train at various stops before the party (exiting an adjacent car and entering the party car when the train stopped).

As soon as they entered the train at Brooklyn Bridge, White, Lovejoy, and Todd ("The Party-throwers" from here on out) began decorating the car for the party. They casually mentioned what they were doing to those who asked. "We're throwing a surprise party. Our friend is boarding the train in a few stops." They began to solicit help from strangers to blow up balloons and tape them to the walls. As the IE Agent "strangers" agreed to help, real strangers began to help as well.

The Party-throwers began to raise their voices and explain to people on the train what was about to happen. "Hey everyone! We're throwing a surprise party and we need your help!" They passed out party hats and noisemakers, and the strangers (both real and planted) eagerly got ready for the party. "Our friend's name is Jesse! He's going to enter from the car over there at the Astor Place stop. One of our friends is with him to make sure he gets on this car." The Party-throwers had the undivided attention of everyone else in the smile-filled car.

"We're throwing a surprise party. Our friend is boarding the train in a few stops."

As the train began to near the Astor Place stop, Agent Todd yelled out the final instructions, "I'll give everyone the signal when he enters the car! We'll yell surprise, and then as soon as the doors close, we'll all sing Happy Birthday together! Remember, his name is Jesse! Okay, here's Astor Place. Shhhh! Shhhhh!" Agent Todd quieted the entire train and the passengers sat in silent, giddy anticipation of Agent (Jesse) Good. At the stop agent Good and Minton (playing the role of Agent Good's friend) exited the adjacent car, walked down the platform, and entered the party car.

"Surprise!" In unison, the train full of strangers shouted out with smiles and laughs. Agent Good stood flabbergasted. Agent Todd counted down, "1, 2, 3, Everyone! Happy Birthday to you . . .", and the entire train sang Happy Birthday to dear Jesse. Everyone clapped and blew their noisemakers with joy. Agent White shouted, "Who wants cupcakes!?" and began to distribute the food to all the hungry passengers. Agent Lovejoy set up the "pin the tail on the donkey"

▼ Strangers and Improv "agents" enjoy the party, complete with cupcakes and games.

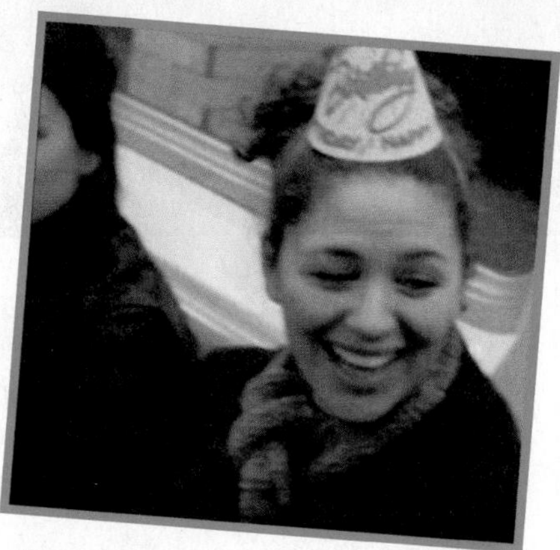

games and a few undercover IE "strangers" began to play, as others looked on with glee. The party throwers began to shout for Agent Good to make a speech, and Jesse delivered a heartfelt thank you to everyone on the train for coming to his party.

On the return trip, the agents threw another surprise party, this time with Agent Richardson as the birthday boy. The results were the same. In a matter of minutes, the train went from quiet and dull, to loud and festive. For both parties, IE Agents had the participation of the entire train. People of all different ages and races joined together in the name of fun. Everyone from the three-year-old Chinese girl and her father to the 60-year-old tourist couple from Holland donned party hats, blew up balloons, and ate cupcakes together. We created a multicultural party for strangers of all ages, and man it was fun. We refer to those we don't know in this report as "strangers," but as these parties prove, there really are no strangers in this world, only potential friends. Sappy? Yeah. True? Absolutely.

Other Highlights

- Agent Richardson declares his birthday cupcake to be "communal," takes a bite out of it, and passes it on. Four strangers take a bite of the same cupcake.
- Woman leaves the train skipping.
- Woman declares, "I have the best story to tell, but none of my friends are ever going to believe this!"
- Before the second party begins, Agent Good gets the ENTIRE train to crouch to the ground for the surprise.

Critical Reading

1. **(a)** What did Improv Everywhere preplan for the "Surprise!" mission? **(b)** What was the mission's goal? **(c) Assess:** How did the preplanned activities help the group reach the mission's goal?
2. **(a) Summarize:** Briefly summarize the ways strangers participated in "Surprise!" **(b) Speculate:** Why do you think the strangers participated?
3. **(a) Describe:** Describe the effect Improv Everywhere's "Surprise!" mission had on its participants. **(b) Evaluate:** What might be the value of such an experience to participants? Explain.

Use these questions to focus a class discussion of "Surprise!":

4. By posting descriptions of missions like "Surprise!" on the Web, how does Improv Everywhere advance its goals?
5. Why do you think groups like Improv Everywhere strive to playfully disrupt people's ordinary routines? What value might exist in these types of activities?

Building Knowledge and Insight

ANCHOR TEXT
Mirror • Courage

Connecting to the Essential Question These poems focus on private emotions, yet reflect a broader social anxiety that was first felt during the 1950s. As you read, look for details that might refer both to an individual and to society at large. Doing so will help you consider the Essential Question: **How does literature shape or reflect society?**

Common Core State Standards

Reading Literature
4. Determine the meaning of words and phrases as they are used in the text, including figurative and connotative meanings; analyze the impact of specific word choices on meaning and tone, including words with multiple meanings or language that is particularly fresh, engaging, or beautiful.

Language
5. Demonstrate understanding of figurative language, word relationships, and nuances in word meanings.
5.a. Interpret figures of speech in context and analyze their role in the text.

Close Reading Focus

Figurative Language

Figurative language is language that is used imaginatively rather than literally. Two types of figurative language, simile and metaphor, compare seemingly dissimilar things:

- A **simile** is a comparison that uses a connecting word such as *like* or *as*: "love as simple as shaving soap."
- A **metaphor** is a comparison that does not use a connecting word. Instead, the comparison is either implied or directly stated: "Your courage was a small coal."

Comparisons such as these are especially useful for poets such as Plath and Sexton, who use language to capture and contain large, powerful, or painful emotions. As you read, notice how each poet uses simile and metaphor to define strong emotions and ideas.

Preparing to Read Complex Texts Poetry uses all the layers of meaning in words, from their *denotation*, or literal definitions, to their *connotations*, or associations. Gather clues to a poem's meaning by **interpreting the connotations** of individual words. To do so, consider the associations and feelings a word calls to mind. For example, Sexton compares being bullied to drinking *acid*—a strong and surprising word. To interpret its connotations, consider why she chose *acid* rather than another word, such as *venom* or *poison.* Consider the range of feelings and meanings the word *acid* carries that other words do not. Then, consider what such a word suggests about the poem's essential meaning, or theme. As you read, use a chart like the one shown to interpret the connotative meanings of individual words.

Attention-Grabbing Word	Associations and Feelings

Vocabulary

The words below are important to understanding the texts that follow. Copy the words into your notebook. Which two words have the same prefix?

preconceptions **transfusion**
endured **transformed**

Sylvia Plath *(1932–1963)*

Author of "Mirror"

Despite her success as a writer, Sylvia Plath lived a short, unhappy life. In many of her poems, she expresses intense feelings of despair and deep inner pain. Born in Boston, Plath wrote poetry and received scholastic and literary awards as a young woman. Her first national publication appeared in the *Christian Science Monitor* in 1950, just after she graduated from high school. Although she had emotional difficulties during her years at Smith College, she graduated with highest honors in 1955. She also studied at Cambridge University in England, where she met and married poet Ted Hughes. Her first book of verse, *The Colossus and Other Poems* (1960), was the only book published during her lifetime. Four more books of poetry and a novel, *The Bell Jar* (1963), were published posthumously. In 1982, Plath was awarded the Pulitzer Prize for her collected poems, making her the first poet to win a Pulitzer Prize after death.

Anne Sexton *(1928–1974)*

Author of "Courage"

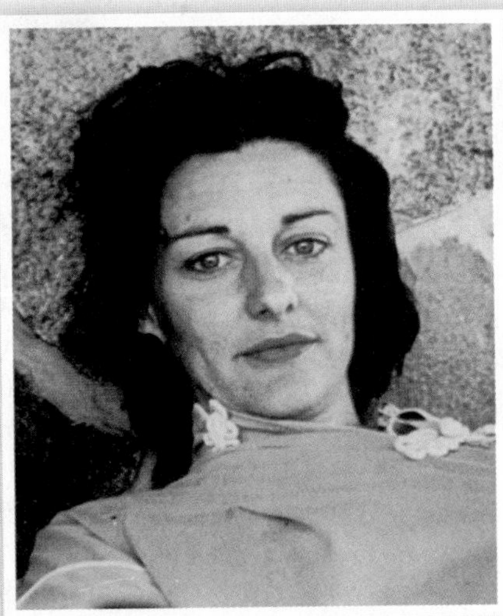

Like her contemporary Sylvia Plath, Anne Sexton led a life marked by mental anguish and profound creativity. Born in Newton, Massachusetts, Sexton married at age nineteen, dabbled in modeling, then gave birth to two daughters. Suffering from severe postpartum depression, Sexton was admitted to a psychiatric hospital for the first of many times in her life. She was encouraged by a doctor to pursue an interest in poetry, and in 1957 enrolled in a local poetry workshop. The quality of her work earned Sexton a scholarship to study with Robert Lowell at Boston University, and by 1960 she had published her first collection, *To Bedlam and Part Way Back.* She won a Pulitzer Prize in 1967. Like other "confessional" poets of the time, Sexton's poems gave readers an intimate and sometimes uncomfortable look at the poet's own troubled psyche.

Mirror

Sylvia Plath

Mirror II, George Tooker, © Addison Gallery of American Art, Phillips Academy, Andover, Massachusetts

▶ Critical Viewing

The artist titled this painting *Mirror II.* What ideas are common to both the painting and Plath's poem? **CONNECT**

Vocabulary

preconceptions (prē′ kən sep′ shənz) *n.* ideas formed beforehand

I am silver and exact. I have no **preconceptions.**
Whatever I see I swallow immediately
Just as it is, unmisted by love or dislike.
I am not cruel, only truthful—
The eye of a little god, four-cornered.
Most of the time I meditate on the opposite wall.
It is pink, with speckles. I have looked at it so long
I think it is a part of my heart. But it flickers.
Faces and darkness separate us over and over.
Now I am a lake. A woman bends over me,
Searching my reaches for what she really is.
Then she turns to those liars, the candles or the moon.
I see her back, and reflect it faithfully.
She rewards me with tears and an agitation of hands.
I am important to her. She comes and goes.
Each morning it is her face that replaces the darkness.
In me she has drowned a young girl, and in me an old woman
Rises toward her day after day, like a terrible fish.

COURAGE

Anne Sexton

It is in the small things we see it.
The child's first step,
as awesome as an earthquake.
The first time you rode a bike,
wallowing up the sidewalk.
The first spanking when your heart
went on a journey all alone.
When they called you crybaby
or poor or fatty or crazy
and made you into an alien,
you drank their acid
and concealed it.
Later,
if you faced the death of bombs and bullets
you did not do it with a banner,
you did it with only a hat to
cover your heart.
You did not fondle the weakness inside you
though it was there.
Your courage was a small coal
that you kept swallowing.
If your buddy saved you
and died himself in so doing,
then his courage was not courage,
it was love; love as simple as shaving soap.
Later,
if you have endured a great despair,
then you did it alone,
getting a transfusion from the fire,

Vocabulary

endured (en do͝ord′) *v.* held up under; withstood

transfusion (trans fyo͞o′ zhən) *n.* the transferring of a life-giving substance from a source to a recipient

Comprehension

According to the speaker, which childhood events require courage?

picking the scabs off your heart,
then wringing it out like a sock.
Next, my kinsman, you powdered your sorrow,
you gave it a back rub
and then you covered it with a blanket
and after it had slept a while
it woke to the wings of the roses
and was **transformed**.
Later,
when you face old age and its natural conclusion
your courage will still be shown in the little ways,
each spring will be a sword you'll sharpen,
those you love will live in a fever of love,
and you'll bargain with the calendar
and at the last moment
when death opens the back door
you'll put on your carpet slippers
and stride out.

Vocabulary
transformed (trans fôrmd′) *adj.* altered; changed

Critical Reading

Cite textual evidence to support your responses.

1. **Key Ideas and Details (a)** In "Mirror", how does the woman "reward" the speaker? **(b) Interpret:** Why do you think she reacts this way?
2. **Key Ideas and Details (a)** To whom does the woman turn? **(b) Interpret:** Why are they called "liars"?
3. **Key Ideas and Details (a)** According to the speaker of "Courage," what happens to sorrow after it sleeps? **(b) Draw Conclusions:** What information does this give you about the speaker's own experience?
4. **Key Ideas and Details (a) Interpret:** What is the "natural conclusion" of old age? **(b) Analyze:** Do you find the response of "you" to this conclusion natural? Explain.
5. **Integration of Knowledge and Ideas** What do the private concerns expressed in these poems suggest about larger issues in society? Explain. In your response use at least two of these Essential Question words: *anxiety, sympathize, identity, collective.* ***[Connecting to the Essential Question: How does literature shape or reflect society?]***

Close Reading Activities

Mirror • Courage

Literary Analysis

1. **Key Ideas and Details (a)** In "Mirror," what is the significance of the word *swallow* (line 2)? **(b)** In what ways does the word *swallow* add to the poem's meaning?
2. **Key Ideas and Details (a) Interpret the connotations** of the word *powdered* in "Courage" (line 32). What associations does the word carry? **(b)** What do these connotations suggest about the poem's essential meaning, or theme?
3. **Craft and Structure (a)** Identify three **metaphors** used in "Mirror." **(b)** What danger or threat does each of these metaphors suggest? **(c)** Which of these dangers comes to pass, and who is the victim?
4. **Craft and Structure (a)** With what **simile** does Plath conclude her poem? **(b)** What two dissimilar things are being compared? **(c)** Why do you think Plath chose to use a simile here—the only one in the poem—rather than a metaphor?
5. **Integration of Knowledge and Ideas (a)** Use a chart like the one shown to identify three metaphors in "Courage." **(b)** Taken together, what do these metaphors reveal about the life that "you" leads?

Metaphor	Things Compared	Significance

Common Core State Standards

Writing
2. Write informative texts to examine and convey complex ideas, concepts, and information clearly and accurately through the effective selection, organization, and analysis of content.

Language
4. Determine or clarify the meaning of unknown and multiple-meaning words and phrases based on *grades 11–12* reading and content, choosing flexibly from a range of strategies.

Vocabulary Acquisition and Use

Sentence Completions Use a vocabulary word to complete each sentence. Explain your choices.

1. The hikers ______ the rain for an hour, then sought shelter in a cave.
2. To keep the trial fair, only jurors with no ______ were chosen.
3. Many actors say that when they step onto the stage, they feel ______.
4. The doctors reported that only a blood ______ would save the patient's life.

Writing to Sources

Informative Text Both "Mirror" and "Courage" address the full sweep of a human life, from youth to adulthood to old age. However, the poets' portrayals of these stages of life are extremely different. Write an **essay** exploring how each speaker sees the process or progress of life. Consider these questions: What words describe each speaker's attitude toward aging? How are these attitudes depicted in the poem's images? Which portrayal is hopeful, and which is full of despair? Why?

Connecting to the Essential Question Some of Theodore Roethke's strongest images are drawn from childhood memories of his father's greenhouse. As you read, look for small-scale details with large-scale meaning. Doing so will contribute to your understanding of the Essential Question: **What is the relationship between literature and place?**

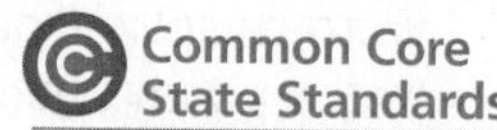
Common Core State Standards

Reading Literature

4. Analyze the impact of specific word choices on meaning and tone, including language that is particularly fresh, engaging, or beautiful.

5. Analyze how an author's choices concerning how to structure specific parts of a text contribute to its overall structure and meaning as well as its aesthetic impact.

Close Reading Focus

Sound Devices

Roethke's poignant, imagistic poetry achieves some of its emotional effect and beauty through **sound devices,** such as the following:

- **Alliteration** is the repetition of a consonant sound at the beginnings of words: "What saint strained so much, / Rose on such lopped limbs to a new life?"
- **Assonance** is the repetition of a vowel sound in stressed syllables with dissimilar consonant sounds: "I quail, lean to beginnings, sheath-wet."
- **Consonance** is the repetition of consonant sounds in stressed syllables in the middle or at the end of words: "The small cells bulge."

In "Cuttings" and "Cuttings (later)," Roethke ponders the microscopic movements of a plant—movements so small in scale that their sounds are undetectable by the human ear. Through his use of sound devices, the poet gives these tiny movements a music all their own, and invites the reader to move in close to hear the delicate strains.

Preparing to Read Complex Texts Sometimes poets dive deep into the complexities of nature, producing images that help readers see both nature and themselves in a new light. In these cases, **using background knowledge** about nature and its processes can help you understand the nuances of a poem. For these poems, refer to the background note or use other resources about cuttings and propagation of plants to add to your understanding. Use a chart like the one shown to apply background knowledge and clarify meaning as you read.

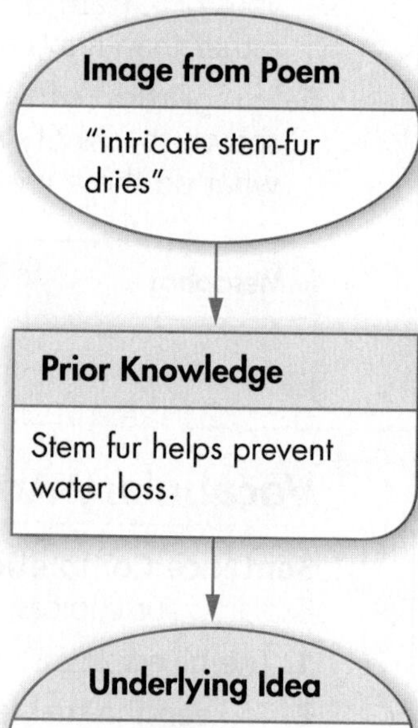
Image from Poem
"intricate stem-fur dries"
Prior Knowledge
Stem fur helps prevent water loss.
Underlying Idea
The plant is in some kind of crisis.

Vocabulary

The words below are important to understanding the texts that follow. Copy the words into your notebook. Which word has multiple meanings?

intricate

seeping

quail

Theodore Roethke

(1908–1963)

Author of "Cuttings" and "Cuttings (later)"

Theodore Roethke (ret′ kē) was born and raised in Saginaw, Michigan, where his family owned several large commercial greenhouses. As a boy, Roethke was a passionate observer of the plants that grew in the greenhouses. He observed nature putting forth roots and blossoms, as well as falling into dormancy and death. These observations later provided him with ideas and inspiration for many of his poems. In 1923, Roethke's father lost his battle with cancer, an event that also heavily influenced Roethke's poetry.

Refuge in Writing Throughout his life, Roethke found it difficult to relate to other people. Poetry and nature gave him a refuge in which to explore various aspects of his own life. Although his style changed throughout his career, the impulse to explore the meaning of subjective, personal experience remained a constant.

First Successes After receiving his education at the University of Michigan and Harvard, Roethke taught writing at Bennington College, Pennsylvania State University, and the University of Washington. A slow, diligent writer, he spent many years assembling poems for his first book. At age thirty-three, he published his first volume, *Open House* (1941), launching a career as one of the most acclaimed poets of his day. He won the Pulitzer Prize for *The Waking* (1953) and the National Book Award for *The Far Field* (1964), which was published after his death. From short, witty poems to complex, philosophical free verse, Roethke's poetry reflects a wide range of feelings and poetic styles.

Roethke published several more books, including *The Lost Son* (1948) and *Words for the Wind* (1958).

A Lasting Influence Theodore Roethke's work was an inspiration both to his contemporaries and to writers today. Remarking on his place in American literature, renowned poet Stanley Kunitz said Roethke "was in possession of a dynasty of extraordinary gifts and powers."

"Art is the means we have of undoing the damage of haste. It's what everything else isn't."

BACKGROUND: When Theodore Roethke's grandparents immigrated to the United States in 1872, they settled in Saginaw, Michigan, where they earned a living by growing and selling plants. Roethke's father and uncle inherited this trade and would go on to own one of the largest greenhouses in the state. As a child, Roethke spent countless hours in this greenhouse, gaining an informal but extensive education in the art and science of gardening. One of the many gardening strategies he learned was how to grow a new plant from a cutting. A cutting—also known as a slip—is a twig, branch, or leaf cut from a mature plant and placed in water or wet sand. Water moves upward through the cutting from its base by a process called diffusion. Diffusion occurs when water molecules move from areas of high concentration to areas of low concentration by passing through the walls of cells. As more and more water enters the cells of the cutting, water pressure builds, which in turn causes the cutting to stand upright. Water pressure also stimulates cell growth, and soon, under the proper conditions, the cutting will sprout new roots and leaves. When the roots are strong enough, the cutting—now a plant—can be potted in soil.

Cuttings

Theodore Roethke

Sticks-in-a-drowse droop over sugary loam,
Their **intricate** stem-fur dries;
But still the delicate slips keep coaxing up water;
The small cells bulge;

One nub of growth
Nudges a sand-crumb loose,
Pokes through a musty sheath
Its pale tendrilous horn.

Vocabulary
intricate (in′ tri kit) *adj.* complex; having many small, interrelated parts

Cuttings (later)

Theodore Roethke

This urge, wrestle, resurrection of dry sticks,
Cut stems struggling to put down feet,
What saint strained so much,
Rose on such lopped limbs to a new life?

I can hear, underground, that sucking and sobbing,
In my veins, in my bones I feel it,—
The small waters **seeping** upward,
The tight grains parting at last.
When sprouts break out,
Slippery as fish,
I **quail,** lean to beginnings, sheath-wet.

Vocabulary

seeping (sēp´ iŋ) *v.* flowing slowly

quail (kwāl) *v.* draw back in fear; lose heart

Critical Reading

Cite textual evidence to support your responses.

1. **Key Ideas and Details** **(a)** In "Cuttings," what are the "delicate slips" doing? **(b) Analyze Cause and Effect:** What are two results of this action?
2. **Key Ideas and Details** **(a) Infer:** What seems to be happening inside the plant? **(b) Interpret:** What details in the poem confirm this observation?
3. **Craft and Structure** **(a)** In line 1 of "Cuttings (later)," what verbs does the poet use to describe what is happening? **(b) Distinguish:** How do these verbs suggest that the second poem is different from the first?
4. **Integration of Knowledge and Ideas** Do you think these poems document observed reality? Explain. In your response use at least two of these Essential Question words: *subjective, objective, scene, clarity, perceptions. **[Connecting to the Essential Question: What is the relationship between literature and place?]***

Cuttings • Cuttings (later)

Literary Analysis

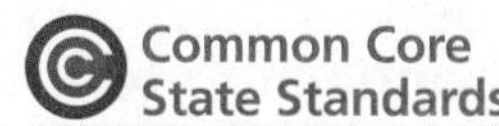

Language
3. Apply knowledge of language to understand how language functions in different contexts, to make effective choices for meaning or style, and to comprehend more fully when reading or listening.

1. **Key Ideas and Details** **(a) Apply background knowledge** to your reading of "Cuttings" to explain the natural processes indicated by the phrases "delicate slips keep coaxing up water" and "small cells bulge"? **(b)** In what way does this process reflect human growth or transformation?
2. **Craft and Structure** Use a chart like the one shown to analyze **sound devices** Roethke uses in these poems. **(a)** Identify one example of **alliteration, assonance,** and **consonance** from either poem. **(b)** Describe how each example brings an image to life or extends the poem's meaning.

	Example	Effect
alliteration		
assonance		
consonance		

3. **Craft and Structure** **(a)** In general, would you describe the sounds of "Cuttings" as easy and fluid or as mildly jarring? Explain. **(b)** How does this sound quality help convey the poem's central message?
4. **Integration of Knowledge and Ideas** Based on these poems, what do you think plant growth would sound like if human ears were sensitive enough to hear it?

Vocabulary Acquisition and Use

Revise for Logic Revise each sentence so that the underlined word is used logically.

1. The dance was so intricate even a beginner could perform it well.
2. If you quail at the mere thought of a horror film, then *Things That Go Bump in the Night* is the movie for you!
3. Seeping water is a sign that your roof is in fine shape.

Writing to Sources

Informative Text Research plant growth in a science book or on a science Web site. Compare and contrast the information in the science text with the depictions in Roethke's poems. Then, write an **essay** in which you evaluate each type of writing. Describe the types of language used in these different contexts as well as the authors' purposes and perspectives. Take a position about which presentation of plant growth is more engaging.

Building Knowledge and Insight

The Explorer • Frederick Douglass

Connecting to the Essential Question These poems express longings for a life or a future that is different from the present. As you read, notice details that speak to longings and hopes. Doing so will help you consider the Essential Question: **How does literature shape or reflect society?**

Common Core State Standards

Reading Literature

4. Analyze the impact of specific word choices on meaning and tone, including language that is particularly fresh, engaging, or beautiful.

5. Analyze how an author's choices concerning how to structure specific parts of a text contribute to its overall structure and meaning as well as its aesthetic impact.

Close Reading Focus

Repetition; Parallelism

Writers, including poets, use various *rhetorical devices* to emphasize messages or evoke emotions in their readers. Repetition and parallelism are two devices that often appear in poetry:

- **Repetition** is the repeating of key words or concepts: "Wee griefs, / Grand griefs. And choices. / He feared most of all the choices. . . ."
- **Parallelism** is the presentation of similar ideas using the same grammatical structures: "When it is finally ours. . . . / when it belongs at last to all, / when it is truly instinct. . . . "

In the first example above, the repetition of *griefs* and *choices* helps communicate the idea that one's grief is related to one's choices. In the second example, the repetition of the grammatical structure *when it* . . . builds a sense of urgency and expectation.

Comparing Literary Works As you read these poems, find examples of repetition and parallelism. Consider the specific purposes—emphasis or emotion—these devices help each poet achieve.

Preparing to Read Complex Texts When poets—and people—repeat words or phrases over and over, they are most likely trying to get your attention. When we read a text silently, though, it can be easy to gloss over repeated elements in order to get more quickly to "the point." As a result, we may miss the point altogether. To give these poems your full attention and to aid your comprehension, **read the poems aloud.** When you encounter repetition, slow down and emphasize it. Listen for the poet's use of repetition, parallelism, and other literary elements in these poems. Use a chart like the one shown to analyze the effects of reading passages aloud.

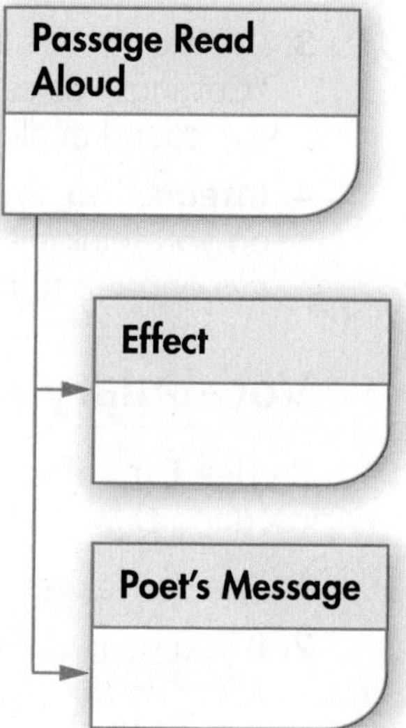

Vocabulary

The words below are important to understanding the texts that follow. Copy the words into your notebook. Which word could be an adjective or a verb?

frayed **gaudy**

wily

Gwendolyn Brooks

(1917–2000)

Author of "The Explorer"

Gwendolyn Brooks was raised in a Chicago neighborhood known as "Bronzeville"—the setting for her first book, *A Street in Bronzeville* (1945). Although her early poems focus on struggling urban blacks who feel uprooted and are unable to make a living, Brooks's own youth was quite different. Her home was warm and her family loving, supportive, and confident that Brooks would find success as a writer. Brooks began writing poetry at the age of seven. Her first published poem, "Eventide," appeared in *American Childhood* Magazine in 1930. When she was in high school, her mother took her to meet Harlem Renaissance poets Langston Hughes and James Weldon Johnson, who encouraged her interests.

Dedication and Recognition By the time she was sixteen, Brooks had published approximately seventy-five poems in local publications. She continued to study, write, and hone her craft. Her first book of poetry garnered critical acclaim. With the publication of her second book, *Annie Allen,* in 1950, she became the first African American writer to win a Pulitzer Prize. Honors and prizes followed throughout her career.

A New Generation Inspired by the civil rights movement of the 1960s—and its new generation of young black activists and artists—Brooks's works became increasingly political and experimental. As noted author Toni Cade Bambara remarked in the *New York Times Book Review,* Brooks's later works were marked by "a new movement and energy, intensity, richness, power of statement and a new stripped lean, compressed style. A change of style prompted by a change of mind."

By the time of her death at the turn of the twenty-first century, Brooks had become one of the most highly regarded poets of our time.

"I WANT
THESE
POEMS TO
BE FREE."

THE EXPLORER

GWENDOLYN BROOKS

Vocabulary

frayed (frād) *adj.* tattered

wily (wī´ lē) *adj.* sly; cunning

Somehow to find a still spot in the noise
Was the frayed inner want, the winding, the frayed hope
Whose tatters he kept hunting through the din.
A satin peace somewhere.
A room of wily hush somewhere within.

So tipping down the scrambled halls he set
Vague hands on throbbing knobs. There were behind
Only spiraling, high human voices,
The scream of nervous affairs,
Wee griefs,
Grand griefs. And choices.

He feared most of all the choices, that cried to be taken.

There were no bourns.[1]
There were no quiet rooms.

---

1. **bourns** (bōrnz) *n.* limits; boundaries.

Critical Reading

1. **Key Ideas and Details** **(a)** What is the "inner want" the speaker expresses? **(b) Interpret:** In what way does the title of the poem relate to the "inner want"?
2. **Craft and Structure** **(a)** What might the explorer's apartment building symbolize? **(b) Interpret:** What might the explorer's actions and feelings symbolize?
3. **Integration of Knowledge and Ideas** Why do you think people often fear making choices?

Robert Hayden *(1913–1980)*

Author of "Frederick Douglass"

Born in Detroit, Robert Hayden had a difficult childhood. He faced poverty, coped with the emotional difficulties of an unstable family, and struggled with extreme nearsightedness. Though his poor vision prevented him from playing sports, it did not stop him from reading. Hayden devoted his days to books, developing an appreciation for the transformative qualities of literature.

Experience, Research, and Art Hayden attended Detroit City College (now Wayne State University). In 1936, he joined the Federal Writers' Project, researching African American history and folk culture. The depth of historical awareness he gained from this research contributed to his poetry and artistry. As a young, politically active writer in the 1930s, he protested both the social and economic conditions of African Americans and what he saw as the nation's inadequate care of the poor.

Hayden was an extremely versatile writer who used a variety of poetic forms and techniques. While working toward his master's degree, he studied under W. H. Auden (p. 773), who influenced Hayden's choices of form and technique.

Publications and Honors During his career, Hayden published several collections of poetry, including *A Ballad of Remembrance* (1962), which won the Grand Prize for Poetry at the First World Festival for Negro Arts in 1966. From 1976 to 1978, Hayden served as Consultant in Poetry to the Library of Congress, a position later known as "Poet Laureate."

Although Hayden sought to undo racial stereotypes and to tell a truthful version of his people's history, he did not believe that race should define a poet. Instead, he believed that identity serves as a starting point from which to offer insights that transcend race and speak to all people.

"[My poetry is] a way of coming to grips with reality . . . a way of discovery and definition."

The Life of Frederick Douglass, #30, Jacob Lawrence, The Jacob and Gwendolyn Lawrence Foundation, Artists Rights Society (ARS), New York

FREDERICK DOUGLASS

ROBERT HAYDEN

BACKGROUND Frederick Douglass (1817–1895) was a leading abolitionist during the 19th century. (See the excerpt from Douglass's autobiography on pages 520–527; see also "Douglass" by Paul Laurence Dunbar on page 636.)

When it is finally ours, this freedom, this liberty,
    this beautiful
and terrible thing, needful to man as air,
usable as earth; when it belongs at last to all,
when it is truly instinct, brain matter, diastole, systole,[1]
reflex action; when it is finally won; when it is more
than the gaudy mumbo jumbo of politicians:
this man, this Douglass, this former slave, this Negro
beaten to his knees, exiled, visioning a world
where none is lonely, none hunted, alien,
this man, superb in love and logic, this man
shall be remembered. Oh, not with statues' rhetoric,
not with legends and poems and wreaths of bronze alone,
but with the lives grown out of his life, the lives
fleshing his dream of the beautiful, needful thing.

1. **diastole** (dī as´ tə lē´), **systole** (sis´ tə lē´) Diastole is the normal rhythmic dilation, or opening, of the heart. Systole is the normal rhythmic closing of the heart.

◀ Critical Viewing
What impression of Douglass does this painting convey? **ANALYZE**

Vocabulary
gaudy (gô´ dē) *adj.* showy in a tasteless way

Critical Reading

1. **Key Ideas and Details (a)** What is the "beautiful and terrible" thing? **(b) Infer:** To whom does it not yet belong?
2. **Integration of Knowledge and Ideas Speculate:** How might Frederick Douglass react to this poem? Explain.
3. **Integration of Knowledge and Ideas** What type of world do the speakers in these poems hope to see realized? Explain. In your response, use at least two of these Essential Question words: *liberty, ambition, vision, lament, idealism.* ***[Connecting to the Essential Question: How does literature shape or reflect society?]***

Cite textual evidence to support your responses.

Literary Analysis

1. **Craft and Structure (a)** Identify an example of **repetition** in the first stanza of "The Explorer." **(b)** How does this repetition help the poet develop a particular idea?
2. **Craft and Structure** Use a chart like the one shown to identify examples of **parallelism** in each poem. **(a)** Note the example of **parallelism** in the last two lines of "The Explorer." **(b)** Identify an example of parallelism in lines 7–14 of "Frederick Douglass." **(c)** Explain how each example of parallelism heightens the emotional energy of the poem.

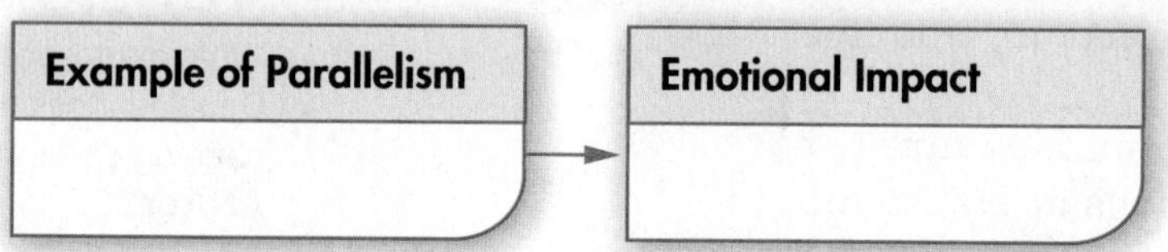

3. **Craft and Structure (a)** What phrase is used to describe Douglass once in line 7 and twice in line 10? **(b)** Why do you think the poet chose to repeat this particular phrase?
4. **Craft and Structure (a)** List lines or phrases from each poem that are particularly striking when **read aloud. (b)** Then, explain how reading the passage aloud helps to clarify its meaning.
5. **Craft and Structure (a)** In what ways does reading aloud emphasize the poets' use of repetition? **(b)** From having read the poems aloud, do you better understand the poets' uses of parallelism? Explain.
6. **Craft and Structure** In your view, which poem lends itself more naturally to an oral reading? Why do you think this is?
7. **Integration of Knowledge and Ideas** Frederick Douglass was an orator, or public speaker, as well as an abolitionist. How does the form of Hayden's poem pay tribute to this aspect of Douglass's life?
8. **Integration of Knowledge and Ideas (a)** Which of the two poems do you find more emotionally moving? Explain. **(b)** Do you attribute this to its message or to the poet's uses of rhetorical devices, such as repetition and parallelism? Explain.

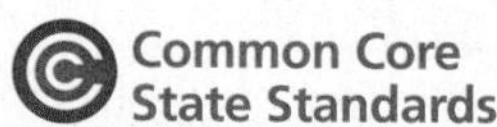

Common Core State Standards

Writing

2. Write explanatory texts to examine and convey complex ideas, concepts, and information clearly and accurately through the effective selection, organization, and analysis of content. *(p. 1069)*

2.b. Develop the topic thoroughly by selecting the most significant and relevant facts, extended definitions, concrete details, quotations, or other information and examples appropriate to the audience's knowledge of the topic. *(p. 1069)*

Language

4. Determine or clarify the meaning of unknown and multiple-meaning words and phrases based on *grades 11–12 reading and content,* choosing flexibly from a range of strategies. *(p. 1069)*

4.a. Use context as a clue to the meaning of a word or phrase. *(p. 1069)*

5. Demonstrate understanding of word relationships. *(p. 1069)*

Vocabulary Acquisition and Use

Word Analysis: Word/Phrase Relationships

The meaning of a descriptive word can change when it is connected to other words in a phrase. For example, the adjective *rigid* means "stiff" in the phrase *rigid posture*, but "harsh" or "severe" in the phrase *rigid rules.* Read each pair of sentences below. Explain how the meaning of the word differs in the context of each underlined phrase.

1. My frayed shirt is soft and comfortable.
   She expressed her frayed emotions in a long letter.
2. Lots of gaudy jewelry made the costume complete.
   The gaudy compliment fell on deaf ears.
3. The wily fox crept close to his prey.
   A thin, wily moon gave little guidance to the midnight travelers.

Vocabulary: Assessing Logic

Each sentence below features an underlined word from the vocabulary list on page 1062. For each item, explain whether the sentence makes sense, given the meaning of the underlined word. If it does not make sense, write a new sentence using the word correctly.

1. It is difficult to coax a frayed piece of thread through the narrow eye of a needle.
2. The wily behavior of the new mayor was reassuring to all those who had voted for him.
3. Our apartment complex has strict rules about holiday decorations: Only gaudy lights and plain green wreaths are allowed.

Writing to Sources

Explanatory Text In an **essay,** examine "The Explorer" and "Frederick Douglass" through two different critical lenses. First, *use a social perspective,* analyzing how each poem reflects the struggles of African Americans during the mid-twentieth century. Then, *use an archetypal perspective,* demonstrating how each poem expresses universal human longings.

Prewriting First, read each poem with the social perspective in mind. Jot down possible connections between details in the poem and issues in mid-1900s America. Then, read each poem from an archetypal perspective, making note of images and symbols with universal power and appeal.

Drafting Begin your essay with a general statement about the poem and the points you will cover. Then, present your material in an organized way: Discuss one poem from both perspectives, and then discuss the other poem from both perspectives; or, apply one perspective to both poems, and then apply the other perspective to both poems.

Model: Using Quotations to Support Interpretation

The poet speaks to and about all humans when she acknowledges the ~~worries, large and small, that make up~~ daily life.
[inserted: "wee griefs" and "grand griefs" ... of]

Using direct quotations supports the interpretation of the poem.

Revising Identify points in your draft at which you make important general statements about the poem. Strengthen your analysis by adding accurate quotations from the poems to support your interpretation.

Connecting to the Essential Question In "One Art," the speaker explores the idea of losing objects, time, and—surprisingly—places. As you read these poems, look for places that have been lost and those that have been found. Doing so will help you consider the Essential Question: **What is the relationship between literature and place?**

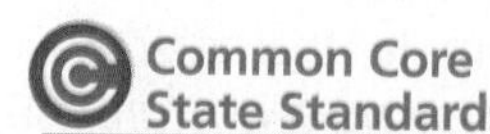

Reading Literature

4. Analyze the impact of specific word choices on meaning and tone, including language that is particularly fresh, engaging, or beautiful.

5. Analyze how an author's choices concerning how to structure specific parts of a text contribute to its overall structure and meaning as well as its aesthetic impact.

Close Reading Focus

Diction; Rhetorical Devices

While Elizabeth Bishop's poems are elegant and carefully crafted, they create the feeling of a conversation between poet and reader. Several literary elements produce this double effect. The first is Bishop's **diction,** or word choice. For example, *master* and *disaster* are the rhyming words that cycle through the *villanelle* "One Art." These are ordinary words, yet their repetition invites readers to see them in new ways. Bishop also draws readers in through her use of **rhetorical devices**—word patterns that create emphasis and stir emotion:

- **Imperatives:** Mild commands invite readers to do or feel certain things. Example: "Lose something every day."
- **Exclamations:** Statements ending in an exclamation point inject an emotional intensity. Example: "Oh, but it is dirty!"
- **Questions:** Questions cast the reader in the role of the speaker's confidant. Example: "Why, oh why, the doily?"

As you read, use a chart like the one shown to note Bishop's use of rhetorical devices and the ways in which they involve the reader in the poems.

Rhetorical Device
Imperative: "Accept the fluster/of lost door keys..."

↓

How It Involves the Reader
The reader is asked to adopt a new attitude toward minor disasters.

Preparing to Read Complex Texts Many poems—including "One Art" and "Filling Station"—are written in sentences and use the same punctuation marks that you find in prose. To *clarify the meaning of a poem,* **read according to punctuation.** As you read these poems, do not pause at line breaks. Instead, pause when you encounter a comma, a colon, a semicolon, a dash, or an end mark.

Vocabulary

You will encounter the words listed here in the texts that follow. Copy the words into your notebook. Which word can be used as either a verb or a noun?

master | **permeated**
intent | **extraneous**

Elizabeth Bishop (1911–1979)

Author of "One Art" and "Filling Station"

Northern Roots The title of Elizabeth Bishop's first poetry collection, *North & South,* reflects the range of both her poetic skill and her world travels. These travels began in Worcester, Massachusetts, where Bishop was born. After the death of her father and the mental collapse of her mother, Bishop was raised by her grandparents. She attended Vassar College, where she founded a literary journal, *Con Spirito,* and began a lifelong friendship with fellow poet Marianne Moore.

Southern Sojourns After graduating from college, Bishop, who was independently wealthy, set out to see the world. She traveled first to France, where she spent a winter in Paris, and then south through the Mediterranean to North Africa. Her poetry from this period is filled with descriptions of sights from her travels—a subject to which she would return, exquisitely, throughout her career.

In 1938, Bishop bought an old house in Key West, Florida, and remained there for several years before heading even farther south. First, she visited Mexico, where she met the poet Pablo Neruda and learned Spanish. She then settled in Brazil, where she lived for almost twenty years. After the devastating loss of a close friend, Bishop returned to the United States, where she spent the rest of her life. She taught at Harvard University from 1970 to 1977.

Poet of Precision Bishop's poetry is celebrated for its precise, true-to-life images and for its polished and often witty language. Her belief that poetry should use the same sentence patterns as good prose gives her verse a conversational quality, though its subject matter is rarely personal. Instead, many of her poems focus on working-class settings such as factories and farms, or on universal human emotions such as grief and longing. Meticulous in the crafting of every line, Bishop wrote slowly and she published sparingly—nevertheless winning the Pulitzer Prize in poetry for *North and South* in 1956, and National Book Awards in 1965 and 1970. By the end of her life, the brilliance of her work had been fully appreciated, and she was hailed as one of the major American poets of the century.

ONE ART

ELIZABETH BISHOP

The art of losing isn't hard to master;
so many things seem filled with the intent
to be lost that their loss is no disaster.

Lose something every day. Accept the fluster
of lost door keys, the hour badly spent.
The art of losing isn't hard to master.

Then practice losing farther, losing faster:
places, and names, and where it was you meant
to travel. None of these will bring disaster.

I lost my mother's watch. And look! my last, or
next-to-last, of three loved houses went.
The art of losing isn't hard to master.

I lost two cities, lovely ones. And, vaster,
some realms I owned, two rivers, a continent.
I miss them, but it wasn't a disaster.

—Even losing you (the joking voice, a gesture
I love) I shan't have lied. It's evident
the art of losing's not too hard to master
though it may look like (*Write* it!) like disaster.

Vocabulary

master (mas´ tər) *v.* become an expert in

intent (in tent´) *n.* purpose or aim

LITERATURE IN CONTEXT

Poetic Structure

The Villanelle

"One Art" is a *villanelle,* a highly structured poem consisting of nineteen lines, two repeating end rhymes, and two refrains. These elements are arranged in a set way, as you can see in "One Art." Notice that the refrains—the first line of the first stanza, and the word *disaster* from the third line of the first stanza—are repeated alternately as the last lines of stanzas 2 through 5, and then repeated together at the end of stanza 6. Notice, too, that every first and third line ends with the *-aster* sound (or its near-rhyme *-uster*) and that every second line ends with the *-ent* sound. When the villanelle first appeared in sixteenth century France, it had a looser structure and focused on pastoral themes. Contemporary poets have used the villanelle to treat a broader range of themes, but within a tighter structure. The modern villanelle allows for slight changes in the refrains, which often signal an evolution in the speaker's thoughts.

Connect to the Literature

What evolution in the speaker's thoughts is evident from the changing refrain in "One Art"? Explain.

◀ **Critical Viewing** Elizabeth Bishop painted this landscape of a mountain valley in Brazil. In what ways does the painting echo the idea expressed in "One Art" of owning a realm? **INTERPRET**

Filling Station

Elizabeth Bishop

Oh, but it is dirty!
—this little filling station,
oil-soaked, oil-**permeated**
to a disturbing, over-all
black translucency.
Be careful with that match!

Father wears a dirty,
oil-soaked monkey suit
that cuts him under the arms,
and several quick and saucy
and greasy sons assist him
(it's a family filling station),
all quite thoroughly dirty.

Do they live in the station?
It has a cement porch
behind the pumps, and on it
a set of crushed and grease-
impregnated wickerwork;
on the wicker sofa
a dirty dog, quite comfy.

Some comic books provide
the only note of color—
of certain color. They lie
upon a big dim doily

Vocabulary
permeated (pʉr′ mē āt′ əd) *adj.* soaked through with

Comprehension
What is the poet's first impression of the filling station?

◀ **Critical Viewing** Could the filling station shown in this painting be the one the speaker describes in the poem? Explain. **MAKE A JUDGMENT**

draping a taboret
(part of the set), beside
a big hirsute begonia.

Vocabulary
extraneous (ek strā´ nē əs) *adj.* unrelated or unconnected

Why the extraneous plant?
Why the taboret?
Why, oh why, the doily?
(Embroidered in daisy stitch
with marguerites, I think,
and heavy with gray crochet.)

Somebody embroidered the doily.
Somebody waters the plant,
or oils it, maybe. Somebody
arranges the rows of cans
so that they softly say:
ESSO—SO—SO—SO
to high-strung automobiles.
Somebody loves us all.

Critical Reading

Cite textual evidence to support your responses.

1. **Key Ideas and Details (a)** In "One Art," what are some things the speaker has lost? **(b) Interpret:** What do you think the speaker means by "practice losing farther, losing faster"? **(c) Make Inferences:** What does the speaker suggest will be the result of such practice?
2. **Key Ideas and Details (a)** According to the speaker, none of the losses has brought what? **(b) Assess:** Do you take this claim at face value, or do you suspect otherwise? Explain.
3. **Key Ideas and Details (a)** In line 14 of "Filling Station," what does the speaker wonder? **(b) Identify:** Cite three details that prompt the speaker to ask this question. Explain.
4. **Integration of Knowledge and Ideas Generalize:** Reread the poem's first and last lines. What might the poet be communicating about the world at large?
5. **Integration of Knowledge and Ideas** Are the places the speaker loses and finds in these poems parts of the actual, physical world, or parts of an emotional world? Explain. In your response, use at least two of these Essential Question words: *landscape, personal, lament, exile. **[Connecting to the Essential Question: What is the relationship between literature and place?]***

Close Reading Activities

One Art • *Filling Station*

Literary Analysis

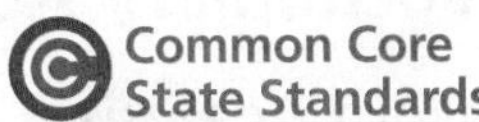

Common Core State Standards

Writing

5. Develop and strengthen writing as needed by planning, revising, editing, rewriting, or trying a new approach, focusing on addressing what is most significant for a specific purpose and audience. *(p. 1078)*

6. Use technology, including the Internet, to produce, publish, and update individual or shared writing products. *(p. 1078)*

Language

4.b. Identify and correctly use patterns of word changes that indicate different meanings or parts of speech. *(p. 1078)*

5. Demonstrate understanding of word relationships. *(p. 1078)*

1. **Craft and Structure** Read "One Art" aloud, pausing at the end of each line. Then, read it aloud according to punctuation. **(a)** What happens to the rhymes when you read the poem in sentences? **(b)** How does reading the poem according to punctuation help you better understand its meaning? Use a chart like the one below to analyze how different approaches to reading affect what you understand about each line.

Single Line	Complete Sentence	Meaning

2. **Craft and Structure** Because of its cycling, repeating form, the *villanelle* "One Art" highlights Bishop's **diction. (a)** What two words does the speaker repeat? **(b)** In what ways do these two words, taken together, capture an important part of the poem's overall meaning? **(c)** How does the repetition of these words subtly contradict this message?
3. **Craft and Structure** **(a)** Identify three **imperatives** in "One Art." **(b)** Why might the speaker urge the reader to do these things? **(c)** Why might the speaker need to address *herself* with these imperatives?
4. **Craft and Structure** Skim "Filling Station," **reading according to punctuation.** Compare the effects of this reading with one in which you follow the line breaks.
5. **Craft and Structure** **(a)** Identify three adjectives, nouns, or verbs that repeat in "Filling Station." **(b)** Do you consider these words particularly "poetic"? Explain. **(c)** Why do you think Bishop chose to repeat such words multiple times?
6. **Craft and Structure** How does Bishop's use of parentheses add to the intimate, conversational quality of her poems?
7. **Integration of Knowledge and Ideas** **(a)** Identify one **exclamation** and one **question** from either "One Art" or "Filling Station." **(b)** Rewrite each as a statement ending with a period. **(c)** Imagine that the poet had used the rewritten statements rather than the originals. How would this have changed the poem or your experience of the poem?

Close Reading Activities Continued

Vocabulary Acquisition and Use

Word Analysis: Latin Word *extra*

The Latin word *extra* means "additional," "outside," or "beyond." In English, *extra* is sometimes used on its own; sometimes used as a root, as in *extraneous*; and often used as a prefix, as in *extraordinary*. For each of the words shown below, write a definition that includes either the word *additional, outside,* or *beyond*. Use a dictionary as necessary to aid your work.

1. extraordinary
2. extrasensory
3. extraterrestrial
4. extrasolar
5. extracranial
6. extracurricular

Vocabulary: Synonyms

Synonyms are words that share the same or similar meanings. Choose the best synonym for each vocabulary word below. Explain your choices.

1. **permeated** **a.** stung **b.** attached **c.** soaked
2. **extraneous** **a.** challenging **b.** irrelevant **c.** dense
3. **master** **a.** learn **b.** spend **c.** choose
4. **intent** **a.** goal **b.** aversion **c.** pretense

Writing to Sources

Explanatory Text Prepare a response to "One Art" and "Filling Station" in more than one genre, or form. Illustrate the poems with drawings, paintings, photographs, or a collage of images from other sources, including the Internet. Then, write an **explanation** of your choices. Finally, combine the images with the text in a poster to display in your classroom.

Prewriting Reread each poem, paying close attention to visual descriptions. Consider the images that form in your mind and how you will communicate themes in visual terms. Decide if your images will summarize the poem, draw conclusions about the poem, or depict your own personal reactions.

Model: Linking Images to Poem

Illustration	Connection to Poem
Photograph of dirt in a field	At first, the viewer of the filling station sees only dirt and grime.

Drafting As you draft your written explanation, refer to your illustration. Explain the thematic connections between the artwork and the poem.

Revising Reread your writing to make sure you have related your ideas to your illustration. Strengthen weak links by adding transitional words or quotations. Then, combine your writing and your illustration into a poster, making sure to observe the principles of design, such as effective use of fonts and white space.

TEXT SET

Literature of Protest

Part 3

Building Knowledge and Insight *The Rockpile*

Connecting to the Essential Question John, the main character in this story, is an outsider in almost all aspects of his life. As you read, look for details that reveal characters as insiders or outsiders. This will help you consider the Essential Question: **How does literature shape or reflect society?**

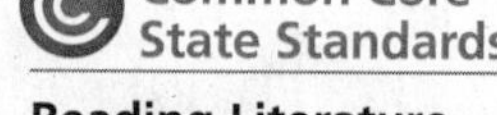

Common Core
State Standards

Reading Literature

3. Analyze the impact of the author's choices regarding how to develop and relate elements of a story or drama (e.g., where a story is set).

5. Analyze how an author's choices concerning how to structure specific parts of a text contribute to its overall structure and meaning as well as its aesthetic impact.

Close Reading Focus

Setting; Symbol

The **setting** of a story is the time and place in which it occurs; it may include details about the weather, physical features of the landscape, and other elements of an environment. "The Rockpile" is set in Harlem during the 1930s. Life in that time and place was influenced by the difficult economic and social realities that people faced.

A story's setting can also serve as a symbol. A **symbol** is a person, place, or object that has a meaning in itself but also suggests a larger meaning. While it is not the story's only symbol, the rockpile that dominates the setting is its most important one. Among other meanings, it can be interpreted as a symbol for violence and failure in the community:

They fought on the rockpile. Sure footed, dangerous, and reckless, they rushed each other and grappled on the heights . . .

As you read, note how the narrator describes the rockpile, the characters that are associated with it, and the events that take place there. These details will help you interpret the symbolic meanings of the rockpile.

Preparing to Read Complex Texts A *cause* is the reason something happens. An *effect* is the result. Often, situations have multiple causes and multiple effects. You will understand the characters and events in a story better if you **identify cause-and-effect relationships** among them. For example, in this story, a child's disobedience results in a series of events that reveal a complicated family dynamic. As you read, use a chart like the one shown to record the reasons for characters' actions and their effects on others.

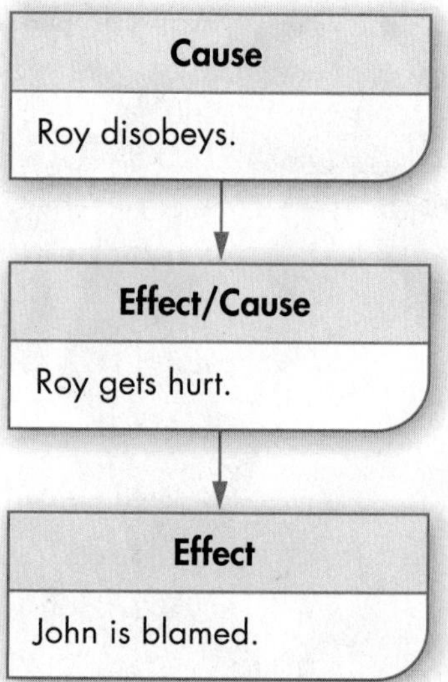

Cause
Roy disobeys.
Effect/Cause
Roy gets hurt.
Effect
John is blamed.

Vocabulary

You will encounter the words listed here in the text that follows. Copy the words into your notebook, sorting them into words you know and words you do not know.

latent
engrossed
jubilant
superficial
perdition

JAMES BALDWIN (1924–1987)

Author of "The Rockpile"

James Baldwin once told an interviewer that he "never had a childhood." Because his stepfather worked long hours as both a preacher and a factory hand, Baldwin was given much of the responsibility for raising his eight half brothers and half sisters. His main leisure activity was reading. He explained, "As [my half brothers and half sisters] were born, I took them over with one hand and held a book with the other . . . ; in this way, in fact, I read just about everything I could get my hands on." Baldwin's love for reading deepened his imagination, planting the seeds of inspiration for his later success as a writer.

A Harlem Childhood Baldwin was born in Harlem, the New York community that served as a cultural center for African Americans during the 1920s and 1930s. As a young boy, it was clear that he had a gift for words, but Baldwin's deeply religious parents disapproved of his interest in literature. At age fourteen, Baldwin followed their wishes and became a preacher. However, encouraged by poet Countee Cullen, who taught in Baldwin's junior high school, and inspired by author Richard Wright, Baldwin decided to devote his life to writing.

The Road to "Writer" For several years, Baldwin worked at odd jobs while writing in his spare time. When he was twenty-four, he won a fellowship that enabled him to live and write in Europe. For the next four years, he lived in Paris where he completed his first novel, *Go Tell It on the Mountain* (1953). The book marked the beginning of a distinguished career that included novels short stories, essays, and plays.

A Powerful Witness Baldwin once said, "One writes out of one thing only—one's own experience. Everything depends on how relentlessly one forces from this experience the last drop, sweet or bitter, it can possibly give." Baldwin's work bears powerful witness to his own experience as an African American. He expresses the need for social justice as well as the universal desire for love. Because his books dig deeply into contemporary life, they are sometimes painful to read, but the pain is always tempered by hope, and by Baldwin's magnificent language.

"It is certain, in any case, that ignorance, allied with power, is the most ferocious enemy justice can have."

ARCO
NO

The Rockpile

James Baldwin

BACKGROUND Even though he spent most of his adult life in Europe, James Baldwin's impassioned voice is full of the rhythms and details of life in Harlem, the New York City neighborhood where he grew up. This story, about a struggling Harlem family, is a strong example of Baldwin's connection to the place that shaped him as both a writer and a person.

Across the street from their house, in an empty lot between two houses, stood the rockpile. It was a strange place to find a mass of natural rock jutting out of the ground; and someone, probably Aunt Florence, had once told them that the rock was there and could not be taken away because without it the subway cars underground would fly apart, killing all the people. This, touching on some natural mystery concerning the surface and the center of the earth, was far too intriguing an explanation to be challenged, and it invested the rockpile, moreover, with such mysterious importance that Roy felt it to be his right, not to say his duty, to play there.

Setting and Symbol
Which unique features of the rockpile are described in the opening paragraph?

Other boys were to be seen there each afternoon after school and all day Saturday and Sunday. They fought on the rockpile. Sure footed, dangerous, and reckless, they rushed each other and grappled on the heights, sometimes disappearing down the other side in a confusion of dust and screams and upended, flying feet. "It's a wonder they don't kill themselves," their mother said, watching sometimes from the fire escape. "You children stay away from there, you hear me?" Though she said "children" she was looking at Roy, where he sat beside John on the fire escape. "The good Lord knows," she continued, "I don't want you to come home bleeding like a hog every day the Lord sends." Roy shifted impatiently, and continued to stare at the street, as though in this gazing he might somehow acquire wings. John said nothing. He had not really been spoken to: he was afraid of the rockpile and of the boys who played there.

Each Saturday morning John and Roy sat on the fire escape and watched the forbidden street below. Sometimes their mother sat in the room behind them, sewing, or dressing their younger sister, or nursing the baby, Paul. The sun fell across them and across the fire escape with a high, benevolent indifference; below them, men and women, and boys and girls, sinners all, loitered; sometimes one of

Comprehension
Where is the rockpile located?

◀ **Critical Viewing** Which details shown in this painting connect to Baldwin's story? **CONNECT**

Vocabulary

latent (lāt′ ənt) *adj.* present but invisible or inactive

Setting and Symbol

Can the tragedy of the boy's drowning in the river be seen as a symbol? If so, of what?

the church-members passed and saw them and waved. Then, for the moment that they waved decorously back, they were intimidated. They watched the saint, man or woman, until he or she had disappeared from sight. The passage of one of the redeemed made them consider, however vacantly, the wickedness of the street, their own latent wickedness in sitting where they sat; and made them think of their father, who came home early on Saturdays and who would soon be turning this corner and entering the dark hall below them.

But until he came to end their freedom, they sat, watching and longing above the street. At the end of the street nearest their house was the bridge which spanned the Harlem River[1] and led to a city called the Bronx; which was where Aunt Florence lived. Nevertheless, when they saw her coming, she did not come from the bridge, but from the opposite end of the street. This, weakly, to their minds, she explained by saying that she had taken the subway, not wishing to walk, and that, besides, she did not live in that section of the Bronx. Knowing that the Bronx was across the river, they did not believe this story ever, but, adopting toward her their father's attitude, assumed that she had just left some sinful place which she dared not name, as, for example, a movie palace.

In the summertime boys swam in the river, diving off the wooden dock, or wading in from the garbage-heavy bank. Once a boy, whose name was Richard, drowned in the river. His mother had not known where he was; she had even come to their house, to ask if he was there. Then, in the evening, at six o'clock, they had heard from the street a woman screaming and wailing; and they ran to the windows and looked out. Down the street came the woman, Richard's mother, screaming, her face raised to the sky and tears running down her face. A woman walked beside her, trying to make her quiet and trying to hold her up. Behind them walked a man, Richard's father, with Richard's body in his arms. There were two white policemen walking in the gutter, who did not seem to know what should be done. Richard's father and Richard were wet, and Richard's body lay across his father's arms like a cotton baby. The woman's screaming filled all the street; cars slowed down and the people in the cars stared; people opened their windows and looked out and came rushing out of doors to stand in the gutter, watching. Then the small procession disappeared within the house which stood beside the rockpile. Then, *"Lord, Lord, Lord!"* cried Elizabeth, their mother, and slammed the window down.

One Saturday, an hour before his father would be coming home, Roy was wounded on the rockpile and brought screaming upstairs. He and John had been sitting on the fire escape and their mother had gone into the kitchen to sip tea with Sister McCandless. By and by Roy became bored and sat beside John in restless silence; and John began drawing into his schoolbook a newspaper advertisement

1. **Harlem River** river that separates Manhattan Island from the Bronx in New York City.

which featured a new electric locomotive. Some friends of Roy passed beneath the fire escape and called him. Roy began to fidget, yelling down to them through the bars. Then a silence fell. John looked up. Roy stood looking at him.

"I'm going downstairs," he said.

"You better stay where you is, boy. You know Mama don't want you going downstairs."

"I be right *back*. She won't even know I'm gone, less you run and tell her."

"I ain't *got* to tell her. What's going to stop her from coming in here and looking out the window?"

"She's talking," Roy said. He started into the house.

"But Daddy's going to be home soon!"

"I be back before *that*. What you all the time got to be so *scared* for?" He was already in the house and he now turned, leaning on the windowsill, to swear impatiently, "I be back in *five* minutes."

John watched him sourly as he carefully unlocked the door and disappeared. In a moment he saw him on the sidewalk with his friends. He did not dare to go and tell his mother that Roy had left the fire escape because he had practically promised not to.

He started to shout, *Remember, you said five minutes!* but one of Roy's friends was looking up at the fire escape. John looked down at his schoolbook: he became **engrossed** again in the problem of the locomotive.

When he looked up again he did not know how much time had passed, but now there was a gang fight on the rockpile. Dozens of boys fought each other in the harsh sun: clambering up the rocks and battling hand to hand, scuffed shoes sliding on the slippery rock; filling the bright air with curses and **jubilant** cries. They filled the air, too, with flying weapons: stones, sticks, tin cans, garbage, whatever could be picked up and thrown. John watched in a kind of absent amazement—until he remembered that Roy was still downstairs, and that he was one of the boys on the rockpile. Then he was afraid; he could not see his brother among the figures in the sun; and he stood up, leaning over the fire-escape railing. Then Roy appeared from the other side of the rocks; John saw that his shirt was torn; he was laughing. He moved until he stood at the very top of the rockpile. Then, something, an empty tin can, flew out of the air and hit him on the forehead, just above the eye. Immediately, one side of Roy's face ran with blood, he fell and rolled on his face down the rocks. Then for a moment there was no movement at all, no sound, the sun, arrested, lay on the street and the sidewalk and the arrested boys. Then someone screamed or shouted; boys began to run away, down the street, toward the bridge. The figure on the ground, having caught its breath and felt its own blood, began to shout. John cried, "Mama! Mama!" and ran inside.

"Don't fret, don't fret," panted Sister McCandless as they rushed down the dark, narrow, swaying stairs, "don't fret. Ain't a boy been

Identifying Cause and Effect
What causes Roy to go down to the street?

Vocabulary
engrossed (en grōst′) *v.* occupied wholly; absorbed
jubilant (jo͞o′ bə lənt) *adj.* joyful and triumphant

DOZENS OF BOYS FOUGHT EACH OTHER IN THE HARSH SUN: . . .

Comprehension
What happens to Roy on the rockpile?

Setting
Which details of Roy's accident reflect the difficulties of life in this place?

Vocabulary
superficial (sōō' pər fish' əl) *adj.* on the surface; shallow

Identifying Cause and Effect
What causes Elizabeth to look "with apprehension" toward the clock?

born don't get his knocks every now and again. *Lord!*" they hurried into the sun. A man had picked Roy up and now walked slowly toward them. One or two boys sat silent on their stoops; at either end of the street there was a group of boys watching. "He ain't hurt bad," the man said, "wouldn't be making this kind of noise if he was hurt real bad."

Elizabeth, trembling, reached out to take Roy, but Sister McCandless, bigger, calmer, took him from the man and threw him over her shoulder as she once might have handled a sack of cotton. "God bless you," she said to the man, "God bless you, son." Roy was still screaming. Elizabeth stood behind Sister McCandless to stare at his bloody face.

"It's just a flesh wound," the man kept saying, "just broke the skin, that's all." They were moving across the sidewalk, toward the house. John, not now afraid of the staring boys, looked toward the corner to see if his father was yet in sight.

Upstairs, they hushed Roy's crying. They bathed the blood away, to find, just above the left eyebrow, the jagged, **superficial** scar. "Lord, have mercy," murmured Elizabeth, "another inch and it would've been his eye." And she looked with apprehension toward the clock. "Ain't it the truth," said Sister McCandless, busy with bandages and iodine.

"When did he go downstairs?" his mother asked at last.

Sister McCandless now sat fanning herself in the easy chair, at the head of the sofa where Roy lay, bound and silent. She paused for a moment to look sharply at John. John stood near the window, holding the newspaper advertisement and the drawing he had done.

"We was sitting on the fire escape," he said. "Some boys he knew called him."

"When?"

"He said he'd be back in five minutes."

"Why didn't you tell me he was downstairs?"

He looked at his hands, clasping his notebook, and did not answer.

"Boy," said Sister McCandless, "you hear your mother a-talking to you?"

He looked at his mother. He repeated:

"He said he'd be back in five minutes."

"He said he'd be back in five minutes," said Sister McCandless with scorn, "don't look to me like that's no right answer. You's the man of the house, you supposed to look after your baby brothers and sisters—you ain't supposed to let them run off and get half-killed. But I expect," she added, rising from the chair, dropping the cardboard fan, "your Daddy'll make you tell the truth. Your Ma's way too soft with you."

He did not look at her, but at the fan where it lay in the dark red, depressed seat where she had been. The fan advertised a pomade[2] for the hair and showed a brown woman and her baby, both with glistening hair, smiling happily at each other.

---

2. pomade (päm ād') *n.* perfumed ointment.

"Honey," said Sister McCandless, "I got to be moving along. Maybe I drop in later tonight. I don't reckon you going to be at Tarry Service tonight?"

Tarry Service was the prayer meeting held every Saturday night at church to strengthen believers and prepare the church for the coming of the Holy Ghost on Sunday.

"I don't reckon," said Elizabeth. She stood up; she and Sister McCandless kissed each other on the cheek. "But you be sure to remember me in your prayers."

"I surely will do that." She paused, with her hand on the door knob, and looked down at Roy and laughed. "Poor little man," she said, "reckon he'll be content to sit on the fire escape *now*."

Elizabeth laughed with her. "It sure ought to be a lesson to him. You don't reckon," she asked nervously, still smiling, "he going to keep that scar, do you?"

"Lord, no," said Sister McCandless, "ain't nothing but a scratch. I declare, Sister Grimes, you worse than a child. Another couple of weeks and you won't be able to *see* no scar. No, you go on about your housework, honey, and thank the Lord it weren't no worse." She opened the door; they heard the sound of feet on the stairs. "I expect that's the Reverend," said Sister McCandless, placidly, "I *bet* he going to raise cain."[3]

"Maybe it's Florence," Elizabeth said. "Sometimes she get here about this time." They stood in the doorway, staring, while the steps reached the landing below and began again climbing to their floor. "No," said Elizabeth then, "that ain't her walk. That's Gabriel."

"Well, I'll just go on," said Sister McCandless, "and kind of prepare his mind." She pressed Elizabeth's hand as she spoke and started

▲ Critical Viewing
Which aspects of this painting are similar to the setting of this story? **ASSESS**

Comprehension
How does Sister McCandless criticize John?

3. **raise cain** slang for "cause trouble."

LITERATURE IN CONTEXT

Cultural Connection

James Baldwin and the Church

Baldwin's choice of words, and often the subject matter of his stories, was influenced by the evangelical church, of which his father was a minister. In this story, many details reflect this influence:

- references to "the good Lord" and "saints"
- reference to the father as "the Reverend"
- mention of prayer services
- the fact that the mother and her friend call each other "Sister"
- conflicts between the family's strict religious values and the temptations of the neighborhood

As a teenager, Baldwin earned renown for his gifts as a preacher. He brought those same gifts, including the use of impassioned, rhythmic language, to his writing, creating prose of great beauty and power.

Connect to the Literature

List two or three examples of Baldwin's rhythmic language in this story.

into the hall, leaving the door behind her slightly ajar. Elizabeth turned slowly back into the room. Roy did not open his eyes, or move; but she knew that he was not sleeping; he wished to delay until the last possible moment any contact with his father. John put his newspaper and his notebook on the table and stood, leaning on the table, staring at her.

"It wasn't my fault," he said. "I couldn't stop him from going downstairs."

"No," she said, "you ain't got nothing to worry about. You just tell your Daddy the truth."

He looked directly at her, and she turned to the window, staring into the street. What was Sister McCandless saying? Then from her bedroom she heard Delilah's thin wail and she turned, frowning, looking toward the bedroom and toward the still open door. She knew that John was watching her. Delilah continued to wail, she thought, angrily, *Now that girl's getting too big for that,* but she feared that Delilah would awaken Paul and she hurried into the bedroom. She tried to soothe Delilah back to sleep. Then she heard the front door open and close—too loud, Delilah raised her voice, with an exasperated sigh Elizabeth picked the child up. Her child and Gabriel's, her children and Gabriel's: Roy, Delilah, Paul. Only John was nameless and a stranger, living, unalterable testimony to his mother's days in sin.

"What happened?" Gabriel demanded. He stood, enormous, in the center of the room, his black lunchbox dangling from his hand, staring at the sofa where Roy lay. John stood just before him, it seemed to her astonished vision just below him, beneath his fist, his heavy shoe.

The child stared at the man in fascination and terror—when a girl down home she had seen rabbits stand so paralyzed before the barking dog. She hurried past Gabriel to the sofa, feeling the weight of Delilah in her arms like the weight of a shield, and stood over Roy, saying:

"Now, ain't a thing to get upset about, Gabriel. This boy sneaked downstairs while I had my back turned and got hisself hurt a little. He's alright now."

Roy, as though in confirmation, now opened his eyes and looked gravely at his father. Gabriel dropped his lunchbox with a clatter and knelt by the sofa.

"How you feel, son? Tell your Daddy what happened?"

Roy opened his mouth to speak and then, relapsing into panic, began to cry. His father held him by the shoulder.

"You don't want to cry. You's Daddy's little man. Tell your Daddy what happened."

Identifying Cause and Effect

How does Gabriel react to Roy's tears?

"He went downstairs," said Elizabeth, "where he didn't have no business to be, and got to fighting with them bad boys playing on the rock-pile. That's what happened and it's a mercy it weren't nothing worse."

He looked up at her. "Can't you let this boy answer me for hisself?"

Ignoring this, she went on, more gently: "He got cut on the forehead, but it ain't nothing to worry about."

"You call a doctor? How you know it ain't nothing to worry about?"

"Is you got money to be throwing away on doctors? No, I ain't called no doctor. Ain't nothing wrong with my eyes that I can't tell whether he's hurt bad or not. He got a fright more'n anything else, and you ought to pray God it teaches him a lesson."

"You got a lot to say now," he said, "but I'll have *me* something to say in a minute. I'll be wanting to know when all this happened, what you was doing with your eyes *then*." He turned back to Roy, who had lain quietly sobbing eyes wide open and body held rigid: and who now, at his father's touch, remembered the height, the sharp, sliding rock beneath his feet, the sun, the explosion of the sun, his plunge into darkness and his salty blood; and recoiled, beginning to scream, as his father touched his forehead. "Hold still, hold still," crooned his father, shaking, "hold still. Don't cry. Daddy ain't going to hurt you, he just wants to see this bandage, see what they've done to his little man." But Roy continued to scream and would not be still and Gabriel dared not lift the bandage for fear of hurting him more. And he looked at Elizabeth in fury: "Can't you put that child down and help me with this boy? John, take your baby sister from your mother—don't look like neither of you got good sense."

ROY OPENED HIS MOUTH TO SPEAK AND THEN, RELAPSING INTO PANIC, BEGAN TO CRY.

John took Delilah and sat down with her in the easy chair. His mother bent over Roy, and held him still, while his father, carefully—but still Roy screamed—lifted the bandage and stared at the wound. Roy's sobs began to lessen. Gabriel readjusted the bandage. "You see," said Elizabeth, finally, "he ain't nowhere near dead."

"It sure ain't your fault that he ain't dead." He and Elizabeth considered each other for a moment in silence. "He came mightly close to losing an eye. Course, his eyes ain't as big as your'n, so I reckon you don't think it matters so much." At this her face hardened; he smiled. "Lord, have mercy," he said, "you think you ever going to learn to do right? Where was you when all this happened? Who let him go downstairs?"

"Ain't nobody let him go downstairs, he just went. He got a head just like his father, it got to be broken before it'll bow. I was in the kitchen."

"Where was Johnnie?"

"He was in here."

"Where?"

"He was on the fire escape."

"Didn't he know Roy was downstairs?"

"I reckon."

"What you mean, you reckon? He ain't got your big eyes for nothing, does he?" He looked over at John. "Boy, you see your brother go downstairs?"

Comprehension
As John faces Gabriel, what sight does Elizabeth remember from her childhood?

"Gabriel, ain't no sense in trying to blame Johnnie. You know right well if you have trouble making Roy behave, he ain't going to listen to his brother. He don't hardly listen to me."

"How come you didn't tell your mother Roy was downstairs?"

John said nothing, staring at the blanket which covered Delilah.

"Boy, you hear me? You want me to take a strap to you?"

"No, you ain't," she said. "You ain't going to taken no strap to this boy, not today you ain't. Ain't a soul to blame for Roy's lying up there now but you—you because you done spoiled him so that he thinks he can do just anything and get away with it. I'm here to tell you that ain't no way to raise no child. You don't pray to the Lord to help you do better than you been doing, you going to live to shed bitter tears that the Lord didn't take his soul today." And she was trembling. She moved, unseeing, toward John and took Delilah from his arms. She looked back at Gabriel, who had risen, who stood near the sofa, staring at her. And she found in his face not fury alone, which would not have surprised her; but hatred so deep as to become insupportable in its lack of personality. His eyes were struck alive, unmoving, blind with malevolence—she felt, like the pull of the earth at her feet, his longing to witness her perdition. Again, as though it might be propitiation, she moved the child in her arms. And at this his eyes changed, he looked at Elizabeth, the mother of his children, the helpmeet given by the Lord. Then her eyes clouded; she moved to leave the room; her foot struck the lunchbox lying on the floor.

Vocabulary
perdition (pər dish′ ən) *n.* complete and irreparable loss; ruin

"John," she said, "pick up your father's lunchbox like a good boy."

She heard, behind her, his scrambling movement as he left the easy chair, the scrape and jangle of the lunchbox as he picked it up, bending his dark head near the toe of his father's heavy shoe.

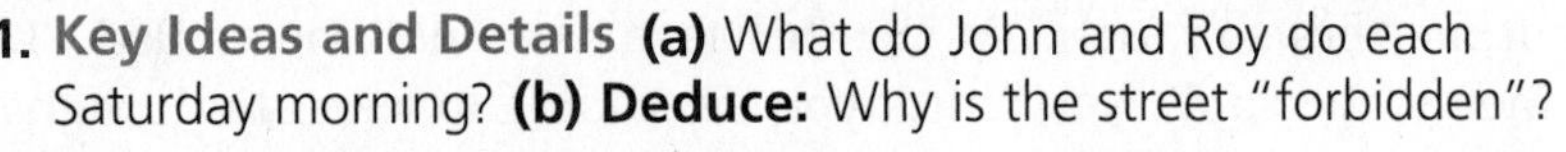

Critical Reading

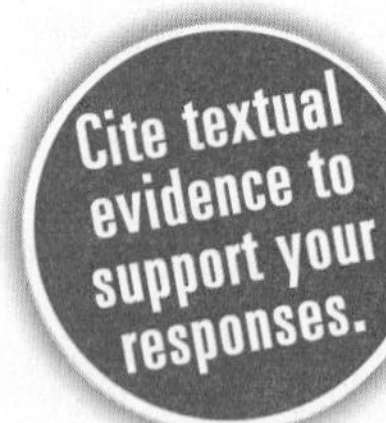
Cite textual evidence to support your responses.

1. **Key Ideas and Details (a)** What do John and Roy do each Saturday morning? **(b) Deduce:** Why is the street "forbidden"?
2. **Key Ideas and Details (a)** How is John related to Gabriel? **(b) Support:** What evidence is there that Gabriel's relationship with John is different from his relationship with the other children?
3. **Integration of Knowledge and Ideas** In which aspects of their lives are the characters in this story insiders or outsiders? Explain. In your response, use at least two of these Essential Question words: *mainstream, identity, community, alienation, prejudice.* ***[Connecting to the Essential Question: How does literature shape or reflect society?]***

Literary Analysis

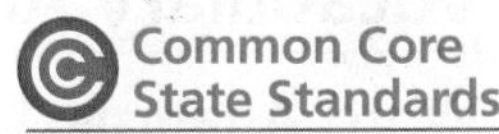

Common Core State Standards

Writing

3. Write narratives to develop real or imagined experiences or events using effective technique, well-chosen details, and well-structured event sequences. *(p. 1092)*

3.b. Use narrative techniques, such as dialogue, to develop experiences, events, and/or characters. *(p. 1092)*

3.d. Use precise words and phrases, telling details, and sensory language to convey a vivid picture of the experiences, events, setting, and/or characters. *(p. 1092)*

Language

1. Demonstrate command of the conventions of standard English grammar and usage when writing or speaking. *(p. 1093)*

4.b. Identify and correctly use patterns of word changes that indicate different meanings or parts of speech. *(p. 1092)*

4.d. Verify the preliminary determination of the meaning of a word or phrase. *(p. 1092)*

5. Demonstrate understanding of word relationships. *(p. 1092)*

1. **Key Ideas and Details** Find three details that describe physical aspects of the story's **setting**—the landmarks of the neighborhood.
2. **Key Ideas and Details** Find three details that describe the psychological aspects of the setting—the mood and atmosphere of the neighborhood.
3. **Key Ideas and Details** **(a)** What are some of the potential dangers the setting presents? **(b)** In what ways do you think this setting has influenced Gabriel and Elizabeth's decisions about how to raise their children?
4. **Key Ideas and Details** **(a) Identify cause and effect** in the events leading to Roy's injury. **(b)** What does Elizabeth say is the real cause of Roy's injury? **(c)** Do you agree with Elizabeth? Why or why not?
5. **Key Ideas and Details** **(a)** What are the causes of Elizabeth's protectiveness toward John? **(b)** What effect does Elizabeth's protectiveness toward John have on Gabriel?
6. **Key Ideas and Details** **(a)** How would you characterize Gabriel? **(b)** What are the similarities and differences between the effects of his presence on Roy, John, and Elizabeth?
7. **Key Ideas and Details** **(a)** How does Gabriel react to Roy's tears? **(b)** What does the effect of Roy's tears on Gabriel suggest about the family dynamic?
8. **Craft and Structure** **(a)** Use a chart like the one shown to analyze the rockpile as the main **symbol** in this story. **(b)** What does the rockpile represent?

The Rockpile			→	What It Represents
What People Say About It	Events Linked With It	Details Used To Describe It	→	

9. **Integration of Knowledge and Ideas** **(a)** How do the neighborhood children behave when playing on the rockpile? **(b)** How does this affect your understanding of the rockpile as both a setting and a symbol of problems within the community?
10. **Integration of Knowledge and Ideas** **(a)** What does "the toe of his father's heavy shoe," mentioned in the last line of the story, symbolize? **(b)** In what way does this symbol capture John's relationship to Gabriel? **(c)** How would you define their relationship at the end of the story?

Close Reading Activities Continued

Vocabulary Acquisition and Use

Word Analysis: Latin Prefix *super-*

The Latin prefix *super-* means "over," "above," or "beyond." English words with this prefix relate to the idea of surface, as in *superficial*, or the idea of extremity, as in *superhero*. Define each underlined word and explain if the prefix relates to surface or extremity. Use a dictionary to check your answers.

1. While supersonic travel is possible, it is not currently a commercial option.
2. The artist frequently superimposes an unusual image over a familiar one.
3. She is gifted with superlative athletic ability.
4. The global summit included leaders from five superpowers.

Vocabulary: Categorizing Vocabulary

For each numbered word, categorize the groups of words that follow as *synonyms, antonyms*, or a combination of both. Explain your choices.

1. **latent** obvious; concealed; dormant
2. **engrossed** distracted; captivated; detached
3. **jubilant** exultant; elated; blissful
4. **perdition** salvation; deliverance; reprieve
5. **superficial** external; profound; peripheral

Writing to Sources

Narrative Text A radio drama can capture the flow and feeling of a story while leaving listeners imaginative space in which to visualize the characters and settings. Adapt "The Rockpile" as a **radio play.** With a group, divide the story into scenes. Individually, choose a scene to develop into a script.

Prewriting Identify the characters from the story that will appear in your scene, and add a narrator to provide background information. Make an outline to list key events that occur in the scene.

Drafting Include stage directions to help actors reflect characters' emotions and to indicate sound effects. Pull dialogue directly from the story, and add description and other dialogue to smooth transitions.

Model: Using Stage Directions

[*From a distance, we hear the jubilant cries of kids playing.*]

JOHN: [*shouting out the window*] Roy, you said five minutes!

[*to himself*] I had enough. [*He slams the window. The sounds are muffled.*]

NARRATOR: John cannot see his brother among the figures in the sun. Then he appears on the other side of the rocks. His shirt is torn and he is laughing.

JOHN: [*opening the window*] Five minutes is up, Roy!

Stage directions add detail to a scene.

Revising Read your draft aloud, listening for a smooth flow of events and clear presentation of characters. Rehearse the finished script with your group and perform it for the class. If possible, record the play, with sound effects, and arrange for it to air on your school or local public radio station.

Conventions and Style: Avoiding Shifts in Verb Tense

Verbs have different forms, called **tenses,** which indicate the time in which an action occurs. If you let verbs shift unnecessarily from one tense to another in your writing, readers will find it difficult to follow your meaning. Generally, use the same tense throughout a piece of writing.

Consistent Tense (past): James Baldwin *lived* in Europe, but he *wrote* about Harlem.

Consistent Tense (present): On Saturday mornings, Roy and John *sit* at the top of the fire escape and *watch* the people below.

Incorrect Verb Shift: On Saturday mornings, Roy and John *sat* at the top of the fire escape and *watch* the people below. (The action takes place at the same time but *sat* is in the past tense and *watch* is in the present.)

If you want to show a change in time, it is appropriate to shift tenses:

Appropriate Tense Shift: "The Rockpile" *is* an example of how Baldwin *used* his life experiences *to write* a story.

Practice In items 1–5, choose the verb that correctly completes each sentence. In items 6–10, correct unnecessary shifts in verb tense.

1. Roy's friends called to him, but John (warns, warned) him not to go.
2. Roy looks at his mother but (says, said) nothing.
3. Elizabeth hopes John (had not had, will not have) a scar.
4. Gabriel's expression (will change, changed) when he saw Delilah.
5. Elizabeth has been protecting John because she (is fearing, fears) Gabriel's anger.
6. Sister McCandless says the scar is gone in a few weeks' time.
7. Although the boys had been fighting a minute before, they disappear when Roy was hurt.
8. Before she left, Sister McCandless is stopping to talk to Gabriel.
9. John had not told his mother Roy is going to play in the street, and he felt guilty.
10. As John picked up the lunchbox, his head nearly touches his father's shoe.

Writing and Speaking Conventions

A. Writing Complete each sentence starter. Use a form of the verb in parentheses and appropriate verb tenses.

Example: The boys played, ______. (fight)

Sentence: The boys played, but then they fought.

1. Roy watched the children play, ______. (join)
2. The boys have been swimming, but ______. (dive)
3. I will unlock ______. (call)
4. Gabriel dropped ______. (kneel)
5. Please turn ______. (look)

B. Speaking Write a brief account from Elizabeth's point of view, explaining what happened after Roy was hurt. Include at least one shift in verb tense to show a change in the time of the action.

Building Knowledge and Insight

Life In His Language

Connecting to the Essential Question In this eulogy, one great writer describes her gratitude to another. As you read, decide whether Morrison speaks as a private individual, as the voice of a community, or both. Doing so will help you reflect on the Essential Question: **How does literature shape or reflect society?**

Reading Informational Text

3. Analyze a complex set of ideas or sequence of events and explain how specific individuals, ideas, or events interact and develop over the course of the text.

5. Analyze and evaluate the effectiveness of the structure an author uses in his or her exposition or argument, including whether the structure makes points clear, convincing, and engaging.

Language

3.a. Apply an understanding of syntax to the study of complex texts when reading.

Close Reading Focus

Eulogy; Mood

A **eulogy** is a literary work written to pay tribute to someone who has died. Eulogies are defined less by their form, which may be a speech, essay, or poem, and more by the subject and occasion of the writing. Usually written shortly after the subject's death, they celebrate the person's strengths, virtues, and accomplishments:

> *That is the astonishing gift of your art and your friendship. You gave us ourselves to think about, to cherish.*

A eulogist creates a **mood,** or emotional quality, that expresses his or her feelings and captures qualities in the person being honored. Mood is evoked through *word choice, rhythms,* and *syntax*, or sentence structure. As you read, note the aspects of James Baldwin's life that Toni Morrison celebrates. Notice, too, the emotions she evokes and the literary devices that add to the feelings.

Preparing to Read Complex Texts One way to understand an essay or a eulogy is to **analyze patterns of organization,** the order and structure of ideas. In this eulogy, Toni Morrison follows a clear pattern when she discusses the "three gifts" that Baldwin gave to the world. The *pattern of threes* is an ancient narrative structure. Fairy tales, folk tales, and myths often tell of three siblings, three tests, and so on. The idea of the three gifts is a part of the Christmas story, to which Morrison alludes. In using this ancient, *archetypal structure*, Morrison both organizes her ideas and communicates a sense of Baldwin's depth as a literary artist. Use a chart like the one shown to analyze the effect of this organizational pattern on Morrison's message.

Gift
1
2
3

↓

Morrison's Explanation
1
2
3

Vocabulary

The words below are important to understanding the text that follows. Copy the words into your notebook. Which word is very similar to the word *scene*?

summation **platitudes**
scenario **appropriate**

TONI MORRISON (b. 1931)

Author of "Life In His Language"

The first African-American woman to win the Nobel Prize in Literature, Toni Morrison is renowned for works that explore the experiences of black women and men, as well as the harsh realities of racism and sexism. She grew up in Lorain, Ohio, nurtured by her family's love of stories, songs, and folktales. These early experiences inspired her to study literature in college and become a professor herself. Later, she worked as an editor, preparing books by such well-known figures as the boxer Muhammad Ali, the writer Toni Cade Bambara, and the activist Angela Davis.

A Novelist's Eye Morrison's career as a writer was launched with the publication of her first novel, *The Bluest Eye* (1970), which depicts the struggle of a black girl who sees beauty as a trait held only by white people. She longs to have the blue eyes of her movie star idol, Shirley Temple. *Sula* (1973) focuses on a friendship that challenges the prejudices of a small community. *The Song of Solomon* (1977) presents a narrator's search for his own identity. *Beloved* (1987), a novel inspired by the true story of Margaret Garner, tells the tale of an escaped slave who was recaptured by her master. *Jazz* (1992) tells a sweeping tale of passion set against the backdrop of Harlem in the 1920s.

Honoring Legacies In addition to novels, Morrison has written literary criticism and children's books. Her writing reflects her deep respect for the wisdom of others, especially generations who have gone before her. She points out that "there is always an elder" in her writing. "These ancestors are not just parents, they are sort of timeless people whose relationships to the characters are benevolent, instructive, and protective, and they provide a certain kind of wisdom." In her essays and interviews, she often pays tributes to writers, like James Baldwin, who have inspired her.

> *"If there's a book you really want to read but it hasn't been written yet, then you must write it."*

LIFE IN HIS LANGUAGE

TONI MORRISON

BACKGROUND One of the great writers of the twentieth century, James Baldwin was an inspiration to many readers and writers. Toni Morrison wrote this essay to pay tribute to his influence on her and the entire literary community.

JIMMY. There is too much to think about you, and too much to feel. The difficulty is your life refuses summation—it always did—and invites contemplation instead. Like many of us left here I thought I knew you. Now I discover that in your company it is myself I know. That is the astonishing gift of your art and your friendship. You gave us ourselves to think about, to cherish. We are like Hall Montana[1] watching "with new wonder" his brother saints, knowing the song he sang is us. "He is us."

I never heard a single command from you, yet the demands you made on me, the challenges you issued to me, were nevertheless unmistakable, even if unenforced: that I work and think at the top of my form, that I stand on moral ground but know that ground must be shored up by mercy, that "the world is before [me] and [I] need not take it or leave it as it was when [I] came in."

Well, the season was always Christmas with you there and, like one aspect of that scenario, you did not neglect to bring at least three gifts. You gave me a language to dwell in, a gift so perfect it seems my own invention. I have been thinking your spoken and written thoughts for so long I believed they were mine. I have been seeing the world through your eyes for so long, I believed that clear, clear view was my own. Even now, even here, I need you to tell me what I am feeling and how to articulate it. So I have pored again through the 6,895 pages of your published work to acknowledge the debt and thank you for the credit. No one possessed or inhabited language for me the way you did. You made American English honest—genuinely international. You exposed its secrets and reshaped it until it was truly modern, dialogic,[2] representative, humane. You stripped it of ease and false comfort and fake innocence and evasion and hypocrisy. And in place of deviousness was clarity. In place of soft, plump lies was lean, targeted power. In place of intellectual disingenuousness and what you called "exasperating egocentricity," you gave us undecorated truth.

Vocabulary

summation (sə mā′ shən) *n.* details stated briefly

scenario (sə nar′ ē ō) *n.* situation

Eulogy

Why do you think the gift of Baldwin's language is particularly important to Morrison?

Comprehension

According to Morrison, what was the first gift Baldwin gave her?

---

1. **Hall Montana** The narrator of Baldwin's novel *Just Above My Head*, who describes the troubled life and death of his brother Arthur, a gospel singer.
2. **dialogic** (dī ə lä′j ik) conversational.

Vocabulary

platitudes (pla´ tə tüdz)
n. tired expressions

appropriate (ə prō´ prē āt)
v. to take or use without permission

You replaced lumbering **platitudes** with an upright elegance. You went into that forbidden territory and decolonized it, "robbed it of the jewel of its naïveté," and un-gated it for black people so that in your wake we could enter it, occupy it, restructure it in order to accommodate our complicated passion—not our vanities but our intricate, difficult, demanding beauty, our tragic, insistent knowledge, our lived reality, our sleek classical imagination—all the while refusing "to be defined by a language that has never been able to recognize [us]." In your hands language was handsome again. In your hands we saw how it was meant to be: neither bloodless nor bloody, and yet alive.

It infuriated some people. Those who saw the paucity of their own imagination in the two-way mirror you held up to them attacked the mirror, tried to reduce it to fragments which they could then rank and grade, tried to dismiss the shards where your image and theirs remained—locked but ready to soar. You are an artist after all and an artist is forbidden a career in this place; an artist is permitted only a commercial hit. But for thousands and thousands of those who embraced your text and who gave themselves permission to hear your language, by that very gesture they ennobled themselves, became unshrouded, civilized.

The second gift was your courage, which you let us share: the courage of one who could go as a stranger in the village and transform the distances between people into intimacy with the whole world; courage to understand that experience in ways that made it a personal revelation for each of us. It was you who gave us the courage to **appropriate** an alien, hostile, all-white geography because you had discovered that "this world (meaning history) is white no longer and it will never be white again." Yours was the courage to live life in and from its belly as well as beyond its edges, to see and say what it was, to recognize and identify evil but never tear or stand in awe of it. It is a courage that came from a ruthless intelligence married to a pity so profound it could convince anyone who cared to know that those who despised us "need the moral authority of their former slaves, who are the only people in the world who know anything about them and who may be, indeed, the only people in the world who really care anything about them." When that unassailable combination of mind and heart, of intellect and passion was on display it guided us through treacherous landscape as it did when you wrote these words every rebel, every dissident, revolutionary, every practicing artist from Capetown to Poland from Waycross to Dublin memorized: "A person does not lightly elect to oppose his society. One would much rather be at home among one's compatriots than be mocked and detested by them. And there is a level on which the mockery of the people, even their hatred, is moving, because it is so blind: it is terrible to watch people cling to their captivity and insist on their own destruction."

Analyze Patterns of Organization

Is the second gift in any way related to the first? Explain.

You gave me a language to dwell in, a gift so perfect it seems my own invention.

Yours was the courage to live life in and from its belly as well as beyond its edges . . .

The third gift was hard to fathom and even harder to accept. It was your tenderness—a tenderness so delicate I thought it could not last, but last it did and envelop me it did. In the midst of anger it tapped me lightly like the child in Tish's womb: "Something almost as hard to catch as a whisper in a crowded place, as light and as definite as a spider's web, strikes below my ribs, stunning and astonishing my heart . . . the baby, turning for the first time in its incredible veil of water, announces its presence and claims me; tells me, in that instant, that what can get worse can get better . . . in the meantime—forever—it is entirely up to me. Yours was a tenderness, a vulnerability, that asked everything, expected everything and, like the world's own Merlin,[3] provided us with the ways and means to deliver. I suppose that is why I was always a bit better behaved around you, smarter, more capable, wanting to be worth the love you lavished, and wanting to be steady enough to witness the pain you had witnessed and were tough enough to bear while it broke your heart, wanting to be generous enough to join your smile with one of my own, and reckless enough to jump on in that laugh you laughed. Because our joy and our laughter were not only all right, they were necessary.

You knew, didn't you, how I needed your language and the mind that formed it? How I relied on your fierce courage to tame wilderness for me? How strengthened I was by the certainty that came from knowing you would never hurt me? You knew, didn't you, how I loved your love? You knew. This then is no calamity. No. This is jubilee. "Our crown," you said, "has already been bought and paid for. All we have to do," you said, "is wear it."

And we do, Jimmy. You crowned us.

---

3. Merlin magician and wise counselor in the legends of King Arthur.

Critical Reading

Cite textual evidence to support your responses.

1. **Integration of Knowledge and Ideas** **Analyze:** Why do you think Morrison addresses her eulogy to Baldwin, rather than to an anonymous listener, or a third party?
2. **Integration of Knowledge and Ideas** American culture places a premium on newness. What does this essay suggest about the importance of past achievements to both individuals and society as a whole? In your response, use at least two of these Essential Question words: *innovation, contribute, legacy, generation.* ***[Connecting to the Essential Question: How does literature shape or reflect society?]***

Close Reading Activities | *Life In His Language*

Literary Analysis

1. **Key Ideas and Details** **(a)** What do you learn about James Baldwin from Morrison's **eulogy**? **(b)** What personal qualities and values does Morrison see in Baldwin that she thinks are especially unique and valuable?
2. **Key Ideas and Details** **(a)** Use a chart like the one shown to analyze the **mood** Morrison creates in this eulogy. Identify four details that add to a particular feeling in the writing. **(b)** Then, list two or three adjectives you feel describe this mood.

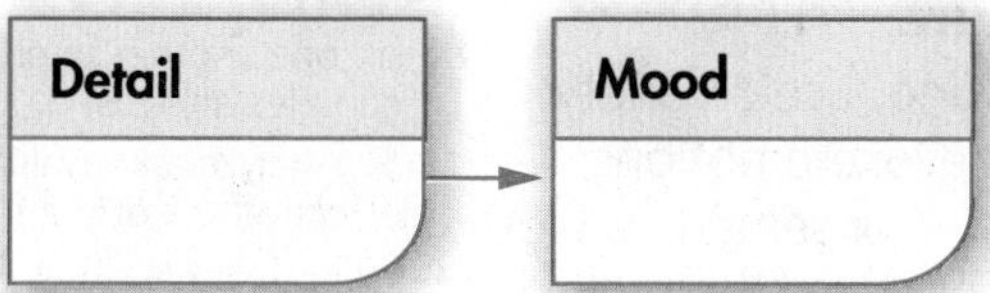

3. **Craft and Structure** **(a)** Identify two examples of unusual *syntax*, or word order. **(b)** Rewrite each example in more common syntax. **(c)** Explain how Morrison's choice of syntax affects the meaning and mood of the writing.
4. **Integration of Knowledge and Ideas** **(a)** Analyze Morrison's **pattern of organization** by defining each of Baldwin's "three gifts." **(b)** Is one of these gifts more or less significant than the others? Explain.

Vocabulary Acquisition and Use

Sentence Completions Use a word from the vocabulary list to complete each sentence logically. Explain your choices.

1. An interesting <u>scenario</u> for a television series would be ______.
2. The <u>summation</u> of a book would include ______.
3. One example of a <u>platitude</u> is ______.
4. A poet might decide to <u>appropriate</u> ______.

Writing to Sources

Informative Text Write an **essay of tribute** to honor a person who has influenced you: someone you know or someone whose art has inspired you. *Organize your essay using a clear pattern of three.* Use Morrison's description of Baldwin's "three gifts" as your model. Include these elements:

- An introduction that identifies your subject and focus
- One paragraph for each of the three elements you will discuss
- A conclusion that summarizes and extends your view of this person

Common Core State Standards

Writing

2. Write informative texts to examine and convey complex ideas, concepts, and information clearly and accurately through the effective selection, organization, and analysis of content.

2.a. Introduce a topic; organize complex ideas, concepts, and information so that each new element builds on that which precedes it to create a unified whole.

2.f. Provide a concluding statement or section that follows from and supports the information or explanation presented.

Language

4.a. Use context as a clue to the meaning of a word or phrase.

ANCHOR TEXTS

Inaugural Address • from *Lett from Birmingham City Jail*

Connecting to the Essential Question Both President Kennedy and Dr. King refer to the protection of human rights as one of America's essential duties. As you read, notice specific actions the authors believe will protect or advance human rights. Doing so will enrich your consideration of the Essential Question: **What makes American literature American?**

Common Core State Standards

Reading Informational Text

2. Determine two or more central ideas of a text and analyze their development over the course of the text, including how they interact and build on one another to provide a complex analysis.

5. Analyze and evaluate the effectiveness of the structure an author uses in his or her exposition or argument, including whether the structure makes points clear, convincing, and engaging.

Close Reading Focus

Rhetorical Devices; Argument/Support Structure

Persuasive writers, such as President Kennedy and Dr. King, use a variety of **rhetorical devices** to clarify and balance ideas and evoke emotions:

- **Parallelism** is the repetition of words, phrases, clauses, or sentences that have the same grammatical structure or the same meaning: "the torch has been passed to a new generation of Americans—born in this century, tempered by war, disciplined by a hard and bitter peace."
- **Antithesis** is a form of parallelism that emphasizes strong contrasts: "Now the trumpet summons us again—not as a call to bear arms, . . . not as a call to battle . . . but [as] a call to bear the burden."

The **organizational structure** of a text adds to its persuasive appeal. King uses an **argument/support** structure, which consists of a series of arguments supported with evidence. By contrast, Kennedy organizes his speech around two **lists**—one a series of pledges, and the other a series of directives, or requests.

Comparing Literary Works As you read, compare each writer's use of rhetorical devices and notice how the different organizational structures add to the power of both texts.

Preparing to Read Complex Texts The main, or central, ideas in a selection are the key points that the writer wants to express. The supporting details are the facts, examples, or reasons that explain or justify these ideas. Use a chart like the one shown to **identify two or more main ideas and supporting details** as you read these selections.

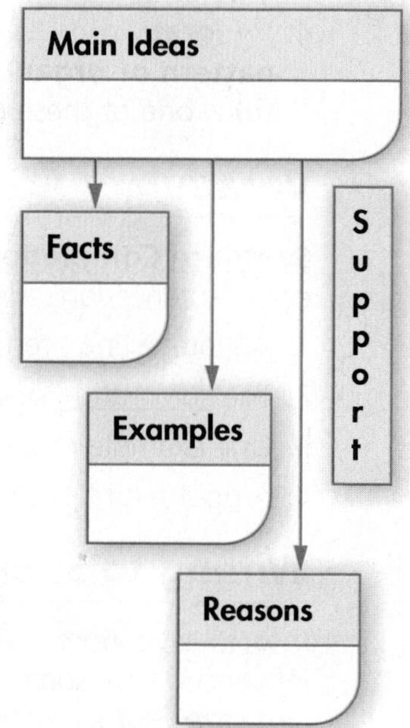

Vocabulary

The words below are important to understanding the texts that follow. Copy the words into your notebook. Which word is a synonym for *destroy*?

alliance
invective
adversary
eradicate
flagrant
profundity

John Fitzgerald Kennedy *(1917–1963)*

Author of **Inaugural Address**

A Tradition of Service John Fitzgerald Kennedy was born into a family with a tradition of public service. His father Joseph served as U.S. Ambassador to Great Britain, and his maternal grandfather was elected mayor of Boston. After graduation from Harvard University, Kennedy served with distinction in the U.S. Navy during World War II. Having barely escaped death in battle, Kennedy returned home as a war hero, and in 1946 he easily won election to the House of Representatives. Kennedy served three terms in the House before he was elected senator from Massachusetts in 1952.

Thirty-Fifth President Eight years later, in 1960, Kennedy won a hard-fought contest for the presidency. At the age of forty-three, he became the youngest person ever to be elected to that office. While he was president, he witnessed events as diverse as the launch of the first communications satellite, *Telstar,* and the signing of the first nuclear nonproliferation treaty with the Soviet Union. The United States teetered on the brink of nuclear war during the Cuban missile crisis and put its first astronaut into orbit around the Earth.

Fallen Leader Tragically, Kennedy was assassinated on November 22, 1963, in Dallas, Texas. Two days after the president's murder, Lee Harvey Oswald, who had been arrested for the crime, was himself assassinated. In 1964, the Warren Commission, charged with investigating the circumstances of Kennedy's murder, ruled that Oswald had acted alone. Nevertheless, conspiracy theories have continued to swirl about the assassination.

"A man may die, nations may rise and fall, but an idea lives on."

INAUGURAL ADDRESS

JOHN F. KENNEDY

BACKGROUND When John F. Kennedy took office in 1961, the United States was locked in a potentially explosive stalemate with the then Soviet Union and its allies. Fierce adversaries in the Cold War, the United States and the Soviet Union were stockpiling nuclear weapons, creating the possibility of a disastrous war that could destroy the earth. In his now-famous inaugural address, Kennedy addressed our nation's fears and reached out to our adversaries, even as he reaffirmed our nation's strength and the ideals of freedom.

Vice President Johnson, Mr. Speaker, Mr. Chief Justice, President Eisenhower, Vice President Nixon, President Truman,[1] *reverend clergy,fellow citizens,* we observe today not a victory of party, but a celebration of freedom—symbolizing an end, as well as a beginning—signifying renewal, as well as change. For I have sworn before you and Almighty God the same solemn oath our forebears prescribed nearly a century and three quarters ago.

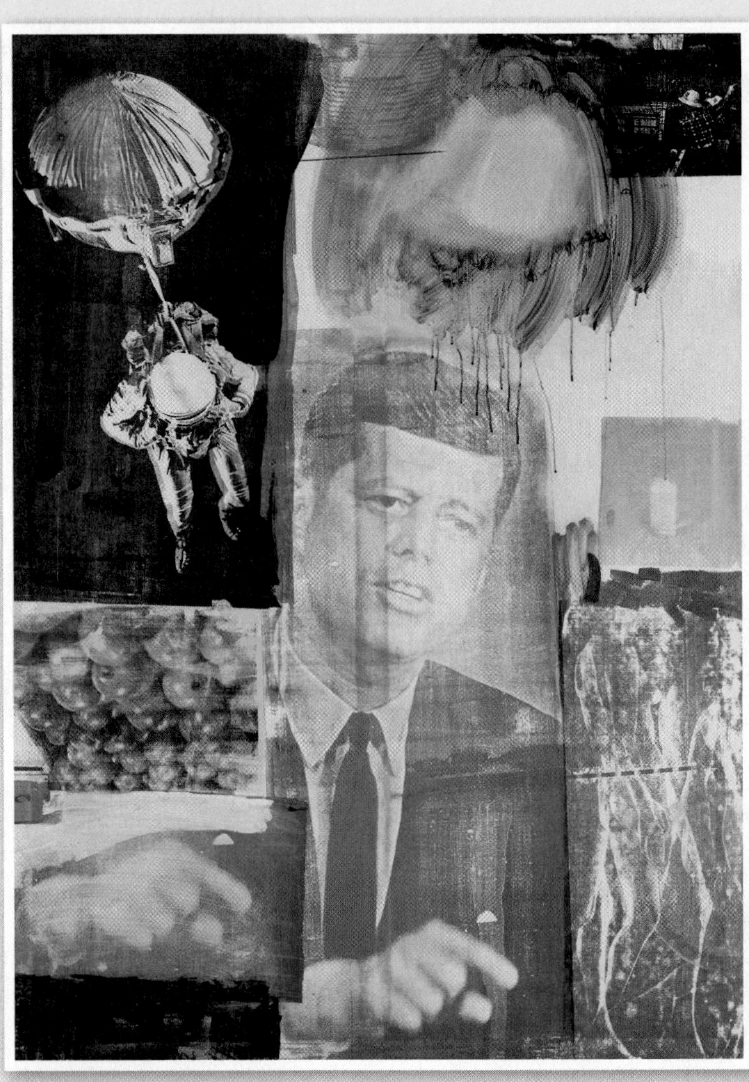

Retroactive I, Robert Rauschenberg, 1964, Wadsworth Atheneum, Hartford, CT, ©Robert Rauschenberg/Licensed by VAGA, New York, NY

▲ **Critical Viewing** What do the images in this montage—and the unfinished quality of the upper right corner—suggest about Kennedy? **[Infer]**

1. **Vice President . . . Truman** Present at Kennedy's inauguration were Lyndon B. Johnson, Kennedy's vice president; 34th president Dwight D. Eisenhower and his vice president, Richard M. Nixon; and 33rd president Harry S Truman.

The world is very different now. For man holds in his mortal hands the power to abolish all forms of human poverty and all forms of human life. And yet the same revolutionary beliefs for which our forebears fought are still at issue around the globe—the belief that the rights of man come not from the generosity of the state, but from the hand of God.

We dare not forget today that we are the heirs of that first revolution. Let the word go forth from this time and place, to friend and foe alike, that the torch has been passed to a new generation of Americans—born in this century, tempered by war, disciplined by a hard and bitter peace, proud of our ancient heritage—and unwilling to witness or permit the slow undoing of those human rights to which this Nation has always been committed, and to which we are committed today at home and around the world.

Let every nation know, whether it wishes us well or ill, that we shall pay any price, bear any burden, meet any hardship, support any friend, oppose any foe, to assure the survival and the success of liberty.

This much we pledge—and more.

To those old allies whose cultural and spiritual origins we share, we pledge the loyalty of faithful friends. United, there is little we cannot do in a host of cooperative ventures. Divided, there is little we can do—for we dare not meet a powerful challenge at odds and split asunder.[2]

To those new States whom we welcome to the ranks of the free, we pledge our word that one form of colonial control shall not have passed away merely to be replaced by a far more iron tyranny. We shall not always expect to find them supporting our view. But we shall always hope to find them strongly supporting their own freedom—and to remember that, in the past, those who foolishly sought power by riding the back of the tiger ended up inside.

To those people in the huts and villages of half the globe struggling to break the bonds of mass misery, we pledge our best efforts to help them help themselves, for whatever period is required—not because the Communists may be doing it, not because we seek their votes, but because it is right. If a free society cannot help the many who are poor, it cannot save the few who are rich.

To our sister republics south of our border, we offer a special pledge—to convert our good words into good deeds—in a new alliance for progress—to assist free men and free governments in casting off the chains of poverty. But this peaceful revolution of hope cannot become the prey of hostile powers. Let all our neighbors know that we shall join with them to oppose aggression or subversion anywhere in the Americas. And let every other power know that this Hemisphere intends to remain the master of its own house.

Antithesis
What contrasting words and phrases does Kennedy use in this paragraph?

Vocabulary
alliance (ə lī′ əns) *n.* union of nations for a specific purpose

Comprehension
What does Kennedy say that Americans dare not forget?

---

2. United . . . Divided . . . split asunder Kennedy echoes the famous lines from Abraham Lincoln's second inaugural address: "United we stand . . . divided we fall."

Vocabulary

invective (in vek´ tiv) *n.* verbal attack; strong criticism

adversary (ad´ vər ser´ ē) *n.* opponent; enemy

To that world assembly of sovereign states, the United Nations, our last best hope in an age where the instruments of war have far outpaced the instruments of peace, we renew our pledge of support—to prevent it from becoming merely a forum for **invective**—to strengthen its shield of the new and the weak—and to enlarge the area in which its writ may run.

Finally, to those nations who would make themselves our **adversary**, we offer not a pledge but a request: that both sides begin anew the quest for peace, before the dark powers of destruction[3] unleashed by science engulf all humanity in planned or accidental self-destruction.

We dare not tempt them with weakness. For only when our arms are sufficient beyond doubt can we be certain beyond doubt that they will never be employed.

But neither can two great and powerful groups of nations take comfort from our present course—both sides overburdened by the cost of modern weapons, both rightly alarmed by the steady spread of the deadly atom, yet both racing to alter that uncertain balance of terror that stays the hand of mankind's final war.

So let us begin anew—remembering on both sides that civility is not a sign of weakness, and sincerity is always subject to proof. Let us never negotiate out of fear. But let us never fear to negotiate.

Rhetorical Devices

How does the list of directives in these four paragraphs add to the persuasive power of the speech?

Let both sides explore what problems unite us instead of belaboring those problems which divide us.

Let both sides, for the first time, formulate serious and precise proposals for the inspection and control of arms—and bring the absolute power to destroy other nations under the absolute control of all nations.

Vocabulary

eradicate (e rad´ i kāt´) *v.* wipe out; destroy

Let both sides seek to invoke the wonders of science instead of its terrors. Together let us explore the stars, conquer the deserts, **eradicate** disease, tap the ocean depths, and encourage the arts and commerce.

Let both sides unite to heed in all corners of the earth the command of Isaiah—to "undo the heavy burdens . . . and let the oppressed go free."[4]

And if a beachhead of cooperation may push back the jungle of suspicion, let both sides join in creating a new endeavor, not a new balance of power, but a new world of law, where the strong are just and the weak secure and the peace preserved.

All this will not be finished in the first 100 days. Nor will it be finished in the first 1,000 days, nor in the life of this Administration, nor even perhaps in our lifetime on this planet. But let us begin.

In your hands, my fellow citizens, more than in mine, will rest the final success or failure of our course. Since this country was founded, each generation of Americans has been summoned to give testimony to

---

3. dark powers of destruction nuclear war.

4. Isaiah . . . free the quotation refers to the passage in Isaiah 58:6.

its national loyalty. The graves of young Americans who answered the call to service surround the globe.

Now the trumpet summons us again—not as a call to bear arms, though arms we need; not as a call to battle, though embattled we are—but a call to bear the burden of a long twilight struggle, year in and year out, "rejoicing in hope, patient in tribulation"[5]—a struggle against the common enemies of man: tyranny, poverty, disease, and war itself.

Can we forge against these enemies a grand and global alliance, North and South, East and West, that can assure a more fruitful life for all mankind? Will you join in that historic effort?

In the long history of the world, only a few generations have been granted the role of defending freedom in its hour of maximum danger. I do not shrink from this responsibility—I welcome it. I do not believe that any of us would exchange places with any other people or any other generation. The energy, the faith, the devotion which we bring to this endeavor will light our country and all who serve it—and the glow from that fire can truly light the world.

And so, my fellow Americans: ask not what your country can do for you—ask what you can do for your country.

My fellow citizens of the world: ask not what America will do for you, but what together we can do for the freedom of man.

Finally, whether you are citizens of America or citizens of the world, ask of us here the same high standards of strength and sacrifice which we ask of you. With a good conscience our only sure reward, with history the final judge of our deeds, let us go forth to lead the land we love, asking His blessing and His help, but knowing that here on earth God's work must truly be our own.

5. **"rejoicing . . . tribulation"** from Romans 12:12. In Paul's letter to the Romans, he calls people to work together in love and mutual respect.

Critical Reading

1. **Key Ideas and Details (a)** What difference does Kennedy stress between the world now and the world as it was during the American Revolution? **(b) Interpret:** How does Kennedy want his audience to respond to this difference?
2. **Integration of Knowledge and Ideas Evaluate:** How effective is the challenge that Kennedy offers in the final paragraphs of the speech? Explain your answer.

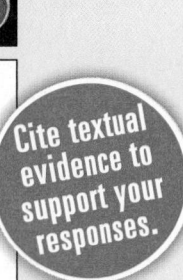

Cite textual evidence to support your responses.

Martin Luther King, Jr. *(1929–1968)*

Author of "Letter from Birmingham City Jail"

Martin Luther King, Jr., was born into a family of ministers: both his father and maternal grandfather were Baptist preachers. At Morehouse College in Atlanta, Georgia, King originally planned to study both medicine and law. However, under the influence of his mentor, the college president and eloquent orator Benjamin Mays, King committed himself to the ministry and to the struggle for racial equality.

Formative Years King prepared for the ministry at Crozer Theological Seminary in Chester, Pennsylvania. Here, the nonviolent philosophy of the Indian leader Mohandas K. ("Mahatma") Gandhi made a critical impression on him. At Boston University a few years later, King earned a doctorate in theology.

Civil Rights Leader King first gained prominence as the leader of the Montgomery Bus Boycott of 1955–1956. Convinced that political and social freedoms were attainable through nonviolence, he led boycotts, marches, and sit-ins to protest segregation, injustice, and the economic oppression of African Americans. A charismatic orator, King soon became known as the most eloquent and influential leader of the civil rights movement. In April 1963, he crystallized the movement's aims and methods in his "Letter from Birmingham City Jail." Four months later, he helped organize the March on Washington, where he delivered his memorable speech "I Have a Dream." Although King stressed nonviolence, he became a martyr for freedom when he was assassinated in Memphis, Tennessee, on April 4, 1968. Before her death in 2006, his widow, Coretta Scott King, worked to keep King's message and achievements alive. The King children continue to carry on their parents' work.

"All labor that uplifts humanity has dignity and importance and should be undertaken with painstaking excellence."

from Letter from Birmingham City Jail

Martin Luther King, Jr.

▲ Martin Luther King, Jr., in a jail cell at the Jefferson County Courthouse in Birmingham, Alabama.

BACKGROUND By the late 1950s, Martin Luther King, Jr., had emerged as a key figure of the civil rights movement. During the Kennedy administration, King was arrested in April, 1963, for protesting racial segregation in Birmingham, Alabama. As he sat in jail, he read a newspaper article in which eight white clergymen criticized him for "unwise and untimely" demonstrations. Without proper writing paper, King drafted a response—this letter—in the cramped margins of that newspaper.

April 16, 1963

I hope the church as a whole will meet the challenge of this decisive hour. But even if the church does not come to the aid of justice, I have no despair about the future. I have no fear about the outcome of our struggle in Birmingham, even if our motives are presently misunderstood. We will reach the goal of freedom in Birmingham and all over the nation, because the goal of America is freedom. Abused and scorned though we may be, our destiny is tied up with the destiny of America. Before the Pilgrims landed at Plymouth we were here. Before the pen of

▲ (left and center) Dr. King is arrested in Montgomery, Alabama (September 3, 1958). (right) Civil rights leaders James Meredith, Martin Luther King, Jr., Roy Wilkins, A. Phillip Randolph, and labor leader Walter Reuther lead a crowd at the March on Washington for Jobs and Freedom (August 28, 1963).

Jefferson etched across the pages of history the majestic words of the Declaration of Independence, we were here. For more than two centuries our foreparents labored in this country without wages; they made cotton king; and they built the homes of their masters in the midst of brutal injustice and shameful humiliation—and yet out of a bottomless vitality they continued to thrive and develop. If the inexpressible cruelties of slavery could not stop us, the opposition we now face will surely fail. We will win our freedom because the sacred heritage of our nation and the eternal will of God are embodied in our echoing demands.

I must close now. But before closing I am impelled to mention one other point in your statement that troubled me profoundly. You warmly commended the Birmingham police force for keeping "order" and "preventing violence." I don't believe you would have so warmly commended the police force if you had seen its angry violent dogs literally biting six unarmed, nonviolent Negroes. I don't believe you would so quickly commend the policemen if you would observe their ugly and inhuman treatment of Negroes here in the city jail; if you would watch them push and curse old Negro women and young Negro girls; if you would see them slap and kick old Negro men and young Negro boys; if you will observe them, as they did on two occasions, refuse to give us food because we wanted to sing our grace together. I'm sorry that I can't join you in your praise for the police department.

Identify Main Ideas and Supporting Details

What are two details King uses to support his main idea about police treatment of protesters?

It is true that they have been rather disciplined in their public handling of the demonstrators. In this sense they have been rather publicly "nonviolent." But for what purpose? To preserve the evil system of segregation. Over the last few years I have consistently preached that nonviolence demands that the means we use must be as pure as the ends we seek. So I have tried to make it clear that it is wrong to use immoral means to attain moral ends. But now I must affirm that it is just as wrong, or even more so, to use moral means to preserve immoral ends. Maybe Mr. Connor and his policemen have been rather publicly nonviolent, as Chief Pritchett was in Albany, Georgia, but they have used the moral means of nonviolence to maintain the immoral end of **flagrant** racial injustice. T. S. Eliot has said that there is no greater treason than to do the right deed for the wrong reason.

I wish you had commended the Negro sit-inners and demonstrators of Birmingham for their sublime courage, their willingness to suffer and their amazing discipline in the midst of the most inhuman provocation. One day the South will recognize its real heroes. They will be the James Merediths, courageously and with a majestic sense of purpose facing jeering and hostile mobs and the agonizing loneliness that characterizes the life of the pioneer. They will be old, oppressed, battered Negro women, symbolized in a seventy-two-year-old woman of Montgomery, Alabama, who rose up with a sense of dignity and with her people decided not to ride the segregated buses, and responded to one who inquired about her tiredness with ungrammatical **profundity**: "My feet is tired, but my soul is rested." They will be the young high school and college students, young ministers of the gospel and a host of their elders courageously and nonviolently sitting-in at lunch counters and willingly going to jail for conscience's sake. One day the South will know that when these disinherited

Vocabulary

flagrant (flā′ grənt) *adj.* glaring, outrageous

profundity (prō fun′ də tē) *n.* intellectual depth

Comprehension

According to King, who are the South's real heroes?

▼ Dr. King at the March on Washington (August 28, 1963)

children of God sat down at lunch counters they were in reality standing up for the best in the American dream and the most sacred values in our Judeo-Christian heritage, and thusly, carrying our whole nation back to those great wells of democracy which were dug deep by the Founding Fathers in the formulation of the Constitution and the Declaration of Independence.

Never before have I written a letter this long (or should I say a book?). I'm afraid that it is much too long to take your precious time. I can assure you that it would have been much shorter if I had been writing from a comfortable desk, but what else is there to do when you are alone for days in the dull monotony of a narrow jail cell other than write long letters, think strange thoughts, and pray long prayers?

If I have said anything in this letter that is an overstatement of the truth and is indicative of an unreasonable impatience, I beg you to forgive me. If I have said anything in this letter that is an understatement of the truth and is indicative of my having a patience that makes me patient with anything less than brotherhood, I beg God to forgive me.

I hope this letter finds you strong in the faith. I also hope that circumstances will soon make it possible for me to meet each of you, not as an integrationist or a civil rights leader, but as a fellow clergyman and a Christian brother. Let us all hope that the dark clouds of racial prejudice will soon pass away and the deep fog of misunderstanding will be lifted from our fear-drenched communities and in some not too distant tomorrow the radiant stars of love and brotherhood will shine over our great nation with all of their scintillating beauty.

Yours for the cause of Peace
and Brotherhood,
Martin Luther King, Jr.

Critical Reading

Cite textual evidence to support your responses.

1. **Key Ideas and Details** **(a)** In the first paragraph, what reasons does King give for his confidence in the outcome of the struggle? **(b) Infer:** Why do you think he emphasizes his attitude about the outcome?
2. **Key Ideas and Details** **Distinguish:** What two points does King make about the means by which a just goal should be reached? Explain.
3. **Integration of Knowledge and Ideas** What do both of these documents suggest are the privileges and obligations of freedom? In your response, use at least two of these Essential Question words: *democracy, liberty, criticize.* ***[Connecting to the Essential Question: How does literature shape or reflect society?]***

Literary Analysis

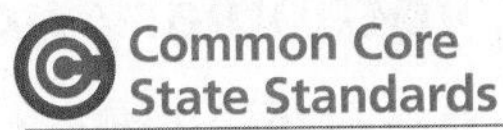

Common Core State Standards

Writing

1. Write arguments to support claims in an analysis of substantive topics or texts, using valid reasoning and relevant and sufficient evidence. *(p. 1114)*

1.d. Establish and maintain a formal style and objective tone while attending to the norms and conventions of the discipline in which they are writing. *(p. 1114)*

Language

3. Apply knowledge of language to understand how language functions in different contexts, to make effective choices for meaning or style, and to comprehend more fully when reading or listening. *(p. 1115)*

4.b. Identify and correctly use patterns of word changes that indicate different meanings or parts of speech. *(p. 1114)*

5. Demonstrate understanding of word relationships. *(p. 1114)*

1. **Key Ideas and Details** What details **support** Kennedy's **main idea** that the task of defending freedom should be welcomed? Explain.
2. **Craft and Structure** **(a)** Identify examples of **parallelism** in the sixth paragraph of Kennedy's inaugural address, beginning "To those old allies . . . ." **(b)** Which of these passages is also an example of **antithesis?** Explain.
3. **Craft and Structure** **(a)** Reread the paragraph on page 1106 in Kennedy's inaugural address that begins "And if a beachhead of cooperation. . . ." Using a chart like the one shown, identify the parallel words and phrases. **(b)** Choose the strongest example and explain your choice.

Parallel Words	Parallel Phrases

4. **Craft and Structure** Identify the two basic **lists** with which Kennedy organizes the majority of the speech.
5. **Craft and Structure** How does the passage that begins "Ask not what your country can do for you . . ." echo and reinforce the two lists Kennedy uses earlier in his speech?
6. **Key Ideas and Details** What supporting details does King give to support his central idea that "One day the South will recognize its real heroes"?
7. **Craft and Structure** **(a)** In King's letter, identify parallelism in the paragraph beginning "If I have said anything in this letter that is an overstatement . . . ." **(b)** What is the effect of this rhetorical device?
8. **Craft and Structure** **(a)** What underlying reason does King point out for the police department's "nonviolent" treatment of the demonstrators? **(b)** What **argument** does King make about this purpose? **(c)** How does he **support** this argument?
9. **Integration of Knowledge and Ideas** **(a)** What double audience, or group of readers, does King address in his letter? **(b)** Which details in the final paragraph show his awareness of both audiences? Explain.
10. **Comparing Literary Works** **(a)** Which text—Kennedy's speech or King's letter—makes more frequent use of parallelism and antithesis? **(b)** Explain why each author's use of these devices is appropriate to the kind of document he is writing and to its method of delivery.

Close Reading Activities Continued

Vocabulary Acquisition and Use

Word Analysis: Latin Root *-vert-* or *-vers-*

The word *adversary* contains the root *-vert-* or *-vers-*, meaning "to switch" or "to turn around." With this root in mind, you might define *adversary* as "a person who has turned against" someone or something. Other words that contain this root include *reverse,* which might be defined as "to turn around again," and *convert,* which might be defined as "to turn with." For each of the words below, write a definition that includes the word *switch* or *turn.* If you are unfamiliar with a word, refer to a dictionary before writing your own definition.

1. introvert
2. divert
3. controversy
4. vertigo
5. invert
6. versatile
7. revert
8. vertical

Vocabulary: Synonyms

For each item, choose the letter of its synonym, and explain your choice.

1. **flagrant: (a)** delicious **(b)** obvious **(c)** contorted
2. **alliance: (a)** contact **(b)** program **(c)** association
3. **profundity: (a)** exploration **(b)** wisdom **(c)** ambiguity
4. **eradicate: (a)** analyze **(b)** redefine **(c)** eliminate
5. **adversary: (a)** antagonist **(b)** friend **(c)** minister
6. **invective: (a)** insult **(b)** apology **(c)** rhetoric

Writing

Argument A letter to the editor is a *formal business letter* written by a member of a community and submitted to a newspaper or magazine for publication. Write a **letter to the editor** commenting on an issue about which you feel strongly. In your letter, keep in mind the needs, views, and prior knowledge of the audience you are addressing.

Prewriting Jot down a list of topics that matter to you. Use a chart like the one shown to list possible ideas and support.

Model: Listing to Generate Ideas

Issue: ______________________________

Statement of Opinion: ______________________________

Support (examples/reasons):

Drafting Craft your claim as a clear, concise statement about the issue that establishes a serious, formal tone. As you draft, support your claim with a variety of examples, reasons, and other details. In addition, use *parallelism* or *antithesis* to boost your letter's persuasive power. Follow correct *business letter format* with a formal inside address, salutation, and closing.

Revising Review your letter to be sure that you have maintained a formal tone while using strong, precise words, a variety of sentence structures, and a form of parallelism. Then, revise for coherence, adding transitional words and phrases as needed to present your argument smoothly and logically.

Conventions and Style: Using Active, Not Passive, Voice

A verb is in the **passive voice** if the action is done to the subject. A verb is in the **active voice** when the subject does the action. Use active voice in your writing whenever you can. It is more economical, forceful, and direct than the passive voice. For example, notice that the sentence using the active voice has two fewer words than the one using the passive voice:

Passive: Nuclear weapons were being stockpiled by the United States and the Soviet Union.

Active: The United States and the Soviet Union were stockpiling nuclear weapons.

Correct Use of Passive Voice

There are exceptions, of course. Some sentences correctly use passive voice verbs because the doer of the action is unknown or unimportant.

- John F. Kennedy was elected in 1960.
- Martin Luther King, Jr., was jailed.

Examples of Passive Voice Verbs	
Past	was held, had been held
Present	is held, has been held, is being held
Future	will be held, will have been held

Practice Identify each sentence as active or passive. If a sentence in the passive voice should be in the active voice, rewrite it.

1. Both groups of countries were being weighed down by the cost of weapons.
2. The torch of freedom was passed by the old generation to a new one.
3. A free society must help the poor.
4. A global alliance is needed to be formed by the nations of the world.
5. King wanted the struggle for civil rights to be won.
6. Oppressed women were symbolized by a seventy-two-year-old from Birmingham.
7. Democracy was established in America.
8. Sit-ins were supported by old and young.
9. The letter was not written by King from his comfortable desk but from jail.
10. King hoped the future would bring an end to racial prejudice.

Writing and Speaking Conventions

A. Writing Rewrite each passive sentence to make it active.

Example: People were called on by President Kennedy to celebrate freedom.

Rewritten Sentence: President Kennedy called on people to celebrate freedom.

1. Citizens were asked by President Kennedy to celebrate freedom.
2. Human life might have been destroyed by nuclear war.
3. King said that nonviolent protesters were mistreated by Birmingham police officers.
4. T. S. Eliot was quoted by Martin Luther King, Jr.

B. Speaking Deliver a formal response to Dr. King's "Letter from Birmingham City Jail." Include reasons for your opinion, and use active voice whenever possible.

Drama is life with the dull bits cut out.

–Alfred Hitchcock

In This Section

For more practice analyzing drama, see page1241.

Defining Drama

A **drama,** or **play,** is a story written to be performed by actors. Unlike a short story or novel, a drama presents action mainly through **dialogue,** the conversation and speeches of characters. A play typically includes several other key literary elements:

- **Plot** is the ordered sequence of events in a play. A play is often divided into large units called **acts,** which are then subdivided into smaller ones called **scenes.**
- **Characters** are the people who participate in the action of the play and are portrayed onstage or onscreen by **actors.**
- **Stage directions** are notes included in the play to describe sets, costumes, lighting, sound, props, and—in some cases—the ways in which actors should move and deliver their lines.

Types of Drama Ever since the development of Western drama in ancient Greece, plays have been divided into two broad categories.

- **Comedy** is drama that ends happily. Comedies may be funny, but humor is not their defining trait.
- **Tragedy** is drama that shows the downfall of a noble but flawed figure called the **tragic hero.**

Note that some plays, including several by Shakespeare, mix elements of both categories, or otherwise bend their definitions.

Modern Realistic Drama While some modern playwrights experiment with fantasy or absurdity, many more write realistic plays that feature recognizable settings and characters. For some modern playwrights, the realistic play is also a vehicle for social and political criticism.

Close Read: Modern Realistic Drama

These elements of modern realistic drama appear in the Model text at right.

Realistic Characters: authentic characters dealing with realistic, if heightened, conflicts *Example: "LAURA: I don't do anything—much. Oh, please don't think I sit around doing nothing!" (Tennessee Williams)*	**Realistic Settings:** the use of familiar, ordinary places, such as a family kitchen, as sites for the action *Example: "[Mrs. Gibbs and Mrs. Webb enter their kitchens and start the day as in the first act.]" (Thornton Wilder)*
Realistic Dialogue: the use of language that reflects how real people speak *Example: "FRIENDLY: What say we grab a little dinner after the show? The 21 Club?" (Heslov and Clooney)*	**Social and Political Criticism:** presentation, through the elements of the play, of the playwright's stand on social or political issues *Example: "Long-held hatreds of neighbors could now be openly expressed, and vengeance taken..." (Arthur Miller)*

Model

About the Text Lorraine Hansberry (1930–1965) was the first African American woman dramatist to have a play produced on Broadway. *A Raisin in the Sun*, which premiered in New York City in 1959, tells the story of the Youngers, an African American family living in Chicago during the late 1940s or early 1950s. The family wants to buy a house in an all-white suburb. In the excerpt, Beneatha is angry at her brother because he has agreed to accept money in exchange for stopping the purchase.

from ***A Raisin in the Sun***
by **Lorraine Hansberry**

BENEATHA: He's no brother of mine.

MAMA: What you say?

BENEATHA: I said that that individual in that room is no brother of mine.

MAMA: That's what I thought you said. You feeling like you better than he is today? [BENEATHA does not answer.] Yes? What you tell him a minute ago? That he wasn't a man? Yes? You give him up for me? You done wrote his epitaph too—like the rest of the world? Well, who give you the privilege?

BENEATHA: Be on my side for once! You saw what he just did, Mama! You saw him—down on his knees. Wasn't it you who taught me—to despise any man who would do that. Do what he's going to do.

MAMA: Yes—I taught you that. Me and your daddy. But I thought I taught you something else too…I thought I taught you to love him.

BENEATHA: Love him? There is nothing left to love.

MAMA: There is always something left to love. And if you ain't learned that, you ain't learned nothing. [looking at her] Have you cried for that boy today? I don't mean for yourself and for the family 'cause we lost the money. I mean for him; what he been through and what it done to him. Child, when do you think is the time to love somebody the most; when they done good and made things easy for everybody? Well then, you ain't through learning—because that ain't the time at all. It's when he's at his lowest and can't believe in hisself 'cause the world done whipped him so. When you starts measuring somebody, measure him right, child, measure him right. Make sure you done taken into account what hills and valleys he come through before he got to wherever he is.

Realistic Characters
The excerpt begins with a typical real-life situation: a sister angry at her brother.

Realistic Settings
The immediate physical setting is an ordinary family home. The realistic historical setting of post–World War II Chicago creates enormous conflicts for the Younger family.

Realistic Dialogue
The characters use informal, ordinary language. Mama, in particular, speaks expressive, nonstandard English.

Social and Political Criticism
By simply telling the Youngers' story, the playwright is implicitly expressing social and political views. Specific speeches, such as Mama's statement that the "world done whipped him so," are more explicit critical statements.

Arthur Miller (1915–2005)

A legend of the modern American theater, Arthur Miller has chronicled the dilemmas of common people pitted against powerful and unyielding social forces. A native New Yorker, Miller lived through bad times as well as good. During the Depression, his family's business went bankrupt. Although Miller graduated from high school in 1932, he was forced to delay his enrollment at the University of Michigan for more than two years in order to raise money for tuition. He did so by working at a variety of jobs, including singing for a local radio station, driving a truck, and working as a stock clerk in an automobile parts warehouse.

Promising Playwright

Miller first began writing drama while still in college. In 1947, his play *All My Sons* opened on Broadway to immediate acclaim, establishing Miller as a bright new talent. Two years later, he won international fame and the Pulitzer Prize for *Death of a Salesman* (1949), which critics hailed as a modern American tragedy.

His next play, *The Crucible* (1953), was less warmly received because of its political content. Miller drew a parallel between the hysteria surrounding the witchcraft trials in Puritan New England and the postwar climate of McCarthyism—Senator Joseph McCarthy's obsessive quest to uncover Communist party infiltration of American institutions.

In the introduction to his *Collected Plays* (1957), Miller described his perceptions of the atmosphere during the McCarthy era and the way in which those perceptions influenced the writing of *The Crucible*. He said, "It was as though the whole country had been born anew, without a memory even of certain elemental decencies which a year or two earlier no one would have imagined could be altered, let alone forgotten. Astounded, I watched men pass me by without a nod whom I had known rather well for years; and again, the astonishment was produced by my knowledge, which I could not give up, that the terror in these people was being knowingly planned and consciously engineered, and yet that all they knew was terror. That so interior and subjective an emotion could have been so manifestly created from without was a marvel to me. It underlies every word in *The Crucible*."

In the Shadows of McCarthyism

During the two years following the publication and production of *The Crucible*, Miller was investigated for possible associations with the Communist party. In 1956, he was called to testify before the House Committee on Un-American Activities (HUAC). Although he had never joined the Communist party, Miller—and many of his contemporaries—had advocated principles of social justice and equality among the classes. He had become disillusioned, however, by the reality of communism as practiced in the Soviet Union. At the HUAC hearings, he testified about his own experiences, but he refused to discuss his colleagues and associates. He was found guilty of contempt of Congress for his silence. The sentence was later overturned.

Hollywood Glamour

In 1956, the spotlight focused on Miller's personal life when he married glamorous film star Marilyn Monroe. Although he wrote very little during their five-year marriage, he did pen the screenplay for a film, *The Misfits* (1961), in which Monroe starred. After the marriage ended, Miller wrote other noteworthy plays, including *After the Fall* (1964), *The Price* (1968), and *The Last Yankee* (1993).

A Voice of Conscience

Arthur Miller died in 2005 at the age of eighty-nine. Playwright Edward Albee said of him, "Arthur never compromised. He never sold out, he never did anything just for that awful word entertainment. . . . He was able to use art and his enormously important social and political points and make them so skillfully that people never thought they were being hit over the head."

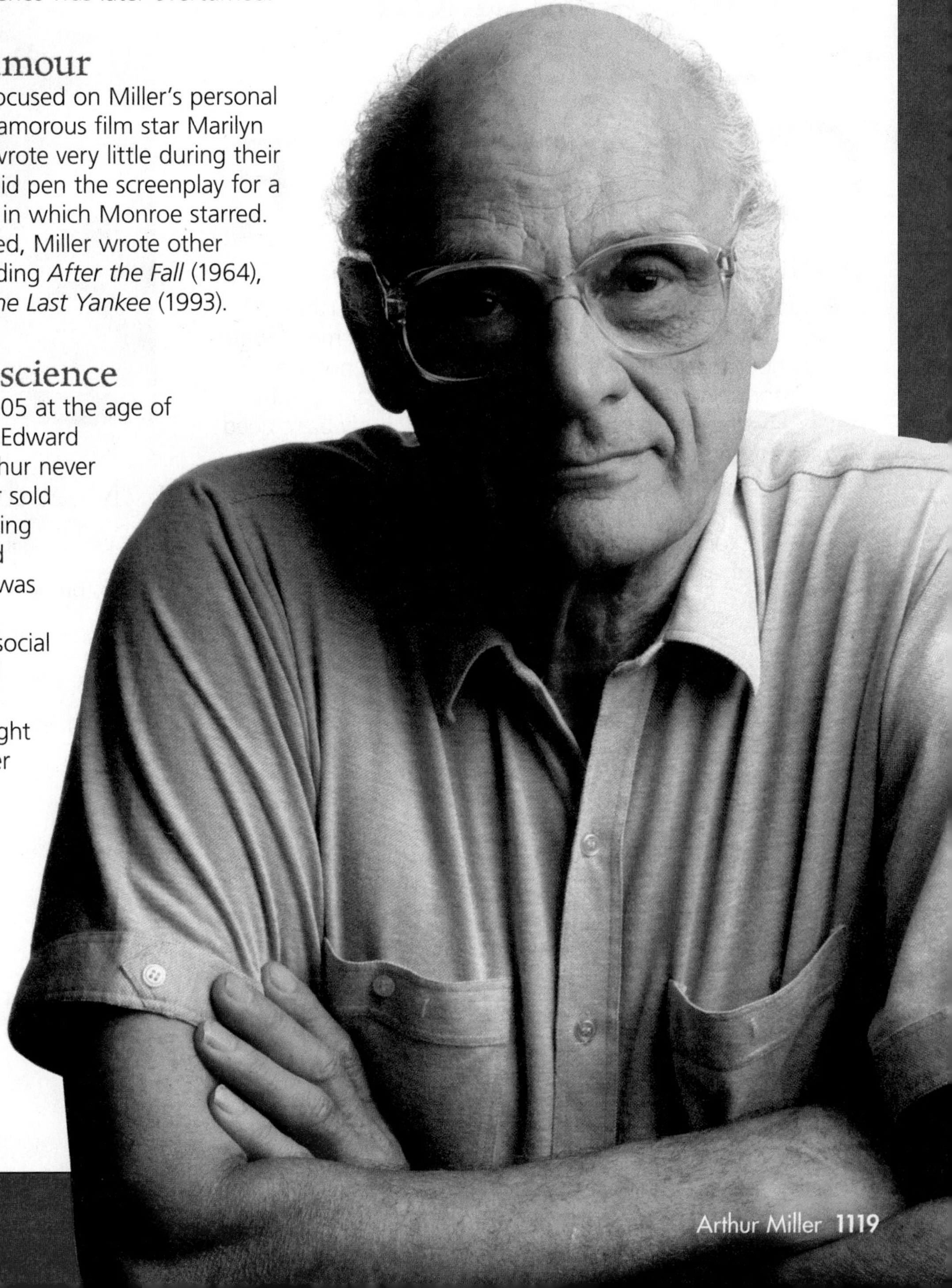

Themes Across Time: Author's Insights

The Words of Arthur Miller on *The Crucible*

The Historical Background of *The Crucible*

In *Echoes Down the Corridor*, published in 2000, Arthur Miller writes: "It would probably never have occurred to me to write a play about the Salem witch trials of 1692 had I not seen some astonishing correspondences with that calamity in the America of the late forties and early fifties. . . . my basic need was to respond to a phenomenon which, with only small exaggeration, one could say was paralyzing a whole generation and in an amazingly short time was drying up the habits of trust and toleration in public discourse.

"I refer, of course, to the anticommunist rage that threatened to reach hysterical proportions and sometimes did. I can't remember anyone calling it an ideological war, but I think now that that is what it amounted to. Looking back at the period, I suppose we very rapidly passed over anything like a discussion or debate and into something quite different, a hunt not alone for subversive people but ideas and even a suspect language."

The Writing of *The Crucible*

Miller explains where his ideas for *The Crucible* came from, saying, "On a lucky afternoon I happened upon a book, *The Devil in Massachusetts*, by Marion Starkey, a narrative of the Salem witch-hunt of 1692. I knew this story from my college reading more than a decade earlier, but now in this changed and darkened America it turned a wholly new aspect toward me, namely, the poetry of the hunt. Poetry may seem an odd word for a witch-hunt, but I saw now that there was something of the marvelous in the spectacle of the whole village, if not an entire province, whose imagination was literally captured by a vision of something that wasn't there. . . .

Meet the Author

Arthur Miller's *The Crucible* failed at the box office in its initial production in 1953, but it has since become one of the most popular American plays of the twentieth century.

"As I stood in the stillness of the Salem courthouse, surrounded by the miasmic swirl of the images of the 1950s but with my head in 1692, what the two eras had in common was gradually gaining definition. In both was the menace of concealed plots, but most startling were the similarities in the rituals of defense and the investigative routines. Three hundred years apart, both prosecutions were alleging membership in a secret, disloyal group; should the accused confess, his honesty could be proved only in precisely the same way—by naming former confederates, nothing less. Thus the informer became the very proof of the plot and the investigator's necessity."

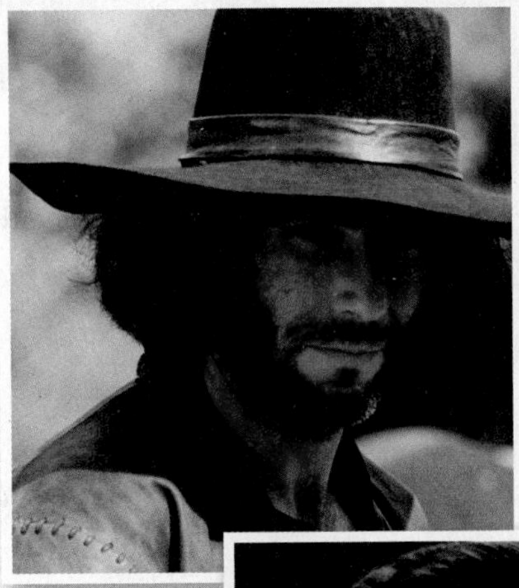

▲ Daniel Day-Lewis as John Proctor and Winona Ryder as Abigail Williams in the 1996 film version of *The Crucible*

How the Play Has Lasted

Musing on the eventual popularity of *The Crucible*, Miller says, "*The Crucible* is my most-produced play, here and abroad. . . . And it is part of the play's history, I think, that to people in so many parts of the world its story seems so like their own. . . . In fact, I used to think, half seriousiy—although it was not far from the truth—that you could tell when a dictator was about to take power in a Latin American country or when one had just been overthrown, by whether *The Crucible* was suddenly being produced there."

Critical Reading

Cite textual evidence to support your responses.

1. **Key Ideas and Details** **(a)** What experience gave Miller the original idea for *The Crucible*? **(b) Infer:** What aspects of this experience helped Miller connect the Salem of 1692 with the United States of the late 1940s and 1950s?
2. **Key Ideas and Details** **(a)** What specific similarities does Miller see between the Salem witch trials of 1692 and the anticommunist hearings of the 1950s? **(b) Speculate:** Why do you think *The Crucible* is Miller's most-produced play?

As You Read *The Crucible* . . .

3. Notice how the conflict in the play can represent a universal conflict.
4. Consider ways in which reading this commentary enhances your experience of the play.

ARTHUR MILLER'S STARS

▶ Dustin Hoffman on the set of *Death of a Salesman* as Willy Loman.

Arthur Miller traveled in the circles of the rich, famous, and celebrated. He was at one time the husband of Marilyn Monroe. He became the father-in-law of Academy Award-winning actor Daniel Day-Lewis. Miller's works also drew actors with major star power, eager for the opportunity to be part of a Miller production.

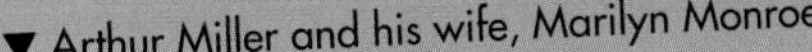

▼ Arthur Miller and his wife, Marilyn Monroe

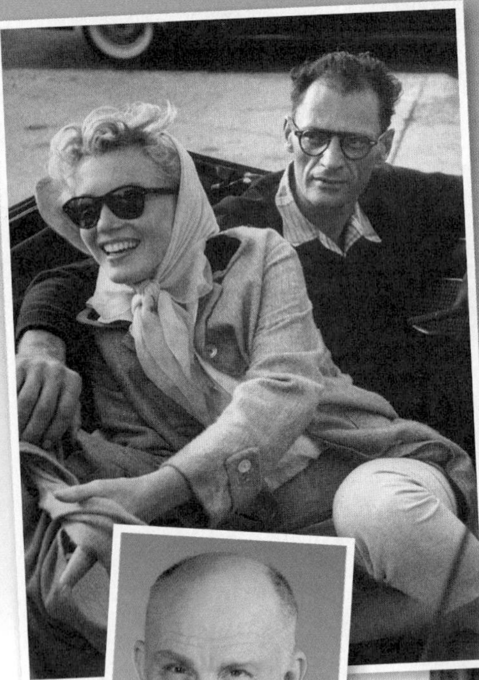

◀ George C. Scott and Arthur Miller

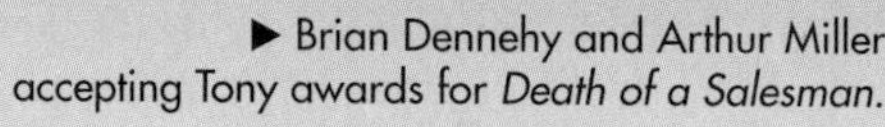

▶ Brian Dennehy and Arthur Miller accepting Tony awards for *Death of a Salesman.*

▲ John Malkovich played Biff Loman

▲ Clark Gable and Marilyn Monroe in Miller's film *The Misfits.*

Building Knowledge and Insight *The Crucible, Act I*

Connecting to the Essential Question In this tragic play, characters must decide what it means to do the right thing. As you read, look for moments when characters must choose between preserving themselves or their ideals. Doing so will help you think about the Essential Question: **How does literature shape or reflect society?**

Close Reading Focus

Plot; Dramatic Exposition

Plot is the sequence of events that happen in a story. Plots follow a series of phases that, taken together, are called the "dramatic arc." Plot is always driven by a *conflict*, or struggle, between opposing forces:

- **Rising Action:** The conflict is introduced and begins to build.
- **Climax:** The conflict reaches its moment of greatest intensity. This is the turning point, when an event signals the final outcome.
- **Falling Action:** The conflict diminishes and approaches resolution.
- **Resolution:** The conflict ends.

In a long, complex narrative such as this play, there may be multiple conflicts. In this play, Miller uses **dramatic exposition,** or prose commentaries, to provide background information about the characters and their world.

Preparing to Read Complex Texts Most plays are written to be performed, not read. When reading drama, it is important to **identify the text structures** that provide different kinds of information. Text structures include *dialogue*, the words spoken by the actors, and *stage directions*, details the playwright includes about the setting and action. Stage directions may be set in italic type or in brackets to distinguish them from dialogue. As you read Act I of *The Crucible,* use a chart like the one shown to examine how information from the two types of text structures contributes to your understanding of the characters.

Reading Literature

3. Analyze the impact of the author's choices regarding how to develop and relate elements of a story or drama (e.g., how the action is ordered).

5. Analyze how an author's choices concerning how to structure specific parts of a text (e.g., the choice of where to begin or end a story, the choice to provide a comedic or tragic resolution) contribute to its overall structure and meaning as well as its aesthetic impact.

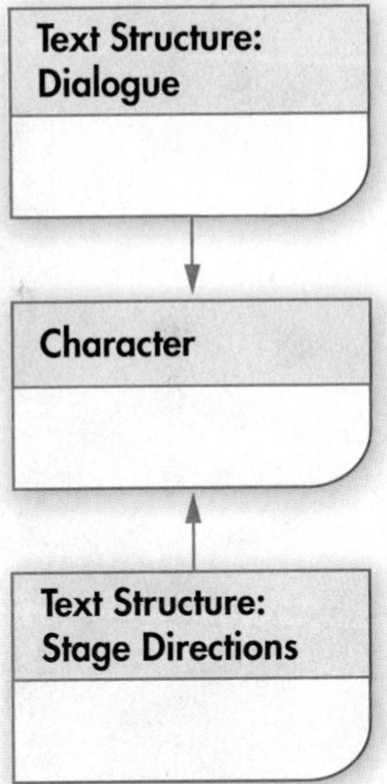

Vocabulary

You will encounter the words listed here in the text that follows. Copy the words into your notebook. Which words have the same suffix and are nouns?

predilection
ingratiating
dissembling
calumny
inculcation
propitiation
evade

The Crucible[1]

Arthur Miller

Background In 1692, the British colony of Massachusetts was convulsed by a witchcraft hysteria that resulted in the execution of twenty people and the jailing of more than 100 others. The incident, though unprecedented for New England, was not unique. During the sixteenth and seventeenth centuries, witchhunts swept through Europe, resulting in tens of thousands of executions. Many of the accused were guilty only of practicing folk customs that had survived in Europe since pre-Christian times. In an era when religion and politics were intertwined, witch hunts were often politically motivated. England's James I, for example, wrote a treatise on witchcraft and sometimes accused his enemies of practicing the black arts. It was a cry that resonated well with a superstitious populace.

For the New England colonies, the witchcraft episode was perhaps inevitable. The colonists endured harsh conditions and punishing hardship from day to day. Finding themselves at the mercy of forces beyond their control—bitter weather, sickness and death, devastating fires, drought, and insect infestations that killed their crops—many colonists attributed their misfortunes to the powers of evil. They were fearful people and believed that witches, servants of the Devil, were real and dangerous. In the small parish of Salem Village, many were quick to blame witchcraft when the minister's daughter and several other girls were afflicted by seizures and lapsed into unconsciousness, especially after it was

---

1. **crucible** (kro͞o′ sə bel) *n.* heat resistent container in which metals are melted or fused at very high temperatures; a severe trial or test.

learned that the girls had been dabbling in fortunetelling with the minister's slave, Tituba. (They were not dancing in the woods, as portrayed in the play.) At first, only Tituba and two elderly women were called witches, but the hunt spread until some of the colony's most prominent citizens stood accused. Many historians have seen a pattern of social and economic animosity behind the accusations, but most scholars feel that mass hysteria was also a strong contributing factor.

A *crucible* is a heat-resistant container in which metals are melted or fused at very high temperatures. The word is used symbolically to suggest a severe trial or test. Miller chose this title well as the play depicts severely trying times. When *The Crucible* was first published, Arthur Miller added a note about the play's historical accuracy: "This play is not history in the sense in which the word is used by the academic historian. Dramatic purposes have sometimes required many characters to be fused into one; the number of girls involved in the 'crying-out' has been reduced; Abigail's age has been raised; while there were several judges of almost equal authority, I have symbolized them in Hathorne and Danforth. However, I believe that the reader will discover here the essential nature of one of the strangest and most awful chapters in human history. The fate of each character is exactly that of his historical model, and there is no one in the drama who did not play a similar—and in some cases exactly the same—role in history."

CHARACTERS

REVEREND PARRIS
BETTY PARRIS
TITUBA
ABIGAIL WILLIAMS
SUSANNA WALCOTT
MRS. ANN PUTNAM
THOMAS PUTNAM
MERCY LEWIS
MARY WARREN
JOHN PROCTOR
REBECCA NURSE
MARTHA COREY
REVEREND JOHN HALE
ELIZABETH PROCTOR
FRANCIS NURSE
EZEKIEL CHEEVER
MARSHAL HERRICK
JUDGE HATHORNE
DEPUTY GOVERNOR DANFORTH
SARAH GOOD
HOPKINS
GILES COREY

(An Overture)

A small upper bedroom in the home of REVEREND SAMUEL PARRIS, *Salem, Massachusetts, in the spring of the year 1692.*

There is a narrow window at the left. Through its leaded panes the morning sunlight streams. A candle still burns near the bed, which is at the right. A chest, a chair, and a small table are the other furnishings. At the back a door opens on the landing of the stairway to the ground floor. The room gives off an air of clean spareness. The roof rafters are exposed, and the wood colors are raw and unmellowed.

As the curtain rises, REVEREND PARRIS *is discovered kneeling beside the bed, evidently in prayer. His daughter,* BETTY PARRIS, *aged ten, is lying on the bed, inert.*

Identifying Text Features

What important information is revealed in the third paragraph of the stage directions?

At the time of these events Parris was in his middle forties. In history he cut a villainous path, and there is very little good to be said for him. He believed he was being persecuted wherever he went, despite his best efforts to win people and God to his side. In meeting, he felt insulted if someone rose to shut the door without first asking his permission. He was a widower with no interest in children, or talent with them. He regarded them as young adults, and until this strange crisis he, like the rest of Salem, never conceived that the children were anything but thankful for being permitted to walk straight, eyes slightly lowered, arms at the sides, and mouths shut until bidden to speak.

Arthur Miller
Author's Insight

Miller once speculated that *The Crucible*, with its large cast, would not be accepted by today's "commercialized" Broadway and was too large for off-Broadway theaters: ". . . what would one do with *The Crucible* on a shoebox stage [off-Broadway] with its twenty-one characters and several sets?"

His house stood in the "town"—but we today would hardly call it a village. The meeting house was nearby, and from this point outward—toward the bay or inland—there were a few small-windowed, dark houses snuggling against the raw Massachusetts winter. Salem had been established hardly forty years before. To the European world the whole province was a barbaric frontier inhabited by a sect of fanatics who, nevertheless, were shipping out products of slowly increasing quantity and value.

No one can really know what their lives were like. They had no novelists—and would not have permitted anyone to read a novel if one were handy. Their creed forbade anything resembling a theater or "vain enjoyment." They did not celebrate Christmas, and a holiday from work meant only that they must concentrate even more upon prayer.

Which is not to say that nothing broke into this strict and somber way of life. When a new farmhouse was built, friends assembled to "raise the roof," and there would be special foods cooked and probably some potent cider passed around. There was a good supply of ne'er-do-wells in Salem, who dallied at the shovelboard[2] in Bridget Bishop's tavern. Probably more than the creed, hard work kept the morals of the place from spoiling, for the people were forced to fight the land like heroes for every grain of corn, and no man had very much time for fooling around.

That there were some jokers, however, is indicated by the practice of appointing a two-man patrol whose duty was to "walk forth in the time of God's worship to take notice of such as either lye about the meeting house, without attending to the word and ordinances, or that lye at home or in the fields without giving good account thereof, and to take the names of such persons, and to present them to the magistrates, whereby they may be accordingly proceeded against." This **predilection** for minding other people's business was time-honored among the people of Salem, and it undoubtedly created many of the suspicions which were to feed the coming madness. It was also, in my opinion, one of the things that a John Proctor would rebel against, for the time of the armed camp had almost passed, and since the country was reasonably—although not wholly—safe, the old disciplines were beginning to rankle. But, as in all such matters, the issue was not clear-cut, for danger was still a possibility, and in unity still lay the best promise of safety.

The edge of the wilderness was close by. The American continent stretched endlessly west, and it was full of mystery for them. It stood, dark and threatening, over their shoulders night and day, for out of it Indian tribes marauded from time to time, and Reverend Parris had parishioners who had lost relatives to these heathen.

The parochial snobbery of these people was partly responsible for their failure to convert the Indians. Probably they also preferred to take land from heathens rather than from fellow Christians. At any rate, very few Indians were converted, and the Salem folk believed that the virgin forest was the Devil's last preserve, his home base and the citadel of his final stand. To the best of their knowledge the American forest was the last place on earth that was not paying homage to God.

For these reasons, among others, they carried about an air of innate resistance, even of persecution. Their fathers had, of course, been persecuted in England. So now they and their church found it necessary to deny any other sect its freedom, lest their New Jerusalem[3] be defiled and corrupted by wrong ways and deceitful ideas.

They believed, in short, that they held in their steady hands the candle that would light the world. We have inherited this belief, and it has helped and hurt us. It helped them with the discipline it gave them. They were a dedicated folk, by and large, and they had to be to survive the life they had chosen or been born into in this country.

Dramatic Exposition

In what ways does this long exposition differ from a typical stage direction?

Vocabulary

predilection (pred′ ə lek′ shən) *n.* preexisting preference

Comprehension

What is a time-honored activity among the people of Salem?

---

2. **shovelboard** game in which a coin or other disk is driven with the hand along a highly polished board, floor, or table marked with transverse lines.
3. **New Jerusalem** in the Bible, the holy city of heaven.

Vocabulary
ingratiating (in grā′ shē āt′ iŋ) *adj.* charming; flattering

The proof of their belief's value to them may be taken from the opposite character of the first Jamestown settlement, farther south, in Virginia. The Englishmen who landed there were motivated mainly by a hunt for profit. They had thought to pick off the wealth of the new country and then return rich to England. They were a band of individualists, and a much more ingratiating group than the Massachusetts men. But Virginia destroyed them. Massachusetts tried to kill off the Puritans, but they combined; they set up a communal society which, in the beginning, was little more than an armed camp with an autocratic and very devoted leadership. It was, however, an autocracy by consent, for they were united from top to bottom by a commonly held ideology whose perpetuation was the reason and justification for all their sufferings. So their self-denial, their purposefulness, their suspicion of all vain pursuits, their hard-handed justice, were altogether perfect instruments for the conquest of this space so antagonistic to man.

The Execution of Stephen Burroughs for Witchcraft at Salem, Massachusetts in 1692, 19th-Century Engraving

But the people of Salem in 1692 were not quite the dedicated folk that arrived on the *Mayflower.* A vast differentiation had taken place, and in their own time a revolution had unseated the royal government and substituted a junta[4] which was at this moment in power. The times, to their eyes, must have been out of joint, and to the common folk must have seemed as insoluble and complicated as do ours today. It is not hard to see how easily many could have been led to believe that the time of confusion had been brought upon them by deep and darkling forces. No hint of such speculation appears on the court record, but social disorder in any age breeds such mystical suspicions, and when, as in Salem, wonders are brought forth from below the social surface, it is too much to expect people to hold back very long from laying on the victims with all the force of their frustrations.

▲ Critical Viewing
This nineteenth-century engraving shows the hanging of the Reverend Stephen Burroughs during the Salem witchcraft trials. What does this image suggest about the condemned man's state of mind? **INFER**

The Salem tragedy, which is about to begin in these pages, developed from a paradox. It is a paradox in whose grip we still live, and there is no prospect yet that we will discover its resolution. Simply, it was this: for good purposes, even high purposes, the people of Salem developed a theocracy, a combine of state and religious power whose function was to keep the community together, and to prevent any kind of disunity that might open it to destruction by material or ideological enemies. It was forged for a necessary purpose and accomplished that purpose. But all organization is and must be grounded on the idea of

4. junta (hoon′ tə) *assembly or council.*

exclusion and prohibition, just as two objects cannot occupy the same space. Evidently the time came in New England when the repressions of order were heavier than seemed warranted by the dangers against which the order was organized. The witch-hunt was a perverse manifestation of the panic which set in among all classes when the balance began to turn toward greater individual freedom.

When one rises above the individual villainy displayed, one can only pity them all, just as we shall be pitied someday. It is still impossible for man to organize his social life without repressions, and the balance has yet to be struck between order and freedom.

The witch-hunt was not, however, a mere repression. It was also, and as importantly, a long overdue opportunity for everyone so inclined to express publicly his guilt and sins, under the cover of accusations against the victims. It suddenly became possible—and patriotic and holy—for a man to say that Martha Corey had come into his bedroom at night, and that, while his wife was sleeping at his side, Martha laid herself down on his chest and "nearly suffocated him." Of course it was her spirit only, but his satisfaction at confessing himself was no lighter than if it had been Martha herself. One could not ordinarily speak such things in public.

Long-held hatreds of neighbors could now be openly expressed, and vengeance taken, despite the Bible's charitable injunctions. Land-lust which had been expressed before by constant bickering over boundaries and deeds, could now be elevated to the arena of morality; one could cry witch against one's neighbor and feel perfectly justified in the bargain. Old scores could be settled on a plane of heavenly combat between Lucifer[5] and the Lord; suspicions and the envy of the miserable toward the happy could and did burst out in the general revenge.

REVEREND PARRIS *is praying now, and, though we cannot hear his words, a sense of his confusion hangs about him. He mumbles, then seems about to weep; then he weeps, then prays again; but his daughter does not stir on the bed.*

The door opens, and his Negro slave enters. TITUBA *is in her forties.* PARRIS *brought her with him from Barbados, where he spent some years as a merchant before entering the ministry. She enters as one does who can no longer bear to be barred from the sight of her beloved, but she is also very frightened because her slave sense has warned her that, as always, trouble in this house eventually lands on her back.*

TITUBA, *already taking a step backward:* My Betty be hearty soon?

PARRIS: Out of here!

TITUBA, *backing to the door:* My Betty not goin' die . . .

PARRIS, *scrambling to his feet in a fury:* Out of my sight! *She is gone.* Out of my—*He is overcome with sobs. He clamps his teeth against them and closes the door and leans against it, exhausted.* Oh, my God! God

Dramatic Exposition
Why is this background knowledge about Salem and the witch hunt important to your understanding of the play?

Plot
What conflict in the Parris household is introduced with Tituba's entrance?

Comprehension
What could now be openly expressed among the residents of Salem?

---

5. Lucifer (lo͞o′ sə fər) the Devil.

Vocabulary

dissembling (di sem′ bliŋ) *n.* concealment of one's real nature or motives

Identifying Text Features

Based on what stage directions have revealed about Abigail's personality, what can you conclude about her "worry" and "apprehension"?

Plot

What problem consumes Parris and a growing number of his neighbors?

help me! *Quaking with fear, mumbling to himself through his sobs, he goes to the bed and gently takes* BETTY'S *hand.* Betty. Child. Dear child. Will you wake, will you open up your eyes! Betty, little one . . .

He is bending to kneel again when his niece, ABIGAIL WILLIAMS, *seventeen, enters—a strikingly beautiful girl, an orphan, with an endless capacity for* **dissembling**. *Now she is all worry and apprehension and propriety.*

ABIGAIL: Uncle? *He looks to her.* Susanna Walcott's here from Doctor Griggs.

PARRIS: Oh? Let her come, let her come.

ABIGAIL, *leaning out the door to call to Susanna, who is down the hall a few steps:* Come in, Susanna.

SUSANNA WALCOTT, *a little younger than Abigail, a nervous, hurried girl, enters.*

PARRIS, *eagerly:* What does the doctor say, child?

SUSANNA, *craning around* PARRIS *to get a look at* BETTY: He bid me come and tell you, reverend sir, that he cannot discover no medicine for it in his books.

PARRIS: Then he must search on.

SUSANNA: Aye, sir, he have been searchin' his books since he left you, sir. But he bid me tell you, that you might look to unnatural things for the cause of it.

PARRIS, *his eyes going wide:* No—no. There be no unnatural cause here. Tell him I have sent for Reverend Hale of Beverly, and Mr. Hale will surely confirm that. Let him look to medicine and put out all thought of unnatural causes here. There be none.

SUSANNA: Aye, sir. He bid me tell you. *She turns to go.*

ABIGAIL: Speak nothin' of it in the village, Susanna.

PARRIS: Go directly home and speak nothing of unnatural causes.

SUSANNA: Aye, sir. I pray for her. *She goes out.*

ABIGAIL: Uncle, the rumor of witchcraft is all about; I think you'd best go down and deny it yourself. The parlor's packed with people, sir. I'll sit with her.

PARRIS, *pressed, turns on her:* And what shall I say to them? That my daughter and my niece I discovered dancing like heathen in the forest?

ABIGAIL: Uncle, we did dance; let you tell them I confessed it—and I'll be whipped if I must be. But they're speakin' of witchcraft. Betty's not witched.

PARRIS: Abigail, I cannot go before the congregation when I know you have not opened with me. What did you do with her in the forest?

ABIGAIL: We did dance, uncle, and when you leaped out of the bush so suddenly, Betty was frightened and then she fainted. And there's the whole of it.

PARRIS: Child. Sit you down.

ABIGAIL, *quavering, as she sits:* I would never hurt Betty. I love her dearly.

PARRIS: Now look you, child, your punishment will come in its time.

But if you trafficked with spirits in the forest I must know it now, for surely my enemies will, and they will ruin me with it.

ABIGAIL: But we never conjured spirits.

PARRIS: Then why can she not move herself since midnight? This child is desperate! *Abigail lowers her eyes.* It must come out—my enemies will bring it out. Let me know what you done there. Abigail, do you understand that I have many enemies?

ABIGAIL: I have heard of it, uncle.

PARRIS: There is a faction that is sworn to drive me from my pulpit. Do you understand that?

ABIGAIL: I think so, sir.

PARRIS: Now then, in the midst of such disruption, my own household is discovered to be the very center of some obscene practice. Abominations are done in the forest—

ABIGAIL: It were sport, uncle!

PARRIS, *pointing at* BETTY: You call this sport? *She lowers her eyes. He pleads:* Abigail, if you know something that may help the doctor, for God's sake tell it to me. *She is silent.* I saw Tituba waving her arms over the fire when I came on you. Why was she doing that? And I heard a screeching and gibberish coming from her mouth. She were swaying like a dumb beast over that fire!

ABIGAIL: She always sings her Barbados songs, and we dance.

PARRIS: I cannot blink what I saw, Abigail, for my enemies will not blink it. I saw a dress lying on the grass.

ABIGAIL, *innocently:* A dress?

PARRIS—*it is very hard to say:* Aye, a dress. And I thought I saw—someone naked running through the trees!

ABIGAIL, *in terror:* No one was naked! You mistake yourself, uncle!

PARRIS, *with anger:* I saw it! *He moves from her. Then, resolved:* Now tell me true, Abigail. And I pray you feel the weight of truth upon you, for now my ministry's at stake, my ministry and perhaps your cousin's life. Whatever abomination you have done, give me all of it now, for I dare not be taken unaware when I go before them down there.

ABIGAIL: There is nothin' more. I swear it, uncle.

PARRIS, *studies her, then nods, half convinced:* Abigail, I have fought here three long years to bend these stiff-necked people to me, and now, just now when some good respect is rising for me in the parish, you compromise my very character. I have given you a home, child, I have put clothes upon your back—now give me upright answer. Your name in the

▼ Critical Viewing

Do you think that Abigail's expression in this image is genuine? **ASSESS**

LITERATURE IN CONTEXT

Social Studies Connection

History Repeats Itself

The Crucible was written in the early 1950s when fear of communism swept America. The fears were understandable—eastern Europe and China had recently fallen to communism—but they were also exploited for political ends. In Congress, a Republican senator named Joseph McCarthy leapt into the limelight when he charged that the State Department had been infiltrated by more than two hundred communists.

Leading a Senate investigation, McCarthy repeatedly charged that those who opposed his hearings were themselves communists; then he investigated them. The parallels between events in Salem, as Miller depicts them, and ongoing events in Congress at the time Miller wrote the play are clear and deliberate.

Connect to the Literature

As you read, look for important parallels between the Senate investigation and the events in *The Crucible*.

town—it is entirely white, is it not?

ABIGAIL, *with an edge of resentment:* Why, I am sure it is, sir. There be no blush about my name.

PARRIS, *to the point:* Abigail, is there any other cause than you have told me, for your being discharged from Goody[6] Proctor's service? I have heard it said, and I tell you as I heard it, that she comes so rarely to the church this year for she will not sit so close to something soiled. What signified that remark?

ABIGAIL: She hates me, uncle, she must, for I would not be her slave. It's a bitter woman, a lying, cold, sniveling woman, and I will not work for such a woman!

PARRIS: She may be. And yet it has troubled me that you are now seven month out of their house, and in all this time no other family has ever called for your service.

ABIGAIL: They want slaves, not such as I. Let them send to Barbados for that. I will not black my face for any of them! *With ill-concealed resentment at him:* Do you begrudge my bed, uncle?

PARRIS: No—no.

ABIGAIL, *in a temper:* My name is good in the village! I will not have it said my name is soiled! Goody Proctor is a gossiping liar!

Enter MRS. ANN PUTNAM. *She is a twisted soul of forty-five, a death-ridden woman, haunted by dreams.*

PARRIS, *as soon as the door begins to open:* No—no, I cannot have anyone. *He sees her, and a certain deference springs into him, although his worry remains.* Why, Goody Putnam, come in.

MRS. PUTNAM, *full of breath, shiny-eyed:* It is a marvel. It is surely a stroke of hell upon you.

PARRIS: No, Goody Putnam, it is—

MRS. PUTNAM, *glancing at* BETTY: How high did she fly, how high?

PARRIS: No, no, she never flew—

MRS. PUTNAM, *very pleased with it:* Why, it's sure she did. Mr. Collins saw her goin' over Ingersoll's barn, and come down light as bird, he says!

PARRIS: Now, look you, Goody Putnam, she never—*Enter* THOMAS PUTNAM, *a well-to-do, hard-handed landowner, near fifty.* Oh, good morning, Mr. Putnam.

PUTNAM: It is a providence the thing is out now! It is a providence. *He goes directly to the bed.*

PARRIS: What's out, sir, what's—?

---

6. **Goody** title used for a married woman; short for Goodwife.

MRS. PUTNAM *goes to the bed.*

PUTNAM, *looking down at* BETTY: Why, *her* eyes is closed! Look you, Ann.

MRS. PUTNAM: Why, that's strange. *To* PARRIS: Ours is open.

PARRIS, *shocked:* Your Ruth is sick?

MRS. PUTNAM, *with vicious certainty:* I'd not call it sick; the Devil's touch is heavier than sick. It's death, y'know, it's death drivin' into them, forked and hoofed.

PARRIS: Oh, pray not! Why, how does Ruth ail?

MRS. PUTNAM: She ails as she must—she never waked this morning, but her eyes open and she walks, and hears naught, sees naught, and cannot eat. Her soul is taken, surely.

PARRIS *is struck.*

PUTNAM, *as though for further details:* They say you've sent for Reverend Hale of Beverly?

PARRIS, *with dwindling conviction now:* A precaution only. He has much experience in all demonic arts, and I—

MRS. PUTNAM: He has indeed; and found a witch in Beverly last year, and let you remember that.

PARRIS: Now, Goody Ann, they only thought that were a witch, and I am certain there be no element of witchcraft here.

PUTNAM: No witchcraft! Now look you, Mr. Parris—

PARRIS: Thomas, Thomas, I pray you, leap not to witchcraft. I know that you—you least of all, Thomas, would ever wish so disastrous a charge laid upon me. We cannot leap to witchcraft. They will howl me out of Salem for such corruption in my house.

Plot

What conflict with the villagers is Parris desperately trying to avoid?

A word about Thomas Putnam. He was a man with many grievances, at least one of which appears justified. Some time before, his wife's brother-in-law, James Bayley, had been turned down as minister at Salem. Bayley had all the qualifications, and a two-thirds vote into the bargain, but a faction stopped his acceptance, for reasons that are not clear.

Thomas Putnam was the eldest son of the richest man in the village. He had fought the Indians at Narragansett, and was deeply interested in parish affairs. He undoubtedly felt it poor payment that the village should so blatantly disregard his candidate for one of its more important offices, especially since he regarded himself as the intellectual superior of most of the people around him.

His vindictive nature was demonstrated long before the witchcraft began. Another former Salem minister, George Burroughs, had had to borrow money to pay for his wife's funeral, and, since the parish was remiss in his salary, he was soon bankrupt. Thomas and his brother John had Burroughs jailed for debts the man did not owe. The incident is important only in that Burroughs succeeded in becoming minister where Bayley, Thomas Putnam's brother-in-law, had been rejected; the motif of resentment is clear here. Thomas Putnam felt that his own name and the honor of his family had been smirched by

Comprehension

Why has Parris sent for Reverend Hale?

the village, and he meant to right matters however he could.

Another reason to believe him a deeply embittered man was his attempt to break his father's will, which left a disproportionate amount to a stepbrother. As with every other public cause in which he tried to force his way, he failed in this.

So it is not surprising to find that so many accusations against people are in the handwriting of Thomas Putnam, or that his name is so often found as a witness corroborating the supernatural testimony, or that his daughter led the crying-out at the most opportune junctures of the trials, especially when—But we'll speak of that when we come to it.

▼ Critical Viewing
Based on this image of Abigail, what role do you think she will play in the accusations of witchcraft in Salem? **SPECULATE**

PUTNAM—*at the moment he is intent upon getting* PARRIS, *for whom he has only contempt, to move toward the abyss:*[7] Mr. Parris, I have taken your part in all contention here, and I would continue; but I cannot if you hold back in this. There are hurtful, vengeful spirits layin' hands on these children.

PARRIS: But, Thomas, you cannot—

PUTNAM: Ann! Tell Mr. Parris what you have done.

MRS. PUTNAM: Reverend Parris, I have laid seven babies unbaptized in the earth. Believe me, sir, you never saw more hearty babies born. And yet, each would wither in my arms the very night of their birth. I have spoke nothin', but my heart has clamored intimations. And now, this year, my Ruth, my only—I see her turning strange. A secret child she has become this year, and shrivels like a sucking mouth were pullin' on her life too. And so I thought to send her to your Tituba—

PARRIS: To Tituba! What may Tituba—?

MRS. PUTNAM: Tituba knows how to speak to the dead, Mr. Parris.

PARRIS: Goody Ann, it is a formidable sin to conjure up the dead!

MRS. PUTNAM: I take it on my soul, but who else may surely tell us what person murdered my babies?

PARRIS, *horrified:* Woman!

MRS. PUTNAM: They were murdered, Mr. Parris! And mark this proof! Mark it! Last night my Ruth were ever so close to their little spirits; I know it, sir. For how else is she struck dumb now except some power of darkness would stop her mouth? It is a marvelous sign, Mr. Parris!

PUTNAM: Don't you understand it, sir? There is a murdering witch among us, bound to keep herself in the dark. PARRIS *turns to* BETTY, *a frantic terror rising in him.* Let your enemies make of it

7. **abyss** (ə bis′) *n.* deep crack in the Earth.

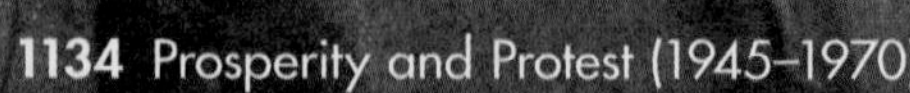

what they will, you cannot blink it more.

PARRIS, *to* ABIGAIL: Then you were conjuring spirits last night.

ABIGAIL, *whispering:* Not I, sir—Tituba and Ruth.

PARRIS *turns now, with new fear, and goes to* BETTY, *looks down at her, and then, gazing off:* Oh, Abigail, what proper payment for my charity! Now I am undone.

PUTNAM: You are not undone! Let you take hold here. Wait for no one to charge you—declare it yourself. You have discovered witchcraft—

PARRIS: In my house? In my house, Thomas? They will topple me with this! They will make of it a—

Enter MERCY LEWIS, *the Putnams' servant, a fat, sly, merciless girl of eighteen.*

MERCY: Your pardons. I only thought to see how Betty is.

PUTNAM: Why aren't you home? Who's with Ruth?

MERCY: Her grandma come. She's improved a little, I think—she give a powerful sneeze before.

MRS. PUTNAM: Ah, there's a sign of life!

MERCY: I'd fear no more, Goody Putnam. It were a grand sneeze; another like it will shake her wits together, I'm sure. *She goes to the bed to look.*

PARRIS: Will you leave me now, Thomas? I would pray a while alone.

ABIGAIL: Uncle, you've prayed since midnight. Why do you not go down and—

PARRIS: No—no. *To* PUTNAM: I have no answer for that crowd. I'll wait till Mr. Hale arrives. *To get* MRS. PUTNAM *to leave:* If you will, Goody Ann . . .

PUTNAM: Now look you, sir. Let you strike out against the Devil, and the village will bless you for it! Come down, speak to them—pray with them. They're thirsting for your word, Mister! Surely you'll pray with them.

PARRIS, *swayed:* I'll lead them in a psalm, but let you say nothing of witchcraft yet. I will not discuss it. The cause is yet unknown. I have had enough contention since I came; I want no more.

MRS. PUTNAM: Mercy, you go home to Ruth, d'y'hear?

MERCY: Aye, mum.

MRS. PUTNAM *goes out.*

PARRIS, *to* ABIGAIL: If she starts for the window, cry for me at once.

ABIGAIL: I will, uncle.

PARRIS, *to* PUTNAM: There is a terrible power in her arms today. *He goes out with* PUTNAM.

ABIGAIL, *with hushed trepidation:* How is Ruth sick?

MERCY: It's weirdish, I know not—she seems to walk like a dead one since last night.

"There are hurtful, vengeful spirits layin' hands on these children."

Arthur Miller

Author's Insight

In *The Crucible*, Miller uses dialogue that sounds like the speech of New England Puritans. Commenting on the language of his plays, Miller wrote: "My own tendency has been to shift styles according to the nature of my subject. . . . I have done this in order to find speech that springs naturally out of the characters and their backgrounds. . . . "

Comprehension

What does Mrs. Putnam believe happened to her babies?

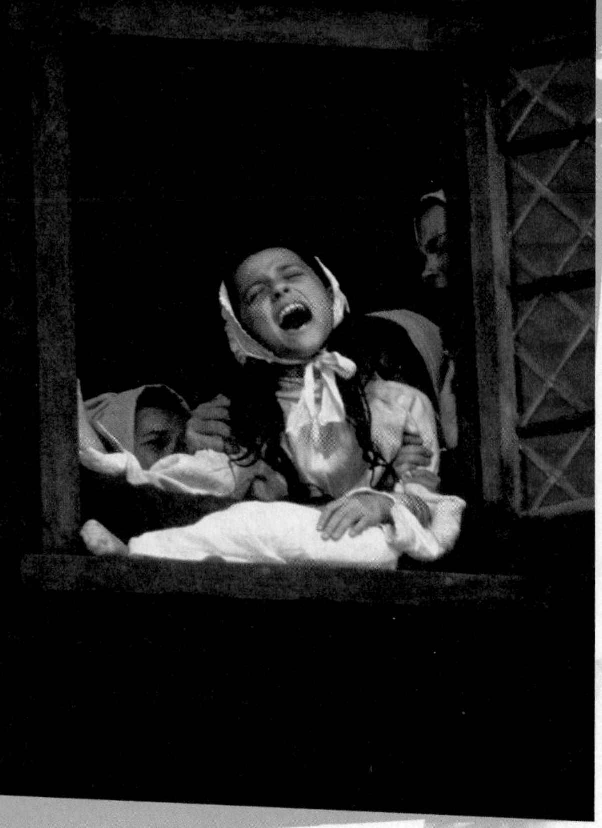

ABIGAIL, *turns at once and goes to* BETTY, *and now, with fear in her voice:* Betty? BETTY *doesn't move. She shakes her.* Now stop this! Betty! Sit up now!

BETTY *doesn't stir.* MERCY *comes over.*

MERCY: Have you tried beatin' her? I gave Ruth a good one and it waked her for a minute. Here, let me have her.

ABIGAIL, *holding* MERCY *back:* No, he'll be comin' up. Listen, now; if they be questioning us, tell them we danced—I told him as much already.

MERCY: Aye. And what more?

ABIGAIL: He knows Tituba conjured Ruth's sisters to come out of the grave.

MERCY: And what more?

ABIGAIL: He saw you naked.

MERCY: *clapping her hands together with a frightened laugh:* Oh, Jesus!

Enter MARY WARREN, *breathless. She is seventeen, a subservient, naive, lonely girl.*

MARY WARREN: What'll we do? The village is out! I just come from the farm; the whole country's talkin' witchcraft! They'll be callin' us witches, Abby!

▲ Critical Viewing
What emotion is conveyed in this image of Betty Parris's attempt to fly? Explain. **INTERPRET**

MERCY, *pointing and looking at* MARY WARREN: She means to tell, I know it.

MARY WARREN: Abby, we've got to tell. Witchery's a hangin' error, a hangin' like they done in Boston two year ago! We must tell the truth, Abby! You'll only be whipped for dancin', and the other things!

ABIGAIL: Oh, *we'll* be whipped!

MARY WARREN: I never done none of it, Abby. I only looked!

MERCY, *moving menacingly toward* MARY: Oh, you're a great one for lookin', aren't you, Mary Warren? What a grand peeping courage you have!

BETTY, *on the bed, whimpers.* ABIGAIL *turns to her at once.*

ABIGAIL: Betty? *She goes to* BETTY. Now, Betty, dear, wake up now. It's Abigail. *She sits* BETTY *up and furiously shakes her.* I'll beat you, Betty! BETTY *whimpers.* My, you seem improving.
I talked to your papa and I told him everything. So there's nothing to—

BETTY, *darts off the bed, frightened of* ABIGAIL, *and flattens herself against the wall:* I want my mama!

ABIGAIL, *with alarm, as she cautiously approaches* BETTY: What ails you, Betty? Your mama's dead and buried.

BETTY: I'll fly to Mama. Let me fly! *She raises her arms as though to fly, and streaks for the window, gets one leg out.*

ABIGAIL, *pulling her away from the window:* I told him everything; he knows now, he knows everything we—

BETTY: You drank blood, Abby! You didn't tell him that!

ABIGAIL: Betty, you never say that again! You will never—

BETTY: You did, you did! You drank a charm to kill John Proctor's wife! You drank a charm to kill Goody Proctor!

ABIGAIL, *smashes her across the face:* Shut it! Now shut it!

BETTY: *collapsing on the bed:* Mama, Mama! *She dissolves into sobs.*

ABIGAIL: Now look you. All of you. We danced. And Tituba conjured Ruth Putnam's dead sisters. And that is all. And mark this. Let either of you breathe a word, or the edge of a word, about the other things, and I will come to you in the black of some terrible night and I will bring a pointy reckoning that will shudder you. And you know I can do it; I saw Indians smash my dear parents' heads on the pillow next to mine, and I have seen some reddish work done at night, and I can make you wish you had never seen the sun go down! *She goes to* BETTY *and roughly sits her up.* Now, you—sit up and stop this!

But BETTY *collapses in her hands and lies inert on the bed.*

MARY WARREN, *with hysterical fright:* What's got her? ABIGAIL *stares in fright at* BETTY. Abby, she's going to die! It's a sin to conjure, and we—

ABIGAIL, *starting for* MARY: I say shut it, Mary Warren!

Enter JOHN PROCTOR. *On seeing him.* MARY WARREN *leaps in fright.*

Identifying Text Features

What do you learn about Abigail from this dialogue?

Comprehension

What does Mary Warren insist the girls do?

WORLD LITERATURE IN CONTEXT

POLITICAL DRAMA

MAXIM GORKY (1868–1936)

Writer Maxim Gorky grew up in Tsarist Russia at a time when millions of Russians lived in poverty. Gorky's parents died when he was young. When Maxim was ten, his grandfather turned him out of the house. Gorky spent his teenage years working at various jobs and tramping across Russia. During this time, he was often homeless but he began writing.

The Lower Depths, Gorky's most famous play, is set in a dark basement and its characters are modeled on the rootless, poverty-stricken people he met during his homeless years. He wrote it for the Moscow Art Theater, whose director, Constantin Stanislavski, was developing a new, realistic style of theater. When the play was first performed in 1902, it caused a sensation. Such an accurate portrayal of Russia's desperate underworld had never been seen on stage and it implicitly challenged the political system. The realistic drama that Gorky and Stanislavski pioneered gave birth to the style of acting that is used today. This style influenced theater around the world.

▲ Still from 1936 film version of *The Lower Depths.*

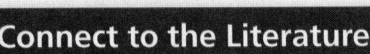

Connect to the Literature

Why would a realistic portrayal of poverty challenge a political system?

Vocabulary
calumny (kal′ əm nē)
n. false accusation; slander

Dramatic Exposition
What important information does Miller reveal about Proctor through this dramatic exposition?

Proctor was a farmer in his middle thirties. He need not have been a partisan of any faction in the town, but there is evidence to suggest that he had a sharp and biting way with hypocrites. He was the kind of man—powerful of body, even-tempered, and not easily led—who cannot refuse support to partisans without drawing their deepest resentment. In Proctor's presence a fool felt his foolishness instantly—and a Proctor is always marked for **calumny** therefore.

But as we shall see, the steady manner he displays does not spring from an untroubled soul. He is a sinner, a sinner not only against the moral fashion of the time, but against his own vision of decent conduct. These people had no ritual for the washing away of sins. It is another trait we inherited from them, and it has helped to discipline us as well as to breed hypocrisy among us. Proctor, respected and even feared in Salem, has come to regard himself as a kind of fraud. But no hint of this has yet appeared on the surface, and as he enters from the crowded parlor below it is a man in his prime we see, with a quiet confidence and an unexpressed, hidden force. Mary Warren, his servant, can barely speak for embarrassment and fear.

MARY WARREN: Oh! I'm just going home, Mr. Proctor.

PROCTOR: Be you foolish, Mary Warren? Be you deaf? I forbid you leave the house, did I not? Why shall I pay you? I am looking for you more often than my cows!

MARY WARREN: I only come to see the great doings in the world.

▼ Critical Viewing
Based on this movie still, do you think Proctor is expressing anger, fear, or another emotion? **INTERPRET**

PROCTOR: I'll show you a great doin' on your arse one of these days. Now get you home; my wife is waitin' with your work! *Trying to retain a shred of dignity, she goes slowly out.*

MERCY LEWIS, *both afraid of him and strangely titillated:* I'd best be off. I have my Ruth to watch. Good morning, Mr. Proctor.

MERCY *sidles out. Since* PROCTOR's *entrance,* ABIGAIL *has stood as though on tiptoe, absorbing his presence, wide-eyed. He glances at her, then goes to* BETTY *on the bed.*

ABIGAIL: Gah! I'd almost forgot how strong you are, John Proctor!

PROCTOR, *looking at* ABIGAIL *now, the faintest suggestion of a knowing smile on his face:* What's this mischief here?

ABIGAIL, *with a nervous laugh:* Oh, she's only gone silly somehow.

PROCTOR: The road past my house is a pilgrimage to Salem all morning. The town's mumbling witchcraft.

ABIGAIL: Oh, posh! *Winningly she comes a little closer, with a confidential, wicked air.* We were dancin' in the woods last night, and my uncle leaped in on us. She took fright, is all.

PROCTOR, *his smile widening:* Ah, you're wicked yet, aren't y'! *A trill of expectant laughter escapes her, and she dares come closer, feverishly looking into his eyes.* You'll be clapped in the stocks before you're twenty.

He takes a step to go, and she springs into his path.

ABIGAIL: Give me a word, John. A soft word. *Her concentrated desire destroys his smile.*

PROCTOR: No, no, Abby. That's done with.

ABIGAIL, *tauntingly:* You come five mile to see a silly girl fly? I know you better.

PROCTOR, *setting her firmly out of his path:* I come to see what mischief your uncle's brewin' now. *With final emphasis:* Put it out of mind, Abby.

ABIGAIL, *grasping his hand before he can release her:* John—I am waitin' for you every night.

PROCTOR: Abby, I never give you hope to wait for me.

ABIGAIL, *now beginning to anger—she can't believe it:* I have something better than hope, I think!

PROCTOR: Abby, you'll put it out of mind. I'll not be comin' for you more.

ABIGAIL: You're surely sportin' with me.

PROCTOR: You know me better.

ABIGAIL: I know how you clutched my back behind your house and sweated like a stallion whenever I come near! Or did I dream that? It's she put me out, you cannot pretend it were you. I saw your face when she put me out, and you loved me then and you do now!

PROCTOR: Abby, that's a wild thing to say—

ABIGAIL: A wild thing may say wild things. But not so wild, I think. I have seen you since she put me out; I have seen you nights.

PROCTOR: I have hardly stepped off my farm this seven month.

Identifying Text Features

What important information about Abigail's behavior is conveyed through stage directions in this scene?

Plot

What conflict exists between Abigail and Proctor?

Comprehension

What does Abigail feel for Proctor?

ABIGAIL: I have a sense for heat, John, and yours has drawn me to my window, and I have seen you looking up, burning in your loneliness. Do you tell me you've never looked up at my window?

PROCTOR: I may have looked up.

ABIGAIL, *now softening:* And you must. You are no wintry man. I know you, John. I *know* you. *She is weeping.* I cannot sleep for dreamin'; I cannot dream but I wake and walk about the house as though I'd find you comin' through some door. *She clutches him desperately.*

PROCTOR, *gently pressing her from him, with great sympathy but firmly:* Child—

ABIGAIL, *with a flash of anger:* How do you call me child!

PROCTOR: Abby, I may think of you softly from time to time. But I will cut off my hand before I'll ever reach for you again. Wipe it out of mind. We never touched, Abby.

ABIGAIL: Aye, but we did.

PROCTOR: Aye, but we did not.

ABIGAIL, *with a bitter anger:* Oh, I marvel how such a strong man may let such a sickly wife be—

PROCTOR, *angered—at himself as well:* You'll speak nothin' of Elizabeth!

ABIGAIL: She is blackening my name in the village! She is telling lies about me! She is a cold, sniveling woman, and you bend to her! Let her turn you like a—

PROCTOR, *shaking her:* Do you look for whippin'?

A psalm is heard being sung below.

ABIGAIL, *in tears:* I look for John Proctor that took me from my sleep and put knowledge in my heart! I never knew what pretense Salem was, I never knew the lying lessons I was taught by all these Christian women and their covenanted men! And now you bid me tear the light out of my eyes? I will not, I cannot! You loved me, John Proctor, and whatever sin it is, you love me yet! *He turns abruptly to go out. She rushes to him.* John, pity me, pity me!

The words "going up to Jesus" are heard in the psalm, and BETTY *claps her ears suddenly and whines loudly.*

ABIGAIL: Betty? *She hurries to* BETTY, *who is now sitting up and screaming.* PROCTOR *goes to* BETTY *as* ABIGAIL *is trying to pull her hands down, calling "Betty!"*

PROCTOR, *growing unnerved:* What's she doing? Girl, what ails you? Stop that wailing!

The singing has stopped in the midst of this, and now PARRIS *rushes in.*

PARRIS: What happened? What are you doing to her? Betty! *He rushes to the bed, crying,* "Betty, Betty!" MRS. PUTNAM *enters, feverish with curiosity, and with her* THOMAS PUTNAM *and* MERCY LEWIS. PARRIS, *at the bed, keeps lightly slapping* BETTY'S *face, while she moans and tries to get up.*

ABIGAIL: She heard you singin' and suddenly she's up and screamin'.

Spiral Review
Context Clues
Use textual clues to define the word *sniveling* as it is used here.

MRS. PUTNAM: The psalm! The psalm! She cannot bear to hear the Lord's name!

PARRIS: No, God forbid. Mercy, run to the doctor! Tell him what's happened here! MERCY LEWIS *rushes out.*

MRS. PUTNAM: Mark it for a sign, mark it!

REBECCA NURSE, *seventy-two, enters. She is white-haired, leaning upon her walking-stick.*

PUTNAM, *pointing at the whimpering* BETTY: That is a notorious sign of witchcraft afoot, Goody Nurse, a prodigious sign!

MRS. PUTNAM: My mother told me that! When they cannot bear to hear the name of—

PARRIS, *trembling:* Rebecca, Rebecca, go to her, we're lost. She suddenly cannot bear to hear the Lord's—

GILES COREY, *eighty-three, enters. He is knotted with muscle, canny, inquisitive, and still powerful.*

REBECCA: There is hard sickness here, Giles Corey, so please to keep the quiet.

GILES: I've not said a word. No one here can testify I've said a word. Is she going to fly again?
I hear she flies.

PUTNAM: Man, be quiet now!

Everything is quiet. REBECCA *walks across the room to the bed. Gentleness exudes from her.* BETTY *is quietly whimpering, eyes shut.* REBECCA *simply stands over the child, who gradually quiets.*

And while they are so absorbed, we may put a word in for Rebecca. Rebecca was the wife of Francis Nurse, who, from all accounts, was one of those men for whom both sides of the argument had to have respect. He was called upon to arbitrate disputes as though he were an unofficial judge, and Rebecca also enjoyed the high opinion most people had for him. By the time of the delusion, they had three hundred acres, and their children were settled in separate homesteads within the same estate. However, Francis had originally rented the land, and one theory has it that, as he gradually paid for it and raised his social status, there were those who resented his rise.

Another suggestion to explain the systematic campaign against Rebecca, and inferentially against Francis, is the land war he fought with his neighbors, one of whom was a Putnam. This squabble grew to the proportions of a battle in the woods between partisans of both sides, and it is said to have lasted for two days. As for Rebecca herself, the general opinion of her character was so high that to explain how anyone dared cry her out for a witch—and more, how adults could bring themselves to lay hands on her—we must look to the fields and boundaries of that time.

As we have seen, Thomas Putnam's man for the Salem ministry was Bayley. The Nurse clan had been in the faction that prevented

Identifying Text Features

How does the combination of stage directions and dialogue reveal Mrs. Putnam's eagerness to see signs of witchcraft?

"I've not said a word. No one here can testify I've said a word."

Comprehension

What is Rebecca Nurse's effect on Betty?

Bayley's taking office. In addition, certain families allied to the Nurses by blood or friendship, and whose farms were contiguous with the Nurse farm or close to it, combined to break away from the Salem town authority and set up Topsfield, a new and independent entity whose existence was resented by old Salemites.

That the guiding hand behind the outcry was Putnam's is indicated by the fact that, as soon as it began, this Topsfield-Nurse faction absented themselves from church in protest and disbelief. It was Edward and Jonathan Putnam who signed the first complaint against Rebecca; and Thomas Putnam's little daughter was the one who fell into a fit at the hearing and pointed to Rebecca as her attacker. To top it all, Mrs. Putnam—who is now staring at the bewitched child on the bed—soon accused Rebecca's spirit of " tempting her to iniquity," a charge that had more truth in it than Mrs. Putnam could know.

MRS. PUTNAM, *astonished:* What have you done?

REBECCA, *in thought, now leaves the bedside and sits.*

PARRIS, *wondrous and relieved:* What do you make of it, Rebecca?

PUTNAM, *eagerly:* Goody Nurse, will you go to my Ruth and see if you can wake her?

REBECCA, *sitting:* I think she'll wake in time. Pray calm yourselves. I have eleven children, and I am twenty-six times a grandma, and I have seen them all through their silly seasons, and when it come on them they will run the Devil bowlegged keeping up with their mischief. I think she'll wake when she tires of it. A child's spirit is like a child, you can never catch it by running after it; you must stand still, and, for love, it will soon itself come back.

PROCTOR: Aye, that's the truth of it, Rebecca.

MRS. PUTNAM: This is no silly season, Rebecca. My Ruth is bewildered, Rebecca; she cannot eat.

REBECCA: Perhaps she is not hungered yet. *To* PARRIS: I hope you are not decided to go in search of loose spirits, Mr. Parris. I've heard promise of that outside.

PARRIS: A wide opinion's running in the parish that the Devil may be among us, and I would satisfy them that they are wrong.

PROCTOR: Then let you come out and call them wrong. Did you consult the wardens before you called this minister to look for devils?

PARRIS: He is not coming to look for devils!

PROCTOR: Then what's he coming for?

PUTNAM: There be children dyin' in the village, Mister!

PROCTOR: I seen none dyin'. This society will not be a bag to swing around your head, Mr. Putnam. *To* PARRIS: Did you call a meeting before you—?

▼ Critical Viewing

How would you characterize John Proctor based on this film still? **GENERALIZE**

PUTNAM: I am sick of meetings; cannot the man turn his head without he have a meeting?

PROCTOR: He may turn his head, but not to Hell!

REBECCA: Pray, John, be calm. *Pause. He defers to her.* Mr. Parris, I think you'd best send Reverend Hale back as soon as he come. This will set us all to arguin' again in the society, and we thought to have peace this year. I think we ought rely on the doctor now, and good prayer.

MRS. PUTNAM: Rebecca, the doctor's baffled!

REBECCA: If so he is, then let us go to God for the cause of it. There is prodigious danger in the seeking of loose spirits. I fear it, I fear it. Let us rather blame ourselves and—

PUTNAM: How may we blame ourselves? I am one of nine sons; the Putnam seed have peopled this province. And yet I have but one child left of eight—and now she shrivels!

REBECCA: I cannot fathom that.

MRS. PUTNAM, *with a growing edge of sarcasm:* But I must! You think it God's work you should never lose a child, nor grandchild either, and I bury all but one? There are wheels within wheels in this village, and fires within fires!

PUTNAM, *to* PARRIS: When Reverend Hale comes, you will proceed to look for signs of witchcraft here.

PROCTOR, *to* PUTNAM: You cannot command Mr. Parris. We vote by name in this society, not by acreage.

PUTNAM: I never heard you worried so on this society, Mr. Proctor. I do not think I saw you at Sabbath meeting since snow flew.

PROCTOR: I have trouble enough without I come five mile to hear him preach only hellfire and bloody damnation. Take it to heart, Mr. Parris. There are many others who stay away from church these days because you hardly ever mention God any more.

PARRIS, *now aroused:* Why, that's a drastic charge!

REBECCA: It's somewhat true; there are many that quail to bring their children—

PARRIS: I do not preach for children, Rebecca. It is not the children who are unmindful of their obligations toward this ministry.

REBECCA: Are there really those unmindful?

PARRIS: I should say the better half of Salem village—

PUTNAM: And more than that!

PARRIS: Where is my wood? My contract provides I be supplied with all my firewood. I am waiting since November for a stick, and even in November I had to show my frostbitten hands like some London beggar!

GILES: You are allowed six pound a year to buy your wood, Mr. Parris.

PARRIS: I regard that six pound as part of my salary. I am paid little enough without I spend six pound on firewood.

Identifying Text Features

What punctuation marks show that Parris interrupts Rebecca?

Comprehension

What hardships does Parris complain of?

PROCTOR: Sixty, plus six for firewood—

PARRIS: The salary is sixty-six pound, Mr. Proctor! I am not some preaching farmer with a book under my arm; I am a graduate of Harvard College.

GILES: Aye, and well instructed in arithmetic!

PARRIS: Mr. Corey, you will look far for a man of my kind at sixty pound a year! I am not used to this poverty; I left a thrifty business in the Barbados to serve the Lord. I do not fathom it, why am I persecuted here? I cannot offer one proposition but there be a howling riot of argument. I have often wondered if the Devil be in it somewhere; I cannot understand you people otherwise.

PROCTOR: Mr. Parris, you are the first minister ever did demand the deed to this house—

PARRIS: Man! Don't a minister deserve a house to live in?

PROCTOR: To live in, yes. But to ask ownership is like you shall own the meeting house itself; the last meeting I were at you spoke so long on deeds and mortgages I thought it were an auction.

PARRIS: I want a mark of confidence, is all! I am your third preacher in seven years. I do not wish to be put out like the cat whenever some majority feels the whim. You people seem not to comprehend that a minister is the Lord's man in the parish; a minister is not to be so lightly crossed and contradicted—

PUTNAM: Aye!

PARRIS: There is either obedience or the church will burn like Hell is burning!

PROCTOR: Can you speak one minute without we land in Hell again? I am sick of Hell!

PARRIS: It is not for you to say what is good for you to hear!

PROCTOR: I may speak my heart, I think!

Plot
How does Parris intensify his conflict with Proctor?

PARRIS, *in a fury:* What, are we Quakers?[8] We are not Quakers here yet, Mr. Proctor. And you may tell that to your followers!

PROCTOR: My followers!

PARRIS—*now he's out with it:* There is a party in this church. I am not blind; there is a faction and a party.

PROCTOR: Against you?

PUTNAM: Against him and all authority!

PROCTOR: Why, then I must find it and join it.

There is shock among the others.

REBECCA: He does not mean that.

PUTNAM: He confessed it now!

PROCTOR: I mean it solemnly, Rebecca; I like not the smell of this "authority."

---

8. **Quakers** members of the Society of Friends, a Christian religious sect that was founded in the mid-17th century and has no formal creed, rites, or priesthood. Unlike the Quakers, the Puritans had a rigid code of conduct and were expected to heed the words of their ministers.

REBECCA: No, you cannot break charity with your minister. You are another kind, John. Clasp his hand, make your peace.

PROCTOR: I have a crop to sow and lumber to drag home. *He goes angrily to the door and turns to* COREY *with a smile.* What say you, Giles, let's find the party. He says there's a party.

GILES: I've changed my opinion of this man, John. Mr. Parris, I beg your pardon. I never thought you had so much iron in you.

PARRIS, *surprised:* Why, thank you, Giles!

GILES: It suggests to the mind what the trouble be among us all these years. *To all:* Think on it. Wherefore is everybody suing everybody else? Think on it now, it's a deep thing, and dark as a pit. I have been six time in court this year—

PROCTOR, *familiarly, with warmth, although he knows he is approaching the edge of Giles' tolerance with this:* Is it the Devil's fault that a man cannot say you good morning without you clap him for defamation? You're old, Giles, and you're not hearin' so well as you did.

GILES—*he cannot be crossed:* John Proctor, I have only last month collected four pound damages for you publicly sayin' I burned the roof off your house, and I—

PROCTOR, *laughing:* I never said no such thing, but I've paid you for it, so I hope I can call you deaf without charge. Now come along, Giles, and help me drag my lumber home.

PUTNAM: A moment, Mr. Proctor. What lumber is that you're draggin', if I may ask you?

PROCTOR: My lumber. From out my forest by the riverside.

PUTNAM: Why, we are surely gone wild this year. What anarchy is this? That tract is in my bounds, it's in my bounds, Mr. Proctor.

PROCTOR: In your bounds! *Indicating* REBECCA: I bought that tract from Goody Nurse's husband five months ago.

PUTNAM: He had no right to sell it. It stands clear in my grandfather's will that all the land between the river and—

PROCTOR: Your grandfather had a habit of willing land that never belonged to him, if I may say it plain.

GILES: That's God's truth; he nearly willed away my north pasture but he knew I'd break his fingers before he'd set his name to it. Let's get your lumber home, John. I feel a sudden will to work coming on.

PUTNAM: You load one oak of mine and you'll fight to drag it home!

GILES: Aye, and we'll win too, Putnam—this fool and I. Come on! *He turns to* PROCTOR *and starts out.*

LITERATURE IN CONTEXT

History Connection

The Inquisition

Miller alludes to the Inquisition, a "court of justice" established by the Catholic Church in the thirteenth century, but he does not describe it. The Inquisition bore some resemblance to the Salem witch hunts of the 1690s and to the Red Scare during the 1950s. In each case, a panel of judges decided allegations of heresy or treason. The Salem judges sentenced some to death, as had the Catholic judges of the Middle Ages. No one died in the 1950s as a result of Senator McCarthy's accusations, but many suffered damage to their personal and professional reputations.

Connect to the Literature

What else might the Salem trials have in common with the Inquisition?

Comprehension

What is a source of disagreement between Proctor and Putnam?

PUTNAM: I'll have my men on you, Corey! I'll clap a writ on you!

Enter REVEREND JOHN HALE *of Beverly.*

Dramatic Exposition
What important information does Miller provide about his view of the world?

Mr. Hale is nearing forty, a tight-skinned, eager-eyed intellectual. This is a beloved errand for him; on being called here to ascertain witchcraft he felt the pride of the specialist whose unique knowledge has at last been publicly called for. Like almost all men of learning, he spent a good deal of time pondering the invisible world, especially since he had himself encountered a witch in his parish not long before. That woman, however, turned into a mere pest under his searching scrutiny, and the child she had allegedly been afflicting recovered her normal behavior after Hale had given her his kindness and a few days of rest in his own house. However, that experience never raised a doubt in his mind as to the reality of the underworld or the existence of Lucifer's many-faced lieutenants. And his belief is not to his discredit. Better minds than Hale's were—and still are—convinced that there is a society of spirits beyond our ken. One cannot help noting that one of his lines has never yet raised a laugh in any audience that has seen this play; it is his assurance that "We cannot look to superstition in this. The Devil is precise." Evidently we are not quite certain even now whether diabolism is holy and not to be scoffed at. And it is no accident that we should be so bemused.

Like Reverend Hale and the others on this stage, we conceive the Devil as a necessary part of a respectable view of cosmology. Ours is a divided empire in which certain ideas and emotions and actions are of God, and their opposites are of Lucifer. It is as impossible for most men to conceive of a morality without sin as of an earth without "sky." Since 1692 a great but superficial change has wiped out God's beard and the Devil's horns, but the world is still gripped between two diametrically opposed absolutes. The concept of unity, in which positive and negative are attributes of the same force, in which good and evil are relative, ever-changing, and always joined to the same phenomenon—such a concept is still reserved to the physical sciences and to the few who have grasped the history of ideas. When it is recalled that until the Christian era the underworld was never regarded as a hostile area, that all gods were useful and essentially friendly to man despite occasional lapses; when we see the steady and methodical **inculcation** into humanity of the idea of man's worthlessness—until redeemed—the necessity of the Devil may become evident as a weapon, a weapon designed and used time and time again in every age to whip men into a surrender to a particular church or church-state.

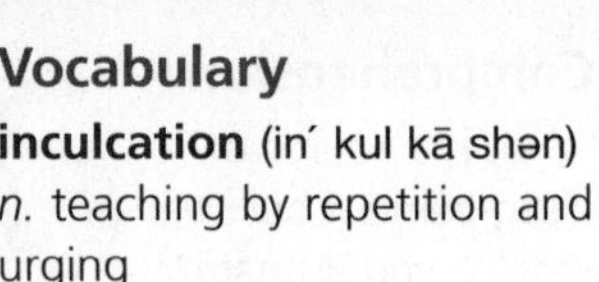

Vocabulary
inculcation (in′ kul kā shən) *n.* teaching by repetition and urging

Our difficulty in believing the—for want of a better word—political inspiration of the Devil is due in great part to the fact that he is called up and damned not only by our social antagonists but by our own side, whatever it may be. The Catholic Church, through its Inquisition, is famous for cultivating Lucifer as the arch-fiend, but the Church's enemies relied no less upon the Old Boy to keep the human mind enthralled. Luther[9] was himself accused of alliance with Hell, and he in turn accused his enemies. To complicate matters further, he believed that he had had contact with the Devil and had argued theology with him. I am not surprised at this, for at my own university a professor of history—a Lutheran,[10] by the way—used to assemble his graduate students, draw the shades, and commune in the classroom with Erasmus.[11] He was never, to my knowledge, officially scoffed at for this, the reason being that the university officials, like most of us, are the children of a history which still sucks at the Devil's teats. At this writing, only England has held back before the temptations of contemporary diabolism. In the countries of the Communist ideology, all resistance of any import is linked to the totally malign capitalist succubi,[12] and in America any man who is not reactionary in his views is open to the charge of alliance with the Red hell. Political opposition, thereby, is given an inhumane overlay which then justifies the abrogation[13] of all normally applied customs of civilized intercourse. A political policy is equated with moral right, and opposition to it with diabolical malevolence. Once such an equation is effectively made, society becomes a congerie[14] of plots and counterplots, and the main role of government changes from that of the arbiter to that of the scourge of God.

The results of this process are no different now from what they ever were, except sometimes in the degree of cruelty inflicted, and not always even in that department. Normally, the actions and deeds of a man were all that society felt comfortable in judging. The secret intent of an action was left to the ministers, priests, and rabbis to deal with. When diabolism rises, however, actions are the least important manifests of the true nature of a man. The Devil, as Reverend Hale said, is a wily one, and, until an hour before he fell, even God thought him beautiful in Heaven.

The analogy, however, seems to falter when one considers that, while there were no witches then, there are Communists and capitalists now, and in each camp there is certain proof that spies of each side are at work undermining the other. But this is a snobbish

Dramatic Exposition
How is Miller's view of the political uses of morality reflected in the play?

Comprehension
According to Miller, on what point does the analogy of the Salem witch hunts to the modern day seem to falter?

---

9. Luther Martin Luther (1483–1546), German theologian who led the Protestant Reformation.
10. Lutheran member of the Protestant denomination founded by Martin Luther.
11. Erasmus Erasmus Desiderius (1466?–1536), Dutch humanist, scholar, and theologian.
12. succubi (suk′ yoo bī) female demons thought to lie on sleeping men.
13. abrogation (ab′ rō gā′ shən) abolishment.
14. congerie (kän′ jə rē′) heap; pile.

Vocabulary
propitiation (prə pish´ ē ā´ shən) *n.* action designed to soothe

objection and not at all warranted by the facts. I have no doubt that people *were* communing with, and even worshiping, the Devil in Salem, and if the whole truth could be known in this case, as it is in others, we should discover a regular and conventionalized propitiation of the dark spirit. One certain evidence of this is the confession of Tituba, the slave of Reverend Parris, and another is the behavior of the children who were known to have indulged in sorceries with her.

There are accounts of similar *klatches*[15] in Europe, where the daughters of the towns would assemble at night and, sometimes with fetishes,[16] sometimes with a selected young man, give themselves to love, with some bastardly results. The Church, sharp-eyed as it must be when gods long dead are brought to life, condemned these orgies as witchcraft and interpreted them, rightly, as a resurgence of the Dionysiac[17] forces it had crushed long before. Sex, sin, and the Devil were early linked, and so they continued to be in Salem, and are today. From all accounts there are no more puritanical mores in the world than those enforced by the Communists in Russia, where women's fashions, for instance, are as prudent and all-covering as any American Baptist would desire. The divorce laws lay a tremendous responsibility on the father for the care of his children. Even the laxity of divorce regulations in the early years of the revolution was undoubtedly a revulsion from the nineteenth-century Victorian[18] immobility of marriage and the consequent hypocrisy that developed from it. If for no other reasons, a state so powerful, so jealous of the uniformity of its citizens, cannot long tolerate the atomization of the family. And yet, in American eyes at least, there remains the conviction that the Russian attitude toward women is lascivious. It is the Devil working again, just as he is working within the Slav who is shocked at the very idea of a woman's disrobing herself in a burlesque show. Our opposites are always robed in sexual sin, and it is from this unconscious conviction that demonology gains both its attractive sensuality and its capacity to infuriate and frighten.

Coming into Salem now, Reverend Hale conceives of himself much as a young doctor on his first call. His painfully acquired armory of symptoms, catchwords, and diagnostic procedures are now to be put to use at last. The road from Beverly is unusually busy this morning, and he has passed a hundred rumors that make him smile at the ignorance of the yeomanry in this most precise science. He feels himself allied with the best minds of Europe—kings, philosophers, scientists, and ecclesiasts of all churches. His goal is light, goodness and its preservation, and he knows the exaltation of the blessed whose intelligence,

---

15. **klatches** (klächz) informal gatherings.
16. **fetishes** (fet´ ish iz) objects believed to have magical power.
17. **Dionysiac** (dī´ ə nis´ ē ak´) characteristic of Dionysus, Greek god of wine and revelry; thus, wild, frenzied, sensuous.
18. **Victorian** characteristic of the time when Victoria was queen of England (1837–1901), an era associated with respectability, prudery, and hypocrisy.

sharpened by minute examinations of enormous tracts, is finally called upon to face what may be a bloody fight with the Fiend himself.

He appears loaded down with half a dozen heavy books.

HALE: Pray you, someone take these!

PARRIS, *delighted:* Mr. Hale! Oh! it's good to see you again! *Taking some books:* My, they're heavy!

HALE, *setting down his books:* They must be; they are weighted with authority.

PARRIS, *a little scared:* Well, you do come prepared!

HALE: We shall need hard study if it comes to tracking down the Old Boy. *Noticing* REBECCA: You cannot be Rebecca Nurse?

REBECCA: I am, sir. Do you know me?

HALE: It's strange how I knew you, but I suppose you look as such a good soul should. We have all heard of your great charities in Beverly.

PARRIS: Do you know this gentleman? Mr. Thomas Putnam. And his good wife Ann.

HALE: Putnam! I had not expected such distinguished company, sir.

PUTNAM, *pleased:* It does not seem to help us today, Mr. Hale. We look to you to come to our house and save our child.

HALE: Your child ails too?

MRS. PUTNAM: Her soul, her soul seems flown away. She sleeps and yet she walks . . .

PUTNAM: She cannot eat.

HALE: Cannot eat! *Thinks on it. Then, to* PROCTOR *and* GILES COREY: Do you men have afflicted children?

PARRIS: No, no, these are farmers. John Proctor—

GILES COREY: He don't believe in witches.

PROCTOR, *to* HALE: I never spoke on witches one way or the other. Will you come, Giles?

GILES: No—no, John, I think not. I have some few queer questions of my own to ask this fellow.

PROCTOR: I've heard you to be a sensible man, Mr. Hale. I hope you'll leave some of it in Salem.

PROCTOR *goes.* HALE *stands embarrassed for an instant.*

PARRIS, *quickly:* Will you look at my daughter, sir? *Leads* HALE *to the bed.* She has tried to leap out the window; we discovered her this morning on the highroad, waving her arms as though she'd fly.

HALE, *narrowing his eyes:* Tries to fly.

PUTNAM: She cannot bear to hear the Lord's name, Mr. Hale; that's a sure sign of witchcraft afloat.

HALE, *holding up his hands:* No, no. Now let me instruct you. We cannot look to superstition in this. The Devil is precise; the marks of his presence are definite as stone, and I must tell you all that I shall not proceed unless you are prepared to believe me if I should find no

Identifying Text Features

What is your impression of Hale based on the dramatic exposition, stage directions, and dialogue?

Comprehension

With what does Hale come prepared?

"I cannot tell. If she is truly in the Devil's grip we may have to rip and tear to get her free."

bruise of hell upon her.

PARRIS: It is agreed, sir—it is agreed—we will abide by your judgment.

HALE: Good then. *He goes to the bed, looks down at* BETTY. *To* PARRIS: Now, sir, what were your first warning of this strangeness?

PARRIS: Why, sir—I discovered her—*indicating* ABIGAIL—and my niece and ten or twelve of the other girls, dancing in the forest last night.

HALE, *surprised:* You permit dancing?

PARRIS: No, no, it were secret—

MRS. PUTNAM, *unable to wait:* Mr. Parris's slave has knowledge of conjurin', sir.

PARRIS, *to* MRS. PUTNAM: We cannot be sure of that, Goody Ann—

MRS. PUTNAM, *frightened, very softly:* I know it, sir. I sent my child—she should learn from Tituba who murdered her sisters.

REBECCA, *horrified:* Goody Ann! You sent a child to conjure up the dead?

MRS. PUTNAM: Let God blame me, not you, not you, Rebecca! I'll not have you judging me any more! *To* HALE: Is it a natural work to lose seven children before they live a day?

PARRIS: Sssh!

REBECCA, *with great pain, turns her face away. There is a pause.*

HALE: Seven dead in childbirth.

MRS. PUTNAM, *softly:* Aye. *Her voice breaks; she looks up at him. Silence.* HALE *is impressed.* PARRIS *looks to him. He goes to his books, opens one, turns pages, then reads. All wait, avidly.*

PARRIS, *hushed:* What book is that?

MRS. PUTNAM: What's there, sir?

HALE, *with a tasty love of intellectual pursuit:* Here is all the invisible world, caught, defined, and calculated. In these books the Devil stands stripped of all his brute disguises. Here are all your familiar spirits—your incubi[19] and succubi, your witches that go by land, by air, and by sea; your wizards of the night and of the day. Have no fear now—we shall find him out if he has come among us, and I mean to crush him utterly if he has shown his face! *He starts for the bed.*

Plot

How does Mrs. Putnam's confession add to the rising action?

REBECCA: Will it hurt the child, sir?

HALE: I cannot tell. If she is truly in the Devil's grip we may have to rip and tear to get her free.

REBECCA: I think I'll go, then. I am too old for this. *She rises.*

PARRIS, *striving for conviction:* Why, Rebecca, we may open up the boil of all our troubles today!

REBECCA: Let us hope for that. I go to God for you, sir.

PARRIS, *with trepidation—and resentment:* I hope you do not mean we go to Satan here! *Slight pause.*

REBECCA: I wish I knew. *She goes out; they feel resentful of her note of*

---

19. incubi (in′ kyo͞o bī) spirits or demons thought to lie on sleeping women.

moral superiority.

PUTNAM, *abruptly:* Come, Mr. Hale, let's get on. Sit you here.

GILES: Mr. Hale, I have always wanted to ask a learned man—what signifies the readin' of strange books?

HALE: What books?

GILES: I cannot tell; she hides them.

HALE: Who does this?

GILES: Martha, my wife. I have waked at night many a time and found her in a corner, readin' of a book. Now what do you make of that?

HALE: Why, that's not necessarily—

GILES: It discomfits me! Last night—mark this—I tried and tried and could not say my prayers. And then she close her book and walks out of the house, and suddenly—mark this—I could pray again!

Old Giles must be spoken for, if only because his fate was to be so remarkable and so different from that of all the others. He was in his early eighties at this time, and was the most comical hero in the history. No man has ever been blamed for so much. If a cow was missed, the first thought was to look for her around Corey's house; a fire blazing up at night brought suspicion of arson to his door. He didn't give a hoot for public opinion, and only in his last years—after he had married Martha—did he bother much with the church. That she stopped his prayer is very probable, but he forgot to say that he'd only recently learned any prayers and it didn't take much to make him stumble over them. He was a crank and a nuisance, but withal a deeply innocent and brave man. In court, once, he was asked if it were true that he had been frightened by the strange behavior of a hog and had then said he knew it to be the Devil in an animal's shape. "What frighted you?" he was asked. He forgot everything but the word "frighted," and instantly replied, "I do not know that I ever spoke that word in my life."

Dramatic Exposition

Which details given in this background information explain Giles Corey's remarks about his wife, Martha?

HALE: Ah! The stoppage of prayer—that is strange. I'll speak further on that with you.

GILES: I'm not sayin' she's touched the Devil, now, but I'd admire to know what books she reads and why she hides them. She'll not answer me, y' see.

HALE: Aye, we'll discuss it. *To all:* Now mark me, if the Devil is in her you will witness some frightful wonders in this room, so please to keep your wits about you. Mr. Putnam, stand close in case she flies. Now, Betty, dear, will you sit up? PUTNAM *comes in closer, ready-handed.* HALE *sits* BETTY *up, but she hangs limp in his hands.* Hmmm. *He observes her carefully. The others watch breathlessly.* Can you hear me? I am John Hale, minister of Beverly. I have come to help you, dear. Do you remember my two little girls in Beverly? *She does not stir in his hands.*

PARRIS, *in fright:* How can it be the Devil? Why would he choose my house to strike? We have all manner of licentious people in the village!

Comprehension

What does Giles believe has made him unable to pray?

HALE: What victory would the Devil have to win a soul already bad? It is the best the Devil wants, and who is better than the minister?

GILES: That's deep, Mr. Parris, deep, deep!

PARRIS, *with resolution now:* Betty! Answer Mr. Hale! Betty!

HALE: Does someone afflict you, child? It need not be a woman, mind you, or a man. Perhaps some bird invisible to others comes to you—perhaps a pig, a mouse, or any beast at all. Is there some figure bids you fly? *The child remains limp in his hands. In silence he lays her back on the pillow. Now, holding out his hands toward her, he intones:* In nomine Domini Sabaoth sui filiique ite ad infernos.[20] *She does not stir. He turns to* ABIGAIL, *his eyes narrowing.* Abigail, what sort of dancing were you doing with her in the forest?

ABIGAIL: Why—common dancing is all.

PARRIS: I think I ought to say that I—I saw a kettle in the grass where they were dancing.

ABIGAIL: That were only soup.

HALE: What sort of soup were in this kettle, Abigail?

ABIGAIL: Why, it were beans—and lentils, I think, and—

HALE: Mr. Parris, you did not notice, did you, any living thing in the kettle? A mouse, perhaps, a spider, a frog—?

PARRIS, *fearfully:* I—do believe there were some movement—in the soup.

ABIGAIL: That jumped in, we never put it in!

HALE, *quickly:* What jumped in?

ABIGAIL: Why, a very little frog jumped—

PARRIS: A frog, Abby!

HALE, *grasping* ABIGAIL: Abigail, it may be your cousin is dying. Did you call the Devil last night?

ABIGAIL: I never called him! Tituba, Tituba . . .

PARRIS, *blanched:* She called the Devil?

HALE: I should like to speak with Tituba.

PARRIS: Goody Ann, will you bring her up? MRS. PUTNAM *exits.*

HALE: How did she call him?

ABIGAIL: I know not—she spoke Barbados.

HALE: Did you feel any strangeness when she called him? A sudden cold wind, perhaps? A trembling below the ground?

ABIGAIL: I didn't see no Devil! *Shaking* BETTY: Betty, wake up. Betty! Betty!

HALE: You cannot evade me, Abigail. Did your cousin drink any of the brew in that kettle?

ABIGAIL: She never drank it!

HALE: Did you drink it?

▶ Critical Viewing

Based on this film still of Abigail, Tituba, and other girls of Salem, how would you describe what actually happened in the woods? **INTERPRET**

Vocabulary

evade (ē vād´) *v.* avoid and escape by deceit or cleverness

---

20. **In nomine Domini Sabaoth sui filiique ite ad infernos** (in nō´ mē nā dō´ mē nē sab´ ā äth so͞o´ ē fē´ lē ē kwā ē´ tā äd in fʉr´ nōs) "In the name of the lord of hosts and his son, get thee to the lower world" (Latin).

ABIGAIL: No, sir!

HALE: Did Tituba ask you to drink it?

ABIGAIL: She tried, but I refused.

HALE: Why are you concealing? Have you sold yourself to Lucifer?

ABIGAIL: I never sold myself! I'm a good girl! I'm a proper girl!

MRS. PUTNAM *enters with* TITUBA, *and instantly* ABIGAIL *points at* TITUBA.

ABIGAIL: She made me do it! She made Betty do it!

TITUBA, *shocked and angry:* Abby!

ABIGAIL: She makes me drink blood!

PARRIS: Blood!!

MRS. PUTNAM: My baby's blood?

TITUBA: No, no, chicken blood. I give she chicken blood!

▼ Critical Viewing

Abigail has accused Tituba of conjuring spirits. What can you infer about Tituba's reaction from her expression here? **INFER**

HALE: Woman, have you enlisted these children for the Devil?

TITUBA: No, no, sir, I don't truck with no Devil!

HALE: Why can she not wake? Are you silencing this child?

TITUBA: I love me Betty!

HALE: You have sent your spirit out upon this child, have you not? Are you gathering souls for the Devil?

ABIGAIL: She sends her spirit on me in church; she makes me laugh at prayer!

PARRIS: She have often laughed at prayer!

ABIGAIL: She comes to me every night to go and drink blood!

TITUBA: You beg *me* to conjure! She beg *me* make charm—

ABIGAIL: Don't lie! *To* HALE: She comes to me while I sleep; she's always making me dream corruptions!

TITUBA: Why you say that, Abby?

ABIGAIL: Sometimes I wake and find myself standing in the open doorway and not a stitch on my body! I always hear her laughing in my sleep. I hear her singing her Barbados songs and tempting me with—

TITUBA: Mister Reverend, I never—

HALE, *resolved now:* Tituba, I want you to wake this child.

TITUBA: I have no power on this child, sir.

HALE: You most certainly do, and you will free her from it now! When did you compact with the Devil?

TITUBA: I don't compact with no Devil!

PARRIS: You will confess yourself or I will take you out and whip you to your death, Tituba!

PUTNAM: This woman must be hanged! She must be taken and hanged!

TITUBA, *terrified, falls to her knees:* No, no, don't hang Tituba! I tell him I don't desire to work for him, sir.

PARRIS: The Devil?

HALE: Then you saw him! TITUBA *weeps.* Now Tituba, I know that when we bind ourselves to Hell it is very hard to break with it. We are going to help you tear yourself free—

TITUBA, *frightened by the coming process:* Mister Reverend, I do believe somebody else be witchin' these children.

HALE: Who?

TITUBA: I don't know, sir, but the Devil got him numerous witches.

HALE: Does he! *It is a clue.* Tituba, look into my eyes. Come, look into me. *She raises her eyes to his fearfully.* You would be a good Christian woman, would you not, Tituba?

TITUBA: Aye, sir, a good Christian woman.

HALE: And you love these little children?

TITUBA: Oh, yes, sir, I don't desire to hurt little children.

HALE: And you love God, Tituba?

TITUBA: I love God with all my bein'.

HALE: Now, in God's holy name—

TITUBA: Bless Him. Bless Him. *She is rocking on her knees, sobbing in terror.*

HALE: And to His glory—

TITUBA: Eternal glory. Bless Him—bless God . . .

HALE: Open yourself, Tituba—open yourself and let God's holy light shine on you.

TITUBA: Oh, bless the Lord.

HALE: When the Devil come to you does he ever come—with another person? *She stares up into his face.* Perhaps another person in the village? Someone you know.

PARRIS: Who came with him?

PUTNAM: Sarah Good? Did you ever see Sarah Good with him? Or Osburn?

PARRIS: Was it man or woman came with him?

TITUBA: Man or woman. Was—was woman.

PARRIS: What woman? A woman, you said. What woman?

TITUBA: It was black dark, and I—

PARRIS: You could see him, why could you not see her?

TITUBA: Well, they was always talking; they was always runnin' round and carryin' on—

PARRIS: You mean out of Salem? Salem witches?

TITUBA: I believe so, yes, sir.

Now HALE *takes her hand. She is surprised.*

HALE: Tituba. You must have no fear to tell us who they are, do you understand? We will protect you. The Devil can never overcome a minister. You know that, do you not?

TITUBA, *kisses* HALE's *hand:* Aye, sir, oh, I do.

HALE: You have confessed yourself to witchcraft, and that speaks a

Identifying Text Features

In what way does the dialogue indicate that Tituba is making things up?

Comprehension

To what does Tituba confess?

Plot

How does Tituba's confirmation of Parris and Hale's suspicions add to the play's rising action?

Identifying Text Features

What do the dialogue and stage directions tell you about the atmosphere on the stage?

wish to come to Heaven's side. And we will bless you, Tituba.

TITUBA, *deeply relieved:* Oh, God bless you, Mr. Hale!

HALE, *with rising exaltation:* You are God's instrument put in our hands to discover the Devil's agent among us. You are selected, Tituba, you are chosen to help us cleanse our village. So speak utterly, Tituba, turn your back on him and face God—face God, Tituba, and God will protect you.

TITUBA, *joining with him:* Oh, God, protect Tituba!

HALE, *kindly:* Who came to you with the Devil? Two? Three? Four? How many?

TITUBA *pants, and begins rocking back and forth again, staring ahead.*

TITUBA: There was four. There was four.

PARRIS, *pressing in on her:* Who? Who? Their names, their names!

TITUBA, *suddenly bursting out:* Oh, how many times he bid me kill you, Mr. Parris!

PARRIS: Kill me!

TITUBA, *in a fury:* He say Mr. Parris must be kill! Mr. Parris no goodly man, Mr. Parris mean man and no gentle man, and he bid me rise out of my bed and cut your throat! *They gasp.* But I tell him "No! I don't hate that man. I don't want kill that man." But he say, "You work for me, Tituba, and I make you free! I give you pretty dress to wear, and put you way high up in the air, and you gone fly back to Barbados!" And I say, "You lie, Devil, you lie!" And then he come one stormy night to me, and he say, "Look! I have *white* people belong to me." And I look—and there was Goody Good.

PARRIS: Sarah Good!

TITUBA, *rocking and weeping:* Aye, sir, and Goody Osburn.

MRS. PUTNAM: I knew it! Goody Osburn were midwife to me three times. I begged you, Thomas, did I not? I begged him not to call Osburn because I feared her. My babies always shriveled in her hands!

HALE: Take courage, you must give us all their names. How can you bear to see this child suffering? Look at her, Tituba. *He is indicating* BETTY *on the bed.* Look at her God-given innocence; her soul is so tender; we must protect her, Tituba; the Devil is out and preying on her like a beast upon the flesh of the pure lamb. God will bless you for your help.

ABIGAIL *rises, staring as though inspired, and cries out.*

ABIGAIL: I want to open myself! *They turn to her, startled. She is enraptured, as though in a pearly light.* I want the light of God, I want the sweet love of Jesus! I danced for the Devil; I saw him; I wrote in his book; I go back to Jesus; I kiss His hand. I saw Sarah Good with the Devil! I saw Goody Osburn with the Devil! I saw Bridget Bishop with the Devil!

As she is speaking, BETTY *is rising from the bed, a fever in her eyes, and picks up the chant.*

BETTY, *staring too:* I saw George Jacobs with the Devil! I saw Goody Howe with the Devil!

PARRIS: She speaks! *He rushes to embrace* BETTY. She speaks!

HALE: Glory to God! It is broken, they are free!

BETTY, *calling out hysterically and with great relief:* I saw Martha Bellows with the Devil!

ABIGAIL: I saw Goody Sibber with the Devil! *It is rising to a great glee.*

PUTNAM: The marshal, I'll call the marshal!

PARRIS *is shouting a prayer of thanksgiving.*

BETTY: I saw Alice Barrow with the Devil!

The curtain begins to fall.

HALE, *as* PUTNAM *goes out:* Let the marshal bring irons!

ABIGAIL: I saw Goody Hawkins with the Devil!

BETTY: I saw Goody Bibber with the Devil!

ABIGAIL: I saw Goody Booth with the Devil!

On their ecstatic cries—

THE CURTAIN FALLS

Critical Reading

Cite textual evidence to support your responses.

1. **Key Ideas and Details** **(a)** What is Betty's condition when the play opens? **(b)** What does Abigail say she and Betty were doing in the forest? **(c) Infer:** What seems to be the main motivation for Reverend Parris's concern about the girls' behavior in the forest?
2. **Key Ideas and Details** **(a)** What do Abigail, Betty, Mercy, and Mary discuss after Reverend Parris leaves his daughter's room? **(b) Interpret:** What events does this scene suggest may occur later in the play?
3. **Key Ideas and Details** **(a)** Who is Reverend Hale? **(b)** Why is he contacted? **(c) Evaluate:** Do you think he is being fair and impartial so far? Why or why not?
4. **Key Ideas and Details** **(a) Summarize:** Summarize Abigail's prior relationship with the Proctors. **(b) Interpret:** What does Betty's revelation about Abigail's actions in the forest suggest about Abigail's feelings for Elizabeth Proctor?
5. **Key Ideas and Details** **(a) Support:** What evidence suggests that sharp divisions exist among the people of Salem Village? **(b) Apply:** Name two others who may be accused. Explain your choices.

Close Reading Activities *The Crucible, Act I*

Literary Analysis

1. **Key Ideas and Details** The **plot** of this play unfolds over four acts. Act I introduces the situation and initial conflicts. Describe the *conflicts* between **(a)** Reverend Parris and the village; **(b)** Abigail Williams and John Proctor.
2. **Key Ideas and Details** Explain how both of the conflicts you identified in response to question 1 contribute to the play's **rising action.**
3. **Key Ideas and Details** In Act I, what seeds of conflict exist among Rebecca Nurse, Reverend Parris, and the Putnams? Explain.
4. **Key Ideas and Details** Use a chart like the one shown to examine how two specific events or characters described in the play's opening **dramatic exposition** are carried through into the action of Act I.

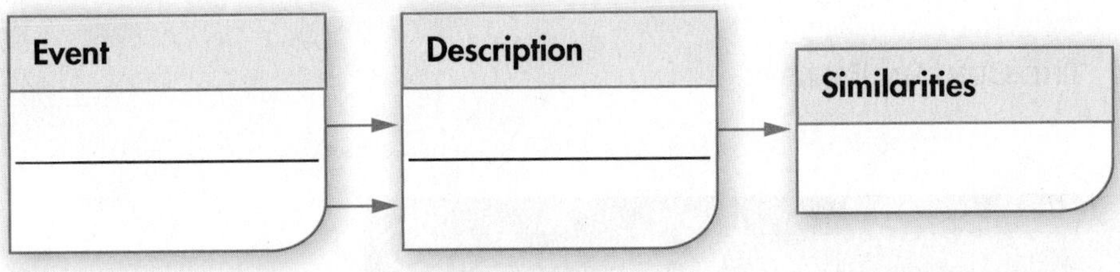

5. **Key Ideas and Details** **(a)** According to the opening dramatic exposition, how did most of the members of Salem feel about the vast forest that surrounded them? **(b)** How do you think these feelings affected the girls' actions in the forest and Parris's reactions to what he saw there?
6. **Key Ideas and Details** **(a)** Reread the dramatic exposition on Thomas Putnam on pages 1133–1134. **(b)** Which details lead you to believe that Putnam will be a fierce figure as the plot unfolds? Explain.
7. **Key Ideas and Details** Explain how the closing scene, in which Abigail and Betty shout the names of the accused, serves as the **climax** of Act I.
8. **Craft and Structure** **(a)** Describe the character of Abigail Williams based on the information provided in Act I. **(b)** Identify which **text structures**—*dialogue* or *stage directions*—provide the meaningful information.
9. **Craft and Structure** What text features provide information about the relationship between Abigail and John Proctor?
10. **Integration of Knowledge and Ideas** **(a)** Which characters depart the Putnam house after Reverend Hale arrives? **(b)** Why do they leave? **(c)** What does this scene suggest about future plot developments?

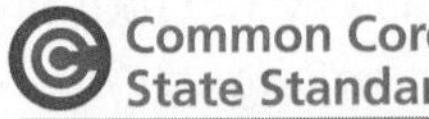

Common Core State Standards

Writing

2. Write informative texts to examine and convey complex ideas, concepts, and information clearly and accurately through the effective selection, organization, and analysis of content. *(p. 1159)*

2.a. Introduce a topic; organize complex ideas, concepts, and information so that each new element builds on that which precedes it to create a unified whole; include formatting. *(p. 1159)*

2.b. Develop the topic thoroughly by selecting the most significant and relevant facts, extended definitions, concrete details, quotations, or other information and examples appropriate to the audience's knowledge of the topic. *(p. 1159)*

2.e. Establish and maintain a formal style and objective tone while attending to the norms and conventions of the discipline in which they are writing. *(p. 1159)*

Language

4.b. Identify and correctly use patterns of word changes that indicate different meanings or parts of speech. *(p. 1159)*

Vocabulary Acquisition and Use

Word Analysis: Latin Root *-grat-*

The Latin word *gratus,* which means "pleasing," is formed with the root *-grat-,* which means "pleasing" or "agreeable." An *ingratiating* attitude, for example, is one intended to please others. Similarly, a *gratuity* is a gift of money given for pleasing service, and *gratitude* is thankful appreciation for gifts received. Explain how the root *-grat-* contributes to the meaning of the following words:

1. congratulate
2. ingrate
3. gratify
4. grateful

Vocabulary: Sentence Completions

Complete each of the sentences below with the appropriate vocabulary word from page 1123. Explain your answers.

1. ______ can destroy a person's reputation.
2. Months of ______ helped me to learn.
3. He hid his true nature by ______.
4. She tried to ______ punishment by lying about her crime.
5. To soothe their gods, they made sacrifices as an act of ______.
6. Her ______ manner pleased the customers.
7. With my ______ for history, I knew I would enjoy *The Crucible.*

Writing to Sources

Informative Text In *The Crucible*, information about the young girls' mysterious ailments and the discovery of witches spreads through conversation and gossip. Stem the flow of misinformation by writing a **newspaper article** reporting on Betty's illness and the subsequent accusations of witchcraft.

Prewriting Review Act I to collect details to cite in your article. Use a chart like the one shown to organize the information.

Drafting Start with the most important information: the Who? What? and When? questions. Add details as you work your way through the article and quote from sources and eyewitnesses. *Maintain a journalistic distance and tone* by avoiding words that reveal your own emotions or attitudes. Finally, write a headline that summarizes the story in a few bold words.

Model: Using a Chart to Organize Ideas

Who is involved?	
What happened?	
When did it happen?	
Where did it happen?	
Why did it happen?	
How did it happen?	

Revising Review your work to make sure you have used correct proper names and accurately quoted witnesses and authorities. If necessary, return to the play to find additional supporting details.

Building Knowledge and Insight *The Crucible, Act II*

Close Reading Focus

Conflict; Biblical Allusions

Conflict is a struggle between opposing forces. There are two broad categories of conflict. In a complex narrative like this play, there are often numerous conflicts, and most characters experience both types:

- An **external conflict** takes place between a character and an external force, such as society, nature, fate, or another person. In Act II, as accusations and hysteria mount in Salem, characters face increasingly dangerous external conflicts with their neighbors, Abigail and the other the accusing girls, and the authorities.
- An **internal conflict** takes place within a character who is torn by his or her own competing or contradictory values or desires. In Act II, deepening external threats create new internal conflicts for characters and magnify those that already exist.

Some of the conflicts in this play arise out of the stern religious world view that defines the Salem community. That world view is not only revealed through characters' actions and descriptions of their lifestyles. It is also revealed through **Biblical allusions,** or references to figures, stories, or settings from the Bible. These Biblical allusions remind characters—and readers—of the religious beliefs on which the Puritan community is based. As you read, notice the conflicts that intensify in Act II and the Biblical allusions that help characters to define, defend, and excuse their actions.

Preparing to Read Complex Texts As you read, help yourself stay alert to important details and changes in characters and situations by **making predictions** about what will happen next. Notice hints the author drops about what might occur and apply your own *background knowledge* and understanding of human nature. As you read, use a chart like the one shown to record and confirm the predictions you make.

Vocabulary

You will encounter the words listed here in the text that follows. Copy the words into your notebook, sorting them into words you know and words you do not know.

pallor
ameliorate
avidly
base
deference
theology

Common Core State Standards

Reading Literature

3. Analyze the impact of the author's choices regarding how to develop and relate elements of a drama.

5. Analyze how an author's choices concerning how to structure specific parts of a text contribute to its overall structure and meaning as well as its aesthetic impact.

7. Analyze multiple interpretations of a drama, evaluating how each version interprets the source text. *(p. 1185)*

Speaking and Listening

1.d. Respond thoughtfully to diverse perspectives; synthesize comments, claims, and evidence made on all sides of an issue. *(p. 1185)*

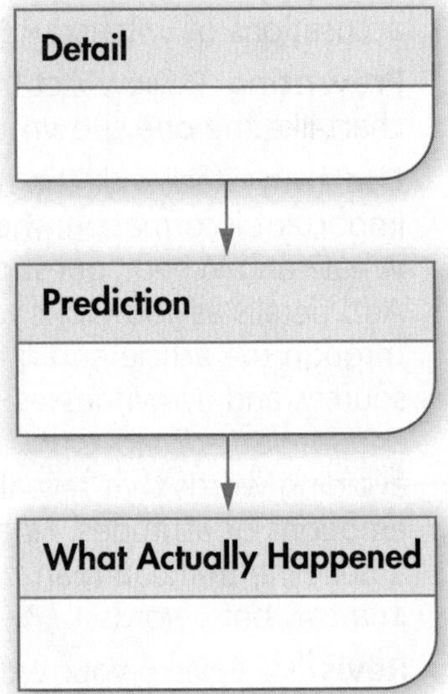

Review and Anticipate

As Act I draws to a close, Salem is in the grip of mounting hysteria. What had begun as concern over the strange behavior of Betty—a reaction that may have stemmed from guilty feelings about her activities in the woods the night before—had swelled by the act's end to a mass hysteria in which accusations of witchcraft were being made and accepted against a growing number of Salem's citizens. Which characters do you think will believe the accusations? Who do you think will be accused next?

The common room of PROCTOR's *house, eight days later.*

At the right is a door opening on the fields outside.
A fireplace is at the left, and behind it a stairway leading upstairs. It is the low, dark, and rather long living room of the time. As the curtain rises, the room is empty. From above, ELIZABETH *is heard softly singing to the children. Presently the door opens and* JOHN PROCTOR *enters, carrying his gun. He glances about the room as he comes toward the fireplace, then halts for an instant as he hears her singing. He continues on to the fireplace, leans the gun against the wall as he swings a pot out of the fire and smells it. Then he lifts out the ladle and tastes. He is not quite pleased. He reaches to a cupboard, takes a pinch of salt, and drops it into the pot. As he is tasting again, her footsteps are heard on the stair. He swings the pot into the fireplace and goes to a basin and washes his hands and face.* ELIZABETH *enters.*

ELIZABETH: What keeps you so late? It's almost dark.

PROCTOR: I were planting far out to the forest edge.

ELIZABETH: Oh, you're done then.

PROCTOR: Aye, the farm is seeded. The boys asleep?

ELIZABETH: They will be soon. *And she goes to the fireplace, proceeds to ladle up stew in a dish.*

PROCTOR: Pray now for a fair summer.

ELIZABETH: Aye.

PROCTOR: Are you well today?

ELIZABETH: I am. *She brings the plate to the table, and, indicating the food:* It is a rabbit.

PROCTOR, *going to the table:* Oh, is it! In Jonathan's trap?

ELIZABETH: No, she walked into the house this afternoon; I found her sittin' in the corner like she come to visit.

PROCTOR: Oh, that's a good sign walkin' in.

Comprehension
At what time of day does this scene take place?

ELIZABETH: Pray God. It hurt my heart to strip her, poor rabbit. *She sits and watches him taste it.*

PROCTOR: It's well seasoned.

ELIZABETH, *blushing with pleasure:* I took great care. She's tender?

PROCTOR: Aye. *He eats. She watches him.* I think we'll see green fields soon. It's warm as blood beneath the clods.

ELIZABETH: That's well.

PROCTOR *eats, then looks up.*

Conflict

As John eats his meal, which details suggest tension in the Proctors' relationship?

PROCTOR: If the crop is good I'll buy George Jacob's heifer. How would that please you?

ELIZABETH: Aye, it would.

PROCTOR, *with a grin:* I mean to please you, Elizabeth.

ELIZABETH—*it is hard to say:* I know it, John.

He gets up, goes to her, kisses her. She receives it. With a certain disappointment, he returns to the table.

PROCTOR, *as gently as he can:* Cider?

ELIZABETH, *with a sense of reprimanding herself for having forgot:* Aye! *She gets up and goes and pours a glass for him. He now arches his back.*

PROCTOR: This farm's a continent when you go foot by foot droppin' seeds in it.

ELIZABETH, *coming with the cider:* It must be.

PROCTOR, *drinks a long draught, then, putting the glass down:* You ought to bring some flowers in the house.

ELIZABETH: Oh! I forgot! I will tomorrow.

PROCTOR: It's winter in here yet. On Sunday let you come with me, and we'll walk the farm together; I never see such a load of flowers on the earth. *With good feeling he goes and looks up at the sky through the open doorway.* Lilacs have a purple smell. Lilac is the smell of nightfall, I think. Massachusetts is a beauty in the spring!

ELIZABETH: Aye, it is.

There is a pause. She is watching him from the table as he stands there absorbing the night. It is as though she would speak but cannot. Instead, now, she takes up his plate and glass and fork and goes with them to the basin. Her back is turned to him. He turns to her and watches her. A sense of their separation rises.

PROCTOR: I think you're sad again. Are you?

ELIZABETH—*she doesn't want friction, and yet she must:* You come so late I thought you'd gone to Salem this afternoon.

PROCTOR: Why? I have no business in Salem.

ELIZABETH: You did speak of going, earlier this week.

PROCTOR—*he knows what she means:* I thought better of it since.

ELIZABETH: Mary Warren's there today.

PROCTOR: Why'd you let her? You heard me forbid her go to Salem any more!

ELIZABETH: I couldn't stop her.

PROCTOR, *holding back a full condemnation of her:* It is a fault, it is a fault, Elizabeth—you're the mistress here, not Mary Warren.

ELIZABETH: She frightened all my strength away.

PROCTOR: How may that mouse frighten you, Elizabeth? You—

ELIZABETH: It is a mouse no more. I forbid her go, and she raises up her chin like the daughter of a prince and says to me, "I must go to Salem, Goody Proctor; I am an official of the court!"

PROCTOR: Court! What court?

ELIZABETH: Aye, it is a proper court they have now. They've sent four judges out of Boston, she says, weighty magistrates of the General Court, and at the head sits the Deputy Governor of the Province.

PROCTOR, *astonished:* Why, she's mad.

ELIZABETH: I would to God she were. There be fourteen people in the jail now, she says. PROCTOR *simply looks at her, unable to grasp it.* And they'll be tried, and the court have power to hang them too, she says.

PROCTOR, *scoffing but without conviction:* Ah, they'd never hang—

ELIZABETH: The Deputy Governor promise hangin' if they'll not confess, John. The town's gone wild, I think. She speak of Abigail, and I thought she were a saint, to hear her. Abigail brings the other girls into the court, and where she walks the crowd will part like the sea for Israel.[1] And folks are brought before them, and if they scream and howl and fall to the floor—the person's clapped in the jail for bewitchin' them.

PROCTOR, *wide-eyed:* Oh, it is a black mischief.

ELIZABETH: I think you must go to Salem, John. *He turns to her.* I think so. You must tell them it is a fraud.

PROCTOR, *thinking beyond this:* Aye, it is, it is surely.

ELIZABETH: Let you go to Ezekiel Cheever—he knows you well. And tell him what she said to you last week in her uncle's house. She said it had naught to do with witchcraft, did she not?

PROCTOR, *in thought:* Aye, she did, she did. *Now, a pause.*

ELIZABETH, *quietly, fearing to anger him by prodding:* God forbid you keep that from the court, John. I think they must be told.

PROCTOR, *quietly, struggling with his thought:* Aye, they must, they must. It is a wonder they do believe her.

ELIZABETH: I would go to Salem now, John—let you go tonight.

PROCTOR: I'll think on it.

ELIZABETH, *with her courage now:* You cannot keep it, John.

PROCTOR, *angering:* I know I cannot keep it. I say I will think on it!

ELIZABETH, *hurt, and very coldly:* Good, then, let you think on it. *She stands and starts to walk out of the room.*

PROCTOR: I am only wondering how I may prove what she told me,

Biblical Allusion

What does Elizabeth's allusion to Moses' parting of the Red Sea reveal about Abigail's new standing in the community?

Making Predictions

Do you think Proctor will go before the court and denounce Abigail? Explain.

Comprehension

According to Elizabeth, how has Mary Warren changed?

---

1. **part like . . . Israel** In the Bible, God commanded Moses, the leader of the Jews, to part the Red Sea to enable the Jews to escape from the Egyptians into Canaan.

Elizabeth. If the girl's a saint now, I think it is not easy to prove she's fraud, and the town gone so silly. She told it to me in a room alone—I have no proof for it.

ELIZABETH: You were alone with her?

PROCTOR, *stubbornly:* For a moment alone, aye.

ELIZABETH: Why, then, it is not as you told me.

PROCTOR, *his anger rising:* For a moment, I say. The others come in soon after.

ELIZABETH, *quietly—she has suddenly lost all faith in him:* Do as you wish, then. *She starts to turn.*

PROCTOR: Woman. *She turns to him.* I'll not have your suspicion any more.

ELIZABETH, *a little loftily:* I have no—

PROCTOR: I'll not have it!

ELIZABETH: Then let you not earn it.

PROCTOR, *with a violent undertone:* You doubt me yet?

ELIZABETH, *with a smile, to keep her dignity:* John, if it were not Abigail that you must go to hurt, would you falter now? I think not.

PROCTOR: Now look you—

ELIZABETH: I see what I see, John.

PROCTOR, *with solemn warning:* You will not judge me more, Elizabeth. I have good reason to think before I charge fraud on Abigail, and I will think on it. Let you look to your own improvement before you go to judge your husband any more. I have forgot Abigail, and—

ELIZABETH: And I.

PROCTOR: Spare me! You forget nothin' and forgive nothin'. Learn charity, woman. I have gone tiptoe in this house all seven month since she is gone. I have not moved from there to there without I think to please you, and still an everlasting funeral marches round your heart. I cannot speak but I am doubted, every moment judged for lies, as though I come into a court when I come into this house!

ELIZABETH: John, you are not open with me. You saw her with a crowd, you said. Now you—

PROCTOR: I'll plead my honesty no more, Elizabeth.

ELIZABETH—*now she would justify herself:* John, I am only—

PROCTOR: No more! I should have roared you down when first you told me your suspicion. But I wilted, and, like a Christian, I confessed. Confessed! Some dream I had must have mistaken you for God that day. But you're not, you're not, and let you remember it! Let you look sometimes for the goodness in me, and judge me not.

ELIZABETH: I do not judge you. The magistrate sits in your heart that judges you. I never thought you but a good man, John—*with a smile*—only somewhat bewildered.

Conflict

What is the source of conflict between Proctor and Elizabeth?

PROCTOR, *laughing bitterly:* Oh, Elizabeth, your justice would freeze beer! *He turns suddenly toward a sound outside. He starts for the door as* MARY WARREN *enters. As soon as he sees her, he goes directly to her and grabs her by the cloak, furious.* How do you go to Salem when I forbid it? Do you mock me? *Shaking her.* I'll whip you if you dare leave this house again!

Strangely, she doesn't resist him, but hangs limply by his grip.

MARY WARREN: I am sick, I am sick, Mr. Proctor. Pray, pray, hurt me not. *Her strangeness throws him off, and her evident* pallor *and weakness. He frees her.* My insides are all shuddery; I am in the proceedings all day, sir.

PROCTOR, *with draining anger—his curiosity is draining it:* And what of these proceedings here? When will you proceed to keep this house, as you are paid nine pound a year to do—and my wife not wholly well?

As though to compensate, MARY WARREN *goes to* ELIZABETH *with a small rag doll.*

MARY WARREN: I made a gift for you today, Goody Proctor. I had to sit long hours in a chair, and passed the time with sewing.

ELIZABETH, *perplexed, looking at the doll:* Why, thank you, it's a fair poppet.[2]

MARY WARREN, *with a trembling, decayed voice:* We must all love each other now, Goody Proctor.

ELIZABETH, *amazed at her strangeness:* Aye, indeed we must.

MARY WARREN, *glancing at the room:* I'll get up early in the morning and clean the house. I must sleep now. *She turns and starts off.*

PROCTOR: Mary. *She halts.* Is it true? There be fourteen women arrested?

MARY WARREN: No, sir. There be thirty-nine now— *She suddenly breaks off and sobs and sits down, exhausted.*

ELIZABETH: Why, she's weepin'! What ails you, child?

MARY WARREN: Goody Osburn—will hang!

There is a shocked pause, while she sobs.

PROCTOR: Hang! *He calls into her face.* Hang, y'say?

MARY WARREN, *through her weeping:* Aye.

PROCTOR: The Deputy Governor will permit it?

MARY WARREN: He sentenced her. He must. To ameliorate it: But not Sarah Good. For Sarah Good confessed, y'see.

PROCTOR: Confessed! To what?

MARY WARREN: That she—*in horror at the memory*—she sometimes made a compact with Lucifer, and wrote her name in his black book—with her blood—and bound herself to torment Christians till God's thrown down—and we all must worship Hell forevermore.

Pause.

2. poppet doll.

Vocabulary

pallor (pal′ ər) *n.* paleness

ameliorate (ə mēl′ yə rāt′) *v.* make better

Arthur Miller
Author's Insight

Miller was fully aware that those who participated in the trials had no perspective on their beliefs or actions. He once wrote: "I spent some ten days in the Salem courthouse reading the crudely recorded trials of the 1692 outbreak, and it was striking how totally absent was the least sense of irony, let alone humor."

Comprehension

What gift does Mary Warren give Elizabeth?

The
American EXPERIENCE

Arthur Miller and the Blacklist

In the late 1940s, the House Un-American Activities Committee developed a "blacklist" of Hollywood screenwriters suspected of being Communists. For many years, film producers used this list to deny employment to these writers.

Arthur Miller himself was called before the House Un-American Activities Committee and asked to name people he had met at a meeting of alleged Communist writers. After refusing, Miller was convicted of contempt; later, he appealed and the contempt charge was overturned.

In 1999, Arthur Miller commented on the relationship between the "Red Scare" and the Salem witch trials. Miller said there were startling similarities in both the rituals of defense and the investigative routines. Three hundred years apart, both prosecutions were alleging membership in a secret, disloyal group.

Connect to the Literature

Which characters in his play resemble Miller in his refusal to answer questions?

PROCTOR: But—surely you know what a jabberer she is. Did you tell them that?

MARY WARREN: Mr. Proctor, in open court she near to choked us all to death.

PROCTOR: How, choked you?

MARY WARREN: She sent her spirit out.

ELIZABETH: Oh, Mary, Mary, surely you—

MARY WARREN, *with an indignant edge:* She tried to kill me many times, Goody Proctor!

ELIZABETH: Why, I never heard you mention that before.

MARY WARREN: I never knew it before. I never knew anything before. When she come into the court I say to myself, I must not accuse this woman, for she sleep in ditches, and so very old and poor. But then—then she sit there, denying and denying, and I feel a misty coldness climbin' up my back, and the skin on my skull begin to creep, and I feel a clamp around my neck and I cannot breathe air; and then—*entranced*—I hear a voice, a screamin' voice, and it were my voice—and all at once I remembered everything she done to me!

PROCTOR: Why? What did she do to you?

MARY WARREN, *like one awakened to a marvelous secret insight:* So many time, Mr. Proctor, she come to this very door, beggin' bread and a cup of cider—and mark this: whenever I turned her away empty, she *mumbled.*

ELIZABETH: Mumbled! She may mumble if she's hungry.

MARY WARREN: But *what* does she mumble? You must remember, Goody Proctor. Last month—a Monday, I think—she walked away, and I thought my guts would burst for two days after. Do you remember it?

ELIZABETH: Why—I do, I think, but—

MARY WARREN: And so I told that to Judge Hathorne, and he asks her so. "Goody Osburn," says he, "what curse do you mumble that this girl must fall sick after turning you away?" And then she replies—*mimicking an old crone*—"Why, your excellence, no curse at all. I only say my commandments; I hope I may say my commandments," says she!

ELIZABETH: And that's an upright answer.

MARY WARREN: Aye, but then Judge Hathorne say, "Recite for us your commandments!"—*leaning* **avidly** *toward them*—and of all the ten she could not say a single one. She never knew no commandments, and they had her in a flat lie!

PROCTOR: And so condemned her?

MARY WARREN, *now a little strained, seeing his stubborn doubt:* Why, they must when she condemned herself.

PROCTOR: But the proof, the proof!

Vocabulary

avidly (av′ id lē) *adv.* eagerly

MARY WARREN, *with greater impatience with him:* I told you the proof. It's hard proof, hard as rock, the judges said.

PROCTOR, *pauses an instant, then:* You will not go to court again, Mary Warren.

MARY WARREN: I must tell you, sir, I will be gone every day now. I am amazed you do not see what weighty work we do.

PROCTOR: What work you do! It's strange work for a Christian girl to hang old women!

MARY WARREN: But, Mr. Proctor, they will not hang them if they confess. Sarah Good will only sit in jail some time—*recalling*—and here's a wonder for you; think on this. Goody Good is pregnant!

ELIZABETH: Pregnant! Are they mad? The woman's near to sixty!

MARY WARREN: They had Doctor Griggs examine her, and she's full to the brim. And smokin' a pipe all these years, and no husband either! But she's safe, thank God, for they'll not hurt the innocent child. But be that not a marvel? You must see it, sir, it's God's work we do. So I'll be gone every day for some time. I'm—I am an official of the court, they say, and I—*She has been edging toward offstage.*

PROCTOR: I'll official you! *He strides to the mantel, takes down the whip hanging there.*

MARY WARREN, *terrified, but coming erect, striving for her authority:* I'll not stand whipping any more!

ELIZABETH, *hurriedly, as* PROCTOR *approaches:* Mary, promise now you'll stay at home—

MARY WARREN, *backing from him, but keeping her erect posture, striving, striving for her way:* The Devil's loose in Salem, Mr. Proctor; we must discover where he's hiding!

PROCTOR: I'll whip the Devil out of you! *With whip raised he reaches out for her, and she streaks away and yells.*

MARY WARREN, *pointing at* ELIZABETH: I saved her life today!

Silence. His whip comes down.

ELIZABETH, *softly:* I am accused?

MARY WARREN, *quaking:* Somewhat mentioned. But I said I never see no sign you ever sent your spirit out to hurt no one, and seeing I do live so closely with you, they dismissed it.

ELIZABETH: Who accused me?

MARY WARREN: I am bound by law, I cannot tell it. *To* PROCTOR: I only hope you'll not be so sarcastical no more. Four judges and the King's deputy sat to dinner with us but an hour ago. I—I would have you speak civilly to me, from this out.

PROCTOR, *in horror, muttering in disgust at her:* Go to bed.

MARY WARREN, *with a stamp of her foot:* I'll not be ordered to bed no more, Mr. Proctor! I am eighteen and a woman, however single!

PROCTOR: Do you wish to sit up? Then sit up.

MARY WARREN: I wish to go to bed!

Conflict
What conflict is developing between the Proctors and their community?

Spiral Review
Text Sructures How do the stage directions here both describe the action and develop the characters?

Comprehension
What evidence does Mary Warren use to prove that Goody Osburn is a witch?

PROCTOR, *in anger:* Good night, then!

MARY WARREN: Good night. *Dissatisfied, uncertain of herself, she goes out. Wide-eyed, both* PROCTOR *and* ELIZABETH *stand staring.*

ELIZABETH, *quietly:* Oh, the noose, the noose is up!

PROCTOR: There'll be no noose.

ELIZABETH: She wants me dead. I knew all week it would come to this!

PROCTOR, *without conviction:* They dismissed it. You heard her say—

ELIZABETH: And what of tomorrow? She will cry me out until they take me!

PROCTOR: Sit you down.

ELIZABETH: She wants me dead, John, you know it!

PROCTOR: I say sit down! *She sits, trembling. He speaks quietly, trying to keep his wits.* Now we must be wise, Elizabeth.

ELIZABETH, *with sarcasm, and a sense of being lost:* Oh, indeed, indeed!

PROCTOR: Fear nothing. I'll find Ezekiel Cheever. I'll tell him she said it were all sport.

ELIZABETH: John, with so many in the jail, more than Cheever's help is needed now, I think. Would you favor me with this? Go to Abigail.

PROCTOR, *his soul hardening as he senses . . .:* What have I to say to Abigail?

ELIZABETH, *delicately:* John—grant me this. You have a faulty understanding of young girls. There is a promise made in any bed—

PROCTOR, *striving against his anger:* What promise!

ELIZABETH: Spoke or silent, a promise is surely made. And she may dote on it now—I am sure she does—and thinks to kill me, then to take my place.

PROCTOR'S *anger is rising; he cannot speak.*

ELIZABETH: It is her dearest hope, John, I know it. There be a thousand names; why does she call mine? There be a certain danger in calling such a name—I am no Goody Good that sleeps in ditches, nor Osburn, drunk and half-witted. She'd dare not call out such a farmer's wife but there be monstrous profit in it. She thinks to take my place, John.

PROCTOR: She cannot think it! *He knows it is true.*

ELIZABETH, *"reasonably":* John, have you ever shown her somewhat of contempt? She cannot pass you in the church but you will blush—

PROCTOR: I may blush for my sin.

ELIZABETH: I think she sees another meaning in that blush.

PROCTOR: And what see you? What see you, Elizabeth?

ELIZABETH, *"conceding":* I think you be somewhat ashamed, for I am there, and she so close.

PROCTOR: When will you know me, woman? Were I stone I would have cracked for shame this seven month!

ELIZABETH: Then go and tell her she's a whore. Whatever promise she may sense—break it, John, break it.

PROCTOR, *between his teeth:* Good, then. I'll go. *He starts for his rifle.*

Making Predictions
Do you think the authorities are more likely to believe Proctor or Abigail? Explain.

"I think you be somewhat ashamed, for I am there, and she so close."

ELIZABETH, *trembling, fearfully:* Oh, how unwillingly!

PROCTOR, *turning on her, rifle in hand:* I will curse her hotter than the oldest cinder in hell. But pray, begrudge me not my anger!

ELIZABETH: Your anger! I only ask you—

PROCTOR: Woman, am I so base? Do you truly think me base?

ELIZABETH: I never called you base.

PROCTOR: Then how do you charge me with such a promise? The promise that a stallion gives a mare I gave that girl!

ELIZABETH: Then why do you anger with me when I bid you break it?

PROCTOR: Because it speaks deceit, and I am honest! But I'll plead no more! I see now your spirit twists around the single error of my life, and I will never tear it free!

ELIZABETH, *crying out:* You'll tear it free—when you come to know that I will be your only wife, or no wife at all! She has an arrow in you yet, John Proctor, and you know it well!

Quite suddenly, as though from the air, a figure appears in the doorway. They start slightly. It is MR. HALE. *He is different now—drawn a little, and there is a quality of deference, even of guilt, about his manner now.*

HALE: Good evening.

PROCTOR, *still in his shock:* Why, Mr. Hale! Good evening to you, sir. Come in, come in.

HALE, *to Elizabeth:* I hope I do not startle you.

ELIZABETH: No, no, it's only that I heard no horse—

HALE: You are Goodwife Proctor.

PROCTOR: Aye; Elizabeth.

HALE, *nods, then:* I hope you're not off to bed yet.

PROCTOR, *setting down his gun:* No, no. HALE *comes further into the room. And* PROCTOR, *to explain his nervousness:* We are not used to visitors after dark, but you're welcome here. Will you sit you down, sir?

HALE: I will. *He sits.* Let you sit, Goodwife Proctor.

She does, never letting him out of her sight. There is a pause as HALE *looks about the room.*

PROCTOR, *to break the silence:* Will you drink cider, Mr. Hale?

HALE: No, it rebels my stomach; I have some further traveling yet tonight. Sit you down, sir. PROCTOR *sits.* I will not keep you long, but I have some business with you.

PROCTOR: Business of the court?

HALE: No—no, I come of my own, without the court's authority. Hear me. *He wets his lips.* I know not if you are aware, but your wife's name is—mentioned in the court.

PROCTOR: We know it, sir. Our Mary Warren told us. We are entirely amazed.

HALE: I am a stranger here, as you know. And in my ignorance I find it hard to draw a clear opinion of them that come accused before the court. And so this afternoon, and now tonight, I go from house to

Vocabulary
base (bās) *adj.* low; mean

Vocabulary
deference (def′ ər əns) *n.* courteous regard or respect

Comprehension
What does Elizabeth fear that Abigail will do to her?

house—I come now from Rebecca Nurse's house and—

ELIZABETH, *shocked:* Rebecca's charged!

HALE: God forbid such a one be charged. She is, however—mentioned somewhat.

ELIZABETH, *with an attempt at a laugh:* You will never believe, I hope, that Rebecca trafficked with the Devil.

HALE: Woman, it is possible.

PROCTOR, *taken aback:* Surely you cannot think so.

HALE: This is a strange time, Mister. No man may longer doubt the powers of the dark are gathered in monstrous attack upon this village. There is too much evidence now to deny it. You will agree, sir?

Vocabulary
theology (thē äl′ ə jē) *n* the study of religion

PROCTOR, *evading:* I—have no knowledge in that line. But it's hard to think so pious a woman be secretly a Devil's bitch after seventy year of such good prayer.

HALE: Aye. But the Devil is a wily one, you cannot deny it. However, she is far from accused, and I know she will not be. *Pause.* I thought, sir, to put some questions as to the Christian character of this house, if you'll permit me.

▼ Critical Viewing
Does Hale, as pictured here, seem sincere? Explain. **MAKE A JUDGMENT**

PROCTOR, *coldly, resentful:* Why, we—have no fear of questions, sir.

HALE: Good, then. *He makes himself more comfortable.* In the book of record that Mr. Parris keeps, I note that you are rarely in the church on Sabbath Day.

PROCTOR: No, sir, you are mistaken.

HALE: Twenty-six time in seventeen month, sir. I must call that rare. Will you tell me why you are so absent?

PROCTOR: Mr. Hale, I never knew I must account to that man for I come to church or stay at home. My wife were sick this winter.

HALE: So I am told. But you, Mister, why could you not come alone?

PROCTOR: I surely did come when I could, and when I could not I prayed in this house.

HALE: Mr. Proctor, your house is not a church; your **theology** must tell you that.

PROCTOR: It does, sir, it does; and it tells me that a minister may pray to God without he have golden candlesticks upon the altar.

HALE: What golden candlesticks?

PROCTOR: Since we built the church there were pewter candlesticks upon the altar; Francis Nurse made them y'know, and a sweeter hand never touched the metal. But Parris came, and for twenty week he preach nothin' but golden candlesticks until he had them. I labor the earth from dawn of day to blink of night, and I tell you true, when I look to heaven and see my money glaring at his elbows—it hurt my prayer, sir, it hurt my prayer.

I think, sometimes, the man dreams cathedrals, not clapboard meetin' houses.

HALE, *thinks, then:* And yet, Mister, a Christian on Sabbath Day must be in church. *Pause.* Tell me—you have three children?

PROCTOR: Aye. Boys.

HALE: How comes it that only two are baptized?

PROCTOR, *starts to speak, then stops, then, as though unable to restrain this:* I like it not that Mr. Parris should lay his hand upon my baby. I see no light of God in that man. I'll not conceal it.

HALE: I must say it, Mr. Proctor; that is not for you to decide. The man's ordained, therefore the light of God is in him.

PROCTOR, *flushed with resentment but trying to smile:* What's your suspicion, Mr. Hale?

HALE: No, no, I have no—

PROCTOR: I nailed the roof upon the church, I hung the door—

HALE: Oh, did you! That's a good sign, then.

PROCTOR: It may be I have been too quick to bring the man to book, but you cannot think we ever desired the destruction of religion. I think that's in your mind, is it not?

HALE, *not altogether giving way:* I—have—there is a softness in your record, sir, a softness.

Comprehension

Why has Proctor avoided attending the church?

WORLD LITERATURE IN CONTEXT

POLITICAL DRAMA

BERTOLT BRECHT (1898-1956)

German playwright and poet Bertolt Brecht began writing in the chaotic years after World War I. Hyperinflation in Germany had severely reduced the value of German money and unemployment had climbed to thirty percent. Brecht pondered how to address the reality of the times. "Can we speak of money in the poetry of iambs?" he asked.

Brecht came to believe an artist's job is to wake people up. He rejected traditional theater where the audience loses itself in the drama. Brecht organized a group of artists who developed a new style of theater. Actors sometimes broke out of character to speak to the audience.

During the early 1930s, Brecht watched with dismay as the Nazis rose to power. In 1933, he and his family fled Germany. While in exile, Brecht completed some of his most important works, including "Mother Courage," a play about the horrors of war.

▲ Production of *Mother Courage*

Connect to the Literature

In what ways can art challenge people to think differently? Explain.

ELIZABETH: I think, maybe, we have been too hard with Mr. Parris. I think so. But sure we never loved the Devil here.

HALE, *nods, deliberating this. Then, with the voice of one administering a secret test:* Do you know your Commandments, Elizabeth?

ELIZABETH, *without hesitation, even eagerly:* I surely do. There be no mark of blame upon my life, Mr. Hale. I am a covenanted Christian woman.

HALE: And you, Mister?

PROCTOR, *a trifle unsteadily:* I—am sure I do, sir.

HALE, *glances at her open face, then at* JOHN, *then:* Let you repeat them, if you will.

PROCTOR: The Commandments.

HALE: Aye.

PROCTOR, *looking off, beginning to sweat:* Thou shalt not kill.

HALE: Aye.

PROCTOR, *counting on his fingers:* Thou shalt not steal. Thou shalt not covet thy neighbor's goods, nor make unto thee any graven image. Thou shalt not take the name of the Lord in vain; thou shalt have no other gods before me. *With some hesitation:* Thou shalt remember the Sabbath Day and keep it holy. *Pause. Then:* Thou shalt honor thy father and mother. Thou shalt not bear false witness. *He is stuck. He counts back on his fingers, knowing one is missing.* Thou shalt not make unto thee any graven image.

HALE: You have said that twice, sir.

PROCTOR, *lost:* Aye. *He is flailing for it.*

ELIZABETH, *delicately:* Adultery, John.

PROCTOR, *as though a secret arrow had pained his heart:* Aye. *Trying to grin it away—to* HALE: You see, sir, between the two of us we do know them all. HALE *only looks at* PROCTOR, *deep in his attempt to define this man.* PROCTOR *grows more uneasy.* I think it be a small fault.

HALE: Theology, sir, is a fortress; no crack in a fortress may be accounted small. *He rises; he seems worried now. He paces a little, in deep thought.*

PROCTOR: There be no love for Satan in this house, Mister.

HALE: I pray it, I pray it dearly. *He looks to both of them, an attempt at a smile on his face, but his misgivings are clear.* Well, then—I'll bid you good night.

ELIZABETH, *unable to restrain herself:* Mr. Hale. *He turns.* I do think you are suspecting me somewhat? Are you not?

HALE, *obviously disturbed—and evasive:* Goody Proctor, I do not judge you. My duty is to add

▼ Critical Viewing

Does this image reflect the qualities you have noticed in Elizabeth up to this point in the play? Explain. **CONNECT**

what I may to the godly wisdom of the court. I pray you both good health and good fortune. *To* JOHN: Good night, sir. *He starts out.*

ELIZABETH, *with a note of desperation:* I think you must tell him, John.

HALE: What's that?

ELIZABETH, *restraining a call:* Will you tell him?

Slight pause. HALE *looks questioningly at* JOHN.

PROCTOR, *with difficulty:* I—I have no witness and cannot prove it, except my word be taken. But I know the children's sickness had naught to do with witchcraft.

HALE, *stopped, struck:* Naught to do—?

PROCTOR: Mr. Parris discovered them sportin' in the woods. They were startled and took sick.

Pause.

HALE: Who told you this?

PROCTOR, *hesitates, then:* Abigail Williams.

HALE: Abigail.

PROCTOR: Aye.

HALE, *his eyes wide:* Abigail Williams told you it had naught to do with witchcraft!

PROCTOR: She told me the day you came, sir.

HALE, *suspiciously:* Why—why did you keep this?

PROCTOR: I never knew until tonight that the world is gone daft with this nonsense.

HALE: Nonsense! Mister, I have myself examined Tituba, Sarah Good, and numerous others that have confessed to dealing with the Devil. They have *confessed* it.

PROCTOR: And why not, if they must hang for denyin' it? There are them that will swear to anything before they'll hang; have you never thought of that?

HALE: I have. I—I have indeed. *It is his own suspicion, but he resists it. He glances at* ELIZABETH, *then at* JOHN. And you—would you testify to this in court?

PROCTOR: I—had not reckoned with goin' into court. But if I must I will.

HALE: Do you falter here?

PROCTOR: I falter nothing, but I may wonder if my story will be credited in such a court. I do wonder on it, when such a steady-minded minister as you will suspicion such a woman that never lied, and cannot, and the world knows she cannot! I may falter somewhat, Mister; I am no fool.

HALE, *quietly—it has impressed him:* Proctor, let you open with me now, for I have a rumor that troubles me. It's said you hold no belief that there may even be witches in the world. Is that true, sir?

PROCTOR—*he knows this is critical, and is striving against his disgust with* HALE *and with himself for even answering:* I know not what I have said, I may have said it. I have wondered if there be witches in the

Conflict

What internal conflict do these stage directions suggest Hale experiences?

Comprehension

What does John Proctor tell Reverend Hale about Abigail Williams?

world—although I cannot believe they come among us now.

HALE: Then you do not believe—

PROCTOR: I have no knowledge of it; the Bible speaks of witches, and I will not deny them.

HALE: And you, woman?

ELIZABETH: I—I cannot believe it.

HALE, *shocked:* You cannot!

PROCTOR: Elizabeth, you bewilder him!

ELIZABETH, *to* HALE: I cannot think the Devil may own a woman's soul, Mr. Hale, when she keeps an upright way, as I have. I am a good woman, I know it; and if you believe I may do only good work in the world, and yet be secretly bound to Satan, then I must tell you, sir, I do not believe it.

HALE: But, woman, you do believe there are witches in—

ELIZABETH: If you think that I am one, then I say there are none.

HALE: You surely do not fly against the Gospel, the Gospel—

PROCTOR: She believe in the Gospel, every word!

ELIZABETH: Question Abigail Williams about the Gospel, not myself!

HALE *stares at her.*

PROCTOR: She do not mean to doubt the Gospel, sir, you cannot think it. This be a Christian house, sir, a Christian house.

HALE: God keep you both; let the third child be quickly baptized, and go you without fail each Sunday to Sabbath prayer; and keep a solemn, quiet way among you. I think—

GILES COREY *appears in doorway.*

GILES: John!

PROCTOR: Giles! What's the matter?

GILES: They take my wife.

FRANCIS NURSE *enters.*

GILES: And his Rebecca!

PROCTOR, *to* FRANCIS: Rebecca's in the *jail!*

FRANCIS: Aye, Cheever come and take her in his wagon. We've only now come from the jail, and they'll not even let us in to see them.

ELIZABETH: They've surely gone wild now, Mr. Hale!

FRANCIS, *going to* HALE: Reverend Hale! Can you not speak to the Deputy Governor? I'm sure he mistakes these people—

HALE: Pray calm yourself, Mr. Nurse.

FRANCIS: My wife is the very brick and mortar of the church, Mr. Hale—*indicating* GILES—and Martha Corey, there cannot be a woman closer yet to God than Martha.

"They've surely gone wild now, Mr. Hale!"

HALE: How is Rebecca charged, Mr. Nurse?

FRANCIS, *with a mocking, half-hearted laugh:* For murder, she's charged! *Mockingly quoting the warrant:* "For the marvelous and supernatural murder of Goody Putnam's babies." What am I to do, Mr. Hale?

HALE, *turns from* FRANCIS, *deeply troubled, then:* Believe me, Mr. Nurse, if Rebecca Nurse be tainted, then nothing's left to stop the whole green world from burning. Let you rest upon the justice of the court; the court will send her home. I know it.

FRANCIS: You cannot mean she will be tried in court!

HALE, *pleading:* Nurse, though our hearts break, we cannot flinch; these are new times, sir. There is a misty plot afoot so subtle we should be criminal to cling to old respects and ancient friendships. I have seen too many frightful proofs in court—the Devil is alive in Salem, and we dare not quail to follow wherever the accusing finger points!

Biblical Allusion
How does Hale use this allusion to the Devil to justify the accusation against Rebecca Nurse?

PROCTOR, *angered:* How may such a woman murder children?

HALE, *in great pain:* Man, remember, until an hour before the Devil fell, God thought him beautiful in Heaven.

GILES: I never said my wife were a witch, Mr. Hale; I only said she were reading books!

HALE: Mr. Corey, exactly what complaint were made on your wife?

GILES: That bloody mongrel Walcott charge her. Y'see, he buy a pig of my wife four or five year ago, and the pig died soon after. So he come dancin' in for his money back. So my Martha, she says to him, "Walcott, if you haven't the wit to feed a pig properly, you'll not live to own many," she says. Now he goes to court and claims that from that day to this he cannot keep a pig alive for more than four weeks because my Martha bewitch them with her books!

Enter EZEKIEL CHEEVER. *A shocked silence.*

CHEEVER: Good evening to you, Proctor.

PROCTOR: Why, Mr. Cheever. Good evening.

CHEEVER: Good evening, all. Good evening, Mr. Hale.

PROCTOR: I hope you come not on business of the court.

CHEEVER: I do, Proctor, aye. I am clerk of the court now, y'know.

Enter MARSHAL HERRICK, *a man in his early thirties, who is somewhat shamefaced at the moment.*

GILES: It's a pity, Ezekiel, that an honest tailor might have gone to Heaven must burn in Hell. You'll burn for this, do you know it?

CHEEVER: You know yourself I must do as I'm told. You surely know that, Giles. And I'd as lief[3] you'd not be sending me to Hell. I like not the sound of it, I tell you; I like not the sound of it. *He fears* PROCTOR, *but starts to reach inside his coat.* Now believe me, Proctor, how heavy be the law, all its tonnage I do carry on my back tonight. *He takes out a warrant.* I have a warrant for your wife.

Comprehension
With what crime is Rebecca Nurse charged?

---

3. as lief (as lēf) *adv.* rather.

PROCTOR, *to* HALE: You said she were not charged!

HALE: I know nothin' of it. *To* CHEEVER: When were she charged?

CHEEVER: I am given sixteen warrant tonight, sir, and she is one.

PROCTOR: Who charged her?

CHEEVER: Why, Abigail Williams charge her.

PROCTOR: On what proof, what proof?

CHEEVER, *looking about the room:* Mr. Proctor, I have little time. The court bid me search your house, but I like not to search a house. So will you hand me any poppets that your wife may keep here?

PROCTOR: Poppets?

ELIZABETH: I never kept no poppets, not since I were a girl.

CHEEVER, *embarrassed, glancing toward the mantel where sits* MARY WARREN'S *poppet:* I spy a poppet, Goody Proctor.

ELIZABETH: Oh! *Going for it*: Why, this is Mary's.

CHEEVER, *shyly:* Would you please to give it to me?

ELIZABETH, *handing it to him, asks* HALE: Has the court discovered a text in poppets now?

CHEEVER, *carefully holding the poppet:* Do you keep any others in this house?

PROCTOR: No, nor this one either till tonight. What signifies a poppet?

CHEEVER: Why, a poppet—*he gingerly turns the poppet over*—a poppet may signify—Now, woman, will you please to come with me?

PROCTOR: She will not! *To* ELIZABETH: Fetch Mary here.

CHEEVER, *ineptly reaching toward* ELIZABETH: No, no, I am forbid to leave her from my sight.

PROCTOR, *pushing his arm away:* You'll leave her out of sight and out of mind, Mister. Fetch Mary, Elizabeth. ELIZABETH *goes upstairs.*

HALE: What signifies a poppet, Mr. Cheever?

Making Predictions
How do you think the poppet will affect Elizabeth's fate?

CHEEVER, *turning the poppet over in his hands:* Why, they say it may signify that she—*he has lifted the poppet's skirt, and his eyes widen in astonished fear.* Why, this, this—

PROCTOR, *reaching for the poppet:* What's there?

CHEEVER: Why—*He draws out a long needle from the poppet*—it is a needle! Herrick, Herrick, it is a needle!

HERRICK *comes toward him.*

PROCTOR, *angrily, bewildered:* And what signifies a needle!

CHEEVER, *his hands shaking:* Why, this go hard with her, Proctor, this—I had my doubts, Proctor, I had my doubts, but here's calamity. *To* HALE, *showing the needle:* You see it, sir, it is a needle!

HALE: Why? What meanin' has it?

CHEEVER, *wide-eyed, trembling:* The girl, the Williams girl, Abigail Williams, sir. She sat to dinner in Reverend Parris's house tonight, and without word nor warnin' she falls to the floor. Like a struck beast, he says, and screamed a scream that a bull would weep to hear. And he goes to save her, and, stuck two inches in the flesh of her belly, he draw a needle out. And demandin' of her how she come to be so stabbed, she—*to* PROCTOR *now*—testify it were your wife's familiar spirit pushed it in.

PROCTOR: Why, she done it herself! *To* HALE: I hope you're not takin' this for proof, Mister!

HALE, *struck by the proof, is silent.*

CHEEVER: 'Tis hard proof! *To* HALE: I find here a poppet Goody Proctor keeps. I have found it, sir. And in the belly of the poppet a needle's stuck. I tell you true, Proctor, I never warranted to see such proof of Hell, and I bid you obstruct me not, for I—

Enter ELIZABETH *with* MARY WARREN. PROCTOR, *seeing* MARY WARREN, *draws her by the arm to* HALE.

PROCTOR: Here now! Mary, how did this poppet come into my house?

MARY WARREN, *frightened for herself, her voice very small:* What poppet's that, sir?

PROCTOR, *impatiently, points at the doll in* CHEEVER'S *hand:* This poppet, this poppet.

MARY WARREN, *evasively, looking at it:* Why, I—I think it is mine.

PROCTOR: It is your poppet, is it not?

MARY WARREN, *not understanding the direction of this:* It—is, sir.

PROCTOR: And how did it come into this house?

MARY WARREN, *glancing about at the avid faces:* Why—I made it in the court, sir, and—give it to Goody Proctor tonight.

PROCTOR, *to* HALE: Now, sir—do you have it?

HALE: Mary Warren, a needle have been found inside this poppet.

MARY WARREN, *bewildered:* Why, I meant no harm by it, sir.

PROCTOR, *quickly:* You stuck that needle in yourself?

MARY WARREN: I—I believe I did, sir, I—

PROCTOR, *to* HALE: What say you now?

HALE, *watching* MARY WARREN *closely:* Child, you are certain this be your natural memory? May it be, perhaps that someone conjures you even now to say this?

MARY WARREN: Conjures me? Why, no, sir, I am entirely myself, I think. Let you ask Susanna Walcott—she saw me sewin' it in court. *Or better still:* Ask Abby, Abby sat beside me when I made it.

PROCTOR, *to* HALE, *of* CHEEVER: Bid him begone. Your mind is surely settled now. Bid him out, Mr. Hale.

ELIZABETH: What signifies a needle?

HALE: Mary—you charge a cold and cruel murder on Abigail.

MARY WARREN: Murder! I charge no—

HALE: Abigail were stabbed tonight; a needle were found stuck into her belly—

ELIZABETH: And she charges me?

Making Predictions
Based on Hale's reaction to Mary Warren's testimony, what do you think will be the fate of those accused?

Comprehension
Who put the needle in the poppet?

HALE: Aye.

ELIZABETH, *her breath knocked out:* Why—! The girl is murder! She must be ripped out of the world!

CHEEVER, *pointing at* ELIZABETH: You've heard that, sir! Ripped out of the world! Herrick, you heard it!

PROCTOR, *suddenly snatching the warrant out of* CHEEVER'S *hands:* Out with you.

CHEEVER: Proctor, you dare not touch the warrant.

PROCTOR, ripping the warrant: Out with you!

CHEEVER: You've ripped the Deputy Governor's warrant, man!

PROCTOR: Damn the Deputy Governor! Out of my house!

HALE: Now, Proctor, Proctor!

▼ Critical Viewing

What thoughts or feelings do the facial expressions of Elizabeth Proctor, the deputy, and Parris convey in this photo? **INTERPRET**

PROCTOR: Get y'gone with them! You are a broken minister.

HALE: Proctor, if she is innocent, the court—

PROCTOR: If *she* is innocent! Why do you never wonder if Parris be innocent, or Abigail? Is the accuser always holy now? Were they born this morning as clean as God's fingers? I'll tell you what's walking Salem—vengeance is walking Salem. We are what we always were in Salem, but now the little crazy children are jangling the keys of the kingdom, and common vengeance writes the law! This warrant's vengeance! I'll not give my wife to vengeance!

ELIZABETH: I'll go, John—

PROCTOR: You will not go!

HERRICK: I have nine men outside. You cannot keep her. The law binds me, John, I cannot budge.

PROCTOR, *to* HALE, *ready to break him:* Will you see her taken?

HALE: Proctor, the court is just—

PROCTOR: Pontius Pilate![4] God will not let you wash your hands of this!

ELIZABETH: John—I think I must go with them. *He cannot bear to look at her.* Mary, there is bread enough for the morning; you will bake, in the afternoon. Help Mr. Proctor as you were his daughter—you owe me that, and much more. *She is fighting her weeping. To* PROCTOR: When the children wake, speak nothing of witchcraft—it will frighten them. *She cannot go on.*

PROCTOR: I will bring you home. I will bring you soon.

ELIZABETH: Oh, John, bring me soon!

PROCTOR: I will fall like an ocean on that court! Fear nothing, Elizabeth.

ELIZABETH, *with great fear:* I will fear nothing. *She looks about the room, as though to fix it in her mind.* Tell the children I have gone to visit someone sick.

She walks out the door, HERRICK *and* CHEEVER *behind her. For a moment,* PROCTOR *watches from the doorway. The clank of chain is heard.*

PROCTOR: Herrick! Herrick, don't chain her! *He rushes out the door. From outside:* Damn you, man, you will not chain her! Off with them! I'll not have it! I will not have her chained!

There are other men's voices against his. HALE, *in a fever of guilt and uncertainty, turns from the door to avoid the sight:* MARY WARREN *bursts into tears and sits weeping.* GILES COREY *calls to* HALE.

GILES: And yet silent, minister? It is fraud, you know it is fraud! What keeps you, man?

PROCTOR *is half braced, half pushed into the room by two deputies and* HERRICK.

PROCTOR: I'll pay you, Herrick, I will surely pay you!

HERRICK, *panting:* In God's name, John, I cannot help myself. I must

"Get y'gone with them! You are a broken minister."

Biblical Allusion

How is Proctor's allusion to Pontius Pilate an insult to Hale?

Comprehension

What happens to Elizabeth Proctor?

---

4. **Pontius** (pän´ shəs) **Pilate** (pī´ lət) Roman leader who condemned Jesus to be crucified.

chain them all. Now let you keep inside this house till I am gone! *He goes out with his deputies.*

PROCTOR *stands there, gulping air. Horses and a wagon creaking are heard.*

HALE, *in great uncertainty:* Mr. Proctor—

PROCTOR: Out of my sight!

HALE: Charity, Proctor, charity. What I have heard in her favor, I will not fear to testify in court. God help me, I cannot judge her guilty or innocent—I know not. Only this consider: the world goes mad, and it profit nothing you should lay the cause to the vengeance of a little girl.

PROCTOR: You are a coward! Though you be ordained in God's own tears, you are a coward now!

HALE: Proctor, I cannot think God be provoked so grandly by such a petty cause. The jails are packed—our greatest judges sit in Salem now—and hangin's promised. Man, we must look to cause proportionate. Were there murder done, perhaps, and never brought to light? Abomination? Some secret blasphemy that stinks to Heaven? Think on cause, man, and let you help me to discover it. For there's your way, believe it, there is your only way, when such confusion strikes upon the world. *He goes to* GILES *and* FRANCIS. Let you counsel among yourselves; think on your village and what may have drawn from heaven such thundering wrath upon you all. I shall pray God open up our eyes.

HALE *goes out.*

FRANCIS, *struck by* HALE'S *mood:* I never heard no murder done in Salem.

PROCTOR—*he has been reached by* HALE'S *words:* Leave me, Francis, leave me.

GILES, *shaken:* John—tell me, are we lost?

PROCTOR: Go home now, Giles. We'll speak on it tomorrow.

GILES: Let you think on it. We'll come early, eh?

PROCTOR: Aye. Go now, Giles.

GILES: Good night, then.

GILES COREY *goes out. After a moment:*

MARY WARREN, *in a fearful squeak of a voice:* Mr. Proctor, very likely they'll let her come home once they're given proper evidence.

PROCTOR: You're coming to the court with me, Mary. You will tell it in the court.

MARY WARREN: I cannot charge murder on Abigail.

PROCTOR, *moving menacingly toward her:* You will tell the court how that poppet come here and who stuck the needle in.

MARY WARREN: She'll kill me for sayin' that! PROCTOR *continues toward her.* Abby'll charge lechery[5] on you, Mr. Proctor!

Making Predictions

What impact do you think the charge of lechery would have on Proctor and his family?

---

5. **lechery** (lech′ ər ē) *n.* lust; adultery—a charge almost as serious as witchcraft in this Puritan community.

PROCTOR, *halting:* She's told you!

MARY WARREN: I have known it, sir. She'll ruin you with it, I know she will.

PROCTOR, *hesitating, and with deep hatred of himself:* Good. Then her saintliness is done with. MARY *backs from him.* We will slide together into our pit; you will tell the court what you know.

MARY WARREN, *in terror:* I cannot, they'll turn on me—

PROCTOR *strides and catches her, and she is repeating, "I cannot, I cannot!"*

PROCTOR: My wife will never die for me! I will bring your guts into your mouth but that goodness will not die for me!

MARY WARREN, *struggling to escape him:* I cannot do it. I cannot!

PROCTOR, *grasping her by the throat as though he would strangle her:* Make your peace with it! Now Hell and Heaven grapple on our backs, and all our old pretense is ripped away—make your peace! *He throws her to the floor, where she sobs, "I cannot, I cannot . . ." And now, half to himself, staring, and turning to the open door:* Peace. It is a providence, and no great change; we are only what we always were, but naked now. *He walks as though toward a great horror, facing the open sky.* Aye, naked! And the wind, God's icy wind, will blow!

And she is over and over again sobbing, "I cannot, I cannot, I cannot," as

THE CURTAIN FALLS

Critical Reading

Cite textual evidence to support your responses.

1. **Key Ideas and Details (a)** What does Mary Warren bring home to Elizabeth Proctor? **(b) Interpret:** What is the significance of this gift?
2. **Key Ideas and Details (a)** What evidence is used to support Abigail Williams's assertion that Elizabeth Proctor is guilty of witchcraft? **(b) Assess:** Do you think the evidence is compelling? Why or why not?
3. **Key Ideas and Details (a)** What does Sarah Good do to save herself from hanging? **(b) Draw Conclusions:** Why would such an action save her?
4. **Key Ideas and Details (a)** According to John Proctor, what is "walking Salem" and writing the law in the community? **(b) Support:** What evidence would support Proctor's assertion?
5. **Key Ideas and Details (a)** Who says the witchcraft trials are "a black mischief"? **(b) Analyze:** What is ironic about that remark?
6. **Key Ideas and Details Analyze:** Why is it surprising that Rebecca Nurse is charged with witchcraft?
7. **Integration of Knowledge and Ideas Evaluate:** Do you find any irony in the fact that Ezekiel Cheever is the one who arrests Elizabeth Proctor? Why or why not?

Close Reading Activities *The Crucible, Act II*

Literary Analysis

1. **Key Ideas and Details** **(a)** What **external conflict** confronts those convicted of witchcraft? **(b)** What **internal conflict** do they face?
2. **Key Ideas and Details** **(a)** What conflicts do Elizabeth and John Proctor struggle with in their relationship? **(b)** Which of these are internal conflicts each character faces alone, and which are external?
3. **Key Ideas and Details** Is it an internal or external conflict, or some combination, that causes Elizabeth's awkward reaction to Proctor's kiss on page 1162? Explain.
4. **Key Ideas and Details** What profound conflict does Proctor note when he confronts Hale with the following words?

   "I'll tell you what's walking Salem—vengeance is walking Salem. We are what we always were . . . but now the little crazy children are jangling the keys of the kingdom . . ."
5. **Key Ideas and Details** What is the nature of the conflict suggested by Proctor's last lines and the last stage directions describing him in Act II?
6. **Key Ideas and Details** **(a)** Note three **predictions** you made about John Proctor in Act II. **(b)** What details led you to make those predictions? **(c)** Were your predictions confirmed by the end of the act? Explain.
7. **Key Ideas and Details** **(a)** What predictions did you make about Elizabeth in Act II? **(b)** What details or events suggested those predictions?
8. **Key Ideas and Details** **(a)** What predictions can you make based on Mary Warren's information about the convictions of Sarah Good and Goody Osburn? **(b)** Is that prediction proved accurate or inaccurate by the arrest of Elizabeth? **(c)** Based on both pieces of information, what predictions can you make about other accusations to come? Explain.
9. **Craft and Structure** Use a chart like the one shown to examine the meanings of **Biblical allusions** in Act II. **(a)** Identify the allusion. **(b)** Determine what the allusion means. **(c)** Explain what it reveals about the character or situation in which it is used.

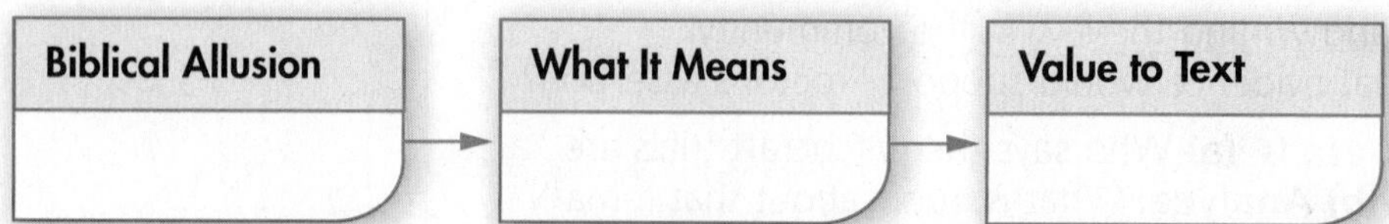

10. **Integration of Knowledge and Ideas** Based on *background knowledge* you acquired in Act I and earlier in Act II, what chance do you think Elizabeth stands in defending herself against Abigail's accusations? Explain, providing supporting evidence.

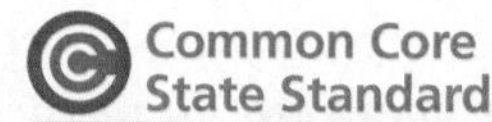

Common Core State Standards

Writing

1. Write arguments to support claims in an analysis of substantive topics or texts, using valid reasoning and relevant and sufficient evidence. *(p. 1183)*

Language

4.a. Use context as a clue to the meaning of a word or phrase. *(p. 1183)*

4.b. Identify and correctly use patterns of word changes that indicate different meanings or parts of speech. *(p. 1183)*

Vocabulary Acquisition and Use

Word Analysis: Greek Suffix *-logy*

The Greek suffix *-logy* means "the science, theory, or study of." When combined with the Greek root *-theo-*, meaning "god," the word *theology* means "the study of religion." Add the prefixes noted below to the suffix *-logy* to generate five science-related terms. Write definitions for all five new words. Use a dictionary if necessary.

1. psych-: *mind*
2. bio-: *life*
3. cardio-: *heart*
4. geo-: *environment or habitat*
5. zoo-: *animals*

Vocabulary: True or False?

Answer each question based on your knowledge of the italicized words. Then, explain your answer.

1. Lying is *base* behavior.
2. If she watches soccer *avidly,* she probably knows very little about it.
3. Rude youngsters show *deference* to elders.
4. A blushing person exhibits a *pallor.*
5. Puritans, in general, analyzed and questioned their *theology.*
6. When you *ameliorate* a situation, you make it better.

Writing to Sources

Argumentative Text Effective persuasive writing in Salem could have saved lives or even more effectively condemned the accused. Assume the persona of a character in the play and write a **persuasive letter** urging another character to take a particular course of action.

Prewriting Review the first two acts of the play, and choose the character and position you will represent. Then, use a chart like the one shown to gather support. Note facts, examples, and personal experiences that will support your persuasive points.

Model: Gathering Evidence

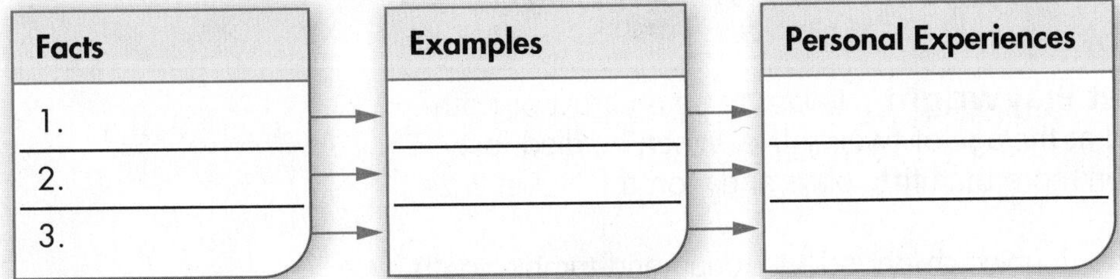

Drafting Organize your letter using one piece of evidence from the chart in each paragraph. Add to the persuasive effect by using *rhetorical devices*, such as *repetition, parallel structures,* and *analogies.*

Revising Reread your letter and assess its effectiveness. Strengthen sections with more specific, emotional language, or with more precise use of rhetorical devices.

Literary History: Drama

▲ **Critical Viewing**
This photograph shows a scene from Tennessee Williams's A Streetcar Named Desire. In what ways does this scene depict the "raw power of human emotion"? **INTERPRET**

Twentieth-Century Drama: America Takes the Stage

It is opening night at the theater. As the curtain rises, you are filled with the anticipation of seeing an exciting new play. No, it is not a big-budget musical with elaborate sets and costumes. It is a night of talk—sometimes loud and angry, sometimes hushed and mournful, but always riveting.

For much of the twentieth century, the theater was the center of American intellectual life. Great plays offered thrilling stories, crackling dialogue, and philosophical truth. The best American playwrights of the twentieth century chronicled different aspects of the American experience.

- **Thornton Wilder** (1897–1975), best known for *Our Town* (1938), revealed the secrets of small-town America.
- **Arthur Miller** (1915–2005) combined politics and realism to give America some of its most moving plays, including *Death of a Salesman* (1949) and *The Crucible* (1953) (see p. 1118).
- **Lorraine Hansberry** (1930–1965) dramatized the lives of African Americans. Her play *A Raisin in the Sun* (1959) was the first drama by a black woman to be produced on Broadway.
- **Edward Albee** (b. 1928) shocked audiences with his psychological dramas, including the harsh and powerful *Who's Afraid of Virginia Woolf?* (1962).

America's First Great Playwright "I want to be an artist or nothing," Eugene O'Neill said at the age of twenty-five. When he died forty years later, he had written more than fifty plays and won the Nobel Prize and four Pulitzer Prizes.

O'Neill's work reflects his troubled childhood and rough-and-tumble youth. He was born in New York City in 1888. In his mid-twenties, hard living landed O'Neill in the hospital, where he pondered his life for the first time: "It was in this enforced period of reflection that the urge to write first came to me," he said.

O'Neill experimented with different styles: realistic, symbolic, and political. *Beyond the Horizon* (1920), his first Broadway play, was a smash hit. *The Iceman Cometh* (1946) tells the stories of dreamers and losers who frequent a waterfront bar. *Long Day's Journey Into Night* (1956), O'Neill's masterpiece, recounts his troubled childhood.

A Woman's Voice Born in 1905 in New Orleans, Lillian Hellman became the most influential female playwright of the twentieth century. Her first play, *The Children's Hour* (1934), is the tale of two teachers whose lives are ruined by malicious accusations. Her best-known work, *The Little Foxes* (1939), takes a harsh look at a rich and powerful southern family. Her political drama *Watch on the Rhine* (1941) warned the world of the dangers of Nazism. By the time of her death in 1984, Hellman had helped shape a golden age in American theater and paved the way for women playwrights to exert influence and express powerful views.

The Raw Power of Human Emotion Born in 1911 in rural Mississippi, Tennessee Williams decided to become a writer while he was still a teenager. His first major play, *The Glass Menagerie* (1945), moved audiences with its compassion for a mother and sister who cling to their ever-fading dreams. In 1947, Williams shocked audiences with *A Streetcar Named Desire,* a hard-hitting story filled with both cruelty and beauty. Its effect on audiences was so great that it inspired dozens of imitations. By the time Williams died in 1983, he had written more than 60 plays and become one of the most important dramatists of all time.

Speaking and Listening: Group Discussion

Comprehension and Collaboration **Analyzing Interpretations** With your class, view two or more productions of *The Crucible.* Consider the 1996 film starring Daniel Day Lewis and Winona Ryder, and the 1967 TV adaptation starring George C. Scott and Colleen Dewhurst. If possible, also view a live stage production. In a small group, discuss the interpretation of the play each version presents. Use questions such as these to focus your discussion:

- Does each production faithfully interpret the play? If so, which elements bring Miller's vision to life? If not, how does the interpretation fail?
- How does each production present the setting? Does it depart in any way from the source material? If so, to what effect?
- Do the actors effectively portray the characters? Are any portrayals misguided? If so, why?
- Do the themes of the play emerge clearly in each adaptation? If not, why not?
- Is one interpretation much better or much worse than the others? If so, why?

Take notes as you converse and work to synthesize, or pull together, the opinions and ideas. Then, prepare a summary of the discussion and share the group's ideas with the class.

Building Knowledge and Insight *The Crucible, Act III*

Close Reading Focus

Characterization; Irony

Characterization is the art of revealing characters' personalities. In **direct characterization,** the author simply tells the reader what a character is like. A playwright may use direct characterization in stage directions, but most dramatic literature requires **indirect characterization** in which characters' traits are revealed through

- the character's words, actions, and appearance;
- other characters' comments;
- other characters' reactions.

Like people in real life, characters in plays are not always what they seem. Fear, greed, guilt, love, loyalty, pride, and revenge are some of the forces that drive human behavior, but they may be masked or hidden. *Characters' motives*—the reasons for their behavior—may be stated directly or suggested through indirect characterization.

Like characters, situations are also not always what they seem. When there is a contrast between expectation and reality, **irony** is at work. With **dramatic irony,** there is a contradiction between what a character thinks and what the audience knows. With **verbal irony,** there is a contrast between what a character says and what is really meant. As you read, notice how you learn about characters. Assess their motivations, and identify the many ironies that swirl around them as dangers in Salem mount.

Preparing to Read Complex Texts In this act, the court proceedings become the focus of attention. As they do, the faulty logic supporting accusations of witchcraft becomes more formalized. The justifications accusers use are examples of *logical fallacy,* arguments that may seem reasonable but are founded on a wrong premise. As you read, **evaluate arguments** used to bring accusations and condemn the innocent. Determine the premise that underlies the accusations and trace the logic that supports the argument. As you read, use a chart like the one shown to assess the arguments presented in Act III.

Common Core State Standards

Reading Literature

3. Analyze the impact of the author's choices regarding how to develop and relate elements of a story or drama (e.g., how the characters are introduced and developed).

6. Analyze a case in which grasping a point of view requires distinguishing what is directly stated in a text from what is really meant.

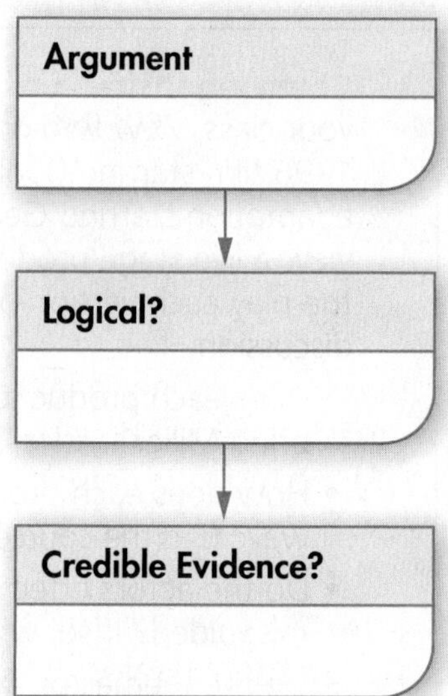

Vocabulary

The words below are important to understanding the text that follows. Copy the words into your notebook. What other words do you know that are related to the word *imperceptible*?

contentious
deposition
imperceptible
anonymity
effrontery
incredulously

Review and Anticipate

Act II ends as Elizabeth Proctor is accused of witchcraft and carted off to jail as a result of the connivance of Abigail Williams. John Proctor demands that Mary Warren tell the court the truth; Mary, though aware of Abigail's ploys, is terrified of exposing her. Do you think John will convince Mary to overcome her fears and testify against Abigail? If he does convince her, how will the judges receive Mary Warren's testimony? Read Act III to see what happens in the Salem courtroom.

The vestry room of the Salem meeting house, now serving as the anteroom of the General Court.

As the curtain rises, the room is empty, but for sunlight pouring through two high windows in the back wall. The room is solemn, even forbidding. Heavy beams jut out, boards of random widths make up the walls. At the right are two doors leading into the meeting house proper, where the court is being held. At the left another door leads outside.

There is a plain bench at the left, and another at the right. In the center a rather long meeting table, with stools and a considerable armchair snugged up to it.

Through the partitioning wall at the right we hear a prosecutor's voice, JUDGE HATHORNE'S, *asking a question; then a woman's voice,* MARTHA COREY'S, *replying.*

HATHORNE'S VOICE: Now, Martha Corey, there is abundant evidence in our hands to show that you have given yourself to the reading of fortunes. Do you deny it?

MARTHA COREY'S VOICE: I am innocent to a witch. I know not what a witch is.

HATHORNE'S VOICE: How do you know, then, that you are not a witch?

MARTHA COREY'S VOICE: If I were, I would know it.

HATHORNE'S VOICE: Why do you hurt these children?

MARTHA COREY'S VOICE: I do not hurt them. I scorn it!

GILES'S VOICE, *roaring:* I have evidence for the court!

Voices of townspeople rise in excitement.

DANFORTH'S VOICE: You will keep your seat!

GILES' VOICE: Thomas Putnam is reaching out for land!

DANFORTH'S VOICE: Remove that man, Marshal!

Comprehension
What accusation does Hathorne make of Martha Corey?

Characterization
What is Giles's motivation for interrupting the court?

GILES' VOICE: You're hearing lies, lies!

A roaring goes up from the people.

HATHORNE'S VOICE: Arrest him, excellency!

GILES' VOICE: I have evidence. Why will you not hear my evidence?

The door opens and GILES *is half carried into the vestry room by* HERRICK.

GILES: Hands off, damn you, let me go!

HERRICK: Giles, Giles!

GILES: Out of my way, Herrick! I bring evidence—

HERRICK: You cannot go in there, Giles; it's a court!

Enter HALE *from the court.*

HALE: Pray be calm a moment.

GILES: You, Mr. Hale, go in there and demand I speak.

HALE: A moment, sir, a moment.

GILES: They'll be hangin' my wife!

JUDGE HATHORNE *enters. He is in his sixties, a bitter, remorseless Salem judge.*

▼ Critical Viewing
Which aspects of the judges' appearance and demeanor, as shown here, would instill fear in the people of Salem? **ASSESS**

HATHORNE: How do you dare come roarin' into this court! Are you gone daft, Corey?

GILES: You're not a Boston judge yet, Hathorne. You'll not call me daft!

Enter DEPUTY GOVERNOR DANFORTH *and, behind him,* EZEKIEL CHEEVER *and* PARRIS. *On his appearance, silence falls.* DANFORTH *is a grave man in his sixties, of some humor and sophistication that does not, however, interfere with an exact loyalty to his position and his cause. He comes down to* GILES, *who awaits his wrath.*

DANFORTH, *looking directly at* GILES: Who is this man?

PARRIS: Giles Corey, sir, and a more **contentious**—

GILES, *to* PARRIS: I am asked the question, and I am old enough to answer it! *To* DANFORTH, *who impresses him and to whom he smiles through his strain:* My name is Corey, sir, Giles Corey. I have six hundred acres, and timber in addition. It is my wife you be condemning now. *He indicates the courtroom.*

DANFORTH: And how do you imagine to help her cause with such contemptuous riot? Now be gone. Your old age alone keeps you out of jail for this.

GILES, *beginning to plead:* They be tellin' lies about my wife, sir, I—

DANFORTH: Do you take it upon yourself to determine what this court shall believe and what it shall set aside?

GILES: Your Excellency, we mean no disrespect for—

DANFORTH: Disrespect indeed! It is disruption, Mister. This is the highest court of the supreme government of this province, do you know it?

GILES, *beginning to weep:* Your Excellency, I only said she were readin' books, sir, and they come and take her out of my house for—

DANFORTH, *mystified:* Books! What books?

GILES, *through helpless sobs:* It is my third wife, sir; I never had no wife that be so taken with books, and I thought to find the cause of it, d'y'see, but it were no witch I blamed her for. *He is openly weeping.* I have broke charity with the woman, I have broke charity with her. *He covers his face, ashamed.* DANFORTH *is respectfully silent.*

HALE: Excellency, he claims hard evidence for his wife's defense. I think that in all justice you must—

DANFORTH: Then let him submit his evidence in proper affidavit.[1] You are certainly aware of our procedure here, Mr. Hale. *To* HERRICK: Clear this room.

HERRICK: Come now, Giles. *He gently pushes* COREY *out.*

FRANCIS: We are desperate, sir; we come here three days now and cannot be heard.

DANFORTH: Who is this man?

FRANCIS: Francis Nurse, Your Excellency.

HALE: His wife's Rebecca that were condemned this morning.

---

1. affidavit (af′ ə dā′ vit) *n.* written statement made under oath.

Characterization

What do you learn about Danforth through direct characterization in these stage directions?

Vocabulary

contentious (kən ten′ shəs) *adj.* argumentative

Comprehension

Why does Giles smile at Danforth?

Evaluating Arguments What is illogical about Danforth's statement to Francis Nurse?

DANFORTH: Indeed! I am amazed to find you in such uproar. I have only good report of your character, Mr. Nurse.

HATHORNE: I think they must both be arrested in contempt, sir.

DANFORTH, *to* FRANCIS: Let you write your plea, and in due time I will—

FRANCIS: Excellency, we have proof for your eyes; God forbid you shut them to it. The girls, sir, the girls are frauds.

DANFORTH: What's that?

FRANCIS: We have proof of it, sir. They are all deceiving you.

DANFORTH *is shocked, but studying* FRANCIS.

HATHORNE: This is contempt, sir, contempt!

DANFORTH: Peace, Judge Hathorne. Do you know who I am, Mr. Nurse?

FRANCIS: I surely do, sir, and I think you must be a wise judge to be what you are.

DANFORTH: And do you know that near to four hundred are in the jails from Marblehead to Lynn, and upon my signature?

FRANCIS: I—

DANFORTH: And seventy-two condemned to hang by that signature?

FRANCIS: Excellency, I never thought to say it to such a weighty judge, but you are deceived.

Enter GILES COREY *from left. All turn to see as he beckons in* MARY WARREN *with* PROCTOR. MARY *is keeping her eyes to the ground;* PROCTOR *has her elbow as though she were near collapse.*

PARRIS, *on seeing her, in shock:* Mary Warren! *He goes directly to bend close to her face.* What are you about here?

PROCTOR, *pressing* PARRIS *away from her with a gentle but firm motion of protectiveness:* She would speak with the Deputy Governor.

DANFORTH, *shocked by this, turns to* HERRICK: Did you not tell me Mary Warren were sick in bed?

HERRICK: She were, Your Honor. When I go to fetch her to the court last week, she said she were sick.

GILES: She has been strivin' with her soul all week, Your Honor; she comes now to tell the truth of this to you.

DANFORTH: Who is this?

PROCTOR: John Proctor, sir. Elizabeth Proctor is my wife.

PARRIS: Beware this man, Your Excellency, this man is mischief.

HALE, *excitedly:* I think you must hear the girl, sir, she—

DANFORTH, *who has become very interested in* MARY WARREN *and only raises a hand toward* HALE: Peace. What would you tell us, Mary Warren?

PROCTOR *looks at her, but she cannot speak.*

PROCTOR: She never saw no spirits, sir.

DANFORTH, *with great alarm and surprise, to* MARY: Never saw no spirits!

GILES, *eagerly:* Never.

PROCTOR, *reaching into his jacket:* She has signed a **deposition**, sir—

Vocabulary
deposition (dep′ ə zish′ ən) *n.* the testimony of a witness made under oath but not in open court

DANFORTH, *instantly:* No, no, I accept no depositions. *He is rapidly calculating this; he turns from her to* PROCTOR. Tell me, Mr. Proctor, have you given out this story in the village?

PROCTOR: We have not.

PARRIS: They've come to overthrow the court, sir! This man is—

DANFORTH: I pray you, Mr. Parris. Do you know, Mr. Proctor that the entire contention of the state in these trials is that the voice of Heaven is speaking through the children?

PROCTOR: I know that, sir.

DANFORTH, *thinks, staring at* PROCTOR, *then turns to* MARY WARREN: And you, Mary Warren, how come you to cry out people for sending their spirits, against you?

MARY WARREN: It were pretense, sir.

DANFORTH: I cannot hear you.

PROCTOR: It were pretense, she says.

DANFORTH: Ah? And the other girls? Susanna Walcott, and—the others? They are also pretending?

MARY WARREN: Aye, sir.

DANFORTH, *wide-eyed:* Indeed. *Pause. He is baffled by this. He turns to study* PROCTOR'S *face.*

PARRIS, *in a sweat:* Excellency, you surely cannot think to let so vile a lie be spread in open court!

DANFORTH: Indeed not, but it strike hard upon me that she will dare come here with such a tale. Now, Mr. Proctor, before I decide whether I shall hear you or not, it is my duty to tell you this. We burn a hot fire here; it melts down all concealment.

PROCTOR: I know that, sir.

DANFORTH: Let me continue. I understand well, a husband's tenderness may drive him to extravagance in defense of a wife. Are you certain in your conscience, Mister, that your evidence is the truth?

PROCTOR: It is. And you will surely know it.

DANFORTH: And you thought to declare this revelation in the open court before the public?

PROCTOR: I thought I would, aye—with your permission.

DANFORTH, *his eyes narrowing:* Now, sir, what is your purpose in so doing?

PROCTOR: Why, I—I would free my wife, sir.

DANFORTH: There lurks nowhere in your heart, nor hidden in your spirit, any desire to undermine this court?

PROCTOR, *with the faintest faltering:* Why, no, sir.

CHEEVER, *clears his throat, awakening:* I—Your Excellency.

DANFORTH: Mr. Cheever.

CHEEVER: I think it be my duty, sir—*Kindly, to* PROCTOR: You'll not deny it, John. *To* DANFORTH: When we come to

Characterization

What is Parris's motive for discrediting Mary Warren in court?

Comprehension

What new testimony does Mary Warren give?

take his wife, he damned the court and ripped your warrant.

PARRIS: Now you have it!

DANFORTH: He did that, Mr. Hale?

HALE, *takes a breath:* Aye, he did.

PROCTOR: It were a temper, sir. I knew not what I did.

DANFORTH, *studying him:* Mr. Proctor.

PROCTOR: Aye, sir.

DANFORTH, *straight into his eyes:* Have you ever seen the Devil?

PROCTOR: No, sir.

DANFORTH: You are in all respects a Gospel Christian?

PROCTOR: I am, sir.

PARRIS: Such a Christian that will not come to church but once in a month!

DANFORTH, *restrained—he is curious:* Not come to church?

PROCTOR: I—I have no love for Mr. Parris. It is no secret. But God I surely love.

CHEEVER: He plow on Sunday, sir.

DANFORTH: Plow on Sunday!

CHEEVER, *apologetically:* I think it be evidence, John. I am an official of the court, I cannot keep it.

PROCTOR: I—I have once or twice plowed on Sunday. I have three children, sir, and until last year my land give little.

GILES: You'll find other Christians that do plow on Sunday if the truth be known.

HALE: Your Honor, I cannot think you may judge the man on such evidence.

Evaluating Arguments
In what way does Danforth's statement represent a logical fallacy?

DANFORTH: I judge nothing. *Pause. He keeps watching* PROCTOR, *who tries to meet his gaze.* I tell you straight, Mister—I have seen marvels in this court. I have seen people choked before my eyes by spirits; I have seen them stuck by pins and slashed by daggers. I have until this moment not the slightest reason to suspect that the children may be deceiving me. Do you understand my meaning?

PROCTOR: Excellency, does it not strike upon you that so many of these women have lived so long with such upright reputation, and—

PARRIS: Do you read the Gospel, Mr. Proctor?

PROCTOR: I read the Gospel.

PARRIS: I think not, or you should surely know that Cain were an upright man, and yet he did kill Abel.[2]

PROCTOR: Aye, God tells us that. *To* DANFORTH: But who tells us Rebecca Nurse murdered seven babies by sending out her spirit on them? It is the children only, and this one will swear she lied to you.

DANFORTH *considers, then beckons* HATHORNE *to him.* HATHORNE *leans in, and he speaks in his ear.* HATHORNE *nods.*

---

2. Cain . . . Abel In the Bible, Cain, the oldest son of Adam and Eve, killed his brother Abel.

HATHORNE: Aye, she's the one.

DANFORTH: Mr. Proctor , this morning, your wife send me a claim in which she states that she is pregnant now.

PROCTOR: My wife pregnant!

DANFORTH: There be no sign of it—we have examined her body.

PROCTOR: But if she say she is pregnant, then she must be! That woman will never lie, Mr. Danforth.

DANFORTH: She will not?

PROCTOR: Never, sir, never.

DANFORTH: We have thought it too convenient to be credited. However, if I should tell you now that I will let her be kept another month; and if she begin to show her natural signs, you shall have her living yet another year until she is delivered—what say you to that? JOHN PROCTOR *is struck silent.* Come now. You say your only purpose is to save your wife. Good, then, she is saved at least this year, and a year is long. What say you, sir? It is done now. *In conflict,* PROCTOR *glances at* FRANCIS *and* GILES. Will you drop this charge?

PROCTOR: I—I think I cannot.

DANFORTH, *now an almost* **imperceptible** *hardness in his voice:* Then your purpose is somewhat larger.

PARRIS: He's come to overthrow this court, Your Honor!

PROCTOR: These are my friends. Their wives are also accused—

DANFORTH, *with a sudden briskness of manner:* I judge you not, sir. I am ready to hear your evidence.

PROCTOR: I come not to hurt the court; I only—

DANFORTH, *cutting him off:* Marshal, go into the court and bid Judge Stoughton and Judge Sewall declare recess for one hour. And let them go to the tavern, if they will. All witnesses and prisoners are to be kept in the building.

HERRICK: Aye, sir. *Very deferentially:* If I may say it, sir. I know this man all my life. It is a good man, sir.

DANFORTH *—it is the reflection on himself he resents:* I am sure of it, Marshal. HERRICK *nods, then goes out.* Now, what deposition do you have for us, Mr. Proctor? And I beg you be clear, open as the sky, and honest.

PROCTOR, *as he takes out several papers:* I am no lawyer, so I'll—

DANFORTH: The pure in heart need no lawyers. Proceed as you will.

PROCTOR, *handing* DANFORTH *a paper:* Will you read this first, sir? It's a sort of testament. The people signing it declare their good opinion of Rebecca, and my wife, and Martha Corey.

DANFORTH *looks down at the paper.*

PARRIS, *to enlist* DANFORTH'S *sarcasm:* Their good opinion! *But* DANFORTH *goes on reading, and* PROCTOR *is heartened.*

PROCTOR: These are all landholding farmers, members of the church. *Delicately, trying to point out a paragraph:* If you'll notice, sir—they've

I tell you straight, Mister—I have seen marvels in this court.

Vocabulary

imperceptible
(im′ pər sep′ tə bəl)
adj. barely noticeable

Verbal Irony

What makes Danforth's statement about the "pure in heart" an example of verbal irony?

Comprehension

What document does Proctor present to the court?

known the women many years and never saw no sign they had dealings with the Devil.

PARRIS *nervously moves over and reads over* DANFORTH'S *shoulder.*

DANFORTH, *glancing down a long list:* How many names are here?

FRANCIS: Ninety-one, Your Excellency.

PARRIS, *sweating:* These people should be summoned. DANFORTH *looks up at him questioningly.* For questioning.

FRANCIS. *trembling with anger:* Mr. Danforth, I gave them all my word no harm would come to them for signing this.

PARRIS: This is a clear attack upon the court!

HALE, *to* PARRIS, *trying to contain himself:* Is every defense an attack upon the court? Can no one—?

Evaluating Arguments

What is faulty about Parris's claim that "all innocent and Christian people are happy for the courts in Salem"?

PARRIS: All innocent and Christian people are happy for the courts in Salem! These people are gloomy for it. *To* DANFORTH *directly:* And I think you will want to know, from each and every one of them, what discontents them with you!

HATHORNE: I think they ought to be examined, sir.

DANFORTH: It is not necessarily an attack, I think. Yet—

FRANCIS: These are all covenanted Christians, sir.

DANFORTH: Then I am sure they may have nothing to fear. *Hands* CHEEVER *the paper.* Mr. Cheever, have warrants drawn for all of these—arrest for examination. *To* PROCTOR: Now, Mister, what other information do you have for us? FRANCIS *is still standing, horrified.* You may sit, Mr. Nurse.

FRANCIS: I have brought trouble on these people: I have—

DANFORTH: No, old man, you have not hurt these people if they are of good conscience. But you must understand, sir, that a person is either with this court or he must be counted against it, there be no road between. This is a sharp time, now, a precise time—we live no longer in the dusky afternoon when evil mixed itself with good and befuddled the world. Now, by God's grace, the shining sun is up, and them that fear not light will surely praise it. I hope you will be one of those. MARY WARREN *suddenly sobs.* She's not hearty, I see.

PROCTOR: No, she's not, sir. *To* MARY, *bending to her, holding her hand, quietly:* Now remember what the angel Raphael said to the boy Tobias.[3] Remember it.

Verbal Irony

In what sense is Proctor's quotation from the Bible ironic?

MARY WARREN, *hardly audible:* Aye.

PROCTOR: "Do that which is good, and no harm shall come to thee."

MARY WARREN: Aye.

---

3. **Raphael . . . Tobias** In the Bible, Tobias is guided by the archangel Raphael to save two people who have prayed for their deaths. One of the two is Tobias's father, Tobit, who has prayed for his death because he has lost his sight. The other is Sara, a woman who is afflicted by a demon and has killed her seven husbands on their wedding day. With Raphael's assistance, Tobias exorcises the devil from Sara and cures his father of blindness.

DANFORTH: Come, man, we wait you.

MARSHAL HERRICK *returns, and takes his post at the door.*

GILES: John, my deposition, give him mine.

PROCTOR: Aye. *He hands* DANFORTH *another paper.* This is Mr. Corey's deposition.

DANFORTH: Oh? *He looks down at it. Now* HATHORNE *comes behind him and reads with him.*

HATHORNE, *suspiciously:* What lawyer drew this, Corey?

GILES: You know I never hired a lawyer in my life, Hathorne.

DANFORTH, *finishing the reading:* It is very well phrased. My compliments. Mr. Parris, if Mr. Putnam is in the court, will you bring him in? HATHORNE *takes the deposition, and walks to the window with it.* PARRIS *goes into the court.* You have no legal training, Mr. Corey?

GILES, *very pleased:* I have the best, sir—I am thirty-three time in court in my life. And always plaintiff, too.

DANFORTH: Oh, then you're much put-upon.

GILES: I am never put-upon; I know my rights, sir, and I will have them. You know, your father tried a case of mine—might be thirty-five year ago, I think.

DANFORTH: Indeed.

GILES: He never spoke to you of it?

DANFORTH: No, I cannot recall it.

GILES: That's strange, he gave me nine pound damages. He were a fair judge, your father. Y'see, I had a white mare that time, and this fellow come to borrow the mare—*Enter* PARRIS *with* THOMAS PUTNAM. *When he sees* PUTNAM, GILES' *ease goes; he is hard.* Aye, there he is.

DANFORTH: Mr. Putnam, I have here an accusation by Mr. Corey against you. He states that you coldly prompted your daughter to cry witchery upon George Jacobs that is now in jail.

PUTNAM: It is a lie.

DANFORTH, *turning to* GILES: Mr. Putnam states your charge is a lie. What say you to that?

GILES, *furious, his fists clenched:* A fart on Thomas Putnam, that is what I say to that!

DANFORTH: What proof do you submit for your charge, sir?

GILES: My proof is there! *Pointing to the paper.* If Jacobs hangs for a witch he forfeit up his property—that's law! And there is none but Putnam with the coin to buy so great a piece. This man is killing his neighbors for their land!

DANFORTH: But proof, sir, proof.

GILES, *pointing at his deposition:* The proof is there! I have it from an honest man who heard Putnam say it! The day his daughter cried out on Jacobs, he said she'd given him a fair gift of land.

HATHORNE: And the name of this man?

This is a clear attack upon the court!

Verbal Irony
What is ironic about Danforth's request for proof from Giles?

Comprehension
What is Giles Corey's defense? Explain.

Arthur Miller
Author's Insight
During the Cultural Revolution in China (1966–1976), Communist party true-believers persecuted intellectuals and artists. Miller wrote how a young Chinese author thought that the courtroom scenes in *The Crucible* were all too familiar: "As she listened to [a production of the play] . . . the interrogations sounded . . . precisely the same as the ones she and others had been subjected to by the Cultural Revolutionaries. . . ."

Vocabulary
anonymity (an´ ə nim´ ə tē) *n.* the condition of being unknown

GILES, *taken aback:* What name?

HATHORNE: The man that give you this information.

GILES, *hesitates, then:* Why, I—I cannot give you his name.

HATHORNE: And why not?

GILES, *hesitates, then bursts out:* You know well why not! He'll lay in jail if I give his name!

HATHORNE: This is contempt of the court, Mr. Danforth!

DANFORTH, *to avoid that:* You will surely tell us the name.

GILES: I will not give you no name. I mentioned my wife's name once and I'll burn in hell long enough for that. I stand mute.

DANFORTH: In that case, I have no choice but to arrest you for contempt of this court, do you know that?

GILES: This is a hearing; you cannot clap me for contempt of a hearing.

DANFORTH: Oh, it is a proper lawyer! Do you wish me to declare the court in full session here? Or will you give me good reply?

GILES, *faltering:* I cannot give you no name, sir, I cannot.

DANFORTH: You are a foolish old man. Mr. Cheever, begin the record. The court is now in session. I ask you, Mr. Corey—

PROCTOR, *breaking in:* Your Honor—he has the story in confidence, sir, and he—

PARRIS: The Devil lives on such confidences! *To* DANFORTH: Without confidences there could be no conspiracy, Your Honor!

HATHORNE: I think it must be broken, sir.

DANFORTH, *to* GILES: Old man, if your informant tells the truth let him come here openly like a decent man. But if he hide in **anonymity** I must know why. Now sir, the government and central church demand of you the name of him who reported Mr. Thomas Putnam a common murderer.

HALE: Excellency—

DANFORTH: Mr. Hale.

HALE: We cannot blink it more. There is a prodigious fear of this court in the country—

DANFORTH: Then there is a prodigious guilt in the country. Are you afraid to be questioned here?

HALE: I may only fear the Lord, sir, but there is fear in the country nevertheless.

DANFORTH, *angered now:* Reproach me not with the fear in the country; there is fear in the country because there is a moving plot to topple Christ in the country!

HALE: But it does not follow that everyone accused is part of it.

DANFORTH: No uncorrupted man may fear this court, Mr. Hale! None! *To* GILES: You are under arrest in contempt of this court. Now sit you down and take counsel with yourself, or you will be set in the jail until you decide to answer all questions.

GILES COREY *makes a rush for* PUTNAM. PROCTOR *lunges and holds him.*

PROCTOR: No, Giles!

GILES, *over Proctor's shoulder at* PUTNAM: I'll cut your throat, Putnam, I'll kill you yet!

PROCTOR, *forcing him into a chair:* Peace, Giles, peace. *Releasing him.* We'll prove ourselves. Now we will. *He starts to turn to* DANFORTH.

GILES: Say nothin' more, John. *Pointing at* DANFORTH: He's only playin' you! He means to hang us all!

MARY WARREN *bursts into sobs.*

DANFORTH: This is a court of law, Mister. I'll have no **effrontery** here!

PROCTOR: Forgive him, sir, for his old age. Peace, Giles, we'll prove it all now. *He lifts up* MARY'S *chin.* You cannot weep, Mary. Remember the angel, what he say to the boy. Hold to it, now; there is your rock. MARY *quiets. He takes out a paper, and turns to* DANFORTH. This is Mary Warren's deposition. I—I would ask you remember, sir, while you read it, that until two week ago she were no different than the other children are today. *He is speaking reasonably, restraining all his fears, his anger, his anxiety.* You saw her scream, she howled, she swore familiar spirits choked her; she even testified that Satan, in the form of women now in jail, tried to win her soul away, and then when she refused—

DANFORTH: We know all this.

PROCTOR: Aye, sir. She swears now that she never saw Satan; nor any spirit, vague or clear, that Satan may have sent to hurt her. And she declares her friends are lying now.

PROCTOR *starts to hand* DANFORTH *the deposition, and* HALE *comes up to* DANFORTH *in a trembling state.*

HALE: Excellency, a moment. I think this goes to the heart of the matter.

DANFORTH, *with deep misgivings:* It surely does.

HALE: I cannot say he is an honest man; I know him little. But in all justice, sir, a claim so weighty cannot be argued by a farmer. In God's name, sir, stop here; send him home and let him come again with a lawyer—

DANFORTH, *patiently:* Now look you, Mr. Hale—

HALE: Excellency, I have signed seventy-two death warrants; I am a minister of the Lord, and I dare not take a life without there be a proof so immaculate no slightest qualm of conscience may doubt it.

DANFORTH: Mr. Hale, you surely do not doubt my justice.

HALE: I have this morning signed away the soul of Rebecca Nurse, Your Honor. I'll not conceal it, my hand shakes yet as with a wound! I pray you, sir, *this* argument let lawyers present to you.

DANFORTH: Mr. Hale, believe me; for a man of such terrible learning you are most bewildered—I hope you will forgive me. I have been thirty-two year at the bar, sir, and I should be confounded were I called upon to defend these people. Let you consider, now—*To* PROCTOR *and the others:*

Vocabulary

effrontery (e frunt′ ər ē) *n.* shameless boldness

Comprehension

According to Danforth, why do people in Salem fear the court?

Evaluating Arguments
In what ways is Danforth's entire argument based on a faulty premise?

And I bid you all do likewise. In an ordinary crime, how does one defend the accused? One calls up witnesses to prove his innocence. But witchcraft is *ipso facto*,[4] on its face and by its nature, an invisible crime, is it not? Therefore, who may possibly be witness to it? The witch and the victim. None other. Now we cannot hope the witch will accuse herself; granted? Therefore, we must rely upon her victims—and they do testify, the children certainly do testify. As for the witches, none will deny that we are most eager for all their confessions. Therefore, what is left for a lawyer to bring out? I think I have made my point. Have I not?

HALE: But this child claims the girls are not truthful, and if they are not—

DANFORTH: That is precisely what I am about to consider, sir. What more may you ask of me? Unless you doubt my probity?[5]

HALE, *defeated:* I surely do not, sir. Let you consider it, then.

DANFORTH: And let you put your heart to rest. Her deposition, Mr. Proctor.

PROCTOR *hands it to him.* HATHORNE *rises, goes beside* DANFORTH, *and starts reading.* PARRIS *comes to his other side.* DANFORTH *looks at* JOHN

4. ***ipso facto*** (ip′ sō fak′ tō) "by that very fact"; "therefore" (Latin).
5. **probity** (prō′ bə tē) *n.* complete honesty: integrity.

▼ Critical Viewing
In this movie still, Danforth conveys a feeling of sympathy, or understanding, for Mary Warren. Compare this portrayal with your own image of Danforth. **COMPARE/CONTRAST**

PROCTOR, *then proceeds to read.* HALE *gets up, finds position near the judge, reads too.* PROCTOR *glances at* GILES. FRANCIS *prays silently, hands pressed together.* CHEEVER *waits placidly, the sublime official, dutiful.* MARY WARREN *sobs once.* JOHN PROCTOR *touches her head reassuringly. Presently* DANFORTH *lifts his eyes, stands up, takes out a kerchief and blows his nose. The others stand aside as he moves in thought toward the window.*

PARRIS, *hardly able to contain his anger and fear:* I should like to question—

DANFORTH *—his first real outburst, in which his contempt for* PARRIS *is clear:* Mr. Parris, I bid you be silent! *He stands in silence, looking out the window. Now, having established that he will set the gait:* Mr. Cheever, will you go into the court and bring the children here? CHEEVER *gets up and goes out upstage.* DANFORTH *now turns to* MARY. Mary Warren, how came you to this turnabout? Has Mr. Proctor threatened you for this deposition?

MARY WARREN: No, sir.

DANFORTH: Has he ever threatened you?

MARY WARREN, *weaker:* No, sir.

Comprehension

sWhat document does Danforth read?

WORLD LITERATURE CONNECTION

POLITICAL DRAMA

FEDERICO GARCÍA LORCA (1898–1936)

Playwright and poet Federico García Lorca was born in a village in southern Spain, a region that had changed little since the Middle Ages. For centuries, the land had been owned by the wealthy and tilled by peasants. As a child, Lorca entertained his family by performing puppet shows. He grew up to write plays that were unique in the Spanish tradition. They were simple and elemental, poetic, and powerful. They spoke of the suffering of people who were not free to express themselves.

In 1931, Spain elected a democratic government and it seemed a freer era had dawned. However, Spain was fiercely divided. In May of 1936, Lorca completed his last play, *The House of Bernarda Alba*, about a tyrannical widow who keeps her five daughters locked in the house. Two months later, before the play could be performed, civil war erupted. Lorca, along with thousands of others, was murdered by fascists. His plays were banned in Spain for many years.

▲ The National Theatre's production of *The House of Bernarda Alba* at the National Theatre, London.

CONNECT TO THE LITERATURE

Speculate about why a government might prevent the performance of a play.

Characterization
What do you think motivates Danforth's repeated questioning of Mary Warren?

DANFORTH, *sensing a weakening:* Has he threatened you?

MARY WARREN: No, sir.

DANFORTH: Then you tell me that you sat in my court, callously lying, when you knew that people would hang by your evidence? *She does not answer.* Answer me!

MARY WARREN, *almost inaudibly:* I did, sir.

DANFORTH: How were you instructed in your life? Do you not know that God damns all liars? *She cannot speak.* Or is it now that you lie?

MARY WARREN: No, sir—I am with God now.

DANFORTH: You are with God now.

MARY WARREN: Aye, sir.

DANFORTH, *containing himself:* I will tell you this—you are either lying now, or you were lying in the court, and in either case you have committed perjury and you will go to jail for it. You cannot lightly say you lied, Mary. Do you know that?

MARY WARREN: I cannot lie no more. I am with God, I am with God.

But she breaks into sobs at the thought of it, and the right door opens, and enter SUSANNA WALCOTT, MERCY LEWIS, BETTY PARRIS, *and finally* ABIGAIL. CHEEVER *comes to* DANFORTH.

CHEEVER: Ruth Putnam's not in the court, sir, nor the other children.

DANFORTH: These will be sufficient. Sit you down, children. *Silently they sit.* Your friend, Mary Warren, has given us a deposition. In which she swears that she never saw familiar spirits, apparitions, nor any manifest of the Devil. She claims as well that none of you have seen these things either. *Slight pause.* Now, children, this is a court of law. The law, based upon the Bible, and the Bible, writ by Almighty God, forbid the practice of witchcraft, and describe death as the penalty thereof. But likewise, children, the law and Bible damn all bearers of false witness. *Slight pause.* Now then. It does not escape me that this deposition may be devised to blind us; it may well be that Mary Warren has been conquered by Satan, who sends her here to distract our sacred purpose. If so, her neck will break for it. But if she speak true, I bid you now drop your guile and confess your pretense, for a quick confession will go easier with you. *Pause.* Abigail Williams, rise. ABIGAIL *slowly rises.* Is there any truth in this?

Dramatic Irony
In what ways do Danforth's statements create dramatic irony?

ABIGAIL: No, sir.

DANFORTH, *thinks, glances at* MARY *then back to* ABIGAIL: Children, a very augur bit[6] will now be turned into your souls until your honesty is proved. Will either of you change your positions now, or do you force me to hard questioning?

ABIGAIL: I have naught to change, sir. She lies.

DANFORTH, *to* MARY: You would still go on with this?

---

6. augur bit sharp point of an augur, a tool used for boring holes.

MARY WARREN, *faintly:* Aye, sir.

DANFORTH, *turning to* ABIGAIL: A poppet were discovered in Mr. Proctor's house, stabbed by a needle. Mary Warren claims that you sat beside her in the court when she made it, and that you saw her make it and witnessed how she herself stuck her needle into it for safe-keeping. What say you to that?

ABIGAIL, *with a slight note of indignation:* It is a lie, sir.

DANFORTH, *after a slight pause:* While you worked for Mr. Proctor, did you see poppets in that house?

ABIGAIL: Goody Proctor always kept poppets.

PROCTOR: Your Honor, my wife never kept no poppets. Mary Warren confesses it was her poppet.

CHEEVER: Your Excellency.

DANFORTH: Mr. Cheever.

CHEEVER: When I spoke with Goody Proctor in that house, she said she never kept no poppets. But she said she did keep poppets when she were a girl.

PROCTOR: She has not been a girl these fifteen years, Your Honor.

HATHORNE: But a poppet will keep fifteen years, will it not?

PROCTOR: It will keep if it is kept, but Mary Warren swears she never saw no poppets in my house, nor anyone else.

PARRIS: Why could there not have been poppets hid where no one ever saw them?

PROCTOR, *furious:* There might also be a dragon with five legs in my house, but no one has ever seen it.

PARRIS: We are here, Your Honor, precisely to discover what no one has ever seen.

PROCTOR: Mr. Danforth, what profit this girl to turn herself about? What may Mary Warren gain but hard questioning and worse?

DANFORTH: You are charging Abigail Williams with a marvelous cool plot to murder, do you understand that?

PROCTOR: I do, sir. I believe she means to murder.

DANFORTH, *pointing at* ABIGAIL, ***incredulously:*** This child would murder your wife?

PROCTOR: It is not a child. Now hear me, sir. In the sight of the congregation she were twice this year put out of this meetin' house for laughter during prayer.

DANFORTH, *shocked, turning to* ABIGAIL: What's this? Laughter during—!

PARRIS: Excellency, she were under Tituba's power at that time, but she is solemn now.

GILES: Aye, now she is solemn and goes to hang people!

DANFORTH: Quiet, man.

HATHORNE: Surely it have no bearing on the question, sir. He charges contemplation of murder.

Evaluating Arguments

On what faulty premise is this argument against Elizabeth based?

Vocabulary

incredulously

(in krej´ o͞o ləs lē) *adv.* skeptically

Characterization

How does Proctor try to shift Danforth's understanding of Abigail?

Comprehension

Of what serious charge do Proctor and Giles accuse Abigail?

DANFORTH: Aye. *He studies* ABIGAIL *for a moment, then:* Continue, Mr. Proctor.

PROCTOR: Mary. Now tell the Governor how you danced in the woods.

PARRIS, *instantly:* Excellency, since I come to Salem this man is blackening my name. He—

DANFORTH: In a moment, sir. *To* MARY WARREN, *sternly, and surprised.* What is this dancing?

MARY WARREN: I—*She glances at* ABIGAIL, *who is staring down at her remorselessly. Then, appealing to* PROCTOR: Mr. Proctor—

PROCTOR, *taking it right up:* Abigail leads the girls to the woods, Your Honor, and they have danced there naked—

PARRIS: Your Honor, this—

PROCTOR, *at once:* Mr. Parris discovered them himself in the dead of night! There's the "child" she is!

DANFORTH— *it is growing into a nightmare, and he turns, astonished, to* PARRIS: Mr. Parris—

PARRIS: I can only say, sir, that I never found any of them naked, and this man is—

DANFORTH: But you discovered them dancing in the woods? *Eyes on* PARRIS, *he points at* ABIGAIL. Abigail?

HALE: Excellency, when I first arrived from Beverly, Mr. Parris told me that.

DANFORTH: Do you deny it, Mr. Parris?

PARRIS: I do not, sir, but I never saw any of them naked.

▼ Critical Viewing

In this scene, Parris and Danforth order Mary to pretend to faint. Analyze this movie still and describe the emotions conveyed by Parris, Danforth, Mary, and the girls. **ANALYZE**

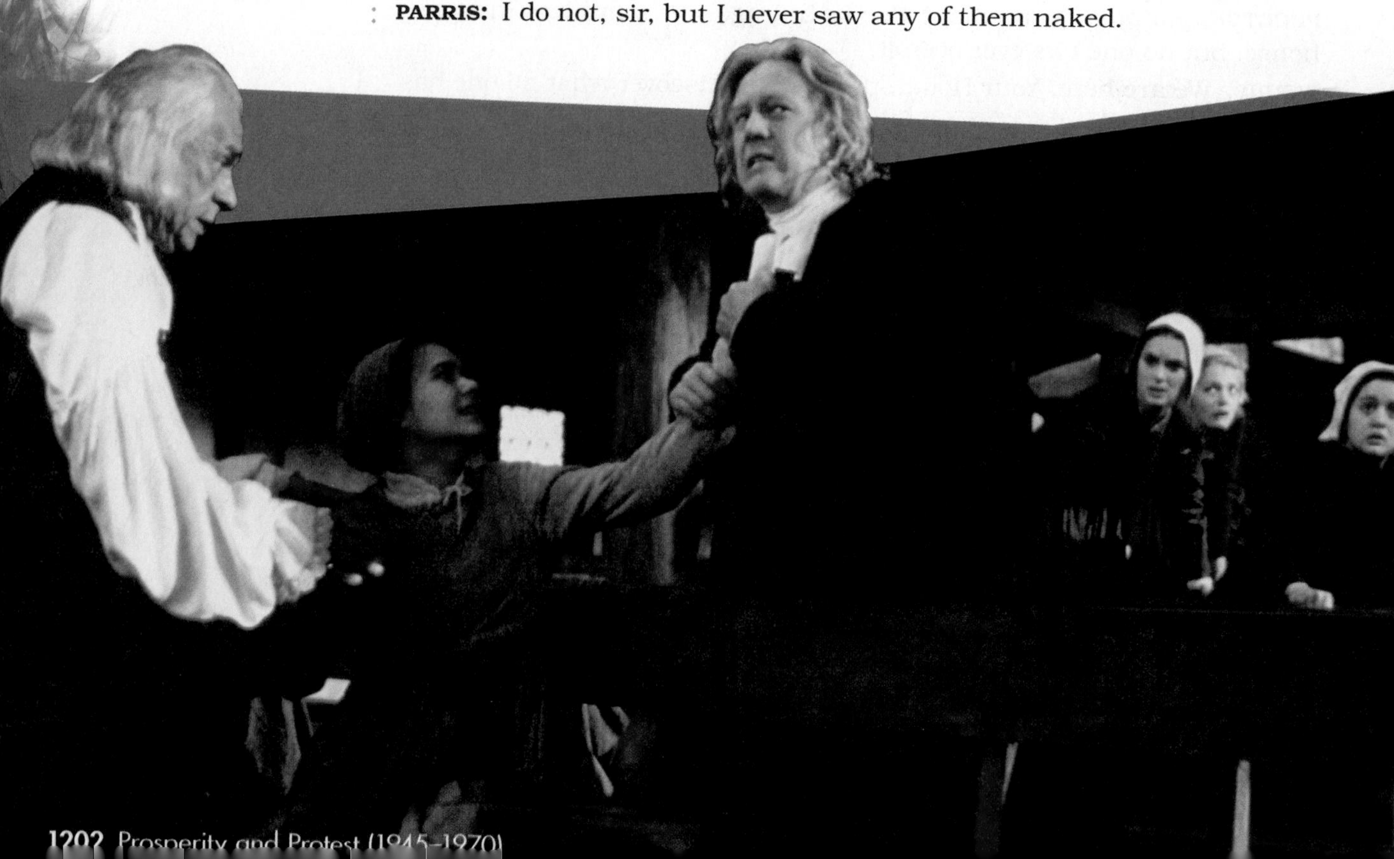

DANFORTH: But she have *danced?*

PARRIS, *unwillingly:* Aye, sir.

DANFORTH, *as though with new eyes, looks at* ABIGAIL.

HATHORNE: Excellency, will you permit me? *He points at* MARY WARREN.

DANFORTH, *with great worry:* Pray, proceed.

HATHORNE: You say you never saw no spirits, Mary, were never threatened or afflicted by any manifest of the Devil or the Devil's agents.

MARY WARREN, *very faintly:* No, sir.

HATHORNE, *with a gleam of victory:* And yet, when people accused of witchery confronted you in court, you would faint, saying their spirits came out of their bodies and choked you—

MARY WARREN: That were pretense, sir.

DANFORTH: I cannot hear you.

MARY WARREN: Pretense, sir.

PARRIS: But you did turn cold, did you not? I myself picked you up many times, and your skin were icy. Mr. Danforth, you—

DANFORTH: I saw that many times.

PROCTOR: She only pretended to faint, Your Excellency. They're all marvelous pretenders.

HATHORNE: Then can she pretend to faint now?

PROCTOR: Now?

PARRIS: Why not? Now there are no spirits attacking her, for none in this room is accused of witchcraft. So let her turn herself cold now, let her pretend she is attacked now, let her faint. *He turns to* MARY WARREN. Faint!

MARY WARREN: Faint?

PARRIS: Aye, faint. Prove to us how you pretended in the court so many times.

MARY WARREN, *looking to* PROCTOR: I—cannot faint now, sir.

PROCTOR, *alarmed, quietly:* Can you not pretend it?

MARY WARREN: I—*She looks about as though searching for the passion to faint.* I—have no *sense* of it now, I—

DANFORTH: Why? What is lacking now?

MARY WARREN: I—cannot tell, sir, I—

DANFORTH: Might it be that here we have no afflicting spirit loose, but in the court there were some?

MARY WARREN: I never saw no spirits.

PARRIS: Then see no spirits now, and prove to us that you can faint by your own will, as you claim.

MARY WARREN, *stares, searching for the emotion of it, and then shakes her head:* I—cannot do it.

PARRIS: Then you will confess, will you not? It were attacking spirits made you faint!

MARY WARREN: No, sir, I—

"... let her pretend she is attacked now, let her faint."

Evaluating Arguments

In what sense does Danforth's question express a logical fallacy?

Comprehension

What do Parris and Hathorne ask Mary Warren to do?

PARRIS: Your Excellency, this is a trick to blind the court!

MARY WARREN: It's not a trick! *She stands.* I—I used to faint because I—I thought I saw spirits.

DANFORTH: *Thought* you saw them!

MARY WARREN: But I did not, Your Honor.

HATHORNE: How could you think you saw them unless you saw them?

MARY WARREN: I—I cannot tell how, but I did. I—I heard the other girls screaming, and you, Your Honor, you seemed to believe them, and I—It were only sport in the beginning, sir, but then the whole world cried spirits, spirits, and I—I promise you, Mr. Danforth, I only thought I saw them but I did not.

DANFORTH *peers at her.*

PARRIS, *smiling, but nervous because* DANFORTH *seems to be struck by* MARY WARREN'S *story:* Surely Your Excellency is not taken by this simple lie.

DANFORTH, *turning worriedly to* ABIGAIL: Abigail. I bid you now search your heart and tell me this—and beware of it, child, to God every soul is precious and His vengeance is terrible on them that take life without cause. Is it possible, child, that the spirits you have seen are illusion only, some deception that may cross your mind when—

ABIGAIL: Why, this—this—is a base question, sir.

DANFORTH: Child, I would have you consider it—

ABIGAIL: I have been hurt, Mr. Danforth; I have seen my blood runnin' out! I have been near to murdered every day because I done my duty pointing out the Devil's people—and this is my reward? To be mistrusted, denied, questioned like a—

DANFORTH, *weakening:* Child, I do not mistrust you—

ABIGAIL, *in an open threat:* Let *you* beware, Mr. Danforth. Think you to be so mighty that the power of Hell may not turn *your* wits? Beware of it! There is—*Suddenly, from an accusatory attitude, her face turns, looking into the air above—it is truly frightened.*

DANFORTH, *apprehensively:* What is it, child?

ABIGAIL, *looking about in the air, clasping her arms about her as though cold:* I—I know not. A wind, a cold wind, has come. *Her eyes fall on* MARY WARREN.

MARY WARREN, *terrified, pleading:* Abby!

MERCY LEWIS, *shivering:* Your Honor, I freeze!

PROCTOR: They're pretending!

HATHORNE, *touching* ABIGAIL'S *hand:* She is cold, Your Honor, touch her!

MERCY LEWIS, *through chattering teeth:* Mary, do you send this shadow on me?

MARY WARREN: Lord, save me!

SUSANNA WALCOTT: I freeze, I freeze!

ABIGAIL, *shivering, visibly:* It is a wind, a wind!

◀ Critical Viewing

Abigail pretends to be under the control of spirits. Does this scene from the movie effectively portray the scene in the play? Explain. **EVALUATE**

Spiral Review

Conflict What conflicts, both internal and external, might Danforth be experiencing in this scene? Explain.

Comprehension

How does Abigail threaten Danforth?

MARY WARREN: Abby, don't do that!

DANFORTH, *himself engaged and entered by* ABIGAIL: Mary Warren, do you witch her? I say to you, do you send your spirit out?

With a hysterical cry MARY WARREN *starts to run.* PROCTOR *catches her.*

MARY WARREN, *almost collapsing:* Let me go, Mr. Proctor, I cannot, I cannot—

ABIGAIL, *crying to Heaven:* Oh, Heavenly Father, take away this shadow!

Without warning or hesitation, PROCTOR *leaps at* ABIGAIL *and, grabbing her by the hair, pulls her to her feet. She screams in pain.* DANFORTH, *astonished, cries, "What are you about?" and* HATHORNE *and* PARRIS *call, "Take your hands off her!" and out of it all comes* PROCTOR'S *roaring voice.*

Characterization

What motivates Proctor to make his confession?

PROCTOR: How do you call Heaven! Whore! Whore!

HERRICK *breaks* PROCTOR *from her.*

HERRICK: John!

DANFORTH: Man! Man, what do you—

PROCTOR, *breathless and in agony:* It is a whore!

DANFORTH, *dumfounded:* You charge—?

ABIGAIL: Mr. Danforth, he is lying!

PROCTOR: Mark her! Now she'll suck a scream to stab me with, but—

DANFORTH: You will prove this! This will not pass!

PROCTOR, *trembling, his life collapsing about him:* I have known her, sir. I have known her.

DANFORTH: You—you are a lecher?

FRANCIS, *horrified:* John, you cannot say such a—

PROCTOR: Oh, Francis, I wish you had some evil in you that you might know me! *To* DANFORTH: A man will not cast away his good name. You surely know that.

DANFORTH, *dumfounded:* In—in what time? In what place?

PROCTOR, *his voice about to break, and his shame great:* In the proper place—where my beasts are bedded. On the last night of my joy, some eight months past. She used to serve me in my house, sir. *He has to clamp his jaw to keep from weeping.* A man may think God sleeps, but God sees everything. I know it now. I beg you, sir, I beg you—see her what she is. My wife, my dear good wife, took this girl soon after, sir, and put her out on the highroad. And being what she is, a lump of vanity, sir—*He is being overcome.* Excellency, forgive me, forgive me. *Angrily against himself, he turns away from the* GOVERNOR *for a moment. Then, as though to cry out is his only means of speech left:* She thinks to dance with me on my wife's grave! And well she might, for I thought of her softly. God help me, I lusted, and there *is* a promise in such sweat. But it is a whore's vengeance, and you must see it; I set myself entirely in your hands. I know you must see it now.

DANFORTH, *blanched, in horror, turning to* ABIGAIL: You deny every scrap and tittle of this?

ABIGAIL: If I must answer that, I will leave and I will not come back again! DANFORTH *seems unsteady.*

PROCTOR: I have made a bell of my honor! I have rung the doom of my good name—you will believe me, Mr. Danforth! My wife is innocent, except she knew a whore when she saw one!

ABIGAIL, *stepping up to* DANFORTH: What look do you give me? DANFORTH *cannot speak.* I'll not have such looks! *She turns and starts for the door.*

DANFORTH: You will remain where you are! HERRICK *steps into her path. She comes up short, fire in her eyes.* Mr. Parris, go into the court and bring Goodwife Proctor out.

PARRIS, *objecting:* Your Honor, this is all a—

DANFORTH, *sharply to* PARRIS: Bring her out! And tell her not one word of what's been spoken here. And let you knock before you enter. PARRIS *goes out.* Now we shall touch the bottom of this swamp. *To* PROCTOR: Your wife, you say, is an honest woman.

PROCTOR: In her life, sir, she have never lied. There are them that cannot sing, and them that cannot weep—my wife cannot lie. I have paid much to learn it, sir.

DANFORTH: And when she put this girl out of your house, she put her out for a harlot?

PROCTOR: Aye, sir.

DANFORTH: And knew her for a harlot?

PROCTOR: Aye, sir, she knew her for a harlot.

DANFORTH: Good then. *To* ABIGAIL: And if she tell me, child, it were for harlotry, may God spread His mercy on you! *There is a knock. He calls to the door.* Hold! *To* ABIGAIL: Turn your back. Turn your back. *To* PROCTOR: Do likewise. *Both turn their backs*—ABIGAIL *with indignant slowness.* Now let neither of you turn to face Goody Proctor. No one in this room is to speak one word, or raise a gesture aye or nay. *He turns toward the door, calls:* Enter! *The door opens.* ELIZABETH *enters with* PARRIS. PARRIS *leaves her. She stands alone, her eyes looking for* PROCTOR. Mr. Cheever, report this testimony in all exactness. Are you ready?

CHEEVER: Ready, sir.

DANFORTH: Come here, woman. ELIZABETH *comes to him, glancing at* PROCTOR'S *back.* Look at me only, not at your husband. In my eyes only.

ELIZABETH, *faintly:* Good, sir.

DANFORTH: We are given to understand that at one time you dismissed your servant, Abigail Williams.

ELIZABETH: That is true, sir.

DANFORTH: For what cause did you dismiss her? *Slight pause. Then* ELIZABETH *tries to glance at* PROCTOR. You will look in my eyes only and not at your husband. The answer is in your memory and you need no help to give it to me. Why did you dismiss Abigail Williams?

ELIZABETH, *not knowing what to say, sensing a situation, wetting her*

Evaluating Arguments
Why does Proctor insist that the court must believe his argument?

Dramatic Irony
Which details in Elizabeth's exchange with Danforth reveal the dramatic irony at work in this scene?

Comprehension
What does Proctor reveal about Abigail?

LITERATURE IN CONTEXT

History Connection

Puritans and Nathaniel Hawthorne

One of the many characters in *The Crucible* who have real historical counterparts is John Hathorne, a judge who takes part in the Salem witchcraft trials. The real Hathorne's most famous descendant was the writer Nathaniel Hawthorne (see p. 271), who lived in Salem during the nineteenth century. Hawthorne used the Puritan colonies of his ancestors as the settings for much of his work. In Puritan rigidity and repression he found an expression for his dark vision of the human soul.

Hawthorne's best-known novel, *The Scarlet Letter*, examines the repressive side of Puritanism and the hypocrisy and pain that such an atmosphere produced. His short stories "Young Goodman Brown" and "The Minister's Black Veil" also focus on New England's Puritan communities.

Connect to the Literature

What inspiration for Hawthorne's dark vision may have come from his Salem ancestor?

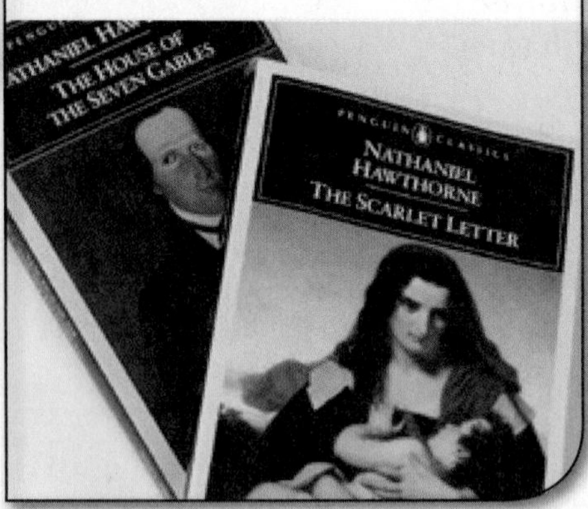

lips to stall for time: She—dissatisfied me. *Pause.* And my husband.

DANFORTH: In what way dissatisfied you?

ELIZABETH: She were—*She glances at* PROCTOR *for a cue.*

DANFORTH: Woman, look at me? ELIZABETH *does.* Were she slovenly? Lazy? What disturbance did she cause?

ELIZABETH: Your Honor, I—in that time I were sick. And I—My husband is a good and righteous man. He is never drunk as some are, nor wastin' his time at the shovelboard, but always at his work. But in my sickness—you see, sir, I were a long time sick after my last baby, and I thought I saw my husband somewhat turning from me. And this girl—*She turns to* ABIGAIL.

DANFORTH: Look at me.

ELIZABETH: Aye, sir. Abigail Williams—*She breaks off.*

DANFORTH: What of Abigail Williams?

ELIZABETH: I came to think he fancied her. And so one night I lost my wits, I think, and put her out on the highroad.

DANFORTH: Your husband—did he indeed turn from you?

ELIZABETH, *in agony:* My husband—is a goodly man, sir.

DANFORTH: Then he did not turn from you.

ELIZABETH, *starting to glance at* PROCTOR: He—

DANFORTH, *reaches out and holds her face, then:* Look at me! To your own knowledge, has John Proctor ever committed the crime of lechery? *In a crisis of indecision she cannot speak.* Answer my question! Is your husband a lecher!

ELIZABETH, *faintly:* No, sir.

DANFORTH: Remove her, Marshal.

PROCTOR: Elizabeth, tell the truth!

DANFORTH: She has spoken. Remove her!

PROCTOR, *crying out:* Elizabeth, I have confessed it!

ELIZABETH: Oh, God! *The door closes behind her.*

PROCTOR: She only thought to save my name!

HALE: Excellency, it is a natural lie to tell; I beg you, stop now before another is condemned! I may shut my conscience to it no more—private vengeance is working through this testimony! From the beginning this man has struck me true. By my oath to Heaven, I believe him now, and I pray you call back his wife before we—

DANFORTH: She spoke nothing of lechery, and this man has lied!

HALE: I believe him! *Pointing at* ABIGAIL: This girl has always struck me false! She has—

ABIGAIL, *with a weird, wild, chilling cry, screams up to the ceiling.*

ABIGAIL: You will not! Begone! Begone, I say!

DANFORTH: What is it, child? *But* ABIGAIL, *pointing with fear, is now raising up her frightened eyes, her awed face, toward the ceiling—the girls are doing the same—and now* HATHORNE, HALE, PUTNAM, CHEEVER, HERRICK, *and* DANFORTH *do the same.* What's there? *He lowers his eyes from the ceiling, and now he is frightened; there is real tension in his voice.* Child! *She is transfixed—with all the girls, she is whimpering, open-mouthed, agape at the ceiling.* Girls! Why do you—?

MERCY LEWIS, *pointing:* It's on the beam! Behind the rafter!

DANFORTH, *looking up:* Where!

ABIGAIL: Why—? *She gulps.* Why do you come, yellow bird?

PROCTOR: Where's a bird? I see no bird!

ABIGAIL, *to the ceiling:* My face? My face?

PROCTOR: Mr. Hale—

DANFORTH: Be quiet!

PROCTOR, *to* HALE: Do you see a bird?

DANFORTH: Be quiet!!

ABIGAIL, *to the ceiling, in a genuine conversation with the "bird," as though trying to talk it out of attacking her:* But God made my face; you cannot want to tear my face. Envy is a deadly sin, Mary.

MARY WARREN, *on her feet with a spring, and horrified, pleading:* Abby!

ABIGAIL, *unperturbed, continuing to the "bird":* Oh, Mary, this is a black art to change your shape. No, I cannot, I cannot stop my mouth; it's God's work I do.

MARY WARREN: Abby, I'm *here!*

PROCTOR, *frantically:* They're pretending, Mr. Danforth!

ABIGAIL *—now she takes a backward step, as though in fear the bird will swoop down momentarily:* Oh, please, Mary! Don't come down.

SUSANNA WALCOTT: Her claws, she's stretching her claws!

PROCTOR: Lies, lies.

ABIGAIL, *backing further, eyes still fixed above:* Mary, please don't hurt me!

MARY WARREN, *to* DANFORTH: I'm not hurting her!

DANFORTH, *to* MARY WARREN: Why does she see this vision?

MARY WARREN: She sees nothin'!

ABIGAIL, *now staring full front as though hypnotized, and mimicking the exact tone of* MARY WARREN'S *cry:* She sees nothin'!

MARY WARREN, *pleading:* Abby, you mustn't!

ABIGAIL AND ALL THE GIRLS, *all transfixed:* Abby, you mustn't!

MARY WARREN, *to all the girls:* I'm here, I'm here!

Comprehension
In what way does Elizabeth's testimony differ from John's?

GIRLS: I'm here, I'm here!

DANFORTH, *horrified:* Mary Warren! Draw back your spirit out of them!

MARY WARREN: Mr. Danforth!

GIRLS, *cutting her off:* Mr. Danforth!

DANFORTH: Have you compacted with the Devil? Have you?

MARY WARREN: Never, never!

GIRLS: Never, never!

DANFORTH, *growing hysterical:* Why can they only repeat you?

PROCTOR: Give me a whip—I'll stop it!

MARY WARREN: They're sporting. They—!

GIRLS: They're sporting!

MARY WARREN, *turning on them all hysterically and stamping her feet:* Abby, stop it!

GIRLS, *stamping their feet:* Abby, stop it!

MARY WARREN: Stop it!

GIRLS: Stop it!

MARY WARREN, *screaming it out at the top of her lungs, and raising her fists:* Stop it!!

GIRLS, *raising their fists:* Stop it!!

MARY WARREN, *utterly confounded, and becoming overwhelmed by* ABIGAIL'S*—and the girls'—utter conviction, starts to whimper, hands half raised, powerless, and all the girls begin whimpering exactly as she does.*

DANFORTH: A little while ago you were afflicted. Now it seems you afflict others; where did you find this power?

MARY WARREN, *staring at* ABIGAIL: I—have no power.

GIRLS: I have no power.

PROCTOR: They're gulling[7] you, Mister!

DANFORTH: Why did you turn about this past two weeks? You have seen the Devil, have you not?

HALE, *indicating* ABIGAIL *and the* GIRLS: You cannot believe them!

MARY WARREN: I—

"You have seen the Devil... have you not?"

PROCTOR, *sensing her weakening:* Mary, God damns all liars!

DANFORTH, *pounding it into her:* You have seen the Devil, you have made compact with Lucifer, have you not?

PROCTOR: God damns liars, Mary!

MARY *utters something unintelligible, staring at* ABIGAIL, *who keeps watching the "bird" above.*

DANFORTH: I cannot hear you. What do you say? MARY *utters again unintelligibly.* You will confess yourself or you will hang! *He turns her roughly to face him.* Do you know who I am? I say you will hang if you do not open with me!

---

7. gulling fooling.

PROCTOR: Mary, remember the angel Raphael—do that which is good and—

ABIGAIL, *pointing upward:* The wings! Her wings are spreading! Mary, please, don't, don't—!

HALE: I see nothing, Your Honor!

DANFORTH: Do you confess this power! *He is an inch from her face.* Speak!

ABIGAIL: She's going to come down! She's walking the beam!

DANFORTH: Will you speak!

MARY WARREN, *staring in horror:* I cannot!

GIRLS: I cannot!

PARRIS: Cast the Devil out! Look him in the face! Trample him! We'll save you, Mary, only stand fast against him and—

ABIGAIL, *looking up:* Look out! She's coming down!

She and all the girls run to one wall, shielding their eyes. And now, as though cornered, they let out a gigantic scream, and MARY, *as though infected, opens her mouth and screams with them. Gradually* ABIGAIL *and the girls leave off, until only* MARY *is left there, staring up at the "bird," screaming madly. All watch her, horrified by this evident fit.* PROCTOR *strides to her.*

▼ Critical Viewing

Examine the girls' expressions in this movie still. What dominant emotions do you think they feel as they follow Abigail's lead? **ASSESS**

Comprehension

What do the girls do to undermine Mary Warren's testimony?

PROCTOR: Mary, tell the Governor what they—*He has hardly got a word out, when, seeing him coming for her, she rushes out of his reach, screaming in horror.*

MARY WARREN: Don't touch me—don't touch me! *At which the girls halt at the door.*

PROCTOR, *astonished:* Mary!

MARY WARREN, *pointing at* PROCTOR: You're the Devil's man!

He is stopped in his tracks.

PARRIS: Praise God!

GIRLS: Praise God!

PROCTOR, *numbed:* Mary, how—?

MARY WARREN: I'll not hang with you! I love God, I love God.

DANFORTH, *to* MARY: He bid you do the Devil's work?

MARY WARREN, *hysterically, indicating* PROCTOR: He come at me by night and every day to sign, to sign, to—

DANFORTH: Sign what?

PARRIS: The Devil's book? He come with a book?

MARY WARREN, *hysterically, pointing at* PROCTOR, *fearful of him:* My name, he want my name. "I'll murder you," he says, "if my wife hangs! We must go and overthrow the court," he says!

DANFORTH'S *head jerks toward* PROCTOR, *shock and horror in his face.*

PROCTOR, *turning, appealing to* HALE: Mr. Hale!

MARY WARREN, *her sobs beginning:* He wake me every night, his eyes were like coals and his fingers claw my neck, and I sign, I sign . . .

HALE: Excellency, this child's gone wild!

PROCTOR, *as* DANFORTH'S *wide eyes pour on him:* Mary, Mary!

Verbal Irony

Which two words in these stage directions are an example of verbal irony? Explain.

MARY WARREN, *screaming at him:* No, I love God; I go your way no more. I love God, I bless God. *Sobbing, she rushes to* ABIGAIL. Abby, Abby, I'll never hurt you more! *They all watch, as* ABIGAIL, *out of her infinite charity, reaches out and draws the sobbing* MARY *to her, and then looks up to* DANFORTH.

DANFORTH, *to* PROCTOR: What are you? PROCTOR *is beyond speech in his anger.* You are combined with anti-Christ,[8] are you not? I have seen your power; you will not deny it! What say you, Mister?

HALE: Excellency—

DANFORTH: I will have nothing from you, Mr. Hale! *To* PROCTOR: Will you confess yourself befouled with Hell, or do you keep that black allegiance yet? What say you?

PROCTOR, *his mind wild, breathless:* I say—I say—God is dead!

PARRIS: Hear it, hear it!

PROCTOR, *laughs insanely, then:* A fire, a fire is burning! I hear the boot

8. anti-Christ In the Bible, the great antagonist of Christ expected to spread universal evil.

of Lucifer, I see his filthy face! And it is my face, and yours, Danforth! For them that quail to bring men out of ignorance, as I have quailed, and as you quail now when you know in all your black hearts that this be fraud—God damns our kind especially, and we will burn, we will burn together.

DANFORTH: Marshal! Take him and Corey with him to the jail!

HALE, *staring across to the door:* I denounce these proceedings!

PROCTOR: You are pulling Heaven down and raising up a whore!

HALE: I denounce these proceedings, I quit this court! *He slams the door to the outside behind him.*

DANFORTH, *calling to him in a fury:* Mr. Hale! Mr. Hale!

THE CURTAIN FALLS

Critical Reading

1. **Key Ideas and Details (a)** Which three depositions are presented to the judges and on whose behalf? **(b) Analyze:** How do the judges discourage defenses of the accused?
2. **Key Ideas and Details (a)** What does John Proctor confess to Danforth? **(b) Interpret:** Why does Proctor make this confession? **(c) Infer:** What does his confession reveal about his character?
3. **Key Ideas and Details (a)** What is the lie Elizabeth Proctor tells Danforth? **(b) Analyze:** What are the consequences of her lie?
4. **Key Ideas and Details (a)** What truth does Mary Warren reveal about her involvement with "spirits"? **(b) Analyze:** Why does she change her testimony and turn on John Proctor?
5. **Key Ideas and Details (a)** What does Hale denounce at the end of Act III? **(b) Evaluate:** Do you find Hale sympathetic? Why or why not?
6. **Integration of Knowledge and Ideas Apply:** Imagine that Elizabeth Proctor had told Danforth the truth. In what way might the outcome of the trials have been different?
7. **Integration of Knowledge and Ideas Assess:** Who bears the most guilt for the fate of those hanged in the Salem witch trials—the girls who accused innocent people or the judges who sentenced them to death?

Cite textual evidence to support your responses.

Close Reading Activities *The Crucible, Act III*

Literary Analysis

1. **Craft and Structure** **(a)** Identify two examples of **direct characterization** Miller uses to describe Giles Corey in stage directions. **(b)** Identify two examples of **indirect characterization**—dialogue or action—that supports this description. Explain your choices.
2. **Craft and Structure** **(a)** Identify three examples of **indirect characterization** that reveal Mary Warren's personality. **(b)** For each example, explain what you learn about her.
3. **Key Ideas and Details** **(a)** What is Elizabeth's *motive* for evading Danforth's questions about Abigail's dismissal from the Proctor household? **(b)** Considering Elizabeth's belief that lying is a sin, what does her evasion suggest about her character, her feelings for her husband, and her understanding of the court proceedings?
4. **Key Ideas and Details** **(a)** What motivates Hale to denounce the proceedings and quit the court? **(b)** How do Hale's character and motivations change from when he first arrives in Salem? Explain.
5. **Craft and Structure** **(a)** Using a chart like the one shown below question 6, list two examples of **dramatic irony** in Act III. **(b)** For each, explain what the audience understands or knows that the characters themselves do not.
6. **Craft and Structure** **(a)** Using the same type of chart, identify two examples of **verbal irony** in Act III. **(b)** Explain what each speaker really means.

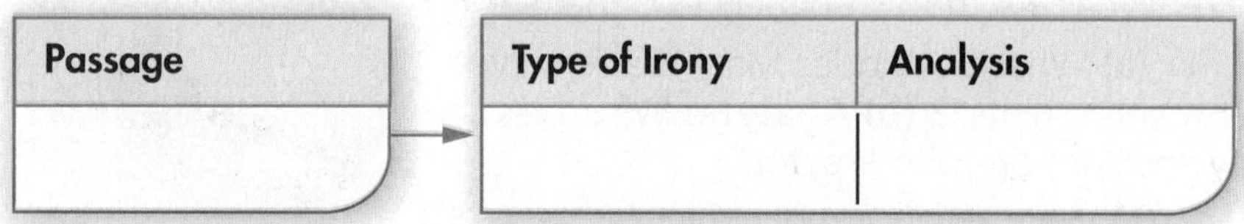

Passage	Type of Irony	Analysis

7. **Craft and Structure** In what ways is the effect of Elizabeth's testimony ironic?
8. **Craft and Structure** What is ironic about Mary Warren's statement, "I—have no power," when she is being interrogated in front of Abigail Williams?
9. **Integration of Knowledge and Ideas** **(a) Evaluate the argument** Judge Danforth uses in the dramatic exchange with Reverend Hale by identifying the erroneous idea that underlies his reasoning about the legal proceedings. **(b)** Is Danforth's argument credible?
10. **Integration of Knowledge and Ideas** In what sense does Danforth's *logical fallacy* have ramifications far beyond the conviction of John Proctor?

Common Core State Standards

Writing

1. Write arguments to support claims in an analysis of substantive topics or texts, using valid reasoning and relevant and sufficient evidence. *(p. 1215)*

1.a. Introduce precise, knowledgeable claim(s), establish the significance of the claim(s), distinguish the claim(s) from alternate or opposing claims, and create an organization that logically sequences claim(s), counterclaims, reasons, and evidence. *(p. 1215)*

1.b. Develop claim(s) and counterclaims fairly and thoroughly, supplying the most relevant evidence for each while pointing out the strengths and limitations of both in a manner that anticipates the audience's knowledge level, concerns, values, and possible biases. *(p. 1215)*

1.e. Provide a concluding statement or section that follows from and supports the argument presented. *(p. 1215)*

Language

5. Demonstrate understanding of word relationships. *(p. 1215)*

6. Acquire and use accurately general academic and domain-specific words and phrases, sufficient for reading, writing, speaking, and listening at the college and career readiness level; demonstrate independence in gathering vocabulary knowledge when considering a word or phrase important to comprehension or expression. *(p. 1215)*

Vocabulary Acquisition and Use

Word Analysis: Legal Terms

The Crucible contains numerous legal terms, specifically words referring to sworn speech. The following Latin roots often form the basis of such words:

-fid- (faith, trust) *-pos-* (to place)
-testis- (a witness) *-jurare-* (to swear)

Use your knowledge of these roots to explain how they contribute to the meaning of the following words. If necessary, use a dictionary to determine the meanings of prefixes or suffixes.

1. affidavit
2. deposition
3. testimony
4. perjury

Then, use a dictionary to find one word containing each of these roots: *-fid-, -testis-, -pos-, -jurare-*. Write a sentence for each new word.

Vocabulary: Synonyms or Antonyms

Review the vocabulary list on page 1186. Then, for each item below, indicate whether the paired words are synonyms or antonyms. Explain your answers.

1. contentious, combative
2. deposition, testimony
3. imperceptible, obvious
4. anonymity, notoriety
5. effrontery, timidity
6. incredulously, disbelievingly

Writing to Sources

Argument A brief is a legal document that contains information about the facts of a case, the legal issues to be decided, and the law the Court ought to apply. An *amicus curiae*—or "friend of the court"—brief is a persuasive document submitted by individuals who are not themselves party to a case. Such briefs are offered in the hope that the court will take their advice. Write a **"friend of the court" brief** as if you were a respected official of a Puritan community near Salem.

Prewriting Review the court scene in Act III from the perspective of someone who shares the Puritan worldview but has no personal involvement in the trial. Use a chart like the one shown to outline your position, evidence, and counterarguments.

Drafting In the first paragraph, explain your position. Then, present arguments and supporting evidence, followed by counterarguments and evidence. Conclude by restating your position and making a final claim.

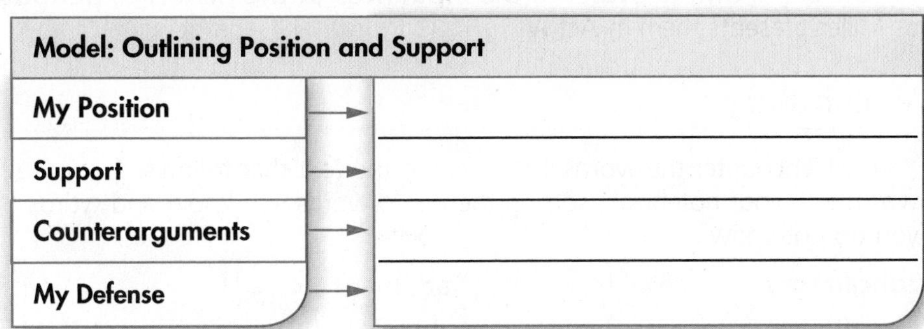

Revising Reread your brief and make sure your word choices are accurate, precise, and vivid. Replace details or words that are inaccurate or vague with better choices.

Building Knowledge and Insight *The Crucible, Act IV*

Close Reading Focus

Tragedy; Allegory

Tragedy is a dramatic form that was first developed in ancient Greece. A tragedy usually has these characteristics:

- The main character is involved in a struggle that ends in disaster. This character, often called the **tragic hero,** is a person of high rank who has the respect of the community.
- The tragic hero's downfall is usually the result of some combination of fate, an error in judgment, and a personality weakness often called a **tragic flaw.**
- Once the tragedy is in motion, the downfall is usually inevitable.
- The tragic hero gains wisdom or insight by the play's end.

Tragedy arouses feelings of pity and fear in the audience. Spectators pity the plight of the main character and fear that a similar fate might befall them. A tragic drama may also suggest that the human spirit is capable of remarkable nobility even in the midst of great suffering.

An **allegory** is a story with more than one layer of meaning: a literal meaning and one or more symbolic meanings. The characters, settings, and themes in an allegory are symbols of ideas and qualities that exist outside the story. *The Crucible* is an allegory, because Miller uses one historical period and setting (seventeenth-century New England) to comment on another (1950s America). The tragedy that occurs in Salem is an allegory for the anti-Communist hysteria that gripped the United States during the 1950s. As you read, notice how the events in Salem echo the events surrounding the McCarthy hearings to tragic effect.

Preparing to Read Complex Texts Arthur Miller brings many areas of Puritan thought to bear on the story of *The Crucible.* These philosophical, political, religious, ethical, and social influences shape the characters, setting, actions, and ultimate meaning of the play. As you read, use a chart like the one shown to **evaluate the influences of the historical period** as Miller presents them in Act IV.

Vocabulary

You will encounter the words listed here in the text that follows. Copy the words into your notebook, sorting them into words you know and words you do not know.

conciliatory **adamant**
beguile **cleave**
retaliation **tantalized**

Common Core State Standards

Reading Literature

3. Analyze the impact of the author's choices regarding how to develop and relate elements of a drama.

6. Analyze a case in which grasping a point of view requires distinguishing what is directly stated in a text from what is really meant.

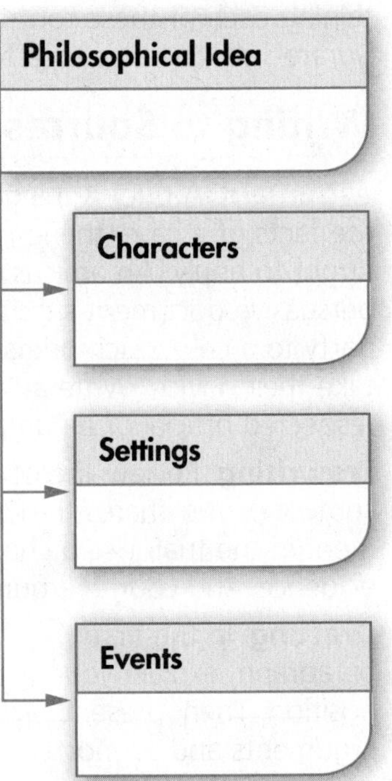

Review and Anticipate

"Is every defense an attack upon the court?" Hale asks in Act III. Danforth observes, "A person is either with this court or he must be counted against it." Such remarks stress the powerlessness of people like John Proctor and Giles Corey against the mounting injustices in Salem. In pursuing justice, their efforts backfire, and their own names join the list of those accused. What do you think the final outcome will be? Who will survive, and who will perish? Read the final act to see if your predictions are correct.

A cell in Salem jail, that fall.

At the back is a high barred window; near it, a great, heavy door. Along the walls are two benches.

The place is in darkness but for the moonlight seeping through the bars. It appears empty. Presently footsteps are heard coming down a corridor beyond the wall, keys rattle, and the door swings open. MARSHAL HERRICK *enters with a lantern.*

He is nearly drunk, and heavy-footed. He goes to a bench and nudges a bundle of rags lying on it.

HERRICK: Sarah, wake up! Sarah Good! *He then crosses to the other benches.*

SARAH GOOD, *rising in her rags:* Oh, Majesty! Comin', comin'! Tituba, he's here, His Majesty's come!

HERRICK: Go to the north cell; this place is wanted now. *He hangs his lantern on the wall.* TITUBA sits up.

TITUBA: That don't look to me like His Majesty; look to me like the marshal.

HERRICK, *taking out a flask:* Get along with you now, clear this place. *He drinks, and* SARAH GOOD *comes and peers up into his face.*

SARAH GOOD: Oh, is it you, Marshal! I thought sure you be the devil comin' for us. Could I have a sip of cider for me goin'-away?

HERRICK, *handing her the flask:* And where are you off to, Sarah?

TITUBA, *as* SARAH *drinks:* We goin' to Barbados, soon the Devil gits here with the feathers and the wings.

HERRICK: Oh? A happy voyage to you.

SARAH GOOD: A pair of bluebirds wingin' southerly, the two of us! Oh, it be a grand transformation, Marshal! *She raises the flask to drink again.*

Comprehension
For whom does Sarah Good mistake Herrick?

HERRICK, *taking the flask from her lips:* You'd best give me that or you'll never rise off the ground. Come along now.

TITUBA: I'll speak to him for you, if you desires to come along, Marshal.

HERRICK: I'd not refuse it, Tituba; it's the proper morning to fly into Hell.

TITUBA: Oh, it be no Hell in Barbados. Devil, him be pleasure man in Barbados, him be singin' and dancin' in Barbados. It's you folks—you riles him up 'round here; it be too cold 'round here for that Old Boy. He freeze his soul in Massachusetts, but in Barbados he just as sweet and—*A bellowing cow is heard, and* TITUBA *leaps up and calls to the window:* Aye, sir! That's him, Sarah!

Evaluating the Influences of the Historical Period

How does Tituba's desire for home reflect historical realities?

SARAH GOOD: I'm here, Majesty! *They hurriedly pick up their rags as* HOPKINS, *a guard, enters.*

HOPKINS: The Deputy Governor's arrived.

HERRICK, *grabbing* TITUBA: Come along, come along.

TITUBA, *resisting him:* No, he comin' for me. I goin' home!

HERRICK, *pulling her to the door:* That's not Satan, just a poor old cow with a hatful of milk. Come along now, out with you!

TITUBA, *calling to the window:* Take me home, Devil! Take me home!

SARAH GOOD, *following the shouting* TITUBA *out:* Tell him I'm goin', Tituba! Now you tell him Sarah Good is goin' too!

In the corridor outside TITUBA *calls on—"Take me home, Devil; Devil take me home!" and* HOPKINS' *voice orders her to move on.* HERRICK *returns and begins to push old rags and straw into a corner. Hearing footsteps, he turns, and enter* DANFORTH *and* JUDGE HATHORNE. *They are in greatcoats and wear hats against the bitter cold. They are followed in by* CHEEVER, *who carries a dispatch case and a flat wooden box containing his writing materials.*

HERRICK: Good morning, Excellency.

DANFORTH: Where is Mr. Parris?

HERRICK: I'll fetch him. *He starts for the door.*

DANFORTH: Marshal. HERRICK *stops.* When did Reverend Hale arrive?

HERRICK: It were toward midnight, I think.

DANFORTH, *suspiciously:* What is he about here?

HERRICK: He goes among them that will hang, sir. And he prays with them. He sits with Goody Nurse now. And Mr. Parris with him.

DANFORTH: Indeed. That man have no authority to enter here, Marshal. Why have you let him in?

HERRICK: Why, Mr. Parris command me, sir. I cannot deny him.

DANFORTH: Are you drunk, Marshal?

HERRICK: No, sir; it is a bitter night, and I have no fire here.

DANFORTH, *containing his anger:* Fetch Mr. Parris.

HERRICK: Aye, sir.

DANFORTH: There is a prodigious stench in this place.

HERRICK: I have only now cleared the people out for you.

DANFORTH: Beware hard drink, Marshal.

HERRICK: Aye, sir. *He waits an instant for further orders. But* DANFORTH, *in dissatisfaction, turns his back on him, and* HERRICK *goes out. There is a pause.* DANFORTH *stands in thought.*

HATHORNE: Let you question Hale, Excellency; I should not be surprised he have been preaching in Andover[1] lately.

DANFORTH: We'll come to that; speak nothing of Andover. Parris prays with him. That's strange. *He blows on his hands, moves toward the window, and looks out.*

HATHORNE: Excellency, I wonder if it be wise to let Mr. Parris so continuously with the prisoners. DANFORTH *turns to him, interested.* I think, sometimes, the man has a mad look these days.

DANFORTH: Mad?

HATHORNE: I met him yesterday coming out of his house, and I bid him good morning—and he wept and went his way. I think it is not well the village sees him so unsteady.

DANFORTH: Perhaps he have some sorrow.

CHEEVER, *stamping his feet against the cold:* I think it be the cows, sir.

DANFORTH: Cows?

CHEEVER: There be so many cows wanderin' the highroads, now their masters are in the jails, and much disagreement who they will belong to now. I know Mr. Parris be arguin' with farmers all yesterday—there is great contention, sir, about the cows. Contention make him weep, sir; it were always a man that weep for contention. *He turns, as do* HATHORNE *and* DANFORTH *hearing someone coming up the corridor.* DANFORTH *raises his head as* PARRIS *enters. He is gaunt, frightened, and sweating in his greatcoat.*

Allegory

How might this description of Salem in chaos warn against anti-communist fear and suspicion in Miller's time?

PARRIS, *to* DANFORTH, *instantly:* Oh, good morning, sir, thank you for coming. I beg your pardon wakin' you so early. Good morning, Judge Hathorne.

DANFORTH: Reverend Hale have no right to enter this—

PARRIS: Excellency, a moment. *He hurries back and shuts the door.*

HATHORNE: Do you leave him alone with the prisoners?

DANFORTH: What's his business here?

PARRIS, *prayerfully holding up his hands:* Excellency, hear me. It is a providence. Reverend Hale has returned to bring Rebecca Nurse to God.

DANFORTH, *surprised:* He bids her confess?

PARRIS, *sitting:* Hear me. Rebecca have not given me a word this three month since she came. Now she sits with him, and her sister and Martha Corey and two or three others, and he pleads with them,

Comprehension

Why are so many cows wandering the roads?

---

1. **Andover** During the height of the terror in Salem Village, a similar hysteria broke out in the nearby town of Andover. There, many respected people were accused of practicing witchcraft and confessed to escape death. However, in Andover people soon began questioning the reality of the situation and the hysteria quickly subsided.

confess their crimes and save their lives.

DANFORTH: Why—this is indeed a providence. And they soften, they soften?

PARRIS: Not yet, not yet. But I thought to summon you, sir, that we might think on whether it be not wise, to—*He dares not say it.* I had thought to put a question, sir, and I hope you will not—

DANFORTH: Mr. Parris, be plain, what troubles you?

PARRIS: There is news, sir, that the court—the court must reckon with. My niece, sir, my niece—I believe she has vanished.

DANFORTH: Vanished!

PARRIS: I had thought to advise you of it earlier in the week, but—

DANFORTH: Why? How long is she gone?

PARRIS: This be the third night. You see, sir, she told me she would stay a night with Mercy Lewis. And next day, when she does not return, I send to Mr. Lewis to inquire. Mercy told him she would sleep in *my* house for a night.

DANFORTH: They are both gone?!

PARRIS, *in fear of him:* They are, sir.

DANFORTH, *alarmed:* I will send a party for them. Where may they be?

PARRIS: Excellency, I think they be aboard a ship. DANFORTH *stands agape.* My daughter tells me how she heard them speaking of ships last week, and tonight I discover my—my strongbox is broke into. *He presses his fingers against his eyes to keep back tears.*

HATHORNE, *astonished:* She have robbed you?

PARRIS: Thirty-one pound is gone. I am penniless. *He covers his face and sobs.*

DANFORTH: Mr. Parris, you are a brainless man! *He walks in thought, deeply worried.*

PARRIS: Excellency, it profit nothing you should blame me. I cannot think they would run off except they fear to keep in Salem any more. *He is pleading.* Mark it, sir, Abigail had close knowledge of the town, and since the news of Andover has broken here—

DANFORTH: Andover is remedied. The court returns there on Friday, and will resume examinations.

PARRIS: I am sure of it, sir. But the rumor here speaks rebellion in Andover, and it—

DANFORTH: There is no rebellion in Andover!

PARRIS: I tell you what is said here, sir. Andover have thrown out the court, they say, and will have no part of witchcraft. There be a faction here, feeding on that news, and I tell you true, sir, I fear there will be riot here.

HATHORNE: Riot! Why at every execution I have seen naught but high satisfaction in the town.

PARRIS: Judge Hathorne—it were another sort that hanged till now. Rebecca Nurse is no Bridget that lived three year with Bishop before

▶ Critical Viewing

What might Parris be saying to Judge Danforth in this court scene from execution day? **SPECULATE** she married him. John Proctor is not Isaac Ward that drank his family to ruin. *To* DANFORTH: I would to God it were not so, Excellency, but these people have great weight yet in the town. Let Rebecca stand upon the gibbet[2] and send up some righteous prayer, and I fear she'll wake a vengeance on you.

HATHORNE: Excellency, she is condemned a witch. The court have—

DANFORTH, *in deep concern, raising a hand to* HATHORNE: Pray you. *To* PARRIS: How do you propose, then?

PARRIS: Excellency, I would postpone these hangin's for a time.

DANFORTH: There will be no postponement.

PARRIS: Now Mr. Hale's returned, there is hope, I think—for if he bring even one of these to God, that confession surely damns the others in the public eye, and none may doubt more that they are all linked to Hell. This way, unconfessed and claiming innocence, doubts are multiplied, many honest people will weep for them, and our good purpose is lost in their tears.

DANFORTH, *after thinking a moment, then going to* CHEEVER: Give me the list.

CHEEVER *opens the dispatch case, searches.*

PARRIS: It cannot be forgot, sir, that when I summoned the congregation for John Proctor's excommunication there were hardly thirty people come to hear it. That speak a discontent, I think, and—

DANFORTH, *studying the list:* There will be no postponement.

PARRIS: Excellency—

DANFORTH: Now, sir—which of these in your opinion may be brought to God? I will myself strive with him till dawn. *He hands the list to* PARRIS, *who merely glances at it.*

Tragedy
How does Parris's description of Proctor suggest some of the qualities of a tragic hero?

Comprehension
What has happened to Abigail?

---

2. **gibbet** (jib′ it) *n.* gallows.

PARRIS: There is not sufficient time till dawn.

DANFORTH: I shall do my utmost. Which of them do you have hope for?

PARRIS, *not even glancing at the list now, and in a quavering voice, quietly:* Excellency—a dagger—*He chokes up.*

DANFORTH: What do you say?

PARRIS: Tonight, when I open my door to leave my house—a dagger clattered to the ground. *Silence.* DANFORTH *absorbs this. Now* PARRIS *cries out:* You cannot hang this sort. There is danger for me. I dare not step outside at night!

REVEREND HALE *enters. They look at him for an instant in silence. He is steeped in sorrow, exhausted, and more direct than he ever was.*

DANFORTH: Accept my congratulations, Reverend Hale; we are gladdened to see you returned to your good work.

HALE, *coming to* DANFORTH *now:* You must pardon them. They will not budge.

HERRICK *enters, waits.*

DANFORTH, ***conciliatory:*** You misunderstand, sir; I cannot pardon these when twelve are already hanged for the same crime. It is not just.

PARRIS, *with failing heart:* Rebecca will not confess?

HALE: The sun will rise in a few minutes. Excellency, I must have more time.

DANFORTH: Now hear me, and **beguile** yourselves no more. I will not receive a single plea for pardon or postponement. Them that will not confess will hang. Twelve are already executed; the names of these seven are given out, and the village expects to see them die this morning. Postponement now speaks a floundering on my part; reprieve or pardon must cast doubt upon the guilt of them that died till now. While I speak God's law, I will not crack its voice with whimpering. If **retaliation** is your fear, know this—I should hang ten thousand that dared to rise against the law, and an ocean of salt tears could not melt the resolution of the statutes. Now draw yourselves up like men and help me, as you are bound by Heaven to do. Have you spoken with them all, Mr. Hale?

HALE: All but Proctor. He is in the dungeon.

DANFORTH, *to* HERRICK: What's Proctor's way now?

HERRICK: He sits like some great bird; you'd not know he lived except he will take food from time to time.

DANFORTH, *after thinking a moment:* His wife—his wife must be well on with child now.

HERRICK: She is, sir.

DANFORTH: What think you, Mr. Parris? You have closer knowledge of this man; might her presence soften him?

PARRIS: It is possible, sir. He have not laid eyes on her these three months. I should summon her.

DANFORTH, *to* HERRICK: Is he yet **adamant**? Has he struck at you again?

Vocabulary

conciliatory (kən sil′ ē ə tôr′ ē) *adj.* tending to soothe anger

beguile (bē gīl′) *v.* trick

retaliation (ri tal′ ē ā′ shən) *n.* act of returning an injury or wrong

adamant (ad′ ə mənt) *adj.* firm; unyielding

HERRICK: He cannot, sir, he is chained to the wall now.

DANFORTH, *after thinking on it:* Fetch Goody Proctor to me. Then let you bring him up.

HERRICK: Aye, sir. HERRICK *goes. There is silence.*

HALE: Excellency, if you postpone a week and publish to the town that you are striving for their confessions, that speak mercy on your part, not faltering.

DANFORTH: Mr. Hale, as God have not empowered me like Joshua to stop this sun from rising,[3] so I cannot withhold from them the perfection of their punishment.

HALE, *harder now:* If you think God wills you to raise rebellion, Mr. Danforth, you are mistaken!

DANFORTH, *instantly:* You have heard rebellion spoken in the town?

HALE: Excellency, there are orphans wandering from house to house; abandoned cattle bellow on the highroads, the stink of rotting crops hangs everywhere, and no man knows when the harlots' cry will end his life—and you wonder yet if rebellion's spoke? Better you should

3. **Joshua . . . rising** In the Bible, Joshua, leader of the Jews after the death of Moses, asks God to make the sun and the moon stand still during a battle, and his request is granted.

Tragedy

According to Danforth, are the events taking place in Salem inevitable? Explain.

Comprehension

Why has Hale returned to Salem?

WORLD LITERATURE IN CONTEXT

POLITICAL DRAMA

WOLE SOYINKA (b. 1934)

Playwright Wole Soyinka grew up in Nigeria, immersed in two cultures. His parents were English-speaking Christians, while his grandparents followed the local Yoruba religion. After attending college in Britain, Soyinka returned to Nigeria, organized a theater troupe, and wrote plays that combine elements of European drama with African folk culture. In 1960, Nigeria won its independence from Britain. Years of political violence followed and a succession of dictators took control of the country. Soyinka wrote political satires that skewered the government, making him powerful enemies. During the 1960s, he was arrested twice and thrown into jail.

Although he has spent much of the last 40 years living in exile, Soyinka has continued writing about Africa. In 1984, he directed the world premiere of *A Play of Giants*, a dark satire about four African dictators visiting New York City. Two years later, Soyinka won the Nobel Prize for Literature.

Connect to the Literature

Why might a playwright choose satire as a form for political commentary?

marvel how they do not burn your province!

DANFORTH: Mr. Hale, have you preached in Andover this month?

HALE: Thank God they have no need of me in Andover.

DANFORTH: You baffle me, sir. Why have you returned here?

HALE: Why, it is all simple. I come to do the Devil's work. I come to counsel Christians they should belie themselves. *His sarcasm collapses.* There is blood on my head! Can you not see the blood on my head!!

PARRIS: Hush! *For he has heard footsteps. They all face the door.* HERRICK *enters with* ELIZABETH. *Her wrists are linked by heavy chain, which* HERRICK *now removes. Her clothes are dirty; her face is pale and gaunt.* HERRICK *goes out.*

DANFORTH, *very politely:* Goody Proctor. *She is silent.* I hope you are hearty?

ELIZABETH, *as a warning reminder:* I am yet six month before my time.

DANFORTH: Pray be at your ease, we come not for your life. We— *uncertain how to plead, for he is not accustomed to it.* Mr. Hale, will you speak with the woman?

HALE: Goody Proctor, your husband is marked to hang this morning *Pause.*

ELIZABETH, *quietly:* I have heard it.

HALE: You know, do you not, that I have no connection with the court? *She seems to doubt it.* I come of my own, Goody Proctor. I would save your husband's life, for if he is taken I count myself his murderer. Do you understand me?

ELIZABETH: What do you want of me?

HALE: Goody Proctor, I have gone this three month like our Lord into the wilderness. I have sought a Christian way, for damnation's doubled on a minister who counsels men to lie.

HATHORNE: It is no lie, you cannot speak of lies.

HALE: It is a lie! They are innocent!

DANFORTH: I'll hear no more of that!

HALE, *continuing to* ELIZABETH: Let you not mistake your duty as I mistook my own. I came into this village like a bridegroom to his beloved, bearing gifts of high religion; the very crowns of holy law I brought, and what I touched with my bright confidence, it died; and where I turned the eye of my great faith, blood

▼ Critical Viewing
From this movie still, what emotions do you imagine John and Elizabeth Proctor are experiencing at this point? **INFER**

flowed up. Beware, Goody Proctor— cleave to no faith when faith brings blood. It is mistaken law that leads you to sacrifice. Life, woman, life is God's most precious gift; no principle, however glorious, may justify the taking of it. I beg you, woman, prevail upon your husband to confess. Let him give his lie. Quail not before God's judgment in this, for it may well be God damns a liar less than he that throws his life away for pride. Will you plead with him? I cannot think he will listen to another.

ELIZABETH, *quietly:* I think that be the Devil's argument.

HALE, *with a climactic desperation:* Woman, before the laws of God we are as swine! We cannot read His will!

ELIZABETH: I cannot dispute with you, sir; I lack learning for it.

DANFORTH, *going to her:* Goody Proctor, you are not summoned here for disputation. Be there no wifely tenderness within you? He will die with the sunrise. Your husband. Do you understand it? *She only looks at him.* What say you? Will you contend with him? *She is silent.* Are you stone? I tell you true, woman, had I no other proof of your unnatural life, your dry eyes now would be sufficient evidence that you delivered up your soul to Hell! A very ape would weep at such calamity! Have the devil dried up any tear of pity in you? *She is silent.* Take her out. It profit nothing she should speak to him!

ELIZABETH, *quietly:* Let me speak with him, Excellency.

PARRIS, *with hope:* You'll strive with him? *She hesitates.*

DANFORTH: Will you plead for his confession or will you not?

ELIZABETH: I promise nothing. Let me speak with him.

A sound—the sibilance of dragging feet on stone. They turn. A pause. HERRICK *enters with* JOHN PROCTOR. *His wrists are chained. He is another man, bearded, filthy, his eyes misty as though webs had overgrown them. He halts inside the doorway, his eyes caught by the sight of* ELIZABETH. *The emotion flowing between them prevents anyone from speaking for an instant. Now* HALE, *visibly affected, goes to* DANFORTH *and speaks quietly.*

HALE: Pray, leave them Excellency.

DANFORTH, *pressing* HALE *impatiently aside:* Mr. Proctor, you have been notified, have you not? PROCTOR *is silent, staring at* ELIZABETH. I see light in the sky, Mister; let you counsel with your wife, and may God help you turn your back on Hell. PROCTOR *is silent, staring at* ELIZABETH.

HALE, *quietly:* Excellency, let—

DANFORTH *brushes past* HALE *and walks out.* HALE *follows.* CHEEVER *stands and follows,* HATHORNE *behind.* HERRICK *goes.* PARRIS, *from a safe distance, offers:*

PARRIS: If you desire a cup of cider, Mr. Proctor, I am sure I—PROCTOR *turns an icy stare at him, and he breaks off.* PARRIS *raises his palms toward* PROCTOR. God lead you now. PARRIS *goes out.*

Vocabulary

cleave (klēv) *v.* adhere; cling

Comprehension

What does Hale urge Elizabeth Proctor to do?

LITERATURE IN CONTEXT

Media Connection

Being Abigail Williams

For more than four decades, no American film director chose to tackle Arthur Miller's challenging stage drama *The Crucible*. Finally, in 1996, Nicholas Hytner enlisted actors including Winona Ryder, Daniel Day-Lewis, and Joan Allen to star in a film based on a screenplay by Miller himself.

Ryder found playing Abigail Williams engrossing and disturbing. "I've heard Abigail called the villain of the piece, but I'm not so sure," she says. "She's never been given any power. . . . Abigail understands that she could get attention and power, so she goes with it. There's always a part of her that knows she is fooling, but I think she was convinced that spirits were attacking her. I see her as insane in a way, but so is the whole town. It's like a disease."

Connect to the Literature

Do you agree with Ryder's assessment of Abigail? Explain.

Alone, PROCTOR *walks to her, halts. It is as though they stood in a spinning world. It is beyond sorrow, above it. He reaches out his hand as though toward an embodiment not quite real, and as he touches her, a strange soft sound, half laughter, half amazement, comes from his throat. He pats her hand. She covers his hand with hers. And then, weak, he sits. Then she sits, facing him.*

PROCTOR: The child?

ELIZABETH: It grows.

PROCTOR: There is no word of the boys?

ELIZABETH: They're well. Rebecca's Samuel keeps them.

PROCTOR: You have not seen them?

ELIZABETH: I have not. *She catches a weakening in herself and downs it.*

PROCTOR: You are a—marvel, Elizabeth.

ELIZABETH: You—have been tortured?

PROCTOR: Aye. *Pause. She will not let herself be drowned in the sea that threatens her.* They come for my life now.

ELIZABETH: I know it.

Pause.

PROCTOR: None—have yet confessed?

ELIZABETH: There be many confessed.

PROCTOR: Who are they?

ELIZABETH: There be a hundred or more, they say. Goody Ballard is one; Isaiah Goodkind is one. There be many.

PROCTOR: Rebecca?

ELIZABETH: Not Rebecca. She is one foot in Heaven now; naught may hurt her more.

PROCTOR: And Giles?

ELIZABETH: You have not heard of it?

PROCTOR: I hear nothin', where I am kept.

ELIZABETH: Giles is dead.

He looks at her incredulously.

PROCTOR: When were he hanged?

ELIZABETH, *quietly, factually:* He were not hanged. He would not answer aye or nay to his indictment; for if he denied the charge they'd hang him surely, and auction out his property. So he stand mute, and died Christian under the law. And so his sons will have his farm. It is the law, for he could not be condemned a wizard without he answer the indictment, aye or nay.

PROCTOR: Then how does he die?

ELIZABETH, *gently:* They press him, John.

PROCTOR: Press?

ELIZABETH: Great stones they lay upon his chest until he plead aye or nay. *With a tender smile for the old man:* They say he give them but two words. "More weight," he says. And died.

PROCTOR, *numbed—a thread to weave into his agony:* "More weight."

ELIZABETH: Aye. It were a fearsome man, Giles Corey.

Pause.

PROCTOR, *with great force of will, but not quite looking at her:* I have been thinking I would confess to them, Elizabeth. *She shows nothing.* What say you? If I give them that?

ELIZABETH: I cannot judge you, John.

Pause.

PROCTOR, *simply—a pure question:* What would you have me do?

ELIZABETH: As you will, I would have it. *Slight pause:* I want you living, John. That's sure.

PROCTOR, *pauses, then with a flailing of hope:* Giles' wife? Have she confessed?

ELIZABETH: She will not.

Pause.

PROCTOR: It is a pretense, Elizabeth.

ELIZABETH: What is?

PROCTOR: I cannot mount the gibbet like a saint. It is a fraud. I am not that man. *She is silent.* My honesty is broke, Elizabeth; I am no good man. Nothing's spoiled by giving them this lie that were not rotten long before.

ELIZABETH: And yet you've not confessed till now. That speak goodness in you.

PROCTOR: Spite only keeps me silent. It is hard to give a lie to dogs. *Pause, for the first time he turns directly to her.* I would have your forgiveness, Elizabeth.

ELIZABETH: It is not for me to give, John, I am—

PROCTOR: I'd have you see some honesty in it. Let them that never lied die now to keep their souls. It is pretense for me, a vanity that will not blind God nor keep my children out of the wind. *Pause.* What say you?

ELIZABETH, *upon a heaving sob that always threatens:* John, it come to naught that I should forgive you, if you'll not forgive yourself. *Now he turns away a little, in great agony.* It is not my soul, John, it is yours. *He stands, as though in physical pain, slowly rising to his feet with a great immortal longing to find his answer. It is difficult to say, and she is on the verge of tears.* Only be sure of this, for I know it now: Whatever you will do, it is a good man does it. *He turns his doubting, searching gaze upon her.* I have read my heart this three month, John. *Pause.* I have sins of my own to count. It needs a cold wife to prompt lechery.

PROCTOR, *in great pain:* Enough, enough—

ELIZABETH, *now pouring out her heart:* Better you should know me!

Tragedy

At this point in the play, how does Proctor view himself? Explain.

Comprehension

Why does Proctor say that he "cannot mount the gibbet like a saint"?

PROCTOR: I will not hear it! I know you!

ELIZABETH: You take my sins upon you, John—

PROCTOR, *in agony:* No, I take my own, my own!

ELIZABETH: John, I counted myself so plain, so poorly made, no honest love could come to me! Suspicion kissed you when I did; I never knew how I should say my love. It were a cold house I kept! *In fright, she swerves, as* HATHORNE *enters.*

HATHORNE: What say you Proctor? The sun is soon up.

PROCTOR, *his chest heaving, stares, turns to* ELIZABETH. *She comes to him as though to plead, her voice quaking.*

ELIZABETH: Do what you will. But let none be your judge. There be no higher judge under Heaven than Proctor is! Forgive me, forgive me, John—I never knew such goodness in the world! *She covers her face, weeping.*

PROCTOR *turns from her to* HATHORNE; *he is off the earth, his voice hollow.*

PROCTOR: I want my life.

HATHORNE *electrified, surprised:* You'll confess yourself?

PROCTOR: I will have my life.

HATHORNE, *with a mystical tone:* God be praised! It is a providence! *He rushes out the door, and his voice is heard calling down the corridor:* He will confess! Proctor will confess!

PROCTOR, *with a cry, as he strides to the door:* Why do you cry it? *In great pain he turns back to her.* It is evil, is it not? It is evil.

ELIZABETH, *in terror, weeping:* I cannot judge you, John, I cannot!

PROCTOR: Then who will judge me? *Suddenly clasping his hands:* God in Heaven, what is John Proctor, what is John Proctor? *He moves as an animal, and a fury is riding in him, a* **tantalized** *search.* I think it is honest, I think so; I am no saint. *As though she had denied this he calls angrily at her:* Let Rebecca go like a saint; for me it is fraud! *Voices are heard in the hall, speaking together in suppressed excitement.*

Vocabulary
tantalized (tan′ tə līzd) *adj.* tormented; frustrated

ELIZABETH: I am not your judge, I cannot be. *As though giving him release:* Do as you will, do as you will!

PROCTOR: Would you give them such a lie? Say it. Would you ever give them this? *She cannot answer.* You would not; if tongs of fire were singeing you you would not! It is evil. Good, then—it is evil, and I do it!

HATHORNE *enters with* DANFORTH, *and, with them,* CHEEVER, PARRIS, *and* HALE. *It is a businesslike, rapid entrance, as though the ice had been broken.*

DANFORTH, *with great relief and gratitude:* Praise to God, man, praise to God; you shall be blessed in Heaven for this. CHEEVER *has hurried to the bench with pen, ink, and paper.* PROCTOR *watches him.* Now then, let us have it. Are you ready, Mr. Cheever?

PROCTOR , *with a cold, cold horror at their efficiency:* Why must it be written?

DANFORTH: Why, for the good instruction of the village, Mister; this we shall post upon the church door! *To* PARRIS, *urgently:* Where is the marshal?

PARRIS, *runs to the door and calls down the corridor:* Marshal! Hurry!

DANFORTH: Now, then, Mister, will you speak slowly, and directly to the point, for Mr. Cheever's sake. *He is on record now, and is really dictating to* CHEEVER, *who writes.* Mr. Proctor, have you seen the Devil in your life? PROCTOR'S *jaws lock.* Come, man, there is light in the sky; the town waits at the scaffold; I would give out this news. Did you see the Devil?

PROCTOR: I did.

PARRIS: Praise God!

DANFORTH: And when he come to you, what were his demand?

PROCTOR *is silent.* DANFORTH *helps.* Did he bid you to do his work upon the earth?

PROCTOR: He did.

DANFORTH: And you bound yourself to his service? DANFORTH *turns, as* REBECCA *Nurse enters, with* HERRICK *helping to support her. She is barely able to walk.* Come in, come in, woman!

REBECCA, *brightening as she sees* PROCTOR: Ah, John! You are well, then, eh?

PROCTOR *turns his face to the wall.*

DANFORTH: Courage, man, courage—let her witness your good example that she may come to God herself. Now hear it, Goody Nurse! Say on, Mr. Proctor. Did you bind yourself to the Devil's service?

REBECCA, *astonished:* Why, John!

PROCTOR, *through his teeth, his face turned from* REBECCA: I did.

DANFORTH: Now, woman, you surely see it profit nothin' to keep this conspiracy any further. Will you confess yourself with him?

REBECCA: Oh, John—God send his mercy on you!

DANFORTH: I say, will you confess yourself, Goody Nurse?

REBECCA: Why, it is a lie, it is a lie; how may I damn myself? I cannot, I cannot.

DANFORTH: Mr. Proctor. When the Devil came to you did you see Rebecca Nurse in his company? PROCTOR *is silent.* Come, man, take courage—did you ever see her with the Devil?

▲ Critical Viewing

Judge Danforth says, "He who weeps for these weeps for corruption." What do you think the people surrounding the condemned are thinking? **ANALYZE**

Comprehension

What sins does Elizabeth think she has committed?

Allegory

How might Proctor's refusal to incriminate others relate to the McCarthy hearings of the 1950s?

"I speak my own sins; I cannot judge another."

PROCTOR, *almost inaudibly:* No.

DANFORTH, *now sensing trouble, glances at* JOHN *and goes to the table, and picks up a sheet—the list of condemned.*

DANFORTH: Did you ever see her sister, Mary Easty, with the Devil?

PROCTOR: No, I did not.

DANFORTH, *his eyes narrow on* PROCTOR: Did you ever see Martha Corey with the Devil?

PROCTOR: I did not.

DANFORTH, *realizing, slowly putting the sheet down:* Did you ever see anyone with the Devil?

PROCTOR: I did not.

DANFORTH: Proctor, you mistake me. I am not empowered to trade your life for a lie. You have most certainly seen some person with the Devil. PROCTOR *is silent.* Mr. Proctor, a score of people have already testified they saw this woman with the Devil.

PROCTOR: Then it is proved. Why must I say it?

DANFORTH: Why "must" you say it! Why, you should rejoice to say it if your soul is truly purged of any love for Hell!

PROCTOR: They think to go like saints. I like not to spoil their names.

DANFORTH, *inquiring, incredulous:* Mr. Proctor, do you think they go like saints?

PROCTOR, *evading:* This woman never thought she done the Devil's work.

DANFORTH: Look you, sir. I think you mistake your duty here. It matter nothing what she thought—she is convicted of the unnatural murder of children, and you for sending your spirit out upon Mary Warren. Your soul alone is the issue here, Mister, and you will prove its whiteness or you cannot live in a Christian country. Will you tell me now what persons conspired with you in the Devil's company? PROCTOR *is silent.* To your knowledge was Rebecca Nurse ever—

PROCTOR: I speak my own sins; I cannot judge another. *Crying out, with hatred:* I have no tongue for it.

HALE, *quickly to* DANFORTH: Excellency, it is enough he confess himself. Let him sign it, let him sign it.

PARRIS, *feverishly:* It is a great service, sir. It is a weighty name; it will strike the village that Proctor confess. I beg you, let him sign it. The sun is up, Excellency!

DANFORTH, *considers; then with dissatisfaction:* Come, then, sign your testimony. *To* CHEEVER: Give it to him. CHEEVER *goes to* PROCTOR, *the confession and a pen in hand.* PROCTOR *does not look at it.* Come, man, sign it.

PROCTOR, *after glancing at the confession:* You have all witnessed it—it is enough.

DANFORTH: You will not sign it?

PROCTOR: You have all witnessed it; what more is needed?

DANFORTH: Do you sport with me? You will sign your name or it is no confession, Mister! *His breast heaving with agonized breathing,* PROCTOR *now lays the paper down and signs his name.*

PARRIS: Praise be to the Lord!

PROCTOR *has just finished signing when* DANFORTH *reaches for the paper. But* PROCTOR *snatches it up, and now a wild terror is rising in him, and a boundless anger.*

DANFORTH, *perplexed, but politely extending his hand:* If you please, sir.

PROCTOR: No.

DANFORTH, *as though* PROCTOR *did not understand:* Mr. Proctor, I must have—

PROCTOR: No, no. I have signed it. You have seen me. It is done! You have no need for this.

PARRIS: Proctor, the village must have proof that—

PROCTOR: Damn the village! I confess to God, and God has seen my name on this! It is enough!

DANFORTH: No, sir, it is—

PROCTOR: You came to save my soul, did you not? Here! I have confessed myself; it is enough!

DANFORTH: You have not con—

PROCTOR: I have confessed myself! Is there no good penitence but it be public? God does not need my name nailed upon the church! God sees my name; God knows how black my sins are! It is enough!

DANFORTH: Mr. Proctor—

PROCTOR: You will not use me! I am no Sarah Good or Tituba, I am John Proctor! You will not use me! It is no part of salvation that you should use me!

DANFORTH: I do not wish to—

PROCTOR: I have three children—how may I teach them to walk like men in the world, and I sold my friends?

DANFORTH: You have not sold your friends—

PROCTOR: Beguile me not! I blacken all of them when this is nailed to the church the very day they hang for silence!

DANFORTH: Mr. Proctor, I must have good and legal proof that you—

PROCTOR: You are the high court, your word is good enough! Tell them I confessed myself; say Proctor broke his knees and wept like a woman; say what you will, but my name cannot—

DANFORTH, *with suspicion:* It is the same, is it not? If I report it or you sign to it?

PROCTOR *—he knows it is insane:* No, it is not the same! What others say and what I sign to is not the same!

DANFORTH: Why? Do you mean to deny this confession when you are free?

PROCTOR: I mean to deny nothing!

DANFORTH: Then explain to me, Mr. Proctor, why you will not let—

Tragedy

In what ways do Proctor's statements here reflect those of a tragic hero?

Comprehension

What does Danforth want Proctor to do?

PROCTOR, *with a cry of his whole soul:* Because it is my name! Because I cannot have another in my life! Because I lie and sign myself to lies! Because I am not worth the dust on the feet of them that hang! How may I live without my name? I have given you my soul; leave me my name!

DANFORTH, *pointing at the confession in* PROCTOR'S *hand:* Is that document a lie? If it is a lie I will not accept it! What say you? I will not deal in lies, Mister! PROCTOR *is motionless.* You will give me your honest confession in my hand, or I cannot keep you from the rope. PROCTOR *does not reply.* What way do you go, Mister?

His breast heaving, his eyes staring, PROCTOR *tears the paper and crumples it, and he is weeping in fury, but erect.*

DANFORTH: Marshal!

PARRIS, *hysterically, as though the tearing paper were his life:* Proctor, Proctor!

HALE: Man, you will hang! You cannot!

Tragedy
What insight does Proctor express?

PROCTOR, *his eyes full of tears:* I can. And there's your first marvel, that I can. You have made your magic now, for now I do think I see some shred of goodness in John Proctor. Not enough to weave a banner with, but white enough to keep it from such dogs. ELIZABETH, *in a burst of terror, rushes to him and weeps against his hand.* Give them no tear! Tears pleasure them! Show honor now, show a stony heart and sink them with it! *He has lifted her, and kisses her now with great passion.*

REBECCA: Let you fear nothing! Another judgment waits us all!

Spiral Review
Biblical Allusion To what does Rebecca Nurse allude in saying, "Another judgment waits us all"?

DANFORTH: Hang them high over the town! Who weeps for these, weeps for corruption! *He sweeps out past them.* HERRICK *starts to lead* REBECCA, *who almost collapses, but* PROCTOR *catches her, and she glances up at him apologetically.*

REBECCA: I've had no breakfast.

HERRICK: Come, man.

HERRICK *escorts them out,* HATHORNE *and* CHEEVER *behind them.* ELIZABETH *stands staring at the empty doorway.*

PARRIS, *in deadly fear, to* ELIZABETH: Go to him, Goody Proctor! There is yet time!

From outside a drumroll strikes the air. PARRIS *is startled.* ELIZABETH *jerks about toward the window.*

PARRIS: Go to him! *He rushes out the door, as though to hold back his fate.* Proctor! Proctor!

Again, a short burst of drums.

HALE: Woman, plead with him! *He starts to rush out the door, and then goes back to her.* Woman! It is pride, it is vanity. *She avoids his eyes, and moves to the window. He drops to his knees.* Be his helper!—What profit him to bleed? Shall the dust praise him? Shall the worms declare his truth? Go to him, take his shame away!

ELIZABETH, *supporting herself against collapse, grips the bars of the window, and with a cry:* He have his goodness now. God forbid I take it from him!

The final drumroll crashes, then heightens violently. HALE *weeps in frantic prayer, and the new sun is pouring in upon her face, and the drums rattle like bones in the morning air.*

THE CURTAIN FALLS

Critical Reading

1. **Key Ideas and Details (a)** Who seeks confessions from Rebecca Nurse and other condemned prisoners? **(b) Infer:** What motivates this person—or people—to seek these confessions?
2. **Key Ideas and Details (a)** What unexpected action does Abigail take in this act? **(b) Draw Conclusions:** Why do you think she does this?
3. **Key Ideas and Details (a)** What decision torments John Proctor? **(b) Interpret:** What conflict does Elizabeth experience as her husband seeks her guidance?
4. **Key Ideas and Details (a)** What does John Proctor have "no tongue for"? **(b) Analyze:** Why does Proctor confess and then retract his confession?
5. **Key Ideas and Details Interpret:** Why does Elizabeth say her husband has "his goodness" as he is about to be hanged?
6. **Integration of Knowledge and Ideas** In the world of the play, are the sacrifices of characters like John Proctor and Rebecca Nurse meaningful and important? If so, to whom? How would you answer this question for the real world? In your response, use at least two Essential Question words: *nobility, lament, idealism, profound, humility.* ***[Connecting to the Essential Question: How does literature shape or reflect society?]***

Cite textual evidence to support your responses.

Close Reading Activities *The Crucible, Act IV*

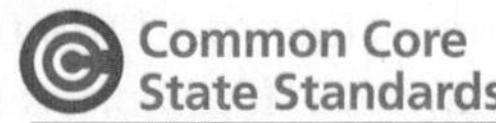

Literary Analysis

1. **Key Ideas and Details** **Evaluate the influence of the historical period** on characters by examining the role of the Puritans' religious views. In what ways do Proctor's religious convictions affect his choice of death over a false confession?
2. **Key Ideas and Details** In what ways do Hale's changing views of the trials reflect influences of the historical period?
3. **Craft and Structure** In what ways is *The Crucible* a **tragedy**? Explain, citing specific traits a dramatic tragedy contains and the effects it has on an audience.
4. **Craft and Structure** **(a)** Who is the **tragic hero** in *The Crucible*? **(b)** Why would this character be considered a tragic hero? **(c)** What other characters in the play could be considered tragic heroes?
5. **Craft and Structure** How is Proctor's downfall in *The Crucible* a combination of **(a)** fate; **(b)** a mistake in judgment; **(c)** a personality flaw?
6. **Craft and Structure** In many ancient tragedies, once the story is under way, the hero's downfall is inevitable. Are the downfalls of John Proctor, Rebecca Nurse, or any of the other characters in this drama inevitable? Explain.
7. **Craft and Structure** Using a chart like the one shown, cite examples from the play that show how ideas such as witchcraft and "the work of the Devil" function in *The Crucible* as an **allegory** for Communism.

Passage From the Text	How It Relates to Communism

8. **Integration of Knowledge and Ideas** **(a)** What does the ending of the play suggest about the value of integrity? **(b)** How might this idea relate to the McCarthy era?
9. **Integration of Knowledge and Ideas** Miller uses the proceedings of the Salem court as an allegory for the hearings conducted by Congress during the late 1940s to mid-1950s. Based on the play's details, what criticisms is Miller making about the way these congressional committees dealt with those it questioned and those who criticized it?
10. Analyze V**isual Information** Explain the dark humor in this cartoon.

Common Core State Standards

Language

4. Determine or clarify the meaning of unknown and multiple-meaning words and phrases based on *grades 11–12 reading and content*, choosing flexibly from a range of strategies. *(p. 1235)*

4.c. Consult general and specialized reference materials, both print and digital, to find the pronunciation of a word or determine or clarify its precise meaning, its part of speech, its etymology, or its standard usage. *(p. 1235)*

5. Demonstrate understanding of word relationships. *(p. 1235)*

▲ "It's Okay—We're Hunting Communists"

From "Herblock Special Report" (W.W. Norton, 1974). Reprinted by permission of the Herb Block Foundation.

Vocabulary Acquisition and Use

Word Analysis: Words from Myths

The word *tantalize* comes from the Greek myth about Tantalus, a man tormented by the gods. Likewise, the word *siren* comes from the myth about the Greek sea nymphs called Sirens, whose sweet singing lured sailors off course. Review the list of mythological characters below. Write a sentence using the word in parentheses that is derived from each character's name.

1. Ceres: Goddess of the harvest (cereal)
2. Titan: A race of giants with brute strength (titanic)
3. Narcissus: A boy punished by the gods for vanity (narcissistic)
4. Mars: God of war (martial)
5. Pan: God who caused fear in herds and crowds (panic)

Vocabulary: Synonyms

Synonyms are words that have the same, or nearly the same, meaning. Review the vocabulary list on page 1216. Then, for each item, select the letter of the word that is the closest in meaning to the first word.

1. **conciliatory: (a)** soothing, **(b)** rude, **(c)** vengeful
2. **beguile: (a)** plead, **(b)** fool, **(c)** straighten
3. **retaliation: (a)** narration, **(b)** restatement, **(c)** revenge
4. **adamant: (a)** calm, **(b)** first, **(c)** stubborn
5. **cleave: (a)** depart, **(b)** grow, **(c)** adhere
6. **tantalized: (a)** freed, **(b)** tempted, **(c)** danced

Using Resources to Build Vocabulary

Theatrical Words: Words for Cueing Actors

In the stage directions, Miller includes modifiers to describe the way he envisions actors speaking, reacting, and moving on the stage. Here are a few of them:

suspiciously (p. 1218)	politely (p. 1224)
instantly (p. 1219)	feverishly (p. 1230)
prayerfully (p. 1219)	hysterically (p. 1232)

Review these words by rereading the relevant lines in the play. Then, use a print or electronic thesaurus to find a synonym for each word. For example, a synonym for *politely* might be *courteously.* On your own paper, rewrite the stage directions in which the word appears, replacing the word with your synonym. Reread the stage directions. In a few sentences, explain why Miller would choose vivid words to direct the speech and movement of actors.

Close Reading Activities Continued

Writing to Sources

Explanatory Text Although Miller wrote *The Crucible* in response to the hysteria caused by the anti-Communist hearings of the late 1940s to 1950s, the themes of the play have endured. Indeed, *The Crucible* remains one of the most-performed plays worldwide. Write an **essay** in which you interpret the play's primary themes and explain how they reflect both the play's historical context and universal human issues.

Prewriting Review the play and briefly summarize the action of each act. Then, generate a list of the themes, or essential ideas, you think are most important. Use a chart like the one shown to examine ideas that reflect the play's historical period and also have a universal application. List characters and situations in the play that exemplify the themes you identify. Then, list events from the world at large that reflect a more expansive, timeless version of the themes.

Model: Identifying Universal Themes

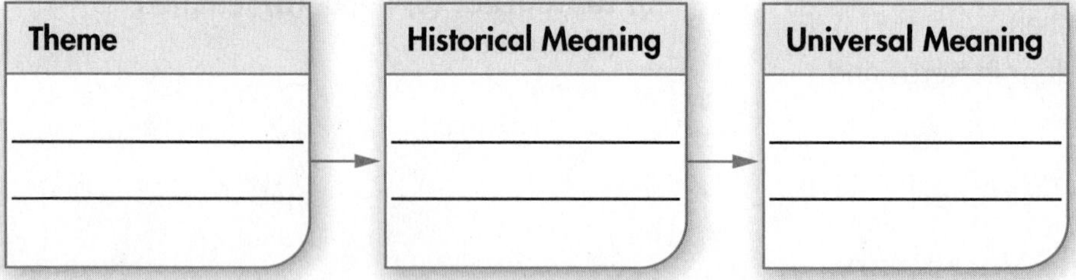

Drafting Organize your essay by focusing on one theme at a time.

- Clearly state the first theme.
- Next, identify the historical context in which the theme is presented. Discuss how the theme has meaning within that context.
- Explain that a universal theme is meaningful to all people in all times and places. Discuss how the theme you chose is relevant to people regardless of where—or when—they happen to live.
- Draw details that illustrate universal thematic appeal from your own experiences and knowledge.

Continue this pattern of organization with the remaining themes. End your essay with a strong conclusion that reviews the themes you discussed, along with your explanations of their universality. To end on a compelling note, suggest current issues or situations that you think might become the next best expression of the play's themes.

Revising As you review your draft, note places where you could clarify the connection between the historical and universal meanings of a theme. Add strong, clear transitions to help guide the reader through your ideas.

Common Core State Standards

Writing

2. Write explanatory texts to examine and convey complex ideas, concepts, and information clearly and accurately through the effective selection, organization, and analysis of content.

2.a. Introduce a topic; organize complex ideas, concepts, and information so that each new element builds on that which precedes it to create a unified whole.

2.b. Develop the topic thoroughly by selecting the most significant and relevant facts, extended definitions, concrete details, quotations, or other information and examples appropriate to the audience's knowledge of the topic.

2.f. Provide a concluding statement or section that follows from and supports the information or explanation presented.

9.a. Apply *grades 11–12 Reading standards* to literature. [RL.11-12.2]

Language

1. Demonstrate command of the conventions of standard English grammar and usage when writing or speaking. *(p. 1237)*

Conventions and Style: Avoiding Sentence Fragments and Run-ons

A **sentence fragment** is a group of words with end punctuation that is missing a subject, a verb, or both. A **run-on sentence** is two or more sentences punctuated as one. Work to avoid these two common errors in your writing.

Correcting Fragments

Fragment: *The Crucible*, a play by Arthur Miller.

Add to another sentence: I enjoyed the production of *The Crucible*, a play by Arthur Miller.

Add a subject or verb: *The Crucible* is a play by Arthur Miller.

Correcting Run-Ons

Run-on sentence: The setting was Salem in 1692 young girls caused much suffering.

1. Add punctuation: The setting was Salem in 1692. Young girls caused much suffering.

2. Add a comma and conjunction: The setting was Salem in 1692, and young girls caused much suffering.

3. Add a semicolon: The setting was Salem in 1692; young girls caused much suffering.

Practice Rewrite each item as a sentence. If an item is a complete sentence, write "Correct."

1. John Proctor, a respected, hard-working farmer, known to be strong and steady.
2. Rebecca Nurse accused one reason may have been resentment against her husband.
3. The Putnams were bitter because they had had eight children yet only one survived birth.
4. The Devil was used as a weapon to control people make them obey out of fear.
5. Reverend Parris believed there were much more sinful households in Salem than his.
6. Giles Corey, at age eighty. Both a nuisance and a brave man.
7. Reverend John Hale arrived in Salem armed with books, he came to fight the Devil.
8. John Proctor appeared. With a testament signed by ninety-one people.
9. Giles refused to name those who gave him information was arrested.
10. John Proctor confessed his own sin. Refused to judge others.

Writing and Speaking Conventions

A. Writing Rewrite the paragraph below, eliminating any fragments and run-ons. You may combine two sentences or break one item into more than one sentence.

Reverend Parris was a straitlaced man. Often felt persecuted by others. His daughter, Betty, lay in bed as if dead then she sat up screaming. After Abigail made accusations. Betty said she saw townspeople with the Devil. Hysteria seemed to spread like a virus through Salem neighboring villages were not affected.

Example: His daughter, Betty, lay in bed as if dead then she sat up screaming.

Rewritten Sentence: His daughter, Betty, lay in bed as if dead; then she sat up screaming.

B. Speaking Deliver testimony from the point of view of one of the characters in the play. Briefly tell what you did and why. Avoid sentence fragments and run-ons as you speak.

POLITICAL DRAMA AROUND THE WORLD

Dramatists around the world and throughout history have used the power of the stage to communicate their ideas about social and political situations.

Comparing Literary Works

The Crucible* • from *Good Night, and Good Luck

Comparing Political Drama Past and Present

The Crucible is part of a tradition of political drama begun by the first Western dramatists, the ancient Greeks. Greek playwrights such as Aristophanes and Sophocles in the fifth century B.C. wrote and staged plays about the politics of war, gender, and politics itself. From the Greeks to Arthur Miller, political drama exhibits the following qualities:

- It reflects the author's political opinions.
- It characterizes a politician or describes a series of political events.
- It questions inequities or injustices in society.
- It examines a political issue from the past or present, or uses past events to comment on current problems.

Today, political drama appears in movies and television programs, as well as stage plays. In their screenplay for the movie *Good Night, and Good Luck* (2005), George Clooney and Grant Heslov, like Arthur Miller before them, focus on the "red scare" of the 1950s. They do so, however, from a very different angle. As you read the excerpt, use a chart like the one shown to compare how Miller and Clooney and Heslov represent political ideas in dramatic form.

Common Core State Standards

Reading Literature
1. Cite strong and thorough textual evidence to support analysis of what the text says explicitly as well as inferences drawn from the text, including determining where the text leaves matters uncertain.

Language
4.c. Consult general and specialized reference materials, both print and digital, to find the pronunciation of a word or determine or clarify its precise meaning, its part of speech, its etymology, or its standard usage.

	Miller	Clooney and Heslov
Specific Political Figures	• Puritan leaders of Salem • Senator Joseph McCarthy	
Specific Events	• Salem witch trials • Senate hearings	
Opinion (stated or implied)	Those instigating both events were blameworthy.	
Critique of Society (stated or implied)	Miller critiques both the individuals who create mass hysteria and the communities that submit to it.	

Gather Vocabulary Knowledge

These selections include forms of *vulnerable, acknowledge, statute,* and *disregard.* Use the following references to explore these words.

- **Book of Quotations:** Use a print or online collection to find a quotation containing one of the words. Explain the meaning of the quotation.
- **Other Related References:** Use resources, such as a visual thesaurus or a vocabulary builder, to learn more about each word's meanings. Create a word map for one of the words, including three synonyms, three antonyms, and a sentence in which you use the word correctly.

George Clooney (born 1961)
Grant Heslov (born 1963)

Co-Authors of ***Good Night, and Good Luck***

▲ George Clooney and Grant Heslov

GEORGE CLOONEY, born in Lexington, Kentucky, has been surrounded by acting, television, and politics all his life. His father, Nick Clooney, was a long-time television newscaster and ran for Congress as a representative from Kentucky in 2004. Clooney had a famous aunt, uncle, and cousin in the film industry. In 1994, he gained national recognition as Dr. Doug Ross on the television drama *ER*.

Acting and Directing Clooney followed his successful television career with critically acclaimed work as a film actor and director. *Good Night, and Good Luck* (2005), about broadcast journalist Edward R. Murrow and his battle against Senator Joseph McCarthy, brings all of Clooney's familial influences together: television, journalism, and politics.

GRANT HESLOV, born in Pittsburgh, Pennsylvania, is an actor, director, and producer who has often worked with George Clooney. Heslov's commitment to producing political drama continues with Clooney. Together, they started Smoke House productions to make smaller films, one of which will tell the story of a man unjustly sent to prison for a murder he did not commit.

GOOD NIGHT, AND GOOD LUCK
Cast of Characters

Good Night, and Good Luck features a clash between two high-profile personalities: Edward R. Murrow, the pioneering 1950s broadcast journalist, and Senator Joseph McCarthy, who pursued an obsessive search for communists in positions of power.

Edward R. Murrow	Journalist, star of television news show *See It Now*
Don Hewitt	Television news executive; director of *See It Now*
Joe Wershba	Television journalist; colleague of Murrow's
Shirley Wershba	Television journalist; colleague of Murrow's
Fred Friendly	Television journalist; colleague of Murrow's
Joseph McCarthy	Senator from Wisconsin who instigated "Red Scare" with his pursuit of supposed communists in the U.S.
William Paley	Chairman of the Board of the CBS television network

from good night, and good luck

George Clooney
Grant Heslov

▲ David Strathairn as Edward R. Murrow

BACKGROUND As this excerpt begins, Murrow's newsroom staff is preparing to air McCarthy's rebuttal to a story Murrow had run about the senator. The story was true and dangerous, for it showed McCarthy to be using unfair, unethical methods. Interestingly, the movie includes historical footage of that rebuttal. Woven into this section of the screenplay is a a verbatim transcript of McCarthy's speech as it aired on Murrow's CBS news show *See It Now* in 1954.

INT.[1] CONTROL ROOM—SHOW NIGHT

This scene will be built with a lot of very tight close ups of crew and reporters. Everyone is very aware of their vulnerability. Cameramen glancing at one another. Stage Manager focusing on the monitor.

Right now it's silent as they wait for MURROW to arrive.

We pull Ed in a close up as he enters into the room and sees the film canisters.

HEWITT. Ed, it's twenty eight minutes. I could clip a little off the end for you to have time to . . .

MURROW. I think we have to leave it alone, Don.

He starts tearing out pages.

Vocabulary
vulnerability (vəln ə rə bil′ ət ē) *n.* state of being open to attack, criticism, or temptation

Comprehension
What is the setting of this scene?

1. **INT** interior.

MURROW (CONT'D)

Very smart, no time for comment . . . when did it come in?

HEWITT. Ten minutes ago. We put it up, I saw the first couple of minutes, you're right.

MURROW. Coming after me?

HEWITT nods.

MURROW (CONT'D)

Joe, have you seen the latest polls? . . . The most trustworthy man in America is Milton Berle.[2]

WERSHBA. Maybe he should do the story.

MURROW. Get him on the line, will ya?

MURROW walks onto the stage. FRIENDLY'S there. Against the back wall are Murrow's team.

MURROW (CONT'D)

Vocabulary

acknowledges (ak näl′ ij əz) *v.* to admit the existence, reality, or truth of something

Fred.

FRIENDLY. What say we grab a little dinner after the show? The 21 Club?

MURROW. Sure.

He sits noticing The Boys. They give little waves, MURROW acknowledges them.

▲ George Clooney directing actors Frank Langella and David Strathairn

MURROW (CONT'D)

What're they here for? "The Monkey and the Bell" show is on stage three.

FRIENDLY. They changed the title. "Goin' Ape."

MURROW. Who's their first guest?

The loudspeaker—"Thirty seconds to Air"

FRIENDLY. After tonight, I hear it's you.

They smile.

FRIENDLY (CONT'D)

Look, there's nothing fun about this one. You've just gotta put your gloves down, stick your chin out and just take it for a whole round. Next week's our round.

MURROW. If I make it up off the mat.

MURROW takes out a cigarette, FRIENDLY lights it.

Loudspeaker—"Twenty seconds to air"

2. Milton Berle (1908–2002) Comedian and first major star of television.

▲ David Strathairn as Edward R. Murrow on the set of *See it Now*

FRIENDLY. You will.

MURROW. Did you see the latest polls, Milton Berle's the most trusted man in America . . .

FRIENDLY. You already did this joke for me . . .

They look at each other.

FRIENDLY (CONT'D)

I'll get Berle on the line.

Loudspeaker—"Ten seconds"

MURROW sits there again in silence. The weight of the world sitting there with him.

STAGE MANAGER. In five, four, three, two . . .

He points to MURROW.

We come up on the monitor as MURROW speaks directly at us.

MURROW. One month ago tonight we presented a report on Senator Joseph R. McCarthy. We labeled it as controversial. Most of that report consisted of words and pictures of the Senator. At that time, we said if the Senator believes we have done violence to his words or pictures, if he desires to speak, to answer himself, an opportunity would be afforded him on this program. The Senator sought the opportunity, asked for a delay of three weeks because he said he was very busy and he wished adequate time to prepare his reply. We agreed. We placed no restrictions on the manner or method of the presentation of his reply and we suggested that we would not take time to comment on this program. Here now is Senator Joseph R. McCarthy, Junior Senator from Wisconsin.

McCarthy begins. As he delivers his rebuttal we will cut to various places that it is airing. For the moment we're right on MURROW as he watches.

Comprehension
What is McCarthy's reason for being on Murrow's show?

▲ Patricia Clarkson as Shirley Wershba and Robert Downey, Jr. as Joe Wershba

MCCARTHY. Good evening. Mr. Edward R. Murrow, Educational Director of the Columbia Broadcasting System, devoted his program to an attack on the work of the United States Senate investigating committee and on me personally as its Chairman. Now, over the past four years, he has made repeated attacks upon me and those fighting communists. Now, of course, neither Joe McCarthy nor Edward R. Murrow is of any great importance as individuals. We are only important in our relations to the great struggle to preserve our American liberties.

CUT TO:[3]

INT. PALEY'S OFFICE

PALEY watches in silence.

Now ordinarily, I wouldn't take time out of the important work at hand to answer Murrow. However in this case I felt justified in doing so because Murrow is a symbol, the leader and the cleverest of the jackal pack which is always found at the throat of anyone who dares expose individual communists and traitors.

Comparing Literary Works
Political Drama
Why do you think the screenwriters chose to include actual footage of McCarthy's rebuttal?

CUT TO:

INT. JOE & SHIRLEY WERSHBA'S NY APT.

Shirley watches.

I am compelled by the fact to say to you that Mr. Edward R. Murrow, as far back as twenty years ago was engaged in propaganda for communist causes. For example, the Institute for International Education of which he was the Acting Director, was chosen to act as a representative by a Soviet agency to do a job which would normally be done by the Russian Secret Police.

3. **CUT TO** Screenwriter's shorthand to indicate a change of scene; the camera "cuts to" a new location.

Back to MURROW on the set.

Mr. Murrow sponsored a communist school in Moscow . . .

This speech will continue but we'll hear MURROW and FRIENDLY talking.

MURROW. When the politicians complain that TV turns the proceedings into a circus, it should be clear that the circus was already there, and that TV has only demonstrated that not all the performers are well trained.

FRIENDLY. We've got him, Ed.

MURROW. If he led with his best.

FRIENDLY. He led with his best.

CUT TO:

INT. PALEY'S OFFICE

MCCARTHY. Now, Mr. Murrow, by his own admission, was a member of the IWW, that's the Industrial Workers of the World, a terrorist organization cited by an Attorney General of the United States . . .

CUT TO:

INT. HALLWAY CBS

It's empty. McCarthy's voice echoing.

MCCARTHY. Now, Mr. Murrow said on this program and I quote, he said, "The actions of the Junior Senator from Wisconsin have given considerable comfort to the enemy."

MURROW walks into the hall followed by FRIENDLY, WERSHBA, MACK; they walk toward us as the speech continues.

MCCARTHY (CONT'D)

That is the language of our statute of treason. If I am giving comfort to our enemies, I ought not to be in the Senate. If on the other hand, Mr. Murrow is giving comfort to the enemies, he ought not to be brought into the homes of Americans by the Columbia Broadcasting System.

As they exit we stay on the empty hallway. We fade to black as McCarthy drones on. WE'LL PLAY AN ALCOA COMMERCIAL HERE

INT. SEE IT NOW SET

We are on the set of *See it Now* as MURROW addresses us directly.

MURROW. Last week, Senator McCarthy appeared on this program to correct any errors he might have thought we made in our report of March 9th. Since he made no reference to

▼ Director George Clooney behind the camera

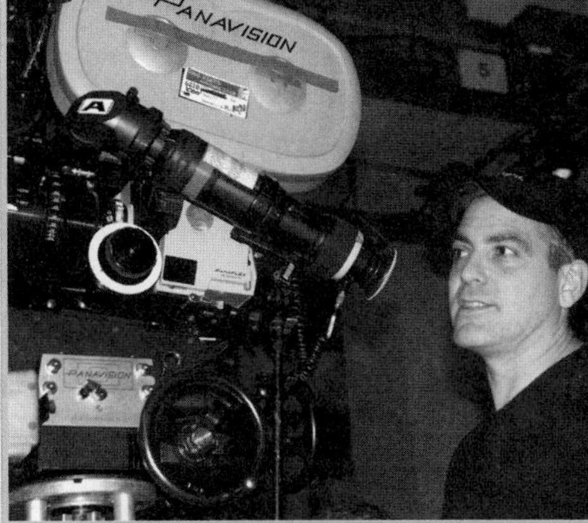

Vocabulary

statute (stach′ o͝ot) *n.* document in which a standard, rule, or law is expressed

Comprehension

What organization does McCarthy say Murrow once joined?

any statements of fact that we made, we must conclude that he found no errors of fact. He proved again that anyone who exposes him, anyone who does not share his hysterical disregard to decency and human dignity and the rights guaranteed by the Constitution must be either a Communist or a fellow traveler. I fully expected this treatment. The Senator added this reporter's name to a long list of individuals and institutions he has accused of serving the communist cause. His proposition is very simple: Anyone who criticizes or opposes McCarthy's methods must be a Communist. And if that be true, there are an awful lot of Communists in this country. For the record, let's consider briefly some of the Senator's charges.

Vocabulary

disregard (dis ri gärd′) *v.* to pay no attention to; ignore

(MORE)

MURROW (CONT'D)

He claimed but offered no proof that I had been a member of the Industrial Workers of the World. That is false. I was never a member of the IWW, never applied for membership.

▲ Grant Heslov as Don Hewitt

CUT TO:

INT. CONTROL BOOTH

We cut to the control booth, PALMER WILLIAMS and company watch on as the broadcast continues.

WILLIAMS. Ready two . . . hold it . . . hold . . . take two . . . tell 'em Ed.

MURROW. The Senator charged that Professor Harold Laski, a British scholar and politician dedicated a book to me. That's true. He is dead. He was a Socialist, I am not. He was one of those civilized individuals who did not insist upon agreement with his political principles as a pre-condition for conversation or friendship. I do not agree with his political ideas. Laski, as he makes clear in the introduction, dedicated the book to me not because of political agreement but because he held my wartime broadcast from London in high regard; and the dedication so reads.

WILLIAMS. Ready on one . . . closer, Charlie . . . take one . . .

CUT TO:

INT. SEE IT NOW SET

Again MURROW addresses us directly.

MURROW. I believed twenty years ago and I believe today that mature Americans can engage in conversation and controversy, the clash of ideas, with Communists anywhere in the world without becoming contaminated or converted. I believe that our faith, our conviction, our determination are stronger than

▲ George Clooney as Fred Friendly and David Strathairn as Edward R. Murrow behind the scenes of *See it Now*

theirs and that we can compete and successfully, not only in the area of bombs but in the area of ideas.

CUT TO:

INT. PALEY'S OFFICE

As PALEY watches on a television.

I have worked for CBS for more than nineteen years. The company has subscribed fully to my integrity and responsibility as a broadcaster and as a loyal American. I require no lectures from the junior Senator from Wisconsin as to the dangers or terrors of Communism—having watched the aggressive forces at work in Western Europe.

CUT TO:

INT. SEE IT NOW SET

Having had friends in Eastern Europe butchered and driven in exile, having broadcast from London in 1943 that the Russians were responsible for the Katyn Massacre—having told the story of the Russian refusal to allow allied aircraft to land on Russian fields after dropping supplies to those who rose in Warsaw and then were betrayed by the Russians.

CUT TO:

INT. BULLPEN

Murrow's team watch.

WERSHBA. (Quietly)
Go Ed.

MURROW. And having been denounced by the Russian radio for

Comprehension
What personal beliefs does Murrow express?

▲ Director Clooney with actor Ray Wise and producer/co-writer Grant Heslov on set

these reports. I cannot feel that I require instruction from the Senator on the evils of Communism.

CUT TO:

INT.* SEE IT NOW *SET

MURROW addresses us directly.

Having searched my conscience and my files, I cannot contend that I have always been right or wise but, I have attempted to pursue the truth with some diligence and to report it, even though as in this case I had been warned in advance that I would be subjected to the attentions of Senator McCarthy. We shall hope to deal with matters of more vital interest to the country next week. Good night. And, good luck.

We go to a commercial. As we hear it play, we see Murrow stand up. He shakes people's hands, there are some pats on the back . . . not victorious . . . not afraid . . . simply a job well done.

Critical Reading

Cite textual evidence to support your responses.

1. **Key Ideas and Details** **(a)** Why was McCarthy invited to speak on Murrow's program? **(b) Draw Conclusions:** What use does McCarthy make of his time on Murrow's program?
2. **Key Ideas and Details** **(a)** What charges does McCarthy make against Murrow, and what is Murrow's response? **(b) Interpret:** Why would McCarthy make such claims against Murrow?

After You Read *The Crucible* • from *Good Night, and Good Luck*

Comparing Political Drama Past and Present

1. **Integration of Knowledge and Ideas** **(a)** Explain Miller's opinion regarding the hysteria surrounding the witch hunt in *The Crucible.* **(b)** What opinions do you think Clooney and Heslov hold about Murrow and McCarthy? Explain. **(c)** Are the authors' views in the two works similar? Explain.
2. **Integration of Knowledge and Ideas** **(a)** The events portrayed in *The Crucible* occurred in the 1600s. What modern political event underlies the play? **(b)** How are aspects of that political struggle dramatized in the screenplay?
3. **Integration of Knowledge and Ideas** **(a)** Does *The Crucible* engage politics of the distant past, the modern era, or both? **(b)** Does the political story in *Good Night, and Good Luck* reflect distant history, modern times, or both? Explain.

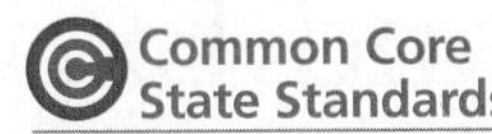

Common Core State Standards

Writing

2. Write explanatory texts to examine and convey complex ideas, concepts, and information clearly and accurately through the effective selection, organization, and analysis of content.

10. Write routinely over shorter time frames for a range of tasks, purposes, and audiences.

Timed Writing

Explanatory Text: Essay

Political playwrights like Miller, Clooney, and Heslov present their own opinions and perspectives through the characters and events of their stories.

Assignment: Write an **essay** in which you analyze the author's political opinions as they are expressed through the two works. Identify the characters in each work that most clearly articulate the political viewpoints of the author or authors. Determine whether those characters are effective or ineffective as the voice of the authors' political views. **[40 minutes]**

Use these questions to focus your analysis.

- Which specific actions or dialogue suggest that a character speaks for the author?
- How do other characters help define these opinions?
- Is drama an effective form for the expression of political views? Explain, citing details of your analysis as support.

As you write, follow the conventions of a strong analytical essay:

- Advance a clear thesis statement.
- Follow a clear organizational plan. Arrange the body of your essay either point by point, or in two sections, one for each play.

USE ACADEMIC VOCABULARY

As you write, use academic language, including the following words or their related forms:

illustrate
convey
contrast
protest

For more information about academic language, see the vocabulary charts in the introduction to this book.

5-Minute Planner

Complete these steps before you begin to write:

1. Read the assignment carefully. Jot down key words and phrases.
2. Scan the selections, looking for details that illustrate the points you want to make. **TIP** As you jot down details from the selections, put points you want to compare or contrast side by side.
3. Decide whether to use point-by-point or two-section organization.
4. Reread the prompt, and draft your essay.

Reading for Information

Analyzing Argumentative and Expository Texts

Theater/Film Review • Feature Article

About the Texts

A **review** is a persuasive nonfiction article in which a writer states an opinion about a work of art. Books, movies, museum exhibitions, plays, concerts, and other artworks or performances are the usual topics of reviews. Reviews usually include a summary of a work; a clear statement of opinion about the work's quality; a quick review device, such as numbered stars; and ticket or contact information.

A **feature article** is a work of nonfiction about a general-interest topic. Unlike news articles that focus on current events, feature articles explore trends, events, or personalities. The basic structure of a feature article includes an attention-grabbing lead, or opening that establishes a theme; a body of facts, anecdotes, quotes, and details; and photos or illustrations of the article's subject.

Common Core State Standards

Reading Informational Text
5. Analyze and evaluate the effectiveness of the structure an author uses in his or her exposition or argument, including whether the structure makes points clear, convincing, and engaging.

Preparing to Read Complex Texts

In feature articles—and especially reviews—a writer builds meaning and a sense of knowledgeable insight by weaving fact and opinion together in an authoritative way. As you read reviews and feature articles, **distinguish between fact and opinion** and assess how the writer applies different types of information to build and support his or her ideas:

- **Facts:** hard data, such as statistics, dates, and events, that can be proved true and do not change with the context
- **Opinions:** statements of belief that cannot be proved true or false; may use language that is evaluative ("too much"; "genuine contribution") or emotional ("powerful"; "silly")

As you read, use a chart like the one shown to identify fact and opinion in the reviews and article.

Facts	Opinions
Summaries:	Evaluative Language:
Dates/Events/People:	Emotional Language:

Content-Area Vocabulary

These words appear in the selections that follow. They may also appear in other content-area texts.

trials (trī´ əlz) *n.* in law, examinations of evidence and charges to determine claims or punishments

accusation (ak´ yo͞o zā´ shən) *n.* act of charging someone with an error

tribunal (trī´ byo͞o´ nəl) *n.* court of justice

adaptation (a dap tā´ shən) *n.* modification of a work for production in another medium

This classic review is by a famous theater critic whose approval or disapproval often determined a play's success.

The New York Times

January 23, 1953

The Crucible

By Brooks Atkinson

The reviewer begins with a general assessment of the play and then follows with a brief summary.

Arthur Miller has written another powerful play. *The Crucible*, it is called, and it opened at the Martin Beck last evening in an equally powerful performance. Riffling back the pages of American history, he has written the drama of the witch **trials** and hangings in Salem in 1692. Neither Mr. Miller nor his audiences are unaware of certain similarities between the perversions of justice then and today.

But Mr. Miller is not pleading a cause in dramatic form. For *The Crucible*, despite its current implications, is a self-contained play about a terrible period in American history. Silly **accusations** of witchcraft by some mischievous girls in Puritan dress gradually take possession of Salem. Before the play is over good people of pious nature and responsible temper are condemning other good people to the gallows.

Having a sure instinct for dramatic form, Mr. Miller goes bluntly to essential situations. John Proctor and his wife, farm people, are the central characters of the play. At first the idea that Goodie Proctor is a witch is only an absurd rumor. But *The Crucible* carries the Proctors through the whole ordeal—first vague suspicion, then the arrest, the implacable, highly wrought trial in the church vestry, the final opportunity for John Proctor to save his neck by confessing to something he knows is a lie, and finally the baleful roll of the drums at the foot of the gallows.

Although *The Crucible* is a powerful drama, it stands second to *Death of a Salesman* as a work of art. Mr. Miller has had more trouble with this one, perhaps because he is too conscious of its implications. The literary style is cruder. . . .

It may be that Mr. Miller . . . has permitted himself to be concerned more with the technique of the witch hunt than with its humanity. For all its power generated on the surface, *The Crucible* is most moving in the simple, quiet scenes between John Proctor and his wife. By the standards of *Death of a Salesman*, there is too much excitement and not enough emotion in *The Crucible*.

As the director, Jed Harris has given it a driving performance in which the clashes are fierce and clamorous. Inside Boris Aronson's gaunt, pitiless sets of rude buildings, the acting is at a high pitch of bitterness, anger and fear. As the patriarchal deputy Governor, Walter Hampden gives one of his most vivid performances in which righteousness and ferocity are unctuously mated. Fred Stewart as a vindictive parson, E. G. Marshall as a parson who finally rebels at the indiscriminate ruthlessness of the trial, Jean Adair as an aging woman of God . . . all give able performances.

As John Proctor and his wife, Arthur Kennedy and Beatrice Straight have the most attractive roles in the drama. . . . They are superb—Mr. Kennedy clear and resolute, full of fire, searching his own mind; Miss Straight, reserved, detached, above and beyond the contention. Like all the members of the cast, they are dressed in the chaste and lovely costumes Edith Lutyens has designed from old prints of early Massachusetts.

After the experience of *Death of a Salesman* we probably expect Mr. Miller to write a Masterpiece every time. *The Crucible* is not of that stature and it lacks that universality. On a lower level of dramatic history with considerable pertinence for today, it is a powerful play and a genuine contribution to the season.

Film Review

Los Angeles Times

Dec. 13, 1996

Hysteria Resides at Heart of Frantic 'Crucible'

KENNETH TURAN

The title identifies the topic of the review and suggests the writer's opinion.

The Crucible, Arthur Miller's play about fear of the devil on the loose in colonial Massachusetts, comes to the screen with powerful credentials: high-profile stars Daniel Day-Lewis and Winona Ryder, the impressive Paul Scofield and Joan Allen in supporting roles, Miller himself doing the screenplay and director Nicholas Hytner in his first film since *The Madness of King George.*

And the play itself, which debuted in 1953, has manifested a powerful durability, selling 6 million copies in paperback in this country alone and allowing Miller to recently claim, "I don't think there has been a week in the past 40-odd years when it hasn't been on the stage somewhere in the world."

But whenever a film has hysteria as its subject, as this one does, the danger exists that it will become hysterical itself, and *The Crucible,* all its promise notwithstanding, falls into that trap with a demoralizing thud. Rife with screaming fits and wild-eyed rantings, this film is too frantic to be involving, too much an outpost of bedlam to be believable.

Part of the difficulty may be inherent in adapting a theater piece to the movies, with Miller himself noting in the introduction to his published screenplay that "the play wants to tell, the movie to show . . . the stage scene is written to be vocally projected onto an audience, a movie scene wants to be overheard." Which makes hysteria on film considerably harder to tolerate than in the stage version.

And, especially in its second half, when Lewis gets warmed up and Scofield and Allen do the brunt of their impeccable work, the film is not without its quietly effective moments. But they are too few and too late to make sufficient headway against the rampant tide of frenzy that is the film's signature emotion.

The madness starts early, as Abigail Williams (Ryder) and her cousin Betty sneak out of their Salem house one night in 1692 and join other young girls for a fairly innocent gathering headed by the slave Tituba (Charlayne Woodard).

While most of the girls are content to wish for help with the boys they have crushes on. Abigail has darker thoughts in mind. But before it's clear what they are, Betty's father, the fatuous Rev. Parris (Bruce Davison) stumbles on their group and Betty is so traumatized at being caught she goes into a trance.

As modern Americans prefer to blame "the government" for all ills, their colonial counterparts put everything on "the devil," and little Betty's spell brings to Salem the respected Rev. Hale (Rob Campbell), a specialist in Satan and all his black arts.

Fearful of being found out. Abigail and her teenage friends raise the stakes by insisting the evil one made them do it. The new sense of empowerment they feel in suddenly being taken seriously encourages them to scream and scream again. Soon the town is rife with accusation and counter-accusation, as the high-decibel charge of witchcraft is manipulated by adults as well as children for their own power and property aims. . . .

Though Ryder's performance is fatally hampered by the one-note nature of her part, her co-star does somewhat better. Always adept at suffering and looking here like the brooding hero of "Mohicans II: The Colonial Years," Day-Lewis gets to fully inhabit his part only in the film's later stages when he attempts to be the community's voice of sanity.

It is no coincidence that both Day-Lewis and Allen, finely drawn as the wife uncertain of her husband's love, flourish in their scenes with Scofield as Judge Danforth, the somber leader of a **tribunal** sent to investigate the witchcraft allegations.

Using his celebrated presence and commanding voice, Scofield emphasizes the sincerity in the judge and makes him a figure of formidable dignity and power, able to wring everything there is out of Miller's artificial lines. Only in Scofield's scenes can director Hytner, whose penchant for high emotion served him better in "King George," be persuaded to pitch things at a human level.

Despite these involving moments, *The Crucible* finally seems too schematic, more useful as an allegory than as drama, and possibly owing that undoubted popularity to its simplistic qualities as much as its insights into group psychology.

It's also interesting to note that many of the original stage reviewers had similar reservations about the play. *The New York Times* said, "There is too much excitement and not enough emotion in *The Crucible,* and the *Herald Tribune's* Walter Kerr called it "a step backward into mechanical parable." Those seeing the new film version will appreciate the wisdom of those words as much as Miller's.

The reviewer quotes historical reviews of the play to support his opinion.

The New York Times

The title clearly shows the reader this profile is about Arthur Miller.

A Rock of the Modern Age, Arthur Miller is Everywhere

By Mel Gussow

When Arthur Miller was in Alaska to receive an award this year, he and a local environmental official went fishing for salmon in Prince William Sound. As they passed an iceberg, Mr. Miller's companion leaned over the side of the boat, chopped off pieces of blue glacial ice and threw them into the bucket with the fish. "That ice is probably millennia old," the playwright said in a recent interview. "Eight-million-year-old ice! It doesn't melt."

If ice can last that long, perhaps that says something about the survival of civilization—and art. Mr. Miller, who has never been known to sidestep a metaphor, smiled and said, "You hang around long enough . . . you don't melt."

In his 60-year career, Mr. Miller has been impervious to winds of fashion and periods of critical neglect. Even when receptivity for his work waned on Broadway, he found an audience in other countries, particularly in England, where he has been honored for his plays and also for his political consciousness.

The writer draws connections between various moments in Miller's career.

Just turned 81, he finds himself in the middle of one of his busiest seasons. Nicholas Hytner's passionate film version of *The Crucible,* starring Daniel Day-Lewis and Winona Ryder, opened this week to generally favorable reviews. In *The New York Times,* Janet Maslin called it a "vibrant" and "beautifully acted" **adaptation** of Mr. Miller's 1953 play about witch hunts and marital betrayal in 17th-century Salem, Mass. Davis Thacker's television film of *Broken Glass* was shown last month on Masterpiece Theater, and his revival of *Death of a Salesman* recently opened at the Royal National Theater in London.

With both the film of *The Crucible* and the television production of *Broken Glass,* there is a trans-Atlantic creative alliance. Each is directed by an Englishman and has a British and American cast. Although Mr. Miller's work has been closely identified with American actors (from Lee J. Cobb to Dustin Hoffman in *Death of a Salesman*), certain English actors have also expressed a natural affinity for his work, including Mr. Day-Lewis and Paul Scofield in *The Crucible* and Michael Gambon, who gave a galvanizing performance in *A View From the Bridge* several years ago at the Royal National Theater.

Analyzing his English connection, Mr. Miller said, "Maybe because of the large amounts of work they do on classical plays, there's an assumption there that fundamentally a play is a metaphor, not simply a series of actions by characters."

From his perspective, his work is not basically naturalistic. With his assent, foreign productions often emphasize the symbolic aspects, as in a Swedish version of *The Last Yankee,* which had a six-foot rose as a life-enhancing emblem at the center of the production. There is no such flower in the text.

In the National Theater production of *Death of a Salesman,* Mr. Thacker has unmoored the play from its realistic roots. On an open turntable stage are aligned artifacts of Willy Loman's life: his old car and refrigerator and beds from Brooklyn to Boston. In a surprising, perhaps temporary turnabout for the playwright, the play and production received mixed reviews from London critics.

The writer is even-handed and fair, presenting both positive and negative reactions to Miller's work.

With the film of *The Crucible,* Mr. Hytner has made the drama more tangible and believable. The film was shot on rugged Hog Island, near Salem, where witch trials took place in the 17th century. Mr. Miller said the location was an asset, counteracting the "tendency to make it a static, photographed stage play." On Hog Island, "the environment kept moving in on you." . . .

Over the years, *The Crucible* has become his most produced play, seemingly transferrable to any country. No matter where it has been done—and he remembered one fanciful production in Georgia in the Soviet Union in which John Proctor was chased by a mob wearing balloon trousers and carrying scimitars—the most important thing is that Proctor is not meant to be heroic. He is "a damaged man" who rises against injustice.

The writer includes telling details that are not general knowledge.

In a recent speech, Robert Brustein said, "I defy you to name a single work of art that has ever changed anything." In response, Mr. Miller said, "I think works of art change the consciousness of people and their estimate of who they are and what they stand for." He pointed to John Steinbeck's *Grapes of Wrath* and to Mark Twain, "who gave America an image of itself, the idea of the innocent American, with his simple-minded appreciation of reality as against the complications of life." . . .

Speaking about his body of work, he said, "I have a feeling my plays are my character, and your character is your fate." Asked if he regretted any of his plays, he said, "That would be like regretting you lost your hair. They're part of my life. Each was terribly important to me at that moment."

As always, he works every day. He is writing a new play and he is revising *The Ride Down Mount Morgan* for its first New York production. And next season there will be a cycle of his plays in New York when he is playwright in residence Off Broadway with the Signature Theater Company.

Suddenly, he repeated his old refrain: "I never had a critic in my corner in this country." When it was pointed out that few playwrights have ever had critical champions, he readily agreed, adding, "As I look back, I honestly feel I have nothing to complain about." But still he keeps complaining.

"Well, yeah," he admitted, with a shrug. "You've got to keep the ball in the air."

Close Reading Activities

Theater/Film Review • Feature Article

Critical Reading

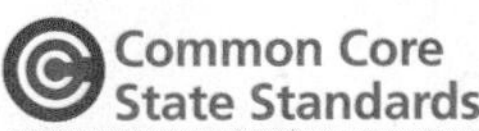

Common Core State Standards

Writing

1. Write arguments to support claims in an analysis of substantive topics or texts, using valid reasoning and relevant and sufficient evidence.

10. Write routinely over shorter time frames for a range of tasks, purposes, and audiences.

Language

4.b. Identify and correctly use patterns of word changes that indicate different meanings or parts of speech.

4.d. Verify the preliminary determination of the meaning of a word or phrase.

1. **(a)** What is Brooks Atkinson's overall **opinion** of the first production of *The Crucible*? **(b)** Cite one element in the play that Atkinson found effective and one he found ineffective. **(c)** For each, identify one piece of evidence Atkinson uses to support his opinion. Explain whether that evidence is a **fact** or another opinion.
2. **(a)** Identify three facts Kenneth Turan presents in the first three paragraphs of his review. **(b)** At what point does he first state an opinion? **(c)** What is that opinion?
3. **(a)** Distinguish between fact and opinion in the feature article by citing two opinions and two facts it presents. **(b)** Overall, does the article rely more heavily on fact or on opinion? Explain.
4. **Content-Area Vocabulary (a)** Explain how the meaning of the Latin word *adaptare* ("fit, adjust") contributes to the meaning of the English word *adaptation*. **(b)** Determine the meaning and parts of speech of the following words derived from the same linguistic source: *adaptable, adaptive, adaptivity.* **(c)** Use a dictionary to verify your preliminary definitions.

 Timed Writing

Argument [40 minutes]

Format

An **argumentative essay** is not a piece of writing in which you start a fight. An argument is a well-reasoned position or opinion. In an essay, you must explain and support your argument.

In 1953, when *The Crucible* premiered, critics had the power to make or break a Broadway play. Today, with the rise of the Internet, social networking sites, and numerous forms of publishing, can any one critic still be as important or as powerful in any art form? Write an **argumentative essay** in which you express and **defend** your opinion on this topic. **Support** your claims with details from the feature article and theater reviews as well as your own observations and experience.

Academic Vocabulary

The prompt does not simply require you to express your personal opinions. Instead, it asks you to **defend** and **support** your views. To do so, cite convincing and varied evidence.

5-Minute Planner

Complete these steps before you begin to write.

1. Read the prompt carefully. List key words.
2. Draft a thesis that clearly responds to the prompt.
3. Skim the text for details you can use as evidence. **TIP** Topic sentences or key ideas are usually stated in either the first or last sentence of a paragraph. Locate details quickly by reading those sentences first.
4. Reread the prompt, and draft your essay.

Writing Workshop

Write an Argumentative Essay

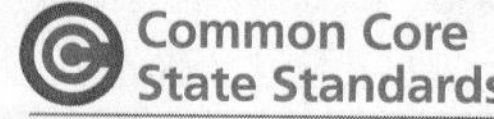

Writing
1. Write arguments to support claims in an analysis of substantive topics or texts, using valid reasoning and relevant and sufficient evidence.
1.a. Distinguish the claim(s) from alternate or opposing claims.
7. Conduct short research projects to answer a question or solve a problem; narrow or broaden the inquiry when appropriate; synthesize multiple sources on the subject, demonstrating understanding of the subject under investigation.

Argument John F. Kennedy and Martin Luther King, Jr., wrote argumentative pieces to convince others to accept their views. Argumentative writing can take many forms, such as speeches, letters, articles, and essays. Argumentative essays are prose works that argue for a claim, using valid reasoning and sufficient, relevant evidence. Follow the steps outlined in this workshop to write an argumentative essay.

Assignment Write an argumentative essay that urges readers to accept your viewpoint on and claims about an issue.

What to Include Your argumentative essay should have these elements:

- A claim that clearly states your position
- Well-organized evidence that supports your argument, such as facts, examples, statistics, and personal experience
- Discussion that defuses or refutes counterclaims and their supporting evidence
- Language that is compelling and convincing
- A concluding statement that follows from and supports your ideas

To preview the criteria on which your argumentative essay may be assessed, see the rubric on page 1263.

Focus on Research

When you write argumentative essays, you should conduct research to locate the following information:

- Evidence to support your claims
- Information to refute or defuse counterclaims

The best evidence will come from valid sources such as reputable, authoritative organizations, books, and websites. Be sure to note all sources you use in your research, and credit appropriately. Refer to the Conducting Research pages in the Introductory Unit as well as the Citing Sources and Preparing Manuscript pages in the Resource section (R21–R23) for information on citation.

Prewriting and Planning

Choosing Your Topic

A good topic for an argumentative essay is an issue that you feel strongly about and that might even affect you personally. It should also be an issue that provokes disagreement. To choose a topic for your argumentative essay, try this strategy:

Make a "news" notebook. Find topics by reading newspapers and magazine editorials, letters to the editor, and op-ed pages. Watch television newscasts and listen to radio talk shows, particularly those that feature experts on both sides of an issue. Record interesting opinions in a news notebook and note your response. Then, review your list, and choose an issue that you find compelling. As you learn more about the topic, your opinion may change.

Source	Topic	Opinion	My Response
Nightly News (7:30 PM)	Community volunteering	PTA leaders believe volunteering should be a requirement for graduation.	It is not volunteering if you have to do it. On the other hand, it could help the community a lot.

Narrowing Your Topic

Focus by looping. Once you have chosen a general topic, a strategy called looping can help you narrow your focus. Freewrite about your broad topic for five minutes. Read what you have written, and then circle the idea that you find most compelling. Then, freewrite for another five minutes about the idea you circled. Repeat the process until you arrive at a manageable topic.

Gathering Details

Compile your evidence. Review the position you stated in your news notebook. Gather evidence to support the position. Use books, newspapers, magazines, Internet sources, and other resources. Look for facts and well-argued opinions.

- A **fact** is a statement that can be proved true. (More than 78% of students were late to school at least once last year.)
- An **opinion** is a judgment or belief that cannot be proved, although it can be supported by facts and arguments. (Students should not have to wake up before 6:00 A.M.)

Analyze both sides of the issue. Use a T-chart to record facts and arguments for and against your position. Prepare counterclaims that will address opinions that contradict yours.

High school should start later in the morning.

Pro	Con
Teenagers are half-asleep at school because they are biologically wired to fall asleep late and wake up late.	Starting school later will create problems for students who do extracurriculars, play sports, or have jobs.

Drafting

Shaping Your Writing

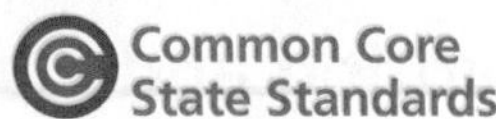

Common Core State Standards

Writing

1.a. Introduce precise, knowledgeable claim(s), establish the significance of the claim(s), distinguish the claim(s) from alternate or opposing claims, and create an organization that logically sequences claim(s), counterclaims, reasons, and evidence.

1.b. Develop claim(s) and counterclaims fairly and thoroughly, supplying the most relevant evidence for each while pointing out the strengths and limitations of both in a manner that anticipates the audience's knowledge level, concerns, values, and possible biases.

1.d. Establish and maintain a formal style and objective tone while attending to the norms and conventions of the discipline in which they are writing.

1.e. Provide a concluding statement or section that follows from and supports the argument presented.

Follow an effective organization. Review your notes. Rank your reasons from most to least convincing. Choose an organization that will highlight your strongest reasons and evidence. This chart shows two structures you might follow.

Introduction:

Include a strong **claim** that identifies the issue and clearly states your position.

Body: Organization A

- Begin with your second strongest reason and evidence.
- Present other reasons and evidence in descending order of strength.
- Present and refute opposing claims, or counterclaims.
- End with your strongest reason and evidence.

Body: Organization B

- Begin with your strongest reason and evidence.
- State and refute the strongest opposing claims, or counterclaims.
- Present other reasons and evidence in increasing order of strength.
- End with your second strongest reason and evidence.

Conclusion:

End with a memorable paragraph that restates your claim and sums up your strongest supporting evidence.

Include sufficient, relevant supporting evidence. Convince readers by making sure you have enough evidence, that it supports your claim, and that it comes from reliable sources.

Maintain a formal style and tone. A calm, formal tone, or attitude, is more persuasive than a reactive emotional one. Maintain a formal style and tone as you draft.

Providing Elaboration

Use effective arguing techniques. You can use these types of reasoning to build a strong case for your claim.

Type of Reasoning	Definition	Example
Inductive Reasoning	Specific facts used to lead to a general truth	Bicycle injury rates in Oaktown decreased when a helmet law was passed. Therefore, a helmet law will help our community prevent bicycle injuries.
Deductive Reasoning	A general truth applied to a specific case	Helmet laws have been shown to reduce accidents. If we had a stronger helmet law, Alicia Martinez would not have been injured last month.

Writers on Writing

Arthur Miller On Using Historical Facts

Arthur Miller is the author of *The Crucible* (p. 1124).

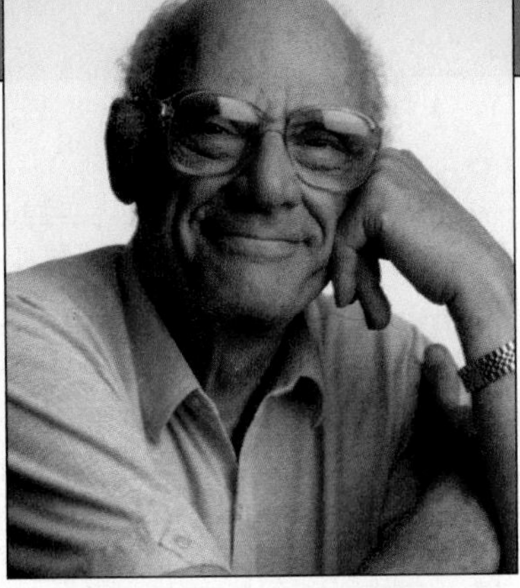

". . . I could not imagine a theatre worth my time that did not want to change the world."

—Arthur Miller

In reading the record [of the Salem witchcraft trials], which was taken down verbatim at the trial, I found one recurring note which had a growing effect upon my concept, not only of the phenomenon itself, but of our modern way of thinking about people, and especially of the treatment of evil in contemporary drama. Some critics have taken exception, for instance, to the unrelieved badness of the prosecution in the play [*The Crucible*]. I understand how this is possible, and I plead no mitigation, but I was up against historical facts which were immutable.

from *The Crucible*

HALE: Man, you will hang! You cannot!

PROCTOR, *his eyes full of tears*: I can. And there's your first marvel, that I can. You have made your magic now, for now I do think I see some shed of goodness in John Proctor. Not enough to weave a banner with, but white enough to keep it from such dogs.

ELIZABETH, *in a burst of terror, rushes to him and weeps against his hand*: Give them no tear! Tears pleasure them! Show honor now, show a stony heart and sink them with it! *He has lifted her, and kisses her now with great passion.*

REBECCA: Let you fear nothing! Another judgment awaits us all!

DANFORTH: Hang them high over the town! Who weeps for these, weeps for corruption! *He sweeps out past them.*

I do not think that either the record itself or the numerous commentaries upon it reveal any mitigation of the unrelieved, straightforward, and absolute dedication to evil displayed by the judges of these trials and the prosecutors. After days of study it became quite incredible how perfect they were in this respect....

No human weakness could be displayed without the prosecution's stabbing into the greater fury. The most patent contradictions, almost laughable even in that day, were overridden with warnings not to repeat their mention.

Revising

Revising Your Overall Structure

Eliminate faulty logic and weak reasoning. When you write argumentatively, you can get carried away with your passionate convictions. Make sure your writing will persuade your reader with careful logical thinking. Review your draft for these common mistakes:

Faulty Logic and Weak Reasoning

Type	Definition	Example
circular reasoning	Supporting a point by simply stating it in other words	"The law *should be amended* because it needs *changing*."
post hoc argument	Assuming that because one event occurs after another, the first event causes the second	"Since she became principal, our school ranking has fallen drastically. She must resign now."
bandwagon appeal	Urging readers to adopt a course of action because "everybody is doing it"	"Every other high school in the county has a soccer team; we need one too."
loaded language	Using words with strong negative or positive connotations to hide weak arguments	"The *ridiculous* new uniforms look *terrible*, so they won't help discipline at all."

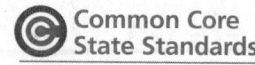

Common Core State Standards

Writing

1.b. Develop claim(s) and counterclaims fairly and thoroughly, supplying the most relevant evidence for each while pointing out the strengths and limitations of both in a manner that anticipates the audience's knowledge level, concerns, values, and possible biases.

1.c. Use words, phrases, and clauses as well as varied syntax to link the major sections of the text, create cohesion, and clarify the relationships between claim(s) and reasons, between reasons and evidence, and between claim(s) and counterclaims.

Language

3.a. Vary syntax for effect.

Revising Your Sentences

Strengthen your transitions. In argumentative writing, good transitions highlight the logic of an extended argument. Both between paragraphs and within them, transitions can make your reasoning more obvious.

Examples:

Transitions that show contrast: *however, although, despite*

Transitions that point to a reason: *since, because, if*

Transitions that signal a conclusion: *therefore, consequently, so, then*

Color-code to check transitions. Circle transitions in your draft. Then, read each paragraph of your essay. Underline in green the places where you set up contrasts, underline in blue where you provide reasons, and underline in red where you have drawn conclusions. In each case, decide whether the transition you have used is effective. Revise or add transitions as needed.

Peer Review: Ask a group of three or four classmates to read your draft and identify places where you might improve your transitions. Make revisions as needed. Then, explain to the group how each of your revisions clarifies your logic or improves the connection between ideas.

Developing Your Style

Using Parallelism

Parallel structure is the repeated use of related ideas in a similar grammatical form. Parallel expressions emphasize your arguments and create a compelling rhythm. If the parallel ideas are in the same sentence, they must have the same grammatical form. Mixing forms is a grammatical error called "faulty parallelism."

Faulty Parallelism	Correct Parallelism
Philadelphia is famous for the First Continental Congress, housing the Liberty Bell, and publishing the country's first newspaper. (one noun and two gerund phrases)	Philadelphia is famous for hosting the First Continental Congress, housing the Liberty Bell, and publishing the country's first newspaper. (three gerund phrases)

Review your draft to identify similar or contrasting concepts. Consider expressing these concepts in parallel form. Phrase the ideas with the same grammatical structure, using similar words, phrases, clauses, or sentences.

Find It in Your Reading

Read or review the Inaugural Address by John F. Kennedy on page 1104.

1. Identify three sentences that use parallelism.
2. Write out the sentences, and underline the parallel elements.
3. Explain the way each sentence uses the same grammatical structure.

Apply It in Your Writing

For each paragraph in your essay, follow these steps:

1. Identify writing that expresses related or contrasting concepts.
2. If these concepts are in different sentences, use parallelism to combine them.
3. If the concepts are in the same sentence, make sure they have the same grammatical structure, as shown:

Faulty Parallelism: *We rowed past the boathouse, under the bridge, and the boat crossed the finish line. (two prepositional phrases and one independent clause)*

Correct Parallelism: *We rowed past the boathouse, under the bridge, and across the finish line. (three prepositional phrases)*

Student Model: Steven Waldorf, Fort Myers, FL

The Internet: Positives Outweigh Negatives

Throughout the course of modern history, technological innovations have revolutionized the world. Of these, few have altered everyday life like the Internet has. From purchasing products to researching information, there is little that cannot be accomplished over the World Wide Web. By making research more convenient and enhancing the speed of communication, the Internet has had an overwhelmingly positive effect on society.

When it comes to writing a research paper or creating a scholastic presentation, the Internet is a tool that puts millions of resources from around the world at your fingertips. With the mere click of a mouse, a researcher can access information on topics ranging from organic chemistry to the American Civil War. Research that once required driving to the library and rifling through hundreds of books can now be conducted in one's own home, and in a fraction of the time. This convenience and ease of use also carries an important implication. Students who live in rural parts of the country, many of whom have traditionally not had as many resources as those who live in suburban or metropolitan areas, can now access the same quality research information. Therefore, students who have previously been at an academic disadvantage now have at their disposal a tool that helps to level the playing field between students from all areas of the country. Overall, the Internet is of tremendous assistance to students everywhere looking for information on scholastic subjects.

Some are quick to point out, however, that the use of the Internet for academic pursuits also has some negative consequences. Research purists often say that information obtained over the Internet is not as accurate as that found in books. This is occasionally the case, but if a researcher uses discretion in the sites from which he or she harvests information, this argument becomes irrelevant. For instance, what difference does it make whether a student uses facts from the Encyclopedia Britannica or from the book's virtual counterpart? Critics also say that information from the Internet is more likely to be plagiarized than material extracted from books. In reality, though, a student who is willing to plagiarize information from the Internet would be just as likely to pass ideas from a book off as his or her own. Furthermore, it is not more difficult to properly cite sources from Web sites than from books or articles. When all the facts are considered, these counterarguments do not hold up to close scrutiny.

Aside from research, the Internet has also revolutionized the way in which people communicate. No longer is it necessary to wait days, even weeks, for letters to travel through the postal system. Now, in literally an instant, written communication can be sent across the country. E-mail can be used to chat with a close relative or to file a complaint with a major corporation. Again, some may claim that this detracts from human-to-human contact. However, there is little empirical evidence to suggest that this impacts society in a harmful way. On the contrary, the Web has opened up a whole new medium by which individuals can correspond with others.

The Internet has had an enormously beneficial impact on the way we conduct research and communicate with one another. Few can argue against the fact that it has made life much easier, particularly for students. Because of this, the Internet has definitely exerted a positive influence on society.

Steven presents a claim that states the opinion that he wants to persuade readers to accept.

Steven gives evidence to support his opinion about the benefits of the Internet.

The writer elaborates on his argument by anticipating counterclaims and answering these in his writing.

Steven appeals to his audience by citing evidence that they are familiar with.

In his conclusion, Steven strengthens his essay by restating his claim and the main points of his argument.

Editing and Proofreading

Check your essay for errors in grammar, usage, punctuation, and spelling.

Focus on punctuation. Make sure you have used commas to separate three or more parallel words, phrases, or clauses in a series.

Words: *The train was crowded, noisy, and slow.*
Phrases: *We toured the town by bus, by car, and by train.*
Clauses: *The survey revealed that most residents support the mayor, oppose the new highway, and plan to vote for the upcoming bond issue.*

Focus on spelling. The sound of *sh* is sometimes spelled *ci*, as in *gracious*, or *ti*, as in *cautious*. Read your essay aloud, listening for words with the *sh* sound. Make sure your spelling of these words is correct.

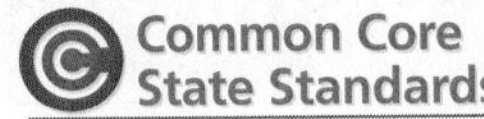

Writing

4. Produce clear and coherent writing in which the development, organization, and style are appropriate to task, purpose, and audience.

5. Develop and strengthen writing as needed by planning, revising, editing, rewriting, or trying a new approach, focusing on addressing what is most significant for a specific purpose and audience.

Language

2.b. Spell correctly.

Speaking and Listening

4. Present information, findings, and supporting evidence, conveying a clear and distinct perspective, such that listeners can follow the line of reasoning, alternative or opposing perspectives are addressed, and the organization, development, substance, and style are appropriate to purpose, audience, and a range of formal and informal tasks.

Publishing, Presenting, and Reflecting

Consider one of the following ways to share and think further about your writing.

Publish in a newspaper. Find out the length requirements for an opinion piece for your local or school newspaper. Modify your essay to meet those requirements and submit it for publication.

Deliver a speech. Use your argumentative essay as the basis for a speech to your classmates or to another audience. Make adjustments to the text to ensure that your audience can follow your line of reasoning and that your content and language are appropriate for the situation. Use eye contact and gestures to add impact to your presentation.

Reflect on your writng. In a writer's journal, jot down your thoughts on the experience of writing an argumentative essay. Begin by answering these questions: How did writing an argumentative essay reinforce or change your opinion? Has any action been taken as a result of your essay? Explain.

Rubric for Self-Assessment

Evaluate your argumentative essay using the following criteria and rating scale.

Criteria	Rating Scale *not very* — *very*
Purpose/Focus: How clear is your claim?	1 2 3 4
Organization: How effectively do you organize your arguments?	1 2 3 4
Development of Ideas/Elaboration: How well do you use a variety of reasons and evidence to support your position?	1 2 3 4
Language: How well do you use parallel structure?	1 2 3 4
Conventions: How correct is your grammar, especially your use of commas?	1 2 3 4

Analyze and Evaluate Entertainment Media

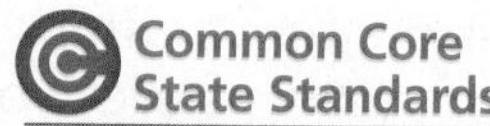

Language
1. Demonstrate command of the conventions of standard English grammar and usage when speaking.

Speaking and Listening
2. Integrate multiple sources of information presented in diverse formats and media in order to make informed decisions and solve problems, evaluating the credibility and accuracy of each source and noting any discrepancies among the data.

Television shows, movies, music videos, podcasts, and radio broadcasts have become constants in American life. All of these broadcast forms present different types of entertainment media—programming explicitly designed for enjoyment rather than for instruction or information. While entertainment media draws people in for fun and leisure, it also conveys powerful messages and can be highly influential in transmitting cultural values.

Types of Entertainment Media

While people may sometimes dismiss entertainment media as frivolous, it is very powerful and can affect how people see the world. You can enjoy a film or a television show but at the same time understand that you are receiving the mediamaker's ideas, values, and perspectives. Just as you think critically when you read a novel, so should you view critically when you watch a movie.

Media Effects The main purpose of nearly all entertainment media is to give viewers an interesting viewing experience; however, these media forms also have profound effects on individuals and the culture. These effects fall into three main categories:

- *To interpret facts.* Movies or TV shows may give viewers new understandings of past or current events. Sometimes, these new understandings are accurate; often, they are not, as media makers emphasize or even distort specific elements for dramatic effect. It is important to know the facts, or use resources to check them, before accepting a view of history or of a current issue as it is presented in entertainment media.
- *To persuade.* Media makers may embed opinions within the elements of an entertainment product. They may depict groups of people in negative ways, fail to provide multiple points of view on a complex problem, or otherwise skew an issue. It is important to be alert to the use of *stereotypes*, *bias*, and other unfair or misleading depictions.
- *To transmit culture and values.* Various forms of entertainment media reflect and shape cultural values and norms. Television sitcoms with morals at the end of each episode or talk radio shows that examine social dynamics are examples of media that reflect and influence cultural values. These media forms can have clear effects on society. For example, in the 1960s and 1970s, television reflected the changing roles of women and minorities in society. These depictions also allowed the culture to arrive at a new understanding of what is "normal." As you watch entertainment media, be alert to portrayals of people that do not reflect the realities in the world around you.

Media Tools and Techniques

Entertainment media use numerous techniques, including those listed here, to make representations more effective or dramatic:

Technique	Description	Example
Special Effects	Visual and audio illusions	Firefighters run in slow motion away from a collapsing building.
Camera Angles	Directions from which a camera operator shoots images	A scene is shot from above to give a bird's-eye view.
Reaction Shots	Shots that show a character's responses	As a girl falls from her horse, the camera pans to her mother's face.
Sequencing	Events arranged in a specific order to tell a story	A flashback interrupts the chronological presentation of events to give the audience background information.
Music	Music used to create a desired mood	As a father and son reunite, soft piano music plays in the background.

Activities: Analyze a Movie, TV Episode, or Skit

Comprehension and Collaboration For Activity A, use an evaluation form like the one below.

A. Choose an example of visual entertainment media, such as a movie or television show, that you enjoy. Examine how the director uses different tools and techniques to shape the content. Present your conclusions to the class, using standard English grammar and usage as you speak.

B. A **parody** is a comic imitation of a serious form. Its purpose is to poke fun at the form itself or the ideas it represents. Locate and watch a parody of a particular type of entertainment media. As you watch, consider the following questions: What qualities in the original are being parodied? How do the media makers create the parody—through visual effects, story line, exaggerated characters, or another element?

Evaluation Form for Entertainment Media

Type of Entertainment Media: ____________________

Name of Movie, Show, or Skit: ____________________

Write a summary of the plot: ____________________

What cultural values are represented in the plot? ____________________

How are certain groups of people represented? ____________________

Identify and describe the technical elements used in the film.

☐ special effects ____________ ☐ camera angles ____________

☐ reaction shots ____________ ☐ sequencing ____________

☐ music ____________________

Which of these technical elements is the most significant? Explain.

____

Language Study

Idioms and Idiomatic Expressions

Idioms are figurative expressions commonly used in conversation and informal writing. Idiomatic expressions do not literally mean what they say. For example, if you *burned the midnight oil,* you stayed up late to work on something. You probably did not not actually rise at midnight to burn oil. To define idioms, look at context clues, or the words and phrases around them. These will help you infer the meanings of unfamiliar expressions.

Consider these examples:

Example	Context Clues
Claire volunteered to be on three committees. Later, she felt that she had bitten off more than she could chew.	The idea that Claire is on three committees helps you understand that the idiom means she had agreed to do too much.
My philosophy is to let sleeping dogs lie rather than to constantly bring up problems.	The words "rather than" set up a contrast. Therefore, you know that *let sleeping dogs lie* means the opposite of "bring up problems."

Common Core State Standards

Language

4. Determine or clarify the meaning of unknown and multiple-meaning words and phrases based on *grades 11–12 reading and content,* choosing flexibly from a range of strategies.

4.a. Use context as a clue to the meaning of a word or phrase.

5. Demonstrate understanding of figurative language, word relationships, and nuances in word meanings.

Practice

Directions: Identify the idiom in each sentence. Then, use context clues to define it.

1. After winning the hot dog–eating contest, Jamal felt under the weather for a day or two.
2. She knew she would have to hit the books tonight if she wanted to do well on the test tomorrow.
3. The instructions made putting the bookcase together seem like a piece of cake, but I knew better from past experience.
4. The ninth-graders are wet behind the ears at first, but they soon get older and wiser.
5. Maria bent over backward to make sure the party was a success.
6. After six days of rainy, cold weather, I felt blue.
7. Sam is too forthright to beat around the bush.

Directions: Complete each **analogy** below. Then, write an explanation of the idiomatic expression and word relationships in each pairing.

1. pouring : "raining cats and dogs" :: _______ : "safe and sound"

   a. loud **b.** secure **c.** wet **d.** friendly

2. "out of hand" : _______ :: "the eleventh hour" : in advance

   a. done with skill **b.** running late **c.** wild **d.** under control

Vocabulary Acquisition and Use: Sentence Completions

Sentence Completion questions appear in most standardized tests. They test not only vocabulary skills but also knowledge of sentence structure. Each item is a sentence with one or more missing words. Your task is to choose the correct word or words to complete each sentence logically.

Practice

This exercise is modeled after the Sentence Completion exercises that appear in the Critical Reading section of the SAT.

Directions: Each of the following sentences is missing one or two words. Choose the word or set of words that best completes each sentence.

> **Test-Taking Tip**
> Eliminate any words with similar meanings, because a single correct answer choice should be obvious.

1. Some __?__ opportunists deprived rural landowners of their legal rights.

A. illiterate
B. rueful
C. unscrupulous
D. convivial
E. morose

2. A lonely countryside can appear to be either beautiful or __?__.

A. desolate
B. punitive
C. repugnant
D. intricate
E. frayed

3. A newcomer would be __?__ by our peculiar local customs and habits.

A. blanched
B. confounded
C. exalted
D. dissuaded
E. permeated

4. If poverty and malnutrition exist, society should attempt __?__ restructuring to solve these problems.

A. contiguous
B. systemic
C. punitive
D. mundane
E. virulent

5. Some downtrodden people __?__ a difficult life of their own .

A. impelled . . . profundity
B. endured . . . volition
C. appeased . . . collusion
D. maneuvered . . . disillusions
E. concocted . . . brazenness

6. Those who did escape poverty proved to be __?__ survivors who shook off the effects of the __?__ surrounding them.

A. intriguing . . . perdition
B. exalted . . . avarice
C. vanquished . . . geography
D. wily . . . malevolence
E. gaudy . . . diligence

From Text to Understanding

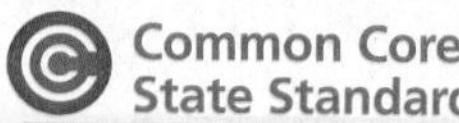

Writing

1. Write arguments to support claims in an analysis of substantive topics or texts, using valid reasoning and relevant and sufficient evidence.

7. Conduct short as well as more sustained research projects to answer a question (including a self-generated question) or solve a problem; narrow or broaden the inquiry when appropriate; synthesize multiple sources on that subject, demonstrating understanding of the subject under investigation.

Speaking and Listening

1. Initiate and participate effectively in a range of collaborative discussions (one-on-one, in groups, and teacher-led) with diverse partners on *grades 11–12 topics, texts, and issues*, building on others' ideas and expressing their own clearly and persuasively.

You have studied each part of Unit 5 as a set of connected texts. In this workshop, you will have the chance to further explore the fundamental connections among these texts and to deepen your essential understanding of the literature and its social and historical context.

PART 1: War Shock

Writing: Argumentative Essay The selections in Part 1 show different intersections between people's lives and World War II. Although the actual field of battle was vast, these texts focus on smaller spaces—ordinary places upon which the war encroached. As you review the Part 1 selections, focusing on the Anchor Text, the excerpt from John Hersey's *Hiroshima*, think about how the settings are tied to the works' themes.

Assignment: Develop a claim that analyzes the use of setting in Hersey's *Hiroshima* and one other selection in Part 1. Why are the settings so important in these works? In what ways do the places themselves inspire the writers? Background material and other Part 1 texts can help you develop your claim, which might resemble the following:

Example: In times of war, all space has the potential to become part of the conflict. Focusing on everyday locations, like Dr. Seuss's easy chair and those painfully detailed in John Hersey's *Hiroshima*, show how writers use setting to illustrate the reach of war.

Read closely. Make a list of guided questions related to the settings of the works. Then, take notes as you review the selections using your questions as a framework.

Evaluate the methods. Notice how authors use adjectives and figurative language to describe concrete physical details. Identify how the description of setting connects to the theme of the work in a clear and significant way.

Show your reasoning. As you write, develop your argument in an organized, methodical way. State your claim, then support it with details and evidence. The structure of your essay should show your thinking in a progression from introduction through development to conclusion.

Focus on word choice. As you write, choose your words with precision. Words specific to war, such as *destruction*, *innocence*, and *inescapable*, can add power to your writing.

Writing Checklist

- ☐ Clear claim

  Identify: ___________

- ☐ References to and thoughtful commentary on quotations from the texts

  Examples: ___________

- ☐ Clear discussion of the author's use of language and style for specific effects

  Examples: ___________

PART 2: Tradition and Rebellion

Research: Documentary Slide Show The selections in Part 2 resonate with the play between expectation and disappointment. Review the Part 2 texts, focusing on the Anchor Text poems, "Mirror" by Sylvia Plath and "Courage" by Anne Sexton, and consider the individual experiences and versions of reality they offer.

Assignment: Work with a partner to create documentary slide shows that present multimedia interpretations of literary works. Develop one presentation about one of the Anchor Text poems, and one about a Part 2 selection that you see as thematically related.

Conduct research and analyze the texts to answer questions such as:

- What is the history of each work?
- What does a close reading of each work reveal about its meaning?

Gather video clips and images such as photographs, paintings, and illustrations. Use sound when possible. Embed the video files or links to videos in your slide show. Share your documentaries with your classmates.

Documentary Production Plan:

- ☐ **Choose the selections.** Choose texts that speak most powerfully to you.
- ☐ **Research the texts' backgrounds.** Find out when they were written and any interesting information about their publication history.
- ☐ **Analyze the texts.** Close-read the texts, drawing parallels between them and making observations about author's style, meaning, and theme.
- ☐ **Research images.** Use the library and the Internet to locate images that reflect the texts' meaning. Include images of the authors.
- ☐ **Choose your format.** Combine video and photographs; create a computer-generated slide show; or make posters.
- ☐ **Put it all together.** Assemble your research, literary analysis, and images, and write a script that tells the story of the works you chose. Read the script aloud while you display images on a computer or posters.

PART 3: Literature of Protest

Listening and Speaking: Roundtable Discussion Review the selections in Part 3, paying special attention to the Anchor Texts, the "Inaugural Address" by John F. Kennedy and "Letter from Birmingham City Jail" by Martin Luther King, Jr. These texts are a clear call to people's better instincts, a call to join the fight against injustice, a call infused with hope even in the face of alarming struggle. These and other Part 3 selections show that acts of protest include speaking and writing, as well as physical resistance.

Assignment: Work with a small group and lead a discussion about how the fight against injustice is engaged in the Anchor Texts by President Kennedy and Dr. King, as well as by a third writer, such as Arthur Miller, author of *The Crucible*. Choose someone to moderate the discussion. Invite classmates to join in with thoughts and questions. You may base your discussion on questions such as the following:

- What is the specific problem?
- How does the writer propose to address the problem?
- How convincing is the writer's approach?
- Is one method of protest more effective than another?
- How is the idea of hope present in these works?

Test-Taking Practice

Reading Test: Prose Fiction

Standardized tests often include **prose fiction** reading selections, passages drawn from novels and short stories. You will be tested on your comprehension of the text as well as your literary analysis skills. Questions will focus on topics such as main ideas, significant details, causes and effects, and author's perspective, as well as theme and underlying meaning.

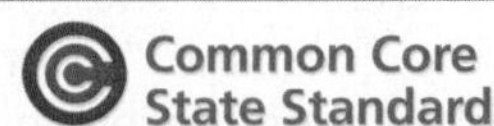

Common Core State Standards

RL.11-12.1, RL.11-12.4, RL.11-12.5; L.11-12.1, L.11-12.4, L.11-12.4.a; W.11-12.2, W.11-12.5.

[For the full wording of the standards, see the standards chart in the front of your textbook.]

Practice

The following exercise is modeled after the ACT Reading Test, Prose Fiction section. The full test has 40 questions.

Directions: Read the following passage from *The First Seven Years,* by Bernard Malamud. Then, choose the best answer to each question.

During the week, by placing here and there a deft question, he managed to get from Miriam some information about Max. It surprised him to learn that the boy was not studying to be either a doctor or a lawyer but was taking a business course leading to a degree in accountancy. Feld was a little disappointed because he thought of accountants as bookkeepers and would have preferred "a higher profession." However, it was not long before he had investigated the subject and discovered that Certified Public Accountants were highly respected people, so he was thoroughly content as Saturday approached. But because Saturday was a busy day, he was much in the store and therefore did not see Max when he came to call for Miriam. From his wife he learned there had been nothing especially revealing about their meeting. Max had rung the bell and Miriam had got her coat and left with him–nothing more. Feld did not probe, for his wife was not particularly observant. Instead, he waited up for Miriam with a newspaper on his lap, which he scarcely looked at so lost was he in thinking of the future. He awoke to find her in the room with him, tiredly removing her hat. Greeting her, he was suddenly inexplicably afraid to ask anything about the evening. But since she volunteered nothing he was at last forced to inquire how she had enjoyed herself. Miriam began something noncommittal but apparently changed her mind, for she said after a minute, "I was bored."

Strategy

Focus on sequence.

- **Underline time words** like dates and time of day, to understand the flow of events.
- **Look for transition words,** such as "then" and "as a result," to further link events together.
- Before answering the questions, reread any section in which you are unsure of the story's progression.

SAT® PREP ACT

1. Which part of Feld's thinking foreshadows the disappointing results of his daughter's date?
   A. his surprise that the boy would not become a doctor or a lawyer
   B. his contentment as Saturday approached
   C. his preoccupation being busy in the store that day
   D. his wife's lack of observance

2. Considering the events of the entire passage, it is most reasonable to infer that Miriam hesitated to say anything about the date after it was over because:
   F. she was reluctant to dash her father's hopes.
   G. she was too tired after work to speak.
   H. the date had been so fulfilling she could not speak.
   J. the date had left her without any opinion of it.

3. As it is used in line 18, the word *inexplicably* most nearly means:
   A. overly exhausted.
   B. unreasonably frightened.
   C. without any motivation.
   D. unable to be explained.

4. Which of the following would be included in a summary of this selection?
   I. Feld had tried to learn more about the boy who was dating his daughter.
   II. Feld did not see his daughter and the boy when they first met.
   III. Feld waited up to find out how the date he arranged had gone.
   F. II only
   G. III only
   H. I and III only
   J. I, II, and III

5. The author provides a visual image to increase the reader's understanding of his characters' motivations by:
   A. describing the differences between professions.
   B. revealing what happened at work that day.
   C. mentioning that Feld's wife was not observant.
   D. describing how Miriam removes her hat when she comes home.

6. According to the narrator, Feld was first upset and then later relieved that Max was an accountant because:
   F. he always wanted his daughter to marry a doctor.
   G. he wanted his daughter to marry someone famous.
   H. he finally learned that accountants were highly respected.
   J. he had hoped his daughter would date someone with his profession.

7. Which element of the author's style helps describe the character of Feld?
   A. a long paragraph of connected thoughts
   B. the character's use of a personal "I"
   C. a disjointed stop/start self-argument
   D. revealing snippets of conversation

8. The details and events in the passage suggest that the friendship between Miriam and her father would most accurately be described as:
   F. tender.
   G. competitive.
   H. intense.
   J. distant.

9. According to the narrator, Feld learned about Max's course of study by:
   A. questioning his daughter.
   B. asking Max directly.
   C. diligent research.
   D. consulting with his wife.

Grammar and Writing: Editing in Context

Editing-in-context segments often appear in the English sections of standardized testing. They are made up of a reading passage with highlighted and numbered areas, some of which contain errors in grammar, style, and usage. For each question, you must choose the best way to correct a given sentence.

Practice

This exercise is modeled after the ACT English Test.

Directions: For each underlined sentence or portion of a sentence, choose the best alternative. If an item asks a question about a numbered portion of the essay, choose the best answer to the question.

Strategy

What is different?
Examine the answer choices with an eye to what makes them different. Various aspects of writing can vary in multiple answers. Make sure each part is effective.

[1]

Flannery O'Connor is perhaps the equal of her contemporary, William Faulkner, but her far smaller output has made her less well known. She wrote in a Southern Gothic style and <u>relies</u> (1) on colorful regional characters and customs. <u>Characters with deformities of body or spirit were often described by O'Connor.</u> (2) This type of character is referred to as a Grotesque character. Ms. O'Connor herself was afflicted with a long-term illness, which made her feel like an outsider, perhaps even an outcast. <u>Like many of her characters.</u> (3) She knew well of what she wrote.

[2]

Though her characters are often misfits, Flannery O'Connor has an underlying sympathy for them. In an effort to point out the spiritual failings of the modern world, O'Connor created characters with dubious moral capacities, <u>not with clear values</u> (4). She had a strong sense of spirituality due to her deeply religious upbringing. She never wrote cloyingly optimistic stories, for her sensibilities <u>runs</u> (5) deeper than a happy surface.

[3]

Ms. O'Connor contracted lupus in 1951. Lupus is a serious and often deadly disease. [6] She died in 1964 at the age of 39, leaving a literary legacy of two novels and 31 short stories. [7]

SAT® PREP ACT

1. **A.** NO CHANGE
   B. relied
   C. has relied
   D. was relying

2. The writer is considering changing this sentence to make a more active statement. Which of the following sentences would do that best?
   F. Were characters with deformities of mind or body often described by O'Connor?
   G. Characters often described by O'Connor had deformities of mind or body.
   H. O'Connor's characters were often described as Grotesque.
   J. O'Connor often described characters with deformities of body or spirit.

3. **A.** NO CHANGE
   B. attach it to previous sentence
   C. attach it to next sentence
   D. OMIT

4. **F.** NO CHANGE
   G. OMIT
   H. not having clear values
   J. not possessing clear values

5. **A.** NO CHANGE
   B. will run
   C. ran
   D. will always run

6. Where in Paragraph 3 would the following best be placed?
   Not long after being accepted into the prestigious Iowa Writer's Workshop,
   A. before the previous sentence
   B. before the first sentence
   C. as part of the previous sentence
   D. after the sentence that follows

7. In reviewing paragraph 3, the writer decides to add more information. What would most benefit the paragraph?
   F. more details about O'Connor's lifetime
   G. more details about O'Connor's published works
   H. more details about O'Connor's mother
   J. more details about O'Connor's love of birds

8. This question refers to the essay as a whole. This short essay would be most accurately categorized as which mode of writing?
   A. informational essay
   B. autobiography
   C. literary criticism
   D. reflective essay

 Timed Writing: Position Statement [30 minutes]

Feld, the hard-working shoemaker in *The First Seven Years*, wants his daughter to marry a highly respected professional. He thinks it is important to move up in society. Others might say that honest work and pride in one's work are more important than social status.

Write an **essay** in which you discuss the ideas of work, career, and status and which is most important in one's life. Back up your opinions with sound reasoning. Remember that there is no right or wrong answer but that your opinion should be clearly stated and supported. This exercise is similar to the optional ACT Writing Test.

Academic Vocabulary

An essay often argues with itself by first presenting one way of looking at an issue, and then refuting that argument with another viewpoint.

Constructed Response

Directions: *Follow the instructions to complete the tasks below as required by your teacher. As you work on each task, incorporate both general academic vocabulary and literary terms you learned in this unit.*

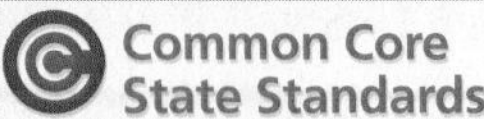
Common Core State Standards

RL.11-12.1, RL.11-12.2; RL.11-12.3; RL.11-12.4, RL.11-12.5; RL.11-12.6; RI.11-12.4; W.11-12.2; W.11-12.4; W.11-12.9a, W.11-12.9b; SL.11-12.4; SL.11-12.6

[For the full wording of the standards, see the standards chart in the front of your textbook.]

Writing

Task 1: Literature [RL.11-12.4, W.11-12.2]

Analyze Word Choice

*Write an **essay** in which you analyze the figurative and connotative language in a story or poem from this unit.*

- Choose a poem or story from this unit that uses figurative and connotative language in a way that is unique and memorable.
- For figurative language, first categorize the type of language used. For example, identify similes, metaphors, idioms, extended metaphors, or personification. Determine the meaning of all examples you cite and offer explanations.
- For connotative language, describe the associations, positive and negative, that a reader would bring to certain words. Then, analyze why the author chose each word or phrase for that particular context.
- Finally, for both types of language, evaluate the effect of word choice on the overall meaning and tone of the work.

Task 2: Literature [RL.11-12.3; W.11-12.2]

Analyze Story Elements

*Write an **essay** in which you analyze the role that setting and character play in driving the plot events in a story from this unit.*

- Choose a story with elements that are clearly or strongly related. For example, you might choose a story with a plot in which the setting is crucial.
- Summarize the story, describing the setting(s) and the major characters.
- Analyze the ways in which setting is essential to the plot of the story. For example, in an adventure story the plot events might hinge on severe weather conditions, high altitude, or heavy snowfall.
- Analyze the ways in which the main characters are crucial to the arc of the story. For example, a reckless climber might take a risk that becomes an inciting event that drives the entire story's action.
- In your conclusion, summarize how the author's choices in creating and developing characters and establishing setting impact the sequence of events in the story.

Task 3: Literature [RL.11-12.5, W.11-12.4]

Analyze Text Structure

*Write an **essay** in which you analyze how an author's choice of structure adds to the overall meaning and impact of a story in this unit.*

- Select a story from this unit in which the choice of structure affects the work's impact and meaning.
- Analyze the author's choices concerning how to structure specific parts of the story. Does the author choose to begin the story in the middle of exciting events or in a more quiet way? Does the author choose a resolution that ties up all loose ends or a resolution that leaves readers guessing? Does the ending emphasize comedic or tragic events?
- Consider how these choices add to the story's meaning and beauty.
- Describe the overall structure of the story. Identify the specific parts of the story you will analyze in depth.
- Evaluate what the specific parts of the story add to the story as a whole.
- Use academic vocabulary, such as *introduction, exposition, rising action, climax,* or *denouement,* in your explanation of structure.
- Organize and develop your ideas logically to produce a clear and coherent essay.

Speaking and Listening

Task 4: Informational Text [RI.11-12.4, SL.11-12.6]

Analyze Word Choice in a Work of Nonfiction

*Deliver an **oral presentation** in which you analyze word choice in a nonfiction work in this unit.*

- Choose a nonfiction work that includes diction you find interesting or challenging.
- Explain the meanings of key words and phrases as they are used in the work. Include explanations of figurative, connotative, and technical meanings.
- Analyze how word choice develops the central ideas of the work in a way that impacts or influences a reader. Include a discussion of specific rhetorical devices that an author uses in the piece, such as parallelism, imperatives, repetition, antithesis, and rhetorical questions.
- To provide support for your analysis, read key passages from the text aloud, stopping to point out examples of interesting word choices, figurative language, and rhetorical devices.
- Draw your audience's attention especially to words and phrases whose meaning the author explores and develops over the course of the work. Then, show how that exploration is connected to the overall meaning of the work. Keep your audience's prior knowledge and understanding of vocabulary in mind as you present.

Task 5: Literature [RL.11-12.4, SL.11-12.4]

Analyze Sound Devices

*In an **oral presentation,** analyze the effect of sound devices in a poem from this unit.*

- Choose a poem in which sound devices play a prominent role in creating an overall effect on the reader.
- Introduce the poem by explaining what sound devices you have found in the poem.
- Recite the poem aloud, emphasizing sound devices, such as alliteration, in your reading.
- Identify the various types of sound devices in the poem, provide examples of each, and explain the overall effect they create for the reader.
- Connect the poet's use of sound devices to the overall mood and meaning of the poem.

Task 6: Literature [RL.11-12.1, RL.11-12.2; SL.11-12.6]

Analyze Theme

*Prepare and present an **analysis** of two themes and their development over the course of a story from this unit.*

- Choose a story from this unit with multiple themes.
- Summarize the story. Then identify at least two of its themes or central ideas.
- Describe whether the themes you have identified are directly stated or implied. If they are directly stated, indicate where in the text this occurs. If they are implicit, indicate the clues that contribute to the theme you inferred. These clues might take the form of lines of dialogue or characters' reactions to events.
- Analyze how the author develops the themes throughout the story using dialogue, characters' actions, or story events. Discuss how the themes interact and build on one another as the story progresses.
- Cite the most significant and relevant quotations from the story to support your analysis.
- Use formal English as you deliver your presentation.

THE ESSENTIAL ?

What is the relationship between place and literature?

The Point of a Place The writers in this unit describe a variety of places—a ruined twentieth-century city, a fragile Puritan village, an ordinary gas station, a greenhouse. Why are settings so critical in literature? In what ways does place itself inspire literary works and contribute to an author's theme or message?

Assignment Choose two descriptions of settings by two different authors from this unit. Write a **comparison-and-contrast essay** in which you analyze each description and compare what the setting adds to each work's overall meaning.

Titles for Extended Reading

In this unit, you have read a variety of literature of the post-war era. Continue to read works related to this era on your own. Select books that you enjoy, but challenge yourself to explore new topics, new authors, and works offering varied perspectives or approaches. The titles suggested below will help you get started.

LITERATURE

Baldwin: Early Stories and Novels
James Baldwin

Fiction James Baldwin is known today as one of the greatest and most influential African American writers, as well as a dedicated civil rights activist. Baldwin's early works reflect the reality of coming of age as an African American in Harlem in the 1950s. Included in this collection is Baldwin's first novel, *Go Tell It on the Mountain.* Largely autobiographical, it reveals many of the author's own feelings and experiences as a teenager.

[Baldwin's short story "The Rockpile" appears on page 1082 of this book. Build knowledge by reading other fiction by this author.]

Anthology of Modern American Poetry
edited by Cary Nelson
Oxford University Press, 2000 **EXEMPLAR TEXT** 

Poetry This collection includes poems by 161 different poets—including poems such as Ezra Pound's "The River Merchant's Wife: A Letter," and selections by newer poets such as Yusef Komunyakaa and Sherman Alexie.

The Adventures of Augie March
Saul Bellow **EXEMPLAR TEXT** 

Novel Growing up poor in Chicago during the Great Depression, Augie March leaves home to try his hand at many different occupations, including dog groomer, shoplifter, and boxing coach. This is the story of Augie's attempt to create a great life for himself.

Death of a Salesman
Arthur Miller **EXEMPLAR TEXT** 

Drama This play relates the end of the life of Willy Loman, an aging salesman who fails to achieve the greatness in life he so longs for.

[Miller's play The Crucible *begins on page 1124 of this book. Build knowledge by reading another play by this playwright.]*

A Raisin in the Sun
Lorraine Hansberry **EXEMPLAR TEXT**

Drama The Youngers family must decide how to spend a $10,000 insurance check in this play, often recognized as the first American drama to realistically portray an African American family.

INFORMATIONAL TEXTS

Historical Texts

A Call to Conscience: The Landmark Speeches of Dr. Martin Luther King, Jr.
Dr. Martin Luther King, Jr.

Speech This collection includes twelve of King's most famous orations, including "I Have a Dream" and "I've Been to the Mountaintop" (delivered the night before his assassination).

Contemporary Scholarship

Patriots: The Vietnam War Remembered from All Sides
Christian G. Appy

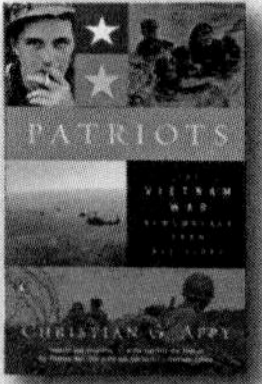

Primary Source The story of the longest military conflict in United States history comes alive through the candid and emotional testimonies of veterans, peace activists, former Vietcong fighters, and others affected by the war.

A Man on the Moon: The Voyages of the Apollo Astronauts
Andrew Chaikin (with a foreword by Tom Hanks)

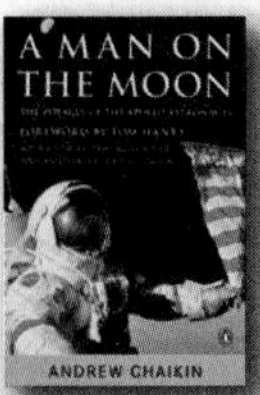

History Through interviews with astronauts and those who supported them from Earth, science writer Andrew Chaikin brings these missions to life, setting them against the backdrop of the war in Vietnam and social unrest in America.

Preparing to Read Complex Texts

Reading for College and Career In both college and the workplace, readers must analyze texts independently, draw connections among works that offer varied perspectives, and develop their own ideas and informed opinions. The questions shown below, and others that you generate on your own, will help you more effectively read and analyze complex college-level texts.

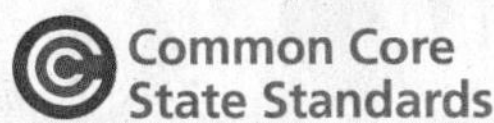

Reading Literature/Informational Text
10. By the end of grade 11, read and comprehend literature, including stories, dramas, and poems, and literary nonfiction, in the grades 11-CCR text complexity band proficiently, with scaffolding as needed at the high end of the range.

When reading analytically, ask yourself...

- What idea, experience, or story seems to have compelled the author to write? Has the author presented that idea, experience, or story in a way that I, too, find compelling?
- How might the author's era, social status, belief system, or personal experiences have affected the point of view he or she expresses in the text?
- How do my circumstances affect what I understand and feel about this text?
- What key idea does the author state explicitly? What key idea does he or she suggest or imply? Which details in the text help me to perceive implied ideas?
- Do I find multiple layers of meaning in the text? If so, what relationships do I see among these layers of meaning?
- Do I find the text believable and convincing? Why or why not?

Key Ideas and Details

- What patterns of organization or sequences do I find in the text? Do these patterns help me understand the ideas better? If so, how?
- What do I notice about the author's style, including his or her diction, use of imagery and figurative language, and syntax?
- Do I like the author's style? Is the author's style memorable? Why or why not?
- What emotional attitude does the author express toward the topic, the story, or the characters? Does this attitude seem appropriate? Why or why not?
- What emotional attitude does the author express toward me, the reader? Does this attitude seem appropriate? Why or why not?
- What do I notice about the author's voice—his or her personality on the page? Do I like this voice? Does it make me want to read on?

Craft and Structure

- Is the work fresh and original? How do I know?
- Do I agree with the author's ideas entirely, or are there elements I find unconvincing?
- Do I disagree with the author's ideas entirely, or are there elements I can accept as true?
- Based on my knowledge of American literature, history, and culture, does this work reflect the American tradition? Why or why not?

Integration of Ideas

New Voices, New Frontiers

Literature of the Contemporary Period 1970–Present

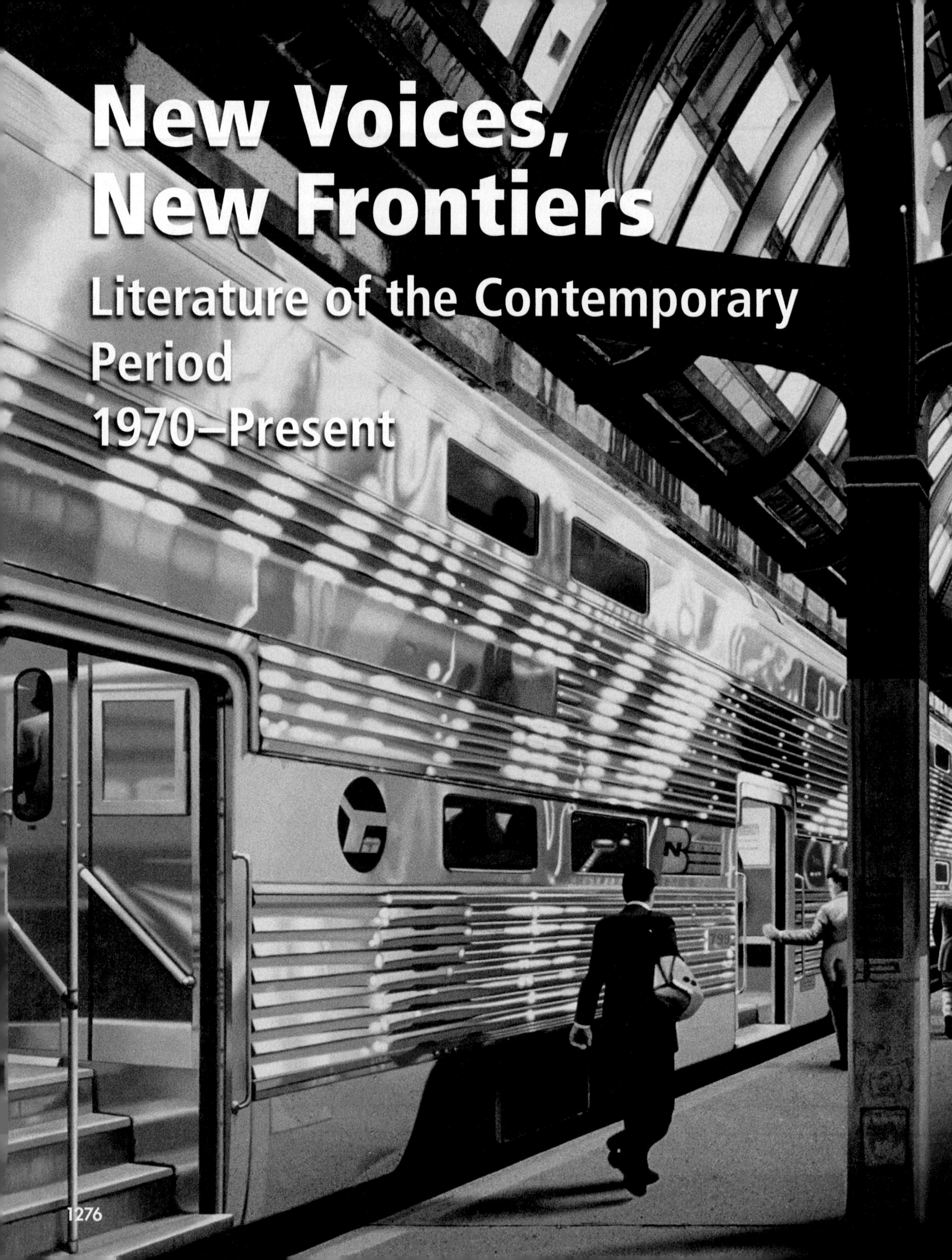

Unit 6

PART 1 TEXT SET

CONTEMPORARY FICTION

PART 2 TEXT SET

CONTEMPORARY POETRY

PART 3 TEXT SET

CONTEMPORARY NONFICTION

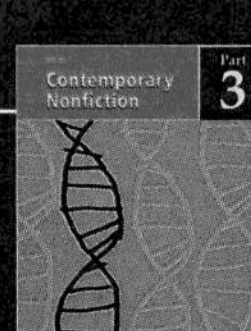

"... Perhaps this is our strange and haunting paradox here in America—that we are fixed and certain only when we are in movement."

— *Tom Wolfe*

CLOSE READING TOOL

Use this tool to practice the close reading strategies you learn.

ONLINE WRITER'S NOTEBOOK

Easily capture notes and complete assignments online.

STUDENT eTEXT

Bring learning to life with audio, video, and interactive tools.

Find all Digital Resources at **pearsonrealize.com**.

Snapshot of the Period

America emerged from the Cold War period as the sole superpower in a dramatically changing world. While national boundaries are still critical, globalization is the new model as the countries of the world become ever more interconnected economically, environmentally, and culturally.

Increasing globalization is due, in large part, to the dawning of the "Information Age" during the second half of the twentieth century. Computers, the Internet, cell phones, and other new technologies change the way people around the world work, play, and communicate. The world has become—simultaneously—more accessible and more complex.

Despite this new global energy, the new millennium opened with shock and sadness for Americans. The terrorist attacks of September 11, 2001, damaged the sense of security that Americans had always enjoyed. Though the world in the twenty-first century offers opportunities, beauty, and inspiration, it also presents individuals with complex questions and uncertainties.

▲ ▶ **(top) Firemen raise the American flag over the rubble of the World Trade Center. (right) The Security Advisory System categorizes the level of terrorist risk.**

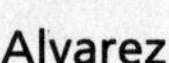
Alvarez

Kunitz

Walker

Carver

Momaday

Tan

As you read the selections in this unit, you will be asked to think about them in view of three key questions:

What is the **relationship** between literature and *place?*

How does **literature** shape or reflect *society?*

What makes **American** literature *American?*

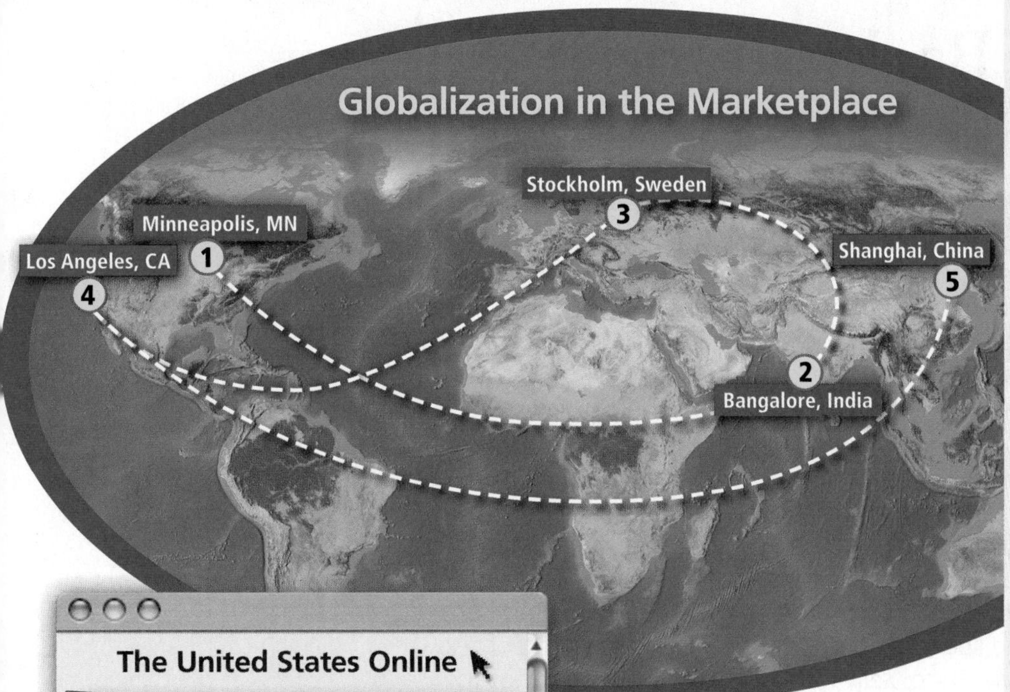

1. A woman in Minneapolis shops for a pair of snowshoes online. She calls a toll-free number on the Web site with questions.
2. A customer-service agent in Bangalore, India answers her questions.
3. The customer's order is received and processed by a computer at the sporting goods company in Stockholm, Sweden. Messages are sent to two locations.
4. A message to the Swedish company's warehouse in Los Angeles tells workers to ship the snowshoes.
5. Another message to a factory in Shanghai, China tells workers to produce more snowshoes and ship them to Los Angeles.

The United States Online

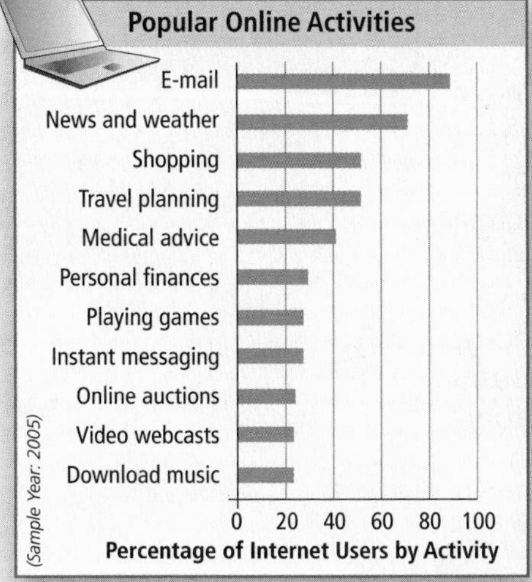

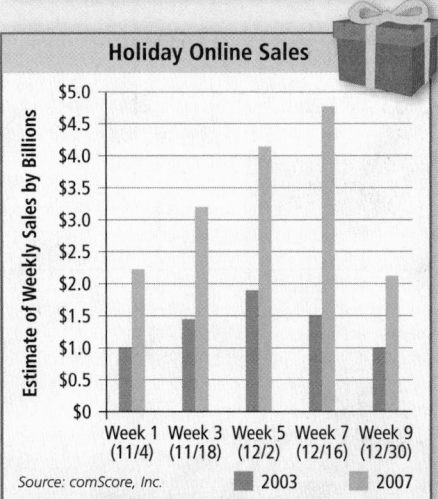

Holiday Online Sales

Estimate of Weekly Sales by Billions

$5.0, $4.5, $4.0, $3.5, $3.0, $2.5, $2.0, $1.5, $1.0, $0.5, $0

Week 1 (11/4) Week 3 (11/18) Week 5 (12/2) Week 7 (12/16) Week 9 (12/30)

Source: comScore, Inc.

2003 2007

Integration of Knowledge and Ideas What does the information presented in the charts and graphs on this page suggest about changing relationships among countries and individuals in the contemporary period? **[Connect]**

Environmental Movement 1970 – Present

1970: The first Earth Day is celebrated on April 22.

1971: Greenpeace Foundation protests U.S. nuclear testing off the coast of Alaska.

1977: Negotiations on the Kyoto Protocol are finalized on December 11. The goal is to reduce greenhouse gases.

1999: For the first time, a mass-produced hybrid vehicle is available in the United States.

2007: The Live Earth concert on July 7 gathers a global audience in support of a campaign to solve the climate crisis.

2007: Al Gore and the Intergovernmental Panel on Climate Change share the Nobel Peace Prize for their roles in climate change education.

Historical Background

The Contemporary Period (1970–Present)

When they created the United States, the American founders set out to build a democratic republic in a natural paradise. They established a great nation, and they foresaw its leadership role, but they could hardly have imagined how interconnected and interdependent all the nations of the world would become by the twenty-first century. At the nation's beginning, Americans celebrated the New World. Now, as part of the global community, Americans are shaping a *new* New World.

Politics and Space The bicentennial of the United States in 1976 highlighted pride in the American accomplishment. Even though the nation was still recovering from the traumas of the Vietnam War and the Watergate affair—the burglary of Democratic Party headquarters that forced the resignation of President Richard Nixon in 1974—Americans celebrated the nation's 200th birthday with great pride. Space exploration, especially the triumph of the space shuttle, offered an escape from politics. The first American woman in space, Sally Ride, was part of the crew of the space shuttle *Challenger* in 1983.

Leadership and Conflict Voters sent Ronald Reagan, the popular governor of California, to the White House in 1980 and again in 1984 with a landslide victory. George Bush, Reagan's vice president, was elected to the presidency in 1988. Seeking reelection in 1992, Bush faced a tough fight against high unemployment, a recession, and growing dissatisfaction with government. Democrat Bill Clinton and his running mate Al Gore—the youngest ticket in American history—won the election. Clinton won reelection in 1996, but in 2000 Al Gore lost to George Bush's son, George W. Bush. In the wake of the terrorist attacks of September 11, 2001, Bush was reelected in 2004. The elections of 2008 resulted in a historic victory with the election of Barack Obama, the nation's first African American president.

TIMELINE

1970

◀ **1970:** Walt Disney World opens in Florida, becoming one of the top travel destinations in the world.

1970: At Kent State University, four students are killed by the National Guard while protesting the Vietnam War.

1971: Chile Poet Pablo Neruda wins the Nobel Prize for Literature.

1972: China President Nixon makes a historic visit to China.

▼ **1972:** Last U.S. combat troops leave Vietnam.

The Computer Age With the introduction of the microprocessor in the 1970s, American life shifted. Computers that began as military and business tools soon became personal companions. The Internet has made information and entertainment available at any time to anyone with a desktop computer, a laptop, or a cellphone. Ever smaller, faster, and easier, technology can now connect anyone with everyone electronically, raising new questions of privacy and personal relations. "Mail" has a new meaning and "text" has become a verb. Workers "telecommute" and fans "download" their favorites. From how your government runs to how you gossip with your friends, computers have transformed virtually every aspect of life in America.

The New Millennium Despite the speed of technological change, however, some of the oldest issues still dominate human affairs. What is our relationship to the natural world? How can people of different cultures live together peacefully? How can people build a better future? One thing is certain: As the new millennium moves forward, America will continue to change and Americans will continue to explore new aspects of life, liberty, and the pursuit of happiness.

Key Historical Theme: Creating the Future

- Americans celebrated two hundred years of progress and democracy during the 1976 bicentennial.
- Americans struggle with political and economic problems at home while dealing with intense international conflicts.
- Americans live in a time of accelerated technological change that makes life easier and raises new questions.
- Americans work toward creating the future while facing persistent issues, such as care of the natural world.

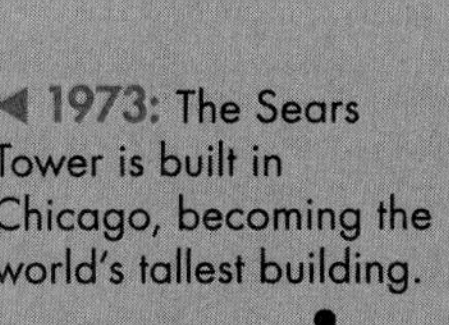

◀ **1973:** The Sears Tower is built in Chicago, becoming the world's tallest building.

◀ **1974:** Nixon resigns as president following exposure of his involvement in the Watergate scandals.

1978

1970: Africa A seven-year drought results in the starvation of 100,000 people.

1975: Francisco Franco dies, ending his dictatorship that began with the Spanish Civil War.

Essential Questions Across Time

The Contemporary Period (1970–Present)

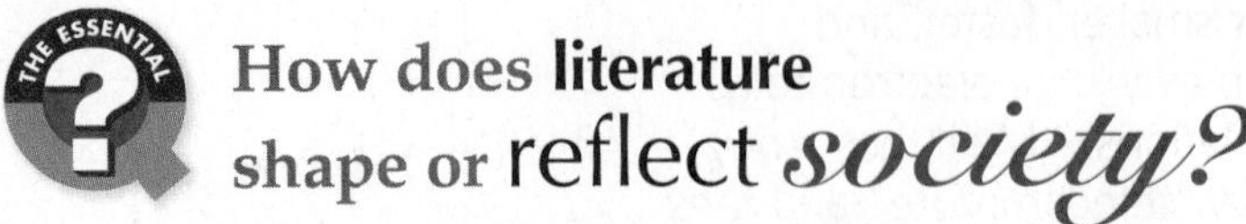
THE ESSENTIAL
How does literature
shape or reflect society?

What social and political events have had the greatest impact on Americans since 1970?

Advance of the Computer Age Digital libraries, electronic voting, global positioning, virtual communities—Americans work, play, think, and even feel differently than did earlier generations. In an increasingly wireless and paperless world, Americans express themselves differently. Change is constant and quick, and many Americans are eager to live on the edge of the latest electronic moment.

Cultural Diversity The 2010 census reported nearly 309 million people in the United States, encompassing a wide spectrum of races and cultural origins. Americans have grown closely attuned to cultural difference and diversity. Historians have revised views of the contributions of individuals once thought to be marginal, and virtually every cultural group has entered into the mainstream of American political, business, and artistic life.

Terrorism The terrorist attacks of September 11, 2001, had an enormous impact on the American consciousness. Americans reacted with anger, fear, appeals for calm, and calls for retaliation. The first decade of the millennium was characterized by an increased sense of vulnerability, more active participation in international affairs, and heightened awareness of the need to resolve the complex situation.

TIMELINE

1978

1978: The Supreme Court upholds affirmative action in *Regents of the University of California v. Bakke.*

1979: **Trinidad** V. S. Naipaul publishes *A Bend in the River.*

1979: **Vietnam** Hundreds of thousands of "boat people" flee Vietnam.

1979: **England** Margaret Thatcher becomes British prime minister. ▶

What values and attitudes have grown out of these events?

Personality vs. Anonymity "On the Internet, nobody knows you're a dog." So goes the caption of a cartoon showing a canine computer user. The cartoon highlights a great advance and a great drawback of the Computer Age. People may express themselves more fully than ever before, but they may also remain, or become, anonymous. Computers have made trust, authenticity, and accuracy major social and cultural concerns.

Materialism and Commercialism While aiding many countries around the world and dealing with economic problems at home, the United States still revels in material progress. Despite ups and downs, commerce fueled by advertising provides most Americans with a high standard of living compared to that of most other nations.

Multiculturalism Once, the "melting pot" image described American life: Immigrants were expected to become indistinguishable from the mass of other Americans. Now, Americans recognize the value of maintaining and savoring the cultural identities of people who are, at the same time, American. Global awareness, too, has made the achievements of cultures around the world not merely exotic but celebrated.

Security Attacked on its own soil in 2001, the nation guards itself with vigilance. Individuals, too, protect themselves from the new computer-assisted crime of identity theft.

The American EXPERIENCE

DAILY LIFE

Blogs: Democratizing the Writing World

The Life You Blog May Be Your Own—in fact, it probably is. Born of the word Weblog—a log or record of activities, thoughts, and comments that anyone may post on the World Wide Web—blogging has become a significant cultural enterprise. Contemporary technology has made it possible for anyone to be published, and millions of people turn themselves into authors every day.

Entering the blogosphere is like having a diary of the world available, the private made public. Want to know what someone in another part of the country had for breakfast? You can certainly find a blog that lets you know. Want to tell the world what you thought of the latest movie? Someone somewhere wants your opinion.

In an age dominated by visual media—movies, television, video, Webcasts—blogging reminds us of the central role that writing still plays in our culture. Of course (like all writing) blogs may be trivial, tedious, self-serving, stupid, or even cruel. They can also be intelligent, incisive, entertaining, and even beautiful.

Political candidates explain themselves in blogs. Teachers expand their lessons in blogs. Artists experiment in blogs, and critics share their insights in blogs. It is even possible to become a professional and blog for a living.

There is a world of words out there in the blogosphere. So blog away!

1981: IBM makes "PC" a household term in America with the release of its first personal computer. ▶

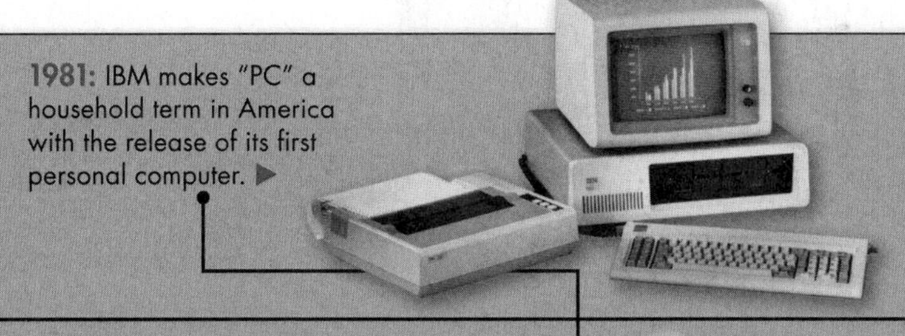

1982: Colombian novelist Gabriel Garcia Márquez wins the Nobel Prize for Literature.

1982: Alice Walker publishes *The Color Purple*.

1984

◀ **1981:** Sandra Day O'Connor becomes the first woman appointed to the U.S. Supreme Court.

▶ **1982:** Vietnam Veterans Memorial is dedicated in Washington, D.C.

How are these values and attitudes expressed in American literature?

Diversity Perhaps nothing characterizes contemporary American literature more clearly than the range of its writers. Authors of every race, age, religion, nationality, culture, occupation, political affiliation, economic class, and level of talent express themselves.

Nonfiction Although fiction continues as a vital literary mode, contemporary readers have a strong appetite for reality-based tales and nonfiction. Autobiography, biography, history, true-life adventures, and stories of ordeals and practical accomplishments fill the bookstores.

Technology New modes of delivery, made possible by computer technology, enable people to read in new ways. Books and periodicals can be read on computer screens, cell phones, and electronic readers. Books, or parts of books, can be ordered and printed on demand.

Themes While American writers continue to explore the fundamental themes that literature has always addressed, some themes have a special appeal in our time:

- **Identity** Personal identity and cultural identity—who we are as individuals and who we are as Americans—are often profound concerns for writers of contemporary fiction and nonfiction.
- **Truth and Illusion** What is true, and how do we know it? In an age when "special effects" can manipulate almost anything, contemporary literature explores what it means to merge reality and imagination.
- **Success** Success—whether material, political, or spiritual—has always been an American preoccupation. Writers are now taking another hard look at it: What makes a person genuinely happy? How do ideas of success affect individuals, communities, or the planet as a whole?
- **Family** Contemporary society is redefining the family, creating the future with new social units. American literature is playing a vital role in examining what a family is and what it can be.

ESSENTIAL QUESTION VOCABULARY

These Essential Question words will help you think and write about literature and society:

virtual (vʉr´ cho͞o əl) *adj.* of, pertaining to, or taking place in cyberspace

diversity (də vʉr´ sə tē) *n.* quality of being varied, not homogenous

spectrum (spek´ trəm) *n.* wide range; complete extent

TIMELINE

1984

1986: **USSR** Chernobyl nuclear disaster spreads a radioactive cloud across Eastern Europe.

1986: The Space Shuttle *Challenger* explodes 73 seconds after launching, killing all seven crew members.

▲ 1987: President Reagan and Soviet leader Mikhail Gorbachev sign the INF treaty, agreeing to ban short-range and medium-range nuclear missiles.

1988: George Bush is elected president. ▼

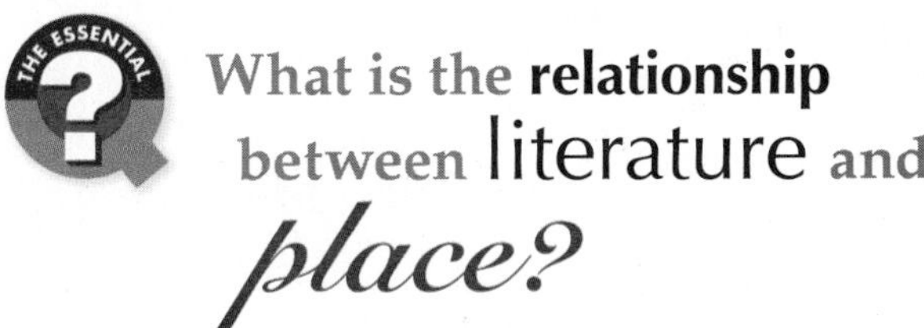

What is the **relationship** between literature and *place?*

What kinds of places do contemporary Americans write about?

Ordinary Places Of course Americans still write about cities and towns, homes and schools, streets and malls. Readers find realistic life in the works of such writers as John Updike, Anne Tyler, Richard Russo, Richard Ford, Edward P. Jones, Michael Chabon, Jhumpa Lahiri, and Annie Proulx.

Ordinary Places Transformed Some writers set their stories in what-if places that have been dramatically, even fantastically, transformed. In Philip Roth's *The Plot Against America* (2004), prejudice and chaos rule the nation. In *The Road* (2006), Cormac McCarthy tracks a grim journey through a post-apocalyptic American landscape.

How does a global awareness show up in American literature?

Green Literature A literary sub-genre emphasizes the relationship of people to the planet as a whole, tackling such topics as pollution and ecoterrorism. "Ecofiction" includes Barbara Kingsolver's *Prodigal Summer* (2000) and T. C. Boyle's *A Friend of the Earth* (2000). In nonfiction, essays by Annie Dillard and John McPhee build on the legacy of Henry David Thoreau. In poetry, natural imagery is at the heart of the verse of Gary Snyder, W. S. Merwin, and A. R. Ammons.

The American EXPERIENCE

A LIVING TRADITION

A. R. Ammons, Emersonian Postmodernist

A. R. Ammons, a North Carolinian, looked at an unusual aspect of the American place. In a long poem called *Garbage* (1993), Ammons takes trash—and the reprocessing of it—as a symbol of our times. Unlike Modernists who strove to create poems that were well-constructed artifacts, Ammons, in good Postmodernist style, creates a talky, sprawling, shifting poem that is itself like a trash heap and that considers, among so many other things, its own making.

Emerson might have blinked and rubbed his eyes if he could have read this poem. However, he might also have recognized in it his own, distinctly American belief in newness.

from "Garbage" by A. R. Ammons

garbage has to be the poem of our time because
garbage is spiritual, believable enough

to get our attention, getting in the way, piling
up, stinking, turning brooks brownish and

creamy white: what else deflects us from the
errors of our illusionary ways . . .

• • •

here is the gateway to beginning, here the portal
of renewing change . . .

1989: China Pro-democracy demonstrations are violently suppressed at Tiananmen Square. ▶

◀ **1989: Germany** The Berlin Wall comes down.

1990: Congress passes the Americans with Disabilities Act, prohibiting discrimination against people with disabilities.

1991: USSR The Soviet Union is dissolved, resulting in the formation of fifteen independent nations.

1991: Middle East Unified forces led by U.S. defeat Iraq in Persian Gulf War.

1991: South Africa Apartheid—the system of racial segregation—is repealed.

1992

How has electronic technology, by changing our surroundings, also changed our literature?

Communication Technology that has made communication faster and easier has altered the limitations of physical space and place.

- *Character to character:* Fictional characters frequently communicate by cell phone, and e-mail is a common plot device.
- *Author to reader:* Authors now use Web sites to explain, expand, and discuss their works with their audiences.
- *Reader to reader:* Readers meet online to discuss books and authors, sharing ideas and opinions.
- *Reader to author:* Readers ask questions, respond, criticize, and make suggestions. This greater interactivity even turns some readers into authors themselves when fans write their own prequels and sequels to their favorite books.

Cultural References Similes, metaphors, allusions, and references of all kinds now often stem from television, movies, and the world of computers. Electronic media have centered themselves in the cultural mainstream, sometimes overshadowing traditional literary sources. Contemporary readers are just as likely to meet a reference to the Starship *Enterprise* as they are to Captain Ahab's *Pequod.* Cultural merging is taking place: In 2007, MtvU, part of the popular MTV Network, chose the renowned postmodern poet John Ashbery to be its first poet laureate.

Cyberliterature Cyberliterature, including hyperfiction and electronic poetry, is literature that is composed and experienced on computers. Hyperfiction offers nonlinear, multi-path, open-ended narratives that enable readers to "travel" around within a story, choosing where they want to go, deciding which characters and themes they want to follow. Electronic poetry uses the visual and aural capabilities of the computer to unfold new and colorful poetic experiences right before the reader's eyes.

ESSENTIAL QUESTION VOCABULARY

These Essential Question words will help you think and write about literature and place:

transform (trans fôrm′) *v.* change the condition, nature, or function of

interactive (in′tər ak′tiv) *adj.* reciprocally active; involving communication between technology and users or among people

global (glō′bəl) *adj.* affecting or including the whole world

1992

1992: Bill Clinton is elected president. ▶

1993: Toni Morrison wins the Nobel Prize for Literature. ▶

1994: **Rwanda** Hundreds of thousands of ethnic Tutsis are killed in the Rwandan Genocide.

1994: **England/France** The Channel Tunnel that crosses the English Channel opens.

1994: **South Africa** Nelson Mandela becomes the first democratically elected president. ▶

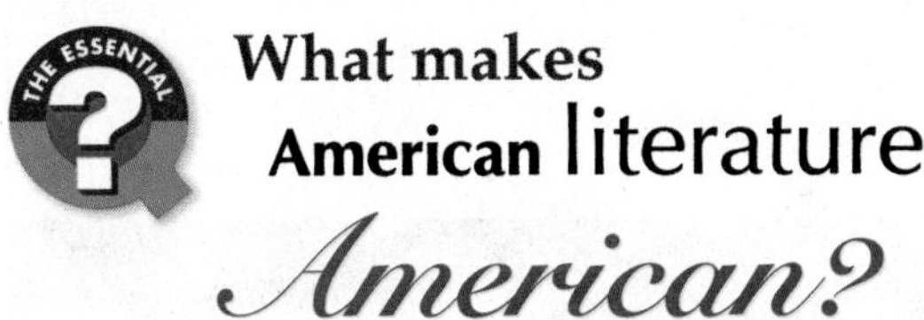

What makes American literature *American?*

What qualities distinguish American literature today?

Cultural Diversity Just as American identity is a unique combination of the nation's mix of people, so is American literature a unique product of that mix. Cross-cultural contributions in subjects, forms, styles, and languages keep American writing alive, open, and adaptable.

Expanding Definition of Literature The definition of literature itself is changing. Just as nonfiction and fiction are merging, so are the "popular" and the "literary." Walk into a bookstore to find a novel that includes recipes, a poem that accompanies a photo essay, a romance that is "based on a true story," a graphic novel that is based on a movie, or a "nonfiction novel" based on a current event. All of it is literature.

Traditional and Postmodern Despite all that is changing, however, the American literary tradition continues to flourish. Writers still produce literature in time-tested forms and styles. Hawthorne would recognize a story by Joyce Carol Oates, and Whitman would celebrate a poem by A. R. Ammons. The co-existence of the traditional and the new has spurred a new vibrancy in American literary life.

The American EXPERIENCE

DEVELOPING AMERICAN ENGLISH

Brave New Words
by Richard Lederer

The history of a living language like English is a history of constant change. Language is like a tree that sheds its leaves and grows new ones so that it may live on. New words, like new leaves, are essential to a living, healthy vocabulary.

Throughout history, as English speakers and writers have met with new objects, experiences, and ideas, they have needed new words to describe them. Nowadays, an average of 5,000 new words enter our language each year! The Anglo-Saxons used a vivid term to describe the great wealth of English—the *word-hoard.*

We needed a name for the system that connects computers around the world. So we combined the Latin prefix *inter,* "together," with the Anglo-Saxon word for a mesh fabric, and—presto!—we came up with the *Internet.*

The study of life on other worlds we have labeled *astrobiology,* from the Greek word parts *astro* ("star") + *bio* ("life") + *logy* ("study of").

The entire chromosomal makeup of an organism we now call the *genome*—a blend of two Greek words, *gene(e)* and *(chromos)ome.*

The brave new worlds of the arts and sciences, technology and medicine make headlines every day, but our English "word-hoard" will never run out of prefixes, suffixes, and roots to identify new concepts.

1995: Amy Tan publishes her third novel, *The Hundred Secret Senses.*

1996: Summer Olympic Games are held in Atlanta, Georgia.

1997: **China** Hong Kong returns to Chinese rule, ending British rule. ▶

1997: A lamb is cloned from a single cell of an adult sheep.

1999: Conflict between Albanians and Serbs in Kosovo leads to a war between Serbia and NATO forces.

2000

The American EXPERIENCE

CONTEMPORARY CONNECTION

Stephanie Strickland: Hypertext Poetry Pioneer

Take the power of poetry to evoke emotion and charge the imagination and combine it with the power of new media and you get what some are calling a new literary genre: hypertext, or electronic poetry. Hypertext poetry presents text with graphics, images, sound, and live links to other texts. By choosing particular links, the reader shapes his or her own reading experience.

Poet Stephanie Strickland is a hypertext pioneer whose works live on the Web. Words dance on the screen, images shimmer, colors swirl. The reader becomes a viewer, a listener, and a participant. An artfully lettered phrase drifts across the screen and turns like a falling leaf while a wave crashes behind it, then more phrases follow.

On the one hand, Strickland simply does what poets have always done, which is engage readers' senses and emotions. However, she uses more than words in her creation of poetry. Readers might wonder, then: Is this a new generation of poetry or a different art form entirely? Just because it is easy to enjoy, is it easy to understand? In an interview in the *Iowa Web Review*, Strickland offers some insight. "My poetry wants to move from static moment to dynamic movement because that is the way the world feels to me."

TIMELINE

2000

▲ **2000:** George W. Bush defeats Al Gore in an extremely close and controversial presidential election.

2001: Hijacked planes crash into the World Trade Center in New York, the Pentagon in Washington, D.C., and a field in Pennsylvania on the same day. Thousands of lives are lost.

2002: The computer industry sells its 1 billionth personal computer, according to a study of worldwide sales.

◀ **2002: Europe** The Euro becomes the official currency of the European Union.

What is "postmodern" in American literature?

"Postmodern" signals works created after Modernism. Here are some of the qualities that help to define postmodern literature:

- **Awareness of Itself** A postmodern work is self-conscious. A postmodern character might refer to the novel he lives in, and a postmodern writer might comment on the story or poem the reader is reading.
- **Release from Meaning** World War II, the atomic bomb, and the Holocaust undercut reliance on rational meaning and the assumption that a work of art could, or needed to, mean anything at all.
- **Interest in Process** A postmodern work is recognized as an ongoing experience. Some works offer alternative versions of themselves.
- **Desire to Revise the Past** A postmodern work does not hesitate to use the past extensively, even re-seeing and rewriting it.
- **Desire to Have Fun** A postmodern work does not take itself so seriously. It may merge "high" and "low" culture. It may feel like a game.

Which American writers are pointing us toward the future?

American writing of extraordinary beauty, passion, imagination, and zest continues to tell us who we are and who we can become:

- Toni Morrison's *Beloved* (1987), an acclaimed narrative of slavery and sacrifice told in a challenging mosaic style
- Andrea Barrett's *Ship Fever* (1996), gripping stories that interweave fiction, history, and science
- Dave Eggers's *A Heartbreaking Work of Staggering Genius* (2000), a postmodern family memoir of profound compassion

Contemporary American poets such as Louise Glück, Ann Lauterbach, Yusef Komunyakaa, and Li-Young Lee provide the verbal soundtrack that will accompany us through the twenty-first century.

ESSENTIAL QUESTION VOCABULARY

These Essential Question words will help you think and write about American literature:

cross-cultural (krôs-kul′chər əl) *adj.* of or relating to different cultures and nations

vibrancy (vī′ brən sē) *n.* radiance, energy, vigor

self-conscious (self-kän′shəs) *adj.* state of being aware of oneself

◀ **2004:** The National Museum of the American Indian opens in Washington, D.C.

◀ **2008:** Barack Obama is elected the first African American president of the United States.

Present

▼ **2003:** 43,435 hybrid electrical vehicles are registered in the United States, a 25.8% increase over the previous year.

2004: Indonesia An earthquake in the Indian Ocean causes a tsunami that claims 186,000 lives.

2005: Hurricane Katrina results in a severe loss of life and property in Louisiana, Mississippi, and Alabama.

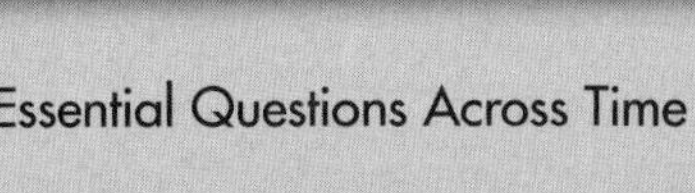

Recent Scholarship

Julia Alvarez

All-American Writer

People often ask me how come I became an American writer. Often there is a tone of surprise. For although I was born in New York City, my Dominican parents returned "home" when I was a month old. I grew up in another culture and language.

I like to respond to the question by saying, I am an all-American writer. My love of stories and many of my characters and even the cadences of my English sentences come from the southern Americas and the musical, rococo extravagances of Spanish; whereas the language I've learned to craft and the literary tradition I've studied comes from the northern part of the Americas. I truly am an all-American writer, in the more expansive, hemispheric sense.

I grew up in a culture, steeped in the oral tradition of storytelling. Stories were shared within a community or family gathering, not through the solitary act of reading. In part, we were living in a repressive dictatorship, where books marked you as an intellectual and a troublemaker. People relied on "Radio Bemba": Radio Big Mouth. Stories were passed on from one teller to another, keeping the love of freedom alive. When we escaped in 1960 leaving everything behind, I carried with me this love and respect for the power of stories.

About the Author

Shortly after her birth, Julia Alvarez moved from New York City to the Dominican Republic with her family. When Alvarez was ten, however, her family was forced to return to the United States because her father was involved in a rebellion against the country's dictator. The sudden change of home and culture was a shock to Alvarez, but she found solace in reading and writing. *In the Time of the Butterflies* and *How the García Girls Lost Their Accents* are among Alvarez's acclaimed novels that reflect these early experiences.

We arrived in a United States that was not very welcoming to foreigners who looked and acted different, who spoke English with an accent. I felt homesick and lost until I discovered the world of written-down stories where everyone was welcomed. I became a reader and again realized the power of stories. Reading, I could become a Danish prince or a young Greek girl wanting to bury her dead brother or an old man on a boat trying to catch a fish. I no longer felt so lonely or lost. The more I read, the more I wanted to contribute to this great circle of storytellers. I had stories to tell and by writing them down I could share them with an invisible community of readers that were to become my new native country.

But I had entered a United States where the civil rights movement was just getting under way. The women's movement, multiculturalism, Native American rights—all these awakenings were still to come. Literature itself reflected these biases. There wasn't a diversity of authors of different traditions and backgrounds in our anthologies and in the curriculum in our classrooms. Since none of the classics we were studying were written by people like me, I began to doubt that I could become an American writer.

But then in one of those anthologies among absent voices and missing stories, I found the Langston Hughes poem, "I, too, Sing America." It was music to my ears. I understood what Mr. Hughes was saying: he was claiming his place in the chorus of American song, an America that was still not listening to him, still treating him as a second-class literary citizen, sent to the kitchen of minor writers, instead of allowing him a place at the table of American literature. But no matter. Mr. Hughes knew that tomorrow he'd be at the table. The fact that Mr. Hughes' poem was in my textbook meant his dream had come true. This was an important voice for a young girl of another culture and language and background with her heart full of dreams to hear.

In my lifetime, I've been lucky enough to experience a sea change in what is considered American literature. When I started writing in the late 60s, the work of my fellow Latina/o writers and other so-called ethnic writers was still considered the province of sociology. But in the late seventies and early eighties, influenced by the opening up of the canon to Afro-American and women's literature, writers of other traditions within the United States were suddenly "discovered." Just as Columbus "discovered" an America that was already home to old cultures and traditions, we who had been writing for several decades began to be welcome at Mr. Hughes' table.

It's an expansion that has enriched American literature—all these varied cadences and stories from so many different traditions. It's a richness that is truly at the heart of America, as Walt Whitman, the quintessential "American" poet, knew way back when he wrote, "I hear America singing, the varied carols I hear." This has always been a country made up of people who came from somewhere else encountering the people who preceded them here. Out of this encounter can come silencing and segregation but also—and this can be our greatness: a more inclusive and astonishingly diverse country and culture. Literature has always been about this multiculturalism, about becoming each other and realizing that we share the same human experience. Stories have always known that the table is wide enough for all of us, Langston Hughes and Walt Whitman and Raymond Carver and Maxine Hong Kingston, and even an all-American writer born in New York City but raised in the Dominican Republic, Julia Alvarez.

There's also room for you. So, pull up a chair because if you want to be a writer, you have to become a reader first.

Collaboration: Speaking and Listening

In her celebration of multiculturalism, Julia Alvarez asserts that "becoming each other" has always been part of the American experience. At the same time, American identity has also been defined by individuality and independence. In a **small group discussion,** examine these two aspects of American life. As a group, choose a moderator to help keep your discussion going and to be sure all opinions are heard. Encourage diverse perspectives from all participants.

Integrate and Evaluate Information

1. Use a chart like the one shown to determine the key ideas expressed in the Essential Question essays on pages 1282–1289. Fill in two ideas related to each Essential Question and note an author closely associated with each concept. One example has been done for you.

Essential Question	Key Concept	Key Author
Literature and Place		
American Literature	Environmental Concerns	Annie Dillard
Literature and Society		

2. How do the visual sources in this section—maps, graphs, timelines, photographs, and artifacts—add to your understanding of the ideas expressed in words? Cite specific examples.
3. Throughout our history as a nation, Americans have valued innovation and progress. Are those values as important in contemporary America as they were in, for example, the nineteenth century? Have other values, such as those involving respect for traditions or a wish to slow the pace of change, arisen to modify the national character? Cite evidence from the multiple sources presented on pages 1278–1289, as well as other materials provided throughout this textbook, in your answer.
4. **Solve a Research Problem** Julia Alvarez explains, "I am an all-American writer, in the ... hemispheric sense." Her complex cultural perspective is part of a broader development in American letters. Research another contemporary author who writes from a similar dual perspective. Write a report of your findings. Integrate information from this textbook and other sources to support your ideas.

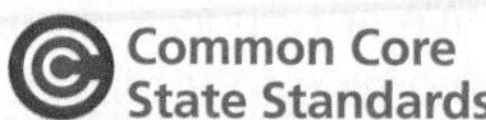

Common Core State Standards

Reading Informational Text

7. Integrate and evaluate multiple sources of information presented in different media or formats as well as in words in order to address a question or solve a problem.

Speaking and Listening

1. Initiate and participate effectively in a range of collaborative discussions with diverse partners on grade 11 topics, texts, and issues.

1.a. Come to discussions prepared, having read and researched material under study; explicitly draw on that preparation by referring to evidence from texts and other research on the topic or issue to stimulate a thoughtful, well-reasoned exchange of ideas.

1.b. Work with peers to promote civil, democratic discussions and decision-making and establish individual roles as needed. *(p. 1291)*

1.c. Ensure a hearing for a full range of positions on a topic or issue; promote divergent and creative perspectives. *(p. 1291)*

Speaking and Listening: Presentation and Discussion

Almost anyone can now shop, meet friends, and pay bills on the Web. Is cyberspace a new place, equal to the real world? Explore this question in an **oral presentation and discussion.**

Answer a Question As the basis for your presentation, create two sets of **travel directions** and maps. For the first set, pick a destination on the Web. Write directions that explain how to get there from a home page. Illustrate the directions with a "map." Then, choose a real-world place. Write directions, with a map, that explain how to get there from school. During your presentation, compare and contrast the sets of directions and maps. Then, conduct a class discussion. As a group, decide whether the virtual world of the Internet is a place equal in any way to the real world.

ESSENTIAL QUESTION VOCABULARY

Use these words in your responses:

Literature and Place
transform
interactive
global

American Literature
cross-cultural
vibrancy
self-conscious

Literature and Society
virtual
diversity
spectrum

TEXT SET

Contemporary Fiction

Part 1

 Themes Across Cultures: Author's Insights

Julia Alvarez Introduces

Antojos

Little did I know when I was writing my short story, "Antojos," that some day it would become the opening chapter of my first novel, *How the García Girls Lost Their Accents.* It makes sense though, that I would begin small—after all, I was an immigrant kid, daring to join my voice to the literature of my new country. As I gained confidence, I would inch forward, chapter by chapter, towards a larger, book-length form, a novel.

I often advise young writers who feel overwhelmed when they begin their first novels to think of each chapter as a short story with a beginning, a middle, and an end. When you finally put all those stories together, you will, of course, have to revise the whole from the perspective of a novel. But you will have written your first draft! This is another version of the writing advice that goes, write your essay, story, poem, word by word, page by page. That assures that each paragraph is beautifully and carefully crafted. Each word counts! Emily Dickinson, one of my favorite writers, once noted that there are "no approximate words in a poem." Now that's a high standard for prose, but a passionate writer doesn't mind a challenge!

But when I began writing "Antojos," I was not plotting a novel. I had been writing many short stories about being an immigrant and arriving in a new country. At some point, I wondered what would it be like for my characters to go back to where they came from? In one of my English classes, we had read a short story by Thomas Wolfe, whose bio mentioned that he'd written a novel titled *You Can't Go Home Again.* Often, in my own return trips to visit family in the Dominican Republic, I had found myself feeling the same thing!

Now I could have written an essay addressing why exactly you can never go back to where you came from. Elaborating central issues. Citing research on returning exiles. Maybe including certain personal experiences that supported my thesis. But that's not how a short story works. You actually play out a situation through characters and actions and see where it takes you! It's like life, you live through an

About the Author

Julia Alvarez is an award-winning and commercially successful novelist, poet, and nonfiction writer. For more information about her, see page 1297.

experience and when you come out the other end and think about it, you go, wow, Better to have loved and lost than never to have loved at all! But that lived experience (that leads to that insight) is what stories are interested in. And that experience, of course, happens to a character. In your life, it's you; in a story, it's someone you make up who might have a lot of you in him or her.

Another way a story speaks is through details and little scenes of dialogue and interaction. In my story, I didn't know why I tacked that Palmolive poster on the cantina post. Sure, I had seen such posters when I traveled in the D.R. (A writer is always "doing research"!) When I was describing the setting in my story, I pulled that little detail from past experience. Once it was in the story, I realized I had one of those "loaded details" that teachers sometimes call "symbols." Just a way of saying, pay attention to this detail. It has something to tell you. But it's never a set meaning. It's rich and ambiguous and shifts with each reading.

Which leads to a final point about stories. They say what can't be put in easy capsule form. They don't have messages. They are luminous and mysterious. You can go home in some ways, and in other ways you can't. But only a story can include all these nuances and feelings and insights in a way that gives us pleasure and deepens our understanding of our lives. You can't sum up a story. You have to be there. And a good writer puts you there, word by word, page by page.

Critical Reading

Cite textual evidence to support your responses.

1. **Key Ideas and Details (a)** According to Alvarez, how do essays and short stories differ? **(b) Speculate:** What kind of understanding might a short story provide about an experience that an essay could not, and vice versa?
2. **Key Ideas and Details (a) Interpret:** What does Alvarez suggest about the connection between authors and their characters? **(b) Speculate:** Do you think most stories contain insights into the lives of their authors? Explain.

As You Read "Antojos" . . .

3. Notice ways in which Alvarez's story speaks through "details and little scenes of dialogue and interaction."
4. Think about ways in which Alvarez's fictional story is reminiscent of her own real life experiences.

Building Knowledge and Insight *Antojos*

Connecting to the Essential Question In this story, a young woman returns to her native country after many years away. As you read, notice details that suggest the people, places, sounds, sights, and tastes Yolanda misses about her homeland. Doing so will help you think about the Essential Question: **What is the relationship between literature and place?**

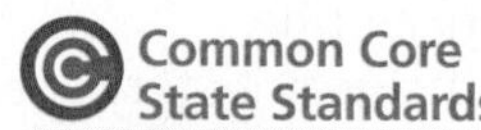

Common Core State Standards

Reading Literature
3. Analyze the impact of the author's choices regarding how to develop and relate elements of a story or drama (e.g., how the action is ordered).
5. Analyze how an author's choices concerning how to structure specific parts of a text contribute to its overall structure and meaning as well as its aesthetic impact.

Close Reading Focus

Plot Devices

While many stories begin at the start of a series of events, some begin *in medias res,* which is Latin for "in the middle of things." Alvarez begins this story with her main character well on her way into the mountains:

> ***For the first time since Yolanda had reached the hills, there was a shoulder on the left side of the narrow road.***

In medias res is a **plot device** writers use to grab readers' interest. Other plot devices are **flashback,** in which a scene from the past interrupts the action, and **foreshadowing,** the dropping of clues to suggest events that have yet to occur. As you read "Antojos," notice how Alvarez uses all of these plot devices to fill in background information, heighten suspense, and add interest and excitement.

Preparing to Read Complex Texts **Making predictions,** or anticipating events, is a useful way to engage with a story and better understand its meaning. To make predictions, consider what you know about the characters and setting and apply your understanding of human nature. In this story, you may also consider background information about the Dominican Republic. As you read, use a chart like the one shown to track and confirm the predictions you make.

Background Knowledge

+

Clues Within the Text

=

Prediction

Vocabulary

The words below are important to understanding the text that follows. Copy the words into your notebook. Which part of speech is the word *collusion*? How can you tell?

dissuade	**machetes**
maneuver	**collusion**
appease	**docile**

JULIA ALVAREZ (b. 1950)

Author of "Antojos"

Poet and fiction writer Julia Alvarez was born in New York City but raised in the Dominican Republic until she was ten years old. When her father's involvement in a plot to overthrow that country's dictator, Rafael Trujillo, was uncovered, the family fled to the United States. "I came into English as a ten-year-old from the Dominican Republic, and I consider this radical uprooting from my culture, my native language, my country, the reason I began writing," Alvarez once explained.

Writing to Ease the Pain While moving to a new country changed her life, Alvarez quickly found her voice as a writer. She said, "I landed, not in the United States, but in the English language. That became my new home . . . ." As a young adult, Alvarez found that writing helped her deal with the pain of adjustment to a new culture and language. After graduating from college, Alvarez earned a masters degree in creative writing at Syracuse University. She went on to join the Kentucky Arts Commission's poetry-in-the-schools program. For two years, she traveled around Kentucky teaching poetry.

"The point is not to pay back kindness but to pass it on."

Writing to Understand For Alvarez, writing "is a way to understand yourself. You learn how you feel about things, but you're also making your little statement about things, and that makes you feel a little bit more powerful." Alvarez's poetry often focuses on her personal experiences as well as her Caribbean heritage. She has published three volumes of poetry: *Homecoming* (1984), *The Other Side* (1995), and *The Woman I Kept to Myself* (2004).

A Storytelling Tradition After *Homecoming* was published, Alvarez began to focus on a new area of writing: fiction. "My own island background was steeped in a tradition of storytelling that I wanted to explore in prose," Alvarez explained. The move to prose proved fruitful, for Alvarez has won fame for four novels rooted in Hispanic American tradition: *How the Garcia Girls Lost Their Accents* (1991), *In the Time of the Butterflies* (1994), *¡Yo!* (1997), and *In the Name of Salomé* (2000). Her fiction, like her poetry, deals with both the immigrant experience and her own bicultural identity.

Antojos[1]

JULIA ALVAREZ

1. **Antojos** (än tō´ hōs) Spanish for "cravings." The story explores additional connotations of the word.

BACKGROUND Alvarez's homeland, the Dominican Republic, won independence in 1844 after a rebellion against Haitian rule. Since then, the country has suffered through dictatorships and foreign domination. One of the most ruthless dictators was Rafael Trujillo, who ruled from 1930 until he was assassinated in 1961. Alvarez's father was part of an underground movement against Trujillo and it was this involvement that forced the Alvarez family to flee the country.

For the first time since Yolanda had reached the hills, there was a shoulder on the left side of the narrow road. She pulled the car over out of a sense of homecoming: every other visit she had stayed with her family in the capital.

Once her own engine was off, she heard the sound of another motor, approaching, a pained roar as if the engine were falling apart. She made out an undertow of men's voices. Quickly, she got back into the car, locked the door, and pulled off the shoulder, hugging her right side of the road.

—Just in time too. A bus came lurching around the curve, obscuring her view with a belching of exhaust, the driver saluting or warning with a series of blasts on his horn. It was an old army bus, the official name brushed over with paint that didn't quite match the regulation gray. The passengers saw her only at the last moment, and all up and down her side of the bus, men poked out of the windows, hooting and yelling, waving purple party flags, holding out bottles and beckoning to her. She speeded up and left them behind, the small compact climbing easily up the snakey highway, its well-oiled hum a gratifying sound after the hullabaloo of the bus.

She tried the radio again, but all she could tune to was static even here on the summit hills. She would have to wait until she got to the coast to hear news of the hunger march in the capital. Her family had been worried that trouble would break out, for the march had been scheduled on the anniversary of the failed revolution nineteen years ago today. A huge turnout was expected. She bet that bus she had just passed had been delayed by breakdowns on its way to the capital. In fact, earlier on the road when she had first set out, Yolanda had passed buses and truckloads of men, drinking and shouting slogans. It crossed her mind that her family had finally agreed to loan her a car because they knew she'd be far safer on the north coast than in the capital city where revolutions always broke out.

The hills began to plane out into a high plateau, the road widening. Left and right, roadside stands began appearing. Yolanda slowed down and kept an eye out for guavas, supposedly in season this far north. Piled high on wooden stands were fruits she hadn't seen in so many years: pinkish-yellow mangoes, and tamarind pods oozing their rich sap, and small cashew fruits strung on a rope to keep them from bruising each other. There were little brown packets of roasted

◀ Critical Viewing
What elements of this artist's portrayal of fruit mirror Yolanda's feelings about guavas? **COMPARE**

Plot Devices
How do the opening paragraphs pull readers into the story?

Comprehension
What political event is occurring in the city as Yolanda drives into the hills?

cashews and bars of milk fudge wrapped in waxed paper and tied with a string, the color of which told what filling was inside the bar. Strips of meat, buzzing with flies, hung from the windows of butcher stalls. An occasional display of straw hats and baskets and hammocks told that tourists sometimes did pass by here. Looking at the stores spread before her, it was hard to believe the poverty the organizers of the march kept discussing on the radio. There seemed to be plenty here to eat—except for guavas.

Plot Devices

What information about Yolanda and her family is conveyed in this flashback?

In the capital, her aunts had plied her with what she most craved after so many years away. "Any little *antojo,* you must tell us!" They wanted to spoil her, so she'd stay on in her nativeland before she forgot where she had come from. "What exactly does it mean, *antojo?*" Yolanda asked. Her aunts were proven right: After so many years away, their niece was losing her Spanish.

"An *antojo*—" The aunts exchanged quizzical looks. "How to put it? An *antojo* is like a craving for something you have to eat."

A cousin blew out her cheeks. "Calories."

An *antojo,* one of the older aunts continued, was a very old Spanish word from before "your United States was thought of," she added tartly. In the countryside some *campesinos*[2] still used the word to mean possession by an island spirit demanding its due.

Her island spirit certainly was a patient soul, Yolanda joked. She hadn't had her favorite *antojo,* guavas, since her last trip seven years ago. Well, on this trip, her aunts promised, Yoyo could eat guavas to her heart's content. But when the gardener was summoned, he wasn't so sure. Guavas were no longer in season, at least not in the hotter lowlands of the south. Maybe up north, the chauffeur could pick her up some on his way back from some errand. Yolanda took this opportunity to inform her aunts of her plans: she could pick the guavas herself when she went up north in a few days.

Vocabulary

dissuade (di swād′) *v.* convince someone not to do something

—She was going up north? By herself? A woman alone on the road! "This is not the States." Her old aunts had tried to **dissuade** her. "Anything can happen." When Yolanda challenged them, "What?" they came up with boogeymen stories that made her feel as if she were talking to china dolls.[3] Haitian hougans[4] and Communist kidnappers. "And Martians?" Yolanda wanted to tease them. They had led such sheltered lives, riding from one safe place to another in their air-conditioned cars.

Plot Devices

What do the warnings of Yolanda's aunts suggest about future events in the story?

She had left the fruit stands behind her and was approaching a compound very much like her family's in the capital. The underbrush stopped abruptly at a high concrete wall, topped with broken bottle glass. Parked at the door was a chocolate brown Mercedes. Perhaps the owners had come up to their country home for the weekend to

---

2. ***campesinos*** (käm′ pe sē′ nōs) "poor farmers; simple rural dwellers" (Spanish).
3. **china dolls** old-fashioned, delicate dolls made of fragile high-quality porcelain or ceramic ware.
4. **Haitian hougans** (o͞o gänz′) voodoo priests or cult leaders.

avoid the troubles in the capital?

Just beyond the estate, Yolanda came upon a small village—ALTAMIRA in rippling letters on the corrugated tin roof of the first house. It was a little cluster of houses on either side of the road, a good place to stretch her legs before what she'd heard was a steep and slightly (her aunts had warned "very") dangerous descent to the coast. Yolanda pulled up at a cantina, the thatched roof held up by several posts. Instead of a menu, there was a yellowing, grimy poster for Palmolive soap tacked on one of the posts with a picture of a blonde woman under a spraying shower, her head thrown back in seeming ecstasy, her mouth opened in a wordless cry. ("Palmolive"? Yolanda wondered.) She felt even thirstier and grimier looking at this lathered beauty after her hot day on the road.

An old woman emerged at last from a shack behind the cabana, buttoning up a torn housedress, and followed closely by a little boy, who kept ducking behind her whenever Yolanda smiled at him. Asking him his name just drove him further into the folds of the old woman's skirt.

"You must excuse him, Doña,"[5] she apologized. "He's not used to being among people." But Yolanda knew the old woman meant, not the people in the village, but the people with money who drove through Altamira to the beaches on the coast. "Your name," the old woman repeated, as if Yolanda hadn't asked him in Spanish. The little boy mumbled at the ground. "Speak up!" the old woman scolded, but her voice betrayed pride when she spoke up for him. "This little know-nothing is Jose Duarte Sanchez y Mella Garcia."

Yolanda laughed. Not only were those a lot of names for such a little boy, but they certainly were momentous: the surnames of the three liberators of the country!

"Can I serve the Doña in any way?" the woman asked. Yolanda gave the tree line beyond the woman's shack a glance. "You think you might have some guavas around?"

The old woman's face scrunched up. "Guavas?" she murmured and thought to herself a second. "Why, they're all around, Doña. But I can't say as I've seen any."

"With your permission—" Jose Duarte had joined a group of little boys who had come out of nowhere and were milling around the car, boasting how many automobiles they had ridden in. At Yolanda's mention of guavas, he sprung forward, pointing across the road

5. Doña (dō′ nyä) "Madam" (Spanish).

LITERATURE IN CONTEXT

Geography Connection

The Dominican Republic

Located in the West Indies, the Dominican Republic takes up the eastern two thirds of the island of Hispaniola. The country is bounded on the north by the Atlantic Ocean; on the east by the Mona Passage, which separates it from Puerto Rico; on the south by the Caribbean Sea; and on the west by Haiti.

In Alvarez's story, Yolanda begins her journey in Santo Domingo, the capital city, which is located on the country's southern coast. Yolanda's journey takes her into the Cordillera Central Range, which includes Pico Duarte, the highest mountain in the Caribbean. The slopes of many of these mountains are covered with dense semi-tropical forests, like those in which Yolanda searches for guavas.

Connect to the Literature

In what ways does the story's setting—both geographical and cultural—contribute to Yolanda's conflict?

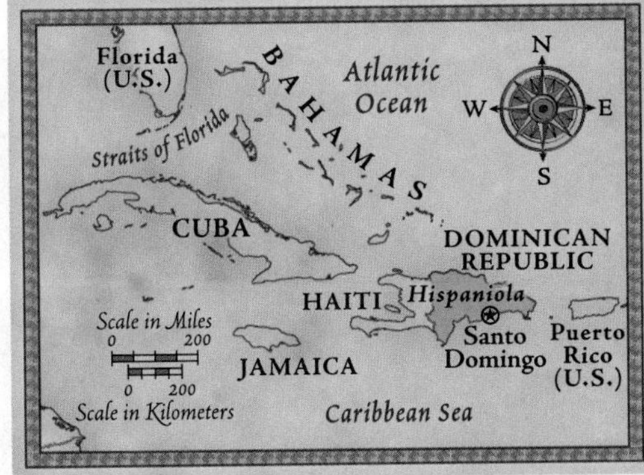

Comprehension

Who does Yolanda meet at the roadside cantina?

towards the summit of the western hills. "I know where there's a whole grove of them." Behind him, his little companions nodded.

"Go on, then!" His grandmother stamped her foot as if she were scatting a little animal. "Get the Doña some."

A few boys dashed across the road and disappeared up a steep path on the hillside, but before Jose could follow, Yolanda called him back. She wanted to go along too. The little boy looked towards his grandmother, unsure of what to think. The old woman shook her head. The Doña would get hot, her nice clothes would get all dirty. Jose would get the Doña as many guavas as she was wanting.

"But they taste so much better when you've picked them yourself," Yolanda's voice had an edge, for suddenly, it was as if the woman had turned into the long arm of her family, keeping her away from seeing her country on her own.

The few boys who had stayed behind with Jose had congregated around the car. Each one claimed to be guarding it for the Doña. It occurred to Yolanda that there was a way to make this a treat all the way around. "What do you say we take the car?"

"*Sí, Sí, Sí,*"[6] the boys screamed in a riot of excitement.

The old woman hushed them but agreed that was not a bad idea if the Doña insisted on going. There was a dirt road up ahead she could follow a ways and then cross over onto the road that was paved all the way to the coffee barns. The woman pointed south in the direction of the big house. Many workers took that short cut to work.

They piled into the car, half a dozen boys in the back, and Jose

6. *Sí, Sí, Sí* (sē) "Yes, Yes, Yes" (Spanish).

▼ Critical Viewing

Do you think the people in this picture have more in common with Yolanda and her family or with the people she meets in the mountains? Explain. **COMPARE**

as co-pilot in the passenger seat beside Yolanda. They turned onto a bumpy road off the highway, which got bumpier and bumpier, and climbed up into wilder, more desolate country. Branches scraped the sides and pebbles pelted the underside of the car. Yolanda wanted to turn back, but there was no room to maneuver the car around. Finally, with a great snapping of twigs and thrashing of branches across the windshield, as if the countryside were loath to release them, the car burst forth onto smooth pavement and the light of day. On either side of the road were groves of guava trees. Among them, the boys who had gone ahead on foot were already pulling down branches and shaking loose a rain of guavas. The fruit was definitely in season.

For the next hour or so, Yolanda and her crew scavenged the grove, the best of the pick going into the beach basket Yolanda had gotten out of the trunk, with the exception of the ones she ate right on the spot, relishing the slightly bumpy feel of the skin in her hand, devouring the crunchy, sweet, white meat. The boys watched her, surprised by her odd hunger.

Yolanda and Jose, partners, wandered far from the path that cut through the grove. Soon they were bent double to avoid getting entangled in the thick canopy of branches overhead. Each addition to the basket caused a spill from the stash already piled high above the brim. Finally, it was a case of abandoning the treasure in order to cart some of it home. With Jose hugging the basket to himself and Yolanda parting the wayward branches in front of them, they headed back toward the car.

When they cleared the thicket of guava branches, the sun was low on the western horizon. There was no sign of the other boys. "They must have gone to round up the goats," Jose observed.

Yolanda glanced at her watch: it was past six o'clock. She'd never make the north coast by nightfall, but at least she could get off the dangerous mountain roads while it was still light. She hurried Jose back to the car, where they found a heap of guavas the other boys had left behind on the shoulder of the road. Enough guavas to appease even the greediest island spirit for life!

They packed the guavas in the trunk quickly and climbed in, but the car had not gone a foot before it lurched forward with a horrible hobble. Yolanda closed her eyes and laid her head down on the wheel, then glanced over at Jose. The way his eyes were searching the inside of the car for a clue as to what could have happened, she could tell he didn't know how to change a flat tire either.

It was no use regretting having brought the car up that bad stretch of road. The thing to do now was to act quickly. Soon the sun would set and night would fall swiftly, no lingering dusk as in the States. She explained to Jose that they had a flat tire and had to hike back to town and send for help down the road to the big house. Whoever tended to the brown Mercedes would know how to change the tire on her car.

Vocabulary

maneuver (mə nōō′ vər) *v.* move something by some plan or scheme

appease (ə pēz′) *v.* satisfy

Spiral Review

Characterization Which details here help you understand how Yolanda and Jose look, behave, feel, and think? Explain.

Plot Devices

How might Yolanda's thoughts about the dangerous mountain roads be a clue to later events?

Comprehension

As Yolanda and Jose start to leave, what happens to the car?

"With your permission," Jose offered meekly. He pointed down the paved road. "This goes directly to the big house." The Doña could just wait in the car and he would be back in no time with someone from the Miranda place.

She did not like the idea of staying behind in the car, but Jose could probably go and come back much quicker without her. "All right," she said to the boy. "I'll tell you what." She pointed to her watch. It was almost six thirty. "If you're back by the time this hand is over here, I'll give you"—she held up one finger "a dollar." The boy's mouth fell open. In no time, he had shot out of his side of the car and was headed at a run toward the Miranda place. Yolanda climbed out as well and walked down a pace, until the boy had disappeared in one of the turnings of the road.

Suddenly, the countryside was so very quiet. She looked up at the purple sky. A breeze was blowing through the grove, rustling the leaves, so they whispered like voices, something indistinct. Here and there a light flickered on the hills, a *campesino* living out his solitary life. This was what she had been missing without really knowing that she was missing it all these years. She had never felt at home in the States, never, though she knew she was lucky to have a job, so she could afford her own life and not be run by her family. But independence didn't have to be exile. She could come home, home to places like these very hills, and live here on her own terms.

Heading back to the car, Yolanda stopped. She had heard footsteps in the grove. Could Jose be back already? Branches were being thrust aside, twigs snapped. Suddenly, a short, dark man, and then a slender, light-skin man emerged from a footpath on the opposite side of the grove from the one she and Jose had scavenged. They wore ragged work clothes stained with patches of sweat; their faces were drawn and tired. Yolanda's glance fell on the **machetes** that hung from their belts.

Vocabulary
machetes (mə shet′ ēz) *n.* large knives with broad blades

The men's faces snapped awake from their stupor at the sight of her. They looked beyond her at the car. "Yours?" the darker man spoke first. It struck her, even then, as an absurd question. Who else's would it be here in the middle of nowhere?

Making Predictions
Based on the description of the men, how do you predict they will respond to Yolanda?

"Is there some problem?" the darker man spoke up again. The taller one was looking her up and down with interest. They were now both in front of her on the road, blocking her escape. Both—she had looked them up and down as well—were strong and quite capable of catching her if she made a run for the Miranda's. Not that she could have moved, for her legs seemed suddenly to have been hammered into the ground beneath her. She thought of explaining that she was just out for a drive before dinner at the big house, so that these men would think someone knew where she was, someone would come looking for her if they tried to carry her off. But she found she could not speak. Her tongue felt as if it'd been stuffed in her mouth like a rag to keep her quiet.

The men exchanged a look—it seemed to Yolanda of **collusion**. Then the shorter, darker one spoke up again, "Señorita,[7] are you all right?" He peered at her. The darkness of his complexion in the growing darkness of the evening made it difficult to distinguish an expression. He was no taller than Yolanda, but he gave the impression of being quite large, for he was broad and solid, like something not yet completely carved out of a piece of wood. His companion was tall and of a rich honey-brown color that matched his honey-brown eyes. Anywhere else, Yolanda would have found him extremely attractive, but here on a lonely road, with the sky growing darker by seconds, his good looks seemed dangerous, a lure to catch her off her guard.

"Can we help you?" the shorter man repeated.

The handsome one smiled knowingly. Two long, deep dimples appeared like gashes on either side of his mouth. "*Americana*," he said to the other in Spanish, pointing to the car. "She doesn't understand."

The darker man narrowed his eyes and studied Yolanda a moment. "*Americana?*" he asked her as if not quite sure what to make of her.

She had been too frightened to carry out any strategy, but now a road was opening before her. She laid her hand on her chest—she could feel her pounding heart—and nodded. Then, as if the admission itself loosened her tongue, she explained in English how it came that she was on a back road by herself, her craving for guavas, her never having learned to change a flat. The two men stared at her, uncomprehendingly, rendered **docile** by her gibberish. Strangely enough, it soothed her to hear herself speaking something they could not understand. She thought of something her teacher used to say to her when as a young immigrant girl she was learning English, "Language is power." It was her only defense now.

Yolanda made the motions of pumping. The darker man looked at the other, who had shown better luck at understanding the foreign lady. But his companion shrugged, baffled as well. "I'll show you," Yolanda waved for them to follow her. And suddenly, as if after pulling and pulling at roots, she had finally managed to yank them free of the soil they had clung to, she found she could move her own feet forward to the car.

The small group stood staring at the sagging tire a moment, the two men kicking at it as if punishing it for having failed the Señorita. They squatted by the passenger's side, conversing in low tones. Yolanda led them to the rear of the car, where the men lifted the spare out of its sunken nest—then set to work, fitting the interlocking pieces of the jack, unpacking the tools from the deeper hollows of the trunk. They laid their machetes down on the side of the road, out of the way. Yolanda turned on the headlights to help them see in the growing darkness. Above the small group, the sky was purple with twilight.

There was a problem with the jack. It squeaked and labored, but the car would not rise. The shorter man squirmed his way underneath

7. **Señorita** (se´ nyō rē´ tä) "Miss" (Spanish).

Vocabulary

collusion (kə lo͞o´ zhən) *n.* secret agreement; conspiracy

docile (däs´ əl) *adj.* easy to direct or manage; obedient

She laid her hand on her chest—she could feel her pounding heart…

Comprehension

What does Yolanda pretend when she is approached by the two men?

and placed the mechanism deeper under the bowels of the car. There, he pumped vigorously, his friend bracing him by holding him down by the ankles. Slowly, the car rose until the wheel hung suspended. When the man came out from under the car, his hand was bloody where his knuckles had scraped against the pavement.

Yolanda pointed to the man's hand. She had been sure that if any blood were going to be spilled tonight, it would be hers. She offered him the towel she kept draped on her car seat to absorb her perspiration. But he waved it away and sucked his knuckles to make the bleeding stop.

Once the flat had been replaced with the spare, the two men lifted the deflated tire into the trunk and put away the tools. They handed Yolanda her keys. There was still no sign of Jose and the Miranda's. Yolanda was relieved. As she had waited, watching the two men hard at work, she had begun to dread the boy's return with help. The two men would realize she spoke Spanish. It was too late to admit that she had tricked them, to explain she had done so only because she thought her survival was on the line. The least she could do now was to try and repay them, handsomely, for their trouble.

"I'd like to give you something," she began reaching for the purse she'd retrieved from the trunk. The English words sounded hollow on her tongue. She rolled up a couple of American bills and offered them to the men. The shorter man held up his hand. Yolanda could see where the blood had dried dark streaks on his palm. "No, no, Señorita. *Nuestro placer.*"[8] Our pleasure.

Yolanda turned to the other man, who had struck her as more pliant than his sterner companion. "Please," she urged the bills on him. But he too looked down at the ground with the bashfulness she had observed in Jose of country people not wanting to offend. She felt the poverty of her response and stuffed the bills quickly into his pocket.

The two men picked up their machetes and raised them to their shoulders like soldiers their guns. The tall man motioned towards the big house. "*Directo, directo,*"[9] he enunciated the words carefully. Yolanda looked in the direction of his hand. In the faint light of what was left of day, she could barely make out the road ahead. It was as if the guava grove had overgrown into the road and woven its mat of branches so securely and tightly in all directions, she would not be able to escape.

But finally, she was off! While the two men waited a moment on the shoulder to see if the tire would hold, Yolanda drove a few yards, poking her head out the window before speeding up. "*Gracias!*"[10] she called, and they waved, appreciatively, at the foreign lady making an effort in their native tongue. When she looked for them in her rear-view mirror, they had disappeared into the darkness of the guava grove.

---

8. *Nuestro placer* (no͞o es´ trō plä ser´) "Our pleasure" (Spanish).
9. *Directo, directo* (dē rek´ tō) "Straight, straight" (Spanish).
10. *Gracias* (grä´ sē äs) "Thank you" (Spanish).

Just ahead, her lights described the figure of a small boy: Jose was walking alone, listlessly, as if he did not particularly want to get to where he was going.

Yolanda leaned over and opened the door for him. The small overhead light came on; she saw that the boy's face was streaked with tears.

"Why, what's wrong, Jose?"

The boy swallowed hard. "They would not come. They didn't believe me." He took little breaths between words to keep his tears at bay. He had lost his chance at a whole dollar. "And the guard, he said if I didn't stop telling stories, he was going to whip me."

"What did you tell him, Jose?"

"I told him you had broken your car and you needed help fixing it."

She should have gone along with Jose to the Miranda's. Given all the trouble in the country, they would be suspicious of a boy coming to their door at nightfall with some story about a lady on a back road with a broken car. "Don't you worry, Jose," Yolanda patted the boy. She could feel the bony shoulder through the thin fabric of his worn shirt. "You can still have your dollar. You did your part."

But the shame of being suspected of lying seemed to have obscured any immediate pleasure he might feel in her offer. Yolanda tried to distract him by asking what he would buy with his money, what he most craved, thinking that on a subsequent trip, she might bring him his little *antojo*. But Jose Duarte Sanchez y Mella said nothing, except a bashful thank you when she left him off at the cantina with his promised dollar. In the glow of the headlights, Yolanda made out the figure of the old woman in the black square of her doorway, waving good-bye. Above the picnic table on a near post, the Palmolive woman's skin shone; her head was thrown back, her mouth opened as if she were calling someone over a great distance.

Making Predictions

Based on your knowledge of the Dominican Republic's economic and political situation, why do you think Jose looks so forlorn?

Critical Reading

Cite textual evidence to support your responses.

1. **Key Ideas and Details (a)** What are *antojos*? **(b) Connect:** What theme does the title of the story stress?
2. **Key Ideas and Details (a) Infer:** What is suggested about the country's political situation by the idea of a "hunger march" taking place in the capital? **(b) Analyze:** What role do economic issues play in this story?
3. **Key Ideas and Details (a) Interpret:** When Yolanda first sees the two men, what does she feel? **(b) Analyze:** Why does she pretend not to speak Spanish?
4. **Integration of Knowledge and Ideas** What details suggest that Yolanda longs for a deeper connection to her homeland? Use at least two of these Essential Question words: *influence, longing, nurture, transformation. **[Connecting to the Essential Question: What is the relationship between literature and place?]***

Close Reading Activities *Antojos*

Literary Analysis

1. **Key Ideas and Details** **(a)** What **prediction** did you make about Yolanda's trip to the north coast? **(b)** What actually happened?
2. **Key Ideas and Details** **(a)** What prediction did you make about the strangers who emerge from the grove? **(b)** Was your prediction confirmed? Explain.
3. **Craft and Structure** **(a)** Make a list of the events in this story as they occur in chronological order. **(b)** At what point in that sequence does Alvarez begin the narration? **(c)** What effect does this use of ***in medias res*** create?
4. **Craft and Structure** **(a)** What does the **flashback** to Yolanda's visit with her aunts reveal about Yolanda's reasons for traveling north? **(b)** Is the author's use of flashback effective? Explain.
5. **Craft and Structure** What does the flashback to Yolanda's visit with the aunts reveal about the family's social and economic circumstances? Explain.
6. **Craft and Structure** **(a)** How else might Alvarez have conveyed the information given in the flashback? **(b)** Is her use of flashback more or less effective than another technique might be? Explain.
7. **Craft and Structure** **(a)** What future event do Yolanda's thoughts about the dangerous mountain roads **foreshadow?** **(b)** In what ways does the author's use of foreshadowing add suspense to this scene?
8. **Craft and Structure** **(a)** Using a chart like the one shown, find two other examples of foreshadowing in the story. List the clues Alvarez provides and the events they hint will happen. **(b)** Do the events unfold exactly as one might expect from the clues? Explain.

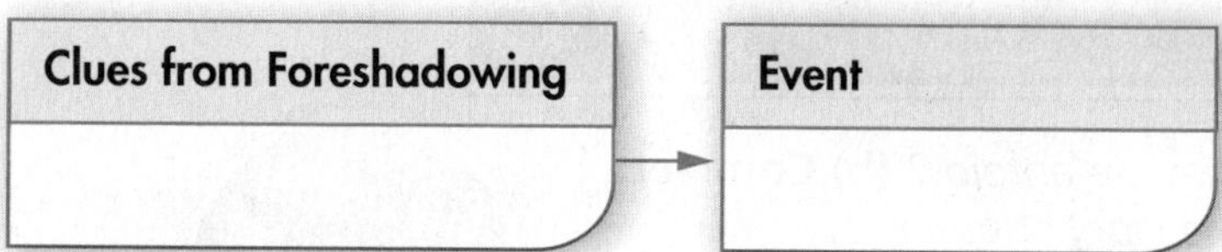

9. **Integration of Knowledge and Ideas** Explain how the author's use of **plot devices** serves two purposes: **(a)** to engage readers; and **(b)** to create a sense of unity and logic in the story.

Writing

3. Write narratives to develop real or imagined experiences or events using effective technique, well-chosen details, and well-structured event sequences. *(p. 1309)*

3.b. Use narrative techniques, such as dialogue, to develop experiences, events, and/or characters. *(p. 1309)*

3.c. Use a variety of techniques to sequence events so that they build on one another to create a coherent whole and build toward a particular tone and outcome. *(p. 1309)*

3.d. Use precise words and phrases, telling details, and sensory language to convey a vivid picture of the experiences, events, setting, and/or characters. *(p. 1309)*

Language

4.a. Use context as a clue to the meaning of a word or phrase. *(p. 1309)*

4.c. Consult general and specialized reference materials, both print and digital, to clarify the precise meaning of a word, its etymology, or its standard usage. *(p. 1309)*

5. Demonstrate understanding of word relationships. *(p. 1309)*

Vocabulary Acquisition and Use

Words from Other Languages: Spanish

Many words, such as *machete, tortilla,* and *sombrero,* come to English directly from Spanish. Use the story context to help you answer these questions about five other Spanish words. Consult a dictionary to check your work.

1. Which English word used in the story probably comes from *guayaba,* the Spanish name for the same tropical fruit?
2. *Cantina,* from the Spanish for "bar" or "tavern," is related to an Italian word for "wine cellar." Which English word probably has a similar origin?
3. In English, a *cabana* or *cabaña* is a small building at a pool or beach. Is that the word's meaning on page 1301? Explain.
4. *Gracias*, the Spanish word for "thank you," comes from the Latin word *gratia*, meaning "pleasing quality, favor, thanks." Which English words probably have a similar origin?

Vocabulary: Synonyms or Antonyms

Categorize each of the following pairs of words as either synonyms or antonyms. Explain your thinking.

1. dissuade, discourage
2. maneuver, reposition
3. appease, arouse
4. machetes, knives
5. collusion, plotting
6. docile, cantankerous

Writing to Sources

Narrative Text In both literature and life, stories are shaped by the points of view of those who tell them. Write a new version of the **story** from the point of view of one of the men who changes Yolanda's tire.

Prewriting Choose the character whose point of view you will use and reread the story considering that perspective. Note details to incorporate and develop. Then, write a brief outline of your new version.

Drafting Write the story from the new point of view. Use sensory details, flashbacks, internal monologue, and dialogue to provide background and flesh out the character's world.

Revising Reread your story, and look for points where you may have strayed from the perspective you have chosen. Delete details the character might not know, and add information to strengthen your use of point of view.

Model: Using Details to Create a Vivid Portrayal

Paulo saw a small white car stuck in the foliage. The tire was busted, and a lady stood there. Her eyes were nervous and black. She reminded Paulo of a cornered chihuahua, and he thought she might bite. He laughed at the thought. "How can we help you, Doña?" he asked.

The inclusion of dialogue and a character's inner thoughts add to the vividness of a narrative.

Building Knowledge and Insight

ANCHOR TEXT

Everyday Use

Connecting to the Essential Question In this story, distance and the passage of time lead a mother and daughter to two very different views of the world. Notice details in the story that suggest how personal relationships reflect social changes. Doing so will help you think about the Essential Question: **How does literature shape or reflect society?**

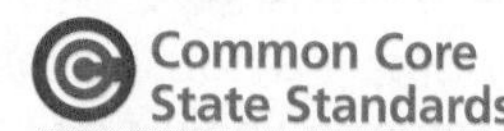

Reading Literature
3. Analyze the impact of the author's choices regarding how to develop and relate elements of a story or drama (e.g., how the characters are introduced and developed).

Close Reading Focus

Characterization; Dialect

Varied types of language are key to the **characterization,** or *development of characters,* in this story. The narrator uses standard English to express her internal thoughts:

> ***I will wait for her in the yard that Maggie and I made so clean and wavy yesterday afternoon.***

However, when she speaks aloud, the narrator uses **dialect,** a language variation specific to the region in which she lives and the ethnic group of which she is a part. The narrator's spoken language also reflects her level of education and other aspects of her character:

> ***"You know as well as me you was named after your aunt Dicie," I said.***

As you read, consider how this duality of language allows readers to develop different perceptions of the narrator than those held by other characters in the story, especially the narrator's oldest daughter.

Preparing to Read Complex Texts As this story opens, you learn that two sisters and their life experiences are quite different. By **comparing and contrasting characters,** or identifying the ways in which they are alike and different, you can uncover the major conflict in the story. Use a Venn diagram like the one shown to note the character traits, such as details in behavior and speech, that separate Dee from Maggie. Consider the ways in which their experiences have shaped their differences.

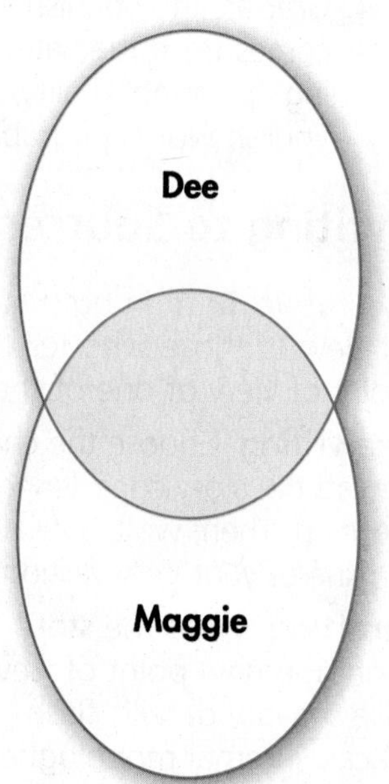

Vocabulary

You will encounter the words listed here in the text that follows. Copy the words into your notebook. Which word is a verb? How can you tell?

homely **cowering**
furtive **doctrines**

Alice Walker *(b. 1944)*

Author of "Everyday Use"

Born in Eatonton, Georgia, Alice Walker was the eighth and youngest child in a family of sharecroppers. Of her childhood, Walker writes, "It was great fun being cute. But then, one day, it ended."

The security of her childhood was challenged by an accident with a BB gun that scarred and nearly blinded her. Eight years old when the accident happened, Walker reports that she did not lift her head for six years. It was not until the family could afford surgery that Walker finally had the scar tissue on her eye removed. With that surgery, her confidence returned.

Civil Rights Walker graduated from high school as both class valedictorian and prom queen. She attended Spelman College, an elite Atlanta school for African American women. While at Spelman, Walker became deeply involved in the civil rights movement. In August 1963, she traveled to Washington, D.C., to take part in the March on Washington for Jobs and Freedom. The guest speaker that day was Dr. Martin Luther King, Jr. Unable to see him through the crowd, Walker perched in a tree to get a better view. From there, she heard Dr. King deliver his famous "I Have a Dream" address.

From Prom Queen to Poet After two years at Spelman, Walker was awarded a full scholarship to Sarah Lawrence College in Bronxville, New York. There, she studied under famed poets Muriel Rukeyser and Jane Cooper, who nurtured her talent. She wrote her first collection of poetry, *Once* (1968), while a student at Sarah Lawrence.

The Color Purple With the publication of her novel *The Color Purple* in 1982, Walker shot to international fame. The novel portrays women who are oppressed by the men in their lives, but go on to find inner strength and personal dignity. Awarded both the Pulitzer Prize and a National Book Award, the book was later adapted into a successful film.

"Everyday Use" explores Walker's maternal heritage, describing the creative legacy of "ordinary" black southern women.

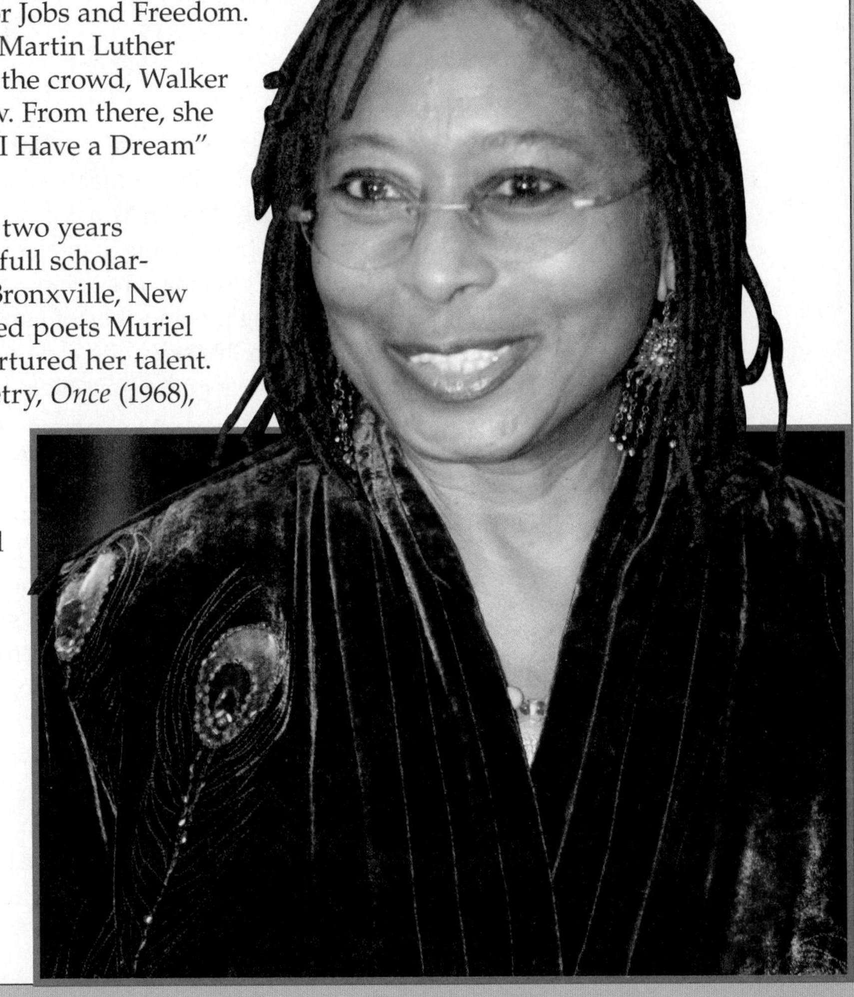

Everyday Use

Alice Walker

BACKGROUND In this story, the narrator's oldest daughter wants an antique butter churn and two quilts—artifacts of her family's history—that she finds in her mother's house. The quilts are especially important items. Like most folk art, quilts serve both practical and aesthetic purposes: keeping people warm, recycling old clothing, providing a focal point for the social gathering of women, preserving precious bits of family history, and adding color and beauty to a home. In this story, the characters' differing attitudes toward the quilts and other objects in the household become critical points of conflict.

I will wait for her in the yard that Maggie and I made so clean and wavy yesterday afternoon. A yard like this is more comfortable than most people know. It is not just a yard. It is like an extended living room. When the hard clay is swept clean as a floor and the fine sand around the edges lined with tiny, irregular grooves, anyone can come and sit and look up into the elm tree and wait for the breezes that never come inside the house.

Maggie will be nervous until after her sister goes: she will stand hopelessly in corners, homely and ashamed of the burn scars down her arms and legs, eyeing her sister with a mixture of envy and awe. She thinks her sister has held life always in the palm of one hand, that "no" is a word the world never learned to say to her.

Vocabulary

homely (hōm′ lē) *adj.* not elegant or polished; crude

You've no doubt seen those TV shows where the child who has

"made it" is confronted, as a surprise, by her own mother and father, tottering in weakly from backstage. (A pleasant surprise, of course: What would they do if parent and child came on the show only to curse out and insult each other?) On TV mother and child embrace and smile into each other's faces. Sometimes the mother and father weep, the child wraps them in her arms and leans across the table to tell how she would not have made it without their help. I have seen these programs.

Sometimes I dream a dream in which Dee and I are suddenly brought together on a TV program of this sort. Out of a dark and soft-seated limousine I am ushered into a bright room filled with many people. There I meet a smiling, gray, sporty man like Johnny Carson who shakes my hand and tells me what a fine girl I have. Then we are on the stage and Dee is embracing me with tears in her eyes. She pins on my dress a large orchid, even though she has told me once that she thinks orchids are tacky flowers.

In real life I am a large, big-boned woman with rough, man-working hands. In the winter I wear flannel nightgowns to bed and overalls during the day. I can kill and clean a hog as mercilessly as a man. My fat keeps me hot in zero weather. I can work outside all day, breaking ice to get water for washing; I can eat pork liver cooked over the open fire minutes after it comes steaming from the hog. One winter I knocked a bull calf straight in the brain between the eyes with a sledge hammer and had the meat hung up to chill before nightfall. But of course all of this does not show on television. I am the way my daughter would want me to be: a hundred pounds lighter, my skin like an uncooked barley pancake. My hair glistens in the hot bright lights. Johnny Carson has much to do to keep up with my quick and witty tongue.

Characterization
What do the details in these paragraphs reveal about the narrator?

But that is a mistake. I know even before I wake up. Who ever knew a Johnson with a quick tongue? Who can even imagine me looking a strange white man in the eye? It seems to me I have talked to them always with one foot raised in flight, with my head turned in whichever way is farthest from them. Dee, though. She would always look anyone in the eye. Hesitation was no part of her nature.

"How do I look, Mama?" Maggie says, showing just enough of her thin body enveloped in pink skirt and red blouse for me to know she's there, almost hidden by the door.

"Come out into the yard," I say.

Have you ever seen a lame animal, perhaps a dog run over by some careless person rich enough to own a car, sidle up to someone

Comprehension
Who are Maggie and her mother waiting to welcome?

who is ignorant enough to be kind to him? That is the way my Maggie walks. She has been like this, chin on chest, eyes on ground, feet in shuffle, ever since the fire that burned the other house to the ground.

Dee is lighter than Maggie, with nicer hair and a fuller figure. She's a woman now, though sometimes I forget. How long ago was it that the other house burned? Ten, twelve years? Sometimes I can still hear the flames and feel Maggie's arms sticking to me, her hair smoking and her dress falling off her in little black papery flakes. Her eyes seemed stretched open, blazed open by the flames reflected in them. And Dee. I see her standing off under the sweet gum tree she used to dig gum out of; a look of concentration on her face as she watched the last dingy gray board of the house fall in toward the red-hot brick chimney. Why don't you do a dance around the ashes? I'd want to ask her. She had hated the house that much.

I used to think she hated Maggie, too. But that was before we raised the money, the church and me, to send her to Augusta to school. She used to read to us without pity; forcing words, lies, other folks' habits, whole lives upon us two, sitting trapped and ignorant underneath her voice. She washed us in a river of make-believe, burned us with a lot of knowledge we didn't necessarily need to know. Pressed us to her with the serious way she read, to shove us away at just the moment, like dimwits, we seemed about to understand.

Why don't you do a dance around the ashes? I'd want to ask her.

Dee wanted nice things. A yellow organdy dress to wear to her graduation from high school; black pumps to match a green suit she'd made from an old suit somebody gave me. She was determined to stare down any disaster in her efforts. Her eyelids would not flicker for minutes at a time. Often I fought off the temptation to shake her. At sixteen she had a style of her own, and knew what style was.

I never had an education myself. After second grade the school was closed down. Don't ask me why: in 1927 colored asked fewer questions than they do now. Sometimes Maggie reads to me. She stumbles along good-naturedly but can't see well. She knows she is not bright. Like good looks and money, quickness passed her by. She will marry John Thomas (who has mossy teeth in an earnest face) and then I'll be free to sit here and I guess just sing church songs to myself. Although I never was a good singer. Never could carry a tune. I was always better at a man's job. I used to love to milk till I was hooved in the side in '49. Cows are soothing and slow and don't bother you, unless you try to milk them the wrong way.

Contrasting Characters
What contrasts between herself and Dee does the narrator describe?

I have deliberately turned my back on the house. It is three rooms, just like the one that burned, except the roof is tin; they don't make shingle roofs any more. There are no real windows, just some holes cut in the sides, like the portholes in a ship, but not round and not square, with rawhide holding the shutters up on the outside. This house is in a pasture, too, like the other one. No doubt when Dee sees it she will want to tear it down. She wrote me once that no matter where we "choose" to live, she will manage to come see us. But she will never bring her friends. Maggie and I thought about this and Maggie asked me, "Mama, when did Dee ever *have* any friends?"

She had a few. **Furtive** boys in pink shirts hanging about on washday after school. Nervous girls who never laughed. Impressed with her they worshiped the well-turned phrase, the cute shape, the scalding humor that erupted like bubbles in lye.[1] She read to them.

Vocabulary
furtive (fur′ tiv) *adj.* sneaky

When she was courting Jimmy T she didn't have much time to pay to us, but turned all her faultfinding power on him. He *flew* to marry a cheap city girl from a family of ignorant flashy people. She hardly had time to recompose herself.

When she comes I will meet—but there they are!

Maggie attempts to make a dash for the house, in her shuffling way, but I stay her with my hand. "Come back here," I say. And she stops and tries to dig a well in the sand with her toe.

It is hard to see them clearly through the strong sun. But even the first glimpse of leg out of the car tells me it is Dee. Her feet were always neat-looking, as if God himself had shaped them with a certain style. From the other side of the car comes a short, stocky man. Hair is all over his head a foot long and hanging from his chin like a kinky mule tail. I hear Maggie suck in her breath. "Uhnnnh," is what it sounds like. Like when you see the wriggling end of a snake just in front of your foot on the road. "Uhnnnh."

Dee next. A dress down to the ground, in this hot weather. A dress so loud it hurts my eyes. There are yellows and oranges enough to throw back the light of the sun. I feel my whole face warming from the heat waves it throws out. Earrings gold, too, and hanging down to her shoulders. Bracelets dangling and making noises when she moves her arm up to shake the folds of the dress out of her armpits. The dress is loose and flows, and as she walks closer, I like it. I hear Maggie go "Uhnnnh" again. It is her sister's hair. It stands straight up like the wool on a sheep. It is black as night and around the edges are two long

Comprehension
What traumatic event occurred in the lives of the mother and her daughters?

1. **lye** (lī) *n.* strong alkaline solution used in cleaning and making soap.

pigtails that rope about like small lizards disappearing behind her ears.

"Wa-su-zo-Tean-o!"[2] she says, coming on in that gliding way the dress makes her move. The short stocky fellow with the hair to his navel is all grinning and he follows up with "Asalamalakim,[3] my mother and sister!" He moves to hug Maggie but she falls back, right up against the back of my chair. I feel her trembling there and when I look up I see the perspiration falling off her chin.

"Don't get up," says Dee. Since I am stout it takes something of a push. You can see me trying to move a second or two before I make it. She turns, showing white heels through her sandals, and goes back to the car. Out she peeks next with a Polaroid. She stoops down quickly and lines up picture after picture of me sitting there in front of the house with Maggie **cowering** behind me. She never takes a shot without making sure the house is included. When a cow comes nibbling around the edge of the yard she snaps it and me and Maggie and the house. Then she puts the Polaroid in the back seat of the car, and comes up and kisses me on the forehead.

Vocabulary

cowering (kou′ ər iŋ) *v.* trembling or cringing, as with fear

Meanwhile Asalamalakim is going through motions with Maggie's hand. Maggie's hand is as limp as a fish, and probably as cold, despite the sweat, and she keeps trying to pull it back. It looks like Asalamalakim wants to shake hands but wants to do it fancy. Or maybe he don't know how people shake hands. Anyhow, he soon gives up on Maggie.

"Well," I say. "Dee."

"No, Mama," she says. "Not 'Dee,' Wangero Leewanika Kemanjo!"

"What happened to 'Dee'?" I wanted to know.

"She's dead," Wangero said. "I couldn't bear it any longer, being named after the people who oppress me."

"You know as well as me you was named after your aunt Dicie," I said. Dicie is my sister. She named Dee. We called her "Big Dee" after Dee was born.

Dialect

How does the narrator's spoken language differ from her narrative voice?

"But who was *she* named after?" asked Wangero.

"I guess after Grandma Dee," I said.

"And who was she named after?" asked Wangero.

"Her mother," I said, and saw Wangero was getting tired. "That's about as far back as I can trace it," I said. Though, in fact, I probably could have carried it back beyond the Civil War through the branches.

"Well," said Asalamalakim, "there you are."

"Uhnnnh," I heard Maggie say.

---

2. **Wa-su-zo-Tean-o** (wä so͞o zō tēn′ ō) African greeting.
3. **Asalamalakim** *Salaam aleikhim* (sə läm′ ä lī′ kēm′) Islamic greeting meaning "Peace be with you."

"There I was not," I said, "before 'Dicie' cropped up in our family, so why should I try to trace it that far back?"

He just stood there grinning, looking down on me like somebody inspecting a Model A car. Every once in a while he and Wangero sent eye signals over my head.

"How do you pronounce this name?" I asked.

"You don't have to call me by it if you don't want to," said Wangero.

"Why shouldn't I?" I asked. "If that's what you want us to call you, we'll call you."

"I know it might sound awkward at first," said Wangero.

"I'll get used to it," I said. "Ream it out again."

Well, soon we got the name out of the way. Asalamalakim had a name twice as long and three times as hard. After I tripped over it two or three times he told me to just call him Hakim-a-barber. I wanted to ask him was he a barber, but I didn't really think he was, so I didn't ask.

"You must belong to those beef-cattle people down the road," I said. They said "Asalamalakim" when they met you, too, but they didn't shake hands. Always too busy: feeding the cattle, fixing the fences, putting up salt-lick shelters, throwing down hay. When the white folks poisoned some of the herd the men stayed up all night with rifles in their hands. I walked a mile and a half just to see the sight.

Hakim-a-barber said, "I accept some of their doctrines, but farming and raising cattle is not my style." (They didn't tell me, and I didn't ask, whether Wangero (Dee) had really gone and married him.)

We sat down to eat and right away he said he didn't eat collards[4] and pork was unclean. Wangero, though, went on through the chitlins[5] and corn bread, the greens and everything else. She talked a blue streak over the sweet potatoes. Everything delighted her. Even the fact that we still used the benches her daddy made for the table when we couldn't afford to buy chairs.

"Oh, Mama!" she cried. Then turned to Hakim-a-barber. "I never knew how lovely these benches are. You can feel the rump prints," she said, running her hands underneath her and along the bench. Then she gave a sigh and her hand closed over Grandma Dee's butter dish. "That's it!" she said. "I knew there was something I wanted to ask you if I could have." She jumped up from the table and went over in the corner where the churn stood, the milk in it clabber by now. She

He just stood there grinning, looking down on me like somebody inspecting a Model A car.

Vocabulary

doctrines (däk′ trinz) *n.* religious beliefs or principles

Comprehension

Why has Dee changed her name?

---

4. collards (käl′ ərdz) *n.* leaves of the collard plant, often referred to as "collard greens."

5. chitlins (chit′ lənz) *n.* chitterlings, a pork dish popular among southern African Americans.

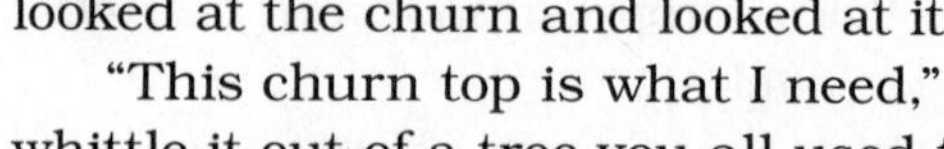

looked at the churn and looked at it.

"This churn top is what I need," she said. "Didn't Uncle Buddy whittle it out of a tree you all used to have?"

"Yes," I said.

"Uh huh," she said happily. "And I want the dasher, too."

"Uncle Buddy whittle that, too?" asked the barber.

Dee (Wangero) looked up at me.

"Aunt Dee's first husband whittled the dash," said Maggie so low you almost couldn't hear her. "His name was Henry, but they called him Stash."

"Maggie's brain is like an elephant's," Wangero said, laughing. "I can use the churn top as a centerpiece for the alcove table," she said, sliding a plate over the churn, "and I'll think of something artistic to do with the dasher."

When she finished wrapping the dasher the handle stuck out. I took it for a moment in my hands. You didn't even have to look close to see where hands pushing the dasher up and down to make butter had left a kind of sink in the wood. In fact, there were a lot of small sinks; you could see where thumbs and fingers had sunk into the wood. It was beautiful light yellow wood, from a tree that grew in the yard where Big Dee and Stash had lived.

After dinner Dee (Wangero) went to the trunk at the foot of my bed and started rifling through it. Maggie hung back in the kitchen over the dishpan. Out came Wangero with two quilts. They had been pieced by Grandma Dee and then Big Dee and me had hung them on the quilt frames on the front porch and quilted them. One was in the Lone Star pattern. The other was Walk Around the Mountain. In both of them were scraps of dresses Grandma Dee had worn fifty and more years ago. Bits and pieces of Grandpa Jarrell's Paisley shirts. And one teeny faded blue piece, about the size of a penny matchbox, that was from Great Grandpa Ezra's uniform that he wore in the Civil War.

"Mama," Wangero said sweet as a bird. "Can I have these old quilts?"

I heard something fall in the kitchen, and a minute later the kitchen door slammed.

"Why don't you take one or two of the others?" I asked. "These old things was just done by me and Big Dee from some tops your grandma pieced before she died."

"No," said Wangero. "I don't want those. They are stitched around the borders by machine."

"That'll make them last better," I said.

"That's not the point," said Wangero. "These are all pieces of dresses Grandma used to wear. She did all this stitching by hand. Imagine!" She held the quilts securely in her arms, stroking them.

"Some of the pieces, like those lavender ones, come from old clothes her mother handed down to her," I said, moving up to touch the quilts. Dee (Wangero) moved back just enough so that I couldn't reach the quilts. They already belonged to her.

"Imagine!" she breathed again, clutching them closely to her bosom.

"The truth is," I said, "I promised to give them quilts to Maggie, for when she marries John Thomas."

She gasped like a bee had stung her.

"Maggie can't appreciate these quilts!" she said. "She'd probably be backward enough to put them to everyday use."

"I reckon she would," I said. "God knows I been saving 'em for long enough with nobody using 'em. I hope she will!" I didn't want to bring up how I had offered Dee (Wangero) a quilt when she went away to college. Then she had told me they were old-fashioned, out of style.

"But they're *priceless*!" she was saying now, furiously; for she has a temper. "Maggie would put them on the bed and in five years they'd be in rags. Less than that!"

"She can always make some more," I said. "Maggie knows how to quilt."

Dee (Wangero) looked at me with hatred. "You just will not understand. The point is these quilts, *these quilts*!"

"Well," I said, stumped. "What would *you* do with them?"

"Hang them," she said. As if that was the only thing you *could* do with quilts.

Maggie by now was standing in the door. I could almost hear the sound her feet made as they scraped over each other.

"She can have them, Mama," she said, like somebody used to never winning anything, or having anything reserved for her.

"I can 'member Grandma Dee without the quilts."

I looked at her hard. She had filled her bottom lip with checkerberry snuff and it gave her face a kind of dopey, hangdog look. It was Grandma Dee and Big Dee who taught her how to quilt herself. She stood there with her scarred hands hidden in the folds of her skirt. She looked at her sister with something like fear but she wasn't mad at her. This was Maggie's portion. This was the way she knew God to work.

When I looked at her like that something hit me in the top of my head and ran down to the soles of my feet. Just like when I'm in church and the spirit of God touches me and I get happy and

Dialect

How does the narrator's speech affect Dee's perception of her?

Contrasting Characters

In what way does the dispute over the quilts reveal the differences between the two sisters?

Comprehension

Why does Dee think Maggie should not have the quilts?

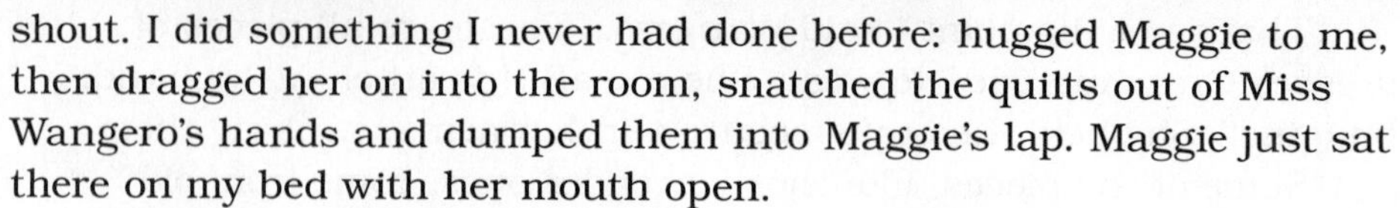

shout. I did something I never had done before: hugged Maggie to me, then dragged her on into the room, snatched the quilts out of Miss Wangero's hands and dumped them into Maggie's lap. Maggie just sat there on my bed with her mouth open.

"Take one or two of the others," I said to Dee.

But she turned without a word and went out to Hakim-a-barber.

"You just don't understand," she said, as Maggie and I came out to the car.

"What don't I understand?" I wanted to know.

"Your heritage," she said. And then she turned to Maggie, kissed her, and said, "You ought to try to make something of yourself, too, Maggie. It's really a new day for us. But from the way you and Mama still live you'd never know it."

She put on some sunglasses that hid everything above the tip of her nose and her chin.

Maggie smiled; maybe at the sunglasses. But a real smile, not scared. After we watched the car dust settle I asked Maggie to bring me a dip of snuff. And then the two of us sat there just enjoying, until it was time to go in the house and go to bed.

Critical Reading

Cite textual evidence to support your responses.

1. **Key Ideas and Details** **(a)** What objects does Dee ask to have? **(b)** What does Dee plan to do with the items? **(c) Evaluate:** What is ironic about her request for these objects and her professed interest in her heritage?
2. **Key Ideas and Details** **(a) Interpret:** What do the quilts symbolize? **(b) Compare and Contrast:** In what ways do the quilts hold different meanings for Dee and for Maggie?
3. **Integration of Knowledge and Ideas** Does this story suggest that there is a personal price for social change—even change for the better? Explain. In your response, use at least two of these Essential Question words: *communication, perspective, compromise, understanding.* ***[Connecting to the Essential Question: How does literature shape or reflect society?]***

Close Reading Activities *Everyday Use*

Literary Analysis

1. **Key Ideas and Details** **(a)** What sort of awareness does each sister have about her heritage? **(b)** To what extent does each sister think it is important to incorporate knowledge of her African heritage into her daily life?
2. **Key Ideas and Details** How would you describe the narrator's relationship with **(a)** Maggie and **(b)** Dee? Use examples from the text to support your answers.
3. **Craft and Structure** Explain how the narrator's internal narrative voice differs from her spoken, external voice.
4. **Craft and Structure** Use a chart like the one shown to identify specific details that portray the narrator. **(a)** Identify each detail you chose as either an example of the narrator's internal voice, using standard English, or an example of her spoken voice, using **dialect. (b)** What do you learn about the narrator through each of these examples?

5. **Craft and Structure** How does her use of these different types of language add to Walker's **characterization** of the narrator?
6. **Craft and Structure** What does the reader learn about Dee through **(a)** the narrator's internal voice and **(b)** spoken dialogue?
7. **Craft and Structure** What does the author reveal about Maggie through **(a)** the narrator's internal voice and **(b)** spoken dialogue?
8. **Integration of Knowledge and Ideas** **(a)** Does Dee/Wangero truly know her mother? Explain. **(b)** How does the duality between the narrator's internal and external expression create different portraits of the narrator for the reader and for Dee?
9. **Integration of Knowledge and Ideas** **Compare and contrast the characters** of Maggie and Dee **(a)** physically, **(b)** intellectually, and **(c)** emotionally.
10. **Integration of Knowledge and Ideas** **(a)** How are Dee and the narrator different from one another? **(b)** How are they alike?

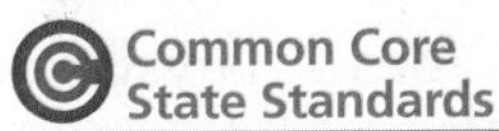
Common Core State Standards

Writing

1. Write arguments to support claims in an analysis of substantive topics or texts, using valid reasoning and relevant and sufficient evidence. *(p. 1322)*

5. Develop and strengthen writing as needed by planning, revising, editing, rewriting, or trying a new approach, focusing on addressing what is most significant for a specific purpose and audience. *(p. 1322)*

Language

1. Demonstrate command of the conventions of standard English grammar and usage when writing or speaking. *(p. 1323)*

4.b. Identify and correctly use patterns of word changes that indicate different meanings or parts of speech. *(p. 1322)*

5. Demonstrate understanding of word relationships. *(p. 1322)*

Vocabulary Acquisition and Use

Word Analysis: Latin Root *-doc- / -doct-*

The word *doctrines*, meaning "teachings, ideas, or beliefs," includes the Latin root *-doc- / -doct-*, meaning "teach." Combine this information with context clues to choose the best word to complete each sentence. Explain your choices.

documents indoctrinate docile documentary

1. We watched a _____ on the history of quilt-making in America.
2. A _____ learner is one who accepts without question anything he or she is taught.
3. The political leader worked to _____ his followers by repeating his ideology at every opportunity.
4. Immigrants were asked to show _____ to prove their citizenship in their original country.

Vocabulary: Analogies

Analogies show the relationships between pairs of words. Complete each analogy using a word from the vocabulary list on page 1310. In each, your choice should create a word pair that matches the relationship between the first two words given. Then, explain your answers.

1. *Laughing* is to *amused* as _____ is to *frightened*.
2. *Comely* is to *stunning* as _____ is to *unattractive*.
3. *Competitive* is to *athlete* as _____ is to *prowler*.
4. *Morals* is to *lessons* as _____ is to *beliefs*.

Writing to Sources

Argument Write a **critical review** of "Everyday Use," explaining whether you think the story is effective. Note your reactions to the story and explain whether the characters are believable and interesting. Consider the story's message, and express your opinion about its importance.

Prewriting Review the story and list your responses, both positive and negative. Beside each item, note the page numbers of appropriate examples. Review your chart, and summarize your opinion in a sentence or two.

Drafting Begin by stating your overall opinion of the story. Then, present a series of paragraphs in which you support your ideas with details.

Revising Evaluate your draft to replace weak modifiers with precise adjectives and adverbs. If necessary, use a print or online thesaurus to locate words that vividly and precisely express your meaning.

Model: Revising to Add Precise Details

Dee, as Wangero, appears ~~nice~~ genuine, but she is ~~really quite~~ insincere. She is not at all interested in ~~the things~~ her heritage, but rather in appearances.

Replacing weak modifiers with specific words makes writing more precise and interesting. Words like *really* do not add meaning to the work.

Conventions and Style: Using Transitional Expressions

To connect ideas in your writing, join one independent clause to another with a **transitional expression.** Transitional expressions are words and phrases that help define specific relationships among ideas. The chart shown here lists common transitional expressions:

Common Transitional Expressions

Intended Meaning	Sample Words or Phrases
Cause-effect	therefore; consequently; as a result
Time	the next step; subsequently
Illustrate	in fact; that is; for example; indeed
Sum up	in conclusion; in summary
Compare	similarly; in the same way
Contrast	however; conversely; on the other hand

Punctuation Tip When you use a transitional expression to join two independent clauses, precede the transition with a semicolon and follow it with a comma.

Connecting Ideas With Transitions

Choppy: Maggie was caught in a fire. She has scars.

Revision with Transition: Maggie was caught in a fire; *consequently*, she has scars.

Choppy: Dee couldn't wait to leave. Maggie likes living with Mama.

Revision with Transition: Dee couldn't wait to leave; *in contrast*, Maggie likes living with Mama.

Practice Rewrite each item using a transitional expression. Punctuate the new sentence correctly.

1. The church raised money. Dee was able to get an education.

2. Maggie was shy. She shuffled when she walked, her head down.

3. Dee liked to read aloud. Maggie read hesitantly, though cheerfully.

4. Dee changed her name. She felt weighed down by her family ancestry.

5. Mama had trouble pronouncing the man's name. Dee said to call him Hakim-a-barber.

Writing and Speaking Conventions

A. Writing Complete each sentence starter. Remember to use a comma after a transitional expression.

1. Maggie is upset by the visit; clearly ______.
2. Dee was not alarmed when the house burned; to be sure ______.
3. Dee insisted she would not bring friends to visit; in fact ______.
4. Dee criticized Jimmy T.; as a result ______.
5. Dee left; after a while ______.

Example: Maggie is upset by Dee's visit; clearly ______.
Complete Sentence: Maggie is upset by the visit; clearly, she feels inferior.

B. Speaking When Dee asked for the quilts, Mama heard something drop. Explain to a partner what happened and why you think the author included this detail. Include at least two transitional expressions in your explanation.

Building Knowledge and Insight

Everything Stuck to Him

Connecting to the Essential Question In this story, an adult daughter struggles to make an emotional connection with her father. As you read, notice how the characters in the story speak—what they say and how they say it. Doing so will help you think about the Essential Question: **What makes American literature American?**

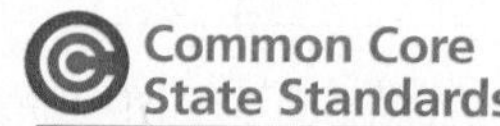

Common Core State Standards

Reading Literature

4. Determine the meaning of words and phrases as they are used in the text, including figurative and connotative meanings; analyze the impact of specific word choices on meaning and tone, including words with multiple meanings or language that is particularly fresh, engaging, or beautiful.

5. Analyze how an author's choices concerning how to structure specific parts of a text contribute to its overall structure and meaning as well as its aesthetic impact.

Close Reading Focus

Author's Style

All writers use language and may even explore similar themes or events. What distinguishes one writer from another is the **author's style**—*how* he or she uses language. Many literary elements, including word choice, sentence length and complexity, types of images, and types of subject matter, contribute to style. Raymond Carver's style, which is one of the most influential in contemporary literature, is marked by certain traits:

- He favors an economy of words and suggests more than he states.
- His restrained use of language creates a distant, almost subdued emotional attitude, or tone.
- He focuses on the lives of the working poor, a recurring theme.
- His characters often seem to struggle, unsuccessfully, to find words to express what they see and feel. They persist in a quiet isolation.

As you read, look for these elements of Carver's intense, pared-down style and think about how they affect the meaning, mood, and power of the story.

Preparing to Read Complex Texts When reading fiction, **asking questions** can clarify your understanding of passages, relationships, or events that may at first seem unclear. For example, in this story, the time frame moves back and forth between an outer story, or *frame story*, narrated by the author, to an inner story narrated by one of the main characters. Clarify your understanding by asking questions about the characters and events. Then, look for details or clues in the writing that help you reach a logical conclusion. As you read, use a chart like the one shown to aid your understanding.

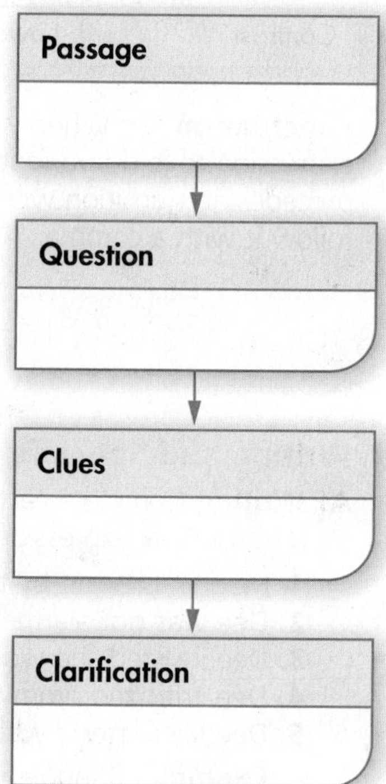

Vocabulary

The words below are important to understanding the text that follows. Copy the words into your notebook. Which one of the words is a multiple-meaning word? Jot down at least two meanings for that word.

coincide **striking**
ambitions **fitfully**

RAYMOND CARVER *(1938–1988)*

Author of "Everything Stuck to Him"

Raymond Carver is one of a handful of authors said to have revitalized the art of short-story writing in the late 1900s. Born in a small Oregon logging town to a mill worker and a waitress, Carver grew up penniless in Washington State. As an adult, he drew heavily from his life in his writings about the hardships of the working poor.

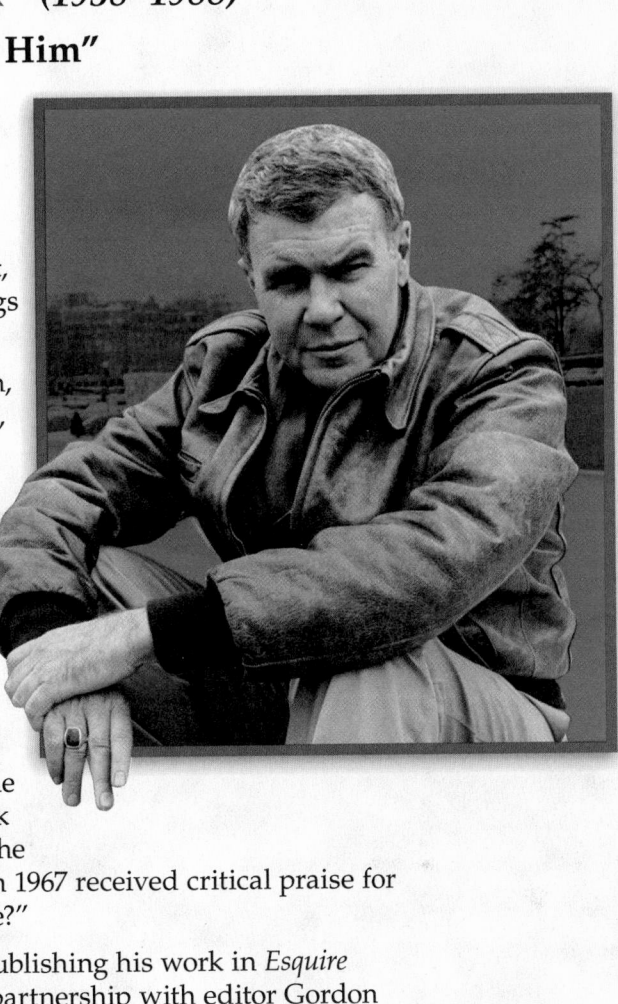

Inauspicious Beginnings At age nineteen, one year after graduating from high school, Carver married his sixteen-year-old sweetheart. By age twenty, he had fathered two children. Struggling to support his family, Carver took on a series of jobs, including work as a janitor, a sawmill worker, and a gas-station attendant.

After moving his family to California in 1958, Carver began studying at Chico State College. There he took a creative writing course taught by the acclaimed novelist John Gardner, who quickly became his mentor. Carver worked nights and took classes during the day. He later attended the prestigious Iowa Writer's Workshop and in 1967 received critical praise for his story "Will You Please Be Quiet, Please?"

A Turning Point In 1971, Carver began publishing his work in *Esquire* magazine, where he began a decade-long partnership with editor Gordon Lish. Lish encouraged a "less-is-more" approach to writing. As a result, Carver's writing became lean and sparse, earning him a reputation as a minimalist. A few years later, Carver published his short-story collection *Will You Please Be Quiet, Please?* and his career took off.

Opening Up In the 1980s, Carver parted ways with Lish, and his work grew more expansive. Then, in 1983, Carver won an award that changed his life. The Mildred and Harold Strauss Livings award brought with it five years of tax-free income and gave Carver financial independence. He earned celebrity treatment, with profiles in the *New York Times Magazine, Vanity Fair,* and *People* magazine. In 1984, his short story collection *Cathedral* was nominated for the Pulitzer Prize.

Carver divorced his first wife in 1982, and in 1988 he married the poet Tess Gallagher. That same year, Carver published his final collection of stories and was inducted into the American Academy and Institute of Arts and Letters. A few months later, at age fifty, Carver succumbed to lung cancer. He is remembered as one of the greatest storytellers of his time.

EVERYTHING STUCK TO HIM

—RAYMOND CARVER—

BACKGROUND This is a **frame story**, or a story within a story. There are many frame narratives in world literature, including the *Arabian Nights* and *The Canterbury Tales*. "The Notorious Jumping Frog of Calaveras County" (p. 576) by Mark Twain is an American example. To be a genuine frame narrative, the introductory story must be of secondary importance to the internal one. Consider whether this is true of Carver's tale.

◀ **Critical Viewing**

How does the setting of the frame story as shown here differ from the setting of the internal story? **COMPARE AND CONTRAST**

She's in Milan for Christmas and wants to know what it was like when she was a kid.

Tell me, she says. Tell me what it was like when I was a kid. She sips Strega,[1] waits, eyes him closely.

She is a cool, slim, attractive girl, a survivor from top to bottom.

That was a long time ago. That was twenty years ago, he says.

You can remember, she says. Go on.

What do you want to hear? he says. What else can I tell you? I could tell you about something that happened when you were a baby. It involves you, he says. But only in a minor way.

Tell me, she says. But first fix us another so you won't have to stop in the middle.

He comes back from the kitchen with drinks, settles into his chair, begins.

They were kids themselves, but they were crazy in love, this eighteen-year-old boy and this seventeen-year-old girl when they married. Not all that long afterwards they had a daughter.

The baby came along in late November during a cold spell that just happened to coincide with the peak of the waterfowl season. The boy loved to hunt, you see. That's part of it.

The boy and girl, husband and wife, father and mother, they lived in a little apartment under a dentist's office. Each night they cleaned the dentist's place upstairs in exchange for rent and utilities. In summer they were expected to maintain the lawn and the flowers. In winter the boy shoveled snow and spread rock salt on the walks. Are you still with me? Are you getting the picture?

I am, she says.

That's good, he says. So one day the dentist finds out they were using his letterhead for their personal correspondence. But that's another story.

He gets up from his chair and looks out the window. He sees the tile rooftops and the snow that is falling steadily on them.

Tell the story, she says.

The two kids were very much in love. On top of this they had great ambitions. They were always talking about the things they were going to do and the places they were going to go.

Vocabulary

coincide (kō′ in sīd′) *v.* to happen at the same time

ambitions (am bish′ ənz) *n.* strongly desired goals

Comprehension

How old were the boy and the girl when they married?

---

1. **Strega** *n.* an Italian herbal liqueur.

Now the boy and girl slept in the bedroom, and the baby slept in the living room. Let's say the baby was about three months old and had only just begun to sleep through the night.

On this one Saturday night after finishing his work upstairs, the boy stayed in the dentist's office and called an old hunting friend of his father's.

Author's Style

Why do you think Carver chooses to name minor characters, while leaving the main characters nameless?

Carl, he said when the man picked up the receiver, believe it or not, I'm a father.

Congratulations, Carl said. How is the wife?

She's fine, Carl. Everybody's fine.

That's good, Carl said, I'm glad to hear it. But if you called about going hunting, I'll tell you something. The geese are flying to beat the band. I don't think I've ever seen so many. Got five today. Going back in the morning, so come along if you want to.

I want to, the boy said.

The boy hung up the telephone and went downstairs to tell the girl. She watched while he laid out his things. Hunting coat, shell bag, boots, socks, hunting cap, long underwear, pump gun.

What time will you be back? the girl said.

Probably around noon, the boy said. But maybe as late as six o'clock. Would that be too late?

It's fine, she said. The baby and I will get along fine. You go and have some fun. When you get back, we'll dress the baby up and go visit Sally.

Vocabulary

striking (strī′ kiŋ) *adj.* very noticeable or impressive

The boy said, Sounds like a good idea.

Sally was the girl's sister. She was **striking**. I don't know if you've seen pictures of her. The boy was a little in love with Sally, just as he was a little in love with Betsy, who was another sister the girl had. The boy used to say to the girl, If we weren't married, I could go for Sally.

What about Betsy? the girl used to say. I hate to admit it, but I truly feel she's better looking than Sally and me. What about Betsy?

Betsy too, the boy used to say.

After dinner he turned up the furnace and helped her bathe the baby. He marveled again at the infant who had half his features and half the girl's. He powdered the tiny body. He powdered between fingers and toes.

He emptied the bath into the sink and went upstairs to check the air. It was overcast and cold. The grass, what there was of it, looked like canvas, stiff and gray under the street light.

Snow lay in piles beside the walk. A car went by. He heard sand under the tires. He let himself imagine what it might be like tomorrow, geese beating the air over his head, shotgun plunging against his shoulder.

Then he locked the door and went downstairs.

In bed they tried to read. But both of them fell asleep, she first, letting the magazine sink to the quilt.

It was the baby's cries that woke him up.

The light was on out there, and the girl was standing next to the crib rocking the baby in her arms. She put the baby down, turned out the light, and came back to the bed.

He heard the baby cry. This time the girl stayed where she was. The baby cried **fitfully** and stopped. The boy listened, then dozed. But the baby's cries woke him again. The living room light was burning. He sat up and turned on the lamp.

Vocabulary
fitfully (fit′ fəl ē) *adv.* without regularity; restlessly

I don't know what's wrong, the girl said, walking back and forth with the baby. I've changed her and fed her, but she keeps on crying. I'm so tired I'm afraid I might drop her.

You come back to bed, the boy said. I'll hold her for a while.

He got up and took the baby, and the girl went to lie down again.

Just rock her for a few minutes, the girl said from the bedroom. Maybe she'll go back to sleep.

The boy sat on the sofa and held the baby. He jiggled it in his lap until he got its eyes to close, his own eyes closing right along. He rose carefully and put the baby back in the crib.

It was a quarter to four, which gave him forty-five minutes. He crawled into bed and dropped off. But a few minutes later the baby was crying again, and this time they both got up.

The boy did a terrible thing. He swore.

For God's sake, what's the matter with you? the girl said to the boy. Maybe she's sick or something. Maybe we shouldn't have given her the bath.

The boy picked up the baby. The baby kicked its feet and smiled.

Look, the boy said, I really don't think there's anything wrong with her.

How do you know that? the girl said. Here, let me have her. I know I ought to give her something, but I don't know what it's supposed to be.

The girl put the baby down again. The boy and the girl looked at the baby, and the baby began to cry.

The girl took the baby. Baby, baby, the girl said with tears in her eyes.

Baby, baby, the girl said with tears in her eyes.

Probably it's something on her stomach, the boy said.

The girl didn't answer. She went on rocking the baby, paying no attention to the boy.

The boy waited. He went to the kitchen and put on water for coffee. He drew his woolen underwear on over his shorts and T-shirt, buttoned up, then got into his clothes.

What are you doing? the girl said.

Going hunting, the boy said.

I don't think you should, she said. I don't want to be left alone with her like this.

Comprehension
What "terrible thing" does the boy do?

Carl's planning on me going, the boy said. We've planned it.

I don't care about what you and Carl planned, she said. And I don't care about Carl, either. I don't even know Carl.

You've met Carl before. You know him, the boy said. What do you mean you don't know him?

That's not the point and you know it, the girl said.

What is the point? the boy said. The point is we planned it.

The girl said, I'm your wife. This is your baby. She's sick or something. Look at her. Why else is she crying?

I know you're my wife, the boy said.

The girl began to cry. She put the baby back in the crib. But the baby started up again. The girl dried her eyes on the sleeve of her nightgown and picked the baby up.

The boy laced up his boots. He put on his shirt, his sweater, his coat. The kettle whistled on the stove in the kitchen.

You're going to have to choose, the girl said. Carl or us. I mean it.

What do you mean? the boy said.

You heard what I said, the girl said. If you want a family, you're going to have to choose.

They stared at each other. Then the boy took up his hunting gear and went outside. He started the car. He went around to the car windows and, making a job of it, scraped away the ice.

He turned off the motor and sat awhile. And then he got out and went back inside.

The living-room light was on. The girl was asleep on the bed. The baby was asleep beside her.

The boy took off his boots. Then he took off everything else. In his socks and his long underwear, he sat on the sofa and read the Sunday paper.

Author's Style

How does this exchange between the boy and the girl reflect the author's unadorned style?

The girl and the baby slept on. After a while, the boy went to the kitchen and started frying bacon.

The girl came out in her robe and put her arms around the boy.

Hey, the boy said.

I'm sorry, the girl said.

It's all right, the boy said.

I didn't mean to snap like that.

It was my fault, he said.

You sit down, the girl said. How does a waffle sound with bacon?

Sounds great, the boy said.

She took the bacon out of the pan and made waffle batter. He sat at the table and watched her move around the kitchen.

She put a plate in front of him with bacon, a waffle. He spread butter and poured syrup. But when he started to cut, he turned the plate into his lap.

I don't believe it, he said, jumping up from the table.

If you could see yourself, the girl said.

The boy looked down at himself, at everything stuck to his underwear.

I was starved, he said, shaking his head.

You were starved, she said, laughing.

He peeled off the woolen underwear and threw it at the bathroom door. Then he opened his arms and the girl moved into them.

We won't fight anymore, she said.

The boy said, We won't.

He gets up from his chair and refills their glasses.

That's it, he says. End of story. I admit it's not much of a story.

I was interested, she says.

He shrugs and carries his drink over to the window. It's dark now but still snowing.

Things change, he says. I don't know how they do. But they do without your realizing it or wanting them to.

Yes, that's true, only—But she does not finish what she started.

She drops the subject. In the window's reflection he sees her study her nails. Then she raises her head. Speaking brightly, she asks if he is going to show her the city, after all.

He says, Put your boots on and let's go.

But he stays by the window, remembering. They had laughed. They had leaned on each other and laughed until the tears had come, while everything else—the cold, and where he'd go in it—was outside, for a while anyway.

Author's Style

Carver is known for his use of "silence." Why do you think the girl does not finish her sentence?

Critical Reading

Cite textual evidence to support your responses.

1. **Key Ideas and Details** **(a)** What is the internal story about? **(b) Draw Conclusions:** Why does the man refer to himself and his family members as "the boy," "the girl," and "the baby"?
2. **Key Ideas and Details** **(a)** To what incident does the title of the story refer? **(b) Infer:** What other significance might the title have?
3. **Integration of Knowledge and Ideas** **(a) Speculate:** What might the young woman have said to her father if she had finished her sentence at the end of the story? **(b) Evaluate:** Do you feel hopeful about the future of the father and daughter's relationship? Why or why not?
4. **Integration of Knowledge and Ideas** Although the frame story is set in Italy, the characters are from the United States. What aspects of their speech strike you as distinctly American? Explain. In your response, use at least two of these Essential Question words: *ornate, vernacular, direct, realistic, regional.* ***[Connecting to the Essential Question: What makes American literature American?]***

Close Reading Activities | *Everything Stuck to Him*

Literary Analysis

1. **Key Ideas and Details** **(a)** What **questions** did you ask to clarify connections between the characters in the external, or *frame*, and internal stories? **(b)** Which details helped you clarify that relationship?
2. **Key Ideas and Details** Note another question you asked about the story, and list the details that answered it.
3. **Craft and Structure** Using a chart like the one shown, describe elements of Carver's **style** and cite examples from the story.

Element	Description	Example
Word Choice		
Sentences		
Details and Images		
Thematic Events		

4. **Integration of Knowledge and Ideas** **(a)** Explain how Carver suggests more than he states in this story. **(b)** What mood does Carver's pared-down style help create?

Vocabulary Acquisition and Use

Use New Words Write a sentence for each word pair in which you use both words correctly.

1. striking / ambitions
2. fitfully / coincide

Writing to Sources

Explanatory Text Write an **analytical essay** in which you examine the story's ending. Consider the following questions as you draft: In what ways does the story end happily? What note of discord is introduced? How is that note introduced? What do you understand about the father and daughter's relationship from earlier details? How is your sense of the ending affected by that understanding?

Begin your essay by stating your position. Then, defend your position with details from the story.

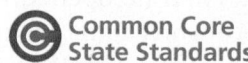

Common Core State Standards

Writing

2. Write explanatory texts to examine and convey complex ideas, concepts, and information clearly and accurately through the effective selection, organization, and analysis of content.

9.a. Apply grades 11–12 Reading standards to literature. [RL.11-12.5]

Language

4. Determine or clarify the meaning of unknown and multiple-meaning words and phrases based on *grades 11–12 reading and content,* choosing flexibly from a range of strategies.

TEXT SET

Contemporary Poetry

Part 2

Building Knowledge and Insight

Traveling Through the Dark • The Secret • The Gift

Connecting to the Essential Question These poems focus on moments of unexpected connections or perceptions. As you read, notice details that express a new understanding. Doing so will help you consider the Essential Question: **How does literature shape or reflect society?**

Reading Literature
1. Cite strong and thorough textual evidence to support analysis of what the text says explicitly as well as inferences drawn from the text, including determining where the text leaves matters uncertain.
2. Determine two or more themes or central ideas of a text and analyze their development over the course of the text, including how they interact and build on one another to produce a complex account.

Close Reading Focus

Lyric Poem; Epiphany

The literary works presented here are lyric poems. A **lyric poem** expresses the thoughts and feelings of a single speaker and often has a lilting, musical quality, as in these lines from Li-Young Lee's "The Gift":

I can't remember the tale,
but hear his voice still, a well
of dark water, a prayer.

Lyric poems are usually relatively short but have great depth. The **theme,** or essential meaning, of such a poem is often multifaceted. The precise, nuanced language of many lyric poems may even help to express multiple themes. In most lyric poems, the theme emerges as a flash of insight or understanding. Although this flash—also known as an **epiphany**—may seem sudden, the details of the poem lead the reader gradually and steadily toward this new understanding. The epiphany is usually accompanied by a shift in perspective: the speaker may face up to a loss, make a decision, or simply see something in a new light. The reader, too, experiences the epiphany alongside the speaker, and comes away from the lyric poem feeling as if he or she has been on a small but meaningful journey.

Preparing to Read Complex Texts Poets rarely spell out their exact meaning in a lyric poem. Instead, it is up to the reader to interpret the poem by noting details and considering the message they collectively present. When **interpreting** lyric poetry, look for a central image or idea that is introduced and revisited throughout the poem. Consider new information about the image that emerges over the course of the poem. As you read, use a chart like the one shown to interpret how key details contribute to the ultimate meaning in each poem.

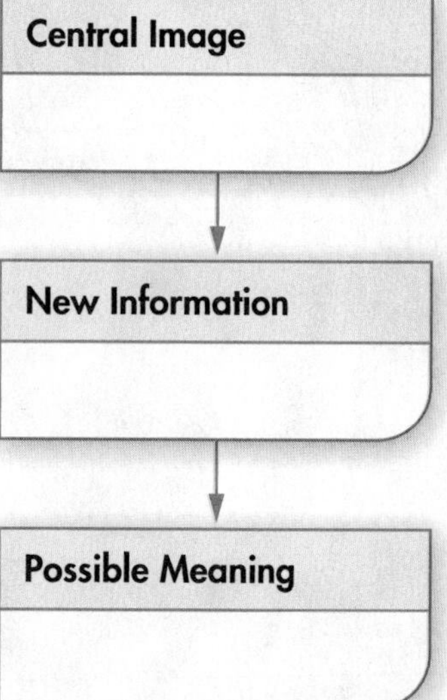

Vocabulary

The words below are important to understanding the texts that follow. Copy the words into your notebook, sorting them into words you know and words you do not know.

swerve **shard**
exhaust

William Stafford

(1914–1993)

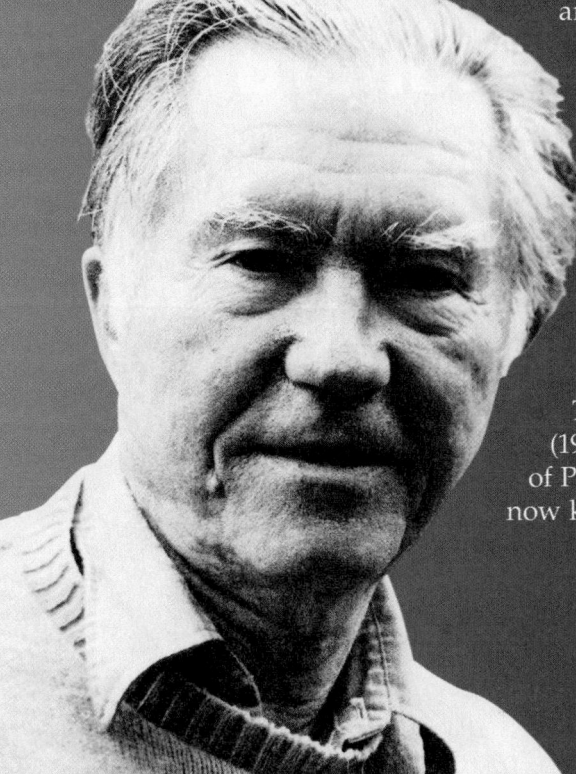

"I have woven a parachute out of everything broken."

Author of "Traveling Through the Dark"

William Stafford grew up in Kansas. When the Great Depression struck, he traveled with his family from town to town selling newspapers, working in the fields, and finding whatever work they could. These childhood experiences would greatly influence Stafford's poetry, both in its themes and its use of unadorned language.

Conscientious Objector A believer in the sanctity of life, Stafford served in World War II as a conscientious objector. In this role, he performed tasks such as fighting fires, building roads, and cultivating crops. Stafford's experiences during this time are described in his memoir, *Down in My Heart*, published in 1947.

After years of working for the U.S. Forest Service, Stafford published his first volume of poetry, *West of Your City* in 1960. He was forty-six years old at the time. In that book and others, Stafford's poems focus on a range of subjects, including the threat of nuclear war and the beauty of nature. His accessible, conversational style invites readers to appreciate the simple elegance of the everyday while considering deeper issues. Writing about Stafford in *Babel to Byzantium,* a book of critical essays, poet James Dickey described Stafford's work as "mystical, half-mocking and highly personal daydreaming about the western United States."

Stafford's other poetry collections include *The Rescued Year* (1966) and *Stories That Could Be True: New and Collected Poems* (1977). In 1970, he was appointed Consultant of Poetry to the Library of Congress, a position now known as Poet Laureate of the United States.

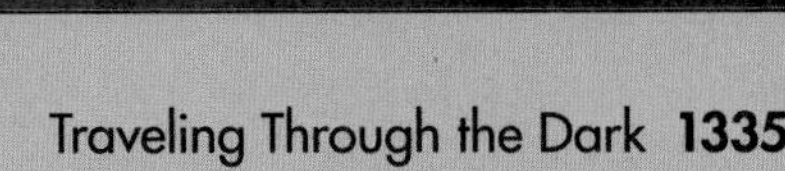

TRAVELING THROUGH THE DARK

William Stafford

Traveling through the dark I found a deer
dead on the edge of the Wilson River road.
It is usually best to roll them into the canyon:
that road is narrow; to **swerve** might make more dead.

By glow of the tail-light I stumbled back of the car
and stood by the heap, a doe, a recent killing;
she had stiffened already, almost cold.
I dragged her off; she was large in the belly.

My fingers touching her side brought me the reason—
her side was warm; her fawn lay there waiting,
alive, still, never to be born.
Beside that mountain road I hesitated.

The car aimed ahead its lowered parking lights;
under the hood purred the steady engine.
I stood in the glare of the warm **exhaust** turning red;
around our group I could hear the wilderness listen.

I thought hard for us all—my only swerving—,
then pushed her over the edge into the river.

Vocabulary

swerve (swʉrv) *v.* turn aside sharply and suddenly

Vocabulary

exhaust (eg zôst′) *n.* discharge of used steam or gas from an engine

Critical Reading

Cite textual evidence to support your responses.

1. **Key Ideas and Details (a)** What discovery does the speaker make when he examines the deer? **(b) Infer:** Why does the speaker hesitate upon making this discovery?
2. **Key Ideas and Details (a) Interpret:** In the fourth stanza, what details make the car seem alive? **(b) Connect:** In what ways does this description echo the speaker's discovery about the deer?
3. **Key Ideas and Details (a) Deduce:** What factors does the speaker weigh in his decision about what to do with the deer? **(b) Analyze:** How does the title reflect the speaker's moral dilemma?

Denise Levertov

(1923–1997)

Author of **"The Secret"**

Born in England, Denise Levertov grew up wandering the parks and museums of London and reveling in her family's private library. By the age of five, she had decided to become a writer, and by seventeen she had published her first poem. Her collection *The Double Image* appeared in 1946, earning the poet recognition in both England and the United States.

Becoming American After serving as a civilian nurse in London during World War II, Levertov married an American writer and moved to the United States. There, she developed a close friendship with the poet William Carlos Williams and studied the works of Emerson and Thoreau. From these writers Levertov learned to pay deep attention to the realities of life, both large and small.

When she came to the United States, Levertov became part of a loosely-organized group known as "The Black Mountain Poets." These writers rejected poetic tradition and embraced a conversational style of writing. In her poem, "The Man," Levertov expresses the force of individualism the Black Mountain poets sought: "you pick out / your own song from the uproar / line by line, / and at last throw back / your head and sing it."

Although her poems cover a broad range of topics—from love to art to politics and war—they are all characterized by a clear, direct voice and a profound reverence for the mystery at the heart of existence. Levertov published more than twenty volumes of poetry during her lifetime, including the award-winning *The Freeing of the Dust.*

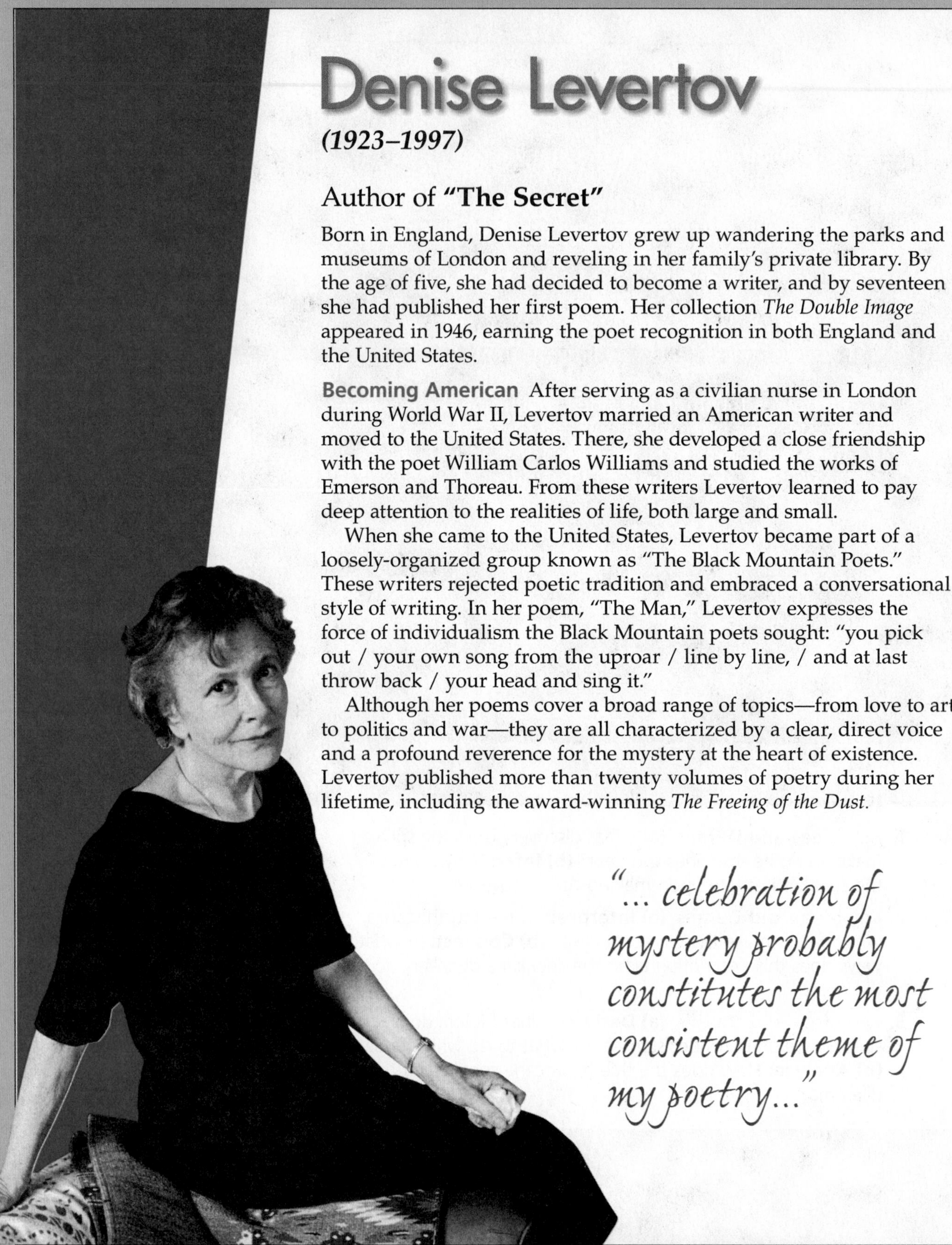

"... celebration of mystery probably constitutes the most consistent theme of my poetry..."

THE SECRET

Denise Levertov

Two Girls Reading, Pablo Picasso, Artists Rights Society (ARS), New York

◀ **Critical Viewing**
This painting by Pablo Picasso is entitled "Two Girls Reading." Does this painting suggest a moment of discovery that is in any way similar to the one described in the poem? **ASSESS**

Two girls discover
the secret of life
in a sudden line of
poetry.

I who don't know the
secret wrote
the line. They
told me

(through a third person)
they had found it

Comprehension
What do two girls discover in a poem?

but not what it was
not even

what line it was. No doubt
by now, more than a week
later, they have forgotten
the secret,

the line, the name of
the poem. I love them
for finding what
I can't find,

and for loving me
for the line I wrote,
and for forgetting it
so that

a thousand times, till death
finds them, they may
discover it again, in other
lines

in other
happenings. And for
wanting to know it,
for

assuming there is
such a secret, yes,
for that
most of all.

Lyric Poem and Epiphany
What sudden understanding does the speaker have about the nature of "the secret of life"?

Critical Reading

Cite textual evidence to support your responses.

1. **Key Ideas and Details** **(a)** Who discovers "the secret" of life, and where? **(b) Assess:** In lines 1–16, how does the speaker seem to feel about this discovery?
2. **Key Ideas and Details** **(a)** For what does the speaker love the secret-finders most of all? **(b) Interpret:** Why does the speaker love the idea that the secret-finders have already lost the secret? **(c) Infer:** Based on this evidence, do you think the speaker herself believes there is a secret?
3. **Integration of Knowledge and Ideas** **Synthesize:** Do you believe there is a secret of life that can be discovered in a sudden moment? Explain.

Li-Young Lee (b. 1957)

Author of "The Gift"

Li-Young Lee was born in Indonesia after his parents were exiled from China. Indonesia proved equally unwelcoming to Lee's father—who was both Christian and pro-Western—and he was imprisoned for nineteen months. After his release, the family moved first to Hong Kong, and then traveled through Macau and Japan. Finally, in 1964, Lee and his family moved to the United States.

Landing in America After a childhood of constant motion, Lee adjusted to a calm life in Pittsburgh, Pennsylvania. As an 11-year-old boy, he met a young woman who would later become his wife and the inspiration for many of his poems. Although Lee's transition to life in the United States was smooth, he still says that he is unable to decide if he should consider himself Chinese, Chinese-American, Asian-American, or American. The search for identity is a recurring theme throughout his work.

Although his father often read poetry aloud, Lee did not begin writing poetry until he was a student at the University of Pittsburgh. After further studies in Arizona and New York, Lee settled in Chicago, where he continues to live and work as a full-time poet. Over the years he has published a number of poetry collections and other works.

Story-Poems Lee's poems are known for their meandering, free-verse style and for the complex web of memories they present. Many of his "story-poems" focus on his childhood experiences as an immigrant and the son of exiles, often recalling, with affection, the strength and gentleness of his father. Influenced by both the Bible and classic Chinese poets, Lee's works have a silent, reverent quality that gives even his most personal subject matter a universal appeal. His many awards include a Lannan Literary Award, a Whiting Writer's Award, three Pushcart Prizes, and a Guggenheim Foundation fellowship.

"The knowledge that it takes to write a poem gets burnt up in the writing of the poem."

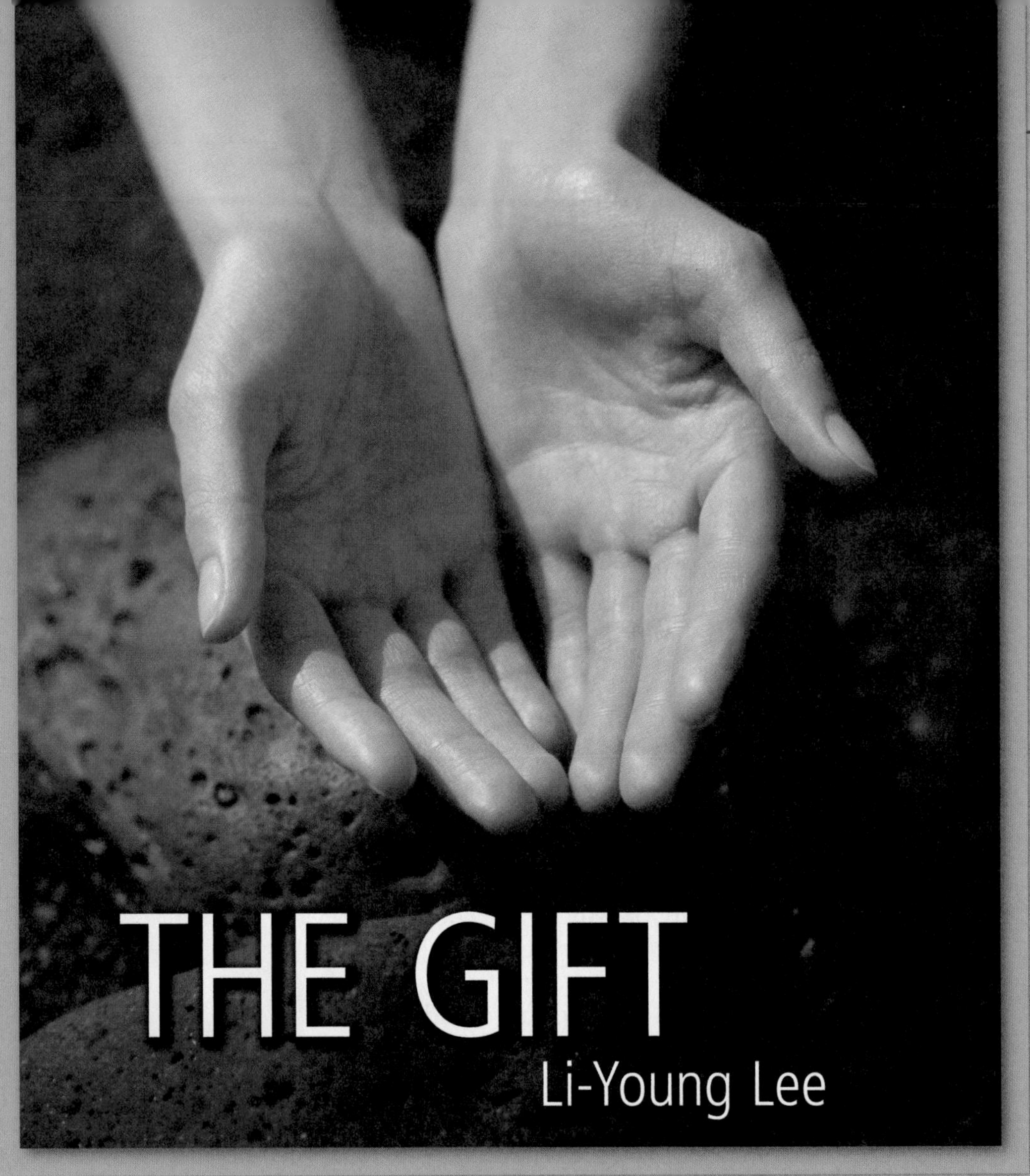

THE GIFT

Li-Young Lee

Interpreting
What central image is presented in the first line of the poem?

To pull the metal splinter from my palm
my father recited a story in a low voice.
I watched his lovely face and not the blade.
Before the story ended, he'd removed
the iron sliver I thought I'd die from.

I can't remember the tale,
but hear his voice still, a well
of dark water, a prayer.
And I recall his hands,
two measures of tenderness
he laid against my face,
the flames of discipline
he raised above my head.

Had you entered that afternoon

you would have thought you saw a man
planting something in a boy's palm,
a silver tear, a tiny flame.
Had you followed that boy
you would have arrived here,
where I bend over my wife's right hand.

Look how I shave her thumbnail down
so carefully she feels no pain.
Watch as I lift the splinter out.
I was seven when my father
took my hand like this,
and I did not hold that shard
between my fingers and think,
Metal that will bury me,
christen it Little Assassin,
Ore Going Deep for My Heart.
And I did not lift up my wound and cry,
Death visited here!
I did what a child does
when he's given something to keep.
I kissed my father.

Vocabulary
shard (shärd) *n.* a sharp fragment of glass or metal

Critical Reading

Cite textual evidence to support your responses.

1. **Key Ideas and Details** **(a)** What does the father do as he removes the boy's splinter? **(b) Analyze:** How does the poem itself mirror this detail?
2. **Key Ideas and Details** **(a)** How does the boy view the splinter when it is set in his hand? **(b) Infer:** Why does the grown speaker refer to the splinter as "Little Assassin" and "Ore Going Deep for My Heart"? **(c) Interpret:** What makes the memory of the splinter meaningful for the speaker?
3. **Integration of Knowledge and Ideas** What do each of these poems suggest about the connections between small events and larger meanings? In your response, use at least two of these Essential Question words: *transform, vision, identity, ambiguity, landscape.* ***[Connecting to the Essential Question: How does literature shape or reflect society?]***

Literary Analysis

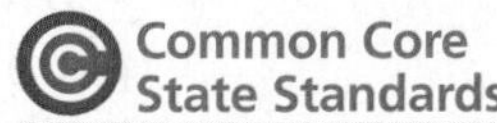

Common Core State Standards

Writing

2. Write explanatory texts to examine and convey complex ideas, concepts, and information clearly and accurately through the effective selection, organization, and analysis of content. *(p. 1345)*

2.c. Use appropriate and varied transitions and syntax to link the major sections of the text, create cohesion, and clarify the relationships among complex ideas and concepts. *(p. 1345)*

Language

4.b. Identify and correctly use patterns of word changes that indicate different meanings or parts of speech. *(p. 1345)*

1. **Key Ideas and Details (a)** In "Traveling Through the Dark," what is the speaker's moral dilemma? **(b)** In line 16, the speaker can "hear the wilderness listen." What is it listening for? **(c)** How does the speaker "answer"?
2. **Key Ideas and Details** In "Traveling Through the Dark," the speaker refers to his hard thought as his "only swerving." Explain the sudden insight, or **epiphany,** the speaker experiences after this "swerving."
3. **Key Ideas and Details (a)** What new understanding does the speaker arrive at in "The Secret"? **(b)** Would you say the theme of this poem centers on a thing, or on a process? Explain.
4. **Key Ideas and Details (a)** "The Gift" tells two mini-stories. What are they? **(b)** Identify two ways in which the speaker is like his father.
5. **Key Ideas and Details (a)** In "The Gift," what paradoxical realization does the speaker make about the removal of splinters? **(b)** How does this realization apply to memories, as well?
6. **Craft and Structure** A **lyric poem** can be thought of as a journey in which the speaker travels through a landscape of nature, memory, spirit, or morality, and returns to the starting point with a new understanding. Using a chart like the one shown, choose one of the poems in this grouping and analyze it from this perspective.

Poem:			
Type of Journey	**Starting Point**	**Events of Journey**	**How Speaker Changes**

7. **Integration of Knowledge and Ideas** Follow these steps to **interpret** each of these lyric poems:
   a. Identify the the central image or event in each poem.
   b. List two pieces of new information you learn about this image over the course of the poem.
   c. Explain how your understanding of the image changes.
   d. Interpret the poem by telling what you think each central image means to the speaker.

Vocabulary Aquisition and Use

Related Words: *Exhaust*

The word *exhaust* derives from the Latin word *exhaustus* meaning "to draw off or out" or "to use up completely." As a noun, the word *exhaust* means "the discharge of used steam or gas from an engine." However, the word may also function as a verb meaning "to empty completely" or "to tire out." Complete each of the sentences below with one of the related words from the list. Explain your choices.

inexhaustible exhausted exhaustion

1. The ______ I felt was due to lack of sleep.
2. By the race's end, the runner was ______.
3. The strength of a fit athlete can seem ______.

Vocabulary: Repairing Logic

Revise each sentence so that the underlined vocabulary word is used logically. Do not change the vocabulary word.

1. If you <u>swerve</u> your car on an icy road, you will most likely get where you are going slowly but surely.
2. After a car has had a tune-up, it should produce a steady stream of black <u>exhaust</u>.
3. Stepping on a <u>shard</u> of glass can be a soothing experience.

Writing to Sources

Informative Text The title of each of these poems has a direct relationship to the poem's meaning. Choose two of the poems, and write an **essay** in which you first **analyze** the relationship between each poem and its title, and then compare and contrast the two title/poem relationships with each other.

Prewriting First, review each poem and decide what you think each title means. Consider whether it has more than one meaning. Use a diagram like the one shown to record your ideas.

Model: Comparing and Contrasting Titles

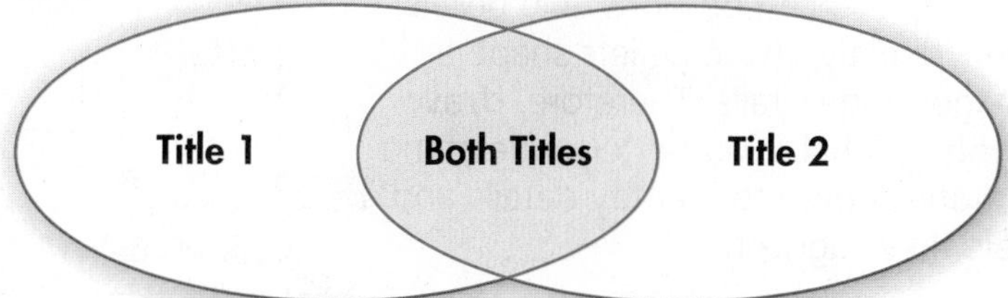

Consider turning each part of the diagram into a section of the essay.

Drafting As you draft, use a logical method of organization. You might discuss the significance of each title in turn and then ways in which the titles are similar and different. Alternatively, you might discuss each key similarity or difference and then draw conclusions about each title.

Revising Clarify the logic of your ideas by adding transitions such as *similarly, equally, to compare, in contrast, in one case,* and *in the other case.*

Building Knowledge and Insight

ANCHOR TEXT
Who Burns for the Perfection of Paper • Camouflaging the Chimera • Streets

Connecting to the Essential Question These poets express ideas about important issues that may prompt readers to think twice about their own views. As you read, look for details that reveal the speaker's beliefs. Doing so will help you consider the Essential Question: **How does literature shape or reflect society?**

Common Core State Standards

Reading Literature
1. Cite strong and thorough textual evidence to support analysis of what the text says explicitly as well as inferences drawn from the text, including determining where the text leaves matters uncertain.
4. Determine the meaning of words and phrases as they are used in the text, including figurative and connotative meanings; analyze the impact of specific word choices on meaning and tone, including words with multiple meanings or language that is particularly fresh, engaging, or beautiful.

Close Reading Focus

Voice; Social Commentary

Just as each person has a distinctive way of speaking, every poet has a unique **voice,** or literary personality. A poet's voice is based on word choice, tone, sound devices, rhyme (or its absence), pace, attitude, and even the patterns of vowels and consonants. Consider these examples:

- *Espada:* No gloves: fingertips required / for the perfection of paper . . .
- *Komunyakaa:* We hugged bamboo & leaned / against a breeze off the river . . .
- *Nye:* . . . the sky which sews and sews, tirelessly sewing, / drops her purple hem. . . .

As you read these poems, note the distinctive voice each one reveals.

Comparing Literary Works Each of these poets uses personal experience as a springboard for **social commentary,** a reflection on a public or political concern. In "Who Burns for the Perfection of Paper," for example, Martín Espada describes an experience from his youth to call attention to a social problem. In "Streets," Naomi Shihab Nye sets her own beliefs about loss and death beside the very different beliefs of others. As you read these poems, identify the particular brand of social commentary each poet offers.

Preparing to Read Complex Texts Poems are almost always subjective—that is, they express the poet's experiences, opinions, and beliefs. While a poet may not always state beliefs directly, those beliefs shape a poem's meaning and are revealed in images and details. Therefore, **drawing inferences about the poet's beliefs** will help you better understand poetry. As you read, use a chart like the one shown to identify details and draw inferences about the implicit beliefs they suggest.

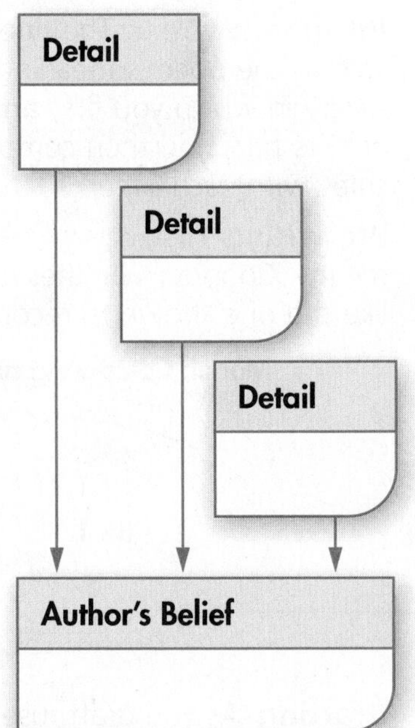

Vocabulary

You will encounter the words listed here in the texts that follow. Copy the words into your notebook, sorting them into words you know and words you do not know.

crevices **refuge**
terrain

Martín Espada *(b. 1957)*

Author of **"Who Burns for the Perfection of Paper"**

Not many lawyers pursue simultaneous careers as poets, but, until 1993, Martín Espada was an exception. Espada was inspired by his father Frank Espada, a photographer based in the New York City borough of Brooklyn. Father and son worked together on a 1981 photo documentary called *The Puerto Rican Diaspora Documentary Project.* A year later, Espada published his first volume of poetry, *The Immigrant Iceboy's Bolero,* which was enhanced by his father's photographs.

Politics and Art A poet of deep social and political consciousness, Espada draws on his Puerto Rican heritage in his work, as well as his experiences as a legal-aid lawyer and activist. His poems celebrate and often lament the experiences of working-class people, especially those of Hispanic descent. He has been acclaimed as "*the* Latino poet of his generation."

To date, Espada has published thirteen books as a poet, essayist, editor, and translator. His many honors include the Paterson Award for Sustained Literary Achievement, the American Book Award, as well as numerous awards and fellowships, including the Robert Creeley Award, the Paterson Poetry Prize, the PEN/Revson Fellowship, and two NEA Fellowships. Espada received the Guggenheim Memorial Foundation Fellowship in 2006. He is a professor of creative writing at the University of Massachusetts at Amherst, where he also teaches the work of Chilean poet Pablo Neruda.

"No change for the good ever happens without being imagined first."

Who Burns for the Perfection of Paper

Martín Espada

At sixteen, I worked after high school hours
at a printing plant
that manufactured legal pads:
Yellow paper
stacked seven feet high
and leaning
as I slipped cardboard
between the pages,
then brushed red glue
up and down the stack.
No gloves: fingertips required
for the perfection of paper,
smoothing the exact rectangle.
Sluggish by 9 PM, the hands
would slide along suddenly sharp paper,
and gather slits thinner than the **crevices**
of the skin, hidden.
Then the glue would sting,
hands oozing
till both palms burned
at the punchclock.

Ten years later, in law school,
I knew that every legal pad
was glued with the sting of hidden cuts,
that every open lawbook
was a pair of hands
upturned and burning.

Vocabulary
crevices (krev′ is iz) *n.* narrow cracks or splits

Yusef Komunyakaa (b. 1947)

Author of "Camouflaging the Chimera"

Yusef Komunyakaa (yōō′ sef kō mun yä′ kä) was born in Bogalusa, Louisiana. In 1965, he joined the army and was sent to Vietnam. He served there as an "information specialist," reporting from the front lines, and editing a military newspaper called the *Southern Cross.* He also earned a Bronze Star. After the war, Komunyakaa pursued his education, earning a B.A. at the University of Colorado, an M.A. at Colorado State University, and an M.F.A. at the University of California, Irvine. In 1977, he published his first collection of poetry, and he has been publishing his poems ever since.

Poet of the Vietnam War Komunyakaa achieved his true breakthrough moment in literature with the 1988 publication of *Dien Cai Dau (Vietnamese for "this crazy head"),* in which he took on the subject of his experiences in Vietnam. "It took me fourteen years to write poems about Vietnam," said Yusef Komunyakaa in 1994, shortly after winning the Pulitzer Prize for *Neon Vernacular,* another poetry collection. "I had never thought about writing about it, and in a way I had been systematically writing around it."

About Komunyakaa's work, the poet Toi Derricotte has written, "He takes on the most complex moral issues . . . His voice, whether it embodies the specific experiences of a black man, a soldier in Vietnam, or a child in Bogalusa, Louisiana, is universal. It shows us in ever deeper ways what it is to be human."

BACKGROUND: THE VIETNAM WAR American involvement in the Vietnam War lasted from 1961 to 1973. The war presented American military forces with the frustrating and terrifying problem of how to fight in dense jungle against the Viet Cong (or VC), an enemy capable of magically "merging" with the landscape. As "Camouflaging the Chimera" demonstrates, part of the answer to this problem involved sending small groups of American soldiers into the jungle to wait in ambush for the elusive enemy.

"Each poem relates to a place—the internal terrain as well as the external terrain..."

Camouflaging the Chimera[1]

Yusef Komunyakaa

We tied branches to our helmets.
We painted our faces & rifles
with mud from a riverbank,

blades of grass hung from the pockets
of our tiger suits. We wove
ourselves into the terrain,
content to be a hummingbird's target.

We hugged bamboo & leaned
against a breeze off the river,
slow-dragging with ghosts

from Saigon to Bangkok,
with women left in doorways
reaching in from America.
We aimed at dark-hearted songbirds.

Vocabulary

terrain (tə rān′) *n.* an area of ground and its features

1. **Chimera** (kī mir′ ə) from Greek mythology, a firebreathing monster with a lion's head, a goat's body, and a serpent's tail.

In our way station of shadows
rock apes tried to blow our cover,
throwing stones at the sunset. Chameleons

crawled our spines, changing from day
to night: green to gold,
gold to black. But we waited
till the moon touched metal,

till something almost broke
inside us. VC struggled
with the hillside, like black silk

wrestling iron through grass.
We weren't there. The river ran
through our bones. Small animals took refuge
against our bodies; we held our breath,

ready to spring the L-shaped
ambush, as a world revolved
under each man's eyelid.

▲ Critical Viewing
How does this photograph reflect the image of soldiers who "wove ourselves into the terrain"? **CONNECT**

Vocabulary
refuge (ref′ yo͞oj) *n.* shelter or protection from danger

Naomi Shihab Nye (b. 1952)

Author of "Streets"

Arab American poet Naomi Shihab Nye spent her teenage years in Jerusalem, far from the cities of St. Louis, Missouri, and San Antonio, Texas, where she had been a child. Her father had emigrated from Palestine and settled in St. Louis, where he and his wife operated stores specializing in imported goods. When Naomi was fourteen, the family moved back to Jerusalem to be near her father's Arab relatives. Nye says the family's years in Jerusalem enabled her to discover her heritage.

Poetry of the Everyday In addition to publishing award-winning volumes of poetry, Nye has also written picture books for children. This versatile writer, whose work is built on the sturdy foundation of everyday experiences, believes that "the primary source of poetry has always been local life, random characters met on the streets, our own ancestry sifting down to us through small essential daily tasks."

"The primary source of poetry has always been local life."

STREETS

Naomi Shihab Nye

A man leaves the world
and the streets he lived on
grow a little shorter.
One more window dark
in this city, the figs on his branches
will soften for birds.
If we stand quietly enough evenings
there grows a whole company of us
standing quietly together.
Overhead loud grackles are claiming
 their trees
and the sky which sews and sews,
 tirelessly sewing,
drops her purple hem.

Comprehension
According to the speaker, what happens when a man leaves the world?

Social Commentary
Does the speaker belong to the group of "some people," or to the group of "others"?

Each thing in its time, in its place,
it would be nice to think the same about people.
Some people do. They sleep completely,
waking refreshed. Others live in two worlds,
the lost and remembered.
They sleep twice, once for the one who is gone,
once for themselves. They dream thickly,
dream double, they wake from a dream
into another one, they walk the short streets
calling out names, and then they answer.

Critical Reading

Cite textual evidence to support your responses.

1. **Key Ideas and Details** **(a)** In "Who Burns for the Perfection of Paper," what was the speaker's first experience with legal pads? **(b)** What was the speaker's later job with legal pads? **(c) Interpret:** What did the speaker learn from the first job?
2. **Key Ideas and Details** **(a)** What word does the speaker use twice to describe cuts on the hands? **(b) Interpret:** What are two possible meanings of this word?
3. **Key Ideas and Details** **(a)** Where does "Camouflaging the Chimera" take place? **(b) Analyze:** What obstacles and burdens does the speaker face?
4. **Key Ideas and Details** **(a)** What runs through the soldiers' bones? **(b) Support:** What other images suggest that the speaker is merging with his surroundings? **(c) Interpret:** What does the speaker mean by his observation that "We weren't there"?
5. **Key Ideas and Details** **(a)** In "Streets," what happens when a man "leaves the world"? **(b) Interpret:** What might these events symbolize?
6. **Key Ideas and Details** **(a)** What do the people who "sleep completely" believe? **(b) Compare:** What do those who "sleep twice" experience? **(c) Speculate:** Who might "they" refer to in line 22?
7. **Integration of Knowledge and Ideas** What do these poems suggest about the power of poetry to convey experience that is both private and public? Explain. In your response, use at least two of these Essential Question words: *transform, alienation, global, awareness, understanding.* ***[Connecting to the Essential Question: How does literature shape or reflect society?]***

Close Reading Activities

Who Burns for the Perfection of Paper • Camouflaging the Chimera • Streets

Literary Analysis

1. **Craft and Structure (a)** Use a chart like the one shown to select the adjective that best describes each poet's **voice. (b)** Then, choose additional adjectives that accurately characterize each voice. Explain your choices.

Adjectives: haunting, meditative, mournful, yearning, reverent, pained

Poet	Voice	Evidence

Additional Adjectives

2. **Integration of Knowledge and Ideas Draw inferences about the poet's beliefs** as they are expressed in these poems. **(a)** In "Camouflaging . . . ," what do you think the speaker feels about the enemy? Explain. **(b)** Do the images suggest that the speaker is opposed to the war? Explain.
3. **Integration of Knowledge and Ideas (a)** Cite two details in "Who Burns . . ." that show the speaker's diligence. **(b)** Based on these details, what beliefs about consumer society do you think the poet holds?
4. **Comparing Literary Works (a)** What "invisible" members of society are brought into focus in each poem? **(b)** Compare and contrast the **social commentary** each poet makes about that group of people.

Vocabulary Acquisition and Use

Synonyms Use a dictionary or thesaurus to choose a synonym for each word below. Then, explain how the synonym suggests different *connotative meanings*, or associations, from those of the original word.

1. crevices **2.** terrain **3.** refuge

Writing to Sources

Informative Text Each of these poems expresses a belief about an aspect of life as it affects a specific group of people. In an **essay,** analyze the way in which each poem's *theme*, or central meaning, is also a comment on life for all people. In your essay, consider the following questions:

- What insights or experiences are described in each poem?
- How do these experiences relate to all people?
- What wish for humanity does each poem express?

Common Core State Standards

Writing

2. Write informative texts to examine and convey complex ideas, concepts, and information clearly and accurately through the effective selection, organization, and analysis of content.

9.a. Apply grades 11–12 Reading standards to literature. [RL.11-12.2]

Language

5. Demonstrate understanding of word relationships and nuances in word meanings.

5.b. Analyze nuances in the meaning of words with similar denotations.

Connecting to the Essential Question In this poem, the speaker revisits a moment from his childhood. As you read, look for specific places that the speaker visits in memory. Doing so will help you think about the Essential Question: **What is the relationship between literature and place?**

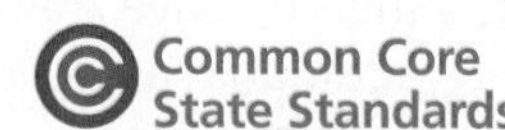

Reading Literature

1. Cite strong and thorough textual evidence to support analysis of what the text says explicitly as well as inferences drawn from the text, including determining where the text leaves matters uncertain.

5. Analyze how an author's choices concerning how to structure specific parts of a text contribute to its overall structure and meaning as well as its aesthetic impact.

6. Analyze a case in which grasping a point of view requires distinguishing what is directly stated in a text from what is really meant.

Close Reading Focus

Free Verse

Free verse is poetry without regular meter or rhyme. Nevertheless, free verse does contain many formal elements. In this poem, the poet uses carefully crafted lines to recreate the rhythms of natural speech or to emphasize meaning. The lines are shaped in one of two ways:

- **End-stopped lines** are lines that complete a grammatical unit, often (although not always) with a punctuation mark at the end. Such lines create a storytelling quality:

  "Repent, ye sinners!" he shouted,
  waving his hand-lettered sign.

- **Enjambed** lines are those that do not end with a grammatical break and do not make full sense without the line that follows:

  . . . They never heard me steal
  into the stairwell hall and climb
  the ladder to the fresh night air.

Enjambed lines help the poet emphasize important words and hint at double meanings. As you read, notice how the lines give shape to the poem and help convey nuances in the poet's meaning.

Preparing to Read Complex Texts Poets writing in free verse often use subtle techniques to emphasize important details. As you read "Halley's Comet," **identify key details,** especially changes in verb tenses and *tone*, or emotional attitude. Consider whether these changes signal a shift in meaning, a shift in point of view, or both. Use a chart like the one shown to record your observations.

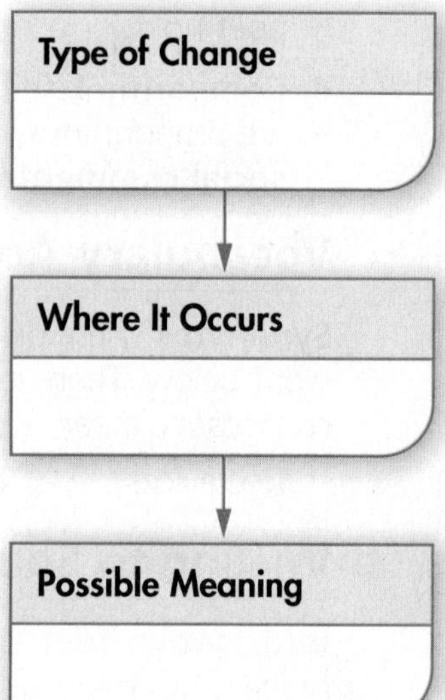

Vocabulary

You will encounter the words listed here in the text that follows. Copy the words into your notebook. What other forms of the vocabulary words do you know?

proclaiming **steal**
repent

Stanley Kunitz (1905–2006)

Author of "Halley's Comet"

Lonely Youth "The deepest thing I know is that I am living and dying at once," Stanley Kunitz once wrote. Indeed, the poet's life was shadowed by death from the beginning as his father died shortly before Kunitz was born. This loss would haunt the poet for nearly a century.

Kunitz was born in Worcester, Massachusetts, where he spent a lonely childhood in a household where birthdays were not celebrated and talk of his father's death not allowed. Kunitz excelled at school, however, and became valedictorian of his class. He attended Harvard University, graduating with highest honors in English.

Poetic Evolution After completing his master's degree at Harvard, Kunitz worked as a newspaper journalist and later moved to a farmhouse in Connecticut. There, he wrote poems and edited reference books. At the age of twenty-five, he published *Intellectual Things,* a volume of poems abstract in theme and formal in style. His next collection, *Passport to the War,* represented his attempt to work out, in verse, the trauma of his childhood. The collection earned high critical praise and paved the way for his third book, *Selected Poems,* which would earn the Pulitzer Prize in 1959.

During his career as a poet, Kunitz taught at a series of prestigious schools, including Yale, Columbia, and Princeton. He was also an avid gardener—"I am never closer to the miraculous as when I am grubbing in the soil," he observed—and a lifelong patron of the visual arts.

As the poet aged, his poetry changed. Kunitz abandoned the distant tone of his early work and adopted a clear, spare style—"almost nonpoetic on the surface," he once described it, but with "reverberations within that keep it intense and alive." His form became freer and looser, his lines shorter, and his subjects more human.

Gifts of Conscience A conscientious objector to World War II, Kunitz was nevertheless drafted and served in the army for several years. Later, during the Vietnam War, Kunitz would become loudly critical of the U. S. government. His commitment to high moral standards and to his own inner truth, however, would lead this same government to name him Consultant in Poetry to the Library of Congress in 1974, and, at the age of ninety-five, the tenth Poet Laureate of the United States.

"The poetry
I admire most is
innocent, luminous,
and true."

Halley's Comet

Stanley Kunitz

BACKGROUND Halley's Comet is the most famous of the periodic comets, appearing in Earth's skies every 75-76 years. This poem centers on its arrival in 1910, when the poet was five years old. The poem also reflects the poet's loss of his father, who died shortly before Kunitz was born. Like much of Kunitz's work, the mood is simultaneously one of darkest doom and brightest hope.

Miss Murphy in first grade
wrote its name in chalk
across the board and told us
it was roaring down the stormtracks
of the Milky Way at frightful speed
and if it wandered off its course
and smashed into the earth
there'd be no school tomorrow.
A red-bearded preacher from the hills
with a wild look in his eyes
stood in the public square
at the playground's edge
proclaiming he was sent by God
to save everyone of us,
even the little children.
"Repent, ye sinners!" he shouted,
waving his hand-lettered sign.
At supper I felt sad to think

Vocabulary
proclaiming (prō klām′ iŋ) *v.* announcing
repent (ri pent′) *v.* feel sorry for what one has done and vow to change one's behavior

that it was probably
the last meal I'd share
with my mother and sisters;
but I felt excited too
and scarcely touched my plate.
So mother scolded me
and sent me early to my room.
The whole family's asleep
except for me. They never heard me steal
into the stairwell hall and climb
the ladder to the fresh night air.

Look for me, Father, on the roof
of the red brick building
at the foot of Green Street—
that's where we live, you know, on the top floor.
I'm the boy in the white flannel gown
sprawled on this coarse gravel bed
searching the starry sky,
waiting for the world to end.

Vocabulary
steal (stēl) *v.* creep

Critical Reading

Cite textual evidence to support your responses.

1. **Key Ideas and Details** **(a)** What is the "wild-eyed" preacher doing in the public square? **(b) Infer:** Why might he be doing this? **(c) Assess:** What effect does the preacher have on the mood of the poem?
2. **Craft and Structure** **(a) Distinguish:** What makes line 27 different from every other line in the poem? **(b) Interpret:** What break or shift in the action of the poem does this mirror?
3. **Key Ideas and Details** **(a) Draw Conclusions:** At the end of the poem, what is the speaker waiting for? Name two possibilities. **(b) Speculate:** Do you think either desire will be fulfilled? Explain.
4. **Integration of Knowledge and Ideas** How does the "place" described in the last seven lines differ from the places mentioned in lines 1–29? Why might the poet have wanted to revisit this particular spot in the landscape of his memories? In your response, use at least two of these Essential Question words: *transformation, awe, lament, personal, fantastic.* ***[Connecting to the Essential Question: What is the relationship between literature and place?]***

Halley's Comet

Literary Analysis

Common Core State Standards

Writing

3. Write narratives to develop real or imagined experiences or events using effective technique, well-chosen details, and well-structured event sequences. *(p. 1361)*

3.e. Provide a conclusion that follows from and reflects on what is experienced, observed, or resolved over the course of the narrative. *(p. 1361)*

Language

4.b. Identify and correctly use patterns of word changes that indicate different meanings or parts of speech. *(p. 1361)*

5. Demonstrate understanding of word relationships. *(p. 1361)*

1. **Key Ideas and Details (a) Identify a key detail**—a change in verb tense—that occurs in line 26. **(b)** How does this change affect your sense of the poem's action?
2. **Craft and Structure** In what ways does the poet's use of **enjambment** in line 4 after the word *stormtracks* add to the meaning of the sentence?
3. **Craft and Structure (a)** What does the teacher tell the class in lines 6–8? **(b)** How is the poet's use of **end-stopped lines** at that point appropriate for the moment being described? **(c)** Explain how those lines are both reassuring and alarming at the same time.
4. **Craft and Structure (a)** What is happening in lines 34–37? **(b)** Why do you think the poet uses end-stopped lines here?
5. **Craft and Structure** Using a chart like the one shown, write three lines from the poem that seem to break in an unusual place. Then, explain how each line break affects the poem's mood or extends its meaning.

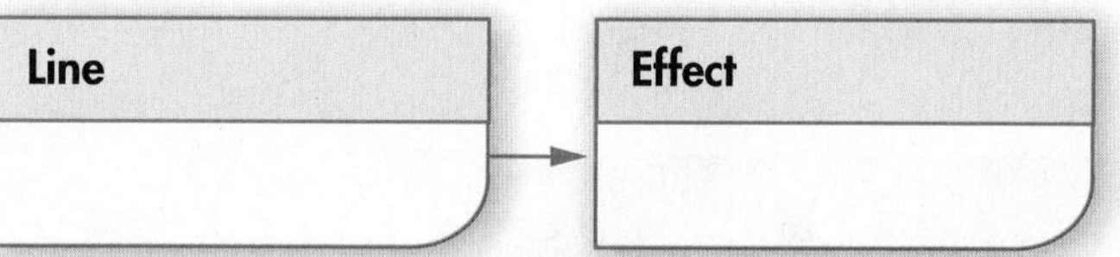

6. **Craft and Structure (a)** Whom does the speaker seem to address in lines 1–29? **(b)** Whom does he address in lines 30–37? **(c)** How does this change affect the *tone* of the poem? **(d)** How does this change affect its meaning?
7. **Craft and Structure (a)** What are the speaker's two primary emotions in the poem? **(b)** How does **free verse** help the poet convey these emotions?
8. **Craft and Structure** Because free-verse poetry does not have a set meter or rhyme, its patterns are sometimes unpredictable. How is the form of "Halley's Comet" related to its content?
9. **Integration of Knowledge and Ideas** This poem moves from a public situation—a classroom—to a private, solitary one. **(a)** Identify a line or a phrase that reflects each situation. **(b)** Identify at least one key detail in each line that clearly expresses the difference in both subject matter and mood.
10. **Analyze Visual Information** Explain the humor in this cartoon.

(left) "Great poem . . . if you're in a coma."

(middle) "You call that a metaphor?!?"

(right) "One word for you, pal: metre!"

Vocabulary Acquisition and Use

Word Analysis: Latin Prefix *pro-*

The Latin prefix *pro-* means "before" or "forward." It can refer to either place or time. The word *proclaim* literally means "to claim or announce before a group"; the word *protract* means "to draw forward in time." For each of the words below, write a definition that includes either the word *before* or *forward*. Then, explain whether the word relates to space, time, or both.

1. protrude
2. provide
3. prospect
4. propose
5. propel
6. prologue
7. promenade
8. prolong

Vocabulary: Word Mapping

Study the word map for the vocabulary word *proclaiming* below. Then, create similar word maps for the words *repent* and *steal*.

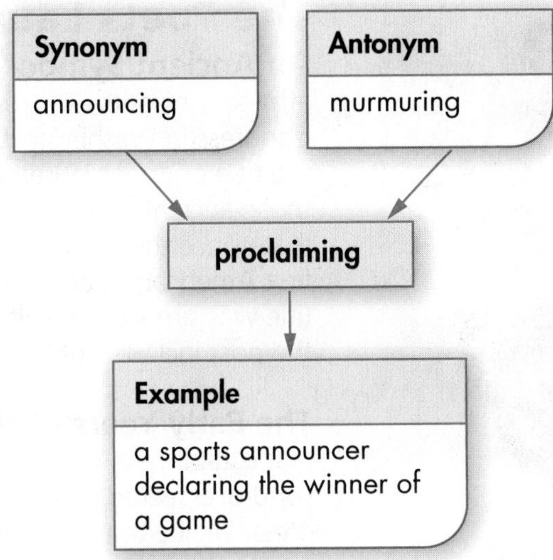

Writing

Narrative Text Children often have their own unique—and inaccurate—interpretations of things. Write an **autobiographical essay** about something you misunderstood or misinterpreted when you were a kid. Try to capture the mix of feelings the misunderstanding evoked or represented at the time, as well as how you feel about it today.

Prewriting For several minutes, write quickly and freely about innocent misunderstandings you held as a child and the incidents that happened to teach you they were incorrect. Choose one to focus on in your essay.

Drafting Organize your essay in chronological order, using a consistent verb tense. After describing your misunderstanding and the related incident, consider how the experience contributed to who you are today.

Model: Using Details to Create a Vivid Portrayal

I was five years old when my father took me to the planetarium. Terror struck me as we entered the enormous domed structure. I looked around, wondering where the spaceship was going to launch and when I would get my helmet. There were hundreds of people sitting in the dim light. Were all these people going to the moon, too?

Adjectives like *enormous* and *dim* portray the speaker's feeling of foreboding.

Revising Share your essay with a classmate to see if he or she can identify with your experience. Elaborate or eliminate details in response to his or her comments.

Brooks

Kunitz

Collins

Glück

Warren

Dove

Being poet laureate made me realize I was capable of a larger voice. There is a more public utterance I can make *as a poet.*

–Rita Dove

The Poets Laureate

An Ancient Symbol The ancient Greeks adorned their heroes—whether athletes or poets—with wreaths made of laurel leaves. Today, the Library of Congress in Washington, D.C., honors one American poet each year with the title of "poet laureate consultant in poetry." The word "laureate" invokes those ancient wreaths of laurels. Although Britain has been naming poets laureate since the year 1630, the United States did not name one until 1937. The first American poet laureate was Joseph Auslander—though at first the official title was simply "consultant in poetry." Famous American poets who have held the post include Robert Frost, Gwendolyn Brooks, and Stanley Kunitz.

The Early Years of the Poetry Consultancy When the position was first established, the consultant was not expected to perform many duties beyond overseeing, in a general way, the poetry collection at the Library of Congress. Unlike the British poet laureate, who is required to write poems for state occasions such as the Queen's birthday, the American laureate has never been asked to write official poetry or preside over events of state. In the beginning, the position was largely honorary.

Over time, some of the appointed poets began to make a larger role for themselves. In 1945, **Louise Bogan,** the first woman named to the post, made audio recordings of poets reading from their work for the Library's poetry archives. She convinced W. H. Auden and T. S. Eliot to record some of their poems and she also recorded her own. **Léonie Adams,** in 1948, was the first to establish the tradition of having a public poetry reading early in the year. When **Robert Frost** was appointed in 1958, he took a more public stance, calling press conferences and speaking with the attorney general on behalf of poet Ezra Pound, who was incarcerated at the time. Shortly after his term expired, Frost read a poem at the inauguration of President John F. Kennedy (see p. 884), thereby bringing poetry into the homes of television viewers across the nation. **Maxine Kumin,** who served in 1981, started a series of women's poetry workshops at the Poetry and Literature Center. **Gwendolyn Brooks,** who, in 1985, became the first black woman to serve in the post, arranged for poetry-reading luncheons and brought poems into elementary schools.

◀ A sampling of poets who have held the post of poet laureate, from top, Gwendolyn Brooks, Stanley Kunitz, Billy Collins, Louise Glück, Robert Penn Warren, and Rita Dove.

The Laureate's Changing Role The poet laureate's job is to promote the enjoyment of poetry throughout America by encouraging people to read and write poetry. Each laureate has interpreted the job in a different way. In 1991, concerned that only a small number of Americans were reading poetry, laureate **Joseph Brodsky** started a program to distribute free poetry books to motels and schools. **Robert Hass** was dubbed the first "activist" laureate in 1995 when he traveled across the country, speaking to civic groups and visiting businesses to raise money for literacy programs.

Two years later, laureate **Robert Pinsky** invited Americans to share their favorite poems by recording them on tape and video. He published them in *An Invitation to Poetry*, a book packaged with a DVD. **Rita Dove,** in 1999, brought children to the Library of Congress to read and record their poems for the archives.

Ted Kooser launched the American Life in Poetry project, which made a poem available every week for newspapers to print, while **Billy Collins** created a Web site where high school students could find a new poem every day of the school year.

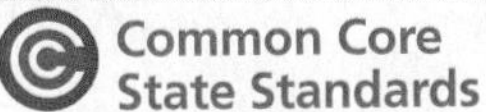

W.11-12.1; SL.11-12.5
[For the full wording of the standards, see the standards chart in the front of your textbook.]

Speaking and Listening: Advertising Campaign

Comprehension and Collaboration Imagine that the office of the poet laureate—the client—has asked your advertising agency to write and design an ad campaign. The goal is to show that poetry is relevant to people's daily lives. With a small group, develop a strategy and materials for an **ad campaign.**

- Advertising is a form of persuasion. Decide how you will use *appeals to logic, emotion, and authority* to develop your content.
- Choose the media you will use: print, radio, television, the Internet, or some combination.
- Consider the populations, or demographics, you will target: students, adults, children, or older people.
- Think about the situations in which people will experience the ads. For example, will they encounter ads on their way to school or work, as they make dinner, or during entertainment or sporting events?
- Design the message and write a slogan to use in a variety of media.

Create preliminary designs for print advertisements and scripts for radio commercials. For television or Web-based videos, make storyboards, or scene-by-scene sketches. Organize your materials and deliver a presentation that will convince the client to hire your agency.

Building Knowledge and Insight

The Latin Deli: An Ars Poetica

Connecting to the Essential Question This poem is a reflection on homesickness, not simply for a prized neighborhood or a person, but for a culture. As you read, note details that reflect different cultures. Doing so will help as you consider the Essential Question: **What is the relationship between literature and place?**

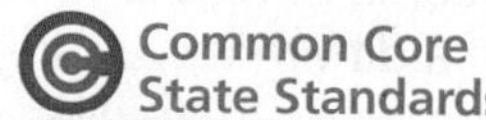

Reading Literature

4. Determine the meaning of words and phrases as they are used in the text, including figurative and connotative meanings; analyze the impact of specific word choices on meaning and tone, including words with multiple meanings or language that is particularly fresh, engaging, or beautiful.

Close Reading Focus

Imagery

Imagery is descriptive language that uses *images*—combinations of words that appeal to the senses and create pictures in the reader's mind. Images draw readers into a literary work by recreating the sensations of actual experience:

> **. . . they walk down the narrow aisles of her store**
> **reading the labels of packages aloud, as if**
> **they were the names of lost lovers: *Suspiros,***
> ***Merengues,* the stale candy of everyone's childhood.**

Images invite the reader into the world of the poem: to walk down the narrow aisle, to scan the shelves of packages, and to murmur the names on the labels. They are the tools by which the poet builds meaning and emotion. As you read, notice how the images accumulate to paint a portrait of a place and a group of people and to, ultimately, convey the poem's essential message.

Preparing to Read Complex Texts Sensory details are words or phrases that appeal to the senses and are the building blocks of images. You will add to your appreciation of poetry if you pay attention to the specific words a poet uses to spark readers' associations of sight, touch, taste, smell, and sound. **Analyze sensory details** by following these steps:

- First, picture in your mind each separate detail.
- Second, consider the details as a group, asking yourself what they have in common and what overall feeling or idea they express.

As you read, use a chart like the one shown to analyze sensory details.

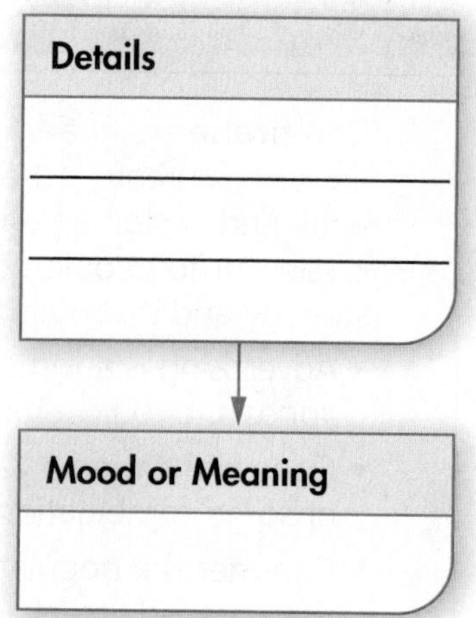

Vocabulary

The words below are important to understanding the text that follows. Copy the words into your notebook. Decide whether all three words have a positive or a negative connotation.

heady **divine**

ample

Judith Ortiz Cofer *(b. 1952)*

Author of "The Latin Deli: An Ars Poetica"

Nomadic Youth Judith Ortiz Cofer was born in Puerto Rico to young parents. To provide for his family, her father gave up his dream of a college education and joined first the United States Army and then the Navy. When he was assigned to the Brooklyn Navy Yard in 1955, the Ortiz family moved to Paterson, New Jersey.

Ortiz Cofer's father spent long stretches of time in Europe. During his absences, her mother would pack up the family and return to Puerto Rico. The constant shuffling made Ortiz Cofer feel like a permanent "new girl." When in the United States, she attended public school, spoke English, and behaved according to the strict social customs of the American Northeast. When in Puerto Rico, she attended a Catholic school and was immersed in a relaxed and colorful Latino culture. This geographically divided life left Ortiz Cofer with a sense of homelessness that would eventually fuel her creativity as a writer.

Putting Down Roots After graduating from Augusta College in 1974, Ortiz Cofer moved to Florida with her husband, Charles Cofer, whom she had married in 1971. She spent the next ten years teaching, earning a master's degree, and discovering poetry. Within several years, she had published three small books of poetry.

In 1984, Ortiz Cofer and her family moved to Georgia, where she continues to live, teach, and write. She is the author of several volumes of poetry, a memoir, a short-story collection, and a collection of essays. She has also published two novels. The second of these, *The Line of the Sun,* was nominated for a Pulitzer Prize in 1989.

Though she writes in all genres, Ortiz Cofer holds poetry especially dear. "It taught me how to write," she says. "Poetry contains the essence of language. Every word weighs a ton."

"I speak English with a Spanish accent and Spanish with an American accent . . . I am a composite of two worlds."

EXEMPLAR TEXT ©

THE LATIN DELI: An Ars Poetica

Judith Ortiz Cofer

BACKGROUND Beginning in the mid-1900s, a stream of immigrants from the Spanish-speaking countries of Latin America and the Caribbean have sought sanctuary of various kinds in the United States. Some flee economic hardship or deprivation; others, political oppression. Still others seek a better education or job training. This *ars poetica,* or poem about the "art of poetry," combines the circumstances of these immigrants with the idea of poetry itself serving as a kind of home. (For more about the literary tradition of the *ars poetica,* see page 1368.)

Vocabulary
heady (hed′ ē) *adj.* strongly affecting the senses; intense

Presiding over a formica counter,
plastic Mother and Child magnetized
to the top of an ancient register,
the **heady** mix of smells from the open bins
of dried codfish, the green plantains[1]
hanging in stalks like votive offerings,
she is the Patroness of Exiles,

1. **plantains** (plan′ tinz) a banana-like fruit used as a cooking staple in tropical regions.

a woman of no-age who was never pretty,
who spends her days selling canned memories
while listening to the Puerto Ricans complain
that it would be cheaper to fly to San Juan[2]
than to buy a pound of Bustelo coffee[3] here,
and to Cubans perfecting their speech
of a "glorious return" to Havana[4]—where no one
has been allowed to die and nothing to change until then;
to Mexicans who pass through, talking lyrically
of *dólares* to be made in El Norte[5]—
all wanting the comfort
of spoken Spanish, to gaze upon the family portrait
of her plain wide face, her **ample** bosom
resting on her plump arms, her look of maternal interest
as they speak to her and each other
of their dreams and their disillusions—
how she smiles understanding,
when they walk down the narrow aisles of her store
reading the labels of packages aloud, as if
they were the names of lost lovers: *Suspiros,*[6]
Merengues,[7] the stale candy of everyone's childhood.
She spends her days
slicing *jamón y queso*[8] and wrapping it in wax paper
tied with string: plain ham and cheese
that would cost less at the A&P, but it would not satisfy
the hunger of the fragile old man lost in the folds
of his winter coat, who brings her lists of items
that he reads to her like poetry, or the others,
whose needs she must **divine**, conjuring up products
from places that now exist only in their hearts—
closed ports she must trade with.

Vocabulary
ample (am′ pəl) *adj.* large

Imagery
To what senses do the images in lines 25–29 appeal?

Vocabulary
divine (də vīn′) *v.* make a guess based on intuition

---

2. **San Juan** capital of Puerto Rico.
3. **Bustelo coffee** (bo͞o stē′ lo) a brand of strong, inexpensive Cuban coffee.
4. **Cubans . . . Havana** Cuba is the westernmost island in the Caribbean Sea; Havana is its capital. When Fidel Castro overthrew the government in 1959, the island's close ties to the United States were severed, and Cuba became a communist state with strong links to the Soviet Union. Since the revolution, thousands of Cubans have emigrated from the country to escape Castro's harsh regime.
5. **El Norte** (el nôr′ tā) "the north" (Spanish); commonly used in Mexico to refer to the United States and Canada.
6. **Suspiros** (so͞o spē′ rōs) "sighs" (Spanish); also, a light, sugary cookie.
7. **Merengues** (me reŋ′ ges) "meringues" (Spanish); sweets made of egg whites and sugar.
8. **jamón y queso** (häm ōn′ ē kā′ sō) "ham and cheese" (Spanish).

WORLD LITERATURE CONNECTION

Ars Poetica

The term *ars poetica* comes from Latin and means "the art of poetry." Today, the phrase describes a statement about what poetry should be. The earliest and most famous *ars poetica* was "Poetics," written by the Greek philosopher Aristotle in 335 B.C. Aristotle laid out his ideas about what makes good art and especially good literature. Writing a century after Sophocles and Euripides had composed their famous tragedies, Aristotle analyzed their plays to derive the "rules"of great drama. He argued art should be an imitation of reality and he judged the quality of art on the basis of that idea.

Three centuries after Aristotle, the Roman poet Horace wrote his own statement on literature. Written in verse, his "Ars Poetica" stressed the importance of harmony and balance in art. Horace said the job of the writer is to delight and instruct at the same time.

▲ Roman poet Horace (65 B.C.– 8 B.C.)

Connect to the Literature

Why does Ortiz Cofer call this poem an *ars poetica*? In what ways does it define poetry?

Critical Reading

Cite textual evidence to support your responses.

1. **Key Ideas and Details** **(a)** What objects are arranged on and around the deli's counter? **(b)** What title is given to the woman who "presides" over the counter? **(c) Interpret:** What do the objects, the title, and the verb "presides" tell you about the woman?
2. **Key Ideas and Details** **(a)** What does the old man read to the woman "like poetry"? **(b) Compare:** How is this object like the poem itself?
3. **Key Ideas and Details** Is this *ars poetica* solely about the art of poetry? Explain.
4. **Integration of Knowledge and Ideas** What geographical, cultural, and emotional boundaries does the poet explore or even merge in this poem? In your response, use at least two of these Essential Question words: *diversity, innovation, transform, global, landscape.* ***[Connecting to the Essential Question: What is the relationship between literature and place?]***

Close Reading Activities

The Latin Deli: An Ars Poetica

Literary Analysis

1. **Key Ideas and Details** **(a)** Identify two words or phrases in the poem that relate to each of the five senses—sight, smell, touch, sound, and taste. **(b)** To which sense would you say most of the **sensory details** in the poem appeal? Explain.
2. **Key Ideas and Details** Choose one word to describe the deli in this poem. Explain your choice.
3. **Craft and Structure** **(a)** Use a chart like the one shown to note five examples of **imagery** in the poem. **(b)** Use the details you have noted to explain the word picture each image creates in your mind.

Image that appeals to . . .				
Sight	**Smell**	**Touch**	**Sound**	**Taste**

4. **Integration of Knowledge and Ideas** **(a)** Identify three images in the poem that have religious overtones. **(b)** How do these images suggest a similarity between the store owner and a religious figure? **(c)** Why is the use of imagery more effective than an outright explanation of such content?

Common Core State Standards

Writing

2. Write informative texts to examine and convey complex ideas, concepts, and information clearly and accurately through the effective selection, organization, and analysis of content.

9.a. Apply grades 11–12 Reading standards to literature. [RL.11-12.4]

Language

4. Determine or clarify the meaning of unknown and multiple-meaning words and phrases based on *grades 11–12 reading and content,* choosing flexibly from a range of strategies.

Vocabulary Acquisition and Use

Sentence Completions Use a word from the vocabulary list on page 1364 to complete each item below. Use each word only once. Explain your choices.

1. The _______ amount of food Betsy prepared would satisfy everyone.
2. The _______ aroma of cooking from the kitchen was wonderful.
3. Based on the smells alone, Maya tried to _______ the ingredients.

Writing to Sources

Informative Text A person who is in exile has been forced by circumstances to leave his or her home. The *connotative meanings* of exile suggest sadness and a longing for the land of origin. Write an **essay** in which you explore the ideas of exile and home in this poem. In your essay, answer the following questions:

- Who is exiled in this poem? From where? Why?
- Which does the deli represent—exile, home, or both?
- What does the poem suggest about language as a kind of home?

CONTEMPORARY CONNECTION

POETRY AND NUMBERS: THE FIBONACCI SEQUENCE

Late in the 12th century, an Italian mathematician named Leonardo of Pisa, also known as Fibonacci (**fib ə nä′chē**), journeyed throughout the Mediterranean to study with the leading mathematicians of the day, especially the Persians al-Karaji and al-Khwarizmi. Fibonacci became convinced that the numeral system the Arab mathematicians were using was far better than the Roman numerals then popular in Europe. Upon his return to Italy, Fibonacci wrote *Liber Abaci*, or *Book of Calculation*, in which he explained the Hindu-Arabic numeral system he had learned from his Persian mentors. The book also included a number sequence that would come to bear Fibonacci's name.

In *Liber Abaci*, Fibonacci proposed a method of calculating the number of rabbits that might result from one set of parents and each subsequent generation in a single year. Although he did not discover this solution, it became known as the Fibonacci sequence. In this sequence, each number after the starting values of 0 and 1 is the sum of the previous two numbers:

0, 1, 1, 2, 3, 5, 8, 13, 21, 34, 55, 89, 144, 233, 377…

The Fibonacci sequence is evident in such marvels of nature as the spiral patterns of nautilus shells, pinecones, and flower petals. It also provides the basis for some traditional poetry, particularly some Sanskrit forms. In recent years, new interest in poetry based on Fibonacci numbers has arisen. In 2006, Gregory Pincus, a writer and librarian from Los Angeles, published a six-line, 20-syllable poem on his blog. He coined his work the "fib."

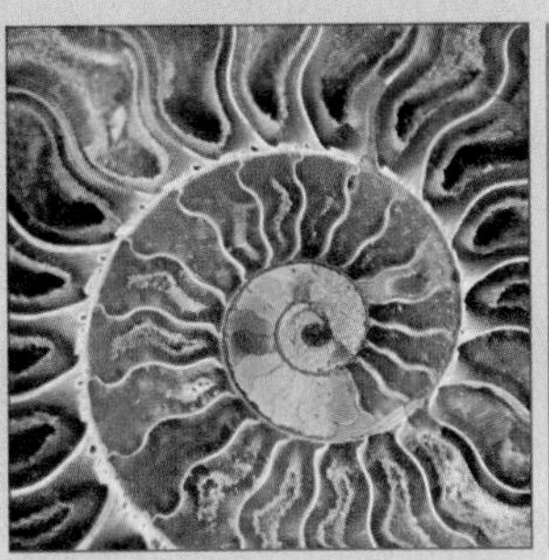

THE FIB

One
Small,
Precise,
Poetic,
Spiraling mixture:
Math plus poetry yields the Fib.

—*Gregory Pincus*

In Pincus's fib, the number of syllables in each line equals the sum of syllables in the preceding two lines. On his blog, Pincus invited others to write and share their fibs and soon these precise little poems were popping up all over the Internet. Several examples of Fibonacci poems appear on the next page.

◀ The Fibonacci Sequence is visible in the spirals of the nautilus shell.

While the numbers of lines and stanzas may vary from fib to fib, all are based on Fibonacci's sequence.

(Ø)
Rain
So
Thick this
Summer day
I can barely see
Ginkgo offer small umbrellas.

—Patricia Lee Lewis

Dig
deep
enough
and you'll find
proof of something said
that must have meant more than it seems,
must have meant something like 'Love' or 'Come back' or 'Yes, now.'

—Athena Kildegaard

Book
Waits
Unread
Paper sits
No words to be found
You left me alone with no Muse

—Patricia Vogel

Critical Reading

1. **Take a Position:** Some readers see similarities between fibs and haiku. Do you agree with this comparison? Explain.

Use these questions to focus a group discussion:

2. Could these writers have expressed the same ideas through another type of writing, or is the form essential to their meaning? Explain.
3. Why do you think a poet, or any artist, might choose to impose constraints, such as a mathematical sequence, on his or her work?
4. In what ways do these poems affect your view of math, poetry, or both? Explain.

TEXT SET

Contemporary Nonfiction

Part 3

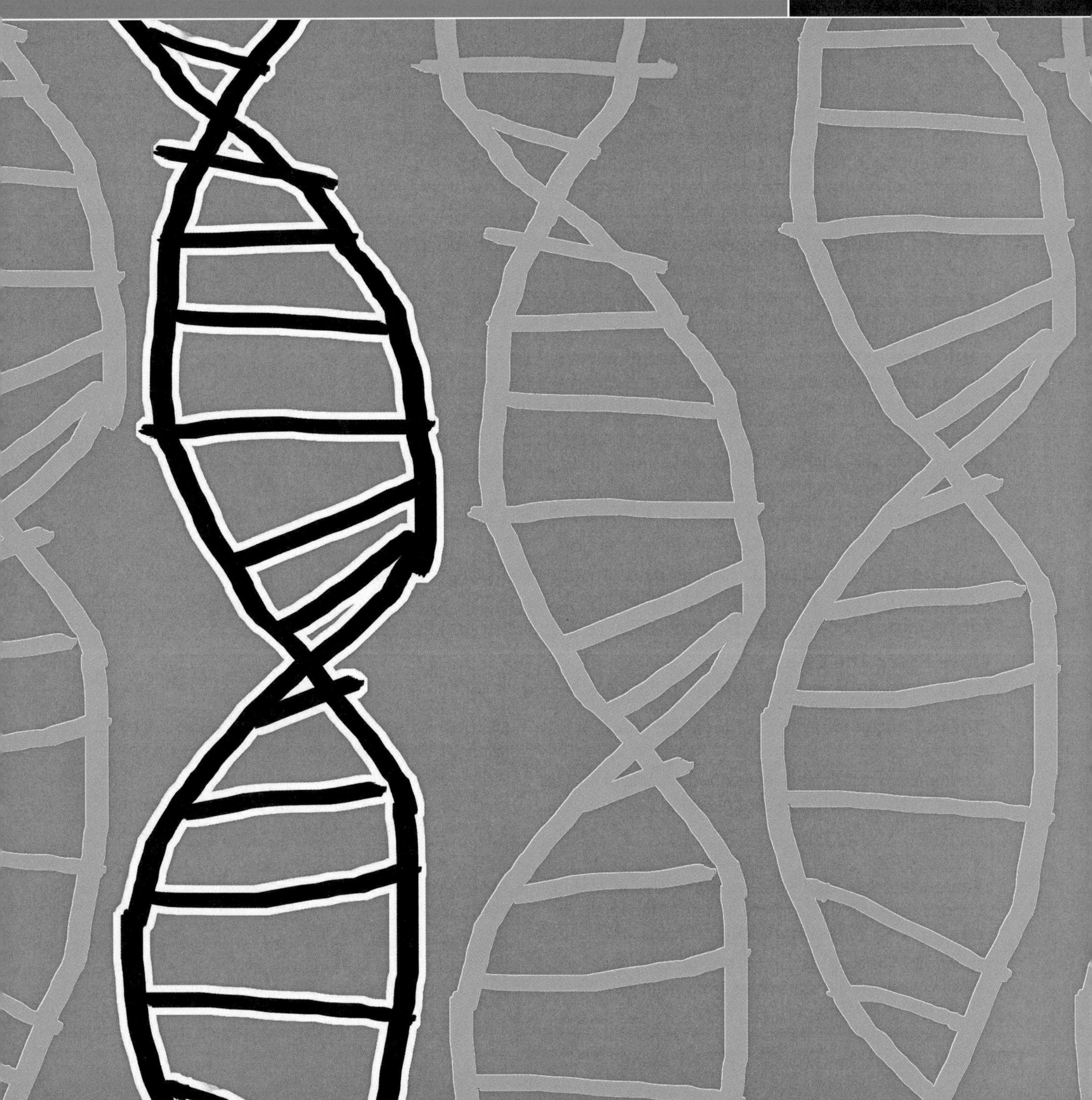

The essay

is a literary device for almost everything about almost anything.

— ALDOUS HUXLEY

In This Section

For more practice analyzing essays, see pages 117, 369, 388, 860, 1410, and 1418.

Defining Essays

An **essay** is a brief nonfiction work about a specific subject. The term was first used in 1580 by the French philosopher Michel de Montaigne, who published a collection of short prose pieces entitled *Essais*. The French word means "attempts" or "tries," and Montaigne used the title to suggest that his discussions were casual explorations of a subject, rather than thorough interpretations. That quality of inquisitive exploration remains a defining feature of the essay form.

Types of Essays Essays are often divided into two main categories, according to the writer's overall approach.

- **Formal essays** are serious explorations of important public topics, such as political, social, or cultural issues.
- **Informal essays,** also called **personal essays,** explore everyday topics in a conversational style. They may also employ a loose structure, circling around a topic and developing ideas in an indirect way.

Within these two broad categories, essays can be further classified according to the **author's purpose:** to inform, to persuade, to tell a story, to convey a sense of place, or to analyze an idea.

- In a **persuasive essay,** the writer tries to convince readers to accept his or her opinion or to take a course of action.
- In a **descriptive essay,** the writer uses sensory details to present a portrait of a person, a place, or an object.
- In an **expository essay,** the writer explains an issue or process.

Close Read: The Essay

These elements of essays appear in the Model Text at right.

Thesis/Central Idea: the author's main idea or essential point *Example: "Trust thyself: every heart vibrates to that iron string." (Ralph Waldo Emerson)*	**Diction and Syntax:** the types of words (diction) and sentence structures (syntax) an author favors *Example: "Reaching for an alliterative onomatope, the poet Milton chose 'melodious murmurs'..." (William Safire)*
Evidence: facts, quotations, data, personal observations, anecdotes, and other details that help to develop and support the author's thesis *Example: "She reads the* Forbes *report, listens to* Wall Street Week, *converses daily with her stockbroker..." (Amy Tan)*	**Tone:** the writer's attitude toward the topic or audience *Example: "...before closing I am impelled to mention one other point in your statement that troubled me profoundly." (Dr. Martin Luther King, Jr.)*

Model

About the Text H. L. Mencken (1880–1956) began his career with a Baltimore newspaper at the age of eighteen and went on to become one of America's legendary journalists. He was especially celebrated for his acute ear for language and his satirical—often biting—commentaries on American cultural life. Mencken's book *The American Language* is now regarded as a classic.

"American Slang," from *The American Language* by H. L. Mencken

What chiefly lies behind [slang] is simply a kind of linguistic exuberance, an excess of word-making energy. It relates itself to the standard language a great deal as dancing relates itself to music. But there is also something else. The best slang is not only ingenious and amusing; it also embodies a kind of social criticism. It not only provides new names for a series of everyday concepts, some new and some old; it also says something about them. "Words which produce the slang effect," observes Frank K. Sechrist, "arouse associations which are incongruous or incompatible with those of customary thinking."

Everyone, including even the metaphysician in his study and the eremite[1] in his cell, has a large vocabulary of slang, but the vocabulary of the vulgar is likely to be larger than that of the cultured, and it is harder worked. Its content may be divided into two categories: (a) old words, whether used singly or in combination, that have been put to new uses, usually metaphorical, and (b) new words that have not yet been admitted to the standard vocabulary. Examples of the first type are *rubberneck,* for a gaping and prying person, and *iceberg,* for a cold woman; examples of the second are *hoosegow, flim-flam, blurb, bazoo* and *blah.* There is a constant movement of slang terms into accepted usage. *Nice,* as an adjective of all work, signifying anything satisfactory, was once in slang use only, and the purists denounced it, but today no one would question "a *nice* day," "a *nice* time," or "a *nice* hotel."...The verb-phrase *to hold up* is now perfectly good American, but so recently as 1901 the late Brander Matthews was sneering at it as slang. In the same way many other verb-phrases, e.g., *to cave in, to fill the bill* and *to fly off the handle,* once viewed askance, have gradually worked their way to a relatively high level of the standard speech. On some indeterminate tomorrow *to stick up* and *to take for a ride* may follow them.

Thesis The author presents a two-part thesis: (a) that slang is a type of linguistic play, and (b) that the best slang carries a distinct note of social criticism.

Evidence Although Mencken is himself an expert on his topic, he uses a quotation from another expert to support his point.

Diction and Syntax Mencken chooses sophisticated words and writes elegant, long sentences. However, he will modify both diction and syntax for effect. (See the short sentence in the first paragraph: "But there is also something else.")

Tone Mencken was famous for his tone, which often combines sharp humor and a sense of intellectual command and boldness.

1. **metaphysician ... eremite** A metaphysician is a type of philosopher; an eremite is a hermit or recluse.

Building Knowledge and Insight *Onomatopoeia*

Connecting to the Essential Question: In this essay, the author explores the connections between the sounds of certain words and their meanings. As you read, notice details that show the author's fascination with words of all kinds. Doing so will help you think about the Essential Question: **What makes American literature American?**

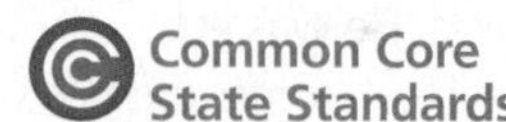

Reading Informational Text

3. Analyze a complex set of ideas or sequence of events and explain how specific ideas, individuals, or events interact and develop over the course of the text.

4. Determine the meaning of words and phrases as they are used in a text, including figurative, connotative, and technical meanings; analyze how an author uses and refines the meaning of a key term or terms over the course of a text.

Close Reading Focus

Expository Essay; Diction

In an **expository essay,** a writer explains a topic or process, or discusses ideas. In this expository essay, William Safire explains the origin, meaning, and uses of *onomatopoeia*—words like *hiss* or *buzz* that sound like what they mean. Expository essays may use other modes, such as persuasion, description, or narration. However, the main emphasis is on explanation. Therefore, when reading expository works, you will find more facts than opinions, as well as definitions, data, and other informative content.

Safire takes a lighthearted approach to his topic. His **diction,** or word choice, combines scholarly and folksy elements, including idioms. **Idioms** are common expressions that have acquired figurative and connotative meanings that differ from their literal meanings:

- **Scholarly, or technical, diction:** "rhetorical bestiary"
- **Folksy, or familiar, diction:** "it had better be spelled right"
- **Idiom:** "slammed the vocabulary <u>right in the kisser</u>"

As you read, notice how Safire's mix of diction allows him to treat his subject with authority, while simultaneously amusing and surprising the reader. Consider how his uses of diction both clarify and serve as examples for the ideas he presents throughout the essay.

Preparing to Read Complex Texts To clarify the main ideas in an expository essay, take time to **paraphrase** any passages that challenge your understanding. When you paraphrase, you restate the author's ideas in your own words. As you read this essay, use a chart like the one shown to paraphrase unfamiliar phrases or whole passages, and track how doing so aids your understanding.

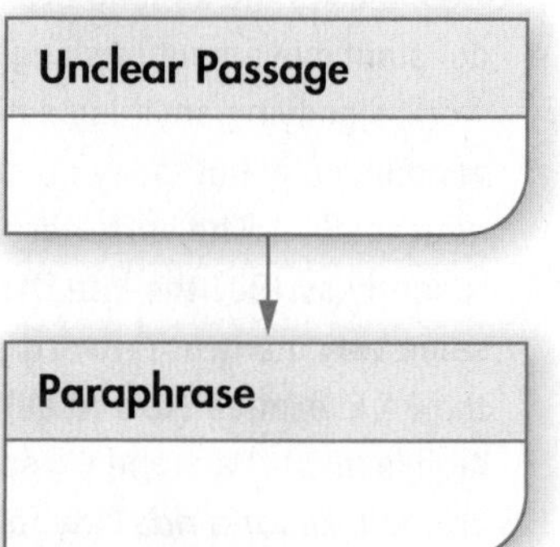

Vocabulary

You will encounter the words listed here in the text that follows. Copy the words into your notebook. Which of the words is a verb? How can you tell?

synonymous **speculation**
derive **coinage**

WILLIAM SAFIRE (1929–2009)

Author of "Onomatopoeia"

When it comes to questions about the use—and misuse—of the English language, few people have more answers or observations than William Safire. A political columnist for the *New York Times* until his retirement in 2005, Safire continues to write the *New York Times Magazine*'s "On Language" column. The column has generated ten books and made Safire the world's most widely read author on the English language.

Safire is a graduate of the Bronx High School of Science, an elite public school in New York City. He attended Syracuse University but dropped out after two years. A generation later, he delivered the commencement address at Syracuse and also became a trustee of the university.

A Career in Writing The 1978 Pulitzer Prize winner for Distinguished Commentary, Safire worked in public relations and television before becoming involved in politics. He worked for Richard Nixon's presidential campaign in 1960 and again in 1968. When Nixon was elected in 1968, Safire became the senior White House speechwriter.

In addition to his writings on language, Safire is the author of three novels, a political dictionary, several anthologies, and other works. In 2006, he was awarded the Presidential Medal of Freedom by George W. Bush.

"Last but not least, avoid CLICHES like the plague."

Blam, 1962, Roy Lichtenstein

▲ **Critical Viewing** What meaning does the onomatopoeia *Blam* convey in this image? **ANALYZE**

ONOMATOPOEIA

William Safire

Background The vocabulary of English is the largest of any language in the world. English readily incorporates new words from a wide variety of sources, including borrowing them from other languages. William Safire, a former presidential speechwriter, describes another way in which English evolves. According to Safire, when we consider onomatopoeia—the figure of speech in which a word sounds like what it means—we discover that new words are not just based on what we experience, but on what we merely imagine.

The word *onomatopoeia* was used above, and it had better be spelled right or one usage dictator and six copy editors will get zapped. That word is based on the Greek for "word making"—the *poe* is the same as in *poetry*, "something made"—and is synonymous with *imitative* and *echoic*, denoting words that are made by people making sounds like the action to be described. (The *poe* in *onomatopoeia* has its own rule for pronunciation. Whenever a vowel follows *poe*, the *oe* combination is pronounced as a long *e: onomato-PEE-ia*. Whenever a consonant follows, as in *poetry* and *onomatopoetic*, pronounce the long *o* of Edgar Allan's name.)

Henry Peacham, in his 1577 book on grammar and rhetoric called *The Garden of Eloquence*, first used *onomatopoeia* and defined it as "when we invent, devise, fayne, and make a name intimating the sound of that it signifieth, as *hurlyburly*, for an uprore and tumultuous stirre." He also gave *flibergib* to "a gossip," from which we derive *flibbertigibbet*, and the long-lost *clapperclaw* and *kickle-kackle*.

Since Willard Espy borrowed the title of Peacham's work for his rhetorical bestiary in 1983, the author went beyond the usual examples of *buzz, hiss, bobwhite* and *babble*. He pointed out that one speculation about the origin of language was the *bow-wow theory*, holding that words originated in imitation of natural sounds of animals and thunder. (Proponents of the *pooh-pooh theory* argued that interjections like *ow!* and *oof!* started us all yakking toward language. Other theories—arrgh!—abound.)

Reaching for an alliterative onomatope, the poet Milton chose "melodious *murmurs*;" Edgar Allan Poe one-upped him with "the *tintinnabulation* of the bells." When carried too far, an obsession with

Vocabulary
synonymous (si nän′ ə məs) *adj.* of the same or almost the same meaning

Vocabulary
derive (di rīv′) *v.* get or receive from a source

speculation (spek′ yə lā′ shən) *n.* a conjecture; a guess

Comprehension
What is the Greek origin of *onomatopoeia?*

words is called *onomatomania;* in the crunch (a word imitating the sound of an icebreaker breaking through ice) Gertrude Stein turned into an *onomatomaniac.*

Vocabulary

coinage (koi′ nij) *n.* a word or expression that has been made up or invented

What makes a word like *zap* of particular interest is that it imitates an imaginary noise—the sound of a paralyzing ray gun. Thus we can see another way that the human mind creates new words: imitating what can be heard only in the mind's ear. The coinage filled a need for an unheard sound and—*pow!*—slammed the vocabulary right in the kisser. Steadily, surely, under the watchful eye of great lexicographers and with the encouragement of columnists and writers who ache for color in verbs, the creation of Buck Rogers's creator has blasted its way into the dictionaries. The verb will live long after superpowers agree to ban ray guns; no sound thunders or crackles like an imaginary sound turned into a new word.

ZAP!

Took me a while to get to the point today, but that is because I did not know what the point was when I started.

"I now zap all the commercials," says the merry Ellen Goodman. "I zap to the memory of white tornadoes past. I zap headaches, arthritis, bad breath and laundry detergent. I zap diet-drink maidens and hand-lotion mavens . . . Wiping out commercials could entirely and joyfully upend the TV industry. Take the word of The Boston Zapper."

Critical Reading

Cite textual evidence to support your responses.

1. **Key Ideas and Details (a)** What is the *bow-wow theory* concerning the origin of language? **(b) Compare and Contrast:** Compare and contrast that theory with the *pooh-pooh theory* of language. **(c) Make a Judgment:** Do you think either of these terms is actually used by linguists? Explain.
2. **Key Ideas and Details (a)** What does Safire find so interesting about the word *zap*? **(b) Analyze:** Why does he believe that this word will "live long after superpowers agree to ban ray guns"?
3. **Craft and Structure Evaluate:** Do you think Safire's humorous style is more or less effective than a more somber explanation would be? Explain.
4. **Integration of Knowledge and Ideas** When someone celebrates language, what other aspects of a culture are they implicitly celebrating? In your response, use at least two of these Essential Question words: *resilience, invention, innovation, diversity, interpretation.* ***[Connecting to the Essential Question: What makes American literature American?]***

Close Reading Activities *Onomatopoeia*

Literary Analysis

1. **Key Ideas and Details** **(a)** Identify four important pieces of information Safire includes in this **expository essay.** **(b)** Classify each item you chose: Is it a fact, a definition, an example, or another form of information?
2. **Craft and Structure** **(a)** Locate two examples of scholarly **diction** Safire uses. **(b)** Locate two examples of folksy, or familiar, diction. **(c)** In what ways does this mix of diction add to the effectiveness of the essay?
3. **Craft and Structure** **(a)** In a chart like the one shown, list two examples of idioms Safire uses in this essay. **(b)** For each, explain its literal and acquired meanings.

Idiom	Literal Meaning	Acquired Meaning

4. **Integration of Knowledge and Ideas** **Paraphrase** the following passages from "Onomatopoeia" as though you are explaining their meaning to a friend: **(a)** "The coinage filled a need . . . right in the kisser"; **(b)** "The verb will live long after . . . imaginary sound turned into a new word."
5. **Integration of Knowledge and Ideas** Choose one paraphrase you wrote and explain how it might help readers understand an idea that was previously unclear.

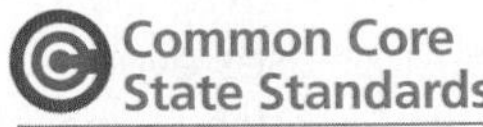

Common Core State Standards

Writing

2. Write informative texts to examine and convey complex ideas, concepts, and information clearly and accurately through the effective selection, organization, and analysis of content.

7. Conduct short research projects to answer a question or solve a problem.

Language

4.a. Use context as a clue to the meaning of a word or phrase.

Vocabulary Acquisition and Use

Sentence Completions Select the word from the list on page 1376 that best completes each sentence. Explain the context clues that support your choice.

1. Hannah ____ great pleasure from her getaways to the mountains.
2. *Supercalifragilisticexpialidocious* is a ____ made popular by a movie.
3. On election night, there was much ____ about the voting results.
4. *Boisterous* is ____ with *rowdy,* which means "loud and unruly."

Writing to Sources

Informative Text Choose a word or phrase in English that you find interesting, odd, or funny. Research the history of the word: its first appearance in the language and changes in its meaning. In an **informative essay,** explain your research. Use a mixture of scholarly diction, familiar diction, and idiomatic expressions.

Building Knowledge and Insight

Coyote v. Acme

Connecting to the Essential Question In this humorous essay, the author uses events in a popular 1950s TV cartoon to make a point about the American legal system. As you read, notice details that mock the legal system. Doing so will help you think about the Essential Question: **How does literature shape or reflect society?**

Reading Informational Text

5. Analyze and evaluate the effectiveness of the structure an author uses in his or her exposition or argument, including whether the structure makes points clear, convincing, and engaging.

6. Determine an author's point of view or purpose in a text in which the rhetoric is particularly effective, analyzing how style and content contribute to the power, persuasiveness or beauty of the text.

Close Reading Focus

Parody; Satire

A **parody** is a comic piece of writing that mocks the characteristics of a literary form, a specific work, or the style of a certain writer. Through the use of exaggeration, a parody calls attention to ridiculous aspects of the original. This essay parodies legal language and argument:

> *My client, Mr. Wile E. Coyote, a resident of Arizona and contiguous states, does hereby bring suit for damages against the Acme Company . . .*

The purpose of this parody is to create **satire,** writing that ridicules the faults of individuals, groups, institutions, or humanity in general. Although satire can be funny, its purpose is not simply to make readers laugh but also to correct the shortcomings that it addresses. As you read, think about the serious point Frazier makes in this parody of a legal document and whether the form and language of satire bring out Frazier's main point effectively.

Preparing to Read Complex Texts This essay is organized using a *cause-and-effect text structure.* The lawyer for Mr. Coyote must prove that the poor design of Acme products (cause) results in injury to Mr. Coyote (effect). To **analyze cause and effect,** look for words and phrases such as *subsequently* and *resulted in* that signal those relationships. Consider how these structural elements help to clarify the comic sequences of events the essay describes and the ideas it expresses. As you read, use a chart like the one shown to outline cause and effect in this essay.

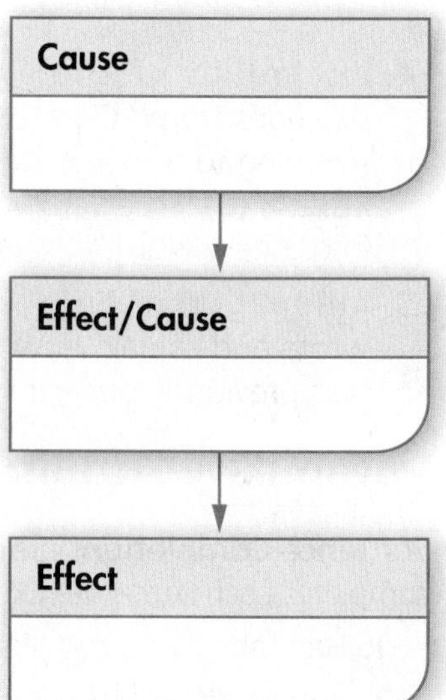

Vocabulary

The words below are important to understanding the text that follows. Copy the words into your notebook. Which word is a synonym for *forcefully*?

contiguous **systemic**
incorporated **emit**
vigorously **punitive**

IAN FRAZIER (b. 1951)

Author of "Coyote v. Acme"

Humorist Ian Frazier was born in Cleveland, Ohio. He is a 1973 graduate of Harvard University, where he wrote for the Harvard *Lampoon,* a humor magazine. After graduating, Frazier joined the staff of *The New Yorker* magazine. He worked there for two decades as a staff writer. His work has also appeared in many other publications, including the *Atlantic,* the *Washington Post Magazine,* and *Outside* magazine.

A Comic Sense Known for both humorous essays and affectionate descriptions of rural and urban America, Frazier brings an irreverant sense of fun to much of his work. "Coyote v. Acme" is typical of his writing: a ludicrous premise packaged in serious style.

Frazier has received many honors for his writing, including the Thurber Prize for American Humor and a 1990 Spur Award for Best Nonfiction from the Western Writers of America. He also has appeared on the National Public Radio program *A Prairie Home Companion* and has acted in two movies, *Smoke* and *Blue in the Face.* His books include *Dating Your Mom* (1986), *Nobody Better, Better Than Nobody* (1987), *Family* (1994), *Coyote v. Acme* (1996), *On the Rez* (2000), *The Fish's Eye* (2002), and *Gone to New York: Adventures in the City* (2005).

"I really like pieces where you start at the beginning, and as you get farther and farther you realize this person has no idea what he's talking about."

COYOTE V. ACME

IAN FRAZIER

BACKGROUND This essay is the fictional opening statement of a lawsuit by Mr. Wile E. Coyote, charging the Acme Company with the sale of defective merchandise. If these names sound familiar, you may remember watching Wile E. Coyote chase the Road Runner around the desert. The Warner Brothers cartoon "Road Runner and Coyote" was popular in the 1950s; more than half a century later, both the coyote and the elusive bird are still going strong. As you read the essay, consider what Frazier is really satirizing—the cartoon character who is his subject or the legal profession.

In the United States District Court,
Southwestern District,
Tempe, Arizona
Case No. B19294,
Judge Joan Kujava, Presiding

WILE E. COYOTE, Plaintiff
—v.—
ACME COMPANY, Defendant

Vocabulary

contiguous (kən tig′ yo͞o əs) *adj.* bordering; adjacent

incorporated (in kôr′ pə rāt′ id) *v.* united or combined to function legally as a business

Opening Statement of Mr. Harold Schoff, attorney for Mr. Coyote: My client, Mr. Wile E. Coyote, a resident of Arizona and **contiguous** states, does hereby bring suit for damages against the Acme Company, manufacturer and retail distributor of assorted merchandise, **incorporated** in Delaware and doing business in every state, district, and territory. Mr. Coyote seeks compensation for personal injuries, loss of business income, and mental suffering caused as a direct result of the actions and/or gross negligence of said company, under Title 15 of the United States Code, Chapter 47, section 2072, subsection (a), relating to product liability.

Mr. Coyote states that on eighty-five separate occasions he has purchased of the Acme Company (hereinafter, "Defendant"), through that company's mail-order department, certain products which did cause him bodily injury due to defects in manufacture or improper cautionary labeling. Sales slips made out to Mr. Coyote as proof of purchase are at present in the possession of the Court, marked Exhibit A. Such injuries sustained by Mr. Coyote have temporarily restricted his ability to make a living in his profession of predator. Mr. Coyote is self-employed and thus not eligible for Workmen's Compensation.[1]

Mr. Coyote states that on December 13th he received of Defendant via parcel post one Acme Rocket Sled. The intention of Mr. Coyote was to use the Rocket Sled to aid him in pursuit of his prey. Upon receipt of the Rocket Sled Mr. Coyote removed it from its wooden shipping crate and, sighting his prey in the distance, activated the ignition. As Mr. Coyote gripped the handlebars, the Rocket Sled accelerated with such sudden and precipitate force as to stretch Mr. Coyote's forelimbs to a length of fifty feet. Subsequently, the rest of Mr. Coyote's body shot forward with a violent jolt, causing severe strain to his back and neck and placing him unexpectedly astride the Rocket Sled. Disappearing over the horizon at such speed as to leave a diminishing jet trail along its path, the Rocket Sled soon brought Mr. Coyote abreast of his prey. At that moment the animal he was pursuing veered sharply to the right. Mr. Coyote **vigorously** attempted to follow this maneuver but was unable to, due to poorly designed steering on the Rocket Sled and a faulty or nonexistent braking system. Shortly thereafter, the unchecked progress of the Rocket Sled brought it and Mr. Coyote into collision with the side of a mesa.[2]

Paragraph One of the Report of Attending Physician (Exhibit B), prepared by Dr. Ernest Grosscup, M.D., D.O., details the multiple fractures, contusions, and tissue damage suffered by Mr. Coyote as

Vocabulary
vigorously (vig´ ər əs lē) *adv.* forcefully or powerfully

▼ Critical Viewing
Based on this single frame of a cartoon, is Mr. Coyote's claim valid? Explain. **MAKE A JUDGMENT**

Comprehension
For what three reasons does Mr. Coyote seek compensation from the Acme Company?

1. **Workmen's Compensation** form of disability insurance that provides income to workers who are unable to work due to injuries sustained on the job.
2. **mesa** (mā´ sə) *n.* small, high plateau with steep sides.

LITERATURE IN CONTEXT

Literature Connection

Parodies in American Culture

There are many famous parodies in American literature, film, and music. Mark Twain's novel *A Connecticut Yankee in King Arthur's Court* parodies the chivalric romance. Stephen Crane's story "The Bride Comes to Yellow Sky" parodies the western.

Popular culture is full of parodies, as well. The films of Mel Brooks satirize absurd aspects of other movies. "Canadian Idiot," a 2006 spoof of the band Green Day's song "American Idiot," is only one of musician "Weird Al" Yankovic's many parodies. "Mockumentaries" such as *Best in Show* and *A Mighty Wind* mimic the documentaries they parody by including fake "confessionals" and pretending to capture actual events.

Connect to the Literature

Parodies are modeled on the pieces they satirize. Which conventions of legal writing does Frazier imitate?

a result of this collision. Repair of the injuries required a full bandage around the head (excluding the ears), a neck brace, and full or partial casts on all four legs.

Hampered by these injuries, Mr. Coyote was nevertheless obliged to support himself. With this in mind, he purchased of Defendant as an aid to mobility one pair of Acme Rocket Skates. When he attempted to use this product, however, he became involved in an accident remarkably similar to that which occurred with the Rocket Sled. Again, Defendant sold over the counter, without caveat, a product which attached powerful jet engines (in this case, two) to inadequate vehicles, with little or no provision for passenger safety. Encumbered by his heavy casts, Mr. Coyote lost control of the Rocket Skates soon after strapping them on, and collided with a roadside billboard so violently as to leave a hole in the shape of his full silhouette.

Mr. Coyote states that on occasions too numerous to list in this document he has suffered mishaps with explosives purchased of Defendant: the Acme "Little Giant" Firecracker, the Acme Self-Guided Aerial Bomb, etc. (For a full listing, see the Acme Mail Order Explosives Catalogue and attached deposition,[3] entered in evidence as Exhibit C.) Indeed, it is safe to say that not once has an explosive purchased of Defendant by Mr. Coyote performed in an expected manner. To cite just one example: At the expense of much time and personal effort, Mr. Coyote constructed around the outer rim of a butte[4] a wooden trough beginning at the top of the butte and spiraling downward around it to some few feet above a black X painted on the desert floor. The trough was designed in such a way that a spherical explosive of the type sold by Defendant would roll easily and swiftly down to the point of detonation indicated by the X. Mr. Coyote placed a generous pile of birdseed directly on the X, and then, carrying the spherical Acme Bomb (Catalogue #78–832), climbed to the top of the butte. Mr. Coyote's prey, seeing the birdseed, approached, and Mr. Coyote proceeded to light the fuse. In an instant, the fuse burned down to the stem, causing the bomb to detonate.

Parody
How does this list of injuries make fun of personal injury claims?

In addition to reducing all Mr. Coyote's careful preparations to naught, the premature detonation of Defendant's product resulted in the following disfigurements to Mr. Coyote:

1. Severe singeing of the hair on the head, neck, and muzzle.
2. Sooty discoloration.

3. **deposition** (dep′ ə zish′ ən) *n.* legal term for the written testimony of a witness.
4. **butte** (byo͞ot) *n.* steep hill standing alone in a plain.

3. Fracture of the left ear at the stem, causing the ear to dangle in the aftershock with a creaking noise.
4. Full or partial combustion of whiskers producing kinking, frazzling, and ashy disintegration.
5. Radical widening of the eyes, due to brow and lid charring.

We come now to the Acme Spring-Powered Shoes. The remains of a pair of these purchased by Mr. Coyote on June 23rd are Plaintiff's Exhibit D. Selected fragments have been shipped to the metallurgical laboratories of the University of California at Santa Barbara for analysis, but to date no explanation has been found for this product's sudden and extreme malfunction. As advertised by Defendant, this product is simplicity itself: two wood-and-metal sandals, each attached to milled-steel springs of high tensile strength and compressed in a tightly coiled position by a cocking device with a lanyard release. Mr. Coyote believed that this product would enable him to pounce upon his prey in the initial moments of the chase, when swift reflexes are at a premium.

To increase the shoes' thrusting still further, Mr. Coyote affixed them by their bottoms to the side of a large boulder. Adjacent to the boulder was a path which Mr. Coyote's prey was known to frequent. Mr. Coyote put his hind feet in the wood-and-metal sandals and crouched in readiness, his right forepaw holding firmly to the lanyard release. Within a short time Mr. Coyote's prey did indeed appear on the path coming toward him. Unsuspecting, the prey stopped near Mr. Coyote, well within range of the springs at full extension. Mr. Coyote gauged the distance with care and proceeded to pull the lanyard release.

▲ Critical Viewing
Describe Mr. Coyote's injuries as shown in this cartoon frame. Use an approach similar to Frazier's. **DESCRIBE**

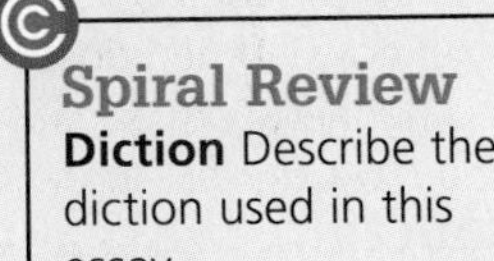

Spiral Review
Diction Describe the diction used in this essay.

Comprehension
Have Acme products performed well for Mr. Coyote? Explain.

Analyzing Cause and Effect

Trace the sequence of cause and effect that results from Mr. Coyote's use of the thrusting shoes.

At this point, Defendant's product should have thrust Mr. Coyote forward and away from the boulder. Instead, for reasons yet unknown, the Acme Spring-Powered Shoes thrust the boulder away from Mr. Coyote. As the intended prey looked on unharmed, Mr. Coyote hung suspended in air. Then the twin springs recoiled, bringing Mr. Coyote to a violent feet-first collision with the boulder, the full weight of his head and forequarters falling upon his lower extremities.

The force of this impact then caused the springs to rebound, whereupon Mr. Coyote was thrust skyward. A second recoil and collision followed. The boulder, meanwhile, which was roughly ovoid in shape, had begun to bounce down a hillside, the coiling and recoiling of the springs adding to its velocity. At each bounce, Mr. Coyote came into contact with the boulder, or the boulder came into contact with Mr. Coyote, or both came into contact with the ground. As the grade was a long one, this process continued for some time.

Vocabulary

systemic (sis tem′ ik) *adj.* of or affecting the entire bodily system

emit (i mit′) *v.* send out or give forth

The sequence of collisions resulted in **systemic** physical damage to Mr. Coyote, viz., flattening of the cranium, sideways displacement of the tongue, reduction of length of legs and upper body, and compression of vertebrae from base of tail to head. Repetition of blows along a vertical axis produced a series of regular horizontal folds in Mr. Coyote's body tissues—a rare and painful condition which caused Mr. Coyote to expand upward and contract downward alternately as he walked, and to **emit** an off-key accordion-like wheezing with every step. The distracting and embarrassing nature of this symptom has been a major impediment to Mr. Coyote's pursuit of a normal social life.

▼ Critical Viewing

Based on this cartoon frame, how worried does Road Runner seem about being Mr. Coyote's "prey"? **DEDUCE**

As the Court is no doubt aware, Defendant has a virtual monopoly of manufacture and sale of goods required by Mr. Coyote's work. It is our contention that Defendant has used its market advantage to the detriment of the consumer of such specialized products as itching powder, giant kites, Burmese tiger traps, anvils, and two-hundred-foot-long rubber bands. Much as he has come to mistrust Defendant's products, Mr. Coyote has no other domestic source of supply to which to turn. One can only wonder what our trading partners in Western Europe and Japan would make of such a situation, where a giant company is allowed to victimize the consumer in the most reckless and wrongful manner over and over again.

Mr. Coyote respectfully requests that the Court regard these larger economic implications and assess punitive damages in the amount of seventeen million dollars. In addition, Mr. Coyote seeks actual damages (missed meals, medical expenses, days lost from professional occupation) of one million dollars; general damages (mental suffering, injury to reputation) of twenty million dollars; and attorney's fees of seven hundred and fifty thousand dollars. Total damages: thirty-eight million seven hundred and fifty thousand dollars. By awarding Mr. Coyote the full amount, this Court will censure Defendant, its directors, officers, shareholders, successors, and assigns, in the only language they understand, and reaffirm the right of the individual predator to equal protection under the law.

Vocabulary

punitive (pyo͞o′ nə tiv) *adj.* punishing or having to do with punishment

Critical Reading

Cite textual evidence to support your responses.

1. **Key Ideas and Details (a)** What happens to Wile E. Coyote's forelimbs when he uses the Rocket Sled? **(b) Support:** What details in this essay suggest that Wile E. Coyote is a cartoon character?
2. **Key Ideas and Details (a)** How often does Wile E. Coyote buy products from the Acme Company? **(b) Support:** Find evidence to explain why he maintains this relationship with Acme, despite the outcomes he has faced with their products.
3. **Key Ideas and Details (a)** What action is Wile E. Coyote seeking from the court? **(b) Make a Judgment:** If you were a member of the jury in this case, what would your verdict be? Explain.
4. **Integration of Knowledge and Ideas** Based on this essay, do you think humorous exaggeration is an effective way to make a serious point? Why or why not? In your response, use at least three of these Essential Question words: *communication, evaluation, perception, transformation, understanding.* ***[Connecting to the Essential Question: How does literature shape or reflect society?]***

Close Reading Activities *Coyote v. Acme*

Literary Analysis

1. **Key Ideas and Details (a)** Summarize the first paragraph of the attorney's opening statement. **(b)** What circumstances caused Wile E. Coyote to sue the Acme Company? **(c)** What words or phrases establish this **cause-and-effect** relationship?
2. **Key Ideas and Details (a)** What specific products caused Mr. Coyote's injuries? **(b)** According to the attorney, how do these injuries affect Mr. Coyote's health and livelihood?
3. **Key Ideas and Details (a)** According to the attorney, what effect will a judgment in favor of his client have on the defendant? **(b)** What larger effect does he believe it will it have on society?
4. **Key Ideas and Details (a)** In "Coyote v. Acme" what type of text does Frazier **parody? (b)** What specific characteristics of the original form's language and types of reasoning does the essay exaggerate?
5. **Key Ideas and Details** How does the topic of this parody—a lawsuit brought by a cartoon character—in and of itself mock the original?
6. **Craft and Structure** Using a graphic organizer like the one shown, list three examples of exaggeration in the essay.

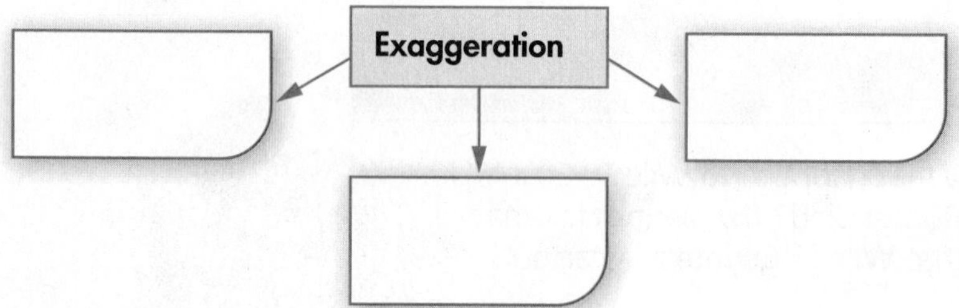

7. **Craft and Structure** In what way is this parody also an example of **satire**—what serious point does Frazier convey through his use of humor?
8. **Key Ideas and Details (a)** Who is the defendant and who is the plaintiff described in this essay? **(b)** Why do you think Frazier chose to parody the opening statement for the plaintiff rather than for the defense?
9. **Integration of Knowledge and Ideas** Americans have been criticized for being excessively "litigious," which means bringing many frivolous or unfounded lawsuits. Based on "Coyote v. Acme," do you think Frazier would agree with that assessment? Explain.
10. **Integration of Knowledge and Ideas (a)** Based on "Coyote v. Acme," what values do you think Frazier considers important? **(b)** What type of society would he support? Defend your answer with details from the text.

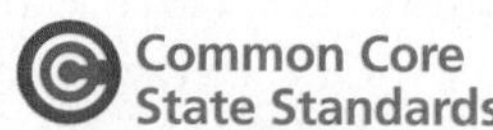

Common Core State Standards

Writing

1. Write arguments to support claims in an analysis of substantive topics or texts, using valid reasoning and relevant and sufficient evidence. *(p. 1391)*

1.a. Introduce precise, knowledgeable claim(s), establish the significance of the claim(s), distinguish the claim(s) from alternate or opposing claims, and create an organization that logically sequences claim(s), counterclaims, reasons, and evidence. *(p. 1391)*

1.c. Use phrases to link the major sections of the text, create cohesion, and clarify the relationships between claim(s) and reasons, between reasons and evidence, and between claim(s) and counterclaims. *(p. 1391)*

Language

4.b. Identify and correctly use patterns of word changes that indicate different meanings or parts of speech. *(p. 1391)*

Vocabulary Acquisition and Use

Word Analysis: Latin Root *-corpus-*

The word *incorporated* includes the Latin root corpus, which means "body." A company that is incorporated is "granted, as a body, certain of the legal powers, rights, privileges, and liabilities of an individual." The root *-corpus-* is often featured in scientific and medical terms. Combine this information about the root *-corpus-* with context clues to choose the best word to complete each sentence below.

corpuscles   corpulent   incorporeal

1. The ____ man began an exercise program to help him lose weight.
2. We learned about the two types of ____ in human blood.
3. In the movie, the woman stared in shock as an ____ figure appeared before her eyes.

Vocabulary: Definitions

Review the vocabulary list on page 1382. Then, choose the definition from the right column that best fits the word in the left column. Explain your choices.

1. systemic	**a.** share a common border
2. incorporated	**b.** inflicting punishment
3. punitive	**c.** spread throughout the body
4. contiguous	**d.** performed with great power
5. emit	**e.** formed into a legal business
6. vigorously	**f.** give off, discharge

Writing to Sources

Argument In his satirical essay "Coyote v. Acme," Frazier parodies aspects of the legal system. Working in groups as teams of attorneys defending the Acme Company, develop a **response to the arguments** presented by the plaintiff's lawyer in "Coyote v. Acme."

Prewriting Work together to develop effective responses to the main arguments presented in the essay. Use cluster diagrams like the one shown to organize your thoughts.

Main Argument
The plaintiff did not use the Acme Rocket Sled properly.

Did not properly follow assembly instructions

Drafting As you draft, use legal language and present your arguments logically and persuasively. Clearly establish cause-and-effect relationships and refute those presented by the plaintiff. Your arguments should appeal primarily to logic, but you can also work in some emotional appeals.

Revising Review your opening statement to make sure that you have clearly answered each of the plaintiff's main arguments. Clarify cause and effect by adding transitional phrases, such as "resulted in" or "due to."

Building Knowledge and Insight

ANCHOR TEXT
One Day, Now Broken in Two

Connecting to the Essential Question In this essay, the writer reflects on the tragic events of September 11, 2001, when the United States suffered terrorist attacks on its own soil. As you read, consider how writings about such public trauma affect individuals and communities. Doing so will help you think about the Essential Question: **How does literature shape or reflect society?**

Common Core State Standards

Reading Informational Text
3. Analyze a complex set of ideas or sequence of events and explain how specific individuals, ideas, or events interact and develop over the course of the text.
5. Analyze and evaluate the effectiveness of the structure an author uses in his or her exposition or argument, including whether the structure makes points clear, convincing, and engaging.

Close Reading Focus

Comparison-and-Contrast Essay

In a **comparison-and-contrast** essay, a writer analyzes similarities and differences between two or more people, topics, or events. Effective comparison-and-contrast essays have the following qualities:

- The discussion is not arbitrary; the two topics genuinely shed light on each other.
- The discussion is balanced; the topics are of equal importance.
- The essay follows an effective organizational structure; the author may alternate between the two topics in a point-by-point organization, or consider each topic as a whole in a block organization.

In this essay, the author compares perceptions of America in the days just after the events of September 11, 2001 and again one year later. As you read, use a chart like the one shown to note the similarities and differences Quindlen discusses. Then, consider whether the comparison-and-contrast structure adds to the essay's clarity and power.

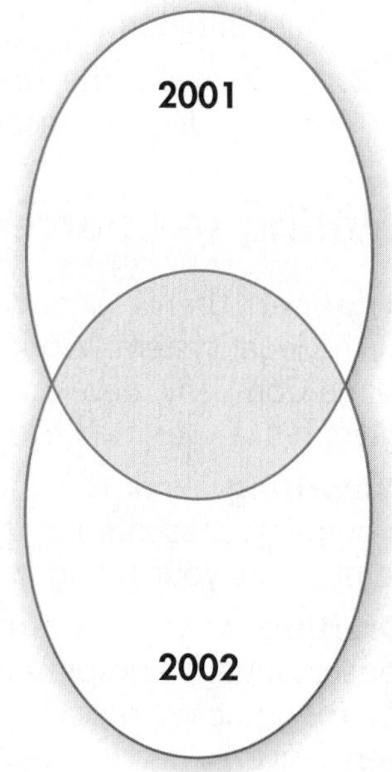

Preparing to Read Complex Texts Many documents that become primary sources begin as private communications in which the writer shares his or her perceptions of historical events. When you read literature about those same events, it can be useful to **relate the literary work to primary sources.** For example, eyewitness accounts of an event may offer useful insights into a literary work about the same topic. As you read, consider how primary source documents, such as those on pages 1401 and 1403, add to your understanding of the ideas Quindlen presents in her essay.

Vocabulary

The words below are important to understanding the text that follows. Copy the words into your notebook and note which words are nouns.

mundane
induce
savagery
revelations
prosperity

Anna Quindlen (b. 1953)

Author of "One Day, Now Broken in Two"

"I show up. I listen. I try to laugh."

Young Reporter As a junior at Barnard College, Anna Quindlen already had a passion for words and an interest in journalism. When her writing professor walked into class with a stack of manila envelopes and encouraged his students to submit their stories for publication, Quindlen did just that. The piece she sent was published soon after in *Seventeen* magazine. This first step launched Quindlen on a successful career as a reporter, columnist, and novelist.

Before she finished college, Quindlen started working part time at the *New York Post*. She took a full-time position at the paper after graduation, and within a few years landed a job at *The New York Times*. In 1986, the *Times* asked Quindlen to write a weekly column.

Life in the 30s Quindlen's column, "Life in the '30s," ran for more than two years. Quindlen's discussions of politics and global issues showed a deep level of insight, but what most attracted critics (and her growing fan base) was her ability to discuss these topics with a personal touch. Her next *Times* column, "Public and Private," won the Pulitzer Prize for Commentary in 1992.

Life as a Novelist In 1995, Quindlen left journalism to devote her time to writing fiction. She went on to publish four bestselling novels: *Object Lessons, Black and Blue, One True Thing,* and *Blessings*. Quindlen's fiction often centers on the dynamics of family relationships, a subject she finds especially compelling.

Today, Quindlen is again an active journalist. She currently writes a column for *Newsweek* magazine entitled "The Last Word" in which she expresses opinions in her distinctive, personal style. "One Day, Now Broken in Two," appeared in *Newsweek* in 2002.

One Day, Now Broken in Two

Anna Quindlen

▲ **Critical Viewing**
In what ways do the two scenes within this image echo Quindlen's ideas in this essay? **ANALYZE**

BACKGROUND This essay was published in *Newsweek* magazine one year after the September 11, 2001, terrorist attacks on the World Trade Center in New York City and the Pentagon building in Washington, D.C. Quindlen's column was part of a commemorative edition of the magazine entitled *America: A Year After.*

September 11 is my eldest child's birthday. When he drove cross-country this spring and got pulled over for pushing the pedal on a couple of stretches of monotonous highway, two cops in two different states said more or less the same thing as they looked down at his license: aw, man, you were really born on 9-11? Maybe it was coincidence, but in both cases he got a warning instead of a ticket.

Vocabulary
mundane (mun dān′) *adj.* commonplace, everyday

Who are we now? A people who manage to get by with the help of the everyday, the ordinary, the mundane, the old familiar life muting the terror of the new reality. The day approaching will always be bifurcated[1] for me: part September 11, the anniversary of one of the happiest days of my life, and part 9-11, the day America's mind reeled, its spine stiffened, and its heart broke.

That is how the country is now, split in two. The American people used their own simple routines to muffle the horror they felt looking at that indelible loop of tape—the plane, the flames, the plane, the fire, the falling bodies, the falling buildings. Amid the fear and the shock there were babies to be fed, dogs to be walked, jobs to be done.

1. **bifurcated** (bi′ fər kā təd) *adj.* divided into two parts.

▲ (left) Firefighters mourn victims of the World Trade Center attack; (center) an impromptu memorial; (right) a firefighter at Ground Zero

After the first months almost no one bought gas masks anymore; fewer people than expected in New York City asked for the counseling that had been provided as part of the official response. Slowly the planes filled up again. A kind of self-hypnosis prevailed, and these were the words used to induce the happy trance: life goes on.

Who are we now? We are better people than we were before. That's what the optimists say, soothed by the vision of those standing in line to give blood and money and time at the outset, vowing to stop and smell the flowers as the weeks ticked by. We are people living in a world of unimaginable cruelty and savagery. So say the pessimists. The realists insist that both are right, and, as always, they are correct.

We are people whose powers of imagination have been challenged by the revelations of the careful planning, the hidden leaders, the machinations[2] from within a country of rubble and caves and desperate want, the willingness to slam headlong into one great technological achievement while piloting another as a way of despising modernity. Why do they hate us, some asked afterward, and many Americans were outraged at the question, confusing the search for motivation with mitigation.[3] But quietly, as routine returned, a new routine based on a new bedrock of loss of innocence and loss of life, a new question crept almost undetected into the national psyche: did we like ourselves? Had we become a people who confused prosperity with probity,[4] whose culture had become personified by oversize sneakers and KFC? Our own individual transformations made each of us wonder what our legacy would be if we left the world on a sunny September day with a "to do" list floating down eighty stories to the street below.

So we looked at our lives a little harder, called our friends a little more often, hugged our kids a little tighter. And then we complained about the long lines at the airport and obsessed about the stock market in lieu of soul-searching. Time passed. The blade dulled. The edges softened. Except, of course, for those who lived through birthdays, anniversaries, holidays, without someone lost in the cloud of silvery dust, those families the living embodiment of what the whole

Vocabulary

induce (in do͞os′) *v.* cause; bring on

savagery (sav′ ij rē) *n.* the condition of being savage or brutal

revelations (rev′ ə lā′ shəns) *n.* things revealed or made known

prosperity (präs per′ ə tē) *n.* the condition of being prosperous, wealthy

Comprehension

In what way will the date of September 11 always be "bifurcated" for Quindlen?

---

2. **machinations** (mak′ ə nā′ shənz) *n.* secret schemes.
3. **mitigation** (mit′ ə gā′ shən) *n.* relief; moderation; lessening of severity.
4. **probity** (prō′ bə tē) *n.* integrity; moral uprightness.

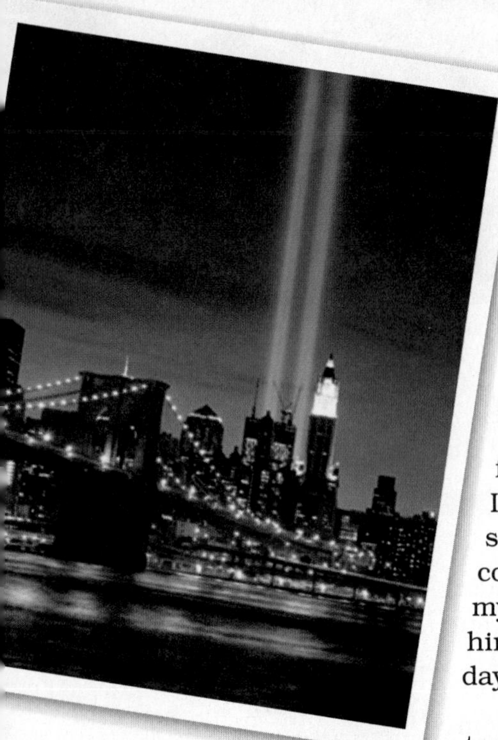

▲ The "Tribute in Light" is an annual remembrance of the 9/11 attacks.

nation had first felt and then learned not to feel.

We are people of two minds now, the one that looks forward and the one that unwillingly and unexpectedly flashes back. Flying over lower Manhattan, the passengers reflexively lean toward the skyline below, looking for ghost buildings. "Is everything back to normal?" someone asked me in another country not long ago, and I said yes. And no. The closest I could come to describing what I felt was to describe a bowl I had broken in two and beautifully mended. It holds everything it once did; the crack is scarcely visible. But I always know it's there. My eye worries it without even meaning to.

On September 10 of last year my daughter and I went to the funeral of a neighbor we both loved greatly. We rushed home so I could go to the hospital, where my closest friend had just had serious surgery. Someone else took the cat to the vet after we discovered that he was poisoned and was near death. That night, as my daughter got ready for bed, I said to her, without the slightest hint of hyperbole,[5] "Don't worry, honey. We'll never again have a day as bad as this one."

Who are we now? We are people who know that we never understood what "bad day" meant until that morning that cracked our world cleanly in two, that day that made two days, September 11 and 9-11. The mundane and the monstrous. "Tell me how do you live brokenhearted?" Bruce Springsteen sings on his new album about the aftermath. September 11 is my boy's birthday; 9-11 is something else. That is the way we have to live, or we cannot really go on living at all.

5. **hyperbole** (hī pur′ bə lē) *n.* exaggeration.

Critical Reading

Cite textual evidence to support your responses.

1. **Key Ideas and Details** **(a)** According to Quindlen, what is the optimists' view of who Americans have become as a result of 9/11? **(b) Compare and Contrast:** What is the pessimists' answer to the same question? **(c) Analyze:** In Quindlen's opinion, which view is correct? Explain.
2. **Key Ideas and Details** **(a)** According to Quindlen, what two questions have Americans asked themselves as a result of 9/11? **(b) Interpret:** Why does she believe it is a mistake to be outraged by the first question?
3. **Integration of Knowledge and Ideas** In the wake of a traumatic event like 9-11, is literature important? Explain. In your response, use at least two of these Essential Question words: *community, insight, perspective, profound. **[Connecting to the Essential Question: How does literature shape or reflect society?]***

Close Reading Activities *One Day, Now Broken in Two*

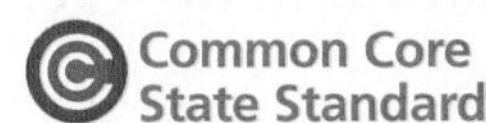

Literary Analysis

1. **Craft and Structure** **(a)** What two perspectives or concepts does Quindlen explore in this **comparison-and-contrast essay? (b)** Does Quindlen's use of comparison-and-contrast text structure genuinely illuminate each perspective? Explain.
2. **Craft and Structure** **(a)** To what object does Quindlen compare life in post 9/11 America? **(b)** In that context, does her use of the word *worries* have more than one meaning? Explain.
3. **Craft and Structure** **(a)** Is the phrase Quindlen uses in her final paragraph—"the mundane and the monstrous"—a useful summary of the comparison and contrast she describes in the essay? Explain. **(b)** Why do you think she leaves that phrase as its own sentence fragment?
4. **Integration of Knowledge and Ideas** **Relate primary sources to a literary work** by listing details from 9/11 primary source documents that offer insight into the outpouring of grief and solicitude that Quindlen refers to in her essay. Read the two primary source articles on pages 1401–1405. Then, use a chart like the one shown to record your observations.

One Day...	Urban Renewal	Playing for the Fighting Sixty-Ninth

Common Core State Standards

Writing

2. Write informative texts to examine and convey complex ideas, concepts, and information clearly and accurately through the effective selection, organization, and analysis of content.

2.e. Establish and maintain a formal style and objective tone while attending to the norms and conventions of the discipline in which they are writing.

Language

4. Determine or clarify the meaning of unknown and multiple-meaning words and phrases based on *grades 11–12 reading and content,* choosing flexibly from a range of strategies.

Vocabulary Acquisition and Use

Use New Words For each item below, write a sentence in which you use the word or word pair correctly.

1. mundane **2.** induce / savagery **3.** revelation / prosperity

Writing to Sources

Explanatory Text Write a **letter** to Anna Quindlen in which you share your thoughts about her essay. Add to the discussion by answering the following questions:

- What is the situation now as Americans look back to 2001 and 2002?
- How might we answer the question "Is everything back to normal?"

As you draft, maintain a formal, objective, and respectful tone in keeping with your audience and purpose.

Primary Sources

Oral History Transcript
Urban Renewal

E-mail
Playing for the Fighting Sixty-Ninth

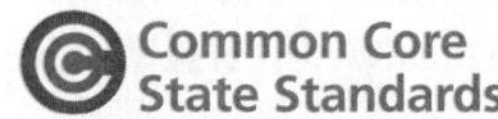

Common Core State Standards

Reading Informational Text
1. Cite strong and thorough textual evidence to support analysis of what the text says explicitly as well as inferences drawn from the text, including determining where the text leaves matters uncertain.

About the Text Forms

An **oral history** is a spoken account of an event by an eyewitness. Oral histories are usually unrehearsed and combine facts with impressions and memories. It was only in the 1900s—with the development of audio recording technologies—that oral histories were first collected and treated as historical records.

An **e-mail** (short for "electronic mail") is a typed message sent through a computer network. E-mails are delivered and received almost instantaneously and can be sent to multiple recipients at once. Because of these two qualities, e-mails can be powerful historical records of dramatic events.

Preparing to Read Complex Texts

Most Americans are aware of the terrorist attacks that took place in New York City and Washington, D.C., on September 11, 2001. Issues that arose as a result of the attacks are still in the news. These texts express the responses of two ordinary people who witnessed some of the events of that day and its aftermath. Their observations suggest, but do not always explicitly state, larger meanings. To gain a deeper understanding, **apply your background knowledge to make inferences and draw conclusions,** interpreting stated details to derive unstated meanings.

- First, take note of incidental details. Consider why the writer or speaker included these details.
- Next, ask yourself what you already know that relates to each detail.
- Finally, apply your background knowledge to each detail to make inferences about the speakers, their connections to larger events, and the extent to which their feelings and experiences represent those of other people across the city, country, and world.

As you read these primary source documents, consider what they illuminate about these dramatic events in America's recent history.

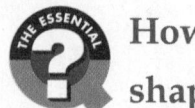

How does literature shape or reflect *society?*

The events described in these documents took place in New York City in the days that followed September 11, 2001. These accounts describe a new and different world. As you read, notice details that tell how both the physical and emotional terrain of New York City changed. Notice, too, how these changes trigger deep feelings in the storytellers.

Note-Taking Guide

Primary source documents are a rich source of information for researchers. As you read these documents, use a note-taking guide like the one shown to organize relevant and accurate information.

1 Type of Document
☐ Newspaper ☐ Transcript ☐ Telegram ☐ Advertisement
☐ Press Release ☐ Journal Entry ☐ E-mail ☐ Editorial

2 Date(s) of Document ______________________

3 Writer or Speaker ______________________

4 Note important details in the text. Then, identify any related background knowledge you already have.

a Important Details ______________________

____

b Related Background Knowledge ______________________

____

5 What broad conclusions can you draw about the speaker, his experiences, or the larger historical event?

____

____

____

____

Using Background Knowledge to Make Inferences and Draw Conclusions For each detail, think about related information you might have gathered from TV reports, newspaper articles, or conversations.

This guide was adapted from the **U.S. National Archives** document analysis worksheet.

Vocabulary

memorials (mə môr′ ē əlz) *n.* objects displayed in memory of a person or event (p. 1401)

homages (äm′ ij əz) *n.* acts showing honor and reverence (p. 1402)

intently (in tent′ lē) *adv.* in a focused, purposeful manner (p. 1402)

fatigues (fə tēgz′) *n.* sturdy clothing worn by soldiers (p. 1403)

intonation (in′ tō nā′ shən) *n.* the quality of playing musical notes in or out of tune (p. 1404)

regiment (rej′ ə mənt) *n.* a military unit (p. 1404)

casualties (kazh′ o͞ol tēz) *n.* members of the armed forces who die in combat (p. 1405)

cadence (kād′ ns) *n.* series of notes or chords near the end of a musical work (p. 1405)

THE STORY BEHIND THE DOCUMENTS

Sean Ramsay

William Harvey

On the morning of September 11, 2001, nineteen members of the extremist group al-Qaeda, based in Afghanistan, boarded and hijacked four American jetliners. They flew two of the planes into the north and south towers of the World Trade Center in New York City; another struck the Pentagon, the U.S. Department of Defense headquarters in Washington, D.C. The fourth crashed in the Pennsylvania countryside after its passengers mounted a defense against the terrorists.

By 10:30 A.M., both Trade Center towers had collapsed, and Americans began their journey through shock, disbelief, horror, anger, and grief. While millions of people sat stunned before TV sets, thousands more sprang into action at the attack sites. In New York City, firefighters, police officers, soldiers, doctors, nurses, emergency medical technicians, and counselors worked tirelessly to rescue victims and treat the injured. College students handed out water and food to the exhausted workers. People collected and delivered boxes of supplies to work stations. Once rescue efforts ceased, the emergency crews, along with scores of skilled volunteers began the grueling work of clearing the smoldering rubble of "Ground Zero," the 16 acres on which the 110-story towers had stood. Behind the scenes, volunteers such as **William Harvey** continued to offer what they could, from massages to music, to soothe the weary bodies and souls of those who labored. William, a freshman at Juilliard Conservatory of Music, offered his musical gifts, and e-mailed home about his experiences. E-mails flew across the country, delivering to distant friends and relatives millions of first-hand accounts of events both horrifying and poignant.

Meanwhile, impromptu memorials in honor of lost loved ones sprang up across the city. These were outward, collective expressions of profound grief. Downtown parks such as Union Square and Washington Square became oceans of flowers, letters, photos, candles, and other mementos. **Sean Ramsay,** a Brooklyn resident and museum exhibit designer, witnessed a remarkable scene at one of these memorials, which he recounts in his oral history.

By now, many of the questions about 9/11 have been answered. We know, for example, that close to 3,000 people from thirteen countries died in the attacks, that more than 400 of these victims were fire-fighters and police officers, and that forty percent of the victims remain either unfound or unidentified. These answers and numbers provide little consolation, though. More comforting are the stories people continue to tell and remember—stories of quiet heroism, tender gestures, and intangible gifts.

URBAN RENEWAL

Sean Ramsay

This story was first told at a storytelling "slam" in New York City, shortly after September 11, 2001. The storyteller, Sean Ramsay, won the contest, and was invited to appear on the public radio show Studio 360. *Following is a transcript of the version of the story he told on the November 3, 2001 episode of that show.*

▼ In the days after the attack, people expressed their grief and sympathy in makeshift memorials.

Sean Ramsay: So, it had been ten days since the tragedy had happened and again I found myself walking towards the promenade on Brooklyn Heights. The Promenade is a walkway on the western edge of Brooklyn that has these sweeping views of the financial district and the Brooklyn Bridge. That is where I had watched events unfold on September 11th. This morning I had gotten there early, and there were a few people sitting on the benches, looking at the skyline, and I was surprised to see that the Promenade was covered with memorials. I had seen on television that there were large displays in Washington Square Park and Union Square, but I guess I just didn't expect to see them here. So, I walked along the walkway and there were these forests of half-melted candles and objects strewn about the ground; there was a plastic child's fireman's helmet with the word "Bravest" written across the front; there were flags strewn up along the railing and there was a small framed quote on the ground by Martin Luther King decrying violence; there were flowers, a fresh vase of white roses, and all sorts of photographs and pictures and children's drawings of the Twin Towers themselves. And as I walked along I noticed there were signs posted along the railing as well, and these signs came in two varieties: one was the quick posters that were obviously put together in the days right after the tragedy—they had a photograph of the person, maybe the first one that could be found, and a quick description of their physical characteristics and

Vocabulary

memorials (mə môr′ ē əlz) *n.* objects displayed in memory of a person or event

Comprehension

What does Ramsay notice on the Promenade?

▲ People posted photos and pleas for the safe return of loved ones.

a phone number. And there were other signs that you saw that were obviously hung up several days later, and they were more like homages. They would have three or four photographs of the loved one that had been lost, with family members or on vacation at the beach, and they were accompanied by messages like, "Katie always had such a great smile. We miss her so." And, "Davey, now you will have to look after us."

I walked along reading these messages and looking at these photographs and I felt an immense sense of loss. You could feel the vacuum of the towers across the water, there on the edge [pause. speaker's voice breaks]. I felt connected to these faces and to these families in a way I hadn't through all the news coverage and all the intellectualizing and all the discussions of war and revenge and vengeance. [speaker's voice trails off]

Vocabulary
homages (äm´ ij əz) *n.* acts showing honor and reverence

And as I walked along having this experience, I noticed that up ahead of me there was a sanitation truck, a small garbage truck, and some sanitation workers along the walkway. They were holding these large plastic bags and then beyond them the walkway was clear, everything had been stripped, no flowers, candles, objects, everything was gone. Obviously they were cleaning things up and I became very angry. I thought, "But it's too soon! We need these things, we need to understand what has happened to us, we need to remember what happened that day." We weren't finished grieving yet, and I wasn't finished grieving yet. And I thought I should say something. I mean I didn't know what to do, I thought that it just . . . it wasn't right that this was happening. I walked over to them not knowing what I would say, I mean I knew these were just people doing their job, but I had to say something . . . as I got close, I realized that they weren't taking the things down.

As I watched, they were taking the plastic bags and one by one they were taking out the photographs and the letters and the signs and they were carefully repairing the torn edges with cellophane tape and attaching them to the railing. Then I watched as they took out the candles and made small groupings. They put toy firetrucks on the ground; they put down the framed photographs; and they hung up the flowers upside down so that they would last longer. And as I watched this I realized that it had rained heavily the night before. Apparently what had happened was the sanitation department had come out and collected all these objects and stored them safely from the rain and this morning was intently and carefully replacing every single one.

Thank you.

Vocabulary
intently (in tent´ lē) *adv.* in a focused, purposeful manner

Playing for the

FIGHTING SIXTY-NINTH

William Harvey

William Harvey was a freshman at Juilliard, a New York City music conservatory, in September, 2001. After the 9/11 attacks, he e-mailed this firsthand account of his experiences to his family in Indianapolis, Indiana. He describes his encounter with members of the "Fighting Sixty-Ninth," the 69th Infantry Regiment of the New York Army National Guard. This regiment—one of the most celebrated in all of American history—was the first military force to secure Ground Zero.

On September 16, 2001, I had probably the most incredible and moving experience of my life. Juilliard organized a quartet to go play at the Armory. The Armory is a huge military building where families of people missing from Tuesday's disaster go to wait for news of their loved ones. Entering the building was very difficult emotionally because the entire building (the size of a city block) was covered with missing posters. Thousands of posters, spread out up to eight feet above the ground, each featuring a different smiling face. I made my way into the huge central room and found my Juilliard buddies.

For two hours we sight-read quartets (with only three people!), and I don't think I will soon forget the grief counselor from the Connecticut State Police who listened the entire time, or the woman who listened only to "Memory" from *Cats*, crying the whole time. At 7:00 P.M., the other two players had to leave; they had been playing at the Armory since 1:00 P.M. and simply couldn't play anymore. I volunteered to stay and play solo, since I had just got there.

I soon realized that the evening had just begun for me: a man in fatigues who introduced himself as Sergeant Major asked me if I'd mind playing for his soldiers as they came back from digging through the rubble at Ground Zero. Masseuses had volunteered to give his men massages, he said, and he didn't think anything would be more soothing than getting a massage and listening to violin music at the same time. So at 9:00 P.M., I headed up to the second floor as the first men were arriving.

From then until 11:30 P.M., I played everything I could do from memory: Bach's *B Minor Partita*, Tchaikovsky's *Concerto*, Dvorak's *Concerto*, Paganini's *Caprices 1* and *17*, Vivaldi's *Winter* and *Spring*, "Theme from *Schindler's List*," Tchaikovsky's *Melodie*, "Meditation"

Vocabulary

fatigues (fə tēgz´) *n.* sturdy clothing worn by soldiers

Comprehension

What event did Juilliard organize?

▶ Rescue workers at Ground Zero

Vocabulary
intonation (in′ tō nā′ shən) *n.* the quality of playing musical notes in or out of tune

Vocabulary
regiment (rej′ ə mənt) *n.* a military unit

from *Thais,* "Amazing Grace," "My Country 'Tis of Thee," "Turkey in the Straw," "Bile Them Cabbages Down." Never have I played for a more grateful audience. Somehow it didn't matter that by the end, my **intonation** was shot and I had no bow control. I would have lost any competition I was playing in, but it didn't matter. The men would come up the stairs in full gear, remove their helmets, look at me, and smile.

At 11:20 P.M., I was introduced to Col. Slack, head of the regiment. After thanking me, he said to his friends, "Boy, today was the toughest day yet. I made the mistake of going back into the pit, and I'll never do that again."

Eager to hear a firsthand account, I asked, "What did you see?"

He stopped, swallowed hard, and said, "What you'd expect to see."

The Colonel stood there as I played a lengthy rendition of "Amazing Grace," which he claimed was the best he'd ever heard. By this time it was 11:30 P.M., and I didn't think I could play anymore. I asked Sergeant Major if it would be appropriate if I played the National Anthem. He shouted above the chaos of the milling soldiers to call them to attention, and I played the National Anthem as the 300 men of the 69th Regiment saluted an invisible flag.

After shaking a few hands and packing up, I was prepared to leave when one of the privates accosted me and told me the Colonel wanted to see me again. He took me down to the War Room, but we couldn't find the Colonel, so he gave me a tour of the War Room. It turns out that the division I played for is the Famous Fighting Sixty-Ninth, the most decorated **regiment** in the U.S. Army. He pointed out a letter from Abraham Lincoln offering his condolences after the

Battle of Antietam . . . the 69th suffered the most **casualties** of any regiment at that historic battle.

Finally, we located the Colonel. After thanking me again, he presented me with the coin of the regiment. “We only give these to someone who’s done something special for the 69th,” he informed me. He called over the division’s historian to tell me the significance of all the symbols on the coin.

As I rode the taxi back to Juilliard—free, of course, since taxi service is free in New York right now—I was numb. Not only was this evening the proudest I’ve ever felt to be an American, it was my most meaningful as a musician and a person as well.

At Juilliard, kids can be critical of each other and competitive. Teachers expect, and in many cases get, technical perfection. But this wasn’t about that. The soldiers didn’t care that I had so many memory slips I lost count. They didn’t care that when I forgot how the second movement of the Tchaikovsky went, I had to come up with my own insipid improvisation until I somehow (and I still don’t know how) got to a **cadence**. I’ve never seen a more appreciative audience, and I’ve never understood so fully what it means to communicate music to other people.

And how did it change me as a person? Let’s just say that, next time I want to get into a petty argument about whether Richter or Horowitz was better, I’ll remember that when I asked the Colonel to describe the pit formed by the tumbling of the Towers, he couldn’t. Words only go so far, and even music can only go a little further from there.

Vocabulary

casualties (kazh´ o͞ol tēz) *n.* members of the armed forces who die in combat

cadence (kād´ ns) *n.* series of notes or chords near the end of a musical work.

Critical Reading

Cite textual evidence to support your responses.

1. **Key Ideas and Details (a) Identify:** What unusual text feature appears in the second paragraph of Ramsay’s story? **(b) Analyze:** How does this feature add to your experience of reading the transcript?
2. **Key Ideas and Details (a)** Name three objects Ramsay sees on the walkway. **(b) Evaluate:** Which object has the greatest emotional impact on you? Why do you think this is so?
3. **Key Ideas and Details (a)** In the e-mail, why does Harvey say he has trouble entering the Armory? **(b) Draw Conclusions:** What does this detail tell you about the situation in New York?
4. **Key Ideas and Details (a)** In what tangible way is Harvey rewarded for his efforts? **(b) Infer:** What intangible gifts does he receive that evening?

Oral History Transcript • E-mail

Comparing Primary Sources

Refer to your Note-Taking Guide to complete these questions.

1. **(a)** Find two details that suggest Ramsay told his story aloud. **(b)** How is the language in Harvey's e-mail similar to and different from Ramsay's?
2. **(a)** Record the final image from each document in a chart like the one shown. Add a note about the background knowledge you bring to the image that helps you understand it. **(b)** Based on the image and on the larger historical event, draw a conclusion about the speaker's experience of events in New York City after 9/11.

	Visual Image	Background Knowledge	Conclusion
Urban Renewal			
Fighting 69th			

3. **(a)** In several paragraphs, explain inferences you drew from each document about the days immediately following 9/11. **(b)** In what ways is the information you derive from these documents similar and different? **(c)** Explain the reasons for these similarities and differences.

Vocabulary Acquisition and Use

Synonyms Replace each italicized word below with a synonym from the vocabulary list on page 1399. Use each word only once.

1. Tribute concerts might be *acts of respect* to great musicians.
2. Someone must *carefully* plan every detail of such an event.
3. Statues of heroes are fine *commemorations* of great achievements.

Content-Area Vocabulary Match each word on the left with a set of words on the right. Explain why the word belongs to that set.

4. fatigues
5. intonation
6. casualties
7. regiment
8. cadence

a. pitch, melody, tempo, dynamics
b. active duty, company, defense

Etymology Study The word *fatigues* comes from the Latin word *fatigare* meaning "to make weary." Use a reference source, such as an etymology dictionary, to explain how the word *fatigues* evolved from its Latin origin. Then, locate another word based on the same root and explain how its meaning is related to that of *fatigues*.

Common Core State Standards

Writing

1. Write arguments to support claims in an analysis of substantive topics or texts, using valid reasoning and relevant and sufficient evidence. *(p. 1407)*

7. Conduct sustained research projects to answer a question or solve a problem; narrow or broaden the inquiry when appropriate; synthesize multiple sources on the subject, demonstrating understanding of the subject under investigation. *(p. 1407)*

8. Gather relevant information from multiple authoritative print and digital sources. *(p. 1407)*

Language

4.c. Consult general and specialized reference materials, both print and digital, to find the etymology of a word.

5. Demonstrate understanding of word relationships.

6. Acquire and use accurately general academic and domain-specific words and phrases, sufficient for reading, writing, speaking, and listening at the college and career readiness level.

Research Task

Topic: The Value and Values of Memorials

The impromptu memorials described by Sean Ramsay and William Harvey embodied a wide range of human values. Throughout history, people have created memorials, whether local or national, spontaneous or planned, temporary or permanent. Why?

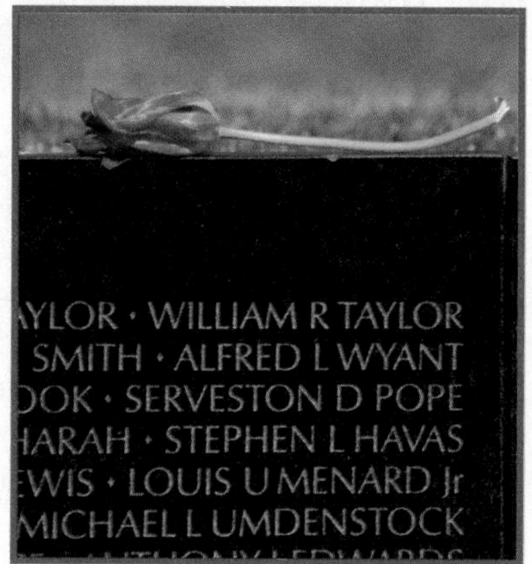

▲ A detail of the Vietnam Veterans Memorial in Washington, D.C., designed by Maya Lin

Assignment: Write a **persuasive article** that takes a stand on the value of a memorial. Conduct research that will allow you to provide an authoritative analysis of this subject. Use a variety of strategies to develop and support your opinion.

Formulate your research plan. To focus your research, pinpoint a specific type of memorial, recalling

- a battle or a war;
- a natural catastrophe or local disaster;
- a landmark event, such as a city founding;
- a heroic individual.

Formulate a meaningful research question. The answer to your research question will be your thesis, or controlling idea.

Gather sources. Use online and library searches to explore multiple sources and perspectives about existing and proposed memorials. Pay special attention to arguments *against* memorials, such as "Money could be better spent." This will help you better anticipate and refute counterarguments when drafting.

Synthesize information. Develop and support your opinion, as opposed to simply restating existing information. To do this, draw inferences from your research:

- What can you infer about people from memorials they create?
- What can you infer about people from their responses when they visit memorials?
- What can you infer about universal human values from the values exhibited or celebrated in memorials?

Organize and present your ideas. Use a variety of formats, including visual elements and rhetorical strategies, to argue for your thesis. For example, graphic organizers may be useful in compiling and presenting responses to counterarguments.

Model: Refuting Counterarguments

Counter-argument	My Response	My Support
Merely another sad reminder of violence	Reminder of the heroism needed to face violence	• Basic emotional need • Shouldn't ignore history • Prevent reoccurrence

RESEARCH TIP

Information from multiple sources may reveal discrepancies. Use asterisks or colored markers to note information from one source—such as a date, name, or cost—that is contradicted in another source.

Use a checklist like the one shown to ensure that your persuasive article is well-researched and well-argued.

Research Checklist

- ☐ Have I answered my main research question?
- ☐ Have I presented adequate support for my opinion?
- ☐ Have I used a variety of formats and rhetorical strategies to argue for my thesis?
- ☐ Have I addressed discrepancies and refuted counterarguments?

Building Knowledge and Insight

Mother Tongue • For the Love of Books

Connecting to the Essential Question The following essays by Amy Tan and Rita Dove explore the idea that the language we grow up with helps shape who we are. As you read, notice details that describe how relationships are strengthened—or weakened—through words. Doing so will help as you consider the Essential Question: **What makes American literature American?**

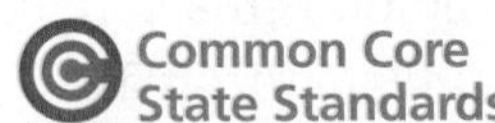

Reading Informational Text

1. Cite strong and thorough textual evidence to support analysis of what the text says explicitly as well as inferences drawn from the text, including determining where the text leaves matters uncertain.

2. Determine two or more central ideas of a text and analyze their development over the course of the text, including how they interact and build on one another to provide a complex analysis; provide an objective summary of the text.

5. Analyze and evaluate the effectiveness of the structure an author uses in his or her exposition or argument, including whether the structure makes points clear, convincing, and engaging.

Close Reading Focus

Reflective Essay

An essay is a short piece of nonfiction in which a writer explores his or her view of a topic. In a **reflective essay,** the writer describes a personal experience, condition, or event and reflects on its larger meanings. For example, Rita Dove focuses on the love of reading she has had since she was a child:

> *. . . always, I have been passionate about books. . . . I loved to feel their heft in my hand . . .*

In most reflective essays, the writer makes connections between personal experience and a larger or more universal idea about life.

Comparing Literary Works These two writers address the same central idea, or **theme:** the struggle to create a true sense of identity. As you read, examine how each writer describes the role played by other people in her creation of a genuine sense of self. Determine if a true sense of identity is to be discovered among our companions, in the recesses of our own privacy, or in some combination of the two.

Preparing to Read Complex Texts Regardless of its specific organizational structure, an effective essay presents ideas in a logical order. To better appreciate this logic and to clarify the meaning of an essay, **outline** the text as you read. Use a simple numbered list like the one shown to identify the central idea of each paragraph. Then, review the outline to trace how the writer sequences two or more central ideas to build meaning. Analyze ways in which these central ideas interact and build upon one another.

Main Ideas
Mother Tongue
1.
2.
3.
Love of Books
1.
2.
3.

Vocabulary

You will encounter the words listed here in the texts that follow. Copy the words into your notebook. Circle the word that is an antonym for *malignant*.

transcribed **daunting**
benign **aspirations**
ecstasy

Amy Tan (b. 1952)

Author of "Mother Tongue"

As a child, Amy Tan—the daughter of Chinese immigrants—answered her mother's Chinese questions in English. Growing up in Oakland, California, Tan continued to embrace typical American values, which she assumed defined her identity.

Early Years Tan's parents both came to America in search of a more peaceful life. Her father left his home to avoid the Chinese Civil War, while her mother found passage to America on the last boat to leave Shanghai before the Communist takeover of 1949. Her parents married and settled in Northern California, where they raised Amy and her two brothers.

Moving Abroad While still in her teens, tragedy struck Tan's family. Within a year, Amy's father and oldest brother both died of brain tumors. Mrs. Tan moved her surviving children to Switzerland, where Amy finished high school.

Changing Careers After graduating from college in America, Tan began a successful business writing career. Though she prospered financially, Tan found her work unfulfilling, and sought relief by playing piano and writing fiction. After publishing several short stories, Tan found an agent, who encouraged her to write full-time.

A Rich Background A trip to China with her mother kindled in Tan an appreciation of her Chinese roots. At the time, she was leaving a successful career as a business writer to become a fiction writer. When she returned to the United States, she began *The Joy Luck Club* (1989), a novel about four Chinese American women and their mothers. The book made Tan a celebrity and was followed by more novels, including *The Kitchen God's Wife* (1991), *The Hundred Secret Senses* (1995), and *The Bonesetter's Daughter* (2001).

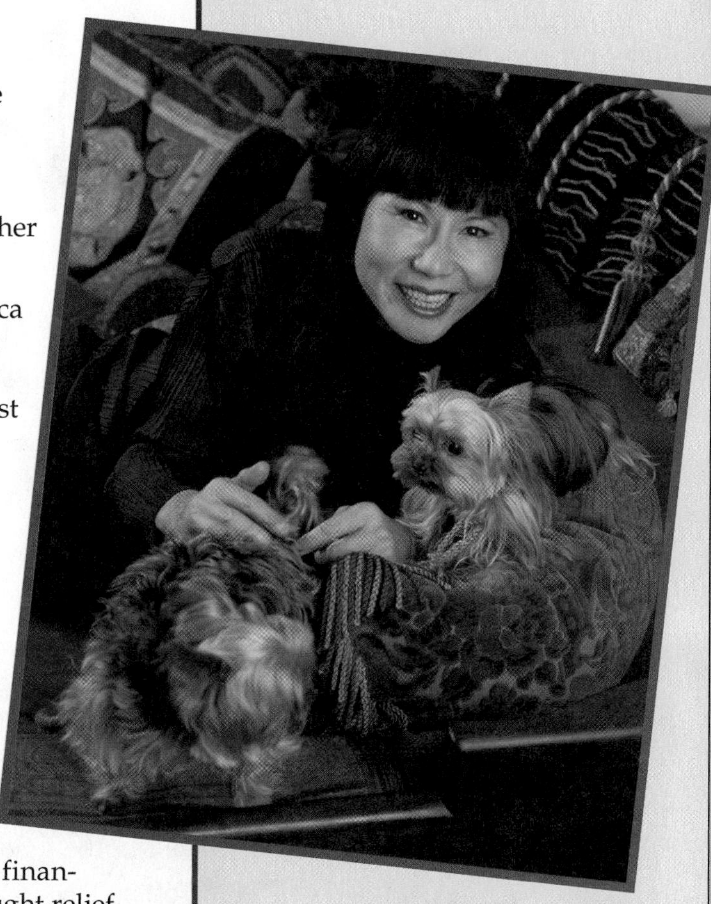

"I have a writer's memory which makes everything worse than maybe it actually was."

Mother Tongue

Amy Tan

I am not a scholar of English or literature. I cannot give you much more than personal opinions on the English language and its variations in this country or others.

I am a writer. And by that definition, I am someone who has always loved language. I am fascinated by language in daily life. I spend a great deal of my time thinking about the power of language—the way it can evoke an emotion, a visual image, a complex idea, or a simple truth. Language is the tool of my trade. And I use them all—all the Englishes I grew up with.

Recently, I was made keenly aware of the different Englishes I do use. I was giving a talk to a large group of people, the same talk I had already given to half a dozen other groups. The nature of the talk was about my writing, my life, and my book, *The Joy Luck Club.* The talk was going along well enough, until I remembered one major difference that made the whole talk sound wrong. My mother was in the room. And it was perhaps the first time she had heard me give a lengthy speech, using the kind of English I have never used with her. I was saying things like, "The intersection of memory upon imagination" and "There is an aspect of my fiction that relates to thus-and-thus"—a speech filled with carefully wrought grammatical phrases, burdened, it suddenly seemed to me, with nominalized forms, past perfect tenses, conditional phrases, all the forms of standard English that I had learned in school and through books, the forms of English I did not use at home with my mother.

Just last week, I was walking down the street with my mother, and I again found myself conscious of the English I was using, the English I do use with her. We were talking about the price of new and used furniture and I heard myself saying this: "Not waste money that way." My husband was with us as well, and he didn't notice any switch in my English. And then I realized why. It's because over the twenty years we've been together I've often used the same kind of English with him, and sometimes he even uses it with me. It has become our language of intimacy, a different sort of English that relates to family talk, the language I grew up with.

So you'll have some idea of what this family talk I heard sounds like, I'll quote what my mother said during a recent conversation which I videotaped and then **transcribed**.

During this conversation, my mother was talking about a political gangster in Shanghai[1] who had the same last name as her family's,

◀ Critical Viewing
Based on this photograph of Amy Tan and her mother, what kind of a relationship do you think they share? Explain. **INFER**

Theme
What theme do you see developing through Tan's thoughts about the use of language?

Vocabulary
transcribed (tran skrībd′) *v.* wrote or typed a copy

Comprehension
How does Tan's language change when she gives her speech?

1. **Shanghai** (shaŋ′ hī′) seaport city in eastern China.

Du, and how the gangster in his early years wanted to be adopted by her family, which was rich by comparison. Later, the gangster became more powerful, far richer than my mother's family, and one day showed up at my mother's wedding to pay his respects. Here's what she said in part:

"Du Yusong having business like fruit stand. Like off the street kind. He is Du like Du Zong—but not Tsung-ming Island people. The local people call putong, the river east side, he belong to that side local people. That man want to ask Du Zong father take him in like become own family. Du Zong father wasn't look down on him, but didn't take seriously, until that man big like become a mafia. Now important person, very hard to inviting him. Chinese way, come only to show respect, don't stay for dinner. Respect for making big celebration, he shows up. Mean gives lots of respect. Chinese custom. Chinese social life that way. If too important won't have to stay too long. He come to my wedding. I didn't see, I heard it. I gone to boy's side, they have YMCA[2] dinner. Chinese age I was nineteen."

You should know that my mother's expressive command of English belies how much she actually understands. She reads the *Forbes*[3] report, listens to *Wall Street Week*,[4] converses daily with her stockbroker, reads all of Shirley MacLaine's[5] books with ease—all kinds of things I can't begin to understand. Yet some of my friends tell me they understand 50 percent of what my mother says. Some say they understand 80 to 90 percent. Some say they understand none of it, as if she were speaking pure Chinese. But to me, my

▼ Critical Viewing

What do these signs in San Francisco's Chinatown district suggest about the multiple "Englishes" spoken there? **DISTINGUISH**

2. **YMCA** Young Men's Christian Association.
3. ***Forbes*** magazine of business and finance.
4. ***Wall Street Week*** weekly television program that reports business and investment news.
5. **Shirley MacLaine's** (mək lānz′) Shirley MacLaine is an American actress who has written several books.

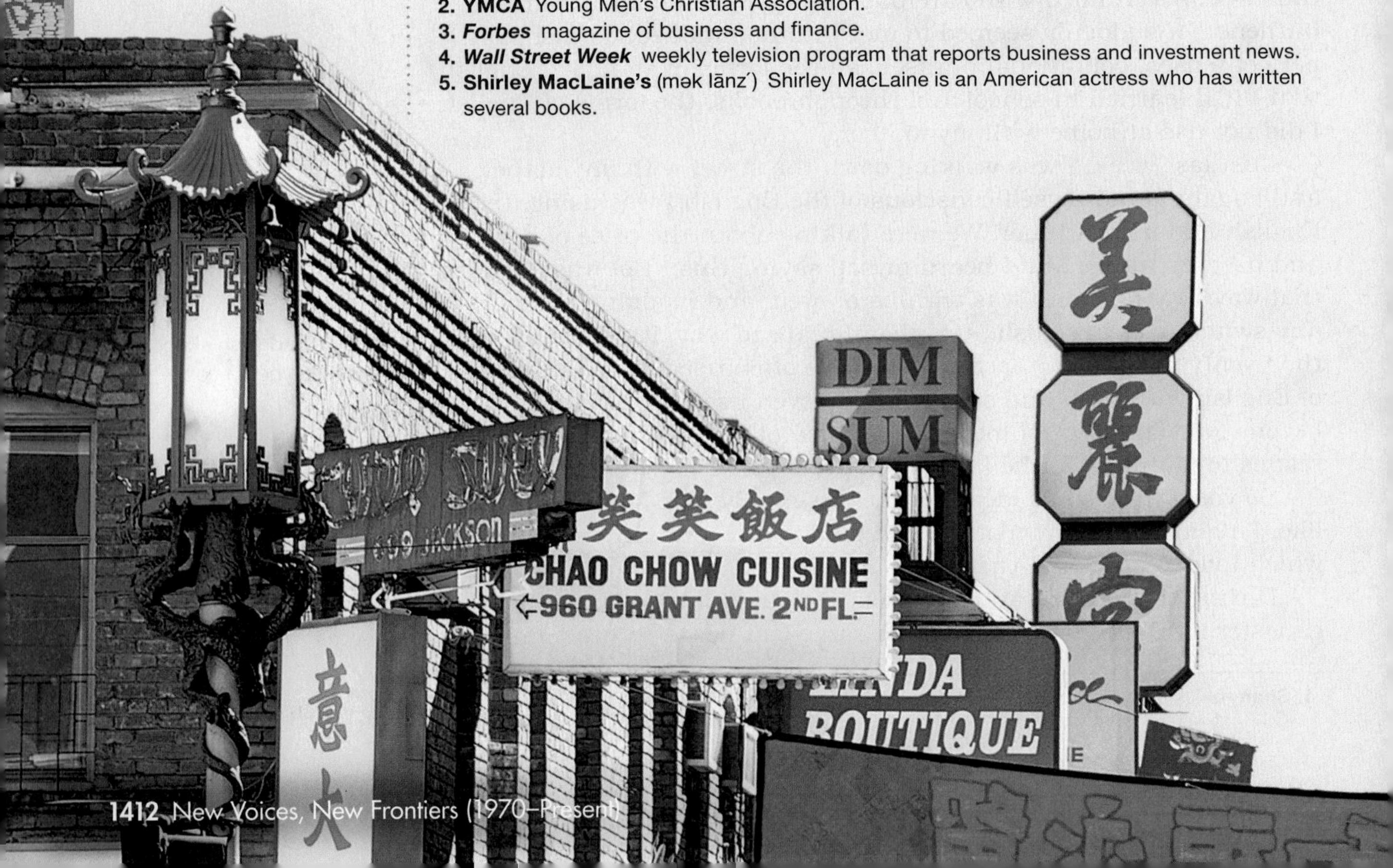

mother's English is perfectly clear, perfectly natural. It's my mother tongue. Her language, as I hear it, is vivid, direct, full of observation and imagery. That was the language that helped shape the way I saw things, expressed things, made sense of the world.

Lately, I've been giving more thought to the kind of English my mother speaks. Like others, I have described it to people as "broken," or "fractured" English. But I wince when I say that. It has always bothered me that I can think of no way to describe it other than "broken," as if it were damaged and needed to be fixed, as if it lacked a certain wholeness and soundness. I've heard other terms used, "limited English," for example. But they seem just as bad, as if everything is limited, including people's perceptions of the limited English speaker.

Reflective Essay
What specific words in this paragraph reinforce the idea that the essay is reflective?

I know this for a fact, because when I was growing up, my mother's "limited" English limited my perception of her. I was ashamed of her English. I believed that her English reflected the quality of what she had to say. That is, because she expressed them imperfectly her thoughts were imperfect. And I had plenty of empirical evidence to support me: the fact that people in department stores, at banks, and at restaurants did not take her seriously, did not give her good service, pretended not to understand her, or even acted as if they did not hear her.

My mother has long realized the limitations of her English as well. When I was fifteen, she used to have me call people on the phone to pretend I was she. In this guise, I was forced to ask for information or even to complain and yell at people who had been rude to her. One time it was a call to her stockbroker in New York. She had cashed out her small portfolio and it just so happened we were going to go to New York the next week, our very first trip outside California. I had to get on the phone and say in an adolescent voice that was not very convincing, "This is Mrs. Tan."

And my mother was standing in the back whispering loudly, "Why he don't send me check, already two weeks late. So mad he lie to me, losing me money."

And then I said in perfect English, "Yes, I'm getting rather concerned. You had agreed to send the check two weeks ago, but it hasn't arrived."

Then she began to talk more loudly. "What he want, I come to New York tell him front of his boss, you cheating me?" And I was trying to calm her down, make her be quiet, while telling the stockbroker, "I can't tolerate any more excuses. If I don't receive the check immediately, I am going to have to speak to your manager when I'm in New York next week." And sure enough, the following week there we were in front of this astonished stockbroker, and I was sitting there red-faced and quiet, and my mother, the real Mrs. Tan, was shouting at his boss in her impeccable broken English.

We used a similar routine just five days ago, for a situation that was far less humorous. My mother had gone to the hospital for an

Comprehension
How does Mrs. Tan's spoken English compare to her understanding of the language?

Vocabulary

benign (bi nīn′) *adj.* not malignant; not cancerous

appointment, to find out about a **benign** brain tumor a CAT scan[6] had revealed a month ago. She said she had spoken very good English, her best English, no mistakes. Still, she said, the hospital did not apologize when they said they had lost the CAT scan and she had come for nothing. She said they did not seem to have any sympathy when she told them she was anxious to know the exact diagnosis, since her husband and son had both died of brain tumors. She said they would not give her any more information until the next time and she would have to make another appointment for that. So she said she would not leave until the doctor called her daughter. She wouldn't budge. And when the doctor finally called her daughter, me, who spoke in perfect English—lo and behold—we had assurances the CAT scan would be found, promises that a conference call on Monday would be held, and apologies for any suffering my mother had gone through for a most regrettable mistake.

I think my mother's English almost had an effect on limiting my possibilities in life as well. Sociologists and linguists probably will tell you that a person's developing language skills are more influenced by peers. But I do think that the language spoken in the family, especially in immigrant families which are more insular, plays a large role in shaping the language of the child. And I believe that it affected my results on achievement tests, IQ tests, and the SAT.[7] While my English skills were never judged as poor, compared to math, English could not be considered my strong suit. In grade school I did moderately well, getting perhaps B's, sometimes B-pluses, in English and scoring perhaps in the sixtieth or seventieth percentile on achievement tests. But those scores were not good enough to override the opinion that my true abilities lay in math and science, because in those areas I achieved A's and scored in the ninetieth percentile or higher.

> I think my mother's English almost had an effect on limiting my possibilities in life as well.

This was understandable. Math is precise; there is only one correct answer. Whereas, for me at least, the answers on English tests were always a judgment call, a matter of opinion and personal experience. Those tests were constructed around items like fill-in-the-blank sentence completion, such as, "Even though Tom was _______, Mary thought he was _______." And the correct answer always seemed to be the most bland combinations of thoughts, for example, "Even though Tom was shy, Mary thought he was charming," with the grammatical structure "even though" limiting the correct answer to some sort of semantic opposites, so you wouldn't get answers like, "Even though Tom was foolish, Mary thought he was ridiculous." Well, according to my mother, there were very few limi-

Reflective Essay

What conflict between her personal sensibilities and the values of society does Tan highlight in this discussion of her English classes?

---

6. CAT scan method used by doctors to diagnose brain disorders.

7. SAT Scholastic Aptitude Test; national college entrance exam.

tations as to what Tom could have been and what Mary might have thought of him. So I never did well on tests like that.

The same was true with word analogies, pairs of words in which you were supposed to find some sort of logical, semantic relationship — for example, "*Sunset* is to *nightfall* as _______ is to _______." And here you would be presented with a list of four possible pairs, one of which showed the same kind of relationship: *red* is to *stoplight, bus* is to *arrival, chills* is to *fever, yawn* is to *boring.* Well, I could never think that way. I knew what the tests were asking, but I could not block out of my mind the images already created by the first pair, "*sunset* is to *nightfall*"—and I would see a burst of colors against a darkening sky, the moon rising, the lowering of a curtain of stars. And all the other pairs of words—red, bus, stoplight, boring—just threw up a mass of confusing images, making it impossible for me to sort out something as logical as saying: "A sunset precedes nightfall" is the same as "a chill precedes a fever." The only way I would have gotten that answer right would have been to imagine an associative situation, for example, my being disobedient and staying out past sunset, catching a chill at night, which turns into feverish pneumonia as punishment, which indeed did happen to me.

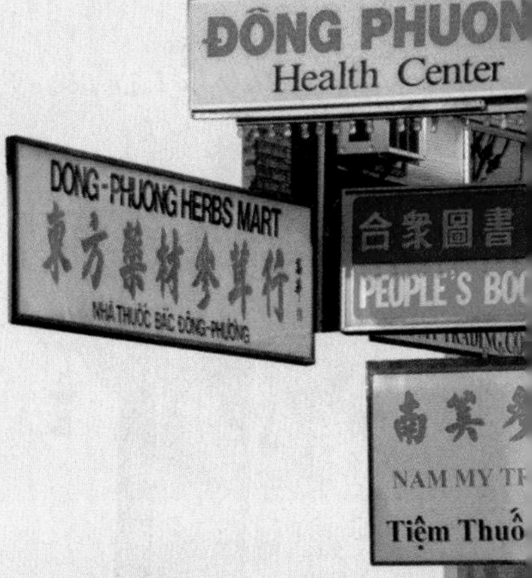

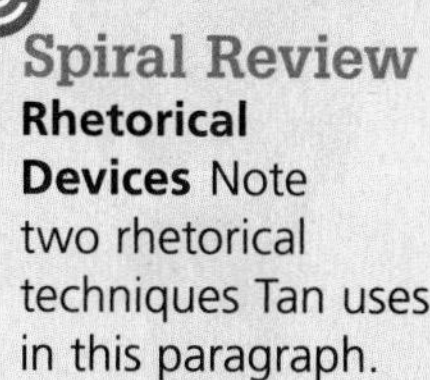

I have been thinking about all this lately, about my mother's English, about achievement tests. Because lately I've been asked, as a writer, why there are not more Asian Americans represented in American literature. Why are there few Asian Americans enrolled in creative writing programs? Why do so many Chinese students go into engineering? Well, these are broad sociological questions I can't begin to answer. But I have noticed in surveys—in fact, just last week—that Asian students, as a whole, always do significantly better on math achievement tests than in English. And this makes me think that there are other Asian-American students whose English spoken in the home might also be described as "broken" or "limited." And perhaps they also have teachers who are steering them away from writing and into math and science, which is what happened to me.

Spiral Review

Rhetorical Devices Note two rhetorical techniques Tan uses in this paragraph.

Fortunately, I happen to be rebellious in nature and enjoy the challenge of disproving assumptions made about me. I became an English major my first year in college, after being enrolled as pre-med. I started writing nonfiction as a freelancer the week after I was told by my former boss that writing was my worst skill and I should hone my talents toward account management.

But it wasn't until 1985 that I finally began to write fiction. And at first I wrote using what I thought to be wittily crafted sentences, sentences that would finally prove I had mastery over the English language. Here's an example from the first draft of a story that later made its way into *The Joy Luck Club,* but without this line: "That was my mental quandary in its nascent state." A terrible line, which I can barely pronounce.

Comprehension

What did Tan's "rebellious" nature move her to do?

Fortunately, for reasons I won't get into today, I later decided I should envision a reader for the stories I would write. And the reader I decided upon was my mother, because these were stories about mothers. So with this reader in mind—and in fact she did read my early drafts—I began to write stories using all the Englishes I grew up with: the English I spoke to my mother, which for lack of a better term might be described as "simple"; the English she used with me, which for lack of a better term might be described as "broken"; my translation of her Chinese, which could certainly be described as "watered down"; and what I imagined to be her translation of her Chinese if she could speak in perfect English, her internal language, and for that I sought to preserve the essence, but neither an English nor a Chinese structure. I wanted to capture what language ability tests can never reveal: her intent, her passion, her imagery, the rhythms of her speech and the nature of her thoughts.

Apart from what any critic had to say about my writing, I knew I had succeeded where it counted when my mother finished reading my book and gave me her verdict: "So easy to read."

Critical Reading

Cite textual evidence to support your responses.

1. **Key Ideas and Details (a)** What does Tan realize while speaking to an audience that includes her mother? **(b) Infer:** What circumstances account for Tan's having developed more than one "English"?
2. **Key Ideas and Details (a)** According to Tan, in what ways do math skills differ from language skills? **(b) Interpret:** In what ways did Tan's sense of different "Englishes" prevent her from answering correctly on grammar and standardized tests?
3. **Key Ideas and Details (a) Summarize:** Summarize one experience Tan had involving her mother's difficulty with Standard English. **(b) Compare and Contrast:** In what ways does Tan's sense of her mother's English differ from the perceptions of strangers?
4. **Key Ideas and Details Evaluate:** What influence has Tan's mother had on her daughter's writing? Support your answer.

Rita Dove *(b. 1952)*

Author of **"For the Love of Books"**

Education Rita Dove was born in Akron, Ohio, to highly educated parents. Encouraged to read from an early age, Dove excelled in school. Upon graduating from high school, she was invited to the White House as a Presidential scholar. Although her first writing efforts—at the age of nine or ten—had been comic books with female superheroes, she turned to poetry in college. Dove attended Miami University in Oxford, Ohio, and graduated with highest honors, winning a Fulbright Scholarship to study in Germany. From there, she continued her education at the famous Writers' Workshop at the University of Iowa.

Teacher and Poet Laureate While teaching creative writing at Arizona State University, Dove gained critical acclaim with several volumes of poetry. In 1987, she won the Pulitzer Prize for *Thomas and Beulah,* a collection of poems based on the lives of her grandparents. In 1993, she was appointed Poet Laureate of the United States, becoming the youngest person ever to hold that position. She has published many volumes of poetry since, including *On the Bus with Rosa Parks* (1999), and *American Smooth* (2004). Dove has also written a play, a novel, and a collection of short stories. "Every time I write a poem," Dove has said, "I try to imagine the reader—the reader that I was—curled up on the couch, at the moment of opening a book and absolutely having my world fall away and entering into another one."

"Poetry is language at its most distilled and most powerful."

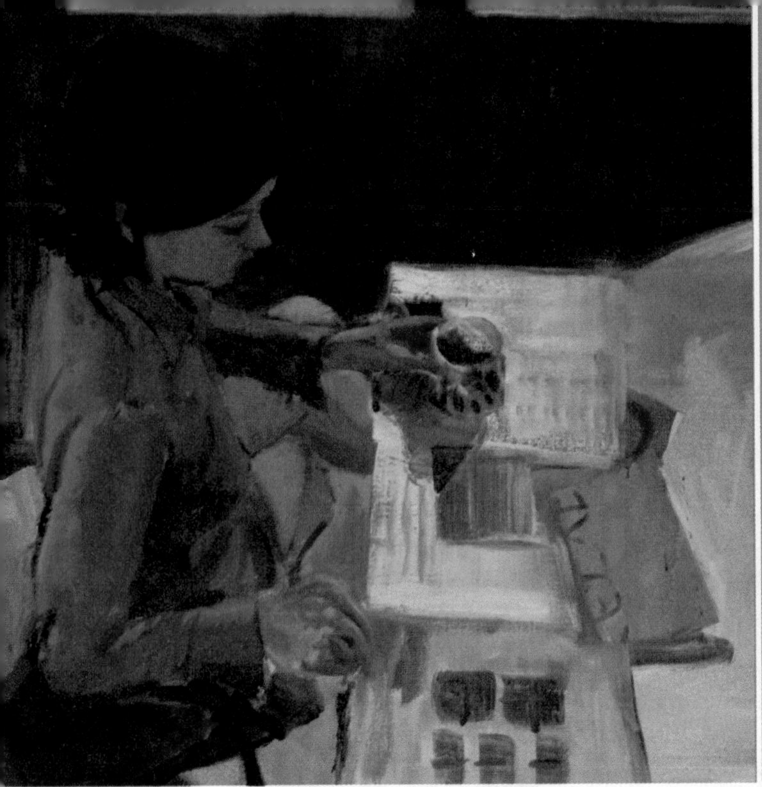

For the Love of Books

Rita Dove

▲ Critical Viewing
Do you think this image expresses the same love of books Dove felt as a child? **CONNECT**

Vocabulary
ecstasy (ek´ stə sē) *n.* a feeling of overpowering joy; great delight

Reflective Essay
Which elements in these first two paragraphs identify this work as a personal essay?

When I am asked: "What made you want to be a writer?" my answer has always been: "Books." First and foremost, now, then, and always, I have been passionate about books. From the time I began to read, as a child, I loved to feel their heft in my hand and the warm spot caused by their intimate weight in my lap; I loved the crisp whisper of a page turning, the musky odor of old paper and the sharp inky whiff of new pages. Leather bindings sent me into ecstasy. I even loved to gaze at a closed book and daydream about the possibilities inside—it was like contemplating a genie's lamp. Of course, my favorite fairy tale was *A Thousand and One Nights*—imagine buying your life with stories!—and my favorite cartoons were those where animated characters popped out of books and partied while the unsuspecting humans slept. In books, I could travel anywhere, be anybody, understand worlds long past and imaginary colonies in the future. My idea of a bargain was to go to the public library, wander along the bookshelves, and emerge with a chin-high stack of books that were mine, all mine, for two weeks—free of charge!

What I remember most about long summer days is browsing the bookshelves in our solarium to see if there were any new additions. I grew up with those rows of books; I knew where each one was shelved and immediately spotted newcomers. And after months had gone by and there'd be no new books, I would think: Okay, I guess I'll try this one—and then discover that the very book I had been avoiding because of a drab cover or small print was actually a wonderful read. Louis Untermeyer's *Treasury of Best Loved Poems* had a sickeningly sweet lilac and gold cover and was forbiddingly thick, but I finally pulled it off the shelf and discovered a cornucopia of emotional and linguistic delights, from "The Ballad of Barbara Fritchie," which I adored for its sheer length and rather numbing rhymes, to Langston Hughes's dazzlingly syncopated "Dream Boogie." Then there was Shakespeare—daunting for many years because it was his entire oeuvre,[1] in matching wine-red volumes that were so thick they looked more like over-sized bouillon cubes than books, and yet it was that ponderous title—*The Complete Works of William Shakespeare*—that enticed me, because here was a lifetime's work—a lifetime!—in two compact, dense packages. I began with the long poem "The Rape of Lucrece" . . . I sampled a few sonnets, which I found beautiful but rather adult; and finally wandered into the plays—first *Romeo and Juliet*, then *Macbeth, Julius Caesar, A Midsummer Night's Dream, Twelfth Night*—enthralled by the language, by the fact that poetry was spinning the story. Of course I did not understand every single word, but I was too young to know that this was supposed to be difficult; besides, no one was waiting to test me on anything, so, free from pressure, I dove in.

Vocabulary
daunting (dônt′ iŋ) *adj.* intimidating

At the same time, my brother, two years my senior, had become a science fiction buff, so I'd read his *Analog* and *Fantasy* and Science Fiction magazines after he was finished with them. One story particularly fascinated me: A retarded boy in a small town begins building a sculpture in his backyard, using old and discarded materials —coke bottles, scrap iron, string, and bottle caps. Everyone laughs at him, but he continues building. Then one day he disappears. And when the neighbors investigate, they discover that the sculpture has been dragged onto the back porch and that the screen door is open. Somehow the narrator of the story figures out how to switch on the sculpture: The back door frame begins to glow, and when he steps through it, he's in an alternate universe, a town the mirror image of his own—even down to the colors, with green roses and an orange sky. And he walks through this town until he comes to the main square, where there is a statue erected to—who else?—the village idiot.

I loved this story, the idea that the dreamy, mild, scatter-brained boy of one world could be the hero of another. And in a way, I identified with that village idiot because in real life I was painfully shy and awkward; the place where I felt most alive was between the pages of a book.

Vocabulary
aspirations (as′ pə rā′ shənz) *n.* strong desires or ambitions

Although I loved books, for a long time I had no aspirations to be a writer. The possibility was beyond my imagination. I liked to write, however—and on long summer days when I ran out of reading material or my legs had fallen asleep because I had been curled up

Comprehension
What made Dove want to be a writer?

---

1. **oeuvre** (ë′ vrə) *n.* all the works, usually of a lifetime, of a particular writer, artist, or composer.

on the couch for hours on end, I made up my own stories. Most were abandoned midway. Those that I did bring to a conclusion I neither showed to others nor considered saving.

My first piece of writing I thought enough of to keep was a novel called *Chaos*, which was about robots taking over the earth. I had just entered third or fourth grade; the novel had forty-three chapters, and each chapter was twenty lines or less because I used each week's spelling list as the basis for each chapter, and there were twenty words per list. In the course of the year I wrote one installment per week, and I never knew what was going to happen next—the words led me, not the other way around.

> . . . I never knew what was going to happen next—the words led me, not the other way around.

At that time I didn't think of writing as an activity people admited doing. I had no living role models—a "real" writer was a long-dead white male, usually with a white beard to match. Much later, when I was in eleventh grade, my English teacher, Miss Oechsner, took me to a book-signing in a downtown hotel. She didn't ask me if I'd like to go—she asked my parents instead, signed me and a classmate (who is now a professor of literature) out of school one day, and took us to meet a writer. The writer was John Ciardi, a poet who also had translated Dante's *Divine Comedy*, which I had heard of, vaguely. At that moment I realized that writers were real people and how it was possible to write down a poem or story in the intimate sphere of one's own room and then share it with the world.

Critical Reading

Cite textual evidence to support your responses.

1. **Key Ideas and Details (a)** Which emotion did Dove feel in the presence of an unopened book? **(b) Interpret:** For Dove, what traits did an unopened book and a genie's lamp share? **(c) Analyze:** What attitude toward the imagination is suggested by this simile?
2. **Key Ideas and Details (a)** What happens in the science fiction story that Dove enjoys so much? **(b) Connect:** Why is the story especially meaningful to Dove?
3. **Key Ideas and Details (a)** Which experience made Dove realize that she could be a "real" writer? **(b) Speculate:** Do you think Dove would have gone on to become a writer if she had not had that experience? Why or why not?
4. **Integration of Knowledge and Ideas** What do these essays suggest about the ways language itself makes or breaks connections among people, both within families and communities? In your response, use at least two of these Essential Question words: *alienation, transformation, community, identity, self-reliance. **[Connecting to the Essential Question: What makes American literature American?]***

Close Reading Activities

Mother Tongue • For the Love of Books

Literary Analysis

1. **Key Ideas and Details** Consult the **outline** you made as you read Amy Tan's essay. **(a)** What central idea does Tan introduce in her first paragraph? **(b)** How does she develop or extend that idea in paragraphs 2 through 4? **(c)** How does Tan's inclusion of her mother's story about the Chinese gangster relate to the ideas with which she introduces the essay?
2. **Craft and Structure** **(a)** In this **reflective essay,** how does Tan describe her changing attitudes toward her mother? **(b)** What role does language play in shaping those attitudes?
3. **Key Ideas and Details** **(a)** What books does Dove say most delighted her as a child? **(b)** What point is Dove making about the imaginative life of a child through this catalog of her favorite literature?
4. **Key Ideas and Details** **(a)** What general question does Dove address in this essay? **(b)** What ultimate insight does Dove state in her final paragraph?
5. **Integration of Knowledge and Ideas** Based on these two examples, why might an author write a reflective essay rather than fiction or poetry to explore a specific subject?
6. **Comparing Literary Works** Compare and contrast the ways in which Tan's and Dove's relationships to words and books shaped their careers as writers. Use a chart like the one shown to organize your thinking.

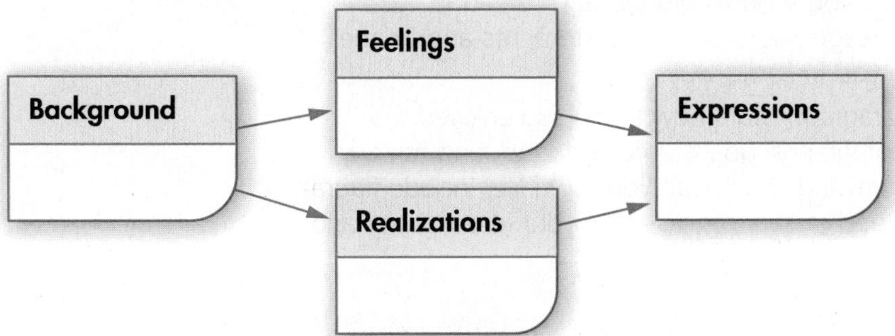

7. **Comparing Literary Works** **(a)** What evidence do you find in these reflective essays related to the **theme** that one must struggle or sacrifice to create a true sense of identity? **(b)** Explain why a reflective essay is a particularly suitable literary form to explore this theme.
8. **Comparing Literary Works** **(a)** In what ways do these authors' inner lives contrast—or conflict—with the outside world? **(b)** What role does writing play in the relationship between each writer's inner and outer life?

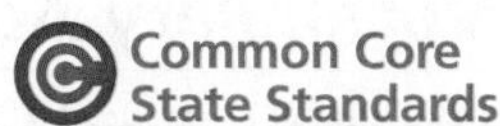

Common Core State Standards

Writing

2. Write informative texts to examine and convey complex ideas, concepts, and information clearly and accurately through the effective selection, organization, and analysis of content. *(p. 1422)*

2.d Use precise language and techniques such as metaphor, simile, and analogy to manage the complexity of the topic. *(p. 1422)*

Language

3. Apply knowledge of language to understand how language functions in different contexts, to make effective choices for meaning or style, and to comprehend more fully when reading or listening. *(p. 1423)*

4.b. Identify and correctly use patterns of word changes that indicate different meanings or parts of speech. *(p. 1422)*

Close Reading Activities Continued

Vocabulary Acquisition and Use

Word Analysis: Latin Root *-scrib-, -script-*

The word *transcribe,* which means "write out or type out in full," is formed from the Latin root *-scrib-,* which means "write." Using each pair of words below, write a sentence that demonstrates the meaning of this root. If necessary, use a dictionary to aid your work.

1. scribble, child
2. prescription, doctor
3. inscription, trophy
4. author, manuscript
5. playwright, script
6. proscription, legislator

Vocabulary: Sentence Completions

Complete each sentence by filling in each blank with a vocabulary word from the list on page 1408. Explain your choices.

1. The idea of speaking in front of so many highly qualified colleagues is ______.
2. The huge hot fudge sundaes sent the children into a state of ______.
3. The kindly old woman had a ______ influence on her children.
4. One of his many ______ is traveling to all seven continents before turning forty.
5. The archaeologist ______ the message that was carved on the wall of the tomb.

Writing to Sources

Informative Text Write a **letter to the author** of the essay you found most interesting. Explain what you liked, what you did not like, and ask any questions you might have.

Prewriting Choose the essay you wish to discuss and reread it. Take notes about the author's message and style. List statements and images that you like, or that disturb you in some way.

Drafting In your opening paragraph, state how much you enjoyed the essay and why. In the body paragraphs, go into greater detail, and ask any relevant questions. Consider drawing parallels to your own life. Include figurative language, such as similes and metaphors, to make your ideas clearer and more interesting. For example, consider modeling a simile after Tan's description of books "so thick they looked more like over-sized bouillon cubes . . ."

Revising Review your letter, and determine whether or not you have used the best language to communicate your thoughts. Replace any vague words with more specific ones.

Model: Revising to Include Precise Language

I enjoyed the way you ~~stated~~ captured your mother's English in the anecdote of the Shanghai gangster. ~~It~~ This example of her speech helped me to see my own prejudices. The ~~point~~ incident you ~~added~~ described with the stockbroker made your mother's struggle very clear.

Replacing vague references with precise words and phrases more accurately conveys ideas.

Conventions and Style: Using Parallel Structure

In your writing, work to express equal ideas using the same grammatical structures. This creates **parallel structure,** the use of similar patterns of words to show that two or more ideas have a close relationship and level of importance. Below are some examples of sentences rewritten to make nouns, phrases, and clauses parallel. Notice that the coordinating conjunction *and* is a clue to the presence of similar ideas in sentences.

Non-Parallel	Parallel
She spoke about her writing, life, and her book.	She spoke about her writing, her life, and her book.
Reading developed her imagination, and it inspired her to become a writer.	Reading developed her imagination and inspired her to become a writer.
She loved reading books, smelled their musky odor, and hearing their crisp pages turn.	She loved reading books, smelling their musky odor, and hearing their crisp pages turn.

Practice Rewrite each item to correct the non-parallel structure.

1. Reading as a child influenced her life and being a writer.
2. Good writers create stories that are believable, vivid, and to be enjoyed.
3. She writes easily, steadily, and in a clear way.
4. Words call up emotions, ideas, and helps to see images.
5. The writer videotaped and then wrote a transcription of the conversation.
6. Having a rebellious nature and adventurous can lead to success.
7. She read books as a child, and wrote them when she was an adult.
8. The teacher says that I have writing ability but I need to follow the rules.
9. She enjoys reading Shakespeare as much as reading science fiction pleases her brother.
10. She was Chinese, a woman, and living in a family as the only daughter.

Writing and Speaking Conventions

A. Writing Use the following items to write sentences with parallel structure.

1. English, Chinese
2. in math, in science, in English
3. judgment, opinion, experience
4. read, listen, talk
5. grades, tests, scores

Example: English, Chinese

Sentence: Mrs. Tan understands English as well as she speaks Chinese.

B. Speaking Deliver an explanation of something you did that you never thought possible, such as writing a prize-winning story or doing well on an achievement test. Use at least two examples of parallel structure.

Connecting to the Essential Question These selections explore the relationship between heritage and homeland. As you read, look for details that reveal the writers' feelings about the settings. Doing so will help you think about the Essential Question: **What is the relationship between literature and place?**

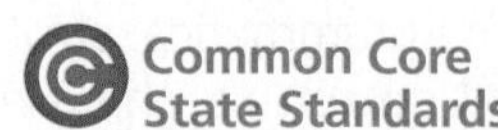

Reading Informational Text
6. Determine an author's point of view or purpose in a text in which the rhetoric is particularly effective, analyzing how style and content contribute to the power, persuasiveness or beauty of the text.

Close Reading Focus

Memoir

Memoirs are nonfiction narratives that recount events in which the writer was a participant or eyewitness. Memoirs are, by definition, acts of memory shaped by literary skill. Often, the memoirist sets personal reflections against historical or cultural landscapes. For example, these lines from Kingston's memoir weave the personal and the historical:

> *These new immigrants had it easy. On Ellis Island*
> *the people were thin after forty days at sea . . .*

Both Kingston and Momaday skillfully incorporate details of culture, place, and history into their recollections of events from their lives.

Comparing Literary Works These selections are now classic works of American memoir, noteworthy in many ways. As you read, consider how the two works are similar and different. For example, the two writers use language very differently. In addition, Momaday relates his experiences from the **first-person point of view.** Kingston, however, uses the **limited third-person point of view,** referring to both herself and her own mother, Brave Orchid, as *she*. As you read these memoirs, examine how the authors' uses of language and choices of point of view help to shape the meaning and power of their work.

Preparing to Read Complex Texts If you have ever loved a pet or listened to relatives tell stories, you can relate to these memoirs. To appreciate these memoirs more deeply, **relate them to your own experience.** As you read, use a chart like the one shown to record the connections you make between the writers' experiences and your own life.

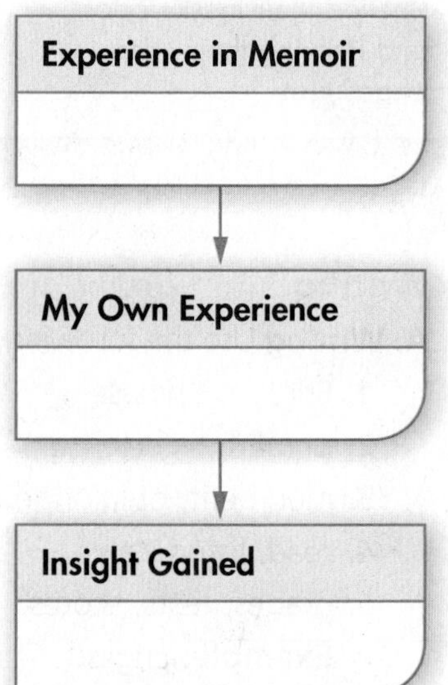

Vocabulary

The words below are important to understanding the texts that follow. Copy the words into your notebook, sorting them into words you know and words you do not know.

inaudibly
gravity
oblivious
pastoral
supple

Maxine Hong Kingston

(b. 1940)

Author of *The Woman Warrior*

"I was born to be a writer," Maxine Hong Kingston once told an interviewer. "In the midst of any adventure, a born writer has a desire to hurry home and put it into words."

Crossing Cultures Although Kingston was born in America, she did not begin describing her adventures in English until she was nearly ten because the language her family spoke at home was Say Yup, a Chinese dialect spoken around Canton, now known as Guangzhou, China. Kingston's parents came from a village near Guangzhou. Her father left first for "the Golden Mountain" of America and settled in New York City. His training as a poet and calligrapher was unmarketable in the United States, so he earned a living working in the laundry business. Kingston's mother, who was trained as a midwife, used the money her husband sent home to run a clinic in their native village. She did so until 1939, when she escaped war-torn China and joined her husband. Not long afterward, the couple resettled in Stockton, California, where Maxine Hong was born.

Building a Love for Story Young Maxine, whose Chinese name is Ting Ting, was a shy and quiet girl who repeated kindergarten because she spoke very little English. While at home, however, she listened intently to the stories told by family members and friends; this love of storytelling later influenced her writing style as Kingston developed her own "talk stories." By the time she was nine years old, she had mastered English and begun writing poetry. Soon, she began to earn straight A's in school.

A Bestseller Kingston shot to success with her first and best-known book, *The Woman Warrior: Memoirs of a Girlhood Among Ghosts*. The subtitle refers to the pale "ghosts" of white America, as well as the ghosts of the narrator's ancestors in China. *The Woman Warrior*, a unique blend of folklore, myth, feminism, and autobiography, won a National Book Critics' Circle Award in 1976.

Kingston earned a National Book Critics' Circle Award a second time, in 1980, for *China Men*, which chronicles the lives of three generations of Chinese men in America. A methodical writer, Kingston labors over numerous revisions to her books. Her latest book is *Veterans of War, Veterans of Peace* (2006), which transforms the horrors experienced by veterans of World War II, Vietnam, and Iraq into words and stories from which they can draw strength.

from The Woman Warrior

Maxine Hong Kingston

▲ Critical Viewing
What is your impression of the relationship between the mother and daughter in this photograph? Explain. **INFER**

BACKGROUND *The Woman Warrior* is an innovative memoir that attempts to capture the experience of growing up in a bicultural world—part Chinese, part American. To accomplish her purpose, Kingston mingles the narrative with "talk stories," tales full of magical events that she heard as a girl from her mother, Brave Orchid. The subtitle of the book, *Memoir of a Girlhood Among Ghosts*, refers both to white America, whose pale inhabitants remind Brave Orchid of ghosts, and to the family's ancestors in China. In this excerpt, Brave Orchid reunites with her sister, one of the ghosts of her past.

When she was about sixty-eight years old, Brave Orchid took a day off to wait at San Francisco International Airport for the plane that was bringing her sister to the United States. She had not seen Moon Orchid for thirty years. She had begun this waiting at home, getting up a half-hour before Moon Orchid's plane took off in Hong Kong.[1] Brave Orchid would add her will power to the forces that keep an airplane up. Her head hurt with the concentration. The plane had to be light, so no matter how tired she felt, she dared not rest her spirit on a wing but continuously and gently pushed up on the plane's belly. She had already been waiting at the airport for nine hours. She was wakeful.

Next to Brave Orchid sat Moon Orchid's only daughter, who was helping her aunt wait. Brave Orchid had made two of her own children come too because they could drive, but they had been lured away by the magazine racks and the gift shops and coffee shops. Her American children could not sit for very long. They did not understand sitting; they had wandering feet. She hoped they would get back from the pay TV's or the pay toilets or wherever they were spending their money before the plane arrived. If they did not come back soon, she would go look for them. If her son thought he could hide in the men's room, he was wrong.

Memoirs

Whose impressions are described in this passage about "her American children"?

"Are you all right, Aunt?" asked her niece.

"No, this chair hurts me. Help me pull some chairs together so I can put my feet up."

She unbundled a blanket and spread it out to make a bed for herself. On the floor she had two shopping bags full of canned peaches, real peaches, beans wrapped in taro leaves,[2] cookies, Thermos bottles,[3] enough food for everybody, though only her niece would eat with her. Her bad boy and bad girl were probably sneaking hamburgers, wasting their money. She would scold them.

Many soldiers and sailors sat about, oddly calm, like little boys in cowboy uniforms. (She thought "cowboy" was what you would call a Boy Scout.) They should have been crying hysterically on their way to Vietnam.[4] "If I see one that looks Chinese," she thought, "I'll go over and give him some advice." She sat up suddenly; she had forgotten about her own son, who was even now in Vietnam. Carefully she split her attention, beaming half of it to the ocean, into the water to keep him afloat. He was on a ship. He was in Vietnamese waters. She was sure of it. He and the other children were lying to her. They had said he was in Japan, and then they said he was in the Philippines. But

Comprehension

Who is Brave Orchid waiting to meet?

---

1. **took off in Hong Kong** After mainland China fell to the Communists in the late 1940s, many native Chinese fled first to Hong Kong (a British colony until 1997) before immigrating to the United States.
2. **taro** (te´ rō) **leaves** leaves of an edible tuberous plant widely eaten in Asia.
3. **Thermos** (thʉr´ məs) **bottles** insulated containers for holding liquids and keeping them warm or cold.
4. **Vietnam** southeast Asian nation where, in the late 1960s when this selection takes place, the U.S. had joined the conflict known as the Vietnam War (1954–1975).

Relating to Your Own Experiences

Can you relate to Brave Orchid's feeling that her family is keeping something from her?

Memoirs

What historical detail does Kingston include in this passage?

when she sent him her help, she could feel that he was on a ship in Da Nang.[5] Also she had seen the children hide the envelopes that his letters came in.

"Do you think my son is in Vietnam?" she asked her niece, who was dutifully eating.

"No. Didn't your children say he was in the Philippines?"

"Have you ever seen any of his letters with Philippine stamps on them?"

"Oh, yes. Your children showed me one."

"I wouldn't put it past them to send the letters to some Filipino they know. He puts Manila[6] postmarks on them to fool me."

"Yes, I can imagine them doing that. But don't worry. Your son can take care of himself. All your children can take care of themselves."

"Not him. He's not like other people. Not normal at all. He sticks erasers in his ears, and the erasers are still attached to the pencil stubs. The captain will say, 'Abandon ship,' or 'Watch out for bombs,' and he won't hear. He doesn't listen to orders. I told him to flee to Canada,[7] but he wouldn't go."

She closed her eyes. After a short while, plane and ship under control, she looked again at the children in uniforms. Some of the blond ones looked like baby chicks, their crew cuts like the downy yellow on baby chicks. You had to feel sorry for them even though they were Army and Navy Ghosts.

Suddenly her son and daughter came running. "Come, Mother. The plane's landed early. She's here already." They hurried, folding up their mother's encampment. She was glad her children were not useless. They must have known what this trip to San Francisco was about then. "It's a good thing I made you come early," she said.

Brave Orchid pushed to the front of the crowd. She had to be in front. The passengers were separated from the people waiting for them by glass doors and walls. Immigration Ghosts were stamping papers. The travellers crowded along some conveyor belts to have their luggage searched. Brave Orchid did not see her sister anywhere. She stood watching for four hours. Her children left and came back. "Why don't you sit down?" they asked.

"The chairs are too far away," she said.

"Why don't you sit on the floor then?"

No, she would stand, as her sister was probably standing in a line she could not see from here. Her American children had no feelings and no memory.

To while away time, she and her niece talked about the Chinese

5. **Da Nang** (dä naŋ) city in central Vietnam that was the site of an important U.S. military base during the Vietnam War; also spelled Danang.
6. **Manila** (mə nil′ ə) capital of the Philippines.
7. **flee to Canada** During the Vietnam War era, thousands of Americans fled to Canada to escape the military draft, even though such draft dodgers were subject to prosecution upon returning to the U.S.

passengers. These new immigrants had it easy. On Ellis Island[8] the people were thin after forty days at sea and had no fancy luggage.

"That one looks like her," Brave Orchid would say.

"No, that's not her."

Ellis Island had been made out of wood and iron. Here everything was new plastic, a ghost trick to lure immigrants into feeling safe and spilling their secrets. Then the Alien Office could send them right back. Otherwise, why did they lock her out, not letting her help her sister answer questions and spell her name? At Ellis Island when the ghost asked Brave Orchid what year her husband had cut off his pigtail, a Chinese who was crouching on the floor motioned her not to talk. "I don't know," she had said. If it weren't for that Chinese man, she might not be here today, or her husband either. She hoped some Chinese, a janitor or a clerk, would look out for Moon Orchid. Luggage conveyors fooled immigrants into thinking the Gold Mountain was going to be easy.

Memoirs
How does Brave Orchid's memory of Ellis Island convey the challenges experienced by immigrants at that place and time?

Brave Orchid felt her heart jump—Moon Orchid. "There she is," she shouted. But her niece saw it was not her mother at all. And it shocked her to discover the woman her aunt was pointing out. This was a young woman, younger than herself, no older than Moon Orchid the day the sisters parted. "Moon Orchid will have changed a little, of course," Brave Orchid was saying. "She will have learned to wear western clothes." The woman wore a navy blue suit with a bunch of dark cherries at the shoulder.

"Moon Orchid will have changed a little, of course."

"No, Aunt," said the niece. "That's not my mother."

"Perhaps not. It's been so many years. Yes, it is your mother. It must be. Let her come closer, and we can tell. Do you think she's too far away for me to tell, or is it my eyes getting bad?"

"It's too many years gone by," said the niece.

Brave Orchid turned suddenly—another Moon Orchid, this one a neat little woman with a bun. She was laughing at something the person ahead of her in line said. Moon Orchid was just like that, laughing at nothing. "I would be able to tell the difference if one of them would only come closer," Brave Orchid said with tears, which she did not wipe. Two children met the woman with the cherries, and she shook their hands. The other woman was met by a young man. They looked at each other gladly, then walked away side by side.

Up close neither one of those women looked like Moon Orchid at all. "Don't worry, Aunt," said the niece. "I'll know her."

"I'll know her too. I knew her before you did."

The niece said nothing, although she had seen her mother only five years ago. Her aunt liked having the last word.

Finally Brave Orchid's children quit wandering and drooped on a railing. Who knew what they were thinking? At last the niece called out, "I see her! I see her! Mother! Mother!" Whenever the doors parted,

Comprehension
Why does Brave Orchid worry about her son?

8. **Ellis Island** island in the harbor off New York City that was the chief U.S. immigration station from 1892 to 1943.

she shouted, probably embarrassing the American cousins, but she didn't care. She called out, "Mama! Mama!" until the crack in the sliding doors became too small to let in her voice. "Mama!" What a strange word in an adult voice. Many people turned to see what adult was calling, "Mama!" like a child. Brave Orchid saw an old, old woman jerk her head up, her little eyes blinking confusedly, a woman whose nerves leapt toward the sound anytime she heard "Mama!" Then she relaxed to her own business again. She was a tiny, tiny lady, very thin, with little fluttering hands, and her hair was in a gray knot. She was dressed in a gray wool suit; she wore pearls around her neck and in her earlobes. Moon Orchid *would* travel with her jewels showing. Brave Orchid momentarily saw, like a larger, younger outline around this old woman, the sister she had been waiting for. The familiar dim halo faded, leaving the woman so old, so gray. So old. Brave Orchid pressed against the glass. *That* old lady? Yes, that old lady facing the ghost who stamped her papers without questioning her was her sister. Then, without noticing her family, Moon Orchid walked smiling over to the Suitcase Inspector Ghost, who took her boxes apart, pulling out puffs of tissue. From where she was, Brave Orchid could not see what her sister had chosen to carry across the ocean. She wished her sister would look her way. Brave Orchid thought that if she were entering a new country, she would be at the windows. Instead Moon Orchid

▼ Critical Viewing

How might life in the city of San Francisco, shown in this image, compare with life in Hong Kong, from where Moon Orchid has just arrived? **COMPARE AND CONTRAST**

hovered over the unwrapping, surprised at each reappearance as if she were opening presents after a birthday party.

"Mama!" Moon Orchid's daughter kept calling. Brave Orchid said to her children, "Why don't you call your aunt too? Maybe she'll hear us if all of you call out together." But her children slunk away. Maybe that shame-face they so often wore was American politeness.

"Mama!" Moon Orchid's daughter called again, and this time her mother looked right at her. She left her bundles in a heap and came running. "Hey!" the Customs Ghost yelled at her. She went back to clear up her mess, talking inaudibly to her daughter all the while. Her daughter pointed toward Brave Orchid. And at last Moon Orchid looked at her—two old women with faces like mirrors.

Their hands reached out as if to touch the other's face, then returned to their own, the fingers checking the grooves in the forehead and along the sides of the mouth. Moon Orchid, who never understood the gravity of things, started smiling and laughing, pointing at Brave Orchid. Finally Moon Orchid gathered up her stuff, strings hanging and papers loose, and met her sister at the door, where they shook hands, oblivious to blocking the way.

"You're an old woman," said Brave Orchid.

"Aiaa. *You're* an old woman."

Vocabulary

inaudibly (in ôd′ə blē) *adv.* in a manner that cannot be heard

gravity (grav′ i tē) *n.* seriousness

oblivious (ə bliv′ ē əs) *adj.* lacking all awareness

Comprehension

What aspect of Moon Orchid's appearance most surprises Brave Orchid?

"But *you* are really old. Surely, you can't say that about me. I'm not old the way you're old."

"But you really are old. You're one year older than I am."

"Your hair is white and your face all wrinkled."

"You're so skinny."

"You're so fat."

"Fat women are more beautiful than skinny women."

The children pulled them out of the door-way. One of Brave Orchid's children brought the car from the parking lot, and the other heaved the luggage into the trunk. They put the two old ladies and the niece in the back seat. All the way home—across the Bay Bridge,[9] over the Diablo hills,[10] across the San Joaquin River[11] to the valley, the valley moon so white at dusk—all the way home, the two sisters exclaimed every time they turned to look at each other, "Aiaa! How old!"

"You're so old . . . How did you get so old?"

Brave Orchid forgot that she got sick in cars, that all vehicles but palanquins[12] made her dizzy. "You're so old," she kept saying. "How did you get so old?"

Brave Orchid had tears in her eyes. But Moon Orchid said, "You look older than I. You *are* older than I," and again she'd laugh. "You're wearing an old mask to tease me." It surprised Brave Orchid that after thirty years she could still get annoyed at her sister's silliness.

9. **Bay Bridge** one of the bridges across San Francisco Bay.
10. **Diablo** (dē äb′ lō) **hills** hills outside San Francisco.
11. **San Joaquin** (wô kēn′) **River** river of central California; its valley is one of the state's richest agricultural areas.
12. **palanquins** (pal′ ən kēnz′) hand-carried covered litters once widely used to transport people in China and elsewhere in eastern Asia.

Critical Reading

Cite textual evidence to support your responses.

1. **Key Ideas and Details (a)** Identify the family members waiting for Moon Orchid at the airport, and briefly describe each one's behavior. **(b) Interpret:** What do Brave Orchid's thoughts about her children's behavior reveal about her?
2. **Key Ideas and Details (a)** How does Brave Orchid try to keep both her sister's plane and her son's ship safe? **(b) Connect:** What does this behavior reveal about Brave Orchid's view of the world?
3. **Key Ideas and Details (a) Interpret:** What is Brave Orchid's main impression when she finally sees Moon Orchid? **(b) Draw Conclusions:** When the two sisters finally meet, why do they speak to each other as they do?
4. **Key Ideas and Details (a) Infer:** What seems to be Brave Orchid's attitude toward America and American culture? **(b) Apply:** What does this selection suggest about the conflicts that face immigrants and the children of immigrants in America?

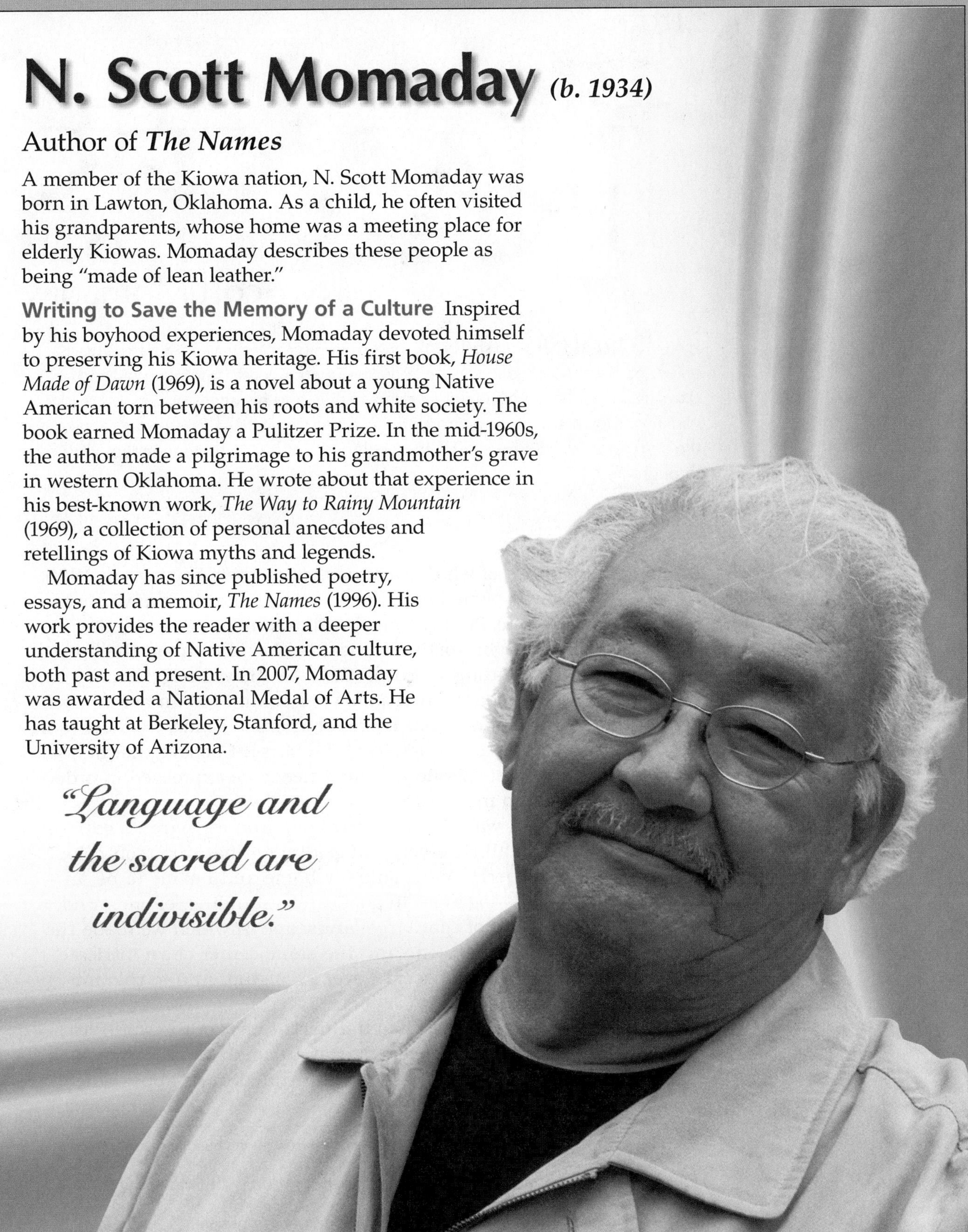

N. Scott Momaday *(b. 1934)*

Author of *The Names*

A member of the Kiowa nation, N. Scott Momaday was born in Lawton, Oklahoma. As a child, he often visited his grandparents, whose home was a meeting place for elderly Kiowas. Momaday describes these people as being "made of lean leather."

Writing to Save the Memory of a Culture Inspired by his boyhood experiences, Momaday devoted himself to preserving his Kiowa heritage. His first book, *House Made of Dawn* (1969), is a novel about a young Native American torn between his roots and white society. The book earned Momaday a Pulitzer Prize. In the mid-1960s, the author made a pilgrimage to his grandmother's grave in western Oklahoma. He wrote about that experience in his best-known work, *The Way to Rainy Mountain* (1969), a collection of personal anecdotes and retellings of Kiowa myths and legends.

Momaday has since published poetry, essays, and a memoir, *The Names* (1996). His work provides the reader with a deeper understanding of Native American culture, both past and present. In 2007, Momaday was awarded a National Medal of Arts. He has taught at Berkeley, Stanford, and the University of Arizona.

"Language and the sacred are indivisible."

from

The NAMES

N. Scott Momaday

BACKGROUND In the book-length memoir from which this excerpt is taken, N. Scott Momaday weaves together poetry, prose, photographs, and drawings, to describe his childhood, his family, and his ancestors. As Momaday explains, Kiowa society is a "horse culture." In this section, Momaday focuses on the story of a favorite horse and the beginnings of his own independent journey through life.

I sometimes think of what it means that in their heyday—in 1830, say—the Kiowas owned more horses *per capita* than any other tribe on the Great Plains, that the Plains Indian culture, the last culture to evolve in North America, is also known as "the horse culture" and "the centaur[1] culture," that the Kiowas tell the story of a horse that died of shame after its owner committed an act of cowardice, that I am a Kiowa, that therefore there is in me, as there is in the Tartars,[2] an old, sacred notion of the horse. I believe that at some point in my racial life, this notion must needs be expressed in order that I may be true to my nature.

It happened so: I was thirteen years old, and my parents gave me a horse. It was a small nine-year-old gelding of that rare, soft color that is called strawberry roan. This my horse and I came to be, in the course of our life together, in good understanding, of one mind, a true story and history of that large landscape in which we made the one entity of whole motion, one and the same center of an intricate, pastoral composition, evanescent,[3] ever changing. And to this my horse I gave the name Pecos.

Vocabulary

pastoral (pas′ tər əl) *adj.* characteristic of rural life; idealized as peaceful, simple, and natural

On the back of my horse I had a different view of the world. I could see more of it, how it reached away beyond all the horizons I had ever seen; and yet it was more concentrated in its appearance,

1. **centaur** (sen′ tôr) *adj.* pertaining to a mythical creature with the head and upper body of a man and the lower body of a horse.
2. **Tartars** (tär′ tərz) *n.* nomadic Turkish peoples who took part in the invasions of Eastern Europe during the Middle Ages.
3. **evanescent** (ev′ ə nes′ ənt) *adj.* transient; tending to fade from sight.

too, and more accessible to my mind, my imagination. My mind loomed upon the farthest edges of the earth, where I could feel the full force of the planet whirling into space. There was nothing of the air and light that was not pure exhilaration, and nothing of time and eternity. Oh, Pecos, *un poquito mas!* Oh, my hunting horse! Bear me away, bear me away!

It was appropriate that I should make a long journey. Accordingly I set out one early morning, traveling light. Such a journey must begin in the nick of time, on the spur of the moment, and one must say to himself at the outset: Let there be wonderful things along the way; let me hold to the way and be thoughtful in my going; let this journey be made in beauty and belief.

I sang in the sunshine and heard the birds call out on either side. Bits of down from the cottonwoods drifted across the air, and butterflies fluttered in the sage. I could feel my horse under me, rocking at my legs, the bobbing of the reins to my hand; I could feel the sun on my face and the stirring of a little wind at my hair. And through the hard hooves, the slender limbs, the **supple** shoulders, the fluent back of my horse I felt the earth under me. Everything was under me, buoying me up; I rode across the top of the world. My mind soared; time and again I saw the fleeting shadow of my mind moving about me as it went winding upon the sun.

When the song, which was a song of riding, was finished, I had Pecos pick up the pace. Far down on the road to San Ysidro I overtook my friend Pasqual Fragua. He was riding a rangy, stiff-legged black and white stallion, half wild, which horse he was breaking for the

▲ Critical Viewing

Using the third paragraph of the essay as a guide, how do you think Momaday would describe this photograph? **HYPOTHESIZE**

Vocabulary

supple (sup′ əl) *adj.* able to bend and move easily; nimble

Comprehension

What is Momaday's idea of a great journey?

rancher Cass Goodner. The horse skittered and blew as I drew up beside him. Pecos began to prance, as he did always in the company of another horse. "Where are you going?" I asked in the Jemez language. And he replied, "I am going down the road." The stallion was hard to manage, and Pasqual had to keep his mind upon it; I saw that I had taken him by surprise. "You know," he said after a moment, "when you rode up just now I did not know who you were." We rode on for a time in silence, and our horses got used to each other, but still they wanted their heads.[4] The longer I looked at the stallion the more I admired it, and I suppose that Pasqual knew this, for he began to say good things about it: that it was a thing of good blood, that it was very strong and fast, that it felt very good to ride it. The thing was this: that the stallion was half wild, and I came to wonder about the wild half of it; I wanted to know what its wildness was worth in the riding. "Let us trade horses for a while," I said, and, well, all right, he agreed. At first it was exciting to ride the stallion, for every once in a while it pitched and bucked and wanted to run. But it was heavy and raw-boned and full of resistance, and every step was a jolt that I could feel deep down in my bones. I saw soon enough that I had made a bad bargain, and I wanted my horse back, but I was ashamed to admit it. There came a time in the late afternoon, in the vast plain far south of San Ysidro, after thirty miles, perhaps, when I no longer knew whether it was I who was riding the stallion or the stallion who was riding me. "Well, let us go back now," said Pasqual at last. "No. I am going on; and I will have my horse back, please," I said, and he was surprised and sorry to hear it, and we said goodbye. "If you are going south or east," he said, "look out for the sun, and keep your face in the shadow of your hat. *Vaya con Dios*."[5] And I went on my way alone then, wiser and better mounted, and thereafter I held on to my horse. I saw no one for a long time, but I saw four falling stars and any number of jackrabbits, roadrunners, and coyotes, and once, across a distance, I saw a bear, small and black, lumbering in the ravine. The mountains drew close and withdrew and drew close again, and after several days I swung east.

The thing was this: that the stallion was half wild, and I came to wonder about the wild half of it...

Memoir

What significant event does Momaday recount in this passage?

Now and then I came upon settlements. For the most part they were dry, burnt places with Spanish names: Arroyo Seco, Las Piedras, Tres Casas. In one of these I found myself in a narrow street between high adobe walls. Just ahead, on my left, was a door in the wall. As I approached the door was flung open, and a small boy came running out, rolling a hoop. This happened so suddenly that Pecos shied very sharply, and I fell to the ground, jamming the thumb of my left hand. The little boy looked very worried and said that he was sorry to have caused such an accident. I waved the matter off, as if it were nothing; but as a matter of fact my hand hurt so much that tears welled up in my eyes. And the pain lasted for many days. I have fallen many times

4. **. . . they wanted their heads** The horses wanted to be free of the control of the reins.
5. **Vaya con Dios** (vī yə kən dē′ ōs) "Go with God" (Spanish).

from a horse, both before and after that, and a few times I fell from a running horse on dangerous ground, but that was the most painful of them all.

In another settlement there were some boys who were interested in racing. They had good horses, some of them, but their horses were not so good as mine, and I won easily. After that, I began to think of ways in which I might even the odds a little, might give some advantage to my competitors. Once or twice I gave them a head start, a reasonable head start of, say, five or ten yards to the hundred, but that was too simple, and I won anyway. Then it came to me that I might try this: we should all line up in the usual way, side by side, but my competitors should be mounted and I should not. When the signal was given I should then have to get up on my horse while the others were breaking away; I should have to mount my horse during the race. This idea appealed to me greatly, for it was both imaginative and difficult, not to mention dangerous; Pecos and I should have to work very closely together. The first few times we tried this I had little success, and over a course of a hundred yards I lost four races out of five. The principal problem was that Pecos simply could not hold still among the other horses. Even before they broke away he was hard to manage, and when they were set running nothing could hold him back, even for an instant. I could not get my foot in the stirrup, but I had to throw myself up across the saddle on my stomach, hold on as best I could, and twist myself into position, and all this while racing at full speed. I could ride well enough to accomplish this feat, but it was a very awkward and inefficient business. I had to find some way to use the whole energy of my horse, to get it all into the race. Thus far I had managed only to break his motion, to divert him from his purpose and mine. To correct this I took Pecos away and worked with him through the better part of a long afternoon on a broad reach of level ground beside an irrigation ditch. And it was hot, hard work. I began by teaching him to run straight away while I ran beside him a few steps, holding on to the saddle horn, with no pressure on the reins. Then, when we had mastered this trick, we proceeded to the next one, which was this: I placed my weight on my arms, hanging from the saddle horn, threw my feet out in front of me, struck them to the ground, and sprang up against the saddle. This I did again and again, until Pecos came to expect it and did not flinch or lose his stride. I sprang a little higher each time. It was in all a slow process of trial and error, and after two or three hours both Pecos and I were covered with bruises

LITERATURE IN CONTEXT

Mythology Connection

The Centaur

In his first paragraph, N. Scott Momaday refers to the Plains Indian culture as "the centaur culture." In alluding to that mythical creature with the upper body of a man and the lower body of a horse, Momaday indirectly places his discussion within the larger context of cultural history. According to Greek myth, centaurs like the one shown below were a race of wild, inhospitable beings who dwelled in the mountains of northern Greece. However, one centaur, Chiron, taught many Greek heroes and was well-known for his wisdom and knowledge of medicine.

Connect to the Literature

Why do you think Momaday calls the Plains Indian culture a "centaur culture" rather than a "horse culture"?

Comprehension

Why were Momaday and Pecos training together?

and soaked through with perspiration. But we had much to show for our efforts, and at last the moment came when we must put the whole performance together. I had not yet leaped into the saddle, but I was quite confident that I could now do so; only I must be sure to get high enough. We began this dress rehearsal then from a standing position. At my signal Pecos lurched and was running at once, straight away and smoothly. And at the same time I sprinted forward two steps and gathered myself up, placing my weight precisely at my wrists, throwing my feet out and together, perfectly. I brought my feet down sharply to the ground and sprang up hard, as hard as I could, bringing my legs astraddle of my horse—and everything was just right, except that I sprang too high. I vaulted all the way over my horse, clearing the saddle by a considerable margin, and came down into the irrigation ditch. It was a good trick, but it was not the one I had in mind, and I wonder what Pecos thought of it after all. Anyway, after a while I could mount my horse in this way and so well that there was no challenge in it, and I went on winning race after race.

I vaulted all the way over my horse...

I went on, farther and farther into the wide world. Many things happened. And in all this I knew one thing: I knew where the journey was begun, that it was itself a learning of the beginning, that the beginning was infinitely worth the learning. The journey was well undertaken, and somewhere in it I sold my horse to an old Spanish man of Vallecitos. I do not know how long Pecos lived. I had used him hard and well, and it may be that in his last days an image of me like thought shimmered in his brain.

Critical Reading

Cite textual evidence to support your responses.

1. **Key Ideas and Details (a)** What inspires Momaday's decision to take a journey? **(b) Draw Conclusions:** What do you think such a journey meant to him, and how did it make him feel?
2. **Key Ideas and Details (a)** What does Momaday trade with Pasqual? **(b) Analyze:** What motivates him to make this trade?
3. **Key Ideas and Details (a) Support:** Provide one detail that shows that Pecos was an extremely good horse. **(b) Infer:** What does the writer mean when he says that he "had used him hard and well"? **(c) Draw Conclusions:** Why do you think Momaday sold Pecos?
4. **Integration of Knowledge and Ideas** Based on these two memoirs, what does the idea of homeland mean? Use at least two of these Essential Question words: *global, natural, formative, environment, exile.* ***[Connecting to the Essential Question: What is the relationship between literature and place?]***

Close Reading Activities

from ***The Woman Warrior*** •
from ***The Names***

Literary Analysis

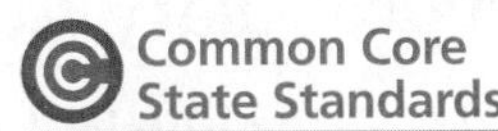

Common Core State Standards

Writing

3. Write narratives to develop real experiences or events using effective technique, well-chosen details, and well-structured event sequences. *(p. 1440)*

3.d. Use precise words and phrases, telling details, and sensory language to convey a vivid picture of the experiences, events, setting, and/or characters. *(p. 1440)*

Language

3.a. Vary syntax for effect; apply an understanding of syntax to the study of complex texts when reading. *(p. 1441)*

4.b. Identify and correctly use patterns of word changes that indicate different meanings or parts of speech. *(p. 1440)*

4.d. Verify the preliminary determination of the meaning of a word or phrase. *(p. 1440)*

1. **Craft and Structure** Using a chart like the one shown, list at least two examples that show how each **memoir** combines historical or cultural elements with personal details from the writer's life.

Historical Details	Personal Details

2. **Craft and Structure** **(a)** Cite two memories Brave Orchid has while waiting at the airport. **(b)** Are these memories typical features of a memoir? Why or why not?
3. **Craft and Structure** **(a)** Whose impressions provide the **limited third-person point of view** in the excerpt from *The Woman Warrior?* **(b)** Explain why this choice of point of view is unusual for any autobiographical work.
4. **Craft and Structure** Brave Orchid is Kingston's mother. What techniques more commonly found in fiction does Kingston use to portray her mother as a literary character?
5. **Craft and Structure** How might Brave Orchid's story have been different if the narrative had been written in her voice, using *I* instead of *she*? Explain.
6. **Key Ideas and Details** **(a)** Identify two events that Momaday describes in this excerpt. **(b)** What connects these events to the cultural theme he introduces in the opening paragraph?
7. **Integration of Knowledge and Ideas** In what specific ways does **relating to your own experiences** help you better understand the feelings and thoughts the writers express in these memoirs? In your answer, mention specific examples from the text.
8. **Integration of Knowledge and Ideas** What similarities or differences did you find between the selections and your own experiences?
9. **Comparing Literary Works** Compare and contrast the effects of each writer's choice of point of view in these memoirs, using these questions to guide you: **(a)** Does the **first-person point of view** bring the reader closer to the narrator than third-person point of view allows? Explain. **(b)** Does the limited third-person point of view allow the writer greater freedom of expression? Explain. **(c)** In which essay do stye and content most effectively communicate the author's purpose? Explain.

Close Reading Activities Continued

Vocabulary Acquisition and Use

Word Analysis: Latin Root *-aud-*

The word *inaudibly* is based on the Latin word root *-aud-,* which means "hear." Words that share this root relate to hearing or sound. For example, *inaudibly* means "in a tone too low to be heard." Apply your knowledge of the root *-aud-* to write definitions for each word listed below. Check your work in a dictionary as needed.

1. audiotape
2. auditory
3. auditorium
4. audition
5. auditor
6. audiology
7. audiophile

Vocabulary: Sentence Completions

Review the vocabulary list on page 1424. Then, complete each sentence with an appropriate word from the list. Explain your choices.

1. The dancer's _____ legs carried her across the stage.
2. ______to passage of time, she worked on into the night.
3. When David replied _____, I asked him to speak up.
4. The ______of the situation silenced all petty bickering.
5. The ______ scene in the painting reminded me of a simpler time.

Writing

Narrative Text Both of these writers share an experience from the past. Choose a significant event that you have experienced and write a brief **memoir** exploring its meaning.

Prewriting Brainstorm for a list of events that affected you earlier in life. For each, write two or three reasons why the event was significant. Decide which event you will write about.

Drafting After describing the event or experience, provide the insight to explain its effect on you. Include details that build the emotional impact of your insight.

Model: Elaborating to Add Emotional Depth

It was during my aunt's visit in the summer of 1996 that I discovered my pride in my Native American heritage. Through her stories about my grandparents and their struggles, I finally learned to celebrate what makes my life different instead of trying to hide it.

Words like *pride*, *finally*, and *celebrate* relate the symbolic meaning of the event.

Revising Ask a classmate to read your draft to see if he or she can identify with your experience. Based on the feedback you receive, revise your draft, adding elaboration to ensure that readers will understand the importance of the event and the feelings it inspired in you.

Conventions and Style: Varying Sentences

In both your personal and academic writing, avoid using the same types of sentences repeatedly. Repetition of the same sentence types diminishes the flow of your ideas and is monotonous for the reader. Instead, work to achieve sentence variety in your writing.

One effective way to add sentence variety is to **vary your sentences' beginnings.** Start by reviewing a draft of your own writing. Examine one paragraph, and bracket the first words of each sentence. Make a list of those words. If you see the same types of words over and over—all nouns or all adverbs, for example—work to break that pattern. The sample sentences below show different types of sentence beginnings:

Types of Sentence Beginnings

Adverb: Suddenly, I realized that my mistake was not that serious.

Direct Object: My mistake, I suddenly realized, was not that serious.

Prepositional Phrase: Above the city lights, we could barely see the silver moon.

Participial Phrase: Working late into the night, I found the solution.

Inverted Subject-Predicate Order: On the table sat a book, a pen, and a rose in a vase.

Practice Revise the following sentences to begin with the part of speech in parentheses, or invert the subject and verb if so indicated.

1. The boy saw his journey would lead him deeper into the desert. (direct object)
2. Pasqual, riding a stallion, was breaking in the horse. (participle)
3. The narrator, wiser, went on alone riding his own horse. (participle)
4. Rolling a hoop, a boy came out of the door. (noun)
5. Mounting a horse during a race wasn't easy. (prepositional phrase)
6. Moon Orchid had shopping bags filled with food on the floor next to her. (prepositional phrase)
7. At the airport were Brave Orchid, Moon Orchid's niece, and Brave Orchid's children. (put subject before predicate)
8. Crowding along the conveyer belts, passengers waited to have their luggage searched. (noun)
9. The sisters stood in the doorway and greeted each other, blocking the way. (participle)
10. Each sister looked surprisingly old to the other one. (adverb)

Writing and Speaking Conventions

A. Writing Write sentences beginning with the following items. Use the item as the part of speech given in parentheses.

1. Silently (adverb)
2. At (prepositional phrase)
3. The settlements (noun)
4. Bruised (participle)
5. Waiting (participle)

Example: Silently

Sentence: Silently, the narrator and his friend rode on together.

B. Speaking Tell a partner or a small group a brief story about a journey. You may use an experience you have had or one you have read about. As you speak, make sure to vary your sentence beginnings.

Analyzing Functional and Expository Texts

Technical Report • Mission Statement

About the Texts

A **technical report** is a document that provides an in-depth explanation of a topic or process related to science or technology. Technical reports are usually written for knowledgeable readers, so they tend to contain advanced language and technical terms. These documents often include

- an introduction;
- a list of numbered parts or sections;
- procedural elements or a description of a process;
- graphics, charts, and other visual presentations of information.

A **mission statement** is a document that expresses in a concise way an organization's purpose, direction, and goals. A mission statement may appear with a brief history of the organization.

Preparing to Read Complex Texts

Documents about scientific or technical topics may contain advanced, specialized concepts with which you are not familiar. Use the following approaches to **clarify** unfamiliar material:

- *Reread* to isolate unfamiliar elements. Focus on elements you do understand, from which you can gather a general meaning.
- Identify familiar words and phrases that serve as *context clues* to help you define unfamiliar terms.

You may also check print or online dictionaries or other sources to define technical terms. As you read, use a chart like the one shown to help as you apply these clarifying strategies.

Strategy	Unfamiliar	Familiar	Clarification
Reread	concatenation of multiple name parts (e.g., first and initial) on a single line.	multiple; first and initial; single line	The names might be combined on a single line.
Use context clues	For purposes of these tabulations; a captured name is considered to be "valid" if . . .	name; valid	Only some names are valid for this study.

Common Core State Standards

Reading Informational Text

4. Determine the meaning of words and phrases as they are used in a text, including technical meanings

Language

4.a. Use context as a clue to the meaning of a word or phrase.

6. Acquire and use accurately general academic and domain-specific words and phrases, sufficient for reading at the college and career readiness level; demonstrate independence in gathering vocabulary knowledge when considering a word or phrase important to comprehension or expression.

Content-Area Vocabulary

These words appear in the selections that follow. They may also appear in other content-area texts.

demographic (dem ə graf´ ik) *adj.* relating to the science of analyzing human populations

aggregates (ag´ rə gits) *n.* groups of distinct things considered together as a whole

cumulative (kyo͞o´ myə lə tiv) *adj.* accumulated; adding up

assimilation (ə sim´ ə la´ sh ə n) *n.* in sociology, the merging of a minority group into mainstream culture

U.S. Census Bureau

Demographic Aspects of Surnames from Census 2000

David L. Word, Charles D. Coleman, Robert Nunziata and Robert Kominski

The introduction gives an overview of the information contained in the report and also focuses on some technical aspects of the research.

This report was issued by the United States Census Bureau, an arm of the federal government that researches and distributes data about the nation's people. The full report is twenty-one pages long.

1. Introduction

This report documents both the overall frequency of surnames (last names), as well as some of the basic **demographic** characteristics that are associated with surnames. **The presentation of data in this report focuses on summarized aggregates of counts and characteristics associated with surnames, and, as such, do not in any way identify any specific individuals. . . .**

3. Characteristics of Surnames

3.1 How many names are there?

The report is organized into numbered and titled sections, making it simpler for readers to navigate the material.

Even after applying various edits and acceptance criteria to the names, there are a sizable number of unique names in the population. Over 6 million last names were identified. Many of these names were either unique (occurred once) or nearly so (occurred 2-4 times) raising questions about the actual validity of the name. Cursory examination of the data indicates that many of these unique names were probably the entire name of the person (first and last, or first, middle initial and last) concatenated into a single continuous string, with some other information. . . .

Table 1 shows the frequency of last names and the numbers of people who are defined by them. Seven last names are held by a million or more people. The most common last name reported was SMITH, held by about 2.3 million people, or about 9 percent of the population. Another 6 names with over a million respondents (JOHNSON, WILLIAMS, BROWN, JONES, MILLER and DAVIS), along with SMITH, account for about 4 percent of the population, or one in every 25 people. There are another 268 last names each occurring at least 100,000 times, but less than 1 million times. Together, these 275 last names, just 4/100,000 of all reported last names, account together for 26 percent of the population, or about one of every four people. On the flip side of this distribution, about 65 percent (or 4 million) of all captured last names were held by just one person, and about 80 percent (or 5 million) were held by no more than 4 people.

The authors provide help in interpreting the chart on the next page.

A discussion of the numerical data presented in this chart appears on the preceding page.

Table 1

Last Names by Frequency of Occurrence and Number of People: 2000

Last Names				People with these Names		
Frequency of Occurrence	Number	Cumulative Number	Cumulative Proportion (percent)	Number	Cumulative Number	Cumulative Proportion (percent)
1,000,000+	7	7	0.0	10,710,446	10,710,446	4.0
100,000-999,999	268	275	0.0	60,091,601	70,802,047	26.2
10,000-99,999	3,012	3,287	0.1	77,657,334	148,459,381	55.0
1,000-9,999	20,369	23,656	0.4	58,264,607	206,723,988	76.6
100-999	128,015	151,671	2.4	35,397,085	242,121,073	89.8
50-99	105,609	257,280	4.1	7,358,924	249,479,997	92.5
25-49	166,059	423,339	6.8	5,772,510	255,252,507	94.6
10-24	331,518	754,857	12.1	5,092,320	260,344,827	96.5
5-9	395,600	1,150,457	18.4	2,568,209	262,913,036	97.5
2-4	1,056,992	2,207,449	35.3	2,808,085	265,721,121	98.5
1	4,040,966	6,248,415	100.0	4,040,966	269,762,087	100.0

4. Methodology of Measuring Names

4.1 Turning names into data

Turning a written name on a census form into usable data for tabulation purposes is a task which involves a number of assumptions and decision rules. This section describes both the operational and logical decision rules used to turn 'names into data'.

The data for this research comes from the written-in names persons provided when they filled out their census form. . . . Obviously, many factors enter into the process of turning a written response on paper into a numerically-coded value. For instance, alternate spellings, including incorrect spellings, random marks on the paper, abbreviations, etc., must all have decision rules associated with them, in order to code them. . . . Transformation of names into data [is] complex, engaging a larger set of rules and procedures. In addition to the possible sources of error already mentioned, a number of other issues relevant to the character strings defining names come into play. This includes things such as: 1) scanning or reading errors by the OCR [Optical Character Recognition] software, 2) mis-keying, 3) respondents entering data into incorrect locations in questionnaires, 4) respondents entering no name or an invalid name, and 5) concatenation of multiple name parts (e.g, first and initial) when they are written in the space for a single name. Each of these problems must be addressed

The authors provide information on research challenges and solutions. This information is helpful to readers who are assessing the data.

either with some kind of editing or resolution rule, or the name must be left as is. It is due to many of these issues that there are a large number of 'names' which occur only once or twice – many of these 'unique' names are variants of more common names which short of inspection on a one-by-one basis, cannot be "corrected" to the character string they actually are supposed to represent.

4.2 Definition of a name

For purposes of these tabulations, a captured name from Census 2000 is considered to be "valid" if it satisfies the following two criteria:

1. Both the first and last names must have at least two alphabetic characters.

2. A first or last name may also be considered valid if it has support in the Social Security Administration's 1998 NUMIDENT file. The NUMIDENT file used in this research is a 5 percent sample of all people who had been issued Social Security numbers as of November 1998. The advantage of using the NUMIDENT file as a benchmark is that individuals receive Social Security cards with the names they provide on their applications. If an individual receives a card with an error in their name, they have an incentive to report the error and have it corrected. Thus, it is assumed that the NUMIDENT file is the most current and correct source for validating names. . . .

The authors do not assume readers' knowledge but provide more information about specialized content.

Records with names that did not satisfy the two criteria were deleted for purposes of these tabulations. For example, names such as A LINCOLN or MISTER T would be ruled invalid because neither the first name A nor the last name T contains two letters, thus violating criterion 1. . . .

Examples of invalid names under criterion 2 are strings such as PERSON (as a first name), ADULT, BABY, HOUSEHOLDER, or SPOUSE. Thus, a census record with the name BABY MILLER would have been dropped from the analysis, because BABY is not supported as a valid name in the NUMIDENT file.

As names become less frequent, the possibility that a string of letters is not a valid name increases. As has been noted, this is due to many factors – misplaced or misscanned letter(s), bad spelling, and a variety of other causes. All names occurring 300 or more times were reviewed for validity, using a series of rules described in section 4.4.5, although certainly this process did not delete or modify all invalid names. However, names occurring fewer than 300 times were not examined at all, because of their large relative volume.

The initial data file used for this report contains 279,132,770 data-defined person records (census records with at least two data fields with valid responses) from an intermediate file created during the processing for Census 2000. After applying the criteria and the edits we developed for improving names, the final number of records for analysis comprises 269,762,087 people, or approximately 96 percent of all people counted in Census 2000.

The Statue of Liberty-Ellis Island Foundation, Inc.

Mission and Background

Mission: To restore and preserve the Statue of Liberty National Monument, which includes, in addition to the Statue itself, Ellis Island and its Museum of Immigration; Custody and control of records, relics and other things of historic interest related to the Statue of Liberty and the millions of immigrants who entered the United States via Ellis Island; To foster, promote and stimulate public knowledge of and interest in the history of the Statue of Liberty and Ellis Island.

This mission statement includes the full range of goals of the foundation.

The National Park Service (NPS), a unit of the United States Department of the Interior, operates both the Statue of Liberty and Ellis Island (the "Monument") and has accepted grants pursuant to an agreement dated October 14, 1983 and subsequent agreements with the Foundation for the restoration and preservation of the Monument.

Background: The first projects of the Foundation from 1982 until 1992 included the restoration of the Statue of Liberty, upgrade of Liberty Island, the preservation of the main building on Ellis Island, upgrading Castle Clinton, and establishment of the Statue of Liberty Museum and the 220,000 square foot Ellis Island Immigration Museum (which has had 25 million visitors since opening). . . .

In 1992 the Foundation launched a project campaign for the restoration and adaptation of the "kitchen and laundry" building, the "bakery and carpentry" building and the "shop" building on Ellis Island. This allowed the museum to expand and establish the Oral History Studio, the Library, Living Theater, Children's Orientation Center and the changing Exhibition Center. It also established new offices for the employees of the NPS.

During 1995 to 2001 the Foundation stepped forward to create the American Family Immigration History Center on Ellis Island and the Internet. The Center contains computerized immigration records (manifests) of 25 million people who arrived in America through the Port of New York between 1892 and 1924. . . . In 2004 the Foundation spearheaded a campaign to make critical safety upgrades to the Statue of Liberty, which was closed to the public after 9/11/01. The Foundation successfully raised the necessary funds and managed the construction work so that the National Park Service/U.S. Department of the Interior could reopen Lady Liberty's doors to the public on August 3, 2004.

In 2007, the Foundation initiated a campaign for The Peopling of America Center (the "Center"). The Center will expand upon the story currently told of the Ellis Island Years (1892-1954) by including the story of those who arrived before Ellis Island and after, right up to the present, becoming citizens, and altering the demographic landscape of America. The Center will follow the arc of the American experience: from immigration, to assimilation, to citizenship, played out in every generation, past, present and future.

The background highlights past achievements and shows how the foundation has grown.

Critical Reading

1. **Key Ideas and Details (a)** Summarize the criteria the Census Bureau used to determine the validity of a name. **(b)** According to the report, what might cause a name to be omitted as invalid? **(c)** Given this criteria, why is it likely that "unique" names are not valid?
2. **Key Ideas and Details (a)** Based on context clues in the report, explain what a "decision rule" is. **(b)** Identify two decision rules the scientists used to turn written responses into quantifiable data.
3. **Key Ideas and Details (a)** In your own words, explain the mission of The Statue of Liberty-Ellis Island Foundation, Inc. **(b)** Identify two details from the "Background" section that best express that mission. Explain your choices.
4. **Content-Area Vocabulary (a)** How do the meanings of the Greek word *demos* ("people") and root *-graph-* ("writing") contribute to the meaning of *demographic?* **(b)** How do the meanings of *demos* and the combining form *-cracy* ("power, might") contribute to the meaning of *democracy*?

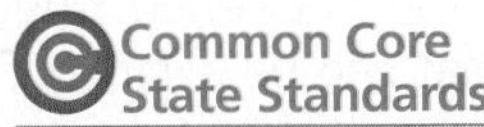

Common Core State Standards

Writing

1. Write arguments to support claims in an analysis of substantive topics or texts, using valid reasoning and relevant and sufficient evidence.

10. Write routinely over shorter time frames for a range of tasks, purposes, and audiences.

Timed Writing

Argument [40 minutes]

Format

In a strong **argumentative essay,** the writer states a position and supports it with evidence. In a Timed Writing sitation, the strongest evidence will be quotations from the texts under discussion.

Both the Technical Report and Mission Statement touch on the idea of heritage. Names represent the heritage of families and ethnic groups, while museums preserve our shared historical and cultural heritage. Write an **argumentative essay** in which you discuss who should bear the most **responsibility** for preserving heritage sites. Consider the government, the general public, non-profit organizations, or another institution. Cite information from the Technical Report and Mission Statement to support your ideas.

Academic Vocabulary

The prompt asks you to discuss issues of **responsibility**, which can mean many different things. In your essay include a brief discussion of how you are applying that term to this topic.

5-Minute Planner

Complete these steps before you begin to write.

1. Read the prompt carefully. Identify key words.
2. Take notes that relate to the prompt. **TIP** Sketch a quick chart to categorize notes that apply to different aspects of the prompt.
3. Reread the prompt, and draft your essay.
4. Before you hand in your essay, check for correct use of the conventions of punctuation and capitalization.

Writing Workshop

Write a Short Story

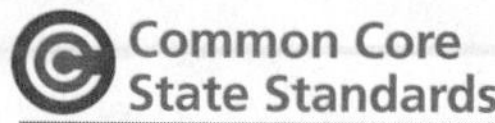

Fictional Narrative Writers create short stories to tell about events that never happened. They use the tools of narrative writing to invent stories that can be exciting, inspiring, or moving. Many short stories focus on a single incident that reveals an insight about a main character. Those insights can give the short story form a surprising depth and relevance. Even though the events are made up, the feelings they generate are real. A good short story can leave a powerful and lasting impression.

Assignment Write a short story that tells about a fictional event in which a central conflict is—or is not—resolved.

What to Include Your short story should have these elements:

- a setting that presents a time and place using concrete sensory details
- a main character who is involved in a conflict or has a problem to be resolved
- a plot that includes a clear sequence of events related to the conflict
- dialogue between characters that moves the plot forward and develops characters' personalities
- effective pacing and plot strategies, such as flashback and foreshadowing

To preview the criteria on which your short story may be assessed, see the rubric on page 1455.

Common Core State Standards

Writing

3. Write narratives to develop real or imagined experiences or events using effective technique, well-chosen details, and well-structured event sequences.

3.a. Engage and orient the reader by setting out a problem, situation, or observation and its significance, establishing one or multiple point(s) of view, and introducing a narrator and/or characters; create a smooth progression of experiences or events.

3.b. Use narrative techniques, such as dialogue, pacing, description, reflection, and multiple plot lines, to develop experiences, events, and/or characters.

3.c. Use a variety of techniques to sequence events so that they build on one another to create a coherent whole and build toward a particular tone and outcome.

Focus on Research

Research can enrich short stories in the following ways:

- by ensuring historical accuracy in a story that is set in a particular time and place
- by adding credible details to descriptions of clothing, scenery, weather, architecture, and food
- by leading to new story ideas

Keep records of your sources when researching for fiction. If you use a direct quote from another source, credit it. However, most of the time your research will be with the aim of gaining general knowledge about a topic so that you can write about it convincingly or accurately in a fictional context.

Prewriting and Planning

Choosing Your Topic

To choose a topic for your short story, use one of these strategies:

- **Make a blueprint.** Sketch a possible setting—anything from a shopping mall to a space station. As you draw, think about events that might unfold there. List three or four ideas and choose one to develop.
- **Focus on a conflict.** Like all writers, you will be influenced by your own life. Make a list about conflicts you have experienced, witnessed, or studied. Consider conflicts between people, between a person and nature, or within a single person. Choose a conflict from your list that you think will make an interesting story.

Narrowing Your Topic

Create a story chart. While anything can happen in fiction, you need to narrow your choices as you organize your story. Make a story chart like the one shown to plan the four stages of your narrative. After you have identified the basic plot events, decide whether you will **foreshadow,** or give hints about what will happen. You might also decide to use **flashbacks,** which give readers information about events that happened before the beginning of the story.

Using a Story Chart

Exposition: Establish the setting, main characters, and set up the conflict.	**Rising Action:** Describe the events that increase the conflict and tension.	**Climax:** Identify the point of greatest tension.	**Resolution:** Tell how the conflict is or is not resolved.
Omar wants to go on a trip. His father will not allow him to go, but he does not explain why.	*Omar wages an all-out campaign at home.*	*Omar's father finally explains his reasoning.*	*Omar respects his father's opinion and decides to wait a year.*

Gathering Details

Interview your characters. The more unique and detailed your characters are, the more interesting they will be for your readers. Conduct an interview with each of your main characters. You might ask a partner to ask you questions while you play the role of each character. Your answers will help you generate specific information. Here are some starter questions:

- Where do you live?
- What is a typical day like for you? What would be a perfect day?
- How would you describe yourself?
- What are your main goals and obstacles?

Drafting

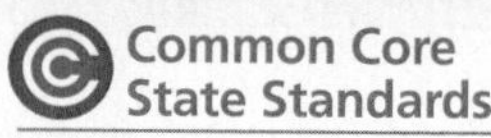

Writing

3.a. Engage and orient the reader by setting out a problem, situation, or observation and its significance, establishing one or multiple point(s) of view, and introducing a narrator and/or characters; create a smooth progression of experiences or events.

Shaping Your Writing

Establish a tense and a point of view. Decide if you will use the past or present tense when you write your story. Also, choose the point of view from which your story will be told. This chart shows three options.

Narrator	Description	Example
First-person	The narrator is a character in the story.	*I knew what I had to do. I had to tell Shana the truth.*
Third-person omniscient	The narrator is outside the story and knows everything that happens.	*Julia was finally ready to tell Shana the truth, but Shana didn't want to hear it.*
Third-person limited	The narrator is outside the story, but only knows what one character does and thinks.	*Julia was finally ready to tell Shana the truth. But would Shana listen?*

3.b. Use narrative techniques, such as dialogue, pacing, description, reflection, and multiple plot lines, to develop experiences, events, and/or characters.

Remember your audience. Keep your readers in mind as you draft your story. Ask yourself these questions:

- Is the opening of my story intriguing enough to grab readers' attention?
- What does my audience need to know to follow the story?
- Have I included enough information to make the setting clear? Do readers need more details about time or place?
- Am I explaining my characters' motivations clearly; can readers understand why characters do what they do?
- Does the action make sense? Do I need to include more information or explanation?

Providing Elaboration

Use dialogue or interior monologue. Incorporating a character's own thoughts and words can add to the portrayal of your characters and make a story more entertaining. Use dialogue between two characters to establish tension and relate plot events. If you are using the first-person point of view, write an interior monologue to share the narrator's private thoughts and feelings about events.

Dialogue	Interior Monologue
"Yeah, right," I laughed. "There's no way I'm going to jump off this cliff." *"I wish we had a choice," said the guide, "but we don't."*	*I looked at the sharp, long drop and the tiny pool of water at the bottom. The guide gave me a vaguely encouraging nod. No way. No way could I jump.*

Writers on Writing

Julia Alvarez On Flashback and Exposition

Julia Alvarez is the author of "Antojos" (p. 1298).

I knew when I titled the story "Antojos" that somewhere in the story I was going to have to give my reader some idea of what the word meant. But where and when? A story doesn't come with footnotes, so anything you want your reader to know you've got to put in a story. The opportunity came when Yolanda is driving in the mountains. We all daydream when we're stuck in a car. So, I have Yolanda flash back to a scene with her aunts in the capital where the Spanish word was explained to her.

from "Antojos"

Left and right, roadside stands began appearing. Yolanda slowed down and kept an eye out for guavas . . .

In the capital, her aunts had plied her with what she most craved after so many years away. "Any little *antojo*, you must tell us!" They wanted to spoil her, so she'd stay on in her nativeland before she forgot where she had come from. "What exactly does it mean, *antojo*?" Yolanda asked. Her aunts were proven right: After so many years away, their niece was losing her Spanish.

> Memories often come as little scenes. It's a good way to give readers background they need. They feel they've been there, too.

"An *antojo*—" The aunts exchanged quizzical looks. "How to put it? An *antojo* is like a craving for something you have to eat."

A cousin blew out her cheeks. "Calories."

> How to show a character's character? There's language (dialogue) but also body language. Instead of a speech tag ("she said"), describe a little gesture that "speaks volumes."

An *antojo*, one of the older aunts continued, was a very old Spanish word from before "your United States was thought of," she added tartly. In the countryside some *campesinos* still used the word to mean possession by an island spirit demanding its due.

Her island spirit certainly was a patient soul, Yolanda joked. She hadn't had her favorite *antojo*, guavas, since her last trip seven years ago. Well, on this trip, her aunts promised, Yoyo could eat guavas to her heart's content.

> At issue in the story is what language Yolanda speaks. This scene, in which a Spanish word has to be explained, "foreshadows"/hints at what's coming.

Revising

Revising Your Overall Structure

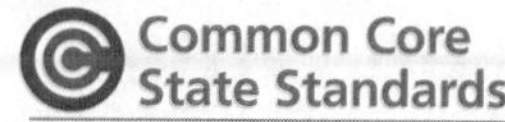

Common Core State Standards

Writing

3.b. Use narrative techniques, such as dialogue, pacing, description, reflection, and multiple plot lines, to develop experiences, events, and/or characters.

3.d. Use precise words and phrases, telling details, and sensory language to convey a vivid picture of the experiences, events, setting, and/or characters.

5. Develop and strengthen writing as needed by planning, revising, editing, rewriting, or trying a new approach, focusing on addressing what is most significant for a specific purpose and audience.

Language

2. Demonstrate command of the conventions of standard English punctuation.

Show instead of tell. Stories are more engaging when the writer shows what is happening rather than simply telling one event after another.

Telling: *Then we had a big argument and got very angry.*

Showing: *He raised his voice, so I raised mine. Soon, we were shouting so loudly our neighbors probably had to turn up the volume on their televisions.*

Follow this strategy to determine if you are showing more than telling:

☆ Place a star next to events in which you show what is happening.

X Place an X next to events that you tell, rather than show.

When you find several Xs in a row, revise to bring your story to life. You might use any of the following techniques:

- Add dialogue to show what people say.
- Use figurative language, including *similes, metaphors,* or *personification,* to heighten descriptions of events, people, or settings.
- Describe specific actions and reactions rather than general emotions.

Model: Revising to Make Writing More Interesting

,as if he expected someone to snatch it away from him at any moment

X Mark ate his dinner rapidly.

"You must have grown up in a big family," she remarked.

Mark looked up, a noodle dangling from his pursed lips.

He slurped, and it disappeared. "Yup," he said.

Kim watched with amusement.

Adding dialogue and descriptive language makes the story livelier.

Peer Review: Exchange drafts with a partner. Identify two or three sections in your partner's story that could be strengthened by showing rather than telling. Provide clear suggestions for improvement strategies.

Revising Your Word Choice

Replace ineffective words. The words in your story work together to create an overall effect. Review your word choices to make sure that each word is pulling its weight. Replace flat or vague words with words that reflect the senses of sight, hearing, touch, smell, or taste.

Revising to Add Sensory Language

Dull: The fire burns at night.
Lively: The crackling fire sprays hot red sparks into the eerie darkness.

Developing Your Style

Using Punctuation in Dialogue

Dialogue conveys the way characters speak. Punctuation can help readers "hear" dialogue. End punctuation—periods, question marks, and exclamation points—affects the tone of a sentence. Other forms of punctuation can also indicate how a character says something.

Rule	Example
Use commas to indicate short pauses.	"Yeah, well, I don't think so."
Use ellipses to show a longer pause or hesitation. Ellipses can also suggest a voice trailing off.	"Well . . . I guess so." "I suppose we could . . ."
Use a dash to indicate a sudden stop, such as an interruption.	"Hey—" "Hurry up, we've got to—"
Use italics to emphasize a word.	"What is *she* doing here?" "What is she doing *here*?"
Use apostrophes to show dropped letters in dialect.	"You're kiddin' me, right?"

Find It in Your Reading

Review the dialogue in "Everyday Use" by Alice Walker.

1. Look for examples of dialogue that are especially vivid or effective.
2. **Discuss:** With a partner, read your favorite examples aloud. Discuss how punctuation contributes to the effect of each example.

Apply It to Your Writing

To improve the dialogue in your story, follow these steps:

1. Read each line aloud. Listen to decide whether it sounds natural. Consider adding punctuation to indicate natural pauses in your character's voice.
2. Decide if there is more than one possible reading for the line. For important lines, consider using italics to show which word the character emphasizes.
3. Be careful not to overuse special punctuation, such as ellipses, dashes, and italics. Limit exclamation points, as well; they are more effective when used sparingly. Reread all of the dialogue in your story, paying attention to the balance of punctuation.

Student Model: Michael Moore, East Stroudsburg, PA

Hallway

Walking through the dimly red corridor in the complex, Gerald found himself surrounded by the uniform shuffling of countless pairs of brown work shoes. Looking down, he saw that his shoes were actually of the same stuff as everyone else's, yet they simply refused to blend in to their surroundings. The rhythmic *THUMP, THUMP, THUMP* was not soothing at all to Gerald, who preferred his own little **tap* interspersed between the monotonous beat.

Michael immediately establishes a clear point of view—limited third person.

Gazing down the seemingly endless straight hallway, he could see the doors, measured off oh so carefully, exactly at ten feet apart. Every so often, as if on cue, a body would turn, leave the line, and meander his way into one of these rooms. As Gerald inched past, pushed along at a pace unbearably slow, he glanced in each room only to see the blank expression on each man's face as he sat down with his wife, son, and daughter. Sometimes there was a dog, sometimes two sons, sometimes even a grandmother. All trifling differences, he thought. But such thoughts are unnecessary, not becoming of oneself. Another person turned in, and another, and another.

Michael uses internal monologue to develop character.

He wondered why the hallway had to be so perfectly, boringly straight. Couldn't they make it curved a little, or have a turn here or there? As he looked behind all he could see was the red hallway filled with pale faces, blank as canvas. He couldn't help but wonder if anyone else thought like he did. I talk to myself in my head, is this normal?

Michael provides vivid details that help readers visualize the scene.

He managed to catch himself considering the silly notion of running, just running to the end of the hallway. He continued walking. The line made a turn at the end of the hallway, seemingly because it had purpose, going up the stairs on the left, but the fact was that there was no other option. It was how it always has been and how it always shall remain, he thought, smiling at himself, smiling at his childishness in thinking he'd break the line. He made the sharp left up the stairs, thinking, as he often did, "A circular staircase would really save space, and be more interesting anyway." But that idea was preposterous, and he soon rid himself of it, as always. Turning into his room, he sat and ate with his family, not speaking a word. "Really, there's nothing to speak about. It's all been said before," he sighed into his food.

Suddenly, he realized himself in the concave reflection of the spoon.

Suddenly, all he could see was the upside-down reflection of himself.

Suddenly, I realized myself in the concave reflection of that spoon.

Suddenly, all I could focus on was the blurry, upside-down ME in that spoon.

A shift to first-person point of view signals a turning point in the plot.

For the complete story, visit www.PHLITonline.com.

Editing and Proofreading

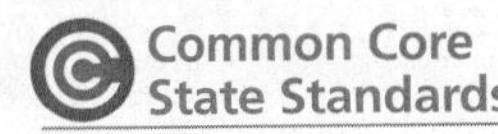

Check your story to eliminate errors in grammar, spelling, or punctuation. Also, be sure that your story is neatly presented and legible.

Focus on punctuation in dialogue. Check that you have punctuated dialogue correctly. Remember to use quotation marks only for direct quotations. Check that you have used commas and capital letters correctly.

Direct Quotation: "We'd better keep practicing," he said.
Indirect Quotation: He said we need a lot more rehearsal.

Focus on spelling. For words ending in silent *-e,* drop the e before adding a suffix beginning with a vowel, such as *-ing, -ed,* or *-es*. For example: *communicate* becomes *communicated, communicating, communicates*. Double-check verbs in the past tense to be sure you have applied this spelling rule.

Spiral Review: Transitional Expressions Earlier in this unit you learned how transitional expressions (page 1323) help connect ideas and reduce choppiness in your writing. Check your story to make sure that you connected ideas correctly with transitional expressions.

Common Core State Standards

Writing

5. Develop and strengthen writing as needed by planning, revising, editing, rewriting, or trying a new approach, focusing on addressing what is most significant for a specific purpose and audience.

6. Use technology, including the Internet, to produce, publish, and update individual or shared writing products in response to ongoing feedback, including new arguments or information.

Language

2. Demonstrate command of the conventions of standard English capitalization, punctuation, and spelling when writing.

2.b. Spell correctly.

Publishing, Presenting, and Reflecting

Consider the following ways to share and reflect on your writing:

Recite your story. Read your story aloud, using appropriate expressions, gestures, pauses, pacing, volume, and body language.

Illustrate and design your story. Use desktop publishing software to create a layout for your story that includes one or more illustrations, as well as an effective type design for the title and text.

Reflect on your writing. Jot down your thoughts about the experience of writing a short story. Begin by answering these questions: Did you always feel in control of the writing process, or did you sometimes feel as if the story took over? Did writing a short story change the way you feel about reading them?

Rubric for Self-Assessment

Evaluate your short story using the following criteria and rating scale:

Criteria	Rating Scale (not very – very)
Purpose/Focus: How clearly do you describe the setting and events in the story?	1 2 3 4
Organization: How effectively do the events and conflict in your story build up to a strong climax and a satisfying resolution?	1 2 3 4
Development of Ideas/Elaboration: How well do you use dialogue to reveal actions and personalities of the characters?	1 2 3 4
Language: How effective are your sentences and their punctuation, both in dialogue and narration?	1 2 3 4
Conventions: How correct is your use of grammar in punctuating dialogue?	1 2 3 4

Compare Print News Coverage

Our world is saturated with broadcast news and information. Television, radio, the Internet, and even cell phones are now vehicles for the delivery of news. However, print media—newspapers and magazines—are still important sources of information, and their online versions extend their reach into the world of electronic media. The ways in which print media cover news stories has significant effects on how the public understands current events.

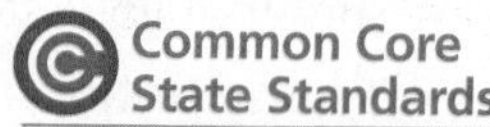

Reading Informational Text

7. Integrate and evaluate multiple sources of information presented in different media or formats as well as in words in order to address a question or solve a problem.

Speaking and Listening

1. Initiate and participate effectively in a range of collaborative discussions with diverse partners on grades 11–12 topics, texts, and issues, building on others' ideas and expressing their own clearly and persuasively.

1.a. Come to discussions prepared, having read and researched material under study; explicitly draw on that preparation by referring to evidence from texts and other research on the topic or issue to stimulate a thoughtful, well-reasoned exchange of ideas.

2. Integrate multiple sources of information presented in diverse formats and media in order to make informed decisions and solve problems, evaluating the credibility and accuracy of each source and noting any discrepancies among the data.

Print Media Genres

There are two main forms of print news media:

Types of Print Media

Newspapers	Magazines
• Daily newspapers present timely coverage of events; many update stories online. • Articles include basic facts and information. • News articles aim to be unbiased. • Photos and captions supplement stories.	• Weekly and monthly magazines target specific topics. • Articles provide in-depth analysis of an event or one aspect of a news story. • Articles include commentary and opinions. • Images provide additional content.

Factors that Shape Print News Coverage

The same news event can be described in many ways, resulting in different messages. The following factors affect the way writers, editors, and news directors shape a story for publication:

- **Purpose:** Most news articles are written to inform, but some media makers may also want to influence opinion or entertain. The purpose of a story will affect the information the reporter writes and the editors include.
- **Author's Perspective:** News articles are meant to be objective. Sometimes, however, a writer may omit certain facts or emphasize others that implicitly express an opinion or shape a particular perception.
- **Audience:** Some publications target specific populations and cater to the interests, needs, or even the biases of those groups. Understanding the target audience can help you identify possible slants in the presentation of a news story.

Aspects of Print News Presentation

News editors organize stories to meet a variety of purposes. As you read, notice how the treatment of the following elements affects your understanding of a news story:

- **Headlines:** The people or groups mentioned in a headline and the use of active or passive voice can affect the meaning. Notice the difference between "President Signs Important War Veterans Bill" and "Key War Veterans Bill Finally Signed into Law."
- **Story Placement:** Placing a story on the front page or burying it in the middle of a paper reflects the level of attention editors think a story deserves.
- **Duration of Coverage:** The length of time a story is covered—a day, a week, a month—also indicates an assessment of its importance.
- **Visual Elements:** Photos shape readers' understanding. The quality of images (flattering, embarrassing, etc.) also has an effect.

Activities: Compare Print Coverage of Same Event

Comprehension and Collaboration For both activities, use an evaluation form like the one shown below.

A. Select a news event and examine its coverage in three different newspapers or magazines. Look for similarities and differences in the ways each publication approaches its coverage, and examine how the coverage emphasizes different elements, including facts. Conduct a group discussion in which members exchange and discuss what they have learned and what ideas they have developed in their own media examinations. Use the Evaluation form below as a guide.

B. Find coverage of the same event in broadcast media (television or radio). Compare the broadcast coverage to the print media versions of the story. Determine if specific information was added or omitted. Write a paragraph explaining your findings.

Evaluation Form for Print Media Coverage

News Event: ______________________

Three Sources in Which It Is Covered: ______________________

Intended Audience of Each Publication: ______________________

How are the headlines different? ______________________

Are the stories placed differently? Explain: ______________________

Do any of the stories seem to favor one side? Explain. ______________________

What information is the same? What is different? ______________________

How does each story provide a different understanding of the event? ______________________

____

Language Study

Cognates

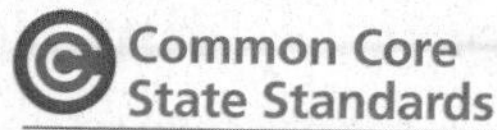

Language
4. Determine or clarify the meaning of unknown and multiple-meaning words and phrases based on *grades 11–12 reading and content,* choosing flexibly from a range of strategies.
4.a. Use context as a clue to the meaning of a word or phrase.
5. Demonstrate understanding of word relationships.

Cognates are words that are essentially the same in different languages. They share origins and meanings and sound and look similar. For example, many English words are rooted in Latin, the same language from which Spanish evolved. Therefore, many English and Spanish words have similar spellings and definitions. You will be better equipped to infer the meaning of a word in one language if you know its definition in another. Study the chart of Spanish words and their meanings shown below.

Spanish Word	Definition
arduo	hard; difficult
beneficio	performing acts of kindness or charity
estudioso	attentive; serious about studying
florido	flushed with rosy color
grave	dignified and serious
indignación	anger caused by something unjust, mean, or unworthy
pedante	someone concerned with formal rules and book learning
perspicaz	shrewd, keen
ubicuidad	appearing to be everywhere at the same time

Practice

Directions: Replace the cognate in each sentence below with a synonym. Explain your answer.

1. Training for the marathon was a highly arduous project.
2. Samara studiously examined the menu before she chose her meal.
3. The judge gravely considered the matter before him.
4. Thanks to the woman's beneficence, the library built its new wing.
5. In the hot room, everyone's cheeks gradually took on a florid hue.

Directions: Evaluate each sentence below and indicate whether the use of the italicized word is logical. If it is logical, explain why. If it is not, rewrite the sentence so that it makes sense.

6. Everywhere I look, that *ubiquitous* weed is flourishing.
7. Dora was easy to trick because she was so *perspicacious*.
8. His *pedantic* approach to playing the game added spontaneity.
9. The injustice of the comment made her *indignant*.

Vocabulary Acquisition and Use: Sentence Completions

Sentence Completion questions appear in most standardized tests. Sentence Completions test your vocabulary skills as well as your understanding of sentence structure. In these types of questions you are given sentences with one or more missing words. Your task is to choose the correct word or words to complete each sentence logically. One method for choosing the correct word involves three steps: (1) Read the whole sentence carefully and identify the idea the missing word should have; (2) Think of a word or words that would have that meaning; (3) Look for those words or synonyms among the answer choices.

Practice

This exercise is modeled after the Sentence Completion exercises that appear in the Critical Reading section of the SAT.

Directions: Each of the following sentences is missing one or two words. Choose the word or set of words that best completes each sentence.

Test-Taking Tip
Monitor your timing. Leave problem questions blank and return to them after you have answered the other questions.

1. Naomi Shihab Nye often writes about people who have been __?__ by the cultures that surround them.

A. dissuaded
B. oppressed
C. maneuvered
D. swerved
E. exhausted

2. Martín Espada writes about the revolutionary struggle in __?__ and moving images.

A. ample
B. heady
C. contiguous
D. mundane
E. striking

3. The life of a poet may often be inspiring, but is sometimes a __?__ struggle.

A. supple
B. pugilistic
C. daunting
D. oblivious
E. synonymous

4. Nye's work has often __?__ the ordinary activities of life and the shared experiences of different cultures.

A. precipitated
B. emitted
C. induced
D. incorporated
E. appeased

5. Are the ideas that form __?__ in our minds the organized sentences of prose or the __?__ of impressions of poetry?

A. benignly . . . aspirations
B. virulently . . . revelations
C. furtively . . . prosperity
D. inaudibly . . . shards
E. ambitiously . . . ecstasy

Text Set Workshop

From Text to Understanding

You have studied each part of Unit 6 as a set of connected texts. In this workshop, you will have the chance to further explore the fundamental connections among these texts and to deepen your essential understanding of the literature and its social and historical context.

Common Core State Standards

Writing

1. Write arguments to support claims in an analysis of substantive topics or texts, using valid reasoning and relevant and sufficient evidence.

7. Conduct short as well as more sustained research projects to answer a question (including a self-generated question) or solve a problem; narrow or broaden the inquiry when appropriate; synthesize multiple sources on that subject, demonstrating understanding of the subject under investigation.

Speaking and Listening

1. Initiate and participate effectively in a range of collaborative discussions (one-on-one, in groups, and teacher-led) with diverse partners on *grades 11–12 topics, texts, and issues*, building on others' ideas and expressing their own clearly and persuasively.

PART 1: Contemporary Fiction

Writing: Argumentative Essay A commonplace object or event can take on deep significance as part of a person's history or heritage. Used as symbols or as elements of characterization, everyday objects have a powerful presence in the works in Part 1. Review the texts in Part 1, paying special attention to the Anchor Text, "Everyday Use," by Alice Walker. Think about how ordinary items or experiences are valued differently by different people.

Assignment: Develop and defend a claim about the ways in which one or more characters in this text set, particularly the Anchor Text, use the past to create a sense of identity. As a way of exploring this idea, consider how an everyday item, experience, or encounter connects a person to his or her heritage. Use textual evidence and background information to support your claim, which might look like the following:

Example: Yolanda's craving for guavas in "Antojos" and Dee's yearning to have Grandma Dee's quilts in "Everyday Use" symbolize two different senses of heritage and identity.

Identify the past and present. Pay attention to the characters' past, as well as present, circumstances.

Identify the ordinary. Read the selections carefully. Look for what the text says about the value of ordinary things.

Craft your claim. Decide what you have concluded about characters, heritage, values, and ordinary things. State your idea in an interesting way.

Structure your writing. As you present and defend your claim, be logical and thorough. Present your thinking in an organized way. Make sure you include all the information your reader will need to understand your argument.

Use new words. As you write, experiment with a broader academic vocabulary. Use thematic words, such as *diversity*, *heritage*, and *assumptions*.

Model: Taking Notes About Passages

Topic: Past and Present

Character name and story:
Dee (Wangero) from "Everyday Use"

Past: Grew up in the rural South; ambitious and intelligent; wished for more in life

Present: Politically and racially aware; adopting new cultural values

PART 2: Contemporary Poetry

Research: Culture Fair Multiculturalism is one of the hallmarks of American literature. The Anchor Text, Yosef Komunyakaa's "Camouflaging the Chimera," is about Vietnam, written by a poet of Trinidadian descent who grew up in Louisiana. Other Part 2 poets are Americans with roots in Indonesia, China, Puerto Rico, England, and Israel.

Review the selections in Part 2, especially the Anchor Text by Komunyakaa. Think about how writers focus on local places and individual experience, yet also manage to speak with a voice that is universal.

Assignment: With a partner, research the literary history, major writers, and important works of two specific American cultural groups represented by the writers in Part 2. Include Yosef Komunyakaa's group as one of your choices. Discuss the similarities and differences between the two groups. Present your research in a display for a Literary Culture Fair, a celebration of American multicultural writing. Use a checklist like the one shown to help organize your research and your presentation.

Literary Culture Fair Checklist

- ☐ **Choose the cultural or ethnic groups.** Choose two heritages represented by the Part 2 writers, including Yusef Komunyakaa. You and your partner may decide that together you will work on both cultural groups, or you may each focus on one.
- ☐ **Make an annotated bibliography.** Conduct research to identify the major writers of that cultural group, both past and present. Create an annotated bibliography in which you list important works and briefly explain their contributions to the American literary scene.
- ☐ **Identify themes, problems, and issues.** Consider the themes that have been particularly important to this group. For example, are these writers concerned with issues of assimilation, racism, family, education, personal happiness, or the American Dream? Describe the stances writers take on these issues.
- ☐ **Research the selection in detail.** Find out more about the writers' selections included in Part 2 as examples of work from their respective groups. Find out more about the style of the poem and the circumstances under which it was written. Devote part of your display to this work.
- ☐ **Research images.** Use the library and the Internet to locate photographs, paintings, and illustrations to enliven your display. You may also include music that is representative of the cultural group you have chosen.

PART 3: Contemporary Nonfiction

Listening and Speaking: Nonfiction Book Club Proposal
The writers in Part 3 share a passion for language. Some are devoted to words, both written and spoken. Others express their thoughts about non-verbal forms of communication, such as music or the power of a kind gesture, in eloquent prose. Language becomes a path to identity, humor, and healing, a path that can span cultural divides.

Review the texts in Part 3, especially the Anchor Text by Anna Quindlen, "One Day, Now Broken in Two." Consider how the selections reflect one of the most basic needs of a writer: to make sense of the world through language.

Assignment: Create a proposal for a nonfiction book club. Select several selections from Part 3, including the Anchor Text, as the first works you will read and study. Choose texts that you think will make an interesting grouping. Explain what is important and engaging about these works and why you will read them together. Prepare a list of sample discussion questions that you would use in your first meeting. Present your completed proposal aloud to the class to convince them to join your group. Encourage classmates' questions and comments about your choices.

Outline for Nonfiction Book Club Presentation

- Which selections did you choose?
- What are your reasons for grouping these texts together?
- What is compelling or interesting about each selection?
- What questions will be used to begin our book discussion?

Test-Taking Practice

Critical Reading: Short Reading Passage

The **short reading passages** of standardized tests require you to read selections that may only be a paragraph or two in length, or about 100 words. They may be poetry or fiction selections, or readings from natural science, social studies, or the humanities. They may include narrative, expository, or persuasive (argumentative) elements. The majority of the questions require extended reasoning in which you analyze and synthesize information. You may also be required to comment on the author's assumptions and style.

RL.11-12.4; RI.11-12.5, RI.11-12.2.c; L.11-12.3; W.11-12.1, W.11-12.5

[For the full wording of the standards, see the standards chart in the front of your textbook.]

Practice

The following exercise is modeled after the SAT Short Passage Critical Reading section. This section usually includes 48 questions.

Directions: Read the following passage from "The Gift" by Li-Young Lee. Then, choose the best answer to each question.

To pull the metal splinter from my palm
my father recited a story in a low voice.
I watched his lovely face and not the blade.
Before the story ended, he'd removed
the iron sliver I thought I'd die from.
I can't remember the tale,
but hear his voice still, a well
of dark water, a prayer.
And I recall his hands,
two measures of tenderness
he laid against my face,
the flames of discipline
he raised above my head.
Had you entered that afternoon
you would have thought you saw a man
planting something in a boy's palm,
a silver tear, a tiny flame.

Strategy

- **Read carefully** to find text directly related to the question.
- **Avoid being misled** by an answer that looks correct but is not supported by information directly stated.
- **Prove your answer** by matching specific details in the text to what a question is asking.

SAT® PREP ACT

1. What literary device does this part of the poem employ?
   A. flashback
   B. in medias res
   C. foreshadowing
   D. hyperbole
   E. chronological order

2. What detail does the poet use to convey his father's character?
   A. his accomplishments
   B. his support of the family
   C. his voice and hands
   D. his face and head
   E. the story he told

3. In line 10 the word "measures" most nearly means
   A. musical divisions
   B. cups or pounds
   C. courses of action
   D. amounts
   E. rulers

4. It can be inferred that the poet's father told him a story to
   A. describe what happened when he put something in his son's palm
   B. tell him about how other men had died from metal splinters
   C. distract him from the pain and worry of the metal splinter
   D. help him remember how his voice was like a deep well
   E. explain how the boy got the metal splinter in his palm in the first place

5. What action would inspire the image of "a man planting" in lines 14–17?
   A. arms held above the boy's head in a gesture of working
   B. someone pushing a tiller through a garden
   C. a quick pulling action
   D. heads leaning together in quiet conversation
   E. the father gently touching the boy's palm

6. How are "a well" and "a prayer" in lines 7–8 related to the father's voice?
   A. They are sacred and inspiring.
   B. They are threatening and desperate.
   C. They are nourishing and appealing.
   D. They are deep and solemn.
   E. They are dark, invisible, and mysterious.

7. Which of these moments could be described as an epiphany for the speaker?
   A. when he realizes he has a metal splinter in the palm of his hand
   B. when he realizes removing something can add something
   C. when he understands that the splinter is finally out of his hand
   D. when he remembers the voice but cannot recall the story
   E. when he thinks about his father's hands beside his face

8. What are "the flames of discipline" mentioned in line 12?
   A. the metal splinters he fears will kill him
   B. his father's strict self-control
   C. his father's words that have scolded him
   D. his father's hands that may have punished him
   E. the dark well water and the prayer his father says

9. What formal element does this poem contain?
   A. The verses are shaped like a sliver.
   B. It has internal rhymes.
   C. It is structured in quatrains.
   D. It is a villanelle.
   E. It contains epic qualities.

10. Which choice best analyzes the poet's use of metal and flame imagery?
   A. He connects the iron splinter to his father's passion and caring.
   B. He links the blade that removes the splinter to the planting of ideas.
   C. He suggests his father's story is about precious metals in a flame.
   D. He indicates that one needs to be hard like metal to endure the heat.
   E. He contrasts tenderness, hardness, and deep emotion.

Grammar and Writing: Improving Paragraphs

Improving paragraphs exercises may appear in the writing sections of standardized tests. They are made up of a reading passage with numbered sentences. The passages are usually drafts of student essays containing errors in grammar, style, and usage. For each question, you must decide which of five possible answers will best correct the given sentence.

Practice

This exercise is modeled after the Improving Paragraphs portion of the SAT Writing Test.

Directions: Questions 1-8 refer to the following draft of a student essay.

[1] Naomi Shihab Nye was born in 1952 in St. Louis, Missouri, published her first poem at age seven, and moved to Jerusalem with her family at age fourteen. **[2]** She ended up in San Antonio, Texas where she lives today. **[3]** Her writing echoes the voices of the Mexican-Americans in her neighborhood. **[4]** It also presents the perspectives of Arab-Americans like herself. **[5]** Her father was a Palestinian and her mother an American citizen. **[6]** Her background gives her a unique perspective on the cultural richness of America.

[7] Nye's career as a writer began with her becoming a speaker, freelancer, and editor after she graduated from Trinity University in 1974. **[8]** Her first collection of poetry explored the differences between cultures. **[9]** Her second collection concerns itself with what is shared between cultures. **[10]** <u>More poems she collected</u> explored the more mature themes of political struggle in the Mideast and the suffering there.

[11] Recently, Nye has expanded beyond writing her own poetry. **[12]** She has written a young adult novel, penned a collection of essays, and a poetry anthology she edited that won many awards.

Strategy

Focus only on the answers provided. As you read the essay, you will notice errors. Do not take time to edit these errors on your own. Select the best version of the answer choices only.

1. Which revision is most needed in sentence 1?

(A) (As it is now)

(B) Naomi Shihab Nye was born in 1952 in St. Louis, published her first poem at age seven and moved to Jerusalem with her family at age fourteen.

(C) Naomi Shihab Nye, born in 1952 in St. Louis, Missouri, then published a poem when she was seven, and moved to Jerusalem with her family at age fourteen.

(D) Naomi Shihab Nye as born in 1952 in St. Louis, Missouri, publishes her first poem at age seven, and moves to Jerusalem with her family at age fourteen.

(E) Naomi Shihab Nye, born in 1952 in St. Louis, Missouri, then published her first poem at age seven.

2. Which sentence would provide the best transition between the first and second paragraphs?
   (A) She has won many awards, including the Pushcart Prize.
   (B) Nye believes that the source of her poetry is the voice of the people combined with her broader background as a professional writer.
   (C) Nye listens to the people around her and tries to incorporate their concerns into her work.
   (D) Moving around a lot has sometimes made Nye feel rootless, which is reflected in her poetry.
   (E) Nye has had many jobs and a good education.

3. In context, which of the following revisions to sentence 7 is most needed to provide variety?
   (A) Delete "with her becoming a speaker, freelancer, and editor."
   (B) Change "her" to "she."
   (C) Add at the end "and she also won the Jane Patterson Award for Poetry."
   (D) Move "after she graduated from Trinity University in 1974" to the start of the sentence.
   (E) Add a semicolon after "editor."

SAT® PREP ACT

4. Which transition would show the relationship between sentences 8 and 9 while uniting them?
   (A) similarily
   (B) therefore
   (C) for example
   (D) in conclusion
   (E) in contrast

5. Which is the best version of the underlined portion of sentence 10?
   (A) More poems in a collection
   (B) Her third collection
   (C) More collected poems
   (D) Nye's next poems
   (E) More poems in her third book

6. Which grammatical or stylistic error is exhibited in sentence 12?
   (A) run-on sentence
   (B) faulty parallelism
   (C) unjustified use of fragments
   (D) misplaced modifier
   (E) use of passive voice

Timed Writing: Position Statement [25 minutes]

Naomi Shihab Nye has said, "Anyone who feels poetry is an alien or ominous force should consider the style in which human beings think. 'How do you think?' I ask my students. 'Do you think in complete, elaborate sentences? . . . Or in flashes and bursts of images, snatches of lines leaping one to the next?' We think in poetry. But some people pretend poetry is far away."

Write an essay in which you agree or disagree with Nye's **perspective** on poetry. Provide reasons for your opinions based on the poetry you have read and your own ideas about the relationship between poetry and life. Use handwriting that is fluent and legible. This assignment is similar to the essay portion of the SAT Writing Section.

Academic Vocabulary

Perspective is both a way of looking at things and a personal definition. In your essay, discuss the author's perspective before stating your opinion.

Constructed Response

Directions: *Follow the instructions to complete the tasks below as required by your teacher. As you work on each task, incorporate both general academic vocabulary and literary terms you learned in this unit.*

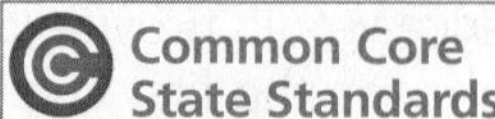
Common Core State Standards

RL.11-12.3, RL.11-12.4, RL.11-12.5, RL.11-12.6; RI.11-12.4, RI.11-12.6; W.11-12.1, W.11-12.2, W.11-12.9.a, W.11-12.9.b; SL.11-12.4, SL.11-12.6

[For the full wording of the standards, see the standards chart in the front of your textbook.]

Writing

Task 1: Literature [RL.11-12.6; W.11-12.2, W.11-12.9.a]

Analyze Point of View

*Write an **essay** in which you analyze the author's point of view as expressed in a literary work from this unit.*

- Identify the story you will discuss and explain why you chose it.
- Express a clear central idea, or thesis.
- Consider the author's diction and tone, as well as his or her use of literary devices, such as hyperbole, understatement, satire, or irony. In all such cases, clearly analyze the relationship between direct statements and their actual meanings. Explain how the true meaning suggests the author's point of view.
- Cite evidence from the story to support your interpretation of meaning and your determination of point of view.
- In your conclusion, restate your central idea.

Task 2: Literature [RL.11-12.4; W.11-12.2]

Analyze Word Choice and Tone

*Write an **essay** in which you analyze the word choice and tone in a literary work from this unit.*

- Identify the literary work you will discuss and explain why you chose it.
- Summarize the work and explain the various types of diction it employs, including figurative or technical language.
- Provide examples from the work of each type of diction you identified. Then, discuss each example in turn. Consider denotative and connotative meanings; figurative meanings; and the impact of each example on the author's overall meaning and tone.
- Conclude with a paragraph or section in which you explain in broader terms the role word choice plays in an author's craft.

Task 3: Informational Text [RI.11-12.6; W.11-12.1, W.11-12.9.b]

Analyze and Evaluate Rhetoric

*Write an **essay** in which you analyze and evaluate the author's rhetoric in a nonfiction work from this unit.*

- Choose a nonfiction work in which the rhetoric is particularly effective. State which work you chose and your reasons for choosing it.
- Include a clear statement of your position—your claim or thesis.
- Discuss the author's purpose for writing the work. Also, explain the author's perspective or point of view on the topic.
- Discuss how the author's rhetoric advances his or her purpose and perspective. Include illustrative examples of specific types of rhetorical devices, such as parallelism, restatement, anaphora, or other rhetorical figures.
- Organize your essay logically, so that the introduction provides information and establishes the reader's expectations, the body paragraphs progress in a clear order, and the conclusion supports the ideas presented earlier.

Speaking and Listening

Task 4: Literature [RL.11-12.3; SL.11-12.4]

Analyze Story Elements

*Deliver an **oral presentation** in which you analyze the development of and relationship among elements of a work of fiction from this unit.*

- Identify the work of fiction from this unit you will discuss. Explain why you chose it.
- Identify three story elements, such as setting, character, and conflict, that you will use as a focus for your presentation. Dicsuss why you chose the three elements rather than other aspects of the story.
- Explain the choices the author made concerning each element. For example, discuss the choice of setting, the order of the action, or the methods by which characters are introduced and developed.
- Explain how the elements you chose combine to create an effective work of fiction.
- Keep your audience in mind as you make your presentation. Provide background information that will help your audience comprehend your analysis.

Task 5: Informational Text [RI.11-12.4; SL.11-12.6]

Analyze Word Choice

*In an **oral presentation,** analyze word choice and meaning in a nonfiction work from this unit.*

- Choose a nonfiction work from this unit that you feel uses noteworthy diction. Identify the work you chose and briefly explain why you chose it.
- Identify three examples of word choice that you feel are particularly effective or critical to the meaning of the work as a whole.
- Cite your choices in context, and then discuss each one separately. Consider their figurative, connotative, or technical meanings.
- Discuss whether the author's use or definition of a key word changes over the course of the work. Explain the effect of any such refinements on the meaning of the work as a whole.
- Use formal English as you deliver your presentation.

Task 6: Literature [RL.11-12.5; SL.11-12.4]

Analyze and Assess Structure

*Prepare and present an **analysis and assessment** of the structure of a literary work from this unit.*

- Choose a literary work with a structure that you feel is closely connected to or helps to convey its meaning. Explain which work you chose and why you chose it.
- Provide a detailed description of the author's structural choices. Use slides, a whiteboard, or hand-outs to present this information clearly and concisely. Discuss how the structural choices of passages or sections contribute to the work's overall structure.
- Discuss how structural choices affect meaning. For example, consider whether structural elements add to a character's complexity or heighten suspense.
- Express your ideas logically so that listeners can easily follow your reasoning.

THE ESSENTIAL Q

What makes American literature American?

Everyday Life A conversation, a journey, a meal, a sunrise—literary versions of such common experiences reveal a great deal about American identity now and throughout history. Does the sight of a bird have a different meaning for a Puritan, a Romantic, a Realist, a contemporary? Are Americans' values different today from what they were in the past?

Assignment Choose an everyday event described in this unit and find a similar event in a previous unit. Write a **comparison-and-contrast essay** in which you discuss the similarities and differences of the passages and explain what each suggests about American identity.

Titles for Extended Reading

In this unit, you have read a variety of literature of the contemporary period. Continue to read works related to this era on your own. Select books that you enjoy, but challenge yourself to explore new topics, new authors, and works offering varied perspectives or approaches. The titles suggested below will help you get started.

LITERATURE

Sailing Alone Around the Room

Billy Collins

Random House, 2001 EXEMPLAR TEXT 

Poetry Billy Collins was the U.S. poet laureate from 2001 to 2003. This collection of poems by Collins, which includes "Man Listening to Disc," covers topics ranging from insomnia to snow days with wit, freshness, and vivid imagery.

The Bluest Eye

Toni Morrison

Vintage, 1970 EXEMPLAR TEXT 

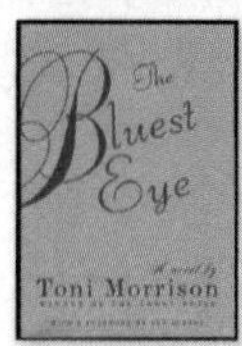

Novel This powerful, disturbing novel explores themes of abuse and the destruction of self-esteem caused by racism. Pecola, a young African American girl during the Great Depression, believes all her troubles would be solved if she only had blue eyes.

Dreaming in Cuban

Cristina Garcia

One World Books, 1992 EXEMPLAR TEXT 

Novel Three generations of Cuban woman from the del Pino family tell their stories of life in Cuba and in exile. Using narratives, love letters, and memories, Garcia brings these troubled but passionate women to life.

The Namesake

Jhumpa Lahiri

First Mariner Books, 2003 EXEMPLAR TEXT 

Novel *The Namesake* explores the life of Gogol Ganguli, a second-generation Indian immigrant who struggles to find his place in his family and in American culture.

Death and the King's Horseman

Wole Soyinka

W. W. Norton, 2002 EXEMPLAR TEXT 

Drama When the king dies in this Nigerian play, his horseman is expected to follow tradition and kill himself. What will happen when the horseman's son arrives from London and a colonial district officer decides to intervene?

Mother Love: Poems

Rita Dove

W. W. Norton, 1996  EXEMPLAR TEXT 

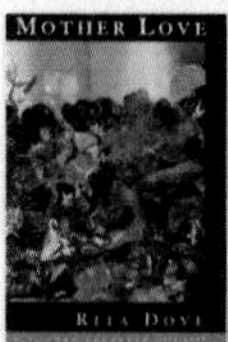

Poetry In this collection, former U.S. poet laureate Rita Dove uses the mythical Greek figures Demeter and Persephone to explore themes of love between mothers and daughters. Included in the collection is "Demeter's Prayer to Hades."

INFORMATIONAL TEXTS

Nonfiction Readings Across the Curriculum

Pearson Prentice Hall

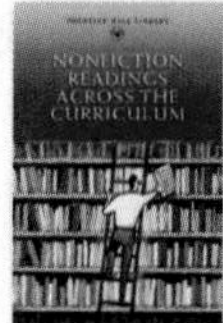

Nonfiction Football great Joe Namath gives players a pep talk. Beverly Cleary tells how she got her start as an author. These and other essays by famous people provide new perspectives on subjects ranging from arts and literature to science, social studies, and sports.

On Nature: Great Writers on the Great Outdoors

edited by Lee Gutkind

Putnam, 2002

Nonfiction This book of contemporary nature essays by some of America's best contemporary authors will appeal to those who love outdoor activities as well as those who prefer getting their [mental] exercise in an armchair with a good book. It features nonfiction by Joyce Carol Oates, Barry Lopez, Mark Doty, Diane Ackerman, John McPhee, and Bill Bryson, among others.

The Tipping Point: How Little Things Can Make a Big Difference

Malcolm Gladwell

Back Bay Books, 2002 EXEMPLAR TEXT

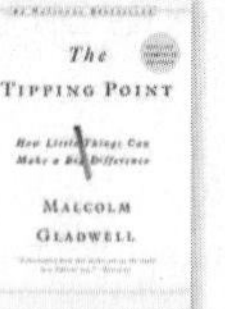

Nonfiction Gladwell suggests that "ideas, messages, and behaviors spread just like viruses," and then uses engaging examples to show how small changes can bring us to the "tipping point," where they transform the world.

Preparing to Read Complex Texts

Reading for College and Career In both college and the workplace, readers must analyze texts independently, draw connections among works that offer varied perspectives, and develop their own ideas and informed opinions. The questions shown below, and others that you generate on your own, will help you more effectively read and analyze complex college-level texts.

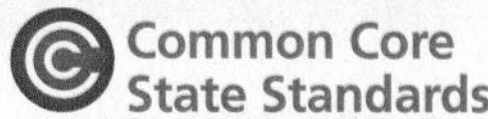

Reading Literature/Informational Text
10. By the end of grade 11, read and comprehend literature, including stories, dramas, and poems, and literary nonfiction, in the grades 11-CCR text complexity band proficiently, with scaffolding as needed at the high end of the range.

While reading analytically, ask yourself...

- What idea, experience, or story seems to have compelled the author to write? Has the author presented that idea, experience, or story in a way that I, too, find compelling?
- How might the author's era, social status, belief system, or personal experiences have affected the point of view he or she expresses in the text?
- How do my circumstances affect what I understand and feel about this text?
- What key idea does the author state explicitly? What key idea does he or she suggest or imply? Which details in the text help me to perceive implied ideas?
- Do I find multiple layers of meaning in the text? If so, what relationships do I see among these layers of meaning?
- How do details in the text connect or relate to one another? Do I find any details unconvincing, unrelated, or out of place?
- Do I find the text believable and convincing?

Key Ideas and Details

- What patterns of organization or sequences do I find in the text? Do these patterns help me understand the ideas better?
- What do I notice about the author's style, including his or her diction, uses of imagery and figurative language, and syntax?
- Do I like the author's style? Is the author's style memorable?
- What emotional attitude does the author express toward the topic, the story, or the characters? Does this attitude seem appropriate?
- What emotional attitude does the author express toward me, the reader? Does this attitude seem appropriate?
- What do I notice about the author's voice—his or her personality on the page? Do I like this voice? Does it make me want to read on?

Craft and Structure

- Is the work fresh and original?
- Do I agree with the author's ideas entirely, or are there elements I find unconvincing?
- Do I disagree with the author's ideas entirely, or are there elements I can accept as true?
- Based on my knowledge of American literature, history, and culture, does this work reflect the American tradition? Why or why not?

Integration of Ideas

Resources

English Glossary

Essential Question vocabulary appears in **blue type**. High-Utility Academic Vocabulary is **underlined**.

A

abeyance (uh BAY uhns) *n.* temporary suspension

absolve (ab ZOLV) *v.* pardon; free from guilt

absurdity (ab SUR duh tee) *n.* nonsense; ridiculousness

accosted (uh KAWST uhd) *v.* approached and spoke to in an eager way

account (uh KOWNT) *n.* a report or description

acknowledges (ak NOL ihj) *v.* to admit the existence, reality, or truth of

acquiesce (AK wee EHS) *v.* agree without protest

adamant (AD uh mant) *adj.* firm; unyielding

adjourned (uh JURND) *v.* closed for a time

advantageous (ad vuhn TAY juhs) *adj.* favorable; beneficial

adversary (AD vuhr sehr ee) *n.* opponent; enemy

adversity (ad VUR suh tee) *n.* hardship; difficulty

affections (uh FEHK shuhnz) *n.* emotions

affliction (uh FLIHK shuhn) *n.* anything causing pain or distress

agape (uh GAYP) *adj.* in surprise; wonder

aggregation (ag ruh GAY shuhn) *n.* group of distinct objects or individuals

agricultural (ag ruh KUHL chuhr uhl) *adj.* with farming as the main way of life

alacrity (uh LAK ruh tee) *n.* speed

alienation (AY lee uh NAY shuhn) *n.* a withdrawing or separation of feeling or affection

alliance (uh LY uhns) *n.* union of nations for a specific purpose

ambiguity (AM buh GYOO uh tee) *n.* state of having two or more possible meanings

ambition (am BIHSH uhn) *n.* strong desire to gain a particular objective; drive to succeed

ameliorate (uh MEEL yuh rayt) *v.* make better

ample (AM puhl) *adj.* large in size; more than enough

analyze (AN uh lyz) *v.* break down a topic into parts and explain them

anarchy (AN uhr kee) *n.* absence of government

ancestor (AN sehs tuhr) *n.* person from whom other people descend

anonymity (an uh NIHM uh tee) *n.* the condition of being unknown

anticipate (an TIHS uh payt) *v.* prepare for or signal something

anxiety (ang ZY uh tee) *n.* state of being uneasy, apprehensive, or worried about what may happen.

apparel (uh PAR uhl) *n.* clothing

apparition (ap uh RIHSH uhn) *n.* act of appearing or becoming visible

appease (uh PEEZ) *v.* satisfy

appendage (uh PEHN dihj) *n.* external part of a plant or animal, such as a tail or a limb

appraise (uh PRAYZ) *v.* evaluate something's worth, significance, or status

apprehension (ap rih HEHN shuhn) *n.* an anxious feeling of foreboding; dread

appropriate (uh PROH pree ayt) *v.* to take or use something without permission

arduous (AHR joo uhs) *adj.* difficult

argue (AHR gyoo) *v.* give reasons for or against; prove by giving reasons

arrange (uh RAYNJ) *v.* put into order or sequence

ascended (uh SEHND uhd) *v.* climbed up

aspirations (as puh RAY shuhnz) *n.* strong desires or ambitions

assault (uh SAWLT) *n.* violent attack

assent (uh SEHNT) *n.* agreement

assess (uh SEHS) *v.* determine importance, size, or value

austerity (aw STEHR uh tee) *n.* sternness in manner or appearance; harshness; severity

auxiliary (awg ZIHL yuhr ee) *adj.* giving help or support

avarice (AV uhr ihs) *n.* greed

aversion (uh VUR zhuhn) *n.* object arousing an intense dislike

avidly (AV ihd lee) *adv.* eagerly

awe (aw) *n.* mixed feelings of fear and wonder

B

base (bays) *adj.* low; mean

beguile (bih GYL) *v.* charm or delight

benediction (behn uh DIHK shuhn) *n.* prayer asking for God's blessing

benevolent (buh NEHV uh luhnt) *adj.* kindly; charitable

benign (bih NYN) *adj.* not injurious or malignant; not cancerous

bequeath (bih KWEETH) *v.* hand down; pass on

blaspheming (BLAS feem ihng) *v.* cursing

brazenness (BRAY zuhn nehs) n. shamelessness; boldness; impudence

brigade (brih GAYD) n. a unit of soldiers

brutal (BROO tuhl) adj. cruel and without feeling; savage; violent

C

cadence (KAY duhns) *n.* a series of notes or chords near the end of a musical work

calamity (kuh LAM uh tee) *n.* disaster; catastrophe

calumny (KAL uhm nee) *n.* false accusation; slander

candid (KAN dihd) *adj.* straightforward

canvass (KAN vuhs) *v.* go through an area asking people for votes, orders, or participation

capable (KAY puh buhl) *adj.* having the skills needed to do something

caper (KAY puhr) *n.* prank

casualties (KAZH oo uhl teez) *n.* members of the armed forces who die in combat

categorize (KAT uh guh ryz) *v.* place in related groups

cavernous (KAV uhr nuhs) *adj.* cavelike; vast

celestial (suh LEHS chuhl) *adj.* of or in the sky, as planets or stars

chaos (KAY os) *n.* disorder of matter and space, supposed to have existed before the ordered universe

chronicles (KRON uh kuhlz) *n.* stories; histories

circumvent (sur kuhm VEHNT) *v.* prevent; get around

civilian (suh VIHL yuhn) *n.* any person who is not a member of the armed forces

classify (KLAS uh fy) *v.* assign to a category

cleave (kleev) *v.* adhere; cling

coinage (KOY nihj) *n.* an invented word or expression

coincide (koh ihn SYD) *v.* to occur at the same time

collective (kuh LEHK tihv) *n.* gathered into a whole

collusion (kuh LOO zhuhn) *n.* secret agreement; conspiracy

commercial (kuh MUR shuhl) *adj.* connected with trade or business

commissioners (kuh MIHSH uh nuhrz) *n.* government officials

commonplace (KOM uhn PLAYS) *adj.* everyday; ordinary

commotion (kuh MOH shuhn) *n.* noisy confusion

community (kuh MYOO nuh tee) *n.* all the people living a particular district, city, or area

compare (kuhm PAIR) *v.* point out similarities or differences

READING AND VOCABULARY HANDBOOK

conciliatory (kuhn SIHL ee uh tawr ee) *adj.* intended to make peace or to reconcile; friendly

conclude (kuhn KLOOD) *v.* reach as a logically necessary end by reasoning

condolences (kuhn DOH luhns ez) *n.* expressions of sympathy

conduct (KON duhkt) *n.* behavior

conflagration (kon fluh GRAY shuhn) *n.* big, destructive fire

conformity (kuhn FAWR muh tee) *n.* action in agreement with generally accepted standards

confounded (kon FOWN dihd) *adj.* confused; dismayed

conjectural (kuhn JEHK chuhr uhl) *adj.* based on guesswork

conjectured (kuhn JEHK chuhrd) *v.* guessed

conjuring (KON juhr ihng) *v.* causing to be; appearing as by magic

consecrate (KON suh krayt) *v.* cause to be revered or honored

conspicuous (kuhn SPIHK yoo uhs) *adj.* obvious; easy to see or perceive

consternation (kon stuhr NAY shuhn) *n.* great fear or shock that makes one feel helpless or bewildered

constitute (KON stuh toot) *v.* serve as the parts or basis of; form; comprise

constitution (kon stuh TOO shuhn) *n.* physical makeup of a person

contentious (kuhn TEHN shuhs) *adj.* argumentative

contiguous (kuhn TIHG yoo uhs) *adj.* bordering; adjacent

contract (KON trakt) *n.* written agreement

contrast (KON trast) *v.* examine to discover differences

convention (kuhn VEHN shuhn) *n.* a meeting attended by members or delegates

conviction (kuhn VIHK shuhn) *n.* strong belief

convivial (kuhn VIHV ee uhl) *adj.* fond of good company; sociable

copious (KOH pee uhs) *adj.* plentiful; abundant

correspond (KAWR uh SPOND) *v.* be in agreement; relate to

countenance (KOWN tuh nuhns) *v.* approve; tolerate

cowering (KOW uhr ihng) *v.* trembling or cringing, as with fear

create (kree AYT) *v.* produce through imaginative skill

crevices (KREHV ihs iz) *n.* narrow openings caused by cracks or splits

critic (KRIHT ihk) *n.* person who disapproves or finds fault

critique (krih TEEK) *v.* examine critically; review

cunning (KUHN ihng) *adj.* skillful in deception; crafty; sly

cyberspace (SY buhr SPAYS) *n.* online world of computer networks

D

daunting (DAWNT ihng) *adj.* intimidating

decorum (dih KAWR uhm) *n.* rightness; suitability

deduce (dih DOOS) *v.* infer from a general principle

defend (dih FEHND) *v.* maintain or support in the face of argument

deference (DEHF uhr uhns) *n.* courteous regard or respect

deficient (dih FIHSH uhnt) *adj.* lacking; not having something needed

define (dih FYN) *v.* tell the qualities that make something what it is

degenerate (dih JEHN uh ruht) *adj.* morally corrupt

dejected (dih JEHK tihd) *v.* in low spirits; downcast; depressed

deliberation (dih lihb uh RAY shuhn) *n.* careful consideration

deposition (dehp uh ZIHSH uhn) *n.* testimony of a witness made under oath but not in open court

depths (dehpths) *n.* deepest areas

derivative (dih RIHV uh tihv) *adj.* not original; based on something else

derive (dih RYV) *v.* trace to or from a source; get by reasoning

describe (dih SKRYB) *v.* represent in words

design (dih ZYN) *v.* create, fashion, execute, or construct according to plan

desolate (DEHS uh liht) *adj.* deserted; isolated

despondent (dih SPON duhnt) *adj.* without courage or hope

despotism (DEHS puh tihz uhm) *n.* absolute rule; tyranny

destitute (DEHS tuh toot) *adj.* living in complete poverty

destruction (dih STRUHK shuhn) *n.* act of demolishing or defeating

detached (dih TACHT) *adj.* not emotionally involved

devise (dih VYZ) *v.* form in the mind by new combinations of ideas; invent

dictum (DIHK tuhm) *n.* formal statement of fact or opinion

differentiate (DIHF uh REHN shee ayt) *v.* recognize a dissimilarity

digress (duh GREHS) *v.* depart temporarily from the main subject

dilapidated (duh LAP uh day tuhd) *adj.* in disrepair

diligence (DIHL uh juhns) *n.* constant, careful effort; perseverance

discern (duh SURN) *v.* perceive or recognize; make out clearly

discord (DIHS kawrd) *n.* difference of opinion; disputing

discretion (dihs KREHSH uhn) *n.* judgment

discriminate (dihs KRIHM uh nayt) *v.* recognize differences between or among things

disdainfully (dihs DAYN fuhl ee) *adv.* showing scorn or contempt

disgrace (dihs GRAYS) *n.* something that brings shame or dishonor

disillusion (DIHS ih LOO zhuhn) *n.* freedom from a false idea; disenchantment

dispatched (dihs PACHT) *v.* sent off, usually on official business

dispersal (dihs PUR suhl) *n.* distribution

disposition (dihs puh ZIHSH uhn) *n.* inclination; tendency

disregard (dihs rih GAHRD) *v.* to pay no attention to; leave out of consideration; ignore

dissembling (dih SEHM buhl ihng) *v.* disguising one's real nature or motives

dissention (dih SEHN shuhn) *n.* disagreement; discord as expressed in intense quarreling

dissuade (dih SWAYD) *v.* convince someone not to do something

distinguish (dihs TIHNG gwihsh) *v.* mark as separate or different

diversity (duh VUR suh tee) *n.* variety; point of unlikeness

divine (duh VYN) *v.* find out by intuition

docile (DOS uhl) adj. easy to direct or manage: obedient

doctrine (DOK truhn) *n.* what is taught

dogma (DAWG muh) *n.* authoritative doctrines or beliefs

dubious (DOO bee uhs) *adj.* questionable; suspicious

duplicate (DOO pluh kayht) *v.* make a copy

duration (du RAY shuhn) *n.* the time during which something continues or exists

dusky (DUHS kee) *adj.* dark; dim; shadowy

dyspepsia (dihs PEHP see uh) *n.* indigestion

E

ecstasy (EHKS tuh see) *n.* a feeling of overpowering joy; great delight

efface (uh FAYS) *v.* erase; wipe out

effigies (eh FIHJ eez) *n.* images or likenesses, especially of people

effrontery (uh FRUHN tuhr ee) *n.* shameless boldness

effuse (ih FYOOZ) *v.* pour out; gush

eloquence (EHL uh kwuhns) *n.* talent for vivid, forceful speech

elusive (ih LOO sihv) *adj.* hard to grasp

embankment (ehm BANGK muhnt) *n.* mound of earth or stone built to hold back water or support or a roadway

embark (ehm BAHRK) *v.* to begin a venture, project, or activity

emigrants (EHM uh gruhnts) *n.* people who leave one place to settle in another

eminence (EHM uh nuhns) *n.* greatness; celebrity

emit (ih MIHT) *v.* utter words or sounds

enamored (ehn AM uhrd) *adj.* charmed; captivated

encroached (ehn KROHCHT) *v.* intruded

endured (ehn DURD) *v.* held up under

engrossed (ehn GROHST) *v.* occupied wholly; absorbed

entreated (ehn TREET uhd) *v.* begged; pleaded

entrenchments (ehn TREHNCH muhnts) *n.* long deep holes with steep sides, used as defense against enemy fire

environment (ehn VY ruhn muhnt) *n.* the surrounding objects or conditions

epitaph (EHP uh taf) *n.* inscription on a tombstone or grave marker

equivocal (ih KWIHV uh kuhl) *adj.*having more than one possible interpretation

eradicate (ih RAD uh kayt) *v.* wipe out; destroy

establishment (ehs TAB lihsh muhnt) *n.* household or business

estimates (EHS tuh mihts) *n.* general, careful calculations

etiquette (EHT uh keht) *n.* appropriate behavior and ceremonies

evacuated (ih VAK yu ayt uhd) *v.* emptied; withdrawn

evade (ih VAYD) *v.* avoid or escape from by deceit or cleverness

evaluate (ih VAL yu ayt) *v.* determine something's significance, worth, or condition through careful study

exalted (ehg ZAWL tihd) *adj.* filled with joy or pride; elated

examine (ehg ZAM uhn) *v.* carefully inquire into a topic

exasperation (ehg zas puh RAY shuhn) *n.* annoyance; frustration

exhaust (ehg ZAWST) *n.* discharge of used steam or gas from an engine

exile (EHG zyl) *n.* the state or period of being banished

expansion (ehk SPAN shuhn) *n.* act or process of increasing in extent, size, or volume

expedient (ehk SPEE dee uhnt) *n.* method used to achieve a goal quickly

expenditures (ehk SPEHN duh churz) *n.* expenses; uses of money or resources

exposures (ehk SPOH zhuhrz) *n.* sections of film on which light falls when a photograph is taken

extort (ehk STAWRT) *v.* obtain by threat or violence

extraneous (ehk STRAY nee uhs) *adj.* unrelated; unconnected

F

fallowness (FAL oh nuhs) *n.* inactivity

fantastic (fan TAS tihk) *adj.* excellent; unbelievable

fastidious (fas TIHD ee uhs) *adj.* careful; meticulous

fatigues (fuh TEEGZ) *n.* sturdy clothing worn by soldiers doing hard work

feigned (faynd) *v.* pretended

fervent (FUR vuhnt) *adj.* extremely passionate; very enthusiastic

finite (FY nyt) *adj.* having measurable or definable limits

fitfully (FIHT fuhl ee) *adv.* characterized by irregular or intermittent activity

flagrant (FLAY gruhnt) *adj.* glaring; outrageous

flourished (FLUR ihsht) *v.* grew strong, healthy, and happy; prospered

fluctuation (fluhk chu AY shuhn) *n.* a change in level or intensity

foothold (FUT hohld) *n.* secure position from which further actions can be taken

forded (FAWRD uhd) *v.* crossed a river at a low point

forestall (fawr STAWL) *v.* prevent by acting ahead of time

formulate (FAWR myuh layt) *v.* express fully and clearly

fortuitous (fawr TOO uh tuhs) *adj.* fortunate

fortune (FAWR chuhn) *n.* wealth; luck

fragmentation (frag muhn TAY shuhn) *n.* act or process of breaking up into parts

frantic (FRAN tihk) *adj.* marked by frenzy

frayed (frayd) *adj.* tattered

freedom (FREE duhm) *n.* not being under another's control

frontier (fruhn TIHR) *n.* border between inhabited regions; a developing region of field of thought

furtive (FUR tihv) *adj.* sneaky

G

garrulous (GAR uh luhs) *adj.* talking too much

gaudy (GAW dee) *adj.* showy in a tasteless way

generalize (JEHN uhr uh lyz) *v.* draw a larger principle from details

genial (JEEN yuhl) *adj.* cheerful; friendly

genre (zhahn ruh) *n.* catagory, or style

global (GLOH buhl) *adj.* spread throughout the world

govern (GUHV uhrn) *v.* to rule; control; manage

grandeur (GRAN juhr) *n.* greatness

grave (grayv) *adj.* serious; solemn

gravity (GRAV uh tee) *n.* seriousness

guile (gyl) *n.* craftiness

H

habitation (hab uh TAY shuhn) *n.* place to live; group of homes or dwellings

hallow (HAL oh) *v.* honor as sacred

handiwork (HAN dee wurk) *n.* work done by the hands; work done personally

harass (HUH ras) *v.* attack; bother

heady (HEHD ee) *adj.* intoxicating

heightened (HY tuhnd) *v.* raised the level of

heritage (HEHR uh tihj) *n.* traits, beliefs, or customs passed on from one's ancestors

homages (HOM ihj uhz) *n.* acts showing honor and reverence

homely (HOHM lee) *adj.* not elegant or polished; crude

huddled (HUHD uhld) *v.* gathered closely; nestled

humor (HYOO muhr) *n.* funny or amusing quality

hypothesize (hy POTH uh syz) *v.* develop a theory about

I

idealism (y DEE uh lihz uhm) *n.* thought based on following standards of perfection or beauty

identify (y DEHN tuh fy) *v.* establish the identity of something

identity (y DEHN tuh tee) *n.* who a person is

illiterate (ih LIHT uhr iht) *adj.* unable to read or write

illustrate (IHL uh strayt) *v.* give examples that support an idea

immigration (ihm uh GRAY shuhn) *n.* act of coming into a foreign country or region to live

imperceptible (ihm puhr SEHP tuh buhl) *adj.* not easy to perceive; unnoticeable

impertinent (ihm PUR tuh nuhnt) *adj.* not showing proper respect; saucy

implore (ihm PLAWR) *v.* ask or beg earnestly; plead

imply (ihm PLY) *v.* hint or suggest

impulsive (ihm PUHL sihv) *adj.* done without thinking

impulsively (ihm PUHL sihv lee) *adv.* spontaneously; suddenly

inanimate (ihn AN uh miht) *adj.* not alive; lifeless

inarticulate (ihn ahr TIHK yuh liht) *adj.* unclearly spoken or expressed

inaudibly (ihn AW duh blee) *adv.* in a manner that cannot be heard

incessant (ihn SEHS uhnt) *adj.* constant; seemingly endless

incorporated (ihn KAWR puh rayt uhd) *v.* organized as a legal corporation

incorrigible (ihn KAWR uh juh buhl) *adj.* impossible to correct; incurable

incredulously (ihn KREHD juh luhs lee) *adv.* skeptically

increment (IHN kruh muhnt) *n.* increase, as in a series

indelible (ihn DEHL uh buhl) *adj.* permanent; that cannot be erased

independence (IHN dih PEHN duhns) *n.* freedom from the control of others

individualism (IHN duh VIHJ u uh LIHZ uhm) *n.* belief that personal freedom is most important

induce (ihn DOOS) *v.* cause; bring about

industry (IHN duh stree) *n.* any branch of business, trade, or manufacturing

ineffable (ihn EHF uh buhl) *adj.* too overwhelming to be spoken

inert (ihn URT) *adj.* motionless

inextricable (ihn EHK struh kuh buhl) *adj.* unable to be separated or freed from

infer (ihn FUR) *v.* derive a conclusion from facts or premises

infinity (ihn FIHN uh tee) *n.* endless or unlimited space, time, or distance

ingratiating (ihn GRAY shee ay tihng) *adj.* charming or flattering

innovation (ihn uh VAY shuhn) *n.* a new idea, method, or device

innumerable (ih NOO muhr uh buhl) *adj.* too many to count

insatiable (ihn SAY shuh buhl) *adj.* constantly wanting more

inscrutable (ihn SKROO tuh buhl) *adj.* not able to be easily understood

inseparable (ihn SEHP uhr uh buhl) *adj.* not able to be divided; linked

insidious (ihn SIHD ee uhs) *adj.* deceitful; treacherous

inspection (ihn SPEHK shuhn) *n.* examination

intent (ihn TEHNT) *n.* purpose or aim

intently (ihn TEHNT lee) *adv.* in a focused, purposeful manner

intercepted (ihn tuhr SEHPT uhd) *v.* seized or stopped something on its way from one place to another

interminable (ihn TUR muh nuh buhl) *adj.* seeming to last forever

interposed (ihn tuhr POHZD) *v.* came between

interspersed (ihn tuhr SPURSD) *v.* placed here and there

intervene (ihn tuhr VEEN) *v.* take action in order to prevent something

intolerable (ihn TOL uhr uh buhl) *adj.* difficult or painful that it cannot be endured; unbearable

intonation (ihn toh NAY shuhn) *n.* the quality of playing musical notes in or out of tune

intricate (IHN truh kiht) *adj.* complex; having many small, interrelated parts

intuitively (ihn TOO uh tihv lee) *adv.* without having to be taught; instinctively

invective (ihn VEHK tihv) *n.* verbal attack; strong criticism

invent (ihn VEHNT) *v.* devise by thinking

investigate (ihn VEHS tuh gayt) *v.* make a systematic examination

J

jocularity (jok yuh LAR uh tee) *n.* joking good humor

jubilant (JOO buh luhnt) *adj.* joyful and triumphant

judge (juhj) *v.* form an estimate or evaluation of something

judgment (JUHJ muhnt) *n.* power to form an opinion well; good sense

justify (JUHS tuh fy) v. prove or show to be just, right, or reasonable

L

label (LAY buhl) *v.* describe or designate

lament (luh MEHNT) *v.* to express sorrow for; mourn aloud for

landscape (LAND skayp) *n.* an area that can be seen at one time from one place

latent (LAY tuhnt) *adj.* present but invisible or inactive

latitude (LAT uh tood) *n.* distance north or south from the equator

levee (LEHV ee) *n.* embankment built along the side of a river to prevent flooding

liberty (LIHB uhr tee) *n.* freedom

license (LY suhns) *n.* freedom from appropriate behavior or speech

licentious (ly SEHN shuhs) *adj.* lacking moral restraint

limber (LIHM buhr) *adj.* flexible

list (lihst) *v.* make a list; enumerate

listed (LIHST uhd) *v.* tilted; inclined

locate (LOH kayt) *v.* find the place of something

longitude (LON juh tood) *n.* distance east or west on the earth's surface

lulled (luhld) *v.* calmed or soothed by a gentle sound or motion

luminary (LOO muh nehr ee) *adj.* giving off light

M

machetes (muh SHEHT eez) *n.* large heavy knives with broad blades

magnanimity (mag nuh NIHM uh tee) *n.* generosity

magnitude (MAG nuh tood) *n.* greatness of size

maledictions (mal uh DIHK shuhnz) *n.* curses

malign (muh LYN) *adj.* malicious; very harmful

malingers (muh LIHNG guhrz) *v.* pretends to be ill

maneuver (muh NOO vuhr) *v.* to move something by some plan or scheme

manifold (MAN uh fohld) *adj.* in many ways

martial (MAHR shuhl) *adj.* relating to war

marvel (MAHR vuhl) *n.* wonderful or astonishing thing

master (MAS tuhr) *v.* become an expert in

media (MEE dee uh) *n.* systems of communication designed to reach the masses

mediator (MEE dee ay tuhr) *n.* one who reconciles opposing groups

melancholy (MEHL uhn kol ee) *adj.* sad and depressed; gloomy

membrane (MEHM brayn) *n.* thin, soft layer serving as a covering or lining

memorials (muh MAWR ee uhlz) *n.* objects displayed in memory of a person or event

meticulous (muh TIHK yuh luhs) *adj.* extremely careful about details

metropolis (muh TROP uh lihs) *n.* large city

migrant (MY gruhnt) *adj.* moving from place to place

monotonous (muh NOT uh nuhs) *adj.* tiresome because unvarying

morose (muh ROHS) *adj.* gloomy; sullen

mundane (muhn DAYN) *adj.* commonplace, everyday, ordinary

munificent (myoo NIHF uh suhnt) *adj.* generous

myriad (MIHR ee uhd) *adj.* countless

N

native (NAY tihv) *adj.* belonging to a place by birth

natural (NACH uhr uhl) *adj.* not man-made or artificial

nostalgia (nos TAL juh) *n.* a longing for something

nuance (NOO ahns) *n.* a slight or delicate variation in tone, color, meaning

O

oblivion (uh BLIHV ee uhn) *n.* condition of being completely forgotten

oblivious (uh BLIHV ee uhs) *adj.* lacking all awareness

obstinacy (OB stuh nuh see) *n.* stubbornness

obstinate (OB stuh niht) *adj.* stubborn

obtuse (uhb TOOS) *adj.* slow to understand or perceive

offensive (uh FEHN sihv) *n.* an attitude or position of attack

ominous (OM uh nuhs) *adj.* threatening; sinister

omnipotent (om NIHP uh tuhnt) *adj.* all-powerful

opposition (op uh ZIHSH uhn) *n.* hostile or resistant attitude toward something

oppressed (uh PREHST) *v.* kept down by cruel or unjust power

optimism (OP tuh mihz uhm) *n.* tendency to be positive

order (AWR duhr) *v.* arrange

ordinances (AWR duh nuhns uhz) *n.* sacraments or religious rites

ostentation (os tehn TAY shuhn) *n.* boastful display

P

pacify (PAS uh fy) *v.* to calm or soothe

pallor (PAL uhr) *n.* paleness

palpable (PAL puh buhl) *adj.* able to be touched, felt, or handled

parsimony (PAHR suh moh nee) *n.* stinginess

pastoral (PAS tuhr uhl) *adj.* characteristic of rural life; idealized as peaceful, simple, and natural

pathos (PAY thohs) *n.* quality that arouses pity, sorrow, or sympathy in others

pedestrian (puh DEHS tree uhn) *adj.* going on foot; walking

pensive (PEHN sihv) *adj.* thinking earnestly; plead

perdition (puhr DIHSH uhn) *n.* complete and irreparable loss; ruin

peremptorily (puh REHMP tuhr uh lee) *adv.* decisively; commandingly

peril (PEHR uhl) *n.* danger

permeated (PUR mee ayt uhd) *v.* soaked through with

perpetual (puhr PEHCH oo uhl) *adj.* lasting forever

persevere (pur suh VIHR) *v.* continue despite hardship; persist

persistent (puhr SIHS tuhnt) *adj.* repeated; continual

personal (PUR suh nuhl) *adj.* belonging to an individual; private

pessimism (PEHS uh mihz uhm) *n.* tendency to be negative

piety (PY uh tee) *n.* devotion to religion

platitudes (PLAT uh toodz) *n.* empty statements; tired expressions

plodding (PLOD ihng) *v.* walking or moving heavily and laboriously; trudging

poignant (POY nuhnt) *adj.* sharply painful to the feelings

poise (poyz) *n.* balance; stability

posterity (pos TEHR uh tee) *n.* all future generations

practicable (PRAK tuh kuh buhl) *adj.* practical, possible

prairie (PRAIR ee) *n.* a treeless, grass-covered plain

precipitate (prih SIHP uh tayt) *v.* cause to happen before expected or desired

preconceptions (prih kuhn SEHP shuhnz) *n.* ideas formed beforehand

predict (prih DIHKT) *v.* foretell on the basis of observation, experience, or reason

predilection (pree duh LEHK shuhn) *n.* preexisting preference

prelude (PREHL yood) *n.* introductory section or movement of a work of music

prescient (PREE shee uhnt) *adj.* having foreknowledge

pervading (puhr VAYD ihng) *v.* spreading throughout

prevalent (PREHV uh lehnt) *adj.* widely existing or occurring

privileges (PRIHV uh lihj uhz) *n.* special rights; advantages

proclaiming (pruh KLAYM ihng) *v.* announcing

procure (pruh KYUR) *v.* bring about through some effort

prodigious (pruh DIHJ uhs) *adj.* of great power or size

profundity (pruh FUHN duh tee) *n.* intellectual depth

profusion (pruh FYOO zhuhn) *n.* abundance; rich supply

propitiation (pruh pihsh ee AY shuhn) *n.* action designed to soothe or satisfy a person, a cause, etc.

propitious (pruh PIHSH uhs) *adj.* favorably inclined or disposed

prospect (PROS pehkt) *n.* something hoped for or expected

prosperity (pros PEHR uh tee) *n.* condition of being successful; wealth

protruded (proh TROOD uhd) *v.* stuck out

prudence (PROO duhns) *n.* carefulness; caution

prudent (PROO duhnt) *adj.* sensible; careful

psychology (sy KOL uh jee) *n.* science dealing with the mind and with mental and emotional processes

punitive (PYOO nuh tihv) *adj.* concerned with punishment

purged (purjd) *v.* cleansed

Q

quail (kwayl) *v.* draw back in fear; lose heart

quench (kwehnch) *v.* satisfy a thirst

quote (kwoht) *v.* speak or write a passage by someone else

R

range (raynj) *n.* distance between certain limits; extent

ravenous (RAV uh nuhs) *adj.* extremely hungry for something

ravine (ruh VEEN) *n.* long, deep hollow in the ground; a gully

realist (REE uh lihst) *n.* person or artist concerned with things as they are, rather than as they could or should be

realistic (REE uh LIHS tihk) *adj.* based on facts; practical

reaped (reept) *v.* gathered; brought in

receipts (rih SEETS) *n.* amounts of money received

recognize (REHK uhg nyz) *v.* perceive clearly

recompense (REHK uhm pehns) *n.* something given or done in return for something else; repayment

recourse (REE kawrs) *n.* access to a form of help or aid

recruits (rih KROOTS) *n.* newly drafted soldiers

rectitude (REHK tuh tood) *n.* correctness; righteousness

redress (rih DREHS) *n.* compensation for a wrong done

refuge (REHF yooj) *n.* shelter or protection from danger

regiment (REHJ uh muhnt) *n.* military unit

regional (REE juh nuhl) *adj.* of or in a particular localized area

regionalism (REE juh nuh LIHZ uhm) *n.* strong or loyal attachment to a certain region or area

relent (rih LEHNT) *v.* become less harsh; be more merciful

reluctant (rih LUHK tuhnt) *adj.* unwilling; disinclined

rendezvous (RAHN duh voo) *n.* meeting place

repeat (rih PEET) *v.* say or state again

repent (rih PEHNT) *v.* feel sorry for what one has done and vow to change one's behavior

repose (rih POHZ) *n.* state of being at rest

repression (rih PREHSH uhn) *n.* restraint

reproduce (REE pruh DOOS) *v.* imitate closely

repugnant (rih PUHG nuhnt) *adj.* offensive; disagreeable

resign (rih ZYN) *v.* accept something as unavoidable; submit oneself to a something negative

resources (rih SAWR sihz) *n.* supplies

retaliation (rih tal ee AY shuhn) *n.* act of returning an injury or wrong

revelations (rehv uh LAY shuhnz) *n.* newly revealed information; disclosures

reverential (rehv uh REHN shuhl) *adj.* showing deep respect and love

revise (rih VYZ) *v.* make a new, improved version

rights (ryts) *n.* that which a person has claim to

rituals (RIHCH oo uhlz) *n.* established forms of ceremonies; ceremonial acts

robust (roh BUHST) *adj.* strong and healthy; full of life

rueful (ROO fuhl) *adj.* feeling or showing someone sorrow or pity

rural (RUR uhl) *adj.* of or relating to the country or agriculture

S

salient (SAY lee uhnt) *adj.* standing out from the rest

salutary (SAL yuh tehr ee) *adj.* beneficial; promoting a good purpose

salvage (SAL vihj) *v.* the saving of goods or materials from waste

satire (SAT yr) *n.* literary work mocking human vices or mistakes

saunter (SAWN tuhr) *n.* a slow, leisurely gait

savagery (SAV ihj ree) *n.* barbarity

scale (skayl) *n.* the extent or size of something

scenario (sih NAIR ee oh) *n.* situation

sediment (SEHD uh muhnt) *n.* material that settles to the bottom of a liquid

seeping (SEEP ihng) *v.* flowing slowly

self-conscious (SEHLF KON shuhs) *adj.* uncomfortable, especially by the presence or the thought of other people

self-reliance (SEHLF rih LY uhns) *n.* dependence on one's own acts

self-reliant (SEHLF rih LY uhnt) *adj.* dependent on one's own acts

sensible (SEHN suh buhl) *adj.* emotionally or intellectually aware

sentience (SEHN shuhns) *n.* capacity for feeling

separate (SEHP uh rayt) *v.* make a distinction between

shard (shahrd) *n.* a fragment or broken piece

shares (shairz) *n.* portions of ownership of a company or a piece of property

sinister (SIHN uh stuhr) *adj.* threatening harm, evil or misfortune

sinuous (SIHN yoo uhs) *adj.* moving in and out; wavy

skyscraper (SKY SKRAY puhr) *n.* very tall building

smite (smyt) *v.* kill by a powerful blow

solemn (SOL uhm) *adj.* serious or grave

somnolent (SOM nuh luhnt) *adj.* sleepy; drowsy

sort (sawrt) *v.* put in place according to kind, class, or nature

sowed (sohd) *v.* scattered; planted

specious (SPEE shuhs) *adj.* seeming to be good or sound without actually being so

spectator (SPEHK tay tuhr) *n.* a person who watches something without taking part in it

speculate (SPEHK yuh layt) *v.* use evidence to guess what might happen

splendor (SPLEHN duhr) *n.* great display of riches; great brightness

squander (SKWON duhr) *v.* spend or use wastefully

stark (stahrk) *adj.* stiff; rigid

state (stayt) *v.* express in words

statute (STACH oot) *n.* the document in which such an enactment is expressed

steal (steel) *v.* creep

stealthily (STEHLTH uh lee) *adv.* slyly or secretively

stirring (STUR ihng) *adj.* busy; full of energy

storytelling (STAWR ee TEHL ihng) *n.* act or art of telling tales or anecdotes

striking (STRYK ihng) *adj.* very noticeable or impressive

structure (STRUHK chuhr) *v.* create a general plot or outline

subject to (SUHB jihkt too) *adj.* likely to be affected by something

sublime (suh BLYM) *adj.* noble; majestic

subsisted (suhb SIHST uhd) *v.* remained alive; were sustained

suburbia (suh BUR bee uh) *n.* region outside of a major city

successive (suhk SEHS ihv) *adj.* following one after another

suffice (suh FYS) *v.* be adequate; meet the needs of

summarily (SUHM uhr uh lee) *adv.* promptly and without formality

summarize (SUHM uh ryz) *v.* briefly state the most important ideas and details

summation (suh MAY shuhn) *n.* summing up; giving all the key details of in a brief form

superficial (SOO puhr FIHSH uhl) *adj.* on the surface; shallow

superfluous (su PUR floo uhs) *adj.* strong belief

supple (SUHP uhl) adj. able to bend and move easily and nimbly

surmised (suhr MYZD) *v.* guessed; concluded

surveyed (suhr VAYD) *v.* measured and marked to show boundaries

swerve (swurv) *v.* to turn aside sharply or suddenly from a straight course

synonymous (sih NON uh muhs) *adj.* equivalent or similar in meaning

systemic (sihs TEHM ihk) *adj.* affecting the entire organism or bodily system

T

taboo (tuh BOO) *n.* something forbidden within a particular society or culture

tactful (TAKT fuhl) *adj.* concerned about upsetting or offending others

tantalized (TAN tuh lyzd) *v.* tormented; frustrated

taut (tawt) adj. tightly stretched

technology (tehk NOL uh jee) *n.* science of the mechanical and industrial arts

tedious (TEE dee uhs) *adj.* long or verbose and wearisome

tempered (TEHM puhrd) *v.* treated to achieve just the right strength or balance

tempest (TEHM pihst) *n.* violent storm with high winds

terrain (teh RAYN) *n.* ground or track of ground, especially with regard to its natural features

terrors (TEHR uhrz) *n.* great fears

theology (thee OL uh jee) *n.* the study of religion

tranquil (TRANG kwuhl) *adj.* calm; quiet; still

transcribed (tran SKRYBD) *v.* wrote or typed a copy

transformed (trans FAWRMD) *adj.* altered; changed

transfusion (trans FYOO zhuhn) *n.* the act of transference or transmission

transient (TRAN shuhnt) *adj.* not permanent

transition (tran ZIHSH uhn) *n.* change or passing from one condition to another

traversed (trav UHRST) *v.* moved over, across, or through

treacherous (TREHCH uhr uhs) *adj.* giving a false appearance of security; dangerous

tremulously (TREHM yuh luhs lee) *adv.* fearfully; timidly

tumultuously (too MUHL choo uhs lee) *adv.* in an agitated way

tyranny (TIHR uh nee) *n.* oppressive power

U

unabated (uhn uh BAY tihd) *adj.* not lessened or reduced

unanimity (yoo nuh NIHM uh tee) *n.* complete agreement

unconscious (uhn KON shuhs) *adj.* having temporarily lost awareness; in a faint

undertaking (UHN duhr tay kihng) *n.* task or challenge

unscrupulous (uhn SKROO pyuh luhs) *adj.* unethical; dishonest

unwonted (uhn WOHN tihd) *adj.* unusual; unfamiliar

urban (UR buhn) *adj.* characteristic of a city

V

validate (VAL uh dayt) *v.* prove to be factual or effective

vanquished (VAN kwihsht) *v.* thoroughly defeated

venerable (VEHN uhr uh buhl) *adj.* commanding respect

verify (VEHR uh fy) *v.* prove to be true by evidence

vernacular (vuhr NAK yuh luhr) *n.* native language

vigilance (VIHJ uh luhns) *n.* watchfulness

vigilant (VIHJ uh luhnt) *adj.* alert to danger

vigorously (VIHG uhr uhs lee) *adv.* forcefully or powerfully

vindicated (VIHN duh kayt ihd) *v.* cleared from blame

virtuous (VUR choo uhs) *adj.* characterized by moral virtue; righteous

virulent (VIHR yuh luhnt) *adj.* extremely hurtful or infectious

vision (VIHZH uhn) *n.* sense of sight; something seen in a dream or the imagination

volition (voh LIHSH uhn) *n.* act of using the will; decision

voluminous (vuh LOO muh nuhs) *adj.* of enough material to fill volumes

votive (VOH tihv) *adj.* designed to accomplish or fulfill a special intention

vulnerability (vuhl nuhr uh BIHL uh tee) *n.* open to moral attack, criticism, temptation, etc

W

wanton (WON tuhn) *adj.* senseless; unjustified

wasteland (WAYST LAND) *n.* land that is uncultivated or barren

wilderness (WIHL duhr nihs) *n.* region with no people living in it

wily (WY lee) *adj.* sly; cunning

wretched (REHCH uhd) *adj.* deeply distressed; miserable

Spanish Glossary

El vocabulario de Pregunta Esencial aparece en **azul**. El vocabulario académico de alta utilidad está **subrayado**.

A

abeyance / suspensión *s.* cesación temporal

absolve / absolver *v.* perdonar; liberar de culpa

absurdity / absurdo *s.* disparate; irracionalidad

accosted / abordó *v.* se dirigió a o habló con alguien de manera vehemente

account / cuenta *s.* informe o detalle

acknowledges / reconoce *v.* acepta la existencia, realidad o verdad de algo

acquiesce / asentir *v.* aceptar sin protesta

adamant / obstinado *adj.* firme; inflexible

adjourned / suspendió *v.* clausuró temporalmente

advantageous / ventajoso *adj.* provechoso; beneficioso

adversary / adversario *s.* opositor; enemigo

adversity / adversidad *s.* desgracia, calamidad

affections / afectos *s.* emociones

affliction / aflicción *s.* algo que causa dolor o angustia

agape / boquiabierto *adj.* con sorpresa; con asombro

aggregation / conjunto *s.* agrupación de objetos o individuos distintos

agricultural / agrícola *adj.* donde la agricultura es el principal medio de vida

alacrity / alacridad *s.* velocidad

alienation / enajenación *s.* distanciamiento o separación de sentimiento o afecto

alliance / alianza *s.* unión de naciones para un fin específico

ambiguity / ambigüedad *s.* estado de tener dos o más significados posibles

ambition / ambición *s.* deseo vehemente de lograr un objetivo específico; ímpetu por triunfar

ameliorate / mejorar *v.* hacer mejor

ample / amplio *adj.* de gran tamaño; más que suficiente

analyze / analizar *v.* descomponer un tema en partes y explicarlas

anarchy / anarquía *s.* ausencia de gobierno

ancestor / antepasado *s.* persona de la que descienden otras personas

anonymity / anonimato *s.* la condición de ser desconocido

anticipate / prever *v.* prepararse para algo o indicar algo

anxiety / ansiedad *s.* estado de sentirse intranquilo, aprehensivo o preocupado por lo que pudiera ocurrir

apparel / vestido *s.* ropa

apparition / aparición *s.* acto de aparecer o hacerse visible

appease / saciar *v.* satisfacer

appendage / apéndice *s.* parte externa de una planta o animal, como una rama o cola

appraise / evaluar *v.* calcular el valor, la importancia o el estatus de algo

apprehension / aprensión *s.* inquietante sensación de premonición; pavor

appropriate / apropiar *v.* tomar o usar algo sin permiso

arduous / arduo *adj.* difícil

argue / argumentar *v.* expresar razones a favor o en contra; comprobar expresando razones

arrange / acomodar *v.* poner en orden o en secuencia

ascended / ascendió *v.* subió

aspirations / aspiraciones *s.* fuertes deseos o ambiciones

assault / asalto *s.* ataque violento

assent / asentir *v.* acordar

assess / evaluar *v.* determinar la importancia, el tamaño o el valor de algo

austerity / austeridad *s.* adustez en la conducta o la apariencia; dureza; severidad

auxiliary / auxiliar *adj.* que brinda ayuda o apoyo

avarice / avaricia *s.* codicia

aversion / aversión *s.* objeto que provoca una fuerte antipatía

avidly / ávidamente *adv.* ansiosamente

awe / asombro *s.* sentimientos encontrados de temor y admiración

B

base / bajo *adj.* ruin; vil

beguile / cautivar *v.* encantar o deleitar

benediction / bendición *s.* plegaria que invoca la gracia de Dios

benevolent / benévolo *adj.* bondadoso; caritativo

benign / benigno *adj.* no injurioso ni maligno; no canceroso

bequeath / legar *v.* transmitir; pasar a otro

brazenness / descaro *s.* desfachatez; atrevimiento; insolencia

brigade / brigada *s.* unidad de soldados

brutal / brutal *adj.* cruel y sin sentimientos; salvaje; violento

C

cadence / cadencia *s.* serie de notas o acordes hacia el final de una obra musical

calamity / calamidad *s.* desastre; catástrofe

calumny / calumnia *s.* falsa acusación; difamación

candid / franco *adj.* sincero

canvass / solicitar *v.* recorrer cierta área solicitando los votos, mandatos o participación de la gente

capable / capaz *adj.* poseer las destrezas necesarias para realizar algo

caper / travesura *s.* picardía

casualties / bajas *s.* miembros de las fuerzas armadas que mueren en combate

categorize / categorizar *v.* colocar en grupos relacionados

cavernous / cavernoso *adj.* que se asemeja a una caverna; vasto

celestial / celestial *adj.* que pertenece o está en el cielo, como los planetas o las estrellas

chaos / caos *s.* desorden de la materia y el espacio, que presuntamente existió antes del universo ordenado

chronicles / crónicas *s.* cuentos; historias

circumvent / circundar *v.* evitar; rodear

civilian / civil *s.* cualquier persona que no es miembro de las fuerzas armadas

classify / clasificar *v.* asignar a una categoría

cleave / asir *v.* adherirse; pegarse

coinage / invención *s.* palabra o expresión inventada

coincide / coincidir *v.* que sucede al mismo tiempo

collective / colectividad *s.* acto de agrupar en un todo

collusion / confabulación *s.* acuerdo secreto; conspiración

commercial / comercial *adj.* relacionado con el comercio o los negocios

commissioners / comisionados *s.* funcionarios de gobierno

commonplace / común *adj.* habitual; ordinario

commotion / conmoción *s.* confusión ruidosa

community / comunidad *s.* todas las personas que viven en un distrito, ciudad o área específica

compare / comparar *v.* señalar las similitudes o las diferencias

conciliatory / conciliatorio *adj.* que busca la paz o la conciliación; amistoso

conclude / concluir *v.* llegar a un fin lógicamente necesario por medio de razonamiento

condolences / condolencias *s.* expresiones de pesar

conduct / conducta *v.* comportamiento

conflagration / conflagración *s.* incendio extenso y destructivo

conformity / conformidad *s.* acción que concuerda con las normas generalmente aceptadas

confounded / confundido *adj.* confuso; consternado

conjectural / conjetural *adj.* basado en la suposición

conjectured / conjeturó *v.* supuso

conjuring / conjurando *v.* invocando; apareciendo como por arte de magia

consecrate / consagrar *v.* motivo para ser venerado u honrado

conspicuous / conspicuo *adj.* obvio; fácilmente visible o perceptible

consternation / consternación *s.* gran temor o conmoción que provoca sentimientos de impotencia e incertidumbre

constitute / constituir *v.* servir de base o parte de algo; formar; abarcar

constitution / constitución *s.* composición física de una persona

contentious / contencioso *adj.* disputable

contiguous / contiguo *adj.* lindante; adyacente

contract / contrato *s.* acuerdo escrito

contrast / contrastar *v.* inspeccionar para descubrir las diferencias

convention / convención *s.* reunión a la que asisten miembros o delegados

conviction / convicción *s.* creencia profunda

convivial / jovial *adj.* que goza de la buena compañía; sociable

copious / copioso *adj.* cuantioso; abundante

correspond / corresponder *v.* concordar; relacionarse con

countenance / aprobar *v.* sancionar; tolerar

cowering / encogiendo *v.* temblando o agachándose, como con miedo

create / crear *v.* producir por medio de habilidad imaginativa

crevices / grietas *s.* estrechas aberturas causadas por resquebraduras o fisuras

critic / crítico *s.* persona que desaprueba o detecta fallas

critique / criticar *v.* examinar críticamente; reseñar

cunning / astuto *adj.* hábil para el engaño; artificioso; taimado

cyberspace / ciberespacio *s.* mundo en línea de redes informáticas

D

daunting / atemorizante *adj.* intimidante

decorum / decoro *s.* rectitud; idoneidad

deduce / deducir *v.* inferir a partir de un principio general

defend / defender *v.* mantener o apoyar en vista de un argumento

deference / deferencia *s.* estimación o respeto cortés

deficient / deficiente *adj.* con falta de; que carece de algo necesario

define / definir *v.* expresar las cualidades que hacen de algo lo que es

degenerate / degenerado *adj.* moralmente corrupto

dejected / abatido *v.* desanimado; cabizbajo; deprimido

deliberation / deliberación *s.* consideración meticulosa

deposition / deposición *s.* declaración de un testigo bajo juramento, aunque no en un tribunal en pleno

depths / profundidades *s.* áreas más profundas

derivative / derivado *adj.* que no es original; que se basa en otra cosa

derive / derivar *v.* rastrear hasta o desde una fuente; obtener por medio de razonamiento

describe / describir *v.* representar en palabras

design / diseñar *v.* crear, elaborar, ejecutar o construir según un plan

desolate / desolado *adj.* abandonado; aislado

despondent / desalentado *adj.* sin valor ni esperanza

despotism / despotismo *s.* dominio absoluto; tiranía

destitute / indigente *adj.* que vive en abyecta pobreza

destruction / destrucción *s.* acto de demoler o abatir

detached / indiferente *adj.* no involucrado emocionalmente

devise / idear *v.* formar en la mente por medio de nuevas combinaciones de ideas; inventar

dictum / dictamen *s.* declaración formal de hecho u opinión

differentiate / diferenciar *v.* reconocer una disparidad

digress / divagar *v.* alejarse temporalmente del tema principal

dilapidated / dilapidado *adj.* ruinoso

diligence / diligencia *s.* esfuerzo constante y minucioso; perseverancia

discern / discernir *v.* percibir o reconocer; distinguir claramente

discord / desacuerdo *s.* diferencia de opinión; disputa

discretion / discreción *s.* Prudencia

discriminate / discriminar *v.* reconocer diferencias entre elementos

disdainfully / desdeñosamente *adv.* que muestra desdén o desprecio

disgrace / ignominia *s.* algo que genera vergüenza o deshonra

disillusion / desengaño *s.* libertad de una idea falsa; desencanto

dispatched / despachó *v.* envió, generalmente en asuntos oficiales

dispersal / dispersión *s.* distribución

disposition / disposición *s.* inclinación; tendencia

disregard / desatender *v.* no prestar atención a; hacer caso omiso de; ignorar

dissembling / disimulando *v.* encubriendo la verdadera naturaleza o los motivos propios

dissention / disensión *s.* desacuerdo; discordia expresada mediante fuertes discusiones

dissuade / disuadir *v.* convencer a alguien de no hacer algo

distinguish / distinguir *v.* marcar como independiente o diferente

diversity / diversidad *s.* variedad; punto de disimilitud

divine / adivinar *v.* averiguar mediante la intuición

docile / dócil *adj.* fácil de dirigir o manejar; obediente

doctrine / doctrina *s.* lo que se enseña

dogma / dogma *s.* doctrinas o credos autorizados

dubious / dudoso *adj.* cuestionable; sospechoso

duplicate / duplicar *v.* hacer una copia

duration / duración *s.* tiempo durante el cual algo continúa o existe

dusky / obscuro *adj.* poco claro; sombrío; tenebroso

dyspepsia / dispepsia *s.* indigestión

E

ecstasy / éxtasis *s.* sentimiento de alegría abrumadora; enorme deleite

efface / tachar *v.* borrar; eliminar

effigies / efigies *s.* imágenes o retratos, especialmente de personas

effrontery / desvergüenza *s.* audacia descarada

effuse / derramar *v.* verter; brotar

eloquence / elocuencia *s.* talento para la oratoria vívida y enérgica

elusive / evasivo *adj.* difícil de comprender

embankment / dique *s.* montículo de tierra o piedra construido para retener agua, o como soporte para una carretera

embark / embarcar *v.* iniciar una empresa, proyecto o actividad

emigrants / emigrantes *s.* personas que abandonan un sitio para establecerse en otro

eminence / eminencia *s.* grandeza; celebridad

emit / emitir *v.* articular palabras o sonidos

enamored / enamorado *adj.* encantado; cautivado

encroached / usurpó *v.* invadió

endured / soportó *v.* aguantó

engrossed / absorto *adj.* completamente ocupado; enfrascado

entreated / suplicó *v.* rogó; imploró

entrenchments / trincheras *s.* zanjas profundas y extensas con paredes empinadas, utilizadas para defenderse del fuego enemigo

environment / entorno *s.* objetos o condiciones circundantes

epitaph / epitafio *s.* inscripción en una lápida o piedra sepulcral

equivocal / ambiguo *adj.* que se puede interpretar de más de una manera

eradicate / erradicar *v.* eliminar; destruir

establishment / establecimiento *s.* casa o negocio

estimates / estimaciones *s.* cálculos generales minuciosos

etiquette / etiqueta *s.* comportamiento correcto y formal

evacuated / evacuó *v.* desalojó; retiró

evade / evadir *v.* eludir o escapar mediante el engaño o ingenio

evaluate / evaluar *v.* determinar la importancia, el valor o la condición de algo estudiándolo detalladamente

exalted / exaltado *adj.* lleno de júbilo u orgullo; regocijado

examine / examinar *v.* indagar detalladamente sobre un tema

exasperation / exasperación *s.* enojo; frustración

exhaust / escape *s.* descarga de vapor o gas ya usado de un motor

exile / exilio *s.* estado o período de destierro

expansion / expansión *s.* acto o proceso de aumentar la amplitud, el tamaño o el volumen

expedient / recurso *s.* método utilizado para alcanzar un objetivo rápidamente

expenditures / desembolsos *s.* gastos; usos del dinero o recursos

exposures / exposiciones *s.* secciones de una película donde se refleja la luz al tomar una fotografía

extort / extorsionar *v.* obtener mediante amenaza o violencia

extraneous / extraño *adj.* no relacionado; desvinculado

F

fallowness / ociosidad *s.* inactividad

fantastic / fantástico *adj.* excelente; increíble

fastidious / exigente *adj.* cuidadoso; meticuloso

fatigues / trajes de fatiga *s.* ropa resistente que usan los soldados para trabajos pesados

feigned / fingió *v.* simuló

fervent / ferviente *adj.* extremadamente apasionado; muy entusiasta

finite / finito *adj.* que tiene límites mensurables o definibles

fitfully / irregularmente *adv.* se distingue por actividad interrumpida o intermitente

flagrant / flagrante *adj.* deslumbrante; escandaloso

flourished / floreció *v.* creció fuerte, saludable y feliz; prosperó

fluctuation / fluctuación *s.* cambio de nivel o intensidad

foothold / asidero *s.* posición estable para emprender acciones subsiguientes

forded / vadeó *v.* cruzó el río en el punto menos profundo

forestall / impedir *v.* prevenir mediante una acción anticipada

formulate / formular *v.* expresar plena y claramente

fortuitous / fortuito *adj.* que ocurre por suerte

fortune / fortuna *s.* riqueza; suerte

fragmentation / fragmentación *s.* acto o proceso de descomponer en partes

frantic / frenético *adj.* marcado por el frenesí

frayed / raído *adj.* andrajoso

freedom / libertad *s.* no estar bajo el control de otros

frontier / frontera *s.* frontera entre regiones deshabitadas; región en desarrollo de un campo de conocimiento

furtive / furtivo *adj.* sigiloso

G

garrulous / gárrulo *adj.* que habla demasiado

gaudy / llamativo *adj.* que llama la atención con mal gusto

generalize / generalizar *v.* llegar a un principio más amplio a partir de detalles

genial / afable *adj.* jovial; cordial

genre / género *s.* categoría o estilo

global / global *adj.* extendido por todo el mundo

govern / gobernar *v.* regir; controlar; manejar

grandeur / grandiosidad *s.* grandeza

grave / grave *adj.* serio; solemne

gravity / gravedad *s.* seriedad

guile / maña *s.* astucia

H

habitation / morada *s.* lugar para vivir; conjunto de casas o viviendas

hallow / venerar *v.* honrar como sagrado

handiwork / manualidad *s.* trabajo hecho a mano; obra hecha con las propias manos

harass / hostigar *v.* acosar; molestar

heady / embriagante *adj.* intoxicante

heightened / enalteció *v.* elevó el nivel de

heritage / patrimonio *s.* rasgos, creencias o costumbres transmitidos de una generación a otra

homages / homenaje *s.* actos que expresan honor y reverencia

homely / sencillo *adj.* que no es elegante ni refinado; tosco

huddled / amontonó *v.* apiñó; acurrucó

humor / humor *s.* cualidad de ser gracioso o divertido

hypothesize / hipotetizar *v.* desarrollar una teoría acerca de algo

I

idealism / idealismo *s.* pensamiento basado en seguir las normas de perfección o belleza

identify / identificar *v.* establecer la identidad de algo

identity / identidad *s.* lo que caracteriza a una persona

illiterate / analfabeto *adj.* incapaz de leer o escribir

illustrate / ilustrar *v.* dar ejemplos para apoyar una idea

immigration / inmigración *s.* acto de llegar a otro país o región para vivir ahí

imperceptible / imperceptible *adj.* difícil de distinguir; desapercibido

impertinent / impertinente *adj.* que no muestra el respeto apropiado; insolente

implore / implorar *v.* pedir o suplicar con devoción; rogar

imply / insinuar *v.* dar a entender o sugerir

impulsive / impulsivo *adj.* que se realiza sin pensar

impulsively / impulsivamente *adv.* espontáneamente; repentinamente

inanimate / inanimado *adj.* sin vida; muerto

inarticulate / inarticulado *adj.* pronunciado o expresado sin claridad

inaudibly / imperceptiblemente *adv.* que no puede ser escuchado

incessant / incesante *adj.* constante; aparentemente interminable

incorporated / constituido *adj.* establecido legalmente como corporación

incorrigible / incorregible *adj.* imposible de corregir; irremediable

incredulously / incrédulamente *adv.* escépticamente

increment / incrementar *v.* aumentar, como en serie

indelible / indeleble *adj.* permanente; que no se puede borrar

independence / independencia *s.* libertad del control de otros

individualism / individualismo *s.* creencia de que la libertad personal es lo más importante

induce / inducir *v.* causar; provocar

industry / industria *s.* cualquier ramo de negocios, comercio o manufactura

ineffable / inefable *adj.* demasiado abrumador para ser expresado

inert / inerte *adj.* sin movimiento

inextricable / inextricable *adj.* que no puede separarse o liberarse de

infer / inferir *v.* derivar una conclusión a partir de hechos o premisas

infinity / infinito *s.* espacio, tiempo o distancia interminable o ilimitado

ingratiating / congraciador *adj.* encantador o halagador

innovation / innovación *s.* una nueva idea, método o dispositivo

innumerable / innumerable *adj.* son tantos que no se pueden contar

insatiable / insaciable *adj.* que constantemente desea más

inscrutable / inescrutable *adj.* que no puede comprenderse fácilmente

inseparable / inseparable *adj.* que no puede dividirse; enlazados

insidious / insidioso *adj.* engañoso; traicionero

inspection / inspección *s.* examen

intent / intención *s.* propósito u objetivo

intently / asiduamente *adv.* de manera concentrada y con un propósito determinado

intercepted / interceptó *v.* capturó o detuvo a algo o a alguien en su trayecto de un lugar a otro

interminable / interminable *adj.* que parece perdurar para siempre

interposed / interpuso *v.* intermedió

interspersed / esparció *v.* colocó por doquier

intervene / intervenir *v.* tomar medidas con el fin de prevenir algo

intolerable / intolerable *adj.* tan difícil o doloroso que resulta insoportable; inaguantable

intonation / entonación *s.* la capacidad de tocar notas musicales de manera afinada o desafinada

intricate / intrincado *adj.* complicado; que tiene muchas partes pequeñas correlacionadas

intuitively / intuitivamente *adv.* que no hace falta aprenderlo; instintivamente

invective / invectiva *s.* ataque verbal; crítica violenta

invent / inventar *v.* crear pensando

investigate / investigar *v.* realizar una inspección sistemática

J

jocularity / jocosidad *s.* buen humor chistoso

jubilant / jubiloso *adj.* alegre y triunfante

judge / juzgar *v.* formar una estimación o evaluación de algo

judgment / juicio *s.* capacidad de formar una opinión apropiadamente; buen razonamiento

justify / justificar *v.* comprobar o demostrar que algo es justo, correcto o razonable

L

label / etiquetar *v.* describir o designar

lament / lamentar *v.* expresar pesar por algo; sufrir en voz alta

landscape / paisaje *s.* área que puede verse a la vez desde un lugar

latent / latente *adj.* presente pero invisible o inactivo

latitude / latitud *s.* distancia al norte o al sur del ecuador

levee / dique *s.* muro construido en las márgenes de un río para detener las inundaciones

liberty / libertad *s.* autonomía

license / libertad de acción *s.* exención de una conducta o lenguaje correcto

licentious / licencioso *adj.* sin refrenamiento moral

limber / flexible *adj.* elástico

list / enumerar *v.* hacer una lista; incluir

listed / inclinado *adj.* ladeado; en declive

locate / ubicar *v.* hallar el lugar de algo

longitude / longitud *s.* distancia este u oeste en la superficie de la Tierra

lulled / arrulló *v.* calmó o sosegó mediante un sonido o movimiento suave

luminary / luminaria *adj.* que irradia luz

M

machetes / machetes *s.* cuchillos grandes y pesados de hoja ancha

magnanimity / magnanimidad *s.* generosidad

magnitude / magnitud *s.* grandeza de tamaño

maledictions / maldiciones *s.* maleficios

malign / maligno *adj.* maléfico; muy dañino

malingers / fingirse enfermo *v.* simular una enfermedad

maneuver / maniobrar *v.* mover algo utilizando un plan o conspiración

manifold / múltiple *adj.* de muchas maneras

martial / marcial *adj.* relativo a la guerra

marvel / maravilla *s.* cosa maravillosa o sorprendente

master / dominar *v.* volverse experto en

media / medios *s.* sistemas de comunicación diseñados para llegar a las masas

mediator / mediador *s.* aquél que reconcilia grupos opositores

melancholy / melancólico *adj.* triste y deprimido; lúgubre

membrane / membrana *s.* capa delgada y suave que sirve de cubierta o forro

memorials / monumentos *s.* objetos que se exhiben en memoria de una persona o suceso

meticulous / meticuloso *adj.* extremadamente cuidadoso de los detalles

metropolis / metrópolis *s.* ciudad grande

migrant / migrante *adj.* que se traslada de un lugar a otro

monotonous / monótono *adj.* tedioso porque no varía

morose / esquivo *adj.* melancólico; retraído

mundane / mundano *adj.* común, cotidiano, ordinario

munificent / munificente *adj.* generoso

myriad / innumerable *adj.* incontable

N

native / nativo *adj.* que pertenece a un lugar por nacimiento

natural / natural *adj.* que no ha sido elaborado por el hombre ni es artificial

nostalgia / nostalgia *s.* sentimiento de añoranza por algo

nuance / matiz *s.* una pequeña o sutil variación en tono, color o significado

O

oblivion / olvido *s.* condición de ser totalmente olvidado

oblivious / abstraído *adj.* falto de todo conocimiento

obstinacy / obstinación *s.* terquedad

obstinate / obstinado *adj.* terco

obtuse / obtuso *adj.* lento para comprender o percibir

offensive / ofensiva *s.* actitud o posición de ataque

ominous / ominoso *adj.* amenazador; siniestro

omnipotent / omnipotente *adj.* todopoderoso

opposition / oposición *s.* actitud hostil o resistente hacia algo

oppressed / oprimió *v.* reprimió mediante un poder injusto o cruel

optimism / optimismo *s.* tendencia a ser positivo

order / ordenar *v.* acomodar

ordinances / ordenanzas *s.* sacramentos o ritos religiosos

ostentation / ostentación *s.* exhibición jactanciosa

P

pacify / pacificar *v.* calmar o apaciguar

pallor / palor *s.* palidez

palpable / palpable *adj.* que puede ser tocado, sentido o manipulado

parsimony / parsimonia *s.* tacañería

pastoral / pastoril *adj.* característico de la vida rural; idealizado como pacífico, sencillo y natural

pathos / pathos *s.* cualidad que inspira lástima, pena o compasión en otros

pedestrian / peatonal *adj.* a pie; caminando

pensive / pensativo *adj.* que piensa intensamente; que suplica

perdition / perdición *s.* pérdida total e irreparable; ruina

peremptorily / perentoriamente *adv.* terminantemente; autoritariamente

peril / peligro *s.* riesgo

permeated / permeó *v.* impregnó

perpetual / perpetuo *adj.* que dura para siempre

persevere / perseverar *v.* continuar a pesar de las penurias; persistir

persistent / persistente *adj.* recurrente; constante

personal / personal *adj.* que pertenece a una persona; privado

pessimism / pesimismo *s.* tendencia a ser negativo

piety / piedad *s.* devoción a la religión

platitudes / trivialidades *s.* declaraciones sin sentido; expresiones desgastadas

plodding / caminar pausadamente *v.* avanzar o moverse pesadamente y con dificultad; recorrer penosamente

poignant / conmovedor *adj.* que hiere profundamente los sentimientos

poise / equilibrio *s.* balance; estabilidad

posterity / posteridad *s.* todas las futuras generaciones

practicable / practicable *adj.* factible, posible

prairie / llanura *s.* planicie cubierta de pasto sin árboles

precipitate / precipitar *v.* provocar que ocurra antes de lo esperado o deseado

preconceptions / preconcepciones *s.* ideas preconcebidas

predict / predecir *v.* vaticinar basándose en observación, experiencia o raciocinio

predilection / predilección *s.* preferencia preexistente

prelude / preludio *s.* parte o movimiento preliminar de una obra musical

prescient / presciente *adj.* que se conoce de antemano

pervading / difundirse *v.* que se esparce a través de

prevalent / extendido *adj.* que existe u ocurre abundantemente

privileges / privilegios *s.* derechos especiales; ventajas

proclaiming / proclamar *v.* anunciar

procure / procurar *v.* llevar a cabo con cierto esfuerzo

prodigious / prodigioso *adj.* de enorme poder o tamaño

profundity / profundidad *s.* profundidad intelectual

profusion / profusión *s.* abundancia; provisión cuantiosa

propitiation / apaciguamiento *s.* acción que busca aquietar o satisfacer a una persona, causa, etc.

propitious / propicio *adj.* favorablemente inclinado hacia o dispuesto a

prospect / prospecto *s.* algo deseado o esperado

prosperity / prosperidad *s.* condición de tener éxito; riqueza

protruded / sobresalió *v.* destacó

prudence / prudencia *s.* cuidado; cautela

prudent / prudente *adj.* perceptible; cauteloso

psychology / psicología *s.* la ciencia que estudia la mente y los procesos mentales y emocionales

punitive / punitivo *adj.* relativo al castigo

purged / purgó *v.* limpió

Q

quail / acobardar *v.* amedrentarse; descorazonarse

quench / aplacar *v.* calmar la sed

quote / citar *v.* decir o escribir un pasaje de la autoría de otra persona

R

range / rango *s.* distancia entre ciertos límites; alcance

ravenous / voraz *adj.* extremadamente hambriento

ravine / cañada *s.* zanja larga y profunda en la tierra; hondonada

realist / realista *s.* persona o artista que se interesa en las cosas como son y no como podrían o deberían ser

realistic / realista *adj.* basado en hechos; práctico

reaped / recolectó *v.* recogió; cosechó

receipts / ingresos *s.* cantidades de dinero recibidas

recognize / reconocer *v.* percibir claramente

recompense / recompensa *s.* algo que se da o se hace como retribución por otra cosa; compensación

recourse / recurso *s.* acceso a cierta forma de ayuda o asistencia

recruits / reclutas *s.* soldados recién alistados

rectitude / rectitud *s.* corrección; probidad

redress / resarcimiento *s.* compensación por un mal cometido

refuge / refugio *s.* amparo o protección del peligro

regiment / regimiento *s.* unidad militar

regional / regional *adj.* de o en un área específica

regionalism / regionalismo *s.* apego intenso o leal a cierta región o área

relent / aplacar *v.* hacerse menos tosco; ser más compasivo

reluctant / reacio *adj.* renuente; maldispuesto

rendezvous / punto de reunión *s.* sitio de encuentro

repeat / repetir *v.* decir o expresar de nuevo

repent / arrepentir *v.* sentir remordimiento por una mala acción y prometer cambiar su comportamiento

repose / reposo *s.* estado de descanso

repression / represión *s.* restricción

reproduce / reproducir *v.* imitar con detalle

repugnant / repugnante *adj.* ofensivo; desagradable

resign / resignar *v.* aceptar que algo es inevitable; someterse a algo negativo

resources / recursos *s.* suministros

retaliation / represalia *s.* acto de desquitarse por un perjuicio o mal

revelations / revelaciones *s.* información recientemente revelada; divulgaciones

reverential / reverencial *adj.* que muestra gran respeto y devoción

revise / revisar *v.* hacer una versión nueva y mejorada

rights / derechos *s.* aquello que una persona puede exigir

rituals / rituales *s.* formas establecidas de ceremonias; actos ceremoniales

robust / robusto *adj.* fuerte y saludable; vigoroso

rueful / desconsolado *adj.* sentir o mostrarle pena o lástima a alguien

rural / rural *adj.* relacionado con el campo o la agricultura

S

salient / sobresaliente *adj.* que se destaca entre los demás

salutary / saludable *adj.* benéfico; que promueve una buena causa

salvage / recuperar *v.* rescatar bienes o materiales de los desechos

satire / sátira *s.* obra literaria que se burla de los vicios o errores humanos

saunter / deambular *s.* paso lento y sin prisa

savagery / salvajismo *s.* barbarie

scale / escala *s.* el alcance o tamaño de algo

scenario / circunstancias *s.* situación

sediment / sedimento *s.* material que se deposita en el fondo de un líquido

seeping / filtrando *v.* fluyendo lentamente

self-conscious / cohibido *adj.* incómodo, especialmente por la presencia de otras personas o lo que ellas piensan

self-reliance / autosuficiencia *s.* dependencia únicamente en los actos propios

self-reliant / autosuficiente *adj.* dependiente únicamente de los actos propios

sensible / sensato *adj.* emocional o intelectualmente razonable

sentience / sensible *s.* que responde a o es conciente de las sensaciones

separate / separar *v.* hacer distinción entre

shard / fragmento *s.* pequeña parte o pedazo roto

shares / acciones *s.* porciones de participación en una compañía o propiedad

sinister / siniestro *adj.* que amenaza con perjuicio, maldad o infortunio

sinuous / sinuoso *adj.* con movimiento serpenteante; ondulante

skyscraper / rascacielos *s.* edificio de gran altura

smite / aniquilar *v.* matar de un fuerte golpe

solemn / solemne *adj.* serio o grave

somnolent / soñoliento *adj.* adormecido; amodorrado

sort / clasificar *v.* ordenar por tipo, clase o calidad

sowed / sembrado *adj.* esparcido; plantado

specious / especioso *adj.* que aparenta estar bueno o sano sin estarlo realmente

spectator / espectador *s.* persona que observa algo sin tomar parte

speculate / especular *v.* usar evidencia para predecir lo que puede ocurrir

speculation / especulación *s.* idea; conjetura

splendor / esplendor *s.* gran exhibición de riqueza; gran brillo

squander / despilfarrar *v.* gastar o derrochar

stark / rígido *adj.* tieso; inflexible

state / establecer *v.* expresar en palabras

statute / estatuto *s.* documento en el cual se expresa la promulgación, aprobación y sanción del mismo

steal / arrastrar *s.* reptar

stealthily / furtivamente *adv.* astuta o disimuladamente

stirring / incitante *adj.* activo; lleno de energía

storytelling / contar cuentos *s.* acto o arte de narrar cuentos o anécdotas

striking / impresionante *adj.* excesivamente llamativo o impactante

structure / estructurar *v.* crear una trama o un esquema general

subject / propenso *adj.* que puede ser afectado por algo

sublime / sublime *adj.* noble; majestuoso

subsisted / subsistieron *v.* permanecieron con vida; soportaron

suburbia / suburbio *s.* región fuera de una ciudad principal

successive / sucesivo *adj.* uno tras otro

suffice / bastar *v.* ser idóneo; satisfacer las necesidades de

summarily / sumariamente *adv.* brevemente y sin formalidades

summarize / resumir *v.* expresar brevemente las ideas y detalles más importantes

summation / recapitulación *s.* compendio; acto de dar todos los detalles principales en forma sucinta

superficial / superficial *adj.* en la superficie; poco profundo

superfluous / superfluo *adj.* innecesario

supple / flexible *adj.* capaz de doblarse y moverse fácil y ágilmente

surmised / conjeturó *v.* adivinó; dedujo

surveyed / deslindó *v.* midió y marcó para mostrar los linderos

swerve / desviar *v.* virar hacia un lado brusca o repentinamente y salirse del rumbo fijo

synonymous / sinónimo *adj.* con significado igual o similar

systemic / sistémico *adj.* que afecta el organismo o sistema físico completo

T

taboo / tabú *adj.* algo prohibido dentro de una sociedad o cultura en particular

tactful / discreto *adj.* que se preocupa por no enfadar u ofender a otros

tantalized / exasperó *v.* atormentó; frustró

taut / tirante *adj.* muy estirado

technology / tecnología *s.* ciencia de las artes mecánicas e industriales

tedious / tedioso *adj.* extenso o verboso y fastidioso

tempered / temperado *adj.* tratado para alcanzar exactamente la fuerza o equilibrio correcto

tempest / tempestad *s.* poderosa tormenta con fuertes vientos

terrain / terreno *s.* tierra o trocha de tierra, principalmente en lo relativo a sus características naturales

terrors / terrores *s.* grandes temores

theology / teología *s.* el estudio de la religión

tranquil / tranquilo *adj.* calmado; quieto; sosegado

transcribed / transcribió *v.* escribió o mecanografió una copia

transform / transformar *v.* cambiar en forma o apariencia

transformed / transformó *v.* cambió la condición o naturaleza de

transfusion / transfusión *s.* acto de transferencia o transmisión

transient / transitorio *adj.* no permanente

transition / transición *s.* cambiar o pasar de una condición a otra

traversed / atravesó *v.* cruzó sobre, a través de, o de un extremo a otro

treacherous / traicionero *adj.* que da una falsa apariencia de seguridad; peligroso

tremulously / trémulamente *adv.* con temor; tímidamente

tumultuously / tumultuosamente *adv.* de forma agitada

tyranny / tiranía *s.* poder opresor

U

unabated / cabal *adj.* no disminuido ni reducido

unanimity / unanimidad *s.* acuerdo total

unconscious / inconsciente *adj.* temporalmente sin conocimiento; desmayado

undertaking / empresa *s.* tarea o desafío

unscrupulous / inescrupuloso *adj.* poco ético; deshonesto

unwonted / inusitado *adj.* inusual; poco familiar

urban / urbano *adj.* característico de una ciudad

V

validate / validar *v.* demostrar que algo se basa en hechos o es efectivo

vanquished / venció *v.* derrotó completamente

venerable / venerable *adj.* que inspira respeto imponente

verify / verificar *v.* demostrar que algo es cierto con evidencia

vernacular / lengua vernácula *s.* idioma nativo

vigilance / vigilancia *s.* cuidado

vigilant / vigilante *adj.* alerta al peligro

vigorously / vigorosamente *adv.* enérgicamente o poderosamente

vindicated / vindicado *adj.* liberado de culpa

virtuous / virtuoso *adj.* que se distingue por sus virtudes morales; con rectitud

virulent / virulento *adj.* extremadamente doloroso o infeccioso

vision / visión *s.* sentido de la vista; algo que se ve en un sueño o en la imaginación

volition / volición *s.* acto de usar la voluntad; determinación

voluminous / voluminoso *adj.* con suficiente material como para llenar volúmenes

votive / votivo *adj.* diseñado para lograr o cumplir una intención especial

vulnerability / vulnerabilidad *s.* exposición a ataques morales, críticas, tentaciones, etc.

W

wanton / displicente *adj.* insensible; injustificable

wasteland / tierra baldía *s.* tierra en su estado natural, sin cultivar

wilderness / tierra salvaje *s.* región en la que no habitan personas

wily / artero *adj.* solapado; astuto

wretched / miserable *adj.* profundamente atormentado; desdichado

Life of the English Language

The life of every language depends on the people who use it. Whenever you use English by asking a question, talking on the phone, going to a movie, reading a magazine, or writing an e-mail, you keep it healthy and valuable.

Using a Dictionary

Use a **dictionary** to find the meaning, the pronunciation, and the part of speech of a word. Consult a dictionary also to trace the word's *etymology*, or its origin. Etymology explains how words change, how they are borrowed from other languages, and how new words are invented, or "coined."

Here is an entry from a dictionary. Notice what it tells about the word *anthology*.

> **anthology** (an thäl′ ə jè) *n., pl.* –gies [Gr. anthologia, a garland, collection of short poems < *anthologos*, gathering flowers < *anthos*, flower + *legein*, to gather] a collection of poems, stories, songs, excerpts, etc., chosen by the compiler.

Dictionaries provide the *denotation* of each word, or its objective meaning. The symbol < means "comes from" or "is derived from." In this case, the Greek words for "flower" and "gather" combined to form a Greek word that meant a garland, and then that word became an English word that means a collection of literary flowers—a collection of literature like the one you are reading now.

Using a Thesaurus

Use a **thesaurus** to increase your vocabulary. In a thesaurus, you will find synonyms, or words that have similar meanings, for most words. Follow these guidelines to use a thesaurus:

- Do not choose a word just because it sounds interesting or educated. Choose the word that expresses exactly the meaning you intend.
- To avoid errors, look up the word in a dictionary to check its precise meaning and to make sure you are using it properly.

Here is an entry from a thesaurus. Notice what it tells about the word *book*.

> **book** *noun* A printed and bound work: tome, volume. See WORDS.
>
> **book** *verb* **1.** To register in or as if in a book: catalog, enroll, inscribe, list, set down, write down. *See* REMEMBER. **2.** To cause to be set aside, as for one's use, in advance: bespeak, engage, reserve. *See* GET.

If the word can be used as different parts of speech, as book can, the thesaurus entry provides synonyms for the word as each part of speech. Many words also have connotations, or emotional associations that the word calls to mind. A thesaurus entry also gives specific synonyms for each connotation of the word.

Activity Look up the words *knight* and *chivalry* in a dictionary. **(a)** What are their etymologies? **(b)** Explain what their etymologies reveal about the development of English. Then, check the word *chivalry* in a thesaurus. **(c)** What are two synonyms for this word? **(d)** In what way do the connotations of the synonyms differ?

The Origin and Development of English

Old English English began about the year 500 when Germanic tribes settled in Britain. The language of these peoples—the Angles, Saxons, and Jutes—combined with Danish and Norse when Vikings attacked Britain and added some Latin elements when Christian missionaries arrived. The result was Old English, which looked like this:

Hwaet! We Gar-Dena in gear-dagum,
peod-cyninga, prym gefrunon,
hu da aepelingas ellen fremedon!

These words are the opening lines of the Old English epic poem *Beowulf*, probably composed in the eighth century. In modern English, they mean: "Listen! We know the ancient glory of the Spear-Danes, and the heroic deeds of those noble kings!"

Middle English The biggest change in English took place after the Norman Conquest of Britain in 1066. The Normans spoke a dialect of Old French, and Old English changed dramatically when the Normans became the new aristocracy. From about 1100 to 1500, the people of Britain spoke what we now call Middle English.

A Knyght ther was, and that a worthy man,
That fro the tyme that he first bigan
To riden out, he loved chivalrie,
Trouthe and honour, fredom and curtesie.

These lines from the opening section of Chaucer's *Canterbury Tales* (c. 1400) are much easier for us to understand than the lines from *Beowulf*. They mean: "There was a knight, a worthy man who, from the time he began to ride, loved chivalry, truth, honor, freedom, and courtesy."

Modern English During the Renaissance, with its emphasis on reviving classical culture, Greek and Latin languages exerted a strong influence on the English language. In addition, Shakespeare added about two thousand words to the language. Grammar, spelling, and pronunciation continued to change. Modern English was born.

But soft! What light through yonder window breaks?
It is the East, and Juliet is the sun!

These lines from Shakespeare's *Romeo and Juliet* (c. 1600) need no translation, although it is helpful to know that "soft" means "speak softly." Since Shakespeare's day, conventions of usage and grammar have continued to change. For example, the *th* at the ends of many verbs has become s. In Shakespeare's time, it was correct to say "Romeo *hath* fallen in love." In our time, it is right to say "he *has* fallen in love." However, the changes of the past five hundred years are not nearly as drastic as the changes from Old English to Middle English, or from Middle English to Modern English. We still speak Modern English.

Old Words, New Words

Modern English has a larger vocabulary than any other language in the world. The *Oxford English Dictionary* contains about a half million words, and it is estimated that another half million scientific and technical terms do not appear in the dictionary. Here are the main ways that new words enter the language:

- **War**—Conquerors introduce new terms and ideas—and new vocabulary, such as anger, from Old Norse.
- **Immigration**—When large groups of people move from one country to another, they bring their languages with them, such as *boycott*, from Ireland.
- **Travel and Trade**—Those who travel to foreign lands and those who do business in faraway places bring new words back with them, such as *shampoo*, from Hindi.
- **Science and Technology**—In our time, the amazing growth of science and technology adds multitudes of new words to English, such as *Internet*.

English is also filled with **borrowings,** words taken directly from other languages. Sometimes borrowed words keep basically the same meanings they have in their original languages: *pajamas* (Hindi), *sauna* (Finnish), *camouflage* (French), *plaza* (Spanish). Sometimes borrowed words take on new meanings. *Sleuth,* for example, an Old Norse word for trail, has come to mean the person who follows a *trail*—a detective.

Mythology contributed to our language too. Some of the days of the week are named after Norse gods—Wednesday was Woden's Day, Thursday was Thor's Day. Greek and Roman myths have given us many words, such as jovial (from Jove), *martial* (from Mars), *mercurial* (from Mercury), and *herculean* (from Hercules).

Americanisms are words, phrases, usages, or idioms that originated in American English or that are unique to the way Americans speak. They are expressions of our national character in all its variety: *easy as pie, prairie dog, bamboozle, panhandle, halftime, fringe benefit, bookmobile, jackhammer, southpaw, lickety split.*

Activity Look up the following words in a dictionary. Describe the ways in which you think these words entered American English.

sabotage *burrito* *moccasin* *mecca* *megabyte*

The Influence of English

English continues to have an effect on world cultures and literature. There are about three hundred million native English speakers, and about the same number who speak English as a second language. Although more people speak Mandarin Chinese, English is the dominant language of trade, tourism, international diplomacy, science, and technology.

Language is a vehicle of both communication and culture, and the cultural influence of English in the twenty-first century is unprecedented in the history of the world's languages. Beyond business and science, English spreads through sports, pop music, Hollywood movies, television, and journalism. A book that is translated into English reaches many more people than it would in its native language alone. Perhaps most significantly, English dominates the Internet. The next time you log on, notice how many Web sites from around the world also have an English version. The global use of English is the closest the world has ever come to speaking an international language.

Activity Choose one area of culture—such as sports, fashion, the arts, or technology—and identify three new words that English has recently added to the *world's* vocabulary.
(a) How do you think non-English speakers feel about the spread of English? **(b)** Do you think English helps to bring people together? Why or why not?

Tips for Improving Fluency

When you were younger, you learned to read. Then, you read to expand your experiences or for pure enjoyment. Now, you are expected to read to learn. As you progress in school, you are given more and more material to read. The tips on these pages will help you improve your reading fluency, or your ability to read easily, smoothly, and expressively. Use these tips as you read daily.

Keeping Your Concentration

One common problem that readers face is the loss of concentration. When you are reading an assignment, you might find yourself rereading the same sentence several times without really understanding it. The first step in changing this behavior is to notice that you do it. Becoming an active, aware reader will help you get the most from your assignments. Practice using these strategies:

- Cover what you have already read with a note card as you go along. Then, you will not be able to reread without noticing that you are doing it.
- Set a purpose for reading beyond just completing the assignment. Then, read actively by pausing to ask yourself questions about the material as you read. Check the accuracy of your answers as you continue to read.
- Use the Reading Strategy instruction and notes that appear with each selection in this textbook.
- Look at any art or illustrations that accompany the reading and use picture clues to help your comprehension.
- Stop reading after a specified period of time (for example, 5 minutes) and summarize what you have read. To help you with this strategy, use the Reading Check questions that appear with each selection in this textbook. Reread to find any answers you do not know.

Reading Phrases

Fluent readers read phrases rather than individual words. Reading this way will speed up your reading and improve your comprehension. Here are some useful ideas:

- Experts recommend rereading as a strategy to increase fluency. Choose a passage of text that is neither too hard nor too easy. Read the same passage aloud several times until you can read it smoothly. When you can read the passage fluently, pick another passage and keep practicing.
- Read aloud into a tape recorder. Then, listen to the recording, noting your accuracy, pacing, and expression. You can also read aloud and share feedback with a partner.
- Use the *Prentice Hall Audio Program Literature Hear It!* to hear the selections read aloud. Read along silently in your textbook, noticing how the reader uses his or her voice and emphasizes certain words and phrases.
- Set a target reading rate. Time yourself as you read and work to increase your speed without sacrificing the level of your comprehension.

Understanding Key Vocabulary

If you do not understand some of the words in an assignment, you may miss out on important concepts. Therefore, it is helpful to keep a dictionary nearby when you are reading. Follow these steps:

- Before you begin reading, scan the text for unfamiliar words or terms. Find out what those words mean before you begin reading.
- Use context—the surrounding words, phrases, and sentences—to help you determine the meanings of unfamiliar words.
- If you are unable to understand the meaning through context, refer to the dictionary.

Paying Attention to Punctuation

When you read, pay attention to punctuation. Commas, periods, exclamation points, semicolons, and colons tell you when to pause or stop. They also indicate relationships between groups of words. When you recognize these relationships you will read with greater understanding and expression. Look at the chart below.

Punctuation Mark	Meaning
comma	brief pause
period	pause at the end of a thought
exclamation point	pause that indicates emphasis
semicolon	pause between related but distinct thoughts
colon	pause before giving explanation or examples

Using the Reading Fluency Checklist

Use the checklist below each time you read a selection in this textbook. In your Language Arts journal or notebook, note which skills you need to work on and chart your progress each week.

Reading Fluency Checklist
❑ Preview the text to check for difficult or unfamiliar words.
❑ Practice reading aloud.
❑ Read according to punctuation.
❑ Break down long sentences into the subject and its meaning.
❑ Read groups of words for meaning rather than reading single words.
❑ Read with expression (change your tone of voice to add meaning to the word).

Reading is a skill that can be improved with practice. The key to improving your fluency is to read. The more you read, the better your reading will become.

Approaches to Criticism

By writing **criticism**—writing that analyzes literature—readers share their responses to a written work. Criticism is also a way for a reader to deepen his or her own understanding and appreciation of the work, and to help others to deepen theirs.

The information in this handbook will guide you through the process of writing criticism. In addition, it will help you to refine your critical perceptions to ensure that you are ready to produce work at the college level.

Understanding Criticism

There are a few different types of criticism. Each can enhance understanding and deepen appreciation of literature in a distinctive way. All types share similar functions.

The Types of Criticism

Analysis Students are frequently asked to analyze, or break into parts and examine, a passage or a work. When you write an analysis, you must support your ideas with references to the text.

Archetypal Criticism Archetypal criticism evaluates works of literature by identifying and analyzing the archetypes contained within them. An archetype, sometimes called a "universal symbol," is a plot, character, symbol, image, setting, or idea that recurs in the literature of many different cultures. Archetypes and patterns of archetypes can be seen as representing common patterns of human life and experience.

Biographical Criticism Biographical criticism uses information about a writer's life to shed light on his or her work.

Historical Criticism Historical criticism traces connections between an author's work and the events, circumstances, or ideas that shaped the writer's historical era.

Political Criticism Political criticism involves viewing an author's work with a focus on political assumptions and content—whether explicit or implicit—and, possibly, assessing the political impact of the work. Similar to historical criticism, political criticism draws connections between an author's work and the political issues and assumptions of the times.

Philosophical Criticism In philosophical criticism, the elements of a literary work such as plot, characters, conflict, and motivations are examined through the lens of the author's philosophical arguments and stances. The critic taking a philosophical approach will analyze philosophical arguments presented in a literary work and determine how those arguments have molded the work.

The Functions of Criticism

Critical writing serves a variety of important functions:

Making Connections All criticism makes connections between two or more things. For instance, an analysis of a poem may show similarities among different images.

Making Distinctions Criticism must make distinctions as well as connections. In an analysis of a poem, a critic may distinguish between two possible purposes for poetry: first, to create an enduring image and, second, to present a deeper meaning.

Achieving Insight By making connections and distinctions, criticism achieves insight. An analysis of a poem may reach the insight that the poem stands on its own as a work of beauty apart from any deeper meaning.

Making a Judgment Assessing the value of a work is an important function of criticism. A critic may assess a work by comparing it with other works and by using a standard such as enjoyment, insight, or beauty.

"Placing" the Work Critics guide readers not by telling them *what* to think but by giving them *terms in which to think.* Critical writing may help readers apply varied perspectives to illuminate different aspects of a work.

Writing Criticism

Like all solid writing, a work of criticism presents a thesis (a central idea) and supports it with arguments and evidence. Follow the strategies below to develop a critical thesis and gather support for it.

Formulate a Working Thesis

Once you have chosen a work or works on which to write, formulate a working thesis. First, ask yourself questions like these:

- What strikes you most about the work or the writer that your paper will address? What puzzles you most?
- In what ways is the work unlike others you have read?
- What makes the techniques used by the writer so well-suited to (or so poorly chosen for) conveying the theme of the work?

Jot down notes answering your questions. Then, reread passages that illustrate your answers, jotting down notes about what each passage contributes to the work. Review your notes, and write a sentence that draws a conclusion about the work.

If your thesis concerns . . .	look for support in the form of . . .
Character	• dialogue • character's actions • writer's descriptions of the character • other characters' reactions to the character
Theme	• fate of characters • patterns and contrasts of imagery, character, or events • mood • writer's attitude toward the action
Style	• memorable descriptions, observations • passages that "sound like" the writer • examples of rhetorical devices, such as exaggeration and irony
Historical Context	• references to historical events and personalities • evidence of social or political pressures on characters • socially significant contrasts between characters (for example, between the rich and the poor)
Literary Influences	• writer's chosen form or genre • passages that "sound like" another writer • events or situations that resemble those in other works • evidence of an outlook similar to that of another writer

Gather Support

Taking Notes From the Work

Once you have a working thesis, take notes on passages in the work that confirm it. To aid your search for support, consider the type of support suited to your thesis, as in the chart.

Conducting Additional Research If you are writing biographical or historical criticism, you will need to consult sources on the writer's life and era. Even if you are writing a close analysis of a poem, you should consider consulting the works of critics to benefit from their insights and understanding.

Take Notes

Consider recording notes from the works you are analyzing, as well as from any critical works you consult, on a set of note cards. A good set of note cards enables you to recall details accurately, to organize your ideas effectively, and to see connections between ideas.

One Card, One Idea If you use note cards while researching, record each key passage, theme, critical opinion, or fact on a separate note card. A good note card includes a brief quotation or summary of an idea and a record of the source, including the page number, in which you found the information. When copying a sentence from a work, use quotation marks and check to make sure you have copied it correctly.

Coding Sources Keep a working bibliography, a list of all works you consult, as you conduct research. Assign a code, such as a letter, to each work on the list. For each note you take, include the code for the source.

Coding Cards Organize your note cards by labeling each with the subtopic it concerns.

Present Support Appropriately

As you draft, consider how much support you need for each point and the form that support should take. You can provide support in the following forms:

- **Summaries** are short accounts in your own words of important elements of the work, such as events, a character's traits, or the writer's ideas. They are appropriate for background information.
- **Paraphrases** are restatements of passages from a work in your own words. They are appropriate for background and for information incidental to your main point.
- **Quotations of key passages** are direct transcriptions of the writer's words, enclosed in quotation marks or, if longer than three lines, set as indented text. If a passage is crucial to your thesis, you should quote it directly and at whatever length is necessary.

Quotations of multiple examples are required to support claims about general features of a work, such as a claim about the writer's ironic style or use of cartoonlike characters.

DOs and DON'Ts of Academic Writing

Avoid gender and cultural bias. Certain terms and usages reflect the bias of past generations. To eliminate bias in any academic work you do, edit with the following rules in mind:

- **Pronoun usage** When referring to an unspecified individual in a case in which his or her gender is irrelevant, use forms of the pronoun phrase he or she. Example: "A lawyer is trained to use his or her mind."
- **"Culture-centric" terms** Replace terms that reflect a bias toward one culture with more generally accepted synonyms. For instance, replace terms such as primitive (used of hunting-gathering peoples), the Orient (used to refer to Asia), and Indians (used of Native Americans), all of which suggest a view of the world centered in Western European culture.

Avoid plagiarism. Presenting someone else's ideas, research, or exact words as your own is plagiarism, the equivalent of stealing or fraud. Laws protect the rights of writers and researchers in cases of commercial plagiarism. Academic standards protect their rights in cases of academic plagiarism.

To avoid plagiarism, follow these practices:

- Read from several sources.
- Synthesize what you learn.
- Let the ideas of experts help you draw your own conclusions.
- Always credit your sources properly when using someone else's ideas to support your view.

By following these guidelines, you will also push yourself to think independently.

Forming Your Critical Vocabulary

To enhance your critical perceptions—the connections you find and the distinctions you make—improve your critical vocabulary. The High-Utility Academic Words that appear in this textbook and are underlined in the Glossary (pp. R1–R13) are useful in critical writing.

Citing Sources and Preparing Manuscript

In research writing, cite your sources. In the body of your paper, provide a footnote, an endnote, or an internal citation, identifying the sources of facts, opinions, or quotations. At the end of your paper, provide a bibliography or a Works Cited list, a list of all the sources you cite. Follow an established format, such as Modern Language Association (MLA) Style or American Psychological Association (APA) Style.

Works Cited List (MLA Style)

A Works Cited list must contain accurate information sufficient to enable a reader to locate each source you cite. The basic components of an entry are as follows:

- Name of the author, editor, translator, or group responsible for the work
- Title
- Place and date of publication
- Publisher

For print materials, the information required for a citation generally appears on the copyright and title pages of a work. For the format of Works Cited list entries, consult the examples at right and in the chart on page R22.

Parenthetical Citations (MLA Style)

A parenthetical citation briefly identifies the source from which you have taken a specific quotation, factual claim, or opinion. It refers the reader to one of the entries on your Works Cited list. A parenthetical citation has the following features:

- It appears in parentheses.
- It identifies the source by the last name of the author, editor, or translator.
- It gives a page reference, identifying the page of the source on which the information cited can be found.

Punctuation A parenthetical citation generally falls outside a closing quotation mark but within the final punctuation of a clause or sentence. For a long quotation set off from the rest of your text, place the citation at the end of the excerpt without any punctuation following.

Special Cases

- If the author is an organization, use the organization's name, in a shortened version if necessary.
- If you cite more than one work by the same author, add the title or a shortened version of the title.

Sample Works-Cited Lists (MLA 7th Edition)

Carwardine, Mark, Erich Hoyt, R. Ewan Fordyce, and Peter Gill. *The Nature Company Guides: Whales, Dolphins, and Porpoises.* New York: Time-Life, 1998. Print.

"Discovering Whales." *Whales on the Net.* 1998. Whales in Danger Information Service. Web. 18 Oct. 1999.

Neruda, Pablo. "Ode to Spring." *Odes to Opposites.* Trans. Ken Krabbenhoft. Ed. and illus. Ferris Cook. Boston: Little, 1995. Print.

The Saga of the Volsungs. Trans. Jesse L. Byock. London: Penguin, 1990. Print.

List an anonymous work by title.

List both the title of the work and the collection in which it is found.

Sample Parenthetical Citations

It makes sense that baleen whales such as the blue whale, the bowhead whale, the humpback whale, and the sei whale (to name just a few) grow to immense sizes (Carwardine, Hoyt, and Fordyce 19–21). The blue whale has grooves running from under its chin to partway along the length of its underbelly. As in some other whales, these grooves expand and allow even more food and water to be taken in (Ellis 18–21).

Author's last name

Page numbers where information can be found

MLA Style for Listing Sources

Book with one author	Pyles, Thomas. *The Origins and Development of the English Language.* 2nd ed. New York: Harcourt, 1971. Print.
Book with two or three authors	McCrum, Robert, William Cran, and Robert MacNeil. *The Story of English.* New York: Penguin, 1987. Print.
Book with an editor	Truth, Sojourner. *Narrative of Sojourner Truth.* Ed. Margaret Washington. New York: Vintage, 1993. Print.
Book with more than three authors or editors	Donald, Robert B., et al. *Writing Clear Essays.* Upper Saddle River: Prentice, 1996. Print.
Single work in an anthology	Hawthorne, Nathaniel. "Young Goodman Brown." *Literature: An Introduction to Reading and Writing.* Ed. Edgar V. Roberts and H. E. Jacobs. Upper Saddle River: Prentice, 1998. 376–385. Print. [Indicate pages for the entire selection.]
Introduction to a work in a published edition	Washington, Margaret. Introduction. *Narrative of Sojourner Truth.* By Sojourner Truth. Ed. Washington. New York: Vintage, 1993. v–xi. Print.
Signed article from an encyclopedia	Askeland, Donald R. "Welding." *World Book Encyclopedia.* 1991 ed. Print.
Signed article in a weekly magazine	Wallace, Charles. "A Vodacious Deal." *Time* 14 Feb. 2000: 63. Print.
Signed article in a monthly magazine	Gustaitis, Joseph. "The Sticky History of Chewing Gum." *American History* Oct. 1998: 30–38. Print.
Newspaper	Thurow, Roger. "South Africans Who Fought for Sanctions Now Scrap for Investors." *Wall Street Journal* 11 Feb. 2000: A1+. Print. [For a multipage article that does not appear on consecutive pages, write only the first page number on which it appears, followed by the plus sign.]
Unsigned editorial or story	"Selective Silence." Editorial. *Wall Street Journal* 11 Feb. 2000: A14. Print. [If the editorial or story is signed, begin with the author's name.]
Signed pamphlet or brochure	[Treat the pamphlet as though it were a book.]
Work from a library subscription service	Ertman, Earl L. "Nefertiti's Eyes." *Archaeology* Mar.–Apr. 2008: 28–32. *Kids Search.* EBSCO. New York Public Library. Web. 18 June 2008 [Indicate the date you accessed the information.]
Filmstrips, slide programs, videocassettes, DVDs, and other audiovisual media	*The Diary of Anne Frank.* Dir. George Stevens. Perf. Millie Perkins, Shelley Winters, Joseph Schildkraut, Lou Jacobi, and Richard Beymer. 1959. Twentieth Century Fox, 2004. DVD.
CD-ROM (with multiple publishers)	Simms, James, ed. *Romeo and Juliet.* By William Shakespeare. Oxford: Attica Cybernetics; London: BBC Education; London: Harper, 1995. CD-ROM.
Radio or television program transcript	"Washington's Crossing of the Delaware." *Weekend Edition Sunday.* Natl. Public Radio. WNYC, New York. 23 Dec. 2003. Television transcript.
Internet Web page	"Fun Facts About Gum." NACGM site. 1999. National Association of Chewing Gum Manufacturers. Web. 19 Dec. 1999 [Indicate the date you accessed the information.]
Personal interview	Smith, Jane. Personal interview. 10 Feb. 2000.

All examples follow the style given in the *MLA Handbook for Writers of Research Papers,* seventh edition, by Joseph Gibaldi.

LITERARY HANDBOOK

APA Style for Listing Sources

Book with one author	Pyles, T. (1971). *The origins and development of the English language* (2nd ed.). New York: Harcourt Brace Jovanovich.
Book with two or three authors	McCrum, R., Cran, W., & MacNeil, R. (1987). *The story of English.* New York: Penguin Books.
Book with an editor	Truth, S. (1993). *Narrative of Sojourner Truth* (M. Washington, Ed.). New York: Vintage Books.
Book with more than three authors or editors	Donald, R. B., Morrow, B. R., Wargetz, L. G., & Werner, K. (1996). *Writing clear essays.* Upper Saddle River, NJ: Prentice Hall. [With eight or more authors, abbreviate all authors after the sixth as "et al."]
Single work from an anthology	Hawthorne, N. (1998). Young Goodman Brown. In E. V. Roberts, & H. E. Jacobs (Eds.), *Literature: An introduction to reading and writing* (pp. 376–385). Upper Saddle River, NJ: Prentice Hall.
Introduction in a published edition	Washington, M. (1993). Introduction. In M. Washington (Ed.), S. Truth, *Narrative of Sojourner Truth* (pp. v–xi). New York: Vintage Books.
Signed article from an encyclopedia	Askeland, D. R. (1991). Welding. In *World Book Encyclopedia.* (Vol. 21. pp. 190–191). Chicago: World Book.
Signed article in a weekly magazine	Wallace, C. (2000, February 14). A vodacious deal. *Time, 155,* 63. [The volume number appears in italics before the page number.]
Signed article in a monthly magazine	Gustaitis, J. (1998, October). The sticky history of chewing gum. *American History*, 33, 30–38.
Newspaper	Thurow, R. (2000, February 11). South Africans who fought for sanctions now scrap for investors. *Wall Street Journal*, pp. A1, A4. [If an article appears on discontinuous pages, give all page numbers and separate the numbers with a comma.]
Unsigned editorial or story	Selective silence [Editorial]. (2000, February 11). *Wall Street Journal*, p. A14.
Signed pamphlet	Pearson Education. (2000). *LifeCare* (2nd ed.) [Pamphlet]. New York: Smith, John: Author.
Filmstrips, slide programs, videocassettes, DVDs, and other audiovisual media	Wallis, H. B. (Producer), & Curtiz, M. (Director). (1942). *Casablanca* [Motion Picture]. United States: Warner.
Radio or television program transcript	Hackett Fischer, D. (Guest), & Hansen, L. (Host). (2003, December 23). Washington's crossing of the Delaware. [Radio series installment]. *Weekend Edition Sunday.* New York: National Public Radio. Retrieved March 6, 2008 from http://www.npr.org/templates/story/story.php?storyId=1573202
Internet	National Association of Chewing Gum Manufacturers. (1999). Retrieved December 19, 1999, from http://www.nacgm.org/consumer/funfacts.html [References to Websites should begin with the author's last name, if available. Indicate the site name and the available path or URL address.]
Work from a library subscription service	Ertman, E. L. (2008 March–April). Nefertiti's eyes. *Archaeology, 61,* 28–32. Retrieved June 18, 2008, from EBSCO Science Reference Center database.
CD	Shakespeare, W. (1995). *Romeo and Juliet.* (J. Simms, Ed.) [CD-ROM]. Oxford: Attica Cybernetics.
Personal interview	[APA states that, since interviews (and other personal communications) do not provide "recoverable data," they should only be cited in text.]

Literary Terms

ALLEGORY An ***allegory*** is a story or tale with two or more levels of meaning—a literal level and one or more symbolic levels. The events, setting, and characters in an allegory are symbols for ideas or qualities. Arthur Miller's play *The Crucible* (p. 1124) is an allegory.

ALLITERATION ***Alliteration*** is the repetition of consonant sounds at the beginning of words or accented syllables. Sara Teasdale uses alliteration in these lines from her poem "Understanding":

> Your spirit's secret hides like gold
>
> Sunk in a Spanish galleon

ALLUSION An ***allusion*** is a reference to a well-known person, place, event, literary work, or work of art. Writers often make allusions to stories from the Bible, to Greek and Roman myths, to plays by Shakespeare, to political and historical events, and to other materials with which they can expect their readers to be familiar. In "The Love Song of J. Alfred Prufrock" (p. 708), T. S. Eliot alludes to, among other things, Dante's *Inferno*, Italian artist Michelangelo, Shakespeare's *Hamlet*, and the Bible. By using allusions, writers can suggest complex ideas simply and easily.

AMBIGUITY ***Ambiguity*** is the effect created when words suggest and support two or more divergent interpretations. Ambiguity may be used in literature to express experiences or truths that are complex or contradictory. Ambiguity often derives from the fact that words have multiple meanings.

See also ***Irony.***

ANALOGY An ***analogy*** is an extended comparison of relationships. It is based on the idea that the relationship between one pair of things is like the relationship between another pair. Unlike a metaphor, an analogy involves an explicit comparison, often using the words *like* or *as.*

See also ***Metaphor*** and ***Simile.***

ANECDOTE An ***anecdote*** is a brief story about an interesting, amusing, or strange event. An anecdote is told to entertain or to make a point. In the excerpt from *Life on the Mississippi* (p. 570), Mark Twain tells several anecdotes about his experiences on the Mississippi River.

ANTAGONIST An ***antagonist*** is a character or force in conflict with a main character, or protagonist. In Jack London's "To Build a Fire" (p. 596), the antagonist is neither a person nor an animal but rather the extreme cold. In many stories, the conflict between the antagonist and the protagonist is the basis for the plot.

See also ***Conflict, Plot,*** and ***Protagonist.***

APHORISM An ***aphorism*** is a general truth or observation about life, usually stated concisely. Often witty and wise, aphorisms appear in many kinds of works. An essay writer may have an aphoristic style, making many such statements. Ralph Waldo Emerson was famous for his aphoristic style. His essay entitled "Fate" contains the following aphorisms:

> Nature is what you may do.
>
> So far as a man thinks, he is free.
>
> A man's fortunes are the fruit of his character.

Used in an essay, an aphorism can be a memorable way to sum up or to reinforce a point or an argument.

APOSTROPHE An ***apostrophe*** is a figure of speech in which a speaker directly addresses an absent person or a personified quality, object, or idea. Phillis Wheatley uses apostrophe in this line from "To the University of Cambridge, in New England":

> Students, to you 'tis given to scan the heights

See also ***Figurative Language.***

ARCHETYPAL LITERARY ELEMENTS ***Archetypal literary elements*** are patterns in literature found around the world. For instance, the occurrence of events in threes is an archetypal element of fairy tales. Certain character types, such as mysterious guides, are also archetypal elements of such traditional stories. Archetypal elements make stories easier to remember and retell. In Moby-Dick (p. 336), Melville uses the archetype of a whale—like the biblical mammal in conflict with Jonah—to address man's conflict with nature.

ARGUMENT See ***Persuasion.***

ASSONANCE ***Assonance*** is the repetition of vowel sounds in conjunction with dissimilar consonant sounds. Emily Dickinson uses assonance in the line "The mountain at a given distance." The *i* sound is repeated in *given* and *distance*, in the context of the dissimilar consonant sounds *g–v* and *d–s.*

ATMOSPHERE See ***Mood.***

AUTOBIOGRAPHY An ***autobiography*** is a form of nonfiction in which a person tells his or her own life story. Notable examples of autobiographies include those by Benjamin Franklin and Frederick Douglass. *Memoirs,* first-person accounts of personally or historically significant events in which the writer was a participant or an eyewitness, are a form of autobiographical writing.

See also ***Biography*** and ***Journal.***

BALLAD A ***ballad*** is a songlike poem that tells a story, often one dealing with adventure and romance. Most ballads include simple language, four- or six-line stanzas, rhyme, and regular meter.

BIOGRAPHY A ***biography*** is a form of nonfiction in which a writer tells the life story of another person. Carl Sandburg's *Abe Lincoln Grows Up* is a biography of President Lincoln.

See also ***Autobiography.***

BLANK VERSE ***Blank verse*** is poetry written in unrhymed iambic pentameter. An iamb is a poetic foot consisting of one weak stress followed by one strong stress. A pentameter line has five poetic feet. Robert Frost's "Birches" (p. 874) is written in blank verse.

CHARACTER A ***character*** is a person or an animal that takes part in the action of a literary work. The following are some terms used to describe various types of characters:

The ***main character*** in a literary work is the one on whom the work focuses. ***Major characters*** in a literary work include the main character and any other characters who play significant roles. A ***minor character*** is one who does not play a significant role. A ***round character*** is one who is complex and multifaceted, like a real person. A ***flat character*** is one who is one-dimensional. A ***dynamic character*** is one who changes in the course of a work. A ***static character*** is one who does not change in the course of a work.

See also ***Characterization*** and ***Motivation.***

CHARACTERIZATION ***Characterization*** is the act of creating and developing a character. In ***direct characterization,*** a writer simply states a character's traits, as when F. Scott Fitzgerald writes of the main character in his story "Winter Dreams" (p. 730), "He wanted not association with glittering things and glittering people—he wanted the glittering things themselves." In ***indirect characterization,*** character is revealed through one of the following means:

1. words, thoughts, or actions of the character
2. descriptions of the character's appearance or background
3. what other characters say about the character
4. the ways in which other characters react to the character

See also ***Character.***

CINQUAIN See ***Stanza.***

CLASSICISM ***Classicism*** is an approach to literature and the other arts that stresses reason, balance, clarity, ideal beauty, and orderly form in imitation of the arts of ancient Greece and Rome. Classicism is often contrasted with ***Romanticism,*** which stresses imagination, emotion, and individualism. ***Classicism*** also differs from ***Realism,*** which stresses the actual rather than the ideal.

See also ***Realism*** and ***Romanticism.***

CLIMAX The ***climax*** is the high point of interest or suspense in a literary work. For example, Jack London's "To Build a Fire" (p. 596) reaches its climax when the man realizes that he is going to freeze to death. The climax generally appears near the end of a story, play, or narrative poem.

See also ***Plot.***

COMEDY A ***comedy*** is a literary work, especially a play, that has a happy ending.

CONFLICT A ***conflict*** is a struggle between opposing forces. Sometimes this struggle is internal, or within a character, as in Bernard Malamud's "The First Seven Years" (p. 1028). At other times, this struggle is external, or between a character and an outside force, as in Jack London's "To Build a Fire" (p. 596). Conflict is one of the primary elements of narrative literature because most plots develop from conflicts.

See also ***Antagonist, Plot,*** and ***Protagonist.***

CONNOTATION A ***connotation*** is an association that a word calls to mind in addition to the dictionary meaning of the word. Many words that are similar in their dictionary meanings, or denotations, are quite different in their connotations. Consider, for example, José García Villa's line, "Be beautiful, noble, like the antique ant." This line would have a very different effect if it were "Be pretty, classy, like the old ant." Poets and other writers choose their words carefully so that the connotations of those words will be appropriate.

See also ***Denotation.***

CONSONANCE ***Consonance*** is the repetition of similar final consonant sounds at the ends of words or accented syllables. Emily Dickinson uses consonance in these lines:

> But if he ask where you are hid
>
> Until to-morrow,—happy letter!
>
> Gesture, coquette, and shake your head!

COUPLET See ***Stanza.***

CRISIS In the plot of a narrative, the ***crisis*** is the turning point for the protagonist—the point at which the protagonist's situation or understanding changes dramatically. In Bernard Malamud's "The First Seven Years" (p. 1028), the crisis occurs when Feld recognizes that Sobel loves Miriam.

DENOTATION The ***denotation*** of a word is its objective meaning, independent of other associations that the word brings to mind.

See also ***Connotation.***

DENOUEMENT See ***Plot.***

DESCRIPTION A ***description*** is a portrayal, in words, of something that can be perceived by the senses. Writers create descriptions by using images, as John Wesley Powell does in this passage from "The Most Sublime Spectacle on Earth," his description of the Grand Canyon:

> Clouds creep out of canyons and wind into other canyons. The heavens seem to be alive, not moving as move the heavens over a plain, in one direction with the wind, but following the multiplied courses of these gorges.

See also ***Image.***

DEVELOPMENT See ***Plot.***

DIALECT A ***dialect*** is the form of a language spoken by people in a particular region or group. Writers often use dialect to make their characters seem realistic and to create local color. See, for example, Mark Twain's "The Notorious Jumping Frog of Calaveras County" (p. 576).

See also ***Local Color.***

DIALOGUE A ***dialogue*** is a conversation between characters. Writers use dialogue to reveal character, to present events, to add variety to narratives, and to arouse their readers' interest.

See also ***Drama.***

DICTION ***Diction*** is a writer's or speaker's word choice. Diction is part of a writer's style and may be described as formal or informal, plain or ornate, common or technical, abstract or concrete.

See also ***Style.***

DRAMA A ***drama*** is a story written to be performed by actors. The playwright supplies dialogue for the characters to speak, as well as stage directions that give information about costumes, lighting, scenery, properties, the setting, and the characters' movements and ways of speaking. Dramatic conventions include soliloquies, asides, or the passage of time between acts or scenes.

See also ***Genre.***

DRAMATIC MONOLOGUE A ***dramatic monologue*** is a poem or speech in which an imaginary character speaks to a silent listener. T. S. Eliot's "The Love Song of J. Alfred Prufrock" (p. 708) is a dramatic monologue.

See also ***Dramatic Poem*** and ***Monologue.***

DRAMATIC POEM A ***dramatic poem*** is one that makes use of the conventions of drama. Such poems may be monologues or dialogues or may present the speech of many characters. Robert Frost's "The Death of the Hired Man" is a famous example of a dramatic poem.

See also ***Dramatic Monologue.***

DYNAMIC CHARACTER See ***Character.***

EPIGRAM An ***epigram*** is a brief, pointed statement, in prose or in verse. Benjamin Franklin was famous for his epigrams, which include "Fools make feasts, and wise men eat them," and "A plowman on his legs is higher than a gentleman on his knees."

EPIPHANY An ***epiphany*** is a sudden revelation or flash of insight. The shoemaker in Bernard Malamud's "The First Seven Years" (p. 1028) experiences an epiphany when he suddenly and thoroughly comprehends that the actions of his apprentice, Sobel, are motivated by his secret love for Miriam.

ESSAY An ***essay*** is a short nonfiction work about a particular subject. Essays can be classified as ***formal*** or ***informal, personal*** or ***impersonal***. They can also be classified according to purpose, such as ***cause-and-effect*** (see the excerpt from "One Day, Now Broken in Two" on p. 1404), ***satirical*** (see "Coyote v. Acme" on p. 1384), or ***reflective*** (see Amy Tan's "Mother Tongue" on p. 1410). Modes of discourse, such as ***expository, descriptive, persuasive***, or ***narrative***, are other means of classifying essays.

See also ***Satire, Exposition, Description, Persuasion,*** and ***Narration.***

EXPOSITION ***Exposition*** is writing or speech that explains, informs, or presents information. The main techniques of expository writing include analysis, classification, comparison and contrast, definition, and exemplification, or illustration. An essay may be primarily expository, as is William Safire's "Onomatopoeia" (p. 1378), or it may use exposition to support another purpose, such as persuasion or argumentation, as in Ian Frazier's satirical essay "Coyote v. Acme" (p. 1384).

In a story or play, the exposition is that part of the plot that introduces the characters, the setting, and the basic situation.

See also ***Plot.***

FALLING ACTION See ***Plot.***

FICTION ***Fiction*** is prose writing that tells about imaginary characters and events. Short stories and novels are works of fiction.

See also ***Genre, Narrative, Nonfiction,*** and ***Prose.***

FIGURATIVE LANGUAGE ***Figurative language*** is writing or speech not meant to be taken literally. Writers use figurative language to express ideas in vivid and imaginative ways. For example, Emily Dickinson begins one poem with the following description of snow:

> It sifts from leaden sieves, / It powders all the wood
>
> By describing the snow as if it were flour, Dickinson renders a precise and compelling picture of it.

See also ***Figure of Speech.***

FIGURE OF SPEECH A ***figure of speech*** is an expression or a word used imaginatively rather than literally.

See also ***Figurative Language.***

FLASHBACK A ***flashback*** is a section of a literary work that interrupts the chronological presentation of events to relate an event from an earlier time. A writer may present a flashback as a character's memory or recollection, as part of an account or story told by a character, as a dream or a daydream, or simply by having the narrator switch to a time in the past.

FLAT CHARACTER See ***Character.***

FOIL A ***foil*** is a character who provides a contrast to another character. In F. Scott Fitzgerald's "Winter Dreams" (p. 730), Irene Scheerer is a foil for the tantalizing Judy Jones.

FOLK LITERATURE ***Folk literature*** is the body of stories, legends, myths, ballads, songs, riddles, sayings, and other works arising out of the oral traditions of peoples around the globe. The folk literature traditions of the United States, including those of Native Americans and of the American pioneers, are especially rich.

FOOT See ***Meter.***

FORESHADOWING ***Foreshadowing*** in a literary work is the use of clues to suggest events that have yet to occur.

FREE VERSE ***Free verse*** is poetry that lacks a regular rhythmical pattern, or meter. A writer of free verse is at liberty to use any rhythms that are appropriate to what he or she is saying. Free verse has been widely used by twentieth-century poets such as Leslie Marmon Silko, who begins "Where Mountain Lion Lay Down With Deer" with these lines:

> I climb the black rock mountain
> stepping from day to day
> silently.

See also ***Meter.***

GENRE A ***genre*** is a division, or type, of literature. Literature is commonly divided into three major genres: poetry, prose, and drama. Each major genre can in turn be divided into smaller genres. Poetry can be divided into lyric, concrete, dramatic, narrative, and epic poetry. Prose can be divided into fiction and nonfiction. Drama can be divided into serious drama, tragedy, comic drama, melodrama, and farce.

See also ***Drama, Poetry,*** and ***Prose.***

GOTHIC ***Gothic*** refers to the use of primitive, medieval, wild, or mysterious elements in literature. Gothic novels feature places like mysterious and gloomy castles, where horrifying, supernatural events take place. Their influence on Edgar Allan Poe is evident in "The Fall of the House of Usher" (p. 292).

GROTESQUE ***Grotesque*** refers to the use of bizarre, absurd, or fantastic elements in literature. The grotesque is generally characterized by distortions or striking incongruities. ***Grotesque characters***, like those in Flannery O'Connor's "The Life You Save May Be Your Own" (p. 1012), are characters who have become bizarre through their obsession with an idea or a value or as a result of an emotional problem.

HARLEM RENAISSANCE The ***Harlem Renaissance,*** which occurred during the 1920s, was a time of African American artistic creativity centered in Harlem, in New York City. Writers of the Harlem Renaissance include Countee Cullen, Claude McKay, Jean Toomer, and Langston Hughes.

HYPERBOLE ***Hyperbole*** is a deliberate exaggeration or overstatement, often used for comic effect. In Mark Twain's "The Notorious Jumping Frog of Calaveras County" (p. 576), the claim that Jim Smiley would follow a bug as far as Mexico to win a bet is hyperbole.

IAMBIC PENTAMETER ***Iambic pentameter*** is a line of poetry with five iambic feet, each containing one unstressed syllable followed by one stressed syllable (˘ ´). Iambic pentameter may be rhymed or unrhymed. Unrhymed iambic pentameter is called blank verse. These lines from Anne Bradstreet's "The Author to Her Book" are in iambic pentameter:

> Ănd fór thy̆, Mótheˇr, sheˇ ălás ĭs póor,
> Whĭch caúsed heˇr thús tŏ sénd theˇe oút ŏf dóor.

See also ***Blank Verse*** and ***Meter.***

IDYLL An ***idyll*** is a poem or part of a poem that describes and idealizes country life. John Greenleaf Whittier's "Snowbound" is an idyll.

IMAGE An ***image*** is a word or phrase that appeals to one or more of the five senses—sight, hearing, touch, taste, or smell.

See also ***Imagery.***

IMAGERY ***Imagery*** is the descriptive or figurative language used in literature to create word pictures for the reader. These pictures, or images, are created by details of sight, sound, taste, touch, smell, or movement.

IMAGISM ***Imagism*** was a literary movement that flourished between 1912 and 1927. Led by Ezra Pound and Amy Lowell, the Imagist poets rejected nineteenth-century poetic forms and language. Instead, they wrote short poems that used ordinary language and free verse to create sharp, exact, concentrated pictures. Pound's poetry (p. 722) provides examples of Imagism.

IRONY ***Irony*** is a contrast between what is stated and what is meant, or between what is expected to happen and what actually happens. In ***verbal irony***, a word or a phrase is used to suggest the opposite of its usual meaning. In ***dramatic irony***, there is a contradiction between what a character thinks and what the reader or audience knows. In ***irony of situation***, an event occurs that contradicts the expectations of the characters, of the reader, or of the audience.

JOURNAL A ***journal*** is a daily autobiographical account of events and personal reactions. For example, Mary Chesnut's journal (p. 495) records events during the Civil War.

LEGEND A ***legend*** is a traditional story. Usually a legend deals with a particular person—a hero, a saint, or a national leader. Often legends reflect a people's cultural values. American legends include those of the early Native Americans and those about folk heroes such as Davy Crockett.

See also ***Myth.***

LETTER A ***letter*** is a written message or communication addressed to a reader or readers and is generally sent by mail. Letters may be ***private*** or ***public***, depending on their intended audience. A public letter, also called a ***literary letter*** or ***epistle***, is a work of literature written in the form of a personal letter but created for publication. Michel-Guillaume Jean de Crèvecoeur's "Letters From an American Farmer" are public letters.

LOCAL COLOR ***Local color*** is the use in a literary work of characters and details unique to a particular geographic area. It can be created by the use of dialect and by descriptions of customs, clothing, manners, attitudes, and landscape. Local-color stories were especially popular after the Civil War, bringing readers the West of Bret Harte and the Mississippi River of Mark Twain.

See also ***Realism*** and ***Regionalism.***

LYRIC POEM A ***lyric poem*** is a melodic poem that expresses the observations and feelings of a single speaker. Unlike a narrative poem, a lyric poem focuses on producing a single, unified effect. Types of lyric poems include the ***elegy***, the ***ode***, and the ***sonnet***. Among contemporary American poets, the lyric is the most common poetic form.

MAIN CHARACTER See ***Character.***

MEMOIR A ***memoir*** is a type of nonfiction autobiographical writing that tells about a person's own life, usually focusing on the writer's involvement in historically or culturally significant events—either as a participant or an eyewitness.

METAPHOR A ***metaphor*** is a figure of speech in which one thing is spoken of as though it were something else. The identification suggests a comparison between the two things that are identified, as in "death is a long sleep."

A ***mixed metaphor*** occurs when two metaphors are jumbled together. For example, thorns and rain are illogically mixed in "the thorns of life rained down on him." A ***dead metaphor*** is one that has been overused and has become a common expression, such as "the arm of the chair" or "nightfall."

METER The ***meter*** of a poem is its rhythmical pattern. This pattern is determined by the number and types of stresses, or beats, in each line. To describe the meter of a poem, you must scan its lines. ***Scanning*** involves marking the stressed and unstressed syllables, as follows:

> Sóon ăs | thĕ sŭn | fŏrsóok | thĕ eás|tĕrn máin
>
> Thĕ péal | ĭng thún | dĕr shóok | thĕ héav'n | lȳ pláin;
>
> —"An Hymn to the Evening," Phillis Wheatley

As the example shows, each strong stress is marked with a slanted line (´) and each weak stress with a horseshoe symbol (˘). The weak and strong stresses are then divided by vertical lines (|) into groups called feet. The following types of feet are common in poetry written in English:

1. ***Iamb:*** a foot with one unstressed syllable followed by one stressed syllable, as in the word "around"
2. ***Trochee:*** a foot with one stressed syllable followed by one unstressed syllable, as in the word "broken"
3. ***Anapest:*** a foot with two unstressed syllables followed by one stressed syllable, as in the phrase "in a flash"
4. ***Dactyl:*** a foot with one stressed syllable followed by two unstressed syllables, as in the word "argument"
5. ***Spondee:*** a foot with two stressed syllables, as in the word "airship"
6. ***Pyrrhic:*** a foot with two unstressed syllables, as in the last foot of the word "imag|ining"

Lines of poetry are often described as iambic, trochaic, anapestic, or dactylic. Lines are also described in terms of the number of feet that occur in them, as follows:

1. ***Monometer:*** verse written in one-foot lines

   > Évĭl
   > Bĕgéts
   > Évĭl
   >
   > —Anonymous

2. ***Dimeter:*** verse written in two-foot lines

   > Thĭs ís | thĕ tíme
   > ŏf thĕ trág|ĭc mán
   >
   > —"Visits to St. Elizabeth's," Elizabeth Bishop

3. ***Trimeter:*** verse written in three-foot lines:

   > Over | the win|ter glaciers
   > I see | the sum|mer glow,
   > And through | the wild-|piled snowdrift
   > The warm | rosebuds | below.
   >
   > —"Beyond Winter," Ralph Waldo Emerson

4. ***Tetrameter:*** verse written in four-foot lines:

   > The sun | that brief | Decem|ber day
   > Rose cheer|less ov|er hills | of gray
   >
   > —"Snowbound," John Greenleaf Whittier

5. ***Pentameter:*** verse written in five-foot lines:

> I doubt | not God | is good, | well-mean|ing, kind,
>
> And did | He stoop | to quib|ble could | tell why
>
> The lit|tle bur|ied mole | contin|ues blind
>
> —"Yet Do I Marvel," Countee Cullen

A complete description of the meter of a line tells both how many feet there are in the line and what kind of foot is most common. Thus, the lines from Countee Cullen's poem would be described as ***iambic pentameter.*** ***Blank verse*** is poetry written in unrhymed iambic pentameter. Poetry that does not have a regular meter is called ***free verse.***

MONOLOGUE A ***monologue*** is a speech delivered entirely by one person or character.

See also ***Dramatic Monologue.***

MOOD ***Mood,*** or atmosphere, is the feeling created in the reader by a literary work or passage. Elements that can influence the mood of a work include its setting, tone, and events.

See also ***Setting*** and ***Tone.***

MOTIVATION A ***motivation*** is a reason that explains a character's thoughts, feelings, actions, or speech. Characters are motivated by their values and by their wants, desires, dreams, wishes, and needs. Sometimes the reasons for a character's actions are stated directly, as in Willa Cather's "A Wagner Matinée" (p. 652), when Clark explains his reception of his aunt by saying, "I owed to this woman most of the good that ever came my way in my boyhood." At other times, the writer will just suggest a character's motivation.

MYTH A ***myth*** is a fictional tale that explains the actions of gods or heroes or the causes of natural phenomena. Myths that explain the origins of earthly life, as do the Onondaga, Navajo, and Modoc myths in this text, are known as origin myths. Other myths express the central values of the people who created them.

NARRATION ***Narration*** is writing that tells a story. The act of telling a story is also called ***narration.*** The ***narrative,*** or story, is told by a storyteller called the ***narrator.*** A story is usually told chronologically, in the order in which events take place in time, though it may include flashbacks and foreshadowing. Narratives may be true, like the events recorded in Mary Chesnut's journal (p. 495), or fictional, like the events in Flannery O'Connor's "The Life You Save May Be Your Own" (p. 1012). Narration is one of the forms of discourse and is used in novels, short stories, plays, narrative poems, anecdotes, autobiographies, biographies, and reports.

See also ***Narrative Poem*** and ***Narrator.***

NARRATIVE A ***narrative*** is a story told in fiction, nonfiction, poetry, or drama. Narratives are often classified by their content or purpose. An ***exploration narrative*** is a firsthand account of an explorer's travels in a new land. Alvar Núñez Cabeza de Vaca's account of his exploration of the wilderness that is now Texas, "A Journey Through Texas," appears on page 48. "The Interesting Narrative of the Life of Olaudah Equiano" (excerpt on p. 170) is a ***slave narrative,*** an account of the experiences of an enslaved person. A ***historical narrative*** is a narrative account of significant historical events, such as William Bradford's *Of Plymouth Plantation.* (p. 58).

See also ***Narration.***

NARRATIVE POEM A ***narrative*** poem tells a story in verse. Three traditional types of narrative verse are ***ballads,*** songlike poems that tell stories; ***epics,*** long poems about the deeds of gods or heroes; and ***metrical romances,*** poems that tell tales of love and chivalry.

See also ***Ballad.***

NARRATOR A ***narrator*** is a speaker or character who tells a story. A story or novel may be narrated by a main character, by a minor character, or by someone uninvolved in the story. The narrator may speak in the first person or in the third person. An ***omniscient narrator*** is all-knowing, while a ***limited narrator*** knows only what one character does.

See also ***Point of View.***

NATURALISM ***Naturalism*** was a literary movement among novelists at the end of the nineteenth century and during the early decades of the twentieth century. The Naturalists tended to view people as hapless victims of immutable natural laws. Early exponents of Naturalism included Stephen Crane, Jack London, and Theodore Dreiser.

See also ***Realism.***

NONFICTION ***Nonfiction*** is prose writing that presents and explains ideas or that tells about real people, places, objects, or events. Essays, biographies, autobiographies, journals, and reports are all examples of nonfiction.

See also ***Fiction*** and ***Genre.***

NOVEL A ***novel*** is a long work of fiction. A novel often has a complicated plot, many major and minor characters, a significant theme, and several varied settings. Novels can be classified in many ways, based on the historical periods in which they are written, the subjects and themes that they treat, the techniques that are used in them, and the literary movements that inspired them. Classic nineteenth-century novels include Herman Melville's *Moby-Dick* (p. 336) and Nathaniel Hawthorne's *The Scarlet Letter* (an extended reading suggestion). Well-known twentieth-century novels include F. Scott Fitzgerald's *The Great Gatsby* and Edith Wharton's *Ethan Frome* (recommended selections for extended reading). A ***novella*** is not as long as a novel but is longer than a short story. Ernest Hemingway's *The Old Man and the Sea* is a novella.

ODE An ***ode*** is a long, formal lyric poem with a serious theme that may have a traditional stanza structure. Odes often honor people, commemorate events, respond to natural scenes, or consider serious human problems.

See also ***Lyric Poem***.

OMNISCIENT NARRATOR See ***Narrator*** and ***Point of View.***

ONOMATOPOEIA ***Onomatopoeia*** is the use of words that imitate sounds. Examples of such words are *buzz, hiss, murmur,* and *rustle.*

ORAL TRADITION ***Oral tradition*** is the passing of songs, stories, and poems from generation to generation by word of mouth. The oral tradition in America has preserved Native American myths and legends, spirituals, folk ballads, and other works originally heard and memorized rather than written down.

See also ***Ballad, Folk Literature, Legend, Myth,*** and ***Spiritual.***

ORATORY ***Oratory*** is public speaking that is formal, persuasive, and emotionally appealing. Patrick Henry's "Speech in the Virginia Convention" (p. 100) is an example of oratory.

OXYMORON An ***oxymoron*** is a figure of speech that combines two opposing or contradictory ideas. An oxymoron, such as "freezing fire," suggests a paradox in just a few words.

See also ***Figurative Language*** and ***Paradox.***

PARADOX A ***paradox*** is a statement that seems to be contradictory but that actually presents a truth. Marianne Moore uses paradox in "Nevertheless" when she says, "Victory won't come / to me unless I go / to it." Because a paradox is surprising, it draws the reader's attention to what is being said.

See also ***Figurative Language*** and ***Oxymoron.***

PARALLELISM ***Parallelism*** is the repetition of a grammatical structure. Robert Hayden concludes his poem "Astronauts" with these questions in parallel form:

> What do we want of these men?
>
> What do we want of ourselves?

Parallelism is used in poetry and in other writing to emphasize and to link related ideas.

PARODY A ***parody*** is a humorous imitation of a literary work, one that exaggerates or distorts the characteristic features of the original.

PASTORAL ***Pastoral*** poems deal with rural settings, including shepherds and rustic life. Traditionally, pastoral poems have presented idealized views of rural life. In twentieth-century pastorals, however, poets like Robert Frost introduced ethical complexity into an otherwise simple landscape.

PERSONIFICATION ***Personification*** is a figure of speech in which a nonhuman subject is given human characteristics. In "April Rain Song," Langston Hughes personifies the rain:

> Let the rain sing you a lullaby.

Effective personification of things or ideas makes them seem vital and alive, as if they were human.

See also ***Figurative Language.***

PERSUASION ***Persuasion*** is writing or speech that attempts to convince a reader to think or act in a particular way. During the Revolutionary War period, leaders such as Patrick Henry, Thomas Paine, and Thomas Jefferson used persuasion in their political arguments. Persuasion is also used in advertising, in editorials, in sermons, and in political speeches. An ***argument*** is a logical way of presenting a belief, conclusion, or stance. A good argument is supported with reasoning and evidence.

PLAIN STYLE ***Plain style*** is a type of writing in which uncomplicated sentences and ordinary words are used to make simple, direct statements. This style was favored by those Puritans who wanted to express themselves clearly, in accordance with their religious beliefs. In the twentieth century, Ernest Hemingway was a master of plain style.

See also ***Style.***

PLOT ***Plot*** is the sequence of events in a literary work. In most fiction, the plot involves both characters and a central conflict. The plot usually begins with an ***exposition*** that introduces the setting, the characters, and the basic situation. This is followed by the ***inciting incident***, which introduces the central conflict. The conflict then increases during the ***development*** until it reaches a high point of interest or suspense, the ***climax***. The climax is followed by the end, or resolution, of the central conflict. Any events that occur after the ***resolution*** make up the ***denouement***. The events that lead up to the climax make up the ***rising action***. The events that follow the climax make up the ***falling action***.

See also ***Conflict.***

POETRY ***Poetry*** is one of the three major types of literature. In poetry, form and content are closely connected, like the two faces of a single coin. Poems are often divided into lines and stanzas and often employ regular rhythmical patterns, or meters. Most poems use highly concise, musical, and emotionally charged language. Many also make use of imagery, figurative language, and special devices such as rhyme.

See also ***Genre.***

POINT OF VIEW ***Point of view*** is the perspective, or vantage point, from which a story is told. Three commonly used points of view are first person, omniscient third person, and limited third person.

In the ***first-person point of view***, the narrator is a character in the story and refers to himself or herself with the first-person pronoun "I." "The Fall of the House of Usher" (p. 292) is told by a first-person narrator.

The two kinds of third-person point of view, limited and omniscient, are called "third person" because the narrator uses third-person pronouns such as "he" and "she" to refer to the characters. There is no "I" telling the story.

In stories told from the ***omniscient third-person point of view***, the narrator knows and tells about what each character feels and thinks. "The Devil and Tom Walker" (p. 228) is written from the omniscient third-person point of view.

In stories told from the ***limited third-person point of view***, the narrator relates the inner thoughts and feelings of only one character, and everything is viewed from this character's perspective. "An Occurrence at Owl Creek Bridge" (p. 480) is written from the limited third-person point of view.

See also ***Narrator.***

PROSE ***Prose*** is the ordinary form of written language. Most writing that is not poetry, drama, or song is considered prose. Prose is one of the major genres of literature. It occurs in two forms: fiction and nonfiction.

See also ***Fiction, Genre,*** and ***Nonfiction.***

PROTAGONIST The ***protagonist*** is the main character in a literary work. In "The Jilting of Granny Weatherall" (p. 834), the protagonist is the dying grandmother.

See also ***Antagonist.***

QUATRAIN See ***Stanza.***

REALISM ***Realism*** is the presentation in art of the details of actual life. Realism was also a literary movement that began during the nineteenth century and stressed the actual as opposed to the imagined or the fanciful. The Realists tried to write objectively about ordinary characters in ordinary situations. They reacted against Romanticism, rejecting heroic, adventurous, or unfamiliar subjects. Naturalists, who followed the Realists, traced the effects of heredity and environment on people helpless to change their situations.

See also ***Local Color, Naturalism,*** and ***Romanticism.***

REFRAIN A ***refrain*** is a repeated line or group of lines in a poem or song. Most refrains end stanzas, as does "And the tide rises, the tide falls," the refrain in Henry Wadsworth Longfellow's poem (p. 260), or "Coming for to carry me home," the refrain in "Swing Low, Sweet Chariot" (p. 534). Although some refrains are nonsense lines, many increase suspense or emphasize character and theme.

REGIONALISM ***Regionalism*** in literature is the tendency among certain authors to write about specific geographical areas. Regional writers, like Willa Cather and William Faulkner, present the distinct culture of an area, including its speech, customs, beliefs, and history. Local-color writing may be considered a type of Regionalism, but Regionalists, like the Southern writers of the 1920s, usually go beyond mere presentation of cultural idiosyncrasies and attempt, instead, a sophisticated sociological or anthropological treatment of the culture of a region.

See also ***Local Color*** and ***Setting.***

RESOLUTION See ***Plot.***

RHYME ***Rhyme*** is the repetition of sounds at the ends of words. Rhyming words have identical vowel sounds in their final accented syllables. The consonants before the vowels may be different, but any consonants occurring after these vowels are the same, as in *frog* and *bog* or *willow* and *pillow.* End rhyme occurs when rhyming words are repeated at the ends of lines. Internal rhyme occurs when rhyming words fall within a line. ***Approximate***, or ***slant***, ***rhyme*** occurs when the rhyming sounds are similar, but not exact, as in *prove* and *glove.*

See also ***Rhyme Scheme.***

RHYME SCHEME A ***rhyme scheme*** is a regular pattern of rhyming words in a poem. To describe a rhyme scheme, one uses a letter of the alphabet to represent each rhyming sound in a poem or stanza. Consider how letters are used to represent the *abab* rhyme scheme rhymes in the following example:

With innocent wide penguin eyes, three **a**
large fledgling mocking-birds below **b**
the pussywillow tree, **a**
stand in a row **b**

—"Bird-Witted," Marianne Moore

See also ***Rhyme.***

RHYTHM ***Rhythm*** is the pattern of beats, or stresses, in spoken or written language. Prose and free verse are written in the irregular rhythmical patterns of everyday speech. Consider, for example, the rhythmical pattern in the following free-verse lines by Gwendolyn Brooks:

Life for my child is simple, and is good.

He knows his wish. Yes, but that is not all.

Because I know mine too.

Traditional poetry often follows a regular rhythmical pattern, as in the following lines by America's first great female poet, Anne Bradstreet:

In critic's hands beware thou dost not come,

And take thy way where yet thou art not known

—"The Author to Her Book"

See also ***Meter.***

RISING ACTION See ***Plot.***

ROMANTICISM ***Romanticism*** was a literary and artistic movement of the nineteenth century that arose in reaction against eighteenth-century Neoclassicism and placed a premium on imagination, emotion, nature, individuality, and exotica. Romantic elements can be found in the works of American writers as diverse as Cooper, Poe, Thoreau, Emerson, Dickinson, Hawthorne, and Melville. Romanticism is particularly evident in the works of the Transcendentalists.

See also ***Classicism*** and ***Transcendentalism.***

ROUND CHARACTER See ***Character.***

SATIRE ***Satire*** is writing that ridicules or criticizes individuals, ideas, institutions, social conventions, or other works of art or literature. The writer of a satire, the satirist, may use a tolerant, sympathetic tone or an angry, bitter tone. Some satire is written in prose and some, in poetry. Examples of satire in this text include W. H. Auden's "The Unknown Citizen" (p. 774) and Ian Frazier's "Coyote v. Acme" (p. 1384).

SCANSION ***Scansion*** is the process of analyzing a poem's metrical pattern. When a poem is scanned, its stressed and unstressed syllables are marked to show what poetic feet are used and how many feet appear in each line. The last two lines of Edna St. Vincent Millay's "I Shall Go Back Again to the Bleak Shore" may be scanned as follows:

> But Í | shall find | the sŭl|len rocks | and skies
>
> Unchanged | from what | they were | when Í | was young.

See also ***Meter.***

SENSORY LANGUAGE ***Sensory language*** is writing or speech that appeals to one or more of the five senses.

See also ***Image.***

SETTING The ***setting*** of a literary work is the time and place of the action. A setting may serve any of a number of functions. It may provide a background for the action. It may be a crucial element in the plot or central conflict. It may also create a certain emotional atmosphere, or mood.

SHORT STORY A ***short story*** is a brief work of fiction. The short story resembles the novel but generally has a simpler plot and setting. In addition, the short story tends to reveal character at a crucial moment rather than developing it through many incidents. For example, Thomas Wolfe's "The Far and the Near" concentrates on what happens to a train engineer when he visits people who had waved to him every day.

See also ***Fiction*** and ***Genre.***

SIMILE A ***simile*** is a figure of speech that makes a direct comparison between two subjects, using either *like* or *as.* Here are two examples of similes:

> The trees looked like pitch forks against the sullen sky.
>
> Her hair was as red as a robin's breast.

See also ***Figurative Language.***

SLANT RHYME See ***Rhyme.***

SONNET A ***sonnet*** is a fourteen-line lyric poem focused on a single theme. Sonnets have many variations but are usually written in iambic pentameter, following one of two traditional patterns: the ***Petrarchan***, or ***Italian***, ***sonnet***, which is divided into two parts, the eight-line octave and the six-line sestet; and the ***Shakespearean***, or ***English***, ***sonnet***, which consists of three quatrains and a concluding couplet.

See also ***Lyric Poem.***

SPEAKER The ***speaker*** is the voice of a poem. Although the speaker is often the poet, the speaker may also be a fictional character or even an inanimate object or another type of nonhuman entity. Interpreting a poem often depends upon recognizing who the speaker is, whom the speaker is addressing, and what the speaker's attitude, or tone, is.

See also ***Point of View.***

SPIRITUAL A ***spiritual*** is a type of African American folk song dating from the period of slavery and Reconstruction. A typical spiritual deals both with religious freedom and, on an allegorical level, with political and economic freedom. In some spirituals the biblical river Jordan was used as a symbol for the Ohio River, which separated slave states from free states; and the biblical promised land, Canaan, was used as a symbol for the free northern United States. Most spirituals made use of repetition, parallelism, and rhyme. See "Go Down Moses" (p. 532) and "Swing Low, Sweet Chariot" (p. 534).

STAGE DIRECTIONS See ***Drama.***

STANZA A ***stanza*** is a group of lines in a poem that are considered to be a unit. Many poems are divided into stanzas that are separated by spaces. Stanzas often function just like paragraphs in prose. Each stanza states and develops a single main idea.

Stanzas are commonly named according to the number of lines found in them, as follows:

1. Couplet: a two-line stanza
2. Tercet: a three-line stanza
3. Quatrain: a four-line stanza
4. Cinquain: a five-line stanza
5. Sestet: a six-line stanza
6. Heptastich: a seven-line stanza
7. Octave: an eight-line stanza

STATIC CHARACTER See ***Character.***

STREAM OF CONSCIOUSNESS ***Stream of consciousness*** is a narrative technique that presents thoughts as if they were coming directly from a character's mind. Instead of being arranged in chronological order, the events are presented from the character's point of view, mixed in with the character's thoughts just as they might spontaneously occur. Katherine Anne Porter uses this technique in "The Jilting of Granny Weatherall" (p. 834) to capture Granny's dying thoughts and feelings. Ambrose Bierce also uses the stream of consciousness technique in "An Occurrence at Owl Creek Bridge" (p. 480).

See also ***Point of View.***

STYLE A writer's ***style*** includes word choice, tone, degree of formality, figurative language, rhythm, grammatical structure, sentence length, organization—in short, every feature of a writer's use of language. Ernest Hemingway, for example, is noted for a simple prose style that contrasts with Thomas Paine's aphoristic style and with N. Scott Momaday's reflective style.

See also ***Diction*** and ***Plain Style.***

SUSPENSE ***Suspense*** is a feeling of growing uncertainty about the outcome of events. Writers create suspense by raising questions in the minds of their readers. Suspense builds until the climax of the plot, at which point the suspense reaches its peak.

See also ***Climax*** and ***Plot.***

SYMBOL A ***symbol*** is anything that stands for or represents something else. A ***conventional symbol*** is one that is widely known and accepted, such as a voyage symbolizing life or a skull symbolizing death. A ***personal symbol*** is one developed for a particular work by a particular author. Examples in this textbook include Hawthorne's black veil and Melville's white whale.

SYMBOLISM ***Symbolism*** was a literary movement during the nineteenth century that influenced poets, including the Imagists and T. S. Eliot. Symbolists turned away from everyday, realistic details to express emotions by using a pattern of symbols.

See also ***Imagism*** and ***Realism.***

THEME A ***theme*** is a central message or insight into life revealed by a literary work. An essay's theme is often directly stated in its thesis statement. In most works of fiction, the theme is only indirectly stated: A story, poem, or play most often has an ***implied theme***. For example, in "A Worn Path" (p. 848), Eudora Welty does not directly say that Phoenix Jackson's difficult journey shows the power of love, but readers learn this indirectly by the end of the story.

TONE The ***tone*** of a literary work is the writer's attitude toward his or her subject, characters, or audience. A writer's tone may be formal or informal, friendly or distant, personal or pompous. For example, William Faulkner's tone in his "Nobel Prize Acceptance Speech" (p. 828) is earnest and serious, whereas James Thurber's tone in "The Night the Ghost Got In" (p. 860) is humorous and ironic.

See also ***Mood.***

TRAGEDY A ***tragedy*** is a work of literature, especially a play, that shows the downfall or death of the main character, or ***tragic hero***.

TRANSCENDENTALISM ***Transcendentalism*** was an American literary and philosophical movement of the nineteenth century. The Transcendentalists, who were based in New England, believed that intuition and the individual conscience "transcend" experience and thus are better guides to truth than are the senses and logical reason. Influenced by Romanticism, the Transcendentalists respected the individual spirit and the natural world, believing that divinity was present everywhere, in nature and in each person. The Transcendentalists included Ralph Waldo Emerson, Henry David Thoreau, Bronson Alcott, W. H. Channing, Margaret Fuller, and Elizabeth Peabody.

See also ***Romanticism.***

College Application Essay

If you are applying for admission to a college, you will probably need to submit an essay as part of your application. This essay will help admissions committee members get a sense of you as a person and as a student. Review the chart at right for general strategies, and follow the guidelines below to produce an effective college application essay.

Strategies for Writing an Effective College Application Essay

- **Choose the right topic**. If you have a choice of essay topics, choose one that truly interests you.
- **Organize.** Use a strong organization that carries the reader from introduction to conclusion.
- **Begin Strongly.** Open with an introduction that has a good chance of sparking the reader's interest.
- **Elaborate.** Be sure to explain why the experiences you discuss are important to you or what you learned from them.
- **Show style.** Bring life to your essay through vivid descriptions, precise word choice, and sophisticated sentence structure, such as parallelism. Consider including dialogue where appropriate.
- **Close with a clincher.** Write a conclusion that effectively sums up your ideas.
- **Do a clean job**. Proofread your essay carefully. It should be error-free.

Selecting a Topic

Read the essay question on the application form with care. Mark key criteria and direction words such as *describe* and *explain*. After you have written a first draft, check to make sure you have met all of the requirements of the question. Your essay has a better chance of succeeding if it meets the requirements exactly.

General Questions About You

The essay question on a college application may be as general as "Describe a significant experience or event in your life and explain its consequences for you." To choose the right topic for such a question, think of an event or experience that truly is meaningful to you—a camping trip, a volunteer event, a family reunion. Test the subject by drafting a letter about it to a good friend or relative. If you find that your enthusiasm for the subject grows as you write, and if your discussion reveals something about your growth or your outlook on life, the topic may be the right one for your essay.

Directed Questions

The essay question on an application may be a directed question, rather than a general question. For instance, you may be asked to select three figures from history you would like to meet and to explain your choices.

In such cases, do not give an answer just because you think it will please reviewers. Rely on your own interests and instincts. Your most convincing writing will come from genuine interest in the subject.

Style

Remember that an essay is a formal document addressed to strangers. Use a formal to semiformal style. Avoid incomplete sentences and slang unless you are using them for clear stylistic effect. Use words with precision, selecting one or two accurate words to express your meaning. Do not use a word if you are unsure of its meaning.

Format

Most applications limit the length of essays. Do not exceed the allowed space or word count. Your college application essay should be neatly typed or printed, using adequate margins. Proofread your final draft carefully. If you submit a separate copy of the essay (rather than writing on the application form), number the pages and include your name and contact information on each page.

Reusing Your Essay

Most students apply to a number of different colleges. Once you have written a strong essay for one application, you may adapt it for others. However, do not submit a single essay to several schools blindly. Always read the application essay question carefully to insure that the essay you submit fulfills all of its requirements.

Workplace Writing

Job Search Document: Cover Letter

A cover letter is a formal letter in which the writer asks to be considered for a job. It usually accompanies, or "covers," a completed job application, a résumé, or both. A good cover letter relates specifically to the job for which the writer is applying.

Write a Cover Letter

Consider a part-time job or a summer job you would like to have. Then, write a cover letter to accompany a job application. Include a header, an inside address, an introductory paragraph, one or two body paragraphs, a closing paragraph, and a signature. Mention your main qualifications, and explain how they make you a good fit for the job.

000 Park Avenue
San Marcos, Texas 00000
512-000-0000
emailaddress@theinternet.com

January 15, 20—

The heading should include the writer's name, address, phone number, e-mail address, and the date of the letter.

Barbara Jones, Director
River Place Day Camp
500 S. Camp Street
Austin, TX 00000

The inside address includes the name, title, and address of the recipient.

Dear Ms. Jones:

I am writing to apply for the position of Activities Coordinator for your summer camp. The job description posted on the Texas Summer Camps job board perfectly parallels my own interests and experience.

As noted on the enclosed résumé, I have four years' experience as a camp counselor, including one as Lead Counselor and one as Assistant Activities Director. In these roles, I learned not only to work as a team leader, but also to help tailor a camp's programs to the needs of its campers. As an education student at Texas State University, I have completed basic education courses as well as electives in counseling, recreational learning, and youth leadership. These courses, along with my volunteer work as an after-school mentor, have sparked my interest in non-classroom education. In fact, I plan to base my entire career on the idea that learning can be fun—and can happen anywhere.

The body paragraph describes how the writer's experiences relate specifically to the job responsibilities.

I hope to help make River Place Day Camp a fun, educational, and well-organized experience for both its campers and its staff. I look forward to meeting with you and discussing my qualifications in more detail.

Sincerely,
Cesar Moreno

Job Search Document: Résumé

A **résumé** is a written summary or outline of a person's job qualifications. It plays a key part in most career or job searches. An effective résumé has the following elements:

- candidate's name, current address, phone number, and e-mail address;
- educational background, work experience, and other relevant life experiences;
- logical organization;
- clearly labeled sections.

Compile a Résumé

Write a résumé to use in a job search. Consider a specific job you would like to pursue. Then, brainstorm for relevant information in your schooling or work experience. Include important details and maintain a professional tone.

As you develop your document, experiment with different fonts to create a professional-looking, readable document.

CESAR MORENO
000 Park Avenue
San Marcos, Texas 00000
512-000-0000 • emailaddress@theinternet.com

Place contact information at the top of the résumé.

EDUCATION

- **Texas State University**, San Marcos, TX
  Bachelor of Science in Education
  Expected: May, 20—
- **Austin High School**, Austin, TX
  Graduated with honors, May, 20—

The headings *Education, Work Experience*, and so on indicate that this résumé is organized by topic.

WORK EXPERIENCE

- **Summer 2008–Summer 2010**
  Camp Lazy J, Fredericksburg, TX
  Camp Counselor: Supervised groups of campers aged 8–12. Served as Lead Counselor in 20– and as Assistant Activities Director in 20–.
- **2009–2010**
  YMCA, Austin, Texas
  Life Guard and Swim Instructor: Guarded weekend free-swim sessions and taught beginning and intermediate youth swim classes.

The items under each topic are bulleted and arranged from most to least recent.

VOLUNTEER EXPERIENCE

- **2009–present**
  San Marcos Community Center, San Marcos, TX
  After-School Mentor: Help elementary and middle school students organize and complete schoolwork, develop skills and interests, and resolve personal issues.
- **2008–2009**
  Stepping Up Preschool, Austin, TX
  Teacher's Aide: Assisted in the 3- and 4-year-old classroom; helped plan and execute special summer programs.

ADDITIONAL SKILLS AND CERTIFICATIONS

- CPR certified, 2007 to the present
- Fluent in Spanish
- Proficient in water sports, including rowing, kayaking, and rafting
- Proficient in Microsoft Word, Excel, and PowerPoint
- Completed childcare training course, YMCA, 2007

REFERENCES
Furnished on request.

A résumé should be no longer than a single page.

Job Search Document: Job Application

Many employers require job applicants to complete a **job application.** A job application is a standard form that asks for particular kinds of information, including the candidate's contact information, education, and work experience.

Complete a Job Application

Consider a part-time job you would like to have. Then, copy and complete the job application shown here using your own information.

Employment Application

PERSONAL INFORMATION

Full Name: Cesar Moreno
Address: 000 Park Ave., San Marcos, TX 00000
Phone Number: (512) 000-0000
E-mail Address: emailaddress@theinternet.com

POSITION AND AVAILABILITY

Position Applied For: Activities Coordinator

EDUCATION

School	Degree/Diploma	Graduation Date
Texas State University Austin High School	B.S./Education diploma	expected 5/20— May, 20—
Additional Skills, Qualifications, Licenses, Training, Awards		
CPR and childcare certified, 2007–present Fluent in Spanish		

Include only relevant information, and condense it to fit the space available.

EMPLOYMENT HISTORY

Present/Last Position and Dates: Camp Counselor, Summer 2006–Summer 2009
Employer: Camp Lazy J
Responsibilities: supervised campers aged 8–12
Supervisor: Mr. Smith
May we contact Supervisor? If so, phone number: yes; (512) 000-0000

Get your former supervisor's permission before responding "yes" to this item.

Previous Position: Lifeguard and Swim Instructor, 2007–2008
Employer: Austin YMCA
Responsibilities: Guarded free-swim sessions; taught youth swim classes
Supervisor: Mrs. Smith
May we contact Supervisor? If so, phone number: yes; (512) 000-0000

Please list additional employment information on a separate sheet of paper.

I certify that the information contained in this application is true and complete. I authorize the verification of any or all information listed above.

Signature: *Cesar Moreno*
Date: January 15, 20—

The applicant's signature gives the employer permission to check the information provided.

Business Communications: Business Letter

Business letters are formal letters in which the content is other than personal. Whatever the subject, an effective business letter has the following elements:

- a heading, inside address, salutation or greeting, body, closing, and signature
- one of several acceptable formats, including *block format,* in which each part of the letter begins at the left margin, and *modified block format,* in which the heading, closing, and signature are indented to the center of the page
- formal and courteous language

Write a Business Letter

Choose one of the following purposes and write a business letter to accomplish it. Include heading, inside address, salutation, body, closing, and signature. Use polite and formal language.

- complain about poor service in a restaurant
- accompany a short story you hope to have published
- praise the work of an artist or musician
- gain support for a beautification plan in your community

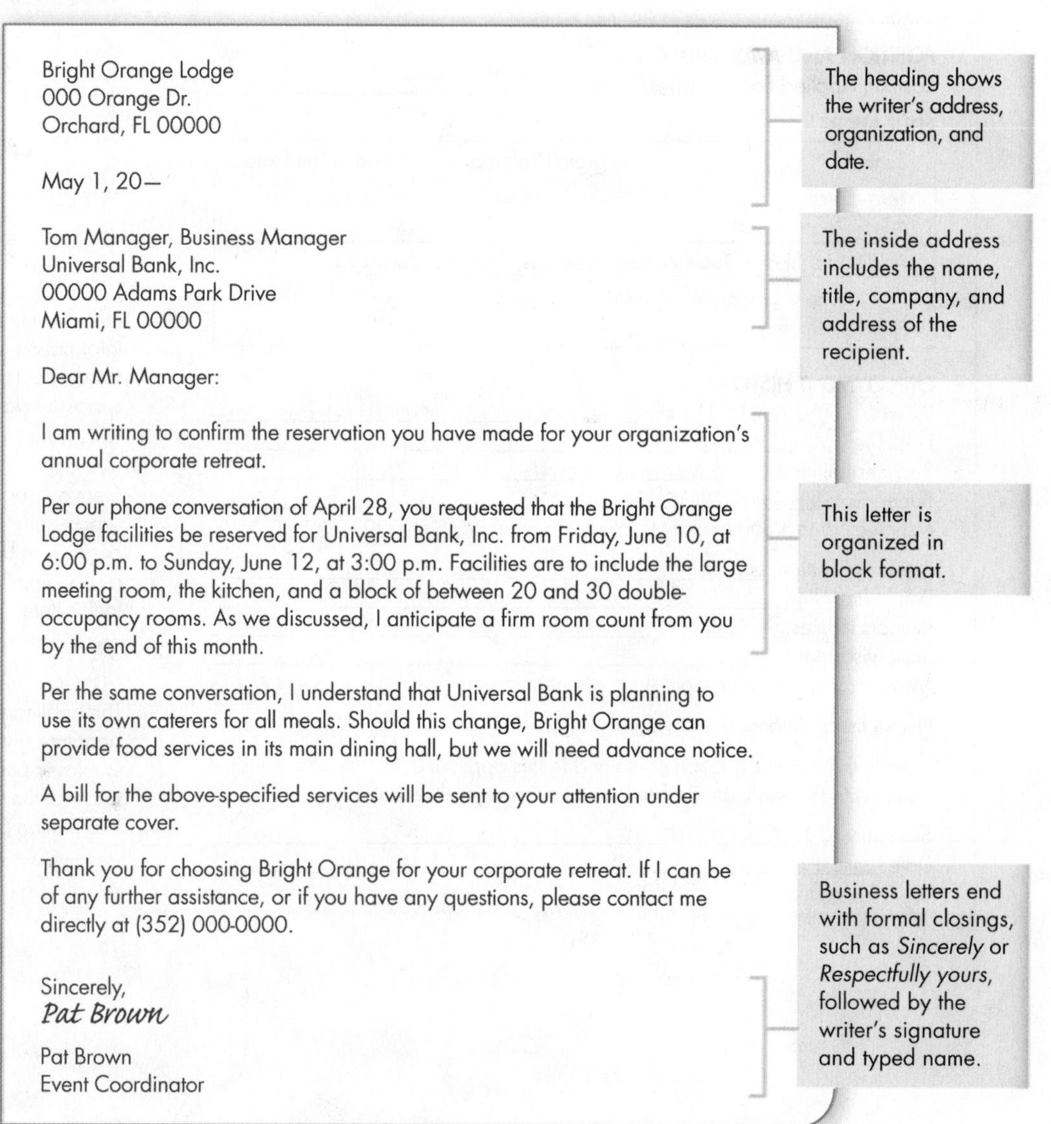

Bright Orange Lodge
000 Orange Dr.
Orchard, FL 00000

May 1, 20—

Tom Manager, Business Manager
Universal Bank, Inc.
00000 Adams Park Drive
Miami, FL 00000

Dear Mr. Manager:

I am writing to confirm the reservation you have made for your organization's annual corporate retreat.

Per our phone conversation of April 28, you requested that the Bright Orange Lodge facilities be reserved for Universal Bank, Inc. from Friday, June 10, at 6:00 p.m. to Sunday, June 12, at 3:00 p.m. Facilities are to include the large meeting room, the kitchen, and a block of between 20 and 30 double-occupancy rooms. As we discussed, I anticipate a firm room count from you by the end of this month.

Per the same conversation, I understand that Universal Bank is planning to use its own caterers for all meals. Should this change, Bright Orange can provide food services in its main dining hall, but we will need advance notice.

A bill for the above-specified services will be sent to your attention under separate cover.

Thank you for choosing Bright Orange for your corporate retreat. If I can be of any further assistance, or if you have any questions, please contact me directly at (352) 000-0000.

Sincerely,
Pat Brown

Pat Brown
Event Coordinator

The heading shows the writer's address, organization, and date.

The inside address includes the name, title, company, and address of the recipient.

This letter is organized in block format.

Business letters end with formal closings, such as *Sincerely* or *Respectfully yours,* followed by the writer's signature and typed name.

Business Communications: Memo

A **memo**—short for *memorandum*—is a brief printed message between co-workers. It usually focuses on information necessary for the completion of a particular task or project. An effective memo has the following elements:

- block organization, with each new element beginning at the left margin
- sender's name, intended audience, date, and topic
- clear and brief description, including statement of actions required

MEMO

TO: Members of the Corporate Retreat Staff
FROM: Ann Smith, Vice President
DATE: May 11, 20—
RE: PLANNING SESSION

Our annual corporate retreat is fast approaching. To ensure that all aspects of the retreat are coordinated, let's meet this Friday, May 14, at 9:00 a.m. in the second-floor conference room.

We will discuss the following topics, so please be prepared to report the status of your assigned area of responsibility.

- finalized dates, times, and location of the retreat (Tom)
- schedule of sessions and events (Bruno)
- presenters and topics (Yolanda)
- caterers and pricing (Barry)
- employee communications — invitations, RSVPs, etc. (DeShon)

I appreciate the many hours you have already invested in the planning process, and hope that our meeting on Friday will be brief and productive.

AS

Most memos follow this format: To, From, Date, and Re (Regarding). The word *re* is Latin for "about." It introduces the subject of the memo.

The body of a memo is brief and informative, and should clearly state a course of action.

Memos are often initialed (either at the conclusion or next to the "FROM" line) in order to indicate that the contents have been approved by the sender.

Business Communications: E-Mail

An **e-mail** is a message sent through an electronic communication system such as a computer network or the Internet. Like a memo, an e-mail may be sent to many recipients at once; however, an e-mail has the added benefit of traveling instantaneously. It can also be used to send an attachment—a file that travels with the e-mail but that must be opened using a separate application. While e-mail messages are often more casual than memos, a workplace e-mail (unlike a personal e-mail) should maintain an appropriately formal tone.

Write a Memo and an E-mail

Choose one of the topics below and write a memo that states the message quickly and efficiently. Then, recast the memo as an e-mail.

- announcement of an upcoming event to members of a club or organization
- reminder to fellow workers in a gift shop about store procedures
- information about a surprise party for a teacher
- details about about transportation to a sports competition

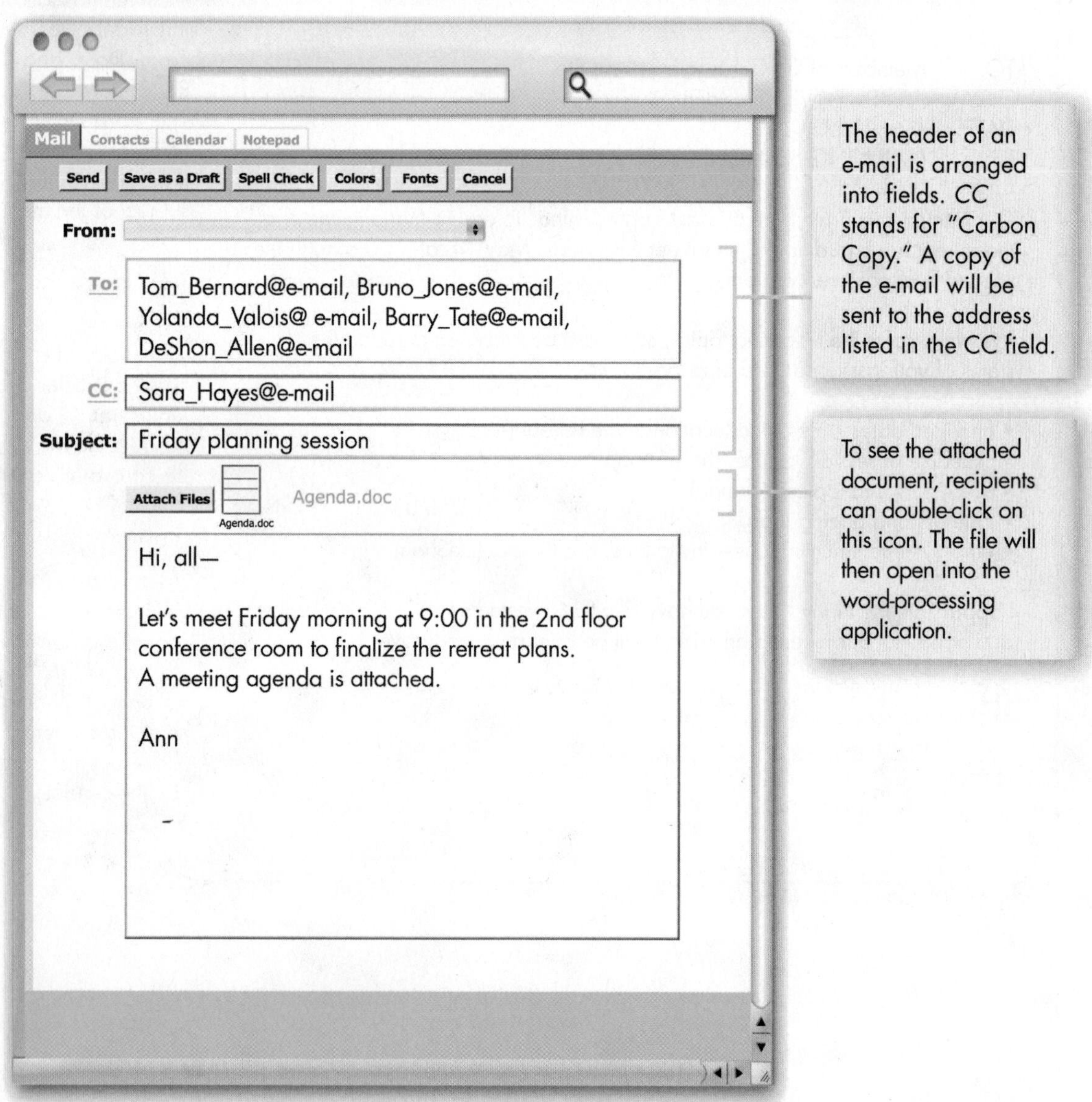

Business Communications: Meeting Minutes

Meeting minutes are notes that tell what transpired at a meeting: what was said, what was decided, and what was left unresolved. Often, the person taking the minutes will jot down abbreviated notes during the meeting, and then rewrite the minutes afterward to distribute to meeting participants.

Write Meeting Minutes

In a small group, conduct a business meeting. Take notes during the meeting. Afterward, write a set of minutes to distribute to your fellow group members.

Meeting to Finalize Corporate Retreat Plans
Friday, May 14, 20–
Main Office, 2nd Floor Conference Room, 9:00 a.m.

Committee Members Present: Ann Smith, Tom Bernard, Yolanda Valois, DeShon Allen
Committee Members Absent: Bruno Jones
Others Present: Sara Hayes, assistant to Ann Smith

Proceedings:
Meeting called to order at 9:00 a.m. by Ann Smith.
Agenda was distributed by Sara Hayes.

First Agenda Item: Retreat dates, times, and location, presented by Tom Bernard.
Tom reported that he has received a letter from Bright Orange Lodge that confirms reservation of their retreat facilities for Universal Bank, Inc. from Friday, June 10, at 6:00 p.m. through Sunday, June 12, at 3:00 p.m. A copy of this letter is attached to the minutes.

Second Agenda Item: Schedule of sessions and events, presented by Ann Smith for Bruno Jones.
Bruno is out of the office today, but e-mailed Ann the finalized retreat schedule. Ann distributed copies of the schedule to all members. MOTION to approve schedule; passed unanimously.

Assessment of the meeting: Members agreed that the retreat promises to be very successful. Jeff congratulated committee members on a job well done.

Meeting adjourned at 10:05 a.m.
Meeting minutes compiled by Sarah Hayes.

The header should include the name of the meeting and its date, location, and time.

These minutes are formatted to show that the meeting followed an agenda.

A *motion* is a proposal to vote on something. All motions and their results should be carefully noted in meeting minutes.

Business Communications: Technical Writing

Technical writing refers to any kind of writing that presents specialized information to help someone perform a task. Scientific reports, troubleshooting guides, assembly instructions, and school handbooks are all examples of technical writing. Although the format varies with the purpose, all technical writing must be clear and easy to use—in other words, "user friendly." It must also be absolutely precise.

Write a Section of a Technical Document

Think of something you know how to do well and write a set of procedures for completing the task. Remember to use specific language that accurately describes the details of the task.

Porterdale Community Library rev. 7/09
Policies and Procedures
Section IV: Collection Maintenance

A page header identifies the publication title, the section, and the revision date.

IV.D. PROCESSING NEW MATERIALS
When new items are delivered to the library, they must be processed, or prepared for use by patrons. The steps for processing a new shipment of items are as follows.

A brief introduction tells the reader what is included in this section.

1. Before unpacking the items:
- **a.** Remove the packing slip from the box.
- **b.** Find the matching order form in the main filing cabinet. Order forms are filed alphabetically by vendor.

2. Unpacking the items:
- **a.** Check each item against both the order form and the packing slip.
- **b.** Place a checkmark on each document next to the title of the item.
- **c.** If all items in the shipment correspond with those on the order form, send the order form and invoice to the business office for payment. The invoice is usually inside the shipment or affixed to the outside in an envelope.
- **d.** If an item is missing or damaged, make a note and/or set the item aside. (See section IV.B. for Ordering and Returning procedures.)

(To process books, see item 3, below. To process other media items, proceed to item 4 on the following page.)

Cross-references and navigational guides are included to help the reader find additional needed information with ease.

3. Processing books:
- **a.** Attach a bar code label to the upper left-hand corner of the front cover.
- **b.** Stamp books with the library name on the front inside cover and back inside cover.
- **c.** Prepare a spine label for books. (See section II.A. for call number designation.) Affix the label to the spine with a label protector.
- **d.** Enter information for the new item into the library catalog database. (See section III.B. for cataloging procedures.)

Tips for Discussing Literature

As you read and study literature, discussions with other readers can help you understand, enjoy, and develop interpretations of what you read. Use the following tips to practice good speaking and listening skills in group discussions of literature.

- **Understand the purpose of your discussion.**

  Your purpose when you discuss literature is to broaden your understanding and appreciation of a work by testing your own ideas and hearing the ideas of others. Be sure to stay focused on the literature you are discussing and to keep your comments relevant to that literature. Starting with one focus question will help to keep your discussion on track.

- **Communicate effectively.**

  Effective communication requires thinking before speaking. Plan the points that you want to make and decide how you will express them. Organize these points in logical order and cite details from the work to support your ideas. Jot down informal notes to help keep your ideas focused.

  Remember to speak clearly, pronouncing words slowly and carefully so that your listeners will understand your ideas. Also, keep in mind that some literature touches readers deeply—be aware of the possibility of counterproductive emotional responses and work to control them.

- **Make relevant contributions.**

  Especially when responding to a short story or a novel, avoid simply summarizing the plot. Instead, consider *what* you think might happen next, *why* events take place as they do, or *how* a writer provokes a response in you. Let your ideas inspire deeper thought or discussion about the literature.

- **Consider other ideas and interpretations.**

  A work of literature can generate a wide variety of responses in different readers—and that can make your discussions really exciting. Be open to the idea that many interpretations can be valid. To support your own ideas, point to the events, descriptions, characters, or other literary elements in the work that led to your interpretation. To consider someone else's ideas, decide whether details in the work support the interpretation he or she presents. Be sure to convey your criticism of the ideas of others in a respectful and supportive manner.

- **Ask questions and extend the contributions of others.**

  Get in the habit of asking questions to help you clarify your understanding of another reader's ideas. You can also use questions to call attention to possible areas of confusion, to points that are open to debate, or to errors in the speaker's points.

  In addition, offer elaboration of the points that others make by providing examples and illustrations from the literature. To move a discussion forward, summarize and evaluate tentative conclusions reached by the group members.

Oral and Visual Communication

You use speaking and listening skills every day. When you talk with your friends, teachers, or parents, or when you interact with store clerks, you are communicating orally. In addition to everyday conversation, oral communication includes class discussions, speeches, interviews, presentations, debates, and performances. The following terms will give you a better understanding of the many elements that are part of communication and help you eliminate barriers to listening by managing any distractions:

Body language refers to the use of facial expressions, eye contact, gestures, posture, and movement to communicate a feeling or an idea.

Connotation is the set of associations a word calls to mind. The connotations of the words you choose influence the message you send. For example, most people respond more favorably to being described as "slim" rather than as "skinny." The connotation of *slim* is more appealing than that of *skinny.*

Eye contact is direct visual contact with another person's eyes.

Feedback is the set of verbal and nonverbal reactions that indicate to a speaker that a message has been received and understood.

Gestures are the movements made with arms, hands, face and fingers to communicate.

Listening is understanding and interpreting sound in a meaningful way. You listen differently for different purposes.

Listening for key information: For example, when a teacher gives an assignment, or when someone gives you directions to a place, you listen for key information.

Listening for main points: In a classroom exchange of ideas or information, or while watching a television documentary, you listen for main points.

Listening critically: When you evaluate a performance, song, or a persuasive or political speech, you listen critically, questioning and judging the speaker's message.

Medium is the material or technique used to present a visual image. Common media include paint, clay, and film.

Nonverbal communication is communication without the use of words. People communicate nonverbally through gestures, facial expressions, posture, and body movements. Sign language is an entire language based on nonverbal communication. Be aware of your nonverbal communication and make sure that your gestures and facial expressions do not conflict with your words.

Projection is speaking in such a way that the voice carries clearly to an audience. It's important to project your voice when speaking in a large space like a classroom or an auditorium.

Viewing is observing, understanding, analyzing, and evaluating information presented through visual means. You might use the following questions to help you interpret what you view:

- What subject is presented?
- What is communicated about the subject?
- Which parts are factual? Which are opinion?
- What mood, attitude, or opinion is conveyed?
- What is your emotional response?

Vocal delivery is the way in which you present a message. Your vocal delivery involves all of the following elements:

Volume: the loudness or quietness of your voice

Pitch: the high or low quality of your voice

Rate: the speed at which you speak; also called pace

Stress: the amount of emphasis placed on different syllables in a word or on different words in a sentence

All of these elements individually, and the way in which they are combined, contribute to the meaning of a spoken message.

Speaking, Listening, and Viewing Situations

Here are some of the many types of situations in which you apply speaking, listening, and viewing skills:

Audience Your audience in any situation refers to the person or people to whom you direct your message. An audience can be a group of people observing a performance or just one person. When preparing for any speaking situation, it's useful to analyze your audience, so that you can tailor your message to them.

Charts and graphs are visual representations of statistical information. For example, a pie chart might indicate how the average dollar is spent by government, and a bar graph might compare populations in cities over time.

Debate A debate is a formal public-speaking situation in which participants prepare and present arguments on opposing sides of a question, stated as a **proposition.**

The two sides in a debate are the *affirmative* (pro) and the *negative* (con). The affirmative side argues in favor of the proposition, while the negative side argues against it. Each side has an opportunity for *rebuttal,* in which they may challenge or question the other side's argument.

Documentaries are nonfiction films that analyze news events or other focused subjects. You can watch a documentary for the information on its subject.

Graphic organizers summarize and present information in ways that can help you understand the information. Graphic organizers include charts, outlines, webs, maps, lists, and diagrams. For example, a graphic organizer for a history chapter might be an outline. A Venn diagram is intersecting circles that display information showing how concepts are alike and different.

Group discussion results when three or more people meet to solve a common problem, arrive at a decision, or answer a question of mutual interest. Group discussion is one of the most widely used forms or interpersonal communication in modern society.

Interview An interview is a form of interaction in which one person, the interviewer, asks questions of another person, the interviewee. Interviews may take place for many purposes: to obtain information, to discover a person's suitability for a job or a college, or to inform the public of a notable person's opinions.

Maps are visual representations of Earth's surface. Maps may show political boundaries and physical features and provide information on a variety of other topics. A map's titles and its key identify the content of the map.

Oral interpretation is the reading or speaking of a work of literature aloud for an audience. Oral interpretation involves giving expression to the ideas, meaning, or even the structure of a work of literature. The speaker interprets the work through his or her vocal delivery. **Storytelling,** in which a speaker reads or tells a story expressively, is a form of oral interpretation.

Panel discussion is a group discussion on a topic of interest common to all members of a panel and to a listening audience. A panel is usually composed of four to six experts on a particular topic who are brought together to share information and opinions.

Pantomime is a form of nonverbal communication in which an idea or a story is communicated completely through the use of gesture, body language, and facial expressions, without any words at all.

Political cartoons are drawings that comment on important political or social issues. Often, these cartoons use humor to convey a message about their subject. Viewers use their own knowledge of events to evaluate the cartoonist's opinion.

Readers theatre is a dramatic reading of a work of literature in which participants take parts from a story or play and read them aloud in expressive voices. Unlike a play, however, sets and costumes are not part of the performance, and the participants remain seated as they deliver their lines.

Role play To role-play is to take the role of a person or character and act out a given situation, speaking, acting, and responding in the manner of the character.

Speech A speech is a talk or address given to an audience. A speech may be **impromptu** or **extemporaneous**—delivered on the spur of the moment with no preparation—or formally prepared and delivered for a specific purpose or occasion.

- ***Purposes:*** the most common purposes of speeches are to persuade, to entertain, to explain, and to inform.
- ***Occasions:*** Different occasions call for different types of speeches. Speeches given on these occasions could be persuasive, entertaining, or informative, as appropriate.

Visual representation refers to informative texts, such as newspapers and advertisements, and entertaining texts, such as magazines. Visual representations use elements of design—such as texture and color, shapes, drawings, and photographs—to convey the meaning, message, or theme.

Grammar, Usage, and Mechanics Handbook

Parts of Speech

Every English word, depending on its meaning and its use in a sentence, can be identified as one of the eight parts of speech. These are nouns, pronouns, verbs, adjectives, adverbs, prepositions, conjunctions, and interjections. Understanding the parts of speech will help you learn the rules of English grammar and usage.

Part of Speech	Definition	Examples
Noun	**Names a person, place, or thing**	
Common	• Names any one of a class of persons, places, or things	writer, country, novel
Proper	• Names a specific person, place or thing	Charles Dickens, Great Britain, *Hard Times*
Pronoun	**Stands for a noun or for a word that takes the place of a noun**	
Personal	• Refers to the person speaking (first person); the person spoken to (second person); or the person, place, or thing spoken about (third person)	I, me, my, mine, we, us, our, ours, you, our, yours, he, him, his, she, her, hers, it, its, they, them, their, theirs, myself, ourselves, yourself, yourselves, himself, herself, itself, themselves
Reflexive	• Names the person or thing receiving an action when that person or thing is the same as the one performing the action	"They click upon *themselves*/ As the breeze rises,..." –Robert Frost
Intensive	• Adds emphasis to a noun or pronoun	"The United States *themselves* are essentially the greatest poem..." –Walt Whitman
Demonstrative	• Singles out specific person(s), place(s), or thing(s)	this, that, these, those
Relative	• Begins a subordinate clause and connects it to another idea in the sentence	that, which, who, whom, whose
Interrogative	• Begins a question	what, which, who, whom, whose
Indefinite	• Refers to a person, place, or thing that may or may not be specifically named	another, everyone, nobody, one, both, few, all, most, none

(Parts of Speech continues)

(continued)

Part of Speech	Definition	Examples
Verb	**Expresses time while showing an action, condition, or the fact that something exists**	
Action	• Tells what action someone or something is performing	gather, read, work, jump, imagine, analyze, conclude
Linking	• Connects the subject with another word that identifies or describes the subject	appear, be, become, feel, look,remain, sound, stay, taste
Helping	• Added to another verb to make a verb phrase	be, do, have, should, can, could, may
Adjective	**Used to describe a noun or pronoun or give it a more specific meaning**	*purple* hat, *happy* face, *this* bowl, *three* cars, *enough* food, *a loud* sound
Adverb	**Modifies a verb, an adjective, or another adverb by telling *where, when, how* or *to what extent***	will answer *soon, extremely* sad, calls *more* often
Preposition	**Relates a noun or pronoun that appears with it to another word in the sentence**	Dad made a meal *for* us. We talked *till* dusk. Bo missed school *because of* his illness.
Conjunction	**Connects words or groups of words**	
Coordinating	• Connects equal words or word groups	bread *and* cheese, brief *but* powerful
Correlative	• Used in pairs to connect equal words or word groups	*both* Luis *and* Rosa, neither you *nor I*
Subordinating	• Indicates the connection between two ideas by placing one below the other in rank or importance	We will miss her *if* she leaves. Hank shrieked *when* he slipped on the ice.
Interjection	**Expresses feeling or emotion**	ah, hey, ouch, well, yippee

Phrases and Clauses

Phrases A **phrase** is a group of words that does not have a subject and verb and that functions as one part of speech.

Prepositional Phrases A **prepositional phrase** is a group of words that includes a preposition and a noun or pronoun.

beyond the horizon **according to** the manager

An **adjective phrase** is a prepositional phrase that modifies a noun or pronoun.

The works **of Benjamin Franklin** appeal to me.

An **adverb phrase** is a prepositional phrase that modifies a verb, an adjective, or an adverb.

I often read **about early American writers.**

Appositive Phrases An **appositive phrase** is a noun or pronoun with modifiers, placed next to a noun or pronoun to add information.

Tamika, **one of my best friends,** is moving away.

Verbal Phrases A **participial phrase** is a participle that is modified by an adverb or an adverb phrase or that has a complement. The entire phase acts as an adjective.

Be alert for snakes **sunning themselves on the rocks.**

A **gerund** is a noun formed from the present participle of a verb (ending in *–ing*). A **gerund phrase** is a gerund with modifiers or a complement, all acting together as a noun.

Her favorite pastime is **hiking in the mountains.**

An **infinitive phrase** is an infinitive with modifiers, complements, or a subject, all acting together as a single part of speech.

I would like **to learn about wilderness survival.**

Clauses A **clause** is a group of words with its own subject and verb.

Independent Clauses An independent clause can stand by itself as a complete sentence.

Henry David Thoreau was considered an eccentric.

Subordinate Clauses A subordinate clause cannot stand by itself as a complete sentence.

Henry David Thoreau, **who did not follow society's rules,** was considered an eccentric.

An **adjective clause** is a subordinate clause that modifies a noun or pronoun by telling what kind or which one.

The journey **that Lewis undertook** was dangerous.

An **adverb clause** is a subordinate clause that modifies a verb, an adjective, an adverb, or a verbal by telling *where, when, in what way, to what extent, under what condition,* or *why.*

As I read the poem, I pictured the Grand Canyon.

A **noun clause** is a subordinate clause that acts as a noun.

Whoever visits the Grand Canyon should remember John Wesley Powell's contributions.

Sentence Structure

Subject and Predicate A **sentence** is a group of words with two main parts: a *subject* and a *predicate.* Together, these parts express a complete thought.

The **complete subject** tells *whom* or *what* the sentence is about. The **complete predicate** tells what the complete subject of the sentence does or is.

Complete Subject **Complete Predicate**

One of those poems | was written by Claude McKay.

The **simple subject** is the essential noun, pronoun, or group of words acting as a noun that cannot be left out of the complete subject. The **simple predicate** is the essential verb or verb phrase that cannot be left out of the complete predicate.

Simple Subject **Simple Predicate**

One of those poems | **was written** by Claude McKay.

Complements A **complement** is a word or word group that completes the meaning of the predicate. There are five kinds of complements: *direct objects, indirect objects, objective complements, predicate nominatives,* and *predicate adjectives.*

A **direct object** is a noun, a pronoun, or a group of words acting as a noun that receives the action of a transitive verb.

Washington Irving used several **pseudonyms.**

An **indirect object** is a noun or pronoun that appears with a direct object and names the person or thing that something is given to or done for.

Folk tales gave **Irving** inspiration for his stories. [The direct object is *inspiration.*]

An **objective complement** is an adjective or noun that appears with a direct object and describes or renames it.

Ms. Gates considers Phillis Wheatley a brilliant **poet.** [The direct object is *Phillis Wheatley.*]

A **predicate nominative** is a noun or pronoun that appears with a linking verb and tells something about the subject.

John Smith became a famous **explorer.**

A **predicate adjective** is an adjective that appears with a linking verb and describes the subject of the sentence.

Smith was **adventurous** and **daring**.

Classifying Sentences by Structure

Sentences are often classified according to the kind and number of clauses they contain. The four basic sentence structures are *simple, compound, complex,* and *compound-complex.*

A **simple sentence** consists of one independent clause.

Alisa enjoys contemporary American poetry.

A **compound sentence** consists or two or more independent clauses.

Alisa enjoys contemporary American poetry, but Joyce prefers earlier works.

A **complex sentence** consists of one independent clause and one or more subordinate clauses.

Alisa, who likes all things modern, enjoys contemporary American poetry.

A **compound-complex sentence** consists of two or more independent clauses and one or more subordinate clauses.

Alisa, who likes all things modern, enjoys contemporary American poetry, but Joyce prefers earlier works.

Paragraph Structure

An effective paragraph is organized around one **main idea,** which is often stated in a topic sentence. The other sentences support the main idea. To give the paragraph unity, make sure the connection between each sentence and the main idea is clear.

Usage

Lessons throughout your literature book will help you with many usage problems. See Unit 1 for help with **using coordinating conjunctions** (p. 31), **using correlative conjunctions** (p. 94), and **using subordinating conjunctions** (p. 155). See Unit 2 for help with **using adjective and adverb clauses** (p. 287), **comparative and superlative adjectives and adverbs** (p. 321), and **using participles, gerunds, and infinitives** (p. 358). In Unit 3 you will find lessons on **misplaced and dangling modifiers** (p. 585) and **introductory phrases and clauses** (p. 613). See Unit 4 for help with **subject-verb agreement problems** (p. 755) and **pronoun-antecedent agreement problems** (p. 911). In Unit 5 you will find lessons on **avoiding shifts in verb tense** (p. 1093), **using active, not passive, voice** (p. 1115), and **sentence fragments and run-ons** (p. 1237). Go to Unit 6 for lessons on **transitional expressions** (p. 1323), using **parallel structure** (p. 1423), and **creating sentence variety** (p. 1441).

Unintended Shift in Person

Do not change needlessly from one person to another. Keep the person consistent in your sentences.

Tara is a good babysitter, but **you** have to pay her well. [shift from third person to second person]

Tara is a good babysitter, but **she** charges high rates. [consistent]

Modifier Placement

To avoid confusion, a modifying word, phrase, or clause should be placed as close as possible to the word or words it is supposed to modify.

We saw a large swan **rowing the boat near the shore.** [misplaced modifier]

Rowing the boat near the shore, we saw a large swan. [correct placement]

Agreement

Subject and Verb Agreement

A singular subject must have a singular verb. A plural subject must have a plural verb.

Daniel cooks chicken tortilla soup to perfection.

The **boys cook** several different casseroles.

A phrase or clause that comes between a subject and verb does not affect subject-verb agreement.

My **sister**, along with her friends, **plays** softball.

Two subjects joined by *and* usually take a plural verb.

The **players** and the **coach take** the game seriously.

Two singular subject joined by *or* or *nor* must have a singular verb.

Neither the **coach** nor the **player is** ready.

Two plural subjects joined by *or* or *nor* must have a plural verb.

The **players** or the **coaches suggest** special plays.

Pronoun and Antecedent Agreement

Pronouns must agree with their antecedents in number and gender. Use singular pronouns with singular antecedents and plural pronouns with plural antecedents.

Kate Chopin became a bold and controversial writer in spite of **her** conservative upbringing.

Writers must be courageous in facing **their** critics.

Use a singular pronoun when the antecedent is a singular indefinite pronoun such as *anybody, each, either, everybody, neither, no one, one,* or *someone.*

Anybody can offer **his or her** help with the report.

Use a plural pronoun when the antecedent is a plural indefinite pronoun (*both, few, many,* or *several.*)

Few of the students offered **their** help.

The indefinite pronouns *all, any, more, most, none,* and *some* can be singular or plural depending on the number of the word to which they refer.

All of the *books* are missing **their** covers.

All of the *book* is ready for **its** final edit.

Using Verbs

Principal Parts of Regular and Irregular Verbs

A verb has four principal parts:

Present	Present Participle	Past	Past Participle
learn	learning	learned	learned
discuss	discussing	discussed	discussed
stand	standing	stood	stood
begin	beginning	began	begun

Regular verbs such as *talk* and *maintain* form the past and past participle by adding *–ed* to the present form. **Irregular verbs** such as *keep* and *give* form the past and past participle in other ways. If you are in doubt about the principal parts of an irregular verb, check a dictionary.

The Tenses of Verbs

The different tenses of verbs indicate the time an action or condition occurred.

The **present tense** is most often used to show one of the following:

Present action or condition:	Jamal **hikes** to the lake. The sky **is** clear.
Regularly occurring action or condition:	Tourists **flock** to the site yearly. **I am** usually tired by 9:00.
Constant action or condition:	The earth **orbits** the sun. Pets **are** good for our health.

The **past tense** is used to express a completed action or condition.

The dog **grabbed** the bone and **ran** away.

The **present perfect tense** is used to express (1) an action or condition that happened at an indefinite time in the past or (2) an action or condition from the past that is continuing into the present.

The mayor **has made** changes in the city code.

My clothes **have been** in the dryer all day.

The **past perfect tense** shows an action or condition completed before another past action or condition.

Micah **had hidden** the gift before he left the house.

The **future tense** is used to show a future action or condition.

The Garcias **will travel** to Rome this summer.

The future perfect tense is used to show a future action or condition that is completed before another future action or condition.

Jess **will have washed** the dishes by the time we return.

Using Modifiers

Degrees of Comparison

Adjectives and adverbs take different forms to show the three degrees of comparison: the *positive,* the *comparative,* and the *superlative.*

Positive	Comparative	Superlative
fast	faster	fastest
crafty	craftier	craftiest
abruptly	more abruptly	most abruptly
bad	worse	worst
much	more	most

Using Comparative and Superlative Adjectives and Adverbs

Use comparative adjectives and adverbs to compare two things. Use superlative adjectives and adverbs to compare three or more things.

The bread is fresher than the rolls.

Of all the foods here, this bread is the freshest.

Using Pronouns

Pronoun Case

The **case** of a pronoun is the form it takes to show its use in a sentence. There are three pronoun cases: *nominative, objective,* and *possessive.*

Nominative	Objective	Possessive
I, you, he, she, it, we, you, they	me, you, him, her, it, us, you, them	my, your, his, her, its, our, their, mine, yours, his, hers, its, ours, theirs

Use the **nominative case** for the *subject* or for a *predicate nominative.*

They worked together to write the play. [subject]

The biggest theater fan is **he.** [predicate nominative]

Use the **objective case** for a *direct object,* an *indirect object,* or the *object of a preposition.*

Jamal drove **me** to the game. [direct object]

Aunt Lil bought **us** the tickets. [indirect object]

The fans cheered for **her.** [object of preposition]

The **possessive case** is used to show ownership.

I think the blue jacket is **his.**

Commonly Confused Words

Diction refers to word choice. The words you choose contribute to the overall effectiveness of your writing. One aspect of diction has to do with choosing between commonly confused words, such as the pairs listed below.

affect, effect

Affect is almost always a verb meaning "to influence." *Effect* is usually a noun meaning "result." Effect can also be a verb meaning "to bring about" or "to cause."

An understanding of T.S. Eliot's multiple allusions can *affect* one's appreciation of his poetry.

In Cather's story, the concert has a profound *effect* on Aunt Georgina.

The aim of persuasive writing is often to *effect* a change in the attitudes of the audience.

farther, further

Use *farther* when you refer to distance. Use *further* when you mean "to a greater degree."

In "A Worn Path," the *farther* Phoenix Jackson travels, the more her determination grows.

In his speech, Patrick Henry urges his countrymen to trust the British no *further.*

good, well

Use the predicate adjective *good* after linking verbs such as *feel, look, smell, taste,* and *seem.* Use *well* whenever you need an adverb.

At the end of "Winter Dreams," Devon implies that Judy does not look as *good* as she used to.

Anne Tyler writes especially *well* about ordinary people and family relationships.

its, it's

Do not confuse the possessive pronoun its with the contraction it's, which stands for "it is" or "it has."

One memorable line in Emerson's poem "The Rhodera" is "Beauty is *its* own excuse for being."

Wallace Stevens's "Anecdote of the Jar" suggests that *it's* impossible to mediate completely between the wilderness and the world of civilization.

set, sit

Set is a transitive verb meaning "to put (something) in a certain place." Its principal parts are *set, setting, set, set. Sit* is an intransitive verb meaning "to be seated." Its principal parts are *sit, sitting, sat, sat.*

Phillis Wheatley's poem is so complimentary to Washington that it seems to *set* him on a pedestal.

As Mrs. Mallard *sits* upstairs alone, she contemplates the death of her husband.

Editing For English Language Conventions

Capitalization

First Words

Capitalize the first word of a sentence.

Compare and contrast the works of Poe and Emerson.

Capitalize the first word of a direct quotation.

Bill asked, "**W**hat are the similarities?"

Proper Nouns and Proper Adjectives

Capitalize all proper nouns.

Carl **S**andburg **N**ovember **H**arvard **U**niversity

Capitalize all proper adjectives.

Turkish heritage **P**uerto **R**ican writers

Academic Course Names

Capitalize course names only if they are language courses, are followed by a number, or are preceded by a proper noun or adjective.

German **S**ocial **S**cience 101 **H**onors **E**nglish
geometry **p**hysics **l**anguage **a**rts

Titles

Capitalize titles showing family relationships when they refer to a specific person unless they are preceded by a possessive noun or pronoun.

Granny Weatherall my **g**randfather Mammedaty

Capitalize the first word and all other key words in the titles of books, stories, songs, and other works of art.

***T**he **C**rucible* "**M**ending **W**all"

Punctuation

End Marks

Use a **period** to end a declarative sentence or an imperative sentence.

War literature can be quite powerful**.**

Discuss the historical context of Hemingway's story**.**

Use periods with abbreviations.

T.S. Eliot Mr. Shiftlet

Use a **question mark** to end an interrogative sentence.

Why did Mr. Hooper wear the black veil**?**

Use an **exclamation mark** after an exclamatory sentence or a forceful imperative sentence.

Our team won in overtime**!**Come here now**!**

Commas

Use a **comma** before the conjunction to separate two independent clauses in a compound sentence.

I read a story by Eudora Welty**,** and I liked it.

Use commas to separate three or more words, phrases, or clauses in a series.

Benjamin Franklin was a statesman**,** a scientist**,** and a journalist.

Use a comma after an introductory word, phrase, or clause.

When the crew heard Ahab's plan**,** they were stunned.

Use commas to set of nonessential expressions.

Captain Ahab**,** as you know**,** was seeking revenge.

Use commas with places and dates.

Boston**,** Massachusetts November 17**,** 1915

Semicolons

Use a **semicolon** to join closely related independent clauses that are not already joined by a conjunction.

Byron is a point guard**;** Mick usually plays center.

Use semicolons to avoid confusion when items in a series contain commas.

Kevin, the team captain**;** Mr. Reece, the coach**;** and Mr. Jenkins, the assistant coach, had a long talk.

Colons

Use a **colon** before a list of items following an independent clause.

Great literature provides us with many things**:** entertainment, enrichment, and inspiration.

Use a colon to introduce an independent clause that summarizes or explains the sentence before it.

Joleen left for a walk**:** She wanted to clear her mind.

Quotation Marks

Use **quotation marks** to enclose a direct quotation.

"A good poet,**"** Mr. Charles said, **"**uses words skillfully and carefully.**"**

An **indirect quotation** does not require quotation marks.

Mr. Charles said that good poets use words skillfully and carefully.

Use quotation marks around the titles of short written works, episodes in a series, songs, and titles of works mentioned as parts of collections.

"Winter Dreams**"** **"**Go Down, Moses**"**

Italics

Italicize the titles of long written works, movies, television and radio shows, lengthy works of music, paintings, and sculptures.

Mary Poppins *House by the Railroad*

For handwritten material, you can use underlining instead of italics.

The Great Gatsby Aida

Dashes

Use **dashes** to indicate an abrupt change of thought, a dramatic interrupting idea, or a summary statement.

I told my teacher—and I was being entirely sincere—that I loved studying American drama.

Parentheses

Use **parentheses** to set off asides and explanations when the material is not essential or when it consists of one or more sentences.

The chair of the city council **(**she also happens to be our neighbor**)** explained the new ordinance to us.

In the example above, the sentence in parentheses interrupts the larger sentence, so it does not have a capital letter and a period. When a sentence in parentheses falls between two other complete sentences, it should start with a capital letter and end with a period.

My family often travels to El Paso. **(**It is the nearest large city.**)** We like to shop there.

Apostrophes

Add an **apostrophe** and an *s* to show the possessive case of most singular nouns and of plural nouns that do not end in –s or *–es*.

Taylor**'**s poetry women**'**s hats

Names ending in *s* form their possessives in the same way, except for classical and biblical names, which add only an apostrophe to form the possessive.

Adams**'**s letter Achilles**'** death

Add an apostrophe to show the possessive case of plural nouns ending in *–s* and *–es*.

the boys**'** ambition the Cruzes**'** house

Use an apostrophe in a contraction to indicate the position of the missing letter or letters.

We**'**ve been studying the works of Edgar Allan Poe.

Brackets

Use **brackets** to enclose a word or words you insert in a quotation when you are quoting someone else.

Columbus's journal entry from October 21, 1492, begins as follows: "At 10 o'clock, we arrived at a cape of the island **[**San Salvador**]**, and anchored, the other vessels in company."

Ellipses

Use three **ellipses** to indicate where you have omitted words from quoted material.

It was Thoreau who wrote, " **. . .** if one advances confidently in the direction of his dreams, **. . .** he will meet with a success unexpected **. . . .**"

In the example above, the four dots at the end of the sentence are the three ellipses plus the period from the original sentence.

Spelling

Spelling Rules

Learning the rules of English spelling will help you make **generalizations** about how to spell words.

Rules for Spelling with Word Parts

The three word parts that can combine to form a word are roots, prefixes, and suffixes. Many of these word parts come from the Greek, Latin, and Anglo-Saxon languages.

The **root word** carries a word's basic meaning.

Root and Origin	Meaning	Examples
-ject- [L.]	to throw	re*ject*
-leg- (-log-) [Gr.]	to say, speak	*leg*al, *log*ic

A **prefix** is one or more syllables at the beginning of a word. A prefix adds to the meaning of the root.

Prefix and Origin	Meaning	Examples
in- (il-, im-, ir-) [L.]	not	*in*human, *il*legal
mono- [Gr.]	alone, one	*mono*poly
over- [A.S.]	above, in excess	*over*flow

A **suffix** is added to the end of a root word and can change the word's meaning or part of speech.

Suffix and Origin	Meaning	Part of Speech
-fy [L.]	to cause to become: clari*fy*	verb
-ish [A.S.]	of, tending to: fool*ish*	adjective
-ism [Gr.]	act, practice, or result of: tru*ism*	noun
-ly [A.S.]	in a manner: quick*ly*	adverb

Rules for Adding Suffixes to Root Words

When adding a suffix to a root word ending in *y* preceded by a consonant, change *y* to *i* unless the suffix begins with *i*.

funny + -est = funniest　　silly + -ness = silliness
modify + -ing = modifying　　cry + -ing = crying

For a root word ending in *e*, drop the *e* when adding a suffix beginning with a vowel.

nature + -al = natural　　seize + -ure = seizure
SOME EXCEPTIONS: courageous, mileage, dyeing

For root words ending with a consonant + vowel + consonant in a stressed syllable, double the final consonant when adding a suffix that begins with a vowel.

slim + -er = slimmer　　permit + -ed = permitted
SOME EXCEPTIONS: rowing, conference

Rules for Adding Prefixes to Root Words

When a prefix is added to a root word, the spelling of the root remains the same.

in- + sincere = insincere　　over- + eat = overeat

With some prefixes, the spelling of the prefix changes when joined to the root to make the pronunciation easier.

in- + pact = impact　　com- + found = confound

Orthographic Patterns

Certain letter combinations in English make certain sounds. For instance, *ph* sounds like *f*, *eigh* usually makes a long *a* sound, and the *k* before an *n* is often silent.

phase　　w**eigh**t　　**kn**eeling

Understanding orthographic patterns such as these can help you improve your spelling.

Forming Plurals

The plural form of most nouns is formed by adding *–s* or *–es* to the singular.

merit**s** sparrow**s**　　American**s**

For words ending in *s, ss, x, z, sh, ch,* add *–es.*

dress**es**　　waltz**es**　　pouch**es**

For words ending in *y* or *o* preceded by a vowel, add *–s.*

way**s**　　rodeo**s**　　bouy**s**

For words ending in *y* preceded by a consonant, change the *y* to an *i* and add *–es.*

quer**ies**　　cemeter**ies**　　luxur**ies**

For most words ending in *o* preceded by a consonant, add *–es.*

potato**es**　　echo**es**

Some words form the plural in irregular ways.

mice　　alumni　　women　　crises

Foreign Words Used in English

Some words used in English are actually foreign words we have adopted. Learning to spell these words requires memorization. When in doubt, check a dictionary.

origami　　desperado　　protégé
laissez faire　　croissant

Index of Authors and Titles

Note: Page numbers in *italics* refer to biographical information for authors, or commentary for titles; nonfiction and informational text appears in red.

Index of Skills

Boldface numbers indicate pages where terms are defined.

Literary Analysis

Comprehension Skills

READING FOR INFORMATION

Analyzing Functional and Expository Text

Primary Sources

READING STRATEGIES

CRITICAL READING

Language Conventions

Vocabulary

Academic Vocabulary

WORD ANALYSIS

LANGUAGE STUDY WORKSHOPS

Writing/Writing to Sources

WRITING APPLICATIONS

WRITING STRATEGIES

Prewriting

Drafting

Student Models

Research

Speaking, Listening, and Viewing

Assessment

Index of Features

Extended Study

Independent Reading

Language Study

Literary Criticism/ Commentary

Literature in Context

Reading for Information

Recent Scholarship

Speaking and Listening

Test-Taking Practice

Themes Across Centuries

Text Set Workshop

Unit Introduction

Writing Workshop

Acknowledgments

Acknowledgments continued from copyright page.

William Harvey "Playing for the Fighting Sixty-Ninth" by William Harvey from *Playing for the Fighting Sixty-Ninth.* Copyright © 2001 by William Harvey. Used by permission.

Historical Museum of Southern Florida "Museum Mission/History" from *http://www.hmsf.org.* Copyright © Historical Museum of Southern Florida. Used by permission.

The Barbara Hogenson Agency, Inc. "The Night the Ghost Got In" by James Thurber. Copyright © 1933, 1961 by James Thurber, © Rosemary Thurber. Used by permission.

Henry Holt and Company, Inc. "Acquainted with the Night" by Robert Frost from *The Poetry of Robert Frost* edited by Edward Connery Latham. Copyright © 1956 by Robert Frost. Copyright 1928, © 1969 by Henry Holt and Co. "The Gift Outright" by Robert Frost from *The Poetry of Robert Frost.* Copyright 1942 by Robert Frost, © 1970 by Lesley Frost Ballantine, © 1969 by Henry Holt & Company. "Stopping By Woods on a Snowy Evening" by Robert Frost from *The Poetry of Robert Frost,* edited by Edward Connery Lathem. Copyright 1951 by Robert Frost, © 1923, 1969 by Henry Holt and Company. Used by permission of Henry Holt and Company, LLC.

Houghton Mifflin Company, Inc. "Ambush" from *The Things They Carried by Tim O'Brien.* Copyright © 1990 by Tim O'Brien. "Ars Poetica" from Collected Poems, 1917–1982 by Archibald MacLeish. Copyright © 1985 by The Estate of Archibald MacLeish. "Courage" by Anne Sexton from *The Awful Rowing Toward God* by Anne Sexton. Copyright © 1975 by Loring Conant, Jr., Executor of the Estate of Anne Sexton. Used by permission of Houghton Mifflin Company. All rights reserved.

Hyperion From *Cold Mountain: The Screenplay* by Anthony Minghella, based on a novel by Charles Frazier. Copyright © 2003 by Anthony Minghellla. Used by permission of Hyperion. All rights reserved.

International Creative Management, Inc. "One Day, Now Broken in Two" by Anna Quindlen from *Newsweek.* Copyright © 2002 by Anna Quindlen. First appeared in *Newsweek.* "Life in His Language" by Toni Morrison from *James Baldwin.* Copyright © 1989 by Toni Morrison. Published in James Baldwin: The Legacy (Quincy Troupe, ed.), Simon & Schuster, 1989. Copyright © 1989 by Simon & Schuster. Used by permission of International Creative Management, Inc.

Athena Kildegaard "untitled" poem by Athena Kildegaard used from *Rare Momentum,* Red Dragonfly Press, 2006, by permission of the author.

The Estate of Dr. Martin Luther King, Jr. c/o Writer's House LLC From "Letter from Birmingham Jail" by Dr. Martin Luther King, Jr. from *A Testament of Hope:The Essential Writings of Martin Luther King, Jr.* Used by arrangement with the Heirs to the Estate of Martin Luther King, Jr. c/o Writers House as agent for the proprietor. Copyright 1963 Martin Luther King, Jr.; renewed 1991 Coretta Scott King.

Galway Kinnell "Reckless Genius" by Galway Kinnell from *http://www.salon.com.* Used by permission.

Alfred A. Knopf, Inc. "Dream Variations" by Langston Hughes from *The Selected Poems of Langston Hughes.* Copyright © 1926 by Alfred A. Knopf, Inc. and renewed 1954 by Langston Hughes. "I, Too" by Langston Hughes from *The Selected Poems of Langston Hughes.* Copyright © 1994 by the Estate of Langston Hughes. "Refugee in America" by Langston Hughes from *The Selected Poems of Langston Hughes.* Copyright © 1943 by The Curtis Publishing Company. "The Negro Speaks of Rivers" by Langston Hughes from *Selected Poems of Langston Hughes.* Copyright © 1926 by Alfred A. Knopf, Inc. and renewed 1954 by Langston Hughes. From "The Woman Warrior" by Maxine Hong Kingston from *The Woman Warrior.* Copyright © 1975, 1976 by Maxine Hong Kingston. "Of Modern Poetry" by Wallace Stevens from *The Collected Poems of Wallace Stevens.* Copyright 1942 by Wallace Stevens and renewed 1970 by Holly Stevens from by Wallace Stevens. "Of Plymouth Plantation" by William Bradford from Of Plymouth Plantation 1620–1647 by William Bradford, edited by Samuel Eliot Morison, copyright 1952 by Samuel Eliot Morison and renewed 1980 by Emily M. Beck. From "Hiroshima" by John Hersey. Copyright 1946 and renewed 1974 by John Hersey. Used by permission of Alfred A. Knopf, a division of Random House, Inc. Excerpt from *The American Language,* 4th Edition by H.L. Mencken. Copyright © 1919, 1921, 1923, 1936 by Alfred A. Knopf, Inc. All rights reserved.

The Landmark Project "Son of Citation Machine and Landmarks Son of Citation Machine Masthead" from *http://citationmachine.net.* Copyright © 2006 by David Warlick & The Landmark Project. Used by permission of The Landmark Project.

League of Women Voters "How to Watch a Debate" from *www.lwv.org.* The material in this publication on "How to Watch a Debate" was excerpted from a League of Women Voters of the United States (LWVUS) online document of the same title, located at www.lwv.org, with express permission of the LWVUS for this one-time use in Pearson Prentice Hall Literature 8e Program. Secondary users must request permission directly from the LWVUS, the copyright owner. Copyright © 2007 League of Women Voters. All rights reserved. Used by permission.

Patricia Lee Lewis "(0)" by Patricia Lee Lewis.

Liveright Publishing Corporation "anyone lived in a pretty how town" by E. E. Cummings from *Complete Poems, 1904–1962.* Copyright 1940, © 1968, 1991 by the Trustees for the E.E. Cummings Trust. "old age sticks" by E. E. Cummings. Copyright 1958 © 1986, 1991 by the Trustees for the E. E. Cummings Trust, from *Complete Poems: 1904–1962* by E. E. Cummings, edited by George J. Firmage. "Frederick Douglass" by Robert Hayden. Copyright © 1966 by Robert Hayden, from *Collected Poems of Rober Hayden* by Robert Hayden, edited by Frederick Glaysher. "Runagate Runagate" by Robert Hayden from *The Collected Poems of Robert Hayden* by Robert Hayden, edited by Frederick Glaysher. Copyright © 1966 by Robert Hayden. "Storm Ending" by Jean Toomer from Cane. Copyright 1923 by Boni & Liveright, renewed 1951 by Jean Toomer. Used by permission of Liveright Publishing Corporation.

Los Angeles Times Syndicate "Hysteria Resides at Heart of the Frantic Crucible" by Kenneth Turan from Los Angeles Times, 12/13/96. Copyright © 1996 The Times Mirror Company, Los Angeles Times. Used by permission.

Ludlow Music c/o The Richmond Organization (TRO) "Dust Bowl Blues" Words and Music by Woody Guthrie TRO-© Copyright 1964 (Renewed) 1977 Ludlow Music, Inc., New York, NY Used by permission.

The Estate of Edgar Lee Masters "Lucinda Matlock" by Edgar Lee Masters from *The Spoon River Anthology.* Permission by Hilary Masters.

The Miami Herald "Crucible Casts a Newly Contempo rary Spell/Free from Chains of McCarthyism, Arthur Miller's Classic Soars" by Rene Rodriguez from *The Miami Herald,* 12/20/96. Copyright © 1996 The Miami Herald. Used by permission.

Milkweed Editions "Museum Indians" by Susan Power from *Roofwalker* (Minneapolis: Milkweed Editions, 2002). Copyright © 2002 by Susan Power. Used with permission from Milkweek Editions.

Navarre Scott Momaday From "The Names" by N. Scott Momaday. Copyright © by N. Scott Momaday. Used by permission.

New Directions Publishing Corporation From "A Retrospect: Few Don'ts By an Imagiste" by Ezra Pound, from *The Literary Essays of Ezra Pound,* copyright © 1935 by Ezra Pound. "Constantly Risking Absurdity" by Lawrence Ferlinghetti from *These Are My Rivers: New and Selected Poems 1955–1993.* Copyright © 1955, 1958, 1959, 1960, 1961, 1964, 1966, 1967, 1968, 1969, 1971, 1972, 1975, 1976, 1977, 1978, 1979, 1981, 1984, 1988, 1993 by Lawrence Ferlinghetti. All rights reserved. "The Great Figure" by William Carlos Williams from *Collected Poems: 1909–1939, Volume I,* copyright © 1938 by New Directions Publishing Corp. "Heat" by H. D. from *Collected Poems, 1912–1944,* copyright © 1982 by The Estate of Hilda Doolittle. "In a Station of the Metro" by Ezra Pound from *Personae,* copyright © 1926 by Ezra Pound. "Pear Tree" by H. D. from *Collected Poems, 1912–1944,* copyright © 1982 by The Estate of Hilda Doolittle. "The Red Wheelbarrow" by William Carlos Williams from *Collected Poems: 1909–1939, Volume 1,* copyright © 1938 by New Directions Publishing Corp. "The Secret" by Denise Levertov from *Poems 1960–1967.* Copyright © 1964 by Denise Levertov Goodman. "This is Just to Say" by William Carlos Williams from *Collected Poems 1909–1939, Volume I,* copyright © 1938 by New Directions Publishing Corp. Used by permission of New Directions Publishing Corp.

New York Times Agency "At the Theater/The Crucible" by Brooks Atkinson from *The New York Times,* January 23, 1953. Copyright © 1953 by the New York Times Co. "Onomatopoeia" originally titled "Zapmanship" by William Safire from *You Could Look It Up.* Copyright 1984, The New York Times. "The Nation: Backing the Attack" from *The New York Times,* September 12, 1943. Copyright © The New York Times. "Rock of the Modern Age, Arthur Miller is Everywhere" by Mel Gussow from *diversityjobmarket.com.* Used by permission and protected by the copyright Laws of the United States. The printing, copying, redistribution, or retransmission of the material without express written permission is prohibited.

Newmarket Press From "Good Night, and Good Luck: The Screenplay and History behind the Landmark Movie". Screenplay by George Clooney and Grant Heslov. Copyright © 2005 by Section Eight Production. Used by permission of Newmarket Press, 18 East 48th Street, New York, New York 10017. www.newmarketpress.com.

Naomi Shihab Nye "Streets" by Naomi Shihab Nye from *Words Under the Words: Selected Poems.* Copyright © Naomi Shihab Nye. Used by permission.

Harold Ober Associates, Inc. "A Black Man Talks of Reaping" by Arna Bontemps from *American Negro Poetry.* Copyright © 1963 by Arna Bontemps. Used by permission of Harold Ober Associates Incorporated.

Gregory K. Pincus "Fib" by Gregory K. Pincus, originally posted online at *http://gottabook.blogspot.com/2006/04/fib.html.* Used by permission of the author.

Popular Photography Magazine From "The Assignment I'll Never Forget" by Dorothea Lange from *Popular Photography,* February 1960, Vol. 46, No. 2. Copyright © Popular Photography, 1960.

Princeton University Press From "Walden" by Henry David Thoreau. Copyright © 1971 by Princeton University Press, 1999 renewed PUP, 1989 paperback edition. Used by permission of Princeton University Press.

Sean Ramsay "Urban Renewal" by Sean Ramsay. Copyright © 2001 by Sean Ramsay. Used by permission.

Random House, Inc. "A Rose for Emily" by William Faulkner from *Collected Stories of William Faulkner* copyright © 1930 and renewed © 1958 by William Faulkner. "The Unknown Citizen", copyright 1940 & copyright renewed 1968 by W.H. Auden from Collected Poems by W.H. Auden. Used by permission of Random House, Inc. "A Raisin in the Sun" by Lorraine Hansberry. Copyright © 1958 by Robert Nemiroff, as an unpublished work. Copyright © 1959, 1966, 1984, by Robert Nemiroff.

Random House, Inc. & Sterling Lord Literistic, Inc. "Man Listening to Disc" by Billy Collins from Random House Trade Paperbacks. Copyright © 2001 by Billy Collins. Used by permission.

Schomburg Center for Research in Black Culture "The Tropics in New York" by Claude McKay from *The Poems of Claude McKay.* Courtesy of the Literary Representative for the Works of Claude McKay, Schomburg Center for Research in Black Culture, The New York Public Library, Astor, Lenox and Tilden Foundations. Used by permission.

Scribner, an imprint of Simon & Schuster "In Another Country" by Ernest Hemingway from *Men Without Woman.* Copyright 1927 by Charles Scribner's Sons. Copyright renewed 1955 by Ernest Hemingway. Used by permission of Scribner, an imprint of Simon & Schuster Adult Publishing Group. "Poetry" by Marianne Moore from *The Collected Poems of Marianne Moore.* Copyright © 1935 by Marianne Moore, copyright renewed © 1963 by Marianne Moore and T.S. Eliot. Used with the permission of Scribner, an imprint of Simon & Schuster Adult Publishing Group.

Simon & Schuster, Inc. "1776" by David McCullough from Chapter 3, "Dorchester Heights." New York: Simon & Schuster, 2005. All rights reserved.

South Florida Water Management District "Kissimmee River Restoration and Upper Basin Initiatives" by Staff from *2007 South Florida Environmental Report.* Copyright © 2007 South Florida Water Management District. Courtesy of South Florida Water Management District. Used by permission.

Donald D. Stanford "Huswifery" from *The Poems of Edward Taylor* ed. by Donald E. Stanford, University of North Carolina Press, 1989. Copyright © 1960, renewed 1988 by Donald E. Stanford.

State of California—Dept. of Parks and Recreation "Archaeological Site Record" from *http://ohp.parks.ca.gov.* Used by permission.

The Statue of Liberty-Ellis Island Foundation, Inc. "Statue of Liberty-Ellis Island Foundation Mission and Background" from *www.statueofliberty.org.* Copyright © The Statue of Liberty-Ellis Island Foundation, Inc. *www.ellisisland.org.* Used by permission.

Sterling Lord Literistic, Inc. "Mission Update blog" by Steve Squyres from *http://athena.cornell.edu/news/mubss/.* Used by permission of SLL/Sterling Lord Literistic, Inc. Copyright by Steven Squyres.

Syracuse University Press "The Iroquois Constitution" from *Arthur C. Parker on the Iroquois: Iroquois Uses of Maize and Other Food Plants, The Code of Handsome Lake; The Seneca Prophet; The Constitution of the Five Nations* by Arthur C. Parker, edited by William N. Fenton (Syracuse University Press, Syracuse, NY, 1981). Copyright © 1968 by Syracuse University Press.

Thompson and Thompson From "The Dark Tower" by Countee Cullen. Published in *Copper Sun* © 1927 Harper & Bros, NY. Renewed 1954 by Ida M. Cullen. Copyrights held by Amistad Research Center, Tulane University. Administered by Thompson and Thompson, New York, NY. Used by permission.

Anthony Thwaite "When I went to visit" by Ki no Tsurayuki translated by Geoffrey Bownas and Anthony Thwaite from *The Penguin Book of Japanese Verse*. Penguin Books copyright © 1964, revised edition 1998. Translation copyright © Geoffrey Bownas and Anthony Thwaite, 1964, 1998. Used by permission.

Charlie Todd "Surprise! Subway Birthday" by Charlie Todd and improve everywhere.com Copyright © 2002. Used by permission of Charlie Todd.

The University of Chicago Press "America's Epic" by James Miller, Jr. from Whitman: A Collection of Critical Essays. Copyright © 1957 by The University of Chicago. © 1962 by Prentice Hall, Inc.

University of Nebraska Press "Crossing the Great Divide" by Meriweather Lewis from *The Journals of the Lewis and Clark Expedition, volume 5*. Edited by Gary E. Moulton, used by permission of the University of Nebraska Press. Copyright © 1988 by the University of Nebraska Press.

University of North Carolina Press "To His Excellency, General Washington" by Phillis Wheatley from *The Poems of Phillis Wheatley*. Edited and with an introduction by Julian D. Mason Jr. Copyright © 1966 by the University of North Carolina Press, renewed 1989. Used by permission of the publisher. www.uncpress.unc.edu.

University of North Texas "Help North Texas Vote" from *http://www.eac.gov*.

Viking Penguin, Inc. "The Turtle (Chapter 3)" by John Steinbeck from The Grapes of Wrath. Copyright © 1939, renewed copyright © 1967 by John Steinbeck. "The Crucible" by Arthur Miller from *The Crucible*. Copyright 1952, 1953, 1954, renewed © 1980, 1981, 1982 by Arthur Miller. Used by permission of Viking Penguin, a division of Penguin Books USA Inc. CAUTION: Professionals and amateurs are hereby warned that "The Crucible" being fully protected under the copyright laws of the United States of America, the British Commonwealth countries, including the Dominion of Canada, and the other countries of the Universal Copyright and Berne Conventions, are subject to royalty. All rights, including professional, amateur, motion picture, recitation, lecturing, public reading, radio, television and cable broadcasting, and the rights of translation into foreign languages, are strictly reserved. Particular emphasis is laid on the question of readings, permission for which must be secured in writing. Any inquiries for The Crucible should be addressed to Viking Penguin, 375 Hudson Street, NY, NY 10014.

Virginia Department of Historic Resources "Virginia Department of Historic Resources Archaeological Site Inventory Form" from Virginia Department of Historic Resources. Used by permission.

Patricia Vogel "untitled" (Fibonacci poem) by Patricia Vogel. Used by permission of the author.

W. W. Norton & Company, Inc. "Halley's Comet" by Stanley Kunitz from *Passing Through: The Later Poems*, New and Selected. Copyright © 1995 by Stanley Kunitz. Used by permission of W.W. Norton & Company, Inc. Copyright © 1985 by Stanley Kunitz. "Who Burns for the Perfection of Paper" by Martin Espada from *City of Coughing and Dead Radiators*. Copyright © 1993 by Martin Espada. Used by permission of W. W. Norton & Company, Inc.

Wesleyan University Press "Camouflaging the Chimera" by Yusef Komunyakaa from *Neon Vernacular*. From Dien Cai Dau (Wesleyan University Press, 1988). Used by permission of Wesleyan University Press.

Wikipedia.org "Kennedy Space Center" from *http://en.wikipedia.org/wiki/Kennedy_Space_Center*; retrieved from http://en.wikpedia.org accessed on 07/06/07. "Atlanta Braves" from *http://en.wikipedia.org/wiki/Atlanta_Braves*; retrieved from http://en.wikpedia.org accessed on 07/06/07. "Mojave Desert" from *http://en.wikipedia.org/wiki/Mojave_desert*; retrieved from http://en.wikpedia.org accessed on 07/06/07.

The Wylie Agency, Inc. "Everything Stuck to Him" by Raymond Carver from *What We Talk About When We Talk About Love*. Copyright © 1981 by Tess Gallagher, used with the permission of the Wylie Agency. "Journey to the Crucible" by Arthur Miller, first published in *The New York Times*, February 8,1953 © 1953 by Arthur Miller. Copyright renewed 2008 by The Arthur Miller Estate, used with the permission of The Wylie Agency Inc.

Yale University Press From "Sinners in the Hands of an Angry God" by Jonathan Edwards from *The Sermons of Jonathan Edwards: A Reader* published by Yale University Press. Copyright © 1999 by Yale University Press. From "Mary Chesnut's Civil War" by Mary Chesnut edited by C. Vann Woodward. Copyright © 1981 by C. Vann Woodward, Sally Bland Metts, Barbara G. Carpenter, Sally Bland Johnson, and Katherine W. Herbert. All rights reserved. Used by permission of the publisher, Yale University Press.

Note: Every effort has been made to locate the copyright owner of material reproduced on this component. Omissions brought to our attention will be corrected in subsequent editions.

ACKNOWLEDGMENTS

Credits

Photo Credits

F & B cover Alan Copson/JAI/Corbis

Lxxii, Universal/Photofest; **lxxiii** TR Universal/Marvel Entertainment/The Kobal Collection/Art Resource; **lxxiii** L Universal/Photofest; **lxxii** Michel Setboun/CORBIS; **lxxv** Paul Knight, Trevillion Images; **lxxvi** Bettmann/Corbis; **lxxvii** TL Time Life Pictures/Time Magazine/Getty Images Inc.; **lxxvii** BR Bettmann/Corbis; **lxxxii** Joseph Sohm/Visions of America/Corbis; **lxxxiii** Lewis H. Hine/George Eastman House/Getty Images, Inc.; **lxxxiv** The Granger Collection, NYC; **lxxxv** Stephen Pierce; **lxxxvii, xi, xii** The Art Archive/Gift of Mrs. Karl Frank/Buffalo Bill Historical Center, Cody, Wyoming/14.86/Art Resource, NY; **xiv–xv** Geoffrey Clements/Corbis; **xlvi–xlvii** gallimaufry/Shutterstock; **xvii–xviii** Bettmann/Corbis; **xxiv–xxv** The Museum of Modern Art/Licensed by SCALA/Art Resource, NY; **xxi–xxii** Drought Stricken Area, 1934 (oil on canvas), Hogue, Alexandre (1898–1994)/Dallas Museum of Art, Texas, USA/The Bridgeman Art Library; **xxvii** Louis K. Meisel Gallery, Inc./Corbis; **0001** The Art Archive/Gift of Mrs. Karl Frank/Buffalo Bill Historical Center, Cody, Wyoming/14.86/Art Resource, NY; **2** TCR Library of Congress; **2** L Buffalo Bill Historical Center/The Art Archive at Art Resource, NY; **2** RCR Portrait of an African, c.1757–60 (oil on canvas), Ramsay, Allan (1713–84) (attr. to)/Royal Albert Memorial Museum, Exeter, Devon, UK/The Bridgeman Art Library; **2** CL Bettmann/Corbis; **2** CR The Granger Collection, NYC; **2** LCL The Granger Collection, NY; **2** TR Courtesy of The Historical Society of Pennsylvania Collection, Atwater Kent Museum of Philadelphia; **2** R Photo by Michael J. Deas/Time Magazine/Time & Life Pictures/Getty Images; **4** R Bettmann/CORBIS; **4** L Bettmann/CORBIS; **5** R Blue Lantern Studio/CORBIS; **5** L The Gallery Collection/CORBIS; **6** L Lee Snider/Photo Images/CORBIS; **6** R The Granger Collection, NYC; **7** T topora/Shutterstock; **7** R Scala/Art Resource, NY; **7** L Bettmann/CORBIS; **8** R istockphoto.com; **8** L Burstein Collection/CORBIS; **9** T istockphoto.com; **9** BR Chris Hillier/CORBIS; **9** BL The Granger Collection, NY; **10** R Blue Lantern Studio/CORBIS; **10** L Bettmann/CORBIS; **10** C Bettmann/CORBIS; **11** L istockphoto.com; **11** R The Granger Collection, NY; **12** T; **12** BR Cynthia Hart Designer/CORBIS; **12** BC The Gallery Collection/CORBIS; **12** BL The Granger Collection, NY; **13** R Francis G. Mayer/CORBIS; **13** L Gerrit Greve/CORBIS; **1** R Prentice Hall; **15** Library of Congress; **17** Smithsonian American Art Museum, Washington, DC/Art Resource, NY; **19** Buffalo Bill Historical Center/The Art Archive at Art Resource, NY; **21** Mary Ann McDonald/Corbis; **23** istockphoto.com; **24** Masterfile; **26** bkgd istockphoto.com; **27** kstudija/Fotolia; **32** BL The Roofwalker, Susan Power. Milkweed Editions. ç 22, Text by Susan Power. Cover and Interior design by Dale Cooney.Cover painting,"Migrations", oil, 1996 by Ojibwe artist Jim Denomie; **32** BR The Grass Dancer, Susan Power. Penguin Putnam, Inc. Copyright ©1994 by Susan Power; **32** T Photo by Rebecca Dallinger; Courtesy of Susan Power; **34** Brooklyn Museum/Corbis; **35** istockphoto.com; **37**; The Old Guitarist, 193, Pablo Picasso, Spanish, 1881–1973, oil on panel 122.9 x 82.6 cm, Helen Birch Bartlett Memorial Collection, 1926.253. Reproduction, The Art Institute of Chicago, ©24Estate of Pablo Picasso/Artists Rights Society (ARS), New York; 38 Buffalo Bill Historical Center; Cody, Wyoming; Gift of Hon. and Mrs. William Henry Harrison; NA. 22.70; **39** DLILLC/Corbis; **41** John Kahionhes Fadden; **42** bkgd istockphoto.com; **42** Corbis; **43** W. Perry Conway/Corbis; **48** Jeremy Woodhouse/Masterfile; **50** Courtesy Catholic Archives of Texas, Austin; **52** Daryl Benson/Masterfile; **53** Jay Krishnan/Shutterstock; **57** T Bettmann/Corbis; **58** Bettmann/Corbis; **60** Bettmann/Corbis; **61** istockphoto.com; **63** The Granger Collection, NY; **68** Ric Francis/epa/Corbis; **69** Denis Scott/Corbis; **70–71** bkgd NASA/Handout/Getty Images; **71** R AP/Wide World Photos; **72** bkgd FILATOV ALEXEY/Shutterstock; **73** Pilgrims Going to Church, George Henry Boughton, Collection of The New-York Historical Society; **75** The Granger Collection, NY; **76** istockphoto.com; **77** Anne Bradstreet, The Tenth Muse Lately Sprung Up in America, Ladonna Gulley Warrick, Courtesy of the artist; **78** BR Dance of Apollo with the Nine Muses (tempera on panel), Peruzzi, Baldassarre (1481–1536)/Palazzo Pitti, Florence, Italy, Alinari/The Bridgeman Art Library; **78** ML Mimmo Jodice/Corbis; **78** T The Granger Collection, NY; **78** BL Demetrio Carrasco CONACULTA-INAH-MEX. Authorized by the Instituto Nacional de Antropologia e Historia; **85** Corbis; **86** Johnson B. Curtis; **87** B istockphoto.com; **87** T istockphoto.com; **89** North Wind Picture Archives; **95** George Washington (1732–99) (colour litho) by John Trumbull (1756–1843) (after) Private Collection/Peter Newark American Pictures/The Bridgeman Art Library; **96** The Granger Collection, NYC; **99** B istockphoto.com; **99** National Portrait Gallery, Smithsonian Institution/Art Resource, NY; **10** Superstock; **14** Bettmann/Corbis; **106** Swim Ink 2, LLC/CORBIS; **18** The New Yorker Collection 200 Frank Cotham from cartoonbank.com; **111** The Granger Collection, NYC; **112** istockphoto.com; **112** bkgd National Archives and Records Adminisitration; **116** The Granger Collection, NYC; **117** The Granger Collection, New York; **118** The Granger Collection, New York; **123** Bettmann/Corbis; **124** New York State Historical Association, Cooperstown, New York; **129** ©ZUMA Press, Inc. / Alamy; **131** ©Bob Daemmrich / Alamy; **132** TL istockphoto.com; **132** Bkgrd; **134** The Granger Collection, NYC; **135** L The Granger Collection, NYC; **135** C The Granger Collection, NYC; **135** R The Granger Collection, NYC; **136** R The Granger Collection, NYC; **136** Photo by Michael J. Deas/Time Magazine/Time & Life Pictures/Getty Images; **137** R The Granger Collection, NYC; **137** C The Granger Collection, NYC; **137** L The Granger Collection, NYC; **138** TL The Granger Collection, New York; **138** TC The Granger Collection, NYC; **138** TR The Granger Collection, NYC; **138** BL Judith Miller/Dorling Kindersley; **138** BR Courtesy of the Bakken Library, Minneapolis; **140** Christie's Images/SuperStock; **142** ©British Museum; **144**; **146** BC istockphoto.com; **146** T ©Richard Cummings/Corbis; **146** BL Accoutrements LLC; **146** BR Liberty Kids is a registered trademark of DIC Entertainment Corp. Used under license. All rights reserved; **148** The Granger Collection, NYC; **149** The Granger Collection, NYC; **151** TL The Granger Collection, NYC; **151** bkgd Seattle Art Museum, Gift of Katherine White and the Boeing Company.Photo by Paul Macapia; **151** BR Seattle Art Museum, Gift of Katherine White and the Boeing Company. Photo by Paul Macapia; **152** The New Yorker Collection 1965 William Hamilton from cartoonbank.com. All Rights Reserved; **153** Hulton-Deutsch Collection/Corbis; **156** BCR AP Photo/Eric Risberg; **156** BR AP Photo/Eric Gay; **156** BCL Bassouls

Sophie/Corbis; **156** BL ©Rune Hellestad/Corbis; **156** CL Bettmann/Corbis; **156** TL Bettmann/Corbis; **156** TR Bettmann/Corbis; **156** CR Getty Images; **156** CCR Hulton Archive/Getty Images; **156** CCL The Granger Collection, New York; **158** AP Photo/Eric Gay; **159** DK Limited/Corbis; **160–161** Michael Storrings; **161** Rivera, Diego (1866–1957). The grinder (La molendera). 1926. Oil on canvas, 35 7/16 x 46 1/16 in. Museo Nacional de Arte Moderno, Instituto Nacional de Bellas Artes, Mexico City, D.F., Mexico. (c)Banco de Mexico Diego Rivera & Frida Kahlo Museums Trust. A **162** ©JUPITERIMAGES/ PHOTOS.COM / Alamy; **162–163** Michael Storrings; **164** ©Imagebroker/Alamy; **166** T Pearson; **166** B From To Tell a Free Story: The First Century of Afro-American Autobiography, 1760–1865. ©1986 by the Board of Trustees of the University of Illinois. Used with permission of the author and the University of Illinois Press.; **167** Courtesy of the Library of Congress; **169** Portrait of an African, c.1757-60 (oil on canvas), Ramsay, Allan (1713–84) (attr. to)/Royal Albert Memorial Museum, Exeter, Devon, UK/The Bridgeman Art Library; **170** The Art Archive/Maritime Museum Kronborg Castle Denmark/Dagli Orti/Art Resource, NY; **171** /©Dorling Kindersley, Courtesy of the Wilberforce House Museum; **171** bkgd From THE WAY WE LIVED IN NORTH CAROLINA edited by Joe A. Mobley. Maps by Mark Anderson Moore. Copyright ©23 by the University of North Carolina Press. Published in association with the North Carolina Department of Cultural Resources, Office of Archives; **172** The Granger Collection, NYC; **175** istockphoto.com; **180** T Bettmann/Corbis; **180** C The Granger Collection, NYC; **180** B The Granger Collection, NYC; **181** T Judith Miller/Dorling Kindersley/Dreweatt Neate; **181** B Profiles in History/Corbis; **183** The Granger Collection, NYC; **184** Library of Congress; **185** Library of Congress; **187** William Manning/Corbis; **191** Photo by Rebecca Dallinger; Courtesy of Susan Power; **206** BR AP Images; **28–29** ©Geoffrey Clements/Corbis; **210** LCL Library of Congress; **210** CL ©Stefano Bianchetti/Corbis; **210** L Smithsonian Institution/Corbis; **210** TL ©adoc-photos/Corbis; **210** CR Bettmann/Corbis; **210** RB The Granger Collection, NYC; **210** TR The Granger Collection, NYC; **210** RCR Amherst College Archives and Special Collections, by permission of the Trustees of Amherst College; 210 TC Cover of Democracy in American by Alexis De Tocqueville, ©1965 by Harper & Row. Publishers, Inc. Reprinted by permission of HarperColins Publishers; **211** RB Bettmann/Corbis; **211** TL Bettmann/Corbis; **211** BL National Museum of American History, Smithsonian Institution; **211** TCR National Museum of American History, Smithsonian Institution; **211** TR Old Sturbridge Village; **211** BCR Science Museum; **211** BC Science Museum; **212** The Granger Collection, NYC; **213** R The Granger Collection, New York; **213** L The Art Archive/Musée du Château de Versailles/Gianni Dagli Orti/Art Resource, NY; **214** R Bettmann/Corbis; **215** R Bettmann/Corbis; **215** L The Granger Collection, NYC; **216** R Bettmann/Corbis; **216** L The Granger Collection, NYC; **217** R Image Source/Corbis; **217** L ©Stefano Bianchetti/Corbis; **217** C The Granger Collection, NYC; **218** T; **218** BR ©Frank Lukasseck/Corbis; **218** BL The Granger Collection, New York; **218** BC The Granger Collection, NYC; **219** L The Granger Collection, NYC; **219** C The Granger Collection, NYC; **219** R The Granger Collection, NYC; **220** L Bettmann/Corbis; **220** R The Granger Collection, NYC; **221** L Bettmann/Corbis; **221** C ©Joseph Sohm/Visions of America/Corbis; **221** North Wind Picture Archives; **222** Aurora/Getty Images; **223** Aurora/Getty Images; **225** ©Private Collection/Photo ©Christie's Images/The Bridgeman Art Library; **227** Bettmann/Corbis; **228** Richard Bowden/Shutterstock; **229** ©Dorling Kindersley; **230** ©Corbis; **233** ©johannesspreter/Fotolia; **234** ©Paul Souders/Corbis; **235** Bettmann/Corbis; **236** ©Phil Schermeister/Corbis; **238** ©Lothar Lenz/zefa/Corbis; **239** ©Zack Seckler/Corbis; **244** B National Portrait Gallery, Smithsonian Institution/Art Resource, NY; **244** T The Granger Collection, NYC; **245** Smithsonian Institution, 95-3550; **246** North Wind Picture Archives; **247** Missouri Historical Society Museum Collections. Photograph and scan ©1998-21, Missouri Historical Society; **248** Library of Congress; **250** T Missouri Historical Society, St. Louis, David Schultz; **250** B The Thomas Gilcrease Institute of Art, Tulsa, Oklahoma; **251** North Wind Picture Archives; **252** R North Wind Picture Archives; **252** L Missouri Historical Society; **253** B Library of Congress; **253** T North Wind Picture Archives; **255** Connie Ricca/Corbis; **257** Corbis; **258** The Art Archive/Whitney Purchase Fund/Buffalo Bill Historical Center, Cody, Wyoming/19.61; **260** ©Craig Tuttle/Corbis; **261** The Granger Collection, NYC; **262** Image copyright ©The Metropolitan Museum of Art/Art Resource, NY; **265** The Granger Collection, NYC; **266** ©Ira Wyman/Sygma/Corbis; **269** Mary Evans Picture Library; **271** Smithsonian Institution/Corbis; **272; 276** Louis R. Linscott and S.B. Goddard & Son Co.; **278; 280** Fenimore Art Museum, Cooperstown, New York; **282** The Puritan, c. 1898, Frank E. Schoonover, Oil on canvas, Collection of The Brandywine River Museum, Gift of Mr. and Mrs. Jacob J. Foster, 1981. ©22 Brandywine Conservancy; **288** Bettmann/Corbis; **289** ©Classic Image/Alamy; **290** BL; **290** bkgd Steven Bourelle/Shutterstock, Inc.; **290** C AIP/The Kobal Collection/Art Resource; **290** BR Accoutrements LLC; **292** Royal Photographic Society/Science & Society Picture Library; **295**; Mary Evans Picture Library; **297; 298; 300; 311** iStockphoto.com; **311** R Adam Woolfitt/Corbis; **312–313** ©Patrick Coughlin/Getty Images; **316** University of Delaware Library, Newark, Delaware; **318** ©The New Yorker Collection 1990 Ed Frascino from cartoonbank.com. All Rights Reserved; **319** Bettmann/Corbis; **322** bkgd ©Aaron/Horowitz/Corbis; **322** BL Bettmann/Corbis; **322** R ©Susan Shacter/Corbis; **324** ©Peter Freed/Corbis; **325** Paul Knight, Trevillion Images; **326** Yolande de Kort, Trevillion Images; **329** Geoff Eley, Trevillion Images; **331** Gaetan Charbonneau/Getty Images; **335** B Bettmann/Corbis; **335** T Bettmann/Corbis; **336** ©1998 Kinuko Y. Craft All Rights Reserved; **338** Bettmann/Corbis; **340** Private Collection/©Bonhams, London, UK/The Bridgeman Art Library; **344** T Frank Greenaway ©Dorling Kindersley, Courtesy of the Town Docks Museum, Hull; **344** BCR Frank Greenaway ©Dorling Kindersley, Courtesy of the Town Docks Museum, Hull; **344** BL Frank Greenaway ©Dorling Kindersley, Courtesy of the Town Docks Museum, Hull; **344** BL David Lyons ©Dorling Kindersley, Courtesy of the Courtesy of the New Bedford Whaling Museum, Massachusetts; **344** TCR Frank Greenaway ©Dorling Kindersley, Courtesy of the Town Docks Museum, Hull; **344** BCR Frank Greenaway ©Dorling Kindersley, Courtesy of the Town Docks Museum, Hull; **344** BR Christian Darkin/Photo Researchers, Inc.; **344** C Courtesy of the New Bedford Whaling Museum; **346** National Maritime Museum; **348** Bettmann/Corbis; **350** Bettmann/Corbis; **352** The Granger Collection, NYC; **356** ©The New Yorker Collection 1998 Arnie Levinfrom cartoonbank.com. All Rights Reserved; **359** ©Mark Karrass/Corbis; **360** ©Lee Snider/Corbis; **362** B; **362** T ©Elisheba Johnson; **363** Bettmann/Corbis; **365** Bettmann/Corbis; **366–368** sanderstock/fotolia; **371** ©Christian Delbert/Fotolia; **371** Leonard Harris/Stock Boston; **374** T Pearson; **375** Courtesy Concord Free Public Library, Concord Massachusetts; **377** The Granger Collection, NYC; **378** Curtis Hamilton (c) Rough Guides; **382** BR Bildarchiv Preussischer Kulturbesitz/Art Resource, NY; **382** BC ©Araldo de Luca/Corbis; **382** BL Pat O'Hara/Corbis; **382–383** TOP BORDER; Curtis Hamilton (c) Rough Guides; **384** MyLoupeRF\UIG/AGE Fotostock America; **388** istockphoto.com; **388** istockphoto.com; **389** bkgd Mitchell, S. Augustus 1792–1868/Library of Congress; **389** Bettmann/CORBIS; **390** The New Yorker Collection 1988 J.B. Handelsman from cartoonbank.com. All Rights Reserved; **393** BL istockphoto.com; **393** bkgd istockphoto.com; **395** istockphoto.com; **396** istockphoto.com; **398–399** Bridget Besaw/Aurora Photos; 40 Bridget Besaw/Aurora Photos; **401** Christie's Images/Corbis; **404** T istockphoto.com; **404** B ©James Marshall/Corbis; **404** T The Granger Collection, NYC; **405** T Property of the Amherst Historical Society.Photo by J.K. Tuthill; **405** B Courtesy of the Emily Dickinson Museum, Amherst, Massachusetts; **406** Amherst College Archives and Special Collections, by permission of the Trustees of Amherst College; **406** Bettmann/Corbis; **48; 410** BPK Berlin/Nationalgalerie, Staatliche Museen/Joerg P. Anders/Art Resource, NY.; **412** istockphoto.com; **413** Heibonsha/Pacific Press Service; **413** Heibonsha/Pacific Press Service; **415** istockphoto.com; **416–417** istockphoto.com; **418** Photo by Maud Kinnell; **422** Library of Congress; **426–427** Janina Dierks/Fotolia; **428** Courtesy of the Library of Congress; **432** The Lawrence Tree,1929, Georgia O'Keeffe, Wadsworth Atheneum, Hartford, CT. The Ella Gallup Sumner and Mary Catlin SumnerCollection, ©1998 The Georgia O'Keeffe Foundation/Artists Rights Society (ARS), New York; **434–435**; Haystack, 1938 (tempera with oil glaze on linen on panel), Benton, Thomas Hart (1889–1975)/Museum of Fine Arts, Houston, Texas, USA, ©DACS/Gift of Mr. Frank J. Hevrdejs/The Bridgeman Art Library International/ ©T.H. Benton and R.P. Benton Testamentar; **436** istockphoto.com; **443** Pearson; **460–461** Bettmann/Corbis; **462** LCL Bettmann/Corbis; **462** T Bettmann/Corbis; **462** CR Bettmann/Corbis; **462** RCR New York Times Co./Getty Images, Inc.; **462** TR The Granger Collection, NYC; **462** L The Granger Collection, NYC; **462** CL Missouri Historical Society; **462** R National Anthropological Archives, Smithsonian Institute, NAA INV 94200; **463** Chas Howson ©Dorling Kindersley; **463** Dave King ©Dorling Kindersley; **463** The Granger Collection, NYC; **463** The British Museum/HIP/The Image Works; **463** Detail from the original painting,The Museum of the Confederacy, Richmond, Virginia, Photography by Katharine Wetzel; **464** L The Art Archive/Bibliothèque des Arts Décoratifs Paris/Gianni Dagli Orti; **464** R Corbis; **465** R The Gallery Collection/Corbis; **465** C Bettmann/Corbis; **465** L Archive Photos/Getty Images; **466** R pinky/Shutterstock; **466** L The Granger Collection, NYC; **467** L The Art Archive/ Art Resource, NY; **467** BR The Gallery Collection/Corbis; **467** CR Six O'Clock, Winter, 1912, John Sloan, The Phillips Collection; **468** istockphoto.com; **468** T; **468** BL Museum of the City of New York/Corbis; **468** The Granger Collection, NYC; **469** L ©Jose Fuste Raga/Corbis; **469** R Columbia Pictures/Photofest; **470** L H. Armstrong Roberts/Corbis; **470** R Underwood & Underwood/Corbis; **471** L Bettmann/Corbis; **471** R The Old Guitarist, **193**, Pablo Picasso, Spanish, 1881–1973, oil on panel 122.9 x 82.6 cm, Helen Birch Bartlett Memorial Collection, 1926.253.Reproduction, The Art Institute of Chicago, ©24Estate of Pablo Picasso/Artists Rights Society (ARS), New York; **472** L ©Deborah Betz Collection/Corbis; **472** C ©Ted Streshinsky/Corbis; **472** R Science Museum/Science & Society Picture Library; **473** R Bettmann/Corbis; **473** L Rue des Archives/The Granger Collection, NYC; **475** Pearson; **476** Bettmann/Corbis; **477** Adoc-photos/Art Resource, NY; **479** Bettmann/CORBIS; **480; 482; 486; 487; 494** B Getty Images; **494** T Mulberry Plantation, Camden, S.C.; **496** Courtesy of the Library of Congress; **50; 53** The Granger Collection, NYC; **55** AP/Wide World Photos; **57** Bettmann/Corbis; **58** Bettmann/Corbis; **59** Bettmann/Corbis; **511** Corbis; **512** Courtesy of the National Museum of the U.S. Army, Army Art Collection.; **513** Museum of the Confederacy, Richmond, Virginia; **519** The National Portrait Gallery, Smithsonian Institution, Washington, D.C./Art Resource, NY; **520** Smithsonian American Art Museum, Washington, DC/Art Resource, NY; **522** The Granger Collection, NYC; **525** A Home on the Mississippi, 1871, Currier & Ives, The Museum of the City of New York, Harry T. Peters Collection; **526** Bettmann/Corbis; **532** Layne Kennedy/Corbis; **533** Corbis; **537** Bettmann/Corbis; **538** Bettmann/Corbis; **540** Corbis; **541** The Granger Collection, NYC; **544** L Shaun Curry/AFP/Getty Images; **544** R Cover design by John Gall. Cover photograph courtesy of National Geographic. Grove Press and imprint of Grove Atlantic, Inc. Distributed by Publishers Group West; **545** Miramax/Photofest; **546** Miramax/Photofest; **546–547** bkgd Purestock/Getty Images; **547** Miramax/Photofest; **548–549** Purestock/Getty Images; **550** T Pearson; **550** B Cover design by Francine Kass.Cover photograph courtesy of the National Portrait Gallery, Smithsonian Institution.W.W. Norton; **553** Hulton Archive/Getty Images; **554** Bettmann/Corbis; **555–556** istockphoto.com; **559** National Portrait Gallery, Smithsonian Institution/Art Resource, NY; **560** T Samir S. Patel; **560** B Samir S. Patel; **563** North Wind Picture Archives; **564** B Corel Professional Photos CD-ROM™; **564** T Courtesy National Archives; **566** Bettmann/Corbis; **566–567** bkgd ©Joseph Sohm/Visions of America/Corbis; **567** The Granger Collection, NYC; **568** bkgd istockphoto.com; **568** Bettmann/Corbis; **570** Minnesota Historical Society/Corbis; **572** Historical Picture Archive/Corbis; **577** The Granger Collection, NYC; **579** The Granger Collection, NYC; **582**; **583** istockphoto.com; **586** T; **588** Rick Friedman/Corbis; **589** T Tom Kelley/Retrofile/Getty Images;

589 B ClassicStock/Fotosearch; 590 T Image of The Advertising Archive; 590 B Image of The Advertising Archive; 592 WALTER SANDERS/Time & Life Pictures/Getty Images; 595; Corbis; 596 bkgd Hans Blohm/Masterfile; 596 Peter Lilja/The Image Bank/Getty Images; 598 istockphoto.com; 600 Shutterstock.com; 602 Paul A. Souders/Corbis; 604 Jeff Curtes/Corbis; 610 Will Datene/Alamy; 616 National Anthropological Archives, Smithsonian Institute, NAA INV 94200; 617 Kansas State Historical Society; 619 Connie Ricca/Corbis; 620 Courtesy of the Lane County Historical Museum; 622 National Portrait Gallery, Smithsonian Institution/Art Resource, NY; 624 Library of Congress; 625 Channel to the Mills, 1913, Edwin M. Dawes, oil on canvas, 51 x 39 1/2 in. Minneapolis Institute of Arts, anonymous gift.; 627 Missouri Historical Society; 629 Afternoon in Piedmont, (Elsie at the Window), c.1911, Xavier Martínez, Collection of The Oakland Museum of California, Gift of Dr. William S. Porter; 631 Hulton-Deutsch Collection/Corbis; 632 Corel Professional Photos CD-ROM™; 635 The Granger Collection, NYC; 636 Bettmann/Corbis; 638 istockphoto.com; 641 Colby College Special Collections, Waterville, ME; 642 Paul Knight, Trevillion Images; 643 istockphoto.com; 644 Photo ©The Metropolitan Museum of Art/Art Resource, NY; 645 National Portrait Gallery, Smithsonian Institution, Washington, D.C./Art Resource, NY; 646 Christie's Images/Corbis; 647 Joel Greenstein/Omni-Photo Communications, Inc.; 651 New York Times Co./Getty Images, Inc.; 652 George Schreiber (194–1977), From Arkansas, 1939, oil on canvas, Sheldon Swope Art Museum, Terre Haute, Indiana; 653 The Granger Collection, NYC; 654–655 The Granger Collection, NYC; 656 Beatriz Schiller/Time & Life Pictures/Getty Images; 656–657 The Granger Collection, NYC; 658 ARS,NYC/photo ©Erich Lessing/Art Resource, NY; 659 The Granger Collection, NYC; 660–661 The Granger Collection, NYC; 669 Pearson; 688–689 Drought Stricken Area, 1934 (oil on canvas), Hogue, Alexandre (1898–1994)/Dallas Museum of Art, Texas, USA/The Bridgeman Art Library; 690 R Library of Congress; 690 C Bettmann/Corbis; 690 L Bettmann/Corbis; 690 T Underwood & Underwood/Corbis; 690 CL Corbis; 690 RCR Corbis; 690 LCL Bettmann/Corbis; 690 CR Hulton Archive/Getty Images; 691 BCB Henry Guttmann/Moviepix/Getty Images; 691 T Chaplin/Photofest; 691 B Warner Bros. Pictures/Photofest; 691 CT United Artists/Photofest; 691 CB MGM/Photofest; 691 TCT; 692 L Bettmann/Corbis; 692 R Hulton Archive/Getty Images; 693 C Bettmann/Corbis; 693 LCorbis; 693 R Mansell/Time & Life Pictures/Getty Images; 694 L Hulton Archive/Getty Images; 694 R FRAN CAFFREY/AFP/Getty Images; 695 L AP Photo; 695 R JazzSign/Lebrecht Music & Arts/Corbis; 696 L Bettmann/Corbis; 696 R Lipnitzki/Roger Viollet/Getty Images; 697 TR Bettmann/Corbis/ ©Salvador Dali, Gala-Salvador Dali Foundation/Artists Rights Society (ARS), New York; 697 BR Bettmann/Corbis; 697 TL Bettmann/Corbis; 697 BL Icon Communications/Archive Photos/Getty Images; 698 T; 698 RT AP Photo; 698 RB Bettmann/Corbis; 698 L Hulton Archive/Getty Images; 699 L Bettmann/Corbis; 699 R The Granger Collection, NYC; 700 R The Granger Collection, NYC; 700 L The Granger Collection, NYC; 701 Radius Images/Alamy; 701 B Richard Peter Snr/Archive Photos/Getty Images; 703 Pearson; 704 Jason Hetherington/Stone/Getty Images; 705 Corbis; 707 Hulton-Deutsch Collection/Corbis; 78 Erich Lessing/Art Resource, NY; 713 T CNAC/MNAM/Dist. Réunion des Musées Nationaux/Art Resource, NY; 713 C The Metropolitan Museum of Art/Art Resource, NY; 713 B Jerry Cooke/Pix Inc./Time Life Pictures/Getty Image; 714 The New Yorker Collection 1994 Bruce Eric Kaplanfrom cartoonbank.com. All Rights Reserved.; 716 Corbis; 717 B Bettmann/Corbis; 717 T Bettmann/Corbis; 719 istockphoto.com/stephen mulcahey; 720 The Granger Collection, NYC; 722 Paul Seheult/Eye Ubiquitous/Corbis; 723 B istockphoto.com/James Pauls; 723 T istockphoto.com/Branko Miokovic; 724 The Metropolitan Museum of Art/Art Resource, NY; 725 age fotostock/SuperStock; 729 Bettmann/Corbis; 730 Mary Evans Picture Library; 731 istockphoto.com/Gary Godby; 732 L istockphoto.com/Vincent Giordano; 732 R C Squared Studios/Photodisc/Getty Images; 733 Mary Evans Picture Library; 735 Mary Evans Picture Library; 736 Mary Evans Picture Library; 738 Mary Evans Picture Library; 740 Mary Evans Picture Library; 742 Underwood & Underwood/Corbis; 747 Mary Evans Picture Library; 751 istockphoto.com; 752 Mary Evans Picture Library; 757 L Bettmann/Corbis; 757 R SuperStock, Inc; 758–759 David Lee/Shutterstock; 760–761 SuperStock, Inc; 766 T Library of Congress; 766 B Corbis; 766 C John Springer Collection/Corbis; 767 Library of Congress; 767 Library of Congress; 767 L Library of Congress; 768 Library of Congress; 771 Sandy Feisenthal/Corbis; 773 Bettmann/Corbis; 774 The Turret Lathe Operator (J.G. Cherry series), 1925, Grant Wood, oil on canvas18" x 24" Cedar Rapids Museum of Art, Cedar Rapids, Iowa,Gift of the Cherry Burrell Charitable Foundation Collection. 75.5.8, ©Estate of Grant Wood/Figge Ar Museum, success; 779 Bettmann/Corbis; 780 Hood Museum of Art, Dartmouth College, Hanover, New Hampshire; gift of Frank L. Harrington, Class of 1924; 785 Bettmann/Corbis; 786 istockphoto.com/Dmytro Konstantynov; 788 B Bettmann/Corbis; 788 T Oscar White/Corbis; 789 istockphoto.com; 791 Untitled, 1964,Alexander Calder, (one of seven lithographs in series), 19 1/2 x 25 1/2" Solomon R. Guggenheim Museum, New York, Gift of the artist, 1965, 65.1736.7. Photo by David Heald, ©The Solomon R. Guggenheim Foundation, New York, ©1998 Estate of; 795 Columbus Museum of Art, Ohio: Gift of Ferdinand Howald 1931.146; 799 Bettmann/Corbis; 800 Military Ambulance, First World War (bodycolour on paper), Simpson, Charles Walter (1885–1971)/Private Collection, ©Chris Beetles, London, U.K./The Bridgeman Art Library; 803 Corbis; 804 Corbis; 805 Corbis; 808 T Pearson; 808 B Random House Inc.; 89 AP Photo; 810 Mary Evans Picture Library; 812 Philip Jones Griffiths/Magnum Photos; 815 Corbis; 816 Snark/Art Resource, NY; 818 San Francisco Museum of Modern Art, Collection of the Sack Photographic Trust; 819 istockphoto.com; 823 Réunion des Musées Nationaux/Art Resource, NY; 824 Markus Amon/The Image Bank/Getty Images; 825 Pierre Vauthey/Sygma/Corbis; 826 age fotostock/SuperStock; 828 ANSA/Corbis; 833 istockphoto.com; 833 Hulton Archive/Getty Images; 834 bkgd istockphoto.com; 834; The Museum of Modern Art/Licensed by SCALA/Art Resource, NY; 839 The Bride, 1886 (w/c on paper), Zorn, Anders Leonard (1860–1920)/©Nationalmuseum, Stockholm, Sweden,/The Bridgeman Art Library International; 840 J. Fishkin/Custom Medical Stock Photo; 847 Philip Gould/Corbis; 848 Miz Emily, Joseph Holston, 24" x 16", Courtesy of Joseph Holston; 852 Georgia Red Clay, 1946, Nell Choate Jones, oil on canvas, 25 x 30 inches, 1989.1.94, Morris Museum of Art, Augusta, Georgia; 859 istockphoto.com; 859 Bettmann/Corbis; 860 My Life and Hard Times Copyright ©1933 by James Thurber. Copyright ©renewed 1961 by James Thurber. Reprinted by arrangement with Rosemary A. Thurber and The Barbara Hogenson Agency.; 862 My Life and Hard Times Copyright ©1933 by James Thurber. Copyright ©renewed 1961 by James Thurber. Reprinted by arrangement with Rosemary A. Thurber and The Barbara Hogenson Agency.; 863 My Life and Hard Times Copyright ©1933 by James Thurber. Copyright ©renewed 1961 by James Thurber. Reprinted by arrangement with Rosemary A. Thurber and The Barbara Hogenson Agency.; 867 Bettmann/Corbis; 867 bkgd Stock Montage, Inc.; 868 Stock Montage, Inc.; 870 istockphoto.com; 873 Bettmann/Corbis; 874 Exactostock/SuperStock; 877 istockphoto.com; 878–879 Destinations/Corbis; 880 Corel Professional Photos CD-ROM™; 882 Fine Art Photographic Library/Corbis; 883 Dante reading from the 'Divine Comedy', detail of Dante Alighieri (1265–1321), 1465 (panel) (detail of 42355), Domenico di Michelino, (1417–91)/Duomo, Florence, Italy/The Bridgeman Art Library; 884 Bettmann/Corbis; 886 The New Yorker Collection 1993 Mick Stevens from cartoonbank.com.All Rights Reserved.; 888 Walter Weissman/Corbis; 889 Jules Feiffer; 890 Jules Feiffer; 891 Jules Feiffer; 892 Jules Feiffer; 893 Jules Feiffer; 894 Jules Feiffer; 895 Aspiration, Aaron Douglas, Fine Arts Museums of San Francisco, Museum purchase; 896 ©Phoebe Beasley; 898 Corbis; 899 Atlantide Phototravel/Corbis; 900 T istockphoto.com; 900 B National Portrait Gallery, Smithsonian Institution/Art Resource, NY; 903 Aaron Douglas, Into Bondage, 1936,60 3/8 x 60 1/2, oil on canvas.In the collection of the Corcoran Gallery of Art, Washington, DC. Museum Purchaseand Partial Gift of Thurlow Tibbs Jr., The Evans-Tibbs Collection. 1996.9; 904 Nobody Around Here Calls Me Citizen, 1943, Robert Gwathmey, oil on canvas, H. 14-1/4" x W. 17" Collection Frederick R. Weisman Art Museum at the University of Minnesota; 906 Girls Skipping, 1949, Hale Woodruff, oil on canvas, 24" x 32", Private Collection. ©Estate of Hale Woodruff/Elnora, Inc.; Courtesy of Michael Rosenfeld Gallery, New York; 912; 912 bkgd age fotostock/SuperStock; 912; 912 title/author/Dover Publication, Inc.; 912 Hill and Wang; 912; 912; 912 Vintage Books; 912; 914 T Christopher Felver/Corbis; 914 B Miriam Berkley/Authorpix; 915 Smithsonian American Art Museum, Washington, DC/Art Resource, NY; 916 The Madonna and Child (detail), 1990, ©Momodou Ceesay; 920 B National Portrait Gallery, Smithsonian Institution/Art Resource, NY; 920 T Corbis; 921 Bettmann/Corbis; 923 B; 923 T Dave G. Houser/Corbis; 924 Hoeing, 1934, Robert Gwathmey, Oil on canvas, 40 by 60 1/4 (11.6 by 153),Carnegie Institute Museum of Art, Pittsburgh, Pennsylvania, Patrons Art Fund, 44.3.Photograph by Richard Stoner, ©Estate of Robert Gwathmey/Licensed by VAGA, New York, NY; 924–925 istockphoto.com; 926 istockphoto.com; 929 Library of Congress; 930 The Granger Collection, NYC; 930–931 bkgd Lake County Museum/Corbis; 931 Hulton Archive/Getty Images; 932–933 Lake County Museum/Corbis; 934–935 Lake County Museum/Corbis; 936 Lake County Museum/Corbis; 941 L Joe Robbins/Getty Images; 941 R The Atlanta Braves/MLB Photos via Getty Images; 947 Pearson; 964–965 The Museum of Modern Art/Licensed by SCALA/Art Resource, NY; 966 L AP/Wide World Photos; 966 CR Everett Collection Inc/Alamy; 966 R Deborah Feingold/Corbis; 966 RCR Flip Schulke/Corbis; 966 CL Peter Turnley/Corbis; 966 LCL Bettmann/Corbis; 966 TL NASA/Photo Researchers. Inc.; 966 TR Time Life Pictures/Time Magazine/Getty Images Inc.; 967 TCT David J. and Janice L. Frent/Corbis; 967 BCB David J. and Janice L. Frent/Corbis; 967 B Hulton Archives/Getty Images Inc.; 967 BC Herbert Orth/Time Life Pictures/Getty Imagess, Inc.; 967 T Herbert Orth/Time Life Pictures/Getty Imagess, Inc.; 967 TC Courtesy of The Peace Corps; 968 R John Springer Collection/Corbis; 968 L Bettmann/Corbis; 969 R Image Source/Getty Images; 969 L Bettmann/Corbis; 970 R Bettmann/Corbis; 970 L Michael Rougier/Time & Life Pictures/Getty Images; 971 L Bettmann/Corbis; 971 R Alfred Pasieka/Photo Researchers, Inc.; 972 T; 972 B Bettmann/Corbis; 973 R Bettmann/Corbis; 973 L Novosti/Photo Researchers, Inc.; 974 L Judith Miller/Dorling Kindersley/Bauman Rare Books; 974 T Bettmann/Corbis; 974 R Hulton Archives/Getty Images; 975 L Bettmann/Corbis; 975 R Charles E. Rotkin/Corbis; 975 C Bettmann/Corbis; 976 R Bettmann/Corbis; 976 L Bettmann/Corbis; 977 C Judith Miller/Dorling Kindersley/Bauman Rare Books; 977 L Bettmann/Corbis; 977 R Bettmann/Corbis; 979 T Sophie Bassouls/Sygma/Corbis; 979 B Playbill, is a registered trademark of Playbill, Inc. All rights reserved. Used by permission.; 980 Adam Woolfitt/Corbis; 981 MPI/Getty Images; 983 Bettmann/Corbis; 984 AP Photo/Stanley Troutman; 986 Corbis; 988 The Granger Collection, NYC; 990–991 The Granger Collection, NYC; 994 The Granger Collection, NYC; 996 Rollie McKenna; 997 Nik Keevil/Alamy; 1002 B Bettmann/Corbis; 1002 T Bettmann/Corbis; 1003 Courtesy Harry S. Truman Library 1004; 1008 Library of Congress; 1009 Choke, 1964, Robert Rauschenberg, Oil and screenprint on canvas, 60" x 48", Washington University Gallery of Art, St. Louis, Gift of Mr. and Mrs. Richard K. Weil, 1972, ©Robert Rauschenberg/Licensed by VAGA, New York, NY; 1011 AP/Wide World Photos; 1012 Deep Fork Overlook, Joan Marron-LaRue, Courtesy of the artist. Gallery is Nedra Matteucci Fine Art, 555 Canyon Rd., Santa Fe, New Mex.55-983-2731; 1017 Black Walnuts, Joseph Pollet, Collection of Whitney Museum of American Art.Purchase and gift of Gertrude Vanderbilt Whitney, by exchange (52.30).Photograph Copyright ©200: Whitney Museum of American Art; 1022 Vlaminck, Maurice de (1876–1958) ARS, NY Banque d'Images, ADAGP/Art Resource, NY; 1027 David Lees/Corbis; 1028 bkgd Shutterstock.com; 1028 Reading by the Oven, 1961 (oil on canvas), Sokolovskaya, Oksana Dmitrievna (fl.1961)/Springville Museum of Art, Utah, USA,/The Bridgeman Art Library; 1029 Shutterstock.com; 1030 istockphoto.com/Robyn Mackenzie; 1032–1033 istockphoto.com; 1034 istockphoto.com/Roel Smart; 1036; 1041 Sean Gallup/Getty Images; 1042 images.com/Corbis; 1044 BC ©Allen Ginsberg/Corbis;

1044 T Bettmann/Corbis; **1044** B Bettmann/Corbis; **1044** TC Timothy Clary/AFP/Getty Images; **1046** Improv Everywhere Productions, Inc.; **1047** Improv Everywhere Productions, Inc.; **1048** Improv Everywhere Productions, Inc.; **1048** Improv Everywhere Productions, Inc.; **1048** Improv Everywhere Productions, Inc.; **1049** Improv Everywhere Productions, Inc.; **1051** T Bettmann/Corbis; **1051** B Ian Cook/Time Life Pictures/Getty Images; **1052** Mirror II, George Tooker, (1920–1938), Egg tempera on gesso panel, 20 x 20 in., 1968.4, Gift of R. H. Donnelley Erdman (PA 1956), ©Addison Gallery of American Art, Phillips Academy, Andover, Massachusetts.All Rights Reserved; **1053** Sunny Forest/Shutterstock; **1054** Sunny Forest/Shutterstock; **1057** Bettmann/Corbis; **1058** 28 Masterfile Corporation; **1059** istockphoto.com/Dar Yang Yan; **1063** Bettmann/Corbis; **1064** istockphoto.com/Valerie Loiseleux; **1065** Pach Brothers/Corbis; **1066**; The Jacob and Gwendolyn Lawrence Foundation/Art Resource, NY Image; **1071** Everett Collection Inc/Alamy; **1072; 1074–1075** Smithsonian American Art Museum, Washington, DC/Art Resource, NY; **1079** Bettmann/Corbis; **1081** Peter Turnley/Corbis; **1082** Push to Walk, collage 48" x 48" ©Phoebe Beasley; **1087** Patti Mollica/SuperStock; **1095** Katy Winn/Corbis; **1096** Bettmann/Corbis; **1099** Walter Daran/Hulton Archive/Getty Images; **1113** Corbis; **1114** Retroactive I,Robert Rauschenberg, 1964, Wadsworth Atheneum, Hartford, CT, Gift of Susan Morse Hilles, ©Robert Rauschenberg/Licensed by VAGA, New York, NY; **1117** Paul Schutzer/Time & Life Pictures/Getty Images; **1118** Flip Schulke/Corbis; **1119** Bettmann/Corbis; **1110** L Bettmann/Corbis; **1110** R Express Newspapers/Staff/Hulton Archive/Getty Images; **1110** C Charles Moore/Black Star/stockphoto.com; **1111** Hulton-Deutsch Collection/Corbis; **1116** Boden/Ledingham/Masterfile; **1118** B Courtesy Everett Collection; **1118** BC Photofest; **1118** TC The Granger Collection, New York; **1118** T Playbill, is a registered trademark of Playbill, Inc. All rights reserved. Used by permission.; **1119** Deborah Feingold/Corbis; **1120** T ©Deborah Feingold/Corbis; **1120** B; **1121** 20th Century Fox, The Kobal Collection/Art Resource, NY; **1121** 20th Century Fox, The Kobal Collection/Art Resource, NY; **1122** RT Punch/Roxbury/Bioskop Film/The Kobal Collection/Art Resource, NY; **1122** BR Dave Allocca/DMI/Time Life Pictures/Getty Images; **1122** LT Paul Schutzer/Time & Life Pictures/Getty Images; **1122** RC Ron Galella/WireImage/Getty Images; **1122** BL Jason Merritt/FilmMagic/Getty Images; **1122** BC Popperfoto/Getty Images; **1124** 20th Century Fox/Photofest; **1128** The Granger Collection, NYC; **1131** Twentieth Century Fox Film Corporation/Photofest; **1132** AP/Wide World Photos; **1134** 20th Century Fox/The Kobal Collection/Art Resource; **1136** Twentieth Century Fox Film Corporation/Photofest; **1137** L Bettmann/Corbis; **1137** R Pathe Contemporary/Photofest; **1138** Getty Images; **1142** Twentieth Century Fox Film Corporation/Photofest; **1145** Musee Conde, Chantilly, France/Bridgeman Art Library, London/New York; **1146** Steve Cole/Photodisc/Getty Images; **1153** Twentieth Century Fox Film Corporation/Photofest; **1154** 20th Century-Fox/Photofest; **1170** Twentieth Century Fox Film Corporation/Photofest; **1171** R Robbie Jack/Corbis; **1171** L Alfredo Dagli Orti/The Art Archive/Corbis; **1172** Twentieth Century Fox Film Corporation/Photofest; **1174** Pocumtuck Valley Memorial Association, Memorial Hall Museum, Deerfield, Massachusetts; **1178** Twentieth Century Fox Film Corporation/Photofest; **1184** Bettmann/Corbis; **1188** Twentieth Century Fox Film Corporation/Photofest; **1198** Twentieth Century Fox Film Corporation/Photofest; **1199** R Robbie Jack/Corbis; **1199** L Archivo Iconografico, S.A./Corbis; **122** Twentieth Century Fox Film Corporation/Photofest; **124** Twentieth Century Fox Film Corporation/Photofest; **129** The Granger Collection, NYC; **1211** Twentieth Century Fox Film Corporation/Photofest; **1221** 20th Century-Fox/Photofest; **1223** Micheline Pelletier/Sygma/Corbis; **1224** Twentieth Century Fox Film Corporation/Photofest; **1226** Reuters/Brad Rickerby; **1229** 20th Century Fox/The Kobal Collection/Art Resource; **1234** "It's Okay-We're Hunting Communists". From "Herblock Special Report (W.W. Norton, 1974). Reprinted by permission of the Herb Block Foundation. **1238; 1240** Fred Prouser/Reuters/Corbis; **1241** Warner Independent/2929 Productions/ The Kobal Collection/Melinda Sue Gordon/Art Resource, NY; **1242** Warner Independent/2929 Productions/The Kobal Collection/Melinda Sue Gordon/Art Resource, NY; **1243** Warner Independent/2929 Productions/The Kobal Collection/Melinda Sue Gordon/Art Resource, NY; **1244** Warner Independent/2929 Productions/The Kobal Collection/Melinda Sue Gordon/Art Resource, NY; **1245** Warner Independent/2929 Productions/ The Kobal Collection/Melinda Sue Gordon/Art Resource, NY; **1246** Warner Independent/2929 Productions/The Kobal Collection/Melinda Sue Gordon/Art Resource, NY; **1247** Warner Independent/2929 Productions/The Kobal Collection/Melinda Sue Gordon/Art Resource, NY; **1248** Warner Independent/2929 Productions/The Kobal Collection/Melinda Sue Gordon/Art Resource, NY; **1259** Deborah Feingold/Corbis; **1274** TCR Time& Life Pictures/Getty Images Inc.; **1276–1277** Louis K. Meisel Gallery, Inc./Corbis; **1278** L Pearson; **1278** B U.S. Department of Defense; **1278** CR Sophie Bassouls/Sygma/Corbis; **1278** CL Keith Bedford/Reuters/Corbis; **1278** R Todd France/Corbis; **1278** LCL Stephen Rose/Liaison/Getty Images; **1278** T Ricky Flores/The Journal News/Corbis; **1279** T istockphoto.com; **1279** B Bob Rowan/ Progressive Image/Corbis; **1280** R Bettmann/Corbis; **1280** L; **1281** Lrudi1976/Fotolia; **1281** R Bettmann/Corbis; **1282** Tim Graham/Corbis; **1283** L Bettmann/Corbis; **1283** C Courtesy of International Business Machines Corporation, International Business Machines Corporation; **1283** R PhotoEdit Inc.; **1284** L Corbis; **1284** R Wally McNamee/Corbis; **1285** R AP Photo/Jeff Widener; **1285** L Peter Turnley/Corbis; **1286** C AP Photo; **1286** L Reuters/Corbis; **1286** R Reuters/Corbis; **1287** Reuters/Corbis; **1288** L AP Photo/The Express-Times, Joe Gill **1288** T; **1288** Andrew Brookes/Corbis; **1289** Car Culture/Corbis; **1289** C Molly Riley/Reuters/Corbis; **1289** R Newscom; **1291** Pearson; **1293** Do It Yourself Landscape (detail), 1962, Andy Warhol. photo: The Andy Warhol Foundation, Inc./Art Resource, NY. ©210 Andy Warhol Foundation for the Visual Arts/ARS, New York; **1294** Daniel Cima; **1295** Leslie Hinrichs/SuperStock; **1297** Pearson; **1298** Will & Deni McIntyre/Getty Images, Inc.; **1298–1299** istockphoto.com/Teresa Hurst; **132** Catherine Karnow/Corbis; **1311** Keith Bedford/Reuters/Corbis; **1312** istockphoto.com/Maksim Sokolov; **1312** istockphoto.com; **1312** istockphoto.com/Emilia Kun; **1318** Erich Lessing/Art Resource, NY; **1325** Sophie Bassouls/Sygma/Corbis; **1326** David Lees/Corbis; **1333** Louis K. Meisel Gallery, Inc./Corbis; **1335** Kit Stafford; **1336–1337** Punchstock; **1338** Christopher Felver/Corbis; **1339** Art Resource, NY; **1341** Donna Lee, courtesy of BOA Editions, Ltd.; **1342** Daniel Aeschlimann/zefa/Corbis; **1347** Shelley Rotner/Omni-Photo Communications, Inc.; **1349** Miriam Berkley/Authorpix; **1350–1351** AP Photo; **1351** istockphoto.com; **1352** James McGoon Photography; **1353–1354** istockphoto.com; **1353–1354** Christie's Images/Corbis; **1357** Stephen Rose/Liaison/Getty Images; **1358–1359** Shutterstock; **1360** 28 Bob Eckstein from cartoonbank.com.All Rights Reserved; **1362** T Library of Congress; **1362** CB AP Photo/TobyTalbot; **1362** CT Christopher Felver/Corbis; **1362** B Christopher Felver/Corbis; **1362** BCB Bettmann/Corbis; **1362** TCT Bettmann/Corbis; **1365** Miriam Berkley/Authorpix; **1366** Jack Gunter/Corbis; **1368** The Granger Collection, NYC; **1370** barneyboogles/fotolia; **1371** B istockphoto.com; **1371** T The Granger Collection, NYC; **1372** C istockphoto.com; **1372** T istockphoto.com; **1372** B Martin Cerny/Fotolia; **1373** Anna Hymas/Science Source/Photo Researchers, Inc; **1377** Alex Gotfryd/Corbis; **1378** Lichtenstein, Roy (1923–1997) ©Copyright Blam, 1962. Oil on canvas, 68 x 80 in. (172.7 x 23.2 cm). Gift of Richard Brown Baker, B.A. 1935. 1995.32.9. Yale University Art Gallery/Art Resource, NY; **1383** James Keyser/Time & Life Pictures/Getty Images; **1384** Warner Bros./Photofest; **1385** Warner Bros./Photofest; **1387** Warner Bros./Photofest; **1388** Warner Bros./Photofest; **1393** AP Photo/STR; **1394** David Butow/CORBIS SABA; **1395** R US Navy Photo/Alamy; **1395** L vario images GmbH & Co.KG/Alamy; **1395** C Reuters/CORBIS; **1396** istockphoto.com; **140** T Delta Hunter; **140** B William Harvey; **141** Michel Setboun/CORBIS; **142** Peter Turnley/Corbis; **143** istockphoto.com/Tomaz Levstek; **144** Peter Turnley/Corbis; **147** James Leynse/Corbis; **149** Todd France/Corbis; **1410** istockphoto.com; **1410** Jim McHugh; **1412** Andrew Gunners/Photodisc/Getty Images; **1415** Rudy Sulgan/Corbis; **1416** Andrew Gunners/Photodisc/Getty Images; **1417** Tim Wright/Corbis; **1418** Morning, 24 (oil on linen), Clarke, Daniel (Contemporary Artist)/Private Collection/The Bridgeman Art Library; **1425** Doug Menuez/Corbis; **1426** Redchopsticks/Photolibrary; **1430–1431** Matt Lambert/Stone/Getty Images; **1433** RCR Sophie Bassouls/Sygma/Corbis; **1433** Sophie Bassouls/Sygma/Corbis; **1434** istockphoto.com; **1435** istockphoto.com; **1437** Museo de Santa Cruz/Bridgeman Art Library, London/New York; **1446** TL istockphoto.com; **1446** TR istockphoto.com; **1451** Daniel Cima

Staff Credits

Dori Amtmann, Tricia Battipede, Rachel Beckman, Nancy Bolsover, Laura Brancky, Odette Calderon, Pam Carey, Kelly Casanova, Geoff Cassar, Jessica Cohn, Kyle Cooper, Sarah Cunningham, Anthony DeSacia, Kim Doster, Irene Ehrmann, Andy Ekedahl, Sandy Engleman, Samantha Fahy, Janet Fauser, Amy Fleming, Pam Gallo, Mark Gangi, Nicole Gee, Susan Graef, Leslie Griffin, Elaine Goldman, Brian Hawkes, Steve Hernacki, Martha Heller, Amanda House, Rick Hickox, Patricia Isaza, Etta Jacobs, Blair Jones, Jim Kelly, Nathan Kinney, Sarah Kraus, Gregory Lynch, Nancy Mace, Jim McPherson, Charles Morris, Pa Moua, Elizabeth Nielsen, Kim Ortell, Kathleen Pagliaro, Jennie Rakos, Sheila Nealon Ramsay, Karen Randazzo, Julianne Regnier, Christopher Richardson, Melissa Schreiner, Hillary Schwei, Jeff Shagawat, Susan Sheehan, Charlene Smith, DeAnn Smith, Sheila Smith, Cynthia Summers, Morgan Taylor, Brian Thomas, Lucia Tirondola, Karen Tully, Merle Uuesoo, Kristen Varina, Jackie Westbrook, Jessica White